MEDIEVAL FRANCE

Garland Encyclopedias of the Middle Ages (Vol. 2)
Garland Reference Library of the Humanities (Vol. 932)

ADVISERS

MEDIEVAL FRANCE

AN ENCYCLOPEDIA

WILLIAM W. KIBLER
GROVER A. ZINN

Editors

LAWRENCE EARP
Associate Editor

JOHN BELL HENNEMAN, JR.
Associate Editor

Garland Publishing, Inc.
New York & London 1995

Library of Congress Cataloging-in-Publication Data

Medieval France : an encyclopedia / William W. Kibler, editor ... [et al.].
       p.   cm. — (Garland reference library of the humanities ; vol. 932. Garland encyclopedias
of the Middle Ages ; vol. 2)
   Includes bibliographical references and index.
   ISBN 0-8240-4444-4
   1. France—Civilization—Encyclopedias.   I. Kibler, William W., 1942- . II. Series: Garland
reference library of the humanities ; vol. 932.   III. Series: Garland reference library of the humanities.
Garland encyclopedias of the Middle Ages ; vol. 2.
DC33.2.M44   1995
944'.003—dc20   95-2617
                                                                                                      CIP

Cover photograph: Morienval. Vaults of ambulatory. Courtesy of Whitney S. Stoddard.
Cover design by Lawrence Wolfson.

Printed on acid-free, 250-year-life paper
Manufactured in the United States of America

CONTENTS

INTRODUCTION

Medieval France: An Encyclopedia is an introduction to the political, economic, social, religious, intellectual, literary, and artistic history of France from the early 5th century to the late 15th. We have sought to present in a single, convenient reference work aspects of medieval France that are otherwise treated in separate scholarly publications. The subject matter is complex and vast, and we therefore make no claims for completeness. We hope, however, to have provided a balanced, informative, and up-to-date reference work that, although directed primarily toward students and the general public, will also provide a useful starting point for scholars in various disciplines.

Entries range from about fifty words to over 3,000. Shorter entries provide ready reference; longer entries explain and interpret major institutions, writers and works, movements, and monuments. The encyclopedia offers a cross-disciplinary focus that promotes the integration of materials, provides a synthetic perspective, and encourages immediate connections among fields often held in isolation. Though scholars using this volume will be familiar with the basic information and bibliography contained in articles that cover their areas of expertise, they will find the articles in fields other than their own to be indispensable for general orientation, interpretation, and bibliography. The index at the end of the volume and cross-referencing at the end of each entry are designed to enhance the cross-disciplinary perspective.

Both "medieval" and "France" require definition. By "medieval," we mean that vast period between the fall of the Roman Empire, with the decline or loss of such Roman institutions as schools, roads, towns, and law—in short, civilization as we conceive it—and the advent of the Renaissance in late 15th-century France. It is a period in which a new and specifically French civilization and identity were forged, in which new institutions were conceived and developed: the universities, the feudal monarchy, scholastic philosophy, Romanesque and Gothic art, western monasticism and mysticism. Paris, which under the Capetians became the capital of a growing dynasty, was the intellectual, artistic, and political center of late-medieval France. But "France" itself is an elusive geographical area during the period in question. For purists, it is no more than the Île-de-France, the region immediately surrounding the capital. But for our purposes, it extends roughly from Brussels to the Mediterranean, from Switzerland to Brittany, and briefly even into Britain: all the area that was dominated by the new court culture that grew out of the Carolingian and Capetian intellectual centers. Individuals who played a dominant role in medieval French political, artistic, or intellectual life, and who are associated chiefly with French cultural centers, whether or not they happened to have been born within the boundaries of contemporary France, are included—for example, Peter Lombard, Thomas d'Angleterre, Thomas Aquinas, Hugh of Saint-Victor, Robert de Courçon, among many others.

Entries are arranged alphabetically. In the listing of literary works, preference has been given to the names of the authors, whenever known, rather than to titles of works. Thus, *Perceval (Conte du Graal)* will be found under CHRÉTIEN DE TROYES and the *Gesta Francorum* under AIMOIN DE FLEURY. The form of the individual's name chosen to alphabetize has frequently proven problematic. At the conception of the project, it was the editors' intention to use the modern French form for all proper nouns, but it quickly became clear that both scholars and the general public would be disoriented, and perhaps shocked, to have to look under GUILLAUME LE BÂTARD for the familiar William the Conqueror, or PIERRE LE CHANTRE for Peter the Chanter. The compromise reached was that we would seek to include that form of the name most familiar to scholars in historical disciplines and to the general public. Thus, all kings of France and England, dukes of Burgundy, and many members of the royal families are found under their Englished form (Charles the Bad, Philip the Bold, Henry II); most theologians and philosophers are anglicized (Philip the Chancellor, William of Champeaux, Thierry of Chartres); while all vernacular authors are found under the usual French form of their name (Marie de France, Thomas d'Angleterre, Peire Cardenal). In all cases, however, the user should try the following equivalencies when the name is not where initially sought: Gautier = Walter; Guillaume/Guilhem = William; Jean = John; Matthieu = Matthew; Philippe = Philip; Pierre/Peire = Peter.

A further complicating factor was whether to alphabetize under the given name or the cognomen. As the article PERSONAL NAMES makes clear, cognomens began to be used only in the 11th century and were generally loconyms common to all people living in a given place, changing as the person changed residence. The personal name remained the individual's chief identification. But, by the 14th century, family names as we know them slowly began to become fixed, so that cognomens vied with personal names in providing identification. Furthermore, many individuals from this period are more readily identified by their cognomens than their personal names (Villon, Deschamps, Ockeghem). So it was decided that individuals whose primary period of activity preceded the 14th century were to be identified by their personal names (Peter of Blois, Renaut de Beaujeu, William of Sens), whereas those who were active principally or wholly in the 14th and 15th centuries are to be found under their cognomens (La Marche, Olivier de; Ockham, William of; Ferrières, Henri de). A few exceptions were made, always with the intention of providing the most accessible and familiar entry (Bernard Gui, Christine de Pizan, René d'Anjou), and usually where the cognomen is still clearly a loconym. The user is encouraged to seek first under the given name, since fully 90 percent of the individuals found herein are so alphabetized, and secondarily under the cognomen.

In the case of anonymous literary works like the *Chanson de Roland* or *Roman de Sidrac*, we have taken the "Chanson de" or "Roman de" as a generic indicator, rather than as a part of the title; these works are listed as *ROLAND, CHANSON DE* and *SIDRAC, ROMAN DE.* French cities are listed under their French spellings, which in only a few cases differ from their English forms (Lyon, Marseille, Strasbourg).

The volume includes maps, genealogies, and illustrations to add a visual dimension that will help cla.ify individual topics and inform the reader. The index at the end of the encyclopedia is intended to guide users to topics that either lack their own entry or are cited repeatedly throughout the volume. The bibliographies appended to the entries are not intended to be exhaustive but instead provide key reference materials that will enable the student and scholar to move quickly and confidently into the matter at hand. They are generally organized as follows: primary sources (editions, then translations where appropriate), followed by secondary scholarship, cited alphabetically by author.

A work of this magnitude requires the collaboration and cooperation of many persons. Our deepest gratitude goes in the first place to the many colleagues who graciously gave of their time and knowledge to write the articles that are the very soul of this enterprise; their names are listed both at the beginning of the volume and after the articles they contributed. In addition to writing key articles, several colleagues provided special assistance in drawing up lists of entries and defining coverage for specific areas: Matilda T. Bruckner for vernacular romance, William W. Clark for art history, Margot Fassler for music, Alan E. Knight for theater, Whitney S. Stoddard for art history, and Roy S. Rosenstein for Occitan poetry. Other colleagues generously contributed some of the photographs used to illustrate this volume: Rebecca Baltzer, Karen Gould, and Joan Holladay. The editors wish to express deep appreciation to Whitney S. Stoddard for making his superb collection of photographs available and to Oberlin College for permitting reproduction of photographs from the Clarence Ward Photograph Collection. Joseph Romano was most helpful in connection with the Ward photographs. The editors wish to thank the following libraries and museums for permission to reproduce items in their collections: Allen Memorial Art Museum, Oberlin College; Archives Nationale, Paris; Bargello, Florence; Biblioteca Medicea Laurenziana, Florence; Bibliothèque de l'Arsenal, Paris; Bibliothèque Municipale d'Arras; Bibliothèque Municipale, Douai; Bibliothèque Nationale, Paris; Beinecke Rare Book and Manuscript Library, Yale University; British Library; Cleveland Museum of Art; The Cloisters, New York; Louvre, Paris; Metropolitan Museum of Art, New York; Museum of Fine Arts, Boston; National Gallery of Art, Washington, D.C.; Pierpont Morgan Library, New York; Walters Art Gallery, Baltimore. Also, Joel Herschman, Virginia Jansen, and the French National Tourist Office permitted reproduction of photographs. Help with typing, bibliography checking, and computer applications was provided by Elisabeth Barret, Mary-Alis Kibler, Jennifer A. Zinn, Thelma Roush, and Terri Mitchell. For timely help in art history, we are particularly grateful to Stacy L. Boldrick and Karen Gould. Finally, this work would never have seen the day without the suggestions, insights, and careful copyediting by Gary Kuris of Garland Publishing. Also at Garland, Helga McCue was instrumental in the early production stages of the encyclopedia, while Eunice Petrini's patience, good humor, eagle-eye, and gentle wisdom proved invaluable in the final editing and assembling of the volume. The University of Texas and Oberlin College provided research assistance to the editors.

ABBREVIATIONS

add.	additional
B.A.R.	British Archaeological Reports
Bibl. mun.	Bibliothèque municipale
Bibl. naz.	Biblioteca nazionale
Bibl. roy.	Bibliothèque royale (Brussels)
Bodl. Lib.	Bodleian Library (Oxford)
B.L.	British Library (London)
B.N.	Bibliothèque Nationale (Paris)
BSAHL	*Bulletin de la Société Archéologique et Historique du Limousin*
c.	century
ca.	circa
CCCM	Corpus Christianorum Continuatio Mediaevalis
CCSL	Corpus Christianorum Series Latina
CDDP	Centre départemental de documentation pédagogique
CESCM	Centre d'Études Supérieures de Civilisation Médiévale (Poitiers)
CNMHS	Caisse Nationale des Monuments Historiques et des Sites
CNRS	Centre National de la Recherche Scientifique
CRAL	Centre de Recherches et d'Applications Linguistiques (Nancy)
CSEL	Corpus Scriptorum Ecclesiasticorum Latinorum
CUER MA	Centre Universitaire d'Études et de Recherches Médiévales d'Aix
Ep.	Epistolae
Fac. de Méd.	Faculté de Médecine (Montpellier)
facs.	facsimile
fl.	flourished
fr.	fonds français

Fr.	French
Gl. kgl. Saml.	Gammel kongelige Samling (Royal Library, Copenhagen)
Gmc.	Germanic
lat.	fonds latin
Lat.	Latin
MGH	*Monumenta Germaniae Historica*
Ms, Mss	Manuscript, manuscripts
nom.	nominative (case)
obl.	oblique (case)
OFr.	Old French
PL	*Patrologia Latina*
PG	*Patrologia Graeca*
Pal. lat.	Palatina latina (Vatican Library)
pl.	plural
PLAC	Poetae Latinae Aevi Carolini
PMLA	*Publications of the Modern Language Association of America*
SATF	Société des Anciens Textes Français
SEDES	Société d'Édition d'Enseignement Supérieur
SEVPEN	Service d'Édition et de Vente des Publications de l'Éducation
sg.	singular
SOBODI	Société Bordelaise de Diffusion des Travaux de Lettres et Sciences Humaines
SPCK	Society for Promoting Christian Knowledge
SS.	Saints
STEM	Società Tipografica Editrice Modenense
UMI	University Microfilms International
vol., vols.	volume, volumes

KINGS, COUNTS, DUKES

(regnal dates)

MEROVINGIANS
Merovech (d. 456)
Childeric I (456–82)
Clovis I (482–511)
Clotar I (511–61)
Chlodomer (511–24); Theuderic I (511–33); Childebert I (511–58); Theodebert I (533–48)

Neustria	*Neustria/Austrasia*	*Austrasia*
Chilperic I (561–84)		Sigibert I (561–75)
		Childebert II (575–95)
		Theodebert II (595–612)
		Theuderic II (612–13)
		Sigibert II (613)
Clotar II (584–629)		
	Dagobert I (629–39)	
Clovis II (637–57)		Sigibert III (632–56)
Clotar III (655–73)		Childeric II (662–75)
Theuderic III (673–90/91)		Dagobert II (675–79)
	Clovis III (691–94)	
	Childebert III (694–711)	
	Dagobert III (711–15)	
Chilperic II (715–21)		Clotar IV (717–19)
	Theuderic IV (721–37)	
	Childeric III (743–51)	

CAROLINGIAN KINGS OF WEST FRANKS/FRANCE

Pepin (III) the Short (751–68)
Carloman (768–71) *and*
Charles I (Charlemagne) (768–814)
Louis I the Pious (814–40)
Charles II the Bald (840–77)
Louis II the Stammerer (877–79)

Louis III (879–82) *and*
Carloman II (879–84)
Charles III the Simple (898–922)
Louis IV d'Outremer (936–54)
Lothair I (954–86)
Louis V (986–87)

ROBERTIAN/CAPETIAN KINGS OF FRANCE

Eudes (888–98)
Robert I (922–23)
Raoul (923–36)
Hugh Capet (987–96)
Robert II the Pious (996–1031)
Henry I (1031–60)
Philip I (1060–1108)
Louis VI the Fat (1108–37)
Louis VII (1137–80)

Philip II Augustus (1180–1223)
Louis VIII (1223–26)
Louis IX (St. Louis) (1226–70)
Philip III the Bold (1270–85)
Philip IV the Fair (1285–1314)
Louis X the Quarrelsome (1314–16)
John I (1316)
Philip V the Tall (1316–22)
Charles IV the Fair (1322–28)

VALOIS BRANCH OF THE CAPETIAN FAMILY

Philip VI (1328–50)
John II the Good (1350–64)
Charles V the Wise (1364–80)
Charles VI (1380–1422)

Charles VII (1422–61)
Louis XI (1461–83)
Charles VIII (1483–98)

COUNTS OF ANJOU

Foulques I le Roux d. (938)
Foulques II le Bon (938–58)
Geoffroi I Grisgonelle (958–87)
Foulques III Nerra (987–1040)
Geoffroi II Martel (1040–60)

Geoffroi III le Barbu (1060–68)
Foulques IV le Rechin (1068–1109)
Foulques V (1109–29)
Geoffroi IV Plantagenêt (1129–51)
Henri (Henry II, king of England) (1151–89)

VALOIS DUKES OF ANJOU

[Also counts of Provence and claimants to Naples]
Louis I (d. 1384)
Louis II (1384–1417)
Louis III (1417–34)
René le Bon (1434–80)
Charles (1480–81)

DUKES OF AQUITAINE/COUNTS OF POITOU

Ebles II (d. ca. 934)
William III (935–63)
William IV Fier à Bras (963–95)
William V the Great (995–1030)
William VI the Fat (1030–ca. 1038)
Eudes I (1038–40)

William VII (ca. 1138–58)
William VIII (Gui-Geoffroi) (1058–86)
William IX (1086–1126)
William X (1126–37)
Eleanor (1137–1204)
[Held by Eleanor's descendants, kings of England,
  until 1453]

COUNTS OF BLOIS and COUNTS OF CHAMPAGNE

Thibaut I le Vieux (d. ca. 940)
Thibaut II le Tricheur (ca. 940–ca. 977)
Eudes I (975–96)
Eudes II (996–1037)   Eudes II count of Champagne (1025–37)
Thibaut III (I of Champagne) (1037–89)
Étienne-Henri (1089–1102)   Hugues I count of Champagne (1093–1125)
Thibaut IV le Grand (1102–52)   Thibaut IV le Grand (II of Champagne) (1125–52)
Thibaut V (1152–91)   Henri I le Libéral count of Champagne (1152–81)
Louis (1191–1205)   Henri II (1181–97)
Thibaut VI (1205–18)   Thibaut III (1197–1201)
Marguerite (1218–25)   Thibaut IV (1201–53)
                                                    (king of Navarre [1234–53])
                                                 Thibaut V (II of Navarre) (1253–70)
                                                 Henri III (I of Navarre) (1270–74)
                                                 Jeanne (m. Philip IV) (1274–1305)
                                                 Louis (X of France) (1305–16)

DUKES (COUNTS) OF BRITTANY

Nominoe (d. 851)   Geoffroi II (Geoffrey Plantagenêt) (1181–86)
Erispoe (851–57)   Arthur I (1186–1203)
Salomon (857–74)   Gui de Thouars (1203–12
    (divided rule [874–88])   Pierre I Mauclerc 1213–37)
Alain I (888–907)   Jean I (1237–86)
Wramaelon (908–19)   Jean II (1286–1305)
    (divided rule [919–36])   Arthur II (1305–12)
Alain II (936–52)   Jean III (1312–41)
    (divided rule [952–70])   Charles de Blois (1341–64)
Conan I (970–92)   Jean IV (1364–99)
Geoffroi I (992–1008)   Jean V (1399–1442)
Alain III (1008–40)   François I (1442–50)
Conan II (1040–66)   Arthur III (Richemont) (1457–58)
Hoel (1066–84)   François II (1458–88)
Alain IV (1084–1112)   Anne (1488–1514) (m. Charles VIII,
Conan III (1112–48)   then Louis XII of France)
Eudon (1148–55)
Conan IV (1155–66)
    (under English rule [1166–81])

DUKES OF BURGUNDY

Capetian Line
Robert I (1032–75)   Eudes III (1192–1218)
Hugues I (1075–78)   Hugues IV (1218–72)
Eudes I (1078–1102)   Robert II (1272–1305)
Hugues II (1102–43)   Hugues V (1305–15)
Eudes II (1143–62)   Eudes IV (1315–49)
Hugues III (1165–92)   Philippe de Rouvre (1349–61)

Valois Line
Philip the Bold (1363–1404)   Charles the Bold (1467–77)
John the Fearless (1404–19)   Marie (m. Maximilian of Austria) (1477–82)
Philip the Good (1419–67)

COUNTS OF FLANDERS

Baudouin I (862–79)
Baudouin II (879–918)
Arnulf I (918–65)
Baudouin III (d. 961)
Arnulf II (965–88)
Baudouin IV (988–1035)
Baudouin V (1035–67)
Baudouin VI (1067–70)
Arnulf III (1070–71)
Robert I the Frisian (1071–93)
Robert II of Jerusalem (1093–1111)
Baudouin VII (1111–19)
Charles the Good (of Denmark) (1119–27)

William Clito (1127–28)
Thierry d'Alsace (1128–68)
Philippe d'Alsace (1168–91)
Baudouin VIII (1191–95)
Baudouin IX (1195–1205)
Jeanne de Constantinople (1205–44)
Marguerite (1244–78)
Gui de Dampierre (1278–1305)
Robert III de Béthune (1305–22)
Louis I de Nevers (1322–46)
Louis II de Mâle (1346–84)
[Thereafter, see dukes of Burgundy]

DUKES OF (UPPER) LORRAINE

Albert of Alsace (d. ca. 1033)
Gerard (1048–70)
Thierry I (1070–1115)
Simon I (1115–39)
Mathieu I (1139–79)
Simon II (1176–1205)
Ferri I (1205–08)
Ferri II (1206–13)
Thibaut I (1213–20)
Mathieu II (1220–50)

Ferri III (1251–1304)
Thibaut II (1304–12)
Ferri IV le Lutteur (1312–28)
Raoul le Vaillant (1328–46)
Jean I (1346–90)
Charles I (1390–1431)
René I d'Anjou (1431–53)
Jean II (1453–70)
Nicolas (1470–73)
René II (1473–1508)

DUKES OF NORMANDY

Robert I (Rollo) (911–28)
William Longsword (928–42)
Richard I (942–96)
Richard II (996–1026)
Richard III (1026–27)
Robert (II) the Magnificent (1027–35)
William the Conqueror (1035–87)

Robert (III) Curthose (1087–1106)
Henry I (1106–35)
Stephen of Blois (1035–44)
Geoffroi IV Plantagenêt (1144–50)
Henry II (1150–89)
*[Held by kings of England to 1204,
     then annexed by kings of France]*

COUNTS OF TOULOUSE (SAINT-GILLES FAMILY)

Raymond I (d. 924)
Raymond II (Pons) (924–ca. 960)
Raymond III (ca. 960–85)
Pons II (985–90)
Guilhem Taillefer (990–1045)
Pons III (1045–60)
Guilhem (d. 1090)

Raymond IV (1090–1105)
Alphonse-Jourdain (1105–48)
Raymond V (1148–94)
Raymond VI (1194–1222)
Raymond VII (1222–49)
Alphonse of Poitiers (1249–71)

POPES
440–1503

(regnal dates)

Leo I (440–61)
Hilary (461–68)
Simplicius (468–83)
Felix III (II) (483–92)
Gelasius I (492–96)
Anastasius II (496–98)
    [Antipope Lawrence (498–99, 501–06)]
Symmachus (498–514)
Hormisdas (514–23)
John I (523–26)
Felix IV (III) (526–30)
    [Antipope Dioscorus (530)]
Boniface II (530–32)
John II (533–35)
Agapitus I (535–36)
Silverius (536–37)
Vigilius (537–55)
Pelagius I (556–61)
John III (561–74)
Benedict I (575–79)
Pelagius II (579–90)
Gregory I (590–604)
Sabinian (604–06)
Boniface III (607)
Boniface IV (608–15)
Deusdedit I (615–18)
Boniface V (619–25)
Honorius I (625–38)
Severinus (640)
John IV (640–42)
Theodore I (642–49)
Martin I (649–53)
Eugenius I (654–57)
Vitalian (657–72)
Adeodatus II (672–76)
Donus (676–78)
Agatho (678–81)
Leo II (682–83)
Benedict II (684–85)
John V (685–86)
Conon (686–87)

[Antipope Theodore (687)]
[Antipope Paschal (687)]
Sergius I (687–701)
John VI (701–05)
John VII (705–07)
Sisinnius (708)
Constantine I (708–15)
Gregory II (715–31)
Gregory III (731–41)
Zacharias (741–52)
Stephen I (II) (752)
Stephen II (III) (752–57)
Paul I (757–67)
    [Antipope Constantine (767–68)]
    [Antipope Philip (768)]
Stephen III (IV) (768–72)
Hadrian I (772–95)
Leo III (795–816)
Stephen IV (V) (816–17)
Paschal I (817–24)
Eugenius II (824–27)
Valentine (827)
Gregory IV (827–44)
    [Antipope John (844)]
Sergius II (844–47)
Leo IV (847–55)
    [Antipope Anastasius Bibliothecarius (855)]
Benedict III (855–58)
Nicholas I (858–67)
Hadrian II (867–72)
John VIII (872–82)
Marinus I (882–84)
Hadrian III (884–85)
Stephen V (VI) (885–91)
Formosus (891–96)
Boniface VI (896)
Stephen VI (896–97)
Romanus (897)
Theodore II (897)
John IX (898–900)

Benedict IV (900–03)
Leo V (903–04)
    [Antipope Christopher (903–04)]
Sergius III (904–11)
Anastasius III (911–13)
Lando (913–14)
John X (914–28)
Leo VI (928)
Stephen VII (VIII) (928–31)
John XI (931–36)
Leo VII (936–39)
Stephen VIII (IX) (939–42)
Marinus II (942–46)
Agapitus II (946–55)
John XII (955–64)
Leo VIII (963–65)
Benedict V (964)
John XIII (965–72)
Benedict VI (973–74)
    [Antipope Boniface VII (974, 984–85)]
Benedict VII (974–83)
John XIV (983–84)
John XV (985–96)
Gregory V (996–99)
    [Antipope John XVI (997–98)]
*Sylvester II (999–1003)
John XVII (1003)
John XVIII (1003–09)
Sergius IV (1009–12)
Benedict VIII (1012–24)
    [Antipope Gregory (1012)]
John XIX (1024–32)
Benedict IX (1032–44, 1045, 1047–48)
    [Antipope Silvester III (1045)]
Gregory VI (1045–46)
Clement II (1046–47)
Damasus II (1048)
Leo IX (1049–54) [Alsace]
Victor II (1055–57)

*Stephen IX (X) (1057–58)
  [Antipope Benedict X (1058–59)]
*Nicholas II (1058–61) [Lorraine or French Burgundy]
  [Antipope Honorius II (1061–64)]
+Alexander II (1061–73)
Gregory VII (1073–85)
  [Antipope Clement III (1080, 1084–1100)]
Victor III (1086–87)
*+Urban II (1088–99)
Paschal II (1099–1118)
  [Antipope Theodoric (1100–01)]
  [Antipope Albert (1101)]
  [Antipope Silvester IV (1105–11)]
Gelasius II (1118–19)
  *[Antipope Gregory VIII (1118–21]
*Calixtus II (1119–24)
Honorius II (1124–30)
  [Antipope Celestine II (1124)]
Innocent II (1130–43)
  +[Antipope Anacletus II (1130–38)]
  [Antipope Victor (1138)]
+Celestine II (1143–44)
Lucius II (1144–45)
+Eugenius III (1145–53)
Anastasius IV (1153–54)

Hadrian IV (1154–59)
Alexander III (1159–81)
  [Antipope Victor IV (1159–64)]
  [Antipope Paschal III (1164–68)]
  [Antipope Calixtus III (1168–78)]
  [Antipope Innocent III (1179–80)]
Lucius III (1181–85)
Urban III (1185–87)
Gregory VIII (1187)
Clement III (1187–91)
+Celestine III (1191–98)
+Innocent III (1198–1216)
Honorius III (1216–27)
+Gregory IX (1227–41)
Celestine IV (1241)
Innocent IV (1243–54)
Alexander IV (1254–61)
*+Urban IV (1261–64)
*+Clement IV (1265–68)
+Gregory X (1271–76)
*+Innocent V (1276)
Hadrian V (1276)
+John XXI (1276–77)
Nicholas III (1277–80)
*Martin IV (1281–85)
+Honorius IV (1285–87)
Nicholas IV (1288–92)
Celestine V (1294)
Boniface VIII (1294–1303)
Benedict XI (1303–04)

*+Clement V (1305–14)
*+John XXII (1316–34)
  [Antipope Nicholas V (1328–30)]
*+Benedict XII (1334–42)
*+Clement VI (1342–52)
*+Innocent VI (1352–62)
+Urban V (1362–70)
*Gregory XI (1370–78)
Roman Line
  Urban VI (1378–89)
  Boniface IX (1389–1404)
  Innocent VII (1404–06)
  Gregory XII (1406–15)[1]
Avignon Line
  +Clement VII (1378–94)
  +Benedict XIII (1394–1417)[2]
  Clement VIII (1423–29)
Pisa Line
  +Alexander V (1409–10)
  John XXIII (1410–15)[3]
Martin V (1417–31)
Eugenius IV (1431–47)
  *[Antipope Felix V (1439–49]
Nicholas V (1447–55)
Calixtus III (1455–58)
Pius II (1458–64)
Paul II (1464–71)
Sixtus IV (1471–84)
Innocent VIII (1484–92)
Alexander VI (1492–1503)
Pius III (1503)

Notes
1. Deposed, Council of Pisa, 1409
2. Deposed, Council of Constance, 1415
3. Deposed, Council of Pisa, 1409, and Council of Constance, 1417; died, 1423

* Popes born in French territory
+ Popes who studied in a French school or university, or were members of a religious community in France

Based on J.N.D. Kelly, *Oxford Dictionary of Popes,* New York: Oxford University Press, 1986.

ARCHITECTURAL TERMS

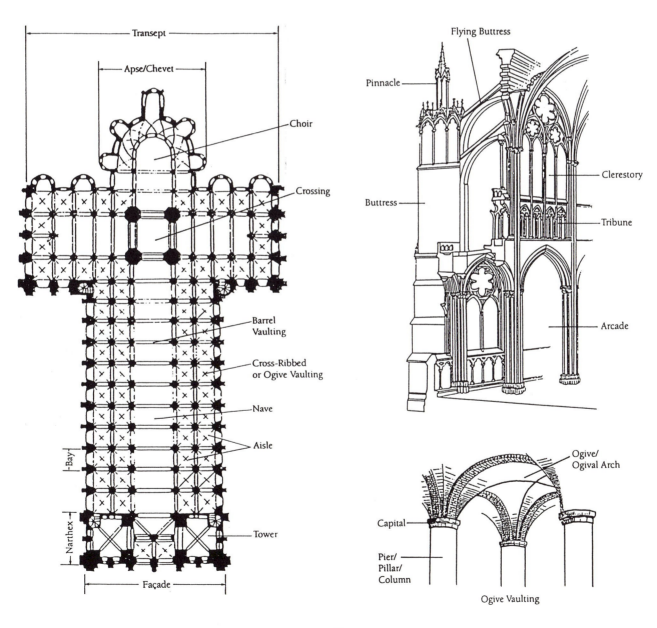

Transept

Apse/Chevet

Choir

Crossing

Barrel Vaulting

Cross-Ribbed or Ogive Vaulting

Nave

Aisle

Bay

Narthex

Tower

Façade

Flying Buttress

Pinnacle

Buttress

Clerestory

Tribune

Arcade

Ogive/ Ogival Arch

Capital

Pier/ Pillar/ Column

Ogive Vaulting

Battlement;
Crenellation

Merlon

Crenel

Ramparts

Meurtrière
(Loophole)

Portcullis

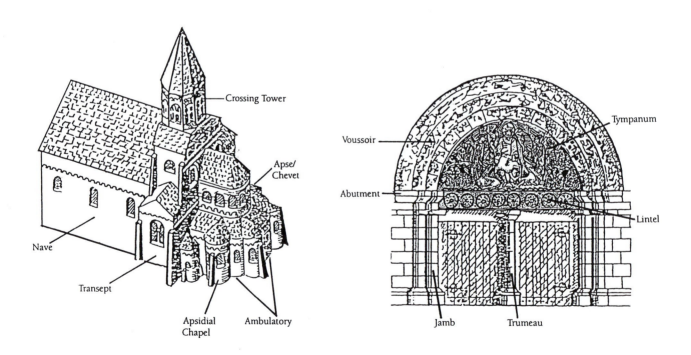

Crossing Tower

Apse/
Chevet

Nave

Transept

Apsidial
Chapel

Ambulatory

Voussoir

Tympanum

Abutment

Lintel

Jamb

Trumeau

MUSICAL TERMS

CANON. A term describing a kind of imitation in polyphonic music. In informal usage, canon or canonic imitation refers to the most common situation, the exact duplication of a leading voice by a follower at a given time interval, e.g., a round like *Frère Jacques*. In more formal usage, canon is a rule whereby one or more unnotated following voices are derived from a notated voice, e.g., *Fuga in diapente* (derived voice proceeds at the interval of a fifth below the given voice); or in the 15th century often in playful terms, e.g., *Vous jeunerez les quatre temps* (derived voice rests four breve measures before following); or *Cancer eat plenus sed redeat medius* (derived voice performs the given voice in retrograde motion, then returns from the end back to the beginning in halved rhythmic values).

COUNTERPOINT. Polyphony; the term derives from *punctus contra punctum*, note against note, by extension melody against melody.

IMITATION. "Imitation" or "melodic imitation" is a technique of polyphonic music involving successive, overlapping statements of a melodic contour by two or more voices.

LIGATURE. A symbol of musical notation encompassing several notes, all sung to the same syllable. The interpretation of rhythmic values in the rhythmic modes depends on certain regularly recurring patterns of ligatures.

MELISMA. In music, a style of text setting that involves singing several pitches to a single syllable. Melismatic text setting is the opposite of syllabic text setting.

MODE. In medieval music theory, "mode" refers according to context either to the church modes or to the rhythmic modes. The medieval church modes can be epitomized as a series of eight scales, two for each of the four final pitches D, E, F, and G, one (authentic) extending above the final, the other (plagal) centered on the final. Some medieval theorists discuss modes in terms of species of the fourth, fifth, or octave, i.e., the particular pattern of tones and semitones that fill those intervals.

MONOCHORD. A simple musical instrument for the examination of musical intervals and tuning, constructed of a single string stretched between two points with a movable bridge.

MONODY. Monophonic vocal music, either plainchant or secular monophony.

MONOPHONY. Music composed of a single line or melody; monophonic music.

PLAINCHANT; PLAINSONG. The monophonic melodies of the church; Gregorian chant.

POLYPHONY. Music composed of several simultaneously sounding lines; polyphonic music.

PROPORTION. A property of musical rhythm exploiting fractional relationships of durations within a voice or between voices. Proportional rhythmic relationships are particularly important in 15th-century music.

SOLFÈGE; SOLMIZATION. A teaching tool attributed to Guido d'Arezzo (early 11th c.). Overlapping scales of six notes, which were named after the initial syllables of the first six lines of the hymn *Ut queant laxis / Resonare fibris* (Ut, Re, Mi, Fa, Sol, La), helped beginners learn to sing. The note names of this system were used in the West throughout the Middle Ages and beyond.

TETRACHORD. In medieval music theory, a scale segment of four notes. The three possible patterns of tones and semitones within a tetrachord (T-S-T; S-T-T; T-T-S) were significant in some descriptions of the church modes.

ACKNOWLEDGMENTS

Full listing and credits for illustrations of manuscripts and art objects. All architectural photographs and plans are fully described, with credits, in individual captions.

p. 5. *The beginning of the section of chansons by Adam de la Halle* in the *Chansonnier d'Arras*. Arras, Bibliothèque Municipale, MS 139 (anc. 657).

p. 28. *A late 15th-century ball (Burgundy, ca. 1469–70) with an alta capella consisting of two shawms and slide trumpet.* Paris, Bibliothèque de l'Arsenal, MS fr. 5073, fol. 117v.

p. 95. *A 14th-century banquet.* Guillaume de Machaut, *Remede de Fortune.* Paris, Bibliothèque Nationale MS fr. 1586, fol. 55r.

p. 114. *The troubadour Bernart de Ventadorn as depicted in a manuscript of his poetry.* Paris, Bibliothèque Nationale MS fr. 854, fol. 26v.

p. 158. *Busnoys's rondeau* Bel Acueil *("Fair Welcome").* The *Mellon Chansonnier.* Yale MS 91, fols. 1v-2. Beinecke Library for Rare Books and Manuscripts, Yale University, New Haven, Connecticut.

p. 173. *Crucifixion.* Upper cover of the binding of the *Lindau Gospels* (French, ca. 870) Gold and jewels, 13³/₄ in. by 10¹/₁₂ in. The Pierpont Morgan Library, New York. M.1, fc.

p. 173. *A Seraph superimposed on the text of the* Sanctus. *Drogo Sacramentary* (French, mid-9th century). Paris, Bibliothèque Nationale MS lat. 9428, fol. 15r.

p. 259. *Illustration of Dufay and Binchois.* In Martin Le Franc, *Champion des dames* (1451). Paris, Bibliothèque Nationale, MS fr. 12476, fol. 98r.

p. 272. *The Battle of Crécy.* Jean Froissart, *Chroniques.* Paris, Bibliothèque Nationale MS fr. 2643, fol. 165r.

p. 287. *Clerics dancing.* Florence, Biblioteca Mediceo-Laurenziana MS Pluteo 29, I, fol. 463r.

p. 318. *Chasse.* Champlevé enamel and copper gilt on wood, 7³/₈ in. high, 17³/₄ in. long. The Metropolitan Museum of Art. Gift of S. Pierpont Morgan, 1917, 17.190.511.

p. 318. *Plaque showing the Pentecost* (Mosan, 1150–75). Champlevé enamel on copper gilt, 11.4 by 11.4 cm. The Cloisters Collection, The Metropolitan Museum of Art, New York, 1965, 65.105.

p. 318. *Cross.* Champlevé enamel and gilding on copper, ca. 1190, 67 by 41.9 cm. Master of the Royal Plantagenet Workshop, France. © The Cleveland Museum of Art, 1994, Gift from J.H. Wade, 23.1051.

p. 319. *Three Worthies in the Fiery Furnace* (Mosan, ca. 1145). Champlevé enamel, 8¹/₈ in. high. Museum of Fine Arts, Boston. The William Francis Warden Fund.

p. 363. Jean Fouquet, *The Right Hand of God Protecting the Faithful,* from the *Hours of Étienne Chevalier* (French, ca. 1452–1460). Tempera and gold leaf on parchment, 5³/₄ by 5³/₄ in. Robert Lehman Collection, The Metropolitan Museum of Art, New York, 1975

p. 397. *Glossa ordinaria* for Daniel 1.1–4 (Paris, mid-13th century). Paris, Bibliothèque Nationale MS lat. 155, fol. 138r.

p. 407. *The Annunciation. Book of Hours* (French, ca. 1230s). The Pierpont Morgan Library, New York. M.92, f. 1v.

p. 408. *The Annunciation,* folio 110r from the *Gotha Missal.* Ink, tempera, and gold on parchment, ca. 1370–75, 10¹¹/₁₆ by 1¹¹/₁₆ in. Jean Bondol, French, late 14th century. © The Cleveland Museum of Art, 1994, Mr. and Mrs. William H. Marlett Fund, 62.287.

p. 480. *Crozier* (French, 12th century). Ivory, 5 in. high. The Bargello, Florence. (Alinari/Art Resource)

p. 480. *Crucifixion.* Crozier (French, 14th century). Ivory, 5³/₁₆ in. high. The Walters Art Gallery, Baltimore.

p. 549. *The Annunciation,* from *Les Belles Heures de Jean, Duc de Berry,* fol. 30r, Pol, Jean, and Herman de Limbourg (French, Paris, ca. 1400–1416). Tempera and gold leaf on parchment, 9³/₈ by 6³/₈ in. The Cloisters Collection, The Metropolitan Museum of Art, New York, 1954.

p. 574. *Guillaume de Machaut composing a lyric.* Guillaume de Machaut, *Remede de Fortune.* Paris, Bibliothèque Nationale MS fr. 1586, 26r.

p. 600. *A celebration of Mass in late 15th-century Paris.* London, B.L. Add. 18192, fol. 110r.

p. 617. *Portrait of Jean Miélot in his study.* Paris, Bibliothèque Nationale MS fr. 9198, fol. 19r.

p. 618. *Bronze openwork disk* (Northern France, 500–600 A.D.). The Metropolitan Museum of Art, New York. Gift of J.P. Morgan, 1917.

p. 618. *Pinned bronze buckle and plaque* (Paris basin, 525–600 A.D.). The Metropolitan Museum of Art, New York. Gift of J.P. Morgan, 1917.

p. 618. *Gold disk fibula* (Niederbreisig, first half 7th century). The Metropolitan Museum of Art, New York. Gift of J.P. Morgan, 1917.

p. 643. Musica *points to the three Boethian levels of Music:* Musica mundana, Musica humana, *and* Musica instrumentalis. Florence, Biblioteca Mediceo-Laurenziana MS Pluteo 29, I, facing fol. 1.

p. 651. *A* joglaresse *dancing and playing bells* (early 12th century). Paris, Bibliothèque Nationale MS lat. 1118.

p. 691. *Luxeuil Miniscule.* St. Augustine, *Sermons* (Luxeuil, second half of 7th century). Beinecke Library, Yale University MS 481, no. 2 (verso).

p. 682. *Carolingian Miniscule. Capitularies of Charlemagne, Louis the Pious, and Charles the Bald* (northeastern France, ca. 873). Beinecke Library, Yale University MS 413, fol. 55r.

p. 682. *Late Caroline Miniscule. Bible* (Aquitaine or Limousin, early 12th century). Beinecke Library, Yale University MS 414, fol. 1r.

p. 682. *Latin translation of Aristotle for the university student in Paris* (Paris, third quarter 13th century). Yale Medical Historical MS 12, fol. 261r. The Beinecke Library, Yale University.

p. 683. *Pecia manuscript of St. Thomas Aquinas with scribe's note.* Aquinas, *Commentary on the Sententiae of Peter Lombard* (Paris, ca. 1270). Beinecke Library, Yale University MS 207, fol. 46r.

p. 694. *Arthurian romances in Gothic script (Vulgate version)* (France, late 13th century). Beinecke Library, Yale University MS 229, fol. 272v.

p. 694. *French translation of Augustine's* De civitate Dei *(The City of God)* (Paris, ca. 1415). Beinecke Library, Yale University MS 215, fol. 145r.

p. 695. Caesar's *Commentaries*, French translation by Jean de Chesne (Bruges, 1476). Beinecke Library, Yale University MS 226, fol. 67.

p. 769. Jean Pucelle, *The Annunciation*, from the *Hours of Jeanne d'Évreux,* fol. 16r (French, 1325–1328). Tempera and gold leaf on parchment, 3⁵/₈ in. by 2³/₈ in. The Cloisters Collection, The Metropolitan Museum of Art, New York, 1954.

p. 790. *Casket-type reliquary. Martyrdom and Burial of Thomas Becket* (Limoges, early 13th century). Cloissoné enamel, 18.4 cm. high by 8.3 cm. deep by 21.2 cm. long. Allen Memorial Art Museum, Oberlin College, Oberlin, Ohio. Gift of Baroness René de Kerchove, 1952.

p. 790. *Reliquary of Sainte Foy* (Conques, 10th century with later additions). Gold and precious stones, 2 ft. 9 in. high. (Alinari/Art Resource).

p. 791. *Stavelot Triptych.* True Cross reliquary (Mosan, 12th century). The Pierpont Morgan Library, New York.

p. 791. *Arm reliquary* (Mosan, ca. 1230). Sleeve: silver over oak; hand: bronze gilt; appliqué plaques: silver gilt, niello; gems; 24¹/₂ in.

high. The Cloisters Collection, The Metropolitan Museum of Art, New York, 1947.

p. 791. *Reliquary shrine of the Virgin and Child*, commissioned by Queen Elizabeth of Hungary (Paris, mid-14th century). Silver-gilt and translucent enamel, 10 in. high. The Cloisters Collection, The Metropolitan Museum of Art, New York, 1952.

p. 792. *Reliquary of St. Stephen* (Mosan, ca. 1220) Silver-gilt, 17 in. high. The Cloisters Collection, The Metropolitan Museum of Art, New York, 1955.

p. 817. *Pentecost*, from *Lectionary from Cluny* (late 11th century). Paris, Bibliothèque Nationale MS nouv. acq. lat. 2246, fol. 79v.

p. 817. *Saint Augustine. Stories in the form of Psalms* (Abbey of Marchiennes, mid-12th century). Douai, Bibliothèque Municipale MS 250, vol. 1, fol. 2r.

p. 818. *Christ in Majesty. Sacramentary of Saint-Étienne at Limoges* (French, ca. 1100). Paris, Bibliothèque Nationale MS lat. 9438, fol. 58v.

p. 818. *Annunciation. Sacramentary* (Mont-Saint-Michel, late-11th century). 2³/₄ in. by 3¹/₄ in. The Pierpont Morgan Library, New York. M.641, f. 24.

p. 819. *Crucifixion. Sacramentary* for use at Reims (Arras or Marchiennes, ca. 1150). 7¹/₈ in. by 4⁵/₈ in. Baltimore, The Walters Art Gallery MS 28, fol. 6v.

p. 879. *Ships being loaded for transport* (French, 14th century). Paris, Bibliothèque Nationale MS fr. 4274, fol. 6r.

p. 891. *Death of Saint Vincent.* Paris, Saint-Germain-des-Prés. Detail of stained glass window. The Walters Art Gallery, Baltimore.

p. 897. *Eagle Vase of the Abbot Suger of Saint Denis* (France, ca. 1140). Bronze and Porphyry. Paris, Louvre. (Giraudon/Art Resource)

p. 897. *Chalice of the Abbot Suger of Saint-Denis*, Widener Collection, © 1994 Board of Trustees, National Gallery of Art, Washington, 2nd/1st century B.C. (cup); 1137–1140 (mounting), sardonyx cup with heavily gilded silver mounting, adorned with filigrees set with stones, pearls, glass insets, and opaque white glass pearls; height: 7¹/₄ in.; diameter at top: 4⁷/₈ in.; diameter at base: 4⁷/₈ in.

p. 901. Nicolas Bataille. *King Arthur* from *The Nine Heroes Tapestries* (French, end of 14th century). Tapestry, 14 ft. by 9 ft. 9 in. The Cloisters Collection, The Metropolitan Museum of Art, New York. The Munsey Fund, 1932, and gift of John D. Rockefeller, 1947.

p. 901. *The Unicorn brought to the castle* from *The Hunt of the Unicorn* (French, late 15th century). Tapestry, 12 ft. by 12 ft. 9 in. The Cloisters Collection, The Metropolitan Museum of Art. Gift of John D. Rockefeller, Jr., 1937.

p. 904. *Women carding, spinning, and weaving wool* (French, 14th century). Paris, Bibliothèque Nationale MS fr. 12420, fol. 71r.

p. 988. *English wool arrived regularly by ship to supply the textile industry of northern France.* Paris, Bibliothèque Nationale MS fr. 2810, fol. 86v.

CONTRIBUTORS

Penelope Adair
University of California,
Santa Barbara

†James W. Alexander
University of Georgia

Peter L. Allen
Pomona College

J. Michael Allsen
University of Wisconsin, Madison

Heather M. Arden
University of Cincinnati

Rosemary Argent
Greenwich, Connecticut

Lawrin D. Armstrong
Simon Fraser University

Robert S. Babcock
Hastings College

Ellen L. Babinsky
Austin Presbyterian Theological
Seminary

Clifford R. Backman
Boston University

Robert L. Baker
Kenyon College

Carl F. Barnes, Jr.
Oakland College

Paul Barrette
University of Tennessee

Keith Bate
University of Reading

Emmanuèle Baumgartner
Paris III, La Sorbonne Nouvelle

Brigitte Bedos-Rezak
University of Maryland,
College Park

George T. Beech
Western Michigan University

Robert A. Bennett
University of Rochester

Rosalind K. Berlow
New York City

Constance H. Berman
University of Iowa

Bradford B. Blaine
Scripps College

Renate Blumenfeld-Kosinski
University of Pittsburgh

Monte L. Bohna
University of Rochester

Stacy L. Boldrick
University of Pittsburgh

Gerald A. Bond
University of Rochester

H. Lawrence Bond
Appalachian State University

Daniel E. Bornstein
Texas A & M University

Constance B. Bouchard
University of Akron

D'A. Jonathan D. Boulton
University of Notre Dame

Maureen B.M. Boulton
University of Notre Dame

Calvin M. Bower
University of Notre Dame

Marjorie N. Boyer
Ann Arbor, Michigan

Susan Boynton
Brandeis University

Nancy Bradley-Cromey
University of Richmond

Annette Brasseur
Université Charles de Gaulle, Lille

Elizabeth A.R. Brown
Brooklyn College,
City University of New York

Matilda T. Bruckner
Boston College

Caroline A. Bruzelius
American Academy in Rome

Lawrence M. Bryant
California State University, Chico

J. Michael Burger
Mississippi University for Women

Glyn S. Burgess
University of Liverpool

E. Jane Burns
University of North Carolina,
Chapel Hill

Paul B. Burrell
University of Cincinnati

Keith Busby
University of Oklahoma

Ardis T.B. Butterfield
Trinity College, Cambridge

William C. Calin
University of Florida

Robert G. Calkins
Cornell University

John B. Cameron
Oakland University

Frank Catania
Loyola University, Chicago

Celia Chazelle
Trenton State College

Frederic L. Cheyette
Amherst College

William W. Clark
Queens College,
City University of New York

Robert Francis Cook
University of Virginia

Rita Copeland
University of Minnesota

Raymond J. Cormier
Wilson College

Didier J. Course
University of Pittsburgh

Eugene L. Cox
Wellesley College

Larry S. Crist
Vanderbilt University

Michael T. Davis
Mount Holyoke College

Luke Demaitre
Lehman College,
City University of New York

Peter F. Dembowski
University of Chicago

Kelly DeVries
Loyola College, Baltimore

Leslie Blake DiNella
University of Pittsburgh

Eglal Doss-Quinby
Smith College

Jean Dufournet
Paris III La Sorbonne Nouvelle

André Duplat
Vesoul, France

Joseph H. Dyer
University of Massachusetts,
Boston

Lawrence Earp
University of Wisconsin, Madison

Marc M. Epstein
Vassar College

Theodore Evergates
Western Maryland College

David Fallows
University of Manchester

Richard C. Famiglietti
Providence, Rhode Island

Steven Fanning
University of Illinois, Chicago

Margot Fassler
Yale Institute of Sacred Music,
Worship and the Arts

Thelma S. Fenster
Fordham University

Donald F. Fleming
University of California,
Santa Barbara

Claude J. Fouillade
New Mexico State University

Paul H. Freedman
Vanderbilt University

Jean M. French
Bard College

Alan Friedlander
Southern Connecticut State
University

Benjamin Garber
Rice University

Richard A. Gerberding
University of Alabama, Huntsville

Paula L. Gerson
International Center of Medieval Art

†Margaret T. Gibson
Manchester University, Emerita

Edmund J. Goehring
University of Georgia

Karen Gould
Austin, Texas

†John L. Grigsby
Washington University, St. Louis

Theresa Gross-Diaz
Loyola University, Chicago

Bernard Guidot
Université de Strasbourg II

Bert S. Hall
University of Toronto

Barbara Hanawalt
University of Minnesota

E. Kay Harris
University of Southern Mississippi

Thomas Head
Washington University, St. Louis

John Bell Henneman, Jr.
Princeton University

Constance B. Hieatt
University of Western Ontario

Richard C. Hoffmann
York University

David F. Hult
University of Virginia

Lois Huneycutt
California State University, Hayward

Sylvia Huot
Northern Illinois University

Thomas M. Izbicki
Johns Hopkins University

Richard A. Jackson
University of Houston

Peter Jeffrey
Princeton University

Scott Jessee
Appalachian State University

Catherine M. Jones
University of Georgia

Michael C.E. Jones
University of Nottingham

William Chester Jordan
Princeton University

Richard W. Kaeuper
University of Rochester

Ernest A. Kaulbach
University of Texas, Austin

Hans-Erich Keller
Ohio State University

F. Douglas Kelly
University of Wisconsin, Madison

William W. Kibler
University of Texas, Austin

Richard Kieckhefer
Northwestern University

Alan E. Knight
Pennsylvania State University

Jelle Koopmans
University of Amsterdam

Maryanne Kowaleski
Fordham University

Jeanne E. Krochalis
*Pennsylvania State University,
New Kensington*

Roberta L. Krueger
Hamilton College

Steven F. Kruger
City University of New York

Norris J. Lacy
Washington University, St. Louis

Richard Landes
Boston University

Michelle I. Lapine
University of Texas, Austin

William MacBain
*University of Maryland,
College Park*

Stephen C. Martin
University of Pittsburgh

E. Ann Matter
University of Pennsylvania

R. Thomas McDonald
Fairleigh Dickinson University

Timothy J. McGee
University of Toronto

James McKinnon
*University of North Carolina,
Chapel Hill*

María Rosa Menocal
Yale University

Emanuel J. Mickel
Indiana University

Stephen Morillo
Wabash College

Thomas C. Moser, Jr.
*University of Maryland,
College Park*

Lynette R. Muir
University of Leeds

John H. Munro
University of Toronto

Lawrence Nees
University of Delaware

Deborah H. Nelson
Rice University

David M. Nicholas
Clemson University

Leah L. Otis-Cour
Castries, France

Willemien Otten
Boston College

William D. Paden
Northwestern University

Franklin J. Pegues
Ohio State University

William A. Percy, Jr.
University of Massachusetts, Boston

Edward Peters
University of Pennsylvania

Wendy E. Pfeffer
University of Louisville

Jean-Louis Picherit
University of Wyoming

Rupert T. Pickens
University of Kentucky

Martin Picker
Rutgers University

Sandra Pinegar
Ohio State University

Steven E. Plank
*Oberlin College Conservatory
of Music*

Elizabeth W. Poe
Tulane University

Cassandra Potts
Middlebury College

Burcht Pranger
University of Amsterdam

Charles Radding
Michigan State University

Nancy F. Regalado
New York University

Kathryn L. Reyerson
University of Minnesota

Earl Jeffrey Richards
*University of North Carolina,
Chapel Hill*

Samuel N. Rosenberg
Indiana University

Roy S. Rosenstein
American College in Paris

Barbara H. Rosenwein
Loyola University, Chicago

Linda M. Rouillard
University of Pittsburgh

Nina Rowe
Northwestern University

Graham A. Runnalls
University of Edinburgh

Hans R. Runte
Dalhousie University

Timothy J. Runyan
Cleveland State University

Jan Ryder
*University of California,
Santa Barbara*

Barbara N. Sargent-Baur
University of Pittsburgh

Francesca Canadé Sautman
*Hunter College,
City University of New York*

Terence Scully
Wilfrid Laurier University

Barbara A. Shailor
Bucknell University

M.B. Shepard
The Metropolitan Museum of Art

Meg Shepherd
University of Leeds

John C. Shidelar
Hood River, Oregon

Leah Shopkow
Indiana University

Michael A. Signer
University of Notre Dame

Julia M.H. Smith
Trinity College

Lesley J. Smith
Linacre College, Oxford University

Nathaniel B. Smith
Franklin & Marshall College

Paul D. Solon
Macalester College

Mary B. Speer
Rutgers University

Whitney S. Stoddard
Williams College

François Suard
Paris IX, Nanterre

Pedro J. Suarez
Boston, Massachusetts

Kristen E. Sukalec
University of Pittsburgh

Robert Sweetman
Institute for Christian Studies, Toronto

Emily Z. Tabuteau
Michigan State University

Heather J. Tanner
University of California, Santa Barbara

William H. TeBrake
University of Maine

Joseph M. Tyrrell
Norfolk, Virginia

Wolfgang G. van Emden
University of Reading

Amelia E. Van Vleck
University of Texas, Austin

Arjo Vanderjagt
University of Groningen

Thomas G. Waldman
University of Pennsylvania

David J. Wallace
University of Minnesota

Lori Walters
Florida State University

Stephen Weinberger
Dickinson College

Ulrike Wiethaus
Wake Forest University

Charity Cannon Willard
Cornwall-on-Hudson, New York

Joan B. Williamson
Long Island University

James I. Wimsatt
University of Texas, Austin

Lenora D. Wolfgang
Lehigh University

Donald L. Wright, Jr.
University of Pittsburgh

Charles R. Young
Duke University

Tony Zbaraschuk
University of Notre Dame

Mark Zier
University of the Pacific

Michel Zink
Collège de France

Grover A. Zinn
Oberlin College

Janice C. Zinser
Oberlin College

Ronald Edward Zupko
Marquette University

A

ABBEVILLE. The town of Abbeville (Somme) was an important center on the Somme River that became the seat of the county of Ponthieu. In 1184, the count recognized a commune that the townspeople had organized some years earlier. The heiress to the county married Ferdinand III of Castile in 1257, and Ponthieu became the dowry of their daughter Eleanor when she married Edward I of England. Abbeville passed back and forth between France and England during the Hundred Years' War and was one of the strategic towns along the Somme that were given to the duke of Burgundy in 1435 subject to repurchase by the king of France. Louis XI exercised this option in 1463, but the town was regained by Burgundy for a few more years before the French king acquired it permanently.

In 1257, Abbeville was the site of negotiations that culminated in an Anglo-French treaty by which Henry III and Louis IX renounced their claims to territories held by the other.

The sole remaining medieval monument in Abbeville is the large church, formerly a collegial, of Saint-Vulfran, whose most notable feature is its Flamboyant façade. The building, which was badly damaged in 1940, was constructed in two periods: the nave and transept from 1488 to 1539; the chevet from 1661 to 1691. In contrast to the lavishly decorated façade with its full complement of sculptures, the post–World War II restorations robbed the interior of any interest.

John Bell Henneman, Jr./William W. Clark

Durand, Georges. "Abbeville, Collégiale Saint-Vulfran." *Congrès archéologique* (Amiens) 99 (1939): 54–95.

Abbeville (Somme), Saint-Vulfran, nave and north aisle. *Photograph: Clarence Ward Collection. Courtesy of Oberlin College.*

ABBO OF FLEURY (ca. 945–1004). Born near Orléans, Abbo entered the Benedictine monastery of Fleury-sur-Loire as a child oblate. After study in Paris and Rome, he returned to Fleury to teach and write. Abbo spent two years in England at Ramsay abbey and was there ordained priest by Archbishop Oswald of York, who had been a monk at Fleury. Upon returning to France, he was elected abbot of Fleury in 988. Abbo died from a wound received in a quarrel over monastic reform while visiting the abbey of La Réole, a dependency of Fleury.

Abbo's writings include scientific treatises (on astronomy, arithmetic, and the *computus*), the *Canones Abbonis* (a collection of conciliar canons and other materials), a work on grammar, the *Vita sancti Edmundi* (written while in England), a brief and incomplete work on lives of the popes, and an *Apologia* concerning a quarrel with Arnoul, bishop of Orléans. Some seventeen letters by Abbo survive. He traveled twice to Rome on behalf of King

Robert II, and he was known as an advocate of ecclesiastical and monastic reform.

Grover A. Zinn

[**See also:** AIMOIN DE FLEURY; HISTORIOGRAPHY]

Abbo of Fleury. *Opera. PL* 139.417–578.
Van de Vyver, A. "Les œuvres inédites d'Abbon de Fleury." *Revue bénédictine* (1935): 125–69.

ABÉLARD, PETER (1079–1142). Much of the life of Abélard, one of the most renowned 12th-century thinkers, is known from his *Historia calamitatum*, written ca. 1133. Born into a minor noble family in Le Pallet, Brittany, in 1079, Abélard embarked on a career as student, then master, in various French schools. He studied with leading masters at three cathedral schools: Roscelin (Loches), William of Champeaux (Paris), and Anselm of Laon (Laon). He himself taught at Paris (Mont-Sainte-Geneviève, Saint-Denis [while a monk there], and the cathedral school at Notre-Dame), Melun, Corbeil, Laon, and the Paraclete (near Troyes). An intellectual combatant, at Paris he challenged Willliam of Champeaux on the existence of universals and at Laon criticized Anselm as lacking theological insight and dialectical skills. Abélard himself was harshly criticized and rebuked. In 1121, a council at Soissons found him guilty of heresy concerning the Trinity and required him to burn his treatise *On the Trinity and Unity of God* (or *Theologia "Summi Boni"*). In the late 1130s, William of Saint-Thierry, deeply troubled by Abélard's *Theologia christiana,* wrote to Bernard of Clairvaux, who had Abélard summoned to a council at Sens in June 1140, where he was charged with heresy. The council condemned nineteen points in Abélard's theology; the pope soon thereafter also condemned Abélard. Following the condemnation at Sens, the Cluniac abbot Peter the Venerable offered Abélard a refuge at Cluny. According to Peter, Bernard and Abélard were reconciled before Abélard died in April 1142 at Saint-Marcel, a Cluniac priory near Chalons-sur-Saône.

While teaching in the schools of Paris, Abélard became involved in a passionate love affair with Héloïse, possibly the niece and certainly the ward of Fulbert, canon of the cathedral of Notre-Dame in Paris. Fulbert engaged Abélard to tutor the brilliant Héloïse, but the two were soon making love, not studying philosophy. Héloïse became pregnant; Fulbert, unsatisfied by the secret marriage of Abélard and Héloïse, had Abélard castrated. Abélard and Héloïse entered the monastic life in 1119, she at the convent of Argenteuil, near Paris, he at the monastery of Saint-Denis, also near Paris. At Saint-Denis, Abélard began teaching again, at the request of students. He earned the monks' enmity by suggesting that the St. Denis to whom their abbey was dedicated was not the same as the mystical author Pseudo-Dionysius the Areopagite, an identification generally accepted in the 12th century.

Abélard's *Historia calamitatum* chronicles the love affair and its aftermath, particularly Abélard's career. A subsequent series of letters exchanged between Abélard and Héloïse reveals her deep attachment to him, his grow-ing concern for her and her sister nuns, and his efforts to provide them with sermons, hymns, and a monastic rule. The authenticity of the correspondence has been challenged in recent years, but the consensus is that the letters represent a genuine exchange between Abélard and Héloïse.

Abélard finally left Saint-Denis and built a hermitage dedicated to the Paraclete at a remote spot near Troyes, where he taught students who sought him out. He later gave the land and buildings to Héloïse and her sister nuns for a convent after they were ejected from Argenteuil by Suger of Saint-Denis. In 1126, Abélard became abbot of Saint-Gildas de Rhuys in Brittany; after an abortive attempt to reform this lax monastic establishment, he fled, probably to Paris and the schools.

An accomplished master of dialectic (logic), Abélard pushed vigorously for questioning in the field of theology, with the goal of arriving at truth through a rigorous examination of conflicting opinions drawn from Scripture and authoritative writings (Augustine, Gregory the Great and other popes, church councils). This approach received classic expression in *Sic et non.* Here, Abélard posed 158 theological questions, gathered statements from the tradition favoring each side of the question, but offered no solution (*sententia*) of the differences in position.

In ethics, Abélard taught a doctrine of intentionality and disinterested love. In *Scito te ipsum,* Abélard argues that the actual deed is morally indifferent; the key to ethical behavior is the intention with which the deed is carried out.

Concerning the doctrine of Christ's atonement, Abélard set forth in his commentary on the Epistle to the Romans a distinctive teaching, often called a "subjective" theory. Abélard argued that the effect of Christ's death was not an "objective" change in the relation of God and humanity (in light of human sin) as presented in Anselm of Bec's *Cur Deus homo.* Rather, Christ's death reveals self-sacrifice and absolute self-giving love, which evokes in the believer a response of total sacrifice and love and effects not a cosmic transaction involving divine justice but a personal and individual transformation of love and intention.

Among Abélard's other writings are an unfinished *Dialogus inter Philosophum, Judaeum, et Christianum,* the *Confessio fidei universalis,* letters, poems, forty-three sermons for use at the Paraclete, an *Apologia,* and *Hexaemeron* (a commentary on the six days of creation in Genesis). Abélard left disciples but no established school. Though he influenced the development of the scholastic method, especially the *quaestio,* in general his contributions to theology were topical and not systematic.

Abélard's poetry reveals exceptional emotional power in lyrics on biblical and religious themes, such as the lament (*planctus*) of David on the death of Jonathan, which he invests with a notable sensibility of personal pain and loss. He wrote other laments, liturgical poems, and a collection of hymns for Héloïse and the nuns at the Paraclete. In a letter, Héloïse remarks that Abélard wrote popular love poems that were the talk of Paris when he and Héloïse were lovers; none survives.

Peter the Venerable transferred Abélard's body to the Paraclete, where it was buried in the church. When Héloïse died in 1163/64, she was buried beside him. Their remains were taken to Paris when the Paraclete was destroyed after the Revolution, and they now rest in a tomb in the cemetery of Père-Lachaise.

Grover A. Zinn

[See also: ANSELM OF BEC; ANSELM OF LAON; ARGENTEUIL; BERNARD OF CLAIRVAUX; HÉLOÏSE; HERESY; PETER THE VENERABLE; PHILOSOPHY; ROBERT OF MELUN; SAINT-DENIS; SCHOLASTICISM; SCHOOLS, CATHEDRAL; SUGER; THEOLOGY; UNIVERSITIES; WILLIAM OF CHAMPEAUX; WILLLIAM OF SAINT-THIERRY]

Abélard, Peter. *Opera omnia*. PL 178.
————. *Petri Abelardi opera*, ed. Victor Cousin. 2 vols. Paris: Durand, 1849–59.
————. *Opera theologica*, ed. Eloi M. Buytaert. 3 vols. CCCM, 11, 12, 13. Turnhout: Brepols, 1969.
————. *Sic et non: A Critical Edition*, ed. Blanche B. Boyer and Richard P. McKeon. Chicago: University of Chicago Press, 1976–77.
————. *Philosophische Schriften*, ed. Bernhard Geyer. 1 vol. in 4 parts. Münster: Aschendorff, 1919–33.
————. *Ethics*, ed. and trans. David E. Luscombe. Oxford: Clarendon, 1971.
————. *Historia calamitatum: texte critique avec introduction*, ed. Jacques Monfrin. 2nd ed. Paris: Vrin, 1962.
————. *The Story of Abelard's Adversities*, trans. Joseph T. Muckle. Toronto: Pontifical Institute of Mediaeval Studies, 1964.
————. *A Dialogue of a Philosopher with a Jew and a Christian*, trans. Pierre J. Payer. Toronto: Pontifical Institute of Mediaeval Studies, 1979.
————. *The Hymns of Abelard in English Verse*, trans. Sister Joseph Patricia. Lanham: University Press of America, 1986.
————. *Dialogus inter Philosophum, Judaeum et Christianum*, ed. Rudolf Thomas. Stuttgart: Fromann, 1970.
Radice, Betty, trans. *The Letters of Abelard and Heloise*. Harmondsworth: Penguin, 1974.
Luscombe, David E. *The School of Peter Abelard: The Influence of Abelard's Thought in the Early Scholastic Period*. Cambridge: Cambridge University Press, 1969.
Weingart, Richard E. *The Logic of Divine Love: A Critical Analysis of the Soteriology of Peter Abailard*. Oxford: Clarendon, 1970.

ABRÈGEMENT DU FIEF. Because of the services and potentially lucrative feudal incidents owed by the holder of a fief, a fief could be abridged in value if it came into the hands of a holder who could not render military service (such as a nonnoble or a cleric) or a corporate body that never died (generally, an ecclesiastical house). When a nonnoble acquired a fief, the circumstance was known as *franc-fief*, and the lord was entitled to a payment, of the same name, to compensate for the abridgment of the fief's value.

When a fief passed from an individual to a corporate body, it was said to change from a state of *main vive* to a state of *main morte*, and this change of status was called *amortissement*. The term *amortissement* also described both the permission required for such a transaction and the payment that the lord required as compensation for the abridgment.

It was not until the 13th century that lawyers began to articulate these principles, perhaps because alienation of fiefs to nonnobles was rare until that time. The French kings, now claiming recognition as supreme suzerains in the feudal hierarchy, began to issue ordinances regarding alienations of feudal property, the first of these being in 1275. Between 1291 and 1313, Philip IV began to use the concept of *abrègement du fief* as a device for raising money. He had commissioners investigate property transactions throughout the realm and levy fines for *franc-fief* and *amortissement* that amounted to several years' revenues of the property in question. In 1321, Philip V regulated all transactions that had occurred in the past sixty years, ordering the church to pay *amortissement* of six years' revenues of fiefs received as gifts and eight years' revenues of fiefs acquired by purchase. The crown made heavy use of *abrègement du fief* as a fiscal device during the 1320s and continued the practice intermittently thereafter, but as regular taxation developed during the Hundred Years' War the exploitation of this source of revenue lost its significance.

John Bell Henneman, Jr.

[See also: FEUDAL INCIDENTS; FEUDALISM; FIEF/FEUDUM]

Carreau, Marie-Elisabeth. "Les commissaires royaux aux amortissements et aux nouveaux acquets sous les Capétiens (1275–1328)." Positions des thèses. Paris: École Nationale des Chartes, 1953 .
Henneman, John Bell. "Enquêteurs-Réformateurs and Fiscal Officers in Fourteenth-Century France." *Traditio* 24 (1968): 309–49.

ABUZÉ EN COURT. This anonymous poem interspersed with prose, preserved in six manuscripts and five incunabula, has been incorrectly attributed to King René d'Anjou or Charles de Rochefort. Written in the third quarter of the 15th century, it is a condemnation of court life in the tradition of Alain Chartier's *Curial* and *Quadrilogue invectif*. Abuzé encounters allegorical figures (Abuz, Folcuider, Temps, Folle Bobance, etc.) and recounts his experiences at court. The work, in the Grand Rhétoriqueur tradition, makes extensive use of rhetorical figures.

William W. Kibler

[See also: CHARTIER, ALAIN; GRANDS RHÉTORIQUEURS; RENÉ D'ANJOU]

Dubuis, Roger, ed. *L'Abuzé en court*. Geneva: Droz, 1973.

ACART DE HESDIN, JEAN (fl. early 14th c.). The *Prise amoureuse*, an allegorical hunt-of-love poem of 1,915 lines, including nine intercalated ballades and nine rondeaux, composed in 1332, is the only known work of this author, whom a manuscript refers to as "hospitalier," presumably a friar living at the foundation of the countess of Artois in Hesdin.

James I. Wimsatt

Acart de Hesdin, Jean. *La prise amoureuse*, ed. Ernest Hoepffner. Dresden: Niemeyer, 1910.

Hoepffner, Ernest. "Zur 'Prise amoureuse' von Jehan Acart de Hesdin." *Zeitschrift für romanische Philologie* 38 (1917): 513–27.

ACCOUNTING. The topic can be divided into the categories of private and public accounting. French royal accounting received considerable impetus from the reign of Philip II Augustus, at which time the careful registration of income and expenses began. A *Chambre des Comptes* would emerge in the early 14th century. However, France did not have an adequate royal budgetary system until after the end of the *ancien régime*. The most advanced private accounting techniques evolved first in medieval Italy and were later best implemented outside Italy in the Low Countries. This is not to say that France did not witness the development of accounting systems, which attained considerable sophistication at markets like the Champagne fairs.

Accounting procedures existed in the context of large rural estates, where *terriers* or *compoti* might provide data on the seed sown, the acreage cultivated, and the yield realized. In the realm of commerce, there survive some few fragmentary private accounts: those of an unknown draper of Lyon for 1320–23, of the notary and draper Ugo Teralh of Forcalquier for 1330–32, of the merchant and draper Jean Saval of Carcassonne, of the Bonis brothers of Montauban in the mid-14th century, and of the merchant Jacme Olivier of Narbonne at the end of the century.

It is generally accepted that the technique of double-entry bookkeeping emerged in Italy in the 13th century. The categories of credits and debits did not exist side by side in the earliest forms of French accounts. In those of Ugo Teralh, debtors wrote in their own obligations. The brothers Bonis kept various books, several of which have survived: a book, labeled C, for credit offered to debtors; a *livre vermeil* for deposits, which also contained the accounts of estates managed by them; a book D, which in part continued C. Forestié has identified additional books A and B, which do not survive but would have preceded book C. The Bonis lent money at interest in addition to their commercial cloth, spice, and pharmaceutical business. Their accounts of credits and debits were not positioned opposite each other but rather consisted of discrete entries in succession. In contrast to the accounts of the Bonis, the account book of Jacme Olivier provided no general accounting of the credits and debits at the end of the volume. However, Olivier provided not only accounts for particular individuals but also for specific voyages, noting the costs of merchandise and shipping. Though not on a par with Italian financial technology, the pressures of complex commercial operations, the existence of associations of multiple partners bringing capital to an affair, and the increased use of delegated authority for administration of property encouraged the development of sophisticated accounting measures in France by the end of the Middle Ages.

Kathryn L. Reyerson

Blanc, Alphonse. *Le livre de comptes de Jacme Olivier, marchand narbonnais du XIVe siècle*. Paris: Picard, 1899.

de Roover, Raymond. "Aux origines d'une technique intellectuelle: la formation et l'expansion de la comptabilité à partie double." *Annales d'histoire économique et sociale* 9 (1937): 171–93, 270–88.

Forestié, Édouard. *Les livres de comptes des frères Bonis, marchands montalbanais*. 2 vols. Paris: Champion, 1890–94.

ACHARD OF SAINT-VICTOR (d. 1170/71). Born in England, Achard became abbot of Saint-Victor, Paris, in 1155, succeeding the community's first abbot, Gilduin. In 1161, Achard was elected bishop of Avranches, a position he held until his death. Fifteen surviving sermons, edited by Châtillon, are important for their presentation of Achard's christology and his theological anthropology.

Grover A. Zinn

[See also: GILDUIN OF SAINT-VICTOR; SAINT-VICTOR, ABBEY AND SCHOOL OF; THEOLOGY]

Achard of Saint-Victor. *Sermons inédits*, ed. Jean Châtillon. Paris: Vrin, 1970.

———. *L'unité de Dieu et la pluralité des créatures* (*De unitate Dei et pluralitate creaturarum*), ed. and trans. Emmanuel Martineau. Saint-Lambert des Bois: Franc-Dire, 1987.

Châtillon, Jean. *Théologie, spiritualité et métaphysique dans l'œuvre oratoire d'Achard de Saint-Victor: études d'histoire doctrinale précédées d'un essai sur la vie et l'œuvre d'Achard*. Paris: Vrin, 1969.

ACROSTIC. Verbal play in which initial or individual letters, taken in order, form a word or phrase—called an acrostic—appears in French texts from about the middle of the 13th century, and the practice continues throughout the medieval period. The acrostic is often a device for naming either poet or patron, as in *Cleomadés*, the *Roman de la Poire*, the *Roman du castelain de Coucy*, and Villon's *Testament*. Stanzaic prayers and hymns to the Virgin are sometimes built on alphabetical acrostics or on the letters in the name "Maria." The acrostic device suggests a growing literacy among the audience for vernacular poetry and an interest in the visual qualities of the written text, especially in cases where the acrostic is highlighted through the use of ornamental initials.

Sylvia Huot

[See also: ANAGRAM; GRANDS RHÉTORIQUEURS; VILLON, FRANÇOIS]

ADALBERO OF LAON (ca. 955–1031). Nephew of Archbishop Adalbero of Reims, Adalbero became bishop of Laon (r. 977–1031), where he was intimately involved in the royal affairs of kings Lothair I, Louis V, Hugh Capet, and Robert II. Adalbero is perhaps most famous for his betrayal of the last Carolingian pretender, Charles of Lorraine, whom he turned over to Hugh Capet (Eastertide, 991); the treason—he had sworn on broken bread and wine to be faithful—recalled that of Judas and gained him the epithet *vetulus traditor* and the nickname Ascelin. His motivations were more pro-Ottonian than pro-Capetian; in 995, he plotted, unsuccessfully, with Otto III and Eudes of Blois, an opponent in the Carolingian struggle, to overthrow the Capetians. Despite his multiple offenses, however, Adalbero survived all the fluctuations in his and the kingdom's fortunes: unlike his more talented contemporary Gerbert of Aurillac, who committed no such treasonous acts, Adalbero was an "insider" in the aristocratic world of northern French episcopal politics. He is the author of a treatise on dialectic, a theological poem, and two satirical poems. His *Carmen ad Rotbertum* contains one of the earliest French articulations of the idea of the "Three Orders" and expresses Adalbero's deeply conservative views and his opposition to the unregal piety of Robert II, who,"ruled over" by Odilo of Cluny, accepted new religious movements like the Peace of God and monastic reform, and raised humble clerics to the ranks of bishop.

Richard Landes

[See also: GERBERT OF AURILLAC; HUGH CAPET; LOTHAIR I; ODILO; ROBERT II THE PIOUS]

Adalbero of Laon. *Poème au roi Robert,* ed. and trans. Claude Carozzi. Paris: Les Belles Lettres, 1979. [Important introduction.]

Coolidge, Robert. "Adalbero, Bishop of Laon." *Studies in Medieval and Renaissance History* 2 (1965): 1–114.

Duby, Georges. *The Three Orders: Feudal Society Imagined,* trans. Arthur Goldhammer. Chicago: University of Chicago Press, 1980.

Heckel, G.A. "Les poèmes satyriques d'Adalbéron." *Bibliothèque de la Faculté des Lettres, Université de Paris* 13 (1901): 49–184.

Oexle, Otto Gerhard. "Die fonktionale Dreiteilung der 'Gesellschaft' bei Adalbero von Laon: Deutungsschemata der sozialen Wirklichkeit im früher Mittelalter." *Frühmittelalterliche Studien* 12 (1978): 1–54.

ADAM DE LA HALLE (ca. 1240–ca. 1285). Dramatist and poet. Also called "Adam le Bossu" or "le Bossu d'Arras" (*bossu* 'awkward' or 'crippled'), Adam de la Halle lived and wrote in Arras during the last third of the 13th century. His modern reputation is based primarily on two plays: a satiric drama, the *Jeu de la feuillée* (1,099 octosyllabic lines), and a work often referred to as a comic opera, the *Jeu de Robin et Marion.* Since *feuillée* has been interpreted to mean the shelter of branches built to house the reliquary of Notre Dame at Pentecost, the *Jeu de la feuillée* is thought to have been composed for performance in the

town of Arras for this festival. This first extant secular drama in French contains little plot, presenting mostly a succession of scenes that tease and ridicule forty-nine named male and female citizens of Arras. The humor of the play depends on exploiting character traits known to the audience, as well as proverbs and puns whose full meaning could be appreciated only by those familiar with the citizenry of Arras. Contemporary documents that contain the names of the characters in the play allow us to date the work to 1276 or 1277. It provides the earliest example on the French stage of the ridicule of the medical profession, which reached its height with Molière. The extant manuscripts preserve some of the music for the songs included in the play.

Closely related to the pastourelle, the *Jeu de Robin et Marion* (780 octosyllabic lines) dramatizes the encounter of a shepherdess and a knight on a spring morning. When his advances are rebuffed, the knight kidnaps the young girl and carries her away on his horse after beating her friend Robin. However, Marion is soon released unharmed, and friends arrive to sing, dance, eat, and play games. Spoken dialogue alternates with singing. When first presented in Arras, the play was preceded by a short dramatic prologue, in which a pilgrim tells of his travels in Italy and says that everywhere he went he heard about a talented, gracious, and noble clerk, native of Arras, loved and hon-

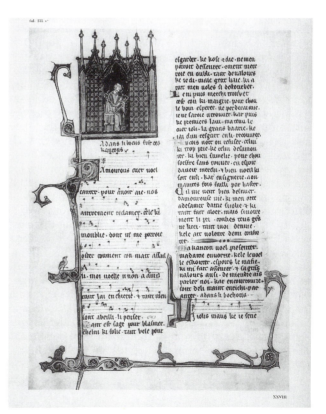

The beginning of the section of chansons by Adam de la Halle in the *Chansonnier d'Arras.* Arras, Bibliothèque Municipale, MS 139 (anc. 657). *Courtesy of Arras, Bibliothèque Municipale.*

ored by the count of Artois because of his poetic and musical talent. The pilgrim states that he visited Adam's tomb the year before and sings two of Adam's songs as examples of his talent.

In addition to the plays, Adam wrote thirty-six chansons, seventeen *jeux-partis*, sixteen rondeaux, five motets, a *congé*, and the first nineteen laisses of an epic poem, the *Roi de Sicile*. Fifteen of the seventeen *jeux-partis* by Adam were composed with Jehan Bretel, who alludes to Adam's superior education, his youth, and his loves. Before 1271, the date of Bretel's death, Adam was already well enough known to write *jeux-partis* with the prince of the Puy. While his chansons written in the tradition of the Provençal love lyric dwell on the suffering endured patiently by a lover whose lady appears indifferent to him, there is no reason to believe that they were based on true feelings.

Although Adam lived and wrote in Picardy for much of his life, the language of his songs reflects relatively few traits of the Picard dialect, whereas the speech of the characters in his plays relies more heavily on dialect and probably resembles the language used in Arras in the 13th century.

In 1276 or 1277, Adam wrote his *Congé* (farewell poem), one of three such poems composed by trouvères (the others are by Jehan Bodel d'Arras and Baude Fastoul). In 156 lines divided into strophes of twelve octosyllabic verses, Adam takes leave for Paris to continue his studies; he expresses his gratitude, good wishes, and regrets to the people of Arras. His departure is by choice and not due to disease, as with the other two *congés*. In *Feuillée*, he also mentions his imminent departure for Paris, though it is not possible to know if he ever actually went.

During his lifetime, Adam's fame stemmed equally from his musical and poetic skills. Many of his melodies and lyrics have been preserved in versions that often resemble each other more closely than is normally the case with trouvère compositions, implying perhaps that they may have been copied from one model even though such a model has not survived. In addition to the typical songs for one voice, Adam also wrote music for five motets for three voices, fourteen rondeaux, and two other refrain songs, suggesting that he probably knew how to read and write music, a rare phenomenon among the trouvères.

Even though he must be considered one of the most versatile poets and composers of his time, no document survives that dates any event in the life of this prolific artist. However, Baude Fastoul, another trouvère of Arras, mentions him in a work dated 1272. Adam died between January 7, 1285, the date of the death of Charles of Anjou, for whom Adam began to compose *Le Roi de Sicile,* and before February 2, 1289, the date on which the copyist Jean Madot, upon finishing a transcription of the *Roman de Troie,* boasts of being the nephew of Adam le Bossu, who had died recently far from Arras.

Deborah H. Nelson

[See also: BAUDE FASTOUL; *CONGÉ*; JEHAN BRETEL; *JEU-PARTI; PASTOURELLE/PASTORELA*]

Adam de la Halle. *Œuvres complètes du trouvère Adam de la Halle: poésies et musique,* ed. Edmond de Coussemaker. Paris: A. Durand et Pedone-Lauriel, 1872.

———. *Le jeu de la feuillée,* ed. Ernest Langlois. Paris: Champion, 1965.

———. *Le jeu de Robin et Marion suivi du Jeu du Pélerin,* ed. Ernest Langlois. Paris: Champion, 1965.

———. *Le jeu de la feuillée* and *Le jeu de Robin et de Marion,* in *Medieval French Plays,* trans. Richard Axton and John Stevens. New York: Barnes and Noble, 1971, pp. 205–302.

———. *The Chansons of Adam de la Halle,* ed. John Henry Marshall. Manchester: Manchester University Press, 1971.

———. *The Lyrics and Melodies of Adam de la Halle,* ed. and trans. Deborah H. Nelson; music ed. Hendrik van der Werf. New York: Garland, 1985.

ADAM DU PETIT-PONT (Adam of Bosham or Adam Balsham; fl. early 12th c.). A shadowy figure, Adam was a dialectician and moral theologian of the speculative school at a time when the most famous names, such as Peter the Chanter and Stephen Langton, were "biblical moral" theologians. Two of his works are preserved for us, an *Ars disserendi* or *dialectica* and *De utensilibus* or *Phaletolum.* Although Adam is praised by a later member of the Petit-Pont school, Alexander Neckham, the adjective *parvipontani* was used as a term of abuse for sophistical hairsplitters.

Lesley J. Smith

[See also: THEOLOGY]

Minio-Paluello, Lorenzo, ed. *Twelfth Century Logic, Texts and Studies I: Adam Balsamiensis Parvipontani Ars disserendi (Dialectica Alexandri).* Rome, 1956.

———. "The *Ars disserendi* of Adam of Balsham 'Parvipontanus.'" *Mediaeval and Renaissance Studies* 3 (1954): 116–69.

ADAM OF SAINT-VICTOR (Adam Precentor; d.1146). Cantor (precentor) at the cathedral of Notre-Dame in Paris by 1107, Adam served in this high office until at least 1133, when he donated his prebend at the cathedral, with all its monies and privileges, to the Augustinian abbey of Saint-Victor and probably took up residence there. Adam was involved in the political embroilments that divided the cathedral clergy in Paris during the first half of the 12th century and found himself on the side of the reformers, an ally of Bishop Stephen of Senlis and the Victorines. He was doubtless involved in the failed attempt to convert the cathedral canons to the common life (ca. 1128).

Adam was known as a great sequence poet by the mid-12th century; his stature as first musician at the cathedral makes it likely that he composed sequence melodies as well. Some texts probably by Adam are *Zima vetus,* and *Mundi renovatio,* both for feasts of the Easter Octave; *Lux iocunda, lux insignis,* for Pentecost; and *Heri mundus,* for St. Stephen. Adam's association with both the cathedral of Notre-Dame and the abbey of Saint-Victor helps explain the fact that both institutions had related yet distinct sequence traditions.

Margot Fassler

[See also: SEQUENCE (LATE)]

Adam of Saint-Victor. *Œuvres poétiques d'Adam de Saint-Victor*, ed. Léon Gautier. Paris: Julien, Lanier, Cosnard, 1894.

———. *Les proses d'Adam de Saint-Victor: texte et musique précédées d'une étude critique*, ed. Eugène Misset and Pierre Aubry. Paris, 1900.

Blume, Clemens, and Henry Marriot Bannister, eds. *Analecta hymnica medii aevi.* Leipzig: Reisland, 1915, 1922, Vols. 54, 55.

Fassler, Margot. *Gothic Song: Victorine Sequences and Augustinian Reform in Twelfth-Century Paris.* Cambridge: Cambridge University Press, 1993.

———. "Who Was Adam of St. Victor? The Evidence of the Sequence Manuscripts." *Journal of the American Musicological Society* 37 (1984): 233–69.

Hegener, Eckhard. *Studien zur "zweiten Sprache" in der religiösen Lyrik des zwölften Jahrhunderts: Adam von St. Viktor—Walter von Châtillon.* Ratingen: Kastellann; Wuppertal: Henn, 1971.

ADELAIDE OF SAVOY (ca. 1098–1154). Queen of France. The daughter of Humbert II, count of Maurienne, and a relation of Pope Calixtus II, Adelaide was born shortly before 1100 and became queen of France in 1114, when she married Louis VI. In twenty-three years of marriage, she bore him six sons and one daughter and had considerable influence at court. After the king's death, she married the constable of France, Matthieu de Montmorency. She died in 1154 at the abbey of Montmartre.

John Bell Henneman, Jr.

Facinger, Marion F. "A Study of Medieval Queenship: Capetian France, 987–1237." *Studies in Medieval and Renaissance History* 5 (1968): 3–47.

ADÈLE OF CHAMPAGNE (ca. 1145–1206). Daughter of Count Thibaut IV of Blois (III of Champagne), Adèle became the third queen of Louis VII in 1160. In 1165, she bore him a long-desired heir, the future Philip II, thereby ensuring the survival of the Capetian dynasty and providing it Carolingian blood, a fact later exploited by royal propaganda. Adèle and her brothers, Henri I (count of Champagne, r. 1152–81) and Thibaut V (count of Blois, r. 1152–91, and royal seneschal)—who married Louis's daughters by Eleanor of Aquitaine—together with Guillaume (bishop of Chartres, r. 1165–68, and archbishop of Sens, r. 1168–75, and Reims, r. 1175–1202) constituted an influential party at the royal court. Adèle and Guillaume shared the regency for Philip II while he was on the Third Crusade (1190–91), but little else is known about her public or private life.

Theodore Evergates

[See also: CAPETIAN DYNASTY; CHAMPAGNE; LOUIS VII; PHILIP II AUGUSTUS]

Baldwin, John W. *The Government of Philip Augustus: Foundations of French Royal Power in the Middle Ages.* Berkeley: University of California Press, 1986.

Facinger, Marion F. "A Study of Medieval Queenship: Capetian France, 987–1237." *Studies in Medieval and Renaissance History* 5 (1968): 3–47.

Lewis, Andrew W. *Royal Succession in Capetian France: Studies on Familial Order and the State.* Cambridge: Harvard University Press, 1981.

Pacaut, Marcel. *Louis VII et son royaume.* Paris: SEVPEN, 1964.

ADÉMAR DE CHABANNES (Ademarus Cabannensis; 989–1034). Son of Limousin aristocrats, monk of Saint-Cybard in Angoulême, educated at Saint-Martial in Limoges, Adémar was a talented and versatile scribe. His autograph manuscripts (over 1,000 folios) include editions, drawings, poetry, liturgy with musical notation, sermons, history, and *computus*. In 1010 at Limoges, at the height of an apocalyptic crisis triggered by Al-Hakim's destruction of the Holy Sepulcher in Jerusalem and various signs, wonders, and natural disasters, he had a vision of a cross planted in the heavens with Christ on it, weeping rivers of tears. Around 1025, he began a history of his time, which survives in three recensions and, in its global scope and popular religious activity, resembles that of Raoul Glaber.

With his ambitions frustrated in Angoulême by the deaths of his abbot and the count of the city, Adémar turned to Limoges, where he strove to become the impresario of the enormously popular cult of St. Martial, writing a new "apostolic" liturgy to accord with a new popular legend that the saint was a companion of Jesus. But on August 3, 1029, the day of the liturgy's inauguration, a prior from Lombardy roundly defeated him in public debate, turning the crowd against the liturgy and ruining its debut. Adémar returned to Angoulême in disgrace and, after defending himself in a circular letter that he never sent, turned to forgery and fiction. He produced a whole dossier of texts—papal letters, conciliar decrees, sermons, interpolations into famous Christian writers, and lengthy accounts of the Peace councils of Poitiers and Limoges in 1031, where "a certain cleric" from Angoulême carries the day for St. Martial. Adémar is perhaps best known for his *Historia* in three books, which traces the history of the Franks from their mythic Trojan beginnings to 1028. In 1032–33, he deposited his life's work at Saint-Martial before going on a terminal pilgrimage to Jerusalem. Given his "mythomania," his work is difficult to interpret, but he is an invaluable source for his period, especially the castellan wars, the Peace of God movement, the rise in relic cults and pilgrimage, and apocalyptic anxieties.

Richard Landes

[See also: ANGOUMOIS; FABLE *(ISOPET)*; HISTORIOGRAPHY; MARTIAL OF LIMOGES; PEACE OF GOD; RAOUL GLABER; TROPES, PROPER]

Adémar de Chabannes. *La chronique d'Adémar de Chabannes*, ed. Jules Chavanon. Paris: Picard, 1897.

Arbellot, J. "Étude historique et littéraire sur Adémar de Chabannes." *Bulletin de la Société Archéologique et Historique du Limousin* 21 (1872): 104–52.

Bachrach, Bernard. "'Potius rex quam esse dux putabatur': Some Observations Concerning Adémar of Chabannes's Panegyric on Duke William the Great." *Haskins Society Journal* 1 (1989): 11–21.

Delisle, Léopold. "Notice sur les manuscrits originaux d'Adémar de Chabannes." *Notices et extraits de la Bibliothèque Nationale* 35 (1895): 241–355.

Gaborit-Chopin, Danielle. "Les dessins d'Adémar de Chabannes." *Bulletin du Comité des Travaux Historiques et Scientifiques* n.s. 3 (1967): 163–225.

Grier, James. "Ecce sanctum quem deus elegit Marcialem apostolum: Ademar of Chabannes and the Tropes for the Feast of Saint Martial." In *Beyond the Moon: Festschrift Luther Dittmer*, ed. Bryan Gillingham and Paul Merkley. Ottawa: Institute of Medieval Music, 1990, pp. 28–74.

Lair, Jules A. *Études critiques sur divers textes des Xe et XIe siècles II: L'Historia d'Adémar de Chabannes.* Paris: Picard, 1899.

Landes, Richard. *The Deceits of History: The Life and Times of Ademar of Chabannes (989–1034).* Forthcoming.

ADENET LE ROI (ca. 1240–ca. 1300). A popular professional poet of the late 13th century, Adenet is known for four major works. He was old enough to have been trained as a court poet before 1261, the year of the death of his first patron, Henri III, duke of Brabant and trouvère. In 1270, he was in Flanders, where he met his new patron, Gui de Dampierre, whom he accompanied to Tunis on the Eighth Crusade. His later travels led him across France and frequently to Paris, the court of Philip the Bold and Marie of France, who also influenced his literary activity. Of the four works known to be by Adenet, only the romance *Cleomadés* can be dated with certainty, to 1285. His earlier production, all chansons de geste, was completed after 1273–74. *Beuvon de Conmarchis* is probably the earliest, followed by the *Enfances Ogier* and *Berte aus grans piés* in that order. The last mention of Adenet appears in a document dated 1297.

Beuvon is considered to be the earliest of Adenet's narratives because of its unpolished style. Typical of the late chanson de geste, the laisses are monorhymed. Adenet adopts, however, the Alexandrine and the short-line refrain of the Guillaume d'Orange cycle. *Beuvon* is a reworking of the *Siège de Barbastre*, containing 3,945 lines and lacking a conclusion. Neither truly romance nor epic, the story exhibits above all a propensity for gallant adventures and praise of women.

Adenet's second narrative, also a reworking, was ordered by Gui de Dampierre and was enjoyed by Queen Marie of France, to whom Adenet sent a copy. Retaining the monorhymed laisse, he reverts to the decasyllabic line without refrains. The *Enfances Ogier* (9,229 lines) imitates the first branch of the *Chevalerie Ogier*. Adenet has considerably improved in skill by concentrating on a few characters. Women retain the place he set for them in *Beuvon de Conmarchis*.

Though the subject matter and form are epic, *Berte aus grans piés* is closer to romance. The monorhymed laisses contain 3,486 Alexandrines. Conciseness and unity characterize this narrative, which has earned praise from critics for its sensitive treatment of the heroine, Berte.

Cleomadés, Adenet's fourth and best-known narrative (twelve manuscripts and three fragments survive), was inspired by Queen Marie and her sister-in-law Blanche of France, widow of the son of King Alfonso X the Wise of Spain, who invited Adenet to compose a story based on the tale of the magic ebony horse from the *Arabian Nights*. Blanche could have come across the legend of the flying horse at Alfonso's court in Spain, which was an important center of cross-cultural transmission from East to West. Surprisingly, Adenet abandons all pretense of creating an epic by choosing rhymed octosyllabic couplets. Aside from the source mentioned above, Adenet included as part of this long romance (18,698 lines) autobiographical information from his travels in Italy.

Son of the powerful Marcadigas, king of Spain, Cleomadés travels across Europe to perfect himself, spending the most time in France, land of honor and courtesy. Envious neighbors, meanwhile, encroach on Marcadigas's territory, leading to war. Cleomadés returns home to head a battalion and establishes his reputation by accomplishing great exploits and leading his countrymen to victory. Three African kings, suitors of Marcadigas's daughters, contrive marvelous automatons to trick the king. As the machines are put to the test, the daughters are overcome with fright and bewilderment. Through the suitors' treachery, Cleomadés is carried off at vertiginous speed by an ebony horse. He lands in Tuscany and falls in love with the king's daughter, Clarmondine. He meets her in her moonlit bedroom, where they confess their love. With her consent, they again take to horse and announce to Clarmondine's parents their intention to marry and govern Spain. But she is soon captured by the traitor Crompart, who schemes to marry his captive. Meanwhile, Meniadus, the king of Salerno, falls in love with the captive and likewise decides to marry her. To save herself, she pretends to go mad. Cleomadés, disguised as a merchant, sets out in search of his beloved. His friend Pinçonnet suggests consulting Meniadus because of his custom of gathering news from travelers. Cleomadés convinces the king that he is a doctor so that he can cure the patient recently gone mad. To accomplish his goal, he must tie the girl to the ebony horse. They soon fly away, enjoying courteous conversation and the pleasure of being together. Back in Spain, the only sad note is the death of Cleomadés's father and Clarmondine's mother. A sumptuous wedding ends the romance. *Cleomadés* is generally rated as Adenet's most successful work.

The advent of Adenet le Roi marks a pivotal moment in the evolution of the chanson de geste. For epic savagery, he has substituted the prestige of courtly conversation. With Adenet, one might venture to say that the epic, as it was known, was buried under the triumph of written romance.

John L. Grigsby

[See also: CHANSON DE GESTE; GIRART D'AMIENS; KING CYCLE]

Adenet le Roi. *Les œuvres d'Adenet le Roi,* ed. Albert Henry. I: *Biographie d'Adenet; La tradition manuscrite.* Rijksuniversitei te Gent. Bruges: De Tempel, 1951. II: *Beauvon de Conmarchis.* Bruges: De Tempel, 1953. III: *Les enfances Ogier.* Bruges: De Tempel, 1956. IV: *Berte aus grans piés.* Brussels: Presses Universitaires de Bruxelles, 1963. V: *Cleomadés.* Vol. 1, Texte; Vol. 2, *Introduction, notes, tables.* Brussels: Editions de l'Université de Bruxelles, 1971.
Adnès, André. *Adenès, dernier grand trouvère: recherches historiques et anthroponymiques.* Paris: Picard, 1971.
Colliot, Régine. *Berte aus grans piés: étude littéraire générale.* 2 vols. Paris: Picard, 1970.

ADMIRAL OF FRANCE. During the late Middle Ages, the admiral had central command of the royal navy of France as well as serving in the military council with the constable, marshals, master of crossbowmen, and, in the 15th century, master of artillery. While the Byzantines, Spanish Muslims, and Sicilian Normans had an admiral as part of their military command earlier in the Middle Ages, the French did not establish such a position until 1244, with the temporary assignment of an admiral over the fleet of the Levant. Only at the end of the century did the post of admiral become permanent.

The earliest appointees were foreigners, generally Genoese or Monagesque sea captains, such as Benedetto Zaccharia, Henri Marchese, and Renier Grimaldi. By the reign of Philip VI, with the admiral now a member of the military hierarchy, the king began to appoint Frenchmen. Philip's first such admiral, the inexperienced Hugues Quieret, was a failure who lost his life when the French fleet met disaster at Sluis in 1340. During the course of the Hundred Years' War, however, the French did produce some able admirals, notably Jean de Vienne, Braquet de Braquemont, Prigent de Coetivy, Jean de Montaubary, and Louis Malet de Graville.

The responsiblities of the French admirals, who were paid extremely well for their services, included overseeing the fleets in the Mediterranean and Atlantic, installing police and judicial officials in the port towns, organizing pay for naval troops, and sitting in judgment over naval illegalities. Lieutenants or vice-admirals frequently assisted them in these duties. Admirals also sat in the Grand' Chambre of Parlement and at the Table de Marbre, a special tribunal for cases involving military, naval, and forestry affairs.

Kelly DeVries

[See also: NAVAL POWER]

Contamine, Philippe. *Guerre, état et société à la fin du moyen âge: études sur les armées des rois de France, 1337–1494.* Paris: Mouton, 1972.
Lot, Ferdinand, and Robert Fawtier. *Histoire des institutions françaises au moyen âge.* 3 vols. Paris: Presses Universitaires de France, 1957–62, Vol. 2.
Luchaire, Achille. *Manuel des institutions françaises.* Paris: Hachette, 1892.
Rosenzweig, Louis. *L'office de l'amiral de France du XIIIe au XVIIIe siècle.* Vannes: Galles, 1856.

ADVOCATUS/AVOUÉ. During the 10th and 11th centuries, it became normal for religious houses to have an *advocatus,* also known as a *custos* or *adjutator.* This advocate was generally a powerful local layman, most commonly a count or duke in the 10th century, although by the late 11th century castellans too might be advocates. The duties of an advocate were to act as a monastery's agent in the outside world and to protect it from its enemies. The monks consulted their advocate before electing a new abbot. A layman who founded or reformed a monastery in the 11th century normally became its advocate. Most advocates seem to have taken their responsibilities seriously and sought to defend "their" monks from other laymen, but the monks relied so much on their advocate that they were virtually helpless if he turned against them.

Although almost all monasteries, including Cluny and her daughters, had advocates in the 10th and 11th centuries, the office became much less common in the 12th century, with the impact of the Gregorian separation of lay and ecclesiastical affairs. Cistercian houses never had formal advocates, but they still hoped for the support and protection of their secular neighbors.

Constance B. Bouchard

[See also: VIDAME]

Bouchard, Constance Brittain. *Sword, Miter, and Cloister: Nobility and the Church in Burgundy, 980–1198.* Ithaca: Cornell University Press, 1987, chap. 5.
Mason, Emma. "Timeo barones et donas ferentes." In *Religious Motivation: Biographical and Sociological Problems for the Church Historian,* ed. Derek Baker. Oxford: Ecclesiastical History Society, 1978, pp. 61–75.

AFFRANCHISSEMENT. Act granting freedom to an unfree person or privileges to a community. In granting freedom to a serf or, in the earlier law, to a slave, *affranchissement* is synonymous with manumission or emancipation. In *affranchissements* from slavery, the legal assimilation of the freedman to the existing free population remained partial under the laws of the state. It was only with the grandchild of the freedman that the last taint of servile status vanished *de jure.* A lord's *affranchissement* of a serf, on the other hand, would transform personal status completely and immediately, but only when the act was properly confirmed by the appropriate superior lord. This was because rights over serfs were ordinarily appurtenant to fiefs. Typically, therefore, an *affranchissement* diminished a fief. It followed that approval was necessary from the superior lord who (or whose ancestor) had granted the fief and who continued to have residual interests in it, such as the right of escheat and relief.

A closely related usage of *affranchissement* is for the act granting liberties or privileges ("franchises") to urban or rural, even servile, communities. The precise number and extent of liberties granted were spelled out in formal charters and differed from community to community depending on the political, social, and economic situation that induced communities to seek and lords to grant the franchises. Since there was much borrowing from one charter to the next, it is possible to talk about a "typical" *affranchissement*, which usually provided for freedom of inheritance, freedom of trade in the protected environment, relaxation of seigneurial taxes and hospitality, reduction of some aspects of military service, and a degree of self-government. In return, either the community made a fixed annual payment to its lord or individuals paid fixed rents to the lord for their tenements in the franchise.

William Chester Jordan

[See also: *HOMME DE CORPS*; SERFDOM/SERVITUDE/ SLAVERY]

Bernard, Pierre. *Étude sur les esclaves et les serfs d'église en France du VIe au XIIIe siècle*. Paris: Société du Recueil Sirey, 1919.

Jordan, William C. *From Servitude to Freedom: Manumission in the Sénonais in the Thirteenth Century*. Philadelphia: University of Pennsylvania Press, 1986.

Mariotte-Lober, Ruth. *Ville et seigneurie: les chartes de franchises des comtes de Savoie*. Annecy: Académie Florimontane, 1973.

AGDE. Founded as a Greek colony (Agathé Tyché) by Phocaens from Marseille in the 6th century B.C., Agde (Hérault) was later a Roman colony and an early bishopric of the Roman church (ca. 450). Ramparts were authorized in 1173 by Louis VII to help defend Languedoc from sea raiders. A Carolingian basilica dedicated to St. Étienne (built 848–72) was replaced in the late 12th century by the current fortified Romanesque cathedral of black lava. A keeplike tower, containing some of the earliest examples of machicolations, was added to its north transept during the Gothic period. Built in the form of a capital T, the church has a wide aisleless nave (100 feet by 50 feet) of six bays, with a transept but no apse.

William W. Kibler/William W. Clark

Bonde, Sheila. *Ecclesiae incastellatae*. Cambridge: Cambridge University Press. Forthcoming.

de Gorsse, P. *Monographie de la cathédrale Saint-Étienne d'Agde*. Toulouse, 1922.

AGEN. A Gallic *oppidum*, Aginnum, and capital of the Nitiobriges, Agen (Lot-et-Garonne) was captured by Clovis I in 506. Made a bishopric in the 10th century, it passed in 1152 with the rest of Aquitaine to Henry II Plantagenêt. After 1271, it was again nominally French but was reoccupied by the English in 1360 and not definitively reunited with France until 1444. The Inquisition was installed in Agen in 1242, leading the new orders to establish religious houses here: the Dominicans (1249), Franciscans (1262), Carmelites (1272), and Augustinians (1290).

The present cathedral of Saint-Caprais, with its 12th-century apse, radiating chapels, and transept, was a parish church until the cathedral of Saint-Étienne was destroyed in the Revolution. Built in the shape of a Latin cross, Saint-Caprais features a broad apse with three radiating chapels. The nearby chapter house has an impressive Romanesque façade. The double-aisled brick church of Notre-Dame-des-Jacobins, with ogival vaulting, is an important example of 13th-century Toulousan Dominican architecture. Like other Dominican foundations, it has a flat chevet and two equal naves divided by pillars. The Tour du Chapelet is a reminder of the 14th-century medieval city walls.

William W. Kibler/William W. Clark

Crozet, René. "Agen, Saint-Caprais." *Congrès archéologique (Agenais)* 127 (1969): 82–97.

Terpak, Frances. "The Role of the Saint-Eutrope Workshop in the Romanesque Campaign of Saint-Caprais in Agen." *Gesta* 25 (1986): 185–96.

———. "The Architecture and Sculpture at Saint-Caprais in Agen." Diss. Yale University, 1987.

AGENAIS. Centered on the city of Agen in southwestern France, the seat of the bishopric and county, the Agenais comprised an irregular territory lying between the rivers Garonne and Dordogne. On the west, it included the town of Marmande; on the east, the towns of Tournon and Puymirol; and on the south, Moissac and Auvillars.

From the 9th through the 12th century, the Agenais fell under the authority of the dukes of Gascony and Aquitaine. In 1196, to secure peace on his southern borders, Richard the Lionhearted granted the Agenais in fief to Count Raymond VI of Toulouse. This transfer brought the Agenais into the center of the turbulent events that commenced with the Albigensian Crusade in 1209 and concluded with the victory of France in the Hundred Years' War. Simon de Montfort attacked the region in 1212, capturing the fortress of Penne d'Agenais, where Cathar heretics were found and burned. In 1219, the crusading army of the future Louis VIII of France assaulted Marmande, which suffered pillage and massacre. By the Treaty of Meaux in 1229, Raymond VII of Toulouse retained the Agenais. On his death in 1249, it was occupied by his son-in-law Alphonse of Poitiers, brother of Louis IX.

The Agenais remained thereafter an object of contention between France and England, where Henry III asserted his claims as duke of Aquitaine. In 1259, the Treaty of Paris conceded the Agenais to England should Alphonse of Poitiers die without heirs. This eventuality came to pass in 1271, but the county was not restored to Edward I of England until 1279. Quarrels between Edward and Philip the Fair rekindled hostilities in the Agenais; from 1293, French seneschals and English administered portions of the disputed territory. The Agenais suffered heavily during the Hundred Years' War. Restored to England briefly by the Treaty of Brétigny in 1360, it returned definitively to France in 1370. At the close of the Middle Ages, the Agenais, like the Quercy, recovered slowly from rural depopulation and economic depression.

Alan Friedlander

[See also: ALBIGENSIAN CRUSADE; ALPHONSE OF POITIERS; LOUIS VIII; MONTFORT; SAINT-GILLES]

Andrieu, Jules. *Histoire de l'Agenais*. 1893; repr. Marseille: Lafitte, 1976.

Marboutin, J. R. *Histoire de l'Agenais*. Agen: Saint-Lanne, 1941–42.

Ourliac, Paul, and Monique Gilles. *Les coutumes de l'Agenais*. Vol. 1, Montpellier: Société d'Histoire du Droit, 1976; Vol. 2, Paris: Picard, 1981.

Samazeuilh, Jean-François. *Histoire de l'Agenais, du Condomois, et du Bazadais*. 2 vols. Auch: Foix, 1846; repr. Marseille: Lafitte, 1980.

AGINCOURT. The greatest English victory of the Hundred Years' War came when France was divided by the Armagnac-Burgundian feud. Henry V seized this opportunity to invade France and forcibly reassert a dubious claim to the French throne. Henry captured Harfleur and then marched north toward Calais. On October 25, 1415, a hostile force cut off his route. An exhausted English force of 1,000 men at arms and 6,000 archers confronted perhaps 25,000 French. Henry shrewdly profited from the restricted, muddy terrain and so deployed his troops to defeat an adversary ill served by a divided command. English archers provoked the overconfident French into an assault that squandered their numerical advantage, allowing the outnumbered but disciplined English to encircle and destroy the uncoordinated French mass. At least 5,000 French died and many French peers were captured, while English casualties were trivial. The dramatic victory proved crucial to Henry's ambitions. With Armagnac forces devastated, he was emboldened to undertake the occupation of Normandy and to conclude an alliance with Burgundy. The resulting Treaty of Troyes gave him widespread recognition as the legitimate heir to the throne of France.

Paul D. Solon

[See also: ARMAGNACS; BOUCICAUT; CHARLES VI; HENRY V; HUNDRED YEARS' WAR]

Burne, Alfred Higgins. *The Agincourt War*. London: Eyre and Spottiswoode, 1956.

Hibbert, Christopher. *Agincourt*. Philadelphia: Dufour, 1964.

Jacob, Ernest Fraser. *Henry V and the Invasion of France*. New York: Macmillan, 1950.

Jarman, Rosemary Hawley. *Crispin's Day: The Glory Of Agincourt*. Boston: Little, Brown, 1979.

Keegan, John. *The Face of Battle*. New York: Viking, 1976.

AGRICULTURE. Throughout the Middle Ages, a huge majority of France's population was engaged in agriculture; land with the laborers on it remained the primary source of wealth even after towns, commerce, and industry revived later in the period. From late antiquity to the 9th century, although there were some independent peasant holdings, agriculture was generally practiced on great estates or villas that were the successors of Roman villas. These estates, organized and worked under a system called manorialism, tended to be self-sufficient, having little recourse to trade and producing for all their own needs. A small surplus went to support the warrior or clerical owner, but few of the villas were large enough to have supported a great man and his retinue through a twelve-month period; to live off their estates, early-medieval lords had to move from one to the next during the year.

Ownership of such estates and rights to the tenancies within them became more fragmented as the centuries passed; by the 12th century, inefficiencies of scale and the numerous middlemen who had inserted themselves between peasants and owners often meant that what remained of the old Carolingian villa produced little for its owners. In the 10th and 11th centuries, however, this situation began to be alleviated by an expansion of cultivation into nearby forest and waste, where new fields, called by such names as *appendariae* or *bordariae*, were both more fertile and more profitable. Lords attempted to reap benefits from the expanded tillage by instituting new types of taxation (based on the *bannum*), by building new mills, ovens, and winepresses, and by encouraging the settlement of forested areas. It was frequently the lords who instigated the foundation of new villages in forest and waste, which would yield them considerable revenues, or who encouraged settlement in reclaimed coastal and riverine marshes.

The main crop produced by medieval agriculture was cereal, but cereal production was practiced within a mixed system of pastoralism and animal husbandry, gardening, viticulture, and, along the Mediterranean coastline, olioculture. Relative dependence on cereals and pastoralism as well as the details of agricultural organization varied with local conditions in each of the numerous *pays,* or regions, but two major zones of agriculture can be distinguished: the flat wheat-producing plain of the north and the more rugged, often mountainous sheep- and rye-producing regions of the south. Several varieties of wheat, sometimes mixed together, along with rye, oats, barley, and pulses (peas, beans), were produced. The Romans and Christianity had encouraged the spread of viticulture throughout France, even into regions today considered wholly unsuited to wine production. Particularly in the early Middle Ages, when yields from the fields were low, there was considerable dependence by all areas on hunting and fishing, and on the forest surrounding cultivated areas for pasture for pigs and products like nuts, berries, and honey. Later, although the clearing of forest and increased limitations on its use came at a time in the central Middle Ages that is associated with increased agricultural yields, the growing difficulty of access to forest resources must have made the famines of the early 14th century even more devastating.

In the early Middle Ages, the major tool for cultivation was the Roman, or scratch, plow (*araire*), which was usually pulled by two oxen over fields made roughly square, since they were plowed across and then again at right angles to the original plowing. Even in later centuries, the scratch plow and the accompanying two-year rotation course would be favored particularly in the Midi, where soils were light and dry, and wherever rural populations were too poor to adopt the heavier, more expensive wheeled plow, which needed more animal power for traction than the scratch plow. During the early period, the organization of tillage was generally on a two-year, two-course rotation in which winter wheat was sown in one of two fields each fall, while the other lay fallow for the entire year. Small bits of outfield or garden plots around homesteads may have been planted with pulses or oats in the spring. Yields were poor—generally no more than 2.5- or 3-to-1 yield to seed.

Probably even in the late Roman period, wherever there was sufficient spring and summer rain, some spring sowing was done along with the more usual fall planting, or if winter crops failed. Later, in heavily populated areas of the north (as documented in the 9th-century ecclesiastical surveys of great estates called polyptychs), the spring planting was gradually incorporated into some variation of a three-course, three-field rotation. In this rotation scheme, one field was planted to winter wheat, one to a spring crop like oats, and only a third of the field was left fallow each year. In many areas, this three-field system was probably introduced after clearance of additional land from forest and waste to make a third field. Even where it was introduced without an associated expansion of arable land, such a three-course rotation effectively increased the total arable land under cultivation in any year. Unless other improvements in agricultural practice were also introduced, the new rotation methods would not have improved production for long, for yields should have dropped on fields expected to produce in two out of three instead of one out of two years. Instead, in this period, not only did older fields produce slightly more often, but yield/seed ratios actually appear to have increased to about 4 to 1 by the 14th century. These higher yields are significant, since they produced a doubling of net yields or consumable produce from earlier gross yields of 2.5 to 1. Yields were maintained partly due to more frequent plowing of the fallow lands and the introduction of spring crops, such as oats and pulses, which had nitrogen-fixing capability. More important were better iron tools, which allowed clearance of new lands, and the introduction of the heavy, wheeled plow, or *charrue*. In addition to wheels, this plow had an iron cutting knife, or coulter, which went ahead of the share to cut open the soil, an iron share, and an iron or wooden moldboard, which turned over the sod completely in one direction or the other. This meant that it dug deeper into the soil to turn over the sod sufficiently to increase the fertility of existing tillage, and it could be used for tilling the heavier soils of river valleys previously inaccessible to agriculture. The disadvantage of the new plow was that it required eight oxen or a pair of horses to pull it, an expense that often must have been shared among villagers. It was also considerably harder to turn this plow. The shape of holdings in fields needed to be changed to the long, slightly S-shaped strips familiar from aerial photographs;

except where it was introduced in entirely noval lands, this must have meant a considerable redistribution of village lands when the new plow was adopted. The new wheeled plow was frequently pulled by horses, an innovation that was possible only after the introduction of the horse collar, better hitching methods, and iron horseshoes. The use of horses thus, like the plow itself, required increased availability of iron and is linked to increased iron production and the burgeoning of forges throughout the countryside during this period. The horses used to pull these plows, like the mounts of the warriors who owned the estates, were fed oats, a spring crop, so that the introduction of horse power in the fields also probably encouraged the spread of the new three-course rotation.

These interrelated innovations in agricultural practice and technology appeared in France between the years 950 and 1150, particularly in the region north of the Loire, and would be distributed fairly widely in north and central France (although much less so in the Midi, where soil and climate were not appropriate) by the 12th and 13th centuries. They marked what has rightfully been called the "Agricultural Revolution of the Middle Ages." This revolution was accompanied by considerable demographic growth, by a widespread expansion of the total area under cultivation in France, by the building of castles by territorial lords, by increased agricultural yields, and by a revival of towns and specialized artisanship in those towns. Much of this revolution, which took place in the 10th and 11th centuries, is undocumented, for there is a dearth of records for the period during and after the 9th-century invasions. Until recently, historians gave credit for the agricultural revolution to monks, particularly the new monks of the 12th century. More recent studies instead show that anonymous peasants needing more land for their families, hermits going out to live alone in the forest, and lords intent on getting a share of the profits of expansion by encouraging settlement advance and technological innovation were all more important than the religious orders.

By the 12th century, for which documents are much more abundant, the major parts of this transformation had taken place. Secondary improvements continued into the 13th century and were often promoted by the new monastic groups. They included the consolidation of fragments of old estates, the elimination of middlemen from claims to the produce of estates, the building and improvement of mills, an improved ratio of animals to arable land through the introduction of transhumance, and the beginnings of selective breeding of animals. Efficiencies were also created when monastic owners of the new consolidated estates of the central Middle Ages cultivated their great demesnes or granges with hired laborers or domestic servitors or lay brothers. However, this last was a short-lived phenomenon, for by the 14th century such demesnes had been rented out to farmers at a fixed rent or in sharecropping contracts.

By the 13th century, the rural world was considerably different from that of the early Middle Ages. The old villa and the social structure associated with it had broken down, as manorialism was replaced by seigneurialism. Peasants were no longer on the verge of starvation but were able to support a growing population of townspeople. Remaining forest was less dense and was threatened more from demand for building materials and fuel for the towns than by clearance; contention over forest rights increased. Pigs grazing in forest, the major protein source for the earlier period, were replaced by transhumant sheep moved seasonally from region to region. There was a shift in diet, not just from pork to lamb, but general improvement—from a diet often based entirely on cereals to one including much more meat, cheese, and other animal products, as well as increasingly good and abundant wines. Other demand, particularly for industrial materials, such as wool, hides and leather, dyes, hemp, flax, and parchment for book and document making, was also beginning to influence rural production.

By the late 12th century, there were indications of problems to come. For instance, peasant cultivators were already finding that not all the newly cleared and drained lands were fertile or reliable enough to provide a livelihood and were abandoning some of them. Grants of frequently flooded but extremely fertile river-valley fields were often made to monks and other religious groups who could keep up the dikes and absorb the risks of crop failure. Near the great cities, some owners and peasants ceased cereal production altogether in favor of commercial production for market, particularly of wines, dyestuffs, and garden produce, making themselves wholly dependent on grain shipments, which in times of dearth would not be forthcoming. Population continued to grow, although by 1300 the pace of that growth was falling off. From that date on, there are indications of feeble attempts to again breach what remained of the great medieval forests or to reclaim land on the coasts. A series of poor harvests, warfare, famine, and increasing malnutrition left the population particularly susceptible to the Black Death in 1348. Afterward, despite population losses, rural prosperity only gradually declined. With a smaller labor force was seen the abandonment of the least productive lands, the renting out of demesnes, and increasing interest in animal husbandry.

In the late 14th and the 15th century, agriculture came more under the control of the wealthiest peasants, who farmed or sharecropped the demesnes. Lords abandoning the countryside for the towns, depended increasingly on seigneurial rights and dues, or on fixed rents. With the exception of the importation into the Midi of new crops and irrigation practices from Arab-controlled parts of Spain in this later period, and except in the vicinity of the great cities whose markets encouraged new forms of cropping, medieval agricultural practice remained more or less unchanged from the 13th through the early-modern centuries.

Constance H. Berman

[See also: ANIMALS (DOMESTIC);
BAN/BANALITÉ; CLIMATE; *DÉFRICHEMENT*; GRANGE;
MÉTAYER/MÉTAYAGE; POPULATION AND
DEMOGRAPHY; RURAL SOCIAL STRUCTURE;
TRANSHUMANCE; *VILLENEUVE*]

Berman, Constance H. *Medieval Agriculture, the Southern French Countryside, and the Early Cistercians*. Philadelphia: American Philosophical Society, 1986.

Bloch, Marc. *French Rural History: An Essay in Its Basic Characteristics*, trans. Janet Sondheimer. Berkeley: University of California Press, 1970.

Duby, Georges. *Rural Economy and Country Life in the Medieval West*, trans. Cynthia Postan. London: Arnold, 1968.

———. *The Early Growth of the European Economy: Warriors and Peasants from the Seventh to the Twelfth Century*. Ithaca: Cornell University Press, 1979.

———, and Armand Wallon, eds. *Histoire de la France rurale des origines à 1340*. Paris: Seuil, 1975.

Faucher, Daniel. *Géographie agraire: types de culture*. Paris: Librairie de Medicis, 1949.

Fourquin, Guy. *Histoire économique de l'Occident médiévale*. Paris: Colin, 1979.

Higounet, Charles. *Paysages et villages neufs du moyen âge*. Bordeaux: Fédération Historique du Sud-Ouest, 1975.

Slicher van Bath, Bernard H. *The Agrarian History of Western Europe: A.D. 500–1850*, trans. Olive Ordish. London: Arnold, 1963.

Villages désertés et histoire économique, XIe–XVIIIe siècles. Paris: SEVPEN, 1965.

White, Lynn, Jr. *Medieval Technology and Social Change*. Oxford: Clarendon, 1962.

AIDES. The feudal obligation of a vassal to render "aid and counsel" to his lord gave rise not only to the specific "feudal aids" payable on designated occasions but also to military service and pecuniary assistance demanded at other times. Aside from feudal *aides* generalized to include subjects who were not royal vassals, we find, as early as Philip II, *aides de l'ost*, payments in lieu of military obligations. Occasional levies called *aides* gave way to more frequent and controversial ones after 1294, when France was frequently at war and the king's finances badly stretched.

Among the terms used for tax in the early 14th century, "war subsidy" was most common, but *aide* was also used in this sense. The word gradually began to refer mainly to indirect taxes on the sale of merchandise, supplanting *maltôte*, which also applied to indirect taxes but carried with it a sense of unjust exaction. Up to 1360, however, *aides* had no very specific meaning when not referring to one of the customary feudal aids. In December of that year, the need to raise a substantial sum for the ransom of King John II led the crown to establish three regular indirect taxes. One of these, which applied specifically to salt, retained the old name of *gabelle*. The other two were a tax on wine (at first about 8 percent but later raised to 25 percent on retail sales) and a general value-added tax on other commodities. Since the occasion was a royal ransom, these taxes amounted to a feudal aid generalized to affect the whole population.

Collected through the 1360s as the *aides pour la délivrance*, these taxes remained in force for all but two of the next fifty-seven years and after 1369 were called the "aids for the war." Thereafter, the term always referred to these taxes and rarely to anything else. Royal indirect taxes being contrary to the traditions of Languedoc, the Estates of that region arranged in 1362 to replace them with an equivalent amount paid as a lump sum and apportioned locally.

Regular taxation came to a halt during the civil wars of the early 15th century, the *aides* being canceled in 1417. For the next two decades, the Estates General occasionally granted *aides*, but they were unpopular with the towns, and regional assemblies usually changed them to another form of tax. The Estates of 1436 restored the *aides* and *gabelle*, and this time the format was not altered and the crown continued to collect them. Languedoc, once again, replaced them with a substitute now actually called the *equivalent*. These taxes now became a permanent feature of the royal fiscal system.

John Bell Henneman, Jr.

[See also: FEUDAL AIDS]

Brown, Elizabeth A. R. *Politics and Institutions in Capetian France*. Aldershot: Variorum, 1991.

Henneman, John Bell. *Royal Taxation in Fourteenth Century France: The Captivity and Ransom of John II, 1356–1370.* Philadelphia: American Philosophical Society, 1976.

Viard, Jules. "Les ressources extraordinaires de la royauté sous Philippe VI de Valois." *Revue des questions historiques* 44 (1888): 167–218.

Vuitry, Adolphe. *Études sur la régime financier de la France avant la Révolution de 1789.* nouv. ser. 2 vols. Orléans: Colas, 1873–83.

AIGUES-MORTES. A royal port built on the Mediterranean coast in the 13th century, Aigues-Mortes was founded because no existing major ports or towns with access to good harbors on the Mediterranean coast of France were susceptible to decisive royal penetration before the end of the reign of Louis VIII. Even when, in the late 1220s and 1230s, the crown made inroads into the independence of a few of these towns after the Albigensian Crusade, it was felt, given the legacy of hostility from the war, that a distinctly royal port would be advantageous. The transformation of this desire into reality came about as a result of Louis IX's need for an embarkation point for the soldiers who accompanied him on his first crusade (1248–54). Beginning in earnest in the mid-1240s, the king's men laid out a small town about 20 miles east of Montpellier, in an area facing saltwater lagoons and stagnant pools, which together account for the name given to the settlement, Aigues-Mortes ("Dead Waters"). Laid out on a square grid, the town was a typical foundation of the 13th century except for the extraordinary degree of royal interest in its success. It was heavily fortified with both impressive walls—originally in wood, in the 1270s rebuilt in stone—and an imposing tower, the Tour de Constance, set slightly apart from the walls themselves.

Dredging and canal building were employed to control silting and to give access to the sea. Even at its best, however, the inner harbor could not handle large ships. These were obliged to anchor in the open sea, where they were subjected to the heavy winds characteristic of that part of the Mediterranean.

Aigues-Mortes (Bouches-du-Rhône), city walls. *Photograph: Clarence Ward Collection. Courtesy of Oberlin College.*

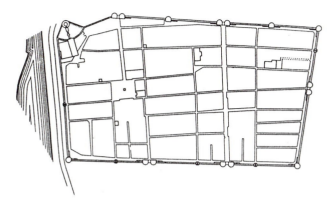

Aigues-Mortes, city plan. After Stierlin.

The townsmen who inhabited Aigues-Mortes received an enormous number of privileges to stimulate the prosperity of the foundation. For example, every ship that came within sight of the port had to put in at Aigues-Mortes. Self-government, on the other hand, was severely circumscribed by the presence of a resident royal governor.

For all its limitations as a physical site, Aigues-Mortes was an important outpost of royal power in the later 13th and early 14th century. No estimate of the number of inhabitants is absolutely trustworthy, but a resident population of 1,000–3,500 seems reasonable. During periods of peak use, such as embarkations for crusades (1248, 1270), this number swelled. Royal fiscal accounts show that the crown expended considerable revenue in keeping the walls in repair and the harbor open. High officials in the government may even have entertained the possibility of diverting a freshwater river to Aigues-Mortes, since the natural water supply was insufficient for a large town.

In the course of the 14th century, older and better ports on the Mediterranean coast either came under French rule or succumbed to more effective royal control. Since the oligarchies of these towns had always resented the favored status of Aigues-Mortes and since the crown, once it established effective control, no longer doubted its ability to work through these oligarchies whenever it needed to discharge obligations that required the use of ports, Aigues-Mortes gradually decreased in importance as a commercial center and as an object of special royal encouragement. It is no doubt due to this decline that the extensive city walls and fortifications of Aigues-Mortes remain largely intact and that the original grid plan of the town is still respected. Together, they make Aigues-Mortes one of the finest surviving examples of 13th-century fortified town planning.

William Chester Jordan

[See also: CRUSADES; LOUIS IX]

Inventaire général des monuments et richesses artistiques de la France. *Gard. Canton d'Aigues-Mortes.* 2 vols. Paris: Imprimerie Nationale, 1973.

Jordan, William. "Supplying Aigues-Mortes for the Crusade of 1248: The Problem of Restructuring Trade." In *Order and Innovation in the Middle Ages: Essays in Honor of Joseph R. Strayer*, ed. William Jordan, Bruce McNab, and Teofilo Ruiz. Princeton: Princeton University Press, 1976, pp. 165–72.

———. *Louis IX and the Challenge of the Crusade: A Study in Rulership.* Princeton: Princeton University Press, 1979.

Salch, Charles-Laurent. *L'atlas des villes et villages fortifiés en France.* Strasbourg: Pubitotal, 1987, pp. 76–85.

Sournia, Bernard. "Les fortifications d'Aigues-Mortes." *Congrès archéologique (Pays d'Arles)* 134 (1976): 9–26.

AIMOIN DE FLEURY (ca. 960–ca. 1010). The son of an aristocratic family in Périgord, Aimoin entered the Benedictine monastery of Fleury-sur-Loire as a child and took monastic vows between 969 and 978. His major writings made important contributions to the development of historiography and hagiography in medieval France. The *Historia (Gesta) Francorum* is a history of the Franks from their beginnings to Pepin the Short, written with the purpose of supporting the Capetian claim to the throne and utilized later by the authors of the chronicles of Saint-Denis and the *Grandes chroniques de France.* Aimoin's *Vita Abbonis*, written in the early 11th century, depicts the life of Abbot Abbo of Fleury, who died in 1004. Books 2 and 3 of the *Miracula sancti Benedicti* form the third major work by Aimoin. Continuing the work of Adrevald de Fleury, Aimoin carries the account of miracles associated with St. Benedict through the period of the abbacy of Abbo.

Grover A. Zinn

[See also: ABBO OF FLEURY; ANDRÉ DE FLEURY; *GRANDES CHRONIQUES DE FRANCE*; HAGIOGRAPHY; HISTORIOGRAPHY]

Aimoin de Fleury. *Opera. PL* 139.617–870.

———. *Les miracles de saint Benoît*, ed. Eugène de Certain. Paris: Renouard, 1858.

Bautier, Robert-Henri. "L'historiographie en France aux Xe et XIe siècles (France Nord et de l'Est)." In *La storiografia altomedioevale, 10–16 aprile 1969.* Spoleto: Presso la Sede del Centro, 1970, pp. 793–850.

Vidier, Alexandre C.P. *L'historiographie à Saint-Benoît-sur-Loire et les Miracles de saint Benoît.* Paris: Picard, 1965.

AIMON DE VARENNES (fl. late 12th c.). The poet Aimon de Varennes informs the reader that his romance *Florimont* was written for love of his lady in 1188. After apologizing for his nonnative French, he tells how Florimont's initial success is disrupted by betrayal of his secret love. Once cured of lovesickness, "Povre Perdu" goes to Phelipople and ultimately triumphs, marries the king's daughter, and becomes the grandfather of Alexander the Great. Much of *Florimont* recalls *Partonopeu de Blois*, while mixing in memories of voyages, local legends, and oriental stories, along with other literary sources. Like 12th-century romancers in general, Aimon uses common forms and materials renewed by his own (re)inventions.

Matilda T. Bruckner

[See also: GRECO-BYZANTINE ROMANCE]

Aimon de Varennes. *Florimont: Ein altfranzösischer Abenteuerroman,* ed. Alfons Hilka. Göttingen: Niemeyer, 1932.

Bruckner, Matilda T. "*Florimont:* Extravagant Host, Extravagant Guest." *Studies in Medieval Culture* 11 (1977): 57–63.

Fourrier, Anthime. *Le courant réaliste dans le roman courtois en France au moyen âge, I: Les débuts(XIIe siècle).* Paris: Nizet, 1960, pp. 447–85.

AIOL. Composed in Picardy during the first third of the 13th century, this chanson de geste (10,983 assonanced lines) is unusual in that the first part is mainly in decasyllables with the rare caesura 6/4, while line 5,367 and thereafter are Alexandrines. Scholars assume that the poet was not comfortable with the decasyllable, a traditional meter of this genre, and gradually moved to one that allowed more latitude.

The poem recounts how Aiol obtains the reinstatement of his father, Elie, a brother-in-law of the king, banished from the court of Charlemagne's son, Louis, by the intrigues of the traitor Makaire de Losane, who is drawn and quartered at the end. Aubri de Trois-Fontaines links *Aiol* to the Garin de Monglane cycle; indeed, the topic must already have been widespread in the mid-12th century, since Aiol is mentioned by Guiraut de Cabrera (d. ca. 1160) in his *Ensenhamen* as well as by Raimbaut d'Aurenga in a poem dated 1165. *Aiol* exists in a single manuscript in French, B.N. fr. 25516; it was adapted twice into Middle Dutch in the 13th century; into Italian by Andrea da Barberino (ca. 1370–post 1431) in his *Aiolfo;* and into Spanish, in the second of six romances about the noble knight Montesinos.

Hans-Erich Keller

Normand, Jacques, and Gaston Raynaud, eds. *Aiol, chanson de geste.* Paris: Firmin Didot, 1877.

Delbouille, Maurice. "Problèmes d'attribution et de composition: 1. De la composition d'*Aiol.*" *Revue belge de philologie et d'histoire* 11 (1932): 45–75.

Finet van der Schaaf, Baukje. "Les deux adaptations en moyen néerlandais de la chanson d'*Aiol.*" In *Au carrefour des routes d'Europe: la chanson de geste.* 2 vols. Aix-en-Provence: CUER MA, 1987, Vol. I, pp. 489–512.

Melli, Elio. "Nouvelles recherches sur la composition et la rédaction d'*Aiol* et d'*Elie de Saint-Gilles.*" In *Essor et fortune de la chanson de geste dans l'Europe et l'Orient latin: Actes du IXe Congrès International de la Société Rencesvals.* Modena: Mucchi, 1984, pp. 131–49.

AIRAINES. The church of Notre-Dame at Airaines (Somme) was given to the Cluniac monks of Saint-Martin-des-Champs in Paris in 1118 or 1119, although the present building was built only ca. 1130–40. The most interesting and oldest aspect of Airaines is the four-bay nave. While the rectangular side aisles are covered with groin vaults, the main nave is one of the earliest rib-vaulted structures in northern France. These vaults, domical in shape, were inspired either by such early examples in Normandy as the chapter house at Jumièges or by the nearly contemporary (but partly rebuilt) vaults at Lucheux (Somme). The transept at Airaines was partly rebuilt in the 13th century. The partially collapsed crossing vault was not rebuilt, whereas the rectangular chevet was rebuilt after the fire of 1422 and damaged again in the 16th century when the tower collapsed. The church still houses a rare, rectangular baptismal font, dated by some scholars to the 11th century.

William W. Clark

Aubert, Marcel. "Airaines." *Congrès archéologique (Amiens)* 99 (1936): 459–67.

AIRVAULT. The former abbey church of Saint-Pierre at Airvault (Deux-Sèvres) was founded under the patronage of Aldéarde, the late 10th-century viscountess of Thouars. This community of Augustinian canons regular experienced a period of revival and expansion in the late 11th century under Abbot Pierre de Saine-Fontaine, who initiated the construction of a new church (consecrated 1110).

The building has an apse with an ambulatory and three radiating chapels, a transept with apsidioles off each arm, and a nave with aisles; it is preceded by an inexplicably off-center narthex. In the 13th century, the square pillars of the transept and choir were reconstructed in the Gothic style. Likewise, the apse, choir, and nave were revaulted in the Angevin manner—the aisles, however, retain their original barrel vaults—and a bell tower with spire was added.

The heavily ornamented interior displays work from both the Romanesque and Gothic periods. Historiated capitals depict biblical scenes, the occupations of the months, and scenes of knights in combat. Engaged statues include representations of St. Peter, the Virgin, St. John, and various animals. Throughout the building, vegetative and purely ornamented forms encrust moldings and keys.

In the north arm of the transept is a cenotaph to Pierre de Saine-Fontaine (12th c.). Nearby conventual buildings include the remains of a 15th-century Flamboyant cloister.

Nina Rowe

Grosset, Charles. "Étude sur les sculptures romanes d'Airvault." *Bulletin de la Société des Antiquaires de l'Ouest* 4th ser. 3 (1955): 41–47.

Rhein, André. "Airvault." *Congrès archéologique (Angers-Saumur)* 77 (1910): 119–29.

AIX-EN-PROVENCE. The historic capital of Provence, Aix (Bouches-du-Rhône) has its origin in a Celto-Iberian fortress founded in the 4th century B.C. on the plateau north of the present-day city. That stronghold was destroyed in 123 B.C. by the Romans under Sextius Calvinus, who, attracted by the site's thermal springs, founded the first

Roman settlement in Transalpine Gaul, Aquae Sextiae. This settlement became the capital of Gallia Narbonensis Secunda, but was abandoned and used as a quarry after being sacked by Lombards in 574. Aix was a preferred residence of the counts of Aragon in the 12th and 13th centuries, then of the counts of Anjou. King René d'Anjou made it his headquarters in 1471, but after his death in 1480 in Aix the city was merged with France. Its university was founded in 1409.

The 13th-century Gothic chapel of the knights of Saint-Jean-de-Malte, with its fortified apsidal tower, was built ca. 1285 in the form of a Latin cross; its bell tower dates from 1376. The church of Saint-Sauveur is an amalgam of styles, from a 5th-century baptistery surrounded by eight recuperated Roman columns, through a 12th-century Provençal Romanesque south aisle, a 13th-century Gothic central nave and apse (ca. 1285), to a 16th-century Flamboyant façade. The 15th-century triptych of the Burning Bush within the church depicts King René and his queen, Jeanne, kneeling to either side of the Virgin, who holds the Child Jesus. Adjacent to Saint-Sauveur is a charming late 12th- and early 13th-century Romanesque cloister with delicately carved capitals.

William W. Kibler

[See also: RENÉ D'ANJOU]

Benoît, Fernand. "Cathédrale Saint-Sauveur," "Église de la Madeleine," "Saint-Jean de Malte." *Congrès archéologique (Aix-en-Provence, Nice)* 95 (1932): 9–41.

AIX-LA-CHAPELLE (Aachen). Site of Charlemagne's royal residence. Located in North Rhine–Westphalia, Germany, Aix was described by Carolingians as the second Rome, the new Jerusalem. The area earned the name Aquae Grani ("waters of Granus," whence Aix or Aachen) from the Romans for its warm baths and the god whom the native Celts had worshiped there. The Carolingian palace, begun ca. 785, included a great hall with living quarters for the royal family and rooms for administrative activities, a large bath, and the still-extant, sixteen-sided chapel with its octagonal dome.

Although initially Charlemagne had no permanent residence but traveled with his court throughout the realm, as his reign progressed he passed an increasing portion of every year at Aix. The palace became the center not only of imperial administration but of cultural and intellectual life: among the scholars associated with the palace school were the Anglo-Saxon Alcuin, the Goth Theodulf of Orléans, the Frank Einhard, and the Italians Paul the Deacon and Paulinus of Aquileia. Their writings, together with the impressive productions of the scribes and artists also linked with the court at Aix, marked the beginning of the Carolingian renaissance.

After Charlemagne's death, Aix-la-Chapelle remained a principal royal and imperial residence until the later 9th century, when its importance declined with the breakup of the empire.

Celia Chazelle

[See also: ALCUIN; EINHARD; THEODULF OF ORLEANS]

Bullough, Donald. "*Aula renovata*: The Carolingian Court Before the Aachen Palace." In *Carolingian Renewal: Sources and Heritage*. Manchester: Manchester University Press, 1991, pp. 123–60.

Flach, Dietmar. *Untersuchungen zur Verfassung und Verwaltung des Aachener Reichsgutes von der Karolingerzeit bis zur Mitte des 14. Jahrhunderts*. Göttingen: Vandenhoeck and Ruprecht, 1976.

Hugot, Leo. "Die Pfalz Karls des Grossen in Aachen." In *Karl der Grosse: Lebenswerk und Nachleben*, ed. Wolfgang Braunfels et al. 5 vols. Düsseldorf: Schwann, 1965, Vol. 3, pp. 534–72.

Sullivan, Richard E. *Aix-la Chapelle in the Age of Charlemagne*. Norman: University of Oklahoma Press, 1963.

ALAIN DE LILLE (ca. 1115/20–1203). Known throughout the later Middle Ages as *Doctor universalis*, Alain was probably born in the city of Lille (Nord), though the Île-de-la-Cité in Paris has also been proposed. He became a Cistercian shortly before his death; when his body at Cîteaux was exhumed in 1960, his age was put in the eighties, and his height at about 5 feet.

An anecdotal life sometimes appended to commentaries and frequently found in early printed editions of the *Parabolae* is late and untrustworthy. We have no contemporary record of where Alain studied, or of any ecclesiastical benefits he enjoyed. His early literary and theological works, however, imply a Paris training, and reliable 13th-century sources list him among the masters there. Study before 1150 at the Benedictine abbey of Bec has been suggested, but there is no proof.

Alain seems to have been based in the southwest by the 1160s and to have written extensively against the Cathars in that region. Manuscripts of his works often call him Alainus de Podio, implying a connection with Le Puy, and two 13th-century manuscripts call him Alain of Montpellier. His *De fide catholica contra haereticos* was dedicated to Guilhem VIII, count of Montpellier (r. 1172–1202); in four books, it argues successively against Cathars, Waldensians, Jews, and Muslims. His *Distinctiones dictionum theologicarum* was dedicated to Abbot Ermengaud of Saint-Gilles (r. 1179–95). The *Liber poenitentialis* is dedicated to Archbishop Henry Sully of Bourges (r. 1183–93), and his brief commentary on the Song of Songs was written for the prior of Cluny.

With a few exceptions, the dates and chronology of Alain's works are far from certain, but the earliest are generally thought to be the *Regulae caelestis iuris* (ca. 1160), also known as *De maximis theologicis*, which treated theology as an exact science, with scientific rules based on geometry, and the summa *Quoniam homines* (1160–65), an incomplete work discussing God and the Trinity, angels and humanity, according to the rules of logic. Some themes are repeated in the brief *De virtutibus et vitiis et de donis Spiritus Sancti*. His shorter theological works include numerous *Sermones diversi*, commentaries on the Lord's Prayer and the Apostles' and Nicene creeds, several short pieces on angels, including *De sex alis cherubim* (sometimes accompanied by a drawing), and the rules of celestial law, which made use of geometrical principles in its discussion of the heavens. A few hymns are also ascribed to Alain of which the best known is *Omnis mundi creatura*.

The Latin *Parabolae* are a collection of maxims in elegiac verse, similar in approach to the *Distichs* of Cato and also designed for use in Latin classes in the schools. They were frequently copied from the 12th through the 15th century, and early printed editions are common.

All of Alain's major works enjoyed wide European circulation throughout the Middle Ages. Many were innovative tools for clergy. His *Liber poenitentialis* built on the tradition of pentitential canons to present the first known manual for confessors. The *Ars praedicandi*, which applied rhetorical methods and techniques to the construction of forty-eight sample sermons, is the earliest known preaching manual. And the *Distinctiones dictionum theologicarum* was an alphabetical index of biblical words covering scriptural and theological topics, with appropriate quotations.

The earliest of Alain's literary works is usually considered to be the *De planctu Naturae*, written probably before 1171. Like Boethius's *De consolatione Philosophiae*, it is written in the mixture of verse and prose known as Menippean satire. The Goddess Nature, God's vicar, appears to the dreaming poet, robed in all creation, with signs of the zodiac in her crown and a flowery meadow at her feet. Only her heart, where man resides, is muddied and torn. She explains to him the ways in which he has violated the natural order, in thoughts and in deeds. The vividness of the condemnation of "unnatural" sex in the fifth prose and metrum led some medieval commentators to describe the work as *Contra sodomitam,* but all vices, including the ultimate corruption, of language and thought, are described at length and condemned. Good love is the offshoot of Venus and Hymenaeus, god of marriage. Evil love, Jocus, was begotten when Venus abandoned Hymenaeus for Anti-Genius. The remedy is provided at the end of the work, when Hymenaeus appears with a train of virtues. Nature's vicar, Genius, then appears, order is restored, and the poet awakens. An epilogue, *Vix nodosum valeo*, on the superiority of virgins to matrons, has traditionally been ascribed to Alain but seems more of a parody than a conclusion to the work.

In the epic Latin poem *Anticlaudianus*, usually dated ca. 1179–83, Nature is viewed more philosophically, and the allegory is more clearly and consistently developed. Nature, assisted by Nous, explains the making of the physical universe, with much material on astronomy and cosmology drawn from Bernard Silvestris. The Seven Liberal Arts build her a chariot in which to explore the universe.

The *Anticlaudianus* and the *De planctu* survive in over 150 manuscripts each and were read throughout medieval Europe as part of the advanced rhetoric curriculum in schools and universities. The *Anticlaudianus* was translated into German by Henry of Mursbach and received a detailed commentary by Raoul de Longchamp ca. 1212–25. Several commentaries on the *Anticlaudianus* and the *De planctu Naturae* remain in manuscript.

The figures of Nature and Genius in the *De planctu*, and Nature in the *Anticlaudianus*, had great influence on allegorical dream visions in the later Middle Ages. Guillaume de Lorris and Jean de Meun used them in the *Roman de la Rose*. It was to Genius that the lover made his confession in Gower's 14th-century *Confessio Amantis*. Alain is also frequently cited in later medieval treaties on dictamen and rhetoric as a model of modern poetic style.

Jeanne E. Krochalis

[See also: BERNARD SILVESTRIS; LIBERAL ARTS; *ROSE, ROMAN DE LA*]

Alain de Lille. *Opera omnia. PL* 210.
———. *Anticlaudianus: texte critique, avec une introduction et des tables*, ed. Robert Bossuat. Paris: Vrin, 1955.
———. *Alain de Lille: textes inédits avec une introduction sur sa vie et ses œuvres*, ed. Marie-Thérèse d'Alverny. Paris: Vrin, 1965.
———. *Anticlaudianus, or the Good and Perfect Man*, trans. James J. Sheridan. Toronto: Pontifical Institute of Mediaeval Studies, 1973.
———. *The Art of Preaching*, trans. Gillian R. Evans. Kalamazoo: Cistercian, 1981.
———. *Plaint of Nature*, trans. James J. Sheridan. Toronto: Pontifical Institute of Mediaeval Studies, 1980.
Evans, Gillian R. *Alan of Lille: The Frontiers of Theology in the Later Twelfth Century.* Cambridge: Cambridge University Press, 1983.
Häring, Nikolaus. "Alan of Lille, De Planctu Natural." *Studi Medievali* ser. 3, 19 (1978): 797–879.
Jauss, Hans-Robert. "La transformation de la forme allégorique entre 1180 et 1240: d'Alain de Lille à Guillaume de Lorris." In *L'humanisme médiéval dans les littératures romanes du XIIe au XIVe siècle, colloque de Strasbourg, 1962*, ed. Anthime Fourrier. Paris: Klincksieck, 1964, pp. 107–46.
Raynaud de Lage, Guy. *Alain de Lille, poète du XIIe siècle.* Montreal: Institut d'Études Médiévales, 1951.
Roussel, Henri, and François Suard, eds. *Alain de Lille, Gautier de Châtillon, Jakemart Gielée et leur temps: actes du Colloque de Lille, octobre 1978.* Lille, 1980.
Wetherbee, Winthrop P. *Platonism and Poetry in the Twelfth Century: The Literary Influence of the School of Chartres.* Princeton: Princeton University Press, 1972.
Ziolkowski, Jan. *Alan of Lille's Grammar of Sex: The Meaning of Grammar to a Twelfth-Century Intellectual.* Cambridge: Medieval Academy of America, 1985.

ALANI (Alans). The only non-Germanic settlers in the western Roman Empire during the so-called barbarian invasions, the Alani spoke an Indo-Iranian language. They were living as nomads in southern Russia when the arrival of the Huns in the 370s caused groups of them to move west, along with many Germanic tribes. With the Vandals and Visigoths, they entered Gaul in the early 5th century, and groups of them settled around Orléans and subsequently moved into Armorica (Brittany) in the later 5th century; others settled around Toulouse and Narbonne. They generally received land grants from the Roman authorities. Their small numbers, lack of a strong tribal structure, abandonment of their nomadic ways, and adoption of Christianity led to the swift assimilation of the Alani in the mixed culture of Gaul, and they ceased to be seen as a distinct people by the end of the 5th century. The chief traces of their existence in Gaul are in the personal name Alain and the many place-names with *Alan-* or *Alain-* as a component. They may have had a role in the development of the "Aquitanian" style of art and the rising importance of cavalry and cavalry tactics in later centuries; they perhaps contributed elements to the Arthurian legends.

A substantial body of Alani remained with the Vandals, with whom they soon assimilated. Vandal kings carried the title King of the Vandals and Alans from ca. 419 to the end of the Vandal kingdom. Other Alani were prominent in the political and military affairs of the eastern Roman Empire in the middle third of the 5th century, and others settled in northern Italy under Roman authority.

Steven Fanning

Bachrach, Bernard S. *A History of the Alans in the West.* Minneapolis: University of Minnesota Press, 1973.

ALARD DE CAMBRAI (fl. mid-13th c.). In the 13th century, Alard de Cambrai translated into French verse the *Moralium dogma philosophorum* of Guillaume de Conches. In the teachings of the resulting *Dits ou moralités des philosophes*, each proverb is attributed (wrongly) to a classical philosopher, commented on, and adapted to the needs of the knightly society for which Alard wrote.

Claude J. Fouillade

[See also: WILLIAM OF CONCHES]

Alard de Cambrai. *Le livre de philosophie et de moralité*, ed. Jean-Charles Payen. Paris: Klincksieck, 1970.

ALBA/AUBE. The Provençal *alba* (OFr. *aube*) is a lyric monologue or series of monologues, possibly originating in a popular tradition indigenous to practically every culture, that expresses in its most typical form the sadness of lovers who, having spent the night together, must part and/or the concern of the watchman, whose duty it is to warn them of the fast-approaching day. The Provençal dawn song contains a refrain consisting minimally of the word *alba* and occasionally uses *alba* as a generic designation. Its French counterpart, remaining closer to popular sources, makes no such use of *aube*. Whereas only five *aubes* survive, four of them anonymously, eighteen *albas* are preserved, thirteen of which are attributed. Music accompanies one *aube* and two *albas*. Though apparently never popular in Italy, the form was adopted by the German Minnesänger as the *Tagelied*. The troubadours, notably Guiraut Riquier, developed several variations on the standard dawn-song theme, such as the counter-*alba*, in which the solitary lover longs for the coming of night, when he will be united with his beloved, and the religious *alba*, in which the dawn becomes a metaphor for the Day of Judgment.

Elizabeth W. Poe

[See also: GUIRAUT RIQUIER; TROUBADOUR POETRY; TROUVÈRE POETRY]

Riquer, Martín de, ed. *Las albas provenzales.* Barcelona, 1944.
Poe, Elizabeth W. "The Three Modalities of the Old Provençal Dawn Song." *Romance Philology* 37 (1984): 259–72.
———. "La transmission de l' 'alba' en ancien provençal." *Cahiers de civilisation médiévale* 31 (1988): 323–45.
Woledge, Brian. "Old Provençal and Old French." In *Eos: An Enquiry into the Theme of Lovers' Meetings and Partings at Dawn in Poetry*, ed. Arthur T. Hatto. The Hague: Mouton, 1965.

ALBERT THE GREAT (Albertus Magnus; ca. 1200–1280). Now remembered as a theologian and philosopher, this teacher of Thomas Aquinas is perhaps most original in his scientific works. Albert was born into a noble family in Lauingen on the Danube, near Ulm. He studied at Bologna and Padua, where he entered the Dominican order in 1222. His theological training was in Germany, but ca. 1241 he went to Paris, where from 1245 to 1248 he was a Dominican regent master and taught his most famous pupil, Thomas Aquinas. In 1248, he and Thomas went to Cologne to start a new Dominican *studium generale*. In 1253–56, he was provincial of the German Dominican province, journeying to Rome in 1256 to defend the mendicants against the attacks of William of Saint-Amour and his followers. In 1260, he agreed to take the see of Ratisbon, simply to sort out its administrative disorder. He resigned two years later to return to Cologne and teaching. There was to be no peace: in 1264–66, he taught at the Dominican house in Würzburg; in 1268, he was at Strasbourg and elsewhere; in 1269–80, he was based in Cologne (where he is buried), although he attended the second Council of Lyon (1274) and was in Paris in 1277 to take part in the arguments over Aristotelian and Averroist doctrine.

Albert, known as *Doctor universalis* or *Doctor expertus*, has suffered from the proximity of his gifted pupil, Thomas, in particular from comparison with Thomas in theology and philosophy. Albert is a less systematic thinker than Thomas and less comprehensive. But this is to misjudge his gifts, which were much more for personal observation, new information, and experimentation. He was much more influential in the natural sciences, especially biology and zoology, where his warmth comes through with a sense of his own observations, than in theology.

Albert was fascinated by the created world and wanted to know all about it. The sheer amount and variety of his work make him difficult to classify and assess: some is simple collation, some is close analysis. In the mold of a Paris master, he wrote biblical commentaries, a commentary on the *Sententiae* of Peter Lombard, theological tracts, and questions. He commented on the whole of Aristotle and used him for work on the natural sciences and psychology. Although he could use and understand philosophical principles, he is not a philospher through preference; he prefers to use philosophy as a tool in other, more interesting, fields.

Lesley J. Smith

[See also: AQUINAS, THOMAS; ARISTOTLE, INFLUENCE OF; PHILOSOPHY; THEOLOGY]

Albert the Great. *Opera omnia,* ed. Auguste Borgnet. 38 vols. Paris: Vivès, 1890–99.
————. *Opera omnia ad fidem codicum manuscriptorum edenda.* Monasterii Westfalorum: Institutum Alberti Magni, 1951– . [15 vols. of a projected 40 have appeared to date.]
————. *On the Intellect and the Intelligible (Book I).* In *Selections from Medieval Philosophers,* ed. Richard McKeon. 2 vols. New York: Scribner, 1929–30, Vol. 1, pp. 326–75.
De Libéra, Alain. *Albert le Grand et la philosophie.* Paris, 1990.
Glorieux, Palémon. *Répertoire des maîtres en théologie de Paris au XIIIe siècle.* 2 vols. Paris: Vrin, 1933, Vol. 1, pp. 62–77. [Complete listing of works.]
Ostlender, H., ed. *Studia Albertina: Festschrift für Bernhard Geyer.* Münster: Aschendorff, 1952.
van Steenberghen, Fernand. "Albert le Grand et l'Aristotélisme." *Revue internationale de philosophie* 34 (1980): 566–74.
Weisheipl, James A. *Albertus Magnus and the Sciences: Commemorative Essays 1980.* Toronto: Pontifical Institute of Mediaeval Studies, 1980.
Zimmerman, Albert, ed. *Albert der Grosse, seine Zeit, sein Werk, seine Wirkung.* Berlin: De Gruyter, 1981.

ALBI. The city of Albi (Tarn) in southern France, whose name became associated with heresy, crusades, and the Inquisition, remained until the 11th century a town of modest size and importance. It was endowed with a bishopric from the 5th century and in 778 became the seat of a county. Following the collapse of Carolingian authority, Albi fell under the power of the counts of Toulouse-Rouergue, who administered it through hereditary viscounts. The viscounts thereafter extended their domains through marriages, culminating with the union of Viscount Raymond-Bernard, called Trencavel, and Ermengarde, heiress of the counties of Carcassonne, Béziers, and Agde (ca. 1066).

The power of the viscounts of Albi, however, did not efface that of the bishops, who retained broad regalian rights and secular jurisdiction. After 1066, the overextension of the Trencavels allowed the bishops to achieve practical autonomy and effective control over their city. At the same time, the burghers, whose numbers and importance increased with growing economic prosperity, allied with the bishops in their struggle for autonomy. During the Albigensian Crusade (1209–29), the burghers and bishop alike collaborated faithfully with Simon de Montfort, and in 1220 Bishop Guilhem Peire recognized the citizens' rights in a charter of liberties and franchises.

The political crisis of Albi came in the reign of Bishop Bernard de Castanet (r. 1277–1308) with the end of the alliance between the bishop and burghers. The latter, seeking increased independence, appealed to the royal government. Bishop Bernard responded by using the power of the Inquisition. In 1299 and 1300, thirty-two of the leading citizens were arrested and condemned for involvement with heresy. Thereafter, the fate of the Albigeois became a rallying point in the great struggle of the Midi against the Inquisition. Both the episcopal and communal power emerged from this struggle diminished; effective authority passed after 1320 to the government of the king, which retained control of Albi through the crises of the Hundred Years' War and the 15th century.

Alan Friedlander

Albi (Tarn), Sainte-Cécile, chevet. *Photograph courtesy of Alinari/Art Resources.*

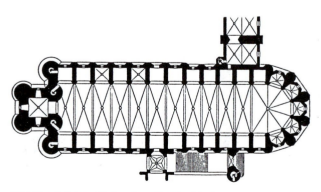

Albi (Tarn), Sainte-Cécile, plan. After Stoddard.

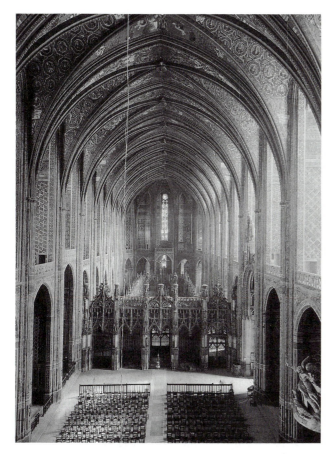

Albi (Tarn), Sainte-Cécile, nave. *Photograph courtesy of Alinari/Art Resources.*

The cathedral of Sainte-Cécile at Albi stands as a monumental symbol of the crusade against the Albigensian heresy in southern France. It was begun in 1282 in the wake of extirpation of the heresy by Bernard de Castanet, bishop of Albi and inquisitor of Languedoc, to be a fortress as well as a cathedral. Although it was built primarily in the 14th century from 1282 to 1347, its massive military appearance remains its major characteristic.

The cathedral is a single-nave structure of red brick whose compact mass is broken only by a tall tower rising from a square base at the west end. The exterior presents a regular alternation of the rounded buttresses that rise from splayed feet up the 130-foot height of the cathedral, with wall surfaces broken by narrow windows. The main entrance is on the south side through the Porch of Dominic of Florence, bishop of Albi from 1397 to 1410. This portal represents the artistic contrasts found in Albi cathedral, since it connects a sturdy crenellated tower that was once part of the surrounding fortification wall with the ornate 15th-century openwork carving of the four arches above the entrance portal.

The vast space of the single nave without aisles or transepts dominates the interior. It is 320 feet long, 63 feet wide, and the vaults reach to 100 feet high. Wall partitions that correspond to the external buttresses create twelve bays with side chapels surmounted by galleries. The ribs of the vaults, which are continued down the partitions by colonnettes, add definition to the bays. The main vaults are supported by the smaller vaults of the chapels, as well as by external buttresses.

Late Gothic decoration of the 15th and 16th centuries brings a delicacy to the appearance of the interior. The Amboise family, who were bishops at Albi at this period, commissioned painters, primarily from Italy, to cover the vaults and walls. A *Last Judgment* is on the west wall, and Old and New Testament subjects, painted by Bolognese artists between 1508 and 1514, adorn the vaults. The choir screen is a late 15th-century masterpiece of intricately carved canopies, pinnacles, and sculpted figures. This decoration transforms a fortress-cathedral of the 13th and 14th centuries into a refined expression of Late Gothic taste.

Karen Gould

[See also: ALBIGENSIAN CRUSADE; SAINT-GILLES; TRENCAVEL]

Biget, Jean-Louis. *Histoire d'Albi.* Toulouse: Privat, 1983.
————. "Un procès d'inquisition à Albi en 1300." *Cahiers de Fanjeaux* 6 (1971): 273–341.
Davis, Georgene W. *The Inquisition at Albi, 1299–1300: Text of Register and Analysis.* New York: Columbia University Press, 1948.
Hauréau, Barthélemy. *Bernard Délicieux et l'Inquisition albigeoise (1300–1320).* Paris: Hachette, 1877.
Mâle, Émile. *La cathedrale d'Albi.* Paris: Hartmann, 1950.
Neirinck, Danièle. "Les impôts directs communaux à Albi du XIII siècle au milieu du XIV siècle (calculs, composantes, évolution)." In *Actes du 102e Congrès National des Sociétés Savantes, Limoges, 1977: Section de Philologie et d'Historie jusqu'à 1610.* Paris: Bibliothèque Nationale, 1979.

ALBIGENSIAN CRUSADE. Name given to the series of military campaigns that began in the spring of 1209 as part of the effort to eradicate the Cathar heresy, an important center of which was the town of Albi in southern France.

France's Languedoc and Midi regions, together with northern Italy, had long offered fertile ground to religious heterodoxy. Geography played a key role in this. These regions' traditional involvement in the diverse cultural, commerical, and intellectual life of the Mediterranean exposed them to a steady stream of new religious and philosophical thought; and their relative lack of, or freedom from, an effective centralized political authority, a situation owing much to the disjointed topography of the territories, made it easy for dissenting ideas to take root. Not only did none of the established religious or civil authorities have the *de facto* power to suppress heresy when it appeared, but their very inability to exert that power inevitably inspired many local inhabitants to question the *de jure* authority of their supposed leaders. In a world where popular belief in such things as a "pure" river's inability to receive the "corrupt" body of an accused criminal (the underlying assumption behind trials by ordeal), the failure to exert power made it easier for people to doubt the validity of the authority in whose name that power was supposedly levied.

Heretical movements appeared in southern France as early as 1120, but an identifiable Catharism cannot be detected until the 1140s and 1150s. Despite its rigors, Catharism appealed to all social levels, including the nobility in Languedoc, and to men and women alike. Its fast-growing popularity led the church to organize episcopally directed preaching missions, and the Third Lateran Council in 1179 enjoined all believers to give their bishops aid in the struggle to root out the heresy, including physical force. But force was not used at once. Instead, preachers like St. Dominic and his followers were dispatched, courts of inquiry (the early Inquisition) were established, and ineffective or corrupt bishops were deposed. By 1204, however, Pope Innocent III decided that stronger measures were needed and called upon the Capetian king Philip II Augustus to take arms against the rebels. Philip demurred, citing his current difficulties with King John of England, and matters came to a standstill as papal energies were drawn to the tangled affairs of the Fourth Crusade then getting underway in Venice.

On January 14, 1208, however, a papal legate in Languedoc was murdered, and suspicion fell upon the count of Toulouse, Raymond VI, widely reputed to have Catharist sympathies. Innocent proclaimed a crusade against the heretics, whom he regarded as a worse threat to Christendom than even the Muslims, and against their protectors and those who tolerated the presence of heterodoxy. By the spring of 1209, a large army had convened, drawn from across Europe. Raymond of Toulouse submitted to the church and underwent a penitential scourging, but others fared worse. The viscount of Béziers and Carcassonne, who was also lord of the territory surrounding Albi, saw his lands invaded and his subjects fiercely cut down. Simon de Montfort, a middling baron from the Île-de-France and a leader of the crusade, took command of the Trencavel lands and turned Béziers into the base from which annual campaigns against the remaining heretics were launched.

Political and strategic matters quickly became complicated. Raymond of Toulouse's failure to fulfill his penitential vows drew Simon's angry attention, and when he directed the crusade against Toulouse throughout 1211 and 1212 Simon found himself battling the king of Aragon, who had come to the aid of Raymond, his brother-in-law. This king, Peter the Catholic, was at that time one of Christendom's great champions, having played a role in the decisive Battle of Las Navas de Tolosa against the Muslims of Spain, which had effectively broken the power of the Islamic princes over the bulk of the peninsula, and his opposition to Simon gave the pope an excuse to abolish the crusade privileges bestowed upon those fighting the Cathars. Innocent by this time wanted desperately to raise soldiers for another crusade to the Holy Land and felt that the drawn-out Cathar affair undermined his hopes. Simon, however, defeated Peter at the Battle of Muret in September 1213, leaving the Aragonese ruler dead on the field and the crusading army in control of most of Raymond's lands in southern France.

The towns of the region, regardless of their religious attitudes, then rebelled against Simon's growing authority, which they viewed as an unwarranted abrogation of their traditional independence. When Simon was killed in a skirmish outside Toulouse in 1218, few mourned. The new pope, Honorius III, restored crusader privileges to those involved in the fight against the Cathars but with little result. Matters remained stalemated until 1226, when King Louis VIII of France led his own crusading force southward, as much in the hope of securing a Capetian outlet to the Mediterranean as out of a desire to defend orthodoxy. The Treaty of Meaux-Paris, signed in early 1229, formally ended the Albigensian Crusade by restoring the Toulousan count (Raymond VII, by this time) to at least part of his lands and by establishing a Capetian foothold in the south. Catharism itself, however, survived well into the 14th century, especially in remoter towns and villages.

The Albigensian Crusade showed the impotence of crusading as a solution for deeply rooted heresy and pointed the way to the need for a different sort of response—the Inquisition. The ways in which political and dynastic concerns affected crusader efforts, usually for the worse, were also amply illustrated; and the crusade's most lasting consequence was the effective halting of Catalan claims of overlordship north of the Pyrénées and the establishment of Capetian power throughout Languedoc, the Midi, and eventually Provence.

Clifford R. Backman

[See also: AGENAIS; ALBI; BÉZIERS; CATHARS; DOMINICAN ORDER; HERESY; INQUISITION; LOUIS VIII; MONTFORT; MURET; TRENCAVEL]

Le Roy Ladurie, Emmanuel. *Montaillou: Catholics and Cathars in a French Village, 1294–1324*, trans. Barbara Bray. London: Scolar, 1978.

Mundy, John H. *The Repression of Catharism at Toulouse: The Royal Diploma of 1279*. Toronto: Pontifical Institute of Mediaeval Studies, 1985.

Roquebert, Michel. *L'épopée cathare: 1198–1212*. 3 vols. Toulouse: Privat, 1970–86.

Strayer, Joseph Rees. *The Albigensian Crusade*. New York: Dial, 1971.

Wakefield, Walter L. *Heresy, Crusade and Inquisition in Southern France, 1100–1250*. London: Allen and Unwin, 1974.

ALBRET. The lords of Albret ("Lebret," "La Bret"), vassals of the dukes of Aquitaine, belonged to one of the most important families in Gascony. Their original seat was Labrit (Landes), but eventually they considered Casteljaloux (Lot-et-Garonne) their chief residence. They bore an unusual coat of arms, *de gueules plain*, devoid of heraldic devices, and five of them were named Bernard-Aiz (a spelling now considered preferable to the more common Bernard-Ezi, which derived from the Latin genitive).

Amanieu V (d. 1240) was a first cousin of Isabelle d'Angoulême, queen of England. Amanieu VII (d. 1326), Edward I's occasional ambassador to the pope, became rector of the northern papal states for Clement V and served

France in the Anglo-French war of Saint-Sardos (1323–25). His son Bernard-Aiz V (d. 1359), son-in-law of the count of Armagnac, switched sides several times during the preliminaries of the Hundred Years' War. He fought for Edward III at Poitiers and was rewarded with a pension of 1,000 pounds.

Bernard-Aiz V's son Arnaud-Amanieu (d. 1401) paid homage to the Black Prince in 1363 and fought as his vassal in Castile (Nájera, 1367). The inability of the Black Prince to continue his pension made him receptive to the overtures of Charles V of France. In 1368, Arnaud-Amanieu married Charles V's sister-in-law Marguerite de Bourbon and was promised a substantial pension. He later became *Grand Chambellan de France*.

Arnaud-Amanieu's son, Charles I (d. 1415), grew up at the French court as a "companion" to the dauphin (Charles VI) and was named constable of France in 1403. As partial payment for his royal pension, he received the county of Dreux in 1407. Considered a member of the Armagnac party, he was replaced as constable in 1411 but regained the post in 1413 and was killed at Agincourt. His son Charles II (d. 1471) sired Alain le Grand (d. 1522), whose son Jean married the queen of Navarre in 1484.

Richard C. Famiglietti

[See also: ARMAGNAC; ARMAGNACS; CHARLES V THE WISE; CHARLES VI; HUNDRED YEARS' WAR]

Dubois, Jean. "Inventaire des titres de la maison d'Albret." *Recueil des travaux de la Société d'Agriculture, Sciences et Arts d'Agen* 2nd ser. 16 (1913): 1–212.

Luchaire, Achille. "Notice sur les origines de la maison d'Albret (977–1270)." *Bulletin de la Société des Sciences, Lettres et Arts de Pau* 2nd ser. 2 (1872–73): 24–40, 99–124.

Marquette, Jean-Bernard. "Les Albret." *Cahiers du Bazadais* 30 (1975): 5–52; 31 (1975): 55–107; 34 (1976): 117–203; 38 (1977): 211–374; 41 (1978): 377–536; 45/46 (1979): 539–886.

———. *Le trésor des chartes d'Albret*. Paris: Bibliothèque Nationale, 1973, Vol. 1.

ALCUIN (Albinus Alcuinus; ca. 735–804). Born in Northumbria, Alcuin became the primary teacher of Charlemagne's palace school. Alcuin was educated under Bishop Egbert of York and saw himself in the intellectual tradition of the Venerable Bede. He met Charlemagne in Italy in 771 and represented him on a mission to Offa of Mercia in 790 and at the councils of Frankfurt (794) and Aachen (799). Ordained deacon but never priest, Alcuin was abbot of several French monasteries and made the abbey of Saint-Martin of Tours an important center of Carolingian learning. His writings include biblical commentaries (on Genesis, the Psalms, Ecclesiastes, the Song of Songs, some New Testament epistles, and the Gospel of John), liturgical treatises, hagiography, poems, many letters, tractates against the Spanish Adoptionists, a treatise on the phases of the moon, and school texts. These last, covering the Trivium (grammar, rhetoric, and dialectic), are in the form of dialogues between Alcuin and his pupils, including "a Saxon," "a Frank," and Charlemagne. At court, Alcuin was called "Flaccus" after the Roman poet Horace. His greatest legacy to medieval France was a tradition of school learning continued by his students Louis the Pious and Rabanus Maurus. He died at the monastery of Saint-Martin.

E. Ann Matter

[See also: ANTICHRIST; CHARLEMAGNE; LOUIS I THE PIOUS; PHILOSOPHY; RABANUS MAURUS]

Alcuin. *Opera*. PL 100–01; MGH PLAC II, pp. 160–351; MGH Ep. IV.

Cavadini, John. *The Last Christology in the West: Adoptionism in Spain and Gaul 785–820*. Philadelphia: University of Pennsylvania Press, 1993.

Duckett, Eleanor Shipley. *Alcuin, Friend of Charlemagne: His World and His Work*. New York: Macmillan, 1951.

Wallach, Luitpold. *Alcuin and Charlemagne: Studies in Carolingian History and Literature*. Ithaca: Cornell University Press, 1959.

ALEMANNI. The Alemanni or Alamanni ("All Men") were a confederation of Germanic tribes first mentioned in A.D. 213 as fighting against the Roman Empire; they raided both Italy and Gaul in the 3rd and 4th centuries. In the early 5th century, they were able to cross the Rhine, and the decline of the western Roman Empire in the middle of that century allowed them to expand westward to the Vosges and into Alsace. Colliding with Frankish expansion, they were defeated by Clovis I in the mid-490s at Zülpich (Tolbiac). Afterward, most of the Alemanni were under Frankish authority.

Although the fortunes of the Alemanni were generally linked to those of the Frankish kingdom of Austrasia, they did enjoy a measure of self-rule under native dukes subordinate to the Merovingians, and they came to dominate southwestern Germany and northern Switzerland along the Jura mountain range. The Alemanni were included in the kingdom of Louis the German in the Treaty of Verdun in 843 and later were attached to Germany rather than to France, forming the core of the later duchy of Swabia. In the Merovingian period, Alemannia was a sort of eastern frontier of the Frankish kingdom, and the Alemanni gave their name to the French words for Germany (*Allemagne*) and for Germans (*allemands*).

Steven Fanning

[See also: CLOVIS I; FRANKS; MEROVINGIAN DYNASTY]

James, Edward. *The Franks*. Oxford: Blackwell, 1988.

Musset, Lucien. *The Germanic Invasions*, trans. Edward and Columba James. University Park: Pennsylvania State University Press, 1975, pp. 80–83.

ALEXANDER III (d. 1181). Pope. When Pope Hadrian IV died in 1159, the majority of the cardinals elected the chancellor of the Roman church, the Sienese Rolando Bandinelli, to succeed him as Alexander III. The emperor

Frederick I Barbarossa, offended by Rolando's conduct at the Diet of Besançon earlier that year, supported the rival claim of Cardinal Octavian. Despite support by the Norman king of Sicily, William I, and by the cities that formed the Lombard League, in 1162 Alexander was forced to take refuge in France, where he conducted councils at Montpellier (1162) and Tours (1163). Although Louis VII, fearing to alienate his mighty vassal Henry I Plantagenêt of England, adhered to Alexander, he also was reluctant to offend Barbarossa. Alexander also found himself caught between princes when in 1170 Louis demanded in vain that the pope condemn Henry for the murder of Thomas Becket. (Alexander had advised Thomas against challenging the Plantagenêt monarch, one of his allies.) This difficult situation was resolved when an impoverished pope and the emperor, who had been defeated by the Lombard League at Legnano, were reconciled in the Peace of Venice (1177). Alexander returned to Rome, where in 1179 he held the Third Lateran Council. Its canons, which imposed penalties on violators of the Truce of God and regulated clerical discipline, became part of the canon law. So did many of Alexander's decretals, which clarified points of law for judges-delegate throughout Christendom.

Thomas M. Izbicki

[See also: CANON LAW; TRUCE OF GOD]

Boso. *Boso's Life of Alexander III*, trans. G.M. Ellis. Oxford: Blackwell, 1973.

Tanner, Norman P., ed. *Decrees of the Ecumenical Councils.* 2 vols. London: Sheed and Ward, 1990, Vol. 1, pp. 205–25. [Third Lateran Council—1179.]

Baldwin, Marshall. *Alexander III and the Twelfth Century.* Glen Rock: Newman, 1968.

Robinson, I.S. *The Papacy, 1073–1198.* Cambridge: Cambridge University Press, 1990.

Somerville, Robert. *Pope Alexander III and the Council of Tours.* Berkeley: University of California Press, 1977.

ALEXANDER OF HALES (ca. 1185–1245). Theologian. Alexander's early life is conjectural: born probably in Hales (now Hales Owen), in the English Midlands, he studied arts, then theology, in Paris, from around the turn of the century. From 1226 to 1229, he was a canon of Saint Paul's, London, although he remained in Paris. He was one of four masters sent to Rome by the University of Paris in 1230 to represent its case in the famous dispute (which led to strike and dissolution) with the French king. Gregory IX's bull *Parens scientiarum* (1231), arising out of the dispute, was partly Alexander's work. In 1231, he was made canon of Lichfield and archdeacon of Coventry. At the height of his career, in 1235, he joined the fledgling Franciscan order (apparently breaking off a sermon he was preaching, taking the habit, and returning to finish the sermon), thus giving the Franciscans their first holder of a magisterial chair in the University of Paris. He was active in teaching for the Franciscans and as an adjudicator of disputes until his sudden death, probably of an epidemic disease, in Paris in 1245.

The catalogue of Alexander's works is unclear. He is best remembered today for introducing commentary on Peter Lombard's *Sententiae* into the Paris theology syllabus. His own *Sententiae* gloss, the earliest we possess, survives in more than one version, apparently being student *reportationes* of his lectures. A set of *Quaestiones disputatae* "antequam esset frater" belongs to him, but a *Summa theologiae* begun by Alexander was finished by William of Melitona, John of La Rochelle, and other members of the "Franciscan school" that Alexander headed. It is thus a useful summary of 13th-century Franciscan ideas. The same group of friars was responsible for an exposition of the Franciscan *Rule*, in 1242.

With William of Auvergne, Alexander (known as *Doctor irrefragibilis*), was the first Paris master to use Aristotle in the service of theology; and, like William, he used Aristotle's ideas in a framework of traditional Augustinian orthodoxy. Alexander's main sources are Augustine, Pseudo-Dionysius, Boethius, and the "moderns" of the 12th century: Bernard of Clairvaux, Gilbert of Poitiers, Anselm, and others.

Alexander's prosaic style makes it difficult for us today to appreciate his enormous contemporary success, although his structured and ordered approach remains a key feature of his work. Bonaventure was of one of the succeeding generation who revered Alexander, suggesting that his teaching in person may have been more gripping than the remnant left to us.

Lesley J. Smith

[See also: ARISTOTLE, INFLUENCE OF; BONAVENTURE; FRANCISCAN ORDER; *PARENS SCIENTIARUM*; PETER LOMBARD; THEOLOGY; WILLIAM OF AUVERGNE]

Alexander of Hales. *Glossa in Sententias*, ed. P. Doucet. 4 vols. Florence: Ex Typographia Collegii S. Bonaventurae, 1951–57.

———. *Questiones disputatae "antequam esset frater."* 3 vols. Florence: Ex Typographia Collegii S. Bonaventurae, 1960.

———. *Summa theologica*, ed. Bernardini Klumper. 4 vols. Florence: Ex Typographia Collegii S. Bonaventurae, 1924.

———. *Summa theologica. Indices in tom. I–IV,* ed. Constantini Koser. Grottaferrata (Rome): Editiones Collegii S. Bonaventurae ad Claras Aquas, 1979.

Catania, F.J. *Knowledge of God in Alexander of Hales and John Duns Scotus.* Kalamazoo: Medieval Institute, 1966.

Herscher, I. "A Bibliography of Alexander of Hales." *Franciscan Studies* 5 (1945): 434–54.

Huber, Raphael M. "Alexander of Hales O.F.M. (ca. 1170–1245): His Life and Influence on Medieval Scholasticism." *Franciscan Studies* 26 (1945): 353–65.

Principe, Walter H. *The Theology of the Hypostatic Union in the Early Thirteenth Century.* 4 vols. Toronto: Pontifical Institute of Mediaeval Studies, 1963–75, Vol. 2: *Alexander of Hales's Theology of the Hypostatic Union.*

ALEXANDER NECKHAM (1157–1217). Alexander Neckham (or Nequam, a nickname meaning "worthless") was born in England at St. Alban's and traveled to read arts at Paris ca. 1175. He returned to England to teach at Dunstable (ca. 1182) and St. Alban's (ca. 1185–90), then studied theology at Oxford (ca. 1190–97). Around 1200, he entered the order of Augustinian Canons, acted as a papal judge-delegate in 1203 and 1205, and was made abbot of Cirencester in 1213. He died in Kempsey, Worcestershire.

Like other "encyclopedists" in England and France at this time, Alexander wanted to know everything. He belonged to a group of Oxford scientists whose knowledge and methods were the best in Europe. He wrote biblical commentaries, consulting Jews for this purpose, and learned some Hebrew, and he wrote on grammar and natural science. Alexander's two major works, *De nominibus utensilium* and *De naturis rerum*, show his encyclopedic learning by defining long lists of words and thus describing everyday objects (saddles, clothing, beds), technology (goldsmithing, manuscript copying, agricultural tools), the liberal arts, buildings and their furnishings, and the like. He also versified Aesop's Fables (*Novus Aesopus*) and was the author of a poem, *De laudibus divinae sapientiae*, and biblical commentaries. An Augustinian theologian who used Aristotle in his science, he complained, while abbot, that religion and study were becoming incompatible—creeping professionalism even in the 12th century.

Lesley J. Smith

Neckam, Alexander. *Alexandri Neckam De naturis rerum libri duo: With the Poem of the Same Author, De laudibus divinae sapientiae*, ed. Thomas Wright. London: Longman, Green, Longman, Roberts, and Green, 1863.
———. *Speculum speculationum*, ed. Rodney M. Thomson. Oxford: Oxford University Press, 1988.
Holmes, Urban Tigner, Jr. *Daily Living in the Twelfth Century: Based on the Observations of Alexander Neckam in London and Paris*. Madison: University of Wisconsin Press, 1952.
Hunt, Richard W. *The Schools and the Cloister: The Life and Writings of Alexander Nequam (1157–1217)*, ed. Margaret Gibson. Oxford: Clarendon, 1984.

ALEXANDER ROMANCES. Alexander the Great (356–323 B.C.), king of Macedonia (336–23 B.C.) and in the Middle Ages considered one of the Nine Worthies, became the subject of a fantastical biography by the Pseudo-Callisthenes in the 2nd century A.D. Julius Valerius's 4th-century Latin translation of this Greek biography, as summarized in a 9th-century *Epitome*, was the principal source of the medieval French *Roman d'Alexandre*, a long poem resulting from a compositional process spread over most of the 12th century.

The earliest extant Old French poem was composed by Albéric de Pisançon in his native Franco-Provençal dialect (Dauphinois), in the first third of the 12th century; only one manuscript fragment, 105 octosyllables arranged in fifteen monorhymed laisses, survives. Albéric's name is known only thanks to the German priest Lamprecht, who translated most (or even all; the life is unfinished) of Albéric ca. 1155. A generation or so later, ca. 1160, an anonymous decasyllabic poem in the dialect of Poitou drew on Albéric to give an account of the conqueror's youth (*enfances*). To this were added two poems: the first, by Lambert le Tort de Châteaudun, narrates Alexander's adventures in the East (*Orient*) up to his arrival in Babylon; a separate, anonymous, branch treats the hero's death (*mort*). These three poems (*enfances, Orient, mort*) were combined, resulting in two manuscripts totaling 6,015 and 9,947 lines, respectively.

After another short interval, Alexandre de Paris, from Bernay in Normandy, rewrote the earlier compilation in twelve-syllable laisses (hence the term "Alexandrine"), adding a previously separate account of a raid on Gaza, the *Fuerre de Gadres*, by a certain Eustache (ca. 1155). Alexandre's work is found in seventeen manuscripts; in the critical edition, the poem is arranged thus:

Albéric (*enfances*)	Br. I, first half	1,656	Alex.
linked to	I, middle	1,009	
the *Fuerre de Gadres*	I, last quarter	619	
the *Fuerre de Gadres*	II, first two-thirds	1,424	
linked to	II, last third	676	
Lambert (*Orient*)	III	7,839	
mort Alexandre	IV	1,709	
		14,932	Alex.

Branch III, the core of the romance, is composed largely of extraordinary adventures, including Alexander's exploration of the depths of the sea in a bathysphere, and of the heavens, harnessed to a flock of birds. Dalliance with exotic and amorous—and dangerous—damsels is of course not lacking. The Middle Ages saw in Alexander the epitome of chivalry and the model of valor (*prouesse*) and generosity (*largesse*).

Alexandre's *Alexandre*, like earlier versions, is a formal anomaly in medieval French literature; though composed in laisses, which are elsewhere used only for the chanson de geste, thematically the poem is a romance, treating the story of a single hero, from birth to death, and not a single episode or series of episodes in which the hero opposes what could be deemed societal enemies. The *Roman d'Alexandre* is thus much more an adventure romance than a biography, classified generally among the Romances of Antiquity because of its subject matter. Its oriental setting was to have an important influence on many Old French romances.

A number of poems were subsequently composed in the north about episodes of the hero's career and are usually found interpolated into the *Roman d'Alexandre* text or at least contained in *Roman d'Alexandre* manuscripts. Among these are Jean Le Névelon's *Venjance Alixandre* (last quarter of the 12th c.; 1,936 lines), Gui de Cambrai's *Vengement Alixandre* (before 1191; 1,806 lines); the anonymous *Prise de Defur* (before 1257; 1,654 Alexandrines); the *Voyage d'Alexandre au Paradis terrestre* (1270–1350; 503 Alexandrines); and Jacques de Longuyon's *Vœux du paon* (ca. 1312), with its continuations by Jean Brisebarre, *Restor du paon* (before 1338), and Jean de Le Mote, *Parfait du paon* (1340). An independent Anglo-Norman Life of Alexander was composed by Thomas of Kent. After 1206, the poem was put into prose, with a second redaction between 1252 and ca. 1290 and a third in the 14th century (total of eighteen manuscripts), with editions through the 16th century.

Larry S. Crist

[**See also:** ANTIQUITY, ROMANCES OF; LE MOTE, JEAN DE; VOW CYCLE]

The Medieval French Roman d'Alexandre. 6 vols. I. *Text of the Arsenal and Venice Versions*, ed. Milan S. La Du. Princeton: Princeton University Press, 1937; II. *Version of Alexandre de Paris: Text*, ed. E.C. Armstrong, D.L. Buffum, Bateman Edwards, and L.F.H. Lowe. Princeton: Princeton University Press, 1937; III. *Version of Alexandre de Paris: Variants and Notes to Branch I*, ed. Alfred Foulet. Princeton: Princeton University Press, 1949; IV. *Le roman du Fuerre de Gadres d'Eustache*, ed. E.C. Armstrong and Alfred Foulet. Princeton: Princeton University Press, 1942; V. *Version of Alexandre de Paris: Variants and Notes to Branch II*, ed. E.C. Armstrong and Frederick B. Agard. Princeton: Princeton University Press, 1942; VI. *Version of Alexandre de Paris: Introduction and Notes to Branch III*, ed. Alfred Foulet. Princeton: Princeton University Press, 1976; VII. *Version of Alexandre de Paris: Variants and Notes to Branch IV*, ed. Bateman Edwards and Alfred Foulet. Princeton: Princeton University Press, 1955.
Gui de Cambrai. *Le vengement Alexandre*, ed. Bateman Edwards. Princeton: Princeton University Press, 1928.
Ham, Edward Billings, ed. *Five Versions of the* Venjance Alixandre. Princeton: Princeton University Press, 1935.
Jehan le Nivelon. *La venjance Alixandre*, ed. Edward Billings Ham. Princeton: Princeton University Press, 1931.
Peckham, Lawton P.G., and Milan S. La Du, eds. *La prise de Defur* and *Le voyage d'Alexandre au Paradis terrestre*. Princeton: Princeton University Press, 1935.
Thomas of Kent. *The Anglo-Norman Alexandre (Le roman de toute chevalerie)*, ed. Brian Foster. 2 vols. London: Anglo-Norman Text Society, 1976–77.
Cary, George. *The Medieval Alexander*. Cambridge: Cambridge University Press, 1956.
Frappier, Jean. "*Le Roman d'Alexandre* et ses diverses versions au XIIe siècle," and Jean-Charles Payen, "*Alexandre en prose*." In *Grundriss der romanischen Literaturen des Mittelalters*, Vol. 4: *Le roman jusqu'à la fin du XIIIe siècle, t. 1 (Partie historique)*. Heidelberg: Winter, 1978, pp. 149–67, and *t. 2 (Partie documentaire)*. Heidelberg: Winter, 1984, nos. 20–32 (pp. 75–80), 176 (p. 119), 236 (pp. 134–35), 304 (pp. 152–53), 392 (pp. 187–88), 492 (pp. 213–14).
Meyer, Paul. *Alexandre le grand dans la littérature française du moyen âge.* 2 vols. Paris: Vieweg, 1886.

ALEXANDRE DU PONT (fl. mid-13th c.). Alexandre's *Roman de Mahomet*, a 1,997-line poem composed in Laon (Aisne) in 1258, is a free adaptation of the *Otia de Machomete* written by Gautier de Compiègne after 1137. It is preserved by a single manuscript, B.N. fr. 1553. The prophet's mythical biography is enhanced by colorful portrayals painted by a longwinded writer, a knowledgeable craftsman of epic poetry, who gave free rein to his moralizing bent.

Annette Brasseur

Alexandre du Pont. *Le roman de Mahomet de Alexandre du Pont*, ed. Yvan G. Lepage. Paris: Klincksieck, 1977.

ALEXIS, GUILLAUME (ca. 1425–1486). A Benedictine monk in the abbey of Lyre in Normandy, Guillaume Alexis (also spelled Alecis) was a prolific writer whose vigorous style derives at once from innovation and variety in rhyme schemes and from his mordant, outspoken moralizing and railing against vainglory. His first poem, *L'ABC des doubles* (1451), uses a complex rhyme scheme based on the letters of the alphabet to offer moral advice. Several of his works, notably the *Blason des faulses amours*, the *Débat de l'omme et de la femme*, and the *Débat du mondain et du religieux*, present cynical views of love. He is often compared with Villon, as some of his poems intersect thematically with Villon's; the direction of influence between the two poets has yet to be clarified.

Janice C. Zinser

[**See also:** VILLON, FRANÇOIS]

Alexis, Guillaume. *Œuvres poétiques de Guillaume Alexis, prieur de Bucy*, ed. Arthur Piaget and Émile Picot. 3 vols. Paris: Société des Anciens Textes Français, 1896–1908.

ALGER OF LIÈGE (ca. 1050–ca. 1131). As deacon and *scholasticus* of Saint-Bartholomew in Liège, and later canon of Saint-Lambert and secretary to Bishop Otbert after 1101, Alger became the leading master in Liège and was involved in major controversies. His *Liber de misericordia et iustitia* addressed questions in the conflict between Bishop Otbert and adherents of the Gregorian reform movement; *De sacramentis corporis et sanguinis dominici* was a product of the debate in Liège occasioned by Rupert of Deutz's eucharistic doctrine. In 1121, Alger entered the Benedictine abbey of Cluny, where he died ca. 1131.

Grover A. Zinn

[**See also:** GREGORIAN REFORM]

Alger of Liège. *De sacramentis corporis et sanguinis dominici.* PL 180.739–854.
———. *Liber de misericordia et iustitia.* PL 180.857–968.
———. *Letters*, ed. Philippus Jaffé. In *Monumenta Bambergensia, Bibliotheca Rerum Germanicarum* 5 (1869): 262–67, 373–79.
Häring, Nicholas M. "A Study in the Sacramentology of Alger of Liège." *Medieval Studies* 20 (1958): 41–78.
Le Bras, Gabriel. "Le *Liber de misericordia et iustitia* d'Alger de Liège." *Nouvelle revue historique de droit français et étranger* 45 (1921): 80–118.
Van Engen, John. *Rupert of Deutz*. Berkeley: University of California Press, 1983, pp. 168–73. [On Alger's *De sacramentis corporis et sanguinis dominici*.]

ALISCANS. A 12th-century epic of 8,435 decasyllabic lines divided into rhymed laisses, *Aliscans* offers variations on material in the latter part of the *Chanson de Guillaume*: the death of Vivien; the flight of Guillaume to Orange; the battles against Desramé and his monstrous pagans, with final victory won for Guillaume by the heroic exploits of Rainouart; Rainouart's exclusion from the celebrations that follow; the reconciliation; and finally his baptism, knighting, and marriage to Aelis, the king's daughter and Guillaume's niece. Different in *Aliscans* is the early announcement, before Rainouart has proved himself, that he will wed Aelis.

Joan B. Williamson

[See also: *GUILLAUME, CHANSON DE*; GUILLAUME D'ORANGE CYCLE]

Holtus, Günter, ed. *La versione franco-italiana della "Bataille d'Aliscans": Codex Marcianus fr. VIII, 252*. Tübingen: Niemeyer, 1985.

Régnier, Claude, ed. *Aliscans*. 2 vols. Paris: Champion, 1990.

Newth, Michael A., trans. *The Song of Aliscans*. New York: Garland, 1992.

ALLEU/ALLOD. An allod was freehold land, land that the possessor owned outright, without owing dues, rents, or homage for it. "Allodial land" in Merovingian times generally referred to inherited property, as opposed to property one had purchased, but soon came to mean any land owned outright. Although scholars used to describe peasants as primarily renting their land and nobles as holding theirs in fief, they now argue that all sectors of society owned much allodial land throughout the Middle Ages.

Constance B. Bouchard

Duby, Georges. *Rural Economy and Country Life in the Medieval West*, trans. Cynthia Postan. London: Arnold, 1968.

Evergates, Theodore. *Feudal Society in the Bailliage of Troyes Under the Counts of Champagne, 1152–1284*. Baltimore: Johns Hopkins University Press, 1975.

ALPHONSE OF POITIERS (1220–1271). Count of Toulouse. Alphonse was the brother of Louis IX (St. Louis) and was himself one of the great territorial princes of the 13th century. When they came of age, the younger sons of Louis VIII were provided for by means of apanages, territorial holdings of considerable extent. Alphonse, who was invested with the apanage of Poitou in 1241, immediately ran up against serious problems. Poitou and its southern marches constituted a region that had seen an English army of invasion a generation before. Nobles in the region were fiercely independent, and many had rallied to the English king, their former overlord, in 1214. They had been defeated, but the region remained discontented. So long as their new lord was the French king, a remote figure, discontent did not become open rebellion; but in 1241, when authority was given over to the cadet prince Alphonse at a great festival in Saumur in the heartland of Poitou, the occasion was interpreted as a direct challenge to the independence and authority of the native nobility. Alphonse's first

years as count of Poitou were thus checkered by the necessity of putting down a rebellion in which the rebels received both the support of the English and the encouragement of the count of Toulouse. The rebellion failed, but it pointed up the precariousness of Capetian rule in the southwest.

Alphonse's holdings were vastly increased in the south in 1249 on the death of his father-in-law, the erstwhile rebel Count Raymond VII of Toulouse. Raymond's heir, as provided by the Treaty of Meaux-Paris (1229) that ended the Albigensian Crusade, was his daughter Jeanne, Alphonse's wife. Although he was with his brother on crusade at the time of Raymond's death, Alphonse's interests were protected by the decisive action of his mother, the regent Blanche of Castile. Reacting swiftly to information that some southerners were refusing to adhere to the transfer of the deceased count's lands to Alphonse, she made a show of force and quickly won their capitulation.

The biography of Alphonse, therefore, is largely the history of his attempts to govern his apanage and the diverse lands that fell to his administration from the holdings of the count of Toulouse. Back from crusade in 1250, he set about ruling these vast territories, which included, besides Poitou and Toulouse, Saintonge, Auvergne, and part of the Rhône Valley. In addition to resident administrators (*sénéchaux, viguiers,* and *bayles*), he employed *enquêteurs*, investigators modeled on his brother's *enquêteurs*, whose duty it was to investigate periodically complaints against his government. He had commissioned a handful of these agents in 1249 at the time of his departure on crusade. He extended the commissions in 1251 to all the lands inherited from the count of Toulouse; and he used the *enquêteurs* regularly thereafter. Their work went a long way toward assuaging the discontent in his territories.

Though governing from Paris, Alphonse took an active, almost obsessive interest in the details of administration, as his surviving administrative correspondence and his excellent accounts demonstrate. He monitored closely the activities of his provincial officials and took a judicious interest in the workings of the high court or parlement of Toulouse.

It is difficult to get a nuanced sense of Alphonse as a man. Although briefly a crusader, he seems on the whole to have been conventionally pious. He detested Judaism and vigorously exploited the wealth of the Jews in his domains; but he did not disdain to use a Jewish physician when he had some painful eye trouble. There is an element of closefistedness in his character, although it would be wrong to call him a miser. He seems to have enjoyed a happy married life. Despite the fact that she bore him no children, Alphonse never deserted Jeanne, and both went on St. Louis's last crusade (1270). Both died on the trip homeward (1271) within a few days of each other. Their holdings escheated to the crown.

William Chester Jordan

Boutaric, Edgard. *Saint Louis et Alfonse de Poitiers*. Paris: Plon, 1870.

DeVic, Claude, and Jean Vaissete. *Histoire générale du Languedoc*, ed. Ernest Molinier. New edition. Toulouse: Privat, 1879, Vol. 7.

Fournier, Pierre-François, and Pascal Guébin, eds. *Enquêtes administratives d'Alfonse de Poitiers*. Paris: Imprimerie Nationale, 1959.

ALTA CAPELLA. A standard grouping of musical instruments in the late Middle Ages. The *alta capella* was employed by 15th-century courts and cities to provide *haute musique* ("loud music") for dancing, ceremony, and enter-

A late 15th-century ball (Burgundy, ca. 1469–70), with an *alta capella* consisting of two shawms and slide trumpet. MS fr. 5073, fol. 117v. *Courtesy of the Bibliothèque de l'Arsenal, Paris.*

tainment. The ensemble was typically made up of three or four minstrels who played shawms, slide trumpets, sackbuts, and bombardes. Until late in the 15th century, much of the repertory of *alta* musicians was improvised; one instrumentalist played the *cantus firmus* (frequently a standard *basse danse* tune), while the others improvised counterpoint around it.

J. Michael Allsen

[See also: *BASSE DANSE*; MUSICAL INSTRUMENTS]

Brown, Howard Mayer. "Alta." In *The New Grove Dictionary of Music and Musicians*, ed. Stanley Sadie. London: Macmillan, 1980, Vol. 1, pp. 292–93.
Duffin, Ross W. "The *trompette des menestrels* in the 15th-Century *alta capella*." *Early Music* 17 (1989): 397–402.
Polk, Keith. "The Trombone, the Slide Trumpet, and the Ensemble Tradition of the Early Renaissance." *Early Music* 17 (1989): 389–97.

AMADAS ET YDOINE. The original version of this anonymous Anglo-Norman romance was written between 1190 and 1220, perhaps earlier. Considerable fragments have survived in two Anglo-Norman manuscripts and a complete version (7,912 lines) in a Picard manuscript from Arras (MS P; B.N. fr. 375), dated 1288. *Amadas* was relatively popular, especially in England; it was alluded to in subsequent texts and its hero was cited in lists of famous lovers.

Ydoine is the daughter of the Duke of Burgundy; Amadas, the son of the duke's seneschal. Ydoine sends her suitor out into the world to win martial renown, but when the duke marries his daughter to the Count of Nevers, Amadas falls into insanity. However, with the assistance of three sorceresses, Ydoine conserves her virginity. The countess cures the young man of his madness, and he rescues her after she has been abducted by a demon. Ydoine then arranges for her marriage to be annulled so she can wed her true love.

Amadas et Ydoine is filled with fine speeches, courtly elegance and descriptions of contemporary life. The author takes a number of themes or conventions literally—lovesickness, love madness, death and rebirth, woman's manipulation and deceit, enchantments, the supernatural—and, extending them to their extreme limits, explores what, both as fact and metaphor, they imply. Following in the tradition of the Tristan romances and Chrétien, the *Amadas* poet seeks to provide ideals of courtly conduct in order that the social code be respected and that true love flourish.

William C. Calin

[See also: ANGLO-NORMAN LITERATURE; ANTIFEMINISM; IDYLLIC ROMANCE]

Arthur, Ross G., trans. *Amadas et Ydoine*. New York: Garland, 1994.
Reinhard, John R., ed. *Amadas et Ydoine, roman du XIIIe siècle*. Paris: Champion, 1926.
Calin, William. "*Amadas et Ydoine*: The Problematic World of an Idyllic Romance." *Continuations: Essays on Medieval French Literature and Language in Honor of John L. Grigsby*, ed. Norris J. Lacy and Gloria Torrini-Roblin. Birmingham: Summa, 1989, pp. 39–49.
Reinhard, John R. *The Old French Romance of Amadas et Ydoine: An Historical Study*. Durham: Duke University Press, 1927.

AMALARIUS OF METZ (ca. 775–ca. 850). The most influential and controversial liturgist of the Carolingian age and the major western Christian propagator of an allegorical understanding of the liturgy. Born near Metz and educated in the school of Alcuin, Amalarius held many positions of importance: archbishop of Trier (811–13), Charlemagne's ambassador to Constantinople (813), and archbishop of Lyon (835–38). It was in this last position, which he held for only three years, that Amalarius became a controversial figure. His highly allegorical liturgical writings, which stressed a polyvalent, many-tiered understanding of ritual, were attacked by the deposed bishop Agobard of Lyon, to whose place Amalarius had been appointed. Because of Agobard's influence, Amalarius was subsequently condemned by the Synod of Quierzy (838) and deposed from his bishopric. In spite of this judgment, the liturgical writings of Amalarius, especially the *Liber officialis* (823), were widely read throughout the Middle Ages. His emphasis on the flexibility of meaning in the liturgical mysteries helped to bring about a shift toward liturgical devotion; this in turn aided the development of late-medieval forms of piety. Amalarius's allegories are difficult, however, and are still in need of detailed study from the point of view of ritual and symbolic thought.

E. Ann Matter

[See also: FLORUS OF LYON; LITURGICAL COMMENTATORS]

Amalarius of Metz. *Amalarii episcopi, opera liturgica omnia,* ed. Jean-Michel Hanssens. 3 vols. Vatican City: Biblioteca Apostolica Vaticana, 1948–50.

Cabaniss, James A. *Amalarius of Metz.* Amsterdam: North Holland, 1954.

Hesbert, René-Jean. "L'antiphonaire d'Amalaire." *Ephemerides liturgicae* 94 (1980): 176–94.

Schnusenberg, Christine. *The Relationship Between the Church and the Theatre: Exemplified by Some Writings of the Church Fathers and by Liturgical Texts Until Amalarius of Metz.* Lanham: University Press of America, 1988.

AMANT RENDU CORDELIER. The full title of this tale, *L'amant rendu cordelier en l'observance d'amour,* summarizes its 234 *huitains,* a dream vision in which an unhappy lover confesses his troubles (presenting a bittersweet critique of love's service) to the prior of a Franciscan house, before entering the order. Once the lover takes his vows, however, the narrator awakens and contrasts the lover's sufferings to bitter monastic penance, thus wittily coming out in favor of love. Originally attributed to Martial d'Auvergne, the anonymous text (tentatively dated 1440–50) is now associated with the literary circle of Pierre de Hauteville (d. 1447).

Wendy E. Pfeffer

Montaiglon, Anatole de, ed. *L'amant rendu cordelier à l'observance d'amour, poème attribué à Martial d'Auvergne.* Paris: Didot, 1881.

AMBROSIUS AUTPERTUS (d. 784). Author of an influential commentary on the Apocalypse. Born in Provence in the first half of the 8th century, Autpertus entered the monastery of San Vincenzo on the Volturno, near Benevento, in 754. Ordained a priest, he became abbot of his community in 777 but was opposed by a Lombard faction and forced to abdicate. He died on his way to Rome to testify about another dispute in his community.

Autpertus's commentary on the Apocalypse, an ecclesiological interpretation synthesized from Primasius, Tyconius, Augustine, Victorinus, and Jerome, circulated widely in medieval France and was a major source for later exegetes. Autpertus also wrote an allegory based on Prudentius, prayers, sermons, and saints' lives.

E. Ann Matter

[See also: BIBLE, CHRISTIAN INTERPRETATION OF]

Ambrosius Autpertus. *Opera,* ed. Robert Weber. *CCCM* 27, 27A, 27B. Turnhout: Brepols, 1975–79.

———. *Oratio summa et incomprehensibilis natura,* ed. V. Federici. *Fonti per la storia d'Italia* 58 (1925): 3–15.

Leclercq, Jean. "La prière au sujet des vices et des vertus." *Studia anselmiana* 31 (1953): 3–17.

Leonardi, Claudio. "Spiritualità di Ambrogio Autperto." *Studi medievali* 3rd ser. 9 (1968): 1–13.

Winandy, Jacques. *Ambroise Autpert, moine et théologien.* Paris: Plon, 1953.

AMI ET AMILE. This 3,504-line chanson de geste (divided into 177 decasyllabic laisses partly assonanced, partly rhymed, and each concluding with a six-syllable, feminine *vers orphelin*), composed ca. 1200, tells the story of the superhuman friendship of two young nobles, Ami and Amile. Born on the same day in different families, they are physically identical. At the age of fifteen, they meet and become sworn friends and companions. After entering the service of Charlemagne, they quickly distinguish themselves. Ami obtains the hand of Lubias, lady of Blaye and niece of a traitor, Hardré. It is a disastrous marriage. Meanwhile, a daughter of Charlemagne, Belissant, having fallen hopelessly in love with Amile, sneaks into his bed and lets herself be seduced by him. The lovers are denounced by Hardré, always envious of the friends' success. Amile must prove his innocence in a judiciary duel. Ami replaces him in this duel, swearing (rightly) that he has never slept with Belissant. He wins the duel, and Charlemagne offers him the hand of Belissant. Since he accepts, despite the admonishment by an angel, he commits technical bigamy and becomes a leper. Although protected by his young son, Gérard, he is driven out of his home by the evil Lubias. Accompanied by two ever-faithful servants, he wanders in search of Amile, now happily married to Belissant. Following a series of adventures, the two friends meet. An angel appears again to Ami to show him the only remedy against his shameful disease: Amile must sacrifice his two young sons and wash his friend in their blood. The superhuman friendship cannot be refused anything, and Amile does as he is told. Ami recovers immediately. God, rewarding the father's heroic act, restores his children to life. Shortly after, Ami and Amile die in Lombardy upon their return from the pilgrimage to Jerusalem. They are buried in Mortara.

The exact origin of this work cannot be determined, but it is obvious that folkloric, hagiographic, romance, and epic elements entered into its composition. The legend, preserved in at least two Latin and numerous foreign versions, was popular, surely because of its strong thematic components: the absolute friendship of the identical "twins," the Isaac-like child sacrifice, the miraculous cure from leprosy, and probably the absolute dichotomy between the good (Ami, Amile, Belissant, Gérard, faithful servants) and the evil (Hardré and Lubias). All these components are, however, well integrated into the King Cycle.

The story is also preserved in a late 12th-century Anglo-Norman romance, *Amis e Amilun,* and a 15th-century miracle play, as well as in unpublished versions in prose. The chanson de geste of *Jourdain de Blaye* is a continuation of *Ami et Amile*. Its protagonist is the grandson of Ami. The two works form a little "Blaye Cycle."

Peter F. Dembowski

[See also: ANGLO-NORMAN LITERATURE; CHANSON DE GESTE; KING CYCLE; MIRACLE PLAYS]

Dembowski, Peter F., ed. *Ami et Amile, chanson de geste*. Paris: Champion, 1969.
Fukui, Hideka, ed. *Amys e Amillyoun*. London: Anglo-Norman Text Society, 1990. [Edition of Anglo-Norman version.]
Danon, Samuel, and Samuel N. Rosenberg, trans. *Ami and Amile*. York: French Literature, 1981.
Dufournet, Jean. *Ami et Amile, une chanson de geste de l'amitié*. Paris: Champion, 1987. [Bibliography, pp. 121–27.]

AMIENS. Throughout the Middle Ages, Amiens (Somme) was an important artistic center known for its architecture, sculpture, manuscript illumination, and painting. The cathedral is the city's outstanding monument. After a fire in 1218, rebuilding commenced ca. 1220 and was substantially completed by 1269. The architect, Robert de Luzarches, was succeeded by Thomas de Cormont and his son Renaud, who finished the upper levels and chevet. Additions included 14th-century chapels in the nave, two western towers, and reconstruction of the spire over the crossing after a 1528 fire.

Amiens represents the epitome of French Gothic architecture. The double-aisled, rib-vaulted cathedral has seven bays in the nave, four in the choir, a slightly projecting transept, and a chevet with seven radiating chapels. The 3:1 proportion of vault height to nave width, and the elevation, whose arcade equals the combined height of the triforium and clerestory, accent the verticality. Piers, ribs, and tracery of clerestory windows convey an impression of lightness and skeletal linearity. Most of the medieval stained glass has been destroyed.

On the exterior, the flying buttresses and sculptured portals typify the Gothic style. The west façade, dated ca. the 1230s, with three recessed porches, is the most unified iconographic and stylistic ensemble of French Gothic sculpture. The central portal depicts the Last Judgment in the tympanum with the famous trumeau of Christ, *Beau Dieu*,

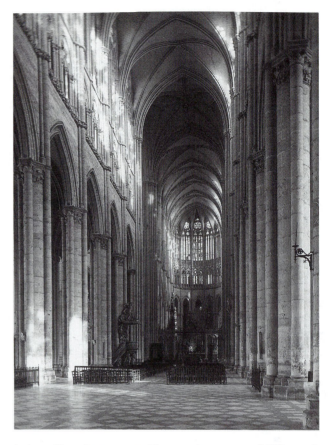

Amiens, Notre-Dame, nave. *Photograph courtesy of Whitney S. Stoddard.*

and jamb figures of the Apostles. The left portal is dedicated to St. Firmin, the first bishop-martyr of Amiens, with other local saints on the jambs. The Virgin is honored on the right door with a tympanum depicting her death and coronation and jamb figures representing an infancy cycle. The piers and basements contain statues and reliefs of prophets, Virtues and Vices, and signs of the zodiac and months. The heavy drapery with broad angular folds enhances the direct presentation of iconographic themes.

The south portal of ca. 1270 features a trumeau statue of the Virgin and Child, *Vierge Dorée*, and scenes from the life of St. Honoré, a 6th-century bishop of Amiens, in the tympanum. Swaying poses, delicate faces, and complex drapery characterize this elegant Gothic style. Two 13th-century bishops have bronze slab tombs in the nave. Two chapels of ca. 1375 contain statues of Charles V and his sons. John Ruskin called the late 15th- and early 16th-century carved choir screen and stalls the "Bible of Amiens" because of their wealth of scriptural subjects. The 13th-century edifice, its sculptured portals, and Gothic furnishings make Amiens one of the great medieval churches.

Karen Gould

[See also: CORMONT; GOTHIC ARCHITECTURE; GOTHIC ART; ROBERT DE LUZARCHES]

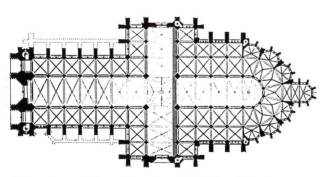

Amiens (Somme), Notre-Dame, plan. After Addis and Murray.

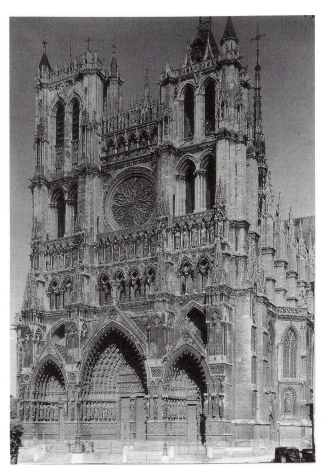

Amiens (Somme), Notre-Dame, façade. *Photograph: Clarence Ward Collection. Courtesy of Oberlin College.*

Hubscher, Ronald, et al. *Histoire d'Amiens.* Toulouse: Privat, 1986.

Jantzen, Hans. *High Gothic: The Classic Cathedrals of Chartres, Reims and Amiens.* New York: Pantheon, 1962.

Thiébaut, Jacques. *Les cathédrales gothiques en Picardie.* Amiens: Centre Régional de Documentation Pédagogique d'Amiens, 1987.

ANAGRAM. A word or phrase formed by transposing the letters of another word or phrase, anagrams appear in French texts from the mid-13th century and were generally used to identify the poet, the patron, or the poet's lady. Anagrams can be embedded in specified lines of text or in individual words or phrases. Although poets give instructions for the solution of anagrams, these are sometimes so complicated that the puzzles remain unsolved. It may be necessary to split letters in half (e.g., forming two *i*'s from an *n*) or to invert them (forming a *u* from an *n*). Particularly elaborate anagrams appear in the *Roman de la Poire,* the *Bestiaire d'amour rimé,* and the works of Guillaume de Machaut and Christine de Pizan. Earlier examples of devices related to the anagram include Jean Renart's use of wordplay to name himself at the end of the *Guillaume de Dole* (early 13th c.) and Tristan's adoption of the pseudonym Tantris in Thomas d'Angleterre's *Roman de Tristan* (mid-12th c.). Anagrams reflect delight in the manipulation of the written word, an index of increasing literacy within the aristocratic audience for vernacular poetry.

Sylvia Huot

[**See also:** ACROSTIC]

ANALECTA HYMNICA MEDII AEVI. The largest printed collection of medieval Latin liturgical poetry, edited by Guido Maria Dreves, Henry Marriott Bannister, and Clemens Blume. The volumes are organized in several ways: some are devoted to a single genre, others to a particular genre of poetry from one region, others, more rarely, to the works of a particular poet or group of poets. In general, hymns are found in Vols. 2, 4, 11, 12, 14, 16, 19, 22, 23, 27, 41a, 43, and 51; sequences in Vols. 7, 8, 9, 10, 34, 37, 39, 40, 41a, 42, 44, 53, 54, and 55; tropes in Vols. 47 and 49; rhymed offices (*hystoriae*) in Vols. 5, 13, 17, 18, 24, 25, 26, 28, 41a, and 45a. Also included are religious songs and motet texts, rhymed prayers, and rhymed psalter texts. The index, prepared by Max Lütolf, contains alphabetized incipits for all texts and indices for genre and for liturgical assignment. *Analecta hymnica* can be supplemented by the index in Chevalier's *Repertorium hymnologicum;* trope texts are now being edited in the several volumes of the *Corpus troporum.* Although *Analecta hymnica* remains useful, many of the sources listed in the lemmata are misdated, and there are frequent errors in the reporting of variants.

Margot Fassler

[**See also:** CONDUCTUS; HYMNS; RHYMED OFFICE; SEQUENCE (EARLY); SEQUENCE (LATE); TROPES, ORDINARY; TROPES, PROPER; VERSUS]

Chevalier, Ulysse. *Repertorium hymnologicum: catalogue des chants, hymnes, proses, séquences, tropes en usage dans l'église latine depuis les origines jusqu'à nos jours.* Vol. 1, Louvain: Lefever, 1892. Vol. 2, Louvain: Polleunis & Ceuterick, 1897. Vol. 3, Polleunis & Ceuterick, 1904. Vol. 4, Louvain: François Ceuterick, 1912. Vol. 5, Brussels, Société des Bollandistes, 1921. Vol. 6, Brussels, Société des Bollandistes, 1920.

Corpus troporum. Stockholm: Almqvist and Wiksell, 1975, 1976, 1980, 1982, 1986 (2 vols.), 1990.

Dreves, Guido Maria, Clemens Blume, and Henry Marriot Bannister, eds. *Analecta Hymnica Medii Aevi.* 55 vols. Leipzig: Fues's Verlag, 1886–90 (vols. 1–8); Leipzig: Reisland, 1890–1922 (vols. 9–55).

Lütolf, Max, ed. *Analecta Hymnica Medii Aevi: Register.* 3 vols. Bern: Francke, 1978.

ANDRÉ DE FLEURY (d. ca. 1050–60). A monk of the Benedictine abbey of Fleury-sur-Loire, André wrote Books 4–7 of the *Miracula sancti Benedicti,* continuing the work of Aimoin de Fleury. André expanded the account beyond miracles to include events relating to the monastery locally and elsewhere. He also wrote a life of Gauzlin, abbot of Fleury 1004–30.

Grover A. Zinn

[See also: AIMOIN DE FLEURY; HAGIOGRAPHY]

Aimoin de Fleury. *Les miracles de saint Benoît,* ed. Eugène de Certain. Paris: Renouard, 1858.
Bautier, Robert-Henri. "L'historiographie en France aux Xe et XIe siècles (France Nord et de l'Est)." In *La storiografia altomedioevale, 10–16 aprile 1969.* Spoleto: Presso la Sede del Centro, 1970, pp. 793–850.
Vidier, Alexandre C.P. *L'historiographie à Saint-Benoît-sur-Loire et les Miracles de saint Benoît.* Paris: Picard, 1965.

ANDREAS CAPELLANUS (André le Chapelain; fl. late 12th c.). Author of a treatise on the art of love, *De amore* (or *De arte honeste amandi*), composed for a certain Gautier. Andreas's identity remains enigmatic. He has most frequently been identified with a chaplain of the same name in the service of Marie de Champagne, the daughter of Louis VII and Eleanor of Aquitaine and the patroness of Chrétien de Troyes.

De amore, preserved in over thirty manuscripts and collections, is composed of three books. The first expounds the nature of love; the second, in a series of twenty-one judgments attributed to some of the noblest ladies of France (Eleanor of Aquitaine, Marie de Champagne, Elizabeth of Vermandois, and others), tells how to maintain love; and the third condemns love. The entire treatise shows the influence of Ovid's *Ars amatoria* and *Remedia amoris,* as well as an intimate knowledge of the casuistry and rhetorical traditions of the medieval Latin school system. Its interpretation, however, like that of Chrétien's *Chevalier de la charrette,* remains problematic. Modern critics are divided as to whether to take the work seriously or read it ironically. If Andreas's intention was to produce a treatise on the practice of (courtly) love, then how can one explain the antifeminism of the final book? Was this true remorse or an ironic stance to avoid ecclesiastical condemnation?

The work was translated into Franco-Italian prose in the second half of the 13th century and into Old French by Drouart la Vache in 1290. It also made its way into Catalan, Italian, and German.

William W. Kibler

[See also: ANTIFEMINISM; COURTLY LOVE; DROUART LA VACHE; JEAN DE MEUN; OVID, INFLUENCE OF]

Andreas Capellanus. *Andreae Capellani regii Francorum De amore libri tres,* ed. E. Trojel. Copenhagen: Libraria Gandiana, 1892.
———. *The Art of Courtly Love,* trans. John J. Parry. New York: Columbia University Press, 1941.
———. *Traité de l'amour courtois,* trans. Claude Buridant. Paris: Champion, 1974.
Karnein, Alfred. "La réception d'André le Chapelain au XIIIe siècle." *Romania* 102 (1981): 324–51, 501–42.
Kelly, F. Douglas. "Courtly Love in Perspective: The Hierarchy of Love in Andreas Capellanus." *Traditio* 24 (1968): 119–47.
Monson, Don A. "Andreas Capellanus and the Problem of Irony." *Speculum* 63 (1988): 539–72.

ANDREW OF SAINT-VICTOR (d. 1175). Biblical exegete who provided the most sustained treatment of the Hebrew Bible according to the literal sense since the time of St. Jerome (4th–5th c.). Born probably in England, Andrew entered the abbey of Saint-Victor in Paris and studied under Hugh of Saint-Victor. He later returned to England as abbot of Wigmore, a house of regular canons in Herefordshire.

Andrew was influenced by Hugh's emphasis on the importance of the literal sense of Scripture as the foundation for understanding the allegorical and moral senses. In contrast to Hugh's interest in the threefold interpretation of Scripture, Andrew wrote exegetical treatises only on the Hebrew Bible, with the literal sense his only focus. His commentaries on the Octateuch, Historical Books, Wisdom Books, Minor Prophets, and Isaiah, Jeremiah, Ezekiel, and Daniel have been preserved. These commentaries indicate that Andrew consulted with Jews in the vernacular and then translated their interpretations into Latin. It is not likely that he had extensive knowledge of biblical or postbiblical Hebrew. From Andrew's commentaries, however, we learn about Jewish liturgical practices and mourning customs. Richard of Saint-Victor wrote *De Emmanuele* condemning Andrew's acceptance of Jewish teachings about Isaiah 7:14, an important messianic prophecy for Christians. But Andrew did not accept all Jewish explications in uncritical fashion. He considered Jewish claims about messianic deliverance and restoration of the sacrificial cult in Jerusalem to be "fables." Andrew's writings influenced Peter Comestor, Peter the Chanter, Stephen Langton, and Herbert of Bosham.

Michael A. Signer

[See also: HERBERT OF BOSHAM; HUGH OF SAINT-VICTOR; PETER COMESTOR; PETER THE CHANTER; RICHARD OF SAINT-VICTOR; STEPHEN LANGTON]

Andreas de Sancto Victore. *Expositio in Ezechielem,* ed. Michael A. Signer. CCCM 53E. Turnhout: Brepols, 1991.
———. *Expositio super Danielem,* ed. Mark Zier. CCCM 53F. Turnhout: Brepols, 1990.
———. *Expositio super heptateuchum,* ed. Charles Lohr and Ranier Berndt. CCCM 53. Turnhout: Brepols, 1986.
———. *Expositiones historicae in Libros Salomonis,* ed. Ranier Berndt. CCCM 53B. Turnhout: Brepols, 1991.
Berndt, Ranier. *André de Saint-Victor (†1175). Exégète et théologien.* Turnhout: Brepols, 1992.
Signer, Michael A. "Peshat, Sensus Litteralis and Sequential Narrative: Jewish Exegesis and the School of St. Victor in the 12th Century." In *The Frank Talmage Memorial Volume,* ed. Barry Walfish. 2 vols. Haifa: Haifa University Press, 1993, vol. 1, pp. 203–16.

Smalley, Beryl. *The Study of the Bible in the Middle Ages.* 3rd ed. Oxford: Blackwell, 1983, chap. 4.

Zweiten, Jan W.M. "Jewish Exegesis Within Christian Bounds: Richard of St. Victor's *De Emmanuele* and Victorine Hermeneutics." *Bijdragen* 48 (1987): 327–35.

ANDRIEU CONTREDIT D'ARRAS (d. 1248?). Author of twenty-three conventional songs, with the melody extant for eighteen, including twenty love songs, one *lai*, one pastourelle, and one *jeu-parti*, written with Guillaume le Vinier. Andrieu is cited in the royal accounts for 1239 as a soldier-poet who enlisted as a crusader, although no evidence exists to prove that he actually went to Jerusalem.

Deborah H. Nelson

Andrieu Contredit d'Arras. *The Songs*, ed. and trans. Deborah H. Nelson, music arranger Hendrik van der Werf. Amsterdam: Rodopi, 1992.

Angers (Maine-et-Loire), château, ramparts, and moat. *Photograph: Clarence Ward Collection. Courtesy of Oberlin College.*

ANGERS. Situated on both banks of the River Maine, five miles north of its confluence with the Loire, Angers (Maine-et-Loire) is rich in monuments exhibiting a Gothic style, Angevin Gothic, that is quite different from the Early and High Gothic of the Île-de-France. Besides the famous 14th-century tapestries of the Apocalypse exhibited inside the castle, Angers has a series of buildings that reveal both the uniqueness and the quality of this local, western French style and its evolution over a span of a hundred years.

Angers had long been governed by the counts of Anjou, some of whom had been dukes of Normandy and Aquitaine, counts of Brittany, and kings of England. Geoffroi IV Plantagenêt was the father of King Henry II of England, who was the husband of Eleanor of Aquitaine and father of Richard I the Lionhearted. In 1204, Angers surrendered to the Capetian king Philip II Augustus, and later in the century Louis IX had vast walls built to protect Angers. These walls were flattened to create the boulevards surrounding the city.

The powerful castle of Angers was begun under Count Foulques III Nerra to protect Anjou from the Normans. After surrender to the Capetians, Louis IX rebuilt Foulques's castle in whitestone with contrasting bands of black slate on two levels, and the seventeen semicircular towers were crowned by overhanging turrets. In the course of the 14th and 15th centuries, the dukes of Anjou continued to embellish the castle: Louis II, nephew of the French king Charles V, and his wife, Yolande d'Aragon, added the Gothic chapel, and their son, the "good duke" René d'Anjou, constructed comfortable living quarters overlooking the Maine. Parts of the castle were dismantled during the Wars of Religion of the 16th century, but much remains of this magnificent example of medieval military architecture.

The three square bays of the nave of the cathedral of Saint-Maurice, which were vaulted with domical, ribbed vaults between 1149 and 1153, exhibit the beginnings of Angevin Gothic. The exterior walls of the nave, with evenly spaced wall buttresses, belong to the 12th-century cathedral, which may have been connected to a choir and short transept with chapels excavated in 1902. This 11th-century nave was covered with either a wooden roof or domes rising from pendentives (the span of 50 feet is too wide for a barrel vault). The single-nave vessel appears often in the Romanesque of the region; the single nave, vaulted with domes, can be found in the Dordogne (Cahors, Souillac) up through western France (Périgueux, Angoulême to Fontevrault, 35 miles southeast of Angers). In the mid-12th-century campaign of the cathedral of Angers, new, large wall buttresses were added to the exterior corners of the three bays, while new thick responds with multiple colonnettes supported the transverse, diagonal, and longitudinal ribs of the four-part vaults. These domical vaults have stylistic connections with those in the north and south tower of Chartres cathedral (1134 and after 1145); the elevation of Angers exhibits connections with the nave of Le Mans. In spite of these relationships to Chartres, to Le Mans, and to the cupolas on the pendentives of Fontevrault, Saint-Maurice is a creative synthesis of Romanesque and Early Gothic characteristics.

Between the completion of the nave of Saint-Maurice in the mid-12th century and the construction of its transepts and choir in the 13th, several monuments in Angers reveal stages in the evolving Angevin Gothic. At Saint-Martin, excavated by an American team under George H. Forsyth, Jr., a small Merovingian church of the 7th century was enlarged in two campaigns in the 9th and 10th centuries by the addition of crossing, transepts, and choir with chapels on the ends of each. Surmounting the crossing was a wooden tower. In the 11th century, the lower section of the crossing tower was reinforced. Finally, after the middle of the 12th century, a new Gothic choir was constructed in two stages: the western square bay and the eastern bay and apse. This western bay is crowned by a domical vault supported by two transverse ribs, two wall ribs, two diagonal ribs, ridge ribs, and two ribs springing from a column between the windows. Thus, twelve ribs strengthen the webbing of the vault. The middle bay is

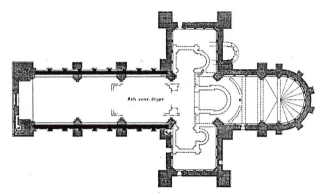

Angers, Saint-Maurice, plan. After Conant.

Angers, Saint-Maurice, nave elevation and section. After Losowska.

more domical in profile and with the same number but thinner ribs. The windows of the middle bay are considerably larger. Finally, the eastern apse has five even larger windows with more complicated frames of three colonnettes supporting the archivolts. This choir, ca. 1150–80, led stylistically to the vaulting of the transept and choir of the cathedral of Angers in the first half of the 13th century.

One other monument in Angers was built before the transept and choir of the cathedral, the Hospice Saint-Jean. Founded in 1180 with a papal bull and two charters signed by King Henry II in 1181, the Hospice consisted of a three-aisled rectangle of eight bays, square chapel, cloister, and separate granary. The room for the sick has aisles and nave of the same height covered with four-part, domical vaults with thin rounded ribs. Used as a hospital until 1865, the spaces were originally divided into wards by screens. The elegance of the ribs is the main characteristic of the Angevin style in the late years of the 12th century.

The four square bays, which comprise the transept and choir of the cathedral of Angers, reveal the stylistic influence of Saint-Martin and the Hospice. The ribs are a simple torus molding under the domical vaults, which are doubled or widened for the transverse and wall ribs. Eight-part vaults of diagonals, ridge ribs, and liernes spring to the central keystone from the keystone of the wall (or longitudinal) rib. The marked domical profile, the thin rib, and eight-part vaults are exactly like the eastern bay of the choir of Saint-Martin. Transept and choir of the cathedral were built in the first half of the 13th century; the narrow bay and apse date from the second half of the 13th century.

One outstanding example of Angevin Gothic remains to be discussed: the choir of the Benedictine monastery of Saint-Serge. The plan consists of a four-bay nave with smaller aisles, all the same height. Nave bays and the three western bays are capped with eight-part, domical vaults with thin, rounded ribs—transverse, longitudinal, ridge, diagonals, and two ribs springing from the keystone of the longitudinal ribs. The carved and polychromed keystones capture eight ribs. With ribs of different lengths, the bay becomes domical in shape with the ribs visible on the top of the vaults. Flanking the nave and aisles are chapels of two bays at a higher level. A small square apse extends eastward. The ribs multiply in the eastern half of the apse,

eastern bays of the aisles, and eastern bay of the north chapel. The proliferation of ribs by the addition of more liernes exhibits, together with the thinness of the nave supports, the decorative delicacy of the structure.

It is the Angevin Gothic of the choir of the cathedral, of Saint-Martin, and of Saint-Serge that spreads beyond the walls of Angers and to the south of the Loire River. Angevin Gothic is a unique style, found only in areas around Angers and to the south. Little attention is given to the exteriors, since no flying buttresses were utilized. Often, these buildings consist of a single nave or interior spaces of the same height with emphasis on elaborate vaulting.

In the nave and crossing of the cathedral of Saint-Maurice are floral capitals vaguely following the Corinthian type, often with human heads and elaborately carved abaci. The west portal of the cathedral is based on the west-central portal of Chartres. Christ in Majesty, surrounded by the four Evangelists, is located in the tympanum. The lintel and trumeau were destroyed in the 18th century to enlarge the entrance to the cathedral. The figure style resembles that of some of the sculpture on the archivolts of the three west portals and on the tympana of the side portals of Chartres. This sculptural campaign is probably contemporary with or slightly later than the vaulting of the nave of the cathedral (1149–53).

Carved capitals in the choir and apse of Saint-Martin are mostly nonfigurative. In the apse and eastern bay, six statues once stood on columns with capitals and visually supported the ribs. In style, they appear to date ca. 1180. They are now in the Yale University Museum.

The ornamental and figurative sculpture on capitals, keystones of some arches, and on all complicated keystones of each vault of the choir of Saint-Serge echoes, in its detailed carving and polychromy, the elegance of the architecture.

Whitney S. Stoddard

[See also: ANJOU; APOCALYPSE TAPESTRY; GOTHIC ARCHITECTURE]

Forsyth, George H., Jr. *The Church of St. Martin at Angers: The Architectural History from the Roman Empire to the French Revolution.* Princeton: Princeton University Press, 1953, esp. pp. 167–86, figs. 200–07.

Mussat, André. *Le style gothique de l'ouest de la France (XIIe–XIIIe siècles).* Paris: Picard, 1963, esp. pp. 173–239.

Sauerländer, Willibald. *Gothic Sculpture in France 1140–1270.* London: Thames and Hudson, 1972.

Urseau, Charles. *La cathédrale d'Angers.* Paris: Laurens, 1927.

ANGLO-NORMAN LITERATURE. The conquest of England by William, duke of Normandy, in 1066 had consequences in linguistic and literary development no less far-reaching than in the political, economic, and social domains. For over 300 years, a dialect of French was to be the official language of the ruling class in both church and state. That dialect, deriving principally from the western (Norman) French of William's followers, was destined to become for a time one of the most important literary languages of northern Europe. Cut off from its continental roots by the natural barrier of the English Channel and forced into an uneasy cohabitation with the Anglo-Saxon dialects of the resident English aristocracy and merchant class, it proceeded to develop along independent lines and within little more than a generation had produced a written form recognizably different from its continental cousin. These differences not only are apparent in phonology, morphology, and syntax but extend to metrical form and syllabic count. Thus, from the early 12th century on, it becomes necessary to distinguish between continental Norman and what for want of a better name has come to be called Anglo-Norman. The advent of the Angevin dynasty in 1154 with the coronation of Henry II brought new and varied continental influences to bear upon the dialect and its literature. Anglo-Norman writers begin to be conscious of the "insular" nature of their dialect, and some continental writers poke fun at Anglo-Norman speech habits. A third phase begins with the loss of the continental provinces by King John in 1204. Deprived of their continental fiefs, the Anglo-Norman barons identify increasingly with their English counterparts, with whom there has been much intermarriage, and the linguistic tide slowly but inexorably turns in favor of English. There is evidence that English is already the dominant vernacular even among the upper classes in the early 13th century, but Anglo-Norman remains a convenient lingua franca for administrative purposes, having a much wider currency than Latin and the advantage of being understood by the literate in all parts of the kingdom at a time when dialectal differences make English unsuited to this task. In literature, the fateful step is taken by Chaucer in the latter part of the 14th century, when he chooses English as his vehicle of expression. His contemporary John Gower writes chiefly in French, but already a literary French greatly influenced by continental models and far removed from the heavily anglicized patterns of Anglo-Norman in its decline. When Henry Bolingbroke assumes the crown of Richard II in 1399, he is the first monarch since Edward the Confessor (d. 1066) to use the English language for everyday discourse.

Several problems arise in determining what comprises Anglo-Norman literature. Some continental texts, such as the *Vie de saint Alexis* and the *Chanson de Roland,* are preserved in manuscripts executed by Anglo-Norman scribes. Others, such as Wace's *Roman de Brut* and Benoît de Sainte-Maure's *Chronique des ducs de Normandie,* were written at the behest of Henry II and other powerful figures in the Anglo-Norman *regnum,* or were intended to engage their attention, but these are Anglo-Norman neither in language nor in place of origin. Marie de France represents something of a grey area. She claims to be "from France" but appears to have written most if not all of her work in England, and her language shows some slight insular influence.

From its beginnings in the early years of the 12th century, with the "scientific" *Cumpoz* and *Bestiaire* of Philippe de Thaün and Benedeit's highly imaginative *Voyage de saint Brendan,* to the prose and poetry of John Gower in the latter half of the 14th century, Anglo-Norman literature has been distinguished by its variety, its richness, and its originality. That it differs in some respects from continental literature of the same period is hardly surprising, since it sprang from another soil and was fed by different streams. Like the dialect itself, it was a graft from a very different culture. Patronage plays a significant role in its development, and the disparate tastes and requirements of the various patrons, Normans, Angevins, Anglo-Normans, and Anglo-Angevins, clerical and lay, exerted a marked influence on the form and content of the works commissioned by them, or written to court their favor. The "didactic" and "practical" quality of much Anglo-Norman literature has frequently been cited. The principal genres are the chronicle, the romance, the saint's life, and what might loosely be termed moral literature. There are no chansons de geste as such, and until the ballades of John Gower at the end of the Anglo-Norman literary period there is little evidence of a strong lyric tradition. What has survived is often political rather than personal in inspiration and accords with what has been seen as the Anglo-Norman predilection for affairs of state and lineage over those of the heart.

Chronicles. The earliest surviving chronicle in French is the Anglo-Norman *Estoire des Engleis* (ca. 1140) by Gaimar, who makes it clear that this is the second part of a tripartite structure involving a history of the ancient Britons (commonly referred to as a *Brut*), a history of the English, and a contemporary history from the time of the Conquest. Gaimar uses both the *Anglo-Saxon Chronicle* and Geoffrey of Monmouth's recently completed *Historia regum Britanniae* as sources. The latter work, although written in Latin, must also be seen as belonging to the Anglo-Norman corpus, since it was to play such a significant role in popularizing Celtic myth and legend in the Anglo-Norman *regnum* and beyond. Gaimar's *Estoire,* the only section of his planned work to survive in completed form, uses the octosyllabic rhyming-couplet pattern established by the *Brendan.* In both form and content, Gaimar's influence was probably felt by the Norman Wace, whose *Brut* may well have led to the eclipse of that of his predecessor. Wace's second section, the *Roman de Rou,* giving an account of the dukes of Normandy rather than of the kings of England, was in its turn supplanted by Benoît de Sainte-Maure's *Chronique des ducs de Normandie,* a work likewise destined to remain unfinished. A series of *Bruts* in verse and later in prose continues through the 13th and

14th centuries, each one updated to include contemporary material. Among the more interesting are that by Peter of Langtoft (d. 1307?) in laisses of Alexandrine lines, an account of the reign of Edward I that was to become the source for all subsequent chroniclers, and the *Scalacronica* of Sir Thomas Gray of Heton (d. 1369), beginning not with the fall of Troy but with that of Lucifer, and continuing to the year 1362.

Not all Anglo-Norman chronicles took such a long view of history. Jordan Fantosme records only the troubled years 1173 and 1174 of Henry II's reign, but he does so more as creative writer than as historian, emphasizing the human weaknesses of his protagonists and the vicissitudes of fortune. Unlike Gaimar and Wace, he writes for the most part in rhyming Alexandrines grouped in laisses. The *Histoire de Guillaume le Maréchal* (1226), commissioned by Guillaume's eldest son soon after his father's death in 1219, marks a return to the octosyllabic couplet. This work, composed by a Norman writer, is a kind of official biography, beginning with the subject's childhood during the reign of Stephen and continuing through the reign of Henry II. It details Guillaume's close association with Henry, the Young King, and continues on through the turbulent reigns of Richard I and John, ending with Guillaume's regency and finally his death. Its 19,254 lines not only contain a vast amount of historical information, but are enlivened by well-observed miniatures of daily life and especially of children. The *Croisade et mort de Richard Cœur de Lion*, a prose work of undetermined date (possibly mid-13th c., but perhaps as late as 1320), is based on several sources, chief among these the Latin chronicle of Roger Howden. It chronicles Richard's participation in the Third Crusade, beginning in 1186 and ending with his death in 1199 from an arrow wound received on a battlefield in Normandy.

Romances. As a general rule, Anglo-Norman romances depart markedly from their continental counterparts in both form and content, perhaps owing to differences in social organization arising from the Conquest. All land, and hence power, derived ultimately from William, who granted land in tenure only, and from his successors. This centralized power structure eliminated to a large extent local wars among the barons, which were in any case expressly prohibited by Henry II. In consequence, an important concern is the maintenance of feudal rights in face of usurpation and the consolidation of such rights through successive generations. It is no surprise, then, that the majority of romances composed for Anglo-Norman patrons should stress the rights of inheritance, the establishment of solid family ties, and the avoidance of adulterous relationships, however courtly, that might endanger legitimacy. Where continental romances examine the tensions between the claims of the individual and the demands of society, especially within that most personal and intimate domain, the love relationship, Anglo-Norman writers are more inclined to tell tales of disinheritance, exile, struggle, and return. Where Chrétien and others, building on the troubadour discovery of sexual love as an ennobling power, concentrate largely on the hero's efforts to win or win back his lady, their insular counterparts stress the high moral courage of the hero, which results in his reinstatement in

his patrimony, the triumph of justice, of right over wrong. Love is understood not as an end in itself but as a means to establish a lineage, the promise of generations to come. In respect of male-female relations, the ethos of these more typically Anglo-Norman romances is closer to that of the chansons de geste and to the teachings of the medieval church. In the *Roman de Horn* (ca. 1170), the work of a certain Master Thomas, the exiled hero in his attempts to vindicate himself and regain his lost kingdom finds himself pitted against the might of the "Saracens," a convenient catchall for pagan tribes. There is a continuing love interest, but it is far from courtly. The women actively woo the handsome hero and indulge in amorous fantasies while he attends to more important concerns.

The "courtly" tradition is not absent, however, and may even be said to flourish during the reign of Henry II. In addition to the *Lais* of Marie de France, which may date from as early as 1160, this tradition is represented by two other important texts: the *Tristan* of Thomas (mid-12th c.?) and the Oxford version of the *Folie Tristan* (late 12th c.?). Those works whose influence was felt far beyond the Anglo-Norman *regnum* are unconnected with the Anglo-Norman preoccupation with feudal land rights. The theme of exile and return is recurrent, but it is less a physical exile than an alienation from society and the real world where true union can be achieved only in death. *Amadas et Ydoine* (ca. 1190–1220), like Chrétien's *Cligés* (with which the Anglo-Norman author was probably unacquainted), appears to be an attempt to present the Tristan-Iseut problem in a manner less disruptive of social norms. Its explicit references to the Tristan legend claim for its protagonists a moral superiority over the more famous couple, and the author boasts that their love, rooted in nature rather than a magic potion, was also more profound and true. Ydoine rejects adultery as a solution for her situation and, unlike Fenice, preserves her virginity until such time as her marriage can be dissolved. A high moral tone combined with subordination of the love interest to that of *compagnonnage* is exhibited also by *Amis e Amilun* (late 12th c.), in which hagiographic as well as epic elements are present. This octosyllabic version is probably earlier than and independent of the French *Ami et Amile*. Hue de Rotelande's *Ipomedon*, for its part, seems almost to lampoon the "courtly" tradition, naming the unapproachable lady "La Fière" and interjecting bawdy comments that bespeak an iconoclastic approach to one of the principal literary topoi of the day, that of the beautiful but haughty princess wooed by a lover of supposedly inferior rank.

Those love-centered romances, whatever their position on *fin'amor*, share with the vast majority of continental romances the fluid octosyllabic couplet form that by mid-century had become traditional for virtually all court-oriented poems. What is curious is that many of the Anglo-Norman poems whose principal interest is not love but rather feudal rights, inheritance, and family tend later to abandon this form in favor of rhyming laisses composed of decasyllabic or Alexandrine lines. Among the latter are the *Roman de Horn* mentioned above, Thomas of Kent's *Roman de toute chevalerie* (1175–85?; also known as the

Anglo-Norman Alexander), and *Boeve de Haumtone* (early 13th c.). Their form suggests that they were intended, like the chansons de geste, to be recited or sung to a wider audience in the great hall rather than in the *chambre* or *soler*, a tradition that may have continued longer in England than on the Continent. Still other romances, notably *Waldef* (late 12th c.), the *Lai d'Haveloc* (ca. 1200), and *Gui de Warewic* (ca. 1230), marry the octosyllabic form to the characteristic Anglo-Norman content. In the case of *Gui de Warewic*, the theme of exile and return is interrelated at first with that of a highly conventional portrayal of *fin'amor*, but devotion to the lady as spur to heroic deeds is eventually superseded in Gui's case by devotion to God, and the romance acquires hagiographic overtones. In the case of *Fouke FitzWarin*, an early 14th-century prose rendering of a lost mid-13th-century poem in octosyllabic couplets tracing the vicissitudes of the FitzWarin family from the time of the Conquest through the reign of King John, the generic distinction between romance and chronicle is decidedly blurred.

Saints' Lives. The *Voyage de saint Brendan* by Benedeit, dated variously between 1106 and 1121 depending on whether the original dedicatee is believed to be the first or second wife of Henry I, is the first long narrative poem in French to use the octosyllabic rhyming couplet. Combining adventure and a taste for the exotic with a didactic purpose that seems never far below the surface of most Anglo-Norman works regardless of genre, it relates the voyage of the abbot Brendan, with fourteen chosen monks and three last-minute intruders, to the Earthly Paradise. Based on an Irish *immram* (voyage tale), this is also the first French vernacular text to make use of Celtic lore, which was to be so significant an element in later medieval literature.

That Anglo-Normans show a predilection for treating the lives of British or English saints is not surprising. Local saints are at once a source of pride and profit. The shrines of St. Alban, St. Edmund the King, St. Edward the Confessor, and above all St. Thomas Becket, martyred in 1170 and canonized in 1173, were favorite pilgrimage sites. All have one or more *Lives* translated from the original Latin into Anglo-Norman. Denis Piramus, a monk who by his own confession had dabbled in courtly love poetry before seeing the error of his ways, wrote a *Life* of St. Edmund the King (ca. 1173), and the noted 13th-century chronicler Matthew Paris (d. 1259) composed *Lives* of St. Alban, St. Edward, and the recently canonized St. Edmund of Abingdon. St. Thomas Becket was the subject of several Latin *Lives* and at least three French *Lives* written within a few years of his martyrdom in 1170. A Norman, Guernes de Pont-Sainte-Maxence, wrote two of them in five-line stanzas of monorhyme Alexandrines, and Beneit, a monk of Saint-Albans, composed a *Life* in six-line tail-rhyme stanzas. Other local saints recorded in Anglo-Norman legends are St. Osyth (late 12th c.), St. Audrey of Ely (early 13th c.), and the Irish St. Modwenna (early 13th c.), whose *Life* is written in monorhyme octosyllabic quatrains. St. Richard of Chichester (d. 1253) is the subject of a Latin *Life* by his confessor written between 1262 and 1270 and translated on request by Peter of Peckham.

The saints of the early church are not neglected, however. Although probably written on the Continent, the *Vie de saint Alexis* is preserved in a number of Anglo-Norman manuscripts, the finest from the famous abbey of Saint Albans. The *Vie de saint Laurent* (mid-12th c.) is the oldest French version of that legend. St. Catherine of Alexandria, one of the most popular saints of the Middle Ages, is the subject of at least three Anglo-Norman *Lives*, one of which, preserved only in a fragment (John Rylands Library fr. 6), may be as early as the *Voyage de saint Brendan*. Its use of varied meters has led to the suggestion that it may have been intended for some kind of dramatic presentation. The second, dating from the latter half of the 12th century, is one of four Anglo-Norman hagiographical works written by women within a period of no more than a century. Its author is Clemence, a nun of Barking, and despite its obvious piety it displays to a remarkable degree the influence of courtly literature of the period and, in particular, both the concept of reciprocal love and its rhetoric associated with the *Tristan* of Thomas. The third is a late 13th-century work on the "Mystic Marriage" of St. Catherine with Christ, a kind of "Enfances sainte Catherine" preserved in a 14th-century cursive manuscript (Additional 40143) in the British Library. Toward the end of the 12th century, Simon de Freine wrote a *Vie de saint Georges* in heptasyllabic couplets and Guillaume de Berneville his *Vie de saint Gilles* in the more traditional octosyllabic form. Early in the 13th century, Chardri (an anagram of Richard?) treated the "oriental" themes of *Josaphat* and the *Set dormanz*. The anonymous *Vie de saint Jean l'Aumônier* (ca. 8,000 ll.) may also be attributed to this period or shortly after, and the *Vie de saint Grégoire le Grand* (ca. 2,950 ll.) by Frère Angier, author of a translation (ca. 24,000 ll.) of St. Gregory's *Dialogues*, is thought to date from 1216.

Moral Literature. Saints' lives form only a part of the considerable volume of moral and religious literature in Anglo-Norman. The earliest translation into French of a book of the Bible is that of the *Proverbes de Salomon*, which Samson de Nanteuil prepared (ca. 1150) for Aeliz de Condet, possibly as a kind of moral instruction manual for her son Roger. Composed of nearly 12,000 octosyllabic couplets, it is preserved in only one manuscript (B.L., Harley 4388). The *Jeu d'Adam*, probably from the same period, is an imaginative dramatization (the earliest with exclusively French dialogue) of the story of the Fall. It covers also the killing of Abel by his brother, Cain, and ends with a procession of the prophets foretelling the coming of the Redeemer, the New Adam. Stage directions are given in Latin, and each section begins with the relevant Scripture reading also in Latin. The Oxford and Cambridge *Psalters* and the *IV livre des reis* are prose translations that date from the late 12th century, as does Simon de Freine's *Roman de Philosophie* or *Roman de Fortune*, an adaptation of Boethius that shows considerable interest in science and the observation of natural phenomena. The *Espurgatoire saint Patrice*, generally attributed to Marie de France, is a verse rendering of a Latin text from the late 12th or early 13th century recounting the knight Owein's visit to Purgatory, Hell, and the Earthly Paradise, while the Anglo-Norman *Lettre du Prêtre Jean*, which defies generic classification, appears to be the first vernacular adaptation of this curious late 12th-century document. Its interest in the exotic recalls the *Brendan*, but its general tone owes more to satire than to piety. Chardri's *Le petit plet*, a dialogue between a youth and an old man on problems of life, love, friendship, and death, is also from the turn of the century.

The Fourth Lateran Council (1215) and the subsequent Council of Oxford (1222) led to an outpouring of sermons and guides to the spiritual life emphasizing penitence and personal piety. The popularity of the *Mirour de seinte Eglyse* (or *Speculum Ecclesiae*) by St. Edmund of Abingdon (d. 1240) can be measured by the vast number of extant Latin, French, and English manuscripts. The work is a systematic guide to true Christian living through a combination of self-awareness and the contemplation of God. A printed version was made as late as the 16th century. Robert Grosseteste (d. 1253), chancellor of Oxford University and later bishop of Lincoln, wrote the *Chasteau d'amour*, a short religious allegory showing the influence of scientific theories on his theological thought; it was sufficiently well regarded to merit a translation into Latin and several into English. The anonymous *Manuel des péchés* (ca. 1260) was likewise popular, but the need for a Latin version was apparently not felt. Peter of Peckham's *Lumere as lais* and *Le secré des secrés* are also associated with this movement toward individual piety, and later Nicole Bozon, author of eleven short saints' lives, composed the heavily allegorical *Char d'orgueil* and *Passion* written in quatrains of Alexandrine lines, the *Proverbes de bon enseignement* in approximately octosyllabic couplets, a series of didactic *Contes* in prose, sermons in verse, and a number of poems to the Blessed Virgin in a variety of meters. Henry of Lancaster's *Seyntz medicines* (1352), a lengthy prose allegory presenting the Seven Deadly Sins as seven wounds each in need of a specific treatment, continues this tradition, which culminates in Gower's *Mirour de l'omme* (ca. 1376–79), a poem of some 30,000 octosyllabic lines detailing the corruption of the world and the way to reform through the help of God and the intercession of the Blessed Virgin.

William MacBain

[See also: *AMADAS ET YDOINE*; *AMI ET AMILE*; BENEDEIT; BENOÎT DE SAINTE-MAURE; BOZON, NICOLE; FRENCH LANGUAGE; GEFFREI GAIMAR; *GUILLAUME LE MARÉCHAL, HISTOIRE DE*; HISTORIOGRAPHY; HUE DE ROTELANDE; *JEU D'ADAM*; JORDAN FANTOSME; MARIE DE FRANCE; MORAL TREATISES; PHILIPPE DE THAÜN; ROMANCE; SAINTS' LIVES; WACE]

Blacker, Jean. *The Faces of Time: Portrayal of the Past in Old French and Latin Historical Narrative of the Anglo-Norman Regnum*. Austin: University of Texas Press, 1994. [We are indebted to Prof. Blacker for allowing access to her manuscript in advance of publication.]

Crane, Susan. *Insular Romance: Politics, Faith, and Culture in Anglo-Norman and Middle English Literature*. Berkeley: University of California Press, 1986.

Dean, Ruth J. "The Fair Field of Anglo-Norman: Recent Cultivation." *Medievalia et Humanistica* 3 (1973): 279–97.

Harvey, Carol J. "The Anglo-Norman Courtly Lyric." *Journal of the Rocky Mountain Medieval and Renaissance Association* 7 (1986): 27–40.

Kibbee, Douglas A. *For to Speake French Trewely: The French Language in England, 1000–1600: Its Status, Description and Instruction*. Amsterdam: Benjamins, 1991.

Legge, M. Dominica. *Anglo-Norman in the Cloisters: The Influence of the Orders upon Anglo-Norman Literature*. Edinburgh: Edinburgh University Press, 1950.

———. *Anglo-Norman Literature and Its Background*. Oxford: Clarendon, 1963.

Pope, Mildred K. *From Latin to Modern French with Especial Consideration of Anglo-Norman*. Manchester: Manchester University Press, 1934.

Stone, Louise W., and William Rothwell. *Anglo-Norman Dictionary*. London: Modern Humanities Research Association, 1977–.

Vising, Johan. *Anglo-Norman Language and Literature*. London: Oxford University Press, 1923.

West, Constance B. *Courtoisie in Anglo-Norman Literature*. Oxford: Blackwell, 1938.

The Anglo-Norman Text Society has to date published forty-nine volumes in its regular series, and ten volumes in the Plain Texts series. Oxford: Blackwell, 1945–75; London: Anglo-Norman Text Society, 1976–.

ANGLURE, OGIER D' (ca. 1360–after 1412). Ogier VIII, lord of Anglure in Champagne, traveled to Rhodes, Jerusalem, Cairo, and Cyprus in 1395 and 1396. His prose account, *Le saint voyage de Jherusalem du seigneur d'Anglure*, is extant in two manuscripts, providing two distinct versions. He furnishes a wealth of historical and geographical information on the areas visited, as well as numerous insights into everyday life.

Claude J. Fouillade

Anglure, Ogier d'. *Le saint voyage de Jherusalem du seigneur d'Anglure*, ed. François Bonnardot and Auguste Longnon. Paris: Didot, 1878.

———. *The Holy Jerusalem Voyage of Ogier VIII, Seigneur d'Anglure*, trans. Roland Browne. Gainesville: University Press of Florida, 1975.

ANGOULÊME. The cathedral of Angoulême (Charente), the fourth since Roman times, retains much of its former majesty despite the unfortunate restorations of Abadie in the 19th century. Begun ca.1110, it belongs to a distinctive group of churches characterized by a single nave covered with a series of domes. The western bay, with its simple arches and massive supports, is among the earliest of this type; however, its primitive austerity was altered by Abadie to harmonize with the two succeeding bays. The "Byzantine" crossing is an Abadie invention; of the four radiating chapels, only that of the northwest is original. The bell tower of the north transept, with its light-filled base, rich carvings, octagonal cupola, and elegant five-storied exterior, is striking in its boldness.

The entire western façade displays a grand theme of triumph, beginning with the Mission of the Apostles in the false tympana and culminating in the apparition of the Son of Man surrounded by the symbols of the four Evangelists

Angoulême (Charente), Saint-Pierre. *Photograph courtesy of Whitney S. Stoddard.*

and attendant angels. The sculpture of the upper level, the most accomplished of the several campaigns, shows affinities with the art of Languedoc. Abadie additions include the superstructure, with its gable and flanking turrets, the sculpture of the central tympanum, that of St. George and St. Martin, and the head of Christ.

Jean M. French

[See also: ANGOUMOIS; PÉRIGUEUX]

Daras, Charles. *La cathédrale d'Angoulême, chef-d'œuvre monumental de Girard II.* Angoulême: Corignan et Lachanaud, 1942.

Dubourg-Noves, Pierre. *Iconographie de la cathédrale d'Angoulême de 1575 à 1880.* 2 vols. Angoulême: Société Archéologique et Historique de la Charente, 1973.

Sauvel, Tony. "La façade de Saint-Pierre d'Angoulême." *Bulletin monumental* 103 (1945):175–99.

Serbat, Louis. "Angoulême." *Congrès archéologique (Angoulême)* 79 (1913): 3–36.

ANGOUMOIS. The Angoumois was a small county in west-central France of only modest importance in medieval times. On its borders lay Poitou to the north, the Limousin to the east, the Périgord to the south, and the Saintonge-Aunis to the west. Since the French Revolution, it has been part of the department of the Charente. Owing to its small size and its proximity to larger territorial states, it did not give rise to a feudal principality of any consequence save for brief periods in the late 9th and early 12th centuries. Nor did it become an ecclesiastical center of any more than regional importance. In early Roman times, the Angoumois belonged to the jurisdiction of the Santones (Saintes, Saintonge), then in the 4th century it broke away as a separate *civitas* centered on the town of Angoulême. Early tradition credited a 4th-century St. Ausonious with being the first bishop, though the first attested one is St. Cybard (d. 581). The bishopric of Angoulême belonged to the archdiocese of Bordeaux.

Almost nothing is known of the Angoumois under the Merovingians save that Angoulême, its only town of any size, was fortified by the 7th century and formed part of the duchy of Aquitaine. Armies of Pepin the Short conquered the province in the 760s preparatory to a century of Carolingian rule. After heavy damage by 9th-century Viking raids, recovery began later in the century with the establishment of Vulgrin I as count of Angoulême (r. 867–86) by Charles the Bald. Vulgrin not only restored order in the Angoumois but annexed the neighboring counties of Périgord and Agen to the south and possibly the Saintonge to the west and began the hereditary dynasty of the counts of Angoulême later called Taillefer. For a brief moment, Angoulême was the capital of a major territorial principality of west-central France, but Vulgrin's successors not only were unable to preserve it intact but could not resist the counts of Poitou/dukes of Aquitaine, who extended their power over the Angoumois in the 11th century.

The county became part of the Plantagenêt empire in the later 12th century, though its counts led bitter Aquitanian resistance to their rule. King John of England's abduction in 1200 of Isabelle, heiress of the county of Angoulême, led to Capetian intervention and the ousting of the English. After John's death in 1216, Isabelle's marriage with Hugues X de Lusignan, her intended husband prior to her abduction, contributed to the creation of a powerful feudal state ruled by the united Taillefer-Lusignan dynasty, which controlled the counties of the Aunis, Saintonge, La Marche, and Angoulême in the early 13th century. Capetian power gradually prevailed, however, and the Angoumois was integrated into the royal domain in 1314. Several monasteries flourished in the medieval Angoumois, most notably those of Cellefrouin, Saint-Étienne-de-Baigne, Saint-Amant-de-Boixe, and the oldest, Saint-Cybard-d'Angoulême. A monk of this latter abbey, Adémar de Chabannes (d. 1034), here wrote the chronicle that is the most important surviving source for the history of Aquitaine from the 9th to 11th century.

George T. Beech

[See also: ADÉMAR DE CHABANNES; ANGOULÊME; AQUITAINE; LUSIGNAN]

Boisonnade, Prosper. *L'ascension, le déclin et la chute d'un grand état féodal du Centre-Ouest: les Taillefer et les Lusignan, comtes de la Marche et d'Angoulême et leurs relations avec les Capétiens et les Plantagenêts 1137–1314.* Angoulême: Société Archéologique et Historique de la Charente, 1935, 1943.

Boussard, J. *Historia pontificum et comitum Engolismensium.* Paris: Argences, 1957.

Debord, André. *La société laïque dans les pays de la Charente Xe–XIIe siècles.* Paris: Picard, 1984.

Depoin, Joseph. "Les comtes héréditaires d'Angoulême de Vulgrin Ier à Audouin II, 869–1032." *Bulletin de la Société Archéologique et Historique de la Charente* (1904).

Histoire du Poitou, du Limousin et des pays charentais. Publiée sous la direction de Édmond-René Labande. Toulouse: Privat, 1976.

ANIMALS (DOMESTIC). Except for the Roman introduction of chickens, domestic animals in medieval France were little different from those of prehistoric times or, except for their smaller size, from domestic animals today. From early on, dogs were bred for hunting and herding and horses for riding and pulling; religious prohibitions prevented the use of either for food. Improved breeding of other species occurred from the central Middle Ages. Although the military and agricultural usefulness of the horse increased tremendously with the early-medieval introduction of horseshoes, horsecollars, and stirrups, most peasants continued to use oxen for plowing; asses served as pack animals (in the Midi they were widely used for hauling salt) and as riding animals for clerics and women. The preference for cattle, despite the higher speeds and greater strength of the horse, was due to the high cost of feeding the latter, particularly over the winter; even with cattle, there was a tendency to sell extra animals before winter, and considerable profits were made by urban dealers having access to winter feed who bought cattle in the fall from peasants and then sold them back for the spring plowing. Cows were kept primarily for the young they produced rather than for their limited milk production. Because large animals competed with humans for food (there was tension between the needs for sufficient livestock to manure the fields, for pasture for that livestock, and for arable for cereals), small-animal husbandry generally predominated in food production. In the earliest period, pigs, being adaptable, were the primary source of meat; they were able to live in a wild state on acorns and nuts in the forest but were also kept by town dwellers. As forests disappeared and their use became more controlled in the central Middle Ages, and as demand for meat, cheese, wool, leather, and parchment increased, sheep and goats became increasingly important in the rural economy, as did the practice of transhumance. Chickens, ducks, geese, and peacocks are mentioned by Carolingian sources, and rabbits appear to have been domesticated during this period.

Constance H. Berman

[See also: AGRICULTURE; *PÂTURAGE*; TRANSHUMANCE]

Duby, Georges. *Rural Economy and Country Life in the Medieval West*, trans. Cynthia Postan. London: Arnold, 1968.

Slicher van Bath, Bernard H. *The Agrarian History of Western Europe: A.D. 500–1850*, trans. Olive Ordish. London: Arnold, 1963.

ANJOU. Originally a relatively small *pagus* (administrative county) centered on the town of Angers at the confluence of the Loire and Mayenne rivers, Anjou expanded throughout the 11th century to become one of the major principalities of France. Under strong counts, Anjou was able to dominate much of western Francia independently of the king of France. From this base, the Plantagenêts were able to conquer Normandy and England, acquire Aquitaine by marriage, and establish the Angevin empire of the 12th century. After the king of France conquered the continental portions of this empire in 1202–04, the stable administrative institutions found there influenced the development of the Capetian kingdom.

In the 9th century, Anjou was merely a part of a larger lordship given to the Robertian family by Charles the Bald to defend against Viking attacks. Its chief city, Angers, was administered for the Robertians by a viscount, one of whom, Foulques le Roux (ca. 888–941), usurped the title of count by 930. Under his descendants, Anjou expanded beyond its original boundaries—sometimes by military conquest, often by marriage alliances. Before the end of the 10th century, Anjou had absorbed the Mauges and dominated Nantes in Brittany to the west, Vendôme to the east, and Loudun and the Gâtinais in the south.

Count Foulques Nerra (r. 987–1040) and his son Geoffroi Martel (r. 1040–60) were the true architects of Angevin expansion into a major power. By military victories, Nerra was able to maintain control of Nantes and the Mauges and to conquer Saintes, Saumur, and a major part of the Touraine. By diplomatic means, he dominated Vendôme and Maine. Geoffroi Martel capped Angevin expansion into the Touraine by capturing Tours from the count of Blois in 1044. This union with the Touraine made Anjou a major power in western Francia. Angevin control over the conquered territories was marked by an ambitious program of castle building, creating a complex system of defense in depth. Angevin domination was ensured as long as the lords of these castles were loyal to the count of Anjou.

Under the weak and unpopular rule of Geoffroi le Barbu (r. 1060–68), however, the system broke down. In the midst of a civil war between Geoffroi and his younger brother, Foulques le Rechin (r. 1068–1109), the Angevin barons increased their own power to the detriment of the count. By the time Foulques finally seized the countship in 1068, the Angevin state had been seriously weakened. He spent most of his reign trying to reassert his authority while successfully fighting off Norman advances into Maine. Although Angevin domination of outlying regions receded, control over the heartland of Anjou and the Touraine was maintained.

From this territory, Foulques le Rechin's successors, Foulques V (r. 1109–29) and Geoffroi Plantagenêt (1129–51), were able to reassert comital authority over the bar-

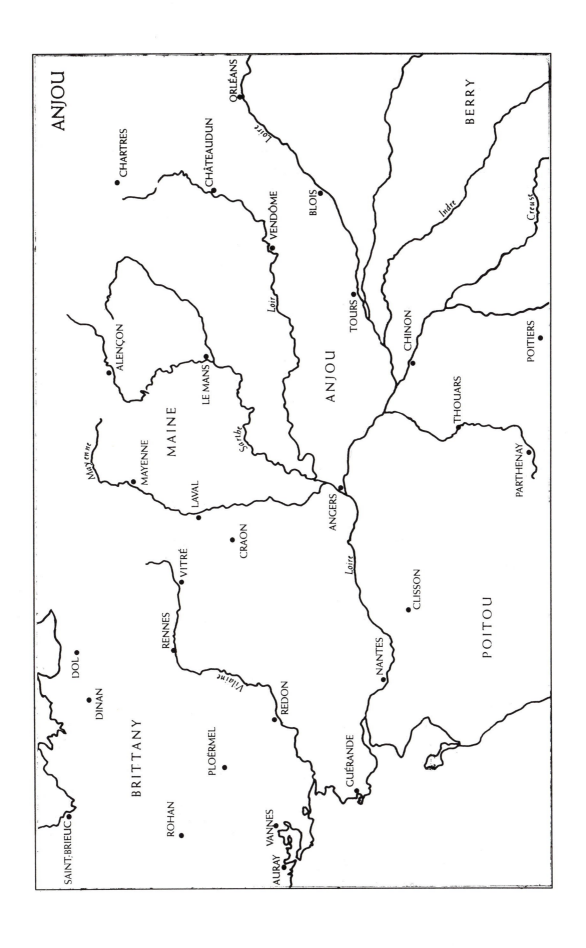

COUNTS OF ANJOU
(Original Dynasty)

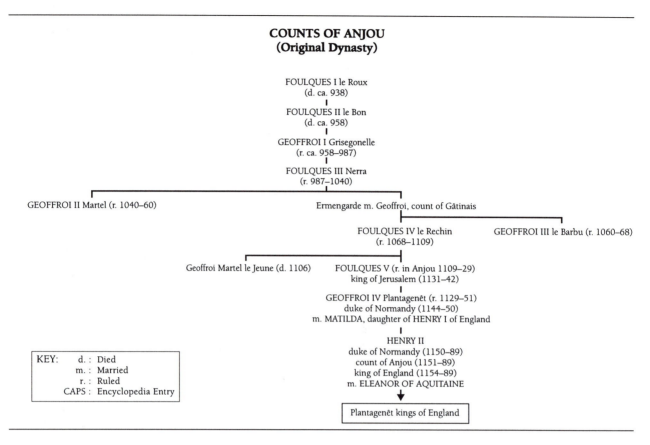

FOULQUES I le Roux
(d. ca. 938)

FOULQUES II le Bon
(d. ca. 958)

GEOFFROI I Grisegonelle
(r. ca. 958–987)

FOULQUES III Nerra
(r. 987–1040)

GEOFFROI II Martel (r. 1040–60)

Ermengarde m. Geoffroi, count of Gâtinais

FOULQUES IV le Rechin
(r. 1068–1109)

GEOFFROI III le Barbu (r. 1060–68)

Geoffroi Martel le Jeune (d. 1106)

FOULQUES V (r. in Anjou 1109–29)
king of Jerusalem (1131–42)

GEOFFROI IV Plantagenêt (r. 1129–51)
duke of Normandy (1144–50)
m. MATILDA, daughter of HENRY I of England

HENRY II
duke of Normandy (1150–89)
count of Anjou (1151–89)
king of England (1154–89)
m. ELEANOR OF AQUITAINE

Plantagenêt kings of England

KEY: d. : Died
      m. : Married
      r. : Ruled
      CAPS : Encyclopedia Entry

ons. Maine was effectively united with Anjou by the marriage of Foulques V to the heiress of that county. In 1128, his heir, Geoffroi Plantagenêt, married Matilda, daughter and heiress of Henry I, king of England and duke of Normandy. Geoffroi, count of Anjou, Maine, and Touraine, thus had a claim to both England and Normandy. The claim was frustrated, however, when Stephen of Blois, King Henry's nephew, seized the English throne in 1135. Geoffroi, forced to fight for his wife's inheritance, conquered Normandy in 1144. The war in England continued for another decade.

When Geoffroi's son Henry became count of Anjou in 1151, he also governed Normandy and pursued his claim to England. The following year, Henry gained the vast duchy of Aquitaine by marrying its heiress, Eleanor. As the result of a political settlement with Stephen, he secured the throne of England in 1154. Anjou thus became part of an enormous territory, including all of England and most of western France, ruled by one man and sometimes called the "Angevin empire." Following a flexible Angevin model, rather than the more tightly controlled Anglo-Norman model, monarchs made little attempt to integrate Anjou into a unified Plantagenêt state. Anjou was ruled by the Plantagenêt kings of England until 1202, when Philip Augustus (r. 1180–1223) captured Angers from John of England. From that point on, the history of Anjou is part of the history of France.

Scott Jessee

[See also: ANGERS; COUNT/COUNTY; FOULQUES; GEOFFROI; HENRY II; JOHN I LACKLAND]

Bachrach, Bernard S. "The Idea of the Angevin Empire." *Albion* 10 (1978): 293–99.

Dunbabin, Jean. *France in the Making: 843–1180.* Oxford: Oxford University Press, 1985.

Gillingham, John. *The Angevin Empire.* New York: Holmes and Meier, 1984.

Guillot Olivier. *Le comte d'Anjou et son entourage au XIe siècle.* 2 vols. Paris: Picard, 1972.

Hallam, Elizabeth, ed. *The Plantagenet Chronicles.* New York: Weidenfeld and Nicolson, 1986.

Halphen, Louis. *Le comté d'Anjou au XIe siècle.* Paris: Picard, 1906.

ANJOU, HOUSES OF. After acquiring the county of Anjou from the Plantagenêt kings of England in the early 13th century, French kings twice assigned the county as an apanage to a younger son. The first house of Anjou was established by Charles I (1227–1285), the youngest brother of Louis IX, who also acquired Provence by marrying Béatrice, the youngest daughter of the count.

With papal backing, Charles I in 1266 invaded the Regno, as the kingdom of Sicily and its mainland province were called. With his victories at Benevento (1266) and Tagliacozzo (1268), Charles carried out Innocent IV's de-

HOUSES OF ANJOU

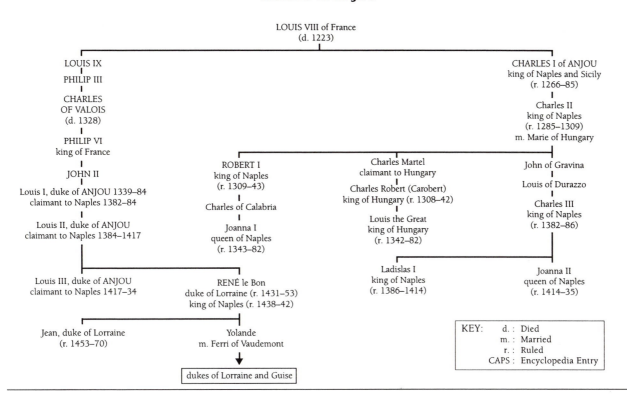

LOUIS VIII of France
(d. 1223)

LOUIS IX
|
PHILIP III
|
CHARLES
OF VALOIS
(d. 1328)
|
PHILIP VI
king of France
|
JOHN II
|
Louis I, duke of ANJOU 1339–84
claimant to Naples 1382–84
|
Louis II, duke of ANJOU
claimant to Naples 1384–1417

ROBERT I
king of Naples
(r. 1309–43)
|
Charles of Calabria
|
Joanna I
queen of Naples
(r. 1343–82)

Charles Martel
claimant to Hungary
|
Charles Robert (Carobert)
king of Hungary (r. 1308–42)
|
Louis the Great
king of Hungary
(r. 1342–82)
|
Ladislas I
king of Naples
(r. 1386–1414)

CHARLES I of ANJOU
king of Naples and Sicily
(r. 1266–85)
|
Charles II
king of Naples
(r. 1285–1309)
m. Marie of Hungary

John of Gravina
|
Louis of Durazzo
|
Charles III
king of Naples
(r. 1382–86)
|
Joanna II
queen of Naples
(r. 1414–35)

Louis III, duke of ANJOU
claimant to Naples 1417–34

RENÉ le Bon
duke of Lorraine (r. 1431–53)
king of Naples (r. 1438–42)

Jean, duke of Lorraine
(r. 1453–70)

Yolande
m. Ferri of Vaudemont
↓
dukes of Lorraine and Guise

KEY: d. : Died
        m. : Married
        r. : Ruled
        CAPS : Encyclopedia Entry

sire to "exterminate that brood of vipers," the German Hohenstaufen dynasty, which had acquired the Regno in 1194 and had seriously threatened the papal states. As the new king of Sicily, Charles I continued the bureaucracy and system of taxation established by earlier Norman and Hohenstaufen kings. His ambitious plans led to the diversion to Tunis of Louis IX's last crusade and to a projected attack on the recently restored Byzantine state at Constantinople.

His oppressive government, marked by heavy taxation, led to the rebellion against Charles I in 1282 known as the Sicilian Vespers. The ensuing war (1282–1302) pitted Aragon, to whose royal house the Sicilians had entrusted themselves, Genoa, and Byzantium against Naples, the mainland part of the Regno, supported by France, Venice, and the papacy. Charles II (r. 1285–1309), who retained Provence and Naples but had to return Anjou to France, concluded the Peace of Caltabellota with Frederick III of Sicily in 1302, but intermittent conflict between the mainland and island parts of the old Regno continued until 1442, when Alfonso V of Aragon seized the kingdom of Naples.

The older son of Charles II, known as Charles Martel, married the heiress of Hungary and established an Angevin dynasty there. Charles Martel's grandson Louis the Great (r. 1342–82) added Poland to his dominions in 1370. The younger son of Charles II, Petrarch's friend Robert (r. 1309–43), reigned in Naples and Provence and led the resistance of the Italian Guelfs against the invasion of the emperor

Henry VII. Robert's son, Charles of Calabria, became *signore* of Florence from 1325 to 1328. The latter's daughter, Joanna I (1326–1382), succeeded her grandfather Robert and married her cousin Andrew of Hungary, whose murder in 1345 many blamed on Joanna. Her long reign was troubled by the rebellious nobles of the Regno and an invasion by Louis of Hungary, who pressed his claim to the succession.

In France, King John II the Good created the second house of Anjou by bestowing the county on his son Louis I (1339–1384) as an apanage. Louis's Italian ambitions were fueled by the papal Schism of 1378, as the French-backed antipope Clement VII hoped for French military assistance against Rome. The childless and oft-married Joanna I of Naples was induced to name Louis as her heir, but her cousin of the Hungarian line Charles of Durazzo seized Naples and reigned as Charles III (r. 1382–86) after capturing and murdering Joanna. Charles III was succeeded by his son Ladislas (r. 1386–1414) and daughter Joanna II (r. 1414–35), during whose reign the Regno disintegrated.

The second house of Anjou, which had seized Provence, continued to claim Naples. Louis I, who failed to dislodge Charles of Durazzo, died in Italy in 1384. His claims passed on to his son Louis II (d. 1417) and grandson Louis III (d. 1434). The latter's brother René (d. 1480) had married Isabelle, the heiress of Lorraine, which with its dependencies he added to Anjou, Maine, and Provence—the inheritance from his brother. René seemed about to realize his family's Neapolitan claims when Joanna II adopted him as heir in 1434. He actually ruled in Naples from 1438 until expelled four years later by Alfonso of Aragon. An ineffectual ruler, René never returned to Italy, and after abdicating Lorraine to his son Jean he turned in his old age to the pursuit of art and literature.

William A. Percy, Jr.

[See also: CHARLES I; NORMANS IN SICILY; RENÉ D'ANJOU]

Léonard, Émile G. *Les Angevins de Naples*. Paris: Presses Universitaires de France, 1954.

ANNE OF BEAUJEU (ca. 1461–1522). Duchess of Bourbon. Anne of France, the oldest child of Louis XI and Charlotte of Savoy, was born ca. 1461 and was married in 1474 to Pierre de Bourbon, lord of Beaujeu, a prince who gave her father able service. She inherited much of her father's ability and, while still in her early twenties, had to act as guardian for her brother, Charles VIII, who became king at the age of thirteen. Despite considerable opposition, she and Pierre retained custody of the young king, skillfully managed the Estates General of 1484, and defeated a princely uprising. For five years, she exercised considerable authority over the French government. In 1488, when her husband inherited the duchy of Bourbon and her brother reached the age of eighteen, her political influence diminished.

John Bell Henneman, Jr.

[See also: BOURBON/BOURBONNAIS; CHARLES VIII]

Pelicier, Paul. *Essai sur le gouvernement de la dame de Beaujeu (1483–1491)*. Chartres: Garnier, 1882.
Pradel, Pierre. *Anne de France, 1461–1522*. Paris: Publisud, 1986.

ANNE OF BRITTANY (1477–1514). Duchess of Brittany and queen of France. The oldest daughter of François II, duke of Brittany, and Marguerite de Foix, Anne of Brittany was born at Nantes on January 26, 1477. At the death of her father in September 1488, she became duchess of Brittany, the heiress of a strategic territory and much sought after as a bride. The autonomy of her duchy was severely threatened, and she finally married Charles VIII of France in December 1491, seven weeks before her fifteenth birthday. Between the ages of sixteen and twenty-two, the young queen experienced repeated pregnancies, but no child lived more than a few years and none survived Charles VIII, who died in 1498. Charles was succeeded by Louis XII, his father's second cousin and an old acquaintance of Anne's, although fifteen years her senior. She married Louis in January 1499 and bore him four children, of whom two daughters survived. The older one, Claude, was married to Francis, duke of Angoulême, who succeeded Louis as king in 1515. Their son, Henry II, inherited Brittany from Claude and finally brought the duchy under the direct rule of the French crown. Anne of Brittany, beloved as the last ruler of independent Brittany, died at Blois in January 1514, so did not live to see her daughter reign as queen of France.

John Bell Henneman, Jr.

[See also: BRITTANY (genealogical table); CHARLES VIII; FRANÇOIS II]

Gabory, Émile. *Anne de Bretagne: duchesse et reine*. Paris: Plon, 1941.
Labande-Mailfert, Yvonne. *Charles VIII et son milieu (1470–1498)*. Paris: Klincksieck, 1975.
Le Boterf, Hervé. *Anne de Bretagne*. Paris: France-Empire, 1976.
Le Roux de Lincy, Antoine. *Vie de la reine Anne de Bretagne*. 4 vols. Paris: Curmer, 1860–61.

ANNE OF KIEV (fl. 11th c.). Queen of France. In 1051, after marrying one or possibly two short-lived German princesses, Henry I (1031–1060) married Anne, daughter of Grandduke Jaroslav of Kiev. She was the mother of Henry's children and the regent for his son Philip I. A year after Henry's death, she married Raoul of Valois.

Constance B. Bouchard

Caix de Saint-Aymour, Amédée de. *Anne de Russie, reine de France et comtesse de Valois*. 2nd ed. Paris: Champion, 1896.
Dhondt, Jean. "Sept femmes et un trio de rois." *Contributions à l'histoire économique et sociale* 3 (1964–65): 35–70.
Facinger, Marion F. "A Study of Medieval Queenship: Capetian France, 987–1237." *Studies in Medieval and Renaissance History* 5 (1968): 3–47.

ANONYMOUS 4 (fl. second half of the 13th century). The English author or compiler of an unattributed treatise on music that probably dates from the 1280s is designated Anonymous 4 after the ordering of *anonymi* in the first volume of Coussemaker's *Scriptorum de musica medii aevi*. Anonymous 4 is the sole source for almost all our knowledge of historical individuals of the Notre-Dame School because he gives an apparently chronological listing of significant individuals working in Paris from the late 12th to the late 13th century, up to and including Franco of Cologne. He knew Léonin by reputation and could describe in detail musical works of Pérotin. His knowledge of other Parisian *magistri* leaves little room to doubt his presence in Paris sometime in the mid- to late 13th century, possibly as a student at the university. A secondary source for Garlandian modal theory, the treatise further appears to be either an adaptation to insular practices or a substantially original extension of Garlandian modal theory independent from developments in Paris.

Sandra Pinegar

[See also: FRANCO OF COLOGNE; LÉONIN; NOTRE-DAME SCHOOL; ORGANUM; PÉROTIN]

Coussemaker, Charles Édmond Henri de, ed. *Scriptorum de musica medii aevi nova series a Gerbertina altera.* Paris: Durand, 1864–76, Vol. 1, pp. 327–65.

Reckow, Fritz. *Der Musiktraktat des Anonymus 4.* Wiesbaden: Steiner, 1967.

Yudkin, Jeremy, trans. *The Music Treatise of Anonymous IV: A New Translation.* Neuhausen-Stuttgart: American Institute of Musicology, 1985.

ANONYMOUS OF BÉTHUNE. A native of Artois in the service of Robert VII of Béthune, this author composed two prose histories, the *Histoire des ducs de Normandie et des rois d'Angleterre* (ca. 1220) and the *Chronique française des rois de France* (ca. 1223). The *Histoire* takes a Plantagenêt slant; the *Chronique* reflects a French viewpoint and is notable for its inclusion of a version of the Pseudo-Turpin chronicle. These works belong to the rising genre of vernacular prose histories composed for the French and English elite. There is no complete edition of the *Chronique*.

Leah Shopkow

Anonymous of Béthune. *Chronique française des rois de France,* ed. Léopold Delisle. Extracts in *Recueil des historiens de Gaulle et de la France* 24, pt. 2 (1904): 750–75, 929–40.

———. *Histoire des ducs de Normandie et des rois d'Angleterre,* ed. Francisque Michel. Paris: Société de l'Histoire de France, 1840.

ANSELM OF BEC (or Canterbury, or Aosta; 1033–1109). Anselm of Bec was born in Aosta, Italy. After the death of his mother, he left for Burgundy and France, where he was attracted to the monastic life and entered the remote monastery of Bec in Normandy in 1059. His countryman Lanfranc of Pavia (d. 1089) was prior at Bec and taught grammar and logic. Anselm became Lanfranc's student, then his assistant, and finally a fellow teacher. When in 1063 Lanfranc became abbot of Saint-Étienne, Caen (before becoming archbishop of Canterbury in 1070), Anselm succeeded him as prior at Bec and became abbot after the death of the monastery's founder, Herluin, in 1078. As abbot, he paid frequent visits to England to inspect the lands owned by Bec. While at Bec, Anselm wrote works of a mixed devotional and philosophical nature: *De grammatico* (1060–63), a linguistico-philosophical treatise about the term "grammarian"; *Monologion,* a soliloquy on proving the existence of God by reason alone; *Proslogion,* an improved version of the *Monologion;* and three treatises, *De veritate, De libertate arbitrii,* and *De casu diaboli.* During this period, he also wrote his *Orationes sive meditationes.*

Anselm succeeded Lanfranc as archbishop of Canterbury in 1093. Before long, he clashed with King William II Rufus over such issues as church property, the right of appointment to ecclesiastical offices, and the recognition of Urban II as pope. Another contentious issue was Anselm's wish to travel to Rome to receive the token of his episcopal dignity, the *pallium,* directly from the pope. In the end, Anselm did not go, yet he did succeed in preventing the king from usurping the right of investiture. There followed a period of relative calm during which Anselm published his *Epistola de incarnatione verbi* in 1094 and started work on his *magnum opus, Cur Deus homo.* In the meantime, Anselm's relations with the king had once more become strained; in 1098, he went in exile to Rome, where he completed *Cur Deus homo.* He also attended the Council of Bari, at which he defended the "double procession" of the Holy Spirit (from the Father and the Son) against the Greeks (later published as *De processione Spiritus Sanctus*).

Following William Rufus's death in 1100, Anselm returned to England. After a peaceful interval, he collided with the new king, Henry I, over old issues, such as homage and investiture. From 1103 until 1106, he lived in exile, mainly in France, and returned to England only after a compromise had been reached with the king. He died in 1109 at Canterbury, having completed in 1108 his *De concordia* (on the concordance of foreknowledge and predestination and the grace of God with free will).

Anselm's writings are marked by a balance between rational argumentation and contemplative intensity. Claiming in his *Proslogion* to prove the existence of God by one single argument and by reason alone, he takes his starting point in a negation of that existence. This negation has to be seen as a dialectical-intellectual game within the monastic context in which it serves the aim of bringing out the presence of the divine. The fool who denies the existence of God is met with the argument that God is that than which no greater can be thought. The logical implications of this formula are such as to exclude the possibility of God's nonexistence. As a consequence, God's presence, which in the beginning of the treatise had been phrased in terms of monastic desperation, frustrated by an inaccessible light, gains clarity and offers joy to the meditating mind. *Cur Deus homo* follows the same pattern. The accusation by the infidels that the Christian concept of incarnation is primitive is met by an analysis of the beauty of God's order. God is bound by intrinsic necessity to keep his order intact and save humanity, which for its part is bound to make satisfaction for its sin. The two elements come together in the necessary appearance of a God-man, who is no other than Christ.

Anselm's dense style of argumentation is further developed in his treatises on truth, on the will, and on the fall of the Devil. In conformity with his monastic way of life, it is the real truth and the real existence of justice that count most. As a result, the freedom of will is the freedom to do the right thing. By the same token, the freedom to sin turns out to lack a real object—injustice having no subsistence of its own—and therefore to be illusory.

Although Anselm has always been held in high esteem, his philosophical and theological influence has been limited mainly to the so-called ontological proof of God's existence and the argument of *Cur Deus homo.* The *Orationes sive mediationes,* on the other hand, were widely read all through the Middle Ages.

Burcht Pranger

[**See also:** LANFRANC OF BEC; PHILOSOPHY; THEOLOGY]

Anselm of Bec. *S. Anselmi Cantuariensis archiepiscopi opera omnia*, ed. Franciscus S. Schmitt. 6 vol. Stuttgart: Fromann, 1968.

———. *Anselm of Canterbury*, ed. and trans. Jasper Hopkins and Herbert Richardson. 4 vols. 2nd ed. New York: Mellen, 1975–76.

———. *The Prayers and Meditations of St. Anselm*, trans. Benedicta Ward. Harmondsworth: Penguin, 1973.

Eadmer. *The Life of St. Anselm, Archbishop of Canterbury by Eadmer*, ed. and trans. Richard W. Southern. Oxford: Clarendon, 1972.

Campbell, Richard. *From Belief to Understanding: A Study of Anselm's* Proslogion *Argument on the Existence of God*. Canberra: Faculty of Arts, Australian National University, 1976.

Hopkins, Jasper. *A Companion to the Study of St. Anselm*. Minneapolis: University of Minneapolis Press, 1972.

Evans, Gillian R. *Anselm and Talking About God*. Oxford: Clarendon, 1978.

Southern, Richard W. *Saint Anselm: A Portrait in a Landscape*. Cambridge: Cambridge University Press, 1990.

Vaughn, Sally N. *Anselm of Bec and Robert of Meulan: The Innocence of the Dove and the Wisdom of the Serpent*. Berkeley: University of California Press, 1987.

ANSELM OF LAON (ca. 1050–1117). As schoolmaster at the cathedral of Laon, Anselm stands at the beginning of an era that saw the expansion of literacy and intellectual training beyond the cloister walls, reaching out to a burgeoning urban population. Through a curriculum that focused on the study of the Bible and basic Christian principles of belief and daily living, Anselm helped to channel both the spiritual awakening that was sweeping Europe and the ecclesiastical reform that was an important focus of the Gregorian papacy.

Anselm composed commentaries on several books of the Bible, including Isaiah, Matthew, the Psalms, the Song of Songs, the opening chapters of Genesis, and Revelation. With his brother Ralph and a younger contemporary, Gilbert the Universal (later schoolmaster at Auxerre and then bishop of London), Anselm began to compile a commentary that was to become the standard (*Glossa ordinaria*) for the Bible by the end of the 12th century. Anselm and his associates digested, abbreviated, supplemented, and otherwise edited the vast deposit of commentaries produced by the Christian authors of late antiquity and the Carolingian era, placing the longer comments in the broad margins of Bibles designed for this purpose and the shorter comments between the lines of the biblical text itself. Anselm was responsible for the *Glossa ordinaria* for the Psalms, for the epistles of Paul, and perhaps for the Fourth Gospel as well.

Equally important were Anselm's collections of theological opinions (*sententiae*). They ranged over the whole spectrum of Christian teaching, from God and Creation to redemption and the sacraments, but focused on such current issues as the nature of marriage and relations with Jews, who had been severely persecuted in the wake of the First Crusade.

Anselm was one of the more successful scholars in addressing the need for a trained and competent clergy, able to deal with the needs of the newly emerging society. Some of the most distinguished theologians of the 12th century studied with him, including Gilbert of Poitiers and William of Champeaux. However influential Anselm was as the central figure of a school for teaching, he did not establish a school of thought characterized by a common set of assumptions.

Mark Zier

[See also: BIBLE, CHRISTIAN INTERPRETATION OF; GILBERT OF POITIERS; *GLOSSA ORDINARIA*; SCHOLASTICISM; SENTENCE COLLECTIONS; THEOLOGY; WILLIAM OF CHAMPEAUX]

Anselm of Laon. *Sententie divine pagine* and *Sententie Anselmi*, ed. Franz P. Bliemetzrieder. In *Anselms von Laon systematische Sentenzen*. Münster: Aschendorff, 1919.

Bliemetzrieder, Franz P., ed. "Trente-trois pièces inédites des œuvres théologiques d'Anselme de Laon." *Recherches de théologie ancienne et médiévale* 2 (1930): 54–79.

Lottin, Odon, ed. "Nouveaux fragments théologiques de l'école d'Anselme de Laon." *Recherches de théologie ancienne et médiévale* 11 (1939): 305–23; 12 (1940): 49–77; 13 (1946): 202–21, 261–81; 14 (1947): 5–31.

Bertola, Ermenegildo. "Le critiche di Abelardo ad Anselmo di Laon ed a Guglielmo di Champeaux." *Rivista di filosofia neo-scolastica* 52 (1960): 495–522.

Cavallera, Ferdinand. "D'Anselme de Laon à Pierre Lombard." *Bulletin de littérature ecclésiastique* 41 (1940): 40–54, 102–14.

Colish, Marcia. "Another Look at the School of Laon." *Archives d'histoire doctrinale et littéraire du moyen âge* 53 (1986): 7–22.

Flint, Valerie I.J. "The 'School of Laon': A Reconsideration." *Recherches de théologie ancienne et médiévale* 43 (1976): 89–110.

Ghellinck, Joseph de. *Le mouvement théologique du XIIe siècle*. 2nd ed. Bruges: De Tempel, 1948.

Landgraf, Artur Michael. *Introduction à l'histoire de la littérature théologique de la scolastique naissante*, ed. Albert-Marie Landry, trans. Louis-B. Geiger. Montreal: Institut d'Études Médiévales, 1979.

Smalley, Beryl. *The Study of the Bible in the Middle Ages*. 3rd ed. Oxford: Blackwell, 1983.

Weisweiler, Heinrich. "Le recueil de sentences 'Deus de cuius principio et fine tacetur' et son remaniement." *Recherches de théologie ancienne et médiévale* 5 (1933): 245–74.

ANTICHRIST. Medieval eschatology held that just before the end of the world a great adversary would arise, the Antichrist, who would initiate the most terrible persecution of all, tempting even the saints themselves. Although the term "Antichrist" appears in the New Testament only in the Epistles of John (1 John 2:18, 4:3; 2 John 7), and is thus a relatively late addition to early Christian eschatology, subsequent commentators interpreted other biblical prophecies of a last persecutor as referring to this same Antichrist: Daniel 7–12, Matthew 24:15, 2 Thessalonians 2:3–8, Revelation 13:11–18. By the patristic period, the Antichrist had become a central element of Christian eschatological teachings, discouraging apocalyptic hopes by describing in lurid and supernatural terms the hideous persecution of the just that will occur before the final Parousia and Redemption. In some versions, there were two Antichrists: an imperial one (Nero *redivivus*) and a Jewish one (born of the tribe of Dan in Babylon). Because this latter figure would be a false Christ, taking over the temple, establishing himself as God, and forcing all the nations to circumcise, this teaching effectively branded any Jewish messianic figure as Antichrist, thus guaranteeing Christian hostility to Jews at the End Time.

And yet, while this element of the Antichrist legend grew greater over time, that of an imperial Antichrist was transformed into its opposite. By interpreting Paul's references in 2 Thessalonians to a "man of sin [or lawlessness]" as Antichrist, the "rebellion" as the collapse of public order, and the "obstacle" to Antichrist as the existence of the Roman Empire, patristic exegetes provided the most conservative form of Christian eschatology: even before Constantine, it was incumbent on good Christians to pray for the continued strength of the Roman Empire. This proimperial eschatology eventually produced the legend of the Last Emperor, himself a supernaturally powerful man who would unite Christendom and rule in peace and justice for 120 years (*Tiburtine Sybil*, ca. 350; *Revelations of Methodius*, ca. 650). At the end of his reign, he would lay down his crown at Golgotha in Jerusalem, thus abdicating and bringing on the reign of Antichrist.

Antichrist imagery flourished throughout the medieval centuries. Earlier exegetes, such as Gregory the Great, Bede, Alcuin, and Haimo of Auxerre, elaborated on his attributes, leading to Adso's highly influential *Libellus de Antichristo* (ca. 950). In the 12th century, ecclesiastical writers like Otto of Freising and Rupert of Deutz elaborated on aspects of the Antichrist's career; dramas like the *Ludus de Antichristo* revealed to laypeople the terrifying details of his career. Indeed, Antichrist imagery appears in every medium of high- and late-medieval culture—theology, visions, polemic, art, drama, history.

Because Antichrist was to be born in Babylon and rise to power only in his thirtieth year, one way to make apocalyptic pronouncements was to announce his birth in the East, thus placing the final events within the lifespan of those now alive, although not immediately (e.g., Martin of Tours, ca. 390). Although such speculation was regularly discouraged (the passage on Martin's belief was censored from Sulpicius Severus's *Dialogues* for centuries), it crops up perennially. When Bernard of Clairvaux and Norbert of Xanten met ca.1125, Norbert declared, as had Martin, that Antichrist would reveal himself in the present generation.

At the same time, because the Epistles of John spoke of an Antichrist and his precursors, the antichrists, there was a wide range of accusations that polemicists could make against their enemies. One could, for example, disapprove of improper religious fervor (such as a mass pilgrimage to Jerusalem in 1033), without condemning it *per se*, by claiming that it was "beating down a path for Antichrist." Such accusations, traditionally reserved for heretics and foreign enemies, reached new heights in the Investiture conflict, where both pope and emperor called each other Antichrist. Joachim of Fiore, by identifying a hidden Antichrist working inside the church, prepared the way for the spiritual movements of the later Middle Ages, from the Spiritual Franciscans in the 13th century to the conciliar movements of the 15th, to view the church as the seedbed for Antichrist, in some cases identifying a specific pope, such as Boniface VIII, as Antichrist. The smear became so common that modern historians have a tendency to dismiss it as a mere topos, a possibly anachronistic elevation, particularly for the period before the 12th century.

Richard Landes

[See also: FRANCISCAN ORDER; MILLENNIALISM; RAOUL GLABER]

Aichele, Klaus. *Das Antichrist-dramas des Mittelalters der Reformation und Gegenreformation.* The Hague: Nijhoff, 1974.

Emmerson, Richard K. *Antichrist in the Middle Ages: A Study of Medieval Apocalypticism in Art and Literature.* Seattle: University of Washington Press, 1981.

———, and Bernard McGinn, eds. *The Apocalypse in the Middle Ages.* Ithaca: Cornell University Press, 1993.

Lerner, Robert E. "Refreshment of the Saints: The Time After Antichrist as a Station for Earthly Progress in Medieval Thought." *Traditio* 32 (1976): 99–144.

———. "Antichrists and Antichrist in Joachim of Fiore." *Speculum* 60 (1985): 553–70.

McGinn, Bernard. *Visions of the End: Apocalyptic Traditions in the Middle Ages.* New York: Columbia University Press, 1979.

Rauh, Hans Dieter. *Das Bild des Antichrist im Mittelalter: Von Tyconius zum deutschen Symbolismus.* Münster: Aschendorff, 1973.

Verhelst, Daniel. "La préhistoire des conceptions d'Adson concernant l'Antichrist." *Recherches de théologie ancienne et médiévale* 40 (1973): 52–103.

ANTIFEMINISM. Although the classical roots of medieval antifeminism are many, the most important classical author is St. Jerome, whose *Contra Jovinianum* (A.D. 393) brings together most of the Greek and Roman arguments against marriage and against women. Misogyny pervades medieval ecclesiastical writing—letters, sermons, theological tracts, discussions of canon law, scientific works, and philosophy. But antifeminism is an element that can be found in almost any work, even those generally considered profemale, such as *Aucassin et Nicolette*.

In medieval Latin literature, the arguments of St. Jerome were used by Héloïse to dissuade Abélard from marriage and by John of Salisbury in his *Policraticus*. One model of antimatrimonial satire is *De coniuge non ducenda* (ca. 1225–50), a skillfully drafted discussion of the disadvantages of marriage. The classic 13th-century complaint against women is the Latin *Lamentationes* (ca. 1290) of Matheolus, a cleric who lost his source of income when his ecclesiastical superiors discovered that his wife had previously been married, which status made Matheolus a bigamist in the eyes of the church. His tirade on the victimization of men by women was translated into French (1371–72) by Jean Le Fèvre. Even Andreas Capellanus, whose 12th-century *De arte honeste amandi* (*Art of Courtly Love*) is often taken as a rulebook for the favorable treatment of women, devotes the final third of his effort to arguments against marriage and womankind.

French literary works of the 12th and especially 13th centuries give the theme free rein. Criticism of women cites their lecherousness, garrulity, and insatiability. Woman is instability personified, contradictory at every turn. Even courtly romances, though claiming to elevate the status of women, can use the themes of antifeminism. An example is the romance of *Amadas et Ydoine*. The anonymous author, attempting to praise his heroine, Ydoine, does so by describing all the things she is not, and the reader is provided with a long litany of woman's failings. Irony is a favorite authorial tool used to attack women; one example among many is the title of the late 14th-century *Quinze joies de mariage*.

Antifeminism is pervasive in the fabliaux, where woman is a favorite object of satire, portrayed with all her "failings," particularly lechery, gluttony, and garrulity. Popular texts, *dits* like the *Dit des cornetes*, the *Contenance des fames*, or the *Évangile aux femmes*, use arguments initiated by Jerome, found repeated in medieval Latin literature and in the fabliaux to criticize women; rare is the popular text that praises the female sex. Proverbs of the period enshrine the theme of antifeminism in popular wisdom. The emphasis in proverbial literature is on the mutability of women; "Cueur de femme est tost mué" is a typical example. These proverbs are often cited in French literary works.

The *Roman de la Rose* also includes the theme. Although Guillaume de Lorris implied that women have bad features, Jean de Meun exploited antifeminism with a vengeance. Most notable in this vein is the long tirade by the Jealous Husband on female vices (ll. 8,437–9,330), repeating all the characterizations seen in other French and Latin literary works. Jean's antifeminism later raised the ire of Christine de Pizan, leading to the celebrated "Quarrel of the Rose."

The popularity of antifeminist arguments in the Middle Ages is not necessarily proof of rampant misogyny. One must be wary of attributing to authors the opinions expressed by characters in their works. Antifeminism, however, was a literary theme appreciated by medieval audiences and much exploited by medieval authors.

Wendy E. Pfeffer

[See also: ANDREAS CAPELLANUS; CHRISTINE DE PIZAN; JEAN DE MEUN; LE FÈVRE (DE RESSONS), JEAN; PROVERB; QUARREL OF THE *ROMAN DE LA ROSE*; *QUINZE JOIES DE MARIAGE*; ROSE, *ROMAN DE LA*]

Jodogne, Omer, ed. "L'édition de l'Évangile aux femmes." In *Studi in onore di Angelo Monteverdi*. Modena: Società Tipografica Editrice Modenese, 1959, Vol. 1, pp. 353–75.

Matheolus. *Les Lamentations de Matheolus et le Livre de leesce de Jehan le Fèvre, de Resson* (*poèmes français du XIVe siècle*), ed. A.-G. von Hamel. 2 vols. Paris: Bouillon, 1892–1905.

Rigg, A. G., ed. *Gawain on Marriage: The Textual Tradition of the "De coniuge non ducenda" with Critical Edition and Translation*. Toronto: Pontifical Institute of Mediaeval Studies, 1986.

Bloch, R. Howard. *Medieval Misogyny and the Invention of Western Romantic Love*. Chicago: University of Chicago Press, 1991.

Ferrante, Joan M. *Woman as Image in Medieval Literature from the Twelfth Century to Dante*. New York: Columbia University Press, 1975.

Friedman, Lionel J. "Jean de Meun, Antifeminism and 'Bourgeois Realism.'" *Modern Philology* 57 (1959): 13–23.

Hicks, Eric, ed. *Le débat sur le Roman de la Rose*. Paris: Champion, 1977.

Rogers, Katherine M. *The Troublesome Helpmate: A History of Misogyny in Literature*. Seattle: University of Washington Press, 1966.

ANTIPHON. Word deriving from the Greek adjective *antiphonos*, the neuter plural of which became the Latin substantive *antiphona* (OFr. *antifone*). Appearing for the first time in a Christian context in the latter half of the 4th century, "antiphon" denoted either a short musical refrain or a manner of performance using that refrain. Apart from the fact that two choral groups were involved, it is not clear how the antiphon interacted with the psalmody at this early period. By the 8th century, "antiphon" usually meant a short textual-musical unit of one to four phrases intended to be sung at the beginning and end of a psalm and possibly intercalated a number of times between verses.

Evidence from Syria implies that the earliest antiphons were nonbiblical and that they played a role in doctrinal controversies. The earliest reference to antiphons in Gaul occurs in the *Institutes* of John Cassian (ca. 360–ca. 435), an eastern monk who seems to assume that his western counterparts already understood their use in the Divine Office. Antiphons appear also in the Office prescribed by the monastic rules of Caesarius and Aurelian, bishops of Arles in the first half of the 6th century (r. ca. 500–43 and 546–51, respectively).

The melodies to which the verses of the psalms are sung have cadences designed to lead smoothly into the beginning of the antiphon, thus implying that at one time the antiphon was repeated between at least some verses of the psalm. Tonaries, catalogues of antiphons grouped according to the psalm tone appropriate to each, record the repertoire of antiphons as early as the first third of the 9th century, but the notated sources begin only ca. 1000, with the Antiphoner of Hartker (St. Gall, Stiftsbibliothek 390–91). The earliest source of the texts without music is the Antiphoner of Compiègne (B.N. lat. 17436), from the last third of the 9th century.

The antiphons for ordinary weekdays, which consist of a psalm hemistich set to a primarily syllabic melody, may represent the oldest layer of the repertoire. Some antiphons that consist solely of the word *alleluia* may be contemporary with them. Other antiphon texts are drawn from other books of the Bible and, in the case of saints' Offices, from the hagiographical literature. Successive antiphons for some later Offices were composed in ascending order of the eight modes. Antiphons with rhymed metrical texts enjoyed great popularity in the high Middle Ages. Certain processional chants and a special group of pieces in honor of the Blessed Virgin were called "antiphons," even though most were not associated with the singing of psalms. Typically, these newer antiphons can be distinguished by their fuller melodic development.

Two of the chants of the Mass, the Introit and the Communion, originated as antiphons with psalm verses. Both are associated with movement: the entrance of the clergy and the congregation's movement to the altar for communion.

Joseph Dyer

[See also: MAGNIFICAT; O ANTIPHONS]

Apel, Willi. *Gregorian Chant.* Bloomington: Indiana University Press, 1958, pp. 392–404 [Office antiphons], 305–12 [Introits and Communions].

Claire, Jean. "Les répertoires liturgiques latins avant l'Octoéchos. I: L'office férial romano-franc." *Études grégoriennes* 15 (1975): 11–193.

de Vogüé, Adalbert. "Le sens d'antifana et la longueur de l'office dans la *Regula Magistri.*" *Revue bénédictine* 71 (1961): 119–24.

Nowacki, Edward. "The Gregorian Antiphons and the Comparative Method." *Journal of Musicology* 4 (1985–86): 243–75.

ANTIQUITY, ROMANCES OF. The three Romances of Antiquity, the *Roman de Thèbes* (ca. 1152), the *Roman d'Énéas* (ca. 1160), and the *Roman de Troie* by Benoît de Sainte-Maure (ca. 1165), made classical antiquity accessible to a vernacular audience. All are linked to the literary currents of the court of Henry II and Eleanor of Aquitaine and are based on classical epics: Statius's *Thebaid,* Virgil's *Aeneid,* and the late-antique accounts of the Trojan War by Dares and Dictys, respectively. In their concerns (celebrating ancient heroes and civilization as forerunners of the present) and techniques (rewriting, rearranging, and medievalizing classical material), they form a coherent body of texts. They appear together in some manuscripts (e.g., B.N. fr. 60).

The *Roman de Thèbes* (10,562 lines) popularized the traditional romance form of the octosyllabic rhymed couplet. Its prologue characterizes the concerns of the genre of Romances of Antiquity as a whole. The poet, identified in the first line as he "who is wise," has the duty to share his knowledge in order to be remembered forever. Homer, Plato, Virgil, and Cicero are adduced as examples of men who did just that. This list exemplifies the *translatio studii* topos, a concept central to the Romances of Antiquity: civilization began in Greece, moved to Rome, and has now arrived in French-speaking territory. The subject matter is worthy since

it derives from ancient *auctores;* it also teaches a moral lesson, which for *Thèbes* is inherent in the story of Oedipus and his sons, Eteocles and Polynices, who begin a civil war after Oedipus's abdication. One should not act against nature—this is in fact the final lesson pronounced by the *Thèbes* poet. Whether this lesson refers to Oedipus's incestuous marriage or to the dangers of waging war is not clear. In any case, the poet accentuates the ravages of war and in particular denounces the horrors of fratricidal, that is, civil war. Although the story is set in antiquity and the characters are called "pagans," many features are medieval: people go to church, there are convents and archbishops, medieval weapons and armor. The tragic love story between Atys and Ismene, not found in Statius's *Thebaid,* inaugurated the strong love interest evident in later romances.

In the *Roman d'Énéas* (10,156 lines), love plays an especially important role and is, for the first time, expressed in the Ovidian forms that later become commonplace. Unlike *Thèbes, Énéas* has no prologue but starts with the prehistory of Aeneas's voyage, the Trojan War. A digression recounts the Judgment of Paris: the three goddesses who were present at the origin of the Trojan War seem to provide the structural principle for the romance. In the promises made to Paris, Venus gives passion (i.e., Dido) to Aeneas; Athene oversees Aeneas's victorious battle against Turnus; and Juno is responsible for Aeneas's winning of Lavinia and the all-important *demesne,* the land that will be Rome. On the whole, the story line follows Virgil's *Aeneid,* but the medieval poet adds a lengthy development on the love between Lavinia and Aeneas. Monologues and dialogues spin out the growing love between the two, and Lavinia often takes the initiative. The poet clearly wants to celebrate the success of a dynastic marriage, perhaps not unlike that of Henry II and Eleanor of Aquitaine. Thus, in contrast to the *Aeneid,* which ends with Aeneas's killing of Turnus, the *Énéas* closes with the joyous description of Aeneas's and Lavinia's wedding and the celebration of their lineage, which engendered the founders of Rome. Other important additions to Virgil include long passages describing marvelous works of art, such as Pallas's tomb.

Benoît's *Roman de Troie,* with 30,316 lines by far the longest of the Romances of Antiquity, tells the story of the Trojan War from Jason's winning of the Golden Fleece to the homecoming of the Greek heroes and Odysseus's tragic death at the hands of Telegonus, the son he had by Circe. Benoît's lengthy prologue, introduced by the topos of the duty of imparting one's knowledge to others, justifies in detail his rejection of Homer as an authoritative source: he was not a participant in the Trojan War. Dares and Dictys, on the other hand, Benoît insists, fought by day and wrote by night. Benoît thus accepts the claims of these late-antique writers as authentic. The story of how their texts came to light underlines the continuity of the geographical and linguistic *translatio* of his source, which ensures Benoît's own authority.

From a didactic perspective, the numerous diplomatic missions and attendant discourses could provide models of political behavior to a medieval audience, while the story of Troilus and Briseida posed the problematics of prowess in war and love. The theme of Briseida's inconstancy, taken up later by Boccaccio, Chaucer, and Shakespeare, led Benoît to some misogynistic tirades, which he interrupted only to praise Eleanor of Aquitaine.

All three romances brought pagan antiquity into medieval literature and thus participated in the "renaissance of the 12th century." Their adaptations of Latin epics introduced new concepts of love and history underlining the disruptive power of war in both domains.

Renate Blumenfeld-Kosinski

[See also: ALEXANDER ROMANCES; BENOÎT DE SAINTE-MAURE; OVIDIAN TALES; ROMANCE]

Benoît de Sainte-Maure. *Le roman de Troie*, ed. Léopold Constans. 6 vols. Paris: Didot, 1904–12.

Raynaud de Lage, Guy, ed. *Le roman de Thèbes*. 2 vols. Paris: Champion, 1968.

Salverda de Grave, Jean-Jacques, ed. *Le roman d'Énéas*. 2 vols. Paris: Champion, 1964.

Coley, John S., trans. *Le roman de Thèbes* (*The Story of Thebes*). New York: Garland, 1986.

Blumenfeld-Kosinski, Renate. "Old French Narrative Genres: Towards a Definition of the Roman Antique." *Romance Philology* 34 (1980): 143–59.

Cormier, Raymond. "The Problem of Anachronism: Recent Scholarship on the French Medieval Romances of Antiquity." *Philological Quarterly* 52 (1974): 145–57.

Faral, Edmond. *Recherches sur les sources latines des contes et romans courtois du moyen âge*. Paris: Champion, 1913.

Petit, Aymé. *Naissances du roman: les techniques littéraires dans les romans antiques du XIIe siècle*. 2 vols. Paris and Geneva: Champion-Slatkine, 1985. [With bibliography.]

ANTI-SEMITISM. Anti-Semitism or, more properly for the Middle Ages, anti-Judaism, was the set of attitudes toward Jews that derived from regarding their religion as inferior to Christianity and themselves as the heirs of deicides. By their persistence in adhering to their religion, Jews, it was widely believed, convicted themselves as approvers of the killing of Jesus. Modern anti-Semitism, contrary to medieval anti-Judaism, is rooted in an ethnic notion of Judaism. Modern anti-Semites regard converts to Christianity from Judaism and their lineage as Jews or as having "Jewish blood" and, therefore, as objects of contempt. Yet there is little evidence that converts or their offspring faced such hatred in the Middle Ages, a few isolated incidents aside, until the huge wave of forced conversions in Spain in the late 14th century and after.

Medieval religious attitudes toward Jews were mediated by the political, social, and economic concerns of various segments of the Christian population in France. Consequently, neither governmental nor popular actions against the Jews should be ascribed merely to religious bigotry. It would nonetheless be naive to think that such actions can be explained without recourse to the fact of religious hostility.

As early as Agobard of Lyon, or even earlier in stories by Gregory of Tours, many of the higher clergy in France articulated theological positions stressing the inferiority of contemporary Judaism. One commonplace asserted that the wine of Sinai had degenerated into the vinegar of postbiblical Judaism. Some French theologians and canonists also shared with people untrained in formal theology cruder attitudes toward Jews and Judaism, attitudes rooted in the notion of the inferiority of Judaism and the corruption of morals that that inferiority was said to imply. The solidarity of the Jewish communities in the face of this contempt savored of clannishness to many critics, and the clannishness savored of a dangerous attraction to secrecy. By the end of the 12th century, many Frenchmen had come to accept the idea that the Jews ritually reenacted the crucifixion of Jesus by kidnaping innocent Christian children to torment *in occulto*. By the end of the 13th century, there is abundant evidence of the widespread acceptance of the notion that Jews indulged in secret curses and slurs of the Christian religion in their religious books, notably the Talmud; that they were required to ingest innocent Christian blood for secret rituals; and that they contrived to get their hands on and desecrate the consecrated host of the Christian eucharist. They were said to lead simpleminded people, particularly servingwomen and wet nurses in their employ, away from the Christian faith. The men were stereotyped as excessively wealthy and avaricious moneylenders and as occasional seducers of Christian women.

It is impossible to know what proportion of the Christian population in France, or anywhere else for that matter, indulged in these attitudes, whether urban anti-Judaism was more intense than rural, whether class or level of education worked effectively to mitigate or exacerbate attitudes. Many high churchmen and many kings did not take certain of the charges seriously. While Philip Augustus, for example, believed that Jews carried out ritual murders, Louis IX seems never to have countenanced the allegation. Nonetheless, actions taken by the royal government, by baronial, ecclesiastical, and municipal authorities, and by vigilantes point up the pervasiveness of these attitudes. Segregation of Jews from Christians became widespread and was increasingly stringent from the 12th through the 14th century. Judicial murders of Jews, tolerated by the count of Blois in 1171 and by ecclesiastics in Troyes in 1288, originated from charges of malicious murder against them. Philip the Fair himself permitted the execution of a Jew of Paris in 1290 for allegedly desecrating the host. And large-scale massacres in 1321 were founded on the rumor of a plot between lepers and Jews, supported by the Muslims of Granada, to poison the wells of France. Expulsion, the ultimate policy of governments hostile to Jews, secured to the lords who pursued it in France the seizure and liquidation of Jewish property to their profit.

William Chester Jordan

[See also: CLOTHING, JEWISH; JEWS; PHILIP IV THE FAIR]

Jordan, William Chester. *The French Monarchy and the Jews from Philip Augustus to the Last Capetians*. Philadelphia: University of Pennsylvania Press, 1989.

Langmuir, Gavin. "Anti-Judaism as the Necessary Preparation for Anti-Semitism." *Viator* 2 (1971): 383–90.

Poliakov, Léon. *The History of Anti-Semitism, I: From the Time of Christ to the Court Jews*, trans. Richard Howard. New York: Vanguard, 1965.

Trachtenberg, Joshua. *The Devil and the Jews: The Medieval Conception of the Jew and Its Relation to Modern Antisemitism.* New Haven: Yale University Press, 1944.

ANZY-LE-DUC. The priory of Anzy-le-Duc (Saône-et-Loire), constructed in the second half of the 11th century, has a five-bay nave, flanked by aisles—all groin-vaulted. Two short barrel-vaulted transepts open off the crossing. In spite of the relatively small size of Anzy, the interior appears wide because of the ample nave arcades and the direct clerestory windows. The crisp ashlar masonry emphasizes the mural nature of the thick walls. The south flank of the priory reveals the simple massing of nave above aisles, the penetrating transept, and the crowning three-storied, octagonal tower above the crossing. Projecting buttresses and punctured windows animate the surfaces.

The most dramatic part of Anzy-le-Duc is its east end. The plan, which is identical to that of Charlieu and related to that of Cluny II, calls for six apsidioles: two opening off the transept arms, two off the bays flanking the fore choir (chapels in eschelon), and one off the choir. When viewed from the side, the apsidioles climb dramatically to three different heights and extend eastward in four different planes.

Fine capitals decorate each nave pier. Starting in the second bay from the façade, sutures, or breaks in the

Anzy-le-Duc (Saône-et-Loire), priory, chevet. *Photograph courtesy of Whitney S. Stoddard.*

masonry, descend. Masonry above and to the west of this suture is a later campaign. The west portal depicts Apostles on the lintel, the Ascension in the tympanum surrounded by Elders of the Apocalypse in the archivolts. Edson Armi argued that the lintel, capitals, and archivolts were carved by two distinct sculptors whose work at Anzy predates the famous choir capitals of Cluny III. The Mont-Saint-Vincent Master created the crude portal of Mont-Saint-Vincent, the inner narthex lintel and tympanum of Charlieu, and the lintel of Anzy-le-Duc. The Avenas Master, deriving his name from a fine altar at Avenas south of Cluny, carved sculpture on the portal of Mâcon, Anzy-le-Duc (archivolts and capitals), and Perreay-les-Forges before continuing to work at Vézelay and Cluny III.

The dates of this sculpture depend upon the dating of the Cluny III choir capitals, which varies from 1085 to 1150. The capitals are probably slightly later than the Cluny III portal of 1109–13; if this conclusion is correct, the Anzy-le-Duc sculpture can be dated in the early 12th century.

In addition to nave capitals and façade portal, there are two other later portals: one in a museum in Paray-le-Monial and the other in a building south of the priory.

Whitney S. Stoddard

Armi, E. Edson. *Masons and Sculptors in Romanesque Burgundy.* 2 vols. University Park: Pennsylvania State University Press, 1983, Vol. 1, pp. 14–15, 21, 37–38, 41–42; Vol. 2, pp. 84a, b, 85d, 89a, b, 116b.

Pendergast, Carol. *The Romanesque Sculpture of Anzy-le-Duc.* Diss. Yale University, 1974.

———. "The Lintel of the West Portal at Anzy-le-Duc." *Gesta* 15 (1976): 135–42.

Porter, Arthur K. *Romanesque Sculpture of the Pilgrimage Roads.* 2 vols. Boston: Marshall Jones, 1923, Vol. 1: *Text*, pp. 120–22, 130; Vol. 2: *Illustrations*, pp. 17–24, 95–99.

Stoddard, Whitney S. *Monastery and Cathedral in France.* Middletown: Wesleyan University Press, 1966, pp. 52, 58, 78; figs 62, 64, 73, 74, 107.

APANAGE. From *apaner*, to endow with a means of subsistence, the word apanage, appanage, or appannage is used for a province or jurisdiction, or later for an office or annuity, granted (with the reservation that in the absence of direct heirs the land escheated to the crown) to the younger children of royalty to compensate them for not receiving the throne and to preserve peace and love in the family. Robert II (r. 996–1031), son of Hugh Capet, stopped partitioning the realm, as the Frankish kings had done, and began crowning his eldest son during his lifetime, a practice continued until the reign of Philip Augustus. He gave Burgundy to his second son. Like many of their predecessors and successors, the next monarchs provided for their younger sons by marrying them to rich heiresses so that they did not have to diminish the royal domain by enfeoffing part of it to a relative.

Beginning with the sons of Blanche of Castile and Louis VIII (r. 1223–26), apanages became normal in France. By installing their sons as rulers, monarchs could control newly acquired outlying areas, as northern French nobles had long done. In 1237, Robert got Artois; Alphonse (who married the heiress of the last count of Toulouse), received Poitou and Auvergne; and the posthumous Charles, Anjou. The royal line of Bourbon dates from 1272, when the heiress of the Bourbonnais, Beatrice of Navarre, married Robert, sixth son of St. Louis, who had received the county of Clermont as an apanage. Philip IV's brother Charles, who received Valois, fathered the house that came to the throne in the person of his son Philip VI in 1328.

A number of these early grants escheated to the crown when the cadet branches died off: Poitou and Auvergne, for example, at the death of Alphonse in 1271. In 1316, the law of succession was interpreted to exclude women not only from the throne but from succession to apanages as well. The younger sons of John II (r. 1350–64), Philip and John, received Burgundy and Berry, respectively, ruling them virtually as independent fiefs. Thereafter, royal princes with apanages tended to become peers; by the accession of Charles V in 1364, when the heir apparent began to receive the Dauphiné, which Philip VI had purchased from the last dauphin, Humbert II, in 1349, younger sons regularly received duchies.

Louis XI (r. 1461–83) brought these virtually independent territories to heel after his father had expelled the English, their frequent allies, from Aquitaine in 1453. The later dukes of Burgundy tried to transform their holdings, having acquired other adjacent principalities on each side of the imperial border, into a resurrected Middle Kingdom that was broken up only after the defeat of Charles the Bold in 1477. Provence, ruled by successive houses of Anjou, only escheated when the last duke, King René, whom Louis XI had forbidden to remarry, died childless in 1480. The crown seized the vast Bourbon apanage after its duke rebelled in the 1520s. The holders of apanages, however rich and powerful, never again threatened the unity of France.

The Angevin and Plantagenêt kings also established apanages in England. Whereas John Lackland received only money and the overlordship of Ireland, Henry III's brother Richard got Cornwall and his younger son Edmund, Lancaster. After Edward I conquered Wales and formally made his eldest son prince there in 1301, it became customary to give younger sons York, Lancaster, Gloucester, or Bedford as ducal apanages, but they never had aspirations to become independent as their counterparts did in France.

Pedro J. Suarez

[See also: ALPHONSE OF POITIERS; ANJOU, HOUSES OF; BERRY; BOURBON/BOURBONNAIS; CHARLES THE BOLD; DREUX; ÉVREUX; JOHN THE FEARLESS; PHILIP III THE BOLD; VALOIS DYNASTY]

Lewis, Andrew. *Royal Succession in Capetian France*. Cambridge: Harvard University Press, 1981.
Wood, Charles T. *The French Apanages and the Capetian Monarchy, 1224–1328*. Cambridge: Harvard University Press, 1966.

APOCALYPSE TAPESTRY. On April 7, 1377, the accounts of Louis I, duke of Anjou and brother of King Charles V, mention a payment of 1,000 francs to Nicholas Bataille for two tapestries of the "Story of the Apocalypse." In January 1378, fifty francs were paid to Hennequin de Bruges for the design and cartoons. The entire set originally involved seven pieces and probably eighty-four scenes altogether. In spite of the loss of several scenes, the tapestries, now displayed in the castle of Angers, remain one of the most ambitious tapestry projects ever undertaken and still measure some 354 feet long by over 13 feet high. They were among the first storied tapestries, as tapestry design had been previously restricted to geometric and animal patterns.

In the Book of Revelation, the last book of the Bible, also known as the Apocalypse of St. John, the angel of Christ reveals the events of the Apocalypse, or the end of time, to St. John. Representations were popular in 13th- and 14th-century Apocalypse manuscripts, and the duke of Anjou borrowed a manuscript of the historiated *Apocalypse* (now B.N. fr. 403) from his brother the king to use as a model. All scenes run from left to right and with alternating red and blue backgrounds. The first three pieces have solid backgrounds, while those of the final four pieces are strewn with flowers, stylized animals, and scrollwork to break the monotony. Each piece originally seems to have held a figure in an architectural setting to one side, then continued with two registers of seven scenes each for the narration, with a band of angels above to represent the heavens, and a band of plants below for the earth. St. John appears in all of the scenes, which closely follow the text of the Apocalypse. The arms of Louis I of Anjou and Marie of Brittany, the wife of Louis, appear in the banners held by angels.

Stacy L. Boldrick

[See also: TAPESTRY]

Planchenault, René. *L'Apocalypse d'Angers*. Paris: Caisse Nationale des Monuments Historiques, 1966.
Souchal, Geneviève F. *Les tapisseries de l'Apocalypse à Angers*. Milan: Hachette-Fabbri-Skira, 1969.

APOCRYPHAL LITERATURE. Biblical books not regarded as inspired, and hence excluded from the sacred canon, appeared in the early Christian centuries in response to pious curiosity about Jesus, his family, and his companions. From the point of view of medieval literature, four Greek texts are of prime importance: the 2nd-century *Book* (or *Protevangelium*) *of James* and the *Gospel of Thomas*, which deal with the childhood of Mary and the birth and infancy miracles of Jesus; the 6th-century *Gospel of Nicodemus*, which supplements the gospel accounts of the Passion; and the 7th-century *Assumption of the Virgin*, which describes the death, funeral, and miraculous assumption of Mary. The *Nicodemus* was translated into Latin in the later 6th century and again a century or so later, while the stories from the *Gospel of Thomas* and the *Book of James* were combined in the 8th or 9th century into a new Latin collection called the *Gospel of Pseudo-Matthew.* This in turn was the source of the *Gospel of the Nativity of Mary.*

Apocryphal legends first appeared in French in the 12th century, in Wace's *Conception,* which includes the story of the three Marys and the birth, childhood, and assumption of the Virgin. Similar material appeared in three texts dubiously attributed to Gautier de Coinci a half-century later. Quite different versions of this material occur in the 13th-century *Roman de saint Fanuel* and *Histoire de Marie et de Jésus.* The childhood miracles of Jesus were recounted in verse in Old French and Anglo-Norman and in three distinct versions in Provençal. There are ten poems on the Passion (which was usually completed by one of four versions of the Descent into Hell), as well as three translations of the *Gospel of Nicodemus.* In 1357, Jean de Venette compiled most of the legends into his long poem *Histoire des glorieuses Maries.* Apocryphal material also supplemented the more strictly biblical narratives of Herman de Valenciennes, Geoffroi de Paris, Roger d'Argenteuil, and Macé de la Charité. Prose versions of the legends appear from the middle of the 13th century, usually in collections of saints' lives but independently as well.

Maureen B.M. Boulton

[See also: *ENFANCES*; MORAL TREATISES; WACE]

Boulton, Maureen, ed. *The Old French Évangile de l'enfance: An Edition with Introduction and Notes.* Toronto: Pontifical Institute of Mediaeval Studies, 1984.

Chabaneau, Camille, ed. "Le Romanz de saint Fanuel." *Revue des langues romanes* 28 (1885): 157–253.

Ford, Alvin, E., ed. *Évangile de Nicodème: les versions courtes en ancien français et en prose.* Geneva: Droz, 1973.

———, ed. *La vengeance de Nostre-Seigneur: The Old and Middle French Prose Versions: The Version of Japheth.* Toronto: Pontifical Institute of Mediaeval Studies, 1984.

Frank, Grace, ed. *Le livre de la Passion, poème narratif du XIVe siècle.* Paris: Champion, 1930.

Reinsch, Robert. *Die Pseudo-Evangelien von Jesu und Marias Kindheit in der romanischen und germanischen Literatur.* Halle: Niemeyer, 1879.

APOLLONIUS DE TYR. The legend of Apollonius of Tyre, which involves the incestuous love of a father for his daughter, was immensely popular in the Middle Ages. There are some sixty Latin texts, and at least six French prose versions from the 14th and 15th centuries. Its influence on later works, such as *Belle Helaine de Constantinople,* the *Roman du comte d'Anjou,* and Philippe de Beaumanoir's *La Manekine,* is manifest.

William W. Kibler

[See also: BEAUMANOIR, PHILIPPE DE RÉMI, SIRE DE; *FLOIRE ET BLANCHEFLOR*]

Lewis, Charles B., ed. "Die altfranzösischen Prosaversionen des Appollonius-Romans." *Romanische Forschungen* 34 (1915): 1–277.

Zink, Michel, ed. and trans. *Le roman d'Apollonius de Tyr.* Paris: Union Générale d'Éditions, 1982.

APPATIS. Military law and custom provided a procedure known in Old French as *appatis* to regulate the behavior of troops living off the land in friendly territory. A special levy on the local inhabitants to support military forces, it generally involved requisitioning supplies. While the affected populations might regard *appatis* as thinly disguised extortion, it did provide an orderly, legal means of supplying troops without resort to outright pillage.

John Bell Henneman, Jr.

Keen, Maurice. *The Laws of War in the Later Middle Ages.* London: Routledge, 1965.

AQUINAS, THOMAS. (ca. 1224–1274). The only medieval philosopher whose ideas command an active following in the 20th century. The symmetry of Thomas's methodical synthesis of traditional Christian (Augustinian and Platonist) theology with Aristotelian methods and categories may be thought of at once as the zenith of medieval scholastic thought and its downfall. Thomas's apparently comprehensive, even-tempered certainties, the product of method and reason, continue to attract those seeking answers to the problems of faith.

Thomas was born in Roccasecca, near Monte Cassino, Italy, the youngest son of Count Landulf of Aquino, a relative of the emperor and the king of France. He was schooled at Monte Cassino, where his family hoped he would become abbot, and later (1240) studied arts at Naples. Thomas's love of Christian learning urged him to join the Dominican order. His family opposed his becoming a mendicant, when the wealth of the Benedictines beckoned, and kept him prisoner, fruitlessly, in Roccasecca for fifteen months. In April 1244, he joined the Dominicans and was sent to Paris (1245–48) to study theology with Albert the Great. In 1248, he accompanied Albert to the new Dominican *studium* at Cologne, but by 1252 he was back in Paris as lecturer at Saint-Jacques, the Dominican convent. Here he defended mendicant poverty against the attacks of William of Saint-Amour and his followers, writing *Contra impugnantes Dei cultum.* He became master of theology (his formal degree having been delayed by the dispute) in 1256. From 1259 to 1269, he taught at Dominican houses in Italy: Anagni, Orvieto, Santa Sabina and the *studium generale* in Rome, and Viterbo. In 1269, just before the condemnation of Aristotelian errors by Étienne Tempier, he returned to Paris but was moved once more, to establish a Dominican *studium* in Naples, in 1272. He was traveling again, to the Second Council of Lyon, when he died at Fossanuova, on March 7, 1274.

Thomas, known as *Doctor angelicus* and *Doctor communis,* is renowned for his massive output, which was remarked upon in the evidence for his canonization. He was said to dictate seamlessly to several secretaries at once, each writing a different work. He wrote biblical commentaries, at least one commentary on the *Sententiae* of Peter

Lombard, commentaries on much of Aristotle and the *liber de causis*, disputed and quodlibetal questions, and other works common to a Paris master, as well as short tracts in answer to specific questions, whether in opposition to the Averroists or Avicebron, for instance, or in reply to the duchess of Brabant on government. Aware of the inadequacy of western knowledge of Aristotle, he had William of Moerbecke (1215–1286) translate or retranslate many of his works, leaving a valuable legacy for later scholars. But Thomas's name is almost synonymous with his *Summa theologica* (or *Summa theologiae*), which, together with the earlier *Summa contra Gentiles,* is a massive statement of the whole of Christian theology. The *Summa* is in three parts, the first (*prima*) dealing with God *in se*, the second dealing first (*prima secundae*) with God's relations with humanity and second (*secunda secundae*) with humanity's relations with God, and the third (*tertia*) with Christ and the sacraments as the path for the human return to God. (The plan is similar to Peter Lombard's *Sententiae* but in three unequal books rather than four.)

Although Thomas's place in the hierarchy of medieval philosopher-theologians is secure, he is perhaps recognized today more for his system and clarity than for his originality of thought. As we learn more about earlier 13th-century scholastics, we see Thomistic ideas in prototype or isolation. His gift was in a synthesis of what had previously tended to the imposition of Aristotelian categories of thought within a Platonist Christian worldview. He brought the so-called scholastic method of argument and truth seeking to its finest honing.

Although Thomas is not generally remembered for his spirituality and is not a mystical theologian in the style of Bonaventure, he was nevertheless revered in his lifetime for his holiness, simplicity, and devotion. Quiet (he was nicknamed "the dumb ox") and unassuming, he had powers of concentration that took on a semimiraculous quality for the secretaries who worked with him. He was canonized in 1323.

Thomas was not without his critics. Some of his positions were condemned by Bishop Étienne Tempier in 1270 and 1277, by Robert Kilwardby in the latter year, and by John Peckham in 1284; but his opinions were officially imposed on the Dominican order in 1278. The Roman Catholic church considers his teaching an authentic expression of doctrine, and canon law makes study of his works the accepted basis for theology.

Lesley J. Smith

[See also: ALBERT THE GREAT; ARABIC PHILOSOPHY, INFLUENCE OF; ARISTOTLE, INFLUENCE OF; DOMINICAN ORDER; ÉTIENNE TEMPIER; HUGUES DE SAINT-CHER; MAGIC; PHILOSOPHY; SCHOLASTICISM; THEOLOGY; WILLIAM OF SAINT-AMOUR]

Thomas Aquinas. *Summa theologiae,* ed. Dominican Fathers of the English Province. 60 vols. Cambridge: Blackfriar's, 1964–76. [Latin text and English translation, introductions, notes, appendices, and glossaries.]
——. *Somme théologique* (*Summa theologiae*). 61 vols. Paris, 1925–72. [Latin-French with commentaries.]
——. *Quaestiones quodlibetales 1–2: English Quodlibetal Questions 1–2*, trans. Sandra Edwards. Toronto: Pontifical Institute of Mediaeval Studies, 1983.
——. *Basic Writings of Saint Thomas Aquinas*, trans. Anton Pegis. 2 vols. New York: Random House, 1945.
——. *On the Truth of the Catholic Faith* (*Summa Contra Gentiles*), trans. Anton C. Pegis, James Anderson, Vernon J. Bourke, and Charles J. O'Neil. 5 vols. Garden City: Hanover House, 1955–57.
Chenu, Marie-Dominique. *Toward Understanding Saint Thomas,* trans. Albert M. Landry and Dominic Hughes. Chicago: Regnery, 1964.
Farrell, Walter. *A Companion to the Summa.* 4 vols. New York: Sheed and Ward, 1941–42.
Glorieux, Palémon. *Répertoire des maîtres en théologie de Paris au XIIIe siècle.* 2 vols. Paris: Vrin, 1933, Vol. 1, pp. 85–104. [Complete listing of works.]

AQUITAINE. Aquitaine, in southwestern France, was the largest and one of the most important provinces in France during the Middle Ages. It gave rise to successive regional governments and a distinctive civilization that long resisted efforts of northern kings to subdue and integrate its population into the life of the French monarchy and nation. Nonetheless, Aquitaine was anything but a clearly defined geographical entity, nor did it have a homogeneous population. Save for the Atlantic coast in the west, it lacked natural geographical boundaries. Its borders therefore fluctuated under the pressure of historical events, and it is sometimes difficult to know just which counties and regions it included. Medieval Aquitaine was in fact an artificial conglomeration of smaller regions that themselves did have some linguistic, cultural, and ethnic unity. Bearing in mind the periodic changes, we may describe medieval Aquitaine as extending from its northern limits in Poitou south of the Loire to Gascony in the south and from the coast eastward to the Massif Central. It grouped together more than a dozen counties: in the north, Poitou and Berry; in the center, La Marche, Limousin, Angoumois, Saintonge, Aunis, Bordelais, Périgord, and Uzerches; and in the south, Agenais, Quercy, Rouergue, and Auvergne. As disparate as its population was its physical environment. In climate, soil, topography, vegetation, and its range of agricultural systems, Aquitaine was a composite of different regions.

The beginnings of medieval Aquitaine go back to the Roman conquest and occupation. By the 4th century, the Romans had for administrative reasons divided southwestern France, aside from the Narbonne region, into Aquitania Prima and Secunda, Bourges being the capital of the first and Bordeaux of the second. This political division disappeared after the Germanic invasions and settlement of the 4th and 5th centuries, but the church perpetuated it through medieval and into modern times in its ecclesiastical organization, with Bourges becoming the see of a vast archdiocese in south-central France and Bordeaux the center of the western archdiocese that included the dioceses of Poitiers, Saintes, Angoulême, Périgueux, and Agen. The christianization of Aquitaine began in the later 4th century and continued through the early-medieval period with the

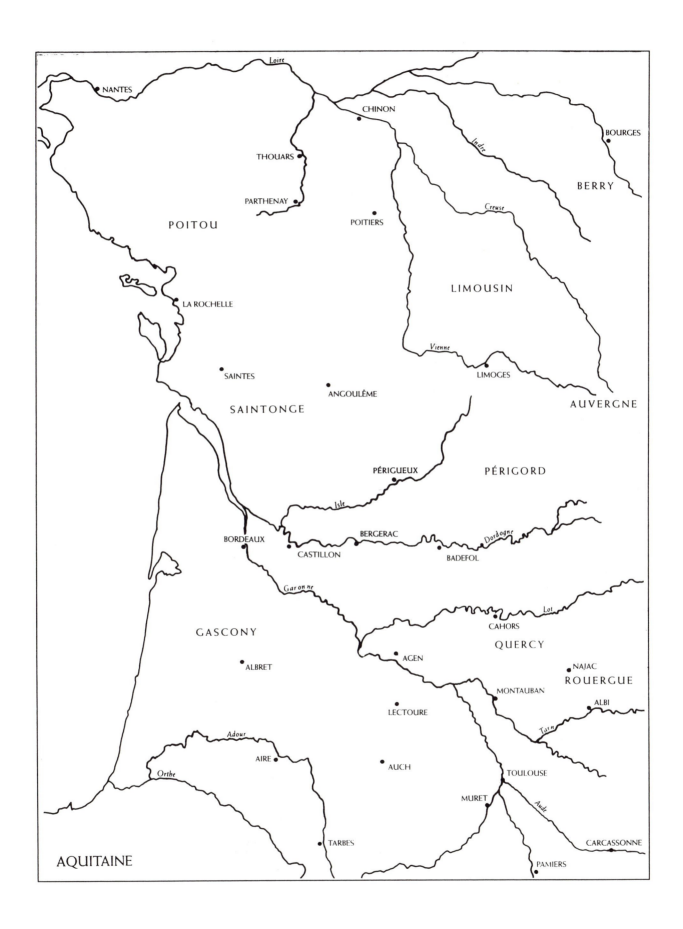

NANTES

Loire

CHINON

BOURGES

BERRY

THOUARS

Indre

PARTHENAY

Creuse

POITOU

POITIERS

LIMOUSIN

LA ROCHELLE

Vienne

SAINTES

LIMOGES

AUVERGNE

ANGOULÊME

SAINTONGE

PÉRIGUEUX

PÉRIGORD

Isle

BORDEAUX

BERGERAC

Dordogne

CASTILLON

BADEFOL

Garonne

Lot

CAHORS

GASCONY

QUERCY

ALBRET

AGEN

NAJAC

ROUERGUE

MONTAUBAN

LECTOURE

ALBI

Adour

Tarn

AIRE

AUCH

Orthe

TOULOUSE

MURET

Aude

TARBES

CARCASSONNE

AQUITAINE

PAMIERS

establishment not only of the bishoprics in Aquitanian towns but also monasticism and the parish system in the rural areas. As a result of the 5th-century invasions, most of Roman Aquitaine became part of the ephemeral Visigothic kingdom of southern Gaul and Spain (406), but the Frankish conquest under Clovis I installed the Franks as rulers of the region after the Battle of Vouillé (near Poitiers) in 507. The failure of the Franks to settle in substantial numbers in Aquitaine, combined with the repeated division of their kingdom under the later Merovingians, meant that Frankish rule and influence were minimal during the 6th and 7th centuries. A distinctive Aquitanian civilization took shape during this time, characterized on the one hand by its fidelity to the Roman past in language, education, laws, institutions of local government, coinage, business customs, and the like and on the other by its Christian character. For a brief period at the beginning of the 8th century, the Aquitanians, profiting from the dynastic troubles of the Merovingian kings, acquired political autonomy with the founding of the first medieval duchy of Aquitaine by Duke Odo (ca. 720).

This was only an interlude. Two foreign invasions put an end to Aquitanian independence by the later 8th century. Gascon immigrants from the Pyrénées had already occupied much of southern Aquitaine as far north as Bordeaux in the late 6th century and were followed in the 720s by Muslim invaders, whose northern advance was stopped at the Battle of Poitiers in 732. Charlemagne firmly implanted Frankish control and reorganized the duchy into the subkingdom of Aquitaine, ruled by his son, Louis (781). The Carolingian hold on Aquitaine was in its turn weakened by the Viking invasions in the mid-9th century. Striking sporadically for the next century and a half up major river valleys from the Loire to the Garonne, the Vikings attacked not only coastal areas but also far inland, devastating towns, dispersing populations, and disrupting ecclesiastical life in both the monasteries and the secular church. In the confusion and destruction of the later 9th century, Carolingian kings gradually abandoned the province, and the kingdom of Aquitaine, barely a century old, came to an end.

Recovery began with the reestablishment of the duchy of Aquitaine in the mid-10th century, when the dynasty of the counts of Poitiers, in the far northern part of the province, gained possession of the ducal title. Successive descendants, all named William, ruled the duchy for nearly two centuries until extinction of the male line at the death of William X in 1137. Under the Poitevin count-dukes, the duchy of Aquitaine became one of the greatest territorial principalities in France, reaching its high point in power and prestige under the rule of William V the Great (r. 995–1030) and Guy-Geoffrey (William VIII, r. 1058–86). The latter completed the unification of the previously independent duchy of Gascony with Aquitaine in 1058 and thereby made his line rulers of western France from the Loire to the Pyrénées. Nonetheless, it was precisely at this time that the dukes of Aquitaine saw their authority increasingly challenged internally by the growing power of regional aristocracies centered in the stone castles built in great numbers during this period. In the

end, these feudal nobles seriously undermined ducal authority.

The 11th and 12th centuries were a time of sustained population and economic expansion leading to the widespread clearance of previously waste lands, foundation of new towns, and beginnings of foreign trade. The same period witnessed the introduction of church reform led by the Gregorian movement and the expansion of Benedictine, Cluniac, and Cistercian monasticism. Pope Urban II pointedly appealed to and counted on Aquitanians to support his call for the crusade in 1096. Aquitanian civilization flowered in two other senses at the end of the 11th century: first, architecturally, in the appearance of many great Romanesque cathedrals and monastic churches; second, in the beginning of a new vernacular (Occitan) literature as exemplified by the earliest surviving troubadour poems of William the Troubadour (Guilhem IX, duke of Aquitaine, r. 1086–1126). During his reign, Poitiers, the capital of the duchy, became one of the leading towns of western Europe.

The failure of William X to leave a male heir at his death in 1137 led to foreign domination from which the Aquitanians never recovered. The marriage of William's daughter and heiress, Eleanor, to Louis VII of France placed the duchy under French rule for fifteen years, but Eleanor did not produce a male heir and their union ended in divorce in 1152. This Capetian interlude had little impact on the duchy. Within months, however, Eleanor married the count of Anjou and duke of Normandy, Henry Plantagenêt, and in 1154, when the latter made good his claim to the English throne, Eleanor became queen for a second time and her duchy fell under English overlordship. Aquitanian resistance prompted Henry to install their son Richard as duke of Aquitaine, but later familial rebellions against Henry's rule compromised the Angevin efforts to subjugate the duchy. After Richard's accession to the English throne in 1189, Eleanor became duchess of Aquitaine once again, but after her death in 1204 the duchy passed to the English crown.

For the next 250 years, English rule in Aquitaine was challenged by the French kings, who finally, in 1453, succeeded in driving out their perennial foes and imposing their own authority. Philip Augustus began the French offensive in 1202, when he invoked feudal custom to disinherit King John, his vassal for Aquitaine, and confiscate his duchy. In subsequent invasions, royal armies conquered Poitou and Saintonge in northern Aquitaine as well as Normandy, Anjou, and Maine. The Treaty of Paris of 1259 confirmed these losses and left the English ruling over a duchy of greatly reduced size, comprising mainly lands south of Bordeaux. Despite these wars, Aquitaine enjoyed a period of prosperity in the 13th century in the form of rural and urban expansion (e.g., the founding of the *bastides*) and above all in the wine trade with England. The volume of wine exported to England through Bordeaux reached enormous proportions at this time.

The longstanding English-French antagonism erupted in the late 1330s, when Philip VI and Edward III made aggressive moves against each other, marking the beginning of the Hundred Years' War. In the early hostilities, the outcome was indecisive, with territorial gains for both

DUKES OF AQUITAINE
FROM THE HOUSE OF POITOU

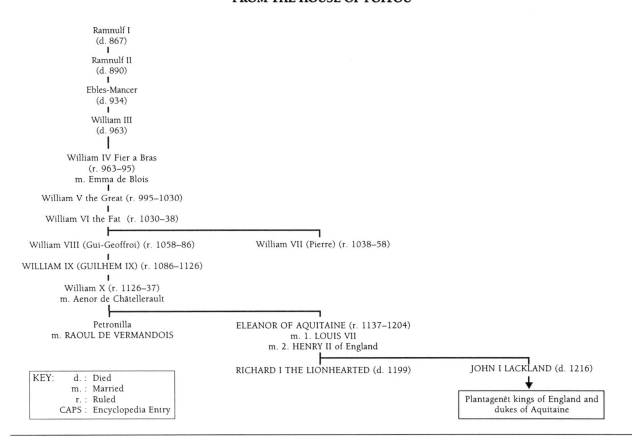

Ramnulf I
(d. 867)

Ramnulf II
(d. 890)

Ebles-Mancer
(d. 934)

William III
(d. 963)

William IV Fier a Bras
(r. 963–95)
m. Emma de Blois

William V the Great (r. 995–1030)

William VI the Fat (r. 1030–38)

William VIII (Gui-Geoffroi) (r. 1058–86)   William VII (Pierre) (r. 1038–58)

WILLIAM IX (GUILHEM IX) (r. 1086–1126)

William X (r. 1126–37)
m. Aenor de Châtellerault

Petronilla   ELEANOR OF AQUITAINE (r. 1137–1204)
m. RAOUL DE VERMANDOIS   m. 1. LOUIS VII
                                             m. 2. HENRY II of England

RICHARD I THE LIONHEARTED (d. 1199)   JOHN I LACKLAND (d. 1216)

KEY:	
d. :	Died
m. :	Married
r. :	Ruled
CAPS :	Encyclopedia Entry

Plantagenêt kings of England and
dukes of Aquitaine

sides. But then the Black Prince assumed command of the English forces in 1355 and won an astounding victory, capturing the French king at the Battle of Poitiers in 1356. The Treaty of Brétigny in 1360 restored the earlier English losses and made the Black Prince, named prince of Aquitaine in 1362, the ruler of an immense principality covering nearly one-third of France. For a decade, Prince Edward ruled in high style over a virtually independent state, but his severe tax levies aroused indigenous resistance and the French once again intervened. Between 1368 and 1374, they regained most of their losses from the Treaty of Brétigny and reduced the English holdings to mere fragments of their once extensive duchy. The last phase of the Hundred Years' War, beginning in 1429, saw the French wear down English defenses, and with their loss of Bordeaux in 1453 the English were definitively expelled from Aquitaine. As was true for most parts of France, the period of the Hundred Years' War was a time of misery and hardship in Aquitaine quite apart from losses suffered in the wars. Plague, periodic famine, widespread brigandage, and economic decline made the later Middle Ages a dark period in Aquitanian history.

George T. Beech

[See also: AUVERGNE; BASTIDE; EDWARD, THE BLACK PRINCE; ELEANOR OF AQUITAINE; GASCONY; GUILHEM IX; HUNDRED YEARS' WAR; LOUIS I THE PIOUS; LOUIS VII; LUSIGNAN; RICHARD I THE LION HEARTED; SAINT-SARDOS]

Auzias, Léonce. *L'Aquitaine carolingienne 778–987.* Toulouse: Privat, 1937.

Dhondt, Jan. *Études sur la naissance des principautés territoriales en France IXe–Xe siècles.* Bruges: De Tempel, 1948.

Histoire de l'Aquitaine. Publiée sous la direction de Charles Higounet. Toulouse: Privat, 1971.

Renouard, Yves. *Études d'histoire médiévale.* 2 vols. Paris: SEVPEN, 1968.

Rouche, Michel. *L'Aquitaine, des Visigoths aux Arabes 418–781: essai sur le phénomène régional.* Paris: Touzot, 1979.

Trabut-Cussac, Jean-Paul. *L'administration anglaise en Gascogne sous Henry III et Édouard I de 1254 à 1307.* Geneva: Droz, 1972.

Vale, Malcolm G. A. *English Gascony, 1399–1453: A Study of War, Government and Politics During the Later Stages of the Hundred Years' War.* London: Oxford University Press, 1970.

ARABIC INFLUENCE ON LITERATURE. The nature and depth of the Arabic impact on medieval European civilization are a source of controversy. The rapid conquests of Muslim armies in the 8th and 9th centuries altered the political configurations of southern Europe and the Mediterranean basin; well into the subsequent centuries, even when Muslim-held territories were retrenching, the ethnic, religious, and cultural landscapes were also considerably altered. The Arabic role in the history of the Iberian peninsula and of Sicily is a major area of scholarly inquiry, but the relationship of these European-Arabic cultures with medieval French civilization is far less studied, primarily because Muslim political domination of territories that were to become modern France was brief: the advance of the Muslim armies was arrested by Charles Martel at Poitiers in 732. Nevertheless, because national frontiers were far from firmly established, because much of Europe's Arabic culture was in the fluid form of translations or oral tradition and was during roughly the 10th through 12th centuries, at a peak of prestige, and because travel in and out of Muslim-held territories was widespread, for both peaceable and bellicose reasons, medieval French *belles lettres* are best understood in the context of a Europe with an influential Arabic presence.

To a large extent, French epic poetry depends on the epochal events of the Muslim conquests of southern Europe for its inspiration, although the narrations of events and the descriptions of the Arab enemies—in many cases, both at several centuries remove—are often transformed into quasimythological versions, as in a text like the *Chanson de Roland*. Other epic texts reflect the ambiguous relationship with the Saracen enemy in narrative and descriptive detail that is less distant and transformed: the cycle of Guillaume d'Orange, for example, features recognizable historical events and characters. In both cases, a minority of scholars perceive a rich, more directly literary influence from Arabic epic narrations and other literary forms, from themes, images, and characters to such details as the names of swords of the French-Christian heroes. In both cases, too, the rich "background" provided by centuries of interaction with "Saracens," who had become a fixture of the European scene, is manipulated in these literary texts to work out historical-ideological and metaliterary issues. This kind of multitiered interaction can be seen most clearly in a work like *Aucassin et Nicolette*, whose hero has an Arabic-like name, whose heroine is an abducted Saracen, and whose themes reflect historical events and literary issues. The work, moreover, is dependent for its background, as are many others in Old French literature, on the complex and variable relationships between the "French"-Christian and the "Spanish"-Arabic worlds: trading partners, culturally interdependent, yet often in a state of military or ideological conflict.

The most debated "origins" question in Romance literatures concerns the courtly vernacular lyric of Provence. The earliest and, more recently, most controversial of the theories is that it is, at least in part, of Andalusian provenance (al-Andalus being the Arabic name for Spain). While this so-called "Arabist theory" has shown a number of variations since it was first proposed in the 16th century, it currently centers on the preexistence of an Arabic-Romance courtly lyric with striking thematic and formal affinities with the poetry that would arise in Provence in the late 11th century and transform European poetry thereafter. It is argued that, in the period immediately before the birth of Provençal courtly poetry and through its heyday during the next century and a half, the Hispano-Arabic world was closely linked to it both politically and culturally (Guilhem IX of Aquitaine, for example, was closely involved with al-Andalus in battle and in marriage) and that the innovative Andalusian *muwashshaha*, an Arabic lyric genre whose final half-strophe was often in the Spanish Mozarabic dialect and which was at its peak of popularity, would have been heard in courts throughout the "frontier" territories frequented by the earliest generations of troubadours.

The least disputed area of incursion of Arabic material into northern European culture is that which derived from the translations that proliferated primarily from the 11th through the 14th centuries, with the most famous and productive centers being Toledo and, under Frederick II, Sicily. The earliest major French figure in this vast commerce in the sciences, philosophy, and medicine was Gerbert of Aurillac, who would become Pope Sylvester II. He traveled to Catalonia in the 10th century to study mathematics and astronomy, both areas in which the Arabs were in the vanguard. Also noteworthy is Peter the Venerable, the influential abbot of Cluny, whose trip to Spain in the mid-12th century yielded, among many other riches, a Latin translation of the Qur'an, the first into a language other than Arabic. Much of the intellectual life of Europe at this time is in fact centered on translated philosophical texts. Not only were Plato and Aristotle an integral part of the Arabic tradition that was eventually made available to a Latin West that had long since lost access to them, but so too were the critical works of Andalusian and other Jewish and Muslim philosophers, such as Avicenna, Maimonides, and, most of all, Ibn Rushd (Averroes). Some scholars believe that much of the 12th-century renaissance in France resulted from upheavals in technology, institutional structures, and philosophy brought about by the reintroduction of the Aristotelian corpus that derived from translations from Arabic materials.

María Rosa Menocal

[See also: ARABIC PHILOSOPHY, INFLUENCE OF]

Boase, Roger. *The Origin and Meaning of Courtly Love: A Critical Study of European Scholarship*. Manchester: Manchester University Press, 1976.

Daniel, Norman. *Heroes and Saracens: An Interpretation of the Chansons de Geste*. Edinburgh: Edinburgh University Press, 1984.

Makdisi, George. *The Rise of Colleges: Institutions of Learning in Islam and the West*. Edinburgh: Edinburgh University Press, 1981.

Menocal, María Rosa. *The Arabic Role in Medieval Literary History*. Philadelphia: University of Pennsylvania Press, 1987.

Metlitzki, Dorothee. *The Matter of Araby in Medieval England*. New Haven: Yale University Press, 1977.

Watt, W. Montgomery. *The Influence of Islam on Medieval Europe*. Edinburgh: Edinburgh University Press, 1972.

ARABIC PHILOSOPHY, INFLUENCE OF. Less than a century after the death of Muhammad in 632, most of Spain had come under Muslim jurisdiction, while inroads had been made into the areas of Narbonne and Carcasonne and even into south-central France, until Charles Martel turned the tide at Poitiers and Tours in 732. As the Muslims were consolidating their power, they were also changing the *lingua franca* of the Byzantine and Roman-Visigothic empires that they had superseded. Arabic, however, had no religious and philosophical texts of its own besides the Qur'an. Thus, Arabic intellectual activity in the sciences and in philosophy began with translation of the Greek writings of the very civilizations that had been overrun. The ensuing work helped make Arabic into a medium for absorbing and developing originally non-Muslim scientific and scholarly concepts and ideas and for transmitting this new synthesis to Latin Christendom.

In the East, this intellectual work was stimulated by the 'Abbasid caliphs of Baghdad in the second half of the 8th and the 9th centuries, beginning with al-Mansur and Harun al-Rashid and finding its culmination in the rich patronage of al-Ma'mun. Al-Ma'mun scoured libraries in the formerly Hellenistic Middle East and even in Byzantium for Greek scientific and philosophical works that were then translated into Arabic. Especially for this purpose, he instituted at Baghdad the influential *Bait al-Hikmah* ("House of Knowledge" or "Wisdom"); here worked for a time Hunain ibn Ishaq, a Nestorian Christian, who besides putting many Greek texts into Arabic also developed a methodology for precise translation. In the course of a century and a half, much of the work of Plato, Aristotle, Porphyry, Hippocrates, Galen, Nicolaus, Albinus, Nemesius of Emesa, and parts of Plotinus and Proclus were made available to Muslim scholars. The intensive contacts between the East and the West of the Muslim sphere of influence soon ensured the availability of these texts throughout the Arabic-speaking world. Many were translated again, this time into Latin, and in the late 12th and the 13th centuries they entered western Europe—at first Italy and especially France—via Sicily and Spain for the use of Latin Christian scholars.

In the Spanish West of the Arabic world, interest in scholarship and learning began in earnest under the Umayyad rulers at the end of the 9th century, but it was not until the end of the 10th century that Cordova became a center of Muslim culture and learning that could rival Baghdad. Caliph al-Hakam II's library at Cordova in the third quarter of the 10th century is said to have contained around 500,000 volumes. Toledo, too, was a repository of learning, especially of the sciences (including astronomy) and medicine. Thus, philosophy came relatively late to Muslim Spain. But, once it arrived, it exerted enormous influence on western Christianity. In the East, crusading Franks tended to destroy the cultural infrastructure—for example, after the fall of Tripoli they destroyed the 100,000-volume library that had been assembled by Abu Talib. In

the West, however, the victorious Spanish and French largely saved the Muslim inheritance and incorporated it into Christendom. In its turn, the scholastic movement in medieval French schools and universities played a decisive role in the preservation and synthesis of this Greco-Arabic knowledge.

The place of philosophy in medieval Islam—at least until the synthetic work of al-Ghazali (Algazel; 1058–1111) and the condemnation for heresy of Ibn Rushd (Averroes; 1126–1198) at Cordova in 1195—differed from that in western Christendom. Latin Christians, following the lead of Augustine of Hippo, who associated the term *theologia* with pagan religious rites and Neoplatonist religious thought, preferred the term *vera philosophia* for reflections on the moral Christian life and its thought, and they used such words as *doctrina* and *studia sacrae scripturae* for exegetical studies of the Bible. It was not until Peter Abélard in the 12th century that the term *theologia* again began to receive currency as a description of a specific subject of pious scholarly endeavor. Yet even then, philosophy and theology were still practiced by the same group of people: Christian monks and clerics, whether in monasteries or at the ecclesiastically dominated cathedral schools and later the universities. On the other hand, in 'Abbasid Baghdad and Umayyad Spain a clearcut division was made—not generally to the liking of religious leaders—between Islamic theology ('*ilm al-kalam*) and philosophical discussion (*al-falsafa*). *Kalam* was the study of the Word of God revealed in the Qur'an and of the Hadith (the traditional account of the prophet Muhammad's sayings and actions); *falsafa* concerned itself with natural-scientific and philosophical knowledge deriving mostly from Greek but also from Persian and Indian non-Arabic sources. Unlike its place in the Latin world, philosophy here was not the prerogative of theologians but was associated closely with the study of medicine, astronomy, and mathematics. This is illustrated clearly by the medical interests of such important philosophers as Ibn Sina (Avicenna; 980–1037) and Ibn Rushd.

The first intellectual contacts of French scholars with Arabic learning were restricted to scientific fields. Paradigmatic is the case of Gerbert of Aurillac (ca. 945–1003), who studied mathematics and astronomy in Catalonia between 967 and 970, albeit not from the Arabic sources but from Latin translations collected in the library of the monastery of Ripoll. Arabic medical works, among others, were soon to be translated by Constantinus Africanus (d. ca. 1087), a Muslim who had been converted to Christianity. He is famous for his *Pantegni*, a reworking of 'Ali ibn al-'Abbas's *Kitab al-maliki*. This work was to help William of Conches (ca. 1085–ca.1154) in his formulation of a new philosophy of nature, which was criticized forcibly by William of Saint-Thierry (1070/90–1148) for its strong materialism and its independence from theology. William of Conches's *Dragmaticon*, which incorporates Greek and especially Arabic ideas, substantially influenced the cosmological and encyclopedic writings of Alain de Lille (ca. 1115/20–1203) and Thomas de Cantimpré (1201–ca.1270). In general, it might be said that the influx of Arabic medical and astronomical writings helped develop an awareness in medieval Europe—especially in the 12th-century French schools—that the cosmos and the natural world could be understood without recourse to Christian mystical and religious interpretations of the Middle Platonist or Neoplatonist sort.

Another important aspect of these early contacts between French and Muslim scholars was the apologetic one. Peter the Venerable (1092/94–1156), reform abbot of Cluny, held a high regard for "Saracen" learning and wrote that Christians had gone to Muslim Spain to seek out manuscripts on the liberal arts and "physics" (the study of nature). Peter's main purpose in stimulating the translation of Arabic texts into Latin, however, lay in trying to understand Islamic religion in order thereby to find ways of converting the Muslims. Translations of the Qur'an and of other Islamic religious writings were collected with Peter's polemical and apologetic writings against Islam to form the so-called *Corpus/Collectio Toletanum/a*. This collection was employed extensively to counter Islam throughout the Middle Ages; it was still being quoted by Nicholas of Cusa, Denis the Carthusian, and Torquemada in the 15th century.

From ca. 1150, translations began to appear of Arab philosophers and of arabicized Greek authors. Central to this movement was the Spanish city of Toledo, which had been taken by the Christians in 1085. While scientific works continued to receive attention, Dominicus Gundissalinus (d. after 1181), archdeacon of Toledo, in collaboration with Ibn Dawud (Avendeath; fl. 1150), was perhaps the greatest of the early translators of Muslim and Jewish philosophical works. He translated works by Ibn Sina, al-Ghazali, and the Jewish thinker Ibn Gabirol (Avicebron; ca.1021–ca.1058), but no doubt his most important work was a synthesis of Arabic and Latin scholarship in four of his own works: *De anima, De unitate, De divisione philosophiae,* and *De processione mundi.* Through this work, western philosophers of the Middle Ages were stimulated to discuss psychological, noetic, and epistemological problems in the context of a Neoplatonic Avicennan reading of Aristotle. Traces of Gundissalinus's efforts can be found in a succession of authors from William of Auvergne (1180/90–1249) to Bonaventure (ca. 1217–1274), Albert the Great (ca. 1200–1280) and Thomas Aquinas (ca. 1224–1274). The Jewish philosopher Moses Maimonides (1135–1204), who wrote in Arabic, was also translated and often used. Aquinas derived his third way of proving that God exists from Maimonides's analysis. The Neoplatonism of Ibn Sina, al-Ghazali, and Ibn Gabirol's *Fons vitae* found fertile ground in the developing Augustinian, Pseudo-Dionysian, Chartrian, and Victorine Platonist interpretations of Christian theology; for example, a form of Ibn Gabirol's doctrine on matter was fundamental to Bonaventure's conception of all created beings, including souls and angels, as partly material, and thus made its way into Franciscan spirituality.

Increasingly, western scholars began to be interested in the Aristotelian corpus. A generation after Gundissalinus, translations from the Arabic were taken up with great vigor by Michael Scot (d. ca. 1236), who worked in Spain but also in the scientific environment of the Sicilian court of Frederick II of Hohenstaufen. To get an impression of the influx of Latin versions of the Arabic Aristotle and his Muslim commentators in the University of Paris, the following can be noted. The Statutes of the Arts Faculty in 1255 prescribed the study of Aristotle from the following works (the availability of a translation from the Arabic is noted in parentheses): *Ethics, Physics* (translated by Gerard of Cremona and Michael Scot), *Metaphysics* (translated by Michael Scot, who also translated Ibn Rushd's great commentary on it), *De animalibus* (translated by Michael Scot), *De caelo* (translated by Gerard of Cremona and Michael Scot), *Metereologica* (translated by Henricus Aristippus and Michael Scot), *De anima* (translation by Michael Scot, who also translated Ibn Rushd's commentary on it), *De generatione et corruptione* (translated by Gerard of Cremona), the Pseudo-Aristotelian *De causis,* actually by Proclus (translated by Gerard of Cremona), *De somno* (translation of Ibn Rushd's epitome, perhaps by Michael Scot), the Pseudo-Aristotelian *De plantis* actually by Nicolaus Damascenus (translated by Alfred of Sareshel), *De memoria* (translation of Ibn Rushd's epitome, perhaps by Michael Scot), *De differentia* (translated by John of Seville), *De morte,* and the logical works (some translations from Arabic available). Some of these works were also translated directly from the Greek, but those from the Arabic can be shown to have been immensely popular by the number of manuscripts that have come down to us. From this list, it can also be learned that at Paris by the mid-13th century Avicennan Neoplatonism had made way for an Averroistic interpretation of Aristotle, in particular of the *Metaphysics* and *De anima.*

Perhaps the most important philosophical debate of the second half of the 13th century was the Parisian controversy between Siger de Brabant (ca. 1240–ca. 1284) and Thomas Aquinas, on the noetic problem of the structure and the function of the soul. Much of the argument was based on the various interpretations of texts of Aristotle, his Greek and Arab commentators, and to a lesser extent of Muslim thinkers. Siger agreed with Ibn Rushd that for all people there is one intellect, which comes from without and joins with the different activities of the human body (life and sensation) to become a composite soul (*anima composita*). The intellect, however, does not become an integral part of the body, because it would then not be able to be separated from it; it operates much in the way—Siger here adopts Aristotle's famous analogy in *De anima*—of a sailor on a ship. It thus follows that it is not the individual human being who thinks but rather the unitive intellect *in* the human being. According to Aquinas, this is a misrepresentation of Aristotle, and thus philosophically untenable, and it also leads to conflict with Christian theology, that is, with regard to individual human responsibility and in the end beatitude for the personal soul.

The strong rationalism and the secularizing naturalism of Ibn Rushd's interpretation of Aristotle and that of the Latin Averroists, such as Siger, indeed brought on the infamous condemnation of 219 propositions by Étienne Tempier, bishop of Paris, in 1277. Yet Jean de Jandun (ca. 1289–1328) continued to defend Ibn Rushd's interpretations of Aristotle. Compelled to flee Paris because of his defense of Marsilius of Padua's *Defensor pacis*, he went to Ferrara and became the great stimulator of North Italian Averroism in the 14th and 15th centuries.

A different aspect of Arabic influence on medieval French thinking is by way of the Catalan polymath Ramon Lull (ca. 1232–1316). Lull's system is decidedly nonscholastic in method, and this can account for its popularity in mystical and even in courtly circles outside the academic system of medieval universities. When he was just over thirty years old, Lull dedicated his life to serving God by taking it upon himself to convert the Muslims. He spent a decade in Mallorca learning Arabic, studying Latin Christian theology and philosophy, and reading Muslim authors. Lull himself was a prolific author in Arabic, Catalan, and Latin; besides mystical and philosophical works, he wrote romances and even a handbook of chivalry. The Arabic elements in his universalist philosophy of Christian Neoplatonism and his project of transforming courtly love into religious mysticism—a kind of philosophy of love—derive especially from such authors as Ibn Sina and al-Ghazali. Lull's creation of a "dynamic" metaphysics and epistemology shows great affinity with and may even have been derived from the ideas of Lull's Muslim contemporary Ibn Sab'in (d. 1270) of Murcia. Lull later taught at Paris, Montpellier, and Naples, and his works were widely distributed throughout France and Europe. He taught especially against Averroism and adhered to a curious amalgam of Arabic and Latin Neoplatonism.

Although Lull's philosophical system and his polemical thought were adopted by many in France, they became the object of virulent controversy at the end of the 14th century. A Dominican inquisitor of Aragon, Nicolas Eymerich, in 1376 obtained a papal bull that prohibited teaching Lullism, and between 1395 and 1402 Jean Gerson, chancellor of the University of Paris, forbade Lull's works. Still, Lullism continued to have its adherents: through the work of the Neoplatonist Heimeric van de Velde (1395–1460), who had studied at Paris and later taught at Cologne, it influenced deeply the thought of Nicholas of Cusa and through him Leibniz and a whole string of thinkers leading to Hegel at the beginning of the 19th century.

Arjo Vanderjagt

[See also: ABÉLARD, PETER; ALAIN DE LILLE; ALBERT THE GREAT; AQUINAS, THOMAS; ARABIC INFLUENCE ON LITERATURE; ARISTOTLE, INFLUENCE OF; CHARLES MARTEL; ÉTIENNE TEMPIER; GERBERT OF AURILLAC; MAIMONIDES, INFLUENCE OF; PETER THE VENERABLE; PLATO, INFLUENCE OF; PSEUDO-DIONYSIUS THE AREOPAGITE; SIGER DE BRABANT; UNIVERSITIES; WILLIAM OF AUVERGNE; WILLIAM OF CONCHES; WILLIAM OF SAINT-THIERRY]

Daiber, Hans. "Lateinische Übersetzungen arabischer Texte zur Philosophie und ihre Bedeutung für die Scholastik des Mittelalters: Stand und Aufgaben der Forschung." In *Rencontres de cultures dans la philosophie médiévale: traductions et traducteurs de l'antiquité tardive au XIVe siècle*, ed. Jacqueline Hamesse and Marta Fattori. Louvain-la-Neuve: Institut d'Études Médiévales, 1990, pp. 203–50.

Jolivet, Jean. "The Arabic Inheritance." In *A History of Twelfth-Century Western Philosophy*, ed. Peter Dronke. Cambridge: Cambridge University Press, 1988, pp. 113–48.

Makdisi, George. *The Rise of Humanism in Classical Islam and the Christian West*. Edinburgh: Edinburgh University Press, 1990.

Peters, Francis E. *Aristotle and the Arabs: The Aristotelian Tradition in Islam*. New York: New York University Press, 1968.

Urvoy, Dominique. *Penser l'Islam: les présupposés islamiques de l'art de Lull*. Paris: Vrin, 1980.

Watt, W. Montgomery. *The Influence of Islam on Medieval Europe*. Edinburgh: Edinburgh University Press, 1972.

ARBITRATION OF DISPUTES. While the ordeal, the *placitum* or formal public court hearing, and the feudal court have been seen as the normal ways in which medieval people resolved disputes, there has been a growing appreciation of the role of arbitration in dispute settlement. Descriptions of such settlements appear primarily in ecclesiastical charters and most often concern property disputes.

Arbitration occurred throughout much of the Middle Ages, but it seems that it was particularly during the high Middle Ages that adversaries preferred to turn to a third party to resolve their dispute. Although public officials could serve as arbitrators, they did so rarely. Instead, arbitrators tended to be the prominent and powerful men of the district who were frequently identified simply as *boni viri*.

Three characteristics of arbitration settlements stand out. First, despite the weight of the evidence, arbitrators most often recommended a compromise. With each side receiving some satisfaction, there was less likelihood that the dispute would be renewed. Second, in order to ensure the stability of the settlement, great care was taken to have it witnessed by as many people as possible. In some cases, a settlement might be held in more than one location. Finally, the guarantors (*fideiussores*) often committed themselves and their property to ensure the compliance of the disputants to the settlement.

Despite the inherent fragility of such settlements, arbitration proved to be a remarkably successful pragmatic means of ending disputes.

Stephen Weinberger

Davis, Wendy, and Paul Fouracre, eds. *The Settlement of Disputes in Early Medieval Europe*. Cambridge: Cambridge University Press, 1966.

Weinberger, Stephen. "Cours judiciaires, justice et responsabilité sociale dans la Provence médiévale: IXe–XIe siècles." *Revue historique* 267 (1982): 273–88.

White, Stephen D. "Pactum . . . legum vincit et amor judicium: The Settlement of Disputes by Compromise in Eleventh-Century Western France." *American Journal of Legal History* 22 (1978): 281–308.

ARCHER/BOWMAN. Archers and archery were a traditional part of the French army during the Middle Ages. The bow was first used by the Franks in the 4th century but did not become a required arm of the Frankish infantry until the time of Charlemagne. These early archers generally were equipped with a short bow of simple wood construction. But in the following centuries bows were improved by the addition of horn, sinew, and glue in a composite construction complete with angled ears to give more pull to the bowstring. By the 11th century, archers had become a designated unit within the French army, differing in responsibility, status, arms, and armor from the regular infantry unit. Rarely were archers mounted, and then only for transportation to and from the battlefield.

With the influx of crossbows, the use of short bows died out in French armies, and by the 13th century they were not considered a weapon of war in most parts of Europe. However, they did persist as hunting weapons. During the late Middle Ages, the crossbow dominated the archery of the French army, although some French military leaders attempted to hire groups of short- and longbowmen from Scotland and mounted archers from Spain and Italy.

Archers were seen as unchivalric participants of battle and frequently were massacred by opposing forces if captured.

Kelly DeVries

[See also: ARMOR AND WEAPONS; CROSSBOW]

Bradbury, Jim. *The Medieval Archer.* New York: St. Martin, 1985.
Contamine, Philippe. *War in the Middle Ages,* trans. Michael Jones. London: Blackwell, 1984.
Lake, Frederick H., and Harold F. Wright. *A Bibliography of Archery.* Manchester: Simon Archery Foundation, 1974.
Nicolle, David C. *Arms and Armour of the Crusading Period, 1050–1350.* 2 vols. White Plains: Kraus, 1988.

Argentan (Orne), Saint-Germain. *Photograph: Clarence Ward Collection. Courtesy of Oberlin College.*

ARGENTAN. Virtually leveled in World War II, this Norman town nonetheless has important vestiges of two late-medieval churches. In addition, the 15th-century Tour Marguerite is a remnant of the late-medieval city walls, and the 14th-century castle includes the remains of a 12th-century keep. The church of Saint-Germain preserves a beautiful porch in Flamboyant Gothic style (14th c.); the six-bay nave with its triforium and the polygonal apse with its double deambulatory and apsidal chapels are likewise Flamboyant. The vaulting in the choir features unusual pendant keystones. Saint-Germain preserves some remarkable 15th-century stained glass as well. The 14th-century chapel of Saint-Nicolas has been heavily restored.

William W. Kibler/William W. Clark

Prieur, Lucien. "Argentan." *Congrès archéologique (Orne)* 111 (1953): 84–112.

ARGENTERIE. *See* HÔTEL DU ROI

ARGENTEUIL. A suburb of Paris on the Seine, Argenteuil (Val d'Oise) was during the Middle Ages the site of a Benedictine priory of women. Its early history is sketchy, though it was in existence by the late 7th century; it is mentioned only rarely in the succeeding centuries. At the beginning of the 12th century, Abbot Suger of Saint-Denis claimed that from its foundation the priory had belonged to his abbey. He produced a charter of the emperors Louis I and Lothair I to support his claim, and in 1129 Argenteuil was "returned" to Saint-Denis and the nuns expelled. There is, however, evidence that Suger fabricated the story and the document that supported his claim. It was to this priory that Abélard led Héloïse after their marriage; it was where she took the veil; and she was the superior when the nuns were expelled.

From the mid-12th-century, the church at Argenteuil claimed to possess the relic of the Holy Tunic, the seamless robe that Christ had at the Crucifixion and that the monks claimed had been given to the priory by a daughter of Charlemagne. Though in the Middle Ages the priory possessed extensive domains, from the time of the Hundred Years' War it suffered losses. In 1686, Argenteuil was joined to the royal foundation at Saint-Cyr. At the Revolution, the priory was suppressed and destroyed, and today only a few fragments of sculpture remain.

Thomas G. Waldman

[See also: HÉLOÏSE; SAINT-DENIS; SUGER]

Waldman, Thomas. "Abbot Suger and the Nuns of Argenteuil." *Traditio* 41 (1985): 239–72.

ARISTOCRATIC REVOLT. Potential for the resort to force of arms characterized 15th-century French politics. Great magnates and princes of the blood regularly assembled coalitions of lesser men anxiously seeking patronage and protection. Those who openly challenged royal authority in 1439, 1465, and 1488 typically cloaked their rebellion in a demand for "reform" but were motivated less by ideology than self-interest. Wishing to dominate rather than resist the monarchy, such rebels demanded a role in crown governance and access to crown resources.

The Praguerie, named in memory of the Hussite revolt, occurred when peers acted to restrain Charles VII, who had been emboldened by the Treaty of Arras and his recent recapture of Paris. At the Estates General of 1439, Charles had threatened princely autonomy by outlawing private armed forces. The duke of Bourbon and others seduced the youthful dauphin, Louis, into joining them in open revolt. Skirmishes in Poitou, Auvergne, and the Bourbonnais restored crown authority by June 1440, but the price of peace was the delay of military reform as well as the provision of *pensions* and seats in the royal council for many of the rebels.

In 1465, peers again united in an inaptly named Ligue du Bien Publique to restrain a monarch whose reach exceeded his grasp. Nominally led by Louis XI's brother, Charles of France, the League was dominated by the dukes of Bourbon and of Brittany and by Charles the Bold, then count of Charolais. Louis's army restored his authority in the Bourbonnais and succeeded in holding Paris after the indecisive Battle of Montlhéry (July 16, 1465). Compelled to compromise nonetheless, Louis, in the treaties of Conflans and Saint-Maur, promised to restore the *pensions* and positions of many he had injudiciously ruined upon his accession to the throne as well as to grant his brother the apanage of Normandy and to reconcile himself to the dukes of Brittany and Burgundy.

As late as 1488, a similar revolt occurred, in the so-called Guerre Folle, when the dukes of Brittany and of Orléans challenged the regency of Anne of Beaujeu. The subsequent attachment of Brittany to the royal domain, however, ended the era of armed defiance of royal authority by eliminating the last great independent principality. Henceforth, rebels, such as the duke of Bourbon in 1525, would be viewed not as disobedient vassals but as traitors deserving exile or execution rather than reconciliation.

Paul D. Solon

[See also: CHARLES VII; CHARLES THE BOLD; FRANÇOIS II; LOUIS XI]

Cuttler, Simon H. *The Laws of Treason and Treason Trials in Later Medieval France.* Cambridge: Cambridge University Press, 1982.

Jouanna, Arlette. *Le devoir de révolte: la noblesse française et la gestation de l'état moderne, 1559–1661.* Paris: Fayard, 1989.

Leguai, André. *Les ducs de Bourbon pendant la crise monarchique du XVe siècle.* Paris: Société des Belles Lettres, 1962.

Lewis, Peter S. *Later Medieval France: The Polity.* New York: St. Martin, 1968.

———, ed. *The Recovery of France in the Fifteenth Century.* New York: Harper and Row, 1972.

Vaughn, Richard. *Valois Burgundy.* London: Lane, 1975.

ARISTOTLE, INFLUENCE OF. The importance of the introduction of translated works of the Greek philosopher Aristotle (384–322 B.C.) into medieval Christian thinking is one of the most often stated and least clear aspects of 13th-century history.

Aristotle's *Categories (Praedicamenta)*, *On Interpretation (Perihermeneias)*, *Topics*, and *Prior Analytics* were widely known through the 6th-century Latin translations of Boethius. With his translation of Porphyry's *Isagoge*, they were the source of Aristotelian ideas in the West until the translation of Averroes's commentary on Aristotle by Michael Scot, at the Sicilian court of Frederick II, in the first third of the 13th century. By 1250, most of the works of natural philosophy, logic, and metaphysics were translated and were basic texts for the arts faculty in Paris. The anonymous *Liber de causis*, thought to be by Aristotle, was also highly influential, although it is in fact Platonic. By ca. 1240, the *Rhetoric*, *Ethics* (very influential), *Politics*, and *Economics* were also available, mostly through translations by James of Venice. In the mid-13th century, Thomas Aquinas and Albert the Great (the greatest Christian Aristotelian philosophers of the theology faculty; the most important Aristotelians in arts were Boethius of Dacia and Siger de Brabant) recognized the need for better translations, and Thomas persuaded William of Moerbecke (1215–1286) to revise and retranslate much of the work. In fact, however, Aristotelian ideas long were best known through Averroes and Avicenna.

The two key theological problems that Aristotle raised were the eternity of the world (an affront to the Creation) and the notion of the unity of the intellect (which, if true, would deny the resurrection of the individual person). As well, later readers of Averroes thought that he taught a double-truth theory: that some things might be true for philosophy but not for theology, and that in such cases philosophy should have priority.

The public or private teaching of Aristotle in theology was first prohibited at the Council of Sens in 1210. Robert de Courçon's statutes (1215) for the University of Paris forbade the teaching of the *Metaphysics* and all books on physics and natural science; the works on logic were allowed. This was restated in Gregory IX's bull *Parens scientiarum* (1231). The tide was irresistible, however, and in 1255 the statutes of the university allowed all of Aristotle's works to be taught. The first theologians to use Aristotle in theological works were Alexander of Hales, Philip the Chancellor, and William of Auvergne, all writing at the beginning of the 1230s, soon after the new Latin translations appeared. All were orthodox theologians who chose from Aristotle whatever suited their purposes, without engaging with the implications of his doctrines as a whole.

Thomas Aquinas, and to some extent Albert the Great before him, made the exemplary synthesis of Christian and Aristotelian ideas, but some of Thomas's propositions were condemned as errors by Bishop Étienne Tempier at Paris, in 1270 and again in 1277. It was not until Thomas's canonization in 1323 that the final nail in the anti-Aristotelian coffin was driven.

It can be argued that what Aristotle provided, and what was so much needed, was a means of approach rather than particular ideas. His ideas of logical argument and of categories, and his four causes (formal, material, final, efficient), were taken up zealously. God could be defined as the First Cause, the Uncaused Causer. The joy of Aristotle, and the danger, was his comprehensiveness: he had addressed almost every branch of knowledge; this held deep appeal for the medieval sense of the unity and knowability of the world.

The followers of strictly Aristotelian ideas were known as Latin Averroists, from their use of Averroes's *Commentary*.

Lesley J. Smith

[See also: ALBERT THE GREAT; ALEXANDER OF HALES; AQUINAS, THOMAS; ARABIC PHILOSOPHY, INFLUENCE OF; ÉTIENNE TEMPIER; GILES OF ROME; *PARENS SCIENTIARUM*; PHILIP THE CHANCELLOR; PHILOSOPHY; SIGER DE BRABANT; WILLIAM OF AUVERGNE]

ARLES. The city of Arles (Bouches-du-Rhône) remained in the shadow of Marseille until 46 B.C., when Julius Caesar established a colony of Roman veterans on the left bank of the Rhône, called Arelate. Arles developed rapidly under his successors, serving as an important communications link between Italy and Spain. Its bishopric was founded in the 1st century by St. Trophimus. By the 2nd century A.D., it had acquired substantial defensive walls and major public-works projects and had supplanted Marseille as the leading Mediterranean port. Arles became the principal residence of the emperor Constantine I the Great (ca. 280–337) and was the birthplace of Constantine II (317–340). In 314, it was the site of the church synod called by Constantine I to deal with the Donatist controversy.

Following the collapse of the western Roman Empire, Arles became the capital of the Visigothic leader Euric, and in 536 it came under the control of the Franks. In the early 8th century, Arles was plundered by the Muslims and became a center for Provençal rebels; Charles Martel had to subdue the town twice before securing control over the region.

Arles was to play a central role in the history of medieval Provence. It was a major commercial center, and in 972 its count, Guillaume II, drove the Muslims from their base at Garde-Freinet. The archbishops of the city were leading figures in the Peace Movement and the reform of the church in the 11th century. In the 12th century, Arles became a free city ruled by a *podesta*, a status it retained until the French Revolution.

Stephen Weinberger

The church of Saint-Trophime at Arles, built during the first quarter of the 12th century, is one of the most important Romanesque churches of southern France. It consists of nave and two aisles, each originally terminated in the east by two apsidioles and the semicircular choir. The nave is tall, thin, and aspiring with high and wide nave arcades surmounted by a single clerestory window above a horizontal band of ornament. Nave piers have double responds on all four faces: supporting the nave arcade, the diaphragm arch over the aisles, and the colonnettes and capitals above the inner respond, which in turn supports the continuous horizontal frieze by pointed barrel vaults, while the aisles are vaulted by three-quarters of a barrel vault, strengthened by diaphragm arches behind each pier. If Burgundian ideas come down the Rhône Valley, they are overwhelmed by Roman influences in forms and decoration to create a distinct regional, Provençal Romanesque style.

In the mid-15th century, the shallow Romanesque east end of Arles was replaced by a deep, handsome Flamboyant choir, ambulatory, and radiating chapels. Ribs melt into the masonry of vaults, and moldings take on a life of their own. This new east end resulted in the destruction of a large crypt completed in 1152 to receive the relics of Trophimus.

The cloister for the Augustinian canons of Saint-Trophime is the most important of the many cloisters in Provence. Indeed, it can be argued that the north gallery of the Arles cloister is the finest in western Europe, if the criteria for judgment include architecture and sculpture and their total interrelationship, as well as the consistency and the high quality of the sculpture. The north gallery, dating from the late 1140s to early 1150s, is vaulted by a three-quarter barrel, which drops lower on the garden side of the cloister, necessitating exterior wall buttresses. Each corner pier of the north gallery has three figures with relief sculpture between them, which visually support the diagonal arch and the two transverse arches, while the two intermediate piers have single projecting figures supporting the transverse arch and recessed flanking figures.

Trophimus is on the northwest corner pier, and St. Stephen, to whom the church was first dedicated, is on the northeast. They are flanked by Peter and Paul. The intermediate piers contain Christ between two pilgrims, which combine Christ meeting the Apostles on the road to Emmaus and the Pilgrimage to Santiago de Compostela. The eastern, intermediate pier depicts Christ between James and Thomas.

Two sculptors appear to be responsible for the monumental sculpture in the north gallery. One, influenced by the sculpture of Saint-Gilles-du-Gard, carved, in order, small Christ, Peter, Paul, John, James; the other, more influenced by western French sculpture, created Stephen, Trophimus, Christ, two pilgrims, and Thomas. The Peter-Paul Master carved more of the historiated capitals. In the east gallery (1150s–60s), the capitals depict scenes from the Incarnation and the Passion of Christ. More sculptors were involved, and some relationship with Italian sculpture is evident.

The south and east galleries are Gothic, dating from the late 13th and 14th centuries. Encrusted with a thick layer of gypsum, they are difficult to interpret. The façade portal of Saint-Trophime is a paradox. Although dramatic in thematic concept, the execution is often uninspired. The single portal, added to the older façade, is in the form of a projecting portico supported by six columns. Its de-

Poly, Jean-Pierre. *La Provence et la société féodale: 879–1166.* Paris: Bordas, 1976.

Sautel, Gérard. *Les villes du Midi méditerranéen au moyen âge: aspects économiques et sociaux (IXe–XIIIe siècles).* Brussels: Société Jean Bodin, 1955.

Stoddard, Whitney S. *Monastery and Cathedral in France.* Middletown: Wesleyan University Press, 1966, pp. 65, 77; figs. 85, 105.

———. *The Façade of Saint-Gilles-du-Gard.* Middletown: Wesleyan University Press, 1973, pp. 198–297; figs. 241–417.

ARLES-SUR-TECH. Situated along the Tech River in Roussillon, the abbey of Sainte-Marie d'Arles (Pyrénées-Orientales) boasts a rich history that is still visible in the abbey church and cloister. Founded in 778 as Sainte-Marie de Vallespir at the ancient Roman baths of Arles (Amélie-les-Bains), the Benedictine community was decimated by invasions during the 9th century. Relocated to its present site, the monastery entered a period of protection and prosperity in the 10th and 11th centuries. In 1078, further protection was afforded the abbey when it came under the authority of Cluny. The 12th and 13th centuries saw increasing profits and new construction, due in part to the rich mines of iron, silver, and copper in the area.

Architecturally, little appears to have survived from the late 9th-century foundation, with the possible exception of the unusual western orientation of the church. The plan of the surviving church, roughly dated by a 1046 consecration, follows a typical basilican format with nave, two side aisles, and three corresponding semicircular apses. The nave arcade on rectangular piers supports a high clerestory with twelve windows. Highly unusual are the three niche chapels that are carved out of the massive eastern wall. When the structure was refurbished around the time of the 1157 consecration, a larger and higher arcade was integrated with the older one, providing additional support for a new vaulted ceiling. Both arcades are visible today. A beautiful Gothic cloister of white marble and double columns that reflect Languedoc models was the final, major addition to the complex under the successful abbacy of Raimond de Bach (r. 1261–1303).

Arles-sur-Tech is most renowned for its 11th-century façade. A rare example of a Lombard-type façade in Roussillon, it includes several series of blind arcades that dominate the exterior. Significant examples of pre-Romanesque sculpture decorate the small central window and the tympanum. The tympanum in particular features a fine example of early sculpture depicting Christ and the symbols of the Evangelists inscribed within a cross. The focus on a decorative and two-dimensional patterning of the figures is typical and derives from techniques native to ivory- and metalworking. This approach to sculpture had an unusually long life at Arles-sur-Tech, as evidenced by the 1211 tomb of Guillaume Gaucelme, now embedded in a wall within the church.

Fragmentary evidence remains of wall painting in the central niche of the eastern end. The representation of the

Arles (Bouches-du-Rhône), Saint-Trophime, cloister, pier. St. Peter. *Photograph courtesy of Whitney S. Stoddard.*

sign is clearly inspired by the façade of Saint-Gilles-du-Gard, which in turn is based on Roman monuments like the arches at Saint-Rémy or Orange.

Paul, a less sensitive replica, in reverse, of the Saint-Gilles Paul, served as model for six of the other seven Apostles carved by a less skilled sculptor. Peter is the work of a third sculptor. The Paul Master seems to have carved the tympanum, and the Peter Master the lintel. The base of the trumeau and some capitals and socles appear to have been carved by an Italian sculptor. The entire portal seems to have been sculpted rapidly by four artists, most likely in the 1170s but certainly by July 30, 1178, for the coronation in Saint-Trophime of Frederick as king of Burgundy.

Whitney S. Stoddard

[See also: PROVENCE; SAINT-GILLES-DU-GARD]

Borg, Alan. *Architectural Sculpture in Romanesque Provence.* Oxford: Clarendon, 1972, pp. 13, 61–70, 107–08, 110–13; figs. pp. 57–67.

Labande, Léon-Honoré. *L'église Saint-Trophime d'Arles.* Paris: Laurens, 1930.

Last Judgment, often found on the entrance wall of churches, included Christ in Majesty in the hemidome and, below, cherubim and seraphim in adoration. The artistic activity of Sainte-Marie d'Arles also extended to the glorification of the saints Abdon and Sennen, whose relics were housed at the abbey.

Leslie Blake DiNella

Carbonell-Lamothe, Yvette. "Pyrénées-Orientales: Arles-sur-Tech, église Sainte-Marie, travaux de restauration." *Bulletin monumental* 144 (1986): 342–43.

Ponsich, Pierre. "L'abbaye de Saint-Marie d'Arles." *Congrès archéologique* (1954): 347–77.

"Le portail dans l'art roman du Midi de l'Europe." *Cahiers de Saint-Michel de Cuxa* 8 (1977).

ARMAGNAC. The lands that came to comprise the county of Armagnac in southwestern France formed part of the great duchy of Gascony in Aquitaine. In the early 10th century, the eastern portion of the duchy was detached to form the large county of Fézensac, centered on the town of Vic-Fézensac and including the archiepiscopal city of Auch. The county of Fézensac in turn was dismembered by the creation of the county of Astarac and, in the middle of the 10th century, by the detachment of its western region as the county of Armagnac. The small county, whose chief towns were Riscle and Aignan, retained these dimensions until the death of the the the last count of Fézensac, Astronove II. In 1119, his widow married Géraud III of Armagnac, reuniting the two counties.

Among the early counts of Armagnac, the most notable was Bernard II Tumapaler (1014–1080), whose attempt to succeed to the duchy of Aquitaine-Gascony was defeated in 1054. During the 12th and 13th centuries, the counts of Armagnac-Fézensac were noted as vassals of their principal overlord, the king of England; Count Bernard-Aiz V was conspicuous in the service of Henry III at Taillebourg in 1242. This traditional alliance ended in the 14th century, as the counts acquired fiefs directly under the lordship of France, most significantly the county of Rodez, added in 1302 through the marriage of Count Bernard VI. Bernard VI, disputing the succession of the viscounty of Béarn, also initiated the great quarrel with the counts of Foix. Thereafter, the history of Armagnac is dominated by this rivalry and by the counts' determined alliance with the cause of the French monarchy against the English. Count Jean I (r. 1319–73), royal lieutenant in Languedoc, vainly opposed the Black Prince's raid in 1355. Bernard VII, constable of France, murdered in 1418, animated the anti-Burgundian party known as the Armagnacs. The reign of Count Jean V brought the downfall of the house of Armagnac. Charged with rebellion against the king, he was besieged and assassinated at the castle of Lectoure in 1473. The domains of Armagnac passed to the family of d'Albret and finally to the monarchy with the accession of Henry IV in 1589.

Alan Friedlander

[See also: ALBRET; ARMAGNACS; FOIX]

Badout, Louis. "La chute de la maison d'Armagnac." *Bulletin de la Société Académique des Hautes-Pyrénées* (1982–83): 130–42.

Baqué, Z. "Les comtes d'Armagnac." *Bulletin de la Société Archéologique Historique Littéraire et Scientifique du Gers* (1944–48). [Series of continuing articles.]

Bordes, Maurice. *Histoire d'Auch et du pays d'Auch.* Roanne: Horvath, 1980.

Samaran, Charles. *La maison d'Armagnac au XVe siècle et les dernières luttes de la féodalité dans le Midi de la France.* Paris: Picard, 1907.

ARMAGNACS. During the summer of 1411, the name Armagnacs began to be used by the Parisians for the faction supporting the duke of Orléans against the duke of Burgundy, John the Fearless. The origin of this ducal struggle was the murder of Louis of Orléans in 1407 at the instigation of Burgundy. At the Peace of Chartres (March 9, 1409), the king pardoned Burgundy, saying that the murder was committed for the good of the kingdom. He commanded Louis's sons Charles, duke of Orléans, and Philip to swear not to pursue vengeance, but the feud did not end.

The nickname reveals the strong influence within the group of Count Bernard of Armagnac, son-in-law of the duke of Berry. Bernard became important when he joined Berry on April 15, 1410, in an alliance with the dukes of Orléans and Brittany and the counts of Alençon and Clermont, aimed against Burgundy and called today the League of Gien. At this time, a marriage was arranged between Bernard's daughter Bonne and Charles d'Orléans. Civil war was averted by the Peace of Bicêtre, announced by the king on November 2, 1410. It was the quick result of a royal threat to confiscate the property of members of the league.

The duke of Orléans initiated new strife on January 30, 1411, with a kidnaping and then began to skirmish with the Burgundians in Picardy. On July 14, Orléans and his brothers sent the king the "Manifesto of Jargeau," which claimed that the royal pardon to Burgundy in 1409 was against divine law and the oaths given at Chartres were therefore invalid. Hostilities resumed, and in October the Armagnacs took Saint-Denis and the bridge of Saint-Cloud. Intercepted letters proved Berry's complicity with their faction, and two royal armies marched against him (November–December 1411 and May–July 1412). After a long siege at Bourges, the king's son, the duke of Guyenne, negotiated a treaty that Berry accepted on July 15, 1412. The more formal Treaty of Auxerre followed on August 22.

The ensuing delicate balance was upset when Burgundy incited the riot of the Cabochiens in Paris in April 1413. Named for the butcher who led them, the Cabochiens were the popular faction of the Burgundian party in Paris. The fall of the Cabochiens in August and Burgundy's flight resulted in a period of Armagnac influence, during which the king led a military campaign against John the Fearless that ended with the Peace of Arras (September 1414; finalized February 22, 1415). The duke of Guyenne sought to curb the influence of the Armagnacs, but his death allowed them much greater freedom to act. Bernard of Armagnac was named constable of France and became the leader of his party with the departure, in 1417, of Louis II of Anjou, a bitter enemy of Burgundy. Berry had died in 1416, and the dukes of Orléans and Bourbon, taken captive at Agincourt, were still prisoners in England. In April 1417, Bernard engineered the exile of the queen, Isabeau of Bavaria, who was plotting against the supremacy of his party. She was rescued, however, and set up a rival government in Troyes. In May 1418, the Burgundians attacked Paris, and on July 12, two days before the entry of Burgundy and the queen, Bernard was put to death. During the invasion in May, one of his partisans had spirited away the dauphin, the future Charles VII, who then became head of the anti-Burgundian party. After this time, the faction continued to be called the Armagnacs.

Richard C. Famiglietti

[See also: CABOCHIENS; CHARLES VI; HUNDRED YEARS' WAR; ISABEAU OF BAVARIA; JOHN, DUKE OF BERRY; JOHN THE FEARLESS; LOUIS, DUKE OF GUYENNE]

Caillet, Louis. "Le traité d'Arras de 1414 d'après un nouveau texte aux archives de Lyon." *Mémoires de l'Académie des Sciences, Lettres et Arts d'Arras* 2nd ser. 40 (1909): 220–35.

Durrieu, Paul. "Acte original de la ligue de Gien (1410)." *Mémoires de la Société Nationale des Antiquaires de France* 54 (1893): 167–204.

Famiglietti, Richard C. *Royal Intrigue: Crisis at the Court of Charles VI 1392–1420.* New York: AMS, 1986.

Mirot, Léon. "Autour de la paix d'Arras (1414–1415)." *Bibliothèque de l'École des Chartes* 75 (1914): 253–327.

———. "Autour de la paix de Chartres, 9 mars 1409." *Annales de Bourgogne* 3 (1931): 305–42.

ARMOR AND WEAPONS. The armor worn in France throughout the medieval period was directly derived from that worn in the Migrations Period by the leaders of Germanic war bands, and its basic structure, which included a shield, helmet, and coat, changed little between ca. A.D. 100 and 1150. In the early period, the shield (Lat. *scutum,* OFr. *escu*) was normally constructed of wood covered with leather and reinforced with strips of bronze or iron centered on a hemispherical metal boss that covered the grip. Down to ca. 1000, the shield was usually ovoid or round and about three feet in diameter. A round shield of similar construction continued to be used by infantry into the 15th century, but a longer and narrower shield of Byzantine origin, shaped like an elongated almond, was introduced in the 11th century for use by heavy cavalry and predominated from ca. 1050 to 1150. The normal type of helmet (MHG *helm,* OFr. *helme,* MidFr. *heaume*) in the period before 1150 took the form of a more or less convex cone, most commonly constructed from four or more triangular sections of metal or some other hard material bound by iron bands. It was usually supplied with a nasal bar and until ca. 750 with hinged cheek plates as well.

The coat was almost always made of mail (OFr. *maille*), a mesh of interlocking iron rings of uniform size. The names most commonly given to the mail coat in the period before ca. 1300 were derived from the Old Germanic word *brunaz* 'bright': Lat. *brunia,* OFr. *brunie* or *bro(i)gne.* Down to ca. 800, no protection for the neck was generally worn, but in the 9th century it became customary to wear a mail hood with attached shoulder cape over or partially under the mail coat and under the helm. This caped hood was apparently known as the *halsbergen* 'neck guard' in Frankish and by a derivative word variously spelled *halberc, halbert, (h)auberc,* etc. in Old French. This word (in English in the form "hauberk") has been applied since at least the 17th century to the mail coat or *brogne* itself, but this was an error of the antiquarians, and historically it had designated only the caped hood as long as the latter was still in use—that is, until the 14th century. The hood proper, which was often attached directly to the *brogne,* was called the *coiffe,* and from the 12th century onward the *brogne* with attached *coiffe* was called an *haubergonne.*

Helmets and mail coats were expensive, and before ca. 800 they were worn only by kings, nobles, and their most distinguished companions-in-arms. In the 9th century, however, they came to be distributed to the ordinary members of royal and noble military retinues, newly named vassals, and from ca. 950 they were to be characteristic of knights, who were always expected to appear for battle in the most complete and up-to-date armor.

The period 1150–1220 saw the first major changes in the form of armor used in France since the Frankish conquest. Most of these changes were in the direction of increased protection for the body, already begun with the adoption of the long shield. In the late 12th century, the sleeves of the *brogne* were extended from the elbows to the wrists and finally acquired attached mittens. Mail leggings, or *chausses,* though occasionally worn earlier, similarly came into general use among knights ca. 1150 and were worn to ca. 1350. Also ca. 1150 began the custom of wearing a surcoat (OFr. *surcote, cote a armer*)—a loose, generally sleeveless cloth coat probably borrowed from the Muslims—over the coat of mail. The surcoat was universally adopted by ca. 1210 and worn thereafter until ca. 1410. Throughout this period, it was commonly emblazoned with its wearer's heraldic "arms," but these new ensigns were primarily displayed on the shield—which between 1150 and 1200 also lost its traditional boss, between 1150 and 1220 was made progressively shorter and wider, and between 1200 and 1250 was given an increasingly triangular shape through the leveling of its upper edge.

Although the traditional conical helm continued in use until ca. 1280, several new forms emerged in this period that were destined to supersede it. The most important were the flat-topped "great" helm, which between 1180 and 1220 evolved to enclose the whole head in a cylinder of steel pierced only by slits for seeing and holes for breathing, and the close-fitting hemispherical bascinet, which emerged ca. 1220. The great helm survived with little further structural change from 1220 to 1400, and from ca. 1300 its apex was often provided with a distinctive heraldic "crest" (*cimier*) of wood or boiled leather, worn primarily in the tournaments to which, by 1380, the helm was restricted. The bascinet was at first worn under the helm and over the coif of the mail hood, but from ca. 1260 the hood was increasingly replaced with a mail curtain (the *camail* or *aventail*) suspended from the outside of the bascinet, and the bascinet thus augmented gradually replaced the clumsy great helm as the principal defense for the head in real warfare. In consequence, the bascinet became steadily larger and more pointed, and acquired in the last decade of the 13th century a movable "visor" (*vissere*) to protect the face.

The eight decades between ca. 1250 and ca. 1330 witnessed a major change in the history of European armor, stimulated in large part by the development of weapons capable of piercing mail: the gradual introduction of pieces of plate (at first of whalebone, horn, and boiled leather, as well as of the iron and steel that ultimately prevailed) to cover an ever larger part of the mail. By 1330, every part of the body of a knight was normally protected by one or several plates, including a poncholike "coat of plates" concealed by the surcoat. By 1410, the various pieces of plate, including a breastplate and backplate instead of the earlier coat of plates, were all connected by straps and rivets in an articulated suit, or "harness," of polished steel. After ca. 1425, this "white" armor was usually worn without a surcoat or any other covering.

The adoption of elements of plate to protect the body steadily reduced the importance of the shield, which between 1250 and 1350 diminished steadily in size until it was only about 16 inches in height. Even this diminished shield was finally abandoned between 1380 and 1400. A new form of shield called the *targe*, of similar size and structure but roughly rectangular in outline, concave rather than convex, often deeply fluted and cusped, and provided with a notch, or *bouche*, for the lance, was introduced in the same two decades, but it was used primarily in tournaments, and knights of the 15th century seem to have done without any shield in battle.

The only offensive weapons commonly borne by the Frankish warriors who seized power in Gaul in the 5th century were the lance, or *framea*, of sharpened ash; the barbed javelin, or *ango*; and the throwing ax, or *frankisca*. The lance or spear, whose more expansive form, equipped with an iron head, was destined to displace the sharpened form and survived with little basic change until the end of the Middle Ages and beyond—for many centuries the only weapon generally available to ignoble as well as noble warriors.

Kings and the leaders of war bands also carried swords, usually of the long, straight, double-edged type called in Latin *spatha*, first developed by the Celts of Gaul ca. 400 B.C. and later borrowed by Germans and Romans. As the Old French use of *espee* for "sword" suggests, the *spatha* (whose blade was ca. 30 inches long) was ancestral to most of the later forms of sword developed in western Europe, of which some thirty-three types and subtypes have been recognized by scholars, four of them antedating A.D. 600. Around 600, the Frankish king and nobles temporarily abandoned both *spatha* and *frankisca* in favor of a machetelike single-edged sword called a *saxo*, whose 18-inch blade permitted it to be used for stabbing and even

throwing as well as slashing; but under Viking influence the *spatha*, which the Scandinavians had continued to use and develop, was reintroduced into Frankish lands and quickly became the principal weapon not only of the rulers and nobles but of the rank-and-file members of the new heavy-cavalry units ancestral to the knights of the 10th and later centuries.

Lesser weapons were also employed by knights after 1050. Special forms of ax, hammer (*bec*), mace, club, and flail were introduced in the 12th and 13th centuries to supplement the sword, but it was only after 1300 that these were both fully developed and commonly used. Most knights and squires also carried a stiff dagger on their sword belt after ca. 1350. All of the knightly weapons were used by the nonknightly combatants who could acquire them, but among the base-born infantrymen a number of weapons scorned by the knightly class were also employed. The simple bow, despised by most Germanic tribes outside of Scandinavia, was little used in France outside of Normandy before the 14th century, when six mounted archers were included in the "lance," or standard tactical unit of the royal army. The crossbow, or *arbaleste*, was reintroduced into France ca. 950 and was commonly used thereafter to ca. 1550, primarily by special infantry units placed from ca. 1200 to 1534 under the overall authority of a grand master of the crossbowmen (*arbalest[r]iers*). After ca. 1350, the bow and crossbow were supplemented on occasion by a primitive handgun. In addition to these projectile weapons, the infantryman of the 14th and 15th centuries had at his disposal new forms of polearm, which were in essence lances with special forms of head.

D'A. Jonathan D. Boulton

[See also: ARCHER/BOWMAN; ARTILLERY; CAVALRY; CROSSBOW; WARFARE]

Blair, Claude. *European Armor, Circa 1066 to Circa 1700.* London: Batsford, 1958.

Buttin, François. *Du costume militaire au moyen âge et pendant la Renaissance.* Barcelona: La Academia, 1971.

Martin, Paul. *Arms and Armour from the 9th to the 17th Century*, trans. René North. Rutland: Tuttle, 1968.

Oakeshott, R. Ewart. *The Sword in the Age of Chivalry.* London: Lutterworth, 1964.

Todd, Malcolm. *Everyday Life of the Barbarians: Goths, Franks, and Vandals.* London: Batsford, 1972.

ARMS (HERALDIC). The term "arms" (Lat. *arma*, Fr. *armes*, *armoiries*, or *blasons*) was used from the late 12th century for a design of fixed elements in a fixed arrangement and fixed colors, conventionally covering the whole surface of a shield or flag, consistently and uniquely employed at any particular time within a particular kingdom or province by a single person, lineage, or corporation as a mark of identity and authority and heritable according to local rules comparable with those governing the inheritance of real property. The design almost always consisted of a colored background, or "field," and one or more objects, or "charges," placed upon it, both depicted in one or two strongly contrasting colors, or "tinctures." The charges could take the form of simple geometrical shapes, such as a cross, band, chevron, or quarter, or of stylized representations of beasts, plants, or objects, usually drawn from a conventional repertory. The repertory of tinctures, charges, and partitions, and the language of "blazon" used to describe them, was developed gradually in the period between 1130 and 1300, mainly by heralds, and it changed little between 1300 and 1500.

Down to ca. 1500, simple arms, representing a single lineage, office, or corporate entity, normally included only one or two distinct forms of charge. In families, such simple arms were in principle borne in France from ca. 1170 "plain," or undifferenced, only by the heir of the first user, in keeping with the principle of primogeniture; all younger sons in every branch and generation were obliged in theory to add permanent marks of difference, or "brisures," to their fathers' arms, and even the heirs apparent had to add a temporary mark during their fathers' lifetimes. After 1300, the arms of princes and barons became still further complicated as increasing numbers of them combined on the same shield steadily growing numbers of simple arms, representative of different principalities and baronies they possessed or claimed. After 1350, these arms were usually arranged on "quarters" of the shield, whose number after 1430 often grew beyond four.

Arms, as defined above, first appeared in France and neighboring countries in the 1130s. Although they were at first displayed primarily on the shields and flags actually borne in battle, their form and use before ca. 1250 are known to us largely from seals, on which they were commonly portrayed from ca. 1135 either on the effigy of the owner or on a representation of the shield alone. The earliest arms often incorporated emblems used before 1135 on seals, coins, or flags, and some princes adopted two distinct armorial designs, one representing their person and, when inherited by their descendants, their patrilineage, and usually displayed on their shield; the other representing their principal dominion, and usually displayed on their banner. The practice of adopting such jurisdictional arms gave rise after 1200 to the idea that arms could be adopted to represent other types of office, jurisdiction, or corporation and to the use of initially dynastic arms as arms of territorial jurisdiction.

Until ca. 1160, the use of arms in France was confined to princes, but after 1160 it spread gradually downward through the ranks first of the military nobility, among whom it became virtually universal by 1260, then of the rest of society, in which it always remained relatively limited. In northeastern France, where these developments occurred first, arms were adopted by lesser barons and knights banneret between 1160 and 1220, by simple knights between 1180 and 1220, and by simple esquires between 1220 and 1260. All of these men used their arms on a real shield as well as on the purely pictorial one represented on their seal, but the existence of the latter led to the gradual adoption of arms by both individuals and bodies who had no occasion to appear in battle: by married women of the upper and middle nobility after 1180, though rarely before 1230; by prelates after 1210, though rarely before 1250; by lesser clerics, especially after 1350; by men of the bourgeoisie after 1300; and by guilds after 1250, though rarely before 1350. Although the arms of nobles were normally designed by professional heralds, down to 1500 lawyers generally maintained that new arms could be adopted at will by anyone, so long as they were different from all existing arms within the kingdom. Even peasants used quasiarmorial seals.

At first used primarily as marks of identity, after 1240 arms were increasingly displayed on every type of object, both as a mark of ownership and as an element in the scheme of decoration. This usage reached its height in the 14th century, which was the last in which arms played an important role on the field of battle.

D'A. Jonathan D. Boulton

[See also: LIVERY, BADGES, AND COLORS; MOTTO/*DEVISE*; SEALS AND SIGILLOGRAPHY]

Brault, Gerard J. *Early Blazon: Heraldic Terminology in the Twelfth and Thirteenth Centuries*. Oxford: Oxford University Press, 1972.

Galbreath, D.L., and Léon Jéquier. *Manuel du blason*. Lausanne: Spes, 1977.

Pastoureau, Michel. *Traité d'héraldique*. Paris: Picard, 1979.

———. *L'hermine et le sinople: études d'héraldique médiévale*. Paris: Léopard d'Or, 1982.

Pinoteau, Hervé, Michel Pastoureau, and Michel Popoff, eds. *Les origines des armoiries*. Paris: Léopard d'Or, 1983.

ARNAUT DANIEL (fl. 1180–1200). The troubadour Arnaut Daniel was admired by Dante, Petrarch, and Pound as much for his technical virtuosity as for his notorious difficulty. Little can be said for certain about his life, except that his literary reputation as a bold if hermetic poet was well established by 1195, when he appears in the Monk of Montaudon's satiric gallery of troubadours. According to his *vida*, he was a noble from Ribérac in the Dordogne, but this assertion, like that of the *razo* that links him to Richard the Lionhearted, cannot be substantiated. Both the *vida* and the Monk of Montaudon's portrait rightly note that Arnaut Daniel delighted in composing difficult rhymes. His nineteen surviving poems, all but one of which are love songs, attest this penchant for *caras rimas* (difficult rhymes). Arnaut's craft is emblazoned throughout by the daring innovations of the *trobar ric* style. His word choices are unusual, his images unfamiliar, his sound patterns harsh, his poetic rhythms broken. The global effect of his lyrics is always striking, often jarring. No doubt, this originality earned him the respect of subsequent writers, but it has also contributed to his reputation as an obscure poet. An example of Arnaut's brilliant creativity was his invention of the sestina.

Roy S. Rosenstein

[See also: SESTINA; TROUBADOUR POETRY]

Arnaut Daniel. *Arnaut Daniel: il sirventese e le canzoni*, ed. Mario Eusebi. Milan: Scheiwiller, 1984.

————. *Le canzoni di Arnaut Daniel*, ed. Maurizio Perugi. Milan: Ricciardi, 1978.

————. *Arnaut Daniel: canzoni*, ed. Gianluigi Toja. Florence: Sansoni, 1960.

————. *The Poetry of Arnaut Daniel*, ed. and trans. James J. Wilhelm. New York: Garland, 1981.

ARNULF. Name of three counts of Flanders. Arnulf I the Great (885–965, r. 918–65), also known in his last years as "the Old," "the Rich," or "the Lame," was the son of Count Baudouin II. After the death of his younger brother in 933, he ruled an area that included his family's ancestral lands in western and southwestern Flanders, Boulogne, Tournai, territories around Saint-Omer and Thérouanne, and perhaps Ghent. A reformer of the Flemish abbeys and a skilled diplomat, he allied with the counts of Vermandois to check the rising power of the dukes of Normandy. The west Frankish king Lothair gave him the title *princeps*, previously held only by Hugues le Grand, count of Paris, and established the principle that all feudal bonds in Flanders passed through the *princeps* and ultimately to the king. Arnulf's son, Baudouin III, predeceased him, and Lothair arranged the succession of Baudouin's son, Arnulf II (ca. 961–988, r. 965–88). Arnulf II's rule witnessed the beginning of serious conflicts in Flanders between the counts' two feudal lords: the king of France, who occupied southeastern Flanders as a condition of permitting Arnulf's accession, and the Holy Roman emperor, lord of the territory east of the Scheldt. Arnulf II married the daughter of King Berengar II of Italy in 976 and died prematurely in 988. Arnulf III (r. 1070–71) was the son of Count Baudouin VI. He ruled only a few months before being killed in battle by his uncle Robert the Frisian, who usurped the countship.

David M. Nicholas

[See also: FLANDERS]

Ganshof, François L. *La Flandre sous les premiers comtes.* Brussels: Renaissance du Livre, 1943.

Koch, A. C. F. "Het graafschap Vlaanderen van de 9de eeuw tot 1070." In *Algemene Geschiedenis der Nederlanden.* 2nd ed. Haarlem: Fibula-van Dishoeck, 1982, Vol. 1, pp. 354–83.

ARNULF OF LISIEUX (Bishop of Lisieux, r. 1141–81). Arnulf was born into an Anglo-Norman family that included several members of the clergy. Not much is known of his early life, though he probably studied at Chartres, in Italy, and at Paris. He held an archdeaconry at Sées and was often in the service of the English king Henry I, though after his death in 1135, like most of the Norman clergy, he supported the claim of Stephen to the English throne. Arnulf was a staunch supporter of Pope Innocent II during the schism of 1130, and his earliest extant writing is directed against Gérard, bishop of Angoulême, who had supported the antipope Anacletus II. Freely elected bishop of Lisieux by the cathedral chapter in 1141, he often tried to reconcile the interests of the kings of France and England and was one of the ecclesiastical leaders of the Second Crusade. In his own diocese, Arnulf is best remembered for his support of the regular canons and the rebuilding of the cathedral at Lisieux. In his last years, he lost the confidence of Henry II, and his stance during the Becket controversy was criticized by the archbishop's partisans. He retired to the abbey of Saint-Victor in Paris, where he died in 1181. His letters, which he collected, are an important source for mid-12th-century history.

Thomas G. Waldman

Arnulf of Lisieux. *The Letters of Arnulf of Lisieux*, ed. Frank Barlow. London: Royal Historical Society, 1939.

ARRAS. The city of Arras (Nord) and the surrounding region, Artois, derive their names from the Gallic tribe known as the Atrebates. After a bishopric established in the 6th century by St. Vaast was removed to Cambrai, a cathedral chapter remained at Arras as the nucleus of the medieval *cité*. Some distance away, a monastery honoring the memory of St. Vaast was founded in the 7th century and richly endowed by the Frankish kings. The medieval *ville* developed around the monastery and grew rapidly thanks to a favorable location near intersecting trade routes.

The Vikings seriously damaged the town in the 880s, but it recovered after the counts of Flanders absorbed Artois in the 10th century. Arras became an important center for the production and marketing of woolen cloth at an earlier date than the more famous Flemish towns. This cloth was traded actively by the early 11th century. By 1137, merchants of Arras were carrying their goods to the fairs of Champagne, and in the last decades of the 12th century they were doing business as far afield as Genoa. Location on the route between Flanders and Champagne favored the economy of Arras, but after ca. 1220 the Italians began to cut into the carrying trade, eventually developing a sea route to Flanders that bypassed the town. Arras then became an important center of moneylending, making available vast sums to towns and princes. When warfare, economic distress, and diminished population afflicted the town in the 14th century, Arras coped with the situation by adapting the technology of cloth production to the manufacture of tapestries for the luxury trade. For a time, the name Arras became virtually synonymous with tapestry.

Artois passed to the French crown as the dowry of Queen Isabelle de Hainaut in 1180. In 1194, Philip II granted Arras a charter, under which a group of *échevins* (municipal magistrates) ruled the town. It was modified in 1302 to accommodate excluded elements that were showing discontent, but the ruling oligarchy of wealthy entrepreneurs enjoyed remarkable continuity, with one family being represented in the urban government most of the time between 1111 and 1450. This patriciate seems to have originated among the petty officials of the abbey of Saint-Vaast, who gradually accumulated enough capital to embark on large-scale cloth production, then large-scale moneylending, and finally the production of tapestries.

In 1435, Arras was the site of a major peace conference among England, France, and Burgundy. The resultant Franco-Burgundian treaty helped the French emerge victorious in the Hundred Years' War.

Arras is known today for its network of connecting Late Gothic city squares and the medieval and Renaissance houses that line them. The main squares were commercial centers lined by shops. Their recessed lower story permitted the arcaded gallery that protected shoppers and goods from the rain.

Prior to the French Revolution, Arras possessed one of the largest and most famous Gothic cathedrals in northern France. This extraordinary structure was begun ca. 1160 at the east end. Shortly after the construction of the crypt, which had an ambulatory with a single polygonal chapel, the plan was enlarged and expanded. The original scheme called for broad bays of four stories (vaulted aisles and galleries topped by a continuous wall passage and clerestory windows). The change in the design is clearly visible in the contrast between the single, large, round-headed windows of the ambulatory and the elaborate triplet pattern of the gallery and clerestory. The result was an elegant and elaborate design matched in height by the broadly projecting transept arms, which, like those at Laon, had terminal towers. Some of the capitals from this lavishly appointed building are preserved in the municipal museum.

John Bell Henneman, Jr./William W. Clark

[See also: ARTOIS; TAPESTRY; WOOL TRADE]

Berger, Roger. *Littérature et société arrageoises au XIIIe siècle.* Arras: Commission Départementale des Monuments Historiques du Pas-de-Calais, 1981.

Bigwood, Georges. "Les financiers d'Arras." *Revue belge de philologie et d'histoire* 3 (1924): 465–519, 769–814; 4 (1925): 109–19, 379–421.

Dickinson, Jocelyne G. *The Congress of Arras: A Study in Medieval Diplomacy.* Oxford: Clarendon, 1955.

Héliot, Pierre. "La cathédrale d'Arras." *Archéologie* 39 (1971): 56–59.

———. "Les anciennes cathédrales d'Arras." *Bulletin de la Commission Royale des Monuments et des Sites* 4 (1953): 9–109.

Huignard. "Arras: les places; l'ancienne abbaye de St-Waast; cathédrale." *Congrès archéologique (Amiens)* 99 (1936): 173–86.

Lestocquoy, Jean. "Étapes du développement urbain d'Arras." *Revue belge de philologie et d'histoire* 23 (1944): 163–86.

———. *Patriciens du moyen âge: les dynasties bourgeoises d'Arras du XIe au XVe siècle.* Arras: Commission Départementale des Monuments Historiques du Pas-de-Calais, 1945.

Reynolds, Robert L. "Merchants of Arras and the Overland Trade with Genoa, XIIth Century." *Revue belge de philologie et d'histoire* 9 (1930): 495–533.

Serbat, Louis. "Quelques églises anciennement détruites du nord de la France." *Bulletin monumental* 88 (1929): 365–435.

ARRAS, JEAN D' (fl. late 14th c.). Author of the prose romance *Mélusine* (1393). Written at the behest of Marie, duchesse of Bar, for her brother, Jean, duke of Berry,

Mélusine recounts the marvelous origins of the powerful noble family of Lusignan. There are ten 15th-century manuscripts, a 1478 Geneva printed edition, and numerous reprints, as well as an English translation from 1500. Coudrette's verse romance *Mélusine* was possibly inspired by Jean d'Arras.

The founding mother of the Lusignan line, the fairy Mélusine, whose name derives possibly from "mère des Lusignan," has been cursed by her mother to become a serpent from the waist down on Saturdays. Concealing the secret from her husband, Raimondin, who promises never to see his wife on that day, Mélusine bears him ten sons, eight of whom are marked with a fantastic trait, and brings the family great prosperity; she builds the Lusignan's castle in Poitou. But Raimondin breaks his promise and learns Mélusine's secret, remaining silent at first. When he learns that his son Geoffrey has burned the abbey of Maillezais, thus killing one of his sons, he furiously blames his wife and curses her. His betrayal turns Mélusine forever into a huge serpent, who leaves her family but returns periodically to haunt the castle.

Roberta L. Krueger

[See also: LUSIGNAN]

Arras, Jean d'. *Mélusine: roman du XIVe siècle par Jean d'Arras,* ed. Louis Stouff. Dijon: Bernigaud and Privat, 1932.

Coudrette. *Le roman de Mélusine ou Histoire de Lusignan,* ed. Eleanor Roach. Paris: Klincksieck, 1982.

Harf-Lancner, Laurence. *Les fées au moyen âge: Morgane et Mélusine. La naissance des fées.* Paris: Champion, 1984.

Perret, Michèle. "Le lion, le serpent, le sanglier. . . ." In Jean d'Arras, *Le roman de Mélusine ou l'histoire des Lusignan,* trans. Michèle Perret. Paris: Stock, 1979, pp. 313–32.

ARRIÈRE-BAN. Just as the word *ban* sometimes referred to a military summons of the king's vassals, so the *arrière-ban* (Lat. *retrobannum*) conveyed a summons to his rear vassals—those owing service to an intermediate lord rather than to the king directly. In actual fact, when Philip IV and his successors used the *arrière-ban*, it went well beyond the world of purely feudal relations and called to service all men able to bear arms. In principle, it was a somewhat archaic device for mustering substantial numbers of fighting men in an emergency. The *arrière-ban* never completely lost this connotation, but if applied to more than a very local area it would have produced a horde of untrained, ill-equipped people. Its real purpose was largely fiscal. During its period of greatest use, the first half of the 14th century, it was used to impress people with a sense of emergency and to facilitate the collection of money in commutation of actual military service.

John Bell Henneman, Jr.

[See also: BAN/BANALITÉ]

Henneman, John Bell. *Royal Taxation in Fourteenth Century France: The Development of War Financing, 1322–1356.* Princeton: Princeton University Press, 1971.

Strayer, Joseph R., and Charles H. Taylor. *Studies in Early French Taxation*. Cambridge: Harvard University Press, 1939.

ARS ANTIQUA. An antithesis to the term Ars Nova, Ars Antiqua designates music written before the late teens of the 14th century, at which time music and its theory began to incorporate innovations championed as new and modern. In the seventh and last book of his *Speculum musicae* (completed ca. 1325) Jacques de Liège looked back upon the generation of Pseudo-Aristotle (Lambertus) and Franco of Cologne, active in the second half of the 13th century, as the representatives of an Ars Antiqua or Ars Vetus in music for which he had greater respect and admiration than the new music of his own day. There is also attributed to Philippe de Vitry a treatise entitled *Ars nova*, for which there is only a fragmentary set of sources, that deals with an Ars Vetus before introducing the innovations of the Ars Nova. The theoretical principles of the Ars Vetus in this treatise deal largely with such matters as solfège, intervals, and the monochord.

What is now designated Ars Antiqua has come to include (1) the sacred, Latin-texted repertory of organa, clausulae, conductus, and motets of the Notre-Dame School, which may be dated from ca. 1160 to 1250; (2) indigenous English polyphony, which has Latin and some French texts, extending from the earliest Worcester Fragments to about the middle of the 14th century, when the impact of the continental Ars Nova becomes apparent in extant insular sources; (3) the large and predominately vernacular motet collections of the second half of the 13th century, such as those in the Montpellier and Bamberg codices; and (4) theoretical writings about temporally measured music (*musica mensurabilis*) that do not include notational principles and innovations described in the treatise entitled *Ars nova*.

Sandra Pinegar

[See also: ARS NOVA; MUSIC THEORY; NOTRE-DAME SCHOOL; PHILIPPE DE VITRY]

Anderson, Gordon A. "Ars antiqua." In *The New Grove Dictionary of Music and Musicians*, ed. Stanley Sadie. London: Macmillan, 1980, Vol. 1, pp. 638–39.

Besseler, Heinrich. "Ars antiqua." In *Die Musik in Geschichte und Gegenwart*. Kassel: Bärenreiter, 1949–86, Vol. 1, pp. 679–97.

Gallo, F. Alberto. *Music of the Middle Ages II*, trans. Karen Eales. Cambridge: Cambridge University Press, 1985.

ARS NOVA. A term taken from notational theory of the early 14th century to describe the musical style of the 14th century in France. The period after the death of Machaut is now more frequently labeled Ars Subtilior.

Some sources attach the name Ars Nova to a music-theory treatise apparently dependent on the teachings of Philippe de Vitry. The term seems further justified by the elderly Jacques de Liège, who unfavorably contrasts works of a new generation of composers, representatives of the Ars Nova, with works of the old school (what we call the Ars Antiqua) in Book 7 of his *Speculum musicae* of 1325. Finally, a letter of Pope John XXII (1324–25) proscribes the application of certain musical techniques, some of which are recognizably characteristic of the Ars Nova, to church music.

The "new art" (more properly "new technique") originally concerned the notation of rhythm. Building upon the foundation of Franco of Cologne's notational theory (ca. 1280), Jehan des Murs—the role of Philippe de Vitry is unclear—took Franco's principles of imperfection (in triple meter, subtracting a third part of a note) and alteration (in triple meter, doubling the value of a note to fill two beats of a three-beat unit) and systematically applied them to both longer and shorter note values, thereby vastly increasing the repertory of rhythmic durations available to the composer. A new note shape, the minim, was introduced for the short values. The full admission of duple ("imperfect") divisions alongside the old triple ("perfect") divisions is a principal characteristic of Ars Nova notational theory, and the system provides for the notation of works in our modern time signatures of 9/8, 6/8, 3/4, and 2/4. Finally, by means of notes written in red instead of black ink, provision was made for changing between perfect and imperfect time within a work, although composers did not fully exploit ramifications of this innovation until the late 14th-century Ars Subtilior.

The first practical source of Ars Nova music is a beautifully illuminated manuscript of the *Livres de Fauvel* (B.N. fr. 146; ca. 1318). Alongside musical insertions of Ars Antiqua motets and conductus are isorhythmic motets of the early Ars Nova. Although no works are attributed in the manuscript, some are probably by Philippe de Vitry. The isorhythmic motet provided the perfect expression for Ars Nova notational developments, exploiting a wide range of durational values in rigorously logical musical works laid out hierarchically with very slow note values in the tenor and fast note values in the motetus and triplum.

Besides the isorhythmic motet genre, the Ars Nova also contributed innovations in the chanson genres. The manuscript of the *Roman de Fauvel* contains a fascicle of chansons in dance forms by Jehannot de Lescurel (d. 1304?). These works, including one three-voice and thirty-one monophonic chansons, are noticeably more florid and rhythmically varied than comparable works of the 13th century (e.g., the rondeaux of Adam de la Halle). Jehannot's cultivation of dance lyrics set to advanced rhythms announced a shift of emphasis in the secular song. All that remained after further consolidation of the poetry of the dance lyrics as the fixed forms—ballade, rondeau, and virelai—was the musical addition of an untexted accompanying voice, a step probably taken ca. 1340 by Guillaume de Machaut.

Around 1350, with the mature polyphonic fixed-form chansons of such composers as Machaut and Pierre des Molins, the mature isorhythmic motets of Philippe de Vitry, Machaut, and others, and the authoritative summa of the notational system found in the *Libellus cantus mensurabilis* of Jehan des Murs, the Ars Nova entered its high phase. In the course of the 1370s, 1380s, and 1390s, developments in the notation of extremely complex rhythms preoccupied composers particularly in the south, at the courts of Gaston Phoebus at Béarn, the popes at Avignon, and John I of Aragon. This phase is now most often called the Ars Subtilior.

Lawrence Earp

[See also: ARS ANTIQUA; ARS SUBTILIOR; *FAUVEL, ROMAN DE; FORMES FIXES*; ISORHYTHMIC MOTET; MACHAUT, GUILLAUME DE; MUSIC THEORY; PHILIPPE DE VITRY]

Fuller, Sarah. "A Phantom Treatise of the Fourteenth Century? The *Ars nova.*"*Journal of Musicology* 4 (1985–86): 23–50.

Huglo, Michel. "De Francon de Cologne à Jacques de Liège." *Revue belge de musicologie* 34–35 (1980–81): 44–60.

Leech-Wilkinson, Daniel. "Ars Antiqua—Ars Nova—Ars Subtilior." In *Antiquity and the Middle Ages: From Ancient Greece to the 15th Century*, ed. James McKinnon. Englewood Cliffs: Prentice-Hall, 1990, pp. 218–40.

Le Roman de Fauvel in the Edition of Mesire Chaillou de Pesstain: A Reproduction in Facsimile of the Complete Manuscript Paris, Bibliothèque Nationale, Fonds Français 146. Introduction by Edward H. Roesner, François Avril, and Nancy Freeman Regalado. New York: Broude, 1990.

ARS SUBTILIOR. A term coined by Ursula Günther to distinguish the style of French music cultivated approximately during the time of the papal Schism (1378–1417) from the earlier Ars Nova. As with Ars Nova, the name derives from treatises on musical notation. Most Ars Subtilior works were written in the south of France, at the court of Aragon, or in northern Italy. The musical style, seen in fixed-form chansons as well as in motets, is characterized primarily by extreme rhythmic complexity, including frequent changes of meters, conflicting meters in different voices, complex proportional relationships, and "displacement syncopation," in which a prevailing meter (e.g., 6/8 in modern transcription) is displaced by one or two eighth notes for a lengthy passage. The music requires a vast assortment of notational symbols, including red notation, note heads with odd hooks and tails, and complex time signatures. Composers who cultivated this style include Matheus de Sancto Johanne, Solage, Cuvelier, Jacob de Senleches, Johannes Ciconia, and the Italians Mateo da Perugia and Philippus de Caserta.

Lawrence Earp

[See also: ARS NOVA; CICONIA, JOHANNES; COMPOSERS, MINOR (14TH CENTURY); *FORMES FIXES*; ISORHYTHMIC MOTET; JACOB DE SENLECHES; MATHEUS DE SANCTO JOHANNE]

Günther, Ursula. "Das Ende der *ars nova.*" *Die Musikforschung* 16 (1963): 105–21.

Strohm, Reinhard. *The Rise of European Music 1380–1500.* Cambridge: Cambridge University Press, 1993.

ARTEVELDE. A politically important family of 14th-century Ghent. A legendary figure in Flemish history, Jacques van Artevelde (ca. 1290–1345) became extraordinary captain of Ghent in 1338, at the outbreak of the Hundred Years' War. Ghent and Flanders were caught between the demands of the French kings, feudal overlords of the Flemish counts, and the dependence of the Flemish cities on English wool for their cloth industries. Van Artevelde was a wealthy broker and dealer in foodstuffs, perhaps with ties to the brewers' guild. Under his captaincy, Ghent dominated the other cities of Flanders and the countryside, and he attempted to control Count Louis of Nevers, who managed to escape to France. Jacques van Artevelde led Flanders into an open English alliance, but a truce in 1340, renewed in 1342, contributed to a lessening of tensions in Flanders and deprived him of the justification for his extraordinary magistracy. Van Artevelde had come to power with the assistance of the weavers' guild, the largest occupational group in Ghent, but he associated all groups in a unity regime: the "small guilds," whose members worked for a local market, the aristocratic landowners, and the weavers' often bitter rivals, the fullers. He is for this reason often portrayed as a democratic reformer; in fact, he became dictator in Ghent, where he maintained his position only by violence and an enormous bodyguard. He ferociously suppressed rebellions against his authority in the smaller Flemish towns and became a personal friend of King Edward III of England. In 1344–45, he supported weaver regimes throughout Flanders in denying a wage increase to the less affluent fullers. He survived a coup attempt in early 1343 but was deprived of his captaincy in the spring of 1345. Personal rivals, including the dean of the weavers' guild, used the rumor that he wanted to recognize the Prince of Wales as count of Flanders as a pretext for assassinating him on July 17, 1345.

The youngest son of Jacques van Artevelde, Philippe (1340–1382), had an obscure early career in which he played no political role. He became confiscation commissioner of Ghent in December 1381, when a rebellion against Count Louis II (de Male) had already been in progress for more than two years. He became captain, the office that his father had held, on January 24, 1382, as the count was on the verge of starving Ghent into submission. Philippe's power was based more exclusively than his father's had been on the support of the weavers, and he seems to have objected in principle to French influence in Flanders. After using his first month in power to exterminate personal rivals, notably the eldest sons of men involved in the plot to assassinate his father, Philippe began negotiating for an English alliance, then captured Bruges in a surprise attack on May 3 and forced Count Louis II, who had been in that city, to flee to France. Although he controlled Flanders and styled himself "regent" from that point, the English help never materialized. The forces of Louis II, his son-in-law and eventual successor, Philip the Bold, duke of Burgundy, and King Charles VI of France invaded Flanders and crushed the Flemings on November 27, 1382, at the Battle of Roosebeke, where van Artevelde lost his life.

David M. Nicholas

[See also: FLANDERS]

Nicholas, David. *The van Arteveldes of Ghent: The Varieties of Vendetta and the Hero in History.* Ithaca: Cornell University Press, 1988.

Carson, Patricia. *James van Artevelde: The Man from Ghent.* Ghent: Story, 1980.

van Werveke, Hans. *Jacques van Artevelde.* Brussels: Renaissance du Livre, 1942.

ARTHUR. Legendary Dark Age king of Britain, Arthur of Avalon was a major inspiration to French vernacular writers from the 12th through the 14th century. Recent research indicates there may have been a late 5th- or early 6th-century warlord around whom popular legends amalgamated, but if such a man did exist he was neither a king nor named Arthur. Given a historical cachet by the Latin fictions of Geoffrey of Monmouth's *Historia regum Britanniae* (ca. 1136), which was translated into French by Wace in 1155, Arthur appears first in romance in the works of Chrétien de Troyes (ca. 1165–90). The power of Chrétien's imaginary constructs, particularly the Lancelot-Guenevere love story and the Grail quest, inspired countless imitators and continuators. Arthur was counted as one of the Nine Worthies during the Middle Ages.

William W. Kibler

[See also: ARTHURIAN COMPILATIONS; ARTHURIAN VERSE ROMANCE; *CHEVALIER AU PAPEGAUT*; CHRÉTIEN DE TROYES; GAWAIN ROMANCES; GEFFREI GAIMAR; GIRART D'AMIENS; GRAIL AND GRAIL ROMANCES; *PERCEFOREST*; *PERCEVAL CONTINUATIONS*; POST-VULGATE ROMANCE; *PROSE TRISTAN*; RAOUL DE HOUDENC; TRISTAN ROMANCES; VULGATE CYCLE; WACE]

Lacy, Norris J., et al., eds. *The New Arthurian Encyclopedia.* New York: Garland, 1991.

ARTHURIAN COMPILATIONS. A number of authors, beginning in the late 13th century, compiled lengthy bodies of French Arthurian material, drawn from earlier sources and often assembled with little concern for coherent organization. The *Roman de Roi Artus* of Rusticiano da Pisa, an Italian writing in French during the late 1270s or the 1280s, includes the entire romance of *Palamedes* as well as numerous adventures of Branor le Brun, Tristan, Lancelot, and other knights. A century later (ca. 1391), Jehan le Vaillant de Poitiers produced a vast work consisting of a *Brut* followed by miscellaneous stories about Arthurian characters. Around 1470, Michot (or Michel) Gonnot drew material from the *Prose Tristan*, the Vulgate Cycle, and other romances of the preceding century to assemble his compilation. The dimensions of these works were prodigious, so much so that during the 16th century Rusticiano's was divided and published as two distinct romances, *Guiron le Courtois* and *Meliadus*.

Norris J. Lacy

[See also: *PROPHÉCIES DE MERLIN*; PROSE ROMANCE]

Pickford, Cedric E. "Miscellaneous French Prose Romances." In *Arthurian Literature of the Middle Ages: A Collaborative History*, ed. Roger Sherman Loomis. Oxford: Clarendon, 1959, pp. 348–57.

ARTHURIAN VERSE ROMANCE. The history of Arthurian romance from the end of the 12th century through most of the 13th is dominated by Chrétien de Troyes. When Chrétien died, probably in the 1180s, he left behind four complete romances of about 6,000 lines each (*Erec et Enide, Cligés, Lancelot,* and *Yvain*), and a fifth, unfinished at 9,234 lines (*Perceval*). The renown of these poems was unparalleled in French literature, their popularity being attested by reference, allusion, quotation, translation, and adaptation. Verse romance after Chrétien may be seen as a response or reaction to the works of the master.

The two or three decades following Chrétien's death are peculiarly wanting in Arthurian verse romance. This may be historical accident, of course, in that little has survived, but it does look as if authors at the end of the 12th and very beginning of the 13th century had difficulty coping with the overwhelming reputation of Chrétien. Only Renaut de Beaujeu's *Bel Inconnu* and a number of shorter poems can be assigned with any probability to this period. Renaut's full-length romance is at once clearly different from Chrétien's and yet owes a good deal to him. Two short so-called lais, *Cor* and *Mantel*, not actual *lais bretons* as written by Marie de France, are variations on a chastity-test theme in which many of the ladies of Arthur's court prove to have been unfaithful to their partners. The poems are humorous and border occasionally on the obscene, perhaps surprising for such early texts. Two anonymous *lais bretons*, *Tyolet* and *Melion*, are Arthurian in their setting rather than in their essence, although *Tyolet* is quite clearly derived from Chrétien's *Perceval*. The Gawain romances, *Mule sans frein* and *Chevalier à l'épée* also date from ca. 1200. Finally, the first two continuations of Chrétien's *Perceval* may have been composed in their first versions about the turn of the century.

The 13th century saw the composition of *Meraugis de Portlesguez* by Raoul de Houdenc, *Gliglois, Durmart le Gallois, Yder* (all probably before 1220), the Occitan *Jaufre* (ca. 1230), *Fergus* by Guillaume le Clerc, the *Chevalier aux deux épées* or *Meriadeuc* (before 1250), *Floriant et Florete,* the *Merveilles de Rigomer* (before 1268), *Claris et Laris,* and *Escanor* by Girart d'Amiens (before 1282). These poems have many features in common with the Gawain romances. The only Arthurian verse romance written in the 14th century is Froissart's *Méliador*, which can better be seen as an anachronism than the last example of the genre.

Raoul de Houdenc's *Meraugis de Portlesguez*, of 5,938 lines, is notable for its discussion of courtly virtues articulated through the rivalry of two friends, Meraugis and Gorvain Cadrut, for the love of Lidoine. Raoul, perhaps the most talented of those writing in Chrétien's wake, is one of the first to accept the challenge laid down by

Chrétien. For Raoul, the decision to write an Arthurian romance meant acknowledging a debt to the master while realizing the necessity to do something different. Raoul's Arthurian romance is playful, the humor ranging from light burlesque to broad farce.

Gliglois is a romance of 2,942 lines concerned with the rivalry of Gawain and his squire, Gliglois, for the love of the aptly named Beauté. Gawain relies on his reputation, assuming that this will be sufficient to win him the lady; Gliglois, on the other hand, serves her patiently and eventually wins her love. *Gliglois* is unusual in that it is a "realistic" poem without any fantastic or supernatural events and none of the usual adventures of Arthurian romance. It is also, by virtue of Gliglois's success and Gawain's failure, an exceptionally "meritocratic" romance.

The influence of Chrétien de Troyes is strangely lacking in *Gliglois*. The same cannot be said of the 16,000-line *Durmart le Gallois*, whose author is heavily indebted to *Erec et Enide*, *Yvain*, and *Cligés* in particular. Much of the narrative of *Durmart* is based on Durmart's quest for the love of the Queen of Ireland, whom he has never seen but of whose extraordinary beauty he has heard tell. The scene in which Durmart wins a sparrowhawk for her makes conscious use of the famous episode in *Erec et Enide*. After many adventures, Durmart marries the queen, founds an abbey, and frees Rome from the pagans. Unusual are the Irish setting and the general lack of humor and burlesque (save perhaps the sight of King Nogant fleeing from Durmart on a camel).

The very beginning of *Yder* is missing. The extant 6,769 lines relate how the illegitimate Yder attempts to win the love of Queen Guenloie. This he eventually does, marries her, and then brings about the wedding of his father and mother, thus legitimizing his own birth. *Yder* is remarkable for its unflattering portrayal of the Arthurian court: there are hints of an amorous relationship between Yder and Guenevere, and Arthur and Kay are positively obnoxious characters rather than the ineffective king and caustic seneschal found elsewhere. In other respects, particularly in its preservation of the Yder-Guenevere story, *Yder* is archaic and shows evidence of otherwise lost traditions.

Fergus, by Guillaume le Clerc, is a romance of 7,012 lines set in Scotland, which may well have been written between 1237 and 1241 for the Balliol family as an ancestral romance in support of territorial claims. Political associations apart, this romance again shows the pervasive presence of Chrétien, and Fergus has even been called a "new Perceval." Certainly, *Perceval*, *Yvain*, and *Erec et Enide* provided Guillaume with material for much of the poem, which is centered on the love of Fergus and Galiene. *Fergus* is an excellent postclassical romance, full of humor and told in a lively manner.

The hero of the *Chevalier aux deux épées* is Meriadeuc, from whom the romance takes its alternative title. This poem of 12,352 lines has a complex plot, the main part of which concerns the love of Meriadeuc for Lore of Caradigan and Meriadeuc's search for his own identity. Meriadeuc's father had been unwittingly slain by Gawain, who is eventually reconciled with the hero. Meriadeuc marries Lore, and Gawain consummates his love for a girl he had cham-

pioned earlier. The *Chevalier aux deux épées* is typical of romances of the period and of the compositional techniques of romance in general, reworking episodes and motifs found elsewhere into a tightly knit and satisfying whole.

Floriant et Florete (8,278 lines) is one of the rare later romances that reverts to the marriage-crisis-resolution structure found in Chrétien's *Erec* and *Yvain*. Floriant, posthumous son of a king of Sicily, is abducted by Morgan the Fay, educated, and sent to Arthur's court. After defending his mother against the Emperor of Constantinople, Floriant marries Florete; like Erec, Floriant takes his wife with him to prove his prowess after he has been accused of *recreantise*. The end of the romance is lacking. It is evident that the basic central structure of *Floriant et Florete* is that of *Erec et Enide*, and indeed there are many verbal echoes from this and Chrétien's other romances. The use of material provided by Chrétien, in *Floriant et Florete* and elsewhere, ranges from the use of motifs and entire narrative segments down to verbatim quotation.

The *Merveilles de Rigomer*, by an author known simply as Jehan, is an incomplete romance of 17,271 lines and has often been regarded as a degenerate example of the last stages of Arthurian verse romance. However, seen in the light of its relationship to Chrétien and the prose romances, it can better be regarded as an example of the creative reception of existing models. It has a double plot, the first involving Gawain's quest to free the imprisoned Lancelot, and the second, Arthur's restoration of her inheritance to the heiress of Quintefuele. One of the most remarkable features of the *Merveilles de Rigomer* is its bestiary of fantastic creatures, such as talking birds, flame-breathing panthers, and a man-eating falcon. Its treatment of the Arthurian material is burlesque and often outrageous.

The most distinctive feature of both *Claris et Laris* and *Escanor* is perhaps their complex narrative structure, based on a series of multiple quests. Although these two lengthy romances (30,369 and 25,936 lines, respectively) have long been regarded, like the *Merveilles de Rigomer*, as degenerate and rambling, their qualities can be seen in a different light when the influence of the prose romances is taken into account. Since they make extensive use of narrative techniques and characters from the prose tradition, they can in many respects be regarded as prose romances in verse.

Recent study of these romances stresses their "epigonal" relationship to Chrétien's *œuvre* with particular reference to audience reaction. Authors make such frequent and subtle use of Chrétien's works that it must be assumed that audiences were aware of this and listened to the romances against the background of Chrétien. There were many ways for Arthurian authors to respond to the phenomenon of Chrétien: they could attempt, although they rarely did, to do blatantly otherwise than he had done; they could attempt various degrees of burlesque and parody; they could write severely didactic works using Arthurian material as sugar for the pill. The Chrétien epigones usually deal less with the fundamentals of human existence than did Chrétien, and their productions are frequently lighthearted and self-consciously literary. It has recently been argued that many of these romances were written directly, but not exclusively, for the Anglo-Angevin court and that they had a strong political function, strengthening dynastic and territorial claims on both national and regional levels. If this is true, then part of their audience must be sought in England and they need to be placed at least partly in a British historical and cultural context. Whatever the case, they are finally beginning to attract the attention they deserve from scholars, and the yoke of the odious comparison with Chrétien is at last slowly being cast off.

Keith Busby

[See also: CHRÉTIEN DE TROYES; GAWAIN ROMANCES; GIRART D'AMIENS; GUILLAUME LE CLERC; *JAUFRE*; RAOUL DE HOUDENC; RENAUT DE BEAUJEU; ROMANCE]

Adams, Alison, ed. *Yder*. Cambridge: Boydell and Brewer, 1983.

Alton, Johann, ed. *Li romans de Claris et Laris*. Tübingen: Bibliothek des litterarischen Vereins in Stuttgart, 1884.

Bennett, Philip, ed. *Mantel et Cor: deux lais du 12e siècle*. Exeter: University of Exeter, 1975.

Foerster, Wendelin, ed. *Li chevaliers as deux espees*. Halle: Niemeyer, 1877.

———, ed. *Les merveilles de Rigomer*. 2 vols. Dresden: Gesellschaft für romanische Literatur, 1908–15.

Gildea, Joseph, ed. *Durmart le Gallois*. 2 vols. Villanova: Villanova University Press, 1965–66.

Girart d'Amiens, ed. *Der roman von Escanor von Gerard von Amiens,* ed. Henri Michelant. Tübingen: Bibliothek des litterarischen Vereins in Stuttgart, 1886.

Guillaume le Clerc. *Fergus*, ed. Wilson Frescoln. Philadelphia: Allen, 1983.

Livingston, Charles H., ed. *Gliglois*. Cambridge: Harvard University Press, 1932.

Tobin, Prudence Mary O'Hara, ed. *Tyolet and Melion*. In *Les lais anonymes des XIIe et XIIIe siècles*. Geneva: Droz, 1976.

Williams, Harry F., ed. *Floriant et Florete*. Ann Arbor: University of Michigan Press, 1947.

Busby, Keith. *Gauvain in Old French Literature*. Amsterdam: Rodopi, 1980.

Lacy, Norris J., Douglas Kelly, and Keith Busby, eds. *The Legacy of Chrétien de Troyes*. 2 vols. Amsterdam: Rodopi, 1988–89.

Schmolke-Hasselmann, Beate. *Der arthurische Versroman von Chrestien bis Froissart*. Tübingen: Niemeyer, 1980.

ARTILLERY. Playing a major role in medieval warfare, artillery evolved parallel to the art of fortification. Although Roger Bacon introduced gunpowder to the West ca. 1260 and the English used cannon at Crécy in 1346, it took a further century of experimentation before cannon supplanted *trébuchet* (i.e., tension) artillery. Improvement of explosives, projectiles, and guns was impeded by the difficulties in obtaining adequate amounts of matériel and equipment. But by 1400 cannon had come into regular use, and the final campaigns of the Hundred Years' War made their superiority unmistakable. Either protecting sappers or breaching walls themselves, they became an indispensable tool in sieges. In response, defense tactics and military architecture changed rapidly after 1450. Governments were compelled to modernize fortifications, and every town was driven to acquire artillery for its own defense.

Following French use of artillery at Formigny (1450) and Castillon (1453), where cannon were shown to be useful on the field as well as in siege warfare, the Valois monarchy led the way in the perfection of technology, in the development of an institutional infrastructure, and in the exploitation of the full potential of the new arms. Gaspard Bureau, *maître de l'artillerie* for Charles VII, formed a permanent force of cannoniers that grew steadily thereafter. Limited range, inadequate rates of fire, and immobility limited reliance on artillery for the remainder of the 15th century, and cannon remained auxiliary to cavalry and infantry in the army of Louis XI. Only the triumphs of Charles VIII, who made dramatic use of artillery in Brittany and in the Italian campaign of 1494, removed all doubt that only armies with adequate artillery could hope to prevail in modern warfare.

Paul D. Solon

[See also: ARMOR AND WEAPONS; RECONQUEST OF FRANCE; WARFARE]

Contamine, Philippe. *Guerre, état et société à la fin du moyen âge: études sur les armées des rois de France 1337–1494*. Paris: Mouton, 1972, p. 757.

———. *War in the Middle Ages*, trans. Michael Jones. London: Blackwell, 1984.

De Lombars, Michel. *Histoire de l'artillerie française*. Paris: Charles-Lavanzelle, 1984.

Patrick, John Merton. *Artillery and Warfare During the Thirteenth and Fourteenth Centuries*. Logan: Utah State University Press, 1961.

Vale, Malcolm G.A. *War and Chivalry*. Athens: University of Georgia Press, 1981.

ARTOIS. Named after the ancient Gallic tribe of the Atrebates, the important cloth-producing region of northern France known as Artois belonged to the counts of Flanders for much of the Middle Ages but became the dowry of Isabelle de Hainaut when she married Philip II in 1180. Her son, Louis VIII, inherited Artois but arranged for it to pass after his death to Robert, the oldest of his cadet sons as one of the earliest apanages.

Robert I of Artois accompanied his brother Louis IX on crusade and died in Egypt in 1250. His son, Robert II, also met a violent end, at the Battle of Courtrai in 1302, and succession to the county was disputed between his daughter Mahaut, countess of Burgundy, and Robert III (1287–1342), the child of Robert II's only son. Philip IV decided for Mahaut (d. 1329), but intermittent strife continued for a generation. Of the next four kings, the only one to favor Mahaut was Philip V, who had married her daughter Jeanne (d. 1330). Their two daughters, Jeanne and Marguerite, were married, respectively, to Eudes IV, duke of Burgundy, and Louis I, count of Flanders. These two important princes thus acquired a vested interest in the succession of Mahaut's descendants, creating an awkward situation for Charles IV and Philip VI, two kings who were close friends of Robert III.

Feeling certain of royal support, Robert demanded his inheritance from Philip VI after the death of his cousin Jeanne in 1330, but the opposition of Burgundy and Flanders led the king to rule against him, whereupon Robert turned rebel and recognized Edward III of England as king of France. The two daughters of Philip V succeeded in turn as countess of Artois. Marguerite, by then dowager countess of Flanders, died in 1382, followed two years later by her son Louis II of Flanders. Artois was one of several important lands inherited by the heiress of Flanders, Marguerite (d. 1405), wife of Philip the Bold, duke of Burgundy. For a century, Artois was part of the Burgundian state. Louis XI was able to occupy the county in 1482, but in the crown's ensuing struggles with the Habsburgs, who had inherited the Burgundian Netherlands, the latter regained Artois and held it until the 17th century.

John Bell Henneman, Jr.

[See also: ARRAS; BURGUNDY; FLANDERS]

Cazelles, Raymond. *La société politique et la crise de la royauté sous Philippe de Valois*. Paris: Argences, 1958.

Hirschauer, Charles. *Les états d'Artois de leurs origines à l'occupation française, 1340–1640*. Paris: Champion, 1923.

Lestocquoy, Jean. *Histoire de la Flandre et de l'Artois*. Paris: Presses Universitaires de France, 1949.

Wood, Charles T. *The French Apanages and the Capetian Monarchy, 1224–1328*. Cambridge: Harvard University Press, 1966.

ARTS DE SECONDE RHÉTORIQUE. The term *seconde rhétorique* is used in several 15th-century French poetic treatises in three senses: to mean verse as opposed to the *première rhétorique* of prose, vernacular rhetoric rather than Latin, and poetry written by the laity rather than by *clercs*. The first such treatise, *L'art de dictier*, was written by Eustache Deschamps in 1392, although the *Prologue* written by Guillaume de Machaut in the 1370s to introduce his complete works perhaps has a competing claim as the first vernacular treatise on the art of poetry. The other *Arts* include Jacques Legrand's *Des rimes* (1405), *Les règles de la seconde rhétorique* (1411–32), Baudet Harenc's *Le doctrinal de la seconde rhétorique* (1432), *Traité de l'art de rhétorique* (1450?), Jean Molinet's *L'art de rhétorique* (1493), *Traité de rhétorique* (1495–1500), and *L'art et science de rhétorique vulgaire* (1524–25). Most of these survive in only a single manuscript, but there are signs of borrowing or of a common model among several. Five authors refer to the *puys d'amour*, which makes it likely that their treatises represent rules of versification drawn up for the judges and competitors in those contests. Others, including Deschamps, Legrand, and Molinet, claim to be writing at the request of aristocratic or even royal patrons, presumably in order to teach them the practical skills of lyric poetry. The works come mainly from northern France, but also from Chalon-sur-Saône and Lorraine.

The majority of the treatises are simply manuals of lyric versification. Their structure typically consists of a short introduction followed by a description, with examples, of a range of rhyme schemes and poetic forms. Five also contain rhyming and spelling lists and, in one case, glossaries of proper nouns and obscure vocabulary. The examples they cite include poems by Machaut, Froissart, and Deschamps, as well as poems from the *puys*. The anonymous 1450 *Traité* also appends a separate collection of lyrics. Molinet's *L'art de rhétorique* is the best organized; the 1524–25 treatise copies it closely, and there are further correspondences with Deschamps, the 1450 treatise, and Baudet Harenc. The anonymous 1411–32 treatise presents an interesting history of vernacular poetic masters from Guillaume de Lorris to Froissart and Deschamps.

Few of the treatises offer any kind of poetic philosophy. In fact, most distinguish their humbler purposes (versification) from instruction in poetry. The case is different for Machaut and Deschamps. Machaut claims the agency of "Sens," "Rhétorique," and "Musique" in his powers of composition, giving pride of place to Music. Deschamps similarly emphasizes music, placing poetry under the category of *musique naturelle*, as opposed to *musique artificielle*, or art music. This has been taken by some scholars to signal a radical departure from traditional medieval views of the relation between music and poetry. Others, however, argue that there is no contradiction between Deschamps and Jean de Garlande's description of rhythm as a species of music and Jean Molinet's equation of rhythm and *rhétorique vulgaire*. According to such a view, Deschamps exalts poetry by appealing to its traditional relation to music, not by denying that relation.

Ardis T.B. Butterfield

[See also: DESCHAMPS, EUSTACHE; GRANDS RHÉTORIQUEURS; HERENC, BAUDET; JEAN DE GARLANDE; MACHAUT, GUILLAUME DE; MOLINET, JEAN; VERSIFICATION]

Dragonetti, Roger. "'La poésie . . . ceste musique naturele': essai d'exégèse d'un passage de *L'Art de dictier* d'Eustache Deschamps." In *Fin du moyen âge et renaissance: mélanges de philologie française offerts à Robert Guiette*. Antwerp: De Nederlandsche Boekhandel, 1961, pp. 49–64.

Langlois, Ernest, ed. *Recueil d'arts de seconde rhétorique*. Paris: Imprimerie Nationale, 1902.

Stevens, John. "The 'Music' of the Lyric: Machaut, Deschamps, Chaucer." In *Medieval and Pseudo-Medieval Literature: The J. A.W. Bennett Memorial Lectures (Perugia, 1982–1983)*, ed. Piero Boitani and Anna Torti. Cambridge: Brewer; Tübingen: Narr, 1984, pp. 109–29.

Zumthor, Paul. *Le masque et la lumière: la poétique des grands rhétoriqueurs*. Paris: Seuil, 1978.

ASPREMONT. A late 12th-century chanson de geste of some 11,000 decasyllabic rhyming lines, *Aspremont* is preserved in multiple manuscripts, a number of which were copied in England and Italy. In Italy, the poem gave rise to Franco-Italian adaptations and the *Cantari d'Aspramonte* and Andrea da Barberino's *Aspramonte* in prose; through its Anglo-Norman connection, the story appears in Denmark, Norway, and Iceland.

The epic treats Charlemagne's defense of southern Italy from a Saracen invasion. Charles is aided by the rebel baron Girart de Fraite, who proves his loyalty when Christendom is in danger, and young Roland, who performs his first acts of prowess.

Aspremont is important for the splendor of its traditional, rhetorical style in celebration of heroism and for its "correction" of the *Chanson de Roland*, its notion of a more perfect Christian universe, one without pride or division, supposed to have existed prior to the events of Roncevaux, when Roland was young and Charlemagne in his prime.

William C. Calin

Brandin, Louis, ed. *La chanson d'Aspremont, chanson de geste du XIIe siècle*. 2 vols. Paris: Champion, 1919–21.

Newth, Michael A., trans. *The Song of Aspremont (La chanson d'Aspremont)*. New York: Garland, 1989.

Calin, William. "Problèmes littéraires soulevés par les chansons de geste: l'exemple d'*Aspremont*." In *Au carrefour des routes d'Europe: la chanson de geste*. 2 vols. Aix-en-Provence: CUER MA, 1987, Vol. 1, pp. 333–50.

Mandach, André de. *Naissance et développement de la chanson de geste en Europe*. Geneva: Droz, 1975–80, Vols. 3–4: *Chanson d'Aspremont*.

Van Waard, Roelof. *Études sur l'origine et la formation de la Chanson d'Aspremont*. Groningen: Walters, 1937.

ASSEMBLIES. Historians of political institutions have long been attracted to medieval assemblies, studying them for evidence of the origins of modern parliamentary bodies. Assemblies convened by princes were special gatherings, generally much larger than the small group of advisers that met frequently to conduct regular business, yet both might be called "court" or "council."

Scholars have tended to treat assemblies as precursors of, or substitutes for, Estates or parliamentary bodies. They have made distinctions between parliaments and preparliaments, between consultative and deliberative bodies, between counsel and consent. They have argued over whether assemblies were judicial, legislative, or financial in function, whether they were representative or not, whether they were imposed on rulers or exploited by them. This entire scholarly enterprise has carried with it much ideological baggage, and the character of the inquiry has varied greatly from nation to nation. Assemblies have especially interested historians of law and politics, who have generally emphasized their function or purpose in some legal/constitutional context.

The assemblies held in medieval France were in fact so varied as to defy simple classification. With roots that lay deep in the culture of the past, they often convened for purposes that had no obvious connection with the modern constitutional model. Over time, some of them evolved their own traditions and acquired unforeseen functions that might or might not have implications for future political institutions.

Perhaps the earliest type of assembly was the convocation of military followers, originally a tribal war band. Great military convocations were common under the Carolingians. As ethnic distinctions blurred and royal authority became fragmented, the meetings of the 10th and 11th centuries generally were assemblies of a land or region, concerned with maintaining the fragile peace. Being concerned with maintaining or restoring order, they retained a military character but also began to exercise functions that we would describe as judicial. Both the early tribal assemblies and the later peace assemblies were occasions that might involve hard negotiating to resolve conflicts among competing interests, but such discussions took place behind the scenes and the plenary assemblies themselves were rituals of consensus. When held under the auspices of a king or great territorial lord, they were celebrations of the ruler's majesty.

Although extraordinary and ceremonial occasions, regional assemblies that dealt with problems of a recurring nature gradually showed signs of customary procedures and institutional evolution. Those "courts" concerned with maintaining order in the south were the first assemblies in France (12th and 13th centuries) to include urban representatives.

Because the power of kings and lords long required an element of public visibility, these rulers, who were constantly on the move, continued to use assemblies of various kinds to affirm loyalty and acknowledge their power. In northern France, festival courts reinforced a royalist culture of chivalry. But as the royal government grew larger in the 13th century, it became more costly and created more political strains. As it became more difficult to celebrate a consensus and exclude partisanship, the crown made less use of assemblies for several generations. Contentious matters increasingly came before the standing body of judicial experts that became the Parlement de Paris. When Philip IV turned again to large assemblies after 1300, they served their traditional purpose of celebrating royal power and majesty, presenting a consensus in the face of his adversaries, initially Pope Boniface VIII. Philip and his sons, however, soon experimented with other uses for assemblies, although always trying to maintain control of the proceedings and use them to reinforce royal authority.

These assemblies of the 14th century now generally included the elected representatives of towns, and they began to be organized as Estates. Those who attended them were not always content with the rhetoric of consensus. Purely ceremonial assemblies did not cease to occur, but the most conspicuous gatherings of the late Middle Ages were those like the Estates, concerned with money and political policy, or the Parlement, concerned with judicial matters. When judicial questions merged with political debate, or when a ceremonial expression of royal power was called for, the kings generally preferred to use the Parlement as their forum.

John Bell Henneman, Jr.

[See also: *CONSEIL*; ESTATES (GENERAL); ESTATES (PROVINCIAL); PARLEMENT DE PARIS; PEACE OF GOD]

Bisson, Thomas N. "Celebration and Persuasion: Reflections on the Cultural Evolution of Medieval Consultation." *Legislative Studies Quarterly* 7 (1982): 181–204.

Henneman, John Bell. "Representative Assemblies and the Historians." *Legislative Studies Quarterly* 7 (1982): 161–76.

ASTRONOMICAL AND NAVIGATIONAL INSTRUMENTS. The Middle Ages have left a variety of instruments intended to measure celestial phenomena. Most were based on Hellenistic predecessors, but some were invented or developed during the medieval period. Arabic scholars served as the principal means of transmitting knowledge of these instruments and their design principles to the West.

To tell time by celestial means requires at least a simple sundial, and this was frequently incorporated into the architectural detail of churches. An excellent specimen is the angel holding a sundial found on the south tower of Chartres cathedral (12th c.). Portable sundials for travelers also were fabricated.

The astrolabe was the next most common instrument. By measuring the angle above the horizon of the sun or a selected star, the astrolabe projects onto a celestial map the position of the body and thus allows the observer to read the time of day from a dial or graph. Indeed, the astrolabe dial is the ancestor of the analogue clock face. The most common subtype of astrolabe was a simplified version without the celestial map, called the mariner's astrolabe. The spread of astrolabes stimulated interest in precise astronomical tables giving the position of the sun, and sometimes other celestial bodies, for each day of the year. One of the earliest was produced at Montpellier by Robert de Montpellier in 1141.

Southern France was the source of several other astronomical instruments as well. Robertus Anglicus, writing at Montpellier ca. 1276, described a form of quadrant (*quadrans vetus*) whose ultimate origins lie in India. Shortly thereafter, a member of the scholarly Provençal family of translators Yacob ben Machir ibn Tibbon (Prophatius Judaeus; d. ca. 1304), developed the "quadrant of Israel" incorporating features from astrolabes. It later was known as the "new quadrant" (*quadrans novus*). Another Jewish scholar born in Languedoc, Levi ben Gershom, invented ca. 1342 a simplified form of measuring device, the cross-staff or Jacob's staff, later favored by mariners. Sightings from the cross-staff or the mariner's astrolabe were referred to tables like that mentioned above to determine latitude while at sea. These instruments remained in common use into the 17th century.

A novel navigational instrument appeared in the 12th century, the magnetic compass. Although there is still controversy over how the compass reached Europe, its Chinese origin is indisputable. The earliest European description comes from an English scholar resident in Paris, Alexander Neckham, writing in 1187. The earliest complete treatise on the compass was composed by the French soldier Pierre de Maricourt (Petrus Peregrinus) in 1269.

Medieval adaptations of earlier instruments include the addition of a sighting tube to the armillary sphere. Resembling a modern telescope but lacking lenses, the tube was apparently used to better orient the sphere to the north celestial pole by sighting Polaris in isolation from its surrounding stars. The earliest representation of such a device is in a manuscript by Gerbert of Aurillac (930–1003), later Pope Sylvester II. Perhaps related to the sighting tube was the nocturlabe, or nocturnal, a device with a dial and a sighting hole. One aligned pointers on the device with stars in the circumpolar constellations and read the time from a dial.

Bert S. Hall

Gunther, Robert T. *Early Science in Oxford.* 15 vols. Oxford: Clarendon, 1920–40, Vol. 2: *Astronomy* (1927).

North, J.D. "The Astrolabe." *Scientific American* 230 (1974): 96–106.

Poulle, Emmanuel. "Le quadrant nouveau médiéval." *Journal des savants* (1964): 148–67, 182–214.

———. *Les instruments astronomiques du moyen âge.* Paris: Brieux, 1983.

ASTRONOMY. *See* LIBERAL ARTS

ATHIS ET PROPHILIAS. A verse romance from the end of the 12th century by Alexandre (de Bernay?), extant in two versions of varying length. It relates the friendship of the Athenian knight Athis and the Roman Prophilias and their common love for the beautiful Cardionès.

Keith Bate

Alexandre. *Li romans d'Athis et Prophilias*, ed. Alfons Hilka. 2 vols. Halle and Dresden: Gesellschaft für romanische Literatur, 1912–16.

AUBERT, DAVID (b. before 1413, fl. 1453–79). Born into a family of prosperous, literate public servants, Aubert became a prolific calligrapher, translator, and literary adapter at the Burgundian court. Books copied by his father, Jean Aubert, and a brother of the same name are also known. In 1463, Aubert is mentioned as one of the duke of Burgundy's scribes for the first time. He is especially known for copies of *Charles Martel* (Brussels, Bibl. Roy. 6–9) and *Perceforest* (Paris, Arsenal, 3483–94), and for his compilations, the *Croniques et conquestes de Charlemaine* (Bibl. Roy. 9066–68), begun for an early sponsor, Jean V de Créquy, but completed for Philip the Good, and for a *Chronique des empereurs* (Arsenal 5089). Some twenty manuscripts are attributed to his hand. In 1469, after Philip the Good's death, he helped inventory the ducal library.

Charity Cannon Willard

[See also: *AYMERI DE NARBONNE*; *PERCEFOREST*]

Cockshaw, Pierre. "La famille du copiste David Aubert." *Scriptorium* 22 (1968): 279–87.

Delaissé, L. M. J. *La miniature flamande, le mécénat de Philippe le Bon.* Brussels: Bibliothèque Royale, Belgique, 1959.

Doutrepont, Georges. *La littérature française à la cour des ducs de Bourgogne.* Paris: Champion, 1909.

AUCASSIN ET NICOLETTE. *Chantefable* of the early 13th century. Extant in only one manuscript (B.N. fr. 2168), this anonymous work is one of the most unusual and, for modern audiences, one of the most popular of all Old French texts. It consists of twenty-one verse sections alternating with twenty in prose. It is normally dated to the first half of the 13th century, but a possible allusion in Section 24 to the *écu*, a coin minted only after 1266, would produce a later date and one that is not unsuited to the spirit of the text. The Picard dialectal features in the late 13th-century manuscript seem to reflect the original area of composition. The possible allusion in line 2 of Section 1 to an old man (*viel antif*, a disputed reading) has been seen as relating to the author of the text. Whoever he was, the latter would have been a sophisticated minstrel or more likely a cleric (cf. the distinction between "handsome clerics" and "old priests" in Section 6).

The story is one of thwarted lovers who eventually live happily ever after. Aucassin, son of the Count of Beaucaire, loves Nicolette, Saracen goddaughter of the viscount of the town. Aucassin is rightly convinced that Nicolette is of noble birth, but his parents make every effort to keep the lovers apart and finally both are imprisoned. Nicolette, who is in many ways the dominant character in the relationship, escapes, and after Aucassin's release the lovers are reunited in a bower constructed by Nicolette. Attempting to leave France by sea, they are driven by a storm to the curious land of Torelore, where Aucassin, suddenly becoming more assertive, deals roughly with the king, who is lying in childbed, and intervenes in a ritualistic war fought with a variety of soft foodstuffs. His injection of violence proves successful but unpopular. The inhabitants, who, unlike Aucassin's parents, recognize Nicolette's noble birth, want to throw him out and keep Nicolette for the king's son. The land of Torelore is then attacked by pirates, who place Nicolette and Aucassin on different ships. A storm drives Nicolette's ship to the "cité de Cartage" (normally interpreted as Cartagena in Murcia province, Spain), where she discovers that she is the long-lost daughter of the king. Aucassin's ship takes him back to Beaucaire, where he becomes count. The lovers are united and marry, once Nicolette, disguised as a jongleur, discovers Aucassin's whereabouts.

In recent years, it has frequently been maintained that the principal driving force of the text is parody, directed against contemporary literary genres, such as the epic, the romance, and the saint's life. But it is rather the comic potential of these genres that seems to be exploited, and throughout the text the author's humor is the most distinctive feature, not his attack on the works of other writers. A further dimension of the plot is the twenty-year war between the Count of Beaucaire and the Count of Valence (occasionally seen as a reflection of the Albigensian Crusade), and much of the early comedy centers on Aucassin's refusal to participate in his father's war, then in his willingness to do so provided he has a kiss from his beloved Nicolette. When he does fight, he puts an end to the war in remarkably quick time, dragging his father's enemy to him by the nose piece of his helmet. But because of his father's refusal to keep his side of the bargain, he soon releases his captive. Other sources of comedy are scenes like Aucassin's encounter with Nicolette's godfather, to whom he explains that he would prefer to live in Hell with Nicolette than to spend his days in Paradise without her (Section 6); the meeting of Nicolette and later Aucassin with a group of shepherds (18, 22); the lovers' futile conversation about the nature of true love, conducted through the crack in the wall of Aucassin's prison (14); Aucassin's arrival at Nicolette's bower with a dislocated shoulder (24–26); his treatment of the King of Torelore, whom he calls the "son of a whore" (29–30); and Nicolette's search for Aucassin disguised as a jongleur. She sings to him of their love without his ever realizing who she is (39).

If there is any deeper significance to the text, it lies in the author's treatment of the generation gap, in the comic exploitation of the futility of war, and in Aucassin's failure to make his ideals coincide with reality. But in spite of his scandalous rejection in the name of love of the principles of feudal society, Aucassin becomes on the death of his father an ideal ruler who keeps his domain safe from war (34). In addition, in spite of his obsessive love for a Saracen captive, he has chosen a partner who is right for him and for society.

The author refers to his text as a *cantefable* (41, l. 24), presumably a term he invented to cover the mingling of verse and prose. The *fable* is the narrative itself, which is closely associated with the lyrical and musical elements in the text. Each verse section is prefaced by the formula *Or se cante*, and some musical notation is contained in the manuscript. Analogues for the mingling of verse and prose can be located in other literatures (e.g., Arabic, Celtic, Chinese, Latin, Provençal), and one finds, for example, a good number of songs performed by the characters in Jean Renart's *Guillaume de Dole*. But the use of the seven-syllable line for the assonanced verse sections and the roughly equal dose of verse and prose have no clear equivalents. Thematically, there are links with other French texts, such as *Floire et Blancheflor, Piramus et Tisbé*, and the Tristan romances, but everything suggests an author with a highly original mind and a superb command of the themes and conventions of contemporary literature.

Glyn S. Burgess

Cobby, Anne E., ed., and Glyn S. Burgess, trans. *The Pilgrimage of Charlemagne and Aucassin et Nicolette.* New York: Garland, 1988.

Dufournet, Jean, ed. *Aucassin et Nicolette: édition critique.* 2nd ed. Paris: Garnier-Flammarion, 1984.

Roques, Mario, ed. *Aucassin et Nicolette: chantefable du XIIIe siècle.* 2nd ed. Paris: Champion, 1935.

Sargent-Baur, Barbara Nelson, and Robert F. Cook. *Aucassin et Nicolete: A Critical Bibliography.* London: Grant and Cutler, 1981.

AUDEFROI LE BÂTARD (fl. first third of the 13th c.). One of the trouvères of Arras. The compositions attributed to him, all surviving with their melodies, include ten *chansons d'amour*, a *jeu-parti*, a lyrico-narrative dialogue with a forlorn lover, and five *chansons de toile*. The last constitute Audefroi's only notable contribution, representing a unique attempt to renew that apparently old genre, partly through innovations in meter and homophony but chiefly through narrative amplification and an accumulation of detail.

Samuel N. Rosenberg

[See also: *CHANSON DE TOILE;* TROUVÈRE POETRY]

Audefroi le Bâtard. *Die Lieder und Romanzen des Audefroi le Bastard, kritische Ausgabe nach alle Handschriften*, ed. Arthur Cullmann. Halle: Niemeyer, 1914.
van der Werf, Hendrik, ed. *Trouvères-Melodien II.* Kassel: Bärenreiter, 1979, pp. 446–82.
Zink, Michel. *Belle: essai sur les chansons de toile, suivi d'une édition et d'une traduction.* Paris: Champion, 1977. [Includes melodies.]

AUGUSTINE, RULE OF ST. From about the 12th century onward, some religious communities in the West took as their guide the *Rule of St. Augustine.* This document has a complicated history, analyzed by Luc Verheijen. In its generally received form, the *Rule* was composed of two major elements: the *Ordo monasterii*, probably sketched out by Augustine's friend Alypius and given final form by Augustine, and the so-called *Praeceptum*, a set of rules for the organization and discipline of a community, written by Augustine. In the medieval period, the received text of the *Rule* reduced the *Ordo monasterii* to the first sentence of that text. In the manuscript tradition, the *Praeceptum* also appears in a form with feminine, not masculine, pronouns and is often attached to Augustine's Letter 211, an admonitory epistle sent to a group of female ascetics. Both sections of the *Rule*, but especially the *Praeceptum*, had provisions for liturgy, food, clothing, manual labor, and the like, but these were frequently set aside in favor of local customaries developed in light of specific Benedictine or Cistercian practices that were more suited to the situation in northern Europe.

However complicated and obscure the pre-12th-century history of the *Rule of St. Augustine* may be, the influence of that text on medieval religious life was profound. Most orders of regular canons, as at Prémontré or Saint-Victor, followed the *Rule*, and when St. Dominic found it necessary to choose from an existing rule for the Order of Preachers (Dominicans), he turned to the Augustinian rule. The *Praeceptum* was first set out in the context of Augustine's own concern with the formation of a community of priests living a life dedicated to poverty and a fully common life in his episcopal household in Hippo. Thus, the later history of the *Rule* as a guide for communities of priests was a faithful echo of its origin in the creative days of the formation of the ascetic-monastic ideal in the West, even before the time of St. Benedict and his own immensely influential *Rule.*

Grover A. Zinn

[See also: AUGUSTINIAN FRIARS/HERMITS; DOMINICAN ORDER; MONASTIC RULES AND CUSTOMARIES; PRÉMONTRÉ; REGULAR CANONS; SAINT-VICTOR, ABBEY AND SCHOOL OF]

Verheijen, Luc. *La règle de saint Augustin.* 2 vols. Paris: Études Augustiniennes, 1967.
Zumkeller, Adolar. *Augustine's Ideal of the Religious Life*, trans. Edmund Colledge. New York: Fordham University Press, 1986. [With English translations of the *Ordo monasterii, Praeceptum,* and Letter 211.]

AUGUSTINIAN CANONS. *See* REGULAR CANONS

AUGUSTINIAN FRIARS/HERMITS. In 1256, Pope Alexander IV ordered several groups of hermits in northern Italy to unite under the authority of the *Rule of St. Augustine* and to model their life according to the *Constitutions* of the Dominican order, which also followed the Augustinian *Rule.* These groups of hermits thus came under the influence of the mendicant ideal and soon moved to cities. The new order quickly spread to France, Spain, Germany, and England; like the Dominicans and Franciscans, the Augustinian Friars quickly established houses of study at university centers and became major participants in late-medieval university life.

Grover A. Zinn

[See also: ALEXANDER NECKHAM; *AUGUSTINE, RULE OF ST.,* DOMINICAN ORDER; UNIVERSITIES]

AULNAY-EN-SAINTONGE. Situated on the important Roman road that connects the Île-de-France to the southwest via Tours and Poitiers, Aulnay (Roman Aunedonacum) is the site of an important pilgrimage church on the route to Santiago de Compostela. Little is known about the construction of the church of Saint-Pierre-de-la-Tour, which dates most probably to the middle of the 12th century, when the regional Romanesque of Poitou and Saintonge was at its height. This richly sculpted church is located outside the town in the midst of an ancient cemetery in which Roman burials have been found.

The exterior gives an impression of squat massiveness, reinforced by the crossing tower, whose upper level and steeple are later additions. The central apse contains some of the most harmonious sculpture at Aulnay: in the space between the window and the flanking colonnettes, the sculptor has placed a series of eight graceful figures set in foliage. But the glory of Aulnay lies in the sculptures of the south and west portals. The south portal consists of four richly sculpted archivolts, peopled by figures carved in a squat and stolid manner to match the shape of the

Aulnay-en-Saintonge (Charente-Maritime), Saint-Pierre, south portal. *Photograph courtesy of Whitney S. Stoddard.*

stones. The innermost archivolt contains six animal figures in a swirl of scrollwork reminiscent of Arabic art. The second archivolt contains twenty-four haloed saints; the third has the twenty-four Elders from Revelation; and the final archivolt is a bestiary of fanciful animals that suggests the Feast of Fools or humanity's constant struggle with its bestial nature. This theme may be echoed in the second archivolt of the central portal of the west façade, where we find armed Virtues trampling the Vices. The third archivolt depicts the Wise and Foolish Virgins. The style here, with its graceful and elongated figures, is very different from that of the south portal. The flanking portals of this façade show the crucifixion of St. Peter and Christ in Majesty.

The interior of Saint-Pierre consists of a five-bay nave with narrow side aisles, a transept, and a deep choir. Quatrilobed columns with richly sculpted capitals carry broken barrel vaults. One famous capital shows three elephants; others have griffins, fantastical animals, and monsters; but the most celebrated shows the sleeping Samson being bound by Delilah while a Philistine is cutting his hair with enormous shears.

William W. Kibler

Chagnolleau, J. *L'église d'Aulnay.* Grenoble, 1938.
Lefèvre-Pontalis, E. "Aulnay-de-Saintonge." *Congrès archéologique* (Angoulême) 79, (1912): 95–111.

AUMÔNIER/AUMÔNERIE. The Latin title *elemosinarius,* from which the Old French *almosn(i)er* or *aumosnier* and its English equivalent, "almoner," are derived, was applied from an early date to the official of a religious house who was charged with the distribution of alms (*almosnes, aumoesnes,* derived through Latin from Greek *eleemosune* 'compassion, charitable gift'). By the 14th century, a similar officer, normally a cleric of some sort, had come to be attached to the households of many princes and prelates, where he often functioned as a sort of chaplain as well. Great princes sometimes maintained a whole corps of almoners, who together formed a department of their household or chapel called the *aumosnerie.* In the household of the king of France, this department was called the *grande aumosnerie de France,* and its chief officer, who was normally a prelate, bore the title *grand aumosnier de France.*

D'A. Jonathan D. Boulton

AURAY. The town of Auray (Morbihan) was the site of a battle, fought on September 29, 1364, that brought an end to a war of succession in the duchy of Brittany that had lasted for twenty-three years and established as duke Jean IV of the Montfort family. The opposing claimant, Charles de Blois, had French support, and his army contained the celebrated Bertrand du Guesclin and most of the great lords of Brittany. Jean de Montfort could count on only one major Breton lord, Olivier de Clisson, but he had with him three renowned English captains—John Chandos, Hugh Calverly, and Robert Knolles.

While Montfort's forces besieged Auray, his enemies attacked in an effort to raise the siege, but they met with overwhelming defeat, as Charles was killed and Du Guesclin captured. Chandos and his compatriots are credited with the decisive role in the victory, while Clisson, who lost an eye in the battle, won his reputation as a courageous warrior.

Auray has only one building with vestiges of its medieval past, the former Chapel of the Holy Spirit. Although radically transformed into a military hospital after 1831, fragments of the late 13th-century window tracery and other elements of the chapel are still visible. Most remarkably, the late 13th- or early 14th-century oak roof is still intact.

John Bell Henneman, Jr.

[See also: BRITTANY; CHARLES DE BLOIS; GUESCLIN, BERTRAND DU; JEAN IV]

La Borderie, Arthur de. *Histoire de Bretagne.* Rennes: Vatar, 1899, Vol. 3.
Luce, Siméon. *Histoire de Bertrand du Guesclin et de son époque . . . 1320–1364.* Paris: Hachette, 1876.
Mouton, Benjamin. "Auray: Chapelle du Saint-Esprit." *Congrès archéologique* (Morbihan) 141 (1983): 28–33.

AURELIAN OF RÉÔME (fl. late 9th c.). The *Musica disciplina,* a collection of theoretical texts drawn from a wide variety of disparate sources, is attributed to one

Aurelian of Réôme. The manuscript tradition and the compiler's relation to the Benedictine house of Saint-Jean de Réôme suggest the treatise originated in the late 9th century, probably in Burgundy.

The compilation is one of the earliest collections of music theory treating medieval liturgical practice. It begins (Chapters 2–7) with an extended essay on music as a liberal art, basically a collection of material drawn from Boethius and glosses on *De institutione musica*, from Cassiodorus, and from Isidore. A chapter on the modes follows, which, while a curious compilation of sources, is an important witness to modal terminology of the Carolingian era. The core of the collection (Chapters 8–18) presents a primitive theoretical tonary—a discussion of each mode, or "tone"—citing over a hundred examples of liturgical melodies in all genres. A chapter on the psalm tones follows, which in the earliest manuscripts includes musical notation in paleo-Frankish neumes, the only place any form of musical notation is found. The treatise concludes (Chapter 20) with an essay concerning genres of liturgical melodies and an epilogue.

The centonate nature of the treatise itself is reflected in the manuscript tradition, for only three sources contain the work as a whole, while over twenty codices contain pieces from the whole. It is by no means clear if these "pieces" are excerpted from *Musica disciplina* or if they have an independent textual history. Aurelian's compilation is nevertheless a major accomplishment in the history of medieval music theory, for through this collection one can establish the nature of texts that were being read and circulated in the 9th century.

Calvin M. Bower

[See also: MUSIC THEORY; MUSICAL NOTATION (NEUMATIC)]

Aurelian of Réôme. *Musica disciplina*, ed. Lawrence Gushee. N.p.: American Institute of Musicology, 1975.
———. *The Discipline of Music (Musica Disciplina)*, trans. Joseph Ponte. Colorado Springs: Colorado College Music Press, 1968.
Bernhard, Michael. "Textkritisches zu Aurelianus Reomensis." *Musica disciplina* 40 (1986): 49–61.
———. "Das musikalische Fachschriftum im lateinischen Mittelalter." In *Geschichte der Musiktheorie*. Darmstadt: Wissenschaftliche Buchgesellschaft, 1990, Vol. 3: *Rezeption des antiken Fachs im Mittelalter*, ed. Frieder Zaminer, pp. 37–103.

AUSTRASIA. Austrasia, "the eastern land," was the northeastern region of the Frankish kingdom. It stretched from near the Seine to the Rhine and included the important Meuse and Moselle river valleys. In general, its population was more Germanic-speaking and Germanic in culture than the other regions of the Frankish kingdom, and in fact it included most of the Franks themselves. It was especially the region inhabited by the Ripuarian, or Rhineland, Franks, and the *Lex Ribuaria* was for Austrasia. The Carolingians and their early supporters were Austrasians.

Austrasia first appears in the sources in the later 6th century as the kingdom of Childebert II (r. 575–95), and it was not truly based on the divisions of the Frankish kingdom among the sons of Clovis I in 511 or the sons of Clotar I in 561. It probably had its origins with the 5th-century kingdom of the Rhineland Franks centered on Cologne and taken over by Clovis I. From the later 6th century, Austrasia was seen as a distinct region within the Merovingian kingdom, with its own administration led by an Austrasian mayor of the palace even when it did not have its own king. With the Carolingian and Austrasian triumph in 687, it no longer enjoyed a separate administration, though Austrasians dominated early Carolingian government.

Much of later Merovingian history can be seen as a struggle for domination between the magnates of Austrasia and those of Neustria, which was more Roman in language, culture, and population. More than a century of Neustrian supremacy ended with the victory of the Austrasian mayor Pepin II at Tertry in 687. Most of Austrasia was allotted to Lothair I by the Treaty of Verdun (843), and it comprised most of the kingdom that went to his son Lothair II in 855, which then came to be called Lotharingia, or Lorraine. However, some of western Austrasia was assigned in 843 to Charles the Bald, who ceded the region to Hugues l'Abbé. It later made up most of the lands of Herbert II of Vermandois, but at his death in 943 his lands were divided among his heirs, as well as Hugues le Grand and King Louis IV.

Steven Fanning

[See also: CAROLINGIAN DYNASTY; LORRAINE; MEROVINGIAN DYNASTY]

Dhondt, Jan. *Études sur la naissance des principautés territoriales en France (IXe–Xe siècles)*. Bruges: De Tempel, 1948.
Dunbabin, Jean. *France in the Making, 843–1180*. Oxford: Oxford University Press, 1985.
Ewig, Eugen. "Die fränkischen Teilungen und Teilreiche (511–613)," "Die fränkischen Teilreiche im 7. Jahrhundert (613–714)," and "Descriptio Franciæ." In *Spätantikes und fränkisches Gallien: Gesammelte Schriften (1952–1973)*. 2 vols. Munich: Artemis, 1976, Vol. 1, pp. 114–230, 274–78.
James, Edward. *The Franks*. Oxford: Blackwell, 1988.

AUTUN. Saint-Lazare at Autun (Saône-et-Loire) exemplifies the Burgundian Romanesque style. Construction began ca. 1120 south of the cathedral of Saint-Nazaire, which the new church, consecrated in 1130, replaced. Building was almost complete by 1146, when the relics of St. Lazarus were translated. Work continued with completion of the west porch, additions of flying buttresses in the 13th century, and building of towers and side chapels off the aisles in the 15th and 16th centuries.

The elevation, vaulting, and architectural details show the influence of Cluny. The plan features a nave of seven bays flanked by single aisles, projecting transept arms, and a choir of two bays with single aisles. Small apses terminate the aisles with a larger central apse behind the altar. The three-story elevation has a lower arcade with pointed arches that is twice the height of the upper stories, a triple-

Autun (Saône-et-Loire), Saint-Lazare, west-portal tympanum, Last Judgment. *Photograph courtesy of Whitney S. Stoddard.*

Autun, Saint-Lazare, nave wall. *Photograph courtesy of John B. Cameron.*

arched passage for the triforium, and a clerestory with a single opening in each bay. A pointed barrel vault spans the nave, transept, and choir. The aisles are groin-vaulted, and a dome on squinches surmounts the crossing. Fluted pilasters of classical inspiration extend from the springing of the transverse ribs of the vaults through the compound piers of the arcade.

The sculptural program of Saint-Lazare has exterior decoration on the west-façade tympanum and north-transept portal along with about fifty capitals and the tomb with relics of St. Lazarus on the interior. The west tympanum is still *in situ*; fragments and some of the capitals are preserved in the upper sacristy and the Rolin Museum. The inscription GISLEBERTUS HOC FECIT on the west tympanum identifies the sculptor, and his work displays a consistent style and quality. In the Last Judgment of the west tympanum, the static abstract presence of Christ at the center contrasts with the active elongated figures of the elect and the damned to the sides. The expressive quality of Gislebertus's sculpture appears in the contortions of the damned and in the gentle touch with which angels raise the elect. This artistic range continues in the historiated capitals, where Gislebertus depicts torment, as in the Suicide of Judas or the tender bond between the Virgin and Child in the Flight into Egypt. The reclining Eve from the lintel of the north portal, a rare medieval portrayal of a female nude, is both sensuous and sensitive. Because of the unity of its architecture and sculpture, Autun is one of the best preserved and most outstanding monuments of Romanesque art in France.

Karen Gould

[See also: GISLEBERTUS; ROMANESQUE ART]

Grivot, Denis, and George Zarnecki. *Gislebertus, Sculptor of Autun.* New York: Orion, 1961.

AUVERGNE. Region of central France, comprising roughly the present-day *départements* of Puy-de-Dôme, Cantal, and Haute-Loire. Auvergne formed part of the subkingdom of Aquitaine under the young Louis the Pious (779–840; king of Aquitaine from 781). In the late 9th century, it became part of the dominions of the duke of Aquitaine, William I the Pious (d. 918).

By ca. 986, Gui (Wido), the hereditary viscount at Clermont, had taken the title of count. From this same family came also the 10th- and 11th-century bishops of Clermont. Nevertheless, the count's regional power was weak, while the dukes of Aquitaine—a title now held by the counts of Poitou—were only nominal overlords. Political and economic power in the 10th and 11th centuries was exercised by numerous castellans, aristocratic families who held and resided in castles. Their impact was great enough to shift settlement patterns: the earlier villages of the fertile plains gave way to nucleated villages centered on hilltop castles. Important patrons of monasteries and cathedral chapters, Auvergnat castellan families swelled the archives of houses like Brioude and Sauxillanges.

Continuous wars between castellan groups in the 10th through early 12th centuries were part of ongoing processes of feuding and peacemaking. New forms of peace were created. Gerald of Aurillac (d. 909), whose *Vita* by Odo of Cluny (d. 942) presented one of the first models of a warrior saint, was an Auvergnat aristocrat. Early and important peace councils met in Auvergne: at Laprade ca. 975/80 (probably the first instance of the Peace of God) and at Saint-Paulien ca. 993/94).

When Eleanor of Aquitaine married Henry II Plantagenêt in 1152, Auvergne became part of the Angevin empire. In 1189, however, Henry recognized the suzerainty of Philip Augustus (d. 1223) over the region. Auvergne subsequently became an apanage (part of the royal domain given out to a cadet of the royal house). Thus, in 1225, Louis VIII (d. 1226) granted the region to his son Alphonse (d. 1271), while in 1360 it was among the territories given to John, duke of Berry.

Barbara H. Rosenwein

Baudot, Anne M. and Marcel, eds. *Grand cartulaire du Chapitre Saint-Julien de Brioude: essai de restitution.* Clermont-Ferrand: Imprimerie Générale, 1935.

Doniol, Henri, ed. *Cartulaire de Brioude.* Clermont-Ferrand: Thibaud, 1861.

Fournier, Gabriel. *Le peuplement rural en basse Auvergne durant le haut moyen âge.* Paris: Presses Universitaires de France, 1962.

Lauranson-Rosaz, Christian. *L'Auvergne et ses marges (Velay, Gevaudan) du VIIIe au XIe siècle: la fin du monde antique?* Le Puy-en-Velay: Cahiers de la Haute-Loire, 1987.

AUVERGNE, MARTIAL D' (ca. 1430/35–1508). A native of Paris and procurator at the Parlement de Paris after 1458, Martial d'Auvergne is best known for the prose *Arrêts d'Amour* (ca. 1460). In this work, which grew out of the Quarrel of the *Belle dame sans merci,* Martial narrates a series of fifty-one fictional trials before the Court of Love. After a lively and often realistic presentation of opposing arguments in appropriate jargon, the cases are closed by unappealable decisions: Love's decrees (*arrêts*). No manuscripts survive, but the work was frequently printed in the late 15th and early 16th centuries.

Martial's *Vigiles de Charles VII* (1477–83), a long poem in honor of the late king (d. 1461), incorporates a chronicle of his reign with alternating allegorical passages lamenting the "good old days." The *Matines de la Vierge* alternates passages relating the life and miracles of Mary with intimate insights into Martial's own life. He may also be the author of a *Danse des femmes,* on the model of the *Danse macabre des hommes.*

William W. Kibler

[See also: *AMANT RENDU CORDELIER;* HERENC, BAUDET; QUARREL OF THE *BELLE DAME SANS MERCI*]

Martial d'Auvergne. *Les arrêts d'Amour,* ed. Jean Rychner. Paris: Picard, 1951.

———. *Les matines de la Vierge,* ed. Yves Le Hir. Geneva: Droz, 1970.

Piaget, Arthur. "La *Belle dame sans merci* et ses imitations." *Romania* 34 (1905): 416–28.

Puttonen, Vilho. *Études sur Martial d'Auvergne.* Helsinki, 1943.

AUXERRE. Situated on the left bank of the Yonne, medieval Auxerre (Yonne) grew from the Roman Autessiodurum, founded on the site of the Gallic settlement of Autricum. Sources on early Christian activity mention the martyrdom of Priscus (late 3rd c.) and the establishment of early church leadership under Peregrinus and Germain (418–48). One of the seven cities of the civil province Lugdunensis Quarta in 400, Auxerre and its see came under Frankish control in the 6th century. The episcopal domain, established by 700 and restored in the 10th century, changed hands a number of times before being reunited to France under Charles V in 1370. In the Middle Ages, the Benedictine abbey at Auxerre was celebrated for its schools, founded in the 11th century. In the late Middle Ages, the flourishing religious communities in Auxerre began to decline, due largely to the Hundred Years' War and the Wars of Religion. However, much of the medieval fabic of the city remains.

With its asymmetrical west front of one bulky tower and series of blind canopies, the former cathedral of Saint-Étienne dominates the city. Its 11th-century painted crypt is 40 feet wide and divided into a nave and two side aisles

Auxerre (Yonne), Saint-Étienne, chevet section. After King.

by two rows of early compound piers. In the upper church, with its three-story elevation, the 13th-century Gothic choir has quadripartite rib vaulting, with sexpartite vaults in the nave. The base of the west portals (ca. 1285–1385) carry Old Testament and other scenes in relief, framed by quatrefoils and trefoils. The painted vaults of the crypt, dated to ca. 1100, feature Christ and angels on horseback and were probably executed under Bishop Humbaut. Stained glass from the 13th–16th centuries can be found in the east end. The treasury features medieval enamels, manuscripts, and miniatures.

Built from the 12th century to the 16th, the church of Saint-Eusebius has a Romanesque nave, but little else remains from the medieval period. In contrast, much of the abbey church of Saint-Germain survives. Founded in the early 6th century, the abbey initially consisted of a basilica with a number of tombs in an above-ground crypt built beyond the east end. Royal patronage financed much of the early construction. Conrad, uncle of Charles II the Bald, ordered a wax model of the basilica to ensure the outcome of his funds before building took place. The abbey church originally had a bell tower in front of the church, three parallel apses, cruciform piers, and a tower-framed façade. The abbey church has a 9th-century crypt with Carolingian frescoes and an upper church with a 13th-century choir and 15th-century nave.

Stacy L. Boldrick

Denny, Don. "A Romanesque Fresco in Auxerre Cathedral." *Gesta* 25 (1986): 197–202.
Louis, René. *Autessiodurum christianum: les églises d'Auxerre des origines au XIe siècle.* Paris: Clavreuil, 1952.
Vallery-Radot, Jean, Marcel Aubert, Paul Deschamps, and Jean Lafond. "Auxerre." *Congrès archéologique* 116 (1958): 26–96.

AVALLON. The church of Saint-Lazare at Avallon (Yonne) is a modification of Romanesque Vézelay, 8 miles west. The nave and aisles were constructed in the 1140s in front of an older sanctuary and crypt. The nave consists of five bays flanked by aisles, with a nave arcade, blank wall above it, and a clerestory. Nave and aisles are crowned by groin-domed vaults. The elevation replicates that of the church of La Madeleine at Vézelay, but the spaces of Avallon are thinner and taller than those of Vézelay. This slight shift in proportions is the result of domical profiles of vaults in each bay. No capitals animate piers, as in Vézelay.

The choir is 30 feet lower than the pavement in the western bay of the nave. A series of steps, adjacent to the nave piers, lowers the level. This change is echoed by the lowering of the molding that establishes the bottom of the clerestory. This simplified variant of the Vézelay interior elevation, combined with sensitive treatment of a difficult site, makes Avallon an interesting structure.

Only two of the three west portals have survived, and only one of the seven jamb statues is *in situ*. The tympanum of the right portal depicts the Adoration of the Magi, Journey of the Magi, and the Magi before Herod. Although related to Vézelay sculpture, figures are thinner and more attenuated. Ornament, smothering bases and archivolts, represents the late, baroque flowering of Romanesque Burgundian sculpture. The lone jamb figure is clearly influenced by the west portals of Chartres, finished by the mid-1140s, but the head remains Burgundian.

Whitney S. Stoddard

[See also: VÉZELAY]

Lasteyrie, Robert de. *L'architecture religieuse en France à l'époque romane.* Paris: Picard, 1929, pp. 433–34, 599.
Porter, A. Kingsley. *Romanesque Sculpture of the Pilgrimage Roads.* 2 vols. Boston: Marshall Jones, 1923, Vol. 1, p. 130; Vol. 2, pp. 137–41.
Stoddard, Whitney S. *The Sculptors of the West Portals of Chartres Cathedral.* New York: Norton, 1987.

AVENAS. Located on the Roman road from Lyon to Autun, Avenas in Beaujolais is the site of a 12th-century church whose Romanesque altar is one of the finest sculpted altars of medieval France. Carved in white limestone, it depicts

Avenas (Rhône), altar. *Photograph courtesy of Whitney S. Stoddard.*

Christ in a mandorla surrounded, on two levels, by the twelve apostles holding books representing their writings. On the left lateral face are depicted scenes from the life of the Virgin, and on the right face is King Louis VII offering the church of Avenas to the chapter of Saint-Vincent of Mâcon.

William W. Kibler

AVESNES. The Avesnes family of Hainaut became involved in dynastic quarrels there and in Flanders and Holland. Jacques d'Avesnes was a vassal of both Count Baudouin V of Hainaut and his brother-in-law, Count Philippe d'Alsace of Flanders, in the late 12th century. The family's fortunes were made when Burchard d'Avesnes married Marguerite, sister and eventual successor (1244–78) of Countess Jeanne of Flanders (r. 1206–44). In 1219, however, he was imprisoned and his marriage to Marguerite declared invalid. After Marguerite's remarriage to Guillaume de Dampierre, the Avesnes and Dampierre families quarreled over her inheritance. In 1246, Louis IX of France awarded rule of Flanders to the Dampierres and of Hainaut to the Avesnes, but neither party accepted the decision, and they continued to fight over imperial Flanders, which had been unaffected by it. During the struggles between the Flemish count Gui de Dampierre and King Philip IV of France during the 1290s, the Avesnes naturally followed France. Jean d'Avesnes had married Aleid of Holland, sister of Count William II, which formed the basis for the dynastic union of Holland, Zeeland, and Hainaut under the Avesnes in 1299. The direct line of the family was extinguished in 1345, when William II was succeeded by his sister Marguerite, the wife of the emperor Louis of Bavaria, and her son William III, whose rule unleashed civil warfare in Holland. The Bavarian Avesnes ruled Holland, Hainaut, and Zeeland until these principalities were absorbed into the Burgundian state in 1433.

David M. Nicholas

Algemene Geschiedenis der Nederlanden. 2nd ed. Haarlem: Fibula-Van Dishoeck, 1982, Vols. 1–4.

Duvivier, Charles. *Les influences française et germanique en Belgique au XIIIe siècle: la querelle des d'Avesnes et des Dampierre jusqu'à la mort de Jean d'Avesnes (1257).* Brussels: Falk, 1894.

Jansen, H. P. H. *Hoekse en Kabeljauwse Twisten.* Bussum: Van Dishoeck, 1966.

Pirenne, Henri. *Histoire de Belgique.* Brussels: Lamertin, 1922, 1929, Vols. 1–2.

Vaughan, Richard. *Valois Burgundy.* Hamden: Archon, 1975.

AVIGNON. The Roman city of Avenio seemed destined to mediocrity before the arrival in France of the papal court in the early 14th century. Thereafter, however, it grew to be the leading city of the Vaucluse and one of the richest of France. Its prosperity in the late Middle Ages is attested even today by its impressive, well-preserved ramparts (over two miles long), its many churches and chapels, but espe-

Avignon (Vaucluse), Papal Palace. *Photograph courtesy of Karen Gould.*

cially by the enormous papal palace. The bridge of Saint-Bénézet, celebrated in song, was constructed between 1177 and 1185, rebuilt in the 13th century, but later largely destroyed by flooding. Only four spans of the original twenty-two remain.

The Palais des Papes is actually two palaces around a large courtyard. With its high walls with arcades, its turreted entrance, and its large rectangular towers at either end (the eight-storied Tour de Trouillas and Tour des Anges), the palace is more a fortress than a residence. It is indeed an excellent example of 14th-century military architecture. The large but austere Palais Vieux was begun in 1335 by Pierre Poisson for Pope Benedict XII. Centered on its cloister, the first floor includes the butlery, the consistory, garderobe, treasury, library, and several chapels. Of particular interest are the superposed chapels of Saint-Jean and Saint-Martial, which were decorated with frescoes of court life by Matteo di Giovanetti da Viterbo for Clement VI. Other frescoes by Giovanetti are preserved in the Chambre du Cerf and Salle de la Grande Audience in the Palais Neuf. The upper floor of the Palais Vieux includes the major reception rooms as well as the private apartments of the popes.

The sumptuous L-shaped Palais Neuf, begun in 1345 by Jean de Loubière for Pope Clement VI, communicates directly with the Palais Vieux. It includes large reception rooms as well as apartments for visiting dignitaries. The elegant Chapelle Clémentine, reached by the Grand Staircase, was reserved for special ceremonies. Its nave is 50 feet wide, but its vaults reach only 62½ feet, because it was constructed over the Salle de la Grande Audience and its roof could not extend beyond that of the other buildings in the complex. After the departure of the papacy in the late 14th century, the palace fell into disrepair and was eventually used as a prison—a use that saved it from destruction in the Revolution.

Churches in Avignon include Saint-Agricol (14th–16th c.), with a Flamboyant portal whose tympanum depicts the Incarnation; Saint-Didier (1325), with a magnificent altar frontal by François Laurana (15th c.) depicting Christ carrying the Cross; Saint-Pierre, rebuilt after 1358; the late 14th-century convent of the Celestines; and the chapel of Saint-Nicolas. But the most important medieval church is the Romanesque Notre-Dame-des-Doms. It consists of a nave of five aisleless bays with four western ones vaulted by pointed barrel vaults strengthened by double transverse arches and the eastern bay capped by a cupola supported by eight relieving arches. The east end consisted originally of a semicircular apse but was altered by the addition of one bay plus a polygonal apse in the 17th century. The eastern cupola is enclosed in an octagonal lantern.

The west end of Notre-Dame-des-Doms consists of a low chamber with a squarish higher room above, which is crowned by a cupola on squinches. This whole narthex has a four-storied bell tower rising above the cupola. A porch with engaged half-columns supporting a classical entablature was added to the narthex. This last element can be found on numerous Provençal churches. However, the narthex with bell tower is not typically Provençal.

The nave displays wide bays, partially obstructed by additions to the piers to support a 17th-century balcony. From this balcony, one can clearly see the colonnettes, capitals, and impost blocks that animate the outer responds and visually support the floral cornice, which runs the length of the nave. The ornament of the nave and the exterior of the lantern are strongly related to that of Roman monuments. According to Alan Borg, Notre-Dame-des-Doms was constructed in the late 11th century.

Besides the ornamental sculpture of Notre-Dame-des-Doms, there is the Episcopal Throne in the nave and fine marble capitals from the destroyed cloister, both historiated and floral, which are now in the Musée des Beaux Arts in Avignon, as well as in museums in Aix-en-Provence, Marseille, Lyon, Cambridge, New York, and Philadelphia. Like Arles, this cloister has ornamented capitals on the garden side and mostly historiated ones on the gallery side. The cloister was created in the late 1150s.

Whitney S. Stoddard

[See also: AVIGNON PAPACY; CLEMENT VI]

Borg, Alan. *Architectural Sculpture in Romanesque Provence.* Oxford: Clarendon, 1972.

Labande, Léon-Honoré. "L'église Notre-Dame-des-Doms d'Avignon." *Bulletin archéologique du Comité des Travaux Historiques et Scientifiques* (1906): 282–365.

———. "Guide archéologique du congrès d'Avignon." *Congrès archéologique* (1909).

AVIGNON PAPACY. The Avignon papacy has suffered both from Petrarch's description of it as "Babylon" and

from invidious comparisons with the reforming popes of earlier centuries. Recent scholarship has offered a more balanced assessment of the 14th-century popes without masking the complacency, fiscalism, and nepotism prevalent at Avignon. The papal court was not an appendage of the French monarchy; but its ethos was predominantly French in the largest sense, reflecting the origins of the popes and most of their cardinals.

A strong Capetian influence can be traced in the curia in the second half of the 13th century, when several French popes reigned and the papacy became entangled in the Angevin domination of Naples. The transfer of the papacy to Avignon, however, resulted from the defeat of Boniface VIII (r. 1295–1303) by Philip IV the Fair and the king's domination of Clement V (r. 1305–14). Failing to elect one of themselves to succeed Benedict XI (r. 1303–04), the cardinals had chosen the archbishop of Bordeaux, who even before his coronation as Clement V acquiesced to Philip's desire that the ceremony be held in his presence at Lyon. Philip imposed his will on a timid and ailing pontiff. The papal bull *Clericis laicos* (forbidding secular rulers from taxing clerics without papal consent) was revoked, and *Unam sanctam* (asserting papal supremacy in temporal as well as spiritual matters) was given an evasive interpretation. Only in helping deny the imperial crown to Charles of Valois, Philip's brother, did the pope frustrate the Capetian king's desires.

Clement never felt able to go to Rome, a dangerous city. While preparing for the Council of Vienne (1311), he resided in Avignon in Provence, an Angevin fief just outside France. The council condemned several errors, including those ascribed to the béguines; but Clement had to wrest final consent to the dissolution of the Templars, against whom Philip IV was proceeding, from a secret consistory. The canons of the Council of Vienne were revised for inclusion in the *Constitutiones clementinae,* the last official collection of medieval canon law. Its emphasis on orthodoxy, obedience, and coercion of dissidents would be typical of the Avignon popes.

Clement died at Carpentras in 1314; a long conclave, dominated by French cardinals, finally named Jacques Duèze, who reigned as John XXII (r. 1316–34). In his pontificate, Avignon became the papal residence, a center of government, finance, trade, and theological debate. To maintain a court so far from Rome, to which it was supposed to return some day, John expanded and regularized papal patronage of benefices, as well as the fees and taxes collected by the curial bureaucracy. At the same time, special commissions began trying to resolve numerous theological issues. Among the writers condemned were Jean de Pouilli, a Parisian master who questioned the papacy's ability to concede pastoral powers to the friars, and the Dominican mystic Meister Eckhart. After a long series of inquiries, a posthumous condemnation was decreed for Peter Olivi, a Franciscan who had espoused Joachite views, strict poverty, and his own version of papal infallibility, which would safeguard recent papal endorsements of the belief that Christ and the Apostles had no property rights. John, with the acquiescence of Michael of Cesena, the Franciscan minister general, began proceedings for heresy against the Spiritual wing of the order, especially in southern France; but the pope soon decided that any Franciscan doctrine of poverty was subversive. When Michael found the pope adamant about revoking past papal pronouncements on this subject, he and William of Ockham fled to Germany, taking refuge with the emperor Louis of Bavaria, John's most bitter political foe.

John was on good terms with Philip V of France, but his relations with the empire had deteriorated rapidly. Clement V had supported Robert of Sicily, an Angevin, against Emperor Henry VII, despite having favored that Luxembourg prince's election as King of the Romans. After Henry's death, the papacy temporized among the rival claims of Luxembourg, Habsburg, and Bavaria. In 1327, Louis of Bavaria, deciding that John was his chief foe, marched on Rome. The Eternal City fell, and an antipope was installed there. Louis's vicar for the city was Marsilius of Padua, whom John had condemned for arguing on the basis of reason and revelation that a lay monopoly on coercive jurisdiction would bring peace to Italy. William of Ockham argued that John's errors concerning apostolic poverty made him a heretic. Although Louis's campaign failed and his antipope became John's prisoner, the polemics of the king's apologists would continue to haunt the papacy. Their credibility was boosted by John's short-lived effort to challenge accepted ideas about the beatific vision.

John's successor, Jacques Fournier, an experienced inquisitor, reigned as Benedict XII from 1334 to 1342. During his pontificate, pope and cardinals began building permanent palaces at Avignon, as if the curia never would return to Rome. Benedict, however, kept a stricter rein on the life of the court than had Clement or John. He also attempted reform of monastic communities, often in a peremptory manner. The pope inherited his predecessor's quarrel with Louis of Bavaria, but French influence foiled negotiations for peace. This old sore would continue to fester until, during the next pontificate, Charles of Luxembourg displaced Louis as emperor.

Benedict, like many popes of that period, cherished the hope of launching a successful crusade. This was foiled when the Valois succession in France was disputed by both Charles of Navarre and Edward III of England. Philip VI had the pope's favor for a time, but he wished to keep the funds raised for the crusade for wars nearer home. Benedict's best efforts to reconcile Philip with Edward failed, leaving the English convinced that the Valois interest dominated Avignon. Edward, moreover, allied himself with Louis of Bavaria and used antipapal legislation to pressure the clergy into helping fund his campaigns.

When Benedict died in 1342, the cardinals quickly agreed on Pierre-Roger de Beaufort, who reigned as Clement VI from 1342 to 1352. Pierre-Roger had been a Benedictine, a theologian and preacher, an archbishop of Rouen, and a servant of the French crown. Despite the ravages of the Hundred Years' War and the eruption of the Black Death in 1348, Clement's pontificate would be regarded as the great age of the papal court at Avignon. The city of Avignon was purchased from the Angevins, as if the papacy never would leave. The papal palace was expanded,

harboring an elegant court, one that contrasted sharply with Benedict's austerity. The best artists, musicians, and writers were employed. In this period, Petrarch enjoyed papal benefactions, even as he wrote poems about Laura, described his ascent of Mount Ventoux, and criticized his master. The ceremonies of the papal chapel were conducted decorously under Clement's supervision, and he preached on important occasions. Nor did the pope neglect the welfare of his subjects during the plague years, burying the dead and caring for the survivors.

The papal palace, however, was not sufficient to contain the entire court and bureaucracy. The papal household alone employed many lay and ecclesiastical functionaries, who, besides caring for the pontiff, entertained his most important guests. A Dominican served as master of the sacred palace, teaching theology and delivering opinions on disputed points of doctrine. The cardinals had their own households, where young clerics might start their quest for advancement. All of these households overlapped with the curial apparatus.

The chancery handled the most important correspondence, including responses to petitions for favors from throughout Christendom. The chancery also examined the fitness of clerics lacking university degrees for the benefices they sought. All documents concerned with private interests were subject to taxation on a set schedule of fees. The chamber received revenues, audited accounts, and resolved disputes concerning these transactions. The penitentiary handled cases concerning matters of conscience, granted routine dispensations, and maintained a staff of confessors able to deal with the major languages of Europe. The papal system of justice still employed judges-delegate conducting hearings throughout Christendom, but a liberal policy of receiving appeals combined with a desire for decisions by the highest tribunals encouraged litigants to carry an increasing volume of business to Avignon. Many princes, prelates, and ecclesiastical corporations retained permanent proctors at the curia. Others employed those who clustered around the tribunals. The highest court was the consistory, that is, the pope and cardinals meeting as a tribunal; but most cases were handled by such bodies as the Rota, whose decisions provided precedents for canonists to study. An entire tribunal existed just to verify documents presented by litigants, but forgery remained common. Bribery and nepotism flourished, helping to give the curia a bad name.

Clement's reign, despite the purchase of Avignon, saw the papacy become preoccupied with Italian politics, leading eventually to efforts to return it to Rome. Cola di Rienzo rose and fell as tribune of the Roman people. Papal legates made efforts to gain control of the turbulent cities of the papal states, many the domain of tyrants. The Visconti rose to power in Milan, and the papacy vacillated over whether to accept their regime as legitimate. Visconti domination drove Florence, once the heart of the Guelf alliance, to renew its ties with the Angevins. Naples, however, fell into the incompetent hands of Joanna, granddaughter of Robert the Wise. Without effective Angevin support and unable to rely on Clement, Florence began its own campaign to dominate all of Tuscany. None of these tensions prevented the pope from organizing a short-lived Latin League to campaign against the Turks; but rivalries between Genoa and Venice prevented it from exploiting its initial success. The rising tensions in Italy were the background of Gil Albornoz's campaign to win control of the papal states for Clement's successor, Innocent VI (r. 1352–62). That native of the Limousin, a more austere and reforming pontiff than his predecessor, poured money into his legates' campaigns. Fiscalism predominated, although some of the curia's income went into bribing free companies turned loose in a lull in the Hundred Years' War to leave Avignon alone. Albornoz won sufficient success to prepare the way for a brief return of the papacy to Rome in the reign of Urban V (r. 1362–70). Urban, however, left part of the bureaucracy at Avignon, evidence of French reluctance to face the perils of Italy. Pressure for a more permanent return persisted from figures as different as Petrarch and Bridget of Sweden.

The decisive decade for the Avignon papacy was the 1370s. Urban's successor, Gregory XI (r. 1370–78), a nephew of Clement VI, was modest, pious, and learned but lacking in resolution. Sufficient resolution to return the papacy to Rome was provided by Catherine of Siena, who lectured the pope on his duty both through letters and in person. The divisions of the curia about a return can be seen in the contemporaneous building campaigns of Gregory around Avignon and in Rome. Both helped exhaust a papal treasury already drained by the benefactions of Urban V. Other distractions were provided by Anglo-French tensions, war with Florence, and the pope's efforts to suppress the Waldensians of Provence. At last, Gregory agreed to go to Rome. He left in 1376; but, once more, part of the curia remained in Avignon. The pope entered Rome in 1377, and he remained there until his death the next year. The Limousin and Gallican factions in the College of Cardinals, unable to elect a cardinal from either group in the tumultuous atmosphere of Rome, whose populace feared another flight to Avignon, chose a curial official, Bartolomeo Prignano, who became Urban VI (r. 1378–89).

Matters might have reached peaceful resolution had Urban VI proved reasonable. His efforts to reform the cardinals, however, were tactless, and his temper was violent to the point of seeming insanity. The cardinals, even the few Italian ones, fled Rome. They met in Fondi, in Joanna's Neapolitan kingdom, and chose Robert of Geneva as Clement VII (r. 1378–94). After failing to drive Urban VI from Rome, Clement returned to Avignon. The princes of Europe held inquiries into the cases for the two pretenders; but the choice between Rome and Avignon tended to follow the lines of alliances in the Hundred Years' War. Despite loud cries for unity, Christendom remain divided for four decades until the Conciliar Movement healed the rupture, though not before a third papal line was begun at the Council of Pisa (1409). The papacy never would regain the degree of control it had exercised from the palace at Avignon in the days of Clement VI. Avignon itself would remain a papal possession until the time of the French Revolution, when it was annexed by the First Republic.

Thomas M. Izbicki

[See also: AVIGNON; BÉGUINES; CLEMENT V; CLEMENT VI; *CLERICIS LAICOS*; CONCILIAR MOVEMENT; FRANCISCAN ORDER; NICHOLAS OF CLAMANGES; OCKHAM, WILLIAM OF; PHILIP IV THE FAIR; TEMPLARS; URBAN V]

Baluze, Étienne, ed. *Vitae paparum avenionensium.* 4 vols. Paris: Letouzey et Ané, 1914–27.

Coogan, Robert, trans. *Babylon on the Rhone: A Translation of Letters by Dante, Petrarch, and Catherine of Siena on the Avignon Papacy.* Potomac: Studia Humanitatis, 1983.

Wright, John, trans. *The Life of Cola di Rienzo.* Toronto: Pontifical Institute of Mediaeval Studies, 1975.

Guillemain, Bernard. *La cour pontificale d' Avignon (1309–1376): étude d'une société.* 2nd ed. Paris: Boccard, 1966.

Mollat, Guillaume. *The Popes at Avignon 1305–1378,* trans. Janet Love. London: Nelson, 1963.

Origo, Iris. *The Merchant of Prato: Francesco di Marco Datini.* New York: Knopf, 1957.

Renouard, Yves. *The Avignon Papacy 1305–1403,* trans. Denis Bethell. Hamden: Archon, 1970.

Tierney, Brian. *Origins of Papal Infallibility 1150–1350.* Leiden: Brill, 1972.

AYCELIN DE MONTAIGU. An important noble family from Auvergne that held lands near Billom (Puy-de-Dôme), the Aycelin produced a series of influential prelates and royal councilors in the 14th century. Pierre Aycelin, who was a contemporary of Philip III (r. 1270–85), left the family lordships to his eldest son, Guillaume, while several younger sons pursued ecclesiastical careers. Hugues, a Dominican, became a cardinal in 1288; Jean became bishop of Clermont; and Gilles, an accomplished lawyer, became archbishop of Narbonne in 1290 and archbishop of Rouen in 1311.

Gilles Aycelin, an important adviser of Philip IV the Fair (r. 1285–1314), had to act with circumspection during Philip's conflicts with the papacy. As archbishop of Narbonne, he favored an ecclesiastical rather than a secular trial when Philip arrested his suffragan, Bernard Saisset, bishop of Pamiers, on charges of treasonable conduct in 1301. In Philip's final conflict with Boniface VIII in 1303, Gilles supported the plan to bring the pope to trial for heresy before a church council. During the pontificate of Clement V (r. 1305–14), when Philip IV moved to have the Templars condemned for heresy, Clement made Aycelin president of the papal commission to investigate the order. Before his death in 1318, the archbishop established the Collège de Montaigu, later one of the most prominent colleges in the University of Paris.

Guillaume Aycelin had two sons, Gilles, lord of Montaigu, and Albert, bishop of Clermont (r. 1307–28). Two generations later, the family produced two additional prelates. The elder of these, another Gilles (d. 1378), served briefly as royal chancellor in 1357 and was bishop of Thérouanne. A younger brother, Pierre, served as chancellor to John, the young duke of Berry (1357–60), and then entered the service of Charles V. He became bishop of Laon, and therefore a peer of France, in 1370 and subsequently a cardinal.

Pierre Aycelin de Montaigu became associated with those advisers of Charles V known as the Marmousets, a loose alliance of financial officers and military commanders. The faction, and its leader, Olivier de Clisson, constable of France, competed for power with the dukes of Berry and Burgundy in the early years of Charles VI's reign (r. 1380–1422). On November 2, 1388, the cardinal of Laon proposed in the royal council that Charles dismiss the dukes and assume personal control of the government. Aycelin died six days later, amid widespread suspicions of poison. A subsequent remark by Clisson suggests that Pierre had indeed been the spokesman of the Marmousets when he made his proposal. He was the last member of the family to hold a powerful position, as the male line ended with the death of his nephew Louis, lord of Montaigu, in 1427.

Franklin J. Pegues

[See also: CHARLES VI; MARMOUSETS; PHILIP IV THE FAIR]

Henneman, John Bell. "Who Were the Marmousets?" *Medieval Prosopography* 5 (1984): 19–63.
McNamara, Jo Ann. *Gilles Aycelin: The Servant of Two Masters.* Syracuse: Syracuse University Press, 1973.
Pegues, Franklin J. *The Lawyers of the Last Capetians.* Princeton: Princeton University Press, 1962.

AYE D'AVIGNON. Preserved complete in a single manuscript (B.N. fr. 2170), this anonymous late 12th-century chanson de geste of some 4,132 Alexandrines combines epic and romance characteristics. Starting as an epic attached to the small Nanteuil Cycle (thematically related to the Rebellious Vassal Cycle), it tells, in outline, of the marriage of the eponymous heroine to Garnier de Nanteuil and the maneuvers of the treacherous clan of Ganelon to secure the marriage for one of its members instead. They succeed in buying the favor of Charlemagne and in capturing Aye; she spends some time as prisoner of a virtuous Saracen king, Ganor, who wishes to marry her. Rescued by Garnier in disguise, Aye returns to Avignon with him and gives him a son, Gui. The Ganelonides succeed in treacherously killing Garnier and bribing Charlemagne to give his widow to their leader, Milon. Ganor, who had earlier abducted Gui, now returns to the rescue with the youth, who kills Milon in battle; Ganor, having proved himself worthy of Aye's love and been converted, marries her.

The interest of this action-packed poem lies in the dovetailing of the romantic story of Ganor's love and his suit for Aye's hand into an epic (the inevitable passivity of the beautiful heiress being the unifying link) and in the poet's transcendance of the normal epic assumption that Saracens and Christians have clear and opposite moral roles: here, the boundaries are intriguingly smudged.

Wolfgang G. van Emden

[See also: CHANSON DE GESTE; NANTEUIL CYCLE; REBELLIOUS VASSAL CYCLE]

Borg, Sam J., ed. *Aye d'Avignon: chanson de geste anonyme.* Geneva: Droz, 1967.
van Emden, Wolfgang G. "*Aye d'Avignon*: à propos d'une étude récente." *Studi francesi* 76 (1982): 69–76. [Responds to E.R. Woods.]
Woods, Ellen Rose. *Aye d'Avignon: A Study of Genre and Society.* Geneva: Droz, 1978.

AYMERI DE NARBONNE. An epic poem of 4,708 rhymed decasyllables from the early 13th century, *Aymeri* tells how Charlemagne, returning from Spain distressed by the disaster of Roncevaux, discovers the rich and admirably fortified Saracen city of Narbonne. In vain, he proposes to grant it to any knight capable of conquering it: all the heroes are tired and discouraged. Only the young Aymeri, pushed by his father, Hernaut de Beaulande, is willing to attack this seemingly impregnable place. He succeeds thanks to his military talent and, finally, the help of Charlemagne's army. After the death of his parents, his advisers urge him, as the only son, to take a wife and recommend Hermengarde, sister of the king of the Lombards, Boniface. A series of adventures of his delegation to Pavia is followed by others of Aymeri himself and his companions; an agreement is at last reached between Boniface and the Narbonnais, and Hermengarde and Aymeri are betrothed. However, while he is returning to Narbonne with his fiancée, Saracens besiege the city; Aymeri liberates it with the help of an army of his uncle, Girart de Vienne, after a violent battle in which he is seriously wounded. Once Aymeri is healed, the marriage takes place in Narbonne, and Aymeri, who lives for a hundred years, has seven sons and five daughters with Hermengarde.

Although inspired by previous poems, the work is remarkable for several scenes, particularly Charlemagne's despair at his barons' refusal of the yet unconquered fief of Narbonne. *Aymeri* is preserved in five manuscripts of the 13th and 14th centuries; the poem has been little modified, since the manuscripts closely follow its composition. However, there exist two 15th-century prose versions, the second of which was partially inserted in David Aubert's *Croniques et conquestes de Charlemaine* (1458). In addition, in the Venice Codex Marcianus fr. IV (ca. 1300), a version of the poem in Franco-Italian immediately follows the *Chanson de Roland*; this version is even more considerably altered in the cyclic Tuscan poem *La Spagna* (1350–80), and it also exists independently in a poem called *Amerigo di Nerbona* (ca. 1380). The "matter" of Aymeri also passed into Andrea da Berberino's huge prose compilation *I reali di Francia* (1380–1420) and in a second, later work by the same author, *Le storie Nerbonesi*. The Occitan "chronicle" by the Pseudo-Filomena (early 13th c.) contains an important sequence reminiscent of Aymeri's conquest of, and investiture with, Narbonne.

Hans-Erich Keller

[See also: BERTRAND DE BAR-SUR-AUBE; GUILLAUME D'ORANGE CYCLE; *NARBONNAIS*]

Demaison, Louis, ed. *Aymeri de Narbonne*. 2 vols. Paris: Didot, 1887. [Vol. 1 has an important introduction and the edition of the prose versions (pp. cclii–cclxxxii).]

Cadalano, Michele, ed. *La Spagna*. 3 vols. Bologna: Carducci, 1939.

Schneegans, F. Eduard, ed. *Gesta Karoli Magni ad Carcassonam et Narbonam*. Halle: Niemeyer, 1898.

B

BADEFOL, SEGUIN DE (ca. 1331–1366). A soldier of fortune who became notorious as a captain of freelance troops (*routiers*) in the 1360s, Seguin de Badefol was the second of four sons of a middling noble from Périgord. Born in the ancestral castle at Badefol-sur-Dordogne, Seguin fought on the French side at Poitiers in 1356, but the king's capture there led to a truce and an end to the payment of troops. Badefol was soon at the head of a *route*, or company, numbering about 2,000 men and nicknamed the Margot. This company joined with other bands in 1360 to form a large force, called the Tard-Venus, that pillaged eastern France. They captured Pont-Saint-Esprit on the Rhône in December and demanded a large payment before leaving. For most of 1361, Badefol's troops ravaged the Velay and lower Languedoc before local resistance induced the Margot to withdraw toward Auvergne and the Lyonnais.

A number of bands combined early in 1362 to form the "Great Company," which decisively defeated a royal army at Brignais on April 6. This engagement left southeastern France exposed to brigandage. In September 1363, Badefol took Brioude, which served as his base for eight months until he agreed to evacuate the town for a payment of 40,000 gold florins. He soon found another lucrative base, Anse, on the Saône north of Lyon, which his troops captured in November 1364. Badefol styled himself "captain of Anse for the king of Navarre," seeking a veneer of legality based on an earlier offer of employment by Charles the Bad, king of Navarre. In his name, the Margot terrorized a large region before finally evacuating Anse for another 40,000 florins in September 1365.

To rid the country of *routiers*, the French crown offered them large sums to join an expedition to Spain. Using this plan as a pretext, Badefol went to Navarre to seek rewards from the king. Charles the Bad, however, was offended by his demands and had him poisoned in January 1366.

John Bell Henneman, Jr.

[See also: BRIGAND/BRIGANDAGE; BRIGNAIS]

Descroix, Bernard. *Seguin de Badefol: "ce fils d'iniquité"—qui fit trembler Anse et la France entière.* Lyon: Société d'Archéologie du Beaujolais, 1986.

Guigue, Georges. *Les Tard-Venus en Lyonnais, Forez, et Beaujolais.* Lyon: Vitte et Perrussel, 1886.

Henneman, John Bell. *Royal Taxation in Fourteenth Century France: The Captivity and Ransom of John II 1356–1370.* Philadelphia: American Philosophical Society, 1976, Chap. 5.

BAILLI/BAILLIAGE. In medieval rural lordships, a familiar manorial officer known as the bailiff (Fr. *bailli*) often acted as manager of an estate. When employed by the French crown in the 12th century, the *bailli* was a salaried judicial officer who inspected the work of the *prévot*, who farmed the revenues of the royal domain and rendered justice at a local level. In 1190, when Philip II was leaving on crusade, he established regulations covering the duties of the *baillis*, who increasingly resembled the English itinerant justices.

In 1204, Philip II gained possession of Normandy, where *baillis* had begun to be associated with a geographical area. Over the next fifteen years, the *bailli* in royal lands gradually lost the character of an itinerant justice and became the administrator of a district called the *bailliage*. Well paid, he represented the king in judicial, military, and financial matters, receiving appeals from lesser jurisdictions. By the late 13th century, a specialized subordinate, the "receiver," assumed most financial duties. During the 14th century, a system of royal judges took over some of the judicial business of the *bailliage*, and because of the endemic warfare of that period the *bailli* concentrated increasingly on military matters. Whereas the early 13th-century *baillis* were drawn mainly from the middling nobility of the old royal domain in the Île-de-France, many of them in the late 14th century were natives of their *bailliage*. This district, and its southern counterpart, the *sénéchaussée*, remained the basic provincial administrative unit of late-medieval France.

John Bell Henneman, Jr.

[See also: *PRÉVÔT/PRÉVÔTÉ*; ROYAL ADMINISTRATION AND FINANCE; SÉNÉSCHAL]

Baldwin, John W. *The Government of Philip Augustus: Foundations of French Royal Power in the Middle Ages.* Berkeley: University of California Press, 1986.

Fesler, James. "French Field Administration: The Beginnings." *Comparative Studies in Society and History* 5 (1962–63): 76–111.

Lot, Ferdinand, and Robert Fawtier. *Histoire des institutions françaises au moyen âge.* 3 vols. Paris: Presses Universitaires de France, 1957–62, Vol 2: *Institutions royales* (1958).

Strayer, Joseph R. *The Administration of Normandy Under Saint Louis.* Cambridge: Harvard University Press, 1932.

Waquet, Henri. *Le bailliage de Vermandois aux XIIIe et XIVe siècles.* Paris: Champion, 1919.

BALLADE. The ballade evolved from the courtly chanson in the late 13th century and was originally meant to be sung. By the late 14th century, with the separation of text and music, it became *littera sine musica*. As defined by Eustache Deschamps in his *Art de dictier et de fere chançons* (1392), the ballade may consist of three stanzas, eight to ten lines each, with seven to eleven syllables per line. A one-line refrain concludes each stanza; it is syntactically joined to the preceding phrase and rhymes with one of the two preceding lines. A typical eight-line strophe has one of the following rhyme schemes, sung to two melodic phrases:

ab ab bc bC / ab ab cc dD / ab ab cd cD
   A A B   A A B   A A B

Other common forms include *septains* in ababbcC, *neuvains* in ababccdcD, *dizains* in ababbccdcD, *onzains* in ababccddedE, and *douzains* in ababbccddedE. Most ballades end with an *envoi* that reproduces the rhyme scheme of the second half of the stanzas and frequently begins with the apostrophe *Prince*.

Eglal Doss-Quinby

[See also: *FORMES FIXES*]

Poirion, Daniel. *Le poète et le prince: l'évolution du lyrisme courtois de Guillaume de Machaut à Charles d'Orléans.* Paris: Presses Universitaires de France, 1965, pp. 361–95.

BALLETTE. Under the rubric "ballettes," MS Douce 308 (Oxford, Bodleian Library, ca. 1300) groups monodic songs, most often composed of three stanzas, generally three to four lines each, rhyming aa(a)b. The meter of each line varies from seven to twelve syllables. A one- to three-line refrain, which may also precede the first verse, is repeated at the end of each strophe. Its metrical and rhyme structure need not correspond to that of the stanzas, although a typical two-line refrain (AB/BB/CB) is usually linked, through its rhyme scheme, to the last line of each strophe. Ballettes were seemingly meant to accompany dancing.

Eglal Doss-Quinby

Bec, Pierre. *La lyrique française au moyen âge (XIIe–XIIIe siècles): contribution à une typologie des genres poétiques médiévaux.* 2 vols. Paris: Picard, 1977–78, Vol. 1, pp. 228–33.

BAN/BANALITÉ. The *ban* (Lat. *bannus, bannum*) was the royal power to command and punish. The Merovingians employed it primarily to summon free men to military service; the Carolingians extended it to include royal protection of the defenseless (churches, widows, orphans, minors) and jurisdiction over crimes of violence, such as assault, rape, and arson. The counts exercised the ban by delegation in public courts until the 10th century; thereafter, the ban devolved to castellans, great landlords, and monasteries with immunities or their lay advocates.

As the *ban* was privatized, military service fell for the most part to a professional class of knights who served their immediate lords. Philip IV later reestablished the principle of the *arrière-ban* (Lat. *retrobannum*), service owed the king from the feudal tenants of his direct vassals, and in the 14th century the commutation of the *arrière-ban* became an important source of royal taxes.

For nonnobles, the *ban* became a district in which all residents, no matter who their landlord, performed labor services, such as maintenance of roads, bridges, or castles, and abided certain monopolies (*banalités*). Georges Duby coined the phrase "banal lordship" (*seigneurie banale*) to describe this new, nonlanded form of lordship, and the concept has been adopted by most historians, although the medieval terms most often used in that sense were *districtus* and *potestas* (in the north) and *mandamentum* (in the south).

By the 12th century, *banalités* consisted of two types of economic rights possessed by some landlords. The first was the monopoly of the local mill, oven, and winepress: local residents were compelled to use those services (*per bannum*) in return for a payment in kind (e.g., every sixth loaf of bread or one-twentieth of the wine or flour processed). Such indexed revenues were important economic resources at a time of expanding population and agrarian production but relatively fixed rents. Even lords who granted generous community franchises often retained the *banalités* of their townsmen. The second type of *banalité* was the *banvin*, the lord's exclusive right to sell wine (*ad bannum*) during a prescribed period, usually just before or after a new vintage.

Theodore Evergates

[See also: *ARRIÈRE-BAN*; SEIGNEUR/SEIGNEURIE]

Duby, Georges. *Rural Economy and Country Life in the Medieval West*, trans. Cynthia Postan. London: Arnold, 1968.

Fossier, Robert. *Histoire sociale de l'Occident médiéval.* Paris: Colin, 1970.

Ganshof, François Louis. *Frankish Institutions Under Charlemagne*, trans. Bryce and Mary Lyon. New York: Norton, 1968.

Van de Kieft, C. "Monopole de vente du *Gruit* et droit de ban." *Acta Historiæ Neerlandica* 1 (1966): 67–81. [Historiographical review.]

BANKING AND MONEYLENDING. The early admixture of banking functions helps to explain the disagreement among financial historians regarding the origins of banking in the Middle Ages. Three in particular have attracted attention: deposit banking, moneylending, and exchange. All three activities can be documented in medieval France. Usher argued that the deposit function was primordial in the development of banking. Sayous acknowledged the existence of the deposit function as typical of banking but offered the hypothesis that before bankers achieved the public confidence necessary to attract deposits, their primitive function was that of lending money. With the passage of time, according to Sayous, those loan bankers became credit bankers and changers. In the opinion of de Roover, it was foreign exchange that would give rise to modern banking techniques.

Pawnbroking, common in most French towns, was frequently the domain of the Jews, who served both urban and rural clienteles. Funds moved frequently via exchange between Italy and France, Paris and the Champagne fairs in the 13th and 14th centuries. From ca. 1260, the fairs developed the function of financial clearinghouse. Towns like Montpellier and Perpignan acted as intermediaries in the late Middle Ages in financial networks linking the Hispanic world with Bruges and northern France. Papal financial operations from the capital of Avignon crisscrossed medieval France in the 14th century.

From the 13th century until 1307, the Temple in Paris functioned as the French royal bank; Jews and Italians were also prominent on the national lending scene. French kings, notoriously short of funds, borrowed frequently and were not adverse to confiscating assets of their creditors to increase royal revenues. While Louis IX legislated against any interest as usury, French kings in the 14th century sanctioned interest rates of between 15 and 20 percent. Medieval France lagged behind Italy and the Low Countries in the sophistication of its private and public financial institutions.

Kathryn L. Reyerson

Bizaguet, Armand. "Les origines des institutions et des mécanismes bancaires en Europe occidentale: de la banque romaine à l'empire napoléonien." *Revue internationale d'histoire de la banque* 9 (1974): 17–79.
———. *The Dawn of Modern Banking.* New Haven: Yale University Press, 1979.
Reyerson, Kathryn L. *Business, Banking and Finance in Medieval Montpellier.* Toronto: Pontifical Institute of Mediaeval Studies, 1985.

BANNERET. The word *banneret* was coined in France under Philip II to describe knights or esquires who, as the commanders of military units of about ten to a hundred men (typically including some other knights or esquires), displayed their personal heraldic arms on the large rectangular flag called a "banner" (*bannière*) rather than on the small triangular lance-pennon carried by knights and esquires of the rank and file. Down to 1438, *chevalier* and *escuier* (or *damoiseau*) *banneret* constituted the highest

noble pay grades in the royal army, above those of *chevalier simple* or *bachelier* and *escuier simple*, but like the proportion of knights the proportion of bannerets of both grades in the royal armies diminished steadily between 1340 (when it was 1.5 percent) and 1411 (when it was 0.3 percent), and these grades were finally suppressed.

D'A. Jonathan D. Boulton

Contamine, Philippe. *Guerre, état et société à la fin du moyen âge: études sur les armées des rois de France 1337–1494.* Paris: Mouton, 1972.

BANQUETING. Banqueting in medieval France called for a group of separately served courses with several dishes to a course—as many as fifteen in each of three to five courses at 15th-century courts, with forty items in a course reported for the spectacular Pheasant Banquet given by Philip the Good in 1454. Fortunate banqueters might be given something resembling a modern "Chinese" banquet or Swedish smorgasbord, but those sitting at the highest table would have been offered the choicest selection. Others may have been served a quarter or less of the items listed on banquet menus. These menus included a high proportion of game, especially game birds, with more elaborate stews and pastries than those found on more modest menus, and they usually omitted the primarily vegetable pottage, made with greens, peas, or beans, that was the usual basis, or sole ingredient, aside from bread and drink, of everyday meals.

The order of service may seem odd by modern standards, and it varies in different times and places. Sometimes, a sort of hors d'œuvres course came first; at other times, banquets began, as in England, with the most basic meats and pottages. In most cases, delicacies, often sweet, came last, followed by spiced wine and wafers, and/or fur-

A 14th-century banquet as depicted in a manuscript of Guillaume de Machaut's *Remede de Fortune.* BN fr. 1586, fol. 55. *Courtesy of the Bibliothèque Nationale, Paris.*

ther *confits* and so on to end the meal. But it was between the courses, usually before the last full course, that the most striking feature of a banquet appeared: the *entremets*, usually edible but presented primarily as entertainment. Decorated pies were used as *entremets* for centuries, but anything unusual could count as such a diversion, ranging from a jellied fish to a skit involving live human players. The most famous examples of this genre are the roast swans and peacocks reclothed in their own feathers, often seen in pictures of such banquets.

Constance B. Hieatt

[See also: BEVERAGES; COOKING; MEALS]

Gottschalk, Alfred. *Histoire de l'alimentation et de la gastronomie depuis la préhistoire jusqu'à nos jours.* 2 vols. Paris: Hippocrate, 1948.

LaFortune-Martel, Agathe. *Fête noble en Bourgogne au XVe siècle.* Montreal: Bellarmin, 1984.

La Marche, Olivier de. *Mémoires d'Olivier de la Marche, maître d'hôtel et capitaine des gardes de Charles le Téméraire,* ed. Henri Beaune and J. d'Arbaumont. 4 vols. Paris: Société de l'Histoire de France, 1883–88.

Scully, Terence, ed. "*Du fait de cuisine,* par Maistre Chiquart 1420." *Vallesia* 40 (1985): 101–231.

Wheaton, Barbara K. *Savoring the Past: The French Kitchen and Table from 1300 to 1789.* Philadelphia: University of Pennsylvania Press, 1983.

BAR-LE-DUC. The county of Bar-le-Duc was created primarily from allodial lands located between Champagne, Burgundy, Lorraine, and Luxembourg. In ca. 960, Frederick I, duke of Upper Lorraine, in order to check incursions from Champagne, built a fortress on the Ornain River that he called Bar (Lat. *barra* 'barrier') and settled his knights on confiscated lands of the nearby abbey of Saint-Mihiel. Bar and its adjacent lands passed to his great-granddaughter Sophie (d. 1093), who first adopted the title countess of Bar.

A line of energetic successors steadily expanded the county by usurpation, conquest, purchase, and marriage. By the mid-12th century, the county had become an important, autonomous principality between France and Germany, although it always was dominated by French cultural and political interests. Count Renaud II (r. 1149–70) married Agnès de Champagne, sister of Queen Adèle and Count Henri I of Champagne. His second son, Renaud, became bishop of Chartres (r. 1182–1217). The prestige of the counts of Bar was such that, when the barons of Champagne sought someone to lead them on the Fourth Crusade after the death of their own count, they asked first the duke of Burgundy, then Count Thibaut I of Bar (r. 1191–1214). Mindful of his own brother Henri I's death on the Third Crusade, Thibaut declined.

Counts Henri II (r. 1214–39) and Thibaut II (r. 1239–91) significantly increased the political role of Bar in eastern France. By awarding substantial fiefs and by purchasing the homages of important nobles in the frontier region, they effectively preempted further eastward expansion by

Champagne. In 1297, royal forces invaded Bar after Count Henri III (r. 1291–1302) supported his father-in-law, King Edward I of England, against Philip IV, and in 1301 the entire county west of the Meuse River, including the city of Bar, became a fief (*Barrois mouvant*) held from the French crown. The counts continued to figure prominently in French affairs and even married into the royal family. In 1354, they acquired the ducal title and became peers of France. Following the loss of the duke's four sons at the battles of Nicopolis and Agincourt, Bar passed indirectly to a grandson, René d'Anjou (r. 1430–80).

Theodore Evergates

[See also: *ALLEU*/ALLOD; COUNT/COUNTY; RENÉ D'ANJOU]

Collin, Hubert. "Le comté de Bar au début du XIVe siècle." *Bulletin philologique et historique du Comité des Travaux Historiques et Scientifiques* (1971): 81–93.

Grosdidier de Matons, Marcel. *Le comté de Bar des origines au traité de Bruges (vers 950–1031).* Paris: Picard, 1922.

Parisse, Michel. *Noblesse et chevalerie en Lorraine médiévale.* Nancy: University of Nancy, 1982.

Poull, Georges. *La maison ducale de Bar: les premiers comtes de Bar (1033–1239).* Rupt-sur-Moselle: Poull, 1977.

BARLAAM ET JOSAPHAT. Name given to three 13th-century poems and three prose tales based on the life of the Buddha. From elements of the legendary life of the Buddha, an original *Barlaam et Josaphat* was composed between the 5th and 7th centuries in Palestine. The work spread throughout the Christian world through translations in most European languages of the Latin version (ca. 1050), of which almost a hundred manuscripts survive. In French, there are three rhymed versions, by a certain Chardri (1,477 octosyllabic couplets in Anglo-Norman, before 1216), by Gui de Cambrai (6,467 octosyllabic couplets in the Picard dialect, after 1209), and an anonymous version (first quarter of the 13th c.) of 6,113 octosyllabic couplets without dialectal markings (two manuscripts and two fragments, ed. Sonet 1949, 1950). There are also three anonymous prose versions, written in the Champagne dialect between 1199 and 1229 (fourteen manuscripts, ed. Mills), translated from a Greek fragment (early 13th c.), and derhymed from the anonymous verse text (three manuscripts, ed. Sonet 1952).

Despite all his efforts, Avennir, king of India, fails in shielding his son Josaphat from the influence of the Christian religion and from the teachings of the anchorite Barlaam, who succeeds in converting his pupil. Having received half the kingdom from his father, Josaphat establishes Christianity in his realm but then spends the rest of his life with Barlaam in the desert.

A number of tales embedded in this story (e.g., *Le lai de l'oiselet, Le dit de l'unicorne*) appear also in most of the common medieval collections of legends, exempla, and sermons, in Latin and in the vernacular. In France, the story of Josaphat is also told in the *Mystère du roy Advenir* by Jean du Prier (ed. Meiller) and in a *Miracle de Nostre*

Dame par personnages (B.N. fr. 819; 15th c.). The legend is also found in an Occitan version in prose from the late 13th or early 14th century.

Hans R. Runte

[See also: EXEMPLUM; MIRACLE PLAYS; MYSTERY PLAYS; *SEVEN SAGES OF ROME*]

Mills, Leonard R., ed. *L'histoire de Barlaam et Josaphat: version champenoise.* . . . Geneva: Droz, 1973. [Based on Apostolicana Vaticana, Reg. lat. 660.]

Sonet, Jean, ed. *Le roman de Barlaam et Josaphat.* Namur: Bibliothèque de la Faculté de Philosophie et Lettres, 1949, Vol. 1: *Recherches sur la tradition latine et française.* [Includes edition of the fragments of the anonymous rhymed version (Besançon 552 and Cividale del Friuli B24).]

——, ed. *Le roman de Barlaam et Josaphat.* Namur: Bibliothèque de la Faculté de Philosophie et Lettres, 1950, Vol. 2: *La version anonyme française.* Part 1: *Texte critique.* [Based on Tours 949.]

——, ed. *Le roman de Barlaam et Josaphat.* Namur: Bibliothèque de la Faculté de Philosophie et Lettres, 1952, Vol. 2: *La version anonyme française.* Part 2: *Études critiques et mise en prose.* [Based on Lyon 867.]

BARON/BARONY. The Latin *baro* (pl. *barones*), probably derived from a Germanic word whose basic sense was "man as distinct from woman," was rarely used in documents before ca. 1030 and was almost always used in that sense. In the half-century after 1030, however, *baro* appeared with rapidly increasing frequency in diplomatic documents composed in northern France and its cultural colonies, primarily to designate the principal vassals, or "men," of both the princes and the castellans who emerged in the same period. By 1120, its Old French derivative *ber(s)* (oblique *baron*) had come to be used adjectivally to characterize personages of high rank or honor, including kings, saints, and even Christ.

In the second half of the 12th century, the sociopolitical use of both *baro* and *ber(s)* was regularized and restricted upward. In the language of the royal chancery, the expression *barones regni* replaced the traditional *proceres regni* as the designation of the leading magnates, who were soon defined as those who held one of a certain set of major castellanies or still larger dominions in fief immediately of the crown. These dominions, which included all of the duchies in France and many of the counties and viscounties, acquired the generic title "barony" (OFr. *baronnie* etc., Lat. *baronia*), and baronial fiefs were said to be held "in" or "by barony." Within certain of the greater principalities, themselves baronies of the realm, the more important fiefs, including all dependent counties and viscounties, were similarly recognized as baronies, and their lords as barons, of the principality.

Although all dukes, counts, and viscounts were barons on one level or the other, the title "baron" was applied after 1180 especially to those barons who had no higher title of dignity—i.e., the more important castellans, of whom there were probably between 300 and 400 in the whole kingdom. In the 13th century, the word "barony" came to be treated as a specific title, applicable to the name of a simple baron's principal dominion on the model of "county" (e.g., *la baronnie de Coucy*). For some reason, "baron" itself remained a purely generic title until the 16th century, and simple barons continued to employ a style of the form *N, sire de X*, common to all minor lords after ca. 1200. The feminine title "baroness" (Lat. *baronissa*, OFr. *barnesse*) did not appear until ca. 1220, but thereafter it was increasingly applied as a generic title to the wives, widows, and heiresses of barons.

D'A. Jonathan D. Boulton

[See also: KNIGHTHOOD; NOBILITY; PEER/PEERAGE]

Boulton, D'A.J.D. *Grants of Honor: The Origins of the System of Nobiliary Dignities of Traditional France, ca. 1100–1515.* Forthcoming.

Guilhiermoz, Paul. *Essai sur l'origine de la noblesse en France au moyen âge.* Paris: Picard, 1902.

Westerblad, C.A. *Baro et ses dérivés dans les langues romanes.* Uppsala: Almqvist, 1910.

BASIRON, PHILIPPE (Phelippon, Philippon de Bourges; ca. 1450–1491). Composer, musician, and cleric. Basiron first appears as a choirboy in the records of the Sainte-Chapelle in Bourges in 1458. He maintained a lifelong association with this institution, which was closely tied during Basiron's lifetime to both Charles VII (r. 1422–61) and Louis XI (r. 1461–83). Basiron was granted a vicariate at the Sainte-Chapelle in 1467 and served for most of his career as master of the chapel choirboys. Basiron, or "Phelippon," was the composer of over a dozen surviving works, including a *L'homme armé* Mass and seven Burgundian chansons.

J. Michael Allsen

[See also: CYCLIC MASS]

Higgins, Paula. "Tracing the Careers of Late Medieval Composers: The Case of Philippe Basiron of Bourges." *Acta Musicologica* 62 (1990): 1–28.

Picker, Martin. "Basiron, Philippe." In *The New Grove Dictionary of Music and Musicians*, ed. Stanley Sadie. London: Macmillan, 1980, Vol. 2, pp. 240–42.

BASOCHE. In the early 15th century, the law clerks of Paris and other cities organized professional associations called basoches, one of whose functions was the staging of dramatic spectacles. In Paris, each high court of justice had its Basoche, the primary ones being those of the Parlement (the Palais de Justice) and the Châtelet (the high criminal court). By the end of the century, there may have been as many as 10,000 Basochiens in Paris. The Basoche had its own administrative and judicial structure, with a king, a chancellor, and a high court.

The Basochiens assembled at special times, such as Mardi Gras, to stage a variety of spectacles, including *tableaux vivants,* burlesque lawsuits called *causes grasses* ("fat" cases, because they were presented at carnival time), and plays, such as moralities, farces, and *sotties.* The Basoche also contributed comic plays to the performances of *mystères* organized by the Confrérie de la Passion. The Enfants-sans-souci, the principal Parisian company performing *sotties,* may have been part of the Basoche. Authors who were not law clerks, such as Pierre Gringore, also appear to have written for the Basoche. Some critics, in particular Howard Graham Harvey, argue from the records of Parlement and from evidence drawn from late-medieval plays that the Basoche had taken on the "more or less exclusive privilege of staging comic plays in Paris." While professional entertainers, students, and others also put on comic plays, the Basoche had a crucial influence on the development of satiric theater in medieval France.

Heather M. Arden

[See also: BAUDE, HENRI; CONFRÉRIE DE LA PASSION; COQUILLART, GUILLAUME; FARCE; *SOTTIE;* THEATER]

Fabre, Adolphe. *Les clercs du palais.* 2nd ed. Lyon: Scheuring, 1875.
Harvey, Howard Graham. *The Theatre of the Basoche.* Cambridge: Harvard University Press, 1941.

BASSE DANSE. An elegant, choreographed procession dance of the 15th and early 16th centuries. The favorite dance in the courts of France, England, and Spain, it was closely related to the Italian *bassadanza.*

Although the earliest mention of the *basse danse* is in a poem by Raimon de Cornet (ca. 1320), nothing is known of the dance steps until the early 15th century, when a number of tunes and choreographies were preserved in manuscripts. From these instruction manuals, we know that each *basse danse* employed a combination of five steps: *révérence, branle, simples, double,* and *reprise.* Each choreography had a unique sequence and length and was paired with a particular tune of exactly the correct number of notes to fit the dance steps.

In the later 16th century, the *basse danse* lost its individual choreography and was performed with a continuous repetition of a set sequence of steps to music of uniform-length phrases.

Timothy J. McGee

[See also: *ALTA CAPELLA;* DANCE]

Brainard, Ingrid. "Bassedanse, Bassadanza and Ballo in the 15th Century." In *Dance History Research: Perspectives from Related Arts and Disciplines,* ed. Joann W. Kealiinohomoku. New York: Committee on Research in Dance, 1970, pp. 64–79.
Bukofzer, Manfred F. "A Polyphonic Basse Dance of the Renaissance." In *Studies in Medieval and Renaissance Music.* New York: Norton, 1950, pp. 190–216.
Crane, Frederick. *Materials for the Study of the Fifteenth Century Basse Danse.* Brooklyn: Institute of Mediaeval Music, 1968.

Heartz, Daniel. "The Basse Dance: Its Evolution Circa 1450–1550." *Annales musicologiques* 6 (1958–63): 287–340.

BASTIDE. Fortified community in western France. In Aquitaine, preceding the Hundred Years' War, along the Anglo-French border both English and French kings or their officials founded fortified towns, usually in contracts (called in French *pariage*) with Cistercian and other monastic houses on lands that had formerly been granges under the direct cultivation of the monks. These fortified towns, or large villages, of the late 13th and early 14th centuries differ from the *villeneuves* in that they were founded on land that was already under cultivation by religious houses rather than in forest or waste and are thus not part of the earlier *défrichement* (deforestation) movement. Detailed plans for the setting out of such towns and for the attraction of settlers frequently accompany the *pariage* contracts. The success of such ventures varied considerably; some never attracted more than a few settlers, while others survive as thriving market towns to this day. Their striking characteristics, evident on plans or in aerial photos, include a compact grid of lots laid out on streets meeting at right angles within the fortifications and a large market square with covered market and arcades surrounding the central square with adjacent parish church.

Constance H. Berman

[See also: *PARIAGE; VILLENEUVE*]

Beresford, Maurice. *New Towns of the Middle Ages: Town Plantation in England, Wales, and Gascony.* New York: Praeger, 1967.
Higounet, Charles. *Paysages et villages neufs du moyen âge.* Bordeaux: Fédération Historique du Sud-Ouest, 1975.

BAUDE, HENRI (ca. 1430–ca. 1496). Henri Baude had a turbulent career as legal agent for Charles VII in the Bas-Limousin and as magistrate in the Paris courts. Baude composed rondeaux, ballades, epistles, and a satirical morality performed by the Basoche in 1486. Among his longer works are the *Testament de la mule Barbeau,* a satire of the courts, and the *Lamentations Bourrien,* satirizing ecclesiastics. Referring to current events in 15th-century France, his poetry is reminiscent of Villon's. The most original effort by this admittedly minor poet are his *Dictz moraux pour faire tapisserie,* short poems to be used as subjects for wall hangings.

Wendy E. Pfeffer

[See also: BASOCHE; GRANDS RHÉTORIQUEURS; VILLON, FRANÇOIS]

Baude, Henri. *Les vers de maître Henri Baude, poète du XVe siècle, recueillis et publiés avec les actes qui concernent sa vie,* ed. Jules Quicherat. Paris: Aubry, 1856. [Incomplete and noncritical edition.]
———. *Dictz moraux pour faire tapisserie,* ed. Annette Scoumanne. Geneva: Droz, 1959.

BAUDE FASTOUL (d. 1272). Just before entering the Beaurains leprosarium in 1272, the trouvère Baude Fastoul addressed a *congé* to his countrymen and benefactors in Arras. It reveals an original writer, capable of talking about his disease with humor while subjecting himself to God's will with resignation and trust.

Annette Brasseur

[See also: *CONGÉ*; JEHAN BODEL; *PUY*]

Ruelle, Pierre, ed. *Les congés d'Arras (Jean Bodel, Baude Fastoul, Adam de la Halle)*. Paris: Presses Universitaires de France and Brussels: Presses Universitaires de Bruxelles, 1965, pp. 107–26. [Based on MS G (B.N. fr. 25566).]

Guesnon, Adolphe. "Baude Fastoul et les congés." In *Mélanges Wilmotte 2*. Paris: Champion, 1910, pp. 726–49.

BAUDOUIN. Name of nine counts of Flanders between the 9th and 13th centuries. Baudouin I (d. 879), known as "Iron Arm," was already count of the small *pagus Flandrensis*, centered on Bruges, when he seduced Judith, daughter of Charles the Bald and widow of King Aethelwulf of Wessex. His son, Baudouin II (865–918, r. 879–918), was the true founder of the fortunes of his dynasty, consolidating its hold on the Courtrai, Aardenburg, and Cassel areas and initiating Flemish efforts to expand into areas of predominantly Romance settlement, Arras and the Vermandois. Baudouin III (d. 962), son of Count Arnulf I and grandson of Baudouin II, shared governance with his father but predeceased him.

Baudouin IV (977–1035, r. 988–1035), nicknamed "With the Handsome Beard," was one of the most noteworthy Flemish counts. His domain was in the Germanic areas bordered roughly by Bruges, Ghent, Lille, and Saint-Omer, which were then Flemish. He concentrated his attentions on expanding eastward. He faced a rebellion in the Courtrai area in the 990s, and the problems between the French- and Germanic-speaking parts of his county plagued him. After the threat of the 990s had passed, Baudouin divided most of Germanic Flanders, but not the south, into large *châtellenies*. Baudouin IV fought the emperor Henry II in the early 11th century, but in 1011 Henry enfeoffed him with Valenciennes and the northern coastal parts of Flanders, which formally made the Flemish count a vassal of both France and the empire. In 1028, he faced a rebellion from his son, the future Baudouin V, who had married Adèle, daughter of the French king Robert the Pious. In 1030, Baudouin fortified Audenarde, and by 1034 the Flemings had gained effective control of "imperial Flanders," the southeastern lands between the Scheldt and the Dendre.

Baudouin V (r. 1035–67) generally continued his father's policies. He lost several wars but was a superb diplomat who raised the prestige of Flanders to new heights and consolidated his internal administration. He founded several towns and acquired Aire-sur-la-Lys and Lille, becoming known as "Baudouin of Lille." Much of the thrust of his policy was toward the southwest, as he built a Norman alliance and extended his own territories in that direction.

In 1050, Richilde, widow of Count Herman of Hainaut, agreed to marry Baudouin's minor son, whom the emperor invested in 1056 as Baudouin VI of Flanders and Baudouin I of Hainaut. When Henry I of France died in 1060, Baudouin V of Flanders, as the late king's brother-in-law, became guardian of the eight-year-old King Philip I. Baudouin VI (r. 1067–70) was an able man, but he died prematurely. Baudouin VII (r. 1111–19) was the son of Count Robert II. His reign was marred by war with his mother, Clemence. Baudouin's chief adviser was his cousin Charles of Denmark, who succeeded him.

Baudouin VIII (r. 1191–94), who was also Baudouin V of Hainaut, succeeded his uncle, Philippe d'Alsace, as count of Flanders. Although Philip II of France recognized Baudouin VIII, his price of recognition was keeping extensive territories in southern Flanders. His son Baudouin IX (r. 1194–1206) ruled in Hainaut as Baudouin VI (1195–1206). He quickly recovered much of the territory lost to the French crown and made an English alliance. Baudouin departed on crusade in April 1202. He became ruler of the Latin kingdom of Constantinople in 1205 and governed Flanders through a regency council, but word reached Flanders in February 1206 of his death in captivity.

David M. Nicholas

[See also: FLANDERS]

de Hemptinne, Th. "Vlaanderen en Henegouwen onder de erfgenamen van de Boudewijns, 1070–1244." In *Algemene Geschiedenis der Nederlanden*. 2nd ed. Haarlem: Fibula-van Dishoeck, 1982, pp. 372–98.

Dunbabin, Jean. *France in the Making, 843–1180*. Oxford: Oxford University Press, 1985.

Ganshof, François Louis. *La Belgique carolingienne*. Brussels: Renaissance du Livre, 1958.

Koch, A. C. F. "Het graafschap Vlaanderen van de 9de eeuw tot 1070." In *Algemene Geschiedenis der Nederlanden*. 2nd ed. Haarlem: Fibula-van Dishoeck, 1982, Vol. 2, pp. 354–83.

BAUDOUIN DE CONDÉ (ca. 1250–early 14th c.). Born into a family from Condé-sur-Escaut (Hainaut), this minstrel at the court of Marguerite of Flanders (d. 1280) was particularly famous in his time. For the edification of the great of this world, he wrote twenty-four *dits* in octosyllabic verse, notable for their multifarious inspiration: cautionary reflections (*Li vers de droit*), stories of unrequited love (*Li prisons d'amours*), satires on the vices of the age (*Li contes de l'aver*), religious verse (*Li Ave Maria*), gruesomely realistic description (*Dit des trois mors et des trois vis*). These topics are often obfuscated by excessive wordplay and metrical acrobatics.

Annette Brasseur

[See also: *DIT*; FABLIAU; PRAYERS AND DEVOTIONAL MATERIALS]

Baudouin de Condé. *Dits et contes de Baudouin de Condé et de son fils Jean de Condé*, ed. Auguste Scheler. 3 vols. Brussels: Devaux, 1866–67. [Based on MS A (B.N. fr. 1446).]

Ribard, Jacques. *Un ménestrel du XIVe siècle, Jean de Condé.* Geneva: Droz, 1969, pp. 72–85, 392–405.

BAUDOUIN DE SEBOURC. A mid-14th-century northern French chanson de geste loosely attached to the Crusade Cycle. Its 25,778 lines, in Franco-Picard dialect, were probably composed in Hainaut, possibly at Valenciennes. There are two manuscripts, B.N. fr. 12552 and 12553. The hero is a composite figure; in other 13th- and 14th-century Crusade epics, the name is given to the third Frankish king of Jerusalem (Baldwin of Le Bourg, 12th c.), but there is some evidence for independent legends about a Picard adventurer called Baudouin de Sebourc. Sebourg is a village in what is today the Département du Nord.

The poem has relatively brief sections set in the Middle East, but only its ending leads, artificially, into the roughly contemporary crusade poem *Le Bâtard de Bouillon.* Most of the action takes place in northern France or the Low Countries and concerns the adventures of Baudouin's youth. The hero is treated according to the conventions of the late epics rather than historically. Baudouin is separated from his family as a child and spends many years wandering before at last avenging the treachery of the villainous Gaufroi and becoming a crusader. Some of his adventures derive from folklore, others—the visit to Hell, the moving of a mountain by prayer—from literary tradition. The hero's martial and sexual exploits (he has thirty bastards) are presented with a verve and piquancy of expression that have given the work an outstanding reputation among the poems of its genre and period.

Robert Francis Cook

[See also: CRUSADE CYCLE; LATE EPIC]

Boca, Louis-Napoléon. *Li romans de Bauduin de Sebourc, IIIe roy de Jherusalem.* 2 vols. Valenciennes: Henry, 1841.

Cook, Robert Francis, and Larry S. Crist. *Le deuxième cycle de la croisade.* Geneva: Droz, 1972.

Duparc-Quioc, Suzanne. *Le cycle de la croisade.* Paris: Champion, 1955.

Labande, Edmond-René. *Étude sur Baudouin de Sebourc.* Paris: Droz, 1940.

BAUDRI OF BOURGUEIL (Baldricus Burgulianus; 1045–1130). An important representative of the humanistic revival of the early 12th century in the Angers region, Baudri was born at Meung-sur-Loire. He studied at Angers under Marbode of Rennes and, according to Dronke, with the poet Geoffroi de Reims. He was elected, ca. 1080–82, abbot of the Benedictine foundation of Saint-Pierre-de-Bourgueil, a place that he described in a verse letter to the nun Emma as having charming landscape but little learning, where onions were commoner than stylus and tablet. In 1107, he became archbishop of Dòl-de-Bretagne. His diocese did not appeal to him, and he traveled in England and Normandy while bishop. The journeys are recorded in his *Itinerarium.*

Baudri's best-known prose work is the Latin *Historia Hierosolymitana,* an account of the First Crusade written shortly after 1107, based on the French *Histoire anonyme de la première croisade.* He also wrote a life of Robert d'Arbrissel for the abbess of Fontevrault. As a poet, he is noted for his correspondence with a number of learned females, including the nun Emma and Adèle, countess of Blois, daughter of William the Conqueror and mother of King Stephen. His longest poem is a 1,366-line description—whether real or imaginary has been debated—of Adèle's palace and chamber with its zodiac on the ceiling, world map on the floor, statues of the Liberal Arts, Philosophy, and Medicine around the bed, and tapestries of Old Testament, Greek, Trojan, and Roman myths and history around the walls. Other substantial works include a moralized mythology, drawing on his favorite classical author, Ovid.

Baudri's shorter poems are chiefly to and about students and friends from his clerical circle and the female convent of Le Ronceray at Angers. He carefully preserved even the short verses that he wrote for mortuary rolls. His religious verse includes a dedicatory poem for the church of Saint-Samson-sur-Rille. His history of the bishops of Dol is lost, but a *vita* of St. Samson and an account of the translation of the head of St. Valentine survive. In all, 256 Latin poems by Baudri are known today.

Jeanne E. Krochalis

[See also: HILDEBERT OF LAVARDIN; LIBERAL ARTS; MARBODE OF RENNES]

Baudri de Bourgueil. *Opera. PL* 166.1049–212.

———. *Carmina,* ed. Karlheinz Hilbert. Heidelberg: Winter, 1979.

———. *Les œuvres poétiques de Baudri de Bourgueil,* ed. Phyllis Abrahams. Paris: Champion, 1926.

———. Poems 50–64. In *Medieval Latin Poems of Male Love and Friendship,* trans. Thomas Stehling. New York: Garland, 1984.

Dronke, Peter. *Medieval Latin and the Rise of the European Love Lyric.* Oxford: Clarendon, 1965, Vol. 1: *Problems and Interpretations,* pp. 209–12, 216–17.

Ghellinck, Joseph de. *L'essor de la littérature latine au XIIe siècle.* 2nd ed. Brussels: Desclée, De Brouwer, 1955.

BAYEUX. The Treaty of Saint-Claire-sur-Epte (911) included Bayeux as one of the places named as a settlement for the Viking leader Rollo. With its strategic position, Bayeux continued to gain importance under the dukes of Normandy but experienced much destruction in the process. Not until the 11th century could restoration of the cathedral take place under Bishop Hugues (r. 1015–49), when Normans began to fund ecclesiastical buildings. By the end of the Hundred Years' War, the English had evacuated and left the area desolate. Today, the city retains much of its medieval fabric, including the cathedral of Notre-Dame, some timber-framed houses, and of course the Bayeux Tapestry.

Notre-Dame-de-Bayeux stands on the site of a Roman temple and later sanctuaries (tradition holds that St. Exupère founded an oratory here), but little documentary evidence survives prior to the 11th century. Orderic Vitalis

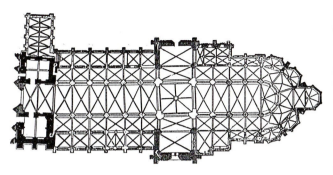

Bayeux (Calvados), Notre-Dame, plan. After Valery-Radot.

notes that Odo, bishop of Bayeux, consecrated the church in 1076 and finished it in 1087, having "endowed it abundantly with many riches and ornament." In 1105, Henry I of England stormed the city and burned the church, and another fire in 1159 initiated the restoration of most of the building. Only Odo's crypt and the west towers survived the 12th century.

Most of the 11th- and 12th-century Romanesque portions remain visible inside the building in the intricate sculpture of the nave arcade, the crypt, and the west towers, but later alterations irretrievably transformed the exterior of the church into a Gothic building with 13th-century tracery, gables, flying buttresses, and 15th-century central tower.

Despite stylistic differences, both Gothic and Romanesque portions conform to a high degree of ornamentation. On the exterior, late 13th-century Gothic work sheaths parts of the Romanesque west towers, and two false blind portals frame the three actual portals that lead into the nave with double side aisles. Only the center portal directly introduces the visitor to the longitudinal space. Cluster piers and subtly molded round-headed arches delineate the six bays of the nave, vaulted with early 13th-century quadripartite rib vaults. Large Gothic clerestory widows illuminate the richly carved surface of the Romanesque arcade: tooled reticulated work covers the entire surface of the walls with complex interlacing, interwoven and overlapping patterns, a variety of arch moldings, and molded architraves with figural and fantastic subjects. Framed figural sculpture, of bishops and nonwestern characters, resides in isolation in the spandrels.

A balustrade with arcade provides a visual transition between the round-headed arcade below and grand lancet windows at clerestory level. Later 13th-century transept arms support a 19th-century tower, reconstructed to avoid total collapse. In the south transept, the Gothic portal tympanum displays the life of St. Thomas Becket. The 13th-century choir has an ambulatory, radiating chapels, and extended chevet. Here, engaged shafts extend from floor to clerestory, where each shaft springs into transverse and diagonal ribs. Medallions pierce the surface of the spandrels throughout the choir arcade, and figural sculpture features Old and New Testament scenes along with the

Bayeux, Notre-Dame, chevet. *Photograph: Clarence Ward Collection. Courtesy of Oberlin College.*

Bayeux, Notre-Dame, nave. *Photograph courtesy of Whitney S. Stoddard.*

legend of SS. Vigor and Loup on the south side of the choir. The 11th-century crypt holds carved capitals.

Of conventual buildings, a late 12th- or early 13th-century chapter house survives, as well as a treasury. The Grand Seminary, known as the Centre Guillaume-le-Conquérant, displays the entire 231 feet of the Bayeux Tapestry.

Stacy L. Boldrick

[See also: BAYEUX TAPESTRY; NORMANDY; ROMANESQUE ARCHITECTURE]

Baylé, Maylis. "La cathédrale [de Bayeux] à l'époque de Guillaume le Conquérant et de ses fils." *Art de Basse-Normandie* 76 (1978–79).

Beaurepaire, François de. *Sources médiévales de l'histoire de Normandie dans les bibliothèques de Bayeux.* Saint-Lô: Société d'Archéologie et d'Histoire de la Manche, 1966.

Musset, Lucien. *Normandie romane.* 2 vols. La Pierre-qui-vire: Zodiaque, 1967, Vol. 1.

Thirion, Jacques. "La cathédrale de Bayeux." *Congrès archéologique* 132 (1978).

Vallery-Radot, J. *La cathédrale de Bayeux.* 2nd ed. Paris: Laurens, 1958.

BAYEUX TAPESTRY. Produced in England between 1066 and 1083, the Bayeux Tapestry illustrates Harold Godwinsson's visit to Normandy and the invasion of England by William the Conqueror. Technically an embroidery, the hanging gained the label of "tapestry" from centuries of French references to *tapis,* an all-inclusive label for designed textiles. Eight joined strips of linen (19 inches in width by 231 feet in length) hold the main narrative, embroidered in eight colors of wool thread. Brief Latin inscriptions identify the portrayed events. The border of grotesque animal figures, landscape elements, and battle scenes between nudes offers a running commentary on the main events and ancillary relationships with literary themes. Scholarship suggests that the patron of the embroidery was Odo of Bayeux, half-brother of William the Conqueror and bishop of Bayeux in the late 11th century. Although displayed in the 15th century on the feast of relics in Bayeux cathedral, the original function of the tapestry remains a subject of speculation, with the possibility of contexts religious (the cathedral of Bayeux) and secular (a great hall).

Stacy L. Boldrick

[See also: BAYEUX]

Bertrand, Simone. *La tapisserie de Bayeux et la manière de vivre au onzième siècle.* La Pierre-qui-vire: Zodiaque, 1966.

Brown, Shirley Ann. *The Bayeux Tapestry: History and Bibliography.* Woodbridge: Boydell, 1988.

Wilson, David M. *The Bayeux Tapestry.* New York: Knopf, 1985.

BAYONNE. The only fortress of any consequence in southwestern France, Lapurdum, now Bayonne (Pyrénées-Atlantiques), was the principal port of the Roman province of Novempopulania. Fortified by the 1st century B.C., it experienced attacks by Visigoths, Basques, Moors, and Normans. When Charlemagne's kingdom of Aquitanie was broken up, Bayonne became the capital of the county of Labourd, which was attached to Gascony in the 12th century. It prospered as a whaling, fishing, and shipbuilding center under Norman rule, from 1154 until the end of the Hundred Years' War, when it was captured by Jean de Dunois (1451).

The Château-Vieux (12th and 15th c.), built on Roman foundations, is a square fortress with corner towers. It was here that Bertrand du Guesclin was imprisoned to await ransom. The Château-Neuf was constructed in 1489. The cathedral of Sainte-Marie is one of the finest in southwestern France. Begun in 1213 on the site of a Roman temple, it was built over two centuries in imitation of northern Gothic churches. South of the church are the 14th-century cloisters, with elegant wide bays.

William W. Kibler/William W. Clark

Lambert, Élie. "Bayonne." *Congrès archéologique* (*Bordeaux et Bayonne*) 102 (1939): 507–70.

BAZAS (Gironde). The ancient *oppidum* of Cossium, former capital of the Vacates, became one of the principal towns of the Roman province of Novempopulania. It was raised to a bishopric in the 5th century and is mentioned by Gregory of Tours. The Gothic cathedral of Saint-Jean-Baptiste, begun in 1233 and continued into the 14th century, is built over an 11th-century Romanesque church destroyed by the English in 1198. It consists of a long (274-foot) and narrow (76-foot) aisled nave of eleven bays, a choir with ambulatory and five radiating chapels, but no transept. The blind triforium with a flattened arch in each bay is an unusual feature possibly imported from the Parisian area. Three portals on the west façade, dedicated to the Last Judgment, the Dormition and Coronation of the Virgin, and the life of St. Peter, preserve remarkable examples of 13th-century Gothic sculpture. Attacked by the Huguenots in 1577 and 1578, the precious sculpture was saved only by a ransom of 10,000 crowns raised by parishoners. The cathedral was extensively restored between 1583 and 1635, following the Wars of Religion.

William W. Kibler/William W. Clark

Gardelles, Jacques. "La cathédrale de Bazas." *Congrès archéologique* (*Bordelais et Bazadais*) 145 (1987): 21–37.

BÉARN. The viscounty of Béarn in Gascony, created in the 9th century, consisted of two principal valleys, the Aspe and the Ossau, draining the northern slopes of the Pyrénées and extending northwest into the lower lands of the Oloron and Pau rivers. Béarnese rulers of the 10th and 11th centuries joined in Navarrese and Aragonese military expeditions against the Muslims and gravitated primarily in an Aragonese political orbit from the late 11th century to the early 13th, when Catalano-Aragonese influence in Languedoc was abruptly ended by the victory of the Albigensian crusaders. In 1170, rights to the viscounty of Béarn passed to members of a Catalan noble lineage, inaugurating a period of relatively weak vice-comital rule. In 1221, Guillem Ramon de Montcada, viscount of Béarn, confirmed important additions to the *Fors d'Oloron*, an 11th-century legal charter. The enhanced text lay the groundwork for the celebrated *Fors de Béarn* and led to the establishment of the "estates" of Béarn, an association of nobles, nonnobles, and churchmen whose consultations with the viscount were institutionalized in the late 14th century. Béarn vacillated between allegiance to the kingdom of France and to the English dukes of Aquitaine from 1228 to 1364, when Viscount Gaston Phoebus declared Béarn independent of England.

John C. Shidelar

Dumonteil, Jacques, and Bernard Cheronnet. *Le fors d'Oloron: édition critique réalisée pour le 9e centenaire de la "Poblation."* Oloron: "Ouvrage publié avec le concours de la municipalité d'Oloron-Sainte-Marie," 1980 (1981).

Tucoo-Chala, Pierre. *La vicomté de Béarn et le problème de sa souveraineté des origines à 1620.* Bordeaux: Bière, 1961.

BEAUCAIRE. The town of Beaucaire (Gard) was the site of a fortress guarding the eastern border of Languedoc. It lay on the right bank of the Rhône, a river that for much of the Middle Ages marked the frontier of the realm in southeastern France. After lower Languedoc was taken over by the French crown in 1229, the district was administered by a royal seneschal whose military headquarters were at Beaucaire, while the judicial and administrative seat lay at Nîmes, farther west.

John Bell Henneman, Jr.

[See also: *AUCASSIN ET NICOLETTE*]

BEAULIEU-SUR-DORDOGNE (Corrèze). The 12th-century church with magnificent sculptured portal, chapter house, several reliquaries, and a beautiful Virgin and Child covered in silver repoussé are all that remain of the Benedictine abbey of Saint-Pierre, founded on the banks of the Dordogne in the 9th century and affiliated to Cluny at the end of the 11th. Typically Limousin in detail, the abbey church emulates the plan of the great pilgrimage churches: wide, groin-vaulted side aisles, galleries (albeit small and dark), transept with apsidioles, ambulatory with three radiating chapels. An octagonal dome, irregular in shape, crowns the crossing. The façade dates from the 13th century (with later modifications) and the attached bell tower from the 14th.

The format of the south portal (ca. 1130–40) appears to follow that of Moissac; the imagery, however, is novel. Most striking are the appearance of the bare-breasted Christ displaying his wounds, the prominence accorded the Cross, the seven gesticulating figures beneath the Apostles, and the double lintel arrangement of apocalyptic and exotic beasts. The theme of the tympanum, based on Matthew 24 and elements from the Apocalypse, is the Second Coming, which precedes the final Judgment. The reliefs of the porch evoke the penitential season of Lent. The whole may be seen as an affirmation of church doctrines threatened by heretical attack.

Jean M. French

Christe, Yves. "Le portail de Beaulieu, étude iconographique et stylistique." *Bulletin archéologique du Comité des Travaux Historiques et Scientifiques* 6 (1971): 57–76.

French, Jean M. "The Innovative Imagery of the Beaulieu Portal Program: Sources and Significance." Diss. Cornell, 1972. [Summarized in *Studies in Medieval Culture* 8–9 (1976): 19–30.]

Klein, Peter K. "'Et videbit eum omnis oculus et qui eum pupugerunt.' Zur Deutung des Tympanons von Beaulieu." In *Florilegium in honorem Carl Nordenfalk octogenarii contextum*, ed. Per Bjurstrom, Nils-Goran Hokby, and Florentine Mutherich. Stockholm: Nationalmuseum, 1987, pp. 123–44.

Maury, Jean, Marie-Madeleine Gauthier, and Jean Porcher. *Limousin roman*. La Pierre-qui-vire: Zodiaque, 1960.

Vidal, Marguerite, Jean Maury, and Jean Porcher. *Quercy roman*. La Pierre-qui-vire: Zodiaque, 1969.

BEAUMANOIR, PHILIPPE DE REMI, SIRE DE (ca. 1250–1296). Jurist, author, and royal official, Beaumanoir came from the village of Remy, near Compiègne, where his family held a fief from the abbey of Saint-Denis. He was the second son of Philippe de Remi (ca. 1205–ca. 1265), who served as *bailli* of Gâtinais for Robert, count of Artois, from 1237 to 1250. By 1255, the father had apparently built a manor house on the property, for he then styled himself "lord of Beaumanoir," a title that passed to his heir, Girard, then to the younger Philippe at Girard's death. Beaumanoir *fils* began his administrative career in 1279 as *bailli* of Clermont-en-Beauvaisis for Robert, count of Clermont. In 1283, he completed the *Coutumes de Beauvaisis*, a systematic treatise on customary law composed in Francien prose with strong traces of Picard. Beaumanoir declares in his prologue that it is essential to write down the legal customs of the region so that they can be maintained without change "because, since memories are fleeting and human lives are short, what is not written is soon forgotten." His book was widely copied in the Middle Ages (thirteen manuscripts extant, ten or eleven other copies known to be lost) and is today considered the most significant work on French customary law of the 13th century. In 1284, Beaumanoir was knighted and entered royal administration; he served as seneschal of Poitou (1284–87) and Saintonge (1287–89), then as *bailli* of Vermandois (1289–91), Touraine (1291–92), and Senlis until his death (1292–96).

Since the 1870s, a substantial body of narrative and lyric poetry has been attributed to the author of the *Coutumes*: two romances in octosyllabic verse, *La Manekine* (8,590 lines) and *Jehan et Blonde* (6,262 lines), both signed

Phelippe de Remi; at least three *chansons courtoises*, two naming the poet Phelippe de Remi; a moralistic fabliau, *Fole Larguece*; and several shorter poems, including a *Salu d'amours* signed Phelippe de Beaumanoir, two *fatrasies*, and an *Ave Maria*. Traditional scholarship holds that Beaumanoir composed most of these works as Philippe de Remi while in his twenties, between 1270 and 1280, and assumed the name Philippe de Beaumanoir only in 1279, when he turned his energies to law and administration. Some recent scholars, troubled by the unusual productivity of such a young man and by the disparity between courtly and legal subjects, prefer to attribute all the poetry to the father and date it between 1237 and 1262. A major factor underlying the revisionist attribution is the revival of a turn-of-the-century Germanist argument that Rudolf von Ems used both romances as sources for his *Willehalm von Orlens*, completed before 1243. Attribution and dating of the poetry remain open questions.

La Manekine is a pious adventure romance based on the folklore motif of "The Maiden Without Hands," also treated in the somewhat later *Belle Helaine de Constantinople* and *Lion de Bourges*. A Hungarian princess who cuts off her right hand rather than marry her father incestuously is set adrift and lands in Scotland, where she marries the king, only to be betrayed by his mother; set adrift again, she lands in Rome, where she is miraculously healed, reunited with her husband, and reconciled with her father. *Jehan et Blonde*, perhaps based in part on the *Roman de Horn* and deeply influenced by the romances of Chrétien de Troyes, tells the story of an impecunious French knight, Jehan, who rises in the world by serving as squire to the Count of Oxford and winning the love of Blonde, the count's daughter; it can be read as a how-to manual for success at court and for moral behavior by lordly vassals. The 15th-century prose romance *Jehan de Paris* is a free adaptation of *Jehan et Blonde*.

Mary B. Speer

[See also: *BELLE HELAINE DE CONSTANTINOPLE*; CUSTUMALS/*COUTUMIERS*; *FATRAS/FATRASIE*; *JEHAN DE PARIS, ROMAN DE*; LAW AND JUSTICE; PRAYERS AND DEVOTIONAL MATERIALS; REALISTIC ROMANCES; *RESVERIE*; WAUQUELIN (DE MONS), JEAN]

Philippe de Remi, sire de Beaumanoir. *Œuvres poétiques*, ed. Hermann Suchier. 2 vols. Paris: SATF, 1884–85, Vol. 1: *La Manekine*, Vol. 2: *Jehan et Blonde; poésies diverses*. [Based on the unique MS (B.N. fr. 1588).]

————. *La Manekine: roman du XIIIe siécle,* trans. Christiane Marcello-Nizia. Paris: Stock, 1980. [Modern French.]

————. *Philippe de Remi's "La Manekine,"* ed. and trans. Irene Gnarra. New York: Garland, 1990.

————. *Jehan et Blonde de Philippe de Rémi: roman du XIIIe siècle,* ed. Sylvie Lécuyer. Paris: Champion, 1984. [Modern French trans., 1987.]

————. "Les chansons de Philippe de Beaumanoir," ed. Alfred Jeanroy. *Romania* 26 (1897): 517–36. [From B.N. fr. 24406.]

————. *Coutumes de Beauvaisis,* Vol. 1 and 2: ed. Amédée Salmon. Paris: Picard, 1899–1900 [English trans. by F.R.P. Akehurst. Philadelphia: University of Pennsylvania Press, 1992]. Vol. 3: *Commentaire historique et juridique par Georges Hubrecht*. Paris: Picard, 1974.

Dufournet, Jean, ed. *Un roman à découvrir: "Jean et Blonde" de Philippe de Remy (XIIIe siècle)*. Paris: Champion, 1991.

Gicquel, Bernard. "Le *Jehan et Blonde* de Philippe de Rémi peut-il être une source du *Willehalm von Orlens*?" *Romania* 102 (1981); 306–22.

Shepherd, M. *Tradition and Re-Creation in Thirteenth-Century Romance: "La Manekine" and "Jehan et Blonde" by Philippe de Rémi*. Amsterdam: Rodopi, 1990.

BEAUNE. Built on the site of prehistoric springs, the Roman town of Belina or Belnocastrum prospered from stock breeding, agriculture, and viticulture. It was fortified at the time of the Germanic invasions (3rd–4th c. A.D.) and became a county during the Carolingian period. In the Middle Ages, it was one of the favorite residences of the dukes of Burgundy. It was chartered by Duke Eudes in 1203 and made a parliamentary seat in 1227. The city walls, largely intact today, were built in 1368. After the death in 1477 of Charles the Bold, last duke of Burgundy, it took Louis XI five weeks to subdue the city.

As a religious center, Beaune was home to Benedictines, Dominicans, Franciscans, and Carthusians. The Romanesque church of Notre-Dame, begun in 1120 under Bishop Étienne de Bâgé, is a typical Cluniac large-porched structure. The ambulatory and three separated radiating chapels are pure Romanesque; the High Romanesque nave, which resembles Autun and Cluny III, has pointed barrel vaulting, while the side aisles have rib vaulting. The crossing tower features Gothic bays over Romanesque blind arcades. The church of Saint-Nicolas, rebuilt in the 13th century, retains a Romanesque tower, porch, and sculpted portal. Within the town, one can admire a number of 12th- and 13th-century houses with linteled windows, a chapter house with a façade dated to the 13th century, and a rectangular belfry of 1403.

Beaune's celebrity today comes primarily from its hospital, or Hôtel-Dieu, founded in 1443 by Nicolas Rolin, chancellor of Duke Philip the Good. A marvel of Flemish Late Gothic style, it was designed by the Brabantine archi-

Beaune (Côte d'Or), Hôtel-Dieu, courtyard. *Photograph courtesy of Joan A. Holladay.*

Beaune (Côte d'Or), Hôtel-Dieu. *Photograph courtesy of Whitney S. Stoddard.*

tect Jean de Visscher (or Wiscrère). The exterior is picturesque, with its high-pitched roof covered with multicolored glazed tiles, its wooden galleries, dormer windows, lacework leaden ornamentation, and gilded vanes. The main ward inside is 172 feet long under an impressive polychromed timber roof in the form of an upturned ship's keel. Within is the magnificent *Last Judgment* by Rogier van der Weyden, commissioned by Rolin in 1443 for the high altar of the main ward.

William W. Kibler/William W. Clark

[See also: BURGUNDY; CHARLES THE BOLD; HOSPITALS; TONNERRE; VAN DER WEYDEN, ROGIER]

Rhein, André. "Beaune: collégiale Notre-Dame," "Beaune: église Saint-Nicolas," and "Beaune: Hôtel-Dieu." *Congrès archéologique* (Dijon) 91 (1928): 267–88, 316–26.

BEAUNEVEU, ANDRÉ (d. 1402). Sculptor and painter active in Flanders and in France during the last third of the 14th century. Beauneveu was commissioned to carve a tomb figure of Charles V in 1364 and is documented as embellishing the duke of Berry's château at Mehun-sur-Yèvre with sculptures and paintings in 1386. The duke's inventories state that he also painted the miniatures of prophets and Apostles at the beginning of the duke's psalter (B.N. fr. 13091). These miniatures are executed in *grisaille*, in a style emulating the volumetric effects of sculpture, for which Beauneveu was renowned. He has also been credited with painting the *Parement de Narbonne* in the Louvre and miniatures in the *Très belles heures de Notre Dame* in Paris (B.N. n.a. lat. 3093), but these attributions remain controversial.

Robert G. Calkins

[See also: JOHN, DUKE OF BERRY]

Meiss, Millard. *French Painting in the Time of Jean de Berry: The Late Fourteenth Century and the Patronage of the Duke.* 2nd ed. 2 vols. London: Phaidon, 1969, Vol. 1, pp. 37, 45, 135, 147–49.
Scher, Stephen. "André Beauneveu and Claus Sluter." *Gesta* 7 (1968): 3–14.
Troescher, Georg. *Die burgundische Plastik des ausgehenden Mittelalters und ihre Wirkungen auf die europäische Kunst.* 2 vols. Frankfurt am Main: Prestel, 1940.

BEAUVAIS. In the first half of the 13th century, the chapter of Saint-Pierre in Beauvais (Oise) decided to replace a church that had been destroyed twice by fire, once in 1180 and again in 1225. Identifying sources of income for this

Beauvais (Oise), Saint-Pierre, chevet. *Photograph: Clarence Ward Collection. Courtesy of Oberlin College.*

project, the chapter also agreed to devote one-tenth of its revenue for the next ten years to the building of a magnificent church, the cathedral of Saint-Pierre. A papal legate approved the plan in 1245.

The foundation for the choir and apse was laid in 1238; had the catheral been completed as originally planned, it would have been the largest Gothic cathedral in the world. The irregular placement of pillars and buttresses, specified by the ambitious architectural plan, resulted in structural weaknesses. The roof caved in twice, in 1247 and 1284. The unfinished cathedral is 239 feet long and 160 feet high. The choir alone is 121 feet in length. Its vaulting, supported by twelve double flying buttresses, opens on an ambulatory by a succession of triangular arcades. A 14th-century clerestory, situated within the three bays, is composed of triangular and trefoil arches. Above the seven ambulatory chapels and the rectangular chapels are a blind triforium and a clerestory of the 13th century. This clerestory is surmounted by a series of windows ornamented with full and quarter-trefoils and a rose window in foliated tracery.

At the west end, adjoining the transept, is the nave of an earlier cathedral, known as Notre-Dame de la Basse-Œuvre. The oldest religious edifice in Beauvais, this church was established 987–88 by Hervé, bishop of Beauvais. The materials for its construction were probably taken from Roman ramparts.

Also at Beauvais is the church of Saint-Étienne, Beauvais's first Christian edifice. It was destroyed by the Normans in 859 and after reconstruction was damaged twice by fire. In 997, Bishop Hervé undertook its restoration. It offers an early example of cross-ribbed vaulting. Its nave and transept with a central bell tower are from the 12th century.

E. Kay Harris

[See also: CHAMBIGES, MARTIN; GOTHIC ARCHITECTURE]

Ajalbert, Jean. *Beauvais*. Paris: Morancé, 1927.
Leblond, Victor. *La cathédrale de Beauvais*. Paris: Laurens, 1926.
Marsaux, M. le chanoine. "Beauvais." *Congrès archéologique* (*Beauvais*) 72 (1905): 1–31.
Mesqui, Jean. *Île-de-France gothique*. 2 vols. Paris: Picard, 1988, Vol. 1, pp. 70–104.

BEDFORD, JOHN OF LANCASTER, DUKE OF (1389–1435). The third son of Henry IV of England, John spent his youth serving with distinction on campaigns in Scotland, Wales, and France. He became regent in France in 1422 and proved himself an excellent general and administrator, though he failed to secure the conquests of Henry V. Maintaining an English alliance with Burgundy was the keystone of his policy. To that end, he signed an alliance with Brittany and Burgundy at Amiens in 1423 and married Anne de Bourgogne in June 1424. Paris, which had accepted Henry V out of Burgundian fidelity, he left essentially self-governing and concentrated on Normandy. Seek-ing loyalty there, he governed generously through an unusually disciplined administration. He continued to exert military pressure against the Valois, but even his greatest victory, at Verneuil in 1424, proved indecisive. After his defeat at Orléans in 1429 and the death of his wife in 1432, he faced the prospect of a rapprochement between Charles VII and the duke of Burgundy. Bedford's failure to prevent this confirmed his incapacity as a diplomat, though he succeeded in holding Normandy. His death, on the eve of the Treaty of Arras, symbolized the doomed hopes of the Anglo-French kingdom.

Paul D. Solon

[See also: CHARLES VII; HUNDRED YEARS' WAR; ORLÉANS CAMPAIGN; PHILIP THE GOOD]

Allmand, C.T. *Lancastrian Normandy, 1415–1450*. Oxford: Clarendon, 1983.
Newhall, R.A. *Muster and Review: A Problem of English Military Administration, 1420–1440*. Cambridge: Harvard University Press, 1940.
Williams, Ethel Carleton. *My Lord of Bedford, 1389–1435*. London: Longman, 1963.

BEDFORD MASTER. An anonymous artist named after a book of hours (B.L. add. 18850) that he illuminated for John of Lancaster, duke of Bedford and regent of France, between 1422 and 1435. He also began a breviary for the duke known as the Salisbury Breviary (B.N. lat. 17294), which remained unfinished. His style is close to that of the Boucicaut Master of about a decade before.

Robert G. Calkins

[See also: BOUCICAUT MASTER; MANUSCRIPTS, PRODUCTION AND ILLUMINATION]

Spencer, Eleanor. "The Master of the Duke of Bedford: The Bedford Hours." *Burlington Magazine* 107 (1965): 495–502.
———. "The Master of the Duke of Bedford: The Salisbury Breviary." *Burlington Magazine* 108 (1966): 607–12.
———. *The Sobieski Hours: A Manuscript in the Royal Library at Windsor Castle*. London: Academic, 1977.

BÉGUINES. Pious laywomen who chose to live a holy life, but not in a convent as members of a regular ecclesiastical order. Béguines emerged in the 12th century as part of a new form of piety that sought to imitate the poverty of Christ and the earliest Christians. These women lived either in groups or alone, mostly in urban centers; by the early 13th century, a strong women's movement had evolved in Germany, the Netherlands, and France. Exemplifying religious zeal for a Christian life of chastity and poverty, they lived either from alms or from the work of their hands. Early on, such work often involved the carding of wool, spinning, and weaving. Later béguine occupations included the teaching of children, care of the sick in hospitals, and prayers for the souls of the dead.

In the late 12th and early 13th centuries, these women were called "béguines," a derisive term conveying the suspect, even heretical, character of their piety in the judgment of their social peers and ecclesiastical authorities. By the second half of the 13th century, however, the term was applied, with a positive connotation, to women who lived a religious life together in a house, most often called a béguinage, or to women who lived as religious solitaries. The solitary béguine could live as a recluse, mendicant, itinerant teacher, or preacher. The name was also given to those suspected of heresy. The béguines were thus viewed with both suspicion and admiration.

The problems attending the béguine life surfaced as early as 1215, when the Fourth Lateran Council forbade the founding of new religious orders; the béguine houses had no existing general ecclesiastical structure. Legitimate recognition would be available if the houses were somehow understood to be annexes of male monasteries, or if the women in the houses could support themselves in strict enclosure without depending on alms, that is, if the women were wealthy enough themselves or if the houses found a wealthy patron to endow them. In 1216, however, through Jacques de Vitry's appeal to Pope Honorius III, béguines in Liège, in the kingdom of France, and in the German empire, received permission to live in communities that were connected to no established religious order and conformed to no extant monastic rule. In 1233, Pope Gregory IX published the bull *Gloriam virginalem*, which formally approved of these groups of virgins living holy lives. With this official recognition, houses of béguines began to proliferate.

In France, the proliferation is most notable in the north, where by the mid-13th century there is evidence for the existence of béguines in four important areas. The earliest mention of a béguinage in northern France occurs in Cambrai in 1236, when Godfrey of Fontaines, bishop of Cambrai (r. 1220–37), indicated his intention to support a community of pious women. In 1239, a hospital was founded for béguines in Valenciennes. A church was built for béguines in Douai in 1245, and béguines are mentioned in a document from Lille dated 1247. These communities had powerful protection from members of the clergy, particularly Godfrey of Fontaines and other bishops who with abbots and parish priests gave public support to the spiritual béguine life. Support from secular guardians, who furnished lands and buildings and convinced local magistrates to support these houses for béguines, was crucial for the survival of the communities. The most powerful protection came from the Capetians. Beginning with Louis IX, the French crown founded and supported a number of béguine houses, and Louis's heirs continued the support with royal revenues. The largest of these houses was the great béguinage of Paris, which, according to Louis's confessor, housed close to 400 women. During the reign of Philip IV the Fair, the crown made certain that papal privileges and exemptions continued to benefit the Paris béguinage and ensured the construction of a chapel for them in which a priest was to celebrate Mass once a year.

The evidence for this kind of support is crucial, because by the mid-13th century public opinion regarding the béguines took on hostile overtones. In 1274, in light of this growing antipathy, the Council of Lyon repeated the proscriptions of the Fourth Lateran Council against the founding of new orders. In addition, the council declared that any orders founded since 1215 without papal approval were forbidden and dissolved. Béguines, however, never claimed to be an order, and particular houses took refuge in letters of protection from the pope, bishops, and civil magistrates. The most serious attack came in 1312 from the Council of Vienne, which promulgated two decrees. *Cum de quibusdam mulieribus* explicitly condemned the status of béguine, citing it as being in violation of the Fourth Lateran ban of new orders, and yet closed with an "escape clause" that conceded that truly pious women might be allowed to live in communal houses. The other decree, *Ad nostrum*, identified in catastrophic fashion the béguines with the organized heretical sect of the Free Spirit. The failure of the Vienne council to develop a workable distinction between truly pious and heretical béguines resulted in what was tantamount to a war on béguines, especially in Germany. In France, however, they may have fared better because of support and protection from their powerful patrons in the French court, nobility, and ecclesiastical hierarchy.

Ellen L. Babinsky

[See also: GODFREY OF FONTAINES; JACQUES DE VITRY; LOUIS IX; MARIE D'OIGNIES: NUNNERIES: PHILIP IV THE FAIR; WOMEN, RELIGIOUS EXPERIENCE OF]

Delmaire, Bernard. "Les béguines dans le nord de la France au premier siècle de leur histoire (vers 1230–vers 1350)." In *Les religieuses en France au XIIIe siècle*, ed. Michel Parisse. Nancy: Presses Universitaires, 1985.

Le Grand, Léon. "Les béguines de Paris." In *Mémoires de la Société de l'Histoire de Paris et de l'Île-de-France*. Paris: Champion, 1893, Vol. 20.

McDonnell, Ernest W. *The Beguines and Beghards in Medieval Culture with Special Emphasis on the Belgian Scene*. New Brunswick: Rutgers University Press, 1954.

BELLE HELAINE DE CONSTANTINOPLE. A lengthy (14,000–18,000 lines) and convoluted romance of Byzantine inspiration, *Belle Helaine* was a popular story, composed first in verse (1250–60; three 15th-c. manuscripts) and later reworked in prose, notably by Jean Wauquelin. Telling the story of a heroine whose right hand is cut off to avoid her identification, the anonymous Tourangeau author used assonanced Alexandrines to disguise his adventure romance as a chanson de geste.

Wendy E. Pfeffer

[See also: BEAUMANOIR, PHILIPPE DE REMI, SIRE DE]

Ruths, R. *Die französische Fassungen des* Roman de la belle Helaine. Diss. Greifswald, 1897.

BELLS. The early history of Christian church bells is obscure. One cannot credit the medieval view that they were introduced by St. Paulinus (d. 431), who never mentioned them in his writings. The notion apparently stems from the coincidence that *campana* and *nola* are common terms for church bells and that Paulinus was bishop of Nola in Campania. Monastic rules in the 4th century already indicate that the monks were assembled for prayer and meals by a signaling device, but this was probably a wooden gong (*sematron*) rather than a metal bell. Gregory of Tours (d. 594) mentions bells on a number of occasions, and it is clear that they were regularly employed in churches of the Carolingian period, perhaps influenced in this respect by Irish and English missionaries. (Another common medieval term for bell, *clocca*, the origin of the French *cloche*, derives from the Gaelic *clog*.) Bells rapidly became an important part of medieval life. They increased in size and number, and great towers were built to house them; they were blessed in an elaborate ritual, given affectionate names, and made to ring on numerous prescribed occasions. They signaled the beginning of Mass and the canonical hours, the time of curfew and of the Angelus; they welcomed princes and bishops and sounded the "passing bell" and the "death knell"; and their primitive efficacy against evil spirits was called upon as they were rung to ward off storms and plague.

In the later Middle Ages, many of their functions came to be shared by the bells of civic bell towers, and great mechanical clocks became a feature of cathedral and town hall alike. The ritual use of bells at Mass is itself a late development, with the most prominent instance of this, that at the elevation of the host, originating in 13th-century Paris; this could be done from a special bell in a tower surmounting the crossing of the church or by a small bell (*tintinnabulum*) held by the acolyte. As a sign of mourning, all church bells were silent from the end of the *Gloria in excelsis* on Holy Thursday to its beginning on Holy Saturday; in their place, some sort of wooden rattle or clapper was used.

James McKinnon

[See also: MUSICAL INSTRUMENTS]

Price, Percival. *Bells and Man*. Oxford: Oxford University Press, 1983.

Smits van Waesberghe, Joseph. *Cymbala: Bells in the Middle Ages*. Rome: American Institute of Musicology, 1951.

BENEDEIT (early 12th c.). An Anglo-Norman poet. Benedeit's *Voyage de saint Brendan* is a 1,834-line retelling in Anglo-Norman verse of the 9th- or 10th-century *Navigatio sancti Brendani*. The author is intriguingly referred to as "Li apostoiles danz Benedeiz." The poem (first quarter of the 12th c.), preserved in four complete manuscripts, is one of the first to use the octosyllabic rhyming couplet. The text relates a legendary voyage by Brendan and his monks from Ireland to Paradise. Paradise is represented as an idyllic garden reached after a seven-year period of wandering that includes a meeting with Judas, who recounts his sufferings vividly. The poem reflects genuine voyages of discovery by early Irish monks but can also be read symbolically as the quest for happiness and eternal life in a world beset with dangers and difficulties. Those with true faith achieve their ends.

Glyn S. Burgess

[See also: ANGLO-NORMAN LITERATURE]

Benedeit. *The Anglo-Norman Voyage of St. Brendan*, ed. Ian Short and Brian Merrilees. Manchester: Manchester University Press, 1979.

BENEDICT, RULE OF ST. The monastic rule that was most frequently followed by French abbeys during the Middle Ages was written in Italy in the early 6th century by Benedict of Nursia, the abbot of Monte Cassino. It was written for his own monastery and probably for a handful of neighboring houses. St. Benedict relied in part on the slightly earlier *Rule of the Master* and incorporated large amounts of Scripture into his *Rule*, but it was his unique blend of practicality and moderation in a community designed to be almost a family of monks under a fatherly abbot, that made it widely adopted. This *Rule* was popularized at the end of the century by Pope Gregory the Great (r. 590–604), who wrote a Life of Benedict as Book 2 of his *Dialogues*.

Benedict's focus was on humility and obedience. The *Rule* laid out the steps of humility, likened to Jacob's ladder, and provided for the monk to climb that ladder under the fatherly direction of an abbot to whom the *Rule* gave full authority, always with the stipulation that he was responsible for the monks' souls before God as well as his own. The *Rule* stressed that the monks should give up normal physical pleasures, from fancy clothes to red meat, and drew a sharp dividing line between the world within the cloister and the always dangerous world outside. The monks especially had to give up individual property, and could not even receive gifts from their secular relatives without the abbot's permission. Benedict assumed that some monks would enter the house as adult converts, but many would arrive as boys, their parents' offering to the monastery, and be brought up and educated by the monks. When the abbot died, according to the *Rule of St. Benedict*, the monks of the house would elect a new one, preferably unanimously, but certainly by the choice of the "wiser part."

Constance B. Bouchard

[See also: BENEDICT OF ANIANE; BENEDICTINE ORDER; MONASTIC RULES AND CUSTOMARIES; MONASTICISM]

Benedict of Nursia. *La règle de Saint Benoît*, ed. Adalbert de Vogüé. Paris: Cerf, 1972.

De Vogüé, Adalbert. *Community and Abbot in the Rule of Saint Benedict*. 2 vols. Kalamazoo: Cistercian, 1979–88.

Knowles, David. *Christian Monasticism*. New York: McGraw-Hill, 1969.

Lawrence, Clifford H. *Medieval Monasticism: Forms of Religious Life in Western Europe in the Middle Ages*. 2nd ed. London: Longman, 1989.

BENEDICT OF ANIANE (d. 821). The *Rule of St. Benedict* was popularized in France in the early 9th century in large part due to the efforts of Benedict of Aniane. He founded the monastery of Aniane in the diocese of Montpellier, ca. 779. Although initially he seems to have sought to establish an especially rigorous form of monastic life there, within ten years he decided instead to adopt the *Rule of St. Benedict.*

Under Louis the Pious, Benedict was encouraged to establish Benedictine monasticism at all monasteries in Aquitaine. In a synod at Aix-la-Chapelle in 817, Benedict spelled out legislation on how the *Rule of St. Benedict* was to be followed, with an emphasis on seclusion, discipline, and moral conversion. His purpose was to create uniformity among all Benedictine houses: *una regula, una consuetudo.* He greatly increased the emphasis on liturgy and prayers for the dead and also made some modifications, such as allowing Frankish monks more clothing than the *Rule,* written in Italy, had countenanced. Benedict assembled a group of a dozen monasteries, all uniformly following the *Rule,* into a monastic "family," including Inde, the imperial model monastery near Aix-la-Chapelle. Although the uniformity quickly broke down after Benedict's death, his idea of monasteries organized as a family later influenced the Cluniacs and ultimately the Cistercians.

Constance B. Bouchard

[See also: *BENEDICT, RULE OF ST.;* BENEDICTINE ORDER; MONASTICISM]

Ardo. *Vita Benedicti abbatis Anianensis et Indensis.* In *MGH SS* 15.200–20.

Lackner, Bede K. *The Eleventh-Century Background of Cîteaux.* Washington, D.C.: Cistercian, 1972.

Lourdaux, William, and Daniel Verhelst, eds. *Benedictine Culture, 750–1050.* Louvain: Louvain University Press, 1983.

BENEDICTINE ORDER. When St. Benedict of Nursia wrote his monastic rule for Monte Cassino, in the early 6th century, he had no intention of founding an order. But from the 7th century onward, the *Rule* was adopted at a large number of French houses. Institutional ties among these houses were rare, however, and if the abbot of one Benedictine house became abbot of another as well such a tie rarely lasted more than a generation. Benedict of Aniane, with his family of monasteries established in 817, and Cluny with its permanent priories of the 10th and 11th centuries, were exceptions. Almost every house of Black Monks, as the Benedictines were often called, followed the *Rule* somewhat differently.

Cîteaux, mother house of the Cistercian order, which began to spread in the first decades of the 12th century, began the first institutionalized, organized system of affiliated monasteries within Benedictine monasticism. In the 13th century, those houses of Black Monks that had not been affiliated with any other order created their own group, called the Benedictine order, although they certainly had no exclusive claim to Benedict's *Rule.* The Fourth Lateran Council of 1215 ordered all unaffiliated monasteries to group together for a chapter general meeting every four years, in imitation of the Cistercian annual meeting; a number of independent houses long resisted such bonds.

Constance B. Bouchard

[See also: BENEDICT OF ANIANE; *BENEDICT, RULE OF ST.;* CISTERCIAN ORDER; CÎTEAUX; CLUNY; MONASTICISM; NUNNERIES]

Knowles, David. *Christian Monasticism.* New York: McGraw-Hill, 1969.

Lawrence, Clifford H. *Medieval Monasticism: Forms of Religious Life in Western Europe in the Middle Ages.* 2nd ed. London: Longman, 1989.

Lourdaux, William, and Daniel Verhelst, eds. *Benedictine Culture, 750–1050.* Louvain: Louvain University Press, 1983.

BENEFICE (NONECCLESIASTICAL). A *beneficium* (*benefice* in modern French and English) was originally, under the Carolingians, a grant of land that the kings made to their counts to hold as long as the counts held office. It referred to land that belonged to one lord but that was delegated to someone else for a temporary period, in return for certain services. Monasteries, too, might grant parts of their lands *in beneficium* to their secular neighbors, usually for a specified period of time (say, the layman's lifetime) and for an annual fee.

The benefice system by which kings and churches rewarded the services of their friends became a common part of more private transactions during the 10th and 11th centuries. By the mid-11th century, a benefice became in most cases indistinguishable from a fief, which a noble or knight held permanently by hereditary right from a noble lord, as long as he promised fidelity and performed homage for the land. The terms *beneficium* and *feudum* (fief) began to be used interchangeably.

Constance B. Bouchard

Dunbabin, Jean. *France in the Making, 843–1180.* Oxford: Oxford University Press, 1985.

Poly, Jean-Pierre, and Eric Bournazel. *La mutation féodale, Xe–XIIe siècles.* Paris: Presses Universitaires de France, 1980.

BENOÎT DE SAINTE-MAURE (fl. 1160–70). Little is known about Benoît de Sainte-Maure that does not emerge directly from his texts. The author of the *Roman de Troie* names himself in line 132 as Beneeit de Sainte-More, and as Beneit in lines 2065, 5093, and 19,207. He praises Eleanor of Aquitaine in the *Roman de Troie* and flatters Henry II in the other text of which he is believed to be the author, the *Chronique des ducs de Normandie.* Here, the author is identified simply as Beneit from Touraine (albeit in summary passages that may not be by the author himself), who, it is presumed, took over for the aged Wace when the latter abandoned his *Roman de Rou,* also a history of the dukes of Normandy. Benoît's *Chronique* has 44,542 lines in octosyllabic rhymed couplets. It begins with the creation and division of the world and ends with the death of Henry I of England. The Latin chronicles of Dudo de Saint-Quentin and Guillaume de Jumièges provided much of the material. But Benoît also invented long discourses for his historical characters and inserted countless proverbs into his narrative. As in the Romances of Antiquity, anachronism and medievalization are rampant. The romance form of the *Chronique* suggests that it was part of the repertoire of texts recited in a courtly milieu. The *Chronique*, together with Wace's *Rou*, is an excellent example of the desire of a new dynasty (as the Angevins with Henry II were in England) to celebrate their roots and their history in vernacular texts that would be accessible not only to a learned clerical audience but also to the aristocracy.

Renate Blumenfeld-Kosinski

[See also: ANTIQUITY, ROMANCES OF; *ESTRABOT*; HISTORIOGRAPHY; WACE]

Benoît de Sainte-Maure. *Chronique des ducs de Normandie*, ed. Carin Fahlin. 3 vols. Uppsala: Almqvist and Wiksell, 1951–67. [A fourth volume of notes was published by Sven Sandqvist in 1979 with the same publisher.]
———. *Le roman de Troie*, ed. Léopold Constans. 6 vols. Paris: Didot, 1904–12.

BERENGAR OF TOURS (ca. 1000–1088). Born at Tours, Berengar studied at Chartres under Fulbert and returned to Tours to become *scholasticus* at Saint-Martin's in 1031 and archdeacon of Angers in 1041. During and after his studies, Berengar displayed a penchant for appealing to reason rather than to church authorities, a characteristic that perhaps led him to question the specifics of eucharistic theology, the doctrine of the Real Presence. Details of Berengar's beliefs must be gleaned from the writings of his opponents and his own obscure treatise, *De sacra coena* (ca. 1065–70), a polemic against one of his most vociferous adversaries, Lanfranc of Bec. For Berengar, the doctrine of the Real Presence seems to have meant that a spiritual or intellectual presence was added to the bread and wine but that their substance did not change. Thus, he is credited with having initiated the first heresy in the history of eucharistic theology.

Berengar attracted many disciples, who were eager to defend him in the debate over the eucharist. His teachings, however, were countered by numerous tracts written by his adversaries, most notably Lanfranc of Bec, and were condemned by a series of councils: at Rome in 1050, Vercelli in 1050, Paris in 1051, and Rome in 1059 and 1079. At the council of 1079, Berengar signed a profession of faith containing the first official use of the words *substantialiter converti*. Returning to France after the council of 1079, Berengar retired to the island of Saint-Côme near Tours, where he died in 1088. In addition to *De sacra coena*, Berengar's extant work includes correspondence, refutations of Lanfranc, accounts of the various synods, and a poem, *Iuste iudex Iesu Christe*.

E. Kay Harris

[See also: FULBERT OF CHARTRES; HERESY; LANFRANC OF BEC]

Berengar of Tours. *De sacra coena*, ed. Martine Matronola. Milan: Societa Editrice "Vitae Pensiero," 1936.
Didier, Jean-Charles, and Philippe Delhaye. "Hugues de Breteuil, évêque de Langres (d. 1050): Lettre à Bérenger de Tours sur la présence réelle." *Revue des études augustiniennes* 16 (1981): 289–331.
Montclos, Jean de. *Lanfranc et Bérenger: la controverse eucharistique du XIe siècle*. Louvain: Spicilegium Sacrum Lovaniense, 1971.
Southern, Richard W. "Lanfranc of Bec and Berengar of Tours." In *Studies in Medieval History Presented to Maurice Powicke*, ed. Richard W. Hunt et al. Oxford: Clarendon, 1948, pp. 27–48.

BERENGUER DE PALAZOL (Palau, Palol). Described by the author of his *vida* as a poor knight from Catalonia, the troubadour Berenguer de Palazol remains, despite repeated attempts at identification, undatable. If, as seems likely, Berenguer composed his few surviving *cansos* in the 13th century, his work offers nothing that is thematically, metrically, or stylistically original.

Elizabeth W. Poe

Berenguer de Palazol. "The Troubadour Berenguer de Palazol: A Critical Edition of His Poems," ed. Terence H. Newcombe. *Nottingham Mediaeval Studies* 15 (1971): 54–95.
———. *Berenguer de Palol*, ed. Margherita Beretta Spampinato. Modena: Società Tipografica Editrice Modenese, 1978.

BÉRINUS, ROMAN DE. Based on a rhymed version (ca. 1252) of which only two fragments survive, the prose *Roman de Bérinus* (ca. 1350–70) by an unknown Burgundian, fuses narrative elements taken from a variety of sources into the episodic story of the Roman merchant and king of Blandie, Bérinus, and his son, Aigres, who, among other adventures, beheads his father (to save him from being prosecuted for defrauding the imperial treasury) and marries the Roman emperor's daughter. *Bérinus* is loosely modeled on the didactic frame narrative of the *Roman des sept sages de Rome*; its linear structure and literary purpose, however, relate it more closely to the *roman d'aventures*. There are four 15th-century manuscripts and one fragment of the prose *Bérinus*, and four early printings (first half of the 16th c.).

Hans R. Runte

[See also: *SEVEN SAGES OF ROME*]

Bossuat, Robert, ed. *Bérinus: roman en prose du XIVe siècle*. Paris: SATF, 1931 (Vol. 1), 1933 (Vol. 2). [Based on B.N. fr. 777.]
Furnivall, Frederick James, and Walter George Boswell Stone, eds. *The Tale of Beryn . . . with an English Abstract of the French Original and Asiatic Versions of the Tale by William Alexander Clouston*. London: Early English Text Society,

1909. [In the past, attributed to Chaucer; corresponds to paragraphs 48–208 of the Bossuat edition.]

BERNARD DE SOISSONS

BERNARD DE SOISSONS (fl. 13th c.). Mentioned in texts of 1282 and 1287 as master mason of the cathedral of Reims, Bernard de Soissons supervised construction of the vaults of the five western nave bays and a major portion of the façade. His image, which was set into the now destroyed labyrinth of the cathedral, showed him drawing a circle with a large compass, indicating that he designed the west rose window. Although Bernard's work in the upper levels of the nave consciously continued the forms of the earlier cathedral masters, his expansive rose composition reveals the impact of "modern" Rayonnant models, particularly the transepts of Notre-Dame in Paris.

Michael T. Davis

[See also: PARIS; REIMS]

Branner, Robert. "The Labyrinth of Reims Cathedral." *Journal of the Society of Architectural Historians* 31 (1962): 18–25.

Demaison, Louis. "Les maîtres de l'œuvre de la cathédrale de Reims." *Congrès archéologique* 78 (1911): 151–69.

Ravaux, Jean-Pierre. "Les campagnes de construction de la cathédrale de Reims au XIIIe siècle." *Bulletin monumental* 135 (1979): 7–66.

Reinhardt, Hans. *La cathédrale de Reims: son histoire, son architecture, sa sculpture, ses vitraux.* Paris: Presses Universitaires de France, 1963.

Salet, Francis. "Le Premier Colloque International de la Société Française d'Archéologie (Reims): chronologie de la cathédrale." *Bulletin monumental* 125 (1967): 347–94.

BERNARD GUI

BERNARD GUI (Bernardus Guidonis; ca. 1261–1331). Historian, inquisitor, and bishop, Bernard was a Dominican who rose through the ecclesiastical ranks in southern France, in Limoges, Castres, Albi, and Carcassonne. He was inquisitor at Toulouse from 1307 to 1323. Between 1317 and 1321, he also served Pope John XXII on diplomatic missions in Italy and Flanders. All of Bernard's writings were in Latin. Though most were of a historical nature, he also produced several works of theology (*De articulis fidei, De peccato originali*), liturgy (*De ordinatione officii missae*), and hagiography (*Legenda sancti Thome de Aquino, Speculum sanctorale*). The *Speculum*, a collection of a number of saints' lives in four parts, was extremely popular in its day. His most important work is the still unpublished *Flores chronicorum* (ca. 1316), a history of the papacy from the birth of Christ to Clement V. This work, known in over fifty manuscripts (some now lost), went through ten revisions, the latest of which continues the history to 1331 (John XXII). Already in the 14th century, it was translated into Occitan (B.N. fr. 24940) and twice into French (four manuscripts). Other historical works by Bernard include treatises on the Roman emperors (*Imperatores Romani*, over forty manuscripts), on the kings of France (*Reges Francorum*, which exists in four revisions and two French translations), and on the Dominican order (catalogues of provincial priors, monographs on individual houses, acts of General Chapters, etc.).

Especially noteworthy is Bernard's history of the Inquisition (*Practica officii Inquisitionis*; ca. 1314–16; four manuscripts), which includes an important section on such heretical groups as Manichaeans, Vaudois, Pseudo-Apostles, béguines, relapsed Jews, and sorcerers. He also composed local histories of the cities in which he lived: Limoges, Toulouse, and Lodève. In spite of the great popularity of his work in the late Middle Ages, as evidenced by the numerous manuscripts and the translation of much of his œuvre into French by Jean Golein for Charles V, few of Bernard's works have found modern editors. He was a diligent compiler and accurate researcher, keen to tease the truth from contradictory sources. Traveling from monastery to monastery, Bernard assembled evidence, interviewed witnesses, and verified his sources at every step. As information accumulated, he prepared copious lists, edited, revised, and expanded. Faced with mountains of material, he regularly composed abridged versions of his most important works. Bernard's lack of literary skill is compensated for by his careful preservation of significant documents and information whose original sources have been lost.

Grover A. Zinn

[See also: AVIGNON PAPACY; DOMINICAN ORDER; GOLEIN, JEAN; INQUISITION]

Bernard Gui. *Practica Inquisitionis heretice pravitatis*, ed. C. Douais. Paris: Picard, 1886.

———. *Manuel de l'inquisiteur*, ed. and trans. G. Mollat. 2 vols. Paris: Champion, 1926–27.

Delisle, Léopold. "Notice sur les manuscrits de Bernard Gui." *Notices et extraits des manuscrits de la Bibliothèque Nationale* 27 (1885): 169–455.

Thomas, Antoine. "Bernard Gui, frère prêcheur." *Histoire littéraire de la France* 35 (1921): 139–232.

Vernet, A. "La diffusion de l'œuvre de Bernard Gui d'après la tradition manuscrite." *Cahiers de Fanjeaux* 16 (1981): 221–42.

BERNARD OF CHARTRES

BERNARD OF CHARTRES (d. 1124–30). Most of our knowledge of Bernard comes through John of Salisbury's *Metalogicon*. John studied with Gilbert of Poitiers, William of Conches, and Richard the Bishop, who were all Bernard's pupils at Chartres when he was chancellor of the schools. Not only was John's knowledge secondhand, but his *Metalogicon* has an ulterior motive: he is not merely describing Bernard for archival reasons but wishes to contrast his good, old teaching methods with the newfangled approach of the Cornificians. It is difficult, then, to be certain how far to trust John's encomium.

John counted Bernard the best Platonist of his time, although to us he seems less interesting than Gilbert of Poitiers or Thierry of Chartres (who is unlikely to have been his younger brother, as is sometimes asserted). He seems to have had no academic contact with the great scholars of his day, William of Champeaux, Roscelin, or

Anselm of Laon. Like all the Chartrians, he got his Plato through Neoplatonist sources, chiefly Chalcidius, Boethius, and Eriugena. His work survives only in fragments quoted by John of Salisbury, though a possible set of glosses on the *Timaeus* by Bernard is now in print. Famous for his cultivation of faith and goodness, as well as simple academic brilliance, Bernard is perhaps best remembered today for reporting the aphorism that compared scholars of the modern age to dwarfs standing on giants' shoulders—their further vision was the result of their elevated viewpoint, not their greater acumen (*Metalogicon* 3.4).

Lesley J. Smith

[See also: CHARTRES; ERIUGENA, JOHANNES SCOTTUS; GILBERT OF POITIERS; JOHN OF SALISBURY; PHILOSOPHY; PLATO, INFLUENCE OF; THIERRY OF CHARTRES]

Bernard of Chartres. *Glosae super Platonem*, ed. Paul Edward Dutton. Toronto: Pontifical Institute of Mediaeval Studies, 1991.

Dutton, Paul Edward. "The Uncovering of the 'Glosae super Platonem' of Bernard of Chartres." *Mediaeval Studies* 46 (1984): 192–221.

Gilson, Étienne. "Le platonisme de Bernard de Chartres." *Revue néo-scholastique de philosophie* 25 (1923): 5–19.

BERNARD OF CLAIRVAUX (1090/91–1153). Born in Fontaines near Dijon and educated with the canons of Saint-Vorles in Châtillon-sur-Seine, Bernard entered the Cistercian monastery of Cîteaux, together with thirty companions, in 1112. In 1115, he founded the monastery of Clairvaux. From this remote corner of the civilized world, he intervened in matters both political and ecclesiastical. In 1128, at the Synod of Troyes, he obtained recognition for the *Rule* of the new order of Knights Templar. In 1130, he supported Innocent II against Anacletus II in the dispute over papal succession, and a few years later he supported Innocent in the conflict with Arnold of Brescia. In 1145, a pupil of his became Pope Eugenius III. Besides continuing to mediate in all kinds of conflicts, Bernard energetically preached the Second Crusade and lived to witness its utter failure in 1148.

Bernard presided over the enormous expansion of the Cistercian order. The first houses founded from Cîteaux—La Ferté, Pontigny, Morimond, and Clairvaux—became centers from which hundreds of monasteries spread over all of western Europe. As abbot of Clairvaux, an obscure Cistercian settlement on the border of Burgundy and the Champagne, Bernard traveled widely, not only advising bishops and princes but also raising his voice on delicate doctrinal isssues. Lacking the modern dialectical skills of his opponents, he focused his criticism on their alleged deviations from traditional theological methods. At the Council of Sens (1141), his intervention decided the fate of Abélard, and a few years later, at the Council of Reims, he spoke out against Gilbert of Poitiers. Bernard was canonized in 1174 and created a doctor of the church in 1830.

Bernard's *œuvre* consists of treatises, many sermons, and letters. His most famous work is the series of sermons on the Song of Songs (*Sermones super Cantica canticorum*), left unfinished at his death. In it, he deals with a variety of themes from the behavior of monks to the mystical union between the Bridegroom from the Canticle (Christ) and the Bride (Bernard, or the church). The method applied to the Canticle text is based on the medieval exegetical scheme of the fourfold meaning of Scripture: literal, allegorical, moral, and mystical. However, unlike earlier medieval commentators on the Canticle, such as Bede, Bernard never loses sight of the literal, dramatic power of the Canticle text. Isolating one textual fragment or even a single word, he then creates clusters of associations with other biblical and patristic writings. The result is a rich and a meticulously organized text that could be used both by the monks as an amplification of their ritual form of life and by a wider literate public, both clergy and lay, for literary enjoyment and religious insight.

Many of Bernard's other sermons follow the cycle of the liturgical feast days (*Sermones per annum*), such as the Annunciation, Christmas, Epiphany, Easter, the Assumption. Noteworthy for their poetic quality and intensity, Bernard's sermons on the Virgin Mary contributed to the development of mariological devotion in the later Middle Ages.

In his treatises, Bernard deals in a more thematic way with the issues of monastic life and of religion in general. A treatise on the steps of humility, *De gradibus humilitatis et superbiae*, is a commentary on a passage from the Benedictine *Rule*. A treatise on love, *De diligendo Deo*, describes the journey toward God, who is to be loved because of himself with a love that is "measure without measure" (*modus sine modo*). Bernard combines the relentless desire for God characteristic of the monastic life with the stability of its goal. The long treatise on consideration, *De consideratione*, dedicated to Pope Eugenius III, outlines the ideal portrait of a pope while offering theological and mystical reflections on the knowledge of God.

In his many letters, Bernard often takes circumstantial matters as a point of departure for reflection. His first letter is, like his *Apologia*, a fierce attack on the luxuriousness of the Cluniac (or, more widely, Benedictine) way of life. This critical attitude was based on Bernard's own Cistercian predilection for simplicity and austerity in art. The lengthy Letter 190, to Innocent II, is directed against Abélard on the occasion of the latter's condemnation at the Council of Sens, depicting him as a dangerous innovator whose application of reason to matters of faith threatens religious stability. In fact, it is Bernard's concern about the legitimacy of his own monastic way of life in the light of the Christian tradition and culture, rather than the motives of his opponent, that comes to the fore. Yet in spite of his claim that he, unlike Abélard, is staying within the bounds of the Christian tradition, Bernard is to be seen as part of the general renaissance of the 12th century. In defending the quality of his own ascetic life, he cherished a sophistication that many of his contemporaries sought in the further refinement of reasoning and art.

Burcht Pranger

[See also: ABÉLARD, PETER; CISTERCIAN ART AND ARCHITECTURE; CISTERCIAN ORDER; GILBERT OF POITIERS; MONASTICISM; WILLIAM OF SAINT-THIERRY]

Bernard of Clairvaux. *Sancti Bernardi opera omnia*, ed. Jean Leclercq, Charles H. Talbot, and Henri Rochais. 8 vols. Rome: Editiones Cistercienses, 1957–78.
———. *Selected Works*, trans. Gillian R. Evans. New York: Paulist, 1987.
Bredero, A.H. *Études sur la Vita prima de S. Bernard*. Rome, 1960.
Casey, M. *Athirst for God: Spiritual Desire in Bernard of Clairvaux's Sermons on the Song of Songs*. Kalamazoo: Cistercian, 1988.
Duby, Georges. *Bernard de Clairvaux et l'art cistercien*. Paris: Arts et Métiers Graphiques, 1976.
Evans, Gillian R. *The Mind of Bernard of Clairvaux*. Oxford: Clarendon, 1983.
Gilson, Étienne. *The Mystical Theology of St. Bernard*, trans. A.H.C. Downes. London: Sheed and Ward, 1940.
Leclercq, Jean. *Recueil d'études sur saint Bernard et ses écrits*. 3 vols. Rome: Edizioni di Storia e Letteratura, 1966–92.
———. *Monks and Love in Twelfth-Century France: Psycho-Historical Essays*. Oxford: Clarendon, 1979.
Pranger, M. Burcht. *Bernard of Clairvaux and the Shape of Monastic Thought: Broken Dreams*. Leiden: Brill, 1994.

BERNARD SILVESTRIS (d. ca. 1159). Bernard probably taught in the cathedral school at Tours in the second third of the 12th century, where one of his students was Matthieu de Vendôme. The dedication of his longest and most important work, the *Cosmographia*, to Thierry of Chartres, has led some scholars to confuse him with John of Salisbury's beloved teacher Bernard of Chartres, who would have been a generation older than Silvestris. If, as seems likely, Bernard was also trained at Tours, he would have studied under Hildebert of Lavardin.

Bernard's earliest works are a commentary on the first six books of Virgil's *Aeneid* and another, incomplete, on Martianus Capella. The commentary on Plato's *Timæus* mentioned in the Martianus commentary has not been identified. In his elegiac poem *Mathematicus*, Bernard discusses destiny and necessity in mathematical terms. Also at least partly his is the *Experimentarius*, a work taken from Arabic sources on cosmography. Two short opuscules derived from problems in Quintilian and Seneca are also usually attributed to him: respectively, *De gemellis* and *De paupere ingrato*.

The *Cosmographia* (ca. 1147–48) has two parts, *Megacosmos* and *Microcosmos*. In the first part, Nature approaches Nous, the personification of the divine eternal mind of God, whom she begs to improve the physical universe. Nous separates the four elements, gives matter form from divine ideas, and shapes the world soul. The new universe is described in detail. *Microcosmos* depicts the formation of humankind. Nature encounters Genius, and they set out to seek Urania and Physis, who will guide them through the heavens to find man's soul and bring it back to earth. The title is explained: man is the world in little.

Though the work has multiple sources, including Boethius, Martianus Capella, and ancient and Arabic scientific sources, the basic concept is apparently original with Bernard. His poem circulated widely—over fifty copies survive in European libraries—and influenced the two most widely read 12th-century allegorical visions of nature, the world, and humanity: Alain de Lille's *De planctu Naturae* and *Anticlaudianus*. In the rhetorical work of Matthieu de Vendôme, he is frequently cited for his excellence of style.

Jeanne E. Krochalis

[See also: ALAIN DE LILLE; HILDEBERT OF LAVARDIN; THIERRY OF CHARTRES]

Bernard Silvestris. *Cosmographia*, ed. Peter Dronke. Leiden: Brill, 1978.
———. *The Commentary on the First Six Books of the* Aeneid *of Vergil Commonly Attributed to Bernardus Silvestris*, ed. Julian Ward Jones and Elizabeth Francis Jones. Lincoln: University of Nebraska Press, 1977.
———. "Il 'Dictamen' di Bernardo Silvestre," ed. M. Brini Savorelli. *Rivista critica di storia della filosofia* 20 (1965): 182–230.
———. "Un manuale de geomanzia presentato da Bernardo Silvestre de Tours (XII secolo): l'*Experimentarius*," ed. M. Brini Savorelli. *Rivista critica di storia della filosofia* 14 (1959): 283–341.
———. *The Cosmographia*, trans. Winthrop P. Wetherbee. New York: Columbia University Press, 1973.
Stock, Brian. *Myth and Science in the Twelfth Century: A Study of Bernard Silvester*. Princeton: Princeton University Press, 1972.

BERNART DE VENTADORN (fl. ca. 1145–1180). With Jaufre Rudel, Bernart de Ventadorn was one of the most popular and most imitated of the 12th-century troubadours. His romanticized biography, or *vida*, says that he was of humble origins but rose to sing his love for the wife of the lord of Ventadorn. Aside from links to the Ventadorn castle and school, which are clear from his name and style, Bernart sang at the court of Count Raymond V of Toulouse and probably also visited England, perhaps in the entourage of Eleanor of Aquitaine. The *vida* further tells us that he retired to the Cistercian abbey of Dalon, but this, like the reports of his early years, has not been documented.

Of his lyric production, some forty-one songs survive, all but three of which are love songs, or *cansos*. (Two of the three *tensos*, or debate poems, are of less than certain attribution.) Eighteen of Bernart's songs are preserved with their music. Bernart sang in the clear style called *trobar leu*. His *cansos* are characterized by the melodious language, nostalgic tone, vivid imagery, and musical virtuosity that won him imitators among medieval poets. But it is their lyrical intensity and emotional span that have especially earned him admirers in our own time.

Roy S. Rosenstein

[See also: TROUBADOUR POETRY]

The troubadour Bernart de Ventadorn as depicted in a manuscript of his poetry. BN fr. 854, fol. 26v. *Courtesy of the Bibliothèque Nationale, Paris.*

Bernard de Ventadour. *Chansons d'amour,* ed. Moshé Lazar. Paris: Klincksieck, 1966.
———. *The Songs of Bernart de Ventadorn,* ed. Stephen G. Nichols, Jr., et al. Chapel Hill: University of North Carolina Press, 1962.
Kaehne, Michael. *Studien zur Dichtung Bernarts von Ventadorn.* Munich: Fink, 1983.
Scherner-Van Ortmerssen, Gisela. *Die Text-Melodiestruktur in den Liedern des Bernart de Ventadorn.* Münster: Aschendorff, 1973.

BERNAY. The church of Sainte-Croix at Bernay (Eure) was begun in 1374. The choir was completed without aisles by the end of the 14th century, as were four arcades, the north crossing, the north aisle of the nave, and the principal entrance. The nave, built during the first part of the 15th century, features intersecting, ribbed vaulting. Sainte-Croix contains the tombstone of Guillaume d'Auvillars, abbot of Bec (1418), and large statues (15th c.) of the Apostles and Evangelists. These stand against the pillars of the nave and choir. The aisles and radiating chapels were constructed in the 19th century.

A Benedictine abbey was founded at Bernay in the beginning of the 11th century by Judith de Bretagne, wife of Richard II, duke of Normandy. Constructed in stone, the abbey church included a nave, seven bays with aisles,

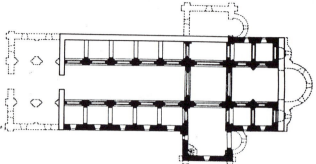

Bernay (Eure), plan of abbey church. After Musset.

a transept, a choir of two bays that culminated in an apse in cul-de-four (vaulting formed by a semicupola). The choir is flanked by two aisles with apsidioles. Fragments from Gallo-Roman constructions were used for the foundation. Despite modifications and attempts at destruction and reconstruction, this abbey church of Bernay is one of the most interesting monuments of Romanesque architecture in Normandy.

E. Kay Harris

Porée, A. Notice in *Congrès archéologique (Caen)* (1908).
———. "Nouvelles observations sur l'église abbatiale de Bernay." *Bulletin monumental* (1911).

BÉROUL (fl. late 12th c.). Nothing is known of Béroul other than that he was the author of a late 12th-century Tristan verse romance. He twice names himself in his surviving text. Owing to certain stylistic inconsistencies and even factual contradictions within the poem, some scholars have concluded that his *Tristan* is the work of two authors, or even more. Such suggestions remain unproved, however, and a good many scholars have argued the case for single authorship.

Béroul clearly composed the poem during the second half of the 12th century, but the date or even decade remains in question; some have contended that it was as early as 1165, while others, concluding that line 3,849 of the poem refers to an epidemic that attacked the Crusaders at Acre in 1190–91, assign the poem to the last decade of the century. The *Tristan* is preserved in fragmentary form in a single manuscript (B.N. fr. 2171) that was copied during the second half of the 13th century. The beginning and end of the poem are both missing, leaving a single long fragment of nearly 4,500 lines of octosyllabic narrative verse; in addition, the manuscript contains a number of lacunae, and the text is obviously defective in many passages.

The poem belongs to what is generally called the primitive or common version (as opposed to the courtly version) of the Tristan legend. That is, it is presumed that this text derives from an earlier, noncourtly stage of the legend, whereas that of Thomas d'Angleterre integrates the work thoroughly into the current of courtly love.

Béroul's extensive fragment begins with the famous encounter of Tristan with Iseut under the tree in which her husband, Marc, is hiding to trap them; they see his reflection in the water and speak in such a way as to allay his suspicions. The poem continues with the episode in which the dwarf spreads flour on Iseut's floor in order to detect Tristan's footprints (should he visit her at night); the scene in which Tristan, having been taken prisoner, asks permission to enter a chapel and pray, whereupon he leaps to freedom from a window; Marc's delivering Iseut to a colony of lepers (for their pleasure and her punishment) and Tristan's rescue of her; the lovers' miserable life in the forest (including Marc's discovery of them, as they sleep with a bare sword between them, and his erroneous conclusion that they are guiltless); their eventual repentance, caused by the waning of the love potion (which, in this tradition, had been made to be effective for three years); and the long episode in which Iseut, tested in the presence of Arthur and his knights, succeeds in exonerating herself by swearing an equivocal oath. At the end, Tristan ambushes and kills one of the lovers' enemies and brings his hair to show Iseut; when he arrives, they discover another of their enemies spying on them, Tristan immediately kills him, and the text breaks off in mid-sentence.

As in the Tristan tradition in general, Béroul's narrative presents a cyclical form: whether physically separated, threatened by Marc or their enemies, or resolved to reform, the young lovers repeatedly fall back into their sinful ways; Marc becomes suspicious, initially refuses to believe he is being betrayed, and is finally convinced; after a period of separation or abstinence on their part, the cycle repeats itself. Most often, the lovers have in fact no great desire to reform, and when they do they are motivated by less than noble impulses. Yet despite their sin and despite the fact that they both betray Marc (Iseut is his wife, while Tristan is both his vassal and his nephew), the sympathies of the author and of the reader remain with the couple, both because their enemies are presented as despicable and jealous characters and because Béroul frequently insists that God favors the lovers and will punish those who oppose them.

The Tristan is a highly ironic and ambiguous text. Appearances are always deceiving: when the lovers appear most innocent, they are consistently the most guilty. When Marc thinks them innocent, he is being deceived or else, as in the episode where they sleep with a naked sword between them, he is misinterpreting the evidence. Tristan is a trickster who clearly takes pleasure in deception, as, for example, when, disguised as a leper, he explains to Marc that he was infected by his unnamed lady, who resembled Iseut and whose husband was a leper.

Despite the potential tragedy of the lovers' passion, Béroul's poem is characterized by humor and, in many passages, by a tone far more reminiscent of the fabliau than of the courtly romance. His style is lively and engaging, bearing many of the marks (such as frequent addresses to Seigneurs) of both public presentation and authorial personality. Despite numerous textual problems, the poem as we have it holds considerable charm and appeal.

Although Béroul's composition is incompletely preserved, the Tristrant of Eilhart von Oberge, written before 1190, presents the common version of the Tristan story in the form of a complete romance. Although Eilhart's German text abridges or omits some episodes found in Béroul's, the two works appear to have at very least a common source, and it has sometimes been suggested that Eilhart adapted the story directly from Béroul's account of the lovers.

Norris J. Lacy

[See also: *FOLIES TRISTAN; PROSE TRISTAN;* THOMAS D'ANGLETERRE]

Béroul. *Le roman de Tristan,* ed. Ernest Muret. Paris: Didot, 1913, 4th rev. ed. L. M. Defourques. Paris: Champion, 1962.
———. *The Romance of Tristran,* ed. and trans. Norris J. Lacy. New York: Garland, 1989.
Walter, Philippe and D. Lacroix, trans. *Tristan et Iseut: les poèmes français, la saga norroise.* Paris: Livre de Poche, 1989.
Raynaud de Lage, Guy. "Faut-il attribuer à Béroul tout le *Tristan?" Moyen âge* 64 (1958): 249–70; 67 (1961): 167–68; 70 (1964): 33–38.
Reid, Thomas Bertram Wallace. *The "Tristan" of Béroul: A Textual Commentary.* New York: Barnes and Noble, 1972.

BERRY. The region just south of the Loire and to the west of Burgundy originally inhabited by the people known as the Bituriges Cubi, Berry englobes the modern departments of the Cher and Indre and includes neighboring parts of Loiret, Indre-et-Loire, and Creuse. It formed part of the Roman imperial province of Aquitania Prima, of which its chief *civitas,* Bourges, became the capital. According to legend, St. Ursinus founded an archbishopric in Bourges during the 3rd century.

On the fall of the western Roman Empire, Berry became a part of the Visigothic kingdom and then of the Frankish subkingdom, later the duchy, of Aquitaine. In 926, King Raoul suppressed the countship of Bourges, after which no major feudal power emerged to complement that of the town's archbishops. This lack resulted in encroachments by the dukes of Aquitaine and the counts of Anjou and Blois.

In 1101, Eudes Harpin de Dun, viscount of Bourges, sold his office to King Philip I, who reasserted the royal presence, but the royal holdings in Berry were granted in 1137 to Eleanor of Aquitaine as a dowry upon her marriage to the future Louis VII. In 1152, she carried them with her when she married the future Henry II of England. French royal presence returned in 1200, when King John of England returned the holdings to Philip II, who, in 1201, having appointed a royal *bailli* for the region, granted them to Eleanor's granddaughter, Blanche of Castile, upon her marriage to the future Louis VIII. Royal control increased from that time on.

In the 14th and 15th centuries, Berry increased in importance to the monarchy. Declared a duchy in 1360, it was given in apanage to John (d. 1416), third son of John II and a famous patron of the arts.

From 1418 to 1436, with Paris in hostile hands, the province sheltered the royal government of Charles VII, "le roi de Bourges." On the death of Duke John's daughter, Marie, in 1434, the duchy was rejoined to the crown, only to be granted out again in 1461 by Louis XI to his brother, Charles, who exchanged it for Normandy at the end of his rebellious *Guerre du Bien Publique* in 1465. It was next granted to Louis's sainted daughter, Jeanne la Boiteuse, who, repudiated by her husband, Louis XII, in 1499, founded in Bourges the order of the Annonciade. The title was often borne after that by members of the immediate family of the reigning monarch.

R. Thomas McDonald

[See also: BOURGES; JOHN, DUKE OF BERRY]

Devailly, Guy. *Le Berry du Xe au milieu du XIIIe siècle.* Paris: Mouton, 1973.
Raynal, Louis. *Histoire de Berry.* Bourges: Vermeil, 1845.

BERSUIRE, PIERRE (ca. 1290–1362). Encyclopedist, moralist, and translator born probably in the Vendée region, Bersuire entered the Franciscan order before joining the Benedictines. His early career (ca. 1320–ca. 1350) was spent amid the fervent intellectual climate of the papal court at Avignon, where he enjoyed the protection and extensive library of Cardinal Pierre des Prés of Quercy, and it was here that he produced his major Latin works. Bersuire came ca. 1350 to Paris, where he seems to have studied theology late in life. He was accused of heresy, imprisoned, and eventually released through the intervention of the new king, John II the Good. In 1354, he was made prior of the Benedictine abbey of Saint-Éloy in Paris, a benefice he held until his death. Both in Avignon and Paris, Bersuire frequented the leading intellectuals and scientists of his day, among them the Italian humanist Petrarch, the surgeon Gui de Chauliac, the English Dominican Thomas Waleys, the musician Philippe de Vitry, and the poet Guillaume de Machaut.

Bersuire's works comprise voluminous original treatises in Latin on moral theology and translations into French. None of his works has been preserved complete or in an autograph manuscript. Of his Latin works, the *Reductorium morale* and *Repertorium morale* have survived fairly intact, while the *Breviarium morale* and *Cosmographia* (or *Descriptio mundi*) have not been positively identified. The encyclopedic *Reductorium* and *Repertorium* are extensive biblical commentaries designed to organize and locate material for preaching. The *Reductorium* is so named because its purpose was to "reduce" to its moral interpretation all that was known or could be known about God, nature, and the world, both visible and invisible. The first thirteen books (ca. 1340), which survive in only one complete exemplar, were based largely on Bartholomew the Englishman's *Liber de proprietatibus* and cite hundreds of classical and medieval *auctores*. The final three books were composed later and circulated independently: *De natura mirabilibus* (1343–45) is a moralization of the marvels of the natural world, drawing especially upon the legends of the Poitou region and the *Otia imperialia* of Gervais of Tilbury; *Ovidius moralizatus* (or *De fabulis poetarum*) is a moralizing commentary on Ovid's *Metamorphoses*, for which Bersuire drew upon, among other sources, the French *Ovide moralisé*; and *Super totam Bibliam* offers moral interpretations of the best-known Old and New Testament episodes.

The *Repertorium morale* is an alphabetical listing of several thousand biblical words of all sorts (proper and common nouns, verbs, adverbs, etc.), each of which is accorded a moralizing interpretation. This work, if printed today, would run to over twenty octavo volumes. Bersuire's usual procedure is to list all the different meanings the word has in Scripture, which are followed by a series of short rhymed statements, each expounded by reference to the Bible, the fathers, theological commentators, or even pagan authors. The lost *Breviarium morale* was perhaps a general introduction to the *Reductorium* and *Repertorium*.

Between 1354 and 1356, Bersuire undertook at the behest of King John a translation into French of the three decades (1, 3, 4) of Livy's *Ab urbe condita* then known. The principal source for late-medieval knowledge of Roman history, the translation survives in some eighty manuscripts and was possibly reworked by Laurent de Premierfait. An important glossary of technical words, many forged by Bersuire, precedes the translation proper.

An important compiler of received knowledge rather than an original thinker, Bersuire was a significant moralist and polemicist, who frequently castigated abuses of ecclesiastical and political offices. With his translation of Livy, his friendship with Petrarch, and his frequent citations of classical authorities, he can be seen as a precursor of humanistic thinking in France.

Grover A. Zinn

[See also: *OVIDE MORALISÉ*; PREACHING; PREMIERFAIT, LAURENT DE; TRANSLATION]

Bersuire, Pierre. *Opera omnia.* Cologne: Friessem and Fromart, 1712.
———. *Reductorium morale: Liber XV, cap. II–XV, "Ovidius moralizatus,"* ed. Joseph Engels. Utrecht, 1962. [Based on the Paris printed edition of 1509.]
Samaran, Charles. "Pierre Bersuire." *Histoire littéraire de la France* 39 (1962): 259–450.

BERTHA OF HOLLAND (fl. late 11th c.). Queen of France. As part of the peace agreement of 1072 between King Philip I (r. 1060–1108) and Robert the Frisian, Robert married his stepdaughter Bertha to the king. She was daughter of Florence, count of Holland. Although she became the mother of Philip's heir, Louis VI, Philip repudiated her in 1092 for Bertrade de Montfort, saying Bertha was too fat.

Constance B. Bouchard

Dhondt, Jean. "Sept femmes et un trio de rois." *Contributions à l'histoire économique et sociale* 3 (1964–65): 35–70.
Duby, Georges. *The Knight, the Lady, and the Priest: The Making of Modern Marriage in Medieval France*, trans. Barbara Bray. New York: Pantheon, 1983, Chap. 1.
Facinger, Marion F. "A Study of Medieval Queenship: Capetian France, 987–1237." *Studies in Medieval and Renaissance History* 5 (1968): 3–47.

BERTRADE DE MONTFORT (fl. late 11th–early 12th c.). Queen of France. The daughter of Simon I, lord of Montfort, Bertrade was first the wife of Foulques IV le Rechin, count of Anjou. Her son, Foulques V, count of Anjou (1109–29), became king of Jerusalem (1131–43).

In 1092, Bertrade left Foulques IV for Philip I, the king of France (r. 1060–1108), whom she bore two sons and a daughter. Because their marriage was regarded as bigamous, she and Philip faced repeated excommunications between 1094 and 1104, and the kingdom was for a time under interdict. Bertrade influenced royal policy, shared in the profits of simony, and was much feared. Reportedly behind the death of her stepson Geoffroi d'Anjou in 1106, she plotted against Philip's heir, the future Louis VI, whom she was said to have tried to poison.

In spite of Philip's repeated promises to live apart from her, and his reconciliation with the church in 1104, Bertrade signed documents as queen until the end of the reign. After Philip's death, she retired to Fontevrault and was still alive in 1115.

R. Thomas McDonald

[See also: LOUIS VI THE FAT; PHILIP I]

Facinger, Marion F. "A Study of Medieval Queenship: Capetian France, 987–1237." *Studies in Medieval and Renaisssance History* 5 (1968): 3–47.

BERTRAN DE BORN (ca. 1150–1215). The feudal lord of Hautefort in the Périgord is remembered as the warmongering troubadour because of Dante's presentation of him in *Inferno* 18. 118–23 and his own political satires, or *sirventes*, in praise of discord and strife. In his lyrics, Bertran claimed that the active life is lived fully only on the battlefield. But this stance was in part literary pose. Though he cut a quarrelsome figure in the personal and political struggles of his time, the historical Bertran de Born was throughout his long life a benefactor of the church, and he was, like Bernart de Ventadorn, a Cistercian monk at Dalon for his last twenty years.

Bertran's latest editors accept some forty-seven of the songs attributed to him (forty-three certain; four doubtful). Throughout, he upholds the virtues of war, particularly courage and generosity. This martial worldview is expressed through moral aphorisms or direct language sometimes seconded by violent imagery. Even in his few love lyrics, Bertran voices his disapproval of an imperfect, unheroic society. As both lover and warrior, the poet's persona embodies the knightly values whose absence all around him he satirically laments. His *sirventes*, *cansos*, and *planhs* are all directed toward realizing those consummate moral and social ideals of the courtly world.

Roy S. Rosenstein

[See also: TROUBADOUR POETRY]

Bertran de Born. *The Poems of the Troubadour Bertran de Born*, ed and trans. William D. Paden, Tilde Sankovitch, and Patricia H. Stäblein. Berkeley: University of California Press, 1986.

———. *L'amour et la guerre: l'œuvre de Bertran de Born*, ed. Gérard Gouiran. Aix-en-Provence: Université de Provence, 1985.

Dauzier, Martine. *Le mythe de Bertran de Born*. Paris: Presses de l'Université de Paris-Sorbonne, 1986.

BERTRAND DE BAR-SUR-AUBE (fl. late 12th c.). A well-born cleric, by his own account, Bertrand claims to have composed the chanson de geste *Girart de Vienne* at Bar-sur-Aube in Champagne. The poem, which dates ca. 1180, is preserved in five manuscripts and consists of just under 7,000 decasyllabic lines arranged in 192 rhymed laisses. It belongs in some sense to both the Rebellious Vassal and the Guillaume d'Orange cycles. Girart becomes an uncle of Aymeri de Narbonne, Guillaume's father. His youth at Charlemagne's court is characterized by capricious and unjust treatment from the emperor, who later besieges Vienne for seven years but is finally reconciled to the hero, acknowledging that he has been in the wrong. This will become a pattern paradigmatic for the epics of revolt. But Bertrand is also influenced by the contemporary romances: the siege (for which Bertrand followed an earlier and more savage chanson de geste, now lost) becomes partly a romanticized account of the origin of the friendship of Roland and Oliver, here on opposite sides, and the former's betrothal to Aude (with obvious reference to the *Chanson de Roland*).

References to Bertrand in other poems testify to his fame as both trouvère and jongleur. At the end of *Girart de Vienne*, a passage found in all the extant manuscripts announces a poem on Aymeri de Narbonne. The epic of that name has been attributed to Bertrand in consequence, but the matter is debated. Bertrand is important for his probably original division of epic material into three *gestes*, or cycles, linked with his connection of a traditional rebel to the loyal clan of Guillaume d'Orange; he is also a skillful *remanieur* able to combine the epic and the romance, with an unusual interest in motivation and indeed psychology.

Wolfgang G. van Emden

[See also: CHANSON DE GESTE; *GIRART DE ROUSSILLON*; GUILLAUME D'ORANGE CYCLE; REBELLIOUS VASSAL CYCLE]

Bertrand de Bar-sur-Aube. *Girart de Vienne*, ed. Wolfgang G. van Emden. Paris: Société des Anciens Textes Français, 1977.

Kibler, William W. "Bertrand de Bar-sur-Aube, Author of *Aymeri de Narbonne*?" *Speculum* 48 (1973): 277–92.

van Emden, Wolfgang G. "*Girart de Vienne*: problèmes de composition et de datation." *Cahiers de civilisation médiévale* 13 (1970): 281–90. [Builds on work by René Louis cited in *Girart de Roussillon* bibliography.]

BERZÉ-LA-VILLE. About six miles southeast of the abbey of Cluny lies the small farm or grange of Berzé-la-Ville. In

Berzé-la-Ville (Saône-et-Loire), grange, apse. *Photograph courtesy of Whitney S. Stoddard.*

the early 12th century, thirty granges around Cluny supplied food for the large monastic community. Inside the chapel of this grange are the finest extant Burgundian mural paintings. Christ in Majesty, surrounded by the twelve Apostles, is seated on a throne inside an almond-shaped mandorla. The inclusion of the twelve Apostles rather than symbols of the four Evangelists suggests a connection with Rome. On the spandrels below the semicupola are holy virgins and martyrs holding lamps, and around the base are nine half-length saints. The martyrdoms of SS. Blaise and Lawrence are depicted within niches on the sides of the choir.

The Berzé muralist painted figures in reds, greens, purple, and white against a blue background. The dark blue sets off the figures in warm tonalities. The figure of Christ has the same frontal pose as does the Vézelay Christ, yet the anatomical articulation of the figure is more emphasized in the fresco. There seem to be strong connections between Cluny and painting in Rome ca. 1100, with its Byzantine flavor.

The martyrdom of St. Lawrence exhibits the compositional sensitivity of the Romanesque muralist. The painter is given a space framed by columns supporting capitals and an arch. The lower part of the mural is filled by the flattened grill with the nude martyr being consumed by flames. In his pose, the Roman delegate repeats the curve of the arch. The backs and heads of the executioners repeat the shape of silhouettes of column, capital, and arch, while diagonals unite the composition. Painting and architecture are united. The architecture of the two-storied grange, like the figures in the murals, is carefully articulated by many planes in space. The exterior resembles the first Romanesque style, with masonry pilasters or wall buttresses and arched corbel tables. The interior walls have multiple arches and responds.

Dating Berzé-la-Ville is difficult. The spread among scholars is from the end of the 11th century to the middle of the 13th. Since Hugues, abbot of Cluny 1049–1109, probably used Berzé for retreat, and since the style of the frescoes is related to dated manuscripts of ca. 1100 or the following decade, Berzé-la-Ville may have been constructed and painted in the early 12th century.

Whitney S. Stoddard

Armi, C. Edson. *Masons and Sculptors in Romanesque Burgundy.* 2 vols. University Park: Pennsylvania State University Press, 1983.

Demus, Otto. *Romanesque Mural Painting.* New York: Abrams, 1970, pp. 98–100.

Koehler, Wilhelm. "Byzantine Art and the West." *Dumbarton Oaks Papers* 1 (1941): 63–87.

Schapiro, Meyer. *The Parma Ildefonsus: A Romanesque Illuminated Manuscript from Cluny.* New York: College Art Association, 1964.

Stoddard, Whitney S. *Monastery and Cathedral in France.* Middletown: Wesleyan University Press, 1966.

BESTIARY. A treatise on animals, usually offering a symbolic or allegorical interpretation of their traits. Old French bestiaries derive ultimately from the *Physiologus*, a Greek text that originated in Alexandria in late antiquity and was translated into Latin sometime between the 4th and the early 6th centuries. The *Physiologus* consists of descriptions of birds, animals, and stones, based largely on legend and subjected to allegorical interpretation. Vernacular bestiaries can feature moral, spiritual, or amorous allegory.

Four French bestiaries survive from the 12th and early 13th centuries. The oldest is the Anglo-Norman bestiary of Philippe de Thaün, dedicated to Adeliza (Aaliz) de Louvain, second wife of Henry I of England, and dating from ca. 1125. The bestiary of Gervaise was produced toward the beginning of the 13th century; those of Guillaume le Clerc (also known as Guillaume le Normand) and Pierre de Beauvais were completed within the first two decades of the century. The best known is that of Guillaume le Clerc, which was one of the most important vernacular sources for the *Physiologus* material. In all four of these examples, the salient feature of a bird or animal becomes an allegory for some element in sacred history or the life of Christ, or for the salvation of the soul.

Bestiary material also appears in vernacular encyclopedias, such as Brunetto Latini's *Li livres dou tresor* and the *Livre des propriétés des choses*, a 1372 translation by

Jean Corbechon of Barthélemy l'Anglais's *Liber de proprietatibus rerum*.

The principal examples of love allegory in the bestiary tradition are Richard de Fournival's *Bestiaire d'amours*, dating from the mid-13th century; the related *Response au bestiaire*; and the *Bestiaire d'amour rimé*, a verse adaptation of Richard's *Bestiaire*. In these texts, the birds and animals retain their traditional attributes; but instead of figuring events in sacred history or aspects of the moral and spiritual life of the soul, the creatures of the natural world are interpreted as representing aspects of the love relationship. For example, the weasel, said to conceive through the ear and give birth through the mouth, is treated in religious bestiaries as an allegory for the Virgin Mary. Richard de Fournival, however, makes of the weasel a figure for the recalcitrant lady: she receives her would-be lover's request through the ear and gives birth through the mouth to her refusal.

Bestiary allusions appear in many works, such as Nicole de Margival's *Dit de la panthère d'amours*, in which the beloved lady is represented as a panther and the enemies of love as a dragon. The trouvères incorporated bestiary allusions into their songs; in *Aussi com l'unicorne sui*, Thibaut de Champagne compares his lovesick state to that of a unicorn, lured to its death in the lap of a maiden.

Bestiaries are usually illustrated. The spiritual bestiary of Guillaume le Clerc is often provided with two-part miniatures, each representing both the animal in question and its allegorical significance. For example, the pelican is shown feeding its babies with its blood, accompanied by an image of the Crucifixion; the turtledove mourning its mate is accompanied by an image of Ecclesia mourning the death of her bridegroom, Christ. Illustrations of the *Bestiaire d'amours* do not manifest this two-part format, but the lover and lady are sometimes included in the miniature along with the animal.

Sylvia Huot

[See also: GUILLAUME LE CLERC; PHILIPPE DE THAÜN; PIERRE DE BEAUVAIS; RICHARD DE FOURNIVAL]

Bianciotto, Gabriel, and Michel Salvat, eds. *Épopée animale, fable, fabliau: actes du IVe Colloque de la Société Renardienne.* Paris: Presses Universitaires de France, 1984.

McCullough, Florence. *Medieval Latin and French Bestiaries.* Chapel Hill: University of North Carolina Press, 1960.

BETROTHAL AND MARRIAGE CONTRACTS. Under Roman and canon law, the institution of marriage had a contractual dimension that influenced Merovingian practices. Betrothal became part of Frankish marriage customs, often formalized by written contract between families. Upon betrothal under Roman law, pledges or earnest money (*arrhae*) were often made. In the Middle Ages, families might enter into contracts of betrothal promising young children in future marriage, although the church prohibited the formal marriage of girls under twelve and boys under fourteen. Churchmen often were present at the passage of betrothal and marriage contracts, with the actual ceremony performed at the church door before a nuptial Mass.

In southern France in the high and late Middle Ages, marriage contracts were drawn up before a notary. The contract might open with the constitution of dowry by the bride's family, followed by the bride's donation of herself (implying individual consent) to her future husband with a promise of loyalty. The groom then made the same commitment and gave acquittal for the receipt of the dowry. He then proceeded in some contracts to make a *donatio propter nuptias* (OFr. *augment*), with the projected return of both dowry and *augment* to his widow secured by his own property. Finally, he renounced any legal recourse to invalidate obligations. The ceremony of marriage generally followed shortly after the contractual arrangements had been concluded.

Kathryn L. Reyerson

[See also: DOWRY; MARRIAGE, CLANDESTINE]

Duby, Georges. *The Knight, the Lady and the Priest: The Making of Modern Marriage in Medieval France*, trans. Barbara Bray. New York: Pantheon, 1983.

Ganshof, François Louis. "Le statut de la femme dans la monarchie franque." *Recueils de la Société Jean Bodin* 12 (1962): 5–58.

Gaudemet, Jean. "Le legs du droit romain en matière matrimoniale." In *Il matrimonio nella società altomedievale.* Spoleto: Presso la Sede del Centro, 1977, pp. 139–89.

Herlihy, David. *Medieval Households.* Cambridge: Harvard University Press, 1985.

Hilaire, Jean. *Le régime des biens entre époux dans la région de Montpellier du début du XIIIe siècle à la fin du XVIe siècle.* Montpellier: Causse, Graille and Castelnau, 1957.

Shahar, Shulamith. *The Fourth Estate: A History of Women in the Middle Ages.* London: Methuen, 1983.

Wemple, Suzanne. *Women in Frankish Society: Marriage and the Cloister, 500 to 900.* Philadelphia: University of Pennsylvania Press, 1981.

BEVERAGES. Water was just as important a means to slake thirst in the Middle Ages as it is today. And just as we must today be cautious about the source of potable water, so six hundred years ago streams and rivers running through urban areas tended to become too polluted to afford safe drinking water. Normally, the dug well was vital to any community. People who had access to a spring or a fountain could consider themselves fortunate: their water was valued for its clarity and its dependable purity.

Water was not considered to be a proper beverage at meals. To accompany food and to aid digestion, a mildly fermented drink of some sort was usually available. The presence of alcohol reduced the risk of bacterial contamination in a beverage. Depending upon both tradition and the strengths of regional agriculture, this drink varied in France among beer (Ofr. *cervoise*), used generally in northeastern areas and in Paris when wine was unavailable, and wine elsewhere. In neither case was the alcoholic content high; proper storage was difficult and expensive, and the product was retailed as soon as it was drinkable. A good number of popular "recipes" were compiled during the period on ways to cure spoilage in stored wines. Two varieties of beer were recognized: a better grade, from barley or spelt, and a small beer, from wheat and rye, oats, vetch, and virtually any other grain. Just as today, the reputation of wines depended upon their geographical source. The Burgundian vineyards produced the most valued, but imported wines, from Greece, Cyprus, or Palestine, had a certain vogue.

Cider and mead (*hydromel*, from a fermented mixture of honey and water, particularly in its flavored forms as *medon* and *bergerasse*) enjoyed local appeal in northern France.

Certain special wines were customarily served as aperitifs, cordials, and digestives at formal meals. For instance, *grenache* was commonly used to "open the stomach" in such meals. Medical faith in the power of spices, both to promote digestion and to ensure a healthy balance of corporal humors, led to the elaboration of fortified wines, such as *hypocras* (in which name the authority of Hippocrates is apparent) and *claret*. Flavoring was also provided wines by wormwood (absinthe), aloes, hyssop, myrtle, anise, rosemary, cubebs, sage, and musk.

A number of other beverages derived as well from the realm of medicine, often by way of their use as ingredients in special cookery. Natural fruit juices, *poiré* and *prunellé*, for example, and in particular citric juices because of their bitterness, were so used from the end of the 14th century. Finely ground flower petals lent a scent and flavor to water. Normally available for finger washing during a meal, an infusion of rose petals (*eaue rose*) enjoyed extensive use particularly in its distilled form, first as a medically prescribed therapeutic beverage, then as a beverage consumed for the maintenance of good health, and finally as a culinary ingredient. The techniques of the still, or alembic, provided the medieval physician with *aqua vitae* from various wines; but thirsty people soon realized that what was beneficial for the sick could be equally salutary for anyone.

Terence Scully

[See also: BANQUETING; COOKING; MEALS]

Gottschalk, Alfred. *Histoire de l'alimentation et de la gastronomie depuis la préhistoire jusqu'à nos jours.* 2 vols. Paris: Hippocrate, 1948, Vol. 1, pp. 257–352.
Glixelli, S. "Les contenances de table." *Romania* 47 (1921): 1–40.

BÉZIERS. Occupying a fortified site on hills overlooking the Orb River, Béziers (Hérault) was an important center of commerce and administration in medieval France. Under the Carolingians, Béziers became the seat of a county, and then (ca. 880) a viscounty under the counts of Toulouse. A series of marriages brought Béziers into the assemblage of territories controlled by the Trencavel family in 1066.

The authority of the viscounts remained paramount in the city until the 12th century. Their subsequent difficulties and conflicts with the counts of Toulouse and

Barcelona allowed the power of the bishop and commune to emerge. By the end of the 12th century, Béziers had become a co-seigneurie, five of its *bourgs* recognizing the sole authority of the bishop. The commune of Béziers first appeared in 1131. Tensions between the viscount and burghers reached a peak in 1167, when the citizens murdered Viscount Raymond Trencavel in the church of the Madeleine. Béziers, under its consuls, enjoyed a well-developed municipal organization throughout the 13th century; in 1280, the artisanal classes gained entry into the consulate through the system of *échelles*, which grouped them into several ranks or grades and accorded to each a position in the consulate.

Béziers suffered heavily during the Albigensian Crusade. Taken by assault on July 22, 1209, it was pillaged and the church of the Madeleine, within which townsmen had taken refuge, was burned. Despite dramatic accounts, the extent of this massacre should not be exaggerated. Bézier's economic growth and the prosperity of its leading families continued unaffected, and the 13th century witnessed the period of greatest brilliance for the city. It emerged as a center of textile production and possessed an important *studium* of civil law. Social conflicts, notably the violent popular uprising led by Bernard Porquier in 1381, agitated Béziers in the 14th century. At the end of the Middle Ages, however, Béziers recovered an important position, particularly through the favor of Charles VII, who located there his Parlement from 1425 to 1429.

Little that is medieval remains of the burned church of the Madeleine. The church of Saint-Aphrodise preserves a Romanesque crypt, nave, and aisles, wedded to a Gothic choir. More significant are the Romanesque church of Saint-Jacques and the fortified Gothic church of Saint-Nazaire. Saint-Jacques contains a five-sided apse in southern Romanesque style, with a sculpted decor inspired by classical art, as at Alet. Saint-Nazaire, recently restored, has two fortified towers on the west façade separated by a machicolated arcade under an enormous rose window. Only fragments of the crypt (9th–10th c.) and Romanesque choir and tower antedate the destruction of the town in 1209; the transept dates from the 13th century and the nave from the 14th. There are stained glass from the 14th century and important murals dated to 1347. The 15th-century octagonal sacristy and chapter house are unusual.

Alan Friedlander

[See also: ALBIGENSIAN CRUSADE; LANGUEDOC; TRENCAVEL]

Gramain, Monique. "'Castrum,' structures féodales et peuplement en Biterrois au XIe siècle." In *Structures féodales et féodalisme dans l'Occident méditerranéen (X–XIII siècles)*. Rome: École Française de Rome, 1980, pp. 119–34.
Lablaude, Pierre. "Béziers." *Congrès archéologique (Montpellier)* 108 (1950): 323–42.
Sabatier, Ernest. *Histoire de la ville et des évêques de Béziers.* Béziers: Carrière, 1854.
Sagnes, Jean. *Histoire de Béziers.* Toulouse: Privat, 1986.
Vidal, Henri. "La coutume de Béziers (1185–94)." *Recueil de mémoires et travaux publié par la Société du Droit et des*

Institutions des Anciens Pays de Droit Écrit, fasc. 11 (1980): 23–40.

———. *Episcopatus et pouvoir épiscopal à Béziers à la veille de la Croisade Albigeoise, 1152–1209.* Montpellier: Université de Montpellier, 1951.

BIBLE, CHRISTIAN INTERPRETATION OF.

BIBLE, CHRISTIAN INTERPRETATION OF. Put together over centuries and argued over for longer, full of inconsistencies, contradictions, obscurities, peculiar vocabulary and syntax, ancient poetry, and tribal law, the Bible is an interpreter's dream: a source that claims to be authoritative—the written Word of God—and to be both necessary and sufficient for the salvation of the believer. Generations of scholars have exercised their learning and ingenuity on this text of texts.

The medieval West was not, then, unusual in its fascination with the Bible as a starting point for commentary and interpretation. Its particular interest for students of interpretation (or "exegesis," after the Greek term) lies not only in studying the methods in which medieval biblical scholars worked but also in trying to discern links between exegesis and everyday life. Medieval society was a Christian society, inasmuch as the ruling societal myth was Christian. With few exceptions, everyone was considered to be Christian. Rulers were Christian princes, and the church held, or attempted increasingly to abrogate to itself, temporal as well as spiritual powers. In such circumstances, the teachings of the Bible, as laid down by authoritative scholarship, had pertinence for an audience wider than academic theologians or devout laypeople.

Over the period A.D. 500–1500, the circumstances of biblical interpretation varied a great deal, moving from Carolingian schools, through monasteries, to secular (i.e., religious but nonmonastic) schools and universities. By the mid-13th century, the interpretation of the Bible had become the preserve of professional theologians, working in universities and generally members of the mendicant orders. Scholastic "questions" from this period ask *who* could interpret the Bible: any believers or only trained interpreters? While theologians had to admit that the Holy Spirit could move any simple believer to a correct understanding of the Word of God, they nevertheless inclined firmly toward professionalization and credentialism.

Before considering how medieval interpreters went about their work, we must ask what exactly was the Bible at this time. The Bible as a physical object rarely existed in one single volume (called a "pandect"), or even two—Old Testament and New. It was much more likely to come in sets of books on the lines established by Cassiodorus in the 6th century. Six-volume sets of Pentateuch, History books, Minor Prophets, Major Prophets, Gospels, and finally Acts, Epistles, and Revelation were common. As the canon of the Old Testament varied in the Hebrew and Greek traditions, some books, such as Maccabees, might be included although they were understood to be apocryphal. The order of books was not always consistent.

Of the translations of the Bible into Latin, the most common was that of Jerome, known now as the Vulgate. By the 13th century, it was rare to find a Bible that was not Jerome's translation, accompanied by his prefaces to each book or group of books and including his *Liber de nominibus hebraicis,* an alphabetical list explaining the meaning of biblical proper nouns.

Interpretation of the Bible came in a number of forms. Jerome and Augustine, almost exact contemporaries, were foundational for Christian biblical interpretation, and yet their surviving writings show us the range of possibilities for the work of an exegete. Jerome was even in his lifetime acknowledged as the supreme linguist and translator, whose knowledge of the biblical text was unparalleled. Apart from his translation, he is known for his letters on theological issues but also for his series of commentaries on the whole Bible. Augustine had different gifts. He did not have Jerome's linguistic skills; his direct commentaries on biblical books are few. Rather, his biblical interpretation comes out in his sermons (which are largely exegeses of texts), treatises on theological issues, and works that respond directly to issues of the day. Augustine *uses* the Bible and exegesis in his work as a bishop, whereas Jerome expounds the Bible in a more detached and scholarly fashion.

Jerome and Augustine are just two of the fathers of the church whose biblical interpretation was crucial for the Middle Ages. Other common Latin and Greek patristic authors were Gregory the Great, Gregory Nazianzus, Ambrose of Milan, Cassiodorus, Origen, John Chrysostom, John Damascene, Bede, Isidore of Seville, and later Rabanus Maurus. The work of those who had gone before was crucial to the medieval method. In the worldview of the Middle Ages, truth was attained by accretion rather than by the overthrow of one system by another. Truth must also have stood the test of time—the very fact of longevity was important. Continued approbation over generations of the church was in itself a test of rightness. Thus, one was on safe ground in using the interpretations of the fathers.

Classical authors, such as Cicero and Seneca, were also utilized to support arguments, but not without reservations. Plato and Aristotle had the biggest influence of any non-Christian sources. The lexicographical interests of some Christian scholars and the stubborn opacity of some Old Testament texts led to consultation with Jews, but this was never a widespread practice; for most people, Jerome was enough of a source for the Hebrew meaning. However, Philo Judaeus, Josephus, Rashi, and Maimonides were known and used. Although Arabic scientific work circulated from the 12th century onward, it had little direct influence on biblical interpretation.

Biblical interpretation could take a variety of forms, from a commentary to be read alongside the text of a whole book or set of books, to a sermon explaining and expounding a few verses. Extended commentaries often appear under such generally interchangeable titles as *Expositiones, Commentaria, Glossa,* or *Postilla.* Titles are not a medieval notion—these tend to be later additions—and the usual medieval description for such a work is, for example, *In Genesim* ("On the Book of Genesis").

Perhaps the biggest medieval innovation in biblical exegesis was a matter not of content or style but of layout, culminating in the production of biblical texts with integrated commentary known as the *Glossa* or *Glossa ordinaria* (the "Gloss" or "Ordinary Gloss"). From the Carolingian period onward, we have books of the Psalms and the Epistles with marginal glosses. The style itself was not new—it was also used for ancient texts—but it was adapted to the Bible with great success. Between 1140 and 1170, a large number of Bibles were produced, made with a planned page layout for integrated patristic interlinear and marginal glosses that are remarkably standardized. Sometime between the Carolingian books and these planned, mass-produced volumes, the text of the glosses and the page format had been decided upon. We know little about this process of evolution, although it has long been associated with Anselm of Laon. We must, however, bear in mind that each biblical book or set of books has a different exegetical history; the manner and type of glossing is not the same all the way through. Moreover, although Laon may have had a large part to play in producing the text, it was in Paris that many glossed Bibles of this period originate. Paris became a renowned center for book production, and it was perhaps the quantity and quality of glossed Bibles made here in these years that fueled its reputation.

How the *Glossa* was used, and what effect it had on subsequent medieval exegesis, is still a moot point. The surge in the production of texts of the *Glossa* coincides with the rise of secular schools, where reference books would be highly useful tools. The patristic texts chosen for inclusion in the *Glossa* are, as far as we can tell without a modern critical edition, conservative. We can therefore see the *Glossa* either as petrifying the accepted range of interpretation of a particular passage of Scripture or as collecting the standard exegesis and putting it to one side so that scholars could move on in other directions. Depending on one's point of view, the *Glossa* gives the fundamental norms of interpretation, or it gives the old-fashioned approach. Its usefulness must vary according to the knowledge and skill of its user.

After the 1170s, new copies of the *Glossa* become rare. They are replaced by the *Historia scholastica* of Peter Comestor (a sort of digest and paraphrase of the Bible that was immensely popular among students), the *Sententiae* of Peter Lombard, and later by the biblical commentaries of Stephen Langton and the Dominican master Hugues de Saint-Cher, whose postilla on the whole Bible were immensely successful. These, in their way, are the *Glossa ordinaria* of the 13th century.

The *Glossa*, then, was the standard first step for biblical interpreters of the 12th century. They might use it to produce their own exegeses of the text, whether in sermon form or continuous commentary. The production of biblical commentaries remained the standard form of professional development for aspiring theologians. As part of the higher degree in theology at the University of Paris, the premier European institution for the study of theology in the 12th and 13th centuries, every student had to "read," that is, lecture on, at least one book of the Old Testament and one of the New.

How was the Bible interpreted? The usual generalization is that exegesis is made according to the "senses" of Scripture. The number and exact nature of these senses varies with time and commentator, but the basic division is into a literal or historical sense and a moral or allegorical sense. This dichotomy is generally linked to the prevailing practices and theological preferences of the early Christian church at Antioch, which held to the literal sense, and at Alexandria, which preferred allegory. In this vein, the main early interpreters of the Antiochene school were John Chrysostom and Theodore of Mopsuestia; the leading Alexandrine exegete was Origen.

Over time, the picture grows more complicated, with the spiritual sense dividing into further categories, so that, for instance, John Cassian held to a ninefold sense of Scripture. However, the classic formulation for the Middle Ages is a fourfold sense of Scripture, enshrined in a verse attributed to Augustine of Dacia:

Littera gesta docet, quid credas allegoria,
Moralis quid agas, quo tendas anagogia.

("The literal [or historical] sense teaches us about what things were done; the allegorical sense tells us what we should believe; the moral [or tropological] sense tells us what to do; and the anagogical sense tells us about our heavenly ends.")

A common medieval example of a word glossed according to the four senses is taken from John Cassian. "Jerusalem" in the literal sense is the city in the Holy Land; in the allegorical sense, it is the Church Militant on earth; tropologically, it stands for the faithful believer; anagogically, it is the heavenly city of Jerusalem. In a sense, the three "spiritual" definitions are arbitrary; they are not the only expositions of "Jerusalem" according to these senses that one might find in medieval exegesis. Indeed, there were books of "distinctions" (*distinctiones*) that gave lists of words, arranged alphabetically, defined according to various senses of Scripture; different definitions may be given for any one word in any one sense.

Furthermore, this neat division cannot be taken to be a description of the reality of exegesis. First, it is *not* the case that exegetes go through each pericope (short section of text), interpreting it according to one sense after the other. The closest one can get to that are the commentaries of Stephen Langton, which proceed according to a general "literal" sense and then to a blanket "allegorical" or "moral" one. Langton's method enabled his commentaries to circulate in various forms, some with both senses of Scripture present, others with only the literal or only the allegorical. But Langton is an exception. Generally, commentators jump from one sense to another, depending on the passage in question and their aim in making the exegesis: a commentator beginning a scholarly consideration of a text may begin with a lexicographical survey (included in the literal sense); but a commentator whose purpose is exhortation will use the allegorical or tropological senses.

Second, not all pericopes, as Hugh of Saint-Victor noted, are suitable for interpretation according to every sense of Scripture. Some appear to have no historical sense, as they are simply untrue or so obscure as to be incomprehensible. Others are only fruitful in an anagogical understanding.

Medieval exegesis cannot be easily characterized and divided into periods when literal or spiritual senses prevailed. In the best cases, interpreters were fluid in their use of Scripture and were always conscious of the task of strengthening the faithful in their beliefs. They write with the needs of their audience in mind and so will shift between senses or through metaphors in order to make a point, or to wrestle a Christian meaning from a pericope.

Third, the meaning of the senses—what each of them included by definition—varied over time. For instance, before the middle of the 13th century the literal sense came to encompass not only a lexical exposition of the text, as well as "what happened" in the historical or narrative sense, but also whatever meaning the author intended, even when that intention was a metaphor or allegory. This shift in definition was possibly to counteract criticism that interpreters could prove anything by recourse to the spiritual senses; it led to fears for orthodoxy. Right doctrine must have its roots in the literal sense of Scripture. The literal sense provided the foundations for the house of interpretation. In order to allow christological (a passage that foreshadows the coming of Christ) and typological (an Old Testament passage acting as an extended metaphor for a New Testament scene or theme) interpretation of the Old Testament, which no Christian medieval exegete would have considered anything but foundational, commentators had to include an allegorical interpretation in the basic meaning of the literal sense. This was, for them, a "commonsense" extension of the definition of literalness: much of the point of the Old Testament is to pave the way for the New.

Much has been made of supposed differences in exegesis between that of the monasteries and that of the schools and later the universities, with the work of the Augustinian abbey of Saint-Victor in Paris standing as a kind of bridge between the two. Such a distinction must be made with care. It is not a simple question of different texts, sources, methods, and procedures. If the distinction is to be found anywhere, it is in the use and goal of the interpretations: why they were made, who was to read them, why they read them. A biblical commentary made in a monastery as an aid to contemplation, for example, will differ in tenor and style from one made in a mendicant school as a friar's preaching tool. In fact, we know little about why biblical commentary was done and what purpose many of the vast, repetitive volumes of exegesis were intended to serve.

From the later 13th century, the place of the Bible as a source of revelation and in theology and devotion was overshadowed by increased interest in science, the natural order, observation, and experiment and by the production of devotional literature inspired by direct revelation, written by or for laypeople. Many of these spiritual texts are in the vernacular, and this fact, together with other devotional aids and translations, even of the biblical text itself, illuminates a shift in the place of "professional" biblical interpretation from the center of the Christian life—a shift that Protestantism would move to redress in the 16th century.

Lesley J. Smith

[See also: ANSELM OF LAON; BIBLE, JEWISH INTERPRETATION OF; BIBLE, LATIN VERSION OF; BIBLICAL TRANSLATIONS; GILBERT OF POITIERS; *GLOSSA ORDINARIA*; HUGH OF SAINT-VICTOR; HUGUES DE SAINT-CHER; PETER COMESTOR; PETER LOMBARD; POPULAR DEVOTION; SAINT-VICTOR, ABBEY AND SCHOOL OF; SCHOLASTICISM; SCHOOLS, CATHEDRAL; SCHOOLS, MONASTIC; SENTENCE COLLECTIONS; STEPHEN LANGTON; THEOLOGY; UNIVERSITIES]

Lampe, G.W.H., ed. *The Cambridge History of the Bible.* 3 vols. Cambridge: Cambridge University Press, 1969–70, Vol. 2: *The West from the Fathers to the Reformation.*
Lubac, Henri de. *Exégèse médiévale.* 2 vols. in 4 parts. Paris: Aubier, 1959–64.
Riché, Pierre, and Guy Lobrichon, eds. *Le moyen âge et la Bible.* Paris: Beauchesne, 1984.
Smalley, Beryl. *The Study of the Bible in the Middle Ages.* 3rd ed. Oxford: Blackwell, 1983.
Vernet, André, and Anne-Marie Genevois. *La Bible au moyen âge.* Paris: CNRS, 1989.

BIBLE, JEWISH INTERPRETATION OF. The study and exposition of the Hebrew Bible was one of the fundamental activities of the Jewish community in medieval France. The biblical text, understood as the "Written Torah," was augmented by an "Oral Torah," which according to Jewish teaching had been transmitted from God to Moses and then through a chain of tradition to the ancient rabbis. The rabbis in France received this "Oral Torah" in the form of written documents—Mishnah, Talmud, and Midrash—composed in the land of Israel and Babylonia between the 3rd and 6th centuries. The task of the medieval rabbi was to harmonize the interpretations of the "Written" and "Oral" Torahs with the praxis of Jewish life.

Jews in medieval France studied Scripture in their academies and also heard Scripture read and expounded during their daily and Sabbath liturgy. Scriptural study thus inspired various genres of rabbinic literature: the biblical commentary, the homily, *responsa* (legal decisions by rabbis), and the liturgical poem. Biblical commentary was never fully separated from other branches of Jewish learning.

In northern France (Champagne, Île-de-France, Lorraine), Jewish learning emerged during the 10th and 11th centuries and was shaped largely by the texts and traditions transmitted by the more ancient Jewish communities in the Rhineland cities of Speyer, Worms, and Mainz. Drawing upon the writings of Jews in Italy and the Byzantine empire, these communities focused their efforts almost entirely on the classical canon of rabbinic literature and developed the Midrash, or homiletic exposition of the Bible and liturgical poetry.

By contrast, the communities in southern France (Provence, Languedoc) had experienced Jewish settlement since late antiquity. Mediterranean commerce and exposure to the Islamic empire opened these communities to a broader sphere of influences from outside the rabbinic canon. The flowering of biblical scholarly activity in southern France began in the mid-12th-century migration of significant scholarly families from Spain in the aftermath of the Almohade invasions. These scholars brought the Spanish tradition of Jewish biblical exegesis with its highly developed use of the linguistic sciences of lexicography and grammar. In addition, the philosophical and poetic traditions of the Judeo-Islamic world had a significant impact on these French communities. It was in Narbonne that most of the Jewish philosophical works written in Arabic, such as Maimonides's *Guide to the Perplexed*, were translated into Hebrew. Southern France thus became a center for the integration of philosophical topics into biblical exegesis. Also by the mid-12th century, the first groups of scholars engaging in mystical interpretation of Scripture began to flourish in Provence.

Both northern and southern French centers of Jewish exegesis were profoundly affected by contacts with the surrounding Christian culture. On occasion, Christian scholars actively solicited Jewish insight for their own exegesis. Examples of these exchanges are Abbot Stephen Harding of Cîteaux's invitation to Jews for discussions or Andrew of Saint-Victor's incorporation of "Traditions of the Jews" into his biblical commentaries. Christian evangelization often called upon Jews to defend their interpretations of Scripture. These challenges led to the composition by Jews of polemical treatises that refuted christological explications of the Hebrew Bible. Many scholars also argue that the contact with Christianity, particularly in northern France, was one of the primary motivations for the development of *peshat* ("plain" or "contextual meaning") exegesis.

The development of biblical exegesis in northern France may be divided into three periods: the 11th century, characterized by the compilation of Old French glosses on Hebrew Scripture and the exegesis of Rabbi Solomon ben Isaac of Troyes (Rashi; 1040–1105); 1100–75, marked by the development of an exegesis of the Hebrew Bible independent of rabbinic allegorization; and 1175–1300, showing the evolution of a dialectical method that harmonized Rashi with contradictory authorities in classical rabbinic literature, the composition of polemical treatises, and the compilation of Old French–Hebrew glossaries.

The earliest example of exegetical activity in northern France seems to have been a group of scholars called *Poterim* ("translators"), whose primary activity was the assembling of lists of words in Hebrew and Old French for teaching children. The unique aspect of the *Poterim* seems to be their focus on the language of Scripture and not on the broader dimensions of the Bible and rabbinic literature.

Rashi gave the basic shape to northern French biblical exegesis. He left Troyes to study in the academies of the Rhineland, where scholars had been compiling notebooks, or *quntresim*, of exegesis on the Talmud. This Talmud commentary focused on clarifying the language of the dialectical arguments within the text. Rashi brought this style of interpretation, which focused on clarification of the sequence of argument, back to Troyes. On the basis of the *quntresim* of his teachers, Rashi wrote a commentary on almost all the tractates of the Babylonian Talmud. This vast project guaranteed that his writings would comprehend the full spectrum of rabbinic learning. Drawing upon the linguistic works of the *Poterim* and the tradition of Talmudic commentary in the Rhineland, he developed a hermeneutics that harmonized the Hebrew Bible with the rabbinic tradition.

Rashi wrote commentaries on the entire Hebrew Bible (except Ezra-Nehemiah, Chronicles, and the Book of Job). One of his fundamental principles was to balance the lexical boundaries of the biblical words or phrases against a variety of potential interpretations from rabbinic literature. He described his approach in the following way: "There are many Aggadic Midrashim, and our Rabbis have previously set them in proper order in Genesis Rabbah and other Midrash collections, and I have come for the plain meaning of the biblical text and for the Aggadoth which settles the words of the Scriptural text in their proper order" (Genesis 3.8). Rashi used the Hebrew phrase unique to his writings, *Peshuto shel Miqra* (translated "plain meaning"), to describe his goal. The goal of the exegete was to examine the sequence of biblical phrases in context and then turn to rabbinic sources that would be adapted to interpret the phrases. Rashi thus focused on narrative aspects of the text, through the sequence of words, joining the "plain meaning" and rabbinic authorities.

Rashi's commentaries generally provide an introduction to each biblical book. In most cases, the introduction is part of the comment on the initial verse. It describes the purpose of the book and gives some details about its author. In these, Rashi employs material from rabbinic literature but adapts it for his own purpose.

Rashi's biblical commentaries were the subject of glosses produced by scholars of the next generation, who saw themselves free to explore the lexical level of the text independently of rabbinic literature. Rashi's younger colleague Rabbi Joseph ben Simon Kara (b. ca. 1060/70) also traveled to the academies in the Rhineland. He wrote glosses on the Pentateuch and full commentaries on the Prophetic and Historical Books and the Writings. He also wrote commentaries on synagogue poetry that contained exegesis of Scripture. Joseph Kara distinguished himself from Rashi by his focus on the biblical text independent of rabbinic literature. In his commentaries, Kara attempts to engage the reader of a biblical verse directly through a series of questions and answers that lead to a comprehension of the entire passage.

By the mid-12th century, Rashi's grandsons, Rabbi Jacob ben Meir of Ramerupt (1100–1171) and Rabbi Samuel ben Meir (Rashbam; 1080–1160), had become the most prominent rabbinic authorities in France. In his commentary on the Pentateuch, Rashbam indicates that he wishes to continue the work of his grandfather Rashi. He focused on the *Peshat*, or plain, meaning of the biblical text. He extends the meaning of *Peshat* by claiming to seek the *'Iqqar Peshuto*, the fundamental plain meaning, of the Bible. This means that he seeks the explanations of difficult words or phrases by connecting them with passages from the same context. Rashbam does not rely on classical rabbinic interpretations but rather refers to human custom and the natural world in his commentaries.

The focus on explaining the biblical text independent of rabbinic tradition continued in the work of two other scholars, Rabbi Joseph of Orléans, also known as Joseph Bekhor-Shor, and Rabbi Eliezer of Beaugency. Joseph of Orléans's primary focus was on discerning the continuous narrative of the biblical text. His commentary also includes polemics against Christian allegorical interpretations of the Hebrew Bible that indicate his knowledge of the text of the Latin Vulgate and some of the most common Christian typological interpretations. Rabbi Eliezer of Beaugency's commentaries on Isaiah, Ezekiel, and the Minor Prophets reveal a striking independence from classical rabbinic interpretations. His emphasis is on the historical background of the Prophets and their visions and on the historical aspects of the prophetic texts.

In the mid-12th century, the Spanish-born Rabbi Abraham ibn Ezra (1089–1164) came to Rouen. His influence on contemporary French biblical exegesis is difficult to determine, but his later influence was extensive. He wrote commentaries on almost all books of the Bible. Ibn Ezra, however, incorporates rabbinic traditions in commentaries that range from philological notes to long scientific treatises. His commentary on the Song of Songs is the most original; in it, he proposes three levels of meaning: the lexical, the narrative, and the historical allegory.

After the development of *Peshat* exegesis during the 12th century, the dialectical Talmudic commentary called *Tosafot* seems to have become dominant. Collections of the biblical comments of these Talmudic masters have been preserved, printed under the titles *Da'at Zeqenim* ("Opinions of the Elders"), *Hadar Zeqenim* ("The Glory of the Elders"), and *Moshav Zeqenim* ("Dwelling Place of the Elders"). In addition, some collections can be ascribed to a single author, such as *Sefer HaGan* by Rabbi Aaron ben Yossi Ha-Cohen or *Minhat Yehudah* by Judah ben Eliezar (fl. 1300). Their biblical comments, usually based on Rashi's explanation, offer a harmonization of his comment with other passages in rabbinic literature.

The concept of assembling previous exegetical work also appears in the polemical treatise *The Book of Joseph the Zealot* by Joseph ben Nathan Official (fl. 1260–70). His polemical treatise, arranged according to the order of the books of the Hebrew Bible, refutes Christian allegorical interpretations with philological and rational arguments. Each chapter is augmented by a narrative that sets the stage for the argument: a conversation with a bishop; an argument with a mendicant; or a discussion with nobility.

Yet another series of exegetical collections from the 13th century comprise glossaries, probably influenced by Rashi's Old French glosses. These dictionaries provide the word in biblical Hebrew, an Old French translation in Hebrew characters, and the Old French in Latin characters. At times, several Old French explanations are proposed for a single biblical phrase.

Jewish intellectual activity in southern France may be divided into two periods: 900–1150 and 1150–1350. The conquest of the Almohades drove Jews educated in the Judeo-Islamic methods of exegesis into Provence, particularly Narbonne, in the mid-12th century. Even before the Spanish-educated Jews arrived, however, Provence hosted Jewish communities that produced literary works in traditional genres of rabbinic literature, such as legal codes, Talmudic commentary, and scriptural exegesis. From 1150 to 1350, the study of the Bible continued with careful attention to linguistic problems and was enhanced by the assimilation of philosophical investigation into Jewish religious thought. Jewish biblical studies during the 10th century in Provence focused on the collection of rabbinic *Aggadah,* or nonlegal material. Rabbi Moses Ha-Darshan ("the Preacher") of Narbonne is the main literary source. Scholars have ascribed two collections to him, *Midrash Bereshit Rabbati* and *Midrash Tadshe.*

The arrival of the Kimchi family changed the direction of biblical exegesis in southern France. Joseph (1105–1170) and his two sons, Moses (d. 1190) and David (d. 1235), brought with them the Spanish tradition of grammar, lexicography, and philosophical learning. These approaches contrasted with the homiletical or allegorical traditions that had dominated biblical studies in previous generations. Joseph Kimchi believed that the foundation of biblical exegesis lay in the knowledge of grammar. From his commentaries on the Pentateuch, Job, and Proverbs, as well as citations of his commentaries on the Prophets by his son David, we can observe Joseph's gift for resolving exegetical problems through a proper understanding of grammar and syntax. He also pursued the broader horizons of biblical meaning that were available through a rationalist approach to exegesis, and he utilized both grammar and rational analysis to refute Christian interpretations of the Hebrew Bible. He wrote *Sefer HaBerit* ("The Book of the Covenant") as an apologetic work proving the truth of Judaism. During this same period, Rabbi Jacob ben Reuben wrote an anti-Christian treatise in Gascony, the *Milchamot HaShem* ("The Wars of the Lord"). The spirit of religious polemic and apologetic, so much part of the broader Christian ambience in mid-12th-century southern France, pervaded Judaism as well.

The most extensive exegetical writings of the Kimchi family come from David. His systematic treatise on textual criticism of the Bible, *Et Sofer* ("The Scribe's Pen"), describes manuscript variants and the problems of the Massorah (the traditional consonantal Hebrew text as furnished with vowels by medieval scribes). His grammar book, *Sefer Mikhlol* ("The Compendium"), contained both a dictionary and a description of Hebrew grammatical rules. He wrote commentaries on Genesis, all the Prophets, the Psalms, Proverbs, and Chronicles, as well as allegorical commentaries on the Garden of Eden, Cain and Abel, and the first chapter of Ezekiel. Like his father, David Kimchi actively pursued polemics against Christian allegorical interpretations of the Hebrew Bible. Many of these polemical interpretations appear in his commentary on Psalms.

During the 12th and 13th centuries, Jewish communities in Provence witnessed the development of two genres related to biblical exegesis. Beginning in Posquières, Jewish esoteric, or mystical, speculation resulted in the composition of the first treatises on that subject. The doctrines developed in these circles would lead to the production of mystical writings in Gerona and throughout Spain in the 13th and 14th centuries. Jacob ben Abba Mari Anatoli (fl.

1300) composed one of the first works of Jewish sermonic literature, *Malmad HaTalmidim* ("Goad for Students"). Arranged according to the weekly Pentateuch reading, Anatoli provided moral lessons in the form of model sermons for preaching. This work, although not formally biblical exegesis, would have great influence on the development of sermonic literature and biblical exegesis in the centuries to follow.

Michael A. Signer

[See also: BIBLE, CHRISTIAN INTERPRETATION OF; JEWS; MAIMONIDES, INFLUENCE OF]

Angus, A.I. "Rashi and His School." In *World History of the Jewish People*, ed. Cecil Roth. New Brunswick: Rutgers University Press, 1966, Vol. 2: *The Dark Ages: Jews in Christian Europe, 711–1096*, pp. 210–48.

Grabois, Aryeh. "The *Hebraica Veritas* and Jewish-Christian Relations in the 12th Century." *Speculum* 50 (1975): 613–34.

Hailperin, Herman. *Rashi and the Christian Scholars*. Pittsburgh: University of Pittsburgh Press, 1963.

Rosenthal, Erwin I.J. "The Study of the Bible in Medieval Judaism." In *The Cambridge History of the Bible*. Cambridge: Cambridge University Press, 1969, Vol. 2: *The West from the Fathers to the Reformation*, ed. G.W.H. Lampe, pp. 252–79.

Shereshevsky, Esra. *Rashi: The Man and His World*. New York: Sepher-Herman, 1982.

Signer, Michael A. "*Peshat, Sensus Litteralis* and Sequential Narrative: Jewish Exegesis and the School of St. Victor in the 12th Century." In *The Frank Talmage Memorial Volume*, ed. B. Walfish. 2 vols. Hanover: University Press of New England, 1992–93, Vol. 1, pp. 203–16.

Talmage, Frank E. *David Kimhi: The Man and the Commentaries*. Cambridge: Harvard University Press, 1975.

Twersky, Isidore. "Aspects of the Social and Cultural History of Provençal Jewry." In *Jewish Society Through the Ages*, ed. Haim Hillel Ben-Sasson and Samuel Ettinger. New York: Schocken, 1971, pp. 185–207.

Zinn, Grover A. "History and Interpretation: 'Hebrew Truth,' Judaism, and the Victorine Tradition." In *Jews and Christians: Exploring the Past, Present and Future*, ed. James Charlesworth. New York: Crossroad, 1990.

BIBLE, LATIN VERSION OF. Although the Bible was written mostly in Hebrew and Greek, the world of early Christianity was chiefly one of Roman imperialism, so a Latin translation was imperative. Until the translation made by Jerome (ca. 342–420), referred to as the Vulgate, a number of other Latin versions were in circulation in the early church. Generally referred to as the Old Latin (*Vetus Latina*) versions, their translations of the books of the Old Testament were made from the Greek translation known as the Septuagint rather than from the original Hebrew. The Old Latin Bible was thus the work of many hands and a number of revisions over the course of the 2nd century A.D.; hence, different traditions of the text existed, particularly in North Africa and Italy. The language of the Old Latin

versions is somewhat odd, reflecting the Greek original, which it sometimes merely transliterates rather than translates, and its popular audience, rather than the Latin style of the cultured elite. No complete manuscript of the Old Latin Bible has survived; the Bible (the word is plural in the Greek) was made up of separate volumes, and pandects (Bible in a single volume) were a later development.

The varying forms of translation and difficulties in the Latin text persuaded Jerome, at the behest of Pope Damasus I, to undertake a new translation, this time from the original languages. This Vulgate text (*vulgata* 'popular') became the standard Bible in the Latin West from about the 6th century to the Reformation. However, although he is responsible for the majority of the text, Jerome is not the sole author, nor did he accord each book the same attention. Since the text of the Old Latin Old Testament was a translation of a translation, Jerome concentrated his energies here. Most of the Vulgate Old Testament is his work, with the exception of the Psalter (which is a corrected Old Latin text) and the five books that were included in the canon by Greek-speaking Jews but were not in the Hebrew canon: Wisdom, Ecclesiasticus, Baruch, 1 and 2 Maccabees. These retain the Old Latin text.

The text of the Psalter, with its varying traditions, involved more than one attempt at a solution. It is possible that the text of the Roman Psalter (that one commonly used by all the churches in Rome) is Jerome's first, hurried, attempt at a translation. His first definite attempt is the Gallican Psalter, based on the Hexapla text of manuscripts collected by Origen at Caesarea (known as Hexapla from its six-column format for comparing Hebrew and Greek texts). This was the version preferred by Alcuin, and, since it was, broadly, the text of the 13th-century Paris Bible and the basis of the first printed Bibles, it was the normal text for centuries. Jerome's final attempt at a Psalter translation, the "Hebrew," is so called because Jerome made it afresh, from the original Hebrew. This never (except for a time in Spain) achieved the popularity of the Gallican Psalter translation.

For the New Testament, Jerome himself seems merely to have revised the Gospels, perfunctorily at times, with the Greek text in hand. The rest of the books were revised by other scholars whose identities remain unknown, although the earliest references to the revised text are found in Pelagius. As well, Jerome wrote a series of prologues to the books or groups of books of the entire Bible, and these were commonly circulated with the text itself, becoming almost an integral part of it. The order of the books is variable.

Jerome seems to have begun the project with the simplest task, the revision of the Gospels, ca. 382. The Gallican Psalter was completed ca. 392, and the Hebrew Psalter and the rest of the Old Testament were done by ca. 407. The new version was not an immediate success, although by the late 6th century it seems to have become the standard text, a position that it retained until the Reformation. It was declared the authentic biblical text by the Council of Trent in the 16th century.

Lesley J. Smith

[See also: BIBLE, CHRISTIAN INTERPRETATION OF; BIBLE, JEWISH INTERPRETATION OF]

Berger, Samuel. *Histoire de la Vulgate pendant les premiers siècles du moyen âge.* Paris: Hachette, 1893.

Fischer, Bonifatius. *Lateinische Bibelhandschriften im frühen Mittelalters.* Freiburg: Herder, 1985.

———. *Beiträge zur Geschichte der lateinischen Bibeltexte.* Freiburg: Herder, 1986.

———. *Novae concordantiae Bibliorum Sacrorum iuxta Vulgatam versionem critice editam.* 5 vols. Stuttgart: Frommann-Holzboog, 1977.

———, with Herman J. Frede, Jean Gribomont, H. F. D. Sparks, Walter Thiele, eds. *Biblia Sacra iuxta Vulgatam versionem.* 2 vols. 3rd ed. Stuttgart: Deutsche Bibelgesellschaft, 1985.

Lampe, G.W.H., ed. *The Cambridge History of the Bible.* 3 vols. Cambridge: Cambridge University Press, 1969–70, Vol. 2: *The West from the Fathers to the Reformation.*

Stegmüller, Frederick. *Repertorium biblicum medii aevi.* 11 vols. Madrid: Matriti, 1940–80.

Smalley, Beryl. *The Study of the Bible in the Middle Ages.* 3rd ed. Oxford: Blackwell, 1983.

Vernet, André, and Anne-Marie Genevois. *La Bible au moyen âge.* Paris: CNRS, 1989.

BIBLE MORALISÉE. Name given to a group of illustrated adaptations of the Bible first composed in Latin in the 13th century and translated into French in the 14th. The text consists of quotations from the Old and New Testaments that do not flow continuously. These are accompanied by commentary in the form of allegorical interpretations or moral applications of the biblical text and illustrated by some 5,000 miniatures. The *Bible moralisée* is to be distinguished from the *Bible historiale figurée,* a 14th-century compilation of similar nature but composed of different texts and commentaries.

Maureen B.M. Boulton

Berger, Samuel. *La Bible française au moyen âge: étude sur les plus anciennes versions de la Bible écrites en langue d'oïl.* Paris: Imprimerie Nationale, 1884.

Delisle, Léopold. "Livres d'images destinées à l'instruction religieuse et aux exercices de piété des laïcs." *Histoire littéraire de la France* 31 (1893): 213–85, esp. 218–46.

Laborde, Alexandre de. *La Bible moralisée, conservée à Oxford, Paris et Londres: reproduction intégrale du manuscrit du XIIIe siècle.* 5 vols. Paris: Société de Reproductions de Manuscrits à Peintures, 1911–27.

BIBLICAL TRANSLATION. Exact translations of biblical texts were rare in Old French. Prepared for a lay audience, many "translations" were actually adaptations or paraphrases or included extensive commentaries. Still others drew on noncanonical sources, especially the apocryphal texts dealing with the life of the Virgin and the childhood of Jesus.

Translations of the Bible into French appeared first in England in the 12th century. The so-called "Psalters" of Cambridge and Oxford were produced in prose before 1200 and perhaps before 1150. The former, based on the Hebrew Psalter, is really a gloss on the Latin text, while the latter, based on the Gallican Psalter, is a continuous translation. Verse translations—the *Sauter en frounceys* and Sanson de Nanteuil's *Proverbes de Salomon*—appeared in England in the second half of the century. These were followed in the latter 12th century by prose versions of the Books of Kings and the Apocalypse. The *Quatre livres des rois* is much less literal than the Psalters; it includes continuous commentary on the text but is of particular importance for the force and elegance of its style. In the enormously popular *Apocalypse,* on the other hand, text and commentary are subservient to the sumptuous illustrations.

On the Continent, the 12th century saw the translation of a different selection of individual books, with enough commentary to place them in an exegetical tradition. Evrat's *Genèse* (1198) includes symbolic explanations and moral applications. Landri de Waben's *Cantique des cantiques* (1176–81) is a poetical paraphrase of the Latin text with interpretations according to the four senses of Scripture. The anonymous *Exodus* and the French version of the psalm *Eructavit* sometimes attributed to Adam de Perseigne are both allegorical in nature. In the latter part of the century, Herman de Valenciennes made the first attempt at an "integral text" of the Bible. His *Roman de Dieu et de sa mère* (also called *Roman de sapience*), is a poem in epic laisses that draws on both testaments and incorporates much legendary material about the life of Mary, drawn from apocryphal accounts of her childhood, marriage, and assumption. His work survives in over thirty-five manuscripts.

Biblical translation flourished in the 13th century, which saw the appearance of no fewer than five verse renderings as well as the scholarly prose version known as the "Thirteenth-Century Bible" or the "Paris Bible." This last was produced under the aegis of the University of Paris toward the middle of the century. It was the work of several translators and was not entirely original, for it incorporated earlier versions of Psalms and the Apocalypse. At the end of the century, its text was combined with Guyart des Moulins's *Bible historiale* (a translation of Peter Comestor's *Historia scholastica*) to form the *Bible historiale complétée.* This text, used in many illustrated Bibles, provided the basis for the *Bible historiale figurée* and for the 14th-century *Bible moralisée.*

Most of the biblical works in verse are more properly described as adaptations. The first successors to Herman de Valenciennes's version were two anonymous renderings written in the early 13th century. One of these (B.N. fr. 763) is fairly faithful to the Vulgate for the Old Testament but incorporates legendary material in the New and ends abruptly with a brief account of the Passion. The other poem (B.N. fr. 898 and 902), written in epic style, covers only the Old Testament, but a prose version of this text (B.N. fr. 6260 and 9562) is virtually complete. Geoffroi de Paris's *Bible des sept estats du monde* (B.N. fr. 1526; ca. 1243) is quite different in character, consisting of a collage of independent texts, many of them apocryphal, arranged in sequence to constitute a sort of biblical legendary. Jean Malkaraume's *Bible* from the middle of the century is generally more faithful to the Vulgate, but it incorporates extraneous material as diverse as *Piramus et Thisbé,* the *Roman de Troie,* and the apocryphal genealogy of the Virgin. The last, longest, and most nearly complete of the verse Bibles was produced by Macé de la Charité between 1283 and the early 14th century. Like its principal source, Peter of Riga's *Aurora,* this version stresses the allegorical meaning of the biblical text. With the later addition of an allegorical exegesis of the Apocalypse, the whole runs to some 43,000 octosyllabic lines and is preserved in a single manuscript (B.N. fr. 401).

Alongside the "integral texts," individual books of the Bible continued to draw translators' attention. Guillaume le Clerc produced his verse *Tobie* at the beginning of the 13th century. Near the middle of that century, Gautier de Belleperche rendered the Book of Maccabees in epic style, producing the 23,000-line octosyllabic *Roman de Judas Machabée.* His poem was completed in 1280 by Piéros du Riés, who may also have written a second, shorter version of the same book in 1285, the *Chevalerie de Judas Machabée et de ses nobles frères.* Two anonymous prose translations of Maccabees appeared in this period, as well as prose versions of Judges, Kings, Genesis, and Proverbs. The popularity of the Apocalypse was unrivaled, and the 12th-century prose translation was followed by seven others, as well as two verse versions. A second rhymed Psalter was made in the second half of the 13th century, and translations of the penitential psalms were frequently copied in books of hours.

In the Midi, the work of translation was closely associated with the activities of the Cathars and the Waldensians. Interest centered on the New Testament, particularly the Gospels. The earliest surviving text is a fragment of a literal rendering of the Gospel of John from the second half of the 12th century. The Languedocian New Testament dates from the early 13th century, while the Vaudois New Testament exists in a mid-15th century manuscript. The Provençal Gospels, with their pronounced popular character, appeared late in the 13th century. The Old Testament is represented only by the 14th-century *Livre de Genesi,* which completed sacred history with apocryphal legends.

Maureen B.M. Boulton

[See also: APOCRYPHAL LITERATURE; BIBLE, LATIN VERSION OF; *BIBLE MORALISÉE;* DIDACTIC LITERATURE (OCCITAN); TRANSLATION]

Gautier de Belleperche et Piéros du Riés. *Roman de Judas Machabée,* ed. Jean-Robert Smeets. 2 vols. Assen: van Gorcum, 1991.

Herman de Valenciennes. *Li romanz de Dieu et de sa mère,* ed. Ina Spiele. Leiden: Universitaire Pers, 1975.

Macé de la Charité. *La Bible,* ed. H. C. M. van der Krabben and Jean-Robert Smeets. 7 vols. Leiden: Universitaire Pers Leiden, 1964–.

Berger, Samuel. *La Bible française au moyen âge; étude sur les plus anciennes versions de la Bible écrites en langue d'oïl.* Paris: Imprimerie Nationale, 1884.

Bonnard, Jean. *Les traductions de la Bible en vers français au moyen âge.* Paris: Imprimerie Nationale, 1884.

BINCHOIS, GILLES (Gilles de Bins dit Binchois; ca.1400–1460). Together with his contemporary Guillaume Dufay, Binchois had a profound effect on continental musical style in the early 15th century. As a member of the Burgundian court for nearly thirty years, Binchois was the strongest single influence on the development of the centrally important repertory of Burgundian chansons.

Binchois was probably born in Mons, into a bourgeois family. The earliest documents regarding his musical career are at the the church of Sainte-Waudru in Mons, where he was organist ca.1419–23. He served briefly as a musician, and possibly as a soldier, to William de la Pole, earl of Suffolk, during the middle 1420s, when Suffolk was resident in Paris. Documents pertaining to an assassination attempt on Philip the Good, duke of Burgundy, show that Binchois composed at least one song, now lost, for Suffolk. By ca. 1425, Binchois was a member of the choir of the Burgundian court, an association that continued for the rest of his career. Unlike the majority of early 15th-century composers, Binchois was never ordained as a priest, nor did he have a university degree. This did not, however, preclude him from service as a chaplain to the duke of Burgundy. He was also able to secure profitable prebends in Bruges, Mons, Cassel, and Soignies, which added to his considerable salary from the duke.

Binchois died in retirement at Soignies in 1460. His music was renowned throughout Europe, and in the *Champion des dames* (ca. 1442) by the Burgundian poet Martin Le Franc he was lauded with Dufay as one of the leading musicians of the day. It is apparent from Dufay's emotional *déploration* on Binchois's death that Dufay knew and respected his contemporary's music. Binchois's death is also lamented in a ballade by his younger colleague Johannes Ockeghem. Although Binchois's songs were outdated in style by the time of his death, they remained popular as subjects for polyphonic elaborations until the end of the 15th century.

Binchois composed a great deal of sacred music, much of it presumably for services in the ducal chapel of Burgundy. Over two dozen surviving Mass Ordinary movements are ascribed to him, but none of the surviving movements appears to have been part of a cyclic Mass. Most of the Mass music is set in a simple style, often resembling contemporary English music in its counterpoint and in its use of texture changes. There are over thirty additional sacred works by Binchois, mostly settings of the Magnificat, antiphons, and hymns. Several of these works are set in *fauxbourdon,* and as in the Mass settings most of them are in a simple style, suggesting day-to-day use in chapel services. Two of his more ambitious sacred works, however, were apparently written for specific events or personages. Binchois's only isorhythmic motet, *Nove cantum/Tanti gaude* (incomplete in its unique source), was written for the baptism of Philip the Good's short-lived son Antoine in 1431. The triplum text of this motet provides a list of Binchois's musical colleagues at the Burgundian court. His *Domitor Hectoris* was apparently written in 1438 to honor Nicholas Albergati, cardinal of the Holy Cross of Jerusalem and the pope's envoy in the delicate three-way peace negotiations among Burgundy, France, and England.

It was Binchois's songs that had the widest circulation and the broadest influence. Nearly sixty surviving songs may be attributed to him, forty-six of which are rondeaux. With the exception of *Files a marier*, Binchois's texts are couched in the language of courtly love, an idiom perfectly suited to the chivalric Valois aesthetics of the Burgundian court. Among the lyrics set by Binchois are three texts by prominent 15th-century poets, *Dueil angoisseux* by Christine de Pizan, *Triste plaisir* by Alain Chartier, and *Mon cuer chante joyeusement* by Charles d'Orléans. Virtually all of his songs are set in a three-voice texture that is entirely dominated by the melody of the uppermost voice. Binchois was unequaled among 15th-century composers as a creator of flowing, arch-form melodies. His rondeaux and ballades feature a carefully contrived formal balance between sections, and the approach to tonality is strikingly modern. The high quality and reputation of his songs and his musical leadership at the court of Burgundy during the apex of its political and artistic power ensured Binchois's strong influence on the next generation of Franco-Flemish composers, including Ockeghem and Antoine Busnoys.

J. Michael Allsen

[See also: *CONTENANCE ANGLOISE*; DUFAY, GUILLAUME; *FAUXBOURDON*; ISORHYTHMIC MOTET; PHILIP THE GOOD]

Binchois, Gilles. *Die Chansons von Gilles Binchois*, ed. Wolfgang Rehm. Mainz: Schott, 1957.

———. *The Sacred Music of Gilles Binchois*, ed. Philip R. Kaye. Oxford: Oxford University Press, 1992.

Fallows, David. "Binchois, Gilles de Bins." In *The New Grove Dictionary of Music and Musicians*, ed. Stanley Sadie. London: Macmillan, 1980, Vol. 2, pp. 709–22.

Kemp, Walter H. *Burgundian Court Song in the Time of Binchois: The Anonymous* Chansons *of El Escorial MS V.III.24*. Oxford: Clarendon, 1990.

Slavin, Dennis. *Binchois' Songs, the Binchois Fragment, and the Two Layers of Escorial A*. Diss. Princeton, 1987.

———. "Some Distinctive Features of Songs by Binchois." *Journal of Musicology* 10 (1992): 342–61.

BIOGRAPHY. In contrast to classical and medieval Greco-Latin tradition and to subsequent development of the genre from the Renaissance on, French medieval secular biography is relatively poor. It appears as if the luxuriant growth of hagiography has stifled the urge to describe nonsaintly lives. Furthermore, it is difficult to distinguish, particularly in the earlier period, between the specifically biographic and the more general historical, didactic, and moral writing that might include biographical accounts of heroes who, today at least, are not considered saints. It can be said that until the end of the 14th century collections of the lives of famous persons belonged chiefly if not exclusively to the clerical—i.e., Latin—tradition. The beginning of this medieval, christianized tradition probably can be traced back to St. Jerome's *De viris illustribus* (ca. 342–420).

The same applies to individual biographies. There is hardly anything in French literature of the 11th, 12th, and 13th centuries that could be compared with the properly biographical *Vita Karoli magni imperatoris* by Einhard (ca. 770–840). But many elements of this monument of secular biography, with its conscious imitation of Suetonius and wealth of details about both the public and private life of the emperor, were either directly or indirectly "borrowed" in such immensely popular works as the Pseudo-Turpin Chronicle (Latin version ca. 1140; seven Old French translations in the course of the 13th c.). Pseudo-Turpin's account was incorporated into the *Grandes chroniques de France* by the monks of Saint-Denis. By 1274, most of this great historical compilation was translated into French. Philippe Mouskés's *Chronique rimée* (continued to 1243) devotes almost a third of its 31,256 lines to the life and deeds of Charlemagne. He takes his material from an Old French version of Pseudo-Turpin, as well as from the less authentic chansons de geste. Dealing with these forms of Charlemagne's biography, we must be mindful that there might have been an important hagiographic element contributing to its popularity, for Charlemagne was formally canonized.

Similar problems of genre are encountered in another work that, from a modern point of view, should certainly be qualified as biographical: Jean de Joinville's *Histoire* (or *Vie*) *de saint Louis*. Asked (ca. 1309) to write a memorandum on the life of the saintly king to serve in the canonization process, Joinville (1225–1317) composed a lively account of his companion, which is also the first serious autobiography in French, since Jean talks interestingly and abundantly about his own life.

In the Occitan domain, there is a curious biographical subgenre. The 13th-century *vidas* are usually brief prose notes on troubadours' lives preceding the poems of a given troubadour, often paraphrasing information culled from the poems. About a hundred such biographies have come down to us, all but two anonymous.

The 15th century witnessed the development of the secular biography proper. There is no doubt that the impetus came, at least in part, from the immense success of Boccaccio's *De casibus virorum illustrium* (1355–60). The purpose of this collection of lives of men and women from Adam to such contemporaries as Charles I of Anjou or Philippa of Catania is moral as well as biographical. As the *casus* of the title indicates, Boccaccio wished to offer a moral commentary on the fickleness of Fortune. The immensely popular *De casibus* was translated by Laurent de Premierfait at the beginning of the 15th century as *Des cas des nobles hommes et femmes*, further contributing to the popularity of the biographic-moral genre.

In 1405, Christine de Pizan (ca. 1364–ca. 1430) composed in prose her *Livre de la Cité des Dames* (1405), containing a long "catalogue" of illustrious ladies of all epochs. Christine was inspired by Boccaccio's *De claris mulieribus* (completed after 1362). Her book, again, is not a pure biography (if such a thing exists) but chiefly a defense of women from misogynous attacks. Christine also wrote the *Livre des fais et bonnes meurs du sage roy Charles V* (1404), in which she uses historical sources and court documents as well as personal reminiscences. The main purpose is not so much historical as biographico-panegyric. Largely panegyrical also is the *Livre des fais du bon messire Jehan le Maingre, dit Bouciquaut*, composed anonymously between 1407 and 1409, during the life of the protagonist. This lengthy prose panygeric has occasionally been attributed to Christine de Pizan, but this identification is generally rejected. The main purpose of this biography seems to be to exalt the chivalric ideal of the times.

The century ends with a far more realistic portraiture of Louis XI and other nobles in the *Mémoires* (completed in 1498) by Philippe de Commynes. The realism and vivacity of the biographical elements in this work foreshadow the triumph of biography during the Renaissance.

Peter F. Dembowski

[See also: CHRISTINE DE PIZAN; COMMYNES, PHILIPPE DE; EINHARD; GUERNES DE PONT-SAINTE-MAXENCE; *GUILLAUME LE MARÉCHAL, HISTOIRE DE*; HISTORIOGRAPHY; JOINVILLE, JEAN DE; *VIDAS* AND *RAZOS*]

Christine de Pizan. *The Book of the City of Ladies*, trans. Earl Jeffrey Richards. New York: Persea, 1982. [*La Cité des Dames* still awaits a modern critical edition.]

Egan, Margarita, trans. *The Vidas of the Troubadours*. New York: Garland, 1984.

Joinville, Jean de. *Vie de saint Louis*, ed. Noel L. Corbett. Sherbrook: Naaman, 1977.

Lalande, Denis, ed. *Le livre des fais du bon messire Jehan le Maingre, dit Bouciquaut*. Geneva: Droz, 1985.

Laurent de Premierfait. *Laurent de Premierfait's Des cas des nobles hommes et femmes. Book I, Translated from Boccaccio*, ed. Patricia May Gathercole. Chapel Hill: University of North Carolina Press, 1968. [The whole of *Des cas* still awaits a critical edition.]

BLACK DEATH. Beginning in late 1347, most of western Europe was attacked by a pandemic that overshadows both the earlier outbreaks in 6th- and 7th-century eastern Gaul and the recurrent epidemics from the 14th through the 16th centuries. The plague later acquired the labels "bubonic" and "black," for the swellings and hematomas it caused, but it was called the "Great Pestilence" by contemporaries. It originated in the Far East and was spread by the rat-flea as carrier of the *pasteurella pestis*. Landing in Marseille in December 1347, the disease swept along the coast and up the Rhône, entering Avignon within the next month. By August 1348, it had ravaged Languedoc and reached Bordeaux, overran Provence and Burgundy, and entered Paris. Before year's end, it raged through Normandy and the northern counties.

Populous, weakened by famines, and distressed by war, France suffered the highest mortality. Fatalities ran between one-fifth of the pontifical courtiers to over half of the population in many rural parishes from Anjou to Savoy. In Paris, Jean de Venette recalled, over 500 dead were buried each day. Religious communities were afflicted dis-proportionately, with several monasteries in the south decimated or exterminated. The poor were defenseless, but even the noble were not exempt: Philip VI's queen, Jeanne of Burgundy, and her daughter-in-law Bonne de Luxembourg succumbed in the last weeks of the pandemic. Many fell ill but lived, and some of these left poignant testimonies, notably the mystic friar Jean de Roquetaillade and the papal physician Gui de Chauliac.

Distinguishing between pneumonic and bubonic plague, Chauliac reported that in the former, more contagious and prevalent in winter, people died within three days after running a high fever and spitting blood; in the latter, the victims often survived after developing abscesses, particularly in the armpits and groin. The vast medical literature generated by the pestilence, including an official report by the University of Paris made at the request of Philip VI, was largely sterile. Scientific attempts to determine the causes, while more rational than the popular explanations, hinged on humoral theories and astrological beliefs. Prescriptions offered, at best, commonsensical precautions and palliation; at worst, they recommended such dangerous procedures as bleeding and the lancing of buboes. Many physicians evidently labored heroically, for the profession suffered more from a severe decline in numbers than from a crisis of credibility.

The socioeconomic and cultural consequences of the Black Death, ranging from inflation and class changes to mass psychoses and a preoccupation with mortality, cannot always be isolated from the impact of the Hundred Years' War and of subsequent epidemics. Among the immediate effects, however, may be counted an extension of the Truce of 1347, a setback for constitutional reforms, and the outbreak of the flagellant movement, which, though banned from the realm, raged in the fringe regions of Flanders, Hainaut, and Lorraine.

Luke Demaitre

[See also: DISEASES; MILLENNIALISM; POPULATION AND DEMOGRAPHY]

Gui de Chauliac. *Ars chirurgicalis* II.ii.5, trans. and annotated by Michael McVaugh. In *A Source Book in Medieval Science*, ed. Edward Grant. Cambridge: Harvard University Press, 1974, pp. 773–74.

Biraben, Jean-Noel. *Les hommes et la peste en France et dans les pays européens et méditerranéens*. 2 vols. Paris: Moulton, 1975–76. [Exhaustive bibliography in Vol. 2, pp. 186–413.]

Emery, Richard W. "The Black Death of 1348 in Perpignan." *Speculum* 42 (1967): 611–23.

Henneman, John Bell. "The Black Death and Royal Taxation in France, 1347–1351." *Speculum* 43 (1968): 405–28.

Lucenet, Monique. *Les grandes pestes en France*. Paris: Aubier, 1985.

BLANCHE OF CASTILE (1188–1252). At the age of twelve, Blanche of Castile, the daughter of Alfonso VIII of Castile, was married to Prince Louis of France, who would reign briefly as Louis VIII (1223–26). Louis's early death while on the Albigensian Crusade left the throne to their young son, Louis IX. The regency was entrusted not to a male relative or a council of barons but to Blanche.

In the first years of her regency, Blanche was confronted with armed rebellions intended to displace her and with the serious possibility of a reversal of French successes in the southern lands that had been conquered in the Albigensian Crusade. She triumphed in both cases. Gifted with an iron will and clever in her ability to cultivate allies but careful not to link her fortunes too closely to any baronial house, such as the house of Champagne, through a hasty remarriage, she pursued a policy of divide-and-conquer against the rebellious barons. Their uprisings and shows of force never achieved a decision in their favor. Blanche's success against the baronial opposition in the north was both cause and effect of her maintenance of French dominance in the south. The swiftness and decisiveness of her actions against the northerners induced the southern nobles to negotiate their grievances; and the army that had been left in the south at her husband's death remained, despite some difficulties, loyally commanded and in firm control. By 1229 and the Treaty of Meaux-Paris, the opposition in Languedoc acknowledged its defeat. The prestige of victory in the south encouraged loyalty and support in the north when the crown had to respond to new baronial demonstrations against it in the 1230s led by, among others, the titular count of Brittany, Pierre Mauclerc.

Blanche's regency was distinguished by a balanced foreign policy. On the one hand, the traditional enemy, the English, never effectively made inroads into those provinces, like Normandy, that they had lost in 1204. On the other hand, she made no concerted effort to eject the English from their remaining territories in Aquitaine. In the war of words and sometimes of men between the emperor Frederick II and the papacy, she kept to a neutral path.

In the later 1230s down to 1244, Blanche's role in government gradually diminished. Her son reached adulthood, married, and became more active, especially in military affairs. This translation of power was not entirely easy. There was mutual dislike between Blanche and her son's wife, Marguerite of Provence; Blanche also vigorously opposed Louis's decision in 1244 to take the crusader's vow. Nonetheless, she remained a close political adviser to the king, far closer than his wife, and Louis entrusted the reins of government to Blanche when he embarked on crusade in 1248.

As a deeply devout and morally strict woman, an enthusiastic patroness of the church, especially the Cistercian order, and a Castilian who grew up in an environment of fierce commitment to the holy war of reconquest in Spain, Blanche's opposition to her son's crusade remains something of a puzzle. But however she felt about his enterprise in the abstract, she devoted her full energies to making certain that he was well supplied and that he need not trouble himself about governance at home while he fought in the East. She managed to negotiate a two-year extension of the clerical income tax of one-tenth in order both to finance the war effort and to replenish the king's coffers after the disastrous early phase of the crusade that saw Louis captured and ransomed in Egypt. She acted with her characteristic firmness in 1249, on the death of the count of Toulouse, when a movement took shape to turn aside the settlement of 1229 that designated her son Alphonse to be the new count of Toulouse. She thought well of the so-called Pastoureaux (1251), Flemish and northern French rustics who proclaimed themselves crusaders determined to rescue and otherwise aid the king. But when bands of these forces rioted in Paris and pillaged other towns, it was she who authorized and oversaw their destruction. Blanche died in November 1252. When her son, still in the Holy Land, received the news some months later, he succumbed to a grief so profound that it troubled all who knew and loved him.

William Chester Jordan

[See also: LOUIS VIII; LOUIS IX]

Sivéry, Gérard. *Blanche de Castille.* Paris: Fayard, 1990.

BLOIS. Originally one of six *pagi* dependent on Chartres, Blois (Loir-et-Cher) became the center of a county in the 9th century. The dukes of France installed a viscount there and later assigned the county to one of their vassals, Thibaut le Vieux, viscount of Tours (r. 908–40). His son, Thibaut I le Tricheur, created a powerful principality in the middle Loire Valley by adding the counties of Blois and Chartres to that of Tours (r. 940–ca. 975). Blois became the natural center of these lands, especially after the loss of Tours to the Angevins (1044), as the counts had few lands or vassals in Chartres, which was dominated by its bishop and cathedral chapter.

Count Eudes II (r. 996–1037) began to reorient the dynasty in 1021, when he claimed succession, through his grandmother Liedgard of Vermandois, to the counties of Meaux and Troyes in Champagne. To soften King Robert's opposition to the impending encirclement of the royal domain, Eudes enlisted Fulbert, bishop of Chartres, to plead his case as rightful heir and loyal vassal. Having succeeded in planting the house of Blois in Champagne, Eudes then managed to link the two lands through Berry by marrying the last heiress of Sancerre (ca. 1030). The eastward thrust of the Thibaudians was reinforced by the loss of Tours and the subsequent acquisition by marriage of two additional counties in Champagne, Bar-sur-Aube and Vitry, under Thibaut III (I of Champagne, r. 1037–89).

Thibaut's elder son, Étienne, became count of Blois-Chartres-Meaux (r. 1089–1102), while the younger, Hugues, was granted Troyes, Bar-sur-Aube, and Vitry (r. 1093–1125). Étienne is best known for his marriage to William the Conqueror's daughter, Adèle, and his ignominious departure from the First Crusade on the eve of Antioch's capitulation. Although his motives are now better understood, contemporary derision forced his return to the Levant to complete his crusade vow. Despite courageous service on the Crusade of 1101, and his execution in captivity, chroniclers relished retelling his earlier misdeeds. Count Hugues likewise perished overseas, on his third expedition.

Étienne's eldest son, Thibaut IV le Grand (II of Champagne, r. 1102–52), inherited the patrimony of Blois-Chartres-Meaux, then in 1125 acquired the counties of his uncle Hugues, who had disowned his own son. Thibaut was a major personage of the time: among the most powerful French princes and a firm supporter of Bernard of Clairvaux, he was, according to Gerald of Wales, an ideal prince. His decision to shift his energies from the confines of the Loire Valley to the more promising counties of Champagne, where he established the international fairs, dramatically transformed the house of Blois: Champagne passed to his eldest son, Henri I, and became a major principality, while the counties of Blois-Chartres, shorn of their accretions, receded to second-tier standing. Thibaut's younger brother, Étienne, who had been sent to England to make his fortune at the court of their uncle Henry I, became King Stephen of England (r. 1135–54) but failed to install a dynasty there.

From 1152, the counts of Blois-Chartres were steadily drawn into the royal orbit. Thibaut V le Bon (r. 1152–91), who was appointed royal seneschal (1154) and who married Louis VII's daughter, Alis, by Eleanor of Aquitaine (1164), regularly attended the king. He accompanied Philip Augustus on the Third Crusade and died at Acre. His son, Count Louis (r. 1191–1205), deprived of a role at court (the office of seneschal was left vacant), encouraged the development of his towns by franchising, among others, Blois, Châteaudun, and Clermont-en-Beauvaisis (which he acquired through his wife) in 1196/97. Blois, however, with a population under 10,000, remained small compared with its neighboring rivals Tours, Orléans, and Chartres. The count's resources, concentrated in the county of Blois, were inadequate to raise the town of Blois to any significant level of administrative, commercial, or cultural importance. That Louis became one of the organizers and leaders of the Fourth Crusade was due entirely to his close familial tie with the count of Champagne. Louis supported the diversion of that expedition to Constantinople and led an assault against the city walls. Awarded the duchy of Nicaea in October 1204, he died in combat the next spring at Adrianople.

Thibaut VI (r. 1205–18) maintained the family crusading tradition by serving in the Albigensian Crusade and at Las Navas de Tolosa, but he died without issue after contracting leprosy and the counties reverted to his father's sisters: Marguerite took Blois (r. 1218–25) while Isabelle took Chartres (r. 1218–56). Both counties became direct royal fiefs in 1234, when Louis IX purchased their homages from the count of Champagne. Although Chartres was sold to Philip IV in 1286, Blois passed by marriage to the Châtillon family and was inherited by its eldest sons through the next century. Count Louis IV of Blois died at Crécy, and his sons led royal forces against the English. Gui II de Châtillon, count of Blois (1381–97), who subsidized Froissart's researches for Book 3 of his *Chroniques*, sold Blois to Charles VI's brother, Louis of Orléans, in 1391.

The château of Blois, which dominates the bluffs above the Loire, was begun by Thibaut I in the 10th century. Nothing, however, remains of his fortress in the Renaissance château now on its site. The Tour de Foix and Salle des États, with its timber vaulting, are all that still stand of a 13th-century reconstruction. Charles d'Orléans, the poet and son of Louis of Orléans, began construction in 1440 on what was destined to become the current château, which was a favored residence of French Renaissance kings. The church of Saint-Nicolas preserves a transept, lantern tower, and ambulatory from the first campaign of construction (1138–86) and has a nave, side aisles, and façade with towers from ca. 1210.

Theodore Evergates

[See also: CHAMPAGNE; CHARLES D'ORLÉANS; CRUSADES; THIBAUT]

Brundage, James A. "An Errant Crusader: Stephen of Blois." *Traditio* 16 (1960): 380–95.

Chédeville, André. *Chartres et ses campagnes (XIe–XIIIe s.)*. Paris: Klincksieck, 1973.

Devailly, Guy. *Le Berry du Xe siècle au milieu du XIIIe*. Paris: Mouton, 1973.

Dunbabin, Jean. *France in the Making, 843–1180*. Oxford: Oxford University Press, 1985.

Hallam, Elizabeth. M. *Capetian France, 987–1328*. London: Longman, 1980.

Soyer, Jacques. *Étude sur la communauté des habitants de Blois jusqu'au commencement du XVIe siècle*. Paris: Picard, 1894.

Werner, Karl Ferdinand. "Untersuchungen zur Frühzeit des französischen Fürstentums, 9. bis 10. Jahrhundert." *Die Welt als Geschichte* 19 (1959): 146–93.

BLONDEL DE NESLE (fl. 1180–1210). An early trouvère, Blondel was part of the lyric coterie that included Conon de Béthune, Gace Brulé, and the Châtelain de Coucy. No doubt noble, he may have been Jean II, lord of Nesle from 1202 to 1241, but there is no firm evidence. His two dozen poems date from ca. 1180 to 1200–10; all preserved with music, they are courtly love songs in a style derived from the Provençal tradition. Often repeated since its appearance in the mid-13th-century *Récits* of the Ménestrel de Reims, the story of Blondel's daring rescue of Richard the Lionhearted from captivity in Austria seems groundless.

Samuel N. Rosenberg

[See also: TROUVÈRE POETRY]

Blondel de Nesle. *Die Lieder des Blondel de Nesle*, ed. Leo Wiese. Dresden: Gesellschaft für romanische Literatur, 1904.

van der Werf, Hendrik, ed. *Trouvères-Melodien I*. Kassel: Bärenreiter, 1977, pp. 3–122.

BOECI. The fragmentary Occitan paraphrase of Boethius's *De consolatione Philosophiae* is regarded as the oldest literary text preserved in the language, written, perhaps, ca. 1000–30. In 258 lines of epic verse, the fragment narrates Boethius's imprisonment and then describes the visit of Lady Philosophy, as in Book 1 of the *De consolatione*.

William D. Paden

[See also: BOETHIUS, INFLUENCE OF; DIDACTIC
LITERATURE (OCCITAN)]

Lavaud, René, and Georges Machicot, eds. *Boecis*. Toulouse:
Institut d'Études Occitanes, 1950.
Schwarze, Christoph, ed. *Der altprovenzalische Boeci*. Münster:
Aschendorff, 1963.

BOETHIUS, INFLUENCE OF. The late Roman philosopher, translator, and political figure Boethius (480–534) belongs to the group of late-antique scholars who conveyed to the earlier Middle Ages the techniques and principles of classical learning. His work lies in four distinct areas: (1) *Logic.* Boethius provided and improved texts and commentaries in the Aristotelian tradition, which were gradually recovered by the Carolingians to form the basis of the "old logic" (*logica vetus*) and constituted the *logica nova* of the 12th-century schools. (2) *De arithmetica* and *De institutione musica.* Both treatises made available Greek numerical theory, on which scholars from the 11th century onward (such as Guido of Arezzo) could base their discussions. (3) *Five theological tractates*, called the *Opuscula sacra.* Written as a contribution to debate on the nature of Christ, these were a rare example of theological questions subjected to logical analysis, with no appeal to the authority of Scripture or the church. As such, they caught the attention of Johannes Scottus Eriugena and the Carolingian school of Auxerre. Whether or not they were known to Anselm of Bec, his philosophical theology is in the same tradition. A new critique was offered by Gilbert of Poitiers and others in Paris in the 1140s, and the first tractate was analyzed a century later by Aquinas. (4) *De consolatione Philosophiae.* Boethius's masterpiece was written (or presented as having been written) in his last months as a prisoner of King Theoderic in Pavia. The *Consolation* is Boethius's debate with himself on the meaning of life. What is the value of wealth and learning, the justification of moral acts, the role of chance in a divinely ordered universe? In Boethius's concluding words, "God sees all." His relation to God is that of the philosopher: there is no reference to Christ. Thus, the *Consolation* has no point of contact with the *Opuscula sacra*; instead, it rehearses the literary and philosophical commonplaces of the classical world. The work was endlessly fascinating to medieval readers, from Alcuin onward. In particular, Book 3, meter 9 (*o qui perpetua mundum ratione gubernas*), conjured up a Platonist universe in which there was every temptation to cast the Holy Spirit as the *anima mundi.* Equally influential were the myths (e.g., Orpheus: 3.12) and legends (e.g., Ulysses: 4.3), the fragments of classical geography, and the well-honed moral epigrams. The *Consolation* was always good value as a child's schoolbook, the next step after the *Disticha Catonis.*

By ca. 1300, the Dominican Nicholas Trivet had written the definitive commentary on the *Consolation*, and translations were appearing in the European vernaculars (e.g., Jean de Meun, Chaucer). Such a book might be lavishly illustrated, and it might also carry extensive additional commentary. In broad terms, in the 14th and 15th centuries it was the French who preferred the luxury "coffee-table" edition, while the Germans (especially the Carthusians) provided extensive new and spiritual annotation. Even in the 16th century, Queen Elizabeth I filled her leisure hours by providing a new English translation: the *De consolatione Philosophiae* was still considered an edifying work suitable for an aristocratic young lady.

Margaret T. Gibson

[See also: *BOECI;* CHARTRES; JEAN DE MEUN;
PHILOSOPHY; TRANSLATION]

Courcelle, Pierre. *La Consolation de Philosophie dans la tradition littéraire.* Paris: Études Augustiniennes, 1967.
Gibson, Margaret T., ed. *Boethius: His Life, Thought and Influence.* Oxford: Blackwell, 1981.
————, and Lesley J. Smith. *Codices Boethiani*, 6 vols. Forthcoming.
Kaylor, Noel Harold, Jr. *The Medieval* Consolation of Philosophy: *An Annotated Bibliography.* New York: Garland, 1993.

BONAGUIL. Located on a promontory of rocks that have broken from a plateau, the castle of Bonaguil (Agenais) is encircled by the valley of the Thèze and Lémance. The promontory offers protection for the castle except on the north side, where it is still attached to the plateau. Bonaguil's history dates back to the 13th century, to a frontier post that probably became the north section of the existing pentagonal keep. The castle came into the possession of the powerful Roquefeuil family in the 15th century and was remodeled ca. 1480 to resist cannon. To the north, its walls are more than 13 feet thick. Its transformation manifested the family's "will to power." Between 1445 and 1482 and under the direction of Jean de Roquefeuil, the keep became a structure with a ground floor and two stories, illuminated by immense windows and furnished with fireplaces. A crenellated parapet bordered the roof. Stairs cut into the stone provided access to the fortress. Thereafter, Jean's sons Berengier and Brigon continued adding buildings, towers (most notably a 30-foot square tower), and levered bridges. The principal entrance was changed from the west to the north side of the castle.

E. Kay Harris

Lauzin, P. *Le château de Bonaguil en Agenais: description et histoire.* 2nd ed. Paris: Champion, 1884.
Marboutin, C. "Bonaguil." *Congrès archéologique (Figeac, Cahors, Rodez)* (1937).
Pons, M. *Bonaguil, château de rêve: essai sur le château de Bonaguil dans le Haut-Agenais.* Toulouse: Privat, 1959.

BONAVENTURE (John of Fidanza; ca. 1217–74). Bonaventure was born in Bagnoregio, near Viterbo, and sources say that he fought his well-to-do family to enter the Franciscan order; this he did in Paris, probably in 1243. Legend has it that as a child he was miraculously cured by St. Francis's intervention. He was educated in the Franciscan friary in Bagnoregio and moved to Paris for the arts course ca. 1234. He studied theology in the Franciscan school under Alexander of Hales, John of La Rochelle, William of Melitona, and Odo Rigaldus; his wide use of the Dominican Hugues de Saint-Cher suggests that he may have been Hugues's pupil as well. He was made regent master, probably in 1253, but formal acceptance for him and for Thomas Aquinas was delayed until October 1257 by the dispute between secular masters and the mendicants.

In February 1257, Bonaventure was made minister-general of the Franciscans, on the suggestion of John of Parma, who had resigned under pressure from Pope Alexander IV. His nomination suggests that the divide between the two wings of the order (Conventual and Spiritual) was not yet unbridgeable, since John was later characterized as a Spiritual and Bonaventure a Conventual. As a master, he composed a commentary on Peter Lombard's *Sententiae* (by far his longest and most systematic work) and biblical commentaries, as well as various theological "questions."

Bonaventure's accession to the minister-generalate effectively ended his academic career, but he continued to write devotional works. His writing is marked by a lucid latinity and deep devotion, qualities that he could also bring to academic argument. He combined academic discipline with fervent piety: for Bonaventure, more clearly than for any other scholastic theologian, the point of any theology was the building up of the life of faith and prayer. After a visit to La Verna, in Italy, in 1259, he began to write mystical texts of great influence; he had, in the Franciscan tradition, a particular devotion to the Passion.

During the 1260–70s, he worked to defend the order, which did not practice the absolute poverty of its founder, against charges of hypocrisy, especially by his *Apologia pauperum* (1270). His aim was to reinterpret Francis's *Testament* for subsequent generations. He was called the "second father of the order," because of his attempt to produce a theology of the Franciscan life. On the publication of his new *Life of Francis* (1266), all previous Lives were ordered to be destroyed, as had happened similarly when Humbert of Romans had produced his new *Life of Dominic* (1260). Bonaventure was made Cardinal-Bishop of Albano in 1273; he died unexpectedly at the Second Council of Lyon in 1274.

Bonaventure's theology is traditionally Augustinian. He is willing to make use of whatever tools come to hand, and to this end he was prepared to use Aristotle, but he held no specifically "Aristotelian" opinions. As well as Aristotle, his sources include Pseudo-Dionysius the Areopagite's *Celestial Hierarchy*, John Damascene, Boethius, and mystical "moderns" like Richard of Saint-Victor. For Bonaventure, theology was so far above philosophy in purpose that there could be no difficulty deciding between faith and reason. This is not to say that faith is irrational; in cases of apparent disagreement, faith is clearly acting out of a different rationality. He made careful distinction among the object of faith *per se,* which is God, who can be known directly (the "believable" or "credible" thing); the object of faith as known through the authority of Scripture; and the object of faith as investigated in theological inquiry. Theology's task is not superior to either revelation or Scripture, or undermining of it, but is intended to cast a new light—that of intelligibility—on the search for God.

Bonaventure, known as *Doctor devotus* and *Doctor seraphicus,* saw the Son of God as the pattern for life on earth, and his theology is particularly Trinitarian—indeed, he described many things in threes. For instance, he developed a theology-spirituality of the triple way: the purgative way, moved by the prick of conscience; the illuminative way, moved by the light of the intellect; and the unitive way, moved by the flame of wisdom.

The obviously devotional stance of Bonaventure's work has sometimes led to his being unfavorably compared with Thomas Aquinas; the two are better seen as complementary than as comparable.

Lesley J. Smith

[See also: ALEXANDER OF HALES; FRANCISCAN ORDER; HUGUES DE SAINT-CHER; MATTHEW OF AQUASPARTA; MYSTICISM; PHILOSOPHY; RICHARD OF SAINT-VICTOR; THEOLOGY]

Bonaventure. *Opera omnia,* ed. PP. Collegii a S. Bonaventura. 11 vols. in 28. Ad claras Aquas (Quaracchi): Typographia Colegii S. Bonaventurae, 1882–1902.

———. *Sermones dominicales,* ed. Jacques-Guy Bougerol. Grottaferrata (Rome): Collegio S. Bonaventura, Padri Editori di Quaracchi, 1977.

———. *Saint Bonaventure's Disputed Questions on the Mystery of the Trinity,* trans. Zachary Hayes. St. Bonaventure: Franciscan Institute, St. Bonaventure University, 1979.

———. *The Works of St. Bonaventure,* trans. José de Vinck. 5 vols. Paterson: St. Anthony Guild, 1960–70.

———. *What Manner of Man? Sermons on Christ by St. Bonaventure,* trans. Zachary Hayes. Chicago: Franciscan Herald, 1974.

Bougerol, Jacques-Guy. *Introduction à Saint Bonaventure.* Paris: Vrin, 1988.

———. *Introduction to the Works of Bonaventure,* trans. José de Vinck. Paterson: St. Anthony Guild, 1964.

———. *St. Bonaventure et la sagesse chrétienne.* Paris: Seuil, 1963.

———. *Lexique saint Bonaventure.* Paris: Éditions Franciscaines, 1969.

Chavero Blanco, Francisco de Asis, ed. *Bonaventuriana: miscellanea in onore di Jacques-Guy Bougerol.* 2 vols. Rome: Antonianum, 1988.

Cousins, Ewert H. *Bonaventure and the Coincidence of Opposites.* Chicago: Franciscan Herald, 1978.

S. Bonaventura 1274–1974. 5 vols. Grottaferrata (Rome): Collegio S. Bonaventura, 1973–74.

Hayes, Zachary. *The Hidden Center: Spirituality and Speculative Christology in St. Bonaventure.* New York: Paulist, 1981.

BONIFACE VIII (d. 1303). Pope. When Celestine V renounced the papacy in 1294, the cardinals elected Benedetto Gaetani, a noblemen from Anagni, who reigned as Boniface VIII. Gaetani had been a legate to France, where he silenced temporarily the complaints of the masters at

Paris about the privileges given the friars by the popes. As pontiff, Boniface took charge of the curia and attempted to prevent war between Edward I of England and Philip IV the Fair of France by forbidding, in the bull *Clericis laicos,* lay taxation of the clergy without papal consent. This attempt to deny him the fiscal resources for war caused Philip to prohibit the export of bullion from France. Pressed by this embargo, by French propaganda, and by his own feud with the Colonna family, Boniface made peace with Philip. Neither pope nor king, however, would remain conciliatory. In 1298, Boniface incorporated *Clericis laicos* into his *Liber sextus decretalium.* In 1300, the pope felt buoyed by the success of his holy year and by French reverses in Flanders. Philip, however, took the offensive against the pope, arresting in 1301 the bishop of Pamiers in violation of canon law, which reserved jurisdiction over the episcopate to the Holy See. A second propaganda war ensued, in which most of the French clergy backed the king, even though Boniface's constitution *Unam sanctam* claimed that obedience to the pope was necessary for salvation. In 1303, Sciarra Colonna and Guillaume de Nogaret, one of Philip's advisers, seized Boniface in his palace in Anagni. Although a mob forced the conspirators to release the pope, he died soon after, a broken man, and France would be dominant in its relationship with the papacy for the next seventy-five years.

Thomas M. Izbicki

[See also: *CLERICIS LAICOS;* NOGARET, GUILLAUME DE; PHILIP IV THE FAIR; *UNAM SANCTAM*]

Boniface VIII. *Les registres de Boniface VIII: recueil des bulles de ce pape publiées ou analysées d'après les manuscrits des archives du Vatican,* ed. Georges Digard et al. 4 vols. Paris: Thorin, 1884–1939.

Boase, T.S.R. *Boniface VIII.* London: Constable, 1933.

Rivière, Jean. *Le problème de l'église et de l'état au temps de Philippe le Bel: étude de théologie positive.* Louvain: "Spicilegium Sacrum Lovaniense" Bureaux, 1926.

BOOK OF HOURS. A late-medieval prayer book used by the laity, particularly common in France and the Netherlands. In the 13th century, the Little Office of the Blessed Virgin was frequently bound together with the psalter to create the psalter-hours. The psalter was soon dropped and the Little Office became itself the core of a prayer book for lay use that consisted primarily of devotional items that had been added to the monastic office in the 9th and 10th centuries. While there was much variation in the makeup of these books, a nucleus of items appeared in most: the calendar, a lesson from each of the four Gospels, the two Marian prayers *Obsecro te* and *O Intemerata,* the Little Office, the penitential psalms, short offices of the Holy Spirit and the Cross, the Office of the Dead, and a series of "suffrages" (prayers to popular saints).

The book of hours allowed the devout member of the laity to follow a daily regimen of prayer that was similar to that of the monks and clergy but much shorter and lacking in its complex day-to-day variation. Books of hours survive in great numbers. While the more lavishly illustrated examples—such as the *Grandes Heures* and the *Très Riches Heures* of the Duke of Berry, the *Heures de Catherine de Clèves,* or the *Grandes Heures de Rohan*—were owned by the nobility, members of the literate middle class had their own more modestly decorated copies. The genre is of immense importance in the history of art and in fact was the principal vehicle of late-medieval painting. France was preeminent in this respect, particularly in the later 14th and earlier 15th centuries. Among the more important illustrations generally found in books of hours are the portraits of the four Evangelists, a series of eight scenes from the life of the Virgin Mary illustrating the Little Office, the depiction of David in Prayer illustrating the penitential psalms, and a great variety of depiction for the Office of the Dead.

James McKinnon

[See also: CALENDAR, LITURGICAL; DIVINE OFFICE; LITURGICAL BOOKS; LITURGICAL YEAR]

Bishop, Edmund. "On the Origin of the Prymer." In *Liturgica Historica: Papers on the Liturgy and Religious Life of the Western Church.* Oxford: Oxford University Press, 1918, pp. 211–37.

Calkins, Robert G. *Illuminated Books of the Middle Ages.* Ithaca: Cornell University Press, 1983.

Leroquais, Victor. *Les livres d'heures manuscrits de la Bibliothèque Nationale.* 2 vols. Paris: Macon, 1927. *Supplément.* Paris: Macon, 1943.

Wieck, Roger S. *Time Sanctified: The Book of Hours in Medieval Art and Life.* New York: Braziller, 1988.

BORDEAUX. Originally a Gallic settlement, Bordeaux (Gironde) became a prosperous commercial center under Roman domination and the capital of Aquitania Secunda. Attracted by its wealth, Visigoths, Muslims, and Vikings laid siege to it over the early centuries of the Middle Ages. Around 630, King Dagobert made his brother Charibert subking for Aquitaine, with Bordeaux as his capital. Muslim incursions from Spain in the course of the 8th century effectively weakened the influence of Bordeaux in Aquitanian politics, in favor of Poitiers farther to the north.

In 1137, the marriage of Eleanor, the only heir of Duke Guilhem IX of Aquitaine, to the future King Louis VII of France was celebrated in Bordeaux. With her divorce and subsequent marriage to Henry II Plantagenêt, Bordeaux and all of Aquitaine fell under foreign dominance. It was during this period that Bordeaux red wine, which had been introduced by the Romans, came to be especially appreciated by the Norman Plantagenêts. During the Hundred Years' War, Bordeaux was the capital of Guyenne and served as an important staging center for English troops. Edward the Black Prince set up his court and headquarters in the city. Only in 1453, with the Treaty of Bordeaux that marked the end of the Hundred Years' War, did the city again come under French domination. Today the port city of Bordeaux is rich in 18th-century architecture. Nevertheless, the spires of its medieval bell towers and churches recall the city's first golden age, in the 14th century, as well as its earlier importance on the pilgrimage route to Compostela.

Cathédrale Saint-André. Despite the Gothic superstructure (ensemble primarily 13th-c., with later revaulting), the broad single nave of seven bays is more closely related to regional Romanesque, parts of which remain, and contrasts with the northern Gothic format of the lofty choir and transept (blind triforium, large windows, classic ambulatory with five radiating chapels). The west wall retains important 11th-century architectural elements; the major sculptured portals are the two transept portals (14th-c.) and the celebrated mid-13th-century "Royal Portal." Four statues of the same era adorn the beautifully proportioned chevet. Within the cathedral are 14th-century alabaster statues of "Notre-Dame de la Nef" and St. Martial. Fragments from the 14th-century cloister (destroyed 1865), as well as fifty-five 12th-century capitals from the cathedral complex, are in the Musée d'Aquitaine. The freestanding bell tower, to the southeast of the cathedral, is attributed to Archbishop Pey (Pierre) Berland (begun ca. 1440; present spire is 19th-c.).

Saint-Seurin. All that survives of the Romanesque collegiate church are the crypt (subsequent modifications), vestiges of 11th-century walls, and the western tower porch (important early capitals) partially hidden behind the 19th-century neo-Romanesque façade. The present structure is essentially Gothic: rectangular choir of two bays covered with rib vaults (late 12th-c.); nave of five bays (first bay contemporary with the choir; subsequent bays 13th- and 14th-c.); sculptured south portal (13th-c.) within a Renaissance porch. The original proportions and simplicity have been altered by the infilling of the nave, reworking of supports, and addition of chapels. Notable are the episcopal throne, the wooden stalls of the canons (both 15th-c.), a beautiful alabaster Virgin and Child (14th-c.), and two alabaster retables.

Sainte-Croix. The former Benedictine abbey church has undergone modifications. The basic format was determined by the 11th-century construction (wide nave and side aisles, extended transept, timber roof). Twelfth-century campaigns include the transformation of the chevet and transept (principal apse, two transept apsidioles), considerable modification of nave supports and crossing (important series of capitals, the finest of Languedocian influence), and the richly sculptured façade with its impressive south tower. The whole was vaulted in the late 12th and 13th centuries (Gothic capitals), the north transept reconstructed, and the side-aisle windows remade; subsequent changes include the high windows of the nave and Burguet's reworking of the apse.

The most dramatic modification is Abadie's 19th-century "restoration" of the west façade. Most of the present sculpture is his, as is the north tower. Intact, for the most part, is the projecting central block, suggestive of a triumphal arch, framed by bundles of decorated columns. Both architectural format and decoration are inspired by the Saintonge. A number of the voussoirs are original, including some of the Elders of the Apocalypse and zodiac signs of the large central portal, and representations of Avarice and Luxuria in the lateral blind arches.

Saint-Michel. A longtime dependency of Sainte-Croix and the largest of Bordeaux's parish churches, the present church (vestiges of Carolingian and Romanesque structures excavated) was begun ca. 1357, with the bulk of its construction dating from the second half of the 15th century. Three polygonal apsidal chapels correspond to the nave and wide side aisles. The choir has three bays; the nave, four. The transept arms terminate in high gables flanked by turrets and pinnacles with sculptured portals at the bases (sculpture of the south portal reworked in the 18th c.). The numerous chapels are primarily 16th-century. Subsequent restorations include 19th-century revaulting of the structure. A bombardment in 1940 destroyed the major part of the stained glass. There are three Late Gothic sculptures: a large Deposition of 1495, a poignant Pieta (late 15th-c.), and St. Ursula sheltering her companions under her mantle. The freestanding bell tower, built over the ossuary of the parish cemetery by Jean Lebas of Saintes and his son (1472–92), is the highest in southwestern France (also transformed by Abadie).

Sainte-Eulalie. Little remains of the church consecrated in 1175. The present composite structure, originally conceived as a hall church, dates from the 13th to the 16th centuries, with additions and restorations, including the new façade of 1901. The polygonal apse was built in 1476; the majority of the buttress statues appear to be of the same period.

Saint-Pierre. Built in the 14th and 15th centuries, the church was almost entirely restored at the end of the 19th. It conserves, however, its elegant pentagonal chevet, the Flamboyant west portal, the lower part of the walls of the south side aisle, and the beautiful south portal.

Saint-Eloi. Founded in the 12th century, the church occupied an important site near the ramparts, city gate, and route to Compostela; however, the present church dates from the Late Gothic period. It is composed of a nave with a single wide side aisle and a pentagonal chevet with bell tower. The upper part of the façade was reconstructed in 1828 by Poitevin.

Civil Architecture. The gate of Saint-Eloi, used by pilgrims on their way to Compostela, was converted (15th–17th c.) into a belfry (the "Grosse Cloche"); the Porte Cailhou, transformed into a triumphal memorial in 1495, was restored in the 19th century.

Jean M. French

[See also: AQUITAINE; DAGOBERT I; EDWARD, THE BLACK PRINCE]

Brutails, Jean-Auguste. *Les vieilles églises de la Gironde.* Bordeaux: Feret, 1912.

Congrès archéologique (Bordeaux et Bayonne) 102 (1941).

Dubourg-Noves, Pierre. *Guyenne romane.* La Pierre-qui-vire: Zodiaque, 1969.

Gardelles, Jacques. *Bordeaux cité médiévale.* Bordeaux: Horizon Chimérique, 1989.

———. *La cathédrale Saint-André de Bordeaux: sa place dans l'évolution de l'architecture et de la sculpture.* Bordeaux: Delmas, 1963.

Higounet, Charles, et al. *Bordeaux pendant le haut moyen âge*. Bordeaux: Fédération Historique du Sud-Ouest, 1963.

BOSCHERVILLE. Saint-Martin-de-Boscherville (Seine-Maritime) is one of the last great Norman examples of 12th-century Romanesque architecture. In contrast to the founding of the majority of great Norman abbeys, the foundation of Boscherville abbey was neither royal nor ducal, but seigneurial; the seigneurs of Tancarville owned the land. The complex history of the edifice has yet to be fully explained. A charter, dated to 1053–66, mentions that a chamberlain of William the Conqueror, Raoul de Tancarville, had replaced the small church of Saint-George with a larger edifice in the form of a cross. There, he installed a community of regular canons of the order of St. Augustine. Subsequently, the Benedictines replaced the Augustinians. The abbey was virtually destroyed during the Revolution; only the church and the chapter house escaped.

In construction, the abbey church is similar to certain Norman churches: Cérisy-la-Forêt, Saint-Nicholas de Caen, Saint-Gabriel, and Lessay. It comprises a nave of eight bays, a transept with a small apse at each arm, a choir of two bays bordered by aisles, a straight chevet, and an apse. The cross-ribbed vaulting that exists today in the nave is not original. Each arm of the transept is subdivided in height at the level of the triforium by a gallery supported by a central column. Semicircular vaulting covers the two bays of the choir. The façade consists of a central door, two-story windows, two corner towers, and a central square tower that culminates in an octagonal spire. The chapter house, located at the north arm of the transept, opens to the east by three bays. Arcades are supported by pillars with historiated capitals. The interior exhibits ribbed vaulting and column statues. A frieze runs along the walls, the work of Abbot Victor, completed ca. 1170.

E. Kay Harris

Besnard, A. *Monographie de l'église et de l'abbaye Saint-Georges de Boscherville*. Paris: Lechevalier, 1899.
Lapeyre, André. *Des façades occidentales de Saint-Denis et de Chartres aux portails de Laon*. Paris: Université de Paris, 1960.
Michon, Louis-Marie. "L'abbaye de Saint-Georges de Boscherville." *Congrès archéologique* (Rouen) 89 (1926): 531–49.

BOUCICAUT. The sobriquet Boucicaut was given to members of the Le Meingre family of Touraine, two of whom served as marshals of France during the Hundred Years' War. The elder Jean le Meingre, who was probably born in the decade before 1320, served as an esquire in the campaigns of the 1330s and was one of the many people of undistinguished birth who rose to positions of power under King John II. He was serving as seneschal of Toulouse when the Battle of Poitiers (September 1356) decimated French leadership. Appointed to one of the vacant posts of marshal, he held that office until shortly before his death in early 1368.

Boucicaut was already advanced in years when his son, the younger Jean le Meingre (1366–1421), was born

at Tours. By the age of eighteen, the young Boucicaut had fought in his first campaign and served as a chamberlain to the duke of Burgundy. In 1391, he became a marshal of France, the post he held for twenty-seven years. He also served as governor of Dauphiné (1399–1407) and of Genoa (1401–09). Although he was celebrated in the annals of French chivalry (*Livre des fais du bon messire Jehan le Maingre, dit Bouciquaut*, found in a single manuscript; 1406–09), historians remember him today for his role in two French military disasters, the battles of Nicopolis (1396) and Agincourt (1415), at both of which he was taken prisoner. He died a captive in England in 1421. His younger brother Geoffroy le Meingre was known as "le petit Boucicaut."

John Bell Henneman, Jr.

[See also: AGINCOURT; MARSHAL; NICOPOLIS]

Lalande, Denis, ed. *Le livre des fais du bon messire Jehan le Maingre, dit Bouciquaut*. Geneva: Droz, 1985.
Bozzolo, Carla, and Hélène Loyau. *La cour amoureuse dite de Charles VI*. Paris: Léopard d'Or, 1982, Vol. 1: *Étude et édition critique des sources manuscrites*.
Lalande, Denis. *Jean II le Meingre, dit Boucicaut (1366–1421): étude d'une biographie héroïque*. Geneva: Droz, 1988.

BOUCICAUT MASTER. An anonymous manuscript illuminator active in Paris during the first two decades of the 15th century, named for the patron of his most elaborate work, a book of hours illuminated for Jean le Meingre II, marshal of Boucicaut (Paris, Musée Jacquemart André 2). Sometimes associated with Jacques Cœur from Bourges, he is believed to have headed a large and prolific atelier; his style dominated French manuscript illumination into the 1420s.

Robert G. Calkins

[See also: BEDFORD MASTER; CŒUR, JACQUES; MANUSCRIPTS, PRODUCTION AND ILLUMINATION]

Durrieu, Paul. "Le Maître des Heures du maréchal de Boucicaut." *Revue de l'art ancien et moderne* 19 (1906): 401ff.
———. "Les Heures du maréchal de Boucicaut du Musée Jacquemart André." *Revue de l'art chrétien* 63 (1913): 73–81, 145–64, 300–14; 64 (1914): 28–35.
Meiss, Millard. *French Painting in the Time of Jean de Berry: The Boucicaut Master*. London: Phaidon, 1968.
Panofsky, Erwin. *Early Netherlandish Painting*. 2 vols. Cambridge: Harvard University Press, 1953, Vol. 1, pp. 53–61.

BOULOGNE-SUR-MER. Situated near the narrowest point of the Channel, Boulogne (the Roman Gesoriacum) was the major crossing point to Roman Britain. Part of Belgica Secunda and then of the Merovingian kingdom of Neustria, it became the center of the Carolingian *pagus Bononiensis*. After its destruction by the Norse, it reappeared in the late 9th century and was promptly absorbed by Count Baudouin II of Flanders.

After 962, Boulogne was ruled by the descendants of Baudouin's younger son. Count Eustache II (r. 1049–93) wedded an English princess and played a major role in the Norman Conquest of 1066. His granddaughter, Matilda (Mahaut), joined the countship with the English crown by her marriage to King Stephen, but the death of their son, Eustache IV, in 1153, left their daughter, Marie, a nun, the sole heiress. Her forced marriage to Mathieu d'Alsace, younger son of the count of Flanders, began a series of female inheritances that carried the Boulonnais to various families while the collateral male lines established overseas dynasties.

King Philip Augustus seized Boulogne in 1212, when Count Renaud joined forces with John of England but then granted it to his legitimized son, Philippe Hurepel, Renaud's son-in-law. The imposing 13th-century fortifications of the *haute-ville* survived the bombardments of World War II. The 14th century saw Boulogne face to face with English-occupied Calais and, in its last decades, as a base for diplomatic activities to end the Hundred Years' War.

In 1416, Boulogne was seized by the Burgundian duke John the Fearless, an action confirmed by the marriage of Michelle, daughter of King Charles VI, to Philip the Good, heir of Burgundy (1419) and by the Treaty of Arras (1435). After the death of Charles the Bold, last duke of Burgundy (1477), King Louis XI was able to take the fortress. He united it to the royal domain, compensating Bertrand VI, count of Auvergne, with Lauragues and making the town a fief held of Notre-Dame-de-Boulogne, thus avoiding earthly homage.

The cult of Notre-Dame-de-Boulogne was extremely popular in the later Middle Ages. It centered on a miracle-working statue said to have drifted into port in the 7th century on a crewless ship. The abbey of Notre-Dame, which was elevated to the status of cathedral in 1567, was sold after the French Revolution and demolished, with the exception of its 12th-century crypt, which survives under the 19th-century cathedral. The only other medieval structure in Boulogne, the transept and chevet of the church of Saint-Nicolas, was rebuilt in the Flamboyant Gothic style between 1567 and 1604.

R. Thomas McDonald

Dhondt, Jean. "Recherches sur l'histoire du Boulonnais et de l'Artois au IVe et Xe siècle." *Mémoires de l'Académie d'Arras* 4th ser. 1 (1941–42): 9–13.

Héliot, Pierre. "L'église Saint-Nicolas de Boulogne avant la Révolution." *Revue du nord* 19 (1933): 269–86.

——— "Boulogne-sur-Mer, église Saint-Nicolas." *Congrès archéologique* (Amiens) 99 (1936): 371–77.

Lestocquoy, Jean. *Histoire de la Picardie et du Boulonnais.* Paris: Presses Universitaires de France, 1970.

BOURBON/BOURBONNAIS. The Bourbonnais in central France, lying southeast of Berry and north of Auvergne, with Moulins (Allier) as its principal town, was the site of a lordship in the 10th century, centered on the castle of Bourbon-L'Archambaud. It was long a fief of the French crown. The population included free peasants and a network of lesser seigneuries with servile tenants. Although the region produced cereal grains, it was best known for the highly regarded wines of Saint-Pourçain, its principal commercial product.

The male line of the ruling house of Bourbon-Dampierre came to an end in 1249 with the death of Archambaud IX, who was succeeded by his older sister Mahaut and then a younger sister, Agnès. The latter's daughter Beatrix married Robert, count of Clermont-en-Beauvaisis, the sixth son of Louis IX and Marguerite of Provence. The couple inherited the Bourbonnais at the death of Agnès in 1283. Their son Louis I (1280–1342) inherited the Bourbonnais from Beatrix in 1310 and Clermont from Robert in 1318. In 1327, King Charles IV traded his county of La Marche to Louis for Clermont and made Louis duke of Bourbon. Soon thereafter, the duke became a peer of France. Louis's son Pierre I (r. 1342–56) married Isabelle de Valois, sister of Philip VI, and their daughter Jeanne married Philip's grandson, the future Charles V, in 1350.

Jeanne's brother, Duke Louis II (1337–1410), with his close connections to the royal house, was a figure of importance in French political life and in the institutional life of the Bourbonnais. At the national level, he held important military commands under Charles V and led a crusade to North Africa in 1390. As one of Charles VI's uncles, he played a prominent role in the royal council but avoided the factionalism that led to the dismissal of two royal uncles in 1388 and of their rivals in 1392. Only in the 15th century did he join the growing anti-Burgundian party. Although as prodigal as his Valois cousins, Louis began adding lands to his duchy and established administrative institutions modeled on those of the crown, such as the judicial Grands Jours in 1371 and a *Chambre des Comptes* at Moulins in 1374. Nevertheless, the Bourbonnais suffered terribly from the ravages of undisciplined soldiers (*routiers*). Conditions became even worse when the next duke, Jean I (1382–1434), was captured at Agincourt in 1415 and spent the rest of his life as a prisoner in England.

Under Charles I (r. 1434–56) and Jean II (r. 1456–88), the duchy of Bourbon participated in the 15th-century revival of France. By marriage and other means, the dukes had added Forez, Beaujolais, Auvergne, and Montpensier to their possessions, and Jean II ruled a powerful apanage. Although occasionally rebellious, he was usually loyal to Louis XI, whose daughter Anne married his brother and successor, Pierre de Beaujeu. As the crown gradually gained control of Burgundy, Anjou, Provence, Brittany, and Orléans, the Bourbon lands constituted the largest block of nonroyal holdings in France by 1500. When the daughter of Anne and Pierre married her cousin Charles of Bourbon-Montpensier, their combined holdings constituted a serious threat to the monarchy, but the rebellion and subsequent disgrace of Charles in the 1520s brought an end to the independent history of the Bourbonnais.

Meanwhile, a younger son of Louis I, Jacques, count of La Marche (d. 1362), founded a cadet line of the house of Bourbon that was to have a great future. His son married the heiress of Vendôme, and this county passed to the couple's younger son, Louis (d. 1446), whose descendant would inherit the French throne as Henry IV in 1589.

John Bell Henneman, Jr.

[See also: ANNE OF BEAUJEU; LOUIS XI; VENDÔME]

Leguai, André. *Le Bourbonnais pendant la guerre de cent ans.* Moulins: Imprimeries Réunies, 1969.

BOURGEOISIE. As urban life gradually revived in France between the late 10th and the 12th centuries, one widespread development was the settlement of mercantile communities adjacent to fortified places, such as a walled *cité*. These settlements often were known as *bourgs*, and their inhabitants became known as *bourgeois* (Lat. *burgenses*). These bourgeois generally took the lead in pursuing urban self-government, obtaining charters restricting seigneurial authority, and in some circumstances forming communes.

As their communities became larger and their rights and privileges better defined, *bourgeoisie* came to signify more than just a collective noun for bourgeois. It implied citizenship in a particular community possessing specific rights. These rights varied from one place to another, as did the conditions one had to meet in order to acquire bourgeois status. A common requirement was residence in the community for a year and a day, but the period might be as long as ten years. Some towns required a substantial payment for admission to bourgeois status. In others, it could be obtained by marrying into a bourgeois family.

There were legal and economic advantages to having the status of bourgeois in a town with extensive privileges, and the bourgeois of royal towns could claim to be subject to the king's jurisdiction when they were in other parts of the kingdom. During the mid-13th century, when royal officials found pretexts for expanding the king's jurisdiction, the government began to offer "letters of bourgeoisie," which declared the recipient a bourgeois of a royal town even when not a resident of it. In principle, this privilege could not apply to people living in the lands of a territorial lord with high justice, but the presence of significant numbers of so-called *bourgeois-le-roi* in nonroyal lands could lead to interventions by royal officials that might seriously undermine seigneurial jurisdiction.

Predictably, letters of bourgeoisie aroused opposition, and in 1287 Philip IV issued an ordinance intended to curb abuses and regulate the *droit de bourgeoisie*. For a man to be admitted as a bourgeois of a particular town, he had to buy or build a domicile of a certain value and either he or his wife had to reside there from November through June. If he or his wife owned property in nonroyal lands, that property was subject to the jurisdiction of the local lord with high justice.

This ordinance, and another one issued thirty years later by Philip V, reduced the attractiveness of letters of bourgeoisie, and they seem not to have become as widespread as some 19th-century historians believed. They did not disappear, however, and the crown employed them as a device for extending protection to, or extracting "protection money" from, certain people. The kings of the early 14th century, for instance, required Italian merchants in France to purchase letters of bourgeoisie for a sum equal to 5 percent of their property—a thinly disguised tax known as the *boite aux Lombards*.

John Bell Henneman, Jr.

[See also: *CITÉ*; COMMUNE; TOWNS]

Chabrun, César. *Les bourgeois du roi.* Paris: Rousseau, 1908.

BOURGES. Situated on a hill at the confluence of the Auron and Yèvre rivers, Bourges (ancient Avaricum) was the chief town of the Bituriges Cubi in pre-Roman Gaul. It became the capital of the imperial province of Aquitania Prima and of the medieval province of Berry. It was also the seat of an archbishopric founded, according to tradition, in the 3rd century by St. Ursinus.

At the fall of the western Roman Empire, Bourges was occupied by the Visigoths and then by the Franks and preserves much of its fortifications from this period. It was given a count, but that office was suppressed by King Raoul in 926 and was replaced by a viscountship. In the absence of any major secular powers in the region, its archbishops came into prominence as hosts to synods in 1031, 1225, and 1276 and built, between 1135 and 1324, the main structure of the magnificent five-aisled cathedral that dominates the old quarter of the town.

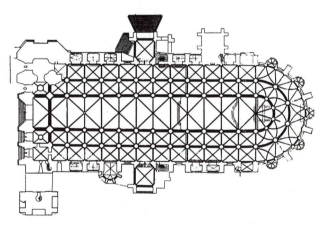

Bourges (Cher), Saint-Étienne, plan. After Branner and Capron.

In 1101, the viscountship was purchased from Eudes Harpin de Dun by King Philip I, presaging a rebirth of royal influence in Bourges. Although Berry was given in dowry to Eleanor of Aquitaine and Blanche of Castile, Philip Augustus established a *bailli* in Bourges, and royal influence increased in the 13th century.

In the 14th and 15th centuries, royal attention focused on the area. Berry was made a duchy for John (d. 1416), third son of King John II, whose sepulchral monuments grace the cathedral, and passed to his daughter Marie (d. 1434). Charles VII during the darkest days of the

Bourges (Cher), Saint-Étienne, south flank. *Photograph courtesy of Whitney S. Stoddard.*

Hundred Years' War established his royal government south of the Loire and became known as *le roi de Bourges* from his residence in the town. It also became the center of the financial dealings of Jacques Cœur, whose house still stands there. The Estates met in Bourges in 1422, as they had in 1316 and 1317, and in 1438 the city was host to an ecclesiastical assembly that resulted in the proclamation of the Pragmatic Sanction defining the "Gallican liberties" of an autonomous French church.

Louis XI was born near Bourges and established a university there in 1463. His daughter, St. Jeanne of France (of Valois), lame and repudiated by her husband, Louis XII, in 1499, resided in Bourges as duchess of Berry and there founded her order of the Annonciade. After 1500, the town resumed its role as a local center.

R. Thomas McDonald

Bourges has preserved two major medieval monuments: the cathedral of Saint-Étienne and the house of Jacques Cœur. The cathedral is one of the most audacious designs of the 12th century, the culmination of half a century of experimentation. The first builder-designer, who worked from 1195 to 1214, conceived this mighty, five-aisled building as a monospatial structure spreading laterally to the equivalent of its height. Construction started

Bourges, Saint-Étienne. *Photograph courtesy of Whitney S. Stoddard.*

Bourges, Saint-Étienne, inner aisle and nave. *Photograph: Clarence Ward Collection. Courtesy of Oberlin College.*

The five-aisle plan translates into five west portals, producing one of the most elaborate sculptural ensembles of the period. While the west-façade sculpture must date close to the mid-13th century, there is clear evidence that the decisions as to subjects of the portals was made much earlier, probably in conjunction with the planning of the stained-glass program. Throughout, Bourges gives evidence of careful, integrated planning of architecture, stained glass, and sculpture, including the jubé (most of which is now found in the Louvre). The care in planning is illustrated by the decisions made concerning quality of stone and quarry sources.

Of the many other medieval churches in Bourges, only the unusual tympanum of the west portal of Saint-Ursin continues to fascinate. The royal palace, which once housed a magnificent chapel, is known only through drawings and the statues preserved in the local museum. In the house of Jacques Cœur, however, Bourges preserves the most splendid surviving townhouse of 15th-century France. Many of the details, such as fireplaces, stained-glass windows, and the painted ceiling of the family chapel, are well preserved.

William W. Clark

[See also: AQUITAINE; BERRY; CHARLES VII; CŒUR, JACQUES; JOHN, DUKE OF BERRY]

Bayard, Tanya. *Bourges Cathedral: The West Portals*. New York: Garland, 1976.

Blanc, Annie, Pierre Lebouteux, Jacqueline Lorenz, and Serge Debrand-Passard. "Les pierres de la cathédrale de Bourges." *Archéologia* 171 (1982): 22–35.

Branner, Robert. *The Cathedral of Bourges and Its Place in Gothic Architecture*, ed. Shirley Praeger Branner. Cambridge: MIT Press, 1989.

Michler, Jurgen. "Zur Stellung von Bourges in der gotischen Baukunst." *Wallraf-Richartz Jahrbuch* 41 (1980): 27–86.

von Konradsheim, G.C. "La famille monumentale de la cathédrale de Tolède et l'architecture gothique contemporaine." *Mélanges de la Casa de Velazquez* 11 (1975): 545–63.

Wolfe, Maury, and Robert Mark. "Gothic Cathedral Buttressing: The Experiment at Bourges and Its Influence." *Journal of the Society of Architectural Historians* 33 (1974): 17–27.

BOUVET, HONORÉ (ca. 1340–ca. 1405). Long misnamed Bonet, this orator, diplomat, and administrator was a longtime prior of the Benedictine abbey of Sellonet (Basse-Alpes). Associated with the house of Anjou and a student at the University of Avignon, he became Doctor of Decretals in 1386. His *Arbre des batailles* (1387), a commentary on the international laws of war, influenced by the Bolognese law professor John of Legnano, was dedicated to Charles VI. It included a portrait of the philosopher king as opposed to the tyrant. The over sixty extant manuscripts show it as his most successful work. His *Somnium super materia schismatis* (1394), on the papal Schism, led to a sermon on the subject that he preached before Wenceslas, king of the Romans, as Charles VI's representative (1399).

In the *Apparicion maistre Jehan de Meun* (1398), dedicated to the duke of Orléans, the Schism and other

Bourges, Saint-Étienne, main roof. *Photograph: Clarence Ward Collection. Courtesy of Oberlin College.*

with the crypt, necessitated by expansion of the site beyond the Gallo-Roman city wall, and included the remarkable pyramidal elevation reaching five stories in height. The lower level included the ambulatory and radiating chapels; the intermediary level (the inner aisle) has a full three-story elevation, which is revealed by the extraordinary height of the main nave piers. The daring and complexity of the design is matched by the audacious engineering of the structure, supported by steep, thin flying buttresses. The second builder, who took over after completion of the chevet, continued the pyramidal spatial scheme but increased the size and thickness of the flying buttresses, as well as reinforcing the chevet buttresses by adding an upper layer to both ranks, probably in response to problems at Notre-Dame in Paris.

In spite of Branner's attempt to link the Bourges designer to areas outside of Paris, it was the scheme of Notre-Dame that served as the starting point for the Bourges design. On the other hand, the builder is the most original designer of his generation. He borrows from a number of sources but synthesizes them into his unique design. The audacity of the design, as well as its exterior profile, may partly explain why this most magnificent spatial achievement of Gothic architecture was so seldom imitated.

contemporary problems are discussed in the hope that the prince would seek remedies for them. Jean de Meun appears in a vision to discuss these problems because Bouvet was living at the time in the poet's former Parisian house.

Charity Cannon Willard

Bouvet, Honoré. *L'apparicion maistre Jehan de Meun*, ed. Ivor Arnold. Paris: Faculté des Lettres de l'Université de Strasbourg, 1926.
———. *L'arbre des batailles*, ed. E. Nys. Brussels: Muquardt, 1883.
———. *The Tree of Battles*, ed. and trans. George William Coopland. Liverpool: University Press, 1949.
Coville, Alfred. *La vie intellectuelle dans les domaines d'Anjou-Provence de 1380 à 1435.* Paris: Droz, 1941, pp. 214–318.

BOUVINES. On Sunday, July 27, 1214, a massive and violent battle took place at the bridge of Bouvines, south of Tournai, in the county of Flanders. On one side fought the German emperor, Otto IV of Brunswick; William, earl of Salisbury and half-brother of King John of England; Ferrand of Portugal, count of Flanders and Hainaut; William, count of Holland; and Henri I, duke of Brabant. Also present were the rebellious nobles of France, Renaud de Dammartin, count of Boulogne, and Hugo, the baron of Boves. Opposing them was the king of France, Philip Augustus. Backing Philip morally and financially was Pope Innocent III; the prince-bishop of Liège, Hugues de Pierrepont, also sent troops to fight for the French.

The two armies joined in a tripartite battle. The allied left wing, composed mostly of Flemish mounted knights under Ferrand, met a similarly composed French right wing. In the center, Otto IV, with German knights and infantry, faced Philip with his strongest soldiers. Finally, the allied right wing, composed largely of English and Boulognese infantry under Renaud de Dammartin, faced a similar French force. Before long, it became apparent that the strength and unity of the French army, more experienced in military affairs, having fought frequently in tournaments and in the Crusades, were superior to that of the allied armies. The battle lasted only three hours; the allied left wing was defeated and their center fled, leaving only Renaud de Dammartin's troops to continue the battle. But despite a valiant effort on their part, the Boulognese eventually succumbed to the continual French attacks. Philip Augustus and the French were victorious.

Many contemporary chroniclers compare the Battle of Bouvines to a tournament, describing the brilliance of the armor and the grandeur of the heraldic banners, which included the fleur-de-lis, the oriflamme of Saint-Denis, and the German imperial eagle with dragon. Few died on either side, with an estimated death toll of 169 allied knights but only two French knights. Henri of Brabant, Hugo de Boves, and Otto fled from the battlefield, while at least five counts (Ferrand of Portugal, William of Salisbury, Renaud de Dammartin, William of Holland, and Otto of Tecklenburg), twenty-five other nobles, and 139 knights were captured and imprisoned.

The loss at Bouvines meant the end of Otto IV. By 1215, Frederick II of Sicily, an opposing candidate to the imperial throne, had the acceptance of all of Germany, and Otto's reign ended. The failure of Bouvines also forced King John of England, then campaigning in Poitou, to return home and later to conclude the Peace of Chinon, which virtually ended England's chance to regain its Angevin lands. For his victory, Philip gained not only continued papal friendship, the English lands in France, and an alliance with Germany, but effective control over the rich but troublesome Low Countries.

Kelly DeVries

[See also: PHILIP II AUGUSTUS]

Cartellieri, Alexander. *Die Schlacht bei Bouvines (27 Juli 1214) in Rahmen der europaischen Politik.* Leipzig: Dyksche Buchhandlung, 1914.
Duby, Georges. *Le dimanche de Bouvines.* Paris: Gallimard, 1973.
Lot, Ferdinand. *L'art militaire et les armées au moyen âge.* 2 vols. Paris: Payot, 1946, Vol. 1.
Oman, Sir Charles. *A History of the Art of War in the Middle Ages.* 2nd ed. London: Methuen, 1924, Vol. 1.
Verbruggen, J.F. *The Art of Warfare in Western Europe During the Middle Ages*, trans. Sumner Willard and S.C.M. Southern. Amsterdam: North Holland, 1977.

BOZON, NICOLE (fl. 1280–1320). An English Franciscan and prolific author, Bozon wrote four allegorical poems, including the *Char d'orguel*, several poems in honor of the Virgin, the *Proverbes de bon enseignement*, seven verse sermons, and eleven saints' lives. He is best known for his prose *Contes moralisés*, which set forth the properties of an animal, plant, or stone as the basis for a moral lesson confirmed with an exemplum or fable. Although not actual sermons, these *contes* served as preaching materials.

Maureen B.M. Boulton

[See also: ANGLO-NORMAN LITERATURE; SERMONS IN VERSE]

Bozon, Nicole. *Les contes moralisés*, ed. Lucy Toulmin Smith and Paul Meyer. Paris: Société des Anciens Textes Français, 1889.
———. *Three Saints' Lives by Nicholas Bozon*, trans. Mary Amelia Klenke. St. Bonaventure: Franciscan Institute, 1947.
———. *Seven More Poems by Nicolas Bozon*, trans. M. Amelia Klenke. St. Bonaventure: Franciscan Institute, and Louvain: Nauwelaerts, 1951.

BRABANT. A predominately French-speaking territory located in the central Low Countries, the duchy of Brabant came into being when Godefroi I le Barbu, count of Louvain and Brussels, was enfeoffed with the margraviate of Antwerp by the emperor Henry V in 1100 and given the title of duke. In 1190, Henri I (r. 1183–1235) took the title duke "of Brabant," a regional designation first used in 1086. Brabant was entirely in the empire, but its population was Romance in the south and Germanic in the north.

The towns of Brabant were still small in the early 12th century but then grew rapidly, rivaling the Flemish cities in the international marketplace during the 13th century. Henri I sided with the English and Flemings at Bouvines, but thereafter the dukes of Brabant maintained correct relations with their French and Flemish neighbors, concentrating on territorial expansion in the east and promoting urban development. The towns were assimilated peacefully into the governance of the duchy in a series of power-sharing arrangements in 1312, 1314, and particularly the Joyeuse Entrée of January 1356.

Duke Jean III (r. 1312–55), the last of his line, abandoned his predecessors' neutrality to pursue an active military and diplomatic policy. He allied briefly with the English against King Philip VI, but in 1347 he married his daughter and eventual heiress, Jeanne, to the pro-French Wenceslas of Luxembourg. Jeanne continued to rule after Wenceslas's death until 1406. But in 1390, she designated her niece, Marguerite of Flanders, and Marguerite's husband, Philip the Bold of Burgundy, her successors, but she outlived them both and was succeeded by Antoine, their younger son. Brabant was incorporated into the Burgundian state when Antoine's line failed in 1430.

David M. Nicholas

Byl, Raymond. *Les juridictions scabinales dans le duché de Brabant (des origines à la fin du XVe siècle)*. Brussels: Presses Universitaires de Bruxelles, 1965.

Martens, Mina. *L'administration du domaine ducal en Brabant au moyen âge (1250–1406)*. Brussels: Academie Royale de Belgique, 1954.

Smets, Georges. *Henri I, duc de Brabant, 1190–1235*. Brussels: Lamertin, 1908.

Uyttebrouck, André. *Le gouvernement du duché de Brabant au bas moyen âge (1355–1430)*. 2 vols. Brussels: Éditions de l'Université de Bruxelles, 1975.

Vanderkindere, Léon. *La formation territoriale des principautés belges au moyen âge*. 2 vols. Brussels: Lamertin, 1902.

BRAINE. The Premonstratensian abbey church of Saint-Yved at Braine (Aisne) is important for its plan, its elevation, and the extraordinary richness of its sculptural deco-

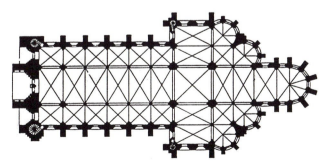

Braine (Aisne), Saint-Yved, plan. After King.

Braine, Saint-Yved, chevet and south transept. *Photograph: Clarence Ward Collection. Courtesy of Oberlin College.*

ration, all of which demonstrate that there were no influences from Cistercian churches on Premonstratensian buildings. New analysis of the documents places the construction between 1176 and 1208. The most notable feature of the plan is the arrangement of double chapels angled in the space between the transept and the chevet, an arrangement that was repeated in a number of other buildings. The presence of the open lantern tower, like the three-story elevation with wall passage, suggests influences from the destroyed Benedictine abbey of Saint-Vincent at Laon. Indeed, the destroyed westwork of Saint-Yved, now known only through imprecise documents, might have been influenced by the westworks of Noyon and Laon. For all the local sources, however, the originality of the designer in his interpretation of the rich regional decorative traditions sets the building apart. The remains of two west portals, a Coronation of the Virgin (reinstalled on the interior of the church) and a Hell (in the museum in Soissons), suggest links to sculpture at Laon, while the stained glass is related to that of Saint-Remi at Reims.

William W. Clark

[See also: LAON; REIMS]

Caviness, Madeline H. "Saint-Yved of Braine: The Primary Sources for Dating the Gothic Church." *Speculum* 59 (1984): 524–48.

———. *Sumptuous Arts at the Royal Abbeys in Reims and Braine: ornatus elegantiae, varietate stupendes.* Princeton: Princeton University Press, 1990.

McClain, Jeroldean. "A Modern Reconstruction of the West Portals of Saint-Yved at Braine." *Gesta* 24 (1985): 105–19.

———. "Observations on the Geometric Design of Saint-Yved at Braine." *Zeitschrift für Kunstgeschichte* 49 (1986): 92–95.

Wochnik, F. "St. Yved zu Braine und die mittelalterlichen Nachfolgebauten (Das Schema von Braine)." *Analecta praemonstratensia* 58 (1982): 252–63.

BRASSART, JOHANNES (ca. 1396?–1455). Composer, musician, and cleric. Brassart was probably born in Lowaigne, near Limbourg. His earliest documented position was at Saint-Jean l'Évangéliste in Liège. He was briefly in Rome during the pontificate of Martin V (ca. 1425) and in 1431–32 served in the papal chapel of Eugenius IV, where he was a colleague of Guillaume Dufay. Brassart was a member of the chapel at the Council of Basel (1433–37) and also served as a senior member of the chapels of Emperor Sigismund (d. 1438), King Albrecht II (d. 1439), and King Frederick III (later emperor). Brassart held canonries at the church of Our Lady in Tongeren and at the collegiate church of Saint-Paul in Liège. Over thirty compositions by Brassart survive, primarily polyphonic Mass movements and motets, similar in style to works of his more famous contemporary Dufay.

J. Michael Allsen

[See also: DUFAY, GUILLAUME; *FAUXBOURDON*; ISORHYTHMIC MOTET]

Brassart, Johannes. *Opera omnia*, ed. Keith Mixter. 2 vols. N.p.: American Institute of Musicology, 1965–71.

Wright, Peter. "Johannes Brassart and Johannes de Sarto." *Plainsong and Medieval Music* 1 (1992): 41–61.

Starr, Pamela. "Communication." *Plainsong and Medieval Music* 1 (1992): 215–16.

BREAD. Bread was the basis of every meal in the Middle Ages: in France, other foods were summed up in the word *companage*, "what accompanies the bread." It was usually made from wheat, rye, or maslin (mixed wheat and rye), but barley and oats, among other grains, were also sometimes used. The best wheat bread, the kind that appeared most often on the tables of the rich, was described as "white." The brown, or "bis," bread, likely to be the fare of the household help and often used for "trencher" bread (a slice on which a diner could put pieces of meat, etc., as we use plates), might be either whole wheat or maslin. Rye bread, apt to be the food of peasants but not confined to any one class, was usually classified as "black." Bread was made simply from flour and water, with or without a leavening of sourdough or yeast—usually derived from beer brewing. Unleavened bread was baked on a hearthstone or grill into flat breads or wafers, while leavened bread was generally baked in an oven. All standard loaves were round, whether they were small individual rolls (*miches*) of white bread or large rye loaves.

Constance B. Hieatt

[See also: COOKING; MEALS; MILLS AND MILLING]

Bautier, A. M. "Pain et pâtisserie dans les textes médiévaux latins antérieurs au XIIe siècle." In *Manger et boire au moyen âge: actes du Colloque de Nice (15–17 octobre 1982)*. Nice: Faculté des Lettres et Sciences Humaines, 1983.

Stouff, Louis. *Ravitaillement et alimentation en Provence aux XIVe et XVe siècles.* Paris: Mouton, 1970.

BRÉTIGNY. A village in the Beauce, Brétigny (Eure-et-Loire) was the site of an important treaty between England and France. Concluded on May 8, 1360, it ended the first phase of the Hundred Years' War. Having captured John II in 1356, Edward III had negotiated two draft treaties with the French, but when the second was rejected he invaded France in 1359. Unable to force a decisive battle or capture a major town, Edward agreed to the Treaty of Brétigny, which French historians have considered a disaster for their country. It was, in fact, less harsh than the rejected draft of 1359. It provided for major cessions of territory in southwestern France, giving England a large duchy of Aquitaine that would be held in full sovereignty without feudal ties to the French crown. John II would be released in return for a ransom of 3 million *écus* (500,000 pounds sterling), 20 percent to be paid before his release and the remainder in six annual installments. The banished supporters of the rival kings would recover their property, and Edward III would abandon his claim to the throne of France. Although ratified at Calais in October 1360, when John was released, the treaty was not implemented in every detail, and war resumed in 1369.

John Bell Henneman, Jr.

[See also: EDWARD III; HUNDRED YEARS' WAR]

Le Patourel, John. "The Treaty of Bretigny, 1360." *Transactions of the Royal Historical Society* 5th ser. 10 (1960): 19–39.

Petit-Dutaillis, Charles, and P. Collier. "La diplomatie française et la traité de Brétigny." *Moyen âge* 2nd ser. 1 (1897): 1–35.

BRIDGES. *See* TRAVEL

BRIENNE. A little town in Champagne, Brienne (Aube), was the seat of an important noble family that played a prominent role in the Crusades and furnished three constables of France. Gautier III, count of Brienne (d. 1205), fought in the Holy Land and later claimed the kingdom of Sicily through his wife. One of his relatives, Jean de Brienne, was elected king of Jerusalem in 1209. His daughter married the emperor Frederick II, who forced him to cede his rights to Jerusalem, but Jean later went to Constantinople, where he ruled the Latin Empire for a number of years during the minority of Baudouin II. His descendants Raoul I and Raoul II, counts of Eu and Guines, were constables of France in 1327–44 and 1344–51, respectively. Meanwhile, the senior line of the family, descended from Count Gautier III, had acquired by marriage the title of duke of Athens. Gautier VI of Brienne, duke of Athens, became constable of France in 1356 and died in the Battle of Poitiers in September of that year.

John Bell Henneman, Jr.

BRIGAND/BRIGANDAGE. In military terminology, the brigand was a professional foot soldier whose protective garb, a leather jacket covered with metal rings (*brigandine*), was lighter and cheaper than the hauberk of chain mail worn by knights. Troops of this sort served in the army of Philip II and again during the early stages of the Hundred Years' War. After the mid-14th century, "brigand" began to acquire the pejorative meaning that it has had ever since.

People began to associate brigands with other foot soldiers, *pillars*, who served a knight and foraged for supplies. Too often, these *pillars* looted and "pillaged" the local property rather than following the legal procedure of levying *appatis* on the populace. Especially in unfriendly territory, *pillars* were more inclined to obtain supplies by outright theft than by observing legal niceties. The familiar military garb made it easy to confuse them with those foot soldiers known as brigands.

As the word "brigandage" evolved, it acquired two dimensions. It came to refer to violent, felonious conduct by undisciplined soldiers, but it also described similar behavior by rural folk reduced to desperation by the soldier-brigands. This second type, the bandit-brigands, could constitute a serious social uprising if assembled in sufficient numbers. In a number of cases, they were called *tuchins*, a term associated particularly with disorders in Languedoc in 1383–84.

Pillaging by soldiers was originally a symptom of poor discipline, but the problem of discipline was soon eclipsed by that of pay. Increasingly, soldier-brigands tended to be unpaid or unemployed troops—professional soldiers from abroad or uprooted petty nobles from French border districts. They first became a major problem in the years 1357–69, a relative lull in the hostilities between England and France, when brigandage helped to hasten the establishment and financing of a salaried royal army. Generally operating as "freelance" companies, or *routes*, these *routiers*, as they were called, served under colorful if bloodthirsty leaders like Seguin de Badefol, John Hawkwood, Arnaud de Cervole, and Perrin Boias. They would occupy some stronghold and terrorize the surrounding region until paid a large sum to leave and go elsewhere. Late in 1360, Badefol and Hawkwood took Pont-Saint-Esprit on the Rhône and extorted a large sum from the pope before leaving. In 1362,

Badefol and Boias, cornered at Brignais near Lyon, defeated a royal force.

The depredations of the *routiers* finally produced two responses by the French crown. One was to pay them to go on a foreign expedition. The other was to establish a regular salaried army that would provide steady employment for the best troops and could be used to defeat or drive out the others. Both policies cost money, and they led the French to pay high taxes in peacetime (when the danger of unemployed troops was always worst).

These remedies brought some relief to the French countryside in the later 14th century, but the fiscal and military system collapsed during the princely civil wars after 1400, and a new wave of brigandage became especially severe after the Franco-Burgundian treaty of 1435. In this period, the companies were called *écorcheurs* ("flayers") and had such leaders as Rodrigo de Villandrando and Étienne de Vignolles. At length, the crown restored internal order by resorting to the remedies first used in the 1360s: sending large numbers of troops on an expedition against the Swiss in 1444 and then establishing a regular, paid force of men-at-arms (the Compagnies d'ordonnance) in 1445.

John Bell Henneman, Jr.

[See also: *APPATIS*; BADEFOL, SEGUIN DE; BRIGNAIS; CERVOLE, ARNAUD DE; LA HIRE; VILLANDRANDO, RODRIGO DE]

Denifle, Heinrich. *La désolation des églises, monastères et hôpitaux en France pendant le guerre de cent ans.* 2 vols. Paris: Picard, 1897–99.

Guigue, George. *Les Tard-Venus en Lyonnaise, Forez, et Beaujolais.* Lyon: Vitte and Perrussel, 1886.

Monicat, Jacques. *Les Grandes Compagnies en Velay.* Paris: Champion, 1928.

Tuetey, Alexandre. *Les écorcheurs sous Charles VII.* 2 vols. Montbéliard: Barbier, 1874.

Wright, Nicholas A. R. "'Pillagers' and 'Brigands' in the Hundred Years War." *Journal of Medieval History* 9 (1983): 15–25.

BRIGNAIS. The small fortified town of Brignais (Rhône) near Lyon was the site of an important 14th-century battle. In 1362, eastern France was menaced by numerous unemployed soldiers (*routiers*), who had combined to form the "Great Company," led by Seguin de Badefol, Perrin Boias, and Perrin de Savoie. John II appointed Jean de Melun, count of Tancarville, to be royal lieutenant in the region, and he assembled a force of several thousand men who besieged these brigands at Brignais. Entrenched in a favorable position, the outnumbered *routiers* withstood the assault of the royal troops on April 6, 1362, and won a crushing victory in which the leading royal commanders were killed or captured. This battle represented the nadir of French military fortunes in the 14th century and hastened the establishment of a regular salaried royal army at the end of 1363.

John Bell Henneman, Jr.

[**See also:** BADEFOL, SEGUIN DE; BRIGAND/BRIGANDAGE]

Descroix, Bernard. *Seguin de Badefol: "ce fils d'iniquité"—qui fit trembler Anse et la France entière.* Lyon: Société d'Archéologie du Beaujolais, 1986.

BRIOUDE. The church of Saint-Julien in Brioude (Haute-Loire) was erected in the early 5th century upon the site of its patron's martyrdom. It soon became a center for pilgrimage, and in the Merovingian era St. Julien's cult rivaled that of St. Martin. Destroyed by Muslims, the church was rebuilt in the late 8th century, and in the 9th century a college of canons was founded here.

The present structure is the result of a series of building campaigns. In the late 11th and early 12th centuries, the narthex and the nave were constructed. The choir, with ambulatory and five radiating chapels, dates from the end of the 12th century, and the two side porches are from the early 13th. After 1259, the nave was rib-vaulted and rose windows and bays in the Gothic style were added.

The interior is highly ornamented. Sculpted capitals throughout the church include figures of angels, Evangelists, sirens, centaurs, antique masks, and knights in combat. Walls and columns also exhibit remains of polychrome figures and decorative motifs in vermilion, pink, fiery yellow, grey, green, and violet. An important 12th-century fresco cycle in a chapel off the south aisle depicts Christ in Majesty surrounded by angels and personifications of the Virtues and Vices.

The façade dates from the mid-19th century, as do the west tower and most of the bell tower over the crossing.

Nina Rowe

Blanc, Alphonse. *Brioude et sa région.* Brioude: Tissandier, 1944.

Jalenques, Joseph. "La basilique Saint-Julien de Brioude." *Almanach de Brioude et de son arrondissement* 38 (1958): 13–26.

Lefèvre-Pontalis, Eugène. "Les dates de Saint-Julien de Brioude." *Congrès archéologique* (Le Puy) 71 (1904): 542–55.

Quarré, Pierre. "Saint-Julien de Brioude et l'art roman auvergnat." *Almanach de Brioude et de son arrondissement* 49 (1960): 59–72.

BRITTANY. Culturally and politically, Brittany has always been one of the most distinctive regions of France. From prehistoric times onward, maritime trade and migration routes along the Atlantic coasts of Europe were as important as landward links with central-northern France: throughout the Middle Ages, Brittany was open to influence and pressure from both the British Isles and from France. The union of the Breton duchy with the French crown in 1532 confirmed the predominance of French political and cultural influences and ended a millennium of intermittent conflict between the two.

The Roman name for the region was Armorica. Profound but poorly documented changes during and after the collapse of Roman rule in Gaul transformed Armorica into Britannia Minor, Brittany, a name first encountered in Gregory of Tours. Migration from the British Isles brought settlers into the three western *civitates* (Osismiorum, capital Carhaix, later Brest; Curiosolitarum, capital Corseul then Alet; Venetum, capital Vannes), areas already affected by economic recession, administrative and military reorganization, and coastal raiding. In these *civitates*, medieval administrative geography only partly respected Roman antecedents. The immigrants' contribution to the culture here is most evident in language and place-names. Philologists disagree about the respective contributions of imported Brittonic and indigenous Gaulish to the Breton language, but the predominance of places with names in *plou-*, *lan-*, and *tre-* points to close affinities with Cornwall and Wales, where these place-name elements are also widespread. Their distribution, together with later formations in *loc-* and *ker-*, is, roughly, west of the rivers Couësnon and Vilaine and in the Guérande peninsula. Also characteristic of the Breton-speaking region is the plethora of obscure local saints represented in church dedications, many of which recur in Wales and Cornwall.

There is scant archaeological or documentary evidence for the Merovingian period; it is known that the Bretons were divided into several principalities with hereditary ruling families. Merovingian sources comment on Breton raiding into the Frankish-controlled counties of Nantes and Rennes. Later Breton hagiographical traditions are unanimous in portraying early Breton churches as monastic communities founded by aristocratic or royal saints of Welsh or Irish descent; the Merovingian church tried without success to assert its authority over them.

Carolingian efforts to protect Frankish ecclesiastical interests in the border area and to realize claims inherited from the Merovingians to hegemony over the Bretons began when Pepin III sacked Vannes in 751/53; the border march was possibly established at this time. Victorious campaigns to subdue the Bretons in 786 and 799 were only temporarily successful: several revolts are recorded in the early 9th century. Louis the Pious (r. 814–40) tried to integrate Brittany into the Carolingian empire, as witness imperial diplomas issued for Breton monasteries, references to Frankish counts in Breton-speaking areas, and the appointment in 831 of the Breton Nominoe as imperial *missus* in Brittany. After 840, Nominoe's position changed; despite some initial support for Charles the Bald (r. 840–77) in the civil wars of 840–43, he raided western Neustria repeatedly thereafter until his death in 851. His ejection in 849 of all the bishops of Breton-speaking sees (Vannes, Alet, Quimper, Saint-Pol, and Dol) became a *cause célèbre*. Charles the Bald was badly defeated by the Bretons in 845 and 851, the latter defeat inflicted by Nominoe's son and successor, Erispoe (r. 851–57). Territorial concessions and the promise of a marriage alliance placated Erispoe, but peace was ended by his assassination by his cousin and successor, Salomon (r. 857–74). Salomon joined in the revolts of Neustrian magnates in 858–63 and again raided Neustria in 865–66. Additional grants of Frankish lands in 863 and 867 extended Breton rule yet farther into Neustria; in all, Charles the Bald yielded the pays de Retz (Rais) and the counties of Nantes, Rennes, Avranches, Coutances, and

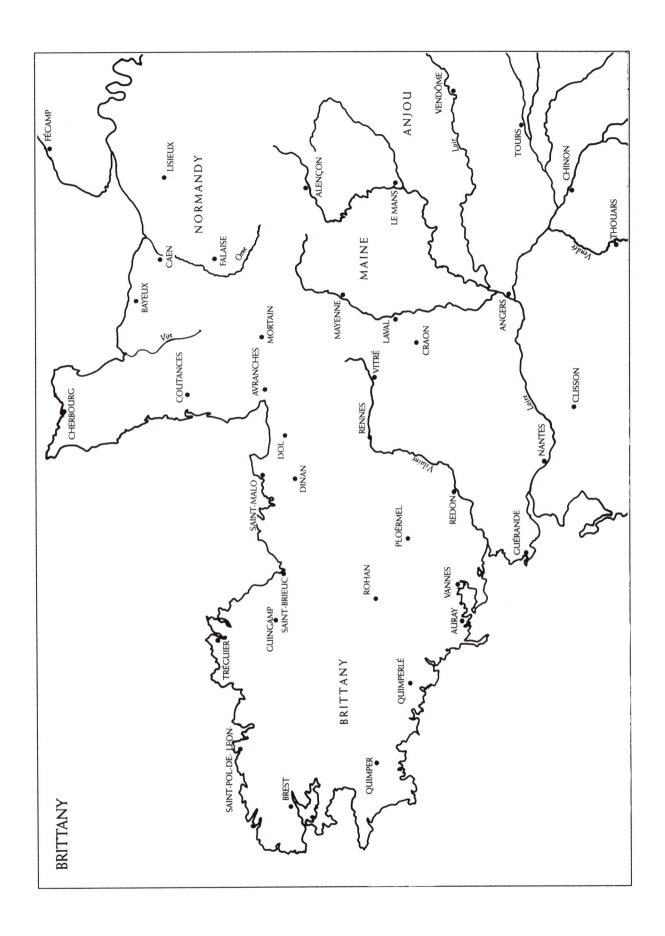

BRITTANY

western Anjou to the Bretons. Salomon's virtual independence from Frankish control was symbolized by his efforts to extract the Breton church from its dependence on the archbishop of Tours, creating instead a Breton archbishopric at Dol, and by the title *rex* given to him in some Breton charters. There are, nevertheless, clear signs of Frankish influence within Brittany, especially in the records of the monastery of Redon in southeastern Brittany and in the manuscripts and writings surviving from Landévennec on the west coast. A distinctive Breton social organization based on the community of the *plebs* (Breton *plou*), in which the *machtiern* was a powerful figure, is evident in southeastern Brittany in the 9th century; affected by the growth of Redon's lordship, it is not traceable after the 10th century.

With the exception of Alain I (r. 888–907), Salomon's successors found it increasingly difficult to retain control over all of Brittany and to keep the Vikings out. From ca. 915, the region was almost entirely in Viking hands and Breton leaders and churchmen were in exile. Alain II (r. 936–52) returning from England in 936, took back Brittany, including Nantes, Rennes, and the pays de Retz. Occasional raids from Normandy continued until 1014, but Alain II began to restore the Breton church and may have been the founder of the medieval bishoprics of Saint-Brieuc and Tréguier. His duchy had much in common with other 10th-century territorial principalities, with a basis of Carolingian administrative practices.

By the end of the 10th century, Alain II's successors had lost the ducal title to the counts of Rennes, whose weak authority was virtually nonexistent in western Brittany and in Nantes. The emergence of powerful castellanies further altered the political geography of Brittany. Throughout the later 10th and 11th centuries, the counts of Rennes and of Nantes were caught up in the territorial ambitions of the counts of Blois and of Angers and, increasingly, the dukes of Normandy. William I the Conqueror already had Breton vassals by 1066, several of whom he endowed with English lands. The honor of Richmond, granted to the sons of Eudo de Penthièvre, uncle of Conan II (r. 1040–66), remained in the hands of the Breton ducal family until 1399.

Norman lordship over Brittany was intensified by Henry I. Henry II integrated Brittany fully into the Angevin empire: in 1166, the betrothal of Constance, infant daughter of Henry's vassal Duke Conan IV (r. 1155–66), to Henry's young son Geoffroi gave Henry the excuse to rule Brittany directly until Geoffroi came of age in 1181. The firm rule of Henry, Geoffroi (r. 1181–86), and the duchess Constance (d. 1201) did much to strengthen ducal power as revolts were crushed and a ducal administration established similar to that in other provinces of the Angevin empire. The *Assize of Count Geoffrey* (1185) changed rules of inheritance to reduce the fragmentation of fiefs and thereby to safeguard military services. Henry II tried to revive the claim for a separate Breton archbishopric, but in 1199 Innocent III definitively quashed Dol's claims. The territorial extent of Brittany—the Breton west plus the counties of Rennes and Nantes—has not changed since unified as an Angevin province.

King John's imprisonment and murder of Geoffroi's posthumous son, Arthur (1186–1203), gave Philip Augustus the opportunity to bring Brittany under Capetian influence. In 1212, he married the Breton heiress Alix to his relative Pierre Mauclerc, who performed liege homage for Brittany but after 1226 oscillated between allegiance to England and France. With the help of French-trained administrators, Mauclerc (r. 1212–37) and his son Jean I (r. 1237–86) took strenuous measures to build up ducal demesne, revenues, and judicial and fiscal administration, to curtail seigneurial independence, and to assert control over the church, particularly episcopal appointments and temporalities. By the 14th century, ducal power was established and an effective household-based administration with a network of local officials put in place.

The 12th- and 13th-century growth in ducal resources coincided with Brittany's belated economic expansion as land was cleared for exploitation, notably by the Cistercians and Hospitalers, and new urban markets founded. Breton participation in trade (salt from the Guérande peninsula, wine from Burgundy, Caen stone) encouraged the growth of ports in French-speaking eastern Brittany. By the 14th and 15th centuries, towns along the northern and western coast were also engaged in the carrying trade south to Gascony and Portugal, north to Flanders, and across the Channel to southern England, especially Cornwall, where Breton and Cornish were mutually intelligible languages. Increasing quantities of Breton canvas and leather products were exported.

Trade significantly altered the linguistic balance between French and Breton, as French spread outward from major towns. In eastern Brittany, the linguistic frontier had greatly receded by the end of the Middle Ages. The Breton aristocracy had adopted French language and culture from the 11th century; with French and Latin as the languages of administration, Breton was a low-status tongue. It was used by the church for preaching; Breton literature survives from the 15th century onward and is mostly devotional.

When Jean II (r. 1286–1305) was created a peer of France in 1297 and his right to the ducal title finally recognized by the royal chancery, Brittany was opened to an even greater degree of French cultural influence and royal control. Military service was expected of the Breton duke, Breton cases were heard in the royal Parlement, royal ordinances were extended to Brittany, and, although the ducal right to strike coin was recognized by the crown, it was carefully monitored lest royal coinage be affected. Growing French control nevertheless provoked a reaction, and in the 14th century royal intervention was restricted. Ducal administrators developed notions of the duke's inalienable regalian rights and validated them by reference to the independent Breton kingdom believed to have existed in the early Middle Ages.

The balance of royal and ducal interests was shattered when Jean III died in 1341, leaving a disputed succession. For the rest of the Middle Ages, the problems of an uncertain succession were worked out against the backdrop of the Hundred Years' War. In the Arrêt de Conflans (1341), Philip VI ruled in favour of Jeanne de Penthièvre and her

RULERS OF BRITTANY OF THE HOUSE OF DREUX

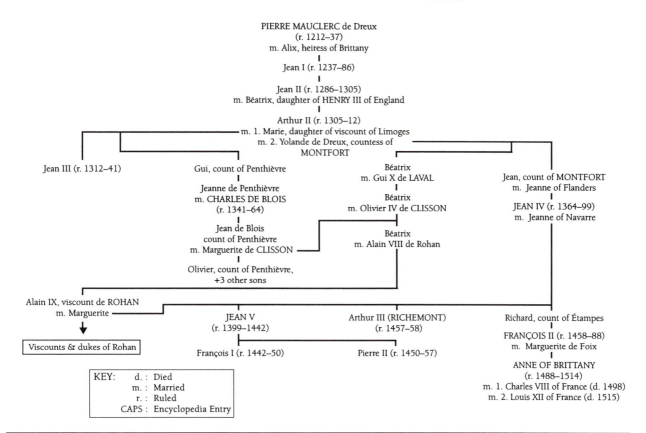

PIERRE MAUCLERC de Dreux
(r. 1212–37)
m. Alix, heiress of Brittany

Jean I (r. 1237–86)

Jean II (r. 1286–1305)
m. Béatrix, daughter of HENRY III of England

Arthur II (r. 1305–12)
m. 1. Marie, daughter of viscount of Limoges
m. 2. Yolande de Dreux, countess of MONTFORT

Jean III (r. 1312–41)

Gui, count of Penthièvre

Jeanne de Penthièvre
m. CHARLES DE BLOIS
(r. 1341–64)

Jean de Blois
count of Penthièvre
m. Marguerite de CLISSON

Olivier, count of Penthièvre,
+3 other sons

Béatrix
m. Gui X de LAVAL

Béatrix
m. Olivier IV de CLISSON

Béatrix
m. Alain VIII de Rohan

Jean, count of MONTFORT
m. Jeanne of Flanders

JEAN IV (r. 1364–99)
m. Jeanne of Navarre

Alain IX, viscount de ROHAN
m. Marguerite →
Viscounts & dukes of Rohan

JEAN V
(r. 1399–1442)

François I (r. 1442–50)

Arthur III (RICHEMONT)
(r. 1457–58)

Pierre II (r. 1450–57)

Richard, count of Étampes

FRANÇOIS II (r. 1458–88)
m. Marguerite de Foix

ANNE OF BRITTANY
(r. 1488–1514)
m. 1. Charles VIII of France (d. 1498)
m. 2. Louis XII of France (d. 1515)

KEY: d. : Died
m. : Married
r. : Ruled
CAPS : Encyclopedia Entry

husband, Philip's nephew Charles de Blois, in preference to the late duke's half-brother, Jean de Montfort. After Montfort's death in 1345, Edward III intervened as guardian of his son, the future Jean IV. The Breton civil war (1341–64) was a convenient theater for Anglo-French hostilities. The defeat and death of Charles de Blois (Auray, 1364) led Charles V to recognize the Montfort claim and left the duchy exhausted by ravaging, coastal pillaging, the collapse of central authority, and arbitrary exactions by both sides. Jean IV (r. 1364–99) had the delicate task of balancing the economic advantages of friendly relations with England with the need to keep on cordial terms with France. He and his son Jean V (r. 1399–1442) had to reassert ducal authority in the face of the Breton aristocracy, among whom the Penthièvre claim still had supporters and several of whom found employment in French service (Bertrand du Guesclin, Olivier de Clisson, and Arthur de Richemont among others). However, they were able to take advantage of the weakness of the French crown to create an effectively independent, well-administered duchy in which the duke's regalian prerogatives were stressed by fostering a sense of Breton national identity, adopting royal ceremonial, and refusing liege homage. Frequent meetings of the Breton Estates (an advisory, legislative, and until 1492 judicial body) furthered ducal sovereignty. The Breton church was similarly inde-

pendent: Breton clergy did not attend French ecclesiastical assemblies, and the Pragmatic Sanction of Bourges was not applicable in Brittany; the papacy negotiated directly with Brittany and appointed only Bretons to Breton benefices. The establishment of the University of Nantes in 1460 symbolized this independence.

Regalian claims culminated during the reign of the incompetent and untrustworthy Duke François II (r. 1458–88), who came into direct conflict with the revived royal power of Louis XI and Charles VIII. After participating in several of the princely revolts against Louis XI, the duke tried to create alliances with Maximilian of Austria and Edward IV of England, but in 1480 Louis XI bought out the Penthièvre claim to the duchy and attracted discontented Breton nobles into his service. When Charles VIII finally attacked Brittany in 1488, François II had an empty treasury and was left without effective support from either his allies or his subjects. Forced to conclude peace, he died shortly thereafter, leaving as heir his daughter Anne (r. 1488–1514), who continued the fighting until 1491. The treaties that accompanied her marriages first to Charles VIII (1491) and then to Louis XII (1499) stipulated terms for the incorporation of the Breton duchy into the kingdom of France.

When the Breton Estates voted for perpetual union with France in 1532, the judicial, fiscal, and ecclesiastical liberties of the duchy were safeguarded. The status of Brittany under the *ancien régime* was thus established; with its foundations in the Middle Ages, Brittany's cultural identity has long outlived the loss of political independence.

Julia M.H. Smith

[See also: ANNE OF BRITTANY; AURAY; CHARLES DE BLOIS; CLISSON; FRANÇOIS II; JEAN IV; JEAN V; NANTES; RENNES; RICHEMONT, ARTHUR DE]

Brunterch, Jean-Pierre. "Puissance temporelle et pouvoir diocésain des évêques de Nantes entre 936 et 1049." *Mémoires de la Société d'Histoire et d'Archéologie de la Bretagne* 61 (1984): 29–82.

Delumeau, Jean, ed. *Histoire de la Bretagne*. Toulouse: Privat, 1969.

Fleuriot, Léon, and Pierre-Roland Giot. "Early Brittany." *Antiquity* 51 (1977): 101–16.

Chédeville, André, and Hubert Guillotel. *La Bretagne des saints et des rois, Ve–Xe siècles*. Rennes: Ouest-France, 1984.

Chédeville, André, and Noël-Yves Tounerre. *La Bretagne féodale, XIe–XIIIe siècles*. Rennes: Ouest-France, 1987.

Davies, Wendy. *Small Worlds: The Village Community in Early Medieval Brittany*. London: Duckworth, 1988.

Galliou, Patrick, and Michael C. E. Jones. *The Bretons*. Oxford: Blackwell, 1991.

Jones, Michael. *Ducal Brittany 1364–1399: Relations with England and France During the Reign of Duke John IV*. Oxford: Oxford University Press, 1970.

———. *The Creation of Brittany: A Late Medieval State*. London: Hambledon, 1988.

Kerhervé, Jean. *L'état breton aux 14e et 15e siècles: les ducs, l'argent et les hommes*. 2 vols. Paris: Maloine, 1987.

La Borderie, Arthur de, and Barthélemy Pocquet. *Histoire de Bretagne*. 6 vols. Rennes: Plihon et Hervé, 1896–1914, Vol. 3 (1899).

Leguay, Jean-Pierre, and Hervé Martin. *Fastes et malheurs de la Bretagne ducale, 1213–1532*. Rennes: Ouest-France, 1982.

Le Patourel, John. "Henri II Plantagenêt et la Bretagne." *Mémoires de la Société d'Histoire et d'Archéologie de la Bretagne* 58 (1981); repr. in his *Feudal Empires Norman and Plantagenet*. London: Hambledon, 1984.

Lewis, Peter S. "Breton Estates." In *Essays in Later Medieval French History*. London: Hambledon, 1985, pp. 127–38.

Pocquet du Haut-Jussé, Barthélemy. "Le grand fief breton." In *Histoire des institutions françaises au moyen âge*, ed. Ferdinand Lot and Robert Fawtier. Paris: Presses Universitaires de France, 1957, Vol 1: *Institutions seigneuriales*, pp. 267–88.

Smith, Julia M. H. *Province and Empire: Brittany and the Carolingians*. Cambridge: Cambridge University Press, 1992.

BROU. The church of Brou (Ain), near Bourg-en-Bresse, was constructed by Marguerite of Austria in fulfillment of a vow made by her mother-in-law, Marguerite de Bourbon. The conventual buildings for the Augustinian com-

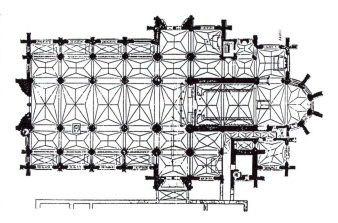

Bourg-en-Bresse (Ain), Church of Brou, plan. After Nodet.

munity were erected between 1506 and 1512, with the church following between 1513 and 1523. Loys van Boghem, the Flemish master mason, realized a design of spatial balance and clarity in the Latin-cross plan and two-story elevation that is divided by a balustraded walkway at mid-height.

The understatement of the architecture showcases the liturgical furniture, including the jubé and choirstalls; lavishly sculpted retables, such as the Seven Joys; the rich stained glass, whose program revolves around the Resurrection and particularly the aristocratic tombs of Marguerite de Bourbon, Duke Philibert le Beau of Savoy, and Marguerite of Austria. Designed in 1516 by Jean de Bruxelles, with the effigies cut 1526–31 by Conrad Meyt, the tombs rival those of the dukes of Burgundy in splendor. The tombs of Philibert and Marguerite of Austria are unusual in their inclusion of two *gisant* figures, the corpse in a burial shroud below and the deceased lying in state in ceremonial costume above.

Michael T. Davis

Frankl, Paul. *Gothic Architecture*. Harmondsworth: Penguin, 1962.

Nodet, Victor. *L'église de Brou*. Paris: Laurens, 1928.

Sanfacon, Roland. *L'architecture flamboyante en France*. Laval: Presses de Université de Laval, 1971.

Vitry, Paul. "L'église de Brou." *Congrès archéologique (Lyon et Mâcon)* 98 (1935): 261–65.

BRUGES. The Flemish commercial city of Bruges was the chief port of northern Europe in the 14th and 15th centuries. By the second half of the 9th century, it was the administrative center of the *pagus Flandrensis*, the nucleus from which the counts extended their power. The counts had a fortification there by 892. Its name means "bridge" or "harbor," although Bruges is not known to have had commercial significance before the 11th century. By the 12th century, it had an active trade with England and at the fairs of Champagne. The rise of the sea level gave Bruges easy access to overseas trade. As the waters receded, Bruges founded Damme and Sluis as outports where merchandise would be discharged for eventual consignment in the halls of Bruges and undertook continual dredging operations against the silting of the Zwin River, which linked the city with the sea.

Bruges led the Flemings in rebellion against the incursions of Philip IV of France into Flanders in 1302 and became involved in the revolt of maritime Flanders between 1323 and 1328 as a result of the count of Flanders's attempt to limit the city's monopolies at Sluis. After this rebellion failed, Bruges generally supported the Flemish counts unless pressure was applied from Ghent, joining only reluctantly in the effort to suppress the cloth industries of the smaller communities. Particularly during the Flemish rebellion of the 1380s, Bruges favored the count except when garrisons of Ghent were in the city.

Bruges was the wealthiest Flemish city, although it was smaller than Ghent, reaching a maximum population of around 35,000 in 1340 and declining thereafter in the wake of plague and civil conflict. The development by the Italians of vessels that could make voyages from the Mediterranean to the North Sea ports made Bruges the "marketplace of the medieval world." During the 14th century, various Italian groups, together with the Castilians, the merchants of the German Hanse, and the English, had resident colonies at Bruges. Virtually all the seaborne trade of Flanders went through the city. Although Bruges had a substantial textile industry, commercial wealth and its small-volume luxury industry were more important, and its occupational structure was thus more diversified than those of Ypres and Ghent, its neighbors and frequent rivals.

Bruges reached the height of its commercial prosperity and political importance in the 15th century. The Burgundian counts spent most of their time there and at Brussels. Under the patronage of their court, music and the plastic arts flourished at Bruges. In the 15th century, Bruges was the center of Flemish painting, boasting such masters as Jan van Eyck (ca. 1380–1441), Petrus Christus (d. ca. 1473), Hans Memling (ca. 1430–1494), Hugo van der Goes (ca. 1440–1482), and Gérard David (ca. 1460–1523). But the continued silting of the Zwin, the advantages of Antwerp, the Flemish wars after 1477, and piracy all contributed to the rapid decline of Bruges, and after 1500 its only economic role was as a regional market for west Flanders. It continued, however, to exercise considerable political power as one of the four "members" of Flanders, along with its castellany, the "Franc" of Bruges.

The 13th-century bell tower of Bruges is, at 268 feet, the tallest in Belgium. The basilica of the Holy Blood (Saint-Sang) was begun ca. 1150 to house a vial of Christ's blood brought back from the Crusades by Thierry d'Alsace, count of Flanders. Its lower chapel retains its Romanesque character, but most of the basilica was rebuilt in the later Middle Ages in Flamboyant style. The nearby Hôtel de Ville (1376–1420) is an excellent example of secular Gothic architecture. Its six tall windows and three turrets give its façade a strong sense of verticality. The Bruges béguinage was founded in 1245 by Marguerite de Constantinople, countess of Flanders, but its buildings are largely postmedieval. Other medieval buildings in Bruges include the church of Notre-Dame (largely 13th c.), which houses the tombs of Charles the Bold (d. 1477) and his daughter, Marie de Bourgogne; the church of Saint-Sauveur, founded in the 10th century; and the Gothic lockhouse of the former inner harbor (Minnewater).

David M. Nicholas

[See also: BÉGUINES; BURGUNDY; FLANDERS; GHENT; VAN EYCK, JAN; YPRES]

de Roover, Raymond. *Money, Banking and Credit in Mediaeval Bruges.* Cambridge: Mediaeval Academy of America, 1948.

Gilliodts-van Severen, Louis. *Inventaire des archives de la ville de Bruges. Section première: inventaire des chartes.* 7 vols. Bruges: Gaillard, 1871–78.

Häpke, R. *Brügges Entwicklung zum mittelalterlichen Weltmarkt.* Berlin: Curtius, 1908.

Prevenier, Walter, and Willem Blockmans. *The Burgundian Netherlands.* Cambridge: Cambridge University Press, 1985.

van Houtte, Jan A. *Bruges: essai d'histoire urbaine.* Brussels: Renaissance du Livre, 1966.

BRUN DE LA MONTAGNE. An incomplete 14th-century verse romance preserved in a single manuscript (B.N. fr. 2170), *Brun de la Montagne* recounts in ca. 4,000 lines the adventures of Brun, whose destiny is foretold at his birth by three fairies. The first predicts his beauty; the second, his prowess. The third announces that he will be irremediably hapless in love (and, indeed, he is called "Tristan" for this reason). Much of the story of Brun, before it breaks off, is occupied by lengthy accounts of adventures and combat. The text offers a number of Arthurian echoes in addition to the Tristan agnomen, but it is fundamentally a non-Arthurian composition.

Norris J. Lacy

Meyer, Paul, ed. *Brun de la Montagne.* Paris: Didot, 1875.

BRUNETTO LATINI (ca. 1220–1294). Brunetto Latini was active in Florentine public life as a *notario*, or lawyer, by 1254. In 1260, he was sent as ambassador by the Florentine commune to King Alfonso X the Wise of Castile, with the aim of enlisting this Guelf monarch in the struggle against Manfred and the Ghibellines. According to his *Tesoretto* (ll. 123–62), Brunetto was returning from this embassy when he met a student from Bologna in the Pass of Roncevaux who told him of the Guelf defeat at Montaperti (September 4, 1260). Brunetto then spent six years of exile in France until the defeat and death of Manfred at Benevento (February 28, 1266). On returning to Florence, he held a series of important public offices and was frequently consulted by the Florentine government. While in France, Brunetto had written his *Rettorica*, a translation of and commentary on the first seventeen chapters of Cicero's *De inventione*. He later continued this effort at public education by translating a number of Ciceronian orations into Italian and composing his *Sommetta*, a collection of letters for teaching *ars dictaminis*. Brunetto died in 1294 and was buried at Santa Maria Maggiore, Florence.

During his years of exile in France, Brunetto visited friars at Montpellier (according to *Tesoretto*, ll. 2,539–45) and wrote notarial letters at Paris (September 1263) and Bar-sur-Aube (April 1264) that are probably to be associated with the commercial fairs that drew many Italians on business. He may have lived in Paris, but it seems more likely he lived among Italian notaries and moneylenders in Arras: his encyclopaedic *Tresor* was composed and dictated in the Picard dialect of this region. Brunetto's two most important and influential works were written in France. The Italian *Tesoretto*, a dream poem indebted to the first part of the *Roman de la Rose*, ends incomplete after 2,944 lines. The didactic ambitions of this work, which are cramped by its seven-syllable couplets, are satisfied by the *Livres dou tresor*, an encyclopedic compilation in French prose. In a celebrated passage in the first chapter, Brunetto explains his choice of the vernacular, appealing to his present circumstances and the widespread popularity of French: *Et se aucuns demandoit pour quoi cis livres est escris en roumanç, selonc le raison de France, puis ke nous somes italien, je diroie que c'est pour .ii. raisons, l'une ke nous somes en France, l'autre por çou que la parleure est plus delitable et plus commune a tous langages* (1.1.7). ("And if anyone should ask why this book is written in Romance according to the usage of the French, even though we are Italian, I would say that there are two reasons: one, that we are in France, the other, that French is more pleasant and has more in common with all other languages.")

Although the *Tresor* is written in French, Brunetto explains that it is designed to assist those wishing to serve an Italian commune rather than a French king (3.73.5–6). Its three books observe a distinction between theoretical (Book 1) and practical (Books 2 and 3) philosophy that derives from Eustratius's Greek commentary on the *Nichomachean Ethics*. Their contents (with major sources in parentheses) are as follows: Book 1, theology (Isidore of Seville), universal history (Bible, Isidore of Seville, Paulus Orosius, Peter Comestor, Geoffrey of Viterbo, Honorius of Autun), physics (Gossoiun, *Image du monde*; *Roman de Sidrac*); geography (Solinus); agriculture and house building (Palladius); natural history (Solinus; *Physiologus*; Ambrose; Isidore; *De bestiis*); Book 2, ethics and economics (Herman the German's *Compendium Alexandrinum*; Isidore; French translation of William of Conches, *Moralium dogma philosophorum*; Martin of Braga, *De quattuor virtutibus*; Albertano of Brescia, *Ars loquendi et tacendi*; Peraldus, *Summa aurea de virtutibus*); Book 3, rhetoric (Cicero, *De inventione*; Boethius, *De rhetoricae cognitione*; *Li fet des Romains*), politics (*Oculus pastoralis*; John of Viterbo, *De regimine civitatum*; official documents of the Commune of Siena).

Brunetto's *compilatio* surpasses its models in its simplicity and in its choice of important passages. The *Tresor* was extremely popular and survives in seventy-three manuscripts. An Italian translation called the *Tesoro*, once attributed to Bono Giamboni but now regarded as Brunetto's own work, survives in forty-four manuscripts, and there are versions in Latin, Provençal, Castilian, Catalan, and Aragonese.

The *Tresor*'s first critics were its scribes, who were often moved to amend its style and doctrine; some families of manuscripts contain extensive interpolations. Several *Tresor* manuscripts reached England: Thomas of Woodstock, duke of Gloucester (murdered 1397), owned a copy, and John Gower used the *Tresor*'s discussion of rhetoric in his *Confessio Amantis*. The poet Alain Chartier, the chronicler Aimery du Peyrat, and the compilers of the *Leys d'amors* all made good use of the *Tresor*. But its most famous reader was Dante Alighieri, who acknowledges Brunetto in *Inferno* 15 as one who taught him *come l'uom s'etterna* ("how man makes himself eternal," l. 85); Brunetto speaks of his *Tesoro* as the work *nel qual io vivo ancora* ("in which I still live," l. 120).

David J. Wallace

[See also: *IMAGE DU MONDE*; *SIDRAC, ROMAN DE*]

Brunetto Latini. *Li livres dou tresor de Brunetto Latini*, ed. Francis J. Carmody. Berkeley: University of California Press, 1947.

———. *The Book of the Treasure* (*Li livres dou tresor*), trans. Paul Barrette and Spurgeon Baldwin. New York: Garland, 1993.

———. *Il tesoretto*, ed. and trans. Julia Bolton Holloway. New York: Garland, 1981.

Holloway, Julia Bolton. *Brunetto Latini: An Analytic Bibliography*. Wolfeboro: Grant and Cutler, 1986.

BRUNHILDE (ca. 545/50–613). A daughter of the Visigothic king Athanagild, Brunhilde became the wife of the Merovingian king Sigibert I of Metz. After her husband's death in 575, she continued to play a leading role in Frankish royal affairs as the wife of Merovech, the son of Sigibert's brother Chilperic I by his first wife, Audovera, and therefore her own nephew, and as regent for her son Childebert II of Austrasia (r. 575–95) and Burgundy (r. ca. 590–95), her grandsons Theudebert II of Austrasia (r. 596–612) and Theuderic II of Burgundy (r. 596–613), and her great-grandson Sigibert of Burgundy (r. 613). During her reign, she was in correspondence with Pope Gregory I and clashed with the Irish monk Columban, whom she banished from Burgundy in 612.

After repudiating Audovera, Chilperic I married Brunhilde's sister Galswintha but then murdered her, perhaps at the instigation of a third consort, Fredegunde, which set off a feud matching Chilperic and Fredegunde on the one hand and Sigibert and Brunhilde on the other. This feud lasted for three generations and led to the assassinations of both Chilperic and Sigibert. Brunhilde's domination of her grandson Theudebert II and her attempt to romanize the royal administration led the Austrasian aristocrats, especially Arnulf of Metz and Pepin I of Landen, to expel her. She moved to Burgundy, where she held a commanding position over Theuderic II. In 612, she temporarily reunified Burgundy and Austrasia, but again the Austrasians refused to accept her and called in Clotar II of Neustria, the son of Chilperic and Fredegunde, who took over Burgundy as well. Clotar had Brunhilde killed by being dragged to death by a wild horse to which she had been tied.

Steven Fanning

[See also: FREDEGUNDE; GREGORY OF TOURS; MEROVINGIAN DYNASTY]

Gregory of Tours. *Liber historiae Francorum*, trans. Bernard S. Bachrach. Lawrence: Coronado, 1973.
———. *History of the Franks*, trans. Lewis Thorpe. Harmondsworth: Penguin, 1974.
James, Edward. *The Franks*. Oxford: Blackwell, 1988.
Nelson, Janet L. "Queens as Jezebels: The Careers of Brunhild and Balthild in Merovingian History." In *Medieval Women*, ed. Derek Baker. Oxford: Blackwell, 1978, pp. 31–77.
Wood, Ian. *The Merovingian Kingdoms, 450–751*. London: Longman, 1994.

BRUNO (ca. 1030–1101). Founder of the Carthusian order. Originally from Cologne, Bruno served as canon, schoolmaster, and eventually chancellor at the cathedral of Reims; he may even have been offered the archiepiscopal office ca. 1081. Fleeing the city for a life in the "desert," he settled as a hermit at Sèche-Fontaine, attached to the monastery of Molesme; but he did not find the isolation he sought there and finally established a hermitage on a nearly inaccessible massif at La Grande Chartreuse, in the Alps, in 1084. Bruno believed that hermits needed a rule, decrying those who practiced what he considered an anarchical life, and that isolation and autonomy were necessary to keep away the influence of the secular world. After a few years, Pope Urban II summoned Bruno from La Grande Chartreuse to the papal curia; the pope then tried to name him bishop of Reggio. Instead, Bruno retired to a hermitage in Calabria, where he died in 1101.

Constance B. Bouchard

[See also: CARTHUSIAN ORDER; MONASTICISM]

Wigo. *Chronique des premiers chartreux*, ed. André Wilmart. *Revue Mabillon* 16 (1926): 77–142.
Bligny, Bernard, ed. *Recueil des plus anciens actes de la Grande-Chartreuse (1086–1196)*. Grenoble: The Author, 1958.
———. *Saint Bruno: le premier chartreux*. Rennes: Ouest-France, 1984.
———, and Gerald Chaix, eds. *La naissance des Chartreuses: Actes du VIe Colloque International d'Histoire et de Spiritualité Cartusiennes*. Grenoble: n.p., 1984.

BUEIL. The lords of Bueil in Touraine played an important role as military commanders in late-medieval France. Jean III (1346–91) commanded important contingents of royal troops over a twenty-year period beginning in 1368 and served as a royal seneschal in Languedoc between 1374 and 1382. His brother, Pierre, was bailiff of Touraine for nineteen years and was a partisan of Louis I of Anjou and then Louis of Orléans in the rivalries among royal princes. Jean IV, also a supporter of Orléans, rose to the position of

master of crossbowmen in the 1390s but met his death at Agincourt in 1415. His brother Hardouin, bishop of Angers, became guardian of his young son. Jean V (ca. 1406–1477) fought in the Battle of Verneuil (1424), served under La Hire and Jeanne d'Arc, and participated in most of the remaining campaigns of the Hundred Years' War. Although he joined the princely rebellion of 1440 (the *Praguerie*), he became reconciled with Charles VII, who named him admiral of France in 1450. In 1461, however, the new king, Louis XI, relieved him of this office when he ousted most of his father's leading officers.

In his subsequent retirement, Jean V composed his famous *Le Jouvencel* (ca. 1466)—part autobiographical reflection, part art of warfare, all couched as a *roman à clef*. Much is borrowed from Christine de Pizan's *Livre des fais d'armes* and other sources, but there are many personal insights into 15th-century life and warfare. *Le Jouvencel* faithfully describes in prose the ideal warrior as he was conceived during the reigns of Charles VII and Louis XI. It was popular, with at least thirteen manuscripts preserved, as well as five printed editions between 1493 and 1529.

John Bell Henneman, Jr./William W. Kibler

[See also: HUNDRED YEARS' WAR]

Jean de Bueil. *Le Jouvencel par Jean de Bueil, suivi du commentaire de Guillaume Tringant*, ed. Camille Favre and Léon Lecestre. 2 vols. Paris: Renouard, 1887–89.
Contamine, Philippe. *Guerre, état et société à la fin du moyen âge: études sur les armées des rois de France 1337–1494*. Paris: Mouton, 1972.
Coopland, George William. "*Le Jouvencel* (Re-Visited)." *Symposium* 5 (1951): 137–86.
Jauernick, Stéfanie. *Studien zu Jean de Bueil "Le Jouvencel": Untersuchungen zum französischen Prosaroman der zweiten Hälfte des 15. Jahrhunderts*. Wiesbaden: Steiner, 1975.

BURGUNDIAN CHRONICLERS. The dukes of Burgundy, Philip the Bold (1342–1404), John the Fearless (1371–1419), Philip the Good (1396–1467), and Charles the Bold (1433–1477), all exhibited great interest in history not only by collecting historical writings but also by appointing official court chroniclers and serving as patrons to writers who wrote historical accounts. These numerous writers approached their task with differing degrees of objectivity. Some were admitted propagandists, while others set out to alter the truth while appearing serious and competent. Some were excellent writers, while others became bogged down in artificial rhetoric. As a group, they left an invaluable record of the Burgundian court, which has given this time and place prestige, importance, and influence; and the style and comprehensiveness of their writings have influenced subsequent chroniclers and historians.

Froissart traced the beginnings of the power of the house of Burgundy, and the future chroniclers of Burgundy imitated and claimed to continue his work. The first was Enguerrand de Monstrelet, a native of Picardy, whose accounts cover the years 1400–44. Although present at the meeting between Philip the Good and Jeanne d'Arc, he did not record any of the conversation, claiming a lapse of memory. Matthieu d'Escouchy, from Hainaut, continued the narrative to 1461. Slightly livelier and less partisan, he describes spectacular feasts and celebrations, including the famous Pheasant Banquet (1454).

The most renowned of these chroniclers, Georges Chastellain received his appointment as official historiographer of the Burgundian court from Philip the Good in 1455. In the prologue to his chronicle, Chastellain defined for himself the role of historian, aiming for impartiality and objectivity. Sincere, independent, and truthful, he nevertheless tried to dwell on the strong points of the reigning family while minimizing the weak ones. He documented his accounts thoroughly from contemporary works and from personal contact with those who were making history. His narrative begins with the murder of John the Fearless at Montereau in 1419 and ends, uncompleted, in 1474. Chastellain's official successor was Jean Molinet (1433–1507), who assumed the title of official historiographer in 1475, having worked with Chastellain for many years. In his chronicle, which covers the years 1474–1506, he also attempts objectivity but obviously favors his patron.

Although Olivier de La Marche (1425–1502), friend and colleague of Georges Chastellain, was never appointed official historiographer, his memoirs cover the years 1435–88. He witnessed both the grandeur and dismemberment of the empire acquired by the dukes. He organized many entertainments at court, including the Pheasant Banquet. He was particularly talented at describing feasts, tournaments, customs, and clothing.

Among the other chroniclers of the house of Burgundy are Edmundus de Dynter, Le Fèvre de Saint-Remy, Jacques du Clercq, Jean de Wavrin, Jean de Haynin, Hugues de Tolins, and Philippe Wielant.

Deborah H. Nelson

[See also: CHASTELLAIN, GEORGES; DU CLERQ, JACQUES; FROISSART, JEAN; HISTORIOGRAPHY; LA MARCHE, OLIVIER DE; MOLINET, JEAN; VOW CYCLE]

Doutrepont, Georges. *La littérature française à la cour des ducs de Bourgogne.* Paris: Champion, 1909.

BURGUNDY. The region that medievalists today generally call Burgundy is the duchy of Burgundy: the area located between the Saône and the Loire, stretching from a little south of Sens and Troyes to north of Lyon. The duchy's major cities were Dijon and Autun; its bishoprics were Autun, Auxerre, Chalon-sur-Saône, Langres, Mâcon, and Nevers. (Dijon became a bishopric only in the early 18th century.) Located halfway between Paris and the Mediterranean, the duchy of Burgundy is often considered the cultural and religious heart of France.

Burgundy is a watershed where waters divide for the Atlantic (via the Loire), the English Channel (via the Seine), and the Mediterranean (via the Rhône). In the center of the duchy rises the Morvan, a wild area, even today, of granite mountains. On the eastern edge, the floodplain of the Saône has worn away the limestone deposited over the granite, making an abrupt drop, the Côte. Here, the good drainage and the morning sun falling on the grapes have produced superb wines, which have been traded throughout Europe since Roman times. In the economic expansion of the high Middle Ages, Burgundy became especially noted as a wine-growing region. Because the rivers of northern Burgundy drain into the Seine, it was easy for growers to load their barrels on barges and float them downstream to the profitable markets at Paris. A chronicler of the late 13th century commented that in the region around Auxerre no one grew grain, only grapes.

Burgundia was also used in the Middle Ages to describe regions other than the duchy of Burgundy. The name derives from the Burgundians, one of the Germanic tribes that settled in the Roman Empire in the 5th century, who established a kingdom that lasted close to a century; centered at Geneva, it stretched down the Rhône to Lyon and south toward Arles, and north from Lyon along the Saône Valley as far as Dijon. The sons of Clovis conquered Burgundy in the 530s, and, with Neustria and Austrasia, it became one of the three principal divisions of Frankish territory. Frankish Burgundy was a large area, comprising most of the Loire and Rhône-Saône river basins, stretching from Orléans, the capital, to Arles and the Mediterranean. It was divided by the sons of Louis the Pious at the 843 Treaty of Verdun. Charles the Bald received as one part of his share essentially what became the duchy of Burgundy, the region between the Saône and the Loire. The rest of Burgundy was subject to Lothair I and the empire: the area south along the Rhône from Lyon to Arles, and also the region around Geneva and Besançon, where the original Burgundian kingdom had been established five centuries earlier. Imperial Burgundy was further divided in the late Carolingian period into upper, or trans-Saône, Burgundy, the northeast portion, and the southern part, called variously lower, or cis-Jurane, Burgundy or Provence.

Lower Burgundy, which had become subject to Charles the Bald when he took the imperial throne in 875, became an independent kingdom in 879 under Boso (r. 879–87), Charles's brother-in-law and the first non-Carolingian king in the west for a century. At the same time, Boso's brother, Richard le Justicier, was establishing ducal power in French Burgundy, the region taken by Charles the Bald in 843. This duchy was ill defined in the late 9th and 10th centuries, but by the time of Richard's death in 922 his rule had been established in the area which was considered the duchy of Burgundy throughout the high Middle Ages, plus the regions of Troyes and Sens.

Boso's nine years as king of lower Burgundy were marked by constant wars with the Carolingians, French dukes, and even his brother, Richard. But in 890, three years after Boso's death, his son Louis succeeded to his father's kingdom. In 900, Louis also became king of Italy, and in 901 he was crowned emperor. Louis's success was short-lived. In 905, he was captured and blinded by Berengar, his principal Italian rival. Louis l'Aveugle retreated to his capital of Vienne, where he lived until 928,

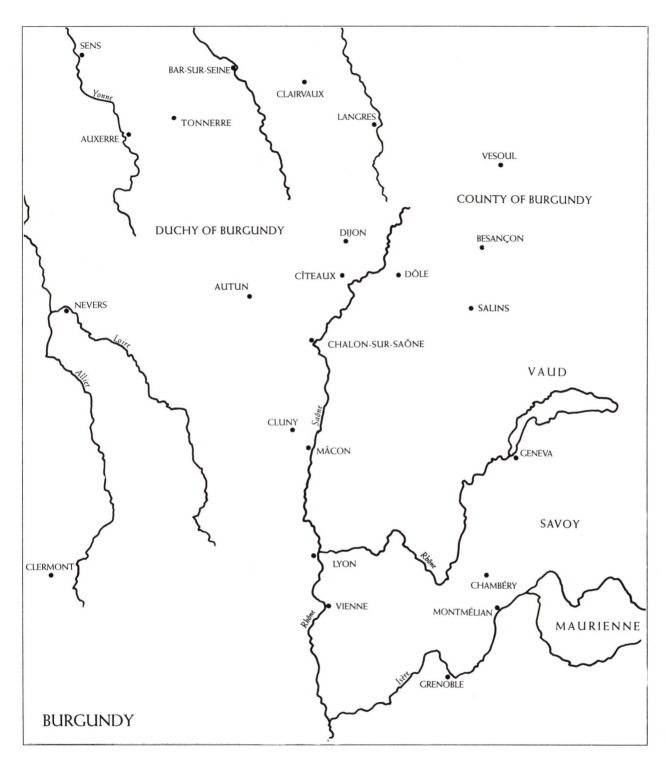

BURGUNDY

but the kingdom of lower Burgundy was never again an independent entity.

In the meantime, upper or trans-Saône Burgundy had also become an independent kingdom in 888, under Rudolph I, of the Welf family. The Rudolphian kings took over lower Burgundy as well after the death of Louis l'Aveugle in 928. Their kingdom continued to be independent until 1032, when Rudolph III died without sons, and the whole region, from his capital at Besançon to Lyon and to Arles, was reabsorbed into the empire.

The French duchy of Burgundy was ruled, after the death of Richard le Justicier, by his son Hugues le Noir and nephew Giselbert. Hugues le Grand, father of Hugh Capet, also exercised authority in Burgundy. After Giselbert's death

CAPETIAN DUKES OF BURGUNDY

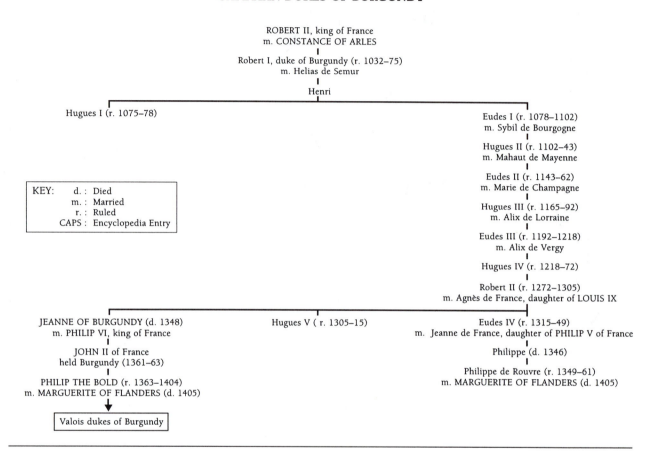

ROBERT II, king of France
m. CONSTANCE OF ARLES

Robert I, duke of Burgundy (r. 1032–75)
m. Helias de Semur

Henri

Hugues I (r. 1075–78)

Eudes I (r. 1078–1102)
m. Sybil de Bourgogne

Hugues II (r. 1102–43)
m. Mahaut de Mayenne

Eudes II (r. 1143–62)
m. Marie de Champagne

KEY: d. : Died
m. : Married
r. : Ruled
CAPS : Encyclopedia Entry

Hugues III (r. 1165–92)
m. Alix de Lorraine

Eudes III (r. 1192–1218)
m. Alix de Vergy

Hugues IV (r. 1218–72)

Robert II (r. 1272–1305)
m. Agnès de France, daughter of LOUIS IX

JEANNE OF BURGUNDY (d. 1348)
m. PHILIP VI, king of France

Hugues V (r. 1305–15)

Eudes IV (r. 1315–49)
m. Jeanne de France, daughter of PHILIP V of France

JOHN II of France
held Burgundy (1361–63)

Philippe (d. 1346)

PHILIP THE BOLD (r. 1363–1404)
m. MARGUERITE OF FLANDERS (d. 1405)

Philippe de Rouvre (r. 1349–61)
m. MARGUERITE OF FLANDERS (d. 1405)

Valois dukes of Burgundy

in 956, the duchy was taken by Hugh Capet's brother Otto, who married Giselbert's daughter, and, after Otto's death, by Henri, another brother of Hugh Capet. The Capetian dukes continued to rule Burgundy until the mid-14th century. When Henri died in 1002, however, there was initially a war between his nephew, King Robert II, and his stepson, Otto-William. Otto-William had become count of Mâcon by marriage and called himself count of Burgundy as well, but he was unable to defeat the king's forces. He settled for Mâcon and the territory east of the Saône that he was able to control under the authority of the Rudolphian kings; his descendants greatly increased their authority in this region after 1032. King Robert II made his son Robert duke in Burgundy during his own lifetime.

Once established under its own dukes, the French duchy of Burgundy was able to maintain its political identity in the 11th, 12th, and 13th centuries. Besides the dukes, the most powerful figures were the counts of Chalon, of Mâcon, and of Auxerre, Nevers, and Tonnerre. The last three counties were usually in the hands of one person in this period, although Tonnerre had been an independent county until the middle of the 11th century; younger brothers of the counts of Nevers took the other two counties for their lifetimes, but they then reverted to the main line of the family.

The dynasty of the Capetian dukes of Burgundy ended in 1361, and the duchy was taken by the crown. In 1363, it became an apanage of Philip the Bold, son of the Valois king John the Good. Burgundy reached the height of its glory under the Valois dukes. Under Philip the Bold (r. 1363–1404), the duchy grew by the addition of the county of Nevers, which had once been attached to the duchy but had become separated in the 13th century, and by the Franche-Comté of Burgundy and the counties of Flanders and Artois. All these territories were part of the inheritance of Philip's wife, and he succeeded in 1384, when his father-in-law died. The Franche-Comté was essentially the western part of what had once been the Rudolphian kingdom of Burgundy. Succeeding dukes, John (r. 1404–19), Philip the Good (r. 1419–67), and Charles the Bold (r. 1467–77), made Burgundy the capital of a powerful principality that stretched across northeastern France. It included, as well as the duchy and the county of Burgundy, much of Lorraine, Luxembourg, Hainaut and Brabant, and Flanders. The dukes of Burgundy supported the English during the Hundred Years' War.

The Valois dukes of Burgundy were important patrons of music, supporting trumpeters and minstrels as well as the singers and composers of the chapel. During much of the 15th century, the musical institutions of the court of Burgundy were the richest in Europe, surpassing those of war-torn France. Numerous composers were employed at Burgundy, including Binchois, the Englishman Robert Morton, Dufay (an honorary appointment), Hayne van Ghizeghem, and Busnoys. The last Burgundian duke, Charles the Bold (r. 1467–77) was himself a harpist and composed chansons.

When Charles the Bold died without sons in 1477, the entire principality of Burgundy was claimed by Maximilian, the imperial heir, who married Charles's daughter Marie. However, prolonged wars between Maximilian and France led to a division of the principality, including a reseparation of the duchy of Burgundy, which remained under the authority of the French king, from the Franche-Comté, which remained in the empire.

While Burgundy was politically one of the most important parts of France during the Middle Ages, it was even more significant as a religious center. At the beginning of the Middle Ages, some of the earliest and most influential monasteries, such as Saint-Maurice-d'Agaune or Saint-Germain-d'Auxerre, were located in the Merovingian kingdom of Burgundy. The Cluniac and Cistercian monastic orders, two of the most influential of the high Middle Ages, were both founded in Burgundy; Cluny was founded not far from Mâcon in 909, and Cîteaux was founded a short distance south of Dijon, in the diocese of Chalon, in 1098. Molesme, the house from which Cîteaux's first monks had come, was also Burgundian, having been founded in the diocese of Langres in 1075. The most important of Cluny's priories and of Cîteaux's daughter houses, including her "four eldest daughters," La Ferté, Pontigny, Clairvaux, and Morimond, were all located in Burgundy. The reform of the religious life had probably the greatest impact in Burgundy of any region of France; by the end of the 12th century, there were essentially no colleges of secular canons left in the duchy, other than the cathedral chapters; the rest had all been reformed as monasteries or houses of canons regular. Dukes and counts from the 10th century on, castellans beginning in the 11th century, and knights in the 12th century were all generous donors to Burgundian monks and canons.

Burgundian churches were also influential architecturally, especially in the 12th century. Abbey churches like Vézelay, La Charité, and Cluny (the last of which was destroyed under Napoléon, although a few portions remain), all built in the first decades of the 12th century, represent the fullest development of the Romanesque style. The sculpture that decorated these and other churches, such as the 12th-century cathedral of Autun, is marked by elongated figures, full, detailed drapery, and an impression of dignity. The first Gothic cathedral is normally considered to be that of Sens, built on the northern edge of Burgundy in the middle of the 12th century.

Constance B. Bouchard

[See also: AUTUN; BINCHOIS, GILLES; BRUGES; BUSNOYS, ANTOINE; CHARLES THE BOLD; CISTERCIAN ORDER; CLUNIAC ORDER; CORDIER, BAUDE; DIJON; DUFAY, GUILLAUME; FRANCHE-COMTÉ; HAYNE VAN GHIZEGHEM; PHILIP THE BOLD; PHILIP THE GOOD; VÉZELAY; WINE TRADE]

Bligny, Bernard. "Le royaume de Bourgogne." In *Karl der Grosse, Lebenswerk und Nachleben*, ed. Wolfgang Braunfels. 4 vols. Düsseldorf: Schwann, 1965, Vol. 1, pp. 247–68.

Bouchard, Constance B. "The Bosonids: Or Rising to Power in the Late Carolingian Age." *French Historical Studies* 15 (1988): 407–31.

———. *Sword, Miter, and Cloister: Nobility and the Church in Burgundy, 980–1198*. Ithaca: Cornell University Press, 1987.

Chaume, Maurice. *Les origines du duché de Bourgogne*. 4 vols. Dijon: Jobard, 1925–31.

Duby, Georges. *La société aux XIe et XIIe siècles dans la région mâconnaise*. 2nd ed. Paris: SEVPEN, 1971.

Jarr, Eugène. *Formation territoriale de la Bourgogne*. Paris: Poisson, 1948.

Marix, Jeanne. *Histoire de la musique et des musiciens de la cour de Bourgogne sous le règne de Philippe le Bon (1420–1467)*. Strasbourg: Heitz, 1939.

Petit, Ernest. *Histoire des ducs de Bourgogne de la race capétienne*. 6 vols. Paris and Dijon: Le Chevalier et Darantière, 1885–98.

Poupardin, René. *Le royaume de Bourgogne (888–1038)*. Paris: Champion, 1907.

Richard, Jean. *Les ducs de Bourgogne et la formation du duché du XIe au XIVe siècle*. Paris: Société des Belles Lettres, 1954.

Vaughan, Richard. *Valois Burgundy*. London: Archon, 1975.

Wright, Craig. *Music at the Court of Burgundy 1364–1419: A Documentary History*. Henryville, Ottawa, and Binningen: Institute of Mediaeval Music, 1979.

BUSNOYS, ANTOINE (Busnois; ca. 1430–1492). French composer in the service of the Burgundian court. His works, of which three-voice chansons are most numerous, typify the Franco-Burgundian style in the third quarter of the 15th century.

Busnoys's name indicates that he or his family came from Busne (Pas-de-Calais), a town in northeastern France. Nothing is known of his early life and education, but in 1461 he was recorded as a chaplain at Saint-Gatien in Tours, at which time he was involved in an attack on a priest and was excommunicated. He did not remain in disgrace for long, since he soon became a singer and minor cleric at the royal abbey of Saint-Martin in Tours and in April 1465 was promoted from the position of choir clerk to subdeacon there. At Tours, he was a colleague and perhaps a student of the famous composer Johannes Ockeghem, master of the French royal chapel and treasurer of the abbey of Saint-Martin. In September 1465, Busnoys sought and received the post of master of the choirboys at Saint-Hilaire-le-Grand, Poitiers, which he held until July 1466.

In his motet *In hydraulis*, which pays homage to Ockeghem, Busnoys describes himself as "unworthy musician of the illustrious count of Charolais," referring to Charles the Bold, son of Philip the Good, duke in June 1467. Busnoys was listed as a singer in Charles's private service in March 1467, and he continued in that position

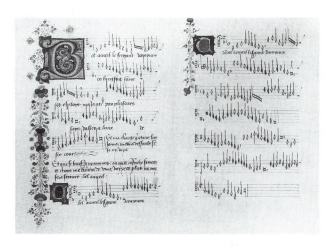

Busnoys's rondeau *Bel Acueil* ("Fair Welcome"), the Mellon Chansonnier. MS 91, fols. 1v–2. *Courtesy of Beinecke Library for Rare Books and Manuscripts, Yale University, New Haven, Connecticut.*

when Charles succeeded his father as duke in June 1467. Busnoys was officially admitted to the ducal chapel in 1471 and, with other members of the chapel, followed Charles on most of his military campaigns, but probably not the last, the disastrous battle at Nancy in 1477, at which Charles was killed.

After Charles's death, Busnoys served his daughter, Marie de Bourgogne, and her consort, Maximilian of Austria, whom she married in 1478. He remained a member of the Habsburg-Burgundian chapel in the Netherlands until it was temporarily disbanded in 1483 after Marie's death. He is listed in court documents of that time as a "priest-chaplain."

Busnoys's subsequent activities are uncertain, but they may have included a visit to Italy, since some works with Italian texts are attributed to him and his music was widely disseminated there. At the time of his death in 1492, he was choirmaster at Saint-Sauveur in Bruges.

Busnoys's reputation as a composer during his later years and after his death was exceeded among his contemporaries only by that of Ockeghem. The theorist Johannes Tinctoris dedicated his treatise on the modes (1476) jointly to Ockeghem and Busnoys, and as late as 1529 Pietro Aron called him "a great man and an excellent musician."

Busnoys was also an outstanding poet. A friend of Jean Molinet, with whom he exchanged poems, he undoubtedly wrote many of the texts he set to music, in the tradition of such earlier poet-musicians as Adam de la Halle and Guillaume de Machaut. His works include two Masses for four voices (*L'homme armé*, *O crux lignum*), a Credo, a Magnificat, eight motets (mostly four-voice), two hymns, and some seventy-five secular pieces, almost all French rondeaux and virelais. His music is characterized by its triadic sonority, strong harmonic progressions, clear structure, and extensive use of imitation, securing for him a central position in the evolution of musical style from Dufay to Josquin.

Martin Picker

[See also: BURGUNDY; OCKEGHEM, JOHANNES]

Busnoys, Antoine. *Collected Works.* New York: Broude Trust, 1990. Parts 2 and 3: *The Latin-Texted Works,* ed. Richard Taruskin.

Higgins, Paula M. "Antoine Busnois and Musical Culture in Late Fifteenth-Century France and Burgundy." Diss. Princeton University, 1987.

———. "*In hydraulis* Revisited: New Light on the Career of Antoine Busnois." *Journal of the American Musicological Society* 39 (1986): 36–86.

Perkins, Leeman L. "The *L'homme armé* Masses of Busnoys and Ockeghem: A Comparison." *Journal of Musicology* 3 (1984): 363–96.

Taruskin, Richard. "Antoine Busnoys and the *L'homme armé* Tradition." *Journal of the American Musicological Society* 39 (1986): 255–93.

BUTLER OF FRANCE. The butler (*bouteiller*) originally was a household officer concerned with supplying wine (and revenues from wine) from the king's estates. In the 11th century, the holder of this position was recognized as one of the "great officers of the crown," like the seneschal and constable. Beginning in 1130, the position was held for several generations by members of an important seigneurial family from Senlis that took the surname of Le Bouteiller. For a thirty-year period beginning in 1317, the king's chief financial adviser (Henri de Sully, then Mile de Noyers) held the position of "Grand Butler." Thereafter, it gradually became largely honorific, as the butlers never succeeded in carving out a permanent political or administrative role for themselves.

John Bell Henneman, Jr.

C

CABOCHIENS. The butchers and flayers of Paris, nicknamed the Cabochiens after one of their leaders, Simon Caboche, created a reign of terror in Paris in 1413, evidently at the instigation of the duke of Burgundy, who hoped to thwart the plans the duke of Guyenne was forming against him.

On April 28, some of Burgundy's officers led the Cabochiens on a rampage against the Bastille and the residence of the duke of Guyenne, arresting a number of Guyenne's officers whom they considered traitors. On May 11 and 22, more prisoners were taken, including the queen's brother. The actions of the Cabochiens were successful because Charles VI, often ill during this period, issued no order against them. At their request, Charles held a *lit de justice* in the Parlement on May 26 and 27, promulgating a list of reforms that a government-sponsored commission had been working on for several months. The list, still unfinished, contained 258 articles and was written in the form of a royal ordinance, dated May 25, 1413. Historians have called it the *Ordonnance Cabochienne*. The commission, using more than twenty old reform ordinances as sources, dealt with every facet of government. The general objective of the *Ordonnance* was to bring money back into the king's coffers and prevent the dilapidation of his resources.

The excesses committed in the summer of 1413 alienated many Parisians from the Cabochiens. This, along with the king's willingness to negotiate with the Armagnacs and allow the duke of Guyenne to free the prisoners taken in the spring, led to the fall of the Cabochiens. Their silent partner, John of Burgundy, was fearful of the duke of Guyenne's revenge and fled Paris. On September 5, 1413, the *Ordonnance Cabochienne* was revoked in its entirety because it had been published in haste without proper deliberation in the royal council or the Parlement and because it contained a final clause that "injured" the king's authority.

Richard C. Famiglietti

[See also: ARMAGNACS; CAUCHON, PIERRE; CHARLES VI; JOHN THE FEARLESS; LOUIS, DUKE OF GUYENNE]

Coville, Alfred. *Les Cabochiens et l'ordonnance de 1413*. Paris: Hachette, 1888.

———. *L'Ordonnance Cabochienne*. Paris: Picard, 1891.

Famiglietti, Richard C. *Royal Intrigue: Crisis at the Court of Charles VI 1392–1420*. New York: AMS, 1986.

CAEN. The medieval city of Caen (Calvados) gained importance in the 11th century owing to the favor of William the Conqueror, who established his base there for the governance of lower Normandy. Around the middle of the century, the duke built a castle and enclosed the town with walls, and shortly afterward he and his wife, Matilda, founded two monasteries at Caen. A short distance from the sea and situated where the Orne and the Odon rivers join, Caen enjoyed a flourishing trade, and the conquest of England in 1066 contributed to its prosperity. The excellent limestone of the area was for centuries one of Caen's chief exports; it was even transported to England to rebuild the cathedral of Canterbury and palace of Westminster. Through the 12th century, Caen remained the military and administrative center of lower Normandy, and the supreme court of justice and finances, the Échiquier de Normandie, was held there.

Caen's administrative importance declined after the conquest of Normandy in 1204 by the French king Philip II Augustus, but the town continued to prosper: cloth manufacturing became an especially important industry. The 13th and 14th centuries saw the flowering of High Gothic and Flamboyant Gothic architecture, best represented in Caen by the church of Saint-Pierre. During the

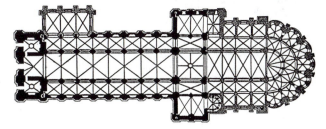

Caen (Calvados), plan of Saint-Étienne. After Conant.

Caen, Saint-Étienne, façade. *Photograph courtesy of Whitney S. Stoddard.*

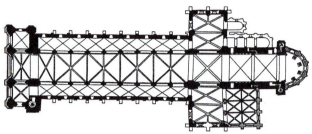

Caen, La Trinité, plan. After Musset.

Hundred Years' War, the town suffered much damage at the hands of the English, who were resolved to win back their French possessions. Sacked in 1346 and 1417, Caen served as the base for the English conquest and occupation of Normandy between 1417 and 1450. One positive outcome of the English possession of Caen was the duke of Bedford's foundation of its university in the 1430s. After the Battle of Formigny in 1450, Caen, with the rest of Normandy, returned to the French.

Cassandra Potts

In the last quarter of the 11th century, William the Conqueror transformed the site on the River Orne into a forest of Norman architecture. Despite destruction from World War II, well-preserved Norman Romanesque and Gothic structures surround vestiges of the Conqueror's 11th-century fortress. Conveniently and strategically located, Caen also served as a place of atonement for the Conqueror and Queen Matilda. Between 1059 and 1065, Matilda founded the Abbaye-aux-Dames with its church of La Trinité. By 1063, William followed his wife with the foundation of the Abbaye-aux-Hommes, including the church of Saint-Étienne at the other end of Caen. The town grew between the two abbeys and fortress.

Built in one campaign, the sleek, rectilinear surface of the west façade of Saint-Étienne stretches to three stories before the western towers, topped with 17th-century spires, begin. Four massive buttresses and a series of regular round-headed windows divide the west front into three sections, which correspond to the interior space with nave and side aisles. Inside the nave, alternating cluster piers delineate eight bays and a three-story elevation with arcade, triforium gallery, and clerestory with wall passage. The vaulted ceiling from 1130 is one of many subsequent alterations in the 11th-century fabric, which ends with the short transept arms. In the 13th century, Master William (whose tombstone can be found in the south part of the choir) replaced the original Romanesque choir with a Gothic chevet that retains the three-story elevation but departs from the original apse-in-echelon plan. Some conventual buildings of the Abbaye-aux-Hommes survive from the 13th to 15th centuries, and other portions were rebuilt in the 18th century.

At the far end of the rue Saint-Pierre, La Trinité (dedicated 1066) offers an alternative to the austerity of Saint-Étienne. While the west front shares the twin-tower design with Saint-Étienne, an accurate 19th-century reconstruction of molded blind arcades and windows achieves an exciting balance with variation in size and ornament. The narthex is lost. Although the central-portal tympanum sculpture is a 19th-century addition, much 11th- and 12th-century sculpture survives within the fabric: fanciful corbels line the exterior, and creatures reside in ambulatory capitals and one of the crypt capitals. The nave is notable for its great length and width, and the two-story elevation sports a false triforium on exterior and interior. Despite periodic campaigns of construction from 1059 until 1130, La Trinité is remarkably coherent in execution. Only a few parts of the church date from later than the 11th century: the 12th-century (1125–30) apse with semiambulatory and concurrent alterations in the transept arms, a 13th-century chapter house off the south arm, and modern apsidal chapels adjoining the the north arm. A black-marble slab designates the remains of Queen Matilda near the entrance to the choir.

Founded by monks of Saint-Étienne, the 11th-century parish church of Saint-Nicolas retains the Romanesque choir of Saint-Étienne and the narthex of La Trinité but is built on a smaller scale. Decoration, though minimal throughout most of the building, is explosive in the east end. Some vaults and spires are 13th- and 15th-century alterations.

Other ecclesiastical buildings in Caen include Saint-Pierre, a Gothic and Renaissance church (13th–15th c.), Saint-Jean (14th–15th c.), Saint-Sauveur (14th–15th c.), and, within the ramparts, the chapel of Saint-Georges (Romanesque nave). Of civic structures, 12th-, 14th-, and 15th-century walls surround the Conqueror's fortress, later transformed into the château of Philip Augustus and captured by the English, who founded a university there in 1432. The château was heavily restored after World War II.

Stacy L. Boldrick

[See also: BEDFORD, JOHN OF LANCASTER, DUKE OF; NORMANDY; RECONQUEST OF FRANCE; ROMANESQUE ARCHITECTURE]

Baylé, Maylis. *La Trinité de Caen: sa place dans l'histoire de l'architecture et du décor romans.* Geneva: Droz, 1979.

de Boüard, Michel. *Le château de Caen.* Caen: Centre de Recherches Archéologiques Médiévales, 1979.

Désert, Gabriel, ed. *Histoire de Caen.* Toulouse: Privat, 1981.

Jouet, Roger. *La résistance à l'occupation anglaise en Basse-Normandie (1418–1450).*

Lambert, Elie. "Caen roman et gothique." *Bulletin de la Société des Antiquaires de Normandie* 43 (1935).

Musset, Lucien. *Caen: ville d'art.* Colmar-Ingersheim: SAEP, 1971.

———. *Normandie romane.* 2 vols. La Pierre-qui-vire: Zodiaque, 1967.

Serbat, Léon. "Caen." *Congrès archéologique (Caen)* 75 (1908): 3–132.

CAESARIUS OF ARLES (ca. 470–542). Reforming bishop, exemplar of pastoral care, popular preacher, monk, and advocate of monasticism. Born near Chalon-sur-Saône, Caesarius was a monk at Lérins from ca. 490 to 497, when he was ordained priest at Arles. In 502, he became bishop of Arles and in 514 was made primate of Gaul. Revered for his personal holiness, his benevolence, and his pastoral care, Caesarius was made a saint of the Catholic church after his death. An Augustinian in theology, he was influential in the Second Council of Orange (529), which established the accepted interpretation of Augustine's teaching on grace and salvation against the Semi-Pelagianist

views of Faustus of Riez and John Cassian. Caesarius wrote a rule for monks (for a community under his nephew) and a rule for nuns (for a convent in Arles in which his sister, Caesaria, was abbess). Some 238 of his sermons survive and provide important documentation of church life in 6th-century Gaul.

Grover A. Zinn

[See also: ARLES; CASSIAN, JOHN; CONVENT ARCHITECTURE; FAUSTUS OF RIEZ; LÉRINS]

Caesarius of Arles. *Opera,* ed. G. Morin. *CCSL* 103–04. Turnhout: Brepols, 1953.

———. *Caesarius of Arles: Sermons,* trans. Mary Magdeleine Mueller. 3 vols. New York: Fathers of the Church, 1956–73.

Daly, W.M. "Caesarius of Arles, a Precursor of Medieval Christendom." *Traditio* 26 (1970): 1–28.

McCarthy, Maria Caritas. *The Rule for Nuns of St. Caesarius of Arles: A Translation with Critical Introduction.* Washington, D.C.: Catholic University of America Press, 1960.

CAHORS. Built on the site of a sacred spring, Cahors (Lot) was a flourishing commercial and university city during the Middle Ages. Thanks to the presence of the Lombards and the Templars, the principal moneylenders of the period, Cahors was one of the largest cities in 13th-century France. It was ceded to the English by the Treaty of Brétigny (1360) and was decimated during the Hundred Years' War. However, it still retains several of its medieval monuments, most prominent of which are the cathedral of Saint-Étienne, the Pont Valentré, and the churches of Saint-Barthélemy and Saint-Urcisse.

The cathedral of Saint-Étienne (main altar consecrated in 1119) is a harmonious fusion of two regional architectural features: the single nave (unusually wide at Cahors) covered by a series of domes and the apse with radiating chapels but no ambulatory. Successive alterations and additions to the east end, beginning in the late 13th century, have partially obscured this unity. The massive, fortresslike façade was added in the 14th century; the Flam-

Cahors (Lot), Pont Valentré. *Photograph courtesy of William W. Kibler.*

boyant Gothic cloister, once richly ornamented, dates from 1504.

The beautiful Romanesque north portal suggests affiliations with both the southern tradition of Moissac and the first flowering of the northern Gothic. Unusual in the tympanum is the combination of theophanic vision (the Ascension) with narrative scenes from the martyrdom of St. Stephen. The porch and exterior wall have been overrestored in this century.

The Pont Valentré, despite the loss of its barbican, remains one of the most impressive examples of military architecture of the 14th century.

Jean M. French

[See also: PÉRIGUEUX; QUERCY]

Bratke, Elke. *Das Nordportal der Kathedrale Saint-Étienne in Cahors.* Freiburg im Breisgau: Rauscher-Druck, 1977.

Durliat, Marcel. "La cathédrale Saint-Étienne de Cahors, architecture et sculpture." *Bulletin monumental* 137 (1979): 285–340.

Rey, Raymond. "Cahors." *Congrès archéologique* (*Figeac, Cahors et Rodez*) 100 (1937): 216–65.

Vidal, Marguerite, Jean Maury, and Jean Porcher. *Quercy roman.* La Pierre-qui-vire: Zodiaque, 1969.

CALAIS. Originating as a fishing village along the northern coast of France, Calais (Pas-de-Calais) began to prosper first under Arnulf I, count of Flanders, who in 938 gave the village and nearby land to the monks of Saint-Bertin, and later under Gérard de Gueldre, the count of Boulogne, who in 1224 fortified it and established it as a town. In 1346, Calais was besieged by Edward III in one of the early engagements of the Hundred Years' War. Fresh from victory at the Battle of Crécy, the English army besieged Calais because of its strategic location, lying only twenty-three miles from Dover, and because of its proximity to their allies in the southern Low Countries. The English forces, perhaps numbering 30,000, constructed large siegeworks that completely cut the town off from all land and most sea commerce. Calais was besieged for nearly a year. Its inhabitants held out, hoping for relief from their king, Philip VI. Finally, in July 1347, Philip arrived at Calais with a relief army, but he was unable to raise the siege. The French retreated to Paris, and the town surrendered on August 4, 1347. The captors exiled all French citizens of the town, replacing them with English merchants and soldiers.

Calais remained an English possession for more than 200 years, despite several attempts to return it to French control, including another extended but unsuccessful siege in 1435–36 by Philip the Good, duke of Burgundy. In 1558, it was recaptured by François de Lorraine, duke of Guise.

Kelly DeVries

[See also: CRÉCY; HUNDRED YEARS' WAR; PHILIP VI]

Daumet, Georges. *Calais sous la domination anglaise.* Arras: Répessé-Crépel, 1902.

DeVries, Kelly. "Hunger, Flemish Participation and the Flight of Philip VI: Contemporary Accounts of the Siege of Calais, 1346–47." *Studies in Medieval and Renaissance History* 12 (1991): 129–81.

Lennel, F. *Histoire de Calais.* 2 vols. Calais: Peumery, 1910.

Viard, Jules. "Le siège de Calais." *Moyen âge* 40 (1929): 129–89.

CALAIS, JEAN DE (fl. early 15th c.). A poem of some 410 lines in the *Jardin de plaisance*, Calais's *Lamentations* is a series of dialogues that a certain Jehan holds with Reason and Fortune. The protagonist, hiding in a monastery from the persecution of the authorities, is abandoned by all save his faithful wife. His only crime was to have loved his king. Reason encourages him and Fortune assures him that the real cause of his suffering was that he followed foolish counsel. Droz and Piaget have tentatively identified the Jehan of the poem with Jean de Calais, a rich Parisian bourgeois who in 1430, during the English occupation, participated in a plot against Henry VI, favoring the return of Charles VII (the so-called *conjuration dauphinoise*). The plot was discovered and several persons were arrested and executed. Jean was liberated upon payment of a large sum of money. The Jean de Calais mentioned by Villon (*Testament* 173) is another person.

Peter F. Dembowski

Calais, Jean de. *Lamentations.* In *Le Jardin de plaisance et fleur de rethorique. Reproduction en fac-similé de l'édition publiée par Antoine Vérard vers 1501.* Paris: Didot, 1910, f. 136v°–139r°. [text.]

Droz, Eugénie, and Arthur Piaget. *Introduction et notes.* Paris: Champion, 1925, pp. 260–61 [Commentary on 1910 ed.]

Longnon, Auguste. *Paris pendant l'occupation anglaise (1420–1436): documents extraits de la chancellerie de France.* Paris: Champion, 1878, pp. 301–08.

CALENDAR, LITURGICAL. "Calendar" has three distinct meanings. In the broadest sense, it refers to the astronomical calendar that provides the context for the other meanings; it is also applied to the annual cycle of ecclesiastical festivals; and it refers to the document that appears at the beginning of a liturgical book.

The astronomical calendar in use throughout western Europe in the Middle Ages is the Julian calendar, so-called for its establishment under Julius Caesar in 46 B.C. It defines a year as consisting of 365 and a quarter days, requiring an additional day every fourth, or leap, year. (This is some eleven minutes longer than the true astronomical year, creating the need for the corrections of the Gregorian calendar worked out under Pope Gregory XIII in 1582: the omission of ten days in October 1582 and the subsequent omission of the leap year in years divisible by 100 but not 400.) The Julian calendar utilized the twelve months of modern usage but had no weeks. The seven days of the week, named after the seven planets as then understood, were added in the 2nd century. The seven-day week, long maintained in the Jewish calendar, greatly influenced the Christian calendar, which replaced the Sabbath by Sunday as the principal day.

The annual round of liturgical dates is divided into a temporal and a sanctoral cycle. The temporal cycle, or temporale, consists of Sundays and the feast days commemorating the events of the life of Jesus Christ. There is a lesser sequence of fixed dates associated with Christmas and the Epiphany, December 25 and January 6; and a major sequence associated with Easter, which is celebrated on the Sunday after the first full moon of spring. The precise calculation of Easter's date, involving differences over the astronomical calendar and other issues, was the subject of intense controversy in the early Middle Ages. The sanctoral cycle, or sanctorale, includes the feast days of saints; these are celebrated on the date of their death, a practice stemming from the fact that the early sanctorale is derived from the Martyrology, itself originating as a calendar commemorating the date and place of a martyr's passion. The temporal and sanctoral festivals were interspersed in the early-medieval liturgical books but eventually separated.

The calendars that preceded liturgical books generally devoted one page to each month beginning with January. One line, in turn, was devoted to each day of the month, giving the name and type of its feast, or left blank if none occurred. In the left-hand margin were three columns of numbers and letters. The inner one gave the date of the month, usually according to the Roman system of nones, ides, and kalends. A second gave the so-called dominical letters, a series of the first seven letters of the alphabet, repeated continuously over the twelve months of the year; thus, whatever letter stood next to the first Sunday of a given year would point to the remainder of its Sundays. Finally, the outer column of numbers called the "golden numbers," encoded the annual lunar tables in such a way so that if they were used in conjunction with the dominical letters a knowledgeable person could calculate the date of Easter for any year.

In the later Middle Ages, calendars were often the subject of special artistic attention, displaying two twelve-fold series of illustrations: the signs of the zodiac and the labors of the month. The latter in particular were sometimes splendidly executed, as in the celebrated full-page miniatures of the *Très Riches Heures* of John of Berry. These book paintings, in turn, influenced some of the earliest easel paintings, like Breugel's great series on the months of the year.

James McKinnon

[See also: BOOK OF HOURS; CANONICAL HOURS; DIVINE OFFICE; MASS, CHANTS AND TEXTS]

Frere, Walter. *Studies in Early Roman Liturgy.* London: Oxford University Press, 1930, Vol. 1: *The Kalendar.*
MacArthur, A. Allan. *The Evolution of the Christian Year.* London: SCM, 1953.
Thurston, Herbert. "Calendar." In *The Catholic Encyclopedia.* New York: Appleton, 1908, Vol. 3, pp. 158–66.

CAMBRAI. Capital of a Frankish kingdom destroyed by Clovis in the early 6th century, Cambrai (Nord) was attached to Lotharingia in the division of Charlemagne's empire in 843. The cathedral of Cambrai, destroyed in the aftermath of the French Revolution, was one of the largest and most important Gothic structures in northern France. It was built in three major phases, beginning with the west tower in 1148, a scheme that was revised after the partial collapse of the tower in 1161. Before the nave was completed, ca. 1180, the transept was begun. It was completed in the early 13th century and the chevet built 1220–50. Our knowledge of the church comes from a series of drawings and the plan by Boileux that has been shown to be accurate. The drawing of the exterior from the east by van der Meulen shows details of the chevet and transept; but the only known interior view of the nave is one made during the destruction that shows the interior elevation of the tower.

William W. Clark

Branner, Robert. "The Transept of Cambrai Cathedral." In *Gedenkschrift Ernst Gall*, ed. Margarete Kuhn. Berlin: Deutscher Kunstverlag, 1965, pp. 69–85.
Héliot, Pierre. "La nef et le clocher de l'ancienne cathédrale de Cambrai." *Wallraf-Richartz Jahrbuch* 18 (1956): 91–110.
Thiébaut, Jacques. *La cathédrale disparue de Cambrai et sa place dans l'évolution de l'architecture du nord de la France.* Diss. Université de Lille, 1975.
———. "L'iconographie de la cathédrale disparue de Cambrai." *Revue du Nord* 58 (1976): 406–33.

CAMPIN, ROBERT (ca. 1376–1444). Late-medieval painter whose career is shrouded in mystery because of limited archival information and few attributed works. He is known principally for his famous pupil Rogier van der Weyden. Campin's reputation in Tournai as a master is substantiated by the positions he held: subdeacon of the goldsmith's guild, head of the painter's guild, and one of the stewards to the city in charge of finances and accounts. Tournai's relationship with the Burgundian court ultimately affected Campin's production. In one of his earlier works, the *Entombment Triptych* (1415–20), Campin displays a knowledge of the italianate painters of the court, such as Malouel and Bellechose, in his use of gold background and treatment of the angels. Court patronage, however, did not provide the artists of Tournai with a steady source of income. Instead, they belonged to guilds and served the city and local clients. Campin's most famous work and the one that epitomizes his style is the *Merode Altarpiece* (ca. 1425), now at the Cloisters in New York. Commissioned by the Ingebrecht family, who appear at the left of the panel, the triptych demonstrates Campin's skill with disguised symbolism. The composition teems with mundane objects that acquire meaning in the presence of the divine. Sadly, Campin's career suffered greatly in the 1430s, when the pro-Burgundian faction in Tournai snatched power away from the guilds. In the midst of the conflict, Campin was arrested and, though he was eventually set free, his career never recovered.

Michelle I. Lapine

[See also: VAN DER WEYDEN, ROGIER]

Frinta, Mojmír S. *The Genius of Robert Campin.* Paris: Mouton, 1966.

Snyder, James. *Northern Renaissance Art.* New York: Abrams, 1985.

CANON LAW. The medieval church was governed by universal canon law and local laws and customs. The former was taught at the universities, especially in Bologna and Paris. It was divided into *ius antiquum,* the conciliar canons, papal decretals (many of them spurious), and patristic texts included in Gratian's *Decretum,* a private (i.e., not ecclesiastically sanctioned) collection from the 12th century, and *ius novum,* recent canons and decretals. Collecting of decretals began as a private endeavor, but the papacy took an interest early in the 13th century. Ultimately, there were three official collections, promulgated to the universities, the *Liber extra* or *Gregorian decretals* of Gregory IX (1234), the *Liber sextus decretalium* of Boniface VIII (1298), and the *Constitutiones clementinae,* left unpromulgated on the death of Clement V in 1314 and reissued by John XXII in 1317. (Other papal decrees, or *extravagantes,* were collected unofficially.) The greatest number of the texts in these collections concerned the discipline and business of the clergy. Teaching from these texts and commenting on them made the canonists important figures in medieval political and ecclesiological theory. Canonistic science was brought into pastoral care through the *summae confessorum,* handbooks, many of which were composed by friars to guide priests in hearing confessions and assigning penance. The Roman curia supplemented universal canon law with collections of its own regulations and decisions of its tribunals, especially the Rota. Local canon law continued to exist in a subordinate role; and numerous synods and provincial councils issued regulations, applying the universal canon law or dealing with regional problems.

Thomas M. Izbicki

[See also: BONIFACE VIII; CLEMENT V; GRATIAN; GREGORY IX; LAW AND JUSTICE]

Corpus iuris canonici, ed. Emil Friedberg. 2 vols. Leipzig: Tauchnitz, 1879; Graz: Akademische Druck und Verlagsanstalt, 1955.

Brundage, James. *Law, Sex and Society in Medieval Europe.* Chicago: University of Chicago Press, 1987.

Kuttner, Stephan. *Harmony from Dissonance: An Interpretation of Medieval Canon Law.* Latrobe: Archabbey, 1955.

Ullmann, Walter. *Law and Politics in the Middle Ages: An Introduction to the Sources of Medieval Political Ideas.* Ithaca: Cornell University Press, 1975.

CANONICAL HOURS (DIVINE OFFICE). The form of service, comprising psalms, hymns, readings, and prayers, designated for the sanctification of specific hours of the day. The two chief types, monastic and secular (for secular clergy), arose to accommodate the particular needs of these communities; their differences reside primarily in the number and arrangement of the items.

As early Christianity existed under constant threat of persecution, most assemblies occurred in the evening, and out of these vigils the most important Hours developed. The 4th century saw important steps toward the formation of the Offices. Drawing from eastern rites, Ambrose (340–397) brought the antiphonal performance of psalms and the singing of hymns to the service; in turn, the flourishing of monastic life at this time generated a need for a measure of uniformity in the celebration of the Hours. This standardization was achieved in large part through adoption of the *Rule of St. Benedict,* although Benedictine practice was but one of many uses; variants persisted throughout the Middle Ages, particularly in the Franciscan and Dominican communities.

The Divine Office consists of a daily cycle of seven Hours in addition to Compline, the night office. The "named" or Greater Hours are Vespers, Matins, and Lauds, performed at sunset, night, and before Mass, respectively. These three emerged out of the vigils of the earliest Christian services and are the most elaborate musically. The Lesser Hours—Prime, Terce, Sext, and None—are celebrated at about 6 A.M., 9 A.M., noon, and 3 P.M. and are linked symbolically to the moments of the Passion and, in some regions, the periods of salvation history. The frequency and arrangement of these periods of common prayer draw their inspiration from two biblical passages: the exhortation from Luke 18:1 to pray always, and Psalm 118 (119):164: "Seven times a day I praise you."

By the end of the 13th century, the Offices were contained in three books: Breviary, Antiphonary, and Choir Psalter. The Breviary, designated for the officiating priest, generally included Proper items only (those specific to a given feast day or liturgical season). The Antiphonary was the principal choir book and contained all of the Proper items; the Choir Psalter supplemented this with the Common items of the Office, which were fixed regardless of the season or feast day. It was only later that almost all of the texts were merged into the portable form of the Breviary, suitable for private devotions.

Edmund J. Goehring

[See also: BENEDICT, RULE OF ST.; LITURGICAL BOOKS]

Bradshaw, Paul F. *Daily Prayer in the Early Church: A Study of the Origin and Early Development of the Divine Office.* New York: Oxford University Press, 1982.

Vogel, Cyrille. *Medieval Liturgy: An Introduction to the Sources,* rev. and trans. William G. Storey. Washington, D.C.: Pastoral, 1986.

CANTUS CORONATUS ("crowned song"). Prize-winning songs in the *puys* were said to be "crowned," and 13th- and 14th-century manuscripts identify about thirty songs as *chansons couronnées.* The theorist Johannes de Grocheio (fl. ca. 1300) identified the highest-level secular songs as *cantus coronatus,* works that maintained elevated courtly poetic language and melody. His examples, *Ausi comne* *unicorne* (King of Navarre) and *Quant li roussignol* (Chastelain de Coucy?) were composed by noble trouvères. In 15th-century music, the term has been applied to series of long notes marked by fermatas, perhaps indicating passages of improvised vocal ornamentation.

Lawrence Earp

[See also: GROCHEIO, JOHANNES DE; *PUY*]

van der Werf, Hendrik, and Wolf Frobenius. "Cantus coronatus." In *Handwörterbuch der musikalischen Terminologie,* ed. Hans Heinrich Eggebrecht. Wiesbaden: Steiner, 1971– . 12 pp. (1983).

CANTUS FIRMUS. A preexisting segment of music, usually extracted from Gregorian chant, upon which a new polyphonic composition is based. The use of a *cantus firmus* provided the earliest means of constructing polyphony and remained important as a compositional procedure in France throughout the Middle Ages. *Cantus firmi* extracted from Notre-Dame organa of the late 12th and early 13th centuries provided the foundation voice for the earliest motets, the most progressive polyphonic form of the 13th century. The *cantus firmus* was subjected to strict rhythmic patterning, and the preexisting segment of music lent the authority of the sacred chant to new compositions based on it. By the latter part of the 13th century, composers occasionally employed secular *cantus firmi*. Often, the texts of the upper voices of a motet were related to the word or words identifying the *cantus firmus* in a complementary or ironic fashion. Use of a *cantus firmus* continued in isorhythmic motets of the 14th and 15th centuries, as well as in the unified cyclic Mass of the 15th century.

Lawrence Earp

[See also: CYCLIC MASS; ISORHYTHMIC MOTET; MOTET (13TH CENTURY); NOTRE-DAME SCHOOL]

CAPETIAN DYNASTY. The Capetians, called in the Middle Ages the "third race" of French kings, coming after the Merovingians and Carolingians, ruled France in unbroken succession from 987 to 1328. (The first kings from the lineage had already ruled briefly a century before Hugh Capet's accession in 987 on the death of Louis V: Eudes [r. 888–98] and his brother Robert I [r. 922–23].) The term "Capetian" was coined in the French Revolution, but the "third race" was a recognized entity 800 years earlier; the epithet "Capet," meaning a cap or cape, was attached to Hugh Capet in the 13th century. Although the Capetian line is considered to have ended with the advent of the Valois in 1328, in fact the Valois and all succeeding French monarchs through Louis XVI were descended in the male line from Hugh Capet.

For the first century or so of Capetian rule, the kings exercised little authority outside the restricted area surrounding their capital at Paris. The counts of Blois and Troyes, whose counties flanked royal Francia, were more powerful in many respects. Yet the Capetians had succeeded the Carolingians with an almost theocratic aura as God's anointed administrators of justice, and they had several advantages that the Carolingians and Ottonians, or for that matter most ducal or comital lineages, lacked.

First, they managed to produce a male heir in every generation. Although the kings from Hugh Capet through Louis VII in the 12th century all practiced anticipatory succession, associating their oldest sons on the throne with them before their deaths, no other family challenged the Capetian claim to royal rule after the end of the 10th century. The production of an heir was, however, sometimes difficult, as in the case of Louis VII, whose only son was born to his third wife, after he had divorced his first wife, Eleanor of Aquitaine, and his second, Constance of Castile, had died. Second, the Capetians were believed capable of healing scrofula, "the king's evil," by their touch; Robert II was first credited with this ability at the beginning of the 11th century. Third, they had few internal quarrels, unlike, for example, the Plantagenêt kings of England. Some of the kings (Hugh Capet, Philip I, Louis VII) had only one legitimate son, thus eliminating sibling quarrels. In other cases, younger sons were given territory of their own. Robert II had his second surviving son, Robert, succeed to Burgundy while Henry I, his oldest surviving son, was designated the royal heir; the Capetian dukes of Burgundy ruled until the middle of the 14th century. Henry in turn married his second son to the heiress of Vermandois. The kings did not divide the central family patrimony, which was attached to the crown from the time Capetian rule began and went whole to the oldest son, but they found it useful to distribute newly acquired territories, like Burgundy, to cadets. The vast territorial acquisitions of the kings in the 13th century made possible the birth of the most developed form of this practice, the apanage system.

While building their political power, the Capetians enjoyed better relations with the church than did other western kings. They did not, like the German emperors, become embroiled in the investiture issue or in the delicate question of secular justice for ecclesiastics, as did the English kings. Philip I worked out a compromise with the pope on royal investiture of bishops that anticipated the Concordat of Worms between the pope and the emperor (1122). Popes fleeing Italy or archbishops fleeing England routinely sought refuge in France in the 12th century.

When French kings were excommunicated in the 11th and 12th centuries, it was for their matrimonial difficulties, not for open breaks with the ecclesiastical hierarchy. Robert II married his cousin Bertha, the widowed countess of Blois, in 996 but was ultimately forced to separate from her on grounds of consanguinity. His grandson Philip I repudiated his first wife in 1092 for an alliance with Bertrade de Montfort, an alliance that he was able to have recognized eventually but that caused him a good deal of difficulty. Philip II's most serious differences with the papacy stemmed from the repudiation of his queen, Ingeborg of Denmark, in 1193.

Although Philip I, excommunicated at the time, could not go on the First Crusade, Louis VII and Philip II were leaders of the Second and Third Crusades, respectively,

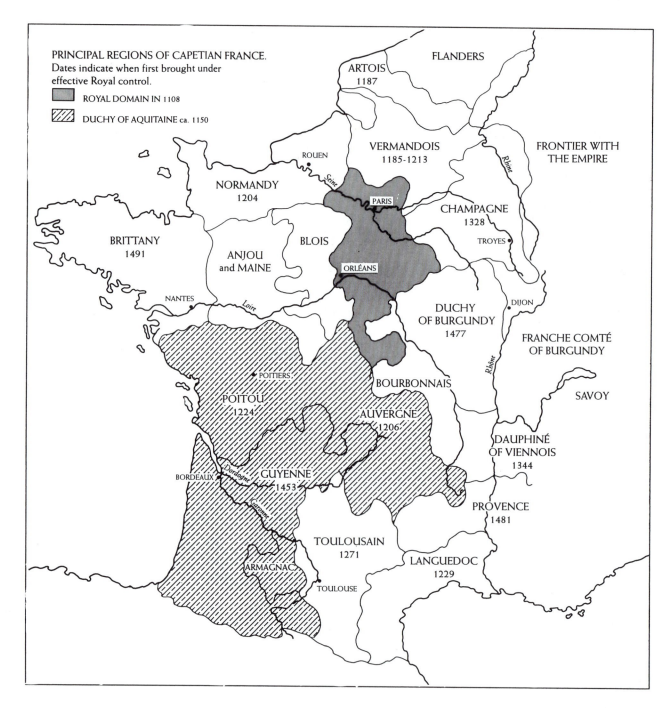

PRINCIPAL REGIONS OF CAPETIAN FRANCE.
Dates indicate when first brought under
effective Royal control.

▨ ROYAL DOMAIN IN 1108

▨ DUCHY OF AQUITAINE ca. 1150

FLANDERS

ARTOIS
1187

ROUEN

VERMANDOIS
1185-1213

FRONTIER WITH
THE EMPIRE

NORMANDY
1204

PARIS

CHAMPAGNE
1328

TROYES

BRITTANY
1491

BLOIS

ANJOU
and MAINE

ORLÉANS

NANTES

DUCHY
OF BURGUNDY
1477

DIJON

FRANCHE COMTÉ
OF BURGUNDY

BOURBONNAIS

POITIERS

SAVOY

POITOU
1224

AUVERGNE
1206

DAUPHINÉ
OF VIENNOIS
1344

BORDEAUX

GUYENNE
1453

PROVENCE
1481

ARMAGNAC

TOULOUSAIN
1271

LANGUEDOC
1229

TOULOUSE

and most of the crusading activity of the 13th century
was led or influenced by Louis IX. In 1303, Philip IV did
make an open break with the papacy, when he captured
Boniface VIII, but by then the Capetians had the support
of the French bishops. Succeeding popes at Avignon were
firmly under the influence of the French kings, even
though their see was officially in the empire, not the
French kingdom.

Despite their good relations with the church, the
Capetians were not great ecclesiastical patrons. Dukes and
counts were much more generous to the French monaster-

ies. Long after kings and popes had agreed on the minimal
role the kings were to play in the selection of new bishops,
the crown still attemped to influence episcopal elections
and to seize episcopal property during a vacancy. The 12th-
and 13th-century monarchs issued diplomas of confirmation and immunity for an increasing number of churches,
but this practice was tied more closely to the spread of
their political power than to religious sentiment. The ecclesiastical hierarchy was, however, practical enough to recognize that the French kings were the best friends it was
likely to have.

CAPETIAN DYNASTY I
(The Early Capetians)

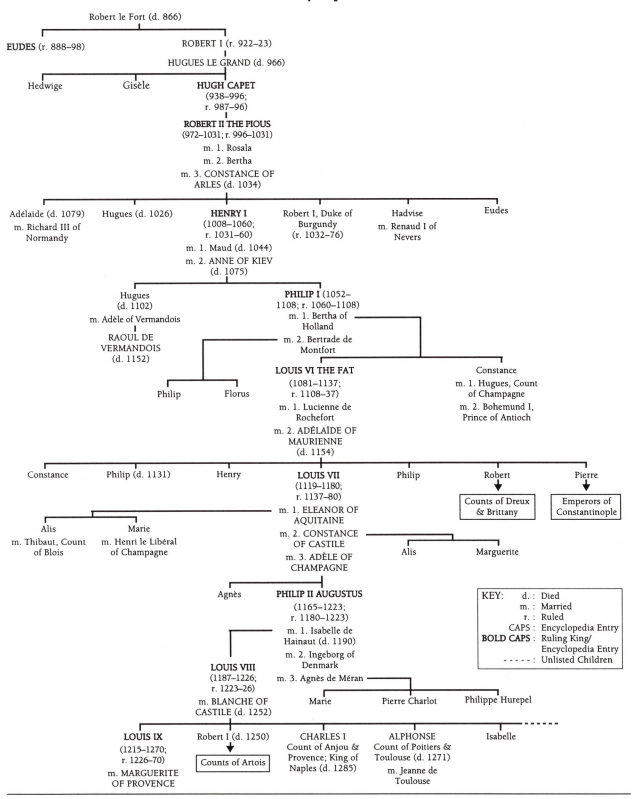

KEY:
d. :	Died
m. :	Married
r. :	Ruled
CAPS :	Encyclopedia Entry
BOLD CAPS :	Ruling King/ Encyclopedia Entry
- - - - - :	Unlisted Children

CAPETIAN DYNASTY II
(Descendants of Louis IX)

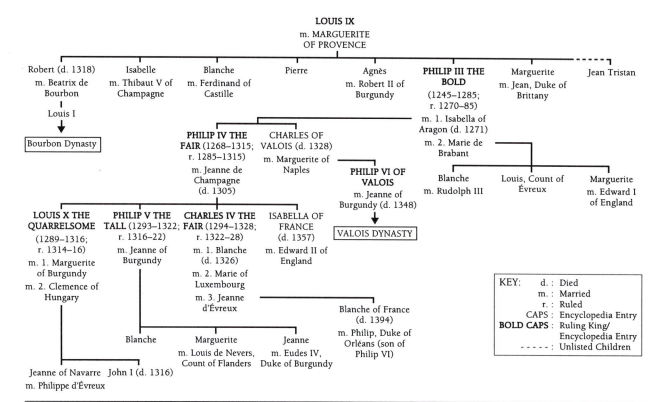

The Capetians rose from obscurity to unquestioned power in the space of three centuries. The kings of the 11th century added political and territorial influence to Hugh Capet's legacy, but Louis VI (r. 1108–37), is usually considered to have reestablished French royal power. Louis, who was fortunate in having a laudatory biographer in his friend Suger, abbot of Saint-Denis, was effective in making the king's vassals recognize royal suzerainty; the great lords of France presented the Capetians with few problems after the first decades of the 12th century. His greatest territorial triumph was acquiring Aquitaine for his son, Louis VII (r. 1137–80), by marrying him to Eleanor, heiress to the vast duchy. This triumph lasted only for fifteen years, however; Louis divorced Eleanor on grounds of consanguinity in 1152, although the real reason seems to have been her failure to produce a son. She brought Aquitaine to her new husband, Henry II of England, and English control of Aquitaine was to last for 300 years. Because of this loss, and his involvement in the unsuccessful Second Crusade (1147), Louis VII is often seen as a weak king. But he should be credited with establishing excellent relations with both the secular and ecclesiastical powers of the kingdom and with laying the foundations for the achievements of his son, Philip II Augustus (r. 1180–1223).

Philip reorganized the government, using a system of royal officers to oversee estates and courts. He relied espe-cially on nonnobles, men who owed their position to the king, rather than on the sometimes dangerously independent nobles who had earlier served as royal officials. After the loss of the French royal archives at the Battle of Fréteval in 1194, Philip set up an efficient royal chancery, which remained at Paris rather than traveling with the king. He was able to generate enough revenues to pay for expensive wars against England, cultimating in the Battle of Bouvines (1214), where he took Normandy from King John.

The governmental organization of the early 13th century laid the basis for the reign of Philip's grandson, Louis IX (r. 1226–70), the most celebrated of the Capetians. Louis, the only king of the high Middle Ages to be sainted, is known especially from the biographical portrait by his close friend Joinville. Though revered more for his personal qualities, his dispensing of justice, and his crusading activities than for administrative innovation, he presided over a well-organized government. The Parlement de Paris became the highest judicial court in France, to which the decisions of all other courts could be appealed.

During the 13th century, the issue of the "dynastic legitimacy" of the Capetians began to be important. After nearly three centuries of rule, no one was likely to challenge their dynasty, but at a time when the kings were greatly expanding their territory beyond Francia it became important to establish that they were the heirs to Charlemagne. The tombs of both Capetians and Carolingians at the abbey of Saint-Denis were rebuilt and carefully rearranged. Most of the queens of France were construed as being in some way Charlemagne's descendants.

Louis IX's grandson, Philip IV the Fair (r. 1285–1314), has had none of the personal appeal of St. Louis, with his suppression of the Templars, battles with the papacy, wars with the English, and repeated devaluations of the currency. But he presided over a France that was firmly united. When the third and last of his sons, Charles IV, died without sons of his own in 1328, no parts of the kingdom broke away, and no one from outside the lineage claimed the throne. The only question was whether succession should go to a woman, or, as it eventually did, to Philip VI, first cousin of Charles IV and first of the Valois kings.

The history of the kingdom of France in the central Middle Ages has to be considered in relationship to the history of its ruling family. Between 987 and 1328, these rulers went from being one family of princes among many to being the leaders of the highly centralized government of one of Europe's most powerful countries.

Constance B. Bouchard

[See also: ALBIGENSIAN CRUSADE; APANAGE; AVIGNON PAPACY; ELEANOR OF AQUITAINE; HUGH CAPET; LAW AND JUSTICE; LOUIS VI THE FAT; LOUIS VII; LOUIS VIII; LOUIS IX; PHILIP I; PHILIP II AUGUSTUS; PHILIP III THE BOLD; PHILIP IV THE FAIR; ROBERT II THE PIOUS; SUGER]

Brown, Elizabeth A.R. *The Monarchy of Capetian France and Royal Ceremonial.* London: Variorum, 1991.

Joinville, Jean de. *The History of St. Louis,* trans. Joan Evans. New York: Oxford University Press, 1938.

Suger. *Vie de Louis VI le Gros,* ed. and trans. Henri Waquet. Paris: Champion, 1929.

Baldwin, John W. *The Government of Philip Augustus: Foundations of French Royal Power in the Middle Ages.* Berkeley: University of California Press, 1986.

Dunbabin, Jean. *France in the Making, 843–1180.* Oxford: Oxford University Press, 1985.

Fawtier, Robert. *The Capetian Kings of France: Monarchy and Nation, 987–1328,* trans. Lionel Butler and R. J. Adam. New York: St. Martin, 1960.

Hallam, Elizabeth M. *Capetian France, 987–1328.* London: Longman, 1980.

Lewis, Andrew W. *Royal Succession in Capetian France: Studies on Familial Order and the State.* Cambridge: Harvard University Press, 1981.

Spiegel, Gabrielle M. "The *Reditus regni ad stirpem Karoli Magni:* A New Look." *French Historical Studies* 7 (1971): 145–74.

Strayer, Joseph R. *The Reign of Philip the Fair.* Princeton: Princeton University Press, 1980.

CAPITULARY. The documents recording the legislative acts of certain Carolingian kings, which contemporary sources refer to as capitularies (Lat. *capitulare,* pl. *capitularia*), earned this name because their contents were often organized into series of short articles, or chapters (Lat. *capitula*). Although capitularies have survived from the time of Carloman (r. 741–47) and Pepin III (r. 741–68), the number of such texts sharply increased under Pepin's son Charlemagne (r. 768–814), as one element in his effort to improve the administration of the vast realm that he came to control. Writing was always of marginal importance in the government of Charlemagne, however; the foundation of law remained what it had been under earlier Frankish monarchs, the king's oral pronouncement based on the royal ban, his absolute power to command. The capitulary possessed no legislative power in itself but merely set forth what the monarch had proclaimed. Furthermore, although the king might consult with his lay and ecclesiastical magnates, at least through Charlemagne's lifetime there is no evidence that their consent was necessary in order for a capitulary to be valid. It is only in some capitularies produced under Louis the Pious (r. 814–40) that the assembly's consensus seems to have become a more vital element of lawmaking. This occurred at the time of a decline in royal authority and a rise in the power of the nobility. While the practice of issuing capitularies continued under Louis the Pious, after the breakup of the empire in 843 (Treaty of Verdun) capitularies are found only from west Francia during the reign of Charles the Bald (r. 840–77). They disappeared even from there shortly after Charles's death in 877.

The peripheral importance of writing to legislative activity under Charlemagne and his successors helps to explain the erratic manner in which Carolingian capitularies have survived. Provisions for the preservation of copies of these documents in the palace archives became common only under Louis the Pious and Charles the Bald and even then were inconsistent. To a great degree, the capitularies have come down to us only because of records preserved by *missi dominici,* representatives of the king who circulated them in the realm. The capitularies that still exist, largely thanks to such collections, take a variety of forms but in general are devoted to specific issues needing attention, both secular and ecclesiastical in character. Some deal with such concerns to the church as the role of images and the propriety of their worship, or the organization of monastic and canonical life; others note matters to be discussed at later assemblies, amend the realm's systems of law, or contain instructions to *missi dominici* or to counts in different parts of the empire.

Among the most important of the capitularies from Charlemagne's reign are the Capitulary of Heristal (779), which aimed at wide-reaching reform of lay and church administration in his realm; the *Admonitio generalis* of 789, a program of ecclesiastical reform that, among other things, provided regulations for the establishment of schools near cathedrals and monasteries; the Programmatic Capitulary of 802, concerning the new situation created by the imperial coronation in 800; and the Capitulary of Thionville (805), which sought to deal with the weakening of Charlemagne's power toward the end of his life and the corresponding increase in corruption among local officials.

Celia Chazelle

Boretius, Alfred, and Victor Krause, eds. *Monumenta Germaniae Historica Legum sectio II: Capitularia regum Francorum.* 2 vols. Hanover: Imprensis Bibliopolii Hahniani, 1883–97.

Ganshof, François L. *Recherches sur les capitulaires.* Paris: Sirey, 1958. [Extract in *Revue historique de droit français et étranger* 35 (1957): 33–87, 196–246.]

Loyn, Henry R., and John Percival. *The Reign of Charlemagne: Documents on Carolingian Government and Administration.* New York: St. Martin, 1975.

McKitterick, Rosamond. *The Carolingians and the Written Word.* Cambridge: Cambridge University Press, 1989.

――――. *The Frankish Church and the Carolingian Reforms, 789–895.* London: Royal Historical Society, 1977.

――――, ed. *The Uses of Literacy in Early Medieval Europe.* Cambridge: Cambridge University Press, 1990.

Schneider, Reinhard. "Zur rechtlichen Bedeutung der Kapitularientexte." *Deutsches Archiv für Erforschung des Mittelalters* 23 (1967): 273–94.

CAPUCIATI. The Capuciati exemplify the mix of politics and religion, of lay religiosity and social revolution, that characterizes the high Middle Ages. In 1182, responding to an infestation of brigands in the wake of the Plantagenêt-Capetian wars, a carpenter from Le Puy named Durand Dujardin had a vision of the Virgin telling him to form a brotherhood of peace. This confraternity of humble men wearing white hoods (*capuciati*) took a collective oath to go to Mass, to forgive each other all sins, and to renounce gaming, blaspheming, and frequenting taverns. Their numbers grew with astonishing rapidity, spreading throughout the central and southern provinces of France (Berry, Limousin, Gascony, Aquitaine, Provence). Chroniclers initially praised the movement and admired the piety of these laymen, and both lay and ecclesiastic nobles in their regions supported them. Within a year, the sworn Peace militias of the Capuciati had defeated several armies of brigands, slaughtering thousands.

Flushed with success, the Capuciati extended their definition of plunder to include prelates and nobles who exploited their serfs; they even invoked Adam and Eve as proof that all should be free and equal. This may be the earliest reference we have to the invocation of the Creation myth among European commoners to denounce aristocratic privilege; in later peasant revolts (England in 1381, Germany in 1525), we hear the ditty: "When Adam delved and Eve span/Who was then the Gentleman?" It is noteworthy that in all three cases these revolts of the commoners were preceded by translations of the Bible into the vernacular (by Waldo in the 1170s, Wyclif in the 1370s, Luther in 1521).

The aristocracy, perceiving the threat, turned against the Capuciati. Chroniclers denounced their "madness" and branded them heretics; and the brigands, now with the assistance of the nobility, took vengeance for their earlier defeats, massacring the Capuciati both on the battlefield and in their towns. Hugh of Noyers, a bellicose lord of royal lineage, became bishop of Auxerre in 1183, defeated the upstart peasants, and condemned them to go for a full year without covering their heads. By 1185, there seems to

be no trace left of the Capuciati. Their fate recalls that of the peasant *coniuratio* of 859 in Neustria, formed to defend against Viking raiders but wiped out by the local aristocracy for engaging in a collective oath, as described in the *Annales sancti Bertiniani.* But the overall dynamics reflect changes in both the religious and social situation in Europe after the millennium. In its ideology of peace, its collective oaths, and its popular militias, the movement was closely related to the early 11th-century Peace of God, although unlike this clerically led movement the Capuciati arose from the ranks of lay commoners.

Richard Landes

[See also: BRIGAND/BRIGANDAGE; HERESY; MILLENNIALISM; PEACE OF GOD; POPULAR DEVOTION; WALDO/WALDENSES]

Duby, Georges. *The Three Orders: Feudal Society Imagined,* trans. Arthur Goldhammer. Chicago: University of Chicago Press, 1978, pp. 327–36.

Luchaire, Achille. *Social France at the Time of Philip Augustus,* trans. Edward B. Krehbiel. New York: Holt, 1912, pp. 12–19.

CARCASSONNE. Situated in a strategic position on the Aude River between the Toulousain and the Mediterranean port of Narbonne, the city of Carcassonne (Aude) served throughout the Middle Ages primarily as a military stronghold and center of administration. Occupied at least since the 1st century A.D. by the Romans, Carcassonne was a major Visigothic stronghold after the 5th century, before becoming one of the largest walled cities in western Europe during the later Middle Ages. In the Carolingian period, the fortress of Carcassonne became the seat of a county; a comital dynasty appeared in the early 9th cen-

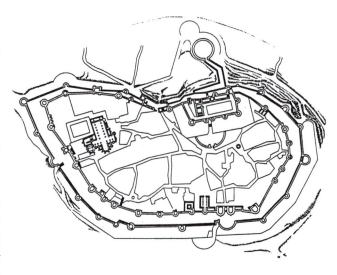

Carcassonne (Aude), plan of upper city. After Stierlin.

Carcassonne, upper city ramparts. *Photograph courtesy of Rebecca A. Baltzer.*

particularly as a center of textile manufacture, reached its height in the first half of the 14th century. After 1350, the city declined rapidly both in commercial and military importance. The raid of Edward, the Black Prince, in 1355 again left the *bourg* destroyed; in 1384, complicity in the revolt of the Tuchins subjected the burghers once more to crippling penalties.

Alan Friedlander

The city consists of a rectangular castle, 247 feet by 148 feet, and double curtain walls separated by grassy lists; the outer ramparts (about 5,000 feet long) have some twenty reinforcing towers or strongholds, and the inner ramparts (about 3,600 feet), twenty-five. The so-called Palace of the Viscounts was actually built, according to Héliot, in the 13th century by Simon de Montfort and especially Louis IX. Constructed of rough-worked sandstone, it is surrounded on three sides by a deep moat and protected by nine towers. Its main entry, between two half-round towers, is defended by a bridge and a semicircular barbican. Within, in lieu of a central keep, is an open courtyard flanked by a high watchtower. Construction on the walls was continued under Louis's son Philip III, who was responsible for several of the more remarkable towers, notably the Tour du Trésaur and Tour de l'Inquisition. A number of the towers have their own well and could be independently defended in the event other sections fell. The principal entry to the town, the Porte de l'Aude, was defended by a series of barbicans and outer works; those entering were required to approach first parallel to the line of defense, then perpendicular to it, thus exposing themselves to fire from every angle.

In its present state, and in spite of major restorations by Viollet-le-Duc in the 19th century, Carcassonne is one of the finest examples of a medieval walled city. Its ramparts and towers, with their crenellations, arrow loops, embrasures, potlug holes, hoarding, walks, and battlements, provide an outstanding example of medieval military architecture.

William W. Kibler

[See also: ALBIGENSIAN CRUSADE; LANGUEDOC; TRENCAVEL]

Finó, J.-F. *Forteresses de la France médiévale: construction, attaque, défense.* 3rd ed. Paris: Picard, 1977.

Guilaine, Jean, and Daniel Fabre. *Histoire de Carcassonne.* Toulouse: Privat, 1984.

Hauréau, Barthélemi. *Bernard Délicieux et l'Inquisition albigeoise (1300–1320).* Paris: Hachette, 1877.

Héliot, Pierre. "L'âge du château de Carcassonne." *Annales du Midi* 78 (1966): 7–21.

Mahul, Alphonse. *Cartulaire et archives des communes de l'ancien diocèse et de l'arrondissement administratif de Carcassonne.* 7 vols. Paris: Didron, 1857–82.

Poux, Joseph. *La cité de Carcassonne, histoire et description.* 5 vols. Toulouse: Privat, 1922–38.

tury. During the 11th and 12th centuries, Carcassonne was at the center of the vast domains controlled by the family of Trencavel. The city, twice lost and regained by the viscounts, played a pivotal role in the struggles between the counts of Toulouse and Barcelona.

The Albigensian Crusade of 1209 ended the dynasty of the Trencavels. Under Simon de Montfort and, after 1226, the king of France, Carcassonne became the seat of a *sénéchaussée.* In 1240, the final attempt of the young Raymond Trencavel to recover his domains failed in the desperate siege of Carcassonne. Trencavel's retreat left the *bourg*, which had joined his rebellion, abandoned and destroyed. It remained depopulated until 1248, when Louis IX had it reconstructed on the left bank of the Aude. At the end of the 13th century, the *bourg* was again the center of agitation, led by Bernard Délicieux against the Inquisition in the Midi. In 1305, fifteen burghers, including the consuls, were hanged for attempted insurrection and treason against the king of France.

Although Carcassonne never achieved the importance of Béziers, Narbonne, or Nîmes, its economic prosperity,

CARLOMAN. Name of several Carolingian rulers. The first Frankish ruler to bear the name Carloman was the eldest son of Charles Martel, mayor of the palace in the united Frankish kingdom. After Charles's death in 741, this Carloman became mayor of Austrasia, while his brother, Pepin III, received the mayoralty of the kingdom of Neustria. Since the Merovingian monarchs were then virtually powerless, the mayors were the most important officials in the land. Carloman and Pepin cooperated to extend their authority, quelling uprisings and supporting the church's efforts to spread Christianity in the region. In 743, they together reestablished a Merovingian, Childeric III, on the throne, vacant since 737. In 747, Carloman abdicated in favor of his brother in order to become a monk. He died in 754 in a monastery at Vienne, three years after Pepin had deposed Childeric and claimed the crown for himself.

The second Carloman was Pepin's younger son. When Pepin, now king of the Franks, died in 768, Carloman was given the more central territories and Charles, the future Charlemagne (742–814), the eldest, received lands encircling those of his brother. The two rulers did not get along, but Carloman's death in 771 permitted Charles to reunite the kingdom. Sometimes called Carloman II to distinguish him from his uncle, the younger Carloman was the first to reign as king. A century later another Carloman (d. 884), son of Louis II, reigned briefly. These two Carlomans should not be confused with King Carloman of Bavaria and Italy (d. 880) or Carloman (d. 876), the son of Charles the Bald.

Celia Chazelle

[See also: CAROLINGIAN DYNASTY]

Hlawitschka, Eduard. "Die Vorfahren Karls des Grossen." In *Karl der Grosse: Lebenswerk und Nachleben*, ed. Wolfgang Braunfels, et al. 5 vols. Düsseldorf: Schwann, 1965–68, Vol. 1, pp. 51–82.
Lot, Ferdinand. *Les destinées de l'empire en occident de 395 à 888*. Paris: Presses Universitaires de France, 1928.
McKitterick, Rosamond. *The Frankish Kingdoms Under the Carolingians, 751–987*. London: Longman, 1983.
Riché, Pierre. *The Carolingians: A Family Who Forged Europe*, trans. Michael Allen. Philadelphia: University of Pennsylvania Press, 1993.

CARMELITE ORDER. The religious order of Our Lady of Mount Carmel, popularly known as the Carmelites, originated in Palestine during the period of the Crusades and under the impetus of monastic and ascetic reform, although it claimed continuity with earlier hermits living on Mount Carmel and even with the prophet Elijah and his followers. Founded ca. 1154, with the earliest rule formulated in 1209 by Albert of Vercelli, Latin patriarch of Jerusalem, the Carmelites emphasized strict asceticism, abstinence from meat, a semi-eremitic life, and total poverty, much in line with other 12th-century monastic foundations and reforms. Their *Rule* was approved by Pope Honorius III in 1226. With the collapse of the crusader states and the crusading movement generally, the Carmelites moved to Europe and reorganized themselves after the pattern of the mendicant orders (Dominicans and Franciscans). They

changed from a movement dedicated to prayer and solitude into an order centered on an urban ministry, with preaching and care of the poor. A female branch of the order was established in the Low Countries in the mid-15th century and has continued as one of the most ascetic and enclosed of the modern female religious orders. Like other mendicant orders, the Carmelites began to seek a university education for their members so as to carry out preaching and missionary work, and the order gradually became clericalized. The quest for education and the acquisition of property for their urban mission led to tension with the original ideal of total poverty and solitude. The 16th century saw a major renewal and reform of the order in both its male and female branches.

Grover A. Zinn

[See also: CRUSADES; DOMINICAN ORDER; FRANCISCAN ORDER; MONASTICISM]

Smet, Joachim. *The Carmelites: A History of the Brothers of Our Lady of Mount Carmel, ca. 1200 A.D. Until the Council of Trent*. Chicago: "privately printed," 1975.

CAROLINGIAN ART. Although members of the Carolingian dynasty ruled in France from 751 to 987, artistic production was concentrated between the last quarter of the 8th century and the end of the 9th. This period witnessed an explosive increase in artistic production in many areas, notably architecture, monumental painting, book production, ivory carving, and many forms of metalwork, and it can fairly be said that Carolingian art laid the foundation for later medieval developments. Little remains today of the monumental arts, although many literary sources describe buildings and their decoration, and considerable evidence has been recovered from archaeological investigation, so that the numerous and often perfectly preserved examples of the "minor arts" give the fullest and clearest picture of Carolingian art as a whole.

The very term "Carolingian art," derived from the ruling dynasty, reflects a tradition of seeing the art of the period as primarily stimulated by centralized royal patronage, and indeed monarchs and ecclesiastical figures in the immediate royal circles were prominent and influential sponsors of artistic projects. On the other hand, much artistic production was spread widely throughout the kingdom, especially in the northern regions, and shows relatively little influence from courtly subjects or styles. Although the Carolingian monarchs clearly revived the ancient tradition of the ruler as patron and often subject of important artistic projects, the early-medieval tradition of artistic production being carried on in monasteries was also continued. Courtly and monastic patronage and production are often inseparable, with monasteries often producing works of art for or at the behest of the monarch.

For a variety of reasons, it seems that artistic production played an especially important role during the Carolingian period, often expressing contemporary political and theological circumstances, a phenomenon encouraged by the debate about the proper role of images in the

Christian church, which from 726 to 843 dominated the Byzantine world. There, the conflict between those who favored the veneration of holy images, or icons, as central elements of Christian cult and those, known as Iconoclasts, who opposed such practices and sought to destroy such images or circumscribe their use called for a western and especially Carolingian reaction. In 792, Archbishop Theodulf of Orléans drafted the first of a series of lengthy Carolingian treatises devoted to religious art. His work, now known as the *Libri Carolini* and in fact the most extensive early-medieval text concerning art, was originally designed to express an official Frankish viewpoint that images should be neither venerated nor destroyed and that they could help to instruct the faithful. The emphasis on didactic art that could convey an important message became a leading feature of Carolingian art, sometimes joined with a growing ability to evoke personal empathetic responses to the image. Images thus assumed a place of special significance, enhanced by the tendency to make grand artistic works to mark special personal and political moments.

The first important Carolingian building in France was the new monastery church at Saint-Denis, begun at the death of King Pepin to house his tomb, and completed and dedicated by his son Charlemagne in 775. Excavations suggest that the basilican church had a large transept, a feature previously contained only in the apostolic basilicas of St. Paul in Rome, and thus announcing a major feature of Carolingian artistic production, the relationship to early Christian and papal Roman art. The feature of the transept seems to have become common, even standard, in later Carolingian basilicas. The great basilica built during the 790s by Angilbert at Saint-Riquier (Centula) in northeastern France, now known from extensive literary descriptions and from some postmedieval drawings, had not only a transept but also several massive towers. An outstanding source of information for architecture and many other subjects is the famous Plan of Saint-Gall, a detailed layout of buildings for a monastery in Switzerland designed ca. 820, and probably reflecting building ideas more widely current throughout France as well as other parts of the Carolingian world. Not all ecclesiastical buildings were basilicas. The famous octagonal palace chapel built by Charlemagne at Aix-la-Chapelle in the 790s is not in France, but a contemporary central plan structure was erected by Archbishop Theodulf of Orléans at Germigny-des-Prés, and Charles the Bald built a magnificent palace chapel in the Aix-la-Chapelle tradition at Compiègne, consecrated in 877.

Few Carolingian mural paintings survive in France, but the extensive decorations in Switzerland, Italy, and Germany support the evidence of the crypt of the church of Saint-Germain at Auxerre that mural painting was produced in large amounts and achieved a high level. A special feature of Carolingian mural decoration is the use of mosaic at Aix-la-Chapelle (Aachen) and probably at Compiègne. The late 8th- or early 9th-century mosaic apse from Theodulf's oratory at Germigny has an unusual subject, the Ark of the Covenant as described in the Old Tes-

Crucifixion. Upper cover of the binding of the *Lindau Gospels*, Morgan MS M1. Gold and jewels, c. 870. *Courtesy of the Pierpont Morgan Library, New York.*

A Seraph, superimposed on the text of the *Sanctus*, Drogo Sacramentary. MS lat. 9428, fol. 15. *Courtesy of the Bibliothèque Nationale, Paris.*

tament, with statues of winged cherubim. Such an unprecedented subject for treatment in a major apse surely reflects the contemporary debate about images in the Christian church and stems directly from the patron's special interests.

Some of the most famous works of Carolingian art are illuminated manuscripts, which survive in large numbers and are often nearly perfectly preserved. Best known are the groups of books that can be closely associated with rulers, especially Charlemagne and Charles the Bald, and that appear to have been produced by scribes and painters directly attached to the royal entourage. The books for Charlemagne include the Gospel lectionary written by Godescalc (B.N. n.a. lat. 1203), datable 781–83, whose colophon employs one of the earliest examples of Carolingian minuscule script and which has elaborately ornamental frames for every page of text as well as impressively large portraits of Christ and the four Evangelists bearing many stylistic and iconographic connections with the 6th-century mosaic art of Ravenna. A slightly later group of books connected with Charlemagne and produced after the establishment of the royal court at Aix-la-Chapelle in 795 make a tighter group, including the Harley Gospels (B.L. Harley 2788), Soissons Gospels (B.N. lat. 8850), Abbeville Gospels, and Lorsch Gospels (Bucharest and Vatican Pal. lat. 50). Some features of the style, iconography, and layout of these books were followed by later groups associated with such monarchs as Charles the Bald, for example, the great *Codex aureus* from Saint-Emmeram of ca. 870 (Munich, Clm. 14000), and also by manuscripts produced at Reims, Fulda, Tours, and other monasteries, which from the second quarter of the 9th century produced luxury manuscripts in large numbers. With Reims is associated a dynamic and expressive, sketchy style of drawing whose greatest representative is the Utrecht Psalter; with Tours is especially associated a series of Bible manuscripts containing extended narrative sequences for scenes from Genesis, Exodus, and other biblical books.

Carolingian production of luxury manuscripts is most often associated with the great Gospels and Bibles but also includes a variety of other texts, some of which are of classical and early Christian origin, such as the comedies of Terence, the astronomical works of Aratus, and the *Psychomachia* of Prudentius; these clearly followed, to some degree, surviving ancient illustrated manuscripts. New pictorial schemes were developed as well. Several Sacramentaries received extensive cycles of illustrations for the first time, and the sequence of extraordinary acrostic poems written in the 820s by Rabanus Maurus of Fulda, *De laudibus sanctae crucis*, were designed from their inception for elaborate pictorial illustration and survive in several luxurious 9th-century manuscripts.

The altar was a preoccupation of Carolingian religious thought, which focused to a great degree on the eucharistic sacrifice, and it is therefore no surprise that architecture often made provision for multiple altars, each of which was required to contain at least one relic, and that a large amount of luxury art was produced for use on the altar. The great silver-gilt and enamel altar made by Vuolvinus and another artist for San Ambrogio in Milan in the mid-9th century probably draws upon French precedents and represents a type of altar decoration that must have been widespread. Altar books included not only Gospels and Psalters but Sacramentaries and prayer books, decorated with elaborate gold and jeweled or ivory covers of which one of the most spectacular is the cover with the crucifixion image of the Lindau Gospels, a work of the second half of the 9th century. Reliquaries were made in large numbers, still for the most part in the form of boxes or chests. A distinctive Carolingian type of object is represented by reverse-carved rock crystals, produced primarily in the general area of Lorraine. Generally decorated with the Crucifixion scene and clearly meant for the altar, the most spectacular of the group is decorated with eight scenes of the story of Susanna and appears to have been especially meant for the use of the king.

Although carved ivories were common in late antiquity, virtually none had been produced before the revival of the technique at the end of the 9th century in works generally associated with Charlemagne's circle. Well over a hundred 9th-century ivory carvings survive, some close transcriptions of early Christian models but others strikingly inventive in style and iconography, as, for example, a superb group close to Charles the Bald that draws upon the expressive style of the Utrecht Psalter. The largest surviving group of ivories decorate a throne made probably in eastern France for Charles the Bald and now preserved in the Vatican as the *Cathedra Petri*, including a remarkable group of twelve Labors of Hercules.

Lawrence Nees

[See also: AUXERRE; CAROLINGIAN DYNASTY; CHARLEMAGNE; CHARLES THE BALD; GERMIGNY-DES-PRÉS; IVORIES; LATIN POETRY, CAROLINGIAN; *LIBRI CAROLINI;* MANUSCRIPTS, PRODUCTION AND ILLUMINATION; PALEOGRAPHY AND MANUSCRIPTS; PEPIN; RABANUS MAURUS; RELICS AND RELIQUARIES; SAINT-DENIS; SAINT-RIQUIER; THEODULF OF ORLÉANS; TOURS/TOURAINE]

Braunfels, Wolfgang. *Die Welt der Karolinger und ihre Kunst.* Munich: Callwey, 1968.

Horn, Walter, and Ernest Born. *The Plan of St. Gall.* Berkeley: University of California Press, 1979.

Hubert, Jean, Jean Porcher, and Wolfgang Fritz Volbach. *The Carolingian Renaissance.* New York: Braziller, 1970.

Mütherich, Florentine, and Joachim E. Gaehde. *Carolingian Painting.* New York: Braziller, 1976.

Périn, Patrick, and Laure-Charlotte Feffer, eds. *La Neustrie: les pays au nord de la Loire de Dagobert à Charles le Chauve.* Rouen: Musées et Monuments Départementaux de Seine-Maritime, 1985.

CAROLINGIAN DYNASTY. Named after its most illustrious member, Charles (Lat. *Carolus*) the Great, or Charlemagne (742–814), the Carolingian family originated in the intermarriage of the Austrasian noble families of Pepin I of Landen (d. 640) and Arnulf of Metz (d. ca. 645). By the 9th century, their descendants ruled an area encompassing portions of modern East Europe and most of the western part of the Continent. From Pepin III's coronation in 751 until the early 10th century, there was always at least one Carolingian on a western throne.

Carolingian fortunes were initially advanced by the Merovingian king Clotar II (r. 584–629), who named Pepin of Landen mayor of the palace (*major domus*) of Austrasia for his help in uniting the Frankish kingdoms of Austrasia and Neustria. Under Pepin I, the post of mayor developed into the most powerful office in the Frankish regions. Such was the position's importance that when Pepin's son, Grimoald, became mayor on his father's death, he had his own son adopted by the reigning Merovingian king in order to place him in line for the throne. This was a maneuver that other Frankish nobles could not tolerate, however, and it led to Grimoald's murder in 656.

Despite this temporary setback for the Carolingians, Pepin I's grandson and duke of Austrasia, Pepin II of Heristal, managed to gain the mayoralty of both Austrasia and Neustria in 687. In contrast to Grimoald, he did not then seek access to the throne but limited himself to the office of *major domus,* a vantage point from which he was able to expand his hold on Frankish territories. His death in 714 precipitated a period of friction within the kingdom, as a power struggle opposed his sole surviving yet illegitimate son, Charles (later Martel), to Pepin's widow, Plectrude. It was only after defeating the forces of Plectrude and other opponents that Charles attained the political authority of his father.

Charles Martel proved a forceful leader of the Franks, strengthening their territorial claims through victories over other Germanic groups as well as over Muslims from Spain. Above all, his military prowess is epitomized by his defeat of a Muslim advance near Poitiers, in October 732. Although scholars debate the significance of that episode— subsequent engagements were necessary in the 8th and early 9th centuries before Muslim raids into the Frankish realm ended—it came to be viewed among western writers as the turning point in the West's struggle against Islam. This was the battle for which Charles received the nickname Martel ("the Hammer") in the 9th century.

The rudimentary administrative machine available to Charles allowed him to maintain only a loose control of the Frankish territories, and it was largely to preserve his grip on them that, as had Pepin II, he lent his support to the church and to its missionary work in the eastern regions. Like his father, Charles considered the church an instrument to further his own ends. He secularized ecclesiastical property to remunerate his supporters, appointed laymen to head abbeys and sees, and otherwise exercised his power, as he saw it, to name and to depose bishops. Such measures made for an incoherence in ecclesiastical organization that would be rectified only through the reforms of Charles's successors.

Upon Charles's death in 741, the kingdom was divided between his legitimate sons, Carloman (d. 754), the eldest, and Pepin III. The two brothers cooperated closely in governing the area left to them. In 743, they placed another Merovingian, Childeric III, on the royal throne, vacant since 737, as a measure to suppress rebellious sentiment among noble factions. In 747, Carloman felt called to the religious life and abdicated in Pepin's favor, leaving him mayor of a reunited realm. By 751, Pepin had asked Pope Zachary I to support his decision to depose Childeric and take the crown for himself, a move accomplished in November of that year. The new king, his wife, and sons, the first-born Charles (later Charlemagne) and a second Carloman, were anointed by Pope Stephen II in 754, who acclaimed Pepin and his sons "patricians of the Romans" in recognition of their special role in protecting Rome, and, at the same time, of the Holy See's new political orientation away from the East and toward northwestern Europe.

As mayor of the palace and king, Pepin supported, if only to a limited extent, Boniface's program to reform the Frankish church along Roman lines, which included efforts to improve clerical discipline and training. This was of fundamental importance to the surge in cultural and intellectual activity after Pepin's death, the Carolingian renaissance.

When Pepin III died in 768, his kingdom was shared between Charles and Carloman; the territories of the former encircled those of the latter. Friction existed between the two brothers, but Carloman died in 771, leaving Charles the sole monarch. Charlemagne's reign, first as king and from 800 as emperor in the West, witnessed a dramatic increase in the lands under Frankish control, the evolution of an administrative machine to govern this territory, and the cultural and intellectual developments that marked the Carolingian renaissance. During the first thirty years of his rule, Charles was involved in almost constant warfare: in 774, he defeated the Lombards; in 787, Duke Tassilo of Bavaria was overcome, though not decisively; campaigns in the 790s brought the conquest of the Avars; reprisals were launched against the rebellious Bretons during the later 8th century; in the early 9th century, engagements with Muslims led to the formation of the Spanish March along the Pyrénées. Above all, Charles faced the hostility of the Saxons to the east, whom he struggled to subdue from 772 until 804—through forced conversions, mass executions, and deportations as well as through battle. By the time these wars of conquest ceased in the early 9th century, the Carolingian territories extended from the English Channel to southern Italy, and from the Atlantic into eastern Germany.

Under Charlemagne, the basic units in the governance of so vast a realm were the counties, each headed by a member of the upper aristocracy given the title of count. The count maintained the peace, promulgated and enforced the laws, administered justice, and levied taxes. Government operated primarily at this local level, and ultimately the court had only limited control over the counts. The chief link between them and the central administration were the *missi dominici,* noble laymen, bishops, and occasionally abbots chosen to be the king's representatives, who undertook tours of inspection for him throughout the realm. They investigated charges of misconduct by local officials, assisted in certain judicial proceedings, heard new oaths of loyalty to the sovereign, and published new laws. The laws that the *missi* circulated and royal directives to

ANCESTORS OF CHARLEMAGNE

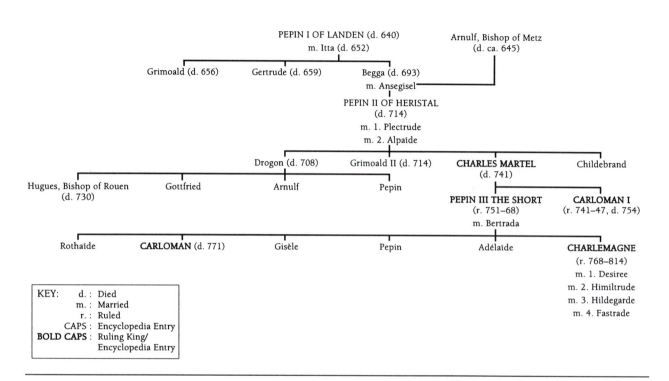

KEY:
d. : Died
m. : Married
r. : Ruled
CAPS : Encyclopedia Entry
BOLD CAPS : Ruling King/
Encyclopedia Entry

them were often recorded in documents known as capitularies, among them such important works from Charlemagne's reign as the Capitulary of Heristal (779) and the *Admonitio generalis* (789). Yet then, as previously among the Franks, the foundation of legislative action was the king's spoken word. The capitularies from Charlemagne's court were merely records of what he had orally decreed and carried no legislative weight in their own right. This legislative and administrative activity was matched by the cultural and intellectual revival of the same period, forwarded by the artists and scholars—Alcuin, Theodulf of Orléans, Paul the Deacon, Paulinus of Aquileia, and others—who gathered around Charlemagne.

All of these developments cast light on the motivations for Charlemagne's coronation as emperor of the West by Pope Leo III, on Christmas Day, 800, in St. Peter's, Rome. Whether the idea for the move came from the papal or the Carolingian court—a point debated by scholars—it suited both parties' interests. Even before 800, Carolingian writers had been evolving a concept of Charlemagne as the successor to Constantine I and the leader of a new Christian-Roman empire in the West. For the papacy, on the other hand, the coronation underscored Charles's special role as protector of western Christendom, at a time when papal authority was particularly threatened.

It is uncertain whether Charlemagne initially viewed the imperial title as a personal honor or one to be passed on to an heir. No arrangement was made concerning it in the *Divisio regnorum* of 806, which decreed that after his death the empire be partitioned among his legitimate sons,

Charles the Younger (d. 811), Pepin (d. 810), and Louis (778–840; later known as "the Pious"); but the inheritance of the imperial crown may have been something that even then Charlemagne intended to settle later. By 813, Charles the Younger and Pepin were dead, however, and in September Louis was crowned co-emperor. He became sole emperor upon his father's death in January 814.

The reign of Louis the Pious witnessed probably the peak of the Carolingian renaissance in arts and letters as well as the implementation of important religious and administrative reforms; but it also saw the political crises emerge that led to the empire's dissolution. The political turmoil of the 830s stemmed partly from the disaffection of aristocratic groups over Louis's ecclesiastical reforms and partly from problems caused by his plans for the succession.

The terms of the inheritance were first outlined in the *Ordinatio imperii* of 817. Whereas Charlemagne had arranged the imperial succession only a year before his death, Louis the Pious made this from the start a basic element of his plans. The *Ordinatio* stipulated that each of his sons—Lothair I (795–855), Pepin of Aquitaine (800–838), and Louis (804–876; later known as "the German")—receive a portion of the empire to govern, while Italy remained under Louis the Pious's nephew, Bernard. But the imperial crown was bestowed immediately on Lothair I alone, who was to rule the empire's most important territories, including Aix-la-Chapelle and Rome, and to exercise supremacy over his brothers and Bernard. Although Louis the German and Pepin were too young to react to these plans, the *Ordinatio*

DESCENDANTS OF CHARLEMAGNE

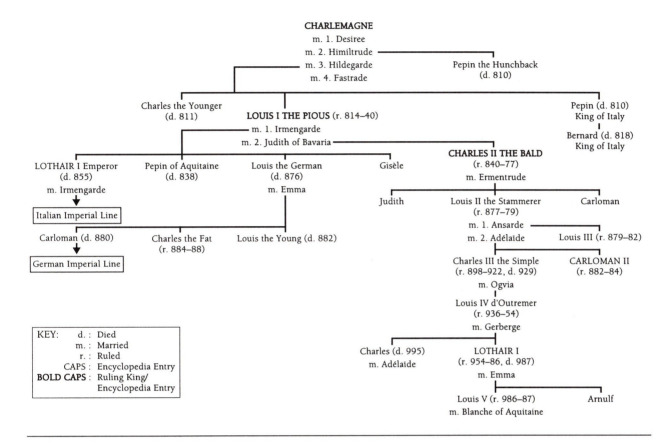

provoked Bernard to revolt in 817. The rebellion was crushed and its instigator blinded, a punishment from which he died.

Difficulties for Louis the Pious increased with the birth in 823 of Charles (later known as "the Bald") to his second wife, Judith. (The three older sons were by his first spouse, Irmengarde.) A revised scheme of inheritance gave to Charles lands previously intended for his older brothers. Coming on top of existing tensions between Louis and Lothair I, this drove Lothair and his supporters to revolt in 830. Over the next several years, conflicts between the aging emperor and one or more of his sons plagued the empire. Although Louis managed to regain political control in 834 and confined Lothair to Italy, strife among Lothair, Louis the German, and Charles the Bald flared after their father's death in 840. The written records that were made of one attempted accord between Louis the German and Charles, the Oaths of Strasbourg of 842, provide unique evidence of the French and German vernaculars of the day; but the agreement failed to achieve a lasting peace. In 843, the Treaty of Verdun ended the ideal of a united empire by dividing it into separate kingdoms for Louis the Pious's surviving sons: to Charles went the western regions, to Louis the German the eastern territories, and to Lothair the middle

section. Yet this only temporarily ended the conflict. The tensions among the brothers, along with such external threats as Viking raids, undermined the authority of the Carolingian monarchs and encouraged the rise of aristocratic factions. The church's authority in secular affairs also grew, as it increasingly claimed a right to intervene in political issues.

After Lothair I's death in 855, his kingdom was shared among his three sons. Italy was given to the eldest, Louis II (d. 875), who had received the imperial crown in 850, while Lothair II (d. 869) obtained the kingdom of Lorraine and Charles (d. 863) the kingdom of Provence. Charles of Provence's realm was partitioned after his death between his two brothers. When Lothair II died, however, Louis II was too busy battling the Muslims in southern Italy to be a serious contender for his lands, and the Treaty of Meerssen (870) split them between Louis the German and Charles the Bald. The boundaries thus formed are the basis for those between France and Germany today.

Emperor Louis II died in 875, leaving no male heirs, and Charles the Bald gained the title of emperor and the realm of Italy. Since Louis II's brothers also had lacked sons who could inherit (the church had thwarted Lothair II's attempt to divorce his wife and marry a mistress who had borne him a son), the rule of Lothair I's line ceased.

The political chaos of the decades after 840 was offset, in Charles the Bald's kingdom, by the continued flourishing of artistic and intellectual activity. Charles's court rivaled those of his father and grandfather in the renown of the theologians it attracted, among them Hincmar of Reims and Johannes Scottus Eriugena, and in the impressive artwork associated with his reign, but this was the last great center of learning and art linked with the Carolingian dynasty. Toward the end of the 9th century, continued Viking raids and the rising power of local aristocracy speeded the disintegration of the central administrations in the eastern and western kingdoms. When the death of the West Frankish king in 884 left only an infant as heir, the great clerics and laymen of that realm turned to the emperor Charles the Fat, king of the East Franks, who thereby reunited virtually the entire area of Charlemagne's empire, but when Charles the Fat was deposed in 887 the West Frankish nobility gave the crown to a non-Carolingian. The Carolingians returned to power in the western territory with the enthronement there of Charles the Simple (r. 898–922) and later with the reigns of Louis IV d'Outremer (r. 936–54), his son Lothair (r. 954–86), and his grandson Louis V (r. 986–87). Louis V was the last ruler of the line, and after his death the kingdom passed to Hugh Capet.

In the East Frankish realm, Charles the Fat was succeeded in 887 by Arnulf of Carinthia (r. 887–99), the illegitimate son of Charles's older brother, Carloman, and then by Louis the Child (r. 899–911), Arnulf's son and a minor when he came to the throne. When Louis died, the nobles elected Conrad of Franconia.

Celia Chazelle

[See also: CAPITULARY; CAROLINGIAN ART; CHARLEMAGNE; CHARLES II THE BALD; CHARLES MARTEL; LATIN POETRY, CAROLINGIAN; LOTHAIR I (EMPEROR); LOTHAIR I (KING); LOUIS I THE PIOUS]

Braunfels, Wolfgang, et al., eds. *Karl der Grosse: Lebenswerk und Nachleben.* 5 vols. Düsseldorf: Schwann, 1965–68.

Bullough, Donald A. *Carolingian Renewal: Sources and Heritage.* Manchester: Manchester University Press, 1991.

Ganshof, François L. *The Carolingians and the Frankish Monarchy: Studies in Carolingian History*, trans. Janet Sondheimer. London: Longman, 1971.

Godman, Peter. *Poets and Emperors: Frankish Politics and Carolingian Poetry.* Oxford: Clarendon Press; New York: Oxford University Press, 1987.

———, and Roger Collins, eds. *Charlemagne's Heir: New Perspectives on the Reign of Louis the Pious (814–840).* Oxford: Clarendon Press, 1990.

Halphen, Louis. *Charlemagne and the Carolingian Empire*, trans. Giselle de Nie. Amsterdam: North-Holland, 1977.

Lebecq, Stéphane. *Les origines franques: Ve–IXe siècle.* Paris: Seuil, 1990.

McKitterick, Rosamond. *The Frankish Church and the Carolingian Reforms, 789–895.* London: Royal Historical Society, 1977.

———. *The Frankish Kingdoms Under the Carolingians, 751–987.* London: Longman, 1983.

Nelson, Janet L. *Charles the Bald.* London: Longman, 1992.

Noble, Thomas F.X. *The Republic of St. Peter: The Birth of the Papal State, 680–825.* Philadelphia: University of Pennsylvania Press, 1984.

Riché, Pierre. *The Carolingians: A Family Who Forged Europe*, trans. Michael I. Allen. Philadelphia: University of Pennsylvania Press, 1993.

CARON, FIRMINUS (fl. late 15th c.). Composer active in the years 1460–80, to judge from the sources and styles of his music. None of the proposed identifications has the correct first name, as attested by the generally reliable Johannes Tinctoris and by one musical source. A Firminus Caron was a senior musician at Amiens Cathedral in 1422, too early to be our composer, though conceivably related to him. Given the large number of musical institutions for which no adequate documentation survives, it should be no surprise that direct biographical information is lacking for an important and influential composer.

Caron's known works comprise five Mass cycles (surviving only in Italian manuscripts) and some twenty French chansons. His Mass *L'homme armé* shows the distinct influence of Guillaume Dufay (d. 1474), as does his rondeau *Du tout ainsy.* Two of his songs set poetry by Alain Chartier. His prime distinction is in certain songs that were repeatedly copied: *Accueilly m'a la belle* (nine sources), *Cent mille escus* (fifteen sources), *Le despourveu* (eleven sources), and particularly *Helas que pourra devenir* (twenty-one sources)—this last being an extreme case of the intricate close imitation with offbeat rhythms that he so often explored in his music.

David Fallows

Caron, Firminus. *Les œuvres complètes de Philippe (?) Caron*, ed. James Thomson. 2 vols. Brooklyn: Institute of Mediaeval Music, 1971–76.

Thomson, James. *An Introduction to Philippe (?) Caron.* Brooklyn: Institute of Mediaeval Music, 1964.

CARTA CARITATIS. Relations among houses of the Cistercian order were governed by the *Carta caritatis*, drawn up probably in 1114, when Cîteaux founded Pontigny, its second daughter house. This document, intended as a basis for regulating the relations between the New Monastery of Cîteaux and her daughters, emphasized the uniformity of practice at Cistercian houses and the mutual love that should bind them together. Like most of the early institutes of the Cistercian order, the *Carta caritatis* was produced by Abbot Stephen Harding (r. 1108–33).

Constance B. Bouchard

[See also: CISTERCIAN ORDER; MONASTICISM; STEPHEN HARDING]

Bouton, Jean de la Croix, and Jean Baptise Van Damme, eds. *Les plus anciens textes de Cîteaux.* Achel: Commentarii Cistercienses, 1974.

Auberger, Jean-Baptise. *L'unanimité cistercienne primitive: mythe ou réalité?* Achel: Commentarii Cistercienses, 1986.

CARTHUSIAN ORDER. The monastery of La Grande Chartreuse, the mother house of the Carthusian order, was founded by St. Bruno in 1084, high in the Alps north of Grenoble. Bruno was assisted in this foundation by Bishop Hugues I of Grenoble (d. 1132). The house always retained many eremitical elements; the monks lived in individual cells, although they met together for Matins and Vespers every day and for a walk once a week. In their search for isolation, the monks avoided parish responsibilities and prayers for the dead other than their own monastic brothers and indeed even tried to avoid visitors. Like the Cistercians, the Carthusians relied for agricultural labor on *conversi*, men who had left the world though not living a life of constant prayer. The purpose, again, was to be self-sustaining so as to minimize contact with the outer world.

In the 12th century, all Carthusian houses were founded far from any settlements, although in the 13th century new houses began to be founded just outside of cities. The order always remained small. By the end of the Middle Ages, Carthusian houses (or "Charter houses") were found as far away as Hungary, England, and Portugal, but the Carthusians never attained the popularity of their contemporaries the Cistercians. The order was widely admired for its holiness of life and attracted new members primarily from within the church, especially the more intellectual sector. Unlike every other medieval monastic order, it never needed reform.

Constance B. Bouchard

[See also: BRUNO; GRENOBLE; MONASTICISM]

Bligny, Bernard, ed. *Recueil des plus anciens actes de la Grande-Chartreuse (1086–1196).* Grenoble: Allier, 1958.
———. *Saint Bruno: le premier chartreux.* Rennes: Ouest-France, 1984.
———, and Gérald Chaix, eds. *La naissance des Chartreuses: Actes du VIe Colloque International d'Histoire et de Spiritualité Cartusiennes.* Grenoble: n.p., 1984.

CARTULARY. For a notary, the cartulary is the book of notes, first drafts, or summaries of charters issued by him as a quasipublic or public authority. He could consult those notes when necessary to authenticate a contract that he or one of his predecessors had written up. Another type of cartulary is strictly private; these began to be drawn up in earlier times (although the 12th and 13th centuries were the heyday of such compilations) by monastic and other ecclesiastical corporations, universities, and powerful families intent on gathering evidence of their rights and landholdings by copying into parchment codices, or occasionally rolls, private charters, royal diplomas and papal bulls, and other materials (e.g., *censiers*, or rent books) concerning that family, abbey, or bishopric and its holdings in a particular district. The relationship between the private cartulary and the original charters and other documents was often complex. In some cases, the first drafts were made directly into the volume and then charters were copied out for the parties involved; more often, the cartulary constitutes the copy (or even reconstruction, sometimes forgery) of documents written down at a considerably earlier date.

Constance H. Berman

[See also: CHARTER]

Pryor, John H. *Business Contracts of Medieval Provence.* Toronto: Pontifical Institute of Mediaeval Studies, 1981.

CAS ROYAUX. The development and expansion of royal justice in the 13th century led the French crown to extend royal jurisdiction at the expense of others, like the church or the great seigneurs. One of the methods was to place more emphasis on the category of cases known as *cas royaux*, in which only royal courts had jurisdiction. The concept was not new, but the ability of royal courts to claim such a monopoly and enforce it with respect to an expanding list of cases came only during the 13th century. The *cas royaux* included those involving *lèse majesté*, rebellion, counterfeiting the royal seal or coinage, violation of royal safeguard, the conduct of royal officials, amortissements, peerages, and royal forests.

John Bell Henneman, Jr.

Perrot, Ernest. *Les cas royaux.* Paris: Rousseau, 1910.

CASSEL. The town of Cassel (Nord), a stronghold in medieval Flanders that Count Arnulf I rebuilt after the Norse raids of the 9th century, was the scene of two important battles. The first of these was in 1071, when Robert the Frisian defeated the forces of Philip I of France and thereby secured the county of Flanders. The second battle occurred in 1328, after Count Louis I appealed for help to the new king of France, Philip VI. A rebellion of several years' duration had forced Louis out of Flanders, and Philip VI, who lacked a clear title to the throne and needed the count's support, agreed to render aid. The Flemings had shocked the French with their victory at Courtrai in 1302, and when they attacked the royal army near Cassel on August 23, 1328, they achieved some initial success. The French, however, with critical assistance from the count of Hainaut, overcame early reverses and won a decisive victory, effectively restoring Louis to his county and strengthening Philip's position at home.

John Bell Henneman, Jr.

Lucas, Henry S. *The Low Countries and the Hundred Years War, 1326–1347.* Ann Arbor: University of Michigan Publications, 1929.

CASSIAN, JOHN (d. 435). Essentially nothing is known of the early life of this important figure in the development of Christian monasticism in southern France. Born probably in the Roman province of Scythia Minor (present-day Romania), Cassian appears ca. 385 as a member of a monastic community in Bethlehem; in 385, or shortly thereafter, he and a friend named Germanus left for a "tour" of the monastic settlements in Egypt, where they discussed such matters as ascetic discipline and prayer with desert monks. By 399 or 400, Cassian and Germanus had left Egypt, probably because of controversy over the theology of Origen. In Constantinople, Cassian was ordained deacon by John Chrysostom and then, in 405, went on to Rome. By 410–15, Cassian was at Marseille in southern Gaul, where he founded two monasteries, one for women, the other for men.

Cassian's fame rests on two books that he wrote after settling at Marseille: the *Institutes* and the *Conferences*. The *Institutes* was composed at the request of Castor, bishop of Apt, who had decided to found a monastery. In Books 1–4, Cassian deals with the dress, prayer, and rules for monks in community and draws extensively on his Egyptian experience. Books 5–12 are each devoted to one of the eight capital sins (gluttony, lust, covetousness, anger, melancholy, accedia, vanity, and pride), their symptoms, and their remedies; in this, as in many other aspects of his spirituality, he follows the Greek monastic author Evagrius. In the *Conferences*, Cassian claims to be recounting conversations held several decades earlier with Egyptian desert ascetics. The twenty-four conferences are concerned primarily with the techniques of bodily and spiritual discipline that lead to effective prayer, and thus contemplation. Within the monastic life, Cassian distinguishes an "active life," which he understands as the pursuit of virtue and flight from sin, from the "contemplative life," the life of quietness, prayer, and contemplation. Drawing again upon Evagrius, Cassian sees the goal of the active life as *apatheia* (Evagrius's Greek term for a state of passionlessness or detachment) or "purity of heart" (Cassian's usual term for the same state; cf. Matthew 5:8, "Blessed are the pure in heart for they shall see God"). This state of tranquillity, purity, and freedom from distraction is the starting point for concentration, interiorization, and advancement in prayer leading toward the experience of divine presence.

Cassian also wrote an anti-Nestorian christological treatise (*De incarnatione*) and in his thirteenth *Conference* opposed Augustine's ideas about grace by suggesting that the human will has some independent role in salvation (a position later known as Semi-Pelagianism).

Cassian's influence on western monasticism and spirituality was profound and lasting. His monastic regulations and spirituality influenced Benedict of Nursia and many later monastic writers. His transmission of the ideas of Evagrius, especially on *apatheia* or purity of heart, was crucial for western spirituality. The *Rule of St. Benedict*'s requirement that the *Conferences* be read to the monks during meals ensured that generations of monks would be shaped by the ideals of asceticism and prayer that Cassian had gleaned from the desert ascetics.

Grover A. Zinn

[See also: CAESARIUS OF ARLES; MONASTICISM; MYSTICISM]

Cassian, John. *Opera*. PL 49–50.
———. *Opera*, ed. Michael Petschenig. *CSEL* 13, 17. Vindobonae: apud C. Geroldi filium, 1886–88.
———. *John Cassian: Conferences*, trans. Colin Luibheid. New York: Paulist, 1985.
Chadwick, Owen. *John Cassian: A Study in Primitive Monasticism*. 2nd ed. London: Cambridge University Press, 1968.
———. *Western Asceticism*. Philadelphia: Westminster, 1958. [Translation of selected *Conferences*.]
Rousseau, Philip. *Ascetics, Authority and the Church in the Age of Jerome and Cassian*. Oxford: Oxford University Press, 1978.

CASTEL, JEAN (ca. 1425–1476). Grandson of Christine de Pizan and son of another Jean Castel, secretary of the French dauphin, the future Charles VII, Castel became a Cluniac monk at Saint-Martin-des-Champs ca. 1439. In 1461, Louis XI transferred there from Saint-Denis the official chronicles of France and appointed Castel an official chronicler. In 1468, he composed for Jean de Bellay, bishop of Poitiers, his *Spécule des pécheurs*, a long moralizing poem. He also exchanged ballades with Georges Chastellain. He was named king's secretary in 1470 and two years later was nominated abbot of Saint-Maur-des-Fossés, where he spent his last years. Castel is the presumed author of a *Mirouer des dames et damoyselles et de tout le sexe femenin*, a meditation on worldly vanity written in a mixture of French and Latin. Although he is mostly forgotten today, Martin Lefranc considered him one of the best poets of the day and Jean Molinet spoke of his importance as a historian.

Charity Cannon Willard

Castel, Jean. *Lo specchio delle dame et altri testi del XI sec.*, ed. G. A. Brunelli. Florence: Sansoni, 1958.
Bossuat, Robert. "Jean Castel, chroniqueur de France." *Moyen âge* 64 (1958): 285–304, 499–538.
Brunelli, G. A. "Jean Castel et le 'Mirouer des Dames.'" *Moyen âge* 62 (1956): 93–117.

CASTELLAN/*CHÂTELAIN*. Commander of a castle. Originally the deputy of a superior, the castellan became largely independent during the proliferation of castle building after the year 1000. Behind the protection of their walls, they could defy superiors and subjugate the local rural population within their district. By the end of the 11th century, castellans, with the help of warrior bands often garrisoned in the castles, exercised extensive judicial and economic authority (*bannum*) over the surrounding region. They constituted a middle-level aristocracy between the dukes, counts, and viscounts on the one hand and the *milites* (knights) on the other. For the remainder of the Middle Ages, the title of castellan could indicate anything from a local lord to a petty official (similar to a *prévôt*) to a courtly sinecure.

Richard Landes

[See also: CASTLE; FEUDALISM; KNIGHTHOOD; NOBILITY; SEIGNEUR/SEIGNEURIE]

Aubenas, Roger. "Les châteaux forts des Xe et XIe siècles." *Revue historique du droit français et étranger* 4th ser. 17 (1938): 548–86.

Beech, George. "A Feudal Document of Early Eleventh Century Poitou." In *Mélanges d'histoire médiévale dédiés a René Crozet.* Poitiers: Centre d'Études Supérieures de Civilisation Médiévale, 1966. Vol. 1, pp. 203–13.

Bouchard, Constance. "The Origins of the French Nobility: A Reassessment." *American Historical Review* 86 (1981): 501–32.

Debord, André. *La société laique dans la Charente.* Paris: Picard, 1985.

CASTLE.

CASTLE. Fortifications were ubiquitous throughout medieval Europe, but "castle" (Fr. *château* from Lat. *castellum*) generally applies to a specific type of fortification that first appeared in France in the 10th century. The development of castles was linked to the changes in society during the "Feudal Age" following the breakup of Carolingian power. Growing out of the military needs of the great princes and seigneurs, castles were not simply fortresses but centers of political, economic, and social life as well. They profoundly influenced the development of the French countryside during the high Middle Ages.

Originally, the most common fortifications of the early Middle Ages were the massive walls of Roman cities, such as Poitiers and Le Mans, fortified in the 3rd century. Smaller fortifications were constructed throughout the Merovingian and Carolingian periods, many of them to serve as temporary refuges for the rural population. The Carolingians claimed a monopoly on military construction, but the collapse of Carolingian power led to the need for local defense and the proliferation of a new type of fortress.

At its simplest, this new fortress consisted of an earthen mound, or "motte," surrounded by a ditch and a wooden rampart, the "bailey." Often a tower of wood or stone, called the "donjon" (Lat. *dungio*), appeared on the mound. It was designed to provide both a residence and a defense for the lord of the castle. Remains of mottes are especially numerous in France, with one modern *département* alone having seventy-seven. While most of the construction was originally of wood, stone became the most common material in the late 11th and early 12th centuries.

Function rather than appearance distinguished the castle from other fortifications. The castle's military and political role can best be illustrated by the career of Count Foulques Nerra of Anjou (r. 987–1040), sometimes called "the Builder" because of his innovative use of stone castles. In his strategy, castles were built to ensure communications with far-flung possessions threatened by enemies. His interlocking network of fortifications, each constructed a day's ride from the next, created a "defense in depth" for the Angevin heartland. Although it ensured the external security of Anjou, the system generated an internal danger: the growing power of the castellans entrusted with the castles. After 1060, many Angevin castles slipped from the count's control into that of castellans acting as independent seigneurs. Of diverse origins, the seigneurs used their castles to establish their own authority over the neighboring territory. For them, the castle was not exclusively a military installation. The birthplace of the lineage, castles gave their possessors a particular place in the feudal hierarchy. Seigneurs exercised power that had once pertained to kings and royal officials over the people of the surrounding countryside. The growth of rural population and trade often focused on the location of castles and parish churches, thoroughly disrupting the settlement pattern inherited from late antiquity.

Tension between counts seeking to maintain public authority and fortified seigneurs seeking to enhance their own independence was typical of much of France. As in Anjou, the princes of the great territorial principalities had to struggle, not always successfully, to reestablish their control over the seigneurs. Castle architecture became increasingly complex from the 12th to 13th centuries. The donjon was no longer a residence but now had several stories with thicker walls. Eventually, it became merely one of the towers of the enclosing wall. Inner walls were added, as well as massive defenses to protect the gates. Elaborate crenellations, machicolations, and turrets to aid the defenders gave the appearance most often associated with medieval castles. All of these precautions became obsolete with the widespread use of gunpowder in the 14th and 15th centuries, and castles became simply country residences for the nobility. As such, they remained symbols of seigneurial rights until the French Revolution.

Scott Jesse

[See also: CASTELLAN/*CHÂTELAIN*; CHÂTEAU-GAILLARD; MILITARY ARCHITECTURE]

Babelon, Jean-Pierre, ed. *Le château en France.* Paris: Berger-Levrault, 1986.

Bachrach, Bernard S. "The Angevin Strategy of Castle-Building in the Reign of Fulk Nerra, Count of the Angevins, 987–1040." *American Historical Review* 88 (1983): 533–60.

Fournier, Gabriel. *Le château dans la France médiévale.* Paris: Aubier Montaigne, 1978.

Salch, Charles-Laurent, et al. *L'atlas des châteaux forts en France.* Strasbourg: Publitotal, 1977.

CATALONIA.

CATALONIA. Catalonia, a region whose name derives from the proliferation of castles during the 11th century, is situated in the northeast corner of the Iberian peninsula. It comprises four modern provinces in Spain (Barcelona, Tarragona, Gerona, and Lérida), plus Andorra and the adjacent French *département* of the Pyrénées-Orientales. Mountains divide the region into valleys that drain into the Mediterranean Sea either directly or via the lower Ebro River.

From the 5th century, Visigoths inhabited Catalonia's Roman cities (e.g., Barcelona, Tarragona, Gerona), which declined in population with economic stagnation; during Muslim invasions of the 8th century, many Christians sought refuge in high mountain villages, concentrating populations there. In 795, Charlemagne designated northern Catalonia as the "Spanish March" of his Frankish kingdom, in anticipation of military victories over local Muslim rulers. Through the intervention of Alcuin, the Adoptionist teachings of Bishop Felix of Urgel were condemned in the late 8th century; subsequently, Roman orthodoxy gained ground in the Catalonian church over Mozarabic influences. The 9th century saw the emergence of an indigenous Hispano-Gothic ruling aristocracy, which intermarried with the southern French nobility and remained loyal to the Frankish kingdom.

As the caliphate of Cordova disintegrated into petty kingdoms, the military advantage shifted to Christian forces. From the early 11th century, the Catalonian nobility profited from trade in arms and export of mercenary services to the Muslim south. The gold they received in exchange contributed to an economic revival both in Catalonia and in western Europe generally.

Catalonia's social order was severely disrupted in the early 11th century by the deterioration of the authority of the count of Barcelona. Local strongmen usurped the authority of the count by constructing castles from which they subjugated a heretofore largely free peasantry. By the end of the 11th century, the rule of law was generally replaced by a new system of military alliances cemented by bonds of fealty and grants of fiefs. Such social and political turmoil inspired the Truce of God movement in Catalonia beginning in 1027.

During the 12th century, the count of Barcelona succeeded in redirecting the energy of Catalonia's military class toward the expansion of his influence and power within the region of Catalonia and beyond its boundaries. In 1137, Ramon Berenguer IV acquired political control of the inland kingdom of Aragon through his marriage to Queen Petronilla. His descendants from 1180 on were known as "count-kings" (of Barcelona-Aragon).

Prior to the Albigensian Crusade, the influence of the House of Barcelona extended north and east of the Pyrénées to the Occitan region of Béarn, Foix, and Toulouse and to Provence. However, the defeat of Count-king Peter I in the Battle of Muret in 1213 effectively ended Catalonia's political influence in Occitania, and under James I the nobility redirected its military attention toward the reconquest of Muslim Spain and the projection of Catalonian influence in the eastern Mediterranean. Nominal suzerainty of the Capetian monarch over the count-kings of Barcelona ended with the Treaty of Corbeil in 1258.

John C. Shidelar

[See also: LANGUEDOC; SPANISH MARCH]

Bisson, Thomas N. *The Medieval Crown of Aragon: A Short History.* New York: Oxford University Press, 1986.
Bonnassie, Pierre. *La Catalogne du milieu du Xe à la fin du XIe siècle.* Toulouse: Association des Publications de l'Université de Toulouse-LeMirail, 1975–76.

CATHARS. Cathari (Greek for "pure ones") was the least offensive of many names for members of a dualist heresy that spread through much of western Europe in the later 12th and 13th centuries. They were also known as Bulgari, *bougres*, buggers (from the Bogomils of Bulgaria), Albigenses (from their stronghold in Albi), and Manichaei (from their alleged dualist ancestors in late antiquity). Despite the survival of some Cathar texts (Gnostic "scriptures" from late antiquity, rituals, the *Book of Two Principles*), the movement is known largely from church documents, such as chronicles, theological invective, and inquisitorial transcripts. As a result, almost everything about the movement is a matter for scholarly dispute. Some historians place its origins in the early 11th century, when popular "heresies" that reject the church first begin to appear in the West; these, they argue, are the result of missionaries of the 10th-century Bogomil heresy from Bulgaria. But none of these cases shows explicit evidence of either dualism or eastern influence. That first appears in the documents of the mid-12th century, when the Cathars seem to be spreading at alarming speed. It is in many cases difficult to judge whether a movement's rejection of ecclesiastical media of salvation and emphasis on asceticism come from a desire to replicate the spirituality of the Apostles or from a dualist ideology. Indeed, the Cathars present themselves as apostolic communities.

Like the Gnostics of late antiquity, the Cathars believed that evil was an independent force in the universe, that it was Satan who in fact had created the physical universe (hence, the God of Genesis), which he used as a prison in which to trap souls, which would continue to transmigrate from incarnation to reincarnation until they had escaped the tentacles of the Evil One. Procreation merely perpetuated Satan's work, and Cathar adepts refused not only all sexual contact but the eating of anything that came from coition, such as meat, cheese, and eggs (but not fish, which they believed reproduced spontaneously). These beliefs were expressed in mythical accounts of the Creation, in which Satan was alternately a fallen angel, a younger brother of Christ, or, in the case of radical dualists, a direct rival of God. This literature focused far more on the evil God and his minions, rulers of this world, than on the good God.

Unlike earlier "heretics," the Cathars developed an independent ecclesiastical structure. The first sign of this alternative church appeared in the Rhineland (1143) and rapidly spread throughout western Europe. By 1165, there were public debates at Lombers (near Albi) between Cathar leaders and Catholic bishops. A decade or so later, first in Italy, then in Languedoc, an eastern envoy named Nicetas converted many to a more radical brand of dualism. This doctrinal source of divisiveness was soon amplified by a Donatist-like controversy over the moral purity of certain Cathari, including the man who had administered the *consolamentum* to Nicetas.

Despite this apparent internal strife, the Cathar movement continued to gain adherents throughout Europe. Persecution in the northern regions, however, tended to push them southward to the more tolerant climes of Occitania, where they became a large minority of the population or even in some places a majority, as in Foix. They gained adherents from among all sectors of the population, urban and rural, peasant, artisan, merchant, and noble;

the high numbers of artisans in the early movement led the northern French to name them *texerant* ("weavers"). The movement spread particularly effectively through women, who turned their households into centers of Cathar preaching and learning. The role of women in the movement led the Inquisition to demand oaths of loyalty to the church from boys over twelve years old but from girls over eight.

The Cathar church was structured in several layers. At the top was a relatively clear-cut ecclesiastical hierarchy, presided over by bishops who administered the *consolamentum* to the "perfects." The perfects adhered to a rigidly ascetic code: apostolic poverty, regular fasts, monthly public confession, constant prayer, and avoidance of physical contact with the opposite sex, killing, swearing of oaths, and foods associated with coition. The perfects often traveled about, preaching to, praying for, and confessing the faithful. Laypeople in general were not expected to live up to the standards of the perfects and took the *consolamentum* only shortly before death. While not allowed to address God as "Our Father," hence to pray, they were to attend sermons and confess regularly (*melioramentum*). A group known as the "believers" took a more active role in the support of the perfects and may even have been able to say the Lord's Prayer.

Beyond these groups was a large number of sympathizers who, out of conservatism or fear, may have remained Catholic but who nevertheless admired the perfects for their spiritual discipline and found the mythical theodicy attractive. It was thus impossible for contemporaries, and so much the more for modern historians, to have a sense of how numerous and influential the Cathars were. It seems clear, however, that the moral and ascetic contrast between the way of life of the Cathar and the Catholic clergy worked decisively to the advantage of the former in drawing the loyalty of the laity.

The new sect's popularity and absolute rejection of the Catholic church posed a grave threat. Early efforts to resist their advances in the area of their greatest strength, Languedoc, failed: Cistercians, licensed as papal legates, rode horses and dressed in rich ecclesiastical vestments, thus failing to win much popular support for their brand of Christianity against the simply dressed, pedestrian Cathars. Although the "apostolic" Waldensians were ready and willing to go into battle against the Cathars, clerics were too suspicious to let them. Even Dominic, whose career began with bringing a Cathar back to the church and who adopted poverty so as to debate more effectively with Cathars (1206), failed to bring about lasting results. The papacy, prompted to take extreme action, launched the Inquisition with the papal bull *Abolendam* in 1184 and called in 1208 upon the king of France to fight the Cathars in Languedoc.

The Catholics eventually won the long and brutal Albigensian Crusade, which resulted in the royal annexation of Languedoc (1229) and the formation of the papal Inquisition to root out "heresy" in the region (1233–34). The battle went on throughout the 13th century: in 1244, some 200 Cathars were captured at Montségur and burned; 178 were burned in Verona in 1278; and the last Cathar bishop was captured in Tuscany in 1321. But in the late 13th century, several revivals took place in the Pyrénées, and in the early 14th century the village of Montaillou in the Pyrénées had a healthy Cathar presence. Cathars and their mysterious beliefs continued to hold fascination for religious seekers, inspiring such esoterics as the anthroposophist Rudolf Steiner (1861–1925) and the Nazi Otto Rahn.

Richard Landes

[See also: ALBIGENSIAN CRUSADE; DOMINICAN ORDER; HERESIES, APOSTOLIC; HERESY; INQUISITION; LANGUEDOC; POPULAR DEVOTION; WALDO/WALDENSES]

Wakefield, Walter L., and Austin Evans, eds. and trans. *Heresies of the High Middle Ages*. New York: Columbia University Press, 1969. [Translates many important documents.]

Cathares en Languedoc. Cahiers de Fanjeaux 3. Toulouse: Privat, 1968.

Lambert, Malcolm. *Medieval Heresy*. 2nd ed. Oxford: Blackwell, 1992.

Le Roy Ladurie, Emmanuel. *Montaillou: Catholics and Cathars in a French Village, 1294–1324*, trans. Barbara Bray. London: Scolar, 1978.

Loos, Milan. *Dualist Heresy in the Middle Ages*, trans. Iris Lewitova. Prague: Akademia, 1974.

Moore, R.I. *The Origins of European Dissent*. New York: St. Martin, 1977.

Wakefield, Walter L. *Heresy, Crusade and Inquisition in Southern France, 1100–1250*. London: Allen and Unwin, 1974.

CATHERINE OF FRANCE (1401–1438). Queen of England. The daughter of Charles VI and Isabeau of Bavaria, Catherine was married to Henry V of England in 1420 as part of the settlement that made Henry heir to the French throne. Soon after giving birth to the future Henry VI, the young queen was widowed. She subsequently married Owen Tudor, earl of Richmond, and their grandson became Henry VII of England.

John Bell Henneman, Jr.

CAUCHON, PIERRE (ca.1371–1442). Born near Reims, Pierre Cauchon studied at Paris and became university rector in 1403. He supported the Cabochien revolt, helped write the famous *Ordonnance* of 1413, and entered Burgundian service. He was appointed bishop of Beauvais in 1420. Driven from his see in 1429, he had political and personal motivations for his leading role in the condemnation of Jeanne d'Arc. Bishop of Lisieux after 1432, he served the cause of Henry VI of England until his death. Infamous for his treatment of Jeanne d'Arc, Cauchon is better remembered as a political cleric typical of the late-medieval church.

Paul D. Solon

[See also: JEANNE D'ARC; LISIEUX]

Neveux, François. *L'évêque Pierre Cauchon*. Paris: Denoel, 1987.

Sarrazin. *Pierre Cauchon, juge de Jeanne d'Arc*. Rouen: Champion, 1901.

Wolff, Philippe. "Le théologien Pierre Cauchon de sinistre mémoire." In *Économies et sociétés au moyen âge: mélanges offerts à Édouard Perroy*. Paris: Publications de la Sorbonne, 1973.

CAUDEBEC-EN-CAUX. Longtime capital of the Pays de Caux, Normandy, the little town of Caudebec-en-Caux (Seine-Maritime) has two significant medieval monuments. The Maison des Templiers, with its well-preserved gable-end walls, is a rare example of 13th-century civil architecture. The Flamboyant Gothic church of Notre-Dame (1426–84), miraculously spared when the town was burned in 1940, was called by Henry IV the "prettiest chapel in my kingdom." The western façade features a rose window above three exquisitely carved Flamboyant porches, which recall those at Saint-Maclou in Rouen. A bell tower, attached to the south side, is capped by an unusual three-tiered octagonal spire that recalls the papal tiara. The triple nave (185 feet by 72 feet), with three-story elevation of arcades, triforium, and clerestory windows, is typically Flamboy-

Caudebec-en-Caux (Seine-Maritime), Notre-Dame, nave. *Photograph: Clarence Ward Collection. Courtesy of Oberlin College.*

ant. Notre-Dame preserves a magnificent ensemble of 15th- and 16th-century stained glass, including windows devoted to John the Baptist, Our Lady, and SS. Michael, Catherine, and George. There also survive impressive late-medieval statues in wood and stone.

William W. Kibler/William W. Clark

Steinke, William A. "The Flamboyant Gothic Church of Caudebec-en-Caux: A Neglected Masterpiece of French Medieval Architecture." Diss. New York University, 1982.

CAVALRY. Military units on horseback are often seen as the supremely characteristic form of medieval warfare. Glorified in chivalric literature, the image is one of medieval armies composed primarily of knights engaged in mounted shock combat and of medieval wars won by these cavalry forces. Until the 12th century, however, mounted shock combat was impossible. Throughout the Middle Ages, fighting on foot and sieges against fortifications dominated warfare, with the horsemen playing only a subsidiary role.

Although the Franks were excellent horsemen, and Merovingian armies had many cavalry units, drawn not only from among the Franks but also from the remnant of Roman forces as well as from other Germanic peoples, most of the wars of this period centered on the taking and holding of fortified sites, both cities and *castra*. The decisive military forces thus were the engineers and footmen who weakened and stormed the defensive works, with horsemen playing virtually no role in this sort of fighting. Moreover, even in battles in the open field, cavalry was usually ineffective against well-trained and disciplined foot soldiers in prepared defenses. The role of the cavalry was usually limited to areas where its mobility was helpful: in reconnaissance, patrol duty, prevention of encirclement, feigned retreats to draw the enemy from its lines, flank attacks, and pursuit. While aristocrats reveled in hunting on horseback and received careful training in horsemanship, they usually dismounted and fought on foot throughout the Merovingian, Carolingian, and post-Carolingian periods.

The development of mounted shock combat was delayed until the 12th century, when technology finally permitted it. The stirrup, introduced in western Europe by ca. 700, was not used in warfare until the 10th century. In the 12th century, cantles to keep the horseman from being pushed off the rear of the saddle were introduced, along with high, wraparound pommels to protect his groin and abdomen and double girths to hold the saddle firmly on the horse. At last, a horseman with lance clutched firmly to his side could make a charge at full speed with a reasonable hope of success and survival.

Steven Fanning

[See also: ARMOR AND WEAPONS; COURTRAI; HUNDRED YEARS' WAR; WARFARE]

Bachrach, Bernard S. "Animals and Warfare in Early Medieval Europe." *Settimane di studio del Centro Italiano di Studi Sull'Alto Medioevo* 31 (1985): 707–64.

———. "'Caballus et Caballarius' in Medieval Warfare." In *The Study of Chivalry, Resources and Approaches,* ed. Howell Chickering and Thomas H. Seiter. Kalamazoo: Medieval Institute, 1988, pp. 173–211.

———. "Charlemagne's Cavalry: Myth and Reality." *Military Affairs* 47: 181–87.

———. "Charles Martel, Mounted Shock Combat, the Stirrup and Feudalism." *Studies in Medieval and Renaissance History* 7 (1970): 49–75.

———. *Merovingian Military Organization, 481–751.* Minneapolis: University of Minnesota Press, 1972.

CENS. Fixed sum paid annually by a tenant in recognition of an ultimate right or proprietorship. In practice, the *cens* (Lat. *census*) constituted a small, unchanging rent. In the 9th century, it was collected primarily from nondomainal property, such as vineyards, fields, and newly cleared land. By the 12th and 13th centuries, it had become a type of tenure known as the *censive* and distinguished from feudal tenure, for which service was required, and allodial tenure, which was free from both rent and service. All kinds of urban as well as rural property could be held for *cens.*

Since the *cens* was fixed and hereditable, the inflationary environment of the high Middle Ages often made it profitable for tenants to sublease their *censives* at higher rents, while landlords attempted to limit the duration of tenure (e.g., to one or two lifetimes) and to tax transfers beyond the original tenant family. Transfer taxes in effect compensated for the fixed low rate of the *cens.* Landlords with large numbers of *cens*-paying tenants often compiled rent books, called *censiers.*

Theodore Evergates

Fossier, Robert. *Polyptyques et censiers.* Turnhout: Brepols, 1978.

Fourquin, Guy. "Le temps de la croissance." In *Histoire de la France rural,* ed. Georges Duby and Armand Wallon. Paris: Seuil, 1975, Vol. 1: *La formation des campagnes françaises des origines au XIVe siècle,* pp. 165–68.

———. *Lordship and Feudalism in the Middle Ages,* trans. Iris and A. L. Lytton Sells. New York: Pica, 1976.

CENT BALLADES, LES. Composed at the end of the 14th century by Jean de Saint-Pierre, the seneschal of Eu, in collaboration with Philippe d'Artois, count of Eu, Boucicaut le Jeune, and Jean de Crésecque, the *Cent ballades* is a variation on the poetic love debate. In the first fifty ballades, an old knight gives advice to a young man on how to make war and how to love by avoiding Fausseté and seeking out Loyauté. Later, the young man encounters a woman, La Guignarde, who insists that Fausseté brings more joy to love the Loyauté. Puzzled by the conflicting advice, he decides to consult the opinions of the count of Eu, Boucicaut, and Crésecque, all of whom opt for Loyauté. In the final ballade, the four authors ask all lovers to respond to the dilemma. Thirteen answers complete the work, with most pronouncing in favor of Loyauté. In the six manuscripts that preserve the work, the ballades are organized into groups of four with seven different forms, making four series of twenty-eight, twenty-eight, twenty-eight, and sixteen poems, respectively, with the same succession of forms in each.

Deborah H. Nelson

Raynaud, Gaston, ed. *Les cent ballades.* Paris: Didot, 1905.

CENT NOUVELLES NOUVELLES, LES. In the early 1460s, amusing after-dinner stories were told at the court and in the presence of Philip the Good, duke of Burgundy (1396–1467). Sometime later, before the duke's death, an anonymous author-compiler wrote down these hundred prose tales, attributing the telling of them to thirty-five *conteurs.* Thirteen of the stories are ascribed to the duke himself, fifteen to monseigneur de la Roche (Philippe Pot), ten to Philippe de Laon, and others to various of the duke's aristocratic friends and courtiers. Two tales are anonymous, and the author himself "tells" five. The latter is doubtless responsible for giving a sense of unity to those basically diverse stories. They come to us in one manuscript (Glasgow, Hunter 252) and an incunabulum (Paris: Antoine Vérard, 1486).

The only *conteur* with a well-established literary reputation mentioned is Antoine de La Sale (ca. 1385–1461), who "tells" the fiftieth story. Because of that, it was long thought that he was the author-compiler of the collection. This attribution is no longer accepted, nor is that of authorship to Philippe Pot.

The origins of those tales are varied and impossible to pin down. The idea of a collection of a hundred *nouvelles* was doubtless much influenced by the *Decameron,* well known in the French-speaking lands through the translation by Laurent de Premierfait (1414), but the *Cent nouvelles* owe little directly to Boccaccio. A more likely literary source is the *Liber facetiarum* by Poggio (Gian Francesco Poggio Bracciolini; 1380–1459). Their real origin, however, must be sought in the local, popular, oral tradition. For the most part, they are tales of the fabliaux kind (e.g., the nineteenth story is, in fact, the well-known fabliau of "The Snow Child"). Racy, farcical, joyful, and occasionally crude, they deal with the eternal comedy of adultery and sex, with its cuckolded husbands, easygoing girls, lusty clerics, crafty and lecherous wives, all placed in a panorama of the social classes: monks, nuns, knights, merchants, bourgeois, and peasants.

Besides their powers to amuse, the real value of the *Cent nouvelles* lies in the documentary character of many of these stories. Under their amusing and irreverent form, we can find a great deal of *realia* of the everyday life in Brabant (where the stories were apparently told), Flanders, Hainaut, Holland, and the north of France. The authenticity of the settings is enhanced by the authenticity of the language. The anonymous author-compiler was a man of obvious talent with an excellent ear for the spoken word. There is no doubt that this collection is one of the most important monuments of Middle French prose.

Peter F. Dembowski

[See also: FABLIAU; LA SALE, ANTOINE DE; PREMIERFAIT, LAURENT DE; VIGNEULLES, PHILIPPE DE]

Champion, Pierre, ed. *Les cent nouvelles nouvelles.* 3 vols. Paris: Champion, 1928. [Text heavily amended, with an excellent introduction and notes; the third volume reproduces one hundred miniatures.]

Sweester, Franklin P., ed. *Les cent nouvelles nouvelles.* Geneva: Droz, 1966. [More faithful to the manuscript; corrects some errors of the above.]

Diner, Judith B., trans. *The One Hundred New Tales (Les cent nouvelles nouvelles).* New York: Garland: 1990.

Dubuis, Roger. *Les cent nouvelles nouvelles et la tradition de la nouvelle en France au moyen âge.* Grenoble: Presses Universitaires, 1973.

Knudson, Charles. "Antoine de la Sale, le duc de Bourgogne et les *Cent nouvelles nouvelles.*" *Romania* 53 (1927): 365–73.

CERCAMON (fl. 1137–49). Little may be said for certain about the life of this early troubadour. His pseudonym ("Search the World") tells us nothing about his origins, and the author of his brief *vida* says simply that Cercamon was a Gascon jongleur. References in his songs to the death of Guilhem X, count of Poitiers, and to the Second Crusade allow us to date his production to the second quarter of the 12th century. His *vida* also tells us that Cercamon wrote songs and *pastorelas.* None of the latter have survived, but among his seven authentic lyrics we find the first *planh,* the first *tenso,* and the first two *sirventes,* as well as three love poems. However, much of the assessment of his originality is based on the perhaps unreliable statement in the *vida* of Marcabru that Cercamon was his master. Many recent scholars think, rather, that it was Cercamon who was the disciple, in which case some of the innovations attributed to Cercamon should be credited instead to Marcabru. In any event, Cercamon's poetry resembles closely that of his fellow moralist and Gascon contemporary in that both denounce the miserly nobles and their deceitful debauchery, which undermines true love.

Roy S. Rosenstein

[See also: MARCABRU; TROUBADOUR POETRY]

Cercamon. *Les poésies de Cercamon,* ed. Alfred Jeanroy. Paris: Champion, 1922.

———. *The Poetry of Cercamon and Jaufre Rudel,* ed. and trans. George Wolf and Roy Rosenstein. New York: Garland, 1983.

———. *Il trovatore Cercamon,* ed. Valeria Tortoreto. Modena: STEM Mucchi, 1981.

CERVERÍ DE GIRONA (fl. ca. 1259–82). Listed alternatively by medieval scribes as Guillem de Cervera, the Catalan troubadour Cerverí de Girona was a prolific craftsman given to experimentation with genre and rhyme. His work comprises 114 lyric pieces, five narrative poems, and a long moralizing satire called the *Proverbis.*

Elizabeth W. Poe

[See also: TROUBADOUR POETRY]

Cerverí de Girona. *Obras completas,* ed. Martín de Riquer. Barcelona: Instituto Español de Estudios Mediterráneos, 1947.

CERVOLE, ARNAUD DE (ca. 1320–66). Soldier of fortune. Arnaud de Cervole, the younger son of a minor lord from Périgord, acquired the title of archpriest of Velines (Dordogne) and is generally known as "the Archpriest." A prominent military commander in the mid-14th century, he gained notoriety as a captain of *routiers* (freelance soldiers) in the decade after 1356. Apparently a protégé of King John II's cousin Charles of Spain (constable of France, 1351–54), Cervole served as royal lieutenant between the Loire and Dordogne rivers during most of 1351. He began to act independently after the constable's murder but soon received a royal pardon and the lordship of Châteauneuf-sur-Charente. He fought for the king in 1355 and 1356.

The defeat and capture of John II at Poitiers in September 1356 brought an end to regular payment of troops, as England and France sought to negotiate a treaty. Unemployed soldiers, as companies of *routiers,* began to support themselves by pillage and extortion, and Cervole quickly became one of their most prominent captains. In 1357, his troops descended the Rhône and caused havoc in Provence for more than a year. Between 1358 and 1361, the Archpriest campaigned in Berry and Nivernais before turning his attention to Burgundy. Although he quickly turned to brigandage when not employed, Cervole was always ready to accept royal employment, and he fought for the crown at the unsuccessful Battle of Brignais (1362) and the successful one at Cocherel in Normandy (1364). As part of a royal project to send the *routiers* eastward on crusade in 1365, Cervole led a force into the empire, where his troops ravaged Alsace and threatened nearby districts. He was threatening Savoy in the spring of 1366 when he was killed by one of his own men on May 25.

John Bell Henneman, Jr.

[See also: BRIGNAIS]

Cherest, Aimé. *L'Archiprêtre: épisodes de la guerre de cent ans au XIVe siècle.* Paris: Claudin, 1879.

CESARIS, JOHANNES (fl. early 15th c.). Composer documented at the Sainte-Chapelle, Bourges (1407–08), and perhaps at Angers cathedral (1417). In his *Champion des dames* (ca. 1442), Martin Le Franc described Cesaris as one of the composers who "astonished Paris" in the years ca. 1400. Seven French songs and one Latin motet survive, showing a marvelous resourcefulness and variety of style.

David Fallows

Reaney, Gilbert, ed. *Early Fifteenth-Century Music.* Vol. 1. N.p.: American Institute of Musicology, 1955.

Besseler, Heinrich. "Cesaris." In *Die Musik in Geschichte und Gegenwart.* 17 vols. Kassel: Bärenreiter, 1949–86, Vol. 2 (1952), cols. 983–89.

CHAALIS. Notre-Dame-de-Chaalis (Oise), a Cistercian abbey in the Gothic style near Senlis, was founded on January 9, 1137, by Louis VI in memory of Charles the Good of Flanders, who had been killed in 1127. The site had previously been occupied by a Benedictine priory founded by Renaud de Mello on his return from the First Crusade and was dependent upon Vézelay. The Cistercian refoundation was a dependency of Pontigny (Yonne). The first abbot, André de Baudemont, had been seneschal for Thibaut IV, count of Blois.

The abbey, suppressed in 1791, is now in ruins. Of the first church erected in the 12th century, there are no remains. The second church, begun by Abbot Adam ca. 1202, survives in fragmentary form: the apse and south transept have been destroyed down to their foundations, but parts of the north transept and fragments of the claustral buildings adjacent to it survive. The church was consecrated on October 20, 1219. Abbot Adam was buried in front of the main altar, and numerous tombs of other abbots, as well as those of thirteen bishops of Senlis and aristocratic patrons, once filled the church. An abbot's chapel located to the east of the church and built ca. 1245–50 is intact, though it was heavily restored in the 19th century. The conventual buildings erected beginning in 1736 now house collections belonging to the Jacquemart-André Museum, and the abbey as a whole is the property of the Institut de France.

The abbey church is notable for its size (almost 270 feet long, with a nave 46 feet wide) and the unusual character of the transept, which had polygonal terminations with seven chapels in each arm. Although often associated with the rounded transepts of Valenciennes, Tournai, Cambrai, and Saint-Lucien at Beauvais, there are important differences between the design of the monastery church and these other monuments in northern France; the transept design seems to have been inspired instead by the chevet of its mother house, Pontigny, begun ca. 1186–1210. Prior to the Revolution, a similar arrangement could be found at the destroyed abbey of Quincy (Yonne), also a daughter of Pontigny.

Caroline A. Bruzelius

[See also: LOUIS VI THE FAT; PONTIGNY; VÉZELAY]

Aubert, Marcel, and La Marquise de Maillé. *L'architecture cistercienne en France*. 2 vols. Paris: Éditions d'Art et d'Histoire, 1943, Vol. 1, pp. 287–89.

Bruzelius, Caroline. "The Transept of the Abbey Church of Chaalis and the Filiation of Pontigny." *Mélanges Anselme Dimier* 3 (1982): 447–54.

Lefèvre-Pontalis, Eugène. "Chaalis." *Bulletin monumental* 66 (1902): 448–87.

Mesqui, Jean. *Île-de-France gothique*. 2 vols. Paris: Picard, 1988, Vol. 1, pp. 127–35

CHACE. A musical composition employing strict canonic imitation at the unison, usually in three voices: the medieval analogue to *Frère Jacques*. Probably derived from 13th-century techniques of voice exchange found in some organa and motets, the earliest complete French *chaces* appear in the first quarter of the 14th century. The name probably refers to the manner in which voices "chase" each other, often employing hocket effects. *Se je chant mains que ne sueil* is a text on hunting, subject matter suggested by the term itself. Around the middle of the 14th century, Machaut wrote a ballade in the form of a *chace*, and employed *chaces* in two of his *lais*, one of which uses three-voice unison canons to symbolize the Trinity ("Car cil .iij. font toute une essance").

Lawrence Earp

[See also: HOCKET; MACHAUT, GUILLAUME DE]

Kuegle, Karl. "Die Musik des 14. Jahrhunderts: Frankreich und sein direkter Einflußbereich." In *Die Musik des Mittelalters*, ed. Hartmut Möller and Rudolf Stephan. Laaber: Laaber, 1991, pp. 352–84.

CHAISE-DIEU. The Benedictine abbey of Chaise-Dieu (Haute-Loire) was founded in 1044 by St. Robert of Turlande, a canon of Brioude, who retired to these forested heights to lead a life of prayer and penance. Chaise-Dieu reached its apogee in the 12th and 13th centuries, when it had over 200 monks and was at the head of a community of ten abbeys and some 300 priories. The new abbey church of Saint-Robert, begun in the early 14th century under Abbot Pierre-Roger de Beaufort (later Pope Clement VI), is in the severe Gothic style of southern France. The western façade consists of two fortified towers joined by an arcade. The nave is unusually vast (241 feet by 79 feet by 59 feet) and flanked by side aisles of the same height. There is no transept or ambulatory, and the chevet ends with chapels opening directly onto the choir. The choir screen is 15th-century, as are the 144 carved oak choirstalls given by Abbot André de Chanac (r. 1378–1420). The 15th-century wall painting of the Dance of Death (6 feet by 86 feet) is an important representation of this popular Late Gothic theme. Its three panels show Death inviting the powerful, the bourgeois, and the peasantry to dance. Only two wings remain of the 14th-century Gothic cloister that abutted the south aisle of the church.

In the Middle Ages, Chaise-Dieu was a thriving artistic center that sent architects and sculptors far afield. The monastery was sacked by Huguenots in 1562 during the Wars of Religion, beginning a long period of decline, culminating in the desecrations of the Revolution.

William W. Kibler/William W. Clark

Erlande-Brandenberg, Alain. "L'abbatiale de la Chaise-Dieu." *Congrès archéologique (Velay)* 133 (1975): 720–55.

CHÂLONS-SUR-MARNE. Although there are text references to earlier Carolingian and Romanesque buildings, the oldest parts of the present cathedral of Saint-Étienne at Châlons-sur-Marne (Marne) are part of the crypt and the north tower flanking the chevet, which should be dated ca. 1150. The tower contains some of the earliest stained glass in Champagne. Repairs to the old building began in 1205 and were financed by income from the relic of St. Stephen acquired in 1204. Serious construction, begun probably after a fire in 1230, proceeded slowly; the north transept and porch were in progress 1260–65. Construction of the choir began in 1285 but was finished only in the later 17th century, following partial construction of the nave in the 15th and erection of the classical façade early in the 17th. The confused building history has been admirably analyzed by Ravaux.

In contrast to the cathedral, the important parish church of Notre-Dame-en-Vaux is a remarkably homogeneous construction of the later 12th century. The lower parts of the transept and the two chevet towers are close in style to the cathedral tower and probably survived the collapse of the old church in 1157. Through the 1160s and 1170s, donations to the fabric financed construction of the lower nave and aisles, although the upper parts and the four-story chevet must have been constructed only after lengthy disputes of income and finances were settled in 1187. The chevet of Notre-Dame and the two upper stories of the nave are closely modeled on the new chevet of Saint-Remi in Reims. In spite of destruction to the exterior and heavy-handed restorations to the interior, Notre-Dame preserves a series of elegant, crisply carved foliate capitals that predict the marvelously inventive architectural decoration of the cloister. Fragments of the 12th-century cloister were excavated, and the site was turned into a museum to display them. The number and diversity of subjects in the statue columns and historiated capitals make this one of the most important sculptural discoveries of the century. Five major styles have been discerned, yet the placement marks indicate that the whole project was constructed simultaneously.

Two other parish churches in Châlons merit mention: Saint-Jean and Saint-Alpin, both of which existed by 1028. Saint-Jean has later 11th-century aisles, which were vaulted in 1671, an early 13th-century chevet, and a 14th-century façade. It was scrupulously restored in the 19th century, while Saint-Alpin was nearly destroyed. The mid-12th-century work here, however, was inspired by Notre-Dame. The main nave and façade were built 1160–75, and vaults were added ca. 1230 to a scheme never planned for them. The apse was replaced ca. 1500, and there was disfiguring work in the 18th and 19th centuries.

William W. Clark

[See also: REIMS]

Prache, Anne. "L'église Notre-Dame-en-Vaux de Châlons." *Congrès archéologique* (*Champagne*) 135 (1977): 279–97.
———. "Notre-Dame-en-Vaux de Châlons-sur-Marne: campagnes de construction." *Mémoires de la Société d'Agriculture, Commerce, Sciences et Arts du Département de la Marne* 81 (1966): 29–92.
Pressouyre, Sylvia. *Images d'un cloître disparu: Notre-Dame-en-Vaux à Châlons-sur-Marne.* Paris: Cuenot, 1976.
Ravaux, Jean-Pierre. "La cathédrale de Châlons-sur-Marne." *Congrès archéologique* (*Champagne*) 135 (1977): 360–400.
———. "La cathédrale gothique de Châlons-sur-Marne." *Mémoires de la Société d'Agriculture, Commerce, Sciences et Arts du Département de la Marne* 91 (1976): 171–227; 92 (1977): 115–55.
———. "Les cathédrales de Châlons-sur-Marne avant 1230." *Mémoires de la Société d'Agriculture, Commerce, Sciences et Arts du Département de la Marne* 89 (1974): 31–70.

CHAMBERLAIN. Officer of the royal bedchamber. The 11th and 12th centuries distinguished the bedchamber (*cubiculum*) from the chamber (*camera, chambre*). The *chambrier* (*camerarius*), head of the chamber, seems to have supervised the furnishing and upkeep of the palace and royal wardrobe, arranged the king's *gîtes* (travel lodgings) and guarded the treasury and archives, then housed in the *camera*.

When the institutions of the monarchy reorganized and developed, the *chambrier* lost his guardianship of the treasury and archives. Displaced when the *camera* absorbed the *cubiculum*, he also lost his domestic functions and became a bureaucrat, the *chambrier de France*. Still a great officer of the crown, he had charge of selling licenses to those who made or sold clothing in and around Paris. Such merchandise was inspected by his agents, and his justice was rendered in the Grand Palais.

The *chambellan de France* (*grand chambellan*) was originally head of the bedchamber. He enjoyed income from various *métiers* and after the 14th century continued to perform certain domestic duties when the king was in Paris. The king also had a *chambellan de Normandie*. The duke of Berry had a *chambellan de Poitou* and a *chambellan de Berry et Auvergne*.

The Valois kings' bedchamber (*chambre*) was supervised on a daily basis by a *premier chambellan* and a rotating group of ordinary chamberlains. The *premier chambellan* carried the royal privy seal and kept for himself some of the money charged for its use. The chamberlains played a role when the king received homage, for this customarily took place in the bedchamber. Royal chamberlains, always knights, were so regularly in the king's company that he often made them councilors.

The duke of Burgundy's chamberlains attended his *coucher*. His *premier chambellan* kept his privy seal and the key to his bedchamber.

Richard C. Famiglietti

Favier, Jean. *Un conseiller de Philippe le Bel: Enguerran de Marigny.* Paris: Presses Universitaires de France, 1963.
Lacour, René. *Le gouvernement de l'apanage de Jean, duc de Berry 1360–1416.* Paris: Picard, 1934.
Lot, Ferdinand, and Robert Fawtier. *Histoire des institutions françaises au moyen âge.* 3 vols. Paris: Presses Universitaires de France, 1957–63.
Luchaire, Achille. *Manuel des institutions françaises: période des Capétiens directs.* Paris: Hachette, 1892.

CHAMBIGES, MARTIN (d. 1532). Known during his lifetime as *supremus artifex*, Martin Chambiges must be viewed as one of the most gifted architectural designers in Late Gothic France. A Parisian, Chambiges is first mentioned between 1489 and 1494 as the master mason charged with completing the south transept of Sens cathedral. This commission was symptomatic of Chambiges's major works, which comprised additions to 12th- and 13th-century edifices. His personal style, evolved from an original fusion of High and Rayonnant Gothic elements with forms derived from the contemporary Parisian milieu, is distinguished by its disciplined visual richness and exuberant plasticity.

In 1499–1500, Chambiges was called in as a consultant on the foundations of the collapsed Pont-Notre-Dame in Paris. His evident structural expertise and proven ability to work harmoniously yet creatively with older structures doubtless led to his appointment in 1500 as master mason of Beauvais cathedral, where he supervised construction of the north and south transepts and the eastern bay of the nave. Soon after his arrival in Beauvais, he appears to have begun the new choir of the parish church of Saint-Étienne, while his design for the north transept of Sens (after 1500) was executed under the direction of an assistant, Cuvelier. Chambiges's activity was extended to Troyes cathedral, for which he authored plans for a new west façade in 1502–03. The triple-portal and twin-towered scheme of Troyes looks back to such High Gothic models as Paris or Reims, but the projection and recession of buttresses and portals as well as the deeply excavated statue niches, framed by sharpened moldings and nodding ogee canopies, vigorously animate the façade.

Chambiges has been credited with additional works, including the west rose of the Sainte-Chapelle, the portal of the Dominican church, and the parish church of Saint-Gervais-et-Protais in Paris, although documentary evidence is absent and stylistic demonstrations are inconclusive. The influence of his architecture was felt strongly in Troyes, where masons from the cathedral workshop adopted the flat east end, steep two-story elevation, and undulant piers of Saint-Étienne, Beauvais, for the churches of Saint-Pantaléon, Saint-Jean-au-Marché, and Saint-Nicolas. Martin Chambiges died on August 29, 1532, and was buried west of the crossing in Beauvais cathedral.

Michael T. Davis

[See also: BEAUVAIS; GOTHIC ARCHITECTURE; PARIS; SENS; TROYES]

Murray, Stephen. *Building Troyes Cathedral: The Late Gothic Campaigns.* Bloomington: Indiana University Press, 1987.
———. *Beauvais Cathedral: Architecture of Transcendence.* Princeton: Princeton University Press, 1989.
———. "The Choir of Saint-Étienne at Beauvais." *Journal of the Society of Architectural Historians* 36 (1977): 111–21.
Sanfaçon, Roland. *L'architecture flamboyante en France.* Laval: Presses de l'Université, 1971.
Vachon, Marius. *Une famille parisienne de maîtres maçons aux XVe, XVIe, XVIIe siècles: les Chambiges.* Paris: Librairie de la Construction Moderne, 1907.

CHAMBRE DES COMPTES. The French monarchy long lacked a central auditing agency like the English exchequer to monitor collection of its "ordinary" or domanial revenues. The Chambre des Comptes finally filled this need. From the mid-12th century, the crown entrusted its finances to the Knights Templar, who maintained a banking establishment in Paris. This tradition caused the royal treasury to be organized like a bank in which the king had the largest account. The receipt of revenues and the payment of salaries often involved simply the transfer of funds from one account to another. Except in the case of Normandy, where the French government inherited an exchequer established by the Anglo-Norman kings, royal officers in the field, who sent revenues to the Temple, had their accounts audited by the royal council, which had special clerks assigned to work at the Temple. By the late 13th century, these financial specialists were being called the *curia in compotis*. From ca. 1297, they audited accounts twice a year, after St. John's (June 24) and Christmas.

In 1295, Philip IV removed his treasure from the Temple and placed it in the fortress of the Louvre. He returned it to the Temple in 1303 but ordered its final removal in 1307. Between 1295 and 1307, the royal financial administration was dominated by the Guidi brothers of the Florentine firm of Francezi. Their deaths coincided roughly with the final removal of funds from the Temple, and Enguerran de Marigny became effective head of royal finances. The financial specialists received accounts for audit in a room of the royal palace that became known as the Chambre des Comptes, and they began to be identified collectively by the same name, although still only a subcommission of the royal council, consisting of about sixteen people.

Several years after the fall of Marigny, Philip V issued the important ordinance of Vivier-en-Brie (1320), which first gave official structure to the Chambre des Comptes, requiring it to audit accounts, judge cases arising from accountability, and maintain registers of documents bearing on finance. For the next twenty-five years, under Henri de Sully and then Mile de Noyers, the Chambre des Comptes became an important organ of the government, and for a time in the 1340s the leaders, or "sovereigns," of the Chamber were virtually synonymous with the royal council. Thereafter, however, the Chamber suffered political eclipse.

Consisting of eleven clerks and eight masters of accounts in 1320, the Chamber grew by about 50 percent in the next two decades but was reduced to twelve clerks and seven masters in 1346. In 1381, the Chamber acquired a president (then an ecclesiastic), and a second (lay) president was added in 1400. The personnel was stabilized in 1408, when the Chamber consisted of two presidents, eight masters, twelve clerks/auditors, two "correctors," plus notaries and ushers. Following the Burgundian (and later English) occupation of Paris in 1418–20, the Chamber in Paris represented the Anglo-Burgundian government, and Charles VII established a rival body at Bourges. After he regained Paris in 1436, a single Chambre des Comptes resumed normal operations in Paris.

At the very time that it was becoming a stable institution in the later 14th century, the Chambre des Comptes was losing its central position in royal finance. First, the currency was put under a separate organ, then the increasingly regular "extraordinary" taxes, such as the *aide*, *taille*, and *gabelle*, came under the authority of the *généraux* of the emerging Cour des Aides. The crown's domainal revenues, over which the Chamber retained control, fell in both relative importance and absolute value. By 1400, the role of the Chambre des Comptes was much reduced from what it had been sixty years earlier.

John Bell Henneman, Jr.

[See also: *AIDES; CONSEIL; GÉNÉRAUX*]

Cazelles, Raymond. *La société politique et la crise de la royauté sous Philippe de Valois.* Paris: Argences, 1958.

Favier, Jean. *Un conseiller de Philippe le Bel: Enguerran de Marigny.* Paris: Presses Universitaires de France, 1963.

Jassemin, Henri. *La Chambre des Comptes de Paris au XVe siècle, précédé d'une étude sur les origines.* Paris: Picard, 1933.

Lot, Ferdinand, and Robert Fawtier. *Histoire des institutions françaises au moyen âge.* 3 vols. Paris: Presses Universitaires de France, 1957–63, Vol. 2: *Institutions royales* (1958).

CHAMPAGNE. The county of Champagne was a classic feudal principality of the high Middle Ages and among the most powerful of the realm. The counts, commanding almost 2,000 direct feudal tenants, from great barons to simple knights, created a sophisticated and well-run government. Their farsighted economic policies led to the vigorous development of both the countryside and their castle towns and to the establishment of fairs that made Champagne the center of international trade and finance. The counts were also noted supporters of reformed monasteries, primarily the Cistercians, and patrons of writers, of whom Chrétien de Troyes was the most illustrious. The proximity of Champagne to the royal domain and intimate ties between the comital family and the Capetians led to close, though not always amicable, relations between the two lands and resulted in the county's ultimate attachment to the royal domain.

As an open region east of Paris bounded by the rivers Aisne, Marne, and Yonne, Champagne lacked a natural center. In the late Roman Empire, northern Champagne was part of a frontier province facing Germanic tribes on the Rhine, while southern Champagne belonged to an interior province centered at Lyon. The church observed that division in creating two archiepiscopal sees, at Reims and Sens. Under the Franks, southern Champagne entered the Burgundian orbit; the northern area, with its chief city of Reims, fell under the sway of royal Francia. Remi baptized Clovis (ca. 496) at Reims, and later Archbishop Hincmar (845–882) made his city the preferred site of royal coronations and its most prestigious monastery, Saint-Remi, the royal necropolis. The cathedral school of Reims enjoyed wide repute from the 9th century, producing such influential personages as Gerbert (later Pope Sylvester II) and Fulbert (later bishop of Chartres).

The collapse of Carolingian government brought political fragmentation to Champagne: numerous counties and lesser lordships, monasteries with immunities, and episcopal cities all resisted integration into larger territorial units. The prelates of Reims and Châlons-sur-Marne, the major urban centers of Champagne, assumed control of their cities and surrounding counties, in effect displacing secular authority from most of northern Champagne. In the 10th century, the house of Vermandois acquired the counties of Meaux and Troyes by marriage, but on the death of Étienne, count of Meaux-Troyes (r. 995–1019/21), those counties passed to his closest heir, Eudes II, count of Blois (r. 996–1037). Eudes's son, Thibaut III of Blois (I of Champagne; r. 1037–89), acquired the adjacent counties of Bar-sur-Aube and Vitry through marriage to Alix de Valois and thus held the four old counties of southern Champagne that would later become the core of the new county of Champagne.

At Thibaut's death, however, the counties of Champagne were temporarily divided between his sons: Meaux remained with the eldest, Étienne-Henri, count of Blois (r. 1089–1102), while Troyes, Bar-sur-Aube, and Vitry passed to the youngest, Hugues (r. 1093–1125). Since Count Hugues's most important urban center and principal residence was the city of Troyes, it became the *de facto* capital of southern Champagne. Count Hugues's young nephew, Thibaut IV of Blois (II of Champagne; r. 1102–52), spent much time in Champagne in his capacity as count of Meaux, and thus it was natural that when Hugues disowned his own son on suspicion of illegitimacy, he transferred his three counties to Thibaut (1125).

Thibaut le Grand continued his uncle's support of the Cistercians, who were rapidly expanding in eastern France under Bernard of Clairvaux's leadership. The count offered secure routes to merchants traveling through the county and supervised trade fairs for the exchange of merchandise. Those Champagne fairs, later organized into a cycle of six terms that rotated between Troyes, Bar-sur-Aube, Provins, and Lagny, became in the course of the 12th century the center of international trade between northern Europe and the Mediterranean. The fairs also served as a financial clearinghouse for princes, aristocrats, and merchants through the 14th century, long after the Atlantic shipping route had displaced the overland trade routes converging in Champagne.

Thibaut's rapprochement with King Louis VI had long-term consequences for Champagne. The count served as guardian to young Louis VII, whom he escorted to Bordeaux for marriage with Eleanor of Aquitaine (1137); and despite a falling out that resulted in the destruction of Vitry by a royal army (1142/43), Thibaut restored good relations with the king, even entrusting his young son Henri to Louis's entourage on the Second Crusade. That crusade experience forged a bond that later permitted Henri and his brother Thibaut to marry Louis's two daughters by Eleanor, while the king in turn married their sister Adèle (of Champagne). Their brother Guillaume, in part because of the royal connection, enjoyed rapid promotion in the church as bishop of Chartres (1165–68), then as archbishop of Sens (1168–75) and Reims (1176–1202).

Largely because of Thibaut's attention, Champagne had become by his death the most promising of his lands.

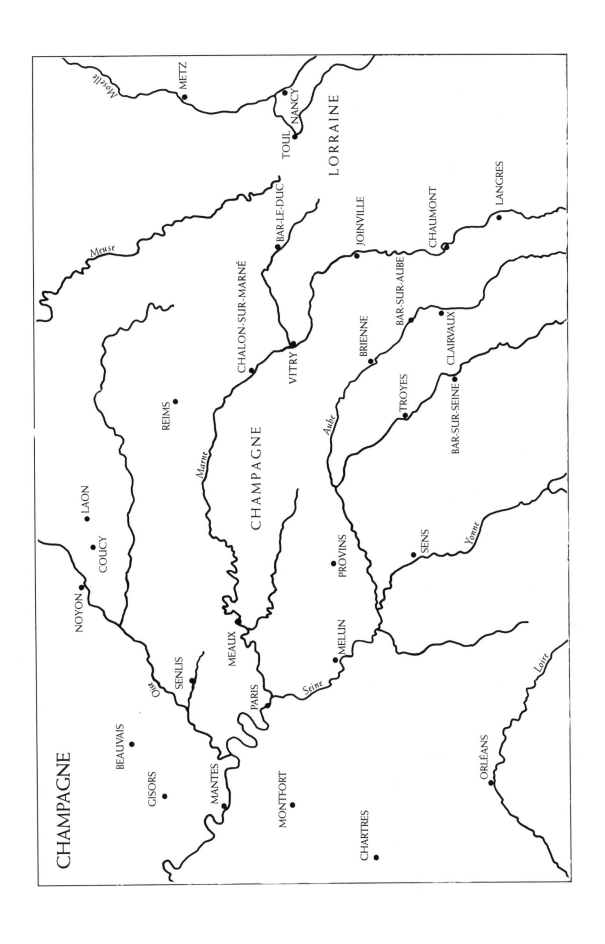

Not surprisingly, his eldest son, Henri, born and raised in Champagne and associated early in its governance, chose it as his inheritance, leaving Blois-Chartres and Sancerre to his younger brothers, Thibaut and Étienne. The Champagne lands of Henri I le Libéral (r. 1152–1181) consisted entirely of fiefs held from ten lords, of whom the most important were the king (for Meaux), the duke of Burgundy (for Troyes), the archbishop of Reims (for Vitry), and the bishop of Langres (for Bar-sur-Aube). Over his disparate lands, the count created a new territorial unit, the county of Champagne, by imposing a single administrative system of castellanies (districts of his own feudal tenants) and *prévôtés* (districts of his domainal lands). The organization of the new principality is best seen through the only surviving administrative record from his rule, the census of his feudal tenants known as the *Feoda Campanie* (1170s), which furnishes the names and military obligations of his barons and knights in each of the twenty-six Champagne castellanies. No doubt, his officials kept equally exact but routine, and therefore expendable, financial accounts of his domain and fair revenues.

Count Henri actively attracted immigrants to clear lands, to create new villages, and to settle in his castle towns. Only two of his towns, however, could approach the size of the neighboring episcopal cities like Reims, Châlons-sur-Marne, and Sens: his capital of Troyes and Provins (which was becoming a second capital), with populations of ca. 15,000 and 10,000, respectively. The growing fairs of Champagne complemented the essentially rural economy of the county and contributed substantial revenues to the comital treasury. The count's coins, minted at both Troyes and Provins, circulated widely in northern France, and the *provinois* even acquired international currency through the fairs.

Henri le Libéral was well known for his generosity to the church, as his 400-odd extant charters testify, and founded a number of collegial chapters, of which Étienne of Troyes and Quiriace of Provins served his administrative needs. Henri and Marie also were noted patrons of writers whose interests ranged from spirituality to poetry and romance. Besides Chrétien of Troyes, the best known included Pierre de Celle, Gautier d'Arras, and Gace Brûlé, none of whom, however, were in residence at the count's court.

Henri II (r. 1181–97) ruled only briefly in Champagne (1187–90). His mother was regent while he was a minor (r. 1181–87) and after he left on the Third Crusade in the company of his uncles, counts Thibaut V of Blois and Étienne de Sancerre, and a large army of Champenois. Henri cooperated closely with his uncle Richard the Lionhearted and, after marrying Isabelle, queen of Jerusalem, assumed leadership of the westerners defending what little remained of the crusader states after Saladin's conquests.

Henri II's younger brother, Thibaut III (r. 1197–1201), is remembered chiefly as one of the organizers of the Fourth Crusade, with his cousin Louis, count of Blois, and his brother-in-law Baudouin, count of Flanders. Thibaut's marshal, Geoffroi de Villehardouin, supervised the logistical arrangements, including the treaty with Venice for the construction of ships, and later recorded his memoirs of that crusade as the *Conquête de Constantinople*. Count Thibaut, however, died shortly before the expedition departed. To his young widow, Blanche of Navarre, fell the daunting task of defending Thibaut's posthumous son's inheritance against Henri II's daughter by Isabelle. Although Henri II had designated Thibaut as successor in Champagne, should Henri not return, no one had foreseen Henri II's marriage overseas nor Thibaut's own untimely death without a male heir.

Countess Blanche's regency for Thibaut IV (1201–22) was a trying period for Champagne. After almost eighteen years under Marie of France (also known as Marie de Champagne), the barons did not relish another long regency, especially by a foreign-born woman. There was regional resentment, too, as Thibaut III had begun to expand comital authority in southeastern Champagne at the expense of formerly independent baronial families. Ultimately, Blanche's determination prevailed. A series of treaties with Philip II, for which she paid dearly, placed Thibaut IV under royal protection. When Érard de Ramerupt, scion of the prominent Brienne family, claimed Champagne through his wife, Henri II's daughter Philippa, the king convened a royal court at Melun (1216) where the peers of the realm (first mentioned here) declared for Thibaut IV. Brienne and his disgruntled supporters attempted a military solution, but a brief civil war (1216–18) left Blanche victorious on the field of battle as well. In May 1222, Blanche handed her son a county not only intact but with a baronage finally subdued.

Thibaut IV le Chansonnier (r. 1222–53) is often depicted as a songwriter of distinction but as an otherwise incompetent leader who committed serious gaffes, such as abandoning Louis VIII at the siege of Avignon (1226) and dallying with the regent queen, Blanche of Castile. In fact, Thibaut IV made significant contributions to the governance and prosperity of the county. He steadily expanded the county eastward, often in competition with the count of Bar-le-Duc, by awarding new fiefs and by purchasing the *mouvance* of others. He consolidated both central and local administration. A "governor" exercised executive authority in the count's absence, and financial "receivers" supervised the comital finances. *Baillis* oversaw the castellanies and *prévôtés* and convened courts of the first instance. The supreme court of Champagne, the Jours of Troyes, met regularly from this time, although its decisions are known only from a later compilation known as the *Coutumier* of Champagne (ca. 1290).

The 1230s brought important changes to the county. In 1230–31, Thibaut franchised his castellany towns after they had vigorously resisted an invasion by French barons led by Pierre Mauclerc, duke of Brittany, to avenge Thibaut's abandonment of their conspiracy against Blanche of Castile. The count commuted *tailles* and personal restrictions to a wealth-based tax, and he granted a large measure of self-governance exercised by elected mayors and councils. Since the franchises included the towns and their surrounding districts, they applied to most of the count's nonfeudal tenants. A number of barons subsequently franchised their own tenants. Those who were not franchised in the course of the 13th century, primarily tenants on church lands,

HOUSE OF BLOIS–CHAMPAGNE

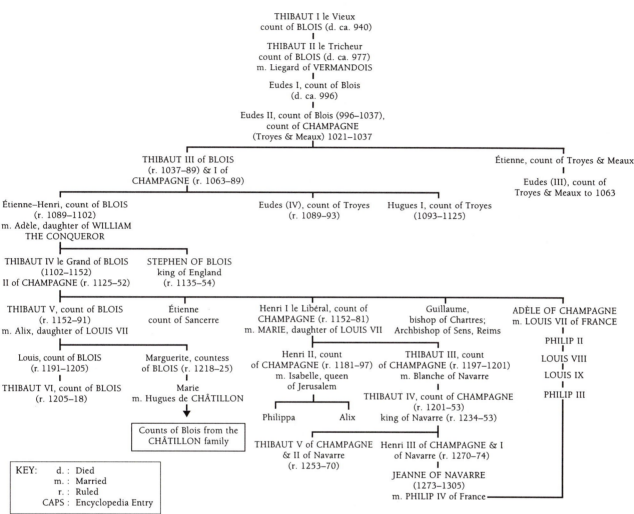

and who therefore retained the old personal liabilities and restrictions, later were stigmatized as "serfs."

In 1234, Alix, queen of Cyprus, the second daughter of Henri II, arrived in Champagne claiming the county as her inheritance. Thibaut bought her off for £40,000 and a pension, but unable to find the ready cash, he sold the *mouvance* of Blois (and Sancerre) to Louis IX, thus severing the historic tie between Blois and Champagne. In the same year, however, Thibaut acquired his mother's inheritance, the kingdom of Navarre, where he and his successors spent many years.

The county achieved its ultimate shape under Thibaut IV. His sons, Thibaut V (r. 1253–70) and Henry III (r. 1270–74), brought Champagne under increasing royal influence. Thibaut V, having married Louis IX's daughter, maintained a residence in Paris, while Henri affianced his daughter Jeanne (b. 1273), heiress of Champagne, to a son of Philip III. With Jeanne's marriage to the future Philip IV

(1284), Champagne lost its independence. Philip III already had issued directives to the *baillis* of Champagne, and soon the *Jours* of Troyes were staffed by royal officials and the county administered as a royal province. Title to both Champagne and Navarre passed through Jeanne to her son Louis X, then to his daughter Jeanne, who was dispossessed of Champagne by Philip V (1316). Charles IV assigned most of the county in dower to his wife (1325) and had the comital archives transferred to Paris.

As a royal province, Champagne suffered misfortune. Heavy taxation spawned an antiroyal league of nobles (1314). The decline of the fairs as trading centers weakened the county's economic vitality. Plague and the Jacquerie, which flared along the Marne and particularly in Meaux, destabilized the social order. And by the 1370s, the Hundred Years' War brought its ravages to Champagne. A demographic decline of 50 percent and more, especially in the towns, forced the abandonment of many villages.

Only in the late 15th century did some semblance of order return to this once prosperous province.

Theodore Evergates

[See also: BLOIS; THIBAUT; THIBAUT DE CHAMPAGNE]

Arbois de Jubainville, Henri d'. *Histoire des ducs et des comtes de Champagne*. 7 vols. Paris et Troyes: Schulz-Thuillié-Bouquet, 1859–66.

Benton, John F. "The Court of Champagne as a Literary Center." *Speculum* 36 (1961): 551–91.

———. "Philip the Fair and the *Jours* of Troyes." *Studies in Medieval and Renaissance History* 6 (1969): 281–344.

———. "Recueil des actes des comtes de Champagne, 1152–1197" [A "preedition" of 732 acts of Count Henry I, Countess Marie, and Count Henry II. On deposit at the Library of Congress and selected university libraries.]

Berlow, Rosalind K. "The Development of Business Techniques Used at the Fairs of Champagne." *Studies in Medieval and Renaissance History* 8 (1971): 3–32.

Bur, Michel. *La formation du comté de Champagne, v. 950–v. 1150*. Nancy: Université de Nancy, 1977.

Chapin, Elisabeth. *Les villes de foires de Champagne*. Paris: Champion, 1937.

Corbet, Patrick. "Les collégiales comtales de Champagne (v. 1150–v. 1230)." *Annales de l'Est* 29 (1977): 195–241.

Crubellier, Maurice, ed. *Histoire de Champagne*. Toulouse: Privat, 1975.

Desportes, Pierre. *Reims et les Rémois aux XIIIe et XIVe siècles*. Paris: Picard, 1979.

Evergates, Theodore. *Feudal Society in the Bailliage of Troyes Under the Counts of Champagne, 1152–1284*. Baltimore: Johns Hopkins University Press, 1975.

———, ed. and trans. *Feudal Society in Medieval France: Documents from the County of Champagne*. Philadelphia: University of Pennsylvania Press, 1993.

———. "The Chancery Archives of the Counts of Champagne." *Viator* 16 (1985): 161–79.

Longnon, Auguste, ed. *Documents relatifs au comté de Champagne et de Brie, 1172–1361*. 3 vols. Paris: Imprimerie Nationale, 1901–14.

———. *Rôles des fiefs du comté de Champagne sous le règne de Thibaut le Chansonnier, 1249–1252*. Paris: Menu, 1877.

Patault, Anne-Marie. *Hommes et femmes de corps en Champagne méridionale à la fin du moyen âge. Annales de l'Est* 58 (1978).

Portegoie, Paulette, ed. *L'ancien coutumier de Champagne (XIIIe siècle)*. Poitiers: Oudin, 1956.

CHAMPEAUX. The legendary founding of the church at Champeaux (Seine-et-Marne) was as a Benedictine monastery in the 7th century, although nothing remains to confirm the story. By 1065, the monks had been replaced by canons, and by 1124 at the latest Saint-Martin at Champeaux belonged to the bishop of Paris. This association explains why the church has close architectural ties to Notre-Dame at each of its three phases of construction. Parisian associations are least visible in the transept, which dates to ca. 1160, although the capitals do relate to examples from Paris. The three-story nave at Champeaux, based directly on the nave of Notre-Dame, was probably begun ca. 1180. The alternating single and double columns reflect the six-part vaults; the original second story had a tracery oculus—the round outer frame is still visible—that must have resembled the design of the third story of the cathedral elevation. Exterior flying buttresses appear in every other bay of the nave at Champeaux, making them among the earliest to be based on the Paris nave design. The deep chevet of Champeaux was built in the early 13th century and again reveals close ties to Paris, although less obviously to Notre-Dame. Saint-Martin at Champeaux is an important example of the impact of Parisian cathedral design on properties outside the city.

William W. Clark

[See also: PARIS]

Bonno, A. "La collégiale royale de Saint-Martin de Champeaux." *Bulletin de la Société d'Histoire et d'Archéologie de Provins* 3 (1898–99): 55–150.

Gusman, P. "L'église collégiale de Champeaux." *Gazette des beaux-arts* ser. 3, 26 (1901): 154–61.

Jacquet, M. *The Nave Capitals of the Collegial of Saint-Martin of Champeaux*. Diss. Courtauld Institute, 1978.

Messelet, Jean. "Le collégiale Saint-Martin de Champeaux." *Bulletin monumental* 84 (1925): 253–82.

CHANCELLOR. The most important of the king's household officers, the chancellor was responsible for the preparation, publication, and preservation of royal documents. The title, *cancellarius*, derived from scribes who sat behind a screen (*cancelli*) in Roman lawcourts, but the office in its medieval form originated with Charlemagne. Then, most literate men were clerics, and the king's chapel provided the personnel. Ecclesiastics administered the office until the 14th century. Second only to the constable in prestige, the chancellor enjoyed far greater constitutional importance and influenced justice, finance, and diplomacy through his administration of crown communications and precedence within council. With the growth of government after 1100, the Capetians often found the office too dangerous to fill and suspended it in 1227. Its administrative functions were diverted to the *garde des sceaux* ("keeper of the seals"). Louis X restored the office in 1314 and began appointing laymen. Louis XI, 150 years later, provided lifetime tenure for the office.

The chancellery developed into a formidable institution in which a growing bureaucracy of secretaries (fifteen clerical before 1300, over 150 lay and clerical by 1360) operated with ever more rigid procedures. They drafted documents in accordance with formularies dating from Merovingian times. After editing and verifying texts, they transcribed them with distinctive scripts in prescribed forms, such as diplomas, letters patent, or *mandements*, and sealed them with appropriate ribbons and waxes (e.g., green wax for the permanently effective *ordonnances*) to ensure their authenticity, signify their importance, and preclude forgery. Finally, texts were proclaimed in formal assemblies and dispatched. Many, but not all, texts were thereafter preserved in the Trésor des Chartes or synopsized in its annual registers.

In 1482, Louis XI codified chancellery staffing and practices in the *ordonnance* of Plessis-les-Tours. The institution continued to grow, but the office of chancellor itself was reduced to a judicial function as chief magistrate. Kings appointed jurists to the office but suspended their nonjudicial functions in favor of the *garde des sceaux*. After 1550, the "great" chancellery lost its effective monopoly on governmental correspondence. Its productions were complemented by those of the "little" chancelleries of the parlements and the Chambre des Comptes and its administrative functions supplanted by those of the king's household secretaries who emerged as independent ministers of state.

Paul D. Solon

Danbury, Elizabeth. "The Chanceries of England and France." In *England and Her Neighbors, 1066–1453: Essays in Honour of Pierre Chaplais*, ed. Michael Jones and Malcolm Vale. London: Hambledon, 1989.

Lot, Ferdinand, and Robert Fawtier. *Histoire des institutions françaises au moyen âge.* 3 vols. Paris: Presses Universitaires de France, 1957–63.

Michaud, Hélène. *La grande chancellerie et les écritures royales au XVIe siècle.* Paris: Presses Universitaires de France, 1967.

CHANDOS HERALD (fl. late 14th c.). Herald for Sir John Chandos, constable of Aquitaine, the so-called Chandos Herald was frequently used as a messenger between disputing parties in the Hundred Years' War. Working, like Froissart, from personal reminiscences as well as interviews with those who lived the events described, he composed ca. 1385 a *Vie du Prince Noir* in some 4,200 rhymed octosyllables. It records the principal events of the Black Prince's life and extols his prowess and piety. Froissart drew extensively upon his account of the Spanish expedition and Battle of Nájera in 1367. The poem is extant in a single manuscript in Worcester College, Oxford.

William W. Kibler

[See also: EDWARD, THE BLACK PRINCE]

Chandos Herald. *Life of the Black Prince by the Herald of Sir John Chandos*, ed. and trans. Mildred K. Pope and Eleanor C. Lodge. Oxford: Clarendon, 1910.

CHANSON DE GESTE. A long narrative poem celebrating the exploits (Lat. *gesta*) of famous national heroes, particularly Charlemagne. As the word *chanson* implies, at least at the beginning these epic poems were sung or chanted in public, rather than read silently in private chambers.

The chanson de geste could vary in length, from the celebrated *Chanson de Roland's* 4,002 lines in editions of the Oxford manuscript to some of the later epics, which number in the tens of thousands of lines. Most lines follow an established form: ten syllables with a caesura, or pause, after the fourth (sometimes the sixth) syllable. Rhyme did not appear until near the end of the 12th century. Until then, assonance sufficed to separate strophes of unequal length, called "laisses." The early *Gormont et Isembart* counts only eight syllables per line, while the *Voyage de Charlemagne* and many later poems survive in dodecasyllables, or Alexandrines. The songs connected with the hero Guillaume are characterized by a short refrain, *le vers orphelin*, of four syllables, which is sporadically attached to the end of laisses.

Controversy still rages on the manner in which the chanson de geste was born. Three early poems typify the problem: the *Chanson de Roland,* the *Chanson de Guillaume,* and *Gormont et Isembart.* All three portray events that transpired in the 8th or 9th centuries, yet their earliest documentary evidence dates from the late 11th or early 12th century. Scholars of the 19th century sought to explain how the kernel of historical truth underlying such poems could have reached their authors, and in such a distorted form; they concluded that the extant epics stand in a long line of oral narrative poems, called *cantilènes,* originating at the time of, or immediately subsequent to, the events portrayed. These anonymously composed short poems were later combined into the longer poems that survived. This view is today labeled "Traditionalist."

A positivist reaction led by Joseph Bédier at the start of the 20th century rejected the continuous poetic tradition in favor of a literate, cultured poet, the trouvère, composing onto parchment like any modern writer—though for singing by a performer, the jongleur. The individual creator thus replaced the vague group contributors. Few critics have equaled the influence that Bédier had upon literary history; his persuasiveness and clarity of style persuaded most scholars to his theories. Bédier's famous opening of his four-volume study of *Les légendes épiques* set forth in a nutshell the basis for his theory: "Au commencement était la route" ("In the beginning was the [pilgrimage] road"). Truly positivistic, Bédier accepted only tangible evidence in the elucidation of his theory of origins. He rejected outright any notion of *cantilènes* and thus of the existence of oral tradition as bearer of the legends. Epic poems first appeared not in the 9th century, according to Bédier, but in the 12th and thereafter. The poets' sources were in Latin chronicles that related the Carolingian events that provided the historical kernel; Bédier connected these with monasteries along the pilgrimage routes of Europe, which claimed to have in their possession relics from celebrated heroes. To draw pilgrims to their institutions, the custodians of these venerated objects prepared publicity in the form of the chansons de geste. Bédier insisted upon the near-contemporaneity of the written text and the creation of the surviving epic, while his predecessors (and followers) believed that one way or another, and probably through oral tradition, the event was borne over centuries through history.

Bédier's view, labeled "Individualism," dominated scholarship until a "Neotraditionalist" current was inaugurated in 1955 by the publication of Jean Rychner's *Essai sur l'art épique des jongleurs.* Rychner relied on the notion that the feudal civilization in which the chanson de geste was born created and consumed "literature" orally. Not only did audiences listen to the singing of the poems, but the poets actually created this highly formulaic poetry in the act of singing. In the wake of Albert Lord's discoveries about Yugoslav singers of tales still thriving in pre-Nazi Europe, Rychner showed how a poet could memorize motifs, themes, and formulae and skillfully recombine them for oral presentation, recomposing the poem each time he sang it, using his own stock of formulae. Thus are explained in great part the vexing contradictions that appear in almost all the story lines of the epic, the numerous exhortations to listen carefully, and the apparent repetitions.

In the late 1950s, Ramón Menéndez Pidal returned to theories expounded as early as the 19th century concerning the oral origins of the *Chanson de Roland*. He had investigated the manner in which Spanish epic had been born at the moment of the historical event. In 1924, he published *Poesia juglaresca y juglares*, demonstrating that Spanish literature cultivated short, totally epic poems and setting forth the hypothesis that French literature undoubtedly passed through a period that mirrored this archaic phase. After Rychner's book, Menéndez Pidal's inquiries into the neotraditionalism of the French epic, particularly in the *Roland*, gave impetus to the growing orality movement. The debate is of importance, for how we view the very nature of the early chansons de geste depends on the answer: are we dealing with literature (in the sense of works composed of letters) at all, or with an ever-changing tradition of sung epic that has no definitive form but exists in a multiplicity of performances, one of which is accidentally preserved in each manuscript manifestation?

No matter its origins, scholars have had to admit the influence of handwriting, courtly romance, and other literary phenomena in the chansons de geste by the end of the 12th century. As the "classical" epic appeared to be dying, efforts were made to preserve its traditional *matière* by creating and copying accretions, which led to the formation of cycles. An early attested recognition of the division into cycles is recorded by Bertrand de Bar-sur-Aube in the prologue to *Girart de Vienne* (early 13th c.). He discerned three: the *gesta* (deeds) of Charlemagne (the King Cycle), of Doon de Mayence (the Rebellious Vassal or Doon de Mayence Cycle), and of Garin de Monglane (the Guillaume d'Orange Cycle). Aside from the allusion to Charles in the King Cycle, the hero mentioned by Bertrand is not the most famous but rather an ancestor of the principal protagonist of each cycle. To give each hero a glorious past, these authors invented histories of their ancestry. In addition to Bertrand's divisions, modern scholars have discerned the *gestes* of the Crusades (of which the most famous is the imaginative *Chevalier au Cygne*) and those of Lorraine, Blaye, Nanteuil, and Saint-Gilles.

The masterpieces of the genre are generally considered to be the earlier poems: the *Chanson de Roland,* the *Chanson de Guillaume,* and *Gormont et Isembart,* from the early 12th century, and *Raoul de Cambrai, Girart de Roussillon, Aliscans,* the *Couronnement de Louis,* the *Charroi de Nîmes,* and the *Prise d'Orange* from the late 12th or early 13th century. Throughout the cycles, traits of the genre may be distinguished. The matter is generally grave in tone and women play a dependent role, particularly in the earlier poems. At the heart of the tale are the battle and accompanying motifs: arms and armor, the warhorse, and formulaic acts of combat. The typical jongleur organized his materials so as to recite the events in a linear story without flashbacks or such withholding devices as interlacing, popular in the prose romances. Often, too, the story commences *in medias res.* The narrator's voice could be heard infrequently but with considerable authority to comment on the events, characters, or outcome. If the *Roland,* for example, portrays two fairly unified actions (Roland's defeat, Charles's victory), poems of the Guillaume legend tend to be episodic, even contradictory, despite their generally shorter length. Some lack a unified plot entirely, such as the *Couronnement de Louis* and the *Moniage Guillaume.*

In a second generation of chansons de geste, composed in the late 12th and 13th centuries, the influence of romance was strongly felt, and women and the fantastic came to play significant roles. Totally absent in *Gormont et Isembart,* more masculine than feminine in *Guillaume,* women came to play major roles in such epics as *Raoul de Cambrai,* the *Prise d'Orange,* and *Aye d'Avignon.* The motif of the Saracen princess who converts to Christianity is important in many epics, but love themes always remain secondary to those of battle. Woman is an object of possession, identified generally with the fief and marriage, and is never an object of desire for her own sake. Increasing interest in the marvelous can be seen in *Huon de Bordeaux,* which places in the foreground a handsome magician and dwarf, Auberon, who will, he claims, take a seat next to God when he decides to depart this world. Even later epics (also called *chansons d'aventure*), such as *Tristan de Nanteuil* and *Lion de Bourges,* feature extraordinary adventures throughout the known (and imagined) world, played out by a cast that includes invulnerable heroes, seductive damsels, angels, shapeshifters, magicians, dwarfs, giants, and fabulous beasts.

Since the 15th century, several notable attempts to revive the epic as a viable genre have failed: among others, Ronsard's *La Franciade,* Voltaire's *La Henriade,* and Hugo's *Légende des siècles.* When the Middle Ages were rediscovered in the 19th century, reaction extended far beyond literary circles into the realm of politics, architecture, and the military. Louis-Napoléon attempted to restore the spirit of epic crusades by venturing into Syria and Crimea. Intellectuals seized upon the epic as a model of the French heritage. While the Round Table was vigorously hailed as a precursor of democracy, the courtly practice of adultery seemed scandalous. To counter the spread of illicit relations, moralists praised the virtues of the epic hero. The scholarly methodology applied to the epic has had handsome rewards. Aside from the variety of approaches that have been useful for other genres, the question of orality has been particularly rich. The study of a warrior society in which the mode of literary consumption was oral has led to new definitions of the process of thinking as well as to surprising cultural ramifications of reliance on voice rather than writing.

William W. Kibler

[See also: ADENET LE ROI; CRUSADE CYCLE; *ENFANCES*; GUILLAUME D'ORANGE CYCLE; JONGLEUR; KING CYCLE; LATE EPIC; LORRAINE CYCLE; NANTEUIL CYCLE; REBELLIOUS VASSAL CYCLE; *ROLAND, CHANSON DE*; SAINT-GILLES CYCLE]

Bédier, Joseph. *Les légendes épiques*. 4 vols. 3rd ed. Paris: Champion, 1926–29.

Boutet, Dominique. *La chanson de geste: forme et signification d'une écriture épique du Moyen Âge*. Paris: Presses Universitaires de France, 1993.

Boyer, Régis, et al. *L'épopée*. Turnhout: Brepols, 1988.

Bulletin bibliographique de la Société Rencesvals. Paris: Nizet, 1958– .

Farrier, Susan. *The Medieval Charlemagne Legend: An Annotated Bibliography*. New York: Garland, 1993.

Heinemann, Edward A. *L'art métrique de la chanson de geste: essai sur la musicalité du récit*. Geneva: Droz, 1993.

Martin, Jean-Pierre. *Les motifs dans la chanson de geste: définition et utilisation*. Lille: Centre d'Études Médiévales et Dialectales, 1992.

Menéndez Pidal, Ramón. *La Chanson de Roland y el neotradicionalismo: orígenes de la épica románica*. Madrid, 1959; French trans., Irénée-Marcel Cluzel, 2nd ed. rev. with René Louis. *La Chanson de Roland et la tradition épique des Francs*, Paris: Picard, 1960.

Rychner, Jean. *La chanson de geste: essai sur l'art épique des jongleurs*. Geneva: Droz, 1955.

Suard, François. *La chanson de geste*. Paris: Presses Universitaires de France, 1993.

CHANSON DE TOILE.

CHANSON DE TOILE. This lyrico-narrative genre, indigenous to northern France and with no counterpart in Provençal poetry, which might be translated as "weaving song," is represented by a score of compositions, mostly anonymous, preserved in 13th-century songbooks or as interpolations in romances (especially Jean Renart's *Guillaume de Dole*). Four anonymous pieces and all of the later, more elaborate ones by Audefroi le Bâtard survive with melodies. The origin and function of the songs (also known as *chansons d'histoire*) are murky and controversial; the genre appears to have arisen at the time of the early epics as an accompaniment to women's spinning and weaving. The texts are simple, brief stanzaic tales of frank and insistent, "precourtly," desire related from the point of view of a young noblewoman.

Samuel N. Rosenberg

[See also: AUDEFROI LE BÂTARD; TROUVÈRE POETRY]

Bec, Pierre. *La lyrique française au moyen âge (XIIe–XIIIe siècles)*. 2 vols. Paris: Picard, 1977–78, Vol. 1, pp. 107–19.

Rosenberg, Samuel N., and Hans Tischler, eds. *Chanter m'estuet: Songs of the Trouvères*. Bloomington: Indiana University Press, 1981, pp.12–24, 245–48.

Toja, Gianluigi. "Antiche reliquie della poesie epica francese nelle *chansons d'histoire*." *Medioevo romanzo* 10 (1985): 37–59.

Zink, Michel. *Belle: essai sur les chansons de toile, suivi d'une édition et d'une traduction*. Paris: Champion, 1977. [Includes melodies.]

CHARITÉ-SUR-LOIRE.

CHARITÉ-SUR-LOIRE. The priory of Notre-Dame at Charité-sur-Loire (Nièvre) was among the largest Cluniac foundations. Its first church, built in the second half of the 11th century, was modeled on Cluny II and featured an apse echelon of three apses to either side of a larger central apse. Soon after the dedication in 1107, remodeling influenced by Cluny III enlarged the church. The double-aisled nave was lengthened to eleven bays, and the choir was extended by an ambulatory with five radiating chapels. An imposing narthex was begun, but only one tower was constructed in the second half of the 12th century. Although parts of the church were destroyed, the tower and apse show rich architectural detailing with cusped arches reflecting Moorish influence.

Karen Gould

Vallery-Radot, Jean. "L'ancienne prieurale Notre-Dame à La Charité-sur-Loire: l'architecture." *Congrès archéologique (Nivernais)* 125 (1967): 43–85.

CHARLEMAGNE.

CHARLEMAGNE (742–814). The Frankish king and later emperor who gave his name to the Carolingian empire was born to Pepin III the Short and Bertrada in 742. In accordance with Frankish custom, on Pepin's death in 768 his realm was divided between his legitimate male offspring, Charles and his younger brother, Carloman. Carloman received the central provinces of the kingdom; Charles's territories, including Thuringia, Frisia, parts of Alemannia, Austrasia, and Neustria, encircled those of his brother. The brothers did not get along, but Carloman died in 771 and Charles took over his lands, setting aside his brother's two sons. From then until his own death in 814, Charles was the sole ruler of the Franks. At its peak, the realm, which with his imperial coronation in 800 came to be regarded as the Christian-Roman empire in the West, comprised portions of modern East Europe and most of the western area of the Continent. Charles's achievements as king and emperor—his extension of the lands under his rule, his efforts to protect and reform the church, and his fostering of a cultural and intellectual revival—inspired western monarchs throughout the rest of the Middle Ages. They justly earned him the name of Charlemagne (Lat. *Carolus Magnus*), or Charles the Great.

For thirty years after Carloman's death, Charlemagne expanded the frontiers of his realm and strengthened his hold on the conquered regions. In 774, he conquered Lombardy and took the title king of the Lombards. He subdued Bavaria, though not decisively, in 787; during the 790s, efforts to protect the Carolingians against Muslim incursions led to the annexation of the territory along the Pyrénées that became the Spanish March. Further campaigns in the 790s crushed the Avars, while from 772 to 804 Charlemagne strove to conquer the Saxons on the eastern boundaries of his realm. The long-term struggle against the Saxons provoked the Carolingians to try a variety of strategies to win control, including forced baptisms, mass executions and deportations, and settlement of Franks in the area.

The large area under Charlemagne's authority was tied socially to the royal power through the system of benefices, lifetime grants to nobles of lands in different parts of the realm in return for oaths of vassalage and services to the monarch, particularly military service. As under earlier Frankish kings, administration still operated primarily at the local level. The main instrument of local government during Charlemagne's reign was the count, who within his county exercised the absolute power of the royal ban on the king's behalf. But local government was linked to the central administration by the annual assemblies of the most powerful aristocrats and by the *missi dominici,* magnates selected as the king's representatives who undertook for him regular tours of inspection throughout the kingdom. One method used to instruct the *missi* in their duties as well as to promulgate new legislation involved documents known as capitularies, which issued from Charlemagne's court at a rate far surpassing anything seen under earlier Frankish rulers. Legislative authority, however, continued to rest with the king's oral pronouncement and was based on the royal ban, not on the capitularies.

Charlemagne was crowned emperor of the Romans by Pope Leo III on Christmas Day 800, in St. Peter's, Rome. Whether the papal or the Frankish court instigated the move, it is clear that for some years previously Carolingian churchmen, such as Alcuin, had been developing a concept of Charlemagne's role as the successor to the first Christian emperor, Constantine I, and the leader of a new Christian-Roman empire in the West. The decision to bestow the imperial title on Charles was inspired by such thinking and, in Rome, by the political difficulties of the pope, threatened by hostile factions within Rome that sought his deposition.

The imperial coronation testified not only to Charlemagne's success at increasing the territory under his authority but also to his work on behalf of the church. Ecclesiastical reform was a major subject of several capitularies issued before 800, among them the *Admonitio generalis* (789) and the Capitulary of the Council of Frankfurt (794). In addition to the efforts in these documents to regulate the lives of clergy, monks, and female religious, to reform the ecclesiastical hierarchy, to ensure that the clergy knew the basic articles of the Christian faith, and to provide guidelines for the religious conduct of the laity, certain of the capitulary decrees and the very proliferation of such texts testify to a new drive, encouraged by Charlemagne, to make the written word the keystone of his administration. That drive—despite the problems that Charlemagne himself encountered in his own efforts to learn to write, according to his biographer, Einhard—built upon, but vastly exceeded in scope, anything under Charles's father, Pepin III. The degree to which Charlemagne and his churchmen perceived mastery of written language as the hallmark of his court is manifested in the *Libri Carolini,* completed in 793. Encompassing 228 pages in the current printed edition, this massive treatise, in which Charlemagne is presented as the one who speaks, denounces the Byzantine empire for its inferiority to the Carolingians on a host of issues; but most fundamentally, it rebukes the eastern government for its failure to understand Scripture, because of the Greeks' inability to match the Carolingians in their command of the written word.

The importance that Charlemagne and his court attached to the skills relating to written language fueled the artistic and intellectual "renaissance" that occurred during his reign, again beginning even before his imperial coronation. The prose writings and poetry by scholars from all over Europe who joined Charles's court circle— the Anglo-Saxon Alcuin, the Visigoth Theodulf of Orléans (author of the *Libri Carolini*), the Italians Paul the Deacon and Paulinus of Aquileia, the Frank Einhard, and others—and the creations of Carolingian artists during the same years, show a sophistication, a subtlety in their use of earlier texts and artistic productions, and an innovativeness that scholars are only starting to appreciate fully. The artistic and intellectual achievements that Charlemagne fostered laid the groundwork for the accomplishments in the same areas under his son Louis the Pious (778–840), yet Louis inherited an empire that, in other ways, was showing signs of strain. During the last decade of Charles's reign, with the end of the wars of conquest and the flow of revenue from them, the Carolingian empire experienced increasing corruption and disaffection among its aristocracy. Charlemagne responded in part by reemphasizing older, Frankish traditions, and thus in accordance with Frankish custom the *Divisio regnorum* of 806 arranged that after Charles's death his territories be divided among his legitimate sons, Charles the Younger (d. 811), Pepin (d. 810), and Louis, each of whom he had already appointed to be king of part of the empire. No attempt was made at the time to ensure the empire's continued unity, nor was a plan set forth for transmission of the imperial title.

By 813, Charles the Younger and Pepin were dead, however, and Louis the Pious received the imperial crown in September of that year. He became sole emperor in the West when Charlemagne died, in January 814.

Celia Chazelle

[See also: ALCUIN; CAROLINGIAN ART; CAROLINGIAN DYNASTY; EINHARD; LATIN POETRY, CAROLINGIAN; *LIBRI CAROLINI*; LATIN POETRY, CAROLINGIAN; LOUIS I THE PIOUS; MILLENNIALISM; PEPIN; THEODULF OF ORLÉANS]

Braunfels, Wolfgang, et al., eds. *Karl der Grosse: Lebenswerk und Nachleben.* 5 vols. Düsseldorf: Schwann, 1965–68.

Bullough, Donald A. "*Europae Pater:* Charlemagne and His Achievement in the Light of Recent Scholarship." *English Historical Review* 85 (1970): 59–105.

Council of Europe. *Karl der Grosse: Werk und Wirkung.* Catalogue to exhibition, Aix-la-Chapelle, 1965. Düsseldorf: Schwann, 1965.

Folz, Robert. "Charlemagne and His Empire." In *Essays on the Reconstruction of Medieval History*, ed. Vaclav Mudroch and G.S. Couse. Montreal: McGill-Queen's University Press, 1974, pp. 86–112.

Ganshof, François L. *The Carolingians and the Frankish Monarchy: Studies in Carolingian History*, trans. Janet Sondheimer. London: Longman, 1971.

Halphen, Louis. *Charlemagne and the Carolingian Empire*, trans. Giselle de Nie. Amsterdam: North-Holland, 1977.

McKitterick, Rosamond. *The Frankish Church and the Carolingian Reforms, 789–895*. London: Royal Historical Society, 1977.

———. *The Frankish Kingdoms Under the Carolingians, 751–987*. London: Longman, 1983.

———. *The Carolingians and the Written Word*. Cambridge: Cambridge University Press, 1989.

Nees, Lawrence. *A Tainted Mantle: Hercules and the Classical Tradition at the Carolingian Court*. Philadelphia: University of Pennsylvania Press, 1991.

Riché, Pierre. *The Carolingians: A Family Who Forged Europe*, trans. Michael I. Allen. Philadelphia: University of Pennsylvania Press, 1993.

Werner, Karl Ferdinand. "Important Noble Families in the Kingdom of Charlemagne: A Prosopographical Study of the Relationship Between King and Nobility in the Early Middle Ages." In *The Medieval Nobility: Studies on the Ruling Classes of France and Germany from the Sixth to the Twelfth Century*, ed. and trans. Timothy Reuter. Amsterdam: North-Holland, 1978, pp. 137–202.

CHARLES I (1226–1285). Count of Anjou and king of Sicily. The brother of Louis IX, Charles was intended for a career in the church, but the death of another brother, Jean, transformed his life. In 1246, the crown decided to grant Charles an apanage of the counties of Anjou and Maine, originally intended for Jean. Earlier that year, Charles had married Béatrice de Provence, a marriage that gave him effective, although theoretically temporary, authority in the county of Provence. Charles thus became an important territorial prince in both northern and southern France. He made several efforts to consolidate and expand his authority. For example, after his return in 1250 from his brother's first crusade (1248–54), he intervened in a succession crisis in Hainaut but failed to secure the county for himself (Treaty of Péronne, 1256). He was more successful in maintaining his authority in Provence despite the fierce independence of key Provençal cities, especially Marseille, reduced by Charles to submission in the later 1250s, and the vigorous, sometimes military, efforts of his mother-in-law and his wife's sisters, the queens of England and France, to secure their rights in the county after Béatrice's death.

The main theater of Charles's operations was Italy. It was he who accepted the invitation of the papacy to deliver the Holy See from the Hohenstaufen threat in southern Italy and Sicily in the 1260s and, in doing so, carved out a huge zone of influence for himself in the central Mediterranean. Besides defeating the Hohenstaufen and becoming king of Sicily in 1266 (though resistance continued until 1268), he became the effective ruler (senator) of Rome, imperial vicar in Tuscany, protector and governor of several important north Italian towns, overlord of Albania, and, after he took command of his brother's second crusade (1270), the possessor of important concessions in Tunisia.

In 1277, Charles secured the rights of Marie of Antioch to the throne of the kingdom of Jerusalem, a symbolic indication of the scale of his ambitions in the Mediterranean. Charles also began seriously to make preparations for the invasion of the Greek empire, which had recently been reconquered by the Paleologoi after the Frankish domination (1204–61) following the Fourth Crusade. He was thwarted in this final design by trouble in Sicily, the great nativist uprising (1282) known as the Vespers. Moreover, the king of Aragon, whose marriage to a Hohenstaufen princess gave him claims in Sicily, supported the uprising. French royal aid to Charles, to counter that support, culminated in the crusade against Aragon (1285), during which King Philip III of France, Charles's nephew, perished. Charles himself died early in the same year, leaving a much less able son as his successor and a tangle of problems not fully resolved until the end of the Middle Ages.

William Chester Jordan

[See also: ANJOU, HOUSES OF; SICILIAN VESPERS]

Baratier, Édouard, ed. *Histoire de la Provence*. Toulouse: Privat, 1969.

Jordan, Édouard. *Les origines de la domination angevine en Italie*. Paris: Picard, 1909.

Richard, Jean. *Saint Louis: roi d'une France féodale, soutien de la Terre Sainte*. Paris: Fayard, 1983.

Runciman, Steven. *The Sicilian Vespers: A History of the Mediterranean World in the Later Thirteenth Century*. Cambridge: Cambridge University Press, 1958.

CHARLES II THE BAD (1332–1387). King of Navarre. The son of Philippe d'Évreux and Jeanne, daughter of Louis X of France, Charles succeeded his father as count of Évreux in 1343 and became king of Navarre (as Charles II) when his mother died in October 1349. Although he became a bitter enemy of the royal house of Valois, whose propagandists accused him of many nefarious deeds and plots, Charles was a popular young man who commanded a considerable political following in the 1350s. Not until the 16th century did he appear as "El Malo" in Navarrese historiography, but this sobriquet gained wide acceptance among subsequent generations of royalist or nationalist historians in France.

The Évreux family had serious grievances against the Valois monarchy, which kept possession of Jeanne's inheritance of Champagne and Brie, never relinquished to her the promised compensation, Angoulême, and remained dilatory in providing the revenues that were to have replaced these territories. The northwestern nobles, disaffected for much of Philip VI's reign, had many connections to the house of Évreux, which had cultivated clients among them. Other critics of the monarchy were genuine reformers whose intellectual wing was based in the Collège de Navarre in Paris, a longtime recipient of Évreux patronage.

The Valois rulers made efforts to cultivate their Évreux cousins. Philip VI, as an aging widower, married Charles's teenaged sister Blanche in 1349, and Charles himself married Jeanne, the eldest daughter of John II, a few years later. These overtures, however, did not defuse the grievances, and the delays in paying his wife's large dowry embittered Charles further. John II aggravated the bad royal relations with the northwestern nobility by summarily executing the constable Raoul de Brienne in 1350. The new constable, John's inexperienced young favorite Charles of Spain, received lavish royal gifts, including the county of Angoulême, which Charles the Bad considered to be rightfully his own. With considerable sympathy from critics of the regime, Charles had the constable murdered in January 1354, thus beginning a decade of rebellion against his father-in-law.

To shield himself from royal wrath, Charles called on the English for aid, and John II had to conclude the Treaty of Mantes (February 1354), which pardoned Charles and his followers and granted him substantial new lands in lower Normandy in return for his definitive renunciation of Champagne and Brie. Charles then proceeded to disrupt Anglo-French negotiations at Avignon and bring troops to Normandy, where he hoped to cooperate with an English invasion. When contrary winds kept Edward III from coming, Charles had to conclude a less advantageous treaty with John II at Valognes (September 10, 1355). The king of Navarre remained a magnet for discontented elements in northwestern France and apparently tried to subvert the dauphin, John's eldest son, into rebelling against his father.

Increasingly bitter toward his son-in-law, John II suddenly arrested Charles at Rouen in April 1356, executing several of his followers and placing him in prison. Normandy was swept by civil war, and in September John and his supporters suffered devastating defeat by the Prince of Wales near Poitiers. With John II now a captive, the dauphin's weakened government faced a large array of critics, some of whom demanded the release of Charles the Bad.

Released by his friends in November 1357, Charles resumed his role as a leader of forces opposed to the crown, yet within a year his position had eroded. Nobles in particular and reformers generally became attracted to the dauphin's camp after the hostility of the Parisians toward nobles drove a wedge between noble and bourgeois reformers. Charles the Bad became suspect because he cooperated with the Parisians and because his negotiations with the English indicated an interest in partitioning France. He and his supporters failed to prevent the release of John II via the Treaty of Brétigny. An uneasy peace with John ended when the king bestowed Burgundy on his son Philip the Bold in 1363. Charles asserted a claim to Burgundy, and with the new hostilities thousands of unemployed soldiers (*routiers*) claimed to be fighting in his name.

At the end of 1363, the Estates General of northern France established a tax to support a regular salaried army. In the spring of 1364, as Charles V was succeeding John II on the French throne, this new army, commanded by Bertrand du Guesclin, won a crushing victory over the forces of Charles the Bad at Cocherel in Normandy. This campaign broke the power of the Navarrese party in Normandy and around Paris. Charles was forced to accept the southern barony of Montpellier and relinquish some of his family's Norman strongholds.

After this time, Charles played a diminished role in French politics, although a scandal came to light in 1378 that implicated him in plots against the crown. With the dissidents who formerly supported him now firmly in the royal camp, Charles was restricted to his role as ruler of a minor Spanish kingdom.

John Bell Henneman, Jr.

[See also: CHARLES V THE WISE; ÉVREUX; GUESCLIN, BERTRAND DU]

Bessen, David M. *Charles of Navarre and John II: Disloyalty in Northern France 1350–1360.* Diss. University of Toronto, 1983.

Cazelles, Raymond. *Société politique, noblesse et couronne sous Jean le Bon et Charles V.* Geneva: Droz, 1982.

Henneman, John Bell. *Royal Taxation in Fourteenth Century France: The Captivity and Ransom of John II 1356–1370.* Philadelphia: American Philosophical Society, 1976.

Secousse, Denis F. *Recueil de pièces servant de preuves aux Mémoires sur les troubles excités en France par Charles II dit le Mauvais, roi de Navarre et comte d'Évreux.* Paris: Durand, 1755.

CHARLES II THE BALD (823–877). King of the West Franks. Charles II the Bald was the only son of Emperor Louis the Pious (r. 814–40) by his second wife, Judith. Three other sons, Lothair I (d. 855), Pepin of Aquitaine (d. 838), and Louis the German (d. 876), had been born to Louis's first wife, Irmengarde. The terms of inheritance outlined in the *Ordinatio imperii* of 817 had divided governance of the empire among Lothair, Louis the German, and Pepin and indicated that Lothair, the eldest, would exercise supremacy as sole heir to the imperial title. But the arrival of a fourth son prompted Louis the Pious to revise his scheme by designating lands for Charles from among those of his half-brothers. The subsequent clashes of Louis the Pious with reformers at his court and with his older sons, along with the struggles for power among his children, created a turmoil that eventually destroyed the empire's unity. In 843, the Treaty of Verdun divided the empire into three separate kingdoms for Charles, Lothair, and Louis the German, with Charles allotted the western third of the empire.

Charles's rule in west Francia was highlighted early on by an assembly at Coulaines (843), at which the king promised to safeguard the rights of his subjects and in return requested their counsel and aid. This pact represented a new step in relations between Carolingian monarch and aristocracy. Although throughout his reign Charles's authority was threatened by his brothers, aristocratic factions, and Viking raids along his coasts, his court remained culturally the most brilliant center of his day in the West, attracting such theologians as Hincmar of Reims and Johannes Scottus Eriugena. Moreover, Charles managed to secure and even extend his power. By the Treaty of Meerssen (870), he and Louis the German shared the territories of their nephew Lothair II, who had ruled Lorraine from 855 to 869. When Emperor Louis II died in 875, Charles the Bald gained the kingdom of Italy and the imperial title. In 877, having decided to conduct an expedition into Italy against the Muslims, he held an assembly at Quierzy remembered for its guarantee of the rights of blood relations in the inheritance of offices and properties vacated during his absence. Charles the Bald died October 6, 877, before his return from Italy. His son, Louis the Stammerer, succeeded to the throne of west Francia.

Celia Chazelle

[See also: ERIUGENA, JOHANNES SCOTTUS; HINCMAR OF REIMS; NITHARD; PHILOSOPHY]

Gibson, Margaret, and Janet Nelson, eds. *Charles the Bald: Court and Kingdom*. Oxford: British Archaeological Reports, 1981.

Tessier, Georges, Arthury Giry, Ferdinand Lot, and Maurice Prou, eds. *Recueil des actes de Charles II le Chauve, roi de France*. 3 vols. Paris: Imprimerie Nationale, 1943–65.

McKitterick, Rosamond. *The Frankish Kingdoms Under the Carolingians, 751–987*. London: Longman, 1983.

Nees, Lawrence. *A Tainted Mantle: Hercules and the Classical Tradition at the Carolingian Court*. Philadelphia: University of Pennsylvania Press, 1991.

Nelson, Janet L. *Charles the Bald*. London: Longman, 1992.

Riché, Pierre. *The Carolingians: A Family Who Forged Europe*, trans. Michael I. Allen. Philadelphia: University of Pennsylvania Press, 1993.

CHARLES IV THE FAIR (1294–1328). King of France. Charles, the youngest son of Philip IV, acceded to the throne in 1322 after the death of his elder brother, Philip V, whose only children were daughters and so excluded from the throne. Early in his reign, Charles IV executed an obstreperous southern notable, Count Jourdain de l'Isle, and firmly established his authority by a subsequent progress through the south.

Charles dissipated some of the respect he enjoyed by employing unpopular and dubious means to strengthen his finances. He sold offices, manipulated the coinage, and hounded Christian debtors who owed money to Jews whose account books had been confiscated by the crown in 1306. He continued the process, begun by his brother, of collecting the fines that had been imposed on Jews who had returned from exile in 1315 but who were accused in 1321 of having plotted with lepers to poison the wells in France. In 1322, large numbers of Jews emigrated; whether this was under an order of expulsion issued by the king is uncertain.

Territorial ambitions and jurisdictional squabbles led Charles into war with England and military intervention in Flanders during his short reign. The war with England, which began in 1323 and produced a French invasion of Guyenne, had more success than the Flemish campaign.

Owing to the overthrow of Edward II of England by his wife, Isabella (Charles's sister), in 1327, the peace that ended the English war resulted in a 50,000-mark payment to the French crown and small territorial concessions in the Agenais.

The king relied on the advice of his uncle, Charles of Valois, on most matters and entrusted him with important military duties and a principal role in negotiating with the pope over a proposed crusade. Some scholars feel that Charles IV expressed interest in a crusade chiefly as a ruse to raise money for more pressing foreign and domestic objectives. Others recognize the force of financial concerns in his hard bargaining with the pope but see no necessary contradiction between these concerns and a genuine interest in promoting a crusade. In any case, no serious crusade took place.

Charles's first wife, Blanche d'Artois, had been implicated in an adultery scandal that rocked the royal household in 1314. After that marriage was annulled in 1322, he married Marie de Luxembourg, who bore a son who died in infancy and then herself died in 1324. Charles then married Jeanne d'Évreux, who bore only daughters. When Charles died on February 1, 1328, at Vincennes, the succession was uncertain until the magnates rallied to his cousin Philip of Valois.

William Chester Jordan

[See also: CHARLES OF VALOIS; ISABELLA OF FRANCE; PHILIP V THE TALL; PHILIP VI; SAINT-SARDOS; VALOIS DYNASTY]

Jordan, William Chester. *The French Monarchy and the Jews from Philip Augustus to the Last Capetians*. Philadelphia: University of Pennsylvania Press, 1989.

Langlois, Charles-Victor. *Saint Louis, Philippe le Bel, les derniers Capetiens directs: 1226–1328*. Paris: Hachette, 1901.

CHARLES V THE WISE (1338–1380). The third French king of the Valois line, Charles V was born on January 21, 1338, the oldest son of John II and Bonne de Luxembourg. He was the first heir of a French king to be styled dauphin of Viennois. Charles owes much of his reputation to Christine de Pizan, who depicted him as a prudent and skillful ruler despite chronic poor health. His reign as king (1364–80) was a time of success for France, in contrast to those of his predecessor and successor, but some recent scholars have questioned how much of the success can be attributed to his abilities.

Charles had an eventful political career before becoming king. In 1355, he was implicated in conspiracies against his father fomented by Charles the Bad, king of Navarre. In 1356, after the defeat and capture of John II at Poitiers, Charles was left to face attacks on the government from partisans of Charles the Bad, genuine political reformers, and ambitious men who hoped to oust unpopular royal financial officers and take their place. Nonnobles were increasingly hostile to nobles, while much of the nobility of northern and western France had been hostile to the Valois monarchy for years.

As royal lieutenant and later regent in the name of his captive father, Charles had to deal with a serious crisis in the years 1356–58. Riot and rebellion in Paris, independent military action by the forces of Charles the Bad, and the savage uprising against nobles known as the Jacquerie all contributed to this crisis, as did a seriously unstable currency and the ravages of unemployed companies of soldiers (*routiers*). Throughout the period, the Estates General convened repeatedly, but the militance of the urban representatives soon alienated the nobles, who slowly gravitated into the royalist camp.

After Charles regained Paris in 1358, the royal government began to recover its authority and institute reforms. A new English invasion in 1359–60 failed to capture any major towns, and the Treaty of Brétigny in 1360 secured John II's release. To pay his ransom, stabilize the currency, and deal with the brigandage of *routiers*, the crown was able to establish substantial regular taxes in 1360 and 1363, and these financed the troops that won a major victory over the Navarrese at Cocherel on May 6, 1364. Charles V, who had just succeeded his father as king, inherited a favorable situation and a reform-minded royal council led by Guillaume de Melun, archbishop of Sens. Charles continued to cultivate the newly royalist nobility of the north and west, who began to provide the bulk of his military leaders. His brother Louis I of Anjou became royal lieutenant in Languedoc, providing energetic leadership there for most of the reign.

As king, Charles profited from two important international developments, both of them in 1369. His brother Philip the Bold married the heiress of Flanders and Artois, thus denying these strategic lands to a potential English suitor. In Spain, Bertrand du Guesclin, the victor of Cocherel, helped establish a pro-French candidate on the throne of Castile, giving Charles an ally with an important fleet. At home, Charles lured into the French camp Olivier de Clisson, who brought with him a host of Breton knights who played a vital role in the French army. The king also cultivated discontented Gascon magnates, accepting their appeal against the English regime in Aquitaine, thus reopening the Hundred Years' War in 1369, when France was able to win quick victories. Aided by a Castilian naval victory off La Rochelle in 1372 and the policy, promoted by Clisson, of avoiding pitched battles, France reduced the English possessions in France to a few coastal enclaves by the end of the reign.

Charles V made his two great mistakes in 1378. One was the attempted confiscation of Brittany, which cost him the valuable military services of the Breton magnates. The other was his quick recognition of the questionable papal election of Clement VII, which brought about the Great Schism. A pious ruler with a strong sense of royal majesty and duty, Charles had profited greatly from the taxes enacted toward the end of his father's reign, but he felt uneasy about their rightness. An important intellectual in his circle, Nicole Oresme, had written a French version of Aristotle's *Politics* in which he strongly criticized taxation. In this climate of opinion, Charles, on his deathbed, canceled the *fouage* (hearth tax), which had financed his victorious armies.

Although clearly not as able a leader as traditionally portrayed, Charles V was a successful ruler who picked effective subordinates, encouraged needed reforms, and had the skill to use rather than antagonize the politically most influential groups in his kingdom.

John Bell Henneman, Jr.

[See also: GUESCLIN, BERTRAND DU; HUNDRED YEARS' WAR; JACQUERIE; LIBRARIES; MARCEL, ÉTIENNE; ORESME, NICOLE]

Babbitt, Susan M. *Oresme's "Livre de politiques" and the France of Charles V*. Philadelphia: American Philosophical Society, 1985.

Cazelles, Raymond. *Société politique, noblesse et couronne sous Jean le Bon et Charles V*. Geneva: Droz, 1982.

Delachenal, Roland. *Histoire de Charles V*. 5 vols. Paris: Picard, 1909–31.

Dodu, Gaston. "Les idées de Charles V en matière de gouvernement." *Revue des questions historiques* 110 (1929): 5–46.

Henneman, John Bell. *Royal Taxation in Fourteenth Century France: The Captivity and Ransom of John II, 1356–1370*. Philadelphia: American Philosophical Society, 1976.

CHARLES VI (1368–1422). Charles VI (r. 1380–1422) was born in Paris on December 3, 1368, to Charles V and Jeanne de Bourbon. He was crowned king on November 4, 1380. His father had stipulated that during his minority the oldest of his paternal uncles, Louis I of Anjou, was to be regent, but Anjou agreed under pressure, on October 2, 1380, that Charles VI be declared of age and the kingdom ruled in his name according to the advice of all four royal uncles. In 1388, influenced by a plan set in motion by Olivier de Clisson, Charles VI took control of the government himself. The counselors he then favored, scornfully called Marmousets by the dukes, initiated a program of reform that was cut short by the onset of his mental illness on August 5, 1392.

This crisis enabled the dukes to regain their power. The king considered himself recovered within five weeks, but other psychotic episodes followed. Charles VI suffered from recurring persecutory delusions and exhibited forms of behavior commonly observed today in schizophrenics. There was often no clearly visible line of demarcation to distinguish his schizophrenic thought patterns from "sane" ones. Since he often seemed able to function, he was allowed to continue to rule with full power, his royal prerogative protected by the sacred character of French kingship. Despite a manifest desire to be a good king, Charles VI made many important decisions while his thinking was disordered, and this soon upset the equilibrium of his government.

His mental illness caused him to deal in an inconsistent and questionable manner with the assassination of his brother, Louis of Orléans, in 1407. The consequence was almost constant civil war that exacerbated the persecutory delusions suffered by the king, for suspicion of treason was everywhere. This atmosphere also had the effect of making the king's schizophrenic thinking often seem sane.

In an attempt to protect the monarchy from control by either the Burgundians or the Armagnacs (the Orléanist party), the king's eldest son, Duke Louis of Guyenne, sought to form a separate royalist party. These efforts, spoiled by the invasion of Henry V of England and by Louis's own death in December, were not continued by the dauphin Charles (later Charles VII), who fled Paris as it fell to the Burgundians on May 29, 1418. He did not return until 1437.

The dauphin Charles and the Armagnacs found support in each other for their demands. The government was anxious for the dauphin to return to the royal court, but reconciliation became impossible after he sanctioned the assassination of John the Fearless, duke of Burgundy, at Montereau in September 1419 and then committed treason by usurping royal authority to call himself regent of France. As a result, Charles VI accepted the Anglo-French-Burgundian Treaty of Troyes in May 1420 and married his daughter Catherine to Henry V. The treaty declared Henry heir to the French throne with the powers of regent, but preserved Charles VI's rights and authority. Charles VI survived Henry and died at the Hôtel de Saint-Pol on October 21, 1422.

Richard C. Famiglietti

[See also: ARMAGNACS; CATHERINE OF FRANCE; CLISSON; HENRY V; JOHN THE FEARLESS; LOUIS, DUKE OF GUYENNE; MARMOUSETS]

Autrand, Françoise. *Charles VI*. Paris: Fayard, 1986.

Famiglietti, R. C. *Royal Intrigue: Crisis at the Court of Charles VI 1392–1420*. New York: AMS, 1986.

Grandeau, Yann. "La mort et les obsèques de Charles VI." *Bulletin philologique et historique du Comité des Travaux Historiques et Scientifiques* (1970): 133–86.

Hindman, Sandra L. *Christine de Pizan's "Epistre Othea": Painting and Politics at the Court of Charles VI*. Toronto: Pontifical Institute of Mediaeval Studies, 1986.

Rey, Maurice. *Les finances royales sous Charles VI: les causes du déficit (1388–1413)*. Paris: SEVPEN, 1965.

CHARLES VII (1403–1461). One of the best known but least understood of the medieval kings of France, Charles VII was the eleventh child of Charles VI and Isabeau of Bavaria. That he would become king or be immortalized by his association with Jeanne d'Arc and the reconquest of France was unimagined during his youth. Becoming dauphin in 1417 after the unexpected deaths of older brothers, he entered the political scene in one of the darkest periods of French history. In 1418, upon escaping a Burgundian coup in Paris, he became head of a government in exile dominated by the Armagnac faction. His ill-advised role in the assassination of the duke of Burgundy in 1419 united the English and Burgundians, and they sought to disinherit him in the 1420 Treaty of Troyes. When Charles did become king in October 1422, he controlled only the third of the realm south of the Loire. He indiscriminantly accepted a wide range of supporters and advisers, whom he only slowly learned to control. Denied access to Paris and derisively called "king of Bourges,"

Charles courted provincial estates and the *bonnes villes*. His actions foreshadowed the administrative decentralization of his later reign.

After years of catastrophic defeats, the appearance of Jeanne d'Arc marked a turning point in Charles's fortunes. Her victories at Orléans and Patay brought Charles to Reims for a coronation in July 1429. By 1435, he brought Burgundy to a separate peace in the Treaty of Arras, which allowed the Valois reentry into Paris in 1436. A contentious decade of reform passed before Charles could complete the reconquest of France. The Pragmatic Sanction of Bourges in 1438 affirmed royal control of the French episcopacy and ecclesiastical revenues, and, at the Estates of 1439, Charles increased taxation and attempted to outlaw unauthorized armed forces. The military anarchy of the brigandage (*écorcherie*) and the revolt of his son, the future Louis XI, and many peers in the Praguerie posed a new crisis that took all of Charles's tactical and diplomatic skills to overcome. Influenced by his mistress Agnès Sorel, he settled on his two reliable advisers: Pierre de Brézé and the constable Richemont, and by 1445 he was able to implement his program. In 1449, the revitalized Valois army renewed the war, and by 1453 the English had been driven from Normandy and Guyenne.

Consolidating his authority for the rest of his years, Charles easily disciplined such restive princes as the count of Armagnac and the duke of Alençon, used the courts to reconcile a nation embittered by civil war, and perfected the administrative structures that had brought him victory. Only his son, the future Louis XI, impatiently waiting in Burgundian exile, celebrated his death. Sometimes called "the Victorious," Charles was a man who preferred negotiations to war and judiciously waited to exploit his enemies' divisions. He is better remembered as "The Well-Served" king, skilled in the selection and management of advisers who helped him construct a new monarchy out of the cruel necessities of a lifelong struggle to reunite France.

Paul D. Solon

[See also: ARISTOCRATIC REVOLT; ARMAGNACS; *COMPAGNIES D'ORDONNANCE*; JEANNE D'ARC; JOHN THE FEARLESS; MONTEREAU; ORLÉANS CAMPAIGN; RECONQUEST OF FRANCE; RICHEMONT, ARTHUR DE; TREMOILLE, LA]

Beaucourt, Gaston du Fresne de. *Histoire de Charles VII*. 4 vols. Paris: Librairie de la Société Bibliographique, 1881–91.

Lewis, Peter S. *Later Medieval France: The Polity*. London: Macmillan, 1968.

Perroy, Edouard. *The Hundred Years War*. Bloomington: Indiana University Press, 1951.

Vale, Malcolm G. A. *Charles VII*. Berkeley: University of California Press, 1974.

Vallet de Viriville, Auguste. *Histoire de Charles VII, roi de France, et de son époque: 1403–1461*. 3 vols. Paris: Renouard, 1862–65.

CHARLES VIII (1470–1498). The son of Louis XI of France and Charlotte of Savoy, Charles VIII was thirteen when his father and mother died; the young king's guardian was his twenty-one-year-old sister Anne, supported by her husband, Pierre de Bourbon, lord of Beaujeu. Louis XI had been an effective but unpopular king, in whose reign the burden of taxation had increased dramatically. The great magnates, led by Louis of Orléans, who was next in line for the throne, wished to gain control of the government. The Estates General met at the beginning of 1484, and Anne and Pierre managed the proceedings skillfully, sacrificing some unpopular officials from the previous reign and accepting a large reduction in the principal royal tax. Later, they overcame an uprising of the princes known as the Guerre folle ("Mad War").

After 1488, as Charles VIII gained increasing control over affairs, Anne and Pierre slipped into the background. The death of François II of Brittany in the same year left the duchy to his eleven-year-old daughter Anne. In 1491, Charles VIII married her in hopes of securing Brittany for the crown. The young queen bore him several children but none lived very long. To marry Anne of Brittany, Charles first had to divest himself of young Margaret of Austria, to whom he had an unconsummated proxy marriage. He also wanted her father, the emperor Maximilian, to stop interfering with his Italian ambitions, and in order to appease the Habsburgs he had to surrender Artois and the Franche-Comté, both parts of the former Burgundian state.

A pious monarch with a strong sense of the historic mission of the French kings to reform the church and defend Christendom, Charles also had a tenuous claim to the kingdom of Naples. These considerations and the urgings of Italian exiles led him to plan a massive invasion of Italy. After careful preparations, he entered the peninsula in 1494 with a large army. He met little effective opposition and succeeded in taking Naples, but a coalition of Italian and foreign powers intervened against him, and the French had to fight their way back home. While planning a second expedition, Charles died at Amboise on April 7, 1498, after suffering an apparently minor blow to the head. His Italian invasion had ushered in the international wars of the early-modern period; his death marked the end of the senior branch of the Valois line of kings.

John Bell Henneman, Jr.

[See also: ANNE OF BRITTANY; ARISTOCRATIC REVOLT]

Labande-Mailfert, Yvonne. *Charles VIII et son milieu (1470–1498): la jeunesse au pouvoir.* Paris: Klincksieck, 1975.

————. *Charles VIII: le vouloir et la destinée.* Paris: Fayard, 1986.

Major, J. Russell. *Representative Institutions in Renaissance France 1421–1559.* Madison: University of Wisconsin Press, 1960.

Pelicier, Paul. *Essai sur le gouvernement de la dame de Beaujeu (1483–1491).* Paris, 1882.

————, ed. *Lettres de Charles VIII, roi de France.* 5 vols. Paris: Renouard, 1898–1905.

CHARLES DE BLOIS (ca. 1319–1364). Duke of Brittany. Charles de Blois was a younger son of Gui de Châtillon,

count of Blois, and Marguerite de Valois, sister of King Philip VI. In June 1337, he contracted a marriage with Jeanne, countess of Penthièvre (1322–1384), niece of the childless duke of Brittany Jean III. The duke preferred Jeanne as a successor over his half-brother, Jean de Montfort, but he never made a public declaration of his preference. When he died in April 1341, the decision was left to the king and peers of France, who convened in September and awarded Brittany to Jeanne and Charles.

In the meantime, Montfort had seized major Breton towns and enlisted the support of Edward III of England. Most of the great Breton lords were pro-French and supported Charles, but many of them died in 1347 at La Roche-Derrien, when he was badly defeated and captured by the English commander Thomas Dagworth. Montfort having died in 1345, England now backed his young son, Jean. Charles secured his release in 1356 but had to promise not to take arms against the English, who now had a strong foothold in Brittany. The duchy was excluded from the Anglo-French treaty of 1360, and by 1362 young Jean de Montfort was old enough to fight in Brittany on his own behalf. With the crucial support of some veteran English captains, Jean won a decisive victory at Auray in 1364, where Charles lost his life. Although his widow had to recognize Jean IV as duke of Brittany in 1365, the Blois-Penthièvre faction remained an important opposition party in Brittany for another sixty years.

Charles had a reputation for piety and sanctity, and in 1371 his son-in-law, Louis of Anjou, promoted an unsuccessful movement to have him canonized as a saint.

John Bell Henneman, Jr.

Jones, Michael. *The Creation of Brittany: A Late Medieval State.* London: Hambledon, 1988.

La Borderie, Arthur de, and Barthélemy Pocquet. *Histoire de Bretagne.* 6 vols. Rennes: Plihon et Hommay, 1896–1914, Vol. 3 (1899).

Luce, Siméon. *Histoire de Bertrand du Guesclin et de son époque.* Paris: Hachette, 1876.

Plaine, François, ed. *Monuments du procès de canonisation du bienheureux Charles, duc de Bretagne, 1320–1364.* St. Brieuc, 1921.

CHARLES D'ORLÉANS (1394–1465). Son of Valentina, daughter of the duke of Milan, and Louis, duke of Orléans and brother of King Charles VI. In 1407, Louis was murdered by John the Fearless, duke of Burgundy, and Valentine died at Blois the following year. In 1406, Charles had married Isabelle, widow of Richard II of England and daughter of Charles VI. The year after her death in 1409, he married Bonne d'Armagnac. Captured by the English at the Battle of Agincourt in 1415, Charles spent the next twenty-five years in England in the custody of several noblemen. Bonne died in France during this period. Released in 1440, Charles returned joyfully to France and soon afterward married fourteen-year-old Marie de Clèves, niece of Philip of Burgundy, who had helped to arrange his release. After a period of political involvement, he spent most of his remaining years at Blois, where two daughters and a son who was to become King Louis XII were born.

During the last fifteen years of his life at Blois, Charles received many visitors, who joined with members of his household to participate in poetry contests. Samples of this literary activity have survived in a manuscript (B.N. fr. 25458) that served as Charles's personal album, in which he recorded in his own hand his own poems, had some entered by scribes, and also invited members of his entourage and visitors to make contributions. Included in this collection are poems by important political figures of the day, by writers with established reputations, and even by the itinerant poet and sometime criminal François Villon, who may have received a small allowance while living at the court. Charles often proposed the first line of a rondeau or ballade and asked his entourage to write a poem following the restrictions of the prescribed form. It was under these circumstances that Villon wrote *Je meurs de suef auprés de la fontaine,* probably in 1457 or 1458. Villon's other poem in the collection, *Épître à Marie d'Orléans,* was probably composed to celebrate the birth of Charles's daughter in December 1457. The wit and good-natured bantering found in the poems written at the court of Blois serve as evidence of an unusually pleasant and relaxed atmosphere, in which poetry writing was an agreeable pastime.

Charles and his two younger brothers, Philippe and Jean, received a traditional medieval education under the direction of a private tutor. Writing in verse seems to have come naturally, since the first work attributed to Charles, *Le livre contre tout péché,* was written at the age of ten. His numerous poetic works include the *Complainte de France,* written in 1433 after he had been in England for many years; *Retenue d'amours,* composed prior to his capture; the *Songe en complainte* (1437), a 550-line sequel to *Retenue d'amours;* eighty-nine chansons and five complaintes written in England, perhaps after Bonne's death; 123 ballades written mostly during but also after his captivity; four *caroles;* and 435 rondeaux written mostly at Blois. In addition to the poems in French, about 125 in English, many with French counterparts, are attributed to him with increasing confidence.

Charles d'Orléans is known particularly for his use of allegory and the introspective nature of his poetry. Recurring themes in his ballades and rondeaux include exile, the passage of time, the flight of love, life as a prison, old age, the decomposition of the human body, and melancholy. He may be one of the best known and least appreciated French poets. Nearly every anthology of French poetry includes a few of his ballades and rondeaux, especially the ubiquitous *Le temps a laissié son manteau.* Many literary historians refer patronizingly to the charm and superficiality of his poetry and the seeming ineffectiveness of his life, echoing Gaston Paris's assessment that Charles was merely a child with a gift for polished verse, who never understood his role in life. Scholars long considered Charles the last courtly poet, using outmoded medieval conventions to express traditional clichés, while they lionized Villon as a fresh and original forerunner of modern poetry. In addition, because so much biographical infor-

mation is available, scholarship has often been stifled by the attempt to tie Charles's creative work to his life. Recently, however, scholars have taken a closer look at his poetry, have become aware of the libraries to which he had access in both England and France, and consequently have begun to discover in many of his poems a new depth and complexity never before suspected. He is now often classed as a precursor of some of the 19th-century romantic and symbolist poets, especially Baudelaire. His *nonchaloir* has been likened to the "spleen" of later times.

Charles's poems have been translated into English, Dutch, Italian, and Romanian. In addition, scholarly books about his life and works have been published in Japanese, Polish, and Russian.

Deborah H. Nelson

[See also: ARMAGNACS; CHARTIER, ALAIN; *JARDIN DE PLAISANCE ET FLEUR DE RÉTHORIQUE*; RÉGNIER, JEAN]

Charles d'Orléans. *Charles d'Orléans, Poésies,* ed. Pierre Champion. 2 vols. Paris: Champion, 1923–27, Vol. 1: *La retenue d'amours, ballades, chansons, complaintes et caroles;* Vol. 2: *Rondeaux.*

——. *Le manuscrit autographe des poésies de Charles d'Orléans,* ed. Pierre Champion. Paris: Champion, 1907.

——. *The French Chansons of Charles d'Orléans with the Corresponding Middle English Chansons,* ed. and trans. Sarah Spence. New York: Garland, 1986.

Champion, Pierre. *La vie de Charles d'Orléans.* Paris: Champion, 1911.

Fox, John. *The Lyric Poetry of Charles d'Orléans.* Oxford: Clarendon, 1969.

Nelson, Deborah H. *Charles d'Orleans: An Analytical Bibliography.* London: Grant and Cutler, 1990.

Planche, Alice. *Charles d'Orléans, ou la recherche d'un langage.* Paris: Champion, 1975.

Steele, Robert, and Mabel Day. *The English Poems of Charles d'Orléans.* London: Oxford University Press, 1941.

Yenal, Edith. *Charles d'Orléans: A Bibliography of Primary and Secondary Sources.* New York: AMS, 1984.

CHARLES MARTEL (ca. 688/9–741). The founder of the Carolingian dynasty, Charles Martel was the dominant figure of western Europe in the first half of the 8th century. As sole mayor of the palace, he ruled the Frankish kingdom as a virtual monarch, and in his active career he reestablished Frankish unity and restored Frankish authority over most of the surrounding regions. His most celebrated victory was over a Muslim raiding expedition, near Poitiers in 732, the first serious check on the advance of Islam in Europe. His activities paved the way for the even greater careers of his son Pepin the Short and his grandson Charlemagne.

Charles was the illegitimate son of Pepin II of Heristal, the last of the Pippinid, or Arnulfing, mayors of the palace. Pepin II's death in 714, with the only legitimate heirs his young grandchildren, led to an intense power struggle within the Frankish kingdom and invasions by Frisians and Aquitanians. Aided by the powerful Austrasian relatives of his mother, Alpaide, Charles was able to defeat his opponents and by 723 had established himself as the sole mayor of the palace under the nominal kingship of the Merovingian Theuderic IV.

Charles, now usually styled *princeps*, then extended his rule over the neighboring regions, waging successful campaigns against the Frisians, Saxons, and Alemanni. As part of his effort to dominate the Germanic territories, he supported Anglo-Saxon missionaries, especially the disciples of Willibrord in Frisia and Boniface in Thuringia and Hesse. Boniface's close ties to the papacy led to warm relations between Charles and popes Gregory II and Gregory III.

The advance of the Muslims into southern France after the fall of the Visigothic kingdom threatened the Aquitanians, whose duke, Eudes, appealed to Charles for military assistance. The victory won by Charles at Moussais, near Poitiers, on October 25, 732, was not the battle that saved Europe from Islam, but it did lead to his being given the sobriquet Martel—from the Latin *martellus* 'hammer'—in the 9th century. His campaigns in the south for the rest of the 730s did halt Muslim advances and led to his conquest of Provence, which realized the old Frankish dream of gaining direct access to the Mediterranean. Charles, however, was not able to bring Aquitaine fully under his authority. He paid for manpower for his many wars in the 730s in part by appropriating church lands and giving them to his military followers, supposedly to be held from the church. Historians consider these grants the beginning of feudal institutions in the Frankish kingdom.

King Theuderic IV died in 737. Charles did not allow a Merovingian successor to be recognized, and he ruled the last four years of his life without a nominal king. In 739, Pope Gregory III recognized Charles's position as the most powerful Christian ruler of western Europe by appealing to him for assistance against the Lombard king Liutprand. But Charles and Liutprand were close allies, and this initial effort to bring in the Franks as papal allies against the Lombards failed.

Charles's death in 741 temporarily broke the unity of the Frankish kingdom. His elder son, Carloman, was made mayor over Austrasia, Alemannia, and Thuringia, while the younger, Pepin the Short, received Neustria, Burgundy, and Provence. Charles was buried in Merovingian royal style at Saint-Denis.

Steven Fanning

[See also: CAROLINGIAN DYNASTY; MAYOR OF THE PALACE]

Wallace-Hadrill, J.M., ed. and trans. *The Fourth Book of the Chronicle of Fredegar with Its Continuations.* London: Nelson, 1960.

Gerberding, Richard A. *The Rise of the Carolingians and the "Liber Historiæ Francorum."* Oxford: Clarendon, 1987.

McKitterick, Rosamond. *The Frankish Kingdoms Under the Carolingians, 751–987.* London: Longman, 1983.

Riché, Pierre. *The Carolingians: A Family Who Forged Europe,* trans. Michael I. Allen. Philadelphia: University of Pennsylvania Press, 1993.

Roi, Jean-Henri, and Jean Devoisse. *La bataille de Poitiers.* Paris: Gallimard, 1966.

CHARLES OF VALOIS (1270–1325). Father of King Philip VI. The third son of Philip III, Charles became associated with the county of Valois in northern France, which he received as an apanage in 1285. His territorial interests and ambitions, however, extended over a much larger area. In 1282, Peter III of Aragon had invaded Sicily, which was ruled by Charles's granduncle, Charles I of Anjou. The ensuing diplomatic crisis pitted the papacy and the French crown against Aragon in a war (1285) that has been called a crusade. To cement the papal-French alliance, Charles of Valois was to receive the crown of Aragon. French defeat in the war rendered his claim to the title empty, but his renunciation of it in 1295 required considerable diplomatic maneuvering, including the release of Charles II of Anjou, then a hostage in Aragon (1288). In 1290, Charles of Valois married his first wife, Marguerite, the daughter of Charles II, through whom he received the counties of Anjou and Maine.

In the course of his career, Charles also laid claim to the Byzantine empire (since 1261 again in the hands of the Greeks) and put himself forward for the imperial title in Germany. Active militarily on behalf of Pope Boniface VIII in northern Italy, he managed to overcome Florentine resistance to the pope, but his Italian expedition was cut short in 1301, when his brother, Philip IV of France, came into conflict with Boniface. He served Philip in his wars, commanding forces in Guyenne in 1295 and in Flanders in the 1290s and the first two decades of the 14th century.

After the death of Philip IV in 1314, Charles of Valois became a principal counselor to the new king, Louis X (r. 1314–16), and was instrumental in the execution of Enguerran de Marigny, his late brother's financial adviser. Less intimate with Louis X's brother and successor, Philip V (r. 1316–22), he reemerged as a close adviser to the youngest of his nephews, Charles IV (r. 1322–28). In his later years, Charles of Valois seems to have been deeply drawn to the idea of mounting a crusade and pledged in 1323, at age fifty-three, to undertake one. His plans were thwarted first by the king's difficult negotiations with the pope on how to finance an expedition and then by Anglo-French hostilities.

Charles appears to have been a literate and cultured prince who patronized a number of authors and may have been an author of verses himself, but it was in politics that he wanted to make his mark. Although he was the son and brother of kings, the uncle of three kings, and the father of Philip VI, who established the Valois line on the French throne, Charles himself, despite his many claims, died in December 1325 without ever gaining a royal title.

William Chester Jordan

[See also: ANJOU, HOUSES OF; PHILIP IV THE FAIR; VALOIS DYNASTY]

Petit, Joseph. *Charles de Valois (1270–1325).* Paris: Picard, 1900.

CHARLES THE BOLD (1433–1477). Duke of Burgundy. Charles was the last of the four Valois dukes of Burgundy, whose state, based in the Netherlands, became a European power in the 15th century. Although his French sobriquet,"le Téméraire," means "the Rash," Charles has usually been called "the Bold" in English, and his most recent biographer has emphasized the greater appropriateness of the latter name.

The historiography of Charles, inextricably bound up with that of his great antagonist, Louis XI of France, has long relied on colorful but inaccurate narrative sources. Charles hated and feared Louis, but his international ambitions were almost all directed toward the empire rather than France, and it was enemies in the empire, not Louis XI, who eventually caused his ruin.

Charles succeeded his father, Philip the Good, on June 15, 1467, inheriting a state that included most of the Low Countries and a southern cluster of lands around the duchy of Burgundy. Between these two large parcels lay Alsace and Lorraine, both of which Charles tried to acquire, although not placing great emphasis on linking up his lands into a compact territory. He also pursued territorial ambitions in the northern Low Countries and in Savoy to the south. His great desire was to gain a crown, preferably the imperial title. In his elaborate diplomacy, his only child, Mary, was a valuable pawn as Europe's most marriageable heiress.

Allied with Edward IV of England, Charles waged inconclusive border warfare with France in the years 1471–75 while he pursued his imperial ambitions. He gradually overhauled the Burgundian army, turning it into a professional body. By 1475, he had occupied Lorraine and had a virtual protectorate over Savoy and the Vaud. Throughout his career, his treatment of towns was harsh, as at Liège in 1468. Townsmen feared him greatly and resisted him bitterly, as at Beauvais in 1472 and Neuss in 1475. A coalition of imperial cities at last determined to drive him from Alsace and Lorraine. At the beginning of March 1476, a largely Swiss army defeated him at Grandson on Lake Neuchâtel. On June 22, a far more serious defeat at Morat (Murten) removed Savoy from Burgundian control. To recover Lorraine, Charles rebuilt his forces and laid siege to Nancy in November. Marching to the rescue at the end of the year, the Swiss won their third victory in ten months on January 5, 1477, a battle in which Charles met his death.

John Bell Henneman, Jr.

Vaughan, Richard. *Charles the Bold: The Last Valois Duke of Burgundy.* New York: Barnes and Noble, 1974.

CHARLIEU. The Cluniac priory of Saint-Fortunat at Charlieu (Loire) is known for its Romanesque church with sculptural decoration. The church, which replaced a 10th-century structure, was begun ca. 1030, dedicated in 1094, and received a narthex ca. 1135–40. Although it survives in fragmentary form, the church had a tunnel-vaulted nave with clerestory, transept, and central apse with added apsidiole. The inner portal sculpture represents the Ascen-

Charlieu (Loire), Notre-Dame, north portal, Christ in Majesty. *Photograph courtesy of Joan A. Holladay.*

sion with Christ in a mandorla supported by two angels and Apostles in an arcade on the lintel. The narthex with a room above has a lateral entrance whose sculptured tympanum depicts the Apocalyptic Christ in a patterned Late Romanesque style.

Karen Gould

Sunderland, Elizabeth. *Charlieu à l'époque médiévale.* Charlieu: Société pour la Connaissance de Charlieu, 1971.

CHARLOTTE OF SAVOY (1439–1483). Queen of France. The youngest daughter of Louis, duke of Savoy, and Anne of Cyprus, Charlotte of Savoy became queen of France through her marriage to Louis XI (r. 1461–83). Louis had married her in 1451, when she was twelve years old and he was still dauphin. At that time, he was feuding with his father, Charles VII, who opposed the marriage. The marriage failed to convert the duke of Savoy into an ally, as Louis had hoped, but Charlotte bore him several children, including the future Charles VIII in 1470. The queen's death late in 1483 prevented her from playing a role in the power struggles that followed the death of her husband.

John Bell Henneman, Jr.

CHARNY, GEOFFROY DE (d. 1356). Geoffroy de Charny, lord of Pierre-Pertuis, died guarding the king's standard at the Battle of Poitiers. His *Livre de chevalerie* is a prose text that deals with the instruction of a young knight. He is also the author of another *Livre* on the same subject written in verse, as well as the *Demandes pour la joute, les tournois et la guerre,* which takes the form of questions to members of the Order of the Star on points of chivalry. In all three works, he is concerned with degrees of honor and achievement in chivalry.

Claude J. Fouillade

Geoffroy de Charny. *Livre de chevalerie*, ed. Joseph K. de Lettenhove. In *Œuvres de Froissart*. Brussels: Devaux, 1873, 1875, Vol. 1:3, pp. 463–533. [Prose *Livre*.]

Piaget, Arthur. "Le livre de messire Geoffroi de Charny." *Romania* 26 (1897): 399–410. [Partial transcription of verse *Livre*.]

Keen, Maurice. *Chivalry*. New Haven: Yale University Press, 1984.

CHARROI DE NÎMES. This epic poem of 1,486 assonanced decasyllabic lines, one of the oldest of the Guillaume d'Orange Cycle (after 1150), tells of the conquest by ruse of the city of Nîmes. The poem's rich thematics link traditional epic matter with 12th-century problems: the duties of king and vassal, the situation of the young fiefless knight, the problem of crusade. Capetian policy itself, with the expeditions of Louis VI and Louis VII to the south of France, may even have its role, intersecting with the theme of pilgrimage to Saint-Gilles.

The structure of the text, the diversity of tone, and the novelty of the role accorded Guillaume make the *Charroi* one of the cycle's most original poems. The first half of the work is a stirring encounter between King Louis the Pious and his vassal, who requests recompense for his services; the second is a lively and sometimes humorous tale of conquest. Nowhere else are Guillaume's heroic qualities so in evidence: not only an invincible warrior, he is also an epic poet, recounting with moving vigor the deeds of Béranger or exhorting his men to crusade with his account of Saracen atrocities. Thanks to suggestions from his nephew Bertrand, this bard is also a counselor of mythic stature: so that peace may reign in the kingdom, the wise vassal must ask to conquer his fief from the Saracens. Finally, Guillaume's doubts and hesitations when he is faced with knightly challenges provide him a new depth of characterization.

François Suard

[See also: CHANSON DE GESTE; GUILLAUME D'ORANGE CYCLE]

McMillan, Duncan, ed. *Le charroi de Nîmes: chanson de geste du XIIe siècle*. 2nd ed. Paris: Klincksieck, 1978.

Frappier, Jean. *Les chansons de geste du cycle de Guillaume d'Orange*. 2 vols. Paris: Société d'Édition d'Enseignement Supérieur, 1965, Vol. 2, pp. 179–253.

Mancini, Mario. *Società feudale e ideologia nel Charroi de Nîmes*. Florence: Olschki, 1972.

CHARTER. Record of a private contract, act, or transaction, most often a donation, sale, exchange, will, or marriage agreement, written in Latin (or occasionally the vernacular) on parchment by a cleric or notary. The legal force of the private charter, written up by monastery or bishop or powerful lord, was ambiguous and changed over the centuries. At first, its value lay primarily in the fact that it listed witnesses to the act or deed, who could be called forward in the event of a dispute. The legal force of the private contract gradually came to lie in the contract itself, and demands would be made for the written document to be produced in cases of disputes; eventually, it was the seals of public authorities—bishops, abbots, lords, and even ladies—affixed to it that gave it its force. Charters written by notaries, found earliest in the towns of the Midi, contain the much wider range of business transactions found among townsmen; the authenticity of charters written up by notaries lay in the notary's possession of his cartulary notes, which could be used as proof of its authenticity.

Constance H. Berman

[See also: CARTULARY; NOTARIES]

CHARTIER, ALAIN (ca. 1385–ca. 1430). Author and diplomat, known chiefly for his controversial poem, the *Belle dame sans merci,* and for his talent as an orator. A native of Bayeux, Alain Chartier studied at the University of Paris, earning the title of "maistre." Early in his career, in the period between 1409 and 1414, Chartier worked in the household of Yolande d'Anjou, mother of King René and of Marie d'Anjou, who was betrothed to the future Charles VII in 1413. Charles's presence at the Angevin court gave him occasion to acquaint himself with Chartier's talents. By 1417, Chartier was in the service of the dauphin as notary and secretary, serving also for a time King Charles VI.

For a decade beginning in 1418, Chartier's life followed the wandering of the exiled dauphin through Berry and Touraine, areas withstanding the Anglo-Burgundian onslaught. In addition to routine duties as secretary and notary, Chartier's later service to Charles included ambassadorial functions on missions during 1425 to the emperor Sigismund's court in Hungary and to the Venetian senate in an effort to convince Sigismund to side with the French against the English. In 1428, at the court of James I of Scotland, Chartier helped to renew relations between France and Scotland and to negotiate the marriage between James's daughter Margaret and the dauphin Louis. During these missions, Chartier provided eloquent introductory discourses opening the diplomatic exchanges.

From 1420 on, Chartier held various ecclesiastical offices. In 1420, he was named canon of Notre-Dame of Paris, although he was unable to assume the responsibilities of the office because of the Burgundian occupation of the city. In 1425, he was named curate of Saint-Lambert-des-Levées near Angers; in 1426, he was granted the prebendal canonry of Tours; and in 1428, he was appointed chancellor of Bayeux. An epitaph engraved in 1458 mentions that he was archdeacon of Paris.

It is generally assumed that Chartier died ca. 1430, since his signature does not appear on any royal document after 1428; *L'esperance,* begun in 1428, was never finished; and shortly after July 17, 1429, he sent a letter to Sigismund recounting Jeanne d'Arc's achievements and the consecration of Charles VII in Reims. By 1432, Chartier's brother had succeeded him as curate of Saint-Lambert-des-Levées. Record of a tombal inscription suggests that he was buried in the church of Saint-Antoine in Avignon, although the reason for his presence in Avignon at the time of his death is unknown.

An active and valued royal servant who held important ecclesiastical positions, Chartier was also a master of prose both in Latin and French and an accomplished poet. The range of style, form, and subject matter in Chartier's work is impressive.

His most controversial, celebrated, and imitated work, the *Belle dame sans merci* (1424), begins with a conventional situation: the wandering, mournful narrator overhears an exchange between a disconsolate lover and his lady. The language the lover uses to persuade the lady of his love and to ask for hers in return reveals that he has been cast in the old mold, in which the lady either granted such requests or maintained a neutral distance. Chartier's *belle dame* reserves her right to refuse and to disabuse the lover of his belief in the power of his own courtly rhetoric. To the lover, who says he will die if she does not take pity on him, she suggests that he is succumbing to a metaphor, since she has seen no one actually die of unrequited love. To his persistent and sometimes accusatory pleas, she affirms that her indifference is neither cruel nor harmful. She counsels him to be reasonable and to take her refusal in stride. The narrator suggests at the close of the work that the lover did in fact die as a consequence. He asks lovers to shun meddlers and braggarts who have done harm to the cause of love; and he asks women not to be as cruel as the *belle dame sans merci*.

The reaction in courtly circles to the *Belle dame sans merci* attests both to the continuing hold that convention had at court in determining codes of amorous conduct and to Chartier's innovative view of these codes. By the following year, while on his mission to Hungary, Chartier was summoned to appear before a "Court of Love" because of objections women at the French court had made to his work. Chartier defended himself from a distance, composing *L'excusacion aux dames* (1425), in which the God of Love accuses the author of wrongs against love's rights. The author responds that, while in some women pity is so deeply hidden as to be invisible, he maintains confidence in love itself. He also claims that he had merely recorded the exchange between lover and lady. It is not known to what extent his *Excusacion* won him forgiveness at court.

The *Lay de Plaisance* (1414) and numerous short lyrics composed thoughout his career show Chartier's mastery of poetic conventions in portraying states of love. Two amusing debate works, the *Débat des deux fortunés d'Amour* (1425) and the *Débat du réveille-matin* (uncertain date), present divergent and unreconciled views on the value and nature of love. More frequently, Chartier's poems rely heavily on convention, while introducing new vantages or combining other concerns with the subject of love. Just as the *Belle dame sans merci* moves outside of convention to challenge it, the *Livre des quatre dames* (1416), composed in the wake of the French disaster at Agincourt, intertwines love stories with the moral and political elements of a national tragedy. The traditional springtime *locus amoenus* in this work, replete with the amorous diversions of a shepherd and shepherdess, provides the backdrop for the sorrowful tales of four women whom the narrator encounters. Each woman describes the fate of her beloved at Agincourt: the lover of the first has

been killed, the second lady's lover has been taken prisoner, the fate of the third lady's lover is unknown, and the fourth lady's lover has disgraced himself by fleeing the battlefield. They ask the narrator to say which of them is to be pitied the most. He confesses inability to judge and refers debate to his own lady in writing.

Chartier rarely supplies resolutions to the debates related in many of his works. The *Débat du hérault, du vassault et du villain* (ca. 1421–26) explores but does not resolve the conflict between generations and between social classes. His best-known prose work, the *Quadrilogue invectif* (1422), is also cast in the form of a debate. Lady France, disheveled and tattered, eloquently inveighs against her three "children," asking them to account for their role in the lamentable state of the nation. The Knight, the Cleric, and the Peasant present in turn excuses, accusations, and expressions of despair. No single estate is to bear the burden of blame at the end of the *Quadrilogue*, yet it is clear that each must assume a share of responsibility and that the divisive forces that cause them to rail against one another need to be eliminated through concern for the common good. Chartier seems to have borrowed from his Latin to provide the first known occurrence of the word *patrie* in this work, as well as the concept of a socially and politically unified France.

While the *Quadrilogue* remains Chartier's best-known prose work in French, the complexity of his concern for the political and spiritual welfare of his compatriots is best seen in the *Livre de l'esperance ou Le livre des trois vertus*, a work begun in 1428 and left unfinished. Interspersing with lyric interludes extensive prose dialogue between the author's personified faculty of Understanding and personifications representing Hope and Faith, Chartier explores many seemingly unanswerable questions about the turmoil and moral decline in France. Having chased away the specters of Melancholy, Indignation, Mistrust, and Despair, whose cumulative influence had brought Understanding to the brink of suicide, Faith and Hope, chiefly the latter, provide extensive lessons to aid in Understanding's recovery. His memory is reawakened to allow him to apply the lessons of secular and biblical history, recounted through numerous exempla, to the current state of affairs in France and to his own spiritual state. Even in its unfinished form, *L'esperance* is a summa of Chartier's own erudition, put to the task of resolving the political turmoil of his time or, at least, of finding an appropriate spiritual context in which to understand it.

Numerous other works, in Latin and French, also bear witness to Chartier's versatility as a writer. Life as a courtier is criticized in the *Curial* (*De vita curiale*), written after 1422. The *Epistola ad regem* (1418), *Epistola ad Universitatem Parisiensem* (1420), and *Epistola ad detestacionem belli gallici et suasione pacis* (ca. 1422–24) display strongly held political convictions. A number of his diplomatic orations survive, no doubt because of their eloquence: *Oratio ad imperatorem* (1425), *Oratio ad regem Romanorum* (1425), *Persuasio ad Pragenses in fide deviantes* (1425), and the *Discours au roi d'Ecosse* (1428). A number of shorter, more personal Latin prose works bear the clear influence of Cicero: *Invectiva contra ingratum amicum* (ca.

1425), *Invectiva contra invidium et detractorem* (ca. 1425), and *Epistola ad fratrem suum iuvenem* (uncertain date).

The large number of manuscripts, early printed editions, and imitations of Chartier's works attests to his continuing popularity as an author well into the 16th century and beyond.

Janice C. Zinser

[See also: *ABUZÉ EN COURT*; AUVERGNE, MARTIAL D'; CARON, FIRMINUS; CHARLES D'ORLÉANS; HERENC, BAUDET; *JARDIN DE PLAISANCE ET FLEUR DE RÉTHORIQUE*; LE FRANC, MARTIN; QUARREL OF THE *BELLE DAME SANS MERCI*; RÉGNIER, JEAN]

Chartier, Alain. *Les œuvres latines d'Alain Chartier*, ed. Pascale Bourgain-Hemeryck. Paris: CNRS, 1977.
———. *Le quadrilogue invectif*, ed. Eugénie Droz. 2nd ed. Paris: Champion, 1950.
———. *The Poetical Works of Alain Chartier*, ed. J. C. Laidlaw. Cambridge: Cambridge University Press, 1974.
———. *Poèmes par Alain Chartier*, ed. J.C. Laidlaw. Paris: Union Générale d'Éditions, 1988.
———. *Le livre de l'esperance*, ed. François Rouy. Diss. Université de Paris, 1967.
Champion, Pierre. *Histoire poétique du XVe siècle*. 2 vols. Paris: Champion, 1923, Vol. 1, pp. 1–165.
Hoffman, E. J. *Alain Chartier: His Work and Reputation*. New York: Wittes, 1942.
Rouy, François, ed. *L'esthétique du traité moral d'après les œuvres d'Alain Chartier*. Geneva: Droz, 1980.
Walravens, C. J. H. *Alain Chartier: études biographiques, suivies de pièces justificatives, d'une description des éditions et d'une édition des ouvrages inédits*. Amsterdam: Meulenhoff-Didier, 1971.

CHARTRES. Originally the capital of the Carnutes, Chartres (Eure-et-Loire), called Autricum by the Romans, was one of the main centers of Gallic Druidism. Indeed, the cathedral of Notre-Dame was founded on the site of a Druidic sanctuary. The town was sacked on several occasions: by the Burgundians (600), Aquitainians (743), and the Vikings (858, 963). In 1360, Edward III's siege of Chartres was his last military action before the Treaty of

Chartres, Notre-Dame, west façade. *Photograph courtesy of Whitney S. Stoddard.*

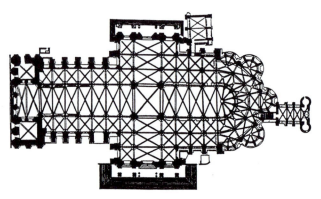

Chartres (Eure-et-Loir), plan of Notre-Dame. After Burckhardt and Merlet.

Brétigny. The English occupied Chartres from 1417 to 1432, when it was recaptured by Jean de Dunois.

Chartres was one of the leading intellectual centers in France in the 11th and 12th centuries, renowned for its humanistic studies. Founded probably in the 10th century, the cathedral school rose to prominence under bishops Fulbert (d. 1028) and Ivo (d. 1116). The influence of Plato, Boethius, and Macrobius, as well as a solid grounding in the classical authors, characterized humanistic studies here. The masters at Chartres sought through their studies and writings to demonstrate the essential harmony between faith and reason, between revealed truths and Platonic cosmology. In the universals controversy, the Chartrians inclined to realism. Important masters at Chartres include

Bernard of Chartres, Gilbert of Poitiers, and Thierry of Chartres; among leading students were William of Conches, Bernard Silvestris, and Clarembald of Arras. John of Salisbury was bishop of Chartres from 1176 until his death in 1180.

Two important Gothic monuments are located at Chartres: the famous cathedral of Notre-Dame and the Benedictine abbey church of Saint-Père-en-Vallée. These structures represent stylistic developments in Gothic art from the mid-12th century through the early 14th.

Notre-Dame at Chartres is one of the great Gothic cathedrals. The earliest part of the extant structure is the west façade and narthex, constructed ca. 1140–60 following a fire in 1134, which destroyed the façade of the Romanesque church. It consisted of two bell towers connected by a triple-portal entrance, the Royal Portal. Sculpture articulates the entire façade. Old Testament figures are placed on the jambs, whose historiated capitals contain New Testament scenes. Christ in Glory appears on the central tympanum, and the Ascension is depicted on the north portal. The south portal is dedicated to the Virgin enthroned with Christ on the tympanum, where the Seven Liberal Arts in the archivolts attest to the intellectual importance of the school of Chartres. The volumetric figures with calm demeanor exemplify the Early Gothic style.

Above the Royal Portal are three stained-glass windows depicting the Tree of Jesse (north), Christ's childhood and ministry (center), and a Passion cycle (south). These windows along with a Virgin and Child, *Notre-Dame de la Belle Verrière*, now in the south-choir aisle, are important examples of 12th-century stained glass, notable for their vibrant blue color.

Another fire in 1194 destroyed the cathedral except for the west façade with narthex and the crypt. The new cathedral was substantially complete by the dedication in 1260. Later additions included the 14th-century chapter house with chapel of Saint-Piat east of the chevet, the 15th-century Vendôme chapel along the south aisle, and the north-tower spire constructed by Jean Texier (Jean de Beauce) in 1507–13.

Chartres represents a classic design of a Gothic cathedral. The basilica plan has a nave of seven bays with single aisles and a double-aisled choir of four bays terminating in a chevet with radiating chapels. The projecting transept arms almost bisect the longitudinal axis. Quadripartite rib vaulting provides structural and aesthetic unity. In the elevation, the arcade and clerestory are equal in height. The piers and engaged ribs emphasize vertical lines, which the triforium arcade balances horizontally. The clerestory windows of double lancets surmounted by a rose allow light to permeate the interior. Systematic use of exterior wall and flying buttresses support the effects of light and verticality.

The iconographic programs of Gothic sculptural façades are developed in the north and south transepts. On the north, the central portal is dedicated to the Virgin with her death, assumption, and coronation on the tympanum. The left portal contains infancy scenes on the jambs and tympanum, while the right portal has Old Testament figures with the Judgment of Solomon on the tympanum. The south façade places the Last Judgment in the center

Chartres, Notre-Dame, west façade, central portal, Christ in Majesty. *Photograph: Clarence Ward Collection. Courtesey of Oberlin College.*

with a martyrs portal on the left and a confessors portal on the right. Additional sculpture fills the transept porches. The north- and south-central portals were carved ca. 1200–15 in a style whose clinging drapery accentuates the plastic forms. In the slightly later sculpture of the south-side portals (ca. 1220), the north-side portals (ca. 1230), and the mid-13th-century porches, the drapery falls in heavier vertical folds.

Chartres preserves the greatest amount of French Gothic stained glass *in situ*, with 173 windows. Donors represent a microcosm of medieval society, including craft guilds, clergy, nobility, and royalty. The varied subjects depict saints, biblical episodes and figures, and historical legend, as in the Charlemagne window. Lower-level windows are composed in medallions; higher windows usually contain large figures. Rich red, blue, yellow, and green predominate. As a total ensemble of architecture, sculpture, and stained glass, Chartres expresses the spiritual and aesthetic vision of the Gothic cathedral.

The abbey church of Saint-Père in Chartres is a composite of several periods. The west-tower porch is dated ca. 990. The church without transept extends along a longitudinal axis of nave and choir flanked by single aisles. The elevation of the six-bay nave constructed ca. 1210–40 is similar to Chartres cathedral. The lower level of the

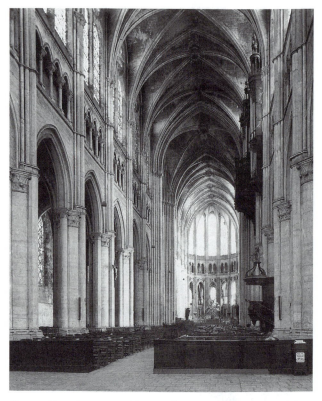

Chartres, Notre-Dame, nave. *Photograph courtesy of Whitney S. Stoddard.*

choir retains its 12th-century plan of five bays terminating in a hemicycle with side and radiating chapels. Its upper stories were rebuilt ca. 1260–1300 in the Rayonnant style. The glazed clerestory of choir (ca. 1270 reusing glass ca. 1245), chevet (ca. 1295–1300), and nave (ca. 1300–15) shows developments in stained-glass composition and technique combining *grisaille* and colored panels. Together, the cathedral of Notre-Dame and the abbey of Saint-Père show the importance of Chartres as an artistic center in the Gothic period.

Karen Gould

[See also: BERNARD OF CHARTRES; BERNARD SILVESTRIS; BOETHIUS, INFLUENCE OF; CLAREMBALD OF ARRAS; DUNOIS, JEAN, COMTE DE; FULBERT OF CHARTRES; GILBERT OF POITIERS; GOTHIC ARCHITECTURE; GOTHIC ART; IVO OF CHARTRES; MACROBIUS, INFLUENCE OF; PLATO, INFLUENCE OF; ROMANESQUE SCULPTURE; SCHOOLS, CATHEDRAL; STAINED GLASS; WILLIAM OF CONCHES]

Branner, Robert, ed. *Chartres Cathedral.* New York: Norton, 1969.

Chédeville, André, et al. *Histoire de Chartres et du pays chartrain.* Toulouse: Privat, 1983.

Clerval, Jules Alexandre. *Les écoles de Chartres au moyen âge (du Ve au XVIe siècle).* Paris: Picard, 1895.

Héliot, Pierre, and Georges Jouven. "L'église Saint-Pierre de Chartres et l'architecture du moyen âge." *Bulletin archéolo-*
gique du Comité des Travaux Historiques et Scientifiques n.s. 6 (1970): 117–77.

Lillich, Meredith P. *The Stained Glass of Saint-Père de Chartres.* Middletown: Wesleyan University Press, 1978.

van der Meulen, Jan. *Chartres: Biographie der Kathedrale.* Cologne, 1984.

———. *Chartres: Sources and Literary Interpretation: A Critical Bibliography.* Boston: Hall, 1989.

CHASTELAINE DE VERGY. This anonymous romance of 948 octosyllabic lines was written between 1203 and 1288. It turns on a series of broken promises. A knight, having sworn never to reveal his love for the Chastelaine, is obliged to confess it to the Duke of Burgundy because of the infatuation he has inspired in the duchess. He is thus caught between his promise to his lady and his allegiance to his lord. The jealous duchess contrives to extract the secret from her husband, who is caught between his promise and his loyalty to the duchess. When the duchess reveals her knowledge of the secret love to the Chastelaine, the latter becomes so distraught she dies. After her maid explains the cause of her death to her lover, he stabs himself. The duke, realizing his role in the tragedy, kills his wife and buries the three victims before departing on crusade.

The tale has inspired various interpretations, from *roman à clef,* to a retelling of traditional themes, to a criticism of *fin'amor.* It has also been suggested that the jealous duchess belongs more to the fabliau than to the courtly romance. One of the most intriguing of medieval tales, it continues to inspire diverse interpretations.

Charity Cannon Willard

[See also: COURTLY LOVE]

Arrathoon, Leigh A., ed. and trans. *The Lady of Vergy.* New York: Cross-Cultural Communications, 1984.

Stuip, R.E.V., ed. *La Chastelaine de Vergi, édition critique du ms. B.N. f.fr. 375 . . . suivie de l'édition diplomatique de tous les manuscrits connus du XIIIe et du XIVe siècle.* The Hague: Mouton, 1970.

Whitehead, Frederick, ed. *La Chastelaine de Vergi.* Manchester: Manchester University Press, 1944.

Lakits, Pál. *La Châtelaine de Vergi et l'évolution de la nouvelle courtoise.* Debrecen: Kossuth Lajos Tudomanyegyetern, 1966.

Zumthor, Paul. "De la chanson au récit: la *Chastelaine de Vergi.*" *Vox Romanica* 27 (1968): 77–95.

CHASTELLAIN, GEORGES (1415–1475). Born in Flanders at Alost, Georges Chastellain studied at the University of Louvain and went to war against the French under Philip the Good. After ten years in France in the service of Charles VII (1435–46), he returned to Burgundy, where he served in many capacities at court before Philip appointed him official chronicler of the house of Burgundy in 1455. Reappointed in 1467 by Philip's successor, Charles the Bold, who named him a knight of the Golden Fleece in 1473, he continued his work until his death. Although his chronicles are considered his most important contribution, he left numerous literary works, virtually all of which reflect his interest in court life and exhibit the same didactic, moralistic tone. His two historical or political morality plays, the *Mort du duc Philippe* and the *Paix de Péronne*, were both presented in 1468 for Charles the Bold. The first memorializes the death of Charles's father, and the second celebrates the brief truce between Charles and King Louis XI of France.

Chastellain's many poems represent a change in form but not in substance. The *Epistre au bon duc Philippe de Bourgogne* praises the duke and advises him on his duties. *Rhythmes sur le trespas du bon duc de Bourgongne* laments the death of Philip the Good, while *Souhaits au duc Charles de Bourgogne* looks ahead to the reign of Charles the Bold. *Le prince*, reflecting the intense political conflict between Charles and Louis XI, sparkles with the passionate anger of the author toward the French king. Chastellain the poet was never far from Chastellain the chronicler.

Deborah H. Nelson

[See also: BURGUNDIAN CHRONICLERS; MESCHINOT, JEAN]

Chastellain, Georges. *Œuvres de Georges Chastellain*, ed. Joseph Kervyn de Lettenhove. 8 vols. Brussels: Heussner, 1863–66.
———. *Chronique*, ed. J. C. Delclos. Geneva: Droz, 1991. [Book 4, based on London B.L. Add. 54156.]
Doutrepont, Georges. *La littérature française à la cour des ducs de Bourgogne*. Paris: Champion, 1909.

CHASTELLAIN, PIERRE (fl. second half of the 15th c.). Little is known of the life of the poet Pierre Chastellain. In the service of King René d'Anjou, he spent four years in Rome (1450–54). After his return to France, he completed the two poems definitely attributed to him: *Le temps perdu* and *Le temps recouvré*. These semiautobiographical works, inspired by such writers as Vincent of Beauvais, Jean de Meun, and Michault Taillevent, reflect on the poet's past and offer long and sometimes cynical meditations and digressions on themes of poverty, aging, and death.

Chastellain has occasionally but unconvincingly been identified with a certain Jehan Vaillant, a lyric poet in the entourage of Charles d'Orléans.

Norris J. Lacy

Chastellain, Pierre. *Les œuvres de Pierre Chastellain et de Vaillant, poètes du XVe siècle*, ed. Robert Deschaux. Geneva: Droz, 1982.
Champion, Pierre. *Histoire poétique du XVe siècle*. 2 vols. Paris: Champion, 1923, Vol. 1, pp. 339–92.

CHÂTEAU-GAILLARD. One of the first European castles raised in the style of the crusader fortifications of the Holy Land. Built at Eure in Normandy in 1196–98 at the behest of the English king Richard the Lionhearted, Château-Gaillard stands on a precipitous cliff 300 feet above the Seine River. The castle consists of three baileys arranged in a line, with a donjon, which may have been a later addition, standing on the edge of the precipice, principally within but also projecting outside of the inner bailey. Five years after its construction, Château-Gaillard was besieged by Philip Augustus. Building his own siegeworks of trenches and towers, Philip began his assault on the castle. Using siege engines, sappers, and mines, the French took their prize in March 1204, but not before suffering high casualties. Château-Gaillard was besieged several times during the Hundred Years' War. In 1418, the French lost the castle

Château-Gaillard (Eure), ruins of castle. *Photograph courtesy of William W. Kibler.*

to Henry V's English forces after six months of siege; in 1420, the French retook it, although the English regained it soon thereafter. Finally, in 1449, Charles VII restored it to French control.

Kelly DeVries

Dieulafoy, Marcel. *Le Château-Gaillard et l'architecture militaire au XIIIe siècle.* Paris: Klincksieck, 1898.

Fournier, Gabriel. *Le château dans la France médiévale.* Paris: Aubier Montaigne, 1978.

Héliot, Pierre. "Le Château-Gaillard et les fortresses des XIIe et XIIIe siècles." *Château-Gaillard* 1 (1962): 53–75.

Ritter, Raymond. *Châteaux, donjons et places fortes: l'architecture militaire du moyen âge.* Paris: Larousse, 1953.

Toy, Sidney. *A History of Fortification from 3000 B.C. to A.D. 1700.* London: Heinemann, 1955.

CHÂTEAU-LANDON. Of the medieval monuments of Château-Landon (Seine-et-Marne), only the church of Notre-Dame retains its architectural interest. To a late 11th- or early 12th-century nave, a broad transept and open, spacious triapsidal chevet was added in the 1130s–40s. The chevet is of particular interest as a good surviving example of the regional traditions in decoration manifested in the 12th-century additions to the church of Saint-Denis.

William W. Clark

Deshoulières, François. "Château-Landon, église Notre-Dame." *Congrès archéologique* (Orléans) 93 (1930): 242–59.

Serbat, Louis. "Excursion à Larchant, Château-Landon, Ferrières-en-Gâtinais." *Bulletin monumental* 75 (1911): 285–305.

CHÂTEAUDUN. Now a sleepy provincial town, Châteaudun (Eure-et-Loir) was an important center in the Middle Ages, with an imposing château that commanded the river below. The château retains a 12th-century donjon and a 15th-century wing with a private chapel.

The most interesting of the remaining churches is La Madeleine, which has a 12th-century nave started on an ambituous scale with double aisles on the north, or town, side. The plan, which initially called for an ambulatory around the chevet, was curtailed with a simple polygonal apse. The elaborate acanthus capitals in the nave recall Parisian work of the third quarter of the 12th century; several are particularly close to examples in the churches of Saint-Denis and Saint-Pierre-de-Montmartre in Paris; others are related to a series of acanthus capitals in the Loire Valley. The south nave wall reveals that rib vaulting was initially planned but like the elaborate east end was abandoned prior to completion, although the aisles have their original vaults. A curious mid-12th-century portal on the south side was rediscovered in 1885. Major repairs were necessary in the 16th and 17th centuries and in the aftermath of World War II.

First mentioned in 1037, the church of Saint-Valérien was built in the 12th century and given rib vaults in the later years of that century. Heavily remodeled in 1491 and again in 1591, the aisles nevertheless preserve groin-vaulted bays. The flat chevet was covered by an elaborate ten-part rib vault. In all, Saint-Valérien is related to architectural practices slightly to the east, perhaps ultimately owing to Sens, in which naves were given six-part vaults matching double aisle units.

William W. Clark

Baratte-Bévillard, Sophie. "La sculpture monumentale de la Madeleine de Châteaudun." *Bulletin archéologique* n.s. 8 (1972): 105–25.

Grant, Lindy. "Aspects of the Twelfth-Century Design of La Madeleine at Châteaudun." *Journal of the British Archaeological Association* 3 (1982): 23–34.

Lesueur, F. "Châteaudun, château." *Congrès archéologique* (Orléans) 93 (1930): 476–520.

Outardel, Georges. "Châteaudun, monuments religieux." *Congrès archéologique* (Orléans) 93 (1930): 442–76.

CHÂTILLON. Taking its name from the castle of Châtillon-sur-Marne (Marne), the Châtillon family served as castellans there for the counts of Champagne, who held the fortress in fief from the archbishops of Reims. The first member of the family known to hold this office was Gui (fl. 1059–87), from whom descended a line of knights whose sphere of activity and influence soon passed beyond the borders of Champagne. By 1127, Henri I de Châtillon was lord of Montjay, located about 18 miles from Paris.

The office of castellan of Châtillon was hereditary and included rights and property that formed the nucleus of a castellany that must be distinguished from the more important count's castellany of Châtillon, which included the donjon and the town and continued to exist as a separate entity. The holdings at Châtillon eventually were among the less important possessions of the family, which advanced to a higher social level through the marriage, in the early 1160s, of Gui II to Adèle de Dreux, granddaughter of King Louis VI. At the time, Gui was already lord of strategically located Montjay, and the marriage served a political purpose for both Adèle's uncle, Louis VII, and her father, Robert I de Dreux.

The children of Gui II and Adèle included Gaucher III, who married the heiress to the county of Saint-Pol, and Robert (d. 1215), who became bishop of Laon in 1210. Gaucher III was *bouteiller* of Champagne, seneschal of Burgundy by 1193, and in 1210 one of the leaders of the royal army. He fought heroically at Bouvines in 1214. His sons, Gui III and Hugues I, married descendants of Louis VI, heiresses, respectively, to the counties of Nevers and Blois. Gui III (d. 1226) left a son who died childless, but from his daughter Yolande, countess of Nevers and wife of the lord of Bourbon, descended the dukes of Bourbon and Bar and the later dukes of Burgundy. From Hugues I descended the counts of Porcien and the counts of Saint-Pol. The latter line ended with another Gui, who died in England as a hostage ca. 1363. His sister's marriage brought Saint-Pol into the house of Luxembourg.

Gaucher de Châtillon (d. 1329), called (perhaps erroneously) Gaucher V, was a grandson of Hugues I. He united the two castellanies of Châtillon by receiving from Philip

IV in 1290 the rights that had belonged to the counts of Champagne, whose heiress was Philip's queen. By the end of 1303, he had returned the count's castellany to the king in exchange for other lands and rights, some of which were combined with his newly purchased lordship of Château-Porcien to form, by royal grant, the county of Porcien. Gaucher also held the office of constable, both for Champagne and for France. The counts of Porcien and the lords of Dampierre were descended from his son Gaucher. Jacques de Châtillon, lord of Dampierre and admiral of France, died at Agincourt in 1415. From Constable Gaucher's son Jean, lord of Châtillon (d. 1363), descended a line that died out in the second half of the 15th century.

Richard C. Famiglietti

Bur, Michel. *La formation du comté de Champagne*. Nancy: Annales de l'Est, 1977.

Corvisier, Marie-Anne. "Le comté de Blois sous les Châtillon: édition du cartulaire de 1319." Positions des thèses. Paris: École Nationale des Chartes, 1976, pp. 45–50.

Du Chesne, André. *Histoire de la maison de Chastillon-sur-Marne*. Paris: Cramoisy, 1629.

Savietiez, Charles. "Dampierre-de-l'Aube et ses seigneurs." *Revue de Champagne et de Brie* 20 (1886): 96–114, 246–60, 345–54, 434–45; 21 (1886): 240–72.

CHÂTILLON-SUR-SEINE. In the high Middle Ages, the small town of Châtillon-sur-Seine (Côte-d'Or), a former center of Gallic and Gallo-Roman activity, enjoyed the protection of a château owned by the bishops of Langres. According to tradition, one of them, St. Didier, founded the oratory of Sainte-Marie-du-Château in the 4th century. In 868, during the Viking invasions, the relics of St. Vorles (d. 592) were transported to the oratory at the instigation of Isaac le Bon, bishop of Langres. This translation is the origin of the church of Saint-Vorles, built in the last years of the 10th century.

The original plan of the church was distorted by careless construction, particularly in the chevet, and parts of the church have been gutted; yet one of its most distinctive features is still easily recognized: the transept or massive transversal, situated in front of the nave, perhaps inspired by Carolingian *églises-porches*. The transept includes a crossing covered by a cupola and two projecting cross-bars, vaulted in semicircular Romanesque arches. Of the original choir, only the principal apse remains. In the Lombard style, which is exceptional for this northern part of Burgundy, Saint-Vorles displays unwieldy and massive internal structures with minimal decoration.

E. Kay Harris

Deshoulières, François. "Église Saint-Vorles." *Congrès archéologique* (Dijon) 91 (1928): 184–205.

CHAUVIGNY. Built on a spur over the Vienne, Chauvigny (Vienne) preserves the remains of four medieval fortresses, a testimony to its military importance in the period. The Château Baronnial was begun in the 11th century, when

Chauvigny (Vienne), view of town. *Photograph courtesy of Whitney S. Stoddard.*

Chauvigny was a possession of the bishops of Poitiers. It has a massive square 12th-century keep with flanking turrets. The Château d'Harcourt (13th–15th c.) belonged to the viscounts of Châtellerault and retains its entry tower and impressive ramparts. Ruins of the Château de Mauléon (12th and 15th c.) and the square keep of the Château de Gouzan (11th c.) are still evident. The Romanesque church of Saint-Pierre, founded by the lords of Chauvigny, was begun in the 11th century and completed with an impressive 13th-century double-bayed bell tower. The interior is remarkable for the richness and originality of the sculpted and polychrome capitals in the choir. All are naively carved but enormously expressive; some are grotesques (dragons, monsters), but most are biblical, including such motifs as the Annunciation, Adoration of the Magi, and Presentation in the Temple. The triple-apsed Romanesque church of Notre-Dame likewise preserves important sculpted capitals but is more remarkable for the late 14th- or early 15th-century mural of Christ Bearing His Cross, attended by numerous civil and religious leaders.

William W. Kibler/William W. Clark

Crozet, René. *Chauvigny et ses monuments: étude archéologique*. Poitiers, 1958.

CHEVALERIE OGIER. Early 13th-century chanson de geste. Ogier, originally a legendary hero of the Ardennes region (*Ogier* [*Ar*]*denois*), the heartland of the Carolingians, has often been confused with the historical Autcharius Francus, who defended the rights of the children of Charlemagne's younger brother, Carloman (d. 771), when he accompanied them to the Lombard king Desiderius in Pavia. From this confusion sprang the dichotomy of Ogier: on the one hand, he is one of Charlemagne's most loyal peers, attested as such in the *Nota Emilianense* (ca. 1070), the falsification of Saint-Yrieux (ca. 1090), the *Chanson de Roland*, and the *Voyage de Charlemagne*; on the other hand, the tradition of a rebel is found since the *Conversio Othgerii militis* of the abbey of Saint-Faron at Meaux (ca. 1070–80).

Ogier as a rebel is the subject of the *Chevalerie Ogier*, which was probably composed by a certain Raimbert de Paris. In 12,346 assonanced decasyllables, the poem tells how Ogier, son of King Godefroy of Denmark, is left as hostage and educated at Charlemagne's court and is later knighted by the emperor during a fierce battle against the Saracens under the walls of Rome. He becomes an intractable rebel after his bastard son Bauduinet is killed by Charlemagne's son Charlot over a game of chess, a crime left unpunished by the king. Ogier eludes the Frankish army thanks to his miraculous horse, Broiefort; he turns quite ferocious, finally holing up in Castel Fort, where he sustains a seven-year siege. The only survivor, he escapes but is found, exhausted, by Turpin, whom Charlemagne puts in charge of the prisoner at Reims. After seven years in prison, a Saracen invasion makes his help necessary. Ogier kills the Saracen king and saves France. Charlemagne and Charlot hold his stirrups after his safe return; Ogier then weds the daughter of the king of England, whom he had freed from the Saracens, and receives from Charlemagne the fiefs of Hainaut and Brabant. At his death, he is buried in Meaux.

The *Chevalerie Ogier* is a romanticized reworking of a lost 12th-century epic known only from a *remaniement* in Alexandrines of the 14th century (still unpublished), a lost poem in decasyllabic laisses (ca. 1350) recognizable in Jean d'Outremeuse's *Myreur des histors* in prose (second half of the 14th c.), and the prose romance *Ogier le Dannoys* (15th c.). The first *branche* seems to be preserved in Adenet le Roi's *Enfances Ogier* (ca. 1290) as well as—though differently—in Book 3 of the Norwegian *Karlamagnús saga*, the Danish *Karl Magnus Krønike*, and the Franco-Italian *Uggeri il Danese*.

Hans-Erich Keller

[See also: OUTREMEUSE, JEAN D'; REBELLIOUS VASSAL CYCLE]

Cremonesi, Carla, ed. *Le Danois Ogier: Enfances—Chevalerie, Codex Marciano XIII.* Milan: Cisalpino-Goliardica, 1977.

Eusebi, Mario, ed. *La chevalerie d'Ogier de Danemarche.* Milan: Cisalpino, 1963.

Rossellini, Aldo, ed. *La "Geste Francor" di Venezia: edizione integrale del Codice XIII del Fondo francese della Marciana.* Brescia: La Scuola, 1986. [*Enfances Ogier*, pp. 505–49; *Chevalerie Ogier*, pp. 569–634.]

Goose, André. "*Ogier le Danois*, chanson de geste de Jean d'Outremeuse." *Romania* 86 (1965): 145–98.

Le Gentil, Pierre. "Ogier le Danois, héros épique." *Romania* 78 (1957): 199–233.

Renier, Rodolfo. "Ricerche sulla leggenda di Uggeri il Danese in Francia." *Memorie della R. Accademia di Torino, scienze morali, storiche e filosofiche* 2nd ser. 41 (1891): 389–459.

Togeby, Knud. *Ogier le Danois dans les littératures européennes.* Copenhagen: Munksgaard, 1969.

Voretzsch, Carl. *Über die Sage von Ogier dem Dänen und die Entstehung der Chevalerie Ogier: Ein Beitrag zur Entwicklung des altfranzösischen Heldenepos.* Halle: Niemeyer, 1891.

CHEVALIER AU BARISEL. Also known as *Le conte du barril*, this pious tale from the early 13th century is transmitted to us in three versions. In a little more than 1,000 octosyllabic couplets, the poet tells of an evil knight who has nothing but disdain for his fellow man, who has no interest in religion, and who has been in a state of sin for thirty years. Prodded by his men into accompanying them to visit a saintly hermit, he finds himself telling his sins. The hermit suggests a number of penances. The knight turns them all down as too troublesome. He does accept an easy one—to fill up a bowl (*barisel* 'keg, cask') with water. But the task turns out to be difficult; indeed, no water will stay in the container. At the end of a year of effort, transformed into a haggard, poverty-stricken man, he reappears at the hermit's dwelling. The hermit is filled with grief at the thought that the knight will go to Hell, and this compassion causes the knight to repent and weep. One tear falls into the *barisel* and fills it up. In conclusion, the poet reminds us that God is always ready to forgive repentant sinners. The tale is told with economy, yet with lively dialogue and craftsmanlike presentation of the transformation of the hero.

Paul Barrette

Bates, Robert Chapman, ed. *Le conte dou barril, poème du XIIIe siècle par Jouham de la Chappele de Blois.* New Haven: Yale University Press, 1932.

Lecoy, Félix, ed. *Le chevalier au barisel, conte pieux du XIIIe siècle.* Paris: Champion, 1967.

LeMerrer-False, Madeleine. "Contribution à une étude du 'Chevalier au Barisel.'" *Moyen âge* 77 (1971): 263–75.

Payen, Jean-Charles. "Structure et sens du 'Chevalier au Barisel.'" *Moyen âge* 77 (1971): 237–62.

CHEVALIER AU PAPEGAUT. Found in a single manuscript (B.N. fr. 2154), the early 15th-century prose romance *Le Chevalier au Papegaut* contains a series of adventures from a number of earlier romances, here assigned to Arthur. Arthur leaves his kingdom in the hands of King Lot to answer the call of a distressed damsel. Traveling incognito, his first adventure is to win a parrot, which will be a comic presence throughout the romance. After a series of complicated and amazing adventures on both land and sea, Arthur rescues the princess Flordemont and returns home. This complex but humorous romance appears to have had no influence on subsequent Arthurian literature.

Joan B. Williamson

Heuckenkamp, Fernand, ed. *Le chevalier au Papegau nach der einzigen Parisen Handschrift zum ersten Mahl herausgegeben.* Halle: Niemeyer, 1896.

Vesce, Thomas E., trans. *The Knight of the Parrot (Le chevalier du Papegau).* New York: Garland, 1986.

CHILDERIC I (ca. 436–482). The father of Clovis I and the first fully historical figure of the Merovingian dynasty, Childeric I was one of several chieftains of the tribes of the Salian Franks of northern Gaul, with his power based on Tournai, in modern Belgium. He made his group of Salian Franks important in the affairs of northern Gaul and set the stage for the greater career of his son.

Childeric's own career is poorly known, but in broad terms it prefigures that of Clovis. He came to power by 463 and appears to have been a loyal federate of the Roman Empire. He supported Roman military operations in northern Gaul all the way to the Loire—fighting under Aegidius against the Visigoths at Orléans in 463 and under Count Paul against the Saxons at Angers in 469. He also opposed the Alani at Orléans. He may have held Roman authority in the province of Belgica Secunda, and Frankish legends also report an eight-year exile that he may have spent in Thuringia. Childeric left a good reputation among the Christians of northern Gaul.

What was probably his grave was discovered outside the walls of Roman Tournai in 1653. Reflecting the mixed nature of his career, the grave produced a signet ring bearing his name and the Latin title *rex*, the remains of the uniform of a Roman official, and Frankish weapons. Most of the items were stolen in 1831.

Steven Fanning

[See also: FRANKS; MEROVINGIAN DYNASTY]

Gregory of Tours. *History of the Franks*, trans. Lewis Thorpe. Harmondsworth: Penguin, 1974.

James, Edward. *The Franks*. Oxford: Blackwell, 1988.

Martindale, J.R. "Childericus I." In *Prosopography of the Later Roman Empire*. London: Cambridge University Press, 1980, Vol. 2: *A.D. 395–527*, pp. 285–86.

Wood, Ian. *The Merovingian Kingdoms, 450–751*. London: Longman, 1994.

Zöllner, Erich. *Geschichte der Franken bis zur Mitte des sechsten Jahrhunderts*. Munich: Beck, 1970.

CHILDHOOD. In medieval France, people defined childhood according to the Roman categories of the Ages of Man: early childhood ended at age seven, and puberty was legally established at age twelve for girls, fourteen for boys. A great deal of legal capacity and responsibility was already attributed to children and adolescents in medieval France. A child of seven could be engaged to be married, enter minor clerical orders, hold a benefice without cure of souls, and sometimes be held responsible for crimes. On reaching puberty, an individual might marry, confirm a religious vocation, hold a benefice with cure of souls, be a witness in civil cases, and consistently be held responsible for crimes. Yet a person was not considered to have reached full adulthood until the age of twenty-five, and the word *adolescens* might qualify men as old as thirty.

The care and treatment of children are documented sparsely until the late Middle Ages, from which period date texts concerning children of the aristocracy and bourgeoisie. Babies then usually received a ritual bath immediately after birth and were baptized the following day. They were breast-fed on demand by the mother or sometimes a wet-nurse and given gruel until about age two, when they adopted an adult diet. Babies were swaddled for the first year, then dressed in loose robes. Children played with dolls, balls, hobby horses, and tops and at such games as hide-and-seek, hopscotch, and blind-man's-bluff. Although childraising was more a female than a male concern, fathers often participated in all the tasks of childraising except, apparently, hygiene. By the age of seven, many children, if not enrolled in a school, were sent outside the family—to train to be a knight, to enter clerical or religious orders, to train as an apprentice, or to work directly—according to the social status of the child's family.

About one out of three children fell victim to the high infant-mortality rate before the age of five. This fact, among others, has led some historians, like Philippe Ariès, to argue that parent-child relationships could not have been very intense, but recently such historians as Emmanuel Le Roy Ladurie and Danièle Alexandre-Bidon have emphasized the warmth and intensity of parental attachment evident in many texts.

Leah L. Otis-Cour

[See also: EDUCATION; FAMILY AND GENDER (BOURGEOISIE)]

Alexandre-Bidon, Danièle, and Monique Closson. *L'enfant à l'ombre des cathédrales*. Lyon: Presses Universitaires de Lyon/CNRS, 1985.

Metz, René. "L'enfant dans le droit canonique médiéval: orientations de recherche." In *Recueil de la Société Jean Bodin*. Brussels: Éditions de la Librairie Encyclopédique de Bruxelles, 1976, Vol. 36: *L'enfant*.

CHILPERIC I (ca. 537–584). The youngest son of the Merovingian king Clotar I, Chilperic I was king of the Franks first at Soissons and then at Paris. A panegyric by Venantius Fortunatus lauds Chilperic for his power and intellectual achievements, but the more famous work of Gregory of Tours condemns Chilperic as the "Nero and Herod of our time."

Upon the death of Clotar I in 561, Chilperic received a kingdom centered on Soissons, but most of his reign was consumed in warfare to gain a larger realm at the expense of his brothers Charibert, Guntram, and Sigibert. Chilperic's responsibility for the murder of his Visigothic wife, Galswintha, and the subsequent elevation of the low-born Fredegunde as his chief wife intensified his struggle with his brother Sigibert I, who was married to Galswintha's sister Brunhilde. After Sigibert's assassination in 575, Brunhilde married Chilperic's son Merovech, whom Chilperic later had killed. By the time of Chilperic's own assassination in 584, two decades of internecine struggle had left him in control of the largest of the four Merovingian kingdoms, comprising Neustria and Aquitaine.

In spite of Gregory's hostile account, it is clear that Chilperic possessed a keen mind. He composed verse and hymns, wrote a book questioning the Trinity, added letters to the Roman alphabet that more accurately reflected Frankish pronunciation, and added a provision to Salic Law permitting daughters to inherit ancestral lands if no brothers were alive.

Steven Fanning

[See also: BRUNHILDE; FREDEGUNDE; MEROVINGIAN DYNASTY]

Gregory of Tours. *History of the Franks*, trans. Lewis Thorpe. Harmondsworth: Penguin, 1974.

Ewig, Eugen. "Die fränkischen Teilungen und Teilreiche (511–613)." In *Spätantikes und fränkisches Gallien: Gessamelte Schriften (1952–1973)*. 2 vols. Zurich and Munich: Artemis, 1976, Vol. 1, pp. 135–41.

James, Edward. *The Franks*. Oxford: Blackwell, 1988.

Wallace-Hadrill, J.M. *The Long-Haired Kings and Other Studies in Frankish History*. London: Methuen, 1982, pp. 185–206.

CHINON. The town and castle of Chinon (Indre-et-Loire), located in Touraine, was the site of a truce concluded in 1214 between Philip II Augustus and John Lackland of England following the French victories of that summer.

Chinon's major claim to fame, however, arises from events that occurred during Charles VII's residence there in 1428–29. Charles concluded a treaty with James I of Scotland that arranged for the marriage of James's daughter Margaret to the five-year-old heir to the French throne, the future Louis XI. In September, Charles convened the Estates General at Chinon in a rare gathering that included representatives from nearly all parts of France then under his control and granted him a substantial tax without demanding ratification by regional estates. In the ensuing months, the English besieged Orléans, and there was every prospect that they would take this critical city. Charles VII was still at Chinon during late February 1429, when Jeanne d'Arc arrived at his court and launched her brief but spectacular public career by persuading him to let her accompany the troops who would make a final effort to relieve Orléans.

One of the largest castles in western Europe, Chinon is in actuality the ruins of three separate fortifications, divided by deep moats: the 13th-century Fort-Saint-Georges, built by Henry II Plantagenêt and named for the patron of England, with its principal fortifications to the east; the 12th- and 14th-century Middle Castle, with its well-preserved clock tower; and the Château de Coudray, constructed by Philip Augustus in the 13th century. Within the town are the medieval churches of Saint-Maurice (12th–16th c.), Saint-Étienne (15th c.), and Saint-Mexme (10th, 11th, and 15th c.).

John Bell Henneman, Jr.

[See also: CHARLES VII; ESTATES (GENERAL); JEANNE D'ARC]

CHIVALRY. The word *chevalerie*, related to *chevalier* 'knight,' has been used as a collective noun, to refer to a body of knights, or to all knights, or to an entire social order—all members of the class from which knights were drawn. Yet it also meant a set of values, a collection of virtuous qualities that became a code of conduct for those who belonged, or aspired to belong, to the aristocracy of mounted warriors. Modern writers usually refer to chivalry in this sense.

Some of these values have been associated with all warrior societies. Others survived into modern times because of their appeal to social elites. The true age of chivalry, however, fell between 1100 and 1500, and the incubator, if not the birthplace, of chivalry was France. To understand chivalry is to understand the "chivalric virtues," but different sources in different periods gave them different emphasis, reflecting the agenda of the writers. There are three main types of sources: ecclesiastical, literary/romantic, and instructional treatises. In them, we find six major virtues, of which two had almost universal acceptance: prowess (a combination of courage and style) and loyalty. Almost as important was *largesse*, which drew support from different groups for different motives. The virtue of courtesy appeared later and survived longer than the others, but its meaning varied greatly. A fifth virtue, associated with words like "honor" and "glory," was of greater importance in some periods than in others. Finally, an imprecise concept of good birth and virtuous behavior was embodied in the word *franchise*.

Huizinga contended that this value system became divorced from "harsh realities" in the declining civilization of the later Middle Ages. Recent scholars, who tend to refute Huizinga, have had to evaluate chivalry in its social and cultural context over successive centuries. The most admired chivalric virtue was prowess, a quality esteemed in fighting men for centuries and not specific to the heyday of the medieval knight. Loyalty had roots in the war bands of early Germanic society and remained important under the Carolingians. By the 11th century, most warriors were men who owed a lord personal service, and loyalty was an important virtue.

Perceptions of loyalty and disloyalty evolved over time. Early epic literature often portrayed faithful warriors who were wronged by their lords. By the 12th century, however, villains of the stories were knights who betrayed their lords. By the 14th century, treason was a crime against the king associated with *lèse-majesté*. Loyalty, then, was a reciprocal obligation between a warrior and his lord, which evolved into an obligation to the king, who was increasingly the embodiment of a state. Finally, loyalty was a reciprocal obligation among the members of the lay orders of knighthood that proliferated in the 14th and 15th centuries.

The virtue of generosity, or *largesse*, doubtless originated in the distribution of booty among members of a war band, but it acquired new economic significance in the 11th century, when the knight had become a trained warrior requiring a strong war-horse and expensive equipment. Knighthood now became an increasingly aristocratic occupation, and those without sufficient lands could be properly equipped only through their lord's generosity. If *largesse* was important to the poorer knights, it also received emphasis from the troubadours, who sang or recited epic tales to noble audiences. Since their livelihood depended on the generosity of their listeners, they had a particular economic stake in promoting *largesse* and making stinginess a mark of unknightly behavior.

In the dangerous and disorderly 11th century, lords seeking to build up a cavalry force turned increasingly to feudal institutions. The spread of the fief reinforced the tendency of noble lineages to consolidate their positions by leaving most of the family patrimony to a single heir. Hundreds of noble families produced sons trained as knights but lacking any prospect of an inheritance. These unmarried landless knights, the "youth" described by Georges Duby, posed a threat to public order and induced the church to accelerate its efforts to regulate warfare. From the dawn of the 11th century, the church promoted a peace movement aimed at protecting the defenseless against the depredations of warriors. Toward the end of the century, it began promoting the Crusades, one objective of which was to direct aggressive fighting men away from Catholic Europe and into projects that served the Christian church. The influence of the church on chivalry has been debated: did ecclesiastical writers describe anything approaching reality, or only an ideal? Certainly, sources emphasize the idea of knighthood as an order of society with a Christian calling, and they present the view that proper knightly behavior required the considerate treatment of noncombatants, with an obligation to defend the weak against the strong. This principle, an important addition to the values of chivalry, was embodied in the virtue of courtesy.

Courtesy is generally associated with the proper treatment of women, but it was not restricted to this sense in 12th-century literature. In many romances, the knight-errant is recognizable as a landless noble "youth." The heroes displayed the chivalric virtues, treating kindly those who were defenseless, defeating opponents who violated chivalric norms, and being rewarded with the hand of an heiress or a respected position in royal service.

As knights became recognized as part of the nobility, and as some nonnobles became wealthier and no longer economically inferior to the knights, chivalry began to acquire greater class-consciousness. High birth grew in importance, especially as a qualification for membership in one of the chivalric orders. Toward the end of the Middle Ages, an increasingly literate aristocracy grew more interested in the culture and literature of ancient Rome, and Roman influences began to supplant those found in the medieval romances. The result was a stronger interest in honor and military discipline, while courtesy became more and more restricted to relations with other members of one's own class, particularly women.

An earlier Roman influence, that of law, had made its presence felt by the 13th century, producing a gradual codification of the rules governing warfare. This *ius militare* was a legal manifestation of chivalric principles, but it dealt only with the relations among members of the military class. The church's earlier concern for the defenseless

nonwarrior was relegated to the background in the later Middle Ages, and in this sense Huizinga may have rightly perceived a distortion of former ideals.

Chivalry acquired more elaborate and ceremonial trappings, especially the tournaments, which still provided the essential military training that had called them into being ca. 1100. The elaborate display did not mean that chivalry had lost touch with reality. As long as kings needed warriors with the equipment and training of a knight, the chivalric lifestyle was an essential element in providing the necessary pool of personnel. What had changed was the attitude toward depredations by undisciplined warriors. In the 15th century, such brigandage was a felonious infringement of the king's monopoly in matters of war and peace. Three centuries earlier, when that monopoly was inconceivable, undisciplined violence by troops drew criticism for violating the Christian knight's obligations toward noncombatants.

John Bell Henneman, Jr.

[See also: LAY ORDERS OF CHIVALRY; NOBILITY; PEACE OF GOD; TREASON; WARFARE]

Duby, Georges. "Dans la France du Nord-Ouest. Au XIIe siècle: les 'jeunes' dans la société aristocratique." *Annales, Économies-Sociétés-Civilisations* 19 (1964): 835–46.

Huizinga, Johan. *The Waning of the Middle Ages: A Study of the Forms of Life, Thought, and Art in France and the Netherlands in the XIVth and XVth Centuries*, trans. F. Hopman. London: Arnold, 1924.

Keen, Maurice. *Chivalry*. New Haven: Yale University Press, 1984. [Extensive bibliography.]

———. *The Laws of War in the Late Middle Ages.* London: Routledge and Kegan Paul, 1965.

Painter, Sidney. *French Chivalry: Chivalric Ideas and Practices.* Ithaca: Cornell University Press, 1940.

Vale, Malcolm. *War and Chivalry: Warfare and Aristocratic Culture in England, France, and Burgundy at the End of the Middle Ages.* London: Duckworth, 1981.

CHRÉTIEN DE TROYES (fl. 1165–91). Although Chrétien wrote lyric poetry in the troubadour and trouvère traditions, he is known principally for his Arthurian romances, where he appears to have treated for the first time, in French at least, the chivalric quest, the love of Lancelot and Guenevere, and the Grail as a sacred object. He also emphasized the problematic side of the love of Tristan and Iseut and may have contributed to the spread of this legend in French in an early work that is lost today.

Although the chronology of his writings is uncertain, the order of composition of his major romances seems to be as follows: *Erec et Enide, Cligés, Le chevalier de la charrette (Lancelot), Yvain (Le chevalier au lion)*, and *Le conte du graal (Perceval)*. He may also have written *Philomena*, an adaptation of the Ovidian story of Philomela (*Metamorphoses* 6.426–74), and *Guillaume d'Angleterre*, a saint's life told like an adventure romance. The prologue to *Cligés* refers to works Chrétien wrote in his early years: *Philomena* ("de la hupe et de l'aronde") and another, lost, on the tale of Pelops ("de la mors de l'espaule"), as well as French versions of Ovid's *Ars amatoria* and *Remedia amoris,* and a Tristan story, concerning which, curiously, Chrétien does not mention Tristan himself: "del roi Marc et d'Iseut la blonde." He is also the author of two courtly chansons in the trouvère tradition.

Chrétien names as patrons Marie de Champagne, the first daughter of Eleanor of Aquitaine and Louis VII of France, who, he writes, gave him the *matiere* and *san* for the *Charrette*, and Philippe d'Alsace, count of Flanders, who gave him "the book" for the *Conte du graal.* Philippe died in the Holy Land in 1191, which may explain why the romance is incomplete. But there is also evidence that Chrétien died before completing it. The last 1,000 lines of the *Charrette* were written by the otherwise unknown Godefroi de Leigni, who names himself in the epilogue and says that he is following Chrétien's plan for the romance. The *Charrette* plot is referred to three times in *Yvain*, and it is likely that Chrétien worked on the two romances at about the same time; this may explain why he left the completion of the *Charrette* to another, whose work he supervised while himself completing *Yvain*.

Erec treats the love of Erec and Enide. In the first part, Erec successfully completes the combat for the sparrowhawk and brings Enide to Arthur's court, where they marry. A dispute between husband and wife breaks out in the second part because Erec abandons deeds of prowess, notably in tournaments, to dally with his wife. Erec and Enide set out in quest of reconciliation, after which they return to Arthur's court and are crowned king and queen there upon the death of Erec's father.

Cligés also has two parts. The first relates how Alixandre, the first son of the Emperor of Constantinople, goes to Arthur's court to test his mettle, falls in love with Gauvain's sister, Soredamors, and helps put down an insurrection by one of Arthur's vassals. Alixandre and Soredamors then marry. The second part recounts the career of their son, Cligés. Alixandre's younger brother, Alis, had been crowned emperor during his older brother's absence. The latter relinquished the throne after Alis had promised not to marry so as to allow Cligés to succeed him. But Alis breaks his word by marrying Fenice. Fenice and Cligés fall in love. At the end of a complicated plot, including a magic potion, a false death, and a secret hideaway, Alis dies and Cligés and Fenice are united in matrimony.

The *Charrette* tells the first known version of the love of Lancelot and Guenevere. The queen is abducted by Meleagant to the land of Gorre. Lancelot, known as the Knight of the Cart after riding in that infamous conveyance, succeeds in saving her from her captors while liberating Arthur's subjects held captive with her.

Yvain tells how the hero knight wins the hand of Laudine, the lady of the magic fountain, by defeating and mortally wounding her husband. After this courtly variant of the Widow of Ephesus tale, Yvain neglects to return to her after more than a year of following tournaments, then goes mad when she repudiates his love. A quest ends with their reconciliation. During the quest, Yvain aids, befriends, and is accompanied by a lion— whence his sobriquet: the Knight with the Lion. *Yvain*

offers interesting parallels and contrasts in plot, structure, and theme with *Erec.*

Chrétien's last major work, the incomplete *Conte du graal,* or *Perceval,* relates how a young, naive squire rises to prominence through combat and love, then fails in the adventure at the Grail Castle because an earlier wrong or "sin" committed against his mother ties his tongue, preventing him from asking the questions he should. The Grail Castle is closed to him, and, as he later learns, great misfortune spreads through the land because of his fault, affecting orphans, widows, and others whom the knight should protect. Perceval sets out to right the wrong. After five years of wandering, during which time he forgets God, Perceval finds himself and God again at his uncle's hermitage, where he also learns of his fault. Interlaced with Perceval's quest are the adventures of Gauvain, accused of murder, and later obliged to seek the Bleeding Lance, which was also found in the Grail Castle during Perceval's visit there. The romance breaks off while relating his remarkable adventures.

Chrétien's romances each average about 7,000 lines and comprise two parts, with the exception of the *Conte du graal,* which extends to somewhat more than 10,000 lines, an apparently more complex variant of the two-part narrative structure. All are written in octosyllabic rhymed couplets, but without the regular alternation between masculine and feminine rhymes that came to characterize classical Alexandrine couplets. Of more importance for the evolution of French romance from verse to prose was Chrétien's extensive use of the "broken" couplet. Before Chrétien, rhymed couplets in French tended to be taken as wholes, so that no sense or breath arrest took place other than on the even-numbered line. Chrétien favored "breaking," whereby the arrest occurred on the odd-numbered line. This reduced the formality of verse enunciation and, besides the freedom it allowed the writer, was a step toward the transition to prose romance in the 13th century.

Chrétien is remarkable for his self-conscious artistry. He seems to have been proud of his achievement, judging by the evidence of the prologues written to almost all his works, as well as by interventions wherein the narrator comments on his art, ideas, and narratives. He knew that his works contributed to fostering French civilization, especially its chivalric and intellectual features. The *Cligés* prologue in particular stresses and conjoins aristocratic *chevalerie* and learned *clergie.* Whatever he may have understood specifically by these ideals, it is clear that they vouchsafed a civilization that came to France from Greece and Rome. However, the prologues to *Erec* and the *Charrette* are most explicit regarding the art of romance, which Chrétien helped define and illustrate. They identify three major features of Chrétien's art: *matiere, san,* and *conjointure.*

The question of Chrétien's putative sources is complex. He refers to written sources in the prologues to *Cligés* and the *Conte du graal;* his Ovidian tales also illustrate his use of traditional written sources. However, the Arthurian *matiere* is explained by its origins in Celtic legend. Chrétien mined oral traditions for his tales. The prologue to *Erec* mentions the jongleurs who had related the story before him, and other sources refer to itinerant storytellers who told marvelous stories about Arthur, Tristan and Iseut, and other Celtic heroes and heroines. We know little about these stories. None has survived in its original state. It is generally believed that they provided the Round Table, as well as most of the names of knights and ladies; the motif of the quest as a passage into the otherworld—the world of the dead, of adventure, of marvelous love between a man and a woman who is not mortal—was probably drawn from Celtic traditions circulating in Chrétien's time. Earlier versions probably had a mythological basis, but Chrétien most likely knew or understood little about it. One clear example of the "Celticity" of Chrétien's sources is the quest in *Erec*. Erec and his wife have a misunderstanding about his love for her. They both set out on a quest and encounter many adventures that test Erec's prowess and Enide's love. The final adventure in the quest is with the count Limors, readily understandable to French ears as "the Dead." During the couple's return, they encounter the adventure known as the Joy of the Court. A huge knight does battle in a magic garden of eternal spring. Whenever he defeats an opponent, the latter loses his head, which is then fixed on a stake in the garden. Erec's victory ends the custom and releases joy in the garden and the outside world. Rituals of combat and death, following prescribed custom, were known in Celtic tradition as *geis*. In Chrétien's romances, they become the more or less euhemerized adventures of questing knights. The inexplicability of such adventures accounts for their marvelous quality.

The *san* that Chrétien says he received for the *Charrette* from Marie de Champagne seems to imply context, significance, an informing idea that is drawn out of the *matiere* to explain it in a manner comprehensible to Chrétien's audiences. In the *Charrette*, for example, the bringing together of Lancelot and Guenevere as lovers has generally been taken to imply that Marie's *san* was what is today called courtly love—an ennobling love shared by the queen and her lover. That Chrétien makes a mystery of Lancelot's name until near the midpoint of the romance suggests that his audiences did not know who Lancelot was until Guenevere names him for the first time while he is fighting for her liberation.

The *Charrette* begins with a quest for Guenevere after her abduction. The knight who liberates her and others entrapped in the kingdom of Gorre makes it obvious early in the narrative that he loves the queen in a most extraordinary way. He is willing to compromise his honor in the eyes of all if it serves her liberation by mounting the shameful cart in order to find her again. Although Lancelot is subject to fits of despair and self-forgetfulness, nothing prevents him from carrying out his service and liberating the queen. In fact, his love seems rather to make it possible for him alone to accomplish the quest. He meets numerous adventures along the way, including a damsel who offers her love if he will protect her from a would-be rapist; the lifting of a mysterious tomb that only the knight able to liberate the queen can open; and the crossing of a sword-bridge on bare hands and knees. Lancelot's return to Arthur involves his own abduction and a great tournament that demonstrates anew his service for the queen.

Much ink has flowed in efforts to determine whether Chrétien approved or disapproved of the adulterous liaison between Lancelot and Guenevere. Basic to the dispute is the presumed adulterous character of courtly love. Courtly love, as a term, is a modern invention. In the Middle Ages, writers spoke of *fin'amors*, stressing the adaptability of love to different contexts, environments, and social circumstances. The basic features seem to have been the joy it produced and the resulting good that accrued to the lovers and the world in which they lived. Chrétien affirms Lancelot's joy, as well as his accomplishments, despite the difficulties the love causes him.

A striking feature of Chrétien's romances is the close relation obtaining between love and prowess. Prowess is not only prowess in arms but the sum of those qualities that represent worth in the knight or lady—the *chevalerie* of the *Cligés* prologue. Arms may demonstrate worth, but so may the quality of love the knight and lady share. Chrétien's courtly chansons evince an effort to overcome the constraints of human passion and make it enhance individual worth and serve noble ends, most notably by the rejection of the irrational features of Tristan and Iseut's love. The rejection also occurs in the romances, especially *Cligés*. It is important to note that, in both the broader medieval context and in Chrétien's own romances, adultery is not predominant, despite the example of Lancelot and Guenevere. More striking, in a medieval context, is the emphasis on conjugal love. The notion must have seemed much more original in the 12th century than it may appear today, after centuries of love stories. That marriage could be more than a social or family obligation is obvious in Chrétien. Erec chooses his bride without consulting his family, and so does Yvain. And there is no sense of forced marriage except for Fenice in *Cligés*, and that marriage does not succeed precisely because it is forced and because the husband, Alis, in marrying, violates an oath made to his brother and thus threatens the succession of his brother's son, Cligés, to the throne.

Marital problems do arise, but they are also solved. Chrétien insists on a certain equality between the spouses. Not that he meant a contractual equality in any modern legal sense but rather a natural, noble equality that was tried and tested in conflict with the outside world and in the resolution of disputes that occur in the marriage.

The word *conjointure* occurs only once, at least in the sense used to describe romance narrative—in the prologue to *Erec*. Chrétien distinguishes his "very beautiful" *conjointure* from the stories about Erec told by storytellers, who were wont, he says, to take apart and leave out material (*depecier et corronpre*) that belonged in the tale. This seems to mean that Chrétien's romance puts the story together as it should be, omitting nothing essential. That "putting together" would include both *matiere* and *san*. This appears to be the case in *Erec*, whose first part combines two stories, the sparrowhawk episode and the hunt for the white stag, to each of which Enide, because of the qualities that make her desirable as a spouse, provides a denouement. In the sparrowhawk contest, Erec proves that Enide is the most beautiful woman, and Arthur bestows the "kiss of the white stag" on her for the same reason.

Enide's beauty comprehends qualities of body, vestment, and, most importantly, mind and mentality that make her exemplary of perfect womanhood. In the aristocratic world of medieval romance, where everyone of worth is "naturally" on a pedestal, Erec and Enide come together out of admiration and a kind of noble affinity. By the identification of the qualities of persons—the invention of those qualities in source material and their elucidation in romance narrative—Chrétien brings together the disparate elements of the storytellers' versions and fills out the missing features in his new romance. The *molt bele conjointure* depends on the disparate elements of romance marvels, reveals the ideal truth perceived in them by 12th-century civilization, and articulates a new, marvelous narrative. Once the exceptional quality of that narrative was recognized—apparently as early as *Cligés*—a new genre had emerged. The word *roman*, which first meant "in the French language," came to mean "romance" as a narrative recounting marvelous adventures that express an aristocratic ethos. That achievement was Chrétien's.

Chrétien's popularity in his own day is attested both by the unusually large number of surviving manuscripts of his romances—an average of seven for the first four, and as many as fifteen for the *Conte du Graal*—and the enduring influence he had on the romancers who succeeded him. While such writers as Jean Renart and Gautier d'Arras deliberately set out to rival him, others more wisely welcomed his influence in their work. His most influential romances were the two he left unfinished: the *Chevalier de la charrette* and the *Conte du Graal*. The latter spawned a series of verse continuations in the early 13th century, while both provided inspiration for the immensely successful *Lancelot-Grail* or *Vulgate Cycle* of the second quarter of the same century. The Grail story was also reworked independently by the anonymous author of the *Perlesvaus*.

F. Douglas Kelly

[See also: ARTHURIAN VERSE ROMANCE; COURTLY LOVE; GAUTIER D'ARRAS; GAWAIN ROMANCES; GRAIL AND GRAIL ROMANCES; *OVIDE MORALISÉ; PERCEVAL CONTINUATIONS;* RAOUL DE HOUDENC; VULGATE CYCLE; WACE]

Chrétien de Troyes. *Christian von Troyes, Sämtliche Werke,* ed. Wendelin Foerster. 4 vols. Halle: Niemeyer, 1884–99.
———. *Œuvres complètes,* ed. Daniel Poirion, et al. Paris: Gallimard, 1994.
———. *Romans,* ed. Michel Zink, et al. Paris: Librarie Générale Française, 1994.
———. *Les chansons courtoises de Chrétien de Troyes,* ed. Marie-Claire Zai. Bern: Lang & Lang, 1974.
———. *Arthurian Romances,* trans. D. D. R. Owen. London: Dent, 1987.
———. *The Complete Romances of Chrétien de Troyes,* trans. David Staines. Bloomington: Indiana University Press, 1990.
———. *Arthurian Romances,* trans. William W. Kibler. Harmondsworth: Penguin, 1991.
Busby, Keith, Terry Nixon, Alison Stones, Lori Walters, eds. *Les manuscrits de Chrétien de Troyes/The Manuscripts of Chrétien de Troyes.* 2 vols. Amsterdam: Rodopi, 1993.

Kelly, F. Douglas. *Chrétien de Troyes: An Analytic Bibliography.* London: Grant and Cutler, 1976.
Reiss, Edmund, Louise Horner Reiss, and Beverly Taylor. *Arthurian Legend and Literature: An Annotated Bibliography.* Vol. 1: *The Middle Ages,* New York, London: Garland, 1984.
Frappier, Jean, *Chrétien de Troyes: l'homme et l'œuvre.* Paris: Hatier, 1968 (English trans. by Raymond J. Cormier, Athens: University of Ohio Press, 1982).
Lacy, Norris J. *The Craft of Chrétien de Troyes: An Essay on Narrative Art.* Leiden: Brill, 1980.
Topsfield, Leslie T. *Chrétien de Troyes: A Study of the Arthurian Romances.* Cambridge: Cambridge University Press, 1981.
Kelly, Douglas, ed. *The Romances of Chrétien de Troyes: A Symposium.* Lexington: French Forum, 1985.
Lacy, Norris J., Douglas Kelly, and Keith Busby, eds. *The Legacy of Chrétien de Troyes.* 2 vols. Amsterdam: Rodopi, 1987–88.

CHRISTINA MIRABILIS (1150–1224). Blessed Christina was born in the town of Saint-Trond. After the death of her parents, she took to tending sheep and eventually lived as a laywoman at the monastery of Sainte-Catherine. Christina's life is described in a *vita* composed by Thomas de Cantimpré. Unlike other women mystics of her era, Christina focused exclusively on extreme physical phenomena to express her spirituality. Her extraordinary charismatic gifts—salamandrism, clairvoyance, bodily elongation, levitation, agility—served the community as a reminder of Purgatory and an exhortation to live a life free of sin while still in this world. Her *vita* constitutes a transitional type of saint's biography, in that it mixes an earlier focus on revelations about Purgatory with a 13th-century concern with biographical information and mystical phenomena.

Ulrike Wiethaus

[See also: HAGIOGRAPHY; MYSTICISM; SAINTS' LIVES; WOMEN, RELIGIOUS EXPERIENCE OF]

Pinius, J., ed. *Vita Christinae Mirabilis. Acta sanctorum* (July 24) 5 Iulius (1868): 637–60.
Thomas de Cantimpré. *The Life of Christina of Saint Trond by Thomas de Cantimpré,* trans. Margot H. King. Saskatoon: Peregrina, 1986.
Bynum, Caroline Walker. *Holy Feast and Holy Fast: The Religious Significance of Food to Medieval Women.* Berkeley: University of California Press, 1987.
Deschamps, J. "Een Middelnederlandse Prozavertaling van de 'Vita Sanctae Christinae Mirabilis' van Thomas van Cantimpre." *Jaarboek van de Federatio der Geschieden Oudheidkundige Kringen in Limburg* 30 (1975): 69–103.

CHRISTINE DE PIZAN (ca. 1364–ca. 1430). France's first woman of letters was in fact born in Italy, where her father, Tommaso de Pizzano of Bologna, was employed by the Venetian Republic. Soon after Christine's birth, her father was appointed astrologer and scientific adviser to the French king Charles V, so the family established itself in Paris in the shadow of the French court. Christine's early taste for study was interrupted by marriage at sixteen to Étienne du Castel, a young notary from Picardy, who was soon given a promising appointment to the royal chancellery. This happy marriage was interrupted ten years later by the husband's unexpected death, leaving Christine to support three children and a widowed mother. She found herself in a world that had little respect for women, where she was cheated at every turn. She found comfort in study and in writing poetry to express her grief and she soon discovered a talent for writing verse in the fixed forms popular in her day.

Her writing brought her into contact with the court of Louis of Orléans, to whom she dedicated several works, beginning with a narrative poem, the *Épistre au Dieu d'Amour* (1399), which makes fun of fashionable young men who pretend to *fin'amor* while reading Ovid and Jean de Meun. This work was followed by other narrative poems: the *Dit de Poissy* (1401), *Le Débat des deux amants*, *Livre des trois jugemens*, and *Dit de la pastoure* (1403). These eventually led to even more ambitious allegorical poems, the semiautobiographical *Chemin de long estude* (1402–03), which also commented on society's current troubles and proposed an international monarchy, and a lengthy account of the role of Fortune in universal history, the *Mutacion de Fortune* (finished at the end of 1403).

It was also to Louis of Orléans that Christine dedicated an equally ambitious work in poetry and prose, the *Épistre Othea* (ca. 1400) combining a commentary on classical mythology with advice to a young knight. It was one of her most popular works. As the duke was unwilling to find a place in his household for Christine's son, Jean du Castel, after 1404 no further works were dedicated to him. At about this same time, Christine was commissioned by the duke of Burgundy, Philip the Bold, to write a biography of the late king, the *Faits et bonnes meurs du sage roy Charles V* (1404), her first work entirely in prose.

Slightly earlier, her views on Jean de Meun and the *Roman de la Rose* had involved Christine in a debate with members of the royal chancellery, Jean de Montreuil and Gontier and Pierre Col, who admired Jean de Meun's erudition, whereas she saw his unfortunate influence on society's attitudes toward women. Christine did not start the debate, as was formerly thought, but she moved it from a private theoretical discussion to a wider audience by giving copies of the letters it inspired to the queen and the provost of Paris (1402), a gesture that added to her literary reputation and marked her first important defense of her sex against traditional misogynistic literature. It also inspired her to compose three later works: the *Dit de la Rose*, a long poem written in the midst of the debate; the *Cité des dames*, inspired largely by Boccaccio's *De claris mulieribus*, in a certain sense a rewriting of it from a feminine point of view; and the *Livre des trois vertus* (1405), offering advice to women of all classes in an interesting commentary on contemporary French society.

The year 1405 marked a turning point in France's affairs, an open break between the political ambitions of

the dukes of Orléans and Burgundy, inspiring Christine to write a letter to the French queen, Isabeau of Bavaria (October 5), begging her to act as savior of the country. The letter had little effect on the queen, but it focused Christine's attention on matters of public interest, inspiring the *Livre du corps de policie* (1407), on the ideal of the perfect prince, the first of several works directed to the dauphin Louis of Guyenne. These also included the *Livre des fais d'armes et de chevalerie* (ca. 1410), based on Vegetius and on Honoré Bouvet, outlining the essentials of military leadership and stressing international laws to govern warfare. With affairs in France steadily worsening, in 1410 she addressed a letter to the elderly duke of Berry, King Charles VI's uncle, begging him to act to save the country. A civil uprising, the Cabochien revolt, led her to appeal once more to Louis of Guyenne in the *Livre de la paix* (1412–14). This prince appeared to be developing qualities of leadership, but his untimely death (December 1415) added to France's chaos following the defeat at Agincourt. This disaster inspired Christine's *Épistre de la prison de vie humaine*, addressed to Marie de Berry, duchess of Bourbon, but speaking to all women who had suffered losses at Agincourt and indeed to widows and bereaved women of all wars.

As violence in Paris increased, Christine sought refuge in a convent, probably the abbey of Poissy, where her daughter had been a nun for many years. There, she wrote the *Heures de contemplation de Notre Dame*, possibly at the time of her son's death in 1425. Her hopes for France were unexpectedly renewed by the appearance of Jeanne d'Arc, who inspired her final poem, the *Ditié de Jehanne d'Arc*, written shortly after the coronation of Charles VII at Reims in July 1429.

The date of Christine's death is unknown, but Guillebert de Mets, writing memories of Paris in 1434, refers to her in the past tense.

Although not French by birth, Christine wrote many pages inspired by her concern for France; as the mother of three children, her views on education of the young were considerably in advance of her times; as a woman obliged to make her own way in an unfriendly society, she courageously raised her voice in protest against traditional misogyny. She is an unusually interesting witness of her times. Her works were printed and read well into the 16th century, providing for her the earthly fame she, like other early Renaissance writers, so greatly desired.

Charity Cannon Willard

[See also: BIOGRAPHY; BOUVET, HONORÉ; CABOCHIENS; COURTESY BOOKS; JEAN DE MEUN; LE FRANC, MARTIN; QUARREL OF THE *ROMAN DE LA ROSE*; WERCHIN, JEAN DE]

Christine de Pizan. *Œuvres poétiques*, ed. Maurice Roy. 3 vols. Paris: Didot, 1886–96.

Bornstein, Diane, ed. *Ideals for Women in the Works of Christine de Pizan*. Detroit: Michigan Consortium for Medieval and Early Modern Studies, 1981.

Kennedy, Angus J. *Christine de Pizan: A Bibliographical Guide*. London: Grant and Cutler, 1984.

Richards, J. E. *Reinterpreting Christine de Pizan.* Athens: University of Georgia Press, 1991.

Solente, Suzanne. "Christine de Pizan." In *Histoire littéraire de la France.* Paris: Imprimerie Nationale, 1974, Vol. 40.

Willard, Charity C. *Christine de Pizan: Her Life and Works.* New York: Persea, 1984.

CHRISTMAS OCTAVE. *See* Liturgical Year

CHRODEGANG OF METZ (d. 766). A member of the Frankish royal court under Charles Martel and Pepin III, Chrodegang became bishop of Metz in 753 and also served as papal legate to the Franks. He founded two monasteries, at Gorze and Lorsch, but is perhaps best known for his efforts to regularize the life of the canons (i.e., priests) of his cathedral in Metz. His *Rule for Canons* was declared authoritative by the imperial Synod of Aachen in 816. It imposed some elements of a shared common life for cathedral canons but allowed them to possess private property and live in private dwellings.

Grover A. Zinn

[See also: *AUGUSTINE, RULE OF ST.*; REGULAR CANONS]

Saint Chrodegang, communications présentées au colloque tenu à Metz à l'occasion du douzième centenaire de sa mort. Metz: Éditions le Lorraine, 1967.

CHURCH, INTERIOR. The earliest Christian churches were simply assembly rooms in domestic dwellings, whether Roman tenements or court-centered villas like that excavated at Dura-Europos. Their liturgical arrangements and furnishings amounted to little more than a wooden table, serving as an altar at one end of the room. This changed dramatically with the emancipation of the church begun under Constantine in 313. By the end of the century, every town and city had at least one impressive stone basilica with an elaborately appointed interior. The liturgical functions were carried out in the east end of these buildings (although the congested city of Rome lagged behind other areas in the matter of orientation, as much for practical as symbolic reasons). The east end culminated in an apse; at the center of it the bishop sat on the *cathedra* ('chair'), while his clerical colleagues sat to either side of him on the *synthronon*, semicircular benches lining the inner walls of the apse. The altar was just to the west of the bishop, who stepped up to it to celebrate the eucharist facing the congregation. The altar retained its relatively small size for centuries, more cubular than oblong in shape, although it came to be of stone and to contain the relics of some martyr. The altar might be covered with rich cloth, but there were few objects on it beyond the chalice and a book for the biblical readings.

The apsidal east end of the basilica was slightly elevated and enclosed by waist-high stone partitions called *cancelli*, creating the sanctuary area. The term *cancelli*, which refers to wooden latticework, indicates the origi-nal structure of these barriers; it accounts for the Old French and current English word "chancel." The chancel barriers were frequently surmounted by decorative pillars and an architrave, while the modest-sized altar was made prominent by the baldochin, a stone canopy supported by pillars. Two important modifications to the basic arrangement were the addition of the ambo, a pulpit for reading and chanting, in the 6th or 7th century under Byzantine influence, and the roughly contemporary extension of the chancel barriers into the nave in order to accommodate singers and the entry procession of the clergy.

The essentials of this arrangement persisted well into the Middle Ages, particularly in Italy. A fundamentally different one can be observed in the enclosed choir of the late-medieval cathedrals and collegiate churches of the north. To some extent a by-product of the development of Romanesque and Gothic architecture in France, this arrangement was achieved by walling-in the entire sanctuary area at the east end of the church, separating it from the nave on the west and the ambulatory that surrounded it on the north, south, and east. At the east end of the enclosed area was the high altar; just to the west of it was an open space for the attendant clergy, called the presbytery; and to the far west, the choir stalls, two sets of benches facing each other. In the later Middle Ages, the walls of the choir, generally called screens, might boast splendid sculpture on their exterior facing the ambulatory, as at Chartres and Amiens, while the portion facing the nave, called the *jubé* in France, was surmounted by a gallery that frequently supported a great organ.

The high altar was now oblong in shape with painted panels or a sculptured wall at its back, the retable or reredos. The celebrating priest faced the altar with his back to the other participants, and the bishop sat on the *cathedra* at the north side of the presbytery. On the altar, in addition to chalice and book, there was a crucifix and candles, the number of them varying according to the solemnity of the occasion. Lighted candles began to appear on the altar in the 11th or 12th century; in the early Middle Ages, they had been carried by acolytes before the entering bishop and placed on the floor near the altar, sometimes to be extinguished after the reading of the gospel. There was no ambo in the northern arrangement, but rather one or more lecterns for readers and cantors; a common decorative feature of lecterns was to shape the book support as a large bronze eagle, symbolizing the Gospel of John.

The enclosed choir excluded the laity from much of the liturgical action. To remedy this, an altar on which to celebrate Mass for the people was erected in the nave just to the west of the *jubé*. During the Enlightenment, the *jubé* was dismantled in most French churches and replaced by wrought-iron gates through which one could observe the ceremonies.

James McKinnon

[See also: VESTMENTS, ECCLESIASTICAL]

Braun, Joseph. *Der christlicher Altar in seiner geschichtlichen Entwicklung.* 2 vols. Munich: Koch, 1924.

CISTERCIAN ART AND ARCHITECTURE 225

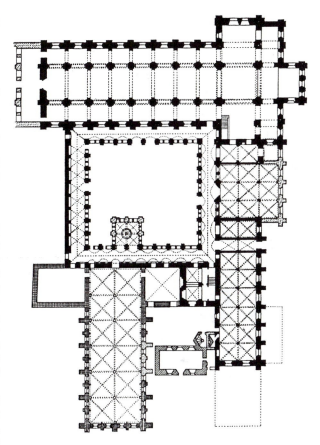

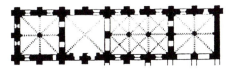

Fontenay (Côte d'Or), Cistercian monastery, plan. After Aubert.

Chastel, André, et al. *Histoire générale des églises de France.* (Vol. 1) and *Dictionnaire des églises de France.* (Vols. 2–5). Paris: Laffont, 1966–71.

Dendy, D. R. *The Use of Lights in Christian Worship.* London: SPCK, 1959.

Heitz, Carol. *Recherches sur les rapports entre architecture et liturgie à l'époque carolingienne.* Paris: SEVPEN, 1963.

Krautheimer, Richard. *Early Christian and Byzantine Architecture.* 4th ed. with Slobodan Curcic. London: Penguin, 1986.

Mathews, Thomas. *The Early Churches of Constantinople: Architecture and Liturgy.* University Park: Pennsylvania State University Press, 1971.

CICONIA, JOHANNES (ca. 1370–1412). Composer and music theorist born in Liège. Ciconia was probably the most important single influence in the unification of Italian and French musical styles that took place ca. 1400. His birth date, long thought to be ca. 1335, is now widely agreed to have been nearer 1370 (most literature published before 1985 must be treated with caution). By 1391, he was a singer in Rome; the texts of several songs, particularly *Una panthera* and *Le ray au soleyl*, show that he must have been at the Visconti court in Pavia later in the 1390s; from 1401 until his death, he was a beneficed singer at Padua cathedral.

Ciconia's musical works include at least ten Mass movements, eight motets, sixteen Italian songs, and four French songs. The motets, in an apparently novel style, include several written for important public events in Padua, including the episcopal installations of both Albano Michele (1406) and Pietro Marcello (1409); others praise Francesco Zabarella and members of the Carrara family. Among his early songs, the virelai *Sus un' fontayne* includes exact quotes from three songs by Philipoctus de Caserta and stands as one of the most complex examples of what is known as the Ars Subtilior. His extraordinary last songs include settings of Leonardo Giustinian (*O rosa bella* and *Con lagrime bagnandome nel viso*) and Domizio Brocardo (*Lizadra donna*). Here, there is a virtually unprecedented degree of text expression, heightened by sequential repetition. Of his two surviving music theory treatises, *De proportionibus* is a later adaptation of a chapter from his larger *Nova musica.*

David Fallows

Ciconia, Johannes. Nova musica *and* De proportionibus:*New Critical Texts and Translations on Facing Pages*, ed. Oliver B. Ellsworth. Lincoln: University of Nebraska Press, 1993.
———. *The Works of Johannes Ciconia,* ed. Margaret Bent and Anne Hallmark. Monaco: Oiseau-Lyre, 1985.
Fallows, David. "Ciconia padre e figlio." *Rivista italiana di musicologia* 9 (1976): 171–77.

CISTERCIAN ART AND ARCHITECTURE. The Cistercians produced art that reflects the purpose of their order, which was to revive the true spirit of Benedictine monasticism. As eloquently stated by St. Bernard, their artistic ideals focused on simplicity that eschewed excessive richness in materials or decoration. At the same time, the Cistercians maintained flexibility in their interpretation of these standards, so that Cistercian art in France adopts regional styles and becomes more elaborate in the progression from Romanesque to Gothic.

The original ideals of early French Cistercian architecture are best preserved in the Burgundian abbey of Fontenay, founded in 1118 as a daughter house of Clairvaux. The church dates from 1139–47, and the other structures are also of this period. The church has a simple façade with a single portal and a few plain windows in the upper story. The nave of eight bays with single aisles is spanned by a pointed barrel vault. The transept of two bays has a rectangular apse and chapels opening off its east side. The beauty derives from the simple lines, balanced proportions, and the play of light on surface. The location of the cloister, chapter house, monks' dormitory, refectory, and other build-

Le Thoronet (Var), Cistercian abbey, cloister. *Photograph courtesy of Whitney S. Stoddard.*

Nave of the Cistercian abbey church of Le Thoronet. 12th century. *Photograph courtesy of Whitney S. Stoddard.*

ings are rationally conceived according to a basic Cistercian plan that facilitated the principal activities of worship, contemplative reading, and manual labor.

Other French Cistercian abbeys adapted this plan with regional modifications, as seen, for example, in the Provençal convents at Sénanque and Le Thoronet dating from the second half of the 12th century. While these small, austere churches conform to the Cistercian rule, both have a semicircular apse. Sénanque has a cupola over the crossing, and the double columns in the cloisters have more elaborate vegetal covering.

The spread of the Cistercian order coincided with the spread of Gothic architecture, and most French Cistercian building utilizes "simplified Gothic" style, which featured cross-rib vaulting, more foliate carving, and increased luminosity. Royaumont, founded by St. Louis in 1228, illustrates these features. Although the church itself does not survive, its plan is known and the well-preserved conventual buildings show its style. Instead of the simple apse, it had a two-bay choir with ambulatory and radiating chapels. The slender proportions of architectural members are typical of the linear features of Rayonnant Gothic.

As time progressed, the Cistercians also introduced more sculpture and stained glass into their building programs. Because of their devotion to the Virgin, most convents had at least one statue representing the Virgin and Child or other Marian themes. Carved altar frontals, such as the early 14th-century retable from Fontenay with a central Crucifixion surrounded by scenes from Christ's life, were also used. Stained glass was in the *grisaille* technique without color. Cistercian *grisaille* windows feature beautifully designed foliate or abstract patterns, which were probably intended to enhance contemplation and meditation.

The Cistercians also produced illuminated manuscripts. Their most notable works emanated from the scriptorium at Cîteaux and other Burgundian abbeys in the 12th century. Some of these manuscripts follow Cistercian decorative edicts by using a monochrome style where the emphasis is on page design, calligraphed script, and arabesque initials. Other Cistercian manuscripts utilize illumination with tinted drawings, as in the Bible of Stephen Harding. The initials constructed of human figures in some of the Cîteaux manuscripts display an inventiveness and humor that reveal an added dimension of Cistercian spirituality.

Karen Gould

[See also: BERNARD OF CLAIRVAUX; CISTERCIAN ORDER; CÎTEAUX; FONTENAY; LONGPONT; NOIRLAC; OURSCAMP; PONTIGNY; ROYAUMONT; SÉNANQUE; SILVACANE; THORONET, LE]

Aubert, Marcel. *L'architecture cistercienne en France.* 2 vols. Paris: Vanoest, 1947.

Dimier, Anselme, and Jean Porcher. *L'art cistercienne: France.* Paris: Zodiaque, 1963.

Zakin, Helen Jackson. *French Cistercian Grisaille Glass.* New York: Garland, 1979.

Zaluska, Yolanta. *L'enluminure et le scriptorium de Cîteaux au XIIe siècle.* Nuits-Saint-Georges: Cîteaux, 1989.

CISTERCIAN ORDER. Within fifteen years of Cîteaux's foundation by Robert of Molesme in 1098, the monastery began to found daughter houses, as more monks came to join the New Monastery than could be accommodated there. Between 1113 and 1115, the "four eldest daughters" of Cîteaux were founded, La Ferté, Pontigny, Clairvaux, and Morimond. Relations among all these houses were spelled out in the *Carta caritatis* (1114), which emphasized the mutual love and obligations binding them together.

The Cistercian order grew quickly, as all four daughter houses began founding daughters of their own, and Cîteaux founded additional houses. The earliest houses were all located in the French duchy of Burgundy, but within a short period Cistercian houses were being founded in other parts of France and in England, Germany, and Italy. A brief and unsuccessful attempt was made in the 1150s to restrict the size of this rapidly growing order. Each of the Cistercian houses had its own abbot, who was supposed to visit the abbot of his mother house once a year and in turn was also supposed to visit annually each of the daughter houses that his own monastery had founded. An annual chapter-general brought together the abbots of all the houses at Cîteaux.

From the beginning, the Cistercian order distinguished itself by a greater austerity of life than many other Benedictine monks. They took almost exclusively adult converts, rather than child oblates. Cistercian houses were founded far from the cities, and the monks emphasized manual labor rather than performance of the liturgy. The land they received was organized into granges. The monks tried to practice direct cultivation of their fields, rather than relying on the rents and dues of peasant tenants, and thus by the 1130s had established the institution of *conversi,* men without an educational background who still wished to live apart from the world; these *conversi* worked the monks' fields.

The Cistercians became the most influential of the new monastic orders of the 12th century, due in part to the perceived holiness of their way of life and in part to the charisma of their most famous member, Bernard, first abbot of Clairvaux (r. 1115–53).

Constance B. Bouchard

[See also: *BENEDICT, RULE OF ST.*; BERNARD OF CLAIRVAUX; *CARTA CARITATIS;* CÎTEAUX; CLUNIAC ORDER; FONTENAY; HAGIOGRAPHY; ISAAC OF STELLA; MONASTICISM; PONTIGNY]

Bernard of Clairvaux. *Sancti Bernardi opera omnia,* ed. Jean Leclercq, C.H. Talbot, and H. Rochais. 8 vols. Rome: Editiones Cistercienses, 1957–78.

Bouton, Jean de la Croix, and Jean-Baptise Van Damme, eds. *Les plus anciens textes de Cîteaux.* Achel: Commentarii Cistercienses, 1974.

Marilier, Jean, ed. *Chartes et documents concernant l'abbaye de Cîteaux, 1098–1182.* Rome: Editiones Cistercienses, 1961.

Auberger, Jean-Baptiste. *L'unanimité cistercienne primitive: mythe ou realité?* Achel: Commentarii Cistercienses, 1986.

Berman, Constance H. *Medieval Agriculture, the Southern French Countryside, and the Early Cistercians: A Study of Forty-three Monasteries.* Philadelphia: American Philosophical Society, 1986.

Bouchard, Constance B. *Holy Entrepreneurs: Cistercians, Knights, and Economic Exchange in Twelfth-Century Burgundy.* Ithaca: Cornell University Press, 1991.

Goodrich, W.E. "The Cistercian Founders and the Rule: Some Reconsiderations." *Journal of Ecclesiastical History* 35 (1984): 358–75.

Lekai, Louis J. *The Cistercians: Ideals and Reality.* Kent: Kent State University Press, 1977.

CITÉ. The word *cité* (Lat. *civitas*), or city, described the urban center of the administrative districts of Gaul in the Roman Empire and the Frankish kingdom. The Roman *civitas,* however, included the surrounding district, and the two formed a single administrative unit. In the late Roman and Merovingian periods, the urban *civitas* capitals survived as centers of royal and ecclesiastical administrations as well as the focus of commercial activity, providing a framework for the unity of the heterogeneous population of the Frankish kingdom.

The barbarian invasions of the 3rd and 4th centuries led to the rapid construction of walls around the capitals of the *civitates,* and these walls gave security to the inhabitants. The capitals continued to function as administrative headquarters for the civil bureaucracy, and the church likewise took refuge behind the protective walls. The cities became the residences of bishops and the centers of diocesan organization. Thus, a permanent and important population became fixed and protected in the *civitas* capitals, and the cities survived. They also remained at the center of the network of roads and waterways, dominating the trade and commerce of the region. The *cités* provided the political, social, economic, and religious focus for the Frankish kingdom. In Gaul, most of the *cités* that the Romans had not walled disappeared by the end of the 6th century.

In the Merovingian kingdoms, the *cités* were the centers of royal administration. From these cities, the counts (*comites*), supported by garrisons of troops, presided over the local administration for the kings, collecting taxes, administering justice, and assembling the local levies for the royal army while also keeping a close eye on the powerful bishop. Most of the royal mints were also located in these cities. Church life was focused on the *cité*. It was the residence of the bishop and his assisting clergy, the home of the major churches and the site of the major cults of the saints, whose festivals provided a strong sense of cohesion for the surrounding population. Down to the mid-7th century, the Merovingian kings resided in the *cités*, especially Paris, Rouen, Metz, Soissons, Tours, and Orléans, which were the centers of their political activity.

Despite the overwhelmingly rural character of the population of the Frankish kingdom as a whole, the cities exercised a preponderant role in its affairs. The control of the small enclosed cities meant the control of the political, military, and ecclesiastical centers of life, and warfare in this period was concerned largely with the capture and holding of the *cités*.

Steven Fanning

[See also: BASTIDE; BOURGEOISIE; COMMUNE; TOWNS]

Bullough, Donald A. "Social and Economic Structure and Topography in the Early Medieval City." *Settimane di studio del Centro Italiano di Studi sull'Alto Medioevo* 21 (1974): 351–99.

Ewig, Eugen. "Résidence et capitale pendant le haut moyen âge." In *Spätantikes und fränkisches Gallien, Gesammelte Schriften (952–1973)*, ed. Harmut Atsma. 2 vols. Zurich and Munich: Artemis, 1976, pp. 383–89.

James, Edward. *The Origins of France from Clovis to the Capetians 500–1000*. New York: St. Martin, 1982.

Wood, Ian N. "Early Medieval Devotion in Town and Country." In *The Church in Town and Countryside*, ed. Derek Baker. Oxford: Blackwell, 1979, pp. 61–76.

CÎTEAUX. Sixteen miles south-southeast of Dijon, Cîteaux is the mother house of the Cistercian order, founded here in 1098 by Robert of Molesme (d. 1111), St. Albéric (d. 1109), and St. Stephen Harding (d. 1134). The first years were difficult, but with the arrival of St. Bernard in 1112 or 1113 fortune shone on the new foundation. He became abbot in 1115, and soon the first four "daughters of Cîteaux" were born: La Ferté, Pontigny, Clairvaux, and Morimond. By the turn of the 13th century, Cîteaux was "mother" to over 1,000 religious establishments in France alone. Little remains of the original abbey: a 12th-century chapel now disaffected, a vaulted hall, and portions of the Gothic cloister.

William W. Kibler/William W. Clark

[See also: BERNARD OF CLAIRVAUX; CISTERCIAN ORDER; MONASTICISM; PONTIGNY; ROBERT OF MOLESME; STEPHEN HARDING]

Pressouyre, Léon, and Terryl N. Kinder, eds. *Saint Bernard et le monde cistercien*. Paris: CNMHS, 1992.

CIVRAY. The squat, four-bay, 12th-century Romanesque church of Saint-Nicolas of Civray (Vienne) is anomalous in the Poitou region. Triangular pendentives, each with a crudely sculpted grotesque, support an unusual octagonal tower over the square crossing of the transept. Wall paintings on the south arm of the transept (late 13th or early 14th c.) celebrate the life of St. Gilles.

The western façade exhibits a decorative and iconographic program of striking richness and exceptional quality. A cornice divides the space into two levels, each of which is further subdivided by three arches. The moldings around the central door depict Christ in Majesty surrounded by the four Evangelists, the parable of the wise and foolish virgins, the Assumption of the Virgin, and the signs of the zodiac. The flanking arches in the ground level include scenes of St. George fighting the dragon, a demon devouring the host, acrobats, a tightrope walker, and human busts.

On the upper level, to the left, is a heavily mutilated equestrian sculpture—possibly an allegory of Constantine crushing paganism. The upper-central arch exhibits the vic-

Civray (Vienne), façade. *Photograph courtesy of Whitney S. Stoddard.*

tory of Virtue over Vice. The right arch shows the legend of St. Nicolas saving three women from prostitution and representations of four Apostles. Historiated capitals throughout the program depict single figures and biblical scenes.

Nina Rowe

Crozet, René. "Le décor sculpté de la façade de l'église de Civray." *Revue de l'art ancien et moderne* 66 (1934): 97–110.

Seidel, Linda. *Songs of Glory: The Romanesque Façades of Aquitaine.* Chicago: University of Chicago Press, 1981, pp. 27, 43, 48, 65.

Thirion, Jacques. "Civray." *Congrès archéologique (Poitiers)* 109 (1951): 331–55.

CLAREMBALD OF ARRAS

CLAREMBALD OF ARRAS (ca. 1110–after 1170). A pupil of Thierry of Chartres and Hugh of Saint-Victor, Clarembald was a Neoplatonist philosopher and theologian. His life centered on Arras, where he was provost ca. 1152–56 and archdeacon until his death. Summoned ca. 1160 to direct the school at Laon, he relinquished the post as soon as he decently could.

Clarembald taught philosophy but is best known as a theologian, especially for his commentary on Boethius's *De Trinitate,* written for the elucidation of young monks. He also commented on Boethius's *De hebdomadibus (Opus. Sac.* 3) and Genesis 1. Though he was not an adventurous thinker—his ideas depend largely on Thierry of Chartres— his polished, clear style and vast knowledge of sacred and secular tradition give his works a personal stamp.

In the Chartrian mold, Clarembald got his Platonism from Chalcidius and was heavily influenced by Boethius. He was a Realist, who viewed God as the Form of all being. God is pure form, pure act, pure entity, pure and simple being; God is therefore a Unity to which all other creation owes its being.

Lesley J. Smith

[**See also:** CHARTRES; HUGH OF SAINT-VICTOR; PHILOSOPHY; THEOLOGY; THIERRY OF CHARTRES]

CLAUDIUS OF TURIN

CLAUDIUS OF TURIN. A biblical exegete and theologian during the reign of Louis the Pious, Claudius was born near Seo de Urguel and studied in the school of Felix, one of the theologians attacked by Alcuin as "Adoptionist," before traveling to the classroom of Leidradus in Lyon. He also spent some years in the palace school at Aix-la-Chapelle, where he brought together *catenae* on earlier commentary on many books of the Bible, notably the Heptateuch (of which Deuteronomy and Numbers do not survive), Matthew, and the Pauline epistles. Most of these influential texts remain unedited. Claudius was appointed bishop of Turin by Louis the Pious ca. 818. Almost immediately, he began a war of words against the cult of relics he found flourishing in that city. His iconoclastic writings are perhaps of most interest, but these survive mainly in the writings of his opponents Sungal and Jonas of Orléans.

E. Ann Matter

[**See also:** ALCUIN; BIBLE, CHRISTIAN INTERPRETATION OF; JONAS OF ORLÉANS; LOUIS I THE PIOUS; THEOLOGY]

Claudius of Turin. *Opera. PL* 50, 104; *MGH Ep.* 4.

Bellet, P. "Claudio de Turin, autor de los commentarios *In Genesim et Regum* del Pseudo Euquerio." *Estudios biblicos* 9 (1950): 209–23.

———. "El *Liber de imaginibus sanctorum,* bajo el nombre de Agobardo de Lyon, obra de Claudio de Turin." *Analecta sacra Tarraconensia* 26 (1953): 151–94.

Italiani, Giuliana. *La tradizione esegetica nel* Commento ai Re *di Claudio di Torino.* Florence: Cooperativa Editrice Universitaria, 1979.

Souter, Alexander. *The Earliest Latin Commentaries on the Epistles of St. Paul.* Oxford: Clarendon, 1927.

CLAUSULA

CLAUSULA. In 12th- and 13th-century music, a clausula (pl. clausulae) was a melismatic passage of plainchant set in the two-part (later sometimes three-part and rarely four-part) polyphony of the Notre-Dame School. The added part (the duplum) moved predominantly note-against-note to the plainchant melisma, a texture termed "discant" style. Some melismas, such as *In seculum* from the Gradual *Hec dies* and *Latus* from the Alleluia *Pascha nostrum,* were frequently set as independent clausulae because their length and melodic properties lent them well to this treatment. The primary Notre-Dame manuscripts (W1, F, and W2) are the main sources for clausulae, and together they transmit some 900 two-part discant passages, many embedded in organa. In W1 and F, there are also separate fascicles containing independent clausulae in series, each of which maintains the liturgical order of the organa to which they belong.

In the clausulae identified as the earliest, the tenor usually is notated as rhythmically equal longs without any pattern. Somewhat later, the longs of the tenor became differentiated in length. Finally, both the tenor and the duplum were subject to modal rhythm, moving rhythmically at about the same pace. One of the most important innovations in the composition of clausulae was repeating the tenor, either with the same rhythmic pattern or with a different, contrasting one. This led to repetition in which the rhythmic pattern overlapped repetition of the melismatic melody, a device that proved to be the precursor of isorhythm, which was of great importance to the musical style of the Ars Nova in the 14th century. Texting the duplum of a clausula created the earliest motets.

Sandra Pinegar

[**See also:** CONDUCTUS; ISORHYTHMIC MOTET; MOTET (13TH CENTURY); NOTRE-DAME SCHOOL; ORGANUM]

Flotzinger, Rudolf. *Der Discantussatz im Magnus Liber und seiner Nachfolge.* Vienna: Böhlaus, 1969.

Smith, Norman E. "Some Exceptional Clausulae of the Florence Manuscript." *Music and Letters* 54 (1973): 405–14.

CLEMENT IV (r. 1265–68). Pope. After Urban IV died in 1264, the conclave in 1265 elected one of his cardinals, Guy Foulques, to succeed him as Clement IV. The new pope was a native of Languedoc and the author of one of the earlier legal opinions on the Inquisition. He had served as a papal legate to England during a baronial rebellion against Henry III. As a subject of Louis IX of France and of his brother Alphonse, the Capetian count of Toulouse, the new pope favored the efforts of their brother, Charles of Anjou, to conquer the kingdom of Naples. Clement agreed to finance Charles's campaign against Manfred, the illegitimate son of the emperor Frederick II; and he crowned Charles king of Sicily at the Lateran in 1266. After Manfred's death, the brutality of the Angevin army moved the pope to protest to the king, but papal support of Charles continued during the war against Conradin, Frederick's surviving grandson, to whose execution Clement gave tacit consent. Clement also rejected overtures from the Byzantine emperor Michael VIII Palaeologus, who was trying to avoid an Angevin attack on Constantinople. Papal financial support of Charles's ambitions led Clement to expand the papacy's claims to appoint to vacant benefices. His successor Gregory X (r. 1271–76) temporarily would reduce Angevin influence in the curia.

Thomas M. Izbicki

[See also: CHARLES I; LOUIS IX]

Jordan, Édouard, ed. *Les registres de Clément IV (1265–1268): recueil des bulles de ce pape publiées ou analysées d'après les manuscrits originaux des archives du Vatican.* Paris: Thorin, 1893.

Nicolas, César Augustin. *Un pape Saint-Gillois: Clément IV dans le monde et dans l'église, 1195–1268.* Nîmes: Imprimerie Générale, 1910.

CLEMENT V (r. 1305–14). Pope. After the death of Boniface VIII in 1303, his successor, Benedict XI (r. 1303–04), sought a compromise with Philip IV the Fair of France while condemning Guillaume de Nogaret's actions at Anagni. When Benedict died, Bertrand de Got, archbishop of Bordeaux, was elected as a compromise candidate in 1305. As a subject of both Edward I in Aquitaine and of Philip, the new pope, Clement V, was in a position to reconcile old foes. Clement, however, beginning with his being persuaded to be crowned in Lyon, in the presence of the French king, not at Vienne, soon proved himself compliant to most of Philip's wishes. This compliance was based partly on the pope's ill health and partly on Philip's frequent threats to have Clement's prececessor Boniface VIII condemned for various crimes and vices. Clement canceled *Clericis laicos* and interpreted *Unam sanctam* in an evasive manner. Other concessions included dropping proceedings against Nogaret and consenting reluctantly to French efforts to dissolve the Templars and confiscate their wealth. Clement also increased French influence in the curia by creating a majority of non-Italian cardinals and avoiding a journey to Rome. Clement did, however, work to have Henry of Luxembourg, not

Charles of Valois, Philip's brother, elected King of the Romans. Clement V's Council of Vienne (1311–12) acted to condemn various groups, including the béguines and beghards, for heresy; but it did not wish to suppress the Templars. Instead, Clement had that act ratified in a secret consistory. The acts of the council and other papal decrees, including the revocation of *Clericis laicos*, were inserted into the *Constitutiones clementinae*, the last official collection of medieval canon law, prepared in Clement's lifetime but issued after his death by his successor, John XXII.

Thomas M. Izbicki

[See also: AVIGNON PAPACY; BÉGUINES; BONIFACE VIII; *CLERICIS LAICOS;* NOGARET, GUILLAUME DE; PHILIP IV THE FAIR; TEMPLARS]

Registrum Clementis papae V. 9 vols. Rome: Ex Typographia Vaticana, 1884–88.

Tanner, Norman P., ed. *Decrees of the Ecumenical Councils.* 2 vols. London: Sheed and Ward, 1990, Vol. 1, pp. 336–401. [Council of Vienne, 1311–12].

Lizerand, Georges. *Clément V et Philippe IV le Bel.* Paris: Hachette, 1910.

Mollatt, Michel. *Le concile de Vienne.* Louvain-la-Neuve: Université Catholique de Louvain, 1978.

CLEMENT VI (r. 1342–52). Pope. Clement VI has been described as the most typical of the Avignon popes, especially as a lover of luxury. Petrarch denounced Clement as Nimrod, even while accepting benefices from him. Pierre-Roger de Beaufort, the future Clement VI, was born into a noble family in Limousin. As a second son, he was dedicated to the church, entering the abbey of Chaise-Dieu in the Auvergne. Pierre-Roger was sent to Paris to study, and he became a theologian and a noted preacher. As a professor, he made his name by defending the privileges of the clergy before an assembly held at Vincennes by Philip VI, the first Valois king of France, in 1329. Pierre's ecclesiastical promotions included elevation to prior, abbot, and bishop, including the archbishopric of Rouen (1330). Philip VI employed Pierre-Roger as a councilor and administrator. Despite difficult relations with John XXII and a role as go-between for Philip and Benedict XII, Pierre-Roger was made a cardinal in 1338.

Elected pope in 1342, Pierre-Roger reigned as Clement VI. The papal palace in Avignon, begun by Benedict XII, was expanded and made into a showplace, a home of art, music, ceremony, and feasting. A powerful Limousin faction was created in the College of Cardinals. Clement made himself popular through his patronage of scholars and students, but this bounty required further expansion of the curia's fiscalism. Clement took pleasure in religious ceremonies and in preaching on state occasions. When the Black Death struck Avignon, however, the pope remained in the city, seeing to the burial of the dead and the welfare of the survivors. Clement was less kind to the bands of flagellants who descended on Avignon in 1349, ordering them dispersed as a threat to order.

In the political sphere, Clement, despite the ravages of the Hundred Years' War, formed a Latin League against Turkish pirates; but its initial success was insufficient to spark a crusade. Clement opposed the intervention of Charles IV of Luxembourg in Italy. Although Avignon was purchased from the Angevin monarchy, the pope welcomed the collapse of Cola di Rienzo's domination of Rome. His lack of interest in returning the papacy to Italy was one reason for Petrarch's denunciation of him.

Thomas M. Izbicki

[See also: AVIGNON PAPACY]

Clement VI. *Clément VI (1342–1352): lettres closes, patentes et curiales se rapportant à la France*, ed. Eugène Déprez et al. 3 vols. Paris: Boccard, 1901–61.
———. *Clément VI (1342–1352): lettres secrètes et curiales intéressant les pays autres que la France*, ed. Paul Lecacheux et al. 4 vols. Paris: Boccard, 1902–55.
Coogan, Robert, trans. *Babylon on the Rhone: A Translation of Letters by Dante, Petrarch, and Catherine of Siena on the Avignon Papacy*. Potomac: Studia Humanitatis, 1983.
Wood, Diana. *Clement VI: The Pontificate and Ideas of an Avignon Pope*. Cambridge: Cambridge University Press, 1989.

CLÉRIADUS ET MÉLIADICE. A lengthy prose romance from the middle of the 15th century that deals with the love of Clériadus, son of the Count of Asturias, and Méliadice, daughter of King Philippon of England. The narrative, which takes place variously in England, Spain, and Cyprus, is largely given over to adventures in which Clériadus proves himself worthy of the love of Méliadice. The work, found in nine manuscripts and five early printed editions, was popular in its day.

Keith Busby

Zink, Gaston, ed. *Clériadus et Méliadice: roman en prose du XVe siècle*. Geneva: Droz, 1984.

CLERICIS LAICOS. In February 1296, Pope Boniface VIII issued his constitution *Clericis laicos*, which forbade lay powers to tax the clergy without papal consent. This decree was intended to deprive Philip IV the Fair of France and Edward I of England of the fiscal resources for war. *Clericis laicos* closed loopholes in the canon law, which had permitted the clergy to make "voluntary" offerings to kings. Its text also was inflammatory, opening with a claim that the laity always had been hostile to the clergy. Apologists for the lay powers would respond by denouncing the ambition and greed of the clergy. *Clericis laicos* set Robert Wichelsey, archbishop of Canterbury, in opposition to Edward; but the French clergy rallied behind Philip. Pressed by troubles with the Colonna family at home and by a French embargo on the export of bullion in 1297, Boniface issued *Etsi de statu,* which permitted the French monarchy a discretionary power to tax the clergy for the defense of the realm. Despite this check, Boniface incorporated *Clericis laicos* into his *Liber sextus decretalium* (1298). Philip IV, aware of this, later

pressured Clement V into revoking this canon. The canonists, however, continued commenting on the text, emphasizing the inability of the clergy to evade canon law by passing their obligations on to their lay dependents.

Thomas M. Izbicki

[See also: BONIFACE VIII; PHILIP IV THE FAIR; *UNAM SANCTAM*]

Izbicki, Thomas M. "*Clericis laicos* and the Canonists." In *Popes, Teachers and Canon Law in the Middle Ages: Festschrift for Brian Tierney*, ed. Stanley Chodorow and James R. Sweeney. Ithaca: Cornell University Press, 1989, pp. 179–90.
Tierney, Brian. *The Crisis of Church and State, 1050–1300.* Englewood Cliffs: Prentice-Hall, 1964, pp. 172–79.

CLERMONT-FERRAND. Since Roman times, when it was named Augustonemetum, Clermont (Puy-de-Dôme) has been the major city of Auvergne. Christianized in the mid-3rd century by St. Austremoine, one of the "seven apostles

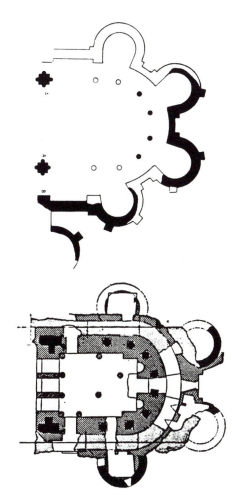

Clermont-Ferrand (Puy-de-Dôme), Notre-Dame, reconstructed plans of 10th-century chevet and crypt. After Ranquet.

Clermont-Ferrand, Notre-Dame-du-Port, nave elevation and section. After Losowska.

Clermont-Ferrand, Notre-Dame-du-Port, south portal. *Photograph courtesy of Whitney S. Stoddard.*

of Gaul," the city was dominated by its bishops, who exercised the most effective political power throughout the Middle Ages. Although destroyed by Pepin the Short in 761 and pillaged by the Normans in 854 and 916, Clermont regained its prominence in the mid-10th century, as witnessed by the building of a new cathedral in the 940s. In 1095, at the Council of Clermont, Pope Urban II issued his call to Christian warriors to wrest the Holy Land from the Muslims, and the age of the Crusades was born.

Following several setbacks in his attempts to seize control of Clermont from the bishop, the count of Auvergne, Guillaume VI, established a fortified *bourg* at Montferrand, 2 miles to the northeast, in the 1120s. This local conflict was played out against a background of international politics, for the count was the vassal of the duke of Aquitaine, Henry II Plantagenêt, after 1152 the king of England, while the bishop was supported steadfastly by Philip II Augustus. Repeated comital assaults finally led to Philip's aggressive armed intervention, and by 1213 the city and region were firmly under royal control. Montferrand, sold to Philip IV the Fair in 1292, became the seat of royal administration. In 1630, however, it was joined administratively to Clermont, hence the name Clermont-Ferrand, and gradually declined into little more than a distant suburb of the larger city.

The architecture of Clermont-Ferrand offers a kaleidoscope of styles that reflects both stylistic developments over time as well as the city's location between northern and southern France. The crypt of the cathedral, dedicated in 946, is one of the earliest examples in Europe of a plan with an ambulatory and radiating chapels. A fully developed version of this scheme appears at Notre-Dame-du-Port, one of the quintessential examples of the vital school of Romanesque architecture and sculpture that flourished in Auvergne in the late 11th and early 12th centuries. The elevation and fully vaulted structure of Notre-Dame-du-Port are connected closely to the so-called pilgrimage-road basilicas of the Loire Valley and Languedoc, such as Saint-Martin at Tours, Sainte-Foy at Conques, or Saint-Sernin at Toulouse. The powerful, thick-set figures that inhabit the capitals and the south portal relate as well to the work at Toulouse and Conques.

The Gothic made its first tentative inroads into Clermont with the arrival of the mendicant orders in the early 13th century, but, as seen in the chapels of the Franciscans and Dominicans, it was limited to such details as crocket capitals and pointed arches. With the reconstruction of the cathedral, the architecture of Paris and the Île-de-France was transplanted to Auvergne. Begun in 1248 by Jean Deschamps, who drew upon such recent projects as the nave chapels of Notre-Dame (Paris), the new work at Saint-Denis, the Sainte-Chapelle, and Beauvais cathedral, Clermont's verticality, thin walls, and luminous windows broke emphatically with previous Auvergnat traditions to establish a clear manifestation of episcopal authority allied staunchly to the French crown. The cathedral workshop also seems to have erected a new chapel for the Franciscans between 1264 and 1284, now engulfed in the Préfecture. However, in keeping with the order's statutes, the church eschews architectural elaboration in favor of a simple single vessel covered by ribbed vaults, a scheme repeated for the Carmelite house (1329), today the parish church of Saint-Genès. Notre-Dame in Montferrand (ca. 1300–16th c.), constructed as a single-nave edifice, reflects not only the impact of monastic ideas on secular church architecture but also building traditions from southern France.

Michael T. Davis

[See also: CONQUES; CRUSADES; JEAN DESCHAMPS; PARIS; PHILIP II AUGUSTUS; PHILIP IV THE FAIR; ROMANESQUE ARCHITECTURE; SAINT-DENIS; TOULOUSE; TOURS/TOURAINE]

Craplet, Bernard. *Auvergne romane*. 3rd ed. La Pierre-qui-vire: Zodiaque, 1962.

Davis, Michael. "The Choir of the Cathedral of Clermont-Ferrand: The Beginning of Construction and the Work of Jean Deschamps." *Journal of the Society of Architectural Historians* 40 (1981): 181–202.

Ranquet, Henri du. *La cathédrale de Clermont-Ferrand*. 2nd ed. Paris: Laurens, 1928.

Rouchon, Gilbert. *Notre-Dame de Clermont, son chapitre, sa cathédrale, son quartier*. Clermont-Ferrand: Imprimerie Générale, 1934.

Tardieu, Ambroise. *Histoire de la ville de Clermont-Ferrand*. 2 vols. Moulins: Desrosiers, 1870–71.

Vieillard-Troiekouroff, May. "La cathédrale de Clermont du Ve au XIIIe siècles." *Cahiers archéologiques* 11 (1960): 199–247.

Welter, Louise. "Le chapitre cathédrale de Clermont, sa constitution, ses privilèges." *Revue d'histoire de l'église de France* 41 (1955): 5–42.

CLÉRY. The collegiate church of Notre-Dame de Cléry (Loiret), located in a small village just south of Orléans, has been an important site of Marian devotion since the late 13th century and enjoyed lavish support by the kings of France. During the first decade of the 14th century, a new church, whose bell tower still survives on the north flank, was erected with the assistance of Philip IV the Fair. After its destruction by the English in 1428, Cléry was rebuilt by Charles VII and Dunois. By 1449, construction had reached the north-transept portal under the direction of Pierre Chauvin, master of the works of the duchy of Orléans, and in 1482 Louis XI, who is buried at Cléry, inaugurated the addition of the four western bays of the nave.

Despite its adoption of such up-to-date Flamboyant style features as double-curved tracery and continuous moldings, Cléry is characterized by decorative severity, a disciplined order of forms, and conscious retrospection. The plan, with its nonprojecting transept and ambulatory without chapels, seems a simplified version of Notre-Dame in Paris. Similarly, the cylindrical piers and taut membranous wall surfaces of the two-story elevation continue ideas that had been part of Parisian architecture since the late 12th century.

Michael T. Davis

Cléry (Loiret), Notre-Dame, nave. *Photograph: Clarence Ward Collection. Courtesy of Oberlin College.*

[See also: GOTHIC ARCHITECTURE; PARIS]

Jarry, Eugène. "Cléry." *Congrès archéologique (Orléans)* 93 (1930): 302–21.

Jarry, Louis. *Histoire de Cléry et de l'église collégiale et chapelle royale de Notre-Dame de Cléry*. Orléans: Herluison, 1899.

Sanfaçon, Roland. *L'architecture flamboyante en France*. Quebec: Presses de l'Université de Laval, 1971.

CLIMATE. Though directly implicated in the rise or fall of some of the great civilizations of the past, climate had only an indirect effect on public affairs in medieval France. Its primary significance lay in the fact that it directly touched the lives of ordinary people. Despite the reappearance of cities and urban life during the later Middle Ages, the vast majority of those living in medieval France continued to be peasants, the producers of the food and fiber essential for maintaining themselves and everyone else. More than any other environmental factor, climate provides the limits within which agriculture can be practiced. The patterns of temperature, precipitation, and wind direction and velocity that constitute climate play a major role in determining what can be planted and when, as well as how much emphasis can be placed on livestock.

As it does today, France during the Middle Ages straddled three climatic zones. The mildest, known as the Mediterranean climate, encompassed the Mediterranean coastal lowland and the lower Rhône Valley. Here, mist and moisture from the Atlantic alternated with dry winds from the Sahara to form cool, damp winters and hot, dry summers. This pattern supported an agricultural complex of wheat or barley, planted in a winter cycle, supplemented by olives and vines, the classic Mediterranean triad. Because of the annual summer drought, the primary livestock were sheep and goats, taken from lowland winter pastures to highland summer pastures in an ancient pattern known as transhumance. At the other extreme were scattered locations in the high Alps and Pyrénées that experienced a northern or Alpine climate. With snow on the ground for much of the year and only short, cool summers, the possibilities for agriculture were limited to the grazing of cattle, sheep, and goats, supplemented by limited production of rye and oats in favored locations.

The remainder and by far the greatest proportion of France lay within the temperate zone, so called because it experienced extremes neither of temperature nor of precipitation. Not only could peasants in this zone practice a traditional agricultural complex of summer crops and heavy dependence on cattle, from the 9th century onward they added a winter planting cycle as well. Because soils over much of this zone were heavier and thicker with a higher organic content than was found in the Mediterranean zone, new agricultural implements were necessary to put them into production effectively. The development of the moldboard plow by the 9th century helped to make the temperate region of France one of the richest agricultural regions of Europe by the high Middle Ages.

Though the gross features of climate during the Middle Ages were not significantly different from those today, there were some variations over the period that seriously affected the production of food and fiber. These variations can be grouped as follows: 400 to 750, cool and wet; 750 to 1200, warm and dry; 1200 to 1350, cool and wet; and 1350 to 1550, warmer but continued wet. Variations in precipitation usually affected agriculture more directly than did temperature variations. Too much precipitation might reduce the harvest in temperate Europe, while drier conditions might have the same effect in Mediterranean Europe. Indeed, one of the best-documented harvest failures to strike temperate Europe occurred in 1315, a year that saw much higher than average precipitation in northern France and surrounding areas.

William H. TeBrake

[See also: AGRICULTURE; FAMINE; TRANSHUMANCE]

Alexandre, Pierre. *Le climat en Europe au moyen âge: contribution à l'histoire des variations climatiques de 1000 à 1425, d'après les sources narratives de l'Europe occidentale.* Paris: École des Hautes Études en Sciences Sociales, 1987.

Lamb, Hubert H. *Climate: Present, Past and Future.* 2 vols. London: Methuen, 1977, Vol. 2: *Climatic History and the Future,* pp. 423–73.

Le Roy Ladurie, Emmanuel. *Times of Feast, Times of Famine: A History of Climate Since the Year 1000,* trans. Barbara Bray. Garden City: Doubleday, 1971.

CLISSON. The village and castle of Clisson (Loire-Atlantique) became the seat of a family important in 14th-century Brittany. Lords of Clisson appear in monastic documents as early as the 11th century, but their precise genealogy before the 14th century remains uncertain.

The Clisson family rose to wealth and prominence through a succession of brilliant marriages. Around 1200, Guillaume I was ranked as a baron. His grandson Olivier I acquired the important castle of Blain from his mother and rebelled against the duke of Brittany until the latter forced him into retirement in 1262. His successor, Olivier II (d. ca. 1295), acquired lands in lower Normandy through marriage, and ca. 1300 his son Guillaume married Isabelle de Craon, linking the Clisson to her important Angevin family.

The two sons of this marriage, Olivier III and Amaury, were active on opposite sides in the Breton war of succession that began in 1341 and lost their lives as a consequence. Olivier III in 1330 married Jeanne de Belleville, heiress to important lordships in northern Poitou, just south of the Clisson family lands. After Olivier's execution for treason in 1343, the French crown confiscated their lands. Jeanne fled to England, where her surviving son, Olivier IV (1336–1407), was raised as a partisan of the English-backed claimant to Brittany, fighting on his side in the victorious Battle of Auray (1364) that won him the ducal title as Jean IV.

By this time, Olivier IV had inherited lands given to his mother by the English and had reacquired the vast family holdings previously confiscated by the French. He married Béatrix de Laval, a cousin of Duke Jean, further increasing his wealth and prestige. In the later 1360s, however, Olivier IV grew increasingly hostile to the English and became a strong supporter and military adviser of Charles V of France. By 1370, his estrangement from Jean IV had become a bitter feud that would last for twenty-five years. His sound tactical sense, his expertise with fortifications, and his almost legendary ferocity in battle made him the most prestigious military commander of his day, and after the death of Charles V he became constable of France and a leading councilor of Charles VI.

In his twelve years as constable, Clisson headed a political faction known as the Marmousets, who opposed the dukes of Berry and Burgundy at the French court. In 1392, he was the intended victim of a bungled assassination attempt that the king blamed on the duke of Brittany. On the ensuing punitive expedition against Jean IV, Charles VI became psychotic, and the royal dukes quickly seized power and ousted Clisson from the office of constable.

Returning to Brittany, Clisson waged bitter war against the duke until 1395, in alliance with his sons-in-law, Alain VIII de Rohan and Jean de Blois, count of Penthièvre, who had married his daughters Beatrix and Marguerite, respectively. After peace was made, he returned to ducal favor but continued to annoy Jean IV and Jean V with litigation until his death on April 23, 1407, his seventy-first birthday.

The last male member of the family, Olivier IV had amassed a great fortune, and some of Europe's most important figures owed money to his estate. Through his older daughter, the Rohan family acquired two-thirds of this wealth and became the greatest noble family of Brittany. Olivier's younger daughter, the countess of Penthièvre, inherited her father's propensity for feuding and litigation and brought ruin on her family by inducing her sons to kidnap Jean V in 1420.

John Bell Henneman, Jr.

[See also: AURAY; BRITTANY; CONSTABLE OF FRANCE; CRAON; HUNDRED YEARS' WAR; JEAN IV; MARMOUSETS]

Bruel, François-Louis. "Inventaire de meubles et de titres trouvés au château de Josselin à la mort du connétable de Clisson (1407)." *Bibliothèque de l'École des Chartes* 66 (1905): 193–245.

Buteau, Michèle. "La naissance de la fortune de Clisson." Unpublished *Mémoire de Maîtrise*, Université de Vincennes, 1970 (available at Vannes, Archives Départementales du Morbihan).

Gicquel, Yvonig. *Olivier de Clisson, connétable de France ou chef du parti breton?* Paris: Picollec, 1981.

Henneman, John Bell. "Reassessing the Career of Olivier de Clisson, Constable of France." In *Law, Custom, and the Social Fabric in Medieval Europe: Essays in Honor of Bruce Lyon*, ed. Bernard Bachrach and David Nicholas. Kalamazoo: Medieval Institute, 1990, pp. 211–33.

Lefranc, Abel. *Olivier de Clisson, connétable de France.* Paris: Retaux, 1898.

CLOCKS AND TIMEKEEPING. Devices to measure and indicate time are descended from astronomical instruments and, like most complex devices, tend to have a history that is international in character. The emergence of a purely mechanical timekeeper in the 14th century, the weight-driven clock, marks a triumph of medieval ingenuity. The French contribution to this development seems to have been in the construction of elegant timepieces and the refinement of mechanisms originally invented elsewhere in Europe.

Monastic houses served as the context out of which mechanical clocks developed. Water clocks with alarm mechanisms attached were used from the 11th century onward to awaken the brothers for midnight services. The rules of Saint-Victor in Paris, for example, made the registrar, a subsacristan, responsible for calibrating and adjusting the water clock, while archaeological remains of Saint-Villers abbey dated 1267–68 show a detailed tablet on stone for this task. The only surviving manuscript illustration of a medieval water clock is found in a French *Bible moralisée* of ca. 1285. In his addition to the *Roman de la Rose*, Jean de Meun shows Pygmalion as possessing domestic versions of these alarm "clocks."

The earliest known examples of purely weight-driven clocks are English (Norwich, 1325; Saint Albans, ca. 1330) and Italian (Milan, 1333?; Padua, 1364), but the speed with which these new devices spread was remarkable. Their acceptance was no doubt enhanced by the fact that the weight-driven mechanism could be made quite large and could drive all manner of ancillary machinery, especially puppet jackwork and bell-ringing devices. The new clocks quickly became objects of royal, noble, and municipal pride, either in the form of gigantic tower clocks or fine miniature chamber clocks. Froissart's poem *L'orloge amoureus* (1369) describes the new machine in detail and praises it lavishly. The cathedral at Strasbourg had an elaborate astronomical clock whose fame extended the breadth of Europe. To punish the rebellious burghers of Courtrai, Philip the Bold of Burgundy in 1382 confiscated their tower clock and put it to use in his own capital, Dijon. An inventory of the possessions of King Charles V in 1380 gives evidence of several chamber clocks in fine metalwork. A similar inventory of 1430 shows the first evidence for spring-driven clocks among the possessions of the duke of Burgundy.

The making of astronomical clocks, timekeepers accurate enough to be useful for observational purposes, was the epitome of the clockmaker's craft. Jean Fusoris (ca. 1365–1436), a physician and canon at Reims and later at Notre-Dame in Paris, was also the headmaster of a shop making instruments and clocks. His astronomical timepiece for the chapter at Bourges (ca. 1423) functioned until the 19th century.

In France, the clock was also adopted as a symbol of the virtue of temperance and the quality of wisdom. Manuscript illuminations of Christine de Pizan's *Épistre Othea* (ca. 1400) show Temperance adjusting a large clock. The image became conventional in Burgundy toward 1450, when Temperance came to be shown with clock, bridle and bit, spurs, eyeglasses, and a windmill. A French translation of Heinrich Suso's *Horlogium Sapientiae*, done in the early 1460s, shows Solomon as a clock repairman and Lady Wisdom surrounded by timekeeping instruments. These illustrations show how integral the clock had become to the European sense of order in natural and human affairs.

Bert S. Hall

Bedini, Silvio, and F. Maddison. *Mechanical Universe: The Astrarium of Giovanni de'Dondi.* Philadelphia: American Philosophical Society, 1966.

Drover, C.B. "The Thirteenth-Century 'King Hezikiah' Water Clock." *Antiquarian Horology* 12 (1980).

Landes, David. *Revolution in Time: Clocks and the Making of the Modern World.* Cambridge: Harvard University Press, 1984.

Poulle, Émanuel. *Un constructeur d'instruments astronomiques au XVe siècle: Jean Fusoris.* Paris: Champion, 1963.

White, Lynn T., Jr. "The Iconography of *Temperantia* and the Virtuousness of Technology." In *Action and Conviction in Early Modern Europe: Essays in Memory of E.H. Harbison*, ed. Theodore K. Rabb and Jerrold E. Seigel. Princeton: Princeton University Press, 1969.

CLOTAR II (584–629). The son of Chilperic I and Fredegunde, Clotar II reunified the Merovingian kingdoms in 613 and passed on the kingdom intact to his son Dagobert I. It was during Clotar's reign that the Frankish aristocracy emerged as a major partner with the monarchy in the administration of the kingdom.

Clotar II succeeded to the kingship at the age of four months, upon the assassination of his father. Fredegunde held together a reduced kingdom for him until he came of age. After 600, he repeatedly tried and failed to take over Austrasia and Burgundy. But in 612, as Brunhilde fell from power, the magnates of those regions accepted Clotar as king, and he ordered the execution of Brunhilde after her capture (613). Immediately afterward, in October 614, Clotar held a great council of lay and ecclesiastical leaders at Paris; the edict issued in this assembly confirmed the power that local nobles had acquired over the appointment of both bishops and secular officials. Under Clotar II, Neustria, Austrasia, and Burgundy each usually had its own administration under a mayor of the palace. Clotar recognized the Austrasian desire for autonomy by associating his son Dagobert I with him as subking there in 622.

Steven Fanning

[See also: AUSTRASIA; BRUNHILDE; FREDEGUNDE; MEROVINGIAN DYNASTY]

Wallace-Hadrill, J.M., trans. *The Fourth Book of the Chronicle of Fredegar with Its Continuations.* London: Nelson, 1960.
James, Edward. *The Franks.* Oxford: Blackwell, 1988.
Wallace-Hadrill, J.M. *The Long-Haired Kings and Other Studies in Frankish History.* London: Methuen, 1962, pp. 206–31.
Wood, Ian. *The Merovingian Kingdoms, 450–751.* London: Longman, 1994.

CLOTHING, COSTUME, AND FASHION. Medieval clothing in Gaul was a combination of earlier Germanic apparel with Roman fashions introduced during the Roman occupation of Gaul (52 B.C.–ca. A.D. 486). The Frankish settlers protected themselves against the cold by wearing tight-fitting garments and fur mantles and wrapping their legs in skins. The Romans introduced looser-fitting tunics and more flowing garments for both men and women.

Peasants wore working shoes with heavy soles (often of wood), a snood cap fastened under the chin, a leather belt over a simple knee-length smock (*sayon*), usually of linen, and wrapped leg coverings. Their clothing, which is well represented on the calendar pages of books of hours and in sculpted Labors of the Months, changed little throughout the medieval period.

Dress for the upper classes varied more from epoch to epoch. The Merovingian period appropriated many items of earlier Gallo-Roman dress, notably the flowing tunic and mantle. The tunic extended in ample folds to the ground and was generally gathered by a large belt or girdle, which could be adjusted for a longer or shorter waist. Multiple tunics were often worn, with the sleeves of the undertunic extending to the wrist, while those of the outer tunic, of a different color, ended at the elbow. The mantle was full and open in the front; it was secured by a clasp or brooch, often at the shoulder. Women wore a square of white or colored material over the head, secured by a circlet, often ornamented with jewels. Hair was worn long and usually braided; for festive occasions, it was intertwined with ribbons and gold threads. Heavy necklaces of gold disks, brooches of enamelwork or encrusted with precious and semiprecious stones, earrings set with stones cut *en cabochon*, rings, and bracelets were all favored by upper-class women. Colors were bright and showy. Rich materials from the Byzantine East, combining Christian symbols and floral patterns in elaborate pictorial and geometric designs, were highly favored. Sometimes, both warp and weft were linen, but linen and wool were often used in combination. Silk was especially prized.

In the Carolingian period, fashion changed little: long doubled tunics were still in vogue, as were the rich eastern materials. Edges of mantles and tunics were frequently trimmed with wide bands of embroidery; jewel-studded girdles were worn just above the hips. Women still wore their hair long and braided, but after the 8th century it became fashionable to hide the hair under long veils or hoods.

With the advent of the Capetians (987), styles became simpler and more severe. Men and women both adopted the *bliaut*, a long straight garment with flowing sleeves. The dress for men consisted of a thigh-length *bliaut* over a linen shirt with long sleeves; linen, wool, or silk hose (*chausses*) in a solid color or striped horizontally with various hues; and a mantle or cloak. The *bliaut* was gathered by a leather belt; the bejeweled belts and heavy necklaces of earlier periods were abandoned. The sleeves of the *bliaut* were wide and funnel-shaped until ca. 1080–90, when they were drawn tightly against the wrists. The mantle was fastened with leather bands decorated with fringes and clasped at the right shoulder. The male *bliaut* remained short for the 11th century but was lengthened in the 12th, with the result that men's and women's fashions were nearly identical until the late 13th century, consisting for both sexes of *chainse*, *bliaut*, and *manteau*.

Women wore two dresses, one over the other. The underdress, called a *chainse* or *chemise*, was slash-waisted, long-sleeved, and trailing to the ground; it was made of fine linen, silk chiffon, or cotton knit. The outer *bliaut* was close-fitting at the waist, flared at the hips, with full and open sleeves. The collar was decorated with embroidered designs. The torso of the overlayed dress was worn close to the body and was gathered at the sides. A long silk, wool, linen, or leather belt worn on the *bliaut* was wrapped twice around the waist and then reached the floor. After the 11th century, the sleeves became longer and funnel-shaped, allowing the *chemise* underneath to be seen. The *bliaut* was fastened at the waist by a double belt of cloth, tied now instead of sporting a bejeweled buckle. The mantle was generally fastened in the center at the breast, and a fine linen veil, which also covered the neck and shoulders, was worn on the head. This veil was the precursor to the wimple. Women still wore their hair long and parted in the middle, with two braids, sometimes joined in the back and often intertwined with ribbons, trailing nearly to the ground.

The Crusades in the 12th century introduced fashions and fabrics of oriental origin: silk became more widely used, and cotton materials were first used in France. New materials included *samite*, a heavy silk; *cendal*, a thinner silk like that of today; *pers*, a blue material; *camelin*, a camel's-hair fabric; cotton *fustaine*; and woven-wool *serge*. The crusading knight wore a short *bliaut* over his armor, usually decorated with the Crusader's Cross and gathered at the waist by a cloth or leather belt. Another fashion introduced by the crusaders and pilgrims was the wearing of a purse (*ausmoniere*) attached to the belt or girdle; it was often distinguished by lavish needlework. Fashion demands in the wake of the Crusades became so exacting that it became profitable for the first time for artisans and craftsmen to mass-produce clothing, accessories, and jewelry in specialized workshops in the larger cities of the industrialized north. Trade guilds favored specialization and highly skilled workmanship.

By the 13th century, the *bliaut* was replaced by the *surcot* for both men and women, sometimes with short sleeves, but even sleeveless. For men, it was split in front and extended just below the knees, while for women it was bell-shaped, closed, and floor-length. Women's clothing was now fitted to emphasize the shape of the female body: slim waists, tiny feet, narrow hips, and small bosom. To make the *surcot* more snug above the waistline, it became fashionable to slit the sides of the *chemise* and *surcot* from the waist to the armpit; the openings were then laced, but a little bare flesh was permitted to show. Sleeves were tight at the wrists and were buttoned or sewed together after the garment was put on. The *chemise* could be dipped in saffron for color and to provide a pleasant odor. Gloves as we know them first came into fashion for ladies of the upper nobility in the 12th century. Buttons were used on some clothing from the 13th century, but most medieval clothing was laced or held together by pins and brooches.

In the 13th century, young girls still wore their hair long and unbraided, but women's hair was generally hidden modestly under long veils or wimples. All this began to change late in the 13th century, when elaborate hairdos became the rage. Instead of braids, hair was rolled and worn in a bun either over the ears or behind the head. The bun was retained by a net called a *crispine* or *crispinette*, which for wealthy women might include gold threads or bands. A veil and wimple were sometimes worn over this elaborate hairdo, gathered by a jeweled circlet. Women used white powder and rouge on their faces, and older women might dye their hair to prevent its turning gray.

Extravagances in dress were condemned by moralists and religious leaders, and sumptuary laws were passed limiting the varieties and numbers of items of clothing a person could own. But even the saintly Louis IX admonished his courtiers to dress well, so that their wives would cherish them more and their people respect them.

In the late 14th century, male courtiers adopted a much shorter form of clothing, a doublet over long tight hose, which would remain in vogue until the 17th century. Although this was the first step in the direction of modern dress, the sharp break with the past brought accusations of indecency. The hose were made of expensive fabrics and were often particolored—that is, a different color was used for each leg. However, the long *bliaut* did not entirely disappear, as elderly men and even the kings from Philip VI to Charles V preferred traditional dress, particularly in the wake of Pope John XXII's condemnation of modern clothing as indecent. Imitating the kings, judges, lawyers, university intellectuals, and administrators all wore the long traditional robes, as did commoners and bourgeois. Only fashionable courtiers wore the effete shorter clothing.

Thin-soled leather shoes were a mark of distinction, being worn only by the wealthy. Sandals and wooden clogs were worn by commoners and peasants. Shoe shapes were simple and practical through the 13th century, but in the 14th century the mode was for pointed toes, which became exaggeratedly long in the *poulaine*, whose point was turned up like a ship's prow. Toes were often stuffed to maintain their shape. In the late 15th century appeared the *hennin* for women, a towering conical headdress as much as a yard tall; it was worn inclined to the rear, and from its peak fluttered a thin veil. The first of the high, elaborate hairdos to gain notoriety was the two-horned *escoffion*, popular ca. 1380–1410.

Because of the abundance of late-medieval tapestries, books of hours, and similar visual sources, the fashions of the 15th century are those most remembered today. All of the luxury fabrics, such as damask, brocade, and velvet from Florence, were widely used, along with imitations of oriental silks that were fabricated in Lyon and Tours after the opening of fabric workshops there under Louis XI in 1466 and in 1480. The dukedom of Burgundy was particularly wealthy and reputed for its magnificent fashions.

Donald L. Wright, Jr.

[See also: ARMOR AND WEAPONS; CLOTHING, JEWISH; JEWELRY AND METALWORKING; TEXTILES; VESTMENTS, ECCLESIASTICAL; WOOL TRADE]

Beaulieu, Michèle. *Le costume antique et médiéval*. 4th ed. Paris: Presses Universitaires de France, 1967.

———. "Le vêtement." In *La France et les Français*. Encyclopédie de la Pléiade (1981), pp. 237–52.

———, and Jeanne Baylé. *Le costume en Bourgogne de Philippe le Hardi à la mort de Charles le Téméraire (1364–1477)*. Paris: Presses Universitaires de France, 1956.

Demay, Germain. *Le costume au moyen âge d'après les sceaux*. Paris: Dumoulin, 1880.

Ruppert, Jacques. *Le costume*. 5 vols. Paris: Flammarion, 1931, Vol. 1: *L'antiquité et le moyen âge*.

CLOTHING, JEWISH. The Fourth Lateran Council of 1215 forced Jews to wear a distinguishing mark on their clothing that in France often took the form of a circular badge of red and white. Otherwise, their clothing was much like that worn by Christians, since religiously mandated elements of everyday dress were relatively few, strongly conservative, and for the most part unobtrusive. A beard and sidelocks (*pe'ot*) were traditionally required for men, but in the Middle Ages they were never exaggerated in the manner of those worn by Hasidic men in eastern Europe in the 16th to 20th centuries. Fringes (*ziziot*) knotted in a specific way were required on each corner of any four-cornered garment worn by a man; since few medieval garments were four-cornered, medieval Jews regularly wore a special fringed undergarment (*arbah kanfot, tallit kattan*) to ensure the observance of the commandment. Headcovering practices varied widely in medieval France, so except for certain occasions Jews would not have been particularly distinguishable on this basis.

Jewish women had no distinctive clothing *per se*, but married women were required to cover the hair, and men and women alike were enjoined to dress modestly. Both men and women were also prohibited from using certain fabrics by the biblical injunction against the commingling of wool and linen in garments.

Thus, Jews would not have stood out dramatically from their neighbors. Christian illuminators often needed to invent exotic, orientalizing, or bizarre garb when they wished to identify Jews in a negative or mocking way. Yet Jews observed another, less obvious admonition with regard to clothing, based on a traditional interpretation of Leviticus 18:3, which prohibits the emulation of the practices of the "nations" among which Jews find themselves. This was interpreted by medieval teachers, following Talmudic dicta, as a prohibition of the hairstyles, the fashions of dress, and the customs of headcovering of the dominant population. As a result, the garments of the masses throughout the Middle Ages seem to have been relatively conservative due to a concerted attempt at retrograde fashion in order to stay "a few steps behind" the Christian population and thus distinguish themselves.

Christian manuscripts tend to depict such Jews: mostly men appear, and these are bearded. If they are intended to represent the tormentors of Jesus, or the collective "Jews" of the New Testament narrative, they wear homespun, peasant-style clothes, breeches, tunics, occasionally hooded. Their heads are covered by soft-peaked hats or hoods turned back. Other biblical Jews—prophets and Pharisees—as well as contemporary Jews are depicted in full-length tunics and cloaks, generally fastened at the shoulder.

Strikingly different is the image we receive from medieval Jewish manuscripts. There, Jews of both sexes wear tunics, cinched at the waist with belts or accompanied by an outer coat with tapering sleeves. Women's hairdress is varied and in some cases quite fashionable, utilizing hair nets, hats, and chin pieces in much the same way, though with some time lag, as such elements were popular in England and France. Though married women are inevitably depicted with hair covered, Jewish manuscripts give the impression that men went bareheaded most of the time.

The manuscript depictions are confirmed in the biblical and Talmudic commentaries of Rashi (ca. 1039–1104), which provide details of Jewish dress, as well as some description of the processes of tailoring, laundering, and perfuming garments. Although information about clothing is never systematically presented in his commentaries, it is from his work in particular that one gets a sense of

Jewish attitudes toward clothing: clothes, Rashi tells us, honor the man—they constitute his "glory"—and should be well cared for, clean, and neat. Rashi describes three layers of clothes: a shiftlike undergarment, an outer robe with attached hose, and a coat of silk or other material, closed with cords hanging around the waist. He mentions puttees worn about the legs, and kneebreeches for men, belted with a string pulled through a hem about the waist, and presumably worn under the robe. The rounded cloak was known to Rashi, and he mentions cloaks of various weights to accommodate fluctuations in weather.

Rashi describes women's fashion more extensively. He discusses many more hairstyles than can be observed in manuscripts: woolen caps or snoods covered with a thin scarf, lace headdresses, headbands made of gold interlaced with silk threads, hats made of the ribs of feathers, and even hairpins are described in detail. He catalogues a variety of jewlery, from the pins or brooches used to fasten cloaks, to jeweled belts, perfume flasks, strings of pearls, amulets, and chokers to close the necks of gowns. Jewelry made by goldsmiths was peddled from door to door and kept in special jewelry boxes. Women and even young girls had their ears pierced, but girls did not begin to wear earrings until they were older. Rashi disapproves of "immodest" modes of dress. A woman who wears garments with slashed sleeves, so that she goes "'with her armpits uncovered' in the manner of the Gentile women in France, whose [bare] flesh can be seen from their sides" gives her husband grounds for divorce. Here, we can witness both the inherent conservatism fostered by the prohibition of Leviticus 18 and the stratification of Jewish society, in which such garments were worn by certain individuals, particularly those moving in "elite" circles in contact with Christians.

Rashi mentions both soft-laced shoes and harder shoes fastened with a buckle or clasp, all pulled on by means of a loop at the heel. Some shoes are described as having wooden soles, which would have to be planed to even them when they started to wear. To others, iron taps were affixed. There were open-toed and open-backed shoes, and in the case of heavier shoes or poor weather socks were worn.

Certain specialized garments were reserved for liturgical use. The *tallit*, the four-cornered prayer-wrap, with the four requisite *ziziot* and large enough to cover "one's head and most of his body," was worn by the precentor at the synagogue for nearly every liturgical occasion and by all married men at morning prayers in synagogue or the home. In some locales, it was worn by boys from the age of religious majority (age thirteen—called *Bar Mizvah*) and in others by boys even below that age. Each morning, *tefillin*, leather boxes containing verses from the Pentateuch (Exodus 13:1–6; Deuteronomy 6:4, 11:13–21) written by a Torah scribe, were bound by all males above the age of thirteen to the upper arm by leather thongs, and around the forehead, for morning prayers, in accordance with the rabbinic interpretation of Deuteronomy 6:8. Finally, there was the special robe (*sargenes* or *kittel*), symbolic of humility and purity, which both echoed components of the garments of the priests in the Jerusalem Temple and served as one of the actual burial garments. This was worn by men at their weddings and thereafter on the High Holidays, at Passover, and for burial. There was no distinctive clerical dress, although regional custom might dictate variations on the basic themes.

Marc M. Epstein

[See also: CLOTHING, COSTUME, AND FASHION; JEWS; MANUSCRIPTS, HEBREW ILLUMINATED]

Metzger, Therese and Mendel. *Jewish Life in the Middle Ages.* New York: Alpine, 1982.
Rubens, Alfred. *A History of Jewish Costume.* New York: Funk and Wagnalls, 1967.
Shereshevsky, Esra. *Rashi, the Man and His World.* New York: Sepher Hermon, 1982.

CLOVIS I (ca. 466–511). The most important of the Merovingian kings, Clovis I was the unifier of the Franks, the conqueror of most of Gaul, and the real founder of the kingdom of the Franks under Merovingian rule. He was also the first Christian king of the Franks. He is the possessor of a reputation for astonishing ruthlessness, brutality, and unscrupulousness.

Upon the death of his father, Childeric I, in 482, Clovis succeeded as chieftain over the group of Salian Franks settled around Tournai, in modern Belgium. He began his conquests in 486 by defeating Syagrius, an independent ruler over northern Gaul. This victory made Clovis the master of Gaul north of the Loire, the later Neustria, and he transferred his capital to Soissons, accompanied by his Frankish entourage.

The chronology and sequence of events of most of the rest of Clovis's reign are unclear and highly debated. Essentially, he became the sole Frankish king by eliminating the kings of other bands of Salian Franks through attack, treachery, and deceit. By similar means, he also rose to mastery over the Ripuarian, or Rhineland, Franks. Through a series of bitter and closely contested battles, he brought the Alemanni and Thuringians under his authority as well.

In the course of one of his battles against the Alemanni, at Zülpich (Tolbiac) in the mid-490s, Clovis converted to orthodox Christianity. This was not a sudden move, however. Like his father, Childeric, Clovis had been careful to maintain good relations with Christian authorities in his lands, and he had also married an orthodox Christian, the Burgundian princess Clotilde. The conversion of Clovis and some of his followers had little immediate effect on their pagan and polygamous habits, nor did it immediately christianize the Frankish people, but it did make Clovis the hero of orthodox Christians in Gaul.

Clovis exploited this position to gain his greatest victory. He attacked the Arian Visigoths, who controlled Gaul south of the Loire as well as Spain. In 507, Clovis defeated their army at Vouillé, near Poitiers, and in the ensuing campaigns his forces swept over most of southern Gaul. Only the military intervention of Theodoric the Ostrogoth preserved Septimania for the Visigoths and prevented the Franks from gaining the Mediterranean. Nonetheless, Clovis was the master of almost all of Gaul. For a time, he even exacted tribute from the Burgundians.

After the victory over the Visigoths, Clovis was given some sort of official recognition by the Byzantine empire, which began a century-long tradition of Frankish-Byzantine cooperation, and he moved his capital to Paris. The years after 507 saw two of his most notable achievements. It was he who probably issued the Salic Law for his Salian Franks and all those living north of the Loire, and in 511, at Orléans, he presided over the first great church council of the Frankish kingdom.

Clovis was the master of a heterogeneous population. Franks and other Germanic peoples were in the northeast, northern Gaul was Gallo-Roman but relatively barbarized and included Franks as well, and the south was thoroughly romanized. His administration continued Roman practices; Clovis worked closely with the Gallo-Roman aristocrats, while his military was primarily Frankish. Upon his death in 511, in proper Frankish fashion his kingdom was divided equally among his four sons. The Frankish kingdom was not united again until 558, by his youngest son, Clotar I.

Most of our knowledge of Clovis comes from the writings of Gregory of Tours, three-quarters of a century after the king's death. Despite the obvious greed and treachery of his hero, Gregory was impressed by Clovis's promotion of orthodox Christianity, especially in the face of the detested Arians. Gregory hailed Clovis as a new Constantine and praised him in terms borrowed from biblical laud for King David. The name "Clovis," which evolved into the French name "Louis," was itself a French form of his correct Frankish name, Chlodovech (Chlodwig in German).

Steven Fanning

[See also: FRANKS; MEROVINGIAN DYNASTY; POPULAR DEVOTION]

Gregory of Tours. *History of the Franks,* trans. Lewis Thorpe. Harmondsworth: Penguin, 1974.
James, Edward. *The Franks.* Oxford: Blackwell, 1988.
Martindale, J.R. "Chlodovechus (Clovis)." In *Prosopography of the Later Roman Empire.* 3 vols. in 4. London: Cambridge University Press, 1980, Vol. 2: *A.D. 395–527,* pp. 288–90.
Tessier, Georges. *Le baptême de Clovis.* Paris: Gallimard, 1964.
Wood, Ian N. "Gregory of Tours and Clovis." *Revue belge de philologie et d'histoire* 63 (1985): 249–72.
———. *The Merovingian Kingdoms, 450–751.* London: Longman, 1994.

CLUNIAC ORDER. When Duke William I the Pious of Aquitaine (d. 918) and his wife founded the monastery of Cluny in 909, it was not with the expectation that they were founding an order. Rather, they were establishing a monastery like several that had already been established in Burgundy in the second half of the 9th century, such as Vézelay and Pouthières, where monks of a regular life would live and pray, at least theoretically free from the outside interference of bishop or count.

Cluny followed the Benedictine *Rule,* but like all Benedictine houses it adopted its own particular customs, or *consuetudines,* which regulated many of the details of daily life not spelled out in the *Rule.* At Cluny, tremendous emphasis was given to the liturgy, including prayers for the dead—both monks and secular friends of the monastery. As the reputation of the monks' holiness spread, laypeople made generous gifts to the monastery, hoping to be associated with the monks and with St. Peter, their patron. It also became increasingly common for a layperson who controlled a monastery that had lost its regularity of life to give it to the abbot of Cluny for reform. In such a case, Cluny's abbot would become abbot, at least temporarily, of this monastery as well as of Cluny. Such a practice had a long history; houses needing reform had long been put under the direction of the abbot of a nearby house of undoubted regularity. When Cluny was first founded, its abbot, Berno, continued to be abbot of Baume, his original house, even though Cluny and Baume had separate abbots after his death. During the 10th century, Cluny's abbots undertook the reform of some several dozen houses, many in Italy or in Auvergne. In the late 10th and 11th centuries, many old monasteries in Burgundy, closer to Cluny, were similarly reformed. Although some, such as Paray-le-Monial or La Charité, remained permanently under Cluny's abbot, many others, such as Saint-Bénigne of Dijon or Bèze, had their own abbots again after a short period. In the late 11th century, other monasteries, like Vézelay, were added to the lists of dependent abbeys that popes periodically confirmed to Cluny, even though they always had their own abbots. In the 12th century, perhaps 1500 houses can be considered Cluniac.

By the first generation of the 12th century, however, the Cluniacs were being outcompeted for the affections of their Burgundian secular neighbors by the new order of the Cistercians. Though Cluny had not declined from its own standards of holiness, many people, both monastic and lay, were arguing that true spirituality lay in poverty more than in liturgical observance. Cluny's magnificent church, the largest in Christendom, was completed in the first decade of the century, and laypeople continued to make gifts to the house, but the overall level of generosity never again achieved that of ca. 1000, as potential donors made more of their gifts to the new monastic orders or to the regular canons.

Abbot Peter the Venerable of Cluny (r. 1122–56) carried out a long correspondence with Abbot Bernard of Clairvaux (r. 1115–53), the most visible spokesman of the Cistercian order, on the relative merits of their ways of monastic life. Although Bernard always argued that the Cistercians were more austere and closer to Benedict's *Rule*, the two men became friends, and, partly in imitation of the Cistercians, Peter adopted some of their system of economic organization to deal with financial difficulties at Cluny.

By the end of the 12th century, again in imitation of Cîteaux, Cluniac monasteries were for the first time being organized into a true order, with institutionalized relations among the houses that followed Cluny's interpretation of Benedictine monasticism. This organization took its final form in 1231, and chapters-general and organized regional leadership took the place of the personal relations between Cluny's abbot and the monasteries affiliated with Cluny. During the 14th and 15th centuries, economic dif-

ficulties multiplied, and a number of powerful men with no interest in furthering the monastic life took the post of abbot.

Constance B. Bouchard

[See also: *BENEDICT, RULE OF ST.*; CISTERCIAN ORDER; CLUNY; HUGUES DE CLUNY; MONASTICISM; ODILO; ODO; PETER THE VENERABLE]

Bernard, Auguste, and Alexandre Bruel, eds. *Recueil des chartes de l'abbaye de Cluny.* 6 vols. Paris: Imprimerie Nationale, 1876–1903.

Hallinger, Kassius, ed. *Consuetudines Cluniacensium antiquiores cum redactionibus derivatis.* Sieburg: Schmitt, 1983.

Maurier, Martin and André Duchesne, eds. *Bibliotheca Cluniacensis.* Mâcon: Protat, 1915.

Peter the Venerable. *The Letters of Peter the Venerable*, ed. Giles Constable. Cambridge: Harvard University Press, 1967.

Bouchard, Constance B. "Merovingian, Carolingian and Cluniac Monasticism: Reform and Renewal in Burgundy." *Journal of Ecclesiastical History* 41 (1990): 365–88.

Constable, Giles. "Cluniac Administration and Administrators in the 12th Century." In *Order and Innovation in the Middle Ages: Essays in Honor of Joseph R. Strayer*, ed. William C. Jordan, Bruce McNab, and Teofilo F. Ruiz. Princeton: Princeton University Press, 1976, pp. 17–30.

Hunt, Noreen. *Cluny Under Saint Hugh, 1049–1109.* Notre Dame: University of Notre Dame Press, 1968.

Rosenwein, Barbara H. *Rhinoceros Bound: Cluny in the 10th Century.* Philadelphia: University of Pennsylvania Press, 1982.

———. *To Be the Neighbor of Saint Peter: The Social Meaning of Cluny's Property, 909–1949.* Ithaca: Cornell University Press, 1989.

CLUNY. Though the great monastery of Cluny (Saône-et-Loire) is in ruins today, it is important historically for the tremendous influence it had as both a political and an economic center. Kenneth John Conant dedicated his life to the study of the site, and it is through his reconstructions that one can understand the monastic complex as it once was.

The community was founded in 909 by Duke William I the Pious of Aquitaine and his wife, with Berno (r. 910–27), abbot of nearby Baume, as the first abbot. Berno constructed the first church on the site, Cluny I (915–27). No archaeological remains indicate the structure of this original church. Berno's successor, St. Odo (r. 927–42), obtained papal privilege to bring other monasteries under the authority of Cluny. The expansion of the order under Odo necessitated the need for a larger church. In 955, construction of Cluny II was begun (dedicated 981, completed ca. 1040). The church had a seven-bay nave, side aisles, and a narthex. It was crossed by a long and narrow transept and ended in a long choir complex with stepped apses. The building was probably barrel-vaulted. The most influential abbot from this period was St. Odilo (r. 994–1049), who was instrumental in peacemaking efforts of bishops and kings and instituted the feast of All Souls.

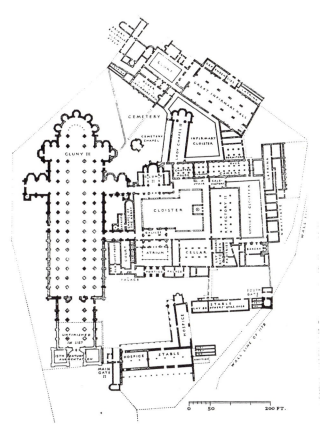

Cluny (Saône-et-Loire), plan of monastery, ca. 1157. After Conant.

Cluny, abbey church, reconstructed view by Kenneth J. Conant. *Courtesy of Medieval Academy of America.*

Nothing remains of Cluny II, but small churches like the nearby Chapaize (ca. 1050) and Romainmoutier in Switzerland (ca. 1080) probably reflect, on a modest scale, its appearance.

Cluny reached its apogee under the direction of St. Hugues de Cluny (r. 1049–1109). By the 1080s, there were 200 monks at Cluny, as opposed to seventy in 1042, and the decision was made to build a third, larger church. The massive Cluny III was begun under Hugues's direction in 1088; its main altar was consecrated by Pope Urban II in 1095, and most of the church, except the nave vaults, was finished by the time of Hugues's death in 1109. The church was completed in 1130, when it was dedicated by Innocent II. During this period of power and prestige, Cluny had some 1,500 daughter houses throughout France, Germany, and Spain.

From porch to apse, Cluny III extended 455 feet (an addition to the porch was made in the 12th century and augmented in the 13th, resulting in a total length of 617 feet). The eleven-bay nave was flanked by double aisles. The eastern end of the nave was intersected by two transepts of unequal length, thus creating a plan based on the shape of the archiepiscopal cross. Two chapels extended from each transept arm and the apsed ambulatory had five radiating chapels. Covered by a system of pointed arches and barrel vaulting, the building reached an astounding

height of almost 100 feet at its peak. Light entered the church on three levels: directly through the clerestory windows, indirectly through the high windows under the groin vaults of the inner aisles, and through the lower windows of the outer aisles. On the basis of measurements made on the site and the study of 18th-century plans, Conant has concluded that the master of Cluny III followed the proportional principles of the Golden Section.

The exterior silhouette of the building was articulated by four principal bell towers, one square (over the crossing of the main transept) and three octagonal (capping the small transept, and atop the arms of the main transept). Towers on the western façade were erected after 1200.

Nine capitals from the hemicycle in the sanctuary of the choir survive in the Musée du Farinier at Cluny. These date probably from the first quarter of the 12th century and represent biblical scenes, the Seasons, the Virtues, and the Tones of Plainsong. Though sculptural remains from Cluny III are scant, ornamentation at other Romanesque churches in Burgundy can provide a sense of its once extensive decorative program.

Under the abbacy of Hugues, the rest of the monastic complex was greatly expanded, on a scale proportional to that of the new monumental church. A large hospice (36 by 163 feet) was built in the great forecourt of the monastery, as was a stable at least 100 feet long. In 1080, the

Cluny (Saône-et-Loire), abbey church, south transept. *Photograph courtesy of Whitney S. Stoddard.*

refectory for the monks was trebled in size and decorated with an immense fresco painting of the Last Judgment.

Cluny's last great abbot was Peter the Venerable (r. 1122–56), who gave sanctuary to Abélard and engaged in debates with Bernard of Clairvaux concerning Cluniac and Benedictine observance.

Ravaged by the Wars of Religion and progressively demolished for its stone between 1798 and 1812, almost nothing of Cluny III survives save the south tower of the main transept and a later side chapel built by Cardinal de Bourbon in the Burgundian Gothic style (1456). One can, however, gain a sense of this once magnificent Romanesque basilica through smaller-scale churches apparently close in style, such as Paray-le-Monial and the cathedral at Autun.

Nina Rowe

[See also: AUTUN; BRUNO; CLUNIAC ORDER; CONSTRUCTION TECHNIQUES; HUGUES DE CLUNY; ODILO; ODO; PARAY-LE-MONIAL; PETER THE VENERABLE; SOUVIGNY]

Conant, Kenneth John. *Cluny: les églises et la maison du chef d'ordre.* Mâcon: Protat, 1968.
Current Studies on Cluny. Special issue of *Gesta* 27.1/2 (1988).
Magnien, Émile. *Cluny, l'abbaye, la ville, la région: guide historique et touristique.* Mâcon: Combier, 1957.
Virey, Jean. *L'abbaye de Cluny.* Paris: Laurens, 1950.

COATS OF ARMS. *See* ARMS, HERALDIC

CODEX CALIXTINUS. *See* LIBER SANCTI JACOBI

CŒUR, JACQUES (ca. 1395–1456). The most important businessman of medieval France, Jacques Cœur was born into a wealthy family in Bourges. By 1430, he was established as a financier, merchant, and master of France's Levantine trade, and he soon became a favorite of Charles VII. Royal *argentier* after 1438 and ennobled after 1441, he reorganized Valois coinage and finances and served as royal commissioner in financial and commercial negotiations. His vast financial, commercial, and industrial empire eventually made him the wealthiest man in Europe. During this period, he built a house in Bourges that symbolized his magnificence and remains a monument of Gothic architecture. His most significant public action was to finance the reconquest of Normandy and Guyenne, but by 1451 his wealth and pride had won him the envy and resentment of both crown and nobility. Charles VII found it easier to ruin than repay his greatest creditor. Arrested on the absurd charge of having poisoned the king's mis-

Bourges (Cher), Hôtel Jacques Coeur, courtyard. *Photograph courtesy of Whitney S. Stoddard.*

tress, Agnès Sorel, Jacques Cœur was condemned for ir- regularities in fact typical of contemporary public finance. His holdings were confiscated by the crown, and he was imprisoned until 1454, when he escaped to Rome, where Calixtus III gave him command of a papal fleet. He died on campaign against the Turks at Chios in November 1456.

Paul D. Solon

[See also: BOURGES; CHARLES VII]

Dauvet, Jean. *Les affaires de Jacques Cœur: journal du Procureur Dauvet, procès-verbaux de séquestre et d'adjudication*, ed. Michel Mollat, Anne-Marie Yvon-Briand, Yvonne Lanhers, Constantin Marinesco. 2 vols. Paris: Colin, 1952–53.
Kerr, Albert Boardman. *Jacques Cœur: Merchant Prince of the Middle Ages.* New York: Scribner, 1927.
Mollat, Michel. *Jacques Cœur.* Paris: Aubier, 1988.

COINS/COINAGE. *See* CURRENCY

COLIN MUSET (fl. 2nd third of the 13th c.). Trouvère- jongleur of the second third of the 13th century. Colin has been credited with a score of lyrics, varied in genre and unusually reflective of the poet's life; about half survive with music. He was from Lorraine, of humble condition, and made his living as an itinerant entertainer. Colin was inventive in compositional form and original in substance, less concerned with the constraints of courtly love than with the delights, real or imagined, of a freer sensuality. Apart from love, his themes include the pleasures of the table, spring, and revery, the satisfactions and difficulties of a minstrel's calling, the avarice of some patrons, the animation of tournaments. The texts are striking in their relatively abundant concrete detail and unhindered self- expression; the genres are no less so, including as they do such rare ones as the *lai/descort* and *reverdie*. Colin Muset is perhaps the most markedly individual of the trouvères.

Samuel N. Rosenberg

[See also: TROUVÈRE POETRY]

Colin Muset. *Les chansons de Colin Muset*, ed. Joseph Bédier. 2nd ed. Paris: Champion, 1938.
Rosenberg, Samuel N., and Hans Tischler, eds. *Chanter m'estuet: Songs of the Trouvères.* Bloomington: Indiana University Press, 1981, pp. 450–64.
van der Werf, Hendrik, ed. *Trouvères-Melodien II.* Kassel: Bärenreiter, 1979, pp. 435–45.

COLMAR. Located on the plain of Alsace near the foot- hills of the Vosges, Colmar (Haut-Rhin) dates back to at least the 13th century and possibly much earlier. Although the date of the first Christian settlement in the south of Alsace has not been attested, it is known that in 823 Benedictine monks of the abbey of Münster arrived, and they had founded a religious establishment west of the Harbourg by 865. A charter from the 10th century records a donation from Empress Adelaïde for the foundation of the priory of Saint-Pierre. Among the many medieval build- ings that have been preserved are the church of Saint- Martin, a cloister and chapel of a former Dominican mon- astery now incorporated in the Musée d'Unterlinden, a Franciscan house (now Saint-Matthieu), and a second church associated with the Dominicans.

The present Saint-Martin (1237–1366) replaced a 10th-century church. The transept was built first, followed by the nave, and then the choir near the end of the 14th century. The transept and nave seem to be the work of one architect, perhaps Master Humbert. In fact, on the south side a statue of Master Humbert with his square drawing- board adorns the portal of Saint-Nicolas. The nave com- prises six bays, flanked by aisles on the north and south. The 14th-century octagonal choir by Guillaume de Marbourg features three bays, a series of interconnecting chapels, and an octagonal chevet and is surrounded by an ambulatory, unusual for Alsace. Four columns stationed at the crossing support 15th-century vaulting. Sculpted tym- pana, the Adoration of the Magi and the Last Judgment, rose windows, and windows with triple and double lan- cets adorn the façades. Medieval sculpture on display in- cludes a 13th-century and a 14th-century Virgin and Child, figures of the Apostles (14th c.), and Crucifixion with the Virgin and St. John (14th c.).

To the northwest, the Musée d'Unterlinden incorpo- rates the cloister and chapel of a former Dominican mon- astery. The chapel contains engravings by Martin Schongauer (ca. 1420–91); panels from the altar frontal of the Dominican church by the School of Schongauer (1480); the Bergheim predella (1460); a diptych of SS. Catherine and Laurence; and a statue of the Annunciation (15th c.). The basement contains, among the museum's archaeologi- cal collection, a Gallo-Roman mosaic (3rd–4th c.).

A second Dominican church was built between 1283 and 1295. Damaged by fire in 1458 and subsequently used as a corn market, the church was completely restored in the late 19th century. The nave, with six bays, is almost square. One of the prominent features of the Dominican church is its stained-glass windows, which depict the life of Christ, the saints with their attributes, and Ulrich and Agnes von Heckenheim, founders of the monastery. In the cloister are frescoes of the Resurrection of Christ, attrib- uted to Urbain Huter (15th c.).

Saint-Matthieu, once a Franciscan church, is located in the north part of Colmar and contains good 14th and 15th century glass and a 15th-century choir screen. Al- though its history reaches back to the 10th century, the present chapel of Saint-Pierre is the work of an 18th-cen- tury architect, J.J. Sarger of Colmar.

E. Kay Harris

Anstett, Peter. *Das Martinsmünster zu Colmar: Beitrag zur Geschichte des gotischen Kirchenbaus im Elsass.* Berlin: Mann, 1966.
Herzog, Émile. *Colmar: guide historique et artistique.* Colmar: Hartmann, 1932.

COLOMBE, JEAN (fl. late 15th c.). A prolific manuscript illuminator active in Bourges from 1463 to ca. 1493. Colombe is best known for the miniatures he painted in the *Très Riches Heures* of the duke of Berry, left incomplete by the Limbourg brothers in 1416, which he finished ca. 1485 for Charles I, duke of Savoy. Among numerous other manuscripts, he illuminated the *Heures de Louis de Laval* (B.N. lat. 920), an *Apocalypse* in the Escorial (I.B.3), and the *Missal de Jean Cœur*, archbishop of Bourges (New York, Pierpont Morgan Library, Glazier 49).

Robert G. Calkins

[See also: MANUSCRIPTS, PRODUCTION AND ILLUMINATION]

Schaeffer, C. "Œuvres du début du la carrière de l'enlumineur Jean Colombe."*Cahiers d'archéologie et d'histoire du Berry* 35 (1973 [1974]): 45–57.
———. "Nouvelles observations au sujet des *Heures de Louis de Laval*." *Arts de l'Ouest* 1–2 (1980): 33–80. [With bibliography.]

COMITES. The *comites* (pl. of Lat. *comes* 'companion'), or "counts," were the chief representatives of royal power on the local level in the Frankish kingdom. Appointed by the king and serving directly under him, the *comites* were virtual viceroys in their districts, the *civitates*. These royal officials of the early Middle Ages gave rise to the counts of the high Middle Ages, who presided over often semi-independent counties, attached to the king by ties of vassalage and perhaps even of loyalty. But they were far removed from the *comtes* of the *ancien régime*, holders of this title of nobility conferred by the king.

The *comites* were originally recipients of the title *comes* from the Roman emperor in recognition of their being close associates, or companions, of his. Constantine the Great (r. 306–37) began to attach official duties to the title. By the 5th century, a great variety of *comites* appeared in the bureaucracy and military, including the *comites civitatum*, who governed the *civitates*, the subdivisions of the province. The Germanic kingdoms created in the territory of the western Roman Empire in the 5th and 6th centuries, including that of the Franks, adopted this official along with the rest of the Roman administration in their lands.

The *comites* served at the pleasure of the king, although they were often members of the local aristocracy. In the *civitas*, they exercised all royal functions. They were delegated the royal *bannum*, the right to command all subjects. They collected tolls and taxes, presided over the royal court (the *mallus* or *placitum*), supervised mints and markets, assembled local levies for the royal armies and sometimes even led them into war. They were generally responsible for law and order. *Comites* served without salary but were compensated by receiving a portion of legal fines and compositions (the *fredus*) and a third of the revenues of specifically reserved royal lands. In the Carolingian period, the *comites* also disseminated and enforced royal capitularies and decrees, as well as administered oaths of fidelity.

In the Germanic regions of the Frankish kingdom, the *comes* was called *grafio*. The *comites* were assisted by *vice comites* (viscounts), whom they appointed, as well as by vicars who administered the subdivisions of the *civitates*.

Steven Fanning

[See also: *CITE*; COUNT/COUNTY; DUKE/DUCHY]

Ganshof, François-Louis. *Frankish Institutions Under Charlemagne*, trans. Bryce and Mary Lyon. New York: Norton, 1968.
James, Edward. *The Origins of France from Clovis to the Capetians, 500–1000*. New York: St. Martin, 1982.
McKitterick, Rosamond. *The Frankish Kingdoms Under the Carolingians, 751–987*. London: Longman, 1983, pp. 87–91.
Murray, Alexander Callander. "The Position of the *Grafio* in the Constitutional History of Merovingian Gaul." *Speculum* 61 (1986): 787–804.

COMMUNE. Communes were sworn associations of rural or urban dwellers designed to provide collective protection from seigneurial authority. The earliest development of self-governing cities occurred in the later 11th century between the Loire and the Rhineland, as well as in northern Italy. A French urban commune typically consisted of a royal charter proclaiming the peace of the city, a belfry, and a town seal that permitted it to deal as a peer with seigneurial powers. Possessing these, a town could then organize and govern itself, generally by means of a mayor and twelve notables (Lat. *scabini*, Fr. *échevins*). The urban territory became officially a "peace zone." Responsibility for enforcing order and judging violators fell to the commune, as did collection of taxes and the payment of dues to the king or local lord. These urban franchises were available to all residents, including those who, fleeing servitude in the countryside, remained for a year and a day.

Economic and political forces at the turn of the millennium set the communal movement in motion. Enterprising lords hoping to develop underpopulated areas attracted immigrants by offering various franchises, thereby providing an escape from the more onerous aspects of the seigneurial *ban*. Those who settled around some privileged fortifications (*bourg*, *cité*, castle) became wealthier and more numerous, overshadowing the habitations of the lay or clerical lords who had first encouraged their association. By the years ca. 1100, conflicts between the growing urban collectivity and the interests of the traditional possessors of power reached a critical stage that dictated new agreements. Where the agglomerations were relatively new, lords granted liberties without much difficulty (Le Huy, 1066). Older urban communities with enlightened lords followed suit. Communal movements often gained support from the monarchy, which, outside its own cities, favored counterweights to its refractory nobility.

The self-assertion of the inhabitants became more violent, however, when lords refused to relinquish traditional authority, and the communal movement took over some of the revolutionary aspects of the Peace of God. Communes engaged all inhabitants in a communal oath, thus substituting a horizontal and egalitarian form of association for the more traditional hierarchical ones of the aristocracy. Within the commune, each member was subservient to the other as a brother. On the ideological level, the notion of "peace" played so fundamental a role that in some charters *pax* and *communa* are synonymous terms.

The word "commune" sometimes had stronger connotations. At Laon in the 12th century, the conservative cleric Guibert de Nogent found it a hateful novelty, while the populace considered it the rallying cry to insurrection. The charter and seal of a city constitute elements of a later, more normative phase of the movement, visible attributes of rights achieved in an era when legal thought played a minor role. The belfry, however, represents the original strength of the movement: the right to sound the bell of alarm and convocation institutionalized the cry of "*communa*," giving members the right to summon the collectivity to deliberate or fight for their peace. Such communes could lead to bloody insurrections, although such violence was not especially common or successful. But their frightening example must have played a role in any negotiation process; and violent hostility between lords and communes recurred throughout the Middle Ages.

Communes continued to form through the 12th and early 13th centuries, and in the reign of Louis IX there were over thirty-five of them in the regions directly north of Paris. They gradually became more established, with a hierarchy of guilds structuring relationships between segments of the population, often concentrating authority in the hands of a clique of ruling families. Communes began to decline after the 13th century, with European economic growth generally. Hardening class distinctions weakened their collective spirit, and communal governments fell into serious debt. By ca. 1300, some cities, such as Sens, Compiègne, Meulan, and Senlis, accusing their leaders of corruption and embezzlement, requested the king and Parlement to dissolve their communes. The disorder and heavy fiscal demands accompanying the Hundred Years' War destroyed some communes but revived the spirit of self-defense and insurrection in others. Although never regaining their institutional weight during the rise of the modern state, communes have retained an almost mythic place in the social imagination of the French.

Richard Landes

[See also: BASTIDE; BOURGEOISIE; *CITÉ*; TOWNS]

Ennen, Edith. *The Medieval Town.* Amsterdam: North-Holland, 1978.

Kennely, Dolorosa. "Medieval Towns and the Peace of God." *Medievalia et Humanistica* 15 (1953): 35–53.

Petit-Dutaillis, Charles. *The French Commune in the Middle Ages,* trans. Joan Vickes, Amsterdam: North-Holland, 1978.

Pirenne, Henri. *Medieval Cities.* Princeton: Princeton University Press, 1925.

Vermeesch, Albert. *Essai sur les origines et la signification de la commune dans le nord de la France (XIe et XIIe siècles).*

Heule: International Commission for the History of Representative and Parliamentary Institutions, 1966.

COMMYNES, PHILIPPE DE (ca. 1447–1511). A member of the Flemish nobility, Commynes was first an important official of Charles the Bold of Burgundy and then afterward served as chamberlain, counselor, and confidant of Louis XI of France. His experiences in both capacities are the subject of his *Mémoires,* written between 1489 and 1498. Commynes's memoirs are one of the first examples of the memoir-as-history, a genre that was to be highly popular in the Renaissance.

Commynes was the son of Colard van den Clyte, a functionary of the dukes of Burgundy. Commynes took his name from Comines near Lille, the holding of his uncle, who raised him from the age of seven. From 1464, he was an intimate adviser of the future Duke Charles the Bold. In July 1472, Commynes defected from the Burgundian side, perhaps for mercenary motives, and entered the service of the king of France, who compensated him with new titles and the holding of Talmont (a territory with 1,700 dependent fiefs), a pension, and, upon his marriage in 1473, the territory of Argenton. The relationship between Louis and Commynes was close; contemporaries noted that he was like the king's alter ego, and as Louis lay paralyzed on his deathbed, Commynes was the only person able to interpret his gestures and noises.

After the death of Louis in 1483, however, Commynes's position deteriorated; he was driven from the court and, between 1487 and 1489, imprisoned. He lost both Talmont and Argenton. In prison, Commynes underwent the religious conversion that explains the moralist tone of his memoirs. Commynes began composing them while still in exile, completing the first five books by 1490. After his rehabilitation, he continued working, completing Book 6 in 1493. Between 1494 and 1495, he accompanied Charles VIII on his disastrous Italian campaign, which became the subject of Book 7. The last book was completed shortly after the death of Charles VIII in 1498.

The *Mémoires* are an eyewitness account of a turbulent and crucial period of French and Flemish history, when the Burgundian dukes were attempting to establish their independence of the kings of France, and the kings were struggling to consolidate and centralize their political control. Commynes's intent was to present events as moral lessons about proper governance; his work is a mirror for princes. He wanted to see rational government and, to that end, to have diplomacy replace reliance on military might. No ruler in this violent age, therefore, was wholly admirable, not even Louis, whom Commynes loved. Commynes deliberately altered events to suit his didactic purposes; the *Mémoires* are factually treacherous. But they do shed light on rapidly changing 15th-century politics and political ideas.

Both the frank and factual quality of the *Mémoires* and its larger philosophical concerns have ensured the popularity of the work. Six manuscripts survive (only one of which contains Book 8), while the first printed edition was published in 1524, only twenty-six years after

Commynes laid down his pen. This has been followed by more than a hundred editions and translations.

Leah Shopkow

[See also: BIOGRAPHY; BURGUNDIAN CHRONICLERS; HISTORIOGRAPHY]

Commynes, Philippe de. *Mémoires*, ed. Joseph Calmette and Georges Durville. 3 vols. Paris: Champion, 1924–25.
———. *Philippe de Commynes: Mémoires*, ed. Bernard de Mandrot. 2 vols. Paris: Picard, 1901–03.
———. *The Memoirs of Philippe de Commynes*, ed. Samuel Kinser, trans. Isabelle Cazeaux. 2 vols. Columbia: University of South Carolina Press, 1969–73.
Dufournet, Jean. *La destruction des mythes dans les "Mémoires" de Philippe de Commynes*. Geneva: Droz, 1966.
———. *La vie de Philippe de Commynes*. Paris: Société d'Édition d'Enseignement Supérieur, 1969.
———. *Études sur Philippe de Commynes*. Paris: Champion, 1975.

COMPAGNIES D'ORDONNANCE. Units of the regular French army established in the 15th century. By 1400, independent mercenary companies had come to dominate warfare. The greatest challenge facing the Valois monarchs became the need to control their own armed forces, which often ravaged France in periods of chaos, such as the *escourcherie* ("slaughter") of 1435. In the spring of 1445, Charles VII disbanded as many of these companies as possible and commissioned a limited number of captains to assemble new commands to be garrisoned in frontier towns where they were to be regularly paid and supplied. These new *compagnies d'ordonnance* were composed of up to a hundred *lances fournies*, each of which theoretically represented one man-at-arms, two archers, and three servants as well as their horses. The key element in the reform was less military than administrative, as the crown worked through regular musters, inspections, and payments by commissioners, comptrollers, and treasurers of war to enhance military discipline. The force never attained its proposed maximum of 12,000 men, *ordonnance* soldiers often relapsed into indiscipline, and the companies sometimes proved more loyal to their commanders than their kings, but they nonetheless represented a dramatic improvement and became the backbone of royal armies for the next century.

These units of heavily armored cavalry and mounted archers were tactically conservative even in the 15th century, but their permanent readiness made them the decisive force in the campaigns of the late Hundred Years' War. Other princes, such as the dukes of Brittany and Burgundy, soon imitated the innovation, and the companies enjoyed rising social and military prestige for the remainder of the century. Appointment to command or serve in the companies became a key form of princely patronage. Such service was ultimately restricted to the most privileged echelons of society. After 1500, the spread of firearms rendered heavy armor useless, and the emergence of modern light-cavalry and infantry formations ended the tactical preeminence of the companies. The traditional characterization of the companies as the first standing army in Europe is perhaps too simplistic, but the significance of the innovation is undeniable. In regularizing military service as a remunerative career, professionalizing the art of war, and providing a device for the cooptation of the medieval aristocracy into the disciplined service of the modern state, they represented a decisive breach with the medieval traditions of war.

Paul D. Solon

[See also: BRIGAND/BRIGANDAGE; CHARLES VII; WARFARE]

Contamine, Philippe. *Guerre, état et société à la fin du moyen âge: études sur les armées des rois de France 1337–1494*. Paris: Mouton, 1972.
———. *War in the Middle Ages*, trans. Michael Jones. London: Blackwell, 1984.
Solon, Paul. "Valois Military Administration on the Norman Frontier, 1445–1461: A Study in Medieval Reform." *Speculum* 51 (1976): 91–111.
Vale, Malcolm G.A. *War and Chivalry: Warfare and Aristocratic Culture in England, France, and Burgundy at the End of the Middle Ages*. Athens: University of Georgia Press, 1981.

COMPLANT/MÉPLANT. The complant, or *méplant*, contract (Lat. *medium vestum*) was used primarily to put land back into cultivation or to convert arable or waste to viticulture, or to make such capital improvements as the construction or repair of mills, although a variation was also used for animal husbandry. Its terms involved a grant of land by owner to laborer for a term of years during which the laborer was to clear it, enclose it and plant vines, or build a mill on it. Generally, costs were borne by the laborer, as were any profits, for the term of the contract. At the end of the term specified (three, five, seven years, or longer), the land with improvements was divided in half between the original owner and the improving laborer, and each henceforth owned half of the holding as an allod. Such contracts were used frequently in the 11th and 12th centuries as a means of instigating reclamation and land improvement.

Constance H. Berman

COMPOSERS, MINOR (14TH CENTURY). Virtually no music manuscripts supply composer attributions until late in the 14th century. Although many early 14th-century composers are named in the texts of two isorhythmic motets (*Musicalis scientia/Sciencie laudabili* and *Apollinis eclipsatur/Zodiacum signis*), we cannot identify specific works by them, except for some isorhythmic motets of Philippe de Vitry and the complete works of Guillaume de Machaut. For the late 14th and early 15th centuries, ascriptions in the Chantilly codex (Chantilly, Musée Condé 564) and the Modena manuscript (Modena, Biblioteca Estense, α.M.5,24) together supply about forty names of composers of French music.

Pierre des Molins and Matheus de Sancto Johanne were with King John II in captivity in England from 1357 to 1359. Pierre's ballade *De ce que foul pense*, probably written in England, was the most widely transmitted musical work of the 14th century. To judge from the style of his five surviving works, Grimace was a contemporary of Machaut (d. 1377). His virelai *A l'arme, a l'arme* exhibits realistic vocal effects, a lover's emergency call to arms to his lady. Jean Vaillant (fl. ca. 1360–90), teacher at a singing school in Paris, may have served John, duke of Berry. His virelai *Par maintes foys*, which imitates birdcalls, was widely transmitted in the 14th century, even supplying the music for a contrafact by Oswald von Wolkenstein. Jean de Susay, active in the 1380s, is represented in Chantilly by one ballade close in style to Machaut and two ballades in a more complex Ars Subtilior style. He is also credited with the composition of one Gloria, possibly written for Avignon.

A center of composition for the Ars Subtilior was the papal court at Avignon. Magister Franciscus may have served under popes Gregory XI and Clement VII and perhaps can be identified as the F. Andrieu who composed a lament on the death of Machaut to texts by Eustache Deschamps, *Armes, amours/O flour des flours*. Pykini, whose virelai in the Chantilly codex was possibly written for Pope Clement VII, probably served at Pamplona in the court of King Charles II of Navarre in the years 1374–87.

Hasprois (fl. 1378–1428), from Arras, who served Clement VII and Benedict XIII from 1393 until 1403, was earlier in the service of King Charles V. One of his ballades, the complex *Puisque je sui fumeux*, was probably written for Eustache Deschamps's society of *fumeux*. Haucourt (fl. 1390–1410) also sang in the chapels of popes Clement VII and Benedict XIII, and Matheus de Sancto Johanne served Clement VII in the years 1382–86. Johannes de Bosco (d. 1406?), a singer in Clement's chapel in 1391, also served Duke Louis I of Anjou, and followed Pope Benedict XIII from court to court later in the century. Other members of the papal choir at Avignon who cultivated complex Ars Subtilior chansons include Goscalch (fl. 1385–95), whose one ballade in Chantilly, *En nul estat*, is rhythmically one of the most complex compositions of the Ars Subtilior, and Philippus de Caserta.

A number of composers represented in the Chantilly codex are linked to the Francophile court of Aragon. Gacian Reyneau served at Aragon from 1398 until 1429. His rondeau *Va t'en mon cuer* looks forward to the simpler style of the early 15th century. Trebol (alias Borlet), composer of the virelai *He, tres doulz roussignol*, served under Martin I of Aragon in 1409. Trebor, perhaps the same person as Trebol, worked for Gaston Phoebus at Foix and later at Aragon under King John I. One of his ballades, *Passerose de beauté*, was written for the wedding of John, duke of Berry, to Jeanne de Boulogne on May 25, 1389. Three of the ten compositions of Solage (fl. 1370–90) were also destined for the duke of Berry. His rondeau *Fumeux fume*, written for Deschamps's society of *fumeux*, exploits surprising chromaticism and a low range unusual in 14th-century music.

Cuvelier (fl. 1372–87), *faiseur* to Charles V of France and author of a chronicle on Bertrand du Guesclin (1387),

composed three complex ballades found in the Chantilly codex. Hymbert de Salinus, a member of the generation of composers who formed the transition from the Ars Subtilior style to the simpler style of the early 15th century, wrote *En la saison*, a ballade on a text by Cuvelier praising Olivier du Guesclin. Philippe Royllart, whose only known composition is the widely transmitted and influential isorhythmic motet *Rex Karole/Letitie pacis* in honor of King Charles V, is another late 14th-century composer of unknown origin.

The Modena manuscript, copied in Bologna in 1410/11, contains French chansons from the courts of popes Alexander V and John XXIII. Matheo da Perugia (d. ca. 1418), an Italian composer who probably assembled the manuscript, is represented by over thirty compositions, at least twenty-two of which are French chansons in 14th-century style. Other Italian composers writing French chansons were associated with the antipope Alexander V; for example, eight French chansons by Anthonello de Caserta are found in the Modena manuscript. His *Beauté parfaite* sets a ballade text by Machaut, and *Dame d'onour* quotes from Vaillant's *Par maintes foys*, evidence of the continuing influence of French music in Italy.

Benjamin Garber

[See also: ARS SUBTILIOR; CESARIS, JOHANNES; CICONIA, JOHANNES; COMPOSERS, MINOR (15TH CENTURY); CORDIER, BAUDE; CUVELIER; EGIDIUS DE MURINO; JACOB DE SENLECHES; MATHEUS DE SANCTO JOHANNE; PHILIPPUS DE CASERTA; TAPISSIER, JOHANNES]

Apel, Willi, ed. *French Secular Compositions of the Fourteenth Century*. 3 vols. N.p.: American Institute of Musicology, 1970–72.

Basso, Alberto, ed. *Dizionario enciclopedico universale della musica e dei musicisti*. 13 vols. Turin: Unione Tipografico-Editrice Torinese, 1983–90.

Greene, Gordon, ed. *French Secular Music*. 5 vols. Monaco: Oiseau-Lyre, 1981–89.

Hirshberg, Jehoash. *The Music of the Late Fourteenth Century: A Study in Musical Style*. Diss. University of Pennsylvania, 1971; Ann Arbor: UMI, 1971.

Sadie, Stanley, ed. *The New Grove Dictionary of Music and Musicians*. 20 vols. London: Macmillan, 1980.

Tomasello, Andrew. *Music and Ritual at Papal Avignon, 1309–1403*. Ann Arbor: UMI Research Press, 1983.

COMPOSERS, MINOR (15TH CENTURY).

Around 200 15th-century composers are known from musical manuscripts across Europe. Over two-thirds of them are French or Franco-Flemish, reflecting the fact that this was an age in which the Franco-Flemish school dominated music in all European countries except England. But it is also a century in which musical manuscripts from France and modern Belgium are in disastrously short supply, as can be seen from the survey of source origins in Vol. 5 of the Illinois *Census-Catalogue*; a vast majority of the surviving sources are from Italy or from eastern countries.

It is also a century in which the composer's name was only intermittently valued. Many musical sources never name a composer: there is no name among the forty-three works of the Chansonnier Cordiforme (Savoy, 1470s), the fifty-six in the Wolfenbüttel chansonnier (Loire Valley, 1460s), or the thirty-three of the Copenhagen chansonnier (Loire Valley, 1470s), to take only three of the most famous manuscripts. Turning to some of the largest manuscripts, we find only three names among the 240 pieces in Trent 91 (northern Italy, 1470s), and the few names among the 106 pieces in the Laborde chansonnier (Loire Valley, mainly 1470s) are nearly all added later.

The names of several important composers survive in only a single manuscript. Without the manuscript Q15 (1420s–30s) in the Bologna conservatory, we would know nothing of Johannes de Lymburgia, whose three dozen works evidently had a wide influence, and we would know little of the early sacred work of the leading composer of the time, Guillaume Dufay. Without MS. Canon. Misc. 213 of the Bodleian Library, we would lose the names of over twenty early 15th-century composers and have little idea of the achievement of such major figures as Pierre Fontaine, Nicolas Grenon, Jacobus Vide, Richard Loqueville, and Gilet Velut, not to mention Carmen, Tapissier, and Cesaris, later praised by Martin le Franc as the leading composers in Paris ca. 1400. Without that manuscript, we also would have lost most of the early secular work of both Dufay and Binchois, music that establishes their reputation as the finest song composers of the century.

There is also a fair number of evidently famous and distinguished composers for whom there is no identifiable music. The theorist Tinctoris in the 1470s asks whether there could be anybody who does not know the fine music of Jacobus Carlerius; elsewhere, he mentions Courbet as though he were a household name, an impression reinforced by the position allotted to him in Compère's motet *Omnium bonorum plena* (ca. 1472). Payments for copying entered in two of the most distinguished musical establishments of the century, Cambrai Cathedral and Saint-Donatien in Bruges, mention substantial sacred works by Bauduin Mijs, Pasquin, Rasse de Lavanne, Johannes Fremiel, Alanus de Groote, Petit Jehan, and Heniart; the last two are now known from one slender secular piece each. Gafforius mentions Guillaume Guarnier (fl. 1470s) as *optimus contrapunctista* and names one of his Masses, Vincenzo Calmeta calls him a superb composer who taught the poet Serafino dall'Aquila, and as late as 1548 Heinrich Faber cites him as a composer of the highest distinction. Ramos de Pareja praises his teacher Johannes de Monte, presumably from Mons and perhaps active in the middle years of the century. Other such composers are mentioned in the writings of Simon Greban and Guillaume Crétin. Similarly, the poor source situation may explain why the greatest composer of the late 15th century, Josquin des Prez, was apparently born ca. 1440 though not a note of his music can be dated with any confidence earlier than ca. 1475, when he was already a middle-aged man by the standards of his time.

Moreover, the slender survival of documentary material from 15th-century France means that there are evidently famous composers for whom there is no biographical material. Barbingant may be a classic example: he is known from three songs and two Mass cycles, but his music strongly suggests that he was a substantial influence on the young Ockeghem and probably on Busnoys and Compère as well. There is a good case for believing that Barbingant was the main composer in Paris in the years ca. 1450. Johannes Tourant (fl. 1450–70) has yet to be located in any document, despite an impressive output of three Mass cycles and fifteen smaller pieces, some found in many sources. Yet another example is the prolific Caron.

On another front, there are major courts and churches for which no useful information survives. René d'Anjou had such a fine musical establishment at his death in 1480 that Louis XI appropriated the entire choir and installed it at the Sainte-Chapelle in Paris, remarking that it contained the finest singers of the time. Almost accidental documentation tells us that René was the only man to have served as patron to the two greatest composers of the century, Dufay and Josquin. Only the slenderest information survives about the evidently generous musical patronage of Jean II, duke of Bourbon (d. 1488), though it is all but certain that he employed two of the finest song composers of that generation, Hayne van Ghizeghem and Loyset Compère.

Music history is one of the smallest and most recent humanistic disciplines; many sources of information remain virtually untouched by researchers. Only within the last few years has exploration of the material at Bourges thrown light on the musical patronage of John, duke of Berry, producing the first biographical information on many eminent composers in the Bodleian manuscript. Recent research in the Vatican archives has brought valuable new details about the lives of such figures as Arnold and Hugo de Lantins, Pulloys, and Busnoys.

For all those reasons, it is often hard to qualify a composer as "minor" in the 15th century. Any newly discovered musical source or any newly explored documentary information could radically change the picture, though all those that now seem likely to have been significant have been mentioned here. The reader can find articles in *The New Grove Dictionary* on all known composers before 1450 and most of those from the second half of the century; there is more recent material on some of them, plus a few extra entries, in the *Dizionario enciclopedico universale*. The Illinois *Census-Catalogue* gives full information on the known manuscripts containing their work.

David Fallows

[See also: BASIRON, PHILIPPE; BINCHOIS, GILLES; BRASSART, JOHANNES; BUSNOYS, ANTOINE; CARON, FIRMINUS; CICONIA, JOHANNES; COMPOSERS, MINOR (14TH CENTURY); CORDIER, BAUDE; DUFAY, GUILLAUME; OCKEGHEM, JOHANNES; PULLOYS, JOHANNES; TINCTORIS, JOHANNES]

Basso, Alberto, ed. *Dizionario enciclopedico universale della musica e dei musicisti.* 13 vols. Turin: Unione Tipografico-Editrice Torinese, 1983–90.

Kellman, Herbert, and Charles Hamm, eds. *Census-Catalogue of Manuscript Sources of Polyphonic Music, 1400–1550,*

Compiled by the University of Illinois Musicological Archives for Renaissance Manuscript Studies. 5 vols. Neuhausen: Hänssler, 1979–88.

Sadie, Stanley, ed. *The New Grove Dictionary of Music and Musicians.* 20 vols. London: Macmillan, 1980.

Strohm, Reinhard. *The Rise of European Music, 1380–1500.* Cambridge: Cambridge University Press, 1993.

COMPUTUS. Treatise for calculating the dates of religious festivals, especially Easter. The Catholic church's use of both a solar and lunar calendar made the calculation of the dates of religious festivals a complicated matter; to assist the faithful in these calculations, the *computus* was devised, a work providing the information needed to determine when Easter and other mobile feasts would fall in a given year. Examples exist in Latin, Bede's *De temporum ratione* (725) being the best known.

This pseudoscientific genre found proponents, particularly in the Norman realm. Philippe de Thaün drafted the first vernacular *computus*, *Li cumpoz*, in Anglo-Norman (1113 or 1119); he was followed by Ralph of Lenham, author of a *Kalender* (1256; 1,330 lines; three manuscripts). An anonymous *Traité du comput* was written in Évreux before 1267, and there exists an Occitan *computus* (170 lines; two manuscripts) by Raimon Féraut (last quarter of the 13th c.). Of these texts, perhaps only that by Ralph of Lenham was destined for a lay audience.

Wendy E. Pfeffer

[See also: PHILIPPE DE THAÜN]

Philippe de Thaün. *Comput (MS BL Cotton Nero A.V)*, ed. Ian Short. London: Anglo-Norman Text Society, 1984.

Rauf de Linham. *Kalender*, ed. Tony Hunt. London: Anglo-Norman Text Society, 1983.

Brunel, Clovis. "Le comput en vers provençaux attribué à Raimon Féraut." *Annales du Midi* 36 (1924): 269–87.

COMTE D'ARTOIS, ROMAN DU. A 15th-century prose romance that recounts the adventures occasioned by the apparently impossible demands the Count of Artois, a perfect knight and courtly lover, makes upon his wife. Direct address to the reader, a favorite device of the author, shows his concern to rouse interest and stimulate imagination. Unaffected dialogues and lyrical soliloquies interspersed with ejaculatory remarks felicitously break up a narrative that might otherwise be weighed down by ponderous latinate rhetoric. The romance, relatively short by contemporary standards (only ca. 150 pages in its modern edition) is preserved in three 15th-century manuscripts.

Annette Brasseur

Seigneuret, Jean-Charles, ed. *Le roman du comte d'Artois.* Geneva: Droz, 1966.

COMTE DE POITIERS, ROMAN DU. A wife wrongly accused of adultery (ll. 1–1,230), a town conquered for the love of a young lady (ll. 1,230–1,719)—these two themes are the matter of a brief adventure romance inspired by the same model as Gerbert de Montreuil's *Roman de la Violette.* The influence of the chanson de geste and the courtly romance can be felt in this hybrid work, written in northern France ca. 1235–40, where a bawdiness worthy of the fabliaux and an epic style do not in the least hamper the expression of refined feelings and didactic intentions, both moral and religious. The poem is found in a single manuscript, Paris, Arsenal 3527.

Annette Brasseur

[See also: GERBERT DE MONTREUIL]

Malmberg, Bertil, ed. *Le roman du comte de Poitiers, poème français du XIIIe siècle.* Lund: Gleerup; Copenhagen: Munksgaard, 1940.

Fahlin, C. "Les sources et la date du *Roman du comte de Poitiers.*" *Studia Neophilologica* 13 (1940–41): 181–225.

CONCILIAR MOVEMENT. Conciliarism, like papalism, had its roots in the medieval heritage, especially in the diverse texts found in Gratian's *Decretum.* The dominant ecclesiology from Gratian to the Great Schism was papalist; but key texts suggested that popes had erred in the past— and could again. Critics, among them the emperor Frederick II, argued for convocation of a general council to correct a pope; and a different group, many masters at the University of Paris, were episcopalists, defending the rights of bishops and curates against the encroachments by the friars that the papacy had authorized. The earliest episcopalist, William of Saint-Amour, was driven into exile; and Jean de Pouilli was condemned for heresy by Pope John XXII. These privileges, too, found apologists, especially among the Dominicans, including Hervaeus Natalis and Pierre de la Palu, prominent figures at Avignon. Other controversies, especially those concerned with Franciscan poverty, helped shape opinion on papal and conciliar power. Even condemned writers like William of Ockham and Marsilius of Padua continued to be read, especially in Paris.

These arguments over poverty and privileges paled before the problems that arose in 1378 with the outbreak of the Great Schism. Christendom became divided between two pretenders to the papal throne. The princes chose sides, supporting either Urban VI (r. 1378–89) or Clement VII (r. 1378–94), usually along the lines of their alliances in the Hundred Years' War. Efforts to end this crisis, vindicating the cherished ideal of ecclesiastical unity, were complicated by the interests of princes and prelates; and a deeper critique of the institution than that of popular heresy appeared in the universities. John Wyclif in England and somewhat later John Hus in Bohemia argued that the corrupt, indulgence-selling church of their time was not the True Church. Nor could sinful priests celebrate the sacraments validly. These doctrines won popular support in the Lollard and Hussite movements; and some of the clergy realized that solution of the Schism had to be coupled with reform of the institution and defense of the faith.

The conciliar movement, which sought to accomplish these goals through convocation of a general council, was slow to appear. A council first was suggested in 1378 by the Italian cardinals. More detailed proposals were prepared in Paris by the theologian Henry of Langenstein and the canonist Conrad of Gelnhausen. Obstacles to holding a council lay in the canon law, which required convocation of such an assembly by the pope, and in the policies of princes. Most notably, Charles V expelled from Paris all those masters who would not support Clement VII, the claimant resident at Avignon. Langenstein and Gelnhausen left for Germany, where conciliarism soon took root.

From 1378 to the end of the 14th century, other solutions to the Schism were sought, especially through mutual renunciation by both pretenders, which would safeguard the benefices of clergy adhering to either. The French, divided between Burgundian and Armagnac interests, sought a solution in partial or complete "subtraction of obedience" from the two pretenders, the latter approach a policy promoted for the duke of Berry by Simon de Cramaud. This period saw a revival of episcopalism at Paris, which helped prepare the way for the emergence of Gallicanism by linking the interests of the secular clergy, especially their attacks on the privileges of the mendicants, with the interests of the French crown. None of the proposals for subtraction of obedience moved Clement's successor, the Aragonese Benedict XIII (r. 1394–1417). Efforts to coerce him led only to his flight from Avignon. When Benedict and the fourth Roman claimant Gregory XII (r. 1406–15) failed to meet and discuss the means of ending the Schism, the cardinals on both sides agreed to summon the Council of Pisa (1409). Gregory sought refuge with the Malatesta of Rimini, and Benedict fled to Peñiscola in Catalonia.

At Pisa, under the presidency of Simon de Cramaud, conciliarism emerged as the dominant justification for the council's efforts to reunify Christendom. Two strands of conciliarism, canonistic and theological, met in the representatives of the Italian and French universities. Canonistic conciliarism was represented among others by Francesco de Zabarella, whose *Tractatus de schismate*, in its final form, made wide claims for both cardinals and council. The heart of his argument was the comparison of the church with a corporation, which was able to depose its rector, the pope, if he endangered its welfare. This doctrine emerged from canonistic discussion of cathedral chapters, from Augustine's statement that Peter received the keys as the church's representative, and from precedents in Gratian's *Decretum* describing past instances of popes falling into error. The theological approach leaned more heavily on Scripture, especially on Paul's reprehending Peter for breaking off contact with the gentile converts. The chief proponents of this viewpoint, Pierre d'Ailly and Jean Gerson, emphasized the visible church as the Mystical Body of Christ. The council, representing that body, could remove an erring pope. Corporation theory also can be found influencing this line of thought, and these theologians made frequent use of texts from canon law. Both schools thought equity justified holding a council even in the absence of a pope.

The Council of Pisa, identifying obstruction of reunification with heresy, declared both claimants deposed; but their first pope of unity, Alexander V, died soon after his election. His successor, the antipope John XXIII, could not win universal acceptance. Gerson and d'Ailly became convinced that another council was needed; and they helped persuade Sigismund of Luxembourg, King of the Romans, that John should be pressed to summon one. Already driven from Rome by the Angevin king of Naples, John was forced to acquiesce. When the Council of Constance began in 1414, the pope found himself regarded as dispensable. His flight from Constance ended in imprisonment, but the assembly had been forced to guarantee its own continuation. The decree *Haec sancta* (1415) embodied the classic tenets of conciliarism—that the council represented the church; that it had power from Christ to act for unity, defense of the faith, and reform; and that even a true pope was bound to obey. The cardinals present were apprehensive about the projected scope of reform and their role in electing the next pope; but the only real dissenter, the Dominican general Leonardo Dati, was moved by fear that Gerson's episcopalist leanings would lead to an attack on the friars. Gerson, however, was too busy trying to have Jean Petit condemned for his defense of the murder of Louis of Orléans as tyrannicide to attack the privileges of the mendicants forcefully.

The council pressed on toward unity. John XXIII and Benedict XIII were deposed. Gregory XII abdicated, after issuing a *pro forma* convocation of the council. The assembly also condemned the errors of Wyclif, whose bones were unearthed for cremation, and burned John Hus and Jerome of Prague as heretics. It nearly failed, however, when arguing whether reform should precede or follow election of a pope. At last, a compromise permitted enactment of some reforms before a special electoral college began its conclave. The chief of these decrees, *Frequens* (1417), mandated holding a regular series of councils to supervise the papacy. Afterward, the electors chose Oddo Colonna, who became Martin V (r. 1417–31). Martin negotiated a series of concordats with the nations present in Constance—English, French, German, Spanish and Italian—which promised further reforms and other concessions. He followed the dictates of these pacts and those of the Council of Constance throughout his reign, but he frustrated the efforts of some present at the Council of Pavia-Siena (1423–24) to further curb the papacy's power. An impression that Martin opposed reform and conciliar authority, which was especially prevalent at the University of Paris, together with political problems in Italy and the Hussite domination of Bohemia, would cause problems for his successor, Eugenius IV (r. 1431–47).

Eugenius inherited the most recent unsuccessful crusade against the Hussites and a council summoned to meet at Basel. The pope wished to transfer the assembly to Italy to negotiate reunion with the Greeks; but the papal legate, Giuliano Cesarini, thought negotiations with the Hussites more crucial. The assembly resisted transfer or dissolution, restating *Frequens* and then *Haec sancta* as a justification. The council flourished as it pursued successfully an agreement with the more moderate party among the

Hussites. Eugenius, hard pressed by foes in Italy and a refugee from riots in Rome, was forced to authorize continuation of the council.

These confrontations led to a flurry of apologetic writing. The most important work was Nicholas of Cusa's *De concordantia catholica*, which balanced hierarchy and consent through a mechanism for the representation of lower ranks at each higher level of the ecclesiastical apparatus. The general council, in a spirit of concord, would reform the church. Nicholas, however, was not interested in any confrontation of pope and council. Instead, when the assembly debated making Eugenius's newly appointed presidents take the oath of incorporation, binding them and their master to obey conciliar decrees, he sided with Cesarini, who sought a compromise solution of the problem.

The council refused their advice, and the pope soon gave up any effort to be accommodating. The council's decision to curtail the curia's collection of annates without any compensation only made matters worse. So did Eugenius's inability to understand the conciliar viewpoint. The pope found few allies at Basel outside of Dominicans like Juan de Torquemada, who were confronted with renewed attacks on the privileges of the friars. A fight over the site of a council of union with the Greeks, however, drove Cesarini, Nicholas of Cusa, and others into the papal camp. The new leadership of the council derived largely from France and Savoy; and their justifications, in purely theological terms, were prepared by John of Segovia, who represented the theological conciliarism of Gerson. The final break came when the assembly insisted that the council meet in Avignon or Savoy, over the objections of both Eugenius and the Greeks.

Eugenius replied by calling a council to meet in Ferrara; and the Greeks, along with the minority party from Basel, went there. Later, at Florence (1439), the council would decree a short-lived union between East and West, which acknowledged papal primacy over the entire church. Basel would respond by declaring conciliar supremacy a dogma, decreeing the deposition of Eugenius and electing as pope Amadeus VIII of Savoy, who became Felix V. Eugenius condemned his opponents in the bull *Moyses,* which dismissed *Haec sancta,* the chief prop of Basel's new dogma, as merely the act of one obedience in the Great Schism, and launched a diplomatic offensive against them. England and Burgundy supported Eugenius. Other princes, including the king of France and the powers of the empire, temporized, often maintaining a neutral stance and proposing a council that would absorb the assemblies at Florence and Basel. Papal diplomats slowly won them over, often more by bribery than by the effectiveness of their arguments. At the same time, a new generation of papalists, led by Torquemada, advanced refutations of conciliarism and new defenses of papal primacy. Finally, the last of the princes, those in Germany, embraced Eugenius's successor, Nicholas V (r. 1447–55). Felix resigned his claim. Even the remainder of the Basel assembly gave up, and nominal unity was restored.

The Renaissance papacy, freed of the threat from the Council of Basel, would act increasingly like a secular monarchy; but even before the Reformation it did not go uncriticized. Conciliar thought and demands for reform flourished, even in the curia. Conciliarism endured, moreover, in Paris as a constituent element in Gallican thought, influencing the development of Monarchomach theory. Fear of a council like that at Basel would slow the papacy's response to the Reformation, putting off wide consultation on defense of the faith and reform until Paul III (r. 1534–49) summoned the Council of Trent in 1545.

Thomas M. Izbicki

[See also: AVIGNON PAPACY; D'AILLY, PIERRE; GALLICANISM; GERSON, JEAN; GRATIAN; HENRY OF LANGENSTEIN; PEACE OF GOD; SUBTRACTION OF OBEDIENCE; WILLIAM OF SAINT-AMOUR]

Juan de Torquemada. *A Disputation on the Authority of Pope and Council*, trans. Thomas M. Izbicki. Oxford: Blackfriars, 1988.

Nicholas of Cusa. *Catholic Concordance*, trans. Paul Sigmund. Cambridge: Cambridge University Press, 1991.

Alberigo, Giuseppe. *Chiesa conciliare: identità e significato del conciliarismo* . Brescia: Paideia, 1981.

Black, Antony. *Monarchy and Community: Political Ideas in the Later Conciliar Controversy 1430–1450.* Cambridge: Cambridge University Press, 1970.

Christianson, Gerald. *Cesarini, the Conciliar Cardinal: The Basel Years 1431–1438.* St. Ottilien: Eos Verlag der Erzabtei, 1979.

Congar, Yves. "Aspects ecclésiologiques de la querelle entre mendiants et séculiers dans la seconde moitié du XIIIe et le début du XIVe siècle." *Archives d'histoire doctrinale et littéraire du moyen âge* 38 (1961): 35–151.

Crowder, C.M.D. *Unity, Heresy and Reform, 1378–1460: The Conciliar Response to the Great Schism.* New York: St. Martin, 1977.

Oakley, Francis. *Council over Pope? Towards a Provisional Ecclesiology.* New York: Herder and Herder, 1969.

Spinka, Matthew. *Advocates of Reform from Wyclif to Erasmus.* Philadelphia: Westminster, 1953.

Tierney, Brian. *Foundations of the Conciliar Theory.* Cambridge: Cambridge University Press, 1955.

Ullmann, Walter. *The Origins of the Great Schism.* London: Burns, Oates and Washbourne, 1948.

CONCORDAT OF AMBOISE. In an ordinance issued at Amboise on October 13, 1472, Louis XI proclaimed in France a concordat with Pope Sixtus IV that the pope had published two months earlier. Its language closely resembled that of papal proposals in the years since 1438, when the Pragmatic Sanction of Bourges had sharply reduced the authority of the papacy over the French church. The "Gallican liberties" embodied in the Pragmatic Sanction gave the French church, particularly the episcopate, considerable independence from both the pope and the king. It was strongly supported by the Parlement de Paris, but Louis XI, on becoming king in 1461, had alternately canceled it, restored it, and ignored it. He preferred to deal with the pope rather than to concede liberties to his own clergy.

The Concordat of 1472, which historians once thought was never enforced, prefigured the more famous Concordat of Bologna (1516), in that the pope and the king arranged for a joint hegemony over the French clergy, primarily with regard to episcopal appointments. Although the relations between Louis XI and Sixtus IV often were bitter during the succeeding decade, the Concordat of Amboise remained the *de facto* arrangement for handling bishoprics, and it enabled the monarchy to strengthen its control over the French church.

John Bell Henneman, Jr.

[See also: GALLICANISM; PRAGMATIC SANCTION OF BOURGES]

Ourliac, Paul. "The Concordat of 1472: An Essay on the Relations Between Louis XI and Sixtus IV." In *The Recovery of France in the Fifteenth Century*, ed. Peter S. Lewis. New York: Harper and Row, 1971, pp. 102–84.

CONDÉ, JEAN DE (ca.1280–ca.1345). The son of poet Baudouin de Condé, Jean served in the court of the counts of Hainaut. Seventy-seven of his poems are extant, mostly in octosyllabic couplets. They comprise numerous didactic works, five fabliaux, and allegorical and moral narratives. Didactic subjects include advice to rulers, the estates, death, reflections on the nature of love, social and antifraternal satire, and religion and ethics. Several of the narratives have love subjects, and there is a love debate in the most famous of Jean's works, the *Messe des oisiaus et li plés des chanonesses et des grises nonnains*. But he was by no means a love poet and did not write lyrics. His several works called *lais* do not use the lyric form.

James I. Wimsatt

[See also: *DIT*; FABLIAU]

Scheler, Auguste, ed. *Dits et contes de Baudouin de Condé et de son fils Jean de Condé.* 3 vols. Brussels: Devaux, 1866–67. [Vols. 2–3 contain Jean's poetry.]

Ribard, Jacques. *Un ménestrel du XIVe siècle: Jean de Condé.* Geneva: Droz, 1969.

CONDUCTUS. A Latin poem relying on syllable count and rhyme that was set to either monophonic or polyphonic music, the conductus (pl. conductus) was one of the predominant musical genres of the 12th and early 13th centuries. Its main function was to substitute or supplement parts of liturgical services, often in processions. Many polyphonic conductus served as replacements for the *Benedicamus Domino*, with which all Offices end, because they conclude or rhyme with those words. These probably were for Vespers or Matins of important feasts. Directions in some liturgical dramas refer to the music sung during stage processions as conductus. Surviving Marian, political, and admonitory texts suggest that conductus also served for private devotion, commemoration of significant events, and learned editorial commentary. The largest extant source is the Florence codex (Biblioteca Mediceo-Laurenziana, Pluteo 29,1) of Parisian origin ca. 1250.

It is controversial whether the music composed for conductus was sung in equal units of time for each syllable ("isochronous") or rhythmically modal, with the syllables rendered in patterns of long and short notes. The music theorist Anonymous 4 describes the declamatory, hymnlike, and usually strophic polyphonic conductus (e.g., the three-part *Deus in adiutorium*) appropriate for less accomplished clerics to sing, and through-composed ones with large, untexted (i.e., melismatic) sections known as caudae (e.g., Pérotin's *Salvatoris hodie*) for well-trained singers.

A number of troubadour and trouvère chansons have been identified as tenors of conductus, such as *A l'entrada del tens clar* in the three-part *Veris ad imperia*. A few conductus quote music and words of sequences, but perhaps the outstanding interrelation between conductus and other genres is that among their caudae, the untexted clausulae of the Notre-Dame School, and the motet, which originated by texting clausulae and became the preeminent genre in the 13th century. A famous instance is the final cauda of *Dic Christi veritas*, which was texted by Philip the Chancellor as *Bulla fulminante*.

Sandra Pinegar

[See also: ANONYMOUS 4; CLAUSULA; FRANCO OF COLOGNE; MOTET (13TH CENTURY); PÉROTIN; PHILIP THE CHANCELLOR; RHYTHMIC MODE; VERSUS]

Anderson, Gordon A. *Notre-Dame and Related Conductus: Opera omnia.* 9 vols. Henryville: Institute of Mediaeval Music, 1981–86.

Falck, Robert. *The Notre Dame Conductus: A Study of the Repertory.* Henryville: Institute of Mediaeval Music, 1981.

Reckow, Fritz. "Conductus." In *Handwörterbuch der musikalischen Terminologie*, ed. Hans Heinrich Eggebrecht. Wiesbaden: Steiner, 1971–. 11 pp. (1973).

Schrade, Leo. "Political Compositions in French Music of the Twelfth and Thirteenth Centuries: The Coronation of French Kings." *Annales musicologiques* 1 (1953): 9–53.

CONFRÉRIE DE LA PASSION. Most religious confraternities in France considered organizing performances of plays as supplementary to their main *raison d'être*. The Paris Confrérie de la Passion was, however, established primarily to put on mystery plays, either on the Passion or the Resurrection, or other saint plays. Their statutes, approved by Charles VI, who had seen their plays earlier, were published in 1402. Their activities originally centered on the hall and courtyard of the Hôpital de la Trinité, but by 1538 they were also using the Hôtel de Flandre. From 1548, they occupied the well-known Hôtel de Bourgogne. In spite of the terms of their statutes, it seems certain that they also performed comic as well as religious plays. Some of these performances took place indoors, in the Hôpital de la Trinité, on a stage estimated to have measured about 40 by 20 feet; others were clearly outdoors, in a theater in the round. The Confrérie must have had a repertoire of plays, but only one surviving manuscript, of the anonymous *Vie de saint Louis* (Paris, ca. 1470; three days, 19,000 lines), bears an explicit mention of the society. Its best-documented performances date from the middle of the 16th century, when several large-scale mysteries were organized at the Hôtel de Flandre. In 1539, a Passion play was put on; a description of the *montre* of the preceding day has survived. In 1541, the Confrères presented the *Actes des Apôtres*, which took four months of rehearsals, and whose performance extended over thirty-five days from May 8 to September 25. The following year, 1542, they put on a similar massive play, the *Mistère du Viel Testament*, which started on May 9 and ended October 22. This successful performance led to the printing of the 50,000-line text, several copies of which have survived. Contemporary documents contain descriptions of certain aspects of these productions.

In 1548, the Parlement de Paris published its edict forbidding the performance of *mystères sacrés*; in the same year, the Confrérie moved to the Hôtel de Bourgogne and continued to put on plays, though now entitled *comédies* and *tragi-comédies*. Though the Paris edict had little immediate effect in the provinces, the Confrérie de la Passion, as it had done from its foundation in 1402, changed with the times. Its history is a microcosm of the history of medieval French drama.

Graham A. Runnalls

[See also: BASOCHE; MYSTERY PLAYS; THEATER]

Frank, Grace. *The Medieval French Drama.* 2nd ed. Oxford: Clarendon, 1960.
Petit de Julleville, Louis. *Les mystères.* 2 vols. Paris: Hachette, 1880, Vol. 1, pp. 412–39.
Rey-Flaud, Henri. *Le cercle magique.* Paris: Gallimard, 1973, pp. 230–53.

CONGÉ. The *congé*, or farewell poem, was a literary genre specific to the town of Arras in the 13th century. In 1202, Jehan Bodel, and in 1272, Baude Fastoul, both suffering from leprosy, sent their fellow citizens a poem to *demander* or *rover congié* ("ask for permission to leave"). Their example was followed in 1276 or 1277 by Adam de la Halle, who was leaving his city in perfect health. The three poets borrowed the form of the *Vers de la Mort* by Hélinant de Froidmont: octosyllabic twelve-line stanzas made up of two sestets with an aabaab/bbabba rhyme pattern. All the themes of this new genre are already to be found in Jehan Bodel's *Congés*. But if the problem of salvation was paramount in Bodel's and Fastoul's concerns, Adam de la Halle intended above all to rebel against the injustice and scandalmongering that prevailed in Arras. The allegorical entities (*Cuer* 'Heart'; *Pitié* 'Pity'; *Anui* 'Pain' . . .) that his predecessors, taking their cue from Hélinant, had called upon at the beginning of their stanzas, were now out of place in a work that went beyond the bounds of the *congé*: a literary genre that was originally lyrical had become, with Adam de la Halle, essentially satirical.

Annette Brasseur

[See also: ADAM DE LA HALLE; BAUDE FASTOUL; JEHAN BODEL]

Foulon, Charles. *L'œuvre de Jehan Bodel.* Paris: Presses Universitaires de France, 1958, pp. 707–66.
Dufournet, Jean. *Adam de la Halle à la recherche de lui-même ou le jeu dramatique de la feuillée.* Paris: Société d'Edition d'Enseignement Supérieur, 1974, pp. 50–55.
Ruelle, Pierre, ed. *Les congés d'Arras (Jean Bodel, Baude Fastoul, Adam de la Halle).* Paris: Presses Universitaires de France, 1965. [Based on MS. A (Arsenal 3142) and G (B.N. fr. 25566).
Zink, Michel. "Le ladre, de l'exil au royaume; comparaison entre les congés de Jean Bodel et ceux de Baude Fastoul." In *Exclus et systèmes d'exclusion dans la littérature et la civilisation médiévales.* Aix-en-Provence: CUER MA, 1978, pp. 71–88.
Zumthor, Paul. "Entre deux esthétiques: Adam de la Halle." In *Mélanges de langue et de littérature du moyen âge et de la Renaissance offerts à Jean Frappier.* 2 vols. Geneva: Droz, 1970, Vol. 2, pp. 1155–71.

CONON DE BÉTHUNE (fl. ca. 1180–1219/20). Now remembered as one of the classic generation of trouvères that included Gace Brulé and the Châtelain de Coucy, Conon, born into a noble family of Artois, was better known during his lifetime as warrior, diplomat, and statesman. A participant in the Third Crusade, he was a major figure in the Fourth, esteemed by the French for his wisdom and eloquence in dealing with recalcitrant allies. After the capture of Constantinople, he served the Latin (Flemish) emperors devotedly and was even named regent of the empire in 1219.

Ten songs, all preserved with their melodies, may be attributed to Conon with reasonable certainty. These include two crusade songs and a satirical love dialogue, along with *chansons d'amour* of an unusually personal stamp. One poem is particularly remarkable for evoking the difference between Conon's dialect and that of the royal court.

Samuel N. Rosenberg

[See also: CRUSADE SONGS/*CHANSONS DE CROISADE*; TROUVÈRE POETRY]

Conon de Béthune. *Les chansons de Conon de Béthune,* ed. Axel Wallensköld. Paris: Champion, 1921.
Rosenberg, Samuel N., and Hans Tischler, eds. *Chanter m'estuet: Songs of the Trouvères.* Bloomington: Indiana University Press, 1981, pp. 182–94.
van der Werf, Hendrik, ed. *Trouvères-Melodien I.* Kassel: Bärenreiter, 1977, pp. 283–314.
Gennrich, Friedrich. "Zu den Liedern des Conon de Bethune." *Zeitschrift für romanische Philologie* 42 (1922): 231–41.

CONQUES. The town of Conques (Aveyron), situated in a remote valley along the mountainous route from Le Puy to Moissac, is the site of the former Benedictine abbey of Sainte-Foy. With its huge sculptured tympanum and magnificent treasury, the abbey provides perhaps the most

Conques (Aveyron), Sainte-Foy. *Photograph courtesy of Whitney S. Stoddard.*

Conques (Aveyron), Sainte-Foy. *Photograph courtesy of Whitney S. Stoddard.*

complete experience of a medieval pilgrimage church. The dates of construction are controversial. If erected, according to the texts, during the abbacy of Odolric (1031–60), it would be one of the first, following Saint-Martin of Tours, of the great "pilgrimage"-type churches. Several writers, however, have cited archaeological factors, such as variation in stone and configuration of the chevet, to extend construction into the 12th century. Small in comparison with other churches of this type, the nave of six bays is elegant in line and bold in the verticality of its proportions. The transept is wide; a lantern tower surmounts the crossing above 14th-century ribbed vaults. The chevet unites two distinct types: chapels in eschelon opening off the transept and ambulatory with three radiating chapels.

The towers of the western façade are a 19th-century addition. The tympanum of the Last Judgment, retaining significant traces of polychromy, is one of the most celebrated in all of Romanesque sculpture. Christ the Judge, right arm raised in blessing, the left lowered in rejection, forms the center of a great diagram of salvation and damnation. Directly below his feet, St. Michael confronts a demon. The elect advance with dignity, seeking the Paradise of Abraham's bosom; the damned are shoved into Hell, where sinners and tormentors are graphically ren-

dered. St. Foy, worker of miracles and deliverer of captives, intercedes for humankind. Inscribed banderoles and gables reinforce and expand the message. The figures are weighty, their faces impassive; the presentation is direct, vivid, and anecdotal.

The contrast between the sober façade and the rich tympanum, and discrepancies within the tympanum and its frame, have fostered various hypotheses regarding the original disposition of the portal—which may well have included the beautiful Annunciation and the figures of Isaiah and John the Baptist now mounted on the internal face of the north-transept façade.

Tympanum of the Last Judgment, Conques, ca. 1130–35. *Reprinted by permission of Giraudon/Art Resource, New York.*

Of the splendid objects in the remarkable treasury, the oldest and most venerated is the 10th-century gold reliquary statue (head and some jewels are earlier) containing the relics of St. Foy, brought from Agen to Conques by subterfuge. Part of the Romanesque cloister of Abbot Bégon (r. 1087–1107) is still preserved.

Jean M. French

[See also: RELICS AND RELIQUARIES; ROMANESQUE ARCHITECTURE]

Aubert, Marcel. *L'église de Conques.* 2nd ed. Paris: Laurens, 1954.

Bernoulli, Christoph. *Die Skulpturen der Abtei Conques-en-Rouergue.* Basel: Birkhauser, 1956.

Bousquet, Jacques. *La sculpture à Conques aux XIe et XIIe siècles: essai de chronologie comparée.* 2 vols. Lille: Service de Reproduction des Thèses, Université de Lille III, 1973.

Desjardins, Gustave. *Cartulaire de l'abbaye de Conques-en-Rouergue.* Paris, 1879.

Gaillard, Georges, et al. *Rouergue roman.* La Pierre-qui-vire: Zodiaque, 1963.

CONSANGUINITY. One of the chief preoccupations of medieval church law was consanguinity, the degree of relationship between two people such that a marriage between them would be incestuous. Roman law had forbidden marriages between people related "within four degrees." The Romans had calculated degrees by counting from one prospective partner back to the common ancestor and then down to the other partner, so that first cousins were considered related within four degrees. By the 8th century, however, the church defined consanguinity as residing within seven degrees and changed the method of calculating degrees by counting back only to the common ancestor; hence, sixth cousins were considered related within seven degrees. These two changes vastly increased the number of people to whom one was theoretically too closely related to marry. Although the nobility initially tried to avoid consanguineous unions, not wanting to have a carefully arranged marriage broken up by the bishop, by the 12th century they frequently married their distant cousins deliberately. Then, if they decided they wanted a divorce, they could "discover" the consanguinity and have their marriage annulled. To discourage this divorce on demand, the Fourth Lateran Council of 1215 cut back the forbidden degrees from seven to four, although continuing to calculate degrees by counting back to the common ancestor.

Constance B. Bouchard

Bouchard, Constance B. "Consanguinity and Noble Marriages in the Tenth and Eleventh Centuries." *Speculum* 56 (1981): 268–87.

Brundage, James A. *Law, Sex, and Christian Society in Medieval Europe.* Chicago: University of Chicago Press, 1987.

Duby, Georges. *Medieval Marriage: Two Models from Twelfth-Century France,* trans. Elborg Forster. Baltimore: Johns Hopkins University Press, 1978.

———. *The Knight, the Lady, and the Priest: The Making of Modern Marriage in Medieval France,* trans. Barbara Bray. New York: Pantheon, 1983.

Freisen, Joseph. *Geschichte des kanonischen Eherechts.* Paderborn: Schöningh, 1963.

CONSEIL. The word *conseil* presents problems for students of medieval political institutions, for it corresponds to two English words, "counsel" (advice) and "council" (deliberative body), while also having, in the medieval setting, a close connection with words that we translate as "court." Early Capetian kings conducted their business with the help of a small body of close advisers called the *curia regis.* Vassals who owed the king "counsel" were an important element in this body, but only a few were continually with the king. By the later 11th century, the most stable group of advisers came from the royal household, first the "great officers" and later on people with special expertise in legal or financial matters. When some important business, usually involving military operations, brought together many royal vassals, the small *curia* became, for the moment, a much larger assembly.

By the late 12th century, Langmuir has shown, this larger assembly was called a *curia* ("court") when its business was primarily judicial and a *concilium* when it deliberated on a major project of common interest, such as a crusade. When the judicial specialists began to act as a separate, sedentary body under Louis IX, the small body that remained with the king tended increasingly to be called his "council" rather than *curia regis.* Yet the Latin word *concilium,* when used in the French vernacular (*concile*) came to refer exclusively to councils of the church. The word *conseil* (Lat. *consilium* 'advice') meant not only "advice" but also "advice-giving bodies." By the 14th century, a royal council was called not only *conseil* in French but also *consilium* where Latin still was used.

In the 14th century, the documents began to identify as royal councilors those who sat on the king's *conseil.* From the disputed succession of Philip V in 1316 until the late stages of the Hundred Years' War, kings often had to appoint councilors who reflected the political mood of the kingdom. For a time ca. 1340, Philip VI's council consisted exclusively of the "sovereigns" of the Chambre des Comptes, but discontent with the financial administration led him to abandon this experiment after 1343. For decades thereafter, frequent changes of councilors reflected the power of interest groups, although there was one period of relative stability (1359–74) when the body was dominated by Guillaume de Melun, archbishop of Sens.

Under Charles VI, the council was one arena for the power struggle between successive dukes of Burgundy and their rivals at court. In 1388, the anti-Burgundian faction called the Marmousets persuaded the king to oust his uncle Philip the Bold, duke of Burgundy, from the council. In 1406, the council, which had risen to more than fifty in number, was reduced by about half, a "reform" that purged most of the supporters of John the Fearless, duke of Burgundy. After many similar episodes, the council was more fully under royal control by the later 15th century.

John Bell Henneman, Jr.

[See also: ASSEMBLIES]

Cazelles, Raymond. "Les mouvements révolutionnaires du milieu du XIVe siècle et le cycle de l'action politique." *Revue historique* 227 (1962): 279–312.

———. *Société politique, noblesse et couronne sous Jean le Bon et Charles V.* Geneva: Droz, 1982.

Langmuir, Gavin I. "Concilia and Capetian Assemblies, 1179–1230." *Album Helen Maud Cam 2 (Studies Presented to the International Commission for the History of Representative and Parliamentary Institutions,* 24 [1963]): 27–63.

Nordberg, Michael. *Les ducs et la royauté: études sur la rivalité des ducs d'Orléans et de Bourgogne, 1392–1407.* Norstedt: Svenska Bokforlaget, 1964.

Valois, Noël. *Le conseil du roi aux XIVe, XVe, et XVIe siècles.* Paris: Picard, 1888.

CONSTABLE OF FRANCE. The office of constable (Fr. *connétable*), which came to signify the chief commander of the French royal army, originated with the "count of the stable" (*comes stabuli*), an officer in the household of 9th- and 10th-century monarchs. This apparently modest position grew into an important one as heavy cavalry became the essential element in military operations. War-horses and their equipment were increasingly expensive; their care and maintenance became a correspondingly important responsibility. Household officials whose duties were related to military activities tended to acquire more prestige than those concerned with domestic duties, especially if the household happened to be that of a ruler.

During the reign of Philip I (1060–1108), the constable emerged as one of the four "great officers" of the crown, who witnessed royal enactments and provided one stable element in a royal entourage of continually changing composition. At first, the chief among these officers, even in military affairs, was the seneschal. Only after 1191, when Philip II let that office remain vacant, did the constable become the leader of the royal military forces.

In the 11th and 12th centuries, the constables were drawn from the nobility of the Île-de-France, most frequently from the Montmorency family. Nobles of the north and east began to dominate the office in the late 13th century, and three members of the Brienne family held it in the 14th. The Hundred Years' War made the position extremely important. The three most celebrated constables of that period were Bretons—Bertrand du Guesclin (1370–80), Olivier de Clisson (1380–92), and Arthur de Richemont (1425–58). These men were of progressively higher economic and social position, and Richemont ended his days as duke of Brittany. Thereafter, the constable was usually a member of the great nobility.

John Bell Henneman, Jr.

Lemarignier, Jean-François. *Le gouvernement royale aux premiers temps capétiens (987–1108).* Paris: Picard, 1965.

Lot, Ferdinand, and Robert Fawtier. *Histoire des institutions françaises au moyen âge.* 3 vols. Paris: Presses Universitaires de France, Vol. 2: *Institutions royales* (1958).

CONSTANCE OF ARLES (d. ca. 1034). Queen of France. King Robert II (996–1031) married his third wife, Constance of Arles, ca. 1005. She was the mother of all his children: Hugh, who died young in 1025; Henry I (1031–60), the next French king; Robert, who became duke of Burgundy; Odo; Adélaïde, who married Count Baudouin of Flanders; and probably Hadwidis, who married Count Raynaud of Nevers. Constance was the daughter of Count Guillaume II of Arles and of Adélaïde-Blanche of Anjou. She had a reputation for a ferocious temper. She seems to have wanted her third son, Robert, to succeed in 1031 rather than Henry, and she even waged a brief war against her sons in that year.

Constance B. Bouchard

Dhondt, Jean. "Sept femmes et un trio de rois." *Contributions à l'histoire économique et sociale* 3 (1964–65): 35–70.

Facinger, Marion F. "A Study of Medieval Queenship: Capetian France, 987–1237." *Studies in Medieval and Renaissance History* 5 (1968): 3–47.

Lot, Ferdinand. *Les derniers Carolingiens.* Paris: Bouillon, 1891, Appendix 9.

Pfister, Christian. *Études sur le règne de Robert le Pieux (996–1031).* Paris: Vieweg, 1885.

CONSTANCE OF CASTILE (d. 1160). Two years after his divorce from Eleanor of Aquitaine in 1152, Louis VII (r. 1137–80) married Constance, daughter of Alfonso VII of Castile. She died in 1160, giving birth to a daughter. It is ironic that the woman Louis married after divorcing Eleanor for consanguinity was just as closely related: she was his third cousin.

Constance B. Bouchard

Facinger, Marion F. "A Study of Medieval Queenship: Capetian France, 987–1237." *Studies in Medieval and Renaissance History* 5 (1968): 3–47.

CONSTRUCTION TECHNIQUES. The history of construction in medieval France can be divided into two major periods. The first, embracing the 5th century into the 12th, is characterized by the survival and variations on the building techniques, as well as many of the ornamental forms, of Roman architecture. The second, the Gothic era of the 12th century to the early 16th, witnessed the advent of innovative methods of building and design and led to a dramatic change in the status of the architect.

The architectural record of France prior to the 9th century is fragmentary. With the collapse of coherent imperial authority in the West and the spread of Christianity in the 3rd and 4th centuries, the church and in particular its bishops emerged as the primary sponsors of major projects. At Cahors, Bishop Desiderius enclosed the city within defensive walls and built aqueducts in the 6th century, while Sidonius Apollinaris, the late 5th-century bishop of Clermont, erected a luxurious villa complete with baths and a swimming pool. However, church structures, not public works, were the primary focus, with the basilica and centralized baptistery serving as the major building types. In the laying out of ecclesiastical complexes, it has been argued that early-medieval masons employed Roman planning strategies based on harmonic proportions, but it is more likely that the simple geometric ratios that order the designs represent the habits of craft practice rather than a conscious continuation of past architectural principles.

In terms of actual construction techniques, political fragmentation produced increased variety. Rather than the Roman system of mass-producing standardized elements, such as columns or capitals, which were stockpiled at the quarry and later shipped to specific sites, building was conditioned by local materials and models. Nevertheless, it appears that many Roman building practices were continued, albeit on a decidedly less monumental scale. Masons continued to build using a rubble wall construction faced with cut-stone patterns, seen in the crypt walls at Jouarre (7th c.) or Notre-Dame de la Basse-Œuvre, Beauvais (late 10th c.), which were composed of *opus recticulatum* in the Roman manner, or stucco, as at Saint-Laurent, Grenoble (8th c.). The more impressive structures often incorporated spolia, for example, the cathedral of Vienne (5th c.), Selles-sur-Cher (mid-6th c.), or as at Jouarre imitated Roman columns and capitals. The sensibilities and renowned skill of "Gallic" masons are showcased in the baptistery of Saint-Jean, Poitiers (7th c.), where the pilasters, pediments, moldings, and geometrical designs set into the wall fabric become surface embroidery rather than structural articulation.

The loss or abandonment of pozzolan concrete as a primary building material had enormous technological consequences. Although masonry vaults and domes were erected from the 5th century (baptistery of Fréjus) through the 7th century (Jouarre), the weak lime mortar used in place of pozzolan limited their scale, and large interior spaces were covered by timber roofs. Yet, despite their structural simplicity, early-medieval French buildings contributed new elements to the language of architecture. Monumental towers were erected at Saint-Martin, Tours (5th c.), in response to defensive and liturgical requirements and as a mark of the church's distinction as the burial site of St. Martin. Spacious crypts were created around the tombs of saints, seen at Notre-Dame-de-Confession at Saint-Victor, Marseilles (5th c.), or Saint-Germain, Auxerre (6th c.), or as privileged burial sites, such as Jouarre. The elaboration of interior space and the creation of an impressive exterior silhouette were to occupy architects throughout the remainder of the Middle Ages.

In the Carolingian period of the late 8th and 9th centuries, architectural practice was invigorated by a new wave of Roman retrospection. In the abbeys of Saint-Denis (754–75) or Saint-Riquier at Centula (790–99), the basilican plan with a transept, likely based on Constantine's St. Peter's in Rome, reappeared, but both buildings sported multiple

Flying buttresses, Chartres cathedral. *Photograph courtesy of William W. Kibler.*

exterior towers. In addition to their ideological message, these plans reveal a greater coherence in planning. A consistent set of geometrical proportions governs the design, with the result that each constituent space is related to the larger whole. In a similar vein, Carolingian construction achieved a greater degree of precision as builders turned increasingly to stone as the primary building material in contrast to the irregular rubble technique of previous centuries. At Saint-Philibert-de-Grandlieu (814–ca. 847), which combined stone, brick, and rubble, the masonry is laid in regular courses and ashlar blocks are used to articulate piers and arches. Despite these advances, however, the essential structural characteristics of Carolingian architecture remain virtually unchanged. While walls grew more massive, the main interior spaces were roofed in timber. The combination of groin and barrel vaults, small domes on squinches, and horseshoe arches at Theodulf's oratory at Germigny-des-Prés (806) hints at the absorption of external influences, probably from Byzantine architecture, but the Carolingian masons of Neustria never developed a structural complexity and spatial monumentality comparable with that of their eastern Mediterranean counterparts.

The quickening of France in the 11th and 12th centuries stimulated a burst of building that produced rapid technical development. Although each region of France tended to develop its own more or less distinctive traditions, Romanesque architecture can be characterized by massive walls and a complex structure that supported stone vaults. As the term "Romanesque" implies, this architecture approaches that of Rome in its monumental scale and its mastery of masonry construction. Related to the Roman *opera*, its muscular walls were built of rubble faced with brick or ashlar blocks and articulated by applied shafts and arcades.

The realization of many buildings must be understood as a collaboration between learned clerics and stonemasons. Cluny III, begun in 1095, was planned by the monks Gunzo and Hezelo, who drew upon their sophisticated knowledge of geometry, music, Vitruvius, and number symbolism to create a design whose order at once ensured stability, achieved beauty, and symbolized divine perfection. But once these programmatic decisions were made, the master mason set out the plan at full scale by means of ropes, a measuring rod, or simple pacing off, and his workshop then raised the structure according to long-established masonry traditions that did not require the guidance of intellectuals. While there were infinite variations, in general southern French Romanesque employed continuous courses of uniform bricklike masonry articulated by corbel tables and bands and emphasized vertically continuous elements. On the other hand, northern Romanesque techniques differentiated stone types, distinguishing frame from fill, tended to break the elevation into separate parts and stressed horizontal divisions.

Architectural ideas were transmitted over significant distances, as shown by the appearance of the "pilgrimage roads" plan and elevation at Saint-Martin in Tours, Saint-Martial in Limoges, Sainte-Foy in Conques, and Saint-Sernin in Toulouse during the last third of the 11th century. However, the repetition of this scheme, in which the main choir space was ringed by an ambulatory and radiating chapels and the elevation was composed of an arcade and gallery, was likely the result of patronal interchange rather than of migrating gangs of masons. To the contrary, Romanesque workshops, so far as we know, maintained a regional focus. One of the ateliers at Cluny III can be followed throughout Burgundy, where they built sections of churches at Charlieu, Anzy-le-Duc, Macon, Perrecy-les-Forges, Vézelay, and Paray-le-Monial.

The mastery of masonry vaulting was the most significant technological stride made by Romanesque builders. The first completely vaulted structures, including Cluny II (ca. 1010) and Saint-Bénigne, Dijon (1001–18), probably drew upon slightly earlier Lombard models. In the course of the 11th and early 12th centuries, each region seems to have developed its own response to the new technology. Spacious domed churches rose at Angoulême, Cahors, and Périgueux in Aquitaine. Hall churches appeared in Poitou. In Burgundy, pointed barrel vaults were introduced in the churches of Cluny III, Autun, and Paray-le-Monial; transverse barrel vaults covered the nave of Saint-Philibert at Tournus; while the nave of Vézelay received a groin vault.

Norman churches, such as Bernay and Jumièges, retained timber ceilings through the 11th century but during the first quarter of the 12th introduced the ribbed groin vault at Saint-Étienne and Sainte-Trinité, Caen. Vaults appeared in combination with a variety of wall systems. At Dijon, the barrel vaults were supported by a vaulted gallery, but their weight reduced the windows to small openings. Such later examples as Saint-Sernin, Toulouse, and Conques retained galleries to buttress their barrel-vaulted naves but eliminated windows. In the "thick-wall" system of the Caen churches, a muscular wall, honeycombed with passages, was developed in depth while the "thin-wall" structure of Jumièges or Saint-Martin-de-Boscherville achieved stability through vertical masonry spines applied to the interior and exterior while emphasizing mural planarity. One of the stimuli to the widespread experimentation in Romanesque architecture may have been a search to combine the fireproof stone vault with greater interior illumination.

During the 1130s in the area around Paris, a new style began to take shape. Combining diverse Romanesque structural elements, such as the ribbed groin vault and pointed arches, this architecture, exemplified by the new choir of the abbey of Saint-Denis (1140–44), achieved a breathtaking spaciousness and visual lightness. In the course of the following century, master masons exploited the structural advantages of the ribbed groin vault to eliminate progressively solid areas of stone and transform the wall into a glazed membrane. With the invention of the flying buttress in the mid-12th century and the introduction of tracery in the early 13th, French architecture combined stupendous size with small-scale effects that effectively expressed transcendental spirituality and intimidating ecclesiastical power.

In writing about the reconstruction of Saint-Denis, Abbot Suger remarked that his master mason laid out the choir through his arithmetical and geometrical cunning. As plans became ever more complex, including congregational and clerical spaces, peripheral aisles for circulation, and a multitude of secondary chapels, and elevations grew taller yet more finely detailed, the master mason increasingly turned to drawing as a tool for design and to ensure precise execution. Small-scale preliminary sketches and full-scale plans of such elements as piers, window-tracery patterns, and flying buttresses were drawn in temporary tracing houses or on the floors and walls of the buildings themselves. Parchment drawings, which served as show plans to a patron as well as project blueprints, survive from the mid-13th century, although their previous existence is likely. The illustrations of church plans, stonecutting, and surveying procedures in the sketchbook of Villard de Honnecourt (ca. 1230) disclose the centrality of geometry to all aspects of the architectural endeavor.

Faced with the daunting task of erecting monumental buildings with the greatest possible speed and economy, Gothic masons evolved a system of production based, as in Roman architecture, upon standardized forms. At Chartres, Soissons, and Cologne, the prefabrication, which extended to pier components, vault ribs, triforium shafts, and window tracery, permitted the separation of cutting and placement procedures. These elements could thus be prepared during the winter months, when inclement weather halted active construction, then rapidly installed. Amiens cathedral (begun 1221) reached an even higher degree of rationalization, likely based on production models offered by the local textile industry: the nave piers were assembled from only three elements, the engaged piers from two, and the wall-masonry courses were regularized. A complete uniformity of stonework was achieved at the Sainte-Chapelle in Paris (1241–48).

These new production techniques led to a greater specialization and division of labor as well as a marked rise of the master mason's social status. He increasingly focused on the graphic design of forms and the coordination of production activity at the quarry and in the lodge, leaving the actual cutting of stone to a second-in-command, the *appareilleur*. From the mid-13th century on, the stratified workshop organization, together with the use of drawing as a standard procedure, allowed the architect to supervise several projects simultaneously. The names of masters were now recorded in building records, their achievements celebrated on tombstones and in inscriptions. Pierre de Montreuil, a Parisian master who died in 1267, was vaunted as a "teacher of masons" (*doctor lathomorum*); the Late Gothic architect Martin Chambiges, who oversaw major projects in Beauvais, Sens, and Troyes, was called *supremus artifex* during his lifetime. No longer a mere craftsman, the Gothic master mason brought his awesome structures into being through his practical organizational abilities, his technical skills, and his gift of design, which seemed a reflection of divine creativity.

Michael T. Davis

[See also: CHAMBIGES, MARTIN; CLUNY; CONQUES; CONVENT ARCHITECTURE; DIJON; GERMIGNY-DES-PRÉS; GOTHIC ARCHITECTURE; JOUARRE; MENDICANT ART AND ARCHITECTURE; PIERRE DE MONTREUIL; PREMONSTRATENSIAN ARCHITECTURE; ROMANESQUE ARCHITECTURE; SAINT-DENIS; TOULOUSE; TOURNUS; VÉZELAY; VILLARD DE HONNECOURT]

Armi, C. Edson. *Masons and Sculptors in Romanesque Burgundy: The New Aesthetic of Cluny III.* 2 vols. University Park: Pennsylvania State University Press, 1983.

Barral i Altet, Xavier, ed. *Artistes, artisans, et production artistique au moyen âge.* 3 vols. Paris: Picard, 1986–90.

Bony, Jean. *French Gothic Architecture of the Twelfth and Thirteenth Centuries.* Berkeley: University of California Press, 1983.

Bucher, François. "Medieval Architectural Design Methods, 800–1560." *Gesta* 11 (1972): 37–51.

Conant, Kenneth J. *Carolingian and Romanesque Architecture, 800–1200.* 3rd ed. New York: Penguin, 1974.

Fitchen, J. *The Construction of Gothic Cathedrals: A Study of Medieval Vault Erection.* Oxford: Clarendon, 1961.

Harvey, J.H. *The Medieval Architect.* London: Wayland, 1972.

Hubert, J., J. Porcher, and W.-F. Volbach. *Europe of the Invasions,* trans. S. Gilbert and J. Emmons. New York: Braziller, 1969.

Kimpel, Dieter. "Le développement de la taille en série dans l'architecture médiévale et son rôle dans l'histoire économique." *Bulletin monumental* 135 (1977): 195–222.

———, and Robert Suckale. *Die gotische Architektur in Frankreich, 1130–1270.* Munich: Hirmer, 1985.

Mark, Robert. *Gothic Structural Experimentation.* Cambridge: MIT Press, 1982.

———, ed. *Architectural Technology up to the Scientific Revolution.* Cambridge: MIT Press, 1993.

Pevsner, Nikolaus. "The Term Architect in the Middle Ages." *Speculum* 17 (1944): 549–62.

Recht, Roland, et al. *Les bâtisseurs des cathédrales gothiques.* Strasbourg: Editions les Musées de la Ville de Strasbourg, 1989.

CONTENANCE ANGLOISE. The term appears in a passage from Martin Le Franc's *Champion des dames* (ca. 1440):

Et ont pris de la contenance
Angloise, et ensuy Domstable,
Pour quoy merveilleuse plaisance
Rend leur chant joieux et notable.

("They have taken on the *English way* and have followed Dunstable, in order that wondrous consonance might make their music joyous and renowned.") Martin thus documents the influence of English musical style upon Dufay, Binchois, and other Franco-Burgundian composers during the second quarter of the 15th century. By mid-century, the impact of English music may be discerned in the fluid

Illustration of Dufay and Binchois in a manuscript of Martin Le Franc's *Champion des dames,* 1451. BN fr. 12476, fol. 98. *Courtesy of the Bibliothèque Nationale, Paris.*

melodic style, harmonic writing, and mensural practices of continental composers.

J. Michael Allsen

[See also: BINCHOIS, GILLES; DUFAY, GUILLAUME]

Fallows, David. "The *contenance angloise:* English Influence on Continental Composers of the Fifteenth Century." *Renaissance Studies: Journal of the Society for Renaissance Studies* 1 (1987): 189–208.

Strohm, Reinhard. "The Close of the Middle Ages." In *Antiquity and the Middle Ages, from Ancient Greece to the 15th Century,* ed. James McKinnon. Englewood Cliffs: Prentice-Hall, 1990.

CONTRAFACTUM. Adaptation of a new text to an old melody, a common practice in medieval music, seen in 13th-century motets, as well as in troubadour and trouvère songs. An example of a work that was subject to many *contrafacta* is Bernart de Ventadorn's *Can vei la lauzeta mover,* whose melody was adapted to seven additional texts, including *Quan vei l'aloete mover, Plaine d'ire et de desconfort,* and sacred texts like *Seyner, mil gracias ti rent* and *Quisquis cordis et oculi.* In the 14th century, several polyphonic French chansons were provided with sacred Latin *contrafacta* in German areas.

Lawrence Earp

CONVENIENTIA. A transaction of promise (Lat. *convenio*) between two equal parties expressed in a written contract called *convenientia* was used widely among nobles and churchmen in southern and central France in the central Middle Ages to seal agreements, often in place of homage or other feudal transactions. The mutuality and equality of such contracts are striking and in considerable contrast to the unequal relationships usually believed to be expressed by vassalage or feudalism. The *convenientia* has been used to argue for the nonexistence of feudalism in these regions (where, though, a *fevum* contract did exist, it was used to record transactions in which tenants were granted land for cultivation rather than to exchange property among warriors). Such *convenientia* contracts were used, for instance, in compromise settlements after arbitration of disputes between monasteries over pastoralism, in negotiation of marriage contracts between the children of elites, in mutual-aid compacts between warriors (who in fact may have been of unequal power but treat one another as equals), and for the granting of castles by one knightly family to another.

Constance H. Berman

Magnou-Nortier, Elisabeth. *Foi et fidélité: recherches sur l'évolution des liens personnels chez les Francs du VIIe au IXe siècle.* Toulouse: Association des Publications de l'Université de Toulouse–Le Mirail, 1976.

Ourliac, Paul. "La 'convenientia.'" In *Études d'histoire du droit privé offertes à P. Petot.* Paris: Montchrestien, 1959, pp. 413–22.

CONVENT ARCHITECTURE. There have been no systematic analyses of the architecture of women religious in France, and few studies of convents include a concern for the special character of female religious life, as distinct from that of monks. In particular, the architectural implications of strict enclosure (*clausura*), which separated women from the external world, have not been examined, nor has the important and complicated issue of the architectural implications of enclosure for the relationship of women religious to the clergy and liturgy.

The reasons for this neglect are many. With the exception of a few royal or noble foundations (Longchamp, Lys, Maubuisson), convents were often small and poor and have therefore rarely attracted the attention of art historians, who have wanted to study large and significant monuments. At these sites, architectural elaboration was usually confined to one or two details, such as a tracery window (La-Cour-Notre-Dame in the diocese of Sens). The vast majority of convents were destroyed in the Revolution, or the churches and conventual buildings were converted to other purposes. Furthermore, enclosure discourages the study of the few medieval convents that are again in operation. It is probably also true that the lack of interest in convents has historical roots in misogyny.

An examination of the earliest rule specifically for women religious, that of Caesarius of Arles, indicates that the concept of enclosure originated in the early centuries of Christianity. Although there were also a number of double communities for men and women in these centuries, such as that of St. Paulinus at Nola, female monasticism normally took the form of separate establishments with a small number of male clergy in attendance to administer the sacraments. Above all, the monastic administration in women's orders was not centralized: there was therefore always a wide range of arrangements and solutions for women religious, ranging from one or several women practicing a religious vocation in a home to huge convents with several hundred nuns. Since these orders rarely possessed the unified organizational structure of their male counterparts, there is hardly ever the architectural consistency that can be found among many male houses, especially among the Cistercians and Carthusians. For women's monasteries, the annual visitation, performed by male counselors or ministers often outside the order, tended to concern observance of the rule, not issues of architectural conformity. The requirements of enclosure were interpreted differently by each order and reached particular complexity in convents that had both male and female communities, such as Fontevrault and Saint-Louis-de-Poissy.

During the 13th century, the requirements of strict enclosure became increasingly rigid and universal; Poor Clares were known as among the most austere and enclosed of the female orders, even though their churches were open to the lay public. The revival and reaffirmation of strict enclosure, which culminated in Boniface VIII's bull *Periculoso* of 1298 and were to a large extent based on the rule of the Poor Clares, universalized regulations concerning convents. The abbeys had to incorporate new strictures concerning barriers, turning wheels, grills, and gates that would ensure the separation of women from the outside world while allowing necessary supplies to be sent to the community. In some orders, such as the Cistercians, which prohibited the public from access to the church, the issues of enclosure were in some respects simplified: the churches of Cistercian women were often small chapels or simple rectangular structures, rarely with aisles or transepts. The only separations that were required were thus those between the clergy and the nuns. On the other hand, the churches at Fontevrault and Poissy, as well as many Clarissan convents, had to accommodate both male and female monastic communities, as well as the lay public and the clergy. These multiple audiences would have led to a series of screens or spatial divisions that are as yet imperfectly understood. It is evident, however, that as a result of enclosure women religious often could not see the altar or had only a partial view and could therefore not participate visually in the Mass, and in particular the elevation of the host.

Caroline A. Bruzelius

[See also: CAESARIUS OF ARLES; FONTEVRAULT; FRANCISCAN ORDER; MENDICANT ART AND ARCHITECTURE; NUNNERIES; WOMEN, RELIGIOUS EXPERIENCE OF]

de Fontette, M. *Les religieuses à l'âge classique du droit canon: recherches sur les structures juridiques des branches féminines des ordres.* Paris: Vrin, 1967.
Desmarchelier, M. "L'architecture des églises des moniales cisterciennes: essai de classement de différents types de plans." In *Mélanges à la mémoire du père Anselme Dimier,* ed. Benoit Chauvin. 3 vols. in 6 parts. Pupillin, Arbois: Chauvin, 1982–87, Vol. 3, part 5, pp. 79–121.
Gesta 31.4 (1992). [Entire issue dedicated to convent architecture.]

CONVENTS. *See* NUNNERIES

COOKING. Most cooking in medieval France was done in a pot over a fire, suspended by a hook or held up by a trivet. Into this cauldron went such vegetables as cabbages, onions, peas or beans, and/or cereal grains, with or without meat or fish—along with water. The result could be a porridge, soup, or stew—or even, if the household was well provided, something resembling what is still called *pot au feu,* yielding a substantial piece of meat as well as soup. Herbs, especially parsley, frequently flavored the resulting *pottages,* some of which might be spiced in a well-to-do household and/or thickened with bread or eggs. A really well-equipped kitchen also had a spit, on which to roast meats and poultry, and perhaps a grill for broiling and a low-sided pan for frying: fried dishes seem to have been more common in France than in England and northern European countries, but they were rarely to be found in peasant households and generally constituted special treats.

Only the largest households had their own ovens. Some baking could be done directly on the hearth, but generally pastries—meat or fish pies being the most important type—were taken out to a communal oven for baking or purchased from a bakeshop, as bread often was in the towns. The food of the nobility and prosperous bourgeoisie was an elaborated version of what everyone else ate, utilizing more fresh (as against salted or dried) meat and fish and developing such elegant specialties as colored meat and fish jellies and the various dishes based on ground meat in almond milk that found their way to Europe from the Near East. Still, the early recipe collections originating in such wealthy households invariably begin with directions for simpler pottages.

Constance B. Hieatt

[See also: BANQUETING; BEVERAGES; BREAD; DIET AND NUTRITION; FOOD TRADES; MEALS]

Brereton, Georgine E., and Janet M. Ferrier, eds. *Le menagier de Paris.* Oxford: Clarendon, 1981.
Lambert, Carole, ed. *Le recueil de Riom et la manière de henter soutillement: un livre de cuisine et réceptaire sur les greffes du XVe siècle.* Montreal: Ceres, 1987.
Scully, Terence, ed. *The Viandier of Taillevent.* Ottawa: University of Ottawa Press, 1988.
Mennell, Stephen. *All Manners of Food: Eating and Taste in England and France from the Middle Ages to the Present.* Oxford: Blackwell, 1985.
Gottschalk, Alfred. *Histoire de l'alimentation et de la gastronomie depuis la préhistoire jusqu'à nos jours.* 2 vols. Paris: Hippocrate, 1948; Vol. 1, pp. 257–352.
Mulon, Marianne, ed. "Deux traités inédits d'art culinaire médiéval." *Bulletin philologique et historique* (1971 for 1968): 369–435.

COQUILLART, GUILLAUME (1452?–1510). First a lawyer in Paris, then an official of Reims cathedral, Coquillart wrote mock court cases and humorous debates and monologues: *Plaidoyé* and *Enqueste d'entre la simple et la rusée* (1478–79), *Droitz nouveaulx* (1480?), *Débat des dames et des armes* (1498?), and *Monologue Coquillart.* Four other dramatic monologues expressing the tribulations of lovers caught in the act and a sequel to the *Droitz nouveaulx* have also been attributed to him.

Coquillart treats domestic or erotic subjects in a mock-serious style. His first three works, written for the Basoche of Paris, use legal language and procedure to resolve such cases as that of the bourgeois wife who sues her chambermaid for alienating her lover's affections. The *Droitz nouveaulx,* Coquillart's most popular work, is a legalistic compilation of such cases; *Plaidoyé* and *Enqueste* examine the claims of two women disputing possession of one man. The *Débat des dames et des armes,* which argues whether a prince should devote himself to war or women, was probably written for the entry of Louis XII to Reims, where Coquillart held important ecclesiastical and municipal posts. His works, full of verve, gaiety, and bawdy language, mock the foibles and foolishness of his contemporaries.

Heather M. Arden

[See also: BASOCHE]

Coquillart, Guillaume. *Œuvres: suivies d'œuvres attribuées à l'auteur,* ed. Michael J. Freeman. Geneva: Droz, 1975.
———. *Les droitz nouveaulx,* ed. and trans. Maria Luisa Miranda. Rome: Bonacci, 1988.

CORBIE. At the confluence of the Ancre with the Somme, Corbie (Somme) is the site of one of the most influential Benedictine abbeys of the Carolingian period. Founded in 657 by St. Balthild, wife of Clovis II, it was headed briefly by Charlemagne's cousin St. Adalard. It was here that Paschasius Radbertus wrote the first theological treatise on the eucharist. All that remains of the powerful abbey are portions of the abbey church of Saint-Pierre, begun in 1498 in Flamboyant Gothic style, and the Romanesque church of Saint-Étienne, with a 13th-century portal of the Coronation of the Virgin.

William W. Kibler/William W. Clark

Gaillard, L., and J. Daoust, eds. *Corbie, abbaye royale.* Lille: Facultés Catholiques, 1963.
Héliot, Pierre. *L'abbaye de Corbie, ses églises et ses bâtiments.* Louvain: Publications de l'Université de Louvain, 1957.

CORDIER, BAUDE (d. 1397/98). Composer and harp player, now believed to be identifiable with Baude Fresnel of Reims, harpist and *valet de chambre* to the court of Burgundy from 1384 until his death in 1397/98. Of his music, eight songs survive only in sources from the second quarter of the 15th century; but one Gloria appears in the 14th-century Apt manuscript and two unusually mannerist songs—*Tout par compas,* written in the shape of a circle, and *Belle bonne sage,* written in the shape of a heart—appear in the Chantilly manuscript (Musée Condé 564, ca. 1400).

David Fallows

Reaney, Gilbert, ed. *Early Fifteenth-Century Music.* Vol. 1. N.p.: American Institute of Musicology, 1955.
Wright, Craig. *Music at the Court of Burgundy, 1364–1419.* Henryville: Institute of Mediaeval Music, 1979.

CORMONT. Name of two Gothic architects, Thomas and Renaud. The inscription in the Amiens cathedral labyrinth related that Thomas de Cormont succeeded the first master mason, Robert de Luzarches, who began construction of the Gothic edifice in 1220. In turn, Thomas was followed by his son, Renaud, who brought the cathedral to completion and placed the labyrinth plaque in 1288.

Because Thomas de Cormont appears to have followed the plans and retained the forms of Robert de Luzarches, a precise determination of the work of these two Amiens masters remains elusive. Thomas is most frequently attributed with the construction of the ambulatory chapels, sections of the transepts, and west façade in the later 1230s and early 1240s. Numerous similarities in structure, decoration, and tracery patterns led Robert Branner to propose Thomas as the designer of the Sainte-Chapelle in Paris, erected 1241–48.

During a long career between 1245/50 and 1288, Renaud de Cormont built the upper levels of the Amiens choir according to a set of radically different architectural premises. Instead of his predecessors' clear articulation of the elevation's components, Renaud blurred the distinction between stories by setting the same number of units in the triforium and clerestory and by glazing the triforium. His highly decorative vocabulary, seen in the pierced gables of the choir clerestory, the openwork tracery of the flying buttresses, the gablelike moldings that crown the choir triforium openings, and the star vault of the crossing, imparts a sense of metallic fantasy to his architecture. However, Renaud's daring reduction of the mass of the supporting masonry armature and dissolution of the wall into expansive glazed surfaces led to problems of stability that plagued the Amiens chevet for the next three centuries.

Michael T. Davis

[**See also:** AMIENS; PARIS; ROBERT DE LUZARCHES]

Branner, Robert. *Saint Louis and the Court Style in Gothic Architecture.* London: Zwemmer, 1965.
Durand, Georges. *Monographie de l'église cathédrale Notre-Dame d'Amiens.* 2 vols. Paris: Picard, 1901–03.
Erlande-Brandenburg, Alain. "La septième colloque internationale de la Société Française d'Archéologie: la façade de la cathédrale d'Amiens." *Bulletin monumental* 135 (1977): 253–93.
Kimpel, Dieter, and Robert Suckale. *Die gotische Architektur in Frankreich, 1130–1270.* Munich: Hirmer, 1985.
Murray, Stephen. "Looking for Robert de Luzarches: The Early Work at Amiens Cathedral." *Gesta* 29 (1990): 111–31.

CORONATION/CONSECRATION OF KINGS. From the anointing of Pepin the Short in 751 to the end of the Middle Ages, the Frankish and French kings were formally invested with their office by means of inaugural rituals that consisted mainly of consecration (or sacring—anointing with chrism) and coronation (*sacre et couronnement* in modern French, and *consecratio, inauguratio,* or *coronatio* in medieval texts). The rituals quickly became essential to accession to the throne.

The crowning of a king was originally a secular act and the sacring an ecclesiastical one. At first, the two were often administered in different times and places. From the coronation of Louis the Pious in 816, both rituals were sometimes performed together, and from 856 to 877 Hincmar, archbishop of Reims, composed texts that wove these two elements into a unified ceremony. Some prayers and benedictions adopted, adapted, or composed by Hincmar remained permanently in the French ceremony.

For centuries, there was little to differentiate the ceremony in France from that of other countries, nor was there a set place for the coronation of French kings until 1129 (Philip, eldest son of Louis VI). Thereafter, all medieval ceremonies took place in Reims; the archbishop of Reims was normally the coronator. The French rite came to be set apart from that of other monarchies with the adoption of the legend of the Holy Ampulla (the vial of

Holy Chrism purportedly sent from Heaven when St. Remi baptized Clovis I), which was closely associated with Reims. The Holy Chrism is first mentioned in connection with a coronation ceremony in 1131 (Louis VII). Before the end of the 13th century, the legend of the ampulla had been fully incorporated into the French rite. More than anything else, this miraculous chrism created a "royal religion" in France, and the French ceremony was sometimes called an eighth sacrament. The monarch's ability to touch for scrofula after his sacring was considered a proof of his legitimacy and of the efficacy of royal unction. The Holy Chrism was never used on those occasions when a queen was anointed and crowned.

By the end of the Middle Ages, the coronation ceremonial was a protracted liturgical event that included many prayers and benedictions, unction, and investiture with the symbols of knighthood (boots or sandals, and spurs) and of royal office (sword, royal mantle, ring, scepters, crown). The ceremony closed with a Mass and was followed by a postcoronation banquet.

The constitutive aspect of the coronation ritual was extremely important in the high Middle Ages, and no one fully possessed the royal title until he was anointed and crowned. The early Capetians crowned their successors as co-kings to solve the problem of succession and to establish the dynasty firmly upon the throne. The coronation ceased to be juridically necessary, but the circumstances of Charles VII's coronation in 1429 show that it remained indispensable. This, coupled with the requirement that the officiant be an archbishop or bishop, inextricably bound the secular office of government to the Christian religion and flavored the character of medieval French kingship.

Richard A. Jackson

[See also: ENTRIES, ROYAL]

Bouman, Cornelius A. *Sacring and Crowning: The Development of the Latin Ritual for the Anointing of Kings and the Coronation of an Emperor Before the Eleventh Century.* Groningen: Wolters, 1957.

David, Marcel. "Le serment du sacre du IXe au XVe siècle: contribution à l'étude des limites juridiques de la souveraineté." *Revue du moyen âge latin* 6 (1950): 5–272.

Folz, Robert. *The Coronation of Charlemagne, 25 December 800*, trans. J. E. Anderson. London: Routledge and Kegan Paul, 1974.

Jackson, Richard A. *Vive le Roi: A History of the French Coronation from Charles V to Charles X.* Chapel Hill: University of North Carolina Press, 1984.

Schramm, Percy Ernst. *Der König von Frankreich: Das Wesen der Monarchie vom 9. zum 16. Jahrhundert.* 2nd ed. 2 vols. Weimar: Böhlaus, 1960.

CORVÉE. Forced labor service. From Late Latin *corrogare* 'to requisition,' corvées in effect had already been institutionalized in the late Roman Empire. Often reluctant and inefficient *coloni* had to perform a prescribed number of days' work without pay for their landlords. Due from certain categories of people to private proprietors, these services were distinguished from the *opera officialis* that certain freemen had to perform for the state. Frankish kings continued this system. *Coruada* was used in one of Charlemagne's capitularies for a day's work without pay that a man performed for his lord. Feudal nobles appropriated these Frankish usages, dividing them into fixed and exceptional, requisitioned only when normal means proved insufficient. Whether real (attached to the land) or personal, corvées forced labor from servile or free tenants but not from noble vassals. They consisted of repairing roads, bridges, castles, levees, or dikes; felling trees; threshing and carting grain and other materials; or even delivering letters—in return for any of which tasks the lords may have supplied food and drink. When they covered field work on the lord's demesne, plowing and harvesting predominated. Especially in the later Middle Ages, corvées were commuted to money payments, an act that removed any question of stigmatization through an indication of the servility often attached to them, after which inflation reduced them. Royal corvées, however, were instituted in the 17th century and, along with certain unrepealed and much-resented seigneurial ones, lasted until the French Revolution.

Less common and onerous than manual labor and carriage (the duty to help transport with carts, draft animals, and wheelbarrows), a specialized corvée consisted of serving in the host and the guard (watch and ward).

William A. Percy, Jr.

COUCY. A town and barony in the Laonnais region, Coucy (Aisne) first became prominent under Thomas de Marle, who was lord of the place between 1116 and 1130 and a brutal warrior against whom Louis VI of France campaigned repeatedly at the behest of the clergy. Thereafter, the lords of Coucy tended to be loyal to the king without surrendering their spirit of independence. Enguerrand III the Great (1191–1243) turned the family castle into an enormous fortress. His daughter Alix married the count of Guines, and when the male line of the family died out in 1311, their son succeeded as Enguerrand V.

Enguerrand VII (b. 1340; lord of Coucy 1346–97) was a hostage in England in the 1360s and married the daughter of Edward III. In 1376, he returned to France, becoming a major military commander under Charles V and Charles VI. Like many nobles from northern France, he had been associated with Charles the Bad of Navarre in the faction opposing the ruling house of Valois and in later life was linked with the faction at court that supported Olivier de Clisson against the dukes of Berry and Burgundy. Yet he managed not to become too closely tied to any faction and retained the respect of all parties. Besides serving the French crown, he participated in crusades in 1390 and 1396. The latter campaign, which culminated in the disastrous Battle of Nicopolis in Hungary, led to his death in captivity. Enguerrand VII was the last male member of the Coucy family; his daughter Marie sold the lordship to the duke of Orléans.

The château of Enguerrand III, a masterpiece of military architecture, covered a vast site and stood on an easily defensible position, which may explain why, aside from repairs and rebuilding of the gateways and the donjon by Enguerrand VII in the 14th century, the complex survived largely intact until World War I. The original structure had some twenty-eight towers and walls that stretched for almost a mile. The château itself sits on the northern promontory of the site and is separated from the lower court, the bailey, by a trench, the whole dominated by the huge circular donjon. Two other deep trenches separate the bailey from the town and the town from the plateau. The parish church was built in the 12th and 13th centuries but extensively altered in the 16th.

John Bell Henneman, Jr./William W. Clark

[See also: MARMOUSETS; NICOPOLIS]

Barthélemy, Dominique. *Les deux âges de la seigneurie banale: pouvoir et société dans la terre des sires de Coucy, milieu XIe–milieu XIIIe siècle.* Paris: Publications de la Sorbonne, 1984.

Chaurand, Jacques. *Thomas de Marle, sire de Coucy, sire de Marle: seigneur de la Fere, Vervins, Pinon et autres lieux.* Marle: Syndicat d'Initiative, 1963.

Dufour, Étienne. *Coucy-le-Château et ses environs.* Soissons: Nougarède, 1910.

Enaud, François. *Coucy.* 2nd ed. Paris: CNMHS, 1978.

Lefèvre-Pontalis, Eugène. *Le château de Coucy.* Paris: Laurens, 1913.

Lepinois, Eugène de Bouchère de. *Histoire de la ville et des sires de Coucy.* Paris: Dumoulin, 1859.

Mesqui, Jean. *Île-de-France gothique.* 2 vols. Paris: Picard, 1988, Vol. 2, pp. 134–59.

Salch, Charles-Laurent. *L'atlas des villes et villages fortifiés en France.* Strasbourg: Pubitotal, 1987, pp. 176–78.

Tuchman, Barbara W. *A Distant Mirror: The Calamitous Fourteenth Century.* New York: Knopf, 1978.

COUCY, CHÂTELAIN DE (d. 1203).

An outstanding early trouvère, Guy de Thourotte was governor of Coucy castle in Picardy from 1186 until his death as a crusader. Of more than thirty compositions ascribed to him in medieval songbooks, only fifteen or so seem authentic. All texts survive with music, and all pieces are courtly chansons in a style derived from the Provençal tradition. Like his friend and fellow trouvère Gace Brulé, the Châtelain sings invariably of love, but his songs are more poignant than despairing and suggest an erotic reality. By the end of the 13th century, the Châtelain had been mythified into a great tragic lover, whom Jakemes, an otherwise unknown writer, made the hero of his *Roman du castelain de Coucy et de la dame de Fayel.*

Samuel N. Rosenberg

[See also: GACE BRULÉ; REALISTIC ROMANCES; TROUVÈRE POETRY]

Châtelain de Coucy. *Chansons attribuées au Chastelain de Couci,* ed. Alain Lerond. Paris: Presses Universitaires de France, 1963.

van der Werf, Hendrik, ed. *Trouvères-Melodien I.* Kassel: Bärenreiter, 1977, pp. 186–282.

COUNT/COUNTY.

The 174 administrative counties, or *pagi*, into which France was divided in 950 began to disintegrate between ca. 980 and 1030, and many of the banal powers formerly reserved to the count were progressively usurped by the lesser nobles who throughout France began to carve out zones of command around the castles they either seized from the count or built for themselves. The period 1025–1125 was characterized by a constant struggle not only between the rising castellans and the counts, who sought to reestablish some sort of authority over them, but also among neighboring counts in many regions, who commonly struggled for control of castellanies whose territories fell partly or wholly outside the traditional boundaries of their county.

When the social and political structures crystallized once again in the 12th century, there were still about a hundred dominions bearing the title "county" (OFr. *conté,* Old Occitan *comtat*) in the kingdom, but they were now, like the kingdom as a whole, federal dominions whose boundaries were usually those of the castellanies and baronies whose lords had been persuaded to hold them in fief from the count, and they were held together largely by those new feudo-vassalic bonds.

The new federal counties varied greatly in extent, from the princely counties of Champagne and Toulouse, more than 12,300 square miles in area, to the tiny castellanial counties of Dammartin and Gaure, with areas of less than 100 square miles.

The 102 counties of 1100 were held by seventy-six counts (OFr. *cuens, conte,* Old Occitan *comte*), including the king and seven bishops, and the sixty-seven lay counts other than the king belonged to forty-six distinct patrilineages. Although the nature and extent of their authority varied almost as much as their wealth, all counts were relatively important lords—significantly richer on average than viscounts or simple barons. By 1200, all counties had come to be regarded as fiefs dependent either on the kingdom or on one of the great principalities, so that from 1202 there were three distinct classes of count: those who were barons and peers of the realm, those who were only barons of the realm, and those who were peers and (or) barons of a principality. From ca. 850, the wives and widows of the more important counts of southern France used the title "countess" (Lat. *comitissa,* Old Occitan *contesa*), and by 1100 the Old French *contesse* was also in general use in the north.

Between 1100 and 1500, the essential nature of the French county changed little. Some sixty-seven of the 102 counties of 1100 survived to 1500, most with only minor modifications of their boundaries, but others lost their comital title through annexation to a demesne. After 1237, new baronial counties were normally created by royal letters. The kings created some thirty-seven new counties in this way between 1314, when Beaumont-le-Roger was created, and 1498, and the number of counties was further affected by changes in the boundaries of the kingdom and the evolution of five counties into duchies between 1360 and 1498. As a result of all these changes, the total number of counties in France dropped to eighty-four by 1327, but rose again to ninety-five in 1422 and 105 in 1498. The number of counts also tended to decline down to 1327, as certain powerful princes, especially the king and members of the royal house of Capet, accumulated growing numbers of counties. The eighty-four counties of 1327 were held by only fifty-two counts, including thirty-nine lay barons and twenty-seven non-Capetians, but thereafter all three numbers fluctuated only slightly down to 1515.

D'A. Jonathan D. Boulton

[See also: *COMITES*; DUKE/DUCHY; KNIGHTHOOD; NOBILITY]

Boulton, D'A.J.D. *Grants of Honour: The Origins of the System of Nobiliary Dignities of Traditional France, ca. 1100–1515.* Forthcoming.

Dhondt, Jan. *Études sur la naissance des principautés territoriales en France (IXe–Xe siècles).* Bruges: De Tempel, 1948.

Feuchère, P. "Essai sur l'évolution territoriale des principautés françaises du Xe au XIIIe siècle." *Moyen âge* 58 (1952): 85–117.

Guilhiermoz, Paul. *Essai sur l'origine de la noblesse en France au moyen âge.* Paris: Picard, 1902.

COUR DES AIDES. See Généraux

COURONNEMENT DE LOUIS.

This epic, one of the oldest of the Guillaume d'Orange Cycle (pre-1150; 2,670 assonanced decasyllables), is anchored in history. Acquainted with Carolingian chronicles, such as Einhard's *Vita Karoli* and Thegan's *Vita Hludowici*, its author alludes to Charlemagne's association of his son Louis with the throne at Aix-la-Chapelle in 813; but he is just as sensitive to the political preoccupations of his own day: imperial claims and the expansion of Capetian power, which, under Louis VII, was still weak.

The poem has five episodes. In the first, Guillaume thwarts a would-be usurper, Hernaïs d'Orléans, who sought to profit from Louis's inexperience (ll. 1–241). The second begins with Guillaume's pilgrimage to Rome and ends with his victory over the Saracens and Corsolt. The hero is about to marry King Gaifier's daughter when messengers call him back to help Louis (242–1,386). Guillaume frees his lord and kills the usurper Acelin (1,387–1,960). A fourth episode has the hero traveling throughout the kingdom to pacify it; attacked by Acelin's father, Richard of Normandy, he captures him and turns him over to Louis, who imprisons him for life (1,961–2,197). All that is left for Guillaume is to negate Gui the German's claims on Rome (2,198–2,631), before a short conclusion informs us that Guillaume will never cease having to come to his lord's rescue.

Above all, the *Couronnement* proposes a model of royal power in its dealings with the great vassals. Essentially symbolic, royal power derives its practical efficacy from a harmonious collaboration with the knightly class, represented here by Guillaume's lineage, which alone permits it to fulfill its obligations: providing a balance of power within the kingdom, protecting the church, fighting the infidels, and laying imperial claims. This explains the apparently diffuse structure of the poem. Guillaume's fidelity to his lord is tested over time in analogous but never identical circumstances. A number of threads, always centered on the hero, are woven through the episodes; there is no need to posit an earlier, more unified version of the poem.

François Suard

[See also: *CHARROI DE NÎMES*; EINHARD; GUILLAUME D'ORANGE CYCLE; *PRISE D'ORANGE*]

Lepage, Yvan G., ed. *Les rédactions en vers du Couronnement de Louis.* Geneva: Droz, 1978.

Frappier, Jean. *Les chansons de geste du cycle de Guillaume d'Orange.* 2 vols. Paris: SEDES, 1965, Vol. 2, pp. 47–178.

COURTESY BOOKS.

Broadly defined as vernacular works for lay audiences that teach etiquette, comportment, and moral values according to gender and social class, courtesy books include works in a variety of genres written from the 12th to the 15th century. Drawing on biblical and historical exempla, the dicta of Cato and Solomon, precepts of the church fathers, proverbs, and contemporary literature and customs, the authors of courtesy literature defined appropriate behavior for men and women of a specified rank.

Among the oldest vernacular didactic works is the Occitan *ensenhamen* of Garin le Brun (second half of the 12th c.); eight other courtly didactic poems of this genre are extant. The oldest estates poem, the *Livre des manières* by Étienne de Fougères (late 12th c.), dedicated to the countess of Hereford, expounds the roles and laments the failings of kings, clergy, knights, peasants, bourgeois, and both virtuous and immoral women.

Courtesy literature flourished in the 13th century, as the royalty and the aristocracy sought to foster noble conduct in their families. St. Louis wrote separate letters of instruction to his son and to his daughters. At the behest of Philip III, Egidio Colonna (Giles of Rome) wrote *De regimine principum* for the future Philip IV the Fair. Translated into French in the late 13th century as the *Livre du gouvernement des rois*, this work has chapters on the domestic duties of women and the education of children, as well as on the rectitude of princes and civil and military government. A royal "mirror" for princesses, the *Speculum dominarum* by Durand de Champagne, was translated into French as the *Miroir des dames* in nine 14th- and 15th-century manuscripts before its adaptation by Ysambert de Saint-Léger in the Renaissance. Two works addressed to the lesser nobility, the anonymous *Urbain li Courtois* (second half of the 13th c.; eight manuscripts) and the *Enseignements de Robert de Ho* (1260?), conveyed lessons in courtesy and comportment from father to son: honor God and parents, avoid taverns and loose women, don't scratch in public. Both of these short treatises were composed in Anglo-Norman in octosyllabic rhyming couplets. Other late-medieval treatises on manners are preserved in only a single manuscript each: the *Apprise de nurture* (237 lines), *Bon enfant* (eighty-nine lines), *Edward* (332 lines), and *Petit traitise de nurture* (190 lines).

Following the lead of Perceval's mother in Chrétien's *Conte du graal*, poems like Raoul de Houdenc's *Roman des eles* (first third of the 13th c.) and *Ordene de chevalerie* (second half of the 13th c.) instructed knights in the moral lessons of chivalry. Three brief poems about table manners, the *Contenances de table*, dating from the late 13th to the 15th century and deriving from a Latin model linked to the *Liber faceti*, counseled cleanliness and polite behavior at table.

Courtesy literature sharply segregated roles for men and women, as seen in Robert de Blois, who wrote didactic verse for aristocratic patrons in the mid-13th century. His *Enseignement des princes* is a sober Christian allegory of princely virtues; the *Chastoiement des dames* alternates between stern moralizing and courtly banter about women's amorous activities. The enticing threat of female sexuality is a recurrent motif in these works: in *Urbain*, men are advised to marry illiterate women, who are more likely to be faithful.

Female instruction is the principal aim of two late 14th-century treatises. The *Livre du chevalier de la Tour Landry* (1371–72), written for his daughters by a knight of considerable standing who fought for France in the Hundred Years' War, contains 128 chapters that warn against impropriety and extol courtesy, modesty in dress, and especially chastity and marital fidelity. The Knight offers a frank depiction of sexual temptations and of the violent punishments—beatings, death—that follow women's disobedience. His examples, which the narrator says have been supplied by two priests and two clerics, are drawn from stock biblical and historical sources, fabliaux, and contemporary life. In a lengthy debate with her husband near the work's conclusion, the Knight's wife condemns courtly love as a dangerous trap for women. The Knight claims to have written a similar book for his sons, but only this one to his daughters has survived, in at least twenty-one French manuscripts, two English translations (one by Caxton in 1484), and a German printed edition.

In the *Menagier de Paris* (1392–94), a wealthy elderly bourgeois of Paris sets forth a compendium of moral wisdom and household management for his young wife, providing exhaustive details about housekeeping, gardening, cooking, the training of servants, horses, and hawking. As staunchly moral as the Chevalier de la Tour-Landry, the Menagier tries to show compassion for his wife's youth, insisting that he would never attempt to test her as Griselda had been tried. The Knight's and the Menagier's books paint a somber picture of the constraints placed on young women and offer revealing portraits of male attitudes about female instruction in late-medieval society.

Christine de Pizan was the first woman to write a courtesy book for other women. Her *Trésor de la cité des dames ou Le livre des trois vertus* (1405) was written for Marguerite of Burgundy, wife of the dauphin, Louis of Guyenne. The book defines the moral virtues and duties of women of all conditions and ranks: unmarried and married women, widows, princesses, women of rank, nuns, bourgeois and peasant wives, even prostitutes. Christine's message to women is no less conservative than that of her male predecessors, although her style is more refined. Like the Chevalier de la Tour Landry, she sternly condemns amorous intrigues and lauds chastity, marital fidelity, and obedience. She advocates that women of all classes aid their husbands in their duties, however exalted or humble they may be. Christine also sets forth principles for the instruction of princes, knights, and men of all classes in the *Livre du corps de policie* (1407). A century later, Anne de Bourbonnois adapted Christine's precepts for noblewomen, along with those of St. Louis, in her book of instruction for her daughter, Susanne de Bourbon, in the *Enseignements d'Anne de France* (ca. 1504–05).

Medieval courtesy books continued to be read in the Renaissance, when several appeared in printed editions and served as sources for Renaissance treatises on gentility. Their popularity attests to the tensions and anxieties that surround the transformation of social roles. Far from being always predictable compendia of stereotypes, these diverse works offer historians and literary critics complex views of daily life and customs and sexual and social mores, as well as ironic commentary about human nature.

Roberta L. Krueger

[See also: CHRISTINE DE PIZAN; DIDACTIC LITERATURE (OCCITAN); ÉTIENNE DE FOUGÈRES; GILES OF ROME; LA TOUR LANDRY, GEOFFROI DE; *MENAGIER DE PARIS*; RAOUL DE HOUDENC; ROBERT DE BLOIS]

Anne de France. *Les enseignements d'Anne de France, duchesse de Bourbon et d'Auvergne à sa fille Susanne de Bourbon,* ed. Alphonse Martiel Chazaud. Moulins: Desrosiers, 1878.

Brereton, Georgine E., and Janet M. Ferrier, eds. *Le menagier de Paris.* Oxford: Clarendon, 1981.

Christine de Pizan. *The Treasure of the City of Ladies or the Book of the Three Virtues,* trans. Sarah Lawson. Harmondsworth: Penguin, 1985.

Étienne de Fougères. *Le livre des manières,* ed. R. Anthony Lodge. Geneva: Droz, 1979.

Garin le Brun. "L'Enseignement de Garin le Brun," ed. Carl Appel. *Revue des langues romanes* 33 (1889): 404–32.

Glixelli, Stefan. "Les contenances de table." *Romania* 47 (1921): 1–40.

Louis IX. "Les *Enseignements* au Prince Philippe." In *La vie en France au moyen âge de la fin du XIIe au milieu du XIVe siècle d'après des moralistes du temps,* ed. Charles-Victor Langlois. Paris: Hachette, 1925, pp. 35–46.

Robert of Blois. *Robert de Blois: son œuvre didactique et narrative . . . suivie d'une édition critique . . . de l'Enseignement des Princes et du Chastoiement des Dames,* ed. John Fox. Paris: Nizet, 1950.

Molenaer, Samuel Paul, ed. *Li livres du gouvernement des rois: A XIIIth Century French Version of Egidio Colonna's 'De Regimine Principum.'* New York: Macmillan, 1899.

Montaiglon, Anatole de, ed. *Le livre du chevalier de la Tour Landry pour l'enseignement de ses filles.* Paris: Bibliothèque Elzevirienne, 1854.

Parsons, H. Rosamund, ed. *Urbain le Courtois.* In "Anglo-Norman Books of Courtesy and Nurture." *PMLA* 44 (1929): 383–455.

Raoul de Houdenc. *"Le roman des eles"; The Anonymous "Ordene de Chevalerie,"* ed. Keith Busby. Amsterdam: Benjamins, 1983.

Young, Mary-Vance, ed. *Les enseignements de Robert de Ho, dits Enseignements Trebor.* Paris: Picard, 1901.

Ysambert de Saint-Léger. *Le miroir des dames,* ed. Camillo Marazza. Lecce: Milella, 1978.

Bornstein, Diane. *The Lady in the Tower: Medieval Courtesy Literature for Women.* Hamden: Archon, 1983.

Hentsch, Alice Adèle. *De la littérature didactique du moyen âge s'adressant spécialement aux femmes.* Halle: Cahors, 1903.

Nicholls, Jonathan. *The Matter of Courtesy: Medieval Courtesy Books and the Gawain-Poet.* Woodbridge: Brewer, 1985.

COURTLY LOVE. The expression "courtly love" does not date to the Middle Ages. It was in all likelihood first used by the eminent 19th-century French medievalist Gaston Paris in the context of a two-part article devoted to romances of the Round Table that appeared in 1881 and 1883. Paris's discussion of love focused upon Chrétien de Troyes's *Lancelot,* the first extant medieval work telling of the adulterous relationship between Arthur's queen, Guenevere, and Lancelot, premier knight of the court. For Paris, the importance of Chrétien's account was in the delineation of a particular type of love relationship that can be explained neither by its putative Celtic sources nor by any historically sanctioned theological or social attitude toward love and marriage. He sharply distinguishes it, most notably, from the brutal spontaneity of the most famous medieval story of adulterous passion, that of Tristan and Iseut, as well as from Chrétien's other romances, such as *Erec et Enide* and *Yvain,* which propose an ideal of wedded love. Specific to the Lancelot-Guenevere affair is its very artificiality, a sense of refinement that Paris qualifies as "excessive and bizarre" (*Romania* 10: 469). The idolatrous passion of Lancelot for Guenevere entails a type of rule-oriented behavior, predicated upon the superiority of the beloved and the lover's efforts to gain her favor. Although Paris cites the *Lancelot* as the first narrative fiction to glorify "courtly" love, the emotional construct was not necessarily Chrétien's invention; the romance conveyed an "absolute" vision of the lover "such as it had long before been conceived in lyric poetry and dreamed about, if not brought to realization, in life" (*Romania* 12: 517). The tradition of love literature thus initiated in 12th-century lyric and romance continued in an unbroken line through to the 15th century in a variety of genres—lyric poetry, romance, short story, debate—that were the stock-in-trade of vernacular authors of the period, including many of France's most illustrious: Guillaume de Lorris, Thibaut de Champagne, Richard de Fournival, Adam de la Halle, Guillaume de Machaut, Jean Froissart, Charles d'Orléans, Alain Chartier.

Paris lists four characteristics of the type of love in question: (1) it is furtive and illegitimate, for such a desire founded in the perpetual fear of loss or distancing, requiring a constant sacrifice of oneself, could not take place in a context of public possession (i.e., marriage); (2) the lover, however great a knight, is always an inferior, while the beloved is haughty, capricious, and disdainful; (3) knightly deeds are conceived as a means of increasing one's value in the service of love, thus exalting the love relationship itself; and (4) "love is an art, a science, a virtue, which has its rules just as chivalry and courtliness have theirs." When Paris proceeds to summarize these qualities by coining the phrase "*courtly* love," it should be clear that he is establishing, through his use of italics, a precautionary critical distance. For his purposes, the phrase translates the vaguely paradoxical nature of this construct, uniting as it does the social or communal (courtly) and the personal (love); the playfully rule-oriented and the serious; the sensual and the mystical.

Paris depends for much of his material upon a text roughly contemporary to Chrétien's *Lancelot,* considered by many to be a serious treatise on the subject, Andreas Capellanus's Latin *De amore* (frequently translated as *The Art of Courtly Love*). In a series of fictional judgments pronounced by "authorities" like Eleanor of Aquitaine and her daughter Marie of Champagne (the patron to whom Chrétien's romance was dedicated), the treatise provides an outline of some of the cultural and social problems encountered in love relationships along with an enumeration of the rules and regulations themselves (e.g., "he who is not jealous cannot love"). This work, divided into three books, on the model of Ovid's *Ars amatoria,* itself remains highly ambiguous, however, for the third book functions as a palinode of the first two, a vociferous condemnation of the frivolity—indeed, the moral perniciousness—of such love relationships.

Paris's felicitous expression seems to have gained immediate acceptance, becoming common currency in discussions of medieval love literature: finally, a term was available to denote a phenomenon that had intrigued 19th-century scholars dating as far back as Stendhal's famous 1822 *Essai sur l'amour.* Although many had spoken of the appearance of a new type of romantic love in early 12th-century France, Gaston Paris gave it a name. As the use of the expression spread, however, so did its application become increasingly normative. The most influential account of courtly love since Gaston Paris, the one that has been read by generations of scholars and students as the "last word" on the subject, is C.S. Lewis's *Allegory of Love,* published in 1936: "The sentiment, of course, is love, but love of a highly specialized sort, whose characteristics may be enumerated as Humility, Courtesy, Adultery, and the Religion of Love" (p. 2).

Early scholarship, taking the courtly-love paradigm as a sociological given, a real-life phenomenon fostered in the "courts of love," steered the question of origins in a multitude of directions. How could such a strikingly new way of expressing and codifying male-female relations have appeared from nowhere? Where did it come from? Answers to the latter question were proposed over the first half of this century, ranging from Neoplatonism to Arabic poetry, from Cathar heresies rampant in the south of France (prior to their extirpation in the Albigensian Crusade) to a rediscovery of Ovidian poetry. Historically oriented studies have attempted to demonstrate the appropriateness of courtly love's appearance at a time when feudal society was entering a new phase, in which a recently achieved economic and political stability gave rise to interconnected sociocultural phenomena: widespread civilizing impulses, an extensive network of literary patronage, and a generation of young disinherited nobles in search of a fortune and a family. Feminist critics have more recently debated the influence of noblewomen in the conception and reception of the courtly ideal. No single theory has gained general acceptance, nor is there likely to be any consensus, as this side of the debate has been eclipsed by other issues.

The most vigorous work in recent years has tended to negate the validity of the expression itself. Preeminent among such critics, D.W. Robertson issued a strong challenge to those who believe in the existence of courtly love, basing his argument upon a Christian interpretation of medieval society. The criticism aimed at eliminating courtly love as a part of our literary vocabulary centers principally upon three issues. The first is terminological, arising from the fact that "courtly love" is a 19th-century concoction and not genuinely medieval. The second issue stems from the observation that what we know as courtly love is found almost exclusively in literary texts and is nowhere substantiated in legal, theological, or historical writings. Indeed, much of what is depicted in the courtly-love literature must be labeled either illegal or immoral when measured against the mores of medieval society. The third aspect of the criticism arises from an ethical and rhetorical interpretation of the texts themselves. Works like *Lancelot*, which seem to depict an antisocial "religion of love," are actually to be understood ironically, as the parodic presentation of idolatrous cupidity, for (so the argument goes) no medieval Christian audience could tolerate the serious depiction of such otherwise immoral behavior.

Jean Frappier has been the most effective defender of courtly love. While admitting the expression's lack of authenticity, he has convincingly demonstrated that the Middle Ages did have a term for the concept in question: *fin'amors*, or "pure love." The charge that the term's inauthenticity entails that of the concept is thus without substance, and the question becomes one of deciding how to redefine an expression that has become indispensable to our common critical vocabulary. As for the second critique, to expect socially orthodox behavior in the literature is to misunderstand the very status of vernacular courtly lyric and romance as escapist forms of literary creation cultivated in many cases at the margins of the dominant (theological and political) power structures and all that this status implies in terms of wish-fulfillment, personal fantasy, and potentially antiestablishment tendencies. Finally, Frappier's answer to the problem of the texts' irony, framed as a rhetorical question, is succinctly cogent: "How [or, we might add, why] could one mock or parody something that never existed?" (Frappier, p. 64).

The crux of the matter is not so much that the concept designated by the expression "courtly love" never existed, but that common usage of it needs to be subjected to as much caution as Andreas Capellanus's seemingly authoritative treatise. In this, the criticisms of "courtly love" are not totally foundationless, for they underscore a problem inherent in Gaston Paris's initial definition and more fully elaborated in C. S. Lewis's categorical restatement: a failure to differentiate lyric from narrative, subjective expression from fictional event, rhetoric from reality. As a complex of thematic elements and rhetorical figures that appears to have found its first formulation in the lyric poetry of the troubadours, thence gravitating to the courts of northern France, "courtly love" is first and foremost the expression of a male subjectivity confronted with the joyous exaltation and pain of erotic desire, accompanied by a consequent fear of isolation and potential loss. Elaboration of love on the psychological level tends to glorify its status as a sublimating virtue, while metaphoric developments of its enslaving power, frequently drawn from the registers of armed combat or imprisonment, abound. When transferred to a narrative setting, a fictional pretext for the lover's isolation needs to be found: hence, the frequently exploited theme of adultery. Adulterous relations are, to be sure, a recurring theme in troubadour lyric as well, but to assert that adultery is a constitutive element of courtly love is to mistake the incidental for the essential.

Short of extending the definition of "courtly love," it is impossible to account for the broad spectrum of literary creations, both in France and elsewhere in Europe, that developed the exalted expression of love-longing in both ironic and spiritual directions. Such divergent works as the lyric corpus of Jaufre Rudel, Thomas's *Tristan*, and Guillaume de Lorris's *Roman de la Rose*, all seminal items in the "courtly love" canon, scarcely present similar attitudes toward love. Adultery is central to *Tristan*, nonexistent in the other two. The particularity of the love object in *Tristan* and the *Rose* contrasts with the immateriality of Jaufre's beloved. Another work, the anonymous 13th-century *Chastelaine de Vergy*, seemingly a classic example of the paradigmatic situation described by Gaston Paris, all but eradicates the social aspects of the lovers' situation (the adulterous triangle) as it highlights the theoretical ramifications of the knight's unfortunate revelation of the furtive love affair: the Châtelaine dies for no other fictional reason than her inner disappointment at the breach of secrecy. Secrecy is no longer a fictional means to an end (maintaining the love relationship), but an end in its own right. By contrast, *Cele qui ne pooit oïr parler de foutre*, one of the many fabliaux predicated upon courtly stereotypes, pokes fun at the hypocritical courtly injunction toward proper speech by juxtaposing it with the pleasure of the uncourtly sexual act. The literary masterpieces that appeared elsewhere in Italy (Dante, Boccaccio), Germany (Gottfried von Strassburg, Wolfram von Eschenbach), and England (Chaucer) adapted French and Occitan courtly models to their own social and cultural needs.

To eliminate the term, to insist that there is no such tradition with specific rhetorical and thematic topoi, would be to impoverish our understanding of many works that presuppose a familiarity with its stereotyped erotic themes and vocabulary. This is especially true of those works, often written late in the Middle Ages, that maintain an ambivalent or overtly satirical stance toward the idealized tenets of courtly love service. How otherwise are we to comprehend the disintegration of the tradition in the 15th century, most tellingly displayed in Alain Chartier's oblique condemnation of unrewarded love service in *La belle dame sans merci* and the extended debate to which it gave rise? Unless one sees love rhetoric itself as a form of poetic imprisonment, how to detect the transgressive satire of François Villon's bitter legacy to his apparently unfaithful "Love," his "dear rose"—neither his heart nor his liver, but a "large silk purse," figure of another part of the poet's anatomy?

David F. Hult

[See also: ANDREAS CAPELLANUS; ARABIC INFLUENCE ON LITERATURE; CHRÉTIEN DE TROYES; DROUART LA VACHE]

Boase, Roger. *The Origin and Meaning of Courtly Love: A Critical Study of European Scholarship.* Manchester: Manchester University Press, 1977.

Burns, E. Jane, and Roberta L. Krueger, eds. "Courtly Ideology and Woman's Place in Medieval French Literature." Special Issue of *Romance Notes* 25. (Spring 1985).

Duby, Georges. "Dans la France du nord-ouest, au XIIe siècle: les jeunes dans la société aristocratique." *Annales: Economies—Sociétés—Civilisations* 19 (1964): 835–46.

Frappier, Jean. *Amour courtois et table ronde.* Geneva: Droz, 1973.

Köhler, Erich. "Observations historiques et sociologiques sur la poésie des troubadours." *Cahiers de civilisation médiévale* 7 (1964): 27–51.

Lewis, C.S. *The Allegory of Love.* Oxford: Clarendon, 1936.

Newman, Francis X., ed. *The Meaning of Courtly Love.* Albany: State University of New York Press, 1968. [Articles by D.W. Robertson, Jr., C. Singleton, W.T.H. Jackson, J. F. Benton, and T. Silverstein.]

Paris, Gaston. "Études sur les romans de la table ronde: *Lancelot du Lac.*" *Romania* 10 (1881): 465–96; 12 (1883): 459–534.

COURTOIS D'ARRAS. The earliest and most original dramatization of the parable of the prodigal son (Luke 15:11–32), *Courtois d'Arras* was composed in Arras by an unknown author in the first quarter of the 13th century. There are no stage directions in the 664-line play, though six narrative verses introduce the central episode of Courtois's riotous living in the tavern, where he is tricked and robbed by two prostitutes and the innkeeper. The realism and humor of this scene, reminiscent of other 13th-century Arras plays by Jehan Bodel and Adam de la Halle, form a dramatic and metrical contrast to the subsequent lamentations of the destitute youth. Prodded by hunger, Courtois sincerely repents his folly and, recognizing his sin of pride, returns humbly to his father.

The biblical "famine in the land" is replaced in this play by the hero's own ravenous hunger. The inedible piece of bread given him by his new master and the dry, inedible peapods that the swine are trampling are an expressive contrast with the *pain et pois* ("bread and peas") he had rejected in his father's house. The opening and closing dialogues between the father and the unsympathetically portrayed elder brother frame the threefold central action of worldliness, repentance, and reconciliation, a pattern followed by many later miracle and morality plays. The pattern is symbolized here by Courtois's three coats: the fine one he loses in the tavern, the ragged garment he wears as a swineherd, and the new robe given him on his return home to his father.

Lynette R. Muir

Faral, Edmond, ed. *Courtois d'Arras.* 2nd ed. Paris: Champion, 1922.

Axton, Richard, and John Stevens, trans. *Courtois d'Arras.* In *Medieval French Plays.* Oxford: Blackwell, 1971, pp. 137–64.

COURTRAI. On July 11, 1302, outside the town of Courtrai in the county of Flanders, a rebellious force of Flemish townspeople defeated a large French army composed mainly of mounted knights.

Under the direct rule of Philip IV, who had imprisoned their count, Gui de Dampierre, in 1297, the Flemings resented their subjection to the monarchy. In 1302, artisans in Bruges massacred a French force sent to put down a rebellious element. Gathered from all the towns and rural areas of Flanders, a newly formed army, led by a son and grandson of the imprisoned count, began advancing against French castles and garrisons in the county, arriving at the castle outside Courtrai on June 26.

A French army under the leadership of Robert d'Artois, composed of about 2,500 knights and accompanied by a support troop of many light infantry and Italian mercenary crossbowmen, arrived on the field of Courtrai on July 8. Robert faced 8,000–15,000 Flemish infantry and very few knights. Although the Flemish army was larger, the French troops were better armed and more experienced. The Flemings, however, held the better ground with their backs to a river, and had dug ditches in the field to hinder cavalry charges.

On July 11, the battle began with crossbowmen exchanging ineffective fire. Robert then sent his French infantry into battle. Although this infantry was effective, almost to the point of victory, Robert recalled them so that he could finish off the Flemings with his knights. The French knights charged repeatedly, but the Flemish infantry held, and the knights fell with little impact upon the Flemish lances and *godedags*, a curious weapon that combined features of the spear and mace. The French losses were great: between 40 and 50 percent of their knights died, including Robert d'Artois. Hundreds of their golden spurs (awarded for victories in tournaments) were collected by the Flemings and hung in the cathedral of the Virgin in Courtrai.

Kelly DeVries

Johnstone, Hilda, ed. and trans. *Annales Gandenses*. London: Oxford University Press, 1951.

Funck-Brentano, Frantz. *Philippe le Bel en Flandre: les origines de la guerre de cent ans*. Paris: Champion, 1896.

Verbruggen, J.F. *The Art of Warfare in Western Europe During the Middle Ages,* trans. Sumner Willard and S.C.M. Southern. Amsterdam: North-Holland, 1977.

———. *De slag der guldensporen, bijdrage tot de geschiedenis van Vlaanderens vrijheidsoorlog, 1297–1305.* Antwerp: Standard-Boekhandel, 1952.

COUTANCES. The city of Coutances (Manche) existed from Roman times (when it was called Constantia) and became a bishopric in the early Middle Ages. In the 9th century, Coutances fell to Norman invaders. By the 11th century, the city regained its position as a religious center; a Norman Romanesque cathedral replaced the edifice that the Vikings had razed ca. 900.

A fire in 1218 severely damaged the Romanesque church, but the new Gothic cathedral constructed during the 13th century encases part of the Romanesque structure and essentially follows its plan and dimensions. The Gothic cathedral consists of a nave of seven bays with side aisles, to which chapels were added between the buttresses in the late 13th and early 14th centuries; a short transept with crossing tower and added porches; and a three-bay choir surrounded by an ambulatory merging with radiating chapels, to which a projecting central chapel was added in the 14th century. The elevation is three-story in the nave and two-story in the choir.

While some features, especially the unity of choir aisles and chapels, are reminiscent of French Gothic cathedrals, such as Bourges, many elements reflect traditions of Norman architecture. Both the interior and exterior display ample linear detailing as seen on the two-tower west façade. The dominant octagonal crossing tower is outstanding in both its construction on pendentives and its interior and exterior articulation.

Fifteen 13th-century stained-glass windows are preserved in the transept, ambulatory, and upper choir, including representations of SS. Thomas of Canterbury, George, and Blaise, as well as the Last Judgment in the south transept. Sculpture from the west façade was destroyed during the Revolution, but the tympana of the north and south transept porches have early 13th-century sculpture of the Virgin with Angels and the Apocalyptic Christ.

Karen Gould

Colmet-Daage, Patrice. *La cathédrale de Coutances*. Paris: Laurens, 1933.

Musset, André. "La cathédrale Notre-Dame de Coutances." *Congrès archéologique* (*Cotentin et Avranchin*) 124 (1966): 57–69.

Coutances (Manche), Notre-Dame, chevet. *Photograph: Clarence Ward Collection. Courtesy of Oberlin College.*

COUTUMES. When rural lords, lay and ecclesiastical, levied exactions on the rest of the population without clear legal authority, they justified them as being "customary." These customary dues, or *coutumes* (Lat. *consuetudines*), ranged from payments in money or in kind, such as tolls (giving the modern English "customs"), taxes, and fines, to services, such as demesne work or road and fortification building. In many cases, these represented forms of payment for protection and were disputed in principle by neither side. But at the beginning of the 11th century, the terms *malae* or *novae consuetudines* appear with increasing regularity, designating the exactions demanded by a more aggressive aristocracy, especially the new castellan class.

Among the burdens placed on the population, and often levied without discrimination on free and servile peasants, perhaps the most significant were rights of justice, a development associated with the collapse of the *pagus*, the basic unit of the Carolingian judicial system. These seigneurial rights, which derived from the acquisition of the royal ban (power to command) by the more powerful lords, characterized the French rural world from the 11th century on; and only their conversion into monetary payments eroded by inflation alleviated this burden. Officially, these "feudal rights" were abolished only by the revolutionary decrees of August 4, 1789.

Coutumes may also refer to the local practices established in individual monasteries as additions to or variations from a rule, such as the *Rule of St. Benedict*.

Richard Landes

[See also: SEIGNEUR/SEIGNEURIE]

Duby, Georges. *The Early Growth of the European Economy.* Ithaca: Cornell University Press, 1974.

———. *Rural Economy and Country Life in the Medieval West,* trans. Cynthia Postan. Columbia: South Carolina University Press, 1968.

Lemarignier, Jean-François. "La dislocation du *pagus* et le problème des *consuetudines*: Xe–XIe siècles." In *Mélanges d'histoire dédiés à Louis Halphen.* Paris: Presses Universitaires de France, 1951.

———. "Political and Monastic Structures in France at the End of the Tenth and the Beginning of the Eleventh Centuries." In *Lordship and Community in Medieval Europe,* ed. Fredric Cheyette. New York: Holt-Rinehart-Winston, 1968, pp. 100–27.

COUVIN, WATRIQUET BRASSENIEX DE (fl. 1319–29).

Attached to the households of Gui de Châtillon, count of Blois, and his great-uncle Gaucher de Châtillon-sur-Marne, the minstrel Watriquet de Couvin left thirty-three poems, most dated between 1319 and 1329. Most of his works are occasional pieces composed for noble households, moral treatises, and allegorical *dits* in the tradition of the *Roman de la Rose,* but included in the extant corpus are two fabliaux and an obscene *fatras.* The titles of these pieces frequently indicate clearly their didactic bent: *Mireoirs as princes, De loiauté, Li despis du monde, De haute honneur, De Fortune,* and so on. Watriquet took much pride in his profession and was among the first writers in French to compile collections of his poems to be offered to various noblemen.

Deborah H. Nelson

[See also: *DIT; FATRAS/FATRASIE*]

Couvin, Watriquet Brasseniex de. *Dits de Watriquet de Couvin,* ed. Auguste Scheler. Brussels: Devaux, 1868.

Huot, Sylvia. *From Song to Book: The Poetics of Writing in Old French Lyric and Lyrical Narrative Poetry.* Ithaca: Cornell University Press, 1987, pp. 224–32.

Langlois, Charles-Victor. "Watriquet, ménestrel et poète français." In *Histoire littéraire de la France.* Paris: Imprimerie Nationale, 1921, Vol. 35, pp. 394–421.

CRAMAUD, SIMON DE (1345–1423).

Archbishop and cardinal. The son of a petty seigneur from the Limousin, Simon de Cramaud became one of the most influential French prelates of the later Middle Ages. Educated in law at Orléans, he began teaching canon law at Paris when he was about thirty years old. A member of the royal household and council in the late 1370s, he entered the service of John, duke of Berry, after Charles V died in 1380. He served as bishop of Agen (1382–83), Béziers (1383–85), and Poitiers (1385–91, 1413–23). He became patriarch of Alexandria (1391–1409) and archbishop of Reims (1409–13) and was named a cardinal in 1413. He was Berry's chancellor for five years (1386–91) and spent many years on the council of Charles VI. Politically, he followed his patron in supporting the duke of Burgundy against the Marmousets and Orléanists at court, but when John the Fearless succeeded his father as duke of Burgundy in 1404, Berry (and therefore Cramaud) shifted to the Orléanist party. Soon, Cramaud was on a list of counselors whom Burgundy considered his enemies.

Because the duke of Berry was the French prince most committed to ending the papal Schism, Simon de Cramaud assumed a leading role in the unionist policies of the French crown. More than any other person in Europe, he succeeded in articulating, over a fifteen-year period, the *via cessionis* that called for the abdication of both popes. A skillful politician, he presided over several major councils of the Gallican church and over the Council of Pisa in 1409–10, as well as performing important diplomatic missions on behalf of church union. His influential treatise *De subtraccione obediencie* (1397) was a crucial document in the campaign to persuade the princes of Europe to endorse the *via cessionis* and the sanctions to enforce it.

John Bell Henneman, Jr.

[See also: JOHN, DUKE OF BERRY; MARMOUSETS; SUBTRACTION OF OBEDIENCE]

Auber, Charles-Auguste. "Recherches sur la vie de Simon de Cramaud." *Mémoires de la société des antiquaires de l'ouest* 7 (1840): 249–380.

Kaminsky, Howard. "Cession, Subtraction, Deposition: Simon de Cramaud's Formulation of the French Solution to the Schism." *Studia Gratiana* 15 (1972): 295–317.

———. *Simon de Cramaud and the Great Schism.* New Brunswick: Rutgers University Press, 1983.

CRAON.

A town and castle in northwestern Anjou, Craon (Mayenne) gave its name to one of the most important families of northwestern France. Like many other such families, the lords of Craon can be traced to a castellan of the mid-11th century. They served the counts of Anjou and by the 13th century were hereditary seneschals of Anjou and lords of Chantocé, Ingrande, Sablé, Briole, and Châteauneuf-sur-Sarthe. They intermarried with the great seigneurial families of neighboring regions, such as the Clisson, Lusignan, and Laval. Amaury IV (d. 1373) was the last male member of the senior line. His sister Isabelle, who succeeded him, was the wife of Louis I, lord of Sully, and their daughter, Marie, married Guy VI de La Tremoille, bringing with her an inheritance that made the fortune of her husband's family. Cadet lines in the 14th century included the viscounts of Châteaudun, the lords of La Suze, and the lords of La Ferté-Bernard. The last male heir of each of these lines died at Agincourt in 1415. The inheritance of the La Suze line passed through a woman to Gilles de Laval, lord of Rais and marshal of France. The line of La Ferté-Bernard produced the Pierre de Craon whose scandal-ridden life included a bungled attempt to assassinate his second cousin, Olivier de Clisson, constable of France, in 1392. This act triggered the ill-fated royal expedition against Brittany during which Charles VI had his first attack of mental illness.

John Bell Henneman, Jr.

[See also: CLISSON; RAIS, GILLES DE]

Bertrand de Broussillon, Arthur. *La maison de Craon, 1050–1480: étude historique, accompagnée du cartulaire de Craon.* 2 vols. Paris: Picard, 1893.
Charles, Robert. *Histoire de la Ferté-Bernard.* Paris: Menu, 1876.

CRÉCY. In July 1346, King Edward III opened a new phase of the Hundred Years' War by landing in Normandy with an army of 15,000 men. By the end of July, the English had captured Caen and then marched to the east to secure other towns in Normandy. Finally, on August 24, they were attacked by the French at Crécy-en-Ponthieu. The French force, under the leadership of their king, Philip VI, numbered 40,000. Given the larger French numbers, the English dismounted and took a defensive position on higher ground to await an attack. The battle began in the late afternoon with a relatively ineffective exchange of archery fire between the English longbowmen and the mercenary Genoese crossbowmen. This lasted only a short time, but the French knights grew impatient. Recognizing their superior numbers and anticipating a quick victory, they charged through their own archers into the lines of dismounted English, commanded in part by Edward, the Black Prince. After an uphill charge through continuous English archery fire, with their lines confused and in disarray, these knights encountered the English soldiers. Despite constant pressure on the English line, the knights were unable to pierce it and the attack failed, with the French suffering heavy casualties. By midnight, the French army, including the king, retreated from the battlefield. The English rested for a few days, then marched to Calais, which they besieged for nearly a year before capturing it.

Kelly DeVries

[See also: CALAIS; HUNDRED YEARS' WAR; PHILIP VI]

Burne, Alfred Higgins. *The Crécy War.* London: Oxford University Press, 1955.
Favier, Jean. *La guerre de cent ans.* Paris: Fayard, 1980.
Oman, Charles. *A History of the Art of War in the Middle Ages.* Boston: Houghton Mifflin, 1924, pp. 124–47.
Perroy, Édouard. *The Hundred Years War,* trans. W. B. Wells. London: Eyre and Spottiswoode, 1951.

CRÉTIN, GUILLAUME (ca. 1460–1525). One of the Grands Rhétoriqueurs, Crétin was a prolific author of *épîtres* and other *poèmes de circonstance*, texts addressed to nobles in an attempt to please or curry favor. He composed many religious poems and even undertook a verse translation of Gregory of Tours, which he was unable to complete. Crétin also wrote a *Débat de deux dames sur le passetemps de la chasse des chiens et oyseaulx*, a text that continues a poetic debate begun some time before: is it better to hunt with dogs or with falcons? This composition was published only after Crétin's death. He was much admired in his day, and his style, particularly his *rimes équivoques*, was praised by Crétin's most influential contemporaries.

Norris J. Lacy

[See also: GRANDS RHÉTORIQUEURS; OCKEGHEM, JOHANNES; VERSIFICATION]

Crétin, Guillaume. *Œuvres poétiques de Guillaume Crétin,* ed. Kathleen Chesney. Paris: Didot, 1932.
Zumthor, Paul, ed. *Anthologie des Grands Rhétoriqueurs.* Paris: Union Générale d'Éditions, 1978, pp. 175–203.

CRIME AND PUNISHMENT. Fifth-century Gaul saw the opposition between the Roman and the barbarian, especially Frankish, criminal-law systems. In Roman society, criminal justice was the affair of the state and the responsible individual. The state prosecuted individuals accused of crimes against the state and public order (treason, sacrilege) or against property (theft) and people (murder, assault). The means of proof was rational (largely testimony), and punishment included execution, imprisonment, banishment, and corporal punishment. Criminal justice in the Frankish kingdom, on the other hand, was conceived of much as civil justice, as a matter in which two families confronted one another. The traditional ven-

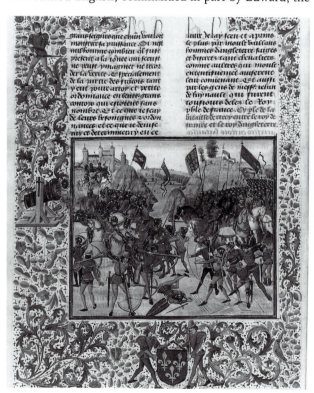

"The Battle of Crécy," Froissart's *Chroniques.* BN fr. 2643, fol. 165. *Courtesy of the Bibliothèque Nationale, Paris.*

geance sought (*faida*) was replaced with monetary compensation (*wergeld*) detailed in exhaustive lists. The procedure was accusatory, and proofs invoked were co-oaths (families and neighbors swearing to the honor of the accused) and ordeals.

The feudal period saw the rise of seigneurial and ecclesiastical jurisdiction, in criminal as well as civil matters. The high and late Middle Ages saw three fundamental changes: the development of municipal courts, the growth of royal justice, which tended to overshadow the old seigneurial jurisdictions, and the reintroduction of Roman principles of justice, especially of procedure, at first through the church and canon law, then also through royal justice and some lower courts, especially in towns. With the strengthening of the notion of the state, inquisitory procedure began to supplement and then to replace the old accusatory procedure. Testimony and confession, both sometimes induced by torture, replaced co-oaths and ordeals as proof, and the practice of appeal was introduced. Individual responsibility tended to replace collective responsibility, and the intention of the accused became as important a factor as the facts of the crime.

With the growth of public authority, persons accused of crimes against religion (sacrilege, witchcraft, blasphemy), against public authority (treason, counterfeiting), and against public order (procuring, concubinage, gaming, sodomy) were prosecuted, as well as those having committed crimes against people (homicide) and property (theft). The principal forms of capital punishment were decapitation, hanging (especially for theft), and burning (for heresy, witchcraft, and sodomy). Corporal punishment was reintroduced; the most common mutilation was the cutting off of ears, normally for theft. Whipping was a common punishment, as was being exposed at the pillory for several days. Banishment was frequent; imprisonment, however, was rarely used as punishment. Confiscation of goods often accompanied other punishments, especially when the accused was noble or in cases of heresy, usury, or suicide. Fines were common, and the sum varied greatly; sixty *sous*, the standard fine in Frankish times, remained the most common.

Leah L. Otis-Cour

Gonthier, Nicole. *Délinquance, justice et société en Lyonnais (fin XIIIe–début XVIe siècles)*. Thesis. Lyon (Lettres), 1988.
Laingui, André, and Arlette Lebigre. *Histoire du droit pénal*. 2 vols. Paris: Cujas, 1979–80.

CROISADE CONTRE LES ALBIGEOIS, CHANSON DE LA.

A historical epic retelling the events of the Albigensian Crusade, the *Chanson* is an invaluable historical and literary resource. The author of the first 131 laisses (2,772 lines), Guilhem de Tudela (fl. first quarter of the 13th c.), began writing in 1210 and ceased in spring 1213; he is a relatively impartial though dry reporter of events. Approving of the crusade, condemning the heretics, he defends, however, southerners whose orthodoxy was unquestionable. In 1228, an anonymous author continued Guilhem's story. Sympathetic to the southern cause, he recounts in

detail those events to which he was an eyewitness; the style is more animated and much more dialogue is reported. His story stops in the midst of a description of the 1218 siege of Toulouse.

Using as model the *Chanson d'Antioche*, the work is composed of 9,582 Alexandrine lines, divided into 214 assonanced laisses; the last line of each laisse (of only six syllables) links to the next, *capcaudada* in Guilhem de Tudela's portion, *capfinida* in the second part of the work. Only one manuscript is extant (B.N. fr. 25425), with pen-and-ink illustrations, dated ca. 1275. Two prose chroniclers of the Albigensian Crusade appear to have had access to this text for their redactions.

Wendy E. Pfeffer

[See also: FOLQUET DE MARSELHA]

Guilhem de Tudela *and* Anonymous. *La chanson de la croisade albigeoise*, ed. Eugène Martin-Chabot. 3 vols. Paris: Les Belles Lettres, 1957–1961.
———. *La chanson de la croisade albigeoise*, trans. Henri Gougaud. Paris: Berg, 1984.
D'Heur, Jean-Marie. "Sur la date, la composition et la destination de la *Chanson de la croisade albigeoise* de Guillaume de Tudèle." In *Mélanges d'histoire littéraire, de linguistique et de philologie romanes offerts à Charles Rostaing*, ed. Jacques De Caluwé et al. Liège: Association des Romanistes de l'Université de Liège, 1974, pp. 231–66.
Ghil, Eliza Miruna. *L'âge de parage: essai sur la poétique en Occitanie au XIIIe siècle*. New York: Lang, 1989.

CROSSBOW. The *arbalète*, or crossbow, was a mechanical bow that became the standard archery weapon in France during the Middle Ages. The basic construction of the weapon was a small bow attached to a stock that provided a groove for the bolt and handle, with a bowstring that was held in place ready for release by a trigger mechanism.

Descended from the ancient Greek *gastraphetes* (or "belly bow"), the *arbalète* became popular in western Europe during the late 11th century. Because of its brutality in war, both Pope Urban II (r. 1088–99) and the Second Lateran Council (1139) condemned its use among Christians. However, this condemnation was rarely heeded as the *arbalète* became increasingly popular in Europe. This was especially the case in France, where most kings and nobles used crossbowmen in their armies between the 12th and 15th centuries, frequently employing mercenary crossbowmen, principally Italians, when they failed to recruit sufficient numbers of these troops from among their own subjects. These troops were used tactically at the beginning of a battle and on the flanks as harassers of opposing forces.

By the late Middle Ages, the *arbalète* had increased in use and efficiency. The composite crossbow, made of horn, sinew, and glue, was considerably more powerful than earlier bows. Stirrups, windlasses, and *cranequins* were added to the stock to enable the bow to be strung with greater tension, increasing immensely the power of the pull. Improvements to the release mechanism and to the bolt also added to the efficiency of the weapon. By the early 13th century, castles were being designed with openings for *arbalètes* and ships were being outfitted with the weapon, and during the reign of Philip the Fair the offices of master and clerk of crossbowmen were established to oversee the military organization and pay of these troops. The master of crossbowmen who eventually became the military leader over the entire infantry was often not a professional soldier, and the units of French or mercenary crossbowmen frequently in battle were confused, disorganized, and at odds with the other infantry or cavalry troops.

By the mid-14th century, crossbows were being replaced in defense of castles by small-caliber cannons, and a decline in the craft was also apparent. Steps were taken to halt this decline—Charles V in 1384 prohibited the playing of any game except with bow or crossbow, and Charles VII in the 1440s set up companies of *franc-archers* who used the weapon—but ultimately the *arbalète* could not survive the late 15th-century influx of handguns. By 1550, the weapon had disappeared from the battlefield.

Kelly DeVries

[See also: ARCHER/BOWMAN]

Bradbury, Jim. *The Medieval Archer.* New York: St. Martin, 1985.

Contamine, Philippe. *War in the Middle Ages*, trans. Michael Jones. London: Blackwell, 1984.

Foley, V., G. Palmer, and W. Soedel. "The Crossbow." *Scientific American* 252 (1985): 104–10.

Nicolle, David C. *Arms and Armour of the Crusading Period, 1050–1350.* 2 vols. White Plains: Kraus, 1988.

Payne-Gallwey, Ralph. *The Crossbow.* London: Longmans, 1903.

CRUSADE CYCLE. This group of chansons de geste about the First and Third Crusades dates from the 12th, 13th, and 14th centuries. It is usually divided into two parts, a First Crusade and a Second Crusade Cycle; the poems of the second cycle are a partly revised, extended version of the first. (A state intermediate between the two cycles also has been preserved.) The texts are all in twelve-syllable rhymed laisses; they vary from about 2,000 lines to 10,000 and more. In its most developed form, the cycle counts some 60,000 lines. It has come under extensive critical scrutiny only recently.

Thirteen separate poems, or branches, are usually counted in the First Crusade Cycle. Their chronological order is roughly as follows: *Chanson d'Antioche* (late 12th c.); *Chanson de Jérusalem, Chétifs, Chevalier au Cygne, Enfances Godefroi de Bouillon, Naissance du chevalier au Cygne* (*Les Enfants-Cygnes*) (all probably early 13th c.); *Fin d'Elyas, Retour de Cornumaran* (13th c.); and the continuations of the *Chanson de Jérusalem: Chrétienté* [i.e., conversion of] *Corbaran, Prise d'Acre, Mort Godefroi, Chanson des rois Baudouin,* and the "Second Continuation," which has several forms and brings the story of the Crusades down to the time of Saladin; the latter branches are known in varying versions from the late 13th or early 14th century. There are also two abbreviated prose versions of parts of the First Crusade Cycle, one from the late 13th century and one from the 15th. The latter has been published as the *Geste du Chevalier au Cygne.*

The Second Crusade Cycle, elaborated during the first half of the 14th century, includes a vast reworking of the narrative material of the first cycle (edited as the *Chevalier au Cygne et Godefroid de Bouillon,* 35,180 lines, two versions) and two loosely attached continuations, *Baudouin de Sebourc* (25,778 lines) and the *Bâtard de Bouillon* (6,546 lines).

The development of the First Crusade Cycle followed the usual rules for the extension and reworking of epic material. The oldest poem, *Antioche,* describes the preparations for the First Crusade, the crusaders' departure, their stay in Constantinople, and the successful campaign against the city of Antioch. This poem inspired works that stretch both forward and backward in narrative time, treating the subsequent capture of the Holy City (*Chanson de Jérusalem*) and then evoking both the ancestors and descendants of Godefroi de Bouillon (a sequence observed also in the growth of the Guillaume d'Orange Cycle). Hence, the oldest poems in the cycle as we have it are those that actually recount events of the First Crusade, the capture of Antioch and of Jerusalem. On the other hand, later works in the cycle, the group that tells the Swan Knight story, describe the rise of the house of Bouillon through the adventures of the legendary Elyas and the other Swan Children, victims of an evil stepmother who steals the magical chains that allow them to change in and out of human shape. Elyas, accompanied by a brother in bird form, saves the Countess of Boulogne from death, marries her, and after engendering the lineage of Godefroi and the Latin kings of Jerusalem, himself falls victim to a taboo deriving from folklore: he disappears when his wife is unable to refrain from asking him the fatal question of his origins.

Other prologues to the *Antioche-Jérusalem* core tell the story of the youthful Godefroi's exploits, which prefigure his role as first king of Jerusalem (a historically inaccurate title). The most recent poems of the First Crusade Cycle, on the other hand, are the "Jerusalem Continuations," which carry the Crusade story on beyond the crucial campaigns of the First Crusade. In the earliest continuations, Godefroi captures the city of Acre (Saint-Jean d'Acre, Akka); the great Saracen leader Corbaran (whose name recalls that of the emir Kerbogha) converts to Christianity; and Godefroi is poisoned by a jealous cleric. The later continuations are more closely tied to history, seeming at some points to derive from the text known as the *Chronique d'Ernoul.* They pay little attention to the Second Crusade but show an early concern with the downfall of the Latin kingdom of Jerusalem and its associated states, a concern that was to be developed at some length in the 14th-century Second Crusade Cycle.

The poem of the *Chétifs* ("captives"), the age and origins of which are debated, is heavily laced with folklore and oriental motifs; although it comes between *Antioche* and *Jérusalem* in the cyclical manuscripts, it is probably somewhat later in date. Recounting not the events of the Crusade but rather the adventures of Christian knights taken prisoner at the Battle of Civetot, it shares characteristics of the *chansons d'aventures*. The Crusade Cycle is thus a patchwork of relatively independent chansons, gathered more or less systematically into a single but far-from-seamless sequence, over several decades starting at the end of the 12th century. Earlier scholarship posited a historically accurate early version of the *Chanson d'Antioche* attributable to a participant in the Antioch campaign, called "Richard the Pilgrim." In the absence of any positive evidence for Richard's existence or that of his poem, it is preferable to consider the Crusade epics as the products of a later period. They reflect not actual experience but a mythical view of the Crusades expressed through techniques typical of the chansons de geste. While the known text of *Antioche* does contain some passages that are historically correct, thanks probably to the influence of the chronicles, it is clear that much of its narrative, and nearly all of the cyclical poems that derive from it, are based on literary motifs. The Crusade Cycle embodies a legendary view of Christian military and moral superiority, and of Godefroi de Bouillon and his family, that was current in northern Europe some time after the events.

The London and Turin manuscripts of the First Crusade Cycle preserve a lengthy set of continuations, the "Second *Jerusalem* Continuations," that date from about the turn of the 14th century. Their content matches that of the earlier continuations in part, with numerous additions. These manuscripts offer a transitional state of the cycle. Much of their matter is preserved, in rewritten form, in the huge *Chevalier au cygne et Godefroid de Bouillon*, the core of the Second Crusade Cycle, which had attained its fully elaborated state by the middle of the century. It recounts the stories told in the First Crusade Cycle with often fanciful continuations. The independent poems *Baudouin de Sebourc* and the *Bâtard de Bouillon*, loosely associated with the Second Crusade Cycle, describe new, and often burlesque, adventures of knights of the lineage of Godefroi. A final "branch," known only in a 15th-century prose version, is dedicated to a legendary biography of Saladin; there are indications that it continued the Crusade story down to the fall of Jerusalem and the extinction of the house of Bouillon in the East. There are parallels with William of Tyre and "Ernoul," but most of the Second Crusade Cycle is a combination of common literary motifs.

The Crusade Cycle of chansons de geste embodied and transmitted a coherent myth of crusader character and action in a popular literary form. Its texts were copied, translated (most notably into Middle Dutch), and collected as late as the 16th century, and derivative prose versions were among the more frequently printed early French books. Its manipulations of history are highly revealing of attitudes toward the Crusades from the 12th century onward.

Robert Francis Cook

[See also: *BAUDOUIN DE SEBOURC*; CHANSON DE GESTE; GODEFROI DE BOUILLON; LATE EPIC]

Mickel, Emanuel J., and Jan A. Nelson, eds. *The Old French Crusade Cycle*. 9 vols. University: University of Alabama Press, 1977–.

Bender, Karl-Heinz, and Hermann Kleber. *Le premier cycle de la croisade. De Godefroy à Saladin: entre la chronique et le conte de fées*. Heidelberg: Winter, 1986.
Cook, Robert Francis. *"Chanson d'Antioche," chanson de geste: le cycle de la croisade est-il épique?* Amsterdam: Benjamins, 1980.
———, and Larry S. Crist. *Le deuxième cycle de la croisade*. Geneva: Droz, 1972.
Duparc-Quioc, Suzanne. *Le cycle de la croisade*. Paris: Champion, 1955.

CRUSADE SONGS/*CHANSONS DE CROISADE*. The twenty-nine extant French crusade songs span the hundred years of the Second to Seventh Crusades; the thirty-five Occitan pieces include both earlier and later compositions. The latter, almost all the work of well-known troubadours, from Marcabru to Guiraut Riquier, belong to the lyric genre of the *sirventes* and deal with political, moral, or religious aspects of the Crusades, exhorting or rebuking. The French corpus is much more varied in form and, especially, in content. While over a third of the pieces are anonymous, many, most notably four by Thibaut de Champagne, stem from famous trouvères. In addition to composing polemical and hortatory songs of the Occitan type, the northern poets were concerned with the impact of the Crusades on their lives as lovers. Indeed, half of the corpus expresses, usually in the style of the *grand chant courtois*, the stress caused by the conflicting demands of love and religious duty, and the pain of separation from the beloved; two of the songs develop the separation theme from the woman's point of view.

Samuel N. Rosenberg

[See also: TROUBADOUR POETRY; TROUVÈRE POETRY]

Bédier, Joseph, and Pierre Aubry, eds. *Les chansons de croisade, publiées avec leurs mélodies*. Paris: Champion, 1909.
Jeanroy, Alfred, ed. *La poésie lyrique des troubadours*. 2 vols. Toulouse: Privat; Paris: Didier, 1934, Vol. 2, pp. 200–12.
Bec, Pierre. *La lyrique française au moyen âge (XIIe–XIIIe siècles): contribution à une typologie des genres poétiques médiévaux*. 2 vols. Paris: Picard, 1977–78, Vol. 1: *Études*, pp. 150–58; Vol. 2: *Textes*.

CRUSADER ART AND ARCHITECTURE. The term "crusader art" refers to works produced in the Latin Kingdom of Jerusalem during the Frankish colonial period from 1099 to 1291. Due to the assimilation and interpretation of artistic elements by westerners within the Latin Kingdom, along with the fragmentary state of some works of art and architecture, much crusader art escapes stylistic definition and attribution to workshop and patron. Early approaches to crusader art involved polarized categories of "eastern" and "western," which reduced multicultural works to products of one homogeneous group. Recognition of the many groups in the Frankish kingdom and inquiries into definitions of ethnicity have recently contributed to more careful approaches to assessment of the artistic practices and products in the Latin Kingdom.

This article will raise the questions that must be posed in order to gain an understanding of the complicated field. To start, the complex composition of the crusader environment and its chronological bounds must be acknowledged. What characteristics make a work of art a work of crusader art? How does crusader art change? Crucial questions center on definitions of crusader art, characteristics of these works, and their place of production. Such definitions must involve careful consideration of format, iconography, and technique. Inquiries into the roles played by western groups and Byzantium, the locations of major centers (the Holy Land or Constantinople), and the differences between artistic production and artistic centers in the 12th and 13th centuries must also be considered.

The Holy Land and the Mediterranean had long been an environment shared by Jews, Christians, and Muslims. Within the Christian population alone, distinct cultures were found in the variety of Christian sects, such as Orthodox Christians, Maronites, Jacobites, Melchites, Nestorians, Coptic Christians, Armenians, and Syrian Christians. Likewise, the Islamic world was unified politically only in the 12th century under Saladin. Even the westerners represented a variety of ethnicities, from Normans to Icelanders to southern Italians. In Sicily and Cyprus, colonization under the Normans in the 11th century had already instigated the meeting of Arab, Byzantine, and Norman cultures, artistic techniques, and products.

Crusaders called this variegated world *Outremer* ("Overseas"), a term used in reference to controlled states, especially the Latin Kingdom of Jerusalem, that included Lesser Armenia, the County of Edessa, the County of Tripoli, and the Principality of Antioch. The formal initiation of the Latin Kingdom began in 1099 with the capture of Jerusalem and the slaughter of all those non-Westerners who sought refuge within the walls of the Temple of Jerusalem. As for artistic activity, scholarship supports a later date for the formation and establishment of workshops and interest in patronage. Thus, artistic activity of the crusaders falls within two periods: from the early 12th century until the taking of Jerusalem by Saladin in 1187, and from 1191, when Acre became the new capital of the kingdom, until 1291, when Acre fell.

In the 19th century, scholarship of the French colonial mindset used selective stylistic or iconographic characteristics to polarize works of crusader art into ill-defined categories of "East" and "West." Such approaches have been overturned. A work of crusader art must be produced during the period of the Latin Kingdom, and its artistic production must involve at least one westerner. In many cases, a western or Byzantine donor can be identified or suggested due to sufficient documentation. A decisive application of ethnic labels must, however, be used with care, especially when labeling artist or workshop and locating the region of production. Careful investigation into iconographic elements problematic for the Orthodox church but part of western formal vocabulary may also contribute to the attribution of work to a regional workshop.

Due to westerners' lack of familiarity with new materials, many works of architecture and sculpture incorporate techniques native to the Latin Kingdom and suggest the cooperative efforts of local workshops. Other works, such as manuscript illuminations, icons, wall paintings, mosaics, and ivories, can be ascribed either to one particular culture (or in some cases to one workshop) on the basis of technique or use of iconographic elements, or to a mélange of workers of diverse ethnic backgrounds. In these media, Latin or Greek inscriptions offer clues to the circumstances of production.

In Jerusalem, the architecture of the Holy Sepulcher exemplifies the complex interchanges between cultures. For the crusaders, the building came to symbolize Jerusalem and the Latin Kingdom, as the number of holy sites grew and pilgrims assigned new meanings to sites within and outside the Sepulcher. Since the construction of the first building under the emperor Constantine, the Holy Sepulcher marked the site of Christ's burial, and subsequent destruction initiated the rebuilding financed by Constantine IX Monomachus. The domed structure was characteristic of Byzantine architecture, with a polygonal apse and three separate spaces for small chapels. Through alteration, the crusaders attempted to transform the building into a Benedictine pilgrimage church, changing the orientation of the altar from west to east and adding radiating chapels. Such alterations conform to western requirements for churches, but the building techniques come from a variety of sources. Rib vaulting is native to the crusader kingdom, the horizontal masonry is French, the flat roofs of the transepts resemble Palestinian buildings, and a tall Aquitinian dome surmounts the structure. The building also gained an additional function, when it served as a place of coronation and celebration of the anniversary of the taking of Jerusalem in 1099.

Another 12th-century monument that defies attribution to a single cultural group is the *Melisende Psalter* (B.L., Egerton 1139; ca. 1131–43). Its elaborately carved ivory cover studded with enamels, twenty-four full-page introductory miniatures, and eight illuminated initials suggest that a number of artists contributed to the psalter, which illustrates the high level of opulence in luxury goods desired by members of the aristocracy associated with crusader society. Though the psalter was initially attributed to the patronage of Queen Melisende (r. 1131–61), lack of evidence and the number of cultural elements point toward the probability of another patron. Such features as the Latin signature of the artist Basilius, the text of the calendar with English saints, the Byzantine dress of the character in the roundels of the ivory cover, and western iconographic elements may not easily offer a name or label for artists and patron, but they do suggest that the agents of production were many and mixed.

Joint patronage produced works that reflect the fusion of cultures and also their distinctiveness. In 1169, King Amalric I and the Byzantine emperor Manuel Comnenus commissioned mosaics that featured a variety of subjects with Byzantine and western elements in the church of the Nativity in Bethlehem. In the nave, the representation of the seven ecumenical councils on the south wall and the six provincial councils on the north wall are Greek in origin, relating to a profession of faith to bring out the condemnation of heresies. Greek inscriptions name the figures representing each council. Beneath these mosaics were the ancestors of Christ with Latin inscriptions that led to the west wall, which held a Tree of Jesse, a typically western iconographic element.

Also at Bethlehem, arcade columns in the nave carry paintings by a number of artists. A thickly painted holy figure graces each column. Saints from diverse geographic areas include Macarius, Anthony Abbot and Euthymius (hermit saints), George (English), Cosmas and Damian (Syrian), Canute and Olaf (Scandinavian), Fusca (Venetian), and St. Margaret of Antioch. One column bears an entire group, identified with Greek inscriptions: Mary the mother of James, Salome, Mary Magdalene, and the Virgin Mary. Another column holds both St. Leo and St. Anne. Kneeling donors underline the function of the columns as votive paintings. Named in Latin, Greek, or both, these figures most immediately illustrate the significance and interdependence of religious and cultural roots for natives as well as for many foreigners and at the same time attest to the communal representation of these roots in crusader society.

During the first period of the Latin Kingdom, the Haram in Jerusalem had been transformed into the Templar headquarters and the site of an Augustinian house. After the fall of Jerusalem in 1187, many of the Christian buildings in the Haram were dismantled and the fragments were reused in the Aqsa mosque, the Dome of the Rock, the entrance to Bab as-Silsilah, and many other Islamic structures. The carving of these pieces are all of high quality, ranging from twisted columns to "wet leaf" acanthus capitals with the sinuous delicate leaf forms carved in relief. Due to the fragmentary nature of the material, however, the composition of the "Temple" workshop remains a matter for speculation, although scholars trace the subsequent migration of artists to southern Italy. In addition to the Temple Workshop, the figural capitals intended for the church of the Annunciation at Nazareth and two lintels over the main entrance to the Holy Sepulcher remain important works in a corpus of crusader sculpture.

When the capital moved to Acre in 1191, artistic activity lapsed until ca. 1250. The crusade of Louis IX and his presence at Acre (1252–54) brought greater support for the Latin Kingdom and motivated patronage, which may account for the greater number of surviving manuscripts and icons from this period. One of Louis IX's commissions for an Old French Bible, the Arsenal Bible (Paris, Bibliothèque de l'Arsenal 5211), shares features with frescoes in Constantinople. Louis IX also initiated investment in increased fortifications of such major sites as Caesarea, Jaffa, Sidon, and later in the century the capital of Acre.

A number of 13th-century icons have been characterized as the product of western artists because of certain unorthodox representations of Byzantine dress and the inclusion of western emblems. Due in part to the scanty remains of comparative material, such as monumental painting, and to the stylistic variety of local workshops, firm attributions of groups of icons to one location are not always possible. Applications of simple "eastern" or "western" labels do not take into consideration local commercial workshops that produced marketable icons for one ethnic group or another.

The Latin Kingdom was not the monolithic culture that westerners have wished to project. The diverse ethnic fabric demanded variety in patronage, eclectic artistic activity, and a broad range of artistic products. Distinct differences between the crusader world in the 12th and 13th centuries may hamper the search for continuity of workshops and patrons but at the same time underline the necessity of acknowledging the complex social, political, and economic circumstances surrounding the production of crusader art.

Stacy L. Boldrick

[See also: CRUSADES; ROMANESQUE ART]

Buchthal, Hugo. *Miniature Painting in the Latin Kingdom of Jerusalem*. Oxford: Clarendon, 1957.

Buschhausen, Helmut. *Die süditalienische Bauplastik im Königreich Jerusalem, von König Wilhelm II. bis Kaiser Friedrich II*. Vienna: Verlag der österreichischen Akademie der Wissenschaften, 1978.

Folda, Jaroslav, ed. *Crusader Art in the Twelfth Century*. Oxford: British Archaeological Reports, 1982.

Goss, Vladimir P., and Christine Verzàr Bornstein, eds. *The Meeting of Two Worlds: Cultural Exchange Between East and West During the Period of the Crusades*. Kalamazoo: Western Michigan University, 1986.

Hunt, Lucy-Anne. "Art and Colonialism: The Mosaics of the Church of the Nativity in Bethehem (1169) and the Problem of 'Crusader' Art." *Dumbarton Oaks Papers* 45 (1991): 69–85.

Hutter, Irmgard. *Byzanz und der West: Studien zur Kunst des europäischen Mittelalters*. Vienna: Verlag der österreichischen Akademie der Wissenschaften, 1984.

Kenaan-Kedar, Nurith. "Local Christian Art in Twelfth-Century Jerusalem." *Israel Exploration Journal* 23 (1973): 167–75, 221–29.

Kühnel, Gustav. *Wall Painting in the Latin Kingdom of Jerusalem*. Berlin: Mann, 1988.

Pringle, Denys. *The Churches of the Crusader Kingdom of Jerusalem: A Corpus*. Cambridge: Cambridge University Press, 1993.

Setton, Kenneth M., ed. *A History of the Crusades*. 2nd ed. 6 vols. Madison: University of Wisconsin Press, 1974, Vol. 4: *The Art and Architecture of the Crusader States*, ed. H.W. Hazard.

Weitzmann, Kurt. *Studies in the Arts of Sinai*. Princeton: Princeton University Press, 1982.

Wilkinson, John. *Jerusalem Pilgrimage, 1099–1185*. Cambridge: Cambridge University Press, 1988.

CRUSADES. The long series of military campaigns that aimed to expand the borders of Latin Christendom against international Islam and to defend Europe against residual paganism and resurgent heresy on the local scene. Drawing inspiration from earlier western notions of just war or divinely sanctioned war, the crusaders acted in the firm belief that their goals—the principal one, especially for the people of feudal France, being the recovery of the Holy Land—not only were justified in God's eyes but were in fact God's explicit wish. *Deus vult!* ("God wills it!") became their battle cry, which could be heard from the 11th century through the 15th. The campaigns against Palestine and Egypt, the Spanish *Reconquista*, the wars against paganism in Lithuania, the struggle to stamp out Catharism in southern France, and the 13th-century papal effort to topple the Hohenstaufen regime in southern Italy all form part of crusade history; but the repeated efforts to regain and defend the Holy Land are the center of the story, insofar as French military involvement and popular support are concerned. That support remained surprisingly constant over the centuries, despite the repeated failure of the campaigns themselves. Only the first four Crusades are examined here in any detail. But French enthusiasm for crusading, while it may never again have reached the extraordinary level of explosive energy that inaugurated the First Crusade, lasted well into the age of gunpowder.

The passion for crusading arose from a passionate desire for peace. The decay of Carolingian power in France in the 9th and 10th centuries amid endemic civil strife and renewed foreign invasion brought stable social and economic life to a virtual standstill in some parts of the realm. Famine and disease spread as brutal private wars engulfed the countryside. Desperate for peace, Frankish peasants and village artisans organized an impromptu series of mass protests that came to be known as the Peace of God movement. These were highly emotive, popular demonstrations, in which bishops paraded the relics of local saints, led prayers for peace, and condemned Europe's warrior caste for its senseless shedding of Christian blood. Among some segments of the Frankish populace, these emotions were inspired by a belief in approaching Armageddon, although the extent to which apocalyptic convictions played a role is still disputed. Proclamations from Peace councils announced the inviolability from harassment of the Christian populace—especially of widows and children, the clergy, and those undertaking pilgrimage to holy sites—on penalty of excommunication. Having outlawed violence against particular persons considered holy, the councils soon took the next step and established the Truce of God, which condemned warfare on holy days as well. The Peace and Truce of God were essential precursors to the crusade phenomenon, since they established the precedent of the church being the arbiter of legitimate warfare.

The rapidly progressing Gregorian reform movement likewise influenced crusade ideology. Reforms like outlawing simony, demanding a celibate clergy, and condemning lay investiture increased popular support for the institutional church that had long been on the wane. The Papal Election Decree of 1059 finally secured the independence of the Holy See from imperial control and gave it the opportunity to exert its new-found strength by promoting a European-wide movement to complete the reformation of the Christian world by ensuring, by force if necessary, Christians' right to undertake unmolested pilgrimages to the site of Christ's birth, miraculous works, and death. Pilgrimage, and the cult of the saints to which it was linked, was a particularly popular devotional exercise among the peoples of the feudal north. Whether as voluntary exercises or as required penitential works, these arduous and dangerous journeys to holy sites figured large in Europe's spiritual life, and pilgrimage routes to popular sites like Canterbury, Rome, Santiago de Compostela, or Jerusalem itself often were filled with hundreds, if not thousands, of the devout. Reports of Muslim harassment of pilgrims en route to the Holy Land, and of the Egyptian caliph 'al-Hakim's 1009 slaughter of the Christian populace of Jerusalem and destruction of the Holy Sepulcher, struck European minds with horror. These reports were grossly exaggerated, but a certain amount of anti-Christian violence did occur with some frequency, usually by Arab or Turkish brigands acting independently rather than by state forces themselves. To defend the holy pilgrims as well as the Holy Land itself, the church considered it well within its rights to summon the military caste of Latin Christendom to lead a divinely sanctioned war to liberate Palestine, rescue the Christian populace held in what was believed to be servitude, and guarantee the safety of pilgrimage routes.

The First Crusade (1095–99) was the only complete success. Pope Urban II at the Council of Clermont (November 27, 1095) called specifically upon the people of France to "enter the road to the Holy Sepulcher and win back the Holy Land from the wicked race" of the Turks. The main army, trailing a rag-tag group of peasants led by the zealot Peter the Hermit, set off by land for Constantinople, from which, urged on by their nervous Byzantine hosts, they moved southward across Anatolia. Amid extraordinary hardship, they liberated city after city (the battle for Tripoli being the most difficult) before finally entering Jerusalem in July 1099. In their zeal, the crusaders sacked the city brutally, killing Jews and Muslims alike. When the fighting ceased, the army organized the resettlement of the Holy Land into four major Christian states: the principalities of Edessa, Antioch, and Tripoli and the kingdom of Jerusalem.

The Second Crusade (1147–49) was a fiasco. The fall of Edessa to the Mosul-based Turkish warlord 'Imad ad-Din Zengi raised fears for the remaining three Christian states. France's Louis VII determined to seize the advantage from the papacy and to lead the new campaign himself. This crusade would be, he hoped, a wholly French affair. The revered abbot of Clairvaux, Bernard, was conscripted to preach and raise recruits—which he did with great success. The soldiers gathered at Paris and set off for the East, by land once again, trailing a German contingent that had taken the cross despite French hopes to exclude them. Most of the German forces were cut down in Asia Minor. Popular tales of Louis's errant wife Eleanor of Aquitaine's scandalous behavior while traveling with the army have been exaggerated, but she does appear to have complicated tactical and diplomatic matters along the way with her willful behavior. The French army, arriving safely in Jerusalem, made the disastrous decision to march against Damascus, whose Arab ruler was actually allied with the Christians against Zengi's successor Nur ad-Din. Caught between the crusaders and Nur ad-Din's forces, the Damascenes sided with the Turks and forced the withdrawal of the French troops. Defeated on the battlefield, the crusaders returned home humiliated and confronted with angry demands for an explanation of their heavy losses.

The Third Crusade (1189–92) hoped to restore Europe's tarnished reputation by removing the new Muslim leader 'Al-Nasir Salah ad-Din (Saladin), who had come up from Egypt to unite the territories from the Nile to Aleppo under his control. At the Battle of Hattim (July 1187), Saladin had routed the army of the kingdom of Jerusalem and become master of all the Holy Land. This setback triggered the Third Crusade. Led jointly, if somewhat chaotically, by France's Philip II Augustus, England's Richard I the Lionhearted, and imperial Germany's Frederick I Barbarossa (who died en route), the crusaders fought surprisingly well against high odds and managed to secure Christians' right of free entry to Jerusalem, although the city remained under Saladin's control.

The Fourth Crusade (1202–04) was doomed from the start. Prompted by Innocent III's desire to reassert papal control of crusading after the two preceding monarchical efforts, the Crusade was preached throughout Europe by envoys from Rome. The crusaders gathered at Venice, whose government had contracted in advance to transport and supply the expected number of recruits. Too few crusaders enlisted to meet the Venetian bill, however, which necessitated a change of plans. Venice offered to forgive the crusaders' debt if they agreed to restore Zara, a Dalmatian colony formerly subject to Venice, to their control. With no alternative, the crusaders took Zara by force, even though it was a Christian city. Innocent responded by excommunicating the entire army. Hoping to restore themselves to the church's good graces, and spurred on by the promise of aid from the exiled claimant to the Byzantine throne in return for their help in ousting his rival, the crusaders then sailed to Constantinople, which they sacked in April 1204 and pillaged ruthlessly. Constantinople remained under Latin control until 1261. Content with their success in returning the Orthodox East to western rule, the crusaders never continued on to the Holy Land.

France's sainted Louis IX led two crusades against Islam (1248–54 and 1270) and had earlier sent a third crusade force against the Cathar heretics in southern France. Both of his overseas campaigns began in high hopes and ended miserably. After a well-executed assault on Damietta in mid-1249, delay and confusion set in, and Louis's army wasted five months sitting passively in the Nile delta. Strategic miscalculation in 1250 resulted in the defeat of his entire army at Mansourah and in Louis's own capture by the forces of the Egyptian sultan. After his ransom, Louis spent four years overseeing the refortification of Acre, Caesarea, Jaffa, and Sidon, before returning to France and devoting himself to civil reforms. Determined to make up for his failure, though, Louis launched a new campaign in 1270, which aimed first at the seizure of Tunis before advancing toward Egypt and the Holy Land itself. Louis fell ill in Tunis, however, and died on August 25, after which his demoralized army returned to France.

The lasting consequences of the Crusades for France, as for the rest of the Latin Christian world, had little to do with the political or military aspects of the wars. Their effect on the Holy Land itself was slight. Indeed, to most of the larger Muslim world the battle to control Palestine was a relatively minor frontier struggle far removed from the center of Islamic life. Economically, the Crusades served as a catalyst for the growth of European commerce by contributing to the evolution of advanced systems of finance and capital administration; they also helped to expand western markets for eastern goods like spices, textiles, metalwork, and glassware. Inevitably, for the feudal north, the increased contact with the Greek, Jewish, and Islamic worlds introduced new ideas and methods into the European tradition—new technologies, new scientific concepts, new philosophical traditions, new artistic methods and techniques. But many of these developments were already well underway in the Mediterranean parts of Europe prior to the Crusades, and it would be a mistake to overemphasize the Crusades' importance in this regard. Indeed, the cultural influence of the Crusades has been greatest in later centuries, in the way that the conflicts have been remembered and either romanticized or vilified in the Christian and Islamic worlds. In popular western culture, they have come to be synonymous with chivalry and pageantry, the medieval world's ill-fated but noble attempt to rescue its spiritual homeland from the hands of foreign tyrants; to much of the Muslim world, they have been regarded, just as erroneously, as the clearest example of naked western aggression and hypocrisy, a cultural wounding from which Islam has yet to recover fully. Neither view is accurate.

For France, the most important legacy of the Crusades was the impetus they gave to the expansion of the kingdom's borders southward to the Mediterranean. The strategic need for a Mediterranean harbor from which to launch further Crusades (and to participate directly in the burgeoning maritime trade) provided a justification for Capetian expansion into the Midi, Languedoc, and Provence—and the crusade against the southern Cathars provided the vehicle for it. French churches acquired innumerable relics from the East, which augmented popular piety and enriched many ecclesiastical houses. Historical writing and poetry in France drew considerable inspiration from the crusade movement; the sheer scope of the enterprise excited the imagination of numerous writers, among them Guibert de Nogent, Jean de Joinville, Geoffroi de Villehardouin, and the anonymous author of the *Chanson d'Antioche*.

Clifford R. Backman

[See also: ALBIGENSIAN CRUSADE; CRUSADE CYCLE; CRUSADE SONGS/*CHANSONS DE CROISADE*; CRUSADER ART AND ARCHITECTURE; EUGENIUS III; GREGORIAN REFORM; GUIBERT DE NOGENT; HISTORIOGRAPHY; INNOCENT III; JOINVILLE, JEAN DE; LOUIS VII; LOUIS IX; MILLENNIALISM; PEACE OF GOD; PHILIP II AUGUSTUS; PILGRIMAGE; TRUCE OF GOD; VILLEHARDOUIN, GEOFFROI DE]

Joinville and Villehardouin. *Chronicles of the Crusades,* trans. Margaret R.B. Shaw. Harmondsworth: Penguin, 1963. [Provides two vivid narratives: Villehardouin's exculpatory account of the Fourth Crusade and Joinville's laudatory biography of Louis IX.]

Odo of Deuil. *De profectione Ludovici VII in Orientem,* ed. and trans. Virginia G. Berry. New York: Columbia University Press, 1953. [A detailed, insightful account of Louis VII's failed Second Crusade.]

Housley, Norman. *The Avignon Papacy and the Crusades, 1305–1378.* Oxford: Oxford University Press, 1986.

Powell, James, ed. *Muslims Under Latin Rule, 1100–1300.* Princeton: Princeton University Press, 1990.

Prawer, Joshua. *Histoire du royaume latin de Jerusalem,* trans. G. Nahon. 2 vols. Paris: CNRS, 1969–70. [The most wide-ranging study of the most important of the crusader states.]

Richard, Jean. *Louis IX: Crusader King of France,* ed. Simon Lloyd, trans. Jean Birrell. Cambridge: Cambridge University Press, 1992.

Riley-Smith, Jonathan. *The Crusades: A Short History.* New Haven: Yale University Press, 1987. [The best single-volume survey.]

Setton, Kenneth M., ed. *A History of the Crusades.* 2nd ed. 6 vols. Madison: University of Wisconsin Press, 1969–89.

CUNAULT. The town of Trèves-Cunault (Maine-et-Loire) owes its origin to the monks of Noirmoutier, who, taking refuge from the Normans, settled in Cunault (846–57). The priory, established around the turn of the millennium, flourished in the 12th century thanks to the political and economic importance of the north bank of the Loire and an influx of pilgrims venerating the reputed marriage band of the Virgin. The oldest part of the church of Notre-Dame de Cunault is the mid-11th-century bell tower. Supported by four pillars, joined by arches, it has an octagonal cupola. The square upper portion is ornamented with a series of blind arches interspersed with Romanesque pilasters and colonnettes and is crowned by a 15th-century spire. The chevet (ca. 1140) is the oldest part of the church proper. Here, an ambulatory with three radiating chapels encircles a blind apse. The building's long nave is flanked by aisles whose first three bays carry eight-branch, 13th-century Angevin vaults. Sculpted capitals with interlaced vegetal designs and images of monsters and chimeras cap columns throughout the church. A formerly painted and gilded wooden shrine (13th c.) holds the relics of St. Maxenceul. In the tympanum on the façade sits a Virgin flanked by two angels (possibly late 13th c.).

Nina Rowe

[See also: ANGERS]

Brincard, Baronne. *Cunault: ses chapiteaux du XIIe siècle.* Paris: Picard, 1937.

Rhein, André. "Cunault." *Congrès archéologique (Angers et Saumur)* 77 (1910): 138–47.

Herbécourt, Pierre d'. *Anjou roman.* La Pierre-qui-vire: Zodiaque, 1959.

Mussat, André. *Le style gothique de l'ouest de la France (XIIe–XIIIe siècles).* Paris: Picard, 1963.

CURIA REGIS. Although most commonly used for courts of the Norman kings of England, the Latin term *curia* ac-quired a general usage for any court of a feudal lord and his vassals, including any meeting, whether for social, judicial, or political affairs. In France, *curia* tended to refer to the king's council acting in a judicial capacity. Rarely did all the twelve peers, as they came to be called, convene, much less meet together with lesser lords or prelates, because the kingdom was so loosely united and royal power so limited before the 13th century.

By the 13th century, the Capetian monarch was recognized as suzerain over a great number of direct and sub-vassals. The *curia regis* decided cases between the king and those who held directly from him while cases between his vassals-in-chief and their vassals were settled in their courts, until St. Louis (r. 1226–70) insisted on the right of appeal to his court in cases of denial of justice or *faux jugement* in the feudal courts. Often, he sat with his judges, who became specialized as the Parlement de Paris and broke off from the less specialized *curia regis,* which handled fiscal affairs as well as general policy. During the reign of St. Louis's grandson Philip the Fair (1285–1314), the Chambre des Comptes also broke off from the *curia* to handle fiscal affairs, and the Estates General evolved perhaps on the model of the English Parliament as a sort of great council with prelates and representatives of the lower clergy, peers and representatives of the lower nobility, and representatives of the towns. It asserted on occasion the power to approve taxes and legislate as well as to advise on policy. Under Charles VII (1422–1461), the Estates General, which granted permanent taxes (*taille* and *gabelle*) for the army, lost control of the purse.

William A. Percy, Jr.

[See also: CHAMBRE DES COMPTES; *CONSEIL;* PARLEMENT DE PARIS]

CURRENCY. The Frankish monarchy inherited late Roman coinage and continued production of a small gold coin known as the *triente.* While appropriate for large-scale trade, gold coins represented too much wealth to be useful in ordinary transactions by small consumers. Trade tended increasingly to be local and small in scale, requiring a coin of less value. Late in the 8th century, Charlemagne introduced a new monetary system featuring a silver penny (Lat. *denarius,* OFr. *denier*) weighing about 1.7 grams. Twelve of these equaled a shilling (Lat. *solidus,* OFr. *sol* or *sou*), and twenty shillings equaled one pound (Lat. *libra,* OFr. *livre*). Only the *denier* was an actual coin during the Carolingian period. The *sol* and *livre* were "money of account," denominations used for record keeping when large sums were involved.

The Carolingian reform was so successful that a system of pounds, shillings, and pence prevailed throughout Europe for 1,000 years. Centralized Carolingian power declined, however, and soon there were many different coinages from the mints of kings, lords, and bishops. While all used the same accounting system, the value and silver content of the *denier* might vary considerably from one minting authority to another. Since money of account was based on the local *denier*, the amount of silver represented by a pound also varied from place to place. Coins received in any transaction had to be converted to local money of account for record-keeping purposes. Four pounds of Paris, *livres parisis* (l.p.), for instance, corresponded in value to five pounds of Tours, *livres tournois* (l.t.). As the volume and geographical scope of commerce began expanding in the 11th century, the moneychanger became an important figure.

This commercial revival also created demand for a stable currency. In various parts of France, especially Normandy, the inhabitants paid a "money tax" to the territorial lord in return for his promise not to alter the silver content of the coinage. Fearful that a new coinage might cheat them, people in some regions demanded that the design as well as the alloy be conserved, or even that no new coins be issued.

By the 13th century, the royal currency was far more important than others in France, and Louis IX was able to insist that royal coins circulate everywhere in the realm while others were valid only in the territory subject to the jurisdiction of the particular minting authority. Some nonroyal currencies survived in the 14th century, and Philip V was unsuccessful when in 1321 he asked for a tax to pay for buying these out. Even the crown could not establish a single money of account. The *livre tournois*, not the pound of Paris, was preferred in most of the realm.

For centuries the silver *denier* was the largest circulating coin, although its actual silver content varied widely by the 13th century. The increased range and volume of trade finally made it desirable again to have coins of greater value. After a brief experiment in the 1260s, the French crown resumed minting gold in the 1290s. Its most successful new coin, however, was the *gros tournois* issued by Louis IX in 1266. It represented twelve deniers in money of account and contained 4.2 grams of silver (the *denier* now having only 26 percent of the silver contained in its Carolingian predecessor).

The silver content and official valuation of a particular coinage in money of account became a matter of such contention that some technical discussion is necessary here. In France, the standard for measuring the intrinsic value of silver coins was the mark of Troyes, containing 4,608 grains of pure silver. The mints used *argent-le-roi*, which had a fineness of .958 (23/24), but if alloyed with other metals its silver content would be reduced. A coinage had three important characteristics. The *prix* was the official valuation of the coin in money of account. The *taille* was the number of coins minted (literally, "cut") from a mark of silver. The *titre* was the alloy or silver content of the coin expressed in units of twenty-four grains called *deniers* (the word also used for penny). The 14th-century monarchy incorporated these three characteristics into a formula that yielded an ordinal numeral called the *pied de monnaie*. The *pied* divided by four equaled the minted value of a silver mark, in *livres tournois*. If, for example, the royal mints issued *gros tournois* on the twelfth *pied*, a mark of silver would produce three l.t. in coins, or sixty *gros* valued at one *sol* each.

The government could alter the *pied* by changing one of its components. Lowering the *titre* (debasement) or raising the *prix* (overvaluing) would each raise the *pied* and "weaken" the coinage by producing a greater amount of currency, in money of account, from the same quantity of silver. The coinage of Louis IX on the twelfth *pied* (to use the later terminology) long remained the standard for "strong" money. Weakening the coinage, which had the effect of increasing the money supply, was inflationary and recognized as such, but there were reasons why it might take place.

Mints were expected to be self-supporting, so coins actually issued were given an official value (*prix*) that exceeded the cost of the bullion. The difference, known as the *monnayage*, was made up of two parts—the relatively consistent *brassage*, which represented the cost of minting, and a second component, *seigneuriage*, which was the profit of the lord operating the mint. To issue "strong money," the royal mints had to buy silver for less than three l.t. per mark. If bullion were scarce and it cost more to attract it to the mints, the mints would lose money unless the *pied* were raised. One purpose of the old regional money taxes was to keep the mints solvent without weakening the coinage.

Most lords with mints, however, were not content merely to break even. As long as the *seigneuriage* remained modest and stable (another objective of the money taxes), few questioned the seigneurial right to profit from the mints, but the 14th-century monarchy had heavy military expenses and tried to use mint profits as a fiscal expedient, raising the *pied* to increase *seigneuriage*. After considerable outcry, Philip VI returned the *pied* to the level of St. Louis in 1330–33, but then the mints ran afoul of a bullion shortage and actually had to close from 1335 to 1337.

With the outbreak of the Hundred Years' War, Philip had to reopen his mints and needed the revenue from *seigneuriage*. By 1343, he had weakened the currency to the sixtieth *pied*. The demand for reform again led the king to strengthen the money, but when he suddenly adopted the fifteenth *pied*, the effect was profoundly deflationary and he soon had to weaken the currency again.

Under John II the Good, the currency was a major political issue. Innumerable changes geared to the level of commercial activity created such confusion that people now demanded "sound" (i.e., stable) money more than "strong" money. The leading theoretician of the period, Nicole Oresme, denounced the whole idea that currency was a private seigneurial right and insisted that it belonged to the whole community. The monetary chaos reached its height in the later 1350s. Then, in 1360, the requirements of the king's ransom led to the establishment of substantial regular taxes and a reform of the currency that placed the silver coinage on the twenty-fourth *pied* and established a new gold coin, the *franc*, that would equal one *livre tournois* in money of account. Regular taxation kept the kings from seeking high mint profits, and the reform of 1360 remained in force, with small modifications, for over fifty years. The civil wars and financial chaos of the early 15th century produced another generation of monetary confusion like that of 1337–60. Not until the later 1430s was the currency stabilized again.

Manufacture of coins at the mints was entrusted to specialists called moneyers who enjoyed a number of important, mostly fiscal, privileges. A few randomly selected coins from each issue, sent to Paris in a sealed box, were inspected to ensure accuracy and honesty at the mints. One or more specialists in the Chambre des Comptes exerted centralized control over the currency, and toward the late 1340s a subcommittee of the Chambre obtained official status as the Chambre des Monnaies, which maintained regular records after 1356.

John Bell Henneman, Jr.

[See also: MINTS]

Bisson, Thomas N. Conservation of Coinage: Monetary Exploitation and Its Restraint in France, Catalonia, and Aragon (c. A.D. 1000–c. 1225). Oxford: Clarendon, 1979.

Bridrey, Émile. La théorie de la monnaie au XIVe siècle: Nicole Oresme; étude d'histoire des doctrines et des faits économiques. Paris: Giard, 1906.

Cazelles, Raymond. "Quelques réflexions à propos des mutations de la monnaie royale française (1295–1360)." Moyen âge 72 (1966): 83–105, 251–278.

Miskimin, Harry A. Money, Prices and Foreign Exchange in Fourteenth Century France. New Haven: Yale University Press, 1963.

Watson, Andrew. "Back to Gold—and Silver." Economic History Review 20 (1967): 1–34.

CUSTOMS DUTIES. Throughout the Middle Ages, seigneurs and towns levied tolls and duties on passing commerce, but not until the later 13th century did the monarchy attempt, in any systematic way, to exact payments on goods passing across the frontiers of the kingdom.

For the customs to become a significant source of revenue, the king had to develop a specialized branch of the government in charge of ports et passages, and this customs service really dates from the reign of Philip IV, one of whose officers, Pierre de Chalon, was the first specialist in ports et passages. The first type of customs duty was based on the prohibition of exports. When France and England went to war in 1294, their respective kings undertook to raise revenue by prohibiting the export of wool and woolens. Those wishing to be excused from this prohibition, generally Italian merchant companies, had to buy a license from the crown, and the revenue from this source was in effect a customs duty on exports. It brought Philip IV considerable revenue in the early 14th century but had declined in value to 8,000 livres parisis in 1331 and only 2,000 l.p. by 1344. This tax was known as haut passage.

The improved machinery that Chalon established in the ports et passages administration made it possible to establish, in 1324, a second type of customs duty, this one a general tax on exports amounting to four deniers per pound, i.e., 1²/₃ percent of the value of exported goods. This tax, known as the droit de rève, also began as a measure to finance war. It was worth 60,000 livres tournois in 1332 and 40,000 l.t. in 1344. The rève was

incorporated into another duty, the imposition foraine, in 1369, but it was in force under Charles VI as a separate tax once more.

The imposition foraine, established in 1361, was the principal customs duty of late-medieval France. Like the others, it was levied on goods exported from the realm. When the aides were established late in 1360 to raise money for the ransom of King John II, they took the form of a 5 percent tax on the sale of goods. To prevent evasion of this tax in border areas, the crown imposed a tax of the same rate on goods leaving the kingdom. When, in 1362, Languedoc arranged to pay a different form of tax in lieu of the aides, the imposition foraine ceased to be levied on goods leaving Languedoc but was now levied on goods passing into Languedoc from parts of the kingdom that were subject to the aides. Replacement of this indirect tax in Languedoc thus created an internal customs barrier. In general, the imposition foraine was canceled and reestablished when the aides were, but because it gave rise to complaints that it damaged commerce, it was canceled on several other occasions, only to be revived with modifications when the absence of this export tax encouraged evasion of the aides.

John Bell Henneman, Jr.

[See also: AIDES]

Bigwood, Georges. "La politique de la laine en France sous les règnes de Philippe le Bel et de ses fils." Revue belge de philologie et d'histoire 15 (1935): 79–102, 429–57; 16 (1936): 95–118.

Henneman, John Bell. "Taxation of Italians by the French Crown, 1311–1363." Mediaeval Studies 31 (1969): 15–43.

Strayer, Joseph R. "Pierre de Chalon and the Origin of the French Customs Service." In Festschrift Percy Ernst Schramm zu seinem siebstgsten Geburtstag von Schulern und Freunden zugeeignet, ed. Peter Classen. Wiesbaden: Steiner, 1964.

Vuitry, Adolphe. Études sur le régime financier de la France avant la Révolution de 1789. Nouv. ser. 2 vols. Orléans: Colas, 1878–83.

CUSTUMALS/COUTUMIERS. Throughout the Middle Ages, the law of France was based primarily on custom rather than written law. Beginning at the end of the twelfth century, with the Très ancien coutumier of Normandy, the customs of various regions began to be recorded in writing. These descriptions, known as "custumals," were private compilations, though regional courts came to treat those of Normandy and Brittany as virtually official sources of law. The authors are often unknown; when they can be identified, they were usually royal or princely judicial officials. Most custumals described the law of northern France; the south, the pays de droit écrit ("land of written law"), where Roman law formed the basis of local custom, produced few. A custumal might describe the law of a province, or a smaller region, or even of a town.

The most admired single custumal of the high Middle Ages is the Coutumes de Beauvaisis by Philippe de Beaumanoir (1283). The Summa de legibus (or Grand coutumier) of Normandy was written a few decades earlier; its unknown author rivals Beaumanoir in his ability to analyze the custom of his province. Another notable custumal is the *Établissements de saint Louis* (ca. 1270); despite its name, this work was not ordained by the king, and it incorporates slightly earlier custumals of the Orléanais and of Anjou and Touraine, rather than describing the customs of the Île-de-France. The *Très ancienne coutume de Bretagne* dates from ca. 1330. Jacques d'Ableiges wrote the misnamed *Grand coutumier de France* (ca. 1387–89), which describes merely some aspects of the custom of Paris. Several custumals were heavily influenced by Roman law, including the *Conseil à un ami* of Pierre de Fontaines, a jurist who wrote to describe Picard custom for a local noble (ca. 1253). Jean Boutillier, royal *bailli,* who wrote the *Somme rurale* to aid nonlawyers in understanding the law of the region around Tournai (1395), has been accused of not understanding the Roman law he cites. The *Livres de justice et de plet* (ca. 1254–60), although it claims to record Orléanais custom, consists of little more than excerpts from Roman legal sources.

These and most other private compilations of regional customs were made in the 13th or 14th century. Few appear thereafter, and the law of significant portions of northern France remained unrecorded. By the mid-15th century, the need for an official record of every regional custom led Charles VII to order *baillis* and seneschals to compile custumals for their districts in order to avoid uncertainty about what the law was and consequent delays in legal process (1454). Progress was at times slow, but by the late 16th century the task had been accomplished. The products of this second wave of redaction, often known as *coutumes réformées,* remained in force, with few modifications, until the Revolution replaced regional customs with a national code based on Roman law.

Emily Z. Tabuteau

[See also: BEAUMANOIR, PHILIPPE DE REMI, SIRE DE; DOWRY; HISTORIOGRAPHY]

Philippe de Remi, sire de Beaumanoir. *Coutumes de Beauvaisis,* ed. Amédée Salmon. 2 vols. Paris: Picard, 1899–1900. [trans. by F.R.P. Akehurst. Philadelphia: University of Pennsylvania Press, 1992.]

Tardif, Ernest Joseph, ed. *Coutumiers de Normandie.* Rouen Cagniard, 1881.

Besnier, Robert. *La coutume de Normandie: histoire externe.* Paris: Sirey, 1935.

Caswell, Jean, and Ivan Sipkov. *The Coutumes of France in the Library of Congress.* Washington, D.C.: Library of Congress, 1977.

CUVELIER (fl. late 14th c.). The author of the *Chronique de Bertrand du Guesclin* (ca. 1385), a 24,346-line French poem, Cuvelier is otherwise unknown. His subject, Du Guesclin (ca. 1324–1380), a minor Breton nobleman, rose through military service during the Breton wars of succession, campaigns in Spain, and the Hundred Years' War to become constable of France. Cuvelier's Bertrand is an epic hero: physically ugly but noble in character, fearless and cunning in war but generous to the common people.

Though unreliable, the *Chronique* was popular; thirteen manuscripts survive, including those of a prose epitome done in 1387 for Jean d'Estouteville.

Leah Shopkow

[See also: COMPOSERS, MINOR (14TH CENTURY); GUESCLIN, BERTRAND DU; HUNDRED YEARS' WAR]

Cuvelier. *La chanson de Bertrand du Guesclin de Cuvelier,* ed. Jean-Claude Faucon. 3 vols. Toulouse: Éditions Universitaires du Sud, 1990–91.

Faucon, Jean-Claude. "Un imagier de la guerre de cent ans." *Littératures* (*Toulouse*) 9–10 (1984): 13–22.

Levine, Robert. "Myth and Antimyth in *La vie vaillante de Bertrand du Guesclin.*" *Viator* 16 (1985): 259–75.

CYCLIC MASS. The term "cyclic Mass" generally refers to polyphonic settings of most or all of the five principal items of the Ordinary of the Mass (Kyrie, Gloria, Credo, Sanctus-Benedictus, Agnus) as a musically unified entity.

The cyclic Mass became an important musical form only in the 15th century, but its roots can be traced back to the 13th, when the diverse chants of the Ordinary began to be collected into cycles. In 14th-century France, and possibly Italy and Spain as well, this practice was extended to the assembling of independent polyphonic Mass movements into cycles (Masses of Tournai, Toulouse, Barcelona, and the Sorbonne). However, only one such Mass seems to have been conceived in its entirety by a single composer: the *Messe de Nostre Dame* by Guillaume de Machaut (ca. 1300–1377). Even in this case, there is no clear internal unity among its six movements (which include a final *Ite missa est*), except that all are for four voices and are in Machaut's characteristic style. These movements fall into two distinct groups: the Kyrie, Sanctus, Agnus, and Ite employ plainsong *cantus firmi* from the Ordinary and are structured by similar isorhythmic procedures, while the Gloria and Credo are without *cantus firmi* or isorhythm, although they are structurally and texturally related to each other.

The use of the same thematic material in two mass movements (usually Gloria-Credo or Sanctus-Agnus) first appeared in England ca. 1400. Cyclic unification of such Mass-pairs was achieved through a common "motto" opening and/or plainsong *cantus firmus* in the tenor. Mass-pairs are not yet cyclic Masses, but the principles of musical unification employed in them were soon extended to embrace most or all of the Ordinary. Thus, the earliest true cyclic Masses, dating ca. 1420, are also English: the *Missa Alma redemptoris mater* by Leonel Power (ca. 1375–1445) and the *Missa Rex seculorum* and *Missa Da gaudiorum* by John Dunstable (ca. 1380–1453). All three masses are for three voices, consist of four movements (lacking the Kyrie, not always set in English cyclic Masses, or the Agnus), and employ the same chant in the tenor of all movements. It is this chant for which the Mass is named. By 1450, English composers had also composed cyclic Masses for four voices, many of which included the Kyrie. The most influential such work is the anonymous *Missa Caput* (formerly attributed to Dufay but recently shown to be an English work), which was taken as a model for like-named Masses by the later Netherlands masters Johannes Ockeghem (ca.1420–1497) and Jacob Obrecht (ca.1450–1505).

Guillaume Dufay (1397–1474) was the first continental composer to write cyclic Masses of the English type. His earliest masses, for three voices, include the Kyrie but lack unifying themes. His later ones, however, are for four voices and are based on unifying *cantus firmi* placed in the tenor. These borrowed melodies are not only sacred (*Missa Ecce ancilla, Missa Ave Regina celorum*) but also secular (*Missa Se la face ay pale, Missa L'homme armé*). Dufay was probably the first composer to base cyclic Masses on secular themes. In his *Missa Se la face ay pale*, Dufay took as a model one of his own chansons, while his *Missa L'homme armé* may have initiated the tradition of composing Masses on this particular popular song that was followed by generations of composers throughout the 15th and 16th centuries, including Ockeghem, Antoine Busnoys (ca. 1430–1492), Firminus Caron (fl. ca. 1460–80), Guillaume Faugues (fl. ca. 1460), Johannes Regis (ca. 1425–96), Johannes Tinctoris (ca. 1435–1511), Obrecht, Josquin des Prez (ca. 1440–1521), Pierre de la Rue (ca. 1460–1518), Antoine Brumel (ca. 1460–ca. 1520), Jean Mouton (ca. 1459–1522), Cristóbal de Morales (ca. 1500–53), Giovanni da Palestrina (1525–1594), and many others.

Following Dufay's example in his *Missa Se la face ay pale*, many 15th-century composers chose polyphonic models for their Masses, incorporating into them various themes and even whole polyphonic complexes from those models. (Dufay had done this but sparingly.) An outstanding example is Ockeghem's *Missa Fors seulement*, based on his own rondeau. This Mass stands on the borderline between the *cantus firmus* Mass and what might be called the "parody" or "imitation" Mass, which were terms actually applied to such works in the 16th century. It may be defined as a Mass based on the entire polyphonic complex of a preexistent composition.

Ockeghem also pioneered a type of cyclic Mass based on procedures other than the sharing of melodic material. His *Missa Prolationum* consists almost entirely of double mensuration canons, only two voices of which are notated and which are to be read in different mensurations (i.e., divisions of the measure, such as 3/4, 4/4, 6/8, and 9/8), while his *Missa Cuiusvis toni*, musically unified only by a vague related "motto" in each movement, is notated in such a way that it may be sung in more than one mode.

Jacob Obrecht specialized in Masses with multiple *cantus firmi*. His masterpiece in the genre is his *Missa Sub tuum presidium*, which combines a principal *cantus firmus*

(after which the Mass is named) with cumulative additions, so that each movement is scored for one voice more than the preceding. Thus, it progresses from a three-voice Kyrie to a seven-voice Agnus that combines five different plainsongs.

The greatest master of the cyclic Mass in the 15th century, but belonging more to the Renaissance than the Middle Ages, was Josquin des Prez, whose more than twenty Masses range from strict *cantus firmus* types (including two Masses on *L'homme armé*) to Masses based on free paraphrases of plainsong (*Missa Ave maris stella, Missa Pange lingua*), on *cantus firmi* derived from sol-fa syllables (*Missa La sol fa re mi, Missa Hercules dux Ferrarie*), on canonic procedures (*Missa Ad fugam, Missa Sine nomine*), and at least one that comes close to being a full-fledged "imitation" mass (*Missa Mater patris*, based on a motet by Brumel).

Other important continental composers of cyclic Masses in the late 15th and early 16th centuries, besides those mentioned, include Johannes Martini (ca. 1450–1517), Loyset Compère (ca. 1450–1518), and Johannes Ghiselin (ca. 1455–ca. 1511). Most of these composers were French or Netherlandish (the Netherlands then being a dependency of Burgundy and dominated by the reigning French culture). Despite its medieval, liturgical origins, the cyclic Mass is the principal large musical form of the 15th and 16th centuries and emblematic of the flowering of French musical culture at the end of the Middle Ages and in the early Renaissance.

Martin Picker

[See also: *CANTUS FIRMUS;* CARON, FIRMINUS; DUFAY, GUILLAUME; MACHAUT, GUILLAUME DE; OCKEGHEM, JOHANNES; REGIS, JOHANNES; TINCTORIS, JOHANNES]

Bukofzer, Manfred. *Studies in Medieval and Renaissance Music.* New York: Norton, 1950.

Burkholder, J. Peter. "Johannes Martini and the Imitation Mass of the Late Fifteenth Century." *Journal of the American Musicological Society* 38 (1985): 470–523.

Finscher, Ludwig. *Die Musik des 15. und 16. Jahrhunderts.* 2 vols. Laaber: Laaber, 1990.

Leech-Wilkinson, Daniel. *Machaut's Mass.* Oxford: Clarendon, 1990.

Planchart, Alejandro E. "Guillaume Dufay's Masses: Notes and Revisions." *Musical Quarterly* 58 (1972): 1–23.

Reese, Gustave. *Music in the Renaissance.* rev. ed. New York: Norton, 1959.

Sparks, Edgar. *Cantus Firmus in Mass and Motet, 1420–1520.* Berkeley: University of California Press, 1963.

Strohm, Reinhard. *The Rise of European Music, 1380–1500.* Cambridge: Cambridge University Press, 1993.

D

DAGOBERT, PSEUDOCYCLE OF. The Frankish king Dagobert I (r. 622–38/39) was the inspiration for a revival of the French epic around the middle of the 14th century for reasons that have not always been understood, although they are clearer when viewed in the context of the reign of Charles V (r. 1364–80). *Florent et Octavien*, the first of this group of late epics to have Dagobert's reign as a background, was followed by *Charles le chauve, Ciperis de Vignevaux, Florence de Rome,* and *Theseus de Cologne.* It was once thought that these poems derived from a lost primitive Merovingian cycle, although no evidence of this exists. There is no doubt, however, that during the later Middle Ages Dagobert was honored as the founder of the abbey of Saint-Denis; the legend was encouraged by the monks there, who had produced a *Gesta Dagoberti* (ca. 835) that became an important source for their *Grandes Chroniques de France,* wherein Dagobert is held up as a model for princes.

Dagobert already figures in the opening lines of the 13th-century octosyllabic *Octavien,* but his role becomes more important in the 14th-century Alexandrine version, which dates from the troubled times after the French defeat at Poitiers, when Edward III of England and Charles the Bad of Navarre were both claiming rights to the French throne. It was under these distressing circumstances that Charles V developed a program of propaganda to make clear his indisputable claim to the throne, including his descent from Dagobert.

In *Florent et Octavien,* the first of the series to support this claim, Octavien, emperor of Rome and friend of Dagobert, comes to his aid when Paris is threatened by an invasion of the pagan Wandres, who bear a certain resemblance to the invading English. He is seconded by one of his twin sons, Florent, who was separated from his father soon after birth but is reunited during this conflict in a dramatic episode. At a bleak moment, Dagobert prays to St. Denis for help against the foe, vowing to endow a monastery in his honor. St. George soon appears, accompanied by St. Maurice, to rescue the situation.

Charles le chauve (sometimes called *Dieudonné de Hongrie*) develops the ancestry of Dagobert, beginning with his imaginary great-grandfather Melisant de Hongrie, who adopts the name Charles le chauve when converted to Christianity. His son, Philippe, becomes the father of Dieudonné, who is in his turn the father of Dagobert. The author of this extravagant genealogy claims the authority of a Latin source he consulted at Saint-Denis. Dieudonné becomes king only after extraordinary adventures fighting the Saracens, but nothing further is learned of him because the end of the single manuscript (B.N. fr. 24372) is missing.

Theseus de Cologne depicts the final years of Dagobert. Now grown old, he is called upon to rescue the king of Cologne, Foridas, father of Theseus. St. Denis appears as mediator of a dispute between Theseus and Dagobert's son, Ludovis (Clovis II). Before the end of the poem, Dagobert, who has now reigned for eighty years, dies, leaving his throne to Ludovis. (The historic Dagobert died by the age of thirty.)

When viewed in the context of the times that produced these tales, this pseudogenealogy is no more exotic than the Chevalier au Cygne's or Melusine's or, indeed, the Trojan origin of France, all popular in their day. Equally important is the personality of Dagobert in Charles V's successful program of propaganda to restore the morale of his subjects after the disaster of Poitiers and Étienne Marcel's civil uprising, encouraged by the King of Navarre's pretentions to the throne. Charles V's direct descent from Dagobert was an important element in this propaganda.

Charity Cannon Willard

[See also: CHARLES V THE WISE; DAGOBERT I; *FLORENCE DE ROME; FLORENT ET OCTAVIEN; GRANDES CHRONIQUES DE FRANCE*]

Bossuat, Robert. "*Florent et Octavien,* chanson de geste du XIVe siècle." *Romania* 73 (1952): 289–331.
——. "*Charles le chauve,* étude sur le déclin de l'épopée française." *Lettres romanes* 7 (1953): 107–32, 187–99.
——. "Theseus de Cologne." *Moyen âge* 65 (1959): 97–133, 293–320, 539–77.
——. "Le roi Dagobert, héros de romans du moyen âge." *Comptes rendus de l'Académie des Inscriptions* (1964): 361–67.

Willard, Charity C. "*Florent et Octavien:* The Fourteenth-Century Poem." *Olifant* 14 (1989): 179–89.

DAGOBERT I (608–638/39). The son of Clotar II, Dagobert I was king of Austrasia (from 622) and then also king over Neustria and Burgundy after the death of his father in 628/29. He is the last Merovingian who is seen as a strong, active, and effective ruler over all of the Frankish kingdoms.

Dagobert was associated with Clotar II as subking of Austrasia, ruling from Metz, before moving to Paris upon his succession in Neustria and Burgundy. However, the particularism of the regions of the kingdom remained strong, and he made his younger brother Charibert (d. 632) subking in southern Aquitaine and established his young son Sigibert III as subking in Austrasia in 634. The powerful aristocracy that was so visible in the reign of Clotar II retained and enlarged its position, especially under the youthful subkings.

Dagobert left a reputation for personally supervising royal officials throughout his lands and personally giving judgments in legal cases. From his position as the source of justice, he saw to the promulgation of the Lex Ribuaria for the Austrasians, and perhaps he played a role in the codification of the laws of the Alemanni and the Bavarians. He exercised supervision of the church in his kingdom, saw to the appointment of bishops of good quality, and supported missionary efforts among the Frisians. Dagobert gave lavish endowments to the church of Saint-Denis (which he founded ca. 624 and where he was buried), which promoted its role as the center of the royal cult. He maintained Frankish control over the Bretons, Gascons, and Bavarians and campaigned successfully against the Visigoths. He failed, however, in his expeditions against the Wends, who were threatening Thuringia, and the Basques remained an unchecked menace to Aquitaine.

When Dagobert died in 638/39, he was succeeded by his sons, the nine-year-old Sigibert III in Austrasia and portions of Aquitaine and the five-year-old Clovis II in the other regions. The young kings were under the tutelage, and thus the domination, of the nobles of their kingdoms, especially the mayors of the palace, and the decline of the Merovingian monarchy under the "do-nothing kings" (*les rois fainéants*) began.

Steven Fanning

[See also: DAGOBERT, PSEUDOCYCLE OF; DENIS; MEROVINGIAN DYNASTY]

Bachrach, Bernard S., trans. *Liber historiæ Francorum.* Lawrence: Coronado, 1973.
Wallace-Hadrill, J.M., trans. *The Fourth Book of the Chronicle of Fredegar with Its Continuations.* London: Nelson, 1960.
James, Edward. *The Franks.* Oxford: Blackwell, 1988.
Wallace-Hadrill, John Michael. *The Long-Haired Kings, and Other Studies in Frankish History.* London: Methuen, 1962, pp. 206–31.
Wood, Ian. *The Merovingian Kingdoms, 450–751.* London: Longman, 1994.

D'AILLY, PIERRE (1350–1420). D'Ailly studied at the Collège de Navarre in Paris and received the master of arts degree in 1368. He lectured at the Sorbonne on Peter Lombard's *Sententiae* in 1375 and promoted Ockham's teaching. In 1381, he became doctor of theology and canon in Noyon. He was rector of the college from 1384 to 1389 and befriended Jean Gerson, his most celebrated pupil. In 1389, he was made chancellor of the University of Paris. From 1389 to 1395, he became influential in Charles VI's court as the king's confessor and almoner. Appointed bishop of Le Puy in 1395, he never entered the see; in 1397, he was made archbishop of Cambrai. He attended the Council of Pisa in 1409 but supported the newly elected Alexander V unenthusiastically. Alexander's successor, the antipope John XXIII, utilized D'Ailly at the Council of Rome in 1411 and named him cardinal in 1412. The following year, he was appointed papal legate to Emperor Sigismund, subsequently playing a prominent role in the Council of Constance (1414–17). He presided over the first session without a pope in residence and supported the primacy of the general council over the pope. As president of the commission of faith, he examined John Hus and witnessed his condemnation in 1415. Martin V, elected by the council as the sole legitimate pope, appointed D'Ailly as legate to Avignon. He died there in 1420.

D'Ailly devoted most of his public life to ecclesiastical reform and to healing the Great Schism by means of a general council. Nevertheless, his writings covered a wide range of topics, including *Quaestiones* on Lombard's *Sententiae* (1390); a large collection of sermons; numerous ecclesiological and legal tracts (many of them later included with Jean Gerson's works), such as *De materia concilii generalis, Tractatus super reformatione ecclesiae,* and *Tractatus de ecclesiae autoritate*; treatises on the soul and the sacraments; a concordance of astronomy; and his famous *Imago mundi,* later owned and annotated by Columbus, who found it to confirm a western passage to India.

H. Lawrence Bond

[See also: CONCILIAR MOVEMENT; GERSON, JEAN; OCKHAM, WILLIAM OF; PHILOSOPHY; UNIVERSITIES]

D'Ailly, Pierre. *De materia concilii generalis, Tractatus super reformatione ecclesiae,* and *Tractatus de ecclesiae autoritate.* In Jean Gerson. *Opera omnia,* ed. Louis E. Dupin. 5 vols. Antwerp: Sumptibus Societatis, 1706, Vol. 2.
———. *Ymago mundi de Pierre d'Ailly,* ed. and trans. Edmond Buron. 3 vols. Paris: Maisonneuve, 1930.
Glorieux, Palémon. "L'œuvre littéraire de Pierre d'Ailly: remarques et précisions." *Mélanges de science religieuse* 22 (1965).
Oakley, Francis. *The Political Thought of Pierre d'Ailly: The Voluntarist Tradition.* New Haven: Yale University Press, 1964.
Salembier, Louis. *Le cardinal Pierre d'Ailly.* Tourcoing: Georges Frère, 1932.

DAME À LA LYCORNE, ROMAN DE LA. A lengthy mid-14th-century romance (8,575 octosyllabic lines) with twenty-five inserted lyrics in *formes fixes* and one inserted prose letter. It is found in a single manuscript (B.N. fr. 12562), where it is illuminated with 102 miniatures. The *Dame à la lycorne* is a late expression of traditional courtly themes, whose hero seems clearly inspired by Chrétien de Troyes's *Yvain, le chevalier au lion*. The inserted lyrics are a way for the two lovers to communicate their true sentiments in a discreet manner.

William W. Kibler

[See also: CHRÉTIEN DE TROYES; *FORMES FIXES*]

Gennrich, Frederick, ed. *Le romans de la dame a la lycorne et du biau chevalier au lyon.* Dresden: Gesellschaft für romanische Literatur, 1908.

Boulton, Maureen B.M. *The Song in the Story: Lyric Insertions in French Narrative Fiction, 1200–1400.* Philadelphia: University of Pennsylvania Press, 1993.

DAMOISEL/DAMOISEAU. *See* ESQUIRE

DAMPIERRE. A noble family from Champagne, the Dampierres were counts of Flanders from 1246 to 1384. Guillaume de Dampierre in 1223 became the second husband of Marguerite, countess of Flanders and Hainaut (1244–1278). His descendants fought the Avesnes family, descended from her first marriage, until 1323. After Gui de Dampierre became count in 1278, Flanders was embroiled in continuous difficulties with King Philip IV of France, who clearly hoped to add it to the royal domain. Although the famous Battle of Courtrai in 1302 was a Flemish victory, the peace of 1305 gave the monarchy major territorial concessions and a huge indemnity.

Gui de Dampierre died in 1305 and was succeeded by his son, Robert III de Béthune, who was caught between French claims and his subjects' desires for autonomy. Divisions within the Dampierre family made his position difficult. The quarrel with the Avesnes family ended in 1323 with their claims on Holland and Hainaut conceded. Robert's son, Louis de Nevers (1323–1346), was loyal to his French overlords. Louis de Male (1346–1384) was the most independent of the Dampierre counts, but also the last; in 1369, he married his daughter to Philip, duke of Burgundy, and they succeeded him in Flanders in 1384.

David M. Nicholas

[See also: FLANDERS]

Duvivier, Charles. *Les influences française et germanique en Belgique au XIIIe siècle: la querelle des d'Avesnes et des Dampierre jusqu'à la mort de Jean d'Avesnes (1257).* Brussels: Falk, 1894.

Luykx, Theo. *Het grafelijk geslacht Dampierre en zijn strijd tegen Philips de Schone.* Louvain: Davidsfonds, 1952.

Nowé, Henri. *La bataille des éperons d'or.* Brussels: La Renaissance du Livre, 1945.

Vandermaesen, M. "Vlaanderen en Henegouwen onder het Huis van Dampierre, 1244–1384." In *Algemene Geschiedenis der Nederlanden.* 2nd ed. Haarlem: Fibula-Van Dishoeck, 1982, Vol. 2, pp. 399–440.

DANCE. Throughout the Middle Ages, dance was an important part of both religious worship and secular recreation. Sacred and secular documents, iconographic depictions, and literary references bear witness that dance played a central role in the lives of all classes of people throughout the medieval period.

From as early as the 4th century, there is documentation that dances were a part of the sacred celebrations on Easter, Pentecost, Christmas, and certain saints' days. It is not always clear at what point in the services dancing was involved; the most frequent references are to dancing in processions. But it could also have been involved more centrally in the services. A mid-13th-century statement by the troubadour Tezaur of Peire de Corbian confirms that by then dance was present during parts of the Mass: "Lords, now I know very divinely indeed how to . . . dance the 'Sanctus' and the 'Agnus' and the 'Cunctipotens.'"

Between the 6th and 17th centuries, the church frequently forbade dance on certain occasions. In 1208, for example, the bishop of Paris declared it improper to dance the *carole* in processions, and in 1209 the Council of Avignon issued an edict against dancing *caroles* on the vigils of saints' days, calling the dance "obscene motion." In 1325, the general chapter in Paris forbade clerics, under pain of excommunication, from participating in dances, with the exceptions of Christmastime and the feasts of St. Nicholas and St. Catherine. The injunctions seem to be intended to regulate the use of dance during sacred ceremonies and to purge it of improper content, in both text and movement, but there is no suggestion that dance was unwelcome in the church. Its presence is recorded in official French church documents into the 17th century.

A repertory of music for sacred dancing can be found in the approximately eighty Latin monophonic rondeaux preserved in 13th-century French sources from the cathedral of Notre-Dame in Paris. The rondeau is described ca. 1300 as a "round dance" (*rotundellus*) by Johannes de

Clerics dancing. MS Pluteo 29,I, fol. 463. *Courtesy of the Biblioteca Mediceo-Laurenziana, Florence.*

Grocheio in his treatise on music, and he explains that its music is distinguished from other types of dance in that the melody used for the refrain is similar to that of the verse (see Example 1). In conformity with the 1325 edict cited above, the majority of the Latin rondeaux texts are for Advent and Christmas, with several each for St. Nicholas and St. Catherine, although there exist rondeaux for other feasts as well. Some of the rondeau texts specifically mention dance: *Leto leta concio, hac die resonet tripudio* ("Let the joyful company this day resound in a joyful dance"); and an illumination in the major manuscript source depicts clerics in a "round" formation, probably dancing.

Example 1. MS Pluteo 29, I, fol. 471–471v. *Courtesy of the Biblioteca Mediceo-Laurenziana, Florence.*

I

Nicholaus pontifex	Nicholas the pontiff
Nostrum est refugium;	Is our refuge;
Clericis ac laicis	To clerics and laity
Sit semper remedium;	May he always be a remedy;
Clericorum est amator,	He is the patron of clerics,
Laicorum consolator,	The consolation of the laity,
Omniumque conformator,	And the guiding light of all,
In omni angustia,	In all our trials;
Nicholae, Nicholae,	*Nicholas, Nicholas,*
Nicholae.	*Nicholas.*

II

In sua infantia	While still an infant
Celebrat ieiunium,	He kept strict fastings,
Fons et caput dicitur	He who is said to be the fount
Confessorum omnium;	And head of all confessors;
Hic in cunis abstinebat,	In his cradle he abstained from food,
Quod mamillas non suggebat,	For he sucked not his nurse's breasts,
Nisi semel nec edebat	Nor did he eat except once only
Quarta, sexta feria.	On Wednesdays and Fridays.
Nicholae, Nicholae,	*Nicholas, Nicholas,*
Nicholae.	*Nicholas.*

III

Suscitavit clericos	He raised up the clerics
Occisos invidia,	Killed in envy,
Quos occidit carnifex	Whom the butcher killed
cum sua nequitia;	In his wickedness;
Tres puellas maritavit,	He allowed three maidens marriage,
De peccatis observavit,	And saved them from sin,
Paupertatem relaxavit	When he mitigated their poverty
Auri data copia.	By giving them bags of gold.
Nicholae, Nicholae,	*Nicholas, Nicholas,*
Nicholae.	*Nicholas.*

Translation from Gordan A. Anderson, *Notre-Dame and Related Conductus, Opera omnia*, vol. 8, p. xlii.

Secular dance music is frequently referred to in the troubadour literature as an important part of the minstrel's art. A poem by the late 12th-century troubadour Jaufre Rudel mentions dances along with other poetic and musical forms performed at court: ". . . minstrels who are in the palace play *descorts* and *suns* and *lais* and *danses* and *cansonz de gesta* on the *viula*. No one will ever see such a celebration again." It is significant that the account relates that the minstrels perform all of these musical forms on the vielle (or fiddle), a bowed string instrument similar in some ways to the later violin. From other references and pictorial evidence, we know that this was the favorite instrument for performing all types of music in the 12th and 13th centuries.

Although only a small repertory has survived, poetic and musical, for the dance forms, the literature attests the vast popularity of all the dances in the courtly circles from the 11th to the late 14th century. Typical is the reference by Jean Maillart in his *Roman du comte d'Anjou* (ca. 1300), which includes dances within a courtly setting of various musical performances: "Then the linen was taken up, and when they had washed their hands, the *caroles* began. Those ladies who had sweet voices sang loudly: everyone answered them joyfully, anyone who knew how to sing, sang thus. . . . Some sang *pastourelles* about Robichon and Amelot, others played on vielles *chansons royales* and *estampies*, dances and *notas*. On lute and psaltery, each according to his preference [played] *lais* of love, *descorts* and ballades in order to entertain those who were ill."

Many more references to dance can be found, often in conjunction with instruments. But dances are also mentioned as songs to be sung without instruments, as in Raimon de Cornet's poem (ca. 1320): "A jongleur would rapidly learn stanzas and many little verses, cansos, and *basses danses*." This reference is the first known mention of the *basse danse*, which would become quite popular as an instrumental form in the 15th and 16th centuries. The implication here is that in the 14th century the *basse danse* was a vocal form, but none is known to have survived.

In spite of the number of dance names that are found in the sources, we have detailed information about only a few. Those that were also poetic forms are discussed in poetry treatises, such as the *dansa*, described in the Catalan treatise *Doctrina de compondre dictatz* (ca. 1300): "If you wish to compose a *dansa*, you should speak well and pleasingly of love in whatever state of mind that you may be in. And you should compose it with three stanzas, and no more, with a *repost*, with one or two *tornadas*, as you may think fit; it should always have a new tune. . . . A *dansa* is so called because it is normally sung while dancing, hence it should should have a pleasing tune; and it is sung with instruments and pleases everyone who sings and hears it." In this case, we have a clear picture of the *dansa*; it is unfortunate that none of the melodies for this poetic form has come down to us. Not all descriptions are so detailed; the early 14th-century treatise *Leys d'amors* by Guillaume Molinier supplies the name of a dance form called the *bal*, which was usually "composed as an instrumental tune and then supplied with words," but no further information is given. A vocal composition from the same time was known as "ballade," having a form related to the rondeau, and this may be what is referred to in the treatise.

The other source of description of late-medieval dance forms is Grocheio's music treatise, which identifies the secular dances "round" (*rotundellus*), *estampie* (*stantipes*), *carole* (*ductia*), and *nota*. The form of the secular round (rondeau) is the same as the sacred form discussed above; the music for both the *estampie* and *carole* is distinct from that of the rondeau in that they have separate melodic material for the verse and refrain. Further, both *estampie* and *carole* have separate vocal and instrumental forms, the main difference being that for the vocal dances a single musical setting is repeated with each new verse, whereas the instrumental dances are composed of many sets of musical verses all ending with the same refrain.

Grocheio describes the *estampie* as a complicated dance, remarking that it causes young men and women to concentrate because of its difficulty. The *Doctrina* adds the information that its poetic subject is to center on "love and homage" and supports Grocheio's description of the *estampie*'s difficult nature by stating that it requires more "vigor" in singing than do other songs. Seven complete instrumental *estampies* survive, as well as twenty-six *estampie* texts, two with music. The most famous medieval *estampie*, *Kalenda Maya*, is reported to have been both a vocal and instrumental composition; the text is said to have been written by the troubadour Raimbaut de Vaqueiras (ca. 1155–1205), to a melody he heard performed on the fiddle by two jongleurs at the court of Montferrat.

Although the *carole* was one of the two most popular dance forms from the 11th to the 14th century, little is known of its music or steps. Caroling is found frequently in the literature as a part of the picture of courtly entertainment and pastoral relaxation, as in the 13th-century romance *Guillaume de Dole* by Jean Renart: "Hand in hand . . . before the tent, in a green pasture, the maidens and young men have begun the *carole*." Reference to "hand in hand" suggests that the *carole* was danced in the round, a fact confirmed by Grocheio, who also implies that the difference between it and round dance (rondeau) was that the round dance was danced completely in round formation, while the *carole* could also use other formations, including that of a line, as in Philippe de Remi's *La Manekine* (ca. 1270): "Such a *carole* had never been seen, nearly a quarter league long." In performance, the dance leader would sing the *carole* verses and all of the dancers would reply with the refrain. Numerous French *carole* texts survive from these centuries, but we do not have even one musical example either of a text setting or an instrumental *carole*.

About the *nota*, little is known beyond the enigmatic statement by Grocheio that it had a musical form that was in some ways similar to the instrumental *estampie* and *ductia* ("either a form of *carole* or an incomplete *estampie*"). Jean Maillart's reference to it, cited above, where the *nota* is listed with *caroles*, *estampies*, and *dansas*, indicates that the *nota* was definitely a separate form. Only two examples are known to have survived, both from the 13th century: *La Note Martinet* and a piece by Adam de la Bassée, canon at Saint-Pierre in Lille. His composition is identified as "a Notula on the composition that begins 'to play and dance. . . .'" The two compositions have only vague reference to the verse-refrain format of the *estampie* and *carole* and are formally quite different from one another, leaving little opportunity to draw conclusions as to what a *nota* was. I have speculated that perhaps *nota* was a term for those dances that had unique forms but bore some resemblance to the *estampie* and *carole*.

Most of the literary evidence and references are to courtly circles, but there is the constant suggestion that similar dances were also danced by the lower classes, especially the *carole*, although the absence of material does not allow us to know how they differed.

Because the dance forms discussed above were closely related to the troubadour and trouvère lyric tradition, they began to wane through the 14th century as the social and political organization of France changed. One of the changes in courtly life was the introduction of dancing masters and the sophisticated *basse danse*, in which the steps for each dance were individually choreographed. Some of the earlier dance names are occasionally found in the literature throughout the 15th century, but by then they had lost their social status. From the early 15th century, all the earlier dance forms were overshadowed as the *basse danse* became the most popular and fashionable court dance of the century.

Timothy J. McGee

[See also: *BASSE DANSE; ESTAMPIE*; GROCHEIO, JOHANNES DE; MUSICAL INSTRUMENTS; RONDEAU]

Anderson, Gordon A. *Notre-Dame and Related Conductus: Opera omnia*. 9 vols. Henryville: Institute of Mediaeval Music, 1979–86, Vol. 8.

McGee, Timothy J., ed. *Medieval Instrumental Dances*. Bloomington: Indiana University Press, 1989.

———. "Medieval Dances: Matching the Repertory with Grocheio's Descriptions." *Journal of Musicology* 7 (1989): 498–517.

Page, Christopher. *The Owl and the Nightingale: Musical Life and Ideas in France 1100–1300*. London: Dent, 1989.

———. *Voices and Instruments of the Middle Ages*. London: Dent, 1987.

Rokseth, Yvonne. "Danses cléricales du XIIIe siècle." *Mélanges 1945 des publications de la Faculté des Lettres de Strasbourg*. Paris, 1947, pp. 93–126.

Sachs, Curt. *World History of the Dance*. New York: Norton, 1937.

DAUPHIN. The dominical title *dauphin* (Lat. *delphinus*) was borne from 1281 by the count of Clermont-en-Auvergne (who styled himself "dauphin of Auvergne") and from 1282 by the count of Vienne and Albon in the kingdom of Arles (who styled himself "dauphin of Viennois"). Derived from the personal name Dauphin, invariably borne either as a second forename or as a surname by the counts of the latter line from 1132 to 1282, it was apparently misinterpreted as a title. The corresponding jurisdictional title Dauphiné (Lat. *delphinatus*) appeared for the first time in 1285 and was thereafter applied to the whole estate of the dauphin. In July 1349, the last independent dauphin of Viennois, Humbert II de la Tour-du-Pin, despairing of an heir and deeply in debt, ceded the Dauphiné to Philip VI, who bestowed it upon his grandson, the future Charles V of France. In the following year, Charles became heir apparent to the throne, but it was not until he, as king, granted the Dauphiné to his own firstborn son, the future Charles VI, shortly after his birth in December 1368, that the delphinal dignity began to be treated as a distinctive attribute of the status of *primogenitus regis*, or firstborn son of the king. All subsequent heirs apparent to the throne, including the first five sons of Charles VI, were given the dignity of dauphin of Viennois at either birth or succession to the status of *primogenitus*.

D'A. Jonathan D. Boulton

[See also: DAUPHINÉ/VIENNOIS]

Boulton, D'A. Jonathan D. *Grants of Honour: The Origins of the System of Nobiliary Dignities of Traditional France, ca. 1100–1515*. Forthcoming.

Prud'homme, Auguste. "De l'origine et du sens des mots dauphin et dauphiné et leurs rapports avec l'emblème du dauphin en Dauphiné, en Auvergne et en Forez." *Bibliothèque de l'École des Chartes* 54 (1893): 429–56.

DAUPHINÉ/VIENNOIS. The region that came to be known as the Dauphiné is bounded by the Rhône and Savoie on the west and north, by Italy on the east, and by Provence on the south. From the 5th century, it formed part of a succession of kingdoms known as "Burgundy" or "Arles and Vienne" (so named after the two cities that disputed the claim to be its capital). After 1032, this kingdom passed in theory under the direct authority of the Holy Roman emperor, but in fact it continued to be controlled by regional magnates. One of these, Archbishop Brochard of Vienne, gave comital authority over the northern part of the Viennois to the count of Savoy, while giving the southern part, with the title of count, to Guigues le Vieux (d. 1060/70), lord of Vion and Albon. This was the beginning of the Viennois as a political entity, but not until Guigues IV (d. 1142) does the name Dauphin appear, as a surname (Guigo Dalphinus). The reasons for this surname are unknown, but since Guigues's mother was English and had a cousin named Dolfin, she was probably responsible.

The rulers of the Viennois, while annexing the adjoining territories (the Briançonnais, Grésivaudan, Embrunais, Gapençais, and the baronies of La Tour-du-Pin, Montauban, and Mévouillon), continued to call themselves "count of Vienne and Albon" until the late 13th century, when *dauphin* first became a title and Dauphiné the name of the principality. The acquisition of the Dauphiné by the king of France occurred in 1349, after Humbert II sold it to Philip VI, who bestowed it upon his grandson, the future Charles V. Charles was thus the first dauphin belonging to a French royal family, and the royal heir apparent thereaf-

ter received the title, underlining the importance of this extension of French sovereignty beyond the Rhône. Under Dauphin Louis II (r. 1440–57), the future King Louis XI, the final important annexations (Valentinois and Diois) to the Dauphiné took place. The mother house of the Carthusian order, La Grande Chartreuse, was founded near Grenoble in 1084, as were the Hospitalers of Saint-Anthoine at about the same time in the Viennois. Several well-known troubadours came from the southern Dauphiné, and in 1339 a university was founded at Grenoble.

Eugene L. Cox

[See also: DAUPHIN]

Bautier, Robert-Henri, and Janine Sornay. *Les sources de l'histoire économique et social du moyen âge*. I. *Provence, Comtat Venaissin, Dauphiné, et états de la maison de Savoie*. Paris: CNRS, 1968.

Bligny, Bernard, ed. *Histoire du Dauphiné*. Toulouse: Privat, 1973.

Chevalier, Cyr Ulysse. *Regeste dauphinois, ou répertoire chronologique et analytique des documents imprimés et inédits relatifs à l'histoire du Dauphiné des origines chrétiennes à l'année 1349*. 5 vols. Valence: Imprimerie Valentinoise, 1913–26.

Sclafert, Thérèse. *Le Haut-Dauphiné au moyen âge*. Paris: Sirey, 1926.

DAUREL ET BETON. A single 14th-century manuscript (B.N. nouv. acq. fr. 4232) preserves 2,200 lines of this Occitan chanson de geste in rhymed laisses (the first five in Alexandrines, the rest decasyllabic), composed ca. 1150–68. His father, Boves d'Antona, having been cruelly betrayed, Beton passes his *enfance* in Babylonian exile with the jongleur Daurel, who sacrifices his own child to save Beton. In a unique Odyssean prelude to Beton's revenge, Daurel recites the tale of betrayal before the traitor himself.

Amelia E. Van Vleck

Kimmel, Arthur S., ed. *A Critical Edition of the Old Provençal Epic Daurel et Beton*. Chapel Hill: University of North Carolina Press, 1971.

DAVID OF DINANT (fl. early 13th c.). A philosopher whose thought is known only obliquely or from fragments. The Council of Sens in 1210 ordered David's works to be burned. Only a few fragments are extant (*De divisionibus*). David is also paraphrased by Albert the Great, who attacked his views fiercely. It is hard to reconstruct David's thought, but he seems to have developed his ideas, particularly on being and essence, from a close knowledge of Aristotle, whom he translated and commented upon (the *Quanternuli*). His views were instrumental in the prohibition of Aristotle's works at the University of Paris.

Nothing is known of David's life, except that he was probably from Dinant in modern Belgium, and his title, *magister*, suggests a university education. In a letter of Innocent III (1206), he is called "our chaplain."

Lesley J. Smith

[See also: ARISTOTLE, INFLUENCE OF; PHILOSOPHY]

DECRETALS. Many of the most important papal documents of the Middle Ages were decretals, especially those rescripts offering legal advice to papal judges-delegate. The decretals of popes like Alexander III and Innocent III were collected by private individuals, and later the papacy promulgated official collections to the universities for teaching purposes. Some of these decretals, like Innocent III's *Per venerabilem*, concerned with the legitimization of a French nobleman's bastard son, were intended to create new law. Other papal bulls, like Boniface VIII's *Clericis laicos*, were constitutions, imposing law on the universal church on the pope's initiative.

Thomas M. Izbicki

[See also: CANON LAW; *CLERICIS LAICOS*; INNOCENT III; LAW AND JUSTICE]

Friedberg, Emil, ed. *Quinque compilationes antiquae necnon Collectio canonum lipsiensis.* Leipzig: Tauchnitz, 1882.
Duggan, Charles. *Twelfth-Century Decretal Collections and Their Importance in English History.* London: Athlone, 1963.
Tierney, Brian. "*Tria quippe distinguit iudicia:* A Note on Innocent III's Decretal *Per venerabilem.*" *Speculum* 37 (1962): 48–59.

DEDICATION OF THE CHURCH. In the Middle Ages, every cathedral and monastic or parish church was dedicated by a bishop in accordance with an ornate and venerable ceremony that has been substantially modified only since the Second Vatican Council (1962–65). The feast of the dedication in the Roman rite existed by the early 6th century, and its shape in later centuries, after it had been transported north of the Alps, can be studied in *Ordo romanus* 4 and, most importantly, in *Ordo romanus* 42, along with the Gallican-influenced *Ordo romanus* 41, which dates from the second half of the 8th century. A fusion of the Gallican and Roman ceremonies is represented in pontificals dating from the 10th century onward and in the pontifical of Guillaume Durand, bishop of Mende, compiled 1293–95.

The anniversary of the dedication of its church was of primary importance in the calendar of each community and was celebrated each year by the Mass and Office for the feast of the Dedication of the Church (often known by the incipit of its introit: *Terribilis est*); in addition, the feast of a cathedral might well be honored in secular churches throughout the diocese. The particular date of the dedication can therefore often be useful in helping to determine the origin of a liturgical manuscript. In many churches, the feast of the Dedication was celebrated at the Octave of the feast of the patronal saint, or soon after. Tropes and sequences, as well as other devotional texts and music, were written for the dedication throughout the later Middle Ages, and their texts, along with the numerous sermons written for the occasion, form a significant commentary upon changing interpretations of the feast.

Margot Fassler

Andrieu, Michel. *Les* Ordines romani *du haut moyen âge.* 5 vols. Louvain, 1931–61.
———. *Le pontifical romain au moyen âge.* 4 vols. Vatican City: Biblioteca Apostolica Vaticana, 1940, Vol. 3: *Le pontifical de Guillaume Durand.*
Benz, S. "Zur Geschichte der römischen Kirchweihe nach den Texten des 7. bis 9. Jahrhunderts." In *Enkainia: Gesammelte Arbeiten zum 800–jährigen Weihegedächtnis der Abteikirche Maria Laach am 24. August 1956*, ed. Hilarius Emonds. Düsseldorf: Patmos, 1956, pp. 62–109.
Fassler, Margot. *Gothic Song: Victorine Sequences and Augustinian Reform in Twelfth-Century Paris.* Cambridge: Cambridge University Press, 1993, pp. 211–40.
Forgeur, R. "Dedicatio Aquensis." *Scriptorium* 42 (1988): 76–83.
Michaud, J. "Dedicaces en Poitou: faste des cérémonies (c.800–c.1050)." *Bulletin de la Société des Antiquaires de l'Ouest et des Musées de Poitiers* 15/2 (1977): 143–62.

DÉFRICHEMENT. Literally, the clearing away of brush; more generally, any reclamation of arable land from the waste. The major medieval rural expansion, although dated slightly differently from region to region, from 1000 to 1300, is called the *grands défrichements*. This conquest of France's "internal frontiers" has been used to explain the urban growth of the central Middle Ages, for agricultural surplus was needed to support town specialists and it was assumed that "frontier" lands were more fertile, gave higher yields and so on. Its chief architects were thought to be the new monks of the period, such as the Cistercians, who advertised their practice of manual labor and claimed to found their abbeys "far from cities." But the correlations between monks and clearance and between clearance and town growth were much less direct than once thought. Rural expansion began first on the margins of settlement, carried out by the population of overcrowded villages, who licitly or illicitly felled, drained, and cultivated surrounding wastelands, adding extra bits of land to their fields, or creating the new fields and holdings, called *appendariae* or *bordariae*, adjoining old village lands. More striking was the assarting and draining that occurred in the great forests and wastes beyond or between existing villages, affirmed by new place-names like Artigue, Finage, and Bordage. Although the older Benedictine monasteries were sometimes the lords involved in the founding of new villages in forest and waste, the actual work of reclamation was carried out by peasant settlers; moreover, where forest clearance was not a planned activity it was the work of hermits, charcoal burners, pastoralists, and other anonymous forest folk. The great expanses of land that the new monks like the Cistercians came to hold were not gained at the expense of forest but were purchased from these earlier cultivators and settlers.

Constance H. Berman

[See also: AGRICULTURE; CISTERCIAN ORDER; GRANGE; *VILLENEUVE*]

Berman, Constance H. *Medieval Agriculture, the Southern French Countryside, and the Early Cistercians*. Philadelphia: American Philosophical Society, 1986.

Duby, Georges. *Rural Economy and Country Life in the Medieval West*, trans. Cynthia Postan. Columbia: University of South Carolina Press, 1968.

Higounet, Charles. *Paysages et villages neufs du moyen âge*. Bordeaux: Fédération Historique du Sud-Ouest, 1975.

DENIS. Patron saint of France and bishop of Paris. The earliest Life of the saint, known from its incipit as the *Gloriosae* (ca. 500), stated that Denis (Dionysius) had been sent to preach to the pagans by a "successor of the Apostles." Settling in Paris, he built a church and performed many miracles. Because of his success, he and his companions, the priest Rusticus and the deacon Eleutherius, were tortured and executed. However, they never ceased to confess their belief in the Trinity and their faith in the Lord. The pagans had planned to throw their bodies into the Seine, but a pious matron took them and buried them six miles from Paris. There she built a mausoleum and later a basilica, where miraculous cures occurred.

This text, or a version of it, was known to Gregory of Tours, who stated in his *Liber historiae Francorum* that seven bishops were sent from Rome to Gaul at the time of the emperor Decius (r. 249–51). The *vita* of St. Geneviève (ca. 520) recounts that it was at Geneviève's urging that the Parisians built ca. 475 the first church in honor of the saint and that it was St. Clement of Rome (pope, 90–100) who had sent Denis to Gaul. (The earliest episcopal list from Paris, too, mentions that Denis was the first bishop of Paris.) The cult of the saint thus seems to have been in existence by the late 5th century and the first Passion shortly afterward.

The early 9th-century Passion *Post beatam et gloriosam* added the details that Denis of Paris was the same as the Dionysius the Areopagite converted in Athens by the Apostle Paul (Acts 17:34); that he was consecrated bishop by Pope Clement as he passed through Rome; that the martyrs were executed on a hill a mile from Paris (i.e., Montmartre); that after his decollation, the saint picked up his head and carried it two miles; and that the matron who buried the saint was called Catulla after "Catullacus," the old name for Saint-Denis.

It was probably in response to the apostolic character of the saint that in 827 the Byzantine emperor Michael the Stammerer sent a manuscript of the works of Pseudo-Dionysius the Areopagite to Louis the Pious, who gave it to the abbey of Saint-Denis. Its abbot, Hilduin (r. 814–40), translated the works of Pseudo-Dionysius from Greek into Latin; his *Passio sanctissimi Dionysii* explicitly joined Denis of Paris to Dionysius the Areopagite. Hilduin added, too, that the night before Denis was executed, as he was

St. Denis between angels, from Reims cathedral. *Photograph courtesy of Joan A. Holladay.*

celebrating Mass in prison with his disciples, just as he was about to receive the sacrament, Christ came and took the eucharist from his hand and gave it to him himself. The next day, after the execution, Denis picked up his head and, carrying it, walked five miles from Montmartre to Saint-Denis.

Although the legend had its critics, it was quickly accepted and appears among the lessons of the Roman breviary and the liturgy of Saint-Denis. The abbey, founded by King Dagobert I ca. 624, was especially favored by the Carolingians. Denis developed from being the patron of a monastery to a saint who was the object of a special devotion from the kings of France and in turn accorded them and their country a special protection. This protection was connected first with King Dagobert, whose devotion to the saint was portrayed in a series of apocryphal tales in the *Gesta Dagoberti*.

From the time of Hugh Capet (r. 987–96), a royal flag was deposited at Saint-Denis, a flag that was later identified with the Oriflamme, the flag given to Charlemagne by the pope. In 1124, when Louis VI prepared to march against the emperor Henry V, he came to the abbey, took the abbey's standard from the altar, and announced that the saint was the special protector of the realm. The royal flag and the abbey's standard were eventually viewed as one and the same, and the saint was credited with bringing victory to the armies of the kings of France.

It was to accommodate the crowds that flocked to the tomb of the saint that Abbot Suger of Saint-Denis (r. 1122–51) enlarged the abbey church and translated the relics of the saint to a new altar. By the 13th century, chroniclers at the abbey had woven together the legend of St. Denis and the history of France. Notable texts in this development are the *Vita et actus beati Dionysii*, the *Vie de saint Denis*, and the *Grandes Chroniques de France*. In this process, St. Denis became not only the patron and protector of the French kings, but of France itself. His feast day is October 9.

Thomas G. Waldman

[See also: DAGOBERT I; *GRANDES CHRONIQUES DE FRANCE*; HILDUIN OF SAINT-DENIS; ORIFLAMME; PSEUDO-DIONYSIUS THE AREOPAGITE; SAINT-DENIS; SUGER]

Acta Sanctorum, Oct. IV, 696–855.

BHL 1, 328–30.

Lacaze, Charlotte. *The "Vie de St. Denis" Manuscript: Paris, Bibliothèque Nationale, MS. fr. 2090–2092.* New York: Garland, 1979.

Liebman, Charles J. *Étude sur la vie en prose de Saint-Denis.* Geneva: Humphrey, 1942.

Loernetz, Raymond J. "La légende parisienne de saint Denys l'aréopagite: sa genèse et son premier témoin." *Analecta bollandiana* 69 (1951): 217–37.

Spiegel, Gabrielle M. "The Cult of Saint Denis and Capetian Kingship." *Journal of Medieval History* 1 (1975): 43–69.

DENIS PIRAMUS (fl. late 12th c.). A cleric, probably from the abbey of Bury-Saint-Edmunds (Suffolk), Denis tells us in the opening lines of his Anglo-Norman *Vie seint Edmunt le rei* (after 1170, possibly 1190–1200) that he spent his early years at court, where he composed various forms of courtly verse. He has been identified with a certain "magister Dionisius," a monk of St. Edmund's abbey mentioned in documents between 1173 and 1200. Denis's work on Edmund (king of East Anglia, martyred 870) was commissioned by the "segnur" of the abbey for which Edmund was patron saint. It recounts, in about 4,033 octosyllabic lines, the saint's early life as well as his death and miracles and combines elements of hagiography, history, and romance. Denis's version seems independent of the other versions of the legend, that of Gaimar, the anonymous quatrain redaction, and the continental prose life.

Glyn S. Burgess

[See also: SAINTS' LIVES]

Piramus, Denis. *La vie seint Edmund le rei: poème anglo-normand du XIIe siècle,* ed. Hilding Kjellman. Göteborg: Wettergren and Kerber, 1935.

Loomis, G. "The Growth of the Saint Edmund Legend." *Harvard Studies and Notes* 14 (1932): 83–115.

Saxo, Henry E. "Denis Piramus: *La vie seint Edmunt.*" *Modern Philology* 12 (1915): 345–66, 559–83.

DESCHAMPS, EUSTACHE (ca. 1346–ca. 1406). Born near Reims at Vertus, in the family home burned in 1380 by the English, Deschamps says that he long applied himself to grammar and logic. He later studied law, probably at Orléans. From 1360, Deschamps was in the service of high nobility, and in 1367 he joined the king's retinue. For most of his life thereafter, he was attached in various capacities to Charles V, and to Charles VI and his brother Louis d'Orléans, as well as to other great personages. From 1375, his name appears in the records as *bailli* of Valois; he became *bailli* of Senlis in 1389. Married ca. 1373, he had two sons and a daughter, his wife dying in childbirth, probably in 1376. He did not remarry.

Until his final years, Deschamps associated with a wide circle of nobility and important figures, and much of his poetry deals with current political and social events. His works also show that he knew many poets of the time: he writes of a joke that Oton de Granson played on him, composes a ballade in praise of Chaucer and another poem praising Christine de Pizan (in response to a poem of praise from her), and in other works speaks of Philippe de Vitry, Jean de Garencières, and most of the poets of the *Cent ballades*. But his most important literary association was with his fellow Champenois Guillaume de Machaut, who figures prominently in several of his works and whose death he laments in a double ballade with the refrain, *La mort Machaut, le noble rethouryque.* He may have been a nephew of Machaut, whom he credits with "nurturing" (educating?) him. Accordingly, his poetry is mostly in the fixed forms that Machaut popularized. But Deschamps writes more on moral and topical subjects than on his mentor's predominating subject, love, and he did not write long *dits amoureux* comparable with Machaut's.

Deschamps's bulky *œuvre* is almost all preserved in a single thick manuscript compiled a few years after his death (B.N. fr. 840). Ballades predominate, 1,017 surviving. In addition, there are 171 rondeaux, eighty-four virelais, 139 *chansons royales*, fourteen *lais*, and fifty-nine other pieces, including twelve poems in Latin. His one important prose piece is the *Art de dictier et de fere chançons* (1392), probably written to instruct one of his "great lords" in the composition of lyrics; it is the only extant treatise on the art of poetry from 14th-century France. Notable is Deschamps's classification and discussion of poetry without music as "natural music"; musical notation is for him "artificial music." The treatise otherwise concentrates on illustrating the ballade, virelai, rondeau, and *lai*.

Neither of Deschamps's two extant long poems was completed, and in both cases rubrics state that death prevented the author from finishing them. The *Fiction du lyon* is a beast-fable on political events in France, with Charles VI presented as Noble the Lion, Charles the Bad of Navarre as Renard the Fox, and Richard II of England as the Leopard. Deschamps's *Miroir de mariage* is his longest poem by far, 12,004 lines in octosyllabic couplets. Drawing on standard writings against matrimony like St. Jerome's *Adversus Jovinianum*, it opens with a discussion of friendship, which leads to the main question, whether a young man named Franc Vouloir (Free Will) should marry. While such friends as Desir and Folie advise him to take a wife, Repertoire de Science (Wisdom) counsels against it in a long enumeration of the dangers and ills of carnal marriage. He contrasts spiritual marriage, which Franc Vouloir eventually chooses. The work ends with a poorly integrated review of history, interrupted at the Treaty of Brétigny (1360). The *Miroir* has been thought an important source for Chaucer's *Canterbury Tales*, but this is questionable.

The great bulk of poetry preserved in the major Deschamps manuscript, edited in eleven impressive volumes, his ballade to Chaucer, his wit, and his interest in current affairs have made Deschamps seem a more important poet than he was. Had it not been for a literary friend who gathered his works together after his death and had them copied, there would remain little evidence of his versifying. Much of the work is journalistic, and virtually none of the alleged influence on Chaucer is sure. Nevertheless, Deschamps was undoubtedly a master of the ballade, and his reports of quotidian incident, dialogues, petitions to his patrons, observances of ceremonial events, and a great variety of other discourses in ballade form are often amusing and well done. Without his work, we would certainly know much less about public life and literature in late 14th-century France.

James I. Wimsatt

[See also: ANTIFEMINISM; *ARTS DE SECONDE RHÉTORIQUE*; BALLADE; *JARDIN DE PLAISANCE ET FLEUR DE RÉTHORIQUE*]

Deschamps, Eustache. *Œuvres complètes d'Eustache Deschamps*, ed. Auguste Queux de Saint-Hilaire and Gaston Raynaud. 11 vols. Paris: Didot, 1878–1903. [Vol. 11 includes biographical study and survey of sources.]

Hoepffner, Ernest. *Eustache Deschamps: Leben und Werke.* Strassburg: Trübner, 1904.

Thundy, Zacharias. "Matheolus, Chaucer, and the Wife of Bath." In *Chaucer Problems and Perspectives*, ed. Edward Vasta and Zacharias Thundy. Notre Dame: Notre Dame University Press, 1979, pp. 24–58.

DEVISE. *See* MOTTO/*DEVISE*

DIDACTIC LITERATURE (OCCITAN). Although two of the earliest works in Occitan are religious, the *Chanson de sainte Foy* and *Boeci*, moral and didactic literature did not develop fully until after the Albigensian Crusade. In addition to short lyrics on religious subjects, there were translations of apocryphal gospels (*Évangile de l'enfance* and *Gospel of Nicodemus*), various poems dedicated to the Virgin's joys and sufferings, and a number of saints' lives (*Vie de saint Honorat* by Raimon Féraut; *Vie de saint Georges*; *Vie de sainte Marguerite*; *Vie de saint Alexis*; *Vie de saint Trophime*). From the 14th century come paraphrases and translations of Latin prayers, such as the Credo and Lord's Prayer, and of the psalms.

Moral and didactic poetry is well represented by the *sirventes* of the troubadours, particularly Arnaut de Mareuil, Guiraut de Borneilh, Peire Cardenal, and Guiraut Riquier. Moral poems directed to a specific class (women, jongleurs, young nobles) are called *ensenhamens*. Many, such as Arnaut's *Razos es e mezura*, offer advice on proper conduct in society. The Catalan troubadour Amanieu de Sescars's *Ensenhamen de la donzela* gives advice to young girls concerning clothing, games, and proper deportment at church; in his *Ensenhamen del escudier*, a master advises his protégé on how to succeed in love. *Ensenhamens* destined for jongleurs, notably that by Guiraut de Cabrera (*Cabra joglar*, ca. 1165), offer intriguing details on the way of life and the repertories of these entertainers. An important scientific and encyclopedic work is Matfre Ermengaud's 35,600-line *Breviari d'Amor*. There also exist separate treatises on birds, medicine, surgical techniques, and astrology.

Didactic literature is written more often in verse than in prose. However, there are several fragmentary translations of the New Testament, including the famous *Bible Vaudoise* from the late 13th century (preserved in a 15th-century manuscript) and an "Albigensian New Testament." Numerous saints' lives and religious legends were rendered into prose as well as verse, including "St. Patrick's Voyage to Purgatory" and "The Voyage of St. Brendan." Monastic rules and statutes were frequently translated into the vernacular, or occasionally even composed in Occitan. Prose translations of classical texts, such as Seneca's *Proverbs* and Cato's *Distichs*, are also known. Numerous charters were written in the vernacular, and we have important *coutumiers* (lists of local laws and customs) for Bordeaux, Avignon, Limoux, Agen, Albi, and Tarascon, among other southern cities.

William W. Kibler

[See also: APOCRYPHAL LITERATURE; COURTESY BOOKS; *LEYS D'AMORS;* MATFRE ERMENGAUD; MORAL TREATISES; PRAYERS AND DEVOTIONAL MATERIALS]

Anglade, Joseph. *Histoire sommaire de la littérature méridionale au moyen âge.* Paris: Boccard, 1921.

Berger, Samuel. "Les Bibles provençales et catalanes." *Romania* 18 (1889): 353–422.

Monson, Don A. *Les "Ensenhamens" occitans: essai de délimitation du genre.* Paris: Klincksieck, 1981.

DIET AND NUTRITION. An understanding about the nature of food in late-medieval France derived ultimately, along with all medical knowledge, from Greek doctrine as amplified by Arab physicians and philosophers. Central to the learning of medical practitioners was a set of notions about the nature of human beings and how this nature could be affected by everything in their environment. In a large sense, the relationship of a person to the environment was what was understood by the term "diet." The compendia of medical doctrine and its distillation in the more popular health handbooks, the *tacuina sanitatis,* and the ubiquitous *regimines sanitatis,* invariably contained a series of chapters that set forth highly practical advice on diet—what we might today term "lifestyle": how the individual could maintain a healthy personal balance of humors by avoiding certain dangers (e.g., by refraining from sexual intercourse during the dry period of summer). That most of the advice offered in the handbooks under the rubric "diet" is negative reflects a fundamental attitude: health is the natural state, diet offers the means to maintain health and avoid sickness. "Diet" in a more modern acceptation, as a temporary regimen followed specifically in order to correct an aberration, is applied to food only in the sense that it could also be used with regard to any other factor affecting health.

Among the wealthier classes, whether "diet" had to do with a "way of living" or a "way of feeding," medical doctrine ultimately defined it. For the wealthy, a diet of specific foods could be of several sorts. It could designate those foods that were consumed habitually and in the belief that they would not normally harm a person's health. Choice of foods was extensive and of relatively great variety: extant recipe collections show that the wealthy could choose from among breads, wines, leafy and root vegetables, peas, beans, rice, many fruits and nuts, some berries, meats of all domesticated and game animals, a broad range of freshwater and sea fish, and domestic and imported herbs and spices, including sugar, to provide appetizing colors and flavors. The wealthy in the late Middle Ages enjoyed a nutritious and varied diet of habitual foods. Therapeutic diet was dealt with in most medical treatises. Prescribed by a physician or surgeon for a patient, this diet was designed, as it is today, to counter the effects of a disease, particularly by restoring an ideal balance of humors. Finally, diet could also be defined as a set of recommended foods for any individual, those that should preserve health. Given the natural temperament of patrons, physicians specified which foods they could safely ingest, because of their properties, and which they should avoid, considering them to constitute a potential danger to patients.

Among the relatively poor, only the first two sorts of diet were current. Concerning the first, it is generally surmised that people habitually ate what they could afford to eat in order to sustain themselves. The staples of this diet were probably bread, beer or wine, stewed vegetables (especially onions, leeks, cabbages), local fish, and some meat (especially chicken and pork). The full details of this diet and its nutritional value are still being studied, but we may assume that the foods of the poor varied according to the times.

Terence Scully

[See also: BANQUETING; BEVERAGES; BREAD; COOKING; FOOD TRADES]

Gottschalk, Alfred. *Histoire de l'alimentation et de la gastronomie depuis la préhistoire jusqu'à nos jours.* 2 vols. Paris: Hippocrate, 1948, Vol. 1, pp. 257–352.

DIGULLEVILLE, GUILLAUME DE (1295–1358). Guillaume, son of Thomas of Digulleville (Degulleville or Deguileville), Normandy, lived as a monk in the Cistercian abbey of Chaalis, Île-de-France, from 1326 until his death. He is known for his dream-allegory moral poems. Inspired by Jean de Meun's *Roman de la Rose* and perhaps by other allegories, he created a trilogy on the Piligrimage of Life theme, in which divine grace, nature, and the virtues and vices are personified. He composed the *Pèlerinage de vie humaine* in a first version in 1330–31, with a recension in 1355, and the *Pèlerinage de l'âme* between 1355 and 1358. He wrote a summary of both the second version of the *Pèlerinage de vie humaine* and the *Pèlerinage de l'âme* that survives in its entirety in only one manuscript. In 1358, he wrote the third part, the *Pèlerinage Jhesucrist.* He also composed a series of Latin poems intended for inclusion at the end of the *Pèlerinage de l'âme,* but these remain unpublished, as does the 1355 recension of the *Pèlerinage de vie humaine.* He wrote a further allegorical poem in French, the *Roman de la Fleur de lys.* This last work, which survives in two manuscripts, explains the origins and symbolism of the arms of France as a defense of the French royal dynasty against the claims of Edward III. Digulleville's popular pilgrimage trilogy, surviving in more than seventy-five manuscripts, inspired Chaucer, Lydgate, and Bunyan. The poems show the way to salvation through obedience to the church, its sacraments, and its principles. The first work takes a Pilgrim-monk from a prenatal vision of the New Jerusalem to his death, with authorial digressions of an encyclopedic nature along the way. In the second pilgrimage, the Pilgrim's soul visits the places on earth where he had sinned, the cemetery where his body rots, and Hell with its torments of the damned, ending in Purgatory. The third part is a life of Christ.

Joan B. Williamson

[See also: DUPIN, JEAN; PURGATORY]

Digulleville, Guillaume de. *Le pèlerinage de vie humaine, Le pèlerinage de l'âme, Le pèlerinage Jhesucrist,* ed. Jacob Stürzinger. 3 vols. London: Roxburghe Club, 1893, 1895, 1897.

Faral, Edmond. "Guillaume de Digulleville, moine de Chaalis." *Histoire littéraire de la France.* Paris: Imprimerie Nationale, 1962, Vol. 39, pp. 1–132.

Huot, Sylvia. *The* Romance of the Rose *and Its Medieval Readers: Interpretation, Reception, Manuscript Transmission.* Cambridge: Cambridge University Press, 1993, pp. 207–38.

Piaget, Arthur. "Un poème inédit de Guillaume de Digulleville: *Le roman de la Fleur de lys.*" *Romania* 63 (1936): 317–58.

DIJON. A small city during the Gallo-Roman epoch, Dijon (Côte-d'Or) was fortified by the emperor Aurelian ca. 273. The dukes of Burgundy made Dijon their capital in the second quarter of the 12th century, and it continued to be the Burgundian capital throughout the Middle Ages. Unlike most capitals of dukes and counts, it was not a cathedral city—the dukes may even have chosen it for this reason. Its chief church was the Benedictine abbey of Saint-Bénigne, which had been founded as an abbey church ca. 525 upon the presumed tomb of the saint (2nd c.). At the end of the 10th century, Saint-Bénigne was reformed to Cluny's *ordo* at the instigation of Bruno, bishop of Langres. Under the abbacy of William of Volpiano, it became the most important 11th-century reforming center in northern Burgundy. Saint-Bénigne became a cathedral when Dijon was made a bishopric. In the mid-15th century, Philip the Good built a magnificent palace at Dijon, the towers of which still stand.

Constance B. Bouchard

Destroyed by fire in 1137, the city was rebuilt by Duke Hugues II. Under Philip the Bold (1342–1404), John the Fearless (1371–1419), and Philip the Good (1396–1467), the splendors of the Burgundian court reached their height, but the death of Charles the Bold at the Battle of Nancy (1476) left the Valois dukes without a male heir; and Louis XI, who, in spite of protestations of the states of Burgundy, seized the province, set up a parlement at Dijon, and refortified the city.

The present-day cathedral of Saint-Bénigne was restored at the end of the 9th century but then fell into ruin. After attaching itself to the community at Cluny, the monastery soon became one of the strongest and most prosperous of the Cluniac houses. A vast rotunda flanked by two towers marks the western end of this five-bayed basilica (constructed 1002–18). The polygonally apsed choir has no ambulatory and is flanked by two apsidioles. The crypt, circular in plan and containing the remains of the tomb of St. Bénigne, is notable for its column capitals ornamented with geometric, Carolingian-style motifs and schematic human silhouettes. Damaged by fires and repaired throughout the 12th and 13th centuries, the church was rebuilt 1281–1325 in Burgundian Gothic style. A number of associated monastery buildings (11th–13th c.) survive.

The church of Notre-Dame (1230–51), designed in the style of Saint-Bénigne, is a fine example of early 13th-century Burgundian Gothic. It has a long nave (215 feet) flanked by aisles and crossed by a transept and a choir without an ambulatory or radiating chapels. Typical of the style, the building is covered with six-part vaulting, and the graceful colonnettes of the triforium are ornamented with human faces. The west front has a deep triple porch, above which are two arcaded galleries separated by three broad friezes, each richly decorated with human and animal grotesques. The church displays the Jacquemart bell, which was carried off from Courtrai in 1382 by Philip the Bold.

Built before 1103 over the tombs of two 6th-century saints, the church of Saint-Philibert was rebuilt and restored after the 1137 fire. The 12th-century groin-vaulted basilica has a five-bay nave with aisles and a choir and is crossed by a transept. The façade is pierced by a late 12th-century Gothic rose window, and the porch dates from the same period. Above the crossing are a cupola and a 15th-century Flamboyant bell tower. In spite of these later additions, the building is fundamentally a Romanesque structure. Saint-Philibert is particularly associated with the municipal life of Dijon. Under its porch, the *vicomte mayeur* and the magistrates of Dijon were elected.

Philip the Bold established a Carthusian monastery, the Chartreuse de Champmol, in 1383 to ensure a proper burial for himself and his successors. All that remains of the once lavishly decorated building (torn down in 1793) is the entrance portal with its sculptural group by Claus Sluter (1395–1404). Here, Philip the Bold and his wife, Marguerite of Flanders, presented by their patron saints, John the Baptist and Catherine, kneel in attendance to the Virgin and Child. The fact that all of the figures here are on the same scale visually creates a link between the temporal realm of the ducal couple and the world of the divine. The tombs and altarpieces once inside the building are now housed in the museum at Dijon. In the adjacent courtyard stands the *Well of Moses,* also by Sluter. Originally the base of a Cavalry, a hexagonal pedestal rising from the well is surrounded by statues of Moses, David, Jeremiah, Zachariah, Daniel, and Isaiah.

Nina Rowe

[See also: BURGUNDY; SLUTER, CLAUS; WILLIAM OF VOLPIANO]

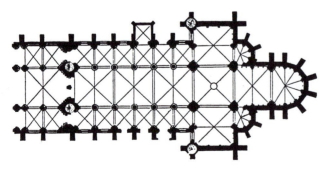

Dijon (Côte d'Or), Notre-Dame, plan. After Losowska.

Bulst, Niethard. *Untersuchungen zu den Klosterreform Wilhelms von Dijon (962–1031)*. Bonn: Röhrscheid, 1973.

Chaume, Maurice. *Les origines du duché de Bourgogne*. 4 vols. Dijon: Jobard, 1925–31.

Chompton, Louis. *Histoire de l'église Saint-Bénigne de Dijon*. Dijon: Jobard, 1900.

Flipo, Vincent. *La cathédrale de Dijon*. Paris: Laurens, 1928.

Oursel, Charles. *L'église Notre-Dame de Dijon*. Paris: Laurens, 1938.

Poinssot, Claude. "Le bâtiment de dortoir de l'abbaye de Saint-Bénigne de Dijon." *Bulletin monumental* 112 (1954): 303–30.

Quarré, Pierre. *La chartreuse de Champmol: foyer d'art au temps des ducs valois*. Dijon: Musée de Dijon, 1960.

———. *Dijon*. Paris: Hachette, 1961.

Richard, Jean. *Les ducs de Bourgogne et la formation du duché du XIe au XIVe siècle*. Paris: Société des Belles Lettres, 1954.

Vallery-Radot, Jean, Marcel Aubert, et al. "Dijon." *Congrès archéologique (Dijon)* 91 (1928): 9–147.

Vaughan, Richard. *Valois Burgundy*. London: Archon, 1975.

DIPLOMA. Under Roman law, most transactions had required a written record, or diploma. These records became much less common in the early Middle Ages, and the *carta* became not a binding legal instrument so much as a record or reminder that an agreement had taken place. Almost all diplomas that survive from before the end of the 12th century are from ecclesiastical archives. The growing literacy of the 12th century led to a great increase in the number of written records. By the early 13th century, kings and popes were keeping chancery records of the diplomas they issued.

Constance B. Bouchard

Bullough, Donald A., and R. L. Storey, eds. *The Study of Medieval Records: Essays in Honour of Kathleen Major*. Oxford: Clarendon, 1971.

Clanchy, Michael T. *From Memory to Written Record: England, 1066–1307*. Cambridge: Harvard University Press, 1979.

van Caenegem, R. C. *Guide to the Sources of Medieval History*. Amsterdam: North-Holland, 1978.

DISEASES. A general assessment of health problems in medieval France awaits systematic collation of written and physical evidence. At present, acute fatal diseases, with the exception of epidemics, as well as ailments considered minor or inevitable (e.g., measles in childhood or rheumatism in old age) are overshadowed by severe chronic illnesses. In learned writings on medical practice and in popular traditions of saints' cults, fevers predominate. This was not a mere catchall of symptoms but a true category of diseases whose essence was a process of "overheating" and whose branches stretched from ague and influenza to meningitis and typhoid. Professional medicine and folk religion diverged in their ranking of a second group, with digestive complaints more common for patients and obstetrical problems most baffling for physicians.

Of the maladies that eluded human treatment, some gained special notoriety under the name of a patron healer. Regular references to *le mal St. Quentin* or *St. Eutrope* indicate that dropsy, a form of edema often caused by malnutrition, was widespread. More notorious was epilepsy, *le grand mal* or *le mal St. Jean* or *St. Eloi* (*Leu, Loup*); in spite of the belief that it was both contagious and mental, the falling sickness was often feigned by beggars. Disorders with a relatively low profile in our principal sources of information include such modern threats as cancer, cardiac impairment, and even tuberculosis, which scattered evidence suggests may have been a most insidious and particularly French scourge. Far more than a respiratory affliction of the poor, it caused a host of other ills ranging from insanity to sterility, it cut short the career of the great physician-surgeon Henri de Mondeville, and it plagued the house of Valois.

Perhaps the most historically important disease is smallpox, of which one epidemic accompanied the Huns ca. 450, another sapped the Merovingians (according to Gregory of Tours), and a third probably claimed Hugh Capet in 996. Frequent outbreaks occurred in the 13th century, in the wake of intensified travel. By the 15th century, variola had become endemic, for children succumbed while adults survived contagion by having acquired immunity, as did Charles V and Charles VIII. The latter contracted *la vérole* in 1494, on his march on Naples, from where his soldiers would spread a new "pox," *la grosse vérole* or "the French disease"—syphilis.

Luke Demaitre

[See also: BLACK DEATH; FAMINE; LEPROSY; MEDICAL PRACTICE AND PRACTITIONERS; MEDICAL TEXTS; SCROFULA]

Ackernecht, Erwin. *History and Geography of the Most Important Diseases*. New York: Hafner, 1965.

Henschen, Folke. *The History and Geography of Diseases*, trans. Joan Tate. London: Longman, 1966.

Sendrall, Marcel, et al. *Histoire culturelle de la maladie*. Toulouse: Privat, 1980.

Sigal, Pierre André. "Miracles et guérisons au XIIe siècle." *Annales: Économies—Sociétés—Civilisations* 24 (1969): 1522–39.

von Kraemer, Erik. *Les maladies désignées par le nom d'un saint*. Copenhagen: Munksgaard, 1949.

Wickersheimer, Ernest. "Les secrets et les conseils de maître Guillaume Boucher et ses confrères: contribution à l'histoire de la médecine à Paris vers 1400." *Bulletin de la Société Française d'Histoire de la Médecine* 8 (1909): 199–305. [111 case histories.]

DISPUTATIO. See SCHOLASTICISM

DIT. As used by 13th-century authors, *dit* seems to designate a work treating, in the first person, subjects of general interest, generally directed to a popular audience. *Dits* treat topics as varied as women (good or bad), the churches of

Paris, the butchers, bakers, or weavers of that city, or recent events (e.g., *Dit de la mort de Philippe de Grève*). Many have literary merit and can also be useful historical documents. Rutebeuf used the genre for his political broadsides (e.g., *Dit des cordeliers*). Many 13th-century *dits* are anonymous, written in octosyllabic couplets, but other forms of versification are found, especially in Rutebeuf's *dits*.

The nature of the genre changed over time. *Dit* came to designate longer works, a change that may have begun with Jean de Condé, whose *dits* vary from sixty-six (*Dit de bonne chere*) to 2,352 lines (*Dit dou chevalier a le mance*), or with his contemporary, Watriquet de Couvin (fl. 1319–29). These longer *dits*, narrative rather than descriptive, were directed largely to a courtly audience. The genre continued to flourish in the 14th century, notably in the hands of Guillaume de Machaut and Jean Froissart, authors of *dits amoureux,* combining elements of romance, allegory, and lyric.

Wendy E. Pfeffer

[See also: CONDÉ, JEAN DE; COUVIN, WATRIQUET BRASSENIEX DE; FROISSART, JEAN; MACHAUT, GUILLAUME DE; RUTEBEUF]

Cerquiglini, Jacqueline. "Le clerc et l'écriture: le *Voir Dit* de Guillaume de Machaut et la définition du *dit*," and Poirion, Daniel. "Traditions et fonctions du *dit poétique* au XIVe et au XVe siècle." In *Literatur in der Gesellschaft des Spätmittelalters*, ed. Hans Ulrich Gumbrecht. Heidelberg: Winter, 1980, pp. 151–68 and 147–50.

Ribémont, Bernard, ed. *Écrire pour dire: études sur le dit médiéval.* Paris: Klincksieck, 1990.

DIVINE OFFICE. In the Middle Ages, the word "office" had more or less the same connotations as the modern word "liturgy." Since the Middle Ages, however, the meaning of "office" has contracted to refer only to the daily cycle of services marking the chief hours of the day, excluding the Mass and the other sacramental celebrations, such as baptism or ordination.

The content of these daily services included a great deal of psalmody, which included the singing of the psalms, canticles (psalmlike poems from the other books of the Old and New Testaments), and nonscriptural hymns. There were also readings from the Bible and other holy books, prayers and blessings, and processions to different parts of the church (e.g., altars, the main cross, the baptistery) or other sites of religious significance, such as shrines or cemeteries. The methods of singing the psalms varied. In what may have been the oldest method, responsorial psalmody, a soloist (an ordained reader or cantor) sang the verses alone or perhaps with one or a few other soloists. After each verse, the congregation or a choir responded with an unvarying refrain, often but not always a verse from the same psalm. This type of psalmody, common by the 4th century, may have given rise to more complex types of psalmody that still survive in the eastern rites, which can involve alternation between two choirs, each with its own soloist and refrain. In the West, by the early Middle Ages,

such methods gave way to the simpler one known as antiphonal psalmody: two choirs sang the verses in alternation, ending with the Gloria patri, and then joined together on the refrain or antiphon at the very end. On a high feast, the antiphon would also be sung at the beginning, but on an average day only its intonation or opening words would be sung by a soloist. Even simpler was direct psalmody, when the entire psalm was simply chanted straight through, without alternation or refrain, either by a soloist or by the entire choir.

The actual number of services per day varied much from one liturgical tradition to another, but it was often influenced by symbolic or allegorical considerations, based on mystical numbers (cf. Psalm 119:164), themes of light and darkness, prayer times mentioned in the Bible (e.g., Daniel 6:10; Acts 2:15, 3:1, 10:3–9), and the chronology of the Passion of Jesus—the third hour, when he was crucified; the sixth hour, when "there was darkness over the whole land"; the ninth hour, when he died; the evening, when he was buried; early Sunday morning, when he rose from the dead (cf. Mark 15:25–16:9).

There were many different traditions for celebrating the Divine Office in Gaul before the establishment of the Roman liturgy in Carolingian times; it is thus misleading to lump them all together, as is generally done, under the term "Gallican rite." Among the earliest sources is the *De institutis coenobiorum* of John Cassian (ca. 360–435), who had lived as a monk in both Egypt and Palestine prior to becoming abbot of a monastery in Marseille. His recollections from his own observation were widely read and profoundly influenced many of the major liturgical traditions of the West. Cassian described the Egyptian practice as following a plan revealed by an angel, consisting of two main services—cockcrow (early morning before dawn) and evening—each with twelve psalms, suggesting the ideal of praying twenty-four hours a day. The more complex Palestinian practice, as Cassian remembered it, added to these two services celebrations at the third, sixth, and ninth hours, with three psalms each, and with all-night vigils on Fridays, which were divided into three sections with three psalms and three readings each.

An office following the Egyptian plan was celebrated at the monastery of Lérins, founded by Cassian's disciple Honoratus (d. 429/30); evidence of it is preserved in the monastic *Rules of the Holy Fathers* from the 5th and 6th centuries and, in much more developed form, in the monastic writings of two bishops of Arles: Caesarius (r. 503–42), who had been a monk at Lérins, and Aurelian (r. 546–51).

In 567, a council in Tours decreed that the cathedral office in that city follow the Egyptian structure of twelve psalms morning and evening, though up to thirty psalms could be sung on long winter nights. The careful adjustment of psalmody to the length of the night was a feature of other Gallican liturgical traditions, such as the office outlined in the monastic rule of the Irish monk St. Columban (d. 615), who founded the monasteries at Luxeuil and Bobbio. Though Columban was aware of multiple traditions, he advocated a daily cursus of six hours: three during the day with three psalms each, and three during the night: services at the beginning and middle of the night with twelve psalms each, and a vigil service with twenty-four to thirty-six psalms depending on the season, thirty-six to seventy-five on Saturdays and Sundays (always arranged in groups of three).

By the 8th century, religious reformers increasingly sought to supplant the indigenous Gallican traditions with usages derived from the liturgical tradition of Rome. Bishop Chrodegang of Metz (d. 766), and the Anglo-Saxon missionary St. Boniface (680–754) were two of the early champions of the Roman liturgy. King Pepin the Short (r. 751–68), after meeting Pope Stephen II in 754, inaugurated a royal policy of romanizing the liturgy in the Frankish kingdom, a policy continued by his son Charlemagne (r. 771–814). The new Romano-Frankish liturgy of the hours took two basic forms: the Monastic Office, based on the prescriptions of the 6th-century *Rule of St. Benedict* (regarded as the Roman monastic rule) and the cathedral or secular Roman Office, to be used by nonmonastic clergy (first described in detail by Amalarius of Metz). These two traditions shared much common material and were similar in structure though they differed in the arrangement of antiphonal psalms; the Monastic Office also used some direct psalmody, while the Roman did so only in the Office of the Dead.

In both the Monastic and the Roman Offices, Sundays and major feasts began with Vespers the preceding evening. Most days, however, began with a long vigil service, Matins, recited in the night hours leading up to sunrise. Like the Palestinian vigil described by Cassian, Matins was divided into three sections, or nocturnes, after a brief introduction featuring the Invitatory Psalm 94 and a hymn. (Vulgate psalm numbers are used in this article.) Probably because a monk or cleric was considered late if he arrived after the invitatory psalm, the performance of this psalm was not modernized to the standard antiphonal method. The verses were sung by two soloists in alternation with the choir, which responded by alternating two forms of the refrain: the complete refrain and the second half of it. Special melodies were used that were more complex than the simple tones of antiphonal psalmody. The text, too, was not updated to the Latin Vulgate, as were the other psalms; an Old Latin or pre-Vulgate text is used even today. In the Monastic Office, Psalm 3 was chanted in direct psalmody before Psalm 94.

The Egyptian practice number of twelve psalms was preserved in the first nocturne of Roman Matins but split between the first two nocturnes of the Monastic. In both traditions, the psalms were arranged into three groups, each with its own refrain or antiphon. The Monastic third nocturne, unlike the Roman, used Old Testament canticles instead of psalms; the specific texts varied with the season. In both traditions, the antiphonal psalms of Matins were assigned mostly in numerical order, omitting those that would be sung at other hours during the day. However, the Roman Office began with Psalm 1, the Benedictine with Psalm 20, though both ended on Saturday with Psalm 108. Following the psalmody were readings from the Old Testament (first nocturne), hagiographical or heortological writings related to the day (second nocturne), and homi-

lies of the church fathers on the Gospel of the day (third nocturne). Each reading was followed by a responsory, sung responsorially even though only a minority of responsory texts were taken from the psalms. The monastic office concluded with the reading of the Gospel itself, but in nonmonastic churches this was typically read only at Mass.

Following Matins was the service of Lauds, marking sunrise; its antiphonal psalms were chosen because their texts were considered appropriate to the theme of morning praise. Following a nigh-universal Christian tradition, the last "psalm" actually consisted of three psalms (148–50) sung as one. The third "psalm" of the Roman Office actually combined Psalms 62 and 66, while the fourth "psalm" in both traditions was actually an Old Testament canticle. The reading at Lauds, as at the other offices throughout the day, was a mere capitulum—a sentence quoted usually from the Epistle of the day, which was read in its entirety only at Mass. This was followed by a brief responsory in the Monastic Office; after that both traditions had a strophic hymn. The New Testament canticle *Benedictus* (Luke 1:68–79), sung antiphonally, was a focal point of this service.

The "little hours" of Prime, Terce, Sext, and None marked the first, third, sixth, and ninth hours of daylight, roughly 6 A.M., 9 A.M., noon, and 3 P.M. The community Mass would typically be celebrated after Terce. Each of these offices in theory consisted of three antiphonal psalms sung as one without a break and with only one antiphon, but the specifics differed in the two traditions. Besides segments of Psalm 118, by far the longest in the Psalter, there were numerical series of psalms omitted from Matins and Vespers: Psalms 21–25 in the Roman Office, 1–19 and 119–127 in the Monastic. In both traditions, this was followed by the singing of *Quicunque vult*, the so-called Athanasian Creed. A distinctive feature of Prime in both traditions was the reading of the martyrology for the following day, so that the monks or clergy would know what liturgical celebrations to expect.

At Vespers, the numerical series of psalms was continued from Psalm 109, having been interrupted at Matins with Psalm 108. The high point of this hour was the antiphonal singing of the New Testament canticle *Magnificat* (Luke 1:46–55). Compline, said just before retiring, varied little from day to day. It began with a capitulum of 1 Peter 5:8, the *Confiteor* prayer of sorrow for sin and absolution, then continued with psalms chosen for their special appropriateness to the evening hour, sung antiphonally in the Roman Office with one refrain, directly in the Monastic Office with no refrain. The New Testament canticle *Nunc dimittis* (Luke 2:29–32) was sung antiphonally only in the Roman Office.

Though most French churches followed this outline from the 9th century on, there were many variations from place to place. The choice of readings and chants differed greatly from diocese to diocese and from monastery to monastery. On feasts of saints and other commemorations, different in each local calendar, the usual psalms of each hour were often replaced by others chosen for their textual relevance to the themes of the day. These local uses survived the Middle Ages, lasting until the 18th century, when they were replaced by "neo-Gallican" liturgies inspired by the ideals of the Enlightenment. In the 19th century, under papal pressure, these reformed rites were suppressed and replaced by the official Roman Breviary as revised after the Council of Trent, which itself would be repeatedly revised and reformed during the 20th century.

Even in the Middle Ages, the official arrangement of daily services was not always followed in practice. On fast days, when one often could not eat before None or Vespers, there was an understandable incentive to get through the services early; a relic of this may be seen in the modern English word "noon," derived from the office of None even though it designated the hour that properly belongs to Sext. Similarly, the practice of anticipating Matins and Lauds by celebrating them after Compline enabled one to sleep until Prime. Such tendencies were exacerbated over the course of the Middle Ages, as the amount of material to be got through increased due to the proliferation of devotional accretions. The Pater Noster, Ave Maria, Apostles' Creed, and other prayers came to be recited quietly before and after each service, and such Marian antiphons as *Salve Regina* were regularly sung as each service ended. Votive or devotional offices were widely added to the Office proper, particularly the Little Offices of the Virgin Mary. The Office of the Dead, intended for use only in conjunction with other burial and funeral services, was often recited every day as a penitential exercise. By the 13th century, many clergy avoided the public celebrations of the Office (sometimes paying a vicar to take their place), fulfilling their obligation by reading the texts privately at more convenient times, even if that meant reading through the entire daily cycle at one sitting. In the 16th century, private recitation became the official practice of some religious congregations, such as the Jesuits, and in our day it is still the unofficial practice of most Catholic secular clergy.

Peter Jeffrey

[See also: CANONICAL HOURS; GALLICAN RITE]

Bradshaw, Paul F. "Cathedral vs. Monastery: The Only Alternatives for the Liturgy of the Hours?" In *Time and Community: In Honor of Thomas Julian Talley*, ed. J. Neil Alexander. Washington, D.C.: Pastoral, 1990, pp. 123–36.

———. *Daily Prayer in the Early Church: A Study of the Origin and Development of the Divine Office.* New York: Oxford University Press, 1982.

Clément, J.-M. *Lexique des anciennes règles monastiques occidentales.* 2 vols. Steenbrugge: Abbaye Saint-Pierre, 1978.

Martimort, Aimé Georges, ed. *The Church at Prayer: An Introduction to the Liturgy*, rev. ed., trans. Matthew J. O'Connell. Collegeville: Liturgical, 1986, Vol. 4: *The Liturgy and Time.*

Möller, Hartmut. "Die Feier des Metzer Osteroffiziums im 9. Jahrhundert." In *Feste und Feiern im Mittelalter: Paderborner Symposium des Mediävistenverbandes*, ed. Detlef Altenburg, Jörg Jarnut, and Hans-Hugo Steinhoff. Sigmaringen: Thorbeke, 1991, pp. 309–22.

Salmon, Pierre. *L'office divin au moyen âge: histoire de la formation du bréviaire du IXe au XVIe siècle.* Paris: Cerf, 1967.

Taft, Robert. *The Liturgy of the Hours in East and West: The Origins of the Divine Office and Its Meaning for Today.* Collegeville: Liturgical, 1986.

Winkler, Gabriele. "Über die Kathedralvesper in den verschiedenen Riten des Ostens und Westens." *Archiv für Liturgiewissenschaft* 16 (1974): 53–102.

DOL-DE-BRETAGNE. The Benedictine monastery at Dol (Île-et-Vilaine) was founded in 548 by St. Samson of Caldey, who was fleeing Saxon invaders in Britain. It was raised to an archbishopric in 848 by Nominoë, who was crowned here as king of the Bretons. Until 1159, its bishop was the primate of Brittany. A key frontier fortress, it successfully resisted William the Conqueror in 1075 but was eventually captured by Henry II Plantagenêt in 1164. Along the Grande-Rue are a number of well-preserved medieval houses. The Maison des Palets, with its original round-arched windows, is a singular example of domestic Norman Romanesque architecture that may date back to the 11th century.

The present Norman Gothic cathedral of Saint-Samson is built on the site of a Romanesque cathedral burned by John Lackland in 1203. Its sharply pointed arches and straight east end show English influence. The nave, side aisles, and transept, all dating from the early 13th century, are remarkable for the unusual plan of the pillars and their shafts, which are attached on the east and west but not on the north and south. The choir, side chapels, and rectangular ambulatory are more ornate and date from the late 13th century.

William W. Kibler/William W. Clark

Couffon, René. "La cathédrale de Dol." *Congrès archéologique* (*Haute-Bretagne*) 126 (1968): 37–59.

Prache, Anne. "Les influences anglaises sur l'architecture de la cathédrale de Dol." *Bulletin de la Société Nationale des Antiquaires de France* (1980–81): 290–95.

DOMINICAN ORDER. The Dominican Order of Friars Preachers, founded by the Castilian canon Dominic of Calaruega (1170–1221), represented the fruit of his long labor of preaching (1206–15) among the heretics of southern France. By 1213, his mission knew its first success, a foundation at Prouille that served simultaneously as a convent for women converted from heresy and a base of operations for Dominic and his disciples. By 1215, he and his band of preachers had settled at Toulouse. They assumed the *Rule of St. Augustine* and were confirmed as an order by Pope Honorius III on December 22, 1216. The following year, Dominic split up his small community, sending two groups northward to Paris, another to Spain, leaving a remnant at Toulouse and traveling himself to Rome. Dominic thus transformed his local order of regular canons into an international order.

Between 1217 and 1221, papal bulls came to define Dominic's followers as an order of preachers, whose apostolate concerned "preaching and the salvation of souls," that is, pastoral care administered through preaching and its corollary, hearing confessions. The last two years of Dominic's life were given over to outlining the order's institutional form at its first two General Chapters (1220, 1221).

The pattern of Dominican life and mission was to be formed by a number of legislative sources. In the first place, there was the *Rule of St. Augustine*. Second, there were the customs of the order, drawn in large measure from the Premonstratensians. Third, there were the constitutions created for the order at its General Chapters. A species within the genus of regular, or Augustinian, canons, the Dominicans combined an internal life of communal prayer, weekly chapters, perpetual fast, and the common life with an external apostolate among the faithful centered upon the acts of preaching and hearing confession. Unlike other Augustinian canons, Dominicans were not bound to a single house or community and embraced communal as well as individual poverty, at least after the General Chapter of 1220. This radical approach to poverty associated them with other new orders of the day, the Franciscans above all, but also the Carmelites, Augustinian Hermits, Order of the Sack, and even smaller groups. Finally, Dominicans did away with manual labor as an integral component of their religious life. Manual labor was given over to lay brothers (*conversi*) so that the clerical brothers would be free for the two most important of their communal enterprises, prayer and study in preparation for their external apostolate.

The basic unit of the order was the convent. No Dominican convent could have fewer than twelve clerical brothers. Of these, one was required to function as prior and received this post by election. Another was required to function as lector or teacher and was appointed by the provincial prior. Groups of convents were organized into provinces. By 1221, what we now call France was divided into two provinces: France, roughly coterminus with the *langue d'oïl*, and Provence, roughly coterminus with the *langue d'oc*. Each was administered by a provincial prior elected by the province's conventual priors and two delegates from each convent. The provincial prior was charged with confirming the election of conventual priors, appointing lectors, visiting the province to ensure the maintenance of the constitutions and ordinances of the order, and presiding over the annual provincial chapters.

The provinces of the order together constituted the order as such. At its head was a Master General, elected by the provincial priors and two delegates from each province. Until the 14th century, the Master General had no fixed abode; later, he tended to reside at Rome. His responsibility was to visit the order as a whole, maintain its laws, correct abuses, and preside over the General Chapter, the order's legislative body.

This basic structure applies to the male First Order. A female Second Order was constituted not by convents but by monasteries of strictly enclosed nuns. Living by the same rule and customs, they claimed spiritual direction by their confreres. The constitutions stipulated that a community of at least six brothers should live within and exercise pastoral care of each monastery of Dominican nuns. This heavy pastoral investment in the care of the order's sisters caused anxiety among male Dominicans from time to time. Anxiety reached a peak during the master-generalship of Conrad of Wildeshausen (1242–52), when there was a concerted effort to dissociate the order from its female wing. In the end, the weight assigned to the antiquity of Prouille and the monastery of St. Sixtus in Rome, Dominic's clear commitment to the women of these communities, and the strict enclosure they practiced carried the day. By 1285, a Third Order of lay Dominicans was added, who lived as much as possible in terms of the rule and ordinances of the order, placing themselves under the spiritual direction of the Friars Preachers.

In France, as in other parts of Europe, Dominicans showed a marked predilection for large conventual communities. Saint-Jacques at Paris, for example, counted 120 brothers only a few years (1223) after its foundation (1218). This predilection meant that there developed considerably fewer convents than were to be found in the Franciscan order, the Dominicans' closest analogue. Moreover, it meant that Dominicans preferred large urban centers. A medieval Latin verse had it that:

Bernardus valles, montes Benedictus amabat,
Oppida Franciscus, celebres Dominicus urbes.

("Bernard loved the valleys, Benedict the mountains. Francis the towns, Dominic the great cities.") In the province of France, the Dominicans had by 1250 established themselves at Paris, Lille, Arras, Valenciennes, Amiens, Saint-Quentin, Rouen, Beauvais, Reims, Verdun, Metz, Toul, Besançon, Langres, Troyes, Caen, Lisieux, Coutances, Nantes, Dinan, Dijon, Le Mans, Angers, Tours, La Rochelle, Poitiers, Clermont, Lyon, Lausanne, and Bourges. In the province of Provence, they established themselves at Bordeaux, Bayonne, Périgueux, Limoges, Cahors, Béziers, Carcassone, Perpignan, Narbonne, Montpellier, Le Puy, Valence, Avignon, Toulouse, Marseille, and Nice. Dominican urban preferences were so pronounced that some have thought to be able to follow the pattern of urbanization in 13th-century France by following the expansion of the order.

The medieval history of the southern province is dominated by struggle with the Cathar and Waldensian sects. Provence was home to an extraordinary number of Dominican preachers throughout the 13th and 14th centuries; and preachers of extraordinary gifts were essential to the task of disputing heretics effectively, since they were not limited to the region assigned their home convent. They could go wherever there were heretics to preach to and dispute. Popes consistently commissioned inquisitors for southern France from the time that Gregory IX (r. 1227–34) established the papal Inquisition (1233). Early on, popes began to favor mendicant friars for the task, especially Dominicans. Southern France thus saw a constant stream of Dominican papal inquisitors; one of the most scholarly Dominicans from the southern French provinces, Bernard Gui, produced not only careful historical research but also one of the most influential inquisitorial manuals.

In the province of France, i.e., the northern province, the Dominican experience was rather different, being dominated by study and the looming specter of its most celebrated convent, Saint-Jacques at Paris. This is not to say that there was any lack of spiritual struggle with heretics. The cities of Flanders, in particular, knew their share of heterodox believers. But it was learning, and especially theological learning, that distinguished the history of the Dominican order in northern France.

The order established *studia generalia* to serve as the apex of its educational structure. Each *studium generale* was administered by a regent master assisted by two bachelors; the subject of instruction was theology. Saint-Jacques at Paris housed the first and greatest *studium generale* of the order. In 1229 and again in 1231, it was granted a chair in the theological faculty of the University of Paris. In 1248, Provence received its own *studium* in the convent at Montpellier. In 1303, the newly established province of Toulouse received its own *studium generale* in its convent in Toulouse. After 1260, other types of schools were organized. *Studia naturalium* provided Dominicans an internal organ for the study of philosophy; other special schools were established for the study of logic and still others for the study of foreign languages, such as Greek, Hebrew, and Arabic.

Saint-Jacques's close association with the University of Paris created a fertile field in which to recruit novices for the order. Despite the inclusion of Dominican regent masters within the theology faculty of the University of Paris, the Dominican *studium generale* was imperfectly integrated with the rest of the university. This was particularly clear in the period 1229–31 and again in the 1250s, when the secular masters of the university called strikes that the Dominican masters refused to join. Their lack of solidarity provoked a far-ranging controversy with the secular masters, which came to be fought over mendicant (and by implication papal) claims to a pastoral apostolate and the office of doctor within the church. The controversy lasted intermittently for a century, heating up in the 1250s, again in the 1270s and 1280s, and then again in the years before the Council of Vienne (1311–12). Dominicans and their mendicant allies proved successful in defending themselves and their religious privileges, though their secular opponents created arguments that were more difficult to dispute than is sometimes realized. What is remarkable is the degree to which the French episcopacy either remained neutral in this protracted dispute or supported the Dominicans and their mendicant allies. In general, the French episcopacy looked upon the order with high favor throughout the 13th century.

The list of Dominican masters at Saint-Jacques includes some of the greatest thinkers of the Middle Ages: Albert the Great, Thomas Aquinas, and Meister Eckhart. Moreover, the Dominicans of Saint-Jacques were also responsible for impressive products of communal effort, including a concordance to the Bible and a complete set of postillae for every biblical book (under the direction of Hugues de Saint-Cher). Some even argue that the *pecia* system of manuscript production was developed by and for the needs of the *studium generale* at Saint-Jacques.

In France, as everywhere, the 13th century was a golden age for the Dominican order. The 14th century was less kind, although the order's numbers did not decline until the Black Death (1348). In 1337, in fact, membership in the order achieved its medieval high-water mark (12,000), in a census taken for Pope Benedict XII (r. 1334–42). Nevertheless, the economy of Europe began to stagnate in the late 13th century, and it became more difficult for the order to beg the resources that it needed to remain viable. The depradations of the Black Death only worsened the situation. Entrance standards loosened and study and the choral office were relatively neglected, as friars assiduously traveled their convent's begging routes.

The order began to combat the relaxation of its religious regime under the direction of Raymond of Capua late in the 14th century. He initiated a movement of strict observance of the contemplative and monastic side of Dominican life that burgeoned throughout the 15th century. It led in time to the formation of congregations within the order, that is, groups of Observant convents that existed autonomously within and across the provincial structure of the order. Of particular importance to the French provinces were the Congregation of Holland (1464) and the Congregation of France (1497).

Robert Sweetman

[See also: ALBERT THE GREAT; AQUINAS, THOMAS; *AUGUSTINE, RULE OF ST.;* AUGUSTINIAN FRIARS/HERMITS; BERNARD GUI; FRANCISCAN ORDER; GREGORY IX; HERESY; INQUISITION; MENDICANT ART AND ARCHITECTURE; MONASTICISM; MYSTICISM; PREACHING; REGULAR CANONS; SCHOLASTICISM; UNIVERSITIES; WILLIAM OF SAINT-AMOUR]

Archivum Fratrum Praedicatorum. 1 (1930)– .

Kaeppeli, Thomas. *Scriptores Ordinis Praedicatorum medii aevi.* 3 vols. (A–S). Rome: Sabinae, 1970–81.

Chapotin, Marie Dominique. *Histoire des Dominicains de la province de France: le siècle des fondations.* Rouen: Cagniard, 1898.

Douais, Célestin. *Essai sur l'organisation des études dans l'ordre des Frères Prêcheurs au XIIIe et au XIVe siècle (1216–1342).* Paris: Picard, 1884.

Hinnebusch, William A. *The History of the Dominican Order.* 2 vols. New York: Alba House, 1966.

Mortier, Daniel Antonin. *Histoire abrégée de l'ordre de Saint Dominique en France.* Tours: Marre, 1920.

———. *Histoire des maîtres généraux de l'ordre des Frères Prêcheurs.* 8 vols. Paris: Picard, 1908–20.

Vicaire, Marie Humbert. *Histoire de saint Dominique.* 2 vols. Paris: Cerf, 1984.

DOMMARTIN. The Premonstratensian abbey church of Dommartin (Pas-de-Calais) was one of the largest and wealthiest of the houses founded from Saint-Martin at Laon. The 12th-century church, begun ca. 1160, was destroyed following the Revolution, but analysis of the ruins and excavations have produced an accurate plan (Pontroué) and numerous beautiful foliate capitals, some of which are housed in the museum at Amiens.

William W. Clark

Enlart, Camille. *Monuments religieux de l'architecture romane et de transition dans la région picarde.* Amiens: Yvert et Tellier, 1895.

Pontroué, Pierre. "Quatre ans de recherches archéologiques à l'abbaye de Dommartin." *Bulletin de la Commission Départementale des Monuments Historiques du Pas-de-Calais* 9 (1973): 266–80.

Rodière, Rogier. "Dommartin." In *La Picardie historique et monumental.* Amiens: Musée de Picardie, 1933, Vol. 7: *Le pays de Montreuil,* pp. 194–215.

DOMONT. The church of Sainte-Madeleine at Domont (Val d'Oise), a dependency of the Parisian abbey of Saint-Martin-des-Champs after 1124, has a chevet that dates to 1150–55, although the axial chapel was added later. The transept and nave were rebuilt in the early 16th century, and there were major repairs in the early 18th. Nonetheless, the three-story interior elevation and the barely protruding flying buttresses on the south side (known through prerestoration photographs) link the chevet to the Parisian Early Gothic milieu.

William W. Clark

Plagnieux, Philippe. "Les arcs-boutants du XIIe siècle de l'église de Domont." *Bulletin monumental* 150 (1992): 209–22.

DONATION OF CONSTANTINE. An 8th-century forgery that purports to establish the temporal authority of the papacy, the *Constitutum Constantini* or *Donation of Constantine* is based on legends of Pope Sylvester I that date from the 5th century, found in the *Legenda sancti Silvestri.* Although attributed to the Roman emperor Constantine I, the *Donation* was probably the work of a cleric of the church of the Savior (St. John Lateran). Divided into two parts and addressed to Pope Sylvester, "Constantine" describes his conversion to Christianity in the *Confessio,* and in the second part, the *Donatio* proper, he bestows on Sylvester and his successors a power that matches his own royal authority. While the document outlines or in a sense creates the temporal sovereignty of the pope, it implicitly undercuts this aim by having the power of the papacy derive from the emperor. Because of this ambiguity, the document has been used both to advance and to restrict the autonomy of papal rule. The *Donation* was also instrumental in developing the thesis of inalienability: no ruler had the right to give to others any of his essential governing powers or any of the lands in the royal domain. In the 15th century, Nicholas of Cusa and Lorenzo della Valle determined that the *Donation of Constantine* was not issued by Constantine, a revelation subsequently used by Protestants to argue that papal power was based on falsehoods. The oldest surviving copy of the *Donation* is the 8th-century manuscript B.N. lat. 2777.

E. Kay Harris

[**See also:** *DONATION OF PEPIN*]

Coleman, Christopher B., ed. and trans. *The Treatise of Lorenzo Valla on the Donation of Constantine: Text and Translation into English.* New Haven: Yale University Press, 1922.

Fuhrman, Horst, ed. *Constitutum Constantini.* Hanover: Hahn, 1968.

Ullmann, Walter. *The Growth of Papal Government in the Middle Ages.* 3rd ed. London: Methuen, 1970, pp. 74–86.

DONATION OF PEPIN. An 8th-century document that transferred control of a strip of land in Italy to Pope Sylvester II, effectively establishing the temporal authority of the papacy. In 751, Rome and surrounding areas had been threatened by the Lombard king Aistulf. Since Sylvester was a Byzantine subject, he appealed to Emperor Constantine V for assistance, but to no avail. Seeking protection elsewhere, Sylvester traveled to Ponthion in 754, where he obtained a sworn oath from Pepin III the Short (714–768) to defend the Roman church. After Pepin had defeated Aistulf and the First Peace of Pavia had been concluded in 755, Aistulf refused to abide by the agreement and attacked Rome again. Summoned by Pope Stephen II, Pepin engaged Aistulf in battle once again and defeated him in 756. The Second Peace of Pavia levied heavy penalties against Aistulf. This time, Fulrad, the abbot of Saint-Denis, was charged with the duty of traveling to various cities in Italy to obtain tokens of submission to the pope. Afterward, Fulrad documented the lands that were given or restored to the pope. It is this document that is known as the *Donation of Pepin.* The lands, however, had not belonged to Pepin or to the pope but had been the property of the emperor, who had failed to defend them.

E. Kay Harris

[**See also:** *DONATION OF CONSTANTINE;* PEPIN]

Caspar, Erich. *Pippin and die romische Kirche.* Berlin: Springer, 1914.

Duchesne, Louis M.O. *The Beginnings of Temporal Sovereignty of the Popes, A.D. 754–1073,* trans. Arnold H. Matthew. New York: Benzinger, 1908, pp. 21–48.

Ullmann, Walter. *The Growth of Papal Government in the Middle Ages.* 3rd ed. London: Methuen, 1970, pp. 44–86.

DONNEI DES AMANZ. Composed in the late 12th century, this incomplete and anonymous Anglo-Norman didactic poem has 1,244 octosyllabic lines in the only manuscript in which it is preserved (Cologny-Geneva, Bibliotheca Bodmeriana 82). The narrator overhears a conversation between a young noble and the lady he loves. In his attempts to win his lady's love, the young man cites examples of famous lovers, especially from the Romances of Antiquity. The episode from the Tristan legend cited in lines 919–1,158 is commonly known as *Tristan rossignol.*

Claude J. Fouillade

[**See also:** ANTIQUITY, ROMANCES OF; TRISTAN ROMANCES]

Paris, Gaston, ed. *Le donnei des amants. Romania* 25 (1896): 497–541.

Busby, Keith. "The *Donnei des amants* and Courtly Tradition." *Medioevo romanzo* 14 (1989): 181–95.

DOON DE MAYENCE. A chanson de geste consisting of two parts: *Les enfances Doon* and *Doon de Mayence*. The first part may have been composed after 1250, possibly as late as the early 14th century, and the second part after 1250. The *Enfances* has 6,038 lines and the second part, 5,467, and both are in rhymed Alexandrines. They survive in three manuscripts (Montpellier, Faculté de médecine, H. 247, ff. 1–46, mid-14th c.; Paris, B.N. fr. 12563, 15th c., and B.N. fr. 1637, 15th c., incomplete). This epic enjoyed wide popularity and was printed, in a prose version, during the 16th century and beyond.

Doon defends his mother against the attempts of traitors who want to usurp the family's fief. He spends several years in a forest with his father, who has become a hermit. A rebel vassal of Charles, Doon receives permission to fight the Saxons. He conquers Flandrine and marries her.

This poem makes allusions to *Garin de Monglane*, the *Chevalier au Cygne*, and Chrétien's *Perceval*.

Jean-Louis Picherit

Pey, Alexandre, ed. *Doon de Maience, chanson de geste.* Paris: Vieweg, 1859. [Based on Montpellier H 247.]

DORAT, LE. The collegiate church of Saint-Pierre in Le Dorat (Haute-Vienne) is the most impressive of extant Romanesque churches in the Limousin; elegant decorative arcades and vigorous carving enliven the starkness of the local granite. Most striking are the octagonal lantern tower with its trilobed blind arcade and high spire topped by a gilded angel, the polylobed oculus of the cupola of the crossing, and the scalloped archivolts of the western portal (original ironwork on doors). The entrance bay (cupola beneath a bell tower, lateral arcades) is similar to those of La Souterraine, Saint-Junien, and Bénévent; twelve stairs descend to the pointed barrel-vaulted nave (the narrow side aisles are groin-vaulted), transept with apsidioles, and choir with ambulatory and three radiating chapels. Other notable features include the crypt (11th c.), treasury, early font, and remnants of fortifications (15th c.).

Jean M. French

Fage, René. "Le Dorat." *Congrès archéologique (Limoges)* 84 (1921): 170–200.

Maury, Jean, Marie-Madeleine Gauthier, and Jean Porcher. *Limousin roman.* 3rd ed. La Pierre-qui-vire: Zodiaque, 1990.

Schneider P. *Le Dorat.* La Pierre-qui-vire: Zodiaque, 1964.

DOUIN DE LAVESNE (fl. mid-13th c.). Author of *Trubert*, a poem of 2,984 octosyllables. Masquerading variously as a fool, a carpenter, a doctor, a knight, and a girl, Trubert succeeds in duping the duke and duchess of Burgundy. The poem is violent, anarchic, sometimes obscene, and its central character, amoral. *Trubert* calls itself a fabliau, but it resembles rather a series of fabliaux linked by the figure of Trubert. Composed in the mid-13th century, *Trubert* is found in a single manuscript (B.N. fr. 2188).

Keith Busby

Douin de Lavesne. *Trubert, fabliau du XIIIe siècle*, ed. Guy Raynaud de Lage. Geneva: Droz, 1974.

Badel, Pierre-Yves. *Le sauvage et le sot: le fabliau de Trubert et la tradition orale.* Paris: Champion, 1978.

Gravdal, Kathryn. *Vilain and Courtois: Transgressive Parody in French Literature of the Twelfth and Thirteenth Centuries.* Lincoln: University of Nebraska Press, 1989.

DOWRY. The resources brought by a woman to a marriage for the support of the couple. In early-medieval France, the Frankish brideprice was replaced by the dowry, accompanied at times by the *Morgangabe*, which the groom provided following the consummation of the marriage, and by other family gifts to the bride. The dowry thus came to resemble the Roman *dos*, the gift by the bride or her family to the groom.

In the high and late Middle Ages, the *dos* and a *donatio propter nuptias*, augment, or "dower" were common. Landed or movable wealth might constitute the dowry; women of urban merchant families in southern France often received monetary sums as dowry. In most regions, the real property of a woman's dowry came under her husband's control (*Grand coutumier de France, Coutumes de Beauvaisis*), but she retained some right of approval for the alienation of property. In the case of movables, custom differed. The *Coutumes de Beauvaisis* granted the husband the right to administer movables, as did the *Très ancienne coutume de Bretagne*, but in the south of France the wife tended to retain control of her personal property, or *bona paraphernalia*.

In most regions, a woman could recover her dowry upon death or divorce; on the death of her spouse, the widow was entitled to her dower rights, which usually ranged from one-half to one-third of his property (*Coutumes de Beauvaisis, Les établissements de saint Louis*).

Kathryn L. Reyerson

[See also: BETROTHAL AND MARRIAGE CONTRACTS; WIDOWS AND WIDOWHOOD]

Duby, Georges. *The Knight, the Lady and the Priest: The Making of Modern Marriage in Medieval France*, trans. Barbara Bray. New York: Pantheon, 1983.

Ganshof, François. "Le statut de la femme dans la monarchie franque." *Recueils de la Société Jean Bodin* 12 (1962): 5–58.

Gaudemet, Jean. "Le legs du droit romain en matière matrimoniale." In *Il matrimonio nella società altomedievale.* Spoleto: Presso la Sede del Centro, 1977, pp. 139–89.

Herlihy, David. *Medieval Households.* Cambridge: Harvard University Press, 1985.

Hilaire, Jean. *Le régime des biens entre époux dans la région de Montpellier du début du XIIIe siècle à la fin du XVIe siècle.* Montpellier: Causse, Graille et Castelnau, 1957.

Shahar, Shulamith. *The Fourth Estate: A History of Women in the Middle Ages*. London: Methuen, 1983.

Wemple, Suzanne. *Women in Frankish Society: Marriage and the Cloister, 500 to 900*. Philadelphia: University of Pennsylvania Press, 1981.

DREUX. The Roman city of Durocasses, Dreux (Eure-et-Loir) evolved into a countship by the 10th century. Strategically located between the royal domain, the duchy of Normandy, and the county of Chartres, it was seized by King Robert II ca. 1015 and remained part of the royal domain until the late 12th century. Fortified before 1100, Dreux had a royal mint under Henry I (r. 1031–60) and communal rights, without justice, which were confirmed in a charter of 1180.

The county of Dreux passed to a younger son of Louis VI, Robert (d. 1188), whose descendants held it until the late 14th century. The most notable of these were Philippe, bishop of Beauvais (d. 1217), a bellicose prelate who participated in the Third Crusade with his brother Robert II (d. 1218), and in the Albigensian Crusade and the campaign of Bouvines; Henri, archbishop of Reims (d. 1240), who dared to excommunicate St. Louis; and Pierre Mauclerc (d. 1250), husband of Alix de Thouars, heiress of Brittany. Pierre was renowned for his opposition to the regency of Blanche of Castile, for consolidating his wife's duchy in the interests of their son, for participating in the crusade of Thibaut de Champagne (1239–40), and for donating the magnificent south rose window to the cathedral of Chartres.

The comital line continued until after 1355, when it was disputed by three sisters—Jeanne, Péronelle, and Marguerite. The last two sold their claims to King Charles V in 1377 and 1378, respectively. In 1407, Charles VI granted Dreux to his brother, Louis of Orléans. When the latter's grandson became king in 1498, it returned to the royal domain.

Saint-Pierre is the only medieval church in Dreux to survive the French Revolution. Of the buildings started under Count Robert, only a few sections of wall survive, the rest having been rebuilt in the 13th century. The north transept, four aisle bays, and four ambulatory columns, as well as the buttress piers on the nave, were incorporated in the rebuilding following the damage from the siege of Dreux by Henry IV of England in 1424. Most of the rebuilding was finished by 1498, although the façade was completed only in 1524. The south tower was not finished in time for the dedication in 1540 and so has remained incomplete.

The most important religious structure in Dreux was the now-destroyed collegial church of Saint-Étienne, a royal foundation within the precincts of the château. The church, begun in the 1130s, was intended as the burial church of the counts. Several historiated and foliate capitals from the church have been identified; two are in the local museum, a fragment is at Yale, and several others are either embedded in the repaired château walls or reinstalled in the burial crypt of the Orléans family mausoleum built on the site in the early 19th century. The château is known from early views and from the extensive surviving walls, although no trace of the donjon or other structures remains.

R. Thomas McDonald/William W. Clark

Cahn, Walter. "A King from Dreux." *Yale University Art Gallery Bulletin* 34 (1974): 14–29.

Châtelain, André. *Châteaux forts et féodalité en l'Île-de-France du XIe au XIIIe siècle*. Nonette: Créer, 1983, pp. 351–53.

Gardner, Stephen. "The Church of Saint-Étienne in Dreux and Its Role in the Formulation of Early Gothic Architecture." *Journal of the British Archaeological Association* 137 (1984): 86–113.

Lelièvre, Jean. *L'église Saint-Pierre de Dreux*. Dreux, 1952.

DROIT DU SEIGNEUR. A symbol of abusive or aristocratic domination, the *droit du seigneur*, or *ius primae noctis*, was a custom once thought to have characterized the Middle Ages, whereby a lord might claim sexual relations with the bride of a servile tenant on her wedding night. There is no evidence that any legally recognized exaction of this sort ever existed. Karl Schmidt attempted to prove that all reports of a *droit du seigneur* are to be traced either to pure invention or misinterpretation of marriage taxes. There are, however, some references to a seigneurial abuse (rather than the right) of newly married women in the regions of the Pyrénées. Peasants in Catalonia agitating for an end to serfdom in 1462 complained of this practice and the king of Aragon abolished it, along with other more widely acknowledged servile incidents, in 1486. There is also indication that the same oppressive custom was practiced in Béarn and Bigorre during the 16th century.

In the 18th century, the *droit du seigneur* was denounced in the antifeudal writings of Voltaire, Restif de la Bretonne, and above all by Beaumarchais, in his *Mariage de Figaro*. Controversy erupted during the mid-19th century, when some asserted that most Frenchmen were the descendants of bastards because of the earlier prevalence of the *droit du seigneur*. The abusive right has appeared frequently in what might charitably be called romantic historical fiction. The historical core of this essentially literary and polemical theme is small but not completely fabricated.

Paul H. Freedman

Barthélemy, Anatole de. "Le droit du seigneur." *Revue des questions historiques* 1 (1866): 95–123.

Bascle de Lagrèze, Gustave. *Histoire du droit dans les Pyrénées (Comté de Bigorre)*. Paris: Imprimerie Impériale, 1876.

Hinojosa y Naveros, Eduardo de. "¿Existio en Cataluña el 'ius primae noctis?" *Annales internationales d'histoire* 2 (1902): 224–26.

Litvack, Frances Eleanor Palermo. *Le droit du seigneur in European and American Literature*. Birmingham: Summa, 1984.

Schmidt, Karl. *Jus primae noctis: Eine geschichtliche Untersuchung*. Freiburg im Breisgau: Herder, 1881.

DROUART LA VACHE (fl. late 13th c.). Otherwise unknown, Drouart la Vache names himself in a riddle at the end of his *Livres d'amours*, a Champenois poem of 7,640 octosyllabic verses composed in 1290. It closely follows Andreas Capellanus's *De amore*, of which it is a translation, first defining love, then presenting situations in which love may occur, and finally distinguishing virtuous "pure love" from "mixed love," which is to be condemned. Drouart says that he translated Andreas's book because he found it amusing, and his text is lighter in tone than its source. The *Livres d'amours* exists in a single manuscript (Paris, Arsenal 3122, last quarter of the 13th c.).

Peter L. Allen

[See also: ANDREAS CAPELLANUS; COURTLY LOVE]

Drouart la Vache. *Li livres d'amours de Drouart la Vache*, ed. Robert Bossuat. Paris: Champion, 1926.

Karnein, Alfred. "La réception du *De amore* d'André le Chapelain au XIIIe siècle." *Romania* 102 (1981): 324–51, 501–42.

Sargent, Barbara Nelson. "A Medieval Commentary on Andreas Capellanus." *Romania* 94 (1973): 528–41.

DU CLERCQ, JACQUES (1420–1501). Lawyer, counselor to Philip the Good of Burgundy, and lord of Beauvoir-en-Ternois. Du Clercq's *Mémoires* (1448–67) are a font of local information, sprinkled with material of broader import. Only one manuscript of the *Mémoires*, now partially lost, exists.

Leah Shopkow

[See also: BURGUNDIAN CHRONICLERS; CHASTELLAIN, GEORGES; LA MARCHE, OLIVIER DE; MOLINET, JEAN]

Du Clercq, Jacques. *Des mémoires de Jacques du Clercq*, ed. J.A. Buchon. In *Chroniques de Enguerrand de Monstrelet*. Paris: Verdière, 1826–27, Vols. 12–15.

DUFAY, GUILLAUME (Du Fay, Du Fayt; 1397–1474). Composer, musician, and cleric. During a career that spanned over fifty years, Dufay produced some of the finest music of the late Middle Ages. Contemporary esteem for Dufay and his music was matched only by the reputation of his contemporary Gilles Binchois.

Dufay's life and peripatetic musical career have been outlined to an extent matched by no other 15th-century composer. There are hundreds of surviving documents relating to his career, and gaps in the documentary record are often filled by evidence from the occasional works he composed. According to recent discoveries by Planchart, Dufay was born near Brussels, the illegitimate son of a priest, on August 5, 1397. The earliest documents regarding his musical career date from 1409, when he is listed as a *puer altaris* at Cambrai cathedral. By 1414, he had risen to the rank of *clericus altaris* and had been granted a chaplaincy at Cambrai. His precise whereabouts are unknown over the next few years, but it is likely that he was at the Council of Constance, possibly in the entourage of Pierre d'Ailly, bishop of Cambrai.

During the early 1420s, Dufay was in northern Italy. Two of his earliest datable works were written for the Malatesta family. He returned to France for a time, from 1423 or 1424 until 1426, probably with an eye toward securing prebends in the area of Laon. His rondeau *Adieu ces bons vins de Lannoys* (1426) bade fond farewell to Laon, as he returned once more to Italy. Dufay was in Bologna by early 1426, serving as secretary to Cardinal Louis Aleman, under whom he was ordained in 1427 or 1428. From 1428 until 1433 or 1434, Dufay served popes Martin V (d.1431) and Eugenius IV in the papal chapel, where he was associated with some of the best composers of the day, among them Arnold de Lantins and Johannes Brassart. His output included occasional motets in celebration of Eugenius IV.

Dufay traveled extensively over the next few years. During 1434–35, he was in the employ of the court of Savoy and made at least one extended visit to Cambrai. At Savoy, Dufay met Gilles Binchois for the first time; it was probably this meeting that is documented in Martin Le Franc's *Champion des dames*. He returned to Italy in 1435, rejoining the entourage of Eugenius IV in Florence. Dufay composed the motet *Nuper rosarum flores* in 1436 for the consecration of Florence cathedral by Eugenius. By 1437, he had returned once again to the court of Savoy, composing one of his last isorhythmic motets, *Magnanimae gentis* (1438), in celebration of a peace treaty between Louis, duke of Savoy, and Louis's brother, Philippe, count of Geneva.

By 1439, Dufay had settled once more in Cambrai, although he was frequently absent throughout the rest of his life, both on cathedral business and on a few freelance excursions. Dufay's activities at Cambrai included a wide variety of musical and clerical duties: supervising choirboys and *petits vicaires* and overseeing the revision and editing of the cathedral's choirbooks. Throughout the 1440s, Dufay maintained an unofficial though familiar relationship with Philip the Good, duke of Burgundy, and some of Dufay's liturgical music of this period, including a sizable number of Mass Proper settings, was composed for the Burgundian chapel. Louis, duke of Savoy, continued to woo the composer as well, and during an extended absence from Cambrai, in 1452–58, Dufay was employed by the Savoy court. It was probably during this last Savoy sojourn that Dufay composed most of his late songs. By 1458, Dufay had returned to Cambrai and remained there for the rest of his life, although he maintained contact with several important patrons, including the dukes of Burgundy and Savoy and, indirectly, with young Lorenzo de' Medici of Florence.

When Dufay died on November 27, 1474, he left explicit instructions regarding the music to be sung at his funeral, which was to include his large four-voice setting of the Marian antiphon *Ave regina celorum*. His will attests to a man of considerable means—books, furnishings, property, and money garnered from a lifetime of patronage and shrewd trading in canonical benefices. There is evidence that both Johannes Ockeghem and Antoine Busnoys composed *déplorations* on Dufay's death, although these works are now lost.

Dufay composed in virtually every polyphonic form of the 15th century, and it has recently been discovered that he composed plainchant as well. His works show an impressive command of every compositional technique available to a 15th-century musician: *fauxbourdon,* isorhythmic writing, *cantus firmus* technique, and imitation.

Dufay's thirteen, possibly fourteen or fifteen, surviving isorhythmic motets are among the latest and finest examples of this longstanding compositional tradition. In nearly all cases, they are works written for a specific event or patron, or may be tied to a period in Dufay's career. His earliest isorhythmic motet, *Vasilissa ergo gaude,* continues the tradition of Royllart's *Rex Karole* (written some forty-five years earlier for Charles V). The brilliant *Ecclesie militantis,* a motet written between 1431 and 1433 for Eugenius IV, is Dufay's most complex essay in isorhythm, in six sections, with two tenors based on different chants and three texted upper voices. With *Supremum est mortalibus* (1433) and his later isorhythmic motets, Dufay turned toward a simpler style, based upon English practices, with long upper-voice duets delineating the *talea* structure.

The majority of Dufay's surviving works are sacred: perhaps thirty or more settings of the complete Mass Ordinary, combined Ordinary and Proper, or Proper; nearly forty additional Mass movements; and nearly fifty settings of hymns, Magnificats, and antiphons for the Office and Marian antiphons. During the 1440s, Dufay conceived at least two large cycles of Proper settings, a series of Masses to various martyrs for Cambrai, and a cycle of votive Masses, probably for the Burgundian Order of the Golden Fleece. In the *Missa Se la face ay pale* and *Missa L'homme armé,* possibly written in the 1450s for the Savoy court, Dufay used secular tenors as a unifying device. His latest Mass, the *Missa Ave regina celorum,* was written in 1472 for the dedication of Cambrai cathedral. Dufay foreshadows later practices in Mass composition by quoting and reworking polyphonic material from his own motet *Ave regina celorum* and his *Missa Ecce ancilla.*

In his Office music and nonliturgical Latin works, Dufay sets the chant usually in the uppermost voice, often paraphrased, transforming it into a flowing melody similar to that of his secular songs. The simplest settings are his Office hymns, set in *fauxbourdon.* Some of Dufay's most expressive writing appears in his settings of Marian antiphons. His four-voice *Ave regina celorum* (ca. 1464), sung at Dufay's funeral and reworked in his *Missa Ave regina,* uses the chant melody as a *cantus firmus* and includes emotional prayers on behalf of the composer himself.

There are over eighty surviving songs by Dufay, composed from ca. 1420 to ca. 1465. His earliest songs exhibit a great variety of styles, from the virtuosity and notational complexity of *Resvelliés vous* (1423) to relatively simple works, such as the rondeau *J'atendray tant.* His late songs, such as *Adieu m'amour* or *Par le regart,* products of a composer in his fifties and sixties, are more sedate than the vivacious songs of the 1420s and exhibit careful attention to text expression and formal balance.

Dufay and Binchois were acknowledged by their contemporaries as the best song composers of their generation, but there are striking differences between them. Binchois's nearly sixty songs are more or less unified in style, while Dufay's song style evolved substantially over his career. As in Binchois's songs, Dufay's most frequent subject is courtly love, but his works exhibit great variety, with texts celebrating May Day or New Year's Day (*Ce jour le doibt* and others), honoring patrons (*Resvelliés vous* for Carlo Malatesta), and other subjects. Like those of Binchois, the bulk of Dufay's texts are in fixed forms—rondeau, ballade, and (in later works) *bergerette*—but his songs also include settings of Latin or Italian poetry, including Petrarch's *Vergene bella.*

J. Michael Allsen

[See also: BINCHOIS, GILLES; BRASSART, JOHANNES; *CONTENANCE ANGLOISE;* CYCLIC MASS; *FAUXBOURDON;* ISORHYTHMIC MOTET; PHILIP THE GOOD]

Dufay, Guillaume. *Guillelmi Dufay: opera omnia.* 6 vols. (Vol. 1 in two parts), ed. Heinrich Besseler. Rome: American Institute of Musicology, 1951–66.

Atlas, Allan, ed. *Papers Read at the Dufay Quincentenary Conference, Brooklyn College, December 6–7, 1974.* New York: Department of Music, School of Performing Arts, Brooklyn College, 1976.

Fallows, David. *Dufay.* London: Dent, 1982.

Planchart, Alejandro Enrique. "Guillaume Du Fay's Benefices and His Relationship to the Court of Burgundy." *Early Music History* 8 (1988): 117–71.

———. "The Early Career of Guillaume Du Fay." *Journal of the American Musicological Society* 46 (1993): 341–68.

Wright, Craig. "Dufay at Cambrai: Discoveries and Revisions." *Journal of the American Musicological Society* 28 (1975): 175–229.

DUKE/DUCHY. The Latin word *dux* 'leader,' from which the later title "duke" was derived, was first employed as a formal title in the late 3rd century, when a new type of officer was put in command of all the forces within districts of the empire composed of one or several provinces, each of which included several *civitates,* or city-states. Down to 1344, all later *duces* in Gaul would have a comparable sphere of authority. Under the Merovingians, the *ducatus,* or ducal office, differed from its Roman predecessor primarily in being irregular and in having a much higher place in the hierarchy of dignities, immediately below the (equivalent) dignities of *patricius,* or "patrician," and *rector* and above that of *comes,* or "count."

Like the patriciate and rectorate, the ducal dignity was suppressed under the first Carolingians, but the title *dux* was informally revived in the usage of the classicizing historians of the 9th century as one of several designations for the counts placed in command of the military forces of one of the border districts, or "marches," which like the former ducal commands were composed of several adjacent *pagi,* or counties—the successors of the former *civitates.* In the 10th century, "duke" was adopted in west Francia as a formal title of dignity by the rulers not only of these marches but of several similar groupings of counties formed within the kingdom with or without the consent of the king. Most of these new *ducatus*, or "duchies," had some sort of relationship to one of the principal ethnic groups within the kingdom, and all of them rapidly evolved into hereditary and effectively independent principalities: Francia, Burgundy, Normandy, Brittany, Gascony, Aquitaine, and Gothia. In most of these districts, however, "duke" continued to be used in random combination and alternation with "prince," "marquis," and "count" until the end of the 11th century, when the great princes finally began to settle on either "duke" or "count" as the exclusive expression of their authority (again in the process of redefinition) within each of their dominions. By 1120, only the lords of Burgundy, Normandy, Aquitaine, Gothia (renamed Narbonne), and Brittany retained the title "duke" (Occitan *duc*, OFr. *dus* or *duc*). In the same period, the jurisdictional title "duchy" (Occitan *ducat*, OFr. *duchié*, *duché*) came to be definitively attached to all but the last of these principalities, Brittany, whose lords continued to employ the alternative title "count" until 1280 and were not recognized as dukes by the royal chancery until 1297. The feminine title "duchess" (Lat. *ducissa*, Occitan *duquesa*, OFr. *duchesse* or *duchoise*) was first employed in France by Eleanor of Aquitaine ca. 1150 and after 1200 was normally used by the wives, widows, and heiresses of dukes, who had previously (since ca. 900) borne the title "countess."

After 987, duke was always regarded as the highest-ranking dominical dignity in France after that of king, and when the peerage of France was created in the early 13th century the rulers of all four of the recognized duchies were included among the twelve peers. Indeed, from 1202 to 1498 all strictly French dukes were also peers and all wholly French duchies were peerages of France. The barony of Bourbon was made a duchy and peerage by Charles IV in December 1327. Nine further duchies were erected in a similar way before 1500: Orléans in 1344; Anjou, Berry, Auvergne, and Touraine in 1360; Nemours in 1404; Valois in 1406; Alençon in 1415; and Valentinois in 1498.

D'A. Jonathan D. Boulton

[See also: COUNT/COUNTY; KNIGHTHOOD; NOBILITY; PEER/PEERAGE]

Boulton, D'A. Jonathan D. *Grants of Honour: The Origins of the System of Nobiliary Dignities of Traditional France, ca. 1100–1515*. Forthcoming.

Kienast, Walther. *Der Herzogstitel in Frankreich und Deutschland (9. bis 12. Jahrhundert)*. Munich: Oldenbourg, 1968.

Lewis, Archibald R. "The Dukes in the *Regnum Francorum*, AD 550–751." *Speculum* 51 (1976): 381–410.

DUNOIS, JEAN, COMTE DE (1402–1468). The bastard of Louis, duke of Orléans, Jean was raised in his father's home and became the effective head of the house of Orléans after the capture of his legitimate half-brothers at Agincourt in 1415. Naturally a member of the Armagnac faction, he joined the dauphin Charles's service. His victory at Montargis in 1427 inaugurated a distinguished military career, and his successful defense of Orléans until relieved by Jeanne d'Arc in 1429 ensured his fame. Though he was to play an intermediary role in both the Praguerie (1439) and the *Guerre du Bien Publique* (1465), he was undoubtedly the most loyal and effective Valois commander of the era. His campaigns in the Seine basin culminated in the triumphal royal entry into Paris in 1436. Jean played a major role in the military reforms of the early 1440s, and between 1449 and 1451 he commanded major elements of the armies that reconquered Normandy and Guyenne. Made count of Dunois in 1439 and count of Longueville in 1444, he held important positions in the government of reunited France, serving both abroad as an ambassador and at home as royal commissioner in the arrest of the duke of Alençon and the rehabilitation of Jeanne d'Arc. After a reconciliation in 1465, he served as a key adviser of Louis XI until his death in 1468.

Paul D. Solon

[See also: ARISTOCRATIC REVOLT; JEANNE D'ARC; ORLÉANS CAMPAIGN; RECONQUEST OF FRANCE]

Léon-Martin, Louis. *Dunois, le bâtard d'Orléans*. Paris: Colbert, 1943.

Merouville, M. Caffin de. *Le beau Dunois et son temps*. Paris: Les Sept Couleurs, 1961.

DUNS SCOTUS, JOHN (ca. 1266–1308). Born in Scotland, Duns Scotus probably obtained his early education at the Franciscan convent in Dumfries, where he entered the order by 1280. He was sent to Oxford no later than 1290 to begin his studies and may have received his baccalaureate there. He lectured on the *Sententiae* of Peter Lombard at both Cambridge and Oxford. Ordained at Northampton in 1291, he went to the University of Paris in 1293 to study for the master's degree in theology, but before completing the degree he returned in 1296 to Oxford, where he commented again on the *Sententiae*. Duns Scotus went once more to Paris in 1302 and continued to lecture on the *Sententiae*. He was exiled in 1303, when he opposed Philip IV the Fair's appeal to a general council against Pope Boniface VIII. He returned in 1304, received the master's degree in 1305, and became regent master in the Franciscan chair for the next two years. In 1307, he was sent to teach at the Franciscan house in Cologne, where he died on November 8, 1308.

Possibly nicknamed "the Scot" early on at Oxford, he engaged in theological disputes with such skill and subtlety that he posthumously received the scholastic titles *Doctor subtilis* and *Doctor maximus*. Duns Scotus extended the moderate realism of Albert the Great and Thomas Aquinas but was intent less on constructing a system than on pursuing, often relentlessly, solutions to philosophical and theological problems that he considered to blemish the systems of his predecessors, such as the issues of contingency, individuation, distinctions and univocity of being, the primary object of the intellect, and the relation of love and will to intellect. He took immense pains to distinguish and then properly to reconnect the tasks and provinces of "philosophy" and "theology." He reacted to the efforts of Henry of Ghent and others to reestablish Augustinianism at the University of Paris. Although influenced by Avicenna, he rejected both Augustinian and Aristotelian epistemologies and argued that being, not God or material things or their essences, is the primary object of knowledge. He saw theology as a science whose knowledge provides the "practical" means to reach the soul's supernatural end. He emphasized the special uniqueness, or *haecceitas*, of the individual, because each is the product of God's thoroughly free creative and loving election. He distinguished between nature and will and argued that the will alone possesses fundamental freedom and is the primary rational power. He analyzed the human capacity to love and to experience God. He distinguished the will's inclination to choose what is advantageous from its "affection" toward justice for its own sake, which enables the will to love God for God's sake and not for the soul's advantage alone. Scotus's concept of intellectual intuition explained the capacity of beatific and unique temporal visions of God in contrast with the ordinary process of knowledge through sensory experience. He promoted the doctrine of the Immaculate Conception and maintained that the Incarnation would have occurred regardless of the Fall.

Duns Scotus's principal composition was his commentary on the *Sententiae*. The two chief extant versions are included in the collections *Opus Oxoniense*, especially the *Ordinatio*, and in the *Opus Parisiense*, also known as the *Reporta Parisiensia*, containing notes from students and scribes. The *Tractatus de Primo Principio* and the quodlibetal questions represent his mature theological constructions. He also composed a series of logical commentaries, in the genre of "questions," on Porphyry's *Isogoge* and Aristotle's *Categories*. Especially interesting are his *Collationes*, composed of disputations held at Oxford and Paris. His writings not only influenced later Franciscan theologians, known as the Scotists, but also such diverse figures as Galileo, C.S. Peirce, and Gerard Manley Hopkins.

H. Lawrence Bond

[See also: ALBERT THE GREAT; AQUINAS, THOMAS; PETER LOMBARD; PHILOSOPHY; SCHOLASTICISM; THEOLOGY; UNIVERSITIES]

Duns Scotus, John. *Opera omnia*, ed. Luke Wadding. Lyon: Sumptibus Laurentii Durand, 1639.

———. *Opera omnia*. Vatican City: Typis Polyglottis Vaticanis, 1950–.

———. *Philosophical Writings*, trans. Allan B. Wolter. Indianapolis: Bobbs-Merrill, 1962.

———. *A Treatise on God as First Principle: A Latin Text and English Translation of the De Primo Principio*, ed. and trans. Allan B. Wolter. 2nd ed. Chicago: Franciscan Herald, 1983.

———. *Duns Scotus on the Will and Morality*, ed. and trans. Allan B. Wolter. Washington, D.C.: Catholic University of America Press, 1986.

———. *God and Creatures: The Quodlibetal Questions*, ed. and trans. Allan B. Wolter and Felix Alluntis. Princeton: Princeton University Press, 1975.

Schäfer, Odulfus. *Bibliographia de vita, operibus et doctrina I. D. Scoti saecula XIX–XX*. Rome: Orbis Catholicus, 1955.

Wolter, Allan B. *The Transcendentals and Their Function in the Metaphysics of Duns Scotus*. St. Bonaventure: Franciscan Institute, 1946.

DUPIN, JEAN (1302–1374). Prior of Saint-Martin-des-Champs and then abbot of Cluny (1369–74), Dupin wrote the *Livre de Mandevie* between 1324 and 1340. This allegorical text is composed of eight books, the first seven written partly in prose and partly in verse, and the last entirely in verse (5,062 octosyllables). The author is guided by the knight Mandevie (*mander* 'to improve' + *vie* 'life') along a route where he meets allegorical figures representing the vices and virtues and the various estates of society. The final book, entitled *Mélancolies sur les conditions de ce monde*, is a moral satire that summarizes the contents of the first seven books; here, he abandons the allegorical form and directly attacks the abuses of this world. The work was popular in its day, resulting in a number of manuscripts and two early printed editions, but it is generally condemned today for its banality.

Claude J. Fouillade

[See also: DIGULLEVILLE, GUILLAUME DE]

Dupin, Jean. *Les mélancolies de Jean Dupin*, ed. Lauri Lindgren. Turku: Turun Yliopisto, 1965. [Book 8 only.]

Karl, Ludwig. *Un moraliste bourbonnais du XIVe siècle et son œuvre: Le roman de Mandevie et les Mélancolies de Jean Dupin*. Paris: Champion, 1912.

EAUX ET FORÊTS. Forests, streams, and ponds were an important source of income to any seigneur fortunate enough to possess such resources, and all medieval kings attributed great importance to their forests. To prevent poaching and to administer sales of wood and other sources of revenue, the French crown employed a variety of forestry officials. A well-established local administrative structure was in place throughout the 13th century. Beginning with the reign of Philip IV, the system became more centralized. In March 1302, a royal ordinance on the administration of *eaux et forêts* established a two-tiered structure of "masters" and "guards." The main innovation of this reign, however, was the appointment of Philippe "le Convers" de Villepreux as *enquêteur* of the king's forests. Officials in the field reported to Villepreux, who traveled extensively to investigate the forest administration and eliminate abuses.

Villepreux remained active until 1327, and successors carried on his work until, in 1384, a royal ordinance formally established the position of "sovereign master of waters and forests." This position was abolished in 1413 but reinstated during the period 1428–1575. The *eaux et forêts* administration soon gained judicial responsibilities, and cases involving forest law were heard at the "marble table" in the royal palace.

John Bell Henneman, Jr.

Lot, Ferdinand, and Robert Fawtier. *Histoire des institutions françaises au moyen âge.* 3 vols. Paris: Presses Universitaires de France, 1957–62, Vol. 2: *Institutions royales* (1958).

Pegues, Franklin. *The Lawyers of the Last Capetians.* Princeton: Princeton University Press, 1962. [For the career of Villepreux.]

ÉBREUIL. The former abbey church of Saint-Léger at Ébreuil (Allier) was founded in the 11th century by the monks of Saint-Maixent. In 1180, Gregory VII placed the monastery under the *Rule* of St. Benedict.

Built in the 11th century, the church has a six-bay nave flanked by aisles (the southern aisle was reconstructed in the 18th century) and an apsed choir with ambulatory and five radiating chapels. The transept (the north arm of which is now partially destroyed) is surmounted by a cupola. The chevet, reconstructed in the Île-de-France style (late 12th–early 13th c.), has cross-ribbed vaults and is fortified by flying buttresses.

The western bell tower dates from the 12th century. Above a triple-arcaded porch rise two stories, each articulated by three arches echoing those on the ground level. The tympanum above the main portal displays Christ and two Apostles (12th c.). The walls of the tribune are embellished with late 12th-century wall paintings depicting St. Austremoine, St. Clement, St. Pancrace, the martyrdom of St. Valérie, and the archangels Michael, Gabriel, and Raphael.

Nina Rowe

Génermont, Marcel, and Pierre Pradel. *Allier: les églises de France: répertoire historique et archéologique par département.* Paris: Letouzey and Ané, 1938.

Rhein, André. "Ébreuil." *Congrès archéologique* (Moulin-Nevers) 80 (1913): 100–24.

ECBASIS CAPTIVI. The oldest beast epic known to us today, the 11th-century *Ecbasis captivi* is an important example of the genre. Written in Latin leonine hexameters, the text exists in two manuscripts, both now in the Royal Library, Brussels. The anonymous work seems to have been intended for readers who could appreciate the many references to Horace, Virgil, and Prudentius, to contemporary society, and to monastic life.

The story is told as a fable within a fable. At Eastertime, a calf is caught by a wolf who plans to eat it. The wolf has a dream that night warning him not to eat the calf. Meanwhile, the animals of the village have come to the wolf's cave. In an "inner fable," the wolf explains why he and the fox are enemies. Long ago, when the lion, the king of the beasts, was sick, all the animals except the fox came to him with cures. The wolf suggested that the fox be hanged. Warned by the panther, the fox appeared at court, justifying his absence with a tale of pilgrimage. His proposed cure involved flaying the wolf in order to make a blanket for the king. The fox then usurped the wolf's position as regent. Courtiers entertained the king; birds sang songs comparing the king's suffering to the passion of Christ. The lion recovered, and the animals returned to their homes, scorning the dying wolf. Switching to the outer fable, the story continues: the wolf shows himself to the angry crowd of village animals, thereby allowing the calf to escape. The wolf is impaled by the steer, and the fox writes his epitaph.

Noteworthy is the degree of humanization of the animals, which will be seen again in the *Ysengrimus* and in Old French fable literature, culminating in the *Roman de Renart*.

Wendy E. Pfeffer

[See also: FABLE (*ISOPET*); *RENART, ROMAN DE*; *YSENGRIMUS*]

Voigt, Ernst, ed. *Ecbasis cuiusdam captivi, das älteste Thierepos des Mittelalters*. Strassburg: Trübner, 1875.

Zeydel, Edwin H., ed. and trans. *Ecbasis cuiusdam captivi per tropologiam. Escape of a Certain Captive Told in a Figurative Manner: An Eleventh-Century Latin Beast Epic*. Chapel Hill: University of North Carolina Press, 1964.

ÉCHANSON/ÉCHANSONNERIE.

The Old French title *échanson* was given to the members of the household of a lord who were charged with serving drinks at the lord's table. The closest equivalent title in English is "cupbearer." In the royal household, servants bearing the title *scancio* (from Frankish **skanjo* 'drink-giver') or *pincerna* (a Late Latin word, from a Greek expression meaning "to mix for drinking") appeared under the early Merovingians, and their successors continued to function throughout the medieval period and beyond. The vernacular word was derived from the former title, but in official Latin the title *pincerna* prevailed from the time of the accession of Hugh Capet. Under the Merovingians, the cupbearers were placed under the authority of a *princeps pincernarum*, but under the early Capetians they seem to have been placed under the authority of the *bouteiller*, or butler, and their corps may have formed his whole department. In the ordinance of 1261 governing the royal *hostel* or inner household, the first document to describe the organization of the royal household of the Capetians, the *échansonnerie* or corps of *échansons* constituted one of the six *ministeria* or *mestiers* of the *hostel*, and it retained that standing thereafter. In 1291, the official staff of the *échansonnerie* consisted of five *échansons* (including the *grand échanson*, or head of the corps); four *bouteillers*, or butlers; four *barillers*, or coopers; two *portes-barils*, or barrel bearers; and one *potier*, or potter, but the number of officers tended to grow over time. The *échansons* and *bouteillers* probably served in rotation, as their successors cetainly did, and one was always in the personal service of the king.

D'A. Jonathan D. Boulton

[See also: *HÔTEL DU ROI*]

ÉCHECS AMOUREUX.

A commentary in French on an allegorical poem of the same name in the manner and tradition of the *Roman de la Rose*. This lengthy romance (some 30,000 octosyllabic lines), was composed by a layman between 1370 and 1430 and is extant in five manuscripts of the Bibliothèque Nationale. Built on a personified chess game, the *Échecs* contains a complete worldview—an informative mythography—that makes frequent references to the *Rose*. Close in time to writers following in the wake of the *Rose*, such as Chaucer, Deschamps, and Machaut, the mythography gives a reading that bears witness to its time, is not religiously motivated, and is the only complete explication of any poem in the tradition of the *Rose*. The unknown secular poet drew on many of the same sources as Jean de Meun but also found inspiration in Vincent de Beauvais, Brunetto Latini, and others.

Emanuel J. Mickel

[See also: JEAN DE MEUN]

Jones, Joan M., trans. *The Chess of Love*. Ann Arbor: University Microfilms, 1969.

Badel, Pierre-Yves. *Le roman de la Rose au XIVe siècle*. Geneva: Droz, 1980.

Sieper, Ernst. *Les échecs amoureux: Eine altfranzösische Nachahmung des Rosenromans und ihre englische Übertragung*. Weimar: Felber, 1898, pp. 97–113.

ÉCHIQUIER DE NORMANDIE.

Henry I, king of England and duke of Normandy (r. 1100/06–35), established the Échiquier de Normandie, like its counterpart in England, as a central commision of royal finances. Like the English exchequer, the Norman *échiquier* had two main branches: an auditing board that balanced royal accounts and received revenue owed to the king-duke and a court that sat in judgment of cases concerning royal finance. Under the Anglo-Norman kings, the Norman exchequer generally met twice a year at Caen, although not necessarily at the "hall of the exchequer" that still survives. During each session, royal officials sat at a large table covered with a checkered cloth to reckon and collect the rent owed from specific lands. The checkered cloth, which gave the institution its name (Lat. *scaccarium*, Fr. *échiquier* 'chessboard'), served as a sort of abacus, with counters that were moved and stacked in different columns to demonstrate amounts owed and received. As in England, the financial accounts of the exchequer were later recorded on rolls of parchment, the earliest of which survives for Normandy from 1180, in fragmentary form.

Lot, Ferdinand, and Robert Fawtier. *Histoire des institutions françaises au moyen âge*. 3 vols. Paris: Presses Universitaires de France, 1957–62, Vol. 2: *Institutions royales* (1958).

Luchaire, Achille. *Histoire des institutions monarchiques de la France sous les premiers Capétiens (987–1180)*. Paris: Imprimerie Nationale, 1883.

Tardif, Jules. *Études sur les institutions politiques et administratives de la France: période mérovingienne*. Paris: Picard, 1881.

After the conquest of Normandy by Philip Augustus in 1204, the Norman exchequer was moved first to Falaise and then to Rouen, where it remained, presided over by commissioners from Paris instead of Anglo-Norman lords. The exchequer's financial duties diminished under the French kings, but it remained the chief administrative and judicial body in Normandy.

Cassandra Potts

[See also: NORMANDY]

Stapleton, Thomas, ed. *Magni rotuli scaccarii Normanniae sub regibus Angliae.* 2 vols. London: Nichols, 1840.
Bouard, Michel de. "La salle dite de l'échiquier, au château de Caen." *Medieval Archaeology* 9 (1965): 64–81.
————, ed. *Histoire de la Normandie.* 2nd ed. Toulouse: Privat, 1987.
Haskins, Charles Homer. *Norman Institutions.* Cambridge: Harvard University Press, 1925.
Valin, Lucien. *Le duc de Normandie et sa cour (912–1204): étude d'histoire juridique.* Paris: Larose et Tenin, 1910.

ÉCOUIS. The church of Écouis (Eure) was founded by Enguerran de Marigny ca. 1310 and finished within three years. Its original timbered ceiling was replaced by red brick in the 18th century. The 14th-century statues within are among the masterpieces of Late Gothic sculpture: SS. Nicaise, Marguerite, François, Martin, Laurent, Cécile, Agnès, Jean-Baptiste, and particularly a splendid Véronique displaying the head of Christ on her veil.

William W. Kibler/William W. Clark

[See also: MARIGNY, ENGUERRAN DE]

Régnier, Louis. *L'église Notre-Dame d'Écouis.* Paris: Champion, 1913.

EDUCATION. The educational system in 5th-century Gaul was based on the Greco-Roman model, which, like the Germanic one, was male-oriented. Boys were educated at home until age seven, when they were sent to a primary school to learn to read, write, and count (unless the family had means to provide a private tutor), then at twelve to a secondary school to learn Greek and Latin grammar, and at fifteen possibly to one of the rare centers of higher learning to study rhetoric. These schools declined and eventually disappeared in the following centuries.

Germanic society emphasized the practical education of young men as warriors; their skills were perfected largely through hunting. Christianity reoriented written culture toward the sacred writings and taught the masses through sermons and the liturgy. In the early Middle Ages, centers of learning were primarily religious, both clerical and monastic. Charlemagne issued capitularies requiring each diocese and monastery to have a school. The great monastic schools, such as Saint-Gall and Saint-Riquier, boasted fine libraries. The program studied comprised the Trivium (grammar, logic, and rhetoric) and the Quadrivium (geometry, arith-metic, astronomy, and music); the Carolingian reform of handwriting and the 10th-century introduction of punctuation facilitated reading. But even greater changes were taking place outside the monastery. The church to a large extent succeeded in christianizing the practical warrior education of the military elite through the ideals and institutions of chivalry. Changes in the liturgy emphasized the predominant role of the priest. And the schools that were to be the most influential in the coming centuries, many of which were to develop into universities, were growing in revived urban centers, such as Orléans, Paris, and Montpellier, influenced by the Italian schools in Bologna and Salerno.

Besides these universities, municipal lay schools developed in the 12th century in Flanders and by the 14th in many other regions. These schools, financed by the municipalities, taught the bases of the Trivium. Colleges for poor pupils were founded, often by papal initiative, starting in the 14th century. Children of the humbler classes received practical and manual education in apprenticeships in the trades, and the poorest probably were put to work at about age seven. Also characteristic of the late Middle Ages is the increasing vulgarization of religious knowledge to the laity, as seen in the preaching efforts of the mendicant orders, the foundation of religious communities for laymen, and the proliferation of religious woodcut images and, by the end of the 15th century, of books.

Throughout the Middle Ages in France, the entire Jewish population learned to read in separate schools. There were at all times both supporters and opponents of female education; women were educated largely at home or in convents in the early Middle Ages. In the high and late Middle Ages, while women were generally excluded from the universities, there was nonetheless a tendency to favor some female education, as witness Héloïse and Christine de Pizan and the widespread iconographic motif of the Virgin reading at the moment of the Annunciation.

Leah L. Otis-Cour

[See also: CHARTRES; LIBERAL ARTS; SCHOOLS, CATHEDRAL; SCHOOLS, MONASTIC; UNIVERSITIES]

Initiation, apprentissage, éducation au moyen âge (*Actes du Ier Colloque International de Montpellier* (*Université Paul Valéry*) *de Novembre 1991.* Published as Cahiers du CRISIMA 1. Montpellier: Université Paul Valéry, 1993.
Rouche, Michel. *L'enseignement, des origines à la Renaissance.* Paris: Nouvelle Librairie de France, 1981. [Vol. 1 of *Histoire générale de l'enseignement et de l'éducation en France,* ed. Louis-Henri Parias.]

EDWARD I (1239–1307). King of England and duke of Aquitaine (1272–1307). Henry III of England's grant of Gascony to Edward gave his son the start on a career that was to engage him in the last Anglo-French war of the 13th century. Nonetheless, Edward did not enjoy real control over the administration of Gascony until he became king of England and duke of Aquitaine in 1272. It was in part the tension between these two positions that led to war with Philip IV.

In 1273, Edward did homage to Philip III for Gascony and then visited his duchy, where he captured his rebellious vassal Gaston de Béarn. Their dispute was negotiated to an end in 1278. On leaving for England, Edward appointed his first seneschal, whose administration was unpopular and resulted in a number of cases appealed to the Parlement de Paris, cases that had no grave diplomatic repercussions. Edward himself resolved problems arising from the Treaty of Paris, gaining most notably the Agenais in the Treaty of Amiens (1279). His fortune held when Philip III's death in 1285 kept Edward from having to choose between, on the one hand, the demands of his Gascon vassals not to fight in Aragon and his own policy of peace on the Continent, and, on the other, his duty as a vassal of the king of France to participate in the invasion of Aragon.

Edward's relations with the newly crowned Philip IV appeared amiable in 1286, when he returned to Gascony. Edward performed homage, compromised over Quercy, and mediated between Philip and Aragon. This harmony did not last. From 1292, conflicts between English and French sailors led to appeals to Philip. The issue came to involve Edward's feudal status in Gascony when Philip emphasized an incident between crews of English ships and a ship from Bayonne. The situation that Edward had always sought to avoid was realized. He refused summons to appear before the Parlement de Paris. To Edward, however, the crisis appeared to have been averted in 1294 with a secret arrangement whereby, in return for surrendering Gascony to Philip, Edward would receive back Gascony with Philip's sister Marguerite in marriage. But once Philip took custody of Gascony, he broke this agreement and the war began. Edward's troubles in Scotland and Wales kept him from pursuing his cause forcefully until 1297, when, as an ally of its count, he landed in Flanders. A truce and papal mediation soon followed. Edward married Philip's sister but did not regain all of Gascony until 1303, when rebellion in Bordeaux and his other difficulties brought Philip to hand over Edward's duchy. In 1306, Edward granted Aquitaine and the Agenais to his son, Edward, Prince of Wales. The prince's officials took charge of these lands in 1307, and Edward I died that same year.

Michael Burger

[See also: PHILIP III THE BOLD; PHILIP IV THE FAIR]

Chaplais, Pierre. *English Diplomatic Practice*. London: Her Majesty's Stationer's Office, 1975–82.
———. *Essays in Medieval Diplomacy and Administration*. London: Hambledon, 1981.
Labarge, Margaret Wade. *Gascony, England's First Colony 1204–1453*. London: Hamish Hamilton, 1980.
Prestwich, Michael. *Edward I*. Berkeley: University of California Press, 1988.
Trabut-Cussac, Jean-Paul. *L'administration anglaise en Gascogne sous Henry III et Édouard I de 1254 à 1307*. Geneva: Droz, 1972.
Vale, Malcolm. *The Angevin Legacy and the Hundred Years War, 1250–1340*. Oxford: Blackwell, 1990.

EDWARD II (1284–1327). King Edward I of England relinquished the duchy of Aquitaine to his son, the future Edward II, in 1306. After his father's death the next year, Edward II inherited, along with the English throne, the generations-old quarrel of the Plantagenêts with the kings of France over the family's French lands. In an attempt to secure peace, Pope Boniface VIII had arranged in 1299 a betrothal between Edward and Isabella, daughter of King Philip IV of France; the marriage took place early in 1308. Nonetheless, the fundamental problem of reconciling Edward's status as an independent monarch with his position as vassal of the French king caused two recurrent tensions: conflicts over appeals by Edward's Gascon subjects to the Parlement de Paris and insistence by the French crown that Edward do homage, a claim exacerbated by the rapid turnover of French kings during Edward's reign. France's aid to Scotland in its resistance to Edward added to the difficulties. Official attempts at mediation, as at the Process of Périgueux in 1311, achieved little, but Edward's personal efforts, such as his journey to Paris to do homage in 1313, smoothed over some of the problems.

Ultimately, the tension between the two crowns erupted in the War of Saint-Sardos. In 1323, one of Edward's vassals violently resisted attempts to construct a French royal bastide near the priory of Sardos in the Agenais. This incident and Edward's failure to do homage to King Charles IV of France since the latter's accession in 1322 led Charles to declare Edward's lands forfeit in 1324. Warfare in that year reduced Edward's holdings to a coastal strip running from Bordeaux to Bayonne. In 1325, Queen Isabella traveled to France and negotiated a settlement for Edward with her brother Charles: Edward was to do homage and regain his lost territory. Edward fell ill, and his son, the future Edward III, took his place, after receiving the duchy from his father. Charles failed to return the conquered lands, so in 1326 Edward II resumed administration of Aquitaine. That year, however, Isabella and her lover, Roger Mortimer, invaded England and overthrew Edward II before he could act effectively in the duchy.

Donald F. Fleming

[See also: ISABELLA OF FRANCE; SAINT-SARDOS]

Brown, Elizabeth A.R. "The Political Repercussions of Family Ties in the Early Fourteenth Century: The Marriage of Edward II of England and Isabelle of France." *Speculum* 63 (1988): 573–95.
Chaplais, Pierre. *Essays in Medieval Diplomacy and Administration*. London: Hambledon, 1981.
Fryde, Natalie. *The Tyranny and Fall of Edward II, 1321–1326*. Cambridge: Cambridge University Press, 1979.
Kicklighter, Joseph A. "French Jurisdictional Supremacy in Gascony: One Aspect of the Ducal Government's Response." *Journal of Medieval History* 7 (1979): 127–34.
Labarge, Margaret Wade. *Gascony, England's First Colony 1204–1453*. London: Hamish Hamilton, 1980.

EDWARD III (1312–1377). King of England and claimant to France. The son of Edward II and Isabella of France,

Edward III became king of England in 1327, when his mother led a coup that deposed his father. Through his mother, Edward was the grandson of Philip IV of France and nephew of Louis X, Philip V, and Charles IV. He was therefore nearer in relation to the last Capetians than was Philip VI of Valois. But the successions of Philip V and Charles IV had established precedents excluding the succession of daughters, and the French princes decided in 1328 to exclude those whose claim was through the female line. At that time, and in 1329 and 1331, Edward had rendered homage to Philip VI for his French fiefs, acts implying acceptance of Philip's succession. But despite this Valois diplomatic victory, the issue of Edward's claim to the throne did not disappear, and it became a major subtheme of the Hundred Years' War.

Edward laid claim to the throne in 1337 and by 1340 was using the title "King of France." His reasons for reviving his claim were twofold. First, it transformed the feudal dispute over Gascony that had triggered the war from an unequal contest between the king of France and a rebellious vassal to a contest between equals. Second, it allowed Edward's partisans in such areas as Flanders and Brittany to support his cause without technically rebelling against the throne. It was thus an important diplomatic and propaganda tool in his war with France.

How seriously did Edward take his claim? There is little doubt that his major aim in the war was to defend and secure his patrimony in Gascony, and in a number of negotiations he seemed willing to relinquish his claim to the throne of France in exchange for full sovereignty (rather than feudal tenure) over a Gascony freed of French territorial inroads. Edward was a master opportunist, and keeping his claim alive gave him many opportunities. Yet it is also probable that Edward and many of his English followers thought that his becoming king of two kingdoms was at least within the realm of possibility. Indeed, in the three years after the capture of King John II at Poitiers in 1356, culminating in the campaign against Reims and Paris in 1359, Edward must have felt within reach of this goal. In fact, it was always unlikely that Edward could have been accepted as king by a sufficient number of the French nobility. His great-grandson Henry V actually came closer to making good on the family claim.

Stephen Morillo

[See also: CALAIS; CHARLES V THE WISE; CRÉCY; HUNDRED YEARS' WAR; ISABELLA OF FRANCE; PHILIP VI]

Le Patourel, John. "Edward III and the Kingdom of France." *History* 43 (1958): 173–89.
Perroy, Édouard. *The Hundred Years War*, trans. W. B. Wells. New York: Capricorn, 1965.
Prestwich, Michael. *The Three Edwards: War and State in England, 1272–1377.* New York: St. Martin, 1980.

EDWARD, THE BLACK PRINCE (1330–1376). Son of Edward III of England. Edward of Woodstock, Prince of Wales and Aquitaine, known as the Black Prince, was the eldest son of Edward III and the father of Richard II. He was the chief English commander in France throughout the second phase of the Hundred Years' War (1355–70) and from 1362, by his father's creation, the ruler of Aquitaine, England's greatest possession in France. Like his father first and foremost a warrior, he was regarded by his contemporaries as the model of chivalry and the greatest knight living. His personal prowess aside, he was a competent though not brilliant field commander and was victorious in a series of campaigns in France and Spain. Heir apparent all his life, he died a year before his father, and the throne went to his ten-year-old son, Richard.

Edward's military career began at the age of sixteen, at his father's greatest victory, the Battle of Crécy (1346). After a profitable *chevauchée* (or mounted raid) through Languedoc in 1355, Edward led another the next year into Poitou. Although caught and forced to fight by John the Good, king of France, near Poitiers, he emerged victorious in one of the most spectacular English successes of the war. Outnumbered by perhaps 25,000 French, Edward's 6,000 troops, mostly longbowmen, handily won the Battle of Poitiers on September 19, 1356, capturing thousands of prisoners, including the king of France himself. His second most notable victory, at Nájera (April 3, 1367), was the culmination of a campaign launched into Spain to settle the succession of Castile, and though it resulted in the temporary victory of the pro-English party there and the capture of Bertrand du Guesclin, the constable of France, it also seems to have been in this campaign that Edward contracted the disease that incapacitated him in the last years of his life.

His rule in Aquitaine cannot be called successful; he was never able to discipline the unruly Gascon nobility, and the taxation required for the campaign of Nájera sparked a revolt in 1369 that Edward met with great cruelty, the most notable example of which was the destruction of Limoges. In 1371, in bad health and unable to stem the encroachment of the French into Aquitaine, he returned to England, where he became involved in the domestic politics of the last years of his father's reign until his premature death in 1376.

Monte L. Bohna

[See also: CHANDOS HERALD; CRÉCY; EDWARD III; HUNDRED YEARS' WAR; NÁJERA; POITIERS]

Chandos Herald. *Life of the Black Prince by the Herald of Sir John Chandos,* ed. and trans. Mildred K. Pope and Eleanor C. Lodge. Oxford: Clarendon, 1910.
Barber, Richard. *The Life and Campaigns of the Black Prince.* Woodbridge: Boydell, 1986.
Hewitt, Herbert J. *The Black Prince's Expeditions of 1355–1357.* Manchester: Manchester University Press, 1958.

EGIDIUS DE MURINO (fl. mid-14th c.). Music theorist named as the author of *De motettis componendis,* which gives some simple precepts for the composition of isorhythmic motets. One source names him as the author of the *Tractatus de diversis figuris,* elsewhere ascribed to

Philippus de Caserta. He is praised as a theorist along with Philippe de Vitry and Jehan des Murs in two 14th-century motets that enumerate names of musicians in their texts, *Musicalis scientia/Scientie laudabili* and *Apollinis eclipsatur/Zodiacum signis.* He may be identifiable with the composer Egidius named in the Chantilly codex (ca. 1400) or with a number of other musicians of the same name.

Benjamin Garber

[See also: COMPOSERS, MINOR (14th CENTURY); ISORHYTHMIC MOTET; MUSIC THEORY; PHILIPPE DE VITRY; PHILIPPUS DE CASERTA]

Leech-Wilkinson, Daniel. *Compositional Techniques in the Four-Part Isorhythmic Motets of Philippe de Vitry and His Contemporaries.* 2 vols. New York: Garland, 1989.

EINHARD (ca. 770–840). Frankish scholar and biographer. The author of the 9th-century *Vita Caroli,* the first known western biography of a secular leader since late antiquity, was born to noble parents in the Main Valley. As a boy, Einhard was educated at the monastery of Fulda and soon after 791 went to the palace school at Aix-la-Chapelle, headed by Alcuin. He became a close friend of Charlemagne (r. 768–814) as well as his adviser, official representative, and probably the supervisor of the building program at Aix.

After Charlemagne's death in 814, Einhard remained at the court of Louis the Pious (r. 814–840), as adviser to Louis's eldest son, Lothair I (d. 855). In 830, he retired with his wife, Imma, to a monastery founded by him on lands granted by Louis. The area became known as Seligenstadt (City of the Saints) after the church there that Einhard had dedicated to SS. Marcellinus and Peter and in which he placed relics of the two saints acquired by nefarious means. He died March 14, 840.

Einhard's extant writings include seventy letters, the treatise *Historia translationis BB. Christi martyrum Marcellini et Petri,* the short *Quaestio de adoranda cruce,* and the *Vita Caroli* (ca. 829–36). The biography is based on Einhard's personal knowledge of Charlemagne and events at Aix between his arrival there and 814, as well as on written sources and likely the eyewitness accounts of older members of the court for the years before ca. 791. Composed in an excellent Latin, the *Vita* shows the influence of various classical writers, above all of Suetonius's *De vita Caesarum,* particularly the life of Augustus. Like many Carolingian authors, however, Einhard did not borrow mindlessly from his sources but selected and manipulated his material to accord with what he wanted to say.

Celia Chazelle

[See also: BIOGRAPHY; CHARLEMAGNE]

Einhard. *Einhard: Vita Caroli Magni. The Life of Charlemagne,* ed. and trans. Evelyn Scherabon Firchow and Edwin H. Zeydel. Coral Gables: University of Miami Press, 1972.
Thorpe, Lewis, trans. *Einhard and Notker the Stammerer: Two Lives of Charlemagne.* Harmondsworth: Penguin, 1969.

Beumann, Helmut. *Ideengeschichtliche Studien zu Einhard und anderen Geschichtsschreibern des früheren Mittelalters.* Darmstadt: Wissenschaftliche Buchgesellschaft, 1969.
Fleckenstein, Josef. "Einhard, seine Gründung und sein Vermächtnis in Seligenstadt." In *Das Einhardkreuz: Vortraege und Studien der Muensteraner Diskussion zum arcus Einhardi,* ed. Karl Hauck. Göttingen: Vandenhoeck and Ruprecht, 1974, pp. 96–121.

ELEANOR OF AQUITAINE (1122–1204). When Duke William X of Aquitaine died in 1137, he entrusted his fifteen-year-old daughter and heiress, Eleanor, to King Louis VI. The king quickly arranged to marry her to his own heir, Louis VII (r. 1137–80). Eleanor brought to the marriage the important duchy of Aquitaine, the southwest quadrant of France, which had long been fairly independent of the king.

Eleanor and Louis VII, who succeeded to the throne almost immediately after his marriage, were related within the "forbidden degrees," and their union was thus officially consanguineous. Abbot Bernard of Clairvaux pointed out to them that they were related within "four or five degrees": both were descended from King Robert II, as Eleanor's great-grandmother Hildegard, wife of William VIII of Aquitaine, was the illegitimate daughter of Duke Robert of Burgundy, King Robert's son. However, the royal couple paid little attention to this relationship until, after ten years of marriage, it became clear that Eleanor was not going to produce a son. Their only child so far had been a daughter, Marie.

By 1147, when Eleanor accompanied her husband on the Second Crusade—and was rumored to have flirted with her uncle, Raymond of Antioch—Louis began to express doubts about the legitimacy of their marriage. Although when they stopped in Rome on the way home, the pope urged them not to be concerned about the degree of their relationship (and indeed, promised them a son), Louis continued to worry. Finally, in 1152, after the birth of Alix, their second daughter, he divorced Eleanor on the grounds of consanguinity and shortly thereafter married Constance of Castile.

Louis apparently had not anticipated that Eleanor would herself remarry, but she did so at once, to Henry, the young count of Anjou and duke of Normandy, who became Henry II of England (r. 1154–89) just two years later. She took Aquitaine with her to her new husband, and the duchy remained in English hands until the Hundred Years' War.

Eleanor and Henry had a son, William, within a year—indicating that Louis's failure to have a male heir had not been *her* fault. Although this son quickly died, Eleanor and Henry had four more: Henry, Richard (king of England, 1189–99), Geoffroi, and John (king, 1199–1216). Eleanor retained her title of duchess of Aquitaine even while she was also queen of England, and when her son John succeeded to the English throne she personally did homage for Aquitaine to the French king so that John would not have to do so.

Eleanor seems to have used her position, both as queen of France and as queen of England, to act as a patron of the arts. Louis and Eleanor contributed to the rebuilding of Suger's abbey church of Saint-Denis, often credited with being the first Gothic church, and Eleanor gave the abbey, by her husband's hand, a crystal vase of ancient origin. In England, a whole series of manuscript illuminations, begun after Eleanor married Henry, are believed to have been influenced by artistic styles from the southwest of France. Because her grandfather Guilhem IX wrote troubadour lyrics, some scholars have also thought that Eleanor's court may have influenced the rise of romances and courtly poetry in northern France in the mid-twelfth century.

Eleanor was a formidable woman—Henry II found it necessary to keep her imprisoned for part of their married life—who, as wife of two kings and mother of two more, strongly influenced the politics of both France and England in the 12th century. When she died in 1204, she was buried at the Poitevin foundation of Fontevrault, where Henry and Richard were already buried.

Constance B. Bouchard

[See also: ANJOU (genealogical table); AQUITAINE (genealogical table); CAPETIAN DYNASTY (genealogical table); FONTEVRAULT; HENRY II; LOUIS VII; SAINT-DENIS; SUGER]

Suger. *Vie de Louis de Gros par Suger suivie de l'Histoire du roi Louis VII*, ed. Auguste Molinier. Paris: Picard, 1887.

Duby, Georges. *The Knight, the Lady and the Priest: The Making of Modern Marriage in Medieval France*, trans. Barbara Bray. New York: Pantheon, 1983.

Kibler, William W., ed. *Eleanor of Aquitaine: Patron and Politician*. Austin: University of Texas Press, 1976.

Facinger, Marion F. "A Study of Medieval Queenship: Capetian France, 987–1237." *Studies in Medieval and Renaissance History* 5 (1968): 3–47.

Kelly, Amy Ruth. *Eleanor of Aquitaine and the Four Kings*. Cambridge: Harvard University Press, 1950.

ELECTION. The word "election" has an ecclesiastical meaning, describing the process for choosing abbots and bishops. It also referred to the geographical jurisdiction of the the fiscal officers called *élus*. Yet it had a particular significance when applied to organs of the royal government. It meant the selection of officials on the basis of merit, rather than their being handpicked by the king and a few of his closest advisers. Election was an attempt to eliminate corruption, nepotism, and cronyism. Various ordinances of reform in the 14th and 15th centuries required that officers be "elected" by the royal council, which often contained men who were not of the king's own choosing. In practice, this requirement of election was not always observed, but it was relatively successful in the case of the Parlement de Paris, where "election" became a form of cooptation that gave this court considerable practical independence.

John Bell Henneman, Jr.

Cazelles, Raymond. *Société politique, noblesse et couronne sous Jean le Bon et Charles V*. Geneva: Droz, 1982.

Lot, Ferdinand, and Robert Fawtier. *Histoire des institutions françaises au moyen âge*. 3 vols. Paris: Presses Universitaires de France, 1957–62, Vol 2: *Institutions royales* (1958).

ELEDUS ET SERENE, ROMAN DE. Extant in a single manuscript (B.N. fr. 1943), *Eledus et Serene* is a Picard reworking of an earlier (lost) Occitan adventure tale, possibly in the form of a chanson de geste. The lovers are mentioned in several southern French works, the earliest being Matfre Ermengaud's *Breviari d'Amor* of 1288. Lacking its ending and with important lacunae, the poem nonetheless contains 7,314 octosyllabic couplets in its French version, which was composed in the early 14th century. It may be a fictionalized account of the struggles of the Romans and West Goths with the Vandals.

William W. Kibler

Reinhard, John R., ed. *Le roman d'Eledus et Serene*. Austin: University of Texas Press, 1923.

ELNE. Founded by Celto-Iberians in the 7th century B.C., the *oppidum* of Illiberis occupied a naturally fortified site above the River Tech. Renamed Helena in the 4th century A.D. in honor of St. Helena, the mother of the emperor Constantine, Elne (Pyrénées-Orientales) was the administrative and religious capital of the Roussillon during the Visigothic period. It was made a bishopric in 571, fell to the Muslims in 719, and was recaptured by the Franks fifty years later. Its richer neighbor Perpignan, however, eventually supplanted Elne in the 17th century. The Romanesque cathedral of Sainte-Eulalie, consecrated in 1069, is one of the oldest in France. Its basilica plan, with double-aisled nave and no transept or apse, dates from the 11th century. The chevet is surrounded by the foundations of a Gothic chancel, vestige of a grandiose 14th-century project that was soon abandoned. Only the south tower, decorated with arcatures and Lombard arcades, is original. The side chapels are Gothic. The adjacent cloister (1172–86), is constructed of two sets of twin colonnettes alternating with square pillars of white marble. The historiated capitals, originally polychrome, contain sculpted scenes of a remarkable realism. Only the south walk abutting the church is wholly original (1175); the other parts were reconstructed in the 14th century after the town was sacked in 1285. Of the original two stories, the upper was destroyed in the 19th century.

William W. Kibler/William W. Clark

Durliat, Marcel. "Le mobilier de la cathédrale d'Elne" and "Le cloître d'Elne." *Congrès archéologique (Roussillon)* 112 (1954): 146–60.

Grau, Roger. "La cathédrale d'Elne." *Congrès archéologique (Roussillon)* 112 (1954): 135–45.

ÉLU. When the French crown sought to levy taxes in the early years of the Hundred Years' War, some of the resistance to paying arose from popular distrust of the honesty of the collectors. In 1340, an assembly in northern France promised a tax if its own appointees collected it. In 1345, the king proposed that each region choose the people who would collect the taxes. In 1347–48, the Estates of several regions granted large sums to be collected by their own nominees. In 1355–56, the Estates General of Languedoïl promised taxes to be appointed under the supervision of persons appointed (*élus*) by the Estates. The use of such *élus* not only appeared as a reform to those who distrusted royal officers, but it provided useful new machinery for dealing with "extraordinary" revenues that were becoming increasingly regular. In 1360, when the ransom of John II required collection of the *aides* and *gabelles* on a regular basis, the *élus* became permanent royal officials. An *élu* had responsibility for a geographical district that became known as an *élection*. For most of the 14th century, this term was not used because it coincided with a diocese of the church. Subsequently, however, the units were divided and the *élections* became smaller and more numerous.

John Bell Henneman, Jr.

[See also: ELECTION; *GÉNÉRAUX*]

Henneman, John Bell. *Royal Taxation in Fourteenth Century France: The Development of War Financing, 1322–1356.* Princeton: Princeton University Press, 1971.

EMBER DAYS. *See* LITURGICAL YEAR

ENAMELING. The fusing onto a metallic surface of a vitreous glaze, usually composed of 50 percent sand, 35 percent red lead, and 15 percent soda or potash, stained to various hues by the addition of metallic oxides. This is then cast in a slab, which is reduced to a fine powder and washed to remove impurities. The resultant powder is then

Plaque showing the Pentecost (Mosan 1150–75). Champlevé enamel on copper gilt. *Courtesy of The Cloisters Collection, Metropolitan Museum of Art, New York.*

Chasse. Champlevé enamel and copper gilt on wood. *Courtesy of the Metropolitan Museum of Art. Gift of J. Pierpont Morgan, 1914.*

Enamel: Cross (French, ca. 1190), Champlevé enamel and gilding on copper. *Courtesy of the Cleveland Museum of Art. Gift from J.H. Wade, 23.1051.*

Enamel: Three Worthies in Fiery Furnace (Mosan). *Courtesy of the Museum of Fine Arts, Boston.*

packed into cells on the metallic base, leveled, dried, fired, ground, and polished.

Decorative enameling, practiced by the Celts and Romans in Gaul before the Middle Ages, seems to have been eclipsed during the early-medieval period by inlaid jewelry. Enameling was revived in the 12th century in Limoges and the Rhine and Moselle river valleys. Originally confined to monastic workshops, by the mid-13th century production became commercialized, with a resultant diminution in quality. Most enamelwork, whether monastic or commercial, was for religious purposes: reliquaries, pyxes, gospel covers, censers. Among secular objects, one finds candlesticks, marriage caskets, and heraldic emblems.

The enameling techniques practiced in medieval France were principally *cloisonné* and *champlevé*. In *cloisonné* work, the powdered enamel is placed in separate cells formed from narrow metal strips or wires, to which the fused enamel adheres. These strips form a raised design above the baseplate, to which they are often soldered; the metalwork is ancillary to the enamel. In *champlevé* work, which largely supplanted *cloisonné* by the mid-12th century, the enamel fills cells encised in the baseplate, and the metal (often gold) left after cutting away the cells takes on a design importance of its own, with the metal and enamel playing harmoniously off one another.

Mosan and Rhenish enamels are easily distinguished by their colors, with greens and yellows predominating. A rich blue dominates most Limoges work. Limoges specialized in *champlevé* caskets and reliquaries, to which was often riveted a head or figure in high relief by repoussé (modeling sheet metal with hammer and punches).

In the 14th century, a new style imported from Italy and Spain, *basse-taille*, began to predominate in French production. This is a combination of techniques including

carving, engraving, and enameling. Precious gold or silver was engraved and carved in bas-relief, then transparent enamel was fused level with the uncarved parts, allowing the design to show through. The most splendid example of *basse-taille* is the gold cup commissioned by John, duke of Berry, as a gift for his brother, King Charles V. It is now in the British Museum.

William W. Kibler

Gauthier, Marie-Madeleine. *Émaux limousins: champlevés des XIIe, XIIIe et XIVe siècles.* Paris: Le Prat, 1950.
Maryon, Herbert. "Fine Metal-Work." In *A History of Technology,* ed. Charles Singer. 5 vols. Oxford: Clarendon, 1954–56, Vol. 2: *The Mediterranean Civilizations and the Middle Ages, c. 700 B.C. to c. A.D. 1500,* pp. 449–84.
———. *Metalwork and Enameling: A Practical Treatise on Gold and Silversmiths' Work and Their Allied Crafts.* 5th ed. New York: Dover, 1971.

ENFANCES. The genre in medieval literature in which the legend of the hero is completed by a return to his birth and youth is called *enfances.* Primarily a phenomenon of epic literature as works complete in themselves, *enfances,* composed after the narration of the heroes' adult exploits, seek to outline the origins of their lineage. The mystery of the birth, which frequently involves a fault committed by a supernatural being, is elucidated, often with recourse to folktale and myth. The heroes' first exploits mark them as destined for greatness. Most of the epic heroes are the subject of such treatment of their early lives, for example: the *Enfances de Charlemagne,* the *Enfances Guillaume,* the *Enfances de Vivien,* the *Enfances Ogier,* and the *Enfances Godefroi* in the *Naissance du chevalier au Cygne.* There is often a partial treatment of the theme, as in the figure of Guiot in the *Chanson de Guillaume,* but in these instances the treatment varies, with emphasis on the youth's fear and inability to tolerate hunger. The genre is visible in the apocryphal *Évangiles de l'enfance,* which recount the childhood of Christ, such as the *Protoévangile de Jacques* and the *Livre de la naissance de la bienheureuse Marie et de l'enfance du Sauveur,* and elements persist in romances, where there is a search for the hero's origins (Gauvain, Lancelot, Merlin, Tristan). As an echo of the Middle Ages, Rabelais made the genre larger than life in his parodic genealogy and youthful exploits of first the son, Pantagruel, then the father, Gargantua.

Joan B. Williamson

[See also: APOCRYPHAL LITERATURE; CHANSON DE GESTE]

Combarieu, Micheline de. "Enfance et démesure dans l'épopée médiévale française." *Senefiance* 9 (1980): 405–56. [Issue on *L'enfant au moyen âge.*]
Horrent, Jacques. *Les versions françaises et étrangères des "Enfances de Charlemagne."* Brussels: Académie Royale de Belgique, 1979.
Lods, Jeanne. "Le thème de l'enfance dans l'épopée française." *Cahiers de civilisation médiévale* 3 (1960): 58–62.

Rank, Otto. *Le mythe de la naissance du héros suivi de la légende de Lohengrin.* Paris: Payot, 1983.

ENQUÊTEUR. Beginning ca. 1247, the crown periodically commissioned a small group of special investigators and judges, probably no more than twenty or so at a time, to uncover abuses of power, malfeasance, and other irregularities committed by public officials in France. To Louis IX belongs the credit of creating these *enquêteurs,* although earlier and contemporary rulers in France and elsewhere occasionally commissioned vaguely similar sorts of investigators. Louis's *enquêteurs,* largely Dominican and Franciscan friars, were originally commissioned to receive complaints on the eve of the king's departure for crusade. The courts they held as they traveled about the country were deliberately informal in order to encourage ordinary people to appear before them. Other lords, like the king's brother Alphonse of Poitiers, followed Louis's lead and employed *enquêteurs* in their lands as well. After Louis's return from crusade in 1254, he regularly issued new commissions to panels of *enquêteurs* right up until his death. The same pattern is discernible in the policies of Alphonse.

After the king's death in 1270, *enquêteurs* were retained in the royal administration, and much of their work, even if more formally conducted than in Louis's time, continued in the tradition he set. Although friars were rarely appointed after 1270, the *enquêteurs* continued to investigate abuses of power and initiate salutary reforms. Known as *enquêteurs-réformateurs* on account of this work, their investigative powers could nevertheless be used in less beneficent ways. The later Middle Ages saw the *enquêteurs* employed as agents to mulct local communities and provincial notables, to such an extent that there was sometimes strong opposition to their being commissioned in the first place.

William Chester Jordan

Brown, Elizabeth A.R. "Royal Commissioners and Grants of Privilege in Philip the Fair's France." *Francia* 13 (1985): 151–90.

Fournier, Pierre-François, and Pascal Guébin, eds. *Enquêtes administratives d'Alfonse de Poitiers.* Paris: Imprimerie Nationale, 1959.

Henneman, John Bell. "*Enquêteurs-Réformateurs* and Fiscal Officers in Fourteenth-Century France." *Traditio* 24 (1968): 309–49.

Jordan, William. *Louis IX and the Challenge of the Crusade: A Study in Rulership.* Princeton: Princeton University Press, 1979.

ENSENHAMEN. *See* DIDACTIC LITERATURE (OCCITAN)

ENTRIES, ROYAL. During the 14th century, French towns instituted a unique ceremony for receiving kings and particularly for celebrating the *joyeux avènement* of a new monarch. The ceremony was a composite of ecclesiastical, courtly, guild, and legal-administrative gestures for deal-ing with dignitaries. Because the clergy had always led visiting kings to the central church of a town, the ecclesiastical rites of *adventus regni* supplied a ritual core that the nonecclesiastical participants extended and embellished. From the 1350s, the clergy made new kings confirm their coronation promises to preserve the church and clergy as part of the welcoming ceremony. Secular corporations soon had the promises and privileges given to them by previous kings reenacted and confirmed by the kings they received in their midst. By the middle of the 15th century, the series of encounters between the king and various corporations were considered a single event, the "happy" or "joyous" entry ceremony. This ceremony consisted of extramural urban processions to greet the king, an intramural royal procession with urban escorts, and the production of spectacles along the processional route. In their entries, new kings carried the aura of the coronation throughout the realm, but they also exited from ritual theaters choreographed by clergy and nobility and entered one staged by inhabitants of the civic sphere.

Entry ceremonies were vehicles for urban-style politics of decorum. Various privileged and social groups found a place to assert their identities and to propagate ideas: youth groups greeted kings beyond the city's gates with songs, mock battles, or morality plays; guilds in livery met them to profess loyalty; magistrates in their robes of office rendered obeisance and solicited the confirmation of local liberties. During the 15th century, royal officials and—in cities where they resided—parlements exited the town and joined the celebrations, to acknowledge the king as their head and to receive promises of continuing royal favor. The entry procession grew to become the largest and most frequent form of assembly with the king, and its ordonnance was overseen by the parlements and royal chancery. Its performance was scripted to be a mirror for the prince and a model for the community: a rehearsal for the accord and reciprocity between kings and cities that should guide both of them in mundane political practices.

The ceremony appropriated forms of expression from many quarters. For example, the addition of the canopy over the king in urban processions resulted from the interplay between Corpus Christi celebrations and the occasion of an entry. The feudal *droit de gîte* (hospitality) was one among many precedents for gift giving and hospitality at royal entries. Liturgical and biblical plays augmented the culture of the entry. Poets and clergy advanced the coronation ceremony and the notion of the royal cult in entry pageantry. Communal and juridical corporations set forth their views with equal ardor. The ceremony flourished both because it opened the public space to interplay among social, political, and aesthetic practices and because its form corresponded to the actual social practices and political roles of its participants. Only in the 17th century was the entry confined to a celebration of royal power alone and only then consistently tagged "royal" rather than a "joyous" or "happy" entry.

Records of entries were kept in guild and town registers, royal chanceries, and parlements, as well as occasionally in chronicles. They are among the best sources for street theater, public art and rhetoric, and popular culture generally. Entries flourished in France and throughout Europe in the late Middle Ages because the *bonnes villes* and fledgling royal administrations found them useful ways of defining a state tradition and for establishing a record of political relations. The discourse of the entry ceremony affirmed peace and law; it sought to eclipse the horror of military conquest and sacking. Towns and officials staged them to give form to actions before the ruler and to place their acts securely into the public laws and history of France.

Lawrence M. Bryant

[See also: CORONATION/CONSECRATION OF KINGS; PROCESSION]

Bryant, Lawrence M. *The King and the City in the Parisian Royal Entry Ceremony: Politics, Ritual, and Art in the Renaissance.* Geneva: Droz, 1986.

Coulet, Noël. "Les entrées solennelles en Provence au XIVe siècle." *Ethnologie française* 7 (1977): 68–86.

Guenée, Bernard, and Françoise Lehoux. *Les entrées royales françaises de 1388 à 1515.* Paris: CNRS, 1968.

ERIUGENA, JOHANNES SCOTTUS (810–877). Little is known about the life of this Irish scholar who taught the liberal arts at the court of Charles the Bald in and around Laon in northern France. Although the earlier view of Eriugena as a lonely genius in a barren period has recently been modified, the wealth of his erudition and his remarkable knowledge of Greek make him stand out among his Carolingian contemporaries.

Eriugena first emerges as a participant in the controversy surrounding predestination in 850–51. In his campaign against the monk Gottschalk of Orbais, archbishop Hincmar of Reims asked Eriugena to refute Gottschalk's doctrine of double predestination (to eternal life and to eternal death), which the latter claimed to be the true Augustinian teaching. Eriugena, who is not known to have been a monk or priest, wrote *De divina praedestinatione* in compliance with Hincmar's request. Instead of advocating Hincmar's view of a single predestination, however, Eriugena argues that predestination is nothing more than God's eternal knowledge, and that humans have freedom of choice even after the Fall. After the condemnation of his views at the councils of Valence (855) and Langres (859), Eriugena never returned to the arena of ecclesiastical politics.

For Eriugena's next assignment, Charles the Bald ordered a new translation be made of the works of Pseudo-Dionysius the Areopagite. The Greek texts of this 6th-century Syrian mystic, who was identified with St. Denis, patron of the Franks, had become available through a codex donated by the Byzantine emperor Michael the Stammerer to Louis the Pious in 827. Through his reading and translation of Pseudo-Dionysius, Eriugena was introduced to certain features of Greek theology, such as the unfolding of the universe according to procession and return and the methods of negative and affirmative theology, which he subsequently incorporated into his own thinking. He also translated Maximus the Confessor's *Quaestiones ad Thalassium* and Gregory of Nyssa's *De hominis opificio.*

Eriugena's major intellectual achievement was the *Periphyseon*, or *On the Division of Nature.* This work, written ca. 864–66, is the mature product of his reflections on Greek theology as well as on the western tradition of Augustine and Boethius. Its most impressive feature is its scope: an inclusive treatment of all of nature, under which he classifies both God and creation. Structuring the universe along the lines of procession and return, Eriugena discusses all major theological and philosophical issues of his time in a dialectical fashion. The discussion of nature ranges from God (nature that creates but is not created) through a treatment of the divine ideas (nature that is created and creates) and of spatiotemporal creations (nature that is created and does not create) back to God (nature that does not create and is not created). In addition, his *Expositiones in ierarchiam coelestem* (on Pseudo-Dionysius's *Celestial Hierarchy*) and his homily *Vox spiritualis aquilae* have become famous.

Due to the later association of Eriugena with the heresy of Amalric of Bène, Pope Honorius III in 1225 ordered that all extant copies of the *Periphyseon* be burned. Yet, through direct and indirect influence, Eriugena's voice continued to be heard in the medieval Christian-Platonic tradition. In connection with idealist philosophy and process theology, Eriugena's ideas also stimulate modern thinking.

Willemien Otten

[See also: CHARLES II THE BALD; DENIS; GOTTSCHALK; HINCMAR OF REIMS; PHILOSOPHY; PSEUDO-DIONYSIUS THE AREOPAGITE; THEOLOGY]

Eriugena, Johannes Scottus. *Commentaire sur l'évangile de Jean,* ed. and trans. Édouard Jeauneau. Paris: Cerf, 1972.

———. *De divina praedestinatione liber,* ed. Goulven Madec. CCCM 50. Turnhout: Brepols, 1978.

———. *Expositiones in ierarchiam coelestem,* ed. Jeanne Barbet. CCCM 31. Turnhout: Brepols, 1975.

———. *Periphyseon (De divisione naturae),* ed. I.P. Sheldon-Williams and Ludwig Bieler. 3 vols. Dublin: Dublin Institute for Advanced Studies, 1968–81.

———. *Periphyseon = On the Division of Nature,* trans. Myra I. Uhlfelder with summaries by Jean A. Potter. Indianapolis: Bobbs-Merrill, 1976.

Marenbon, John. *From the Circle of Alcuin to the School of Auxerre: Logic, Theology and Philosophy in the Early Middle Ages.* Cambridge: Cambridge University Press, 1982.

Moran, Dermot. *The Philosophy of John Scottus Eriugena: A Study of Idealism in the Middle Ages.* Cambridge: Cambridge University Press, 1990.

O'Meara, John J., and Ludwig Bieler, eds. *The Mind of Eriugena.* Dublin: Irish University Press, 1973.

Otten, Willemien. *The Anthropology of Johannes Scottus Eriugena.* Leiden: Brill, 1991.

ERWIN DE STEINBACH (fl. late 13th–early 14th c.). Since Johann Wolfgang von Goethe's paean to Erwin de Steinbach in *Von deutscher Baukunst,* published in 1772, the name of this master mason at Strasbourg cathedral has been enshrined in the pantheon of legendary builders. The historical reality of his career can be pieced together from scattered documents and inscriptions: a 1284 contract mentions Erwin as master of the works; a destroyed 1316 inscription in the chapel of the Virgin, erected against the jubé, names him as its builder; and the master of Niederhaslach is identified as the son of Erwin, "once the master of the works at the cathedral of Strasbourg," on his 1330 tomb. The epitaph of an Erwin who was "governor" of the Strasbourg fabric and died on January 17, 1318, may commemorate a financial administrator rather than the builder; the famous 1277 inscription that appended the Steinbach surname to Erwin and credited him with beginning the "glorious work" of the west façade disappeared before 1732 and cannot be verified. Nevertheless, if Erwin was master from the late 1270s into the early 14th century, he would have built a considerable portion of the west front and may well have been the author of Projects B, B1, and D, which are among the most stunning architectural drawings ever produced. Project B, which corresponds closely to the portal zone as built, introduced the dramatic freestanding tracery that screens the masonry of the façade block. Based on the vocabulary of French Rayonnant architecture, these Projects showcase the elaborate optical effects that preoccupied designers in the later 13th century.

Michael T. Davis

[See also: GOTHIC ARCHITECTURE; STRASBOURG]

Geyer, Marie-Jeanne. "Le mythe d'Erwin de Steinbach." In *Les bâtisseurs des cathédrales gothiques*, ed. Roland Recht. Strasbourg: Éditions les Musées de la Ville de Strasbourg, 1989, pp. 322–29.
Recht, Roland. "Dessins d'architecture pour la cathédrale de Strasbourg." *Oeil* 174–75 (1969): 26–33, 44.
———. "Le mythe romantique d'Erwin de Steinbach." *Information d'histoire de l'art* 15 (1970): 38–45.
———. *L'Alsace gothique de 1300 à 1365: étude d'architecture religieuse.* Colmar: Alsatia, 1974.
Will, Robert. "Les inscriptions disparues de la *porta sertorum* ou *Schappeltür* de la cathédrale de Strasbourg et le mythe d'Erwin de Steinbach." *Bulletin de la cathédrale de Strasbourg* 14 (1980): 13–20.

ESQUIRE/*ESCUIER*. By ca. 1100, the term *escuier* (derived from Lat. *scutarius* 'shield man' but normally represented in Latin by *scutiger* 'shield bearer' or *armiger* 'arms bearer') was generally applied, with *va(s)let* 'young vassal' and *damoisel* 'lordling,' to young men serving as apprentices to knights. Down to ca. 1180, most sons of knights who were not destined for a clerical career probably undertook this apprenticeship, and most of those who did so seem to have been dubbed to knighthood around the age of twenty-one. After that date, however, the growing expense of knighthood led increasing numbers of apprentice knights to postpone formal dubbing, or *adoubement*, indefinitely and to serve in battle with less than full equipment through most or all of their lives. Such adult but undubbed noblemen were known at first by a variety of titles, including *valet* and *damoisel* (later *damoiseau*,

Occitan *donsel*), but the first of these titles survived in this sense only in Poitou and Saintonge, and the second only in Burgundy and the south generally. In northern regions, all other titles were entirely replaced ca. 1250 by *escuier*, which gave rise to the English equivalent "esquire" and its shortened form "squire." By 1300, a substantial majority of the male members of the knightly nobility of France never received knighthood, and, according to region, *valet, damoiseau,* or *escuier* had come to be used by these men as a title of nobiliary rank on the model of *chevalier*, in the form N de X, *valet/damoiseau/escuier*. At first, these three equivalent titles designated the lowest grade of the nobility, below that of simple knight, but from ca. 1300 they were increasingly reserved for those undubbed noblemen who were rich enough to serve, like knights, as heavy cavalry; nobles who could not afford to fight in this way were increasingly distinguished by the title "gentleman" (*gentilhomme*), common to all persons of noble or "gentle" birth.

After ca. 1200, adult nobles of the rank of esquire commonly formed part of the household of kings, princes, and barons, performing functions thought to be appropriate to their rank. Some of these were distinguished by special titles, such as the *ecuyer-valet tranchant*, or "cutting squire," who cut his lord's meat.

D'A. Jonathan D. Boulton

Contamine, Philippe. *Guerre, état et société à la fin du moyen âge: études sur les armées des rois de France 1337–1494.* Paris: Mouton, 1972.
Guilhiermoz, Paul. *Essai sur l'origine de la noblesse en France au moyen âge.* Paris: Picard, 1902.

ESTAMPIE. Although few examples survive, we know that the *estampie* was both a poetic form and a dance. The poetry is described in the anonymous *Doctrina de compondre dictatz* (ca. 1300) and the *Leys d'Amors* compiled by Guillaume Molinier during the first half of the 14th century. The subject of the *estampie* was "love and homage"; it was set in couplets with a refrain and possibly one or two *envois*.

The musical *estampie*, described by Johannes de Grocheio (ca. 1300) as having both vocal and instrumental forms, was composed of verses and refrains, with melodies and couplets. The melody of the refrain differs from that of the verse, thus distinguishing the *estampie* from other types of musical dance forms, such as ballade, virelai, and rondeau, in which the melody of the refrain was also used in the verse. Twenty-six poetic texts without music and two with music have been identified as *estampies*, but none seem to have the required refrain. Seven complete instrumental *estampies* and one fragment survive, all conforming to Grocheio's description.

Nothing is known of the steps, but Grocheio described it as a complicated and elegant dance. The word *estampie* may come from the Latin *stante pedes*, meaning standing, or stationary, feet.

Timothy J. McGee

[See also: DANCE; GROCHEIO, JOHANNES DE]

Aubry, Pierre, ed. *Estampies et danses royales, les plus anciens textes de musique instrumentale du moyen âge.* Paris: Fischbacher, 1907.

McGee, Timothy, J., ed. *Medieval Instrumental Dances.* Bloomington: Indiana University Press, 1989.

Streng-Renkonen, Walter O., ed. *Les estampies françaises.* Paris: Champion, 1930.

ESTATES (GENERAL). An assembly of nobles, clergy, and representatives of towns from the whole kingdom or at least most of Languedoil. Although the term was not used until 1484, "the three estates" are mentioned as early as the mid-14th century, and it is convenient to refer to the Estates General when distinguishing assemblies of this type from those of a more restricted social and geographical character.

Great barons and prelates had long attended royal assemblies of one sort or another, and the king had sometimes summoned nonnoble laymen as individuals who were experts on the matter to be discussed. "Estates" applies only to assemblies to which numbers of towns were told to send representatives. Such a summons not only established towns as the voice of the "third estate" (nonnoble laymen), but it also gave assemblies a representative character for the first time. After 1484, nobles and clergy were convened in most districts to choose representatives when the Estates were summoned, but for a long time persons from other than the third estate were summoned as individuals and did not serve as representatives of their social peers.

When the towns began sending representatives, the model for such action was the naming of a proctor (*procurator*) to represent a corporate body's legal interests before a court. Towns gave their representatives a "procuration" empowering them to act on behalf of the town. This fact has persuaded some historians to view the early Estates as analogous to a judicial proceeding subject to the rules of Roman and canon law, but in practice those who attended these assemblies seem not to have accepted that model. Their actions suggest that they understood these assemblies in more traditional, feudal terms, in which an obligation to give counsel was far more meaningful than the right of consent described in Roman law. Particularly when money was at stake, representatives often avoided making a binding commitment to anything for which they had not received precise advance instructions.

The king convened assemblies like the Estates General when he hoped such a body would be useful to him. At rare moments of crisis, the Estates tried to limit the king's authority in some area, but such exceptional action only persuaded the king to call the assembly less frequently. The Estates General was not a body whose function was to limit royal power.

The Estates General first appeared as a sort of propaganda forum in which the royal government hoped to drum up support for some potentially controversial policy. The earliest documented examples of this sort of assembly belong to 1302, 1308, and 1312, when Philip IV sought support for his ecclesiastical policies. Over the next ten years, numerous assemblies of different sorts were convened. A group of assemblies, divided by region and/or the estate in attendance, sometimes had the effect of composing what amounted to an Estates General, but the government was still experimenting.

When asked to grant taxes, the Estates usually avoided a binding commitment. In 1333, 1343, and 1346, the Estates convened, each time to deal with a crisis and with related financial issues. They gave their endorsement to financial arrangements that required subsequent local ratification. At the end of 1347, the Estates General bargained at length over measures to reform the government and agreed in principle to a large tax that, again, would be paid according to the arrangements made at regional Estates.

The Black Death frustrated the work of the Estates of 1347, and the disastrous Battle of Poitiers would do the same to the Estates that met eight years later. The Estates General met frequently during the years of the king's captivity (1356–60) but the efforts of their leaders to intimidate the royal government, and their failure to deliver the taxes they promised, persuaded the crown that they were more troublesome than useful. Meetings in 1363, 1367, and 1369 proved far more helpful to the king, but in the troubled reign of Charles VI, the meetings of the Estates (1381 and 1413) led to large uprisings.

Charles VII had frequent recourse to the Estates (generally of Languedoil only) in the years 1422–39 but still found them reluctant to rise above regional differences and make binding commitments to a royal tax. When they finally did make such a grant, he kept collecting the taxes without recourse to future assemblies. The last two medieval meetings of the Estates General were in 1468, when Louis XI used the meeting as an old-style propaganda forum, and 1484, when his daughter and son-in-law, who had custody of the young Charles VIII, used it to defuse opposition.

The Estates General could prove useful to the king, especially in time of crisis, but it could also prove troublesome. It never acquired a role that made it indispensable and therefore never became a regular institution of the French government.

John Bell Henneman, Jr

[See also: ASSEMBLIES; *CONSEIL*; ESTATES (PROVINCIAL)]

Henneman, John Bell. *Royal Taxation in Fourteenth Century France: The Captivity and Ransom of John, 1356–1370.* Philadelphia: American Philosophical Society, 1976.

Major, J. Russell. *Representative Institutions in Renaissance France 1421–1559.* Madison: University of Wisconsin Press, 1960.

Strayer, Joseph R., and Charles H. Taylor. *Studies in Early French Taxation.* Cambridge: Harvard University Press, 1939.

ESTATES (PROVINCIAL). Representative assemblies of many types and composition flourished in medieval France, becoming more active in the 13th century. In the following two centuries, membership in these meetings was frequently drawn from three social orders, or estates: the clergy, the nobility, and the townspeople. Such assemblies were held at various jurisdictional levels. Those at the provincial level were known as provincial Estates.

The chief importance of French provincial Estates from the royal point of view was that they provided a medium through which the consent of the influential inhabitants of the province could be obtained for extrafeudal taxes so urgently needed during the Hundred Years' War and the turbulent period following. They were important to the inhabitants because, in times of war, they maintained and repaired local transportation routes. They also appointed deputies to present special grievances to the crown and to defend their interests before king and council.

The origins of French provincial Estates were multiple. They appear to have developed from the gradual blending of several main concepts to meet changing conditions. Feudalism, with its network of reciprocal relationships, gave the lord the right to summon his vassals to his court to give him aid and counsel. Many vassals soon saw advantages in attending and claimed the right to be summoned. A feudal council, gradually enlarged to include other men of influence, provided the framework for many, but not all, of the provincial Estates.

Also, the concept was growing throughout medieval Europe that one or more individuals could legally represent and commit their constituents. This depended on the organization of society into corporate groups, such as towns, monastic orders, cathedral chapters, and estates. The representative principle by which individuals could defend the rights of these corporate bodies and represent them at the court of lord or king was derived from Roman and canon law and their use of the power of attorney, through which a person could appoint someone to act for him in a court of law. The new corporate groups gradually obtained the same right and began to appoint proctors (*procuratores*) to act in their name.

By the 11th century, some ecclesiastical writers were describing French society in terms of three functional groups: those who worshiped, those who fought, and those who worked, reflecting roughly the social situation at the time. Thus emerged the belief that there were three estates: the clergy, the nobility, and the third estate. With the subsequent growth of towns and lay education, the third estate became a large conglomerate of diverse groups, chiefly inhabiting the towns. This concept of three estates led to the tripartite division of many of the assemblies that emerged.

In the case of provincial Estates that developed from the feudal council, only direct vassals of the lord were originally summoned. As a class of wealthy burghers emerged whose aid and counsel became valuable, lords gradually began inviting their representatives to attend as well. Delegates from other corporate bodies, such as cathedral chapters and monasteries, were also included.

In the 13th century, the French kings greatly enlarged the royal domain and extended their powers of suzerainty. As they were also fighting larger domestic and foreign wars, their expenses for government and warfare had increased substantially. They could no longer obtain sufficient revenue from the royal domain.

The outbreak of the Hundred Years' War placed even greater demands on the royal treasury. In the mid-14th century, the Estates General, or the regional Estates of Languedoil and Languedoc, were summoned several times to consider taxation. The experiment was unsuccessful because local Estates refused to accept their decisions. The crown then normally imposed and collected taxes without consent until the death of Charles VI. Then the dauphin, seeking recognition as legitimate heir to the throne, resorted once again to the use of Estates General and provincial Estates. Over a fifteen-year period beginning in 1421, he summoned the Estates General or the Estates of Languedoil almost every year. They voted financial assistance, but to collect the money locally usually required negotiating with the provincial and local Estates. After 1439, Charles VII imposed taxes without consulting any central assembly, but, where customary, he continued to summon the provincial Estates to vote their share.

Estates continued to flourish in these regions, fostered by the strong provincial loyalties that characterized late-medieval France. By the late 15th century, some began to assume a stable composition and procedure. They consented to direct and sometimes indirect taxes. They comprised more than half of France, including such important provinces as Normandy and Languedoc. Elsewhere, Estates henceforth met rarely and never became part of the institutional structure.

During the reign of Charles VII, many of the more active Estates established a permanent bureaucracy and archives and levied taxes to support their own and royal expenses. The provincial Estates never challenged the authority of the monarchy and French kings usually accepted their role until well into the 17th century. They provided a useful forum for contact between the king and persons of influence throughout France.

The growth of French representative institutions was part of a trend marked by the development of similar institutions throughout much of Europe during the late Middle Ages. There were similar reasons for these parallel movements: the need by rulers to consult with their subjects and seek their support and money, especially for war; the desire of the politically active classes to act during emergencies, protect their own interests, and restrain princely excesses; and the severe economic, social, political, and demographic crises of the period, which exacerbated the level of warfare and shook the foundations of government.

In France and several other states, these developments occurred primarily at the local and provincial rather than at the national level. Because of the large size of the country, the deep-rooted particularism of the people, and the fact that the local and provincial Estates presented no particular threat to the monarchy, they were much more durable than the central assemblies.

Joseph M. Tyrrell

[See also: ASSEMBLIES; *CONSEIL*; ESTATES (GENERAL); ÉTIENNE DE FOUGÈRES]

Bisson, Thomas. *Assemblies and Representation in Languedoc in the Thirteenth Century*. Princeton: Princeton University Press, 1964.

Cadier, Léon. *Les états de Béarn depuis leurs origines jusqu'au commencement du XVIe siècle*. Paris: Imprimerie Nationale, 1888.

Dussert, Auguste. *Les états du Dauphiné aux XIVe et XVe siècles*. Grenoble: Alliers Frères, 1915.

Gilles, Henri. *Les états de Languedoc au XVe siècle*. Toulouse: Privat, 1965.

Major, J. Russell. *Representative Institutions in Renaissance France, 1421–1559*. Madison: University of Wisconsin Press, 1960.

———. *Representative Government in Early Modern France*. New Haven: Yale University Press, 1980.

Prentout, Henri. *Les états provinciaux de Normandie*. 3 vols. Caen: Lanier, 1925–27.

Thomas, Antoine. *Les états provinciaux de la France centrale sous Charles VII*. Paris: Champion, 1879.

Tyrrell, Joseph M. *A History of the Estates of Poitou*. The Hague: Mouton, 1968.

ESTOUTEVILLE. The Estoutevilles were a great seigneurial family whose senior line was based at Vallemont in the Caux district of eastern Normandy. They claimed descent from a legendary Viking ancestor, Stoot (or Estout) the Dane. Robert I d'Estouteville participated in the Norman conquest of England, and his several sons by a second, Saxon, wife produced the English Stutevill families.

The main line of the Estoutevilles, in Normandy, survived until the 18th century, being loyal to the French crown after royal acquisition of Normandy in 1204. Jean II, lord of Estouteville, was captured by the English at Agincourt in 1415 and lost his lands in the subsequent English conquest of Normandy. His elder son, Louis, however, profited from the French reconquest and regained the family lands, while Jean's younger son, Guillaume (1403–1483), held several bishoprics and abbacies, became archbishop of Rouen and a cardinal, and was a major figure at the papal court for several decades.

The family produced prominent cadet lines, the most important being the lords of Torcy, descended from Estout, a younger son of Jean I, lord of Estouteville (d. 1259). Estout's son, Jean, married the daughter of a constable of France and sired a large and influential family. Their oldest son, Colart (a diminutive of Nicolas), had a military career that spanned half a century (1364–1415), and he became a royal chamberlain and councilor as well as serving fourteen years as seneschal of Toulouse. Among the younger sons were Thomas, bishop of Beauvais; Guillaume, bishop of Évreux and then Auxerre; Jean, lord of Charlesmesnil, a prominent member of the Marmouset party at the French court under Charles VI; Estout, abbot of Cérisy; and Jeannet the younger, lord of Villebon and a member of the royal household. A large number of adult Estoutevilles were active in public life toward the end of the 14th century, but many of them died in the period 1396–1416 and the family never again enjoyed so much influence.

John Bell Henneman, Jr.

La Morandière, Gabriel de. *Histoire de la maison d'Estouteville en Normandie*. Paris: Delagrave, 1903.

ESTRABOT. The *estrabot* was a French lyric of mockery and insult mentioned only by Benoît de Sainte-Maure, Guillaume de Machaut, and perhaps Clément Marot. The two surviving Occitan monorhymed Alexandrine *estribotz* by Peire Cardenal and Palais, from which *estrabot* is probably derived, suggest that it was fixed in form. Its satirical nature has disappeared in the subsequent Spanish *estrambote* and Italian *strambotto*.

Roy S. Rosenstein

Chambers, Frank M. *An Introduction to Old Provençal Versification*. Philadelphia: American Philosophical Society, 1985, pp. 85–86.

Ricketts, Peter T. "L'estribot: forme et fond." In *Mélanges de langue et littérature occitanes en hommage à Pierre Bec*. Poitiers: CESCM, 1991, pp. 475–83.

Vatteroni, Sergio. "Peire Cardenal et *l'estribot*." *Medioevo Romanzo* 15 (1990): 61–91.

ÉTAMPES. Only three bays of the crypt remain of the original church of Notre-Dame-du-Fort in Étampes (Essonne). Founded in the 11th century by Robert II the Pious, the existing church (begun ca. 1140) is unusual in plan. A narthex, flanked on either side by irregularly shaped chapels, precedes the short nave with aisles. The choir (12th–13th c.) has a straight east end and an ambulatory of irregular plan. The early 13th-century western façade is placed obliquely in front of the bell tower, which surmounts the narthex. Its central tympanum depicts the Annunciation, the Visitation, the Nativity, the Annunciation to the Shepherds, and the Flight into Egypt. The portal on the south side of the church is directly dependent on the Royal Portal at Chartres. Here, jamb sculptures of Old Testament figures are crowned by capitals in the form of a frieze representing scenes from the life of Christ. The now mutilated tympanum depicts Christ surrounded by angels.

The church of Saint-Basile has a square bell tower, transept, and façade depicting the Last Judgment, all dating from the 12th century. The rib-vaulted nave, double aisles, and choir with aisles were reconstructed in the 15th century. Renaissance additions include lateral chapels and stained-glass windows.

Other buildings in Étampes include the church of Saint-Martin (begun ca. 1140), which has a dangerously leaning late 12th- or early 13th-century tower; the church of Saint-Gilles, founded in 1123 by King Louis VI; and the huge 12th-century keep, or donjon (ca. 1176–1236), where Philip II Augustus confined his queen, Ingeborg of Denmark, from 1201 to 1213.

Nina Rowe

Guibourgé, Léon. *Étampes, ville royale.* Étampes, 1958.

Lefèvre, Louis-Eugène. *Le portail royal d'Étampes.* 2nd ed. Paris: Picard, 1908.

Lefèvre-Pontalis, Eugène. "Étampes." *Congrès archéologique (Paris)* 82 (1919): 3–49.

Nolan, Kathleen. "Narrative in the Capital Frieze of Notre-Dame at Étampes." *Art Bulletin* 71 (1989): 166–84.

ÉTIENNE DE BOURBON (ca.1190/94–ca. 1261). Born at Belleville-sur-Saône, Étienne studied at Mâcon and later at Paris. He entered the Dominican order in 1223 at Lyon. One of the first inquisitors, Étienne was present at Mont-Aimé in 1239 when 180 heretics were burned to death. After traveling extensively, he retired to Lyon in 1250 to compile a collection of exemplary lives. Combining medieval folkloric images and details with theological interests, the *Tractatus de diversis materiis predicabilibus* is organized according to the seven gifts of the Holy Spirit and is the first representative of this genre. Étienne died before the work was completed. He wrote five sections, on fear, piety, knowledge, fortitude, and wisdom (unfinished). More commonly known as *Tractatus de donis Spiritu Sancti* or *De septem donis Spiritu Sancti*, this work includes the first account of the legendary female pontiff Pope Joan. Étienne's collection includes almost 3,000 stories from a great number of sources. Since his accounts of heroic Christians have affinities with the figures of Arthurian romance, his work registers a movement between and integration of popular and theological literary interests and cultures.

E. Kay Harris

[See also: FOLKLORE; PREACHING]

Étienne de Bourbon. *Anecdotes historiques, légendes et apologues, tirés du recueil inédit d'Étienne de Bourbon, dominican du XIIIe siècle,* ed. A. Lecoy de la Marche. Paris: Renouard, 1877. [Partial edition.]

Munro, Dana Carleton, ed. *Medieval Sermons-Stories: Revised Edition of Monastic Tales of the XIIIth Century.* Philadelphia: University of Philadelphia Press, 1901.

Berlioz, Jacques, and J.L. Eichenlaub. "Les tombeaux des chevaliers de la Table ronde à Saint-Émiland (Saône-et-Loire)?: à propos d'un exemplum d'Étienne de Bourbon." *Romania* 109 (1988): 18–40.

ÉTIENNE DE FOUGÈRES (d. 1178). King's chaplain and member of the chancellery of Henry II Plantagenêt, Étienne de Fougères was appointed bishop of Rennes in 1168. His writings were principally in Latin and, of these, two saints' lives, those of St. Firmatus and Abbot Vitalis of Savigny, survive along with his account of the embellishment of his cathedral at Rennes. The only French poem ascribed to him, the *Livre des manières* (1174–78), is preserved in a single manuscript (Angers 304 [295], fol. 141–50). Dedicated to the countess of Hereford, it is written in the western dialect of the Plantagenêt domain in monorhymed quatrains of eight-syllable lines. Since all of Étienne's other

known writings were in Latin, the possibility exists that the *Livre des manières* is an anonymous translation from a Latin original by Étienne. The *Livre des manières* is the first of a number of Old French texts treating the estates of society. It is divided into two equal parts: lines 1–672 treat the higher orders of society (king, clergy, knights), while lines 677–1,344 discuss the lower estates (peasants, bourgeois, and women). Dividing these sections is the famous quatrain on social order:

> Li clerc deivent por toz orer,
> li chevalier sanz demorer
> deivent defendre et ennorer,
> et li païsant laborer.
> (ed. Lodge, ll. 673–76)

("Clerics should pray for everyone, knights unhesitatingly should defend and honor, and peasants labor.") The purpose of the poem is to summarize the church's teachings on the social and political problems of the day, which Étienne does in a practical rather than theoretical manner. He laments the absence of justice in this world and exposes the dangers of vanity, criticizing the rich for being slaves to money and the church hierarchy for not practicing virtue. Étienne closes by warning against concupiscence and by regretting his involvement with women in his youth.

Claude J. Fouillade

[See also: COURTESY BOOKS; ESTATES (PROVINCIAL); GUILLAUME LE CLERC; GUIOT DE PROVINS; HUGUES DE BERZÉ; JEAN DE MEUN; LI MUISIS, GILLES]

Étienne de Fougères. *Le livre des manières,* ed. R. Anthony Lodge. Geneva: Droz, 1979.

Langlois, Charles-Victor. *La vie en France au moyen âge de la fin du XIIe au milieu du XIVe siècle d'après des moralistes du temps.* Paris: Hachette, 1926.

ÉTIENNE TEMPIER (d. 1279). A former master in the University of Paris, Étienne Tempier became bishop of Paris and then, in 1270 and 1277, issued two condemnations of philosophical errors in the teachings of Parisian masters. The first condemnation, December 10, 1270, specified thirteen philosophical errors identified with the teachings of the so-called Latin Averroists, led by Siger de Brabant, and included such ideas as the oneness of the intellect, the eternity of the world, the mortality of the individual human soul. On March 7, 1277—the third anniversary of the death of Thomas Aquinas—Tempier condemned a list of 219 propositions and declared excommunicated those who held or defended them. This list, hastily compiled and unsystematic in presentation, was composed mostly of Averroist positions but included propositions drawn from Aquinas. Influenced by Franciscan masters and theologians of an Augustinian orientation, this condemnation hastened the separation of philosophical inquiry and theological reflection in the university faculties.

Grover A. Zinn

[See also: AQUINAS, THOMAS; ARABIC PHILOSOPHY, INFLUENCE OF; ARISTOTLE, INFLUENCE OF; PHILOSOPHY; SCHOLASTICISM; SIGER DE BRABANT; THEOLOGY]

Leff, Gordon. *Paris and Oxford Universities in the Thirteenth and Fourteenth Centuries: An Institutional and Intellectual History.* New York: Wiley, 1968.

EUCHARISTIC VENERATION AND VESSELS. The early church looked upon the eucharist more as an action than as an object. Veneration of the host in stasis was a distinctively medieval development. It was given impetus by the controversial views of Berengar of Tours (d. 1088) and the more orthodox responses that followed. Berengar did not altogether deny the Real Presence but held that no material change in the bread and wine was necessary to bring it about. The contrary view, the doctrine of Transubstantiation, was much discussed in the 12th century and defined as official church teaching by the Fourth Lateran Council of 1215. This theological ferment contributed to the popular movement of venerating the divine presence in the consecrated host. A prominent facet of this was an eagerness to gaze upon the host, which led to the ritual of the elevation. This originated in early 13th-century Paris, where the priest kept the host carefully concealed until the moment of consecration, when he held it aloft for all to see. The custom spread rapidly throughout Europe and became, along with the subsequently introduced elevation of the chalice, the dramatic high point of the Mass. Closely related was the feast of Corpus Christi, celebrated on the Thursday after Trinity Sunday; it was fervently championed by St. Juliana of Mont-Cornillon (d. 1258) and established by Pope Urban IV in 1264. The date came to be marked by a festive procession involving the entire population of a town as participants or spectators. The host was carried by the principal clergyman of the area, who stopped at set points to raise it in blessing over the faithful. This is the probable origin of the devotional practice known as the Benediction of the Most Blessed Sacrament. During the late Middle Ages, the ceremony was performed in church each evening after the singing of the *Salve Regina* at the close of Compline; this explains the French term for Benediction, *Salut*, which was applied also to the chant.

The principal eucharistic vessels are the chalice, ciborium, monstrance, and pyx. The chalice, used in the celebration of the Mass, was originally a glass cup similar to those in everyday use but came to be made of precious metal as early as the 4th century. In earlier centuries, the cup was broad, sometimes with handles, as it was used for the communion of the faithful, while it took on its familiar elongated shape in the Middle Ages when communion under the species of wine was reserved to the priest. The ciborium, of early-medieval origin, was shaped like a more ample chalice and was covered with a lid; its function was to store and to transport the hosts before and after consecration. The monstrance, or ostensorium, was used to display the host, as in Corpus Christi processions and at Benediction. Both its earlier form of a vertical glass cylin-der enclosed in a gothic gable and its later form of a flat glass window surrounded by emanating rays were derived from reliquary designs. The pyx was a small box of varying shapes used to house the host. Its most familiar form in later centuries was that of the flat cloth-covered case in which the priest carried communion to the sick; it can also be seen in miniatures of 15th-century French books of hours, suspended over the altar beneath a round canopy.

James McKinnon

[See also: JULIANA OF MONT-CORNILLON; MASS, CHANTS AND TEXTS]

Braun, Joseph. *Das christliche Altargerät in seinem Sein und in seiner Entwicklung.* Munich: Hueber, 1932.

Jungmann, Josef. *The Mass of the Roman Rite: Its Origins and Development,* trans. Francis X. Brunner. 2 vols. New York: Benziger, 1951–55.

EUDES (Odo; ca. 857–898). King of the West Franks (r. 888–98). The first king of the Robertian (Capetian) line, Eudes was the elder son of Robert le Fort, marquis of Neustria. Heroic defender of Paris during the Norse siege of 885–86, he succeeded Hugues l'Abbé (d. 885) as chief defender of Neustria. His prowess, the remoteness of the German Carolingian Arnulf, and the extreme youth of the French Carolingian heir apparent Charles the Simple led to his election as king after the deposition of Charles the Fat (887).

Eudes's election was opposed by Archbishop Foulques of Reims, who, after the king had suffered a series of defeats and when he was faced by a series of revolts, crowned the adolescent Charles the Simple in 893. Civil war engulfed the realm until Charles's submission in 897. Eudes died on January 1, 898, recommending the succession of Charles to his supporters but passing on his vast family lands and power to his brother, the future Robert I.

Eudes was the first of the Capetian kings to be interred at the abbey of Saint-Denis, which was to become the traditional burying place of the dynasty.

R. Thomas McDonald

[See also: ROBERT LE FORT]

Bautier, Robert-Henri. "Le règne d'Eudes (888–898) à la lumière des diplômes expédiés par sa chancellerie." Paris: Comptes Rendus de l'Académie des Inscriptions et Belles-Lettres, 1961.

Favre, Édouard. *Eudes, comte de Paris et roi de France (882–898).* Paris: Bouillon, 1893.

EUDES RIGAUD (d. 1275). Little is known of Eudes's life prior to his becoming a Franciscan ca. 1236, except that he was born in northern France to a devout family of the knightly class. By 1240, he was studying theology at Paris and succeeded John of La Rochelle in the Franciscan chair of theology a few years later. During his regency, ca. 1245, he commented on the first three books of Peter Lombard's

Sententiae and collaborated with three of his Franciscan colleagues in commenting on the *Rule of St. Francis* (*Expositio regulae quaturo magistrorum*). In March 1248, Eudes was elected to the archiepiscopal see of Rouen, where he served until his death.

As archbishop, Eudes served Louis IX on several missions, including the Treaty of Paris (1259), which saw the Plantagenêts cede Normandy to the Capetians. Eudes is perhaps best remembered for the careful records that he kept of his regular visits to the parishes and churches in his archdiocese to inquire into the lives of both clergy and religious. From these records, we get a clear picture of the life of the church in the third quarter of the 13th century (1248–69) and of the controversies and contentions, such as those of the Pastoureaux, that occupied the archbishop.

Mark Zier

[See also: FRANCISCAN ORDER; PASTOUREAUX]

Eudes Rigaud. *The Register of Eudes of Rouen*, ed. and trans. Sidney M. Brown and Jeremiah F. O'Sullivan. New York: Columbia University Press, 1964.

Schneyer, Johannes-Baptist, ed. *Repertorium der lateinischen Sermones des Mittelalters für die Zeit von 1150–1350*. 6 vols. Münster: Aschendorff, 1969–74, Vol. 4, pp. 510–16.

Andrieu-Guitrancourt, Pierre. *L'archévêque Eudes Rigaud et la vie de l'église au XIIIe siècle*. Paris: Sirey, 1938.

Darlington, Oscar G. *The Travels of Odo Rigaud, Archbishop of Rouen (1248–1275)*. Diss. University of Pennsylvania, 1938.

Henquinet, F.M. "Les manuscrits et l'influence des écrits théologiques d'Eudes Rigaud, OFM." *Recherches de théologie ancienne et médiévale* 11 (1939): 324–50.

Principe, W. "Odo Rigaldus, a Precursor of St. Bonaventure on the Holy Spirit as *effectus formalis* in the Mutual Love of the Father and Son." *Medieval Studies* 39 (1977): 498–505.

Thomson, Williell. *Friars in the Cathedral: The First Franciscan Bishops 1226–1261*. Toronto: Pontifical Institute of Mediaeval Studies, 1975, pp. 77–91.

EUGENIUS III (d. 1153). Pope. A disciple of St. Bernard of Clairvaux and a Cistercian abbot of Saints Vincent and Anastasius, Bernard of Pisa became Pope Eugenius III in 1145. Under his pontificate, the first formal crusade bull was issued in 1145. The crusade proved unsuccessful, and subsequently both Roger of Sicily and Louis VII of France urged Eugenius to begin a new one. Eugenius refused to accede to their wishes. Skilled in diplomacy, Eugenius had recognized the anti-Byzantine features of the proposed crusade, and he had no wish to antagonize the Byzantines and their allies. Forced from Rome in 1146 by his archenemy Arnold of Brescia, Eugenius journeyed to France, where he remained until 1148. While there, Eugenius held a synod and a council at Reims. At the council, in 1148, Gilbert of Poitiers, once a student of Bernard of Chartres and later bishop of Poitiers, was charged with heresy. With the help of Roger of Sicily, Eugenius returned to Rome in 1149. In the Treaty of Constance, concluded in 1153, Eugenius and Frederick I Barbarossa reached an important agreement guaranteeing a relationship of mutual as-

sistance. Trained as a Cistercian monk, Eugenius remained a devout religious despite his involvement in the politics of his day. His good friend St. Bernard dedicated *De consideratione* to him. Eugenius died on July 8, 1153, and his cult was authorized in 1872 by Pope Pius IX.

E. Kay Harris

[See also: BERNARD OF CLAIRVAUX; CRUSADES; GILBERT OF POITIERS]

Eugenius III. *Opera. PL* 180.1013–642.

John of Salisbury. *Memoirs of the Papal Court*, ed. and trans. Marjorie Chibnall. London: Nelson, 1956.

Brezzi, Paolo. *Roma e l'impero medioevale, 774–1252*. Bologna: Capelli, 1947.

ÉVREUX. The episcopal city of Évreux (Eure) was the seat of a Norman county in the 11th and 12th centuries before being acquired by the French crown, but it is best known as the center of an apanage that gave its name to a cadet branch of the royal family in the 14th century. In 1307, Philip IV the Fair granted the county as an apanage to his younger brother Louis (d. 1319), and in 1317 Philip V erected Évreux into a peerage.

Louis of Évreux arranged marriages between his children and their royal cousins. His daughter Jeanne married Charles IV, and his son Philippe (1301–1342) married Jeanne (1312–1349), the daughter of Louis X and heiress of Navarre. Philippe and Jeanne continued this policy. Their daughter Blanche (1331–1398) married the much older Philip VI near the end of his life; their son, Charles II the Bad (1332–1387), married the daughter of King John II the Good. Although Jeanne was excluded from the French crown and also from her inheritance of Champagne and Brie, she and Philippe did become rulers of Navarre in 1328. They acquired clients and connections throughout northern and western France as well as in Champagne, attracting followers with grievances against the reigning house of Valois, including a growing body of reformers who wished to overhaul the royal government. They generously endowed the Collège de Navarre at the University of Paris, which became a center for reform-minded preachers and intellectuals in the second half of the 14th century and enjoyed continuing support from the Évreux family.

At his mother's death in 1349, Charles the Bad became king of Navarre, and for the next fifteen years the Évreux family played a major, often disruptive, role in French politics. Charles engineered the murder of the constable of France in 1354 and extorted from the crown the favorable treaties of Mantes (1354) and Valognes (1355). In 1356, John II arrested him for conspiring against the crown, and he spent the next seventeen months in prison. Critics of the monarchy clamored for his release, but after his liberation in 1357 Charles pursued an independent policy that involved a division of the kingdom. He gradually lost the support of the reformers in his party, many of whom rallied to Charles V after the royal army crushed the Évreux-Navarrese forces at Cocherel in 1364. Charles retained some political influence until his last conspiracy was exposed in 1378. His son, Charles III of Navarre (r. 1387–1425), the last male member of the family, ceded Évreux to the crown in 1404.

The most dangerous domestic enemies of the early Valois kings, the Évreux princes played a major role in weakening the monarchy during the mid-14th century, but their legacy was more positive and enduring. Many of their reform-minded followers became associated with the Marmousets, the political faction that brought major improvements in governmental efficiency under Charles V and Charles VI. Reformers associated with the Collège de Navarre enjoyed significant influence at court until well past 1400.

John Bell Henneman, Jr.

Although the town of Évreux was largely destroyed in World War II, some medieval buildings have survived. Overlooking the Eure, a bulky 17th-century mask covers the 12th-century twin towers of the cathedral of Notre-Dame and conceals the edges of the Gothic rose window. This strange façade prepares the visitor for the conglomeration of styles within. In 1119, Henry I of England burned the original church, dedicated in 1076–77. Construction took place sometime in the 12th century, but another fire in 1196 destroyed the fabric above the arcade, as shown by the Romanesque cluster piers and simply molded arcades that subside to late 13th-century triforium and clerestory. This fusion of Gothic and Romanesque elements continues throughout the eight-bay nave with side aisles and 13th–14th-century lateral chapels. The later 13th-century triforium is part of the same building campaign, which continues in the clerestory and choir. The four-bay 13th–14th-century choir terminates in a seven-sided east end with single ambulatory, four radiating chapels, and three-bay chevet. On the exterior, a Flamboyant north-transept portal flaunts lacy gables and crossing tower, in contrast to the 16th-century Renaissance classicism of the west portal. Some heraldic and figural stained glass from the 14th and 15th centuries remains in the ground-level and triforium windows, but modern glass dominates.

On the south side of the cathedral, the 15th-century cloister was originally two stories tall but has been reduced to one. A 15th-century bishop's residence also survives.

Named after the local St. Taurinus, the founder of the diocese of Évreux, the church of Saint-Taurin has a stylistically variegated fabric. The structure consists of elements from the first quarter of the 12th century to the 18th. The 17th–18th-century façade leads to a three-story interior with a Romanesque north elevation and a south elevation from the Renaissance. The 12th-century north elevation has bulky cruciform piers and a round-headed arcade, with a later triforium and clerestory. Three sides of the polygonal east end hold 15th-century stained glass with scenes from the life of St. Taurin. Housed in this east end is the 13th-century gilt-silver reliquary of St. Taurin, produced by a Parisian atelier and representative of ornate Gothic house shrines.

Stacy L. Boldrick

[See also: CHARLES II THE BAD; PHILIP IV THE FAIR; VALOIS DYNASTY]

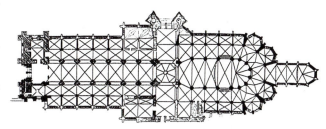

Évreux (Eure), plan of Notre-Dame. After Bonnefant.

Autrand, Françoise. *Charles VI*. Paris: Fayard, 1986.

Bonnefant, Georges. *La cathédrale d'Évreux*. Paris: Laurens, 1925.

Cazelles, Raymond. "Le parti navarrais jusqu'à la mort d'Étienne Marcel." *Bulletin philologique et historique* 2 (1960): 839–69.

——. *Société politique, noblesse et couronne sous Jean le Bon et Charles V*. Geneva: Droz, 1982.

Fossey, Jules. *Monographie de la cathédrale d'Évreux*. Évreux: Imprimerie de l'Eure, 1898.

Solet, François. "La cathédrale d'Évreux: quelques remarques." *Congrés archéologique (Évrecin, Lieuvin, Pays d'Ouche)* 138 (1980): 300–13.

Taralon, Jean. "La châsse de Saint-Taurin d'Évreux." *Bulletin monumental* 140 (1982): 41–56.

——. "L'ancienne église abbatiale de Saint-Taurin d'Évreux." *Congrés archéologique (Évrecin, Lieuvin, Pays d'Ouche)* 138 (1980): 266–99.

EXEMPLUM. Until the 9th century, the exemplum was one of the *figurae sententiae* of Greco-Roman and, since Tertullian, of ecclesiastical rhetoric, a form of simile employed in semantic amplification to offer proof by demonstrating the common characteristics of two or more phenomena. By the 12th century, the use of the exemplum had spread beyond the monastic into the scholastic, urban milieu and into the vernacular; in the 13th and 14th centuries, exempla became themselves text and tale, literary and cultural artifacts assembled and preserved in numerous collections, such as Jacques de Vitry's *Sermones vulgares* and Petrus Alfonsus's *Disciplina clericalis*.

The medieval exemplum has been defined as "a short narrative said to be true and meant to be inserted in an oration (usually a sermon) for the purpose of convincing an audience by means of a salutary lesson" (Bremond, pp. 37–38). It is a didactic, originally oral tale based on pagan, Judeo-Christian, or medieval written and oral traditions or on a preacher's real-life experiences; it often sketches a realistic, sometimes humorous picture of the medieval world. The exemplum illustrates simple moral principles by simple narrative means: it is uncomplicated structurally, and logically it relies on analogy and metonymy. The ease with which it could be used and endlessly repeated precluded, once the standard corpus of stock exempla was established, the renewal and development of the genre beyond the 14th century.

Hans R. Runte

[See also: *BARLAAM ET JOSAPHAT*; JACQUES DE VITRY]

Bremond, Claude, Jacques Le Goff, and Jean-Claude Schmitt. *L'exemplum*. Turnhout: Brepols, 1982.

Schmitt, Jean-Claude. *Prêcher d'exemples: récits de prédicateurs du moyen âge*. Paris: Stock, 1985.

Tubach, Frederic C. *Index exemplorum: A Handbook of Medieval Religious Tales*. Helsinki: Suomalainen Tiedeakatemia, 1969.

Welter, Jean-Thiebaut. *L'exemplum dans la littérature religieuse et didactique du moyen âge*. Paris: Occitania, 1927.

EXPOSITIO MISSAE. The tradition of expounding the meaning of liturgical ceremonies began in the 4th century with the mystagogical catecheses, sermons in which the rites of baptism, confirmation, and the eucharist were explained to newly baptized adult converts. Liturgical commentaries were subsequently written by Pseudo-Dionysius the Areopagite (ca. 500), Maximus Confessor (580–662), Germanus of Constantinople (ca. 640–733), and others. The first western treatise exclusively devoted to liturgy is the *De ecclesiasticis officiis* of Isidore of Seville (ca. 560–636), which in turn served as a source for the *Expositio antiquae liturgiae Gallicanae* attributed to St. Germanus (bishop of Paris 555–76), the only description of a Gallican Mass ordo. But the bulk of *Expositiones missae* dates from the Carolingian period, when the Roman Mass was being assimilated by the Frankish church; these treatises are therefore important sources of information about the texts and ceremonies of the early Franco-Roman Mass and were among the sources consulted by Amalarius of Metz and other Carolingian commentators. By the 12th century, the *Expositiones* were no longer in circulation as such, because they had become incorporated into the canon-law literature and the liturgical book known as the Pontifical.

Peter Jeffrey

[See also: AMALARIUS OF METZ; GALLICAN RITE; MASS, CHANTS AND TEXTS]

Lawson, Christopher M., ed. *Sancti Isidori episcopi Hispalensis: De ecclesiasticis officiis*. CCSL 113. Turnhout: Brepols, 1989.

Ratcliff, E. C., ed. *Expositio antiquae liturgiae Gallicanae*. London: Regnum, 1971.

Schulz, Hans-Joachim. *The Byzantine Liturgy: Symbolic Structure and Faith Expression*, trans. Matthew J. O'Connell. New York: Pueblo, 1986.

Yarnold, Edward. *The Awe-Inspiring Rites of Initiation: Baptismal Homilies of the Fourth Century*. Slough: St. Paul, 1972.

EXULTET. The Easter vigil, celebrated Holy Saturday night and ending Easter morning, began in both East and West with a lamplighting service (*lucernarium*). In some of the western rites, but not originally at Rome, this involved the lighting of a large candle while a deacon sang a special Easter hymn, the *Praeconium Paschale*. There were many texts in use for the *praeconium*, but the one that became the standard medieval text (a Gallican text that came into the Roman rite via the supplement to the Hadrianum sacramentary) began with the words *Exultet iam angelica turba caelorum*. There were multiple melodic traditions, but the one that became standard was closely related to the tone for the Preface of the Mass, that is, the prayer of the priest leading up to the Sanctus. Late in the Middle Ages, this melody was also adapted to another lengthy solo chanted by a deacon, the announcement of the dates of the movable feasts that took place at the bishop's Mass on Epiphany, January 6.

Peter Jeffrey

[See also: GALLICAN RITE]

Baroffio, Bonifazio, Marco Carminati, Marco Gemmani, and Antonello Lazzerini, eds. *Exsultet: la chiesa canta la sua fede: codici e partiture musicali dal VI al XVIII secolo*. Rimini: Meeting per l'Amicizia fra i Popoli, 1990.

Combe, Pierre-Marie. "L'exultet au cœur de la vigile pascale à Lyon." *Études grégoriennes* 10 (1969): 125–39.

Décréaux, Joseph. "Louange de l'abeille dans le sacramentaire carolingien d'Autun." In *Memoriam sanctorum venerantes: miscellanea in onore di Monsignor Victor Saxer*. Vatican City: Pontificio Istituto di Archeologia Cristiana, 1992, pp. 239–43.

Pinell, Jordi M. "La benediccio' del ciri pasqual i els seus textos." In *Liturgica: Cardinali I. Schuster in memoriam*. 2 vols. Montserrat, 1956–58, Vol. 2, pp. 1–119.

F

FABLE (*ISOPET*). Of the celebrated inventor of the genre, Aesop of Thrace (6th c. B.C.), medieval writers and compilers of fables knew little more than the name, from which derives the appellation *Isopets* of the French collections. Most medieval fables belong, in fact, in the Latin tradition of Phaedrus (1st c. A.D.), a naturalized Roman of Thracian origin, whose name had been forgotten by the 10th century. The earliest French version of Aesop's fables appears to be Guillaume Tardif's rendering (before 1498) of Lorenzo della Valle's Latin translation (ca. 1440) of thirty-three Greek fables.

Aesop's fables were eclipsed by Aesopic fables of the Phaedrean kind from the 10th to the 14th century. On Phaedrus's work (some 150 fables) are based four major groups of Latin adaptations: those of Avianus, Adémar de Chabannes, Rufus, and Romulus. Three Latin prose versions are attributed to the legendary Romulus: the *Romulus ordinarius* (eighty-three fables), the *Romulus of Vienna and Berlin* (eighty-two fables), and the *Romulus of Nilant* (fifty-two fables). Two Romulus versions are in verse: the *Romulus of Nevelet* (sixty to sixty-two fables), and Alexander Neckham's *Novus Aesopus* (forty-two fables). The *Romulus of Oxford* (forty-five fables) and the *Romulus of Berne* (thirteen fables) present abridged prose versions. Vincent de Beauvais included twenty-nine Romulean prose fables in his *Speculum historiale* and *Speculum doctrinale*.

The French fable collections are based largely on the Romulus versions: from the *Romulus of Nevelet* derive the *Isopet of Lyon* (sixty fables; one manuscript), the *Isopet I* (sixty-four fables; six manuscripts) and its prose adaptation, the *Isopet III* of Paris (forty-three fables; one manuscript). Neckam's *Novus Aesopus* is the source of the *Isopet II* of Paris (forty fables; two manuscripts) and of the *Isopet of Chartres* (forty fables; one manuscript). Vincent de Beauvais's fables were translated by Jean de Vignay in his *Mireoir historial* (first printed in 1479); an imitation of the *Speculum historiale*, entitled *Rudimentum noviciorum* and containing twenty-nine fables, was printed in Germany in 1475 and translated into French as *La mer des histoires* (1488).

In five manuscripts of the *Isopet I*, the Romulean fables are followed by eighteen fables inspired by Avianus (the *Avionnet*). A further nine fables translated from Avianus are contained in the York Fragment (ed. Warnke), and another twenty-seven are part of Julien Macho's translation (1480) of Steinhöwel's bilingual (Latin-German) edition of 147 fables of various origins, including eighty Romulean fables.

In the history of the French fable, the Anglo-Norman collection by Marie de France (12th c.; twenty-three manuscripts) is of particular importance. While her claim to have translated an English model is being increasingly discounted as an authorial topos of self-justification, she likely knew, or knew of the *Romulus of Nilant*, with which she shares most of the initial forty of her 102–104 fables. Nevertheless, for more than 60 percent of her work no precise sources have been found, a fact that may demonstrate her originality or point speculatively to undocumented influences from as far away as Greece, Arabia, and India. That she greatly enriched the tradition of the Aesopic fable is manifest from the adaptations of her work by Berechiah ben Natronai (*Mischle Shu'alim*), by the compilers of the *Romulus of Robert*, the L(ondon)B(russels)-G(öttingen) fragments and an Italian fable collection, and by the author of the *Promptuarium exemplorum* (ed. Warnke).

The case of Marie de France's fables illustrates that despite a long history of written transmission, the genre is fundamentally an oral one. It shares with popular songs, proverbs, riddles, and fairy and animal tales the common sources of folklore and has, like them, an essentially didactic purpose. The lesson to be drawn from a fable is summarized in an opening "promythium" or in a closing "epimythium," or "moral." In keeping with their didactic function, fables usually adhere to a simple structural paradigm according to which the plot line progresses straightforwardly from (1) the presentation of the characters (mostly but not always animals) and (2) their intentions to (3) their distribution into opposing roles (the strong against the weak, the poor against the rich), and from there to (4) their interaction and (5) its results.

Because of its origins, intent, and structure, the fable is often denied any intrinsic literary value. Only rarely are fables expanded into skillfully told stories in which the artistic purpose outweighs the didactic, or into a vast creation, such as the animal epic of the *Roman de Renart*. While the fable may have had to wait for La Fontaine in the 17th century to be admitted into the French canon of respectable literary genres, its medieval manifestations offer, despite their didactic dryness, invaluable insights into the everyday life of the society they describe and reflect.

Hans R. Runte

[See also: MARIE DE FRANCE; *RENART, ROMAN DE*; VINCENT DE BEAUVAIS]

Bastin, Julia, ed. *Recueil général des Isopets*. 2 vols. Paris: Champion, 1929–30. [Edition of all *Isopets* and of the *Avionnet*.]

Spiegel, Harriet, ed. and trans. *Marie de France: Fables*. Toronto: University of Toronto Press, 1987.

Warnke, Karl, ed. *Die Fabeln der Marie de France*. Halle: Niemeyer, 1898. [Includes edition of the York Fragment of the *Avionnet*, and of the *Promptuarium exemplorum*.]

Martin, Mary Lou, trans. *The Fables of Marie de France: An English Translation*. Birmingham: Summa, 1984.

Carnes, Pack. *Fable Scholarship: An Annotated Bibliography*. New York: Garland, 1985.

FABLEL DOU DIEU D'AMORS. Written in the mid- to late 13th century, probably in Hainaut, the *Fablel* is among the earliest surviving allegorical first-person love visions. It occurs in a single Picard manuscript (B.N. fr. 1553) in 142 monorhymed decasyllabic quatrains. The narrative includes a bird debate and an encounter with the God of Love.

Ardis T.B. Butterfield

Lecompte, I.C., ed. "Le fablel dou Dieu d'Amors." *Modern Philology* 8 (1910–11): 63–86.

Oulmont, Charles, ed. *Les débats du clerc et du chevalier*. Paris: Champion, 1911, pp. 197–216.

Windeatt, Barry A., trans. *Chaucer's Dream Poetry: Sources and Analogues*. Woodbridge: Boydell and Brewer, 1982, pp. 85–91.

FABLIAU. Concentrated in the north of France and dating from the 13th and first half of the 14th centuries, the fabliaux are relatively brief and generally comic tales, composed in the octosyllabic rhymed couplets that are the standard narrative form of the period. Although many Chaucerians designate certain of the stories in *The Canterbury Tales* as fabliaux, the term is more properly, if not exclusively, applicable to a large group of French texts. Over forty surviving manuscripts preserve fabliaux. Some include only a single one alongside texts from other genres; others are veritable compendia of fabliaux, with one (B.N. fr. 837) containing around sixty of the works. A traditional controversy about the fabliaux concerns their public and their fundamental character. Conceptions of the fabliaux were shaped largely by Joseph Bédier's 1893 study. Bédier, who had comparatively little regard for the purely literary merits of the fabliaux but a keen appreciation of their value for social historians, found a correlation between the rise of the genre and the growth of cities and of a thriving bourgeoisie. His conclusion was that, just as the courtly circles had their literature (e.g., courtly romances, cultivated lyric poetry, *lais*), now the bourgeois public had its own. This conception of origins and audiences offered a convenient explanation for the fabliaux' apparent lack of literary pretentions, their frequent choice of middle-class or peasant settings, their frankness in sexual and linguistic matters, and their irreverent and often unsubtle humor. The fabliaux, in other words, were everything the courtly romance was not, and they must therefore belong to a different social class.

In fact, Bédier's views were considerably less categorical than this summary suggests; he acknowledged, for example, that the fabliaux were heard and enjoyed in courtly circles. Nonetheless, what most scholars retained from Bédier's book was a sharp division of literature into courtly and bourgeois genres; and, while a few studies questioned or qualified his theories, they continued to be widely accepted until challenged by Per Nykrog in 1957. Acknowledging most of the characteristics Bédier identified in the fabliaux, Nykrog disagreed that the genre was the product of a bourgeois mentality. Identifying in a number of fabliaux certain situations and formulae that would likely be appreciated only by a courtly audience, he concluded that the fabliaux often exploit or parody courtly texts and situations. They are thus as courtly, in their way, as are romances and *lais*.

Although a necessary corrective to Bédier's theory, Nykrog's study is at times too uncompromising. Numerous fabliaux clearly do not reflect courtly ideals or language, even as parody. The range of fabliau subjects and methods is extraordinarily wide, varying from linguistic playfulness and complex comic developments to unsubtle anecdotes and simple dirty jokes. Some are "courtly" in some sense; others are not, although we have no convincing evidence that even the crude sexual jokes might not appeal to inhabitants of courts. Moreover, as Jean Rychner demonstrated in 1960, we often have two or more variants of the same fabliau, with the situation or the language apparently adapted to different publics.

A second and more persistent controversy concerns the definition of the genre and the precise constitution of the fabliau canon, questions that have never been satisfactorily resolved. Bédier formulated the most frequently quoted definition: *Les fabliaux sont des contes à rire en vers* ("Fabliaux are comic tales in verse"). The generality of this convenient definition holds a certain appeal but also limits its usefulness considerably. Furthermore, the emphasis on humor may raise a question instead of resolving it. The inspiration or purpose of a fabliau is not always easy to define, and it is in any case of questionable value as a generic determinant. If we assume with Bédier that all fabliaux are humorous, we should then routinely exclude from the genre all compositions that we judge to be (for example) primarily moralizing, including a number of texts once published with fabliaux. An example is the well-known *La housse partie*, a work sometimes excluded, despite its cleverness and its general resemblance to fabliaux, simply because it is considered more serious than humorous.

On the other hand, this criterion is not applied uniformly, and scholars often include among the fabliaux a few works that make a serious moral point in a clever fashion. In *Du vilain qui conquis paradis par plait*, the protagonist argues his way into heaven by pointing out that the sins of those already there (e.g., Peter, who denied his Lord) are considerably more serious than his own.

One frequent approach to the problem of definition is to study self-nominated fabliaux, that is, those that describe themselves as being fabliaux. Critics may thus limit themselves to those works, which number about seventy, or they may begin with those in an attempt to define the properties of the genre and then include in the canon other poems that exhibit those same properties. Even this approach is problematical, however, because it assumes that medieval authors possessed both a specific consciousness of literary categories and a precise terminology for them, and the evidence does not convincingly support such an assumption. For example, many of the compositions commonly taken as fabliaux describe themselves in a variety of ways, as fabliaux, fables, *contes* ("stories" or "tales"), *dits* (short narratives), and a number of other terms.

The formulation of a satisfactory definition is by no means a simple matter. In practice, each critic is left to construct a canon. Bédier listed 147 works he considered to be fabliaux; Nykrog expanded that number to 160. Noomen's critical edition of the fabliaux, begun in 1983, will include 127 texts. Most likely, the specific confines of the genre can never be established; at the edges of the genre, at least, works that are presumably fabliaux tend to merge with other forms and types of texts. The solution to the problem of taxonomy is necessarily more pragmatic than technical or scientific: there is a solid core of texts accepted as fabliaux by virtually all critics, and from a study of those compositions we can derive reliable notions of the themes, styles, and techniques characteristic of the genre.

The fabliaux, although related by inspiration and often by specific thematic properties to earlier works from Europe, the classical world, and even the Orient, came into existence in France toward the end of the 12th century. Some scholars identify Jehan Bodel as the first author of fabliaux; Bodel, who died in 1210, was in any case the first whose name is known. Most fabliaux are in fact anonymous, but a number of fabliau authors in addition to Bodel are identified; they include Gautier le Leu, Henri d'Andeli, Eustache d'Amiens, Rutebeuf, Baudouin de Condé, and his son Jean (d. 1346), who was the last known composer of fabliaux.

The shortest of the fabliaux is *Du prestre et du mouton* (signed by one Haiseaus or Haisel) at eighteen lines. The longest run to some 1,300 lines, with the single exception of *Trubert*, a 3,000-line text that is often but not always considered a fabliau. Most contain between a hundred and 300 lines, with the average around 250.

Whether or not the fabliau is taken as a bourgeois genre, it is true that the characters most often belong to the middle class or to peasant society. Only rarely do knights play prominent roles. In some works, such as *De celle qui se fist foutre sur la fosse de son mari*, a knight may appear, but he is often not the protagonist, a role taken in this text by his squire. Similarly, descriptions of activities associated with the nobility are rare but not unheard of: *Le chevalier qui recovra l'amor de sa dame* offers an account of a tournament through which a knight will win a lady's love and is identifiable as a fabliau only because of a ruse perpetrated by the knight in the second half of the poem.

Readers interested in social history will find in these texts fascinating reflections of the daily life of the period. The characters in fabliaux are very often observed working, eating and drinking, and carrying on all the usual activities of middle-class and peasant existence. We have descriptions of houses, towns, professions (notably merchants, millers, and farmers), and leisure activities. References to work, food, and drink are extremely common in the fabliaux, but the activity most frequently depicted is sexual. Of course, sexuality within marriage is hardly ever treated, and sexual satisfaction between spouses is practically unheard of. When it is mentioned at all, marital sex is dismissed with a very few words or else reduced to an emphasis, not on desire or sexual intimacy, but on sex organs. A memorable but not atypical example is the absurd story told in *Les quatre souhaits saint Martin*, where a husband and wife, granted four wishes, initially have their bodies covered with genitals and have to use all their remaining wishes to return to normal.

Much more common is seduction or attempted seduction outside of marriage. This can hardly come as a surprise, not only because sexual humor is almost universally extramarital, but also because fabliau characterizations imply and invite such dalliances. Husbands are routinely presented as cruel or stupid, while many wives are found to be lascivious creatures with gargantuan sexual appetites, either ripe for an adulterous relationship or already embroiled in one. Adultery is a prevalent theme in the fabliaux. Nykrog calculated that sixty-three of his 160 fabliaux dealt with love triangles. Almost invariably, the participants in an adulterous relationship are married women and men other than their husbands, rather than husbands with mistresses. Seducers are never in short supply. Priests attempt the most seductions of married women, but they are rarely successful (only five out of twenty-two times, according to Nykrog). Knights and clerics invariably succeed.

The fabliaux frequently show an interest in language and its uses or misuses. Some are mere puns: in *Estula*, a man calls to his dog, but the dog's name, Estula, also means "Are you there?" and a thief hiding in the garden responds, "Yes, I'm here." Linguistic taboos provide the subject of *La damoisele qui ne pooit oïr parler de foutre*, a work about a young woman who finds the sexual act considerably less offensive than the word. Several texts offer amusing anecdotes that play on the distinction between figurative and literal language. In *Brunain, la vache au prestre*, an avaricious priest tells a naive couple that whatever they give to God will be returned doubly to them; they take his words literally (as indeed he intended) and obediently give the priest their cow, but the tables are turned when the cow comes home later, leading the priest's own.

Revenge is the motivating force in some of the best fabliaux. *L'enfant qui fu remis au soleil* has a woman explain her pregnancy to her husband by noting that a snowflake fell into her mouth and grew inside her; the husband bides his time, eventually sells the child into slavery, and explains his disappearance by insisting that the hot sun melted him. *Le boucher d'Abbeville* deals with a butcher who seeks shelter in a priest's house and takes revenge when the priest refuses it to him; he steals one of the priest's sheep, trades it for lodging, shares the meat, and seduces the priest's maidservant and mistress by offering both of them the sheepskin—which he then sells to the priest himself.

The authors of fabliaux show a keen interest in genitalia. They thus give us works in which genitals talk, multiply, detach themselves from their owners, exhibit prodigious dimensions, and are frequently personified and described in endlessly imaginative ways. At the other end of the thematic and tonal spectrum are texts of subtlety and refinement, even though they are still intended for amusement and often have seduction as their subject. *Guillaume au faucon* presents a young man who is passionately in love with his noble master's wife and who fasts nearly unto death when the lady repels his advances. When her husband asks the reason for William's suffering, the woman, inventing an explanation in order to avoid complications, replies that William has asked for her husband's falcon. Most of this text is indistinguishable from a *lai* or an episode from a courtly romance, but it presents an ingeniously humorous conclusion, turning on the pun involving *faucon* ("falcon" and "false cunt") and on the result of her pretext: he orders her to give the young man what he wants.

A commonplace of fabliau criticism concerns the anticlericalism and antifeminism of these compositions. In the former instance, it is true that the fabliaux are populated with priests who are most often avaricious or lascivious; while the reader never senses that authors are attacking the institution of the church itself, it is indisputably true that priests themselves provide a tempting and popular target for humor. The question of antifeminism is more complex. Certain female characters in the fabliaux are presented as intelligent and virtuous, and the *Borgoise d'Orliens* is treated sympathetically even as she commits adultery while her husband is being brutally beaten nearby. In general, however, the weight of evidence, drawn both from situations and from explicit authorial commentary, suggests a considerably less than favorable view of women, many of whom are explicitly condemned for lasciviousness and deceitfulness. Admittedly, the fabliaux also criticize some men, but it is often for their foolishness in trusting women or allowing themselves to be led astray by them, and the condemnation thus extends to women as well. The most extreme treatment of women is exemplified by *La dame escoilliee*, in which a wife's strong will and presumption are attributed to her having testicles, a graphic organic metaphor for "wearing the pants in the family." Here, though, the metaphor provides the pretext for physical punishment, and a brutal operation is performed to "remove" the offending items. In case she has not learned her lesson, she is told that any repeat of her unacceptable behavior will necessitate additional surgery.

In both theme and technique, the fabliaux exhibit a wide range, as indeed we should expect of a group of some 150 texts composed over a century and a half. Some are little more than dirty jokes; others are sophisticated and subtle compositions that indulge in refined humor. Some append morals (although they often have little or nothing to do with the preceding text), while others tell their story quickly and then stop. Most are simple and economical narratives, stripped of all nonessential material, while a few go to some lengths to establish character or tone. They do not always agree about women, priests, nobles, or other subjects—or especially about the best way to tell a story. What most do agree on is the need to please and amuse their audiences. Even when the authors draw logical moral conclusions from their anecdotes, their primary purpose is in a broad sense entertainment, if not always specifically humor. The fact that they succeeded in most cases is demonstrated by their literary influence on Chaucer, Boccaccio, and other authors, by their preservation and their survival in impressive numbers into the 20th century, and by their continued ability to give us pleasure today.

Norris J. Lacy

[See also: ANTIFEMINISM; BAUDOUIN DE CONDÉ; CONDÉ, JEAN DE; GAUTIER LE LEU; HENRI D'ANDELI; JEHAN BODEL; RUTEBEUF]

Eichman, Raymond, and John Duval, eds. and trans. *The French Fabliaux: B.N. MS. 837*. 2 vols. New York: Garland, 1984–85.

Montaiglon, Anatole de, and Gaston Raynaud, eds. *Recueil général et complet des fabliaux des XIIIe et XIVe siècles*. 6 vols. Paris: Librairie des Bibliophiles, 1872–90.

Noomen, Willem, and Nico van den Boogaard, eds. *Nouveau recueil complet des fabliaux*. 10 vols. Assen: Van Gorcum, 1983– .

Bédier, Joseph. *Les fabliaux: études de littérature populaire et d'histoire littéraire du moyen âge*. Paris: Champion, 1893; 5th ed., 1925.

Lacy, Norris J. *Reading Fabliaux*. New York: Garland, 1993.

Ménard, Philippe. *Les fabliaux: contes à rire du moyen âge*. Paris: Presses Universitaires de France, 1983.

Muscatine, Charles. *The Old French Fabliaux*. New Haven: Yale University Press, 1986.

Nykrog, Per. *Les fabliaux*. Copenhagen: Munksgaard, 1957.

Rychner, Jean. *Contribution à l'étude des fabliaux*. 2 vols. Geneva: Droz, 1960.

FAIRS AND MARKETS. The fair, or *nundinae*, had roots in the Roman era and can be distinguished from the regional weekly market day by its occurrence once a year and for a period of several days. The medieval fair resembled nothing so much as a wholesalers' gathering or merchandise mart, for the fair was geared to an economy that did not support the existence during many centuries of daily retail markets. While for the most humble fair it sufficed to make available a field and some tents, towns with well-established fairs usually provided additional amenities in the form of display rooms and housing for visiting merchants. Taxation was an important element in internal fair organization. Displays and shops were taxed, as were actual sales. Tolls might be charged on merchandise making its way to a fair. French kings conceded fairs as privileges to some locales by regalian right, uncontested except in the case of the most rebellious of lords, such as the duke of Burgundy under Louis XI.

While the Champagne fairs are the most celebrated of all medieval fairs, they were by no means the only such gatherings in France. Mention of fairs and markets in Merovingian France is infrequent, although such venerable fairs as the October Fair at Saint-Denis (founded ca. 635), just north of Paris, are duly famous. Market quarters, often called *portus*, are noted at such Merovingian sites as Champtoceaux on the Loire. The Carolingian period witnessed many markets, often of agricultural dimension, scheduled to coincide with local feast days and sometimes favored by royal privileges. A February fair was added at Saint-Denis in the late 8th century.

One must await the commercial revolution of the 11th century for a flourishing of markets and fairs in medieval France. The Lendit fair in June at Saint-Denis emerged at this time, and by 1070 Italian merchants were frequenting the Saint-Denis fairs. Fairs in Flanders appear in this era. Indeed, small fairs grew up in many regions, Normandy, Brittany, the Touraine, and Anjou being the most important.

Languedoc, with its proximity to the Mediterranean and outlets to international trade, was the site of considerable growth in fairs. Noted from the early 12th century were fairs at such towns as Moissac, Nîmes, Carcassonne, Aniane, Villemagne (Villeveyrac), Montagnac, and Pézénas. Saint-Gilles, where the feast of September 1 took on the dimensions of a fair, was the ongoing focus of southern French commerce, thanks to its connections with Genoa and Pisa in the 12th century. By the 13th century, many fairs were concentrated in small towns of the Hérault and Orb valleys, where connections between the Mediterranean coast and mountainous routes leading to northern France could be made. In the late 13th and early 14th centuries, a cycle of six fairs developed at Pézénas and Montagnac. These fairs became important sites for the repayment of debts in international commerce, particularly for the cloth trade, much in the clearinghouse tradition of the Champagne fairs.

The late Middle Ages witnessed the emergence of new fairs. The fair of Chalon-sur-Saône, the cloth halls of which can be noted in 1244, picked up some of the cloth business between Flanders, northern France, and the papacy at Avignon in the 14th century. The fair of Beaucaire in Languedoc was founded in 1464. The fairs of Geneva took up some further slack from the declining merchandise fairs in Champagne in the 14th century. To counter the shift of north-south trade to routes lying east of royal territory, Louis XI reestablished the fairs of Lyon in 1463, as an alternative to Geneva. The Lyon fairs successfully offered a market in spices and silks until Antwerp came to dominate European commercial and financial markets in the 16th century. While the fair as an economic phenomenon persisted beyond the Middle Ages in

France, the heyday of the fair economy had long passed by the late 15th century.

Kathryn L. Reyerson

[See also: CHAMPAGNE; TRADE ROUTES]

Bresard, Marc. *Les foires de Lyon aux XVe et XVIe siècles.* Paris: Picard, 1914.

Combes, Jean. "Les foires en Languedoc au moyen âge." *Annales: Économies, Sociétés, Civilisations* 13 (1958): 231–59.

Huvelin, Paul. *Essai historique sur le droit des foires et des marchés.* Paris: Rousseau, 1897.

Laurent, Henri. "Droits des foires et droits urbains aux XIIIe et XIVe siècles." *Revue historique de droit français et étranger* 4th ser. 11 (1932): 660–710.

Verlinden, Charles. "Markets and Fairs." In *Cambridge Economic History of Europe.* 8 vols. Cambridge: Cambridge University Press, 1952–78, Vol. 3: *Economic Organization and Policies in the Middle Ages,* ed. M.M. Poston, E.E. Rich, and E. Miller, 1965, pp. 119–53.

FALAISE. Celebrated in legend, the mighty citadel of Falaise (Calvados) is the oldest fortress in Normandy. Built atop a rocky spur (Fr. *falaise*), it was a favorite residence of the Norman dukes. According to legend, it was from the castle windows that Robert le Diable, the younger son of Duke Richard II, spotted the beautiful Arlette, daughter of a rich tanner, doing her washing in the river. Refusing to be carried off in secret, she rode boldly through the castle gates to become the mother of William the Conqueror. It was from Falaise that William launched his invasion of England in 1066. The town was captured by Philip II Augustus in 1204, retaken by Henry V in 1417, and finally rejoined to the French crown by Charles VII in 1450.

The castle is an impressive ruin, dominated by its 12th-century square Norman keep. The curtain walls, main gate, and sixteen flanking towers are 13th-century. Within the town are the Romanesque church of Saint-Gervais (11th c., with a 12th-c. lantern tower), and the Gothic church of La Trinité (13th–16th c.), both of which sustained damage in World War II.

William W. Kibler/William W. Clark

[See also: *ROBERT LE DIABLE;* WILLIAM I THE CONQUEROR]

Berry, Maurice. "Église Saint-Gervais de Falaise." and "Église Sainte-Trinité de Falaise." *Congrès archéologique (Orne)* 111 (1953): 143–80.

Doranlo, M. "Le château de Falaise." *Congrès archéologique (Orne)* 111 (1953): 181–200.

FAMILY AND GENDER (ARISTOCRACY). The word "family" today usually refers to either the nuclear family or an ill-defined group of cousins and in-laws, but there was no word in medieval Latin for either of these meanings, and aristocrats probably did not think in those terms. A *stirps* or *gens*, which we might now translate as "family," was a group that included both the living and the dead and generally was composed of those descended from a common male ancestor and the women who had married into this group.

What we would call family life for a high-medieval French aristocrat was centered on the hereditary castle, which was both a defensible fortress and an elegant home. Until the end of the 12th century, there was generally only one married couple in a castle, the lord and lady, who served as the symbolic parents of everyone living there. With the exception of a few women attending the lady and her own daughters, she was generally the only woman in the castle. All the rest, knights, servants, cooks, chaplains, stablemen, and the like, were men. The knights who served the castellans seem in many cases to have been local men who served until they were too old to fight, perhaps in their thirties, at which time they married and settled down nearby and might in time send their own sons to serve in the castle.

The girls born to the castellan and his lady were raised and educated at home. A girl's most important lessons were in household management, for noble girls married in their teens and were expected to take over administration of a castle. A girl's husband, who might be twice her age, was generally chosen by her parents. A castle's keys hung from its lady's belt as she planned, supervised, and bought the necessary food, clothing, and supplies for everyone who lived there. She kept peace among a castle's inhabitants and even defended it if necessary while her husband was away.

Noble boys spent only the first years of their life at home. By the time they were six or eight, they had been sent to a monastery or cathedral school if their parents intended them for a life in the church; boys entered the ecclesiastical life far more frequently than girls. Those boys who became warriors were generally trained in the castle of an uncle or feudal lord rather than at home. With their knightly training complete, they might spend time on crusade or on the tournament circuit until their fathers died and they inherited. Only at this point did a young noble marry, unless he had found an heiress with her own castle. Until the 13th century, usually only one or two of a castellan's sons ever married.

Constance B. Bouchard

Bouchard, Constance B. "The Structure of a Twelfth-Century French Family: The Lords of Seignelay." *Viator* 10 (1979): 39–56.

Duby, Georges. *The Chivalrous Society*, trans. Cynthia Postan. Berkeley: University of California Press, 1977.

———. *The Knight, the Lady, and The Priest: The Making of Modern Marriage in Medieval France*, trans. Barbara Bray. New York: Pantheon, 1983.

FAMILY AND GENDER (BOURGEOISIE). Socioeconomic status was an important factor in determining family experience among the urban residents of medieval France. The marriages of the patriciate or urban elite, for example, were generally arranged unions heavily influenced by parental desires, business considerations, and property arrangements. Marrying at a younger age (in their mid- to late teens) than women from artisanal families and with access to more comfortable and healthier living conditions, patriciate women had larger families because they experienced a greater number of fertile years and lower infant mortality. The patriciate's greater wealth also made for larger households, since the rich could afford to keep more servants and apprentices.

Most urban inhabitants did not, however, possess the wealth, political power, or social status of the patriciate. Instead of being wealthy merchants, officeholders, or *rentiers*, they worked in the crafts or petty retail trades. These artisanal families, like those of the urban elite, were primarily nuclear in form and were headed by men who first married in their mid to late twenties. But the wives and daughters of these families were more likely to work in the family business or outside of the household, particularly as domestic servants, or in the textile or food trades. Because the economic contribution of artisanal wives to the family income could be substantial, their influence within the family may have differed from that of patriciate women, whose primary financial contribution to the family was their large dowries.

Sons of artisans frequently began an apprenticeship when they were about fourteen and moved away from home to board and train in the homes of their masters. Apprentices also came from outside of the city, migrating along with many other young men and women who were attracted by the economic opportunities offered by towns. Most of these migrants were probably poor rural residents who took low-paying jobs that made it difficult for them to save sufficient funds to marry. They, along with the city's large numbers of apprentices, servants, and widows, accounted for the extraordinarily large number of single people in medieval towns.

Urban economic prosperity or demographic experience could also affect family life. Few urban families, even among the elite, lasted beyond three generations in the male line, especially during the late Middle Ages, when plague elevated urban mortality and family and household size declined. The effect of these factors must, however, have varied regionally, since differences in local custom, law, and economy, particularly between northern and southern France, undoubtedly had a significant impact on family formation, the status of women, and domestic life in medieval towns.

Maryanne Kowaleski

Desportes, Pierre. "La population de Reims au XVe siècle d'après un dénombrement de 1422." *Moyen âge* 72 (1966): 463–509.

Frappier-Bigras, Diane. "La famille dans l'artisanat parisien du XIIIe siècle." *Moyen Age* 95 (1989): 47–74.

Higounet-Nadal, Arlette. *Périgueux aux XIVe et XVe siècles: étude de démographie historique*. Bordeaux: Fédération Historique du Sud-Ouest, 1978.

Howell, Martha. "Rewriting Marriage in Late Medieval Douai." *Romanic Review*. Forthcoming.

Rossiaud, Jacques. "Prostitution, Youth, and Society in the Towns of Southeastern France in the Fifteenth Century." In *Deviants and the Abandoned in French Society: Selections from the Annales,* ed. R. Forster and O. Ranum. Baltimore: Johns Hopkins University Press, 1978, pp. 3–46.

FAMILY AND GENDER (PEASANTRY). The basic unit of the peasant economy and social organization was the family. The basic lines of the household economy and gender roles within it were part of the negotiations that the parents of the bride and groom undertook at the formation of a new marriage. The bride brought to the marriage a dowry that might take the form of money, cattle, land, household goods, or other assets, while the groom guaranteed the support of his wife through marriage (brideprice) in the early Middle Ages or provision of a dower in the later Middle Ages.

The work that the couple engaged in fell into separate spheres. The woman's work was primarily that of the house and village, while the men worked primarily in fields, vineyards, and highways. Women's work included the rearing and training of the children in the household; work with domestic animals, such as cows, pigs, goats, and poultry; production of cheeses, butter, linen and woolen thread, and perhaps bread and beer for the market economy; planting and harvesting from the kitchen garden and the fruit trees; and tending the hearth fire, cooking the meals, and doing the laundry. Housecleaning occupied little time in the rudimentary peasant dwellings. Women did field work on a largely seasonal basis that included weeding, hoeing, and helping with harvesting. Men's work included working with the horses and oxen used for plowing and carting; plowing and other heavy field work; construction, wine production, butchering, road repair, and so on. The roles that men and women played in the household economy were so well defined and so heavily relied upon that when one of the couple died the other most frequently remarried quickly to reestablish the unit.

Although male and female children identified with the roles they would come to play in the household economy when they were toddlers, they evolved only gradually into the tasks they would eventually perform. Thus, boys and girls of five through ten first helped their mothers in such tasks as caring for poultry, picking vegetables and fruits, and fetching water. By the age of ten, male children began to work more with the tasks their fathers assigned, such as herding, goading the ox, and other field work. Only gradually did the older teenaged boys learn to plow and girls to brew or bake.

Barbara Hanawalt

FAMINE. Conditions of death or starvation resulting from crop failure caused by poor weather, infestation by pests, warfare, or other factors were considered famine. Records depict crowds of beggars waiting for food at the gates of monasteries, peasants abandoning holdings to seek food and livelihoods in other districts, distended stomachs from attempts to live on grass and roots, and human flesh hung up for sale in the markets. For the early Middle Ages, such conditions cannot have been markedly different from normal subsistence levels of the populace, which was consistently near starvation, when endemic malnutrition caused high infant mortality and low fertility, and when a diet composed almost entirely of cereals meant that human

productivity and resistance to disease were low. Given the almost total dependence of the agricultural population on cereals and the extremely low yields of agriculture at the time (between 2:1 and 3:1 yield-to-seed ratios being considered normal) any slight worsening of weather, infestation of crops, or other bad luck could cause the inhabitants of a district to begin consuming grain needed for next year's planting, pushing them into even more dire consequences and true famine in the following year if sufficient seed had not been found elsewhere to plant at normal levels. Even the lords could suffer famine insofar as they had to waive payment of rents, tithes, and taxes and hand out food and seed grain, in order to ensure that agricultural laborers did not depart or starve to death. Moreover, even for the lord or ecclesiastical almsgivers, once local reserves were gone there was little possibility of coming to the relief of the local population, for transport and communications were poor. Thus, although the diversity of climate, soils, and topography of France meant that bumper crops in one area might be accompanied by poor harvests in another, famines could be relieved not by importing food but only, to some extent, by people taking to the roads. When year after year of low yields followed one another in many areas, the results could be social unrest and even cannibalism (as was described by the Cluniac monk Raoul Glaber for ca. 1000) or the lowered resistance and susceptibility to diseases that followed the European-wide famines of 1315–17.

Constance H. Berman

[See also: AGRICULTURE; DISEASES]

Duby, Georges. *The Early Growth of the European Economy: Warriors and Peasants from the Seventh to the Twelfth Century,* trans. Howard B. Clarke. Ithaca: Cornell University Press, 1974.

FARCE. Dramatic farces are short comic plays usually involving a trick by which one or more characters deceives another for personal gain. Major popular entertainments in urban areas in the 15th and 16th centuries, they were often played on trestle stages that were quickly set up in streets or squares on holidays. The small number of roles required few actors and few stage props, making the plays easily transportable. Farces were written and played by amateur groups, such as student organizations, municipal confraternities, and trade guilds. The comic theater owes a special debt, however, to the Basoche, or guild of law clerks, a chapter of which was found in every major city in France. It was no doubt the play-loving law clerks who were responsible for the large number of legal themes and courtroom scenes in the farces. When professional acting troupes began to appear in France in the 16th century, they too were avid practitioners of the genre.

The earliest extant play of the farce type is *Le garçon et l'aveugle* (13th c.), in which a boy tricks his blind but miserly master out of both money and clothes. The play's title lacks a genre designation, and it was probably not called a farce. The first recorded use of "farce" to designate a dramatic work is found in a document from Paris dated 1398, which forbids the playing of *jeux de personnages par manière de farces*. There are numerous references in 15th-century documents to the staging of farces, but no plays have survived that antedate the *Farce de maistre Pathelin*, written in the 1460s. About 175 farces have survived from the hundred years following the appearance of *Pathelin*.

Most of these farces portray the comic side of domestic life. The characters are ordinary people who exemplify everyday relationships (husbands, wives, mothers-in-law, neighbors) or who engage in familiar occupations (shoemakers, tailors, tavern keepers, servants). Farces combine dramatic simplicity with brevity to create a rich variety of easily recognizable character types. Among the most prominent are the domineering wife, the henpecked husband, the braggart soldier, and the dull-witted student. Characters of this kind permit quick and usually light satirical thrusts at common social abuses. Though the characters may be familiar, the plots of the plays are not realistic reflections of ordinary events in the lower-middle-class households portrayed. The action of a farce depends on improbable coincidences or unbelievable disguises. Moreover, when one considers that all the roles were played by men, it is easy to see that realism was not a quality that a medieval audience sought in a farce.

The world in which farce characters live is essentially amoral, because their actions have no ultimate consequences. Unlike the morality play, the farce has no heroes and embodies no ideals. Neither is there a higher power to reward good and punish evil. Its characters are wholly absorbed in gaining some immediate material advantage through trickery. The farce world is thus a kind of ethical jungle in which only the cleverest survive. And no character, however clever, is immune to being tricked. The wily lawyer Pathelin, for instance, cheats a clothier out of some expensive cloth, only to be cheated in turn by a simple, but cleverer shepherd. *Maistre Pathelin* exemplifies an axiom of the farce world: *à trompeur, trompeur et demi*.

A large number of farces deal comically with the problems of conjugal relationships. The wife in *Le cuvier* is a domineering woman who makes her timorous husband, Jaquinot, do all the housework—an ignominious role in medieval society. To ensure that he forgets nothing, she has him make a list of the chores. When later she accidentally falls into the washtub, Jaquinot refuses to pull her out because that chore is not on his list. He finally extricates her only after she agrees that he will henceforth be master of the house. Unfaithful and deceptive wives also are a frequent topic of these plays. In *Resjouy d'amours*, the wife hides her lover in a sack when her husband returns home inopportunely. In a fit of suspicion and jealousy, the latter sets fire to the house to smoke out his rival. At his wife's pleading, he saves the sack because it contains all their "worldly goods." When no lover comes out of the burning house, he asks his wife to forgive him for his suspicions. Such plays, while making the spectators laugh, had the effect of ridiculing weak husbands, who were perceived in the Middle Ages as a threat to social order and stability.

Other objects of ridicule in the farces are dull-witted students (*Maistre Mimin*), country bumpkins (*Mahuet*), cowardly soldiers (*Colin, fils de Thévot*), and bombastic lovers (*Les trois amoureux de la croix*). The kind of ridicule such plays utilize may be lightly satirical, but in all cases the comic elements take precedence over the satire.

There is, however, a subgenre of the farce in which social satire was clearly the primary goal of the playwright. This is the allegorical farce, in which the characters are no longer ordinary people who are sometimes foolish, but fools of various stripes in the guise of personified abstractions. The use of such characters allows the playwright to attack the abuses of the powerful behind the mask of folly. One type of allegorical farce is the *farce moralisée*, a good example of which is *Les gens nouveaux qui mangent le monde et le loge de mal en pire*. The *gens nouveaux* are those who have recently acquired wealth and power but who have abandoned traditional values to seek only fame and financial gain. Caring nothing for those they govern, they systematically pillage *le monde* and its resources, making it go from bad to worse. In this caustic satire, the playwright presents the powerful as malicious fools and dramatizes the social effects of their folly.

Another type of allegorical farce is the *sottie*, in which the fools (*sots*) play no role in bringing about the social abuses that are condemned but limit themselves to observing and reporting the follies of the world. The effect of the satire is no less sharp, since their foolish and comic commentary causes spectators to compare the world they know with the utopian dream of an idealized society.

Alan E. Knight

[See also: BASOCHE; *PATHELIN, FARCE DE MAISTRE*; *SOTTIE*; STAGING OF PLAYS; THEATER]

Tissier, André, ed. *Recueil de farces (1450–1550)*. 7 vols. Geneva: Droz, 1986–93.

Bowen, Barbara C. *Les caractéristiques essentielles de la farce française et leur survivance dans les années 1550–1620*. Urbana: University of Illinois Press, 1964.

Knight, Alan E. *Aspects of Genre in Late Medieval French Drama*. Manchester: Manchester University Press, 1983.

Lewicka, Helina. *Études sur l'ancienne farce française*. Paris: Klincksieck, 1974.

Rey-Flaud, Bernadette. *La farce ou la machine à rire: théorie d'un genre dramatique, 1450–1550*. Geneva: Droz, 1984.

FATRAS/FATRASIE. These terms designate two related but distinct poetic forms. Sometimes considered a kind of medieval surrealism, both involve the creation of apparent nonsense, often by such methods as the juxtaposition of incongruities or the attribution of animate characteristics to inanimate objects. The dislocation of logic is limited to themes or images, however, while the grammar and syntax of the poems remain conventional and correct.

Both genres originated in northern France. *Fatrasie* dates from the 13th century; *fatras*, from the 14th and 15th. Most examples are anonymous, but eleven *fatrasies* are from the pen of Philippe de Remi, sire de Beaumanoir.

Both are fixed forms. The form of the *fatrasie* is aabaab/babab (in lines of five and seven syllables). The *fatras* began with two lines (AB) often taken from a popular song. The first of those lines is then repeated as the first line of the body of the poem, while B becomes the last line (thus, AB Aabaab/babaB). Occasional "double *fatras*" occur, with a second stanza constructed on an inversion of the initial distich.

Fatras continued to be composed after the Middle Ages, but they became *fatras possibles*, with simple parody replacing the linguistic inventiveness and "absurd" juxtapositions of the earlier genre.

Norris J. Lacy

[See also: BEAUMANOIR, PHILIPPE DE REMI, SIRE DE]

Porter, Lambert C. *La fatrasie et le fatras: essais sur la poésie irrationnelle en France au moyen âge.* Geneva: Droz, 1960.
Zumthor, Paul. "Fatrasie, fatrassiers." In *Langue, texte, énigme.* Paris: Seuil, 1975, pp. 68–88.

FAUSTUS OF RIEZ (d. ca. 495). British monk of Lérins, bishop of Riez in Provence from ca. 458. Exiled by the Arian Visigoth king Euric from 477 to 485. Faustus was famous for his sermons against Arianism and his articulation of the "Semi-Pelagian" position on predestination. Faustus taught that grace attracts souls to God and that God's foreknowledge does not require predestination. Extant works of Faustus include treatises *De spirito sancto* and *De gratia Dei*, letters, and a collection of sermons that may include works by other authors. In *De spirito sancto*, Faustus argues the materiality of the human soul, a position close to that of the 2nd-century author Tertullian.

E. Ann Matter

[See also: CAESARIUS OF ARLES; CASSIAN, JOHN; LÉRINS; PHILOSOPHY; THEOLOGY]

Faustus of Riez. *Opera.* PL 53, 58.
Tibilette, Carlo, ed. *Pagine monastiche provenzali: il monaschesimo nella Gallia del quinto secolo.* Rome: Borla, 1990. [Selections.]
Koch, A. *Der heilige Faustus, Bischof von Riez.* Stuttgart: Roth, 1895.
Weigl, Gustav. *Faustus of Riez.* Philadelphia: Dolphin, 1938.

FAUVAIN. The *Histoire de Fauvain* or *Dit de Fauveyn* is an animal verse satire (258 octosyllabic lines) in Picard dialect by Raoul le Petit that accompanies a series of forty ink drawings in B.N. fr. 571 (ca. 1326). Evil appears as the traditional figure of a dun-colored she-ass or horse (Fauvain). The beast is ridden by greedy hypocrites; simony, broken promises, refusal to aid the poor, justice miscarried are censured. Although she slays Loyalty, Fauvain dies too, and her soul is shown carried off by the Devil while Loyalty's soul is received by God.

Nancy F. Regalado

[See also: *FAUVEL, LIVRES DE*]

Lângfors, Arthur, ed. *L'histoire de Fauvin: reproduction phototypique de 40 dessins du manuscrit français 571 de la Bibliothèque Nationale (XIVe siècle) précédée d'une introduction et du texte critique des légendes de Raoul le Petit.* Paris: Geuthner, 1914.
Sandler, Lucy Freeman. *Gothic Manuscripts 1285–1385.* 2 vols. London: Harvey Miller/Oxford University Press, 1986, Vol. 1: *Text and Illustrations,* Ill. 246=fp; 150v; Vol. 2: *Catalogue* [description of B.N. fr. 571], pp. 103A–05B. [*Dit de Fauveyn* is described on 104A–05A.]

FAUVEL, LIVRES DE. An allegorical verse satire (3,280 octosyllabic lines) representing the horse Fauvel, harbinger of the Antichrist and emblem of hypocrisy and evil, whose dun color symbolizes vanity (*fauve* suggests *faus* 'false') and whose name spells out his vices: Flattery, Avarice, Unscrupulousness, Villany, Envy, Laxity (*Flaterie, Avarice, Vilanie, Varieté, Envie, Laschetê*).

The anonymous Book 1 of *Fauvel* (1310) was inspired by the discourse of Faus-Semblant in the *Roman de la Rose* and by such animal satires as *Renart le nouvel* by Jacquemart Gielée (1288). Condemning those who show their hypocrisy and greed by "currying Fauvel" (whence our expression "to curry favor"), Book 1 is organized as a traditional estates satire. It describes the upside-down world ruled by Fauvel and denounces corruption, decadence, and abuse of power in the church hierarchy, monastic orders, and the secular world, while commenting specifically on the scandalous charges brought against the Templars in 1307.

Book 2 was completed December 6, 1314, by a royal notary, Gervais du Bus, perhaps also the author of Book 1. Book 2 allegorically describes Fauvel's palace, peopled by Vices, and offers a noble portrait of Lady Fortune—daughter of God, sister of Wisdom, and mistress of the temporal world. Wooed by Fauvel, Fortune exhibits her twin crowns of ephemeral riches and virtuous poverty and her great wheel, whose turning governs the rise and fall of human destinies. Fortune then rejects his suit and, predicting his eventual destruction on the Last Day, she marries him off to Vain Glory. Book 2 gains topical overtones from its allusions to the kingdom of France and from its specific date, a week after the death of Philip IV and the very moment of the disgrace of his powerful minister Enguerrand de Marigny.

In 1316–17, another royal administrator, Chaillou de Pesstain, composed the vastly expanded version of *Fauvel* found in B.N. fr. 146 (1317), the earliest of a dozen manuscript sources. Chaillou borrowed extensively from Huon de Méry's *Tournoiement Antécrist* (ca. 1235) and the *Roman du comte d'Anjou* (1316) by another royal notary, Jean Maillart, to add some 1,800 lines narrating the wedding festivities of Fauvel: an allegorical banquet, a rowdy charivari, a tournament of Vices and Virtues, and a Fountain of Youth, where Fauvel's followers are renewed. Moreover, Chaillou illustrated his version with seventy-seven miniatures and 169 musical interpolations, including thirty-four polyphonic motets in Latin and French, numerous moral-satirical lyrics from the 13th century, and a large number of vernacular pieces in the emerging *forme fixe* lyric genres. These make Fr. 146 the most significant musical source to survive from the first half of the 14th century in France and *Fauvel* the most sumptuously embellished medieval romance. The effect of political reference is enhanced in Fr. 146 by the Parisian setting of the wedding celebration, by insertion of lyrics addressed to Louis X and Philip V, and by compilation of *Fauvel* with political *dits* by Geoffroi de Paris and an anonymous metrical chronicle of the kingdom of France from 1300 to 1316; these transform the moral satire into a festive *admonitio*, or *speculum principis*, a work intended to instruct the prince.

Nancy F. Regalado

[See also: ARS NOVA; *FAUVAIN*; HUON DE MÉRY; MAILLART, JEAN; MARIGNY, ENGUERRAN DE]

Aubry, Pierre, ed. *Le roman de Fauvel: reproduction photographique du manuscrit français 146 de la Bibliothèque Nationale de Paris.* Paris: Geuthner, 1907.

Långfors, Arthur, ed. *Le roman de Fauvel par Gervais du Bus.* Paris: Didot, 1914–19.

Le roman de Fauvel in the Edition of Chaillou de Pesstain: A Reproduction in Facsimile of the Complete Manuscript, Paris, Bibliothèque Nationale, Fonds Français 146. Introduction by Edward Roesner, François Avril, and Nancy Freeman Regalado. New York: Broude, 1990.

Schrade, Leo, and Frank L. Harrison, eds. *The Roman de Fauvel.* In *Polyphonic Music of the Fourteenth Century.* 24 vols. Monaco: L'Oiseau Lyre, 1956, Vol. 1.

Rosenberg, Samuel N., and Hans Tischler, eds. *The Monophonic Songs in the "Roman de Fauvel."* Lincoln: University of Nebraska Press, 1991.

Langlois, Charles Victor. *La vie en France de la fin du XIIe au milieu du XIVe siècle d'après les moralistes du temps.* Paris: Hachette, 1908, 1970, pp. 276–304. [Summary in modern French.]

Paris, Gaston. "*Le roman de Fauvel.*" In *Histoire littéraire de la France.* Paris: Imprimerie Nationale, 1898, Vol. 32, pp. 108–53.

FAUXBOURDON. A quasi-improvisatory practice associated with sacred music by 15th-century Franco-Burgundian composers. The term is associated with a repertory of over 170 surviving pieces, primarily hymns, psalms, Magnificats, and antiphons. The texture was also utilized in Mass movements, particularly in Introits and Sequences, but also in movements of the Ordinary. *Fauxbourdon* is usually notated as two voices, with a verbal cue (*faux bourdon*) indicating that a third voice is to be sung in parallel fourths below the cantus. In the example, Dufay paraphrases the plainchant in the cantus, while the tenor moves primarily in sixths and octaves below, giving the musical effect of a series of first-inversion triads resolving at cadences into sonorities of fifth and octave.

Guillaume Dufay, *Christe redemptor omnium*, *fauxbourdon* setting of verse 2

The simplest surviving *fauxbourdon* settings, such as those by Binchois, may reflect the sort of polyphony extemporized by 15th-century singers of liturgical music. While the precise origins of *fauxbourdon* are debated, it is clear that there was a connection with the similar English practice of singing "faburden." When *fauxbourdon* appears in relatively elaborate compositions, such as Dufay's *Supremum est mortalibus* or *Juvenis qui puellam*, it may have carried extramusical significance as a symbol or as a rhetorical figure in the setting of a humanistic text to music.

J. Michael Allsen

[See also: BINCHOIS, GILLES; DUFAY, GUILLAUME]

Besseler, Heinrich. *Bourdon und Fauxbourdon: Studien zur Ursprung der niederländischen Musik.* rev. ed. Peter Gülke. Leipzig: Breitkopf und Härtel, 1974.

Elders, Willem. "Guillaume Dufay's Concept of Faux-Bourdon." *Revue belge de musicologie* 43 (1989): 173–95.

Trowell, Brian. "Fauxbourdon." In *The New Grove Dictionary of Music and Musicians*, ed. Stanley Sadie. London: Macmillan, 1980, Vol. 6, pp. 433–38.

FEALTY. Fealty (OFr. *feelté*) was the oath of loyalty sworn by important Frankish men to their king from the 7th century. Charlemagne's capitulary of 802 extending that obligation to all free men, in order to reinforce public authority, had the force of generalizing fealty in private contracts, and by the 10th century it regularly supplemented homage. Initially, the oath was a promise not to harm, as indicated in Bishop Fulbert of Chartres's letter to the duke of Aquitaine (1020), but it acquired a more positive sense in the 11th century. As Galbert de Bruges explained (1127), a new vassal would perform homage, then would swear fealty (with his hand on the Gospels or a relic), and finally would be invested with a fief. Fealty in essence conferred a religious guarantee to a secular contract.

Like homage, fealty originally was an exclusive act that evolved to accommodate the increasing complexity of feudal tenure. In the 12th century, vassals with several fiefs often "reserved" their primary fealty for their liege homages. From the 13th century, feudal tenants often sealed charters attesting that they held their fiefs "by faith and homage," and in some cases written instruments even supplanted the acts themselves.

Theodore Evergates

[See also: FEUDALISM; FIEF/*FEUDUM*; FIEF HOLDING; HOMAGE; INVESTITURE (FEUDAL)]

Bachrach, Bernard S. "Enforcement of the *Forma Fidelitatis*: The Techniques Used by Fulk Nerra, Count of the Angevins (987–1040)." *Speculum* 59 (1984): 796–819.

Dunbabin, Jean. *France in the Making, 843–1180.* Oxford: Oxford University Press, 1985.

Fourquin, Guy. *Lordship and Feudalism in the Middle Ages,* trans. Iris and A.L. Lytton Sells. New York: Pica, 1976.

Ganshof, François L. *Feudalism,* trans. Philip Grierson. London: Longman, 1952.

Poly, Jean-Pierre, and Eric Bournazel. *La mutation féodale, XIe–XIIe siècles.* 2nd ed. Paris: Presses Universitaires de France, 1991.

FÉCAMP. A Benedictine abbey on the English Channel in the diocese of Rouen, Fécamp was originally founded as a house for nuns in 664. It was destroyed by the Vikings in 841 and refounded in 1001 by Richard II, duke of Normandy, as a house for monks. The first abbot was William of Saint-Bénigne of Dijon. The most famous member of the community, Jean de Fécamp, became abbot in 1028; Jean's monastic reforms reached far beyond his community. Fécamp was known in the central Middle Ages for liturgical chant and as a pilgrimage center focusing on a relic of the precious blood of Jesus. The church burned in 1168 and was rebuilt at the turn of the 13th century. Fécamp, part of the Maurist reform in the 17th century, was suppressed in the French Revolution.

E. Ann Matter

L'abbaye bénédictine de Fécamp: ouvrages scientifiques du XIIIème centenaire, 658–1958. 4 vols. Fécamp: Durand, 1959–63.

Leclercq, Jean, and Jean-Paul Bonnes. *Un maître de la vie spirituelle au XIe siècle: Jean de Fécamp.* Paris: Vrin, 1946.

FERRAND OF PORTUGAL (1188–1233). Ferrand of Portugal became count of Flanders and Hainaut when he married the young Jeanne de Constantinople, countess of Flanders and Hainaut, in 1212. The marriage was arranged with the permission of Philip II Augustus, who believed that it would secure the two counties for France and also align him to Portugal. Ferrand, however, refused to recognize Philip's sovereignty. In 1212, several kings and nobles, including Emperor Otto IV and King John of England, as well as Ferrand, rose against Philip. Philip defeated his foes at the Battle of Bouvines on July 27, 1214, and captured Ferrand, who was imprisoned in the Louvre until January 6, 1227. He was finally freed when Jeanne threatened to divorce him and marry Pierre de Dreux, duke of Brittany, a match less appealing to the new French king, Louis VIII. Ferrand returned to Flanders, where he continued to rule his two counties until his death in Noyon from hepatitis.

Kelly DeVries

Baldwin, John W. *The Government of Philip Augustus.* Berkeley: University of California Press, 1986.

Dept, Gaston G. *Les influences anglaises et françaises dans le comté de Flandre au début du XIIIe siècle.* Ghent: Van Rysselberghe et Rombaut, 1928.

Goffin, Louis. *Ferrand de Portugal, comte de Flandre et de Hainaut.* Lisbon: Biblioteca de Altos Estudos, 1967.

Luykx, Theo. *Johanna van Constantinople, gravin van Vlaanderen en Henegouwen.* Antwerp: Standaard-Boekhandel, 1946.

Pirenne, Henri. *Histoire de Belgique.* 7 vols. Brussels: Lamertin, 1922, Vol. 1.

FERRIÈRES, HENRI DE (ca. 1315–after 1377). A Norman of noble birth, Henri de Ferrières wrote the *Livres du roy Modus et de la royne Ratio* between 1354 and 1377. Divided into two parts—the *Livre de chasse* and the *Songe de pestilence*—it takes the form of a dialogue between the expert hunter Modus and several disciples. The book, in prose with interspersed verse, is not simply a treatise on hunting, as is often asserted, but also an allegorical work offering a moral reflection on the vices and virtues of the

Fécamp (Seine-Maritime), La Trinité, nave. *Photograph: Clarence Ward Collection. Courtesy of Oberlin College.*

time, based on a symbolic interpretation of the behavior of game animals. Some thirty-six manuscripts survive, many lavishly illustrated.

Annette Brasseur

[See also: GACE DE LA BUIGNE; GASTON PHOEBUS]

Tilander, Gunnar, ed. *Les livres du roy Modus et de la royne Ratio*. 2 vols. Paris: Didot, 1932. [Based on MS A (B.N. fr. 12399).]
———, trans. *Le livre de chasse*. Paris: Nourry, 1931. [Modern French trans.]
Ménard, Philippe. "Littérature et iconographie: les pièges dans les traités de chasse d'Henri de Ferrières et de Gaston Phébus." In *La chasse au moyen âge: actes du Colloque de Nice (22–24 juin 1979)*. Paris: Les Belles Lettres, 1980, pp. 159–88.

FET DES ROMAINS. Written ca. 1213/14 by an anonymous, probably Parisian, author, the *Fet des Romains* is a compilation of Roman historical texts. Sallust's *De coniuratione Catilinae*, Suetonius's *De vita Caesarum*, Lucan's *Pharsalia* (properly called *Bellum civile*), and especially Julius Caesar's *Commentarii de bello gallico* (then believed to have been written by one Julius Celsus) supplied the models for the translation into Old French prose. There are also traces of Flavius Josephus's *Bellum Judaicum*, Peter Comestor, Augustine, and Isidore of Seville. Despite announcements in the prologue that the work will cover all twelve Caesars, the *Fet* is essentially a life of Julius Caesar. The prologue, stressing the civilizing power of literature, the duty to impart one's knowledge to others, and the moral lessons that can be learned from the Romans, borrows heavily from Sallust. The text itself begins with a short overview of Roman history, recounts Caesar's birth (as a Caesarean section, based on Isidore of Seville's *Etymologies*), and then, like Suetonius, skips to Caesar's sixteenth year. The Catiline conspiracy and Caesar's political difficulties are followed by an account of the Gallic Wars which forms the bulk of the 744-page (in the modern edition) book. The civil war is recounted according to Lucan (whose anti-Caesar feelings largely disappear in the translation). The book ends with Caesar's murder.

The *Fet* was extremely popular, in both learned and aristocratic circles, in several countries and over several centuries. Its last period of popularity was in the Burgundy of Charles the Bold. More than sixty manuscripts survive, many of them beautifully illuminated. In one group of manuscripts, the *Fet* is preceded by the *Histoire ancienne jusqu'à César*, an unfinished history of the world that leaves off approximately where the *Fet* begins. Both texts are important because they are among the earliest examples of French prose and of historical texts in the vernacular. The *Fet* is also tied to contemporary politics through two allusions to similarities between Julius Caesar and the French king Philip Augustus. Perhaps the text indirectly supported Philip's expansionist desires. The *Fet* and the *Histoire ancienne* show the strong interest in ancient history as a source for both moral exemplars and a national past.

Renate Blumenfeld-Kosinski

[See also: *HISTOIRE ANCIENNE JUSQU' À CÉSAR*; HISTORIOGRAPHY]

Flutre, Louis Fernand, and K. Sneyders de Vogel, eds. *Li fet des Romains*. Paris: Droz, 1936.
Beer, Jeanette M.A. *A Medieval Caesar*. Geneva: Droz, 1976.
Flutre, Louis Fernand. *Li fait des Romains dans les littératures française et italienne du XIIIe au XVIe siècle*. Paris: Hachette, 1932.
Guenée, Bernard. "La culture historique des nobles: le succès des *Faits des Romains* (XIIIe au XVe s.)." In *La noblesse au moyen âge*, ed. Philippe Contamine. Paris: Presses Universitaires de France, 1976, pp. 261–88.
Meyer, Paul. "Les premières compilations françaises d'histoire ancienne." *Romania* 14 (1885): 1–81.

FEUDAL AIDS. In a feudal relationship, the vassal normally owed his lord "aid and counsel." The first of these originally meant, above all, military service, but it soon included pecuniary assistance as well. The word *aide* began to refer to a variety of taxes or payments to one's lord, and when the latter was a king or territorial prince, the payments were required of many subjects who were not his direct vassals. Four types of *aide*, however, were deeply rooted in the feudal relationship and appeared in customals as the *aides aux quatre cas*. These *aides*, confined to specific situations, were the ones that historians usually call the feudal *aides*. The four "cases" were (1) when a lord's eldest son was knighted, (2) when his eldest daughter was married, (3) when the lord had to be ransomed from captivity, and (4) when he went on crusade and the vassal chose not to accompany him. The first two of these were by nature nonrecurring, while the last was not customary in every part of France. The need for a ransom, while it might never occur, was also capable of occurring more than once. The ransom of a king, generally an expensive matter, required payments that went beyond direct vassals. Two such *aides*—that for Louis IX after 1250 and that for John II after 1360—were major events in the history of royal taxation and affected so many people that it is hardly appropriate to call them feudal *aides* at all.

John Bell Henneman, Jr.

[See also: *AIDES*; FEUDALISM]

Brown, Elizabeth A.R. "Customary Aids and Royal Policy Under Philip VI of Valois." *Traditio* 30 (1974): 191–258.
Henneman, John B. "The French Ransom Aids and Two Legal Traditions." *Studia Gratiana* 15 (1972): 615–629.
———. *Royal Taxation in Fourteenth Century France: The Development of War Financing 1322–1356*. Princeton: Princeton University Press, 1971.

FEUDAL INCIDENTS. In England, the customs that grew out of feudal tenure but were incidental—not essential—to it, are called "feudal incidents." No comparable term exists in French, although similar practices obtained. The three main incidents, relief, marriage, and wardship, arose from the fief grantor's desire to maintain the service owed by fiefs that had become hereditable. Family control over fiefs was much stronger in France than in England, where kings routinely abused their incidental rights. In France, the inheritance tax payable to the feudal lord and called "relief," or *rachat*, generally was exacted only in cases of collateral transfers (i.e., *escheats*), not when fiefs passed to direct heirs, as was the case in England and Normandy. Relief usually amounted to the annual income of the fief. In the 13th century, a tax called the "fifth penny," or *quint*, often was assessed whenever fiefs were alienated to nonnobles.

Restrictions on the marriage of feudal tenants, whether they were widows, minor heirs, or adults, were imposed primarily by kings on their great vassals. Louis VII apparently was the first to object to the proposed marriages, and consequent political alliances, of his vassals inimical to royal interests; his successors remained alert to their vassals' marriage plans, but, unlike English kings, they did not force disparaging marriages on their feudal tenants. The wardship of minors, which in England fell to the feudal lord, was exercised in France by family members, usually the widow or eldest child.

Four *aides* were likewise exacted from feudal tenants but were not properly incidents, as they developed from the obligation of "aid and counsel" to one's lord. A lord could tax his vassals for the knighting of his son, the marriage of his daughter, a crusade, and his own ransom. Philip IV extended the collection of feudal *aides* to rearvassals and even nonnobles, and in the 14th century these exactions served as the basis for national taxation.

Theodore Evergates

[See also: *ABRÈGEMENT DU FIEF; AIDES;* FEUDAL AIDS; FEUDALISM]

Fourquin, Guy. *Lordship and Feudalism in the Middle Ages*, trans. Iris and A. L. Lytton Sells. New York: Pica, 1976.
Ganshof, François L. *Feudalism*, trans. Philip Grierson. London: Longman, 1952.
Strayer, Joseph R. *The Reign of Philip the Fair*. Princeton: Princeton University Press, 1980.

FEUDALISM. A term coined in the 17th century and widely used since the 19th, "feudalism" was intended to describe the practices and institutions associated with the word "fief" (*feudum*). When properly used in this technical sense, feudalism is best described in the entry FIEF HOLDING. In French, the word *féodalité*, which is supposed to refer to feudalism in this sense, has been used imprecisely, even though the French use another word, *féodalisme*, to refer to feudalism in the Marxist sense described below.

Medieval historians have become increasingly disenchanted with the term because it has lost much of its meaning as others have appropriated it to describe things having nothing to do with fiefs. It has been used to refer to decentralized aristocratic regimes, to any militaristic preindustrial society, to medieval conditions generally, and even to anything one considers reactionary. The most important of these developments came with the Marxist use of the term to define a stage in history that preceded capitalism. Feudalism in the Marxist sense generally describes a system of agricultural production in which large numbers of peasants work their own small plots as well as a larger demesne farm owned by a lord. Non-Marxist medieval historians often associate this system with the word "manorialism," described in this volume under AGRICULTURE and especially RURAL SOCIAL STRUCTURE. Many non-Marxists now use "feudalism" in something like the Marxist sense. These include most social scientists and many historians of postmedieval societies, but not non-Marxist medieval historians.

In its narrow, fief-holding sense, feudalism emerged in 11th-century France as a set of private arrangements that filled a void left by the breakdown of public institutions of government and justice. Its roots were both Roman and Frankish, but it took hold most strongly in the regions of greatest Frankish influence, roughly what became known as the Languedoil. Notwithstanding the lamentable cliché "feudal anarchy," feudalism actually prevented the worst excesses of lawlessness and political anarchy, which tended to be most severe in regions, mainly the south, where institutions based on the fief developed only belatedly and incompletely.

As traditional public institutions proved inadequate to maintain public order and achieve nonmilitary resolution of disputes, regional rulers like counts made increasing use of private contractual arrangements to enforce their authority. The rise of the fortified castle, however, often undercut this authority, producing a group of castellans who usurped some of the counts' powers and restricted the geographical area in which they could compel obedience. In this unsettled situation (early 11th century), those who were weak came under the protection of the strong, willingly or otherwise, and those who were strong sought to build up enough military might to protect themselves and their dependents. Both developments gave rise to feudal institutions. A lesser noble with a modest lordship who lacked a fortified house could best find protection by becoming the "man" of a powerful castellan, giving homage and fealty to this lord, and holding his lands henceforth as a fief. The castellan, in building up his own forces, gradually found it expedient to have his military retainers (vassals) supported by lands of their own, so he granted them fiefs subject to homage, fealty, and service. These fief holders generally were far inferior to their lords in wealth and power, but as landlords living off the labor of others they were nonetheless members of a small elite at the top of the social order, and the relationships of fief holding carried some presumption of *social* equality. This fact gave feudalism great flexibility, because it could be used as a device for making alliances and resolving conflicts between lords of roughly equal power. A potentially explosive property dispute could be settled by having one lord hold the land as a fief from the other.

Thus the fief-holding men of a particular castellan might have several different origins: lesser landlords who had chosen, or been forced, to hold their lands as fiefs; fighting men who had been granted fiefs to support them as knights; and neighboring castellans who held fiefs as a result of a transaction that resembled a treaty more than anything else. At the highest level of power were those "territorial princes" whose men included all these types but who also built castles and installed their own castellans, who held them as fiefs. A sufficiently powerful prince could sometimes compel existing castellans to render homage for their substantial possessions and hold them as fiefs.

Because the men who held fiefs from a lord varied greatly in their *de facto* power, it has been difficult to describe accurately the obligations attached to fief holding, and conditions also varied according to period and to local custom. The "classic" formulation of feudal obligations described them as consisting of aid (*auxilium*) and counsel (*consilium*). The former included mounted military service, garrison duty, ceremonial gifts on certain occasions, and the obligation to assist financially if the lord were captured and forced to pay a ransom. "Counsel" referred to advice, sought and given according to custom, and service at the court that important lords maintained to deal with cases involving their men.

Against this view of feudal obligations, we have the different formulation of Fulbert of Chartres (1020), who wrote in purely negative terms, listing the things that a man should not do against his lord. Aside from the fact that Fulbert was writing at a time when feudal institutions were just coming into being as a response to public disorder, it is probable that obligations did vary enormously according to the *de facto* power of the parties involved. If a lord held a castle and his man did not, the feudal obligations of the latter were considerable and were enforceable. If, however, the holder of a fief was himself a castellan, the negative obligations described by Fulbert were as much as could be expected unless, in a particular situation, a castellan perceived that self-interest required him to attend his lord's court or respond with troops to his military summons.

The *de facto* power of a party to a feudal relationship, and with it the character of feudal obligations, could be altered dramatically if the holdings of one party were inherited by a minor or subject to a disputed succession. When succession to a fief was in dispute, the lord could make strenuous demands as his price for investing the successful claimant with the fief. If, however, the lord's position was disputed or fell to a minor heir, those who owed homage gained unusual leverage because their support was so sorely needed.

When it came into being in the 11th century as a revival and reformulation of much older practices, feudalism was an *ad hoc* attempt to cope with the disappearance of public courts and public order. As a device for regulating the relationships among the members of a violent military elite through a network of private contracts, it proved to be a flexible tool for reconstructing a system of public order. By the later 12th century, the French kings and territorial princes had found it a useful system for consolidating their power and providing a framework within which professional soldiers, paid officials, and public courts could be reintroduced. When, in the 13th century, feudal institutions were being elaborated in the legal sources, they were already becoming archaic, since military power, judicial authority, and the maintenance of public order no longer depended primarily on private relationships based on the fief. Nevertheless, the outlook of the nobility and the assumptions that gave rise to the representative and fiscal institutions of the 14th century remained strongly influenced by the feudalism of the 12th.

John Bell Henneman, Jr.

[See also: *ABRÈGEMENT DU FIEF; ALLEU/ALLOD;* BENEFICE (NONECCLESIASTICAL); *CONSEIL;* FEALTY; FEUDAL AIDS; FEUDAL INCIDENTS; FIEF/*FEUDUM;* FIEF HOLDING; *FIEF-RENTE;* HOMAGE; INVESTITURE (FEUDAL); *MOUVANCE;* VASSAL]

Brown, Elizabeth A.R. "The Tyranny of a Construct: Feudalism and Historians of Medieval Europe." *American Historical Review* 79 (1974): 1063–88.

Duby, Georges. *La société aux XIe et XIIe siècles dans la région maconnaise.* Paris: Colin, 1953.

Fourquin, Guy. *Lordship and Feudalism in the Middle Ages,* trans. Iris and A.L. Lytton Sells. New York: Pica, 1976.

Ganshof, François L. *Feudalism,* trans. Philip Grierson. London: Longman, 1952.

FIEF/*FEUDUM*. Revenue-producing property granted to a vassal in return for military service. The term *feudum* became common in the 11th century as it displaced "benefice." Although most fiefs consisted primarily of land, they could be entirely nonlanded (e.g., mills, tolls) or consist simply of a right to collect certain revenues (e.g., rents, taxes). The money fief (*fief-rente,* or *feudum de bursa*) was a cash pension paid from a prince's treasury; the counts of Champagne, for instance, assigned many such fiefs on the taxes they collected at the fairs of Champagne. Whatever the source of revenue, a fief was supposed to produce a regular, fixed income.

In most of France, the large-scale feudalization of land occurred from the late 11th century, as lords at all levels created fiefs from their domainal lands and imposed homage on allodial proprietors. At first, fiefs were considered personal grants, but they quickly became heritable and alienable and consequently evoked an increasingly complex set of customs to govern their circulation. Lords with many vassals often conducted inquests in order to determine the current standing of their vassals and fiefs; they also sought to check the abridgment of fiefs by vassals who subinfeudated (subdivided into rear-fiefs) and alienated their fiefs to nonnobles (churches and townsmen) who could not perform military service. In fact, by the 13th century military service was largely detached from feudal tenure, and fiefs became essentially aristocratic (rent-free and tax-exempt) tenures.

Theodore Evergates

[See also: *ABRÈGEMENT DU FIEF*; BENEFICE (NONECCLESIASTICAL); FEUDALISM; FIEF HOLDING; *FIEF-RENTE*; INVESTITURE (FEUDAL)]

Fourquin, Guy. *Lordship and Feudalism in the Middle Ages*, trans. Iris and A. L. Lytton Sells. New York: Pica, 1976.

Ganshof, François L. *Feudalism*, trans. Philip Grierson. London: Longman, 1952.

Guilhiermoz, Paul. *Essai sur l'origine de la noblesse en France au moyen âge*. Paris: Picard, 1902.

Poly, Jean-Pierre, and Eric Bournazel. *La mutation féodale, XIe–XIIe siècles*. 2nd ed. Paris: Presses Universitaires de France, 1991.

FIEF HOLDING. A new institution emerged in many parts of France during the first half of the 11th century, that of fief holding. This was a personal relationship between two men (or in rare cases a man and a woman) of knightly or noble status. One became the other's "man" (*homo*), promising allegiance in an act of homage, and received a fief in return. The fief was a piece of property, usually land, that the vassal, the man who performed homage, held for his lifetime. It could not be taken from him unless he failed to be faithful to his lord, and it was presumed that his heir would normally take up the same fief, subject to doing homage to the lord's heir.

Although this practice of fief holding was new in the 11th century, it had long roots. The commendation of one man to another had similarities to the process by which Roman clients had commended themselves to powerful men during the Roman Empire, or even that by which serfs had commended themselves to landlords during the early Middle Ages. But what was different here was the presumed social equality between the lord of a fief and the vassal who received that fief, as there had never been between a Roman aristocrat and his clients, much less between a landlord and his serfs. The social equality was reflected in the kiss that was a normal part of the homage ceremony.

Again, there are roots of fief holding in the oath of fidelity that Charlemagne demanded of the freemen of his realm—essentially a "negative" oath, not to harm the king in any way—and in the benefices that Carolingian kings gave to their counts as long as they held their offices. But when fief holding became a fully developed institution in the 11th century, it was not part of any public or governmental function. Rather, it was a private relationship between lords involving personal land-holdings. It was in origin extremely *ad hoc*, used in many cases as a means to cement alliances or to settle disputes.

Princes and kings, however, soon saw the potential advantages of the fief-holding system. William the Conqueror divided all of England into fiefs for his great barons. They themselves had men who held fiefs from them, but the king was the ultimate lord of English territory and reserved the right to decide what to do with a fief when the fief holder died. The French and German kings, because they did not start with a clean slate, as had William in England, had more trouble imposing this concept of fief holding as something evolving from the king. But during the course of the 12th century they were able to persuade most dukes and counts that their duchies and counties were indeed fiefs.

Fief holding, which started as a private relationship between aristocrats in the 11th century and became an instrument of royal power in the 12th, reached its peak in the 13th century, when the obligations of holding a fief were institutionalized, the ceremony of homage became both stylized and elaborate, and long lists of fiefs and fief holders were compiled. By the 14th century, however, fief holding was in decline, as salaries and retainer fees, rather than fiefs, became standard for aristocrats in binding their knights to them, and as kings increasingly exercised royal power directly or through judges and bureaucrats, not through dukes and counts. Fief holding, which is what "feudalism" must be considered to mean if the term has any precise meaning at all—and what the term meant when it was coined in the 17th century—had become an insignificant part of social and governmental relationships by the end of the Middle Ages.

Constance B. Bouchard

[See also: *ABRÈGEMENT DU FIEF*; FEUDALISM; FIEF/*FEUDUM*; *FIEF-RENTE*; INVESTITURE (FEUDAL)]

Brown, Elizabeth A.R. "The Tyranny of a Construct: Feudalism and Historians of Medieval Europe." *American Historical Review* 79 (1974): 1063–88.

Dunbabin, Jean. *France in the Making, 843–1180*. Oxford: Oxford University Press, 1985.

Evergates, Theodore. *Feudal Society in the Bailliage of Troyes Under the Counts of Champagne, 1152–1284*. Baltimore: Johns Hopkins University Press, 1975.

Poly, Jean-Pierre, and Eric Bournazel. *La mutation féodale, Xe–XIIe siècles*. Paris: Presses Universitaires de France, 1980.

Structures féodales et féodalisme dans l'Occident méditerranean (Xe–XIIIe siècles). Paris: CNRS, 1980.

FIEF-RENTE. Fiefs-rente, or money fiefs (Lat. *feudum de bursa*), were created when a lord (usually the king) granted a lump sum of money or designated revenues instead of land in exchange for fealty, homage, and military service. It was a central institution in what has been called "bastard feudalism," existing in a period of transition between predominantly feudal (land-based) military systems and predominantly mercenary ones.

Although in theory identical to a landed fief, *fiefs-rente* tended not to be heritable, were not subinfeudated, nor did they owe feudal *aides* and incidents. The essentially mercenary character of *fiefs-rente* is indicated by the fact that their recipients received not only the lump sum, but daily wages on campaign. Subtract fealty and homage from a *fief-rente* and the result is an indenture contract, widely used, especially by the English, to raise troops in the Hundred Years' War.

The use of *fiefs-rente* peaked in the 13th century. Philip II Augustus, having extended royal financial resources, began competing with Richard I and John of England for a limited pool of mercenaries. The use of *fiefs-rente* shot up on both sides as the kings attempted to secure the loyalty of mercenary troops with bonds of homage and fealty. Their use died out when money and its institutions became common enough that homage and fealty were no longer necessary to ensure a contract.

Stephen Morillo

[See also: *ABRÈGEMENT DU FIEF*; FEUDALISM; FIEF/*FEUDUM*; FIEF HOLDING; INVESTITURE (FEUDAL)]

Lyon, Bryce D. "The Feudal Antecedent of the Indenture System." *Speculum* 29 (1954): 503–11.
———. *From Fief to Indenture*. Cambridge: Harvard University Press, 1957.

FIERABRAS. An anonymous chanson de geste of the King Cycle relating the story of the winning of the Passion relics housed at Saint-Denis. Composed in 6,219 Alexandrines at the end of the 12th century, *Fierabras* shows the beginnings of the decomposition of epic narrative into romantic fantasy, in which locality, place, and action become blurred due to the author's propensity to make light of everything, even cruelty and religious earnestness.

Three years before the Battle of Roncevaux, the emir Balan retires with his army to Spain after ransacking Rome and carrying away the treasure of St. Peter. Charlemagne and his army follow. A series of battles culminates in a lonely duel between Oliver and Balan's giant son, Fierabras, who meets defeat and converts to Christianity, while Oliver is taken prisoner. Most of Charlemagne's peers follow Oliver and are likewise captured by the emir, among others Gui de Bourgogne, with whom Fierabras's sister Floripas had already fallen in love after seeing him fight under the walls of Rome. Love scenes and battles between the Saracens and Christians follow until at last the emir himself is captured. Spain is then divided between Gui (and Floripas) and Fierabras, and Charlemagne has the relics brought to Saint-Denis, where they will be exhibited annually during the Lendit fair. The chest of relics, the true "hero" of the poem, serves to combine (at l. 1,260) two older stories, which narrate the destruction of Rome and duel between Fierabras and Oliver, with a more recent second part inspired by a variety of chansons de geste.

In its Old French version, the poem is preserved in four manuscripts. More often than any other chanson de geste, *Fierabras* has been adapted to different environments and times. The earliest adaptation (5,084 Occitan Alexandrines) was composed between 1218 and 1230 in the Toulouse region. The Italian *Cantari di Fierabraccia e Ulivieri* date from the 15th and 16th centuries. A Middle Dutch version is attested for the 14th century, as is the Middle English *Sir Firumbras* (1357–77). The *Sowdon of Babylon*, narrating the Destruction of Rome episode as well as the romantic second part in Spain, is of the first half of the 15th century. *Fierabras*, the first chanson de geste to find its way into print in the 15th century, was, according to Cervantes, a favorite of Don Quixote.

The most important transformation of the Fierabras story appears in the three-part French prose adaptation, the *Histoire de Charlemagne* by Jehan Bagnyon (Geneva, ca. 1475). The first part deals with the legendary origins of France and traces its history through the reigns of the Merovingians to Charlemagne; Bagnyon dwells on the latter's legendary pilgrimage to Jerusalem and Constantinople by rendering the old poem of the *Voyage de Charlemagne* into prose. The second and longest part narrates the story line of *Fierabras*, and the third summarizes Vincent de Beauvais's version of the Pseudo-Turpin chronicle, with emphasis on the Battle of Roncevaux. An immediate success, the work was frequently reedited through the 19th century.

Hans-Erich Keller

[See also: KING CYCLE; *VOYAGE DE CHARLEMAGNE À JERUSALEM ET À CONSTANTINOPLE*]

Bagnyon, Jehan. *L'histoire de Charlemagne* (*parfois dite "Roman de Fierabras"*), ed. Hans-Erich Keller. Geneva: Droz, 1992.
Bekker, Immanuel, ed. *Der Roman von Fierabras, provenzalisch.* Berlin: Reimer, 1829.
I cantari di Fierabraccia e Ulivieri: Italienische Bearbeitung der chanson de geste Fierabras. Marburg: Elwert, 1881.
Kroeber, A., and G. Servois, eds. *Chanson de Fierabras.* Paris: Vieweg, 1860.
Marinoni, Maria Carla, ed. *"Fierabras" anonimo in prosa: Parigi, B.N. mss.* [*fr.*] *2172, 4969.* Milan: Cisalpino–La Goliardica, 1979.
Miquet, Jean, ed. *Fierabras: roman en prose de la fin du XIVe siècle publié d'après les manuscrits fonds français 4969 et 2172 de la Bibliothèque Nationale à Paris.* Ottawa: Éditions de l'Université d'Ottawa, 1983.
Horrent, Jules. "*Chanson de Roland* et Geste de Charlemagne." In *Les épopées romanes*, ed. Rita Lejeune. Heidelberg: Winter, 1981, pp. 24–25 [*La destruction de Rome*], 34–36 [*Fierabras*].
Mandach, André de. *Naissance et développement de la chanson de geste en Europe.* 6 vols. Geneva: Droz, 1961–93, Vol. 5: *La geste de Fierabras: le jeu du réel et de l'invraisemblable, avec des textes inédits.*

FILLE DU COMTE DE PONTHIEU. The first short story in Old French prose, composed in the early 13th century, the *Fille du comte de Ponthieu* relates the adventures of a noblewoman raped before her bound husband; she then tries to kill her witness. To punish the lady, her father, the count of Ponthieu, condemns her to abandonment at sea, where she is rescued, only to be married to a sultan. Later, she saves her first husband and father-in-law from death and escapes with them to France. The story is retold in the 13th-century chronicle by Ernoul, *Histoire d'outremer et du roi Saladin* and in the 15th-century romance *Jean d'Avesnes*.

Wendy E. Pfeffer

Brunel, Clovis, ed. *La fille du comte de Ponthieu, conte en prose, versions du XIIIe et du XVe siècle.* Paris: Champion, 1923.

Régnier-Bohler, Danielle, trans. "La fille du comte de Ponthieu." In *Le cœur mangé—récits érotiques et courtois, XIIe et XIIIe siècles*. Paris: Stock, 1979, pp. 253–279.

Vitz, E. Birge. "Narrative Analysis of Medieval Texts: *La fille du comte de Ponthieu*." *Modern Language Notes* 92 (1977): 645–75.

FISHING. Fish were an important source of dietary protein and fishing a significant economic activity in France throughout the Middle Ages. Miraculous drafts of fishes met the prayers of Merovingian saints. Charlemagne ordered estate managers to improve fish stocks, while contemporary monasteries employed their own fishers. By then, most observing Christians were emulating the monks in abstaining from meat more than one day in three. Technological inability to fish offshore, to preserve, and to transport fish made the saltwater fishery less important than local freshwater stocks, which came under intense exploitation.

Depending on the size of the watercourse, rights over freshwater fisheries belonged to the king, territorial lord, or local landowner, who managed them as part of his domainal economy. Use of the fishery for substance by ordinary peasants was limited, tacit, and, in the later Middle Ages, ever more restricted. Lords allocated fishing zones (*piscaturae*) to specialized craftsmen in return for payments in kind. The varieties and seasons of local fishes called for various capture techniques: at bridges, mill dams, and sluices, permanent palisaded traps and wicker enclosures took migratory salmon and eels; bow nets, seines, hoop nets, and dip nets, as well as a number of angling methods are commonly recorded. By the 12th century, Norman coastal fishers were sending herring, cod, and various flatfishes to Paris from the English Channel and the North Sea. Their inland counterparts caught trout, pike, bream, and, by the early 1200s, the exotic carp.

People carried eastern European carp westward, for this fish's ability to thrive in the artificial fishponds slowly developed from the impoundments made since the 9th century to power mills. By the mid-13th century, complexes of ponds were being constructed purposely for fish culture in, for instance, Burgundy, Sologne, and Forez. After the fish put on two to four years of growth, the pond was drained to harvest them, seeded to grain for a year or so, then refilled and restocked with fry. Full-grown carp or pike could grace a lord's table or, as those from the many ponds of the last Capetian dukes of Burgundy, yield rich returns from sales to bourgeois merchants or the popes in Avignon. The same pressure of commercial demand caused overfishing of French fish stocks. In 1289, Philip IV initiated royal regulation of fishing gear, seasons, and the size of a legal catch. Probably as effective in changing the role of French fisheries, however, was the late-medieval expansion of the sea fishery, especially after the Dutch learned better ways to preserve herring for shipment inland.

Richard C. Hoffman

[See also: FOOD TRADES; HUNTING AND FOWLING]

FLAGELLANTS. *See* POPULAR DEVOTION

FLAMENCA. An Occitan romance dating from ca. 1240–50, *Flamenca* (also called *Las novas de Guilhem de Nivers*) survives in one manuscript (Carcassonne, Bibl. Mun. 34, formerly 2703) with several important lacunae, including first and last pages. Comprising 8,095 lines of octosyllabic rhymed couplets, this zestful narrative develops with wit and sympathy the stylized motifs of *fin'amors* into a full-length *roman*. It mischievously plays the church and marriage against an "underground" world where love rules.

Flamenca's father, Count Gui de Nemurs, consults his wife and advisers before marrying his daughter to the worthy Archimbaut de Bourbon. Archimbaut's love for his bride soon turns to jealousy. He locks her in a tower with two maids, allowing her out only for church and for medicinal baths. Guilhem de Nivers, the outlandishly perfect man in love with Flamenca by reputation alone, then takes rooms at the local bathhouse. His book-learning abets hypocrisy and his wealth facilitates bribery: he obtains the church office of circulating "the Peace." Each Sunday, the lovers exchange two syllables, finally agreeing to meet in the baths. After four months, Flamenca sends Guilhem and her husband away to prove themselves in tournaments, pledging fidelity to Archimbaut provided he end his jealousy. The men become friends. Archimbaut unwittingly delivers a love poem from Guilhem to his wife. At a final home tournament, Flamenca triumphs more than the men.

Stylistic elements suggest "realism" and hence value as a cultural and historical document. Abundant concrete details enliven lists of spices, musical instruments, songs, gifts; baths are sulfurous; a letter is illuminated. Feast days in the main action correspond exactly to those in the calendar years 1197, 1223, and 1234. Easily drawing on the medieval repertoire of rhetorical figures, the *Flamenca* poet spryly crosses boundaries between the "real," the conventional, and the outrageous.

Amelia E. Van Vleck

[See also: *JOUFROI DE POITIERS*]

Gschwind, Ulrich, ed. *Le roman de Flamenca: nouvelle occitane du XIIIe siècle*. 2 vols. Bern: Francke, 1976.

Hubert, Merton J., ed., and Marion E. Porter, trans. *The Romance of Flamenca: A Provençal Poem of the Thirteenth Century*. Princeton: Princeton University Press, 1962.

Huchet, Jean-Charles, ed. and trans. *Flamenca, roman occitan du XIIIe siècle*. Paris: Union Générale d'Éditions, 1988.

Limentani, Alberto. *L'eccezione narrative: La Provenza medievale e l'arte del racconto*. Turin: Einaudi, 1977.

"Encore une bibliographie pour Flamenca?" *Revue des langues romanes* 92 (1988): 105–23.

FLANDERS. The *pagus Flandrensis* was a district along the North Sea coast from Bruges to the Yser River, first mentioned in the 8th century. The "Flanders" with political and economic power by the 10th century, however, was bordered by the Scheldt (Escaut) on the north, the line of the Scheldt and Dender on the east, and the Canche on the south. While the counts held western and southern Flanders in fief of the French crown, lands in the east were held of the Holy Roman emperor.

The first known count, Baudouin I Iron Arm (d. 879), added the districts of Ghent, Waas, Thérouanne, Aardenburg, and perhaps the Yser and Leie valleys to his lands around Bruges. Baudouin II (d. 918) extended his power southward, and Arnulf I the Great (r. 918–65) took Montreuil, Douai, and Artois. After he died, his principality was divided and only reunited in the 11th century, and the counts' position was never as strong in the south, which had a predominantly Romance-speaking population, as in the north, the home of their dynasty. Baudouin IV (r. 988–1035) was the first Flemish count to control both banks of the Scheldt. Count Baudouin V (r. 1035–67) married his son and successor to the widow of the count of Hainaut, but the two houses were divided after the death of Baudouin VI (Baudouin I of Hainaut) in 1070. His young son Arnulf III's position was usurped by his uncle, Robert the Frisian (count of Flanders 1071–93). Flanders and Hainaut were reunited only in 1191.

The next counts tried to keep the peace with their French lords and Norman neighbors on the south. From the early 12th century, Lotharingia and imperial Flanders, which had dominated the diplomacy of the 11th-century counts, moved into the background, while Flemish policy was increasingly caught between the counts' two other feudal lords: the king of France, from whom they held most of their lands, and the king of England, from whom they held a *fief-rente* and on whom their cities were already dependent by the 12th century for high-grade wool. Foreign interests came to the foreground in 1127, when Count Charles the Good was assassinated by members of his entourage. After a civil war in which the king of France supported William Clito, the nephew and rival of King Henry I of England, and the Flemish cities used the confusion to gain concessions from both sides, the cities and nobles chose as count Thierry d'Alsace, maternal grandson of Count Robert the Frisian.

Thierry d'Alsace (r. 1128–68) pursued a policy of neutrality and internal consolidation. He played the international diplomat, particularly as a crusader, making four trips to Palestine and marrying the daughter of King Foulques V of Jerusalem. In 1156, he married his son Philippe to Elizabeth of Vermandois and his daughter Marguerite to Elizabeth's brother Raoul V. After 1157, Thierry spent most of his time in Palestine, and power was exercised by Philippe, who became count in his own right in 1168. After Raoul V's death, Philippe arranged his widowed sister's marriage to Count Baudouin V of Hainaut. One of the great princes of Europe, Philippe consolidated his authority by promoting economic growth, notably in the foundation of new towns, instituting *baillis*, who took over most of the functions of the now feudalized *châtelains*, and giving new constitutions to the larger cities that strictly subordinated them to the count's administration.

Philippe d'Alsace's two marriages were childless, and he undertook closer relations with the French crown after the young Philip II Augustus, his ward, became king in 1180. He arranged the marriage of his niece Isabelle de Hainaut to the king. But to get this marriage he had to promise as her dowry one-third of his lands, including southern Flanders and Artois. After Elizabeth of Vermandois died in 1182, Philippe's refusal to return Vermandois to her sister led to a war with the French.

After Philippe d'Alsace died in Palestine, he was succeeded by Baudouin V of Hainaut, who ruled in Flanders as Baudouin VIII (r. 1191–95). Although Baudouin VIII had had to surrender Artois to the French crown as the price of the successsion, Baudouin IX (r. 1195–1205) managed to get most of it back by 1200. Baudouin IX became the first Latin emperor of Constantinople, but he died in captivity in the East after a military defeat in 1205, leaving Flanders to his two young daughters. Philip Augustus in 1212 forced the elder, Jeanne (countess 1205–44), to marry Ferrand of Portugal (d. 1233), who quickly took the Anglo-Guelf side in the dispute between King John I and the French. After the Battle of Bouvines (1214), Ferrand was kept in prison until Jeanne accepted the Treaty of Melun, which subordinated Flanders to the French crown. Her death without children in 1244 made her sister Marguerite countess of Flanders. Marguerite's first years were overshadowed by the power struggles of the children of her two marriages, to Burchard d'Avesnes and Guillaume de Dampierre. The countess also fell afoul of the cities, demanding that they contribute to paying her debts to the English king. When they refused, the English embargoed the export of their wool in 1270, and Flanders had to submit to a humiliating peace in 1275.

Long before this, Flanders had developed a precocious economic prosperity. There had been substantial population growth in the vicinity of Ghent as early as the 7th century. Colonization and reclamation were also significant in the 11th century east of Ghent and around Ypres and the coastal area, which led to the development of Bruges as the most important Flemish port. Most other inhabitable areas of Flanders were drained and colonized by the early 13th century, although the sandy and infertile northeast lagged behind. The classic manorial regime declined earlier in Flanders than in neighboring territories. The rural population of maritime Flanders had been free from the beginning, but the development of commercial relations and the advantages gained by the peasants during the clearance movements led to the emancipation of most of the others from labor services by the 13th century except for a few areas in imperial Flanders. The chronology of clearances suggests a strong population growth in the central Middle Ages and relative overpopulation by 1250. Many rural tenements had been subdivided into units that were too small to sustain households, although this in turn promoted efficient agriculture and high seed yields. Flemish farming practice, emphasizing multiple sowings each year and intensive cultivation of the fallow and of industrial and fodder crops and animal husbandry, was the most technically advanced of Europe.

Flemish commerce in the 11th and 12th centuries was chiefly with England for wool and with the Rhineland

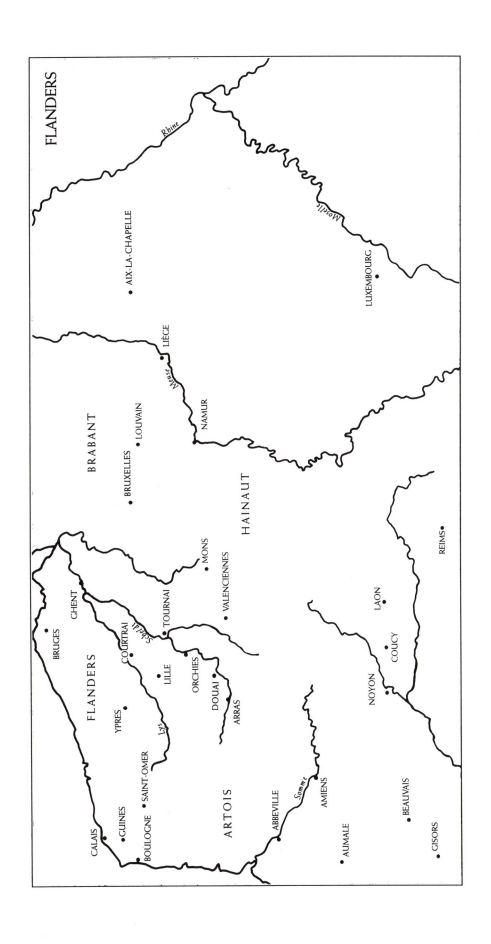

COUNTS OF FLANDERS to 1322

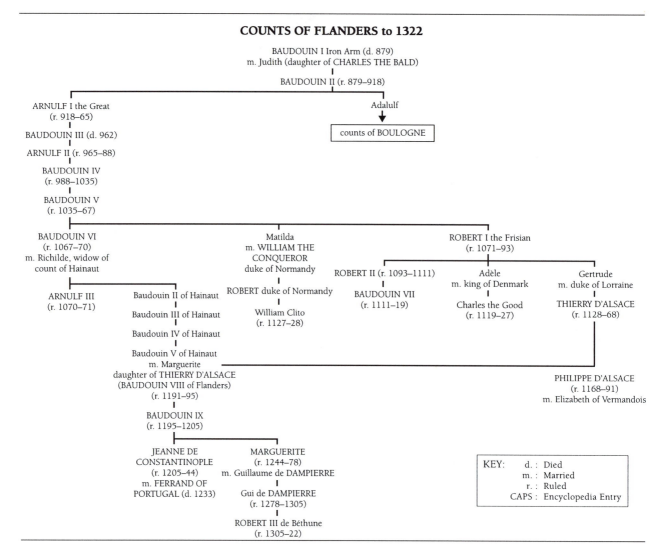

BAUDOUIN I Iron Arm (d. 879)
m. Judith (daughter of CHARLES THE BALD)

BAUDOUIN II (r. 879–918)

ARNULF I the Great
(r. 918–65)

BAUDOUIN III (d. 962)

ARNULF II (r. 965–88)

BAUDOUIN IV
(r. 988–1035)

BAUDOUIN V
(r. 1035–67)

Adalulf

counts of BOULOGNE

BAUDOUIN VI
(r. 1067–70)
m. Richilde, widow of
count of Hainaut

Matilda
m. WILLIAM THE
CONQUEROR
duke of Normandy

ROBERT I the Frisian
(r. 1071–93)

ARNULF III
(r. 1070–71)

Baudouin II of Hainaut

ROBERT duke of Normandy

William Clito
(r. 1127–28)

ROBERT II (r. 1093–1111)

BAUDOUIN VII
(r. 1111–19)

Adèle
m. king of Denmark

Charles the Good
(r. 1119–27)

Gertrude
m. duke of Lorraine

THIERRY D'ALSACE
(r. 1128–68)

Baudouin III of Hainaut

Baudouin IV of Hainaut

Baudouin V of Hainaut
m. Marguerite
daughter of THIERRY D'ALSACE
(BAUDOUIN VIII of Flanders)
(r. 1191–95)

PHILIPPE D'ALSACE
(r. 1168–91)
m. Elizabeth of Vermandois

BAUDOUIN IX
(r. 1195–1205)

JEANNE DE
CONSTANTINOPLE
(r. 1205–44)
m. FERRAND OF
PORTUGAL (d. 1233)

MARGUERITE
(r. 1244–78)
m. Guillaume de DAMPIERRE

Gui de DAMPIERRE
(r. 1278–1305)

ROBERT III de Béthune
(r. 1305–22)

KEY: d. : Died
        m. : Married
        r. : Ruled
        CAPS : Encyclopedia Entry

for wine, in return for which Flanders exported finished cloth. The counts' economic policies included furthering a cycle of five fairs. Flanders became the most densely urbanized region of northern Europe in the 13th and 14th centuries. While Bruges was a largely commercial city, albeit with a substantial textile industry, the prosperity of Ghent, Ypres, and most of the smaller towns was based on the manufacture of cloth—heavy, luxury textiles for export in the case of Ghent and Ypres. The smaller communities, particularly in southern Flanders, used cheaper wools to make lighter textiles for export to Spain and Italy. The mixed cloths of many villages of western Flanders in the late Middle Ages found a considerable export market in the Baltic areas of Germany. Linen was also important in the villages and some of the larger towns, notably Ghent.

The mid-13th century also witnessed the first signs of social conflict in the Flemish cities, which were racked by strikes of textile artisans who resented the domination of the great entrepreneurs. Flanders was struck by the plagues of the late Middle Ages but suffered less than its neighbors. The most severe epidemics seem to have been those

of 1368–69 and 1400, rather than that of 1348–49. By 1469, over one-third of the inhabitants of northern Flanders lived in cities. By this time, however, the great Flemish cities had passed their peak. Considerable industry was moving to the rural areas, and Brabant, Flanders's eastern neighbor, was nearly as densely urbanized.

Countess Marguerite was succeeded by her son, Gui de Dampierre (r. 1278–1305). He was greeted in 1280 with a series of uprisings in the major cities, in which the upper orders, the oligarchies of merchants and landowners who were generally pro-French, were opposed by the artisans and some newly wealthy drapers who were excluded from political participation and cherished Flemish national sentiment. King Philip IV the Fair of France intervened increasingly in the internal affairs of Flanders in the 1290s, hoping to annex Flanders to the crown domain. Gui de Dampierre was subjected to personal humiliations, although he tried until 1297 to remain a loyal vassal; but in early 1297 he renounced his allegiance to Philip and allied with King Edward I of England. The English military failure of that year left Gui isolated; in 1300, he was taken

FLEMISH SUCCESSION IN THE 14th CENTURY

LOUIS I de Nevers
Count of Flanders (r. 1322–46)
m. Marguerite de France, daughter of PHILIP V &
heiress of ARTOIS & the FRANCHE COMTÉ (d. 1382)

LOUIS II de Male (r. 1346–84)
m. Marguerite de BRABANT

MARGUERITE de Male (r. 1384–1405)
Countess of FLANDERS, Nevers, Rethel,
ARTOIS, & FRANCHE COMTÉ
m. (1369) PHILIP THE BOLD (1342–1404),
son of JOHN II of France
Duke of BURGUNDY (1363–1404)

JOHN THE FEARLESS, duke of BURGUNDY,
count of Flanders, Artois, etc. (r. 1404–19)

PHILIP THE GOOD (r. 1419–67)

CHARLES THE BOLD (r. 1467–77)

Antoine, duke of BRABANT (d. 1415)

KEY:	d. :	Died
	m. :	Married
	r. :	Ruled
	CAPS :	Encyclopedia Entry

captive to Paris, and Flanders came under direct French rule. The extreme measures of the French officials provoked a reaction, and in 1302 the French army was defeated in the famous "Battle of the Golden Spurs" near Courtrai. The French returned to the fight, however, and the treaties of Athis (1305) and Pontoise (1312) decreed a huge Flemish indemnity payable to the French, the surrender of the "Walloon" Flemish castellanies of Lille, Douai, and Orchies to the crown, and the restoration of the "Leliaert" (French-sympathizing) patricians who had been overthrown in 1302, but many of whom gradually worked their way back into the town magistracies.

Count Robert III de Béthune (r. 1305–22), Gui's son and successor, was able to restore much of the independence of Flanders, but only at the cost of frequent French military and diplomatic interventions. His grandson and successor, Count Louis de Nevers, came to power after a dispute within his family, was imprisoned by the French briefly at the beginning of his rule, and evidently thought that he owed his position to French help. Louis faced a rebellion in maritime Flanders, including Bruges, between 1323 and 1328, which he was able to crush only with the help of Ghent and the French in 1328. But during the 1330s Louis's entente with Ghent ended as the count tactlessly meddled in municipal affairs. The coming of the Hundred Years' War between England and France caught Flanders between the French sympathies of the count and many wealthy townsmen and the reliance of the great cities on English wool for their draperies. The great cities had taken a leading role in the political affairs of Flanders as early as the crisis of 1127–28, and by the 13th century the "good towns" were meeting in consultation with the counts on all matters of public policy. As an extension of this principle, the cities claimed the right to govern Flanders through the count after 1338, and without him after he fled Flanders in late 1339. Jacques van Artevelde, the captain of Ghent who became the virtual dictator of Flanders, carefully maneuvered Flanders into an English alliance but evidently hoped to convince the count to recognize Ed-

ward III of England as king of France. The English hoped to use Flanders as a base from which to invade France, but this hope failed at the siege of Tournai in 1340. The cities themselves, dominated but not controlled completely by weavers, maintained their rebellion until Ghent was stormed in January 1349.

The new count, Louis de Male (r. 1346–84), imposed loyal regimes in all the cities, generally giving considerable authority to the fullers, a less revolutionary element than the weavers. He gave privileges to foreign merchant colonies in Bruges and confirmed rights given earlier to numerous smaller communities to manufacture certain types of cloth. But there was a disastrous commercial war with the German Hanse between 1358 and 1360, and Flanders had to submit to the Germans' demands after a blockade. Louis's debasements of the coin also contributed to severe inflation and to the problems of Flemish drapers in maintaining their overseas markets. The control of the counter-revolutionary regimes began to fail in 1358, and weaver-dominated regimes were back in control by 1361.

In contrast to what had happened in 1349–50, however, there was no mass proscription of political opponents, and the relations of the cities with the count generally remained correct, although the count did show some favoritism to the fullers, notably in giving them wage increases. Throughout the 14th century, Flanders had become increasingly dependent on imported grain from Germany and France. Louis de Male permitted Bruges, which by now was better disposed to him than was Ghent, to try to evade the monopoly of Ghent on French grain coming down the Lys River by digging a canal into the Lys south of Ghent. The cities had well-defined spheres of influence, and when the workmen of Bruges began digging in the "quarter" of Ghent in the autumn of 1379, the militia of Ghent attacked. The resultant war lasted until the Peace of Tournai (December 18, 1385). Ghent was the only constant opponent of the counts, but at various times it was able to install rebel regimes in Bruges and Ypres and to control the smaller towns and rural jurisdictions, although less effectively than they had done in the time of Jacques van Artevelde.

After the war, Flanders came more completely than ever before into a French orbit. Louis de Male had married his heiress in 1369 to Philip, duke of Burgundy and brother of the French king Charles V. Philip succeeded his father-in-law as ruler of Flanders on January 30, 1384. The Flemish cities were more strictly subordinated to the Burgundian council and Chambre des Comptes. The power of the "four members" of Flanders—Ghent, Bruges, Ypres, and the Franc (*châtellenie*) of Bruges—continued strong during the Burgundian period. Although there were rebellions in the major cities between 1436–38 and 1450–53, the only consequence was the further limitation of the cities' autonomy. With the death of Charles the Bold in 1477 and the succession of his daughter Marie and her husband, Maximilian of Habsburg, the cities again tried unsuccessfully to throw off the foreign ruler. At the end of the 15th century, Flanders was being ruled not by Frenchmen but by a German dynast whose heirs in the Low Countries would be Spaniards.

David M. Nicholas

[See also: ARNULF; ARTEVELDE; BAUDOUIN; BOUVINES; CASSEL; COURTRAI; DAMPIERRE; PHILIP II AUGUSTUS; PHILIP III THE BOLD; PHILIP IV THE FAIR; TEXTILES]

Blockmans, W.P. "Vlaanderen 1384–1482." In *Algemene Geschiedenis der Nederlanden*. 2nd ed. Haarlem: Fibula-van Dishoeck, 1982, Vol. 4, pp. 201–23.

de Hemptinne, Th. "Vlaanderen en Henegouwen onder de erfgenamen van de Boudewijns, 1070–1244." In *Algemene Geschiedenis der Nederlanden*. 2nd ed. Haarlem: Fibula-van Dishoeck, 1982, Vol. 2, pp. 372–98.

Dhondt, Jan. *Les origines de la Flandre et de l'Artois*. Arras: Centre d'Études Régionales du Pas-de-Calais, 1944.

Dunbabin, Jean. *France in the Making, 843–1180*. Oxford: Oxford University Press, 1985.

Faider-Feytmans, G. *La Belgique à l'époque mérovingienne*. Brussels: La Renaissance du Livre, 1966.

Ganshof, François L. *La Belgique carolingienne*. Brussels: La Renaissance du Livre, 1958.

———. *La Flandre sous les premiers comtes*. Brussels: La Renaissance du Livre, 1943.

Koch, A.C.F. "Het graafschap Vlaanderen van de 9de eeuw tot 1070." In *Algemene Geschiedenis der Nederlanden*. 2nd ed. Haarlem: Fibula-Van Dishoeck, 1982, Vol. 2, pp. 354–83.

Nicholas, David. *Town and Countryside: Social, Economic, and Political Tensions in Fourteenth-Century Flanders*. Bruges: De Tempel, 1971.

Nowé, Henri. *La bataille des éperons d'or*. Brussels: La Renaissance du Livre, 1945.

Pirenne, Henri. *Histoire de Belgique*. 7 vols. Brussels: Lamertin, 1922, 1929, Vols. 1–2.

Prevenier, Walter. *De Leden en de Staten van Vlaanderen (1384–1405)*. Brussels: Vlaamse Academie, 1961.

———, and Willem Blockmans. *The Burgundian Netherlands*. Cambridge: Cambridge University Press, 1985.

Quicke, Fritz. *Les Pays-Bas à la veille de la période bourguignonne, 1356–1384*. Brussels: Éditions Universitaires, 1947.

Vandermaesen, M. "Vlaanderen en Henegouwen onder het Huis van Dampierre, 1244–1384." In *Algemene Geschiedenis der Nederlanden*. 2nd ed. Haarlem: Fibula-Van Dishoeck, 1982, Vol. 2, pp. 399–440.

Verhulst, Aadrian. *Histoire du paysage rural en Flandre*. Brussels: La Renaissance du Livre, 1971.

Warlop, E. *The Flemish Nobility Before 1300*. 3 vols. Courtrai: Desmet-Huysman, 1975–76.

FLAVIGNY. Although no longer a major provincial center, Flavigny-sur-Ozerain (Côte-d'Or) retains fascinating medieval monuments and archaeological sites of artistic and historical interest, including the abbey of Saint-Pierre de Flavigny. Established in 719 by Wideradus, a nobleman of Burgundy, the Benedictine abbey was first dedicated to St. Prix, bishop of Clermont and martyr, although St. Peter soon became the dominant titular. Though no structures survive from this early period, as a prestigious monastery Flavigny maintained an important scriptorium by the end of the 8th century. Despite the turmoil of the 9th century, the community succeeded in translating the relics of St. Regina from nearby Alise in 866 under the dynamic abbacy of Ergilo. Subsequent abbots secured the continued prosperity and expansion of Flavigny, and as a town began to form around the abbey from the 10th century onward parish churches and fortifications were constructed. Following occupation by the English in the 14th century, the town was refortified in the late 14th and 15th centuries. In 1644, the Benedictines of Saint-Maur reformed the abbey and occupied it until its demise and sale in the 18th century.

The abbey church of Flavigny, largely ruined today, retains two 8th-century Carolingian crypts, unusual and valuable survivals of early-medieval architecture. The first occupies the lowest level and has been associated with the relics of St. Regina. Originally semicircular in plan with four bays to the west, it was later altered to create a hexagonal terminus. The second, often linked to the 878 dedication by Pope John VIII, is constructed one level up and to the east with two bays, small aisles, and a hexagonal apse. In addition to a Romanesque reworking of the church in the early 11th century, a Gothic campaign of construction is dated 1180–1230. Within the remains of the church and crypt, rare examples of pre-Romanesque and Romanesque sculpture of ornamental vegetal forms on pilasters and capitals are still to be found. A cloister was added ca. 1125, with sculpture in the tradition of Cluny III and Moutiers-Saint-Jean.

The parish church of Saint-Genest, with its narrow nave and refined floral capitals, offers a late example of Burgundian Gothic architecture. It also houses several Burgundian sculptures of the 15th century. A number of medieval houses survive from the 13th century through the 16th, with such architectural details as trilobed arches and mullioned stone windows. Buret-Vitello, an exemplar of Flamboyant Gothic domestic architecture from the late 15th century, includes ogive arches and a statuary niche. During the late-medieval centuries of prosperity, Flavigny was also given the right of fortification. Both the Porte du

Val (13th c. and later) and the Porte du Bourg (mid-15th c.) are valuable survivals of defensive structures.

Leslie Blake DiNella

Bouchard, Constance B., ed. *The Cartulary of Flavigny, 717–1123.* Cambridge: Medieval Academy of America, 1991.

Sapin, Christian. "Saint-Pierre de Flavigny: l'ancienne abbatiale et ses cryptes." *Congrès archéologique* (1986): 97–109.

———. *La Bourgogne préroman.* Paris: Picard, 1986.

———, and Bailey K. Young."The Story of a Medieval Town (Flavigny, France)." *Archaeology* 37 (1984): 26–32.

Stratford, Neil, and Jean Dupont. "Sculptures de Flavigny (Côte-d'Or)." In *Mélanges d'histoire et d'archéologie offerts au professeur K.J. Conant par l'Association Splendide Bourgogne.* Mâcon: Éditions Bourgogne Rhône-Alpes, 1977.

FLODOARD DE REIMS (893–966). Frankish chronicler. The history of west Francia in the first three-quarters of the 10th century is known principally through the *Annales* of Flodoard. This canon of Reims recorded the events from 919 to his own death in 966, focusing on the royal court and the great men of northern Francia. He continued the annals begun by Hincmar of Reims and was succeeded as a chronicler by Richer. Flodoard's other major work was a history of the bishopric of Reims, which also includes many details of 10th-century political history.

Constance B. Bouchard

Flodoard de Reims. *Les annales,* ed. Philippe Lauer. Paris: Picard, 1905.

———. *Historia Remensis ecclesiae.* In *Monumenta Germaniae historica, Scriptores.* Berlin, Hannover, Weimar, 1872–1923, Vol. 13, pp. 409–599.

Dunbabin, Jean. *France in the Making, 843–1180.* Oxford: Oxford University Press, 1985, chap. 2.

FLOIRE ET BLANCHEFLOR. This idyllic romance, based on the story of "Neema and Noam" in the *Thousand and One Nights,* exists in two versions, both anonymous. The earlier (ca. 1160; 3,342 octosyllabic lines in manuscript *A*) is courtly in inspiration and preserved in four manuscripts (*A*: B.N. fr. 375; *B*: B.N. fr. 1447; *C*: B.N. fr. 12562, and, as a fragment, in *V*: Vatican, Palatinus, lat. 1971). A 13th-century reworking, more popular in tone, is preserved in one manuscript and incomplete (3,448 octosyllables; B.N. fr. 19152). Both versions tell of two children born on the same day, one to a pagan queen, the other to a Christian captive, who are brought up together at court and fall in love. King Fénix (Galerïen in the popular version) opposes their union, sells Blancheflor into captivity and tells the hero she has died, building a magnificent tomb to support this fiction. Only when Floire becomes ill does he reveal his deceit. The young man searches through the East and discovers that Blancheflor is held captive by an emir. He bribes a porter with a magnificent goblet, decorated with scenes from the story of Paris and Helen, and is smuggled into the tower in a basket of flowers. He is later discovered by the Emir, who, however, forgives the couple and joins them in marriage. On return to his homeland, Floire becomes king and converts to Christianity.

The popular version stresses the battle skills of the hero but curtails description of objects and settings. Floire wins over the Emir by defending Babylon against his enemy, the story ending with this victory. The courtly version contains references to the works of Ovid, Virgil, and the vernacular Alexander romance *Apollonius de Tyr.* As the owner of the magnificent goblet, Floire becomes part of a heroic line of descent, from Vulcan, its creator, to Aeneas, an earlier owner. The tale's popularity is attested by its translation into a variety of languages, including Dutch, German, Yiddish, Middle English, Italian, and Spanish.

Meg Shepherd

[**See also:** ALEXANDER ROMANCES; APOLLONIUS DE TYR; *AUCASSIN ET NICOLETTE*]

Leclanche, Jean-Luc, ed. *Le conte de Floire et Blancheflor.* Paris: Champion, 1980. [Courtly version.]

Pelan, Margaret M., ed. *Floire et Blancheflor: seconde version: éd. du ms. 19152 du fonds français avec introd., notes, et glossaire.* Paris: Ophrys, 1975. [Popular version.]

Leclanche, Jean-Luc, trans. *Le conte de Floire et Blanchefleur.* Paris: Champion, 1986.

Kibler, William W. "Archetypal Imagery in *Floire et Blancheflor.*" *Romance Quarterly* 35 (1988): 11–20.

Leclanche, Jean-Luc. "La date du conte de *Floire et Blancheflor.*" *Romania* 92 (1971): 556–67.

FLOOVENT. Composed in Burgundy at the end of the 12th century in 2,534 assonanced Alexandrines, the chanson de geste *Floovant* combines the themes of the exiled hero and the Saracen princess who, having fallen in love with the hero, frees him from her father's prison and abandons her religion in order to marry him. It is found in Montpellier 441 and in two fragments in Freiburg (all three of the 14th c.). It was translated into Middle Dutch, Icelandic, and Italian.

King Clovis's son, Floovant, is banished by his father for having cut off his teacher's beard; with his squire, Richier, he enters the service of King Flore of Alsatia, who, upon learning that Floovant has saved his daughter from the Saracens, gives him the sword Joïeuse and the command of an army against the pagan King Galien. Floovant eventually weds the latter's daughter, while Richier, knighted, receives the hand of King Flore's daughter, Florete. When they learn that Clovis has been attacked by Galien at Soissons, Floovant, Richier, and the twelve peers hasten with an army to succor him; then, after a battle in which at one point—unknown to each other—Clovis fights his own son, Galien is killed, and Floovant is crowned Clovis's eventual successor. Attempts to link the story to Merovingian history, especially to Clotar II (584–629) and his son Dagobert I (608–638/39) have failed.

Hans-Erich Keller

Andolf, Sven, ed. *Floovent: chanson de geste du XIIe siècle.* Uppsala: Almqvist and Wiksell, 1941. [With important preface, pp. i–lxii.]

Stricker, Eugen. *Entstehung und Entwicklung der Floovant-Sage.* Tübingen: Heckenhauer, 1909.

FLORENCE DE ROME. A chanson de geste of 6,410 Alexandrine lines from the first quarter of the 13th century, *Florence de Rome* is based on the legend of a virtuous married woman unjustly accused of adultery by her brother-in-law, disowned by her husband, pursued by several men, and falsely charged with murdering a child. She finally enters a convent, receives extraordinary healing powers, and is vindicated when her oppressors, stricken by horrible diseases, confess to their crimes. There are hundreds of versions of this story, both oriental and occidental (the earliest ca. 1150 in the German *Kaiserchronik*). Other names were given to Florence, notably Crescentia, Hildegarde, or Constantia. The poem was reworked in monorhyming quatrains in the 14th century and was also incorporated into the Pseudocycle of Dagobert in several 15th-century manuscripts, including B.N. fr. 24384.

Renate Blumenfeld-Kosinski

[See also: DAGOBERT, PSEUDOCYCLE OF]

Wallensköld, Axel, ed. *Florence de Rome: chanson d'aventure du premier quart du XIIIe siècle.* 2 vols. Paris: Didot, 1909. [Vol. 1 offers a valuable study of the oriental connections of the legend and its spread through Europe.]

Karl, Ludwig. "Florence de Rome et la vie de deux saints de Hongrie." *Revue des langues romanes* 52 (1909): 163–80.

Stefanovic, Svetislav. "Die Crescentia-Florence Sage: Eine kritische Studie über ihren Ursprung und ihre Entwicklung." *Romanische Forschungen* 29 (1911): 461–556.

FLORENT ET OCTAVIEN. One of several late-medieval epics inspired by the deeds of a pseudohistorical King Dagobert and his foundation of the abbey of Saint-Denis near Paris, this one centering on the adventures of the twin sons of a Roman emperor. The mid-14th-century poem of some 18,5000 Alexandrines, based on an octosyllabic 13th-century *Octavien* (5,000 lines), was rewritten in prose for a Burgundian courtier, Jean de Créquy, in 1454. An abbreviated version was printed several times during the 16th century, the last in 1592.

Charity Cannon Willard

[See also: DAGOBERT, PSEUDOCYCLE OF]

Laborderie, N., ed. *Florent et Octavien.* Paris: Champion, 1991.

Bossuat, Robert. "*Florent et Octavien,* chanson de geste du XIVe siècle." *Romania* 73 (1952): 289–31.

Krappe, Alexandre H. "*Florent et Octavien.*" *Romania* 65 (1939): 359–73.

FLORUS OF LYON (d. ca. 860). Deacon and teacher at the cathedral school of Lyon, Florus studied under Leidradus and became a noted exegete, known especially for such *catenae* as his composite of Augustine on the Pauline epistles. Florus supported the rights of the deposed bishop Agobard in 835 and opposed Amalarius of Metz at the Synod of Quierzy in 838. He also played a part in disputes with Gottschalk and Johannes Scottus Eriugena, in both cases supporting Rabanus Maurus.

E. Ann Matter

[See also: AMALARIUS OF METZ; ERIUGENA, JOHANNES SCOTTUS; GOTTSCHALK; RABANUS MAURUS]

Florus. [Works in] *PL* 119, 121; *MGH* PLAC 2.509–66, Stegmüller RB 2.2274–79.

Charlier, C. "Les manuscrits personnels de Florus de Lyon et son activité litteraire." In *Mélanges E. Podechard.* Lyon: Facultés Catholiques, 1945, pp. 71–84.

———. "La compilation augustinienne de Florus sur l'apôtre: sources et authenticité." *Revue bénédictine* 57 (1947): 132–86.

Fransen, I. "Les commentaires de Bède et de Florus sur l'apôtre et saint Césaire d'Arles." *Revue bénédictine* 65 (1955): 262–66.

Wilmart, André. "Sommaire de l'exposition de Florus sur les épîtres." *Revue bénédictine* 38 (1926): 205–16.

FOIX. The last of the great fiefs of the Midi to be restored to the crown, the county of Foix was also one of the last to be created during the Middle Ages. The town and castle of Foix, noted as early as the 7th century, formed part of the large county of Comminges-Couserans. A partition of the inheritance of Count Roger le Vieux in 1002 left the territory of Foix to a cadet, Bernard-Roger, whose sons Roger I (d. 1064) and Pierre-Bernard (r. 1064–70) ultimately assumed the title count of Foix. The domains of the counts included the cities of Foix and Pamiers, the towns of Lézat, Saverdun, and Mazères to the north and Tarascon, Lordat, and Aix-les-Termes to the south. During the Albigensian Crusade, Count Raymond-Roger, whose sister Esclarmonde sheltered and assisted heretics at Pamiers, was a determined enemy of Simon de Montfort. With the elimination of the viscounts Trencavel and the extinction of the house of Toulouse, Foix emerged in the mid-13th century as the most important independent fief in lower Languedoc. In 1290, its territory increased with the marriage of Count Roger-Bernard III to Marguerite, heiress of the viscounty of Béarn.

The apogee of the counts' power came in the 14th century, when they profited from the weakness of royal authority during the Hundred Years' War and the strategic position of their own domains to play a critical role in the politics of the kingdom. Against the determinedly pro-French position of his rivals the counts of Armagnac, the brilliant and lettered Gaston III Phoebus (r. 1343–91) pursued a policy of official neutrality in favor of the English and engaged in frequent hostilities with both the house of Armagnac and the duke of Berry, royal lieutenant of Languedoc. His successor Jean I (r. 1412–36) continued the pro-English alliance until the accession of Charles VII, from whom he accepted the lieutenancy of Languedoc. At the death of François Phoebus (1483), the county of Foix passed to the house of d'Albret and was united to the monarchy with the accession of Henry IV.

Alan Friedlander

[See also: ALBIGENSIAN CRUSADE; GASTON PHOEBUS; LANGUEDOC; TRENCAVEL]

Courteault, Henri. *Gaston IV comte de Foix, vicomte souverain de Béarn, prince de Navarre, 1423–1472.* Toulouse: Privat, 1895.

Tucoo-Chala, Pierre. *Gaston Fébus et la souveraineté de Béarn.* Pau: Marrimpouey, 1981.

———. *Gaston Fébus, un grand prince d'occident au XIV siècle.* Pau: Marrimpouey, 1983.

Wolff, Philippe. "Une ville pyrénéenne du XIII siècle: l'exemple de Foix." *Annales du Midi* 77 (1965): 137–55.

FOLIES TRISTAN. The common subject matter of the Bern *Folie* (Bern MS 354; 584 octosyllables) and Oxford *Folie* (Bodleian Library, d6; 998 octosyllables) is Tristan's return to Iseut conjoined to the motif of feigned madness. The narrative of these two short tales is itself based on another "return": Tristan's evocation, first at Marc's court and then for Iseut and Brangain, of the main events of his past life. Because of the episodes cited, the Bern version is generally associated with the tradition represented by Eilhart and Béroul, while Oxford is related to Thomas d'Angleterre. Thus the two texts are important for reconstituting episodes that are missing in the Béroul and Thomas fragments.

Tristan's hiding behind a mask of madness permits the development, without constraints of decency, chronology, or verisimilitude, of a highly eroticized discourse, which moves without transition from burlesque fantasies and obscenities to lyric laments and the detailed depiction of dream worlds. Marked by the repetition of the verb "to recall, remember" (OFr. *membrer, remembrer*), the *Folies* return obsessively to the main Tristan themes of wounds, lovesickness, self-alienation (of which madness is the sign), unsatisfied desire, and death. They translate another Tristan obsession as well: the impossibility of establishing the veracity of language, especially the language of love. Tristan's words alone are not enough for Iseut to recognize him in either *Folie.* Only the hound Husdent can pick out the hero, who, in the Oxford *Folie,* must revert to his own voice to convince the queen to receive him again.

Emmanuèle Baumgartner

[See also: BÉROUL; THOMAS D'ANGLETERRE; TRISTAN ROMANCES]

Hoepffner, Ernest, ed. *Folie Tristan de Berne.* Paris: Les Belles Lettres, 1934.

———, ed. *Folie Tristan d'Oxford.* Paris: Les Belles Lettres, 1938.

Walter, Philippe, and D. Lacroix, trans. *Tristan et Iseut: les poèmes français, la saga Norroise.* Paris: Livre de poche, 1989, pp. 233–311.

FOLKLORE. Discipline that involves the study of daily life and material culture, symbolic systems, rituals, popular religion, folk medicine, judicial customs, performances, songs, tales, riddles, and many other aspects of life. The study of folklore—which draws on fields as diverse as literature, history, historical anthropology, ethnobotany, art and music history, and sociology—has shed considerable light on medieval French culture.

Historical anthropology, for example, has enabled us to undertake the excavation of a medieval folk culture no longer seen as a jumble of fragments but as an integrated worldview, acting on its environment through rituals and ceremonies and translating that experience through myth and legend. It has also stressed the specificity of the diverse ethnic components, regional cultures, and religious cultures that converged in the French Middle Ages. Archaeology has provided insights into the medieval rural world that have established foundations for understanding the relationship of material culture to beliefs. Examples are Bordenave and Vialle's study of funerary objects and burial practices in the rural areas around Albi (1983) and Chapelot and Fossier's 1980 study of villages that yielded information on patterns of settlement and human bonding. Linguistics is a kind of archaeology of words. Personal names and place-names, words for tools, plants, and trade techniques—all these help document material culture, as well as legends and the mental processes at work in word associations and word play. Facetious or derogatory surnames, for instance, are precious indicators of popular invective systems, exclusion patterns, and animal and plant symbolism.

Iconography is another important source. Its study was long dominated by Christian readings, but from the 1970s on scholarship illuminated the pagan or folk underpinnings of medieval sculptures in both ecclesiastical and secular buildings (e.g., Ross and Sheridan's work on grotesques and gargoyles and the Krauses' on misericords, both 1975). French cities, large and small, are richly adorned with symbolic and functional iconography. The densely coded language of street signs, known mostly through archival records, had been catalogued since the 19th century but not read with respect to folkloristics. Gaibenet's pioneering work (1984) identified images previously thought of as simply bizarre or amusing. Manuscripts, capitals and portals of churches, corner pillars of houses, beams, and lintels came alive with a folk world rife with facetious saints, mythological creatures, wild men, mermaids, the Jack-O'Green, the four outcast sons of Aymon, but also with the symbols of folly and with obscene gestures to ward off evil, along with references to social customs, like the *ius primae noctis.*

Folk practices and customs are known through ample documentation. Letters of pardon refer to the organization of the calendar, feasts, and other aspects of religion. They bring us right into the worldview of the protagonists. A landmark in the study of medieval French folklore was Vaultier's work on letters of pardon during the Hundred Years' War (1965), which incorporated fragmentary information into the standard classification system of folklorists.

Another document of inestimable impact is the 15th-century *Évangiles des quenoilles*, a collection of aphorisms, medical recipes, charms, and beliefs attributed to a group of rural women who are presented as transmitting their knowledge through the sometimes bored or ironic cooperation of a scribe. Jeay's 1982 study raised crucial issues of how to read "folk" against "clerical," direct information against mediated, and how to exercise suspension of disbelief in handling such a source.

Literature provides a wealth of references to songs, legends, and proverbs. Though folk music, like all medieval music, is one of the hardest domains to document, song texts were embedded in medieval narratives and in separate collections, such as the *chansons de toile*. The function of orality in the formation, composition, and transmission of many medieval fictional narratives has been the subject of long debate. This is particularly true of the chanson de geste; the study of its formulaic composition, facilitated by Duggan's use of computers, has prompted serious rethinking of the relationship between oral and written composition and of blithe characterizations of a genre as uniquely "aristocratic" or "popular."

The extensive corpus of exempla, catalogued by Tubach (1969), is replete with material from oral tradition and has generated a renewed interest in the sources and variations of complex folktale cycles and of the relationships and tensions between folk culture and its clerical voicing. The study of hagiography allows us to differentiate saints' cults that can be deemed truly popular from those cults generated from above; an example is historical anthropologist Jean-Claude Schmitt's 1983 study of the local cult of a deceased dog "canonized" by the folk. Feminist studies, often coming from a social-science or art-history perspective, have played a major role in the development of this aspect of medieval folklore, broadening its definition beyond traditional distinctions of rural-urban or elite-folk to include the communities of women. Ashley and Sheingorn, for instance, begin their volume of essays on the place of St. Anne in late-medieval society by stating that their perspective is at the intersection of popular culture, popular piety, and women's studies, informed by cultural and gender studies, and attempts to bridge the gap between popular and elite cultures, between folklore and theology.

The foregoing represents just a sampling of French medieval-folklore scholarship, making reference to trends and issues that reflect to the greatest possible extent on the whole. Other areas that have been studied include public performance, carnival plays and other rituals, fraternities, the folklore of trades, folk medicine, fools and folly, witchcraft and the Devil, demons and ghosts, the legends of Melusine the serpent and Hellekin, leader of the unquiet dead, and tales of Roland leaving his mark on the landscape.

Though fully recognized as a discipline only in the past few decades, the study of medieval French folklore has a venerable history. One of the earliest explicit attempts at gathering folklore from primary sources in an organized way was the 16th-century doctor Laurent Joubert's *Erreurs populaire au fait de la médecine et régime de santé*, whose 1576 edition included catalogues of sundry medical beliefs entitled *Propos vulgaires*, or sayings from the untutored, gleaned at his behest by friends and colleagues. Satirical depictions of Catholic folk practices by Protestant writers and polemicists, such as the erudite Henri Estienne (*Apologie pour Hérodote*), also provided useful insights into the folk religion of the time.

Medieval French folklore became a more densely charted sea with the 19th-century development of folklore studies throughout Europe, in the intellectual context of Romanticism. The upsurge of Germanic nationalism profoundly affected French folklore studies, since German scholars happily annexed France to Germanic culture. An important example of this approach is found in Liebrecht's notes to a partial edition of Gervase of Tilbury's *Otia imperialia*, entitled *Ein Beitrag zu deutsches Mythologie* (1856), a comparative study of medieval traditions with a medley of modern west European folk traditions, many of them French.

Throughout the 19th century, scholarly journals, national, regional, and local, published a plethora of articles on aspects of medieval French folklore, in which philology was dominant. Such medievalists as Joseph Bédier, Gaston Raynaud, and Paul Meyer focused on the role of medieval French fabliaux and other tales in the formation and transmission of the corpus of folktales and legends. Much attention was directed to the question of attributing Indian origins to European tales, and medieval tales generally; such was the argument in Bédier's *Fabliaux* and in Cosquin's 1911 study of the tale of "The Cat and the Candle" (*Romania* 40). Studies on Old French explained *façons de dire*—sayings, idiomatic expressions—and helped explicate the extended meaning of words and the beliefs underpinning them. Meyer and others also devoted attention to medieval medicine and its relationship to folk practices. In the early 19th century, extensive collections of miscellaneous texts were published: comic plays, debates, pamphlets, and broadsides, many of them connected to carnival and other popular feasts. The Romanian folklorist Sainéan studied the history of French slang; the polymath Francisque Michel's commentaries on the *races maudites*—pariah communities, such as the *cagots*, the presumed descendants of lepers—albeit now obsolete in scope and method, raised a question of folk culture and French history that is still discussed by medieval historians.

The early 20th century saw giant leaps in French folkloristics. Van Gennep's *Manuel de folklore français contemporain* (1937–58), still the standard work, provided the calendar and festive structure for the study of isolated folklore manifestations; his discussion included medieval examples. Saintyves, concerned with the survival of pagan practices, treated many themes of medieval hagiography in connection with folklore, such as the cult of St. Christopher, the symbolism of leprosy, virgin births, and protective processions around cities. Another landmark was

Marc Bloch's *The Royal Touch* (1924; trans. 1973). A historian of the of the economic and social relations of feudalism, Bloch studied the healing powers of kings, exploring the connection among the political rituals of the monarchy, its religious content, and the practices of the folk.

Bloch's advances in bringing the discipline of history into the study of medieval folklore and Vaultier's reliance on letters of pardon did not have their full impact until much later, with the "New History." The historian Jacques Le Goff favored a multidisciplinary approach to history that included folklore and its methodologies as valid tools. In his *Time, Work and Culture* (1980), Le Goff discussed the function of blood tabus in certain professions, the connection between official processions and folk religion, dragon lore, and the myth of Melusine, the serpent-tailed woman of dynastic foundation legends. Focused on a specific area and regional culture, Emmanuel Le Roy Ladurie's *Montaillou: The Promised Land of Error* (1978) also joined folklore and history. Based on a 14th-century inquisitor's records of a heresy-hunting expedition in a previously Cathar-Albigensian region, Ladurie combined ethnology, sociology, anthropology, and folklore as domains of the historian. He classified the behaviors of the people of Montaillou according to recognizable folklore categories and discussed beliefs within the broader context afforded by a comparative folkloristic view.

In the 1970s, the study of popular religion and popular religious sensitivity accelerated. The use of clerical writers, theologians, and even inquisitors was being recognized as an important means of retrieving fragments of folk culture. Essays on Languedoc in the 13th and 14th centuries, by Étienne Delaruelle, Bernard Plongeron, and Jean-Claude Schmitt (*Cahiers de Fanjeaux 11* [1985]), examined the saints, feasts, legends, and amulets of popular piety. Ethnologist Claude Gaignebet's *Art profane et religion populaire* (1985) was a syncretic rereading of medieval culture and folklore in which iconography, myth, custom, and literature combined to underscore the pivotal importance of time, the folk calendar, and myth. He reopened the forbidden dossier of obscenity in art and culture, stressed the popular foundations of great texts of medieval literature, and incorporated isolated folk practices into systems of myth and religion, parallel but not always opposed to Christianity. Symbolic and mythical readings of the folk calendar were furthered in Philippe Walter's studies of time and hagiography in medieval narratives, and his dictionary of Christian mythology (1992) provides a useful summary of medieval folklore, myth, and ritual.

Francesca Canadé Sautman

[See also: APOLLONIUS DE TYR; ARTHUR; CHANSON DE GESTE; *CHANSON DE TOILE*; COOKING; CUSTUMALS/*COUTUMIERS*; DANCE; DIET AND NUTRITION; EXEMPLUM; FABLE (*ISOPET*); FABLIAU; GUILD; HAGIOGRAPHY; HEALTH CARE; JONGLEUR; MAGIC; MUSICAL INSTRUMENTS; MUSICAL PERFORMANCE PRACTICE; NECROMANCY; PILGRIMAGE; POPULAR DEVOTION; PROCESSION; PROVERB; RAIS, GILLES DE; *ROBERT LE DIABLE*; ROMANCE; RURAL SOCIAL STRUCTURE; SAINTS, CULT OF; SAINTS' LIVES; THEATER; WITCHCRAFT]

Ashley, Kathleen, and Pamela Sheingorn. *Interpreting Cultural Symbols: Saint Anne in Late Medieval Society*. Athens: University of Georgia Press, 1990.

Bloch, Marc. *The Royal Touch: Sacred Monarchy and Scrofula in England and France*, trans. J.E. Anderson. London: Routledge and Kegan Paul, 1973.

Gaignebet, Claude, and Dominique Lajoux. *Art profane et religion populaire au moyen âge*. Paris: Presses Universitaires de France, 1984.

Jeay, Madeleine. *Savoir faire: une analyse des croyances des "Évangiles des quenouilles" (XVe siècle)*. Montreal: Le Moyen Français, 1982.

Le Goff, Jacques. *Time, Work and Culture in the Middle Ages*, trans. Arthur Goldhammer. Chicago: University of Chicago Press, 1980.

Le Roy Ladurie, Emmanuel. *Montaillou: The Promised Land of Error*, trans. Barbara Bray. New York: Braziller, 1978.

Medieval Folklore. Lewiston: Mellen, 1991– . [Annual.]

Schmitt, Jean-Claude. *The Holy Greyhound: Guinefort, Healer of Children Since the Thirteenth Century*, trans. Martin Thom. Cambridge: Cambridge University Press, 1983.

Walter, Philippe. *Mythologie chrétienne: rites et mythes du moyen âge*. Paris: Entente, 1992.

FOLQUET DE MARSELHA (fl. ca. 1178–95). Son of a rich Genoese merchant, the troubadour Folquet de Marselha was himself a wealthy merchant in Marseille by ca. 1178. Around 1200, he, his wife, and two sons entered the Cistercian abbey of Le Thoronet, of which he became abbot. As bishop of Toulouse from 1205 until his death in 1231, he helped found the Order of Preachers (Dominicans) and organize the Albigensian Crusade. According to the *Chanson de la croisade contre les Albigeois*, Folquet was responsible for the deaths at the stake of 10,000 Albigensians.

Of Folquet's nineteen certain songs, fourteen are love songs (thirteen have music preserved); the others are two crusade songs, two debate poems, and one *planh*. In song as in deed, he praised courtly love before rejecting it, in a learned and literary style that builds on his assimilation of Latin and Occitan *sententiae*. Yet his carefully refined and subtle artistry remains original and abstract, preoccupied with aesthetic and moral issues. His poetry and music were admired and imitated.

Roy S. Rosenstein

[See also: *CROISADE CONTRE LES ALBIGEOIS, CHANSON DE LA*; TROUBADOUR POETRY]

Stronski, Stanislaw, ed. *Le troubadour Folquet de Marseille*. Kraków: Académie des Sciences, 1910.

Locher, Caroline. "Folquet de Marseille and the Structure of the Canso." *Neophilologus* 64 (1980): 192–207.

FONTENAY. Founded by St. Bernard himself in 1118, the abbey of Fontenay (Côte-d'Or) was one of the most

Fontenay, Cistercian abbey church, cloister. *Photograph courtesy of Whitney S. Stoddard.*

Fontenay (Côte d'Or), Cistercian abbey church. *Photograph courtesy of Whitney S. Stoddard.*

prosperous Cistercian foundations in the Middle Ages, with some 300 monks and postulants. The abbey church, begun ca. 1130 thanks to the generosity of Évrard, bishop of Norwich (d. 1150), and consecrated in 1147 by Pope Eugenius III, is one of the oldest Cistercian churches in France. It is marked by the simplicity typical of Cistercian architecture. Constructed on the plan of a Latin cross, the eight-bay nave is covered by pointed barrel vaulting and supported by transverse arches carrying barrel vaults in the side aisles. The flat chevet is lit by triple lancets, symbolizing the Trinity. The spare dormitory has a beautiful 15th-century timbered ceiling in the form of an upturned ship's keel. The elegant cloister and the rib-vaulted chapter house, supported by central piers, are pure Romanesque. Other conventual buildings include a prison, warming room and scriptorium, infirmary, and forge.

William W. Kibler/William W. Clark

[See also: CISTERCIAN ART AND ARCHITECTURE]

Aubert, Marcel. "Fontenay." *Congrès archéologique (Dijon)* 91 (1928): 234–51.
Bégule, Lucien. *L'abbaye de Fontenay.* 4th ed. Paris: Laurens, 1966.

FONTEVRAULT. The 12th-century abbey of Fontevrault (Maine-et-Loire), located near the Loire's confluence with the Vienne, was founded, probably in 1101, by Robert d'Arbrissel as a monastic community for those, especially women, who had been attracted by his preaching. Fontevrault was a "double monastery," with communities of men and women living separate existences but sharing a single church and under the single rule of an abbess. It attracted generous benefactions, notably from Henry II Plantagenêt and his son Richard the Lionhearted, who attributed his release from prison to the nuns' prayers. Both kings were buried at Fontevrault in the *cimetière des rois*, along with Henry's wife, Eleanor of Aquitaine, and his daughter-in-law Isabelle d'Angoulême, who ended her days here as a nun.

The abbey church, consecrated in 1119, is Romanesque in style and has a barrel-vaulted choir with ambulatory and three radiating chapels, a transept likewise barrel-vaulted, and an aisleless nave vaulted with a series of cupolas. This is the northernmost example of this latter stylistic feature, seen so often in southwestern France. The church was transformed into a prison after the Revolution, and its nave was divided into three stories. Restoration was undertaken at the beginning of the 20th century.

Also largely intact are the 16th-century cloister, chapter house, and refectory. Particularly remarkable at Fontevrault is the 12th-century octagonal kitchen, the Tour d'Évrault, each of whose original eight apsidioles had its own chimney. (Three have since disappeared.)

John B. Cameron

[**See also:** ROBERT D'ARBRISSEL]

Crozet, Réne. "L'église abbatiale de Fontevraud." *Annales du Midi* 48 (1936): 113–50.
Erlande-Brandeburg, Alain. "Le 'cimitière des rois' à Fontevrault." *Congrès archéologique (Anjou)* 122 (1964): 482–92.

FOOD TRADES. Most medieval people spent well over half of their incomes on food and drink, making the trade in victuals the most important sector of the medieval economy. In the countryside, both lords and peasants concentrated on the agricultural production of foodstuffs, particularly grains, meat, and grapes for wine. Peasants, many of whom lived on the edge of subsistence, produced most of their own food and often paid their rents or received wage payments in the form of food. By the late Middle Ages, however, an increasingly large number of peasants produced a marketable agricultural surplus, which they either sold to middlemen (like traveling cornmongers) or brought to village and town markets themselves for sale directly to consumers.

Urban inhabitants were the most active traders and consumers in the medieval food trades. Between 25 and 40 percent of townspeople worked in some branch of the trade in victuals. Their occupations ranged from that of the wealthy vintner engaged in the wholesale purchase and sale of large quantities of wine, to the petty huckster who sold onions and garlic from door to door. Grains like wheat, rye, and barley represented the most crucial foodstuffs. A middling-sized town of 3,000 people consumed about 1,000 tons of grain each year, an amount of grain that required about 4,500 acres of arable land. Thus, a large city like Paris, inhabited by over 100,000 people in the early 14th century, had to go far outside its own hinterland to acquire adequate supplies of grain. During times of famine, municipal governments were forced to take spe-

Fontevrault (Maine-et-Loire), abbey kitchen. *Photograph courtesy of Grover A. Zinn.*

Fontevrault, abbey kitchen, vaults. *Photograph courtesy of Whitney S. Stoddard.*

cial steps to prevent hoarding and to secure a regular and cheap supply of foodstuffs. Indeed, the fundamental anxiety over food supply, particularly grain, ensured that the food trades were among the most regulated aspects of medieval town life.

Many of the urban food trades were organized into guilds that shared in the regulation of foodstuffs. Most towns had guilds of bakers, butchers, and vintners; the largest cities possessed even more specialized guilds, like those of the pastry makers at Toulouse or poulterers of Paris. With the exception of those few merchants involved in the profitable long-distance trade in grain, wine, or salt, however, few of the medieval food-trade guilds attained the political power or prestige enjoyed by some of the other craft guilds, such as those in the textile trades. Butchers probably represented the most prosperous food-trade occupation aside from wine and grain wholesalers. Selling both salted and fresh meat, by the piece or on the hoof, butchers also profited from the sale of hides, skins, horns, and animal fat to other craftspeople. Mutton was the most common and cheapest meat they sold; pork was twice as expensive and beef four times as dear as mutton. As stock breeding expanded in the countryside and urban meat consumption increased in the late Middle Ages, the affluence of butchers appears to have grown even more.

Many urban residents produced a good deal of their own food by raising their own chickens, pigs, and even cows, and growing fruits and vegetables in their gardens. Some made their own bread dough (but usually had to take it to the baker for baking). For other essential foodstuffs, townspeople depended largely on the market. Fish, for example, was usually purchased in the marketplace, although inhabitants of coastal communities easily secured their own supplies. The church's ban on meat during Lent, certain feast days, and every Friday and Saturday, made fish an important element in the medieval diet. Because of the risks of spoilage, fresh fish was generally retailed nearby its origins in the sea, rivers, or fishponds. But salted and dried fish were often shipped over long distances and represented a substantial proportion of the maritime trade of port cities and coastal fishing villages.

Spices, oils, and salt were also shipped over long distances. Salt was a particularly valuable and essential foodstuff, since it was used extensively as a seasoning and to preserve meat and fish. Towns and even the national government took advantage of the demand for salt by assessing a salt tax, or *gabelle*, on consumers, which was substantial enough to constitute an important element of urban tax revenues. Indeed, towns benefited from a wide variety of taxes on food and also realized revenues from the rents charged on shops and stalls, the butchers's shambles, and butter cross (where dairy products were commonly sold). Port customs and tolls on exports and imports of wine also represented a significant source of income for many towns and regional governments.

Maryanne Kowaleski

[See also: COOKING; DIET AND NUTRITION; FISHING]

Comité des Travaux Historiques et Scientifiques. *Bulletin philologique et historique*. Actes du 93e Congrès. *L'alimentation*. Paris, 1968.

Duby, Georges. *Rural Economy and Country Life in the Medieval West*, trans. Cynthia Postan. Columbia: University of South Carolina Press, 1968.

Renouard, Yves. "Le grand commerce des vins de Gascogne au moyen âge." *Revue Historique* 211 (1959): 261–304.

Stouff, Louis. *Ravitaillement et alimentation en Provence aux XIVe et XVe siècles*. Paris: Mouton, 1970.

Wolff, Philippe. "L'approvisionnement des villes françaises au moyen âge." In *L'approvisionnement des villes de l'Europe occidentale au moyen âge et aux temps modernes: 5e Journées internationales d'histoire, Flaran, 16–18 Sept. 1983*. Auch: Centre Culturel de l'Abbaye de Flaran, 1985, pp. 11–32.

FORMARIAGE. The marriage or, more exactly, the prohibition of marriage of a rustic living in one seigneurie to a rustic living in another is known as *formariage*, from Latin *foris* 'outside' and *maritagium* 'marriage.' By the 13th century, many jurists argued that, even in the absence of other signs of servile status, liability to this prohibition was a strong presumption of serfdom. Sometimes, the restriction on marriages between serfs and free people is also called *formariage*, but "mixed marriage" is the preferred term for these unions. At any rate, serfs who wanted to enter into marriages of either sort could do so by paying fines, also known under the general rubric of *formariage*, to the appropriate lord or lords.

Regional customs differed about who became the lord of children born from marriages between serfs of different seigneuries and whether children of mixed marriages were serfs at all. With regard to *formariage* narrowly defined, some customs favored the claim of the lord of the father, others that of the lord of the mother, and still others that of the lord of the seigneurie within which the births of the children occurred. Most frequently, these problems were resolved by conventions among lords of neighboring seigneuries to apportion the children according to some simple formula.

A dispensation for a serf to marry a free person was less easy to obtain, because local customs often favored regarding the offspring of mixed marriages as free people. Lords in consequence demanded high fines to obtain the privilege of making mixed marriages. For this and other reasons, popular demands for the abolition of serfdom usually emphasized the desire for freedom of marriage.

William Chester Jordan

[See also: AFFRANCHISSEMENT; SERFDOM/SERVITUDE/SLAVERY]

Bloch, Marc. "Liberté et servitude personelles au moyen-âge." In *Mélanges historiques*. Paris: SEVPEN, 1963, Vol. 1, pp. 286–355.

FORMES FIXES. The "fixed forms" of French lyrical poetry of the 14th and 15th centuries developed from dance lyrics of the 13th century and include principally the ballade, rondeau, and virelai. Different strophic structures characterize each form, but all include a refrain. The poetry served to determine the form of the musical setting, although the *formes fixes* were less frequently set to music after Machaut. Deschamps's *Art de dictier* (1392) provides the first systematic listing of the formal characteristics of the *formes fixes* for the late 14th century. The ballade was most favored by Machaut, Froissart, and Deschamps; 15th-century poets favored the rondeau. Later in the 15th century, the single-strophe virelai, renamed the bergerette, enjoyed a brief flowering.

Lawrence Earp

[See also: ARS NOVA; BALLADE; BUSNOYS, ANTOINE; CHARLES D'ORLÉANS; CHRISTINE DE PIZAN; DESCHAMPS, EUSTACHE; *FAUVEL, LIVRES DE;* FROISSART, JEAN; LESCUREL, JEHANNOT DE; MACHAUT, GUILLAUME DE; PHILIPPE DE VITRY; REFRAIN; RONDEAU; VIRELAI]

Poirion, Daniel. *Le poète et le prince: l'évolution du lyrisme courtois de Guillaume de Machaut à Charles d'Orléans.* Paris: Presses Universitaires de France, 1965.

FOUAGE. The word *fouage* (Lat. *focagium*) meant "hearth tax," but the meaning of "hearth" varied over time and from place to place, as did the way of assessing *fouages*. An important early example of a *fouage* was the money tax in Normandy, where, from the 11th century, the population paid a *fouage* in return for the maintenance of a stable coinage. In this case, the hearth clearly referred to households, as it tended to throughout northern France. Towns sometimes raised municipal taxes through a *fouage*, often in response to demands from reformers who considered it more equitable than indirect taxes that bore on poor consumers.

As royal taxation developed in the 14th century, the *fouage* became the preferred method of payment in Languedoc, especially between 1340 and 1380. Generally, the towns of a district would agree to pay a lump sum assessed among them on the basis of households. Within these towns, the actual tax might take any form. When it was a direct tax, it tended to be assessed on the value of real property (exclusive of rural fiefs or church lands, which rarely lay within a town's jurisdiction anyway). After the mid-14th century, when war and plague had reduced the number of households, hearth counts in Languedoc lost their connection with actual households and became an administrative device for apportioning taxes among the towns.

The *fouage* best known as a royal tax was that enacted by the Estates General of Languedoïl in December 1363 and canceled by Charles V in September 1380. Averaging three francs per household (but graduated from one to nine) and affecting rural lordships as well as towns, this levy paid for the army that scored important victories in the reign of Charles V. It was the ancestor of the royal *taille*.

John Bell Henneman, Jr.

[See also: CHARLES V THE WISE; CURRENCY; *TAILLE*]

Borelli de Serres, Léon. *Recherches sur divers services publiques du XIIIe au XVIIe siècle.* 3 vols. Paris: Picard, 1895–1905.
Brown, Elizabeth A.R. "Taxation and Morality in the Thirteenth and Fourteenth Centuries: Conscience and Political Power and the Kings of France." *French Historical Studies* 8 (1973): 1–28.
Dupont-Ferrier, Gustave. *Études sur les institutions financières de la France à la fin du moyen âge.* 2 vols. Paris: Didot, 1930–32.
Henneman, John B. *Royal Taxation in Fourteenth Century France: The Captivity and Ransom of John II.* Philadelphia: American Philosophical Society, 1976.

FOUCHER DE CHARTRES (ca. 1059–ca. 1127). The author of one of the principal accounts of the First Crusade and the history of the Latin kingdoms in the Near East, Foucher may have been at the Council of Clermont in 1095 when Pope Urban II announced the crusade and soon thereafter accompanied Étienne, count of Blois and Chartres, as his chaplain on the journey to the Holy Land. In 1097, Foucher's fortunes became linked to those of Baudouin I, who became king of Jerusalem in 1100. Foucher began to compose his *magnum opus*, the *Historia Hierosolymitana*, toward the end of 1101; and it is likely that the end of the chronicle in 1127 marks his death.

Mark Zier

[See also: CRUSADES; HISTORIOGRAPHY]

Foucher de Chartres. *Historia Hierosolymitana (1095–1127)*, ed. Heinrich Hagenmeyer. Heidelberg: Winter, 1913.
———. *A History of the Expedition to Jerusalem 1095–1127*, ed. Harold S. Fink, trans. Frances R. Ryan. Knoxville: University of Tennessee Press, 1969.

FOUGÈRES. Located on an escarpment overlooking the Nançon River and strategic crossroads, Fougères (Île-et-Vilaine), an ancient town on the borders of Brittany, has preserved an imposing feudal castle that dates from the 11th century. The castle occupies a slightly lower position than the city and is built almost entirely of schist and granite. The escarpment provides a natural protection for the castle. Additionally, ponds and moats, with levered bridges, surround the fortress; these once provided water to turn the mill, whose wheels can still be seen. In the 12th and 13th centuries, the walls of the bastion measured nearly 20 feet in height, with the towers stretching to nearly 40 feet. Had the castle been provided with palisades, the summit would have been crenellated. Several towers were built, and their entrances barricaded by portcullises and mobile panels. Of those that originally flanked the principal wall, only the Tour du Cadran survives. The keep was 66 feet in diameter, with excessively thick walls. Its exterior was octagonal, but its interior was circular. Only portions of the foundations remain.

Fougères (Île-et-Vilaine), city walls. *Photograph courtesy of William W. Kibler.*

In the 14th century, the bastion was built up, two stories were added to the Tour des Gobelins, and other towers were constructed. One of the new towers, Mélusine, housed an underground dungeon and four hexagonal floors. Two square towers (66 feet by 66 feet), Surienne and Raoul, were added in the 15th century. Also during this period, openings in walls were adapted or created to accommodate cannoniers and archers.

Despite being taken and razed by Henry II Plantagenêt in 1166, much of the fortress has been preserved through extensive and frequent restorations.

                                                            E. Kay Harris

Besnard, Charles. "Le château de Fougères." *Bulletin monumental* 76 (1912): 5–21.

Finó, J.-F. *Forteresses de la France médiévale.* Paris: Picard, 1970.

Gillot, G. *Notice succincte sur le château de Fougères.* Fougères: Imprimerie de La Chronique, 1949.

———. *Fougères, heures épiques, heures tragiques: épisodes de son histoire.* Rennes: Bretonne, 1951.

FOULQUES. Names of counts of Anjou. From the 10th to the 12th century, an extraordinary line of counts transformed Anjou into a major territorial principality. Because of the prevalence of the name Foulques, the family is sometimes referred to as the Fulconian dynasty. Throughout the 11th century, the Fulconians were able to battle both the Anglo-Norman and French kings for control of western Francia.

The real founder of the dynasty was Foulques I le Roux (ca. 888–941), viscount of the city of Angers. By 930, he had usurped the title of count from his Robertian overlords. Angevin expansion began with his son, Foulques II le Bon (r. 941–60), who married the widow of the count of Nantes. While unsuccessful in exerting control over the region, Angevin counts would continue to claim the Nantais.

Foulques II's grandson, Foulques III Nerra (r. 987–1040), although only seventeen at his accession, soon displayed the qualities that enabled him to create what has been called "the first Angevin empire." The central feature of Nerra's success was his rivalry with the count of Blois. Victories at Conquereuil in 992 and Pontlevoy in 1016 gave Nerra control over the Nantais and ended Blésois ambitions in Brittany. Of more importance was Nerra's drive against Blésois lands in the Touraine, which would culminate in the conquest of Tours by his successor. Elsewhere, Nerra extended Angevin domination into Vendôme, the Gâtinais and Maine, and even Aquitaine. Perhaps Nerra's greatest achievement was the construction of a remarkable system of stone castles that ensured the security of his newly expanded realm throughout the 11th century. Despite a reputation for ferocity, he died not in battle but on his way home in 1040 from the last of three pilgrimages he made to Jerusalem.

The rule of Nerra's grandson, Foulques IV le Rechin (r. 1068–1109), saw a reduction of Angevin power. When Count Geoffroi Martel died in 1060 without an heir, the countship went to Martel's nephew, Geoffroi le Barbu. Foulques le Rechin, the new count's younger brother, received only the Saintonge and Viliers and soon lost these to the count of Poitiers. Allying himself with a coalition of barons disgruntled with Count Geoffroi's incompetence, Foulques seized the countship and imprisoned his brother in 1068. The Angevin barons took the opportunity to advance their own interests. Castles became the hereditary fiefs of their lords as they slipped from the count's direct control. As a result, Angevin power suffered a severe blow. Yet the achievement of Foulques IV was genuine: he was able to maintain control over Maine in the face of attacks by the Norman duke William the Conqueror and his sons; and by marrying his second son, Foulques le Jeune, to the heiress of Maine, he prepared the definitive union of Maine and Anjou.

This second son, Foulques V (r. 1109–29), began the restoration of Angevin fortunes by bringing the barons to heel and reasserting comital control over all castles. His marriage to the heiress of Maine effectively united the two counties, while his greatest coup was marrying his son Geoffroi Plantagenêt to Matilda, daughter of King Henry I of England. In 1129, Foulques abdicated in favor of Geoffroi to become king of Jerusalem. Geoffroi would use the solid base left to him by his Fulconian ancestors to lay the foundation of the 12th-century Angevin empire.

                                                            Scott Jessee

[See also: ANJOU (genealogical table); ANJOU, HOUSES OF; GEOFFROI; MATILDA]

Bachrach, Bernard S. *Fulk Nerra, the Neo-Roman Consul 987–1040.* Berkeley: University of California Press, 1993.

———. "The Idea of the Angevin Empire." *Albion* 10 (1978): 293–99.

Dunbabin, Jean. *France in the Making, 843–1180.* Oxford: Oxford University Press, 1985.

Guillot, Olivier. *Le comte d'Anjou et son entourage au XIe siècle.* 2 vols. Paris: Picard, 1972.

Hallam, Elizabeth, ed. *The Plantagenet Chronicles*. New York: Weidenfeld and Nicolson, 1986.

Halphen, Louis. *Le comté d'Anjou au XIe siècle*. Paris: Picard, 1906.

FOUQUET, JEAN (ca. 1420–1481). The most influential painter of the mid-15th century in France, Jean Fouquet infused elements of Italian Renaissance art with his own native French style. He painted a portrait of Pope Eugenius IV (now lost) in Rome before 1447. By 1448, he was working for Charles VII at Tours, and he was appointed as court painter to Louis XI in 1475. He is best known for a book of hours that he illuminated for Étienne Chevalier ca. 1452, fragments of which survive in the Musée Condé at Chantilly. Among the panel paintings that have been attributed to Fouquet are portraits of Charles VII (ca. 1445) and Juvenal des Ursins (ca. 1455), both in the Louvre. Recently, it has been shown that Fouquet was probably not the head of a large, prolific atelier but worked as an independent artist who contributed sporadically to manuscripts from a variety of sources.

Robert G. Calkins

[See also: MANUSCRIPTS, PRODUCTION AND ILLUMINATION]

Jean Fouquet, Hours of Étienne Chevalier. The Right Hand of God Protecting the Faithful. *Courtesy of the Lehman Collection, Metropolitan Museum of Art, New York.*

Clancy, Stephen. *Books of Hours in the* Fouquet Style: *The Relationship of Jean Fouquet and the* Hours of Étienne Chevalier *to French Manuscript Illumination of the Fifteenth Century*. Diss. Cornell University, 1988. [With bibliography.]

Reynaud, Nicole. *Jean Fouquet*. Paris: Éditions de la Reunion des Museés Nationaux, 1981.

Sterling, Charles, and Claude Schaeffer. *The Hours of Étienne Chevalier: Miniatures by Jean Fouquet*. New York: Braziller, 1971.

Wescher, Paul. *Jean Fouquet and His Time*. Basel: Pleiades, 1947.

FOURRIER/FOURRIÈRE. The *fourrier* (related to the verb *fourrager* 'forage') was a member of a corps of servants in the household of great lords and prelates who preceded the lord in his travels and arranged for the lodging of his court. The royal *fourrière*, or corps of *fourriers*, was elevated to the standing of a distinct *ministerium*, or *mestier*, of the royal *hostel*, or inner household, at some time between 1257 and 1261, to replace the *chambre*.

D'A. Jonathan D. Boulton

Lot, Ferdinand, and Robert Fawtier. *Histoire des institutions françaises*. 3 vols. Paris: Presses Universitaires de France, 1957–62, Vol. 2: *Institutions royales* (1958).

FRANC-ARCHERS. On April 28, 1448, Charles VII issued an *ordonnance* requiring every parish to mobilize at local expense an archer for a militia of *franc-archers*. Such men received 9 *livres tournois* per year and a tax exemption for their participation and as much as 4 *livres tournois* per month when on active duty. Theoretically organized into bands of 500 assembled under four generals, each commanding 4,000 men, the envisioned force of 16,000 infantry would serve for provincial defense and in emergencies as reinforcements for the crown's professional forces. Though never fully mobilized, these reserves played a valuable role in the decisive campaigns of the Hundred Years' War.

Though they had proven valuable in the era of national liberation, the *franc-archers* gradually became havens for tax exemption. Units of ill-disciplined men little interested in military service proved inadequate to the needs of a state permanently at war against foreign and domestic enemies. After 1480, the crown relied on mercenaries and neglected the reserves. Despite sporadic reforms, climaxing in the creation of the legions of Francis I, they were rarely mobilized, and their revolutionary potential for universal military service remained untapped for centuries.

Paul D. Solon

Bonnault d'Houet, Marc Louis Xavier, baron de. *Les francs-archers de Compiegne, 1448–1514*. Compiegne: Lefebvre, 1897.

Contamine, Philippe. *Guerre, état et société à la fin du moyen âge: études sur les armées des rois de France*. Paris: Mouton, 1972.

————. *War in the Middle Ages*, trans. Michael Jones. London: Blackwell, 1984.

Esquer, G. "Levée des francs-archers aurillacois au XVe siècle d'après les comptes consulaires d'Aurillac (1451–1493)." *Revue de la Haute-Auvergne* 6 (1904): 297–311.

FRANCHE-COMTÉ. Although the kingdom of trans-Saône Burgundy was absorbed into the Holy Roman Empire upon the death of Rudolph III in 1032, the region continued to have a fairly independent existence until the middle of the 12th century, especially the most western part, which centered on Dôle, Besançon, Vesoul, and Salins. This region became known as the Franche-Comté of Burgundy in the late Middle Ages. The county of Burgundy, as it was called in the 11th and 12th centuries, was ruled for over a century by the descendants of Otto-William (d. 1026), count of Mâcon and claimant to the duchy of Burgundy.

The independence of the county was such that the German emperors felt compelled to reassert their control over it in the 12th century. When Count Raynald III of Burgundy died without sons, the county went to his daughter Beatrix, whom the emperor Frederick Barbarossa married in 1156, thus claiming trans-Saône Burgundy for himself and his descendants.

Although within the empire, the county continued to have closer cultural ties to France than to Germany. In 1384, Philip the Bold, the Valois duke of French Burgundy, also obtained the county of Burgundy via his wife's inheritance. The duchy and county remained united for a century, the period of Burgundy's greatest glory. After the death of Duke Charles the Bold in 1477, his inheritance was claimed both by the French king and by Maximilian, the imperial heir, who married Charles's daughter. In the ultimate division of the legacy, in 1493, the duchy and county were again divided, the Franche-Comté being subjected to imperial Habsburg rule.

Constance B. Bouchard

[See also: BURGUNDY]

Bligny, Bernard. *L'église et les ordres religieux dans le royaume de Bourgogne aux XIe et XIIe siècles.* Paris: Presses Universitaires de France, 1960.

Bouchard, Constance Brittain. *Sword, Miter, and Cloister: Nobility and the Church in Burgundy, 980–1198.* Ithaca: Cornell University Press, 1987.

Mariotte, Jean-Yves. *Le comté de Bourgogne sous les Hohenstaufen.* Paris: Les Belles Lettres, 1963.

Vaughan, Richard. *Philip the Bold: The Formation of the Burgundian State.* Cambridge: Harvard University Press, 1962.

FRANCISCAN ORDER. One of the two major mendicant religious groups, the Franciscan order (officially the *Fratres minores*, "little," or "lesser," brothers) was founded in Italy in the early 13th century by Francis of Assisi and had spread by the 1220s to France and especially Paris, where over the course of time Franciscan masters and students became major forces in the lives of the university and the French church.

An ecstatic mystic, Francis of Assisi (ca. 1181–1226) as a young man experienced a radical conversion in which he embraced a life of total poverty, wandering preaching, service to others, humility, and prayer. From 1209, others were attracted to this life, and Francis formed them into a group committed to his ideals. The first rule (*Regula primitiva*) of 1209 is lost, but Pope Innocent III gave his approval to Francis's way of life and to the role of Francis and his followers as public preachers in 1210. At the Fourth Lateran Council (1215), he declared that they formed an already-existing religious order and thus were not affected by the ban on new religious orders passed by the council. The *Rule* of 1221 (*Regula secunda*) and the *Rule* officially approved by Honorius III in 1223 (*Regula bullata*) are the fundamental rules. In forming his ideal of the religious life, Francis focused on complete poverty, simplicity and humility, and preaching, characteristics that were identified with the "apostolic life" modeled on the lives of Jesus and his disciples. The characteristic that most distinguishes Franciscans from other orders is the insistence from the very founding of the order on complete poverty, not only personal (which was true of monastic orders) but also corporate (which was not true of monastic orders). They were to support themselves by manual labor or by begging, to live in whatever simple lodgings they might find, and to possess neither property nor money. This insistence, fundamental to Francis's vision, later became a point of intense and tragic dispute in the order and the church.

The chapter of 1217, meeting in Assisi, decided to send friars on preaching missions outside Italy and divided the potential mission field into provinces: six in Italy, two (north and south) in France, and one each for Germany, Spain, and the Holy Land. Each province had a provincial minister to supervise the friars, and after the death of Francis a minister general supervised the order. The *Rule* of 1223 called for a meeting of the general chapter every three years, but not until 1239 was this firmly fixed.

Work in the province of southern France went slowly, but by ca. 1220 there were settlements at Mirepoix, Arles, Aix-en-Provence, Montpellier, and Périgueux. In 1222, houses were founded in Draguignan, Nîmes, and Apt. The year 1224 saw foundations in Limoges and Brive, then later at Nice, Bordeaux, La Réole, Saint-Jean-d'Angely, and Le Puy.

The northern province advanced steadily under the leadership of Pacifico, a poet and one of Francis's early converts. By 1218 or 1219, Franciscans were at Paris, and by 1223 there were thirty friars and a convent was being built. After the Paris foundation, houses were started at Le Mans, Bayeux, Vézelay, Chartres, Arras, and Vendôme. Houses were later founded in Nantes, Tours, Rouen, Sézanne (1223–24); Compiègne, Beauvais, and Auxerre (1225); Samur, Angers, and Mirebeau (1226); and Bruges, Ghent, and Ypres (1227). At Francis's death, France was divided into three provinces (France/Paris, Provence, and Aquitaine), with two others soon following, Burgundy and Touraine. In addition to Paris as a major center for study, there were schools for friars in Rouen, Reims, Metz, Bruges, Marseille, Narbonne, Toulouse, and Bordeaux.

Francis's death produced a crisis of definition, for in his last writing, the *Testament*, he had unambiguously insisted yet again on absolute poverty and simplicity for the friars personally and communally. One of Francis's strong supporters, Pope Gregory IX, finally declared the *Testament* nonbinding in its insistence on literal poverty and allowed, in the bull *Quo elongati* of 1230, communities to have buildings, books, furniture, and the like, arguing that they were merely using what others (i.e., ecclesiastics appointed for the purpose or even the pope) owned/possessed "for" them. Rigorists in the order rejected this "compromise" and looked for leadership to John of Parma (minister general 1247–57), while those who favored Gregory IX's move, the so-called Conventuals, found a leader in Bonaventure, the theologian and mystical writer who was minister general 1257–74. Bonaventure, selected to write the official *vita* of Francis, not only defended the theory of the "use" of possessions, arguing that the friars needed large convents, books, vestments, and the like to carry out their ministry; he also defended the mendicants in their conflict with the secular clergy, led by William of Saint-Amour, over the right of the mendicant orders to preach and hear confessions without regard to parish and diocesan boundaries, arguing that the friars were a new order that combined monastic virtue, contemplative prayer, and pastoral care of individuals through preaching and hearing confessions. Conflict with local clergy is regrettable, stated Bonaventure, but the friars make up for the defects of poorly prepared clerics. Increased emphasis upon university studies at the expense of manual labor, and thus full participation as masters and students in university life, was justified by Bonaventure as the necessary preparation for preaching. Unlike Dominicans, who from the beginning had been a clerical order dedicated to doctrinal preaching against heresy, the Franciscans began with a model of lay exhortation to moral conversion, not doctrinal preaching in a clerical mode. Recruiting from the university student body and the conversion of university masters like Alexander of Hales to the Franciscan way ensured the increasing place of studies, and of a clerical elite, in the order.

Some Franciscans, known as "Spirituals," found in the eschatological ideas of the Italian monastic Joachim of Fiore (ca. 1132–1202) a prediction that Francis was the harbinger of a new world order of radical spirituality. Peter John Olivi (1248–1298), a friar from Provence who was trained at Paris and taught at Montpellier and Narbonne, was one of the most forceful of these Spirituals. In his writings, which included a commentary on the Book of Revelation, Olivi joined an intense apocalyptic spirituality, foreseeing a cosmic struggle in which a corrupt church would be replaced by a spiritual church, with an acceptance of the doctrine of the "use" of goods, provided that "use" was in all simplicity and only of necessities.

Dissension and debate over the issue of ownership and property continued within and without the order. The Inquisition sought out and punished Spirituals in southern France. In the early 14th century, Pope Clement V sought to balance acceptance of the Spirituals' criticism of laxity in the order with a need for reconciliation and unity.

Soon, however, Pope John XXII turned the doctrinal and coercive power of the papacy against the Spirituals and attacked their central beliefs and practices in a series of condemnations that led to the isolation and decline of the Spiritual Franciscans, a struggle that cost each side dearly. In addition, John declared heretical the fundamental doctrine agreed to by all Franciscans, that Christ and his disciples had no possessions. Moreover, he forced the Conventuals to accept full ownership of all they possessed, thus reversing previous papal distinctions between "use" and "ownership." At the Council of Constance (1415), the Observants, a group drawing on Spiritualist traditions of austerity, were granted a certain level of independence within the order, with a separate vicar in each province and a vicar general for all provinces, all serving under the minister general of the order. Pope Martin V reinstated in 1428 the distinction between "use" and "ownership" made by Gregory IX. In 1517, the Franciscans were divided into two independent branches, Observants and Conventuals, each with its own minister general, a division that continues to this day.

Several years after Francis attracted his first converts, Clare (ca. 1194–1253), a young woman from a wealthy Assisi family, sought to join Francis's group. In 1212, she was accepted by Francis as a convert and placed for the moment in a Benedictine nunnery. Clare and another young woman were soon living in the church of San Damiano at Assisi as enclosed female religious, dedicated to asceticism and prayer of the strictest kind. Clare was denied the apostolate to the world that Francis found and that she desired; hers was to be an intense dedication to denial and prayer in a strictly enclosed life. This female branch of the Franciscans became known as the "Poor Ladies of San Damiano," later the "Poor Clares" or "Clarisses." At San Damiano, they lived by manual labor or alms, fasted, prayed, accepted the rule of perpetual silence, and refused to accept the usual kind of endowments that supported female religious houses. Later, other houses were forced to accept endowments and property for support, but Clare steadfastly refused what she saw as a compromise with wealth. The first house of Poor Clares in France was established in Reims in 1220 by a group of nuns sent by Clare. Another group went to Béziers in 1240, with the support of Louis IX.

Francis also began what became known as the "Third Order," or Tertiaries, for individuals who were drawn to a new spirituality but did not wish to join either the male or female branches of the Franciscans. These people continued to live in the world, might be married with families, but adopted moderate asceticism and sought to live more virtuously and simply, to be regular in prayer and the sacraments, to aid others, to refuse to bear arms or swear oaths, and to promote peace. Tertiaries were formed into local groups with officers and regulations.

Grover A. Zinn

[See also: ALEXANDER OF HALES; BONAVENTURE; DOMINICAN ORDER; GREGORY IX; MENDICANT ART AND ARCHITECTURE; MILLENNIALISM; MYSTICISM; PREACHING; UNIVERSITIES; WILLIAM OF SAINT-AMOUR]

Archivum Franciscanum historicum 1– (1908–).

Armstrong, Regis J., and Ignatius C. Brady, trans. *Francis and Clare: The Complete Works.* New York: Paulist, 1982.

Burr, David. *The Persecution of Peter Olivi.* Philadelphia: American Philosophical Society, 1976.

Franciscan Studies 1– (1919–).

Lambert, Malcolm D. *Franciscan Poverty: The Doctrine of the Absolute Poverty of Christ and the Apostles in the Franciscan Order, 1210–1323.* London: SPCK, 1961.

Little, Lester K. *Religious Poverty and the Profit Economy in Medieval Europe.* Ithaca: Cornell University Press, 1978.

Moorman, John. *A History of the Franciscan Order from Its Origins to the Year 1517.* Oxford: Clarendon, 1968.

FRANCO OF COLOGNE (fl. 1260–90). No biographical information has come to light that might clarify who Franco was, why he was involved in music and its notation, or when he wrote the music treatise entitled *Ars cantus mensurabilis,* although it would seem certainly to have been in Paris ca. 1280. This treatise attributed to Franco is one of the most important historical documents concerning polyphony in the western tradition. It established fixed relationships among pitch, rhythm, and written symbol comparable to the development of writing as a means of transmitting language, and the principles of notation that it proposed lasted through the 16th century. Franco's achievement was a high degree of rationalization of the written means for communicating musical ideas by which complex rhythmic and polyphonic relationships could be realized in a purely intellectual manner, could be transmitted in a relatively coherent way in writing, and so could be reproduced with some degree of fidelity distant from their inception. More manuscript copies survive for the *Ars cantus mensurabilis* than for any other 13th-century treatise on music, and comparisons among these copies indicate substantial homogeneity in transmission. The treatise displays a detachment and succinctness that are uncharacteristic of 13th-century writing in general.

Sandra Pinegar

[See also: MUSIC THEORY]

Franco of Cologne. *Franconis de Colonia Ars cantus mensurabilis,* ed. Gilbert Reaney and André Gilles. N.p.: American Institute of Musicology, 1974.

Haas, Max. "Die Musiklehre im 13. Jahrhundert von Johannes de Garlandia bis Franco." In *Die mittelalterliche Lehre von der Mehrstimmigkeit,* ed. Frieder Zaminer. Darmstadt: Wissenschaftliche Buchgesellschaft, 1984, pp. 89–159.

Huglo, Michel. "De Francon de Cologne à Jacques de Liège." *Revue belge de musicologie* 34–35 (1980–81): 44–60.

Strunk, Oliver. *Source Readings in Music History.* New York: Norton, 1950, pp. 139–59.

FRANCO-ITALIAN LITERATURE. A collective classification given to a sizable corpus of texts of the late Middle Ages, sharing a north Italian provenance. Genre varies widely, including chansons de geste, romance epics, romans, chronicles, and hagiography; the common element is linguistic hybridism issuing from varying combinations of Old French interference with several north Italian dialects, especially Lombard. As testimony to the prestige with which French language and letters were regarded, Franco-Italian literature offers a unique area of cultural and ideological contact in the cities, courts, and prehumanist centers of northern Italy.

The largest collection of these works, twenty-five manuscripts, is now in the Marciana Library in Venice; sixteen can be traced to the extensive library holdings of Francesco Gonzaga, duke of Mantua. At his death in 1407, an inventory listed some sixty-seven manuscripts *in lingua francigena.* Numerous manuscripts of French chansons de geste and Arthurian romances were also held by the Este court in nearby Ferrara and may have also circulated among other courts of the region, such as the Scaglieri in Verona, Visconti in Milan, and Da Carrara in Padua. It is likely that many of these works were commissioned by such regional potentates for recitation/reading in their opulent courts, precursors to the great Renaissance courts and the Italian masterworks that they in turn fostered, such as Boiardo's *Orlando Innamorato* and Ariosto's *Orlando Furioso.* Formerly regarded as contaminations of both national languages and literatures, Franco-Italian texts were frequently dismissed as by-products of French works disseminated to the south or as primitive versions of Italian works of the following generations. Scholars now recognize the significant literary and linguistic value of many of these texts, particularly the V4 and V7 *Chansons de Roland, Aspremont, Aquilon de Bavière, Entrée d'Espagne,* the *Attila* of Nicholas of Casola, and the works of Nicholas of Verona, which include the sequel to the *Entrée d'Espagne,* the *Prise de Pampelune.* Among other Carolingian works in the Marciana Franco-Italian collection is a vast compilation known as the *Geste Francor,* which includes *Enfances* texts of Roland and Charlemagne; *Aliscans, Gui de Nanteuil, Bues d'Aigremont, Foulque de Candie,* and *Doon de Mayence.* Romance works include *Le roman de Troie, La Folie Lancelot, Florimont, Jugement d'amour,* and *Prophécies de Merlin.* Brunetto Latini's *Li livres dou tresor* and Marco Polo's *Devisement du monde* are likewise classified as Franco-Italian.

The process by which these texts were introduced to northern Italy can be described according to the degree of distance between a "parent" text and its Franco-Italian counterpart. One can hypothesize that French jongleurs traveling to Italy diffused, orally and/or in manuscript form, epic and romance material in the latter 13th and early 14th centuries; scribes and artists then transcribed and illuminated manuscripts in the Veneto-Lombard regions and in Bologna. Belonging to this initial phase are *Aliscans* and the V4 *Roland.* Subsequently, Italian authors began to alter originally French texts to varying degrees in form and content, introducing their own material and dialectal usage; within this group of *remaniements* are *Macaire* and the *Roman de Hector et Hercule.* Finally, scholars agree that such works as the *Entrée d'Espagne* and *Prise de Pampelune* were conceived in Franco-Italian and composed in Italy by Italian writers and can be considered autonomous to the extent that no single model text can be identified.

The prestige of French in northern Italy, particularly among the aristocracy and prosperous mercantile bourgeoisie, is expressed by Brunetto Latini, Florentine mentor of Dante. Justifying his choice of language, he writes in Book 1 of the *Trésor* (1. 7): "Et se aucuns demandoit por quoi cist livres est escriz en romanz selonc le langage des François, puisque nos somes Ytaliens, je diroie que ce est por .ii. raisons; l'une car nos somes en France, et l'autre por ce que la parleüre de France est plus delitable et plus commune a toutes gens." ("And if anyone were to ask why this book is written in Romance according to the language of the French, since we are Italian, I would say that it is for two reasons: one, because we are in France, and the other because the French language is more pleasant and more common among all peoples.") In the *De vulgari eloquentia* (1.10.2), Dante, too, extols the French language, because it is easier and more pleasant than the other two Romance idioms, Provençal and Italian. Plurilingualism was a fundamental ingredient in the evolution of the Romance languages and is present to some degree in many documents of the period, as extant multilanguage texts incorporating *oc, oïl,* and different Italian dialects bear witness.

From a linguistic point of view, Franco-Italian, also called Franco-Venetan and Franco-Lombard according to the regional origin of its Italian infrastructure, remains a source of unresolved questions. Some earlier scholars claimed that it was a spoken, living language arising within specific geographical, cultural, and chronological parameters. As evidence, they cited the Venetian chronicler Martin da Canal: "Et porce que lengue franceise cort parmi le monde et est la plus delitable a lire et a oïr que nule autre, me sui je entremis de translater l'anciene estoire des Veneciens de latin en franceis. . . ." ("And because the French language travels throughout the world and is more pleasant to read and to hear than any other, I have undertaken the translation of the ancient history of the Venetians from Latin into French. . . .") Most scholars now agree that it was a purely literary, artificial language fashioned in an area of northern Italy particularly receptive to French letters and language and that it flourished for about a hundred to 150 years. It then disappeared completely, eclipsed by the proliferating Italian dialects, including Tuscan, later adopted as the national language.

The many unsolved questions surrounding Franco-Italian as a language system are complicated by the fact that one is not confronting a unified, codified system, where a single comprehensive lexicon or grammar might suffice. Instead, there are virtually as many Franco-Italian "languages" as there are surviving texts. This is not to say, however, that it is totally random or without its own regulations. There is significant variation, morphologically and syntactically, from one text to another and not infrequently within a single text. Such ubiquitous variation prompted some scholars to argue that Franco-Italian authors were generally either too ignorant of Old French to employ the language properly, or that they wished, intended, and even believed in some cases that their French was correct. Nicholas of Verona declares in the *Pharsale*: "Car çe ne sai nuls home en Paris ne en Valois/Que non die qe ces vers sont feit par buen françois." ("For I know of no man in Paris or in the Valois/Who does not say that these verses are written in good French.") Others argued that such authors were sufficiently competent to use the language correctly but adopted the hybrid Franco-Italian to accommodate linguistically, as well as thematically, their Italian publics. In the case of the *Entrée d'Espagne*, unmistakable and uncommon erudition lends substantial support to the latter thesis. Recent linguistic work reveals that the two principal language systems are not synchronic. The French element, the *langue écrite,* dates back to the earlier French of the chansons de geste and *romans* and is thus anachronistic in its interaction with the then contemporary Italian of the 13th and 14th centuries, which is entered as a *langue parlée.*

Current research likewise stresses the importance of placing both Franco-Italian language and letters within the complex sociopolitical, cultural, and historical contexts in which they developed. Thus, a Franco-Italian Rolandian work of ca. 1325 is likely to effect some alteration of its 12th-century model in narrative material and character presentation, as well as in ideological orientation. Indeed, one of the most pervasive innovations is the elevation of Roland to new, quasihagiographic heroism, while simultaneously undermining Charlemagne's role in the earlier French poems. Archaic epico-feudal mentalities were to be at least partially recast for reception by different publics in different times.

The cultural and intellectual climate of Venetan-Lombard Italy in the 13th century suggests explanations for such change. Site of one of Europe's oldest universities, Padua was also an important Franco-Italian center. The university began as a *studium* ca. 1220, composed of a group of scholars of canon and civic law, joined by grammarians, dialecticians, and rhetoricians migrating from Bologna. It was most notably the scholars of the Trivium who gave rise to the Prehumanist movement in the region, characterized essentially by its enthusiasm for and emulation of Greco-Roman antiquity. Such individuals as Albertino Mussato and Lovato Lovati recovered texts and documents lost for centuries and composed elegant writings in the style of the ancient *auctores.* There is evidence that Dante and Petrarch were in the region at various times and that the *Divina commedia* was known to the *Entrée's* anonymous Paduan poet. Humanistic traits have been noted in several Franco-Italian texts; scholars trace a direct line between the humanism of Mussato and Petrarch. In the exceptionally active intellectual, artistic, and literary environment of the period, scholars and clerics mingled easily with the nobility and with the less learned but vital sector of the mercantile bourgeoisie. Franco-Italian literature, developed within so fertile an environment and addressed to multiple, heterogeneous publics, expands and enhances the study of both the French and Italian national traditions.

Nancy Bradley-Cromey

[See also: BRUNETTO LATINI; CHANSON DE GESTE; FRENCH LANGUAGE; MARCO POLO]

Baldelli, Ignazio, ed. *Glossarietto francese-veneto*. Paris: Bibliothèque de l'Arsenal, 1961.

Folena, Gianfranco, ed. *Storia della cultura veneta*. 5 vols. Vicenza: Neri Pozzi, 1976, Vol. 2: *Il Trecento*.

Limentani, Alberto, et al., eds. *Essor et fortune de la chanson de geste dans l'Europe et l'Orient latin. Actes du IXe Congrès International de la Société Rencesvals pour l'Étude des Épopées Romanes, Padoue-Venise 29 août–4 septembre 1982*. Modena: Mucchi, 1982, vol. 2, part 4: "Littérature franco-italienne et italienne. Littérature française en Orient Latin, 585–807." [Series of articles on aspects of Franco-Italian.]

Viscardi, Antonio. *Letteratura franco-italiana: testi e manuali*. Modena: n.p., 1941.

FRANÇOIS II (1435–1488). François II, son of Jean IV's fourth son, succeeded his uncle, Arthur III, as duke of Brittany in 1458. Largely brought up at the court of King Charles VII, he played a modest role in the expulsion of the English from France but was not by choice a soldier, nor did he exhibit outstanding gifts in any other direction.

The poet Jean Meschinot (d. 1491), who served in his household, described the ducal court as a "storm-tossed sea where shipwreck frequently occurred." From the beginning of his reign, although he adopted the independent stance characteristic of the house of Montfort in its relations with France, policy seems to have been made by stronger figures who often manipulated the duke.

Among his advisers, there were always discontented refugees from the wrath of Louis XI. These men exercised great influence. Some, like Tanguy du Chastel (d. 1477), were Bretons who had also made careers in royal service. Others, like Jean, count of Dunois, and his son François, Odet d'Aydie, or Jean de Chalon, were strangers. Two major Breton figures provided continuity: Guillaume Chauvin, chancellor 1459–81, who tried to avoid direct confrontation with the French, and Pierre Landois, treasurer 1460–85, who advocated a more aggressive policy and, on occasion, alliance with England. Increasingly, it was Landois, through his control of the purse strings and ruthless promotion of his family and clients, who came to exercise the most influence. In 1481, his feud with Chauvin came to a head with the arrest of the chancellor, who died in jail in 1484. However, in July 1485 a baronial clique, in league with the French, seized Landois in the duke's presence and hurriedly arranged his execution, for which François later pardoned them.

These faction-ridden last years of his reign were increasingly dominated by the question of his succession and fear of France. The duke's first wife and their young son had died by 1469, and in 1471 François took a second wife, Marguerite, daughter of the count of Foix. She bore him two daughters, Anne and Isabelle, in 1477 and 1478. But by the first Treaty of Guérande (1365), in the absence of a legitimate male heir, succession should have reverted to the Penthièvre branch of the ducal family, now represented by Nicole of Brittany, whose claim Louis XI had acquired in 1480. In 1486, as the prospect of conflict grew, the Estates of Brittany promised to support the duke's daughters. A French army invaded in 1487 and again in 1488, when it gained an important victory at Saint-Aubin-du-Cormier over the Bretons and their English and other allies (July 28). In the aftermath of this disaster, François died on September 9, 1488, leaving Anne (aged eleven) and a group of Breton diehards to continue the struggle with France.

Michael C.E. Jones

[See also: ANNE OF BEAUJEU; ANNE OF BRITTANY; ARISTOCRATIC REVOLT; BRITTANY; CHARLES VIII]

Dupuy, Antoine. *Histoire de la réunion de la Bretagne à la France*. 2 vols. Paris: Hachette, 1880.

Labande-Mailfert, Yvonne. *Charles VIII et son milieu (1470–1498)*. Paris: Klincksieck, 1975.

Pocquet du Haut-Jussé, Barthélemy-Amadée. *François II, duc de Bretagne, et l'Angleterre (1458–1488)*. Paris: Boccard, 1929.

FRANKS. The Germanic people known as the Franks expanded their political control out of their original lands of the middle and lower Rhine and in the 6th century created a kingdom that extended over the modern areas of western Germany, the Low Countries, and most of France. Established by Clovis I (d. 511), the Frankish kingdom lasted until the Treaty of Verdun (843) divided it among the three sons of Louis the Pious. It thus gave rise to the medieval kingdoms of both France and Germany. The Franks were always a small minority in their own kingdom, and it is an irony that both France and the French language take their names from the Franks, although there are only a few hundred Frankish words in French and few Franks actually settled in France.

The Franks were a West Germanic people, and the modern Dutch and Flemish languages are direct descendants of Frankish. The Franks (the name means "fierce" or "proud") first appear in historical sources in the 3rd century A.D., as the product of one of the periodic dissolutions and regroupings of Germanic tribal confederations. The late and artificial character of the origin of the Franks left them without a long tribal history, a deficit that was corrected in the 7th century by the myth that they were descendants of Trojans. There also was little cohesion or unity among the Franks, and each of their major branches comprised many subgroups under their own chieftains. The Salian Franks were on the lower Rhine, while the Ripuarians were on the middle Rhine. But there were also many other groups of Franks, among them the Chati, Bructeri, Chamavi, and Amsivarii.

In the later 3rd century and throughout the 5th, the Franks, along with the Alemanni and other Germanic tribes, constantly tested Roman defenses along the Rhine. The Romans generally had the upper hand, and many of the defeated Franks were settled in Roman Germany and northern Gaul as *laeti* (farmer soldiers). The Salians were given land in Toxandria, southwest of the mouths of the Rhine. Many Franks were enrolled in the Roman army and rose to positions of command. Franks could be found in Roman service in Spain, Egypt, Asia Minor, and Mesopotamia.

During the decline of Roman imperial government in the 5th century, the defenses of the Rhine collapsed and the Ripuarian Franks established a strong kingdom centered on Cologne. The band of Salian Franks around Tournai began to rise to prominence under its leaders, the Merovingians Childeric I and his son Clovis I. Clovis brought all of the Frankish tribes under his dominion, along with the neighboring Alemanni and Thuringians and almost all of Gaul. Although he moved his capital first to Soissons and then to Paris, accompanied by his entourage, few other Franks moved with him. The kingdom of the Franks was ruled by a Salian Frank with his mostly Frankish companions and army, but its population and culture were mixed, with Franks themselves forming only a small part of its ethnic composition, though they were dominant in northeastern Gaul and the lower and middle Rhine.

Thus, the kingdom of the Franks, the ensemble of lands subject to the Merovingian kings, including Aquitaine and Burgundy, must be distinguished from the land of the Franks, Francia, which ran from northern Gaul through the Salian and Ripuarian territories—the regions of Neustria and Austrasia. The small numbers of Franks scattered throughout Neustria soon assimilated with the Gallo-Roman population and left little ethnic imprint on the region's culture, other than the Salic Law and an identification as Franks. The word "Frank" lost its ethnic significance during the 6th century and came to be synonymous with "free man"; in France, it came to denote someone from north of the Loire, a Neustrian. In Germany, the Frankish territories preserved their ethnic identity as Franconia (one of the five German "stem-duchies"), while the heart of Lorraine was Austrasia, the land of the Ripuarian Franks.

Steven Fanning

[See also: CHILDERIC I; CLOVIS I; GREGORY OF TOURS; MEROVINGIAN DYNASTY]

Bachrach, Bernard S., trans. *Liber historiae Francorum*. Lawrence: Coronado, 1973.

Gregory of Tours. *History of the Franks*, trans. Lewis Thorpe. Harmondsworth: Penguin, 1974.

James, Edward. *The Franks*. Oxford: Blackwell, 1988.

Wallace-Hadrill, J.M. *The Barbarian West, A.D. 400–1000: The Early Middle Ages*. 2nd ed. New York: Harper and Row, 1962, chaps. 4–5.

Wood, Ian. *The Merovingian Kingdoms, 450–751*. London: Longman, 1994.

FRAUD, COMMERCIAL. Definitions of ethical wrongdoing in medieval France varied according to the legal system, canon, civil, or customary law, or royal legislation under consideration. As a rule in matters of trade, town governments and guilds policed weights and measures and ensured quality control of merchandise for export and local sale. There was concerted effort to protect consumers from fraud. In the south of France, where

Roman law formulae, such as *sine dolo* and *sine ulla fraude*, appeared in 12th-century documents, a theory of fraud developed, giving rise to various remedies of justice including restitution and disbarment from the practice of a particular trade.

While Jehan Boinbroke defrauded his employees in northern Douai, in the south of France, Catalan and local merchants occasionally ran afoul of inspection procedures in spice imports. Several instances of saffron fraud can be reconstructed from 14th-century documents. Adulteration of the spice to increase its weight, through wetting or the admixture of extraneous material, was recorded. Municipal officials often chose to make an example of offenders. In France, as elsewhere in medieval Europe, the maintenance of high ethical standards in business was essential to the medieval system of commerce, which was based on mutual faith and trust.

Kathryn L. Reyerson

Cheyette, Fredric L. "The Sovereign and the Pirates, 1332." *Speculum* 45 (1970): 40–68.

Fransen, Gérard. *Le dol dans la conclusion des actes juridiques: évolution des doctrines et système du code canonique*. Gembloux: Duculot, 1946.

Meynial, Edmond. "Note sur l'histoire du dol et de la violence dans les contrats dans notre ancien droit français." In *Mélanges Paul Fournier*. Paris: Sirey, 1929.

Reyerson, Kathryn L. "Commercial Fraud in the Middle Ages: The Case of the Dissembling Pepperer." *Journal of Medieval History* 8 (1982): 63–73.

FREDEGAR (fl. ca. 642). At some point in the mid-7th century in Burgundy, a chronicler, or chroniclers, assembled a group of six historical works, now known together as *The Chronicles of Fredegar*. The name Fredegar is not found in the medieval manuscripts of this work; it appears first in the 16th century. Historians, however, have kept it as a convenient way to refer to the author, or authors, of this important anonymous source for the history of early-medieval France in the Merovingian period. Fredegar is the most coherent and reliable guide to things Frankish from 591, when Gregory of Tours left off, until 642. A Carolingian continuation of the chronicle is found in some, but not all, of the early manuscripts, and this, too, is an important source for the period up to the first year of Charlemagne's reign (768).

Scholars have focused most intently upon the sixth chronicle (or the fourth book, depending upon how the work is divided), which is Fredegar's original account of his own times. The first five chronicles (or three books) comprise his copying, editing, and interpolating earlier historical works. Fredegar is accurately called a chronicler and not a historian, for though he moves in an orderly chronological fashion his account lacks the comprehensive synthesis of large amounts of material that would elevate him to the company of Bede or Gregory of Tours. His perspective is clearly Burgundian; when he treats matters in that kingdom, he is most detailed and vivid. He also knows a great deal about events in Neustria and Austrasia and, from time to time, adds valuable information concerning Spain, central Europe, and even Byzantium.

Richard A. Gerberding

[See also: HISTORIOGRAPHY]

Krusch, Bruno, ed. "Chronicarum quae dicuntur Fredegarii Scholastici Libri IV cum continuationibus." In *Monumenta Germaniae Historica, scriptores rerum Merovingicarum.* Hanover: Hahn, 1888, Vol. 2, pp. 1–193.
Wallace-Hadrill, J.M., ed. and trans. *The Fourth Book of the Chronicle of Fredegar with Its Continuations.* London: Nelson, 1960.

FREDEGUNDE (d. 597). The most famous of the wives of the Merovingian king Chilperic I, Fredegunde was the mother of Clotar II. The extremely hostile accounts of her by Gregory of Tours and in the *Liber historiae Francorum* have left her with the reputation of being an embodiment of evil, a scheming murderess whose wiles led Chilperic I to commit his worst excesses.

Apparently of low birth, Fredegunde became one of the wives of Chilperic and then rose to the position of queen and chief wife by eliminating her rivals, especially by the murder of Galswintha, which precipitated a long feud with Chilperic's brother Sigibert and his wife, Brunhilde, Galswintha's sister. Fredegunde is blamed for the subsequent assassination of Sigibert, as well as for the torture, murder, and attempted murder of real or perceived opponents, including sons of Chilperic by other wives, Brunhilde and her son Childeric II, as well as bishops, counts, and dukes. After Chilperic's assassination in 584, Fredegunde preserved the kingdom for her son Clotar II during his minority. Despite her evil reputation, Fredegunde was a dominant and capable politician.

Steven Fanning

[See also: BRUNHILDE; CHILPERIC I; MEROVINGIAN DYNASTY]

Gregory of Tours. *History of the Franks,* trans. Lewis Thorpe. Harmondsworth: Penguin, 1974.
James, Edward. *The Franks.* Oxford: Blackwell, 1988.
Wood, Ian. *The Merovingian Kingdoms, 450–751.* London: Longman, 1994.

FREDUS. In Frankish law, the *fredus* was the portion of a fine that was paid to the king, either directly or through his representative, or to those who held immunities. This was a payment for the intervention of the government in the resolution of a dispute, not a penalty or a fine. It usually was one-third of the compensation paid to the injured party, though at times it was a fixed sum. In the later Merovingian period, the *fredus* was primarily a source of revenue for the crown. In the Carolingian period, it was often absorbed into the *bannum*, a royal order to do or not to do something on pain of fine.

Steven Fanning

[See also: BAN/BANALITÉ]

Rivers, Theodore John, trans. *Laws of the Salian and Ripuarian Franks.* New York: AMS, 1986.
Ganshof, François L. *Frankish Institutions Under Charlemagne,* trans. Bryce and Mary Lyon. New York: Norton, 1968.
Goebel, Julius, Jr. *Felony and Misdemeanor: A Study in the History of English Criminal Procedure.* New York: Commonwealth Fund, 1937.

FRÉJUS. Established by Julius Caesar in 50 B.C. and known as the Forum Julii, Fréjus is located in the southeast of France in the department of the Var. From the Roman period, there remain the ruins of a 3rd-century amphitheater, an aqueduct, and some fortifications. A 5th-century baptistery also survives that is significant for several reasons. Formigé's work on the edifice in 1926–27 and 1929–30 demonstrated that the baptistery was erected specifically for the Christian rite. Its style is Merovingian—an octagon built within a square with four rounded apses and four rectangular niches. The floor is of marble, while those of the apses and niches are terra-cotta mosaics.

In the Fréjus baptistery are the only surviving French *dolium* and remnants of a *ciborium*. The *dolium* is a basin built into the floor on the south side, 1 foot 3 inches deep, for a foot-washing ceremony prior to baptism in the Ambrosian rite. The octagonal *piscina* in which the catechumen was immersed is 2 feet 9 inches deep. Only one of the eight columns originally surrounding the *piscina* now remains. From these columns, curtains were hung to protect the modesty of the catechumen. Another curtain divided the baptistery into sex-segregated halves.

The cathedral of Notre-Dame-et-Saint-Léonce, rebuilt by Bishop Riculfus in 975 after the Muslim attack in 915, contained a single nave and one side aisle, which formed the parish church dedicated to St. Étienne. The present narthex dates from the 12th century. The original cathedral dating from the 4th–5th centuries contained a nave and two lower side aisles, a common occurrence in Provence. The cathedral group is completed by a cloister that dates from the 12th and 13th centuries.

Linda M. Rouillard

Donnadieu, Alphonse. *La Pompéi de la Provence: Fréjus.* Paris: Champion, 1928.
Formigé, Jules. *Les monuments romains de la Provence.* Paris: Champion, 1924.
Goettelmann, Paul Augustus. "The Baptistry of Fréjus: A Restoration Based on the Architectural and Historical Evidence." Diss. Catholic University of America, 1933.

FRENCH LANGUAGE. Old French had its origin in the colloquial form of Latin brought to Gaul in the 2nd century B.C. as a consequence of the Roman occupation. With the collapse of the Roman Empire in the 5th century, Germanic groups in great numbers began to enter Gaul, among them the Franks, who settled most thickly in the north. The linguistic evolution of the earlier period, which had included many features shared throughout the empire, gave way to divergence and to the formation of the Romance tongues. The language spoken in Gaul during this period, called Gallo-Roman, gradually underwent considerable dialectal differentiation. By the mid-9th century, two main dialect groups could be found in Gaul: in an area roughly south of the Loire River were the dialects of the Langue d'oc, now called Provençal or Occitan; north of there were the dialects of the Langue d'oïl, the ancestor of modern French.

Stages in the development of the language from colloquial Latin through Middle French are:

Late (or "Vulgar") *Latin:* 2nd century B.C. to 5th century A.D.
Gallo-Roman: end of 5th to mid-9th century
Early Old French: mid-9th to end of 11th century
Old French: 12th and 13th centuries
Middle French: 14th and 15th centuries

By the Carolingian Renaissance (ca. 800), French and Latin were separate languages, though conscious reform rather than natural linguistic evolution may have shaped the Latin used at the time. In 813, the Council of Tours recommended that priests explain the word of God in the language of the people, that is, in the *rusticam Romanam linguam.* In 842, Charlemagne's feuding grandsons paved the way for the division of his land by swearing the Oaths of Strasbourg. The oaths were recorded by another family member, the chronicler Nithard, and have subsequently become the event scholars cite to mark the beginning of the Early Old French period.

A Latin of record, religion, and learning persisted. In the spirit of the Council of Tours, however, inspirational literature began to appear in the vernacular. The earliest surviving example of a saint's life, the *Séquence de sainte Eulalie,* dates from the 9th century.

In England, for more than two centuries after the Norman Conquest of 1066, French was the language spoken by the group of people surrounding the ruler. At first, their dialect must have reflected Norman usage, but nobles arriving later came from other parts of France. As in France itself, the use of French in imaginative works preceded by far its appearance in official documents, for which Latin was preferred. Although many words of French origin entered English, there is little evidence that French became the language of the people. English borrowings into French are rare before the 17th century.

Gallo-Roman and Early Old French. Of the numerous and complex phonological changes that occurred during the early centuries, perhaps the most sweeping were those caused by one or more of the following speech habits: word stress, palatalization, and, beginning in the Early Old French period, vowel nasalization. Along with a tendency to vocalize consonants or to eliminate them without trace, these forces, or their greater impact in Gaul than elsewhere, gave to Old French its distinctive character. They are responsible for the creation of new diphthongs and consonants, as well as for a dramatic loss of syllables. The following discussion offers examples of those changes.

(Phonetic symbols employed are those of the International Phonetic Alphabet. Upper-case letters are used for Latin forms. An asterisk denotes an unattested form. Bracketing indicates unstable sounds that were lost early. The symbol < means "comes from, came from," and > means "becomes, became.")

Two general but highly significant alterations occurred in Vulgar Latin. The Classical Latin distinction in vowel quantity ceded to a system of vowel quality: long vowels closed, high vowels lowered, long and short A fell together, and the Classical Latin diphthongs simplified (except for AU, which was not reduced until the end of the Gallo-Roman period). The second important change was the replacement of the Classical Latin musical, or pitch, accent, by a stress, or tonic, accent. The syllable that received the tonic accent in Latin was retained in Old French, whereas other, weakly stressed syllables tended to be effaced. To that stress system, Germanic speech later contributed its own strong expiratory stress.

Vowels developed according to the degree of stress with which they were uttered. When the strongest degree of stress, called tonic stress, fell on one syllable of a word, other syllables were uttered more weakly. Vowels were altered in measure as they were found in tonic, countertonic (secondarily stressed), or atonic (unstressed) syllables. In most cases, the way in which they developed also depended upon their consonantal environment. Simply put, a group of two consonants (except where the second is an *r* or an *l*) closes a syllable, "checking" or "blocking" a vowel preceding, but just one consonant leaves the syllable open and the vowel is said to be "free."

Diphthongs were created when certain tonic free vowels "broke": ẹ > *ie* (PED EM] > *pied*); / ɔ / > *uo* (SOR OR] > *suor*); ę > *ei* (ME > *mei*); ọ > *ou* (FLOR EM] > *flour*); later, *ei*> *oi* , *uo* > *ue* and *ou* > *eu*. By contrast, in tonic checked position and in syllables bearing secondary stress, the same vowels did not diphthongize.

Because final and intertonic syllables were unstressed, their vowels were especially vulnerable to effacement. Although final *a* remained in the form of /ə/ (as in Eng. *about*: PORTA > *porte*), most other word-final vowels were effaced (PORT[U]> *port*). Most vowels between tonic and countertonic syllables were eliminated (TAB[U]LA > *table*, DEB[I]TA > *dette*); here again, *a* could be more resistant: before an accented syllable *a* > /ə/ (ORNAMENTU > *ornement*), which could stand in hiatus with a following stressed vowel (ARMA[T]URA > *armëure*).

A distinguishing feature of French was the alteration of free *a* in a stressed syllable. In that environment, *a* was raised to ẹ, which later opened to ę in certain situations (MATR[EM] > *mere*, PORTAR[E] > *porter*).

Palatalization, the process by which sounds made with the tongue are altered as the middle or the front of the tongue is lifted toward the hard palate, began in colloquial Latin. The velar consonants *k* (spelled *c*) and *g* are a striking example. The palatalization of *k* and *g* in certain positions in Gallo-Roman resulted in the creation of four new consonants: the fricatives /ts/ (as in Eng. *bits*) and /dz/ (as in Eng. *beds*), and the affricates /tʃ/ (as in Eng. *church*) and /dʒ/ (as in Eng. *judge*): in CENT(EM), /k/(C) > /ts/; in

CANTA(T), /k/(C) > /tʃ/; in GAMB(A), G > /dʒ/, and so on. Similarly, in the groups *kl* and *gl,* the loss of the first element after a vowel produced another new consonant, the palatal liquid /λ/ (as in Ital. *figlio*). Palatalization also occurred when *e* or *i* before *a, o, u* became /j/ (as in Eng. *yes*) after a syllable bearing tonic stress; /j/ then palatalized the preceding consonant, as in the new /ɲ/: VINEA > *vigne* (as in Mod. Fr.).

Palatalization affected vowels as well as consonants. It occurred independently in the raising of /u/ (as in Fr. *ou*) to /y/ (as in Fr. *tu*), but other instances were conditioned by environment and often led to the creation of diphthongs. One such instance is that of tonic free *a* preceded by /k/. In that position, *a* was raised and then diphthongized (CANEM > *chien*). When /k/ and *g* in certain positions were effaced, they left /j/ (spelled *i*), which then combined with a preceding vowel to form a diphthong, as PACARE > *paiier*.

Consonant vocalization (the opening of consonants into vowel sounds) resulted in the formation of new diphthongs, as happened when velarized *l* [ɬ] in preconsonantal position began to vocalize in the 9th century: *a* + /ɬ/ > *au* (ALBA > *aube*); *ę* + /ɬ/ > *eu* (ILL[U]S > *els* > *eus* [*eux*]); ɔ + /ɬ/ > *ou* (FOLL[I]S > *fɔs* > *fous*); *ǫ* + /ɬ/ > *ou* (AUSCULTA[T] > *escoute.* A new triphthong, *eau* (BELL[U]S > *beau*), emerged from *ę* + /ɬ/ preconsonantal.

Consonants in a weak position (those at the end of a word or standing alone between vowels) tended to be eliminated. Final M had been lost in early colloquial Latin, and *m* and *n*, which became final later, likewise fell. Final *t* and *d* after a vowel were effaced early. The sounds *p, b, v* final either remained as [*f*] (*CAP[U] > chef*) or were lost. When intervocalic consonants were lost, the number of syllables in a word was reduced, sometimes through an intermediate situation of vowel hiatus. Intervocalic *p, t, k* and *b, d, g* had already weakened in Vulgar Latin. In Gallo-Roman, *p* and *b* intervocalic were retained as *v* (FABA > *feve*, RIPA > *rive*), but before *o* and *u* they disappeared (TABON[EM] > *taon*), as did /k/ and *g.* Intervocalic *t* and *d* were effaced (MUTAR[E] > *muer*, VIDER[E] > *vĕoir*).

Germanic speech habits, too, influenced the development of French. Whereas Latin *h* had already ceased to be pronounced (HABERE > *aveir, avoir*), the *h* in Germanic words was pronounced (haunitha > *honte*), and the Germanic bilabial *w* became *gu* or *g* : WERRA > *guerre*, WARDA > *garde*.

Nasalization, a phenomenon peculiar to French and Portuguese among the Romance languages, did not begin until the Early Old French period. In general, tonic vowels both free and blocked nasalized before the consonants *m*, *n* and /ɲ/, but countertonic vowels nasalized only in some circumstances. The low vowel *a* nasalized first (as in *tant*), probably in the 10th century, followed by the mid-vowels and eventually the high vowels *i* and /y/ and the diphthongs *ie, oi, ui*, which nasalized toward the end of the 12th century. Nasal consonants also caused diphthongization of tonic free *a* to *ai* (which did not raise to *e*, therefore: MAN(UM) > *main*) and they prevented certain other developments.

French in the 12th Century. Evidence for Old French is contained in a large body of written material of many types, including literary works. Nevertheless, it is not easy to know with precision the exact pronunciation of Old French or the dates and geographical extension of linguistic phenomena. As against the hesitancies of Old French orthographic practice (the same phoneme in the same environment was often represented by different graphies), the rhyme and counting of syllables required by verse are a precious, if not infallible, aid in determining linguistic values.

The preponderance of dialects in the Old French period is a further complicating factor, making it impossible to talk about one Old French pronunciation. The main variants of the Langue d'oïl were Francien and, to its immediate east and much like it, Champenois; to the south were the dialects of Orléans, Bourbonnais, Nivernais, and Berry; others were Anglo-Norman, the dialect spoken in England after the Conquest, and Norman (northwest); Picard, Lotharingian, and Walloon (northeast); Burgundian and Franc-Comtois (southeast); the dialects of Anjou, Touraine, Maine, and Brittany (west); and those of Poitou and Saintonge (southwest). The dialects were marked by regionalisms and may not have been entirely mutually intelligible. Their corresponding written languages, called "scriptas," were colored in varying degrees by dialectal traits but remained understood by speakers in other areas; the scriptas, therefore, were not faithful records of the dialects. The base of the scriptas was from the beginning Francien, the scripta of the Île-de-France region around Paris, and that was so mainly for political and geographical reasons. Modern French is derived from the Francien dialect. The following description of the Old French (Francien) sound system of the late 12th century nevertheless represents a reliable conjecture:

Consonant phonemes: probably twenty-one: /p/, /b/, /t/, /d/, /k/, /g/, /m/, /n/, /l/, /f/, /r/, /v/, /s/, /z/, and /h/ (in words of Germanic origin) and the new consonants /ɲ/, /λ/, /ts/, /tʃ/, /dz/, and /dʒ/. In the 13th century, affricates reduced to their fricative element: /ts/ > /s/, /tʃ/ > /ʃʃ/, /dz/ > /z/, and /dʒ/ > /ʒ/.

Oral vowels: probably the high vowels /i/, /y/, /u/, and /ǫ/, the mid-vowels /ę/, /ę/, /ɔ/, /ø/, and /ə/, and the low vowel /a/. There was a sound longer than /ǫ/ and one longer than /ę/. Oral diphthongs: probably six, that is, /ei/ (in an open syllable, as *rai-son*); /oi/ < /ei/, /yi/ (*nuit*); /au/ (from vocalized /ɬ/; /ię/ (*chief*); /iø/ (*Dieu*); and the triphthong /eau/ (*beaus*). By the end of the 12th century, /ai/ had been reduced to /ę/ in a closed syllable, and /ou/ > /u/. The diphthongs /ue/, /eu/, and the triphthong /ueu/ became /ø/, spelled *eu* or *œ*. There were two nasal monophthongs, /ã/ and /õ/, and two nasal diphthongs, /ię̃/ and /ęĩ/.

In the 13th century, /ǫ/ long free > /ø/ (*flor* > *fleur*), /ǫ/ checked > /u/ (*tor* > *tour*). The first element of the diphthongs /ię/, /ieu/, /oi/, and /yi/ consonantalized, becoming /ję/, /jø/, /wę/, and /ɥi/, respectively. The high vowels /i/ and /ø/ nasalized to /ĩ/ and /ø̃/.

The Francien scripta could employ varying spellings to render each of those phonemes, even in the same text, paragraph, or line. For example, the competing spellings *ilg, lg, lli,* or *illi,* could appear for the new /λ/. Regional scriptas, and dialectal differentiation, added to the variety of graphemes.

Twelfth-Century Morphology and Syntax. Classical Latin was a synthetic language, one in which flexions marked relationships between the parts of a sentence. Modern French, an analytic language, expresses those relationships through the use of particles (e.g., prepositions) and fixed word order. Accordingly, in the development of French the Latin cases, which had been reduced to just the nominative (replacing the Latin nominative and vocative) and oblique (replacing the Latin accusative, genitive, dative, and ablative), probably by the end of the Late Latin period, were gradually lost. The two-case system of the 12th century used *-s* or *-z* alone to mark both case and number in several classes of nouns:

Table 1. *Old French Nouns*

	A. Masc.	B. Masc.	C. Fem.	D. Fem.
Nom. sg	*murs*	*pere*	*rose*	*flors*
Obl. sg.	*mur*	*pere*	*rose*	*flor*
Nom. pl.	*mur*	*pere*	*roses*	*flors*
Obl. pl.	*murs*	*peres*	*roses*	*flors*

Another class of nouns, both masc. and fem., had a nom. sg. form that was always shorter than its other forms (e.g., *ber* —baron, *none* —nonain). Adjectives in Old French tended to precede, not follow, nouns, and most agreed with them in gender and in number.

Among other parts of speech, the Old French system of articles (<[IL]LE) resembled the modern paradigm except for a masc. nom. sg. and pl. form, *li*. The definite article was used in general to individualize a substantive; it did not appear with abstract nouns. The indefinite article *uns* (< UN[U]S) was slower to appear. Old French demonstratives included forms for proximate (*cist* or *cest*; *ceste*) and distant (*cil* or *cel*; *cele*) reference. By the end of the 12th century, the proximate forms had become specialized as adjectives, but *cil* and *cele* functioned equally as pronouns and adjectives.

Certain Old French parts of speech had two sets of forms, tonic and atonic. Tonic forms were relatively more autonomous, appearing in stressed position in a phrase—after a preposition, for example. Atonic forms tended to precede stressed forms, such as verbs. Among personal pronouns, the first two oblique forms were represented by a stressed and unstressed series of forms that did not distinguish between direct and indirect objects: tonic: *mei* (*moi*), *tei* (*toi*), *sei* (*soi*); atonic: *me, te, se*. The system of possessives, too, was divided into tonic and atonic forms, and in the masc. obl. sg. forms *mien* (tonic) and *mon* (atonic) can be seen the origin of the modern French distinction between pronoun and adjective.

As for verb tenses, of the Latin indicative tense forms, active voice, only the present, imperfect, and the perfect persisted into Old French. A new future form was created from the infinitive + present indicative of HABERE (e.g., *chanter + ai > chanterai*) and a compound future perfect was developed (*j'aurai chanté*). A future-in-the-past that could also be used to describe hypothetical or contingent action, the "conditional," was added, built on the infinitive + the imperfect endings of HABERE: *chanter + oie, -ois, -oit,*

etc. The new compound form, the *passé composé*, had mainly present perfect meaning. Thus, in the 12th century Old French had five simple tenses of the indicative: present, imperfect, simple past (*passé simple*), future, and conditional. There were five compound tenses: present perfect, past perfect (formed in two ways, either with the imperfect or the simple past of the auxiliary), a future perfect, and a conditional perfect. The *passé surcomposé* did not begin to appear before the early 13th century.

There were three classes of Old French verbs: I: infinitive in *-er* and *-ier*; II: infinitive in *-ir*, present participle with *-iss*; and, III: infinitive in *-ir, -re, -eir* (> *oir*). The relatively more distinctive personal endings of verbs made expressed subjects less necessary than in the modern language.

Table 2. *Old French Present Indicative*

I. chanter	II. fenir	III. corre
chant	*fenis*	*cor*
chantes	*fenis*	*cors*
chante	*fenist*	*cort*
chantons	*fenissons*	*corons*
chantez	*fenissez*	*corez*
chantent	*fenissent*	*corent*

The simple past presented weak and strong forms. Weak forms included all *-er, -ier*, most *-ir*, and many *-re* verbs. Of the four types of Classical Latin strong perfects, three survived, in altered form, into Old French. Because of the effects of stress, strong forms presented greater paradigmatic variation than weak forms. Syntactically, the simple past was primarily a narrative tense with punctive aspect, but it could also be used descriptively, especially in the earlier period when the imperfect was infrequent. Unlike the modern *passé simple*, the simple past was used in conversation.

Although the imperfect tense had competing dialectal endings in the 12th century, the predecessor of the modern form was common: *vend-eie, vend-eies, vend-ei(e)t, vend-iiens, vend-iiez, vend-eient*.

Of the Classical Latin subjunctive forms, only the present and pluperfect survived into French. The Latin pluperfect subjunctive became the Old French imperfect subjunctive, its endings not very different from the modern imperfect subjunctive.

Middle French. Significant vocalic changes of the Middle French period include the continued reduction of diphthongs to simple vowels (there are no diphthongs in modern French). The diphthong *au* reduced to /ǫ/ and the triphthong *eau* reduced to /eǫ/ very late in this period. Vowels in hiatus were reduced to just their stressed element (*meïsmes > mesmes*). Before a stressed syllable, /ə/ was effaced (*armeüre > armure*). In late Middle French, a process of denasalization began, affecting first the vowels that had been the last to nasalize. Other vowel changes occurred, but it was not until the late 16th century that the vowel system of modern French was in place.

The erosion of final consonants continued in Middle French, encouraged by a shift, evident even in the 12th century, from word to group stress, the pattern of modern French. Under that type of stress, groups of words are run together, making a phrase or locution into a unit. As words are linked, some of their final consonants weaken and disappear; that was the case for final plosives and fricatives before a consonant. Even final consonants preceded by another consonant (and thus supported) were generally effaced in this period. Final *r* weakened.

As for the case system, virtually all texts show traces of it, but none uses case systematically or coherently. The nominative inflection had yielded to the accusative with few exceptions.

Middle French literary practice took advantage of old and new forms, as well as of regionalisms. Although leveling of dialectal features in scriptas had begun early, radiating outward from the area around Paris, a common stock of forms, which included regional variants, nevertheless remained available to writers from all areas. Their use was not necessarily a true indication of the writer's own dialect. Regionalisms like the Picard word-final reduction of *-ié* and *-iée* to *-ie* can be found at the rhyme in texts from many regions. The raising of *a* before /ʒ/ or /ɲ/ was an eastern trait that appeared broadly in literary texts in the form of *-aige* for *-age* and *-aigne* for *-agne* (as *Bretaigne* rhyming with *enseigne*, or *couraige* with *sai je*). In this period, it is not unusual to find rhymes between *-eu* and *-ou* (*gracious*, *gracieux* with *nous*), and *-ui* could rhyme either with *-u* or with *-i*, and both in the same text (*huis* with *lassus*, *je vi* with *bui*). Rhymes also attest the spread later in the period of such Parisian pronunciations as *-ar* for *-er* (as in the rhyme *Robert* with *Lombart*, found in the poetry of François Villon).

Word Order, Sentence Structure, Vocabulary. Word order in Old French was fairly flexible, owing in part to the two-case system. While the modern French order subject-verb-complement was common in both prose and poetry, another order, that of complement-verb-subject (+ possible additional complement), was frequent, particularly in poetry and in main clauses. Thus, the sentence *Ses barons fist li rois venir* means "The king summoned his barons." In Middle French, as use of the case system declined, word order tended to become more fixed.

Parataxis, or the placing together of clauses or phrases without explicit coordinating or subordinating words, was frequent in verse texts of the Old French period. In Middle French, parataxis became rare. On the other hand, the revival of classical studies and with it a taste for latinizing encouraged many writers of Middle French prose to imitate Latin periodic construction.

Although over the centuries French has borrowed vocabulary from other languages, Old French was overwhelmingly a language inherited from colloquial Latin. The Celtic spoken originally by the Gauls contributed words to French, as *vassal*, *cheval*. Low Latin, the written form of Latin which persisted throughout the Gallo-Roman and Old French periods, continued to provide words. Germanic words from many semantic groups passed into French, some in the Vulgar Latin period, others in Gallo-Roman: *heaume*, *guise*, *garnir*, *blanc*, *choisir*, *fournir*, *danser*, *gage*, *guetter* are but a few examples. In the Middle French period, the desire to latinize brought large-scale borrowing from Classical Latin. Borrowings from Italian became more numerous, reflecting Italy's new cultural ascendancy.

Thelma S. Fenster

[See also: ANGLO-NORMAN LITERATURE; FRANCO-ITALIAN LITERATURE; LITURGICAL LANGUAGES; OCCITAN LANGUAGE; *STRASBOURG, OATHS OF*]

Bourciez, Édouard and Jean. *Phonétique française: étude historique*. Paris: Klincksieck, 1967.

Clanchy, M.T. *From Memory to Written Record: England, 1066–1307*. Cambridge: Harvard University Press, 1979.

Einhorn, E. *Old French: A Concise Handbook*. Cambridge: Cambridge University Press, 1974.

Ewert, Alfred. *The French Language*. London: Faber and Faber, 1933.

Gossen, Carl Theodor. *Französische Skriptastudien: Untersuchungen zu den nordfranzösischen Urkundensprachen des Mittelalters*. Vienna: Böhlaus, 1967.

Kibler, William W. *An Introduction to Old French*. New York: Modern Language Association of America, 1984.

Marchello-Nizia, Christiane. *Histoire de la langue française aux XIVe et XVe siècles*. Paris: Bordas, 1979.

Ménard, Philippe. *Manuel du français du moyen âge*. Bordeaux: SOBODI, 1976, Vol. 1: *Syntaxe de l'ancien français*.

Moignet, Gérard. *Grammaire de l'ancien français: morphologie—syntaxe*. Paris: Klincksieck, 1976.

Pope, Mildred. *From Latin to Modern French with Especial Consideration of Anglo-Norman*. Manchester: University of Manchester Press, 1934.

von Wartburg, Walther. *Évolution et structure de la langue française*. Bern: Francke, 1946.

Wright, Roger. *Late Latin and Early Romance in Spain and Carolingian France*. Liverpool: Cairns, 1982.

FROISSART, JEAN (1337–after 1404). The greatest French chronicler, as well as an outstanding poet and romancer, Jean Froissart was born the year the Hundred Years' War began, to a humble bourgeois family of Valenciennes, which lay then outside the French kingdom. After a clerical education, he entered the service of the counts of Hainaut. All his life, Froissart was a servant of powerful nobles. His ability to please his aristocratic patrons and protectors is his chief characteristic as a man and writer. In 1361, he went to England to become one of the *clercs de la chambre* of Philippa of Hainaut, wife of Edward III. He remained in that service until her death in 1369. His stay in England was interrupted by extensive travels to Scotland, to southern France in the suite of the Black Prince, and later, in the retinue of Edward's second son, Lionel, duke of Clarence (patron and protector of Chaucer), to northern Italy, where Lionel married the daughter of the duke of Milan. After the wedding, Froissart traveled to Rome and returned to England via Hainaut and Brabant. These travels doubtless furnished him with the "pan-European" outlook informing much of his *Chronicles*. The youthful service at the very French court of Philippa imprinted in him a permanent, idealized image of a chivalric "paradise lost" so evident in his romance *Meliador*. After the death of Philippa, Froissart returned to his native Hainaut in search of new patrons. His chief benefactors were Robert de Namur (d. 1392); more importantly, Gui II, count of Blois (d. 1397), who in all probability urged him to work on the *Chroniques*; and Wenceslas, duke of Luxembourg and Brabant (d. 1383), who certainly encouraged his poetry, for he was a poet in his own right. We know that Froissart took holy orders and that, in 1373, he received a benefice in Les Estiennes near Mons. In 1384, he became a canon at Chimay. Sometime later, he received another canonry at Lille. He spent the winter of 1388–89 in Orthez, at the splendid court of another aristocratic man of letters, Gaston Phoebus, count of Foix (d. 1391). He traveled to the Low Countries, and in 1394 he briefly revisited England. Little is known about Froissart's declining years. He died some time after 1404.

Froissart's main achievement is *Les chroniques de France, d'Angleterre et de païs voisins . . .*, a history of almost all of western Europe spanning the years 1327 (the accession of Edward III) and ca. 1400 (the death of Richard II). This history, although providing us with an enormous wealth of realistic detail, is written from a distinctive point of view. Like so much of Froissart's poetry, it embodies a frank glorification of an aristocratic, idealized, "international," chivalric life. Up to 1361, his work is a recasting of Jean le Bel's (ca. 1290–1370) *Vrayes chroniques*, which present the first years of the reign of Edward III and the beginnings of the Hundred Years' War. After this date, Froissart follows his own observations, hearsay, and, occasionally, documents. He was certainly conscious of partisan points of view in history and took some pains to ascertain the facts, interviewing eyewitnesses and participants in the events described. He traveled widely to seek out sources and constantly recast the first two books of his *Chroniques* to suit changing political circumstances and the tastes and views of his patrons.

Froissart's *Chroniques* are divided into four books. Book 1 was recast by the chronicler into four redactions. It relates events up to 1369, 1372, or 1377 depending on redactions. After this book, Froissart wrote the independent *Chronique de Flandre*, which relates the disorders occurring in that country between 1378 and 1387. This chronicle was later incorporated into Book 2, which ends with events in 1387; there are two redactions of Book 2. The last two books exist in only one redaction. The third relates events to ca. 1390 and the fourth to ca. 1400.

Froissart's *Chroniques*, an important monument of an elegant and efficient French prose, enjoyed an instant, wide, and lasting success. They were particularly appreciated in England, not only for their pro-English stance (inherited, so to speak, from Jean le Bel), but also for their archaizing, chivalric outlook. The *Chroniques* are a priceless source for the history of the 14th century, especially for the reader who understands the aristocratic vantage point from which Froissart viewed it. One should not expect to find either penetrating explanations of political history or subtle social commentary. Froissart's

views were limited by those of his patrons: he never understood the aspirations and growing power of the bourgeoisie. He had nothing but contempt for the peasant revolt of the French Jacquerie of 1358, or for its English counterpart led by Wat Tyler in 1381. His *Chroniques* give us a vivid mirror of the epoch, the distortions of which can be more easily understood through the ideology informing his poetry.

Froissart wrote lyric verse, narrative-didactic poetry, and a long, rhymed Arthurian romance. His lyrical output is considerable: thirteen *lais*, six *chansons royaux*, forty ballades, thirteen virelais, 107 rondeaux, and twenty *pastourelles*. They come to us in the two manuscripts carefully copied under his supervision (B.N. fr. 830 and 831), which also contain his narrative-didactic poetry. He also wrote several *serventois* in honor of the Virgin. Otherwise, all his lyrical poems, most of which were composed before 1372, celebrate courtly love. In lyrical as well as narrative-didactic poems, his unavowed model was Guillaume de Machaut (ca. 1300–77), but Froissart, as far as we know, composed no music.

Of special historical interest because of their historical *realia* are Froissart's *pastourelles*. The lovestruck shepherds sometimes make historical allusions, and under the easily penetrated fictional cover, six of these *pastourelles* celebrate public events, such as the arrival in Paris of Queen Isabeau (1385), or the marriage of the elderly John, duke of Berry, to the very young Jeanne de Boulogne (1389). The *pastourelles* present real affinities between Froissart's lyric poetry and his *Chroniques*.

Much of Froissart's lyric poetry exists in two "redactions," for many of the poems were not only grouped according to their genre, but also inserted (sometimes slightly modified) in narrative *dits* (called also *dittiés* or *trettiés*). The oldest of them is the *Paradis d'Amour* (1,724 lines with five lyric insertions), an allegorical dream vision (in the manner of the first part of the *Roman de la Rose*) in which the poet-lover encounters in the Garden (Paradise) of Love such traditional figures of the God of Love, Plaisance, Hope, Pity, and Sweet Looks. The protagonist tells the story of his love to the God of Love, recites his poems, and meets his ladylove, who makes him a wreath of daisies. To reward her, the poet recites his ballade *Sur toutes flours j'aimme la margerite*. Her touch wakes him from his delightful dream. What is important in this *dit* is Froissart's explicit connection between the love-dream and the ability and capacity for composing lyric poetry.

The *Orloge amoureus* is the only *dit* written in decasyllabic couplets (unlike the others composed in octosyllables). Its 1,174 verses describe the workings of the clock, then a relatively new invention. In all probability, it was the real Parisian clock in the tower of the Palais Royal on the Île de la Cité that Froissart examined in 1368 during his return trip from Italy. The poet systematically compares his love-filled heart with the "subtlety" of the workings of the clock. Thus, the foliot or bar-balance is Fear, the main weight is Beauty, the mother wheel is Desire, the 'scape wheel is Moderation, the striking wheel is Sweet Talk, and so on. Each part of the mechanism corresponds thus to a "well-working," allegorical system of courtly love. The presentation of the workings of the clock is so detailed and exact that the *Orloge amoureus* was cited and partially translated by an English historian of horology. This *dit* is, like the *Chroniques*, a monument to Froissart's unquenchable curiosity concerning the things of this world.

The *Espinette amoureuse* (4,198 verses with fourteen lyric insertions) offers first a long pseudo-autobiographical introduction describing his childhood and stressing the precocity of his love inclination. Then the poet presents a dream vision in which he encounters Juno, Pallas Athene, Mercury, and Venus. Venus makes him a gift of a "[c]œur gai, joli et amoureus" (l. 547). The rest of the *dit* is quite similar to the *Paradis*. The poet-lover encounters his ladylove, they exchange poems, they dance, but after a while the lady must leave because she is to marry someone else. The poet becomes ill and alternates between hope and despair.

The *Prison amoureuse* (3,895 lines with sixteen inserted poems and twelve letters in prose) tells, under the usual allegorical cover, the real story of Wenceslas of Luxemburg, captured in the Battle of Baesweiler in 1371 and awaiting the ransom money to be paid by his brother, the emperor Charles IV. The seven letters written by Rose (=Wenceslas) and five by Flos (=Froissart) present the backbone of the *dit*. They discuss the subtleties of courtly love. We know that the combination of letters and verse-narration was made popular by Machaut in his *Voir dit* (ca. 1362), but whereas Machaut presents a real plot, in Froissart the plot is replaced by two *exempla*: a pseudomythological love story told by Flos and an allegorical vision experienced by Rose, in which we can made out the real story of the imprisoned Wenceslas.

The *Joli buisson de Jonece* is the longest and most ambitious of Froissart's *dits* (5,442 lines, with twenty-seven inserted poems). It is a dream vision that Froissart, aged thirty-five, had on November 30, 1373. In his dream, populated by mythological and allegorical figures, Youth leads him to an allegorical Bush. Awakened, the poet realizes the real danger and turns his thoughts toward the Virgin, whom he praises in a *lai*. She becomes "li Buissons resplendissans" (l. 5,402) and her Son "[e]st li feus plaisans,/ Non ardans,/Mais enluminans" (ll. 5,407–10).

Like the *Orloge*, the *Temple d'honneur* (1,076 lines) does not contain any inserted lyrics. In this allegorical dream, Honor marries his son, Desire, to Lady Plaisance. Froissart calls this poem not a *dit amoureus*, but *trettié de moralité*. Indeed, most of the *trettié* consists of Honor's long moral sermon on love and marriage. It is quite possible that the *Temple* is indeed an epithalamium celebrating a real couple.

Besides these five *dits*, Froissart composed six shorter lyrico-narrative poems. The *Dit dou bleu chevalier* (504 lines) tells, in a complicated metric scheme, the efforts of the poet to console a lovesick knight dressed in blue (the color of fidelity). The *Joli mois de mai* (464 lines with three lyric insertions) is a purely lyrical composition in which the poet, addressing a nightingale, extolls the beauty of his ladylove. Purely lyrical also is the *Dit de la margueritte* (192 lines): the poet sings the praise of his flower-ladylove. The *Plaidoirie de la rose et de la violette* (342 lines) is a perfect example of Froissart's ability to flatter: these two flowers ask the court of France to decide which of them is more worthy of praise. The court, presided over by "noble et haulte Flour de Lys" (l. 308) and seconded not only by the usual allegorical figures of Prowess, Youth, Sense, Gernerosity, and others, but also by the dukes of Berry, Burgundy, Eu, and La Marche, will some day pronounce a judgment on all flowers, even on Froissart's flower, the daisy.

More apparently autobiographical are the last two *dits* presented without inserted lyrics or mythological allusions. The *Debat dou cheval et dou levrier* (92 lines) shows Froissart returning from Scotland and overhearing a discussion between his horse and his greyhound on the joys and sorrows of their respective existences. The *Dit dou florin* (490 lines) is a debate between Froissart and the last of his coins left from a dissipated fortune. The poet tells us about the eighty *florins* that he received from the count of Foix and, more importantly, informs us that during his stay in Orthez, Froissart read each night, for eleven weeks, a passage of his *Méliador* to the count.

If in his lyric and lyrico-narrative poetry Froissart adheres closely to the literary canons established by Machaut, his verse romance *Méliador* is perhaps more "original," for it is a conscious return to a much earlier tradition. Its other claim to originality lies in Froissart's insertion of seventy-nine lyric poems from the pen of his patron Wenceslas of Luxembourg. While most 14th-century romances are recastings or continuations, usually in prose, *Méliador*'s subject is new, though it is composed in the traditional octosyllabic couplets. The romance of more than 30,000 lines (unfinished and with two lacunae) is set in a youthful Arthurian court and could be called the "enfances de la Table Ronde." It depicts the innumerable adventures, chiefly jousting and chance armed encounters, of innumerable knights-errant, but the main plot is easily discernible: Hermione, princess of Scotland, is promised to the knight who proves himself most valiant in a series of tournaments organized by the ladies. Méliador, son of the duke of Cornwell, is an ideal knight-errant. At the end, he wins not only Hermione but also the Scottish kingdom, while his companions win lesser princesses. *Méliador*, begun in the early 1360s and completed only after the death of Wenceslas in 1383, reflects the geography and ideology of Froissart's early service in Great Britain. As a frank glorification of chivalry, with its implied desire to revive it in Froissart's own time, *Méliador* is a powerful link between his poetry and the greatest accomplishment of his life, his idealizing, and "restoratory" *Chroniques*.

Peter F. Dembowski

[See also: *DIT*; GASTON PHOEBUS; MACHAUT, GUILLAUME DE; *PASTOURELLE/PASTORELA*]

Froissart, Jean. *Les œuvres de Froissart—Chroniques*, ed. Joseph M.B.C. Kervyn de Lettenhove. 25 vols. in 26. Vols. 1–17, Brussels: Devaux, 1867–73; Vols. 18–25, Brussels: Closson, 1874–77. [The only complete, but idiosyncratic, edition of the chronicles.]

———. *Chroniques de Jean Froissart*. 15 vols. Vols. 1–8, part 1, ed. Siméon Luce. Vol. 8, parts 2–11, ed. Gaston Raynaud. Vol. 12, ed. Léon Mirot. Vol. 13, ed. Léon Mirot and Albert Mirot. Vols. 14 and 15, ed. Albert Mirot. Vols. 1–4, Paris: Renouard, 1869–73. Vols. 5–7, Paris: Renouard, H. Loones, successeur, 1874–78. Vols. 8–11, Paris: Renouard, H. Laurens, successeur, 1888–99. Vol. 12, Paris: Champion, 1931. Vols. 13–15. Paris: Klincksieck, 1957–75. [Vols. 1–8 contain Book 1 with variants; Vols. 9–11, Book 2 with variants; Vols. 12–15, most of Book 3 (up to 1389). This "national edition," begun in 1869, is still "in progress."]

———. *Ballades et rondeaux*, ed. Rae S. Baudoin. Geneva: Droz, 1978.

———. *Le paradis d'amour; L'orloge amoureus,* ed. Peter F. Dembowski. Geneva: Droz, 1986.

———. *L'espinette amoreuse*, ed. Anthime Fourrier. Paris: Klincksieck, 1972.

———. *La prison amoureuse*, ed. Anthime Fourrier. Paris: Klincksieck, 1974.

———. *Le joli buisson de Jonece*, ed. Anthime Fourrier. Geneva: Droz, 1975.

———. *"Dits" et "Débats" avec en appendice quelques poèmes de Guillame de Machaut*, ed. Anthime Fourrier. Geneva: Droz, 1979. [Edited here are: *Le temple d'honneur, Le joli mois de may, Le dit de la margueritte, Le dit dou bleu chevalier, Le debat dou cheval et dou levrier, Le dit dou florin, La plaidoirie de la rose et de la violette.*]

———. *Chroniques: début du premier livre: édition du manuscrit de Rome Reg. lat. 869*, ed. George T. Diller. Geneva: Droz, 1972.

———. *Méliador: roman comprenant les poésies lyriques de Wenceslas de Bohême, duc de Luxembourg et de Brabant*, ed. Auguste Longnon. 3 vols. Paris: Didot, 1895–99.

———. *The Lyric Poems of Jean Froissart*, ed. Rob Roy McGregor, Jr. Chapel Hill: University of North Carolina Press, 1975.

———. *Chronicles*, trans. Geoffrey Brereton. Harmondsworth: Penguin, 1968.

Dembowski, Peter F. *Jean Froissart and His* Méliador: *Context, Craft, and Sense*. Lexington: French Forum, 1983.

Shears, Frederic Sidney. *Froissart: Chronicler and Poet*. London: Routledge, 1930.

FULBERT OF CHARTRES (ca 960–1028). Born of humble parents probably in Aquitaine, perhaps Poitou, Fulbert studied at Reims under Gerbert of Aurillac (later Pope Sylvester II), the outstanding master of the day. Fulbert became master of the cathedral school at Chartres in the 990s and served as master and chancellor before becoming bishop of Chartres in 1006. He had a close association with King Robert II the Pious of France, a schoolmate of Fulbert's at Reims. Fulbert was particularly well versed in law and medicine and was familiar with the astronomical works that had been recently translated from the Arabic. Although intellectually conservative (he avoided the new discipline of dialectics), his teaching attracted one of the most dialectical thinkers of the time: Berengar of Tours, condemned for his novel eucharistic opinions.

After the cathedral burned in 1020, Fulbert began a campaign to rebuild it, a project made possible by the generosity of King Canute of England and Denmark, as well as King Robert of France. The new, spacious crypt constructed by Fulbert remains the largest crypt in France and became the basis for all further construction at the site. The new crypt was meant to accommodate the pilgrims who came to venerate the holy relic of the *sancta camisia*, a garment reputed to have been worn by Mary when she gave birth to Jesus; it was enshrined at Chartres from the 9th century forward and is still possessed by the cathedral. Fulbert was an avid promoter of devotion to the Virgin.

Fulbert was also a reformer who campaigned against simony (buying and selling church offices) and clerical marriage. Like most bishops of his day, Fulbert was both a churchman and a feudal lord, and he knew first-hand the tension of dual allegiances. In a well-known letter to Duke William V of Aquitaine, his long-time benefactor, Fulbert explains the meaning of the feudal oath. But in another, he is highly critical of ecclesiastics who are intent on bearing arms rather than on keeping the peace of the church. In several letters, he rebukes Foulques III Nerra, count of Anjou, for his depredations.

Of Fulbert's sermons, the best known is that composed for the feast of the Nativity of the Virgin Mary, in which he recounts the history of Théophile, a Christian who after selling his soul to the Devil was rescued by the Virgin. Fulbert's legend of Théophile is the subject of Rutebeuf's *Miracle de Théophile*. An excellent latinist and one of the best writers of his day, Fulbert left behind a substantial body of correspondence, some 140 letters, with leading churchmen, including abbots Abbo of Fleury, Richard of Saint-Vannes, and Odilo of Cluny. He also wrote several poems and a few other miscellaneous works.

Mark Zier

[See also: ABBO OF FLEURY; ARABIC PHILOSOPHY, INFLUENCE OF; BERENGAR OF TOURS; CHARTRES; GERBERT OF AURILLAC; ODILO; SCHOOLS, CATHEDRAL]

Fulbert of Chartres. *Opera omnia. PL* 141.185–368.

———. *The Letters and Poems of Fulbert of Chartres*, ed. and trans. Frederick Behrends. Oxford: Clarendon, 1976.

MacKinney, Loren Carey. *Bishop Fulbert and Education at the School of Chartres*. Notre Dame: Mediaeval Institute, University of Notre Dame, 1957.

GAB. A word from Old Norse *gabba* meaning originally "to mock, to sneer; a mockery, an insult," it became famous through its peculiar usage in the late 12th-century *Voyage de Charlemagne*: "a boast." Attested as early as the 10th century in Provençal and later in Old French texts, mostly centered in the northwest, the word retained its original meanings until the 16th century, when it finally died out. Because of the renown of the *Voyage*, however, modern scholars tend to recognize "boast" as its most frequent meaning. The episode that celebrates it occurs in Constantinople, where, after a copious dinner well supplied with claret, Charles and the peers make extravagant boasts to while away the time, as is their custom (ll. 448–617). The host, Hugon, places a spy in the chambers and learns that his guests, during their amusements, have insulted him. In rage, he calls upon them to perform their boasts. It takes only three of the *gabs* to prove that the French are superior, so Hugon releases them from further obligation and becomes Charles's vassal. The fame of this adventure has left its mark on *Galien restoré* and may have inspired the poems of the Vow Cycle.

In southern France, the troubadours adopted the word to express themes of boasting, so that scholars may refer to certain songs generically as *gabs*. Although an identifiable autonomous genre was never constituted, an argument for the existence of a latent narrative genre can be made.

John L. Grigsby

[See also: *GALIEN RESTORÉ*; VOW CYCLE; *VOYAGE DE CHARLEMAGNE À JÉRUSALEM ET À CONSTANTINOPLE*]

Von Kraemer, Erik. "Sémantique de l'ancien français *gab* et *gaber* comparée à celles des termes correspondants dans d'autres langues romanes." In *Mélanges de philologie et de linguistique offerts à Tauno Nurmela*. Turku: Annales Universitatis Turkuensis, 1967, pp. 73–90.

GABELLE. The term *gabelle* had widespread use in Mediterranean Europe to describe indirect taxes on the sale of merchandise. In France, after the mid-14th century, it came to refer almost exclusively to a royal tax on salt. Originally a seigneurial right like other mineral resources, salt became an important source of royal revenue after Philip VI's ordinance of March 16, 1341, ordered seizure of salt throughout the kingdom. It was to be stored in royal warehouses and then sold for a profit by royal officials called *gabelliers*. The king established a more permanent administrative structure in 1343, but general hostility to the new tax led Philip to cancel it in 1346–47 in return for grants of war subsidies. The Estates General of December 1355 reimposed the *gabelle* as one of several indirect taxes that soon were canceled because of opposition. It appeared again at Paris in 1358, and the Estates of Languedoc began imposing a *gabelle* on salt after 1359.

The *gabelle*, along with other indirect taxes, became a permanent part of royal finances in December 1360, when the ransom of King John II required heavy regular taxes. Until 1367, it was a 20-percent *ad valorem* tax, but then the crown changed it to a surcharge of twenty-four francs per *muid* of salt.

John Bell Henneman, Jr.

Dupont-Ferrier, Gustave. *Études sur les institutions financières de la France à la fin du moyen âge*. 2 vols. Paris: Didot, 1930–32.

Henneman, John Bell. *Royal Taxation in Fourteenth Century France: The Development of War Financing, 1322–1356*. Princeton: Princeton University Press, 1971.

Meynial, Edmond. "Études sur la gabelle du sel avant le XVIIe siècle en France." *Tijdschrift voor Rechtsgeschiedenis* 3 (1922): 119–62.

Pérousse, Gabriel. "Étude sur les origines de la gabelle et sur son organisation jusqu'en 1380." Positions de thèses. Paris: École Nationale des Chartes, 1898.

GACE BRULÉ (fl. ca. 1185–1210). The most illustrious early trouvère, born into the lower nobility of Champagne, Gace has been credited with the most extensive corpus of monophonic compositions in Old French. The over eighty texts, the great majority surviving with their melodies, are almost all courtly chansons in a style derived from the Provençal tradition. Their usual theme, persistent but unrequited and despairing love for a socially superior lady, is often interwoven with the theme of poetic and musical creation: loving and singing express each other. Though almost nothing is known of Gace's life, it is clear that his circle included other major lyric poets and that his patrons—Marie de Champagne, first of all—were among the most powerful feudal figures of his time. Textual and melodic evidence shows that he was widely admired and emulated by both contemporary and later trouvères, in Germany as well as France.

Samuel N. Rosenberg

[See also: TROUVÈRE POETRY]

Gace Brulé. *Gace Brulé, trouvère champenois: édition des chansons et étude historique,* ed. Holger Petersen Dyggve. Helsinki, 1951.

———. *The Lyrics and Melodies of Gace Brulé,* ed. and trans. Samuel N. Rosenberg, Samuel Danon, and Hendrik van der Werf. New York: Garland, 1985.

van der Werf, Hendrik, ed. *Trouvères-Melodien I.* Kassel: Bärenreiter, 1977, pp. 315–554.

GACE DE LA BUIGNE (1305?–1384?). First chaplain of John II the Good, whom he followed into captivity in England, Gace composed the *Roman des deduis* between 1359 and 1377 as an instruction book for John's youngest son, the future Philip the Bold of Burgundy. Its 12,210 octosyllabic lines can be divided into two parts: a battle of personified virtues and vices, enlivened by occasional hunting scenes, and a debate over the merits of hunting with dogs as opposed to falconry. The second part is particularly vivid, with frequent digressions from Barthélemy l'Anglais's *Encyclopedia* and Henri de Ferrière's *Livres du roy Modus et de la royne Ratio.* The great popularity of this amalgam of hunting advice and ethical instruction is reflected in twenty-one manuscripts and three early 16th-century printed editions.

William W. Kibler

[See also: FERRIÈRES, HENRI DE; GASTON PHOEBUS]

Gace de la Buigne. *Le roman des deduis,* ed. Ake Blomqvist. Stockholm: Almqvist and Wiksell; Paris: Thiebaud, 1951.

Van den Abeele, Baudouin. *La fauconnerie dans les lettres françaises due XIIe au XIVe siècle.* Louvain: Presses Universitaires, 1990.

GAGE. In credit operations of the Middle Ages, the *gage* was surety given in return for a loan (although occasionally a *gage* over property might be given as a pious gift without a loan being made); it was sometimes used as a means of temporarily raising cash and transferring property to the church's safekeeping, especially by pilgrims and crusaders, often with reversion of all rights over a property to that religious house if the pilgrim died en route. In general, there were two types of medieval *gages*—the *mort-gage* (not to be confused with our modern mortgage) and the *vif-gage.* The interest-bearing and onerous *mort-gage* was condemned by 12th-century church councils, which allowed use only of the *vif-gage.* In both transactions, the borrower granted land or other property to the lender in *gage* (Lat. *dono in pignus*), as surety for a loan of a specified amount of cash. By the terms of written contracts for either type of *gage,* the lender enjoyed the fruits of the land or property that had been granted as surety until the loan was redeemed; the term of the loan was usually unlimited and redemption was limited to a certain date or season annually, frequently All Saints' Day. In the *vif-gage,* however, the fruits of the land, or at least a set part of them, served to reduce the amount of the loan so that it was automatically repaid and the land or other property reverted to the original owner after a term of years. In the *mort-gage,* the fruits did not reduce the principal but in effect served as the lender's interest, making the contract usurious and therefore illegal according to ecclesiastics. In northern France, another type of contract, called the constituted rent, in which an individual purchased a set annual income in return for paying an initial sum, began to replace the *gage* contract after ecclesiastical condemnation; in the Midi, the use of the *mort-gage* continued, although disguised as a *vif-gage* in which the fruits of the land were given as a "gift," rather than as interest, to the lender.

Constance H. Berman

Berman, Constance H. "Land Acquisition and the Use of the Mortgage Contract by the Cistercians of Berdoues." *Speculum* 57 (1982): 250–66.

Castaing-Sicard, Mireille. *Les contrats dans le très ancien droit toulousain (X–XIIIe siècle).* Toulouse: Espic, 1957.

Génestal, Robert. *Le rôle des monastères comme établissements de crédit: étudié en Normandie du XIe à la fin du XIIIe siècle.* Paris: Rousseau, 1901.

GAGUIN, ROBERT (1433–1501). As the son of a poor family, Gaguin's early education was provided by Trinitarian brothers devoted to educating poor children. Subsequent studies in Paris were paid for by Isabel of Portugal, duchess of Burgundy. As leader of the Trinitarians and dean of the University of Paris law school (1483–1500), Gaguin went on diplomatic missions for Louis XI and Charles VIII and assisted in recovering captives from infidel hands for the Trinitarians. He also devoted himself to study and writing and was associated with Guillaume Fichet's early printing ventures. He was the author of *De arte metrificandi* (1473), the humanistic *Compendium de Francorum origine et gestis* (1495), a translation of Caesar's *De bello gallico* dedicated to Charles VIII (1485), and an important volume of correspondence with leading humanists published in 1498. His major work, the *Compendium de Francorum origine et gestis* (1495) is a national history of France in ten books, from Pharamond to Charles VIII's Italian expedition. This immensely successful work went through nineteen editions before 1586.

Charity Cannon Willard

[See also: CHARLES VIII]

Gaguin, Robert. *Roberti Gaguini epistoli et orationes*, ed. Louis Thuasne. 2 vols. Paris: Bouillon, 1903–04.

Bossuat, Robert. "Traductions françaises des 'Commentaires' de César à la fin du XVe siècle." *Bibliothèque d'Humanisme et Renaissance* 4 (1944): 373–411.

Simone, Franco. "Robert Gaguin e il suo cenacolo umanistico." *Aevum* 13 (1939): 410–76.

GALBERT DE BRUGES (ca. 1075–ca. 1128). A Flemish chronicler who wrote a gripping eyewitness account of the murder of Charles the Good, count of Flanders, in 1127 and the power struggle involving the Flemish nobility and townsmen that led to the establishment of Thierry d'Alsace as count in 1128. Galbert tells us only that he was a notary in the service of the count, and thus probably a clerk in minor orders rather than a priest or canon. He wrote his first version on wax tablets, then revised and inserted other material into his detailed description of the events of April and May 1127, then wrote a more general discussion of developments in Flanders in the last half of that year. With the renewal of civil strife between February and July 1128, he composed another diary, one that is less detailed than the first and that he left unfinished, a fact perhaps indicating an early death. His history was evidently unread in the Middle Ages for want of a patron willing to overlook its often hostile portrait of figures in authority. A manuscript, now lost, was evidently kept at Bruges, and copies were made in the 16th and 17th centuries.

David M. Nicholas

Galbert de Bruges. *Histoire du meurtre de Charles le Bon comte de Flandre (1127–1128) par Galbert de Bruges*, ed. Henri Pirenne. Paris: Picard, 1891.

———. *The Murder of Charles the Good, Count of Flanders*, trans. James Bruce Ross. Rev. ed. New York: Harper and Row, 1967.

———. *Le meurtre de Charles le Bon*, trans. Jacques Gengoux. Anvers: Fonds Mercator, 1978.

van Caenegem, Raoul C. *Galbert van Brugge en het Recht*. Brussels: Vlaamse Academie, 1978.

GALIEN RESTORÉ. A work in the King Cycle that narrates the tribulations of Galien, Oliver's son by Jacqueline, daughter of Emperor Hugh of Constantinople, and the product of Oliver's *gab* during the visit of Charlemagne and his peers. The poem, dated late 13th or early 14th century, combines several chansons de geste with a rhymed version of the *Chanson de Roland*: Galien arrives at Roncevaux when his father is dying, as is Roland, whose death he also witnesses. In Charlemagne's battle of revenge for Roncevaux, Galien plays a major role; victorious, he then goes off to conquer the castle of Monfusain, which houses Baligant's niece, Guimarde, who subsequently becomes a Christian and Galien's wife. However, news reaches him that his mother is again being harassed by her brothers for bearing an illegitimate child, a fact that had earlier driven the young Galien out of Constantinople; Jacqueline is even accused of having poisoned her father. Galien marches against the city, wins a duel against the emir Burgualant, and is crowned emperor: his honor as well as that of his mother (and Oliver) has thus been "restored." Meanwhile, Charlemagne is still besieging Saragossa; when he learns the emir Baligant is coming to the Saracen Marsile's defense, he asks Galien for help. In the ensuing battle, Ogier le Danois distinguishes himself. Galien's grandfather Renier de Gennes is killed, but Galien nearly kills Baligant himself; finally, Charlemagne kills Baligant in a lengthy duel. While Galien returns to Monfusain to spend a peaceful life with his mother, wife, and young son, Mallart, Charlemagne must announce the tragic death of her fiancé to Galien's aunt, Belle Aude, then, at Laon, judge Ganelon, who, after having escaped into the Ardennes, is recaptured by Thierry and drawn and quartered.

The poem (4,911 Alexandrine lines) is preserved only in a 15th-century copy (University of Oregon, Special Collections CB B 54, formerly Cheltenham 26092), where it immediately follows *Hernaut de Beaulande*, *Renier de Gennes*, and *Girart de Vienne*. A prose version survives in Arsenal 3351 (15th c.) and in an incunabulum of 1521 by Jehan Trepperel; there also exist two prose renderings exclusively devoted to *Galien restoré*, the first in B.N. fr. 1470 (15th c.), the second in an incunabulum by Antoine Vérard (1500) that was frequently reprinted from the 16th century to the 18th.

Galien is a chivalric romance that, despite the constant displacement of the action (Vienne, Jerusalem, Constantinople, Genoa, Spain, Monfusain, etc.), is not without literary merit, thanks to the constant presence of Galien in the narration and his overriding intention: the restoration of his family.

Hans-Erich Keller

[See also: *GAB*; KING CYCLE]

Dougherty, David M., and Eugene B. Barnes, eds. *Le Galien de Cheltenham*. Amsterdam: Benjamins, 1981. [Important introduction, pp. xvi–xxxi.]

Horrent, Jules. "Galien le Restoré." In *La chanson de Roland dans les littératures française et espagnole*. Paris: Les Belles Lettres, 1951, pp. 377–412.

———. "Galien." In *Les épopées romanes*, ed. Rita Lejeune. Grundriß des romanischen Mittelalters 3/1, fasc. 2. Heidelberg: Winter, 1981, pp. 47–48; 3/2, fasc. 2. Heidelberg: Winter, 1985, pp. 58–60.

GALLICAN RITE. When Pepin III the Short (r. 751–68) and his son Charlemagne (r. 771–814) established a uniform, Roman-derived liturgy throughout the Frankish kingdom, the older traditions they were replacing came to be known collectively as the "Gallican" rite, though in fact there was no uniform usage throughout the country but rather a network of more-or-less related local practices. The destruction of Gallican liturgical books was so extensive that we no longer possess the complete rite of any one locality and are forced to reconstruct from a small amount of evidence.

The earliest evidence can be gleaned from writers who lived in Gaulish territory, such as John Cassian (d. 435), Caesarius of Arles (d. 542), and Gregory of Tours (d. 594), as well as from the canon-law literature and decrees of ecclesiastical councils. The oldest actual liturgical book, a palimpsest fragment of the early 6th century, is part of a lectionary that contained biblical readings and refrains for the responsorial psalms at Mass throughout the liturgical year. Other lectionary fragments, as well as Bibles with liturgical rubrics and collections of saints' lives for reading on their feasts, survive from the 7th and 8th centuries.

Better known are the sacramentaries, containing the Proper, or variable prayers, of the Mass and other sacramental celebrations. Palimpsest fragments survive from as early as the 6th century, but most informative are the relatively intact sources of the 8th century, the manuscripts known as Missale Gothicum (from Autun?), Missale Gallicanum Vetus (northeast of Paris?), Bobbio Missal (northern Italy), Missale Francorum (near Corbie?), and Stowe Missal (Ireland). These sources show that Gallican prayers were more prolix than those of the Roman liturgy and that there was much more variety from day to day over the course of the liturgical year. They reveal varying amounts of Roman influence, anticipating the complete romanization of the liturgy that would be in effect by the 9th century. Only one source describes in detail the invariable portions, or Ordinary, of the Gallican Mass—the anonymous *Expositio antiquae liturgiae Gallicanae* attributed to Germanus of Paris but actually dependent on a work of Isidore of Seville. Much less direct evidence survives regarding the chants of the Mass or any part of the Divine Office, though many responsorial refrains are marked in a 6th-century psalter.

As liturgical materials were brought north from Rome to replace the Gallican rite, they were frequently revised and supplemented by Gallican texts and ceremonies. This happened, for instance, in the "8th-century Gelasian" sacramentaries, adaptations of a Roman book that survive only in one manuscript copied in Chelles near Paris. By the 9th century, these sacramentaries were losing ground to the so-called "Gregorian" sacramentaries descended from the archetype known as the "Hadrianum," a manuscript sent to Charlemagne by Pope Hadrian (r. 772–95) but now lost. Some copies include a supplement of non-Roman material (i.e., of Gallican and Mozarabic or Spanish origin), now attributed to the monastic reformer St. Benedict of Aniane (d. 821). By this route, many Gallican texts and practices survived in the medieval liturgy, which as a result was a hybrid of Gallican and Roman traditions. Among the most distinctive Gallican survivals were the episcopal blessings that took place before communion when the Mass was celebrated by a bishop. Many benedictionals—collections of texts for these blessings—still survive (see Moeller). Though absent from the Missale Romanum issued after the Council of Trent (1570), some of them were reintroduced in the reformed Missal issued by Pope Paul VI (1970).

Peter Jeffrey

[See also: CAESARIUS OF ARLES; DIVINE OFFICE; *EXPOSITIO MISSAE*; LITURGICAL BOOKS]

Clercq, C. de, ed. *Concilia Galliae a. 511–695.* Turnhout: Brepols, 1963.

Gamber, Klaus, ed. *Codices liturgici Latini antiquiores.* 2nd ed. 2 vols. Freiburg: Universitätsverlag, 1968, pp. 57–66, 152–93, 230–38.

———. *Ordo antiquus gallicanus: Der gallikanische Messritus des 6. Jh.* Regensburg, 1965.

Moeller, Edmond Eugène, ed. *Corpus Benedictionum Pontificalium.* 4 vols. Turnhout: Brepols, 1971–79.

Munier, C., ed. *Concilia Galliae a. 314–506.* Turnhout: Brepols, 1963.

Bullough, D.A., and Alice L.H. Corrêa. "Texts, Chant, and the Chapel of Louis the Pious." In *Charlemagne's Heir: New Perspectives on the Reign of Louis the Pious (814–840),* ed. Peter Godman and Roger Collins. Oxford: Clarendon, 1990, pp. 489–508.

Gaudemet, Jean. *Conciles gaulois du IVe siècle.* Paris: Cerf, 1977.

GALLICANISM. Doctrine espousing the autonomy of the French church. French defiance of papal authority dates from Carolingian times, but it was during the confrontation (1296–1305) between Philip IV and Boniface VIII that a means of resisting the ultramontane pretentions of the late-medieval papacy was formalized and implemented as doctrine. In such texts as the *Songe du vergier,* royal legists argued that the kings of France drew their authority directly from God, that they held a unique position of independence within Christendom, and that royal temporal concerns were outside papal jurisdiction. The result of this doctrine was the crown's insistence that the French church exercise independent authority over ecclesiastical appointments, religious courts, and church revenues within the realm.

During the Avignonese papacy and ensuing Great Schism (1378–1417), the French played a complex role. Parisian scholars like Jean Gerson perfected the theory asserting the so-called *libertés de l'église gallicane* and simultaneously supported the parallel doctrine of conciliarism, which called for the council of bishops to limit papal prerogative. French monarchs initially supported the Avignonese popes, but by 1398 they temporarily withdrew obedience from both papal claimants. After the Council of Constance (1414–18) reunified the western church, Valois legists and clerics worked to reconcile their dogma with their institutions. At a 1438 synod, Charles VII issued the Pragmatic Sanction of Bourges, which contained twenty-three articles giving Gallicanism legal form. The papacy consistently opposed this legislation, and it was eventually superseded by the Concordat of Bologna of 1516. In this definitive concession to the French crown, the papacy promised to confirm all future royal appointments to ecclesiastical office. As a result, the tradition of Gallican liberties jointly exercised by crown and clergy lapsed in favor of an emphasis on the independent authority of the crown over the French church.

Medieval Gallicanism left a mixed legacy. Although not tempted to support domestic Protestantism, the crown was isolated from the Counter-Reformation church. France never accepted the decrees of the Council of Trent, and the monarchy often supported Protestant princes during the Wars of Religion. Gallicanism reached its fullest statement in the 1682 declaration of the French clergy drafted by Bishop Bossuet, whose four articles, though repealed only eleven years later, remained the basis of French church-state relations until the 20th century.

Paul D. Solon

[See also: AVIGNON PAPACY; CONCORDAT OF AMBOISE; GERSON, JEAN; PRAGMATIC SANCTION OF BOURGES; *SONGE DU VERGIER;* SUBTRACTION OF OBEDIENCE]

Lewis, P.S. *Later Medieval France: The Polity.* New York: St. Martin, 1968.

Martin, Victor. *Les origines du Gallicanisme.* Paris: Bloud et Gay, 1939.

Royer, Jean-Pierre. *L'église et le royaume de France au XIVe siècle d'après le "Songe du vergier" et la jurisprudence du Parlement.* Paris: Librairie Générale de Droit et de Jurisprudence, 1969.

Valois, Noel. *La France et le grand schisme en occident.* 4 vols. Paris: Picard, 1896–1902.

GARENCIÈRES, JEAN DE (1372–1415). Along with Oton de Granson and the poets of the *Cent ballades,* Garencières represents the new generation of knight-poets who appeared at the end of the 14th century. His surviving corpus includes some fifty poems, almost all love lyrics in contemporary *formes fixes*: ballade, rondeau, *lai,* and *complainte.* They are found in a single manuscript (B.N. fr. 19139) along with lyric poems by Alain Chartier and Garencières's friend and protector, Charles d'Orléans, whose poetry was much influenced by that of Garencières.

James I. Wimsatt

[See also: *CENT BALLADES, LES;* CHARLES D'ORLÉANS; *FORMES FIXES;* GRANSON, OTON DE]

Young, Neal Abernathy. *Le chevalier poète Jean de Garencières, sa vie et ses poésiés complètes 1372–1415.* Paris: Nizet, 1953. [Biographical and critical study as well as an edition of the poems.]

GARLANDE. A knightly family of the Île-de-France, the Garlandes appeared in the royal entourage in the 10th century and rose to prominence in the early 12th. At the height of their power (ca. 1112), three Garlande brothers controlled the great royal offices of seneschal, chancellor, and butler.

Paien de Garlande was seneschal in 1101, and his brother Anseau appears in the same office in 1104 and from 1107 until his death in 1118 at the hands of Hugues du Puiset. Two other brothers, Étienne and Gilbert, were respectively chancellor (from 1107) and butler (in 1112).

Another brother, Guillaume, succeeded Anseau as seneschal from 1118 to 1220, when Étienne combined that office with the chancellorship and became the prime royal adviser. In addition to his royal offices, Étienne was archdeacon of Paris, dean of Sainte-Geneviève, and, in Orléans, dean of Saint-Samson, Saint-Avite, and the cathedral. His aspirations to a bishopric, however, were foiled by reformist clerics.

Étienne gained the enmity of the queen, Adelaide of Savoy, and in 1127, when he tried to pass the seneschalship to his son-in-law, he lost his royal offices and waged war against Louis VI until 1132, when he regained the position of chancellor. A year later, he gained revenge on the clerical reformers when his clients assassinated Archambaud, subdeacon of Sainte-Croix of Orléans, and Thomas, prior of Saint-Victor. He did not regain his role as chief royal adviser, for that honor now belonged to Suger, abbot of Saint-Denis.

Étienne faded from sight after this time but left his name to a part of the Latin Quarter of Paris, the *pays de Garlande,* bounded by the rue Saint-Jacques, rue de Fouarre, and rue de Garlande. A Guillaume de Garlande was named by Philip II as one of the caretakers of the kingdom during the king's absence on the Third Crusade (1190–91). Louis IX later imprisoned an Anseau de Garlande for refusing to release hostages held against one of his creditors.

R. Thomas McDonald

GASCONY. Gascony, a large province in southwestern France north of the Pyrénées, had almost nothing to do with northern France during the early Middle Ages. It passed under English rule in the late-medieval period before finally being integrated into the French monarchy in the 15th century. With no clear geographical boundaries other than the Pyrénées in the south and the Atlantic in the west, it did not correspond to a single natural region but was rather a historical creation grouping a collection of counties extending to the Garonne River in the north (the Bordeaux region) and inland to the Languedoc (Toulouse) in the east. Among the best-known counties and viscounties making up medieval Gascony were Armagnac, Bigorre, Comminges, Fézensac, Lomagne, Albret, and Marsan. The present-day departments of the Pyrénées-Atlantiques, Hautes-Pyrénées, the Landes, and the Gers cover most of the territory of medieval Gascony. Ecclesiastically, most of the province lay within the archdiocese of Auch, which broke down into the bishoprics of Bayonne, Comminges, Oloron, Lescar, Tarbes, Dax, Aire, Lectoure, Bazas, and Couserans.

The earliest Gascons (Lat. *Vascones*) were Basques who filtered across the Pyrénées at the end of the 6th century into what had been the Roman Aquitania Prima, eventually settling as far north as the Bordeaux region. The Basque language did not prevail except in a few regions of the Pyrénées; what came later on to be called Gascon was a romance dialect. Gascony formed the southern part of what became the first duchy of Aquitaine created near the end of the 7th century. Saracens overran the province temporarily early in the 8th century, but the Carolingian conquest of the 8th century had more lasting effects. Nonetheless, internal divisions combined with Viking invasions, which struck Gascony as well, in the 9th century weakened the Carolingian government, and toward the middle of the century Gascony emerged as an independent duchy, now separate from Aquitaine, with its capital at Bordeaux. An almost complete lack of documentary evidence makes it difficult to reconstruct the history of the duchy for the next two centuries, yet this was clearly the time when the rise of a dozen regional lordships, such as those of the counts of Bigorre, Armagnac, and Comminges and the viscounties of Lomagne, Oloron, and above all the powerful state of the viscounts of Béarn, took shape and undermined the authority of the duke. In the 1050s, the counts of Poitou/dukes of Aquitaine acquired the ducal title through marriage, forging the great territorial principality of the duchy of Aquitaine-Gascony, centered in Poitiers and Bordeaux. Through the successive marriages of Eleanor, duchess and heiress of Aquitaine-Gascony, to Louis VII of France in 1137, then to Henry Plantagenêt of Anjou in 1152, Gascony passed along with Aquitaine first under Capetian then under English rule. For the next three centuries, the English resisted all efforts of the French to drive them out and maintained their hold on Gascony even when they lost Aquitaine in the north. Only the loss of Bordeaux in 1453 forced them to abandon their holdings to the French kings.

Gascony never proved to be particularly favored ground for monastic foundations in large numbers, yet one should note the success of abbeys, most of them foundations of the 10th to 12th centuries, at Saint-Sever, Sordes, Lescar, Saint-Pe-de-Generes, Saint-Mont, and Sainte-Foi-de-Morlaas. Many northern Europeans came to know Gascony because the northern pilgrimage routes to Santiago in Spain traversed the province.

George T. Beech

[See also: AQUITAINE; ARMAGNAC; FOIX]

Bordes, Maurice, ed. *Histoire de la Gascogne des origines à nos jours.* Roanne: Howath, 1982.
Labarge, Margaret W. *Gascony, England's First Colony 1204–1453.* London: Hamish Hamilton, 1980.
Trabut-Cussac, Jean-Paul. *L'administration anglaise en Gascogne sous Henry III et Édouard I de 1254–1307.* Geneva: Droz, 1972.
Vale, Malcolm G.A. *English Gascony, 1399–1453.* London: Oxford University Press, 1970.

GASTON PHOEBUS (1331–1391). Third count of Foix and lord of Béarn. The prose *Livre des oraisons*, written between 1380 and 1383, a collection of thirty-seven prayers imploring God's pardon for the murder of his own son (in circumstances that are still not understood), would not in itself have ensured its author fame. A fine scholar and musician, a gallant warrior and passionate hunter, Gaston III is known chiefly for his *Livre de chasse*, written be-

tween 1387 and 1391. A genuine treatise of natural science (it was to influence Buffon in the 18th century), nourished with long experience and multifarious memories, it is a profoundly innovative work by a close observer of wildlife who knows how to recreate the exciting atmosphere of the hunting scenes he has lived, thanks to a sense of image and movement. The work was enormously popular, with some forty-four manuscripts extant, about half of which were lavishly illustrated.

Annette Brasseur

[See also: FERRIÈRES, HENRI DE; FOIX; GACE DE LA BUIGNE]

Phoebus, Gaston. *Livre de chasse,* ed. Gunnar Tilander. Karlshamm, 1971. [Based on MS *L* (Leningrad, Hermitage).]
———. *Livre des oraisons,* ed. Gunnar Tilander and Pierre Tucoo-Chala. Pau: Marrimpouey, 1974. [Based on MS *L* (Leningrad, Hermitage).]
Ménard, Philippe. *Littérature et iconographie: les pièges dans les traités de chasse d'Henri de Ferrières et de Gaston Phébus.* Paris: Les Belles Lettres, 1980, pp. 159–88.
Tucoo-Chala, Pierre. *L'art de la pédagogie dans le Livre de chasse de Gaston Fébus.* Paris: Les Belles Lettres, 1980, pp. 19–34.
———. *Gaston Fébus, un grand prince d'occident au XIVe siècle.* Pau: Marrimpouey, 1976.

GAUCELM FAIDIT (fl. 1173–1202). A well-traveled and underappreciated Limousin troubadour, Gaucelm Faidit led an extravagant bohemian life, according to his picaresque *vida* and five *razos*. Historical documents suggest that he was neither poor nor plebeian. In his far-flung wanderings across France, in Italy, to Hungary, and on crusade, he was in contact with fellow troubadours, like Raimbaut d'Aurenga, and trouvères, like Gace Brulé.

His poetic legacy is considerable. Some fifty-four *cansos* survive, including a *rotrouenge* (probably the only French text composed by a troubadour), in addition to nine poetic debates, two crusade songs, the famous *planh* on Richard the Lionhearted, and perhaps one *alba*. These reveal a discreet poet of *trobar leu* in the Ventadorn style, but with occasional *ric* and *clus* refinements perhaps traceable to his contacts with Raimbaut d'Orange.

Roy S. Rosenstein

[See also: TROUBADOUR POETRY]

Gaucelm Faidit. *Les poèmes de Gaucelm Faidit, troubadour du XIIe siècle: édition critique,* ed. Jean Mouzat. Paris: Nizet, 1965.
Paden, William D. "Dramatic Formalism in the Alba Attributed to Gaucelm Faidit." *Neuphilologische Mitteilungen* 83 (1982): 68–77.

GAUCHER DE REIMS (fl. 13th c.). "Gaucher de Reims was master of this church for seven years and worked on the arches." This slim information, taken from the destroyed labyrinth of Reims cathedral, is all that is known about this mason. A 1256 document that mentions a certain "Walterius, master of the fabric of the church of Reims" recently has been interpreted as a reference to Gaucher, but this must remain hypothetical. Gaucher has been seen, notably by Henri Deneux, as the designer of the Gothic cathedral of Reims, but he is most frequently credited with the portals of the west façade, which were erected ca. 1252–65. Thus, despite the tantalizing hints offered by texts and the clear archaeological evidence that the cathedral of Reims was the work of several master masons, the contribution of Gaucher de Reims to this monumental project remains enigmatic.

Michael T. Davis

[See also: JEAN D'ORBAIS; JEAN LE LOUP; REIMS]

Branner, Robert. "The Labyrinth of Reims Cathedral." *Journal of the Society of Architectural Historians* 31 (1962): 18–25.

Demaison, Louis. "Les architectes de la cathédrale de Reims." *Bulletin archéologique du Comité des Travaux Historiques et Scientifiques* (1894): 1–40.

Deneux, Henri. "Chronologie des maîtres d'oeuvre de la cathédrale de Reims." *Bulletin de la Société Nationale des Antiquaires de France* (1920): 196–200.

Ravaux, Jean-Pierre. "Les campagnes de construction de la cathédrale de Reims au XIIIe siècle." *Bulletin monumental* 135 (1979): 7–66.

GAUTIER. *See also* **WALTER**

GAUTIER D'ARRAS. A contemporary and rival of Chrétien de Troyes, Gautier d'Arras identifies himself in two romances as a writer linked to important political and literary courts: *Eracle* was begun for Thibaut V of Blois and his sister-in-law, Countess Marie de Champagne, then completed and dedicated to Baudouin de Hainaut (if Baudouin IV, probable dates are 1164–71; if Baudouin V, somewhat later). *Ille et Galeron*, begun after *Eracle* but possibly finished before it (ca. 1167–70), praises the empress Béatrice de Bourgogne (d. 1184), for whom he started the romance (Chrétien may allude ironically to Gautier's praise in his prologue to the *Charrette*). The romance was completed for Count Thibaut. The poet may be the same man as the Gautier d'Arras who was an officer at the court of Philippe d'Alsace and signed many documents between 1160 and 1185.

Eracle is a hagiographical romance in octosyllabic rhymed couplets that offers a biography of Heraclius, the Roman emperor who recovered from King Cosdroes of Persia and placed in Jerusalem a piece of the Holy Cross. The first half, probably based on oral legends and popular tales, which Gautier weaves together with as much coherence and *vraisemblance* as possible, tells how Eracle uses his miraculous gifts in the service of the Emperor of Rome: Eracle is a perfect judge of jewels, horses, and women. When the emperor must go away, he places his young and beautiful wife, Athanaïs, in a tower under close surveillance. The inevitable happens when she falls in love and manages to start a liaison with Paridés. Eracle informs the emperor and convinces him to unite the two lovers. The second half, based on written sources and more historical in orientation, retells the legend of the cross and St. Cyriacus, to whom is dedicated the main church at Provins in Champagne, and Eracle's expedition, after he himself had become emperor, to return the holy relic to Jerusalem. Gautier thus makes available to a courtly public Latin texts and religious legends worked into a narrative whose use of adventure and the marvelous clearly locates it within the domain of romance, as does the importance given to love in the Athenaïs episode (4,319 lines out of 6,593).

Though apparently part of the *matière de Bretagne*, *Ille et Galeron* retains the Roman and Byzantine orientation of *Eracle*, as it retells and transforms the familiar tale of a man with two wives. Chased out of Brittany, the young Ille takes refuge in France. Knighted, he returns and reconquers his family lands, for which he pays homage to Conain, count of Brittany. Ille falls in love with Galeron, Conain's sister. Their love is mutual, but the difference in their social rank poses an obstacle, until Ille's military service elevates him to the post of seneschal and marriage with Galeron. When Ille subsequently loses an eye (in a tournament according to one manuscript, a battle in another), he fears the loss of Galeron's love, steals away, and fights as mercenary for the Emperor of Rome. Given his prowess, Ille quickly becomes seneschal of Rome and inspires love in Ganor, the emperor's daughter. Galeron, who has searched fruitlessly for her husband, now lives secretly in Rome in the greatest misery. When offered Ganor's hand in marriage, Ille reveals that he is married; only if Galeron cannot be found will he marry Ganor. Just as that ceremony is about to be celebrated, Galeron recognizes her husband. When Galeron assures Ille of her continuing love, they return to Brittany. Their happy life is interrupted when Galeron makes a vow to become a nun, if she survives the difficult birth of a third child. Ille grieves, but is called to fulfill his promise to aid Ganor, now empress and under attack by the Emperor of Constantinople. Ille triumphs, he and Ganor are married in Rome and live happily with their own children and those of the first marriage.

Comparison with Marie de France's *Eliduc*, a *lai* that either furnishes Gautier's model or has a common source, reveals how Gautier has significantly reworked a short tale into an episodic romance whose two parts are clearly related through the key event: Ille's loss of an eye furnishes a crisis that resembles one of the love judgments reported in Andreas Capellanus's *De amore*: can love survive disfigurement? This event and the exploration of Ille's psychology before and after the crisis keep the romance plot squarely situated within the realm of the possible. The marvelous death and rebirth described in *Eliduc* are eliminated, as Gautier d'Arras places his art in the service of mimetic realism. Gautier thus appears as a kind of link between Chrétien and Jean Renart, as Fourrier has suggested. In elaborating the episodes that fill in Ille's story, Gautier demonstrates his ability to reuse materials from a variety of literary traditions (chansons de geste, saints' lives, *Énéas*). A narrator clearly able to please his audience,

Gautier d'Arras plays an important role in the development of a romance tradition oriented toward realism, psychological interest, and contemporary life.

Matilda T. Bruckner

[See also: CHRÉTIEN DE TROYES; GRECO-BYZANTINE ROMANCE; MARIE DE FRANCE]

Gautier d'Arras. *Eracle*, ed. Guy Raynaud de Lage. Paris: Champion, 1976.
———. *Ille et Galeron*, ed. Yves Lefèvre. Paris: Champion, 1988.
Calin, William. "Structure and Meaning in Eracle by Gautier d'Arras." *Symposium* 16 (1962): 275–87.
Fourrier, Antoine. *Le courant réaliste dans le roman courtois en France au moyen âge.* Paris: Nizet, 1960, Vol. 1: *Les débuts (XIIe siècle).*
Haidu, Peter. "Narrativity and Language in Some Twelfth Century Romances." *Yale French Studies* 51 (1974): 133–46.
Nykrog, Per. "Two Creators of Narrative Form in Twelfth Century France: Gautier d'Arras and Chrétien de Troyes." *Speculum* 48 (1973): 258–76.
Zumthor, Paul. "L'écriture et la voix: Le roman d'Eracle." In *The Craft of Fiction: Essays on Medieval Poetics,* ed. Leigh Arrathoon. Rochester: Solaris, 1984, pp. 161–209.

GAUTIER D'AUPAIS (fl. early 13th c.). The author of *Gautier d'Aupais,* an 876-line tale from the first half of the 13th century in a language slightly tinged with Picardisms, certainly was a minstrel from the Île-de-France. Although he employed the monorhymed laisse characteristic of the chanson de geste, we still find the themes, devices, and formulae of the courtly romances in the "Salut d'amour," in the portrayal of Gautier's infatuation, and in the evocation of his lady's emotion.

Annette Brasseur

Faral, Edmond, ed. *Gautier d'Aupais, poème courtois du XIIIe siècle.* Paris: Champion, 1919. [Based on B.N. fr. 837.]

GAUTIER DE COINCI (1177/78–1236). Gautier entered the Benedictine monastery of Saint-Médard in Soissons in 1193, was appointed prior of Vic-sur-Aisne in 1214, and returned to Soissons in 1233 as prior of Saint-Médard. He was a prolific writer, whose works include religious songs, two sermons, and four saints' lives, as well as the *Miracles de Nostre Dame,* for which he is most famous. A series of narrative poems on the birth of Mary, the childhood of Jesus, and the Assumption, and a paraphrase of the Psalm *Eructavit,* appear in some manuscripts of the *Miracles* and are sometimes credited to him. The attribution of the *Saint dent Nostre Seigneur,* a poem about a relic discovered at Soissons, which appears in only two manuscripts, is even less certain.

The *Miracles* (ca. 30,000 lines) are divided into two books organized symmetrically. Each begins with a prologue and a series of seven songs in honor of the Virgin. The first book, begun in 1218 and revised four years later, contains thirty-five miracles and ends with three songs in honor of St. Leocadia. The second book, with twenty-three miracles, was perhaps written between 1223 and 1227. Gautier, who sought to convert the lapsed and strengthen the faith of the believer, intended his collection for an unlearned but aristocratic audience, as he expresses contempt for the *vileins.*

Gautier found his stories in a collection of Latin Marian legends in his monastery at Soissons. Although this manuscript has been lost, enough of its character has been established to determine the way Gautier treated his sources. He did not follow his model slavishly but sometimes expanded it by resorting to other sources and even drew on events of his own life. In most stories, a sinner is saved by a single redeeming virtue, usually devotion to the Virgin. The final sections of the stories, often satirical attacks on all classes of society, are original and of great interest to modern readers. Gautier was a skilled versifier who made frequent use of rich and equivocal rhymes. The reactions of modern critics to this material range from enthusiasm to hostility but depend largely on their appreciation of the genre rather than Gautier's treatment of it.

The songs that begin each book are important in their own right, for they are the best examples of religious lyric poetry from the 13th century. Despite his antipathy to secular literature, Gautier's lyric poetry was strongly influenced by the secular tradition. If his musical compositions were not of the first rank, he was nevertheless a musician of considerable skill and refinement.

Maureen B.M. Boulton

[See also: MIRACLE PLAYS; PRAYERS AND DEVOTIONAL MATERIALS; SAINTS' LIVES; SERMONS IN VERSE; *VIES DES ANCIENS PÈRES*]

Gautier de Coinci. *Les miracles de Nostre Dame,* ed. V. Frederic Koenig. 4 vols. Geneva: Droz, 1955–70.
———. *Miracles de Gautier de Coinci: extraits du manuscrit de l'Ermitage,* ed. Arthur Långfors. Helsinki, 1937.
Drzewicka, A. "La fonction des emprunts à la poésie profane dans les chansons mariales de Gautier de Coinci." *Moyen âge* 91 (1985): 33–51, 179–200.
Ducrot-Granderye, Arlette. *Études sur les Miracles Nostre Dame de Gautier de Coinci.* Helsinki, 1932.
Långfors, Arthur. "Mélanges de poésie lyrique, II, III." *Romania* 53 (1927): 474–538; 56 (1930): 33–79.
Lommatzsch, Ernst. *Gautier de Coincy als Satiriker.* Halle: Niemeyer, 1913.
Verrier, Paul. "La 'Chanson de Notre Dame' de Gautier de Coinci." *Romania* 59 (1933): 497–519; 61 (1935): 97.

GAUTIER DE MORTAGNE (ca. 1090–1174). Born in Flanders, Gautier spent his career in northern France, principally at Laon. He studied at Reims under Alberic, who himself was a student of Anselm of Laon, perhaps the most influential theologian in the early decades of the 12th century. Gautier had a reputation as a stern schoolmaster, first at Laon, then at the abbey school of Sainte-Geneviève in Paris. Gautier became dean of the cathedral of Laon in

1150 and bishop of the diocese in 1155. His legacy includes letters on various theological subjects to Abélard, Hugh of Saint-Victor, and other leading theologians of his day.

Mark Zier

[See also: THEOLOGY]

Gautier de Mortagne. *De coniugo*. PL 176.153–74 (in *Summa sententiarum*); *Liber de Trinitate*. PL 209.575–90.

Ott, Ludwig. "Untersuchungen zur theologischen Briefliteratur der Frühscholastik." *Beiträge der Geschichte der Philosophie des Mittelalters* 34 (1937): 126–347.

GAUTIER DE VARINFROY (fl. 13th c.). In October 1253, the bishop and chapter of Meaux appointed Gautier de Varinfroy master mason of the cathedral, agreeing to pay an annual salary of ten pounds but forbidding him to stay more than two months per year at Évreux, where he also directed the cathedral workshop. Gautier's career appears to have been devoted to the restoration and modernization of older buildings: at Évreux, he constructed the triforium and clerestory of the nave above a Romanesque arcade, while at Meaux he converted the four-story choir into a three-story elevation composed of elaborate panels of tracery. Stylistic analysis further suggests that this master mason rebuilt the upper levels of Saint-Père, Chartres, in the 1240s and restored the western bays of the nave and façade of Sens cathedral following the collapse of the southwest tower in 1268. Gautier's insistence on flat, linear effects, his tracery patterns, and pier design remain firmly within the contemporary idiom of Île-de-France architecture, yet his ability to create smooth transitions between new and older forms demonstrates a remarkable sensitivity and stylistic flexibility.

Michael T. Davis

[See also: ÉVREUX; MEAUX; SENS]

Branner, Robert. *Saint Louis and the Court Style in Gothic Architecture*. London: Zwemmer, 1965.

Kimpel, Dieter, and Robert Suckale. *Die gotische Architektur in Frankreich, 1130–1270*. Munich: Hirmer, 1985.

Kurmann, Peter. *La cathédrale Saint-Étienne de Meaux*. Paris: Droz, 1971.

———. "Gauthier de Varinfroy et le problème du style personnel d'un architecte au XIIIe siècle." In *Les bâtisseurs des cathédrales gothiques*, ed. Roland Recht. Strasbourg: Éditions les Musées de la Ville de Strasbourg, 1989, pp. 186–94.

———, and Dethard von Winterfeld. "Gauthier de Varinfroy, ein 'Denkmalpfleger' im 13. Jahrhundert." In *Festschrift für Otto von Simson zum 65. Geburtstag*, ed. Lucius Grisebach and Konrad Renger. Berlin: Propyläen, 1977, pp. 101–59.

GAUTIER LE LEU (fl. late 13th c.). Although it has been suggested that Gautier Le Leu was a student at Orléans and that later he had some association with the Benedictine abbey of Maroilles, we can be certain only that he was a poet and jongleur of the second half of the 13th century who was the most prolific author of fabliaux. He composed eleven fabliaux, of which eight are extant. His compositions vary in inspiration from obscenity and ferocious social and clerical satire (e.g., *Le prestre teint*) to lively character analysis, as in *La veuve*. This poem features a character related to Chaucer's Wife of Bath and to the Vieille in the *Roman de la Rose*; she reacts to her husband's death by grief more over sexual deprivation than over personal loss, and she quickly and capably sets out to find a replacement. *La veuve* is a small but important contribution to the continuing "Quarrel of the *Romance of the Rose*" that was to rage for centuries in theological and literary circles.

Norris J. Lacy

[See also: FABLIAU]

Livingston, Charles H., ed. *Le jongleur Gautier le Leu: étude sur les fabliaux*. Cambridge: Harvard University Press, 1951.

———. "The Jongleur Gautier le Leu: A Study in the Fabliaux." *Romanic Review* 15 (1924): 1–67.

GAWAIN ROMANCES. Chrétien de Troyes established Arthur's nephew Gawain (Gauvain, Gavain, and other orthographical variants) as one of the major figures of Arthurian romance. Although he had never made Gawain a hero proper, he had allotted half of the narrative to him in his last romance, *Perceval* (ca. 1180). Whereas the majority of post-Chrétien verse romancers continue to use Gawain largely as a foil or adjunct to the hero, a small number do make him the center of attention and the major protagonist, availing themselves of an opportunity left unseized by Chrétien and others. The author of the *Chevalier à l'épée* (end of the 12th c.) in fact claims that he is writing a romance about Gawain because Chrétien had not done so.

The *Chevalier à l'épée* and the contemporaneous *Mule sans frein* can be seen as a pair for a number of reasons: they are both short (1,206 and 1,136 lines, respectively), are of approximately the same date, appear in the same manuscript (Bern, Burgerbibliothek 354), may be by the same author (who signs himself in the latter as Paien de Maisières), and are characterized by the same humorous and burlesque treatment of conventional romance motifs. In the *Chevalier à l'épée*, Gawain becomes enamored of a young woman, attempts to seduce her but is prevented from doing so by a sword that descends from above the bed, loses her to a stranger knight she sees urinating in the bushes, avenges himself on the latter, and then abandons the girl to her own devices. The *Mule sans frein* relates how Gawain braves all kinds of perils (lions, serpents, dwarfs, a beheading test) to retrieve a bridle for a damsel.

The *Vengeance Raguidel*, probably by Raoul de Houdenc, author of another Arthurian romance, *Meraugis de Portlesguez*, is more substantial. Some 6,182 lines long and dating from the first quarter of the 13th century, it concerns the avenging by Gawain of Raguidel, a knight treacherously killed by the wicked Guengasoain. Although

Gawain carries out the vengeance, it is only after forgetting the lance point required to kill the murderer and after a series of sometimes farcical adventures, many of them related to Gawain's various love affairs. The shine is further taken off Gawain's achievement by the fact that he requires the help of another knight, Yder, to avenge Raguidel. Another full-length Gawain romance is the *Atre périlleux* (6,676 lines), dating from the second quarter of the 13th century. In this romance, Gawain finds and kills Escanor, a knight who had abducted Arthur's cupbearer; in the course of the quest, Gawain is confronted with the news of his own death and beheads a devil who had imprisoned a damsel in a tomb (the episode from which the romance takes its title). In addition to Chrétien's romance, the poet of the *Atre périlleux* knows and alludes to *Meraugis de Portlesguez* and the *Vengeance Raguidel*.

The fragmentary *Enfances Gauvain* (712 lines), dating probably from the 1230s, tells the story of Gawain's birth and childhood. According to this poem, Gawain's parents are Arthur's sister, Morcades, and her page, Lot. The child is entrusted to a knight called Gauvain le Brun, who names it after himself and then sets it adrift in a cask; after the boy is rescued by a fisherman, he is brought to Rome and educated by the Pope. Other versions of this story can be found elsewhere, notably in Wace's *Brut*, the *Perlesvaus*, and the Latin romance *De ortu Walwanii*. Writing the *enfances* of a hero who had already become popular was one way of capitalizing on his celebrity; writing about the hero's offspring was another, and that was the option chosen by Robert de Blois in *Beaudous* (third quarter of the 13th c.). Beaudous's mother conceals his lineage from him so that he must win his own fame rather than bask in his father's reflected glory. Beaudous accomplishes much, wins the hand of a beautiful princess, defeats many of Arthur's famous knights, and is reunited with his father; the romance concludes with the double wedding of Beaudous and Gawain. Robert de Blois is known also for didactic works, such as the *Enseignement des princes*, and there is a strong didactic streak in *Beaudous*, particularly in its presentation of chivalry.

Authors clearly expect their audiences to be familiar with Gawain's basic traits, since they rarely take the time to introduce him. He is in many respects a "preformed" character capable of limited development; he is used by authors rather than investigated psychologically. In this sense, the romances that do choose Gawain as a hero are the exceptions rather than the rule, although he plays extensive roles in most Arthurian verse romances.

A number of characteristics are common to most of these romances. First of all, Gawain is confronted at almost every turn with his own reputation as knight and lover: he is the standard to which all knights must aspire and the knight whom all ladies seek to love. When authors in the 13th century begin to treat these aspects of romance in a gently burlesque or sometimes openly parodic light, Gawain, the courtly knight *par excellence*, is himself burlesqued and parodied as a result. Yet the criticism is affectionate. In contrast to the unrepentant sinner of the prose *Queste del saint Graal* and the vindictive rapist and murderer of the *Prose Tristan*, the Gawain of the verse tradition remains an amiable character and a great if flawed knight. The later verse romances that take Gawain as hero suggest that the popularity of the figure was too strong for the attempts to discredit it in the prose tradition. In the last instance, however, it is the variety of uses to which Gawain is put in French Arthurian literature that is significant: foil, hero, villain, to mention only three. This is testimony not only to the conventional nature of romance but also to the differing uses to which convention can be put by authors with different aims and intentions.

Keith Busby

[See also: ARTHURIAN VERSE ROMANCE; GIRART D'AMIENS; RAOUL DE HOUDENC; RENAUT DE BEAUJEU; ROBERT DE BLOIS; ROMANCE]

Johnston, Ronald Carlyle, and D.D.R. Owen, eds. *Two Old French Gauvain Romances: Le chevalier à l'épée and La mule sans frein.* New York: Barnes and Noble, 1973.

Meyer, Paul, ed. "Les enfances Gauvain." *Romania* 39 (1910): 1–32.

Raoul von Houdenc. *Sämtliche Werke*, ed. Mathias Friedwagner. 2 vols. Halle: Niemeyer, 1909, Vol. 2: *La Vengeance Raguidel: Altfranzösischer Abenteuerroman*.

Robert de Blois. *Sämtliche Werke*, ed. J. Ulrich. Berlin: Meyer und Müller, 1889, Vol. 1: *Beaudous*.

Woledge, Brian, ed. *L'atre périlleux*. Paris: Champion, 1936.

Busby, Keith. *Gauvain in Old French Literature*. Amsterdam: Rodopi, 1980.

———. "Diverging Traditions of Gauvain in Some of the Later Old French Verse Romances." In *The Legacy of Chrétien de Troyes*, ed. Norris J. Lacy, Douglas Kelly, and Keith Busby. 2 vols. Amsterdam: Rodopi, 1988, Vol. 2, pp. 93–109.

Schmolke-Hasselmann, Beate. *Der arthurische Versroman von Chrestien bis Froissart*. Tübingen: Niemeyer, 1980.

GEFFREI GAIMAR (fl. 1130–40). Connected with the court of Hugh of Avranches, earl of Chester, Geffrei Gaimar may also have been acquainted with David the Scot, who became bishop of Bangor (1120–39) upon his return to England from the imperial court in Germany. Through his connections with Hugh, Gaimar was asked by Constance, wife of Ralph FitzGilbert, to translate Geoffrey of Monmouth's *Historia regum Britanniae* (ca. 1136). Gaimar's design was to trace history from Jason and the Golden Fleece to the death of King William II Rufus (1100), incorporating a translation of Geoffrey's work; however, the first part was supplanted by Wace's *Roman de Brut*, so that Gaimar's poem survives (in four manuscripts, where it immediately follows the *Brut*) only from the arrival in England in 495 of King Cerdic of Wessex, a relative of Hengist, king of Kent, to the death of William Rufus. This surviving part, drawn up to line 3,594 from a version of the *Anglo-Saxon Chronicle* and thereafter from largely unknown sources, was given the title *Estoire des Engleis* by the scribe of B.L. Royal 13 A xxi (late 13th-c.); its 6,526 lines were composed in octosyllabic rhymed couplets (ca. 1136–40).

Gaimar's narrative qualities are uneven: he is gauche when too close to his source but quite dramatic when he allows himself to indulge in such striking episodes as the story of Haveloc (ll. 96–819), the first known version of the *Lai of Haveloc*, or the poignant episode of Buern Bucecarle (ll. 2,571–720), meant to explain the Danes' conquest of Northumbria in 866. Gaimar's narration of the Danish invasion under Gormont (ll. 3,239–310) is interesting in its own right, since it differs from that found in the *Gormont et Isembart* fragment or Wace's *Brut*; and the description (ll. 4,861–5,029) of the trial of Count Godwine, earl of Wessex, reveals an aspect of Anglo-Norman law that may have been a model for the trial scene in Marie de France's *Lanval*.

Hans-Erich Keller

[See also: HISTORIOGRAPHY; WACE]

Geffrei Gaimar. *L'estoire des Engleis: By Geffrei Gaimar*, ed. Alexander Bell. Oxford: Blackwell, 1960.
Bell, Alexander. "Gaimar as Pioneer." *Romania* 97 (1976): 462–80.
Tatlock, John S.P. *The Legendary History of Britain*. Berkeley: University of California Press, 1950.

GÉNÉRAUX. With the growth of royal taxation after the mid-14th century, both the French crown and its critics groped their way toward a system that would provide honest and efficient collection of these "extraordinary" revenues without depending on traditional domainal officials. Soon after the introduction of *élus* to supervise collection, we find a board of higher supervisory officials, named originally by assemblies of the Estates and later by the crown. Although they were called by various names, the word *généraux* almost always appeared in their title.

The Estates of December 1355 appointed *généraux-surintendants* to supervise taxes. The next few assemblies named similar officials called *généraux-députés*. In 1360, when the crown established the *aides*, it appointed *généraux-trésoriers* to oversee collection of the funds intended for the ransom of John II. At the end of 1363, when the Estates of Languedoïl established the *fouage*, or hearth tax, to finance a royal army, members of the supervisory board were called *généraux-élus*. Finally, when war with England resumed in 1369, a board of *généraux-conseillers* coordinated the administration of taxes.

The three (later four) men who served as "counselors-general" of the *aides* had great authority in the 1370s, being empowered to issue orders in the king's name. Although taxes were canceled in 1380–81, resumption of the *aides* two years later meant the reestablishment of the board of *généraux-conseillers*. In the course of sweeping reforms under the rule of the Marmouset party at court (1388–92), these *généraux* received judicial powers and additional supporting staff. Ordinances of April 1390 and March 1391 began the process of converting them into a body known as the Cour des Aides. This court exercised auditing and judicial functions in matters involving extraordinary revenues (*aides*, *taille*) much as the Chambre des Comptes had done for revenues emanating from the royal domain. Ordinances of 1388 and 1393, which granted fiscal exemptions to categories of nobles, and enactments relating to other privileged groups, ensured that the *généraux* in the Cour des Aides would play an important role in determining cases involving a person's liability to taxes.

John Bell Henneman, Jr.

[See also: *AIDES; ÉLU; FOUAGE*]

Cazelles, Raymond. *Société politique, noblesse et couronne sous Jean le Bon et Charles V*. Geneva: Droz, 1982.
Dupont-Ferrier, Gustave. *Études sur les institutions financières de la France à la fin du moyen âge*. 2 vols. Paris: Didot, 1930–32.
Henneman, John Bell. *Royal Taxation in Fourteenth Century France: The Captivity and Ransom of John II, 1356–1370*. Philadelphia: American Philosophical Society, 1976.
Rey, Maurice. *Le domaine du roi et les ressources extraordinaires sous Charles VI, 1388–1413*. Paris: SEVPEN, 1965.

GENEVIÈVE (ca. 420–ca. 512). Saint and patroness of Paris. When Attila and his Huns threatened Paris in 451, Geneviève, a woman from nearby Nanterre, urged the populace not to abandon their homes but to pray for deliverance. Attila's bypassing of Paris for Orléans was attributed to her prayers. Ten years later, when the city was blockaded by the Franks, she arranged convoys to bring food down the Seine from Troyes to avert starvation. Through her intervention, both Childeric and Clovis treated captured Parisians leniently. At her death, she was interred next to Clovis and his wife, Clotilde, in a basilica built by Clovis on Paris's Mont-Sainte-Geneviève to celebrate his victory over the Visigoths at Vouillé (507). Her reliquary is now in the church of Saint-Étienne-du-Mont.

William W. Kibler

GEOFFROI. A succession of Angevin counts named Geoffroi were instrumental in the development of an Angevin state from the 10th to the 12th century. Through their efforts, Anjou became a major territorial principality and gave rise to the Angevin empire of the 12th century.

Geoffroi I Grisgonelle (r. ca. 958–87) succeeded in dominating Nantes, exerted Angevin influence over Maine, acquired Loudun, and married his son to the heiress of Vendôme. Loyal to his Robertian overlords, he died fighting to make Hugh Capet king of France in 987. He was succeeded by his son Foulques Nerra.

Nerra's son, Geoffroi II Martel (r. 1040–60), consolidated Angevin control over the expanded Anjou left to him by his father. While an active campaigner, conquering Tours in 1044, his greatest accomplishments were in statecraft, creating the essential elements of Angevin government. He skillfully combined the tradition of Carolingian public rights with new feudal elements of vassalage and homage. Expanding the network of castles begun by his father, Martel kept his castellans under tight control. For as long as he was married to Agnes, widow of Duke William the Fat of Aquitaine, he was able to exercise considerable control over that region as well. When the marriage ended in divorce in 1052, he was still able to dominate Vendôme and virtually ruled Maine until his death.

At Martel's death, the countship went to his nephew Geoffroi III le Barbu (r. 1060–68), whose rule was a disaster for Anjou. His incompetence and military ineffectiveness soon alienated the Angevin nobility, including his brother, Foulques le Rechin (r. 1068–1109). After an abortive coup in 1067, Geoffroi was deposed and imprisoned by Foulques in 1068. The civil war between the brothers seriously shook comital control over the lords of Anjou.

By the countship of Geoffroi IV Plantagenêt (r. 1129–51), the authority of the count had been much restored. Geoffroi continued the process of bringing his barons to heel. Aside from internal consolidation of comital power, Geoffroi began a phenomenal expansion of Angevin domination by marrying Matilda, daughter of King Henry I of England, in 1128. When Henry died in 1135, Matilda was the sole heiress to the kingdom of England and the duchy of Normandy. Since the throne was seized by Henry's nephew, Stephen of Blois, Geoffroi had to fight for his wife's inheritance. By 1144, he had gained control of Normandy. The submission of England was left to his son, Henry II Plantagenêt. Although Geoffroi had united a vast territory in western France, he ruled each area separately, under its own law. This was to be the model for the Angevin empire of his son.

Scott Jessee

[See also: ANJOU; FOULQUES; HENRY II; MATILDA]

Bachrach, Bernard S. "The Idea of the Angevin Empire." *Albion* 10 (*1978*): 293–99.

Dunbabin, Jean. *France in the Making, 843–1180*. Oxford: Oxford University Press, 1985.

Guillot, Olivier. *Le comte d'Anjou et son entourage au XIe siècle*. 2 vols. Paris: Picard, 1972.

Hallam, Elizabeth, ed. *The Plantagenêt Chronicles*. New York: Weidenfeld and Nicolson, 1986.

Halphen, Louis. *Le comté d'Anjou au XIe siècle*. Paris: Picard, 1906.

GERBERT DE MONTREUIL (fl. 1220s). A poet at the court of Marie, countess of Ponthieu, to whom he dedicated his *Roman de la Violette* ca. 1220, Gerbert is best known for his continuation of Chrétien de Troyes's *Perceval*. Gerbert's *Continuation* is inserted between the *Second Continuation* and Manessier's conclusion in two Paris manuscripts.

The *Roman de la Violette* (6,654 octosyllables) exploits the same folk motif as Jean Renart's *Guillaume de Dole*: Lisïart de Forez wagers Gérard de Nevers that he can seduce Gérard's ladylove, Eurïaut. By deceit, he discovers that she has a violet-shaped birthmark on her right breast and uses this information to "prove" his success. Thinking her unfaithful, Gérard abandons Eurïaut and weds her only after many adventures and the eventual confession of Lisïart.

Gerbert's *Perceval Continuation* (ca. 1226–30; ca. 17,000 lines) brings Perceval, after numerous adventures designed to show that he is the worthiest knight in the world, to the Grail Castle, where he is about to have the secrets of the Grail revealed to him. However, Gerbert's presumed explanation is replaced, in both manuscripts that contain his poem, by Manessier's continuation and explanation.

William W. Kibler

[See also: CHRÉTIEN DE TROYES; *COMTE DE POITIERS, ROMAN DU;* GRAIL AND GRAIL ROMANCES; *PERCEVAL CONTINUATIONS;* REALISTIC ROMANCES; TRISTAN ROMANCES]

Gerbert de Montreuil. *La continuation de Perceval,* ed. Mary Williams. Paris: Champion, 1922–25, and M. Oswald. Paris: Champion, 1975.

———. *Roman de la Violette,* ed. D.L. Boffum. Paris: Société des Anciens Textes Français, 1928.

GERBERT OF AURILLAC (Pope Sylvester II; ca. 945–1003). Gerbert was born in the Auvergne and educated at the monastery of Saint-Géraud in Aurillac. He studied in Spain at the school in Ausona (Vich) and in 970 went to Rome. He was master of the cathedral school of Reims from 972 to 989, with one brief interruption. One of the leading teachers in his day, he numbered among his students Fulbert of Chartres and the future king Robert II the Pious of France. Gerbert's teaching was notable in that he taught the whole range of the Seven Liberal Arts (Trivium and Quadrivium). However, he was especially interested in literature, logic, scientific observation, and mathematics. He established the logical works of Boethius as essential in the syllabus of studies, and he developed astronomical instruments for observation. He was active in support of Hugh Capet for the French crown and participated in the coronation at Reims in 987. Appointed archbishop of Reims in 991 (an appointment never approved by the pope), he held the position for several years before joining the entourage of Emperor Otto III; he was later appointed archbishop of Ravenna. In 999, he became bishop of Rome, the first Frenchman to so serve. As Pope Sylvester II, Gerbert was a vigorous reformer and an opponent of simony and married clergy. Owing to his mathematical skills, medieval tradition saw him as adept in magic.

Grover A. Zinn

[See also: ARABIC INFLUENCE ON LITERATURE; BOETHIUS, INFLUENCE OF; FULBERT OF CHARTRES; MAGIC; PHILOSOPHY; SCHOOLS, CATHEDRAL]

Marenbon, John. *From the Circle of Alcuin to the School of Auxerre: Logic, Theology and Philosophy in the Early Middle Ages*. Cambridge: Cambridge University Press, 1981.

GERMIGNY-DES-PRÉS. Theodulf, bishop of Orléans, abbot of Saint-Benoît-sur-Loire at Fleury, and an important intellectual at Charlemagne's court, built a villa at Germigny-des-Prés (Loiret). Only the oratory, consecrated in 806, remains. The small square structure composed of nine vaulted compartments with a central tower has single apses projecting from three sides and a triple apse on the east. The horseshoe arches and decoration show Visigothic influence. The central west apse preserves a mosaic of the Ark of the Covenant surrounded by two pairs of angels that reflects Byzantine inspiration. The architectural eclecticism and theological context of the mosaic represent significant aspects of Carolingian culture.

Karen Gould

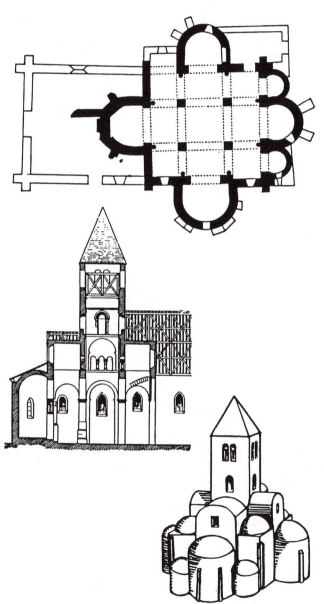

Germigny-des-Prés (Loiret), Carolingian oratory of Theodulf, plan, long section, and reconstructed view from east. After Conant and others.

[See also: CAROLINGIAN ART; THEODULF OF ORLÉANS]

Hubert, Jean. "Germigny-des-Prés." *Congrès archéologique* 93 (1930): 534–37.

GERSON, JEAN (Jean Charlier; 1363–1429). Theologian, scholar, teacher, translator, poet, mystic, and humanist, Gerson was one of the most illustrious and prolific writers of the late Middle Ages. One of twelve children, he grew up in a pious household in Champagne, the son of an educated artisan. Three of his brothers became monks and another a priest. Although his sisters did not enter religious orders, they formed among themselves an informal religious group devoted to prayer and spiritual exercises. Gerson entered the University of Paris in 1377 and received an arts degree in 1381 from the Collège de Navarre. Subsequently, he studied theology and obtained the doctorate in 1392. Tailoring his sermons to his audience, Gerson gained fame as an orator who could preach with eloquence to both kings and the laity at large. He succeeded his friend and mentor Pierre d'Ailly as chancellor of the university in 1395, taking over the duties in the midst of the Great Schism (1378–1417). Although Gerson opposed the withdrawal of French obedience from the Avignon pope, Benedict XIII, and worked to restore it in 1403, he nevertheless sought a reconciliation between the two contending popes by suggesting that both claimants resign. In 1407, the Roman pope, Gregory XII, indicated a willingness to meet with Benedict and discuss mutual resignation. Gerson was chosen to head the French delegation and facilitate the meeting, which was, however, a failure. With the aim of restoring church unity, Gerson supported a move to resolve the conflict through a church council. The Council of Pisa, held in 1409, was not successful. Although it elected a new pope, Alexander V, this strategy served only to introduce a third contender. The Council of Constance (1415–18) finally put an end to the Schism with the election of Martin V. Writing numerous treatises to justify the work of the council, Gerson was an outspoken proponent of conciliarism, setting out the limitations of papal authority.

Gerson was also strenuous in efforts to eradicate heresy. Critical of the writings of Wyclif and Hus, Gerson was an adviser to Pierre d'Ailly, who served on the commission that condemned Hus to death. Also interested in secular affairs, Gerson openly opposed the Burgundian assassination of the duke of Orléans in 1407, attacking and condemning Jean Petit's *Apologia* for favoring tyrannicide in justification of the Burgundian deed. His position so angered the duke of Burgundy, who had previously been one of Gerson's strongest protectors, that he was prevented from returning to Paris after the Council of Constance. Gerson retired to Lyon, living first at a Celestine monastery where his youngest brother, also named Jean, who became his copyist and editor, was prior, and then at the church of Saint-Paul. During his exile, however, Gerson continued to write as he had before on such subjects as spiritual renewal, church reform, Christian education, and the integration of mystical and speculative theology. His writings have not received extensive attention from historians, although they offer insights into the culture of the late Middle Ages. His work, for example, on the Christian education of the young provides important information on medieval attitudes on children and childhood.

Gerson was also a Latin poet of notable talent and skill. Influenced by Petrarch, his eclogue on the Schism is perhaps the first humanist work produced in France. Other works include *De vita spirituali animae*, in which he locates ecclesiastical authority in church councils rather than in the pope; *De unitate ecclesiae*, one of twenty-seven extant treatises on the church; *Mémoire sur la réforme de la faculté de théologie*, which outlines his pedagogy; and informal writings on the spiritual life, such as the *Montagne de contemplation*. Although it is often attributed to him, Gerson did not write the *Imitatio Christi*. Among his last writings is a defense of Jeanne d'Arc, *Puella Aurelianensi* (1429).

E. Kay Harris

[See also: AVIGNON PAPACY; CONCILIAR MOVEMENT; D'AILLY, PIERRE; ERIUGENA, JOHANNES SCOTTUS; MYSTICISM; NECROMANCY; QUARREL OF THE *ROMAN DE LA ROSE*; SCHISM, GREAT]

Gerson, Jean. *Œuvres complètes de Jean Gerson,* ed. Palémon Glorieux. 10 vols. Paris: Desclée, 1960–73.

Combes, André. *La théologie mystique de Gerson.* 2 vols. Rome: Editores Pontificii, 1965.

Delaruelle, Étienne, L.R. Labande, and Papul Ourliac. *L'église au temps du Grand Schisme et de la crise conciliaire (1378–1449).* 2 vols. Paris: Blond et Gay, 1962.

Morrall, John B. *Gerson and the Great Schism.* Manchester: Manchester University Press, 1960.

GESTA FRANCORUM ET ALIORUM HIEROSOLIMITANORUM

(ca. 1101). The earliest account of the First Crusade. The unknown author was a knight in the Italian contingent of Bohemund who wrote in simple, rough Latin. He begins with the Council of Clermont (1095) and ends with the Battle of Ascalon (August 1099). The *Gesta* was reworked by Robert le Moine, Baudri of Bourgueil, and Peter Tudebod and was known by most other writers treating the crusade, including Foucher de Chartres and Raymond d'Agiles, both eyewitnesses themselves. The *Gesta* was also read in its own right; it is extant in seven manuscripts.

Leah Shopkow

[See also: FOUCHER DE CHARTRES; HISTORIOGRAPHY]

Hagenmeyer, Heinrich, ed. *Anonymi gesta Francorum.* Heidelberg: Winter, 1890.

Hill, Rosalind, ed. *Gesta Francorum et aliorum Hierosolimitanorum.* London: Nelson, 1962.

GHENT. Before an abrupt decline after 1356, Ghent (Fr. Gand), a Flemish city at the junction of the Scheldt and Lys rivers, was the second-largest city, after Paris, of medieval northern Europe, with a population of some 50,000. Ghent was important in commerce by the 8th century and had a thriving textile industry by the 12th. By the 13th century, Ghent was governed by the Thirty-Nine, three cooptative boards of councilors who rotated annually and were notoriously corrupt, provoking industrial and political unrest. Ghent maintained a generally royalist posture in the conflicts of the French monarchy with the Flemish count Gui de Dampierre; only a small contingent from Ghent joined Bruges and Ypres in defeating the French at the Battle of the Golden Spurs, Courtrai, in 1302.

During the 14th century, Ghent was governed by two boards of aldermen, and the magistracy was open to all social and professional groups. Occupational guilds other than the exclusive merchant organization of the 13th century were legalized, but only after 1360 were the twenty-six seats on the councils apportioned in a fixed scheme among groups of guilds. The government was dominated by oligarchies within the guilds and members of *poorter* (landowner) families. Ghent developed a substantial shipping trade after 1300, particularly in grain shipped from France down the Scheldt and Lys. But the textile industry, dependent on imported English wool, continued to dominate the city at least through mid-century. Ghent was as cripplingly dependent on England for wool for its textile looms as on France for grain to feed its workers. Thus caught in the Anglo-French struggles of the 1340s, the town fell under the domination of the captain Jacques van Artevelde. After his death, Ghent continued its resistance to the new count, Louis de Male.

When Louis's forces stormed the city in January 1349, they installed a regime based on the fullers' guild, which was less inimical to his authority than that of the weavers, who had dominated Ghent in the 1340s without excluding other groups. The weavers had regained power and barred the fullers from the town councils by 1361. Between 1379 and 1385, Ghent waged another war against the count, who had allowed Bruges to dig a canal toward the Lys with the intention of channeling into it south of Ghent and ending Ghent's lucrative control of the French grain supply. This "Ghent War" did not have the support of the rest of Flanders, although the military power of Ghent kept pro-Ghent factions in power intermittently elsewhere. Ghent and Flanders were thereafter ruled by Louis de Male's Burgundian successors, who slowly limited the cities' autonomy. The textile industry of Ghent, which had gone into a severe decline after 1350, revived somewhat in the 15th century. Although Ghent rebelled in 1438 and 1451–53 against Philip the Good of Burgundy, capitulation was inevitable. Philip and particularly his son, Charles the Bold, attempted to control directly the choice of magistrates in the city, leading to further rebellion against his son-in-law and successor, Maximilian of Habsburg. In the 16th century, Ghent and Flanders were part of a Habsburg state.

David M. Nicholas

Ghent initially grew up around two monasteries, Saint-Pierre, founded by St. Amand in the 7th century, and Saint-Bavon, also founded in the 7th century and rebuilt in the

10th. A third urban center was dominated by the stone castle built ca. 1000 on the site of what is now the castle of the counts of Flanders ('s Gravensteen). In order to assert his authority over the powerful weavers' guild, Philippe d'Alsace, count of Flanders and Vermandois, strengthened and added to the castle after 1180, upon his return from the Third Crusade, using as models the crusader castles of the Near East. It is deeply moated, and the outer curtain wall, with its twenty-four watch towers, forms an oval measuring approximately 165 feet by 200 feet. These curtain walls, reinforced by powerful rectangular buttresses, most supporting the semicylindrical watch towers, are over 6 feet thick. The only entrance, projecting to the east, is a rectangular châtelet terminating in two machicolated turrets supported by buttresses. Within the walls are a massive keep, some 100 feet tall with walls over 6 feet thick, and several residences.

The cathedral of Saint-Bavon, built largely in the 16th century on the site of the 12th-century church of Saint-Jean, houses Van Eyck's *Polyptych of the Mystical Lamb* (1432), a masterpiece of Flemish art. Including no less than 248 figures, it is a *summa* of medieval Christian faith, illustrating salvation history from the Fall to the Redemption. The lower panels show the Mystical Lamb, surrounded by angels, upon an altar. On either side, virgins, martyrs, confessors, hermits, knights, and pilgrims approach the altar across a lushly painted landscape. In the upper panels, Christ sits in majesty, with the Virgin, Adam, and a choir of angels to his left and St. John the Baptist, Eve, and angel musicians to his right. The backs of the panels depict the prophets, the sibyls, the Annunciation, St. John the Evangelist, and St. John the Baptist with the donors, Josse Vijd and his wife, Elisabeth Borluut.

The belfry, built in the 13th and 14th centuries as a sign of the power of the trade guilds, rises some 200 feet above the city. The town retains several medieval guildhalls, markets, and private houses, especially along the Quai aux Herbes (Graslei). The charming Petit Béguinage (Klein Begijnhof), founded by Jeanne de Constantinople in 1234, is an important reminder of this popular form of late-medieval devotion.

William W. Kibler

[See also: ARTEVELDE; BÉGUINES; BRUGES; FLANDERS; JEANNE DE CONSTANTINOPLE; TEXTILES]

Finó, J.-F. *Forteresses de la France médiévale.* Paris: Picard, 1970.

Nicholas, David. *The Metamorphosis of a Medieval City: Ghent in the Age of the Arteveldes, 1302–1390.* Lincoln: University of Nebraska Press, 1987.

———. *Town and Countryside: Social, Economic, and Political Tensions in Fourteenth Century Flanders.* Bruges: De Tempel, 1971.

Pirenne, Henri. *Early Democracies in the Low Countries.* New York: Harper and Row, 1963.

———. *Histoire de Belgique.* Brussels: Lamertin, 1922–29, Vols. 1 and 2.

van Werveke, Hans. *Gand: esquisse d'histoire sociale.* Brussels: Renaissance du Livre, 1946.

GILBERT OF POITIERS (Gilbertus, Gislebertus, or Gillibertus Porreta or Porretanus; also, less correctly, de la Porrée, 1075/80–1154). Gilbert was born in Poitiers and returned there as bishop in 1141 or 1142. After studying the liberal arts and philosophy with Hilary in Poitiers and Bernard in Chartres, he immersed himself in the study of the Bible in Laon. As Anselm of Laon's disciple, Gilbert participated in the great exegetical undertaking that was to culminate in the formation of the *Glossa ordinaria* in Paris during the middle decades of the century. Gilbert's commentaries on the Psalms (before 1117) and on the Epistles of Paul (perhaps a decade later) owed much to Anselm's glosses and to his use of *quaestiones* and *sententiae* to explore theological and pastoral topics. In addition, Gilbert introduced to scriptural exegesis pedagogical techniques, such as the *accessus ad auctores*, used by grammarians to teach works of profane literature. These methods influenced subsequent exegetes: Peter Lombard's biblical commentaries, for example, rely heavily on Gilbert's work.

Gilbert returned to Chartres as a canon and by 1126 was chancellor of the cathedral. (There is no evidence to support the claim that he taught in Poitiers.) Though he certainly taught in Chartres, most contemporary testimony associates Gilbert with Paris, where he is reported teaching grammar, logic, and theology and where he helped promote the biblical glosses that were developing into the *Glossa ordinaria.*

In his commentaries (ca. 1140) on the *Opuscula sacra* of Boethius, Gilbert distinguishes between different aspects of a being: that which a thing is (*id, quod est*) and that by which a thing is what it is (*id, quo est*). The resulting attempt to differentiate among persons, natures, attributes, and essences, when applied to Trinitarian issues, led Gilbert to the brink of disaster. In March 1148, after the Council of Reims, Gilbert's orthodoxy was examined on four counts: that God is not "divinity" or divine nature; that the Persons of the Trinity are not "divinity"; that God's properties are not God and are not eternal; that the divine nature is not incarnate. The theologians present at the consistory never got a chance to debate these propositions fully: when it became clear that the curia sided with Gilbert, Bernard of Clairvaux (appointed to the prosecution) drew up a "confession of faith" of sound spiritual instinct (but loose terminology) that he presented to Eugenius III, in effect pressuring the pope to declare either Gilbert or Bernard a heretic. Eugenius sidestepped the maneuver and made some token pronouncements regarding theological language; Gilbert, acquitted of heresy, declared that he "believed whatever Eugenius believed" and promised to correct any offending passages in his writings. No such "corrections" were ever made, to Bernard's chagrin.

Theresa Gross-Diaz

[See also: ANSELM OF LAON; BIBLE, CHRISTIAN INTERPRETATION OF; CHARTRES; *GLOSSA ORDINARIA*; PETER LOMBARD; PHILOSOPHY; THEOLOGY]

Gilbert of Poitiers. *The Commentaries on Boethius,* ed. Nikolaus M. Häring. Toronto: Pontifical Institute of Mediaeval Studies, 1966.

Colish, Marcia L. "Early Porretan Theology." *Recherches de théologie ancienne et médiévale* 56 (1989): 59–79.

Gross-Diaz, Theresa. *The Psalms Commentary of Gilbert of Poitiers: From* lectio divina *to the Lecture Room.* Leiden: Brill. Forthcoming.

Häring, Nikolaus M. "Handschriftliches zu den Werken Gilberts, Bishof von Poitiers." *Revue d'histoire des textes* 8 (1978): 133–94.

Maioli, Bruno. *Gilberto Porretano: dalla grammatica speculativa alla metafisica del concreto.* Rome: Bulzoni, 1979.

Nielsen, Lauge Olaf. *Theology and Philosophy in the Twelfth Century: A Study of Gilbert of Porreta's Thinking and the Theological Expositions of the Doctrine of the Incarnation During the Period 1130–1180.* Leiden: Brill, 1982.

van Elswijk, H.C. *Gilbert Porreta: sa vie, son œuvre, sa pensée.* Louvain: Spicilegium Sacrum Lovaniense, 1966.

GILDUIN OF SAINT-VICTOR (d. 1155). The first abbot of Saint-Victor, a house of regular canons at Paris founded by William of Champeaux, Gilduin guided the development of the abbey in its crucial early decades. He developed ties with the king, so that the abbey enjoyed royal patronage, and oversaw the erection of the abbey's first buildings. During his abbacy, a group of distinguished canons brought fame to the abbey as a center of biblical study, theological inquiry, and liturgical creativity, along with dedication to the contemplative ideal and to ecclesiastical reform.

Grover A. Zinn

[See also: ADAM OF SAINT-VICTOR; HUGH OF SAINT-VICTOR; SAINT-VICTOR, ABBEY AND SCHOOL OF; WILLIAM OF CHAMPEAUX]

Bonnard, Fourier. *Histoire de l'abbaye royale et de l'ordre des chanoines réguliers de Saint-Victor de Paris.* 2 vols. Paris: Savaète, 1907.

GILES OF ROME (Aegidius Colonna; ca. 1243–1316). One of the most outstanding students of Thomas Aquinas, Giles was born at Rome, perhaps of the Colonna family. Contrary to his family's wishes, Giles embraced the religious life ca. 1258 at the convent of Santa Maria del Populo of the Hermits of St. Augustine. Arriving at Paris ca. 1260, he studied and taught there until 1278. He heard the lectures of Thomas during the latter's second period of teaching at Paris (1269–71) and strenuously defended Thomistic teachings against Bishop Étienne Tempier's condemnation in 1277. This dispute with the bishop occasioned Giles's departure from Paris; the bishop's death helped smooth the way for Giles's return in 1285 as master of theology and the first Augustinian friar to hold a chair in theology at Paris (1285–91).

King Philip III of France had charged Giles with the education of his son, the future Philip IV the Fair, for whom Giles composed perhaps his best-known work, *De regimine principum* (1280). By 1282, the work had been translated into French and in the 14th century was translated into Castilian, Portuguese, Catalan, English, German, and Hebrew. The work was an admirable combination of Aristotelian ethics and Christian moral and spiritual teaching.

Giles maintained good relations with Philip, and in the year following his election to the post of prior-general of the Augustinians (1292) Philip granted the order the Grand Convent of the Augustinians in Paris. In 1295, Pope Boniface VIII, with Philip's consent, elevated Giles to the archiepiscopal see of Bourges. But in the ensuing controversy between Philip and Boniface, Giles sided with Boniface, composing the treatise *De ecclesiastica potestate* (1301)—one of the principal sources for the papal bull *Unam sanctam* (1302) and one of the broadest expressions of papal supremacy in the entire controversy.

Following the death of Boniface, Giles returned to his duties in Bourges. He was active in several controversies at the time, among them the disputes with the Templars and with Peter Olivi. He was active at the Council of Vienne (1311–12) and died a few years later in Avignon.

As a teacher, Giles lectured according to the prescribed course of study, commenting first on the Bible and on the *Sententiae* of Peter Lombard; but his greatest love was philosophy. He left commentaries on many of Aristotle's works on logic, physics, and metaphysics, including the Pseudo-Aristotelian *Liber de causis.* His works were held in such high esteem that the general chapter of his order meeting at Florence in 1287 declared that his "opinions, positions, and conclusions [*sententiae*] both written and yet to be written" were to receive the unqualified assent of all Augustinian teachers and students. The Franciscan philosopher William of Ockham went so far as to speak of Giles as the "Expositor" of Aristotle's *Physics.*

Giles was an independent thinker, and though he shared many ideas with Aquinas he disagreed markedly with him on the relationship between essence and existence. For Giles, these are two separate things, the latter not necessarily implied in the former. In this way, he stressed the contingency of all things on the will of God and enunciated a theme that would become one of the hallmarks of later nominalism.

Mark Zier

[See also: AQUINAS, THOMAS; ARISTOTLE, INFLUENCE OF; AUGUSTINIAN FRIARS/HERMITS; BONIFACE VIII; COURTESY BOOKS; PHILIP IV THE FAIR; PHILOSOPHY; *UNAM SANCTAM*]

Giles of Rome. *De ecclesiastica potestate,* ed. Richard Scholz. Weimar: Böhlaus, 1929.

———. *Errores philosophorum,* ed. Josef Koch, trans. John Riedl. Milwaukee: Marquette University Press, 1944.

———. Sermons. In *Repertorium der lateinischen Sermones des Mittelalters von 1150–1350,* ed. Johannes-Baptist Schneyer. 6 vols. Münster: Aschendorff, 1969–74, Vol. 1, p. 57.

Hocediz, E. "La condemnation de Gilles de Rome." *Recherches de théologie ancienne et médiévale* 4 (1932): 34–58.

Luna, C. "La lecture de Gilles de Rome sur le quatrième livre des sentences: les extraits du Clm 8005." *Recherches de théologie ancienne et médiévale* 57 (1992): 183–255.

Nash, P.W. "Giles of Rome: Auditor and Critic of St Thomas." *Modern Schoolman* 28 (1950): 1–20.

———. "Giles of Rome on Boethius' *Diversum est esse et id quod est.*" *Medieval Studies* 12 (1950): 57–91.

———. "The Accidentality of *Esse* According to Giles of Rome." *Gregorianum* 38 (1957): 103–15.

GILLES DE CHIN (d. 1137). This chamberlain of Count Baudouin IV of Hainaut has left his trace in history and legend. The literature he inspired records his adventures in the Holy Land, as well as in his native Hainaut. His effigy is still to be seen in the chapel of Saint-Calixte in Mons, and his exploits are recalled annually by a procession in nearby Wasmes. Gilbert de Mons recorded his deeds in the *Chronicon Hanoniense* (ca. 1195–1221), and Gautier de Tournai celebrated them in a 13th-century poem of which only a 16th-century manuscript remains. A 15th-century prose version is preserved in two manuscripts, one of which, in Lille (Fonds Godefroy 134), is illustrated by the celebrated Wavrin Master. Marks of ownership further identify it with the Burgundian counselor, historian, and bibliophile Jean de Wavrin. Although the anonymous author of this prose version generally follows the earlier poem, he adds contemporary personages to the story and elaborates scenes from contemporary life. The tale belongs to a group that celebrates local heroes, including Gérard de Nevers, Gilles de Trazignies, and Jacques de Lalaing. Copies of all of these were made in the Lille workshop of the Wavrin Master.

Charity Cannon Willard

Gautier de Tournai. *Histoire de Gille de Chyn*, ed. Edwin B. Place. Evanston: Northwestern University Press, 1941.

Doutrepont, Georges. *Les mises en prose des épopées et des romans chevaleresques du XIVe au XVIe siècles*. Brussels: Académie Royale de Belgique, 1940.

Liégeois, Camille. *Gilles de Chin, l'histoire et la légende*. Louvain: Peeters: 1903.

GIRART D'AMIENS (fl. 1280–1305). A familiar of the courts of Edward I of England and Philip the Fair of France, Girart is known to us only through the prologues of his three lengthy poems. His romance *Escanor* (25,936 octosyllables, with lacunae) was dedicated ca. 1280 to Eleanor of Castile, Edward's queen; *Meliacin* or the *Cheval de fust*, (19,159 octosyllables with twenty-four intercalated lyrics) was composed at the command of Gaucher V de Châtillon shortly after 1285; and *Charlemagne* (over 23,000 Alexandrines; ca. 1303–06) was written for Charles of Valois, brother of Philip the Fair. *Escanor*, perhaps conceived as a sequel to the *Atre périlleux*, is an Arthurian romance whose two main themes are the love affair of Kay and Andrivete of Northumberland and the enmity of Gawain and Escanor. *Meliacin* is a non-Arthurian romance based on the eastern legend of the Ebony Horse (from the *Arabian Nights*), found also in Adenet le Roi's *Cleomadés*. Both poems were inspired by Blanche of France, daughter of St. Louis and daughter-in-law of Alfonso X the

Wise of Spain, after her return to France as a widow. *Charlemagne*, extant in three manuscripts but still largely unedited, is presented as a continuation of Adenet le Roi's *Berte aus grans piés*. It has three principal parts: Charlemagne's youth (inspired by the epic *Mainet*); the exploits of Roland, Ogier, and Naimes, followed by Charlemagne's voyage to the Holy Land; and a rhymed version of the Pseudo-Turpin chronicle.

William W. Kibler

[**See also:** ADENET LE ROI; ARTHURIAN VERSE ROMANCE; GAWAIN ROMANCES]

Girart d'Amiens. *Escanor: roman arthurien en vers de la fin du XIIIe siècle,* ed. Richard Trachsler. 2 vols. Geneva: Droz, 1994.

———. *Meliacin ou Le cheval de fust,* ed. Antoinette Saly. Aix-en-Provence: CUER MA, 1990.

Saly, Antoinette. "La date du *Charlemagne* de Girart d'Amiens." In *Au carrefour des routes d'Europe: la chanson de geste, actes du Xe Congrès International de la Société Rencesvals.* Aix-en-Provence: CUER MA, 1987, Vol. 2, pp. 975–81.

GIRART DE ROUSSILLON. Written anonymously between 1155 and 1180 (probably ca. 1170), this poem in Franco-Provençal consists of some 10,000 decasyllabic lines (with an unusual 6/4 caesura). Preserved in three manuscripts, it features the same 9th-century count of Vienne as do the *Chanson d'Aspremont* ("Girart de Fraite") and *Girart de Vienne. Girart de Roussillon* belongs to the Rebellious Vassal Cycle but uncharacteristically uses the figure of the unjust king not to excuse revolt but to show that, even under the greatest imaginable provocation, a vassal has no right to rebel. King Charles Martel forces Girart to exchange fiancées with him in consideration of release from vassalic duties; he then tries by force to bring Girart back into vassaldom; the resulting civil war ends when God's thunderbolts strike the banners of both armies. It resumes after a murder by some of Girart's relations, whom he refuses, in his pride, to surrender, and leads to appalling slaughter and destruction. Reduced to flight, Girart plots to murder Charles but is converted by a hermit; his long and difficult penance is supported by his wife, who leads him ultimately to the renunciation of secular chivalry and to sanctity.

Girart de Roussillon is remarkable for its insight into human motivation, especially the effects of pride, and for its vividly expressed horror at civil war and its consequences.

Wolfgang G. van Emden

[**See also:** BERTRAND DE BAR-SUR-AUBE; REBELLIOUS VASSAL CYCLE]

Hackett, W. Mary, ed. *Girart de Roussillon.* 3 vols. Paris: SATF, 1953–55.

———. *Langue de Girart de Roussillon.* Geneva: Droz, 1970.

Le Gentil, Pierre. "*Girart de Roussillon:* sens et structure du poème." *Romania* 78 (1957): 328–89, 463–510.

Lot, Ferdinand. "La légende de Girart de Roussillon" and "Encore la légende de Girart de Roussillon: à propos d'un livre récent." *Romania* 52 (1926): 257–95; 70 (1948–49): 192–253, 355–96. [Discusses Louis, below.]

Louis, René. *De l'histoire à la légende: Girart, comte de Vienne, dans les chansons de geste.* 2 vols. Auxerre, 1947.

Pfister, Max. *Lexikalische Untersuchungen zu Girart de Roussillon.* Tübingen: Niemeyer, 1970.

GIRAUT DE BORNELH (fl. ca. 1162–99). Called *maestre dels trobadors* by the author of his *vida,* this prolific and respected singer traveled to the courts of Spain and participated in the Third Crusade. Dante later turned to him for a model of the poet of rectitude. The *vida* also suggests that Giraut was a master in another sense: a teacher. Certainly, his lyrics are the work of a poets' poet, at once learned and elegant. In his approximately seventy-six songs of certain attribution, including some fifty love songs and fifteen moral *sirventes,* Giraut is a difficult poet, concise and cerebral. His cold rhetoric and his obsession with style seem to confirm the *vida's* assertions. Giraut was as much at ease in the hermetic style of *trobar clus,* perhaps in imitation of Raimbaut d'Aurenga, as he was in the clear style of *trobar leu,* which he defends in a debate with Raimbaut. His most successful lyric is the religious *alba Reis glorios,* but he also practiced the *planh, tenso,* crusade song, romance, and *pastorela.*

Roy S. Rosenstein

[See also: TROUBADOUR POETRY; *PASTOURELLE/PASTORELA*]

Giraut de Bornelh. *Giraut de Borneil, maestre dels trobadors: choix de poésies,* ed. James and Claude Dauphiné. Périgueux: Fanlac, 1978.

———. *Sämtliche Lieder des Trobadors Guiraut de Bornelh,* ed. Adolf Kolsen. 2 vols. Halle: Niemeyer, 1910–35.

———. *The Cansos and Sirventes of the Troubadour Giraut de Borneil,* ed. and trans. Ruth V. Sharman. Cambridge: Cambridge University Press, 1988.

Sharman, Ruth V. "Giraut de Borneil: maestre dels trobadors. " *Medium Aevum* 52 (1983): 63–76.

GISLEBERTUS (fl. late 11th–early 12th c.). The west tympanum of Saint-Lazare at Autun bears the inscription GISLEBERTUS HOC FECIT, and this sculptor's career can be traced through stylistic comparisons to Autun. Around 1115, Gislebertus assisted the Master at Cluny working on some capitals and the west portal. He was briefly at Vézelay producing sculpture intended for the west tympanum. His major *œuvre* was at Autun ca. 1125–35, where he carved the Last Judgment of the west tympanum, in the north doorway of which a lintel fragment of Eve remains, and, with assistants, about fifty foliate and historiated capitals. His significance as a Romanesque sculptor arises from the quantity and expressive quality of his work.

Karen Gould

[See also: AUTUN; ROMANESQUE SCULPTURE; VÉZELAY]

Grivot, Dennis, and George Zarnecki. *Giselbertus, Sculptor of Autun.* New York: Orion, 1961.

GISORS. Capital of the Norman Vexin, Gisors (Eure) was the principal base of operations of the Anglo-Normans in their struggles against the Capetian monarchy. A fortress with a double curtain wall was begun here in 1096–97 by the Norman Robert de Bellême on orders from King William II Rufus. For a century, it was the scene of constant strife until finally ceded by Richard I the Lionhearted to Philip II Augustus by the Treaty of Louviers (1196). Richard then immediately built Château-Gaillard to replace it. The extensive remains of the ramparts (built probably under Henry I), of the 12th-century keep (constructed on an irregular octagonal plan upon a 65-foot motte), and of the three-story Tour du Prisonnier (built by Philip Augustus), dominate the present-day town. It is an impressive example of Norman military architecture.

The church of Saint-Gervais-Saint-Protais, constructed from the 12th through the 16th century, witnessed a succession of styles. The nave is largely Renaissance, but the transept tower (12th c.) and choir (13th c.) are significant Gothic structures in the region.

William W. Kibler/William W. Clark

[See also: CHÂTEAU-GAILLARD; LOCHES]

Bruand, Yves. "Le château de Gisors, principales campagnes de construction." *Bulletin monumental* 116 (1958): 243–65.

Mesqui, Jean, and Patrick Toussaint. "Le château de Gisors aux XIIe et XIIIe siècles." *Archéologie médiévale* 20 (1990): 253–318.

Pépin, Eugène. *Gisors et la vallée de l'Epte.* 2nd ed. Paris: Laurens, 1963.

GLOSSA ORDINARIA. The "Ordinary Gloss" is the name generally given to the commentary on the Bible (and the prologues of Jerome) of which manuscripts were commonly produced ca. 1130–1250 and which contained in effect a digest of the opinions of all the important patristic commentators, as well as some selected "moderns" on any given text. It was a reference work for teachers and students of biblical commentary. Once the text had become established, it was largely stable, laid out with a central biblical text and glosses added in the margins and interlinearly. There is no difference, apart from length, between the marginal and interlinear glosses, and they may change places at will.

Jerome, whose translation is the basis for the *Glossa's* Bible text, is also a major source of the individual glosses, along with Ambrose, Augustine, Bede, Cassiodorus, Gregory the Great, Origen, and their 9th-century editor, Rabanus Maurus. These are the main contributors, but others, especially Carolingian authors, are sometimes quoted on particular words or phrases.

By ca. 1490, it was a commonplace that the Carolingian scholar Walafrid Strabo was the compiler of the *Glossa,* but recent scholarship prefers to credit the Psalter, Pauline

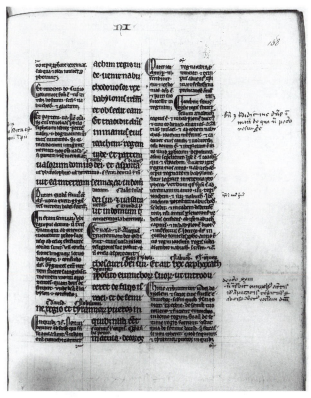

Glossa Ordinaria. Biblical text (large text) and gloss (small text) for Daniel 1.1–4. BN lat. 155, fol. 138. *Courtesy of the Bibliothèque Nationale, Paris.*

Epistles and perhaps the Gospel of John to Anselm of Laon, and the Pentateuch, Jeremiah, and perhaps Joshua to 2 Kings and the Minor Prophets to Gilbert of Auxerre, "the Universal." Anselm's brother, Ralph, may have made the gloss on Matthew. The compilers of the other glosses remain a mystery.

The *Glossa* was taken up by two famous Parisian masters, Gilbert of Poitiers and Peter Lombard. Peter wrote commentaries on the Psalter and the Pauline epistles, which were incorporated into the glossed text as standard (the *Magna glossatura*). Perfecting the characteristic layout, apparently in Paris late in the 12th century, made it the reference tool *par excellence.*

The *Glossa* was printed in many early versions, the first by Adolph Rusch of Strasbourg (1480–81). From the 1495 edition, the *Glossa* was printed together with the postillae of Nicholas of Lyra, and after ca. 1500 an increasing number of interpolations in the printed texts make them unreliable witnesses to the 12th-century versions. The adjective *Ordinaria* was not added to the general term *Glossa* until the 14th century.

Lesley J. Smith

[See also: ANSELM OF LAON; BIBLE, CHRISTIAN INTERPRETATION OF; GILBERT OF POITIERS; PETER LOMBARD; RABANUS MAURUS; WALAFRID STRABO]

GODEFROI DE BOUILLON (ca. 1061–1100). Duke of Lower Lorraine, leader of the First Crusade, and first Latin ruler of Jerusalem, Godefroi was the second son of Count Eustache II of Boulogne and of Ide, daughter of Duke Godefroi II of Lower Lorraine. In 1076, the emperor Henry IV refused him the succession to his grandfather's duchy, but Godefroi finally acceded in 1089.

He participated in the First Crusade in 1096 along with his brothers Eustache III of Boulogne and Baudouin, choosing the land route via Hungary. On arriving at Constantinople, he at first refused the requested oath to the emperor Alexios I Comnenos but consented finally after an attack on the suburbs of the city when the emperor cut off provisions for his forces. Though he did not figure as prominently as the other crusading leaders prior to their arrival at Jerusalem, his forces were the first to break in, and he became the compromise candidate for ruler of the Holy City. Refusing the title king, he became the Advocate of the Holy Sepulcher and secured the Latin position in Palestine by defeating an invading relief army from Fatimid Egypt at Ascalon.

Godefroi's rule was brief and made difficult by the ambitions of the other crusading leaders. He also had to deal with the pretensions to rule of Daimbert of Pisa, the first Latin patriarch of Jerusalem. On his death (July 18, 1100), he was succeeded by his younger brother, Baudouin, who had founded the first of the Crusading States at Edessa and who took the title king of Jerusalem.

Godefroi's life almost immediately became the stuff of legends. He was one of the three medieval members, with Charlemagne and Arthur, of the Nine Worthies and is the principal hero of the Crusade epics, including the 35,000-line *Chevalier au cygne et Godefroid de Bouillon* (1356), the final reworking of the cycle.

R. Thomas McDonald

[See also: CRUSADE CYCLE; CRUSADES; LORRAINE]

Andressohn, John Carl. *The Ancestry and Life of Godfrey of Bouillon.* Bloomington: Indiana University Press, 1947.

GODEFROI DE CLAIR (Godefroi de Huy; d. 1175). A renowned metalworker active in the Meuse Valley during the third quarter of the 12th century, Godefroi de Clair is reputed to have worked for the emperors Lothair II and Conrad III. Although many works have been attributed to him, such as the base of the Cross of Saint-Omer (Saint-Omer, Musée) no documented pieces survive. He may be the goldsmith addressed in a famous exchange of letters between Abbot Willibald of Stavelot and a "Dear Son G," in which the abbot requests objects be delivered that were long overdue and the artist requests payment. Godefroi was a canon in Huy when he died in 1175.

Robert G. Calkins

[See also: ENAMELING; JEWELRY AND METALWORKING]

Collon-Gevaert, Suzanne. *Histoire des arts du métal en Belgique.* Brussels: Palais des Académies, 1951, p. 149. [With bibliography.]

———, Jean Lejeune, and Jacques Stiennon. *A Treasury of Romanesque Art: Metalwork, Illuminations and Sculpture from the Valley of the Meuse.* New York: Phaidon, 1972, pp. 83–84.

Davis-Weyer, Caecilia. *Early Medieval Art 300–1150: Sources and Documents in the History of Art.* Englewood Cliffs: Prentice-Hall, 1971, pp. 170–72.

von Falke, Otto, and Heinrich Frauberger. *Deutsche Schmelzarbeiten des Mittelalters und andere Kunstwerke der Kunst-Historischen Ausstellung zu Dusseldorf 1902.* Frankfurt am Main: Baer, 1904, pp. 61–87.

GODEFROI OF SAINT-VICTOR (ca. 1125–after 1194).

Godefroi of Saint-Victor (not to be confused with another Augustinian canon of the late 12th century, Geoffroy of Breteuil) seems to have studied the Trivium in Paris for some years between 1140 and 1155, when Adam du Petit-Pont was active. By 1160, he had entered the abbey of Saint-Victor, where he received his theological and monastic training. Imbued with the intellectually robust spirit of Hugh and Richard of Saint-Victor, Godefroi found himself forced to leave the abbey under the priorship of Walter, ca. 1180. After Walter's death, Godefroi (ca. 1190) returned and remained at the abbey until his own death.

His liturgical poetry includes verses dedicated to St. Augustine and to the Virgin Mary. Over thirty sermons for feast days survive. Godefroi's major theological works are *Fons philosophiae* and *Microcosmus.* The former, written in 1178, is an elaborate description in verse of a course of study in the liberal arts, Scripture, and theology in Paris, and is much indebted to the program of Hugh of Saint-Victor's *Didascalicon.* The *Microcosmus* contains a moral interpretation of the biblical story of Creation and a consideration of divine grace and will vis-à-vis human desires and emotions. Godefroi develops numerous parallels between human beings (the *microcosmus*) and the created world (*megacosmus*). He strove to give a positive value to nature (as created and as "fallen"), to the human body, to the so-called "mechanical arts," and to classical Roman authors and especially their ethical teaching. This evoked opposition from Walter of Saint-Victor, who brought about Godefroi's ten-year exile to a rural priory. He also wrote on the eucharist and on the symbolic meaning of the parts of Christ's body.

Godefroi's was one of the last voices in the Victorine chorus that sang the praises of what might be styled 12th-century humanism: a protest against the regnant opinion of body-soul dualism and an affirmation of the harmony of nature and grace in Christian life.

Mark Zier

[See also: HUGH OF SAINT-VICTOR; SAINT-VICTOR, ABBEY AND SCHOOL OF; WALTER OF SAINT-VICTOR]

Godefroi of Saint-Victor. *Fons philosophiae,* ed. Pierre Michaud-Quantin. Namur: Godenne, 1956

———. *The Fountain of Philosophy: A Translation of the Twelfth-Century Fons philosophiae of Godfrey of Saint Victor,* trans. Edward A. Synan. Toronto: Pontifical Institute of Mediaeval Studies, 1972.

———. *Godefroy de Saint-Victor: Microcosmus. Texte,* ed. Philippe Delhaye. Lille: Facultés Catholiques, 1951.

Bonnard, Fourier. *Histoire de l'abbaye royale et de l'ordre des chanoines réguliers de Saint-Victor de Paris.* 2 vols. Paris: Savaète, 1907.

Delhaye, Philippe. *Le Microcosmus de Godefroy de Saint-Victor: étude théologique.* Lille: Facultés Catholiques, 1951.

———. "Les sermons de Godefroy de Saint-Victor: leur tradition manuscrite." *Recherches de théologie ancienne et médiévale* 21 (1954): 194–210.

GODFREY OF FONTAINES (d. 1304).

Born near Liège, Godfrey studied at Paris under Henry of Ghent and was a regent master in theology there from 1285 to 1295. He was also canon of Liège, Tournai, and Paris and provost of Saint-Séverin of Cologne. Although elected bishop of Tournai in 1300, he renounced his claims to the episcopate. Both Godfrey and Henry of Ghent actively engaged in the debate between the secular clergy and the mendicant orders, opposing the privileges of the latter. Highly critical of the Augustinian school, Godfrey is generally regarded as an Aristotelian and a Thomist. Although open to Aristotelian thought, he was an independent thinker and differed with Aquinas on a number of issues. Unlike Aquinas, for instance, Godfrey denied the real distinction between essence and existence. No single work sets forth completely either his theology or philosophy; his writings address such subjects as existence, the discord between the mendicants and the secular clergy, and the condemnation by Étienne Tempier, bishop of Paris, in 1277 of 219 theses of the Aristotelian school. Thus, Godfrey's system of thought is integrated with and emerges from his observations on controversial issues of the late 13th century. His major works are his fifteen *Quodlibeta,* composed during his regency and considered a masterpiece in quodlibetical literature.

E. Kay Harris

[See also: ÉTIENNE TEMPIER; HENRY OF GHENT]

Godfrey of Fontaines. *Quodlibeta.* In *Les philosophes belges,* ed. Maurice de Wulf, A. Pelzer, Jean Hoffmans, and Odon Lottin. 5 vols. Louvain: Institut Supérieur de Philosophie, 1904–37.

Wippel, John F. *The Metaphysical Thought of Godfrey of Fontaines: A Study in Late Thirteenth-Century Philosophy.* Washington, D.C.: Catholic University of America Press, 1981.

GOLDEN FLEECE.

The most successful lay order of knighthood founded in France and the principal model for all later orders of its type, the Order of the Golden Fleece (Fr. *Toison d'or*) was proclaimed in Bruges by Philip the Good, duke of Burgundy, on January 7, 1430. Endowed with statutes composed by Jehan Germain on the occasion of its first meeting in Lille on November 30, 1431, it functioned under those statutes, as amended from time to time, until its last meeting in 1559. The order was the first of the fully neo-Arthurian monarchical type to be founded anywhere for half a century, and its statutes were based on those of the two earlier orders still surviving in 1430: the Garter of England (1344/49) and the Collar of Savoy (1364). The order thus took the form of a cooptative corporate society of nobly born lay knights, or "companions" (at first twenty-five, in 1433 raised to thirty), including a hereditary "Chief and Sovereign" (the duke of Burgundy), four corporate officers (chancellor, treasurer, registrar, and king of arms), a corporate seal, a corporate chapel (in the ducal palace at Dijon) in which each companion had his own stall marked with his arms, and a college of canons (initially equal in number to the companions), whose principal function was to offer up prayers and Masses on the companions' behalf. The companions of the order had obligations both to their sovereign and to one another, in life and after death, and the whole order met in occasional (until 1445, annual) "assemblies," which consisted of a business meeting, or "chapter," a banquet, and religious services. The companions wore at all times a collar composed of metallic representations of the ducal badge of a B-shaped *fusil*, or firesteel, and a flint spewing flames, from which depended an effigy of the golden fleece captured by Jason and the Argonauts.

Like its English model, the Order of the Golden Fleece was founded partly to reward and promote chivalrous behavior among its sovereign's noble subjects (especially loyalty to the crown) and partly to increase the prestige of its sovereigns themselves by portraying them in the image of Arthur or Jason at the head of a company of highborn heroes. It was also intended, however, to secure the active service of its companions and to unite the leading members of the separate and formerly antagonistic nobilities of the various Burgundian principalities in the bonds of fraternity.

D'A. Jonathan D. Boulton

[See also: CHIVALRY; LAY ORDERS OF CHIVALRY; PHILIP THE GOOD]

Boulton, D'A.J.D. *The Knights of the Crown: The Monarchical Orders of Knighthood in Later Medieval Europe, 1325–1520.* Woodbridge: Boydell, 1987.

Hommel, Luc. *L'histoire du noble ordre de la Toison d'or.* Brussels: Éditions Universitaires, 1947.

Kervyn de Lettenhove, H. *La Toison d'or.* 2nd ed. Brussels: van Oest, 1907.

Reiffenberg, Baron de. *Histoire de l'ordre de la Toison d'or.* Brussels: Fonderie et Imprimerie Normale, 1830.

GOLDEN LEGEND. See *Legenda Aurea*

GOLEIN, JEAN (ca. 1320–1403). Charles V's most prolific translator, the Carmelite Jean Golein was a master of theology at the University of Paris and an active participant in the university debates over the Great Schism. His translations for the king include the *Flores chronicorum* (*Fleur des chroniques*) and other works by Bernard Gui

(1368), a *Vie de sainte Agnès* (before 1369), the *Collations de Cassien* (1370), Guillaume Durand's *Rationale divinorum officiorum* (1372–74), and the *De informatione principium* (*Livre d'informacion des princes*, 1379).

Wendy E. Pfeffer

[See also: LIBRARIES; SCHISM, GREAT; TRANSLATION]

Delisle, Léopold. *Recherches sur la librairie de Charles V, roi de France 1337–1380.* Paris, 1907, pp. 94–104.

GORMONT ET ISEMBART. An Anglo-Norman fragment of 661 assonanced octosyllables, transcribed in the 13th century and preserved in Brussels, Bibl. Roy. de Belgique, II. 181, *Gormont et Isembart* contains the final episodes of a battle in which the Saracen king Gormont fells every French baron who dares measure swords with him; finally, he is slain by King Louis. Louis, however, ruptures his own midriff and dies several weeks later. The renegade Isembart rallies the Saracens but is killed after four days of a raging battle in which he even unhorses his own father; in the last moments of his life, he reconverts to Christianity.

The whole plot is known thanks to lines 14,053–296 of Philippe Mouskés's *Chronique rimée* (before 1243) and Book 3 of the 1437 German translation of a prose rendering (1405) of a long romance of the 14th century, *Lohier et Mallart.* According to these texts, Isembart (Lohier) is Louis's nephew, who, exiled by court intrigues, abandons his faith and takes refuge in England with the Viking king Gormont. Pushed by Isembart, Gormont lays waste to Isembert's own seigneuries, the Vimeu and the Ponthieu, and burns down the abbey of Saint-Riquier. Since in Geoffrey of Monmouth's *Historia regum Britanniae* (ca. 1136) Isembart already is Louis's nephew, and since the plot is summarized in Hariulf's *Chronique de l'abbaye de Saint-Riquier* (1088), the legend must have originated in the 11th century, possibly even immediately after Louis III's victory over the Vikings at Saucourt-en-Vimeu (August 3, 881). The poem itself must have been composed between 1140 and 1150, probably in the region southwest of Paris.

Hans-Erich Keller

[See also: PHILIPPE MOUSKÉS]

Bayot, Alphonse, ed. *Gormant et Isembart: fragment de chanson de geste du XIIe siècle.* 3rd ed. Paris: Champion, 1931.

Lonigan, Paul R. *The "Gormont et Isembart": Problems and Interpretation of an Old French Epic.* Ann Arbor: UMI, 1976.

Nichols, Stephen G., Jr. "Style and Structure in *Gormont et Isembart.*" *Romania* 84 (1963): 500–35.

Pauphilet, Albert. "Sur la chanson d'Isembart." *Romania* 50 (1924): 169–94.

Vries, Jan de. "La chanson de *Gormont et Isembart.*" *Romania* 80 (1959): 34–62.

GOTHIA. The region called Gothia was one of the major divisions of Carolingian and post-Carolingian Gaul, comprising the coastal region along the Mediterranean from the Rhône to the Pyrénées. It was identical with the earlier Septimania and with the county of Toulouse formed the future Languedoc. The region preserved a strong sense of its Roman and Visigothic past after its annexation by Pepin the Short in the 750s, and it came to be referred to as Gothia as well as Septimania. Its nobles were conscious of being a distinct people, Goths, within the Frankish kingdom, and Visigothic law was observed there for centuries after its incorporation by the Carolingians, under whose rule it was usually a separate administrative unit, as a county, duchy, or march.

In the early Carolingian period, Gothia was frequently linked with the march of Toulouse or the Spanish March, but in the mid-9th century it emerged as a separate march. However, in 924 it was annexed by Raymond III, count of Toulouse, and it remained among the holdings of his successors, who carried the title marquis of Gothia. The population and culture of Gothia soon blended with those of the other Toulousan territories, and by the end of the 11th century Languedoc had emerged.

Steven Fanning

[See also: LANGUEDOC; SEPTIMANIA]

Dhondt, Jan. *Études sur la naissance des principautés territoriales en France (IXe–Xe siècles)*. Bruges: De Tempel, 1948.

Kienast, Walther. *Studien über die französische Volksstämme des Frühmittelalters*. Stuttgart: Hiersemann, 1968, pp. 74–88.

Lewis, Archibald. *The Development of Southern French and Catalan Society, 718–1050*. Austin: University of Texas Press, 1965.

GOTHIC ARCHITECTURE. The term "Gothic," first derisively applied by Italian Renaissance writers, is still the accepted designation for the last phase of medieval art and architecture, lasting from ca. 1140 to ca. 1525. The period is usually divided into four parts, based (incorrectly) on the organic model of growth: Early Gothic (ca. 1140–95); High Gothic (ca. 1195–1225/30); Rayonnant (ca. 1225/30–ca. 1400); and Flamboyant (ca. 1400–1525).

The development of the Gothic style is usually analyzed in terms of specific elements, such as round or pointed arches, rib vaults, tribune galleries, wall passages and triforia, flying buttresses, elevations, and plans. More important than such constructional features, which can also be traced in Romanesque architecture, was the change in the way builders worked within their architectural vocabularies. Prior to the rebuilding of parts of the abbey of Saint-Denis beginning ca. 1140, builders generally borrowed features, more or less unchanged, from other building projects. Builders in the generations that followed Saint-Denis more and more integrated borrowed elements into the total design. It is the cognitive shift and the increasingly comprehensive design sense, together with the unified architectural space in which the parts are subsumed within the whole, that set Early Gothic apart from Romanesque. The change occurred as a series of experiments,

not as an absolute solution. The surviving structures resist easy synthesis and suggest that we must appreciate the staggering variety of experimentation, the excitement of discovery, and the intellectual ferment that resulted in the extraordinary range of Early Gothic architecture; there are as many directions and trends as there are buildings. With the acceptance of a pluralistic approach, we move closer to the reality of the extraordinary variety that characterized the period.

"Early Gothic" is the generally accepted designation for the first phase of the French Gothic style, lasting from its beginning at Saint-Denis, ca. 1140, until the reconstruction of the cathedral of Notre-Dame of Chartres, begun in 1194. The Early Gothic style was initially confined to the areas in and around Paris and those under royal control but quickly lost its Parisian association with the Capetian kings. Architecture ceased to be a craft and became a discipline in the new chevet at Saint-Denis, dedicated in 1144. For the first time, medieval architecture became something other than the sum of a series of parts or sequence of units. The important conceptual shift in the thinking of the second builder at Saint-Denis is that for the first time he faced the challenge of creating an inner spaciousness that fused separate but contiguous units into a single architectural entity. The success of the east end of Saint-Denis lies in the creation and direct expression of a visual logic in the arrangement of every architectural element and a subordination of elements to the unified, total space. In the decade or so following the dedication of the east end of Saint-Denis in 1144, we can find a number of buildings that respond to it in a variety of ways. With few exceptions, the builders react as did builders of previous generations and borrow elements from Saint-Denis in random fashion or attempt to "copy" the east end as they understood it.

The other important achievement of this period is the cathedral of Sens, the first large-scale Gothic space. Detailed analysis of the north wall of the ambulatory at Sens permits us to observe many small changes in the design made during construction, all of them "responses" to Saint-Denis. Sens differs most from Saint-Denis in the large size and ambitious scale of its volumes. The visual logic of the east end of Saint-Denis is explored in varying degrees in other buildings started in the decade 1145–55, such as the cathedrals of Senlis and Noyon, and the new chevet of the abbey church of Saint-Germain-des-Prés in Paris.

The next decade is characterized by experiments in both size and scale, as well as explorations in the creation and application of the system of visual logic that Bony terms the "Gothic grid." Chief among the surviving buildings are the cathedrals of Paris and Laon, four-story elevations that achieve both real and apparent height, respectively. Equally important were the two cathedrals of Cambrai and Arras, now destroyed, massive buildings in which many novel effects of design were explored. The decade also witnessed an increase in the adaptation of Romanesque structural features and solutions to the Gothic vocabulary.

Advanced thinking in the decade ca. 1165–75 is characterized by daring experiments in voiding the wall with

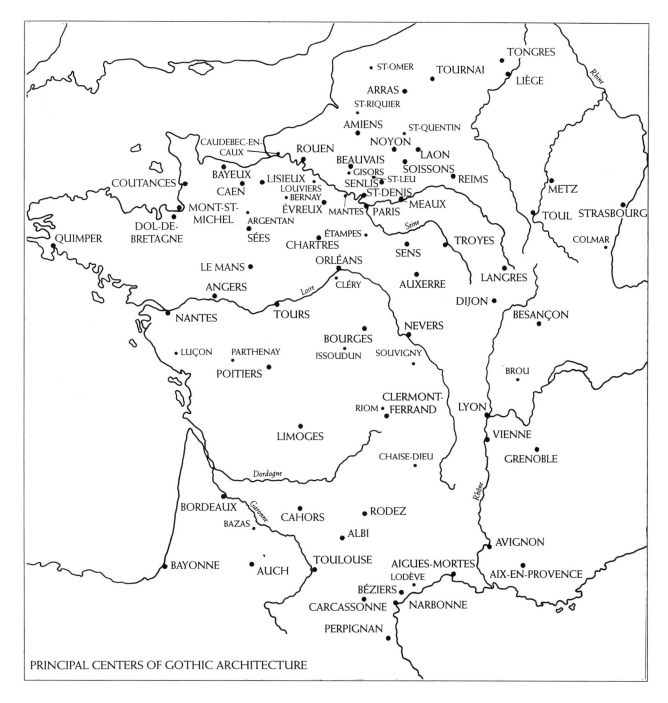

PRINCIPAL CENTERS OF GOTHIC ARCHITECTURE

superposed passages and arcade screens, as in the transept arms of Noyon, the transept chapels at Laon, and the interior of the façade of Saint-Remi at Reims. The period ca. 1175–85 saw those experiments continued but usually on a more modest scale than at Paris or Cambrai, both of which were over 100 feet tall on the interior. Perhaps the most important change that took place in this decade was the systematic application of the flying buttress to the exteriors. The flying buttresses constructed at the lower level of the nave at Notre-Dame in Paris were the first examples to suggest the full potential of the feature. From the moment of their appearance, probably ca. 1175, they had a profound impact on builders and were quickly incorporated at such sites as Mantes, Saint-Remi at Reims, and Canterbury. The evidence suggests that they were added after the fact in a number of other cases, such as the nave at Laon. So profound was the impact of the flying buttress that other structural experimentation for all intents and purposes ceased. The decade ca. 1185–95 saw the continuation of the experiments of the previous decade and was again dominated by the flying buttress. The vocabulary of design solutions was broadened and made ever more complex through the sheer number of buildings, large and small, that were undertaken, but no major new features were introduced.

With the rebuilding of Chartres, begun after the fire of 1194, and of Bourges (ca. 1195), the lines of experimentation can be said to have reached two different but equally important ends. Chartres in particular is separated by scholars from Early Gothic and considered the beginning of a new stylistic trend, commonly called "High Gothic." "High Gothic" is the term for what has long been considered the "classic" moment in French Gothic architecture, that series of cathedrals built in northern France between 1195 and ca. 1225/30. In English, the term carries the added connotation of height. By general agreement, High Gothic begins with the reconstruction of Chartres following the fire of 1194 and continues, for some, with Bourges, begun in 1195, or more often with Soissons, now thought to predate Chartres; then Reims, begun after the fire of 1208, followed by the nave of Amiens, begun by Robert de Luzarches 1218–20, and the chevet of Beauvais, begun ca. 1225.

One can argue with equal validity that Chartres, Bourges, and Soissons, along with others usually excluded, represent the final flowering and full variety of possible solutions available to builders after a half-century of extraordinary architectural experimentation. Bony has characterized Chartres as a radical simplification of ideas from a variety of earlier sources. The design of Soissons is another sort of simplification, but one still firmly rooted in previous experiments. In this line of reasoning, Bourges represents the ultimate complexity coming out of these same experiments. In short, all three are the continuation of Early Gothic experiments.

The importance of Chartres has been exaggerated, both because of its identification during the 19th century as the most sacred shrine of the Virgin in France and because of its proximity to Paris. Its stylistic impact is confined largely to Reims; but the latter's importance as the source for the simplified three-story elevation incorporating bar-tracery windows and double tiers of flying buttresses topped by pinnacles is incontestable. As a solution, the design of Reims is less radical than those adopted at Chartres, Soissons, or Bourges. If it is recognized that the elements at Reims constituted refinements to existing techniques and designs, it, too, becomes the product of builders with full knowledge of previous experiments. The only "dislocation" concerns the cathedrals of Amiens and Beauvais, both of which, but most especially Amiens, are usually included in the "High Gothic" canon. If we recognize, however, that both designs exhibit significant shifts in interest from those of Chartres, Soissons, Bourges, and Reims, even while being influenced by them, then the realization that both herald the new decorative complexity of the Rayonnant becomes possible. Such a reorganization does not privilege them over later Rayonnant solutions any more than over such precedents as Reims; rather, it restores to them a measure of originality.

Thus, it is time to question the whole concept of "High Gothic" and to discard both the deterministic models and concepts of stylistic development based on organic models, as well as value judgments that privilege one aspect of a style above another. The continued use of the construct prejudices an understanding of the Rayonnant as a distinct and independent architectural development based on different values. If we discard the notion of the classic moment of the Gothic style in favor of an understanding of early 13th-century buildings continuing the rich tradition of experimentation, then structures previously relegated to the sidelines and excluded from the "High Gothic" assume their places as varied accomplishments in their own right.

Like most stylistic terms, even "Gothic" itself, "Rayonnant" is a misnomer. Chosen in the 19th century because the rose window was seen as typifying the style, it has come to stand for the new direction in Gothic architecture that manifests itself ca. 1225–30. Rayonnant is the result of a variety of experiments that seem to crystallize in and around Paris, but they would not have been possible without knowledge of comparable experiments at Amiens, Troyes, Saint-Nicaise at Reims, and even Royaumont. The Rayonnant is characterized by a new exploration of the applications of geometry in the design of window tracery and the systematic application of the principles of window-tracery design to the entire building, inside and out. Since the design principles are derived from the elegant screens of window tracery, the emphasis is linear and flat, with a sense of apparent fragility and brittleness, together with an incisive analytical elegance. The fragility of window tracery is nevertheless an illusion that results from its linear qualities and thinness: these thin screens of ornament have withstood countless storms since their creation.

The linear complexity leads to an abrupt and systematic change of emphasis. All of the ornament is on these thin screens of tracery; all forms of plasticity are rejected. The compound piers of Reims and Chartres become the attenuated linear piers of the nave of Saint-Denis. The linear value of the piers runs up the wall, every layer of which receives the same unified treatment of incisively carved yet delicate ornament. The substantial wall structures of previous generations have disintegrated into layers of the thinnest possible tracery. Even wall passages cease to convey depth, because their two surfaces are sharply delineated units of surface pattern superimposed in front of one another. Density and mass even disappear on the exterior, as all surfaces are covered with elegant tracery or thinned down by sheets of tracery gables. The buildings become thin, elegant, elongated, and miraculously insubstantial, as at the Sainte-Chapelle in Paris or Saint-Urbain at Troyes. The patterns are rational, logical, and neat—ceaseless explorations of the almost infinite number of possible patterns to be derived from experiments with the geometry of circles, squares, and triangles. Design becomes a logical process in which a series of similar patterns may be repeated and manipulated through a variety of sizes and scales.

In addition to the extraordinary facility of design found in the Rayonnant, other factors must be considered. The development of elaborate patterns of tracery ornament in the later 1220s and 1230s is matched by a decrease in the size and scale of the buildings, which serves to make the patterns visible, just as the broad double aisles and pyramidal elevations of buildings like Paris and Bourges are abandoned in favor of simpler, more concentrated plans that allow the outer windows to be brought closer to the central space. The result is greater light on the interior from larger windows filled with more complex tracery patterns. The period reveals an almost quantum leap forward in the handling of design complexities, as well as in the carving of complex, multifaceted pieces that make up the tracery puzzle. There is a marked preference for hard, fine-grained limestone that lends itself to fine carving, and we can speculate that there must also have been an explosive development in the production of tools capable of producing the detail demanded. Lastly, there are the economic considerations.

Beginning in the mid-1220s, western Europe entered what is termed a "Little Ice Age," when temperatures year-round grew noticeably colder. Lower temperatures wreaked havoc on agriculture, particularly in northern France, where wine production, heretofore a major industry, practically disappeared. Only the cloth-producing towns in the north escaped economic disaster. In this economic climate, it is important to note that, for all of the complexity of tracery and richness of pattern, a building in the "Rayonnant" style actually requires less stone for construction than an Early Gothic building. The difference becomes clear, for example, if we compare a cross-section and elevation of the nave of Saint-Denis with those of Laon. While they are about the same height, the nave of Saint-Denis is wider yet required only about one-third the stone needed to construct a comparable area at Laon. In addition, the Rayonnant structure seems not only lighter and more open but achieves a greater sense of spatial mystery and illusion.

The Rayonnant period also witnessed a shrinking in scale and complexity that not only reflects the economic realities but serves to make the design itself more visible. And some of the designs were becoming, if less complex, hardly less elegant. The church of Saint-Martin-aux-Bois, for example, has a much simpler and more concentrated plan without an elaborate chevet but uses tall, thin windows surrounded by large areas of masonry. Still, through a skillful juxtaposition of height and narrowness, the builder achieved an elegance of statement. The innumerable Franciscan and Dominican churches of the later 13th and succeeding centuries will use these same principles of design. Their compact preaching halls will eschew elaborate chevet plans in favor of simple apses and will have tall, thin windows in large wall surfaces.

Another important aspect of the Rayonnant is the development of distinctive regional styles, both as a reflection of the creative possibilites inherent in the tracery patterns and as a return to structural systems typical of particular areas. It was common in Normandy, for example, to find wall passages in front of the clerestory windows, as in the Norman Gothic chevets at Bayeux and Coutances or in the church at Norrey. But wall passages in front of clerestory windows were even more common in Norman Romanesque churches from Cerisy-la-Forêt and Saint-Étienne at Caen, as well as in occasional Early Gothic buildings like La Trinité at Fécamp. As was the case in other areas,

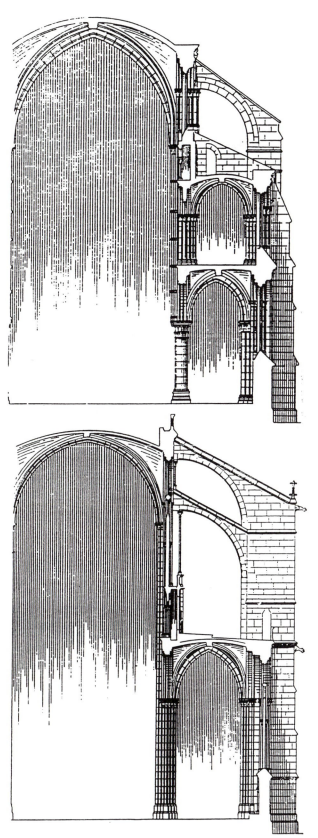

Comparison of the nave sections of Laon cathedral and Saint-Denis. After Dehio.

the traditional structural systems of Romanesque Normandy were updated in the Rayonnant Gothic and outfitted with elaborate tracery patterns in the windows and wall-passage screens to create the distinctive Norman Gothic style.

A similar interest in older structural systems updated and sheathed in complex tracery patterns characterizes the regional styles of Burgundy and Champagne. One thinks of the superposed passages of the apse of Saint-Amand-sur-Fion, which must be a reflection of the design complexity of Saint-Nicaise at Reims, which in turn picks up the lower-level passage in front of windows seen at both Saint-Remi and the cathedral of Reims. Likewise, in Burgundy the distinctive regional variant of Rayonnant Gothic usually includes passages in association with windows, as at Auxerre cathedral, Notre-Dame at Dijon, and the elegant church at Semur-en-Auxois.

In the south, the Romanesque single-nave tradition of Languedoc provided the inspiration for comparable Gothic spatial experiments at Toulouse cathedral, among others. And some of the Angevin experiments with single naves and complex, domed vaults culminates in the extraordinary lightness and openness of Saint-Serge at Angers and Candes, among others, in this particularly experimental region. In short, the regional styles all seem to have more to do with updating older traditions in a climate that favored experimentation in structure and design than with creating styles in reaction to what was emanating from the royal domain.

Discarding the outmoded concept of "High Gothic" and reevaluating Rayonnant Gothic as an equally valid but different approach to design and decoration also permits us to rethink the assessments of previous generations with regard to the last phase of the Gothic style, called "Flamboyant" after the elegant reverse curves used in window tracery that produces patterns resembling tongues of flame. Past generations tended to dismiss the Flamboyant as "decadent" or "baroque." To do so fails to recognize two important aspects of Late Gothic. First, the Flamboyant exists side-by-side with the now conservative Rayonnant. In other words, the Flamboyant is a logical outgrowth of Rayonnant tracery patterns, an outgrowth that does not replace the older patterns but exists with them. More important, in the hands of talented builders the Flamboyant became the means to expand the limits of Gothic illusionism and to question the very tenets of architectural design.

The Hundred Years' War drained the French economy at every level. With resources stretched thin, building activity practically ceased. Many projects were abandoned or languished until the recovery in the late 15th century. Flamboyant tracery patterns began to appear in the last decades of the 14th century, but the major monuments would be created only after the end of the war and would be built in those areas most devastated by battles: Picardy, Champagne, Burgundy, the western valley of the Loire, and Normandy, as well as in Paris itself.

The most identifiable aspect of Flamboyant Gothic is the ogee, or reverse-curve, arch, which first appeared simply as one more variant in the rich Rayonnant vocabulary. But by the 15th-century recovery, the patterns had grown more complex and had begun to be used to impart a sense of dynamics to the lines of the buildings. The ogee arch and the resulting tracery patterns are used to define the style not only because they are so immediately identifiable but because they create a sense of continuous, sinuous movement across the window tracery or around the portals. This dynamism spread to the patterns of vault ribs and even to the design of piers. Abandoning the traditional visual and design limits imposed by the presence of bases and capitals, as well as the volumetrics resulting from colonnettes, the pier could become something dynamic in design with a plan of delicate scallops. The thin vertical lines swirl upward, twisting dramatically and seeming wildly to sprout vault ribs, as in the ambulatory of Saint-Séverin in Paris.

This extraordinary visual fantasy at the same time is accompanied by the increasingly "realistic" depiction of flora and fauna seemingly copied from nature. Already present in the decoration of the Sainte-Chapelle in Paris, this tendency flourished in the 15th century with the creation of designs based on ever more specific fruits, vegetables, and foliage now filled with exotic and monstrous animals whose realistic treatment belies their fantastic origins. The element of fantasy pervades architecture. In this new order, the transept gables of Notre-Dame at Paris become the dissolving openwork screens of Louviers or the façade of Saint-Maclou at Rouen. Visual limits are challenged by illusionary effects, piers without bases or capitals, vault ribs that sprout from walls, scatter across vaults like unchecked foliage and abruptly vanish into other ribs, piers, and walls.

Architectural space becomes more unified into total volumes but also more visionary and illusionistic. In eastern France and in Champagne, this was achieved by using the hall-church scheme with aisles equal or nearly equal in height to the main nave. But the illusionism might also rely on the tall, narrow proportions found in the Rayonnant, a design favored in Parisian churches. The Rayonnant visual linkage of upper zones that suggested a two-storied elevation became reality in such buildings as Notre-Dame at Cléry (1429–85), a royal church on the Loire, and later in Saint-Gervais (1494–1502) and Saint-Étienne du Mont in Paris (after 1494). Moulins cathedral, formerly a collegial church founded in 1468 for the dukes of Bourbon, repeats this Parisian scheme. In Normandy, the traditional three-story elevation is maintained, but the treatment of the second story as a tracery screen obscures its role as the front of a wall passage, as at Caudebec-en-Caux, Saint-Maclou at Rouen, or the new chevet of Mont-Saint-Michel. The extraordinary illusionism that redefines architectural space is not only international (Prague cathedral was begun by a French architect-builder, Matthew d'Arras), but resulted in a number of striking architectural fantasies: Notre-Dame at Cléry (patroned by Louis XI after 1467 and practically made into his private chapel); the church of Brou (1513–32), reflecting the intense love and devotion of Marguerite of Austria for her short-lived marriage to Philibert of Savoy; the pilgrimage church of Notre-Dame de l'Épine in Champagne (in the works in the 1440s); Saint-Pol-de-Léon (begun in 1429); and the rebuilding of Nantes cathedral (begun in 1434). The Flamboyant is the most neglected period of Gothic architecture because of the prejudices of past generations; but the neglect of these highly original and inventive architectural fantasies is unwarranted. The time has come to discard old conceptions and look anew at Late Gothic architecture.

William W. Clark

[See also: AMIENS; ANGERS; AUXERRE; BAYEUX; BOURGES; BROU; CHAMBIGES, MARTIN; CHARTRES; CLÉRY; CORMONT; COUTANCES; DIJON; ERWIN DE STEINBACH; GAUTIER DE VARINFROY; GOTHIC ART; JEAN DE CHELLES; LAON; L'ÉPINE; MENDICANT ART AND ARCHITECTURE; NANTES; NOYON; PARIS; PIERRE DE MONTREUIL; REIMS; ROBERT DE LUZARCHES; ROMANESQUE ARCHITECTURE; ROUEN; SAINT-DENIS; SENS; SOISSONS; TOULOUSE; TROYES]

Bechmann, Roland. *Les racines des cathédrales.* Paris: Payot, 1984.

Bony, Jean. *French Gothic Architecture of the Twelfth and Thirteenth Centuries.* Berkeley: University of California Press, 1983.

Branner, Robert, ed. *Gothic Architecture.* New York: Braziller, 1961.

Focillon, Henri. *The Art of the West,* ed. Jean Bony, 2 vols. Greenwich: New York Graphic Society, 1963.

Frankl, Paul. *The Gothic: Literary Sources and Interpretations Through Eight Centuries.* Princeton: Princeton University Press, 1960.

Grodecki, Louis. *Gothic Architecture.* New York: Abrams, 1978.

Kimpel, Dieter, and Robert Suckale. *Die gotische Architektur in Frankreich, 1130–1270.* Munich: Hirmer, 1985.

Le Goff, Jacques, and René Rémond. *Histoire de la France religieuse. I. Des dieux de la Gaule à la papauté d'Avignon.* Paris: Seuil, 1988.

Mark, Robert. *Gothic Structural Experimentation.* Cambridge: MIT, 1982.

Panofsky, Erwin. *Gothic Architecture and Scholasticism.* Latrobe: Archabbey, 1951.

Radding, Charles, and William W. Clark. *Medieval Architecture, Medieval Learning.* New Haven: Yale University Press, 1992.

Recht, Roland, et al. *Les bâtisseurs des cathédrales gothiques.* Strasbourg: Musées de la Ville de Strasbourg, 1989.

Sanfaçon, Roland. *L'architecture flamboyante en France.* Laval: Presses de l'Université de Laval, 1971.

Wilson, Christopher. *The Gothic Cathedral.* London: Thames and Hudson, 1990.

GOTHIC ART. The origins and development of French Gothic art are closely tied to architecture. Gothic cathedrals and chapels provided the structural context for monumental sculpture and stained glass. Metalwork, ivories, paintings in manuscripts or on panels, and textiles were the furnishings that complemented and completed both religious and secular architecture. The close alliance between architecture and the visual arts appears in the similarity of design principles based on geometric proportions and in representations of architectural motifs and structures in metalwork, ivories, stained glass, and painting.

The beginnings of the Gothic style in stained glass and sculpture are connected with Early Gothic architecture. The chevet of Saint-Denis (ca. 1144) contained stained-glass windows that not only were integral to the more skeletal structural principles but were also a key element in the aesthetics of light articulated by Abbot Suger. The west façade of Saint-Denis contained a sculptural program that represented a departure from Romanesque aesthetic. Two of the three portals had sculpted tympana (the third had a mosaic), and jamb statues were attached to the vertical supports. The placement of sculpture more logically reflected the vertical and horizontal divisions of the architecture, the figures had more spatial autonomy, and the iconographic program was more comprehensive.

Because of the destruction that Saint-Denis suffered during the Revolution, these new elements are best preserved on the west façade of Chartres cathedral (ca. 1150). The three-portal façade with jambs, tympana, and archivolts shows the new stylistic principles. In the central tympanum, the apocalyptic Christ displays a calm visage, and his body has a three-dimensional unity that softly falling drapery articulates. The jamb figures exhibit a tight columnar shape, but their forms are attached in front of the column and not confined within its frame, as was the practice in Romanesque sculpture. Above the portals are three stained-glass windows, famed for the beautiful colors of their glass, especially the blue.

The incipient monumentality of these Early Gothic examples of sculpture and stained glass became apparent in all media of French Gothic art in the years just preceding and following 1200. This period in French Gothic art goes by several names, including the "Year 1200 style" and *muldenfaltenstil* (or "damp-fold style") for the clinging drapery folds with characteristic hairpin loops that cover the figures. Monumental sculpture offers many examples of this stylistic phenomenon. Dating from ca. 1170, the west portal of Senlis cathedral, with the death, assumption, and coronation of the Virgin, clearly shows the plastic, three-dimensional quality of figures revealed through the soft draperies and the tender emotional expression. The north-transept portals at Chartres demonstrate a well-

Dormition of the Virgin. Sculpture from the central portal of the west façade of Senlis cathedral. 13th century. *Reprinted by permission of Giraudon/Art Resource, New York.*

developed version of this style ca. 1200. As sculptural workshops moved to different locations, the style extended to many outlying areas, such as Alsace. The Death of the Virgin tympanum on the south portal of Strasbourg cathedral, carved ca. 1225, is one of the most beautiful monuments of Gothic art. The graceful bodies are revealed through clinging drapery, and the expression of contained grief is especially moving.

The Year 1200 style is evident in other media as well. The formal relationships of metalwork and sculpture make the style especially apparent in altarpieces and reliquaries

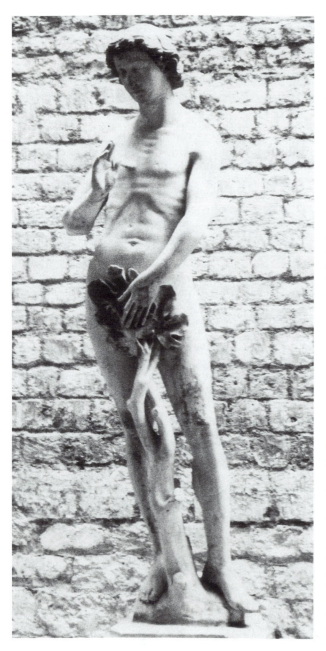

Adam, sculpture from interior of transept of the cathedral of Notre Dame, Paris. 14th century. *Photograph courtesy of Rebecca A. Baltzer.*

by the goldsmith Nicolas de Verdun. Two of his famous works, the Klosterneuburg Altar and the Shrine of the Three Kings at Cologne, display the supple bodies, plastic forms, and clinging drapery. In manuscript illumination, a famous example is the *Ingeborg Psalter,* possibly made in north France ca. 1190 for the second wife of King Philip Augustus, whom he repudiated immediately after their marriage. The monumental figures stand out almost in relief against burnished gold grounds. They have the elongated faces and draperies that fall in looping folds as they articulate and model the substantial bodies.

The first half of the 13th century was a creative period in French Gothic art. It was the time when the great French cathedrals—Chartres, Amiens, Reims, and others—were being built. Sculpture, stained glass, manuscripts, metalwork, and ivories were all components of the cathedral as a multimedia ensemble. Because of factors of time and economics, however, few of these artistic projects were completed as a unified stylistic entity. In addition, destruction and dispersal of these components through the centuries make total reconstruction of any of these monuments virtually impossible.

Chartres cathedral preserves the most unified example of sculpture and stained glass *in situ.* In both cases, stylistic changes occurred from the early to mid-13th century. While much of the sculpture on the north- and south-transept portals reflects the classicizing Year 1200 Style, some of the sculpture of the south porch, which is closer to 1240, displays a style in which the drapery folds are heavier and more angular. Likewise, the earlier lancet windows of the lower story in the nave are medallion windows with linear rendering of drapery and faces. Newer styles in stained-glass composition appear in the clerestory, chevet, and especially the transept, with rose windows and single figures in lancets.

This period witnessed considerable overlapping of styles. The basic features of the Year 1200 style continued well into the century, as seen in such manuscripts as the *Bible moralisée* of ca. 1230 and the *Psalter of Blanche of Castile* associated with the royal court. The layout with superimposed scenes in medallions and the vestiges of the soft drapery with looped folds reveal connections with the Year 1200 style. The drapery, however, is heavier and more broadly linear in its articulation. In sculpture, the Judgment portal on the west façade of Notre-Dame in Paris also shows the weighty angular drapery. The crisp, heavy drapery style appears with greater uniformity in the well-preserved sculpture of the three-portal west façade of Amiens cathedral, also dated ca. the 1230s.

These new stylistic directions converged with the advent of Rayonnant architecture ca. the 1230s, particularly in Paris. The Sainte-Chapelle, the French court chapel, dedicated in 1248, is an outstanding example of the merging of media. The chapel itself is on a smaller scale and gives the impression of being a reliquary turned outside in. In the upper story, the walls have dissolved into a linear skeleton, leaving the stained-glass panels as the surface elements. These tall, thin windows are composed of scenes in medallions. The figure style emphasizes fine lines, delicate features, and angular drapery. The wall surfaces are painted and gilded with decorative patterns. Sculptural figures of the Apostles are now placed on the interior. Their poses have a swaying contrapposto that is accentuated by the play of V-shaped drapery folds. The focal point of the chapel was a great metalwork reliquary to house the relics of the Passion that Louis IX had acquired. It no longer survives, but representations of it show that it repeated the stylistic features of the chapel's architecture and decoration.

Manuscript illumination connected with the Parisian court reflects similar characteristics. As in the St. Louis Psalter or the Sainte-Chapelle Evangeliaries, the figures are placed under architectural arcades that are painted versions of the Rayonnant style. The figures are animated and elegant, with delicate features and complex, usually linear, patterns of drapery folds.

By the beginning of the 14th century, new stylistic tendencies were becoming established in French Gothic art. These interconnected developments included continuing emphasis on smaller scale; use of softer colors; interest in narrative, especially in depicting emotional interaction among figures; and depiction of a more concrete spatial setting for scenes.

In sculpture, the monumental encyclopedic programs of large cathedrals were replaced by smaller freestanding figures in chapels or on altars. The most popular subject became the Virgin and Child. Regardless of media—stone, ivory, or metal—the most familiar representation was the Virgin standing in an exaggerated S-curve pose balancing the small infant Christ child on her hip. The delicate, smiling facial features and complex play of drapery folds created a regal but human figure.

The Virgin and Child or other standing saints were frequent themes in stained glass as well, particularly in Normandy, where a number of examples survive. Painted architectural canopies created connections with the structural setting. *Grisaille* glass and more pastel colors infused buildings with a brighter light that helped to define the increasingly linear quality of architectural details.

The interest in artistic narrative increased. Narrative cycles became more extensive, and the scenes often became more densely crowded with figures. The range of subjects also expanded. Devotional practices associated with popular piety broadened the interest in depicting biblical narrative with an emphasis on Christ's life and passion, as well as saints' lives. The popularity of vernacular literature also promoted illustration of these secular themes, often in lengthy cycles for such works as Arthurian romances. All of these subjects were popular in ivory carvings on polyptychs as well as luxury items, such as boxes, combs, and mirrors.

In manuscript illumination, these elements found their fullest expression. Manuscripts of vernacular literature often contained vivid illustrations of the themes recounted in the text. Devotional manuscripts, especially books of hours, became popular. Jean Pucelle, whose *œuvre* extends from ca. 1320 to 1336, expanded the artistic range of manuscript illumination. In his small book of hours for Jeanne d'Évreux, queen of France, he used a *grisaille* painting technique to endow his figures with a three-dimensional

presence characteristic of sculpture. His scenes, such as the Annunciation, began to situate the figures within believable spatial interiors. He also heightened the emotional level, as seen in the grieving spectators at the Crucifixion and Entombment.

By the middle of the 14th century, realism began to replace courtly elegance in the visual arts. This tendency is most apparent in two areas, portraiture and landscape. Charles V (r. 1364–80) gave particular encouragement to the development of portraiture. The king, with his clearly distinguishable features, especially a long, prominent nose, was depicted in many media. Numerous portraits of Charles V are found in illuminated manuscripts in depictions of the presentation of the book to the king. Although fewer panel paintings survive, this medium experienced a revival, and portrait panels, such as the one of John II the Good (r. 1350–64) in the Louvre, are representative of this artistic trend. Sculptural representations include a pair of figures of Charles V and his queen, Jeanne de Bourbon, now in the Louvre. Portraits also became fashionable in tomb sculpture. One of the most outstanding sepulchral ensembles is the portal sculpture, Moses Well, and tomb of Philip the Bold, duke of Burgundy, at the Chartreuse de Champmol at Dijon, dated ca. 1400. The sculptor, Claus Sluter, created figures whose lifelike veracity enhanced powerful subtlety of expression.

Annunciation, book of hours (Normandy?), 1230s. M92, fol. 1v. *Courtesy of the Pierpont Morgan Library, New York.*

Jean Bondol, Annunciation, Gotha Missal, ca. 1375. Fol. 110. *Courtesy of the Cleveland Museum of Art, Cleveland.*

Realism of landscape setting was also developed in French painting from around the middle of the 14th century. By the early decades of the 15th century, manuscript illumination placed figures in landscape settings with considerable depth, a sense of aerial perspective, and attention to detail. The calendar miniatures by the Limbourg brothers in the *Très Riches Heures*, one of many luxurious manuscripts illuminated for John, duke of Berry, in the early 15th century, are the epitome of these features. The landscape scenes of seasonal activities not only utilize techniques for showing spatial recession but also are so realistic that they include accurate renderings of the duke's numerous castles.

The Limbourg brothers and Claus Sluter typify another aspect of Late Gothic art in France: the influence of styles and employment of artists from across Europe. The Limbourgs and Sluter came from one major artistic center, the Low Countries; southern Europe, especially Italy, exercised a particularly strong influence in southern France, where the Avignon papacy in the 14th century had encouraged the residence of Italian artists who decorated the papal palace. Paris remained important in late-medieval art, but other regions asserted equally strong artistic traditions. In Normandy, renewed architectural activity after the Hundred Years' War brought a resurgence of stained-glass projects in which realism of figure style and details was manifested in the muted colors of the glass.

Illuminated manuscripts, especially devotional books and works of vernacular literature, remained popular. The development of oil painting and the advent of printing, however, caused a decline in manuscript illumination in favor of panel painting, where realism of spatial perspective could be more fully developed. As economy and trade prospered, commercial centers, such as Lyon, created affluent middle-class patrons who could furnish their living quarters with tapestries as well as metalwork and ivory objects. The detailed realism of late French Gothic art continued into the early 16th century, when the classical influences of the Italian Renaissance brought the art of the Gothic era to an end.

Karen Gould

[See also: AMIENS; CHARTRES; ENAMELING; GOTHIC ARCHITECTURE; IVORIES; LIMBOURG BROTHERS; MANUSCRIPTS, PRODUCTION AND ILLUMINATION; JEWELRY AND METALWORKING; MARY, DEVOTION TO; NICHOLAS DE VERDUN; PARIS; PUCELLE, JEAN; REIMS; RELICS AND RELIQUARIES; SLUTER, CLAUS; STAINED GLASS; STRASBOURG; TAPESTRY]

Aubert, Marcel, et al. *Le vitrail français.* Paris: Deux Mondes, 1958.

Avril, François. *Manuscript Painting at the Court of France: The Fourteenth Century (1310–1380).* New York: Braziller, 1976.

Baron, Françoise, et al. *Les fastes du gothique: le siècle de Charles V.* Paris: Réunion des Musées Nationaux, 1981–82.

Branner, Robert. *Manuscript Painting in Paris During the Reign of Saint-Louis.* Berkeley: University of California Press, 1977.

Deuchler, Florens, and Konrad Hoffmann. *The Year 1200.* 2 vols. New York: Metropolitan Museum of Art, 1970.

Erlande-Brandenburg, Alain. *Gothic Art.* New York: Abrams, 1989.

Gaborit-Chopin, Danielle. *Ivoires du moyen âge.* Fribourg: Office du Livre, 1978.

Gauthier, Marie-Madeleine. *Émaux du moyen âge occidental.* Fribourg: Office du Livre, 1972.

Grodecki, Louis, and Catherine Brisac. *Gothic Stained Glass: 1200–1300.* Ithaca: Cornell University Press, 1985.

Koechlin, Raymond. *Les ivoires gothiques français.* 3 vols. Paris, 1924.

Lightbown, R. *Secular Goldsmith's Work in Medieval France: A History.* London: Society of Antiquaries, 1978.

Meiss, Millard. *French Painting in the Time of Jean de Berry.* 5 vols. New York: Phaidon and Braziller, 1967–74.

Plummer, John. *The Last Flowering: French Painting in Manuscripts 1420–1530.* New York: Pierpont Morgan Library, 1982.

Sauerlander, Willibald. *Gothic Sculpture in France, 1140–1270.* London: Thames and Hudson, 1970.

Sterling, Charles. *La peinture médiévale à Paris 1300–1500.* Paris: Bibliothèque des Arts, 1987.

Verdier, Philippe, et al. *Art and the Courts: France and England from 1259 to 1328.* Ottawa: National Gallery of Canada, 1972.

Wixom, William D. *Treasures from Medieval France.* Cleveland: Cleveland Museum of Art, 1967.

GOTTSCHALK (ca. 803–ca. 867/69). Saxon theologian and poet, author of works on predestination that aroused controversy in 9th-century France. Gottschalk was presented by his father, Berno, as an oblate to the Benedictine monastery of Fulda. His boyhood was spent at Fulda, where Rabanus Maurus was abbot, and at Reichenau. In 829, Gottschalk petitioned a church synod at Mainz to be released from his monastic vows, claiming that his profession had not been voluntary and was not binding since there had been no Saxon witnesses present. The synod agreed that Gottschalk could return to secular life but did not agree to return the inheritance given by his father to Fulda. Rabanus Maurus won a reversal of that decision at a synod at Worms. Gottschalk spent the next ten years at Orbais and Corbie, where he dedicated himself to a study of the writings of Augustine. He was ordained a priest in the late 830s, apparently without the approval of the bishop of Soissons, in whose jurisdiction such ordination rested.

During a pilgrimage to Rome in the 840s, Gottschalk taught and preached about predestination in Italy and the Balkans and made visits to Count Eberhard of Friuli and Bishop Noting of Brescia. News of Gottschalk's teachings provoked Rabanus Maurus, who compelled him to return to Francia. In 848, Gottschalk was condemned twice, at synods at Mainz and Quierzy-sur-Oise. The second synod ordered him whipped and imprisoned at the monastery of Hautvillers. His writings were burned, and his ordination to the priesthood was revoked. Gottschalk continued to write, principally on predestination, until his death. A number of influential theologians, including Florus of Lyon, Prudentius of Troyes, and Ratramnus of Corbie wrote in support of Gottschalk's ideas on predestination, although these views were condemned by such important ecclesiastical figures as Amalarius of Metz, Hincmar of Reims, Johannes Scottus Eriugena, and of course Rabanus Maurus. On an official level, Gottschalk's teachings were repeatedly condemned: at the synod of Quierzy-sur-Oise in 853 and at numerous other synods and national councils in the 850s and 860s. An appeal to Rome on Gottschalk's behalf made by Guntbert of Hautvillers in 866 was cut short by the death of Pope Nicholas I.

The theological position that led to this drama is difficult to reconstruct because of the fragmentary nature of Gottschalk's extant writings. It seems to have been a logical derivation from the late writings of Augustine, stressing the point that God had, from eternity, not only foreseen but also predestined either the salvation and damnation of every human being. What was absolutely unacceptable to his contemporaries was the conclusion that Jesus therefore died only for the saved, and that the sacraments, even baptism, were not efficacious for all.

In spite of the condemnation of his contemporaries and the increasingly harsh treatment he received, Gottschalk never renounced his position but continued to write, with increasing complexity, until his death. His later works include speculation on the eucharist, supporting the posi-

tion of Ratramnus of Corbie over that of Paschasius Radbertus; two works on the Trinity, apparently aimed against Hincmar of Reims, and lyrical poems that were especially innovative in their use of rhyme.

E. Ann Matter

[See also: FLORUS OF LYON; HINCMAR OF REIMS; PASCHASIUS RADBERTUS; RABANUS MAURUS; RATRAMNUS OF CORBIE; THEOLOGY]

Gottschalk. *Œuvres théologiques et grammaticales de Godescalc d'Orbais,* ed. Cyril Lambot. Louvain: Spicilegium Sacrum Lovaniense, 1945.
———. "Lettre inédite de Godescalc d'Orbais," ed. Cyril Lambot. *Revue bénédictine* (1958).
Duckett, Eleanor Shipley. *Carolingian Portraits: A Study in the Ninth Century.* Ann Arbor: University of Michigan Press, 1962.
Van Moos, Peter. "Gottschalks Gedicht *O mi custos*—eine confessio." *Frühmittelalterliche Studien* 4–5 (1970–71).
Vielhaber, Klaus. *Gottschalk der Sachse.* Bonn: Rohrscheid, 1956.

GOURNAY-EN-BRAY. The former collegial church of Saint-Hildevert at Gournay-en-Bray (Seine-Maritime) has a six-bay nave flanked by aisles from the early 12th century (with 13th-c. rib vaults), an 11th-century north-transept arm with an eastern apsidal chapel, and a three-bay chevet ending in a flat wall dating from the 11th century. The chevet windows and south transept were rebuilt in the 13th century. Saint-Hildevert is a rare surviving example of a three-story elevation from the early 12th century in upper Normandy.

William W. Clark

Régnier, Louis. "Excursion à Gournay-en-Bray et Saint-Germer." *Annuaire normande* (1903): 67–110.
———. "Gournay-en-Bray, église Saint-Hildevert." *Congrès archéologique* (Beauvais) 72 (1905): 74–80.

GRAIL AND GRAIL ROMANCES. The word *gradalis,* of disputed origin, meaning a kind of serving dish, is attested in medieval Latin as early as 718. A well-known definition from ca. 1200 reads: "A *gradalis,* or in the Latin of Gaul *gradale,* is a wide dish, somewhat deep, in which costly foods in their broth are usually set out for the rich with pieces arranged in order [*gradatim*], one after the other, in different patterns; and in the vernacular it is called a *graalz* [grail]" (Hélinant de Froidmont, 1294). Association of the words for grail with *gradatim* 'by steps, in stages' and the notion of orderly arrangement may originate in a flight of etymological fancy typical of the Middle Ages; but the grail's use in serving food at a rich meal is consistent with the word's earliest occurrences in French, in the decasyllabic *Roman d'Alexandre* (1165–70) and in Chrétien de Troyes's *Perceval,* or the *Conte du Graal* (ca. 1180), as is the implication that a grail was a rare and costly dish that would nevertheless be known in wealthy households in northern France.

In the *Conte du Graal*, Chrétien seems to play familiarity with grails in general against a particular Grail's extraordinary qualities. Four facts distinguish the special Grail that Perceval first sees at the Fisher King's castle. (1) It is valuable beyond measure, made of gold and studded with rare gems. (2) Along with candelabra and a cutting platter, it appears in a procession (not an unusual event at a banquet), but the procession is headed by a squire carrying an amazing Bleeding Lance. (3) It is not used to serve the diners in the main hall but follows the procession into a room beyond. Meat is served from the platter; the Grail passes by at each course but does not stop at the table. (4) It is accompanied by a bright light apparently emanating from within. Later, Perceval learns about the extraordinary food the Grail contains that makes it a "holy thing" (and that might explain the light): neither pike, lamprey, nor salmon, which one might expect to be served in an ordinary grail, but a consecrated Mass wafer, the only sustenance taken for years by a king, Perceval's grandfather, who lives in the inner room.

The Grail is simultaneously an ordinary and a mysterious object. Mystery arises, in fact, because it behaves or is treated in unexpected ways. One of its functions is to provoke inquiry about what makes it mysterious. Perceval ought to ask questions about where the Grail goes and whom it serves, not about its material nature. It is "holy" because of what it conveys, rather than for what it is; the purpose of the questions is thus to draw attention beyond itself toward what lies hidden from view.

Just as Chrétien's Grail is meant to be the object of questions, so he makes of it as well the object of a quest. The Grail Castle and its inhabitants disappear the morning after Perceval's failure; later, reminded of the consequences of his failure, he resolves to search until he finds it again and can ask the right questions in order to heal the wounded Fisher King and restore the Grail kingdom.

In the wake of Chrétien's unfinished *Conte du Graal*, a series of verse continuations arose, which extend Chrétien's story for over 40,000 lines before giving it a form of closure. The theme of the Grail extends through these romances and into several prose reworkings of the legend as well. A decade or so after Chrétien, Robert de Boron (fl. 1190–1210) is the first to turn this Grail (so named, according to Robert, because it brings pleasure [<*agreer*]) into an object that is holy in its own right, the Holy Grail. His writing concretizes associations of the Grail with religious experience that Chrétien leaves poetically implicit. Robert does so by creating a "sacred history" for the Grail and reinforcing its place in Arthurian history by accounting for its presence in Britain. The prose Didot-*Perceval*, written under the influence of the *Second Continuation* as well as Chrétien, is a romance of ambition and failure, for which a Grail quest is an act of atonement; this prose work is the earliest romance to include a successful conclusion to the hero's quest.

The First Continuator, drawing on Chrétien's implication of a quest by Gawain for the Bleeding Lance, elevates the secondary hero to the status of Grail quester; in the endings provided by Manessier and Gerbert de Montreuil, however, the final triumph is reserved for Perceval alone.

Continuing the process of christianization, the *First* and *Second Continuations* identify the Bleeding Lance, ignored by Robert, with the spear of Longinus, thus linking both objects definitively to the Mass. However, the Grail's extraordinary character continues to elevate its sacramental functions. Hardly a chalice destined for service at an "ordinary" Mass, it figures, in the Vulgate Cycle and subsequently, as Chalice *par excellence*, the central material object in a vision of Christ's own service at the altar as Victim and as Priest. Moreover, the goal of the Grail quest can no longer be a dream of heroic liberation but is a pious search for personal worth and purity. Perceval is replaced as the ideal Grail quester by the flawless Galahad; after Galahad witnesses the extraordinary ceremony, the Grail is removed to Heaven, its appropriate abode.

Perlesvaus, another early 13th-century prose romance, incorporates material from Robert de Boron and from Chrétien and the first two Continuators with matter from a wide range of other sources to produce an idiosyncratic and heightened account of the Grail as Mass chalice, the object of the Perceval figure's quest, in which the Crucifixion drama is replayed.

The Grail as a source of plenty is one characteristic that brings its literary manifestations into contact with mythic and folkloric themes and motifs. Among the most evocative and provocative of many possible examples are the *cornu copia*, magic sources of abundance, the vegetative cycle, cycles of destruction and restoration, impotence and fecundity, feminine sexuality. Such resonances enrich the medieval texts poetically, but they do not, in most cases, emerge as a major focus of interest. Nevertheless, they help explain the widespread appeal of the Grail and its continued renewal in literature throughout the Middle Ages and down to the present day.

Rupert T. Pickens

[See also: CHRÉTIEN DE TROYES; GERBERT DE MONTREUIL; *PERCEVAL CONTINUATIONS*; *PERLESVAUS*; PROSE ROMANCE; ROBERT DE BORON]

Frappier, Jean. "Le Graal et ses feux divergeants." *Romance Philology* 24 (1970–71): 373–400.

Imbs, Paul. "L'élément religieux dans le *Conte del Graal* de Chrétien de Troyes." In *Les romans du Graal dans la littérature des XIIe et XIIIe siècles*. Paris: CNRS, 1956, pp. 31–53.

Marx, Jean. *La légende arthurienne et le Graal*. Paris: Presses Universitaires de France, 1952.

———. *Nouvelles recherches sur la littérature arthurienne*. Paris: Klincksieck, 1965.

Owen, D.D.R. "From Grail to Holy Grail." *Romania* 89 (1968): 31–53.

Pickens, Rupert T. "Le conte del Graal (Perceval)." In *The Romances of Chrétien de Troyes: A Symposium*, ed. Douglas Kelly. Lexington: French Forum, 1985, pp. 232–86.

Roques, Mario. "Le nom du Graal." In *Les romans du Graal dans la littérature des XIIe et XIIIe siècles*. Paris: CNRS, 1956, pp. 5–13.

GRAMMAR. *See* LIBERAL ARTS

GRAND MASTER. The position of Grand Master of France, established in 1451, had already existed for a century under other names, the earliest being "sovereign master of the king's household." This personage presided over a household of several hundred people, many of whom were important political figures or influential royal advisers. In the 14th and 15th centuries, when the composition of the royal council often reflected the political mood of the realm more than the king's personal wishes, the king often drew his most trusted advisers from the household. The master of the king's (and dauphin's) household became an important player on the political stage.

John Bell Henneman, Jr.

GRANDES CHRONIQUES DE FRANCE. The official history of the French realm, as kept in French at Saint-Denis from 1285 on, the *Grandes chroniques* presents the history of France as a series of kings' reigns. The first part of the *Grandes chroniques* was the translation, made by the monk Primat ca. 1274, of a Latin chronicle from the early 13th century. This was itself based upon the histories of Aimoin de Fleury and his continuators, Einhard, Pseudo-Turpin, the Astronomer, Suger, Rigord, Guillaume le Breton, and the *Gesta Dagoberti* and the royal Frankish annals, as well as the archival resources of Saint-Denis. By 1285, the *Grandes chroniques* were official.

Anonymous historians continued the text to ca. 1350, using translations of Guillaume de Nangis's lives of Louis IX and Philip III and the chronicles of Géraud de Frachet and Richard Lescot. The chronicle was then continued by outsiders, first by Pierre d'Orgemont, the chancellor of France (to 1384), then by Juvenal des Ursins, archbishop of Reims (to 1402), and finally by the Berry Herald (to 1422). Jean Chartier, a monk at Saint-Denis, wrote the last part of the chronicle (to 1461).

The *Grandes chroniques* are of supreme historical and literary interest, since after 1274 they are contemporary with the events they describe; many manuscripts have survived (the simultaneously-kept Latin chronicle exists only in fragments). They reflect the rich holdings of the library at Saint-Denis, as well as the growth of a powerful tradition of vernacular historical writing under royal auspices.

Leah Shopkow

[See also: HISTORIOGRAPHY]

Viard, Jules M.E., ed. *Les grandes chroniques de France.* 10 vols. Paris: Société de l'Histoire de France, 1920–58.

Béthune, François. "Les écoles historiques de Saint-Denis et Saint-Germain-des-Prés dans leurs rapports avec la composition des *Grandes chroniques de France.*" *Revue d'histoire ecclésiastique* 4 (1903): 24–38, 207–30.

Spiegel, Gabrielle M. *The Chronicle Tradition of Saint-Denis: A Survey.* Brookline: Classical Folia, 1978.

GRANDS RHÉTORIQUEURS. The term "Grands Rhétoriqueurs" is a misnomer, originally used to designate "minor" poets who wrote between Villon and Clément Marot. It has now been more narrowly and fruitfully applied to three closely linked generations of poets from the several duchies and royal territories whose verses appeared between 1470 and 1520, many of whom addressed their works to the others. As a group, they are an important and often neglected link between medieval and Renaissance culture, and their poems reveal important continuity in rhetorical education between the 15th and 16th centuries. They are distinct in their techniques and attitudes from many of their contemporaries.

The list of Grands Rhétoriqueurs has been most recently revised by Paul Zumthor to include the anonymous author of the *Abuzé en court,* Jean Meschinot, Henri Baude, Jean Molinet, Jean Robertet, the anonymous author of the *Lyon couronné,* André de la Vigne, Octavien de Saint-Gelays, Guillaume Crétin, Jean Lemaire de Belges, Jean Bouchet, Destrées, Pierre Gringore, and Jean Marot, of whom the most important are Meschinot, Molinet, Crétin, Lemaire, and Marot.

Artifice is the most obvious feature of these authors' works, and their major difficulty. Favorite techniques include alliteration, *annominatio, amplificatio,* anaphora, and puns. (For example, every one of the thirty-five lines in a ballade by Meschinot begins with *plus.*) Given the politically subordinate positions of most of these poets at court, they were forced to rely on frozen, ritualized, highly oratorical forms that highlight figures of speech and wordplay. Most works seem written for a ducal court and are openly moralizing and didactic. Favored genres include the doctrinal, *débat,* epistle in prose, and ballade and rondeau in verse. Their works frequently rely on praise, ornament, and hyperbole and are replete with allegorical figures borrowed from the *Roman de la Rose.* This situation was guaranteed, as Zumthor has shown, to alienate the writer from his subject, so that the playfulness of the works often masks an attempt to "repersonalize" the writer's relationship to writing. Yet beneath this brittle and gilded surface, one finds some stunningly "original" compositions that go far beyond courtly games.

In one ballade, Meschinot presents a dialogue between France and Louis XI, in which the following exchange takes place after France identifies herself as "La destruicte France./ —Par qui?—Par vous." Tiring of France's reproaches, the king urges her three times to speak more beautifully: "Parle plus beau," to which he must, again three times, hear the same answer, "Je ne puis, bonnement." This skillful use of a refrain can hardly be construed as art for art's sake. The opening of Molinet's *Ressource du petit peuple* (1481–82), from his *Faictz et dictz,* is another striking example of highly rhetorical, moralizing social commentary. Molinet describes the appearance of the *fille de perdicion,* listing her attributes in a classic example of *amplificatio.* Then are listed her companions, both allegorical and historical villains, followed by an enumeration of the afflictions of the people, "et tant exploitèrent de détestables et excécrables faix que l'hystoire au loing récitée donroit piteuses lermes aux yeulx des escoutans." These two typical examples deploy rhetoric to convey a political message rather than to shore up political hierarchies.

The use of allegory reveals similar subtlety. Traditionally, scholars have stressed the indebtedness of the Grands Rhétoriqueurs to the allegory of the *Roman de la Rose*, but this conclusion seems premature. In Meschinot's *Lunettes des princes*, a work typical of the Grands Rhétoriqueurs, Reason appears to the author in a dream. After he addresses Reason, she recollects her thoughts, which had been devastated by Despair, "Lors elle entra dans son endendement,/Qui vuyde estoit et pillé grandement/Par Désespoir." There, she finds only the bread of faith. Meschinot's somber Reason is a far cry from Jean de Meun's Reason, who had expatiated on the ambiguity of language. This difference, moreover, must be stressed in light of the Grands Rhétoriqueurs' frequent exploitation of linguistic ambiguity itself.

A prime example of how ambiguity was manipulated for moralizing ends is found in Octavien de Saint-Gelays's *Epistre en équivoques, au roy Charles* (1493). Homophonic rhymes bring out a political message as unambiguous as the sounds themselves are the opposite:

> Pour contempler vostre immense justice,
> Faites, pour Dieu, que le fleuve juste ysse
> Çà bas sur nous, vos trèshumbles subjectz!
> Tenuz nous ont, ainsi qu'oiseaulx sus getz,
> Division, simes, discorde, envye:
> Remettez nous, noble seigneur, en vye!

This interest in linguistic play can be traced back to the fabliaux, and Molinet, for example, composed an entire ballade whose rhymes are exclusively based on -*vis/t*, -*cu(l)*, and -*c/çon*. The *Art et science de rhétorique vulgaire* (1524–25) provides examples of double and triple verbal ambiguities.

Perhaps due to their penchant for moralizing, the Grands Rhétoriqueurs did not celebrate chivalric ritual and convention with the wholehearted endorsement of Olivier de La Marche, their contemporary at the court of Burgundy. Generally silent on explicitly political topics, they tend to side implicitly with the Burgundian position in the struggle between Louis XI and Charles the Bold. The condemnation of the ravages of war, as found in the *Ressource du petit peuple*, for example, makes its point allusively. By comparison, when Jean Lemaire de Belges celebrates the advantages of French over Italian, his "patriotism" remains largely literary and is not transferred to the French royal house that was invading northern Italy at the time.

Among lyrical genres, the Grands Rhétoriqueurs particularly cultivated funeral laments, whose models were the elegy and *planctus*. They do not stress the same subjects as the contemporary and widely popular *danse macabre*. Crétin's *Translation du chant de misere*, for example, points out that rhetoric has never saved its practictioners from death:

> Les belles fleurs de Tulle et rhetorique
> N'ont point rendu exemptz d'exil mortel
> Ceulx qu'ont instruitz.

This reserve regarding death, so different from contemporary popular accounts, shows that the Grands Rhétoriqueurs, with their rhetorical self-consciousness, could steer between thematic commonplaces and popular stereotypes and still achieve an "original" effect.

The *Arts de seconde rhétorique*, composed in the wake of the poetic works of the Grands Rhétoriqueurs, formalize many of their practices and provide valuable evidence for the intersection of literary theory and practice.

Earl Jeffrey Richards

[See also: *ARTS DE SECONDE RHÉTORIQUE*; CRÉTIN, GUILLAUME; GRINGORE, PIERRE; MESCHINOT, JEAN; MOLINET, JEAN; SAINT-GELAYS, OCTAVIEN DE]

Zumthor, Paul, ed. *Anthologie des grands rhétoriqueurs*. Paris: Union Générale d'Éditions, 1978.

James, Laurence. "L'*objet poétique* des grands rhétoriqueurs." In *Mélanges de langue et de littérature médiévales offerts à Alice Planche,* ed. Maurice Accarie and Ambroise Queffelec. Paris: Les Belles Lettres, 1984, pp. 225–34.

Martineau-Génieys, Christine. *Le thème de la mort dans la poésie française de 1450 à 1550*. Paris: Champion, 1978, pp. 319–51, 429–37.

Zumthor, Paul. *Le masque et la lumière: la poétique des grands rhétoriqueurs*. Paris: Seuil, 1978.

GRANDSON. At Grandson, on Lake Neuchâtel in the Swiss canton of Vaud, Charles the Bold, duke of Burgundy, was attacked on March 3, 1476, by 20,000 troops from a score of mostly Swiss towns. Hoping to lure the advancing pikemen into a trap, Charles withdrew his forces in the center. His infantry on the flanks, who should have enveloped the Swiss, misread the maneuver and broke ranks, then fled in panic when they saw another Swiss column approaching. Its losses were relatively light, but in the rout the Burgundian army abandoned considerable booty to the Swiss.

John Bell Henneman, Jr.

GRANGE. Literally, a barn or farmstead (sometimes fortified), the term "grange" in the 12th century became attached to the large expanses of land forming the agricultural estates of new religious groups, especially the Cistercians, Premonstratensians, and military orders. Such a grange is a large agrarian unit of varying size cultivated under the direct management of its monastic owners, encompassing up to three or more parishes, on which the most up-to-date and rationalized agriculture was practiced in the 12th and 13th centuries. Under optimal conditions, all previous peasant cultivators on grange lands were replaced by a staff of monastic laborers, primarily lay brothers (*conversi*) and hired day workers. The claims of such monks to practice manual labor and found their houses in uninhabited places led most historians until recently to assert that such huge farms resulted from monastic clearance and reclamation; recent studies, however, show that granges were almost always created by repurchase and compacting of smaller holdings previously settled and cultivated by peasants. In many regions, the monastic granges of the Middle Ages became model farms, while their barns were edifices of monumental size.

Constance H. Berman

[See also: CISTERCIAN ORDER; *DÉFRICHEMENT*]

Berman, Constance H. "Fortified Monastic Granges in the Rouergue." In *The Medieval Castle: Romance and Reality*, ed. Kathryn Reyerson and Faye Powe. Dubuque: Kendall-Hunt, 1984, pp. 124–46.

Blary, François. *Le Domaine de Chaalis: XIIe–XIVe siècles. Approches archéologiques des établissements agricoles et industriels d'une abbaye cistercienne.* Paris: Éditions des Travaux Historiques et Scientifiques, 1989.

Higounet, Charles. *La grange de Vaulerent: structure et exploitation d'un terroir cistercien de la plaine de France: XIIe–XVe siècle.* Paris: SEVPEN, 1965.

Horn, Walter, and Ernest Born. "The Barn of the Cistercian Grange of Vaulerent." In *Festschrift Ulrich Middeldorf*, ed. Antje Kosegarten and Peter Tigler. Berlin: De Gruyter, 1968, pp. 24–41.

GRANSON, OTON DE (ca. 1345–1397). Born of a noble family in Savoy and killed in a judicial duel, Granson served as a knight under the counts of Savoy and two kings of England. Froissart praised Granson as *banerés et riche homme durement*, Deschamps was his friend, and after his death Christine de Pizan was his ardent encomiast. She admired both Granson's prowess as knight and his service to womanhood, manifested especially in his poetry. Chaucer praised him as "flour of hem that make in Fraunce." During Granson's long service to Edward III and Richard II, he and Chaucer evidently became close friends; each copies verse by the other. But Guillaume de Machaut was Granson's great model for forms, imagery, and expression. The "Isabelle" he refers to in several poems may be Isabeau of Bavaria, Charles VI's queen. Four manuscript collections have a substantial number of Granson's poems, which have been gathered into an edition that includes ninety ballades, nineteen rondeaux, a virelai, six *complaintes*, a lengthy *pastourelle*, three *lais*, and two *dits amoureux*. The longer *dit*, the *Livre de messire Ode* (2,495 lines), a combination of narrative and inserted lyrics in a dream vision, represents an original development. In general, though, Granson is a skilled amateur whose work is derivative and modest in scope.

James I. Wimsatt

[See also: GARENCIÈRES, JEAN DE; *JARDIN DE PLAISANCE ET FLEUR DE RÉTHORIQUE*]

Granson, Oton de. *Oton de Grandson: sa vie et ses poésies*, ed. Arthur Piaget. Geneva: Payot, 1941. [Full edition of the poetry, along with information on Granson's life, the manuscripts, etc.]

GRATIAN (fl. early 12th c.). The father of the science of canon law remains a shadowy figure. Most of the scanty evidence suggests that he was a monk, possibly affiliated with the monastery of SS. Felix and Nabor in Bologna. The role of Bologna as the nursery of canonistic science lends this tradition credibility. Gratian participated in the larger scholastic culture that produced Peter Abélard's *Sic et non* and Peter Lombard's *Sententiae*. His *Concord of Discordant Canons*, or *Decretum*, had the same purpose as those theological works, the reconciliation of a diverse and often contradictory heritage of thought through the application of dialectic. This private collection combined conciliar canons, papal decretals (many of them spurious), and patristic texts with Gratian's own comments, or *dicta*. Texts marked for exclusion from lectures, called *palae*, or "chaff," included the so-called Donation of Constantine. In its final form, the *Decretum* is divided into a treatise on law, the *Distinctiones*, a series of hypothetical cases; the *Causae*, including a distinct tract on penance; and a sacramental tract, *De consecratione*. The compilation became the first textbook of canon law at Bologna and Paris. The teachers of canon law brought to the interpretation of this work of disciplinary theology the principles and procedures of Roman law, producing a distinctive legal science. Connections between Gratian and the Roman curia are difficult to demonstrate, but students of canon law were presented with a papalist viewpoint on key questions of ecclesiastical structure. Dante would place Gratian in Heaven in the *Paradiso*, as a counterweight to later canonists, some of whom emphasized papal temporal power.

Thomas M. Izbicki

[See also: ABÉLARD, PETER; CANON LAW; CONCILIAR MOVEMENT; IVO OF CHARTRES; LAW AND JUSTICE; PETER LOMBARD]

Corpus iuris canonici, ed. Emil Friedberg. Leipzig: Tauchnitz, 1879, Vol. 1.

Chodorow, Stanley. *Christian Political Theory and Church Politics in the Mid-Twelfth Century: The Ecclesiology of Gratian's Decretum.* Berkeley: University of California Press, 1972.

Kuttner, Stephan. *Harmony from Dissonance: An Interpretation of Medieval Canon Law.* Latrobe: Archabbey, 1955.

Noonan, John. "Gratian Slept Here: The Changing Identity of the Father of the Systematic Study of Canon Law." *Traditio* 35 (1979): 145–72.

GREBAN, ARNOUL (d. before 1473). Author of a well-known *Mystère de la Passion*, Greban was born in Le Mans and studied theology at the University of Paris. From 1450 to 1455, he lived in the cloister of the cathedral of Notre-Dame in Paris, where he was organist and master of the choirboys. It was here that he wrote his Passion play, probably in 1450–52. This work is set in the framework of the *Procès de Paradis*, first introduced by Eustache Marcadé, and its 35,000 lines are divided into four playing days. Despite its variety of styles (sermons, debates, lamentations) and moods (solemn in Heaven, comic in Hell, pathetic in torture scenes), the play exhibits a strong unity. Greban employs many poetic forms and punctuates the action throughout with music. The life of Jesus is presented against the background of a cosmic struggle between the forces of good and evil. This conflict is introduced in the first scenes, where Lucifer rebels against God then out of envy tempts Adam and Eve to fall from grace. Greban's *Passion* was played three times in Paris before 1473. It served as the basis for Jean Michel's Passion play and was adapted for production in a number of other cities.

Alan E. Knight

[See also: MICHEL, JEAN; MYSTERY PLAYS; PASSION PLAYS]

Greban, Arnoul. *Le mystère de la Passion*, ed. Omer Jodogne. 2 vols. Brussels: Palais des Académies, 1965–83.
Champion, Pierre. *Histoire poétique du quinzième siècle*. 2 vols. Paris: Champion, 1923, Vol. 2, pp. 133–88.

GREBAN, SIMON (d. 1473). Presumed author, perhaps in collaboration with his brother Arnoul, of the *Mystère des Actes des Apôtres*, a dramatization in 62,000 lines of the biblical book of Acts. By a complex interweaving of scenes, Greban presents parallel lives of the Apostles dispersed in many countries. He adds many legendary events and spectacular scenes of miracles, martyrdoms, and shipwrecks. The play had complete performances at Bourges in 1536 and Paris in 1541.

Alan E. Knight

[See also: MYSTERY PLAYS]

Lebègue, Raymond. *Le mystère des Actes des Apôtres*. Paris: Champion, 1929.

GRECO-BYZANTINE ROMANCE. Eloquent witnesses to the renaissance of the 12th century and its desire to explore and integrate the riches of the Orient, along with the treasures of its classical past and the *matière de Bretagne*, the Greco-Byzantine romances explore a variety of settings around the Mediterranean basin. While these romances may differ widely in tone and orientation, they each demonstrate the West's fascination with an exotic and fabulous world, opened up by travel reports and crusades, renewed commercial interests, and desire for political expansion. Among the most important are the anonymous *Floire et Blancheflor*, *Guillaume de Palerne*, and *Partonopeu de Blois*, Hue de Rotelande's *Ipomedon* and *Protheselaus*, Aimon de Varennes's *Florimont*, Chrétien de Troyes's *Cligés*, and Gautier d'Arras's *Eracle*.

Matilda T. Bruckner

[See also: AIMON DE VARENNES; CHRÉTIEN DE TROYES; *FLOIRE ET BLANCHEFLOR*; GAUTIER D'ARRAS; *GUILLAUME DE PALERNE*; HUE DE ROTELANDE; *PARTONOPEU DE BLOIS*]

GREGORIAN CHANT. The monophonic chant of the medieval Latin liturgy, sometimes known as "plainchant." Although the term is often used for chant compositions from the later Middle Ages, "Gregorian chant" applies specifically to the music for the Mass and Divine Office according to the Romano-Frankish liturgy as it was codified ca. 800. It excludes other regional chant repertoires (Gallican, Milanese, Visigothic, Beneventan, Aquileian, Ravennate), all of which, with the exception of Milanese, or "Ambrosian," chant, finally yielded to Gregorian chant, a repertoire promoted first by the Carolingians and later spread throughout Europe. The epithet "Gregorian" derives from Pope Gregory I (r. 590–604), who was thought to have played a decisive role in the shaping of western chant and liturgy. A connection between Gregory and the music named after him has never been demonstrated, however. The expression "Gregorian chants" (*gregoriana carmina*) does not antedate the mid-9th century, even though a verse prologue found in earlier books of Mass chants attributes the contents to one "Gregorius presul." It has been argued that this prologue was intended to celebrate the work of Gregory II (r. 715–31) and that the text became associated with his more famous eponymous predecessor.

Although the origins of the medieval Latin chant repertoires are clouded in an obscurity that will probably never be penetrated, a process of growth and transformation can be assumed. The "Proper" chants of the Roman Mass (Introit, Gradual, Tract, Alleluia, Offertory, Communion), which vary according to the season or feast, were undoubtedly introduced singly over a period of time. What is presumably the earliest Mass chant, a responsorial psalm sung between the Scripture readings—predecessor of the musically more elaborate Gradual—existed by the end of the 4th century. Though the custom of singing during the reception of communion dates back to about the same era, a variable cycle of communion chants did not yet exist. The choice always fell on Psalm 34, chosen because of the line "taste and see that the Lord is good." The Offertory chant was probably the last of the Proper chants to be introduced.

A simple explanation of the origin of Gregorian chant is complicated by the existence of a body of music known to modern scholars as "Old Roman" chant. Both share the same texts and the musical traditions are obviously related, but the musical styles rest on different aesthetic foundations. As far as we know, Old Roman chant was sung only in Rome, its oldest witness being a *graduale* copied there in 1071. Scholars have not arrived at a consensus about where and when the Gregorian repertoire received the shape found in the earliest notated manuscripts. Some argue that what we know as Gregorian chant preserves essentially intact the musical repertoire brought from Rome in the late 8th century as part of the Carolingian liturgical reforms and scrupulously guarded by Frankish musicians. Others maintain that the Franks reshaped and adapted the Roman music to their own native idiom. The latter process is difficult to assess in detail, because the earlier Gallican chant, which would presumably have reflected that idiom, disappeared with virtually no trace. Manuscripts from

France and elsewhere attest to the uniformity and stability of the Gregorian musical tradition throughout the Middle Ages. Some of the earliest and best manuscript sources of chant originated in French territory: four of the *Sextuplex* manuscripts and several of the earliest notated *gradualia* from the 10th century (Laon, Bibl. mun. 239; Angers, Bibl. de la Ville 91; and Chartres 47). The first and third of these have been published in facsimile in the series *Paléographie musicale*.

The repertoire may be divided into two large categories: chants for the Mass and those for the Office. The Book of Psalms provides most of the texts. The psalm text can be sung in one of three musical forms: (1) direct, (2) responsorial, or (3) antiphonal. Each has more than one possible realization, but in general it can be stated that (1) involves the continuous recitation of the psalm text by a soloist or chorus, (2) calls for a choral response to the solo singing of a psalm, and (3) implies an alternation between the two choral groups, possibly in conjunction with a soloist. These performance practices were also used with nonpsalmic texts, like hymns, chants of the Ordinary of the Mass, and responsories of the Office.

Eventually, the Proper chants of the Mass consisted of a repertoire of about 600 chants for all feasts of the Lord and Sundays of the year (temporal cycle) and for the commemoration of the saints (sanctoral cycle). Some feasts of the saints had unique chants, while others were supplied from the "common"—chants with texts chosen because of their appropriateness to the category of saint (martyr, virgin, confessor, etc.) being honored. Later in the Middle Ages, this core repertoire was expanded by additions of various types: new compositions in the traditional genres for new feasts; tropes, new musical material—usually with text—prefaced to and inserted between phrases of the preexistent Gregorian melody; prosae or prosulae, new texts fitted to already existing melismas; and independent compositions like the sequence, the Aquitanian *versus*, and liturgical drama. Although the sequence was at first attached to the Alleluia of the Mass, it later became a virtually independent genre with an accentual, rhyming text set to successively repeated musical phrases (aa, bb, cc, etc.).

The Ordinary of the Mass consists of items sung at the eucharist on a daily, or almost daily, basis. The texts of the Kyrie, Gloria, Credo, Sanctus, and Agnus Dei do not vary according to the seasons of the church year or sanctoral celebrations. Whereas the Proper chants are unique—there is, for example, but a single Gregorian melody for "Resurrexi," the Introit of Easter day—settings of Ordinary chants continued to be composed well into the 12th century and beyond. In fact, most of them seem to belong to later compositional layers. Though some melodies for the Ordinary chants are represented in large numbers of sources, others enjoyed only a restricted geographical distribution.

The three most important musical elements of the Divine Office are antiphons used in conjunction with the weekly chanting of the Psalter, responsories sung after readings from the Bible or the fathers of the church, and hymns. Although the antiphon repertoire is large (1,600 or more items), the number of model melodies to which the texts are set is much smaller, amounting to less than three dozen basic types.

Because of the large span of time during which Gregorian chant (in its broadest sense) was composed, stylistic generalities can claim only limited validity. One of the most readily perceived distinctions rests on the relationship between the text and the degree of melodic embellishment it receives. In the simplest style, syllabic chant, each syllable of text corresponds more or less to a single pitch. In neumatic style, most syllables receive melodic figures of two to six pitches. Melismatic style is the most elaborate of all: melodic decoration takes precedence over the declamation of the text. The degree of melodic elaboration depends to a certain extent on the genre: antiphons for ordinary weekdays are syllabic, while Graduals, Alleluias, and Offertory verses tend to melismatic style. The relationship between text and music need not remain exactly the same from phrase to phrase. Although prevailingly syllabic chants, which tend to be relatively short, do not contain melismatic passages, neumatic and melismatic chants frequently have recourse to syllabic style.

The chant was transmitted orally for many centuries. The earliest surviving books with the chant texts date from the 9th century. These have been collected and published by Dom Jean Hesbert under the title *Antiphonale Missarum Sextuplex*. They lack musical notation and indeed were never intended to contain it. The existence of such unnotated *gradualia*, as books of Mass chants came to be called, testifies to continued oral transmission of the melodies.

One of the characteristics of the Gregorian repertoire is the fidelity of its transmission across the regional types of musical notation in which it was written down. These notational signs, known as "neumes," were created specifically for the purpose of ensuring accurate dissemination of the repertoire. All of the notational systems share the same basic principles despite their diverse graphic configurations. The earliest specimens of notation begin to appear sporadically from about the middle of the 9th century. Most of the regional notations are cursive: two or more pitches are joined to form a single graphic gesture. Some (Lorraine, Breton, Aquitanian) portray the melodic movement as a series of discrete dots. All of the early notations are adiastematic, that is, they do not transmit precise pitch levels but only short-range melodic direction involving two to five discrete pitches. Large and small intervals appear as identical shapes on the page. The *podatus* (♪), signifying a rising motion, or the *clivis* (∧), representing a descending motion, could indicate an interval as small as a minor second or as large as a fourth or fifth. The notation did not, moreover, permit the relationship between the last pitch of one neume and the first note of the succeeding neume to be determined.

Some notations incorporated nuances indicating longer rhythmic values and specially shaped "liquescent" neumes, reserved for combinations of consonants (*gn*, *lm*) or vowels (*au*, *ui*) that require special care in pronunciation. In addition, expressive nuances could be signified either by letters above the notation or by special neume symbols (*quilisma*, *oriscus*). Their exact manner of interpretation is subject to speculation, particularly since most of these special signs disappeared in many regions at an early date.

Certain regional notations began to dispose the notes on the page in a manner that reflected the relative size of the intervals separating them. The next step in the development of this "diastematic" notation saw the line that served as the point of reference become etched more deeply into the parchment. A pitch value, usually F or C, was assigned to it and indicated at the beginning of each line of music.

The better to distinguish the two lines, the lower (F) was drawn in red and the upper (C) in yellow or green. Aquitanian manuscripts employ cleffing other than C or F, and sometimes only a B-flat sign under a line is employed. One of the French regional notations, Norman, developed into "square" notation. Placed on a four-line staff drawn in either black or red, it became the standard chant notation of the Roman Catholic church and has continued in use for printed chant books up to the present time. The same notation was adapted for the earliest polyphonic music.

During this period originated the distinction between the new rhythmic polyphony, *cantus mensuratus*, and plainchant (*cantus planus*), sung in relatively equal note values. Chant was sometimes sung in proportional duration values and notated with symbols derived from the mensural polyphonic notation of the 13th century.

One of the important contributions of Frankish monastic musicians was the development of a music theory that sought to classify the new music that had replaced Gallican chant. This process took some time, and it was not until the middle of the 9th century that the first chant treatise, the *Musica disciplina* of Aurelian of Réôme, was written. Frankish music theory combined Byzantine concepts (a system of eight modes) and ancient Greek theory in an original synthesis. The result could hardly claim to be more than an approximate explanation of a repertoire created without reference to an explicit theoretical foundation.

At the beginning of the 11th century, there developed the concept of the hexachord, an ascending pitch set from C to A that could be duplicated on G and F (in the latter case with B-flat). By means of "mutation," one could move from one hexachord to another and remain within a familiar configuration of steps and half-steps. Guido d'Arezzo (ca. 990–1050) assigned syllables (ut, re, mi, fa, sol, la) to each of the steps of the hexachord as an aid to learning new or unknown chants.

It had long been realized that although chants customarily cadenced on one of four finals (D, E, F, G) some chants moved almost exclusively in the tonal space above the final, and others descended frequently beneath it and used fewer notes above the final. The tonal space was delimited by eight modal scales, four of which were "authentic," corresponding to the first category, and the remaining four were "plagal," corresponding to the second. In the fully elaborated system, each scale was composed of a species of fifth and a species of fourth. In the case of the authentic scales, both were found above the final; the plagal scales had a fourth below and fifth above the final.

Though recourse to the manuscripts is essential for historical chant studies, the modern editions published by the monks of Solesmes provide a good introduction to the repertoire. The *Liber usualis* is a diverse collection of chants required for the Mass and for parts of the Office. It includes the complete Office of Matins for certain days as well as other miscellaneous items. The *Graduale Romanum* offers Mass chants for all days of the liturgical year including the weekdays of Lent, which are not included in the *Liber usualis*. Particularly useful for study are the *Graduale Triplex* and the *Offertoriale Triplex*, which contain the chants not only in square notation but also the adiastematic neumes of the manuscripts Laon, Bibl. mun. 239 (10th c.) and Einsiedln, Stiftsbibliothek 121 (11th c.) or Saint-Gall, Stiftsbibliothek 358 (9th c.), written above and below the staff, respectively.

Joseph H. Dyer

[**See also**: GALLICAN RITE; HYMNS; LITURGICAL BOOKS; MASS, CHANTS AND TEXTS; MUSICAL NOTATION (NEUMATIC); O ANTIPHONS; PROSULA; RHYMED OFFICE; SEQUENCE (EARLY); SEQUENCE (LATE); TROPES, ORDINARY; TROPES, PROPER]

Graduale Triplex. Solesmes: Abbaye Sainte-Pierre, 1979.

Hesbert, René-Jean, ed. *Antiphonale Missarum Sextuplex.* Brussels: Vromant, 1935.

Offertoriale Triplex cum versiculis. Solesmes: Abbaye Saint-Pierre, 1985.

Apel, Willi. *Gregorian Chant.* Bloomington: University of Indiana Press, 1958.

Bryden, John R., and David G. Hughes. *An Index of Gregorian Chant.* 2 vols. Cambridge: Harvard University Press, 1969.

Crocker, Richard, and David Hiley, eds. *The New Oxford History of Music.* 2nd ed. Oxford: Oxford University Press, 1990, Vol. 2: *The Early Middle Ages to 1300.*

Hiley, David. *Western Plainchant: A Handbook.* Oxford: Oxford University Press, 1992.

Hoppin, Richard H. *Medieval Music.* New York: Norton, 1978.

Pothier, Joseph. *Les mélodies grégoriennes d'après la tradition.* Tournai: Desclée, 1880.

GREGORIAN REFORM. The reform of the Catholic church named after Pope Gregory VII, one of its most ardent promoters, is customarily defined in terms of the legal and administrative developments that accompanied the rise of the papacy between the papal election decree of 1059 and the First Lateran Council in 1123: the decree proclaimed that the pope was to be elected by the cardinal bishops without lay interference, and the council confirmed the compromise over the lay investiture of bishops hammered out the year before at the Diet of Worms.

Although the most accessible data of the reform comprise a myriad of canonical collections, papal correspondence, polemical tracts, and conciliar documents, it would be a distortion to conclude that the development of the papal monarchy was an end in itself, rather than a response to the spiritual ferment throughout European society that encouraged and even demanded a church that promoted the spirituality described in the Book of Acts, the *vita apostolica*, both for the clergy and the laity. The spirit of the Gregorian Reform in fact arose in the decades preceding 1059 as Cluniac abbots like Odilo and Hugues de Cluny extended monastic reform, and bishops like Bruno of Toul (later Pope Leo IX) undertook the reform of the secular clergy. With Gregory VII, the spirit of reform came explicitly to include the responsibility for justice throughout Christian society, particularly the subservience of secular matters and temporal rulers to spiritual matters and ecclesiastical overlords. The implications of these convictions led by the end of the century to the calling of western Christendom to crusade by Urban II and to the expectation that diocesan clergy would live the common life (regular canons) in keeping with the monastic *vita apostolica*; in the 12th century, at the Diet of Worms and First Lateran Council, they led to a workable solution to the role of the laity in episcopal elections and to the rise of cathedral schools and subsequently universities for the training of the clergy (Bologna, Paris, Oxford); and in the 13th century, they led to Innocent III bestowing kingdoms as fiefs (England, Hungary, Portugal, Aragon), to the provision of adequate support for local parish clergy and pastoral care (Fourth Lateran Council, 1215), and to the new mendicant orders, the Dominicans and Franciscans, obedient directly to the Holy See, that gave shape and expression to a *vita apostolica* suited to the new urban scene.

The importance of the monastic reform at Cluny in the first half of the 11th century lay particularly in the manner by which a network of monasteries, all looking to Cluny as their head, had come to enjoy the *libertas ecclesiae*, an independence from local lay and even episcopal interference. Over the years, this status was reinforced by papal privileges and protections, forging a natural allegiance between the papacy and the Cluniac movement.

At the same time, there was a serious effort in many places at the local level to introduce something of the monastic ideal into the life of the secular clergy: the buying of church offices, simony, and clerical unchastity (nicolaitism), were effectively condemned in places like Toul under Bruno and Milan under the impact of the Patarenes. But these reforms could only be temporary without a fundamental change in the relationship of the church to the institutions of feudalism, in which ecclesiastical appointments at all levels were considered the prerogatives of emperors, kings, and feudal lords and often distributed to relatives or vassals without due consideration for the worthiness of the candidates. Moreover, the goods and properties of churches and monasteries often became the objects of feudal transactions, alienated from their primary purpose of providing stability and sustenance for monks and clergy. This state of affairs, symbolized by lay investiture of clerical office, became the focus of the contest between Pope Gregory VII and Emperor Henry IV.

The impulse for reform gave rise to major developments in the institutions of the papacy. In essence, the papacy had to circumvent the vested interests of the higher clergy and find ways to support and promote reforming impulses from below, requiring strong and centralized institutions that could respond quickly and decisively. Under Leo IX, the college of cardinals became an important extension of papal bureaucracy, as many were deputized to serve as legates throughout Europe from time to time to promote the papal cause. With Nicholas II, the election of the pope was to be made by the cardinal bishops, excluding the direct influence of either the Tuscan nobility or the German emperor. Under Gregory VII, legates became permanent and certain archbishops were appointed as primates for each of the regions of Europe to serve as courts of appeals for the legates. Newly appointed archbishops were required to journey to Rome to receive the *pallium*, the symbol of their office. The rights and privileges accorded to Cluniac foundations in France were extended to the monastery of Hirsau and its daughter foundations in Germany. Urban II, a monk of Cluny, extended the liberties and exemptions of Cluny to many more Cluniac establishments; and Paschal II extended papal protection to Cîteaux in 1100.

The ideals and ambitions of the reformers spurred the development of canon law. In the *Collection in Seventy-four Titles*, compiled under Leo IX, the precedents set down in earlier collections were reorganized to emphasize the primacy of Rome and the reform program. With the passing of time, subsequent collections became the vehicles for the promulgation of new law, such as the collections of Anselm of Lucca (1083) and Deusdedit (1086), which drew on materials beyond the traditional canons. Gregory VII's own *Dictatus papae* (1075) seems to stand at a crucial point in this regard: a brief listing of twenty-seven propositions concerning the authority of the pope, they read like chapter headings for the later collections: only the pope has the right to be called universal; only he can depose or absolve bishops; only he can create new laws; the Roman church has never erred and will never err; the pope has the authority to depose emperors; the pope alone may use the imperial insignia; the pope ought to be judged by no one; the pope can absolve subjects from obedience to wicked rulers. Although much of this legal program existed only in embryo at the end of the 11th century, it expanded dramatically in the 12th and 13th centuries with the *Decretum* of Gratian (1140) and the later compilations of the Decretists and Decretalists.

The implications of the Gregorian vision of a just Christian society incorporated other projects of the late 11th and 12th centuries: the reconquest of Spain, rapprochement with Constantinople and the crusade in the East, the Peace and Truce of God in European territories, the transformation of chivalry according to religious ideals (the Templars and Hospitalers), and the rehabilitation of marriage as a protection for women and families.

Although the reform was not always and everywhere to achieve its goals, it went a long way to establish the *libertas ecclesiae* against the manipulations of the feudal establishment, and it gave a concrete, institutional expression to the very idea of Christendom.

Mark Zier

[See also: CANON LAW; CISTERCIAN ORDER; CLUNIAC ORDER; CRUSADES; DOMINICAN ORDER; FRANCISCAN ORDER; GRATIAN; GREGORY VII; HUGUES DE CLUNY; INNOCENT III; LEO IX; ODILO; PEACE OF GOD; REGULAR CANONS; SCHOOLS, CATHEDRAL; TEMPLARS; TRUCE OF GOD; UNIVERSITIES]

Gilchrist, John T., trans. *Collection in Seventy-four Titles: A Canon Law Manual of the Gregorian Reform.* Toronto: Pontifical Institute of Mediaeval Studies, 1980.

————, ed. *Diversorum patrum sententiae: sive, Collectio in LXXIV titulos digesta.* Vatican City: Biblioteca Apostolica Vaticana, 1973.

Blumenthal, Uta-Renate. *The Investiture Controversy: Church and Monarchy from the Ninth to the Twelfth Century.* Philadelphia: University of Pennsylvania Press, 1988.

Cowdrey, Herbert E.J. *The Cluniacs and the Gregorian Reform.* Oxford: Clarendon, 1970.

————. *Popes, Monks, and Crusaders.* London: Hambledon, 1984.

Fliche, Augustin. *La réforme grégorienne et la reconquête chrétienne (1057–1123).* Paris: Bloud and Gay, 1946.

La preparazione della riforma gregoriana e del pontificato di Gregorio VII: atti del IX Convegno del Centro di Studi Avellaniti. Fonte Avellana: Il Centro, 1985.

Tierney, Brian. *The Crisis of Church and State, 1050–1300.* Englewood Cliffs: Prentice-Hall, 1964.

Ullmann, Walter. *The Growth of Papal Government in the Middle Ages.* 3rd ed. London: Methuen, 1970.

Williams, Shafer, ed. *The Gregorian Epoch: Reformation, Revolution, Reaction?* Boston: Heath, 1964.

GREGORY VII (ca. 1020–1085). Pope. Born of a humble Tuscan family, Hildebrand, the future Gregory VII, came to Rome at an early age and received his education at the monastery of St. Mary's on the Aventine, where it appears he made his monastic profession. He served as chaplain to the reform-minded Pope Gregory VI and accompanied Gregory into exile in Germany when he agreed to step down to end the gridlock of three claimants to the papal throne. After Gregory VI's death in 1047, Hildebrand was at the monastery of Cluny. In 1049, he met bishop Bruno of Toul, now Pope Leo IX, and returned to Rome in his company. Hildebrand served Leo IX and four succeeding reforming popes in various capacities. In 1073, upon the death of Alexander II, Hildebrand was enthroned pope by popular acclamation and took the name Gregory VII.

Like his predecessors, Gregory first wished to reform the clergy in line with the monastic ideal, eliminating the buying of ecclesiastical offices (simony) and enforcing of clerical celibacy. But Gregory broadened the scope of reform to encompass *iustitia*, that is, justice and the proper governance of all of Christian society. For Gregory, this meant that just as spiritual realities took precedence over temporal realities, so, too, spiritual authority preceded temporal authority; not only the clergy but princes, kings, and emperors were to be obedient to the pope. Gregory sketched out the implications of this conviction in the *Dictatus papae* of 1075.

In France, Gregory largely had his way with the higher clergy through his legate, Hugues de Die, who vigorously pursued the reform between 1076 and 1080. In England, William the Conqueror respected the papal decrees regarding clerical celibacy, although he retained the practice of lay investiture without incurring excommunication. But in Germany, where ecclesiastical office and feudal obliga-

tion were closely intertwined in the administration of the realm, and indeed, where Emperor Henry III had not only appointed archbishops but even popes, almost immediately a conflict arose between Gregory and Henry III's son and successor, Henry IV. Henry regularly intervened in ecclesiastical affairs; he considered the upper clergy his vassals and invested them with the insignia of their offices. In the wake of papal criticism of his practices, Henry declared Gregory deposed; Gregory proclaimed Henry excommunicated and suspended German bishops. When Henry sought and received absolution from Gregory in the snows of Canossa in January 1077, Gregory's German allies elected Rudolf of Swabia as antiking without Gregory's consent and initiated a civil war in Germany that lasted until 1080, when Gregory once again excommunicated Henry and recognized Rudolf. Henry, in 1082, appointed an antipope. In 1084, Robert Guiscard and the Normans, on whom Gregory had called to relieve Henry's siege of Rome, looted and set fire to a significant quarter of the city and were forced to leave, taking Gregory with them. Gregory died a few months later at Salerno, exhausted.

However much of a failure Gregory's pontificate may have appeared at the time, Gregory nonetheless established with his new papal administration a mechanism for implementing his ideals; and his archenemy, the German emperor, was never to be so powerful again. In the century and a quarter that followed Gregory's death, the pope would muster all of Christendom to go on crusade for justice in the world; several of the kings of Europe would receive their kingdoms in fief from the pope; and the renewal of the church, both laity and clergy, would be encouraged and broadly supported by the central vision of the papacy.

Mark Zier

[See also: GREGORIAN REFORM; LEO IX]

Gregory VII. *Das Register Gregors VII*, ed. Erich Caspar. In *Monumenta Germaniae Historica, Epistolae selectae*, Vol. 2. Berlin: Weidmann, 1920–23. (Munich: Monumenta Germaniae Historica, 1990.)

————. *The Correspondence of Pope Gregory VII: Selected Letters from the Registrum*, trans. Ephraim Emerton. New York: Columbia University Press, 1932.

————. *The Epistolae Vagantes of Pope Gregory VII*, ed. and trans. Herbert. E. J. Cowdrey. Oxford: Clarendon, 1972.

Arquillière, Henri-Xavier. *Saint Grégoire VII: essai sur sa conception du pouvoir pontifical.* Paris: Vrin, 1934.

Fliche, Augustin. *Saint Grégoire VII.* Paris: Lecoffre, Gabalda, 1928.

Ullmann, Walter. *The Growth of Papal Government in the Middle Ages.* 3rd ed. London: Methuen, 1970.

GREGORY IX (d. 1241). Pope. When Innocent III died in 1216, his successor, Honorius III (r. 1216–27), maintained a conciliatory policy toward the Hohenstaufen. This changed with the election in 1227 of Innocent's nephew, Cardinal Ugolino, who reigned as Gregory IX. Gregory embroiled the papacy in a long-term confrontation with

Emperor Frederick II, his uncle's ward. To prevent Frederick from dominating Rome through his double heritage, imperial and Sicilian, the pope twice found reasons to excommunicate him. Gregory, at the same time, adopted his foe's harsh measures against heretics. This papal policy affected southern France, where in the aftermath of the Albigensian Crusade the Inquisition was entrusted to the new orders of friars, the Dominicans and the Franciscans, not the bishops, with the backing of the Capetian monarchy. (The French crown was the chief lay beneficiary of the repression of the Cathars.) As a cardinal, Gregory had been a friend of St. Francis; but he furthered the clericalization of the Friars Minor by ruling that the *Testament* of their founder, which forbade petitioning the pope to relax the *Rule,* was not legally binding on them. The key legal texts establishing the Inquisition became part of the canon law in the *Liber extra,* or *Gregorian Decretals,* which were edited by the Dominican Raymond of Peñafort from earlier collections and new decrees. This volume was promulgated by Gregory to the universities in 1234. The bull *Parens scientiarum* (1231) made the papacy the arbiter of institutional and doctrinal disputes concerning the University of Paris.

Thomas M. Izbicki

[See also: ALBIGENSIAN CRUSADE; DOMINICAN ORDER; FRANCISCAN ORDER; *PARENS SCIENTIARUM*]

Brooke, Christopher. *Medieval Church and Society: Collected Essays.* New York: New York University Press, 1972, pp. 183–96.

Kuttner, Stephan. "Raymund of Peñafort as Editor: The *decretales* and *constitutiones* of Gregory IX." *Bulletin of Medieval Canon Law* 2 (1982): 65–80.

Landini, Lawrence C. *The Causes of the Clericalization of the Order of Friars Minor 1209–1260 in the Light of Early Franciscan Sources.* Chicago: Pontificia Universitas Gregoriana, Facultas Historiae Ecclesiasticae, 1968.

GREGORY OF TOURS (ca. 538–594). Born Georgius Florentius, the man known as Gregory pursued many careers during his fifty-five years of life: monk, author, builder, administrator, ambassador, propagandist, politician, and bishop of Tours. He was descended from rich and influential families on both his father's and his mother's side. Senators and bishops, especially the bishops of Langres and Tours, hung thick on the branches of his family tree. Destined for the episcopacy, he spent his youth in the care of uncles and cousins, all of whom were important churchmen. In 573, he was elected bishop of Tours, one of the most powerful of all the Frankish sees, holding its episcopal throne until his death in 594.

Gregory vigorously performed his ecclesiastical duties and played an active role in both local and national politics, as he himself tells us. His position often demanded that he stand up for Tours against the Frankish kings, especially Chilperic I (r. 561–84) of Neustria. He seems to have found ample time to write. At one point, he grouped his massive literary output into five major works: ten books

of *Histories,* seven books of *Miracles* (which include four books on the miracles of St. Martin), one on the *Life of the Fathers,* a *Commentary on the Psalms,* and a tract *On the Office of the Church.*

Most famous for his *Histories,* often improperly called *History of the Franks* (though now scholars are gaining a great deal from his other works as well), Gregory is certainly the first writer in medieval France worthy to be called a historian. The *Histories* were not conceived specifically as a "History of the Franks," but within 200 years of their completion this became their most common name. They are by far our most valuable source for Merovingian Gaul; the Frankish Dark Ages would be even darker without them.

Drawing on the Bible, Eusebius, Jerome, Orosius, Sulpicius Severus, Renatus Profuturus Frigeridus, Sulpicius Alexander, and others, Gregory's first four books cover world history from Adam to his own age. Book 5 begins with an elaborate preface and completes the work with accounts of Gregory's own times. The overall result is, especially in the later books, frequently confusing. While perceptive and analytical, Gregory often skips from episode to episode without obvious order or structure. Scholars have tried to present Gregory as a beguiling storyteller, or as an advocate for the earlier and sterner rule the Franks had enjoyed under Clovis, or as a provider of a cure for the disorder of his times, or as the sincere author of an artless reflection of the chaos of Merovingian society in general. A more charitable assessment sees Gregory as intentionally presenting history as chaotic: the very nature of secular history, that is, the story of fallen humanity, is chaos; true order and structure are divine.

Gregory's other works treat the divine. Here, critics have viewed him as a credulous hagiographer, devoid of the analytical intellect obvious in the *Histories.* For Gregory, however, there could be nothing more concrete than God's power evidenced in a miracle. Particularly revealing of Gregory, and of the 6th-century Gallic episcopacy generally, is his attitude toward St. Martin. Martin had been bishop of Tours two centuries before, and that city guarded his relics. Gregory saw himself as Martin's successor; Martin was his present guide. Gregory protected Martin's interests and Martin protected Gregory's city. His relationship to the saint is a poignant reminder that, though remembered largely for having been a historian, Gregory was first and foremost a Christian bishop.

Richard A. Gerberding

Gregory of Tours. *Monumenta Germaniae Historica, Scriptores Rerum Merovingicarum,* ed. Bruno Krusch and Wilhelm Levison. Hanover: Hahn, 1951; and II-2, Hanover: Hahn, 1885.

———. *The History of the Franks,* trans. Lewis Thorpe. Harmondsworth: Penguin, 1974.

Goffart, Walter. "Gregory of Tours and 'The Triumph of Superstition.'" In *The Narrators of Barbarian History.* Princeton: Princeton University Press, 1988, pp. 112-234.

Hellmann, Siegmund. "Studien zur mittelalterliche Geschichtsschreibung, I, Gregor von Tours." *Historische Zeitschrift* 107 (1911): 1–43.

Wallace-Hadrill, J. M. *The Long-Haired Kings.* Toronto: University of Toronto Press, 1982, pp. 49–70.

GRENOBLE. First recorded in 43 B.C. as Cularo, and renamed Gratianopolis, whence modern-day Grenoble (Isère), the city is situated on the confluence of the Drac and the Isère and is surrounded by mountains on each side but the western. Though lacking navigable waterways, Grenoble, with its situation on three Roman trade routes, continued to be a center for trade throughout the Middle Ages. The city was surrounded by an oval rampart, comprising some thirty towers, between A.D. 284 and 293. It was instituted as a bishopric ca. 381, conquered by the Burgundians in the mid-5th century, and annexed by the Franks ca. 543. The Treaty of Verdun (843) saw its acquisition by Lothair, and it was incorporated into the Holy Roman Empire ca. 1032. Grenoble, receiving its first franchise in 1225, was made capital of the Dauphiné in the course of the 13th century and was sold to the king of France in 1349 by the last dauphin of the Viennois, Humbert II (d. 1349).

The cathedral of Notre-Dame (11th–15th c.) is noted for its tabernacle (1445–57) and the magnificent Ciborium, a specimen of ornate Gothic stonework dating 1455–60. The church of Saint-André (early 12th c.–1236), built originally as the dauphin's palace chapel, is joined to the Hôtel de Ville and situated near the ruins of the church of Saint-Jean. The latter's front-entrance carving now decorates the side door of Saint-André. Saint-Laurent (ca. 965) is perhaps the most interesting religious site, due to its antiquity. It was founded as a necropolis upon which the funerary church, the crypt of Saint-Oyand (late 8th–early 9th c.), was built. The capitals of Saint-Laurent date from the 8th century, with work continuing into the 11th. The Benedictines were asked to rebuild the church in 1012. Unfortunately, much of the woodwork and stucco that remained was destroyed in the restorative efforts of the mid-19th century. Two other necropoli are of importance to the Middle Ages. Saint-Antoine is a Merovingian necropolis and the Roman Saint-Ferréol was used continuously up through the Merovingian period.

Opposite the church of Saint-André is the Gothic Ancien Palais des Dauphins. On May 12, 1339, the University of Grenoble was founded by a papal bull. In its collection, the Grenoble museum posesses a Frankish helmet, and the municipal library houses 12th-century illuminated manuscripts from La Grande Chartreuse.

Stephen C. Martin

[See also: CARTHUSIAN ORDER; DAUPHINÉ/VIENNOIS]

Colardell, Renée. *Grenoble aux premiers temps chrétiens: Saint-Laurent et ses nécropoles.* Paris: Imprimerie Nationale, 1986.

Ferrand, Henri. *Grenoble and Thereabouts: Chartreuse, Oisans, Vercors, Belledone, Uriage-les-Bains, Allevard, Trièvres, Salette, Laffrey.* Boston: Medici Society, 1923.

Prudhomme, Auguste. *Histoire de Grenoble.* 1888; Marseille: Lafitte, 1975.

GRINGORE, PIERRE (d. 1538/9). Throughout his life, the Norman poet Gringore (or Gringoire) commented on contemporary problems, amusing and lecturing his public. The twenty-five works attributed to him are predominantly moral writings and plays. Gringore created an enigmatic persona: he was known during his life as Mère Sotte, the character he played in the troupe of fools called the Enfants-sans-souci, but his motto, which appears on a number of his works, was *Raison Par Tout, Tout Par Raison, Par Tout Raison.* Both Victor Hugo (in *Notre Dame de Paris*) and Théodore de Banville put Gringore into their works.

Gringore is best known today for his *sottie*, part of the *Jeu du Prince des Sots et Mère Sotte* (Mardi Gras, 1512). In fast-paced, witty dialogue, Gringore shows how Mère Sotte, disguised as Pope Julius II, attempts to harm the cause of Louis XII by bribing or pressuring Louis's prelates and nobles into supporting the corrupt, bellicose papacy. The *jeu* also includes a *cry* calling all types of fools (the audience) to the play, a morality in which Julius II reappears as the *Homme obstiné*, and a farce to send the audience away laughing. Gringore accomplishes this by showing how women, especially in matters sexual, prefer *Faire* to *Dire.*

Gringore was also the author of a history play, the *Vie monseigneur saint Louis* (ca. 1527). In nine *livres* (6,572 lines), the moral portrait of the most perfect Christian king evolves in scenes of conflict between St. Louis and powerful enemies—his vassals, the English, and the Saracens—interspersed with episodes portraying the foibles and cares of common people. Gringore is also believed to be the author of the *Croniqueurs*, a satiric play written at the beginning of the reign of Francis I. In addition to writing and performing plays, Gringore was a producer and director of spectacles, such as the *couronnement, sacre, et entrée* into Paris of Queen Claude, on May 9, 1517.

Gringore's nondramatic writings include works of a moral nature, those inspired by contemporary events, and pious works. The best known of the moral writings are the *Folles entreprises*, a long indictment of corrupt prelates and noblemen, the *Fantasies de Mère Sotte*, an adaptation of the stories of the *Gesta Romanorum* glossed by Gringore, and the *Menus propos*, a bestiary of love imitating that of Richard de Fournival. (Gringore often adapted, translated, or paraphrased earlier works.) Most of his *œuvres de circonstance* were provoked by the Italian wars: they include the *Entreprise de Venise*, the *Chasse du cerf des cerfs*, and the *Obstination des Suisses.* Gringore's *Blazon des hérétiques* was the first pamphlet to attack Luther. His pious writings include a translation of the Hours of Notre-Dame.

A conservative who saw every question in a moral light, Gringore epitomizes the strengths and weaknesses of the late 15th century. His purely moral writings now have little appeal, but when his point of view was channeled through the stage he produced works of lasting interest.

Heather M. Arden

[See also: GRANDS RHÉTORIQUEURS; HISTORY PLAYS; RICHARD DE FOURNIVAL; SAINT PLAYS; *SOTTIE*]

Gringore, Pierre. Œuvres complètes de Gringore, ed. Charles d'Héricault and Anatole de Montaiglon. 2 vols. Paris: Jannet, 1858–77.

———. Pierre Gringore's "Les fantasies de Mere Sote," ed. Richard L. Frautschi. Chapel Hill: University of North Carolina Press, 1962.

Picot, Émile, ed. Recueil général des sotties. 3 vols. Paris: Didot, 1909–12, Vol. 2, pp. 105–73, 199–244.

Oulmont, Charles. La poésie morale, politique et dramatique à la veille de la Renaissance: Pierre Gringore. Paris: Champion, 1911.

GROCHEIO, JOHANNES DE (fl. ca. 1300). French music theorist, whose treatise *De musica* is our most important source of information on genre distinctions between medieval French secular music with vernacular texts and instrumental music. Grocheio focuses on the musical practice of Paris, distinguishing broadly between monophonic vernacular music (*musica vulgaris*), measured, or polyphonic, music (*musica mensurata*), and sacred music (*musica ecclesiastica*).

Grocheio divides *musica vulgaris* into *cantus* (vocal music without refrain) and *cantilena* (popular dance music with refrain). There are three categories of *cantus*: *gestualis*, *versualis*, and *coronatus*. *Cantus gestualis* refers to French medieval epic, the chanson de geste. Grocheio provides more information than any other source about the performance practice of the epic. *Cantus versicularis* refers to French chansons organized by syllable count and rhyme scheme, that is, the songs of the troubadours and trouvères. *Cantus coronatus* refers to particularly distinguished and elevated examples of *cantus versualis*, the *grands chants courtois*.

Under the term *cantilena*, Grocheio provides us with our best descriptions of popular dance forms, distinguishing *rotundellus* (rondeau), *stantipes* (estampie), and *ductia* (carole), the latter two with both vocal and instrumental forms. He provides a useful distinction between dance forms in which all parts of the song are dependent on the refrain (i.e., rondeau) from those that have additional music not dependent on the refrain (i.e., virelai and ballade). The instrumental *ductia* and *stantipes* are articulated by alternating phrases called *puncta* (each with first and second endings) with the refrain and are best played on the vielle.

For polyphonic music, Grocheio discusses the motet, organum, conductus, and hocket, describing a successive compositional process in which first the tenor voice is organized and then upper voices are built one at a time over the tenor.

Grocheio peppers his treatise with fascinating comments on the social functions of musical forms; for instance, girls and youths in Normandy sing rondeaux at festivals and banquets, *stantipes* turn the souls of the rich from depraved thinking, motets are not suitable for common people, who do not understand their subtleties, but should be performed for the learned.

Lawrence Earp

[See also: *CANTUS CORONATUS*; CHANSON DE GESTE; DANCE; MUSIC THEORY; *PUY*; TROUBADOUR POETRY; TROUVÈRE POETRY]

Grocheio, Johannes de. Die Quellenhandschriften zum Musiktraktat des Johannes de Grocheio, ed. Ernst Rohloff. Leipzig: Deutscher Verlag für Musik, 1972.

———. Johannes de Grocheo: Concerning Music (De musica), trans. Albert Seay. 2nd ed. Colorado Springs: Colorado College Music Press, 1973.

Page, Christopher. "Johannes de Grocheio on Secular Music: A Corrected Text and a New Translation." Plainsong and Medieval Music 2 (1993): 17–41.

———. Discarding Images: Reflections on Music and Culture in Medieval France. Oxford: Clarendon, 1993, pp. 65–111.

Stevens, John. Words and Music in the Middle Ages: Song, Narrative, Dance and Drama, 1050–1350. Cambridge: Cambridge University Press, 1986, pp. 429–34.

GUEBWILLER. Originally a civil *bourg* attached to the nearby abbey of Murbach, Guebwiller (Haut-Rhin) was granted its independence in the 13th century and soon built ramparts, which served the city well against *routiers* in 1376 and Armagnacs in 1445. The church of Saint-Léger is a fine example of early Rhenish style. The Romanesque façade with two dissimilar towers is decorated with Lombard arcading and has a sculpted typanum of Christ enthroned. A porch extends across the entire west side; above it are two levels of arcades, the lower one blind, and a gable with a criss-cross pattern similar to that at Saint-Étienne, Beauvais. The porch, nave, side aisle, and transept are all late 12th-century; The choir and chevet are 14th-century. An octagonal lantern tower has been reconstructed over the crossing. The now disaffected Gothic Dominican church was begun in 1312. It features a vaulted choir and a high nave with timber roof. The stone choir screen (ca. 1461) is rare for Alsace. In the nave are wall paintings showing the Crucifixion, saints' lives, and the mission of St. Dominic; in the north aisle is a famous fresco depicting the vision of St. Catherine of Siena. The Flamboyant Gothic Hôtel de Ville was built in 1514.

William W. Kibler/William W. Clark

[See also: MURBACH]

Deshoulières, François. "Guebwiller." Congrès archéologique (Metz, Strasbourg, Colmar) 83 (1920): 422–37.

Gardner, Antoine. "Le couvent des Dominicains de Guebwiller." Congrès archéologique (Haute-Alsace) 136 (1978): 249–63.

Meichler, Alexandre. "L'église Saint-Léger de Guebwiller." Congrès archéologique (Haute-Alsace) 136 (1978): 264–83.

GUÉRANDE. The Breton town of Guérande (Loire-Atlantique) played a role in both the Viking raids of the 10th century and the Breton civil wars of the 14th, but it is best known for two treaties concluded during the reign of Duke Jean IV of Brittany (r. 1364–99). The first treaty, on April 12, 1365, resulted from the Battle of Auray the preceding September. It secured recognition of Jean IV as duke, while his rivals, Jeanne de Penthièvre and her sons, would be his heirs if he were to have no children. She would render homage to Jean, who had promised her certain revenues secured by lands.

The second Treaty of Guérande (January 15, 1381) ended a rupture between the French king and the duke of Brittany over the latter's support of England against France and Charles V's abortive attempt to confiscate the duchy. It provided for Jean IV to seek and receive a royal pardon and do homage in the manner of his predecessors. He was to exclude all English from his council and his military commands and ally himself to the king of France. Royal princes and important Breton personages swore to uphold this treaty.

The city has preserved, nearly intact, its 14th- and 15th-century walls with flanking towers.

John Bell Henneman, Jr.

Jones, Michael, ed. *Recueil des actes de Jean IV, duc de Bretagne.* 2 vols. Paris: Klincksieck, 1980–83.

GUERNES DE PONT-SAINTE-MAXENCE (fl. 1170s). An itinerant cleric born north of Paris and known as Guernes composed between 1172 and 1174 the first and most important French *Vie de saint Thomas Becket* in 6,180 Alexandrines in monorhymed five-line stanzas. An edifying biography and a well-documented chronicle, this masterpiece, written in terse language and pregnant with emotion, extols the saint's life and describes his recent tragic death (1170). With its fastidious care for accuracy (on-the-spot investigations, personal perusal of written sources), this hagiographical poem, full of evangelical echoes and of outstanding literary quality, has indisputable historic importance. The poem has come down to us in six Anglo-Norman manuscripts, only three of which contain the complete work.

Annette Brasseur

[See also: BIOGRAPHY; HAGIOGRAPHY]

Guernes de Pont-Sainte-Maxence. *La vie de saint Thomas Becket,* ed. Emmanuel Walberg. Paris: Champion, 1936. [Based on MS *B* (Wolfenbüttel, Bibl. de Brunsvick, August. in 4°, 34.6).]
Walberg, Emmanuel. *La tradition hagiographique de saint Thomas Becket avant la fin du XIIe siècle.* Paris: Droz, 1929.

GUERRE DU BIEN PUBLIQUE. *See* ARISTOCRATIC REVOLT

GUERRE FOLLE. *See* ARISTOCRATIC REVOLT

GUERRIC D'IGNY (ca. 1070/80–1157). Born at Tournai, Guerric was probably educated in the cathedral school

there and may have been *magister* in the school before he adopted a solitary life and entered the Cistercian order ca. 1125. He was chosen abbot of Igny in 1138. He is best known for his fifty-four sermons on the feasts of the liturgical year, which demonstrate a mastery of Scripture. Guerric preached a contemplative theology that emphasized Christ's coming into humans in his "spiritual form," as supernatural guide and life-giving grace. Especially important are Guerric's insistence on Mary's maternal role in this in-forming of Christ in humankind and his presentation of the process of illumination in the spiritual development of the individual.

Grover A. Zinn

Guerric d'Igny. Sermons. *PL* 185.11–214.
———. *Liturgical Sermons,* trans. the Monks of Mount Saint Bernard Abbey. 2 vols. Spencer: Cistercian, 1970–71.
Bouyer, Louis. *The Cistercian Heritage,* trans. Elizabeth A. Livingstone. Westminster: Newman, 1958, pp. 190–203.

GUESCLIN, BERTRAND DU (ca. 1320–1380). Constable of France. Bertrand du Guesclin, perhaps the most famous French warrior of the Hundred Years' War, was the first of three distinguished Breton noblemen to serve as constable of France during this conflict. Du Guesclin was born into an old but not very wealthy family. In 1353, he succeeded his father as lord of Broons and a year later was knighted. He began serving the French crown at Pontorson as early as 1351, and for the next thirteen years his military career was confined to Normandy, where he fought for the king against the supporters of Charles the Bad, king of Navarre, and Brittany, where he fought for Charles de Blois against Jean de Montfort, the English-backed claimant to the duchy. In 1357, he led the forces that supplied the besieged city of Rennes. In May 1364, he won a great victory over the Navarrese forces at Cocherel in Normandy after feigning a withdrawal that induced his foes to abandon a superior position. In the same period, he also suffered defeats, as the English captured him at Pas d'Évran in 1359, at the bridge of Juigne in 1360, and at Auray in 1364. In this last battle, Charles de Blois was killed and Montfort became duke of Brittany.

With Normandy and Brittany now pacified, Du Guesclin devoted the rest of the 1360s to service in southern France and Spain. Louis of Anjou, brother of Charles V, was royal lieutenant in Languedoc and needed him to lead numerous *routiers* (unemployed soldiers) outside the realm on campaigns in Provence and Castile. His successful expedition to Spain in 1365 was followed by his defeat and capture at Nájera in 1367. In 1369, however, he returned to Spain and reinstalled a pro-French king on the Castilian throne.

Rarely successful at pitched battles, Du Guesclin was adept at handling bands of *routiers* and fighting with their tactics. In 1370, when a *routier* chieftain, Robert Knolles, was leading an English raid into northwestern France, Charles V summoned Du Guesclin and made him constable. The latter then made a private alliance with Olivier de Clisson, a wealthy Breton lord who had fought against him at Auray and Nájera. Clisson brought powerful contingents of Bretons into the French army, and he and Du Guesclin conquered Poitou and Saintonge in 1371–72. In 1373, they secured Brittany, whose duke had gone over to the English.

For the next five years, the constable led French forces against the English in various parts of France. At the end of 1378, Charles V made the political error of trying to confiscate Brittany. Du Guesclin, one of those charged with implementing this unpopular decision, was reluctant to do so, since many of his old comrades had rallied to the duke. Never popular with the king's nonmilitary advisers, he was nearly removed from office but instead was sent to fight against *routiers* in Auvergne, where he died from an unknown illness (perhaps dysentery) in the summer of 1380 while beseiging the town of Châteauneuf-de-Randon.

Admired by his contemporaries for his military prowess, Du Guesclin earned the titles count of Longueville and duke of Molina. He was buried at Saint-Denis.

John Bell Henneman, Jr.

[See also: CUVELIER; HUNDRED YEARS' WAR]

Cazelles, Raymond. "Du Guesclin avant Cocherel." *Actes du Colloque International de Cocherel* (1964): 33–40.

Dupuy, Micheline. *Bertrand du Guesclin: capitaine d'aventure, connétable de France.* Paris: Perrin, 1977.

Hay du Chastelet, Paul. *Histoire de Bertrand du Guesclin, connétable de France.* Paris: Billaine, 1666.

Jacob, Yves. *Bertrand du Guesclin, connétable de France.* Paris: Tallandier, 1992.

Luce, Siméon. *Histoire de Bertrand du Guesclin et de son époque.* Paris: Hachette, 1876.

GUI DE MORI (fl. second half of 13th c.). Monk or priest who composed the most extensive signed *remaniement* of the *Roman de la Rose.* In refashioning the text of Guillaume de Lorris completed by the anonymous continuation, Gui brought about several major changes: he created a second prologue that contains a system of notation indicating additions, deletions, new rhymes, and "restored omissions"; he introduced an eleventh anticourtly vice, Pride; and he recast the Narcissus episode using Robert de Blois's *Floris et Lyriopé* (ca. 1250).

In his reworking of the section composed by Jean de Meun, Gui continued the tendency to transform the *Rose* into a more clerkly and didactic art of love with a linear rather than digressive structure. Gui reduced allusions to pagan mythology while increasing those dealing with the Bible and the church fathers. Gui cut Genius's speech to one-tenth its original length and suppressed many of the bawdy lines describing the taking of the Rose. In a passage inserted into the God of Love's speech, Gui portrayed himself as the third *Rose* author.

The so-called Tersan manuscript, now lost, contained an early version of Gui's *remaniement.* The most complete text is found in MS 101 of the Municipal Library of Tournai. Either Gui or an anonymous editor reinstated many of the verses originally left out.

Lori Walters

[See also: *ÉCHECS AMOUREUX*; GUILLAUME DE LORRIS; JEAN DE MEUN; ROBERT DE BLOIS; *ROSE, ROMAN DE LA*]

Hult, David F. "Gui de Mori, lecteur médiéval." *Incidences* 5 (1981): 53–70.

———. *Self-Fulfilling Prophecies: Readership and Authority in the First "Roman de la Rose."* Cambridge: Cambridge University Press, 1986, pp. 34–55, 59–60, 63–64.

Huot, Sylvia. *The Romance of the Rose and Its Medieval Readers: Interpretation, Reception, Manuscript Transmission.* Cambridge: Cambridge University Press, 1993, pp. 85–129.

Jung, Marc-René. "Gui de Mori et Guillaume de Lorris." *Vox Romanica* 27 (1968): 106–37.

Langlois, Ernest. "Gui de Mori et le *Roman de la Rose.*" *Bibliothèque de l'École des Chartes* 68 (1907): 1–23.

GUIBERT DE NOGENT (ca. 1064–ca. 1125). Perhaps best known for his autobiography, *De vita sua sive monodiarum suarum libri tres,* and a treatise concerning the veneration of relics, *De pignoribus sanctorum,* this Benedictine monk also wrote a popular history of the First Crusade (*Gesta Dei per Francos*), a moral commentary on Genesis, a handbook for preachers (*Liber quo ordine sermo fieri debeat*), and lesser works.

Born at Clermont-en-Beauvaisis in northern France, Guibert was dedicated by his parents to the monastic life. His father died soon after his birth, and he was raised by his mother, who isolated him from other children. As a young adolescent, he entered the monastery of Saint-Germer-de-Fly, where he studied not only the Bible and theology but also classical authors, especially Ovid and Virgil. In 1104, he became abbot of a small Benedictine house at Nogent-sous-Coucy. There, he wrote his history of the First Crusade and, in 1115, his autobiography. Guibert's attitudes toward his mother, sexuality and sexual sins, cleanliness, and his (and others') visionary experiences are important aspects of the autobiography, which also offers numerous insights into daily life, education, and social and political history. Guibert's treatise on relics attacks the veneration of a supposed tooth of Christ at the abbey of Saint-Médard, Soissons, but it is not a total rejection of either the cult of the saints or the veneration of relics.

Grover A. Zinn

[See also: CRUSADES; HISTORIOGRAPHY; SAINTS, CULT OF]

Guibert de Nogent. *Opera. PL* 166.

———. *Autobiographie,* ed. and trans. Edmond-René Labande. Paris: Les Belles Lettres, 1981.

———. *How to Make a Sermon,* trans. George E. McCracken. In *Early Medieval Theology,* ed. George E. McCracken with Allen Cabaniss. Philadelphia: Westminster, 1957.

———. *Gesta Dei per Francos,* ed. M. Thurot. In *Recueil des historiens des croisades.* 16 vols. Paris: Imprimerie Royale, 1879, Vol. 4: *Historiens occidentaux,* pp. 115–263.

———. *Self and Society in Medieval France: The Memoirs of Abbot Guibert of Nogent,* trans. John F. Benton. New York:

Harper Torchbooks, 1970. [Excellent introduction and bibliography.]

————. *De vita sua sive monodiarum suarum libri tres,* ed. Georges Bourgin as *Histoire de sa vie.* Paris: Picard, 1907.

GUILD. Economic association of traders or artisans. No direct continuity between Roman *collegia* and French medieval guilds can be established. Frankish drinking associations and Carolingian *caritates* (confraternal organizations) provide a chronological intermediary without demonstrated links to the high-medieval guilds. The medieval guild had a primary economic function, often with a religious or confraternal dimension. Separate spiritual confraternities also existed alongside guilds. The oldest French records survive for the *caritet* of Valenciennes (ca. 1050) and the *gilda mercatoria* of Saint-Omer (late 11th c.).

The guild was essentially an association of tradespeople or merchants grouped to supervise production and guarantee quality of merchandise. Close parallels with the northern European *hansas,* groups of traveling merchants who banded together for mutual protection, can be noted.

In the course of the 13th century, trade guilds multiplied in French towns. Associations of bakers, barbers, drapers, spice merchants, moneyers, silversmiths, and other occupations often were incorporated with statutes and a governing hierarchy in the late 13th and 14th centuries. They might impose entry fees. Strict regulations for promotion from apprentice to journeyman and finally to master developed, and in some artisanal occupations the production of a *chef-d'œuvre* became the criterion for master status. Training and expertise were jealously guarded in some trades, with the passage of skills from father to son, inspiring the criticism of monopolistic practices and hereditary membership by the end of the Middle Ages.

The guilds in France often had a role in urban government. The merchant guilds of northern France contributed to the earliest movements of urban communal autonomy. In Languedoc, representation from merchant and artisanal corporations formed the basis of some consulates. By the end of the medieval era, however, royal influence over guilds and town governments was considerable.

Kathryn L. Reyerson

Coornaert, Émile. "Les ghildes médiévales." *Revue historique* 199 (1948): 22–55.

Gouron, André. *La réglementation des métiers en Languedoc au moyen âge.* Geneva: Droz, 1958.

Thrupp, Sylvia L. "The Gilds." In *The Cambridge Economic History of Europe.* 7 vols. Cambridge: Cambridge University Press, 1965, Vol. 3: *Economic Organization and Policies in the Middle Ages,* pp. 230–280.

GUILHEM IX (William IX, 1071–1126). The first troubadour was also the seventh count of Poitiers, ninth duke of Aquitaine, and grandfather of Eleanor of Aquitaine. One of the few who returned to France after the First Crusade (1096–99), he successfully led a crusading army to Spain in 1120. Contemporary anecdotes recall him entertaining crowds with jokes, verses, and stories; some sources style him a reckless, violent, sarcastic infidel who earned his excommunication.

Eleven songs survive, one of doubtful attribution. Though often seeming to parody or recast a preexisting tradition, Guilhem's work lays the foundation for later troubadour song, including the love lyric, satire, and *pastorela*; the figures of warrior and lover, boasting and humility, ribaldry and nascent courtliness are all represented. Three songs addressed to his "companions" jocularly compare women to property (horses, fishing holes, woodlands), subject to legal disputes; in three more, the poet, disguised as a fool or madman, claims prowess in both word games and sexual games. Four meditate more soberly on love, using feudal and natural metaphors; these inaugurate in Occitan the vocabulary and topoi of *fin'amors,* among them the nature introduction, with woods and birdsongs inspiring the poet and the paradoxical joy that cures the sick and drives wise men insane. Natural imagery is not confined to the *exordium*: in a middle strophe, Guilhem compares fragile love to a hawthorn branch that trembles at night in the freezing rain, then gleams with sunlight the next day. The same poem includes indoor, domestic scenes. Recalling a "battle" with his lady that ended in mutual desire, he concludes that words are cheap: "Let others brag of love; *we* have the bread and the knife." A final farewell song recants his youthful frivolity and impiety; throwing off his furs, he relinquishes Poitiers to the care of his old enemy Foulques of Anjou.

Researches into Guilhem's sources of inspiration involve the origins of troubadour poetry itself. In the *pastorela*-like "poem of the red cat" (*Farai un vers, pos mi sonelh*), whose hero feigns muteness (or foreignness) to fool two ladies who abduct him for an eight-day orgy, the words *babariol, babarian* have suggested to some a possible Andalusian-Arabic influence. Guilhem's range of registers is interpreted sometimes as schizophrenia (was he two poets?), sometimes as a progression that invents courtliness in moving from bawdy to idealistic views of love. If his *Farai un vers de dreit nien* mocks distant love:

Anc non la vi ez am la fort; . . .
Quan no la vei, be m'en deport,
No•m prez un jau: . . . /
No sai lo luec ves on s'esta

("I've never seen her and I love her a lot. / . . . When I don't see her, I'm quite happy; / I don't care a rooster. / . . . I don't know where she lives"), then what was its antecedent? This and the "red cat" song were, he claims, composed while sleeping; the two poems thus suggest dream visions. Guilhem's verse often uses long lines of eleven, twelve, or fourteen syllables (with internal rhyme)—lines seldom used by later troubadours. Studies of his verse forms suggest connections with Latin poetry, the liturgy, the popular round dance, and even epic measures. A fragment of his music is preserved as a *contrafactum* in the 14th-century *Jeu de sainte Agnès*; though doubtless adapted, it shows the melody's filiation with monastic music.

Amelia E. Van Vleck

[See also: *JOUFROI DE POITIERS*; REALISTIC ROMANCES; TROUBADOUR POETRY]

Guilhem IX. *The Poetry of William VII, Count of Poitiers, IX Duke of Aquitaine,* ed. and trans. Gerald A. Bond. New York: Garland, 1982.

———. *Guglielmo IX: poesie,* ed. Nicolo Pasero. Modena: Mucchi, 1973.

Bezzola, Reto R. "Guillaume IX et les origines de l'amour courtois." *Romania* 66 (1940): 145–237.

GUILHEM DE MONTANHAGOL (fl. ca. 1233–68).

Troubadour of Toulouse. Active in the courts of Toulouse, Provence, Castile, and Aragon, Guilhem left seven *cansos,* or love songs; six *sirventes,* or satires; and a *partimen,* or dialogue, with Sordello. His death was lamented in a *planh* by his brother-in-law, Pons Santolh. An orthodox Catholic, Guilhem expressed approval during the Albigensian Crusade for a benevolent correction of the Cathars' errors but not for the violent excesses committed by the crusading army. His statement that chastity begins in love has been seen in the tradition leading to the *dolce stil nuovo* but perhaps means only that love is a necessary precondition of fidelity.

William D. Paden

[See also: TROUBADOUR POETRY]

Guilhem de Montanhagol. *Les poésies de Guilhem de Montanhagol, troubadour provençal du XIIIe siècle,* ed. Peter T. Ricketts. Toronto: Pontifical Institute of Mediaeval Studies, 1964.

Riquer, Martín de, ed. *Los trovadores: historia literaria y textos.* 3 vols. Barcelona: Planeta, 1975, Vol. 3, pp. 1429–46.

Topsfield, L.T. "The Theme of Courtly Love in the Poems of Guilhem Montanhagol." *French Studies* 11 (1957): 127–34.

GUILLAUME. *See also* GUILHEM OR WILLIAM

GUILLAUME, CHANSON DE.

Known by a single manuscript in Anglo-Norman dialect (B.L. Add. 38, 663), dated 1225–50, the *Chanson de Guillaume* (3,554 assonanced decasyllables) survives in a reworked and corrupt version. The poem nevertheless preserves many archaic epic traits, a fact that explains the unusual attention it has received since its discovery in the late 19th century and its initial publication in 1901.

The place of the *Chanson de Guillaume* in the development of the epic traditions that make up the Guillaume d'Orange Cycle is important. This poem gives evidence of the mingling of historical traditions relative to Guillaume de Toulouse—e.g., the allusion to the glorious defeat on the Orbieu River in 793—and to his son Bernard of Septimania, nicknamed Naso, with traditions concerning Count Vivien of Tours, lay abbot of Saint-Martin, who died in 851, a victim of betrayal. It is thus at the origin of the cyclic expansion that was to give birth to poems about Vivien and his death at Archamp or Aliscans (*Enfances Vivien, Chevalerie Vivien, Aliscans*). Traditions relative to Orange, the third element in the makeup of the epic character of Guillaume, are likewise present, but as a subtext: it is only in the later part of the poem (G^2) that Orange is substituted for Barcelona as the hero's capital.

The extant version (ca. 1150–75) comprises two parts of different date and provenance. Lines 1–1,980 (known as G^1) might have been composed before 1100. Vivien, Guillaume's nephew, is involved in spite of himself in an unequal battle; his courage inspires the Christian forces, but he is overwhelmed and killed (1–930). A messenger from Vivien reaches Guillaume in Barcelona, and he hastens to the battlefield of Archamp, where he, too, is defeated; he returns to Barcelona with the body of another nephew, Guischard (931–1,228). Guibourc, Guillaume's wife, comforts the hero and encourages him to return to battle, hiding the defeat from the vassals she gathers for the counterattack. All the Frenchmen are killed or captured in this third battle, except Guillaume and his young nephew, Gui; the hero does manage to kill the pagan leader, Desramé (1,229–980).

In the second and later part (G^2), which is frequently in contradiction with the first, Guillaume continues the fight until he kills a second pagan king, Alderufe, while Gui is captured. Guillaume finds Vivien still alive, comforts him as he dies, and then returns to Orange, which is now his capital (1,981–2,213). He announces the new disaster to Guibourc, who urges him to seek help from King Louis (2,214–453). At Laon, Guillaume is initially put off by the king, but his men convince the sovereign while the hero secures the help of the young and powerful Rainouart (2,454–928). Count Guillaume leads his forces to Archamp, where, thanks to Rainouart's extraordinary strength, the prisoners are freed and the Saracens wiped out. Guibourc recognizes Rainouart as her brother, and he is baptized and married to Ermentrude (2,454–3,554).

The primitive nature of lines 1–1,980 is certain; they use the epithet "crooked nose" (*al corb nés*) for Guillaume, draw on the tradition of the siege of Orange, and depict Guillaume's association with Barcelona, a reminiscence of the participation of Guillaume de Toulouse in the conquest of the Spanish March; a refrain of remarkable intensity (*Lunsdi al vespre, Joesdi al vespre, Lores fu mecresdi*) punctuates the action. It makes Vivien an emblem of heroic virtue, whence his authority in the vacuum left when the traditional baronial prerogatives were mocked by Tiébaut and Estourmi.

The character of the second part is fundamentally different, notably in the appearance of Rainouart, who, in heroic-comic vein, nearly supplants Guillaume as hero. It is perhaps the reworking of a poem conceived as a continuation of G^1, a poem that might have been the model for both G^2 and *Aliscans*. Nonetheless, certain scenes are esthetically powerful, such as that at the gate of Orange in which Guibourc rejects her threatened and fleeing husband until, by his valor, he is able to prove his identity. Furthermore, one must question whether the *Chanson de Guillaume* can be considered completed with the death of

Desramé, when Guillaume is alone and numerous Christians are still held by the Saracens; in this case, the model for G² and *Aliscans* could have been at least partially linked to the primitive poem.

Crossroads of the formative elements of the Guillaume cycle, a work rich in passages of beauty, the *Chanson de Guillaume* in the state in which it has come down to us is exasperating for its modern editors, caught between the desire to respect the text and that of finding the original. Readers, on the other hand, will find only pleasure in this unforgettable poem, worthy of comparison with the *Roland*.

François Suard

[See also: *ALISCANS*; GUILLAUME D'ORANGE CYCLE]

McMillan, Duncan, ed. *La chanson de Guillaume.* 2 vols. Paris: SATF, 1949–50.

Suard, François, ed. and trans. *La chanson de Guillaume.* Paris: Bordas, 1991.

Wathelet-Willem, Jeanne, ed. *Recherches sur* La chanson de Guillaume: *études accompagnées d'une édition.* 2 vols. Paris: Les Belles Lettres, 1975.

Bennett, Philip. "La chanson de Guillaume, poème anglo-normand?" In *Au carrefour des routes d'Europe: la chanson de geste. Xe Congrès International de la Société Rencesvals,* ed. Jean Subrenat. 2 vols. Aix-en-Provence: CUER MA, 1987, Vol. 1, pp. 259–81.

Frappier, Jean. *Les chansons de geste du cycle de Guillaume d'Orange.* 3 vols. Paris: SEDES, 1955–83, Vol. 1, pp. 113–233.

GUILLAUME DE LORRIS (fl. 1220–40). The *Roman de la Rose* of Guillaume de Lorris, a poem of 4,028 lines thought to have been written ca. 1225–40, has always been linked to Jean de Meun's *Roman de la Rose,* a poem more than four times the length of Guillaume's and written as its continuation. It is in Jean's poem that the reader learns the names of the authors of the two works and the fact that Guillaume died before completing his *roman,* which he had written some forty years earlier.

Although Jean de Meun's *roman* became one of the most popular works of the Middle Ages, read and cited extensively through the Renaissance and existing in more than 250 manuscripts, Guillaume de Lorris's unfinished poem has captured the imagination of the post-18th-century reading public and remains a source of lively critical debate.

In a prologue of twenty lines, the author discusses the importance of dreams (with a reference to Macrobius) and establishes the dream narrative of the text itself. In the narrative proper, set in springtime, the dreamer discovers an enclosed garden. On the wall of the garden are portrayed Hate, Felony, Baseness, Covetousness, Avarice, Envy, Sadness, Old Age, Hypocrisy, and Poverty—all characters excluded from the inside of the garden. The Dreamer enters through the only gate, guarded by Idleness, a beautiful lady whose day is spent fixing her hair and face. Inside the garden, the Dreamer meets Merriment and his friends Beauty, Wealth, Generosity, Nobility, Courtesy, and Youth.

As the Dreamer makes a tour of the garden, he is stalked by the God of Love and overcome at the Fountain of Narcissus, a spring at the center of the garden whose two brilliant crystals allow one to see all things in the garden. While looking into the crystals, the Dreamer sees a rose, falls in love, and becomes the Lover. The God of Love now takes his new vassal in charge and instructs him carefully in the art of love. The Lover makes an attempt to approach the Rose but is repulsed by Resistance, the figure in charge of the Rose and the precincts within the hedge around her. Dejected by his failure and miserable from the pains of love, the rejected Lover is approached by Reason, described in Boethian terms as a lady of such lineage that she must have come from Paradise, as Nature would not have been able to make a work of such dimension. Reason reproaches the Lover for his foolishness in becoming acquainted with Idleness and explains that the evil he calls love is really madness. Is it wise or foolish to follow what causes you to live in grief, she asks? The Lover reacts angrily to Reason's advice, arguing that it would not be right for him to betray his lord, Love.

The Lover then seeks consolation from a Friend, who advises him that, though Resistance is angry at the moment, he can be overcome by flattery. With the aid of Openness and Pity, who plead for mercy on the Lover's behalf, the Lover once again gains access to Fair Welcome, who is persuaded to allow him to draw ever nearer the Rose, finally bestowing a kiss. Outraged, Slander arouses Jealousy; Shame, and Fear go to awaken the sleeping Resistance. Angry that he has been duped, Resistance chases the Lover from the Rose, and Jealousy builds a prison to keep Fair Welcome locked up. The Lover laments his misery and stresses that he is worse off now than he was before. The poet returns to the contrasting theme of the brevity of love's pleasures and the eternity of grief that follows. The Lover evokes the Wheel of Fortune, comparing Love's treatment of him to Fortune's own behavior. In the midst of further lamenting, the poem breaks off.

From the beginning, the reader of the *Roman de la Rose* is faced with difficulties in understanding Guillaume's poem. The dream-allegory setting implies multiple levels of meaning, in the medieval sense of allegory as saying one thing and meaning another. Macrobius's *Commentary on the Dream of Scipio* demonstrates the medieval concern for the dream and its relationship to other orders of reality. Moreover, the narrator is not merely the author but also the Dreamer and Lover, who operates in an objective world of personifications. Or are the personifications merely devices for the psychological description of the Lover and the Rose? In this question lies one of the most difficult medieval problems concerning the understanding of character and personality. But beyond these questions of form and meaning lie questions raised by the narrative itself. What is this garden the Lover enters—a kind of paradise involving a beautiful, elite society and a new form of love that transcends ordinary morality? Or is it a society obsessed with its own youth and the pleasures of self-gratification, careful to exclude images of Old Age and Poverty from the inner precincts of its own self-interest? Is this a love beyond Reason's comprehension, or is it the self-delusion of youth calling something *amor* that is really *folie*? Is this the meaning of the Fountain of Narcissus for the Lover? Is it really a dangerous fountain that might lead ultimately to death, or are the crystals a gateway to a higher form of love?

Because the poem breaks off with no hint of how it will end, or even how near the end the reader is, scholars have often turned to Jean de Meun's continuation and other texts for help in interpreting Guillaume's formidable *roman*. It is a poem shrouded in mystery and tantalizingly inconclusive.

Emanuel J. Mickel

[See also: COURTLY LOVE; JEAN DE MEUN; *POIRE, ROMAN DE LA*; *ROSE, ROMAN DE LA*; QUARREL OF THE *ROMAN DE LA ROSE*]

Guillaume de Lorris and Jean de Meun. *Le roman de la Rose*, ed. and trans. Armand Strubel. Paris: Livre de Poche, 1992.
———. *Le roman de la Rose*, ed. Félix Lecoy. 3 vols. Paris: Champion, 1965–70.
———. *The Romance of the Rose*, trans. Charles Dahlberg. Princeton: Princeton University Press, 1971.
Arden, Heather. *The Romance of the Rose*. Boston: Twayne, 1987.
———. *The Roman de la Rose: An Annotated Bibliography*. New York: Garland, 1993.
Batany, Jean. *Approches du "Roman de la Rose."* Paris: Bordas, 1974.
Brownlee, Kevin, and Sylvia Huot. *Rethinking the "Romance of the Rose": Text, Image, Reception*. Philadelphia: University of Pennsylvania Press, 1992.
Fleming, John V. *"The Roman de la Rose": A Study in Allegory and Iconography*. Princeton: Princeton University Press, 1969.
Gunn, Alan M.F. *The Mirror of Love: A Reinterpretation of the Romance of the Rose*. Lubbock: Texas Tech Press, 1952.
Lewis, C.S. *The Allegory of Love*. London: Oxford University Press, 1936.
Muscatine, Charles. "The Emergence of Psychological Allegory in Old French Romance," *PMLA* 68 (1953): 1160–82.
Poirion, Daniel. *Le roman de la Rose*. Paris: Hatier, 1973.
Robertson, D.W. *A Preface to Chaucer*. Princeton: Princeton University Press, 1962.
Spearing, Anthony. *Medieval Dream-Poetry*. Cambridge: Cambridge University Press, 1976.

GUILLAUME DE PALERNE. An anonymous Greco-Byzantine romance of the early 13th century, *Guillaume de Palerne* is preserved in a single manuscript, Arsenal 6565. It recounts in 9,664 rhyming octosyllables the adventures of its eponymous hero, who as an infant would have been murdered by his uncle, who wishes to inherit his lands, had he not been aided by a friendly werewolf, which turns out to be the enchanted son of the King of Spain. Raised ignorant of his heritage, Guillaume encounters the beautiful princess Melior, daughter of the Emperor of Rome. After many adventures, he wins her, has his own inheritance restored, and ends the werewolf's enchantment. Influence of the chanson de geste is evident in the style and length of the scenes of combat. An English alliterative version was made in the 14th century, and a French prose reworking by Pierre Durand appeared in the 16th.

William W. Kibler

[See also: GRECO-BYZANTINE ROMANCE; IDYLLIC ROMANCE; MARIE DE FRANCE]

Micha, Alexandre, ed. *Guillaume de Palerne*. Geneva: Droz, 1990]

GUILLAUME DE SAINT-PAIR (fl. 1150–1190). A monk at Mont-Saint-Michel when Robert de Torigni was abbot there (1154–86), Guillaume de Saint-Pair wrote the *Roman du Mont-Saint-Michel*. The poem, in almost 3,800 octosyllabic lines, is divided into three sections, the first two purporting to record the history of the Benedictine monastery, the third describing Mont-Saint-Michel and recounting legends and miracles attached to it.

Norris J. Lacy

[See also: MONT-SAINT-MICHEL]

Guillaume de Saint-Pair. *Roman du Mont-Saint-Michel*, ed. Paul Redlich. Marburg: Elwert, 1894.
Beaurepaire, Eugène de. "Étude sur Guillaume de Saint-Pair." In *Mémoires de la Société des Antiquaires de Normandie*. Caen, 1851, pp. 227–53.

GUILLAUME D'ORANGE CYCLE. The epic cycle of Guillaume d'Aquitaine takes its name from St. Guilhem d'Aquitaine, who was a grandson through his mother of the first Carolingian king, Charles Martel. Named count of Toulouse in 789 by his cousin Charlemagne, Guilhem (OFr. Guillaume) fought for many years against the Muslims, being defeated by them at Orbieu (793) but capturing Barcelona from them in 803. In 804, he retired to the abbey of Aniane. Shortly thereafter, he founded the abbey of Gellone nearby—later renamed Saint-Guilhem-le-Désert in his honor—where he died in 812. Around this saintly hero, there arose in the 12th and 13th centuries twenty-four chansons de geste that fall into two groups: poems devoted to Guillaume himself and those devoted to his father, Aymeri, or other members of his family. The ensemble is known as the Guillaume d'Orange (or William of Orange) Cycle or, alternately, as the Garin de Monglane Cycle, after Guillaume's legendary ancestor. With the exception of the *Chanson de Guillaume*, these poems, grouped in "cyclical manuscripts," constitute the largest and most coherent of the chanson de geste cycles and have much to tell us about the medieval epic.

The manuscript tradition is extensive and attests to both the oral role of the jongleurs and the importance of writing in the elaboration of the poems; ateliers ensured the coherence of the ensemble by creating transitional pieces between the texts. The manuscripts allow us to catch glimpses of earlier redactions and to propose hypotheses on the development of the *geste*. One group, called the "short cycle manuscripts," comprises only poems relating to Guillaume; another group, characterized by the presence of a six-syllable line at the end of each laisse, comprises poems about Aymeri; and the third, called the "long cycle manuscripts," brings together both types of poems. Several manuscript families, the work of three different revisers, can be distinguished; the families *A* ("short cycle") and *B* ("long cycle") have the most coherent groupings and have been used to prepare the standard editions.

Poems About Guillaume. Not counting the *Chanson de Guillaume*, which is not found in the cyclical manuscripts, eleven poems comprise Guillaume's poetic biography. The *Enfances Guillaume* (3,400 lines; 13th c.) tells how Guillaume distinguishes himself from his brothers and wins the heart of Orable. The *Couronnement de Louis*, the *Charroi de Nîmes*, and the *Prise d'Orange*, all closely related and composed between 1150 and 1170, tell of Guillaume's most famous exploits: the wound to the nose by Corsolt, from which the hero received his epithet *al corb nés;* the capture of Nîmes by ruse; the conquest of Orable and her city of Orange. Another ensemble narrates the deeds and passion of Vivien, who will be avenged by his uncle Guillaume and by the giant Rainouart. The *Enfances Vivien* (3,200 lines; 13th c.) tells in a style reminiscent of the adventure romances how Guillaume's nephew Vivien, son of Garin d'Anseüne, is surrendered to the Saracens of Luiserne in exchange for his father, how he miraculously escapes death and succeeds, thanks to help from his family, in recapturing Anseüne. The *Chevalerie* or *Covenant Vivien* (1,918 lines; ca. 1200), much more imbued with epic spirit, explains why Vivien must die in battle. At his knighting, the youthful warrior swears never to retreat a single foot before the pagans and immediately launches a brutal raid into Spain. Desramé of Cordova, the Saracen leader, sets sail to meet him at the field of Archamp. Vivien, fearful of breaking his oath, refuses to send to his uncle Guillaume for help until it is too late. Guillaume joins battle but is soon separated from his nephew.

The end of the battle is recounted in the earliest poem of this group, *Aliscans* (last quarter of the 12th c.). Vivien, overwhelmed by the odds, dies, and Guillaume watches all his companions disappear. He is forced back to Orange, where his wife, Guibourc, allows him to reenter the city only after he has accomplished an act of valor to prove his identity. He seeks aid from King Louis while the Saracens besiege Orange. Helped by the giant Rainouart, Guillaume overcomes the Saracens, and Rainouart, recognized by Guibourc as her brother, marries King Louis's daughter Aelis.

Aliscans and its prologue, the *Chevalerie Vivien*, are reworkings of two different narratives: an account of the exploits and death of Vivien, avenged by Guillaume, and a poem dedicated to the stunning revenge of the Christians, aided by Rainouart, over the Saracens. The *Chanson de Guillaume* (ca. 1150), a noncyclic text, also combines these elements but features an older version of Vivien's exploits.

Rainouart's story continues in the *Bataille Loquifer* (4,180 lines; late 12th c.), which exploits, by adding fanciful elements, the heroic-comic vein represented by this character. Most of the poem is devoted to the combat be-

tween Rainouart and the pagan giant Loquifer, but it also tells of the birth of Rainouart's son, Maillefer, which causes the death of his mother, Aelis. The infant is then stolen by the dwarf Picolet.

Finally, two texts exploit the theme of *moniage*, the hero's renouncing of this world and the adventures that devolve from that choice. The older, the *Moniage Guillaume* (12th c.), of which we have two versions, tells of the hero's rejection by the monks of Aniane, where he had retired to expiate his sins. Instead, he becomes a hermit but is captured by Sinagon of Palerne; finally freed, he returns to his hermitage but must again take up arms to defend his sovereign, Louis, from Ysoré: only then can he end his life in conformity with his wishes. More recent (late 12th or early 13th c.) but placed before the *Moniage Guillaume* in the manuscripts because it tells of events that happened earlier in Guillaume's life, the *Moniage Rainouart* (7,600 lines) develops comic situations that arise from the contrast between the hero's immense size, strength, and simplicity and the demands of monastic life. The monks, who do not hesitate to betray Rainouart to the Saracens, are even more odious than in the *Moniage Guillaume*. Among the many adventures in the poem, one should note the hero's reunion with his son, Maillefer, who had been taken from him in the *Bataille Loquifer*, and his victory over the giant Gadifer.

The cyclical manuscripts attach two later poems to the Guillaume Cycle, *Foulque de Candie* (16,000+ lines; 13th c.), an independent version of Guillaume's battle at Archamp to avenge Vivien, and *Renier* (late 13th c.), which has as its hero Rainouart's grandson and ties this cycle to the Crusade Cycle.

The creation of such a vast cycle is the result of complex processes. Analysis of the poems and the manuscripts reveals what Tyssens calls two "cyclic nuclei." On the one hand are three tales narrating the early epic career of the hero: *Couronnement*, *Charroi*, and *Prise*; on the other, three poems in which Rainouart plays an important role: *Aliscans*, *Bataille Loquifer*, and *Moniage Rainouart*. Then, isolated poems, such as the *Moniage Guillaume*, or poems composed to serve as prologues to texts already in the corpus—the *Enfances Guillaume* prepares the *Couronnement* and the *Prise*, the *Chevalerie Vivien* introduces *Aliscans*, and the *Enfances Vivien* the *Chevalerie*—attach themselves to these nuclei.

The problem of cyclical organization must be distinguished from that of the dating of the poems and their relationship to history. The *Moniage Guillaume* predates the *Moniage Rainouart* but is integrated into the cycle after it. And the *Chanson de Guillaume*, which in its first part includes the most archaic matter, remains apart from the cycle.

There exist traces of earlier legendary activity relative to Guillaume. The *Nota Emilianense* (ca. 1065–75) includes among Charlemagne's peers a *Ghigelmo alcorbitanas*, and a *Guillelmus curbinasus* is supposed to have signed the counterfeited charter of Saint-Yrieix (ca. 1090). The hero's characteristic physical trait, at least in one of its two forms, is thus known by the last third of the 11th century. Moreover, a poem on the siege of Orange, now lost, was composed before 1125, since it is alluded to in the earliest *Vita sancti Wilhelmi.*

Guillaume's epic biography derives from three possible historical sources. Guillaume de Toulouse, Charlemagne's cousin, is mentioned in the panegyric of Louis the Pious, composed after 827 by Ermold the Black, and in the *Life of Louis the Pious* by the Astronomer (after 840). Victor over the Gascons in 790, he suffered a glorious defeat in 793 at the hands of the Saracens, who, after burning the outskirts of Narbonne, marched against Carcassonne; in spite of their numerical superiority, they withdrew into Spain. Ten years later, Guillaume took part in the siege and conquest of Barcelona, before retiring from the world and entering the religious life, first at Aniane in 804, then at Gellone (known today as Saint-Guilhem-le-Désert) in 806, which he founded. It is worth noting in passing that the historical Guillaume's son Bertrand was nicknamed Naso. Traditions centering on the count of Toulouse thus lie behind the battle at Archamp (*Chanson de Guillaume, Aliscans*), the "crooked nose," and the withdrawal from the world (*Moniage Guillaume*). Count Vivien, lay abbot of Saint-Martin of Tours, who died fighting the Bretons under Charles the Bald in 851, was the prototype of Guillaume's illustrious nephew Vivien in the *Chanson de Guillaume.* Finally, the tradition of the siege of Orange may derive from memories of Guillaume I the Liberator, count of Provence, who gained an important victory over the Muslims in 972.

Born of different sources and nourished by events of the 12th and 13th centuries, the poems about Guillaume vary in tone, from the stark heroism of the first part of the *Chanson de Guillaume* to the adventuring spirit of the *Enfances Vivien.* A variety of themes is prominent in the cycle: the unflagging fidelity of the lineage, especially of Guillaume, to the sovereign (*Couronnement, Charroi, Moniage Guillaume*); heroism in the fight against the infidel (*Guillaume, Chevalerie Vivien, Aliscans*); and the relations between love and valor (*Enfances Guillaume, Prise*) and between knighthood and the religious life (the two *Moniages*). The unity of the whole is ensured by Guillaume himself, characterized by the glorious stigmata of his crooked or shortened nose, by the strength of his fists, and by his laughter. By his side, Orable-Guibourc is the guarantor of epic values, who urges her husband to remain faithful to his calling and who will not accept him until he gives proof of his valor. Vivien, the hero of Archamp, is immortalized by his vow, while the giant Rainouart, symbol of brute strength in service of the good, incorporates heroic-comic aspects of which Guillaume himself shows signs.

Poems About Aymeri. The chansons about Guillaume's father and brothers for the most part are not as old as those about the hero. There are nonetheless venerable traditions concerning the Narbonnais lineage, as in the Latin prose *Hague Fragment* (ca. 1000), in which Aymeri and his sons Hernaut, Bernard, and Guibelin, as well as Bertrand the Paladin, confront Borel and his sons. The origin of the Narbonne cycle may thus lie in either a tradition of a siege of Narbonne thwarted by the lineage (source of the second part of the *Narbonnais,* for which there once existed an assonanced version) or the story of the conquest of Nar-

bonne by Aymeri, a tradition following in the wake of Roncevaux.

Among the epics having an archaic substratum are *Girart de Vienne* (ca. 1180), in which the trouvère Bertrand de Bar-sur-Aube links an older poem treating Girart's rebellion against Charlemagne to the Narbonne cycle, and *Aymeri de Narbonne* (before 1200), perhaps by the same poet, a tale of conquest and love, relating the capture of Narbonne as well as Aymeri's marriage to Hermenjart. An even more recent version of the capture of Narbonne is found in the manuscript Venice V[4], which integrates the taking of the city with the *Roland* material, situating it between the capture of Saragossa and the punishment of Ganelon.

The *Narbonnais* (early 13th c.) reflects the siege-of-Narbonne tradition; the *Siège de Barbastre* (7,392 lines; late 12th c.), loosely inspired by the capture of Barbastro by the Christians in 1064, also has archaic elements, including echoes of the siege of Orange. The *Mort Aymeri de Narbonne* (4,176 lines; 12th c.) combines, with its story of the hero's final combats, epic tonality with the exotic, in its introduction of the Sagittaries.

The cycle is completed by poems that tell of the founding hero's ancestors or descendants. *Garin de Monglane* (14,000+ lines; 13th c.) features Aymeri's grandfather. After defeating Charlemagne in a chess match, the emperor authorizes him to win the fief of Monglane; Garin weds Mabile, who bears him four sons: Hernaut de Beaulande (Aymeri's father), Girart de Vienne, Renier de Gennes (Oliver and Aude's father), and Milon de Pouille. In the 14th century, the poem was reworked and an *Enfances Garin* added. Among poems treating Aymeri's descendants, *Guibert d'Andrenas* (2,406 lines; 13th c.) tells of the conquest of a Spanish city by Aymeri's youngest son; the *Prise de Cordres et Sebille* (2,948 lines; 13th c.) makes Aymeri's grandson Bertrand the lord of Cordova. In a final step, in the 14th or early 15th century, the epic of *Girart de Vienne,* reworked and amplified with the story of Hernaut de Beaulande's and Renier's youthful exploits, is associated (in the so-called Cheltenham manuscript) in the *Geste de Monglane* with *Galien restoré.*

The historical basis of the Narbonne poems is less easy to determine than that of the epics about Guillaume. Aymeri recalls no specific model; progressively, however, he becomes associated with several early 12th-century viscounts of Narbonne of the same name. Aïmer goes back perhaps to Hadhemarus, a companion of Guillaume de Toulouse who took part in the Barcelona campaign, then fought at Tortose (809–10).

The differences are great from poem to poem. One can find archaic epic motifs (division of the fief among sons, hero's fury, exaggerated vows), but the cycle is dominated by the spirit of the adventure romance, in the sense that love frequently plays an important role. Several figures predominate: Hernaut de Gironde (Gerona, in Catalonia), a savage and impetuous character; Aymeri, a violent young man in *Girart de Vienne* and a family leader urging his sons to bravery in the *Narbonnais*; the mysterious Aïmer, who vows, like Vivien, to never spend the night in a house and to fight the Saracens to the end.

François Suard

[See also: *ALISCANS; AYMERI DE NARBONNE;* BERTRAND DE BAR-SUR-AUBE; CHANSON DE GESTE; *CHARROI DE NÎMES; COURONNEMENT DE LOUIS; GALIEN RESTORÉ; GUILLAUME, CHANSON DE; MONIAGE GUILLAUME; NARBONNAIS; PRISE D'ORANGE*]

Becker, Philippe-Auguste. *Das Werden der Wilhelm und der Aimerigeste.* Leipzig: Hirzel, 1939.

Bédier, Joseph. *Les légendes épiques.* 4 vols. Paris: Champion, 1908, Vol. 1.

Frappier, Jean. *Les chansons de geste du cycle de Guillaume d'Orange.* 3 vols. Paris: SEDES, 1955–83.

Guidot, Bernard. *Recherches sur la chanson de geste au XIIIe siècle.* 2 vols. Aix-en-Provence: Université de Provence, 1986.

Tyssens, Madeleine. *La geste de Guillaume d'Orange dans les manuscrits cycliques.* Paris: Les Belles Lettres, 1967.

———. "Relectures de la geste des Narbonnais." *Au carrefour des routes d'Europe: la chanson de geste. Xe Congrès International de la Société Rencesvals,* ed. Jean Subrenat. 2 vols. Aix-en-Provence: CUER MA, 1987, Vol. 1, pp. 163–95.

Wathelet-Willem, Jeanne, ed. *Recherches sur* La chanson de Guillaume: *études accompagnées d'une édition.* 2 vols. Paris: Les Belles Lettres, 1975, Vol. 1.

GUILLAUME DURAND (ca. 1230–1296). Liturgist, canon-law scholar, and ecclesiastical judge, Guillaume Durand studied in Paris and Bologna and served in a number of ecclesiastical functions before being chosen bishop of Mende in 1285. Among his legal writings, the *Speculum judiciale* (ca. 1271) is a masterly summation of ecclesiastical juridical practices, the *Speculum legatorum* (1279) analyzes the rights and procedures of legates, and the *Repertorium iuris canonici* is a digest of canon law. Guillaume's most influential work is the *Rationale divinorum officiorum,* which explains liturgical ceremonies for the benefit of both clergy and laity, with special attention to the symbolism of architecture, liturgical vestments and vessels, rituals, and the like. The *Rationale* is divided into eight parts: the church building, orders of clergy (bishop, priest, deacon, etc.), vestments, the Mass, the yearly liturgical cycle, the feast days of saints, *computus,* and calendar. While bishop of Mende, Guillaume produced a revision of the Roman Pontifical (ca. 1293–95) that was used at the papal court and served as the basis of the official text of the Roman Pontifical printed in 1485.

He should not be confused with his nephew, also named Guillaume Durand, who administered the bishopric of Mende in our Guillaume's absence.

Grover A. Zinn

[See also: CANON LAW; *COMPUTUS;* LITURGICAL BOOKS; LITURGICAL COMMENTATORS; MASS, CHANTS AND TEXTS]

Guillaume Durand. *The Symbolism of Churches and Church Ornaments: A Translation of the First Book of the Rationale divinorum officiorum Written by William Durandus,* trans. John Mason Neale and Benjamin Webb. 3rd ed. London: Gibbings, 1906.

———. *Rational ou Manuel des divins offices . . . ou, Raisons mystiques et historiques de la liturgie catholique,* trans. Charles Barthélemy. 5 vols. Paris: Vivès, 1854.

———. *Le pontifical de Guillaume Durand,* ed. Michel Andrieu. Vol. 3 of *Le pontifical romain au moyen âge.* Vatican City: Biblioteca Apostolica Vaticana, 1940.

———. *The Sacred Vestments,* trans. Thomas H. Passmore. London: Sampson Low, Marston, 1899.

Douteil, Herbert. *Studien zu Durantis* Rationale divinorum officiorum *als kirchenmusikalischer Quelle.* Regensburg: Bosse, 1969.

GUILLAUME LE BRETON (fl. 1220s). The author of a Latin chronicle of the kings of France and a Latin poem on Philip II Augustus, the *Philippide* (ca. 1224), Guillaume was Philip's chaplain and tutor to his illegitimate son. His chronicle (1207–20) continues that of Rigord. (A continuation from 1220 to 1222 is almost certainly not Guillaume's work.) There are eight manuscripts, which represent four redactions (1207–27), but Guillaume's work circulated more widely indirectly, for some of his material was incorporated into the *Grandes chroniques de France.* The *Philippide,* extant in three manuscripts, is more detailed than the chronicle.

Leah Shopkow

[See also: HISTORIOGRAPHY]

de la Borde, H. François. *Œuvres de Rigord et de Guillaume le Breton, historiens de Philippe-Auguste.* 2 vols. Paris: Renouard, 1882.

GUILLAUME LE CLERC (1180/91–after 1238). Among the several poets known by this name in the 13th century, the most important is the Norman Guillaume le Clerc, to whom are attributed the *Bestiaire divin,* the *Besant de Dieu,* the *Livre de Tobie,* the *Treize Moz,* and the fabliau *Du prestre et d'Alison.*

The *Bestiaire divin* (ca. 1210) is an allegorizing bestiary of 4,200 octosyllabic lines that shows considerable borrowing from the *Liber de bestiis et aliis rebus,* attributed to Hugh of Saint-Victor. The *Besant de Dieu* is another moralizing work of some 3,755 octosyllabic lines that evokes the miseries of the century, invokes the aid of God for the church, and deplores the lack of a crusade. It was inspired by a reflection Guillaume had one evening: humankind refuses to accept God's invitation to feast. The besant represents the unused talent that the unworthy servant in the parable (Matthew 25:14–30) renders to his lord. The author through moral edification tries to convince his reader of the evils of money and greed. By following Guillaume's advice, men and women have the capability to double their God-given talents.

Lesser works by Guillaume are the *Livre de Tobie,* based on the Book of Tobit and composed for William, prior of Kennelworth, in the first twenty years of the 13th century; the *Treize Moz,* a moral work dedicated to Alexander, bishop of Litchfield and Coventry (1224–38), that draws heavily on the *De contemptu mundi sive de miseria humanae condicionis* of Innocent III; and the fabliau *Du prestre et d'Alison*.

Claude J. Fouillade

[See also: ARTHURIAN VERSE ROMANCE; BESTIARY; PHILIPPE DE THAÜN; *PIERRE DE PROVENCE ET LA BELLE MAGUELONNE*]

Guillaume le Clerc. *Le bestiaire*, ed. Robert Reinsch. Leipzig: Fues's Verlag (O.R. Reisland), 1890.
———. *Le besant de Dieu de Guillaume le Clerc de Normandie*, ed. Pierre Ruelle. Brussels: Éditions de l'Université de Bruxelles, 1973.

GUILLAUME LE MARÉCHAL, HISTOIRE DE.

Commissioned by his eldest son shortly after the hero's death in 1219, the anonymous *Histoire* is one of the earliest and most successful secular biographies. Modeled on contemporary hagiographic literature, its 19,214 octosyllabic lines in the Norman dialect of Old French celebrate the lineage, deeds, and exemplary death of one of the greatest knights of the 12th and early 13th centuries. Preserved by a single manuscript (Cheltenham, Phillips 25155), it includes lengthy accounts of tournaments and is a rich source of information about medieval life and chivalry.

William W. Kibler

[See also: ANGLO-NORMAN LITERATURE; BIOGRAPHY; HISTORIOGRAPHY]

Meyer, Paul, ed. *L'histoire de Guillaume le Maréchal, comte de Striguil et de Pembroke, régent d'Angleterre de 1216 à 1219*. 3 vols. Paris: Renouard, 1891–1901. [Vol. 3 includes introduction and abridged translation into modern French.]
Duby, Georges. *William Marshall: The Flower of Chivalry*, trans. Richard Howard. New York: Pantheon, 1985.
Painter, Sidney. *French Chivalry: Chivalric Ideas and Practices in Mediaeval France*. Baltimore: Johns Hopkins University Press, 1940.

GUIOT DE PROVINS

(fl. ca. 1180–1210). After much success at numerous seigneurial courts, this early trouvère participated in the Third Crusade and then, disillusioned, retired to a monastic life that left him no less disenchanted. Five *chansons d'amour* are attributed to Guiot with reasonable certainty, and late in life he wrote a pious allegorical summing-up, the *Armeüre du chevalier*. His most important work is the 2,686-line *Bible Guiot* (completed ca. 1206), a verbally brilliant and unusually personal satire criticizing feudal figures and mores but directed especially against ecclesiastical powers and monastic orders.

Samuel N. Rosenberg

[See also: ÉTIENNE DE FOUGÈRES; HUGUES DE BERZÉ; TROUVÈRE POETRY]

Guiot de Provins. *Guiot de Provins: Œuvres*, ed. John Orr. Manchester: Manchester University Press, 1915.

GUIRAUT RIQUIER

(fl. 1254–92). The most prolific troubadour after Cerveri de Girona, Guiraut Riquier of Narbonne left 105 compositions in all genres, mostly *vers* and *cansos* (love songs). The poems are dated 1254–92 in a section of troubadour MS *C* (B.N. fr. 856), which purports to be a copy of the troubadour's own autograph book. Guiraut began his career in the court of the viscount of Narbonne, traveled to the Castilian court of Alfonso X the Wise, and returned to the courts of Rodez, Comminges, Astarac, and Narbonne, where he died in 1292. In that year, he lamented that he had come "among the last," meaning perhaps among the last of the troubadours. We have the melodies of forty-eight of his songs. The love songs, dedicated to a lady whose name is concealed by the *senhal*, or sobriquet, *Belh Deport* ("Good Conduct"), lack passionate conviction, but his series of six *pastorelas* are a notable development in the genre: he wove them into a continuing narrative in which he encounters the same shepherdess repeatedly over a period of twenty-two years. Among his epistles are an extended commentary on a *canso* written ca. 1200 by Guiraut de Calanso and a supplication to Alfonso the Wise for recognition of his poetic achievements, with Alfonso's declaration (no doubt written by Guiraut) awarding him the title of *doctor de trobar* ("doctor of poetic composition").

William D. Paden

[See also: TROUBADOUR POETRY]

Guiraut Riquier. *Les épîtres de Guiraut Riquier, troubadour du XIIIe siècle*, ed. Joseph Linskill. London: Association Internationale d'Études Occitanes, 1985.
———. *Guiraut Riquier: las cansos*, ed. Ulrich Mölk. Heidelberg: Winter, 1962.
———. *Guiraut Riquier*, ed. S.L.H. Pfaff. In *Die Werke der Troubadours in provenzalischer Sprache*, ed. Carl A.F. Mahn. 5 vols. Berlin: Duemmler, 1853, Vol. 4.
Bossy, Michel-André. "Cyclical Composition in Guiraut Riquier's Book of Poems." *Speculum* 66 (1991): 277–93.
———, ed. *Tenso* 9, 2 (1994): 103–76. Special issue on Guiraut Riquier.
Riquer, Martín de, ed. *Los trovadores: historia literaria y textos*. Barcelona: Planeta, 1975, Vol. 3, pp. 1609–46.

HADEWIJCH (fl. first half of the 13th c.). Only sparse information about Hadewijch's life is known to us today, although her works greatly influenced Carthusian spirituality and the *Devotio moderna* movement, in particular Ruusbroec (1293–1381) and Jan van Leeuwen (1314–1378). Hadewijch might have been active in either Brussels or Antwerp as a béguine, living together with other women who became her students or, as documented in her moving letters, her enemies. Her writings, all composed in the dialect of Brabant, were produced probably between 1220 and 1240. Hadewijch's work, now considered one of the most remarkable medieval mystical texts in the vernacular, consists of thirty-one letters, forty-five stanzaic poems, fourteen visions, and sixteen poems in rhyming couplets.

All texts focus on *minnemystiek*, or bridal mysticism. They are characterized by the rhetoric of courtly love poetry and a sophisticated understanding of Christian teachings, which testify to Hadewijch's extraordinary education. The key force in Hadewijch's teachings on mystical transformation is *minne*, or Love, allegorized as a fickle and impatient female teacher. According to N. de Paepe, she represents the human capacity to love God. In focusing on *minne* in a sustained and rigorous fashion, the human soul can achieve a state that facilitates the enjoyment of mystical union with Christ in this life.

Ulrike Wiethaus

[See also: MYSTICISM; WOMEN, RELIGIOUS EXPERIENCE OF]

Hadewijch. *Hadewijch: Brieven; Mengeldichten; Strophische Gedichten; Visioenen.* 6 vols. Antwerp: Staandard-Boekhandel, 1924–52.
———. *Hadewijch: The Complete Works*, trans. Columba Hart. New York: Paulist, 1980.
———. *Hadewijch: Strofische Gedichten*, ed. and trans. E. Rombauts and N. de Paepe. Zwolle: Tjeenk Willink, 1961.
Guest, Tanis N. *Some Aspects of Hadewijch's Poetic Form in the "Strofische Gedichten."* The Hague: Nijhoff, 1975.
Milhaven, John G. *Hadewijch and Her Sisters.* Albany: State University of New York Press, 1993.
Weevers, Theodoor. *Poetry of the Netherlands in Its European Context: 1170–1930.* London: Athlone, 1960.

HAGIOGRAPHY. Term (from the Greek *hagios* 'holy,' hence 'saint,' + *graphia* 'writings') referring to the full range of writings about saints, and, by extension, to the study of such works. These usages are of relatively modern vintage. The Greek word *hagiographa*, by contrast, was used in late antiquity to specify one of the three divisions of the Hebrew Scriptures. Similar usage continued in medieval Latin: Notker the Stammerer (d. ca. 890), for example, used *hagiographi* to refer to the "holy writings" of the Bible. The systematic study and criticism of writings about the saints began in the 17th century with the work of clerics of the Congregation de Saint-Maur and the Société des Bollandistes. It was only then that the term came to refer to this new discipline and its subject matter.

Hagiography can be understood only with reference to the concept of sanctity and to the practice of the cult of saints. For medieval Christians, saints were those "holy people" (*sancti, -ae*) who had posthumously entered the Kingdom of Heaven. Only a limited number of such heroes, however, were officially recognized and celebrated by Christian churches. Admission to this canon was controlled by the ecclesiastical hierarchy, bishops in particular, although the papacy exerted ever more control over the processes of canonization from the 12th century onward. Hagiography played a crucial role in this process, for the very composition and use of a hagiographic text implied that its subject had received institutional recognition.

Saints were venerated long after their deaths and thus long after memory of them had faded. The most common type of hagiography, saints' lives (*vitae*), served to record the actions that had formed and demonstrated their holiness. Excerpts from such Lives were often read out as part of the liturgical celebration of a saint's feast. In the mid-9th century, Bertholdus of Micy described the purpose of hagiography:

The churches of the faithful scattered through the world celebrate together with highest praise the fame of holy men. Their tombs, which are wreathed in the metals of gold and silver, as well as in layers of precious stones and a shell of marble, now bear witness to their pious memory. . . . Surely to no less a degree than miracles, which incite the love proffered by the devotion of faithful people, the monuments of letters that are set down on pages also fully satisfy the senses of those who read and hear them. For what has been said and done by the saints ought not to be concealed in silence. God's love provided their deeds to serve as a norm of living for the men of their own times as well as of those years that have since passed; they are now to be imitated piously by those who are faithful to Christ.

The aim of hagiographers was not to produce biography in the modern sense but to portray a saint as an exemplar of the Christian life. Gregory of Tours (d. 594) named a work the *Life of the Fathers* rather than the *Lives of the Fathers* because he deemed most important the "merits and virtues" common to a single ideal of sanctity rather than the diverse singularities of the lives of his many subjects. Hagiographers used stories, known as "types" (*topoi*), that followed a traditional form and were intended to convey a moral message rather than historically accurate information. Hagiographers borrowed phrases, themes, motifs, even verbatim passages from stories from earlier works, adapting them to the specifics of their story. The traditional and even repetitive character that such use of topoi creates is one of the most striking aspects of medieval hagiography.

In addition to exemplary conduct, the "merits and virtues" described by hagiographers also included the miracles that God performed through the saints. Such miracles occurred not only during the lives of the saints, but also posthumously at their tombs or otherwise in relation to their relics. Posthumous miracles included such visible marvels as cures and exorcisms, as well as invisible acts, like the remission of sins. The devout came to the shrines of saints or prayed to them in search of miraculous intercession. Hagiography recorded these aspects of the veneration of the saints through collections of posthumous miracle stories (*miracula*) and accounts of major events in the history of relic cults (*inventiones*, the ritual placement of relics in a shrine that inaugurated their public veneration), and *translationes* (the transfer of relics from one shrine to another).

The origins of hagiography in medieval France must be sought in the Roman province of Gaul, whose ecclesiastical hierarchy was dominated by members of its elite families. Over this well-born company towered the figure of St. Martin of Tours (d. 397), a military officer who underwent a dramatic conversion to Christianity. The former soldier remained a man of action his entire life, becoming in turn a tireless missionary, a severely ascetic monk, and a capable bishop. Martin was recognized as a holy man in his own day; shortly after his death, his devoted disciple Sulpicius Severus (d. 410) composed a record of his life. The work betrays both the sophistication of a

Roman man of letters and the zeal of a religious reformer. Martin's portrait is finely etched with vivid anecdotes recalled by the author himself or by other eyewitnesses. Sulpicius originally intended his work as a guide to the ascetic life for a circle of Gallo-Roman aristocrats who gathered at his home, but it was widely copied and circulated. One of the earliest pieces of hagiography to be composed in what was to become France, this work set the standards for later Latin hagiography and became a virtual mine of topoi.

Over the course of the 5th century, other Gallo-Roman aristocrats, both bishops and hermits, came to be celebrated as saints. An excellent example is provided by the *vita* of Germanus of Auxerre (d. 448), composed a generation after his death by Constantius of Lyon. Writing after the collapse of Roman authority in Gaul, the author sought to provide a model of an efficient and aristocratic bishop who guarded the lives of his flock with charismatic power. An ideal administrator and pastor was thus presented to the contemporary Gallo-Roman elite. The work was written at the request of a bishop of Auxerre and given wide dissemination by another in order to promote the cult of the saint. Hagiography was steadily taking on a public function.

During the 6th century, the Franks tightened their grip on Gaul. The greatest hagiographer of the Merovingian kingdom was Gregory of Tours, who composed eight linked collections of traditions about the saints of Gaul during the last decades of the 6th century. These *libri miraculorum* contained stories of miracles performed by Christian holy people, both during their lives and posthumously at their shrines. The bishop's purpose was above all else pastoral, providing the Roman community of Gaul with a record of its glorious Christian past that would serve as a comfort and a guide in the more difficult present. His work confirms that the veneration of relics had become central to the practice of Christianity, and one of his goals was to endow the cults of local saints with trustworthy histories. In Gregory's eyes, the most important saintly patron of the kingdom was Martin of Tours, whose shrine lay outside the walls of his own see.

Though saints of Frankish origin were conspicuously few in the works of Gregory, the Franks had largely been converted to Christianity. Venantius Fortunatus (d. ca. 601), bishop of Poitiers, celebrated saints among the women of the Frankish aristocracy. Foremost among them was Radegund (d. 587), a queen who had left her husband and the court for ascetic retirement in the convent of the Holy Cross at Poitiers. Fortunatus composed his memorial of Radegund shortly after her death. Over two decades later, Baudonivia, a nun of the Holy Cross, composed a second *vita*. A short time thereafter, an anonymous nun of Chelles wrote of Balthild, another Frankish queen converted to the monastic life. These two women were probably the earliest female hagiographers in the Latin West.

Throughout the 7th century, male members of the Frankish aristocracy entered the monastic life in increasing numbers, perhaps inspired by the almost military discipline of Columbanian monasticism, while others took up careers in ecclesiastical administration. A new type of saint emerged who was representative of and attractive to this ruling elite. Known to historians as *Adelsheilige*, or "noble saints," they included such men as Sulpicius of Bourges and Eligius of Noyon. The hagiographers who recorded their lives had, like Baudonivia, Frankish names, but their works were still influenced by Gallo-Roman literary models provided by Sulpicius Severus and Gregory of Tours.

The contours of hagiography changed dramatically in the 9th century. Ecclesiastical authorities came to rely increasingly on written documentation for the authenticity of saints and their veneration. In the *Admonitio generalis* of 789, Charlemagne renewed a canon borrowed from an ancient collection that ordered that "the false names of martyrs and the uncertain memorials of saints should not be venerated." Five years later, the bishops whom the emperor gathered at Frankfurt were more explicit: "No new saints should be honored or invoked, nor shrines to them erected on the roads. Only those saints are to be venerated in a church who have been chosen on the authority of their Passion or on the merit of their Life." The "Passions and Lives" in question were hagiographic texts. In response to the perceived need for written documentation for the cults of saints, Carolingian clerics produced many works celebrating the saints of the distant past. Hincmar of Reims wrote about Remi, Hilduin of Saint-Denis about Denis, and Alcuin of York about Vedast, to cite only some of the best-known examples. They were forced to piece together bits of written and oral tradition, along with topoi borrowed from ancient and respected works of hagiography. Few contemporaries, however, were celebrated by the Carolingian church as saints, with the exception of those monks and nuns, such as Boniface and Leoba, who served as missionaries in the Christian borderlands. According to one survey, some forty-five Lives had been composed in Neustria during the 7th century to celebrate contemporary figures as saints. By contrast, only ten Lives of such recently deceased saints were written in the 8th century, and the number dropped to a mere eight in the 9th.

The Carolingian period also witnessed the growth of hagiography concerning the posthumous veneration of saints' relics. Monks compiled collections of miracles performed at the shrines of such saints as Benedict of Nursia at the monastery of Saint-Benoît-sur-Loire and Richarius at Saint-Riquier. The enthusiasm for relics was not confined to those saints traditionally enshrined in France. Many relics of martyrs were obtained from Italy and Spain, or even other regions of France. Numerous translation accounts survive that document these journeys. Some authors, such as Einhard, described these relics as the objects of what they termed "holy thefts" (*furta sacra*), a topos that suggested that the relics had been carried off to a new home under the inspiration and guidance of the saints themselves.

The Viking raids of the 10th century caused major disruptions in all phases of public life in France. As numerous monasteries were pillaged or destroyed along the riverways, the relics of many saints were moved to new homes. The story of the wanderings of the monks of Noirmoutier, carrying the relics of their patron, Philibert, as they journeyed as far as Tournus in their search for a safer home, is one of the best known. Relatively few Lives of saints, either historical or contemporary, were composed during this period. The most important exception was Odo of Cluny's *vita* of Gerald of Aurillac. Odo portrayed this count as a novel type of saint, the Christian knight (*miles christianus*). Gerald never entered the religious life, but he practiced a life of prayer and asceticism, while using his political and military power to fight injustice and protect the clergy and the poor. An important part of Odo's message was that a noble might lead a life pleasing to Christ by providing for the peace and defending God's church. Gerald was certainly noble, for Odo went to pains to demonstrate (or, quite possibly, to invent) the fact that the count was descended from St. Caesarius of Arles and thus had both senatorial and saintly blood in his veins. Odo himself was also considered to be a saint, and his Life was composed by a Cluniac monk, John of Salerno. In a sense, these two works portrayed the twin faces of an emerging clerical ideal of the relationship between secular and ecclesiastical aristocracies. Both became influential models: Hariulf of Saint-Riquier (d. 1143) had Gerald in mind when he composed the Life of Arnulf of Soissons, and Raoul Glaber (d. ca. 1046) turned to the *vita* of Odo as a model when portraying Abbot William of Volpiano.

The social and political order of France was radically reshaped in the decades ca. 1000. Many monastic communities underwent reform, and the cults of their patron saints came to be renewed. The dominant hagiographic genre in France in the 11th and 12th centuries comprised collections of posthumous miracles attributed to patrons of monastic houses. These works were specific in their geographical scope: they included stories from a single diocese or a single monastic house and its priories. They intended to tell how a saint aided and protected people who came under his or her patronage. As Letaldus of Micy (d. ca. 1010) wrote, "All people should learn these things, for such miracles as were done in the days of our fathers and are still done for us now do not happen on account of our own merits, but through the kindness of piety and the intervention of those fathers who are provided as intercessors for us." These stories provide in their vivid detail a colorful picture of the social fabric and religious practice of France during these centuries. While 11th-century collections contained many stories in which the saints miraculously chastised their enemies with beatings and even death, those of the 12th century came to focus more on the miraculous cures effected at the shrines.

The oldest known literary document in Old French is a brief hagiographic poem, the *Séquence de sainte Eulalie*, which dates to ca. 880. Significant numbers of vernacular hagiographic works, all in verse, survive from the late 10th, 11th, and 12th centuries; they concern such diverse subjects as St. Léger, a 7th-century bishop of Autun; St. Brendan, an Irish missionary; and St. Mary the Egyptian, a prostitute turned hermit. In general, these works appear to have been performed as a sort of pious entertainment. The moralist Thomas of Chobham exempted jongleurs who performed works about the saints from his general condemnation of that profession. The masterpiece among these works was the *Vie de saint Alexis,* which told of a wealthy young man who left his family to pursue an ascetic life, only to return years later as an unrecognized holy begger living under the steps of his family house. This poem, dating in its earliest form to ca. 1050 and frequently rewritten in later centuries, prefigured the movement of the *vita apostolica.*

The high Middle Ages witnessed the emergence of a variety of new spiritual movements, each of which was accompanied by the development of new types of sanctity recorded in hagiography. The first important development was the Lives of the hermits and wandering preachers associated with the "new monasticism." Monastic reformers like Robert d'Arbrissel (d. 1117) and Stephen of Muret (d. 1124) intended to return to the ascetic practice of the earliest monks in the eastern deserts. Over the previous two centuries, hagiography had come to focus ever more exclusively on the miraculous powers of the saint, but in the lives of these men hagiographers returned to an interest in the spiritual life and ascetic exercises of saints. The Life of Stephen records how hagiography itself played a role in this process, for the saint required that his monks dine in silence, while one of their number read from the *Lives of the Desert Fathers.*

By the late 12th century, the Cistercian order was producing its own distinctive hagiography in France and elsewhere. These works depicted the lives of such abbots as Bernard of Clairvaux (d. 1153) as spiritual ascents to God in a manner characteristic of Cistercian psychology and spirituality. The influence of the eremitic tradition can also be sensed here, as when William of Saint-Thierry reminisced in his Life of Bernard about a sojourn spent with the saint: "I remained with him for a few days, and as I looked about me I thought that I was gazing on a new Heaven and a new earth, for it seemed as though there were tracks freshly made by men of our own day in the path that had first been trodden by our fathers the Egyptian monks of long ago." The Cistercian monks and saints were thus portrayed as imitators of their ancient predecessors. Cistercians also compiled large collections of miracle stories, but these were not associated with specific shrines; rather, they were intended to convey moral messages. The use of miracle stories—some of which were contemporary, others taken from ancient sources—for didactic purposes in the training of monastic novices had been pioneered at Cluny by Peter the Venerable (d. 1156) but was perfected in such Cistercian collections as the *Exordium magnum* and the *Dialogue on Miracles* of Caesarius of Heisterbach (d. ca. 1240).

In the early 13th century, béguinages came to offer women lives of ascetic spirituality that were not strictly cloistered. This new movement was particularly vibrant in the cities of the Low Countries. By the 1230s, Jacques de Vitry and Thomas de Cantimpré had begun to write an influential series of lives that celebrated béguines and nuns in the region of Liège. Their subjects included Marie d'Oignies, Christina of Saint-Trond, Ivetta of Huy, Margaret of Ypres, and Luitgard of Aywières. In championing this novel approach to the religious life, which combined traditional asceticism with charitable works and teaching, these hagiographers provided a model for late-medieval female sanctity whose characteristics included strenuous fasting, ecstatic visions, devotion to the eucharist, and service to the urban poor.

The new religious movement that had perhaps the greatest impact on western Christendom was that of the mendicant orders. Although active in France, they did not number many saints among those members who were associated primarily with that country. While Thomas Aquinas and Bonaventure were masters at the University of Paris, the hagiographic traditions about them come, like the saints themselves, from Italy. As preachers, however, the mendicants represented a vigorous attempt on the part of the ecclesiastical hierarchy to reach the urban laity. Preachers needed collections of exemplary stories of a sort different from those produced for monastic novices. Many such collections were gathered for preaching purposes by Flemish and French mendicants—such as Stephen of Bourbon, Thomas de Cantimpré, and Vincent de Beauvais—which made use of hagiographic traditions. The most influential hagiographic compendium, in France as in the rest of western Christendom, however, was the *Legenda aurea,* completed by Jacobus of Voragine, an Italian Dominican, in 1258 and available in French translation by the end of the century.

One major factor in late-medieval hagiography, the development of papal control over canonization, produced a new genre of hagiographic literature, the *processus canonizationis,* which was the record of the official tribunal that investigated a candidate's holiness. A number of such investigations were conducted in France: of Edmond Rich at Pontigny in 1244–45, Louis IX at Saint-Denis in 1282, Louis of Anjou at Marseille in 1297, Dauphine of Puimichel at Apt and Avignon in 1363, Charles de Blois at Angers in 1371, Urban V at Avignon in 1382 and 1390, and Peter of Luxembourg at Avignon in 1389–90. The frequency of such inquiries at Avignon in the late 14th century can be explained by the dominant position of French clerics in the papal court during its sojourn there. Unsuccessful processes of canonization were undertaken for such French ecclesiasical figures as Robert of Molesme and Étienne de Die. These new procedures also encouraged the composition of more traditional Lives, such as that written by Guillaume de Saint-Pathus about Louis IX, in order to provide evidence of the sanctity of their subjects.

During the 13th and 14th centuries, hagiography composed in French was also taking interesting new directions. Large numbers of verse Lives were composed in this period, some twenty-six of them about female subjects, such as Margaret of Antioch and Catherine of Alexandria. In general, these poets followed the style of contemporary romances, but they also attempted to produce a morally uplifting rival to such secular works. The author of a *Vie de sainte Barbe* claimed, "I want to tell a new kind of story, / Never heard before. / Know that it does not concern Ogier, / Nor Roland, nor Oliver, / But a most holy maiden / Who was very courteous and beautiful." Nor were verse Lives the only hagiography available in French. Collections of miracles performed by the Virgin Mary, the most famous by Gautier de Coinci, began to appear in the late 12th century. The earliest works of French prose hagiography were composed only a couple of decades later. While some were renderings of vernacular verse works, many were translations of Latin texts such as the *Legenda aurea* or the *Lives of the Desert Fathers*. Collections of such texts, called *légendiers*, played a role in the religious instruction of the laity. While most works of vernacular hagiography had their ultimate roots in Latin sources, a few original hagiographic works were composed in French, notably Joinville's highly personal and moving life of Louis IX and Rutebeuf's poem about Elizabeth of Hungary (d. 1231). Hagiographic influence can also be detected in works of other genres, such as the Vulgate *Queste del saint Graal*.

Over the course of the 15th century, the composition of Latin hagiography declined precipitously in France, as did the official recognition by the papacy of the kingdom's inhabitants as saints. This was in part due to the position of France in ecclesiastical politics during the Great Schism and its aftermath. There were some exceptions to the general lack of new French saints: the Dominican reformer Vincent Ferrer (d. 1419) was canonized in 1455; Jeanne-Marie de Maillé (d. 1414) became the focus of a local cult in Touraine, though the papacy never pursued her canonization. Perhaps the most famous French saint of the period, Jeanne d'Arc (d. 1431), was not officially canonized until the 20th century.

Vernacular hagiography, on the other hand, flourished. Many early printed French books contained Lives of the saints and were produced for a thriving market in devotional works intended for the laity. In the early 16th century, a manual of religious practice directed to a female audience reminded its readers, "Our Lord said that the Kingdom of the Heavens is taken by force and, since you do not require ease of your wicked body, you should put before your eyes the example of the blessed saints who have reached Heaven and who have acted for the love of our Lord. . . . Read their stories and consider the constancy of the male and female saints." The Reformation brought with it a radical reaction against the cult of saints, which caused Calvinists to spurn such traditional hagiography. The Wars of Religion, however, spawned the composition of collective biographies of both Huguenot and Catholic "martyrs" that owed much to the medieval genre.

Thomas Head

[See also: ANGLO-NORMAN LITERATURE; BÉGUINES; BENEDEIT; BERNARD OF CLAIRVAUX; CISTERCIAN ORDER; GAUTIER DE COINCI; GREGORY OF TOURS; JEANNE D'ARC; JOINVILLE, JEAN DE; *LEGENDA AUREA*; MARTIN OF TOURS; MIRACLE PLAYS; ODO; PREACHING; RADEGUND; RAOUL GLABER; RUTEBEUF; *SAINT ALEXIS, VIE DE; SAINT LÉGER, VIE DE*; SAINT PLAYS; *SAINTE EULALIE, SÉQUENCE DE*; SAINTS, CULT OF; SAINTS' LIVES; WILLIAM OF VOLPIANO]

Aigrain, René. *L'hagiographie: ses sources, ses méthodes, son histoire*. Paris: Bloud and Gay, 1953.

Bibliotheca Sanctorum. 13 vols. Rome: Instituto Giovanni XXIII della Pontificia Universita Lateranense, Citta Nuova, 1961–70.

Cazelles, Brigitte, trans. *The Lady as Saint: A Collection of French Hagiographic Romances of the Thirteenth Century*. Philadelphia: University of Pennsylvania Press, 1991.

Dalarun, Jacques. *L'impossible sainteté: la vie retrouvée de Robert d'Arbrissel (v.1045–1116) fondateur de Fontevraud*. Paris: Cerf, 1985.

Folz, Robert. *Les saints rois du moyen âge en occident (VIe–XIIIe siècles)*. Brussels: Société des Bollandistes, 1984.

Geary, Patrick. *Furta Sacra: Thefts of Relics in the Central Middle Ages*. 2nd ed. Princeton: Princeton University Press, 1990.

Graus, Frantisek. *Volk, Herrscher und Heiliger im Reich der Merowinger: Studien zur Hagiographie der Merowingerzeit*. Prague: Nakladatelstvi Ceskoslovenske Akademie Ved, 1965.

Head, Thomas. *Hagiography and the Cult of Saints: The Diocese of Orléans, 800–1200*. Cambridge: Cambridge University Press, 1990.

Patlagean, Evelyne, and Pierre Riché, eds. *Hagiographie, cultures, et sociétés: IVe–XIIe siècles. Actes du Colloque organisé à Nanterre et à Paris, 2–5 mai 1979*. Paris: Études Augustiniennes, 1981.

Poulin, Joseph-Claude. *L'idéal de sainteté dans l'Aquitaine carolingienne d'après les sources hagiographiques (750–950)*. Quebec: Presses de l'Université Laval, 1975.

Roisin, Simone. *L'hagiographie cistercienne dans le diocèse de Liège au XIIIe siècle*. Louvain: Bibliothèque de l'Université, 1947.

Stancliffe, Clare. *Saint Martin and His Hagiographer: History and Miracle in Sulpicius Severus*. Oxford: Clarendon, 1983.

Vauchez, André. *La sainteté en occident aux derniers siècles du moyen âge d'après les procès de canonisation et les documents hagiographiques*. Rome: École Française de Rome, 1981.

Vies des saints et des bienheureux, selon l'ordre du calendrier: avec l'historique des fêtes, par les révérends pères bénédictins de Paris. 13 vols. Paris: Letouzey et Ané, 1935–59.

Weinstein, Donald, and Rudolph Bell. *Saints and Society: The Two Worlds of Latin Christendom, 1000–1700*. Chicago: University of Chicago Press, 1982.

HAIMO OF AUXERRE (fl. ca. 840–60). Carolingian exegete of the school of the Benedictine house of Saint-Germain at Auxerre, Haimo was the author of widely read commentaries on the Song of Songs, Revelation, and the Minor Prophets, as well as of many sermons. Commentaries on the Pauline Epistles attributed to Alcuin's pupil Haimo of Halberstadt may also be his. Haimo studied with the Irish grammarian Murethach and was for a time the abbot of the monastery of Sasceium. He brought Carolingian biblical commentary to its most successful and influential point; his skillfully woven composite method was passed on through his pupil Heiric to Remigius of Auxerre. Commentaries on some books of the Bible, notably Genesis, are attributed to both Haimo and Remigius. The writings of Haimo of Auxerre published in the *Patrologia Latina* appear under the name of Haimo of Halberstadt. Haimo's biblical interpretation is only now receiving the scholarly attention it deserves.

E. Ann Matter

[See also: AUXERRE; BIBLE, CHRISTIAN INTERPRETATION OF; REMIGIUS OF AUXERRE]

Haimo of Auxerre. *Opera. PL* 117–18.
———. *Les dix-sept homélies de Haimon*, ed. Karl Storchenegger. Zurich: Juris, 1973.
Contreni, John J. "Haimo of Auxerre, Abbot of *Sasceium* (Cessyles-Bois), and a New Sermon on 1 John V, 4–10." *Revue bénédictine* 85 (1975): 303–20.
———. "The Biblical Glosses of Haimo of Auxerre and John Scottus Eriugena." *Speculum* 51 (1976): 412–34.
Matter, E. Ann. "Exegesis and Christian Education: The Carolingian Model." In *Schools of Thought in the Christian Tradition*, ed. Patrick Henry. Philadelphia: Fortress, 1984, pp. 90–105.
Quadri, Riccardo. "Aimone di Auxerre alla luce dei *Collectanea* di Heiric di Auxerre." *Italia medioevale e umanistica* 6 (1963): 1–48.

HAINAUT. County in the Low Countries, bordering on Flanders. Medieval Hainaut was an agricultural area, centering on the Scheldt, Sambre, and Dendre rivers. Its only large towns were Valenciennes and Mons. Although its population was Romance, Hainaut was entirely in the empire, and its bonds with France, which bordered it on the south, were thus diplomatic rather than dynastic.

Hainaut's first known count was Reginar "au long col," who founded a dynasty that lasted until after 1040. In 1170, Count Baudouin V of Hainaut married Marguerite, sister of the childless Philippe d'Alsace, count of Flanders. Their son ruled Hainaut and Flanders, beginning a dynastic union that persisted until the death of Countess Marguerite in 1278, when Hainaut passed to her grandson, Jean d'Avesnes. Jean's mother had been the sister of Count William II of Holland; at the death of Florence V of Holland in 1299, a dynastic union of Holland and Hainaut began that lasted until Hainaut was incorporated into the Burgundian state in the 15th century.

After the extinction of the Avesnes line in 1345, Hainaut was ruled by the Bavarian descendants of Marguerite, sister of Count William II and wife of the emperor Louis IV. In 1417, Count William IV was succeeded by his daughter Jacqueline, wife of Jean IV, the Burgundian duke of Brabant; but when she left her husband to marry Duke Humphrey of Gloucester in 1422, the Burgundians invaded Hainaut. With Holland and Zeeland, it was annexed formally to the domain of Philip the Good in 1433.

David M. Nicholas

[See also: AVESNES; BAUDOUIN; FLANDERS (genealogical table)]

de Hemptinne, Th. "Vlaanderen en Henegouwen onder de erfgenamen van de Boudewijns, 1070–1244" and Vandermaesen, M. "Vlaanderen en Henegouwen onder het Huis van Dampierre, 1244–1384." In *Algemene Geschiedenis der Nederlanden*. 2nd ser. Haarlem: Fibula-Van Dishoeck, 1982, Vol. 2, pp. 372–440.
Delcambre, Étienne. *Les relations entre la France et le Hainaut (1280–1297)*. Mons: Union des Imprimeries, 1929.
Falmagne, Jacques. *Baudouin V, comte de Hainaut*. Montreal: Presses de l'Université de Montréal, 1965.
Genicot, Léopold. *Études sur les principautés lotharingiennes*. Louvain: Bureau du Recueil, Bibliothèque de l'Université, 1975.
Hasquin, Hervé. *La Wallonie: le pays et les hommes: histoire, économies, sociétés*. Brussels: La Renaissance du Livre, 1975.
Vanderkindere, Léon. *La formation territoriale des principautés belges au moyen âge*. 2 vols. Brussels: Lamertin, 1902.

HARCOURT. The Norman barons of Harcourt (Eure) claimed descent from a 10th-century Viking chief. Over the centuries, the branches of this family became connected to all the important noble houses of Normandy and adjacent regions. Jean II, lord of Harcourt (d. 1302), was admiral of France. His oldest grandson, Jean IV, received the title of count in 1338, but the latter's brother, Godefroi, lord of Saint-Sauveur (Manche), became a chronic rebel against Philip VI and John II of France. The king executed Jean V of Harcourt in 1356 for supporting the party of the king of Navarre against the French crown.

Like many other Norman lords who had been English or Navarrese sympathizers in the 1340s and 1350s, the Harcourts became royalist after 1360. Both Jean VI and his brother Jacques, lord of Montgommery, served the king frequently in war. Jean VII (1370–1452) was captured at Agincourt (1415). His younger son, Louis, was archbishop of Rouen (1409–22). The senior male line of the family ended with Jean VIII's death in battle at Verneuil (1424). The descendants of Jacques, lord of Montgommery, included Jean (d. 1452), archbishop of Narbonne and patriarch of Antioch, whose brother Jacques married the heiress of the Melun family and thus acquired the county of Tancarville. The county of Harcourt itself passed to the house of Lorraine by marriage in 1476.

John Bell Henneman, Jr.

Anselme de Sainte-Marie, Pierre (de Guibours). *Histoire généalogique et chronologique de la maison de France*. 9 vols. 3rd ed. Paris: Compaignie des Libraires Associés, 1726–33.
Delisle, Léopold. *Histoire du château et des sires de Saint-Sauveur-le-Vicomte*. Valognes: Martin, 1867.
La Roque de la Lontière, Gilles-André. *Histoire généalogique de la maison de Harcourt*. 4 vols. Paris: Cramoisy, 1662.

HAUT PASSAGE. *See* CUSTOMS DUTIES

HAYNE VAN GHIZEGHEM (fl. ca. 1465–85). Composer of some of the most successful songs of the late 15th century. First documented in 1457 as a young boy entrusted to the care of the Burgundian court chapel singer Constans van Languebroeck, he appears in the court accounts as a singer and *valet de chambre* from 1467 to 1477, though the style of his music makes it clear that he must have lived for at least another ten years. Of his seventeen songs, all seem to be rondeau settings and are among the most characteristic late examples of that genre. Three had particularly impressive careers: *Amours amours* (seventeen sources); *Allez regretz* (thirty sources, setting a poem by Jean II, duke of Bourbon); and particularly *De tous biens plaine* (twenty-nine sources, and providing the musical materials for nearly sixty later works).

David Fallows

Hayne van Ghizeghem. *Hayne van Ghizeghem: opera omnia*, ed. Barton Hudson. N.p.: American Institute of Musicology, 1977.

HEALTH CARE. Standards of personal and communal health were often minimal in rural settings; they evolved most markedly at such model monasteries as Cluny and, later, under the pressures of urbanization. Their elaboration is documented by prescriptions for good living, descriptive vignettes in poetry and prose, fanciful illuminations in manuscripts, and pragmatic ordinances in archives. Throughout, Mediterranean mainsprings of hygienics were supplemented by local notions, and folk wisdom fused with learned medicine. Preservative and preventive concerns ranged from infancy to old age, from diet to environment, and from homebound routines to distant journeys.

A famous vernacular guide, the *Régime du corps*, accompanied Countess Béatrice de Provence in 1256 on her visit to four queens, her daughters. It shows how private hygiene depended on social standing. For courtiers and prosperous bourgeois, aesthetics tended to prevail over genuine hygienics. For example, the shift from whole grains to white bread was more pronounced in France than elsewhere north of the Alps, but mostly because members of the elite found white bread aesthetically more pleasing and something of a status symbol, rather than for the medically sounder reason that rye bread, widely consumed by peasants, made them more prone to ergotism. Similarly, the upper classes avoided garlic, despite its health benefits (it was legendary as a prophylactic), because it was associated with the poor. Their attitudes toward soap and clothing were similarly inspired. Readily available "Gallic" soap was spurned for exotic soaps from Outremer, because these contained oils rather than tallow. The shape, volume, and variety of clothing were often more important than comfort or cleanliness. Nevertheless, frequent changing of clothes was deemed important, and bathing was less rare than is often assumed. Fetor, skin diseases, and parasites were viewed as traits of those who were not only poor but lazy.

Bathhouses, or "stews," were popular enough to number at least twenty-six in Paris under Philip II Augustus (r. 1180–1223). Royal control was maintained by licensing, but it could extend further, as when Louis X (r. 1314–16) ordered new *étuves* built in Provins to keep up with the growing population. The steady influx of newcomers, the persistence of rural lifestyles, and overcrowding caused health hazards that were not addressed systematically. However, the layout of most towns shows that crafts with noxious byproducts, such as tanning and metallurgy, were kept at the edge of habitation. Sewers were installed before 1250 in Paris, and municipal governments enforced policies for refuse removal and sanitation, including the daily flushing of butchers' and fishmongers' quarters. By the end of the 15th century, authorities began to charge medical experts with inspections of water and food supplies, assessments of the need to quarantine, and public-health services for the poor.

Luke Demaitre

[See also: DISEASES; HOSPITALS; MEDICAL TEXTS; MENTAL HEALTH]

Alebrant (Aldebrandin de Sienne). *Le régime du corps*, ed. L. Landouzy and R. Pépin. Paris: Champion, 1911.

Jarry, Daniel. "Diététique et hygiène aux XIIe et XIIIe siècles." *Languedoc médical* 41 (1958): 5–24.

Loewe, R. "Handwashing and the Eyesight in the *Regimen sanitatis.*" *Bulletin of the History of Medicine* 30 (1956): 100–08.

Thorndike, Lynn. "Sanitation, Baths, and Street Cleaning in the Middle Ages and Renaissance." *Speculum* 3 (1929): 192–203.

Vigarello, Georges. *Concepts of Cleanliness: Changing Attitudes in France Since the Middle Ages*, trans. Jean Birrell. Cambridge: Cambridge University Press, 1988.

HEIRIC OF AUXERRE (841–ca. 876). A student of Lupus of Ferrières and Haimo of Auxerre, Heiric taught Remigius of Auxerre and was a disciple, if not a student, of Johannes Scottus Eriugena. Heiric was one of the major authors who transmitted the ideas of Eriugena to later generations. He was the first master to cite the *Periphyseon*, and one of his homilies makes use of Eriugena's homily on the prologue to John's Gospel. Heiric may have composed a set of glosses, reflecting ideas from Eriugena, on the *Categoriae decem*. Heiric's *Collectanea* contains a set of extracts from classical authors and a set of questions concerning problems of scriptural exegesis. He represents an important link in the intellectual traditions of the 9th-century schools and exemplifies the combination of interests in classical literature, biblical exegesis, and philosophical questions in that period.

Grover A. Zinn

[See also: ERIUGENA, JOHANNES SCOTTUS; HAIMO OF AUXERRE; PHILOSOPHY; REMIGIUS OF AUXERRE; SCHOOLS, CATHEDRAL]

Heiric of Auxerre. *Homiliae per circulum anni*, ed. Richard Quardri. CCCM 116, 116A. Turnhout: Brepols, 1992.

Contreni, John J. *Carolingian Learning, Masters and Manuscripts*. Hampshire: Variorum, 1992.

Jeauneau, Édouard. "Dans le sillage de l'Érigène: une homélie d'Héric d'Auxerre sur le Prologue de Jean." *Studi medievali* 3rd ser. 11 (1970): 937–55.

———. "Héric d'Auxerre disciple de Jean Scot." In *L'école carolingienne d'Auxerre, de Murethach à Remi, 830–908*, ed. Dominique Iogna-Prat, Colette Jeudy, and Guy Lobrichon. Paris: Beauchesne, 1991, pp. 353–70.

———. "Influences érigéniennes dans une homélie d'Héric d'Auxerre." In *The Mind of Eriugena: Papers of a Colloquium,*

Dublin, 14–18 July, 1970, ed. John J. O'Meara and Ludwig Bieler. Dublin: Irish University Press for the Royal Irish Academy, 1973, pp. 114–24.

HELDRIS DE CORNÜALLE (fl. late 13th c.). Otherwise unknown, Heldris de Cornüalle is the author of the *Roman de Silence* (6,706 octosyllabic lines), which survives in a single manuscript (University of Nottingham Mi. LM. 6). The story is of a count of Cornwall who names his daughter "Silence" to hide her gender, since only sons may inherit property. Nature and Nurture debate, and Silence leaves home disguised as a jongleur; returning, (s)he attracts the unwanted sexual advances of Queen Eufeme. Through Merlin's intervention, the unfaithful Eufeme is executed, and Silence, recognized as female, becomes the new queen of England. The ambiguity of the heroine's gender and its relationship to the power of language have attracted critical attention since Thorpe's edition appeared.

Peter L. Allen

Heldris de Cornüalle. *Le roman de Silence: A Thirteenth-Century Arthurian Verse Romance by Heldris de Cornüalle*, ed. Lewis Thorpe. Cambridge: Heffer, 1972.
———. *Roman de Silence*, trans. Regina Psaki. New York: Garland, 1990.

HÉLINANT DE FROIDMONT (1160?–1230?). Before becoming a monk at the abbey of Froidmont in Beauvaisis in 1183, Hélinant studied at Beauvais and was a trouvère at the court of King Philip II Augustus. After his conversion, he composed a Latin semiautobiographical chronicle, as well as a series of sermons and letters in Latin. But he is remembered today for his *Vers de la Mort*, written between 1193 and 1197. This popular poem of fifty stanzas, each of twelve octosyllabic lines, uses the rhyme scheme AAB AAB BBA BBA, which Hélinant is reputed to have invented. This meter became popular among other 13th-century poets writing in a similar didactic vein, such as Barthélemi, a recluse at the abbey of Saint-Fuscien-au-Bois, who composed a *Charité* and a *Miserere*, and Robert le Clerc, who also wrote a poem titled *Vers de la Mort* (Arras, 1269–70). Over sixty works are known to have imitated this meter. Hélinant's message is simple yet powerful. He attempts to convince humankind to abandon, as he has, secular trappings and to think about salvation. Death, he reminds us, is the great equalizer that works ceaselessly at transforming happiness into sorrow. Hélinant then asks Death to go greet the living. The princes of the church and those of secular realms appear in a sort of *danse macabre*. Hélinant enjoins his readers to reject the teachings of ancient philosophers who profess that there is no afterlife. He suggests that humankind, if deprived of hope of a life after death, is no different from the animals. There has to be an afterlife, he concludes, to remedy the lack of justice in the world.

Claude J. Fouillade

[See also: PLANH/COMPLAINTE]

Hélinant de Froidmont. *Vers de la Mort*, ed. E. Walberg. Paris: Droz, 1905.
Blum, Claude. *La représentation de la mort dans la littérature française de la Renaissance*. 2 vols. Geneva: Slatkine, 1989, Vol. 1: *D'Hélinant de Froidmont à Ronsard*.
Paden, William D. "De Monachis rithmos facientibus: Helinant de Froidmont, Bertran de Born and the Cistercian General Chapter of 1199." *Speculum* 55 (1980): 669–85.

HÉLOÏSE (1100/01–1163/64). Héloïse, abbess of the famous monastery of the Paraclete and its six daughter houses, was raised as a possibly illegitimate child in the Benedictine convent of Sainte-Marie of Argenteuil. At the age of seventeen, she continued her studies at her uncle Fulbert's house in Paris, where she was tutored by the theologian Peter Abélard (1079–1142). After a stormy love affair with Héloïse, Abélard offered the Paraclete and its lands as a refuge to Héloïse and her fellow nuns. Pope Innocent II confirmed the donation in 1131. Héloïse left us three letters to Abélard and one letter to Peter the Venerable (ca. 1092–1156). She is mentioned frequently in the cartulary of the Paraclete as a competent and efficient abbess who turned her religious house into one of the most prestigious women's monasteries in France. Its rule stressed the importance of education for all nuns, the unusual relaxation of strict enclosure, and the authority of the abbess over both male and female members of the monastic community.

In Peter Abélard's biographical *Historia calamitatum* and his moving correspondence with her, Héloïse emerges as an articulate and heroic person who equals Abélard in rhetorical sophistication and surpasses him in personal integrity. Her letters reveal a woman of deep love and devotion who remained attached to Abélard with both the bond of friendship and the memory of their earlier passion. Moreover, in her own mind, she was convinced that she had acted throughout the entire affair with disinterested love, devoted only to Abélard, while he had begun with lust only and never achieved her level of disinterested love, even though it was he who had taught her the true understanding of love and friendship.

Ulrike Wiethaus

[See also: ABÉLARD, PETER; ARGENTEUIL; PETER THE VENERABLE]

Abélard, Peter. *Historia calamitatum: texte critique avec introduction*, ed. Jacques Monfrin. 2nd ed. Paris: Vrin, 1962.
Peter the Venerable. *The Letters of Peter the Venerable*, ed. Giles Constable. 2 vols. Cambridge: Harvard University Press, 1967.
Radice, Betty, trans. *The Letters of Abelard and Heloise*. Harmondsworth: Penguin, 1974.
Charrier, Charlotte. *Héloïse dans l'histoire et la légende*. Paris: Champion, 1933.
Newman, Barbara. "Authority, Authenticity, and the Repression of Heloise." *Journal of Medieval and Renaissance Studies* 22 (1992): 121–57.
Pernoud, Régine. *Héloïse and Abélard*, trans. Peter Wiles. London: Collins, 1973.

HENRI D'ANDELI (fl. first half of the 13th c.). Henri was probably a native of Andelys (in Normandy) who studied and later wrote in Paris. His poetic compositions include the *Bataille des vins* (ca. 1225); the *Dit du chancelier Philippe*, a funeral eulogy for the chancellor of Notre-Dame of Paris (d. 1236); and the *Bataille des sept arts*, concerning university disputes during the 1230s. He is, however, best known for the *Lai d'Aristote* (ca. 1220), a fabliau that illustrates the triumph of "nature over nurture." This work has Aristotle rebuke Alexander for forgetting reason and becoming a slave to love; thereafter, seized by lust for Alexander's mistress, the great philosopher allows himself to be saddled and ridden in order to win her favors.

Norris J. Lacy

[See also: FABLIAU; PHILIP THE CHANCELLOR]

Henri d'Andeli. *Le lai d'Aristote d'Henri d'Andeli*, ed. Maurice Delbouille. Paris: Bibliothèque de la Faculté de Philosophie et Lettres de l'Université de Liège, 1951.

HENRY I (1008–1060). The third king of the Capetian line, Henry I (r. 1031–60) was the second son of Robert II and Constance of Arles. After the death of his elder brother, Hugh, in 1025, Henry was crowned in 1027 over the objections of his mother, who preferred her third son, Robert. After Henry succeeded his father, Robert and Constance rebelled with the aid of Eudes II, count of Blois and Champagne. Henry received direct support from Robert the Magnificent, duke of Normandy, and indirect support from the emperor Conrad II, a rival of Eudes in Burgundy and Lorraine, to whose daughter Matilda (d. 1034) Henry was affianced (1033). Henry had to give his brother the duchy of Burgundy, but the deaths of Constance in 1034 and Eudes in 1037 left the king more secure.

In the 1140s, Henry maintained the imperial connection by his marriage with another Matilda (d. 1044), the niece of the emperor Henry III (r. 1039–56). After the death of his Norman ally Robert, Henry supported Robert's illegitimate son and heir, William (r. 1035–87), defeating rebellious vassals at Val-ès-Dunes in 1047. Henry also supported the new count of Anjou, Geoffroi Martel (r. 1040–60), against his enemy Thibaut III of Blois (r. 1037–89), who had succeeded Eudes II. He also maintained his rights and control over the French church in the face of the reforming pope Leo IX (r. 1049–54), while avoiding a direct confrontation.

Henry concluded a new marriage in 1051, with Anne, the daughter of the Russian prince Jaroslaw III of Kiev (r. 1019–54). His heir, the future Philip I, was born in 1052, and Henry arranged for his coronation at Reims in May 1059. In his last years, Henry's deteriorating relations with William the Conqueror led him to invade the duchy twice, but he met defeat at Mortemer (1054) and Varaville (1058). Following his son's coronation, Henry arranged for a regency under Baudouin V of Flanders (r. 1035–67), the husband of Henry's sister Adèle and the father-in-law of William the Conqueror. Soon afterward, the king died prematurely at Vitry-aux-Loges near Orléans (August 4, 1060).

R. Thomas McDonald

[See also: ANNE OF KIEV; CONSTANCE OF ARLES; ROBERT II THE PIOUS]

Soehnee, Frédéric. *Catalogues des actes de Henri Ier, roi de France (1031–1060)*. Paris: Champion, 1907.

HENRY I (1068–1135). As king of England (1100–35), Henry I played a significant role in French warfare and diplomacy, especially after 1106, when he took over the governance of Normandy. Although modern historians have sometimes characterized Henry's rule as harsh and oppressive, contemporaries were struck by Henry's peaceful reign over a land long accustomed to war.

Upon William the Conqueror's death in 1087, Normandy went to Henry's oldest brother, Robert Curthose, and England to the second brother, William II Rufus. Henry inherited 5,000 pounds of silver, out of which he purchased the Avranchin and Cotentin from Robert. King William's invasion of Normandy in 1091 forced Robert to cede captured land, including lands previously sold to Henry. But by 1092, Henry became the overlord of Domfront, which he used as his base to reconquer the Cotentin.

In 1096, Robert pawned Normandy to William and set off on crusade. As Robert was returning in 1100, William was killed in a hunting accident and Henry seized the throne. After trying for a year to capture the crown, Robert agreed to a treaty that recognized Henry as king while Henry renounced most of his Norman possessions. But Robert could not maintain order in Normandy, and when a French bishop wrote requesting help for oppressed Norman churches, Henry received justification for military action. In July 1106, he launched an invasion, and on September 28, in a pitched battle at Tinchebrai, Robert was captured.

Henry could not rest secure in his possession of Normandy. Robert's son, William Clito, also had a claim to the duchy, and Henry also had to contend with baronial revolts and hostile princes. War erupted in 1111 between Henry and Louis VI of France, who allied with the counts of Anjou and Flanders. By 1113, Henry was victorious and Louis was forced to recognize English overlordship in Maine and Brittany. Hostilities resumed in 1116, when Norman barons joined with France, Flanders, and Anjou to revolt in favor of William Clito. With the Flemish count killed in 1119, Henry secured peace with Anjou by marrying his son to Count Foulques's daughter. Defeated both in battle and by the English king's diplomatic skills, Louis complained to the pope about Henry's action, but Calixtus II sided with Henry and by 1120 Normandy was at peace.

Henry's only legitimate son, William, drowned in 1121, reopening William Clito's claim to Normandy. Although Henry suppressed Norman insurrection in 1123–24, Clito's position was strengthened by his marriage to Louis VI's sister-in-law and further enhanced when Louis named him to the Flemish countship. Clito was killed in 1128 while fighting to gain control of Flanders. Henry's second marriage proved childless, and he named his daughter, Matilda, as his successor. Although Henry's barons swore to support her in 1127, they became disenchanted after Matilda married Geoffroi IV, count of Anjou, especially after the couple demanded Normandy in 1135. Matilda retained possession of Normandy after Henry's death but lost the crown of England to Henry's nephew Stephen of Blois.

Lois Huneycutt

[See also: ANJOU; NORMANDY]

Orderic Vitalis. *The Ecclesiastical History of Orderic Vitalis*, ed. and trans. Marjorie Chibnall. 6 vols. Oxford: Oxford University Press, 1972–80.

Hollister, C. Warren. "Courtly Culture and Courtly Style in the Anglo-Norman World." *Albion* 20 (1988): 1–17.

———. *Monarchy, Magnates and Institutions in the Anglo-Norman World*. London: Hambledon, 1986.

Poole, Austin Lane. *From Domesday Book to Magna Carta: 1087–1216*. 2nd ed. Oxford: Oxford University Press, 1964.

HENRY II (1133–1189). King of England. The son of Geoffroi IV, count of Anjou, and Matilda, daughter of Henry I of England, Henry II ruled most of western France, yet despite the power at his disposal faced recurrent conflicts with his lord, the king of France, and his own family. Henry amassed his territories largely between 1150 and 1154, gaining Normandy by grant from his father in 1150 and Anjou by inheritance on Geoffroi's death in 1151. A year later, Henry added the duchy of Aquitaine to his possessions when he married its heiress, Eleanor, shortly after her marriage to Louis VII was annulled; in 1154, England came to Henry on the death of his rival, King Stephen. Louis VII of France organized a coalition to oppose Henry's growing power, but without success; the two kings were reconciled by 1154. Relations between them remained cordial for half a decade. In 1158, Louis betrothed his daughter Marguerite to Henry's eldest son (also Henry), and gave his blessing to Henry's attempts to exert control over Brittany, attempts that soon gained overlordship there for the English king.

This amicable relationship ended in 1159, when Henry asserted his wife's claim to Toulouse, whose count was brother-in-law to Louis. Louis stymied the attack by defending the town in person, setting off a wider conflict, which (despite an abortive peace made in 1160) dragged on until 1161. Henry then concentrated on tightening his grip on his continental domain, deposing the duke of Brittany, Conan IV, in 1166 and betrothing the duke's daughter to his son Geoffroi. In 1167, war between Henry and Louis broke out once more, caused mainly by Henry's intervention in a dispute over the county of Auvergne. Peace came in 1169, and Louis betrothed his daughter Alice to Henry's son Richard.

Henry's next serious conflict was with his family as much as his lord. In 1173, Eleanor and Henry's three el-

dest sons rebelled against him in alliance with Louis; the revolt took two years to put down. War with Louis threatened again in 1177, but the Treaty of Ivry settled outstanding problems, submitting conflicting claims in Auvergne to arbitration. After Louis's death, Henry acted as a distant protector to his heir, Philip II. Further disputes among Henry's sons, largely over the plans for succession after his death, arose repeatedly from 1182, when a revolt in Aquitaine provided the spark. Adopting an anti-Angevin policy, Philip supported Henry the Young King and later Geoffroi against their father, but both sons died unexpectedly before much could be accomplished against Henry II. Philip went to war with Henry in 1187, demanding (among other things) Richard's marriage to Alice. Henry made a counteroffer: his youngest son, John, would marry Alice and receive all the French fiefs except Normandy, which with England would be Richard's. When Richard learned of this plan, he turned against his father and in 1188 allied with Philip; they made war on Henry in 1189. His health failing, Henry had nothing to gain by a war against his chief heir; he submitted on July 4 and died two days later.

Donald F. Fleming

[See also: ANJOU; BRITTANY; ELEANOR OF AQUITAINE; NORMANDY]

Gillingham, John. *The Angevin Empire*. New York: Holmes and Meier, 1984.

Wattern, W.L. *Henry II*. Berkeley: University of California Press, 1973.

HENRY III (1207–1272). In 1216, Henry III, eldest son of King John and Isabelle d'Angoulême, assumed the title king of England, lord of Ireland, duke of Normandy and Aquitaine, and count of Anjou. Even though his father had lost control of Normandy, Anjou, and much of Aquitaine, Henry III continued to press his claims both diplomatically and militarily to all these lands, which he considered his rightful patrimony. Largely unsuccessful, he finally acquiesced to much less in the Treaty of Paris in 1259, though he retained control over Gascony and as duke of Aquitaine was a peer of France. Thus, Henry III continued to be an important baron on the Continent.

Henry was only nine years old when he inherited what was left of his father's feudal empire. His regents were successful in ending the barons' rebellion in England, and Louis of France, son of Philip II Augustus, gave up his claim to the English throne and left the country. When Henry assumed control of the government in 1227, he held England, the Channel Islands, Gascony, and the island of Oléron and continued to try to regain the rest of the lands that he believed belonged to him. His military expeditions of 1230 and 1242 produced no long-term gains, while his diplomatic efforts did not force Louis IX to return the disputed territory. Finally, on December 4, 1259, Henry and Louis signed the controversial Treaty of Paris, in which Henry III recognized Louis's control over Normandy, Anjou, Maine, Touraine, and Poitou, while Henry retained the title duke of

Aquitaine, for which he did homage to Louis. Henry's hold over Aquitaine, however, was limited to Gascony and Oléron. Several of Louis's concessions required negotiations over many years before they were useful to Henry. Within Gascony, some lords remained relatively independent of Henry's control. Also, Louis's role as Henry's liege lord allowed Gascons, unhappy with the settlement of disputes in Henry's courts, to appeal to the Parlement de Paris. This recourse, first used immediately after the treaty's ratification, opened the way for increasing French royal intervention into Gascon affairs.

Henry III can be credited with two changes that strengthened his and his successors' control over Gascony. First, he began the development of a more efficient administration within the county. Second, when Henry gave control of this land to his heir, Edward, he did so with the stipulation that it never be separated from the crown.

Penelope Adair

[See also: GASCONY; LOUIS IX]

Clanchy, Michael T. *England and Its Rulers 1066–1272: Foreign Lordship and National Identity.* Oxford: Blackwell, 1983.

Labarge, Margaret W. *Gascony, England's First Colony 1204–1453.* London: Hamish Hamilton, 1980.

LePatourel, John. "The Plantagenet Dominions." *History: The Quarterly Journal of the Historical Association* (London) 50 (1965): 289–308.

Powicke, F.M. *King Henry III and the Lord Edward: The Community of the Realm in the Thirteenth Century.* 2 vols. Oxford: Clarendon, 1947.

HENRY V (1387–1422). During his ten years as king of England (1413–22), Henry made himself a major force in French politics. He abandoned the traditional Plantagenêt goal of simply guarding English possessions on the Continent and seriously attempted the conquest of France. The sources of this ambitious policy are found in the conjunction of his personal sense of his rights and his shrewd opportunism, when both Burgundians and Armagnacs invited his intervention in France. Henry astutely negotiated with both sides while preparing the invasion of 1415, which destroyed the illusion that he would merely be a tool of either faction. His brilliant campaign marked the military highpoint of the Hundred Years' War for the English. The capture of Harfleur and subsequent victory at Agincourt left France defenseless, the Armagnacs leaderless, and Henry persuaded that he could become king of France with Burgundian support.

Henry returned to France in 1417 with an army of conquest prepared for a war of sieges and organized to remain and garrison captured territories. In January 1419, the capture of Rouen secured Normandy, and by summer the English threatened Paris itself. Henry's combined strategy of warfare and diplomacy triumphed in the Treaty of Troyes (1420), which arranged his marriage to Catherine of France, designated him as regent for the unfortunate Charles VI, and proclaimed him heir to the throne. There-

after, Henry consolidated his hold on Normandy, sought taxes to make the French war self-financing, and pressed to the south in the fruitless search for a decisive victory over the troublesome forces of the dauphin, Charles. Despite the birth in 1421 of an heir to the dual monarchy, the future Henry VI, the Lancastrian edifice proved unstable, for it was built on French divisions that precluded a timely reconciliation. Henry remained dependent on the duke of Burgundy, and his army in Normandy came to be viewed as an occupying force despite his best efforts to win acceptance as the legitimate ruler of the realm and of the duchy.

Henry's premature death of dysentery at Vincennes in 1422 ended a life of unfulfilled promise. However illusory his goals and ephemeral his achievements, he remains a legendary figure in French as well as English history. Neither as cruel as the French remember nor as chivalrous as the English imagine, he was a talented commander who seized a tragic moment in French history to become the most heroic of English monarchs. It would take the Valois a generation to reverse his magnificent accomplishments.

Paul D. Solon

[See also: AGINCOURT; ARMAGNACS; CATHERINE OF FRANCE; CHARLES VI; NORMANDY; ROUEN]

Harriss, G.L., ed. *Henry V: The Practice of Kingship.* London: Oxford University Press, 1985.

Jacob, Ernest Fraser. *Henry V and the Invasion of France.* New York: Macmillan, 1950.

Labarge, Margaret Wade. *Henry V: The Cautious Conqueror.* London: Secker and Warburg, 1975.

Newhall, Richard A. *The English Conquest of Normandy, 1416–1424.* New York: Russell and Russell, 1971.

Wylie, James Hamilton. *The Reign of Henry the Fifth.* 3 vols. Cambridge: Cambridge University Press, 1914–29. [Vol. 3 with W.T. Waugh.]

HENRY VI (1421–1471). The son of Henry V of England and Catherine of France, Henry VI of England was the unfortunate heir to his father's kingdom and conquests. He was born in fufillment of the hopes of the Treaty of Troyes. Within nine months, the deaths of his father and his grandfather made him the only Plantagenêt ever to be widely recognized as king of France. His uncle John, duke of Bedford, regent in France, could not preserve his throne despite Henry's belated coronation in Paris in the aftermath of that of Charles VII in Reims. By 1436, the reconciliation of Charles with the duke of Burgundy left Henry only the duchies of Normandy and Aquitaine as he came of age.

Henry's reign was marked by an admirable devotion to charity, factionalism in England, and a hopeless entanglement in a France he could neither govern nor abandon. Henry sought to reinforce his French position by releasing the duke of Orléans and by negotiating for an Armagnac marriage during the Praguerie, but his greatest success came later with his marriage in 1445 to Margaret of Anjou. The policy of reconciliation it represented having failed, Henry's reign as king of France ended in the disastrous campaigns of 1449–53, when he lost both his father's Norman conquests and his ancestors' duchy of Guyenne.

Henry's incapacity for government became unmistakable when he went insane in autumn 1453. Thereafter, he was little more than a tool in the hands of others. His formidable wife worked ceaselessly for their desperate cause, but Henry was deposed by Edward of York in 1461. Ironically, Margaret then won support from Louis XI, who felt that any prolongation of the Wars of the Roses would preclude English activity in France. However, neither Louis's diplomacy nor French military assistance under Pierre de Brezé could salvage the Lancastrian cause. Restored briefly by Warwick in 1470, Henry was murdered shortly after the death of his son Edward at the Battle of Tewkesbury.

Paul D. Solon

[See also: ARISTOCRATIC REVOLT; BEDFORD, JOHN OF LANCASTER, DUKE OF; CATHERINE OF FRANCE; CHARLES VII; RECONQUEST OF FRANCE]

Griffiths, Ralph A. *The Reign of King Henry VI*. Berkeley: University of California Press, 1981.
Wolffe, Bertram P. *Henry VI*. London: Eyre Methuen, 1981.

HENRY OF GHENT (ca. 1217–1293). Known as *doctor solemnis*, Henry was born at Ghent or Tournai and was regent master in theology at the University of Paris from 1276 to 1292. Although he was also canon of Tournai and archdeacon of Bruges and Tournai, he is best remembered for his active participation in the affairs of the university. An outspoken, independent thinker, Henry not only opposed the Averroists in 1277, but he differed with the Christian Aristotelianism of Thomas Aquinas. A proponent of Augustinianism, Henry attempted to restore Augustinian theology to the prominent place it once had held. Henry's version of Augustinian theology, however, was influenced by both Aristotle and Avicenna. For example, Henry proposed that prototypical ideas or essences were eternally produced by God or emanated from Him, but only by a free act of God did any of these essences achieve actual existence. Thus, by appropriating the Avicennan concept of emanation, Henry described a precarious relation between divine ideas, which exist eternally, and the act of creation, a relation that some of his contemporaries and successors regarded as a threat to the Christian doctrine of creation *ex nihilo*. Henry also held that truth could be known only through divine illumination. Although his ideas met with much criticism, his work influenced nominalism, shaping the thought of such notable theologians as Duns Scotus and William of Ockham. Henry was also opposed to the confessional privileges of mendicant orders; so fervent and extreme was his condemnation of mendicants that he was reprimanded in 1290. His principal works are his disputations, including disputations *de quodlibet*, held between 1276 and 1292.

E. Kay Harris

[See also: GODFREY OF FONTAINES]

Henry of Ghent. *Henrici de Gandavo opera omnia*, ed. R. Macken. 37 vols. to date. Leiden: Brill, 1979– .
Gilson, Étienne. *History of Christian Philosophy in the Middle Ages*. New York: Random House, 1955.
Marrone, Steven P. *Truth and Scientific Knowledge in the Thought of Henry of Ghent*. Cambridge: Medieval Academy of America, 1985.

HENRY OF LANGENSTEIN (Henry Heinbuche of Langenstein, Henry of Hesse; 1325–1397). An eclectic theologian, scholar, and mystic interested in scientific knowledge, Henry of Langenstein entered the University of Paris in 1358 and became regent master of arts there in 1363. He received the doctorate in theology in 1376. Drawn into the ecclesiastical struggle known as the Great Schism, Henry wrote perhaps the first treatise, *Epistola pacis* (1379), that recommended summoning a general council to resolve this conflict. A later work, *Epistola concilii pacis* (1381), set forth the theory of conciliarism and was addressed to secular princes, giving them implicit authority to summon a general church council. Henry then left Paris, perhaps exiled for his views, and lived at the Cistercian monastery at Eberbach, where he wrote *Speculum animae* (1382), a tract on mysticism. Henry was also keenly interested in the sciences. Before becoming a member of the faculty of theology, he wrote *Quaestio de cometa*, inspired by the comet of 1368, and *Tractatus contra astrologus conjunctionistas de eventibus futurorum* (1368). His theological writings also reveal this interest in the sciences. In 1393, Henry was invited to the University of Vienna to oversee its reorganization. While there, he wrote its constitution, translated hymns into German, and wrote numerous other works, including treatises on the church, a Hebrew grammar, and a vast exegesis on Genesis, *Lecturae super Genesim* (1385). Only a small part of Henry's writings have been published.

E. Kay Harris

Lang, Justin. *Die Christologie bei Heinrich von Langenstein*. Freiburg: Herder, 1966.
Pruckner, Hubert. *Studien zu den astrologischen Schriften des Heinrich von Langenstein*. Leipzig: Teubner, 1933.
Steneck, Nicholas H. *Science and Creation in the Middle Ages: Henry of Langenstein (d. 1397) on Genesis*. Notre Dame: University of Notre Dame Press, 1976.

HERALD/HERALDRY. The term "herald" (OFr. *heralt* or *herau[l]t*) was applied from at least 1170 to men (down to ca. 1300 closely associated with minstrels) who specialized in matters associated with the tournament. From 1170 to 1500 and beyond, heralds were regularly sent forth to proclaim tournaments at various courts, returned with the replies of those challenged, and accompanied their lord, often at first in considerable numbers, to the place appointed for the combat. During the tournament, the heralds would announce the combatants as they entered the field, often praising their past performances, and would discuss their merits with fellow heralds and other spectators while each combat was in progress. Their need to be able to identify individual knights gave them a special interest in the cognizances, or "arms," whose use became general among knights between 1160 and 1220, and it is likely that they not merely encouraged the use of such cognizances among those who took part in tournaments but played an important role in designing them and in systematizing their use. From ca. 1250, some heralds kept books or rolls of arms, collected from various sources, to assist them in remembering the hundreds of distinct but often similar arms they encountered in their work, and from ca. 1300 a growing number wrote treatises on the subject. Thus, the word "heraldry" (OFr. *herau[l]die*), which designates the profession of the herald as a whole, came to be used more narrowly to designate the arcane "science" related to the design, description, analysis, and recognition of armorial bearings.

During the later 13th and early 14th centuries, the body of heralds gradually acquired the character of a professional corps, with distinct ranks and jurisdictions granted by the kings and princes who employed them. By 1276, England had been divided into territories presided over by men with the title "king of heralds" (*roi des herauts*) or "king of arms" (*roi d'armes*); a king of the heralds of France (in the narrow sense) is attested in 1318. Within his territory, or "march of arms" (*marche d'armes*), corresponding in France to one of a dozen great principalities or regions, the king of heralds was eventually given the task of overseeing all matters that touched on armorial bearings, nobility, and chivalry. Apprentice heralds were given the title "pursuivant (of arms)" (*poursuivant [d'armes]*), so that "herald (of arms)" became the special title of master heralds who were not yet kings. Like kings of heralds, who took their style from their march, after ca. 1330 simple heralds and pursuivants came to be given special styles at the time of their appointment, the former typically derived from the name of a town, the latter from some device. In 1406, the French heralds were formally united in a college under the presidency of Montjoye, king of arms of the March of France.

Down to 1330, the heralds of all ranks continued to be concerned exclusively with tournaments, but in the 1330s kings began to entrust heralds with diplomatic missions, bearing letters to foreign princes or instructions to ambassadors, and from 1425 they frequently led important embassies. As ambassadors, heralds came to enjoy important privileges and immunities and to constitute an internationally recognized order comparable with the clergy.

D'A. Jonathan D. Boulton

[See also: ARMS (HERALDIC)]

Adam-Even, Paul. "Les fonctions militaires des hérauts d'armes, leur influence sur le développement de l'héraldique." *Archives héraldiques suisses* 71 (1957): 2–33.
Galbreath, D.L., and Léon Jéquier. *Manuel du blason.* Lausanne: Spes, 1977.
Pastoureau, Michel. *Traité d'héraldique.* Paris: Picard, 1979.
Wagner, Anthony Richard. *Heralds and Heraldry in the Middle Ages.* London: Mitford, 1939.

HERBERT OF BOSHAM (b. ca. 1120). Born in Bosham, Sussex, Herbert studied at Paris under Peter Lombard ca. 1150 and later edited Peter's *Magna glossatura* on the Psalter and the letters of Paul. After his studies, Herbert returned to England and entered the service of King Henry II Plantagenêt. He was a member of the household of Thomas Becket when Becket became archbishop of Canterbury. Herbert shared Becket's exile to France (1164–70) and was one of the most ardent supporters of Becket's cause before and after the archbishop's death. Herbert was Becket's instructor in biblical and theological matters and wrote a Latin *vita* of the archbishop. Herbert was given a papal commendation to the position of provost in the cathedral of Troyes, but he seems not to have taken it up. He retired to the Cistercian abbey of Ourscamp as a lay resident in his old age.

Herbert of Bosham is known today for his literal commentary on the Psalms, a commentary based on the Latin translation by Jerome known as the *Hebraica*, so named because it was a fresh translation from the Hebrew. Bosham was greatly influenced by Andrew of Saint-Victor, with whom he may have studied and whose works he certainly knew, especially his emphasis upon the literal-historical sense of the biblical text and the use of Jewish sources for understanding that sense in the Old Testament writings. Herbert went beyond Andrew, however, for he was able to read texts in the Hebrew and thus had access to the written Jewish commentary tradition. He was probably the most accomplished Christian Hebraist (excluding converts from Judaism) between Jerome and the Italian humanists, such as Pico della Mirandola. He corrected Jerome's translation where he thought it necessary and recorded a number of Jewish exegetical points in his own commentary.

Grover A. Zinn

[See also: ANDREW OF SAINT-VICTOR; BIBLE, CHRISTIAN INTERPRETATION OF; BIBLE, JEWISH INTERPRETATION OF; BIBLE, LATIN VERSION OF; PETER LOMBARD]

Loewe, Raphael. "Herbert of Bosham's Commentary on Jerome's Hebrew Psalter." *Biblica* 34 (1953): 44–77, 159–92, 275–98.
Smalley, Beryl. *The Becket Conflict and the Schools: A Study of Intellectuals in Politics.* Oxford: Blackwell, 1973, pp. 59–86.
———. "A Commentary on the *Hebraica* by Herbert of Bosham." *Recherches de théologie ancienne et médiévale* 18 (1951): 29–65.
———. *The Study of the Bible in the Middle Ages.* 3rd ed. Oxford: Blackwell, 1983, pp. 186–95.

HERENC, BAUDET (fl. first half of the 15th c.) A native of Chalon-sur-Saône, Herenc composed ca. 1425 a refutation of Alain Chartier's *Belle dame sans merci*. This poem, apparently very popular (seventeen manuscripts extant), was known under various titles. In a printed version in the *Jardin de plaisance et fleur de réthorique*, its title is the *Parlement d'Amour*. In sixty-eight octosyllabic octets, Baudet describes a vision of a court of love in which the usual allegorical figures (Hope, Desire, Memory, Sweet Thoughts) condemn the lady for having dishonored "the wise and noble gentleman who is more perfect than any other creature" (f. 152 r°).

In 1432, Baudet composed the *Doctrinal de la seconde rhétorique*. Like other *arts poétiques* of the epoch, it contains a dictionary of spelling (containing some 2,700 words), a rhyming dictionary (6,000 words), and, most important, examples of various genres of lyric poetry, such as *lai, chant royal, serventois, pastourelle, sotte amoureuse*, ballade, rondeau, and *fatras*. Patterson considers the *Doctrinal* to be "the clearest, the most intelligent, and the best arranged treatise between the times of Deschamps and Molinet." In 1448, Baudet composed some ballades for Charles d'Orléans, none of which has survived.

Peter F. Dembowski

[See also: *ARTS DE SECONDE RHÉTORIQUE;* CHARTIER, ALAIN; QUARREL OF THE *BELLE DAME SANS MERCI*]

Herenc, Baudet. *Le parlement d'Amour*. In *Le jardin de plaisance et fleur de réthorique*. 2 vols. Paris: Didot, 1910, Vol. 1, f. 139v–142v. [Commentary: Vol. 2, Eugénie Droz and Arthur Piaget, *Introduction et notes*.] Paris: Champion, 1925, pp. 261–62.

———. *Doctrinal de la seconde rhétorique*. In *Recueil d'arts de seconde rhétorique*, ed. Ernest Langois. Paris: Imprimerie Nationale, 1902, pp. xxxii–xlii [commentary], 104–98 [text].

Patterson, Werner Forest. *Three Centuries of French Poetic Theory: A Critical History of the Chief Arts of Poetry in France (1328–1630)*. Ann Arbor: University of Michigan Press, 1935, pp. 121–24.

HERESIES, APOSTOLIC.

Among the most fervent and controversial forms of medieval Christian spirituality was the desire to live the *vita apostolica* ("evangelical life"), modeled on that of the followers of Jesus (Acts 1–4). This generally meant some combination of voluntary poverty, asceticism, manual labor, religious devotion, and preaching. In one sense, nothing could be more orthodox, and many of the most powerful movements of Christian renewal were so inspired. On the other hand, this earliest form of Christianity was too radical for most ecclesiastical structures; indeed, it was impossible for clergy to model themselves too closely on the apostolic life (i.e., living with women, equality of lay and cleric). More troubling, by apostolic standards ecclesiastical wealth and worldly power could be seen as signs of corruption, or worse. In some ways, then, the apostolic life suited laity better, and as such threatened clerical control of religious matters. But ecclesiastical efforts to discipline lay apostolic groups often provoked hostility and even an outright break with the church. In almost every case of an "apostolic heresy," a lay movement started out orthodox in both doctrine and practice but, through a dialectic of conflict with the clergy, came to see the church as the enemy of a true Christian life.

This conflict between lay and clerical interpretations of the *vita apostolica* centered on several interlocking issues, any of which could lead to heresy.

Poverty. The Apostles had held their goods in common and renounced any attachment to material well-being. This voluntary poverty, linked to a renunciation of power and status within society ("pauper" meant "powerless"), became the focus of class hostility: on the one hand, aristocrats who voluntarily gave up their wealth and social power drew devoted disciples and followers from among the populace; on the other, institutions that waxed rich, whether the papacy or a successful monastic reform house, became associated with the corruption of filthy lucre. The stakes involved in poverty, when pushed to ideological extremes by groups like the Spiritual Franciscans, could lead to war of the "poor" against the rich and the clergy.

Manual Labor. Linked to poverty both by its social status and by its renunciation of the privileges of power, the emphasis on "earning one's bread by the sweat of one's brow" became a common refrain. Such an approach was not always apostolic—St. Francis and his followers took poverty to full-fledged mendicancy—but it formed the core of many lay apostolic communities, such as the béguines and Beghards. As such, it posed a threat to ecclesiastical claims embodied in the principle of the three orders: if all should labor and pray, what place is there for clerics who prayed full time and lived off the products of layfolk's labor?

Preaching. The main purpose of the original Apostles was to preach the gospel. But monks, committed to a cloistered apostolic life, could not preach; whereas the secular clergy, alone licensed to preach, were least likely to live the apostolic life and to espouse apostolic values. Pious laymen and laywomen, such as the Waldensians, bound neither by monastic vows nor by clerical commitments, could attract enthusiastic crowds to their sermons, thereby rousing the envy of a less charismatic clergy. The emergence of the preaching orders solved the need for more apostolic preaching in the face of heretical threats to the church. But the career of the Spiritual Franciscans illustrates how difficult it was to negotiate such a solution in practice.

Sacraments and Salvation. In its most extreme form, the apostolic life could lead beyond questions of discipline (preaching, clerical supervision) to that of the church's legitimacy. To some, the very act of living in an apostolic community was the guarantee of salvation; whereas the institutional church, with its sacraments and infant baptism, offered only empty motions with no salvific power. Such an attitude, which was still more extreme than Donatism (a 4th-century heretical movement in North Africa that held that ministers without grace could not validly administer sacraments), clearly took an "apostolic community" over into heresy.

There is little evidence of apostolic "heresies" in the early-medieval period, unless one so interprets such charismatic figures as the "False Christ" of Bourges (described by Gregory of Tours) and Aldebert. The early 11th century saw popular heretical movements and communities that some historians have interpreted as "apostolic"; the 12th century saw the spread of lay communities and movements, first in the preaching of wandering hermits like Henry of Lausanne and Peter de Bruys, later in the Waldensians, Humiliati, and Franciscans. By the 13th century, béguine and Beghard convents had spread throughout much of France and western Europe, providing women and men with an urban form of communal apostolic life. It is arguable that apostolic heresies are the core of most (and of the most successful) medieval popular heresies. On the other hand, they are not found only in "working class" circles; the apostolic ideal inspired some of the most learned thinkers of the high Middle Ages (John Wyclif, Marsilius of Padua, William of Ockham). Apostolic movements are occasionally contrasted with apocalyptic ones, but the original apostolic community was clearly inspired by a sense of the imminent return of Christ, and many subsequent ones were equally so inspired (e.g., Spiritual Franciscans, Hussites). Apostolic movements may in fact represent secondary apocalyptic movements, which, like the original Apostles, formed around an initial disappointment, looking toward a later fulfillment of eschatological hopes. In some cases, such as the béguines of Provence, apocalyptic hopes may have produced the more extreme forms of lay apostolic life.

Richard Landes

[See also: BÉGUINES; FRANCISCAN ORDER; HERESY; MILLENNIALISM; PREACHING; WALDO/WALDENSES]

Chenu, Marie-Dominique. *Nature, Man and Society in the Twelfth Century,* trans. Jerome Taylor and Lester K. Little. Chicago: University of Chicago Press, 1968, pp. 200–70.

Classen, Peter. "Eschatologische Ideen und Armutsbewegungen im 11. und 12. Jahrhundert." In *Povertà e ricchezza nella spiritualità dei secoli XI e XII.* Todi: Accademia Tudertina, 1969, pp. 126–62.

Landes, Richard. "La vie apostolique en Aquitaine au tourant du millennium: Paix de Dieu, culte de reliques et communautés 'hérétiques.'" *Annales* 46 (1991): 573–93.

Little, Lester K. *Religious Poverty and the Profit Economy in Medieval Europe.* Ithaca: Cornell University Press, 1978.

Leyser, Henrietta. *Hermits and the New Monasticism.* London: Macmillan, 1984.

McDonnell, Ernest W. "The Vita Apostolica: Diversity or Dissent." *Church History* 24 (1955): 15–31.

Violante, Cinzio. "La pauvreté dans les hérésies du XIe siècle." In *Études sur l'histoire de la pauvreté,* ed. Michel Mollat. Paris: Publications de la Sorbonne, 1974, pp. 347–69.

HERESY. Term derived from the Greek word for "choice" (*hairesis*). In the early church, the term came to indicate leaders or groups who "chose" rather than "received" their teachings about Christ: heresy was associated with pride rather than the humility and submission of the true Christian. But what were the true teachings? In early Christianity, a charismatic messianic movement with a moral rather than theological message, variations in teaching abounded. The first Christian centuries are marked by constant, often vicious, mutual accusations between groups, as the emerging institutional church attempted to enforce discipline under the principles of "one shepherd one flock" (John 10:16) and "there is no salvation outside the church." For the church, orthodoxy emerged victorious because of its direct links to the "apostolic tradition"; less partisan analyses suggest that orthodoxy was merely the most successful heresy (Bauer). Ultimately, the labels "orthodox" and "heretic" are political, applied by those with enough power to assert their will; rarely if ever would "heretics" call themselves that. Support of Christianity by the emperor Constantine (r. 307–37) transformed the situation: he demanded doctrinal and liturgical unity (hence the councils and creeds of the 4th century); and he introduced the use of state power to "discipline" dissidents. In the early 5th century, Augustine developed an ideology whereby errant Christians could be "compelled to enter the church" out of love for their souls, thus justifying official violence against heretics and schismatics.

Arianism alone of theological heresies survived the fall of Rome in the West, largely because the Goths and Burgundians had converted to it in earlier centuries. Thus, the Germanic kingdoms in southern Gaul, Spain, and Italy were ruled by an Arian and ethnic elite, while the native population remained either Catholic or pagan. After his conversion to Catholicism in the mid-490s, the Frankish king Clovis invoked Arian heresy as a pretext to invade the Visigothic south. But over the next five centuries, despite occasional cases of theological dispute (Adoptionism, Predestination), the church was more concerned with paganism than heresy. The only signs of genuinely Christian dissent come from popular millenarian or apostolic movements that rejected the ecclesiastical hierarchy. The leaders of these groups, like the "False Christ" of Bourges or the prophetess Thiota, arose during periods of need and crisis and used the utopian imagery of imminent salvation and social revolution to mobilize the most basic of urges for liberation from current suffering among the peasantry.

Starting in the early 11th century, documents report incidents of "heretical communities," which, despite some purely elite (canons of Sainte-Croix at Orléans) or popular (peasant Leutard of Vertus) instances, most often seem to have united clergy and laity, aristocrat and commoner alike. The clerics who described these incidents, which range from Lombardy to Aquitaine to Orléans to Champagne and Arras, express alarm at a far-flung and deeply threatening movement. The execution of thirteen canons at Orléans in 1022 by order of King Robert the Pious marks the first time in the Latin church that someone had been executed specifically as a heretic. Despite the tenor of the sources, these earliest heresies are difficult to assess: they may be isolated idiosyncratic instances; they may be part of a larger movement with traveling "leaders." Their prosecution may have been limited to the known case of Orléans; or there may have been widespread, often vigilante, attacks on heretics in which some were killed "merely on account of their pallor" (i.e., they fasted). They may have been influenced by Bogomil preachers from the East, thus expressing dualist tendencies. Many seem to be indigenous movements inspired by some combination of the apostolic life, a rejection of the ecclesiastical and social structures of the day, and a response to the failure of the Peace movement and to the passing of the year 1000. In any case, they all seem marked by strong ascetic tendencies (no meat, sex, or property), iconoclasm (no crucifixes, relic cults, or elaborate liturgies), and a rejection of the ecclesiastical means of salvation (baptism, eucharist).

After the mid-11th century, however, popular heresy all but disappeared for the next half-century. This is explained in part by the appeal of the Gregorian Reform movement within the church, which mobilized great popular support and inspired many potential "heretics" to join. Certainly, the case of the radical and violent Patarines in Italy and that of Ramirhardus, burned as a heretic by the clerics of Cambrai only to be proclaimed a martyr by Pope Gregory VII, illustrate the way in which behavior that would have been deemed heresy by early 11th-century clerics was encouraged by a church dangerously close to Donatism. Perhaps, as well, the more committed "heretical" communities went underground, or, in the case of the hermits, literally into the woods.

Whatever the case, this hiatus was temporary. Beginning in the early 12th century, "heresies" reappeared. These new expressions of religious zeal differ from earlier cases in that they are at once more aggressive and less radical in their rejections of the church. Inspired by a desire for the apostolic life, charismatic preachers, often "returning" hermits, invoked the values of the papally led Gregorian Reform movement—purification of the church and the life of its clergy. But now that the papacy had shifted from its radical reform program into an ongoing struggle with lay rulers over matters like investiture, these same ascetics, their criticism intensified by a sense of betrayal, found themselves outside the bounds of propriety. In some cases, apostolic preaching led to the formation of new religious orders; in others, the matter of heresy lay closer to hand (e.g., Robert d'Arbrissel); and in some, the criticism of lax clergy moved toward a rejection of the church as an institution (Henry of Lausanne, Peter de Bruys). Generally, the more "orthodox" movements tended to withdraw from society and live in cloistered apostolic communities; the more "heretical" tended to proclaim their criticisms of the church to large, agitated crowds.

The most dangerous and widespread of "heresies" in medieval France was that of the Cathars. Unlike earlier cases, the Cathars developed an independent ecclesiastical structure with bishops, cult, sacraments, and ranks of faithful—the latter divided into auditors, believers, and elect or *cathari* ("pure ones"). The first sign of this alternative church appeared in the Rhineland (1143) and rapidly spread throughout western Europe. Celibate, the elect refused any products of copulation, such as meat and milk. Influenced by Bogomil missionaries from Bulgaria, Cathar doctrine was at once apostolic and dualist, viewing the material world (and hence the God of the Old Testament, who created it) as part of the realm of evil. Jesus had a brother, the fallen angel Satan, with whom he was locked in a deadly battle.

The new sect's absolute rejection of the Catholic church, and its facility at gaining not only actual converts but also a broad base of sympathizers among the population, posed a particularly grave threat. In response to persecution in northern France and Germany, Cathars migrated to the more tolerant south of France (site of open debates between Catholic and Cathar preachers), where they had great success among commoners and lay nobility alike. By the end of the 12th century, they constituted a majority in some regions, and the efforts of the papacy and Cistercian abbots to win back the faithful through preaching failed. Even St. Dominic, whose career began with bringing a Cathar back to the church, and who adopted poverty specifically to debate more effectively with Cathars, failed to bring about lasting results. The papacy was prompted to take extreme actions, including the launching of the Inquisition with the papal bull *Ad abolendam* in 1184 and the calling of a crusade in 1208. It was in the aftermath of this war that the papal Inquisition sought to root out the remaining Cathars systematically. In 1244, some 200 were captured at Montségur and burned; but as late as the 15th century, they were still to be found in the Pyrénées (Montaillou) and the western Mediterranean.

Despite the clear-cut doctrinal aberrations of Catharism (some analysts consider it another religion entirely), the basis of most "popular" heresy, where illiterate commoners play a significant but not exclusive role, in medieval France was the split between the egalitarian tendencies of apostolic Christianity and the hierarchical structure of a wealthy and powerful church tied politically and socially to the dominant aristocracy. This traditional configuration, when undermined by the economic changes of the high Middle Ages—rapid urbanization, monetization, commercialization, rise of an urban proletariat, spread of vernacular literacy—made an anticlerical, communitarian Christianity highly appealing to lay folk from the lower classes. The "textual communities" based on evangelical passages provided structure in a changing world and put forth a critique of the powerful, whether nobles, merchants, or prelates.

In the case of "popular heresies," then, the real issue was not doctrinal but social: a generic Donatism (i.e., lay hostility to clergy deemed insufficiently "pure") could, when rebuffed by a clergy intent on maintaining both its religious monopoly and its secular interests, drive the laity to reject sacraments altogether. The Waldensians illustrate both the dangers of lay preaching and the use of vernacular Bibles: doctrinally orthodox, their conflicts with secular clergy eventually led the church to view them as "heretics," while they came to view the church as the "Whore of Babylon." The béguines and Beghards illustrate how even a lay, quietistic movement, willing to submit to clerical supervision, could eventually become entangled in ecclesiastical rivalries (friars vs. regular clergy) and the internal logic of its own mysticism. Both groups, like the Franciscans, eventually split into orthodox and heretical sects.

The Capuciati exemplify the intimate mix of politics and religion, of lay religiosity and social revolution. In 1182, responding to an infestation of brigands in the wake of the Plantagenêt-Capetian wars, a carpenter from Le Puy named Durand Dujardin had a vision of the Virgin telling him to form a brotherhood of peace. This confraternity of humble men who wore white hoods (*capuciati*), rapidly grew in number and spread throughout the central and southern provinces of France. Monastic chroniclers praised the movement and admired the piety of these common laymen; and both lay and ecclesiastic nobles supported them. Within a year, the sworn Peace militias of the Capuciati had defeated several armies of brigands, slaughtering thousands. But flushed with success, the Capuciati extended their definition of plunder to include prelates and nobles who exploited their serfs: they served notice that no lord should demand any exaction beyond his legal due and eventually invoked Adam and Eve as proof that all men should be free and equal. The church rapidly turned against them; chroniclers denounced their raging madness and heresy; and the lay nobles allied with the remaining brigands to wipe them out. They did not survive long enough to be condemned officially by the church as heretics, although the papal bull *Ad abolendam* (1184) seems to allude to them.

Along with these popular heresies, the rebirth of intellectual life, particularly at the University of Paris, produced its own strain of learned heresies. The earliest such case may be the teachings of Berengar of Tours, a product of the school at Chartres who used grammar and dialectic to question the nature of the eucharist in the mid-11th century. Peter Abélard's aggressive dialectical approach to Bible and Creed provoked the wrath of Bernard of Clairvaux, who had Abélard's teachings condemned and burned at the Council of Sens (1140). With the absorption of Aristotle in the 13th century, conflicts between reason and revelation, or philosophy and theology, intensified. Siger de Brabant argued for the doctrine of "double truth" (something can be true in theology but false in philosophy) and articulated a dangerous cosmology: the eternity of the world and the unity of intellect of all humanity denied key church teachings on the Last Judgment and the eternity of the individual soul, which will be rewarded or punished according to its deeds.

The 13th century witnessed the great battle between heresy and orthodoxy on all levels. The Inquisition emerged in the aftermath of the Albigensian Crusade, promulgated by the pope and manned by the new preaching orders, the Dominicans and Franciscans (1229–33). Rapidly spreading and developing their techniques (e.g., torture in 1252), inquisitors sought out and persecuted "heresy" in the most remote places, as at Montaillou. Even a (future) pillar of orthodoxy like Thomas Aquinas had his work condemned and burned in 1277. The aggressive approach of the Inquisition seems to have eliminated the more extreme forms of religious dissent, or at least driven them into hiding. Nevertheless, Waldensian strongholds, particularly in the Massif Central, survived for centuries, providing a welcome soil for the spread of Protestantism in the 16th century.

According to R.I. Moore, the inquisitorial approach derived from "new" bureaucratic elites intent on expanding their power. By rallying society against groups branded impure and dangerous, officials created a sense of beleaguered community that they alone could protect. So successful was this technique that where no real groups existed it was convenient to invent them, targeting marginal groups like Jews, lepers, homosexuals, and single women. The impression that the sources give—that the clergy tried unsuccessfully to restrain rabid mobs infuriated by religious dissidents—may be a mirage. On the contrary, it was the sympathy that apostolic heresies (and even Jews) elicited among the populace that drove the clergy to action against them.

Richard Landes

[See also: ABÉLARD, PETER; ALBIGENSIAN CRUSADE; AQUINAS, THOMAS; BÉGUINES; BERNARD OF CLAIRVAUX; CAPUCIATI; CATHARS; DOMINICAN ORDER; ÉTIENNE TEMPIER; FRANCISCAN ORDER; HERESIES, APOSTOLIC; HOMOSEXUALITY; INQUISITION; LANGUEDOC; MILLENNIALISM; PEACE OF GOD; PETER DE BRUYS; POPULAR DEVOTION; ROBERT D'ARBRISSEL; SCHOLASTICISM; SIGER DE BRABANT; UNIVERSITIES; WALDO/WALDENSES]

Asad, Talal. "Medieval Heresy: An Anthropological View." *Social History* 11 (1986): 345–62.

Bauer, Walter. *Orthodoxy and Heresy in the Earliest Church.* 2nd ed. Philadelphia: Fortress, 1971.

Lambert, Malcolm. *Medieval Heresy: Popular Movements from the Gregorian Reform to the Reformation.* 2nd ed. London: Blackwell, 1992.

Le Goff, Jacques. *Hérésies et sociétés dans l'Europe préindustrielle 11e–18e siècles.* Paris: Mouton, 1968.

Le Roy Ladurie, Emmanuel. *Montaillou: Promised Land of Error,* trans. Barbara Bray. New York: Braziller, 1978.

Little, Lester K. *Religious Poverty and the Profit Economy in Medieval Europe.* Ithaca: Cornell University Press, 1978.

Lourdaux, W., and Daniel Verhelst. *The Concept of Heresy in the Middle Ages (11th–13th c.).* Louvain: Catholic University Press, 1976.

Moore, Robert I. *The Origins of European Dissent.* New York: St. Martin, 1977.

———. *The Origins of a Persecuting Society: Europe in the Twelfth Century.* Oxford: Blackwell, 1987.

———, ed. *The Birth of Popular Heresy.* New York: St. Martin, 1975.

Peters, Edward, ed. *Heresy and Authority in Medieval Europe: Documents in Translation.* Philadelphia: University of Pennsylvania Press, 1980.

Russell, Jeffrey B. *Dissent and Order in the Middle Ages: The Search for Legitimate Authority.* New York: Twayne, 1992.

Stock, Brian. *The Implications of Literacy: Written Language and Models of Interpretation in the 11th and 12th Centuries.* Princeton: Princeton University Press, 1983.

Wakefield, Walter, and Austin Evans, eds. *Heresies of the High Middle Ages.* New York: Columbia University Press, 1969.

HERISTAL. On the Meuse about six miles northeast of Liège, Heristal (modern Herstal) was one of the residences of the Carolingians. The Meuse Valley, a region of many lands belonging to the Pippinid ancestors of the Carolingians as well as to many of their aristocratic supporters, was the center of their early power. Pepin II is sometimes called Pepin of Heristal. It was the principal residence of Charlemagne until 784 and sometimes the site of general assemblies of the Franks, one of which produced the Capitulary of Heristal (779).

Steven Fanning

[See also: PEPIN]

Ewig, Eugen. "Résidence et capitale dans le haut moyen âge." In *Spätantikes und fränkisches Gallien: Gesammelte Schriften (1952–1973).* 2 vols. Zurich: Artemis, 1976, Vol. 1, pp. 390–95.

HILDEBERT OF LAVARDIN (1055/56–1133). Hildebert was born at Lavardin, near Vendôme, but little is known about his early years. In 1091, he was appointed director of the cathedral school at Le Mans, and in 1096 he was elected bishop of Le Mans. Hildebert's ecclesiastical career was fraught with political conflicts. In 1099, for example, William II Rufus, king of England and duke of Normandy, forced Hildebert into exile in England, claiming that the bishop had used his office to launch an attack against William's castle in Le Mans. Hildebert returned to Le Mans in 1100 after William's death. In 1125, he was elected archbishop of Tours. Although much that has been attributed to Hildebert is spurious, he nevertheless left behind a significant body of work that attests to his literary accomplishments. His best-known prose works, however, do not reveal great originality. His *Vita sanctae Radegundis,* for example, is a revision of an account by Fortunatus, whom he credits as his source. *De querimonia et conflictu carnis et spiritus seu animae* is modeled on Boethius's *De consolatione Philosophiae.* More successful as a poet, Hildebert displayed both originality and versatility in his verse. His poems include an account of his exile in England, a eulogy to Berengar of Tours, and descriptions of Rome inspired by his three visits to that city. Using his vast classical knowledge to illustrate religious themes in his poetry, Hildebert is an important representative of the Christian-Latin culture that began to develop at the close of the 11th century.

E. Kay Harris

[See also: BOETHIUS, INFLUENCE OF; LATIN LYRIC POETRY]

Hildebert of Lavardin. *Opera. PL* 171 (1854). 9–1458. [Includes much that is spurious.]
———. *Hildeberti Cenomanensis episcopi carmina minora,* ed. A. Brian Scott. Leipzig: Teubner, 1969.
Dieudonné, Adolphe E. *Hildebert de Lavardin, évêque du Mans, archevêque de Tours (1056–1133).* Paris: Picard, 1898.
Scott, A. Brian. "The Poems of Hildebert of Le Mans." *Medieval and Renaissance Studies* 6 (1968): 42–83.

HILDUIN OF SAINT-DENIS (ca. 775–ca. 855/59). Born of noble parents (his aunt was mother of Louis the Pious), Hilduin was abbot of Saint-Denis near Paris from 814 and then became archbishop of Cologne (842–50) and chancellor of the German emperor Lothair I (843–55). Hilduin studied with Alcuin and was among the scholars associated with the court school of Charlemagne. Hilduin in turn was the teacher of Walafrid Strabo and Hincmar of Reims. Hilduin wrote a *vita* of St. Denis, the patron saint of his monastery (*Passio sanctissimi Dionysii*), in which he identified Denis the martyr with Dionysius the Areopagite, who was converted by St. Paul in Athens; moreover, he

identified that Dionysius with an author now known as Pseudo-Dionysius the Areopagite, the author of an important corpus of mystical writings. During his abbacy at Saint-Denis, Hilduin translated from Greek into Latin a manuscript of the works of Pseudo-Dionysius the Areopagite that had been sent to Louis the Pious by the Byzantine emperor Michael the Stammerer in 827. This rather rough translation was replaced by one made later in the century by Johannes Scottus Eriugena.

Grover A. Zinn

[See also: ALCUIN; DENIS; ERIUGENA, JOHANNES SCOTTUS; HINCMAR OF REIMS; PSEUDO-DIONYSIUS THE AREOPAGITE; SAINT-DENIS; WALAFRID STRABO]

Hilduin. *Opera omnia. PL* 106.9–50.

HINCMAR OF REIMS (ca. 806–882). Carolingian ecclesiastical leader, canonist, and theologian. Educated at Saint-Denis under Abbot Hilduin, who introduced him to the court of Louis the Pious, Hincmar served as archbishop of Reims from 845 to 882 and as political adviser to Charles the Bald ca. 850–76. Hincmar's consecration as archbishop was contested by his predecessor, Ebbo of Reims, who had been deposed in 835. This controversy was typical of Hincmar's involvement in ecclesiastical politics, which included disputes involving popes Leo VI, Nicholas I, Adrian II, and John VIII. Hincmar was a major presence at the condemnation of Gottschalk at the Synod of Mainz in 848. One of Hincmar's works, *Ad reclusos et simplices,* is a refutation of Gottschalk's views on predestination. His most famous work, *De divortio Lotharii,* is a reprimand to Lothair II about his separation from Queen Tetberga. Hincmar also wrote against Lothair's appointment of a candidate to the bishopric of Cambrai and generally upheld the rights of bishops in ecclesiastical appointments. Although known mostly for his political activities, Hincmar also wrote a treatise on the palanquin of Solomon (Song of Songs 3:9–10) which seems to comment on a *carmina figurata* of these verses, making use of a good deal of numerical symbolism.

E. Ann Matter

[See also: CHARLES II THE BALD; CORONATION/CONSECRATION OF KINGS; GOTTSCHALK; SAINT-DENIS; REIMS]

Hincmar of Reims. *Opera. PL* 125–26.
———. *De ordine palatii,* ed. Maurice Prou. Paris: Vieweg, 1884.
———. *Collectio de ecclesiis* and *Ad reclusos et simplices,* ed. W. Grundlach. *Zeitschrift für Kirchengeschichte* 10 (1899): 93–144, 258–309.
Carey, F.M. "The Scriptorium of Reims During the Archbishopric of Hincmar." In *Classical and Medieval Studies in Honor of Edward Kennard Rand,* ed. Leslie W. Jones. New York, 1938.
Devisse, Jean. *Hincmar, archevêque de Reims 845–882.* 3 vols. Geneva: Droz, 1976–79.

Duckett, Eleanor Shipley. *Carolingian Portraits: A Study in the Ninth Century.* Ann Arbor: University of Michigan Press, 1962.

Nelson, Janet L. "Kingship, Law, and Liturgy in the Political Thought of Hincmar of Reims." *English Historical Review* 92 (1977): 241–79.

Schrörs, Johann Heinrich. *Hincmar, Erzbischof von Reims: Sein Leben und Seine Schriften.* Freiburg, 1884.

Taeger, Buckhard. *Zahlensymbolik bei Hraban, bei Hincmar, und im Heliand: Studien zur Zahlensymbolik im Frühmittelalter.* Munich: Beck, 1970.

HISTOIRE ANCIENNE JUSQU'À CÉSAR. Written by an anonymous clerk from Lille ca. 1208–13, the *Histoire ancienne jusqu'à César* was the first universal history in Old French. It covers events from the creation of the world to the invasion of Flanders by Julius Caesar. Based on the historical books of the Old Testament, on Orosius's *Historia adversus paganos*, and on the Old French Romances of Antiquity, the text exists in two versions: at the end of the 14th century, the second redaction suppresses the story of Alexander the Great and adds an extensive account of the Trojan War drawn from Benoît de Sainte-Maure. The *Histoire*, found in over sixty manuscripts, inspired such writers as Christine de Pizan; in many manuscripts, it precedes the *Fet des Romains*. It has been attributed without cause to Wauchier de Denain.

Renate Blumenfeld-Kosinski

[See also: *FET DES ROMAINS*; HISTORIOGRAPHY; LEFÈVRE, RAOUL]

Blumenfeld-Kosinski, Renate. "Moralization and History: Verse and Prose in the *Histoire ancienne jusqu'à César* (B.N. fr. 20125)." *Zeitschrift für romanische Philologie* 97 (1981): 41–46.

Meyer, Paul. "Les premières compilations françaises d'histoire ancienne." *Romania* 14 (1885): 1–81.

HISTORIOGRAPHY. Medieval French historical writing can be divided into two periods. In the 6th through 11th centuries, histories were produced at centers of literacy for various reasons: to continue old works, to imitate historical exemplars, to please a patron, or to assimilate unusual events. Relatively few early works survive, and most are monastic and idiosyncratic in method and content. After the mid-11th century, increased literacy and dependence on written texts brought about a revolution in historical writing. Histories continued to be produced for the old reasons, but new circumstances gave rise to new sorts of narratives written for new audiences by new types of historians in both Latin and the vernacular. In this period, a *culture historique*, to use Bernard Guenée's phrase, emerged.

Although there were historians in France before the Franks arrived—e.g., Prosper of Aquitaine (ca. 455) and Sulpicius Severus (d. 410)—French historical writing really begins with Gregory of Tours (ca. 538–594). His *Histories* is a narrative attempt to come to terms with the impact of the Franks on Christian, Gallo-Roman society. Gregory's other works were largely hagiographic, in keeping with his ecclesiastical focus.

The next Frankish histories, the chronicle of "Fredegar" (covering the years 584–642) and the *Liber historiae Francorum* (covering 640–721) appeared after a century's hiatus. The former was composed in Burgundy, probably ca. 658–60; the latter was written ca. 726 in Neustria. Shortly thereafter, the two chronicles came to Austrasia, where they were interwoven and continued to 751 for Charles Martel's brother and nephew; this compilation is the first "official" Frankish history.

Martel's descendants learned the lesson that whoever sponsored history controlled its contents. The *Annales regni Francorum* (covering 741–829) were probably kept at Charlemagne's court, while his descendants maintained the three continuations. The first part (for 741–835) of the West Frankish continuation, the *Annales Bertiniani*, was not official, but the second (for 835–61), written by Bishop Prudentius of Troyes, and the third (for 862–82), by Archbishop Hincmar of Reims, were, as were the *Annales Xantenses* (covering 790–873), which were partly composed at Aix-la-Chapelle by Gerward, the palace librarian. The East Frankish continuation, the *Annales de Fulda*, was official until 882. Also official were the *Historiarum libri quatuor* of Nithard (d. 844), a layman who wrote at the request of Charles the Bald. The learned environment promoted by the Carolingians contributed to the generation of unofficial histories as well. Frechulf of Lisieux (fl. 825–52) and Ado of Vienne (d. 874) both produced universal chronicles that were learned and extensive, and most Carolingian monasteries kept simple annals, even if many just copied annals that came to hand.

Greater learning also led historians to rediscover biography. The classical biographical tradition was imitated in Einhard's *Vita Caroli* (ca. 830/33) and Paschasius Radbertus's *Vita Adalardi* (after 826) and *Epitaphium Arsenii* (ca. 850). Not all biographies were classicizing, however; the *De Carolo Magno* of Notker the Stammerer (ca. 884/87), for example, is a hodgepodge of fantastical and largely ecclesiastical anecdotes. Charlemagne was celebrated in the *Annales gestis Caroli magni imperatoris* of the Poeta Saxo (late 9th c.) and the *Carmen de Karolo Magno* (ca. 801) attributed to Angilbert of Saint-Riquier (both in verse); Louis I appeared in biographies by Thegan (ca. 848), the Astronomer (after 840), and Ermold Nigel (825–35). The serial biography, the lives of a series of bishops or rulers, was introduced in France ca. 784 by Paul the Deacon in his *Gesta archiepiscoporum Mettensium* (the form is based on the *Liber pontificalis*). It was imitated widely, giving rise to serial biographies of the abbots of Fontanelle (834–45) and of the bishops of Le Mans (832–63), Auxerre (873–76), and Verdun (first redaction ca. 917), among others.

The Viking invasions slowed historical production in France. Reims alone was still active in the 10th century. Flodoard (893–966), the diocesan archivist, wrote a history of the church of Reims and continued the *Annales Bertiniani*; his chronicle was carried forward by the annals of Reims (to 999). Flodoard's work was also a source for Richer de Reims's regnal history of France (ca. 996). Safe from Viking attacks, the historians of Reims documented the chronic political instability of the see, while adding to Hincmar's legacy.

With the Viking threat abating by the 11th century, histories appeared at new regional centers. Saint-Martial in Limoges became active, producing the splendid chronicle of Adémar de Chabannes (988–1035) and annals (to 1060). At Fleury, Abbo (d. 1004) composed a brief serial biography of the popes. His disciple Aimoin wrote Abbo's biography (*Vita Abbonis*, ca. 1005/08), the *Historia Francorum* (a history of the Franks to 654, written ca. 997–99), and Books 2 and 3 of the *Miracula sancti Benedicti*. Helgaud of Fleury (d. 1048) produced a life of Robert II and a history of Fleury, and André de Fleury wrote a biography (ca. 1041) of Abbot Gauzlin. This Fleuriac flurry of history appeared in part to help the monastery claim its independence from the bishops of Orléans. In Normandy, the first historian, Dudo de Saint-Quentin, wrote a serial biography of the first Norman dukes, the *De moribus et actis primorum Normanniae ducum* (ca. 1015–26), concentrating on the conversion of the Normans. A half-century later, Guillaume de Jumièges abridged, secularized, and continued Dudo's work through the Norman Conquest in his *Gesta Normannorum ducum* (1071). Guillaume de Poitiers composed a laudatory biography of the Conqueror ca. 1078, the *Gesta Guillelmi*, using Guillaume de Jumièges as a source. The Conquest inspired the last two histories and probably also encouraged Norman monasteries to begin keeping annals around the same time.

Once established, a regional center might maintain its historiographic vitality for centuries. For example, Saint-Columba in Sens began to keep annals in the 9th century. In the 11th, Odoranus of Sens composed a chronicle, a life of the founder of Saint-Pierre-le-Vif, and a history of that monastery. Around the same time, the *Historia Francorum Senonensis* (1015/34), a chronicle based on the earlier annals of Sens, was created. A century later, Clarius began the chronicle of Saint-Pierre-le-Vif (1108–24). Richer de Sens picked up the Senonais tradition after 1254 with his *Gesta Senoniensis ecclesiae*, while Geoffroi de Coulon continued the tradition at Saint-Pierre with a chronicle (to 1295). These works circulated, spawning new historiographic traditions elsewhere.

By the beginning of the 12th century, this regional pattern was supplemented by broader works. The First Crusade (1095–99), perhaps because it was seen as being triumphantly French, sparked an outpouring of historical writing not confined to any one region. The four surviving accounts of the crusade, the *Gesta Francorum et aliorum Hierosolymitanorum* (ca. 1101), the *Historia Francorum qui ceperunt Jerusalem* of Raymond d'Agiles (after 1102), the *Historia Hierosolymitana* of Foucher de Chartres (begun ca. 1101), and Peter Tudebod's *Historia de Hierosolymitano itinere* (before 1111), were read and then reworked, particularly the anonymous *Gesta*; Baudri of Bourgueil's *Historia Hierosolymitana* (ca. 1107), Robert le Moine's *Hierosolymitana expeditio* (before 1107), and Guibert de Nogent's *Gesta Dei per Francos* (ca. 1108) were all based on the anonymous *Gesta*. The Pseudo-Turpin chronicle, a 12th-century, pseudohistorical, Latin *Chanson de Roland*,

was also probably inspired by the First Crusade. Nor did interest in the crusade cease as it receded in time. Raoul de Caen, a Norman-trained cleric, wrote the *Gesta Tancredi* (after 1112) about Norman exploits in the Middle East. Book 9 of Orderic Vitalis's *Historia Ecclesiastica* is devoted to the crusade. Albert d'Aix wrote the postcrusade history of the Middle East (after 1120), as did Gilo and Fulco in their verse history (mid-12th c.).

Regional histories continued to flourish alongside these broader works. Norman writers were still active. Orderic's *Historia Ecclesiastica* is a universal history from Creation to 1141, but Anglo-Norman affairs predominate after Book 2. Orderic also interpolated Guillaume de Jumièges's work. New histories appeared at Bec; Robert de Torigny wrote a *Gesta* of the abbots, added an eighth book to Guillaume de Jumièges, and began a major chronicle based on the universal chronicle of Sigebert de Gembloux (d. 1112). When Robert became abbot of Mont-Saint-Michel in 1154, he reactivated the local annals and commissioned Guillaume de Saint-Pair to write his French *Histoire de Mont-Saint-Michel* (before 1186). This activity was for the most part not directly inspired by the dukes. Instead, it seems that the Norman historiographic tradition was sufficiently vital to generate new works on its own, though Étienne de Rouen's *Draco Normannicus*, a polemical Latin verse history of Normandy, was written specifically to influence the policy of Henry II of England.

Ducal patronage was clearly behind historical writing in Anjou, however, where the first history is a fragment written by Count Foulques le Rechin (d. 1109). Odo of Marmoutier began the *Gesta consulum Andegavensium*, an unofficial work, at roughly the same time. The *Gesta* was reworked under official auspices; the last versions were done by Jean de Marmoutier (ca. 1170), who dedicated the works to Henry II of England. Where dukes led, kings followed. As part of their efforts to establish their house, the Capetians, too, sponsored history. Abbot Suger (1081–1151), author of the Latin *Vita Ludovici grossi regis* and the unfinished *Vita gloriosissimi Ludovici*, had no formal title, but Rigord, writing at Saint-Denis toward the end of the century, was proclaimed royal chronicler for his *Gesta Philippi Augusti* (ca. 1196). His successor, Guillaume le Breton, author of his own account of Philip II, was also an official historian. From the 13th century on, the Capetians made steady use of Saint-Denis, having learned the old lesson about the value of historical publicity.

While it might seem more suitable to keep royal historians at court, monasteries were still better fit to produce history than anyplace else because of their records and libraries; Saint-Denis was a favorite spot for historical research. Consequently, monasteries continued to produce major historical works: the chronicle of Sigebert de Gembloux (a continuation of Jerome's translation of Eusebius); Robert d'Auxerre's chronicle (1181–1211), which came to supplant Sigebert's; Aubri de Trois-Fontaines's chronicle (1227–51); and Guillaume de Nangis's great chronicle (1285–1300), which supplanted Robert d'Auxerre's in popularity, were all monastic productions.

Nevertheless, the schools of the 12th century, the universities of the 13th, and the friars left their marks on historical writing. The *Historia scholastica* of Peter Comestor (ca. 1169), a biblical history, was intended expressly to assist theological study in the schools. Jacques de Vitry (1160/70–1240), author of the *Historia Hierosolymitana abbreviata*, was a student at Paris under Peter the Chanter. Vincent de Beauvais's enormous universal history, the *Speculum historiale* (1244–60), was the typically scholastic project of a university-trained Dominican; Géraud de Frachet (d. 1266), another Dominican, wrote the *Vitae fratrum* and a universal chronicle based on Robert d'Auxerre, which enjoyed significant unmerited success. The famed Dominican inquisitor Bernard Gui was also a historian; his *Flores chronicorum* (1306–31), a universal chronicle, and the *Reges Francorum* (1312 and 1320) were widely read and translated. To the scholastics, that history had its uses was self-evident.

But not only scholastics and monks felt so; the popularity of vernacular history indicates that laypeople agreed. The earliest examples of vernacular history, the *Brut* (now lost) and *Estoire des Engleis* of Geffrei Gaimar (ca. 1140), the *Brut* (ca. 1155) and *Roman de Rou* (ca. 1160–70) of Wace, the *Chronique des ducs de Normandie* (ca. 1170) and *Roman de Troie* of Benoît de Sainte-Maure, are in verse. So were the *Estoire de la guerre sainte* (ca. 1195), an account of the Third Crusade by Ambroise d'Évreux, and the Crusade Cycle: the *Chanson d'Antioche* and the *Chanson des chétifs* (both reworked in the late 12th century by Graindor de Douai) and the *Conquête de Jerusalem* (ca. 1130). Occitan verse was preferred by Guilhem de Tudela for his *Chanson de la croisade contre les Albigeois* (ca. 1212–13). But by the Fourth Crusade, vernacular historians began to prefer prose, since verse, associated as it was with epics and romances, seemed untruthful. Geoffroi de Villehardouin and Robert de Clari, both writing about the Fourth Crusade, were among the first to write in prose, as did Villehardouin's continuator, Henri de Valenciennes. Geoffrey and Robert were laymen as well; vernacular composition enabled significant numbers of laypeople to read and write history for the first time. However, prose history never completely effaced poetic history, for Geoffroi de Paris, writing ca. 1317, composed a chronicle of his own times in verse.

The audience for vernacular history was sophisticated in its tastes. Highly learned works, such as those of Peter Comestor and Vincent de Beauvais, were quickly translated. Classical history also became available in the form of the anonymous *Fet des Romains* (ca. 1213/14), the *Histoire ancienne jusqu'à César* (ca. 1208–13), and the *Histoire de Jules César* of Jean de Thuin (ca. 1240). These works, all prose, were adaptations and translations of the work of classical historians, notably Lucan. Bernard Gui's histories appeared in French ca. 1368 in Jean Golein's translation. But the choice of language did imply a particular audience. It was thus natural for Guillaume de Puy-Laurens, the chaplain of Count Raymond VII of Toulouse but also an envoy to Innocent IV, to write his *Historia Albigensium* (ca. 1273) in Latin to reach an international audience, while it was equally natural for the anonymous authors of the French verse *Chronique de Saint-Magloire* (after 1307) and the *Petit Thalamus de Montpellier*, an Occitan civic

chronicle probably begun in the 14th century, to write in the language of their anticipated audiences.

The existence of these separate audiences meant that there was always a need for histories in both Latin and the vernacular. The *Grandes chroniques de France*, created ca. 1274, are Primat's French translation of the Latin chronicle of Saint-Denis; the *Grandes chroniques* were then kept in their own right. But the existence of the vernacular text did not mean the monks stopped writing the Latin chronicle. Indeed, both chronicles might be kept by the same person, as was the case with Jean Chartier's (d. 1464), and both were official. Vernacular writers often based their own work on Latin originals or consulted Latin sources. For example, Jean Jouvencel, writing in 1431, abbreviated and translated the Latin chronicle of Saint-Denis, while Guillaume de Nangis (d. ca. 1300), who wrote his long and short chronicles and biographies of Louis IX and Philip III in Latin, translated the short chronicle into French himself. But Latin writers also consulted and sometimes translated vernacular works. Francesco Pippino (d. 1325) translated the *Livre d'Eracles* (ca. 1230), an unwieldy compendium of Middle Eastern history, into Latin for use in his universal chronicle. Historical writing was greatly enriched by this interplay of traditions and languages.

By the later Middle Ages, the habit of writing history was so deeply ingrained that history was written everywhere. Naturally, in a traditional culture in which the past was normative, it continued to be important to control the presentation of the past. Most courts had official historians, frequently the court archivists. The royal court continued to be a major market for history, hence the seven biographies of St. Louis, by Geoffroi de Beaulieu (ca. 1274), Guillaume de Chartres (before 1282), Gilo de Reims (now lost), Guillaume de Nangis (late 13th c.), Jean de Joinville (1272 and 1298–1309), Guillaume de Saint-Pathus (ca. 1302/03)—in both Latin and French—and an anonymous hagiographer of Saint-Denis (ca. 1297), all composed around the canonization process. Royal chroniclers were regularly appointed, sometimes monks from Saint-Denis and sometimes outsiders, such as Jean Castel (1463–76). Even histories that were not directly commissioned by the royal court were written with an eye to publication there. Guillaume Guiart's *Branche de royaulx lignages*, a verse history of the French kings from Philip II (ca. 1306/07), was researched at Saint-Denis and clearly intended for a court audience. Christine de Pizan (1363–ca. 1429) wrote a prose biography of Charles V, which would have interested the court, as well as other works, such as her verse universal history, with a broader appeal. Likewise, the historical works of Gilles le Bouvier (1386–ca. 1455), the Berry Herald, the *Chronique du roi Charles VII*, the *Histoire de Richard II*, and the *Recouvrement de Normandie*, were probably written with the court in mind; Gilles also kept the *Grandes chroniques* for a time (1403–22).

Nowhere was the desirability of controlling history clearer than in the battle between the kings of France and dukes of Burgundy in the 15th century, which turned into a battle of the historians. Pierre le Fruitier dedicated his *Mémoires* (ca. 1409) to the king of France, although he was probably a Burgundian spy at the court, while Jean Mansel wrote his *Fleur des histoires* (before 1454) for Philip the Good. Both Georges Chastellain (1415–1475), author of a chronicle, and Olivier de La Marche (1425–1502), who wrote memoirs, were appointed official historians to the Burgundian dukes. Enguerrand de Monstrelet's chronicles (before 1453) have a Burgundian point of view; Thomas Basin, exiled bishop of Lisieux, wrote pro-Burgundian biographies of Charles VII and Louis XI (1461–91) However, Matthieu d'Escouchy, Enguerrand's continuator (ca. 1465), was a royal procurer in Saint-Quentin, and Philippe de Commynes, a Fleming, favored in his *Mémoires* (after 1489) the French kings he had come to serve.

Even lesser courts generated histories. Lambert d'Ardres wrote his *Historia comitum Ghisnensium* (ca. 1194) for the seigneur of Guines, chronicling the family's history from the 10th century. It is particularly valuable for the light it sheds on nobility and family in the 11th and 12th centuries. Baudouin d'Avesnes, grandson of Baudouin IX of Flanders, commissioned the major French prose omnibus in the 13th century that bears his name. Jean d'Outremeuse (d. ca. 1400), author of a historical poem, the *Geste de Liège*, and a prose history, the *Myreur des histors*, was an official of the count-bishop of Liège. Michel de Bernis wrote a chronicle of the counts of Foix (first edition 1429), as the introduction to his inventory of their archives.

It would be a mistake to see all histories of the later Middle Ages as being created totally by patronage. A more cultivated society meant more room for individual expression. The process really begins with Joinville, who began his memoirs of Louis IX before he was commissioned to write. His writing expresses aristocratic values in an age when these seemed increasingly threatened. Jean le Bel's *Vrayes chroniques* (ca. 1357–70), which concentrate on chivalric deeds far from his native Liège, and Froissart's *Chroniques* (1369–1400), inspired by Jean le Bel, similarly illustrate aristocratic ideals—heroism, the glory of war, valor, courtesy—rather than political truths. The *Livre des faits du bon messire Jean le Meingre, dit Boucicaut* (ca. 1408) and Cuvelier's *Chronique de Bertrand du Guesclin* (ca. 1385) are both moral exemplars, accounts of men widely considered by their contemporaries to have been perfect knights.

The fitting end to this process was the rise of memoirs, the most personal historical works. Memoirs, particularly those of Philippe de Commynes, exemplify the new turn history was taking in the 15th century. Commynes was not the first to write memoirs: he was preceded by Jean de Joinville, Jacques du Clercq (1448–67), Pierre le Fruitier, and Olivier de La Marche, but his memoirs represent something new in France. To Commynes, history was as much moral instruction as a record of the past, an object lesson for the ruler and the citizen. For precisely those reasons, the humanists were urging the teaching and study of history. Commynes's work thus marks the transition from the medieval to the Renaissance view of history.

Leah Shopkow

[See also: ABBO OF FLEURY; ADÉMAR DE CHABANNES; AIMOIN DE FLEURY; ANGLO-NORMAN LITERATURE; BENOÎT DE SAINTE-MAURE; BIOGRAPHY; BURGUNDIAN CHRONICLERS; CHRISTINE DE PIZAN; COMMYNES, PHILIPPE DE; CUVELIER; FROISSART, JEAN; *GRANDES CHRONIQUES DE FRANCE*; GREGORY OF TOURS; GUIBERT DE NOGENT; GUILLAUME DE SAINT-PAIR; HISTORY PLAYS; JEAN LE BEL; JOINVILLE, JEAN DE; LA MARCHE, OLIVIER DE; ORDERIC VITALIS; OUTREMEUSE, JEAN D'; PETER COMESTOR; RIGORD; ROBERT DE CLARI; ROBERT DE TORIGNY; VILLEHARDOUIN, GEOFFROI DE; VINCENT DE BEAUVAIS; WACE]

Archambault, Paul. *Seven French Chroniclers: Witnesses to History*. Syracuse: Syracuse University Press, 1974.

Bautier, Robert-Henri. "L'historiographie en France aux Xe et XIe siècles (France du Nord et de l'Est)" and Ganshof, François L. "L'historiographie franque sous les Mérovingiens et les Carolingiens." In *La storiografia altomedievale*. Spoleto: Centro Italiano di Studi sull'Alto Medioevo, 1970, pp. 631–85, 793–850.

Grundmann, Herbert. *Geschichtsschreibung im Mittelalter*. Göttingen: Vandenhoeck and Ruprecht, 1965.

Guenée, Bernard. *Histoire et culture historique dans l'occident médiéval*. Paris: Aubier Montagne, 1980.

Kervyn de Lettenhove, Joseph M.B.C. *Chroniques relatives à l'histoire de la Belgique sous la domination des ducs de Bourgogne*. 3 vols. Brussels: Hayez, 1870–76.

———. *Istore et chroniques de Flandres*. 2 vols. Brussels: Hayez, 1870–80.

Krueger, Karl H. *Die Universalchroniken*. Turnhout: Brepols, 1976.

McCormick, Michael. *Les annales du haut moyen âge*. Turnhout: Brepols, 1975.

Molinier, Auguste. *Les sources de l'histoire de France des origines aux guerres d'Italie*. 6 vols. Paris: Picard, 1901–06. [Still the place to begin; an updated edition was begun in 1971.]

Sot, Michel. *Gesta episcoporum, gesta abbatum*. Turnhout, Brepols, 1981.

HISTORY PLAYS. One of the primary functions of the theater in late-medieval society was to preserve the memory of significant events by reenacting them in public spectacles. Providing a vivid picture of humankind's origin and destiny, history plays were a mirror in which both the individual and the society found their identities confirmed.

In the Middle Ages, the history of the world was seen as the working out of a divine plan for salvation in a temporal span lying between Creation and Doomsday. In this view, the most important historical events were those recorded in the Bible. Most history plays from the period consequently are dramatizations of biblical events. Because of the centrality of salvation in the medieval concept of history, dramatizations of the life and death of Jesus constitute the most significant group of biblical plays, the Passion plays. These are treated in a separate article.

Much of the Old Testament was dramatized in a lengthy work called the *Mistère du Viel Testament*, a collection of plays on biblical subjects brought together by a compiler around the middle of the 15th century. The episodes are placed in Old Testament order from Creation to the Queen of Sheba's visit to Solomon. This historical sequence is followed by a group of individual plays centering on such characters as Job, Tobias, Judith, and Esther. The authors of the plays made frequent use of legendary material to supplement the biblical narratives. The story of Joseph in Egypt, for example, is set against a conspiracy to poison Pharaoh. The plays circulated widely for more than a century, and the whole compilation was printed at least three times in first half of the 16th century. Direct influence has been found in the Passion plays of Troyes and Valenciennes, as well as in the Chester mystery cycle of England.

An unrelated series of biblical plays comes from Lille, where plays were presented on pageant wagons at an annual procession. These short works were staged individually, with new plays being written each year. Unlike the *Mistère du Viel Testament*, the Lille plays contain no legendary material. The playwrights followed the biblical text closely, adding only material found in the standard biblical commentaries, such as those of Peter Comestor and Nicolas of Lyra. The forty-three Old Testament plays include episodes not found in the *Mistère du Viel Testament*, such as the stories of Gideon, Ruth, Elijah, and Ahab. Similarly, the twenty-one New Testament plays from Lille dramatize a number of scenes not found in the Passion plays.

New Testament history after the Passion is dramatized in the *Mystère des Actes des Apôtres*, attributed to Simon Greban. Comprising some 62,000 lines of verse, this play is the longest of those surviving from the late-medieval period. It was staged in 1536 in Bourges and again in 1541 in Paris. Dramatizing events from the Book of Acts, the play also draws upon postbiblical history and legendary material, presenting the Apostles on their missionary journeys and showing their martyrdoms in faraway lands.

The immediate postbiblical era is represented by the *Vengeance de Jésus Christ*. Little known today, the play was staged relatively often in the 15th and 16th centuries. It survives in two manuscript versions and six early printed editions. Its historical basis is the Jewish War of A.D. 66–70 conducted by the emperor Vespasian and his son Titus, which ended in the siege and destruction of Jerusalem. Woven into the plot are the legendary accounts of the trial and death of Pilate and the miracles of Veronica. In an era when spectators sought realism in the portrayal of historical events, the violence and carnage that accompany the destruction of Jerusalem in this play must have attracted large audiences and may have been a reason for its popularity.

Plays based on the lives of the saints cover much of the period between the 1st and the 15th centuries. Though from our point of view such plays are based on legendary accounts, the original audiences saw them as reenactments of historical events. Because the staging of history plays was costly, they were often subsidized from municipal treasuries. As a consequence, many of them portray the life of a town's patron saint. The town of Seurre, for example, staged the life of its patron, St. Martin, in 1496. A

play by Guillaume Flamant on the life of St. Didier, bishop of Langres, was staged in that city over a three-day period in 1482. In his search for historical realism, the author devoted half the play to battle scenes in which the Vandals besiege and sack the city and in which a Roman army later destroys the invaders.

Late-medieval contemporary history was dramatized in the lengthy *Mistère du siège d'Orléans*. The work is a detailed and historically accurate account of the defense of the city of Orléans against the English in the siege of 1428–29 and of its ultimate deliverance by Jeanne d'Arc. Writing most likely between 1440 and 1467, the anonymous author was possibly a witness to the events. In any case, he also consulted written accounts of the siege for greater historical accuracy. Though the play is patriotic in tone, its characters are unidealized. Jeanne d'Arc is portrayed as a simple, straightforward young girl; the character of the poet Charles d'Orléans, a prisoner of the English at the time, is consonant with what is known of him from other historical sources. Despite the appearance of many well-known historical figures, the play's major protagonist is the city of Orléans itself.

At the other end of the historical spectrum, we find a play that treats the Trojan War. In the late Middle Ages, the French believed themselves to be descended from Trojans who, like Aeneas, had fled the final destruction of their city. No doubt, this presumed ancestry inspired Jacques Milet to write the *Istoire de la destruction de Troye la grant*. The play is based not on Homer but on a medieval Latin account of the conflict. Though there is no record of its having been performed, the text is rich in stage directions and was almost certainly intended for performance. Its survival in a dozen manuscripts and an equal number of early printed editions suggests that it was widely read as well.

The history plays of the late-medieval period, both religious and secular, were dramatic spectacles that served to define the community, to provide individual and group identity, and to reinforce social values.

Alan E. Knight

[See also: GREBAN, SIMON; LA VIGNE, ANDRÉ DE; MYSTERY PLAYS; PASSION PLAYS; PROCESSIONAL THEATER; SAINT PLAYS; THEATER]

de Rothschild, James, ed. *Le mistére du Viel Testament*. 6 vols. Paris: Didot, 1878–91.

Guessard, François, and E. de Certain, eds. *Le mistère du siège d'Orléans*. Paris: Imprimerie Impériale, 1862.

Lebègue, Raymond. *Le mystère des Actes des Apôtres, contribution à l'étude de l'humanisme et du protestantisme français au XVIe siècle*. Paris: Champion, 1929.

Milet, Jacques. *L'istoire de la destruction de Troye la grant*, ed. Marc-René Jung. Forthcoming.

Wright, Stephen K. *The Vengeance of Our Lord: Medieval Dramatizations of the Destruction of Jerusalem*. Toronto: Pontifical Institute of Mediaeval Studies, 1989.

HOCKET. Primarily a compositional or improvisatory technique that creates an exciting and unmistakable texture in polyphonic music from the mid-13th to the late 14th century, hocket (Lat. *hochetus*) can also refer to an independent piece of music in which that texture is predominant or pervasive. Either the notes of one melody may be alternately sung by two different voices or these voices may alternate short phrases that may be imitative of one another. Also, two or three melodies may rhythmically interlock in such a way that much the same effect of rapid, virtuoso note-by-note alternation occurs. The earliest extant hocketing appears in Notre-Dame two-part clausulae, three-part organa, and conductus, while the earliest independent hocket seems to be the *In seculum* added to the modally notated Madrid Codex.

In spite of Pope John XXII's condemnation of hockets and other musical "frivolities" in 1324–25, they can be found later among Machaut's compositions, French chansons and *chaces*, Italian madrigals and *caccias*, and the liturgical polyphony of the Old Hall Manuscript. In some isorhythmic motets of the Ars Nova, hocketing highlights structural points anticipating repetition of the tenor *talea*. Hockets succumbed to changing musical tastes, metamorphosing into antiphonal melodic imitation by the early 15th century.

Sandra Pinegar

[See also: *CHACE;* ISORHYTHMIC MOTET; MOTET (13TH CENTURY); NOTRE-DAME SCHOOL]

Dalglish, William. "The Hocket in Medieval Polyphony." *Musical Quarterly* 55 (1969): 344–63.
Frobenius, Wolf. "Hoquetus." In *Handwörterbuch der musikalischen Terminologie*, ed. Hans Heinrich Eggebrecht. Wiesbaden: Steiner, 1971– . 13 pp. (1988).
Sanders, Ernest H. "Medieval Hocket in Practice and Theory." *Musical Quarterly* 60 (1974): 246–56.

HOMAGE. Homage originated in the Frankish custom of the *immixtio manuum*, by which the king clasped the joined hands of a follower who promised loyal service. The first example of a great lord performing homage occurred in 757, when Tassilo, duke of Bavaria, commended himself "by his hands" to King Pepin. Galbert de Bruges provides the fullest description of the act when he recounts how in 1127 the Flemish barons were received by their new count: they performed homage by placing their hands in his and sealed the relationship by a kiss; they pledged their loyalty (fealty); and the count invested them with their fiefs.

The practice of multiple homages, by which vassals with fiefs from several lords did homage to each, led inevitably to the development of liege (primary) homage from the 11th century: a vassal declared his first loyalty to the lord from whom he held his most important fief. The circulation of fiefs, however, continued to complicate the chain of loyalty, especially as powerful princes forged new political and military alliances by purchasing the homage of barons and knights and demanding that fiefs, rather than tenants, be considered liege. The multiplication of liege fiefs resulted in reservation clauses by which vassals ranked their fiefs, and consequently their loyalties, in order to prevent misunderstandings.

From the late 12th century, those who performed homage often were required by their lords to submit sealed letters confirming that act; later sealed letters could be sent in lieu of the act itself. In the 13th and 14th centuries, lords with large numbers of feudal tenants periodically conducted inquests of their tenants and fiefs; the resultant "books of homages" furnish invaluable information on the nobility of late-medieval France.

Theodore Evergates

[See also: FEALTY; FIEF HOLDING]

Boutrouche, Robert. *Seigneurie et féodalité.* 2 vols. Paris: Aubier, 1968–70.
Fourquin, Guy. *Lordship and Feudalism in the Middle Ages,* trans. Iris and A.L. Lytton Sells. New York: Pica, 1976.
Ganshof, François L. *Feudalism,* trans. Philip Grierson. New York: Harper, 1961.
Lemarignier, Jean-François. *Recherches sur l'hommage en marche et les frontières féodales.* Lille: Bibliothèque Universitaire, 1945.
Poly, Jean-Pierre, and Eric Bournazel. *La mutation féodale, XIe–XIIe siècles.* Paris: Presses Universitaires de France, 1980.

HOMME ARMÉ. A melody used in at least thirty-eight polyphonic Mass cycles of the years ca. 1460–1600, of which about thirty are probably from before 1520; at least nine smaller works incorporate the melody. Conflicting modern theories make the early history of *L'homme armé* hard to see clearly. The tune is in a simple ABA form, and its text warns of the approach of the armed man with his iron breastplate. Many of the Masses appear to be associated with the Burgundian court's Order of the Golden Fleece, though that can hardly be the origin of them all. Plainly, there was an element of friendly emulation among the composers: elements from the cycle by Guillaume Dufay appear to have influenced those of Antoine Busnoys and Johannes Ockeghem. Ideas from the work by Busnoys are taken over by Jacob Obrecht and Josquin des Prez, and so on. The decisive importance of the tune is as a generating factor in the early history of the polyphonic Mass cycle.

David Fallows

[See also: BUSNOYS, ANTOINE; CYCLIC MASS; DUFAY, GUILLAUME; OCKEGHEM, JOHANNES]

HOMME DE CORPS. Common in the north and east of France, the phrase *homme* (or *femme*) *de corps* (Lat. *homo de corpore; femina de corpore*) is one of many words and phrases virtually synonymous with "serf." Like the other synonyms, it emphasizes certain aspects of serfdom. However, unlike some of the synonyms, such as *villein*, which in the earlier Middle Ages could refer to either a free or unfree resident of a manor (*villa*) and came to be interchangeable with "serf" only in the 12th and 13th centuries, *homme de corps* always seems to have been restricted to the unfree population and to a particularly low stratum of the unfree, those who *de jure* had no right of inheritance or freedom of marriage. Most important, in Marc Bloch's words, "the feeling of . . . almost physical compulsion is expressed to perfection in the phrase *homme de corps*." An *homme de corps* was an *homme de corps et de chef*, a person whose body (labor and offspring) and head (his punishment for crime) were in the power and gift of another man. Or he was an *homme propre*, a person who was the property of a lord. A medieval abbot of Vézelay, quoted by Bloch, described his power over his serf in a slightly elaborated version of the formula: "He is mine from the soles of his feet to the crown of his head." Yet, despite the impression of absolute power and physical coercibility that the phrase gives, an *homme de corps* was not a slave. He had recognized personal rights and, despite the principles of the learned law, enjoyed strong customary protections of the real property he worked and the chattels he possessed, just as other serfs had.

William Chester Jordan

[See also: SERFDOM/SERVITUDE/SLAVERY]

Bloch, Marc. *Feudal Society*, trans. L.A. Manyon. 2 vols. Chicago: University of Chicago Press, 1964.

Patault, Anne-Marie. *Hommes et femmes de corps en Champagne méridionale à la fin du moyen-âge*. Nancy: Université de Nancy II, 1978.

HOMOSEXUALITY. The exuberant homosexuality for which the ancient Gauls, like other Celts, were famed seems to have survived or even increased during the Roman occupation but was dampened by Christian conversion. The Germanic invasions demolished imperial and weakened Christian authorities, and the Germans themselves seem to have practiced pederasty but to have disapproved of effeminacy and adult passivity. Neither Franks nor Burgundians legislated against homosexuality, but the Visigothic code of Reccesvinth (ca. 654) stipulated castration as a penalty. Although the Franks adopted Catholic Christianity with its morality that pilloried as the "crime against nature" all nonreproductive forms of sexual expression, including homosexuality, the later Merovingians, and probably their nobles, indulged their sensual appetites freely.

Considerable sexual license continued under the Carolingians (751–987). An erotic element appears in the circle of clerics headed by Alcuin, the "friend of Charlemagne." Alcuin directed his feelings toward his pupils, even bestowing on one a "pet name" from one of Virgil's *Eclogues*. Walafrid Strabo's affection for Liutger was more specifically Christian, presaging Elizabethan love sonnets. His exiled friend Gottschalk penned a tender poem to a young monk, probably at Reichenau.

During the 9th and 10th centuries, in the rude early castles, knights and squires, often sleeping on pallets in the same room and depending on one another for survival, must have formed erotic attachments, a type of situational homosexuality known to armies. Anglo-Norman nobles were particularly reprimanded for homosexuality.

Pederastic poems were part of the renaissance of the 12th century. Marbode of Rennes (ca. 1035–1123), master of the school of Chartres, loved a boy who loved a beautiful girl who was herself in love with Marbode. Marbode's disciple Baudri of Bourgueil (1046–1130) shifted to more openly erotic poetry, with some verses extolling the moral qualities and others the physical charms of the addressee. Hildebert of Lavardin (ca. 1055–1133) reiterated conventional moralizing arguments against the "plague of Sodom," implying that homosexuality was common in his age, but another of his poems boldly denied that male love is a sin and faulted "heaven's council" for calling it one. Allegorical poetry was less favorable to homosexuality. Alain de Lille's *De planctu Naturae* (ca. 1170) indicted humankind for inventing monstrous kinds of love and perverting Nature's laws. Jean de Meun's sequel to the *Roman de la Rose* (ca. 1270) had Nature's Genius liken practitioners of nonreproductive sex to plowmen who till stony ground.

In the 11th century, with Peter Damian condemning sodomy, the church moved to regulate private conduct. The term *sodomia*, which appeared at the beginning of the 13th century, often covered bestiality, homosexual practices, and "unnatural" heterosexual relations of all kinds. Late 11th-century theologians, who advocated the same penalty for all three, associated what came to be called sodomy with heresy and magic. Scriptural commentators in Anselm of Laon's circle linked heresy and sodomy as forms of sacrilege punishable by death.

Before 1200, southern France became a stronghold of heretical Cathars (Albigensians). Because of their similarity to the Bogomils of Bulgaria, they came to be stigmatized as *bougres*, a term that meant first heretic and then sodomite. Catholic authorities charged them with sexual heterodoxy, claiming that unrestrained sexual hedonism was part of their cult. The word itself survives to this day in English as "bugger."

In northern France, Chrétien de Troyes, like the troubadours of Languedoc, sang of love—and its clandestine homoerotic culture. In *Lanval*, Marie de France has Queen Guenevere accuse Lanval of homosexuality after he refuses her advances. In Paris, already a center of academic and political life, Jacques de Vitry denounced the students at the university for practicing sodomy. In 1270, Guillot, in his *Dit des rues de Paris*, cited the rue Beaubourg as an area favored by sodomites. Again in the 15th century, the poet Antonio Beccadelli alluded to the continued homosexual practices of the intellectuals in Paris, and the still obscure jargon of François Villon has also been cited as evidence of that Parisian subculture.

Politics have occasioned accusations of sodomy in many epochs, none more notorious than the trial of the entire order of Knights Templar, Europe's great bankers. The first charges of sexual heterodoxy against the Templars date from 1304 or 1305 in the Agenais. Many witnesses, including some whose testimony is suspect, claimed that the order tolerated as sinless "acts against nature" between members, who were accused of the *osculum infame* at their initiations. Philip IV the Fair pressured Pope Clement V to take action against the Templars, and they were arrested throughout

France in October 1307. Hundreds of episcopal and royal tribunals tallied the wealth of the order, gathered witnesses, heard testimony, and passed judgment. Eventually, about 120 Templars met their deaths in Paris. Only a few of the many who were accused actually confessed to sodomy, but many more confessed to blasphemy and heresy. The guilt of the Templars remains moot to this day. Some may have been involved in homosexual liaisons, but the political atmosphere and controversy surrounding the investigation made impartial judgment impossible.

Philip IV's daughter, Isabella, with the help of her lover, Mortimer, imprisoned and tortured her sodomitical husband Edward II of England.

Prosecutions for sodomy continued sporadically in late-medieval France. In 1317, Robert de Péronne, called de Bray, was burned, and his brother Jean received an unknown sentence the following year at Laon. Arnaud de Vernioles, a subdeacon of Pamiers, was accused of sodomy as well as heresy in 1323–24 and was consigned to a monastery for life. In 1333, in Paris, Raymond Durant was condemned for sex with his male servants but managed to escape. In 1334, Pierre Porier was burned in Dorche. Guillaume Belleti, in Chambéry, escaped with a fine in 1351. Jacques Purgatoire, charged with violent assault, was burned at Bourges in 1435. If his confession is genuine, Gilles de Rais cannot be labeled a victim. The same is true of Benjamin Deschauffours: since the time of Voltaire, his trial has been seen as a classic example of persecution of homosexuals.

A persistent fear of sexuality and the inability to stamp out its proscribed manifestations even, or especially, within the strictly regulated confines of the cloister plagued medieval society, with its celibate clergy. Albert the Great and Thomas Aquinas condemned sodomites to death, and Lucas da Penna (ca. 1320–ca. 1390) even declared that "if a sodomite had been executed, and subsequently several times returned to life, each time he should be punished even more severely if this were possible. . . ." The medieval state, however, lacked the means of carrying out the mass arrests and executions of homosexuals that were to occur in later periods.

William A. Percy, Jr.

[See also: LATIN LYRIC POETRY]

Stehling, Thomas, trans. *Medieval Latin Poems of Male Love and Friendship.* New York: Garland, 1984.

Boswell, John. *Christianity, Social Tolerance, and Homosexuality.* Chicago: University of Chicago Press, 1980.

Courouve, Claude. "Sodomy Trials in France." *Gay Books Bulletin* 1 (1979).

Goodich, Michael. *The Unmentionable Vice.* Santa Barbara: ABC-Clio, 1979.

Payer, Pierre. *Sex and the Penitentials: the Development of a Sexual Code, 550–1150.* Toronto: University of Toronto Press, 1984.

HONORÉ, MASTER (d. ca. 1318). A Parisian illuminator active in the last quarter of the 13th century who intro-duced a new sense of three-dimensional volume to his figures. A copy of Gratian's *Decretals* (Tours, Bibl. mun. 558) contains a statement that the book was purchased from Honoré the illuminator, and an entry in royal accounts of 1296 states that he was the illuminator for the king and suggests that he illuminated the *Breviaire de Philippe le Bel* (B.N. lat 1023). Records indicate that he was dead by 1318. On the basis of stylistic affinities with these manuscripts, the miniatures of a copy of the *Somme le roi* (B.L. Add. 54180) have also been attributed to him.

Robert G. Calkins

Millar, Eric C. *An Illuminated Manuscript of La somme le roy: Attributed to the Parisian Miniaturist Honoré.* Oxford: Roxburgh Club, 1953.

——. *The Parisian Miniaturist Honoré.* New York: Yoseloff, 1959.

HOSPITALS. From their origin as guesthouses for pilgrims and almshouses for the indigent, medieval hospitals offered custodial care rather than therapy. The sick poor received special attention when monastic infirmaries were extended beyond the cloister in early Benedictine communities (Fleury, Centula) and until the heyday of Cluny. French hospitals long retained a religious character in their moral and economic dependence on charity as well as in their staffing and administration. A gradual secularization occurred, however, first with the building of the nonmonastic "Hôtel-Dieu," typically near the gate of such new towns as Troyes or Provins. The number of these foundations increased dramatically after 1100 thanks to the inspiration of the Hospitalers of St. John, seigneurial largesse, and bourgeois initiative. The development of universities opened the door to professional medical assistance with visits by doctors and their students and, apparently, the occasional performance of surgery: this was the case for the hospital of Saint-Esprit in Montpellier, recommended by the pope as a model for all Christendom. By the 15th century, many institutions passed under royal or municipal control and were governed by lay committees. The best-preserved example of this type is the Hôtel-Dieu of Beaune, built between 1443 and 1459 by Nicolas Rolin, chancellor of Burgundy.

If the modern "health-care facility" is focused on the operating room, the heart of the medieval hospice was the sick ward, or *salle.* The great hall was over 300 feet long in the Hôtel-Dieu of Paris and in the one founded at Tonnerre by Marguerite, the wife of Charles of Anjou. While benefactors could claim private quarters, most residents were lodged communally. Two often shared one bed, particularly in the smaller dormitories; curtains would screen each bed in the larger, draftier, and more crowded wards. Some hospitals had isolation wings for contagious patients, the disruptive insane, or children; others, like Saint-Jacques of Valenciennes, turned away incurable patients. Special foundations sheltered lepers, the mentally ill, the old, or, as in the case of the hospice "des Quinze-Vingts" erected by Louis IX in Paris, the blind. In many instances, care and conditions declined from the late Middle Ages on, with the aging of early foundations, the fading of charitable impulses, the overcrowding in epidemics and wars, and—paradoxically—the transition to official control.

Luke Demaitre

[See also: BEAUNE; HEALTH CARE; TONNERRE]

Caille, Jacqueline. *Hôpitaux et charité publique à Narbonne au moyen âge*. Toulouse: Privat, 1978.

Imbert, Jean, and Michel Mollat. *Histoire des hôpitaux en France*. Toulouse: Privat, 1982.

Mundy, John H. "Hospitals and Leprosaries in Twelfth- and Thirteenth-Century Toulouse." In *Essays on Medieval Life and Thought Presented in Honor of Austin P. Evans*, ed. John H. Mundy and R.W. Emery. New York: Columbia University Press, 1955.

Quynn, D. "A Medieval Picture of the Hôtel-Dieu of Paris." *Bulletin of the History of Medicine* 12 (1942): 118–28.

Wickersheimer, Ernest. "Médecins et chirurgiens dans les hôpitaux du moyen âge." *Janus* 32 (1928): 1–11.

HÔTEL DU ROI. The term *hôtel du roi* (Lat. *hospitium regis*) was applied in the period after ca. 1200 to the innermost part of the royal household, or *familia*, comprising those departments (*ministeria* or *métiers*) whose members were still engaged largely in domestic rather than political duties. By 1261, when its organization was first set down in a household ordinance, the *hôtel* consisted primarily of six *métiers*: the *paneterie*, or pantry; the *échansonnerie*, or butlery; the *cuisine*, or kitchen; the *fruiterie*, or fruitery; the *écurie*, or stable; and (replacing the *chambre* after 1257, though the latter effectively remained part of the *hôtel*) the *fourrière*, or foragery. In 1315, a new department was created, the *argenterie*, under the direction of an *argentier du roi*, to supervise the provision of clothing and furnishings to the king. All of these departments, and such non-departmental personnel as the chamberlains, chaplains, physicians, ushers, porters, launderers, messengers, and other minor functionaries in the king's personal service (a total of 165 persons in 1291), were initially placed under the immediate supervision of two officers bearing the title (*grand*) *maître de l'hôtel du roi*, whose offices were eventually conflated into one. The queen, the king's eldest son, and many lesser princes also maintained *hôtels* from the 13th century onward, and they were generally organized along the same general lines as that of the king.

D'A. Jonathan D. Boulton

Lot, Ferdinand, and Robert Fawtier. *Histoire des institutions françaises au moyen âge*. 3 vols. Paris: Presses Universitaires de France, 1957–62, Vol. 2: *Institutions royales* (1958).

HOUDAN. The small city of Houdan (Île-de-France), situated at the confluence of the Vesgre and the Option, preserves a 12th-century keep, the only remains of the castle of the Montforts. The transformation of the keep into a water tower has complicated the study of its interior. Elements of its unusual plan, however, are still discernible. A round

tower approximately 100 feet high and 50 feet in diameter, this keep is flanked by four turrets, each 6 feet 6 inches in diameter, that run the height of the tower. The walls, 12 feet thick, are made of millstone. Conical roofs must have topped the central tower, as they do the turrets. The keep could be accessed only by a door in the north turret situated 20 feet above the level of the soil. This limited and somewhat hidden access encapsulates one of the most striking features of the keep's interior: its complex arrangements for moving from one floor to another. For example, this outer door opens onto a corridor that ends at a stone staircase leading to the first story, a square room whose corners lead to the alcoves of the turrets. This central room, or Grande Salle, served as the lord's. In addition to the corner recesses leading to the turrets, sets of staircases and ladders lead from this room or floor to others. In short, to get from one room to another or into the turrets, one had to pass through the Grande Salle. And it was here that the lord of Montfort resided, since from this vantage he could watch over the comings and goings of all those who entered and in this way could deal with any treasonous activity.

E. Kay Harris

de Dion, A. "Description de la tour de Houdan." *Bulletin monumental* 31 (1865): 392–98.

Finó, J.-F. *Forteresses de la France médiévale*. Paris: Picard, 1970.

HUCBALD OF SAINT-AMAND (ca. 849–930). Music theorist, composer, hagiographer, and author of *De harmonica institutione*, Hucbald was a monk at the abbey of Saint-Amand at Tournai. He studied at Saint-Amand, Nevers, and Saint-Germain of Auxerre, and became a fellow student of Remigius of Auxerre at Fulda. Later, he became director of the school at Saint-Amand, started the school at Saint-Bertin, and helped Remigius to revive the cathedral school at Reims. Hucbald had access to the major ancient works of learning, notably Martianus Capella, Boethius, and Chalcidius's commentary on Plato's *Timaeus*. His own work, however, is original. Adopting the Greek scale transmitted by Boethius (Greater Perfect System), Hucbald described a second tetrachordal system, different from the Boethian tradition, that is built on the tetrachord of the finals D-E-F-G and that became paramount for the development of medieval modal theory. His concern for practical issues is shown by his method of illustrating theoretical points with examples taken from chant repertoire as sung in the monasteries. Hucbald also devised a letter notation, suggesting its simultaneous use with neumes, to indicate their precise musical pitch.

Tony Zbaraschuk

[See also: BOETHIUS, INFLUENCE OF; MUSIC THEORY; MUSICAL NOTATION (NEUMATIC); MUSICAL NOTATION (12TH–15TH CENTURIES)]

Palisca, Claude V. ed., *Hucbald, Guido, and John on Music: Three Medieval Treatises*, trans. Warren Babb. New Haven: Yale University Press, 1979.

HUE DE ROTELANDE (fl. late 12th c.). Anglo-Norman author of *Ipomedon* (10,580 octosyllabic lines) and *Protheselaus* (12,741 octosyllabic lines). Probably a native of Rhuddhan (Flintshire), Hue lived in Credenhill, near Hereford, when he wrote his two romances for local nobility (*Protheselaus* for Gilbert Fitz-Baderon, lord of Monmouth; d. 1191). *Ipomedon*, the earlier of the two, is concerned with the love of La Fière, princess of Calabria, and Ipomedon, son of the King of Apulia. In *Protheselaus*, the hero is the son of Ipomedon and La Fière; he eventually becomes king of Apulia. *Ipomedon*, the finer work, is remarkable for its treatment of the motifs of the Three Day's Tournament and the rescue of the princess by the hero disguised as a madman. Hue de Rotelande is especially gifted as a comic writer, and *Ipomedon* is thoroughly humorous from beginning to end, the humor ranging from whimsicality to open obscenity. While it is not usually possible to show specific sources for the two romances, both owe a good deal to the Romances of Antiquity, the Tristan romances, and the works of Chrétien de Troyes. *Ipomedon*, which is preserved complete in two manuscripts (London, B.L. Cotton Vespasian A VII and Oxford, Bodl. Rawlinson Miscel. D 913), was adapted on three occasions into Middle English.

Keith Busby

[See also: ANGLO-NORMAN LITERATURE; ANTIQUITY, ROMANCES OF; IDYLLIC ROMANCE]

Hue de Rotelande. *Ipomedon, poème de Hue de Rotelande* (*fin du XIIe siècle*), ed. Anthony J. Holden. Paris: Klincksieck, 1979.

———. *Protheselaus, ein altfranzösischer Abenteuerroman*, ed. F. Kluckow. Halle: Niemeyer, 1924.

Calin, William. "The Exaltation and Undermining of Romance: *Ipomedon*." In *The Legacy of Chrétien de Troyes*, ed. Norris J. Lacy, Douglas Kelly, and Keith Busby. 2 vols. Amsterdam: Rodopi, 1987, Vol. 2, pp. 111–24.

Legge, M. Dominica. *Anglo-Norman Literature and Its Background*. Oxford: Clarendon, 1963, pp. 85–96.

HUGH CAPET (ca. 940–996). The son of Hugues le Grand, duke of Francia, Hugh Capet is traditionally considered the founder of the third dynasty of French kings, the Capetians, who ruled, through collateral lines, up to and after the French Revolution. Hugh became duke of Francia and Aquitaine in 961, five years after his father's death. Like his ancestors, the Robertians, Hugh had landholdings and an influence over the Neustrian aristocracy that effectively made him more powerful than the king, Lothair I (r. 954–86). From ca. 980 on, the two were in constant conflict. With the deaths of Lothair (986) and Louis V (987), Hugh rose to the throne (June–July 987) and had his son Robert crowned soon after in Orléans (December 987).

Once king, however, Hugh proved as weak as he had been strong as duke: the last Carolingian claimant, Charles of Lorraine, rebelled against him, and only the treachery of Bishop Adalbero of Laon resolved the conflict (991). The treachery of Arnulf, archbishop of Reims, and the papal deposition of his replacement, Gerbert of Aurillac, set in motion a conflict that marred the remainder of Hugh's reign. Although it had started before he took the throne, the castellan revolution reached a peak in many regions of the kingdom at this point, and the impotence of both royal power and local Carolingian political structures (the *pagus*) drove some areas of his kingdom to seek their own solutions to disorder and violence. Among the most famous and consequential of these efforts was the Peace of God. In October 996, Hugh died on campaign near Tours.

Unable to assert the kind of royal authority at least theoretically available to Carolingians, Hugh sought legitimacy in an alliance with the church, both the episcopacy and the reforming monastic movement, and with some of his most powerful neighbors, such as William V of Aquitaine and Richard II of Normandy, who gave support in exchange for still greater levels of autonomy. As a result, the monarchy underwent a shift in the basis of its authority, from the essentially aristocratic Carolingian model to one more dependent on ecclesiastical legitimation and popular support.

Richard Landes

[See also: ADALBERO OF LAON; CAPETIAN DYNASTY; GERBERT OF AURILLAC; PEACE OF GOD]

Lemarignier, Jean-François. *Le gouvernement royal aux premiers temps capétiens* (*987–1108*). Paris: Picard, 1964.

Lewis, Andrew. *Royal Succession in Capetian France: Studies on Familial Order and the State*. Cambridge: Harvard University Press, 1981.

Lot, Ferdinand. *Études sur le règne d'Hugues Capet*. Paris: Bouillon, 1903.

Sassier, Yves. *Hugues Capet*. Paris: Fayard, 1987.

Theis, Laurent. *L'avènement d'Hugues Capet*. Paris: Gallimard, 1984.

HUGH OF AMIENS (ca. 1080–1164). Born in the area of Ribemont in northern France, Hugh was successively a student at the school of Laon, monk of Cluny, prior of Saint-Martial at Limoges, prior of St. Pancras, Lewes, and the first abbot of Henry I's foundation at Reading, before being elected archbishop of Rouen by the cathedral chapter. He was a strong believer in the rights of the episcopate, and he attempted to make newly elected abbots take a written oath of obedience to him. During the civil war between King Stephen and Empress Matilda, he was one of Stephen's strongest episcopal supporters, even defending him when he seized the castles of some of the English bishops, and he remained on the king's side until Rouen was captured by the Angevins.

In his youth, Hugh went to Rome to be a clerk in the papal curia, and he later served as legate. He was a vigorous judge in ecclesiastical disputes and a generous benefactor of numerous Norman monasteries. Though his personality remains elusive, he was admired by his contemporaries for his knowledge, for he was the author of several works of theology and (possibly) a defense of Cluny against the attacks of the Cistercians. He carried out work on the cathedral at Rouen, and he introduced the feast of the Immaculate Conception (December 8) into Normandy.

Thomas G. Waldman

HUGH OF SAINT-VICTOR (d. 1141). A leading theologian, biblical interpreter, and mystic of the first half of the 12th century, Hugh was the effective founder of the important school of the abbey of Saint-Victor at Paris. Hugh's place of birth is uncertain—evidence supports both Saxony and the Low Countries, with birth in one and early life in the other area a possibility. He came to the new community of regular canons at Saint-Victor, probably in the early 1120s; by 1125, he was writing and teaching and beginning to gain a wide following among students and peers. Hugh was instrumental in asserting the fundamental need to understand the literal, historical sense of the biblical text before undertaking allegorical and moral interpretation. Indeed, his whole exegetical and theological project was founded on the premise that one must understand history, the unfolding of events in time, as the fundamental category for God's revelation in the history of the Jewish and Christian peoples. Hugh sought contemporary Jewish interpretations for understanding the literal sense of the Hebrew Scriptures, and he inspired others, especially Andrew of Saint-Victor and Herbert of Bosham, to pursue more thoroughly the understanding of Scripture through knowledge of the Hebrew language and consultation with Jewish rabbis. In theology, Hugh composed the first *summa* of theology in the Parisian schools, *De sacramentis christianae fidei*, thus paving the way for the long series of *summae* that would characterize much of medieval scholastic theology. His mystical writings, especially the two treatises on the symbolic meaning of Isaiah's vision of the seraphim and the structure of Noah's Ark (*De arca Noe morali* and *De arca Noe mystica*) are some of the first attempts to systematize in treatises teaching on the ascetic-contemplative life. *De arca Noe mystica* describes a complex drawing (meant to be used as a focus for meditation) that presented a visualization of the cosmos, the unfolding of the history of salvation, and the stages of the interior spiritual journey of the individual to contemplative ecstasy. His commentary on the *Celestial Hierarchy* of Pseudo-Dionysius the Areopagite (*In hierarchiam coelestem*) was a major moment in bringing the thought of Pseudo-Dionysius into the mainstream of western theology and mysticism. Hugh based his work upon the 9th-century translation and commentary by Johannes Scottus Eriugena, but the interpretation was stamped with his own distinctive understanding of Dionysius's thought, an understanding deeply influenced by Hugh's Augustinian theology and his own view of the function of symbols in the mediation of divine truth to human beings living in a material world. Hugh's encyclopedic learning is reflected in his *Didascalicon: de studio legendi*, that provides a guide for the student of philosophy (Books 1–3) and the Bible (Books 4–6). In this work, Hugh presents the liberal arts as the remedy for the loss of knowledge and goodness in the Fall, while the mechanical arts (e.g., weaving) provide for the resulting weakness of the human body. The section on reading Scripture outlines Hugh's understanding of a sequence of disciplines of study (history, allegory, and tropology), and gives for each discipline the proper order in which to read the biblical books appropriate for that approach to the interpretation of the text. For the student pursuing the discipline of history, Hugh compiled a *Chronicon* with numerous chronological tables and historical aids; for the student of allegory, his theological masterwork, *De sacramentis christianae fidei*, was intended to serve as an introduction. *De scripturis et scriptoribus sacris*, the preface to Hugh's collection of literal comments on the Pentateuch and other Old Testament books (these comments are printed as *Notulae* in Migne), is modeled on the form of the *accessus ad auctores* then being used by the arts faculty to introduce classical authors and by biblical interpreters to introduce their commentaries. The introduction to Hugh's *Chronicon* contains a treatise on the "art of memory," an important contribution to the memory tradition. Hugh's other works include an unfinished series of sermons on Ecclesiastes; short pieces, extracts, and fragments collected into several books of *miscellania*; short contemplative and theological treatises; several letters; and numerous sermons scattered throughout medieval collections and only recently fully identified.

Grover A. Zinn

[See also: ANDREW OF SAINT-VICTOR; BIBLE, CHRISTIAN INTERPRETATION OF; ERIUGENA, JOHANNES SCOTTUS; LAURENT D'ORLÉANS; MYSTICISM; PSEUDO-DIONYSIUS THE AREOPAGITE; SAINT-VICTOR, ABBEY AND SCHOOL OF; THEOLOGY]

Hugh of Saint-Victor. *Opera*. PL 175–77.

———. *Hugonis de Sancto Victore, Didascalicon: de studio legendi. A Critical Text*, ed. Charles Henry Buttimer. Washington, D.C.: Catholic University Press, 1939.

———. *The "Didascalicon" of Hugh of St. Victor: A Medieval Guide to the Arts*, trans. Jerome Taylor. New York: Columbia University Press, 1961.

———. *Hugh of Saint Victor on the Sacraments of the Christian Faith (De sacramentis)*, trans. Roy J. Deferrari. Cambridge: Mediaeval Academy of America, 1951.

Baron, Roger. *Science et sagesse chez Hugues de Saint-Victor*. Paris: Lethielleux, 1957.

Ehlers, Joachim. *Hugo von St. Viktor: Studien zum Geschichtsdenken und zur Geschichtsschreibung des 12. Jahrhunderts*. Wiesbaden: Steiner, 1973.

Goy, Rudolf. *Die Überlieferung der Werke Hugos von St. Viktor: Ein Beitrag zur Kommunikationsgeschichte des Mittelalters*. Stuttgart: Hiersemann, 1976.

Sicard, Patrice. *Hugues de Saint-Victor et son école*. Turnhout: Brepols, 1991.

Van den Eynde, Damien. *Essai sur la succession et la date des écrits de Hugues de Saint-Victor*. Rome: Apud Pontificium Athenaeum Antonianum, 1960.

Zinn, Grover A. "Mandala Symbolism and Use in the Mysticism of Hugh of St. Victor." *History of Religions* 12 (1972–73): 317–41.

———. "Hugh of St. Victor, Isaiah's Vision, and *De arca Noe*." In *The Church and the Arts*, ed. Diana Wood. Oxford: Blackwell, 1992.

HUGUES DE BERZÉ (1150/55–ca. 1220). The knight Hugues de Berzé was born in the Mâconnais and joined the crusaders in 1201 and again in 1220. Near the end of his life, he wrote his *Bible*, a poem of 1,029 octosyllables preaching reform. Inspired by both the certainty of death and the uncertainty of his times, Hugues criticized the three orders of society, drawing on his own experiences in Constantinople. The *Bible*, which is influenced by the *Bible Guiot* of Guiot de Provins, is an example of the beliefs of a pious layman with a considerable breadth of worldly experience. In addition to the *Bible*, five lyric poems are attributed to him in the *chansonniers*.

Maureen B.M. Boulton

[See also: GUIOT DE PROVINS; MORAL TREATISES]

Hugues de Berzé. *La Bible au seigneur de Berzé*, ed. Félix Lecoy. Paris: Droz, 1938.
Lecoy, Félix. "Pour la chronologie de Hugues de Berzé." *Romania* 67 (1942–43): 243–54.

HUGUES DE CLUNY (d. 1109). The monastery of Cluny reached the peak of its popularity and prestige under the abbacy of St. Hugues (r. 1049–1109). A member of the castellan family of the lords of Semur-en-Brionnais, Hugues was originally put by his parents into the cathedral school of Auxerre, where his great-uncle, also named Hugues, was bishop (r. 999–1039). He left the cathedral school when he was fifteen, against his parents' wishes, to become a monk at Cluny. He soon became prior under Abbot Odilo and then abbot.

As abbot, he ruled a tremendously wealthy monastery, by far the biggest landowner in its region, which held its own courts to resolve legal cases and often found itself in dispute with its seigneurial neighbors. The principle of Cluny's immunity from the bishop of Mâcon, first enunciated in the 10th century, became a principle for which Cluny had to argue strenuously against bishops unwilling to recognize it.

During Hugues's long years as abbot, Cluny reached perhaps the pinnacle of its international prestige. Cluny, which had reformed a number of other monasteries in the 10th and early 11th centuries, was given the direction of a great many more by popes, bishops, and laymen. People as distant as the king of Castile arranged for generous gifts to Cluny. Hugues was asked to lend his assistance to emperors and popes, including being a mediator at Canossa during the Investiture controversy. In his monastery, he sponsored a thorough reworking of Cluniac customaries.

Under Hugues's leadership, the number of monks at Cluny tripled, from about one hundred to 300. Hugues and his brothers established the nunnery of Marcigny in 1055 as a house for the wives and daughters of men who wished to enter the monastery. He sponsored a new and enormous abbey church, called Cluny III by art historians. The church, finished shortly before his death, was the largest church in the West until the late Renaissance.

Constance B. Bouchard

[See also: CLUNIAC ORDER; CLUNY; ODILO]

Odilo. *Vita sancti Hugonis*, ed. Herbert Edward John Cowdrey. In "Two Studies in Cluniac History, 1049–1126." *Studi gregoriani* 11 (1978): 1–297.
Hallinger, Kassius, ed. *Consuetudines Cluniacensium antiquiores cum redactionibus derivatis*. Sieburg: Schmitt, 1983.
Raynald of Vézelay. *Vita*, ed. R.B.C. Huygens. In *Vizeliacensia II. Textes relatifs à l'histoire de l'abbaye de Vézelay*. CCCM 42 supplementum. Turnhout: Brepols, 1980.
Hunt, Noreen. *Cluny Under Saint Hugh, 1049–1109*. Notre Dame: University of Notre Dame Press, 1968.
Rosenwein, Barbara. *To Be the Neighbor of Saint Peter: The Social Meaning of Cluny's Property, 909–1049*. Ithaca: Cornell University Press, 1989.

HUGUES DE SAINT-CHER (ca. 1195–1263). Nothing is known of Hugues's origins, except that he was born in Saint-Cher, not far from Vienne in the south of France. He had become a doctor of canon law and a bachelor of theology even before he joined the Dominicans at Paris in 1225, where he studied under Roland of Cremona, the first Dominican to hold a chair in theology at the University of Paris. Hugues soon set upon a vocation that would make him one of the most prominent churchmen of his day. He first served in an administrative capacity as provincial of the Order for France from 1227 to 1229. Subsequently, he took up the posts of master of theology (1230–36) at the university and prior of the Dominican convent of Saint-Jacques (1233–36). After leaving his posts at the university and the convent, he resumed his duties for the next eight years as provincial-general of the Order of Preachers for the French province, while continuing to maintain a lively interest in the scholarly activities of his order in Paris. He became vicar-general of his order in 1240 and attained his highest administrative post with his selection as the first Dominican cardinal on May 28, 1244.

Hugues played a central role in the study of the Bible and theology in the 13th century. At Saint-Jacques, he assembled a team that produced three works that served as essential starting points for the theologians and preachers of his day: an expanded commentary on the Bible; a version of the Latin Vulgate incorporating a vast series of linguistic notes "correcting" the contemporary version of the text; and the first alphabetical concordance to the Bible. His set of commentaries, known as *Postillae*, use as their starting point the *Glossa ordinaria*, itself a digest of patristic and Carolingian exegesis, and add to it the fruits of the study of the Bible produced from the middle of the 12th century to his own time. His "corrected" Vulgate, the *Correctoria*, gives as full a sense of the literal meaning of the text as was possible for the 13th century, and his

Concordantia greatly facilitated the task of preaching, allowing a relative novice to find his way around in the Bible without having to commit the entire text to memory.

Hugues began his work on the *Correctoria* as early as 1227, although the latest versions of this work date from his years as cardinal (1244–63). The *Postillae* date from his years as master (1230–36), and his *Concordantia* from 1238–40—a work to which some 500 friars contributed. Although the Bible had been given standard chapter divisions by Stephen Langton at the end of the 12th century, Hugues was the first to introduce subdivisions (a,b,c,d,e,f,g), an essential element for his correctoria and concordance.

His *Commentary* on the *Sententiae* of Peter Lombard, dating from his early years as master of theology, was among the first to employ the form of the *quaestio* in preference to a running commentary. In effect, this form signaled a shift away from simply commenting on Lombard's text to rewriting it, a process that was to reach its perfected form a generation later in the *Summa theologica* of Thomas Aquinas.

Among Hugues's more original contributions to theology was his teaching of the "treasury of merits" that held that the superabundance of the merits and good works of Christ, the Virgin, and the saints are at the disposal of the church, in the office of the pope, to distribute to the faithful. With the articulation of the treasury of merits, the theology of indulgences became integral to the practice of private penance.

As cardinal, Hugues worked closely with three popes and served on papal commissions that heard the controversies over Joachim of Fiore, the posthumous champion of the Spiritual Franciscans, in 1255 and William of Saint-Amour, the most vocal critic of the mendicant orders, in 1256. Hugues's eucharistic devotion is epitomized in the feast of Corpus Christi, which he authorized in Liège while legate there between 1251 and 1253 and which was placed in the calendar of the universal church in 1264 by Pope Urban IV, whom Hugues had served.

Mark Zier

[See also: AQUINAS, THOMAS; BIBLE, CHRISTIAN INTERPRETATION OF; BIBLE, LATIN VERSION OF; DOMINICAN ORDER; *GLOSSA ORDINARIA*; PETER LOMBARD; THEOLOGY; URBAN IV; WILLIAM OF SAINT-AMOUR]

Kaeppeli, Thomas. *Scriptores ordinis praedicatorum medii aevi.* 3 vols. Rome: Ad S. Sabinae, 1975–80, Vol. 2, pp. 269–81.
Lerner, Robert E. "Poverty, Preaching, and Eschatology in the Revelation Commentaries of Hugh of Saint-Cher." In *The Bible in the Medieval World: Essays in Memory of Beryl Smalley*, ed. Catharine Walsh and Diana Wood. Oxford: Blackwell, 1985.
Principe, Walter. *The Theology of the Hypostatic Union in the Early Thirteenth Century.* 4 vols. Toronto: Pontifical Institute of Mediaeval Studies, 1970, Vol. 3: *Hugh of Saint-Cher's Theology of the Hypostatic Union.*
Smalley, Beryl. *The Study of the Bible in the Middle Ages.* 3rd ed. Oxford: Blackwell, 1983.

HUGUES D'OIGNIES (fl. first third of the 13th c.) A goldsmith active in the Meuse Valley and a major proponent of the school of metalwork of Entre-Sambre-et-Meuse, Hugues was a prior at Oignies. He is best known for three documented works: a gold and silver cover of a Gospel book, a reliquary for the rib of St. Peter, and the chalice of Gilles de Walcourt, all now in the treasury of the Benedictine convent of the Sisters of Notre Dame at Namur. His works are characterized by the use of *niello* rather than the use of brightly colored enamels of earlier Mosan metalwork.

Robert G. Calkins

[See also: ENAMELING; JEWELRY AND METALWORKING]

Collon-Gevaert, Suzanne. *Histoire des arts du métal en Belgique.* Brussels: Palais des Académies, 1951, pp. 204–14. [With bibliography.]
———, Jean Lejeune, and Jacques Stiennon. *A Treasury of Romanesque Art: Metalwork. Illuminations and Sculpture from the Valley of the Meuse.* New York: Phaidon, 1972, pp. 105–07.
Courtoy, Ferdinand. "Les phylactères d'Hugo d'Oignies." *Bulletin des Musées Royaux* (1930): 93–96.
Mitchell, H.P. "Some Works by Goldsmiths of Oignies." *Burlington Magazine* 39 (1921): 157–69.

HUGUES LE GRAND (d. 956). Duke of Francia, son of Robert I (r. 922–23) and nephew of King Eudes, Hugues played a major role in the French kingdom from 923 to his death.

In spite of his father's death in the Battle of Soissons (June 15, 923), Hugues rallied his army and routed that of the Carolingian king Charles III the Simple (r. 898–922). He was, however, passed over by the rebel magnates who elected his brother-in-law, Duke Raoul of Burgundy, to succeed Robert as their candidate for the throne. Hugues remained loyal to Raoul throughout his reign (923–36), all the while consolidating his position in his father's lands between the Seine and the Loire.

He supported the election of Charles's son, Louis IV (r. 936–54), but soon fell out with the young king. Open warfare between the two in the 940s resulted in the intervention of their joint brother-in-law, Otto I of Germany. Condemned and excommunicated by the Council of Ingelheim (June 948), Hugues finally submitted to Louis in 950. Although friction between the two continued until Louis's death, Hugues supported the succession of Louis's young son, Lothair.

From the accession of Lothair (954) to his own death in 956, Hugues virtually ruled France. To his title of duke of the Franks he added those of duke of Burgundy and of Aquitaine. He left three minor sons: Hugh Capet, duke of Francia and future king, and Otto and Eudes-Henri, successively dukes of Burgundy.

R. Thomas McDonald

[See also: LOTHAIR I (941–986)]

Flodoard. *Les annales*, ed. P. Lauer. Paris: Picard, 1906.

Richer. *Histoire de France*, ed. R. Latouche. 2 vols. Paris: Champion, 1930, Vol. 1; Les Belles Lettres, 1937, Vol. 2.

Lauer, Philippe. *Le règne de Louis IV d'Outremer*. Paris: Bouillon, 1900.

HUGUES LIBERGIER (d. 1263). Mason. Although the abbey church of Saint-Nicaise, Reims, is his only known work, Hugues Libergier was one of the most innovative master masons in northern France during the second third of the 13th century. Construction of the church began in 1231, and by Hugues's death the nave, portals, and two façade towers had been completed. While certain details, such as the use of the *pilier cantonné* and tracery patterns, reveal connections to Amiens, Hugues created an original architecture marked by contrasts of rounded and sharpened forms, of smooth mural surface and brittle calligraphic line. The Saint-Nicaise façade, with a screen of seven gables stretched across the portal zone, exercised a fundamental influence on succeeding designs, including the west façade of the cathedral of Reims and the transepts of Notre-Dame in Paris. Hugues's tombstone, preserved at the cathedral of Reims following the abbey's destruction, depicts the master with the tools of his trade: the graduated rod, compass, and set-square. His academic dress recalls the parallel drawn by Thomas Aquinas between the master mason and the professor and testifies to the contemporary appreciation of the cerebral activity demanded by the design process and building.

Michael T. Davis

[See also: PARIS; REIMS]

Bideault, Maryse, and Claudine Lautier. "Saint-Nicaise de Reims: chronologie et nouvelles remarques sur l'architecture." *Bulletin monumental* 135 (1977): 295–330.

Branner, Robert. *Saint Louis and the Court Style in Gothic Architecture*. London: Zwemmer, 1965.

Givelet, Charles. *L'église et l'abbaye de Saint-Nicaise de Reims: notice historique et archéologique*. Reims, 1897.

Kimpel, Dieter, and Robert Suckale. *Die gotische Architektur in Frankreich, 1130–1270*. Munich: Hirmer, 1985.

HUNDRED YEARS' WAR. The name posterity has bestowed on the series of Anglo-French conflicts that occurred between 1337 and 1453. Two major issues were at stake: the claim of English kings to be rightful kings of France and the irritations arising from the fact that the king of England, as duke of Aquitaine, was a liege vassal of the king of France. The dynastic claim to the French throne was important to Edward III but was at best tenuous in the 15th century. The feudal status of Aquitaine, regarded by some scholars as the key to the whole conflict, was eliminated by the expulsion of the English from southwestern France in 1453.

The Hundred Years' War in fact comprised three wars of particular intensity, each of twenty years' duration, preceded and followed by lesser conflicts. The "Edwardian" war of 1340–60 was dominated by Edward III of England.

The "Caroline" war of 1369–89 was dominated by the military establishment of Charles V of France. The "Lancastrian" war of 1415–35 was dominated by Henry V of England and his brother John, duke of Bedford. Besides these three major conflicts, there was indecisive Anglo-French fighting in the periods 1294–1303, 1323–25, 1337–39, and 1436–44, in addition to the French campaign of reconquest (1449–53), an abortive English invasion in 1475, and various war scares at other times.

The periods of intermittent conflict after 1294 were marked by fairly easy French victories that gave way to stalemate, but each monarchy also suffered one humiliating defeat at the hands of a supposedly inferior neighbor, Flanders (1302) and Scotland (1314), respectively. These were the first of many other European states to be drawn into the Anglo-French struggle over the course of a century.

In 1340, when Edward III first called himself king of France, the opposing kings assembled large and expensive armies that confronted each other without engaging in decisive action, to the annoyance of taxpayers on both sides of the Channel. A war of succession in Brittany broke out in 1341 and breathed new life into the Anglo-French war. France was weakened by a tradition of not collecting taxes in time of truce, and especially by internal divisions in which important segments of the politically influential classes opposed the government. Edward launched two well-organized campaigns, about a decade apart. The first of these, in 1345–47, produced decisive English victories at Auberoche in the southwest (1345), Crécy (1346) and Calais (1347) in the north, and La Roche-Derrien (1347) in Brittany. The crisis caused by the Black Death then intervened, but the second great campaign began in 1355, when the Prince of Wales ravaged upper Languedoc. In the next year, he defeated and captured John II at Poitiers. France was virtually paralyzed by social strife, political rivalries, and an empty treasury, while her captive king attempted to negotiate a treaty.

Six centuries of historical commentary have failed to give a satisfactory explanation for the French defeats. The noble knights, specialists in the traditional tactics of heavy cavalry, seemed reluctant to appreciate the military value of nonnoble infantry, to adapt to the problems posed by new and more powerful missile weapons, and to place coordination and discipline ahead of personal glory or the opportunity for booty. Yet neither the nobility nor heavy cavalry was obsolescent in 1350, as some have claimed, and we still await a convincing explanation of the reasons for their shortcomings in the 14th century.

Financial exigencies may have influenced the war in ways that have not received adequate emphasis. For Edward III, it was cheaper to transport quantities of longbowmen across the Channel than to send an army made up exclusively of heavy cavalry. For the French government in 1357–60, it was financially impossible to assemble a large force and therefore desirable to avoid battle. The pitched battle had been the key to English success. When Edward III, in his final invasion of France (1359–60), failed to bring the French to battle, he had to conclude the Treaty of Brétigny, which gave him possession of all of Aquitaine but was less favorable to him than earlier peace proposals.

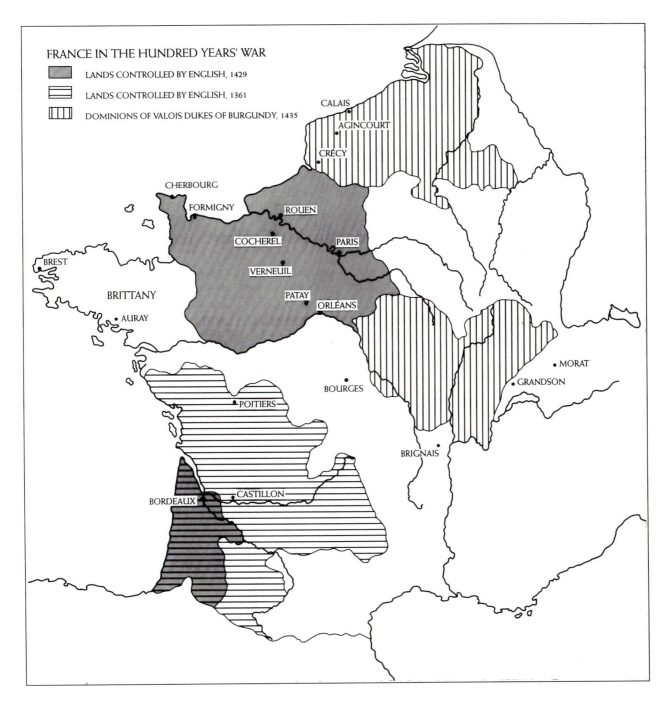

FRANCE IN THE HUNDRED YEARS' WAR

- LANDS CONTROLLED BY ENGLISH, 1429
- LANDS CONTROLLED BY ENGLISH, 1361
- DOMINIONS OF VALOIS DUKES OF BURGUNDY, 1435

The Edwardian war was nevertheless an English victory and a French defeat. When it ended, France was plunged into even greater misery by the ravages of unemployed troops (*routiers*). This scourge forced people to acquiesce to a much higher level of taxation for military purposes than would have been conceivable a few years earlier. Just as important was the crown's *rapprochement* with the disaffected nobility of the north and west. This regional aristocracy became the core of a regularly financed French army at a time when England began to face weak and divided leadership.

The war resumed in 1369, when Charles V agreed to accept appeals from Gascon lords who chafed under English rule. The Caroline war of the next twenty years was bitter and destructive but lacked dramatic battles. Bertrand du Guesclin (constable of France, 1370–80) was a master at the tactics of the *routiers*. His close associate and successor as constable, Olivier de Clisson, exerted a strong influence against pitched battles and commanded the respect of the northwestern nobles. Under these two able Bretons, the French regained large amounts of territory while the English squandered resources on expeditions that inflicted great damage without producing strategic results. Yet England did retain key ports in France, like Bordeaux, Brest, Cherbourg, and Calais, while French attempts to carry the war across the Channel in the 1380s did not succeed.

Peace negotiations in 1389–96 produced a prolonged lull in the war but no definitive settlement, and the advantage in leadership swung back to England. The French military elite suffered dreadful losses on crusade at Nicopolis (1396) and became badly divided during the mental incapacity of Charles VI, as the dukes of Burgundy engaged in a power struggle with the Orléans-Armagnac faction. The English reopened the conflict, inaugurating the Lancastrian war in 1415 and winning a crushing victory at Agincourt in October of that year. The weakened nobility of northwestern France was decimated by death or capture. Leaderless Norman lordships were in no position to halt Henry V's subsequent conquest of the region. Supported by Burgundy after the murder of John the Fearless in 1419, Henry in 1420 secured the Treaty of Troyes, which acknowledged him as heir to the French throne. His early death did not immediately change the situation because his able brother, John of Bedford, continued to advance, defeating the French badly at Verneuil (1424) and overrunning Anjou and Maine.

A new stalemate ensued only after the English failed to take Orléans in 1428–29. In stopping their advance, the French found an unlikely group of leaders: the bastard of Orléans Jean de Dunois, the *routier* captain La Hire, the young, rich, and unstable marshal Gilles de Rais, and, most celebrated of all, the teenaged visionary Jeanne d'Arc. Jeanne's presence seems to have had an inspirational effect on French morale and a correspondingly negative impact on the English. Jeanne was involved in several French victories that culminated in the coronation of Charles VII at Reims, but in 1430 she fell into Burgundian hands, and the English, who accused her of heresy and sorcery, had her executed in 1431.

The pendulum of leadership began swinging back in favor of the French after the ouster of Georges de La Trémoille from court in 1433 and the rise of Arthur de Richemont, who had been constable since 1425 and favored a *rapprochement* with Burgundy. The English did not join in the Franco-Burgundian treaty of 1435, and Bedford's death was a blow to Lancastrian unity. Richemont regained Paris in 1436, but after a new stalemate the two sides concluded a five-year truce in 1444. While the French were rebuilding Charles V's system of regular taxes and a salaried army, England began to suffer from problems resembling those that had afflicted France at the turn of the century—princely rivalries around a weak and mentally unstable king, Henry VI. The French mastery of firearms rivaled the earlier English success with the longbow. When the truce expired, French victories at Formigny (1450) and Castillon (1453) sealed their rapid reconquests of Normandy and Aquitaine, respectively.

No treaty ended the Hundred Years' War, but a new Anglo-Burgundian alliance in the 1470s was thwarted by the erratic but skillful Louis XI. England's recurrent internal problems and the permanence of France's restored fis-

cal and military institutions gave the Valois monarchy strength and stability at last. These factors, and a measure of good luck, permitted the crown to regain control of several important territories—Burgundy (1477), Anjou, Maine, and Provence (1481), Brittany (1491), and Orléans (1498)—and to become a major European power.

John Bell Henneman, Jr.

[See also: AGINCOURT; ARCHER/BOWMAN; ARMAGNACS; ARTILLERY; BADEFOL, SEGUIN DE; BRÉTIGNY; BRIGAND/BRIGANDAGE; CERVOLE, ARNAUD DE; CHARLES V; CLISSON; CRÉCY; DUNOIS, JEAN, COMTE DE; EDWARD III; EDWARD, THE BLACK PRINCE; GUESCLIN, BERTRAND DU; HENRY V; JEANNE D'ARC; JOHN II THE GOOD; JOHN THE FEARLESS; KNOLLES, ROBERT; LA HIRE; LANCASTER, DUKES OF; LOUIS XI; NAVAL POWER; ORLÉANS CAMPAIGN; PHILIP THE BOLD; PHILIP THE GOOD; POITIERS; RAIS, GILLES DE; RECONQUEST OF FRANCE; RICHEMONT, ARTHUR DE; TALBOT, JOHN; VILLANDRANDO, RODRIGO DE; WARFARE]

Contamine, Philippe. *Guerre, état et société à la fin du moyen âge: études sur les armées des rois de France 1337–1494.* Paris: Mouton, 1972.

Favier, Jean. *La Guerre de cent ans.* Paris: Fayard, 1980.

Henneman, John Bell. "The Military Class and the French Monarchy in the Late Middle Ages." *American Historical Review* 83 (1978): 946–65.

Palmer, John Joseph Norman. *England, France and Christendom, 1377–1399.* London: Routledge, 1972.

———, ed. *Froissart: Historian.* Woodbridge: Boydell, 1981.

Perroy, Edouard. *The Hundred Years War*, trans. W. B. Wells. London: Eyre and Spottiswoode, 1951.

HUNTING AND FOWLING. Hunting was an essential part of the aristocratic way of life during the Middle Ages. Charlemagne often journeyed between his scattered hunting lodges in pursuit of the sport and was prepared to go directly into the field after hearing Mass. The Carolingian practice of setting aside tracts of land as royal forest, in which the kings exercised a monopoly on hunting, later spread to the nobles, who established their own forests as protected hunting preserves under the weakened French monarchy. The animals hunted in these forests included several kinds of deer, wild boars, wolves, foxes, otters, and hares. While hunting was considered an activity primarily for males, ladies also joined in fowling, and a falcon poised on the wrist became a recognized symbol of nobility. Royal and other large households had professional huntsmen who provided meat for the table, and peasants also hunted for food where not prohibited by aristocratic monopolies over forests, but these practical uses of hunting were not considered as *la chasse*, which so delighted its participants.

Hunting developed a kind of ritual. Literary descriptions can be found from saints' lives to romances, in which hunting sometimes became a literary motif expanded into an elaborate metaphor. In the Tristan legend, for example, the hero reveals his aristocratic training by teaching the huntsmen of King Marc how to divide the slain stag into portions to be borne in triumphal procession at the conclusion of the hunt. This ceremonious "breaking the stag" is included in the two most influential medieval hunting manuals: Henri de Ferrières's *Livres du roy Modus et de la royne Ratio* (ca. 1354–77) and Gaston Phoebus's *Livre de chasse* (ca. 1389). These describe the seasons for hunting, how various animals should be hunted, types of hunting dogs and their care, and how to make the traps and nets used in some kinds of hunting. The prologues emphasize that hunting keeps the body fit and gives familiarity in the use of arms but that it also has the spiritual benefit of occupying the mind so that the hunter is not tempted to fall into sin. Even though many clergy shared the aristocratic enthusiasm for hunting, various learned traditions against hunting merged in Gratian's *Decretum* (ca. 1140) and formed the basis for ecclesiastical sanctions against hunting, but these sanctions proved ineffective.

One section of Henri de Ferrières's manual is a formal disputation between two ladies on the virtue of hunting with dogs as compared to hunting with birds. Later chapters deal briefly with the selection and training of birds of prey used for hunting, but this manual does not have the detail found in the famous book on falconry written by Emperor Frederick II in the early 13th century. References in literature and representations in art confirm the popularity of fowling, along with hunting, as part of the aristocratic way of life.

Charles R. Young

[See also: FERRIÈRES, HENRI DE; FISHING; GASTON PHOEBUS]

Bise, Gabriel. *Illuminated Manuscripts: Medieval Hunting Scenes*, trans. J. Peter Tallon. Fribourg: Productions Liber SA and Éditions Minerva SA, 1978.

La chasse au moyen âge. Nice: Centre d'Études Médiévales de Nice, 1980.

Thiébaux, Marcelle. "The Medieval Chase." *Speculum* 42 (1967): 260–74.

———. *The Stag of Love: The Chase in Medieval Literature*. Ithaca: Cornell University Press, 1974.

HUON DE BORDEAUX.

HUON DE BORDEAUX. The chanson de geste of *Huon de Bordeaux* (10,553 mostly decasyllabic assonanced lines) may have been composed between 1216 and 1229 or between 1260 and 1268 at the latest. It is conserved in three manuscripts (Tours, Bibl. mun. 936, 13th c.; Paris, B.N. fr. 22555, 15th c.; Turin: Bibl. naz. L. II. 14, MS fr. XXXVI, dated 1311).

Huon and Gérard, sons of Seguin, duke of Bordeaux, do not pay homage to Charlemagne for their fief. Amauri, a traitor, accuses them of rebellion against the emperor. Naimon intercedes and has them both summoned to court. Amauri and Charlot, Charlemagne's son, ambush Huon and Gérard. In the ensuing melee, Huon kills Charlot. The peers intervene, and Huon's life is spared on condition he undertake what appears to be an impossible mission into Saracen land while Gérard watches over their fief. Huon is expected to kill the first pagan he meets in Babylon, to kiss Emir Gaudisse's daughter Esclamonde three times, and to bring back the emir's moustache and three of his teeth. Huon overcomes many obstacles thanks to his companion, Gériaume, and the fairy king Auberon. After numerous adventures, Huon returns to his fief with Esclamonde, now his wife, only to discover that his brother has betrayed him. Huon is thrown in jail, but Auberon intervenes to free him.

Huon de Bordeaux was composed by a talented but unknown author. It is an original and complex poem that successfully renews the genre of the chanson de geste. The author followed the epic literary tradition, using assonance and decasyllabic verse, while at the same time drawing from the romance, especially folk themes and supernatural and fantastic elements. The author must have known a number of French poems, among them the *Chanson de Roland, Fergus,* the *Voyage de Charlemagne, Aye d'Avignon, Ogier le Danois,* and Chrétien de Troyes's *Yvain.*

Huon de Bordeaux enjoyed great popularity in France and abroad beyond the Middle Ages. In the 15th century, it was rewritten both in Alexandrines and in prose and was printed many times until the middle of the 19th century.

Jean-Louis Picherit

[See also: LATE EPIC; *TRISTAN DE NANTEUIL*]

Ruelle, Pierre, ed. *Huon de Bordeaux*. Paris and Brussels: Presses Universitaires de France, 1960. [Based on MS Tours 936.]

Rossi, Marguerite. *Huon de Bordeaux et l'évolution du genre épique au XIIIe siècle*. Paris: Champion, 1975.

Suard, François, trans. *Histoire de Huon de Bordeaux et Aubéron roi de féerie*. Paris: Stock/Moyen Âge, 1983.

———. "Le cycle en vers de *Huon de Bordeaux*." In *La chanson de geste et le mythe carolingien: Mélanges René Louis*. 2 vols. Saint-Père-Sous-Vézelay, 1982, Vol. 2, pp. 1035–50.

HUON DE MÉRY (fl. first half of the 13th c.). Author of the *Tournoiement Antéchrist* (3,546 octosyllables; ca. 1234–40), Huon is known only through topical allusions in this work. He appears to have been a Norman who participated in the wars against Pierre Mauclerc, duke of Brittany, during Louis IX's minority (1232–35). His poem, contemporary with the *Roman de la Rose*, is an allegorical psychomachia opposing the forces of God (the Virtues, archangels, and Arthurian knights) and those of the Antichrist (the Vices, pagan gods, and peasants). In the midst of the battle, the narrator himself is wounded in the eye by Cupid's arrow, which eventually drives him to seek refuge in a monastery. The poem includes direct allusions to Chrétien de Troyes's *Yvain* and to Raoul de Houdenc's *Songe d'enfer.*

William W. Kibler

[See also: CHRÉTIEN DE TROYES; JACQUEMART GIELÉE; RAOUL DE HOUDENC; TOURNAMENT ROMANCES]

Huon de Méry. *Li tornoiemenz Antecrit*, ed. Georg Wimmer. Marburg, 1888.

———. *Le torneiment Anticrist*, ed. Margaret O. Bender. University: Romance Monographs, 1976.

Busby, Keith. "Plagiarism and Poetry in the *Tournoiement Antechrist* of Huon de Méry." *Neuphilologische Mitteilungen* 84 (1983): 505–21.

Emmerson, Richard K. *Antichrist in the Middle Ages: A Study of Medieval Apocalypticism in Art and Literature*. Seattle: University of Washington Press, 1981.

HUON D'OISY (d. 1190). One of the earliest trouvères, Huon was castellan of Cambrai and a member of the upper nobility. He wed the daughter of Count Thierry d'Alsace and was himself lord of Oisy (Pas-de-Calais). He left two poems, both dated 1189. The first is a crusade song in which Huon castigates his nephew, the trouvère Conon de Béthune, for having returned prematurely with Philip II Augustus from the Third Crusade. The second is the *Tournoiement des dames*, which as edited by Alfred Jeanroy has 216 lines (of three, four, six, and seven syllables) divided into eight stanzas of twenty-seven lines each. This unusual and possibly satirical poem recounts a tournament at Lagny in which the participants are all historically identifiable noble ladies of Picardy who are relatives or acquaintances of the poet.

William W. Kibler

[See also: CONON DE BÉTHUNE; TOURNAMENT ROMANCES]

Jeanroy, Alfred, ed. "Notes sur le *Tournoiement des dames*." *Romania* 28 (1899): 232–44.

HUON LE ROI DE CAMBRAI (fl. 13th c.). A number of texts are identified as the work of Huon le Roi, Huon de Cambrai, or Huon le Roi de Cambrai; these are possibly names for the same 13th-century poet. Huon is known to be the author of several religious compositions, including the *Vie de saint Quentin* (4,000+ octosyllables), dedicated to Philip III, and the *Regrés Nostre Dame*. If the several names designate a single person, he also composed ironic or playful texts on religious orders and even on the alphabet, as well as two better-known works, a fabliau entitled *Le male honte* (an ambiguous title that can mean either "the terrible shame" or "Honte's trunk") and *Le vair palefroi*, a courtly *lai* of 1,342 octosyllables that illustrates how a young woman can escape an unfortunate marriage and find true love with the man of her choice.

Norris J. Lacy

Huon le Roi de Cambrai. *Li regrets Nostre Dame*, ed. Arthur Långfors. Helsinki, 1907.

———. *La vie de saint Quentin*, ed. Arthur Långfors and Werner Söderhjelm. Helsingfors: Imprimerie de la Société de Littérature finnoise, 1909.

———. *Le vair palefroi, avec deux versions de La male honte*, ed. Arthur Långfors. Paris: Champion, 1912.

HYMNS. The hymns sung in France during the Middle Ages have their roots in classical Greek songs (*hymnoi*) associated with liturgical ceremonies, especially of libation and sacrifice, and performed either chorally or monodically with instrumental accompaniment. Eastern Christian sources of the 2nd and 3rd centuries record hymns based on both biblical and nonbiblical texts. In the classical and medieval periods, the term *hymnus* may be found loosely applied to a great variety of religious and secular verse, but by the early Middle Ages in the West *hymnus* was most precisely used for the "office hymn": a Latin chant, on almost any religious subject, whose text was composed of a series of metrically identical (or essentially identical) strophes sung to an unvarying melody repeated with each succeeding strophe. Musical settings of true hymns remained uniformly monophonic throughout Europe until nearly the beginning of the 15th century. Vast numbers of Latin hymns, sequences, and tropes were composed in the Middle Ages; one estimate puts their number at nearly 100,000, of which perhaps 20 percent have been printed. Numerous hymnals, collections of hymns for use throughout the liturgical year, survive either as separate manuscripts or as parts of larger manuscripts. While vernacular hymns appear relatively early in Germany and England, true hymns with French texts are rare until the close of the medieval period.

The earliest allusions to hymns in the Christian West occur in the 4th century and suggest that Gaul played a central role in the development and dissemination of the genre. St. Jerome credits Hilary, bishop of Poitiers (ca. 310–66), with writing a *Liber hymnorum*, which has not survived, though several extant hymns are traditionally associated with his name. Another Gaul, Ambrose, bishop of Milan (ca. 340–97) and a great opponent of Arianism, composed hymns to be sung by his congregation. Four well-known works can be attributed to him with confidence, *Aeterne rerum conditor*, *Deus creator omnium*, *Iam surgit hora tertia*, and *Veni redemptor gentium*, with perhaps ten others likely to be Ambrosian.

The church institutionalized the singing of hymns in the first half of the 6th century, in the monastic movements centered in Gaul under the bishops Caesarius and Aurelius of Arles and under Benedict of Nursia. The bishops' closely related *regula* suggest over a dozen different hymns, designated by incipits, for use in services; Benedict's *Rule*, while not specifying particular hymns, declared that one hymn should be sung at each of the eight canonical hours of the daily monastic office and that those sung at the Night Office, Lauds, and Vespers must be Ambrosian. By the 10th century, manuscripts of the Office for secular clergy begin to appear with hymns as well. While some early hymn composers are known by name (e.g., Venantius Fortunatus, bishop of Poitiers ca. 599–ca. 609 and author of *Vexilla regis prodeunt* and *Pange lingua*), the clerics responsible for many popular early hymns, such as *Veni creator spiritus*, *Ave maris stella*, and *Ad cenam agni providi*, remain anonymous.

Helmut Gneuss has reconstructed the modest original collection of hymns implied by the early monastic rules (which he terms the Old Hymnal I), as well as a more elaborate revision of that first collection (Old Hymnal II), introduced in France and Germany by the 8th century. The Old Hymnal I contained about sixteen hymns, while Old Hymnal II contained about twenty-five, mostly from Old Hymnal I but with some additions and deletions. Both early versions were replaced, beginning in the 9th century, by a still more elaborate hymnal, probably originating in France, whose earliest form contained thirty-eight hymns (the New Hymnal).

In the centuries that followed, hundreds more hymns, often reflecting strictly local interests, were added to the core collection to provide for all the feast days and special commemorations of the church calendar. Gneuss lists 133 hymns found in English Benedictine hymnals by the 10th and 11th centuries. Chrysogonus Waddell's study of the development of the 12th-century Cistercian hymnal in France reveals how a conservative hymn repertory might fluctuate in response to changes in monastic thinking. Waddell observes the "pioneer" monks of Molesme, who left that monastery to found the abbey of Cîteaux, arriving at their new site in 1098 with their traditional hymnal of over eighty hymns in hand. This collection was soon abandoned in favor of a much-reduced collection of only thirty-four hymns, which the monks felt was more purely Ambrosian and thus closer to St. Benedict's ideal. When these hymns, amid some liturgical controversy between Bernard of Clairvaux and Peter Abélard, proved inadequate for even the simple services of the Cistercians, a third collection was introduced after 1147 that incorporated all the original thirty-four hymns and twenty-five additional works; none of these was newly composed, but many were anonymously divided, revised, and assigned new melodies and new places in the liturgy.

In the same period, Peter Abélard himself composed over ninety completely new hymns for various occasions that were added to the large hymnal used by the nuns at Héloïse's convent of the Paraclete. In the 13th century, members of the recently founded preaching orders, the Franciscans (including St. Bonaventure) and the Dominicans (including St. Thomas Aquinas), produced new hymns for their own evolving spiritual purposes. As a result of all this activity, a huge body of hymns on many subjects came to exist by the close of the Middle Ages. Joseph Szövérffy, to cite but one example, has compiled 152 hymns written about St. Peter between the 4th and the 16th centuries.

Various poetic meters were used in the composition of medieval Latin hymns, but after the earliest period meters consisted largely of accentual patterns that had developed out of older quantitative classical meters; patterns of stressed and unstressed Latin syllables came regularly to replace the older meters that had been defined by sequences of long and short syllables. Bruno Stäblein lists the eleven most important medieval Latin hymn meters, the commonest being the iambic dimeter line in use as early as Ambrose's compositions. Each hymn strophe contained a series of metrically, or at least syllabically, identical lines. (Hymns written in distichs were the only common exception to this rule.) The number of lines per strophe was not fixed, but within an individual hymn each strophe was constructed like all the others.

The earliest hymnals with music begin to appear in the 11th and 12th centuries. Hymn texts and tunes circulated widely; few hymn tunes are found uniquely linked with particular texts; all hymn texts composed in one meter could in theory be sung to the same melody. Waddell's reconstructed early Cistercian hymnal, for example, contains only nineteen hymn melodies for its thirty-four hymn texts (all but two in iambic dimeter).

Polyphonic hymns proper emerge in France, as in the rest of Europe, only toward the close of the Middle Ages, though certain hymn texts or fragments of texts were earlier used in the composition of motets. Besides a collection of ten hymns for three voices from the late 14th century, probably composed for the papal court in Avignon, multiple-voice hymn settings begin with the French composer Guillaume Dufay (1397–1474). About thirty of his settings survive, all for three voices; they include versions of *Ave maris stella*, *Veni creator spiritus*, and *Pange lingua*. Dufay's hymn settings all tend to follow the same pragmatic pattern: an old liturgical melody is adopted with slight elaboration and two new voices composed in rhythmic parallel to the original melody. Dufay was enormously influential in his own lifetime, and much of the history of the polyphonic hymn in the 15th century consists of contemporary composers writing adaptations of his work.

The vernacular religious song in France has a long if tenuous career, but hymns proper appear only in Latin before the 15th century. The earliest traces of religious songs in the vernacular go back to a four-note fragment of text from the late 8th century and a *cantilena* (without music) in honor of St. Eulalie dated to the first third of the 9th century. By the late 12th and early 13th centuries significant numbers of religious sequences, *lais*, *descorts*, and chansons began to appear, but not hymns strictly speaking. A manuscript (B.N. fr. 964) of 1415 contains the first complete collection of vernacular hymns for the whole cycle of the liturgical year, all based loosely on Latin originals and most in meters appropriate to the old liturgical tunes, as in this version of Ambrose's iambic dimeter *Aeterne rerum conditor.*

(Aeterne rerum conditor,
noctem diemque qui regis
et temporum das tempora,
ut alleves fastidium.)

Tu, des estoilles Conditeur,
Des créans durable lumière,
Crist, Rédempteur et visiteur
De tous, oy nostre humble prière.

Such "translations" became increasingly common through the 15th century, appearing in books of hours and later in 16th-century printed hymn collections.

Thomas C. Moser, Jr.

[See also: *ANALECTA HYMNICA MEDII AEVI;* PRAYERS AND DEVOTIONAL MATERIALS; *SAINTE EULALIE, SEQUENCE DE*]

Dreves, Guido Maria, Clemens Blume, and Henry Marriot Bannister, eds. *Analecta Hymnica Medii Aevi.* 55 vols. Leipzig: Fues's Verlag, 1886–90 (Vols. 1–8); Leipzig: Reisland, 1890–1922 (Vols. 9–55).

Waddell, Chrysogonus, ed. *The Twelfth-Century Cistercian Hymnal.* 2 vols. Trappist: Gethsemeni Abbey, 1984.

Walpole, Arthur Sumner, ed. *Early Latin Hymns.* Cambridge: Cambridge University Press, 1922.

Gastoué, Amédée. *Le cantique populaire en France.* Lyon: Janin, 1924.

Gneuss, Helmut. *Hymnar und Hymnen im englischen Mittelalter.* Tübingen: Niemeyer, 1968.

Messenger, Ruth Ellis. *The Medieval Latin Hymn.* Washington, D.C.: Capital, 1953.

Stäblein, Bruno. *Hymnen: Die mittelalterlichen Hymnenmelodien des Abendlandes.* Kassel: Bärenreiter, 1956.

Szövérffy, Joseph. *A Concise History of Medieval Latin Hymnody.* Leiden: Brill, 1985.

———. *A Mirror of Medieval Culture: St. Peter Hymns of the Middle Ages.* New Haven: Connecticut Academy of Arts and Sciences, 1965.

———. *Repertorium hymnologicum novum.* Berlin: Classical Folia, 1983– .

I

ICONOGRAPHY OF MUSIC. A subdiscipline of musicology that can be practised in two fundamentally different ways. One can view an artwork as no more than a source of evidence for some question of music history, or one can seek first to understand the work on its own terms and look upon any evidentiary finding as a fragile by-product. The former approach was widely employed at an earlier stage, particularly in pursuit of information on the history of medieval and Renaissance musical instruments and instrumental usage. It resulted frequently in naive error due to an insufficient knowledge of artistic style and iconographic convention. The second approach has gained the ascendancy in recent years as music historians have become more sophisticated in the methodology of art-historical iconography. They remain interested in some of the earlier questions and continue to pursue them in a more cautious manner, but more often they show interest in matters of cultural and intellectual history with a musical dimension. Some of the best examples of musical iconography take a single artwork with musical subject matter and seek simply to explore its meaning in the fullest possible sense. The methodology is that of the art historian, but the music historian adds to this the special insights and knowledge of the second discipline.

In addition to the work of individual musicologists, the development of musical iconography owes much to the organization *Répertoire International d'Iconographie Musicale* (founded in 1971 by a group of scholars led by Barry S. Brook), particularly for the numerous national and international conferences it has sponsored. Mention should be made also of the highly respected journal of musical iconography, *Imago Musicae*, edited by Tilman Seebass since its founding in 1984.

James McKinnon

[See also: MUSICAL INSTRUMENTS; MUSICAL PERFORMANCE PRACTICE]

Brown, Howard, and Joan Lascelle. *Musical Iconography.* Cambridge: Harvard University Press, 1972.

McKinnon, James. "Iconography." In *Musicology in the 1980's,* ed. Dallas Kern Holoman and Claude V. Palisca. New York: Da Capo, 1982, pp. 79–93.

IDYLLIC ROMANCE. The idyllic romance (*roman idyllique*) describes the juvenile love of its hero and heroine, whose emotional union is threatened by differences in religious or social background. The variations on this theme include the inappropriate love of a Saracen slave for a Christian knight and the attraction of a lesser noble for a woman of higher rank. Family opposition often leads to separation. Some romances show the departure of the hero to foreign lands, where he proves his worth in combat; others depict the exile of both hero and heroine and their separate struggles against pirates, would-be seducers, and rival knights. However, all ends happily with the reunion and marriage of the couple, once death has overtaken the dissenting parents. The settings of the romances are varied, ranging from a stylized Byzantine or Arthurian background to a more realistic French, German, or Scandinavian context. The plot incorporates traditional themes, including the exile-and-return motif, usually part of the hero's adventures, but sometimes duplicated in the experiences of the heroine. The rivalry between an official and unofficial suitor and the landless knight's achievement on the battlefield, overcoming objections to the young couple's *mésalliance*, are also featured. The idyllic hero's sufferings, based on the Ovidian pathology of love, threaten to keep him from victory. His lady, often indifferent to love at first, also yields to the sweet sickness, sometimes with amusing rapidity. Titles frequently feature the names of both hero and heroine, a device to indicate their equal beauty, worth, and suffering, which has led to suggestions that Chrétien's *Erec et Enide* be labeled an idylic romance.

Floire et Blancheflor (first version, ca. 1160; second version, 13th c.) is a classic combination of the genre's main themes. The hero and heroine, separated by religion but united in the intensity and precocity of their love, are driven apart but reunited through the hero's efforts. Later romances develop the melodrama of the plot, becoming openly parodic in the case of *Aucassin et Nicolette*, which, against a traditional background of exile and reunion, playfully inverts many of the narrative and characterizational conventions of medieval fiction. *Amadas et Ydoine* (1190–1220) plays heavily on the lovesick hero and introduces an atmosphere of magic and the supernatural. Jean Renart's

Escoufle (ca. 1202) traces the love and separation of Guillaume and Aelis, who had been brought up together at the imperial court. Roughly contemporaneous, *Galeran de Bretagne* by a certain Renaut follows the wanderings of the hero, son of the count of Brittany, who had met and fallen in love with Frêne, abandoned by her mother, fearful that the birth of twins would lead to accusations of infidelity. The anonymous early 13th-century *Guillaume de Palerne* tells of Guillaume's love for Melior and his protection in childhood and in his later exile by a werewolf. *Blancandin et l'Orgueilleuse d'Amour* (ca. 1230) is preserved in five manuscripts, one of which (*A*: B.N. fr. 19152) contains a much curtailed version. The lady's hostility to love, reminiscent of La Fière in Hue de Rotelande's *Ipomedon*, is vanquished by the hero's victory over her pagan enemy, King Alimodes. The work was composed by a "mestre Requis," whom Foerster has identified with the author of *Richars li biaus* (in his edition of the latter). In the 15th century, Jean de Créquy produced a prose version of the tale. Robert de Blois's *Floris et Lyriopé* (ca. 1250) has the ill-starred Narcissus as the product of his hero and heroine's youthful liaison. *Cristal et Clarie* (ca. 1268), extant in only one manuscript (Arsenal 3516), depicts the hero's quest for a woman he has glimpsed in a dream. There is disputed attribution of the fabliau *Guillaume au faucon* to the author of this romance. *Sone de Nausay* (late 13th c.) depicts the hero's rejection by the girl he had loved, his pursuit of adventure in England, Scotland, and Norway, his marriage with the daughter of the king of this country, and his elevation to emperor. *Floriant et Florete* (ca. 1250–75) reworks in an Arthurian setting the elopement of its hero and heroine. *Eledus et Serene* has its heroine, a rich princess, fall in love with the son of a count who wins her from her official suitor.

In the 14th and 15th centuries variations on the idyllic theme include *Cleomadès et Clarmondine* by Philippe Camus, *Cleriadus et Meliadice*, *Pamphile et Galatée*, and *Ponthus et Sidoine*.

The *roman idyllique* introduces the poignancy of young love into traditional romance themes, including the hero and heroine's progress toward maturity through the experience of loss and reunion, and their ritual courtship leading to marriage and social integration.

Meg Shepherd

[See also: *AMADAS ET YDOINE; AUCASSIN ET NICOLETTE;* CHRÉTIEN DE TROYES; *ELEDUS ET SERENE, ROMAN DE; FLOIRE ET BLANCHEFLOR; GUILLAUME DE PALERNE;* HUE DE ROTELANDE; *PIERRE DE PROVENCE ET LA BELLE MAGUELONNE;* REALISTIC ROMANCES; ROBERT DE BLOIS]

Lot-Borodine, Myrrha. *Le roman idyllique au moyen-âge.* Paris: Picard, 1913.

Payen, Jean-Charles. "Le moyen âge." In *La littérature française,* ed. Claude Pichois. Paris: Arthaud, 1970, pp. 172–73.

IMAGE DU MONDE. A hugely popular didactic poem by the otherwise unknown Gossuin (or Gautier) de Metz; the dialect is that of Lorraine. It exists in three redactions of various lengths (from 6,600 to over 10,000 octosyllabic lines), of which the first and shortest, supposedly offered in 1246 to Robert d'Artois, brother of St. Louis, was by far the most widely known (sixty-seven manuscripts). The work is divided into three sections: an introduction to science (twenty-one chapters, including twenty-eight illustrations), geography and meteorology (nineteen chapters, nine illustrations), and astronomy (twenty-eight chapters, nine illustrations). Principal sources are Honorius of Autun's *Imago mundi,* Jacques de Vitry's *Historia Hierosolymitana,* Alexander Neckham's *De naturis rerum,* and Alain de Lille's *Anticlaudianus.* Like other encyclopedists of the period, the author treats such diverse subjects as the Seven Liberal Arts, the four elements, the shape of the earth (round), and celestial and terrestrial geography. His influence can be found in Matfre Ermengaud's *Breviari d'Amor,* in the prose *Sidrac,* and in Jehan Bonnet's *Placides et Timeo.*

William W. Kibler

[See also: JEHAN BONNET: MATFRE ERMENGAUD; *SIDRAC, ROMAN DE*]

Langlois, Charles-Victor. *La vie en France au moyen âge, du XIIe au milieu du XIVe siècle.* 4 vols. Paris: Hachette, 1925–28, Vol. 3: *La connaissance de la nature et du monde,* pp. 135–97.

INDULGENCES. Ecclesiastical actions, usually papal or episcopal, granting full or partial remission of the temporal punishment (*poena*), but not the guilt (*culpa*), due to sins. Indulgences appear in the 11th century, become prominent in the 12th, and thereafter form an important part of medieval religious belief and practice. The substitution of a lighter penance (prayers, almsgiving) for a longer or more severe penance can be found in the Carolingian period and even earlier, but this is not the equivalent of an indulgence, which frees a person from the temporal punishment required after confession of sin and priestly absolution.

The first widespread papal grants of indulgences occurred in connection with the Crusades. When calling for the First Crusade in 1095, Pope Urban II declared an indulgence granting full forgiveness (hence a "plenary indulgence") of all temporal punishment for all crusaders who confessed their sins. This had the effect of declaring that a knight who died on crusade would enter Heaven immediately after death, since he would have no temporal penance to carry out.

By the early 13th century, a plenary indulgence could be gained by contributing money, or even advice, toward the Crusades. Somewhat later, papal decrees allowed individuals to purchase letters allowing a confessor to grant the individual possessing the letter a plenary indulgence at the point of death. By the 14th century, it was possible to obtain a letter authorizing even a layperson to read a formula that decreed forgiveness of punishment *and* guilt (at the point of death).

Not all indulgences were full; many offered forgiveness of a finite time of punishment measured in days or in years. Such indulgences might be gained by going on pilgrimage, contributing to church building, attending a church dedication, visiting a shrine at a specific festival, building bridges, and the like. The Fourth Lateran Council (1215) sought to limit the extent of the forgiveness granted by such indulgences, but the tendency was to expand the occasions for granting and the length of penitential time forgiven.

The 14th century saw the development of plenary papal indulgences in connection with specific years for pilgrimage to Rome ("Jubilee Years"). Boniface VIII decreed a plenary indulgence for all Christians who confessed their sins and made pilgrimage to the churches of the Apostles in Rome in the year 1300 (and every hundred years thereafter). Clement VI shortened the interval between Jubilee Years to fifty, while also predicating the papal grant of indulgences on the idea of the "Treasury of Merits" of Christ, whose sacrificial death provided a superabundance of merits that were to be dispensed to the faithful through the authority of the pope, as God's vicar on earth, in granting full and partial indulgences. The Dominican theologian Hugues de Saint-Cher had already linked indulgences to the theory of a "treasury of merits" built up through the merits of Christ, the Virgin Mary, and the saints and administered by the church. Urban VI, in 1389, reduced the Jubilee interval to thirty-three years; Paul II, in 1470, reduced it to twenty-five, which is the modern interval. At this same time, papal privileges were being granted to local churches and shrines to such an extent that the journey to Rome finally became unnecessary for gaining a sufficient indulgence.

An innovation with significant impact on late-medieval and early-modern religious life took place in 1476, when Sixtus IV granted a plenary indulgence for souls in Purgatory and declared that it was possible for the living to obtain indulgences for the dead to shorten their time in Purgatory. From the early centuries, Christian belief and practice asserted that alms and prayers offered by the living could be effective in shortening the time that persons might suffer the purifying fires and pains of purgation before entering Heaven. Sixtus, however, claimed that the papal power extended beyond the span of this life to offer the possibility of remission of temporal punishment for sin to those languishing in Purgatory, and to offer this in return for a money payment or a specific devotional act made by a living individual.

Grover A. Zinn

[See also: HUGUES DE SAINT-CHER; PURGATORY]

Lea, Henry Charles. *A History of Auricular Confession and Indulgences in the Latin Church.* 3 vols. Philadelphia: Lea Brothers, 1896.

Paulus, Nicolaus. *Geschichte des Ablasses im Mittelalter vom Ursprunge bis zur Mitte des 14. Jahrhunderts.* 2 vols. Paderborn: Schoningh, 1922–23.

———. *Indulgences as a Social Factor in the Middle Ages,* trans. J. Elliot Ross. New York: Devin-Adair, 1922.

Southern, Richard W. *Western Society and the Church in the Middle Ages.* Harmondsworth: Penguin, 1970, pp. 136–43.

INNOCENT III (r. 1198–1216). Pope. The period between the death of Alexander III and the election of Lotario dei Seigni as Innocent III in 1198 was comparatively peaceful for the papacy. A series of elderly popes, some members of a party conciliatory to the Hohenstaufen, concentrated on ecclesiastical business, on responding to Saladin's capture of Jerusalem (1187), and on combating the rise of Cathar and Waldensian heresy in southern France. The coronation of Innocent inaugurated a new phase of political activity by the papacy, coupled with further efforts to reform the clergy and launch a crusade.

Lotario, a member of the Roman nobility, had studied theology at Paris and had gained a grounding in canon law. These studies made him a competent theologian, exegete, and preacher; on this traditional basis, he would build new interpretations of old texts, expanding papal jurisdiction "by reason of sin" (*ratione peccati*) into an ability to supervise the princes of Christendom. Lotario's most famous theological work, *De miseria conditionis humanae,* emphasized the brevity and pain of human life; but this may help explain his concept of the clergy, especially the pope, as mediating between God and humanity, able to work for peace and justice, as well as for orthodoxy and reform. Innocent III adopted Bernard of Clairvaux's description of the Roman pontiff as the "vicar of Christ," which became a key papalist term, replacing an older emphasis on the Roman pontiff as vicar of Peter.

Innocent benefited from a crisis of leadership in both the ecclesiastical and secular spheres. Emperor Frederick I Barbarossa's son, Henry VI, had died young, leaving his son, Frederick, heir to Sicily and to a claim on the empire, as the pope's ward. Philip II Augustus of France and John Lackland of England were at odds, and the English nobility was restive. The Byzantine empire was weak, and the crusader states were under siege. The bishops of France were unable to deal with the Cathars, and the Cistercians were losing the influence they had enjoyed when Bernard was alive.

The Roman pontiff intervened in these situations with adroit and persistent efforts, supported by well-reasoned papal letters. Even the legitimation of a French nobleman's bastard could be the occasion for a declaration, in the decretal *Per venerabilem,* that the French kingdom was not subject to the empire. A dispute over the imperial succession in Germany allowed Innocent to keep the Hohenstaufen weak, while establishing a claim that the pope could review the election of a king of the Romans. Frederick II was supported in Sicily but with an intention of keeping the *Regno* separate from the empire. Efforts to reconcile Philip and John were unsuccessful, as the Capetians gained control of Normandy, and Philip refused to take back Ingeborg of Denmark as his wife. On the one hand, through the imposition of an interdict, Innocent was able to compel John to accept Stephen Langton as archbishop of Canterbury and to become a vassal of the Holy See. On the other hand, Innocent supported his new vassal by declaring *Magna carta* void, helping embroil John in a civil war in which the French intervened.

Innocent's crusading policy had mixed fortunes. A Spanish army defeated the Muslims of Spain and North

Africa at Las Navas de Tolosa (1212), but the Fourth Crusade went awry, being diverted to Constantinople by Venice and a refugee prince. The storming and sack of that city in 1204 permanently embittered Byzantine relations with the West, but Innocent, although displeased, agreed to establish a Latin emperor and patriarch there. A less traditional crusade was that against the Cathars, launched by Innocent after the murder of one of his legates by a vassal of the count of Toulouse in 1208. At first, this campaign was led by Simon de Montfort; only after his death would the Capetian monarchy take over, using the crusade to gain control of Languedoc.

A more adventurous policy was implemented in ecclesiastical affairs. Numerous decretals expanded the role of Rome as the arbiter of justice for the clergy. New religious orders, the more mobile mendicant friars, were favored as teachers of sound doctrine in opposition to heresy. Dominic's Order of Preachers (Dominicans) arose in southern France to combat the Cathars; Francis's Friars Minor (Franciscans), dedicated to poverty, arose in urban Italy, which had its own problems with heresy. The secular clergy resented these friars, whose reception of alms diminished the income of parish priests and whose papal privileges undermined old lines of authority. Much of medieval ecclesiology was evolved in disputes over the limits of such interventions in local sees and parishes.

Innocent's last achievement was the great Fourth Lateran Council (1215), which was intended to promote yet another crusade. The assembly legislated for all Christendom. Orthodox doctrine was reaffirmed; preaching was encouraged, even as the proliferation of new orders was discouraged. One canon compelled all believers to confess their sins to their own priests at least once a year, during Lent or Eastertide, and to receive communion, the Easter duty that has remained a part of canon law. These canons and Innocent's numerous decretals became important parts of the first official collection of canon law, the *Gregorian decretals* (1234).

Thomas M. Izbicki

[See also: ALBIGENSIAN CRUSADE; CATHARS; CRUSADES; DECRETALS; INQUISITION]

Lotario dei Segni (Pope Innocent III). *On the Misery of the Human Condition (De miseria humane conditionis)*, trans. Margaret Mary Dietz. Indianapolis: Bobbs-Merrill, 1969.

———. *Die Register Innocenz' III*, ed. Othmar Hageneder and Anton Haidacher with Herta Eberstaller et al. 2 vols. Graz: Böhlau, 1964–79.

Tanner, Norman P., ed. *Decrees of the Ecumenical Councils*. 2 vols. London: Sheed and Ward, 1990, Vol. 1, pp. 227–71. [Fourth Lateran Council—1215.]

Barraclough, Geoffrey. *The Medieval Papacy*. New York: Harcourt, Brace and World, 1968.

Hamilton, Bernard. *The Medieval Inquisition*. New York: Holmes and Meier, 1981.

Imkamp, Wilhelm. *Das Kirchenbild Innocenz' III. (1198–1216)*. Stuttgart: Hiersemann, 1983.

Morris, Colin. *The Papal Monarchy: The Western Church from 1050 to 1250*. Oxford: Clarendon, 1989.

Pennington, Kenneth. "The Legal Education of Pope Innocent III." *Bulletin of Medieval Canon Law* 4 (1984): 70–77.

Tierney, Brian. *The Crisis of Church and State, 1050–1300*. Englewood Cliffs: Prentice-Hall, 1964, pp. 127–38.

Tillmann, Helene. *Papst Innocenz III*. Bonn: Röhrscheid, 1954.

INNOCENT V (d. 1276). Pope. When Gregory X died early in 1276, the first papal election under the provisions of the decree *Ubi periculum* of the Second Council of Lyon (1274) was conducted. The cardinals quickly elected Pierre de Tarantaise, who reigned as Innocent V for fewer than six months. Pierre had become a Dominican in Lyon ca. 1240. He had studied and taught at Paris, composing a well-known commentary on Peter Lombard's *Sententiae*. After helping formulate the Dominican program of studies, twice serving as provincial of France and preaching the crusade for Clement IV, Pierre was elevated by Gregory X to the archbishopric of Lyon in 1272. Made a cardinal in 1273, Pierre took part in the Council of Lyon, preaching the funeral sermon for St. Bonaventure. Gregory had allied himself with Rudolph of Habsburg to diminish Angevin influence on the papacy. Innocent reversed this policy, postponing Rudolph's imperial coronation indefinitely. The new pope did try to continue his predecessor's policy of conciliating the Byzantines, but Charles of Anjou, who had eastern ambitions, pressured him into weakening this effort. When Innocent died, Charles, in gratitude, built his tomb. Leo X beatified Innocent in 1898.

Thomas M. Izbicki

Innocent V. *Innocentii V . . . in IV libros sententiarum commentaria . . .* , ed. Thomas Turco and Johannes Baptista de Marinis. 4 vols. Toulouse: Colomerium, 1649–52.

Gill, Joseph. *Byzantium and the Papacy, 1198–1400*. New Brunswick: Rutgers University Press, 1979.

Laurent, M.-H. *Beatus Innocentius V (Petrus de Tarantasio OP) studia et documenta*. Roma: Sabinae, 1943.

INNS/INNKEEPING. *See* TRAVEL

INQUISITION. In medieval Latin, the term *inquisitio* generally conveyed the sense of investigation or inquest. Charlemagne's agents, the *missi dominici*, conducted inquests; William the Conqueror's survey that produced Domesday Book was an *inquisitio*. Emperor Henry IV encountered opposition from the Saxons when he attempted to conduct an *inquisitio* concerning lost royal rights in Saxony. Thus, the investigation of religious dissent, the practice with which the word "inquisition" has been most closely identified, was in a major sense merely another form of investigation by an authority competent to inaugurate an inquest and carry it out.

Other forms of *inquisitio* included the obligation of bishops to make visitations to the religious institutions of their dioceses and to correct wrongs found during such visitations. Various forms of *inquisitio* were used in the church, usually against erring or criminous clergy, more frequently after 1200. These instances of the term probably echoed older Roman criminal legal procedure, which from the 1st century tended to supplant an older private accusatorial criminal procedure with one in which the magistrate or judge assumed the responsibility for assembling evidence and carrying out a criminal trial. This process was technically known as *cognitio extraordinaria*. In another instance, inquisition might be made into the writings of a scholar accused of error.

With the emergence of formalized and institutionalized papal authority in the 11th century and classical canon law in the mid-12th, other dimensions were added to *inquisitio*. Papally delegated investigators and judges were instituted and in some instances could subdelegate all or part of their judicial authority to others. With the growth of widespread forms of religious dissent, popes urged bishops to investigate heresy in their own dioceses and appointed monastic figures to preach against it. This combination of delegation and appointment was not restricted to matters of dissent, however; popes also appointed preachers of the Crusades and later constituted the Order of Preachers (Dominicans) and delegated judicial authority for other matters as well.

Earlier episcopal attempts to discover heresy were hampered by the survival in many regions of the accusatorial procedure—that is, someone had to accuse publicly those he suspected of heresy. In 1162, however, Pope Alexander III wrote to Henry, archbishop of Reims, ordering an archiepiscopal inquest into reported heresy in Flanders. The next year, at the Council of Tours, Alexander included a canon indicating that heretics were to be sought out by local ecclesiastical authorities. Another canon, c. 10 of Tours, stated that "it is expedient to discover new remedies for new maladies," and some of Alexander III's other correspondence indicates a concern for the secrecy of heretics and could be considered a rationale for requiring the *inquisitio* procedure in this instance.

As for the laity, Alexander also allowed the procedure of denunciation—that is, accusation without the responsibilities normally incumbent on the accuser. This was a form of the *denunciatio evangelica* that with accusation and inquisition came to be regarded as the three standard means of making a crime known to authorities. Denunciations were to be made by suitable people, synodal witnesses—*testes synodales*, a principle laid out in the well-known decretal of Alexander III, *Ad abolendam* of 1184, which also insisted that the ordinaries (bishops) of dioceses conduct hearings of these special witnesses for the purpose of discovering heresy.

As the perception of the extent and danger of heresy increased, more and more severe penalties were imposed by both ecclesiastical and temporal powers for those convicted. Crusades against heretics were launched, and the use of the inquest increased during the pontificate of Innocent III (1198–1216). In 1199, Innocent III appointed the abbots of Cîteaux and other Cistercian monasteries to hold inquests in Metz in matters of dissent, and in the process of rationalizing the prosecution of criminous clerics, Innocent commanded that they be proceeded against by the *inquisitio* method rather than by accusation. Recent scholarship has indicated how important the changing criminal law of clergy now seems to have been for developments in criminal procedure generally.

In the wake of the Albigensian Crusade, the pope and the king of France collaborated upon the general constitution of inquisitorial tribunals throughout the kingdom, established in the *ordonnance Cupientes* of 1229. *Cupientes* established, as Maisonneuve stated, "the inquisitorial procedure, by virtue of which all vassals and officers of the king were obliged specifically to seek out heretics and accomplices to heresy." In the same year, the Council of Toulouse formalized the episcopal inquisition. With the increasing importance of the mendicant orders, particularly the Dominicans, in the early 13th century, mendicant inquisitors joined mendicant confessors and preachers. After the disastrous inquisitorial experiments of Robert le Bougre in 1233–35, Dominicans began to be used regularly as inquisitors, even in episcopal inquisitions.

Inquisitorial tribunals flourished most effectively in the south of France, but in 1310 Marguerite Porete became the first capital victim of the inquisitors at Paris, followed by the destruction of the Templars in 1316. The case of Jeanne d'Arc in 1431 reflects the increasingly prominent role in the inquisitional tribunals not only of the Dominicans but of the faculty of theology at the University of Paris and continued the close collaboration among episcopal, mendicant, and political authorities.

From the 14th century through the 16th, the faculty of theology of Paris provided most of the inquisitorial activity in France.

Edward Peters

[See also: ALBIGENSIAN CRUSADE; ALEXANDER III; BERNARD GUI; HERESY; JEANNE D'ARC; MARGUERITE PORETE]

Barber, Malcolm. *The Trial of the Templars*. Cambridge: Cambridge University Press, 1978.

Lambert, Malcolm. *Medieval Heresy: Popular Movements from the Gregorian Reform to the Reformation*. 2nd ed. Oxford: Blackwell, 1992.

Lea, Henry Charles. *A History of the Inquisition of the Middle Ages*. 3 vols. New York: Harper, 1887.

———. *The Inquisition of the Middle Ages, Its Organization and Operation*. New York: Citadel, 1954.

Maisonneuve, Henri. *Études sur les origines de l'inquisition*. 2nd ed. Paris: Vrin, 1960.

Pernoud, Régine. *Joan of Arc by Herself and Her Witnesses*, trans. Edward Hyams. New York: Stein and Day, 1968.

Peters, Edward. *Inquisition*. Berkeley: University of California Press, 1989.

Somerville, Robert. *Pope Alexander III and the Council of Tours (1162)*. Berkeley: University of California Press, 1977.

Wakefield, Walter L. *Heresy, Crusade and Inquisition in Southern France, 1100–1250*. Berkeley: University of California Press, 1974.

INSTRUMENTS. *See* ASTRONOMICAL AND NAVIGATIONAL INSTRUMENTS

INVESTITURE (FEUDAL). Investiture was the act by which a lord transferred possession of a fief to a vassal. After homage was rendered, the lord would hand his vassal an object, such as a baton, twig, or turf representing the fief. Knights granting their fiefs to monasteries often did so by placing "twig and turf" on the altar. In other cases, a feudal tenant would divest himself by placing his hands in those of the local bishop, who in turn would invest the recipient. With the spread of written homages from the late 12th century, sealed charters transferring title in effect constituted investiture and often replaced the physical act.

Theodore Evergates

[See also: FEUDALISM; FIEF/FEUDUM; FIEF-HOLDING; *FIEF-RENTE*; HOMAGE]

Forquin, Guy. *Lordship and Feudalism in the Middle Ages*, trans. Iris and A.K. Lytton Sells. New York: Pica, 1976.
Ganshof, François L. *Feudalism*, trans. Philip Grierson. New York: Harper, 1961.

INVESTITURE CONTROVERSY. *See* GREGORIAN REFORM

IRMINON, POLYPTICH OF. The "polyptich," a multi-leaved document used from late Roman times through the 14th century, inventoried an estate or seigneurie with tenants, as well as their obligations in kind or in money and services. Irminon, abbot of Saint-Germain-des-Prés, had his survey, the most informative of all those that survive from the early Middle Ages, redacted between ca. 807 and ca. 825, naming approximately 8,000 people residing on the 1,378 farms of the abbey, squeezed into "population islands" surrounded by forests and wastelands. This first comprehensive catalogue treats peasant households (*familia*) in the medieval rather than the classical sense. Cited as units of measurement in the 7th century, *familia*, equivalent to the "hide" in England and the *mansus* in Italy, became generally used in the 8th for a peasant farm. The virtual end of slavery caused the family farm, normally inalienable and inheritable, to become the basic agricultural unit.

Although difficult to read and full of lacunae, Irminon's survey indicates that there were 135 males for every 100 females in the twenty-seven *brevia*, surveys of individual estates held by the abbey, that counted 4,188 males, 3,556 females, with 939 indeterminable as to sex. That ratio was common, except after wars, to most non-European as well as European societies before the 18th century because of high death rates in childbirth and because infanticide of females exceeded that of males. The survey of the landholdings of the Italian monastery of Farfa made between 789 and 822, where males outnumber females by 122 to 100, like other surveys even of late-medieval Europe, almost always provide similar ratios.

In Irminon's polyptich, the average family consisted of 5.75 people, each of whom worked approximately 120 acres. No grandfathers and only twenty-six grandmothers were recorded. Extended lateral families predominated. The 2,006 men and 2,200 boys against 1,975 women and 1,569 girls gives a ratio clearly beneath replacement needs, so that the population must have been shrinking. Marriages were apparently relatively late for females as well as for males, husbands being about nine years older than their wives and many men not marrying at all.

William A. Percy, Jr.

[See also: POPULATION AND DEMOGRAPHY]

Guérard, Benjamin, ed. *Polyptyque de l'abbé Irminon; ou, Dénombrement des manses, des serfs et des revenus de l'abbaye de Saint-Germain-des-Prés sous le règne de Charlemagne.* 2 vols. Paris: Imprimerie Royale, 1844.

ISAAC OF STELLA (after 1100–1169/78). Born in England, Isaac became abbot of the small French Cistercian house of Stella, near Poitiers. Nothing is known of his life before he became abbot, but the nature of his thought and his use of technical theological language strongly suggest that he was a student in the schools of Paris and Chartres. He possibly came to France ca. 1130 and may have embraced the Cistercian life shortly after 1140, perhaps at Pontigny. Isaac was a strong supporter of Thomas Becket in the latter's conflict with the English king Henry II.

Isaac's writings include two widely read letters: *Letter on the Office of the Mass*, an allegorical interpretation of the liturgy, and *Letter on the Soul*, an important contribution to 12th-century theological anthropology. Fifty-five of his sermons survive. Like other Cistercian sermon collections, this one contains not only actual sermons but also literary works that were never given as sermons, despite the fictions of sermonic style. Several series of sermons suggest that Isaac intended them to be seen as a unit on a specific topic. Sermons 1–5 are a commentary on the beatitudes that presents the stages of the spiritual life. Sermons 7–12, 14, and 15, address the fall and redemption of humans in a systematic way. Sermons 18–26 (on the Gospel parable of the sower) form a theological treatise on the divine nature. All of Isaac's sermons address topics of significance for the monastic life, but they do it from a perspective and with theological language shaped by his formation in the schools, for Isaac is a speculative theologian as well as a monastic embarked on a course of asceticism and prayer. Metaphysical and theological questions concerning the cosmos, creation, and redemption, Trinitarian theology, Neoplatonic influences (via Pseudo-Dionysius the Areopagite and Johannes Scottus Eriugena), the Incarnation, and the ultimate return to God (source of all) through Christ's work of redemption—these and other issues are handled with theological insight directed to the final purpose of guiding individuals on the spiritual path of contemplation.

Isaac left Stella ca. 1167 to establish a small monastic house on the desolate island of Ré, off the Atlantic coast near La Rochelle, that was later taken into the Cistercian order. Isaac died there, perhaps as early as 1169 or as late as 1178.

Grover A. Zinn

[See also: CISTERCIAN ORDER; ERIUGENA, JOHANNES SCOTTUS; PSEUDO-DIONYSIUS THE AREOPAGITE; THEOLOGY]

Isaac of Stella. *Sermons on the Christian Year*, trans. Hugh McCaffery. Kalamazoo: Cistercian, 1979. [Only one volume published.]
McGinn, Bernard, ed. *Three Treatises on Man: A Cistercian Anthropology*. Kalamazoo: Cistercian, 1977.
———. *The Golden Chain: A Study in the Theological Anthropology of Isaac of Stella*. Washington, D.C.: Cistercian, 1972.

ISABEAU OF BAVARIA (ca. 1370–1435). Queen of France. Born to Stephen, duke of Bavaria, and Taddea Visconti, Isabeau married Charles VI of France on July 17, 1385. Charles VI had fallen in love with her at their first meeting on July 14 and married her without a marriage contract or dowry. Their relationship was troubled by his schizophrenia, which caused him to have an ambivalent attitude toward her. Isabeau was adept at politics, and on July 1, 1402, Charles empowered her to deal with government business in his absence, aided by the dukes and whichever counselors she wished, but her prerogative was tempered in April 1403, when a group of royal ordinances attempted to achieve a balance of power among the royal relatives.

In 1405, Isabeau's court was accused of moral corruption and the queen herself was rebuked for instigating extravagant fashions by Jacques Legrand, an Augustinian friar. Until recently, historians have considered her frivolous and, more significantly, involved in an adulterous relationship with her brother-in-law, Louis of Orléans. The accusation of adultery first appeared in the anti-dauphin Paris of 1422–29, as part of an effort to throw doubts on the paternity of Charles VII. The myth found expression in the *Pastoralet*, a poem composed at that time to glorify John the Fearless of Burgundy, recently murdered at the dauphin's command.

Politically, Isabeau was quite unsupportive of Louis of Orléans until late 1404 or 1405, and she opposed John the Fearless until he rescued her from the exile imposed by the Armagnacs (Orléanist party) in 1417. Her objective from 1409 until that time had been to set up her eldest son as a replacement for the king during his periods of illness and thus keep the power to govern within the immediate royal family and away from the warring dukes. In January 1418, viewing the king and dauphin as prisoners of the Armagnacs in Paris, Isabeau formed a rival government with John the Fearless in Troyes. The Burgundian invasion of Paris in May 1418 produced a rapprochement between the king and queen but caused the departure of the dauphin, breaking the familial link that was essential to save the independence of the monarchy. Isabeau played an important role in the negotiations that led to the Treaty of Troyes (1420), and her policy of this period, aimed at protecting the monarchy, was long misinterpreted by historians as anti-French. Isabeau died at the Hôtel Saint-Pol in Paris in 1435.

Richard C. Famiglietti

[See also: ARMAGNACS; CHARLES VI]

Famiglietti, R.C. *Royal Intrigue: Crisis at the Court of Charles VI 1392–1420*. New York: AMS, 1986
Grandeau, Yann. "Les dernières années d'Isabeau de Bavière." *Cercle Archéologique et Historique de Valenciennes* 9 (1976): 411–28.
———. "Isabeau de Bavière, ou l'amour conjugal." *Actes du 102e Congrès National des Sociétés Savantes, Limoges 1977, Section de Philologie et d'Histoire jusqu'à 1610* (1979): 117–48.
Kimm, Heidrun. *Isabeau de Bavière, reine de France, 1370–1435*. Munich: Stadtarchiv München, 1969.
Thibault, Marcel. *Isabeau de Bavière, reine de France: la jeunesse 1370–1405*. Paris: Perrin, 1903.

ISABELLA OF FRANCE (1292–1358). Queen of England. The daughter of Philip IV and Jeanne of Navarre, Isabella of France was born at Paris and subsequently became queen of Edward II of England (r. 1307–27) and mother of Edward III (r. 1327–77). Her marriage, which had been under discussion as early as 1298, took place at Boulogne on January 25, 1308. After the execution of Edward's favorite, Piers Gaveston, Isabella played a leading role in mediating between her husband and his nobles (1312 and 1316). A chronicler of dubious reliability, Jean d'Outremeuse, alleged that Isabella was the one who told her father about the adultery of her sisters-in-law.

In 1321, a refusal to admit her to Leeds castle led to a new round of warfare between Edward II and his uncle Thomas of Lancaster, leading to Thomas's execution in March 1322. In September 1324, war broke out with her brother Charles IV of France, and Isabella was sent to negotiate (March 1325), followed by her son, the future Edward III, who did homage to Charles for Aquitaine and Ponthieu (September 14).

Isabella then formed a liaison with the exiled English rebel Roger Mortimer, refused to return to England, and traveled to Hainaut, where the young Edward was betrothed to the count's daughter, Philippa, whose dowry was used to hire mercenaries. Isabella and Mortimer invaded England on September 24, 1326, and the barons rose in favor of her son. Edward II was captured on November 16 and abdicated on January 20, 1327. In September, he was murdered in prison.

Isabella and Mortimer, made earl of March in September 1328, ruled England, making disadvantageous treaties with France (March 1327) and Scotland (May 1328), but on the night of October 18–19, 1330, the young Edward III seized power in a coup. He had Mortimer executed on November 29. Isabella no longer played a major role, although she regained Ponthieu and Montreuil in 1332 and was suggested as a mediator with France in 1348. She died at Hertford on August 23, 1358.

R. Thomas McDonald

[See also: EDWARD II; PHILIP IV THE FAIR; SAINT-SARDOS]

Blackley, F.D., and G. Hermanson. *The Household Book of Queen Isabella of England.* Edmonton: University of Alberta Press, 1971.

Hutchinson, H.F. *Edward II.* New York: Stein and Day, 1972.

ISORHYTHMIC MOTET. A 20th-century term applied to over 200 works of the 14th and early 15th centuries, characterized by a repeating pattern of rhythms (the *talea*) applied to the tenor. The tenor melody (*color*) is usually a *cantus firmus* borrowed from Gregorian chant. Above it, the phrase structure of motetus and triplum voices recurs at the same point above each *talea* statement. A clear hierarchy of rhythms differentiates the voices: the tenor (and contratenor, a fourth voice common by the mid-14th c.) moves at a slow rate, while triplum and motetus move quickly, exploiting rhythmic contrasts allowed by the Ars Nova notational system. The recurring nature of the form is emphasized through hocket, rhythmic sequences, changes in mensuration, or regular changes in texture.

The earliest examples appear as musical interpolations to a lavish copy of the *Livres de Fauvel* (second decade of the 14th c.). A unipartite plan, with constant rhythmic values in the tenor *talea*, is the most common formal disposition in the earliest works. By the second quarter of the century, bipartite motets with diminution were also cultivated, in which rhythmic values of the tenor *talea* are halved for a second section. Later in the century, isorhythmic motets were commonly written in several sections, with rhythmic values diminishing in a numerical ratio, such as 9:4:3:2 (*Portio nature/Ida capillorum* by Egidius de Pusieux; 1342), or even 18:12:10:5:9:10 (*Salve virgo/Vita via* by Billart; ca. 1400). Strict isorhythmic *taleae* appear in all voices after ca. 1350.

As in the 13th-century motet, triplum and motetus declaim different poems. Strophic patterns in the poetry are often reflected in the isorhythmic layout, with a new strophe beginning at the same point in each succeeding *talea*. Most 14th-century isorhythmic motets have Latin texts; the many French-texted motets of Machaut are exceptions, polyphonic settings of courtly poetry written before the consolidation of the fixed forms and the development of polyphonic chansons ca. 1340. Otherwise, motets often served as political or polemical works, perhaps celebrating a pope (Vitry's *Petre Clemens/Lugentium siccentur*) or a king (Royllart's *Rex Karole*), excoriating venal officials at the French court (Vitry's *Garrit gallus/In nova fert*), or lamenting conditions during the Hundred Years' War (Machaut's *Tu qui gregem/Plange regni respublica*).

Early 15th-century isorhythmic motets by Franco-Burgundian composers, such as Johannes Carmen, Nicholas Grenon, and Guillaume Dufay, and the forty anonymous isorhythmic motets in the Cypriot-French codex (Turin, Biblioteca Nazionale, J.II.9), continue many of the style traits established in the late 14th century. Royllart's *Rex Karole* (ca. 1375) served as a compositional model for some of these later works; dramatic rhythmic changes in the upper voices (hocket, rhythmic sequences, mensuration changes, etc.) articulate the midpoint or end of each tenor *talea*.

During the 1420s and 1430s, the isorhythmic motet absorbed foreign stylistic influences. Some works written in Italy by Dufay and by his Franco-Burgundian contemporaries display the influence of Italian motets (e.g., Johannes Brassart's *Ave Maria*), while the latest isorhythmic works by Dufay, Brassart, and Johannes de Sarto adopted English features.

Unlike motets of the preceding century, 15th-century works written in France, Burgundy, and at the French court of the Lusignan in Cyprus are almost exclusively sacred in character, mostly on texts venerating the Virgin. Excluding motets that Dufay and his contemporaries wrote for Italian patrons, there are few overt political or occasional references in these works. By ca. 1450, the isorhythmic motet had effectively disappeared as an independent genre, but its structural principles exerted a continuing influence upon late 15th-century motets and upon the increasingly prominent tenor Mass.

Lawrence Earp/J. Michael Allsen

[See also: ARS NOVA; BRASSART, JOHANNES; CYCLIC MASS; DUFAY, GUILLAUME; *FAUVEL, LIVRES DE*; HOCKET; MACHAUT, GUILLAUME DE; MOTET (13TH CENTURY); PHILIPPE DE VITRY]

Allsen, J. Michael. *Style and Intertextuality in the Isorhythmic Motet 1400–1440.* Diss. University of Wisconsin–Madison, 1992. Ann Arbor: UMI, 1992 [9231671].

Bent, Margaret. "The Late-Medieval Motet." In *Companion to Medieval and Renaissance Music*, ed. Tess Knighton and David Fallows. New York: Schirmer, 1992, pp. 114–19.

Fallows, David. *Dufay.* London: Dent, 1982, pp. 103–23.

Günther, Ursula. "The 14th-Century Motet and Its Development." *Musica Disciplina* 12 (1958): 27–58.

Leech-Wilkinson, Daniel. *Compositional Techniques in the Four-Part Isorhythmic Motets of Philippe de Vitry and His Contemporaries.* 2 vols. New York: Garland, 1989.

ISSOIRE. The former abbey church of Issoire (Puy-de-Dôme), dedicated to St. Austremoine, first bishop of the Auvergne, is the largest of a homogeneous group of Romanesque churches found within a twenty-mile radius of Clermont-Ferrand. With a sober architecture of great formal beauty, enlivened by elegant arcading and mosaics of colored volcanic stones, this group is characterized by a powerful "westwerk," a continuous barrel vault over the nave buttressed by quadrant vaults in the tribune, a multiplication of windows in the choir, and an ambulatory with radiating chapels. Most distinctive is the treatment of the crossing: on the interior, the dome on squinches is carried by Carolingian flying screens (diaphragm arches) and buttressed by the high quadrant vaults of the adjacent transept bays; on the exterior, the raised bays form an oblong lantern supporting the tower. The ornate chevet and powerful crypt are among the most beautiful in the Auvergne. The octagonal tower, the heavy façade, and the interior paint are 19th-century, and the famous historiated capitals of the choir have suffered from mutilation and restoration.

Jean M. French

15th-century stained-glass window of the Crucifixion; a 12th-century belfry, once a part of the city's walls; and an octagonal tower known as the Tour Blanche, built between 1187 and 1195 by Richard the Lionhearted. The tower is located within the castle walls, forming a "spur" in the southeast corner and surrounded on the other three sides by a moat. It had an original height of 99 feet and walls up to 13 feet thick.

Linda M. Rouillard

Erlande-Brandenburg, Alain. "La Tour Blanche à Issoudun." *Congrès archéologique (Bas-Berry)* 142 (1984): 129–38.
Vallery-Radot, Jean. "La Tour Blanche d'Issoudun (Indre)." In *Château-Gaillard, études de castellologie européenne, I: Colloque des Andelys, 30 mai–4 juin 1962.* Caen, 1964, pp. 149–60.

IVO OF CHARTRES (ca. 1040–1116). An outstanding bishop, reformer, canonist, and theologian, Ivo studied at Paris and with Lanfranc at the Norman abbey of Bec. He became prior of Saint-Quentin, an abbey of regular canons in Beauvais, ca. 1078. In 1090, he was made bishop of Chartres, where he remained until his death. While bishop, he compiled three important pre-Gratian collections of canon law: *Collectio tripartia, Decretum,* and *Panormia.* The *Panormia* was the most influential and was used as a source by Abélard and Hugh of Saint-Victor in their writings. Ivo was directly involved in the marriage dispute of King Philip I, as well as other instances of episcopal rulings on marriage law within the church. He was also involved in the Gregorian reform movement and in the regularizing of clerical life through the reform of cathedral chapters and the establishment of houses of regular canons. His correspondence of over 300 letters is a valuable source for knowledge of ecclesiastical and secular matters in his lifetime.

Grover A. Zinn

[See also: CANON LAW; GRATIAN; REGULAR CANONS]

Ivo of Chartres. *Opera.* PL 161–62.
———. *Yves de Chartres: Correspondance 1090–1098,* ed. and trans. Jean Leclercq. Paris: Les Belles Lettres, 1949.
Duby, Georges. *The Knight, the Lady, and the Priest,* trans. Barbara Bray. New York: Pantheon, 1983.

Issoire (Puy-de-Dôme), Saint-Austremoine, chevet. *Photograph courtesy of Whitney S. Stoddard.*

[See also: SAINT-NECTAIRE]

Craplet, Bernard. *Auvergne romane.* La Pierre-qui-vire: Zodiaque, 1962.
Ranguet, H. and E. du. "Abbatiale de Saint-Austremoine d'Issoire." *Bulletin monumental* 94 (1935): 277–313.
Sauget, B. and J.-M. *L'abbaye Saint-Austremoine d'Issoire.* Clermont-Ferrand: Reix, 1989.
Swiechowski, Zygmunt. *Sculpture romane d'Auvergne.* Clermont-Ferrand: Bussac, 1973.
Terrasse, Charles. *Congrès archéologique (Clermont-Ferrand)* 87 (1924): 80–100.

ISSOUDUN. Originally a Gallic settlement, the fortified site of Issoudun (Indre) played a role in the conflict between the Capetian and Plantagenêt dynasties. Part of Eleanor of Aquitaine's dowry to Henry II, it was seized by Philip II Augustus in 1187. Two years later, Richard I the Lionhearted inherited the territory but ceded it to Philip as part of the Treaty of Gisors. In 1195, one of Philip's officers betrayed him and took control of the tower in Richard's name. Philip attacked Issoudun again later in the same year.

Issoudun has several important medieval monuments: the Gothic church of Saint-Cyr, with a beautiful 14th- and

IVORIES. From antiquity through the Middle Ages, ivory was prized as a precious material. Ivory comes from tusks, bones, or teeth of animals. Elephant-tusk ivory is especially valued and was used in the Middle Ages along with whalebone and other materials. The ivory-carving techniques used simple tools similar to those used in woodcarving. In the Middle Ages, ivory was finished by polishing and often painting and gilding. Medieval ivories were also combined with metalwork and jewels.

Carved ivory pieces were used in France throughout the Middle Ages. In the Merovingian period, some ivory

Ivory: Crozier, 12th century, Florence, Bargello. *Photograph by Alinari/ Art Resources.*

carving was essentially a continuation in subject matter, especially religious scenes for liturgical furnishings, from late antiquity in Gaul. Other carvings displayed styles characteristic of Germanic tribes, such as the Franks. Ivory carving was one of many arts that experienced a revival during the Carolingian 9th century. Although production of ivories declined in the turbulent centuries following the fragmentation of the Carolingian empire, ivory carving was continued in French Romanesque art under the auspices of the church. In the Gothic period, ivory carving flourished in France. The Carolingian and Gothic eras were the two outstanding periods for the art of ivories in France.

From the Carolingian period, ivories that have survived were produced mainly as liturgical objects. They fall into the same stylistic categories as other art, such as manuscript illumination, that can be associated with either the court or with important abbeys. Many of the ivories were relief plaques used as book covers. As was typical of arts during the Carolingian renaissance, they were modeled on late-classical ivory diptychs and other objects. In ivories associated with Charlemagne's palace school, figures have a plastic monumentality despite their smaller scale. By contrast, the smaller, more animated figures from the Reims school are comparable with manuscript illumination from this center.

In the Gothic period, ivory carving was extremely popular in France. Paris was probably the leading French center producing Gothic ivories. Increased contacts with the East made the valued elephant ivory available in quan-

tity. A book of occupations, the *Livre des métiers* (1260), lists four categories of ivory carvers: painters and carvers of images, sculptors and crucifix carvers, comb and lantern makers, and those who made knife handles and writing tablets. Other areas in France also were active in the production of ivories, but their portability makes ivory carvings difficult to localize. At the same time, this characteristic made ivories one of the main artistic vehicles in spreading the French Gothic style throughout Europe.

French Gothic ivories can be divided into two basic categories, religious and secular. In both, stylistic characteristics were consistent with other arts, especially sculpture, with which ivory carving has so much in common. Religious ivories included statuettes, especially of the Virgin and Child, portable altars, and liturgical objects, such as pyxes and croziers. Statues of the Virgin and Child usually depicted the crowned Virgin, either standing or seated, holding a playful Christ child. Faces were elegant and delicate, and drapery was often in complex, V-shaped folds. By the 15th century, under the influence of Flemish art, figures of the Virgin became more realistic and "maternal." Portable altars usually had at least two wings. Under frames of Gothic arches, multiple scenes were carved. Passion cycles were common, or sometimes the Virgin and Child was paired with a Crucifixion scene. Figures were lively,

Ivory: Crucifixion, crozier. *Photograph by B. Wag. Courtesy of the Walters Art Gallery, Baltimore.*

and the deep relief carving created a play of light and shadow.

The nobility and also the increasingly prosperous bourgeoisie created a demand for luxury objects, including mirrors, combs, boxes, and ivory tablets. Scenes on these objects often depicted themes from romances and courtly lyric poetry. Among favored subjects were a lovers' tryst and the attack on the Castle of Love, with delicately carved roses serving as the weapons. For both religious and secular ivories, the elegant style of French Gothic art found perfect expression through the medium of ivory with its precious qualities and lustrous glow.

Karen Gould

[**See also:** CAROLINGIAN ART; GOTHIC ART; JEWELRY AND METALWORKING]

Gaborit-Chopin, Danielle. *Ivoires du moyen âge.* Fribourg: Office du Livre, 1972.

Grodecki, Louis. *Ivoires français.* Paris: Larousse, 1947.

Koechlin, Raymond. *Les ivoires gothiques français.* 3 vols. Paris, 1924.

Randall, Richard H., Jr. *Masterpieces of Ivory from the Walters Art Gallery.* New York: Hudson Hills, 1985.

JACOB DE SENLECHES (fl. 1378–95). French composer and harpist, represented in the Chantilly codex by four complex Ars Subtilior songs. Jacob spent a number of years at the court of Aragon and Castile. In 1383, he appears at Navarre, a harpist in the service of Cardinal Pedro de Luna, the future Pope Benedict XIII. His complex and virtuosic virelai *Harpe de melodie*, notated in one manuscript in the shape of a harp, features irregular canonic imitation in the upper voices. Performance instructions call for the singer to accompany himself on the harp.

Benjamin Garber

[See also: ARS SUBTILIOR; COMPOSERS, MINOR (14TH CENTURY)]

Strohm, Reinhard. "*La harpe de mélodie* oder Das Kunstwerk als Akt der Zueignung." In *Das musikalische Kunstwerk: Geschichte, Asthetik, Theorie: Festschrift Carl Dahlhaus zum 60. Geburtstag,* ed. H. Danuser et al. Laaber: Laaber, 1988, pp. 305–16.
Tomasello, Andrew. *Music and Ritual at Papal Avignon, 1309–1403.* Ann Arbor: UMI, 1983.

JACQUEMART GIELÉE (fl. late 13th c.). Author of *Renart le nouvel*, a virulent anticlerical poem (7,862 lines; ca. 1289). Using the characters popularized by the *Roman de Renart*, the Lillois Jacquemart composed an essentially symbolic work in which Renart, as the personification of Satan, seduces humankind through appeals to pride, lust, and gluttony. The secular and regular clergy—and even the mendicant orders—are castigated in traditional terms drawn largely from Huon de Méry's *Tournoiement Antéchrist.*

William W. Kibler

[See also: HUON DE MÉRY; *RENART, ROMAN DE*]

Jacquemart Gielée. *Renart le nouvel par Jacquemart Gielée,* ed. Henri Roussel. Paris: Didot, 1961.

JACQUERIE. The Jacquerie, named for the peasants who led it (popularly termed *Jacques*), was the greatest of late-medieval French rebellions. In a two-week period during late May and early June 1358, widespread violence broke out in and around the Paris basin, including the regions of Champagne, Brie, Picardy, Beauvaisis, and part of Normandy. While the degree to which the Jacquerie was linked to the concurrent revolt of Étienne Marcel in Paris itself is uncertain, the roots of both movements can be found in the conjuncture of political destabilization, social and economic tension, and the stresses of war.

The Jacquerie was said to have begun as a bloody quarrel between some stonecutters and noblemen, but antagonism soon fueled a rising noted for its cruelty and destruction. Although the Jacques had little in the way of political ideology, their militant rural march, under Guillaume Cale, was most often directed against the property and families of the nobility. The rebels received support from some provincial towns and from Paris but were crushed by a resurgent nobility under Charles of Navarre, who had earlier appeared to sanction the Jacques. Thousands of people lost their lives in an aftermath of brutal reprisals by the nobility, known as the Counter-Jacquerie.

The Jacquerie has traditionally been labeled a "class war" or "social rebellion" because of the basic nature of the conflict—nonnobles vs. nobles. Though most of the rebels were from the lower to middle social ranks, brief alliances that transcended any class distinctions emerged to cover particular political needs; communities that were followers of the malcontent Charles of Navarre, such as Paris, thus tended to support or at least tolerate the rebels as a means of protest against earlier actions of the crown. Similarly, Étienne Marcel temporarily aided the Jacques. The tenuous nature of these connections is evident in their short duration and reinforces the degree to which their political programs were not those of the Jacques.

Robert A. Bennett

[See also: CHARLES II THE BAD; CHARLES V THE WISE; MARCEL, ÉTIENNE; MILLENIALISM]

Bessen, David M. "The Jacquerie: Class War or Co-opted Rebellion?" *Journal of Medieval History* 11 (1985): 43–59.

Cazelles, Raymond. "La Jacquerie: fut-elle un mouvement paysan?" *Académie des Inscriptions et Belles-Lettres, comptes rendus* (1979): 654–66.

Flammermont, J. "La Jacquerie en Beauvaisis." *Revue historique* 9 (1879): 123–43.

Luce, Siméon. *Histoire de la Jacquerie.* 2nd ed. Paris: Hachette, 1894.

Medeiros, Marie-Thérèse de. *Jacques et chroniqueurs: une étude comparée de récits contemporains relatant la Jacquerie de 1358.* Paris: Champion, 1979.

Mollat, Michel, and Philippe Wolff. *The Popular Revolutions of the Late Middle Ages,* trans. A.L. Lytton-Sells. London: Allen and Unwin, 1973.

JACQUES DE LIÈGE (Jacobus Leodiensis; ca.1260–after 1330). Author of the *Speculum musice* and other works on music theory. Little is known about Jacques's life. He has been identified with one Jacobus de Oudenaerde, a canon of Liège and, in 1313, a professor at Paris. Jacques's early education in music was in the theories of Franco of Cologne and later Boethius, whose *De institutione musica* he studied at Paris. It was there that the *Speculum musice* was begun, an encyclopedic discussion of speculative music (five books, in which he draws upon the authority of Plato, Boethius, Isidore, Guido d'Arezzo, and John of Afflighem, as well as Aristotle, Robert Kilwardby, Peter Comestor, Johannes de Garlandia, and Franco of Cologne), ecclesiastical chant (one book, treating both Boethian and Guidonian modal theory), and measured music (one book, describing the genres of discant composition and discussing notation). The last two books of the *Speculum* reveal connections with Liège sources and might have been composed in that city. Book 7 was composed chiefly to refute the teachings of the Ars Nova school on rhythm and notation, vindicating such traditional theorists as Franco of Cologne and Magister Lambertus. Overall, Jacques's work is the most cogent and complete statement of the theory and practice of the Ars Antiqua. The *Speculum musice* was formerly attributed to Jehan des Murs, but many of its doctrines contradict Jehan's teaching.

Tony Zbaraschuk

[See also: ARS ANTIQUA; ARS NOVA; FRANCO OF COLOGNE; JEHAN DES MURS; JOHANNES DE GARLANDIA; MUSIC THEORY]

Jacques de Liège. *Speculum musicae,* ed. Roger Bragard. 7 vols. Rome: American Institute of Musicology, 1955–70.

JACQUES DE VITRY (ca. 1160/70–1240). The son of a wealthy bourgeois family in Vitry-en-Perthios near Reims, Jacques studied in Paris at a time when Peter the Chanter, one of the most celebrated preachers of his day, was master of the cathedral school. In 1211, he entered the monastery of Augustinian regular canons dedicated to St. Nicolas in Oignies, not far from Cambrai. Over the next five years, he was close to the lay religious group known as the béguines, whose leader was Marie d'Oignies. During this same period, he became a preacher of crusades, first against the Albigensians in 1213 and then against the infidels in the Holy Land in 1214. His preaching won him the see of Acre on the coast of Palestine. Jacques arrived in Palestine in 1216 and accompanied the armies of the Fifth Crusade at Damietta, 1218–21. Weary of constant strife, Jacques left Acre in 1225 and served Pope Gregory IX in Italy and in the Low Countries over the next three years. In 1228, Gregory appointed him cardinal bishop of Tusculum, and he remained in Rome until his death. Jacques was buried at the monastery in Oignies, where he had begun his ecclesiastical vocation.

Jacques's most significant contribution to the history of the church comprised his collections of sermons intended to serve as models for preachers. One collection, *Sermones dominicales (de tempore),* gives three sermons for each of the Sundays of the ecclesiastical calendar; *Sermones de sanctis* gives 115 sermons for saints' days and special feasts; *Sermones communes et feriales* gives twenty-seven sermons for daily use; *Sermones vulgares* (or *ad status*) gives seventy-four sermons addressing social classes and religious groups. The first small collection of such model sermons was compiled only the generation before by Alain de Lille, and Jacques went far beyond them with his collections, particularly in their homiletic illustrations, or exempla, which provide a wealth of amusing and instructive anecdotes.

Jacques also composed a biography of Marie d'Oignies (1213) that helped gain papal approval for the béguine movement and has since become a valuable historical source for the early days of that controversial movement. Several of his letters date from his sojourn in Palestine (up to 1221), and his *Historia Hierosolymitana abbreviata* in three books recounts not only the history of Jerusalem during the Crusades but also, and perhaps more importantly, the new and often controversial religious movements of the day, such as the béguines, the Humiliati, and even the Franciscans (at least in their more colorful manifestations), as they relate to the renewal of the church and to the success of its mission.

Although Jacques's religious vocation took the more traditional form of an Augustinian canon, both his sympathies for the spiritual revival of his day and his talents as an extraordinary preacher place him firmly in the mainstream of the life of the church in the 13th century.

Mark Zier

[See also: BÉGUINES; EXEMPLUM; MARIE D'OIGNIES]

Jacques de Vitry. *The Historia occidentalis of Jacques de Vitry,* ed. John F. Hinnebusch. Fribourg: University Press, 1972.

———. *Lettres de Jacques de Vitry, 1160/70–1240, évêque de Saint-Jean d'Acre,* ed. R.B.C. Huygens. Leiden: Brill, 1960.

———. *Sermones vulgares.* In *Analecta nouissima spicilegii Solesmensis, altera continuatio,* ed. Jean Baptiste Pitra. 2 vols. Paris: Typis Tusculanis, 1885–88, Vol. 2.

Funk, Philipp. *Jakob von Vitry: Leben und Werke.* Leipzig: Teubner, 1909.

JARDIN DE PLAISANCE ET FLEUR DE RÉTHORIQUE.
Printed in Paris by Antoine Vérard between 1501 and 1503, the *Jardin de plaisance et fleur de réthorique* is a compendium of over 630 ballades, rondeaux, and other short lyric poems and narrative segments from the preceding two centuries.

The compiler, who identifies himself only as "L'Infortuné," dedicates his work to King Louis XII and prefaces the anthology proper with the *Instructif de seconde réthorique*, a treatise on poetic art of some 2,000 lines. Three longer works follow this treatise: the *Doleance de Megere*, written in 1469 by Regnaud Le Queux (whom some argue is the compiler of the *Jardin*); the *Donnet baillé au feu roy Charles huytiesme*, a brief treatise on Latin grammar composed ca. 1491, perhaps by Le Queux; and the *Chastel de joyeuse destinée*, an anonymous allegorical narrative poem of over 4,000 lines, relating a long quest through lands peopled by recognizable allies and adversaries of Love, ending with a vision of Love's palace, a place of *plaisance*, referring no doubt as well to the *jardin de plaisance*, the anthology in which the work is included. After hearing one of their company recount a debate between heart and eye, the lovers dwelling in the garden begin to create ballades and rondeaux both praising and blaming love and women. The women respond, in verse as well, thus carrying forth an exchange of opinion and sentiment extending over some 600 short lyric pieces. Poetic debates and laments on amorous situations are followed by a series of some thirty ballades and a single rondeau. The work is then slowly brought to an unhappy ending through a series of poems relating the obstacles to love. In the end, dying from love, a knight leaves a confession and testament to other lovers. In the work's final poem, he is called the *Oultré d'amours*, the one wronged by Love.

The *Jardin de plaisance* is ineffective as an overall narrative. Its interest resides in its attempt to define and illustrate in the same volume poetic art of the later Middle Ages and in its selection of poets included in the anthology. Written at the request of students of law, the *Instructif* can thus be seen as a handbook for those wishing to avoid pitfalls in composing occasional poetry. It relates poetry to a rhetorical aim and enumerates defects of style, figures of speech, principles of rhyme and versification, poetic genres, and appropriate levels of discourse for speech attributed to characters in moralities, comedies, chronicles, and other prose genres. By a curious tour de force, the *Instructif's* rules are generally given in the form of the genre being defined. Nearly fifty poets are represented in the *Jardin's* anthology, among them Machaut, Deschamps, Chartier, Charles d'Orléans, Granson, Pierre Chastellain, Jean de Calais, Baudet Herenc, Villon, Meschinot, and Molinet. The anthology gives little attention to the then flourishing Grands Rhétoriqueurs, preferring to present the models of the previous tradition.

Janice C. Zinser

Le *jardin de plaisance et fleur de réthorique*. 2 vols. Paris: Didot, 1910 and 1925. [Vol. 1 (1910) is the facsimile edition; Vol. 2 (1925) comprises the introduction and notes by Eugénie Droz and Arthur Piaget.]

JAUFRE. An Occitan quest-romance of 11,000 lines (octosyllabic rhymed couplets), *Jaufre* survives entire in two principal manuscripts (B.N. fr. 2164 and B.N. fr. 12571). Dated either in the 1170s (Rita Lejeune) or 1205–30 (Paul Rémy), the poem is dedicated to a king of Aragon who was generous with jongleurs and "crowned very young."

Jaufre, son of Dozon, arrives to be knighted at Arthur's weakened court just when Taulat offends Arthur by murdering a knight and vowing to repeat this yearly. Jaufre pursues Taulat, vanquishing evildoers all the way and each time sending prisoners and witnesses back to Arthur. After three days without food or rest, he angers Brunissen by sleeping in her orchard. The two fall in love, but Jaufre flees her crazed people's attacks. Eventually vanquishing Taulat, he liberates the wounded knight Melian de Monmelior, whom Taulat has tortured monthly for seven years. This frees his subjects, including Brunissen, from lamentations and compulsive rage. After more otherworldly adventures, Jaufre marries Brunissen at Cardoil. Although often parodic of Arthurian material, *Jaufre* reaffirms the power of true piety against giants, felons, lepers, witches, and devils.

Amelia E. Van Vleck

Brunel, Clovis, ed. *Jaufre, roman arthurien du XIIIe siècle en vers provençaux*. 2 vols. Paris: Didot, 1943.
Keller, Hans-Erich, ed. *Studia Occitanica in memoriam Paul Rémy*. 2 vols. Kalamazoo: Medieval Institute, 1986, Vol. 2: *The Narrative—Philology*.
Arthur, Ross G., trans. *Jaufre: An Occitan Arthurian Romance*. New York: Garland, 1992.

JAUFRE RUDEL (fl. 1120–48). The troubadour Jaufre Rudel, lord of Blaye in the Gironde, sang of earthly love infused by a mystical quest expressed also through his participation in the Second Crusade. Of his six surviving songs of certain authenticity, Jaufre's most successful *canso* is directed to his love from afar, or *amor de loing*, which gives this lyric its leitmotif and keyword. In this song and in *Qan lo rius*, he voices his yearning for a distant love, diversely interpreted by critics as a woman, the Virgin Mary, God, or the Holy Land. Recent scholarship underlines instead the deliberate ambiguity in Jaufre's fusion of linguistic registers and love objects drawn from both profane and sacred traditions. The legend of his love for the Countess of Tripoli dates from the pseudobiographical *vida* and earlier. It has been echoed in every century since the 13th by authors as varied as Petrarch, Stendhal, Rostand, Browning, Heine, Carducci, Pound, and Döblin.

Roy S. Rosenstein

[See also: TROUBADOUR POETRY]

Jaufre Rudel. *The Songs of Jaufre Rudel*, ed. Rupert T. Pickens. Toronto: Pontifical Institute of Mediaeval Studies, 1978.
———. *The Poetry of Cercamon and Jaufre Rudel*, ed. and trans. George Wolf and Roy Rosenstein. New York: Garland, 1983.

————. *Il canzoniere di Jaufre Rudel*, ed. Giorgio Chiarini. Rome: Japadre, 1985.

Rosenstein, Roy. "New Perspectives on Distant Love: Jaufre Rudel, Uc Bru, and Sarrazina." *Modern Philology* 87 (1990): 225–38.

JEAN IV (ca. 1340–1399). Duke of Brittany. Jean was the son of Jean de Montfort, a claimant for the ducal title in 1341. He spent most of his youth in England under the guardianship of Edward III. Following Montfort's capture (1341) and death (1345), Edward helped his widow, Jeanne of Flanders, to maintain their claims. After the Truce of Malestroit (1343), lieutenants occupied parts of Brittany for the English king and his ward. In 1356–57, Jean accompanied Henry, duke of Lancaster, to Brittany and was present at the siege of Rennes.

When negotiations to resolve the disputed Breton succession failed in 1361, Jean returned to Brittany in 1362 and in 1364 won the Battle of Auray, where his rival, Charles de Blois, was killed. The latter's widow, Jeanne de Penthièvre, agreed to peace at Guérande (April 12, 1365) under the aegis of Charles V's representatives. The new duke began a reorganization of his administration and finances, marking a watershed in the duchy's history and giving his reign enduring significance. But his pro-English stance and the presence of a few English counselors proved unpopular. In 1373, he was again forced into exile in England.

An attempt by Charles V to dispossess him (1378) provoked a violent reaction among the Breton nobility, who formed a league and invited Jean to return. After further warfare and the death of Charles V, a second comprehensive treaty was arranged at Guérande (April 4, 1381). Though Jean retained links with England, the failure of the English to return the castle of Brest or to restore fully his lands in England was a longstanding cause of dispute. He rendered moderate aid to the French crown in Flanders in 1383 and in 1386–87 but chiefly pursued policies to enhance an independent and largely neutral stance.

The last twenty years of his reign were also punctuated by a long feud with Jean, count of Penthièvre, Jeanne's son, and his father-in-law, Olivier IV de Clisson (constable of France, 1380–92). In 1387, Jean held Clisson for ransom, and he may have encouraged the murderous attack on him by Pierre de Craon in 1392. In 1395, Philip, duke of Burgundy, arranged a settlement. At the same time, Jean was bound more closely to French interests by the betrothal of his three-year-old heir to Charles VI's daughter, Jeanne de France, in 1392.

Throughout his career, Jean had a tendency to antagonize by an autocratic style of government; however, with increasing wealth, due to financial reforms and the cessation of war, he attracted many able men into his service. His rule advanced ducal authority and prestige and set a pattern for his successors. He was a considerable builder of castles and led a chivalric, courtly life, being especially interested in music. Around 1381, he founded the Order of the Ermine to commemorate his victory at Auray. He was married three times: to Edward III's daughter Mary (d. 1361); to Joan Holland (d. 1384), a step-daughter of Edward, Prince of Wales; and in 1386 to Jeanne, daughter of Charles II of Navarre, who gave him four sons and four daughters.

Michael C.E. Jones

[See also: AURAY; BRITTANY; CHARLES V THE WISE; CHARLES DE BLOIS; CLISSON; GUÉRANDE; HUNDRED YEARS' WAR; LANCASTER, DUKES OF; LAVAL; MONTFORT]

Jones, Michael, ed. *Recueil des actes de Jean IV, duc de Bretagne*. 2 vols. Paris: Klincksieck, 1980–83.

————. *Ducal Brittany 1364–1399: Relations with England and France During the Reign of Duke John IV*. London: Oxford University Press, 1970.

————. *The Creation of Brittany: A Late Medieval State*. London: Hambledon, 1988.

JEAN V (1389–1442). Duke of Brittany. Jean succeeded his father, Jean IV, in 1399. Despite moments of crisis, notably in 1420, when he was held captive for five months by Olivier, count of Penthièvre, in a further twist in the story of the rivalry for the ducal throne after 1341, Jean's reign was less dramatic than that of Jean IV. Internally, the duke's authority was seldom challenged. Taking advantage of the factional quarrels that undermined the French crown and allowed the English to establish their rule in northern France, Jean V normally avoided too close a commitment to any cause and oscillated between an Anglo-Burgundian and a French alliance for many years. This enabled Brittany to avoid the worst consequences of the Anglo-French war. From the vantage point of the early 16th century, the chronicler Alain Bouchart saw Jean's reign as a peaceful golden age.

How far he was personally responsible for this is controversial. Jean V is a shadowy personality when compared with his father or his younger brother, Arthur III (r. 1457–58), who was constable of France 1425–58. The events of 1420 left their mark and encouraged a caution sometimes interpreted as timidity. Recent research shows that the economic advantages of neutrality were not as great as once assumed. Nevertheless, the consolidation and strengthening of the administration begun by Jean IV continued, ably directed by Jean de Malestroit (chancellor, 1408–43) and outstanding financial officers like Jean de Mauléon (*trésorier de l'épargne*, 1405–44). Reform of the army began in 1424–25, and Brittany made diplomatic contacts with many powers in western Europe, especially to promote trade. The ceremonial aspects of ducal rule received new emphasis by a coronation service (1401), reorganization of the household along Burgundian lines (1405), adoption of the title *Dei gratia* in the ducal style, continuing appointments to the Order of the Ermine, and the issue of a gold coinage. When he died, Jean V was exposed "in his royal habit" in imitation of French royal practice. By his marriage to Jeanne de France, he had three sons and four daughters; the future prosperity of his house seemed ensured.

Michael C.E. Jones

[See also: BRITTANY; JEAN IV; RICHEMONT, ARTHUR DE]

Blanchard, René, ed. *Lettres et mandements de Jean V, duc de Bretagne*. 5 vols. Nantes: Société des Bibliophiles Bretons, 1889–95.

Kerhervé, Jean. *L'état breton aux 14e et 15e siècles: les ducs, l'argent et les hommes*. 2 vols. Paris: Maloine, 1987.

JEAN BELETH (fl. 1135–82). Little is known about the life of Jean Beleth. He witnessed a charter in the diocese of Chartres in 1135; was a student of Gilbert of Poitiers in Paris ca. 1141; composed a commentary on the liturgy, the *Summa de divinis officiis*, between 1160 and 1164; and was associated with the church at Amiens in 1182. He is best known for his *Summa*, which stands as the second of three important medieval treatises on the liturgy, the others being those by Amalarius of Metz (9th c.) and Guillaume Durand of Mende (13th c.). His work reads like a report of his lectures, dealing with sacred times, places, and objects from a largely historical point of view. Like many of his contemporaries, Jean is fond of dividing even the smallest of his topics into threes. His reputation as an expert on the liturgy has led to the attribution of many sermons to Jean, although only a few of them are considered authentic.

Mark Zier

[See also: AMALARIUS OF METZ; GUILLAUME DURAND]

Jean Beleth. *Summa de divinis officiis*. PL 202.9–166.

Van den Eynde, Damien. "Précisions chronologiques sur quelques ouvrages théologiques du XIIe siècle." *Antonianum* 26 (1951): 223–46.

JEAN D'ANDELYS (fl. early 13th c.). During the later 12th century, a series of projects at the cathedral of Notre-Dame, Rouen, realized the northwest tower (Tour Saint-Romain) and two new façade portals and launched construction of the four western bays of the nave. However, on April 8, 1200, a fire swept through the city devastating the cathedral. The reconstruction, liberally supported by Jean, duke of Normandy, and Pope Innocent III, was directed by Jean d'Andelys, mentioned as "mason, master of the works" in 1206/07.

Jean incorporated the 12th-century nave piers that had survived the fire and set the new choir atop the Romanesque foundations. His nave was planned as a four-story elevation, including a gallery, in the manner of the cathedrals of Arras, Laon, or Paris; although adopting such modern Gothic features as pointed arches and linear articulation, it retained the imposing heaviness typical of Norman architecture. By 1214, Jean d'Andelys had been succeeded by Enguerrand (Ingelrannus), who, along with the later master Durand, abandoned the galleries to create a three-story nave.

Michael T. Davis

[See also: ROUEN]

Aubert, Marcel. "La cathédrale de Rouen." *Congrès archéologique* (Rouen) 89 (1926): 11–71.

Beaurepaire, Charles. "Notes sur les architectes de Rouen." *Bulletin de la Société des Amis des Monuments Rouennais* (1901): 75–96.

Fauré, André. "Rouen, la cathédrale." In *Dictionnaire des églises de France*. Paris: Laffont, 1968, Vol. 4 B, pp. 132–43.

Loisel, L'abbé. *La cathédrale de Rouen*. Paris: Laurens, 1911.

JEAN DE CHELLES (fl. 13th c.). Jean de Chelles is mentioned by name only in the honorary inscription at the base of the south-transept façade of the cathedral of Paris (*Anno D[omi]ni MCCLVII mense Februario idus secundo [h]oc fuit inceptum Christi genit[ri]cis honore kallensi lathomo vivente Johanne magistro*). On the strength of this evidence, however, he is viewed as the designer of Notre-Dame's north-transept façade, built between ca. 1247/50 and 1257. This original and influential frontispiece combined a screen of gables across the portal, inspired by the west front of Saint-Nicaise, Reims, with the glazed triforium and enormous rose-in-square window derived from the Saint-Denis transepts. Jean's architecture is characterized by its tone of metallic preciosity as well as by its subtle tensions and contrasts, as individual forms achieve a limited independence within a crisply framed rectilinear grid. Attempts have been made to credit Jean de Chelles with the construction of the nave and choir chapels of Notre-Dame adjacent to the north transept, the south transept of Saint-Denis, the royal chapel at Saint-Germain-en-Laye, and the choir of the cathedral of Le Mans, although in the absence of positive documentary proof these attributions must remain speculative.

Michael T. Davis

[See also: PARIS]

Bouttier, Michel. "La reconstruction de l'abbatiale de Saint-Denis au XIIIe siècle." *Bulletin monumental* 145 (1987): 357–86.

Branner, Robert. *Saint Louis and the Court Style in Gothic Architecture*. London: Zwemmer, 1965

Kimpel, Dieter. *Die Querhausarme von Notre-Dame zu Paris und ihre Skulpturen*. Bonn, 1971.

———, and Robert Suckale. *Die gotische Architektur in Frankreich, 1130–1270*. Munich: Hirmer, 1985.

JEAN DE FÉCAMP (ca. 990–1078). An Italian, Jean accompanied his uncle William of Volpiano when the latter came in 989 to reform the abbey of Saint-Bénigne in Dijon. In 1028, Jean was named abbot of Fécamp, which William had reformed in 1006. He wrote an important contemplative treatise, which has survived in three distinct forms: *Confessio theologica* (before 1018), *Libellus de scripturis et verbis patrum* (1030–50), and *Confessio fidei* (ca. 1050). Inspired by the Bible and the church fathers, Jean was a Christ-centered mystic who believed that Jesus was healer and support to sinners. He was also the author of several

Latin poems and corresponded with both William the Conqueror and Pope Leo IX.

Grover A. Zinn

[See also: MYSTICISM; WILLIAM OF VOLPIANO]

Jean de Fécamp. *Opera.* PL 143.797–800; 147.453–58, 463–76.

Leclerq, Jean, and Jean-Paul Bonnes. *Un maître de la vie spirituelle au XIe siècle: Jean de Fécamp.* Paris: Vrin, 1946.

JEAN DE GARLANDE (Johannes de Garlandia; ca. 1195–ca. 1272). Born in England, Jean first studied at Oxford shortly after 1200 and went to Paris in 1217 or 1218, first to complete his studies and then to teach. At Paris, he lived in the Clos de Garlande, from which he derives his name. At the close of the Albigensian Crusade, the papal legate Romain Frangipani commissioned him to teach at the newly formed University of Toulouse (April 2, 1229), together with the Dominican master Roland of Cremona. Jean remained at Toulouse for only a few years. He may have returned to England during the 1230s but in any case was again teaching in Paris by 1241.

Jean's interests ranged primarily over the field of literary studies: etymology, rhetoric, grammar, and poetics. One of his earliest and best-known works, the *Parisiana poetria* (ca. 1220; revised a decade later), was a treatise on the art of poetry in the tradition of Matthieu de Vendôme and Geoffroi de Vinsauf. In this work, he stresses the place of both verse and prose composition in the arts curriculum. From this same period comes his *Dictionarius*, perhaps the first word book to be so entitled. Jean also wrote a brief verse commentary to Ovid's *Metamorphoses*, the *Integumenta Ovidii*, giving interpretations sometimes moral, sometimes scientific or historical, to the fables. Like many of his works, the *Integumenta* presupposes a vast general knowledge of the subject and is not intended for the novice.

Jean was also concerned about the moral formation of his students and wrote several works with that aim, among them the *Morale scolarium* (1241), an admonition on the values and habits of the ideal scholar, and the *Stella maris* (ca. 1249), in praise of the Virgin Mary as a paragon of Christian virtue and action. A later work, *De triumphis ecclesiae* (ca. 1252), is a polemic against pagans and heretics, based on his earlier experiences in Toulouse.

Jean had a prominent reputation in the 13th century. But though his promotion of lay piety was in keeping with the contemporary mission of the Dominicans and Franciscans, his resistance to Aristotelian studies and to the new emphasis on logic in the curriculum bespeak a conservatism more in keeping with the schools of the 12th century than with the universities of the 13th.

Jean must not be confused with the musician of the same name, listed hereunder as Johannes de Garlandia.

Mark Zier

Jean de Garlande. *Morale scolarium of John of Garland (Johannes de Garlandia), a Professor in the Universities of Paris and Toulouse in the Thirteenth Century,* ed. Louis J. Paetow. Berkeley: University of California Press, 1927.

Wilson, Evelyn Faye. *The Stella maris of John of Garland.* Cambridge: Mediaeval Academy of America, 1946.

JEAN DE MEUN (Jehan de Meung; 1235/40–1305). Born at Meung-sur-Loire, Jean Chopinel (or Clopinel) obtained the Master of Arts, most likely in Paris. He dwelt for much of his adult life in the capital, where from at least 1292 to his death he was housed in the Hôtel de la Tourelle in the Faubourg Saint-Jacques. Jean's works exhibit a rich classical and scholastic culture. Among the works he translated into French are Vegetius, *De re militari*, dedicated to Jean de Brienne, count of Eu; Boethius, *De consolatione Philosophiae*, dedicated to Philip the Fair; and the correspondence of Abélard and Héloïse. He also claims two additional translations, which are not extant: versions of Giraldus Cambrensis, *De mirabilibus Hiberniae*, and of Aelred of Rievaulx, *De spirituali amicitia*. More likely than not, Jean was also the author of the satirical *Testament maistre Jehan de Meun* and *Codicile maistre Jehan de Meun*.

But Jean is best remembered as the second author of the *Roman de la Rose*, an allegorical narrative begun by Guillaume de Lorris. This masterwork has survived in over 250 manuscripts. It also had twenty-one printed editions from 1481 to 1538. The *Rose* was translated partially or *in toto* during the medieval period once into Dutch, twice into Italian, and three times into English—the first English fragment is attributed to Chaucer. Jean de Meun influenced Dante, Boccaccio, Machaut, and Froissart; he played a crucial role in the formation of both Chaucer and Gower. Jean's section of the *Rose* became the subject of the first great literary quarrel, at the beginning of the 15th century. Jean de Meun was the first recognized *auctor* and *auctoritas* in French literary history, and his book the first true French classic, glossed, explicated, quoted, indexed, anthologized, and fought over—treated as if it were a masterpiece from antiquity.

Guillaume de Lorris wrote his *Roman de la Rose*, 4,028 lines left unfinished, in the early 1220s. In the decade 1264–74 Jean de Meun brought Guillaume's text to a conclusion. Jean's *Rose*, some 17,722 lines, does not merely complete the earlier poem: he grafts a totally original sequel onto it.

The God of Love comes with his army to succor Guillaume's forlorn Lover. First, False Seeming and Constrained Abstinence slay Foul Mouth, permitting the Lover to speak with Fair Welcome. A pitched battle occurs between the attackers and the defenders of the castle, ending in a truce. Finally, Venus leads a victorious assault, flinging her torch into the sanctuary: the castle bursts into flames, and the Lover wins the Rose.

The action and the allegory no longer play a primary role, as they did for Guillaume de Lorris. They serve as supports, and pretexts, for discourse: exhortations from Reason and Friend to the Lover, False Seeming's confession of his true nature to the God of Love before he is admitted into the army, the Old Woman's exhortation to

Fair Welcome, Nature's confession to her priest, Genius, and Genius's exhortation to the army before the final battle.

The God of Love refers to Jean's book as a *miroër aus amoreus* (l. 10,621). It is, in one sense, a *speculum* or anatomy, a medieval encyclopedia, treating all knowledge, including ethics, economics, cosmology, astronomy, optics, alchemy, and the university. The knowledge in the *speculum*, however, is granted unity and coherence by means of its inclusion under the category of love, which Jean expounds in all facets, both good (sex and reproduction, friendship, justice, the love of reason, one's neighbor, and God) and bad (lust for money, enslavement to Fortune, clerical celibacy, and the hypocrisy and deceit that exist between false lovers and false friends).

That the *Roman de la Rose* is didactic no one denies, but the precise nature of the message, the world vision that Jean de Meun wishes to instill, is subject to controversy. Most scholars believe that Jean transforms and refutes Guillaume de Lorris's *Rose*, that he derides, undermines, and destroys the ideal of *fin'amors* at every turn. One school of thought argues that Jean counters *fin'amors* with a call to procreation, to free love in the service of cosmic plenitude. Another school proposes that Jean treats all his characters, with the exception of Lady Reason, with irony and that his philosophy conforms to orthodox, Augustinian Christianity. The reason scholarly opinion differs so strikingly, why it is so difficult to pin down the author's personal doctrine, lies in the fact that Jean de Meun has chosen to exploit a unique version of narrative technique, quite different from that of his predecessors. Jean distinguishes himself as author from the dreamer-protagonist of his story, proclaimed to be Guillaume de Lorris, thus creating a first level of irony and distance. Second, the dreamer-protagonist, Fair Welcome, and Genius listen to and approve or disapprove of the lengthy discourses listed above, all of which are also presented with comedy and irony. Speakers have a proclivity to contradict themselves, and to cite texts from antiquity that refute rather than support their position. There is no foolproof method for determining which, if any, of the discourses are to be given greater weight than the others; which, if any, carry Jean's own conviction. Readers must judge each of these delegated voices in turn, analyzing the facts and rhetoric, to come to their own conclusions. The result, perhaps intended by Jean de Meun, is a state of doctrinal indeterminacy, in which the Lover and the audience are offered a sequence of philosophies and worldviews. The Lover, in the end, decides—he opens the sanctuary with joy—but the reader-audience is not obliged to applaud his decision. The indeterminacy remains, part and parcel of Jean's text and of a certain late Gothic mentality of which he is the first outstanding master.

Less controversial are the texture and ambience of Jean's imaginative world, a domain in which he is as great an innovator as in narrative technique. Compared with Guillaume de Lorris, Jean is a master of truculent vulgar speech, material detail, and picaresque naturalism. He shifts the audience's perspective from top to bottom, from rose petals to what they hide. A generation before Dante, three generations before Chaucer, Jean juxtaposes lofty and humble registers of style. Scenes, images, and speech once reserved to the fabliaux or excluded from polite letters altogether are now included in a serious work of art, alongside the sublime.

Jean's demystification of courtly love assumes several forms. His characters underscore the role of money in the erotic life, that so often the opposite sex is an object to be purchased, bartered, or exchanged for money or other commodities. The process of reification, and perhaps of antifeminism, is crowned by Jean de Meun's transformation of the woman-rose into a piece of lifeless architecture, a sanctuary, which the Lover pries open with his pilgrim's staff.

Still more striking is the role the author applies to manipulation and duplicity. Speech serves two purposes: to instruct and to trick. All people can be divided into knaves and fools, masters and slaves, deceivers and deceived. The deceivers create illusion by hiding behind masks; it is not easy for the Lover, Fair Welcome, or anyone else to distinguish appearance from reality, the mask from the flesh, the literal bark from an allegorical kernel. The author tells us that, since the end of the Golden Age, dissimulation, violence, and evil are part of the human condition and that we must learn to cope with them. Throughout the *Rose*, he implicitly urges the Lover and the audience to go beyond appearances and seek the truth, to open our eyes and rip aside the mask of falsehood. Knowledge can then lead to action. Some of Jean's characters remain passive, blind, impotent. Others, including the Lover, attain a measure of freedom, becoming masters not slaves, adults not children.

Jean's is a world of comedy. Several of his characters embody comic archetypes derived from the classics of ancient Rome. They are rigid, mechanical, obsessed with their narrow concerns. Furthermore, the narrative line, such as it is, constitutes the triumph of young love over old constraint. In spite of the blocking figures, Venus's torch burns and the story ends, as comedies must, with the couple packed off to bed. Whatever Jean's doctrine, whether for good or ill, the victory of our animal nature is achieved in a denouement of erotic explosion and the exaltation of life. It is for this reason that many scholars, especially in France, associate Jean de Meun with the awakening of humanism, the rebirth of reverence for antiquity, lust for life, and the revaluation of art that are hallmarks of the 12th- and 13th-century renaissance.

William C. Calin

[See also: COURTLY LOVE; GUILLAUME DE LORRIS; *ROSE, ROMAN DE LA*; QUARREL OF THE *ROMAN DE LA ROSE*]

Guillaume de Lorris and Jean de Meun. *Le roman de la Rose*, ed. and trans. Armand Strubel. Paris: Livre de Poche, 1992.

———. *Le roman de la Rose*, ed. Félix Lecoy. 3 vols. Paris: Champion, 1965–70.

———. *The Romance of the Rose*, trans. Charles Dahlberg. Princeton: Princeton University Press, 1971.

Arden, Heather M. *The Romance of the Rose*. Boston: Twayne, 1987.

————. *The Roman de la Rose: An Annotated Bibliography.* New York: Garland, 1993.

Badel, Pierre-Yves. *Le roman de la Rose au XIVe siècle: étude de la réception de l'œuvre.* Geneva: Droz, 1980.

Brownlee, Kevin, and Sylvia Huot. *Rethinking the Romance of the Rose: Text, Image, Reception.* Philadelphia: University of Pennsylvania Press, 1992.

Calin, William. *A Muse for Heroes: Nine Centuries of the Epic in France.* Toronto: University of Toronto Press, 1983, chap. 5.

Fleming, John V. *The Roman de la Rose: A Study in Allegory and Iconography.* Princeton: Princeton University Press, 1969.

Gunn, Alan M. F. *The Mirror of Love: A Reinterpretation of the Romance of the Rose.* Lubbock: Texas Tech Press, 1952.

Payen, Jean-Charles. *La Rose et l'utopie: révolution sexuelle et communisme nostalgique chez Jean de Meung.* Paris: Éditions Sociales, 1976.

JEAN DESCHAMPS (fl. 13th c.). From the inscription on a memorial, we learn that Jean Deschamps began the cathedral of Clermont-Ferrand in 1248 and was buried with his wife, Marie, and their children outside the north portal of the church. Further, Jean Deschamps was hired in 1286 as the head master (*le premier maistre*) of the workshop of Narbonne cathedral, where he labored until 1295. However, based on careful analysis of these edifices, it appears likely that the two texts refer to different, but possibly related, masters.

Jean Deschamps of Clermont may also have been the designer of the choir of the cathedral of Limoges (begun ca. 1265–70). His architecture, connected closely to such major projects in and near Paris in the 1230s and 1240s as the nave chapels of Notre-Dame and the new work at Saint-Denis, combined brittle grids of tracery with undecorated wall surfaces to produce buildings of restrained elegance. Jean Deschamps's activity at Narbonne, confined to the chapels of the north aisle and the transept, lacks a clear "personality," but the approach to pier and tracery design does not reveal close ties to Clermont.

Michael T. Davis

[See also: CLERMONT-FERRAND; GOTHIC ARCHITECTURE; LIMOGES; NARBONNE; PARIS; SAINT-DENIS]

Branner, Robert. *Saint Louis and the Court Style in Gothic Architecture.* London: Zwemmer, 1965.

Davis, Michael. "The Choir of the Cathedral of Clermont-Ferrand: The Beginning of Construction and the Work of Jean Deschamps." *Journal of the Society of Architectural Historians* 40 (1981): 181–202.

————. "Le chœur de la cathédrale de Limoges: tradition rayonnante et innovation dans la carrière de Jean des Champs." *Bulletin archéologique du Comité des Travaux Historiques et Scientifiques* n.s. 22 (1989): 51–114.

Freigang, Christian. "Jean Deschamps et le Midi." *Bulletin monumental* 149 (1991): 265–98.

Ranquet, Henri du. "Les architectes de la cathédrale de Clermont-Ferrand." *Bulletin monumental* 76 (1912): 70–124.

JEAN D'ORBAIS (fl. late 12th–early 13th c.). To Jean d'Orbais has often been attributed the design of Reims cathedral, begun in 1211, where he served as master mason for approximately a decade. One version of the labyrinth inscriptions declared that he began the choir (*encommencea la coiffe*) of the cathedral, and the sketch of his image may show him in the process of laying out the groundplan of the hemicycle. If Jean was the first cathedral master, his architecture can be appreciated as a brilliant blend of tradition and innovation. His plan and features of his elevation, such as the linkage of triforium and clerestory, were influenced by the late 12th-century abbey of Saint-Remi, Reims. At the same time, the introduction of bar tracery in the windows of the cathedral was arguably the most important innovation in 13th-century European architecture, for it formed the basis for new effects of complex linearity, textural consistency and contrast, and countless compositional experiments.

Michael T. Davis

[See also: GAUCHER DE REIMS; GOTHIC ARCHITECTURE; JEAN LE LOUP; REIMS]

Branner, Robert. "Jean d'Orbais and the Cathedral of Reims." *Art Bulletin* 43 (1961): 131–33.

Demaison, Louis. "Les architectes de la cathédrale de Reims." *Bulletin archéologique du Comité des Travaux Historiques et Scientifiques* (1894): 1–40.

Hamann-MacLean, Richard. "Zur Baugeschichte der Kathedrale von Reims." In *Gedenkschrift Ernst Gall.* Munich: Deutscher Kunstverlag, 1965, pp. 195–234.

Salet, Francis. "Le premier colloque international de la Société Française d'Archéologie (Reims): chronologie de la cathédrale." *Bulletin monumental* 125 (1967): 347–94.

JEAN LE BEL (d. ca. 1370). The *Vrayes chroniques* of Jean le Bel is a valuable source for the Hundred Years' War and the Flemish wars of the 14th century. Born in Liège of a patrician family, Jean became a canon of Saint-Lambert. As his contemporaries noted, his clerical career did not prevent him from living like a great noble; Jacques de Hemricourt has left us a portrait of a man with a large retinue, who held court like the bishop himself, wore costly clothing, and thoroughly enjoyed himself doing so.

Jean claims in his writing to have undertaken his chronicle to correct the "false" history of a minstrel, but Jean d'Outremeuse tells us that he wrote at the request of Jean de Beaumont. He wrote in French "prose," primarily from his own experience, which included personal service during Edward III's Scottish campaign of 1327, and probably also from reports by Jean de Beaumont and other members of his circle. He seems to have written all the material up to 1357 sometime during that year and then made additions afterward. He was interested primarily in wars and deeds of chivalry, rather than in politics, like Froissart, who both used Jean's chronicle as a source and continued it, but he is a more careful historian than Froissart, deeply concerned to tell the truth as he saw it. Apart from Froissart, only his compatriot Jean d'Outremeuse and Cornelius Zantvliet seem to have known his work.

Leah Shopkow

[See also: FROISSART, JEAN; HISTORIOGRAPHY; OUTREMEUSE, JEAN D']

Jean Le Bel. *Chronique*, ed. Jules Viard and Eugène Déprez. 2 vols. Paris: Renouard, 1904–05.

Tyson, Diana B. "Jean le Bel: Portrait of a Chronicler." *Journal of Medieval History* 12 (1986): 315–32.

JEAN LE LOUP (fl. early 13th c.). Jean Le Loup served as master mason of Reims cathedral for sixteen years. Several scholars have proposed him as the first of the Reims architects (1211–27), while others have situated his activity in the 1230s and 1240s. Two of the transcriptions of the cathedral labyrinth add that Jean began the portals—but do they refer to the north transept or an early version of the west façade? In the absence of further information, Jean Le Loup, like his fellow masters at Reims Gaucher de Reims and Adam, must remain a name without an identifiable *œuvre*.

Michael T. Davis

[See also: GAUCHER DE REIMS; JEAN D'ORBAIS; REIMS]

Branner, Robert. "The Labyrinth of Reims Cathedral." *Journal of the Society of Architectural Historians* 31 (1962): 18–25.

Panofsky, Erwin. "Über die Reihenfolge der vier Meister von Reims." *Jahrbuch für Kunstwissenschaft* (1927): 55–82.

Reinhardt, Hans. *La cathédrale de Reims: son histoire, son architecture, sa sculpture, ses vitraux.* Paris: Presses Universitaires de France, 1963.

Savy, Paul. "Les étapes de la cathédrale de Reims du XIIIe siècle." *Travaux de l'Académie Nationale de Reims* 154 (1956): 47–63.

JEAN RENART. *See* REALISTIC ROMANCES

JEANNE D'ARC (ca. 1412–1431). The most heroic of France's saints, Jeanne d'Arc was born to a peasant family in Lorraine. At thirteen, Jeanne began hearing the "voices" (of SS. Michael, Catherine, and Margaret) that inspired her. In February 1429, she persuaded a Valois captain to provide an escort for her dangerous journey to the court of Charles VII. At Chinon, Jeanne convinced the king of her divine mission to defeat the English and to assist at his overdue coronation. After formal inquiry into her orthodoxy and chastity, she was given a commanding role in a relief force for Orléans and led reinforcements into the besieged city on April 29. She inspired counterattacks that compelled the English to abandon the siege on May 8. A month later, her army's decisive victory at Patay ensured Valois control over the Loire Valley and destroyed the myth of English invincibility. The subsequent campaign that brought Charles to Reims for a triumphant coronation on July 17 was the high point of Jeanne's meteoric career.

Now a political force, Jeanne became a recognized leader of the court faction favoring renewed war over negotiations with the Anglo-Burgundians. Failure in war soon destroyed her influence. When she was defeated and wounded in an ill-considered assault on Paris in September, Charles arranged a truce and disbanded her army. Though her family had been ennobled, Jeanne was politically isolated and left the court in the spring to bolster Compiègne's resistance to a Burgundian siege. She was captured there on May 24, 1430, and, to his eternal discredit, abandoned by Charles. Jeanne's cross-dressing, claims to divine guidance, and success had aroused suspicions of sorcery, but her subsequent trial and execution for heresy were acts intended primarily to discredit the Valois cause. In response to an accusation by representatives of the University of Paris, her Burgundian captors delivered her for trial at Rouen under the direction of Bishop Pierre Cauchon. Eloquent in testimony and steadfast when threatened with torture, Jeanne submitted only when weakened by illness and faced with execution. Sentenced to a life of imprisonment and penance, she relapsed and was condemned. Courageous to the end, she insisted on her innocence and asked the executioner to hold the cross high so she could see it through the flames. Jeanne remained a controversial figure, and in 1456 Charles VII arranged the annulment of her conviction mainly to clear himself of a suspect association.

Shrouded in myth and exalted by unceasing artistic glorification, Jeanne endures as a figure inspiring even the most skeptical. Her historical importance could be narrowly construed: she was essentially a military figure whose inspirational leadership and ephemeral battlefield success helped restore the prestige of the Valois dynasty, ensuring its survival but not its eventual triumph. Few, however, would restrict themselves to such a reductive assessment. Jeanne's courageous example and her martyrdom assure her an enduring role in modern life, not unlike that played by Roland in the Middle Ages. She has become a symbolic figure emblematic of many and varied hopes. Above all, she is the symbol of 20th-century France at war with both itself and its German invaders. In the late 19th century, the "Maid of Orléans" become a popular heroine who inspired generations of French conservatives in the struggle against the secularism of the Third Republic and reminded all Frenchmen of the need to regain the lost provinces of Alsace and Lorraine seized by Germany in 1870. This popular devotion led to her canonization in the aftermath of the First World War and final confirmation that her greatness transcends if not defies historical analysis.

Paul D. Solon

[See also: CAUCHON, PIERRE; CHARLES VII; CHRISTINE DE PIZAN; RAIS, GILLES DE; WOMEN, RELIGIOUS EXPERIENCE OF]

Doncoeur, Paul, and Yvonne Lanhers, eds. *Documents et recherches relatifs à Jeanne la Pucelle.* 5 vols. Vols. 1–4,

Melun: Librairie d'Argences, 1921–58; Vol. 5, Paris: De Brouwer, 1961.

Tisset, Pierre, and Yvonne Lanhers, eds. *Procès de condamnation de Jeanne d'Arc*. 3 vols. Paris: Klincksieck, 1960–71.

Gies, Frances. *Joan of Arc: The Legend and the Reality*. New York: Harper and Row, 1981.

Margolis, Nadia. *Joan of Arc in History, Literature, and Film: A Select, Annotated Bibliography*. New York: Garland, 1990.

Vale, Malcolm G.A. *Charles VII*. Berkeley: University of California Press, 1974.

Warner, Marina. *Joan of Arc: The Image of Female Heroism*. New York: Knopf, 1981.

JEANNE DE CONSTANTINOPLE (ca. 1200–1244). Countess of Flanders and Hainaut. The older daughter and successor of Baudouin IX of Flanders and emperor of Constantinople, Jeanne became countess when her father died on crusade in 1205/06. Philip II Augustus of France used her long minority to remove much of the threat that he had perceived from Flemish power. The regency lasted until Jeanne was married at Paris in 1212 to Ferrand of Portugal. Allegedly to counteract English influence in Flanders, the crown prince Louis occupied Aire and Saint-Omer before Jeanne and Ferrand were permitted to assume their inheritance. Ferrand quickly allied with the pro-English party in Flanders but was captured by the French at Bouvines (July 27, 1214) and kept in prison until 1227. Jeanne was forced to accept the control of a group of Francophile Flemish nobles. There was some easing of tensions in the 1220s; but to gain the release of Ferrand, to whom she seems genuinely to have been attached, Jeanne had to agree to the Treaty of Melun (1226), which provided an enormous indemnity and subordinated the counts of Flanders to the French crown. Ferrand fought the nobles who had caused his wife trouble during his captivity and forced the count of Holland to do homage to Flanders for Zeeland west of the Scheldt. He died in 1233, and his infant daughter did not live to maturity. In 1237, Jeanne married Thomas of Savoy. She died on December 5, 1244, and was succeeded in Hainaut and Flanders by her sister Marguerite.

David M. Nicholas

[See also: FERRAND OF PORTUGAL; GHENT]

de Hemptinne, Th. "Vlaanderen en Henegouwen onder de erfgenamen van de Boudewijns, 1070–1244." In *Algemene Geschiedenis der Nederlanden*. 2nd ed., Vol. 2, pp. 372–98.

Luykx, Theo. *Johanna van Constantinopel, gravin van Vlaanderen en Henegouwen*. Antwerp: Staandard-Boekhandel, 1946.

JEANNE OF BURGUNDY. Two women named Jeanne of Burgundy, both born in the 1290s, reigned as queens of France in the first half of the 14th century. The older Jeanne was the daughter of Mahaut of Artois, a second cousin of Philip IV, and of Otto IV, count of Burgundy. In 1306, she married the king's second son, who ascended the throne ten years later as Philip V. Two of their children, both

daughters, lived to adulthood. The older, another Jeanne, married Eudes IV, duke of Burgundy, and the younger, Marguerite, married Louis I of Flanders. Mahaut's title to the county of Artois was hotly contested, and Jeanne's husband, daughters, and sons-in-law became involved in this dispute, which split the French royal family. Queen Jeanne died in 1330 at about the age of forty, the year after she had succeeded her mother as countess of Artois.

Jeanne's rival in Artois, her cousin Robert, was a close friend of Charles IV (r. 1322–28) and Philip VI (r. 1328–50), but Philip finally broke with Robert after Jeanne's death, when the county passed to her daughter, the duchess of Burgundy. Philip was extremely close to Eudes IV of Burgundy, who was his brother-in-law. Eudes's sister was the second Jeanne of Burgundy (a granddaughter of St. Louis through her mother, Agnes), who had married Philip of Valois in 1313. After Philip became king in 1328, the queen was a highly influential figure in royal politics. She and Philip corresponded frequently when they were separated, and he delegated important authority to her.

Devoted to all that was Burgundian, Jeanne is said to have strongly disliked people from northwestern France, especially Normans. For much of Philip VI's reign, Burgundians had considerable influence at court, while men of the west were seriously underrepresented. The disaffection of the northern and western nobility, a significant political factor in the reigns of Philip VI and John II, may have been related to the influence that this remarkable queen was able to exert on the policies of her husband and the attitudes of her son.

John Bell Henneman, Jr.

[See also: BURGUNDY (genealogical table); PHILIP VI]

Cazelles, Raymond. *La société politique et la crise de la royauté sous Philippe de Valois*. Paris: Argences, 1958.

JEANNE OF NAVARRE (1273–1305). Queen of France. The daughter of Henri III of Champagne and Navarre and Blanche of Artois, granddaughter of Louis VIII, Jeanne inherited her father's lands in 1274. Plans for her to marry the heirs, first of Edward I of England and then the king of Aragon, failed after problems in Spain led Blanche and Jeanne to seek asylum with Philip III. In May 1275, Blanche put Navarre under Philip's protection and affianced Jeanne to one of his sons. Raised at the French court, Jeanne was declared of age on May 17, 1284, and on August 16 married Philip IV the Fair, who on October 6, 1285, succeeded his father as king. Jeanne was closely involved with the administration of Champagne and Navarre, but Philip effectively controlled them.

Jeanne was a popular queen, and Philip was devoted to her. In 1288, he deferred until after her death collection of money owed for the defense of Navarre. In October 1294, he appointed her regent of France if he died before their eldest son came of age. Her name was associated with Philip's in important acts, and she accompanied him on his grand tour of the Midi in 1303–04. She showed independence in supporting the Franciscan Bernard Délicieux and accepting gifts from citizens of Béziers, whose orthodoxy and loyalty were suspect. She pressed the prosecution of Guichard, bishop of Troyes, accused of cheating her and her mother (and later charged with killing Jeanne by sorcery). A woman of considerable culture, she commissioned Joinville's *Vie de saint Louis*; Ramon Lull and her confessor Durand de Champagne dedicated works to her, and Raymond of Béziers began for her his translation of *Kalila et Dimna*. She was godmother of Enguerran de Marigny's wife, and Enguerran was the officer in charge of Jeanne's pantry before joining Philip's service in 1302.

Jeanne bore Philip four sons and a daughter before dying on April 2, 1305. In her lavish testament, she used 40,000 *livres parisis* and three years' revenues of Champagne, assigned her by Philip, to endow a hospital at Château-Thierry and the Collège de Navarre in Paris. Having rejected burial at Saint-Denis, the royal mausoleum, she was interred at the Franciscan church in Paris.

Elizabeth A.R. Brown

[See also: MARIGNY, ENGUERRAN DE; PHILIP IV THE FAIR]

Arbois de Jubainville, Henry d'. *Histoire des ducs et des comtes de Champagne*. 7 vols. Paris: Durand et Lauriel, 1859–69.
Brown, Elizabeth A.R. *The Monarchy of Capetain France and Royal Ceremonial*. London: Variorum, 1991.
Favier, Jean. *Un conseiller de Philippe le Bel: Enguerran de Marigny*. Paris: Presses Universitaires de France, 1963.
Lalou, Elisabeth. "Le gouvernement de la reine Jeanne, 1285–1304." *Cahiers Haut-Marnais* 167 (1986): 16–30.

JEHAN BODEL (d. 1210). A trouvère from Arras in the second half of the 12th century and one of the most prominent writers of his time. Jehan Bodel's life is only sketchily known—neither the date nor the place of his birth has been established with accuracy.

Jehan Bodel had strong links with the city of Arras and its surroundings. He introduces himself as a minstrel in his *Congés*: he was a member of the Arras minstrel and burgher brotherhood and contributed to the rapid expansion of this society. Stanza 40 of the *Congés* suggests that he was a familiar of the Arras *échevinage*, or town council, to which he was presumably attached. Elated by Foulque de Neuilly's preaching, he was about to follow Baudouin of Flanders, the future conqueror of Constantinople, to the Holy Land, when he began to suffer from the first signs of leprosy. In 1202, he withdrew to a leprosarium in the Arras region, most likely at Grant Val near Beaurains, where he died, according to the death-roll of the brotherhood, between February 2 and June 16, 1210.

Jehan's work has only gradually unveiled its secrets. Long underestimated, it now appears as one of the richest, most original *œuvres* in medieval literature. Because he tackled various genres simultaneously, the chronology of his works is difficult to establish. He is one of the earliest writers of *pastourelles* in *langue d'oïl*; five have been ascribed to him. Such narrative lyrics had already been composed by troubadours, but the Arragese minstrel left his mark upon the genre. Within a conventional framework, he proved original in his skilled composition in a wide range of prosodic structures and in the impression of truthfulness he gives due to subtle characterization and concrete details taken from peasant life.

Slightly different in inspiration were his one fable and eight fabliaux, those merry tales that give full scope to the imagination of an artist aiming at entertaining a noble audience at the expense of the middle class, peasants, women, and churchmen. If not as incisive as Gautier le Leu's, Jehan's fabliaux evince acute observation and a rich experience of the life of Picard peasants and merchants. The genre, free enough to encompass risqué tales and cautionary fables, appealed to this storyteller keen on Gallic mirth: *Jehan Bodiax, un rimoieres de flabiax*, as he called himself.

His versatility led him to widen the scope of his writings. A connoisseur of chansons de geste, he soon realized that the Saxon wars, a landmark in Charlemagne's reign, were a fit subject for a vast epic, and by 1180 he undertook the composition of the *Chanson des Saisnes*, which his disease prevented him from completing. Four drafts of this work are extant, the shortest one known as *A* (4,337 lines) and the longest as *T* (8,019 lines). Analysis shows that later writers tried to bring the unfinished poem to completion after the 12th century. The first 3,307 lines of *A* provide us with a text as close as possible to what Jehan's original work may have been. Here, we can recognize the innovator at once by his art and literary theories as well as his idea of history. In keeping with the Roland tradition of the chanson de geste, he foregrounds Charlemagne but also humanizes the God-chosen emperor, whose character underwent further transformation with the continuators. Nor is Jehan's inspiration purely epic: with the amours of Baudouin, the young Frenchman, romance is woven into the martial narrative, while the comedy peculiar to fabliaux creeps into the episode of Saint-Herbert du Rhin. The poem synthesizes all the components of the author's craftsmanship: a scholarly minstrel, fascinated by history and committed to his times, both an observer of reality and a visionary, but first and foremost a poet capable of breathing life into whatever he portrayed.

Jehan dealt once more with an epic subject in the *Jeu de saint Nicolas*, a semiliturgical drama produced during the *grand siège*, or convention, of the Arras brotherhood, between 1194 and 1202. As in the *Chanson des Saisnes*, the background is the war of Christians and heathens. After an initial victory by the king of Africa's Saracens, the only survivor of the Christian host eventually ensures the triumph of his party, thanks to the protection of the saint; the king and his men convert to Christianity. The *Jeu* is a chanson de geste in miniature. Yet once more, the narrow frame of the genre, the dramatized miracle play, bursts under the poet's creative power. "Throughout the play," Albert Henry writes, "sacred and profane, sublime and comic, marvellous . . . and realistic elements are to be found side by side." In this powerful and original work, a masterpiece of medieval dramatic literature, is reflected the multifarious personality of an author who showed as much sincerity in praising Auxerre wine as in extolling the crusade.

Disease turned Jehan into one of our great lyric poets. When obliged to withdraw from the society of his contemporaries, he wrote a long supplication to his friends and benefactors in his farewell poems (*Congés*), composed in 1202. Taking up the stanzaic form of Hélinant de Froidmont's *Vers de la Mort*, he bade a pathetic farewell to the world in forty-five octosyllabic stanzas. The regret of bygone joys, rebellion against and resignation to his misfortune, faith in God, gratitude to those who harbored him "half sound and half rotten"—all the themes of a new genre are to be found here. A work of harrowing sincerity, the *Congés* stand, in the early 13th century, as the first example of "ordeal lyricism" to be found in so many poets from Rutebeuf to Verlaine.

A teller of spicy stories, the author of a chanson de geste, a skillful dramatist, a lyric poet, and a critic (in the prologue to the *Chanson des Saisnes*, he puts forward a classification of the three principal poetic genres), Jehan Bodel tackled most contemporary forms and achieved creativity in each.

Annette Brasseur

[See also: *CONGÉ*; FABLIAU; KING CYCLE; MIRACLE PLAYS; ROMANCE]

Bartsch, Karl, ed. *Altfranzösische Romanzen und Pastourellen.* Leipzig: Vogel, 1870, pp. 287–91. [Based on MS *F* (B.N. fr. 12645).]

Berger, Roger, ed. *La nécrologie de la confrérie des jongleurs et des bourgeois d'Arras (1194–1361): texte et tables.* Arras: Imprimerie Centrale de l'Artois, 1963.

Bodel, Jehan. *La chanson des Saisnes*, ed. Annette Brasseur. 2 vols. Geneva: Droz, 1989.

———. *La chanson des Saxons*, trans. Annette Brasseur. Paris: Champion, 1992.

———. *Le jeu de saint Nicolas de Jehan Bodel*, ed. Albert Henry. Brussels: Palais des Académies, 1980. [Based on MS *V* (B.N. fr. 25566).]

———. *Les fabliaux de Jean Bodel*, ed. Pierre Nardin. Paris: Nizet, 1965. [Based on MS *A* (B.N. fr. 837).]

———. *Les congés d'Arras (Jean Bodel, Baude Fastoul, Adam de la Halle)*, ed. Pierre Ruelle. Paris: Presses Universitaires de France, 1965, pp. 83–104. [Based on MS. *A* (Arsenal 3142).]

Brasseur, Annette. *Étude linguistique et littéraire de la "Chanson des Saisnes" de Jehan Bodel.* Geneva: Droz, 1990.

———. "Index des rimes de Jehan Bodel." *Olifant* 15 (1990): 211–336.

Foulon, Charles. *L'œuvre de Jehan Bodel.* Paris: Presses Universitaires de France, 1958.

JEHAN BONNET. Otherwise unknown, Jehan Bonnet composed before 1303 a philosophical dialogue in Old French prose, *Placides et Timeo*, extant in two redactions. The author draws extensively on William of Conches's *Philosophia mundi* and *Philosophia secunda* as well as on the *Image du monde* and *Secretum secretorum*. This encyclopedic work touches on questions of natural history, biblical history, astronomy, theology, and philosophy.

William W. Kibler

Langlois, Charles-Victor. *La vie en France au moyen âge, du XIIe au milieu du XIVe siècle.* 5 vols. Paris: Hachette, 1925–28, Vol. 3: *La connaissance de la nature et du monde*, pp. 276–334.

Renan, Ernest. "Dialogue de Placide et Timéo." In *Histoire littéraire de la France.* Paris: Imprimerie Nationale, 1888, Vol. 30, pp. 567–95.

Thomasset, Claude. *Une vision du monde à la fin du XIIIe siècle: Commentaire du dialogue de* Placides et Timéo. Droz: Geneva, 1982.

JEHAN BRETEL (ca. 1200–1271). A wealthy cloth merchant and banker of Arras, Jehan Bretel was also an active member and occasional leader of the poetic circle there, the Confrérie des Jongleurs et des Bourgeois d'Arras. He is sole author of seven lyrics but is known primarily for his *jeux-partis*, of which he co-composed over ninety. His preferred partners in these compositions include Adam de la Halle, Jean de Grieviler, and Lambert Ferri.

Wendy E. Pfeffer

[See also: *JEU-PARTI*; *PUY*]

Jehan Bretel. "Les *chansons* de Jean Bretel," ed. Gaston Raymond. *Bibliothèque de l'École des Chartes* 41 (1880): 195–214.

Lângfors, Arthur, Alfred Jeanroy, and Louis Brandin, eds. *Recueil général des jeux-partis français.* 2 vols. Paris: Champion, 1926, Vol. 1, pp. 86–356.

JEHAN DE PARIS, ROMAN DE. Two manuscripts (B.N. fr. 1465 and Louvain G 54) contain this prose romance (ca. 1495) inspired by Philippe de Beaumanoir's *Jehan et Blonde*. The anonymous author recounts the success of the King of France over the King of England, as both seek the hand of a Spanish princess. The text, written in Lyon, contains references to the marriage of Charles VIII and Anne of Brittany.

Wendy E. Pfeffer

Wickersheimer, Edith, ed. *Le roman de Jehan de Paris.* Paris: Champion, 1923.

JEHAN DES MURS (Johannes de Muris; ca.1300–ca. 1350). Jehan was one of the most important music theorists of the later Middle Ages. His works on musical proportion and mensural notation remained authoritative for two centuries and were more widely distributed than those of any other theorist after 1200. Jehan's works on mathematics and astronomy, such as the *Opus quadripartitum numerorum*, were less influential than his musical writings. Considerable doubt remains as to the titles and authentic versions of Jehan's works. Four treatises are almost certainly authentic, all dating from the 1320s. The *Ars nova musice* (or *Notitia artis musice*) of 1321 stresses in its first part that only the theorist has sufficient wisdom to teach. The second book of the *Ars nova*, entitled *Musica practica*, discusses musical time, measurement, and notation. The *Quaestiones super partes musice* (or *Compendium musicae practicae*) is based largely on the *Ars nova*. The third work, *Musica speculativa secundum Boetium*, is notable for its mathematical methods, such as the use of theorems, in the study of music and became a standard textbook in eastern European universities in the 14th and 15th centuries. Other texts attributed to Jehan include the *Libellus cantus mensurabilis*, written for a nonacademic audience, and the *Ars contrapuncti*. The form, terminology, and theories of Jehan's writings were widely adopted by later writers. Jehan himself built on the style of Franco of Cologne, using Aristotelian concepts and methods of exposition and proof. By not writing on plainchant and by not using the traditional lore about music's utility and classification, Jehan set a precedent for later writers to focus more on the practical problems of contemporary music.

Tony Zbaraschuk

[See also: ARS NOVA; FRANCO OF COLOGNE; MUSIC THEORY]

Michels, Ulrich, ed. *Die Musiktraktate des Johannes de Muris.* Wiesbaden: Steiner, 1970.

JEU D'ADAM. The only extant manuscript of this early vernacular biblical play was copied in southwest France in the second quarter of the 13th century, though the original language was mid-12th-century Anglo-Norman. The play's Latin title, *Ordo representacionis Ade*, has a liturgical flavor, and its three vernacular episodes—the Fall, Cain and Abel, and the Prophets of Redemption—are framed by Latin lections, responsories, and prophecies. Moreover, the Latin stage directions, which prescribe not only costume and decor but movement, formal gesture, and manner of speaking, are reminiscent of church service books. The stage direction *ad ecclesiam* has traditionally been taken to indicate a performance outside the church building, but may designate a *lieu*, or stage location, opposite the synagogue referred to in the stage direction *de sinagoga*. In this case, a performance inside the church would be possible.

The long episode of the Fall (590 of the 944 lines) may be divided into three parts. The first and third, formal in tone and highlighted by choral interventions, are separated by the lively dialogue of the Temptation sequence. In the first part, Adam and Eve, clothed respectively in red and white, are joined in marriage by the Salvator, vested in a dalmatic and referred to thereafter as Figura. (God the Son, the figure of his father [Hebrews 1:3], usually replaces the Father as Creator in art before 1200.) God establishes the relationship of Adam and Eve to each other and then to himself as Creator and feudal overlord; he reminds them that they have free will and gives them Paradise as their fief. In the second part, demons running about the platea, or central playing space, usher in the rare scene of Satan vainly tempting Adam to disobey his lord. Next comes the justly celebrated temptation of Eve by the now flattering and soft-spoken "infernal Don Juan." Eve mimes listening to the advice of an artificial serpent before picking and eating the fatal apple. The last part of the Fall comprises lamentations by Adam, the Expulsion from Paradise, and more lamentations on earth. It ends with Adam and Eve being led off by rejoicing demons to a cacophonous welcome in Hell.

Cain and Abel, representing respectively the wicked who will be damned and the righteous who will be redeemed, are followed by a procession of prophets who foretell the coming of the Redeemer. The play, which is incomplete, breaks off in the scene of Nebuchadnezzar and the fiery furnace. The *Jeu d'Adam* exhibits a wide range of language registers and versification; vivid characterization, especially of Eve and Satan; and a subtle mixture of prophecy, biblical allusions, feudal terms, and internal cross-references. It is one of the most frequently edited, translated, studied, and performed plays from medieval Europe.

Lynette R. Muir

[See also: ANGLO-NORMAN LITERATURE; STAGING OF PLAYS; THEATER]

Noomen, Willem, ed. *Le jeu d'Adam (Ordo representacionis Ade)*. Paris: Champion, 1971.
Muir, Lynette R. *Liturgy and Drama in the Anglo-Norman Adam.* Oxford: Blackwell, 1973.

JEU-PARTI. The occasional *joc-partit*, or *partimen*, of the troubadours blossomed into a 13th-century trouvère corpus of almost 200 *jeux-partis*, about half preserved with music. The earliest are due to Thibaut de Champagne, whose renown no doubt contributed to the genre's success among the poet-musicians of Arras, especially Jehan Bretel and Adam de la Halle. In six alternating stanzas of identical form and of the courtly chanson type, two poets debate a dilemmatic question, normally concerning amorous behavior and often playful as well as reflective of bourgeois circumstances, posed by one of them in the first stanza; then, in separate *envois*, they ask two judges for their verdict, which is never recorded.

Samuel N. Rosenberg

[See also: ADAM DE LA HALLE; JEHAN BRETEL; *TENSO/ DÉBAT*; TROUVÈRE POETRY]

Lângfors, Arthur, Alfred Jeanroy, and Louis Brandin, eds. *Recueil général des jeux-partis français.* 2 vols. Paris: Champion, 1926.
Gally, Michèle. "Les Arrageois et le jeu-parti." *Romania* 107 (1986): 55–76.
Stewart, M.F. "The Melodic Structure of Thirteenth-Century 'Jeux-partis.'" *Acta Musicologica* 51 (1979): 86–107.

JEWELRY AND METALWORKING. As early as the 5th century, the working of precious and nonprecious metals became a leading craft in Gaul. Through contact with peoples from central Asia during the period of migration, the Germanic tribes learned the art of working refined metals. However, the processes used were not always an improvement over earlier Gallo-Roman ones. The earlier *trempe* technique, for example, in which hot metal was dipped in cold water to give the object rigidity, gave way to the *recuit* process, which consisted of heating metal objects several times while letting them cool down between each heating. On the other hand, the development of soldered joints between different metals, metal plating, and inlaying allowed the forging of sturdy, reliable weapons that were largely responsible for Frankish military successes. In this period, iron was still a rare and precious commodity, reserved almost exclusively for military and court use. Most early metalwork therefore consists of the weapons and objects of personal adornment that have been found in large numbers accompanying aristocratic burials of the period.

In jewelry making, early Frankish craftsmen worked most frequently with the *cloisonné* process, which consisted of setting jewels in tiny compartments formed of gold bands or strips soldered to a metal baseplate. The objects thus executed are a combination of primitive and refined ornamentation, good examples of which can be seen in the treasure of the Christian queen Arnegund (d. ca. 565), discovered in a tomb in the church of Saint-Denis. Gold- and silversmiths had high social standing in early-medieval cultures; compensation in silver for the murder of a serf was thirty *sous*, forty for a carpenter, fifty for a blacksmith, but as much as a hundred for a gold- or silversmith.

A model early metalworker was St. Éloi (ca. 588–660), who was born in Limoges and apprenticed there to the master of the mint. After creating two royal thrones of gold and precious stones for Clotar II, he was made head goldsmith of the royal mint at Marseille. After Clotar's death in 629, his son Dagobert I continued to patronize Éloi, naming him bishop of Tournai and Noyon as well as making him one of his chief ministers. Now wealthy, Éloi founded a monastery at Solignac and a convent for women in Paris. With his canonization, the bishop-goldsmith became the patron saint of silver-, gold-, and blacksmiths.

By the 11th and 12th centuries, iron was more generally available, thanks largely to imports from west Africa, and forges could now be found in most rural villages. Although iron was still used primarily for military purposes (weapons and armor for both men and horses), its greater abundance permitted the production of sturdier farming implements, and these led to a revolution in agrarian techniques and productivity during this period. Particularly significant was the development of the wheeled plow, with coulter, share, and moldboard, which allowed farmers to till the heavy soils of northern France efficiently for the first time. Steel, an iron-carbon alloy, is mentioned for the first time in a text from Anjou dated to 1177. By the end of the 12th century, the blacksmith and the miller were the backbone of the typical village hierarchy.

In jewelry making, the process of enameling was rediscovered in the early 12th century, with the *champlevé* technique now predominating, and became widely used for large jewels, brooches, rings, sword handles, and belt buckles. In spite of attempts by the church to limit ostentatious display, ornamental jewels became more and more

refined. Noble men and women alike frequently placed a band of metal or a braided ribbon decorated with pearls and precious stones (*couronne*) on their head. The rising bourgeoisie of the northern cities, frequently as rich and powerful as the noble classes by the 13th century, sought to imitate the nobility in their finery.

Religious devotional practice introduced the rosary, whose beads were made of gold, bone, ivory, coral, mother of pearl, or amber. Enamel, having become too commonplace, fell out of fashion, while diamonds, pearls, and gold and silver decorations were preferred. Upper-class men and women had hands full of rings, and both sexes wore belts, necklaces, bracelets, and metal bands on their head.

The development in the 13th century of guilds led to high degrees of specialization among the metalworking crafts. Knife makers, for example, were divided into two guilds: the cutler and the gold, wood, or ivory handle maker. Toward the end of the Middle Ages, bills of Parlement in 1429 show that goldsmiths were forbidden to work with silver and that distinctions were made between those who worked with various percentages of precious metals.

Didier J. Course

[See also: AGRICULTURE; CLOTHING, COSTUME, AND FASHION; ENAMELING; LIÈGE; MIGRATIONS ART; SOLIGNAC; TOURNAI]

Le fer à travers les âges. Colloque de Nancy, 1965. *Annales de l'Est* 16 (1966).
Lespinasse, René de, and François Bonnardot. *Le livre des métiers d'Étienne Boileau.* Paris: Imprimerie Nationale, 1879.
"Le travail dans la France médiévale." In *La France et les Français.* Encyclopédie de la Pléiade (1981), pp. 196–347.
Wolff, Philippe. "Le moyen âge." In *Histoire générale du travail*, ed. Louis-Henri Parias. 4 vols. Paris: Nouvelle Librairie de France, 1962.

JEWS. Jews settled in what is now southern France in antiquity. New settlements took place in the course of the Middle Ages, although many parts of northern France did not see significant Jewish immigration until the 11th or 12th century. At its height, immediately before 1306, Jewish population reached at least 100,000 (in a total population of 9–12 million) with the vast majority concentrated in the south but with significant settlements in Champagne, Burgundy, and the Île-de-France. Northern French (Tsarfati) Jewry had its strongest ties to the Rhenish communities to the east and provided the pool from which Jews migrated to England after the Norman Conquest (1066). Southern Jews in Languedoc and Provence were in touch with the political, social, economic, and cultural life of other Mediterranean communities, especially in Spain and northern Italy.

A great cultural division distinguished northern Jewry from southern, especially in the centuries after 1096, the period that saw massacres of Jews in the Rhineland and elsewhere in the north in the wake of the Crusades. Society in the north was for the most part provincial, even parochial; there were few large towns. Northern Jews even before the period of the Crusades were noted for their brilliant exegesis of the Bible and for legal(istic) learning in general. Rashi (Rabbi Solomon ben Isaac; 1040–1105) and his followers loom large in this story. Northern Jews also developed a notable martyrocentric self-image, expressed particularly in liturgical poetry. Southern Jews mastered these genres as well but were renowned for their interest in secular subjects, such as philosophy, in the tradition of the Spaniard Maimonides (Moses ben Maimon; 1135–1204). Southern Jews were also well known for their lyric poetry, and southern society in general for its greater cosmopolitanism based on a vibrant urban culture in the coastal cities.

In the Carolingian period, the Jews of the south enjoyed considerable autonomy, and their leading citizen, the so-called *nasi* (loosely translated as "king"), came from a family of considerable influence with Christians and Jews. Later legends told how the Jews of the Narbonnais had supported Charlemagne in his military engagements with the Muslims, and the evident prosperity of the southern communities was supposed to have originated in Charles's gratitude for their support. Jews, however, came under increasing pressure in the 12th and 13th centuries, at first mainly in the north, later in every region where the authority or even influence of the Capetian rulers of France reached. Believing that Jews ritually murdered Christian children, Philip II Augustus expelled his Jews from the royal domain, the Île-de-France, in 1182 but allowed them to return in 1198. From 1198 onward, they were placed under an ever-growing list of restrictions as to occupation, residence, and social and commercial interaction with Christians. By the 13th century, they were confined largely to the business of moneylending.

In 1240, the crown investigated the Talmud at the behest of the pope to determine, among other things, whether it blasphemed Christianity. Two years later, twenty-four cartloads of copies of the book were consigned by royal order to the flames. Philip IV, believing that Jews endeavored to obtain pieces of the eucharistic host in order to desecrate them, put further restrictions on Jewish activities. In 1306, he arrested and seized the property of Jews all over the kingdom and then expelled them. His son Louis X readmitted them for a term of twelve years in 1315, and thousands returned. After anti-Jewish riots associated with a popular movement for crusade (1320) and the rumors of a plot between Jews and lepers to poison the wells in France at the behest of the Muslim ruler of Granada (1321), many Jews were persecuted and fled. Not until 1359 was a reduced number of Jews allowed to return to do business and be taxed. The period of their sojourn was marked by unceasing popular animosity and increasing acts of violence. They were expelled definitively in 1394.

Throughout the period of their settlement in France, Jews governed themselves in internal matters. They had courts that settled disputes over marriage, contracts, ritual law, and so forth. Each community, if of a sufficient size, leased or owned communal sites and buildings, such as synagogues, schools, baths, ovens, and cemeteries. In relations with Christians, however, and in criminal matters, Jews were subject to the jurisdiction of the king or of those lords who had *dominium* over them. Despite the progressively stricter restrictions on residence, it is incorrect to speak of the ghettoization of French Jewry. Jewish neighborhoods almost always had some Christian residents. Nonetheless, Jewish solidarity, reinforced by Christian restrictive legislation on contacts with Christians, was exceptionally strong. Conversion to Christianity, even in times of great violence, seems to have been rare.

William Chester Jordan

[See also: ANTI-SEMITISM; BIBLE, JEWISH INTERPRETATION OF; CLOTHING, JEWISH; MAIMONIDES, INFLUENCE OF; MANUSCRIPTS, HEBREW ILLUMINATED]

Brown, Elizabeth A.R. "Philip V, Charles IV, and the Jews of France." *Speculum* 66 (1991): 294–329.

Chazan, Robert. *Medieval Jewry in Northern France*. Baltimore: Johns Hopkins University Press, 1973.

Jordan, William. *The French Monarchy and the Jews from Philip Augustus to the Last Capetians*. Philadelphia: University of Pennsylvania Press, 1989.

Kriegel, Maurice. *Les Juifs à la fin du moyen âge dans l'Europe méditerranéenne*. Paris: Hachette, 1979.

Schwarzfuchs, Simon. *Les Juifs de France*. Paris: Michel, 1975.

JOHANNES DE GARLANDIA (fl. ca. 1240). An influential music theorist associated with the University of Paris, Johannes is the author of two treatises, *De plana musica* and *De mensurabili musica*, in which he offers important discussions of the Notre-Dame polyphonic repertoire, the systemization of musical intervals, and the codification of the rhythmic modes. His long-enduring system of musical intervals divides consonance and dissonance into "perfect," "imperfect," and "medial" categories. With respect to Notre-Dame polyphony, which he categorized by style as organum, copula, or discant, his treatment of the six rhythmic modes and their notation addressed one of the major innovations of this repertoire.

Steven E. Plank

[See also: MUSIC THEORY; MUSICAL NOTATION; NOTRE-DAME SCHOOL; ORGANUM; RHYTHMIC MODE]

Johannes de Garlandia. *De mensurabili musica*, ed. Erich Reimer. Wiesbaden: Steiner, 1972.

Apel, Willi. *The Notation of Polyphonic Music, 900–1600*. 4th ed. Cambridge: Mediaeval Academy, 1953.

Rasch, Rudolf A. *Iohannes de Garlandia en de ontwikkeling van de voor Franconische notatie*. Brooklyn: Institute of Medieval Music, 1969.

JOHN, DUKE OF BERRY (1340–1416). The son of John II the Good of France and Bonne de Luxembourg, John was born in the castle of Vincennes on November 30, 1340. His father named him count of Poitou in 1356, but when this territory was ceded to England by the treaty of 1360

John became duke of Berry and Auvergne. During the years 1360–64, he was one of the hostages sent to England after the release of his father from captivity.

In 1369, John was charged with guarding the western frontier to keep the English contained within Poitou, and his brother Charles V reassigned him this county as an incentive to recover it from the English. His ineptitude at military strategy soon became clear. In 1374, Charles V's attitude toward John changed, perhaps because of a distaste for his private life. In October, when arranging for the succession, Charles V ordered that John not be one of his son's guardians if the dauphin, the future Charles VI, should succeed to the throne as a minor. Despite some rapprochement between the brothers in 1375 and 1376, John never regained Charles's full confidence. With the accession of Charles VI in 1380, however, John was officially accorded a place in the government and began to act as mediator between his two surviving brothers, the dukes of Anjou and Burgundy.

In November 1380, John was named royal lieutenant-general in Languedoc, where his officers and his policies soon made him unpopular. He rarely visited the Midi personally, and his lack of direct involvement produced near-anarchy in the province. When the king resolved to go to the south in person in 1389, John resigned his lieutenancy. The details of John's political behavior, especially in the years following the assassination of his nephew Louis of Orléans in 1407, show him to have been unethical, unreliable, and selfish. Despite this evidence, contemporaries viewed him as gregarious, eloquent, and philanthropic. He did show both consistency and determination in his ecclesiastical policy, being the French prince most committed to ending the papal Schism.

After April 1404, as the king's sole surviving paternal uncle, John enjoyed a prestigious position and important role at court, serving as mediator between the Burgundian and Armagnac parties, particularly after the murder of the duke of Orléans. He was married twice: in 1360 to Jeanne d'Armagnac and, after her death, in 1389 to Jeanne de Boulogne. He died in Paris on June 15, 1416, leaving no male heirs.

Richard C. Famiglietti

One of the greatest patrons in the history of art, John was an inveterate collector—of books, dogs, castles, tapestries, jewels, and *objets d'art,* whether antique or contemporary. If he overtaxed his people, as has been claimed, it was to transform his immense wealth into works of art. Probably the best-known work commissioned by him is the unfinished *Très Riches Heures* (Chantilly, Musée Condé), illuminated by the Limbourg brothers and Jean Colombe. The famous calendar illuminations in this manuscript picture some of the duke's seventeen castles: Lusignan, Dourdan, Hôtel de Nesle, Clain, Étampes, Saumur, the Louvre, and Vincennes. Another favorite castle, Mehun-sur-Yèvre, dominates the Temptation of Christ scene. Other works illuminated by the brothers include the *Très Belles Heures de Notre Dame* (B.N. lat. 3093) and the *Belles Heures* (New York, The Cloisters). They also contributed a miniature of the duke setting off on a journey in the *Petites Heures* (B.N. lat. 18014) and some scenes in *grisaille* for a *Bible historiale* (B.N. fr. 166). Another famous book of hours associated with the duke is the *Grandes Heures* (B.N. lat. 919), commissioned in 1407 and completed in 1409. Unfortunately, its original sixteen large miniatures, possibly by Jacquemart de Hesdin, who had illuminated the *Heures de Bruxelles* (before 1402) for the duke, have been lost. The list of artists contributing small miniatures reads like a who's who of the day, including the Boucicaut and Bedford Masters, as well as the Pseudo-Jacquemart. Other artists in the duke's employ were his master architect Gui de Dammartin, André Beauneveu, and Jean de Cambrai, who sculpted the duke's tomb.

John's extensive library included thirty-eight chivalric romances, forty-one histories, as well as works by Aristotle, Nicole Oresme, and Marco Polo. His secular books were outnumbered by religious works, especially prayer books: fourteen Bibles, sixteen psalters, eighteen breviaries, six missals, and fifteen books of hours. Of the over 300 illuminated manuscripts in the duke's library, some one hundred are extant today. Most of the other objects in his collections are known to us only through the extensive registers he caused to be kept after 1401.

William W. Kibler

[See also: ARMAGNACS; BEAUNEVEU, ANDRÉ; BOOK OF HOURS; CHARLES VI; COLOMBE, JEAN; ENAMELING; LIBRARIES; LIMBOURG BROTHERS; MEHUN-SUR-YÈVRE; PHILIP III THE BOLD]

Guiffrey, J. *Inventaires de Jean, duc de Berry (1401–1416).* 2 vols. Paris, 1894–96.

Lacour, René. *Le gouvernement de l'apanage de Jean, duc de Berry 1360–1416.* Paris: Picard, 1934.

Lehoux, Francoise. *Jean de France, duc de Berri: sa vie, son action politique.* 4 vols. Paris: Picard, 1966–68.

Longnon, Jean, and Raymond Cazelles. *The Très Riches Heures of Jean, Duke of Berry.* New York: Braziller, 1969.

Meiss, Millard. *French Painting in the Time of Jean de Berry: The Late Fourteenth Century and the Patronage of the Duke.* 2nd ed. 2 vols. London: Phaidon, 1969.

———, and Elizabeth H. Beatson. *The Belles Heures of Jean, Duke of Berry.* New York: Braziller, 1974.

Thomas, Marcel. *The Grandes Heures of Jean, Duke of Berry.* New York: Braziller, 1971.

JOHN I LACKLAND (1167–1216). King of England. The youngest son of Henry II and Eleanor of Aquitaine, John acceded to the English throne in 1199, after the death of his brother Richard. He was immediately confronted with the difficulty of securing English control over Maine, Anjou, and Touraine against the claims of his nephew and rival for the crown, Arthur I, duke of Brittany. The struggle ended in victory for John; as set out in the Treaty of Le Goulet in May 1200, he was acknowledged heir to all continental possessions of his father and brother in return for his recognition of the king of France as his overlord. But following his marriage later that year to Isabelle d'Angoulême, her spurned fiancé, Hugues X de Lusignan, appealed to Philip II Augustus for redress, and the French king summoned John to appear before his court. When John refused, Philip declared forfeit his continental possessions and launched an assault upon Normandy. John's efforts to retain hold of Normandy were thwarted by the defection of the Norman barons to Philip, and in December 1203 he returned to England to reconsider strategy and gather his resources. But Philip's capture of Château-Gaillard, a key stronghold, in March 1204 dealt a major blow to his plans, and the rest of Normandy quickly fell, followed by John's remaining possessions with the exception of portions of Aquitaine. In an expedition in 1206, John regained Poitou, and he spent the following eight years plotting his return to the Continent to take back the rest of his former lands, during which time he built up a key alliance with the Holy Roman emperor Otto of Brunswick. In 1214, he launched his attack from Poitou while Otto invaded from Flanders. But John soon found his expedition collapsing for lack of support, while his hopes were dealt a final blow with the defeat of his allies at the Battle of Bouvines in July 1214. All that now effectively remained to the English crown in France were the lands of Gascony in the southwest.

Whether due to ill fortune or to his own incompetence, John's reign proved the turning point in the efforts of the French kings to break up the Angevin empire and extend their control over the territories of France. In addition, as a consequence of John's defeat at Bouvines the Capetian dynasty emerged as the strongest in Europe, a position it would maintain for another century.

Jan Ryder

[See also: BOUVINES; CHÂTEAU-GAILLARD; GISORS; PHILIP II AUGUSTUS]

Painter, Sidney. *The Reign of King John*. Baltimore: Johns Hopkins University Press, 1949.

Powicke, F.M. *The Loss of Normandy, 1189–1204: Studies in the History of the Angevin Empire*. 2nd ed. Manchester: Manchester University Press, 1961.

Warren, W.L. *King John*. Berkeley: University of California Press, 1978.

JOHN II THE GOOD (1319–1364). King of France, 1350–64. The elder son of Philip VI and Jeanne of Burgundy, John became heir to the throne when his father succeeded to it in 1328. In 1332, John married Bonne de Luxembourg, daughter of the king of Bohemia. Before she died of plague in 1349, Bonne bore him nine children, among whom were the future Charles V and Jeanne, who married Charles the Bad of Navarre.

In the early campaigns of the Hundred Years' War, John's first important command was at the abortive siege of Aiguillon in 1345. He was much attached to his mother and to the strong Burgundian faction in French politics, with which she was aligned. When Philip VI finally tried to mollify the dissident northwestern nobility in the 1340s and reduce the role of Burgundians, John remained linked to the latter in opposition to his father.

John's accession to the throne in 1350, soon followed by the summary execution of the constable Raoul de Brienne, revived the old tension between the Valois monarchy and the northwestern nobles. Leadership of the opposition passed to the Évreux branch of the royal family, headed by Charles of Navarre, who engineered the murder of the new constable, Charles of Spain, in 1354. After two provisional settlements with his dangerous son-in-law, John finally lost patience and arrested Charles in April 1356, executing several of his Norman allies and plunging northwestern France into civil war.

John also attracted criticism for his style of government, which gave great responsibility to the heads of administrative bodies, who tended to be men of modest social origins. Their continuity in office contrasted with that of the royal council, which frequently changed in composition as John had to appoint representatives of political factions rather than trusted men of his own choosing. Reformers on this council resented their lack of control over the administrative bodies. Bourgeois reformers, led by Parisians, harbored personal and political resentments against these royal officials. Noble reformers had an agenda based on class and geography as well as governmental philosophy, while clergy were found in both camps.

These opposition groups both played a role in the Estates General of 1355, but their failure to generate needed revenues provoked the king into policies that alienated both groups during 1356. In September, with an army consisting of his own noble supporters, John II met defeat and capture at the hands of an Anglo-Gascon army at Poitiers. For the next four years, he was a prisoner in England, trying to negotiate a treaty that would secure his release, while his son Charles struggled to preserve some authority for the monarchy in Paris.

As the bourgeois reformers showed increasing hostility to the nobles, and as the nobles became disillusioned with their erratic leader Charles the Bad, the crown managed to recruit important dissident nobles and rebuilt its power around a new coalition. This realignment occurred during the last six years of John's reign, but historians differ as to whether he or his son deserves credit for the royal recovery. Released for a large ransom under the terms of the Treaty of Brétigny in 1360, John had to contend with the violence of thousands of unemployed soldiers. After considering a crusade to lure them away, he secured from the Estates in December 1363 an important new tax, the *fouage*, to finance an army to restore order. Continuing unresolved problems with England were complicated when the king's son Louis, a hostage for his father's ransom, broke parole and fled. John returned to captivity in England and died there in the spring of 1364.

John Bell Henneman, Jr.

[See also: ESTATES (GENERAL); HUNDRED YEARS' WAR; MARCEL, ÉTIENNE; POITIERS; ROYAL ADMINISTRATION AND FINANCE]

Bordonove, Georges. *Jean le Bon et son temps*. Paris: Ramsay, 1980.

Cazelles, Raymond. "Jean II le Bon: quel homme? quel roi?" *Revue historique* 509 (1974): 5–26.

———. *Société politique, noblesse et couronne sous Jean le Bon et Charles V.* Geneva: Droz, 1982.

Deviosse, Jean. *Jean le Bon.* Paris: Fayard, 1985.

Henneman, John Bell. *Royal Taxation in Fourteenth Century France: The Captivity and Ransom of John II, 1356–70.* Philadelphia: American Philosophical Society, 1976.

JOHN OF SALISBURY (ca. 1115–1180). John was born in Old Sarum, England, and entered a clerical career as a young man, studying in the schools of Paris from 1136 until the mid-1140s. There, he heard lectures by Peter Abélard, Robert of Melun, William of Conches, Thierry of Chartres, Gilbert of Poitiers, and other masters of the day. He then traveled to Rome, where he entered the service of the pope. In 1148, he attended the synod at Reims where Gilbert of Poitiers was tried for heresy, a trial that John recounts in his *Historia pontificalis*. In 1153–54, he returned to England, where he served as secretary to Theobald, archbishop of Canterbury, and to his successor, Thomas Becket. John was part of one of the most striking public conflicts of royal and ecclesiastical power in the 12th century, that between Becket and King Henry II Plantagenêt of England. Becket's exile to France took John of Salisbury there as well. John was present in Christ Church cathedral, Canterbury, when Becket was attacked, but he fled the scene before the actual murder. In 1176, John was consecrated bishop of Chartres and died there in 1180. He knew well the worlds of episcopal patronage, education in the schools of Paris, the papal and royal courts, and the web of personal and professional friendships woven by the exchange of letters. Each of these circles influenced his life and writings.

The *Metalogicon*, a spirited defense of the Trivium, with emphasis upon the discipline of logic, is a valuable resource for understanding the world of the 12th-century schools and lists the masters with whom John studied. His *Policraticus* combines political theory, a handbook for government, criticism of court life, and a program of education for courtiers. In the *Historia pontificalis*, John offers a history focused on the papal court from the Synod of Reims (1148) through the year 1152. Among his other writings are a *vita* of Anselm of Bec and a brief *vita* of Becket, probably meant to serve as preface to a collection of the murdered archbishop's letters. Some 325 of John's letters survive.

Grover A. Zinn

[See also: ABÉLARD, PETER; CHARTRES; GILBERT OF POITIERS; LIBERAL ARTS; ROBERT OF MELUN; SCHOLASTICISM; SCHOOLS, CATHEDRAL; THIERRY OF CHARTRES; UNIVERSITIES; WILLIAM OF CONCHES]

John of Salisbury. *Memoirs of the Papal Court*, ed. and trans. Marjorie Chibnall. London: Nelson, 1956.

———. *The Metalogicon of John of Salisbury: A Twelfth-Century Defense of the Verbal and Logical Arts of the Trivium*, trans. D.D. McGarry. Berkeley: University of California Press, 1955.

———. *The Letters of John of Salisbury, 1: The Early Letters (1153–1161)*, ed. W.J. Millor and H.E. Butler, rev. Christopher N.L. Brooke. London: Nelson, 1955.

———. *The Letters of John of Salisbury, 2: The Later Letters (1163–1180)*, ed. W.J. Millor and Christopher N.L. Brooke. Oxford: Oxford University Press, 1979.

Smalley, Beryl. *The Beckett Conflict and the Schools: A Study of Intellectuals in Politics.* Oxford: Blackwell, 1973, pp. 87–108.

Webb, C.C.J. *John of Salisbury.* London: Methuen, 1932.

Wilkes, Michael, ed. *The World of John of Salisbury.* Oxford: Blackwell, 1984.

JOHN THE FEARLESS (1371–1419). Duke of Burgundy. The son of Philip the Bold, duke of Burgundy, and Marguerite of Flanders, John the Fearless was born at Dijon on May 28, 1371, and named count of Nevers in 1384. In 1396, to aid the king of Hungary against the Turks, he led the Franco-Burgundian contingent of the expedition now called the Crusade of Nicopolis. When John inherited Burgundy in 1404, he gave the county of Nevers to his brother Philip. On August 31, 1404, John's daughter Marguerite married the duke of Guyenne, heir to the French throne.

In 1405, John became involved in French politics by opposing the new tax promoted by the duke of Orléans. At the death of his mother on March 21, 1405, John inherited the county of Flanders and found himself at war with the English after they attacked his port of Sluys. His desire to besiege the English stronghold of Calais was thwarted when Louis of Orléans influenced the royal council to refuse him aid. From this point on, a bitter hatred developed between John and Louis. John's tactics were impetuous, risky, and brutal. His demands for reform were made to gain the support of the people, and he was clearly interested more in personal gain than in the kingdom of France or true governmental reform. Because Louis threatened his interests on too many fronts, John had him assassinated in 1407. In his official justification for this act, presented by Jean Petit in Paris on March 8, 1408, John claimed that he had saved the monarchy because Louis had been planning to have the king and his heirs killed in order to take the crown for himself. John received the king's pardon, but the Orléans family was unwilling to accept the decision. The ensuing conflict, called the quarrel of the Burgundians and the Armagnacs, dominated French politics even after John's own assassination at Montereau on September 10, 1419.

Richard C. Famiglietti

[See also: ARMAGNACS; BURGUNDY; CABOCHIENS; CHARLES VI; CHARLES VII; LOUIS, DUKE OF GUYENNE; LOUIS, DUKE OF ORLÉANS]

Famiglietti, R.C. *Royal Intrigue: Crisis at the Court of Charles VI 1392–1420.* New York: AMS, 1986.

Mirot, Leon. "Jean sans Peur de 1398 à 1405 d'après les comptes de sa chambre aux deniers." *Annuaire-Bulletin de la Société de l'Histoire de France* (1938): 129–245.

Pocquet du Haut-Jussé, Barthélémy. "Jean sans Peur: programme, moyens et résultats." *Revue de l'Université de Bruxelles* 7 (1954–55): 385–404.

————. "Jean sans Peur: son but et sa méthode." *Annales de Bourgogne* 14 (1942): 181–96.

Vaughan, Richard. *John the Fearless: The Growth of Burgundy.* New York: Barnes and Noble, 1966.

JOINVILLE, JEAN DE (1225–1317). Joinville's *Vie de saint Louis*, a French prose memoir by a powerful aristocrat, is one of our most valuable accounts of noble society in the 13th century. Joinville's father was seneschal of Champagne, an office he inherited. In 1248, he decided to take part in the Seventh Crusade and thus met St. Louis, becoming a close friend. The two endured captivity together, then Joinville served as royal steward at Acre (1250–54) before returning to France. Joinville began his memoirs of the king in 1272, just after Louis's death, but undertook the second part (composed 1298–1309) when Jeanne of Navarre, wife of Philip IV, requested it.

Joinville's narrative has many virtues. As an important noble, he advised the king during the crusade; as a warrior, he fought in it. Although a close friend, Joinville, unlike other biographers of Louis, respected but was not overawed by the king and sometimes disapproved of his actions, particularly when Louis's saintliness conflicted with what Joinville perceived to be his duties as king, aristocrat, and layman. Louis's decision to go on crusade in 1270 was one such occasion, but there were others. Joinville felt free at the time to speak his mind and records a number of salty interchanges between himself and his ruler. He was also candid about his own prejudices; he defended aristocratic privileges and was contemptuous of bourgeois upstarts. His observations are vivid, and his frankness makes the *Vie* delightful reading.

Joinville's work was overshadowed in his own day by Guillaume de Nangis's biography of Louis; of the three extant manuscripts, only one is medieval, a copy of the presentation manuscript of 1309.

Leah Shopkow

[See also: BIOGRAPHY; HISTORIOGRAPHY]

Joinville, Jean de. *La vie de saint Louis,* ed. Noel L. Corbett. Sherbrooke: Naaman, 1977.

———— and Villehardouin. *Chronicles of the Crusades,* trans. Margaret R.B. Shaw. Harmondsworth: Penguin, 1963.

Billson, Marcus K. "Joinville's *Histoire de Saint-Louis:* Hagiography, History and Memoir." *American Benedictine Review* 31 (1980): 418–42.

Perret, Michèle. "'À la fin de sa vie ne fuz-je mie': Joinville's *Vie de Saint-Louis.*" *Revue des sciences humaines* 183 (1981): 16–37.

JONAS OF ORLÉANS (before 780–ca. 843). Frankish theologian. Born in Aquitaine, Jonas became bishop of Orléans in 818, after its previous bishop, Theodulf, was compromised in the revolt of Bernard of Italy, nephew of Emperor Louis the Pious (r. 814–40). Jonas was involved in the political crises of Louis's reign and in several synods, including the assembly held in Paris in 825 to discuss the problem of image worship in the East and the Paris reform synod of 829. In connection with the synod of 825, Louis the Pious charged Jonas and Archbishop Jeremiah of Sens with preparing for Pope Eugenius II an extract of the council's decrees, which clarified the ways that 9th-century Carolingian views on images and their worship differed from those espoused by the papacy and the Byzantine court.

Jonas's writings also include the treatise *De institutione regia,* composed for Pepin of Aquitaine (d. 838), on the duties of monarchs and the role of bishops in the temporal sphere; *De institutione laicali,* written for Count Matfrid of Orléans, purportedly to explain the obligations of marriage; and *De cultu imaginum,* completed after 840, which defended the cults of relics and the Cross as well as the presence of artistic representations in churches.

Celia Chazelle

Jonas of Orléans. *PL* 106.

————. *A Ninth-Century Political Tract: The "De institutione regia" of Jonas of Orleans,* trans. R.W. Dyson. Smithtown: Exposition, 1983.

Delaruelle, Étienne. "Jonas d'Orléans et le moralisme carolingien." *Bulletin de littérature ecclésiastique* 55 (1954): 129–43.

Reviron, Jean. *Les idées politico-religieuses d'un évêque du IXe siècle, Jonas d'Orléans et son "De institutione regia": étude et texte critique.* Paris: Vrin, 1930.

JONGLEUR. Professional performers best known for propagating the chansons de geste, jongleurs also performed more mundane acts, such as acting, doing stunts, dancing, and bear baiting. Since the jongleurs normally sang the works of another and belonged to a lower class, they are regularly distinguished from the trouvères, who by definition "found," that is, created themselves, the songs they sang and did not participate in the other aspects of the jongleurs' art. Deriving from Old French *jogleor,* itself from Latin *joculator* 'jokester, comedian,' the form *jongleur* dates from the 16th century and is a contamination of *jangler* 'to chat, to gossip.'

The jongleurs' trade apparently emerged about the 8th century, although attestation of the word itself occurs only in the 9th. The church early on recognized the danger of uncontrolled histrionics during holy festivities, but since jongleurs also recited saints' lives ecclesiastical authority began to favor them, and some few acquired prestige. As a rule, however, their low social class made them outcasts, so that they were often rejected and prohibited from participating in the church services.

The 13th century has been labeled the golden age of the jongleur, when he was both respected and admired. Handsome rewards accruing to some attracted recruits from among artisans and peasantry, sometimes including women. Jongleurs amused the common folk by enlivening their fairs, saints' days, and other popular events. Occasions to seek their services abounded: return from battle, dubbing of knights, marriages, funerals. Along with their tales, songs, and acrobatics, they brought dancing, to the consternation of moralists. Jongleurs were often considered a necessary touch of elegance in aristocratic courts. They traveled from castle to castle seeking hospitality and employment. Those permanently hired in the courts were called *ménéstrels*. Typically, the court was seated around the banquet table, and as the meal began a jongleur might recite a romance or announce the serving of the courses. But these were preludes to the core of the contribution, which came after dinner with instrumental music, community singing, and acting.

Jongleurs were rarely paid with money. Their salary consisted above all of food and drink, after which ranked clothing. A lord and his guests occasionally would shower the performers with rich gifts in order to outdo each other. Only then could a jongleur pay off the debts he had accumulated at the tavern or satisfy his family with capon and wine.

In the 15th century, the jongleur art broke up into specialties. Lower status came to those who emphasized acrobatics and prestidigitation; musicians and poets rose in prestige.

John L. Grigsby

[See also: CHANSON DE GESTE; MUSICAL INSTRUMENTS]

Faral, Edmond. *Les jongleurs en France au moyen âge*. Paris: Champion, 1910.

JORDAN FANTOSME (fl. late 12th c.). Author of an Anglo-Norman verse chronicle of some 2,065 lines recounting the barons' revolt against King Henry II Plantagenêt and the incursions into northern England of William the Lion's Scottish irregulars in 1173–74. Most likely, he should be identified with the Jordanus Fantasma who was a pupil of Gilbert of Poitiers in Paris and a clerk at Winchester. Jordan, writing in late 1174 or 1175, is an important contemporary witness to the events described, particularly on the Scottish front. Jordan's *Chronicle* is preserved in two manuscripts, Durham Cathedral Library C. iv. 27 and Lincoln Cathedral Library 104. The poem is divided into 217 laisses; the versification is both experimental and highly original.

William W. Kibler

[See also: ANGLO-NORMAN LITERATURE; HISTORIOGRAPHY; GILBERT OF POITIERS]

Jordan Fantosme. *Jordan Fantosme's Chronicle*, ed. and trans. Ronald Carlyle Johnston. Oxford: Clarendon, 1981.

JOUARRE. The ancient city of Dividorum, in Brie near present-day Meaux, was the site of a prestigious Benedictine abbey for women founded during the Merovingian era, one of the oldest religious foundations in the Île-de-France. Like many old foundations, Jouarre had a series of small churches but never a single large abbey church. Important vestiges of the rectangular crypt (second half of the 7th c.) are preserved behind the 15th-century church. Its two rows of porphyry and jasper columns, surmounted by white

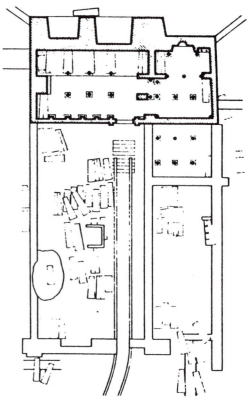

Jouarre (Seine-et-Marne), plan of monastery. After Rousseau.

marble capitals, are noteworthy. In the crypt are also found Merovingian sarcophagi with foliage and cockleshell decorations. The most notable is that of St. Agilbert, 7th-century bishop of Paris. At the head of the tomb is carved Christ in Majesty, while on the two sides dead souls raise their arms in prayer.

All that remains of the 12th-century Romanesque church is the bell tower. The nearby crypt of St. Ébrégésile contains additional Merovingian sarcophagi.

William W. Kibler/William W. Clark

Delahaye, Gilbert-Roland. "Jouarre: état des recherches sur les cryptes mérovingiennes." In *Île-de-France de Clovis à Hugues Capet*. Guiry-en-Vexin: Valhermeil, 1993, pp. 106–10.

Maillé, La Marquise de. *Les cryptes de Jouarre*. Paris: Picard, 1971.

JOUFROI DE POITIERS. An anonymous mid-13th-century romance of some 4,600 rhymed octosyllabic couplets, *Joufroi* recounts the amorous and knightly exploits of an aristocrat who closely resembles the great troubadour Guilhem IX of Aquitaine. A long central episode is dependent on *Flamenca*, while others follow the hero's travels across western France and England. Dubbed knight by the King of England in a manner reminiscent of Chrétien de Troyes's *Cligés*, he returns later to seduce the queen and ends up in a fabliaulike situation, which typifies the tongue-in-cheek humor of the romance. A second particularity is the chatty narrator, who ostentatiously interrupts the tale to seek comments from the audience and especially to relate his own unsuccessful experience with love. The text exists in a single incomplete manuscript (Copenhagen Gl. kgl. Saml. 3555, 8º).

John L. Grigsby

[See also: *FLAMENCA*; GUILHEM IX]

Fay, Percival B., and John L. Grigsby, eds. *Joufroi de Poitiers, roman d'aventures du XIIIe siècle*. Geneva: Droz, 1972.

Noël, Roger, trans. *Joufroi de Poitiers: traduction critique*. New York: Lang, 1987.

Dragonetti, Roger. *Le Gai Savoir dans la rhétorique courtoise: Flamenca et Joufroi de Poitiers*. Paris: Seuil, 1982.

JOURNAL D'UN BOURGEOIS DE PARIS.

The *Journal d'un bourgeois de Paris* provides a highly personal account of Parisian history from 1405 to 1449. It needs to be read together with other contemporary accounts of French life, such as those by the Menagier de Paris, Nicolas de Baye, Clément de Fauquembergue, and Pierre de Fenin. The work presents many puzzling features, including both its title and author. Modern scholars call it a "journal," following Denis Godefroy in 1653. All six surviving manuscripts lack the opening pages of the work, and in some manuscripts overly critical passages have been scraped away rather than simply crossed out. Internal evidence suggests that the author had some connection to the university, but its piecemeal, anecdotal composition and the author's idiosyncratic use of Latin phrases reveal that he was little interested in the categories of sacred history and therefore probably not a professional theologian. His loyalties seem to lie first with the city of Paris rather than the French nation.

Besides detailed reports on epidemics, the weather, and agricultural products, the *Journal* contains a sobering account of Jeanne d'Arc from 1429. She appeared to the author as one of many religious personalities claiming heavenly inspiration. He was dismayed that Jeanne did not renounce her mission after the university apprised her of her theological errors. Though he generally sides with the Burgundians, his description of her execution is deeply moving, and he tells how the executioner raked back the fire to expose *sa pauvre charogne* ("her poor carcass") to the crowd. The *Journal* also recounts the composition of the mural pictures of the *danse macabre* at the church of the Holy Innocents, which served as a model for later artistic versions.

Earl Jeffrey Richards

[See also: JEANNE D'ARC; *MENAGIER DE PARIS*]

Tuetey, Alexandre, ed. *Le journal d'un bourgeois de Paris*. Paris: Champion, 1881. [Based on the Vatican (Reg. Lat. 1923) and Paris manuscripts (B.N., Collection Dupuy 375; B.N. fr. 10145; 3480).]

Shirley, Janet, trans. *A Parisian Journal, 1405–1449*. Oxford: Clarendon, 1968. [From the Vatican manuscript with supplements from the Aix manuscript (Collection Méjanes, MS 316).]

JUGE-MAGE.

Judicial officer in Languedoc. The development of Roman law in Languedoc in the 12th century prepared the way for an administration of justice dispensed by trained jurists distinct from the other functionaries of secular government. With the installation of royal authority in 1226, this judicial administration received organization and a hierarchy of judges, at the head of which appear senior judicial officers in attendance upon the courts of the seneschals. The earliest of these officers, bearing the title *judex senescalli*, appear in the seneschalsy of Beaucaire in 1240 and in that of Carcassonne in 1253. By 1256, the judge of the seneschal of Beaucaire had assumed the name *juge-mage* (*judex major senescalli*). The title was adopted at Carcassonne in 1269 and subsequently in the seneschalsies of Toulouse, Rouergue, and Quercy. The *juge-mage* possessed appellate jurisdiction over the courts of the *juges-ordinaires* and also the exercise of immediate jurisdiction in cases of high justice or of unusual importance in the seneschalsy. He served as a principal counselor to the seneschal and might on occasion act as lieutenant of that officer.

Alan Friedlander

[See also: *JUGE-ORDINAIRE*; LAW AND JUSTICE]

Dognon, Paul. *Les institutions politiques et administratives du pays de Languedoc du XIII siècle aux guerres de religion*. Toulouse: Privat, 1895.

Rogozinski, Jan. "Ordinary and Major Judges." *Studia Gratiana* 15 (1972): 591–611.

Strayer, Joseph R. *Les gens de justice de Languedoc sous Philippe le Bel*. Toulouse: Association Marc Bloch, 1970.

JUGE-ORDINAIRE.

Judicial officer in Languedoc. The title of *judex ordinarius*, deriving from Roman legal procedure, entered the administrative framework of the French monarchy in the 14th century through the usages of ecclesiastical justice. In the definition of the church, it denoted a judge possessing full competence over cases falling within the area of his authority, as the bishop within his diocese. It came, in the secular sphere, to designate judges of the courts of first instance within the royal seneschalsies of Beaucaire, Carcassonne, Toulouse, Rouergue, and Quercy. Although these courts of the *viguiers* existed from the early 13th century, the title *judex ordinarius* was not applied until the establishment in the 1250s of a superior position, that of the *judex major* (*juge-mage*). By 1350, the larger subordinate courts were recognized as the seats of *judices ordinarii*. The *juges-ordinaires* exercised full competence within their districts but were subject in extraordinary cases to the appellate jurisdiction of the *juge-mage* and in general cases to that of the judge of criminal appeals.

Alan Friedlander

[See also: *JUGE-MAGE*; LAW AND JUSTICE]

Dognon, Paul. *Les institutions politiques et administratives du pays de Languedoc du XIII siècle aux guerres de religion.* Toulouse: Privat, 1895.

Gouron, André. "Enseignement du droit, légistes et canonistes dans le Midi de la France à la fin du XIII siècle et au début du XIV siècle." *Recueil de mémoires et travaux publiés par la Société d'Histoire du Droit et des Institutions des Anciens Pays de Droit Écrit* fasc. 5 (1966): 1–33.

Rogozinski, Jan. "Ordinary and Major Judges." *Studia Gratiana* 15 (1972): 591–611.

Strayer, Joseph R. *Les gens de justice de Languedoc sous Philippe le Bel.* Toulouse: Association Marc Bloch, 1970.

JULIANA OF MONT-CORNILLON (1193–1258). Founder of the feast of Corpus Christi, Juliana was born at Retinne near Liège to wealthy parents. Orphaned at the age of five, she was educated at a hospice for lepers in Mont-Cornillon, where she became prioress in 1222. As her anonymous biographer recounts, Juliana's life was marked by numerous crises that forced her to leave the hospice in 1242 and again in 1247–48. Together with a few trusted women friends, she spent the remaining years as a wandering béguine, a Cistercian nun, and finally a recluse. In 1246, Juliana and Prior John composed the Office for Corpus Christi; on June 6, 1247, the feast was celebrated for the first time in Liège; it was officially endorsed in 1264 by Pope Urban IV, with a new Office composed by Thomas Aquinas. A local cult in Juliana's honor was authorized by the Vatican in 1869.

Juliana's *vita* displays few individualistic traits besides her difficult life circumstances and accounts of her *caritas*. Although descriptions of extraordinary mystical feats are lacking, Juliana's spirituality follows generally the paradigmatic pattern of holy women of her era, especially in the form of prolonged and extreme fasting, intense devotion to the eucharist, visualizations of Christ's Passion, and reverence for the priesthood. It is therefore hard to establish how accurately Juliana's biographer captured this remarkable woman.

Ulrike Wiethaus

[See also: MYSTICISM; WOMEN, RELIGIOUS EXPERIENCE OF]

Newman, Barbara, trans. *The Life of Juliana of Mont Cornillon.* Toronto: Peregrina, 1990.

Roisin, Simone. *L'hagiographie cistercienne dans le diocèse de Liège au XIIIe siècle.* Louvain: Bibliothèque de l'Université, 1947.

Voosen, E. "Sainte Julienne de Cornillon." *Collectiana namurcenses* 26 (1922): 248–71.

JUMIÈGES. Founded ca. 654 by St. Filibert, the abbey of Notre-Dame de Jumièges (Seine-Maritime) is today a splendid ruin, its fantastic skeleton defining the skyline by the Seine. Despite being abandoned (14th c.), sacked (16th c.), and used as a quarry (18th c.), much of Notre-Dame, along with its neighbor, Saint-Pierre, and other ecclesiastical buildings survive.

Jumièges (Seine-Maritime), Notre-Dame, nave ruins. *Photograph courtesy of Whitney S. Stoddard.*

A murky history of the early abbey reveals significant ties to the Carolingian dynasty. In 841, Vikings burned the town. Eventually, the dukes of Normandy funded the reconstruction of the abbey churches of Saint-Pierre (completed 990) and Notre-Dame (1037–66) on their original 7th-century sites. Although the adventures of William the Conqueror postponed the dedication of Notre-Dame for a year, to 1067, the Conqueror brought English land and monastic ties to the abbey. The signature of austere, imposing strength common to other Norman buildings is particularly indelible at Notre-Dame. Free from embellishments and figural sculpture, variations in pierced and blind arcades highlight the sides of the western octagonal towers. A single, plain portal and great barrel-vaulted tribune projects one bay between the towers. Within the now roofless nave (which was originally timber and painted), a three-story elevation with arcade, triforium, and clerestory marches on alternating rectangular compound and columnar piers. Only the west wall of the transept tower records its original great height. Apart from the northwest wall of the north transept, very little of the transept arms survives. The east end was rebuilt in the 13th century (1267–78), but archaeological evidence suggests that the 11th-century transepts ended in apsidal chapels and the choir had an ambulatory without radiating chapels. A few figural capitals are in the abbey museum.

A passage and chapter house join Notre-Dame and Saint-Pierre. The western wall and two bays of Saint-Pierre date to the 10th century, and the rest of the structure is 13th-century. A second-story wall passage at the west end and rectilinear east end contains the long, aisleless nave. Of conventual buildings at Saint-Pierre, the 12th-century chapter house, lodgings, and cellars remain.

Founded at the beginning of the 12th century, the parish church of Saint-Valentine held relics of its patron saint from Jumièges. A façade pierced by six windows leads to the six-bay nave with plain arcade, clerestory windows, wooden roof—all Romanesque—and 16th-century choir. The nearby church of Yainville belonged to the monks of Jumièges and shares its 11th-century date. Although comparatively small, the church shares an imposing central tower and solidity with Notre-Dame.

Stacy L. Boldrick

"Jumièges." *Congrès scientifique du XIIIe centenaire.* 2 vols. Rouen, 1955.

Michon, Louis Marie. "Jumièges." *Congrès archéologique (Rouen)* 89 (1926): 587–609.

———, and Roger Martin du Gard. *L'abbaye de Jumièges.* Paris: Laurens, 1927.

Musset, Lucien. *Normandie romane.* 2 vols. La Pierre-qui-vire: Zodiaque, 1967.

Taralon, Jean. *Jumièges.* Paris: Cerf, 1955.

JUVENAL DES URSINS. The name Juvenal des Ursins was assumed by the sons of Jean Jouvenal (1360–1431), a prominent official of Charles VI and Charles VII. They claimed descent from a Neapolitan branch of the Orsini family of Rome. The new name appeared by 1410 and had completely supplanted the old one by 1438. Jean Jouvenal's origins cannot be proved. He came from Troyes, studied civil law at Orléans, was *prévôt des marchands* in Paris (1389–1400), and served as royal lawyer in the Parlement and councillor of Charles VI and of the dukes of Berry, Burgundy, and Orléans. His important role in quelling the Cabochien uprising of 1413 won him the post of chancellor to the duke of Guyenne. He remained Guyenne's councillor after his replacement as chancellor in 1415.

Jean was a high official in the Cour des Aides (1415–18) but left Paris when it fell to the Burgundians in 1418 and joined the cause of the dauphin (later Charles VII). Thereafter, he held high positions in the parlements of Poitiers and Toulouse. He acquired a barony by 1407 and was knighted by 1420.

Jean Jouvenal and Michelle de Vitry had eleven children who survived infancy, four of whom attained prominence. Jean (1388–1473), best known as the author of a chronicle of the reign of Charles VI, was bishop of Beauvais (1432–44) and Laon (1444–49) and then archbishop of Reims (1449–73). He headed the papal commission that pronounced the rehabilitation of Jeanne d'Arc in 1456 and produced a treatise on the duties of the chancellor of France. His brother Guillaume (1401–1472) was a longtime chancellor of France (1445–61 and 1465–72). Michel (b. 1409), served as *bailli* of Troyes; Jacques (1410–1457) held positions in the Parlement de Paris and Chambre des Comptes, was treasurer of the Sainte-Chapelle and archbishop of Reims (1444–49), and finished his career as patriarch of Alexandria with administration of the bishoprics of Poitiers and Fréjus.

Richard C. Famiglietti

Juvénal des Ursins, Jean. *Jean Juvénal des Ursins: écrits politiques,* ed. Peter S. Lewis and A.-M. Hayez. 2 vols. Paris: Klincksieck, 1979–86.

Batiffol, L. *Jean Jouvenel, prévôt des marchands de la ville de Paris 1360–1431.* Paris: Champion, 1894.

Lewis, Peter S. "La noblesse des Jouvenal des Ursins." *L'état et les aristocracies: France, Angleterre, Écosse.* Paris: Presses de l'École Normale Supérieure, 1989, pp. 79–101.

Little, Roger G. *The Parlement of Poitiers: War, Government, and Politics in France 1418–36.* Woodbridge: Boydell and Brewer, 1984.

Valois, Noël. "Note sur l'origine de la famille Juvenal des Ursins." *Mémoires de la Société Nationale des Antiquaires de France* 6th ser. 9 (1900): 77–88.

KING CYCLE. Charlemagne is at the center of the chansons de geste: many of the surviving epics can be grouped around him and even more so around the other rulers of the Carolingian dynasty, fused by time within the person of Charlemagne. Nevertheless, such terms as "King Cycle" or *geste du roi* remain problematic, since the poems about Charlemagne were never systematically grouped in a cycle like those of Guillaume d'Orange. The Charlemagne legend was brought together only later in the hybrid combinations of chanson de geste and verse chronicle composed by Philippe Mouskés in his *Chronique rimée* (completed in 1243) and by Girart d'Amiens in his *Charlemagne* (early 14th c.), and in the Franco-Italian epic cycle of MS Venice XIII (ca. 1350), David Aubert's *Croniques et conquestes de Charlemaine* (completed in 1458), and the Old Norse *Karlamagnús saga* (ca. 1250). The emperor and his peers figure in the chansons primarily thanks to the paramount importance of the *Chanson de Roland*, which furnished to later poets a stereotypical stock of heroes; the catastrophe at Roncevaux forms the backdrop for the organization of the cycle. Compared with other historical figures celebrated in the chansons de geste, however, Charlemagne's mighty personality, his prestige as emperor and king, and the fact that so many events of his life were well known to later generations greatly increased audience interest. Soon after the beginning of the 12th century, legendary stories about the emperor's youth, his pilgrimage to the Holy Land and travel to Constantinople, and his dispute with Ogier and wars against the Saxons were circulating in the form of chansons de geste. Only the epics about his youth constitute a more or less autonomous group, the other legends being simply integrated into the songs about the heroes of Roncevaux. The Latin Pseudo-Turpin chronicle (ca. 1140) already contains, in addition to an exaltation of the military and political service of the suzerain, the story of Ganelon's high treason in betraying Charlemagne's rearguard in the Pyrénées as he was returning from Spain. The influence of the Pseudo-Turpin is felt even later in a series of romanticized poems, such as *Aspremont*, *Gui de Bourgogne*, and *Otinel*. Within the King Cycle, it is the Spanish expedition and, to a lesser degree, the acquisition of the relics of Christ's Passion by the abbey of Saint-Denis

that form a further point of departure for poetic treatment. There is, however, no cohesion among the poems, many of which show centrifugal tendencies and resist a systematic grouping.

Charlemagne's birth is the subject of Adenet le Roi's *Berte aus grans piés* (ca. 1275), which narrates the romantic circumstances that led to the conception of the son of Pepin the Short and Bertha (a Hungarian king's daughter), the future Charlemagne. His youth is related in the fragment *Mainet* (late 12th c.), in which Bertha is poisoned by a servant whose daughter resembled Bertha so much that she could take her place with Pepin in the marital bed and conceive Heudri and Rainfroi (who later poison Pepin). Forced to flee, the young Charles changes his name to Mainet (diminutive of *magne*) and enters the service of the pagan king Galafre of Toledo, whom he helps to win a decisive battle; he obtains the hand of the king's daughter, Galienne, who is baptized and becomes his wife. In the lost *Chanson de Basin* (or *Couronnement de Charlemagne*), preserved in the *Karlamagnús saga* and in Middle Dutch and Middle High German adaptations, the youth Charles, summoned by an angel to go out and steal with the nobleman-turned-thief Basin, overhears a conspirator explaining to his wife the plan to prevent Charles's coronation; he brings down the conspiracy on the occasion of the dedication of the cathedral of Aix-la-Chapelle.

Although the historical Charlemagne was in diplomatic relations with the court of Byzantium, legend allows him also to make a pilgrimage to the Holy Land and travel to Constantinople, as in the *Voyage de Charlemagne*, in which he transports the relics of the Passion to his abbey, Saint-Denis. In *Simon de Pouille*, the Holy Land is the setting for the adventures of the old duke, Simon, of Aymeri of Narbonne's lineage (complete only in B.L. Royal 15 E VI of the 15th c.; 5,100 lines); in this poem, Charlemagne is a remote, prestigious figure, too old to take up arms himself but always willing to help his barons in danger. The liveliest characters in the poem are the converts: Synodos, Emir Jonas of Babylon's seneschal and lord of the castle Abilant; the shipmaster Sorbarrés, who assumes the name Simon the Convert, after Simon de Pouille, when he becomes a Christian; and Jonas's daughter Licoride, who marries Synodos at Saint-Germain-des-Prés at the end of the poem.

The first part of *Fierabras*, whose action takes place in Italy and Rome and revolves around the relics of Christ's Passion, is known today as the *Destruction de Rome* (probably mid-13th c.), preserved in two manuscripts and a fragment. Italy is likewise the setting for Charlemagne's fight against the pagans in *Aspremont* (late 12th c.). The poem is also called the *Enfances Roland*, because Roland forces the emperor to knight him on the battlefield after he has distinguished himself against the pagans and won his sword, Durendal. In the decisive battle, Turpin carries the True Cross, and the emir Agolant is felled by Claron, Milon's son, for the whole clan of Girart de Roussillon has come to fight against the pagans despite its feud with Charlemagne. *Otinel* is another italianate poem of the King Cycle. It deals with the conversion of Otinel, a daring Saracen messenger sent by the pagan emperor Garsile, who, having sacked Rome, has established himself in the fortress Atilie in Lombardy. Otinel's mission is to summon Charlemagne to submit to Garsile and renounce Christianity. Otinel hopes to use this opportunity to avenge his uncle Ferragu, slain by Roland, and comports himself so outrageously at Charlemagne's court that Roland challenges him to a duel, during which Otinel, winning, is suddenly enlightened by the Holy Spirit. Charlemagne offers him his daughter Belissent in marriage with Lombardy as dowry, but Otinel wants first to prove himself an exemplary Christian knight at the siege of Atilie, where he indeed shows himself stronger than Roland, Oliver, and Ogier. Otinel then weds Belissent and becomes king of Lombardy.

The war waged by Jehan in the swashbuckling romantic poem *Jehan de Lanson* (first half of the 13th c.; 6,330 Alexandrines in the most complete manuscript) also takes place in Italy. Jehan, Ganelon's nephew, has obtained from Charlemagne a duchy in southern Italy but converts to paganism; the ungrateful vassal then plots with Ganelon and Alori against his benefactor, after which the latter exiles Alori for murder but Jehan offers him hospitality. Charlemagne sends Roland and the twelve peers against the traitors; although Roland kills Jehan's father, Nivard, the peers are in great danger but are saved thanks to the artifices of the magician Basin of Gennes. This poem makes many borrowings from the *Quatre fils Aymon* and *Maugis d'Aigremont*; Basin, its real hero, is clearly an avatar of the popular and valiant magician Maugis, cousin of Aymon's sons. Among poems having the wars in Italy as subject, *Ogier le Danois*, which takes place in upper Italy from line 3,366 to 9,039 (in a poem of 12,346 lines), should also be mentioned.

Charlemagne's war against Widukind's Saxons was reflected in the lost *Guiteclin de Sassoigne* of the second half of the 12th century, of which only traces remain in the *Karlamagnús saga* and the Middle Dutch *Gwidekijn van Sassen* (late 14th c.); Jehan Bodel's incomplete *Chanson des Saisnes* (late 12th–early 13th c.) represents a courtly as well as satirical reworking of the story.

Aiquin ou la conquête de la Bretagne par le roi Charlemagne (late 12th–early 13th c.; preserved only in an incomplete 15th-c. manuscript, B.N. fr. 2233) narrates Charles's reconquest of Brittany from the Saracen Aiquin while returning with Roland's father and Naimes from a military expedition against the Saxons. Roland, Oliver, Ogier, and the other peers are still too young to participate, although the poem alludes to young Roland's deeds in *Aspremont* and underscores his Breton birth.

In the *Entrée d'Espagne*, composed by a Padovan poet in the early 14th century, Charles, having successfully fought the giant Ferragu, must besiege Pamplona; he has a falling out with Roland because of the latter's unauthorized conquest of the city of Nobles, following which Roland leaves the French camp in a huff. This incomplete poem was continued ca. 1343 in a much purer French by Nicholas of Verona in the *Prise de Pampelune* (also called *Guerre de Spagne*), in which the action continues until after Charlemagne's return from Roncevaux. Between the conquest of Pamplona and the battle of Roncevaux is *Gui de Bourgogne* (first quarter of the 13th c.; preserved in two copies of the same century), an epic with moralistic intent in which the young knights around Gui, whom they elect king of France, are pitted against the old peers surrounding Charles, and Gui in particular against Roland. The action comes to a head at the siege of Luiserne, the last pagan stronghold besides Saragossa. Competition between the armies of "the young" and "the old" barons before Luiserne is so fierce—and the poet does not hide his sympathy for the younger generation—that Charlemagne wishes Luiserne could sink into the sea to end this rivalry. The poet's creative verve gives the stock epic features the charm of novelty, and the vivacity of his dramatic sense carries much of the poem.

The epilogue of the battle of Roncevaux is developed in two poems. *Gaidon* (1230–34; three manuscripts) is a hybrid between the King and Rebellious Vassal cycles. It begins after Ganelon's punishment, which takes place in Spain, where the hero, Thierry (surnamed Gaidon because a jay [OFr. *gai*], once perched on his helmet), is victorious over Pinabel. Because of the intrigues of Ganelon's clan and his own pitiful weakness, Charlemagne neglects those who are loyal to him, among whom are Naimes, Ogier, and Thierry-Gaidon; the latter is pushed into a lengthy feud with the emperor, in which the young knights side with Gaidon while their fathers fight for Charlemagne, as in *Gui de Bourgogne*. However, Gaidon continuously seeks reconciliation and finally succeeds after defeating the implacable traitors. *Anseïs de Carthage* (ca. 1230–50; four 13th-c. manuscripts and several fragments), a chivalric poem in which heroism and love are intertwined, narrates the tragic theme of the loss of a country because of a woman. Charlemagne has regained Spain, and Carthage (= Cartagena) is given to the young Breton knight Anseïs. An embassy led by the old Ysoré de Conimbre (= Coimbra) suggests to Anseïs that he marry Gaudisse, Marsile's daughter, in order to end the war. However, Anseïs seduces Ysoré's daughter Lentisse, and Ysoré goes over to Marsile, who renews the war. Gaudisse falls in love with Anseïs, is baptized, and marries him, while Ysoré and Marsile die in prison and Charlemagne of old age.

A last poem, *Macaire ou la reine Sebile*, deals with an old Charlemagne who has taken a young wife, Sibile, who, according to Alberic des Trois-Fontaines (mid-13th c.), was the daughter of King Desiderius of Lombardy. The Middle High German chronicle of Weihenstephan (14th c.), a Spanish adaptation (manuscript of the 14th c., imprint of 1532), and a Dutch chapbook, the *Historie vander coninghinnen Sibilla* (Antwerp: Willem Vorsterman, ca. 1538) make her the daughter of Emperor Richer of Constantinople. Though not found in the chansons de geste of the King Cycle, Charlemagne's death is treated in the Guillaume d'Orange Cycle, as in the first branch of the *Couronnement de Louis* and especially in the unpublished Franco-Italian *Mort Charlemagne* (Oxford, Bodl. Canonici 54; 13th c.). The British manuscript narrates basically the same events as the *Couronnement*, but where the latter only mentions Charlemagne's death as having occurred while Louis was on pilgrimage to Rome, the *Mort Charlemagne* actually describes his death, foretold to him by an angel during a visit to Saint-Gilles-de-Provence, where he was forgiven, thanks to divine intervention, his mortal sin of having engendered Roland with his sister Berthe.

Hans-Erich Keller

[See also: ADENET LE ROI; *ASPREMONT; AYMERI DE NARBONNE*; CHANSON DE GESTE; CHARLEMAGNE; *FIERABRAS*; FRANCO-ITALIAN LITERATURE; GUILLAUME D'ORANGE CYCLE; JEHAN BODEL; PHILIPPE MOUSKÉS; PSEUDO-TURPIN; REBELLIOUS VASSAL CYCLE; *ROLAND, CHANSON DE; VOYAGE DE CHARLEMAGNE À JÉRUSALEM ET À CONSTANTINOPLE*]

Adenet de Roi. *Les œuvres d'Adenet le Roi*, ed. Albert Henry. I *Biographie d'Adenet; La tradition manuscrite*. Rijksuniversiteit te Gent. Brugge: De Tempel, 1951. II *Beuvon de Conmarchis*. 115 Afl. 1953. III *Les enfances Ogier*. 121 Afl. 1956. IV *Berte aus grans piés*. Université libre de Bruxelles. Brussels: Presses Universitaires de Bruxelles, 1963. V *Cleomadés*. Vol. 1: *Texte*. Vol. 2: *Introduction, notes, tables*, 1971.

Alton, J., ed. *Anseïs von Karthago*. Tübingen: Niemeyer, 1892.

Baroin, Jeanne, ed. *Simon de Pouille*. 3 vols. Paris: Champion, 1978.

Brandin, Louis, ed. *La chanson d'Aspremeont, chanson de geste du XIIe siècle*. 2 vols. Paris: Champion, 1919–21.

Guessard, F., ed. *Macaire, chanson de geste*. Paris: Vieweg, 1866.

—— and Henri Michelant, eds. *Gui de Bourgogne, chanson de geste*. Paris: Vieweg, 1859.

—— and Siméon Luce, eds. *Gaidon, chanson de geste*. Paris: Vieweg, 1862.

Jehan Bodel. *La chanson des Saisnes*, ed. Annette Brasseur. 2 vols. Geneva: Droz, 1989.

Kroeber, A. and A. Servois, eds. *Chanson de Fierabras: Parise la Duchesse*. Paris: Vieweg, 1860.

Mussafia, A. *La prise de Pampelune*. Vienna, 1864.

Myers, John Vernon, ed. *Jehan de Lanson: Chanson de Geste of the 13th Century*. Chapel Hill: University of North Carolina Press, 1965.

Paris, Gaston, ed. "*Mainet*, fragments d'une chanson de geste du XIIe siècle." *Romania* 4 (1875): 305–37.

Speich, Johann Heinrich, ed. *La destructioun de Rome (d'après le ms. de Hanovre IV. 578)*. Bern: Lang, 1988.

Thomas, Antoine, ed. *L'éntree d'Espagne, chanson de geste franco-italienne*. 2 vols. Paris: Didot, 1913.

Horrent, Jules. "Chanson de Roland et Geste de Charlemagne." In *Les épopées romanes*, ed. Rita Lejeune. *Grundriss der romanischen Literaturen des Mittelalters,* Heidelberg: Winter, 1981, 1–51; 3/2, fasc. 2. [A complete bibliography for all chansons de geste mentioned in this article can be found in this volume.]

KNIGHTHOOD. Since 1066, the English word "knight" has been used as the equivalent of the Latin *miles* and the French *cheval(i)er. Miles* had been used from before 500 to ca. 950 to designate a soldier or military retainer of any sort, but after 950, both *miles* and *chevalier* were used especially to designate a particular type of mounted warrior, the professional heavy cavalryman who fought with the expensive armor and weapons traditionally used by Frankish nobles—helm, mail coat, lance, sword—and normally served as a vassal in the retinue of a prince or lesser noble. This type of warrior had apparently arisen under the Carolingians, but it was not until the second half of the 10th century that the vassalic cavalrymen began to emerge as a distinct and increasingly hereditary social category in France, forming a stratum of rural society between the noble landlords and their peasant tenants. Unlike the former, most *milites* in 10th- and 11th-century France came from undistinguished lineages, held little or no land, and possessed no rights of jurisdiction, but unlike the peasants they retained their full rights as freemen, were not tied to the soil or subjected to the jurisdiction of manorial courts, and served their noble lords (in whose households most of them lived) in capacities that were regarded as relatively honorable.

The basic definition of the knight that emerged between 950 and 1000, that of a fully equipped professional heavy cavalryman of free condition, was to change little before 1500, but the status, the number of men who enjoyed it, and the ideology and honor associated with it were to change tremendously during those same five centuries. The 11th century, which saw the creation of a new regime based on the possession of castles and armed retinues, naturally saw a rapid expansion in the number of knights, who were now called upon to garrison castles. It also witnessed the general adoption of the stirrup and the long Byzantine shield and the development both of the massed charge with couched lance and of the form of mock war called a *torneamentum*, or tournament. Finally, in the second half of the century, growing numbers of the nobility, who thought of themselves as warriors and fought in precisely the same way as knights at the head of a company of their knightly vassals, adopted the title *miles* as the formal designation of their social condition. By 1220, virtually all adult members of the old nobility not destined for the clergy assumed the title "knight" when they came of full age and were given the equipment characteristic of knighthood in the rite of *adoubement*. Thus, formal knighthood (Lat. *militia*, OFr. *chevalerie*) united the whole military class.

A social gulf nevertheless continued to exist between noble and nonnoble knights in most regions before ca.

1180, when the two social strata began to merge into a single noble estate. By that date, the great majority of simple knights in France were provided with fiefs and resembled nobles in being landlords, if only of a fraction of a village. The knightly class also benefited from the development of social ideologies that assigned a high function to the status of knight. The first of these, developed between 1025 and 1160 by clerical theorists, tended toward the identification of the body of knights with the second of the three "orders" into which God had divided Christian society, and to assign to knights as such both the military and the governmental functions originally assigned to this theoretical order of "fighters," an order previously identified with the nobility alone. Thus was created the idea of a sacred "order of knighthood" transmitted by knights, and the simple ceremony of *adoubement* was gradually altered under its influence into an elaborate rite of ordination. Between 1170 and 1200, an alternative but not incompatible ideology was developed in the new genre of the romance, in which knighthood was associated with the virtues of the courtly noble whose principal goal was to win honor for himself.

Inspired by these exalted ideas of their profession, in the half-century or so after 1180 the simple knights of France gradually usurped the distinctive attributes of their noble lords, including a dynastic surname and coat of arms, a seal, the personal prefix "lord" (Lat. *dominus*, OFr. *sire* or *messire*), and a fortified residence. By 1270, the king forbade his knightly subjects to dub anyone not of knightly ancestry and declared null the effects of such actions performed by anyone other than himself. The knights and their descendants thus came to form, with the descendants of the princes and castellans, a new and much larger noble estate, so closely identified with knighthood that it was more often called the *chevalerie* than the *noblesse*.

A surprising result of this development was a steady decline, especially after 1250, in the proportion of the male members of this knightly nobility who actually assumed the status and burdens of knighthood. The growing cost both of armor and of the ceremony of *adoubement* placed impossible strains on the finances of the sons of many petty knights, and as their social status was now securely based on descent more and more minor nobles decided to postpone indefinitely their admission to knighthood and remained esquires for most or all of their lives. The absolute number of knights in France declined from a high of perhaps 40,000 in 1180 to between 10,000 and 5,000 in 1300, between 5,000 and 3,000 in 1350, and about 1,000 in 1470, and the proportion of the royal army composed of knights fell from 16 percent in 1340 to 11 percent in 1382 and 3 percent in 1461.

The tradition of receiving knighthood on coming of age around twenty-one was preserved in the middle and especially the upper nobility down to ca. 1500, with the odd result that a status that before 1180 had been associated primarily with petty warriors in the service of nobles was associated between 1300 and 1500 primarily with the heirs of those same nobles. Knights continued to serve in battle with the latest armor, the price of which continued to escalate, down to 1500, and knight banneret and knight

bachelor continued to be recognized as pay grades in the royal army down to 1438, but after 1400 knighthood came to be seen less as a professional than as an honorific status.

D'A. Jonathan D. Boulton

[See also: CHIVALRY; NOBILITY; SEIGNEUR/SEIGNEURIE; WARFARE]

Contamine, Philippe. "Points de vue sur la chevalerie en France à la fin du moyen âge." *Francia* 4 (1976): 255–84.

Duby, Georges. *The Chivalrous Society*, trans. Cynthia Postan. Berkeley: University of California Press, 1977.

Flori, Jean. *L'idéologie du glaive: préhistoire de la chevalerie*. Geneva: Droz, 1983.

———. *L'essor de la chevalerie, XIe–XIIe siècles*. Geneva: Droz, 1986.

Keen, Maurice. *Chivalry*. New Haven: Yale University Press, 1984.

KNOLLES, ROBERT (ca. 1325–1407). One of the most famous leaders of the English Free Companies during the early Hundred Years' War. Knolles rose from the lower ranks of the army, as the English military leaders soon recognized his prowess, knighted him, and constantly requested his assistance in military adventures.

Nothing is known about Knolles's birth, although it is certain that he was not a noble, nor is there anything known about the date or reason for his military muster. He had attained a prestigious reputation as a soldier by 1351, when he fought in the Combat of the Thirty, during which he was captured by the French. In 1356, he led an English force of more than 800 men, which, after the victory at Poitiers, pillaged the coast of Normandy. In 1358, Knolles again commanded a force in France; during the next two years, it sacked the suburbs of Orléans, controlled forty castles in the Loire Valley, and even threatened the pope at Avignon, for which he earned 100,000 crowns in French booty. Knolles joined Edward III on a successful *chevauchée* that pillaged France in 1359–60, ending only with the signing of the Treaty of Brétigny (1360).

Knolles continued fighting through the 1360s, mostly in Brittany. In 1370, he again undertook a *chevauchée* in France, but although this raid succeeded in destroying much of the countryside, at Pontvallain his rearguard was annihilated and he retreated into Brittany. Knolles's military activity then diminished, although he again led *chevauchées* in France in 1379 and in 1380.

In 1380, Knolles retired to a wealthy life in London. Only twice did he come out of retirement to lead English armies: during the 1381 Peasant Revolt, when he was asked to be the leader of the defense of London, and in 1385, when he led a relief force on Damme. He died, an old man, in 1407.

Kelly DeVries

[See also: BRIGAND/BRIGANDAGE; GUESCLIN, BERTRAND DU; HUNDRED YEARS' WAR]

Venette, Jean de. *Chronique*, ed. Richard A. Newhall, trans. Jean Birdsall. New York: Columbia University Press, 1953.

Burne, Alfred. *The Crécy War*. London: Oxford University Press, 1955.

Favier, Jean. *La guerre de cent ans*. Paris: Fayard, 1980.

Seward, Desmond. *The Hundred Years' War*. New York: Atheneum, 1978.

L

LA CEPEDE, PIERRE DE (Ceppede, Cypede; fl. first half of the 15th c.). Marseillais author of a prose romance in French (possibly from an Occitan source), *Paris et Vienne* (1432), about the lovers Vienne, heiress to the Dauphiné, and Paris, her father's vassal, who triumph over adversity through their constancy and valor. The many editions and translations before 1700, including Caxton's, attest to the romance's popularity.

Heather M. Arden

La Cepede, Pierre de. "Der altfranzösische Roman *Paris et Vienne*," ed. Robert Kaltenbacher. *Romanische Forschungen* 15 (1904): 321–647. [Only modern edition.]

Coville, Alfred. *La vie intellectuelle dans les domaines d'Anjou-Provence de 1308 à 1435.* Paris: Droz, 1941, pp. 81–91.

St. Clair, Jeffrey J. "Ideological Structure in *Paris et Vienne*." *Semasia* 4 (1977): 65–99.

LA CHESNAYE, NICOLAS DE (fl. late 15th c.). Author of a 3,650-line allegorical play probably written before 1500, *La condamnation de Banquet*, that shows the fate of seven *bons vivants* who overindulge in food and drink. During the feasting first at Supper's place then at Banquet's, ten terrible maladies, including Gout, Colic, Apoplexy, Jaundice, and Epilepsy, attack and eventually kill most of the revelers. Finally, Supper and Banquet are tried and condemned by Experience. This morality differs from others in the genre by its focus on the physical rather than the moral effects of unwise behavior. A stern warning against excess, it is also a lively and humorous portrait of late-medieval feasting.

Heather M. Arden

La Chesnaye, Nicolas de. *La condamnation de Banquet*, eds. Jelle Koopmans and Paul Verhuyck. Geneva: Droz, 1991.

Parfondry, Max. "*La condamnation de Banquet*, moralité médiévale, et son auteur, Nicole de la Chesnaye." In *Hommage au professeur Maurice Delbouille*, ed. Jeanne Wathelet-Willem. Liège: Cahiers de l'Association des Romanistes de l'Université de Liège, 1973, pp. 251–68.

LA HIRE (ca. 1390–1443). Étienne de Vignolles, called "La Hire" for his temper, was a constant but undisciplined supporter of Charles VII. He fought at many major Valois defeats (Verneuil, 1424; the Battle of the Herrings, 1429) and victories (Orléans, 1429; Tartas, 1442). His chief military achievement was to maintain an army in the field regardless of the cost to those whom he nominally served. Often, this meant that his troops were little more than bandits, but his close association with Jeanne d'Arc has cloaked this ignominy and ennobled an otherwise ruthless personality. *Bailli* of Vermandois after 1429, he died in Montauban in the presence of the king.

Paul D. Solon

[See also: BRIGAND/BRIGANDAGE; HUNDRED YEARS' WAR; MONTMORILLON]

Beaucourt, Gaston du Fresne de. *Histoire de Charles VII.* 6 vols. Paris: Librairie de la Société Bibliographique, 1881–91.

Contamine, Philippe. *Guerre, état et société à la fin du moyen âge: études sur les armées des rois de France 1337–1494.* Paris: Mouton, 1972.

Rohmer, R. "La vie et les exploits d'Étienne de Vignolles, dit La Hire, capitaine gascon et bailli de Vermandois, 1390?–1443." Paris: École Nationale des Chartres, 1907, Positions des thèses, pp. 167–73.

Tuetey, Alexandre. *Les écorcheurs sous Charles VII.* Montbéliard: Barbier, 1874.

LA MARCHE, OLIVIER DE (1425/29–1502). Chronicler and poet of the court of Burgundy. His prose writings, including the *Mémoires* and several treatises and letters on the house of Burgundy, celebrate the splendor of late-medieval chivalric ceremony. La Marche helped supervise court festivities, and he describes them at length, especially the 1454 Pheasant Banquet and celebrations in honor of the Order of the Golden Fleece recorded in an epistle from 1500. His highly personal chronicle of the dukes of Burgundy, written for Philip of Habsburg, duke of Burgundy and grandson of Charles the Bold, covers the period 1435–88.

Among his verse, two works are of special note. The *Parement et triomphe des dames* (1493) enumerates allegorically the aspects of a noblewoman's costume. The *Chevalier délibéré* (1483), a conventional, moralized allegory of human life—written in honor of Charles the Bold and published by Vérard and translated into Dutch, Spanish, and English—explores the theme of death. The narrator undergoes symbolic adventures, encountering Hutin, son of Gluttony, ·the hermit Understanding, and Age. He witnesses several combats and retires to his bed, where he muses on the battles of life.

Earl Jeffrey Richards

[**See also**: BURGUNDIAN CHRONICLERS; VOW CYCLE]

La Marche, Olivier de. *Parement et triomphe des dames*, ed. Julia Kalbfleisch. Rostock: Adler, 1901.
———. *Mémoires et opuscules*, ed. H. Beaune and J. d'Arbaumont. 4 vols. Paris: Champion, 1983–88.
———. *Le chevalier délibéré by Olivier de la Marche, printed at Paris in 1488*, intro. Elizabeth Mongan. Washington, D.C.: Library of Congress, 1945.
Stein, Henri. *Étude biographique, littéraire et bibliographique sur Olivier de la Marche*. Brussels: Hayez, 1888.

LA SALE, ANTOINE DE (1385/86–1460/61). Illegitimate son of a celebrated Gascon mercenary, Bernard de La Sale, Antoine served for most of his life at the court of Anjou, performing administrative and military duties for Louis II, Louis III, and King René. He traveled extensively, especially in Italy. From 1435 to 1446, he served as tutor to Jean de Calabre, René's young son. During this period, he wrote *La Salade* (1440–44), a prose pedagogical treatise that touches on, among other subjects, geography, history, rules of protocol, and military tactics. It is preserved in one complete manuscript (Brussels, Bibl. Roy. 18210–15) and two early printed editions. Incorporated in it are two earlier works by La Sale, sometimes edited separately: *Paradis de la reine Sibylle* and *Excursion aux Iles Lipari*.

In 1448, La Sale entered the service of Louis de Luxembourg, count of Saint-Pol, as tutor to his three children. For his pupils, he composed *La Sale* (1448–51), a second pedagogical treatise, this time in the form of exempla taken from classical and Christian authors to illustrate such virtues as prudence, moderation, justice, pity, and abstinence. This prose work of 167 chapters is extant in two manuscripts (Brussels, Bibl. Roy. 10957, revised by the author's own hand, and Bibl. Roy. 9287–88).

La Sale also composed works of fiction and historiography: *Jehan de Saintré* (1456), *Floridan et Elvide* (1456), *Adicion extraicte des chroniques de Flandres* (1456), *Réconfort à Madame de Fresne* (1457), and *Des anciens tournois et faictz d'armes* (1459). The most important of his works is *Jehan de Saintré*, preserved in ten manuscripts. This substantial prose romance, in which some have wished to see a *roman à clef*, tells of a young page whose love for the Dame des Belles Cousines, coupled with his own natural merits, leads him to become a great knight. When Jehan is away at a tournament, the lady comes to an abbey, where she is seduced by its worldly abbot. The hero himself is beaten by the abbot but eventually has his revenge. The work is an important description of the life of the nobility in the later Middle Ages, gilding its underlying decadence with a still courtly vocabulary. Critics are divided as to whether it promotes or condemns late-medieval chivalry, whether it advances an aristocratic or a bourgeois ideal.

Several works occasionally attributed to La Sale—*Cent nouvelles nouvelles*, *Quinze joyes de mariage*, and *Livre des faits de Jacques de Lalaing*—are no longer widely believed to be by him.

William W. Kibler

[**See also**: RENÉ D'ANJOU]

La Sale, Antoine de. *Œuvres complètes d'Antoine de la Sale*, ed. Fernand Desonay. 2 vols. Paris: Droz, 1935–41, Vol. 1: *La salade;* Vol. 2: *La sale*.
———. *Jehan de Saintré*, ed. Jean Misrahi and Charles A. Knudson. Geneva: Droz, 1965.
———. *Jehan de Saintré, suivi de L'adicion extraicte des croniques de Flandres*, ed. Yorio Otaka. Tokyo: Librairie Takeuchi, 1967.

LA TOUR LANDRY, GEOFFROI DE (ca. 1330–ca. 1405). Prime among 14th-century lay moralists who wrote to ensure the practical, moral, and religious education of their targeted readers, mostly women, is Geoffroi de La Tour Landry, who in 1371–72 wrote his prose *Livre du chevalier de La Tour Landry pour l'enseignement de ses filles*. The prologue states his aims: to teach his daughters the art of storytelling (*roumancier*) and how to conduct themselves and tell right from wrong. The text has 142 chapters and 150 exempla. Each chapter expounds principles of good education and courtesy, comments on a particular vice or virtue, and gives one or two exempla. These, taken from the Bible and from the chronicles of France, England, Greece, and other lands, sometimes refer to contemporary nobles and events. Often profane and realistic, they are developed like a *conte* and take place in the world of the court or the bourgeoisie.

Joan B. Williamson

[**See also**: COURTESY BOOKS]

La Tour Landry, Geoffroi de. *Le livre du chevalier de La Tour Landry pour l'enseignement de ses filles*, ed. Anatole de Montaiglon. Paris: Bibliothèque Elzevirienne, 1854.
Hentsch, Alice Adèle. *De la littérature didactique du moyen âge s'adressant spécialement aux femmes*. Halle: Cahors, 1903.

LA VIGNE, ANDRÉ DE (ca. 1457–ca.1515). Late-medieval poet and playwright. Born between 1457 and 1470 in the port city of La Rochelle, La Vigne was in the service of Marie d'Orléans from ca. 1488 until her death in 1493, when he became secretary to the duke of Savoy. In 1494, in an effort to attract a more powerful protector, he presented a work to King Charles VIII, the *Ressource de la*

Crestienté. This poem is a dream allegory in which the king, in the personage of Magesté Royalle, is shown as the protector of Dame Crestienté, who is in peril. Impressed with La Vigne's talents, Charles appointed him historiographer of his military expedition into Italy to conquer the kingdom of Naples (1494–95). The resulting chronicle, the *Voyage de Naples*, is an eyewitness record of the events of the Italian campaign. Like the *Ressource*, it is written in alternating verse and prose.

In May 1496, La Vigne was invited to the town of Seurre in Burgundy, where he was commissioned to write a play on the life of St. Martin, patron of the town. Within five weeks, he had completed not only the *Mystère de saint Martin*, comprising more than 10,000 lines of verse, but also a comic morality play, the *Aveugle et le boiteux*, and a farce, the *Meunier de qui le diable emporte l'âme en enfer*. The mystery play was written to edify the people with scenes from the holy and devout life of their patron saint. To this end, there are sermons, miracles, and conversions, as well as scenes set in Heaven and Hell. The play is also a rich tapestry of daily life, showing people of all sorts and conditions engaged in their daily tasks. La Vigne portrays this milieu from a variety of stylistic perspectives. He sympathetically treats family difficulties and explores the psychology of suffering; he satirizes the abuses of the powerful, the faults of the clergy, and the venality of the merchant class; he depicts the bombast of braggart soldiers and the antics of drunken messengers. All these strands are woven together in a seamless dramatic action in which the playwright deftly alternates affective and comic scenes for maximum effect.

Toward the end of the century, La Vigne collected a number of his early works in the *Vergier d'honneur*. In 1504, he brought suit against Michel Le Noir, a Parisian printer, to stop an unauthorized edition of this work; the Parlement de Paris issued the injunction. Before the death of Charles VIII in 1498, La Vigne had been appointed secretary to the queen, Anne of Brittany. He remained in this capacity until her death in 1514. His later works included epitaphs for his patrons and other panegyric poems. He wrote two other plays, the *Sotise à huit personnages*, attacking the abuses of his day, and the *Moralité du nouveau monde* against the abolition of the Pragmatic Sanction, as well as political poems. In the *Louenge des roys de France*, for example, he supported Louis XII in his quarrel with the pope. Francis I in the year of his accession (1515) named La Vigne his historiographer and charged him with writing the history of his reign. Since only a few pages of the chronicle were completed, La Vigne is thought to have died shortly after.

André Duplat

[See also: GRANDS RHÉTORIQUEURS; HISTORIOGRAPHY; MORALITY PLAYS]

La Vigne, André de. *Le mystère de saint Martin, 1496*, ed. André Duplat. Geneva: Droz, 1979.

———. *Le voyage de Naples*, ed. Anna Slerca. Milan: Pubblicazioni della Università Cattolica del Sacro Cuore, 1981.

Brown, Cynthia Jane. *The Shaping of History and Poetry in Late Medieval France: Propaganda and Artistic Expression in the Works of the Rhétoriqueurs*. Birmingham: Summa, 1985.

Duplat, André. "La *Moralité de l'aveugle et du boiteux* d'Andrieu de la Vigne: étude littéraire et édition." *Travaux de linguistique et de littérature* 21 (1983): 41–79.

***LAI*, NARRATIVE.** In addition to the twelve *lais* by Marie de France, over twenty Old French texts, the majority of which are anonymous, can be classed as *lais: Amours, Aristote, Conseil, Cor, Desiré, Doon, Espervier, Espine, Graelent, Guingamor, Haveloc, Ignaure, Lecheor, Mantel, Melion, Ombre, Nabaret, Narcisus, Oiselet, Piramus et Thisbé, Trot, Tydorel, Tyolet, Vair Palefroi*. Problems of classification exist, as the term *lai* is found with reference to texts not normally regarded as *lais* (the fabliau *Auberee* appears in one manuscript as the *Lais de dame Aubree*), and the *Lai d'Aristote* has many of the features of a fabliau. Several Old French texts mention *lais* that have not come down to us. A manuscript discovered in Shrewsbury School lists sixty-seven *lais*, most of which are unknown. No clear definition of a *lai* can be given, but in its widest sense the term designates a short narrative in verse. The expression "Breton *lais*," sometimes used to designate the entire corpus, is best reserved for poems that present an amalgam of love and adventure, such as *Desiré, Doon, Espine, Graelent, Guingamor, Melion, Tydorel*, and *Tyolet*. These *lais* often seem to be related to Celtic stories, and it is also possible that they were written under the influence of or in reaction to the *lais* of Marie de France, who has been seen as the inaugurator of the genre in French.

Melion, for example, tells, like Marie de France's *Bisclavret*, of the transformation of a human into a wolf. Melion's wife, who is presented as the daughter of the King of Ireland but who clearly has nonhuman features, requests a piece of the meat of a stag encountered on a hunting trip. To oblige her, Melion is transformed into a wolf by a magic ring, but on his return with the meat he learns that his squire and his wife have left for Dublin. The story then tells of Melion's difficult but successful pursuit ·of his wife and the ring he needs to regain human form. *Espine* relates the adventures of the illegitimate son of the King of Brittany and the daughter of the boy's stepmother by another husband. The two youngsters are brought up together and fall in love at an early age. The main event of the *lai* is the account of the night spent by the hero at the Perilous Ford, where he defeats a knight in red armor and takes his horse, which is such that it does not require food and will disappear when its bridle is removed. He encounters two further knights and finally returns to court with his beloved, who has been miraculously transported to the ford to witness his prowess. The lovers are married, and they retain the horse until the girl removes its bridle out of curiosity, whereupon it disappears.

In comparison with the *lais* of Marie de France, *merveilleux*, or supernatural, elements are generally more in evidence in these *lais*, and there is less emphasis on the birth, nature, and problems of love. But they share with Marie's *lais* many of the themes and the aristocratic personnel: brave and handsome knights and wise and beautiful maidens. The stories are set against a background of the ideals and tensions of courtly society. In *Melion* and *Tyolet*, King Arthur plays a prominent role.

Two of the *lais*, *Narcisus* and *Piramus et Thisbé*, are adapted from tales by Ovid and can be called *Lais* of Antiquity. Some *lais* have a strong didactic intent (*Conseil, Espervier, Ignaure, Trot*). In *Conseil*, a lady who cannot choose among three suitors puts her problem to a knight, whose ability to assess the suitors' characteristics and explain the nature of true love is such that the lady accepts and eventually marries him rather than one of the suitors. *Oiselet* discusses the nature of *courtoisie* and *vilenie* by means of a talking bird that inhabits a garden owned by a wealthy peasant; the peasant is incapable of understanding the values of the noble knight from whom the house and garden had been purchased.

Other *lais* have fundamentally humorous themes and resemble the fabliaux. In *Cor*, a messenger presents King Arthur with a magic drinking horn from which only husbands with faithful wives can drink without spilling the contents. In *Mantel*, a youth offers Arthur a mantle that fits only women who have not been unfaithful. The horn and the mantle prove the widespread infidelity of the ladies at court. *Nabaret* pokes fun at a jealous husband who has married a woman of superior rank. *Lecheor* reduces the whole of knightly aims and activities to the search for sexual gratification. In what is probably the best *lai* of the entire corpus and one that fits into none of the above categories, Jean Renart in the *Lai de l'ombre* presents a verbal duel between a handsome knight and a lady well equipped with arguments to counter his offer of love. Composed from the second half of the 12th century until probably late into the 13th, these *lais* vary in quality, but they represent the earliest form of the short story in French literature.

Glyn S. Burgess

[See also: FABLIAU; MARIE DE FRANCE; OVIDIAN TALES]

Micha, Alexandre, ed. and trans. *Lais féeriques des XIIe et XIIIe siècles*. Paris: Garnier-Flammarion, 1992. [French translations; texts of Tobin edition: *Désiré, Doon, Espine, Graelent, Guingamor, Lecheor, Melion, Nabaret, Trot, Tydorel, Tyolet*.]

Tobin, Prudence M.O., ed. *Les lais anonymes des XIIe et XIIIe siècles*. Geneva: Droz, 1976.

Baader, Horst. *Die Lais: Zur Geschichte einer Gattung der altfranzösischen Kurzererzählungen*. Frankfurt: Klostermann, 1966.

Brereton, Georgine E. "A Thirteenth-Century List of French Lays and Other Narrative Poems." *Modern Language Review* 45 (1950): 40–45.

Donovan, Mortimer J. *The Breton Lay: A Guide to Varieties*. Notre Dame: University of Notre Dame Press, 1969.

Kroll, Renate. *Der narrative Lai als eigenständige Gattung in der Literatur des Mittelalters*. Tübingen: Niemeyer, 1984.

Payen, Jean-Charles. *Le lai narratif*. Turnhout: Brepols, 1975.

Smithers, G.V. "Story-Patterns in Some Breton Lays." *Medium Aevum* 22 (1953): 61–92.

LAI-DESCORT. The *lai-descort* is an independent lyric piece treating the same themes and occurring in the same *chansonniers* as the *canso* and the *grand chant courtois*. Developed in the late 12th or early 13th century, it distinguishes itself from the *canso* on strictly formal grounds: by the variable length of verses and stanzas within the individual text. The *lai-descort* tends to be slightly longer than the *canso*, though the number of stanzas rarely exceeds twelve. Musically, the *lai-descort* is complicated, with a new melody for each stanza. In contrast to the *canso*, it uses few melismas, each syllable corresponding to a single note. Though possibly originating in the south, the genre was practiced simultaneously by both trouvères and troubadours. In the north, it often served as a vehicle for religious expression. In the 14th century, at the hands of Guillaume de Machaut in particular, the structure of the *lai-descort*, or simply *lai*, became more rigid, with stanza divisions into halves and quarters and with the final stanza formally identical to the first. The *lai-descort* should not be confused with the narrative *lai* or the Arthurian *lais* integrated into certain prose romances, nor with the *Lais* ("Legacies") of François Villon.

Elizabeth W. Poe

Bec, Pierre. *La lyrique française au moyen-âge (XIIe–XIIIe siècles): contribution à une typologie des genres poétiques médiévaux*. 2 vols. Paris: Picard, 1977–78, Vol. 1: *Études*; Vol. 2: *Textes*.

LALAING, JACQUES DE (ca. 1420–1453). Born to a noble family still known in Belgium, Lalaing was a model of Burgundian knighthood, according to the *Livre des faits de Jacques de Lalaing* (1470–72), variously attributed to Georges Chastellain, Jean Lefèvre de Saint-Remy, and Antoine de La Sale. It can be compared with two other heroic biographies produced in Burgundy at about the same time, the *Livre des faits de Gilles de Chin* and *Gillion de Trazenies*. In all these works, fiction mixes freely with reality. At the tournament of the Fontaine des Pleurs near Chalons-sur-Saône in 1450, Lalaing took on twenty-one challengers. He was killed by a cannonball at a siege near Ghent in 1453.

Charity Cannon Willard

Le livre des faits de Jacques de Lalaing. In *Œuvres de Georges Chastellain*, ed. Kervyn de Lettenhove. Brussels: Heuser-Devaux, 1866, Vol. 8.

Born, Robert. *Les Lalaing, une grande "mesnie" hennuyère*. Brussels: Éditeurs d'Art Associés, 1986.

Doutrepont, Georges. "Le *Livre des faits du bon chevalier messire Jacques de Lalaing*, une biographie romancée du XVe siècle." *Journal des savants* (1939): 221–32.

LANCASTER, DUKES OF. The first two dukes of Lancaster played prominent roles in France during the Hundred Years' War. Edward III's second cousin Henry of Grosmont (1310–1361) was created duke in 1351, some years after leading a brilliant campaign against the French in Aquitaine. Arriving at Bordeaux on August 9, 1345, he took Bergerac two weeks later, defeated a French army at Auberoche on October 21, and captured La Réole by November 2. These victories reversed the tide of war in the southwest and stripped Languedoc of its forward defensive positions. A decade later, Lancaster was back in France, campaigning successfully in Normandy and Brittany in 1355–57.

In 1359, Henry's daughter Blanche married John of Gaunt (1340–1399), Edward III's fourth (and second surviving) son. When her father and sister died of plague, Blanche inherited vast possessions and Edward created John duke of Lancaster in 1362. John's first leading military role came in the summer of 1369, when he took several thousand men to Calais and ravaged northern France and upper Normandy. Although he did not bring the French to battle, his expedition did force them to give up hopes of attacking England.

In the next five years, Lancaster was extremely active, retaining more soldiers in that time than any other English commander in the 14th century. His principal French expedition was in 1373, when he marched south from Calais in August with a large force, ravaging Picardy and Vermandois. By the end of September, he had passed through Champagne, but the French avoided battle. With colder weather approaching, the alternative to retreat was to pass across the rugged hills and swollen rivers lying between the Seine and English Aquitaine. When he reached Bordeaux near the end of the year, he had lost half his army in a five-month campaign that achieved few military objectives. He would serve again in Aquitaine, but his main concerns after 1373 lay outside France.

John Bell Henneman, Jr.

Fowler, Kenneth. *The King's Lieutenant: Henry of Grosmont, First Duke of Lancaster (1310–1361)*. New York: Barnes and Noble, 1969.

Sherborne, James. "John of Gaunt, Edward III's Retinue, and the French Campaign of 1369." In *Kings and Nobles in the Later Middle Ages: A Tribute to Charles Ross*, ed. Ralph A. Griffiths and James Sherborne. New York: St. Martin, 1986, pp. 41–61.

LANFRANC OF BEC (ca. 1010–1089). Born into a good family in Pavia, Lanfranc was educated in that city and more generally in northern Italy. He left Italy for France while still a young man and made his reputation as an itinerant teacher in the area around Avranches. In 1042, he entered the new monastery at Bec (founded 1041); he was abbot of Saint-Étienne, Caen, in 1063; in 1070, he was made archbishop of Canterbury. He had a dual reputation, first as a teacher and scholar and later as a brilliant administrator and leader.

His scholarship falls into two periods, before and after his entry into Bec. The earlier works, no longer extant, are on the Trivium; after 1042, he devoted himself to theology, writing commentaries on the Psalms and Pauline epistles that circulated widely. About 1063, he wrote a treatise *De sacramento corporis et sanguinis Christi*, against the opinions of Berengar of Tours's *De eucharistia*, and to which

Berengar replied in *De sacra coena*. Berengar's ideas caused widespread antagonism and were finally condemned by Pope Gregory VII in 1079. The issue centers on the changes taking place in the bread and wine of the eucharist in order for them to become the body and blood of Christ. Both Berengar and Lanfranc believed in the Real Presence, but they differed on the necessity and type of any change in the elements, Berengar insisting that no material alteration was needed and Lanfranc arguing for outward identity concealing inner grace. The question was compounded by difficulties of language: no clearer statement of the central issue was to be possible until the introduction of Aristotelian notions of substance and accident in the 13th century.

Lanfranc's leadership of the school at Bec made it into one of the most famous of its day, and pupils included Anselm of Bec, Ivo of Chartres, and Guitmund of Aversa (later Pope Alexander II). He was a valued counselor to Duke William of Normandy (the Conqueror) despite having declared William's marriage invalid.

Lanfranc was a great holder of synods (in 1075, 1076, 1078, 1081), which he used to promulgate canon law, and he was the first to create separate courts of ecclesiastical jurisdiction. His legal turn of mind (he seems to have practiced or at least studied civil law in Pavia) was coupled with a traditionalist viewpoint, so that his outlook reminds us of Carolingian attitudes and practices rather than any innovation. The collection of canon law, the so-called *Collectio Lanfranci*, which Lanfranc brought to Canterbury from Bec, has an old-fashioned cast, in contrast to the *Collection in Seventy-Four Titles (Diversorum patrum sententiae)* or Ivo of Chartres's *Panormia* and other legal works, the new breed of legal collections that it seems Lanfranc preferred to ignore.

As archbishop of Canterbury, Lanfranc replaced many Saxon bishops with Normans, to the displeasure of some in the English church, but in doing so he increased ties with the Continent and with Gregory VII's reforms, with which, at least in the area of the moral reform of the church, he was largely in sympathy. Lanfranc rebuilt the church at Canterbury and established its library. He reestablished many of the old monastic privileges and lands.

Lesley J. Smith

[See also: ANSELM OF BEC; BERENGAR OF TOURS; BIBLE, CHRISTIAN INTERPRETATION OF; CAEN; CANON LAW; IVO OF CHARTRES; THEOLOGY]

Lanfranc of Bec. *Opera.* PL 150. 1–782.
———. *The Letters of Lanfranc, Archbishop of Canterbury*, ed. Helen Clover and Margaret T. Gibson. Oxford: Clarendon, 1979.
Gibson, Margaret T. *Lanfranc of Bec.* Oxford: Clarendon, 1978.
Huygens, R.B.C. "Bérenger de Tours, Lanfranc et Bernold de Constance." *Sacris Euridiri* 16 (1965): 355–403.
Southern, Richard W., ed. *Essays in Medieval History.* London: Macmillan, 1948.

LANGRES. Located fifty miles northeast of Dijon in northern Burgundy, Langres (Haute-Marne) is a fortified town on a spur of land dominating the surrounding plain. In the Middle Ages, Langres served as an advanced, northern fortress for Burgundy. The cathedral of Saint-Mammès is late Burgundian Romanesque in the process of becoming Gothic.

Saint-Mammès was begun after the Early Gothic choir of Saint-Denis (1140–44) and after the start of Sens, the first Early Gothic cathedral. Indeed, parts of Sens are Romanesque, with its ambulatory of groin vaults, which were changed to Gothic ribbed vaults in the late 1140s. Langres is different; it has a Burgundian Romanesque elevation of nave arcade, triforium, and clerestory derived from that of Cluny III, Paray-le-Monial, and Autun. Instead of the vaults being pointed barrels and springing from above the clerestory windows, as at Cluny III and other Burgundian churches, the vaults of Langres are four-part Gothic ribbed vaults that spring from a much lower point in the elevation, from just above the bottom of the clerestory windows. Thus, the greater verticality of the Cluniac churches gives way to a less soaring interior at Langres.

The plan of Langres seems to have been derived from that of Paray-le-Monial, the early 12th-century Cluniac priory. Originally, the nine-bay ambulatory probably had three apsidioles like Paray-le-Monial. These were destroyed in the 14th century when five Rayonnant chapels were added. Short, aisleless transepts are also reminiscent of Paray-le-Monial. However, the six-bay nave and flanking aisles, all vaulted with four-part ribbed vaults, contain the relatively wide interior spaces. The elevation is straight Burgundian Romanesque, with fluted pilasters serving as responds. The Roman-type Corinthian capitals and pilasters animate the piers and triforium area, like the Roman gate in the city. Ribbed vaults resemble those of the Gothic Cistercian abbey of Pontigny.

Langres seems to have been started in the middle of the 12th century and built slowly over the remaining decades of the century. A kind of baroque exuberance manifests itself in the ornate capitals and friezes.

Whitney S. Stoddard

[See also: PARAY-LE-MONIAL; PONTIGNY; ROMANESQUE ARCHITECTURE]

Schlink, Wilhelm von. *Zwischen Cluny und Clairvaux: Die Kathedrale von Langres und die burgundische Architektur des 12. Jahrhunderts.* Berlin: De Gruyter, 1970.

LANGUEDOC. The provinces in southern France that came to be recognized in the Middle Ages as the region of Languedoc formed one of the principal territorial units assembled under the kings of France. The extent of this medieval Languedoc was far wider than that of the later administrative province of the 17th and 18th centuries. Neither did it comprise, however, the totality of the linguistic region of the Langue d'oc (Occitan). Though the Langue d'oc may strictly be said to have extended across the county of Angoulême and the Auvergne, the territories of Languedoc commenced south of the River Dordogne, in the mountains of Auvergne and Burgundy. They were re-flected in the five great seneschalsies—Beaucaire-Nîmes (extending north to Viviers and Le Puy), Carcassonne-Béziers, Toulouse, Quercy, and Rouergue— through which the kings administered them from the 13th century. Throughout the Middle Ages, this region retained an identity based on culture and customary law. Only in the 13th century, however, after prolonged and brutal contact with the people of the north, do the first references occur to the region as an entity distinct and its people as distinguished by their language (*homines nostri idiomatis, videlicet de nostra lingua*). In the 14th century, finally, residents of Carcassonne could refer casually to their region as the *patria* and speak of plans to travel north, *in Franciam*.

With the end of the Roman Empire and the subsequent advance of the Franks under Clovis I, the region fell by the 8th century into two zones: the northern, including the Rouergue, Toulousain, and Albigeois, incorporated into the Frankish kingdoms as part of the territory of the dukes of Aquitaine, and the southern, known as Septimania and extending from the Pyrénées to the Rhône, part of the kingdom of the Visigoths. The Arab invasions that destroyed the Visigothic kingdom reached Septimania in 718, and the area remained under Islamic control until 759, when Pepin III conquered it definitively for the Frankish realm.

Under the empire of the Carolingians, counts were appointed in Septimania and southern Aquitaine, and in the period that followed the decline of imperial authority in the 9th century their successors competed to form the comital dynasties of Languedoc. The most successful of these, the house of Toulouse-Rouergue, came eventually to dominate most of the territory between the Rhône and the Garonne; its downfall in the 13th century marked the end of the effective independence of Languedoc. The prominence of the family began with Fredelon, a Frankish noble confirmed as count of Toulouse by King Charles the Bald in 849. Although his successors suffered a temporary eclipse by the end of the century, they had recovered their possessions and had added the counties of Rouergue, Quercy, Nîmes, and Albi. The second half of the 10th century marked in Languedoc, as elsewhere in France, the disintegration of the central and public authority maintained generally on the level of the county. The possessions of the house of Toulouse broke apart in 919 on the death of Count Eudes, whose eldest son, Raymond, succeeded as count of Toulouse while his brother Ermengaud became count of the Rouergue. In the 11th century, there appeared the first features of what became the regime of feudalism in Languedoc.

The precise nature of Languedocian feudalism poses problems that are yet debated. The older evaluation of such historians as Paul Dognon and Pierre Timbal that the institutions of feudalism in the south scarcely merited the name, Languedoc remaining "practically ignorant of even the concept of feudal law," has been challenged; for Pierre Bonnassie, the historian of the Midi and Catalonia, the practices of feudalism and vassalage appeared in Languedoc in a form quite pure by the beginning of the 12th century. While it is certainly unwise to assume a monolithic definition of feudalism, it is clear that in Languedoc feudal institutions developed more slowly and in a more nuanced

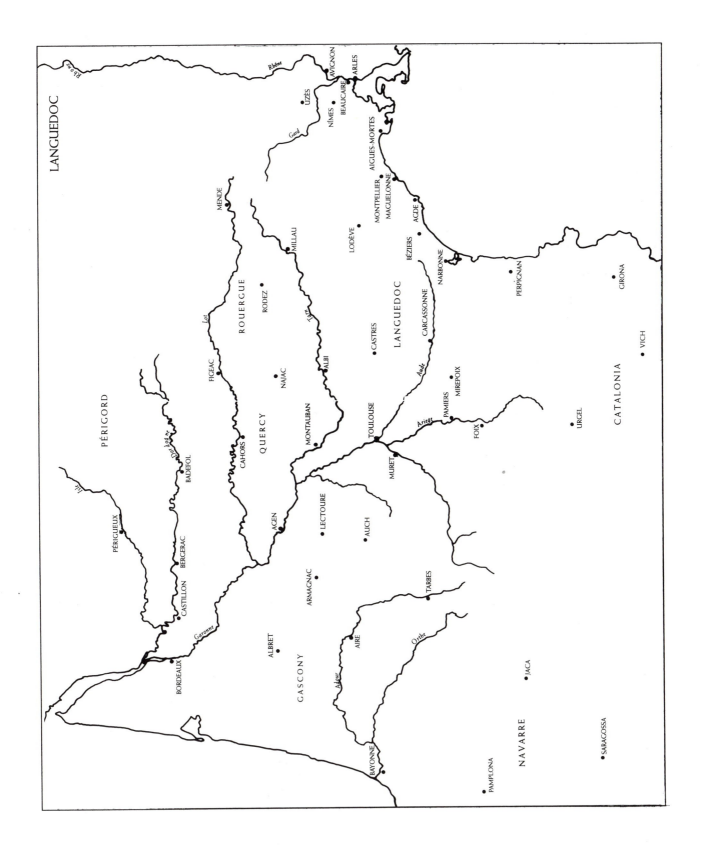

form than that which they took in the north. Two essential features of the prefeudal regime—commerce and a relatively viable circulation of money, and the prevalence of the allod, land possessed in full proprietorship—remained more firmly fixed in the south than elsewhere. These factors both retarded the appearance and diluted the rigor of feudalism in its early stages. Later, the evolution of the customs of Languedoc, particularly their testamentary provisions favoring free distribution of properties, limited the effectiveness of the military aspect of feudalism. By the end of the 12th century, nevertheless, undeniably feudal institutions were in place in Languedoc; certainly, the view of Dognon that even then the power of the count of Toulouse rested on the number of his allods and not on the number of his vassals cannot be maintained. It is significant, nonetheless, that the northerner Simon de Montfort felt it necessary immediately after his conquests to redefine and establish, through the statutes of Pamiers, rigorous feudal obligations for his southern vassals.

Two other features emerged in the 12th century that gave to the society of Languedoc its distinctive physiognomy: customary law based on the Roman codes and the spread of the heretical doctrines known as Catharism. Unlike Catalonia, where Roman legal traditions, maintained by the Visigoths, remained alive, north of the Pyrénées the disorders of the 10th century brought their influence to an end. The reemergence of Roman law in the 12th century can be traced, first in the former region of Septimania, then in the Rouergue, and finally in the Toulousain, through the appearance of advocates (*magistri, causidici*) and of notaries public. The adoption of Roman law, which these and other institutions announced, became established in the 13th century. Promoted by the royal administration and by that of Alphonse of Poitiers, whose interests were served by defining a coherent legal system, and by the creation of great centers of study at the universities of Toulouse and Montpellier, Roman law was accepted as the custom of the Midi. In 1251, an ordinance of Blanche of Castile formally recognized the custom of *droit écrit* as the binding legal system of Languedoc.

Conjointly with the emergence of Roman law came economic expansion and the rise of municipal self-government. This latter, achieved sometimes at the cost of violence (as at Béziers and Nîmes), most often through mutual agreement, appeared typically in the form of governments directed by urban consuls representing the dominant merchant class. The consulates in turn, beginning with that of Arles in 1131, provided ready vehicles for the spread of Roman law. They coincided as well with the growth of the heterodox beliefs of Catharism.

It is possible that Catharism owed its success in Languedoc, as in Lombardy and Catalonia, to the precocious urbanization of the region. Its faith did indeed find a favorable milieu among the artisans, merchants, and notaries of many towns. The indulgent attitude of the Cathar ministers toward commercial activities and usury, as well as their ability to serve as intermediaries and repositories for moneys exchanged, made them attractive to the merchant classes. The causes of the success of Catharism, however, are complex. Its appeal cut across socioeconomic lines, affecting both the nobility and the peasantry. Its greatest sphere of influence within Languedoc was limited to the region of Carcassonne, Albi, part of the Toulousain, and the region of Foix. Major urban and commercial centers, such as Cahors, were barely touched. Clerical laxity may also have prepared the way for Catharism, but it, too, was not unique to those few areas of Languedoc in which the Cathars took root. Catharism in Languedoc, as elsewhere Waldensianism or the movement of the béguines, represented an alternative for those who aspired to a more apostolic conception of the Faith. As such, the weapons that defeated it were not the crusades or the Inquisition but the message and spirituality of the mendicant orders, particularly the disciples of St. Francis. Before its disappearance, however, the persistence of Catharism led Languedoc into a new phase of its history and to unification with the crown of France.

The political history of Languedoc in the century and a half preceding the Albigensian Crusade is dominated by the revival of the house of Toulouse, whose territories from the Quercy to the Rhône were once again united by Raymond IV in 1093, and its struggles against the ambitions of the dukes of Aquitaine to the north and the counts of Barcelona to the south. It is possible, as the Catalan historian Ramon d'Abadal y Vinyals has contended, that the counts of Barcelona entertained no grand design of creating a trans-Pyrénéan principality. Their advance, however, especially after their acquisition of the counties of Provence, Millau, and the Gévaudan in 1112, convulsed the politics of Languedoc. It enabled the lords of lower Languedoc, particularly the Trencavels, viscounts of Albi, Carcassonne, Béziers, and Nîmes, to maintain practical independence of Toulouse. It required the continuous efforts of the able counts of Toulouse Alphonse-Jourdain and Raymond V to withstand the pressure from Catalonia and Aquitaine until the peace of 1190. In 1209, the Albigensian Crusade descended upon Languedoc.

The murder of a papal legate and the inability of the established institutions to deal with Catharism precipitated the initial crusade; the disunity of the great families of Languedoc permitted its success. While Raymond VI of Toulouse stood aside, his sometime vassal Raymond-Roger Trencavel was swept away and his counties occupied by the crusaders. It is not just, however, to ascribe the later triumphs of the northerners under Simon de Montfort to their opponents' ineptitude or the inefficiency of southern feudalism. The military structures of Languedoc consistently placed superior armies in the field, and these armies operated as was expected of medieval hosts. The martial genius of Simon de Montfort and his unorthodox and aggressive tactics at Castelnaudary (1211) and Muret (1213) allowed him briefly to triumph. Ultimately, though the domination of the Montforts was defeated, it prepared the way for the advance of the monarchy under Louis VIII, to whom Amaury de Montfort ceded his rights in 1224.

The final phase of the history of medieval Languedoc begins with the military promenade of Louis VIII in 1226. The Trencavel domains were absorbed and henceforth administered by royal seneschals at Carcassonne and Beaucaire. Rebellions in 1240 and 1242 failed to shake the royal authority, and when Raymond VII of Toulouse died in 1249 he was succeeded by his daughter, Jeanne, and son-in-law, Alphonse of Poitiers, brother of Louis IX of France.

Despite occasional unrest caused by the work of the ecclesiastical Inquisition, Languedoc experienced an era of growth and prosperity under royal rule in the 13th century. The careful policy of Louis IX and Alphonse of Poitiers, respecting local custom and promoting the establishment of *droit écrit*, facilitated the integration of the region into the domains of France. Toulouse, Narbonne, Béziers, Cahors, and other cities enjoyed economic prosperity. The consular regimes, although their independence might be circumscribed, as at Toulouse and Nîmes, were respected, as royal policy encouraged control of the cities by the merchant classes. Agitation by the artisans and trades, nevertheless, increased during the century. Violent upheavals, as at Cahors in 1268–70, were restrained for a time by the establishment of the system of *échelles*, which grouped the artisanal classes into several ranks or grades and accorded to each a position within the consulate. Notwithstanding these concessions, tensions increased into the 14th century; even a small town like Roujan could report in 1320 that the consuls had mistreated the leader of the *populi minuti* and had held him captive with the connivance of the royal bailiff.

The 14th century saw the decline of the general economic prosperity of Languedoc, the breakdown of the social peace maintained by the *échelles* and of the political peace maintained by the royal government. The devastation of the Hundred Years' War was felt most severely in Quercy, Agenais, and the Rouergue, where free companies and mercenary bands added to the destruction. Crop failures, including massive famines in 1332, 1335, 1351, and 1374–76, occurred with increasing frequency and led to the final crisis of medieval Languedoc. The famine of 1374–76, which exacerbated social tensions in the cities, combined with increased demand for taxes by the royal government and the machinations of Gaston Phoebus, count of Foix, to produce an explosion of urban revolts that swept Languedoc from 1378 to 1382. Riots directed against the consuls, the rich, the agents of royal government, and the king's lieutenant the duke of Berry, occurred at Le Puy, Montpellier, Clermont-l'Hérault, Alais, Nîmes, Narbonne, and Béziers. These were followed by the great peasant revolt known as the rebellion of the Tuchins, which was not suppressed until 1384.

In the 15th century, Languedoc recovered something of its economic vitality. Its loyalty to the crown survived the crises of the previous century and preserved for the dauphin Charles a base of support during the 1420s. The last great independent fiefs, the counties of Foix and Armagnac, passed to the family of Albret and Navarre and were united to the crown with the accession of Henry IV.

Alan Friedlander

[See also: ALBIGENSIAN CRUSADE; CATALONIA; CATHARS; FEUDALISM; FOIX; HERESY; MONTFORT; MONTPELLIER; NÎMES; OCCITAN LANGUAGE; SAINT-GILLES; TOULOUSE; TRENCAVEL]

Bisson, Thomas N. *Assemblies and Representation in Languedoc in the Thirteenth Century.* Princeton: Princeton University Press, 1964.

Bonnassie, Pierre. "Du Rhône à la Galice: genèse et modalités du régime féodale." In *Structures féodales et féodalisme dans l'Occident méditerranéen (Xe–XIIIe siècles).* Rome: École Française de Rome, 1980, pp. 17–55.

d'Abadal y Vinyals, Ramon. "À propos de la domination de la maison comtale de Barcelone sur le Midi français." *Annales du Midi* (1964): 315–45.

Devic, Claude, and Joseph Vaissète. *Histoire générale de Languedoc.* 16 vols. Toulouse: Privat, 1872–1904.

Dognon, Paul. *Les institutions politiques et administratives du pays de Languedoc du XIIIe siècle aux guerres de religion.* Toulouse: Privat, 1895.

Higounet, Charles. "Un grand chapitre de l'histoire du XIIe siècle: la rivalité des maisons de Toulouse et de Barcelone." In *Mélanges d'histoire du moyen âge dédiés à la mémoire de Louis Halphen.* Paris: Presses Universitaires de France, 1951, pp. 312–22.

Lewis, Archibald. *The Development of Southern French and Catalan Society, 718–1050.* Austin: University of Texas Press, 1965.

Magnou-Nortier, Elizabeth. *La société laïque et l'Église dans la province ecclésiastique de Narbonne (zone cispyrénéenne) de la fin du VIIIe siècle à la fin du XIe siècle.* Toulouse: Université de Toulouse-le-Mirail, 1974.

Rigaudière, Albert. "Hiérarchie socioprofessionnelle et gestion municipale dans les villes du Midi français au bas moyen âge." *Revue historique* 269 (1983): 25–68.

Strayer, Joseph R. *The Albigensian Crusades.* New York: Dial, 1971.

Wakefield, Walter. *Heresy, Crusade and Inquisition in Southern France, 1100–1250.* Berkeley: University of California Press, 1974.

Wolff, Philippe. *Histoire du Languedoc.* Toulouse: Privat, 1967.

LANGUEDOIL. The term, which appeared only at the end of the Middle Ages, describing that part of France where Old French was spoken: the region of the Langue d'oïl north of the linguistic frontier formed, roughly, by the Cevennes and the Dordogne River. South of that frontier lay the Langue d'oc, where Occitan was spoken. The two regions became subject to many fiscal and administrative distinctions during the Hundred Years' War, and for convenience historians often refer to the Estates General of Languedoil to describe assemblies that did not include representatives of the southern districts.

John Bell Henneman, Jr.

LAON. Laon (Aisne) is dramatically situated atop a fishhook-shaped plateau overlooking the flat plains of northern France. A natural fortress and lookout point, the site has been inhabited since Neolithic times and is identified with the *oppidum* Bibrax mentioned by Caesar. A fortified point in the northern line of defense against barbarian invasions and, later, Viking raids, Laon became the main

Laon (Aisne), Notre-Dame, west façade. *Photograph courtesy of Whitney S. Stoddard.*

Laon is one of the first Early Gothic buildings with a four-story elevation, including arcades and aisles, vaulted galleries connected by platforms across the transept façades, a wall passage that also continued across the transept arms, and clerestory windows. The nave and chevet were covered by nearly square sexpartite vaults, while the transept arms had rectangular quadripartite vaults. Laon cathedral was planned with seven towers, two each on the west façade and both transept façades, as well as the central lantern tower that provides the focus of the interior space. In its measured regularity and expansiveness, as well as its four-story elevation, Laon achieves the appearance of large size and scale, even though it is only about 75 feet tall.

The west façade is characterized by a dramatic interplay of projections and recessions, of porches and doors, arches and windows, that culminates in the enormous rose window and the façade towers that shift from square to octagonal plan. Any sense of the heaviness of walls or buttresses is hidden by pinnacles and gables. The design is enhanced at all levels by sculptural decoration, beginning with the three portals. That on the south contains the oldest sculpture, a cut-down tympanum of the Last Judgment with two archivolts of angels. Additional archivolts and a new lintel showing the Separation of the Saved and the Damned were added when the sculpture was installed ca. 1195–1200. The present statue-columns, like those of the other portals, were created by Geoffroy-Dechaume during the 19th-century restorations.

The central portal is devoted to the Coronation of the Virgin, with the Tree of Jesse, angels, and prophets in the archivolts. The present lintel was created by Geoffroy-Dechaume. From the standpoint of both style and iconography, the most interesting portal at Laon is the north portal of the façade. The tympanum, through careful design, manages to combine the theme of Virgin as the Seat of Wisdom with the Adoration of the Magi, even as the sculptor explores a new sense of spatial expansiveness in the composition and placement of figures. The archivolts show angels, the Triumph of the Virtues over the Vices, and prefigurations of Salvation. The lintel shows the Annunciation, the Nativity, and the Angels appearing to the Shepherds.

Each of the portals is framed by a deep porch topped by a gable with figure sculpture, the subjects of which enhance the portals. For example, above the Last Judgment portal stands St. Michael flanked by two seated angels; above the central portal is a giant Virgin and Child flanked by angels. This suggests that the traditional, but unfounded, identification of the central gable figure above the north portal as St. Proba should be reconsidered; the scene may be the Assumption of the Virgin.

Four ranks of archivolts flank the two lateral lancet windows of the façade and extend the iconographic program to include the Liberal Arts, together with Architecture, Medicine, and Philosophy, flanked by dragons and foliage (north window), and a Creation cycle flanked by eagles and foliage above the Last Judgment portal on the south. Tying the whole façade together are the numerous bands of foliage ornament, punctuated by corbels and consoles, used both to emphasize and to conceal shifts in planes and changes in level. Like the highly colored and

redoubt for the region and one of the favored residences of the Carolingian kings. The 12th-century keep was torn down only in the 1830s. The diocese was created by St. Remi in the late 5th century, but the first mention of a cathedral church is in a poem by Alcuin. The Carolingian church was renovated by Adalbero in the 10th century and damaged during the civil unrest of 1112. The present Gothic cathedral was begun ca. 1155. In addition, Laon had a Benedictine abbey, Saint-Vincent; an Augustinian priory, Saint-Jean; and an important Premonstratensian abbey, Saint-Martin, as well as a Templars church, a leprosarium, and a number of parish churches. Of the medieval churches, only the cathedral, Saint-Martin, and the Templars church survive.

The Gothic cathedral of Notre-Dame was completed in five major periods of construction, between ca. 1155 and ca. 1225. The plan of the first church called for a shallow chevet of three bays surrounded by an ambulatory, hardly enough space for the large numbers of clergy occasioned by prosperity from wine production. Projecting transept arms with two-storied eastern chapels open from the dramatic lantern tower. The long nave ends in the first attempt to rethink the meaning of the façade as an entrance into the church in the 12th century. It was the plan of the two identical transept arms, opening from the crossing, with their large rose windows, that suggested to the builder the repetition of the plan of the nave for the new chevet, both highlighted by their huge rose windows.

Two other 12th-century religious structures survive in Laon, the Templars church and the chapel of the episcopal palace, which also has a 13th-century gallery opening to the north of the cathedral. In the absence of precise documents, the style of the Templars church, an octagonal central-plan structure, suggests that it was constructed ca. 1140–50. While the entrance porch dates a little later, its tribune was added only in the 14th century. Opening to the east of the central octagon is an altar area consisting of a groin-vaulted straight bay and an apse. The central octagon is covered by a ribbed cupola.

The bishop's chapel belongs to a tradition of two-storied chapels, reaching at least as far back as the Carolingian chapel at Aix-la-Chapelle. The Laon chapel is built on a square plan with a projecting eastern apse. The lower story is groin-vaulted, and its four central supports are square piers with half-columns; the upper story is rib-vaulted with a taller center bay resting on four columns. Despite the mix of vaulting techniques, the structure is homogeneous and was built in a single campaign shortly after 1150 by the same builders working in the adjacent cathedral shop.

In the course of urban renewal in the area adjacent to the south side of the cathedral façade, the remains of the early 13th-century hospital came to light, one of the few surviving 13th-century hospitals known.

William W. Clark

[See also: GOTHIC ARCHITECTURE]

Laon, Notre-Dame, transept. *Photograph courtesy of Whitney S. Stoddard.*

Bur, Michel, et al., eds. *Histoire de Laon et du Laonnois.* Toulouse: Privat, 1987.

Clark, William W. "Cistercian Influences on Premonstratensian Church Planning: Saint-Martin at Laon." In *Studies in Cistercian Art and Architecture.* Kalamazoo: Cistercian, 1984, Vol. 2, ed. M. Lillich, pp. 161–88.

———. *Laon Cathedral, Architecture (2), The Aesthetics of Space, Plan and Structure.* London: Miller, 1986.

———, and Richard King. *Laon Cathedral, Architecture (1).* London: Miller, 1983.

Fernie, Eric. "La fonction liturgique des piliers cantonnés dans la nef de la cathédrale de Laon." *Bulletin monumental* 145 (1987): 257–66.

Lambert, Élie. "L'ancienne abbaye de Saint-Vincent de Laon." *Comptes-rendus de l'Académie des Inscriptions et Belles-Lettres* (1939): 124–38.

Saint-Denis, Alain. *L'Hôtel-Dieu de Laon 1150–1300.* Nancy: Presses Universitaires de Nancy, 1983.

movemented linear values of the façade design, the use of sculptural ornament reaches an unprecedented degree of complexity and richness.

The abbey church of Saint-Martin at Laon, second in rank in the Premonstratensian order, dates like the cathedral from the 12th century. It was begun shortly after 1150 on a plan that has often been compared with that of early Cistercian churches. That is, it consists of a flat chevet of two bays, a projecting transept with three contiguous eastern chapels on each arm, and a nine-bay nave. The original plan called for rib vaults only in the chevet and transept chapels; a campaign in the later 12th century increased the height of the transept so that it could be vaulted at the same level as the nave, at which time flying buttresses were added. The superficial resemblance to a Cistercian plan ends when one examines the plan of the chevet in detail and notes that it included three altar niches, a distinctive feature of the Aisne Valley region. Indeed, all of the details of design and structure, from capitals and keystones to wall techniques and exterior moldings, make a strong case for the regional vocabulary. In the end, it is only the plan of the transept and its chapels that might have come from a Cistercian source. Even the richness of the 14th-century façade design argues for the predominance of local traditions.

LAPIDARY. A treatise offering descriptions or allegorical interpretations of precious and semiprecious stones. Medieval French lapidaries fall into two categories: those, deriving ultimately from pagan tradition, which describe the appearance, formation, and properties of stones, and those of the Christian tradition, which include allegorical interpretation. Both traditions are represented by texts in prose and verse. A third type, describing the powers of stones engraved with figures, usually astrological, is much less common.

French lapidaries of the first type are based on a Latin text traditionally attributed to Marbode, who became bishop of Rennes in 1096; some posit as their source a treatise compiled by a King Evax of Arabia. Lapidaries in this tradition list up to sixty stones. The oldest surviving version dates from the early 12th century, making it one of the earliest examples of French translation from the Latin. The entry for each stone includes not only a physical description but also an account of its special properties. Of the sapphire, for example, we are told that it is blue, that it is very precious, and that the best specimens come from Africa; it protects those who carry it from bodily harm or imprisonment, it can cure various ailments, and it is much used by necromancers. The magical and curative properties of stones are an important aspect of lapidary tradition, which teaches that God placed special powers in words, herbs, and stones.

The Marbode tradition is also represented, though less directly, in a prose lapidary of the mid-14th century, falsely attributed to Jean de Mandeville. This text is the only medieval French lapidary to be printed in the 15th and 16th centuries. Lapidary material additionally appears in encyclopedias, such as Jean Corbechon's *Livre des propriétés des choses* (1372), a translation of the *De proprietatibus rerum* of Barthélémy l'Anglais.

The allegorical lapidaries represent a different tradition. Though sometimes drawing on the Marbode tradition, they also rely on biblical exegesis and patristic writings. Lapidaries of this type are limited to stones mentioned in the Bible or in the writings of the church fathers. A common pattern is to focus on the twelve stones figuring in the breastplate of Aaron (Exodus 28:17–20). The stones and precious materials appearing in the walls of the Heavenly Jerusalem (Revelation 21:18–21) are another important source. The earliest French allegorical lapidary is a verse text of the early 13th century. A prose version dating from the 14th century is dedicated to an unspecified King Philip, probably Philip VI.

The allegorical lapidaries describe the appearance and properties of stones but add to that an explanation of each stone's religious significance. Topaz, for example, is said to be yellow, to come from Arabia and the Orient, and to change its appearance according to the phases of the moon; it cures various ailments and protects the chastity of those who carry it. In addition, we learn that it signifies the ninth order of angels and the celestial kingdom; kings should gaze upon it in order to remind themselves that spiritual glory far outweighs the honor and glory of this world.

Lapidary lore also appears in literary texts. The most celebrated stones in medieval French literature are the crystals in Guillaume de Lorris's *Roman de la Rose*; the same text also describes the powers of precious stones worn by Richesse, the personification of wealth. In Nicole de Margival's *Dit de la panthère d'amours*, the presentation of a gold ring set with an emerald occasions a description of the properties of gold, emerald, and diamond, which become allegories for aspects of the love relationship. Thus, while no "lapidary of love" exists as counterpart to Richard de Fournival's bestiary of love, lapidary material does appear in the love poetry of the French Middle Ages.

Sylvia Huot

[See also: BESTIARY; MANDEVILLE, JEAN DE; MARBODE OF RENNES; OUTREMEUSE, JEAN D'; RICHARD DE FOURNIVAL]

Meyer, Paul. "Les plus anciens lapidaires français." *Romania* 33 (1909): 44–70, 254–85, 481–552.
Pannier, Léopold. *Les lapidaires français du moyen âge des XIIe, XIIIe, et XIVe siècles.* Paris: Vieweg, 1882.
Studer, Paul, and Joan Evans. *Anglo-Norman Lapidaries.* Paris: Champion, 1924.

LARCHANT. The 13th-century church of Saint-Mathurin at Larchant (Seine-et-Marne) is notable for two reasons. The first is the consistently high quality of the work, which is attributable to the fact that the church belonged to the chapter of Notre-Dame in Paris, which provided the builders. Second, its role as a pilgrimage site associated with cures for madness is commemorated in a 15th-century wood statue of St. Mathurin healing St. Theodora, afflicted daughter of the emperor Maximilian. The large broad chevet was built at the end of the 12th or early 13th century, while the Virgin Chapel is close to the Rayonnant work in the nave of Saint-Denis. The aisleless nave is notable for its breadth and its double layers of windows, although it has been in ruins since the 17th century.

William W. Clark

Henriet, Jacques. "La chapelle de la Vierge de Saint-Mathurin de Larchant, une œuvre de Pierre de Chelles?" *Bulletin monumental* 136 (1978): 35–47.
———. "Le chœur de Saint-Mathurin de Larchant et Notre-Dame de Paris." *Bulletin monumental* 134 (1976): 289–307.
Verdier, Marc. *L'église Saint-Mathurin de Larchant.* Verneuil l'Étang: Amis des Monuments et des Sites de Seine-et-Marne, 1969.

LASSAY. Textual evidence from the 11th century attests to the construction of a fortress at Lassay (Bas-Maine) that seems to have been larger than the present structure. Built on a bank of granite, the fortress probably incorporated the square in front of the present château. Built of granite and covered by a slate roof, the castle was heavily damaged in 1417 during a siege by the English and was dismantled by Charles VII in 1422. In 1457, Jean de Vendôme obtained authorization from the king to rebuild the castle. The fact that the reconstruction took only a year testifies to the viability of the original structure. The keep, destroyed probably during the events of 1417–22, was not rebuilt.

The castle's bastions rise from the base of the rock, and its towers rise to a height of approximately 43 feet. Two entrances, one for pedestrians and the other for carriages, open on the north side and are equipped with levered bridges. Although no trace of a portcullis exists, hinges from moving panels and the latch bar have survived. The north façade, a vulnerable point of the castle, was later accommodated with openings for artillery.

E. Kay Harris

Beauchesne, Le Marquis de, and E. Lefèvre-Pontaillis. "Le château de Lassay, Mayenne." *Bulletin monumental* 69 (1905).

Vassas, Robert. "Le château de Lassay." *Congrès archéologique* (*L'Orne*) 111 (1953): 206–20.

LATE EPIC. The late narrative poems in chanson de geste form, sometimes called *chansons d'aventures*, extended the life of Old French epic, with significant modifications, well into the Middle French period. The turning point between earlier and later forms of the epic is difficult to fix, but it may conveniently be placed near the middle of the 13th century. With works like *Huon de Bordeaux, Maugis d'Aigremont*, and *Vivien de Monbranc*, the epic texts began to increase in complexity and length, became relatively rigid in form, and showed preference for elements that were less important in earlier epic works, such as love intrigues, comedy, the quest, and the non-Christian supernatural. Like earlier epics, the poems of this period share a fund of names, episodes, motifs, and even formulae. The last original work composed in chanson de geste form was probably the *Enfances Garin de Monglane* (15th c.; the octosyllabic version of *Lion de Bourges* is from the 16th). Numerous verse and prose reworkings continued throughout the 15th century, and the prose versions were widely diffused in printed form from 1478 on, some at last becoming staples of the 19th-century popular literature series known as the Bibliothèque Bleue.

The late epics retain many of the formal aspects of the chanson de geste, including clear laisse division, epic meter (the strongly caesural rhyming Alexandrine is almost universal), formulae, and performer's asides (anticipations and résumés of the action and commentary on it, appeals for money, and so on). Nico van den Boogaard showed the continuity of techniques associated with oral transmission for *Tristan de Nanteuil*, but such techniques are to be found in the group generally. Some texts show a marked tendency to end the laisse with a proverb or sentential commentary on the action.

Much of the action is that found in earlier French epics and indeed throughout all epic literature. The later chansons display examples of heroic solidarity in combat and great if sometimes misplaced concern for knightly conduct. They also spend considerable time on various forms of love, with occasional realistic and comic aspects, and, in the wake of *Huon de Bordeaux*, include magic, monsters, the otherworld, and other preternatural phenomena. Their characters are drawn from several walks of life, not only from the military elite; their heroes are complex beings, shown in a variety of situations and sometimes exhibiting ambiguous moral stances. Comic elements occur, and even predominate, as, for example, in sections of *Baudouin de Sebourc* (ca. 1330–50; 25,778 lines). This combination of fairly traditional form with new content has led Léon Gautier, François Suard, and Robert F. Cook to treat the late epics as belonging to a unified chanson de geste genre, although Gautier thought them degenerate, immoral, and trivial ("ils n'ont de l'épopée que la forme"). Cook follows Jean Subrenat in calling the late texts simply "la chanson de geste de l'époque gothique" and with Suard pleads for their full integration into studies on the genre.

On the other hand, Suard and William Kibler have brought out macrostructural differences between the earlier texts and the later. Kibler finds close parallels between the episodic and agonistic structure of the later texts and the structure of "romance" as defined by Northrop Frye. This has led him to propose treating the 14th- and 15th-century epic or quasiepic texts as a separate genre of broad popular appeal, under the name *chansons d'aventures*. Such a classification has the advantage of lifting the cloud of reproach dating from Gautier's time and allowing empirical work on the late poems to proceed without reference to an idealized concept of French epic.

The works involved are more numerous than is usually stated; Kibler counts twenty-nine chansons dating from the 14th and 15th centuries, including the reworkings of older subject matter (*remaniements*). The addition of epics in Franco-Italian dialect would bring the number up to well over thirty late epic poems that we know to have been in circulation from St. Louis's time to about the end of the Hundred Years' War. This means that 20–25 percent of all medieval French texts in chanson de geste form are "late."

The adventures in the *chansons d'aventures* are stereotyped—kidnapings, treachery, sea voyages, sieges—and usually cyclical: a character is separated from family or beloved, travels (often incognito), and undergoes trials before the inevitable reunion. In turn, the chansons are woven into further cyclical sequences in which the adventures of heroes and heroines are given in succession. Several of them indeed represent prefaces or sequels to earlier works. Along with the expansion of the Guillaume d'Orange Cycle, largely through the creation of a sort of subcycle of adventures for the Monglane family, and the rewriting and loosely conceived filling-in of the Crusade Cycle, there is development of the Nantueil Cycle in the long *Tristan de Nantueil* (mid-14th c.; 23,361 lines) and a small cycle centered on Huon de Bordeaux. Poems with no cyclical attachments also exist.

The late epics, as usually conceived, are immense, with a mean length of about 19,300 lines. The longest is the *Chevalier au cygne et Godefroid de Bouillon* at 35,180 lines; *Lion de Bourges* has 34,298, the revised *Ogier le Danois* about 31,000, and *Baudouin de Sebourc* nearly 26,000. The shortest text considered complete is *Aubéron*, at 2,456 lines; *Florence de Rome* has 4,562 and *Hugues Capet* has 6,381; but some texts (*Ciperis de Vignevaux, Bâtard de Bouillon*) may be incomplete, and the subtexts of the Monglane group are nearer the 2,000–3,000-line length common in earlier works. The huge *Chevalier au cygne* is in fact a 14th-century reworking of the poems of the Crusade Cycle. In such a work, as in *Tristan de Nantueil* or the continuations of *Huon de Bordeaux*, episode and branch are not easily distinguishable, which reminds us that the late works were not necessarily intended or received as wholes.

This in turn raises the questions of the way these chansons were meant to be presented and the form in which they were known to their audiences. Their texts include clear signs of oral transmission in a traditional sense, and although it is sometimes claimed that these must represent only archaizing window dressing, nothing indicates that oral performance of literature died out abruptly in France with the coming of courtly romance. It is likely that the late epics were both recited (perhaps read aloud) and read silently by individuals. Their versification probably responds to traditional concern for a listening audience and cannot be dismissed as merely facile any more than the earlier formulaic texts are merely cliché-ridden. The audience itself has not been identified, but some of the narratorial asides are addressed to a socially mixed group.

Robert Francis Cook

[See also: *BAUDOUIN DE SEBOURC*; CHANSON DE GESTE; CRUSADE CYCLE; DAGOBERT, PSEUDO-CYCLE OF; *HUON DE BORDEAUX*; NANTEUIL CYCLE; *TRISTAN DE NANTEUIL*]

Boogaard, Nico H.J. van den. "Le caractère oral de la chanson de geste tardive." In *Langue et littérature françaises: études réunies par R.E.V. Stuip*. Assen: Van Gorcum, 1978, pp. 25–38.

Cook, Robert Francis. "'Méchants romans' et épopée française: pour une philologie profonde." *Esprit créateur* 23 (1983): 64–74.

———. "Unity and Esthetics of the Late Chansons de Geste." *Olifant* 11 (1986): 103–14.

Gautier, Léon. *Les épopées françaises*. 2nd ed. 4 vols. Paris: Welter, 1878–94.

Kibler, William W. "Bibliography of Fourteenth and Fifteenth Century French Epics." *Olifant* 11 (1986): 23–50.

———. "La 'chanson d'aventures.'" In *Essor et fortune de la chanson de geste dans l'Europe et l'Orient latin: actes du IXe Congrès International de la Société Rencesvals*. 2 vols. Modena: Mucchi, 1984, Vol. 2, pp. 509–15.

———. "Relectures de l'épopée." In *Au carrefour des routes d'Europe: la chanson de geste. Actes du Xe Congrès de la Société Rencesvals*. 2 vols. Aix-en-Provence: CUERMA, 1987, Vol. 1, pp. 103–40.

Suard, François. "L'épopée française tardive (XIVe–XVe s.)." In *Études de philologie romane et d'histoire littéraire offertes à Jules Horrent*. Liège: n.p., 1980, pp. 449–60.

———. "La tradition épique aux XIVe et XVe siècles." *Revue des sciences humaines* 183 (1981–83): 95–107.

LATIN LYRIC POETRY. High-medieval Latin poets studying, working, and writing primarily in France produced a distinctive group of secular personal poems whose sophisticated treatment of style, ideas, forms, and voice won admirers and imitators in the courts as well as in the schools, in the vernacular as well as in Latin. The topic, however, presents many problems of definition, since within medieval Latin culture it is often difficult to separate secular from ecclesiastic, personal from professional, lyric from letter, or France from England.

Despite its popular, personal, and secular traits, this lyric always belonged to the written culture of the schools and always existed in written form. The practice of light poetry accompanied the mastery of Latin, and many high-medieval authors regret the "trifles" (*nugae*) they wrote in their younger years. In the later 11th century, poets already speak of sending and receiving poems both as single texts and in small groups; they also speak of public recitations of poetry. In fact, variants indicate that secular lyric could circulate both as performance and as text. Written copies, often made at first on wax tablets because they were cheap and easily corrected, attained permanent form in authorized copies (such as that of Baudri of Bourgueil), regional collections (such as that of Saint-Omer), and general anthologies (such as those at Oxford). These poetic practices brought criticism, approval, and betterment for the text; amusement, friendship, and favor for the poet; renown, identity, and authority for patron or institution.

Multiple sources for this lyric can be found. Horace and the satirists on the one hand and Ovid on the other had been adapted to the new requirements of the Christian educational system, and they were being widely read in high-medieval France—especially at Orléans, the school most known for its humanist study of the *artes*. A second source lay in Carolingian culture, where secular lyric was written by and for members of the courts of Charlemagne and his successors and where literacy in general and lyric in particular functioned as symbolic markers of power. In a different arena, religious lyric practices offered the secular Latin poet both popular and learned forms (such as the Ambrosian stanza and the sequence, respectively) as well as a cultural rationale for formal experimentation. In one sense, there is thus a continuous tradition in France of secular Latin poets' renewing a genre of playful and personal school poetry that can be traced back to the 4th-century poet Ausonius writing in Bordeaux—though those acts of renewal themselves are significant. In the hands of the new poets, however, such trifling texts became highly successful vehicles for serious treatments of formal, psychological, literary, moral, or political topics.

For the sake of convenience, one can divide the high-medieval secular lyric poets into four "generations." The discussion that follows will give special attention to leading figures of "satire" and "love," the two lyric modes that brought the most prestige and reward. A first generation appeared in France during the last decades of the 11th century led by Marbode of Rennes, praised as the "King of Eloquence," who wrote an extensive body of secular poems while schoolmaster and chancellor at Angers from ca. 1067 to 1096. His collection includes love poems, satires, epigrams, stylistic exercises, personal laments, and poetic letters. Some of his most daring ventures into secular topics and techniques were suppressed in the early 18th century and have become known only recently. The speakers of his love poems return repeatedly to the power and anguish of their desire for young women and men—the latter topic widely treated during this first generation—and it is clear that Marbode's great achievement lies in the depiction and exploration of human nature. Hildebert of Le Mans (or Lavardin) wrote only a small amount of secular poetry, but both his command of Latin poetry and rhetoric and his Christian humanism were widely admired and imitated throughout the 12th century. Others, such as Godefroi of Reims, Raoul of La Tourte, and Baudri of Bourgueil, also made important experiments in Romanesque poetics. Although these poets remain relatively unknown today, their efforts led to a cultural reevaluation of a "modern" secular personal poetry written in Latin.

The texts of the second generation of poets writing during the early decades of the century, when Reformist pressure was greatest in France, have been less well preserved than those of the first. How interesting it would be to see the love songs that Abélard wrote ca. 1120 and that were still being sung decades later; the fervor, eloquence, and learning of his extant religious lyric suggest that they must have been of high quality. Yet even such infamous love lyric was ignored by anthologists. Of the extant love poetry from this second group, that of Abélard's student Hilary of Orléans claims perhaps the most serious attention.

Born and educated in Orléans, Hilary became ca. 1105 a cleric attached to a convent in Angers; his complaint (with an Old French refrain) to Abélard about refusing to teach disobedient students establishes Hilary's presence at the abbey of the Paraclete ca. 1125, and he apparently taught in various schools, including Orléans, for the remainder of his life. In about a dozen love poems, found in a unique manuscript, he uses plain style and simple form, building his songs with rhymed quatrains. Lavishly praising the beauty of beloved nuns and young men, Hilary adopts the position of a humble servant, even describing himself as a feudal vassal on his knees with hands joined. He speaks from the same position in some of his letters, offering *servitium* to those above him, a fact that implies that his originality lay in the ambiguous overlap between sexual and material desires.

Satires began to change during this second generation, with respect to both the poet's persona and his target. The few extant poems in leonine hexameters by Serlo of Bayeux, for instance, announce a new direction with their combination of specific personal content and broad institutional critique. Writing from ca. 1095 to ca. 1115 while archdeacon of Saint-Étienne, Serlo profited under the patronage and suffered under the power of Anglo-Norman rule. In his poems, he details his position outside the ecclesiastic hierarchy, which he bitterly satirizes for gluttony, greed, and debauchery, thus exploiting the Reformist agenda for his own purposes. Serlo's satirical voice (adapted in part from Roman models), which speaks without authority as it speaks against authority, finds a parallel in the more successful works of Peter the Painter, a canon at the monastery of Saint-Omer in Flanders during the first decades of the 12th century. Though he emulates at times cathedral-school satirists in England and France, Peter differs in the subject and object of his satire. He is more conscious than Serlo of his role as an artist and "grammarian man" (*vir grammaticus*) seeking fame and fortune, and he aims at a wider secular target, which includes bad poets (*ioculatores*) on the one hand, ladies and their lovers on the other.

A new satirical form blossomed during the third generation of secular poets in the hands of Hugh (Primas) of Orléans, who stands above the rest in terms of quantity, quality, and influence. Born ca. 1093 and first educated in Orléans, Hugh wrote from the early 1130s to the early 1160s while teaching at schools and serving ecclesiastic magnates at Amiens, Sens, Beauvais, Orléans, Reims, and Paris. Twenty-four poems can be ascribed to him with reasonable assurance, some of which were transmitted, altered, expanded, and imitated by a large number of subsequent poets. The first of the great "Goliardic" poets, Hugh wrote of "wine, women, and song," as well as of dice games, patrons, and books; with biting humor and clever wit, he satirized arrogant ecclesiastics, parodied authoritative texts, and mocked himself. Such topics and tones created the persona—often equated with the person of a learned and irreverent "wandering student" (*clericus vagans*)—that has had enormous appeal for medieval and modern readers. If we look at the texts instead of through them, though, we see a clerical author well established within the French cathedral culture, who completely mastered the demands of both metrical and rhythmic verse, and who displayed great talent and pleasure in the art of rhyming. Contemporary appreciation of the achievements of speaker and writer can be measured by the nickname "Primas" (i.e., ecclesiastic dignitary), which his fellow schoolmen allegedly gave him and which both he and the manuscripts use.

Love lyric continued to be written in this period, in learned and popular forms. Many of the latter remained anonymous and appear scattered throughout anthologies of the 13th century, if they were recorded at all. But we do know well a famous poet of the period whose poems of love and friendship follow the learned forms used by Marbode. Serlo of Wilton, born in England ca. 1110, came to France for schooling, and wrote poetry ca. 1130–60 while teaching in Paris, until he abandoned the schools to spend the remainder of his life as a monk. Using hexameters and distichs, often and variously linked with rhyme and ornamented with rhetorical figures, Serlo wrote almost fifty poetic letters, epigraphs, praise poems, complaints, and epigrams. In many, the speaker addresses or discusses friends and lovers, male and female, and establishes a forceful textual presence with his witty manipulation of language. The confession and display of sexuality seems at times extraordinarily candid, producing a sincere presence that appears to have repelled the few critics who have approached these intriguing and well-crafted poems.

A fourth and final generation of secular poets followed, some of the most famous exercising their talents outside France. Many fine poets, such as the Rheinlander known only as "the Archpoet," were born and employed abroad but received their education and poetic models in France. Yet even the two dominant French lyric poets, Peter of Blois and Walter of Châtillon, spent a considerable amount of their career in courts outside modern France. By the end of the 12th century, the Latin clerical culture had become so homogeneous and "universal" that class or regional identities mattered much less than they had at the beginning.

The rhythmic poems by Peter of Blois, which Walter of Châtillon himself praised, had been presumed lost until recently. Circumstantial but persuasive evidence now suggests that a group of sixteen formally and topically coherent metrical love songs at the beginning of the famous Arundel anthology belong to him; the dozen Christmas songs and satires that follow may be his as well. Born ca. 1135 and educated in France, Peter spent his career as a letter writer and diplomat in the service of Anglo-Norman magnates in Sicily and England before retiring to the monastery and dying ca. 1200. His Arundel poems stand out for their formal virtuosity; the presence of stanzas, refrains, and complex rhyme structure signals a strong influence by vernacular court lyric; yet vocabulary, style, and concepts belong to the school culture. Peter's sophisticated poet-lover treats art and love as natural, serious, and significant activities, a view common in vernacular lyric but rare in Latin poetry.

Walter of Châtillon was the most productive, important, and influential secular Latin lyric poet of the 12th century, composing more than fifty satires, love songs, and hymns. Born ca. 1135 at Lille, he studied and taught in France during the early part of his career, then became associated with the brilliant humanist court of Henry II of England; when Thomas Becket was murdered (1169), he left for posts at Châtillon and then Reims, dying of leprosy ca. 1200. His dozen or so love poems include *pastourelles*, nature poems, and a paean to Love. But despite his constant borrowing from Ovid, Walter was not a love poet, and both tone and form signal his distance from that material. In most of his poetry, in fact, he attacked as satirist and moralist all forms and agents of cupidity. In his earlier poems, he built lively stanzas from the short rhythmic verses (predominantly seven or eight syllables) of the vernacular tradition, often adding a refrain. For his later pieces, he turned to the "Goliardic measure" that the Archpoet had used with such success in the 1060s and that featured long rhythmic verses, simple four-line stanzas, a "Goliardic" speaker similar to that of Hugh Primas, satire, and frequent parody. Walter invented a successful variant by substituting an *auctoritas* for the final line: a hexameter or pentameter taken from a classical or "modern" author—including himself. Widely imitated and anthologized during the 13th century, Walter's poems mark the end of great high-medieval secular personal poetry by signaling the institutional pressures to harmonize the products of the human imagination with a new orthodoxy.

This minor genre does not carry minor significance for an understanding of 12th-century Latin culture, for it affords a privileged view of human and humanistic aspects otherwise difficult to see. By content, the genre portrays, examines, and publicizes the psychological, economic, and social costs imposed upon its own members by the institutional demands. By form, it reveals the centrality, commodification, and ambiguity of wit, since its performative value lay in the demonstration of an ability to manipulate language and form that, when successful, brought authority and employment. There is much to be gained from a comparative study of these Latin versifiers and the troubadours and trouvères, with whom they overlapped and interacted.

Gerald A. Bond

[See also: BAUDRI OF BOURGUEIL; LATIN POETRY, CAROLINGIAN; LATIN POETRY, MEROVINGIAN; OVID, INFLUENCE OF]

Hilary of Orléans. *Versus et ludi; Epistolae; Ludus Danielis Belouacensis,* ed. Walther Bulst and M.L. Bulst-Thiele. Leiden: Brill, 1989.

Hildebert of Lavardin. *Carmina minora,* ed. Brian Scott. Leipzig: Teubner, 1969.

McDonough, Christopher James, ed. *The Oxford Poems of Hugh Primas and the Arundel Lyrics.* Toronto: Pontifical Institute of Mediaeval Studies, 1985.

Marbode of Rennes. "Liebesbriefgedichte Marbods," ed. Walter Bulst. In *Liber Floridus: Mittellateinische Studien,* ed. Bernhard Bischoff. St. Ottilien: Eos Verlag der Erzabtei, 1950, pp. 287–301.

Serlo of Wilton. *Poèmes latins,* ed. Jan Öberg. Stockholm: Almqvist and Wiksell, 1965.

Stehling, Thomas, ed. and trans. *Medieval Latin Poems of Male Love and Friendship.* New York: Garland, 1984.

Bond, Gerald A. "'Iocus Amoris': The Poetry of Baudri of Bourgueil and the Formation of the Ovidian Subculture." *Traditio* 42 (1986): 143–93.

Dronke, Peter. "Peter of Blois and Poetry at the Court of Henry II." *Mediaeval Studies* 38 (1976): 185–235.

Mann, Jill. "Satiric Subject and Satiric Object in Goliardic Literature." *Mittellateinisches Jahrbuch* 15 (1980): 63–86.

Offermanns, Winfried. *Die Wirkung Ovids auf die literarische Sprache der lateinischen Liebesdichtung des XI. und XII. Jahrhunderts.* Wuppertal: Kastellaun, 1970.

Raby, Frederic J.E. *A History of Secular Latin Poetry in the Middle Ages.* 2nd ed. 2 vols. Oxford: Clarendon, 1957.

Rigg, George. "Golias and Other Pseudonyms." *Studi medievali* 18 (1977): 65–109.

Witke, Charles. *Latin Satire: The Structure of Persuasion.* Leiden: Brill, 1970.

LATIN POETRY, CAROLINGIAN. Though Charlemagne reigned from 768 to 814, Carolingian Latin poetry spans the period from 747 (the advent of Pepin the Short and the *Carmina* of Boniface) to 877 (the death of Charles the Bald and the *Eclogues* of Radbod of Utrecht). A capitulary from Charlemagne, the *Epistola de litteris colendis,* issued in 787 for the education of the clergy, characterizes the poetry of the period. Practice in the classic *litterarum studia* was to perfect the composition of poems in praise of the Trinity, Jesus, the Virgin, the saints, holy cities, holy rivers, or ancient Germanic legends. School exercises, called *dictamina,* practiced and perfected according to the rules of the Trivium and Quadrivium, were to serve the study and preaching of Scripture.

Poets of the Roman Empire were models for those of the Holy Roman Empire. A script, Carolingian minuscule, was developed for copying the texts of the classical authors. Charles imported palace preceptors to teach the rules of classical prosody in the palace school at Aix-la-Chapelle. From England came Alcuin and Moduin, named respectively "Flaccus" (Horace) and "Naso" (Ovid) at the imperial court. Charles invited "Pindar" (Theodulf of Orléans) from Spain, and "Homer" (Angilbert) from the old Frankish territories. Paul the Deacon, Peter of Pisa, Paulinus of Aquileia—all three from Lombardy—and a small group from Ireland, including Clement and Dougal, round out the first generation of Carolingian poets.

The *dictamina* of Alcuin and Theodulf incorporate Virgilian, Horatian, or Ovidian quantitative half-lines; but the lines are often stamped with an accentual metric, and scansion is impeded by Carolingian pronunciation of Latin (e.g., *periclum* for *periculum*). For example, *Aeneid* 1.531, resounds in Alcuin's *Verses on the Saints in the Church of York*:

Est antiqua, potens bellis et corpore praestans,
Germaniae populos gens inter et extera regna,
Duritiam propter dicti cognomine Saxi

("Among the peoples of Germania and the foreign powers, there is an ancient race, strong in war and sturdy in body, called Saxons on account of their hardness"); but the *-iae* in *Germaniae* must be scanned as one syllable to make the hexameters work. Theodulf's verses on Palm Sunday,

Gloria, laus et honor tibi sit, rex Christe
redemptor,
Cui puerile decus prompsit osanna pium. . . .

("Let glory, praise, and honor be to You, O Christ, King and Redeemer. Children utter a loyal and well-turned 'Hosanna' to You . . ."), are still chanted in the liturgy of Palm Sunday; but the music does not indicate whether *cui* is pronounced as one syllable or two. It is not important that classical Latin was a "foreign language" to the Carolingian poets; they developed a latinity of their own. Poems composed in acrostics, *carmina figurata*, abecedaria, and aenigmata show the skill and pleasure that Charlemagne's court and the monastic schools took in intricate combinations of letters and in Teutonic-Latin semantics.

Some exquisite pieces came out of this period. In liturgical use today are the anonymous *Veni, creator spiritus* and *Ave, maris stella*, and Paulinus of Aquileia's *Ubi caritas et amor, Deus ibi est*. Something close to Germanic alliteration permeates the anonymous *Debate Between Winter and Spring* over the proper time for the cuckoo to sing:

Ver quoque florigero succinctus stemmate venit,
frigida venit Hiems, rigidis hirsuta capillis.
his certamen erat cuculi de carmine grande

("Spring comes, girdled even in a garland of flowers. Winter comes, completely covered by frozen, frosted hair. Both were to debate a great debate over the song of the cuckoo.")

Walafrid Strabo has some magnificent lines on the cultivation and care of roses: *Iam nisi me fessum via longior indupediret*. An epic, the *Waltharius*, evidences the power and compression of Carolingian poetry:

At vir Waltharius missa cum cuspide currens
evaginato regem importunior ense
impetit et scuto dextra de parte revulso

ictum praevalidum ac mirandum fecit eique
crus cum poblite adusque femur decerpserat
omne. . . .

("Having thrown his spear, the manly Walter ran at the king more savagely with a drawn sword, and attacked. The [king's] shield was ripped away from his right side, and [Walter] struck a huge and awful blow. The [king's] thigh with the hough all the way to the foot, he [Walter] cut off completely. . . .")

Guido d'Arezzo, the 11th-century Benedictine, used the following verses of Paul the Deacon's *Hymn to John the Baptist* to derive the notes of the "great scale":

UT queant laxis REsonare fibris
MIra gestorum FAmuli tuorum,
SOlve polluti LAbii reatum
sancte Johannes.

When compared with the dearth of Latin poetry in the Merovingian period (ca. 482–ca. 751), the poetry of this period deserves the name "Carolingian renaissance." When compared with the brilliance of 12th-century Latin poetry, however, this same poetry may appear unengaging.

Ernest A. Kaulbach

[See also: LATIN LYRIC POETRY; LATIN POETRY, MEROVINGIAN]

Poetae latini aevi carolini, ed. E. Duemmler (Vols. 1–2), Ludwig Traube (Vol. 3), Karl Strecker (Vol. 4). *Monumenta Germaniae Historica*. Berlin: Weidman, 1881–1923.

Strecker, Karl, ed. *Die Lateinischen Dichter des deutschen Mittelalters: Poetarum latinorum medii aevi*. Vol. 6, fasc. 1. Munich: Monumenta Germaniae Historica, 1978.

Raby, Frederic James Edward, ed. *The Oxford Book of Medieval Latin Verse*. Oxford: Clarendon, 1959, pp. 87–132.

Ghellinck, Joseph de. *Littérature latine au moyen âge*. Brussels: Bloud et Gay, 1939, pp. 84–130.

McGuire, Martin R.P., and Hermigild Dressler. *Introduction to Medieval Latin Studies*. 2nd ed. Washington, D.C.: Catholic University of America Press, 1977, pp. 89–99.

Norberg, Dag L. *La poésie latine rythmique du haut moyen âge*. Stockholm: Almqvist and Wiksell, 1954.

Raby, Frederic James Edward. *A History of Secular Latin Poetry in the Middle Ages*. 2nd ed. 2 vols. Oxford: Clarendon, 1957, Vol.1, pp. 178–269.

———. *A History of Christian-Latin Poetry from the Beginnings to the Close of the Middle Ages*. 2nd ed. Oxford: Clarendon, 1953, pp. 155–210.

LATIN POETRY, MEROVINGIAN. The term "Merovingian" not only suggests Christian imperial influence from Ravenna but describes a transition that occurred in the Latin poetry composed in France from ca. 482, the beginning of the reign of Clovis I, until after 751, the advent of Pepin I. At the time that the last of the native, Gallo-Roman rulers was ceding power to the first of the Merovingians, Clovis I (r. 482–511), native Gallo-Roman poetry was in decline.

The Gallo-Latin poets of this period, Virgilius Maro and Theodofrid, are generally cited and then ignored.

Both "Merovaeus" (Gmc. "Merewig"), the legendary founder of the line, and the best-known poet of the period, Venantius Fortunatus, immigrated from Ravenna to the north of France. "Merovingian Latin poetry" refers primarily to that of Venantius (540–600), who continued the tradition of occasional poetry that preceded 482:

> Fortunatus ego hinc humili prece voce saluto
> (Italiae genitum Gallica rura tenent)
> Pictavis residens, qua sanctus Hilarius olim
> natus in urbe fuit, notus in orbe pater.

("I, Fortunatus, here greet you in the speech of humble entreaty/[Rustic Gaul keeps me, Italian born] /Now living at Poitiers, the city where St. Hilary was born long ago,/ Father Hilary known all over the world.") But he also introduces the rhythmic poetry that followed:

> Vexilla regis prodeunt,
> fulget crucis mysterium
> quo carne carnis conditor
> suspensus est patibulo. . . .

("The battle standards of the King march forth,/The sacred sign of the Cross shines./On it, the founder of the flesh hung/In the flesh, suspended on the crosspiece. . . .") The disparate qualities of Merovingian latinity blend in the rhythms of Venantius Fortunatus. His occasional pieces retain the grace of the old Gallo-Roman style of Ausonius (310–ca. 393) (*natus in urbe fuit, notus in orbe pater*); he effaces his personal voice within the requisite formality (*Italiae genitum Gallica rura tenent*). In his rhythmic hymns, he imports imperial legalities from Byzantium by way of Ravenna (*conditor, baiulat*), adopts a warlike spirit from the Sicambrian tribal culture of Clovis I (*vexilla regis prodeunt*), stamps the verses with the meters of St. Ambrose, the teacher of Theodosius (*fulget crucis mysterium*), and converts the Roman sense of military duty into the Christian sense of militancy for Christ:

> Pange, lingua, gloriosi proelium certaminis
> et super crucis tropaeo dic triumphum nobilem,
> qualiter redemptor orbis immolatus vicerit. . . .

("Sing, my tongue, of a glorious battle for the prize;/Speak out a noble triumph about the trophy, the cross:/How the Redeemer of the whole world conquered, by being slain. . . .") *Pange, lingua* would appeal to Christian-Frankish nobles; its sacred septameter, or "Roman Marching Rhythm," stamped into *Pange, lingua, gloriosi proelium certaminis*, would recall the glory days of Roman *imperium*. The iambic tetrameters or octosyllabics in *Vexilla regis prodeunt* imitate the chaste rhythms and images in the hymns of Ambrose of Milan, now in the Frankish antiphoners.

True to the Byzantine-Latin style of the *kallos* (poems of the "beautiful," called *laudes* in Latin), Venantius composed stylized panegyrics of persons, cities, countrysides, and rivers. Like Ausonius, Venantius declaimed the pieces in the presence of the persons or places, while he was traveling from Mainz to Cologne to Trier on his way to the royal city. His occasional *epithalamia* and epitaphs were written for the marriages and deaths of patrons. As bishop of Poitiers at the end of his career, Venantius formed a close friendship with a group of noblewomen and especially with Radegund, wife of Clotar I, who had retired from the savagery of the court into monastic life at the nearby abbey of Sainte-Croix. Venantius's *De excidio Thoringiae* is a celebration of the destruction of the kingdom of Radegund's father, and he versified the narrative of the murder of King Chilperic's fiancée, Galswintha. From Poitiers also came *Vexilla regis prodeunt* and *Pange, lingua*.

The strange poet of Toulouse known as Virgilius Maro or Virgil of Toulouse gives various examples of the *rhythmi* practiced in Gaul, and Theodofrid, abbot of Corbie, has some anthologized verses on the six ages of the world, but the *rhythmi* of Venantius Fortunatus dominate Merovingian Latin poetry.

Ernest A. Kaulbach

[See also: HYMNS; LATIN LYRIC POETRY; LATIN POETRY, CAROLINGIAN; RADEGUND]

Raby, Frederic James Edward, ed. *The Oxford Book of Medieval Latin Verse*. Oxford: Clarendon, 1959, pp.74–76.

Leo, Frederick, ed. *Venanti Honori Clemenianti Fortunati Presbyteri Italici opera poetica*. In *Monumenta Germaniae Historica: Auctores Antiquissimi*. Vol. 4, fasc. 1. Berlin: Weidmann, 1881.

Curtius, Ernst Robert. *European Literature and the Latin Middle Ages*, trans. Willard R. Trask. New York: Harper, 1953, pp. 154–58.

McGuire, Martin R.P., and Hermigild Dressler. *Introduction to Medieval Latin Studies*. 2nd ed. Washington, D.C.: Catholic University of America Press, 1977, pp. 89–99.

Raby, Frederic James Edward. *A History of Secular Latin Poetry in the Middle Ages*. 2nd ed. 2 vols. Oxford: Clarendon, 1957, Vol. 1, pp. 128–46, 153–58.

———. *A History of Christian-Latin Poetry from the Beginnings to the Close of the Middle Ages*. 2nd ed. Oxford: Clarendon, 1953, pp. 86–95.

LAURENT D'ORLÉANS (d. ca. 1325). A Dominican friar and confessor of King Philip III, Laurent completed the *Somme le roi* in 1280 at the king's request. Preserved in about a hundred manuscripts in French, in translations into Flemish, English, Italian, Provençal, and Catalan, and in several incunabula, this lengthy prose work is essentially a treatise on the vices and virtues, drawing on Hugh of Saint-Victor, Guillaume Peyraut's *Summa virtutum*, and the anonymous *Miroir du monde*. It is divided into five sections, on the Ten Commandments, the Twelve Articles of Faith, the Seven Deadly Sins, Virtue (in general), and a treatise on the Seven Virtues derived from the Seven Gifts of the Holy Ghost. This final section, twice as long as the other four combined, also includes a commentary on the Lord's Prayer.

William W. Kibler

[See also: MORAL TREATISES]

Edition being prepared for the Société des Anciens Textes Français series by E. Brayer.

Brayer, Edith. "Contenu, structure et combinaisons du *Miroir du monde* et de la *Somme le roi*." *Romania* 79 (1958): 1–38, 433–70.

Langlois, Charles-Victor. *La vie en France au moyen âge de la fin du XIIe au milieu du XIVe siècle*. 4 vols. Paris: Hachette, 1926–28, Vol. 4: *La vie spirituelle*.

LAVAL. The lordship of Laval (Mayenne) in the county of Maine in northwestern France dates from the mid-11th century. The male line of the original seigneurial family died out in 1213, and the heiress, Emma, married Mathieu II of Montmorency. Their son, Gui VII de Laval, married Philippa, heiress to the important Breton lordship of Vitré, in 1239, thus establishing the house of Laval-Montmorency as an important dynasty in Breton feudal politics. Gui VII died in 1267 while accompanying Charles I of Anjou on his conquest of the kingdom of Sicily. Gui VIII (r. 1267–95) and Gui IX (r. 1295–1333) served kings Philip III and Philip IV on their military campaigns. The family's position in Brittany grew stronger when Gui X married Béatrix, daughter of Duke Arthur II, and his brother Foulques married the heiress of the important barony of Rais (Retz). Gui X died in the Battle of La Roche-Derrien in 1347. His daughter Béatrix married Olivier IV de Clisson, future constable of France, while his two sons succeeded to the lordship successively as Gui XI and Gui XII. The latter (d. 1412) was an important royal commander until Charles V's attempted confiscation of Brittany (1379), after which he served Jean IV and Jean V of Brittany. The Montmorency male line died out with Gui XII, whose daughter Anne married a prominent Breton, Jean, lord of Montfort, Gael, and Lohéac. He took the name Gui XIII but soon died, leaving Anne to administer the family lands for their young son, Gui XIV (d. 1486), during whose long reign Charles VII erected Laval into a county. A younger son, André, lord of Lohéac, became admiral of France in 1437 and in 1439 succeeded his third cousin Gilles de Rais as marshal.

John Bell Henneman, Jr.

[See also: BRITTANY (genealogical table)]

Bertrand de Broussillon, Arthur. *La maison de Laval, 1020–1605: étude historique accompagnée du cartulaire de Laval et de Vitré*. 3 vols. Paris: Picard, 1895–1900.

LAVILLETERTE. The little church at Lavilleterte (Oise) is an almost perfectly preserved country church of the mid-12th century. The nave is flanked by single aisles; all are covered by rib vaults, as are the projecting transept and the simple, flat chevet. The sturdiness of the construction perhaps accounts for the remarkable homogeneity of the structure.

William W. Clark

Prache, Anne. *Île-de-France romane*. La Pierre-qui-vire: Zodiaque, 1983, pp. 249–52.

Régnier, Louis. "L'église de la Villeterte (Oise)." *Congrès archéologique* (*Beauvais*) 72 (1905): 489–522.

LAW AND JUSTICE. To speak of French law is to speak first of the end of the Carolingian state in the late 10th century and the rise of the Capetian kings of France, laboriously establishing their authority in the area around Paris and slowly extending their domain throughout the 11th and 12th centuries. During this period, the customs of feudalism, a legacy of the Carolingians, governed the king's relations with the lay nobility of his domain and with the great ecclesiastical lords—the bishops, abbots, and priors—who were part of the feudal system. The bailiffs of the lay and ecclesiastical lords administered the law that regulated the lives and activities of the agricultural population, law that was embedded in the body of manorial customs that had also come from the distant Carolingian past. During this period, the reviving economic activity of western Europe produced towns that in France would create a new area of law.

It is difficult, therefore, to speak of French law before the 13th century, and by then three other legal systems had become prominent in France and would contribute in various ways to the development of French law. The first of these was the revival of Roman law in Italy in the late 11th and 12th centuries. By the middle of the 12th, this revival, based on renewed interest and study of Justinian's *Corpus iuris civilis* of the 6th century, had spread into southern France. It did not become the sole legal system of southern France but provided important concepts and systematic structure as the customary law became a written law. Along with Roman law came the notary, who as a paralegal agent had a recognized authority to create in writing juridically authentic documents that were accepted in legal disputes as proof, whether they concerned loans, business contracts, marriage agreements, wills, property matters, or a dozen other subjects of legal conflict.

The earliest important center for the study of Roman law in France was Montpellier, where legal scholars like the Italian jurist and glossator Placentinus were at work in the 1160s. In the early 13th century, the Bolognese jurist and professor Francis Accursius produced a gloss on the body of Roman law, a commentary recognized as so complete and superior to all others that the jurists who produced commentaries after Accursius would be called "postglossators." By 1260, Montpellier was the site of a university with a law faculty and students, many of whom as graduates became judges and administrators in southern France as it gradually came under control of the French crown in the 13th century. In coming into the service of the French king, they brought a legal mentality formed by the concepts of Roman law that would influence in many important ways the further development of French law.

A second system of law arose in the 12th century when Gratian, a monk of Bologna, compiled the largest collection of canonical decrees and texts then assembled, a collection that has carried the popular name of the *Decretum*.

Gratian's complete Latin title translated into English is *A Concord of Discordant Canons*. Gratian's collection, inspired by Justinian's codification of Roman law, established the view that as the Roman emperor had been the supreme source of Roman law, so was the pope the supreme legislator for the church and its legal sphere. Canon law dealt with the regulation and ordering of the clergy, the church, and the Christian population of Europe, since the pope claimed exclusive jurisdiction in all matters touching marriage, wills, and areas, such as education and heresy, that concerned the spiritual life of the church.

Canon law, using Roman law principles, terminology, and procedure, soon demonstrated that it was capable of much growth. Later popes added collections of decrees to the *Decretum*, and canon law, like Roman law, became the subject of study in the universities. A large and growing number of young men who chose a clerical life found the study of canon law a key to a successful career in the church. Not only did they enter the administrative and legal services of popes, bishops, and abbots, but they found a large and attractive area for their talents in the service of the kings and lesser rulers of Europe, who could use their literacy and legal training in governmental offices. In France, they found numerous positions of employment in the king's household and in his treasury and accounting department, and especially in the chancery, which issued royal correspondence and helped to frame the king's legislation. Most of all, they entered the Parlement de Paris, the great royal law court, serving as judges, as staff assistants, and in judicial capacities. They brought the influence of both Roman and canon law into the field of royal justice and lawmaking.

The economic development of the 11th and 12th centuries produced a third area of legal activity as the old Roman cities, commercially depressed for centuries, now, along with newly founded towns, established autonomous urban governments with independent judicial institutions. These towns developed a legal system, neither feudal, Roman, nor customary, that administered the legal needs of the urban population and managed often complex relations with the church and the monarchy. Rigaudière has shown how these towns used *avocats-conseillers* to counsel them and to conduct their legal business, many on a permanent basis and others occasionally. These counselors usually held degrees in law, and the number engaged in this kind of work increased steadily from the 13th century through the 15th and beyond. Trained as they usually were in Roman law, they provide a striking example of the use and influence of Roman law in the development of French institutions.

While the 12th century produced the great revival of Roman law and the origins of canon law, only in the 13th century did French customary law come to be written; Roman and canon law provided the inspiration for this activity. Customary law varied from one region of France to another, and the writing of such law took place within regional or provincial boundaries. The results were *coutumiers*, collections of laws, legal customs, ways of holding court and doing justice. Their content was as much procedural as substantive law. The first of these to appear was the *Ancien coutumier de Normandie* in the early part of the 13th century. By the middle of the century, a larger and more complete collection for Normandy appeared under the name of the *Grand coutumier de Normandie*, a volume whose contents would remain applicable for centuries. Pierre de Fontaines, a royal administrator and *bailli* of Vermandois, produced ca. 1258 a *coutumier* for that area called *Conseil a un ami*. The unknown author of the *Livre de jostice et de plet* (1260) addressed the area of Orléans, and the *Établissements de saint Louis* (ca. 1270), far from being an official or royal compilation, contained two anonymous treatises for the Orléannais and the region of Touraine-Anjou.

The most important legal treatise written in medieval France was the great collection of customary law made by Philippe de Beaumanoir ca. 1283, the *Coutumes de Clermont en Beauvaisis*. Beaumanoir became the *bailli* of the count of Clermont in 1279, his first important position, and his book must be considered the result of all that he learned in holding the courts of the count, observing cases in nearby courts, and in frequently attending the Parlement de Paris. He cited more than one hundred cases from his judicial experience to support the rules and precedents that he discussed. And whereas the earlier *coutumiers* contained quotes and texts from Justinian's *Corpus*, comparing Roman with French customary law, Beaumanoir was the first to achieve a successful merging of the two. He believed that for laws to be valid and just they must be made by great counsel, for the common profit of the realm, and for reasonable cause. The idea that laws should be for the common profit is also found in canon and Roman law.

The extent to which Roman and customary law confronted each other in 13th-century France is further illustrated in the work of Jacques de Révigny, the most prominent of the professors in the law school at Orléans. The formal teaching of Roman law at Orléans represented its farthest penetration in northern France, and Révigny was deeply concerned with the connection between the two legal systems. Writing in the 1270s, he gave much attention to the similarities and differences between the two laws and expressed his views in his commentaries on various Roman laws, distinguishing custom from the Roman statute and trying to reconcile the two.

While these developments were taking place in French law, the French king's role as lawmaker or legislator slowly came into prominence. No legislation has survived from the early Capetian kings. Louis VII was the first to issue ordinances, when in 1144 he banished the relapsed Jews from the kingdom and in 1155 established the Peace of God for ten years. Both measures were made with heavy church sponsorship. Apart from the famous ordinance of 1190, providing for the administration of the realm, Philip II Augustus did little more than change succession rules for fiefs and increase the widow's dower in her deceased husband's property. And these two ordinances applied only to the royal domain, not to the entire kingdom.

The king's power to make laws binding on all of his subjects slowly increased through the 13th century. Ideological support came from the study of Roman law, which in its general attitude toward political power revived the image of the prince who was supreme in his legislative authority and by analogy elevated the sovereign power of a king to make laws for the entire realm. Beaumanoir paraphrased the texts of the Code and the Digest in arguing that what pleases the prince is to be held as law or, moving as he could to the feudal context, that as each feudal lord is sovereign in his particular lordship so is the king sovereign over all. But while Louis IX issued ordinances and his son Philip III issued more, the legislation of these kings concerned only the area of public law, the principles and problems of governmental administration. None of their lawmaking addressed the domain of private law, whereby the inhabitants of France sued and were sued in the courts of the king. Certain kings encouraged the further collecting of local customs. Even here, little was accomplished. Philip III sponsored the compilation of the customs of Toulouse, and Philip V in the early 14th century pushed other projects of this kind. Not until the 16th century would progress be made on a complete *coutumier* for all of France.

The greatest progress in medieval French law came in the 13th century. This progress, which concerned procedure as much as legal doctrine, affected justice as much as law. In this century, the judicial duel received the first setback in its long history. Sometimes called "the judgment of God," the judicial duel was the system by which two litigants reached judgment through physical combat. The Burgundians and the Bavarians used it in the 6th century, and though it does not appear in Salic law there are incidents of the practice in Gregory of Tours's *Liber historiae Francorum*. It either subsided or disappeared during the Carolingian period, because legal procedure was more organized and proof consisted of written documents and witnesses. With the disappearance of the Carolingian state in the 10th century, its legal system vanished or weakened and its former territories became counties, duchies, and other feudal lordships, each with its own court in which the judicial duel as a way of settling legal disputes revived and became more frequent.

More is known about the judicial duel in the 13th century because the authors of the *coutumiers* described it in detail for the first time. One could appeal from the "false judgment" of an ordinary tribunal to judgment by combat in the belief that God would give victory to the party who had right on his side. If the combatants were members of the noble class, they would use the weapons of the noble class, the lance and the sword. If the dispute was between a lay noble and a cleric, the latter would be obliged to find a "champion" to fight for him since the clergy were forbidden to shed blood, and the weapons would be nonnoble, that is, the staff and the shield. This would also be the case in battle between a noble and a nonnoble. No vassal could appeal his lord to judgment by combat except in an accusation of crime. Only in the 13th century, when we know most about the judicial duel, did restrictions on its use appear. Beaumanoir listed seventeen cases in which combat could not be used to decide a legal dispute. The resistance to this method of trial came in part from the rising class of professional lawyers in France.

Louis IX was the first king of France to abolish the judicial duel; the occasion for his action was the trial of Enguerrand de Coucy in 1259 on charges of having killed two young clerics. The king ordered an *enquête*, or investigation, to decide the matter, using witnesses and depositions. The baron, through his counsel, argued that he should not have to submit to such process when the accusation touched his person, his honor, and his heritage. Determined to give severe justice for the seriousness of the crime, the king referred to an ancient right of Merovingian kings to put to death without judgment. He knew that he could not do that and sentenced the baron to heavy fines and three years in the Holy Land.

As the result of this case, Louis IX issued an ordinance prohibiting trial by combat throughout his domain in all disputes, and in place of battle he ordered the *enquête*, or proof by witnesses and written instruments. His prohibition of the judicial duel displeased much of the feudal nobility. His son Philip III permitted trial by combat to resume. His grandson Philip IV the Fair kept the prohibition for civil cases but permitted battle in criminal and capital cases. France would wait until the mid-14th century for trial by battle to be finally abolished.

Louis IX also raised to a level of standard procedure the use of the appeal in legal disputes. The ability of a litigant to question the rightness of a judgment in one court and to remove it to a higher court for reconsideration can be found in the Roman Empire and in Salic law. Charlemagne provided for it in a capitulary of 805 whereby one could complain of a judgment and procure letters from the royal palace that would lead to a judicial review of the original decision.

When the Carolingian empire disintegrated, the counts, dukes, and other great lords did not encourage processes from their feudal courts to proceed in appeal to the king's court. And in the early stages of the French monarchy, the king was not strong enough to command his great vassals to let cases proceed upward to his court. But gradually, through the 12th century and into the 13th, the evidence for systematic appeals from lower jurisdictions to the king's court slowly increased until, with the appearance of the earliest records of the Parlement de Paris in the reign of Louis IX, one can see the practice firmly established. The multiplication of appeals was the major reason for the rapid growth of judicial business in the Parlement de Paris in the late 13th century. The vast new urban class as well as the greatly enlarged lower nobility embraced the opportunity for a more certain justice. A remnant of the distant past remained in the 13th-century appeal, when the appellant did not appeal his earlier adversary but rather the earlier judges, or the tribunal, who in giving a bad judgment became the reason for the appeal and the new adversary.

As cases of appeal multiplied, so did the rules governing them. An appellant could not choose the court but was directed by regulations to the next highest tribunal. In 1298, the Parlement de Paris addressed this problem in prohibiting cases from coming directly to it that should first be tried in the court of the *bailliage* or *sénéchaussée*. It also sought to reduce the number of judicial levels created by the seigneurial class, which often exhausted the resources of the appellants before they could reach the highest court. Could one appeal from a judgment of the Parlement de Paris? It answered this question in a general ordinance of 1303, recognizing that it could review its own decisions in a process of emendation.

French law had reached a significant level of growth and sophistication by the early 14th century, largely through the suppression of the judicial duel, the transformation and elaboration of the appeal, and the institution of the *enquête* as the system of proof. Louis IX must receive major credit for these accomplishments. But French law, so far as legal doctrine was concerned, had become an amalgamation of the revived Roman law, with influences from canon law and the great body of customary law.

The working of this amalgamation can be seen in contractual obligations, a field of legal activity that grew at a remarkable rate in the 13th and 14th centuries. The revival of towns and economic activity in the 11th century, a much larger commercial class produced by the new urban centers in the 12th and 13th, and the striking population growth of the same period were basic factors behind the noticeable rise in contractual activity. Beaumanoir in his great law book gave prominent space to contract, and it is a subject that illustrates how Roman law, canon law, and customary law contributed to the theoretical and practical aspects of this field of legal doctrine. Those who judged and those who counseled in cases on contract knew that the language of a contract and its clauses must be clear, so that the business or object sought in the agreement was made certain and could be determined beyond doubt when the need arose. These qualities of the contract made it valid and could in litigation ensure forced execution if required.

A second requirement of the contract as a legal instrument was that the object of its provisions must be possible. If the thing agreed upon did not or could not exist, the contract was invalid. An example without intent of fraud is the agreement to deliver a horse that, unknown to its owner, is already dead. An example involving fraud is the promise to sell a thing that he knows does not belong to him.

The third quality of a valid contract required that it be lawful, that its provisions not go against legal concepts or ideas that were considered mandatory. The most complex of the three conditions, in Christian Europe it played to a more moral than juridical viewpoint. Roman law had taught that the law could not be set aside by the agreement of parties, that a contract made *contra bonos mores* was tantamount to being made *contra legem*. Adopting this view, the medieval church taught that an oath that put the soul or the life of a Christian in peril could only nullify the obligation that it was supposed to enforce. The postglossators of the 13th century and the canonists came together in supporting the view that a contract was invalid if it tended to defeat a law made for the public utility (*utilitas publica*) but its validity was not harmed if it worked against a law that concerned only private utility (*utilitas privata*).

The books written on customary law in the 13th century promoted the view that "agreement conquers law," but they recognized at the same time that the only agree-

ments that should not be kept were those made against Holy Church or the common profit, or against good customs (*contre bonnes meurs*). In this way, customary law supported basic legal concepts that came originally out of Roman and canon law. Customary law also had its own view of "public order" in its treatment of inheritance. The widow whose dead husband's property was sold to satisfy his debts to the king could reclaim parts to fulfill her dower.

Franklin J. Pegues

[See also: BEAUMANOIR, PHILIPPE DE REMI, SIRE DE; CANON LAW; *CAS ROYAUX; COUTUMES; ENQUÊTEUR;* GRATIAN; *JUGE-MAGE; JUGE-ORDINAIRE;* LEGAL TREATISES; LETTERS OF REMISSION; MONTPELLIER; NOTARIES; PARLEMENT DE PARIS; TREASON]

Garward, Claude. *"De grace especial": crime, état et société en France à la fin du moyen âge.* 2 vols. Paris: Publications de la Sorbonne, 1991.

Lot, Ferdinand, and Robert Fawtier. *Histoire des institutions françaises au moyen âge.* 3 vols. Paris: Presses Universitaires de France, 1957–63, Vol. 2: *Institutions royales.*

Olivier-Martin, François. *Histoire du droit français des origines à la Révolution.* Paris: Montchrestien, 1948.

Rigaudière, Albert. "L'essor des conseillers juridiques des villes dans la France du bas moyen âge." *Revue historique de droit français et étranger* 62 (1984): 361–90.

Timbal, Pierre-Clément. *Les obligations contractuelles dans le droit français des XIIIe et XIVe siècles.* Paris: CNRS, 1973.

LAY ORDERS OF CHIVALRY. Between 1325 and ca. 1470, many associations were formed in western Christendom in which membership was restricted to laymen (and more rarely laywomen) of noble birth. As the more important of these bodies were also restricted to men who followed the profession of arms as knights or esquires, and bore the corporate title "order," all such societies came to be loosely designated by the generic term "order of chivalry" (*ordre de chevalerie*). To distinguish them from the older orders of monk-knights like the Templars and Hospitalers, on which some of them were partially modeled, the latter-day societies of lay knights may be termed collectively "lay orders of chivalry."

Four types of true lay order, endowed with corporate statutes intended to govern the lives and activities of members, were founded in our period. (1) The "confraternal order" differed from the normal lay confraternity only in being restricted to nobles and thus had elected officers. (2) The "monarchical order" differed from the confraternal type primarily in having a presidency attached on a permanent and hereditary basis to the crown or, more rarely, dynasty of its princely founder; it gave its president (variously titled "sovereign," "prince," or "chief") powers comparable with those of the "master" of one of the religious orders of knighthood. (3) The "fraternal order" was essentially a temporary society of brothers-in-arms, loosely modeled on the confraternity but intended to exist only for the duration of a particular campaign or crisis. (4) The "votive order" was a temporary society of knights who collectively undertook a vow to accomplish some enterprise (*emprise*) of arms within a specified period of time, typically a year or two. Lay orders of all types commonly took their name from the badge, or *devise*, worn by their members, but some were named after their patron saint. Orders of the first two types were created at least partly to promote chivalrous behavior and activities, but those of the second type, modeled more or less directly on the fictional society of the Round Table, were intended primarily to promote and reward loyalty and service to the crown of the prince-president among the members, usually called "companions."

Orders of all four types were founded in France. Among the confraternal orders, the most important were the Dauphinois Order of St. Catherine (founded ca. 1335), the Barrois Order of St. Hubert (1422), the Comtois Order of St. George de Rougemont (ca. 1440), and the Angevin-Provençal Order of the Crescent (1448). The only monarchical orders certainly established in France before 1578 were the Company of Our Lady of the Noble House of Saint-Ouen (known from its badge as the Company of the Star), founded by King John II as a rival to the English Order of the Garter in 1352, dissolved as a true order on his death in 1364, and completely defunct by 1380; the Order of the Golden Shield, founded by Duke Louis of Bourbon in 1365 and dissolved on or by his death in 1410; the Order of the Ermine, founded by Duke Jean IV of Brittany in 1381 and dissolved as a true order on his death in 1399; the Order of the Golden Fleece, founded by Duke Philip the Good of Burgundy in 1430; and the Order of Messire St. Michael the Archangel, founded by Louis XI in 1469, long maintained in disregard of most of its statutes (which were almost identical with those of the Golden Fleece), and suppressed in 1790. Among the handful of fraternal orders now known are those of the Tiercelet or Young Male Falcon (1377/85), of the Golden Apple (1394), and of the Hound (1416); the votive orders now known include those of the White Lady with the Green Shield of Marshal Boucicaut (1399), of the Prisoner's Iron of Duke Jehan de Bourbon (1415), and of the Dragon of the Count of Foix (ca. 1415).

In addition to the true orders, a number of French princes created what are best termed "pseudo-orders," which were essentially elite bodies of retainers lacking in any corporate statutes or activities. Most prominent among these were the Order of the Belt of Esperance, established by Duke Louis of Bourbon in 1365 and maintained into the 16th century; the royal Order of the Broom-Pod (*Cosse de Geneste*), created by Charles VI ca. 1386 and maintained until his death in 1422; and the Order of the Camail or Porcupine, created by Duke Louis of Orléans ca. 1394 and maintained until 1498.

D'A. Jonathan D. Boulton

[See also: GOLDEN FLEECE; MÉZIÈRES, PHILIPPE DE]

Boulton, D'A. J.D. *The Knights of the Crown: The Monarchical Orders of Knighthood in Later Medieval Europe, 1325–1520.* Woodbridge: Boydell, 1987.

LE FÈVRE (DE RESSONS), JEAN (ca. 1320–ca. 1390). Translator of the *Disticha Catonis, De vetula,* the *Lamentationes Matheoli,* and a selection of liturgical hymns (B.N. fr. 964) into French. Le Fèvre's *Livre de leesce* (1380–87) is a point-by-point refutation of the *Lamentationes.* He also wrote the *Respit de la mort* (1376), in which his knowledge of the Paris courts is seen, and the *Épistre sur les misères de la vie* (unedited) as well as a now lost *Danse macabré.* A translation of the *Ecloga Theoduli* may also be his. Born in Ressons-sur-le-Matz, near Compiègne, Le Fèvre spent his adult life in Paris, where he was royal *procureur* before the Parlement de Paris.

Wendy E. Pfeffer

[See also: ANTIFEMINISM]

Fournival, Richard de. *La vieille, ou les dernières amours d'Ovide: poème français du XIVe siècle,* ed. Hippolyte Cocheris. Paris: Aubry, 1861.

Le Fèvre, Jean. *Le respit de la mort,* ed. Geneviève Hasenohr-Esnos. Paris: Picard, 1969.

———. "Die Übersetzungen der Disticha des Pseudo-Cato: Der Cato Jean Lefevre's," ed. Jakob Ulrich. *Romanische Forschungen* 15 (1904): 70–106.

Matheolus. *Les lamentations de Matheolus et le Livre de leesce de Jehan le Fèvre, de Resson (poèmes français du XIVe siècle),* ed. A.-G. van Hamel. Paris: Bouillon, 1892–1905.

Hasenohr, Geneviève. "La locution verbale figurée dans l'œuvre de Jean Le Fèvre. *Moyen français* 14–15 (1984): 229–81.

LE FRANC, MARTIN (ca. 1410–ca. 1461). Born in Normandy, Martin Le Franc was provost of Lausanne and later, following a persuasive Latin letter on the nature of eloquence that he wrote to the future Pope Felix V, papal secretary. His Latin erudition and original thinking secure his place among 15th-century humanists. Between 1440 and 1442, he composed the *Champion des dames,* a didactic allegorical poem of some 24,000 octosyllabic lines. In it, Le Franc shows himself to be the ally of Christine de Pizan in the persistent Quarrel of the *Roman de la Rose* and perhaps even the adversary of Alain Chartier, author of the *Belle dame sans merci.* Franc Vouloir is the ladies' "champion," whose lessons and battles finally defeat Malebouche of Jean de Meun's romance. In 1447–48, Le Franc wrote another didactic work, the *Estrif de Fortune et de Vertu,* apparently inspired by Petrarch's *De remediis utriusque fortunae.*

Janice C. Zinser

[See also: CHARTIER, ALAIN; CHRISTINE DE PIZAN; JEAN DE MEUN; QUARREL OF THE *ROMAN DE LA ROSE*]

Le Franc, Martin. *Le champion des dames,* ed. Arthur Piaget. In *Mémoires et documents de la Société de la Suisse Romande.* 3rd ser. Lausanne: Payot, 1968, Vol. 8.

Jung, Marc-René. "Rhétorique contre philosophie? un inédit de Martin Le Franc." In *Rhetoric Revalued,* ed. Brian Vickers. Binghamton: Medieval and Renaissance Texts and Studies, 1982, pp. 241–46.

Williams, Harry F. "Structural Aspects of *Le champion des dames*." *Fifteenth Century Studies* 11 (1985): 149–61.

LE MANS. A prehistoric site and perhaps capital of the Gallic Cenomani, Le Mans (Sarthe) was the ancient capital of the county of Maine. It lies in western France between Normandy and the Loire Valley on an important trade route. A major center since Roman times, when it was known as Vindonum, Le Mans was evangelized in the late 3rd century by St. Julien, to whom its Gothic cathedral is dedicated. When the Roman Empire began to disintegrate, the center of population removed from the surrounding plains to the central hilltop and a great wall (late 3rd–early 4th c.) was constructed around the upper town. This wall survives in large part and has recently been disengaged along much of its perimeter. In the Middle Ages, Le Mans was a center of the Norman-Angevin dynasty and a favorite city of Henry II Plantagenêt.

In the 9th century, an important Carolingian cathedral was built in the upper town. This was replaced in the 11th century by a new cathedral building in Romanesque style, parts of which survive today—the side aisles of the nave and important parts of the transept, the latter subsequently remodeled. A contemporary text records the consecration in 1093 and details the construction campaigns of the 11th century. Major fires in 1134 and 1137 greatly damaged this Romanesque structure, and reconstruction was undertaken first in the choir, then in the transept, and finally in the nave. In 1158, the new building was consecrated. The present nave and lower wall of the transept belong to this phase of construction. The original 11th-century choir, as well as its reconstruction after the fires of 1134 and 1137, was limited in its eastern extension by the great Gallo-Roman wall. In the 13th century, this choir must have been considered excessively modest, since the construction of vast Gothic cathedrals had been undertaken in many of the great cities of northern France. In November 1217, Philip II Augustus authorized the destruction of a large section of the venerable Gallo-Roman wall so that the choir could be rebuilt on a vastly larger scale beginning ca. 1221. The new choir was consecrated, and most likely completed, in 1254, since monks at the neighboring monastery of La Couture were authorized as

Le Mans (Sarthe), Saint-Julien, chevet. *Photograph: Clarence Ward Collection. Courtesy of Oberlin College.*

of 1252 by the cathedral chapter to use the quarry at Bernay just west of Le Mans, which had previously served as the principal source of stone for the new cathedral. Seen from the great marketplace immediately to the east and below, this choir is one of the most magnificent structures of Gothic Europe. In addition to the cathedral, Le Mans is rich in medieval monuments from the Romanesque and Gothic periods, such as Notre-Dame-du-Pré, the former abbey church of La Couture, and the former Cistercian abbey of L'Épau.

John B. Cameron

Congrès archéologique (Maine) 119 (1961): 9–142.

Mussat, André. *La cathédrale du Mans.* Paris: Berger-Levrault, 1981.

LE MOTE, JEAN DE (La Motte; fl. mid-14th c.). A poet and composer, Le Mote was active in the Low Countries and England and probably spent time in Paris. Gilles Li Muisis, writing in 1350, names Le Mote with Guillaume de Machaut and Jean de Vitry among the prominent composers of *biaus dis*. His extant works include an elegiac dream vision, the *Regret Guillaume comte de Hainault* (dated 1339), written for the daughter of the dead count, Queen Philippa of England, and two works written in 1340 for Simon de Lille, goldsmith to King Philip VI: a continuation of the romances of Alexander, the *Parfait du paon*, and a religious vision, the *Voie d'enfer et de paradis*. None of his music is extant, and though his long works contain intercalated ballades, a single independent lyric survives, a ballade response to Philippe de Vitry. Vitry had criticized Le Mote's poetry for its bizarre use of names, and Le Mote defends his practice while praising his attacker.

James I. Wimsatt

[See also: ALEXANDER ROMANCES; LI MUISIS, GILLES; VOW CYCLE]

Le Mote, Jean de. *Le parfait du paon*, ed. Richard J. Carey. Chapel Hill: University of North Carolina Press, 1972.

———. *La voie d'enfer et de paradis*, ed. M. Aquiline Pety. Washington, D.C.: Catholic University of America Press, 1940.

———. *Li regret Guillaume, comte de Hainaut*, ed. Auguste Scheler. Louvain: Lefever, 1882.

Wimsatt, James I. *Chaucer and the Poems of "Ch" in University of Pennsylvania MS French 15.* Cambridge: Brewer, 1982, pp. 51–60. [Details about the poet and the ballade exchange with Vitry.]

LE PUY. The volcanic peaks rising from the Auvergnat plain create a dramatic setting for the town of Le Puy-en-Velay (Haute-Loire). This site had religious significance in Roman times, when a temple of Diana may have preceded the church. By the 6th century, Le Puy was the bishopric of Velay. The cathedral dedicated to the Virgin was a major pilgrimage center located on one of the main roads to

Le Puy (Haute-Loire), chapel of Saint-Michel. *Photograph courtesy of William W. Kibler.*

Santiago de Compostela. In 1254, Louis IX's gift of the Black Virgin, obtained while on crusade in the Holy Land, enhanced the religious significance of Le Puy.

The most notable architecture in Le Puy is the cathedral of Notre-Dame, which, along with its subsidiary buildings—cloisters; baptistery, or chapel, of Saint-Jean; and chapter house, or Salle des Morts—formed a fortified complex in the Middle Ages. The present cathedral was built in the 11th and 12th centuries. The earlier part of the structure is the simple cruciform plan formed by the apse, transept, and two eastern bays of the nave. At the east end is a staged tower similar to the one at Saint-Martial, Limoges. The crossing has an octagonal dome, and the nave bays are vaulted with octagonal domes on squinches. In the 12th century, the nave was extended to form a substantial crypt porch over the sloping site.

The cathedral has several features that indicate Moorish influence. The imposing west façade with its steep steps leading to the deep porch has striped ashlar masonry, cusped arches in the blind arcades, and wooden doors with Cufic inscriptions. The construction of the squinches and the carving of about a hundred capitals also display Moorish stylistic connections.

Several frescoes survive in the cathedral and cloisters. Two chapels in the apsidal niches of the north transept have paintings of the three women at Christ's sepulcher and the martyrdom of St. Catherine. Lunettes with the Virgin Enthroned and the Transfiguration are visible in the porch. The Salle des Morts just east of the cloisters contains a Crucifixion that fills the lunette of the south wall. Although they are by various artists, all the frescoes

Le Puy, Notre-Dame, cloister. *Photograph courtesy of Whitney S. Stoddard.*

are from the first half of the 13th century and reflect Italo-Byzantine stylistic features.

Karen Gould

Thiollier, Noël. "Guide archéologique du Congrès du Puy." *Congrès archéologique (Le Puy)* 71 (1904): 3–38.
Fikrī, Ahmad. *Art roman du Puy et les influences islamiques.* Paris: Leroux, 1934.

LEFÈVRE, RAOUL (d. late 1460s). A member of Philip the Good of Burgundy's circle, the Picard Raoul Lefèvre is the author of two romances based on classical materials, the prose *Histoire de Jason* (ca. 1460), which uses the *Ovide moralisé* and *Histoire ancienne jusqu'à César* as sources, and the *Recueil des histoires de Troie* (ca. 1465), based on Boccaccio's *De genealogia deorum*. These works reflect the interest in classical and humanistic subjects at the Burgundian court. Not only did Philip the Good institute the Order of the Golden Fleece (1430), but he also commissioned a series of tapestries celebrating the deeds of Jason and Hercules, the two heroes of Lefèvre's romances. Lefèvre's works were printed by Colard Mansion (1475– 76) and translated into English and printed by William Caxton between 1469 and 1477.

Wendy E. Pfeffer

Lefèvre, Raoul. *L'histoire de Jason: Ein Roman aus dem fünfzehnten Jahrhundert,* ed. Gert Pinkernell. Frankfurt am Main: Athenäum, 1971.
Hale, David G. "The Crisis of Chivalry in *La vie du Prince Noir* and *L'histoire de Jason." Acta* 12 (1988): 95–104.

LEGAL TREATISES. Feudal or customary law existed throughout the Middle Ages. In the course of the 12th century, however, there occurred a revival of Roman law that, after its beginnings at the law school in Bologna, spread from southern to northern France. Everywhere, Roman law penetrated into the schools. In the south of France, where customary law had always been strongly influenced by Roman law, a vernacular summary of the legal Code of Justinian, known as the *Codi,* was made available in the mid-12th century to the laity and judges of Provence.

Two schools, Orléans and Montpellier, developed slowly into leading law schools in the 13th century. Orléans had already produced a useful treatise on Roman law in the 12th century, the *Corpus legum per modum institutiones,* which demonstrated an understanding of Justinian's *Codex.* Montpellier's law school dates from 1160, when Placentinus, who had been educated in Bologna, established himself there.

Although both schools offered a curriculum in canon and civil law, the two most important scholars in these fields did not belong to these institutions. Guillaume de Montlauzun (d. 1343), a Cluniac, wrote commentaries on canon law and the *Sacramentale* (ca. 1317), in which he explains theology to lawyers. Jean Faure discussed civil law in the *Breviarium* (ca. 1325–30), which is a summary of Justinian's *Codex,* and the *Lectura* (ca. 1335–40), a commentary on four books of the *Institutiones,* law textbooks designed for school use.

The *Livre de Jean Roisin* is a practical compilation based on Roman legal ideas that sets out in some 120 chapters the rights of the citizens of Lille. It grew out of acts and charters dating back as far as Philippe d'Alsace (r. 1168–91) but is first mentioned only in 1349.

Claude J. Fouillade

[See also: LAW AND JUSTICE; NOTARIES]

Monier, R., ed. *Le livre Roisin: coutumier lillois de la fin du XIIIe siècle.* Paris, 1932.
Bloch, Marc. *Feudal Society,* trans. L.A. Manyon. Chicago: University of Chicago Press, 1961.

LEGENDA AUREA. The collection of saints' lives known as *Legenda aurea,* or *Golden Legend,* was the most copied text in the Middle Ages, surviving in more than 1,000 manuscripts and translated into nearly all the vernacular languages of western Europe. It was among the first books printed in France in the 15th century and, by William

Caxton, in England. Originally titled *Legenda sanctorum alias Lombardica hystoria*, the *Legenda aurea*—its name attests to its popularity—was composed in Latin ca. 1261–67 by Jacobus of Voragine (Jacques de Varazze; 1228/30–1298). Jacobus, a Dominican and archbishop of Genoa, sought to provide a collection of easily understood texts that would serve to inspire the devotion of the laity. Relying most probably on Vincent de Beauvais's *Speculum historiale*, Jean de Mailly's *Abbreviatio in gestis et miraculis sanctorum*, and Bartholomew of Trent's *Liber epilogorum in gesta sanctorum*, Jacobus chose to add numerous accounts of marvelous and miraculous deeds. His work consists of 182 chapters and follows the order of the liturgical calendar. It reflects the encyclopedic tastes of its age and includes numerous eastern saints' lives as well as western lives written originally in Latin in the early Middle Ages but frequently translated or reworked in the vernacular. The *Legenda aurea* itself was translated into French a number of times, the best-known translation being that by Jean de Vignay; there are three independent Occitan versions. The popularity of the *Legenda aurea* diminished in the 16th century, criticized by reformers for encouraging devotion to the saints rather than to God.

E. Kay Harris

[See also: HAGIOGRAPHY; SAINTS, CULT OF; SAINTS' LIVES; VIGNAY, JEAN DE]

Jacobus of Voragine. *The Golden Legend*, ed. and trans. Granger Ryan and Helmut Ripperger. New York: Longmans, Green, 1941.

Vignay, Jean de. "The Jean de Vignay Version of the Life of Saint Dominic," ed. W.F. Manning. *Archivum Fratrum Praedicatorum* 40 (1970): 29–4. [Partial edition.]

Reames, Sherry L. *The Legenda aurea: A Reexamination of Its Paradoxical History*. Madison: University of Wisconsin Press, 1985.

LEGRAND, JACQUES (ca. 1360–ca. 1418). A member of the Augustinian order, Legrand is the author of the *Sophilogium* (1398–99) and Latin sermons denouncing the corruption of religious and secular authorities. He was also active in the Armagnac faction after the assassination of Louis of Orléans (1407). He is best remembered as the author of the French *Archiloge Sophie* (ca. 1400), dedicated to Louis of Orléans, which treats questions of rhetoric, poetics, and spelling; and the *Livre de bonnes meurs*, dedicated to John, duke of Berry. The *Livre*, a treatise on Christian morality, is divided into five parts, which discuss vice and virtue, the clergy, kings and the nobility, the common people, and death and the Judgment Day.

Claude J. Fouillade

Legrand, Jacques. *L'archiloge Sophie; Livre de bonnes meurs*, ed. Evencio Beltran. Paris: Champion, 1986.

LEO IX (1002–1054). Pope. Born of Alsatian nobility at Egisheim, Bruno, the future Leo IX, was educated from an early age at Toul, by Bishop Berthold. After entering an ecclesiastical career, he accompanied the emperor Conrad II on campaign in Lombardy in 1025 and became bishop of Toul by imperial appointment in 1026. Known for his piety and intelligence, Bruno set out to reform the church in his diocese and took advantage of imperial privileges to achieve his goal. After twenty-two years at Toul, Bruno was elevated to the papal see by his cousin, Henry III, at Worms in 1048. He was the second of four German churchmen so elevated by the emperor.

Taking the name of Leo IX, Bruno immediately set out to reform the church throughout Europe. He traveled widely and spent barely six months in Rome after his coronation. In 1049, he made the first of several trips north of the Alps, heading first to Reims, the principal see of France, where the bishops and abbots of the realm were gathered for a synod. There, he demanded an accounting from suspected simoniacs, those who had bought their ecclesiastical office. Prelates who thought it more discreet not to attend the synod were immediately deposed and excommunicated. Leo enforced his policy for the German realm in a synod held a few weeks later at Mainz.

The following year, at a great synod held in Rome shortly after Easter, Leo took aim at what was considered the other great clerical abuse of the time, clerical incontinence. Scandalized by the sexual mores of many clergy and fired by the monastic ideal, Leo pronounced celibacy to be the norm for the clergy and called for a boycott of priests and deacons who violated this norm.

Leo also dealt with the heresy of Berengar of Tours over the eucharistic presence of Christ and the controversy with Michael Cerularius, the patriarch of Constantinople, over differences in liturgical practice (and implicitly the dignity of Rome), especially the use of leavened or unleavened bread in the eucharist. The Eastern Schism is traditionally dated from this controversy.

Although Leo's reign was marked by many successes, it ended on an ignominious note: in 1053, he led an expedition of Swabian troops to southern Italy to resist the encroachments of the Normans, who crushed the papal army at Civitella and captured Leo. He remained under virtual house arrest near Bari until April 1054. Gravely ill, he returned to Rome just weeks before his death.

Leo IX brought to the papal court some of the most outstanding clerics of his day, among them Hildebrand, the future Gregory VII; Humbert of Silva Candida, his legate to Constantinople; and Peter Damian, a champion of the monastic ideal. It was while Leo was on the papal throne that the cardinal clergy of Rome became more than liturgical functionaries and that the laws of the church were compiled in support of the reform in the *Collection in Seventy-four Titles (Diversorum patrum sententie)*.

Mark Zier

[See also: BERENGAR OF TOURS; GREGORIAN REFORM; GREGORY VII; NORMANS IN SICILY]

Gilchrist, John T., trans. *Collection in Seventy-four Titles: A Canon Law Manual of the Gregorian Reform*. Toronto: Pontifical Institute of Mediaeval Studies, 1980.

————. *Diversorum patrum sententiae: sive, Collectio in LXXIV titulos digesta*. Vatican City: Biblioteca Apostolica Vaticana, 1973.

Garreau, Albert. *Saint Léon IX, pape alsacien, réformateur de l'église, 1002–1054*. Paris: Tolra, 1965.

Krause, Hans Georg. *Das Papstwahldekret von 1059 und seine Rolle im Investiturstreit*. Rome: Abbazia di San Paolo, 1960.

Petrucci, Enzo. *Ecclesiologica e politica di Leone IX*. Rome: ELIA, 1977.

Sittler, Lucien, and P. Stintzi, eds. *S. Léon IX, le pape alsacien*. Colmar: Alsatia, 1950.

LÉONIN (Leoninus; fl. 1154–ca. 1201). Anonymous 4's epithet *optimus organista* ("the best singer/improviser/composer/compiler/notator of organum") assured Léonin a significant place in music history long before any convincing identification of the person was suggested. Since he was responsible for the new polyphonic repertory of the cathedral of Notre-Dame in Paris in the decades after its founding in the 1160s, his place was evidently among the dignitaries of its ecclesiastical hierarchy, but the familiar use of the Latin diminutive of his name, as "Magister Leoninus," in the theoretical treatise of Anonymous 4—the only source for information on his considerable musical achievement—long seemed to belie this. Anonymous 4 credited Léonin with the *Magnus liber organi de gradali et antifonario* some one hundred years after its compilation, a fact that recommends cautious use of his testimony and the need for independent verification. Three major manuscript sources (*W1*, *F*, and *W2*) confirm a repertory of organum that fits Anonymous 4's description of a *Magnus liber organi*, and the melodies of the plainchant that form the basis of that organum match notated plainchant sources used at Notre-Dame. Still, this does not clarify what Léonin's role may have been in making such a book. *Optimus organista* suggests a youthful man in full voice, while the diminutive implies a beloved elder whose practical contributions may have been overshadowed by his administrative usefulness—two very different "portraits" of the individual. It may not have been so much by his initiative as by his approval that modal rhythm became the primary innovation of the Notre-Dame School, and there is no certain evidence that such rhythm was subject to systematic theoretical or notational principles during his lifetime.

Archival evidence only recently brought to light establishes a probable identity for Anonymous 4's Magister Leoninus as Magister Leoninus presbyter, a canon active in the affairs of the cathedral during the late 12th century and a Latin poet whose hexametric Old Testament commentary, *Hystorie sacre gestas ab origine mundi*, was long praised after his death. There is, however, no document, except possibly the treatise of Anonymous 4, to substantiate the involvement of Leoninus presbyter with music at all, a striking omission given the significance of the *Magnus liber organi* and the stature of the poet. Thus, while the search for independent, corroborating evidence continues, the hypothesis that Léonin, known also as Magister Leoninus presbyter, was responsible for the vanguard of virtu-

ally a new era in music with the *Magnus liber organi* should remain compelling.

Sandra Pinegar

[**See also:** ANONYMOUS 4; NOTRE-DAME SCHOOL; PÉROTIN; RHYTHMIC MODE]

Reckow, Fritz. *Der Musiktraktat des Anonymus 4*. Wiesbaden: Steiner, 1967.

Wright, Craig. "Leoninus, Poet and Musician." *Journal of the American Musicological Society* 39 (1986): 1–35.

L'ÉPINE. Commemorating a miraculous appearance of the Virgin, the church of Notre-Dame-de-l'Épine (Marne) was established as a pilgrimage goal in the early 13th century; its popularity reached an apogee in the late Middle Ages, when it attracted the interest and devotion of French monarchs, including Charles VII and Louis XI. Construction of the present edifice advanced in a complex sequence of campaigns. The eastern bays of the nave, begun ca. 1405/

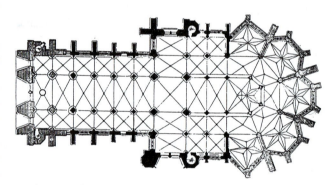

L'Épine (Marne), Notre-Dame, plan. After Chauliat.

10, the transept, and western portions of the choir of ca. 1440 were built in a Late Rayonnant style; the façade, probably inaugurated in the mid-1450s under master mason Florent Bleuet, introduced a Late Gothic Flamboyant vocabulary of decoration. The radiating chapels, ambulatory, and apse were erected from 1509 by Rémy Gouveau, Guichart Antoine, and Antoine Bertaucourt. L'Épine's architectural significance lies not in formal inventiveness but in its masters' skillful combination of structural and compositional ideas from contemporary northern French buildings as well as 13th-century models, particularly the cathedral of Reims. In its plan, with an ambulatory and radiating chapels, three-story elevation, and twin-towered façade, L'Épine was conceived as a cathedral in miniature.

Michael T. Davis

[**See also:** PILGRIMAGE]

Benoist, Luc. *Notre-Dame-de-l'Épine*. Paris: Laurens, 1933.

Prache, Anne. "Un maître maçon du XVe siècle: Florent Bleuet." *Gazette des beaux arts*, 6th ser. 111 (1988): 21–26.

Puiseux, Abbé. *Notre-Dame-de-l'Épine, son histoire, son pèlerinage.* 2nd ed. Châlons-sur-Marne: Imprimerie Martin, 1910.

Villes, Alain. "Notre-Dame-de-l'Épine, sa façade occidentale." *Congrès archéologique* 135 (1977): 779–862.

LEPROSY. Paradox marks the subject of leprosy in medieval France. Though the object of universal dread, the disease was not as widespread as modern images suggest. The symptoms and causes were moralized not only by preachers but also by poets from Béroul to Rutebeuf and in such romances as *Ami et Amile*; yet they were also discussed in rational and scientific terms by medical authors. Physicians urged and applied caution in diagnosis, even if their belief in contagion perpetuated unnecessary fears.

Confirmed patients, officially cast out with funerary rituals and barred from towns, nevertheless roamed the streets freely until they became too numerous or unruly. Lepers were legally "dead to the world" according to a sweeping principle in the Beauvaisis, but local regulations on their property and marital rights varied widely. Deeds of charity, from the foundation of lazar houses to the saintly heroics of Louis IX, contrast with outbursts of popular intolerance. Accused of poisoning wells, lepers at large were attacked by mobs during plagues and sheltered ones were burned under Philip V, who seized their communal assets for his depleted treasury.

Leprosy peaked in France in the 13th century; in the early 1200s, Jehan Bodel and Baude Fastoul poetically bewailed their exile from Arras, where several *maladreries* could have housed them by the end of the century. After 1350, the disease declined markedly for reasons that are not yet fully clear but that included improved diet and hygiene, mortality in epidemics, isolation, and more accurate identification—in which physicians played an increasing role.

Luke Demaitre

[See also: *CONGÉ;* DISEASES; HEALTH CARE; HOSPITALS; MEDICAL PRACTICE AND PRACTITIONERS]

Barber, Malcolm. "Lepers, Jews and Moslems: The Plot to Overthrow Christendom in 1321." *History* 66 (1981): 1–17.

Bourgeois, Albert. *Lépreux et maladreries du Pas-de-Calais (X–XVIIe siècles): psychologie collective et institutions charitables.* Arras: Commission Départementale des Monuments Historiques du Pas-de-Calais, 1972.

Cougoul, Jacques. *La lèpre dans l'ancienne France.* Bordeaux: Delmar, 1943.

Demaitre, Luke. "The Description and Diagnosis of Leprosy by Fourteenth-Century Physicians." *Bulletin of the History of Medicine* 59 (1985): 327–44.

LÉRINS. A small island (now known as Saint-Honorat) in the Mediterranean, just off the French coast at Cannes, Lérins was the site of a monastery founded ca. 410 by Honoratus, who had traveled east on pilgrimage and returned to found a monastic community. The monastery at Lérins combined a community under an abbot with isolated cells for hermits. A major center for monastic training, it provided both monastic leaders and monk-bishops for the church, such as Caesarius of Arles, Hilary of Arles, Vincent of Lérins, and Lupus of Troyes. According to tradition, St. Patrick was trained at Lérins before embarking on his mission to Ireland. Lérins had a strong tradition of intellectual as well as ascetic training, thus presaging the role that later monastic communities would play in preserving and transmitting classical and Christian culture to the Middle Ages and beyond.

Grover A. Zinn

[See also: CAESARIUS OF ARLES; MONASTICISM; VINCENT OF LÉRINS]

LESCUREL, JEHANNOT DE (d. 1303). A trouvère credited with thirty-three chansons, ballades, rondeaux, and *dits*, preserved with music, written to honor several ladies whom he describes with conventional attributes, Lescurel was hanged in Paris in 1303 with several other men for crimes committed against both religious and lay women.

Deborah H. Nelson

[See also: VIRELAI]

Langlois, Charles-Victor. "Jean de Lescurel, poète français." *Histoire littéraire de la France* 26 (1927): 109–15.

LESSAY. A magnificent example of Romanesque architecture, the Abbatiale de la Trinité in Lessay (Manche) was founded in 1056 by a Norman baron, Thurstin Haldup. A certificate of 1080, confirming the foundation and ownership, constitutes the first reference to this Benedictine abbey, built probably at the turn of the century. The church features the first known occurrence of cross-ribbed vaulting in France. Whether this type of vaulting developed in France at this time or was imported from England, after the style of the cathedral of Durham (1093), has been a matter of debate.

One of the most striking traits of the church is its spirit of spacious grandeur effected by three-story columns that rise from the ground to the ceiling without interruption. The nave comprises seven bays with broad arcades. The choir precedes an apse in cul-de-four illuminated by two-story windows. A single stone slab serves as the high altar. To the right of the choir, a baptistery occupies a 15th-century chapel. A circular gallery surrounds the entire church. The typically Romanesque exterior is less original.

The abbey was destroyed in 1356 by Charles the Bad. Reconstruction from 1385 to 1420 meticulously followed the original plan of the church. During World War II, the church was again severely damaged. A comprehensive restoration project, begun in 1945, took twelve years.

E. Kay Harris

Lessay (Manche), abbey church, nave. *Photograph: Clarence Ward Collection. Courtesy of Oberlin College.*

Froidevaux, Yves-Marie. "Église abbatiale de Lessay." *Congrès archéologique* (*Contentin et Avranchin*) 124 (1966): 70–82.
Musset, Lucien. *Normandie romane.* 2 vols. La Pierre-qui-vire: Zodiaque, 1967.
Taralon, Jean, and Pierre Héliot. Notice in *Bulletin de la Société des Antiquaires de la France* (1959).

LETTERS OF REMISSION. The stern justice of late-medieval France was somewhat mitigated by the granting of pardons. Pardons were expensive, with chancery fees alone costing over ten *livres tournois* by 1550, so that only individuals with financial resources and political influence normally obtained them. Individuals charged with capital crimes, such as murder, obtained pardons by requesting the king, chancellor, or other high chancery official to order the notarial preparation of a description of the crime and any extenuating circumstances. This draft was reviewed in council or chancellery and issued as a letter of pardon (*lettre de rémission*), which then had to be ratified by the royal court with jurisdiction over the case. The process of ratification involved a series of hearings and investigations to ensure the accuracy and propriety of the pardon letter. A sort of plea bargaining resulted that often provided for modified punishment and compensation of victims before the case was closed. Most pardon letters were registered in chancellery, where 58,300 are still to be found in the Trésor des Chartes (58 percent of registers after 1300). However unreliable they may be as a statistical indicator of criminality, they comprise an invaluable source of anecdotal information, providing marvelous vignettes of late-medieval France.

Paul D. Solon

[**See also:** LAW AND JUSTICE]

Actes du 107e Congrès National des Sociétés Savantes, Brest 1982. Section de Philologie et d'Histoire jusqu'à 1610. Paris, 1984, Vol 1: *La faute, la répression et le pardon.*
Davis, Natalie Zemon. *Fiction in the Archives: Pardon Tales and Their Tellers in Sixteenth-Century France.* Stanford: Stanford University Press, 1987.
François, Michel. "Note sur les lettres de rémission transcrites dans les registres du Trésor des Chartes." *Bibliothèque de l'École des Chartes* 103 (1942): 317–24.

LEYS D'AMORS. Attributed to Guilhem Molinier, the *Leys* is the art of versification for Occitan poetry drawn up in the 14th century by the *Consistòri de la Subregaya Companhia del Gai Saber.* This group, organized at Toulouse by seven troubadours in the early 14th century, was dedicated to preserving Occitan poetry and the values of *fin'amor.* Theirs was a last-ditch attempt to keep alive a dying art. With French victory in the Albigensian Crusade, love poetry in Occitan was disappearing in favor of moral and didactic works, and works in French. At the *Consistòri's* inaugural meeting on May 1, 1324, its chancellor, Guilhem Molinier, was commissioned to draw up a Code of Poetry, which seems to have been established by 1341. The *Leys* went through successive stages, in both prose and verse. The final stage, in three prose books, was published by Anglade. The first volume is a history of the founding of the *Consistòri,* combined with a treatise on ethics (the nature of God and love, the moral virtues); the second and third include an extensive grammar (phonology, morphology, syntax, with some poetic samples) and an art of poetry (versification, rhymes, and numerous examples of the principal literary genres). The influence of the *Leys* was extensive, well into the 16th century, particularly in Catalonia, and it is credited with keeping Occitan alive as a poetic medium until the end of the Middle Ages.

William W. Kibler

[**See also:** DIDACTIC LITERATURE (OCCITAN); TROUBADOUR POETRY]

Anglade, Joseph, ed. *Las leys d'Amors.* 4 vols. Toulouse, 1919–20.
Lafont, R. "Les *Leys d'Amors* et la mutation de la conscience occitane." *Revue des langues romanes* 77 (1966): 13–59.

LI MUISIS, GILLES (Gilles Li Muisit, 1272–1353). Chronicler and poet. Born into a powerful middle-class family from Tournai, Gilles Li Muisis entered the Benedictine monastery of Saint-Martin in Tournai as a novice in 1289; he later served as its seventeenth abbot. According to some accounts, Gilles studied at the University of Paris. In 1300, he accompanied the abbot Gilles de Warnave to Rome on the occasion of the great pardon instituted by Boniface VIII. Elected abbot of Saint-Martin in 1331, Gilles restored discipline and financial stability to the institution. When blindness overcame him in his late seventies, he dictated his memoirs to Jacques Muevin, his successor. Two cataract operations performed in 1351 restored Gilles's eyesight but hastened his demise.

In his Latin prose chronicles, four volumes of *Tractatus*, Gilles documents his years at Saint-Martin and his first-hand knowledge of Tournai and the county of Flanders. His *Méditations*, a didactic poem composed in French, is a survey of the worldly estates designed to correct the vices of clerical and lay readers. It shows the influence of the Reclus de Molliens and the *Roman de la Rose*, read as a satire of contemporary manners and customs.

Lori Walters

[See also: ÉTIENNE DE FOUGÈRES; LE MOTE, JEAN DE; RECLUS DE MOLLIENS]

Li Muisis, Gilles. *Poésies de Gilles Le Muisis*, ed. Joseph M.B.C. Kervyn de Lettenhove. 2 vols. Louvain: Lefever, 1882.

Badel, Pierre-Yves. *Le roman de la Rose au XIVe siècle: étude de la réception de l'œuvre.* Geneva: Droz, 1980, pp. 74–82.

D'Haenens, Albert. "Gilles li Muisis historien." *Revue bénédictine* 69 (1959): 258–86.

Guenée, Bernard. *Between Church and State: The Lives of Four French Prelates in the Late Middle Ages*, trans. Arthur Goldhammer. Chicago: University of Chicago Press, 1991.

Langlois, Charles-Victor. *La vie en France au moyen âge de la fin du XIIe au milieu du XIVe siècle.* 4 vols. Paris: Hachette, 1926–28, Vol. 2: *D'après des moralistes du temps*, pp. 321–73.

LIBER FORTUNAE. An anonymous treatise on Fortune that its author claims to have composed in prison in the year 1345. He seeks to reconcile the dilemma of Fortune and Divine Providence, by making Fortuna the daughter of God. There follows a display of the banal knowledge a typical cleric possessed, codified according to sins, vices, virtues, and so on. The author knew the *Roman de la Rose*, Boethius's *De consolatione Philosophiae*, the *Disticha Catonis*, the *Somme le roi* of Laurent d'Orléans, the *Elucidarius*, and a goodly number of proverbs. The author's effort to sign his work with an acrostic is a failure. The text, surviving in two manuscripts and a fragment, is some 4,000 rhymed octosyllables in length and evinces both a mediocre style and a poverty of original thought. When the author discovers that he has begun to repeat himself, he brings the poem to a close.

John L. Grigsby

Grigsby, John L., ed. *The Middle French* Liber Fortunae. Berkeley: University of California Press, 1967.

LIBER SANCTI JACOBI. A compilation of five texts, with prefatory letter and addenda, devoted to the cult of the Apostle James the Greater. The texts appear to have been independently composed and then brought together at some time after 1137 and before 1173. The twelve extant manuscript copies contain the compilation entirely or in an abridged version and range in date from the 12th century through the 18th. The earliest manuscript, probably from the early 1140s, is in the Cathedral Archives of Santiago de Compostela. It is uncertain whether or not an earlier exemplar of the compilation existed, and it has not been possible to establish the identity of the authors or compilers of the work.

The compilation was originally called the *Codex Calixtinus* after Pope Calixtus II (r. 1119–24), whose name appears as the author of the prefatory letter and other parts of the texts. This attribution was rejected as early as the 16th century, however, and a more accurate designation for the compilation would be the *Pseudo-Calixtine Compilation*. The name *Liber sancti Jacobi* (*Livre de saint Jacques*, Book of St. James) was adopted by the early 20th century, a choice suggested by the contents of the manuscript and the incipits of Books 2, 3, and 5. The compilation has also been called *Jacobus* in current literature, a name appearing in some of the manuscript copies.

The Compostela manuscript opens with the Pseudo-Calixtine prefatory letter and is followed by Book 1, which contains the liturgy for the three main feasts of St. James with accompanying monophonic music and notation. Book 2 recounts twenty-two miracles of St. James dated from 1080 to 1135. Book 3 gives confusing versions of the arrival of the relics of the saint in Spain. In Book 4 is found the legendary account of the campaigns against the Saracens in Spain waged by the emperor Charlemagne (r. 780–814), which includes the famous story of the ambush and death of Charlemagne's nephew Roland. Known as the Pseudo-Turpin, because it was falsely attributed to Archbishop Turpin of Reims (753–800), this component has a separate manuscript tradition, with well over 200 copies extant. Book 5, referred to as the *Pilgrim's Guide*, provides information for pilgrims traveling from France to Santiago de Compostela to visit the shrine of James. Book 5 ends with a colophon that states that the manuscript "was written in many places, namely in Rome, in the region of Jerusalem, in France, in Italy, in Germany, and in Frisia, and chiefly at Cluny"; it is, however, unclear whether the colophon refers to Book 5, the entire compilation, or some other part of the compilation. The addenda following Book 5 include polyphonic songs with musical notation, an Alleluia and fragments of a Mass, a false papal bull attributed to Pope Innocent II (r. 1130–43), and seven additional miracles, two of them dated 1139 and 1164.

Paula L. Gerson

[See also: CHARLEMAGNE; PILGRIMAGE; PSEUDO-TURPIN]

Whitehill, Walter Muir, ed. *Liber sancti Jacobi, Codex Calixtinus.* 3 vols. Santiago de Compostela: N.p., 1944.

Moralejo, Laso A., C. Torres, and J. Feo, trans. *Liber sancti Jacobi, Codex Calixtinus.* Santiago de Compostela: Consejo Superior de Investigaciones Científicas, Instituto Padre Sarmiento de Estudios Gallegos, 1951.

David, Pierre. "Études sur le livre de St-Jacques attribué au pape Calixte II." *Bulletin des études portugaises et de l'Institut Français au Portugal* 10 (1946): 1–41; 11 (1947): 113–85; 12 (1948): 70–233; 13 (1949): 52–104.

Díaz y Díaz, Manuel C. *El Códice Calixtino de la catedral de Santiago: estudio codicológico y de contenido.* Santiago de Compostela: Centro de Estudios Jacobeos, 1988.

Williams, John, and Alison Stones, eds. *The Codex Calixtinus and the Shrine of St. James.* Tübingen: Narr, 1992.

LIBERAL ARTS. The Seven Liberal Arts were the cornerstones of a classical education in the Middle Ages. The basic three, known as the Trivium, were grammar, rhetoric, and logic or dialectic. After mastering these, a student was ready to proceed to the Quadrivium, which comprised arithmetic, geometry, music, and astronomy. The grouping was established as the core of Christian education in the *Institutions* of Cassiodorus and the writings of Boethius. Their Latin names were all grammatically feminine (Grammatica, Rhetorica, etc.), so when they came to be personified in literature and art they were naturally represented as women.

Between 410 and 439, the North African Martianus Capella wrote *De nuptiis Philologiae et Mercurii*, in which Philology, accompanied by her handmaidens the Seven Liberal Arts, marries Mercury, the god of eloquence. This mixed verse-prose text, in which the Liberal Arts are first presented as female personifications, was enormously popular in the schools for the next millennium. Grammar is a Roman physician, succoring the young; Dialectic has a serpent concealed in her sleeve, as a clever counsel must conceal a crucial point; Rhetoric is armored with her decorative skills; Geometry is a traveler, measuring roads and distances; Astronomy is winged and carries an inlaid metal book; Arithmetic emanates rays; Music has a stringed instrument. Commentaries were written in the 9th century by Dunchad, Johannes Scottus Eriugena, and Remigius of Auxerre, and in the 12th by Bernard Silvestris among others.

In the Carolingian period, two of Charlemagne's court poets, Theodulf of Orléans and the anonymous *Hibernicus exul*, wrote verses on the Liberal Arts, which have sometimes been considered as sources for artistic depictions, possibly in Charlemagne's palace at Aix-la-Chapelle. One of the most widespread brief descriptions of the Liberal Arts occurs in the account of Charlemagne's Spanish campaign ascribed to Archbishop Turpin of Reims (Pseudo-Turpin), a text that first appears in Latin ca. 1138 and was rapidly translated into French and most of the other vernaculars of Europe. In this text, the Liberal Arts were depicted in Charlemagne's palace at Aix-la-Chapelle. The Pseudo-Turpin does not describe the pictorial images but lists the subdivisions of each subject, with some brief interpretation. Grammar and its subdivision orthography

teach one to write down words correctly and then to understand what is written, as church lectors must do. Music is the art of David and the angels; the four lines of a staff signify the cardinal virtues, Prudence, Justice, Fortitude, and Temperance, and the eight notes the beatitudes. Dialectic teaches us to discern right from wrong. Rhetoric teaches us to speak suitably, calmly, and beautifully. Geometry measures spaces, such as cities, fields, and army camps. Arithmetic counts things. Astronomy, here conceived as astrology, tells about lucky and unlucky hours for doing things. Though not depicted, necromancy, or magic, is also discussed briefly. At about the same period, Baudri of Bourgueil (1045–1130) described the chamber of Countess Adèle of Blois, where the decoration included statues of Philosophy, Medicine, and the Seven Liberal Arts surrounding the bed.

Hugh of Saint-Victor's *Didascalicon: de studio legendi* (before 1141), a general introduction to the disciplines necessary for the study of Scripture and theology, presents the Liberal Arts as the remedy for the loss of knowledge and goodness in the Fall, while the mechanical arts compensate for the resulting weakness of the human body. The *Didascalicon* was accompanied in many manuscripts by schematized diagrams of the Arts. But Hugh did not restrict learning to the usual seven. Like the Seven Deadly Sins, the Arts acquired hangers-on and subdivisions. The *Didascalicon* also discussed medicine, magic, and practical arts.

The longest and most carefully integrated 12th-century study of the Liberal Arts was the *Heptateuchon* of Thierry of Chartres (1141), designed to organize learning for the ultimate purpose of understanding philosophy. All seven Arts, even arithmetic and geometry, were useful in understanding the nature of God in different ways. In the late 12th century, Godefroi of Saint-Victor composed an 800-line *Fons philosophiae*, an allegorical dream vision inspired by Hugh, in which philosophy and theology are the crowning intellectual experiences of human life; the Liberal Arts are described at the beginning of the quest.

Alain de Lille's *Anticlaudianus* (ca. 1179–83) describes the Liberal Arts constructing the chariot of Nature. Alain also wrote a short *Rhythmus de incarnatione Christi* on the Incarnation, which defines the usual laws of Nature viewed through the Seven Liberal Arts.

Two closely related 13th-century poems describe the *Mariage des sept arts*. One is by Jehan le Teinturier d'Arras and the other is anonymous. In both, the poet lies in bed and dreams that he is in a flowery meadow where he sees seven beautiful maidens. The eldest, Grammar, is the mother of the others. She announces her intention to marry *un serjant Dieu* called Faith; her daughters follow her example. Rhetoric chooses Alms, a persuasive advocate; Logic chooses Penitence, *uns hardiz avocat*; Arithmetic chooses Confession, who counts sins; Geometry chooses Abstinence, defined as measure; Astronomy chooses Love, who pierces through all the heavens to God; and Music chooses Prayer to praise God. In the anonymous version, Logic, here called Dialectic, chooses Alms, and Rhetoric chooses Obedience. More surprisingly, Astronomy is replaced by Theology. The lady Physic, accompanied in Jehan's version by Theology, appears, and after some discussion the suitors are summoned to celebrate the nuptials.

In the mid-13th century, Gossuin de Metz wrote a popular encyclopedic work in octosyllabic rhyming couplets, *Image du monde*, which was illustrated with forty-six figures referred to in the text. Some manuscripts also illustrate the Liberal Arts; unusually for the tradition, the figures are male. Grammar, as usual, holds a whip, or is accompanied by a male teacher who holds it. Rhetoric is shown as a male cleric arguing, with a ruler or sealed document in his hand. Henri d'Andeli framed his witty analysis of the quarrel between the Arts and the new disciplines of Philosophy and Theology (the ancients and the moderns) at the University of Paris in the verse *Bataille des sept arts* (ca. 1259). Grammar and the traditional literary arts as taught in the schools of Orléans, aided by Donatus, Priscian, Virgil, Ovid, and other authors, do battle with the new university curriculum taught at Paris: Philosophy, Theology, Medicine, and Law, aided by Aristotle and Boethius. The Paris faction is marshaled under the banner of Dialectic, assisted by Rhetoric, elevated (or reduced) to business-letter writing (*ars dictaminis*). The other Arts find practical applications for their traditional skills: Arithmetic counts supplies; Geometry measures encampments and troop movements; Music entertains the army; Astronomy casts the horoscope for the battle. Logic wins, but Henri begs the question by pointing out that, ultimately, no triumph of language is possible without Grammar.

The images in Charlemagne's and Adèle's palaces have not survived, but others have. The best-known images of the Seven Liberal Arts are the figures on the west façade at Chartres (1145–50), where full-length female figures with attributes alternate with male scholars. The traditional figures are unlabeled but are usually assumed to be those used by Thierry of Chartres: Priscian for grammar, Aristotle for dialectic, Cicero for rhetoric, Boethius for Arithmetic, Ptolemy for Astronomy, Euclid for Geometry, and Pythagoras for Music. Personifications of the Liberal Arts also appear on cathedral façades at Auxerre and Sens and on figures around a window in the west end of Laon; the figures in the rose window on the north side have been restored. The gable of the north-transept portal of the cathedral at Clermont-Ferrand shows the Arts as male figures. At Le Puy, there are 15th-century female figures of Grammar, Logic, Rhetoric, and Music in the sacristy. The figures that once stood beneath the Last Judgment at Paris have been destroyed. Those at Loches no longer survive, and the figures in the archivolt of the north portal at Déols were destroyed in 1830.

Manuscript illustrations of the Arts are surprisingly uncommon; few texts of Martianus are illustrated, and no tradition develops. Only a scattering of Martianus manuscripts are illustrated at all, and only a handful of those are French. One 9th-century illustrated French manuscript of Martianus survives (B.N. lat. 7900A) and another from ca. 1100 (Florence, Bibl. Mediceo-Laurenziana MS San Marco 190). Arts also occur in a manuscript from the 11th century, accompanied by verses on the Arts (B.N. lat. 3110); from the 12th, possibly Arras, Bibliothèque de la Ville 599. None of the philosophical studies of the Arts have illustra-

tions, and the only illustrations to the Arts in Alain de Lille's *Anticlaudianus* occur in the German translation. Occasionally, as in Pierpont Morgan MS 222, Boethius is shown with Philosophy and the Seven Arts. Only the *Image du monde* of Gossuin has a traditional picture cycle, which also appears in the Rothschild Canticles and the *Virgiet de solas*.

In other decorative arts, a late 12th-century Limoges enamel casket survives in the Victoria and Albert Museum in London, showing figures of the Arts, Philosophy, and Nature in roundels. Rhetoric is a male, holding scales, but the other Arts are female.

The Seven Liberal Arts in Education: Grammar. The way in which students learned basic Latin changed little throughout the medieval period. The grammars of Donatus (Major and Minor) and Priscian, followed by moral proverbs of the *Distichs* of Cato and the fables of Aesop, Avianus, and Phaedrus remained the core texts; as part of the collection sometimes called the *Auctores octo*, they lasted into Renaissance printed editions, supplemented by two 12th-century texts by French authors: Alain de Lille's *Parabolae* and the collecton of anecdotes called *Moretus*, usually ascribed to Bernard. More recent texts, working specifically with biblical Latin, included studies of words and constructions. The most widely used were by Bede and Alcuin.

In the late 12th century and early 13th, metrical grammars intended for students having advanced beyond Donatus appeared. The two most popular were the *Graecismus* of Eberhardt of Béthune (1212) and the *Doctrinale de puerorum* of Alexander of Villa Dei (1199). The same period saw the more speculative and philosophical grammars of the Modistae, whose inquiries into the nature of language, the modes of being, understanding, and signifying (*modus essendi, intelligendi, et significandi*) were widely read in the 13th and 14th centuries. Chief among them were Peter Helias, Jean de Garlande, and Peter of Spain. Their theories were revived among linguistic philosophers of the 17th and 18th centuries and again among modern-day French and American theoreticians of language, such as Lacan, Derrida, and Jakobsen.

Dialectic, or Logic. Cassiodorus and Martianus Capella both treated dialectic, basing their work on Aristotle, and the Dialectic and Rhetoric that Alcuin composed for Charlemagne and his court had a modest circulation from the 9th through the 11th century, but until the 12th century the core text remained Boethius, *De topicis differentiis*.

Rhetoric. Rhetoric changed and developed, especially from the 12th century on. While Cicero and the *Rhetorica ad Herennium* (thought to be by Cicero as well) continued to be read and commented on, new texts also appeared. Important French authors include Thierry of Chartres, Matthieu de Vendôme, and Jean de Garlande. Geoffroi de Vinsauf, despite his name, was English, but his *Poetria nova* (ca. 1200) circulated widely in glossed manuscripts in France as well as the rest of Europe. From the late 12th century, prose writing was taught especially through the art of official and unofficial letter writing, the *ars dictaminis*.

Arithmetic. Classical arithmetic included number, ratio, and proportion and continued to be studied from such authors as Boethius and Cassiodorus. The introduction of Arabic numerals, which spread slowly from the 13th century on, made computation easier but did little to change the study of numbers. The innovative work was done in the 13th century, when the *Elementa* of Jordannes described experiments with weights and measures, and the practical mathematical treatises of Fibonacci (Leonardo of Pisa) culminated in the Fibonacci series for determining the convergence of a series of ratios.

Geometry. Geometry was studied in Boethius's translation of Euclid and, from the 12th century, in the *Practica geometriae* of Hugh of Saint-Victor. In the 10th century, Gerbert of Aurillac (the future Pope Sylvester II) incorporated practical surveyors' manuals into the study of geometry. Practical geometry also included treatises on the use of measuring instruments and overlapped with astronomy in the treatise on the use of the astrolabe (known from the 10th century) and the equatory of planets. Jordannes and Fibonacci also wrote geometry texts. The geometry of construction and sculpture found its most interesting expression in the *Sketchbook* of the 13th-century designer Villard de Honnecourt.

Astronomy. Astronomy followed the system of planetary relationships worked out in Plato's *Timaeus*, which was known in Latin translation, and the *Almagest* of Ptolemy. Martianus Capella's Book 8 also provided a good discussion of astronomy. Astronomical calculations were necessary for figuring the dates of Easter; Bede's table continued to be used, and others were developed. Gerbert of Aurillac wrote a treatise on the astrolabe. In the 1130s, Bernard Silvestris incorporated astronomical material into his *Cosmographia*, as did Thierry of Chartres in his *Heptateuchon*, and later in the century Alain de Lille discussed astronomy at length in the *Anticlaudianus*. William of Moerbecke translated Aristotle from the Arabic versions, and practical school texts were written in the 13th century by John of Sacrobosco.

Music. Boethius's *De institutione musica* remained the chief textbook throughout the Middle Ages. His discussion, like that of Martianus Capella, was based largely on Pythagorean number symbolism and stressed harmonics. Gregorian chant developed fully in the Frankish kingdom in the 8th century and was written in neumes, which appeared at varying heights and in different shapes above the words, but with no staff lines or clear indication of exact pitch or duration. The alphabet letters taken from Paul the Deacon's *Ut queant laxis* hymn to John the Baptist by Guido d'Arezzo in the 11th century gave the tones ut, re, mi, fa, sol, la, from which the modern scale developed. These could be written on a staff to indicate regular intervals and duration, and by the 13th century neumes had become obsolete.

Jeanne E. Krochalis

[See also: ALAIN DE LILLE; BAUDRI OF BOURGUEIL; BERNARD SILVESTRIS; BOETHIUS, INFLUENCE OF; ERIUGENA, JOHANNES SCOTTUS; GERBERT OF AURILLAC; HUGH OF SAINT-VICTOR; *IMAGE DU MONDE*; JOHANNES DE GARLANDIA; MARTIANUS CAPELLA; MUSIC THEORY; MUSICAL NOTATION (NEUMATIC); MUSICAL NOTATION, 12TH–15TH CENTURIES; PSEUDO-TURPIN; REMIGIUS OF AUXERRE; SCHOOLS (CATHEDRAL); THEODULF OF ORLÉANS; VILLARD DE HONNECOURT]

Jehan le Teinturier d'Arras. *Le mariage des sept arts par Jehan le Teinturier d'Arras,* ed. Arthur Långfors. Paris: Champion, 1923.

Eriugena, Johannes Scottus. *Annotationes in Marcianum,* ed. Cora Lutz. Cambridge: Mediaeval Academy of America, 1939.

Martianus Capella. *De nuptiis Philologiae et Mercurii,* ed. A. Dick. rev. ed. J. Preaux. Stuttgart: Teubner, 1969.

———. *Martianus Capella and the Seven Liberal Arts,* trans. W.H. Stahl, R. Johnson, and E.L. Burge. New York: Columbia University Press, 1971.

Arts libéraux et philosophie au moyen âge. Actes du Quatrième Congrès International de Philosophie Médiévale. Montreal: Institut d'Études Médiévales, 1969.

Bursill-Hal, Geoffrey. *Speculative Grammars of the Middle Ages: The Doctrine of* partes orationis *of the Modistae.* The Hague: Mouton, 1971.

Evans, Michael. "Allegorical Women and Practical Men: The Iconography of the *Artes* Reconsidered." In *Medieval Women,* ed. Derek Baker. Oxford: Blackwell, 1978.

Hughes, Andrew. *Medieval Music: The Sixth Liberal Art.* Toronto: University of Toronto Press, 1974.

Katzenellenbogen, Adolf. *The Sculptural Programs of Chartres Cathedral.* Baltimore: Johns Hopkins University Press, 1959.

———. *Allegories of the Virtues and Vices in Medieval Art.* London: Warburg Institute, 1939.

Murphy, James Gerald. *Medieval Rhetoric: A Select Bibliography.* Toronto: University of Toronto Press, 1971.

———. *Medieval Rhetoric.* Berkeley: University of California Press, 1973.

———, ed. *Medieval Eloquence: Studies in the Theory and Practice of Medieval Rhetoric.* Berkeley: University of California Press, 1978.

Wagner, David L., ed. *The Seven Liberal Arts in the Middle Ages.* Bloomington: Indiana University Press, 1983.

LIBRARIES. The history of libraries in the early Middle Ages is bound up with the decline of the urban schools and educated civic elite characteristic of Roman culture and the emergence of the monastic community and the household of the bishop as centers of intellectual activity in Christian culture. The conversion of intellectuals like Jerome, Augustine, Paulinus of Nola (from Bordeaux), and Sulpicius Severus, the biographer of Martin of Tours, to a monastic or clerical life in the 4th and 5th centuries, together with their use of classical literary culture, shorn of reference to Greek and Roman religion, ensured the continuation of a learned book culture. The fact that Christianity was a religion based on a text, with the consequent need to interpret that text, contributed as well to an emphasis on a literate, book culture for the clerical and monastic elite.

The development of libraries required material resources (a supply of prepared animal skins for parchment; ink, pens, and other writing tools; binding supplies), skilled scribes and artisans to use these resources, the ability to bring these resources and skills together at one place, and the opportunity to obtain exemplars from which to copy texts. The first Christian missionaries to northern Europe brought a foreign language and a foreign religion. Soon, however, the clergy of the bishop's church and the monks in new abbeys were in need of books for liturgical services, collections of sermons, writings of the "authorities" of earlier centuries like Augustine or Jerome, and commentaries on Scripture. Young boys being trained for monastic or clerical service needed instruction in grammar, rhetoric, music, and the other Liberal Arts. Classical poets were copied and imitated; the art of letter writing flourished. All required that books be borrowed and copied and that manuscripts be preserved. Some clue to the nature of early-medieval libraries at a monastery or cathedral can be gleaned from the works cited by an author resident there, but citation from a copy of the full work itself rather than a *florilegium*, or collection of extracts, is not always demonstrable.

With the rise of the Carolingian monarchy and especially during the reign of Charlemagne, new impetus was given to learning, literary culture, books, and libraries. Charlemagne brought a literary-theological scholar from England, Alcuin, to head the palace school. Charlemagne and his successors patronized monasteries and their libraries. The library at the abbey of Saint-Denis, near Paris, had donations from Charles the Bald and perhaps Charlemagne himself, as well as an important Greek manuscript of the works of Pseudo-Dionysius the Areopagite given by Louis the Pious (B.N. gr. 437), who received it from the Byzantine emperor. Charlemagne favored "standardizing" texts of Scripture, the liturgy, and canon law, which meant bringing exemplars from Italy, having them copied, and distributing the copies. The disintegration of the Carolingian empire and Viking and other raids took a toll on books and libraries, but a revival of studies, and libraries, came in the late 10th and 11th centuries, although the rarity of book lists from the period makes reconstruction of holdings difficult. Evidence suggests that the abbeys of Cluny and Saint-Benoît-sur-Loire, among others, had extensive libraries and that they carefully regulated the lending of their books outside the local community. The letters of Peter the Venerable make it clear that Cluny lent books and requested loans from others. Monks also traveled to copy manuscripts: in the late 12th century, the abbot of St. Albans in England wrote to the abbot of Saint-Victor at Paris to ask if a monk might be sent to Saint-Victor to copy some of the works of Hugh of Saint-Victor that were not in the English abbey's collection.

With the growth of cathedral schools in the 11th and 12th centuries, libraries began to develop in these institutions as well. Bishops collected books for the library; scholars and masters bequeathed their personal libraries; patrons donated manuscripts or funds for copying. While archbishop of Reims, Gerbert of Aurillac (the future Pope Sylvester II) asked a friend to copy Caesar's *Bellum Gallicum* for him, and he sought other classical manuscripts at Rome. The library of the cathedral of Chartres was the beneficiary of many bequests of books; ca. 1150, Thierry of Chartres left fifty volumes from his private library, and John of Salisbury, who died as bishop of Chartres in 1180, left his books to the cathedral.

The abbey of Saint-Victor, one of the leading schools of Paris in the 12th century, quickly amassed a significant library through donations and copying. The cathedral of Notre-Dame, Paris, received the library of Peter Lombard, including his set of volumes of the glossed Bible (*Glossa ordinaria*) and Gratian's volume on canon law.

With the growth of the universities and their colleges, new libraries for masters and scholars came into being. The library of the Sorbonne, Paris, originated as the library of a house for poor scholars, established by Robert de Sorbon. Others followed his example of donating books, and by the 13th century the library had over 1,000 volumes. Recent detailed analysis of catalogues of the Sorbonne collection gives a new sense of its development and innovations, such as the division of the library ca. 1292–98 into a large library of chained books, made up of those books most frequently needed by masters and scholars for reference, and a smaller library that continued to lend books to individuals. In 1321, Sorbonne regulations required that the best copies of each work owned by the college be kept in the chained library; the college also required an adequate pledge be deposited when a book was borrowed.

Patronage by kings and nobles had always played an important role in the development of monastic and cathedral libraries, but in the later Middle Ages they were also important as book collectors themselves. Notable French royal and noble bibliophiles were John II the Good, Charles V, John, duke of Berry, and Philip the Bold and Philip the Good, dukes of Burgundy. John II purchased or commissioned manuscript books of religious and secular varieties; he commissioned a translation of the Bible into French and a translation of Livy into French by Pierre Bersuire. His son Charles V took great interest in the royal library and had it installed in a tower of the Louvre. Charles enlarged his collection by purchase, commission, and sometimes confiscation of the library of a defeated enemy. Surviving records give details of purchases of materials for the making of books, binding costs, and payments to illuminators and booksellers. Like his father, Charles had numerous Latin works translated into French for his library, including classical literature, histories, and philosophy.

John, duke of Berry, brother of Charles V, was his equal as a bibliophile and accumulated one of the most important medieval personal libraries. He had an extensive collection of classical literature in Latin and in French translation, but essentially no Greek literature. The duke commissioned numerous works, including some of the most exquisite books of hours of the later Middle Ages. He was also part of a large gift-exchange network among the members of the aristocracy, who presented each other with sumptuous illuminated manuscripts.

Philip the Bold, duke of Burgundy, began one of the great collections of the northern regions, purchasing many devotional texts, histories, and miscellaneous treatises from Parisian booksellers. His descendants continued to enlarge the collection with, among other things, a copy of the works of Christine de Pizan and translations of Boccaccio's *De-*

cameron. The library of the dukes reached its zenith under Philip the Good, who enriched the collection through inheritance, exchanges of gifts, commissions, and purchases. The additions ranged over classical literature, vernacular translations, religious texts, and even books on the Near East.

One cannot close a discussion of medieval libraries without noting developments that greatly facilitated the availability and the ready use of books. The *pecia* copying system for "farming out" the copying of manuscripts by parts greatly speeded up the production of manuscripts for the use of scholars at the University of Paris and elsewhere. This innovation had consequences primarily in the realm of availability, supply, and price. However, another innovation, the development of indices, concordances, and other "finding tools" for the Bible and the works of major authors, facilitated the task of locating passages and "authoritative" citations. What had in the past required feats of memory or the possession of *florilegia* with extracts from the church fathers could now be accomplished by consulting a subject index or a concordance keyed by a standard system of reference marks to pages in a text. Comparing the *Quattuor libri sententiarum* of Peter Lombard, the *Sic et non* of Abélard, or the *Glossa ordinaria* to the Bible, with their full quotations of patristic authorities on each question or each passage of Scripture, to the new "finding tools" of the 13th century underscores the difference that the latter made. The Lombard and his generation sought to "digest" the past (represented by quotations from "authoritative texts") in textual form on the page, reconciling citations from texts as they were presented. The university masters of the 13th century worked out a new way to approach texts in their entirety, but with an ability to interrogate them in a new, more detailed way. It should be noted, also, that in the 14th century the library of the Sorbonne had lists of books in other libraries in Paris, apparently for the use of members of the college who might want to consult books not in the Sorbonne library.

Grover A. Zinn

[See also: ABÉLARD, PETER; CANON LAW; CHARLES V THE WISE; CLUNY; GERBERT OF AURILLAC; JOHN, DUKE OF BERRY; JOHN OF SALISBURY; MANUSCRIPTS, PRODUCTION AND ILLUMINATION; PALEOGRAPHY AND MANUSCRIPTS; PETER LOMBARD; PHILIP THE BOLD; PHILIP THE GOOD; SAINT-VICTOR, ABBEY AND SCHOOL OF; SCHOOLS, CATHEDRAL; SCHOOLS, MONASTIC; THIERRY OF CHARTRES; UNIVERSITIES]

Christ, Karl. *The Handbook of Medieval Library History*, trans. Theophil M. Otto. Metuchen: Scarecrow, 1984.

Reynolds, L.D., and N.G. Wilson. *Scribes and Scholars: A Guide to the Transmission of Greek and Latin Literature*. 2nd ed. Oxford: Clarendon, 1974.

Rouse, Mary A., and Richard H. Rouse. *Authentic Witnesses: Approaches to Medieval Texts and Manuscripts*. Notre Dame: University of Notre Dame Press, 1991.

Stahl, Harvey. "The Problem of Manuscript Painting at Saint-Denis During the Abbacy of Suger." In *Abbot Suger and Saint-Denis: A Symposium*, ed. Paula L. Gerson. New York: Metropolitan Museum of Art, 1986, pp. 163–81.

Thompson, James Westfall. *The Medieval Library*. Chicago: University of Chicago Press, 1939.

LIBRI CAROLINI. The official Carolingian rebuttal to the iconodulist Second Nicene Council (787). Completed in 793 by Theodulf of Orléans, the treatise is divided into four books of chapters attacking *acta* by the eastern council, based on a Latin translation of the council's Greek decrees that had been prepared earlier in Rome. Despite the care taken over the contents and wording of the Carolingian response, evident from the erasures and rewriting still visible on the extant, original manuscript of the *Libri*, the document was never promulgated. The decision not to do so resulted probably from the Carolingians' realization, only after Theodulf had begun his work, that Pope Hadrian I approved of the Second Nicene decrees. The pope's views were made evident in his reply to the Carolingian *Capitulare adversus synodum*, a list of chapter headings to be included in the *Libri Carolini* that was sent to Rome most likely in 792. Once the response to the *Capitulare* had been received, the *Libri* were more or less finished, but under the circumstances Charlemagne did not wish to set himself against Hadrian by presenting him with the treatise.

The Latin rendering of the council's decrees available to Theodulf was flawed at numerous points. Above all, it consistently used the word *adoratio*, which implies the type of worship owed to God alone, to translate references in the Greek to an inferior kind of reverence that the Byzantine iconodules believed was justifiably bestowed on works of art. But although such errors led Theodulf to misunderstand aspects of the eastern position, his teachings in the *Libri Carolini* merit attention in their own right and reveal in their author a carefully developed, highly Augustinian conception of the role and nature of the Christian artistic image, its relation to the spiritual realm, and indeed of the entire world of matter to the sacred.

Celia Chazelle

[See also: THEODULF OF ORLÉANS]

Theodulf of Orléans. *Libri Carolini sive Caroli Magni capitulare de imaginibus*, ed. Hubert Bastgen. Hanover: Imprensis Bibliopolii Hahniani, 1924.

———. *Opus Caroli regis contra synodum (Libri Carolini)*, ed. Ann Freeman. *MGH Legum sectio 3, Concilia 2, Neubearbeitung*. (Forthcoming.)

Chazelle, Celia. "Matter, Spirit, and Image in the *Libri Carolini*." *Recherches augustiniennes* 21 (1986): 163–84.

Freeman, Ann. "Carolingian Orthodoxy and the Fate of the *Libri Carolini*." *Viator* 16 (1985): 65–108.

———. "Theodulf of Orleans and the *Libri Carolini*." *Speculum* 32 (1957): 663–705.

Gero, Stephen. "The *Libri Carolini* and the Image Controversy." *Greek Orthodox Theological Review* 18 (1973): 7–34.

LIÈGE. Liège owes its founding to St. Lambert, bishop of Maastricht, who was martyred (705/06) in an oratory he built here on the banks of the Meuse. His successor, St. Hubert, impressed by miracles, moved the bishopric here from Maastricht ca. 717. Under the powerful Bishop Notger (r. 972–1008), Liège became one of the ecclesiastical principalities of the Holy Roman Empire ca. 980, and the cathedral school that flourished here made Liège the leading intellectual center in the West until it was supplanted by Paris in the 12th century. Liège was granted a communal charter in 1185. In the course of the 13th century, the trade guilds gained considerable power, including the right of self-representation on the city council, which was resented by the nobles and upper classes. In August 1312, the nobles attempted to wrest back power, but their entire armed party was burned in the church of Saint-Martin (the "Male-Saint-Martin"), and in February 1313 the trade guilds and laborers were granted political equality. Privileges were revoked in 1408 after general uprisings in the northern communes, and in 1467–68, during the Burgundian domination of the Low Countries, Charles the Bold ruthlessly sacked and burned the town. After the fall of Burgundian power, Liège was rebuilt under Érard de la Marck (r. 1506–38).

The art of working copper and brass originated in the 11th century at neighboring Huy and led eventually to the establishment in Liège of a flourishing school of liturgical metalwork during the 12th and 13th centuries. The baptismal font by Renier de Huy (fl. 1107–18) in the church of Saint-Barthélémy in Liège is an important example of the earlier, more sober Romanesque style. The font is supported by twelve half-figures of oxen, symbolic of the Apostles, and includes five scenes in high relief, centering on Christ's baptism. Godefroi de Huy employed the more complex *champlevé* technique of enameling his many reliquaries. Nicolas de Verdun, who created the reliquary of Our Lady for the cathedral of Tournai (1205), marks the transition to Gothic style. In the later Middle Ages, Liège's tradition of fine metalworking led to its becoming an important center for the production of armor.

Because of its importance as an intellectual, artistic, and ecclesiastical center, Liège is rich in medieval churches and monuments. The Gothic cathedral of Saint-Paul, founded in 969, was constructed largely in the 13th century. Its treasury contains the gilded silver reliquary of St. Lambert (1512) and the reliquary of Charles the Bold in gold and enamel, offered in atonement for his attack on the city. Saint-Barthélémy, with its massive twin-towered façade in Rhenish Romanesque style, contains the celebrated baptismal font by Renier de Huy. Sainte-Croix, founded by Bishop Notger in 969, is a fine example of Rhenish Romanesque style (ca. 1175). Saint-Denis, founded by Notger in 987, preserves the oldest Romanesque tower in Belgium but was largely rebuilt in the 15th century.

William W. Kibler

[See also: ENAMELING; JEWELRY AND METALWORKING]

Dewez, Louis. *La cathédrale Saint-Paul à Liège*. Liège, 1956.
Gobert, Théodore. *Liège à travers les âges*. 6 vols. Liège, 1924–29.
Kurth, Godefroid. *La cité de Liège au moyen âge*. 3 vols. Liège: Cormaux, 1909–10.

LIMBOURG BROTHERS (fl. late 14th–early 15th c.). Three brothers (Paul, Jean, and Herman), nephews of the painter Jean Malouel, came to Paris from Nijmegen in the Low Countries as youths to serve as apprentices under a goldsmith but had to leave because of the plague. Imprisoned on their way home in 1399, they were ransomed by Philip the Bold, duke of Burgundy, for whom they illuminated a Bible, now lost, between 1400 and 1404. They may have been in the service of John, duke of Berry, by 1405; for him, they produced their most notable works: miniatures in the *Très Belles Heures de Notre Dame* (B.N. n.a. lat. 3093), a miniature of the duke of Berry embarking on a journey in the *Petites Heures* (B.N. lat. 18014), some scenes in *grisaille* for a *Bible historiale* (B.N. fr. 166), the illuminations of the *Belles Heures* (New York, The Cloisters), and, most notably, miniatures in the *Très Riches Heures* (Chantilly, Musée Condé), which remained unfinished in 1416, when all three brothers and their patron appear to have died in an epidemic.

Their miniatures, particularly in the *Très Riches Heures*, are representative of the height of the Interna-

Annunciation, *Les Belles Heures de Jean, Duc de Berry*. The Cloisters Collection, 1954 (54.1.1, fol. 30) *Courtesy of the Metropolitan Museum of Art, New York.*

tional Gothic style in France, combining courtly elegance, sumptuous coloration, and a mixture of fanciful and remarkably naturalistic landscape settings. Although attempts have been made to define the style of each of the brothers, these have not always been successful, and they are generally regarded to have participated collectively on their productions.

Robert G. Calkins

[See also: JOHN, DUKE OF BERRY; MANUSCRIPTS, PRODUCTION AND ILLUMINATION; PHILIP THE BOLD]

Longnon, Jean, and Raymond Cazelles. *The Très Riches Heures of Jean, Duke of Berry.* New York: Braziller, 1969
Meiss, Millard. *French Painting in the Time of Jean de Berry: The Limbourgs and Their Contemporaries.* 2 vols. New York: Braziller, 1974.
———, and Elizabeth H. Beatson. *The Belles Heures of Jean, Duke of Berry.* New York: Braziller, 1974.

LIMOGES. Founded by the Gauls as an *oppidum* overlooking the Vienne River, Limoges (Haute-Vienne) became a crossroads of major highways during the Roman period, when it was known as Augustoritum. With the invasions of the 4th century, the population center shifted eastward toward the cathedral of Saint-Étienne, which became the hub of the *cité*, the bishop acting as the primary authority and protector of the town. The abbey of Saint-Martial was founded with the support of the Carolingian monarchy in 848 at the saint's tomb site, and a second urban agglomeration, the château, soon developed under the control of the abbot and the viscount of Limoges, a vassal of the duke of Aquitaine. This division was formalized by the Treaty of Paris of 1259, by which Louis IX ceded the château to England while the episcopal *cité* remained under French control. Throughout the Middle Ages, Limoges was wracked by rivalry, even open warfare, between its constituent halves. The devastating sack of the *cité* by Edward, the Black Prince, in 1370 during the Hundred Years' War was perhaps Limoges's darkest hour.

Saint-Martial and the cathedral were the premier edifices of the city. The abbey was one of the great monastic centers of medieval Europe, known particularly for its contributions to the development of liturgical music. Rebuilt after a fire of 1053 and destroyed in 1794, Saint-Martial adopted the choir plan with an ambulatory and radiating chapels and vaulted superstructure seen in elite Romanesque churches, such as Saint-Sernin, Toulouse, and Santiago de Compostela. The cathedral of Saint-Étienne belongs to the Gothic period: its western tower was erected ca. 1240 above an early 11th-century porch; the choir was begun ca. 1270 by Jean Deschamps, master mason of Clermont cathedral, or a close follower; the transept and eastern bays of the nave were realized in the early 16th century. In contrast to the northern French pattern of the cathedral, the hall-church scheme of Saint-Pierre de Queyroix (late 13th–early 14th c.) and Saint-Michel-des-Lions (14th–15th c.) looks to architectural traditions of southwestern France.

Medieval Limoges is best known for its exquisite enamels. From the 11th century on, products of the city's workshops, ranging from large reliquaries and liturgical utensils to delicately wrought jewelery, were exported throughout Europe.

Michael T. Davis

[See also: ADÉMAR DE CHABANNES; ENAMELING; HUNDRED YEARS' WAR; JEWELRY AND METALWORKING; MARTIAL OF LIMOGES; RELICS AND RELIQUARIES]

Davis, Michael T. "Le chœur de la cathédrale de Limoges: tradition rayonnante et innovation dans la carrière de Jean des Champs." *Bulletin archéologique du Comité des Travaux Historiques et Scientifiques* n.s. 22 (1989): 51–114.
Ducourtieux, Paul. *Histoire de Limoges.* Limoges: Ducourtieux, 1925.
Fage, René. *La cathédrale de Limoges.* Paris: Laurens, 1926.
Gauthier, Marie-Madeleine. *Émaux limousins champlevés des XIIe, XIIIe et XIVe siècles.* Paris: Prat, 1950.
Grenier, Paul-Louis. *La cité de Limoges, son évêque, son chapitre, son consulat (XIIe–XVIIIe siècles).* Paris: Picard, 1907.
Lasteyrie du Saillant, Robert de. *L'abbaye de Saint-Martial de Limoges: étude historique, économique et archéologique.* Paris: Picard, 1901.
Limouzin-Lamothe, Roger. *Le diocèse de Limoges des origines à la fin du moyen âge.* Strasbourg: Le Roux, 1951.
Verynaud, Georges. *Histoire de Limoges.* Limoges: Centre Régional de Recherche et de Documentation Pédagogiques, 1973.

LIMOUSIN. The Limousin, a large, thinly populated county in northern Aquitaine, was of minor importance in the history of medieval France. Bounded by the counties of Berry and La Marche in the north, Poitou and the Angoumois in the west, Auvergne in the east, and Périgord and Quercy in the south, it corresponded approximately to the modern departments of Haute-Vienne, Corrèze, and Creuse. A hilly region of generally poor soils, the Limousin could sustain only a scattered population; its capital, Limoges, was its only town of any size. Inadequate roads and its location left the region relatively isolated from the main currents of medieval French life, and its principal rulers, the viscounts of Limoges, never became politically powerful, being subject to the authority first of the dukes of Aquitaine and then of the kings of France.

The medieval county descended from the tribal territory of the Celtic Lemovices conquered by Caesar in the 1st century B.C., with Limoges as its capital. Christianization began in the 3rd century, though in the 11th the monks of Saint-Martial of Limoges launched a spectacular campaign claiming that their patron saint was the apostle to the Aquitanians, having been sent there by St. Peter himself. In early times, Limoges became an episcopal see in the archdiocese of Bourges. After the era of the Germanic invasions, the Limousin formed part of the first duchy of Aquitaine; then, after the century of Carolingian rule from the late 8th century to the late 9th, the newly created viscounts of Limoges came under the authority of the counts of Poitou/dukes of Aquitaine until the early 12th century. The Angevins controlled the Limousin in the later 12th century through the marriage of Eleanor, duchess of Aquitaine, with King Henry II of England. In the 13th century, the Capetians conquered it and absorbed it into their royal domain. The Limousin was the site of several famous monastic houses, including Solignac, Beaulieu, Uzerches, Vigeois, Tulle, Grandmont, and Saint-Martial of Limoges. Grandmont, founded by Étienne de Muret in the early 12th century, became the mother house of a new monastic order that spread widely in France and gained the favor of the Angevin kings in particular. Saint-Martial, a Cluniac dependency after the mid-11th century, is well known through the survival of a large part of its magnificent manuscript library of the 10th–12th centuries, the richest of its kind in southwestern France. A number of these manuscripts are of incomparable value for the study of illumination and liturgical drama. Troubadour poetry also flourished in the Limousin, which boasted an unusual number of poets among its native sons, the most famous perhaps being Bernart de Ventadorn. The renown of Limoges enamels, however, overshadowed all other arts during the 12th and 13th centuries, when the industry reached its greatest heights and made the town the most important production center in Europe.

George T. Beech

Aubrun, Michel. *L'ancien diocèse de Limoges des origines au milieu du XIe siècle.* Clermont-Ferrand: Institut des Études du Massif Central, 1981.

Brelingard, Désiré. *Histoire du Limousin et de La Marche.* Paris: Presses Universitaires de France, 1971.

Gaborit-Chopin, D. *La décoration des manuscrits à Saint-Martial de Limoges et en Limousin du IVe au XIIe siècle.* Paris: Droz, 1969.

Labande, Edmond-René, ed. *Histoire du Poitou, du Limousin et des pays charentais.* Toulouse: Privat, 1976.

Lasteyrie du Saillant, Robert de. *Étude sur les comtes et vicomtes de Limoges antérieurs à l'an mil.* Paris: Franck, 1874.

LINEAGE AND INHERITANCE. Medieval nobles took much of their identity from their lineage, those from whom they descended and from whom they had inherited their power and property. One's lineage was a selected group out of all the people one might find in one's family tree, for nobles normally identified only with those ancestors from whom they were descended in the male line, unless at some point the inheritance had gone through a woman or unless one of the male ancestors had married a woman from a much more powerful family.

This agnatic tendency is clearest among royal families and those of the upper nobility. In the 11th and 12th centuries, a lineage's self-identification became closely linked with the hereditary castle, and it became common for the oldest son to inherit the castle and most of his parents' property. Daughters were given dowries, but younger sons were, if possible, not given any land that would be permanently alienated from their older brother's inheritance. An emphasis on male inheritance, however, was well established long before primogeniture became normal practice in the 12th century. In the turbulent 9th and 10th centuries, while men trying to establish a strong position took power and authority from wherever they could find it, whether from their wives, their allies, or their lords, they always intended to pass that authority on to their sons.

Women were a vital component of the continuity of an agnatic lineage. They brought land, prestige, and sometimes princely names to the lineage of men lucky enough to be able to marry wives socially above themselves, as most ambitious medieval men tried to do. Choice of a suitable marriage partner was a complicated decision that might cement an alliance, join warring factions, or create a dynasty. Men always considered their wives to some extent as outsiders, but to their sons these same women were an integral part of their lineage.

The Romans had had a testamentary system, which assumed that a man would leave a will. He was legally supposed to leave a certain minimum of property to his relatives but could dispose of the rest as he wished. From the 8th century on, however, written testaments were rare. They began to be common again only in the 13th century. Medieval men and women assumed that their relatives, in particular their children, would inherit all their property. If they wanted to dispose of some of it elsewhere, say as a gift to a church, they would normally make such a gift during their own lifetimes rather than after their deaths via testament. The force of custom, rather than written law, in determining inheritance meant that in the high Middle Ages there was always ambiguity over the nature of property rights: on the one hand, a man could do with his own property what he liked; on the other, he was expected not to do anything that would disrupt his lineage's inheritance.

Constance B. Bouchard

[See also: BETROTHAL AND MARRIAGE CONTRACTS; DOWRY; FEUDALISM; NOBILITY; SEIGNEUR/SEIGNEURIE]

Bouchard, Constance B. "Family Structure and Family Consciousness Among the Aristocracy in the Ninth to Eleventh Centuries." *Francia* 14 (1986): 639–58.

Il matrimonio nella società altomedievale. Spoleto: La Sede del Centro, 1977.

Reuter, Timothy, ed. and trans. *The Medieval Nobility: Studies on the Ruling Classes of France and Germany from the Sixth to the Twelfth Century.* Amsterdam: New Holland, 1978.

Sheehan, Michael M. "Choice of Marriage Partner in the Middle Ages: Development and Mode of Application of a Theory of Marriage." *Studies in Medieval and Renaissance History* 11 (1978): 1–33.

White, Stephen D. *Custom, Kinship, and Gifts to Saints: The Laudatio Parentum in Western France, 1050–1150.* Chapel Hill: University of North Carolina Press, 1988.

LISIEUX. The diocese of Lisieux (Calvados) was the last founded in Normandy and the only one without a local bishop-saint. The city was an important Gallo-Roman center and seaport on the Touques River even before the arrival of Christianity. Traces of the 3rd-century city walls were found during the rebuilding after 1944. Of the known medieval abbeys and churches in and around Lisieux, only the former cathedral of Saint-Pierre and the Flamboyant church of Saint-Jacques survive.

Saint-Pierre, which dates from the 12th and 13th centuries, was begun during the episcopacy of Arnulf, who had served on the crusade of 1146. Its nave is one of the first Gothic structures in Normandy, although Gothic elements are confined to features of style, columnar supports, pointed arches, and attempts to accomplish the new spatial organization. The technique and structure are typically Norman and have little to do with Île-de-France experiments in lightening the wall. The nave was followed by the transept and straight bays of the chevet near the end of the 12th century; the elegant turning bays, ambulatory, and side radiating chapels announce the Norman regional style of Gothic. The axial chapel was rebuilt under Bishop Pierre Cauchon, now remembered only as one of the condemning judges of Jeanne d'Arc.

The plan of the church consists of an eight-bay nave, flanked by aisles, a projecting transept with eastern aisles and a handsome lantern tower, and a deep chevet with ambulatory and three separated radiating chapels. The elevation has three stories throughout: arcades and aisles, subdivided arcade units open into the unfloored roof space above the aisle vaults, and single clerestory windows. In spite of details associated with the Gothic style, the elevation is a common Norman one updated from Romanesque precedents. Prior to its systematic scrapping after the Revolution, the richly decorated central portal of the west façade was one of the rare sculpted Early Gothic portals in Normandy. The remainder of the façade, including the lateral portals, dates from the 13th century; the south tower is a 17th-century recreation of the original design.

The Flamboyant parish church of Saint-Jacques was begun in 1496 by Guillaume de Samaison and completed in the 1550s. Unfortunately, the original interior decoration, consisting of the elegant Flamboyant stained-glass windows and rich painting on the vaults, all disappeared in 1944. After many years of restoration work, only the skeleton of the original church remains.

William W. Clark

[See also: CAUCHON, PIERRE]

Barral i Altet, Xavier. "Sculptures gothiques inédites de la cathédrale de Lisieux." *Bulletin monumental* 139 (1981): 7–16.

Clark, William W. "Saint-Pierre at Lisieux and the Beginning of Norman Gothic Architecture." Diss. Columbia University, 1970.

———. "The Central Portal of Saint-Pierre at Lisieux: A Lost Monument of Twelfth-Century Gothic Sculpture." *Gesta* 11 (1972): 46–58.

———. "The Nave of Saint-Pierre at Lisieux: Romanesque Structure in a Gothic Guise." *Gesta* 16 (1977): 29–38.

Cottin, François. "Noviomagus Lexoviorum des temps les plus lointains à la fin de l'occupation romaine." *Bulletin de la Société des Antiquaires de la Normandie* 53 (1955–56): 169–96.

Erlande-Brandenburg, Alain. "La cathédrale de Lisieux: les campagnes de construction." *Congrès archéologique* (*Bessin et Pays d'Auge*) 132 (1974): 137–72.

LIT DE JUSTICE. Term originally used to describe the paraphernalia of the king's seat in the Parlement de Paris; by the 15th century, it also designated particularly important royal sessions of this court. Its institutional significance was recognized when, in April 1485, Charles VIII declared that in the Parlement de Paris "and nowhere else is held and must be held our *lit de justice*." As early as 1318, the space where the king sat in the Parlement was referred to as a *lit*, and its imposing features are depicted in a copy of a drawing showing the trial of Robert d'Artois in 1332. The elements of the *lit* (draped backdrop, covering, canopy, and pillows) were similar to those of ordinary beds (*lits*) used for sleeping and ceremonial purposes. Although the parliamentary *lit* was not yet connected terminologically with royal dispensation of justice, Charles V was said to be "holding his justice" when he issued an *ordonnance* on majority in the Parlement in 1375. By 1387, official records of the court referred to the *lit de justice*, used in that year at the trial of Charles of Navarre and regularly set up when the king visited the Parlement (even though records of the court's proceedings did not always mention it). In 1396, a clerk of the court, doubtless influenced by current usage, extended the name by metonymy from apparatus to session, writing that the *lit de justice* was held when Charles VI attended the court to solicit advice concerning a pardon.

The *lit de justice* was soon an established institution: in 1404, Christine de Pizan praised Charles V for holding "the *lit de justice*, in cases reserved for him to decide." Official records applied the term to sessions held in 1413 at which reforming measures pressed by the Cabochiens were registered and then revoked. Contemporaries applied it to the trial of the duke of Alençon at Vendôme in 1458. The sessions termed *lits de justice* were not novel: earlier kings had visited the Parlement to register important *ordonnances* and for important trials. In the new usage, the term designated the most solemn and formal of the king's visits, distinguished from those made to attend pleadings and seek counsel. In the 16th century, it came to be associated particularly with sessions when the king imposed registration of unpopular legislation. Although evidence is sparse for the late 15th and early 16th centuries, the *ordonnance* of 1485 and the declarations of such officials as Claude de Seyssel show that the institution's significance was not forgotten and go far to explain the reappearance of the term to designate solemn royal sessions of the Parlement in 1527 and later years.

Elizabeth A.R. Brown/Richard C. Famiglietti

[See also: LAW AND JUSTICE; PARLEMENT DE PARIS]

Brown, Elizabeth A.R., and Richard C. Famiglietti. *The Lit de Justice: Semantics, Ceremonial, and the Parlement of Paris 1300–1600.* Sigmaringen: Thorbecke, 1994.

Hanley, Sarah. *The* Lit de Justice *of the Kings of France: Constitutional Ideology in Legend, Ritual, and Discourse.* Princeton: Princeton University Press, 1983.

Holt, Mack P. "The King in Parlement: The Problem of the *Lit de Justice* in Sixteenth-Century France." *Historical Journal* 31 (1988): 507–23.

Scheller, R.W. "The 'Lit de Justice,' or How to Sit on a Bed of Estate." In *Annus quadriga mundi: Dertien Opstellen over middeleeuwse Kunst,* ed. J.B. Bedaux and A.M. Koldeweij. Zutphen: Welburg Pers, 1989, pp. 193–202.

LITURGICAL BOOKS. Liturgical books contain the prescribed texts and rubrics for the conduct of worship, including the celebration of the Mass, the observance of the Divine Office, and the administration of the sacraments. Chief among the numerous medieval types are the Lectionary, a descendant of the *Comes,* which contains excerpts (*pericopes*) from Scripture to be used as readings in the daily liturgy of the Mass; the Breviary, which in the 12th and 13th centuries emerged as a single volume incorporating all of the texts of the Divine Office; and the Sacramentary and Pontifical, discussed below.

The earliest forms of Christian worship used the Bible as the primary text and were organized around freely created formulae. By the 3rd century, however, there is evidence of written formulae for the eucharistic celebration, and following the Edict of Milan (313) a process of increasing systematization of the liturgy begins. The first collections to appear, the *libelli missarum,* were small booklets containing prayers for the Mass. Out of these developed the Sacramentaries, the most important of which were the Leonine, the so-called Gelasian (*Vat. Reg.* 316), and the Gregorian. Reflecting the medieval practice of providing a book for each minister, not each liturgical act, the Sacramentary contained the texts required for the presider only; the directions for the performance of the liturgy were found in separate volumes known as "Ordinals (*ordines Romani*). Ordinals accompany both the Gelasian and Gregorian Sacramentaries. It was only in the 12th and 13th centuries that the *ordines* and the Sacramentary were fully merged into a single volume, the Pontifical.

The history of the Sacramentary from the 7th century to the 11th provides witness to the attempts to base liturgical practice throughout Europe on the Roman model, a step encouraged by the Carolingian kings. Yet the shape that the liturgy assumed was from the beginning influenced by local "uses," or variants of the Roman Rite. For example, the Gregorian Sacramentary, which Pope Hadrian I sent Charlemagne in 785–86, contained services for the papal feasts only; Alcuin took on the task of completing and supplementing it by incorporating local uses. One must speak, therefore, of a Romano-Frankish and even a Romano-Germanic liturgy.

Following the period of Pope Gregory VII, the northern influence on Roman liturgy diminished significantly, though by no means entirely. Gallican and Germanic influences are to be found in the most significant and authoritative texts of the time, including the Pontifical of Guillaume Durand (ca. 1293–95), which became the basis for the printed edition of the Pontifical of 1485. The official books that emerged out of the rigid unification of liturgical practices in the Council of Trent were also direct offspring of these Romano-Frankish and Romano-Germanic sources.

Edmund J. Goehring

[See also: CANONICAL HOURS; DIVINE OFFICE; GUILLAUME DURAND; MASS, CHANTS AND TEXTS]

Pfaff, Richard W. *Medieval Latin Liturgy: A Select Bibliography.* Toronto: University of Toronto Press, 1982.

LITURGICAL COMMENTATORS. Throughout much of the Latin Middle Ages, exegetes wrote interpretations of the liturgy, most frequently either to instruct the clergy in the meanings of the texts and music of the Mass and Office or to defend particular theological positions, especially regarding the sacraments. One of the only surviving witnesses to the liturgy of the Gallican church is the commentary of the Pseudo-Germanus, now known to have been written in the 7th century, after the time of Isidore of Seville (d. 636), whose writings are one of its sources. A significant body of early Carolingian commentaries was written apparently for didactic purposes, including works by Leidradus of Lyon (d. 813), Angilbert of Saint-Riquier (d. 814), Magnus of Sens (d. 818), Theodulf of Orléans (d. 821), and Jesse of Amiens (d. 836). Contemporaries of Amalarius of Metz (d. ca. 850), the most important liturgical commentator of the early period, and the following generation constitute a second wave of Carolingian commentators: Agobard of Lyon (d. 840), Rabanus Maurus (d. 842), Walafrid Strabo (d. 849), Florus of Lyon (d. 860), and Remigius of Auxerre (d. 908).

Although the 10th century did not produce significant numbers of commentators—the Pseudo-Alcuin's *De divinis officiis* (before 950) is an important exception—the numbers swelled once again in the wake of the Gregorian reform movement of the later 11th century, with Humbert of Silva Candida (d. ca. 1064), Peter Damian (d. 1072), John of Avranches (d. 1079), and Bernold of Constance (d. 1100); the date of the much copied *Liber quare* remains in doubt, but its earliest source dates from the late 11th century.

Reform, which brought increasing emphasis on the education of priests, helped to inspire the many liturgical commentaries written in France and northern Europe during the 12th century. In addition to the extensive discussions of Rupert of Deutz (d. 1129), *Liber de divinis officiis*; Honorius of Autun (fl. first half of the 12th c.), *Gemma animae, Speculum ecclesiae,* and *Sacramentarium*; Hugh of Saint-Victor (d. 1142), *De sacramentis christianae fidei*; Jean Beleth (d. ca. 1180), *Summa de ecclesiasticis officiis*; the anonymous Pseudo-Hugh of Saint-Victor, *Speculum de mysteriis ecclesiae* (ca. 1160); and Robert Paululus (d. after 1180), *De ceremoniis, sacramentis, officiis et observationibus ecclesiasticis,* are shorter liturgical commentaries found in the writings of Petrus Pictor (fl. ca. 1100), Sigebert de Gembloux (d. after 1112), Odo of Cambrai (d. 1113), Ivo of Chartres (d. 1116), Pseudo-Alger of Liège (*De sacrificio missae*); Hildebert of Lavardin (d. 1133), Drogo of Laon (d. 1135), Isaac of Stella (d. 1169/78), and Stephen, bishop of Autun (d. 1189) *(Libellum de sacramento altaris)*, as well as the *Libellus de canone mystici libaminis*, sometimes attributed to Richard the Premonstratensian (of Wedinghausen?).

Liturgical commentators of the 13th century, most of whom either studied or taught in Paris during some period in their lives, wrote the liturgical *summae* that organized earlier material for teaching and studying in the schools: Sicard of Cremona (d. 1215), Pope Innocent III (d. 1216), Praepositinus of Cremona (d. 1210), William of Auxerre (d. 1231), Guy of Orchelles (d. ca. 1230), Alexander of Hales (d. 1245), Hugues de Saint-Cher (d. 1263), Albert the Great (d. 1280), and Gilbert of Tournai (d. 1284). The culmination of these efforts was the great *Rationale divinorum officiorum* (1285–91) by Guillaume Durand, bishop of Mende (d. 1296). Liturgical commentaries written in the 14th and 15th centuries are less studied than those of earlier periods. Although the importance of liturgical commentators is increasingly recognized, many treatises, including the *Rationale* of Durand, do not yet exist in critical editions.

Margot Fassler

[See also: AMALARIUS OF METZ; *EXPOSITIO MISSAE;* GUILLAUME DURAND]

Fassler, Margot. *Gothic Song: Victorine Sequences and Augustinian Reform in Twelfth-Century Paris.* Cambridge: Cambridge University Press, 1993, chaps. 2–4.

Kaske, Robert. "Medieval Liturgists." In *Medieval Christian Literary Imagery: A Guide to Interpretation.* Toronto: University of Toronto Press, 1988, pp. 64–70.

Pfaff, Richard W. "The *Abbreviatio Amalarii* of William of Malmesbury." *Recherches de théologie ancienne et médiévale* 57 (1980): 77–113; 58 (1981): 128–71.

Reynolds, Roger E. "Liturgical Scholarship at the Time of the Investiture Controversy: Past Research and Future Opportunities." *Harvard Theological Review* 71 (1978): 109–24.

Schaefer, Mary M. *Twelfth-Century Commentaries on the Mass: Christological and Ecclesiological Dimensions.* Diss. University of Notre Dame, 1983, Ann Arbor: UMI, 1983.

Vogel, Cyrille. *Medieval Liturgy: An Introduction to the Sources*, rev. and trans. William G. Storey and Niels Krogh Rasmussen. Washington, D.C.: Pastoral, 1986.

LITURGICAL DRAMA. From the beginning, the liturgy of the medieval church had many dramatic characteristics, but ceremonies that might be called dramas in their own right developed only in the 10th century. One of the first steps in this development was the insertion of tropes into the liturgy. These were short chanted texts that sometimes took the form of dialogues. The Easter trope *Quem quaeritis* represented the dialogue between an angel and the three Marys at the tomb of Christ; the earliest surviving text (ca. 923–34) is from the monastery of Saint-Martial at Limoges. Though at first the trope was only sung, by the end of the century we find it embedded in a short play, the *Visitatio sepulchri*, in which the events of Easter morning were acted out. Some versions of the Easter play include a scene in which Peter and John race to the tomb. Others add a scene in which the risen Christ appears to his followers. These plays were usually inserted into the liturgy at the end of Matins, and, in keeping with the character of the service, they were sung in Latin.

A similar trope sung during the Christmas liturgy was at first a simple dialogue between the three shepherds and the midwives at the manger. This trope, too, became part of a short play, the *Officium pastorum*, though it was never as widespread as the Easter play. Associated with the feast of Epiphany, the *Officium stellae* reenacted the visit of the Magi to Bethlehem and seems to have had a much wider extension than the shepherds play. Some versions of the Magi play add the character of Herod, a few making him the center of the action. These were also sung in Latin, usually at the end of Matins.

Though works of this kind continued to be performed in churches and monasteries all over Europe throughout the Middle Ages, some dramas of a liturgical nature were played outside the context of the liturgy. The richest collection of these is the so-called Fleury playbook, a 12th- or 13th-century manuscript from the monastery of Fleury near Orléans, today called Saint-Benoît-sur-Loire. Of the ten plays included, four are highly developed versions of the Christmas and Easter plays, in addition to four St. Nicholas plays, a *Conversion of St. Paul*, and a *Raising of Lazarus*. The sophistication of these works suggests that they were conceived as theater independent of ritual, rather than as embellishments of the liturgy.

Alan E. Knight

[See also: *SPONSUS*; THEATER; THEATER, LATIN]

Campbell, Thomas P., and Clifford Davidson, eds. *The Fleury Playbook: Essays and Studies.* Kalamazoo: Medieval Institute, 1985.

Flanigan, C. Clifford. "The Liturgical Drama and Its Tradition: A Review of Scholarship 1965–1975." *Research Opportunities in Renaissance Drama* 18 (1975): 81–102; 19 (1976): 109–36.

Young, Karl. *The Drama of the Medieval Church.* 2 vols. Oxford: Clarendon, 1933.

LITURGICAL LANGUAGES. The most important liturgical language in medieval France was Latin. This was true in the Gallican liturgy of the Merovingian period, and it remained true when the Roman liturgy was imported and adapted by the Carolingians. Ecclesiastical Latin was in many respects different from the language of Cicero and other classical writers, yet the literary culture of ecclesiastical Latin was relatively uniform throughout western Europe, from Ireland, Spain, and northern Africa to Poland and Hungary. Spoken Latin, however, differed in pronunciation and vocabulary under the influence of local vernacular languages. By the late Middle Ages, Latin speakers from different parts of Europe did not always find it easy to understand each other. The diversity of pronunciations survived into the early 20th century, when Pope Pius X mandated the use of the Italianate "Roman" pronunciation in the entire Roman Catholic church.

There must have been a time when Christians in the area we now call France worshiped in Greek, the language of the earliest Christian writers of the area, such as Irenaeus, bishop of Lyon (r. ca. 178–ca. 200), who was born and raised in Asia Minor and educated in Rome. But from the time of Hilary, bishop of Poitiers (r. 353–ca. 367), the Gallican church seems to have been uniformly Latin-speaking, and little trace of its earlier Greek period survives in the liturgical sources. The use of the Greek Kyrie eleison in the Mass, Office, and processional litanies was widespread throughout the East and West; the option of using Greek for the readings and Creed of the Easter Vigil is more likely of Roman origin. In the rite for the dedication of churches, the ceremony in which the bishop wrote the Latin and Greek alphabets on the floor is apparently of Gallican origin.

In the Carolingian period, scholarly interest in Greek led to the limited introduction of new Greek elements into the liturgy. Most notable was the *Missa Graeca*, the Ordinary of the Mass sung in Greek. Greek words were also commonly used in the early tropes and sequences, giving an impression of greater erudition than their authors actually possessed.

Few early-medieval Christians knew Hebrew; most of the Hebrew words that survived in the liturgy came by way of Latin translations of the Bible: *Sabaoth* (in the Sanctus; cf. Isaiah 6:3, Romans 9:29), *Adonai* and *Emmanuel* (in the O antiphons of Advent; cf. Exodus 6:3, Isaiah 7:14), *Alleluia* and *Amen* from the Psalms and other liturgical passages (e.g., Deuteronomy 27:15–26). Some of Jesus's own sayings, preserved in the Gospels in the original Aramaic, were also quoted in the liturgy (notably Matthew 27:46 and Mark 15:34 in the Passion readings, Mark 7:34 at baptism). Only in the high Middle Ages did such theologians as Andrew of Saint-Victor (d. 1175) and Nicolas of Lyra (d. 1340) learn enough Hebrew to study the Bible in the original language, though their work had little impact on the liturgy.

French was little used in the medieval liturgy proper, though vernacular glosses on the psalms and other texts doubtless played a role in the way the liturgy was experienced and understood. On the feast of St. Stephen (December 26), the day of the Christmas Octave devoted to the deacons, it was customary to chant the Epistle of the Mass with farses, or tropes, that paraphrased the Latin text in French. Ecclesiastical condemnations of polyphonic music, most notably the *Docta sanctorum patrum* of Pope John XXII in 1322, may imply that ribald French motets were sometimes sung in liturgical contexts. The most important uses of French, particularly in the later Middle Ages, were in the two areas where laypeople had extensive contact with the liturgy: in preaching, though written sermon texts circulated more often in Latin, and in books of hours and other prayerbooks, in which the public liturgy was adapted for use in private prayer and personal devotion.

Peter Jeffrey

[See also: BOOK OF HOURS; DEDICATION OF THE CHURCH; DIVINE OFFICE; MASS, CHANTS AND TEXTS]

Duffin, Ross W. "National Pronunciations of Latin ca. 1490–1600." *Journal of Musicology* 4 (1985–86): 217–26.

Le Vot, Gérard. "La tradition musicale des épîtres farcies de la Saint-Étienne en langues romanes." *Revue de musicologie* 73 (1987): 61–82.

Liebman, Charles J. *The Old French Psalter Commentary: Contribution to a Critical Study of the Text Attributed to Simon of Tournai.* N.p.: By the author, 1982.

Ottosen, Knud. "Le problématique de l'édition des textes liturgiques latins." In *Classica et mediaevalia Francisco Blatt septuagenario dedicata*, ed. O.S. Due et al. Copenhagen: Gyldendal, 1973, pp. 541–56.

Rézeau, Pierre. *Les prières aux saints en français à la fin du moyen âge.* 2 vols. Geneva: Droz, 1982–83.

Sinclair, Keith Val. *Prières en ancien français.* Hamden: Archon, 1978.

———. *French Devotional Texts of the Middle Ages: A Bibliographic Manuscript Guide.* Westport: Greenwood, 1979; first supplement, 1982; second supplement, 1988.

LITURGICAL YEAR. The Christian liturgical year consists of two interacting cycles. Most feasts of the sanctoral cycle fall upon fixed dates, commemorating either the date of a saint's death (*dies natalis*—the "birthday" into heaven) or the anniversary of some other event, such as the dedication of a church or the reburial (translation) of relics. The more important temporal cycle contains mostly movable feasts, which fall on a different date each year, commemorating events in the life of Jesus or in salvation history. As it was celebrated in the Latin Middle Ages, the temporal cycle can be subdivided into several smaller cycles:

(1) *The Paschal cycle*

a. *Easter, Ascension, Pentecost.* The core of the Paschal cycle is the fifty-day period from Easter Sunday to Pentecost, the only part of the Christian liturgical year that is undeniably descended from a Jewish antecedent—the fifty days from Passover to the Feast of Weeks. Because the Resurrection was also commemorated every Sunday, Christians early felt the need to abandon the linkage between Easter and the Jewish date of Passover, so that the annual feast of the Resurrection could always be celebrated on Sunday. By the 3rd century, those few Christians who still celebrated Easter on the Jewish Passover were ostracized as heretics. Even among the majority, however, there was much disagreement on the question of how to calculate the date of Easter Sunday, and to this day the Eastern Orthodox churches differ with Catholics and Protestants on this issue. The complex astronomical calculations involved constituted the medieval science of *computus*, on which many treatises survive.

By the 5th century, the fortieth of the fifty days, always a Thursday, was being specially marked as the day of Jesus's Ascension or return to Heaven (cf. Acts 1:3), though earlier liturgies did not clearly distinguish the Ascension from the Resurrection.

b. *Lent.* Already by the 4th century in most places, Easter was preceded by a forty-day Lent (Quadragesima), during which new converts (catechumens) were prepared for baptism, Christians under penitential discipline (penitents) were expelled from the church, and Christians in good standing practiced fasting and other penances. Because fasting was not permitted on Sundays, however (and in some places also on Saturdays) the actual method of calculating the forty days varied at different times and in different places. The Gallican rite may perhaps have followed the most common custom of beginning Lent on a Monday; by the Carolingian period, the Frankish kingdom followed the Roman calculation of Lent, beginning on Ash Wednesday.

The Lenten period received much of its structure from the ceremonies that were held for adult converts preparing for baptism on Easter. These included (1) lengthy readings of the Scriptures with sermons expounding their meaning (*apertio aurium*); (2) the teaching of the Lord's Prayer, the Creed, and sometimes other texts that would have to be recited from memory prior to baptism (*traditio symboli*); and (3) prayers and exorcisms to free the converts from the power of evil (*scrutinia*). An early practice that was widely used in the West, including at least parts of France, had three such services on the last three Sundays of Lent, marked by Gospel readings with strong baptismal symbolism: the Samaritan woman at the well (John 4:1–42), the blind man healed by washing in a pool (John 9:1–41), the raising of Lazarus (John 11:1–44). But at Rome, these ceremonies with their Gospel readings and parallel communion antiphons were shunted off to weekdays by the 7th century, to make room for a new organizational principle in which the readings and other liturgical texts focused on the patron saints or relics of the stational church—the building (a different one each day) to which the pope and the Roman populace went in procession to celebrate the eucharist. This reorganized Roman Lent was the one adopted in the Frankish kingdom during the Carolingian period. But because each locality had its own church buildings and its own ancient traditions, the choice of stational churches and processional routes to them obviously had to be determined locally.

c. *Holy Week.* The week leading up to Easter, Holy Week, commemorated in detail the events of Jesus's Passion, death, and burial. The classic medieval shape of this week represents a hybrid of differing Gallican and Roman traditions. In the Gallican rite, as at Jerusalem, the Sunday before Easter was Palm Sunday, commemorating the triumphal entry of Jesus into Jerusalem (Matthew 21:1–17). Holy or Maundy Thursday commemorated the Last Supper with the institution of the eucharist and Jesus's washing of his disciples' feet (John 13:1–20), reenacted in the Mandatum or Maundy. Good Friday was the day of Jesus's death, when Gospel accounts of the Passion were read and relics or images of the Cross were venerated. Holy Satur-

day night was the time of the great vigil service leading up to Easter morning, at which a candle was blessed with a lengthy hymn of praise, twelve readings were heard, the catechumens were finally baptized, and the eucharist was celebrated, all closely following the pattern of the Jerusalem liturgy.

The original Roman tradition, best known from the sermons of Pope Leo the Great (r. 440–61), was more austere. The Sunday before Easter was Passion Sunday; on this day, the Passion readings of the Gospel were begun, and they were continued on Wednesday. Thursday was the day for the reconciliation of penitents who had been expelled from the church at the beginning of Lent. Friday featured the Solemn Intercessions, ten prayers for all members of the church as well as for those outside it. Saturday was the day the catechumens recited the Creed, proving they had memorized it (*redditio symboli*).

With the romanization of the Gallican rite, these two traditions were merged. The Sunday before Easter incorporated both the palm procession and the reading of the first Gospel Passion (Matthew), but the name Passion Sunday was moved back to the Sunday before, creating a season of Passiontide that was more solemn than the earlier part of Lent, marked particularly by the veiling of all religious images until Holy Thursday. The Passions of Mark, Luke, and John were read on Tuesday, Wednesday, and Friday, respectively, while Holy Thursday came to include a Mass for the blessing of chrism to be used at the baptisms on Holy Saturday, the Reconciliation of Penitents, a Mass commemorating the Last Supper, and a foot-washing Maundy. Good Friday combined the Solemn Intercessions with the adoration of the Cross. The Easter vigil, which gradually moved from the evening to the morning of Holy Saturday, absorbed both Roman and non-Roman practices, the latter including the starting of a new fire and an elaborate blessing of a candle. After twelve readings from the Old Testament, the new converts would be baptized, putting on long white robes as they emerged from the water. Before the Gospel, they sang the Alleluia in alternation with the priest, suggesting the new song of Psalms 95 and 97 (English 96 and 98). For the first time, they were permitted to stay past the Offertory and to receive communion.

d. *Easter Week.* In the ancient Roman liturgy, the week following Easter focused on the newly baptized converts, who were called *infantes*, newborns in the faith. They assembled daily for further instruction and did not remove their white robes for eight days until the following Sunday (Low Sunday), when the papal liturgy was celebrated at the church of St. Pancras, a child saint. For this reason, the week after Easter became known as the Easter Octave, and the Sunday after Easter came to be known as *Dominica in albis*, and also *Quasimodo*, from the first word of the introit chant ("Like as newborn babes . . ."). Though baptism of adults became rare in the Middle Ages, the readings, chants, and prayer texts of this week, with their frequent references to the milk and honey of the Promised Land, remained in the medieval liturgy.

e. *Additions to Pentecost.* A vigil similar to the one on Holy Saturday was celebrated the day before Pentecost, providing another opportunity for baptisms and emphasizing that Easter and Pentecost mark the beginning and end of the fifty-day period. The parallel with Easter was expanded when, by the 7th century, the week following Pentecost came to be celebrated as the Octave of Pentecost, a kind of eight-day extension of the feast. In the 9th century, by a further development, the Sunday after Pentecost began to be celebrated as Trinity Sunday. Later, the Thursday after Trinity Sunday became Corpus Christi, promulgated by Pope Urban IV in 1264; it was further expanded with a procession and its own octave in 1318.

(2) The Nativity Cycle

The other half of the temporal cycle revolved around Christmas, the feast of Jesus's birth, December 25. The feast originated in the West, with a variety of factors contributing to the choice of date, and by the late 4th century it was being adopted in the East as well. The corresponding eastern feast, January 6, came to be reinterpreted in a variety of ways—as the feast of Jesus's baptism (at Constantinople) or of his first miracle at Cana (in Egypt)—but in the West it was linked to the visit of the Magi to the infant Jesus. The originally brief period of preparation focused on the Annunciation (Luke 1:26–38), but by the 6th century the celebration of this event had been moved to March 25 (the presumed date of Jesus's conception, nine months before Christmas). In the West, this permitted the development of a more extended preparatory period, Advent, lasting five or even six weeks in a kind of second Lent. With the romanization of the liturgy in the Carolingian period, however, the number of weeks was stabilized at four.

By ancient custom, the days after Christmas were used to celebrate the feasts of important saints whose dates of death were unknown: the first martyrs St. Stephen (December 26) and the Holy Innocents (December 28), and St. John the Beloved Disciple (December 27). Two other feasts commemorated saints known to have died during this period, Pope Sylvester I (December 31), and later St. Thomas Becket (December 29). The eighth day, January 1, was celebrated as the Octave of Christmas, with something of a Marian emphasis, in Rome; but in the Gallican rite, as in the East, it was the feast of the Circumcision and naming of Jesus on the eighth day after his birth (Luke 2:21). In this case, it was the Gallican theme of Circumcision and naming that predominated in the medieval period. By the high Middle Ages, the Christmas Octave had become a period of much revelry among the younger clergy. Ritualized role-reversals were popular, with each rank taking over the liturgy for one day. Thus the feast of St. Stephen, a deacon, belonged to the deacons, and the feast of St. John to the priests. On Holy Innocents' day, the acolytes elected one of their own as Boy Bishop (Episcopellus), who even had the right to mint special coins for the occasion. The nadir of this period was the Feast of Fools or Feast of the Ass (variously celebrated on January 1, 6, or 13), which belonged to the subdeacons. The solemn procession featuring a donkey was among the less offensive customs of this day, which extended even to drunkenness, the singing of lewd songs, cross-dressing, and the theft of eucharistic vessels. The more responsible members of the clergy, constantly looking for ways to rein in such juvenile antics, found an effective tool in liturgical dramas that reenacted stories from the Bible.

The Nativity cycle ended on February 2, the fortieth day after December 25, which commemorated both the Presentation of the Infant Jesus in the Temple and the Purification of the Virgin Mary after childbirth, events that are recorded together in Luke 2:22–38. The custom of distributing blessed candles for the procession on this day led to the popular name Candlemas or *Chandeleur*.

(3) The remainder of the temporal cycle

a. *"Ordinary time."* Early on, a variety of systems were used to designate the Sundays throughout the year (nowadays often called "Ordinary time"), those that fell outside the periods of Advent through Epiphany or Septuagesima through Pentecost. The simplest one prevailed, in which the Sundays were numbered after Epiphany (between two and six, depending on the date of Septuagesima) and after Pentecost (between 24 and 28, depending on the dates of Pentecost and the First Sunday of Advent). In some places, the second period was counted as Sundays after Trinity rather than after Pentecost. The liturgical texts for the last Sunday after Pentecost or Trinity emphasized eschatological themes, as this was regarded as the end of the liturgical year, with Advent marking the beginning of the next year.

b. *Ember days.* The four seasons of the year were marked by *Quatuor Tempora* (the "four times"), whose Latin name was corrupted in the vernaculars to Quatember or Embertide. The Wednesday, Friday, and Saturday in each of these weeks was a fast day, recalling an early Christian practice of fasting every Wednesday and Friday. At an early date, the Friday fast was extended through Saturday, which was marked with a vigil Mass during the night leading to Sunday morning, reminiscent of the vigil Masses of Easter and Pentecost. The sermons of Pope Leo the Great tell us that each Ember week was announced the preceding Sunday, and that the Saturday Mass was always celebrated at St. Peter's. It soon became common to schedule ordinations during these weeks: because the ordaining bishop and the candidates were expected to fast, it was convenient to hold the ceremony during a period when everyone was fasting anyway. The practice of holding ordinations during a Saturday vigil Mass also paralleled the celebration of baptism during the Easter and Pentecost vigils. For centuries, there was disagreement as to exactly when to celebrate the Ember weeks, but by the Carolingian period three of them had become linked to other periods that were characterized by fasting: the first week of Lent (with readings recalling biblical personages who fasted forty days in the desert), the Octave of Pentecost (marking the resumption of fasting after the rejoicing of the fifty-day Paschal period), and the third week of Advent (picking up Annunciation themes left over from the earliest form of this pre-Christmas period). The other Ember Week, following the seventeenth Sunday after Pentecost, fell in September, picking up themes of harvest, the Old Testament Fast of the Seventh Month (Leviticus 23:26–43), and paralleling the fasts observed in the eastern church around the feast of the Holy Cross (September 14).

c. *Rogation days*. In times of plague, earthquake, famine, and other hardships, it was a common Christian practice to hold a penitential procession, complete with the chanting of litanies, repetitive prayers invoking God and the saints. Such processions were sometimes repeated on the anniversary of the original event and thus became annual observances. Two such periods became established in the medieval calendar. The Greater, or Roman, Rogations, held on April 25 (coincidentally the feast of St. Mark), were first celebrated, according to a questionable report by Gregory of Tours, by Pope Gregory the Great when a plague was devastating Rome. The Lesser, or Gallican, Rogations, attributed by most sources to the 5th-century bishop Avitus of Vienne, was authorized by a Council of Arles in 511 and thereafter spread throughout Europe. It was celebrated on the three weekdays before Ascension Thursday, except at Milan, where it was moved to after the Ascension (inspired by Matthew 9:14–15). The liturgical books for these days preserve a great number of processional antiphons and litanies that may be survivals of Gallican chant.

Peter Jeffrey

Alexander, J. Neil, ed. *Time and Community: In Honor of Thomas Julian Talley*. Washington, D.C.: Pastoral, 1990.

Farmer, Sharon. *Communities of Saint Martin: Legend and Ritual in Medieval Tours*. Ithaca: Cornell University Press, 1991.

Fassler, Margot. "The Feast of Fools and *Danielis Ludus*: Popular Tradition in a Medieval Cathedral Play." In *Plainsong in the Age of Polyphony*, ed. Thomas Forrest Kelly. Cambridge: Cambridge University Press, 1992, pp. 65–92.

Grégoire, Réginald. *Manuale di agiologia: introduzione alla letteratura agiografica*. Fabriano: Monastero Santo Silvestro Abate, 1987, pp. 117–43.

Gy, Pierre-Marie. "L'Office du Corpus Christi, œuvre de S. Thomas d'Aquin." In *La liturgie dans l'histoire*. Paris: Saint-Paul/Cerf, 1990, pp. 223–45.

Jeffery, Peter. "Litany." In *Dictionary of the Middle Ages*, ed. Joseph Strayer. New York: Scribner, 1986, Vol. 7, pp. 588–94.

Martimort, Aimé Georges, ed. *The Church at Prayer: An Introduction to the Liturgy*, rev. ed., trans. Matthew J. O'Connell. Collegeville: Liturgical , 1986, Vol. 4: *The Liturgy and Time*.

Nocent, Adrian. *The Liturgical Year*. 4 vols. Collegeville: Liturgical, 1977.

Schmidt, Herman A.P., et al. *Hebdomada sancta*. 2 vols. Rome: Herder, 1956–57.

———. *Introductio in Liturgiam Occidentalem*. Rome: Herder, 1960, pp. 500–685.

Talley, Thomas J. "Constantine and Christmas." In *Gratias Agamus: An Ecumenical Collection of Essays on the Liturgy and its Implications*, ed. Wiebe Vos and Geoffrey Wainwright. Rotterdam: Liturgical Ecumenical Center Trust, 1987, pp. 191–97.

———. "The Origin of the Ember Days: An Inconclusive Postscript." In *Rituels: mélanges offerts à Pierre-Marie Gy, O.P.*, ed. Paul De Clerck and Éric Palazzo. Paris: Cerf, 1990, pp. 465–72.

———. *The Origins of the Liturgical Year*. New York: Pueblo, 1986.

LIVERY, BADGES, AND COLORS. From an early date, the members of royal and noble households were paid a regular allowance, or "livery" (OFr. *livrée*), of food, drink, and clothing. In both France and England, the term "livery" came to be applied especially to the clothing distributed, whether by a lord or by a corporation like a confraternity. By ca. 1300, many confraternities distributed liveries of one or several fixed colors, which constituted a sort of uniform for wear on festive or official occasions, and between 1350 and 1400 this practice spread gradually to royal and noble households in France, England, and adjoining regions. By 1300, many confraternities had also adopted distinctive cognizances, often of a quasiheraldic nature, and some of these, at least, took the form of metallic jewels or brooches similar to those distributed to pilgrims at shrines. Comparable ensigns, called *devises* in French and "badges" in English, were first adopted by kings and princes only in the 1360s and soon distributed by them (and after 1370 by growing numbers of barons) not only to household servants but to various classes of retainer and ally as a mark of political adherence. This development seems to have been inspired largely by the distribution of similar badges to the companions of the monarchical orders of knighthood founded between 1347 and 1360, and, like the knightly badges, those distributed as livery were sometimes accompanied by a short inscription or "motto," also called *devise* in French.

In France, after a period of experimentation under Charles V, a revolutionary system of livery colors and badges was introduced into the royal court of Charles VI in 1362, under which all members of the court were constantly dressed in costumes of particular colors and bearing particular badges and mottoes, chosen by the king and his counselors at some point in every year. Some of these badges, like the white winged stag and the sprig of broom, were used continuously, but many others were employed only for one or two years. This system was continued on a reduced scale under Charles VII, and although it was finally abandoned by Louis VI in 1461, the use of livery badges and colors continued into the next century among the nobles of the kingdom. After ca. 1370, livery badges and colors were commonly worn by soldiers and displayed on the long tapering flags under which they fought, the standard and guidon, and these gradually displaced the armorial banner as the principal form of military flag.

D'A. Jonathan D. Boulton

[See also: MOTTO/*DEVISE*]

Beaune, Colette. "Costume et pouvoir en France à la fin du moyen âge: les devises royales vers 1400." *Revue des sciences humaines* 183 (1981): 125–46.

Pastoureau, Michel. *Traité d'héraldique*. Paris: Picard, 1979.

———. "Aux origines de l'emblème: la crise de l'héraldique européenne aux XVe et XVIe siècles." In *Emblêmes et devises au temps de la Renaissance*. Paris: Touzot, 1981.

LOCHES. Commanding the Roman roads from Tours, Angers, and Orléans, Loches (Indre-et-Loire) was fortified by the 6th century, according to Gregory of Tours. This

Loches (Indre-et-Loire), central keep. *Photograph courtesy of William W. Kibler.*

fortress was destroyed by Pepin the Short in 742 but was soon rebuilt. It came through marriage into the possession of Count Foulques I le Roux (ca. 888–941) and was reinforced by Foulques III Nerra (r. 987–1040) in the 11th century. When their descendant Henry II Plantagenêt became king of England in 1152, he added three large semicircular corner towers to the fortifications. The castle was captured from Richard I the Lionhearted by Philip II Augustus after a year's siege and used as a state prison. In the 15th century, Loches became the official residence of Agnès Sorel (ca. 1422–1450), Charles VII's favorite. The 11th-century tower, a rectangle 82 feet long by 43 feet wide with walls 9 feet thick, is one of the earliest and finest examples of a stone keep; it was here that the chronicler Philippe de Commynes, among many others, was incarcerated. Of the original double curtain walls and broad moat (35–40 feet), only one wall still stands. In the 14th century, the Governor's Tower was built, and the entrance was reinforced with a moat and drawbridge. In the 15th century, the curtain walls were joined to the keep by the Tour Neuve. Like the Tour du Prisonnier at Gisors, it has two stone-vaulted levels and a third, timbered story.

William W. Kibler

[See also: GISORS]

Finó, J.-F. *Forteresses de la France médiévale.* Paris: Picard, 1970, pp. 399–403.

LODÈVE. The former cathedral of Saint-Fulcran in Lodève (Hérault) was dedicated to a bishop who died in 1066. The present building dates from the 13th and 14th centuries, but the presence of Gallo-Roman materials in the substructure attests to its antiquity and to the probability of a Carolingian origin. With a length of 165 feet, the interior includes a nave of three bays with ribbed vaulting, bordered by aisles that join chapels from the 14th and 15th centuries. The choir, the most remarkable feature of this building, forms a large, impressive space composed of two bays and a polygonal chevet in nine sections with an abundance of tall windows. The western façade features a superb Gothic rose window and two turrets displaying corbeling and machicolations. Some 188 feet tall, the enormous belfry has doubled bays, which in the upper story are adorned with statues of SS. Fulcran, George, Flour, and Amans and the bishop of Lodève.

E. Kay Harris

Bonnet, E. "Antiquités et monuments du département de l'Hérault." In *Géographie générale du départment de l'Hérault.* 3 vols. Montpellier: Ricard, 1905.

Rey, Raymond. *L'art gothique du Midi de la France.* Paris, 1934.

———. "Lodève." *Congrès archéologique (Montpellier)* 108 (1950): 247–52.

LOGIC. *See* LIBERAL ARTS

LONGPONT. The ruins of the abbey church of Longpont (Aisne) present the most striking example of Cistercian architectural rigor in a High Gothic style. The abbey, founded in 1132 by Gérard and Agnès de Chérisy, was highly favored by the bishops of Soissons and the other nobility of the region. A first provisional chapel was replaced after 1144 by a new church founded by Count Raoul de Vermandois. (The remains of this structure have been detected in a geomagnetic survey, but the site has never been excavated.) Beginning in the last decade of the 12th century (James) or the first decade of the 13th (Bruzelius), the older structure was replaced by the present church, consecrated in the presence of Blanche of Castile and Louis IX in 1227.

The scale of the 13th-century church reflects the renown and wealth of the abbey. Peter the Chanter retired to Longpont from Paris shortly before his death in 1197, and the tomb of the Blessed Jean de Montmirail attracted numerous pilgrims after his death in 1217. The medieval tombs in the abbey church, recorded by Gagnières, presented an important series of ambitious Gothic sculptural compositions.

Although the church has often been described as an example of the decadence of 13th-century Cistercian architecture, it has been demonstrated that the proportional system is identical to that of the buildings associated with Bernard of Clairvaux in the 12th century, such as Fontenay. This indicates that principles of architectural simplicity in the Cistercian order were based on internal proportions as well as on general austerity. The principle of austerity was

Longpont (Aisne), Notre-Dame, nave ruins. *Photograph: Clarence Ward Collection. Courtesy of Oberlin College.*

affirmed at Longpont by the adoption of simple cylindrical supports, a blind triforium, and a reduced clerestory.

Caroline A. Bruzelius

[See also: CISTERCIAN ART AND ARCHITECTURE; ROYAUMONT]

Bruzelius, Caroline. "Cistercian High Gothic: The Abbey Church of Longpont and the Architecture of the Cistercians in the Early Thirteenth Century." *Analecta cisterciensia* 35 (1979): 3–204.

Héliot, Pierre. "Le chœur gothique de l'abbaye d'Ourscamp et le groupe de Longpont dans l'architecture cistercienne." *Bulletin de la Société Nationale des Antiquaires de France* (1957): 146–62.

James, John. "The Canopy of Paradise." *Studies in Cistercian Art and Architecture* 2 (1984): 115–29.

Lefèvre-Pontalis, Eugène. "L'abbaye de Longpont." *Congrès archéologique* 78 (1911): 410–22.

LORDSHIP. See SEIGNEUR/SEIGNEURIE

LORRAINE. A province on the northeastern frontier of the French kingdom, Lorraine takes its name from the state created in 855 for Lothair, the second son of the emperor of the same name. Lotharingia, as it came to be called by the 10th century, comprised the northern third of the middle kingdom set up in 843 by the Treaty of Verdun, which divided the empire of Charlemagne among his three grandsons. It included the watersheds of the Meuse and the Moselle rivers as well as the bishoprics (reading from north to south) of Cologne, Liège, Cambrai, Verdun, Metz, Toul, Strasbourg, Basel, and Besançon.

This region, the heart of the old Frankish homeland, was a major crossroads for east-west and north-south movement and became a region of conflict between the kingdoms of the West Franks (later France) and the East Franks (later the Holy Roman Empire and Germany). The name Lorraine was, by the 12th century, to be restricted to the southern part of the original realm, centered on the bishoprics of Verdun, Metz, and Toul. At about the same time, the town of Nancy became the chief residence of its rulers and was to remain so until the area was officially joined to France in the 18th century.

Rivalry for this rich and strategic region began with the death of King Lothair, its first ruler, in 869. In 870, the Treaty of Meerssen divided the realm between the dead ruler's uncles, Charles the Bald of France (r. 840–77) and Louis the German (r. 840–76). Both Lorraine and the empire were briefly and ingloriously reunited under Charles the Fat between 884 and 887, after which Lorraine retained its identity, with the whole region falling eventually to the East Frankish ruler Arnulf, who reestablished it as a distinct state for his illegitimate son Zwentibold (r. 895–900).

The 10th century saw Lorraine's magnates grow more independent, and they were able to use their geographical situation to advantage by playing off the eastern and western monarchs against each other. This was made easier as the French Carolingian rulers, losing ground in their own realm to the rival Capetian family, sought to regain authority by taking over Lorraine. Even before Zwentibold's death in 900, Charles the Simple had invaded the kingdom at the invitation of its magnates. Crowned king of Lorraine when its lords refused to accept the election of Conrad I in Germany, he held off the German ruler Henry I until after 922, when the French magnates rose against him and took him prisoner. His rival in France, King Raoul, had to concede Lorraine to Henry with the exception of the bishopric of Besançon, which was definitively separated from Lorraine at this time.

Henry I transformed Lorraine into a duchy, which he granted to Gilbert (Giselbert), count of Hainaut, in 925. But the new duke proved disloyal to Henry's son, the emperor Otto I, and in 939 called in Louis IV of France, only to be killed in battle the same year. Otto was eventually to entrust Lorraine to his own brother Bruno, archbishop of Cologne (r. 954–65). It was Bruno who (ca. 960) divided the duchy into Lower (northern) and Upper (southern) Lorraine. The former was granted to Charles, brother and rival of King Lothair and opponent of Hugh Capet in 987; the latter went to Frederick I, count of Bar.

In spite of many attempts during the 11th century to reunite the two duchies, they remained separate. Lower Lorraine, in the course of the 11th century, was transmogrified into the duchy of Brabant after being ruled by such noteworthy figures as Godefroi II le Barbu (d. 1069) and Godefroi IV de Bouillon (d. 1100), the hero of the First Crusade and the last of his line.

In 1046, Emperor Henry III bestowed Upper Lorraine on Albert (Adalbert) of Alsace, who founded a line that

DUKES OF LORRAINE
(Originally Upper Lorraine)

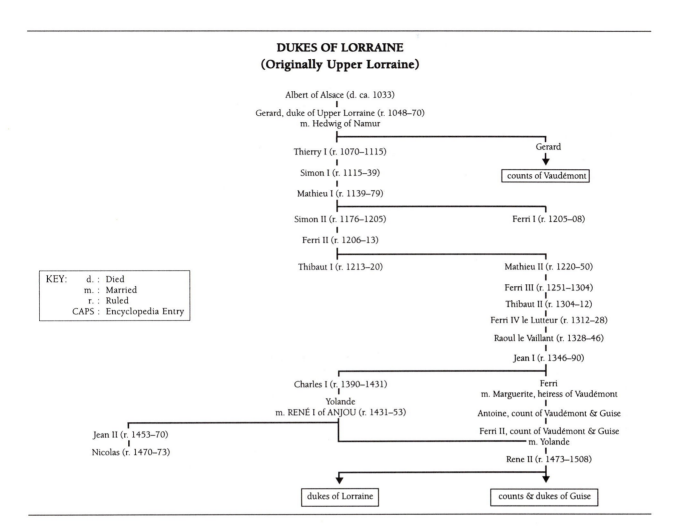

Albert of Alsace (d. ca. 1033)

Gerard, duke of Upper Lorraine (r. 1048–70)
m. Hedwig of Namur

Thierry I (r. 1070–1115)   Gerard

Simon I (r. 1115–39)   counts of Vaudémont

Mathieu I (r. 1139–79)

Simon II (r. 1176–1205)   Ferri I (r. 1205–08)

Ferri II (r. 1206–13)

Thibaut I (r. 1213–20)   Mathieu II (r. 1220–50)

Ferri III (r. 1251–1304)

Thibaut II (r. 1304–12)

Ferri IV le Lutteur (r. 1312–28)

Raoul le Vaillant (r. 1328–46)

Jean I (r. 1346–90)

Charles I (r. 1390–1431)   Ferri
m. Marguerite, heiress of Vaudémont

Yolande
m. RENÉ I of ANJOU (r. 1431–53)   Antoine, count of Vaudémont & Guise

Ferri II, count of Vaudémont & Guise
m. Yolande

Jean II (r. 1453–70)

Nicolas (r. 1470–73)   Rene II (r. 1473–1508)

dukes of Lorraine   counts & dukes of Guise

KEY: d. : Died
        m. : Married
        r. : Ruled
        CAPS : Encyclopedia Entry

ruled in uninterrupted male succession until 1431. Upper Lorraine (henceforth referred to simply as Lorraine) during this time increased its contacts with the French kingdom, with Duke Simon I (r. 1115–39) becoming the vassal of the counts of Champagne for at least part of his lands and with Ferri III (r. 1251–1304) promoting a communal movement by issuing charters modeled on that of Beaumont-en-Argonne. The disintegration of imperial power after the death of Emperor Frederick II (1250) made this movement easier.

In the 14th and 15th centuries, the dukes of Lorraine found themselves confronted with the growing power of the Valois dukes of Burgundy, who had united that duchy to the south of Lorraine with a growing agglomeration of power based on Flanders to their north. The alliance of the Burgundian dukes with the English in the last phase of the Hundred Years' War created in Lorraine the sort of tensions that gave rise to the career of Jeanne d'Arc. In 1431, the year of her execution, Duke Charles II (or I if one does not count the 10th-c. Charles) died with no male heir. This marked the beginning of a disputed succession between the houses of Anjou and Vaudémont. Charles the Bold, duke of Burgundy, and the last of the great independent feudal figures in France, also entered the succession dispute. Having failed to get the emperor Frederick III to recreate a "middle kingdom" in his favor, Charles was killed while attacking Nancy in 1477. The death of the last Angevin claimant, Duke Nicolas, having already taken place in 1473, the house of Vaudémont came to power in the person of Duke René II (r. 1473–1508). He was the ancestor not only of the ducal line until 1738 but also of the house of Guise and of the rulers of Austria after 1780.

R. Thomas McDonald

[See also: BRABANT; CHARLES THE BOLD]

LORRAINE CYCLE. The Lorraine Cycle of chansons de geste consists of four branches preserved in some fifty manuscripts and fragments. The core of the cycle, *Garin le Lorrain* (16,617 lines), was composed in the late 12th century and provides the lineal and thematic superstructure of subsequent poems. Set in the reign of Pepin the Short, the story relates the bitter rivalry between two feudal houses: the worthy Lotharingians (from Lorraine), led by Garin and his brother, Bégon, engage in perpetual struggle with the treacherous Bordelais (from the region of Bordeaux), led by Fromont de Lens and Bernart de Naisil. Succeeding branches prolong the conflict, extending the feud to the children of Garin and Bégon as well as their children's children. Throughout the remarkably lengthy and brutal war, which appears to have no basis in historical fact, Pepin emerges as a weak and avaricious ruler whose efforts often lead to further strife.

Nineteen surviving manuscripts attest to the success of *Garin le Lorrain* in the Middle Ages. Several manuscripts attribute the poem's composition to a certain Jehan de Flagy, who is now believed to have reworked earlier versions. The first 1,000 lines of *Garin* relate the exploits of Duke Hervis de Metz, father of Garin and Bégon and champion of Charles Martel. The greater portion of the text, however, is devoted to the Lorraine-Bordelais feud, which culminates in the deaths of Garin and Bégon. Generally faithful to the early epic tradition, *Garin le Lorrain* is distinguished by its extraordinary geographical precision.

The first continuation, *Gerbert de Metz* (14,795 lines early 13th c.), is never separated from *Garin* in the nineteen extant manuscripts. Here, a new generation of Lotharingians and Bordelais wages war with increasing ferocity. Garin's son Gerbert initially sets out to avenge his father's death with the help of his cousins Hernaut and Gerin, but the mighty feud degenerates into savagery, as Lotharingians and Bordelais alike engage in acts of barbarity, including mutilation, disinterment, and the murder of children. The poem concludes with the death of the Bordelais Fromondin.

The sequel to *Gerbert* comes down to us in two versions, *Anseïs de Metz* (14,597 lines; 13th–14th c., four manuscripts) and *Yon, ou La vengeance Fromondin* (6,672 lines; 13th c.; one manuscript). *Yon*, the earlier of the two, is noted for its incorporation of events and characters from *Raoul de Cambrai*. Both *Yon* and *Anseïs* relate the acts of retaliation that follow Fromondin's death as well as the murder of Gerbert de Metz. Whereas *Yon* ends with Gerbert's demise, *Anseïs* narrates at length the wars of vengeance conducted by Gerbert's son and his allies.

One branch continues the cycle in reverse chronological order by recounting the early exploits of the Lotharingians' illustrious ancestor. *Hervis de Metz* (10,521 lines; three manuscripts), composed after *Gerbert* and probably before its sequels, portrays the father of Garin and Bégon as the son of a noblewoman and her bourgeois husband. Before establishing his status as duke of Metz and Lorraine, the young Hervis passes through a series of romance like adventures, including the purchase and wedding of a beautiful slave who is in reality the Tyrian princess Biatris. *Hervis* is the only poem in the cycle that does not pertain directly to the Lotharingian-Bordelais feud.

The enduring success of the Lorraine Cycle is indicated by the survival of three prose redactions, including the early 16th-century reworking by Philippe de Vigneulles. Fragments in Middle Dutch demonstrate that the cycle was also known in the Low Countries.

Catherine M. Jones

[**See also:** CHANSON DE GESTE; *RAOUL DE CAMBRAI*]

Green, Herman J., ed. *Anseïs de Mes*. Paris: Presses Modernes, 1939.

Herbin, Jean-Charles, ed. *Hervis de Mes*. Geneva: Droz, 1992.

Mitchneck, Simon R., ed. *Yon or La venjance Fromondin*. New York: Institute of French Studies, 1935.

Taylor, Pauline, ed. *Gerbert de Mez*. Namur: Nauwelaerts, 1952.

Vallerie, Josephine E., ed. *Garin le Loheren*. New York: Edwards, 1947.

Gittleman, Anne Iker. *Le style épique dans Garin le Loherain*. Geneva: Droz, 1967.

Guidot, Bernard. "Continuité et rupture: l'univers épique de *Garin le Lorrain* et *Gerbert*." *Olifant* 13 (1988): 123–40.

Jones, Catherine M. *The Noble Merchant: Problems of Genre and Lineage in Hervis de Mes*. Chapel Hill: University of North Carolina Press, 1993.

Suard, François, ed. *La Geste des Lorrains*. Littérales 10. Paris: Université de Paris X, 1992.

Zezula, Jindrich. "L'élément historique et la datation d'*Anseïs de Mes* (Ms. *N*)." *Romania* 97 (1976): 1–22.

LOTHAIR I (795–855). King of Lotharingia and emperor. The eldest son of Emperor Louis the Pious (778–840) and Irmengarde, Lothair I is remembered chiefly for his role in dismembering the empire constructed by Charlemagne. In 817, Louis the Pious sought to ensure the empire's unity after his death by promulgating the *Ordinatio imperii*. This divided the Carolingian territories into kingdoms for Lothair I and his brothers, Pepin of Aquitaine (800–838) and Louis the German (804–876), while leaving Italy under their father's nephew, Bernard. Lothair, who was made co-emperor, was granted the largest, central realm, including Aix-la-Chapelle and Rome. After his father's death, he was to exercise supremacy over his brothers and Bernard.

Difficulties emerged in 817 with the revolt of Bernard, who died after being blinded as punishment. Italy was transferred to Lothair. In 823, the birth of another son, Charles the Bald, to Louis the Pious (by his second wife, Judith) forced the emperor to modify his plans for the inheritance by allotting to Charles lands earlier assigned to his half-brothers. Lothair revolted in 830, and again in 833 with the help of his brothers Louis the German and Pepin. While their father emerged victorious and in 834 confined Lothair to Italy, the remaining years of Louis's reign saw continued political unrest.

Upon Louis's death in 840, Lothair I proclaimed again the *Ordinatio imperii* and turned against his surviving brothers, Louis the German and Charles. The power struggle among those rulers led to the Treaty of Verdun (843), dividing the Carolingian territories into separate kingdoms for Louis, Charles, and Lothair. This testified to the end of the ideal of a united empire, though Lothair retained the imperial title.

Lothair was in conflict with one or both brothers most of the rest of his life. Upon his death in 855, his lands were divided among his sons, Louis II (d. 875), Lothair II (d. 869), and Charles of Provence (d. 863). Louis II alone was left the imperial crown, which he had received in 850.

Celia Chazelle

[See also: CHARLES II THE BALD; LOUIS I THE PIOUS]

Ganshof, François L. *The Carolingians and the Frankish Monarchy: Studies in Carolingian History,* trans. Janet Sondheimer. London: Longman, 1971, pp. 289–302.

McKitterick, Rosamond. *The Frankish Kingdoms Under the Carolingians, 751–987.* London: Longman, 1983.

Nelson, Janet L. *Charles the Bald.* London: Longman, 1992.

Riché, Pierre. *The Carolingians: A Family Who Forged Europe,* trans. Michael I. Allen. Philadelphia: University of Pennsylvania Press, 1993.

LOTHAIR I (941–986). The last significant Carolingian king, Lothair I was the son of Louis IV and Gerberge, sister of the emperor Otto I. He succeeded his father in 954 with the support of Hugues le Grand, who dominated the scene until his death in 956. Hugues's place was taken by Archbishop Bruno of Cologne, Lothair's maternal uncle, who kept a balance between the young king and his first cousin and greatest potential rival, Hugh Capet, the son of Hugues le Grand. From Bruno's death (965) until that of Otto I (973), Lothair kept close ties to the German court.

The rest of his reign was occupied principally in attempts to gain control of Lorraine at the expense of Otto's successors. This policy was opposed by Archbishop Adalbero of Reims and his factotum Gerbert of Aurillac (later Pope Sylvester II), and they looked to Hugh Capet, Lothair's most powerful vassal, for support.

Lothair died in the midst of these tensions on March 2, 986, leaving his throne to his young son, Louis V, whom he had taken care to have crowned in 978 during his own lifetime.

R. Thomas McDonald

[See also: GERBERT OF AURILLAC; HUGH CAPET; HUGUES LE GRAND]

Richer. *Histoire de France (888–995),* ed. and trans. Robert Latouche. 2 vols. Paris: Champion, 1930 (Vol. 1); Paris: Les Belles Lettres, 1937 (Vol. 2).

Halphen, Louis, and Ferdinand Lot. *Recueil des actes de Lothaire et de Louis V.* Paris: Imprimerie Nationale, 1908.

Lot, Ferdinand. *Les derniers carolingiens: Lothaire, Louis V, Charles de Lorraine (954–991).* Paris: Bouillon, 1891.

LOUIS, COUNTS OF FLANDERS. Louis I de Nevers (r. 1322–46), also known as Louis de Crécy, showed himself a loyal French vassal through a turbulent reign, when the powerful Flemish cities generally opposed him. His clumsiness in limiting the privileges of Bruges at Sluis ignited the rebellion of maritime Flanders in 1323, which most of the county except Ghent joined at some point. Only with the help of King Philip VI was Louis able to end the rebellion in 1328. As tensions heightened between France and England in the mid-1330s, the English used a wool embargo to try to force a change of position on Louis de Nevers. The cities were caught between their count's French allegiance and their need for the wool. After Jacques van

Artevelde took power in Ghent in January 1338, Louis de Nevers fled to the French court. Except for two brief periods, he remained away from Flanders until his death at the Battle of Crécy in 1346.

Louis II de Male (1330–1384) was the son and successor of Louis de Nevers and last count of the house of Dampierre. In 1347, the year after his accession, he married Marguerite, daughter of Jean III, duke of Brabant, and by 1349 had ended the rebellion of Ghent. The disputed succession of his father-in-law in Brabant after 1355 involved Louis in a costly war. His fiscal demands placed serious burdens on the cities. To protest Louis's inability to control piracy, the German Hanseatic League, which controlled much of Flanders's foreign supply, blockaded Flanders, and Louis had to agree to the Germans' demands in 1360.

Forced by the strength of representative institutions in Flanders to consult with the cities before levying taxes, Louis had recourse to ruinous devaluations of the coinage, contributing to rampant inflation. A talented administrator who strengthened and professionalized the central court, he confirmed the privileges of numerous small towns throughout Flanders, particularly their right to make textiles that did not imitate those of the great cities, and gave charters to foreign merchants allowing them to maintain resident colonies at Bruges. He favored Bruges over Ghent, and when he allowed Bruges to dig a canal that would cut into the Lys River south of Ghent, challenging the latter city's monopoly on shipping from France, Ghent began a civil war that would last until 1385. Louis died on January 30, 1384, and was succeeded by his son-in-law, Philip the Bold, duke of Burgundy, who in fact had been directing policy in Flanders from 1382.

David M. Nicholas

[See also: DAMPIERRE; FLANDERS (genealogical table); PHILIP THE BOLD]

Blockmans, F. and W.P. "Devaluation, Coinage and Seignorage Under Louis de Nevers and Louis de Male, Counts of Flanders, 1330–84." In *Coinage in the Low Countries (880–1500),* ed. Nicholas J. Mayhew. Oxford: B.H.R., 1979, pp. 69–94.

Nicholas, David. *Town and Countryside: Social, Economic, and Political Tensions in Fourteenth-Century Flanders.* Bruges: De Tempel, 1971.

Pirenne, Henri. *Histoire de Belgique.* 4 vols. Brussels: Lamertin, 1908–12, Vols. 1–2.

Vandermaesen, M. "Vlaanderen en Henegouwen onder het Huis van Dampierre, 1244–1384." In *Algemeen Geschiedenis der Nederlanden.* 2nd ed. Haarlem: Fibula-Van Dishoeck, 1982, Vol. 2, pp. 399–44.

LOUIS, DUKE OF GUYENNE (1397–1415). The eighth child of Charles VI and Isabeau of Bavaria, Louis became their eldest surviving son in 1401 and was named duke of Guyenne, the title by which he was generally known though he was also dauphin. He was called upon to play a central role in the government at an early age because of his father's mental illness.

In December 1409, the queen had Louis removed from her guardianship. He was empowered to summon the council and preside over it when the king and queen were absent, but these sessions were bound by restrictions regarding the execution of important decisions. John the Fearless, duke of Burgundy, Louis's father-in-law, was named his guardian at this time. All of John's decisions in this capacity were subject to royal approval. Louis quickly developed a spirit of independence. In 1412, he disregarded Burgundy's advice and guided the drafting of a treaty with the duke of Berry. Early in 1413, Louis finally decided to take action against Burgundy, based on incriminating information he had been promised. To prevent this, Burgundy fostered the Cabochien uprising in Paris. When the Cabochiens fell and Burgundy fled, the duke of Guyenne was determined on revenge, but his anger was diverted when the Armagnac party sought to diminish his influence. To alarm them, Louis commanded Burgundy to return to Paris. The queen considered this a dangerous move and had him countermand the order, but John the Fearless continued toward Paris, withdrawing only when the king himself spoke out against him. A royal campaign against Burgundy in 1414 culminated in a long and unsuccessful siege of Arras. Negotiations with John began, but the king's mental health worsened. Louis prolonged the negotiations for a final treaty, which he imposed on Burgundy's ambassadors in February 1415. They ratified it before receiving contrary orders from their master.

During 1414 and 1415, Guyenne greatly increased the number of his household officers in an attempt to form a political party that would be neither Burgundian nor Armagnac. In April 1415, he sent the princes of the blood away from Paris, and the king named him captain general of all the frontiers to prepare against an English invasion. He could not, however, prevent the fall of Harfleur to the English in September. Neither Louis nor the king was present at the defeat of their army at Agincourt in October. Louis himself died in December without leaving children. The kingdom then became, more than ever, a victim of the struggle between the Burgundians and the Armagnacs.

Richard C. Famiglietti

[See also: ARMAGNACS; CHARLES VI; ISABEAU OF BAVARIA; JOHN THE FEARLESS]

Famiglietti, Richard C. *Royal Intrigue: Crisis at the Court of Charles VI 1392–1420.* New York: AMS, 1986.

Pannier, Léopold. "Les joyaux du duc de Guyenne, recherches sur les goûts artistiques et la vie privée du dauphin Louis, fils de Charles VI." *Revue archéologique* n.s. 26 (1873): 158–70, 209–25, 306–20, 384–95; 27 (1874): 31–42.

LOUIS, DUKE OF ORLÉANS (1372–1407). The second surviving son of Charles V of France and Jeanne de Bourbon, Louis played a role of great importance during the reign of his brother, Charles VI. His assassination in 1407 caused a war that raged through the rest of Charles's reign and had repercussions lasting well beyond.

Louis was called count of Valois as early as 1375–76. In September 1385, he prepared to leave France to marry Marie, the child queen of Hungary, but Sigismund, son of the emperor Charles IV, took her by force for himself. In 1386, Louis received from his brother hereditary title to the duchy of Touraine and the counties of Valois and Beaumont. In the same year, France began negotiations to marry him to Valentina Visconti, daughter of the ruler of Milan, who came to France as his bride in 1389. On June 4, 1392, Charles VI gave Louis the duchy of Orléans in place of Touraine.

Louis's possession of Asti, as part of Valentina's dowry, drew him into Italian politics, but he went to Italy himself only once during his life, in February and March of 1391. A plan in 1393–94 for him to be infeudated by the Avignonese pope Clement VII with the kingdom of Adria, consisting of the papal states in central Italy, came to nothing.

After the onset of Charles VI's schizophrenia, Louis developed a rivalry with their uncle, Philip the Bold, duke of Burgundy, as both struggled to control royal policy. Their conflict escalated to alarming proportions in 1401, and despite an official settlement of their differences by arbiters in January 1402 they continued to outmaneuver one another. In 1403, Louis prepared for a military expedition to Lombardy to resolve a crisis in Milan and perhaps to pave the way for a return to Rome of the Avignonese pope, Benedict XIII, who was to bestow upon him in return, so it was said, the imperial crown. He abandoned the project, however, early in 1404 while with the pope in southern France. After the death of Philip the Bold (April 27, 1404), Louis was more successful in his quest for riches and power. For the fiscal year of October 1404 to October 1405, he received over 400,000 francs from the king. The proclamation of a new tax in 1405 turned the populace against him, and John the Fearless, Philip's son, became his new rival. Louis was able to keep the royal council full of his partisans, and he worked against John's interests on so many fronts that John finally had him assassinated on November 23, 1407. Louis was considered charming, cultivated, and an eloquent orator, but his cleverness was tainted by a selfish unscrupulousness.

Richard C. Famiglietti

[See also: ARMAGNACS; CHARLES VI; JOHN THE FEARLESS; PHILIP THE BOLD]

Circourt, A. de. "Le duc Louis d'Orleans, frère de Charles VI: ses enterprises au dehors du royaume." *Revue des questions historiques* 42 (1887): 5–67; 45 (1889): 70–127; 46 (1890): 91–168.

Coville, Alfred. *Jean Petit: la question du tyrannicide au commencement du XVe siècle.* Paris: Picard, 1932.

Famiglietti, Richard C. *Royal Intrigue: Crisis at the Court of Charles VI 1392–1420.* New York: AMS, 1986.

Jarry, E. *La vie politique de Louis de France, duc d'Orléans.* Paris: Picard, 1889.

LOUIS I THE PIOUS (778–840). King of the Franks and emperor. Louis the Pious, Charlemagne's third son by his second wife, Hildegarde, was named king of Aquitaine at the age of three. In 806, the *Divisio regnorum* arranged for the succession by dividing the empire among Charlemagne's legitimate sons, Charles the Younger (d. 811), Pepin (d. 810), and Louis. No plan was then announced concerning the imperial title bestowed on Charlemagne in 800, but with the deaths of his brothers, Louis became co-emperor in September 813. He inherited the entire empire upon Charlemagne's death in January 814.

In ca. 794, Louis married Irmengarde, who bore him Lothair I (795–855), Pepin of Aquitaine (800–838), and Louis the German (804–876). She died in 818, a year after Louis the Pious had proclaimed the terms of his sons' inheritance in the *Ordinatio imperii*. An effort to ensure the empire's unity after his death, the document provided that while each son would exercise royal authority over a portion of the Carolingian territories Lothair I would receive the most important lands, including Aix-la-Chapelle and Rome, and he was immediately named co-emperor. After his father's death, he would exercise supremacy over his brothers. Bernard, a nephew of Louis the Pious, would retain the throne of Italy given him by Charlemagne, but he, too, would be subject to Lothair.

Tensions among aristocratic groups aroused by Louis's program of ecclesiastical reforms and disaffection with his plans for the succession underlay the political strife that marked the second half of his reign. The first threat to the emperor's authority came in 817 with a revolt by Bernard, who died after being blinded as punishment. Lothair I was then given Italy to rule, and Louis did penance for Bernard's death at Attigny in 822. More significant for the succession, in 823 Louis's second wife, Judith, gave birth to Charles the Bald (d. 877). In provision for Charles's inheritance, lands previously assigned to his three half-brothers were designated for him to rule. This revision to the *Ordinatio imperii*, in addition to tensions among court factions, precipitated rebellions in the early 830s by Lothair I, his supporters, and his brothers. In 833, Louis the Pious was forced from the throne. Although he regained power in 834 and confined his eldest son to Italy, until Louis's death in 840 the empire remained in turmoil. Its unity survived only until the Treaty of Verdun (843) divided it into separate kingdoms for Lothair I, Louis the German, and Charles the Bald.

Louis the Pious deserves a better reputation than he has generally enjoyed, especially for his efforts to maintain the empire's unity. More clearly than Charlemagne, who initially made no provisions for the imperial succession, Louis held a vision of the office of emperor as a permanent institution in the West. Moreover, it was during his reign that there occurred the true flowering of the Carolingian renaissance begun by Charlemagne. Under Louis, monastic reform was extended throughout the realm, artistic production surged in volume and quality, and religious thought reached a new, high level in writings by such churchmen as Rabanus Maurus and Amalarius of Metz.

Celia Chazelle

[See also: AMALARIUS OF METZ; CHARLES II THE BALD; LOTHAIR I; RABANUS MAURUS]

Cabaniss, Allen, trans. *Son of Charlemagne: A Contemporary Life of Louis the Pious.* Syracuse: Syracuse University Press, 1961.

Ganshof, François L. *The Carolingians and the Frankish Monarchy: Studies in Carolingian History,* trans. Janet Sondheimer. London: Longman, 1971, pp. 261–72.

Godman, Peter, and Roger Collins, eds. *Charlemagne's Heir: New Perspectives on the Reign of Louis the Pious (814–840).* Oxford: Clarendon, 1990.

McKitterick, Rosamond. *The Frankish Kingdoms Under the Carolingians, 751–987.* London: Longman, 1983.

Noble, Thomas F.X. "Louis the Pious and His Piety Re-considered." *Revue belge* 58 (1980): 297–316.

Riché, Pierre. *The Carolingians: A Family Who Forged Europe,* trans. Michael I. Allen. Philadelphia: University of Pennsylvania Press, 1993.

LOUIS VI THE FAT (1081–1137). Son of Philip I and Bertha of Holland and king of France from 1108 to 1137, Louis seems known as much for his corpulence as for his limited, though successful, gain of control over his patrimony, the Île-de-France. Inheriting chaotic political and feudal challenges to royal power, Louis overcame the robber barons and the feudatories' conservative defiance of his nascent challenge to their localized authority. After the death of his first wife, Lucienne de Rochefort, Louis wed Adelaide of Savoy in 1115, who bore him his heir, Louis VII, in 1120.

Louis realized the need to establish his own position in the Île before he could extend royal claims beyond what is traditionally, if erroneously, known as the French royal domain. Toward the close of his reign, he intervened with unprecedented success in the south of France. The marriage of his son and heir, the future Louis VII, to Eleanor, daughter of the duke of Aquitaine, was a sign less of the duke's status than of the rising position of the king. Louis's interference in Flanders and Normandy was less blessed.

If Louis's success in extending his power outside the Île-de-France was ambiguous, his reform of the royal administration was not. The struggle to remove major administrative offices from the hands of their hereditary holders was difficult but eventually triumphant. Louis replaced the old administrative hierarchy with new men drawn from the lower nobility and clergy from the domain. Notable among these new administrators was Abbot Suger of Saint-Denis (1081–1151), the first in a line of great statesmen and royal advisers drawn from the ranks of the clergy, a line that ended with Richelieu, Mazarin, and Fleury. Louis was also the first great royal patron of communes, most of them in and surrounding the royal patrimony.

Louis VI, then, consolidated his power within his ancestral homeland and made its administration more amenable to the royal will, thus laying the foundation upon which his successors would build the French monarchy as a dominant power in western European medieval history.

James W. Alexander

[See also: GARLANDE; SUGER]

Suger. *Vie de Louis VI le Gros*, ed. Henri Waquet. Paris: Les Belles Lettres, 1964.

———. *The Deeds of Louis the Fat*, trans. Richard Cusimano and John Moorhead. Washington, D.C.: Catholic University of America Press, 1992.

Bur, Michel. *Suger, abbé de Saint-Denis, régent de France*. Paris: Perrin, 1991.

de Bayac, Jacques Delperrié. *Louis VI: la naissance de la France*. Paris: Lattès, 1983.

Dunbabin, Jean. *France in the Making, 843–1180*. Oxford: Oxford University Press, 1985.

Fawtier, Robert. *The Capetian Kings of France: Monarchy and Nation (987–1328)*, trans. Lionel Butler and R.J. Adam. London: Macmillan, 1960.

Hallam, Elizabeth. *Capetian France, 987–1328*. London: Longman, 1980.

LOUIS VII (1120–1180). King of France. Crowned in 1137, Louis, the son of Louis VI, continued his father's expansion of royal power, extending his authority beyond the Île-de-France. He cleverly utilized marriage alliances and relations with the French church and with the papacy as instruments of royal policy, notably during the second half of his reign.

Louis's reign to ca. 1152 was not auspicious, characterized by blundering relations with important barons and with the church, a failed marriage to Eleanor of Aquitaine, and an inept crusade. Pacaut, the most perceptive historian of his reign, argues that its unhappy first fifteen years were due primarily to the king's youth and lack of training for the kingship, to which he became heir only upon the death of his older brother. Certainly, these years were marked by impetuosity and bad judgment; but Louis grew to his responsibilities and passed the monarchy to his son, Philip II Augustus, with enhanced prestige and power.

That the monarchy survived the first half of the reign indicates some political ability on the part of the king and his advisers; his domain was surrounded by powerful and dangerous neighbors, the most threatening of which was Normandy (by 1154 united with Anjou), the kingdom of England, and the duchy of Aquitaine. Henry II of England, his continental possessions vastly augmented by his marriage to Eleanor of Aquitaine, Louis's first wife, posed a threat, but he was distracted by internal problems and perhaps uninterested in pushing hostilities with Louis, his feudal overlord, to the point of serious conflict.

Pacaut explained that Louis depended upon cooperation with the church, with the nobility, and with the territorial and administrative base of the Île-de-France to maintain, and eventually to enhance, the royal authority. There were faltering beginnings toward converting the rights of the monarch as feudal overlord to the rights of the king as sovereign, from the powers of the king as a private source of authority to the king as a public authority figure. At the close of his reign, the court was dominated by the relatives of his third wife, Adèle (his second wife, Constance of Castile, had died in childbirth), the counts of Champagne and their entourage. His son by Adèle, Philip II Augustus, associated in the rule of France

in 1179, here began his political experience. The king-designate was now introduced to his need to grow in cunning and in manipulation of family relationships in order to enhance the royal authority. Louis VII was not a great king, but he was a successful one.

James W. Alexander

[See also: ADÈLE OF CHAMPAGNE; CONSTANCE OF CASTILE; ELEANOR OF AQUITAINE; HENRY II]

Bur, Michel. *Suger, abbé de Saint-Denis, régent de France*. Paris: Perrin, 1991.

Dunbabin, Jean. *France in the Making, 843–1180*. Oxford: Oxford University Press, 1985.

Fawtier, Robert. *The Capetian Kings of France: Monarchy and Nation (987–1328)*, trans. Lionel Butler and R.J. Adam. London: Macmillan, 1960.

Hallam, Elizabeth. *Capetian France, 987–1328*. London: Longman, 1980.

Pacaut, Marcel. *Louis VII et son royaume*. Paris: SEVPEN, 1964.

Petit-Dutaillis, Charles. *The Feudal Monarchy in France and England from the Tenth to the Thirteenth Century*, trans. E.D. Hunt. New York: Harper and Row, 1964.

LOUIS VIII (1187–1226). King of France from 1223 until 1226, son of Philip II Augustus, and father of Louis IX. Though a sickly child, nearly dying in 1191, Louis became an ambitious and able soldier, who energetically assisted his father in military activities. (For his prowess, Louis was described by Nicolas de Brai as Louis the Lion.) In 1212, he seized the towns of Aire and Saint-Omer from the rebellious count of Flanders, Ferrand, and in 1215–16 he gathered a large army for an expedition against England.

In 1224, after becoming king, he invaded and took Poitou from the English, and the following year he tried unsuccessfully to conquer Gascony. Perhaps his greatest military victory was against the Albigensian heretics in Languedoc. Beginning in 1218–19, when still prince, Louis continued to fight against the Albigensians as king; in 1226, with papal and comital support, he attacked Languedoc, conquered Avignon, and forced the rest of the south to submit to his rule. He died soon after, on November 8, 1226, leaving the throne to the child Louis IX under the regency of his mother, Blanche of Castile.

Kelly DeVries

[See also: ALBIGENSIAN CRUSADE; BLANCHE OF CASTILE]

Choffel, Jacques. *Louis VIII le Lion*. Paris: Fayard, 1983.

Fawtier, Robert. *The Capetian Kings of France: Monarchy and Nation (987–1328)*, trans. Lionel Butler and R.J. Adam. London: Macmillan, 1960.

Hallam, Elizabeth. *Capetian France, 987–1328*. London: Longman, 1980.

Petit-Dutaillis, Charles. *The Feudal Monarchy in France and England from the Tenth to the Thirteenth Century*, trans. E.D. Hunt. New York: Harper and Row, 1964.

LOUIS IX (1214–1270). King of France and saint. The son of Louis VIII, Louis IX came to the throne as a child in 1226. He spent his early years as king under the tutelage of his mother, Blanche of Castile. Many northern barons resented the assignment of the regency to a woman, let alone a foreigner. Others resented the growing authoritarianism of the crown during the preceding fifty years, the reigns of Philip II Augustus and Louis VIII. Many baronial families in the west nursed grievances from the period of the conquest of the Plantagenêt fiefs in the early years of the century. And in the south, local notables remained unreconciled to the French regime established in the wake of the Albigensian Crusade. These resentments periodically broke into rebellion: the late 1220s and early 1230s saw the crown confronting shifting alliances of northern barons (including the count of Brittany, Pierre Mauclerc) in defense of aristocratic interests. In the opening years of the 1240s, nobles and townsmen in the southwest and Languedoc banded together with the support of the Plantagenêt king of England to undo the conquests of the previous half-century. The crown defeated all these movements. The credit for the early successes goes largely to Blanche of Castile, but gradually in the 1230s her son became the effective ruler of the kingdom.

Married in 1234 to Marguerite of Provence, who came to dislike his mother, Louis remained devoted to Blanche and responsive to her political advice. Only in one matter is there evidence of political disagreement between mother and son: Louis's decision in late 1244 to take the crusader's vow. Despite Blanche's objections, Louis fulfilled the vow after almost four years of preparation that included commissioning *enquêteurs*, or special investigators, to identify the perpetrators of injustices in his government. In addition to the goodwill that these investigations produced, the information allowed Louis to improve the machinery of government by retiring or reassigning certain of his administrators. At the same time, he worked hard to encourage national and international support for his venture and to build a port, Aigues-Mortes, in the south of France for the embarkation of his army, estimated at 15,000–25,000 men.

Louis departed for the Seventh Crusade in 1248, leaving his mother as regent; his wife accompanied him on the expedition. After wintering in Cyprus, he began the invasion of Egypt in May 1249. The crusaders captured the coastal city of Damietta, and then, after a considerable respite, they began the invasion of the Egyptian interior late in the year, continuing into the early months of 1250. Daily running up against fiercer opposition, they were decisively defeated in April at Al-Mansura; Louis and the remnants of his army were captured. After difficult negotiations, the king and his men were ransomed, and many, including the king's two surviving brothers, Alphonse of Poitiers and Charles of Anjou, took ship for Europe. The king and a small group of crusaders, spent the next several years in the Christian states of the Holy Land helping to rebuild fortifications and to formulate effective strategies against the enemy.

The queen-mother died in November 1252. Although he learned of her death in the spring of 1253, it was not until a year later that Louis was persuaded by the steady stream of information that reached him from France that conditions there necessitated his return. Landing at Hyères, not far from Marseille, in July 1254, he began immediately to transform the governance of his realm. Convinced that his failure on crusade was the result of his own sinfulness, and translating this conviction into a decision to live up to his notion of the ideal Christian ruler, he set about restraining the excesses of the Inquisition, reintroducing the *enquêteurs*, reforming the administration of the city of Paris, and, most far-reaching, undertaking a thorough overhaul of royal administrators in the provinces. Louis ceaselessly traversed the realm to hear petitions and do justice personally. Traditional institutions of rule, like Parlement, were improved in their organization and were leavened by his commitment to equity. He worked hard, too, to execute a severely restrictive policy toward the Jews that was in part intended to encourage them to convert.

In the late 1260s, Louis committed himself to another crusade. After considerable preparations, he departed in 1270. His wife remained in France. Following a brief stopover in Sardinia, the army, perhaps 5,000–10,000 strong, launched its attack on Tunis. Before the city could be taken—and in the event it never was—the king died (August 25, 1270). He was succeeded by his son, Philip III. As his bones were being transported to their final rest at Saint-Denis, miracles began to be reported. A few years later, the canonization process began in earnest. In 1297, the former king was raised to the catalogue of saints as St. Louis Confessor.

William Chester Jordan

[See also: ALPHONSE OF POITIERS; BLANCHE OF CASTILE; CRUSADES; *ENQUÊTEUR*; JOINVILLE, JEAN DE; MARGUERITE OF PROVENCE]

Jordan, William C. *Louis IX and the Challenge of the Crusade: A Study in Rulership*. Princeton: Princeton University Press, 1979.

Richard, Jean. *Saint Louis: Crusader King of France*, trans. by Jean Birrell. Cambridge: Cambridge University Press, 1992.

Sivéry, Gérard. *Saint Louis et son siècle*. Paris: Tallandier, 1983.

LOUIS X (1289–1316). King of France. Later known as *le Hutin*, the Quarrelsome, Louis was the eldest son of Philip IV the Fair and Jeanne of Champagne and Navarre. Affianced to Jeanne of Burgundy and Artois before 1300, Louis was married to Marguerite of Burgundy, a granddaughter of Louis IX, on September 23, 1305. At his mother's death in 1305, he became count of Champagne and king of Navarre. During Philip's reign, Louis was dominated by his father, and his stature was compromised when the adultery scandal of 1314, shortly before he ascended the throne, resulted in his wife's imprisonment. Louis's desire to secure annulment of his marriage and replace Marguerite with a suitable wife led him to press for the election of a pope to nullify his marriage. Simultaneously, he began wooing Clemence of Hungary. Marguerite's death in April 1315 was suspiciously fortuitous, and Louis married

Clemence on July 31, 1315. Perhaps because of his marital problems, Louis did not begin using the great seal of France until April 1315, and he was not crowned until August 3, four days after his marriage to Clemence.

Like his personal problems, the political difficulties that Louis inherited from his father dominated his brief reign. Confronted by alliances of subjects discontented by the monarchy's financial policies and infringement of traditional rights, Louis issued numerous charters and dispatched reforming officials in an attempt to satisfy the allies' demands. Hostility toward his father's unpopular ministers, especially Enguerran de Marigny, was galvanized by Louis's uncle Charles of Valois and led to Marigny's execution in April 1315. Conflict with Flanders continued; the French army of 1315 came to be known as "the muddy host" because of its ignominious retreat in the face of ruinous storms.

When Louis died on June 5, 1316, Clemence was pregnant. But before dying the king declared the legitimacy of the daughter, Jeanne, whom Marguerite had borne him in 1312. The succession thus remained unclear, since there was no legal bar to Jeanne's accession. Clemence's son, John I, lived for less than a week, and the throne passed to Louis's brother Philip.

Elizabeth A.R. Brown

[See also: CHARLES OF VALOIS; MARIGNY, ENGUERRAN DE; PHILIP IV THE FAIR]

Artonne, André. *Le mouvement de 1314 et les chartes provinciales de 1315*. Paris: Alcan, 1912.
Brown, Elizabeth A.R. *The Monarchy of Capetian France and Royal Ceremonial*. London: Variorum, 1991.
———. "Kings Like Semi-Gods: The Case of Louis X of France." *Majestas* 1 (1993): 5–37.

LOUIS XI (1423–1483). The eldest son of Charles VII, Louis XI was raised in isolation from his father, and their subsequent animosity made Louis XI a political force long before he ascended the throne. Charged with the defense of Languedoc in 1439, he fell under the influence of rebellious nobles and joined the Praguerie. He was soon forgiven, but the continuing animosity between Louis and Charles seems to have increased after the death of Louis's wife, Margaret of Scotland, in 1445 and Louis retired to his apanage of the Dauphiné in 1447. There he began an apprenticeship for the throne by reforming provincial government. A disobedient remarriage to Charlotte of Savoy completed the family breach, and Louis fled the realm in 1456.

Louis began his reign in 1461 by ambitiously seeking to expand his authority both abroad, through the invasion of Catalonia, and at home, with his vengeful dismissal of his father's advisers and foolish rejection of previous allies. He barely survived the subsequent *Guerre du Bien Publique* and the indecisive Battle of Montlhéry in July 1465, but the rest of the reign was marked by a remarkable ability to learn from his mistakes. Henceforth, Louis handled his domestic adversaries by isolating and destroying each in turn and sought international success through diplomacy rather than war.

By judicious gifts and appointments, Louis reconciled himself to his father's advisers, Dunois and Chabannes and such dangerous peers as the duke of Bourbon. He isolated his brother Charles of France by the award of the apanage of Guyenne. Louis supported first the Lancastrians and then the Yorkists to prevent English intervention in France, subsidized Swiss resistance to Burgundy, and supported Angevin ventures in Italy to secure the southwest. The birth of a son in 1470 (the future Charles VIII), the death of his brother Charles in 1472, the destruction of remaining Armagnac strongholds in 1473, the execution of the count of Saint-Pol in 1475—all these combined to secure Louis's domestic authority.

Thereafter, Louis concentrated on Charles the Bold, duke of Burgundy, who, at Péronne in 1468, had humiliated him by extorting a guarantee of the independence of Flanders. Charles's death in 1477 was Louis's greatest stroke of good fortune. The remaining years of the reign were devoted to the acquisition of Burgundian territories. In these same years, Louis's annexation of Anjou and inheritance of Maine and Provence virtually completed the territorial unification of modern France before his death.

Louis's successes came as a fulfillment of his predecessors' policies. Ugly and socially isolated from his peers, Louis's rejection of medieval courtly behavior, dress, and ritual later endeared him to 19th-century romantics but in his own day alienated many whose help he needed. Louis was not some sort of "New Monarch" but rather an idiosyncratic medieval king whose breaches with convention often proved self-defeating and whose greatest successes came through the traditional means of diplomacy and warfare made possible by the military and fiscal reforms of his less colorful father.

Paul D. Solon

[See also: ARISTOCRATIC REVOLT; CHARLES THE BOLD; CHARLOTTE OF SAVOY; CONCORDAT OF AMBOISE]

Bittmann, Karl. *Ludwig XI. und Karl der Kuhne: Die Memoiren des Phillipe des Commynes als historische Quelle*. Göttingen: Vandenhoeck und Ruprecht, 1964.
Champion, Pierre. *Louis XI*. New York: Dodd, Mead, 1929.
Kendall, Paul M. *Louis XI: The Universal Spider*. New York: Norton, 1970.
Lewis, Peter S. *Later Medieval France: The Polity*. New York: St. Martin, 1968.
Tyrell, Joseph M. *Louis XI*. Boston: Twayne, 1980.

LOUVIERS. Called Loveris in the 9th century, Louviers (Eure) became the seat of the dukes of Normandy; in 1197, it was ceded to the archbishopric of Rouen. The church of Notre-Dame, begun in the late 12th or early 13th century, was extensively remodeled in the 15th. The choir with its flat east end, the nave, and side aisles with triforium and clerestory reflect the original design. A second pair of aisles was added in the 15th century, along with the Flamboyant south porch and north tower (unfinished). The exquisite lacework carving of the porch, with its pinnacles and pendant keys, is more reminiscent of goldsmith's work than of

Louviers (Eure), Notre-Dame, south porch. *Photograph: Clarence Ward Collection. Courtesy of Oberlin College.*

sculpture. The late-medieval stone statuary of the interior is also remarkable.

William W. Kibler/William W. Clark

Verdier, François. "L'église paroissiale Notre-Dame de Louviers" and "Le couvent des pénitents de Louviers." *Congrès archéologique (Évrain, Lieuvin, Pays d'Ouche)* 138 (1980): 9–32.

LUÇON. Luçon (Vendée) first appears in the documentary record in the late 830s as a dependency of the abbey of Saint-Philibert of Noirmoutier. By the 11th century, the fortified village included a parish church of Saint-Philibert and, more importantly, a Benedictine abbey of Notre-Dame. Burned by the count of Poitiers in 1068, the abbey was restored between 1091 and 1121. The Romanesque fabric survives in the north transept, but the main body of the church was raised in campaigns of the 13th (transept, beginning of choir), 14th (nave), and late 14th–early 15th (remainder of choir, sacristy) centuries. With the elevation of Luçon to episcopal rank in 1317, Notre-Dame was designated as the cathedral of the see. While the flat east wall of its choir follows the cathedral of Poitiers, the three-story elevation, which includes a dark triforium and capacious tracery windows, adopts the Rayonnant style of architecture of northern France, perhaps in emulation of other southern cathedrals, such as Bayonne or Bordeaux.

Michael T. Davis

Crozet, René. "La cathédrale de Luçon." *Congrès archéologique* 114 (1956): 41–55.

Dillange, Michel. *Vendée romane.* La Pierre-qui-vire: Zodiaque, 1976.

Du Tressay, Georges Alexandre François Marie. *Histoire des moines et des évêques de Luçon.* Paris: Lecoffre, 1869.

Labande, Édmond-René, ed. *Histoire du Poitou, du Limousin et des pays charentais: Vendée, Aunis, Saintonge, Angoumois.* Toulouse: Privat, 1976.

LUITGARD OF AYWIÈRES (Luitgard of Tongres; 1182–1246). Born into a wealthy family, Luitgard entered the monastery of Sainte-Catherine at Saint-Trond at the age of twelve. Twelve years later, she was elected prioress but chose instead to leave for the Cistercian monastery at Aywières. After a long life of exemplary holiness, Luitgard died among her fellow sisters on July 16, 1246. She eventually became the patron saint of Flanders. Several *vitae* of Luitgard exist, the most notable being composed by Thomas de Cantimpré three years after her death. Luitgard's life was filled with an extravagant array of visions and miracles. The visions include highly abstract apparitions of light, concrete personal admonitions by Christ and by angelic messengers, political and ecclesiastical messages (e.g., asking her to fast for seven years because of the Albigensians), and contacts with souls in Purgatory. Among her miracles are such physical phenomena as levitation, profuse sweating and crying, ecstasies, healing with spittle and the laying on of hands, prophecy, and raptures.

Illiterate and unable to speak French, Luitgard nonetheless contributed powerful images to the growing movement of christocentric mysticism: Christ urges her repeatedly to drink directly from his bleeding wound and receives her heart in his own. Luitgard's *vita* offers remarkable insight into the flourishing communities of spiritual women and their mutual influence on each other. Marie d'Oignies, for example, is present at her deathbed and predicts Luitgard's miraculous activities from beyond the grave. A Cistercian nun, Sybille de Gages, composes a poem in her honor; Luitgard's spirit frequently appears to other nuns in visions.

Ulrike Wiethaus

[See also: MARIE D'OIGNIES; WOMEN, RELIGIOUS EXPERIENCE OF]

Thomas de Cantimpré. *Vita Lutgardis,* ed. Pinius. *Acta Sanctorum* (1867) 3.187–209.

———. *The Life of Lutgard of Aywières,* trans. Margot H. King. Saskatoon: Peregrina, 1987.

Deboutte, A. "S. Lutgarde et sa spiritualité." *Collectanea cisterciensa* 44 (1982): 73–87.

Dinzelbacher, Peter. "Das Christusbild der heiligen Luitgard von Tongeren im Rahmen der Passionsmystik und Bildkunst des 12. und 13. Jahrhunderts." *Ons geestelijk erf* 56 (1982): 217–77.

LUPUS OF FERRIÈRES (Servatus Lupus; ca. 805–862). A leading literary figure of the Carolingian renaissance.

Born into a family with strong ecclesiastical ties, Lupus entered the Benedictine monastery of Ferrières in the 820s and was appointed abbot in 841 by Charles the Bald. He studied with Rabanus Maurus at Fulda (ca. 828–36) and soon showed his ability as an author of Latin prose. He was especially known for his correspondence with many important political and ecclesiastical figures, among them Charles the Bald, Einhard, Hincmar of Reims, and Paschasius Radbertus. His letters, collected by his most famous pupil, Heiric of Auxerre, were widely read and copied. The school under Lupus at Ferrières was a center of study and copying of Latin texts, including works of classical antiquity, especially Cicero. Lupus served as an adviser to Charles the Bald, attended over a dozen ecclesiastical synods, and wrote several saints' lives and a treatise in support of the predestinarian views of Gottschalk of Orbais.

E. Ann Matter

[See also: CHARLES II THE BALD; GOTTSCHALK; HINCMAR OF REIMS; PASCHASIUS RADBERTUS; RABANUS MAURUS]

Lupus of Ferrières. *Servati Lupi epistulae*, ed. Peter K. Marshall. Leipzig: Teubner, 1984.

Beeson, Charles H. *Lupus of Ferrières as Scribe and Text Critic: A Study of His Autograph Copy of Cicero's "De oratore."* Cambridge: Mediaeval Academy of America, 1930.

Gariepy, Robert J. *Lupus of Ferrières and the Classics.* Darien: Monographic, 1967.

Levinson, W. "Eine Predigt des Lupus von Fierrières." In *Aus rheinischer und fränkischer Frühzeit.* Düsseldorf: Schwann, 1948.

Regenos, Graydon Wendell. *The Latinity of the Epistolae of Lupus of Ferrières.* Diss. University of Chicago, 1936.

LUSIGNAN. The castle of Lusignan, near Poitiers, which was fortified ca. 950, gave its name to a family whose members were to become kings of Jerusalem, Cyprus, and Lesser Armenia (Cilicia), as well as counts of La Marche and Angoulême. Situated where Poitou, Saintonge, Angoumois, and the Limousin meet, the Lusignan holdings, although nominally subject to the counts of Poitiers (later dukes of Aquitaine), offered the family opportunities to rise to political prominence during the 11th and 12th centuries.

Three sons of Hugues VIII achieved particular importance. In 1180, Gui de Lusignan married the heiress of the the kingdom of Jerusalem, and he ruled that crusader state from 1185 to 1192 despite losing the capital after the disastrous Battle of Hattim in 1187. Richard the Lionhearted, during the Third Crusade, compensated Gui for the loss of Jerusalem by giving him the newly conquered island of Cyprus, to which his brother Amaury succeeded in 1194. The Lusignans retained Cyprus, but the title of king of Jerusalem passed to the Hohenstaufen family between 1205 and 1268 following the marriage of the heiress, Isabelle (Gui's stepdaughter), to the emperor Frederick II.

In France, the third brother, Hugues IX, had become count of La Marche and sought to join it to Angoulême by betrothing his son and heir, Hugues X, to Isabelle, heiress of Angoulême. This plan was disrupted when Hugues's lord, John, king of England and duke of Aquitaine, married Isabelle himself in 1200, triggering the celebrated conflict that culminated in the seizure of John's French fiefs by Philip II Augustus. After John's death in 1216, Hugues finally did marry Isabelle. Their sons, the unpopular half-brothers of Henry III of England, were resented by the English barons, while the refusal of the Lusignans to render homage to Louis IX's brother Alphonse of Poitiers was a source of Anglo-French conflict in Aquitaine until the defeat of Henry III at Taillebourg in 1242. The turbulent Lusignan family finally sold their rights to La Marche and Angoulême to Philip IV in 1303.

Their cousins ruled Cyprus until 1474 and Lesser Armenia until 1375, while regaining the virtually empty title of king of Jerusalem in 1268. Although Acre was lost in 1291 and Armenia conquered by the Mamluks of Egypt in 1375, the Lusignans in Cyprus maintained these titles in the vain hope that the crusading movement would be revived.

R. Thomas McDonald

[See also: ARRAS, JEAN D']

Garaud, Marcel. *Les châtelains de Poitou et l'avènement du régime féodale, XIe et XIIe siècles.* Poitiers: Société des Antiquaires de l'Ouest, 1967.

Iorga, Nicolae. *Brève histoire de la Petite Arménie.* Paris: Gamber, 1930.

Poute de Puybaudet, G. *Étude sur les sires de Lusignan de Hugues Ier à Hugues VIII (Xe siècle–1177).* Positions des thèses. Paris: École des Chartes, 1896.

Runciman, Steven. *A History of the Crusades.* 3 vols. Cambridge: Cambridge University Press, 1951–54.

Setton, Kenneth M., ed. *A History of the Crusades.* 2nd ed. 5 vols. Madison: University of Wisconsin Press, 1969–89.

LUXEMBOURG. The territory of Luxembourg, part of the duchy of Lorraine, became a distinct political entity in 963 under Sigefroid d'Ardenne. It remained in the imperial orbit until the end of the 12th century, almost completely disintegrating during the long rule of Count Henri IV l'Aveugle (r. 1136–96). His daughter, Ermesinde (r. 1196–1247), whose first husband was the count of Bar, was mainly French in culture and outlook. She and her son Henri V (r. 1247–81) did much to restore the integrity of the county of Luxembourg. Henri's two sons, Henri VI and Waleran, lord of Ligny, died at the Battle of Worringen in 1288, contesting Limbourg against the duke of Brabant. Waleran's descendants, the French branch of the family, were counts of Ligny and Saint-Pol. One of them, Waleran III, served as both Constable and Butler of France in the early 15th century under Charles VI. Another, Louis de Luxembourg, was executed for treason by Louis XI in 1475 after serving as constable.

The older branch of the Luxembourgs had a more glorious future. Of Henri VI's sons, Henri VII (d. 1313) was elected emperor in 1308 and Baudouin became archbishop of Trier. In 1309, Henri VII turned Luxembourg over to his son, Jean l'Aveugle (d. 1346), and the next year made him king of Bohemia. Among Jean's children were the emperor Charles IV (r. 1347–78) and a daughter, Bonne, who married the future John II of France. Although she died before she could reign as queen, Bonne was the mother not only of Charles V but also of Louis I of Anjou, John of Berry, and Philip the Bold, duke of Burgundy and founder of the Burgundian state in the Low Countries.

Wenceslas I (1334–1383), the son of Jean l'Aveugle by his second wife, received Luxembourg from Charles IV in 1353. The emperor raised it to the rank of a duchy in 1354, and Jeanne, wife of Wenceslas, inherited Brabant the next year. Subsequently, he ruled as duke of Brabant and Luxembourg until his death without children. Luxembourg then passed successively to his nephews the emperors Wenceslas II and Sigismund, sons of Charles IV. They rarely appeared in Luxembourg and were chronically short of money. As early as 1388, Wenceslas II pawned the duchy to his nephew Jost of Moravia, who turned it over for awhile (1402–07) to Duke Louis of Orléans. A niece of the emperors, Elizabeth of Goerlitz (d. 1451), held the duchy after 1411 amid growing disorder and the counterclaims of her cousin Elizabeth, Sigismund's daughter. She finally sold her rights to the duke of Burgundy, Philip the Good, who took over Luxembourg in 1443, incorporating it into the Burgundian Netherlands.

John Bell Henneman, Jr.

Gade, John A. *Luxemburg in the Middle Ages.* Leiden: Brill, 1951.

Goedert, Joseph. *La formation territoriale du pays de Luxembourg depuis les origines jusqu'au milieu du XVe siècle.* Luxembourg: Imprimerie Central, 1963.

LYON. Situated at the confluence of the Saône and Rhône, Lugdunum was the capital of Celtic Gaul. Julius Caesar's base camp for the conquest, it was made capital of Roman Gaul in 27 B.C. The five great Roman roads across Gaul—toward Aquitaine, the Atlantic, Rome, Arles, and the Rhine—originated from Lugdunum, and the city held the monopoly for the wine trade of the whole province. A powerful mercantile city, Lyon was also one of the earliest Christian centers in Gaul and the site of the martyrdom of many early Christians in A.D. 177. After the Carolingian era, and for most of the Middle Ages, Lyon was ruled by its bishops; bridges were built over the Saône and Rhône. It was attached to the crown early in the 14th century and was declared a commune in 1312. Its location and commercial importance were at the origin of a semiannual fair created in 1419 by the future Charles VII; after 1463, thanks to the patronage of Louis XI, the fairs were held four times annually and Lyon became one of the leading economic centers of France.

Prosperity brought the construction of many churches and abbeys throughout the Middle Ages, of which the most important are the Gothic cathedral of Saint-Jean and the Franciscan church of Saint-Bonaventure. Saint-Jean, site of the two councils of Lyon (1245 and 1274), was begun in 1165 but not completed until the late Middle Ages. The first campaign of construction (1165–ca. 1180) consisted of the lower parts of the aisleless chevet, aisle chapels flanking the choir, and the east walls of the transepts. The lowest section of the apse has an arcade supported by channeled pilasters that recall the decoration of Cluniac Romanesque churches in Burgundy and monuments in Vienne. By the end of the 12th century, the vaults of the chapels and the clerestory of the choir were completed; the vaults of the choir were finished in the 13th century. The choir is three stories—arcade, triforium, and clerestory—and is considerably lower than the nave.

Work progressed slowly through the 13th century on the transepts, the crossing, and the four-bay nave with six-part vaults. Unusual for the 13th century is the alternating articulation of piers relating to the six-part, ribbed vaults, which is reminiscent of Sens cathedral, which was begun in 1140 and mostly completed by 1200. However, treatment of the clerestory windows is similar to that of monuments in the Île-de-France of the 13th century. Flying buttresses animate the exterior of the nave. The transept arms became towers flanking the crossing.

The 14th-century façade with its two towers is Rayonnant in style, with steep gables filled with stone mullions. The ornamental surfaces recall the Rayonnant transepts of Notre-Dame in Paris.

The church of Saint-Bonaventure, dedicated to the saint who died at the Second Council of Lyon (1274), has preserved its primitive Franciscan plan, with its simple architecture and large central area open to preaching.

Whitney S. Stoddard

Aubert, Marcel. "Lyon Cathedral." *Congrès archéologique* (*Lyon et Mâcon*) 98 (1935): 54–90.

Bégule, Lucien. *La cathédrale de Lyon.* Paris: Laurens, n.d.

Histoire de Lyon, des origines à nos jours. 2 vols. Le Coteau: Horvath, 1990, Vol. 1, *Antiquité et Moyen Âge,* ed. André Pelletier and Jacques Rossiaud.

MACHAUT, GUILLAUME DE (ca. 1300–1377). The greatest French poet and composer of the 14th century. Machaut's narrative *dits* set a style in poetry that would predominate in France and England through the 15th century; his lyrics, many set to music, established and popularized the *formes fixes*; his *Messe de Nostre Dame* is the earliest surviving polyphonic setting of all movements of the Mass Ordinary by one composer; his strong interest in manuscript production made him a prime force in creating an awareness of the artist as a professional figure.

Born near Reims, Machaut probably received a university education in Paris. After his studies, he served from ca. 1323 to the late 1330s as personal secretary and clerk to Jean l'Aveugle of Luxembourg, king of Bohemia. In 1333, Jean procured a canonry at Reims for Machaut, whose name appears regularly in the records of Reims after 1340. With Jean's death in 1346 at the Battle of Crécy, Machaut did not lack for patrons. He composed his *Remede de Fortune* for Jean's daughter, Bonne of Luxembourg, who was also the mother of two of his most important patrons, Charles, duke of Normandy (later Charles V), and John, duke of Berry. Machaut praises Charles in his *Voir dit* (1363–65) and probably composed his last major poem, the verse chronicle *Prise d'Alexandrie* (ca. 1369–71), at his instigation. Machaut dedicated his *Fonteinne amoureuse* to the duke of Berry, and one of the most elaborate manuscripts of Machaut's collected works bears the duke's signature. In the early 1350s, Machaut established an important association with Charles the Bad, king of Navarre, whose family had hereditary connections with Champagne and who had married a daughter of Bonne and King John II. Although he apparently continued to cultivate royal patrons, no major works by Machaut are known after the *Prise*, and public records do not speak of him again until his death in April 1377.

Most of Machaut's poetic and musical production can be dated to the period after he settled at Reims in the late 1330s until ca. 1370. He composed some 420 lyric poems, most in the *formes fixes* of *chant royal* (eight extant), ballade (239), rondeau (seventy-seven), virelai (forty), and *lai* (twenty-three). He also wrote twenty-three motets, nine *complaintes*, eight long and four shorter *dits amoureux*, a poem of comfort and counsel (*Confort d'ami*), the *Prise d'Alexandrie,* as well as a *Prologue* that introduced his late complete-works manuscripts. In total, Machaut produced some 60,000 lines of verse. He set about 140 of his lyrics to music, providing polyphonic settings of forty ballades, twenty-one rondeaux, four *lais*, one virelai, and twenty-three motets and monophonic settings for one ballade, sixteen *lais*, thirty virelais, one *complainte*, one *chant royal,* and two miscellaneous lyrics. The manuscripts also include music for his famous *Messe de Nostre Dame* and a textless three-voice hocket.

Machaut's earliest narrative poem, the *Dit du vergier* (late 1330s; 1,293 lines), is an allegorical dream vision in the tradition of the *Roman de la Rose*. It is a first-person account of an encounter with the God of Love, who together with six youths and six maidens appears to the narrator in a grove. In three lengthy speeches, the god discourses on love and promises to help the narrator in his own amours, if he proves worthy.

The *Jugement du roy de Behaigne* (late 1330s; 2,079 lines) narrates a love debate and its resolution by Jean l'Aveugle. The allusions to this poem and the large number of extant manuscripts (twenty) are evidence that this was the most popular of Machaut's works. The question debated is who suffers more, the knight whose lady has taken a new lover or the lady whose beloved has died. Jean decides in favor of the knight, then entertains both parties at his castle of Durbuy for a week. Elements of verisimilitude and the participation of a historical king bring a new air of realism to the *dit amoureux*.

Remede de Fortune (ca. 1340; 4,300 lines) is arguably the best and most influential French love poem of the 14th century. The Lover/Narrator tells of his long but silent love service to his lady. To pass time, he writes poems in the *formes fixes* about his love and circulates them anonymously, until one day a *lai* comes into his lady's hands. When she asks him who had written it, he is unable to speak and retreats in despondency to the Park of Hesdin, where he delivers a lengthy *complainte* against Love and Fortune. In response, Lady Hope appears and tells him that both Fortune and Love had treated him as well as could be expected. Encouraged by Hope, the Lover finally

Guillaume de Machaut composing a lyric, *Remede de Fortune.* BN fr. 1586, fol. 26. *Courtesy of the Bibliothèque Nationale, Paris.*

goes to his Lady's château and declares his love. Although they exchange rings, the Lady, prompted by the need for discretion and secrecy in love, later ignores him, and the poem ends on an ambiguous note. *Remede de Fortune* is an important didactic poem, serving as a manual for courtiers and providing a poetic and musical model for each of the *formes fixes.* Among the last and best of a line of French love poems that integrated lyrics with narrative, it also provided a model for the nonmusical narratives of such poets as Froissart, Granson, and especially Chaucer.

The *Dit du lyon* (2,204 lines), with the action set on April 2, 1342, is sometimes thought to be the original of Chaucer's lost *Book of the Lion.* The narrator comes onto an island, where he encounters a friendly lion; the lion leads him through a wasteland into a grove, where they are received by a noble lady and her retainers. Here, the narrator observes the love experience of the lion, who is harassed by the persecution of hostile beasts whenever his lady takes her gaze from him. The narrator intercedes on behalf of the lion before returning to his manor.

In the *Jugement du roy de Navarre* (1349; 4,212 lines), Machaut returns to the love debate of *Behaigne* and this time pronounces, through the person of Charles the Bad, king of Navarre, in favor of the Lady. Much more than a simple love debate, the poem is a complex commentary on the role of a poet and poetry in society. An important prologue evokes the Black Death.

The *Dit de l'alerion* (1350s; 4,814 lines) is a bird allegory that presents extensive analogies between birds of prey and women, between hawking and *fin'amors.* The Narrator/Lover tells of four raptors he has acquired, loved, and lost: a sparrowhawk, an alerion (a type of large eagle), an eagle, and a gerfalcon. Like the *Remede,* it is a didactic treatise on love; unlike that poem, it incorporates exempla drawn from historical and literary sources to make its points.

The *Fonteinne amoureuse* (1360–62; 2,848 lines) is a dream vision in which Machaut offers advice to his patron, Duke John of Berry. One night, the Narrator overhears a Lover bemoaning the fact he must go into exile (in actuality, John went to England in 1360 as a hostage after the Treaty of Brétigny) and be separated from his Lady. The next day in a garden, the Narrator and the Lover fall asleep

near a fountain and are visited by Venus, who brings the Lady to comfort her suitor and assure him of her fidelity. The two men awaken and return to the castle; several days later, the Lover crosses the sea, but with joy in his heart.

In his last and lengthiest *dit amoureux,* the *Voir dit* (1363–65; 9,009 lines with intercalated prose letters), Machaut gives a pseudoautobiographical account of an affair with a young admirer, Toute-Belle. A sort of epistolary novel in verse, the work is more likely a fiction than an account of a real affair, though many early scholars sought to see in it a *roman à clef.* It is notable for its verisimilitude and for its apparently parodic depiction of *fin'amors.*

The shorter *dits* include the *Dit de la Marguerite,* the *Dit de la Fleur de Lis et de la Marguerite,* the *Dit de la Harpe,* and the *Dit de la Rose.*

In addition to his *dits amoureux,* Machaut composed two other long poems: *Confort d'ami* (1356–57; 4,004 lines) and *Prise d'Alexandrie* (1369–71; 8,886 lines and three prose letters). The *Confort,* incorporating many exempla, was written to console Charles the Bad, who had been taken prisoner by John II in April 1356. The *Prise* is a verse account of the career of Pierre de Lusignan, king of Cyprus, which culminated with the capture of Alexandria in 1365.

Machaut's musical works fall into three genres: motets, settings of fixed-form lyrics, and Mass. Fifteen of Machaut's motets set French texts, six set Latin texts, and two mix French and Latin. The earliest date we have for a work by Machaut is the Latin motet *Bone pastor Guillerme/Bone pastor qui/Bone pastor,* written for the occasion of the election of Guillaume de Trie as archbishop of Reims in 1324. Most of the remaining motets, dated before ca. 1350, celebrate *fin'amors.* The invective against Fortune in Machaut's most popular motet, *Qui es promesses/Ha Fortune/Et non est,* was known to Chaucer. The last three of Machaut's motets appear to relate to political events of the late 1350s. Formally, the motets use isorhythmic designs based on chant tenors and are evenly divided among bipartite designs with diminution and unipartite designs. Three motets are based on secular tenors in virelai or rondeau form, one of which, *Lasse comment oublieray/Se j'aim mon loyal/Pour quoy me bat mes maris,* sets a 13th-century dance song, the complaint of a *malmariée.*

Machaut is unique among 14th-century composers in his cultivation of the difficult *lai* with music. Although most of the musical *lais* are monophonic, their great length, demanding a half-hour or more in performance, requires an attention to formal balance and development unprecedented in medieval music.

The composition of polyphonic songs based on the *formes fixes* of ballade, rondeau, and virelai, began probably in the 1340s. Several experimental early works give the impression that Machaut was decisive in the development of this new musical style. The mature works, with a highly melismatic text carrying voice accompanied by textless tenor and contratenor, remained standard through most of the 15th century. A small core of works, mostly ballades, circulated widely, reaching Languedoc, Italy, and the empire, especially the popular *De petit po, De Fortune me doy plaindre*, and *De toutes fleurs*. The learned enumeration of mythological characters in the *Voir dit* double ballade *Quant Theseus/Ne quier veoir* and the clear musical setting-off of the refrain are characteristics imitated in later 14th-century ballades.

Machaut's Mass, formerly thought to have been composed for the coronation of Charles V at Reims on May 19, 1364, is now considered to have been composed for a foundation made by Guillaume and his brother Jean for services to commemorate their deaths. The Mass appears to have been performed regularly at these services at the cathedral of Reims until after 1411.

Machaut stands at the culmination of a movement in French literature marked by a growing interest in the manuscript presentation of an author's works. Several manuscripts, prepared at various stages of Machaut's career, collect his complete works, carefully organized into sections by genre, most usually retaining the same order from manuscript to manuscript, with new works added at the end of each series. In general, it appears that each genre is arranged in chronological order. Such complete-works manuscripts had an influence on later poets, such as Froissart and Christine de Pizan; the transmission of musical works after Machaut, however, was confined largely to mixed anthologies.

The Machaut manuscripts are often elaborately illuminated, and the series of illustrations for a given narrative poem was in many cases doubtless determined by the author. The several artists who illustrated Machaut's manuscripts include figures known for their work on manuscripts of kings John II and Charles V. Unfortunately, the original owners of these volumes, except for a posthumous collection belonging to the duke of Berry, have not been conclusively identified.

William W. Kibler/Lawrence Earp

[See also: ANAGRAM; BALLADE; *DIT; FORMES FIXES;* ISORHYTHMIC MOTET; *LAI-DESCORT;* MARGIVAL, NICOLE DE; RONDEAU; VERSIFICATION; VIRELAI]

Machaut, Guillaume de. *Œuvres de Guillaume de Machaut*, ed. Ernest Hoepffner. 3 vols. Paris: Didot, 1908–21.

——. *Guillaume de Machaut: poésies lyriques*, ed. Vladimir Chichmaref. 2 vols. Paris: Champion, 1909.

——. *Guillaume de Machaut: Musikalische Werke*, ed. Friedrich Ludwig. 4 vols. Leipzig: Breitkopf and Härtel, 1926–54.

——. *Polyphonic Music of the Fourteenth Century*, ed. Leo Schrade. Monaco: L'Oiseau-Lyre, 1956, Vols. 2–3: *The Works of Guillaume de Machaut*.

——. *Guillaume de Machaut: Le jugement du roy de Behaigne and Remede de Fortune*, ed. and trans. James I. Wimsatt, William W. Kibler, and Rebecca A. Baltzer. Athens: University of Georgia Press, 1988.

——. *The Judgment of the King of Navarre*, ed. and trans. R. Barton Palmer. New York: Garland, 1988.

——. *Le confort d'ami*, ed. and trans. R. Barton Palmer. New York: Garland, 1992.

Avril, François. *Manuscript Painting at the Court of France: The Fourteenth Century*. New York: Braziller, 1978.

Brownlee, Kevin. *Poetic Identity in Guillaume de Machaut*. Madison: University of Wisconsin Press, 1984.

Calin, William. *A Poet at the Fountain: Essays on the Narrative Verse of Guillaume de Machaut*. Lexington: University of Kentucky Press, 1974.

Cerquiglini, Jacqueline. *"Un engin si soutil": Guillaume de Machaut et l'écriture au XIVe siècle*. Paris: Champion, 1985.

Earp, Lawrence. *Guillaume de Machaut: A Guide to Research*. Forthcoming.

Guillaume de Machaut: poète et compositeur. Paris: Klincksieck, 1982.

Huot, Silvia. *From Song to Book: The Poetics of Writing in Old French Lyric and Lyrical Narrative Poetry*. Ithaca: Cornell University Press, 1987.

Imbs, Paul. *Le Voir-dit de Guillaume de Machaut: étude littéraire*. Paris: Klincksieck, 1991.

Leech-Wilkinson, Daniel. *Machaut's Mass: An Introduction*. Oxford: Clarendon, 1990.

Machabey, Armand. *Guillaume de Machaut: La vie et l'œuvre musicale*. 2 vols. Paris: Richard-Masse, 1955.

Poirion, Daniel. *Le poète et le prince: l'évolution du lyrisme courtois de Guillaume de Machaut à Charles d'Orléans*. Paris: Presses Universitaires de France, 1965.

MACROBIUS, INFLUENCE OF. The commentary by the early 5th-century Latin grammarian Macrobius on the *Somnium Scipionis* from Cicero's *De republica* (Book 6) was one of the most pervasive texts for the transmission of Platonist ideas into the Middle Ages. Itself strongly influenced by Plato and Plotinus, Macrobius's text considers the world as three main Ideas: the Good (or the One, *Tagathen*), the Intelligence (*Nous*), and the Soul (*Psyche*). The Soul contains all individual souls, which descend into bodies made of matter (*hyle*), separating themselves from the First Cause and losing memory of their origins. They can return to the Soul only by the exercise of four sorts of Virtues: political, purifying, contemplative, and exemplary.

Christian theology has always been strongly attracted by Platonist views, and a number of heresies have been merely the incorrect weighting of the division between body and soul as good and bad, which Platonism contends. But the Platonism was rarely direct from the source. In the Middle Ages, as especially in the strong Platonism of the 12th-century Chartrians, the ideas came through Chalcidius's translations of parts of the *Timaeus*, from his commentary on it, and from Macrobius's commentary on the *Somnium Scipionis*, Apuleius's *Golden Ass*, and Boethius's *De consolatione Philosophiae*.

Lesley J. Smith

[See also: BOETHIUS, INFLUENCE OF; CHARTRES; PLATO, INFLUENCE OF]

Macrobius. *Commentarii in Somnium Scipionis*, ed. James Willis. Leipzig: Teubner, 1963.
———. *Commentary on the Dream of Scipio*, trans. William Harris Stahl. New York: Columbia University Press, 1952.

MAGIC. The terms *magica* and *ars magica* were used in medieval Europe primarily for operations that explicitly or implicitly invoked the aid of demons. In the late Middle Ages, a second type of magic, "natural magic," came to be recognized, which relied instead on "occult virtues" within nature; these virtues were inherent in certain herbs, gems, animals, or verbal formulae and could be exploited by those who knew the effects they could produce. While these latinized Greek terms were used chiefly by those with formal education, vernacular words, such as *sorcellerie*, partly overlapped with them in their significance, although the vernacular terms usually referred more unambiguously to maleficent forms of magic.

Magical formulae occur in some medieval medical writings. Magic remedies of antiquity were passed down to the Middle Ages in such writings as the *De medicamentis liber* of Marcellus Empiricus of Bordeaux (ca. 400), a collection of medical *experimenta*. The author's epithet derives from his concern not to ground his work in medical theory but merely to list formulae that he or others have found effective. His *materia medica* includes a wide range of objects with occult virtues: herbs, gems (sometimes enhanced with magical characters), and the bodily parts of animals (bat's blood, mouse's brain, wolf's liver). He tells how a person who has gone bald from bewitchment can restore his hair by rubbing the bald spot with rough linen, then applying a compound of ashes from a lizard, purple wool, and paper, mixed with oil, but in this case the affliction is more obviously magical than the cure. Elsewhere, he recommends procedures for transferring disease to animals; a person suffering from toothache, for example, should spit into the mouth of a frog and implore the frog to assume the toothache. Alternatively, a toothache may be cured by reciting the incantation *Argidam, margidam, sturgidam* seven times under a waning moon, on Tuesday and Thursday. Some of his prescriptions involve ritual observances: the goat's blood collected to treat a stone should be collected by naked boys, and the person who kills the goat must be chaste.

While Marcellus's work is only partly magical in character, and of interest mainly for its illustrative value, Marbode of Rennes's *Liber lapidum seu de gemmis* was a specifically magical compilation of considerable importance, which remained for generations an influential source of information on the occult properties of gems. Marbode probably composed the work in the late 11th century, before becoming bishop of Rennes. He wrote in Latin hexameters, intending his work for a small circle of friends. (Further publication would defile the mysteries: *Nam majestatem minuit qui mystica vulgat*.) Marbode admitted that herbs have great power, but the virtues of gems are greater. Some people may question their powers, but only because powerless imitation gems have misled them. The sapphire, for example, preserves a person from fraud, envy, and terror and can release a captive from prison. An amulet made of gagates ("jet") works against dropsy, while fumigation with this stone is effective against both epilepsy and demons. Indeed, gagates can even counteract magical illusions and incantations. Magnetite, which Circe used *in praestigiis magicis*, can be used to test the fidelity of one's wife: place it against her head while she is sleeping, and if she has been chaste she will embrace you, while if she has committed adultery she will tumble from the bed. A burglar can force all occupants from a house by sprinkling burning coals on the floor and then adding crushed magnetite.

Through the 12th century, medieval writers relied heavily on Isidore of Seville's *Etymologiae* for discussion of magic and its various forms: Rabanus Maurus (in his *De magicis artibus*), Hincmar of Reims, John of Salisbury, and others drew from Isidore, and the survey of magic at the end of Hugh of Saint-Victor's *Didascalicon* stands in this tradition of antimagical literature. Hugh says that magic is "false in what it professes, mistress of every iniquity and malice, lying about the truth and truly harming souls, seduces them from divine religion, promoting the worship of demons, encouraging the corruption of morals, and impelling its followers' minds to every crime and wickedness." He then goes on to divide magic into its branches: *mantice* includes necromancy and divination by the four elements, *mathematica* is the use of horoscopes and other divinatory devices, *sortilegium* is casting of lots, *maleficium* uses demonic incantations and ligatures ostensibly for healing, and *praestigium* deceives the senses by demonic art.

Perhaps the most important theorist of magic in medieval France was William of Auvergne, a theologian and then (from 1228 to 1249) bishop of Paris, who discusses magic extensively, especially in *De universo* 2.3.18–25, and *De fide et legibus* 24 and 27. William presents himself as a pioneer in this area, claiming with slight exaggeration that he has found nothing relevant in earlier writers. What surely is true is that he is the first important theorist in the high Middle Ages to articulate a conception of magic allowing for natural as well as demonic forms. He is also important because in his early years he read widely in the writings of the magicians and astrologers themselves and thus had a clear idea what they were attempting to do.

Like other writers, William recognizes that a great deal of magic is demonic. He tells of one necromantic experiment entitled the Major Circle, in which demon kinds from the four cardinal directions come with retinues of horsemen, musicians, jugglers, and so forth. Another such experiment produces a phantom castle. The magicians may claim they are invoking good spirits, but William is convinced that the angels used are fallen ones, demons who live in the sublunary air and in desert regions (to which magicians often have recourse). He tells how magicians have young boys gaze into mirrors or other reflective surfaces, and after conjurations have been recited some such mediums (perhaps as few as one out of ten) will see apparitions. Plato explained this effect in terms of the soul being turned back on itself so that its own power of divination is enhanced, and William conceded that explanations of this sort were possible, yet he inclined to suppose that demons were generally at work in such magic.

William is more original in recognizing a natural magic—"the part of natural science that is called natural magic" (*De universo* 2.3.21) as an alternative to the demonic sort. Natural magic works with materials rare in Europe but common in and around India. Some substances, however, are presumably available domestically. Magicians kill animals when they are in heat, for example, hoping to extract powerful love potions from their bodies. William cites Pliny's example of the fish called *echineis* or *remora* that can cause a ship to cease moving, and he tells how the gem and herb called heliotrope can make a person invisible. He includes under the heading of natural magic what he calls the *sensus naturae*, which corresponds roughly to extrasensory perception (by which a woman can detect her beloved when he is two miles away, or a dog can identify a thief amid a crowd).

William holds that natural magic is in itself harmless; indeed, God should be glorified for such wonders. Yet it can be used for illicit ends, and in early Christianity it was condemned because it seemed to involve the work of gods and thus led people into idolatry. More fundamentally, he holds that many techniques ascribed to natural magic cannot in fact work unless demons intervene: images, characters, and incantations have no effect in themselves, and if they have efficacy it is only as signals to demons. Words can work only by means of their material (air), their form (sound), or their signification, and William discounts all these possible explanations for the natural efficacy of incantations; air, for example, can kill people only if it is infected with venom from toads, dragons, or plague. (He does grant that names of God seem to have exceptional efficacy, although he says the magicians use a corrupt substitute for the Tetragrammaton.)

Furthermore, William disputes many claims about magic and says that if magic were as powerful as some have claimed any magician could hold the world at his mercy. Yet his skepticism is at times tempered by recollection of the wonders natural magic can accomplish. He doubts that mercury is effective against demons and incantations, until he recalls that a crab suspended in the air deters underground moles and that peony expels demons from possessed people.

Yet many of the pretended accomplishments of magic are mere trickery, exemplified by the use of magic candles that can make a house appear to be filled with serpents, and by illusions comparable with fantastic dreams. Demons often use trickery, as well as the occult powers in nature, in aiding magicians; thus, the demonic entourage

produced by "Major Circle" is merely an illusion, seen only by those inside the magic circle, and the horses that appear leave no hoofprints. Practitioners of natural magic sometimes also deceive people with mere illusions.

Thomas Aquinas discussed magic in various places but most importantly in *Summa contra gentiles* 3.101–05. He tells how magicians make use of herbs and other objects, verbal formulae, figures and characters, images, sacrifices, and astrological observations to discover hidden treasure, foretell the future, open doors, become invisible. Yet he believes the means employed are not a sufficient cause for the effects attained, which require the intervention of demons. The magicians are typically criminal persons using these arts to perform such offenses as adultery, theft, and murder. Elsewhere, however, Thomas deals with the occult virtues in nature in a way that is less hostile and examines the ways in which astral influences can underlie such virtues. While he does not speak of the use of these occult virtues as "natural magic," as other writers did, he manifests an interest in such phenomena and a willingness to acknowledge that many extraordinary effects could be accomplished by means within the natural order.

Nicole Oresme's writings on magic illustrate one possible stance that a late-medieval philosopher and scientist might adopt. Oresme wrote about magic in his treatise *De configurationibus qualitatum et motuum*, in a treatise of 1370 devoted chiefly to astrology, and in a series of *Quodlibeta* on the wonders of nature appended to the treatise of 1370.

Much of the effect of magic he attributes to deception and self-delusion. Yet certain types of magic can have real effect: sometimes, it influences the spirits and senses of the beholder but at other times affects external objects directly. It does so by means of virtues inherent in the magicians' herbs, gems, incantations, and other such means. Unlike such writers as Marsilio Ficino, Oresme does not attribute such magical virtues to the accumulated influence of the stars; instead, he attributes them to the "configuration," or physical qualities, of the objects and formulae used. If incantations have real magical effect, it is because the physical quality of the sound, both the words and the melodies, produces these extraordinary results. Unlike Avicenna and Algazel, he did not acknowledge the direct power of mind over matter, but he did acknowledge the indirect power of the mind: the imagination may be so distorted that it affects the body, which in turn has influence on the air and on other bodies around it. The eye in particular serves as a medium for the transmission of corrupt influences from the imagination, and this effect works most powerfully when a physically and mentally corrupt old woman casts an evil eye on the tender body of an infant.

Oresme is generally skeptical about demonic magic, which he calls *nigromantia*. Here, too, deception and self-delusion play an important role. Nigromancers (or necromancers) commonly use impressionable young boys as mediums; they make these boys stare into polished surfaces in hopes that they will see demons, and often the apparitions cause the mediums to go blind. The nigromancers themselves often show facial distortion and mental alienation during their invocations; they prepare themselves with fasting, and they operate by preference at night, thus encouraging disturbance of body and mind and predisposing the imagination toward delusion. Demonic apparitions may also be caused by melancholy. Repeatedly, following his 13th-century predecessor Witelo, Oresme insisted on finding natural rather than demonic explanations for observed wonders, adding in explanation that "it is better to say this than to ascribe [the effect] to demons." He was aware that Alkindi and Algazel denied that any magic was the work of demons, ascribing it instead to a kind of natural radiation, or to the imaginative powers and virtues of the soul. Yet Oresme himself did not take this extreme position. Even if grudgingly, he admitted that certain effects of magic are so unnatural that they can only be the work of malign or benign spirits. Magicians may succeed in invoking demons. They do not coerce demons; if demons come, it is only with God's permission and with the intention of deceiving their invokers. Magicians' incantations may allure or repel demons, as David's playing on the harp relieved Saul by dispelling demons.

Oresme seems to have interviewed some people who claimed to have magical powers. He tells how he received permission to speak with an accused sorceress, whom he found terrified to the point of incoherence. Again, he tells how certain incantations that magicians perform have never succeeded when he was present. And when he argues that no one can meddle in these arts without incurring some evil, he appeals not only to authority and reason but also to experience.

Richard Kieckhefer

[See also: MARBODE OF RENNES; NECROMANCY; ORESME, NICOLE; WILLIAM OF AUVERGNE; WITCHCRAFT]

Marcellus. *De medicamentis liber*, ed. Georg Helmreich. Leipzig: Teubner, 1889.

William of Auvergne. *Guilielmus Alvernus: Opera omnia*. Paris: Andraeas Pralard [?], 1674.

Flint, Valerie I.J. *The Rise of Magic in Early Medieval Europe*. Princeton: Princeton University Press, 1991.

Hansen, Bert. *Nicole Oresme and the Marvels of Nature*. Toronto: Pontifical Institute of Mediaeval Studies, 1985.

Kieckhefer, Richard. *Magic in the Middle Ages*. Cambridge: Cambridge University Press, 1989.

Peters, Edward. *The Magician, the Witch, and the Law*. Philadelphia: University of Pennsylvania Press, 1978.

Riddle, John M. *Marbode of Rennes' (1035-1123) "De lapidibus" Considered as a Medical Treatise, with Text, Commentary and C.W. King's Translation, Together with Text and Translation of Marbode's Minor Works on Stones*. Wiesbaden: Steiner, 1977.

Thorndike, Lynn. *The History of Magic and Experimental Science*. 2 vols. New York: Macmillan and Columbia University Press, 1923-58.

MAGNIFICAT. One of the three New Testament canticles used in the liturgy, the Magnificat (Luke 1:46-55 with closing doxology) is sung at the climax of Vespers accompanied by the censing of the altar and on high feasts by the ringing of bells. The monastic rule of Aurelian of Arles (d. 551) assigned the Magnificat to the morning office, but the Benedictine *Rule* contains the first reference to its definitive place at Vespers in both the monastic and the secular practice of the Middle Ages. The incantation was not originally attached to the Magnificat but to the verse from Psalm 141 ("Let my prayer be set forth in your sight as incense"), which preceded it.

Like the psalms of the Office, the Magnificat is associated with an antiphon. Besides the antiphons whose texts are drawn from the canticle itself, a large number of antiphons are extracted from the Gospel pericope read at the Mass of the day. These antiphons, together with those for the "Benedictus" canticle of Lauds, are identified by the rubric *in evangelio* in medieval antiphoners. Gospel antiphons exist for Christmas, Epiphany, all of the days of Lent and Paschaltide through Pentecost week, the Sundays after Pentecost and the feasts of saints mentioned in the Gospels. Some of the oldest sources (the antiphoners of Compiègne and Hartker) contain antiphons from Jeremiah during the last two weeks of Lent. The antiphons for Advent are more eclectic in their textual sources, concluding with the O antiphons prescribed for the days preceding Christmas Eve. The antiphons for Saturday Vespers during the summer and fall derive from the concurrent Old Testament readings of the Office.

The elaborate tones to which the Magnificat is sung are probably Frankish (or later) creations designed to enhance the solemnity of the canticle. With the same end in view, some cathedral and monastic choirs "triumphed" (from Latin *trium fare* 'to say three times') the Magnificat antiphon: singing it (1) before the Gloria Patri, (2) before the Sicut erat, and (3) at the conclusion of the canticle. The practice could be further amplified by repeating the antiphon or a portion thereof between all the verses of the canticle.

Joseph Dyer

[See also: ANTIPHON; O ANTIPHONS]

Alonzo, Pio. *L'antifonario dell'ufficio romano*. Subiaco: Tipografia dei Monasteri, 1935, pp. 124-55.

Cabrol, Ferdinand, ed. "Cantiques évangeliques." In *Dictionnaire d'archéologie chrétienne et de liturgie*. 15 vols. Paris: Letouzey et Ané, 1907-53, Vol. 2, Part 2, pp. 1994-99.

Mearns, James. *The Canticles of the Christian Church, Eastern and Western, in Early and Medieval Times*. Cambridge: Cambridge University Press, 1914.

O'Carroll, Michael. "Magnificat." In *Theotokos: A Theological Encyclopedia of the Blessed Virgin Mary*. Wilmington: Glazier, 1982.

MAILLART, JEAN (d. 1327). Member of the chancelleries of Philip III and Philip IV the Fair between ca. 1286 and 1316 and canon of Tournai after 1311. Maillart completed his *Roman du comte d'Anjou* in 1316 after working on it for many years. It is preserved in two manuscripts (B.N. fr. 765 and fr. 4531), and the poem comprises 8,156 lines of octosyllabic rhymed couplets in the standard edition. In spite of its title, the romance recounts the tribulations of the count of Anjou's daughter, who is driven from home by his incestuous advances. She works as a seamstress but is eventually wed to the count of Bourges. Yet another folklore motif has her husband's jealous relatives use an intercepted letter to inform him that his wife has given birth to a monster; a second false letter condemns her and her beautiful son to death. Eventually, the truth is revealed and the moral lesson is drawn that virtue and faith in God will triumph over evil. The theme of the incestuous father is also found in *Belle Helaine de Constantinople, Lion de Bourges*, and Philippe de Beaumanoir's *La Manekine*.

William W. Kibler

[See also: BEAUMANOIR, PHILIPPE DE REMI, SIRE DE; *BELLE HELAINE DE CONSTANTINOPLE*; DANCE; *FAUVEL, LIVRES DE*; LATE EPIC; REALISTIC ROMANCES]

Maillart, Jean. *Le roman du comte d'Anjou*, ed. Mario Roques. Paris: Champion, 1931.
Langlois, Charles-Victor. *La vie en France au moyen âge de la fin du XIIe au milieu du XIVe siècle*. Paris: Hachette, 1926–28, Vol. 1: *D'après des romans mondains du temps*, pp. 260–85.

MAIMONIDES, INFLUENCE OF. Moses Maimonides, who was born in Cordova, Spain, in 1135, and died in Cairo, Egypt, in 1204, was the greatest medieval Jewish theologian and one of the most important medieval Aristotelians. The later Latin scholastics called him Rabbi Moyses instead of the *quidam* ("a certain person") that they generally used for contemporaries, thus showing the esteem in which they held his opinions.

With the exception of the Hebrew *Mishneh Torah*, his codification of Jewish law (introduced by a *Sefer ha-madda*, or "Book of Knowledge," which treats important physical and metaphysical topics), Maimonides's works were written in Arabic. He is most famous for the *Dalalat al-Ha'irin* ("Guide to the Perplexed"), known to scholastics as *Dux neutrorum*. Here, Maimonides discusses at length the problem of the relationship of the God of Aristotle and the philosophers to the God of the Old Testament and the relationship of reason to faith. He maintains not only that God's revelation in the Bible and the Averroistic interpretation of Aristotelian thought are compatible but that the Bible already contains in it the germs of natural reason, from which the Greek philosophic tradition develops. The second important point that Maimonides raises is that of "negative theology"; he explains that when God is named or described, these words have only a causal significance, saying nothing about God but only about that which he causes to exist. Both points can be readily found in many Latin scholastics in French schools and universities of the later Middle Ages.

William of Auvergne (ca.1180–1249), who worked along the lines of the Platonizing thought of Augustine, Boethius, and Anselm of Bec, was most interested in the ideas of the newly accessible Muslim and Jewish Aristotelian tradition. His work helped prepare the way for the synthesis of Albert the Great and Thomas Aquinas. He must be credited with introducing Ibn Gabirol (Avicebron) and Maimonides to thinkers in medieval France, although he does not mention Maimonides by name, presumably because he knew him to be Jewish. Vincent de Beauvais (ca.1190–ca.1264) uses the *Dux neutrorum* a number of times in his *Speculum naturale*, particularly for the cosmology of the first chapter of Genesis. Maimonides was read by Alexander of Hales (ca.1185–1245), who quotes him not by name but as *quidam expositor, licet non sanctus*. After 1230, Maimonides is quoted increasingly by name, apparently first by Roland of Cremona, who was trained at Toulouse ca. 1230–34. Aspects of Maimonides's thought were condemned in Giles of Rome's *Errores philosophorum*, but this did not keep Albert the Great and Thomas Aquinas from using his ideas for the development of their philosophical systems. Albert in particular is intent on only using him as a *philosophus*, and he is evidently straining his intentions when he calls Maimonides's system *prophetia naturalis*. It is in the context of the "natural" proofs for God's existence that Thomas Aquinas seems to have been thinking of Maimonides in the formulation of his "third way." Systematic and extensive use was made of Maimonides's *Dux neutrorum*, and especially of the aspects of his "negative theology," by the German theologian and mystic Meister Eckhart (ca.1260–ca.1328), who was often in Paris. At the end of the Middle Ages and in the Renaissance, Maimonides was still being used by such scholars as Giovanni Pico della Mirandola, Michael Servet, and Jean Bodin.

Arjo Vanderjagt

[See also: ALBERT THE GREAT; ALEXANDER OF HALES; ANSELM OF BEC; AQUINAS, THOMAS; ARABIC PHILOSOPHY, INFLUENCE OF; ARISTOTLE, INFLUENCE OF; BIBLE, JEWISH INTERPRETION OF; BOETHIUS, INFLUENCE OF; GILES OF ROME; PHILOSOPHY; VINCENT DE BEAUVAIS; WILLIAM OF AUVERGNE]

Bacher, Wilhelm, Marcus Brann, David Simonsen, and Jacob Guttman, eds. *Moses ben Maimon: Sein Leben, seine Werke und sein Einfluss*. 2 vols. Leipzig: Fock, 1908–14.
Haberman, Jacob. *Maimonides and Aquinas: A Contemporary Appraisal*. New York: KTAV, 1979.
Kraemer, Joel L., ed. *Perspectives on Maimonides: Philosophical and Historical Studies*. Oxford: Oxford University Press, 1991.
Pines, Shlomo, and Yirmiyahu Yovel. *Maimonides and Philosophy: Papers Presented at the Sixth Jerusalem Philosophical Encounter, May 1985*. The Hague: Nijhoff, 1986.

MAINMORTE. When a peasant tenant died without a direct heir living in his house and ready to assume his tenancy and debts, his property was said to have fallen into "dead hands" (*manus mortua*) and thus reverted to his landlord. In most cases, the heirs living away from home or collateral heirs paid a tax in order to assume possession of the deceased's personal and landed possessions: they forfeited the best animal or, more often, negotiated a cash payment. Although *mainmorte*, along with the *taille* and marriage tax, have been traditionally regarded as characteristic of "serfdom," recent French scholarship has considerably downplayed the servile nature of those taxes. *Mainmorte*, in fact, was similar to the feudal relief in that it represented the landlord's consent to an irregular succession.

Mainmorte is mentioned frequently in the 12th century, when landlords attempted to discourage the emigration of their tenants to new lands and into towns. But it was the newly wealthy townsmen who most strongly resented restrictions on the disposition of their property, and perceptive lords invariably abolished or commuted *mainmorte* in the community franchises of the late 12th and 13th centuries. By the 14th century, those still subject to *mainmorte*, mostly residents of small villages or tenants of conservative lords, were stigmatized as being socially inferior.

Theodore Evergates

Evergates, Theodore. *Feudal Society in the Bailliage of Troyes Under the Counts of Champagne, 1152–1284*. Baltimore: Johns Hopkins University Press, 1975.

Jordan, William Chester. *From Servitude to Freedom: Manumission in the Sénonais in the Thirteenth Century*. Philadelphia: University of Pennsylvania Press, 1986.

Petot, Pierre. "L'origine de la mainmorte servile." *Revue historique de droit français et étranger*. 4th ser. 19–20 (1940–41): 275–309.

MANDEVILLE, JEAN DE (d. 1372). Composed at Liège ca. 1357 by an otherwise unidentifiable English knight-voyager, Mandeville's *Voyages d'outre-mer* was the most popular secular book of its day, surviving in over 250 manuscripts and some ninety incunabula, including translations into Latin, English, Danish, Dutch, German, Italian, Spanish, Czech, and Irish. Of the three distinct versions, the earliest was certainly composed in French on the Continent. An "insular" version, done ca. 1390 in England, is a Middle English classic, whose anonymous author is sometimes considered the "father" of English prose. The *Voyages* popularized the newly discovered wonders of the East, including much fabulous material, and gives a lengthy description of the Holy Land. Mandeville compiled the work at third hand from French translations by Jean Le Long of Saint-Omer (d. 1383) of genuine Latin travel accounts from the early 14th century. Le Long's translations of five Latin travel accounts are found together in several manuscripts, of which the best known is the *Livre des merveilles* (B.N. fr. 2810), copied ca. 1400 for the duke of Burgundy. Mandeville also drew liberally from Vincent de Beauvais's *Speculum naturale*, Marco Polo's *Devisement du monde*, Gossuin de Metz's *Image du monde*, and Brunetto Latini.

Though filled with fabulous accounts, the *Voyages* relates in a simple and unselfconscious prose the sum of medieval knowledge of the world. It explains, for example, why the world is round and incorporates many other accurate observations. Through the centuries, it has been alter-

nately praised for its style and richness and damned for absurdities and plagiarism. The author has on occasion been confused with a Liège physician, Jean de Bourgogne, and with the writer and notary Jean d'Outremeuse. Mandeville is also credited with a French prose lapidary found in 15th-century manuscripts and early printed editions.

William W. Kibler

[See also: BRUNETTO LATINI; *IMAGE DU MONDE*; LAPIDARY; MARCO POLO; OUTREMEUSE, JEAN D'; VINCENT DE BEAUVAIS]

Mandeville, Jean de. *Mandeville's Travels, Texts and Translations*, ed. M. Letts. London: Hakluyt Society, 1953. [Edition of B.N. fr. 4515 and the English "Egerton" translation.]

———. *Mandeville's Travels*, ed. Michael C. Seymour. Oxford: Clarendon, 1967. [Edition of the English "Cotton" translation.]

———. *The Metrical Version of Mandeville's Travels*, ed. Michael C. Seymour. London: Early English Text Society, 1973.

———. *The Travels of Sir John Mandeville*, trans. C.W.R.D. Moseley. Harmondsworth: Penguin, 1983. [Modern English translation.]

De Poerck, Guy. "La tradition manuscrite des *Voyages* de Jean de Mandeville." *Romanica gandensia* 4 (1955): 125–58.

Goosse, A. "Les lapidaires attribués à Mandeville." *Dialectes belgo-romans* 17 (1960): 63–112.

MANEGOLD OF LAUTENBACH (ca. 1045?–before 1109). Manegold of Lautenbach enjoyed a long and varied career that earned him a reputation both as a "master of the modern masters" and as a firm defender of the reforming policies of Pope Gregory VII. Originally from Bavaria and known as the *Teutonicorum doctor*, Manegold seems to have established himself, ca. 1060, as a master in Paris, where one of his disciples was William of Champeaux. Like his contemporary Lanfranc, Manegold traveled from place to place earning his livelihood as a teacher; but unlike his contemporaries, he enlisted the talents of his daughters as instructors. From this early period of his career, Manegold produced commentaries on the Psalms and Matthew.

By ca. 1082, he had entered the convent at Lautenbach in the Haut-Rhin (near Guebwiller), where he published ca. 1085 two substantial pamphlets. The *Liber contra Wolfelmum* is a tract on the proper Christian approach to pagan learning and a critique of the support of the emperor Henry IV given by Wolfelm, bishop of Cologne; the *Liber ad Gebehardum* vigorously supports the papal cause in the controversy between emperor and pope. As this region was a stronghold of the emperor, Manegold seems to have found it expedient to absent himself from Alsace for a few years, and we find him at this time in the small Bavarian town of Raitenbuch. By 1094, Manegold had returned to Alsace, where he established, with the patronage of Buchard de Geberschwihr, a house of regular canons in Marbach, south of Colmar. The special privileges accorded Manegold by Pope Urban II did not endear him to the emperor, and in 1098 Henry IV imprisoned him for a time;

but within a few years (ca. 1103) Manegold had once again assumed his post as provost of Marbach, where he seems to have remained until his death.

Mark Zier

[See also: GREGORIAN REFORM; REGULAR CANONS; WILLIAM OF CHAMPEAUX]

Manegold of Lautenbach. *Liber ad Geberhardum*, ed. K. Francke. *MGH, Libelli de lite* I (1891), pp. 308–40.
———. *Liber contra Wulfelmum*, ed. W. Hartmann. *MGH, Quellen zur Geistesgeschichte des Mittelalters* VIII (1972).
Lottin, Odon. "Manegold de Lautenbach, source d'Anselme de Laon." *Recherches de théologie ancienne et médiévale* 14 (1947): 218–23.
Robinson, I.S. "The Bible in the Investiture Contest: The South German Gregorian Circle." In *The Bible in the Medieval World*, ed. Katherine Walsh and Diana Wood. Oxford: Blackwell, 1985.

MANSE. Historians define a manse (Lat. *mansus*), particularly for the early Middle Ages, as a farmstead with house, associated buildings, fields, rights in common and forest, and so on, of sufficient size to support one peasant family, varying in acreage with the productivity of the soil. In the classical definition of the Carolingian manor or villa, this peasant holding is often contrasted to the lord's reserve, the demesne (*mansus indominicatus*), on which peasants from the surrounding manses were expected to labor; in later documents, the old reserve, or demesne, itself appears to have been called a "manse" or "capmanse" perhaps after it had been cut up into peasant-sized holdings. Even for the early period, there are difficulties with such a definition because of the variability of family size and level of subsistence. For instance, if several days of labor services were owed to the lord by a member or several members of such peasant families, they may have been fed by the lord on those days; subsistence may have been possible on some manses only when agriculture was supplemented by the products of forest, river, and sea. Although the family generally appears to have encompassed only two or at most three generations and several servants, there are also occasional indications that brothers may have held manses in common for some periods. Frequently, even in the classic Carolingian villa, manses are found that may have been large enough to support three or four families; however, some of those families may also have had rights in other manses. In the later period, in addition to the manses in compact villages, there were additional isolated manses located in the interstices between villages; these owed no services to a lord on his reserve but were held as allods by free peasants.

Constance H. Berman

MANSION, COLARD (ca. 1425–after 1484). Copyist of manuscripts and bookseller in Bruges. Mansion is first mentioned as a supplier of books to Duke Philip the Good of Burgundy and Louis de Gruuthuse, bibliophile and host to Edward IV during his exile from England. In 1471–73, Mansion was dean of the Guild of St. John, a corporation of booksellers in Bruges, of which he was also a founding member.

Circumstantial evidence strongly suggests that Mansion and William Caxton were for several years partners in a printing press. No other printers of their day were also translators, providing their texts with original prologues and epilogues. There are some technical similarities in their imprints, and they translated and printed some of the same texts.

Mansion's printing of the French version of Boccaccio's *De casibus virorum illustrium* (1476) was illustrated with nine handsome copperplate engravings, the earliest in any book. His imprint of the *Ovide moralisé* (1484) was apparently a financial failure, which caused him to give up printing.

Charity Cannon Willard

[See also: LEFÈVRE, RAOUL]

Michel, H. *L'imprimeur Colard Mansion et le Boccace de la Bibliothèque d'Amiens*. Paris: Société Française de Bibliographie, 1925.
Painter, George D. *William Caxton*. London: Chatto and Windus, 1976.
Sheppard, Leslie A. "A New Light on Caxton and Colard Mansion." *Signature*, n.s. 15 (1952): 25–39.

MANTES. The collegial church of Notre-Dame at Mantes (Yvelines) was founded by the Montmorency family. The present church was begun with the west façade ca. 1165. The plan was dramatically revised 1175–80, when the wall of the second story was reduced by more than half its thickness as a consequence of the incorporation of the flying buttress. That the nave of Notre-Dame in Paris was the source of this feature is confirmed by the interior el-

Mantes (Yvelines), Notre-Dame, north side. *Photograph courtesy of Whitney S. Stoddard.*

evation of Mantes, which clearly shows the Parisian aesthetic. The main part of the work was completed ca. 1200, although the buttress design was revised again, ca. 1225–30. Two of the western portals survive but without their statue columns and, in the case of the center portal (the Coronation of the Virgin), badly mutilated. The north door (the Three Marys at the Tomb and Christ in Majesty) is the earliest; the south door was rebuilt 1285–1325, during which time radiating chapels were added to the original plan. The building underwent two drastic restorations in the 19th century, although much of the original early 13th-century roof structure survives.

William W. Clark

Bailly, Robert. *La collégiale Notre-Dame à Mantes-la-Jolie.* Mantes, 1980.

Bony, Jean. "La collégiale de Mantes." *Congrès archéologique* (*Paris-Mantes*) 104 (1946): 163–220.

———. *Notre-Dame de Mantes.* Paris: Cerf, 1947.

MANUSCRIPTS, HEBREW ILLUMINATED. The fate of the books of the "people of the book" in medieval France was not a happy one. The "burning of the Talmud" in the Place de Grève on June 6, 1242, was a large-scale destruction of Hebrew books of all kinds. Tractates of the Talmud were certainly among the many volumes consigned to the flames, but illuminated manuscripts for public or personal liturgical use were not spared. Thus, though the Jews were avid consumers of books, we are left with only a fragmentary remnant of what is presumed to have existed. The surviving illuminated manuscripts produced by and for Jews indicate the magnitude of the loss of 1242: though relatively few in number, they can rival the best of the productions of the Latin manuscript workshops of the High Gothic. At the same time, such works remind us that the cultural production of medieval French Jewry was rich, almost as if in defiance of the difficulties under which it flourished. They also testify to the pervasiveness of literary culture among the Jews. Books were not restricted to the elite or to synagogue functionaries, as is evinced by the considerably cruder and more provincial manuscripts that have survived.

A variety of books were illuminated: liturgical works, legal codes, miscellaneous volumes, and presumably marriage contracts as well. The Scroll of the Law itself, read in the synagogue, was required by the legal tradition to remain unadorned, but the majority of surviving French illuminated manuscripts are liturgical—festival prayer books and manuals for the home ritual of Passover. In all of these, the pervasive themes of the Jewish tradition, as dictated by those texts, are illustrated in a distinctively French style. Stylistic content reflects the influence on the illuminations of shifting Jewish demography: manuscripts bear evidence of the assimilation of stylistic conventions from northern and northeastern France, England, and the Germanic lands. The figures depicted in some are replete with the courtly contrapposto of certain Paris schools, or with the stylized hair, beards, and drapery typical of the workshop of Master Honoré. Some examples are so fine that researchers have been moved to assert that they were in fact illuminated by Christian artisans, a view that has both its supporters and detractors among prominent scholars in the field.

Initially, the Hebrew manuscripts may seem surprisingly similar in their iconography to Latin manuscripts. The details seem to devolve from a Christian rather than from any distinctively Jewish milieu. We see a bare-headed Moses, a Solomon bedecked in the trappings of a medieval French monarch, an Aaron whose priestly garb is the typical dress of a medieval French Jew, haloed angels. A depiction of the three Hebrews before Nebuchadnezzer and in the fiery furnace is remarkably similar to a scene from the chronicle of the life of St. Denis (Paris, Bibliothèque Sainte Geneviève 782, fol. 129v); the clothing is the typical "biblical" garb in which figures in Latin Bible illustrations appear, and the architecture is Gothic.

These manuscripts, however, are not mere offshoots of or borrowings from the Christian tradition of illumination. The very fact that the clothing of the figures is the typical garb of Latin Bible illumination is unremarkable in a Christian context, but interesting here. That these clothes are based in some cases upon contemporary Jewish dress heightens the association of the viewer with the figures. The Jews were not merely a minority in medieval France. They were a minority viewed with a mixture of fascination and hostility as the remnants of the ancient Jews. They were occasionally despised, sometimes envied, usually misunderstood. In times of active persecution and relative toleration alike, they felt both ambivalence and defiance toward the majority culture. When "read" against the historical background, the iconography of these works reveals the desire to utilize traditional motifs and even motifs from the dominant Christian culture to protest the circumstances in which the artists and their patrons find themselves and to express eschatological hopes, often for triumph over the persecutors.

In the magnificent *Mishneh Torah* in the Kaufmann collection in Budapest (Budapest, Academy of Sciences, Kaufmann A 77/I–IV), illuminated most probably in Lorraine in the late 13th century, motifs familiar from Christian iconography are used by the Jewish artist in relation to the text in ingenious ways. Samson, the Bible's preeminent Nazirite, appears rending the lion in juxtaposition to the Laws of the Nazirite; a depiction of David harping is juxtaposed with the text's description of the instruments used in the Jerusalem Temple. The Sacrifice of Isaac, with the ram substituting for Isaac, appears immediately following the section of the Code dealing with "sacrifices of substitution." Adam and Eve are represented in the section of the book dealing with trusts and deposits, as theirs was the first violation of the law that prohibits the use of an object entrusted for safekeeping. Such "in-jokes" and other scholarly plays indicate that the patron and the illuminator of this manuscript shared the learned culture of northern French Jewry. The unexpected figure of Judah Maccabee in full knightly armor on the folio describing the rabbinic "chain of tradition" may represent a covert reminder to Jews that their ancient heroes were both sages and military leaders—that there was a "knightly virtue" and "courtesy" both in the study of the Torah and in the battle fought in the name of God. Medieval Jews certainly viewed crusaders as "false knights" for the massacres they inflicted upon innocent Jewish communities. Judas Maccabee, here juxtaposed with the "heroes" of rabbinic culture, is the example *par excellence* of the Jewish "true and perfect knight."

A northern French miscellany of the late 13th century, now in the British Library (Add. 11639), has several series of full-page illustrations of biblical themes, some exquisitely drawn and colored. Though the book has been rearranged over time, so that the illuminations now appear random, one series in particular may be "read" as a unit that forms an iconographic parallel to the dynastic-messianic-eschatological-thrust of an *Avodah* (one of the liturgical texts recited on Yom Kippur, the Day of Atonement) written by Yose ben Yose; the text figures prominently in the manuscript. The *Avodah*, which describes the service of the High Priest in the Jerusalem Temple on Yom Kippur, may have had special significance for a priestly patron. A similar theme is to be found in the magnificent Pentateuch now in the Bibliothèque Nationale, illuminated at Poligny ca. 1300 (B.N. Heb. 36, fol. 283v), in which a full-page miniature of a menorah has, intertwined in its branches, depictions of a number of the same themes found in the British Library miscellany. Here, since the design is a sort of "shorthand," the dynastic-messianic-eschatological theme is more explicit.

What is most telling about these manuscripts is not their quality or style, or even their iconography, but the fact that they are effectively the sole relics of medieval Jewish material culture. The marks of use that they bear offer proof that they were handled familiarly and often. In a given manuscript, the dedication inscription may testify that the book was offered as a wedding present from a bride to her groom, a second layer of "testimony" may be the wine stains on the pages containing the liturgy for the Sanctification (*Kiddush*) of the holiday over wine, and a third layer may be the marks and deletions of the censor. These volumes have traveled through both joy and sorrow; they provide an eloquent metaphor for the situation of the Jews as a minority culture in medieval France.

Marc M. Epstein

[See also: CLOTHING, JEWISH; JEWS; MANUSCRIPTS, PRODUCTION AND ILLUMINATION]

Gutmann, Joseph. *Hebrew Manuscript Painting.* New York: Braziller, 1978.
Narkiss, Bezalel. *Hebrew Illuminated Manuscripts.* Jerusalem: Keter, 1969.
Sed-Rajna, Gabrielle. "The Illustrations of the Kaufmann Mishneh Torah." *Journal of Jewish Art* 6 (1979): 64–77.
———. "The Paintings in the London Miscellany." *Journal of Jewish Art* 9 (1982): 18–30.

MANUSCRIPTS, PRODUCTION AND ILLUMINATION. Throughout the Middle Ages in France, various centers were major producers and decorators (illumina-tors) of manuscripts. These were books handwritten on prepared sheep- or calfskins (vellum or parchment). Until the 13th century, manuscripts were usually produced in the scriptoria of monasteries by monks and nuns, frequently copying earlier examples. In the Gothic period, book production increasingly shifted to urban centers, and books were written and decorated by lay scribes and illuminators, sometimes several working together in workshops. By the 15th century, book dealers or publishers might farm out the book to artisans working separately. At the same time, secular texts, often translated into or written in the vernacular as opposed to the Latin of earlier manuscripts, became increasingly popular among the aristocracy and wealthy bourgeois.

During late antiquity and the Merovingian period, it became customary to enlarge and decorate capital letters beginning major sections of the text. These initials might be decorated with abstract or geometric forms like those found on barbarian metalwork or with whimsical zoomorphic elements made up of animals, fish, and human limbs, as in some Merovingian commentaries on the books of the Bible produced at the monastery at Luxeuil in the 7th century. Inhabited initials, made up of plant forms with animals and humans clambering around in the branches, became prevalent in the Carolingian and Romanesque periods. The "historiated" initial, containing scenes, usually incidents from the Bible, was another Carolingian invention that remained popular throughout the Romanesque and Gothic periods. Miniatures (so called after the *minium*, or red ink, used in their underdrawings) served as pictorial illustrations to the text. They might be full-page frontispieces to the manuscript or major divisions within it, or partial-page illustrations introducing chapters or the relevant portion of the text.

Beginning in the mid-13th century, introductory capital letters began to sprout tendrils, branches, and leaves into the margins around the text, eventually surrounding it and, together with the repetitive strokes of the script and painted horizontal bars, filling out the block of the text (line endings) enhancing the decorative effect of the entire folio. These border decorations then began to serve as a habitat for marginal scenes, cavorting animals, strange hybrids (marginalia, or drolleries), and eventually additional scenes expanding or commenting on the subject matter of miniatures on that or a facing page. In the second half of the 15th century, the foliate borders were often painted illusionistically, depicting flowers and other objects as though they were three dimensional, casting a shadow against a solidly colored background.

Because of liturgical and devotional requirements, different types of manuscripts had a greater currency during different periods of the Middle Ages. During the Carolingian period, Gospel books and full Bibles were produced for imperial use. The Carolingian illuminators, under the influence of early Christian manuscripts, developed lavish copies of the Gospels, particularly at the courts of Charlemagne and of Charles the Bald, containing a tabulation of concordances between the Gospels (Canon Tables), portraits of the Evangelists inspired by late-antique or early Byzantine painting, and a variety of decorative title pages.

The most lavish of these is the *Codex Aureus* of St. Emmeram produced for Charles the Bald (Munich, Bayerische Staatsbibliothek Clm 14000), completed in 870, with numerous gold and purple title pages and a text written entirely in gold. Full copies of the Bible were produced at Saint-Martin at Tours, with pictorial frontispieces, perhaps some emulating lost early Christian models, while others, such as representations of Christ in Majesty, were Carolingian inventions. These frontispieces, perhaps programmatic in their selection, introduced selected books of the Bible. The *Vivian Bible* made for Charles the Bald (B.N. lat. 1) contains eight such frontispieces. The tradition of illustrated Bibles continued in the Romanesque period in volumes that were often large in scale, some with full-page frontispieces, others with decorative or historiated initials opening each book.

Books for the celebration of the Mass, Sacramentaries that later evolved into the Missal, were also developed during the Carolingian period. The most sumptuous of these is a *Sacramentary* made for Archbishop Drogo of Metz (B.N. lat. 9428) containing elaborate historiated or pictorial initials introducing the texts for major feast days and a remarkable series of ornamental folios leading up to a decorative crescendo at the beginning of the Canon of the Mass.

The Psalter, consisting of the Psalms of David, became the most commonly used book for private devotions from the early Middle Ages until the 14th century. With the later addition of Canticles, hymns, a Litany of the Saints, and other prayers, this book formed the basis for the celebration of the Divine Office, which consisted of the eight canonical hours during the day. Psalters were frequently decorated with prefatory scenes from the Old and New Testament, and the eight divisions of the text, corresponding to the eight hours of the day at which they were to be recited, would be introduced by historiated initials. The *Psalter of St. Louis* (B.N. lat. 10525) contains seventy-eight prefatory miniatures.

Transformations of and further additions to the Psalter resulted in the formulation of the book of hours, named after the eight canonical hours during the day in which a section was to be recited. This transformation took place from the 10th to the 13th century, and by the 14th the book of hours supplanted the Psalter as the most popular devotional book. The basic text was the Hours of the Virgin, supplemented by other Hours, such as the Hours of the Cross, as well the Seven Penitential Psalms, an Office of the Dead, prayers to saints, excerpts from the four Gospels, and a calendar indicating the principal feast days of the liturgical year. It became customary to illustrate these books with miniatures depicting the infancy of Christ, the story of his crucifixion, representations of saints, and, for the calendar, scenes of the labors of the months and signs of the zodiac. One of the most remarkable 14th-century books of hours is the minute (3⅝ inches by 2⅜ inches) *Heures de Jeanne d'Évreux*, queen of France (New York, The Cloisters), with miniatures and marginalia attributed to Jean Pucelle executed in *grisaille* between 1325 and 1328. In the 15th century, the most famous book of hours is the one produced for John, duke of Berry, known as the *Très Riches Heures* (Chantilly, Musée Condé), begun by the Limbourg brothers before 1415 and finished by Jean Colombe ca. 1485.

Robert G. Calkins

[See also: BOOK OF HOURS; CAROLINGIAN ART; COLOMBE, JEAN; LIMBOURG BROTHERS; MANUSCRIPTS, HEBREW ILLUMINATED; MEROVINGIAN ART; PALEOGRAPHY AND MANUSCRIPTS; PUCELLE, JEAN]

Avril, François. *Manuscript Painting at the Court of France: The Fourteenth Century (1310–1380)*. New York: Braziller, 1976.

Cahn, Walter. *Romanesque Bible Illustration*. Ithaca: Cornell University Press, 1982.

Calkins, Robert G. *Illuminated Books of the Middle Ages*. Ithaca: Cornell University Press, 1986.

———. *Monuments of Medieval Art*. Ithaca: Cornell University Press, 1985, pp. 201–39.

de Hamel, Christopher. *A History of Illuminated Manuscripts*. Oxford: Phaidon, 1986.

Kessler, Herbert. *The Illustrated Bibles from Tours*. Princeton: Princeton University Press, 1977.

Meiss, Millard. *French Painting in the Time of Jean de Berry*. 5 vols. New York: Phaidon/Braziller, 1967–74.

Mütherich, Florentine, and Joachim Gaehde. *Carolingian Painting*. New York: Braziller, 1976.

Pächt, Otto. *Book Illumination in the Middle Ages*. London: Harvey Miller, 1986.

Plummer, John. *The Last Flowering: French Painting in Manuscripts 1420–1530*. New York: Oxford University Press, 1982.

Porcher, Jean. *Medieval French Miniatures*. New York: Abrams, 1959.

Robb, David M. *The Art of the Illuminated Manuscript*. Cranbury: Barnes, 1973.

Thomas, Marcel. *The Golden Age: Manuscript Painting at the Time of Jean, Duke of Berry*. New York: Braziller, 1979.

MARBODE OF RENNES (ca. 1035–1123). An important representative of the humanistic revival of the early 12th century in the Angers region, Marbode was born at Angers and remained in the cathedral school there as pupil, teacher, and by ca. 1067, master. Among his pupils was Baudri of Bourgueil; he was acquainted with Hildebert of Lavardin, bishop of Le Mans (1096–1125) and Tours (1125–33). Marbode was elected bishop of Rennes in 1096 but retired to Angers shortly before he died.

Marbode's best-known works in the Middle Ages were his hexameter lapidary, written between 1067 and 1081, and his treatise on rhetoric, *De ornamentis verborum*. Over a hundred manuscripts of the Latin text of the lapidary survive. The earliest of the four verse translations into French was by Philippe de Thaün; there are also at least five French prose translations, as well as versions in Spanish, Italian, Provençal, Irish, Danish, and Hebrew.

The *Liber decem capitulorum* (1102) opens with a discussion of subjects that Marbode considered suitable for writing about. The chapters treat time, harlots, good women, old age, fate, the pleasures of the flesh, true friend-ship, good death, and bodily resurrection. Some of his shorter and lighter verses are addressed to nuns and girls at the convent of Le Ronceray at Angers. He also composed hymns and poems on saints, usually in leonine hexam-eters. The only prose works to survive are his letters and a sermon on St. Florent.

Jeanne E. Krochalis

[See also: BAUDRI OF BOURGUEIL; HILDEBERT OF LAVARDIN; LAPIDARY; LATIN LYRIC POETRY; PHILIPPE DE THAÜN]

Marbode of Rennes. *Marbodi episcopi Redonensis Liber decem capitulorum*, ed. Walther Bulst. Heidelberg: Winter, 1947.
———. *Liber lapidum*, ed. J.M. Riddle, English trans. C.W. King. Wiesbaden, 1977.
———. Poems 45–49. In *Medieval Latin Poems of Male Love and Friendship*, trans. Thomas Stehling. New York: Gar-land, 1984.
Bulst, Walther. "Liebesbriefgedichte Marbods." In *Liber Floridus: mittellateinische Studien (Mélanges P. Lehmann)*, ed. Bernhard Bischoff. St. Ottilien: Verlag der Erzabtei, 1950, pp. 287–301.
———. "Studien zu Marbods *Carmina varia* und *Liber decem capitulorum*." *Nachrichten von der Gesellschaft der Wissenschaften zu Göttingen* 2 (1939): 173–241.
Evans, Joan. *Magical Jewels of the Middle Ages and the Renais-sance*. Oxford: Clarendon, 1922. [Includes the Latin (pp. 33–37) and the French translations (pp. 53–67).]
Pannier, Léopold. *Les lapidaires français du moyen âge des XIIe, XIIIe, et XIVe siècles*. Paris: Vieweg, 1882.

MARCABRU (fl. 1130–49). Little can be said for certain about the origins of the troubadour Marcabru. Relying in part on the lyrics, his two *vidas* are probably right to de-scribe him as an early Gascon singer of low birth. Evidence in the songs ties him to courts in southern France and Spain, where he was evidently a jongleur. In some forty-two surviving lyrics, Marcabru is preoccupied largely with social satire and moral allegory. He vehemently denounces a decline in societal mores. One *vida* also describes him as "maligning women and love." But it is still debated whether Marcabru's many pronouncements on love in society are entirely negative or rather idealize love along the lines of a Christian or courtly model. His voice is raw and bitter, his images original and forceful, his language aphoristic and difficult. He is sometimes read as a precursor of the *trobar clus* school. Aside from his thirty-two *sirventes*, his lyrics include the romance *A la fontana del vergier*, the crusade song *Pax in nomine domini*, and the *pastorela Autrier jost' una sebissa*. Marcabru's thematic and stylistic influence on subsequent troubadour song was massive and pervasive.

Roy S. Rosenstein

[See also: TROUBADOUR POETRY]

Marcabru. *Poésies complètes du troubadour Marcabru*, ed. Jean-Marie-Lucien Dejeanne. Toulouse: Privat, 1909.
Harvey, Ruth E. *The Troubadour Marcabru and Love*. London: Westfield College, 1989.
Pirot, François. "Bibliographie commentée du troubadour Marcabru." *Moyen âge* 73 (1967): 87–126. ["Mise à jour," by Ruth E. Harvey and Simon Gaunt. *Moyen âge* 94 (1988): 425–55.]
Thiolier-Méjean, Suzanne. *Les poésies satiriques et morales des troubadours du XIIe siècle à la fin du XIIIe siècle*. Paris: Nizet, 1978.

MARCADÉ, EUSTACHE (d. 1440). Author of a mystery play, the *Vengeance Nostre Seigneur*, and presumed au-thor of the *Mystère de la Passion*, both from Arras. Mar-cadé studied theology and law at the University of Paris and was an official at the Benedictine abbey of Corbie near Amiens. He was later dean of the faculty of ecclesi-astical law in Paris. It was Marcadé who gave the mystery plays their vast dimensions. The *Passion* (25,000 lines) required four days for playing and the *Vengeance* (14,000 lines) three days. He also introduced to the Passion play the theological framework of the *Procès de paradis*, a debate in Heaven between Mercy and Justice, during which God decides to become man. Marcadé's *Passion* celebrates the birth of the church by emphasizing the primacy of Peter. His *Vengeance* shows the origin of the Diaspora by dramatizing the destruction of Jerusalem by the Roman emperor Titus.

Alan E. Knight

[See also: MYSTERY PLAYS]

Marcadé, Eustache. *Le mystère de la Passion, texte du ms. 697 de la Bibliothèque d'Arras*, ed. Jules Marie Richard. Arras: Imprimerie de la Société du Pas-de-Calais, 1893.
Bordier, Jean Pierre. "Rome contre Jérusalem: la légende de la *Vengeance Nostre Seigneur*." In *Jérusalem, Rome, Constan-tinople: l'image et le mythe de la ville au moyen âge*, ed. Daniel Poirion. Paris: Presses de l'Université de Paris–Sorbonne, 1986, pp. 93–124.

MARCEL, ÉTIENNE (1310–1358). A prosperous Pari-sian draper who, as *prévôt des marchands*, led a rebellion against the monarchy in 1357–58. Born into a less wealthy cadet branch of a large and influential family, Marcel was successful in business, a supplier for the royal household, and a respected figure in Paris by the late 1340s. He was elected *prévôt* in 1354. Connected by kinship or marriage to many Parisians who had gained wealth and sometimes ennoblement in royal service, risking disgrace and destitu-tion for corrupt practices but often regaining royal favor, Marcel was perhaps too cautious or too honest to follow their example, and he increasingly resented these rich royal officers from his own circle.

In December 1355, the Estates General met in Paris, and Marcel became the spokesman for the towns of Languedoil, as the assembly worked out an ambitious plan to raise a large tax to support the army, in exchange for governmental reforms and a return to stable currency. Marcel and the Parisians were then staunch supporters of John II in his campaign against the kings of England and Navarre, who had claims to the French throne and sought to partition the realm. By May 1356, however, the tax plan was failing, and without adequate revenues for his troops John II resumed manipulating the currency and restored to power the officials he had agreed to dismiss. These actions caused Marcel to break with the king, no longer providing him with Parisian troops. When John met defeat and capture at Poitiers in September, he had no bourgeois troops but relied solely on nobles.

In the last months of 1356, Marcel seems to have become a partisan of Charles the Bad, the rebellious king of Navarre. An inflammatory Navarrese partisan, Robert Le Coq, dominated the Estates that met after Poitiers, and the urban representatives, led by Marcel, lent at least tacit support to his demands. In December, Marcel organized his first large Parisian street demonstration against the government. He made frequent use of such intimidating tactics in subsequent months.

The Estates obtained a sweeping ordinance of reform in March 1357, but when they failed repeatedly to deliver the taxes needed to prosecute the war, the government ceased to feel bound by the reforms. Marcel and the Parisian crowd became increasingly intimidating, and in February 1358 they murdered two military commanders in the presence of the dauphin Charles, thereby alienating the nobles who had originally spearheaded the reform movement. Marcel and his followers became increasingly radical in their hostility to nobles and gave some support to the Jacquerie of late May. The dauphin, meanwhile, left Paris in March and began to rally noble support. Marcel failed in his effort to organize a league of towns to oppose them, and Paris became increasingly isolated. At the end of July, one of the citizens murdered Marcel, paving the way for the dauphin's triumphant return to the capital.

John Bell Henneman, Jr.

[See also: CHARLES II THE BAD; HUNDRED YEARS' WAR; JACQUERIE; PARIS]

Avout, Jacques d'. *Le meurtre d'Étienne Marcel.* Paris: Gallimard, 1960.

Cazelles, Raymond. *Étienne Marcel: champion de l'unité française.* Paris: Tallandier, 1984.

MARCH. As a defense against external threats to the Carolingian realm, Charlemagne (r. 768–814) established along its frontiers special regions known as marches (Lat. *marca, marcha*). Some of these areas aided the assimilation of rebellious tribes into the Carolingian kingdom, as did the Saxon March, formed in the northeast in the 770s. Other marches included the March of Brittany, to help in the subjugation of the Bretons, the March of Spain, to protect Frankish territories from incursions over the Pyrénées, the March of Friuli, bordering the southern Slavonic regions, and a March of Bavaria.

Each march was organized on a military basis. The "count of the march" (Lat. *comes marcae*, whence "marquis, marquess"), who possessed important military skills, served as commander of the troops stationed there and headed the area's government. His presence, together with that of his garrison, was meant to guarantee the march's stability as well as provide ready forces to deal with problems beyond its boundaries.

Celia Chazelle

[See also: MARQUIS/MARQUISATE]

Bonnassie, Pierre. *La Catalogne du milieu du Xe à la fin du XIe siècle: croissance et mutations d'une société.* 2 vols. Toulouse: Association des Publications de l'Université de Toulouse–Le Mirail, 1975–76.

Deer, J. "Karl der Grosse und der Untergang des Awarenreiches." In *Karl der Grosse: Lebenswerk und Nachleben*, ed. Wolfgang Braunfels, et al. 5 vols. Düsseldorf: Schwann, 1965; Vol. 1, pp. 719–91.

Folz, Robert. *De l'antiquité au monde médiéval.* 5 vols. Paris: Presses Universitaires de France, 1972, Vol. 3, pp. 315–53.

McKitterick, Rosamond. *The Frankish Kingdoms Under the Carolingians, 751–987.* London: Longman, 1983.

Smith, Julia. *Province and Empire: Brittany and the Carolingians.* Cambridge: Cambridge University Press, 1992.

Werner, Karl-Ferdinand. "*Missus, marchio, comes:* entre l'administration centrale et l'administration locale de l'empire carolingien." In *Histoire comparée de l'administration*, ed. Werner Paravicini. Munich: Artemis, 1980, pp. 191–239.

MARCO POLO (1254–1324). Italian-born author of the *Devisement du monde*, a Franco-Italian prose description of his voyages to the East, which included Persia, Armenia, Turkestan, China, Indochina, India, and the Middle East. Between 1270 and 1295, Marco followed the lead of his father and uncle, who in the 1260s had journeyed as far as the court of Kublai Khan on the border of Cathay. The first westerner to traverse the whole of Asia, he spent much time at the court of Kublai and in his service as ambassador. The *Devisement*, essentially a travel account based on personal observations, is nevertheless filled with fabulous descriptions and legends garnered on his voyages. Marco aimed to instruct and entertain an aristocratic audience, which explains why his work has been given little credence by scholars. However, it can still be profitably consulted for its geographical descriptions, and more especially for its accounts of oriental religions and politics.

William W. Kibler

[See also: MANDEVILLE, JEAN DE; OUTREMEUSE, JEAN D']

Marco Polo. *Le devisement du monde, Le livre des merveilles*, ed. A.-C. Moule and Paul Pelliot, trans. Louis Hambis. 2 vols. Paris: Maspero, 1980.

———. *Il Milione, prima edizione integrale*, ed. Luigi Foscolo Benedetto. Florence: Olschki, 1928.

Hérisson, Jean-Luc. *Le devisement du monde.* Paris: Flammarion, 1990.

Olschki, Leo. *Marco Polo's Asia: An Introduction to His "Description of the World" Called "Il Milione."* Berkeley: University of California Press, 1960.

MARGIVAL, NICOLE DE (fl. late 13th or early 14th c.). Author of the *Dit de la panthère d'amours*, the earliest known French poem that combines first-person narrative with a series of lyric insertions composed by the narrator. In addition to citing several songs of Adam de la Halle, the *Roman de la Rose*, and Drouart la Vache's adaptation of Andreas Capellanus's *De amore*, Nicole includes his own corpus of *forme fixe* compositions. The *Panthère*, a rich synthesis of Old French literary traditions—bestiary, lapidary, art of love, allegorical dream vision, lyric forms—was an important influence on Guillaume de Machaut. Nicole is also the author of a *Dit des trois morts et des trois vifs*, an often-used format for a poem warning of the inevitability of death; and he may have composed an art of love, the *Ordre d'amours*.

Sylvia Huot

Margival, Nicole de. *Dit de la panthère d'amours*, ed. Henry A. Todd. Paris: Didot, 1883.

Hoepffner, Ernest. "Les poésies lyriques du *Dit de la panthère d'amours* de Nicole de Margival." *Romania* 46 (1920): 204–30.

Boulton, Maureen B.M. *The Song in the Story: Lyric Insertions in French Narrative Fiction, 1200–1400*. Philadelphia: University of Pennsylvania Press, 1993.

MARGUERITE (1202–1280). Countess of Flanders and Hainaut. Marguerite, sometimes known as Marguerite of Constantinople, where her father Baudouin IX was emperor for a short time, succeeded her sister Jeanne as countess in 1244. Her first marriage, to the Hainaut nobleman Burchard d'Avesnes, was declared invalid by the pope, but her children from it disputed her legacy with the children of her second marriage, to Guillaume de Dampierre, a nobleman of Champagne. Civil war between them erupted in 1244, when she succeeded as countess, and continued until 1257. Marguerite had inherited a substantial debt from Jeanne and added substantially to it, creating antagonism by taxing and borrowing heavily. In 1270, she demanded arrears on a money fief owed to the counts by the English kings, which led to a commercial war won by the English. Marguerite and her son and co-ruler, Gui de Dampierre, tried in 1275 to replace the government of Ghent, which Ghent appealed to the Parlement de Paris as a violation of its charter. Marguerite abdicated in favor of Gui on December 29, 1278. Her most notable accomplishment may have been the abolition of serfdom in 1252 in all lands under the countess's direct control.

David M. Nicholas

[See also: AVESNES; DAMPIERRE; FLANDERS]

Luykx, Theo. *De grafelijke bestuursinstellingen en het grafelijk patrimonium in Vlaanderen tijdens de regering van Margareta van Constantinopel (1244–1278)*. Brussels: Vlaamse Academie, 1978.

Vandermaesen, M. "Vlaanderen en Henegouwen onder het Huis van Dampierre, 1244–1384." In *Algemene Geschiedenis der Nederlanden*. 2nd ed. Haarlem: Fibula-Van Dishoeck, 1982, Vol. 2, pp. 399–440.

MARGUERITE D'OINGT (ca. 1240–1310). Marguerite was born to noble parents in the French Beaujolais region. By 1288, she became prioress of the Carthusian monastery of Poletains at Lyon. Although she was never canonized, a popular cult in her honor flourished until the Revolution, and she was revered as blessed. Marguerite is the only medieval Carthusian woman writer known to us. The *Pagina meditationum*, a response in Latin to a visionary experience during Mass, interweaves liturgical sections with reflections on Christ's Passion and the Last Judgment. In a remarkable passage, Marguerite develops the image of Christ as a woman undergoing the suffering of labor. The *Speculum*, written in Franco-Provençal and dedicated to Hugo, prior of Vallebonne, describes three visions and their meaning. In the first, Christ shows her a book with white, black, red, and golden letters symbolizing his suffering. In the second, the book opens and reveals a vision of Paradise and the heavens, whence all goodness emanates. In the third, she is shown the glorified body of Christ and meditates on its meaning for Christian spirituality. Marguerite's final work is the biography of Béatrice of Ornacieux (ca. 1260–1303/09), a stigmatized nun at the charterhouse of Parmenie, whose cult was recognized by Pope Pius IX in 1869. Also written in the vernacular, the biography stresses Beatrice's intense mystical experiences, including frequent apparitions, the gift of tears, severe acts of penance to ward off the Devil, and eucharistic visions and miracles. Marguerite's christocentric mysticism includes not only Carthusian but also Franciscan and Cistercian elements. Some letters by Marguerite also survive.

Ulrike Wiethaus

[See also: WOMEN, RELIGIOUS EXPERIENCE OF]

Marguerite d'Oingt. *Les œuvres de Marguerite d'Oingt*, ed. Antonin Duraffour, Pierre Gardette, and Paulette Durdilly. Paris: Les Belles Lettres, 1965.

———. *The Writings of Margaret of Oingt, Medieval Prioress and Mystic*, trans. Renate Blumenfeld-Kosinski. Newburyport: Focus Information Group, 1990.

Dinzelbacher, Peter. "Margarete von Oingt und ihre *Pagina meditationum*." *Analecta cartusiana* 16 (1988): 69–100.

Maisonneuve, Roland. "L'experience mystique et visionnaire de Marguerite d'Oingt (d.1310), moniale chartreuse." *Analecta cartusiana* 55 (1981): 81–102.

MARGUERITE OF FLANDERS (ca. 1349–1405). Duchess of Burgundy. Daughter of Louis II de Male, count of Flanders (r. 1346–84), and Marguerite, daughter of Duke Jean III of Brabant, Marguerite was married first to Philippe de Rouvre, duke of Burgundy, who died in 1361, and thereafter in 1369 to Philip the Bold (1342–1404), duke of Burgundy since 1363. Her dowry included Artois and the county of Burgundy from her paternal grandmother, Marguerite d'Artois, and Flanders and Rethel from her father. To get this attractive match, Philip's brother, King Charles V of France, had to return to Flanders the towns and castellanies of Lille, Douai, and Orchies, which had been surrendered to the crown in 1305. Marguerite succeeded her grandmother in 1382 and her father in early 1384, and her husband ruled her lands through her. In 1390, her aunt, Countess Jeanne de Brabant, designated her with Philip as her heirs. In 1391, Marguerite willed her lands to Philip on grounds of their son's immaturity and the skill with which Philip had governed her inheritance. In fact, she survived him by a year, and Flanders passed to that same eldest son, John the Fearless. She and her husband were patrons of the arts, and she frequently acted as regent during his absences. Between 1371 and 1391, Philip and Marguerite had at least eleven children, of whom seven survived into adulthood. Their diplomatic marriages would establish the foundations of the Burgundian power of the 15th century.

David M. Nicholas

[See also: FLANDERS; JOHN THE FEARLESS; PHILIP THE BOLD]

Canat de Chizy, M. "Marguerite de Flandre, duchesse de Bourgogne, sa vie intime et l'état de sa maison." *Mémoires de l'Académie Impériale des Sciences, Arts et Belles-Lettres de Dijon*, 2nd ser. 7 (1958–59): 65–332.

Hughes, Muriel J. "The Library of Philip the Bold and Margaret of Flanders, First Valois Duke and Duchess of Burgundy." *Journal of Medieval History* 4 (1978): 145–88.

Vaughan, Richard. *Philip the Bold: The Formation of the Burgundian State.* Cambridge: Harvard University Press, 1962.

MARGUERITE OF PROVENCE (ca. 1221–1295). Marguerite was the eldest of four daughters of Count Raymond-Berenguer V of Provence. In 1234, at the age of twelve or thirteen, she became queen of France by her marriage to Louis IX. The wedding and her coronation as queen were celebrated at the cathedral of Sens. Eleven children were eventually born to the couple. The marriage was difficult in a number of respects. From the beginning, Marguerite resented and was resented by her mother-in-law, Blanche of Castile; yet she admired Blanche's influence with Louis. She tried to achieve the same position with her son, the future Philip III, but provoked her husband to intervene and have the young Philip's ill-considered oath to obey her until the age of thirty quashed. Though Marguerite by no means lacked in courage or ability (e.g., she successfully preserved order in Damietta in Egypt in 1250 at a particularly difficult moment in her husband's first crusade), Louis almost always ignored her political advice.

After the king's death in 1270, Marguerite became a more active political figure. She was particularly exigent—to the point of raising troops—in defending her rights in Provence, where her husband's brother, Charles of Anjou, maintained his political authority and control of property after his wife's (her sister's) death, contrary to the intentions of the old count, who had died in 1245. Philip III had his hands full in restraining her. Only his death in 1285 and Charles of Anjou's in the same year resolved the situation. At the behest of the new king, Philip IV, she accepted an assignment of income from Anjou as compensation for recognizing the preeminent rights of Charles of Anjou's heirs in Provence. Her last years were spent in doing pious work, including founding in 1289 the Franciscan nunnery of Lourcines, which eventually became a focal point of the cult of her late husband, Louis. Although she does not seem to have testified for her husband's canonization, Marguerite was active in the propagation of his memory: her confessor, Guillaume de Saint-Pathus, for example, wrote an important and reverential biography of the king. Marguerite died on December 30, 1295, nearly two years before the process of canonization was completed.

William Chester Jordan

[See also: LOUIS IX]

Le mariage de saint Louis à Sens en 1234. Sens: Musées de Sens, 1984.

Sivéry, Gérard. *Marguerite de Provence: une reine au temps des cathédrales.* Paris: Fayard, 1987.

MARGUERITE PORETE (d. 1310). Biographical information about Marguerite Porete comes from inquisitorial documents, which tell us that she was a béguine from Hainaut. Quite possibly, she was a solitary itinerant who expounded her teachings to interested listeners. She wrote the *Mirouer des simples ames anienties* in Old French sometime between 1296 and 1306. Since there is no indication that someone else wrote the text of the *Mirouer* from the author's dictation, we can surmise that the author wrote the treatise herself and that she was well educated.

The text received approvals from three orthodox church leaders, one of whom was Godfrey of Fontaines, a scholastic at Paris between 1285 and 1306, who also counseled the author to use caution in her expressions. Approval was not universal, however, and the text was condemned and burned in the author's presence with the orders not to spread her views under threat of being turned over to the secular authorities. Marguerite was arrested at the end of 1308 and remained in prison for a year and a half before being condemned to the flames as a relapsed heretic. Despite the condemnation, the *Mirouer* apparently enjoyed widespread popularity, for in addition to copies made of the text in Old French it was translated into Middle English, Italian, and Latin.

The *Mirouer* is a dialogue among allegorical figures who represent the nature of the relation between the soul and God. The fundamental structure of the discourse is grounded in traditional Neoplatonic philosophy, and courtly language is used to express theological abstractions. The *Mirouer* is a theological treatise that analyzes how love in human beings is related to divine love and how the human soul by means of this relation may experience a lasting union of indistinction with God in this life. The *Mirouer* is also a handbook, or "mirror," that aims to teach the "hearers of the book" about themselves and how to attain union with God.

Ellen L. Babinsky

[See also: BÉGUINES; HERESY; INQUISITION; WOMEN, RELIGIOUS EXPERIENCE OF]

Marguerite Porete. *Le mirouer des simple ames anienties*, ed. Romana Guarnieri and Paul Verdeyen. *CCCM* 69. Turnhout: Brepols, 1986.

———. *The Mirror of Simple Souls*, trans. Ellen L. Babinsky. New York: Paulist, 1993.

Lerner, Robert E. *The Heresy of the Free Spirit in the Later Middle Ages.* Los Angeles: University of California Press, 1972.

Verdeyen, Paul. "Le procès d'inquisition contre Marguerite Porete et Guiard de Cressonessart (1309–1310)." *Revue d'histoire ecclésiastique* 81 (1986): 47–94.

MARIAN ANTIPHONS. Antiphons honoring the Virgin Mary, many with texts from the Song of Songs, that originated in the Divine Office but were often used for separate votive services or commemorations from the early 13th century on. The daily choice of Marian antiphon varied among churches, but the *Salve regina* was sung on Saturday everywhere and was adopted for daily singing by the Cistercians in 1218 and the Dominicans in 1250. In 1246, the Franciscans introduced a seasonal distribution of four commorative antiphons at Compline that was taken over into Roman use and still survives today: *Alma redemptoris mater* from Advent to Purification, *Ave regina* from Purification to Wednesday of Holy Week, *Regina caeli* from Easter Day to the Saturday after Pentecost, and *Salve regina* from Trinity Sunday to the Saturday before Advent. The sources of local French liturgies indicate that Marian antiphons could be sung at various times of the day (e.g., after Lauds or Terce or at the conclusion of a procession) and in various locations in the church: before an image or statue of the Virgin, in the choir, or in a private chapel. In the later Middle Ages, Marian antiphons provided *cantus firmi* for motets; these were often intended for private devotions, as part of votive services commissioned by individual donors.

Susan Boynton

[See also: ANTIPHON; *CANTUS FIRMUS*; DIVINE OFFICE; MARY, LITURGICAL VENERATION OF; MOTET (13TH CENTURY)]

Colette, Marie-Noël. "Le *Salve regina* en Aquitaine au XIIe siècle: l'auteur du *Salve*." In *Cantus Planus*, ed. Lázló Dobszay, Agnes Papp, and Ferenc Sebö. Budapest: Hungarian Academy of Sciences, 1992, pp. 521–47.

Huglo, Michel. "Antiphon." In *The New Grove Dictionary of Music and Musicians*, ed. Stanley Sadie. 20 vols. London: Macmillan, 1979.

Steiner, Ruth. "Marian Antiphons at Cluny and Lewes." In *Music in the Mediaeval English Liturgy: Plainsong and Mediaeval Music Society Centennial Essays,* ed. Susan Rankin and David Hiley. Oxford: Clarendon, 1993, pp. 175–204.

Wright, Craig. *Music and Ceremony at Notre Dame of Paris, 500–1500.* Cambridge: Cambridge University Press, 1989.

MARIE DE FRANCE (fl. 1160–1210). Recognized today among the major poets of the renaissance of the 12th century, Marie de France was equally admired by her contemporaries at court, according to the testimony of Denis Piramus in his *Vie seint Edmunt le rei*. Three works of the period are signed "Marie" and are usually attributed to the same author: the *Lais*, the *Fables*, and the *Espurgatoire saint Patrice*. In the epilogue to the *Fables*, the author adds to her name *si sui de France* (l. 4). This is probably an indication of continental birth, a fact to be remarked if, as seems likely, she was living in England. A number of identities have been proposed for Marie, none of which can be established with certainty: the natural daughter of Geoffroi Plantagenêt (and half-sister of Henry II), abbess of Shaftsbury (1181–1216); Marie de Meulan or Beaumont, widow of Hugues Talbot and daughter of Waleron de Beaumont; and the abbess of Reading (the abbey where the Harley 978 manuscript may have been copied). Identifying her literary patrons is equally problematic. The *Lais* are dedicated to *vus, nobles reis* (l. 43), who may be either Henry II (1133–1189), the most likely candidate, or his son, Henry the Young King (crowned 1170, d. 1183). The Count William named in the *Fables* has been linked to a number of prominent figures, including William Marshal, William Longsword (the natural son of Henry II), William of Mandeville, William of Warren, William of Gloucester, and Guillaume de Dampierre.

Marie's works can be dated only approximately with reference to possible patrons and literary influences. The works themselves suggest that Marie knew Wace's *Brut* (1155) and the *Roman d'Énéas* (1160), an undetermined Tristan romance, classical (notably Ovid) and Celtic sources, but not the romances of Chrétien de Troyes. The *Lais* are therefore dated between 1160 and 1170, the *Fables* between 1167 and 1189, and the *Espurgatoire* after 1189 and probably between 1209 and 1215, since its Latin source, the *Tractatus de purgatorio sancti Patricii* (in the version of Hugh or Henry of Saltrey), has been placed no earlier than 1208.

Five manuscripts contain one or more of Marie's *lais*; only Harley 978 contains a general prologue, which presents the twelve *lais* that follow as a collection specifically arranged by the author (the same manuscript also contains a complete collection of the *Fables*). Marie appears to be the initiator of a narrative genre that flourished between about 1170 and the late 13th century. About forty narrative *lais* are extant. The lyric *lai*, which flourished from the 12th to the 15th century, seems to be an unrelated form.

The prologues and epilogues that frame each of Marie's tales refer to the *lais* performed by Breton storytellers in commemoration of past adventures truly lived. Celtic and English place-names and personal names corroborate Marie's claimed sources: four *lais* take place in Brittany, three in Wales, two in both places, and one in an undetermined

Bretagne. Marie did not simply write down orally circulating stories. Her artfully crafted compositions combine the written traditions of Latin and vernacular writings with the legendary materials of Celtic and popular tales. While it may be impossible to untangle historical reference and literary topos in Marie's repeated claim to retell well-known *lais bretons,* her indications suggest a process of transmission that begins with an adventure heard by Bretons, who then compose a *lai,* sung with harp accompaniment. Marie has heard the music and the adventure, the latter perhaps told as a prelude to the song. She then tells us the adventure in rhymed octosyllables, the form used also in the *Fables* and the *Espurgatoire,* elaborating simultaneously its truth, or *reisun* (cf. the *razos* in the Provençal lyric tradition). The title itself, carefully designated in each case and sometimes translated into several languages, guarantees the authenticity of the process.

The general prologue opens with a traditional exordium on the obligation of writers to share their talents and then cites the authority of Priscian to describe the relationship between ancient and modern writers: do philosopher-poets hide a *surplus* of meaning to be found later in the obscurities of their writing, or do later, more subtle poets add it to their predecessors' works? Scholars have variously interpreted these verses (9–22): we are drawn into the problem of interpretation at the very moment the subject of glossing is introduced by Marie's authorial persona. She then explains the nature of her project: not a translation from the Latin as many have done, but something new, demanding hard labor and sleepless nights, the writing down in rhyme of those adventures commemorated in *lais.* Hoping to receive great joy in return, Marie then offers her collection to an unnamed king. She names herself in the following verses, printed by modern editors as the prologue to *Guigemar* (ll. 3–4) but set off in the manuscript only by a large capital indicating a new section (*G1*).

The twelve *lais* that follow in Harley 978 are *Guigemar* (886 lines), *Equitan* (314), *Fresne* (518), *Bisclavret* (318), *Lanval* (646), *Deus amanz* (254), *Yonec* (558), *Laüstic* (160), *Milun* (534), *Chaitivel* (240), *Chievrefoil* (118), and *Eliduc* (1184). As indicated by the considerable variations in length, the *lais* offer great diversity, but they also operate as a collection unified by the themes of love and adventure. Indeed, they seem to invite exploration as an open-ended set of theme and variations, in which Marie reveals the complexities and varieties of human experience, without trying to contain them within the confines of any single doctrine of love. Heroes and heroines, all noble, beautiful, and courteous, are individualized not by psychological development but by the situations in which they find themselves. Consider the two short anecdotes that constitute *Laüstic* and *Chievrefoil.* Both involve a love triangle: married couple plus lover. *Chievrefoil* relates an episode in the story of Tristan and Iseut, a secret reunion of the lovers vouchsafed during one of Tristan's returns from exile. Whereas Marc here remains ignorant of the tryst, the husband of *Laüstic* discovers his wife's nocturnal meetings with her lover. Although their affair remains innocent, limited to their mutual gaze across facing windows, the angry husband puts an end to their meetings by trapping and

killing the nightingale the lady claims as reason for her nightly visits to the window. When the lady sends to her lover the nightingale's body wrapped in an embroidered cloth, along with a messenger to explain the events, he has a golden box made, adorned with precious stones. The nightingale's body is placed in it, and the reliquary accompanies him wherever he goes—hence the name of the *lai: laüstic* is the Breton word for *russignol* in French, *nihtegale* in English (ll. 3–6).

The emblem that thus closes the *lai* figures the end of the lovers' meetings, though it may also suggest the triumph of continued love, however impossible to realize: optimistic and pessimistic readings of the ending are both possible. The emblem of *Chievrefoil* also testifies to the enduring nature of Tristan and Iseut's love: just as the hazelwood dies (so it was thought) if the honeysuckle growing around it was cut away, so the two lovers would die if separated: *"Bele amie, si est de nus: ne vus sanz mei, ne jeo sanz vus"* (ll. 77–78). But while that phrasing is negative, what we see realized in this episode is the reunion of the lovers thanks to the piece of hazelwood that Tristan prepares as a signal to Iseut, so that the queen will know he must be hiding in the woods near the route of her cortege. Whereas the emblem of *Laüstic* ends the lovers' meetings, *Chievrefoil's* emblem initiates Tristan and Iseut's reunion, as it symbolizes their love. And just as the repetition of characters, scenes, and situations in *Laüstic* and *Chievrefoil* creates doubles, echoes, and contrasts in positive and negative variations at all levels of the text, so the tendency to present and explore different combinations of the same materials characterizes the links between the *lais* and invites readers to analyze their interactions. The arrangement of twelve *lais* in a collection considerably increases the potential for meaning, however elusive that meaning remains in the beautiful obscurities of Marie's text, and begins to give her *lais* the weight and proportion we normally associate with romance.

The brevity of most *lais* limits their plot development to a single anecdote or episode, although in the mid-length and longer *lais,* especially *Guigemar* and *Eliduc,* there may be a fuller elaboration as the characters' love develops through a series of episodes. The type of adventure that appears in the *lais* differs somewhat from that of romance: it does not involve a quest, even in the longer *récits;* the hero is more passive and his experience leads to private fulfillment and happiness; no special relationship exists between the hero's destiny and that of his society.

While some *lais* have marvelous and folktale elements that recall their Celtic sources (e.g., *Guigemar, Yonec, Lanval*), others remain realistically placed in the courtly world of the 12th century (*Equitan, Fresne, Milun, Chaitivel*). All explore the intersection of two planes of existence, where otherness may be magically encountered or simply introduced by the new experience of love. Although efforts to thus categorize the *lais* often remain problematic, leading to overlap, omissions, and the like, they do respond to the sense of intertextual play that links the *lais* across echoes and contrasts.

Marie's art is as carefully crafted as the precious reliquary she describes in *Laüstic.* The economy and brevity of her style are enriched by the subtlety of her narrating voice. Her use of free indirect discourse, in particular, allows her to merge her voice with that of her characters, while maintaining the distinctness of both. Marie's literary art, sustained throughout the collection of twelve *lais*, joins her work to that of the philosopher-poets, described in the general prologue as worthy of glossing and interpretation.

The twenty-three extant manuscripts of Marie's *Fables*, two of which are complete with prologue, epilogue, and 102 fables, attest their popularity. Marie claims to translate from the English of King Alfred's adaptation from Latin. No such translation is known, and Marie may have invented a fictitious source. Her fables derive from the Latin *Romulus* in combination with other traditions: some details bring her collection closer to the Greek fables than to the Latin; evidence of oral tradition is also apparent. Hers is the first known example of Old French *Isopets*. Each short narrative (eight–124 lines) leads to an explicit moral lesson. This framework of moral and social values provides an underlying unity for the diversity of the fables. The political stance is basically conservative, reflecting an aristocratic point of view, but also shows concern for justice available to all classes: social hierarchy should be maintained for the sake of harmony; people should accept their place, as well as their responsibilities. Marie's concern for justice in terms of feudal loyalty between lord and vassal is demonstrated in a number of fables; elsewhere appears a more specific regard for mistreatment of the poor, as in Fable 2, *De lupo et agno*, in which the wolf invents a series of false accusations to justify killing the lamb. Marie's moral targets the abuse of rich robber barons, viscounts, and judges who exploit those in their power with trumped-up charges.

Extant in a single manuscript, the *Espurgatoire* combines in its over 2,000 lines a variety of materials, romanesque, hagiographic, and homiletic. In addition to various anecdotes, the principle narrative concerns the proselytizing efforts of St. Patrick, thanks to whom an entrance to Purgatory for the still-living has been established in a churchyard, in order to strengthen belief in the afterlife. After suitable prayers and instructions, many have descended to witness the tortures of the damned and the delights of the saved. Not all have returned from the perilous journey. The greater part of the story follows in detail the preparation and descent of the knight Owein. Through a series of diabolical torments, Owein is saved each time when he invokes the name of Jesus. Upon his return, he is confirmed in his knightly career, now purified and dedicated to saintly pursuits. The *Espurgatoire* offers one of the earliest vernacular examples of the same visionary tradition that inspires Dante's *Commedia*.

Matilda T. Bruckner

[See also: ANGLO-NORMAN LITERATURE; FABLE (*ISOPET*); GAUTIER D'ARRAS; *LAI*, NARRATIVE]

Marie de France. *Les lais de Marie de France*, ed. Jean Rychner. Paris: Champion, 1969.

———. *Les fables*, ed. and trans. Charles Brucker. Louvain: Peeters, 1990.

———. *The Lais of Marie de France*, trans. Glyn S. Burgess and Keith Busby. Harmondsworth: Penguin, 1986.

———. *Marie de France: Fables*, ed. and trans. Harriet Spiegel. Toronto: University of Toronto Press, 1987.

———. *The Espurgatoire Saint Patriz of Marie de France, with a Text of the Latin Original*, ed. Thomas Atkinson Jenkins. Chicago: Chicago University Press, 1903.

———. *Das Buch vom Espurgatoire s. Patrice der Marie de France und seine Quelle*, ed. Karl Warnke. Halle: Niemeyer, 1938.

———. *The Lais of Marie de France*, trans. Robert W. Hanning and Joan Ferrante. New York: Dutton, 1978.

———. *The "Fables" of Marie de France: An English Translation*, trans. Mary Lou Martin. Birmingham: Summa, 1984.

Burgess, Glyn S. *Marie de France: An Analytic Bibliography*. London: Grant and Cutler, 1977; First Supplement, 1985.

Ménard, Philippe. *Les lais de Marie de France: contes d'amour et d'aventure au moyen âge*. Paris: Presses Universitaires de France, 1979.

Mickel, Emanuel J., Jr. *Marie de France*. New York: Twayne, 1974.

Sienaert, Edgar. *Les lais de Marie de France: du conte merveilleux à la nouvelle psychologique*. Paris: Champion, 1978.

MARIE D'OIGNIES (1177–1213). Mystic and one of the founding mothers of the béguine movement. Testimonies of her life were recorded by Jacques de Vitry (ca. 1215) and Thomas de Cantimpré (ca. 1230/31).

Born in Nijvel (Brabant), Marie was married at the age of fourteen but did not consummate her marriage. Together with her spouse, she practiced the *vita apostolica* and cared for the sick. At the age of thirty, she retired to a cell at the Augustinian monastery of Aiseau-sur-Sambre and gained in stature as a spiritual healer and holy woman. According to her pupil Jacques de Vitry, Marie's spirituality was characterized by eucharistic devotion and christocentrism. She lived a life of strict asceticism, abstained from sleep and food, and frequently experienced visions, ecstasies, and trances. Her death was an example of a saintly *ars moriendi*, surrounded by miracles; most noteworthy perhaps is her feat of three days of incessant chanting and scriptural exegesis performed during ecstasy. Jacques de Vitry stressed Marie's allegiance to the church by structuring her *vita* in two parts: Part 1 records the outline of her life's journey towards holiness and aspects of saintliness; Part 2 describes her interior life according to the seven gifts of the Holy Spirit. As with other texts of this genre, it is difficult to distinguish between Marie d'Oignies as a prototype (exemplum) and her individuality and original contributions to medieval spirituality.

Ulrike Wiethaus

[See also: BÉGUINES; JACQUES DE VITRY; WOMEN, RELIGIOUS EXPERIENCE OF]

Jacques de Vitry. *The Life of Marie d'Oignies*, trans. Margot H. King. Saskatoon: Peregrina, 1986.

Thomas de Cantimpré. *Supplement to the Life of Marie d'Oignies*, trans. Hugh Feiss. Saskatoon: Peregrina, 1987.

Kowalczewski, J. "Thirteenth Century Asceticism: Marie d'Oignies and Liutgard of Aywières as Active and Passive Ascetics." *Vox benedictina* 3 (1986): 20–50.

———. The Life of "Marie d'Oignies." In *Medieval Women's Visionary Literature*, ed. Elizabeth Petroff. Oxford: Oxford University Press, 1986, pp. 179–84.

MARIGNY, ENGUERRAN DE (ca. 1275–1315). Chief minister of Philip IV from 1311 until the king's death on November 29, 1314, Marigny was hanged on April 30, 1315, because of the enmity of Philip's brother Charles of Valois, who wielded great influence over the new king, Louis X. Accusations of financial dishonesty could not be proven, and he and other members of his household and family were convicted on trumped-up charges of necromancy. His power had been immense; he was considered "a second king in France." The *Livres de Fauvel*, attributed to Marigny's chaplain Gervais du Bus, is a scarcely veiled commentary on the overmighty minister and the miseries he was believed to have inflicted on France.

Marigny was a member of the petty nobility of Normandy. His father was a royal officer; his cousin Nicolas de Fréauville was the king's confessor before becoming a cardinal; his brother Philippe, successively archbishop of Sens (1309) and Beauvais (1313), served King Philip in the affairs of Guichard, bishop of Troyes, and the Templars and participated in the judgment of his brother. No theorist or legist, Marigny was a practical man who increased his own fortune as he worked for the king, whose household he entered after serving the king's wife, Jeanne of Champagne and Navarre. In 1304, he was the royal chamberlain, a position that brought him into close contact with the king and enabled him to influence policy; before May 1308, he was made a royal councilor; he was governor of the Louvre; he directed the rebuilding of the royal palace in Paris. His financial acumen, demonstrated early on, led Philip to give him complete control of the kingdom's finances in 1314. He was instrumental in persuading Philip to abandon his vendetta against the memory of Boniface VIII and to accept the assignment of Templar property to the Hospitalers. Preferring negotiated truces to armed conflict, he averted war with the Flemings in 1313 and 1314, having obtained Lille, Douai, and Béthune for France in 1312.

Elizabeth A.R. Brown

[See also: CHAMBRE DES COMPTES; *FAUVEL, LIVRES DE*; PHILIP IV THE FAIR]

Favier, Jean, ed. *Cartulaire et actes d'Enguerran de Marigny.* Paris: Bibliothèque Nationale, 1965.

———. *Un conseiller de Philippe le Bel, Enguerran de Marigny.* Paris: Presses Universitaires de France, 1963.

———. "Les portraits d'Enguerran de Marigny." *Annales de Normandie* 15 (1965): 517–24.

MARMOUSETS. The political faction during the reign of Charles VI that opposed the king's uncles, John of Berry and Philip the Bold of Burgundy, is known to historians as the "Marmousets." This term of derision, meaning "little boys," hence people of no account, was used in the Middle Ages to describe parvenus and upstarts. The Marmousets consisted of two groups who had been prominent in the service of Charles V—financial officers, some of whom were from obscure backgrounds, and military commanders, some of whom were from old and distinguished families.

Although linked politically to Louis of Anjou (d. 1384), the brother of Charles V, and Louis of Orléans (d. 1407), the brother of Charles VI, the Marmousets did not have a powerful princely patron but were led by Olivier de Clisson, constable of France. Other important members of the group were Bureau de La Rivière; Jean Le Mercier; Jean de Montaigu; Pierre de Chevreuse; Pierre "le Begue" de Villaines; Jeannet d'Estouteville, lord of Charlemesnil; Guillaume de Melun, count of Tancarville; Nicolas du Bosc, bishop of Bayeux; Pierre Aycelin, cardinal of Laon; and Guillaume des Bordes.

In 1388, when Charles VI was twenty years old, Clisson and the Marmousets persuaded him to dismiss from his council the uncles who had ruled during his minority and for the next four years they dominated royal policy, promoting reforms and a generally more frugal government. The king, however, was emotionally unstable, and when he suffered an attack of mental illness on an expedition to Brittany in 1392, the royal dukes quickly regained power and dismissed Clisson, Le Mercier, and La Rivière from the government.

John Bell Henneman, Jr.

[See also: CHARLES VI; CLISSON]

Autrand, Françoise. *Charles VI.* Paris: Fayard, 1986.

Henneman, John Bell. "Who Were the Marmousets?" *Medieval Prosopography* 5 (1984): 19–63.

MARQUIS/MARQUISATE. The title "marquis" (OFr. *marchis* or *marquis*, Occitan *marques*) was coined in the early 9th century to describe the counts who had been placed in command of the new multicounty border districts, or "marches," created by Charlemagne. Under Charlemagne himself, these officers were commonly designated by some descriptive phrase, but under his son Louis the Pious three distinctive titles began to be used to designate them: *praefectus marcae* or *limitis* ("prefect of the march" or "border"), *dux* ("duke"), and *marchio* ("march man" or "marquis"). The last of these titles, first attested in 828, was used after 850 with increasing frequency by the West Frankish chancery, along with its adjectival equivalents *marchisus* and *marchensis*.

In the 10th century, the marches that survived were converted into hereditary principalities, but the princes who ruled them and other comparable dominions continued to employ the title *marchio* and its variants, along with the titles *princeps* ("prince"), *comes* ("count"), and in most cases *dux* ("duke"), in various combinations, in reference to the same dominion. The wives and widows of these princes were usually styled *comitissa* ("countess").

This usage persisted until the period 1060–1120, when one by one the princes of France abandoned the title *marchio*, or "marquis," in respect to their French principalities, in favor of either *dux* or *comes*. Between 1120, when the count and marquis of Flanders abandoned the title, and 1504, when a new marquisate was erected in Provence, there was no dominion bearing the title "marquisate" (Lat. *marchionatus*, Fr. *marquisat*) subject to the king of France.

D'A. *Jonathan D. Boulton*

[See also: MARCH]

Boulton, D'A.J.D. *Grants of Honour: The Origins of the System of Nobiliary Dignities of Traditional France, ca. 1100–1515.* Forthcoming.

Dhont, Jean. "Le titre de marquis à l'époque carolingienne." *Bulletin du Cange* 19 (1948): 407–17.

———. *Études sur la naissance des principautés territoriales en France (IXe–Xe siècles).* Paris: De Tempel, 1948.

Kienast, Walther. *Der Herzogstitel in Frankreich und Deutschland (9. bis 12. Jahrhundert).* Munich: Oldenbourg, 1968.

MARRIAGE, CLANDESTINE. According to medieval canon law, the heart of a valid marriage was consent, expressed in the oaths exchanged between the principals. This meant that if a man and woman swore to be true to each other and then proceeded to consummate their union, they were indeed married, even if their wedding was unwitnessed. Such a marriage was termed "clandestine." But the church greatly preferred witnesses, because a clandestine marriage could easily lead to disputes if one or both of the parties later claimed they were not really married at all. Therefore, although clandestine marriages were recognized, and those who had taken part in them could not proceed to marry anyone else, such persons were nevertheless expected to undergo penance to make up for having entered into marriage in an illegal manner.

Constance B. Bouchard

Sheehan, Michael M. "Choice of Marriage Partner in the Middle Ages: Development and Mode of Application of a Theory of Marriage." *Studies in Medieval and Renaissance History* 11 (1978): 1–33.

MARSEILLE. Founded ca. 600 B.C. by Greek traders, Marseille quickly became one of the most important centers for Hellenic commerce in the western Mediterranean. Within a century, Marseille had established colonies of its own, becoming a rival of Carthage. With the expansion of Roman power, the Marseillais served as faithful Roman allies while preserving their autonomy. In 476, the city came under the control of the Visigoths, and then the Burgundians, Ostrogoths, and finally, in 536, the Franks.

Throughout the 5th century, Marseille enjoyed an active trade with the East, North Africa, and Spain and had sizable resident colonies of Greeks, Jews, and Syrians. By the late 6th century, Lombard attacks and internecine rivalry among the Merovingian and then the Carolingian Franks resulted in a prolonged decline for the city. It was only after 972, when the Muslims had been forced from the region, that Marseille began to recover its former economic activity. At the same time, the monastery of Saint-Victor of Marseille became one of the leading forces for Christian reform.

In the 13th century, after short-lived experiments in self-government, Marseille was ruled by the house of Toulouse and then in mid-century by Charles of Anjou as count of Provence. In this period, the city's trade flourished until the Muslims reasserted their control over the Levant. In the 1440s, René d'Anjou again restored the city's commercial prosperity, which continued after Provence was incorporated into the French kingdom in the 1480s.

Stephen Weinberger

The original crypt of the basilica of Saint-Victor in Marseille was carved out of the rock in the early 5th century, when an abbey was founded here by St. John Cassian. His monastery played an important role in early Christendom and was burned several times by invaders. The present building, constructed for the most part after 1201, encloses the 5th-century crypt as well as an 11th-century crypt built over it. The transept and square apse were added by Pope Urban V in 1363, as well as the battlemented curtain wall that surrounds the abbey. The old cathedral of La Major stands a little north of the Vieux Port over vestiges of a 4th-century baptistery. Of the 12th-century church, there remain the transept with its ribbed dome; the apse, of Provençal type, with a ribbed semidome; and a Romanesque altar dedicated to the Virgin Mary.

William W. Kibler

[See also: MEDITERRANEAN TRADE; PROVENCE; RENÉ D'ANJOU]

Baratier, Édouard, et al. *Histoire de Marseille.* Toulouse: Privat, 1973.

Benoît, Fernand. *L'abbaye de Saint-Victor de Marseille et l'église de la Major à Marseille.* 2nd ed. Paris: Laurens, 1966.

Feuher, Paul-Albert. *Le développement urbain en Provence de l'époque romaine à la fin du XIVe siècle.* Paris: Boccard, 1964.

Lesage, Georges. *Marseille angevine, 1264–1348.* Paris: Boccard, 1950.

Rambert, Gaston. *Histoire du commerce de Marseille.* 2 vols. Paris: Plon, 1949–51.

MARSHAL. By the end of the Middle Ages, the marshal had become one of the highest-ranking military officers in France. Before the Crusades, the *mariscalus* had been a monastic officer responsible for provisions. The office became secular by the 11th century, when records from the reign of Henry I tell of a royal marshal whose responsibilities included the provisioning of the military. At this early date, the duties of the office do not appear to be standardized, since during the reigns of Philip II Augustus and Louis VIII the marshal was only an inspector of the royal stables, without responsibilities. It was not until the 14th century that he gained his military command duties, when Philip VI appointed two marshals as second in command of the French army below the constable. Throughout the Hundred Years' War, the marshals held command in the French military organization. Helped by a provost and some lieutenants, they were responsible for recruiting captains, inspecting the troops, and organizing the pay for the army. Perhaps their most important responsibility was keeping order among the soldiers and sitting in judgment over them. Marshals were also responsible for deciding ransoms and carrying out executions. They could also sit in parlement or in council and could be used as diplomatic envoys.

The marshals of the late Middle Ages were an inept group. Leadership quality was often poor and several officeholders failed in their responsibilities. Marshal Arnoul d'Audrehem fell into the hands of Edward, the Black Prince, at the Battle of Nájera in 1367; marshals Jean le Meingre II dit Boucicaut and Pierre de Rochefort were captured by the English in 1415 and 1419, respectively. In 1453, Marshal Philippe de Culant was forced to resign the office in disgrace. At other times, political rivalries and jurisdictional overlaps of military officers prohibited unified military command.

Kelly DeVries

[See also: BOUCICAUT; RAIS, GILLES DE]

Boutaric, Edgard. *Institutions militaires de la France avant les armées permanentes.* Geneva: Megariotis, 1978.

Contamine, Philippe. *Guerre, état et société à la fin du moyen âge: études sur les armées des rois de France, 1337–1494.* Paris: Mouton, 1972.

Lot, Ferdinand, and Robert Fawtier. *Histoire des institutions françaises au moyen âge.* 3 vols. Paris: Presses Universitaires de France, 1957–62, Vol. 2: *Institutions royales* (1958).

Luchaire, Achille. *Manuel des institutions françaises.* Paris: Hachette, 1892.

MARTIAL OF LIMOGES (fl. ca. 250). Saint, missionary, bishop of Limoges. According to Gregory of Tours, Martial of Limoges was one of the seven missionaries active in Gaul ca. 250. Later, a brief *vita* presented him as a disciple of the Apostle Peter, but the cult remained unexceptional until the end of the 10th century, when in conjunction with the Peace movement Martial became one of Gaul's foremost saints. A new story of his origins emerged in which he became Peter's younger cousin, companion of Jesus, towel holder at the Last Supper, witness to the Ascension and Pentecost, and spectacularly successful missionary to all of Gaul. The great success of this legend and the sensational consecration of a new, pilgrimage-style basilica at Limoges in 1028 inspired the monks to promote Martial to the status of apostle. Under the leadership of Adémar de Chabannes, they produced an elaborate apostolic liturgy; but on the day of its inauguration, August 3, 1029, the ceremony was interrupted by a Lombard prior, Benedict of Chiusa, who crushed Adémar and the monks in public debate. Adémar, however, composed forgeries and fictive narratives in which Pope John XIX and various church councils supported his cause; about a century later, the monks of Saint-Martial successfully redeployed these works and established Martial's apostolicity for the next nine centuries. There was a major ostention of the relics in 1388, and by the 16th century the tradition developed—still alive today—of carrying the relics through the city every seven years.

Richard Landes

[See also: ADÉMAR DE CHABANNES; HAGIOGRAPHY; RELICS AND RELIQUARIES; SAINTS, CULT OF]

Vita 1: BSAHL 40 (1892): 238–43; *Vita 2:* Surius, Laurentius. *Vitae sanctorum ex probatis authoribus et MSS. codicibus.* Cologne: Sumptibus Ioannis Kreps et Hermanni Mylii, 1617–18, Vol. 6, pp. 365–74.

Callahan, Daniel. "Sermons of Adémar of Chabannes and the Cult of St. Martial of Limoges." *Revue bénédictine* 86 (1976): 251–95.

Landes, Richard. *The Deceits of History: The Life and Times of Ademar of Chabannes (989–1034).* Forthcoming.

———, and Catherine Paupert, trans. *Naissance d'apôtre: la vie de saint Martial de Limoges.* Turnhout: Brepols, 1991.

Le Maître, Jean Loup. "Les miracles de saint Martial accomplis lors de l'ostension de 1388." *BSAHL* 102 (1975): 67–139.

MARTIANUS CAPELLA (fl. first half of the 5th c.). Between 410 and 439, Martianus Capella wrote his *De nuptiis Philologiae et Mercurii.* This non-Christian allegorical treatise, an encyclopedic work on the Seven Liberal Arts, was to have a widespread influence in the Christian schools of the late Middle Ages, as a source for teaching the Trivium and Quadrivium. The *De nuptiis* is in nine books, the first two describing the allegorical marriage and each of the next seven dealing with one of the liberal arts. In time-honored tradition, Martianus drew his material from a variety of earlier sources, chiefly Apulaius, Varro, Pliny, and Euclid. This (to us) derivative method only heightened its status in the Middle Ages.

Martianus had three clear "vogues": the first was among the scholars of the Carolingian renaissance centered on Charles the Bald. Johannes Scottus Eriugena and Remigius of Auxerre wrote commentaries on Martianus, and it is through Remigius's commentary that the *De nuptiis* became so influential. The second group of admirers were 10th-century Italians, like Notker of Saint-Gall, Rather of Verona, and Luitprand of Cremona. Finally, Martianus was one of the cosmographical authors most admired by the 12th-century Chartrians, like Alexander Neckham (who wrote a commentary), John of Salisbury, and Thierry of Chartres.

Of Martianus himself, little is known, except that he was a Roman citizen who spent most of his life at Carthage. One Victorian scholar, D. Samuel, describing the *De nuptiis* as a "mixture of dry traditional school learning and tasteless and extravagant theological ornament, applied to the most incongruous material, with an absolutely bizarre effect," illustrates the extant to which Martianus's work, with its interweaving of fact and fiction, has become foreign to our sensibility, although some earlier Christian writers, such as Cassiodorus and Gregory of Tours, similarly disliked this hybrid style.

Lesley J. Smith

[See also: ALEXANDER NECKHAM; CHARTRES; ERIUGENA, JOHANNES SCOTTUS; LIBERAL ARTS; REMIGIUS OF AUXERRE; THIERRY OF CHARTRES]

Martianus Capella. *De nuptiis Philologiae et Mercurii*, ed. Adolfus Dick, rev. Jean Preaux. Stuttgart: Teubner, 1983.

———. *The Marriage of Philology and Mercury,* trans. William Harris Stahl and Richard Johnson with E.L. Burge. New York: Columbia University Press, 1977.

Shanzer, Danuta. *A Philosophical and Literary Commentary on Martianus Capella's* De nuptiis Philologiae et Mercurii, *Book 1.* Berkeley: University of California Press, 1986.

MARTIN OF TOURS (ca. 316–ca. 397/400). Martin of Tours was born at Sabaria in Pannonia (today Szombathely, Hungary). Much of his youth was spent in Italy, at Pavia, where his father, a Roman army officer, was posted. At about age fifteen, he joined the army but became increasingly attracted to Christianity. While assigned to Amiens, Martin gave half his cloak to a beggar, who the next night revealed himself in a dream as Christ. Martin was baptized soon after this episode, and at some time after 339 he won release from the Roman army at Worms. He then returned to Italy to see his parents and while there ran into difficulties with the Arians, eventually finding respite as a hermit on the island of Gallinara (now Isola d'Albenga) in the Tyrrhenian Sea. After Hilary of Poitiers returned from exile, Martin joined him (ca. 360) in Poitiers and then founded at Marmoutier the first monastery in Gaul. Acclaimed bishop of Tours by the populace, but against his will, he was consecrated July 4, 372.

Although bishop, Martin lived as a monk, establishing a small hermitage outside of Tours at Ligugé. Considered the founder of monasticism in France, he was known for working miraculous cures and for at least two miracles in which he resuscitated the dead. Martin was also involved in many political and ecclesiastic struggles during his lifetime. He died at Candes, most probably in 397, although some have argued for the year 400. At his death, his body was claimed by the citizens of both Poitiers and Tours, with the relics finally coming to rest in Tours. His cult was popular throughout the Middle Ages, and the small chapel built over his tomb was rebuilt and enlarged a number of times. Martin's *vita* was written by his friend Sulpicius Severus. An account of his miracles was composed by Gregory of Tours.

Paula L. Gerson

[See also: GREGORY OF TOURS; HAGIOGRAPHY; MONASTICISM; PILGRIMAGE; RELICS AND RELIQUARIES; SAINTS, CULT OF; SAINTS' LIVES; TOURS-TOURAINE]

Sulpicius Severus. *Vita sancti Martini. PL* 20.159–222.

———. *Vie de saint Martin*, ed. Jacques Fontaine. 3 vols. Paris: Cerf, 1967–69.

———. *Life of Saint Martin.* In *Writings of Sulpicius Severus,* trans. Bernard Peebles. In *Fathers of the Church,* Vol. 7. New York: Fathers of the Church, 1949.

Gregory of Tours. *De virtutibus beati Martini episcopi.* In *Miracula et opera minora,* ed. B. Krusch (*MGH,* Scriptorum rerum merovingicarum I, 2, 584–661). Hanover, 1885; repr. 1965.

Donaldson, Christopher William. *Martin of Tours: Parish Priest, Mystic and Exorcist.* London: Routledge and Kegan Paul, 1980.

Farmer, Sharon A. *Communities of Saint Martin: Legend and Ritual in Medieval Tours.* Ithaca: Cornell University Press, 1991.

MARY, DEVOTION TO. Over the course of the medieval period, devotion to the mother of Jesus became a focus of Christian belief and practice, affecting liturgy, theology, art, and personal piety. Although Mary is mentioned infrequently in the canonical Gospels, with the exception of the birth-infancy narratives, Christian tradition soon developed a special place for her in literature, devotion, and thought. The apocryphal 2nd-century Greek *Protoevangelium of James* supplies Mary with a biography that makes her a dedicated virgin in the Jerusalem Temple, fed by angels, assigned the sacred task of weaving cloth for the Temple, and, at the end of her service, at age twelve, betrothed to a pious elderly man, Joseph. This same source provides a *vita* of Mary's parents, who are given the names Anna and Joachim. The early life of Mary and her miraculous conception by Anna were frequent subjects for illuminations in late-medieval books of hours, such as the magnificent *Hours of the Virgin* in the *Grandes Heures* of John, duke of Berry.

By the 5th century, Mary was hailed in Christian liturgy and doctrine as *theotokos* (Mother, or bearer, of God), a title confirmed by the Council of Ephesus in 431. Liturgical hymns praised her virginity. In letters and treatises, the monk and Bible translator Jerome argued for Mary's virginity not only before but during and after Jesus's birth ("perpetual virginity"), a view that became dominant in patristic and medieval thought, although opposed in Jerome's time by Helvidius and others. Only gradually did Mary receive recognition in the dynamics of salvation beyond her role as the virgin mother of Jesus and exemplar of the Christian woman dedicated to lifelong virginity. First in the Greek-speaking East, then in the Latin-speaking West, there began to develop the idea of her ability to intervene miraculously to benefit those who gave her special devotion. The legend of Theophilus—5th-century Greek, translated into Latin at the Carolingian court in the 8th century, and versified in French by Rutebeuf as the *Miracle de Théophile* in the latter part of the 13th century—told of a man who, Faust-like, sold his soul to the Devil, only to repent and ask Mary to deliver him from eternal damnation. This she does and is celebrated as the redeemer of captives and helper of the oppressed. This and many similar legends did much to spread the idea of Mary as intercessor and miraculous deliverer.

The special devotion to Mary first flowers in the late 11th and early 12th centuries and can be traced in France in a number of ways: in the collections of Marian miracles; in the prominence of relics, clothing especially, associated with Mary; in the number of churches, particularly cathedrals, dedicated to her; in liturgical texts and innovations as well as popular poetry; in iconographic developments in sculpture and illuminated manuscripts; and in theological treatises and debates.

Relics of the Virgin were primarily clothing, milk, or "separable" body parts, such as teeth or hair. The cathedral of Notre-Dame at Chartres possessed perhaps the most famous Marian relic in France: her tunic, or dress, donated by Charles the Bald in 876. Found unharmed in the crypt after fire destroyed the nave and choir in 1194, it was the focus of pilgrimage and devotion throughout the Middle Ages and remains so today. Laon had a fragment of Mary's clothing and perhaps some of her hair; a convent at Soissons possessed a slipper that was the focus of a healing cult briefly in the mid-12th century. Other sites claimed Mary's milk, a tooth, her belt, and the like.

Chartres, Soissons, and Laon were also foci of another 12th-century Marian phenomenon: the collection of accounts of miracles associated with the relics of a shrine. When Laon cathedral burned in 1112, a group of canons was twice sent on tour to raise money for rebuilding. Taking a collection of relics that included a fragment of Mary's clothing and perhaps strands of her hair, the canons stopped in cities and villages to invite prayers for Mary's intercession and offerings for rebuilding her church at Laon. The miracles and cures on these tours were recorded by Herman, a canon of the cathedral, in *De miraculis sanctae Mariae Laudunensis*. A collection formed at Soissons recorded miracles associated with a slipper. Similar collections were produced at Coutances and Rocamadour, the latter a Marian shrine without a relic but with a miracle-working statue from the 12th century onward. After the fire of 1194 at Chartres, the cathedral clergy, like those at Laon, took relics around the countryside. The miracles were recorded in a book; the contributions helped rebuild the cathedral. The Latin text of the miracles from Chartres was versified in French by Jean le Marchant (ca. 1262) as the *Livre de Notre Dame de Chartres*. The Latin collections of Marian miracles associated with local shrines and relics were combined with other generalized, less-localized miracle stories, and with Marian prayers, chants, poems, and the like to form *Mariales* that were meant to be read publicly or privately on Mary's feast days. These *Mariales* were soon translated into French, a notable example being Gautier de Coinci's *Miracles de Nostre Dame*. Jean de Garlande produced a versified collection of Marian miracles, the *Stella maris*, in 1248–49, while Vincent de Beauvais included a collection of her miracles in his *Speculum historiale*. In the 13th and 14th centuries, collections of Marian miracles provided a rich source of exempla for Dominican and Franciscan preachers.

Several iconographic representations of Mary became widespread and influential "types": the seated Mother and Child; Mary enthroned with Christ in Heaven (the Triumph and the Crowning of the Virgin); the standing Mother and Child; the sorrowing Mary holding the dead body of Christ. Each reflected a doctrinal or devotional attitude. The seated mother holding the child Jesus represented, from the 5th–6th centuries forward, the *theotokos*. It is Mary's awesome role as "birthgiver" of the incarnate deity that dominates this mode of representation. Numerous wooden cult statues took this form in medieval France, e.g., at Rocamadour. A striking example in monumental sculpture is in the tympanum of the right portal of the west façade of Chartres (ca. 1145–55).

The representation of Mary enthroned with Christ in Heaven, found in monumental sculpture of the late 12th and 13th centuries as well as in panel paintings and carved ivory panels throughout the later Middle Ages, emphasizes not maternity but two other themes: regal and triumphant power in a cosmic framework and the association of Mary with the bride and Christ with the bridegroom of the Song of Songs. Although some verses from the Song of Songs had long received a Marian interpretation and the feast of the Assumption had readings from the Song, it was not until the 12th century that the entire Song was given a symbolic interpretation, taking Mary as the bride, earlier interpretations had seen either the church or the individual soul as the bride. The overriding point is Mary's appearance as a woman with her adult son in a position of regal power in Heaven, an image drawing on ideas from courtly romance as well as royal ideology and shaped by the theological concept of the "bride of Christ" in Song of Songs commentaries. Sculpted tympani on the façades of the cathedrals of Senlis (ca. 1170) and Paris (ca. 1210–20) and the north-transept portal of Chartres (1205–10) depict Mary in this triumphant mode and have associated scenes from the death and resurrection-assumption of the Virgin.

The standing Mary with Jesus exemplified by the trumeau statue of the south portal of the cathedral of Amiens (ca. 1250), the *Vierge dorée*, presents Mary as the loving mother playing with her child, thus reflecting her deep human tenderness, connected in devotional piety with her love of all humankind, as shown in the numerous collections of Marian miracles that emphasize devotion to her as the loving mother.

A final widespread image type, the weeping Mary holding the crucified body of Christ, reflects a new 13th-century piety focused on Christ's suffering, Mary's sorrow, and the sorrowing response of the faithful; it was a piety developed especially in Franciscan and Dominican circles. In poetry, the popular *Stabat mater* shows a similar point of view, describing Mary's sorrow as she views the Crucifixion and then the yearning of the believer to share her sorrow.

The medieval church recognized five Marian feast days: Conception (December 8), Nativity (September 8), Annunciation (March 25), Purification (February 2), and Assumption (August 15). In addition, Saturday was especially dedicated to her. The feast day of the Assumption is predicated on an early legend that recounts an angelic vision foretelling Mary's death and then describes the gathering of the Apostles, her death, funeral, burial, and, three days later, the raising of her body by angels to Heaven, where it is reunited with her soul. So Mary was seen to have a special status: not only the virgin mother of Christ, but also, like him, present bodily in Heaven.

The doctrine of the Assumption passed readily into medieval theology and devotion. The doctrine of her Immaculate Conception, which asserts that Mary, unique among humans, was conceived by Anna and Joachim without Original Sin, was controversial, being vehemently rejected by Bernard of Clairvaux, Albert the Great, Thomas Aquinas, and Bonaventure. In the 13th century, the Franciscan theologian Duns Scotus argued in favor of the doctrine; generally, Franciscans favored it while Dominicans opposed it. Popular devotion tended to support it.

Poetry dedicated to Mary found a ready place both in and outside the liturgy. The popular Marian hymn *Ave maris stella* probably dates from the 8th century. Mary, called "Star of the Sea," is described as the virgin mother and Gate of Heaven and is the helper of humans, delivering them from disaster, illness, and oppression through her motherly influence over Jesus. The prayer *Ave Maria,* based on Luke 1:28 and 1:42, appeared first in the Little Office of the Blessed Virgin and then found more general use in the 12th century. The popular *Salve regina* was used in the liturgy at Cluny ca. 1135 and soon found use among the Cistercians and later the Dominicans. The gifted sequence writer Adam of Saint-Victor extolled Mary in theological and poetic paradoxes. In prose, hundreds of sermons praised Mary and explicated her theological significance, devotional importance, and maternal-queenly role.

The prayers to Mary composed by Anselm of Bec had a lasting and determinitive impact on Marian devotion and theology. He spoke of her maternal aspect as both vehicle of the Incarnation and the embodiment of motherly forgiveness and graciousness; he also used the language of courtly romance and queenship to stress her benovolence and status as "redemptrix," as he titled her.

From the 12th century onward, patterns of Marian devotion appeared that utilized repeated formulaic prayers, much on the model of the monastic repetition of the 150 Psalms each week, the repetitive recitation of the Lord's Prayer in devotion or penance, and antiphonal praises to Mary. These prayers were finally reduced to a brief formula consisting of the *Ave Maria,* with inserted *Glorias* and the Lord's Prayer. Finally, a pattern of 150 *Ave Marias,* in fifteen groups of ten each ("decades"), with a focus of meditation for each decade came to be an accepted pattern, with the prayers counted by means of a string of beads that came to be known as a rosary. The association of the origin of the recitation of the rosary with the Dominicans and Dominic is not supported by recent research.

Grover A. Zinn

[See also: ADAM OF SAINT-VICTOR; CHARTRES; COUTANCES; GOTHIC ART; LAON; MARIAN ANTIPHONS; MARY, LITURGICAL VENERATION OF; POPULAR DEVOTION; PREACHING; RELICS AND RELIQUARIES; ROCAMADOUR; RUTEBEUF; SOISSONS]

Gautier de Coinci. *Les miracles de Nostre Dame,* ed. V. Frédéric Koenig. 4 vols. Geneva: Droz, 1955–70.

Herman. *De miraculis s. Mariae Laudunensis.* PL 156.961–1020.

Jean le Marchant. *Le livre de Notre Dame de Chartres,* ed. Pierre Kunstmann. Ottawa: Éditions de l'Université d'Ottawa, 1973.

Liber de miraculis sanctae Dei genitricis Maria, ed. Thomas F. Crane. Ithaca: Cornell University Press, 1925. [Repr. of edition published by Bernard Pez, Vienna, 1731.]

Rutebeuf. *Le miracle de Théophile,* ed. and trans. Jean Dufournet. Paris: Flammarion, 1987.

Graef, Hilda. *Mary: A History of Doctrine and Devotion.* 2 vols. in 1. Westminster: Christian Classics, 1985.

O'Carroll, Michael. *Theotokos: A Theological Encyclopedia of the Blessed Virgin Mary.* Wilmington: Glazier, 1982.

Ward, Benedicta. *Miracles and the Medieval Mind: Theory, Record, and Event, 1000–1215.* Philadelphia: University of Pennsylvania Press, 1982, pp. 132–65.

MARY, LITURGICAL VENERATION OF. Although they all originated in the East and were instituted in Rome in the course of the 7th century, the four great Marian feasts of the church year were well on their way to being firmly established by the late 8th century in what is now modern France: the Feast of the Purification, February 2; the Annunciation, March 25; the Assumption, August 15; and the Nativity of the Blessed Virgin, September 8. January 1, the Feast of the Circumcision and the Octave of Christmas, was also a day for Marian veneration. Already by the 8th century, *Ordines romani* XV and XX testify that an elaborate procession for the Purification was known north of the Alps. Processional antiphons sung at the three other major feasts in manuscripts from the 9th and 10th centuries prove that these feasts had processions, as well as a repertory of chant texts, prayers, and readings. The series of four seasonal Marian antiphons sung regularly at Compline from the 13th century were taken from the repertory of elaborate antiphons composed to frame the performance of of the Magnificat (Luke 1:46–55), sung at Vespers to a series of tones.

Increasing Marian devotion from the 9th century led also to a greater number of celebrations in her honor: major Marian feasts came to be celebrated with Vigils and Octaves, and a votive Mass for the Virgin was instituted in most places for Saturdays throughout the year. With the founding of Cluny and the establishment of an ever larger network of affiliated houses during the 10th century, it became traditional to celebrate a commemorative Office of the Virgin on Saturdays, in conjunction with her Mass, so that Saturday, from first Vespers on Friday until Compline on Saturday evening, was consecrated to the Blessed Virgin in monasteries throughout France. Ordinals and customaries from the 11th century reveal the adoption of the "Little Office of the Virgin" as well, which included a full cycle of hours and was said each day, alongside the *opus Dei.* During this same period, great numbers of hymns, tropes, and sequences were composed for upgraded Marian feasts, embodying a history of the rise of Mary's cult in France in their texts. The intense devotion of the Dominicans and Franciscans to Mary led to greater standardization of texts and music for her celebration from the 13th century onward. Votive Masses for the Virgin, the singing of the Magnificat at Vespers, and the Marian antiphons at Compline served to provide both opportunity and inspiration for later polyphonic music dedicated to her honor.

Margot Fassler

[See also: DIVINE OFFICE; MARIAN ANTIPHONS]

Auniord, Jean-Baptiste, and Robert Thomas. "Cîteaux et Notre Dame." In *Maria: études sur la sainte vierge*, ed. Hubert Du Manoir de Juaye. 7 vols. Paris: Beauchesne, 1949–64, Vol. 2, pp. 579–624.

Duval, André. "La dévotion mariale dans l'ordre des Frères Prêcheurs." *Ibid.*, Vol. 2, pp. 737–82.

Dom Frénaud. "Le culte de Notre Dame dans l'ancienne liturgie latine." *Ibid.*, Vol. 6, pp. 157–211.

Gourdel, Yves. "Le culte de la Très Sainte Vierge dans l'ordre des Chartreux." *Ibid.*, Vol. 2, pp. 625–78.

Leclercq, Jean. "Dévotion et théologie mariales dans le monachisme bénédictin." *Ibid.*, Vol. 2, pp. 547–78.

O'Carroll, Michael. *Theotokos: A Theological Encyclopedia of the Blessed Virgin Mary*. Wilmington: Glazier, 1982.

Wright, Craig. *Music and Liturgy in Notre Dame de Paris (500–1500)*. Cambridge: Cambridge University Press, 1989.

MARY MAGDALENE. Mary of Magdala (Mary Magdalene), a female follower of Jesus in the Gospels, received a medieval *vita* that offered a major expansion upon her appearance in the Gospel narratives. She was venerated especially at two popular French pilgrimage shrines: the Benedictine abbeys of Vézelay and of Saint-Maximin at Aix-en-Provence.

In the Gospels, Mary of Magdala is among the women who travel with Jesus in his ministry (Luke 8:1–2; cf. Matthew 27:55–56), and Jesus is said to have cast seven devils out of her (Luke 8:2 and Mark 16:9). She is present at the Crucifixion (at the foot of the Cross with the Virgin Mary [John 19:25] or looking on from afar with other women [Matthew 27:55–56 and Mark 15:40–41]). She is named among the women who go, after the sabbath, to the sepulcher where Jesus was buried (Matthew 28:1; Mark 16:1; Luke 24:1–10). She is the first to encounter Jesus after the Resurrection (John 20:1–19). These incidents provided the basic narrative of a woman cured of demonic possession who followed Jesus, was present at his death, and was the first to see him resurrected. Indeed, on the basis of the passage in John 20, she is called "the apostle to the Apostles."

In the patristic and early-medieval periods, other Gospel narratives involving Jesus and women were associated with Mary Magdalene. The unnamed woman identified as a sinner (and thus important for the later persona of the Magdalene) who bathes Jesus's feet with her tears and anoints them (Luke 7:30) and the unnamed woman who anoints his head (Matthew 26:6–13) were both identified with Mary Magdalene. She was also identified with Mary of Bethany, the sister of Lazarus and Martha. Not only the name made this identification possible; Mary of

Bethany also anoints Jesus's feet and wipes them with her hair when Jesus visits in her home (John 12:13).

This identification with Mary of Bethany provided Mary of Magdala with a family closely associated with Jesus, for he visited in their home and he raised Lazarus from the dead. The medieval *vita* of Mary extended this family. Mary's rich and noble parents possessed the castle of Magdala and its lands. Mary was betrothed to young John the Evangelist. When he forsook her to follow Jesus, she entered a life of prostitution. Later, cured of demonic possession by Jesus, Mary dedicated herself to his service and became the prototype of conversion, devotion, humility, penance, and contemplative prayer (the latter signified by Mary sitting peacefully at Jesus's feet listening to him while Martha, active, prepares a meal [Luke 10:39–42]).

Following Jesus's ascension, persecution forced Mary, Martha, and Lazarus to flee in a boat, which arrived at Marseille on the south coast of France. Lazarus became bishop of Marseille; Mary became a renowned preacher. Later, she went to Aix-en-Provence and embraced the life of a hermit dedicated to extreme asceticism and prayer. She was fed by angels and allowed her hair to become the covering for her body emaciated from ascetic discipline. (This later ascetic career may owe much to a conflation with the *vita* of St. Mary the Egyptian, a reformed prostitute who went into the desert to perform radical acts of asceticism and penance.)

Veneration of Mary Magdalene at Vézelay seems to have begun in the mid-11th century, when an account of the 8th-century "translation" (by pious theft) of her relics from her tomb in Aix, deserted in the wake of Muslim attacks, was drawn up. Papal confirmation of the possession of her relics by the monks at Vézelay followed. The famous Romanesque church was consecrated by Pope Innocent II in 1131–32; St. Bernard preached the Second Crusade there in 1146.

The monks of Saint-Maximin in Aix retaliated in the late 13th century with the assertion that the monks of Vézelay had taken the wrong body several centuries earlier; Mary's relics were in fact still in the crypt of the abbey church. The presence of these relics, then the site of miraculous cures, was promoted with vigor, and veneration of Mary Magdalene shifted from Vézelay to Aix.

The elaboration of the medieval *vita* of Mary Magdalene and the theft and veneration of her relics at two different sites illustrate two common elements of the hagiographical literature and devotional practice of the medieval period.

Grover A. Zinn

[See also: AIX-EN-PROVENCE; HAGIOGRAPHY; RELICS AND RELIQUARIES; RUTEBUEF; SAINTS, CULT OF; SAINTS' LIVES; VÉZELAY]

Rabanus Maurus. *The Life of Saint Mary Magdalene and Her Sister Saint Martha: A Medieval Biography*, trans. David Mycoff. Kalamazoo: Cistercian, 1989.

Garth, Helen Meredith. *Saint Mary Magdalene in Medieval Tradition*. Baltimore: Johns Hopkins University Press, 1950.

Geary, Patrick. *Furta Sacra: Thefts of Relics in the Central Middle Ages*. rev. ed. Princeton: Princeton University Press, 1990.

Saxer, Victor. *Le culte de Ste. Marie Madeleine en occident: des origines à la fin du moyen âge*. Auxerre: Publications de la Société des Fouilles Archéologiques et des Monuments Historiques de l'Yonne, 1959.

Ward, Benedicta. *Harlots of the Desert: A Study of Repentance in Early Monastic Sources*. Kalamazoo: Cistercian, 1987.

MASS, CHANTS AND TEXTS. The Mass (Latin *missa*) was the term commonly used in the Middle Ages to designate the eucharistic sacrifice that is the principal religious service of Christianity. The service has its origins in the Last Supper of Jesus Christ, described in the three Synoptic Gospels. The term appears as early as the 4th century (St. Ambrose, *missam facere*).

The most basic division within the Mass is that between its first part, the Fore-Mass or Liturgy of the Word, and the sacrificial rite proper that follows. For the early church, these are called the Mass of the Catechumens and the Mass of the Faithful, since the Catechumens, those undergoing instruction before baptism, were dismissed before the onset of the sacred mysteries. The Fore-Mass consisted at first only of an initial greeting from the presiding priest or bishop, readings from Scripture, a discourse (homily or sermon) on the readings, and concluding prayers. This is obviously a service of instruction, altogether appropriate for Catechumens. There were three readings rather than the medieval two: an Old Testament reading, one from an Epistle or the Acts of the Apostles, and one from the Gospels. There were no chants until the later 4th century, when a psalm, the apparent ancestor of the medieval Gradual, came to be a regular feature of the Fore-Mass. Its verses were chanted by the lector and answered by a congregational refrain. A second psalm, the Alleluia psalm, came by the early 5th century to be sung in the church at Jerusalem after the Gradual psalm, as prelude to the Gospel; it was not taken up immediately in the West.

After the dismissal of the Catechumens, the eucharistic rite began with the "prayers of the faithful." Next, the elements of bread and wine were brought in, and the presiding priest said the eucharistic prayer over them. The medieval Latin version of the prayer is present already in the *De sacramentis* of St. Ambrose of Milan (d. 397). Present also in the 4th century was the chanting of the Sanctus and the Lord's Prayer, which formed the high points of a dialogue between celebrant and faithful, sung in all probability to the same simple tones employed in the Middle Ages (see Levy). During the distribution of the eucharist, a communion psalm was sung, generally Psalm 33 (34), with its Verse 8 as congregational refrain: "Taste and see that the Lord is sweet."

Western liturgical sources from the late 5th to early 8th century are sparse, but with the document *Ordo romanus I* we have a highly detailed description of the papal Mass from ca. 700. *Ordo romanus I* is one of the earliest of many *ordines romani*, all existing exclusively in Frankish manuscripts, that not only describe the papal Mass but show how it was imitated and adapted throughout the Carolingian realm in the late 8th and early 9th centuries. The medieval Mass, outlined here in Table 1, is virtually complete in the papal Mass of *Ordo romanus I*.

Table 1.   *The Mass-Prayers, Readings, Chants*

Chants		Prayers and readings
Proper	Ordinary	
Fore-Mass		
Introit		
	Kyrie	
	Gloria	
		Collect
		Epistle
Gradual		
Alleluia-tract		
(Sequence)		
		Gospel
	Credo	
Mass of the Faithful		
Offertory		
		Preface
	Sanctus	
		Eucharistic prayer
		Lord's Prayer
	Agnus Dei	
Communion		
		Postcommunion
	(Ite missa est)	

The distinction between Proper and Ordinary chants, of doubtful application to the ecclesiastical song of the early church, is now of fundamental importance. The texts of the Proper chants relate to a particular feast day so that they change more or less daily, while the texts of the Ordinary chants are the same for every Mass. All the Proper chants of Table 1 are present in *Ordo romanus I*, with the exception of the Sequence, a poetic extension of the Alleluia, that the Franks added in the 9th century. The Introit consisted of an antiphon, a melodious chant of moderate length and elaboration, that was sung as a refrain to a psalm chanted while the pope (later bishop or abbot) processed down the nave of the church to the sanctuary. At Rome, the singing of the Introit and the other Proper chants was the responsibility of the *schola cantorum*, a group of skilled clerical musicians; similar organizations were established in the principal ecclesiastical centers of Francia already before the end of the 8th century. After the declaiming of the Epistle, a member of the *schola* stood on the steps of the ambo to chant the Gradual (called *responsum in Ordo romanus I*). It was starkly different from its 4th-century psalmodic ancestor, consisting in a highly elaborate refrain sung by the *schola* and an equally elaborate single verse sung by the soloist. This was followed by the singing of the Alleluia, or during penitential seasons the Tract; the Alleluia consisted of a rhapsodic refrain sung by the *schola* before and after a solo verse, while the Tract was unique in that it consisted of a series of psalm verses sung to a florid melody without any sort of refrain structure. This group of chants associated with the readings were exceptional in that they accompanied no liturgical action; they were simply listened to by the attendant clergy and congregation.

A celebration of Mass in late 15th-century Paris. B.L. Add. 18192, fol. 110. *Courtesy of the British Library.*

The Offertory was sung as the gifts of bread and wine were presented to the celebrant; it consisted of an elaborate refrain and two or three verses of similar musical complexity; within a few centuries the verses would be dropped with only the refrain retained. The Communion, finally, sung during the distribution of communion as in the early church, closely resembled the Introit with its melodious antiphon sung as a refrain to a chanted psalm (both Introit and Communion would eventually lose most of their psalm verses).

The chants of the Ordinary also were mostly in place at the beginning of the 8th century in Rome; only the Credo, which would follow some three centuries later, was absent. The Kyrie eleison, sung immediately after the Introit, is a radically shortened form of litany that was earlier recited as part of the prayers that concluded the Fore-Mass. Next came the Gloria in excelsis, an ancient hymn that takes its first words from the angelic salutation to the shepherds at Christmas. A comparatively late entry into the Mass, its use was subject for a number of centuries to restrictions; it was limited, for example, to Christmas, or to Masses where a bishop presided. The Sanctus, as in the early church, concluded the Preface, the introductory portion of the eucharistic prayer. The Agnus Dei, finally, sung during the fraction of the host, was introduced only in the time of Pope Sergius I (r. 697–701). Its text, "Lamb of God, who takest away the sins of the world," was adopted as a deliberate act of theological defiance against the Byzantine empire, which recently had forbidden references to Christ as a lamb. (The Ite missa est, intoned by the celebrant to signal the end of Mass, later took on the character of an Ordinary chant when it began to imitate the melodies of the Kyrie.)

While this early-medieval papal Mass (and its Frankish adaptations) retained the essential shape of its 4th-century counterpart, its overall aspect differed dramatically. Aside from the pomp required by the movements of the pope and his retinue, the dominating impression is that created by the nearly continuous choral and solo singing of the *schola cantorum*. The melodies of the Mass Proper, while probably not precisely those we know from the early 10th-century Frankish manuscripts of Gregorian chant, were comparable in format and dimension. The melodies of the Mass Ordinary were simpler than their later counterparts; but still they were sung by the *schola* as discrete musical events, whereas they had originated for the most part as simple congregational contributions to the dialogue with the celebrant. He, too, ceded much of his earlier role as the aural focal point of the ceremony. He continued to exchange greetings with the attendant clergy and people, and he chanted the Preface and Pater noster; but he recited the eucharistic prayers (the medieval Canon) in a subdued tone, and by the end of the 8th century in complete silence. Solemn Mass at the beginning of the 8th century was well on its way to being dominated by ecclesiastical music, a process that would be completed in the late Middle Ages.

The texts, and quite possibly the music, of the Mass Proper achieved their first maturity close in time to the copying of *Ordo Romanus I*. We have the texts in unnotated Frankish graduals from ca. 800 (and their melodies from notated graduals of ca. 900), and we know that the texts existed in Rome in the first half of the 8th century because they appear in the so-called Old Roman graduals, manuscripts that represent the Roman liturgy before its transmission to Francia in the second half of the 8th century. In earlier centuries, the Proper chants had simply been psalms and the first chant books had been psalters, so that clearly a period of intense composition and organization was required to produce the complex system of texts that makes up the early-medieval Mass Proper. Liturgical and musical historians long assumed this period to be the time of Pope Gregory I (590–604), but it appears more likely now to have been the heyday of the *schola cantorum*, the later 7th and earlier 8th centuries.

The essential trait of the Mass Proper is the provision of an appropriate set of chants for each day of the annual cycle, something one might take for granted today, but an innovation in a time when the more normal expectation was a day-to-day selection of antiphons and psalms from an existing repertory. The majority of the new texts were chosen from the time-honored source of the Psalter, but they were short apposite passages, removed from their original context and frequently reshaped to create a workable vehicle for a musical composition. And many texts were fashioned from other biblical sources, for example, evocative lyrics from the prophetic books for the newly created season of Advent, and colorful Gospel narratives for the communion antiphons of the Christmas and Paschal seasons. As for the melodies, one can only assume that this project of textual revision and creation went hand in hand with a similar musical process. What remains a question of the most profound difficulty, however, is how closely these melodies match those in the earliest notated Frankish graduals of nearly two centuries later.

Two major developments altered the external aspect of the Mass in later centuries: the accumulation of tropes and the growth in prominence of the Ordinary. Tropes— preludes, interludes, and postludes of text and music— were freely added to chants of the Proper and Ordinary with the exception of the Credo. They were obviously a creative outlet for active clerical poets and musicians at a time when the core repertory of the Mass was complete. Common already among the 9th-century Franks, troping reached its climax in the great Benedictine monasteries of the 11th century, such as those belonging to the French order of Cluny. The Ordinary, in addition to accumulating tropes, was the beneficiary of numerous new and more elaborate melodies. Both manifestations can be seen as different aspects of a process that at once gave the Ordinary an eminence it had not previously possessed (nor deserved, modern liturgical scholars would say) and allowed it also to share to some extent in the essential characteristic of the Proper, as certain tropes and melodies became associated with particular feast days, or at least classes of festival. In the late Middle Ages, the rise of the polyphonic Ordinary succeeded in eclipsing even the musical significance of the Proper. France was foremost in this movement that created one of the great monuments of western music, the Cyclic Mass, a unified composition in five movements: Kyrie, Gloria, Credo, Sanctus, and Agnus Dei. Guillaume Dufay of Cambrai (d. 1474) was the central figure in establishing the genre.

James McKinnon

[See also: CALENDAR, LITURGICAL; CYCLIC MASS; EUCHARISTIC VENERATION AND VESSELS; GALLICAN RITE; LITURGICAL BOOKS; LITURGICAL LANGUAGES; LITURGICAL YEAR; STATIONS OF THE CROSS; SEQUENCE (EARLY); SEQUENCE (LATE); TROPES, ORDINARY; TROPES, PROPER; VESTMENTS, ECCLESIASTICAL]

Atchley, Edward. *Ordo Romanus Primus*. London: Moring, 1905.
Jeffrey, Peter. "The Introduction of Psalmody into the Roman Mass by Pope Celestine I (422–432)." *Archiv für Liturgiewissenschaft* 26 (1984): 147–65.
Jungmann, Josef. *The Mass of the Roman Rite: Its Origins and Development*, trans. Francis X. Brunner. 2 vols. New York: Benziger, 1951–55.
Levy, Kenneth. "The Byzantine Sanctus and its Modal Tradition in East and West." *Annales musicologiques* 6 (1958–63): 7–68.
McKinnon, James. "The Fourth-Century Origin of the Gradual." *Early Music History* 7 (1987): 91–106.
Martimort, Aimé Georges. "Origine et signification de l'alleluia de la messe romaine." In *Kyriakon: Festschrift Johannes Quasten*, ed. Patrick Granfield and Josef Jungmann. Münster in Westphalia: Aschendorff, 1970, pp. 811–38.

MASSELIN, JEAN (d. 1500). Cleric, lawyer, and historian. Masselin was a canon at the cathedral of Rouen, doctor of civil and canon law, and *officialis* of the archbishop of Rouen when he was chosen to represent the *bailliage* of Rouen at the Estates General that convened at Tours between January and March 1484. His lengthy journal of the proceedings of the Estates, one of the most valuable sources for the history of medieval representative assemblies, remains Masselin's claim to fame, although he later served with distinction as dean of the chapter of Rouen.

John Bell Henneman, Jr.

Bernier, Adhelm, ed. *Journal des États-Généraux de France tenus à Tours en 1484 sous le règne de Charles VIII, rédigé en latin par Jean Masselin*. Paris: Imprimerie Royale, 1835. [Collection of unedited documents.]

MATFRE ERMENGAUD. Author of the *Breviari d'Amor*, an Occitan encyclopedic work in rhyming octosyllabic couplets, dated 1288, preserved entire (35,600 lines) in twelve manuscripts from Languedoc, Toulouse, and Catalonia. The author, otherwise unknown, was a native of Béziers and drew upon the earlier *Image du monde*.

Organized as a "Tree of Love," Matfre's encyclopedia popularizes theology more than science. Beginning at the roots with the Trinity, he discusses angels, demons, the zodiac, and the planets. He provides a cursory account of the natural world. Under "Natural Law," he discusses the proper way to worship God. A section on sin offers portraits of greed and duplicity drawn from contemporary society: the castle lord, the lawyer, the apothecary, the merchant, the gambler. Under "The Love of God," he summarizes the articles of faith and the life of Christ, then several saints' lives.

In the last 8,000 lines, the "Perilhos tractat d'amor de las donas," Matfre uses 266 quotations from troubadour poetry (including his own) to support his precepts. Through imaginary dialogue with Love's followers and critics, he answers questions and objections. The impulse to love, natural but potentially dangerous, must be managed wisely. Ladies should be honored; good love must not be criticized. A 138-line verse letter to his sister, explaining the symbolism of a Christmas capon, follows the *Breviari*.

Amelia Van Vleck

[See also: DIDACTIC LITERATURE (OCCITAN); *ELEDUS ET SERENE, ROMAN DE*; *IMAGE DU MONDE*; MORAL TREATISES]

Matfre Ermengaud. *Le breviari d'amor de Matfre Ermengaud, suivi de sa lettre à sa soeur*, ed. Gabriel Azaïs. 2 vols. Béziers:

Société Archéologique, Scientifique et Littéraire de Béziers, 1862–81.

———. *Le breviari d'amor de Matfre Ermengaud, tome V (27252T–34597T)*, ed. Peter T. Ricketts. Leiden: Brill, 1976.

Laske-Fix, Katja. *Der Bildzyklus des Breviari d'amor*. Munich: Schnell und Steiner, 1973.

MATHEMATICS. *See* LIBERAL ARTS

MATHEUS DE SANCTO JOHANNE (fl. 1365–89).

French composer in the service of King John II during his captivity in England from 1356 to 1359, at the same time as composer Pierre des Molins. Matheus served Louis I of Anjou in 1378 and Pope Clement VII at Avignon from 1382 to 1386. His works, which influenced Philippus de Caserta, show remarkable independence of voices and sophisticated rhythmic proportions.

Benjamin Garber

[See also: ARS SUBTILIOR; COMPOSERS, MINOR (14TH CENTURY); PHILIPPUS DE CASERTA]

Apel, Willi, ed. *French Secular Compositions of the Fourteenth Century*. Vol. 1. N.p.: American Institute of Musicology, 1970.

Greene, Gordon, ed. *French Secular Music: Manuscript Chantilly, Musée Condé 564*. 2 vols. Monaco: Oiseau-Lyre, 1981–82.

MATILDA (Maud; 1102–1167).

Countess of Anjou and claimant to the English throne. After 1121, Matilda was the only surviving legitimate child of Henry I, king of England and duke of Normandy. After the death of her husband, Emperor Henry V of Germany, in 1125, Matilda was reunited with her father, whose barons swore to support her as his heir. In 1128, Matilda married Geoffroi Plantagenêt, count of Anjou.

In 1135, conflict arose between Matilda's father and husband over Normandy. Matilda and Geoffroi were in rebellion when Henry died in December, and this may have contributed to Matilda's loss of the English crown to her cousin Stephen of Blois. Between 1139 and 1148, Matilda was in England, fighting unsuccessfully for the throne, although she did win the right of succession for her son Henry II (r. 1154–89). Matilda then returned to Normandy, where she assisted in the routine business of ducal, and later royal, government.

Although English chroniclers saw Matilda as arrogant and unsuited to rule, she won the approbation of continental writers. A patron of letters, Matilda received dedications from the historical writer Hugues de Fleury and the poet Philippe de Thaün. Upon her death, she bequeathed money to construct a stone bridge across the Seine near Rouen. She had also been a generous patron to Cistercian and Augustinian monasteries but above all to the Benedictines of Bec-Hellouin.

Lois Huneycutt

Barlow, Frank. *The Feudal Kingdom of England, 1042–1216*. 3rd ed. London: Longman, 1972.

Chibnall, Marjorie. "The Empress Matilda and Church Reform." *Transactions of the Royal Historical Society* 5th ser. 38 (1988): 107–30.

———. "The Empress Matilda and Bec-Hellouin." *Anglo-Norman Studies* 12 (1988): 35–48.

MATTHEW OF AQUASPARTA (ca. 1240–1302).

Bonaventure's most famous disciple, Matthew was a gifted Franciscan leader rather than an original theologian or academic. He was born in Aquasparta, near Todi, and became a Franciscan ca. 1254. By 1268, he was studying theology in Paris under John of Peckham and was later Franciscan regent master there. He also taught at Bologna. In 1278–79, he followed John of Peckham as *lector sacri palatii* in Rome, and his ecclesiastical rise continued in regular fashion: he was minister-general of the order in 1287, cardinal in 1288, and cardinal-bishop of Porto and Rufina in 1291, carrying out various missions for Boniface VIII.

Matthew's academic strengths are his clarity of mind and of expression. Largely following and developing Bonaventure (and therefore Augustine) in his thought, he nevertheless gives a lucid restatement of some of the most difficult issues. His own opinions are most evident in the theory of knowledge. However, like Bonaventure, he is Franciscan in believing that the end of human speculation is not knowledge but love of God.

His writings, which were not widely circulated even in his own time, include biblical commentary, a *Sententiae* commentary, quodlibetal questions, disputed questions, and sermons.

Lesley J. Smith

[See also: BONAVENTURE]

Matthew of Aquasparta. *Quaestiones disputatae: De anima separata* [ed. G. Gal], *De anima beata* [ed. A. Emmen], *De ieiunio* [ed. I. Brady], *et De legibus* [ed. C. Piana]. Quaracchi, Florence: Typographia Collegii S. Bonaventurae, 1959.

———. *Quaestiones disputatae de anima XIII*, ed. A.-J. Gondras. Paris: Vrin, 1961.

———. *Quaestiones disputatae de fide et de cognitione*. 2nd ed. Quaracchi, Florence: Typographia Collegii S. Bonaventure, 1957.

———. *Quaestiones disputatae de gratia*, ed. Victorini Doucet O.F.M. Ad Claras Aquas, Florence: Typographia Collegii S. Bonaventurae, 1935.

———. *Quaestiones disputatae de incarnatione et de lapsu aliaeque selectae de Christo et de Eucharistia*, ed. PP. Collegii S. Bonaventurae. 2nd ed. Quaracchi, Florence: Typographia Collegii S. Bonaventurae, 1957.

———. *Quaestiones disputatae de productione rerum et de providentia*, ed. Gedeonis Gal. Quaracchi, Florence: Typographia Collegii S. Bonaventurae, 1956.

———. *Ten Disputed Questions on Knowledge*. In *Selections from Medieval Philosophers*, ed. Richard McKeon. 2 vols. New York: Scribner, 1929–30, Vol. 1, pp. 242–302.

Hayes, Zachary. *The General Doctrine of Creation in the Thirteenth Century, with Special Emphasis on Matthew of Aquasparta.* Munich: Schoningh, 1964.

MATTHIEU D'ARRAS (d. 1352).

Born in northern France, Matthieu d'Arras was in Avignon when hired by Emperor Charles IV to design and build the new cathedral of Prague. He supervised the construction of Saint-Vitus from the laying of its foundation stone on November 21, 1344, until his death, completing eight choir chapels together with the corresponding arcades of the main vessel to the height of the triforium. Although nothing is known of Matthieu's other buildings prior to Prague, his plan for the cathedral reveals a strong influence from Narbonne, the most monumental of recent French episcopal projects. Matthieu's work is often branded as traditional and overshadowed by that of his successor, Peter Parler, yet his piers anticipate Late Gothic design in their compact prismatic forms and reduction of capitals to thin moldings. The subsequent activity of his workshop at the abbey of Sázava, the Celestine church at Oybin, and the Cistercian house of Skalice contributed significantly to the spread of the Gothic style throughout Bohemia.

Michael T. Davis

Bachman, Erich. "Architektur bis zu den Hussitenkriegen." In *Gotik in Böhmen*, ed. Karl M. Swoboda. Munich: Prestel, 1969, pp. 99–109.
Frankl, Paul. *Gothic Architecture.* Harmondsworth: Penguin, 1962.
Héliot, Pierre, and Vaclav Mencl. "Mathieu d'Arras et les sources méridionales et nordiques de son œuvre à la cathédrale de Prague." In *La naissance et l'essor du gothique méridional au XIIIe siècle.* Toulouse: Privat, 1974, pp. 103–25.

MAURICE DE SULLY (ca.1120–1196).

Maurice had a strong episcopal career, culminating in his project to rebuild the Carolingian cathedral of Notre-Dame in Paris, which led to the cathedral we know today. It was begun, but not finished, in his lifetime.

Born at Sully, near Orléans, of humble parents, Maurice was a student of Peter Abélard. By 1147, he was canon and subdeacon of Notre-Dame and master in the cathedral school. Famed for his preaching, he became bishop of Paris in 1160, on the death of Peter Lombard. He made strenuous attempts to reform his diocesan clergy, and was a friend, adviser, and delegate to Louis VII and Philip II Augustus. In the great tradition of scholar-bishops, he tried to continue his studies. His *Sermons on the Gospels* (1168–75), the oldest original prose extant in French, are also among the finest. They were later translated into Latin and English. He also wrote a treatise on the canon of the Mass.

Maurice began the rebuilding of Notre-Dame in 1163 (it was consecrated in 1182); he also rebuilt the episcopal palace. In 1196, he retired to the abbey of Saint-Victor, where he died in the same year.

Lesley J. Smith

[See also: PARIS; SCHOOLS, CATHEDRAL]

Maurice de Sully. *Maurice of Sully and the Medieval Vernacular Homily,* ed. Charles A. Robson. Oxford: Blackwell, 1952.
Longère, Jean. *Les sermons latins de Maurice de Sully, évêque de Paris (1196): contribution à l'histoire de la tradition manuscrite.* Steenbrugis/Dortrecht: In Abbatia S. Petri/Kluwer Academic, 1988.
Martin, Marie-Madeleine. *Un grand évêque d'Occident, Maurice de Sully (XIIe siècle), évêque de Paris, né à Sully-sur-Loire.* N.p.: Reconquista, 1973.
Mortet, V. "Maurice de Sully, évêque de Paris (1160–1196): étude sur l'administration épiscopale pendant la seconde moitié du XIIe siècle." *Société de l'Histoire de Paris et de l'Île-de-France, Mémoires* 16 (1890): 105–318.
Robson, Charles A. *Maurice of Sully and the Medieval Vernacular Homily, with the Text of Maurice's French Homilies, from a Sens Cathedral Chapter MS.* Oxford: Blackwell, 1952.
Zink, Michel. *La prédication en langue romane avant 1300.* Paris: Champion, 1976.

MAYOR OF THE PALACE.

The *maior domus*, "first man of the house," that is, of the palace, was originally the manager of the household and estates of the Merovingian kings. By the early 7th century, he was effectively the head of the royal government, a sort of chief of staff, while also representing the interest of the great noble families, to one of which he belonged. As the Merovingian kings weakened in the mid-7th century, the mayors of the palace became virtual heads of state. In 751, the mayor Pepin the Short overthrew the Merovingian dynasty and arranged for his own election as the first Carolingian king of the Franks.

Mayors were originally estate managers of great landowners, and a *maior domus* supervised the other mayors. At first, the Merovingians had their own *maior domus* to manage all royal estates and revenues, as well as the household. His close association with the king led to his gaining political powers, such as appointing and directing counts and dukes, presiding over the royal court, and commanding the army. He came to be a virtual prime minister for the king. The three Frankish kingdoms of Neustria, Burgundy, and Austrasia frequently had separate administrations headed by their own mayors of the palace, who were from the regional aristocracy and tried to make the office hereditary. Mayors like Ebroin of Neustria and Grimoald of Austrasia occasionally even attempted to install their own sons as kings. The victory of the Austrasian mayor Pepin II at Tertry in 687 led to the single mayorality for all of the Frankish kingdoms, held by a Carolingian, which presaged the establishment of the Carolingian dynasty.

Steven Fanning

[See also: CAROLINGIAN DYNASTY; CHARLES MARTEL; PEPIN]

Gregory of Tours. *Liber historiae Francorum,* trans. Bernard S. Bachrach. Lawrence: Coronado, 1973.

Wallace-Hadrill, J.M., trans. *The Fourth Book of the Chronicle of Fredegar with Its Continuations.* London: Nelson, 1960.

Fouracre, P.J. "Merovingians, Mayors of the Palace and the Notion of a 'Low-Born' Ebroin." *Bulletin of the Institute of Historical Research* 57 (1984): 1–14.

Heidrich, Ingrid. "Les maires du palais." In *La Neustrie: les pays au nord de la Loire de Dagobert à Charles le Chauve (VIIe–IXe siècles),* ed. Patrick Périn and Laure-Charlotte Feffer. Rouen: Les Musées et Monuments Départementaux de Seine-Maritime, 1985, pp. 71–72.

MEALS. In households of comfortable means throughout the medieval period, it seems to have been customary in France to eat two meals each day: at or before midday, a principal meal, called *disner* (the Latin *coena* or *prandium*), was prepared, and toward the end of the day a lesser meal, called *souper* (or *merenda*). At the midday meal, all possible dishes might be served in two or more courses or servings, and, if the occasion lent itself, a proper formal ceremonial at table and in serving could be followed. The evening meal consisted, as the name suggests, primarily of lighter fare, such as sops (in which bread or toast was used to absorb a semi-liquid preparation) and pottages (any preparation whose basis was a broth), these being served with less formality and in fewer courses than the earlier meal. In religious institutions, the same two meals, *disner* and *souper*, were normal as well, although among the poorest in urban and rural communities little evidence exists. Peasants working their fields were likely unwilling to take much time for a substantial midday meal. To these two main meals may have been added two others, depending upon the social circumstances of the individual household: a *desjeunee* (*jentaculum*) and a light collation at bedtime.

Meals in comfortable households normally were eaten at trestle tables, set up for the purpose, spread with a cloth, and dismantled after the meal. Optionally, a long lap cloth at the edge of table functioned as a napkin to wipe fingers and lips. Standard table settings included a valuable container of salt; round pattens of bread (*trancheors*), to hold bits of food as they were eaten; goblets, perhaps shared between two diners; spoons and occasionally knives, a small knife being a personal possession that most individuals brought to a dining table. In formal circumstances, a fanfare announced meals with a summons to wash (the phrase was *corner l'eaue*); because fingers were the primary utensils at a meal, and because platters and bowls of food served more than one guest, cleanliness was emphasized. Collections of *contenances de table* legislated proper behavior of diners in refined society. The amount of service provided to diners varied greatly according to the affluence of the household. Personnel might be responsible for highly specialized functions in the kitchen and hall, such as concocting sauces or carving the master's meats.

By the late Middle Ages, the *Menagier de Paris* and Chiquart's *Du fait de cuisine* show that the sequence of dishes in a formal meal on a meat day (*jour gras*) was more or less fixed as follows: boiled meats (with sauce), preserved meats (with sauce), a puree of greens, pottages (broths or stews), an *entremets* or diversionary preparation (possibly a figure molded out of meat- or pea-paste, possibly a *tour de force* involving a fire-breathing animal or fowl), roast meats and roast fowl (with sauce), wheat porridge (*fromentee*) with venison, pasties, more stews, a rice dish (*blanc mangier*), another *entremets*, cold dishes (jellied meats, galantine), fruit, mulled wine (hippocras or claret), and spiced candies (*dragees*).

To some extent, the sequence of dishes in a meal was determined by medical doctrines on the digestibility of different foodstuffs and their faculty for opening or closing the stomach. Principles in this doctrine held that those foods that were readily digested should be eaten first in a meal in order not to block the passage out of the stomach and so cause a corruption of the food already digested there; and further that those foods functioning as aperitives of the stomach or as digestives should be taken at the most suitable times. Boiled meats, having the warm and moist quality of the human body, should be served in the initial course; roasts and venison, both being relatively drier in nature, should be consumed later in a meal; hippocras and candies were universal digestives, considered central to any dessert.

The relative importance of the two regular meals might vary depending upon the events of the day. In particular, the exertions of a tournament made it advisable that the midday meal be somewhat less heavy than normal, and that *souper* be correspondingly more substantial.

The church's rules on fasting during penitential seasons and on certain days of the week (usually Wednesday, Friday, and Saturday) led to the development of menus from which the meat of four-footed animals, and their products (such as milk and grease), were absent. Such lean meals, with their dependence upon peas, poultry, fish, and almonds (the latter, like modern American peanuts, ground, substituting for milk and butter), came to occupy a large place in the diet of the period. Because meat was the dominant foodstuff in the meal in an aristocratic or wealthy bourgeois household, professional cooks had to maintain two distinct sets of menus in their repertoire, a meat menu and its lean counterpart.

Terence Scully

[See also: BANQUETING; BEVERAGES; BREAD; COOKING; DIET AND NUTRITION; FOOD TRADES]

MEAUX. Originally an *oppidum* of the Gallic Meldi tribe, Meaux (Seine-et-Marne) was made a bishopric in the 4th century; capital of Brie, it lay within the jurisdiction of the counts of Champagne, who granted it a charter in 1179. Along with the rest of Champagne, Meaux was reunited to the French crown in 1285. During the Hundred Years' War, the city saw the crushing of the Jacquerie in 1358; although the town was burned, the cathedral was somehow spared. There are remains of the Gallo-Roman city walls, and recent archaeology has revealed a number of early churches. The cathedral of Saint-Étienne, begun ca. 1180, was continued in various Gothic styles into the 16th century. Its triportaled façade (14th–16th c.) is pure Flamboyant, but 13th-century sculpture from the earlier campaign was successfully reemployed in the central (Christ in Majesty) and south portals (dedicated to the Virgin). Only the north tower was completed. The north-transept portal has a 12th-century statue of St. Stephen, and both portals contain bas-reliefs showing scenes of his life. The south transept, both interior and exterior, is a beautiful example of Rayonnant Gothic. Below its enormous rose is a delicately carved openwork triforium that opens onto the lancet windows. The interior consists of a lofty, well-lighted nave with impressive double side aisles, transept, and Rayonnant Gothic chancel with double ambulatory and five apsidal chapels, built by an architect inspired by Soissons.

The adjacent rectangular chapter house, with its four corner turrets, is a rare example of 13th-century capitular architecture. Thought to have been originally the chapter's tithe barn, it is a three-story rectangular structure, consisting of a cellar, a ground floor with ogival vaulting, and an upper room with wooden ceiling, which is reached by a covered exterior staircase (15th c.). Nearby, the episcopal palace (15th–17th c.) preserves a 12th-century chapel.

William W. Kibler/William W. Clark

Deshoulières, François. *La cathédrale de Meaux*. Paris: Laurens, 1921.

Formigé, Jules. *Cathédrale de Meaux: histoire et développements*. Pontoise, 1917.

Kurmann, Peter. *La cathédrale de Meaux: étude architecturale*. Geneva: Droz, 1971.

MEDICAL PRACTICE AND PRACTITIONERS. The image of premodern medicine is skewed to the extent that our evidence is scriptural rather than material and discursive or demonstrative rather than factual. It remains difficult to do justice to the varied group of men and women who catered to the health needs of most people and who were far less marginal throughout the Middle Ages than their modern counterparts. They ranged from herbalists to bath attendants and from midwives to miracle workers, but in France their protagonist, as the successor to the Roman *medicus*, was the *mège* (metge, metgesse) or *mire* (miresse). Together with popular medicine in general, this figure was eclipsed, more completely than the analogous *læce*, or "leech," in England, by the learned physician or doctor and his Latin writings.

The sources from the first two-thirds of the medieval millennium are meager, yet they reveal some persistent characteristics of French medical practice. A disproportionate prominence of royal patients, the influence of imported healers and Mediterranean traditions, and a preference for palliative therapy over more aggressive intervention: all these features are personified by the physician who attend to Theuderic I of Austrasia, the son of Clovis. Anthinus, a Byzantine exile sent to Metz by the Ostrogothic king Theodoric, left prescriptions that are nutritional rather than medicinal. When native practitioners first became literate, they drew on classical traditions not only through

Gallo-Roman schools, as at Marseille or Autun, but also through monastic infirmaries. By the 10th century, as we learn from a personal appeal by Charles the Simple and a heralded visit by Bishop Adalbero of Verdun, the oracle and mecca for health seekers was the center of Salerno, where cures as well as care revolved around a "regimen," or dietary governance. The propagation of Salernitan wisdom, even across the Channel, was aided by emanations from Chartres and by such individuals as the monk Baudouin, French physician to Edward the Confessor.

Until close to 1100, the majority of acute and chronic ailments that demanded more intense attention seem to have been treated by monks, faith healers, good Samaritans, and part-time practitioners. A rising demand for more specifically trained and dedicated "professionals" is reflected in the 12th-century complaint by the Welsh visitor Giraldus Cambrensis that the wandering monks of Cîteaux and Clairvaux treated the populace "not with fresh drugs, selected syrups, or medicines compounded according to the art, but only with collected and assorted herbs of the fields, as if this would seem to be something unusual." A contemporary, the satirist Guiot de Provins, clearly differentiated unschooled practitioners, the *medicus* and the apothecary, from the physician who had been academically trained at Salerno or Montpellier and who commanded a higher honorarium.

A literate instruction in health care was virtually inaccessible to anyone outside the clergy. Members of this class, however, faced ethical problems when they wished to apply their schooling, particularly to lucrative transactions, surgical treatments, and such unseemly activities as gynecology or even diagnosis by uroscopy. The practice of medicine by clerks was initially proscribed at church councils on French soil (at Clermont in 1130 and at Tours in 1163) and formally prohibited in 1219, but, paradoxically, it remained more prevalent—and far more physicians held prebends or church benefices—in France than elsewhere until the 15th century. As further ironies, even here the secularization of medicine was the result less of ecclesiastical restrictions than of incorporation in the universities, and it did not preclude the special deference that academically trained physicians showed to clerical prerogatives in their refusal to treat the critically ill before they had gone to confession.

As the professionalization of medicine evolved in the university, it accentuated the social ranking of practitioners on the basis of literacy. The teaching of the art became paramount, and the title of "doctor" appeared more coveted than those referring to healing. Nevertheless, the exercise of the art remained the object of school statutes that required experience as an integral part of training, of many scholastic writings devoted to diagnostic techniques and therapeutic procedures, and of the professors' careers and communal actions outside academe. Once they had gained control of instruction, the incorporated physicians aimed for the regulation of all practice by means of licensing. An avowed concern with the public welfare as well as a drive for control, if not for monopoly, culminated at Paris between 1332 and 1352 in a bitter campaign of the faculty against two dozen unlicensed practitioners. On account of their Latin book learning and their practice with oral advice rather than with manual intervention, doctors deemed themselves above surgeons, unlike in Italy; the distance was more pronounced in Paris than at Montpellier.

Even within the craft of surgery, there was a stratification based as much on education as on activities. In his *Livre des métiers,* the *prévôt* of Paris under Louis IX, Étienne Boileau, distinguished between the *barbier-clerc,* or surgeon-barber, "of the long robe" and the lowlier *barbier-laic,* or barber-surgeon, "of the short robe." The former, who seemed as much at ease in the royal court as downtown, claimed greater respectability on account of their knowledge of medical theory; their ambitions gained momentum after 1295, when Lanfranc of Milan introduced academic surgery to Lyon and to Paris; and they were recognized as a faculty by King John in 1356. Most illustrious among these master surgeons were Henri de Mondeville and Gui de Chauliac, distinguished by their books no less than by their care of kings and popes. A larger group was that of the barber-surgeons, whose chief customers were merchants, sailors, and other travelers; from 1311 on, they were allowed, after examination by four sworn masters, to provide such health-related services as cupping and bloodletting; incorporated in Paris since 1361, in 1372 they received from King Charles V permission to extend their activities to the treatment of "boils, tumors, and open wounds if these are not mortal."

Documented practitioners, whatever their educational level, were naturally concentrated at noble courts and in urban centers. Their services, less often as providers of care to the community than as expert witnesses at trials, examiners of alleged lepers, and inspectors of health conditions, were engaged by municipalities mainly from the 15th century on, later than in Italy. Such services may not have received generous compensation, and bourgeois patients were perhaps not the most profitable ones. While doctors to notables could accumulate considerable fortunes, urban practitioners appear to have been of modest average means. One may be surprised to learn that in Paris the majority of them paid low taxes, and in Toulouse one-half were characterized as "poor devils."

Luke Demaitre

[See also: BLACK DEATH; DISEASES; HEALTH CARE; HOSPITALS; LEPROSY; MEDICAL TEXTS; MENTAL HEALTH; SCROFULA]

Biller, P. "*Curate infirmos*: The Medieval Waldensian Practice of Medicine." In *The Church and Healing*, ed. W.J. Sheils. Oxford: Blackwell, 1982, pp. 345–78.

Bouteiller, Marcelle. *La médecine populaire d'hier et d'aujourd'hui.* Paris: Maisonneuve et Larose, 1966.

Bullough, Vern L. *The Development of Medicine as a Profession.* Basel: Karger, 1966.

———. "Training of the Nonuniversity-Educated Practitioners in the Later Middle Ages." *Journal of the History of Medicine* 14 (1959): 446–58.

Contreni, John. "Masters and Medicine in Northern France During the Reign of Charles the Bald." In *Charles the Bald: Court and Kingdom*, ed. Margaret Gibson and Janet Nelson. Oxford: B.A.R. International Series, 1981, pp. 333–50.

———. "The Study and Practice of Medicine in Northern France During the Reign of Charles the Bald." *Studies in Medieval Culture* 6–7 (1976): 43–54.

Demaitre, Luke. "Theory and Practice in Medical Education at the University of Montpellier in the Thirteenth and Fourteenth Centuries." *Journal of the History of Medicine* 30 (1975): 103–23.

Jacquart, Danielle. *Le milieu médical en France du XIIe au XVe siècle.* Geneva: Droz, 1981.

Kibre, Pearl. "The Faculty of Medicine at Paris, Charlatanism, and Unlicensed Medical Practices in the Later Middle Ages." *Bulletin of the History of Medicine* 27 (1953): 1–20.

MacKinney, Loren. *Early Medieval Medicine, with Special Reference to France and Chartres.* Baltimore: Johns Hopkins University Press, 1937.

———. "Tenth-Century Medicine As Seen in the *Historia* of Richer of Rheims." *Bulletin of the History of Medicine* 2 (1934): 347–75.

Wakefield, Walter. "Heretics as Physicians in the Thirteenth Century." *Speculum* 57 (1982): 328–31.

MEDICAL TEXTS. With the rise of the universities in the 13th century, an increasing number of medical texts become available to students and scholars along with such classics as Avicenna's *Canon,* Galen's *Ars parva,* and Hippocrates's *Aphorismi* or *Pronostica.* The great majority of authors of medical texts were conferred degrees by the University of Montpellier, where the best medical teaching among all nineteen French universities was available. The broad body of known medical texts reveals the most common preoccupations of both the authors and readers. They can be divided as follows: (1) commentaries dealing with problems of medical doctrine; (2) practical books, such as diets written for an individual, *Consilia* with diagnosis and prescriptions for certain illnesses, and *Experimenta,* such as Arnaud de Villeneuve's *Tractatus de diversitatum infirmitatum,* which recorded various types of diseases witnessed by a doctor; (3) general treatises, including such encyclopedias as Ricardus Anglicus's *Micrologus* and Bernard de Gordon's *Lilium Medicine*; (4) treatises dealing with one medical specialty, such as *De pulsibus, De febribus* (14th-c. plague literature belongs to this category); and (5) texts related to antidotes and medications.

Medicine and surgery were one and the same discipline until the 13th century. One of the most influential medical treatises of the period, Henri de Mondeville's *Chirurgie,* composed in Latin and then translated in an abridged form (B.N. fr. 2030), treats not so much of surgery, as the title might suggest, but of potions, ointments, cosmetic treatments, and recipes for treating specific ailments. The official surgeon of King Philip IV, Henri had studied at Montpellier and often exercised his trade on the field of battle. Only with the *Chirurgia magna* of Gui de Chauliac (1300–1368) do we encounter a medical text devoted purely to surgery. Gui studied at Montpellier and practiced at Avignon, where he was the doctor to three popes, Clement VI, Innocent VI, and Urban V. His work was translated into French in the

14th century, as well as into Occitan, Dutch, Middle English, and Hebrew; it was first printed at Venice in 1498. Jacques Despars, who practiced medicine in the entourage of Philip the Good of Burgundy, devoted thirty years (1432–53) to the *Commentarius in Canones Avicennae*, his *summa* of the medical knowledge of the 15th century, which included quotations from Greek and Arabic writers, problems of doctine, and practical examples.

Although over 80 percent of all medical texts were written in Latin, some practical texts dealing with health, hygiene, or the plague were composed in the vernacular, in both verse and prose: among the more important are the anonymous 13th-century Anglo-Norman *Novele chirurgie*, Jean Falco's *Notables déclaratifs sur le Guidon*, and Jean le Lièvre's *Petit traictié sur le fait du nombre de la déclairacion des vaynes qui sont assises sur le corps de la personne*. Along with these should be mentioned Jean Sauvage's *Trésor des povrez* or *Réceptaire de Jean Sauvage*, a 14th-century verse and prose translation of Pierre d'Espagne's *Thesaurus pauperum*. It is a compilation of remedies of all sorts and provenances.

Claude J. Fouillade/William W. Kibler

[See also: HEALTH CARE; HOSPITALS; MEDICAL PRACTICE AND PRACTITIONERS]

Hieatt, Constance B., and Robin F. Jones, eds. *La novele chirurgerie*. London: Anglo-Norman Text Society, 1990.

Mondeville, Henri de. *La chirurgie de maître Henri de Mondeville*, ed. Alphonse Bos. 2 vols. Paris: Didot, 1897–98.

Jacquart, Danielle. *Le milieu médical en France du XIIe au XVe siècle*. Geneva: Droz, 1989.

MEDITERRANEAN TRADE. The Romans bequeathed a Mediterranean trade network to medieval southern France. Salvian, Caesarius of Arles, and Gregory of Tours mentioned Syrian, Jewish, and Greek merchants in Mediterranean French towns in the 5th and 6th centuries, indicating a persistence of international trade, though of what volume and importance is not known. In addition, ships with Mediterranean goods—oils, wines, pottery—made their way to Brittany and Britain. Coins minted in Provence have been found as far afield as Sutton Hoo. The succeeding centuries witnessed a decline in French Mediterranean trade, but some international exchange may have continued under Charlemagne, who recognized Viking ships, initially mistaken for Jewish, African, or British merchant vessels, off the Mediterranean coast of France. Diplomatic exchanges, if not actual trade, existed between Charlemagne and the Abbasid caliph Harun-al-Rashid.

Little evidence survives for 10th- and early 11th-century French Mediterranean trade. With the 11th century, however, coastal shipping can be documented, and by the end of the century, merchants of such towns as Montpellier were recorded in the Levant. Mediterranean trade overall revived substantially in the 11th century under the leadership of the Italo-Byzantine towns of Italy. The Genoese and the Pisans established commercial hegemony over the Mediterranean coast of France during the mid-12th century. The Rhône town of Saint-Gilles was the center of Italian trading efforts in southern France. In exchange for products of the East, Europeans could offer expensive spices and fabrics, raw materials, wool cloths, iron for military purposes, wood, and slaves.

During the Third Crusade, Conrad de Montferrat granted tax exemption and free circulation to bourgeois of Saint-Gilles, Montpellier, Marseille, and Barcelona in return for aid against Saladin. Gui de Lusignan accorded similar privileges at Saint-Jean-d'Acre and elsewhere within the Latin kingdom of Jerusalem. However theoretical these concessions, given the recent loss of territory, they represent the beginning of commercial emancipation from Italian domination. The 1220s witnessed a series of treaties of nonaggression and commerce among towns of Languedoc and Provence. The great natural port of Marseille became a hub of wide-ranging trade among southern France, the ports of Bougie and Ceuta in North Africa, and the Levant. Exports of northern French and Flemish cloth, along with substantial credit activities in the form of money-exchange contracts, underlay the Levant connections out of Marseille. Reexport of eastern products, silks in particular, was directed to North Africa. The heyday of Marseille came to an end with its conquest by Charles I of Anjou in 1262. From that date until at least the mid-14th century, it was Montpellier, trading out of the French port of Aigues-Mortes, that would dominate western trade with the Levant.

French Mediterranean trade underwent numerous changes in the later 13th and 14th centuries. In the western Mediterranean, southern French trade linked Montpelliérains and Marseillais with outlets in Majorca, Naples, Sicily, and Sardinia. North African contacts moved farther east to Algiers and Collo once the Aragonese were implanted at Ceuta. In the eastern Mediterranean, crusading losses on the Syrian mainland meant that trading activities were forced back on the islands of Cyprus and Rhodes. Additional eastern Mediterranean trading destinations included Armenia, Alexandria, and the Byzantine empire. Papal prohibitions of trade with the infidel did not hinder southern French Mediterranean commerce, but this trading network was further disrupted with the breakup of the Mongol empire in Asia beginning in the 1330s.

Economic problems in the 14th century, the Black Death, and the Hundred Years' War occasioned decline in French trade. The Italian towns remained strong competitors, as did the Majorcans and the Aragonese, particularly from their expanding port of Barcelona.

Kathryn L. Reyerson

[See also: AIGUES-MORTES; MARSEILLE; MERCHANTS; MONTPELLIER; TRADE ROUTES]

Dupont, André. *Les relations entre les cités maritimes de Languedoc et les cités méditerranéennes d'Espagne et d'Italie du Xe au XIIIe siècle*. Nîmes: Chastanier et Alméras, 1942.

Heyd, Wilhelm. *Histoire du commerce du Levant au moyen âge*. 2 vols. Leipzig: Harrassowitz, 1885.

Lopez, Robert S., and Irving Raymond. *Medieval Trade in the Mediterranean World*. New York: Columbia University Press, 1955.

Pryor, John. *Commerce, Shipping and Naval Warfare in the Medieval Mediterranean.* London: Variorum, 1987.

Rambert, Gaston. *Histoire du commerce de Marseille.* 2 vols. Paris: Plon, 1949–51.

Reyerson, Kathryn L. "Le rôle de Montpellier dans le commerce des draps de laine avant 1350." *Annales du Midi* 94 (1982): 17–40.

———. "Medieval Silks in Montpellier: The Silk Market ca. 1250–ca. 1350." *Journal of European Economic History* 11 (1982): 117–40.

———. "Montpellier and the Byzantine Empire: Commercial Interaction in the Mediterranean World Before 1350." *Byzantion* 48 (1978): 456–76.

Schaube, Adolf. *Handelsgeschichte der romanischen Völker des Mittelmeergebiets bis zum Ende der Kreuzzüge.* Munich: Oldenbourg, 1906.

MEHUN-SUR-YÈVRE. The little town of Mehun (Cher) on the Yèvre just north of Bourges, has three medieval monuments: the remnants of John, duke of Berry's castle, illustrated in his *Très Riches Heures* in a miniature by Paul de Limbourg; the collegial church of Notre-Dame; and the Porte de l'Horloge, a vestige of the 14th-century ramparts. An older castle was sumptuously rebuilt between 1367 and 1390 by John, and here he received important artist friends, among them the writer Froissart, the Limbourg brothers (miniaturists), and the sculptor and architect André Beauneveu, who worked on the reconstruction under the general direction of Gui de Dammartin. Built on a trapezoidal plan, Mehun was distinguished by its light and airy Gothic upper level, which may have inspired Chambord. John bequeathed the castle to his grandnephew Charles VII, who was crowned (1422) and died (1461) here. Charles was visited at Mehun-sur-Yèvre by Jeanne d'Arc in 1429–30.

The Romanesque church of Notre-Dame, built in the form of a horseshoe, was begun in the 11th century. A Flamboyant chapel was added in the 15th century.

William W. Kibler/William W. Clark

[See also: BEAUNEVEU, ANDRÉ; JOHN, DUKE OF BERRY; LIMBOURG BROTHERS]

Deshoulières, François. "Mehun-sur-Yèvre, église collégiale Notre-Dame." *Congrès archéologique (Bourges)* 94 (1931): 329–37.

Gauchery, Robert. "Mehun-sur-Yèvre, château." *Congrès archéologique (Bourges)* 94 (1931): 338–45.

MELUN. The town and viscounty of Melun (Seine-et-Marne) in the Île-de-France produced a noble house that rose to prominence in 14th-century France. Tracing their ancestry to the 10th century, the viscounts of Melun were well established by the early 13th. Adam II (d. 1217) accompanied the future Louis VIII on several campaigns, and his brother Jean became bishop of Poitiers. Adam III (d. 1247) left four sons, two of whom successively held the vice-comital title, while a third, Simon, became lord of La Louppe and Marcheville and was a marshal of France before being killed at Courtrai in 1302. Simon's brother, the viscount Adam IV (d. 1304), had four sons, two of whom, Guillaume and Philippe, became archbishop of Sens, while the oldest, Jean I, enhanced the family's fortune by marrying the heiress to the Norman lordship of Tancarville.

The children of this marriage brought the family to the height of its prestige. They were associated with the reforming party in northwestern France. The oldest son, Jean II, viscount of Melun and count of Tancarville (d. 1382), was a royal chamberlain and prominent military commander under kings John II and Charles V. His brother Adam, lord of Château-Landon (d. 1362), was first chamberlain and a leading royal adviser. The third brother, Guillaume (archbishop of Sens, 1345–76), was perhaps the dominant figure in the royal council between 1359 and 1374. Raymond Cazelles called him the "Richelieu of the 14th century." Guillaume IV, who held the family titles for over thirty years until his death at Agincourt in 1415, was a leading figure in the court faction known as the Marmousets, which inherited much of the program of the earlier reforming party. Guillaume IV, who was also butler of France, left no male heir. His daughter Marguerite married into a cadet line of the Harcourt family of Normandy.

John Bell Henneman, Jr.

[See also: CHARLES V THE WISE; *CONSEIL*; MARMOUSETS]

Cazelles, Raymond. *Société politique, noblesse et couronne sous Jean le Bon et Charles V.* Geneva: Droz, 1982.

MENAGIER DE PARIS. A rich householder of Paris ca. 1394 composed for his young wife a prose work on how to achieve a successful and happy marriage. Incomplete, this treatise provides moral teaching with accompanying exempla and practical instructions on the supervision of the household. Also included is detailed information on gardening for both flowers and vegetables, the care of dogs and horses, falconry, the hiring and mangement of servants, and cooking (which comprises marketing, devising menus, and many recipes). The *Menagier* is in the genre of educational treatises for women and sheds light on late-medieval bourgeois life and the tradition of the popular tale. It survives in three manuscripts.

Joan B. Williamson

[See also: COURTESY BOOKS; *JOURNAL D'UN BOURGEOIS DE PARIS*]

Brereton, Georgine E., and Janet M. Ferrier, eds. *Le menagier de Paris.* Oxford: Oxford University Press, 1981.

MENDICANT ART AND ARCHITECTURE. From the time of their founding in the early 13th century, the Dominican and Franciscan orders played an important role in France. Paris, especially the university, was a major center for both orders, and both also benefited from royal pa-

Toulouse (Haute-Garonne), Dominican church, section, elevation and isometric. After Duret.

Dominican church. *Photograph courtesy of Whitney S. Stoddard.*

tronage, but the mendicants could be found throughout France. Several difficulties are encountered, however, in studying their impact on French art and architecture. Because of their mendicancy and vows of poverty, their conventual structures and furnishings, which emphasized function and simplicity, did not conform to particular stylistic characteristics. The orders did not produce their own art but rather relied on secular artisans. And finally, they preferred urban centers, where many of their buildings and possessions have been destroyed or dispersed. Despite these limitations, several approaches provide insight into their influence on late-medieval French art.

Because so many mendicant structures have been destroyed, knowledge of French mendicant architecture is based on a few surviving buildings, primarily in southern France, and on plans and drawings. For example, none of the four Dominican churches in Paris is extant, but plans reveal that the major church of the Jacobins had parallel naves supported by center piers.

This type of plan recurs in one of the most impressive surviving mendicant churches in France, the Dominican church of the Jacobins in Toulouse. In this late 13th-century edifice, the long nave of six rib-vaulted bays is supported by central columns and terminates in a polygonal choir. Although other double-nave Dominican churches were built in France, as at Agen, the Dominicans and Franciscans favored simple structures with a large single nave that either had a flat roof or was vaulted, as in the

now destroyed church of the Cordeliers (Franciscans) at Toulouse.

In some cases, royal patronage promoted more elaborate architecture. In 1295, Charles II, count of Provence, entrusted to the Dominicans a foundation dedicated to St. Madeleine at Saint-Maximin. The church, built during the 14th century, had a long nave with double aisles, a polygonal apse with two diagonally placed chapels, and a three-story elevation reminiscent of Gothic architecture in northern France. French mendicant architecture, though it lacks common stylistic features, reflects the way in which the demands of function, practicality, and patronage were adapted to a particular situation.

Although the mendicants stressed simplicity and poverty, their churches were furnished with appropriate devotional paintings, sculpture, and other objects. Unfortunately, because few of these art forms have survived *in situ*, direct evidence for the character of visual arts associated with the French mendicants is limited. The Franciscans and Dominicans had a great impact on popular piety and the iconography of devotional art that it inspired in the later Middle Ages. Their influence is apparent in French manuscript illumination, especially in liturgical and devotional books whose usage indicates Franciscan or Dominican connections. The late 13th-century north French *Psalter and Hours of Yolande de Soissons*, for example, shows Franciscan inspiration in miniatures of St. Francis preaching to the birds, the magus kissing the Christ child's foot, and the image of the Tree of Life. Many French manuscripts from the 13th century on utilize similar iconographic motifs. The illumination of the *Belleville Breviary* of ca. 1325, produced for a Dominican, is associated with Jean Pucelle. The complexity of the didactic imagery, including three lost miniatures that can be reconstructed from a prefatory explanatory text, may reflect the Dominican mission of teaching and explicating theological issues. The cycle representing the articles of faith was the model for illustration in several other French devotional manuscripts. The mendicants thus had a pervasive and diverse influence on French art, architecture, and iconography in the late Middle Ages.

Karen Gould

[See also: AGEN; DOMINICAN ORDER; FRANCISCAN ORDER; PUCELLE, JEAN; TOULOUSE]

Durliat, M. "Le rôle des ordres mendiants dans la création de l'architecture gothique méridionale." In *La naissance et l'essor du gothique méridional au XIIIe siècle*. Toulouse: Privat, 1974, pp. 71–86.

Gould, Karen. *The Psalter and Hours of Yolande de Soissons*. Cambridge: Medieval Academy of America, 1978.

Lambert, E. "L'église des Jacobins de Toulouse et l'architecture dominicaine en France." *Bulletin monumental* 104 (1946): 141–86.

Montagnes, Bernard. *Architecture dominicaine en Provence*. Paris: CNRS, 1979.

Sandler, Lucy Freeman. "Jean Pucelle and the Lost Miniatures of the Belleville Breviary." *Art Bulletin* 66 (1984): 73–96.

Sundt, Richard A. "The Jacobin Church of Toulouse and the Origins of Its Double-Nave Plan." *Art Bulletin* 71 (1989): 185–207.

MENTAL HEALTH. In medieval scholastic theory and in everyday practice, functional intelligence and "normal" behavior enjoyed greater latitude than today, yet their impairment was also extended to disease categories that ranged from lovesickness to rabies and from incubus to epilepsy. The understanding and treatment of aberrations readily fell in the realm of religion because of the affinity between mind and soul, the moralization of conduct, and the mysteries of mental processes. Nevertheless, physicians and laypeople recognized the role of natural factors, including a person's history, environment, and bodily condition—primarily soundness of the brain and balance of the humors. Somatic and psychological considerations shaped most rules of mental hygiene and explanations of dementia. The *frénésie* of Robert de Clermont, son of Louis IX, was attributed to blows he received on the head during a joust. The decline of Charles VI into *manie* was blamed on excess humidity inherited from his mother, troubles with his nobles, and an ensuing excess of black bile.

Dynastic streaks of madness were paralleled by more widespread disorders, as suggested by mass hysterias in 9th-century Dijon, recurring episodes of St. Anthony's Fire (*le mal des ardents*), and the misery of pilgrims to a hundred shrines. Mental maladies ranked high among the reasons for visiting the tombs of St. Martin and other prominent healers. Early specialists in miraculous psychotherapy, led by St. Acaire and St. Mathurin, received competition from such aptly named saints as Aimable at Riom (Auvergne) and Front and Mémoire at Périgueux. Pilgrimages appear routinely in the poignant dossiers of the insane, who, after being convicted of a major crime, were granted a royal pardon.

Attitudes toward the mentally ill in medieval France appear to have been more relaxed and humane than in other regions and in later France. There is far less evidence of confinement in "fool's cells" than, for example, in Germanic lands. The mentally ill were considered best served by family care; if they became *furieux*, they could be tied or locked up only with official permission. For the indigent, cities not only founded hospitals but also subsidized clothing and other expenses, even for pilgrimages and votive offerings, as evident in the accounts of Lille. Communal care of the mentally ill was further provided by special fraternities, such as that of St. Hildevert at Gournay.

Luke Demaitre

[See also: HEALTH CARE; HOSPITALS; MEDICAL PRACTICE AND PRACTITIONERS]

Beek, Henri Hubert. *Waanzin in de Middeleeuwen*. Haarlem: De Toorts, 1969.

Chaput, B. "La condition juridique et sociale de l'aliéné mental." In *Aspects de la marginalité au moyen âge*, ed. Guy Allard. Montreal: L'Aurore, 1975, pp. 38–47.

Geremek, Bronislaw. *The Margins of Society in Late Medieval Paris*, trans. Jean Burrell. Cambridge: Cambridge University Press, 1987.

Jackson, Stanley W. "Unusual Mental States in Medieval Europe. I. Medical Symptoms of Mental Disorder, 400–1100 A.D." *Journal of the History of Medicine* 27 (1972): 262–97.

MERCHANTS. In the Roman world, mercantile activities were stigmatized. In medieval France, after the Frankish conquest, the few references to merchants cite primarily foreigners: Syrians, Greeks, Jews. There are few details regarding an indigenous merchant community. Under the Carolingians, the Rhadanite Jews were still a factor, and along with them one finds mention of palace merchants purveying supplies to the itinerant royal court. At Aix-la-Chapelle under Louis the Pious, there was mention of residences of merchants. By and large, the fate of merchants was that of towns under the Carolingians: little accommodation was made for either.

Pirenne and later historians have linked the urban revival and the growth of a merchant class in the late 10th and 11th centuries to the recovery of international trade in Europe. As has been demonstrated by Lestoquoy and Espinas for northern French towns like Arras, long-distance commerce and the settling down of the itinerant merchants were not the only causes of the reemergence of towns. Demographic growth of the local, previously agricultural, community furnished candidates for the merchant class. Northern French merchants were actively patronizing the Champagne fairs by the end of the 12th century, while their high-quality wool cloths joined Flemish products as premier French exports in the Mediterranean world. Southern French merchants followed in the footsteps of Italians to participate in this trade. Merchant wealth led to the acquisition of real estate in town and countryside, as well as to marital alliances with the increasingly impoverished nobility.

Merchants and artisans were sufficiently numerous and powerful to be politically active in the 11th century in communal revolutions in such towns as Le Mans and in the 12th century in the establishment of southern French consulates. The political activities of merchant elites received the positive endorsement of the French kings from Louis VI through Louis VIII. The financial needs of Louis IX and his conservative stance on usury led to a more exploitative attitude. By the reign of Philip IV, the urban autonomy of French mercantile communities had fallen victim to the expansion and intrusion of royal government, but the basic alliance between bourgeoisie and king would survive the Middle Ages.

Kathryn L. Reyerson

[See also: CHAMPAGNE; FAIRS AND MARKETS; MEDITERRANEAN TRADE; TEXTILES; TRADE ROUTES; WINE TRADE; WOOL TRADE]

Espinas, Georges, Lucien Fèbvre, and Jean Lestoquoy. "Fils de riches ou nouveaux riches." *Annales: Économies, Sociétés, Civilisations* 1 (1946): 139–53.

Le Goff, Jacques. *Marchands et banquiers au moyen âge.* Paris: Presses Universitaires de France, 1956.

Pegolotti, Francesco Balducci. *La pratica della mercatura,* ed. Allan Evans. Cambridge: Mediaeval Academy of America, 1936.

Wolff, Philippe. *Commerces et marchands de Toulouse (vers 1350–vers 1450).* Paris: Plon, 1954.

MEROVINGIAN ART. The term "Merovingian art" should refer to all the arts produced in the territories dominated by kings of the Merovingian family from Clovis in the late 5th century to the deposition of the last Merovingian king by the Carolingian, or Arnulfing, family in 751. In art-historical writing, however, the term's use is commonly both contracted and expanded. It is contracted by restriction to the architecture, sculpture, and painting produced for Christian purposes, material dating primarily from the 7th and 8th centuries, and by the exclusion of much of the metalwork of the 6th century, relegated to the "migrations arts." On the other hand, the term is expanded to connote an artistic style distinct from the developed Carolingian court styles with their more classicizing appearance, even if the work in question dates from the early 9th century, so that some of the best-known examples of "Merovingian illumination" date from the second half of the 8th and even from the early 9th century.

Not even one surviving intact building can be confidently termed Merovingian. The only likely candidate is the baptistery of Saint-Jean in Poitiers, a central-plan structure richly decorated with colored masonry patterns and elements of Roman architecture, such as pedimental gables and "Corinthian" capitals and pilasters; but the date of the building remains controversial, and it may well be earlier or later than the Merovingian period. Some fragments of Merovingian masonry, like the elaborate carving and coursing of the 7th-century wall at Jouarre, clearly testify to a high level of craftsmanship. Literary sources, especially the writings of Gregory of Tours, make it clear that many churches were built and often richly decorated. The most famous example is the church of "La Daurade" in Toulouse, elaborately covered with gold and figural mosaics; one of the more intriguing is Gregory's reconstruction of his own church of Saint-Martin at Tours after its destruction by fire in 558, whose painted decoration Venantius Fortunatus described at length ca. 590. Many Merovingian cathedrals and other churches, including that of Paris, survived for centuries, being generally replaced with large Romanesque and Gothic churches in the later Middle Ages.

In contrast to the dearth of surviving architectural works, abundant sculpture survives from the Merovingian period. Among the best-known works are three 7th-century sarcophagi from the monastery of Jouarre, which show a high standard of ornamental carving and epigraphy for the tomb of Abbess Theodechilde, and elaborate and inventive Last Judgment and theophanic Christ images on the tomb of Bishop Agilbert. The early 7th-century sculptures of the "Hypogée des Dunes," or Memoria of Abbot Mellebaudis, at Poitiers, an underground burial chamber and chapel, are a rich mixture of ornamental and figural carvings, the latter including perhaps the remains of a monumental Crucifixion group as well as fragments of carved sarcophagi. The importance of sarcophagi as a locus for carving, and for devotion, is clearly a direct inheritance from the late Roman and early Christian period; carved stone and plaster sarcophagi with primarily ornamental decoration, often with apotropaic significance, were produced in great numbers during the period.

Merovingian painting survives only in the form of manuscript illumination; all the mural paintings attested by literary sources have been lost. It seems likely that most of the books were produced at such great monastic scriptoria as Luxeuil and Corbie, originally founded as part of the Irish missionary activity on the Continent in the 7th century, as well as at Laon and other centers not yet identified. In comparison with contemporary Irish and Anglo-Saxon illumination, the Merovingian works often seem simple and even clumsy, dominated by simple color schemes and for the most part decorated with zoomorphic and vegetal patterns derived from late antiquity, and especially applied to initial letters and to framing of text pages. Whereas most decorated insular books of the period are liturgical or altar books, however, surviving Merovingian manuscripts are commonly doctrinal works, commentaries on Scripture, encyclopedias of Isidore, and even secular law books—library rather than altar books, in other words, whose decoration at any period is generally less elaborate, painstaking, and costly.

A notable feature of Merovingian art was the production of magnificent gold and jeweled metalwork for ecclesiastical purposes. Techniques and styles developed for luxurious secular objects during the "Migration" period, especially garnet and enamel *cloisonné* work, were adapted for use in chalices, croziers, crosses, and reliquaries. Among these the most notable include the small fragment of the large cross made by St. Eligius, metalworker and bishop of Noyon in the 7th century (B.N., Cabinet des Médailles), and the slightly later reliquary casket made by Undiho and Ello for the priest Teuderigus (Saint-Maurice-d'Agaune, Treasury). The association of these works with known artists bears witness to the high prestige of this form of artistic work, a prestige clearly inherited from pre-Christian Frankish traditions.

Lawrence Nees

[See also: JOUARRE; MANUSCRIPTS, PRODUCTION AND ILLUMINATION; MIGRATIONS ART; PALEOGRAPHY AND MANUSCRIPTS; POITIERS]

James, Edward. *The Franks.* Oxford: Blackwell, 1988.

Nees, Lawrence. *From Justinian to Charlemagne: European Art 565–787: An Annotated Bibliography.* Boston: Hall, 1985.

Périn, Patrick, and Laure-Charlotte Feffer. *Les Francs.* Paris: Colin, 1987.

———, eds. *La Neustrie: les pays au nord de la Loire de Dagobert à Charles le Chauve.* Rouen: Musées et Monuments Départementaux de Seine-Maritime, 1985.

Salin, Édouard. *La civilisation mérovingienne d'après les sépultures: les textes et le laboratoire.* 4 vols. Paris: Picard, 1950–59.

MEROVINGIAN DYNASTY. The first dynasty of kings to rule over the Franks became known as the Merovingians. Their realm included not only most of modern France but western Germany and the Low Countries. The first Merovingian to rule over this area was Clovis I (r. 482–511), and the last was Childeric III, who was overthrown by the Carolingian mayor of the palace Pepin the Short in 751. The Merovingians are considered to be the "first race" of French kings, and their long retention of an old Germanic aristocratic hair fashion led to their being called "the longhaired kings." Their reputation is one of cruelty, violence, immorality, and fraticidal warfare. The term "Merovingian" is also applied to the period of Frankish history from 482 to 751, as well as to the culture and civilization of the lands under the control of the Merovingians.

The Merovingians were named for Merovech, a semilegendary figure who was the father of Childeric I. Their origins are as chieftains of one of the many bands of Salian Franks living to the west of the lower Rhine, with their own center around Tournai and Cambrai, along the modern frontier between France and Belgium, in an area known as Toxandria. It is likely that all of the Salian chieftains were related, and their power would have been that of priest-judges. The Merovingians became true kings by two means. Childeric I, and perhaps Merovech before him, was an active ally of the Roman Empire and was himself a Roman official. He would thus have been influenced by Roman concepts of kingship. The takeover of the Roman administrative structure of Gaul by Clovis I put him in the legal position of the Roman emperor there. Thus, from the beginning of the Frankish kingdom, there were in theory no constitutional restrictions on the power of the kings. The only limitation on their will was the willingness of their subjects to tolerate their actions. Merovingian kingship was, as it has been said, "absolutism tempered by assassination."

It was Clovis I who made the spectacular rise from being the leader of the Salian Franks around Tournai to becoming the founder of the Frankish kingdom. By warfare, deceit, and treachery, he unified all of the Frankish tribes under his authority and conquered northern Gaul after his defeat of Syagrius in 486 and southern Gaul after his defeat of the Visigoths in 507. He also established his dominion over the Alemanni and the Thuringians. By the end of his reign in 511, Clovis ruled over a kingdom stretching from Germany to the Atlantic to the Pyrénées, in which the Franks were only a small minority within a largely Gallo-Roman population. Clovis adopted the Roman administrative structure intact, and he worked closely with the Gallo-Roman aristocracy of his lands. The differences between Frank and Roman were further reduced by his conversion to orthodox Christianity.

These characteristics were continued after Clovis by his sons, Theuderic, Chlodomer, Childebert I, and Clotar I. In accordance with Frankish custom, they received equal portions of their father's lands. Although there were then four independent Merovingian kingdoms, there was only one kingdom of the Franks. The next half-century saw the conquest of the Burgundian kingdom by the sons of Clovis (534), but it also witnessed vicious warfare within the family that led to the extinction of the lines of three of the brothers and the reunification of the Merovingian kingdoms by Clotar I from 558 to 561. At his death, however, there was another quadripartite division of the kingdom among his sons, Charibert I, Sigibert, Guntram, and Chilperic I. Another half-century of bloody warfare among the Merovingians ensued, and it was Chilperic I's son Clotar II who again reunited all the kingdoms (613). During this second major division, the four great distinct regions of the Frankish kingdom emerged: Neustria, Austrasia, Burgundy, and Aquitaine. They were to have a strong sense of identity as well as yearnings for autonomy. From time to time, Austrasia received a son of the Merovingian king as an autonomous ruler. Yet with or without their own kings, Austrasia, Neustria, and Burgundy usually had their own royal administration under the direction of a mayor of the palace.

Clotar II and his son Dagobert I continued to rule in the strong Merovingian tradition, but the rising power of the aristocracy, led by mayors of the palace, was already evident. After the death of Dagobert in 639, the position of the Merovingian kings declined rapidly, and they fell under the domination of the aristocracy and the mayors of the palace. Merovingian reigns tended to follow the pattern of a weak or sickly king's death at an early age, leaving minor heirs under the tutelage of the magnates. The unification of the Frankish kingdom by Clotar II had the accidental effect of eliminating relatives as fellow kings, who in the past had served as guardians of such heirs. In addition, the Merovingians often married low-born women who

MEROVINGIAN DYNASTY

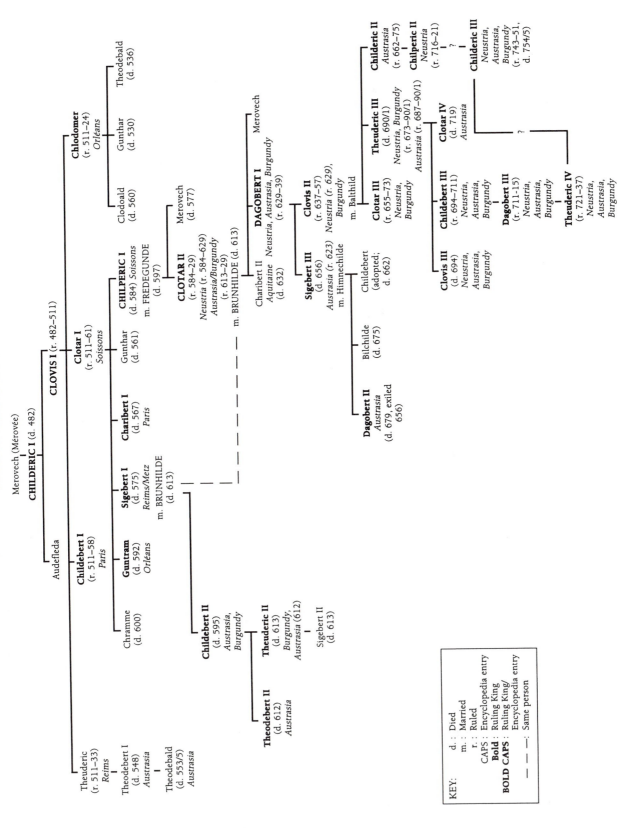

KEY:

- d. : Died
- m. : Married
- r. : Ruled
- CAPS : Encyclopedia entry
- **Bold** : Ruling King
- **BOLD CAPS** : Ruling King/ Encyclopedia entry
- — — — : Same person

lacked powerful kinsmen who might have provided support for the queen and her children on such occasions. Generous land grants to favorites, especially aristocrats, had, moreover, steadily reduced the material resources, and thus the power, of the kings.

The Merovingian kings after Dagobert I are traditionally seen as puppets of the mayors of the palace, as "do-nothing kings" (*rois fainéants*). It is true that the Merovingian decline tempted ambitious mayors like Ebroin of Neustria (d. 680) and Grimoald of Austrasia (d. 656) to plot to put up their own sons as kings, but aristocratic rivalries and strong loyalties to the Merovingian dynasty thwarted these efforts. Some of the later Merovingians were not mere puppets. Childeric II of Austrasia (r. 662–75) was important enough to be murdered in a vendetta, and for a time Theuderic III (r. 673–90/91) actually did rule rather than merely reign.

However, from the victory of the Austrasian mayor Pepin II in 687, the future of the Frankish kingdom was in the hands of the Pippinid-Carolingians. Charles Martel ruled without a Merovingian king on the throne from 737 to his death in 741, but the absence of a legitimate king provided an excuse for rebellions. Carloman and Pepin the Short were obliged to restore a Merovingian, Childeric III, to the throne in 743, but by 751 Pepin was secure enough to depose Childeric and arrange his own election as king of the Franks, thus ending the Merovingian dynasty and inaugurating that of the Carolingians. The Merovingians did not die out. They were forcibly removed in a *coup d'état*.

Steven Fanning

[See also: AUSTRASIA; CHARLES MARTEL; CHILDERIC I; CHILPERIC I; CLOTAR II; CLOVIS I; DAGOBERT I; FRANKS; MAYOR OF THE PALACE; PEPIN]

Gregory of Tours. *Liber historiae Francorum*, trans. Bernard S. Bachrach. Lawrence: Coronado, 1973.
———. *History of the Franks*, trans. Lewis Thorpe. Harmondsworth: Penguin, 1974.
James, Edward. *The Franks*. Oxford: Blackwell, 1988.
Wallace-Hadrill, J.M. *The Long-Haired Kings and Other Studies in Frankish History*. London: Methuen, 1962, chap. 7.
Wood, Ian. *The Merovingian Kingdoms, 450–751*. London: Longman, 1994.

MESCHINOT, JEAN (ca. 1420–91). Born in the region of Nantes, this soldier-poet has been characterized as a "Grand Rhétoriqueur Breton," belying the theory that such poets came from humble origins. An impoverished nobleman, Meschinot served five dukes of Brittany, notably Pierre II and Arthur III, although he was official poet for François II, celebrating his marriage with Isabelle de Foix in 1471. His political poetry, in particular twenty-five ballades against Louis XI exchanged with Georges Chastellain at the time of the Guerre du Bien Publique, shows him to have been a *poète engagé*. His principal work, the *Lunettes des princes* (1461–65), is not, as has been suggested, a breviary for princes but rather a meditation on spiritual salvation for the noble soul, every human's most precious

possession, regardless of station in life. The spectacles (*lunettes*) in question are given to the poet by Reason in order better to read a book on Conscience she gives him. This poem of 3,076 verses with a short prose interlude consists of a brief autobiographical opening and the poet's long dialogue with the four cardinal virtues: Prudence, Temperance, Fortitude, and Justice. It reflects the late-medieval taste for *miroirs* and *parements* but perhaps also the popularity of the earlier *Traité des quatre vertus* by the Pseudo-Seneca (Martin of Braga). Boethius is an immediate source for the poet's reflections. Although little-read today, the *Lunettes* is preserved in four manuscripts, and twenty-two editions printed between 1493 and 1539.

Charity Cannon Willard

[See also: CHASTELLAIN, GEORGES; GRANDS RHÉTORIQUEURS; *JARDIN DE PLAISANCE ET FLEUR DE RÉTHORIQUE*]

Meschinot, Jean. *Les lunettes des princes*, ed. Christine Martineau-Génieys. Geneva: Droz, 1972.
Champion, Pierre. *Histoire poétique du XVe siècle*. 2 vols. Paris: Champion, 1923, Vol. 2, pp. 189–238.
La Borderie, Arthur de. "Jean Meschinot, sa vie et ses œuvres." *Bibliothèque de l'École des Chartes* 56 (1895): 99–140, 274–317, 601–38.

MÉTAYER/MÉTAYAGE. *Métayage* is the agricultural regime apparently imported from Italy that became increasingly predominant in the French Midi in the later Middle Ages; it is comparable with *fermage* in the north. Small plots (fields, gardens, orchards, vineyards), medium-sized farms, and large holdings (monastic granges or the demesne land of large estates) all came to be cultivated under *métayage*. Contracts for *métayage* were established for a set term during which tenant farmers (*métayers*) cultivated land by sharecropping rather than for fixed annual rents. Like those holding land for rents (under *baux à cens*), and unlike the dependent peasants attached to the manses of traditional estates, *métayers* had no hereditary rights to the land, although rental terms could be relatively long: twenty to thirty years, a tenant's lifetime, or even several lifetimes. Under *métayage*, the owner generally provided a farm with farmstead, livestock, equipment, seed, and sometimes even food for the start-up year; the tenant agreed to maintain the farm, equipment, and buildings in good condition and to split both income and expenses of a holding in a set proportion (often half and half, hence *métayage*) with the owner. Actual proportions due to owner and *métayer* varied widely, depending on the quality of the land involved and on the availability of land and labor locally; instances are recorded for southern France in which no *métayer* would take up offers of even 19/20ths of the produce of extremely poor land. The institution of *métayage* has often been heralded as indicative of the transformation of lords into city-dwelling *rentiers*, but this interpretation is now being questioned. In periods of improving yields, a division of output must have appeared advantageous to owners, who were obviously anxious to profit from increased production on their land. Owners must still have had to supervise their holdings closely to assure themselves that they were actually getting their share of the produce. This may explain why such sharecropping agreements were often eventually transformed into leases for fixed rents, either in money or in kind. In addition to their use for land cultivation, contracts of *métayage* were widely used for animal husbandry.

Constance H. Berman

[See also: AGRICULTURE]

Duby, Georges. *Rural Economy and Country Life in the Medieval West*, trans. Cynthia Postan. Columbia: University of South Carolina Press, 1968.

———, and Armand Wallon, eds. *Histoire de la France rurale des origines à 1340*. Paris: Seuil, 1975.

Fourquin, Guy. *Histoire économique de l'Occident médiévale*. Paris: Colin, 1979.

Sicard, Germain. *Le métayage dans le Midi toulousain à la fin du moyen âge*. Toulouse: Subiron, 1956.

METZ. An important center of Frankish power on the Moselle River, Metz (Moselle) was the capital of Austrasia and the center of power of the Arnulfing-Pippinid ancestors of the Carolingians. It also was the principal city of the kingdom of Lorraine and later of the duchy of Upper Lorraine.

Divodurum, the capital of the Celtic tribe of the Mediomatrici, was a heavily romanized and substantial city with temples, aqueduct, baths, and amphitheater, located in the later Roman province of Belgica Prima. With its strong walls, it survived the invasions of the 5th century and became renowned for its many churches and monasteries. After the division of the lands of Clotar I among his sons in 561, the region that was soon to be called Austrasia was allotted to Sigibert I, who eventually made Metz his residence. Thereafter, strong feelings of autonomy usually meant that Austrasia had its own king residing at Metz, with a palace and royal administration under a mayor of the palace. The bishop and mayor of the palace represented the powerful Austrasian aristocracy, and the Arnulfing-Pippinid family dominated both offices.

Bishop Arnulf and the mayor of the palace Pepin I were leaders of the opposition to Sigebert's wife, Brunhilde; Pepin's son Grimoald, mayor of the palace at Metz (d. 656), attempted to place his own son on the Austrasian throne. Pepin II conquered Neustria in 687 and began the family's domination of the entire Frankish kingdom. The Pippinids were aided by their control of the bishopric of Metz, not only with Arnulf (d. 626) but with Chlodulf in the mid-7th century, Chrodegang (d. 766), Angilramn (d. 791), and Drogo (d. 855), and also by the support of allied aristocratic families in the Meuse-Moselle region between Metz and Verdun.

The Carolingians stressed their ties to Metz by promoting the cult of their ancestor, Bishop Arnulf. Charlemagne had his wife, Hildegard, and several of their children who died in infancy buried in the abbey of Saint-Arnoult (Arnulf), which was also the final resting place for Louis I the Pious. When Charlemagne's kingdom was divided by the Treaty of Verdun (843), Metz was made capital of Lotharingia. In the 12th century, Metz declared its independence from the dukes of Lorraine and set itself up as a city-state ruled by a chief magistrate chosen from among the wealthy patrician families.

The cathedral of Saint-Étienne in Metz is 13th-century, the result of reconstruction in Gothic style that united two earlier churches. The two flanking towers, one of which serves as the town's belfry, were begun at this time but not completed until the 15th century. The height of the nave (138 feet) is striking, second only to that of Beauvais. It is lit by a remarkable ensemble of stained-glass windows, installed from the 13th century to the 20th. The large 14th-century rose on the west façade is the work of Hermann of Münster.

Other medieval churches include Saint-Pierre-aux-Nonnains, reputedly the oldest surviving church in France, having been founded in the 7th century as a Benedictine abbey church; Saint-Maximin (late 12th c.); the octagonal church of the Templars (early 13th c.); Saint-Martin (13th–15th c.); and Saint-Eucaire, with its handsome 12th-century bell tower and 13th-century façade.

Steven Fanning

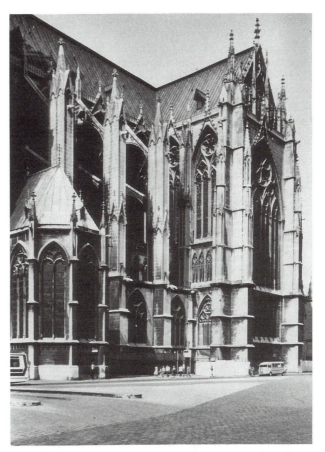

Metz (Moselle), Notre-Dame, south flank. *Photograph courtesy of Joan A. Holladay.*

[**See also:** AUSTRASIA; BRUNHILDE; MAYOR OF THE PALACE; VIGNEULLES, PHILIPPE DE]

Dollinger-Léonard, Yvette. "De la cité romaine à la ville médiévale dans la région de la Moselle et la Haute Meuse." *Studien zu den Anfängen des europäischen Städtwesens* 4 (1958): 195–201.

Ewig, Eugen. *Spätantikes und fränkisches Gallien: Gesammelte Schriften (1952–1973).* Zurich: Artemis, 1976, pp. 385–86.

Gerberding, Richard A. *The Rise of the Carolingians and the "Liber historiae Francorum."* Oxford: Clarendon, 1987.

Le Moigne, François-Yves, ed. *Histoire de Metz.* Toulouse: Privat, 1986.

McKitterick, Rosamond. *The Frankish Kingdoms Under the Carolingians, 751–987.* London: Longman, 1983.

Oexle, Otto Gerhard. "Die Karolinger und die Stadt des heiligen Arnulf." *Frühmittelalterliche Studien* 1 (1967): 250–364.

MÉZIÈRES, PHILIPPE DE (1327–1405). Born in Mézières in Picardy, Philippe was a soldier of fortune, then an advocate on the diplomatic and political levels of a crusade to regain Jerusalem for Christendom. He founded the chivalric Order of the Passion of Jesus Christ, was chancellor of Cyprus under Peter I, was a citizen of Venice, knew popes Urban V and Gregory XI and was a friend of Petrarch, and served as counselor to Charles V of France from 1373 until 1380, when he withdrew to the convent of the Celestines in Paris. Here, he wrote the major part of his work, in both French and Latin prose, remaining at the convent until his death. His first known work is the Latin *vita* (1366) of his spiritual adviser, Peter Thomas. He wrote on the feast of Mary's Presentation at the Temple, achieving celebration in the West of this originally eastern feast. Three of his treatises depict the order he had founded: *Nova religio milicie Passionis Jhesu Christi pro acquisicione sancte civitatis Jherusalem et Terre Sancte*, extant in two versions written in 1368 and 1384, respectively, but copied together in the only surviving manuscript; the *Sustance de la chevalerie de la Passion de Jhesu Crist en françois* (ca. 1389–94); and the *Chevalerie de la Passion de Jhesu Crist,* written in 1396 shortly before the Battle of Nicopolis. The *Livre sur la vertu du sacrement de mariage* (1384–89) contemplates the mystical union of Christ with the church and the human soul and includes the famous exemplum of "patient Griselda," translated by Philippe from the Latin of his friend Petrarch. The *Songe du vieil pèlerin*, an allegorical pilgrimage finished in 1389, points out the evils of the world and suggests remedies. His 1395 letter to Richard II of England urges the king to wed Isabella of France as a means to European peace. All of Philippe de Mézières' major works urge the social and political stability of Europe necessary for his long-sought but never to be realized crusade.

Joan B. Williamson

Mézières, Philippe de. *Campaign for the Feast of Mary's Presentation,* ed. William E. Coleman. Toronto: Pontifical Institute of Mediaeval Studies, 1981.

———. *Letter to King Richard II,* ed. and trans. G.W. Coopland. New York: Harper and Row, 1976.

———. *Le songe du vieil pèlerin,* ed. G.W. Coopland. 2 vols. Cambridge: Cambridge University Press, 1969.

———. *La sustance de la chevalerie de la Passion de Jhesu Crist en françois: Philippe de Mézières and the New Order of the Passion,* ed. Abdel Hamid Hamdy. 3 vols. Alexandria: Alexandria University Press, 1964–65. [Transcription of Ashmole 813.]

———. *Vita sancti Petri Thomae,* ed. Joachim Smet. Rome: Institutum Carmelitanum, 1954.

Iorga, Nicolae. *Philippe de Mézières (1327–1405) et la croisade au XIVe siècle.* Paris: Bouillon, 1896.

MICHAULT, PIERRE (late 15th c.). A poet attached to the court of Burgundy, Michault composed the *Procès d'honneur féminin,* a judicial allegory; the *Dance aux aveugles* (1464), a variation on the *danse macabre* featuring the blind Cupido, Fortune, and Atropos; the *Doctrinal du temps présent* (1466), a moralized satire in prose and verse modeled on the *Doctrinale* of Alexander of Villa Dei; and the *Complainte sur la mort d'Ysabeau de Bourbon.* These works reflect important variations on standard 15th-century themes: the quarrel between the champions and detractors of women, the dance of death, court life.

Earl Jeffrey Richards

[**See also:** QUARREL OF THE *BELLE DAME SANS MERCI*]

Michault, Pierre. *Œuvres poétiques,* ed. Barbara Folkart. Paris: Union Générale d'Éditions, 1980.

MICHEL, JEAN (d. 1501). Author of a *Mystère de la Passion* played at Angers in 1486, Michel practiced medicine in that city, serving for a time as doctor to the dauphin, infant son of Charles VIII. He was also a regent of the University of Angers. Michel based his Passion play on Days 2 and 3 of Arnoul Greban's *Passion,* expanding them to four days and 30,000 lines. Thus, the work treats only the adult life of Jesus from baptism to death, omitting both his childhood and the Resurrection. In addition, Michel suppressed the *Procès de paradis,* affirming that the Incarnation had been decided from all eternity. Stressing the moral aspects of the story, he amplified the sermons of Jesus and expanded the roles of three principal characters: Mary Magdalene, Lazarus, and Judas. He incorporated the oedipal legend associated with Judas, in which he kills his father and marries his mother. The other two roles exemplify the importance of repentance for the sinner. Michel's *Passion* continued to be played to the mid-16th century and was sometimes "completed" by the addition of Days 1 and 4 from Greban's play.

Alan E. Knight

[**See also:** GREBAN, ARNOUL; MYSTERY PLAYS; PASSION PLAYS]

Michel, Jean. *Le mystère de la Passion*, ed. Omer Jodogne. Gembloux: Duculot, 1959.

Accarie, Maurice. *Le théâtre sacré de la fin du moyen âge.* Geneva: Droz, 1979.

MIÉLOT, JEAN (fl. 15th c.). Translator, copyist, illuminator. A native of Gueschard in Picardy, near the residence of the dukes of Burgundy at Hesdin, Miélot was later canon of Saint-Pierre in Lille and, from 1449 to 1467, honorary secretary of Duke Philip the Good. This appointment followed his translation for the ducal library of the *Miroir de la salvation humaine* (1448), the first of a series of translations that included not only such religious texts as the *Vie et miracles de saint Josse* (1449) or the *Sermons d'un Franciscain sur l'oraison dominicale* (1457) but also, shortly after the Pheasant Banquet (1454), several crusading texts, such as the *Advis directif pour faire le voyage d'oultremer* and a *Description de la Terre Sainte* by the Dominican missionary Bouchard, and certain classical texts, such as the *Romuléon*, a Roman history by Roberto della Porta of Bologna (1465) and, for Charles the Bold, the *Épistre de Cicéron à son frère Quintus* (1472). He was also a calligrapher, on occasion an illustrator, and a director of a workshop in Lille that prepared manuscripts of these translations, which, it has been suggested, contributed to the development of French prose.

Charity Cannon Willard

Portrait of Jean Miélot in his study. BN fr. 9198, fol. 19. *Courtesy of the Bibliothèque Nationale, Paris.*

Bossuat, Robert. "Jean Miélot, traducteur de Cicéron." *Bibliothèque de École des Chartes* 99 (1938): 82–124.

Delaissé, L.M.J. *La miniature flamande, le mécénat de Philippe le Bon.* Brussels: Bibliothèque Royale, 1959.

Perdrizet, Paul. "Jean Miélot, l'un des traducteurs de Philippe le Bon." *Revue de l'histoire littéraire de la France* 14 (1907): 472–82.

Wilson, Adrian L. *A Medieval Mirror.* Berkeley: University of California Press, 1984.

MIGRATIONS ART. The term usually used to refer to art produced by and for the "new peoples," primarily Germanic, who entered the former territory of the Roman Empire as federate allies, mercenaries, raiders, and ultimately as settlers. In France, the migration of new peoples on a large scale is a phenomenon primarily of the 5th century, prior to the establishment of dominant Frankish power throughout most of the country, and the conversion of the Franks to Christianity, ca. 500. By convention, however, "migrations art" refers to ornamental metalwork primarily of non-Christian function and subject matter down to the 7th century. Furthermore, it has become clear that this migrations art is by no means a collection of tribal artistic traditions but rather the product of considerable interchange among Germanic peoples and between the new settlers and indigenous inhabitants; migrations art was not brought to the former Roman territories by new settlers but created there.

The bulk of the migrations art consists of weapons and objects of personal adornment, such as pins, brooches, and buckles, which have been recovered in vast numbers from graves of the period. Important artistic work must also have been undertaken in building (such as royal and aristocratic halls), in wood sculpture, and especially in textiles; that the medium of metalwork alone has survived in quantity gives it undue importance. In addition, the concentration upon elaborate metalwork does not indicate that only portable arts were produced because the artists and their patrons were nomadic. Nonetheless, this metalwork is characteristic of the period, and the great luxury objects played a major role in displaying social patterns and status. Archaeologists and art historians have organized the metalwork of the 5th to early 7th centuries according to technical and stylistic criteria and have concentrated attention on the objects using gold and jewels rather than the far more numerous examples in iron and bronze. Most objects fall within the categories known as chip carving, Polychrome Style, Style I, and Style II. All of these terms are used for objects produced and found from Scandinavia to Italy and from Spain to the Black Sea basin, and for none of them does France appear to have been the most original or productive center, although it certainly participated actively in the development.

Chip carving developed along the eastern borders of the Roman Empire, including the Frankish regions of the lower Rhine, in the late 4th century, in connection with cast-bronze objects made for soldiers; it involved hand-chiseling of abstract patterns into the metal. The starting point of the tradition is Roman in both design and tech-

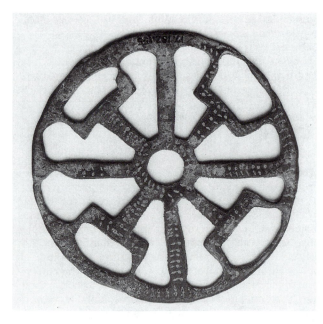

Bronze openwork disk. 500–600 A.D. Northern France. New York: Metropolitan Museum of Art. Gift of J.P. Morgan, 1917. *Courtesy of the Metropolitan Museum of Art.*

filigree. Patterns are primarily abstract or geometric, and the emphasis on precious materials ensures that this class of objects has royal and aristocratic associations. The greatest French examples of this technique are the sword fittings and other objects from the tomb of Clovis's father, Childeric I, last pagan Frankish king, a tomb excavated at Tournai in 1653 and usually dated to 481. Here, the color is restricted to the red garnets, now set closely together to make whole fields of red divided only by thin sheets of gold. This polychrome *cloisonné* style continued well into the 6th century in such luxury objects as the disc brooches founded in the tomb of the Christian Queen Arnegund (probably died ca. 565) excavated in the church of Saint-Denis.

Style I and Style II metalwork focuses upon animal forms. Style I clearly developed in northern Europe, perhaps in Scandinavia and England, in the early 6th century and spread rapidly across France and the Continent. It primarily used compact animals and animal parts, which were treated in a progressively more abstract and decorative manner. Style II now seems likely to have developed in Lombard Italy in the late 6th century, whence it rapidly spread northward into Germany and France. It essentially involves the combination of animal forms with complex ribbon-interlace patterns of Mediterranean origin. Both animal styles were used not only in the decoration of commonplace objects in base metals but also in combination with polychrome *cloisonné* techniques in a series of objects of stunningly inventive virtuosity, examples of which are again provided from Arnegund's burial. Ultimately, such decorative styles were adopted for Christian art in reliquaries and other sacred objects of high status.

Lawrence Nees

nique, and the bulk of the material, executed in base metals, was used widely throughout the military class. In contrast, the Polychrome Style, developed in eastern Europe by the 4th century, used red garnets, glass, and other colored gems set onto gilt backgrounds as small separate cells, or *cloisons*, often surrounded with gold granulation and

Pinned bronze buckle and plaque. 525–600 A.D. Paris basin. New York: Metropolitan Museum of Art. Gift of J.P. Morgan, 1917. *Courtesy of the Metropolitan Museum of Art.*

Gold disk fibula. First half of 7th century. From Neiderbreisig. New York: Metropolitan Museum of Art. Gift of J.P. Morgan, 1917. *Courtesy of the Metropolitan Museum of Art.*

[See also: JEWELRY AND METALWORKING;
MEROVINGIAN ART]

Haseloff, Günther. "Salin's Style I." *Medieval Archaeology* 18
(1974): 1–15.
Lasko, Peter. *The Kingdom of the Franks: Northwest Europe
Before Charlemagne.* London: Thames and Hudson, 1971.
Nees, Lawrence. *Justinian to Charlemagne: European Art, 565–
787: An Annotated Bibliography.* Boston: Hall, 1985.
Périn, Patrick, and Laure-Charlotte Feffer. *Les Francs.* Paris:
Colin, 1987.
Roth, Helmut. *Kunst der Völkerwanderungszeit.* Supplement-
band 4 of *Propylaen Kunstgeschichte.* Frankfurt am Main:
Propylaen, 1979.

MILITARY ARCHITECTURE.

Both the castle complex and urban defenses in medieval France relied upon strong walls and gateways designed to prevent entrance to enemies and ensure access for allies. River towns and ports had fortified bridges and special defenses. *Bastide* towns, fortified towns of French origin, were forms of military architecture on the grand scale of the urban landscape. Designs of temporary defensive or offensive war machines, technological innovations, and social and economic factors all affected the construction of these works.

During the 12th and 13th centuries, building techniques and weapons improved due to the increased exchanges between cultures and technological advances in metallurgy. More town walls and castles were made of stone, and designs of defensive fortifications aspired to incorporate the idea of effective counterattacks.

In the first half of the 13th century, advances in the design and construction of main gateways included the addition of flanking towers and added height to three or four stories in total. Portcullises, machicolations, meurtrières, and two-leaved doors helped to defend the gateway passages. A system of shod-iron portcullises operated by ropes and pulleys stood in front of the door, and machicolations opening out into the vault or roof of the gateway stood either between the portcullis and the door or in front of the portcullis. The gateway held two or three sets of these defenses, with an additional machicolation at the gate itself. Such protection deterred surprise attacks and allowed inspection of those entering.

Fortified bridges from the 13th century were protected on the far side by a barbican or tête-du-pont. At Tournai, a fortified bridge protected the curtain walls on either side of the River Scheldt. The surviving Pont des Trous is a three-span covered bridge, pierced by loopholes on both sides and defended by a strong square tower at either end. At Cahors, the enormous six-span Pont Valentré has a tower at each end and a third tower over the middle of the bridge. A fortified gateway in each tower is defended by an embattled parapet, and the two end towers also have machicolations.

In the early 13th centuries, new fortified towns called *bastides* were planned in southwest France and in England and Wales. The prototype of the *bastide* was Montauban, founded in 1144 by Alphonse-Jourain, count of Toulouse, to guard the road to Toulouse. Its grid plan with market square was copied by princes, counts, and minor lords throughout the 13th century. Many *bastides* held strategic positions on the frontiers of principalities, especially on the border between the county of Toulouse and the duchy of Aquitaine, but the main purposes of the *bastides* were to attract population to the frontiers and to provide the founder with a political base.

Stacy L. Boldrick

[See also: BASTIDE; CAHORS; CARCASSONNE; CASTLE;
CHÂTEAU-GAILLARD; WARFARE]

Enlart, Camille. *Manuel d'archéologie française depuis les temps
mérovingiens jusqu'à la Renaissance: architecture civile et
militaire.* 2 vols. Paris: Picard, 1932.
Higounet, Charles. "Zur Siedlungsgeschichte Sudwestfrankreichs
vom 11. bis zum 14. Jahrhundert." *Vortrage and Forshungen*
18 (1975).
Toy, Sidney. *Castles: A Short History of Fortifications from 1600
B.C. to A.D. 1600.* Toronto: Heinemann, 1939.
Trabut-Cussac, J.P. "Bastides ou forteresses?" *Moyen âge* 60
(1954): 81–135.

MILLENNIALISM.

Literally, millennialism (also millenarianism, chiliasm) refers to the belief, expressed in the book of Revelation, that Christ will establish a 1,000-year reign of the saints on earth before the Last Judgment. More broadly, millennialists expect a time of supernatural peace and abundance here on earth. Both usages reflect the eschatological belief that at the end of time God will judge the living and the (resurrected) dead. This belief in ultimate divine justice has provided the solution to the problem of theodicy for countless generations of Christians suffering under hardship and oppression.

In most early forms, millennial beliefs were anti-imperial, even antiauthoritarian: as the messianic vision of Isaiah 2:4 depicts, the instruments of war and domination will be beaten into instruments of peace and prosperity. Apostolic Christianity demonstrates all of the key traits of apocalyptic millenarian groups: the rhetoric of the meek versus the powerful, of the imminence of the Lord's Day of wrath and the coming Kingdom of Heaven; the shift from a disappointed messianic hope (Crucifixion) to a revised expectation (Second Coming or Parousia); a following among common, working people; the rituals of initiation into a group preparing for and awaiting the End; the fervent spirituality and radical restructuring of community bonds; and the prominence of women visionaries.

As Christianity evolved from a charismatic cult on the fringes of society into a self-perpetuating institution eager to live in harmony with Rome, the hopes of apocalyptic millenarianism embarrassed church leaders who emphasized that Jesus's kingdom was "not of this world." With the advent of imperial Christianity, millenarianism was pushed to the margins of acceptable Christian thought.

As a result, as early as the 2nd century, two of the principal themes of medieval millennialism emerged: the use of chronology to postpone the End, thus encouraging patience, and the transformation of the Roman Empire into a positive force. The former teaching invoked a sabbatical millennium that would come in the year 6000 after Creation; ca. A.D. 200, the first Christian chronology placed the Creation in 5500 B.C., thus providing a buffer of 300 years until the year A.D. 500. The latter interpreted Paul's reference to an obstacle to the "man of iniquity" (2 Thessalonians 3:4) to mean that as long as the Roman Empire endured, the Antichrist could not come. This pro-Roman eschatology would, after the mutual conversion of Rome to Christianity and Christianity to imperialism, produce the myth of the Last Emperor, a superhuman figure who would unite all of Christendom, rule in peace and justice for 120 years, and finally abdicate his throne.

But both these approaches merely delayed the problem: despite pagan and Christian belief in *Roma eterna*, the empire (especially in the West) was doomed; and, coincidentally, the year 6000 grew inevitably closer, transforming an antiapocalyptic chronology into an apocalyptic one. Jerome and Augustine reoriented Latin thought on the millennium in two ways. Jerome introduced a new set of calculations, which placed the Creation in 5199 B.C., delaying the year 6000 another three centuries. Augustine went farther, arguing that no historical event or chronology can be intepreted apocalyptically and that the millennium was not a future event but already in progress—the millennium began at the time of Jesus. To explain why the evils of war, hatred, injustice, and poverty continued unabated, Augustine introduced the concept of the Two Cities: a heavenly city, the celestial Jerusalem, where the millennium was already manifest, and the terrestrial Babylon, the time-bound city of violence and oppression in which the millennium was not visible.

Augustine's opposition to millennial thought so dominated the theological writings of the early Middle Ages that many historians think that it actually disappeared. But there are signs of its presence, both in the activity of antiecclesiastical prophets like the "False Christ" of Bourges described by Gregory of Tours (*Histories* 10.25) and in the antiapocalyptic uses of chronology. In the 8th century, Bede and Carolingian historians shifted the dating system again, this time to *anno Domini*.

It is surely no accident that Charlemagne took up the imperium in the absence of a legitimate emperor in Byzantium, and thus assumed the role of continuator of the Roman Empire, on the first day of the year A.D. 800, or 6000 *annus mundi*. With the apocalyptic dimension of the deed eliminated from the documentation, modern historians have analyzed this pivotal moment in western history without any awareness of its background. It has gone down in history as the Coronation of the year 800, not 6000 *annus mundi*.

Charlemagne's coronation contributed two essential elements to European millennialism. He "transferred" the empire, with all its apocalyptic and millennial freight, to the West, and he shifted the chronological hopes for the Apocalypse from 6000 *annus mundi* to the year A.D. 1000, a date at once millennial (the end of the sixth age, dawn of the sabbatical era) and Augustinian (the end of the millennium of the church). Germany and France of the year 1000

illustrate the two directions of millennial symbolism: whereas the emperor Otto III manipulated every aspect of the imperial variety of millennialism (*renovatio imperii Romani*, opening Charlemagne's tomb on Pentecost of 1000), King Robert II the Pious of France, second ruler of a new and still uncertain dynasty and excommunicate in 1000, presided over a kingdom marked by the social turmoil of the castellan revolution. Here, apocalyptic and millennial symbols were generated from below, especially in the earliest popular religious movement of the Middle Ages, the Peace of God. This conciliar movement, which mobilized huge crowds at open-air revivalist gatherings in the collective pursuit of God's peace on earth, may have been the earliest sustained millenarian movement that joined all levels of society. It appeared in two waves, each in the decades before the millennium of the Incarnation (1000) and the Passion (1033), first south of the Loire, then throughout France.

When the year 1000 passed without the Parousia, there was a sea-change in millennial hopes. The period after the year 1000 saw much vaster millennial movements, often approved by ecclesiastical authorities—popular crusades, Joachites, Flagellants, the Peace Movement. Some of these movements were broadly based, militant, and hostile to ecclesiastical authority, the wealthy, and Jews, thus bringing out the most revolutionary elements of millennialism.

But the more documentable, and in some ways more surprising, aspect of medieval millennialism was its use by lay and ecclesiastical elites to buttress their own authority. Starting with the Gregorian Reform in the 11th century, papal reformers used apocalyptic imagery both to attack their enemies as Antichrist and to wrap their own efforts in messianic promises. Similarly, royal and even comital courts used eschatological prophecy as propaganda. Dynastic publicists often painted their patrons in the imagery of the Last Emperor—the Norman William the Conqueror consciously used themes from Revelation (his crown, his Doomsday book) to buttress his conquest of England. Supporters of Thierry d'Alsace, count of Flanders, responding to the seemingly apocalyptic civil war of 1127–28, disseminated prophecies claiming that Thierry's (Carolingian) dynasty was the last barrier to Antichrist.

Millennial hopes and ambitions reached new levels as a result of the work of Joachim of Fiore (d. 1202). Joachim was the first theologian to reject Augustine and return to a notion of a future earthly age of bliss. Joachim revitalized every aspect of medieval millennialism: within decades of his death, prophecies attributed to him began to circulate that people identified with current events, mystical numerology, Franciscans and Dominicans, Holy Roman emperors, and popes all became elements in vast and ever-shifting predictions of imminent apocalypse. Chronological calculations fixed on 1250, then 1260 as the beginning of the new age; the Franciscan order split over interpretations of Joachite prophecy, one branch becoming inquisitors, the other, revolutionary millenarians; angelic popes and messianic emperors (some dead but returning), vied among lay and clerical constituencies for a following. In France, the imagery of millennialism continued to influence political discourse throughout the remainder of the

Middle Ages. The catastrophes of the 14th century—the Hundred Years' War and the Black Death—renewed fervor for the final, divine intervention.

The hopes and expectations of the Christian Apocalypse offered the outlines of a powerful if ultimately impractical, and hence suicidal, ideology of social revolution to the peasants and the urban poor of France in the later Middle Ages. The thousands of shepherds, or Pastoureaux, who swept through the French countryside in 1251 and again in 1320, were convinced that they were God's chosen instrument to free the Holy Land, thus bringing about the Parousia. While none ever reached the Holy Land, they traveled in bands throughout the kingdom of France, amazing some with their piety, all the while slaughtering clerics, Jews, and university intellectuals. Similar apocalyptic ideas regarding the election of the poor to usher in God's kingdom motivated other popular insurrections and probably inspired the great Jacquerie of 1358.

Modern historians, limited by the nature of the documentation, tend to emphasize "political" or imperial millennialism in their analyses. The presence and strength of popular and revolutionary millennialism, rarely reported except by hostile clerical sources or by later spokesmen eager to downplay millenarian origins, are more difficult to assess. If one limits oneself only to explicitly millenarian groups, the numbers are few; if one identifies such groups by their patterns rather than their or others' claims about them, they are far more numerous. Given how dangerous even proimperial millennialism could be (e.g., Spiritual Franciscans or John of Roquetaillade), the prominence of conservative millennialism in medieval thought may testify to the ineradicable nature of its appeal to the populace at large. In short, millennial beliefs and aspirations must be ranked among the most profound and versatile of medieval ideologies of social change.

Richard Landes

[See also: ANTICHRIST; ANTI-SEMITISM; BLACK DEATH; CHARLEMAGNE; CRUSADES; GREGORIAN REFORM; HERESIES, APOSTOLIC; JACQUERIE; PASTOUREAUX; PEACE OF GOD; POPULAR DEVOTION; RAOUL GLABER]

Bietenhard, Hans. "Millennial Hope in the Early Church." *Scottish Journal of Theology* 6 (1953): 12–30.

Cohn, Norman R.C. *The Pursuit of the Millennium.* Rev. ed. New York: Oxford University Press, 1970.

Daniels, Theodore T. *Millennialism: An International Bibliography.* New York: Garland, 1992.

Emmerson, Richard K., and Bernard McGinn. *The Apocalypse in the Middle Ages.* Ithaca: Cornell University Press, 1993.

Fredriksen, Paula. "Apocalypse and Redemption in Early Christianity: From John of Patmos to Augustine of Hippo." *Vigiliae christianae* 45 (1991): 151–83.

Fried, Johannes. "Endzeiterwartung um die Jahrtausendwende." *Deutsches Archiv für Erforschung des Mittelalters* 45.2 (1989): 385–473.

Landes, Richard. "Lest the Millennium Be Fulfilled: Apocalyptic Expectations and the Pattern of Western Chronography, 100–800 CE." In *The Use and Abuse of Eschatology in the Middle Ages,* ed. W. Verbeke, D. Verhelst, and A. Welken-huysen. Louvain: Catholic University Press, 1988, pp. 141–211.

———. "Millenarismus absconditus: l'historiographie augustinienne et le millénarisme du haut moyen âge jusqu'en l'an mil." *Moyen âge* 98 (1992): 355–77; 99 (1993): 1–26.

Lerner, Robert E. "Refreshment of the Saints: The Time After Antichrist as a Station for Earthly Progress in Medieval Thought." *Traditio* 32 (1976): 99–144.

McGinn, Bernard. *Visions of the End: Apocalyptic Traditions in the Middle Ages.* New York: Columbia University Press, 1979.

Reeves, Marjorie. *Joachim of Fiore and the Prophetic Future.* London: SPCK, 1976.

St. Clair, Michael J. *Millenarian Movements in Historical Context.* New York: Garland, 1992.

Williams, Ann, ed. *Prophecy and Millenarianism: Essays in Honour of Marjorie Reeves.* Harlow: Longman, 1980.

MILLS AND MILLING. Taken to mean the mechanical devices and processes utilized in the preparation of foodstuffs and manufactured goods, mills and milling experienced notable technical developments during the Middle Ages. The forces that stimulated technological innovation and the full impact of that innovation upon medieval industry, economy, and life are matters of debate, but what can be shown here is the variety of mechanisms and their uses, as well as their ingenuity. French millers clearly made significant contributions.

Roman Gaul doubtless received the full range of ancient milling technologies, including not only human- and animal-driven grinding and crushing machines, used, respectively, to make flour and oil, but also the water-powered grain mill employing a vertical axle that in turn moved the flat-rotating grinder. Nowhere was this latter machine used more effectively than in the 4th century at Barbegal, near Arles, where a concentration of sixteen grinders, each driven by its own wheel, produced what is now reliably estimated to be nine tons of flour in a twenty-four-hour day. The continued and expanded use of water-powered grain mills is traceable through the Merovingian, Carolingian, and subsequent medieval periods in France, in some cases displaying an intensity of industrialization more pronounced than elsewhere in Europe. Nothing in the 9th-century sources compares, for instance, with the eighty-four mills at work on the monastic properties of Saint-Germain-des-Prés at the time of Abbot Irminon (r. 800–25) or the fifteen mills ordered to produce the flour for 450 loaves of bread per day in Abbot Adalhard of Corbie's statutes of 822.

Among the innovations relating to water-powered mills was their location not just on streams, or near streams and fed by sluices, but also as floating mills anchored in riverine currents or tidal estuaries, as stationary mills built over sluices through which tidal pools were drained, and as bridge mills constructed normally on pilings associated with the arches and cutwaters of a bridge. All of these variations are to be found in Europe by the 12th century, with France showing particular adaptability, the most fully documented examples being bridge mills, origins of which can be traced there back to the 11th century (e.g., Jumièges, ca. 1020; Angers and Mayenne, 1028) and the earliest illustrations of which appear, however schematic or fanciful, in French manuscripts (e.g., the *Légende de saint Denis*, 1317).

Major innovations are also to be seen in the utilization of water-powered machinery in processes other than grinding grain. Crucial here is the translation of the rotary motion of the wheel into reciprocating motion, as of a hammer, vertical or recumbent, made possible by cams located on the horizontal axle of the vertical water-wheel. This is first indicated in an architectural plan produced for the abbot of Saint-Gall ca. 820, in which the hammers adjoin a brewery and thus are seemingly intended for use in the preparation of the malt (beer mash). The earliest documentary references to working beer mills anywhere are from mid-9th-century France (e.g., Évreux, 862; Vaux-sur-Somme, 867); hammers are not always specified (grinding was a practical, if less efficient, alternative in the reduction of the malt), but water power is clearly indicated by the hydrographical context of the relevant entries in the documents. Pounding action is undoubted in the fulling and hemp mills that appeared during the 11th century in the manufacture, respectively, of cloth and cordage in Italy and France, as at Lérins (1040); in the tanning mills, for crushing the bark, that made their appearance in the 12th century in France, as at Charment, near Paris (1138); and in the metallurgical industry. The latter experienced the first certain use of water-powered hammers and bellows, also operated by cams, by the 13th century in Sweden (1224), France (the Dauphiné, 1226), and Germany (ca. 1270). Other uses of water power to which French millers significantly contributed include wood sawing (first documented at Évreux, 1204; first illustrated by Villard de Honnecourt, ca. 1235) and paper making (in Italy and Spain, late 13th c.; in France, at Troyes, 1338).

Worthy of note here is the appearance in medieval Europe of the windmill, perhaps from eastern origins or, certainly in its distinctive western form, as an independent invention. This consisted of wind vanes set vertically upon a horizontal axle that was geared to the vertical axle and the working parts, all located, until the early 15th century, in a structure that could be pivoted upon a post to face the wind. Such mills are now identifiable in mid-12th-century England and were at work by the early 13th century grinding grains in France, as at Arles (1202). Not to be ignored in the tradition of medieval European and French milling is a simpler but geographically adaptable kind of water mill employing a horizontal waterwheel whose vertical axle turned the grinder without the intervention of gears. Notable, too, are distinct improvements throughout the period in the design of manually operated devices, such as flat-rotating grinders, edge rollers, cranked or treadled whetstones and lathes, water-raising mechanisms, and hoists for heavy materials.

The technical variety and advances in medieval milling and related machinery are clearly discernible. The ingenuity involved is admirable. And both of these are nowhere more evident than in France.

Bradford B. Blaine

[See also: BREAD]

Bautier, Anne-Marie. "Les plus anciennes mentions de moulins hydrauliques industriels et de moulins à vent." *Bulletin philologique et historique* (1960): 567–626.

Boyer, Marjorie N. *Medieval French Bridges: A History.* Cambridge: Mediaeval Academy, 1976.

Forbes, Robert J. "Power," and Bertrand Gille, "Machines." In *A History of Technology*, ed. Charles Singer et al. 5 vols. Oxford: Clarendon, 1954–58, Vol. 2: *The Mediterranean Civilizations and the Middle Ages, c. 700 B.C. to c. A.D. 1500*, pp. 589–662.

Holt, Richard. *The Mills of Medieval England.* New York: Blackwell, 1988.

Reynolds, Terry S. *Stronger than a Hundred Men: A History of the Vertical Water Wheel.* Baltimore: Johns Hopkins University Press, 1983.

White, Lynn, Jr. *Medieval Technology and Social Change.* Oxford: Oxford University Press, 1962.

MINING AND METALS. France possesses no precious-metal resources and little copper. Iron ores are abundant, and there are regional deposits of lead, zinc, and coal. All of these were exploited during the Middle Ages.

Evidence for ironworking exists from Merovingian France onward. By the reign of Charlemagne, Frankish iron weapons and armor were so famous that exports had to be forbidden. Decorative ironwork was also widely practiced, as on the hinges and scrollwork of the western portals of Notre-Dame in Paris (13th c.). At Liège, we find from the late 14th century evidence of blast furnaces blown by water-powered bellows. Gunpowder weapons made of iron came to join traditional weapons as the major product of the iron industry.

Bronze, a mixture of copper and tin, is a prehistoric alloy much used in medieval Europe for artistic purposes. Although dependent on imported raw materials, French artisans excelled in bronze castings, especially in bells, which remain one of the highest expressions of this art. From the 15th century, bronzework was dominated by the demand for cannons, which are cast by the same technique as bells.

Brass, a metal sometimes confused with bronze, is an alloy of copper and zinc; it is much more difficult to produce. France's abundant supplies of calamine (zinc carbonate) made it a center for brass production. Noteworthy in the French-speaking world was the city of Dinant, across the imperial frontier in the Meuse Valley. *Dinanderie* products were highly famed until the industry was dispersed in the sack of 1466.

Lead was widely used in the Middle Ages. In sheets, it served for roofing and guttering, while it could be cast into decorative objects from baptismal fonts to small medallions. Common pewter, an alloy of lead and tin, was frequently used for tableware. Lead bullets and shot, along with cast iron, replaced stone pellets as the preferred missiles in firearms in the 15th century. France's lead resources were among the best of any European region.

In the 12th century, the coalfields in the Low Countries near Liège began to be worked. Here, and in the valleys reaching westward to Charleroi and Mons, the technical pinnacle of medieval coal exploitation was reached; workings extended beneath the local water table, giving rise to sophisticated pumps and drainage tunnels. Coal was shipped via river barge to distant markets, but by the late 15th century it was also consumed locally as a metallurgical fuel.

The absence of precious metals had an effect on French legal history relating to mining. Roman law had regarded mineral rights, especially to precious metals, as an imperial monopoly, to be consigned in return for royalties. England and the empire followed Roman precedent. Yet France's minerals, especially coal and zinc (the latter unrecognized as a metal during this period), were unmentioned by the Roman legists. Astute feudal lords, such as the dukes of Burgundy and counts of Hainaut, asserted their claims in the absence of royal prerogatives, but by the 15th century the crown was asserting some measure of regalian right over minerals.

Bert S. Hall

[See also: BELLS]

Bromehead, Cyril N. "Mining and Quarrying to the Seventeenth Century," and Robert J. Forbes, "Metallurgy." In *A History of Technology*, ed. Charles Singer et al. 5 vols. Oxford: Clarendon, 1954–58, Vol. 2: *The Mediterranean Civilizations and the Middle Ages, c. 700 B.C. to c. A.D. 1500*, pp. 1–80.

Malherbe, R. "Historique de l'exploitation de la houille dans le pays de Liège jusqu'à nos jours." *Mémoires de la Société Libre d'Émulation de Liège* 2 (1862). [There is little recent research on this important topic.]

Salin, Edouard. *La civilisation mérovingienne*. Paris: Picard, 1957, Vol. 3: *Les techniques*.

Viollet-le-Duc, Eugène E. "Plomberie." In *Dictionnaire raisonné de l'architecture française du XIe au XVIe siècle*. Paris: 1864, Vol. 7.

MINTS. The control of mints was in theory a royal prerogative in medieval France, but the early-medieval kings gradually lost control of the monopoly of minting. The Edict of Pîtres of Charles the Bald in 864 represents a last attempt to enforce royal control over minting; thereafter, bishops, abbots, dukes, and counts minted their own coinage. In spite of efforts by such kings as Louis IX and Philip IV, there remained between thirty and forty baronial silver coinages in medieval France in the early 14th century. Some, such as the Melgorian coinage of lower Languedoc, enjoyed wide regional circulation and considerable stability of precious-metal content over many centuries. By 1300, the royal Tournois and Parisis coinages were nonetheless the dominant systems of exchange in the kingdom.

Mints, whether baronial or royal, suffered the vicissitudes of fluctuating precious-metal supplies and changing royal and baronial politics, which led frequently to the debasement of coinage. Gold and silver coin were minted under the Merovingians; a monometallic silver standard persisted from the Carolingian period until the reintro-

duction of gold coinage in the 13th century again created a bimetallic royal monetary system.

Coinage profits were generated on several levels. Some precious metal was accumulated at the mint in the discards of the refinement process. The political authority in charge of the mint received a percentage of the coins struck, perhaps one of each twelve *deniers*, as seigniorage. The costs of processing were generally deducted from the precious-metal stocks at acquisition.

By the 14th century, mints had a complex administrative hierarchy and trained technical personnel. Mintmasters, guardians, and officers were charged with supervisory responsibilities; moneyers and workers designed and minted the actual coins. Once the precious metal had been sufficiently purified, according to the standard of fineness in use, minting was divided into two technological processes: the creation of dies or molds and the striking of coins. A Chambre des Monnaies was created by ordinance in 1348 as an advisory group to the Chambre des Comptes or the king's council for royal coinage.

Kathryn L. Reyerson

[See also: CURRENCY]

Castaing-Sicard, Mireille. *Monnaies féodales et circulation monétaire en Languedoc (Xe–XIIIe siècles)*. Toulouse: Association Marc Bloch, 1961.

Fournial, Étienne. *Histoire monétaire de l'Occident médiéval*. Paris: Nathan, 1970.

Spufford, Peter, and N.J. Mayhew, eds. *Late Medieval Mints: Organization, Administration and Techniques*. Oxford: B.A.R. International Series, 1988.

MIRACLE PLAYS. Miracle plays are dramatizations of two types of religious narrative material: miraculous events performed by the Virgin Mary in response to requests from a believer in difficulty, or episodes from the life of a saint during which miraculous events occur. Plays called *miracles* were especially popular in France during the 13th and 14th centuries, a period that corresponds not only with the growth of the cult of the Virgin Mary, but also with the increase in the number of religious *confréries* and trade guilds, which were largely responsible for performing these plays. Miracle plays had a double attraction: they were religious works set in the real, secular world, and they were in essence dramatic, since by definition their action led to a theatrical, supernatural climax.

Miracle plays in France form a bridge between liturgical drama and the mystery plays. Latin liturgical drama included miracle-type plays, such as the *Iconia sancti Nicolai*, on which legend vernacular plays were later written. After the 14th century, many so-called mystery plays were based on material, like saints' lives, that in the previous century would have been called *miracles* by their authors. Thus, the label "miracle play," both then and now, corresponds not only to a type of dramatized material but also to a period.

The great majority of surviving miracle plays come from the 14th century, but two 13th-century texts, and a few from the 15th and 16th centuries, have also come down to us. Jehan Bodel's *Jeu de saint Nicolas* (Arras; 1194–1202; 1,538 lines) is arguably the best and most original of all miracle plays. It dramatizes one of the several legends associated with the saint—his power to protect, and even multiply, any treasure entrusted to him—but sets the action in a crusading context. The Saracen king who announces that his treasure is to be guarded merely by a statue of Nicolas is testing the claims of the only survivor of a Christian army that his forces have been shown defeating. The thieves, whose attempt to steal the treasure is thwarted by the brusque intervention of Nicolas, appear as the cheating, drinking, gambling, and argumentative habitués of an Arras tavern. The play, which has provoked many studies, is complex and many-layered: serious yet comic, epic yet grotesque, exotic yet realistic. Rutebeuf's *Miracle de Théophile* (Paris; ca. 1260; 660 lines), a more uniform, poetic, even literary play, dramatizes the legend of Théophile, who sells his soul to the Devil in order to regain a bishopric he once turned down.

The collection of plays known as the *Miracles de Nostre Dame par personnages* (Paris; 1339–82; forty plays of 1,000–3,000 lines each), preserved in one fine illustrated manuscript (B.N. fr. 819–20) is all that survives from the 14th century. A new play was performed each year, early in December, by the Confrérie Saint Éloi, the patron of the Guild of Parisian Goldsmiths, probably in the Guild Hall. The collection illustrates the remarkable versatility of the miracle-play format: almost any secular narrative that involves a man or woman who prays to the Virgin and who overcomes an obstacle in an unexpected manner can be incorporated into a *Miracle de Nostre Dame par personnages*. The variety of sources used by the authors of these plays is enormous; in every case, the text is the dramatization of previously nondramatic narrative material. Thus, although many plays are based on saints' lives (*Étienne, Panthaléon, Ignace, Valentin, Laurent, Alexis*), or on well-known legends associated with the Virgin Mary, often drawn from Gautier de Coinci (*L'enfant voué au diable, L'abbesse enceinte délivrée, La nonne qui laissa son abbaye, Le paroissien excommunié*), many others derive from secular literature, such as epic (*Ami et Amile*), romance (*La reine de Portugal, Robert le diable, L'impératrice de Rome, Le roi Thierry*), or historical romance (*Berthe femme du roi Pépin, Le baptême de Clovis, La reine Bautheuch et ses fils*). In one instance, the *Enfant ressuscité*, the play is based on a "real" documented recent miracle.

Each year for much of the 14th century, the Parisian Goldsmiths saw a dramatization of one of the most popular tales of their time. The diversity of the sources, however, is belied by the homogeneity of the collection. Every one of the plays follows the same pattern; some authors no doubt contributed several works; certainly, the authors were familiar with the texts that had preceded theirs. In addition to the normal narrative framework of any miracle play, the *Miracles de Nostre Dame par personnages* have a number of elements in common: a sermon (either before the play proper or incorporated into the action); frequent prayers to the Virgin; scenes set in Heaven in which Notre Dame urges God to intervene in the predicament of some-

one who prays to her, even if that person is the most wicked sinner; scenes in which Notre Dame descends to Earth, accompanied by angels (occasionally including St. Éloi) who sing a rondeau. Other frequently recurring scenes show childbirth, imprisonment, and tortures. The quality of the texts is variable: some are poorly constructed, provide little character development, and fail to integrate the traditional elements in a convincing manner; but others, such as the *Enfant ressuscité* and the *Femme sauvée du bûcher*, are vivid examples of almost realist drama. The collection as a whole provides a remarkable picture of life in 14th-century France.

Several of the *Miracles de Nostre Dame par personnages*, had they survived independently from the collection, would now be considered as mystery plays, especially the saint plays, such as *Saint Valentin*. This fact underlines the somewhat arbitrary nature of labels as used both now and at the end of the Middle Ages. Few miracle plays survive from the 15th century; one rare exception is the play about a pregnant abbess and her miraculous delivery, found among the processional plays from Lille. But critics have not failed to note the relatively short texts, under 2,000 lines, preserved in early 16th-century printed editions, that in their scope, subject matter, and treatment resemble the Goldsmiths' miracle plays. These include the *Miracle de saint Nicolas et d'un Juif*, the *Chevalier qui donna sa femme au diable*, the *Femme qui se voulut abandonner au péché*, and the so-called *Mystère de saint Christofle*. The original versions of these plays were undoubtedly composed long before they were printed and probably should be attached to the corpus of surviving miracle plays.

Graham A. Runnalls

[See also: *AMI ET AMILE*; *BARLAAM ET JOSAPHAT*; CONFRÉRIE DE LA PASSION; GAUTIER DE COINCI; JEHAN BODEL; LITURGICAL DRAMA; MYSTERY PLAYS; RUTEBEUF; SAINTS' LIVES; THEATER]

Paris, Gaston, and Ulysse Robert, eds. *Les miracles de Nostre Dame par personnages*. 8 vols. Paris: Didot, 1876–93.

Runnalls, Graham A., ed. *Le miracle de l'enfant ressuscité*. Geneva: Droz, 1972.

Frank, Grace. *The Medieval French Drama*. 2nd ed. Oxford: Clarendon, 1960.

Jeanroy, Alfred. *Les quarante miracles de Nostre Dame*. In *Histoire Littéraire de la France*. Paris: Imprimerie Nationale, 1959, Vol. 39, pp. 23–91.

Runnalls, Graham A. "Medieval Trade Guilds and the *Miracles de Nostre Dame par personnages*." *Medium Aevum* 39 (1970): 257–87.

MISSI DOMINICI. The Carolingian system of royal messengers, generally referred to by the Latin term *missi dominici*, developed under the early Carolingian mayors of the palace but was first exploited by Charlemagne (r. 768–814). During his reign, these king's representatives made regular visits throughout the kingdom as a means of linking local government and the central administration.

This was one way in which Charlemagne sought to maintain control over the wide-ranging territories under his authority, for which he had only a rudimentary political organization that relied heavily on local powers.

Not a separate class of officials, the *missi* were chosen from lay and ecclesiastical magnates, usually counts and bishops, more rarely abbots. Each group of *missi,* including both a layperson and a churchman, was assigned to cover a defined area, the *missaticum,* where they exercised the royal authority on the king's behalf. They might investigate the conduct of government officials in the region (especially if abuses by them had been reported), transmit new royal decrees to local magnates, hear new oaths of allegiance to the sovereign, and assist local counts in the administration of justice.

By the end of Charlemagne's reign, four journeys a year to a given *missaticum* was the norm, so that the obligation to undertake the trips represented a significant commitment of time away from the other duties of the *missus* as a member of the secular or ecclesiastical nobility. This problem, together with the large size of the area for which a group of *missi* was responsible and the difficulty of enforcing its decisions on local magnates, limited the system's effectiveness.

Celia Chazelle

Ganshof, François L. *Frankish Institutions Under Charlemagne,* trans. Bryce Lyon and Mary Lyon. Providence: Brown University Press, 1968.

———. "The Use of the Written Word in Charlemagne's Administration." In *The Carolingians and the Frankish Monarchy: Studies in Carolingian History,* trans. Janet Sondheimer. London: Longman 1971.

Halphen, Louis. *Charlemagne and the Carolingian Empire,* trans. Giselle de Nie. Amsterdam: North-Holland, 1977.

McKitterick, Rosamond. *The Frankish Kingdoms Under the Carolingians, 751–987.* London: Longman, 1983.

———. *The Carolingians and the Written Word.* Cambridge: Cambridge University Press, 1989.

MOISSAC. (Tarn-et-Garonne). The fame of the former Benedictine abbey of Saint-Pierre at Moissac, a major stop on the route to Santiago de Compostela, rests with the sculpture of the south portal and with the late 11th-century cloister, one of the oldest and most complete Romanesque cloisters in France.

Alternating single and double marble columns carry the seventy-six capitals of the four cloister galleries; the pointed arches and upper walls are a 13th-century restoration. On the piers are marble reliefs of Abbot Durandus de Bredon, first Cluniac abbot of Moissac, and nine Apostles. Reliefs and capitals are related to contemporary Toulousan ateliers at Saint-Sernin and the cloister of La Daurade.

The Romanesque church was consecrated in 1063. The domed church of the following century was reconstructed after the Hundred Years' War in the southern Gothic style. On the exterior, the lower walls are Romanesque; the upper, in brick, are 15th-century.

Moissac (Tarn-et-Garonne), sculpture of the prophet Jeremiah. *Photograph courtesy of Rebecca A. Baltzer.*

The dates of the west tower and the famous south portal have not been satisfactorily determined. The projecting porch—with representations on its lateral walls of Avarice and Luxuria, Dives and Lazarus, the death of the evil rich man and his torture in Hell (west wall); the Annunciation (Gabriel is replaced), the Visitation, and scenes from the infancy of Christ (east wall)—was presumably added during the abbacy of Roger (1115–31), whose statue flanks the central porch.

An apocalyptic vision of the Second Coming fills the huge tympanum: the Majestic Christ, enthroned and crowned, holding the Book of Life on his left knee, his right hand raised in blessing, dominates the entrance to the Heavenly Jerusalem. Symbols of the four Evangelists and two elongated seraphim form a framing mandorla; twenty-four Elders strain to regard the central vision. The figures are in high relief; the carving is crisp, precise, and vigorous. Flanking the doorway are St. Peter, patron saint of the abbey, and the prophet Isaiah. On the central face of the trumeau are three pairs of lions and lionesses, their bodies crossed in a vertical "triple-x" composition. On the

Moissac, Saint-Pierre, south portal. *Photograph courtesy of Whitney S. Stoddard.*

Moissac, Saint-Pierre, cloister. *Photograph courtesy of Rebecca A. Baltzer.*

west lateral face is St. Paul; on the east, the most elegant figure in all of Romanesque art, the prophet Jeremiah unwinding his scroll. The cusped trumeau and jambs, as well as the regality of Christ and the Elders, recall the exoticism of Islamic Spain; the richness of pose and the details of robes, crowns, and book are solidly within the Languedocian tradition.

Other notable features include a lapidary museum; a 12th-century Crucifixion in wood; a Pieta with donor (1476); a Flight into Egypt (15th c.); an Entombment from the tomb of Abbot Pierre de Caraman (15th c.); and a Merovingian sarcophagus.

Jean M. French

Klein, Peter K. "Programmes eschatologiques, fonction et réception historiques des portails du XIIe s.: Moissac—Beaulieu—Saint-Denis." *Cahiers de civilisation médiévale* 33 (1990): 317–49.

Mezoughi, Noureddine. "Le tympan de Moissac: études d'iconographie." *Cahiers de Saint-Michel de Cuxa 9* (1978): 171–200. [Includes a survey of iconographic studies.]

Moissac et l'Occident au XIe siècle: actes du Colloque International de Moissac, 1963. Toulouse: Privat, 1964.

Rupin, Ernest. *L'abbaye et les cloîtres de Moissac.* Paris: Picard, 1897.

Schapiro, Meyer. "The Romanesque Sculpture of Moissac." In *Romanesque Art: Selected Papers.* New York: Braziller, 1977.

Vidal, Marguerite, Jean Maury, and Jean Porcher. *Quercy roman.* 3rd ed. La Pierre-qui-vire: Zodiaque, 1959.

MOLINET, JEAN (1453–1507). Molinet was born at Desvres in the Pas-de-Calais and studied in Paris. He became court historiographer for Charles the Bold, duke of Burgundy, in 1475 after the death of Georges Chastellain, his protector and the previous historiographer. In addition to compiling the official chronicles for his patrons, Molinet wrote verse and prose in many forms: plays, a prose adaptation of the *Roman de la Rose* with moral commentary, occasional poems, religious and allegorical pieces, *débats*, and some obscene verse. Like his fellow Rhétoriqueur poets, he played with etymologies and puns, described marvels, and used allegory and mythological allusion as moral examples. In a poem to the Virgin, all the words in each of the five stanzas of *huitains* begin with the appropriate letter of her name: M, A, R, I, E. What we tend to see as tricks and excesses were derived from the Rhétoriqueurs' conviction that the physical world is an analogue of the spiritual; what we view now simply as convention, for them was necessary commensurability. Even the individual letters of the language had significance. Both Maurin and Zumthor point to the worldview of these poets, essential for understanding their work.

Paul B. Burrell

[See also: BURGUNDIAN CHRONICLERS; CHASTELLAIN, GEORGES; GRANDS RHÉTORIQUEURS; HISTORIOGRAPHY; *JARDIN DE PLAISANCE ET FLEUR DE RÉTHORIQUE*; OCKEGHEM, JOHANNES; *ROSE, ROMAN DE LA*; VERSIFICATION]

Molinet, Jean. *Chroniques*, ed. Georges Doutrepont and Omer Jodogne. 3 vols. Brussels: Palais des Académies, 1935–37.
———. *Faictz et dictz*, ed. Noël Dupire. 3 vols. Paris: Didot, 1936–39.
———. *Plusieurs ditz de la manière d'aucunes femmes*, ed. M. de Grève. Brussels: Palais des Académies, 1961.
Dupire, Noël, *Jean Molinet: la vie—les œuvres*. 2 vols. Geneva: Droz, 1932.
Jodogne, Omer. "Les 'Rhétoriqueurs' et l'humanisme: problème d'histoire littéraire." In *Humanism in France*, ed. A.H.T. Levi. Manchester: Manchester University Press, 1970.
Sautman, Francesca. "'Des vessies pour les lanternes': Villon, Molinet, and the Riddles of Folklore." *Neophilologus* 69 (1985): 161–84.

MONASTIC RULES AND CUSTOMARIES. The first monks lived either as solitaries or under the direct supervision of an *abba* ('father'). This seems to have been the case with the first known European monastic house, Marmoutier, established in 361 by Martin of Tours. As monasticism developed into a permanent institution, the charisma of a spiritual master was supplemented by written legislation regulating the common life in the monastery. As de Vogüé has shown, the earliest sources of such monastic guidelines (Pachomius, Basil, Augustine), all written ca. 400, exercised a decisive influence on the subsequent tradition. Quotations from them appear in later monastic rules, which also borrow among themselves to a striking degree. This reflects the eclectic nature of monastic establishments until the triumph of the *Rule of St. Benedict* in the 9th century.

About 300 monastic rules were written between the end of the 4th century and last half of the 7th. The majority provide no more than the barest suggestions for the regulation of life within the monastery. They vary considerably in length and detail, from the succinct *De ordine monasterii* (by Augustine, or from his circle) to the enormous *Rule of the Master*, whose ninety-five chapters legislate on every conceivable aspect of monastic discipline. (Benedict's *Rule* is little more than one-third the length of the Master's.) The *Rule for Virgins* (ca. 534) by Caesarius of Arles is the first rule written for female religious. Its prescriptions for the Divine Office are thought to reflect the lost tradition of Lérins, an island monastery off the coast of Provence near Cannes, founded ca. 410 by Honoratus.

The origin of the monastic customaries coincides with the activity of Carolingian reformers, led by Benedict of Aniane (d. 821), to impose the *Rule of St. Benedict* everywhere in the Frankish empire. The customaries make specific, detailed applications of the *Rule* to the circumstances present in a single monastery or a group of monasteries. They not only interpret and supplement the directives of the *Rule* but can actually alter Benedict's careful equilibrium, as happened with the large quantity of liturgical obligations required by the customs in force at Cluny. A common customary imposed the influence of the great monasteries like Cluny, Saint-Benoît-sur-Loire, and Cîteaux on daughter houses. The monastic customaries can profitably be studied as a source of information on contemporary social and cultural life.

Joseph H. Dyer

[See also: *BENEDICT, RULE OF ST.*; BENEDICT OF ANIANE; CISTERCIAN ORDER; CLUNY; LÉRINS; MONASTICISM]

Desprez, Vincent, ed. *Règles monastiques d'Occident (IVe–VIe siècle): d'Augustin à Ferréol*. Begrolles-en-Mauges: Abbaye de Bellefontaine, 1980.
Franklin, Carmela, et al., eds. *Early Monastic Rules: The Rules of the Fathers and the Regula Orientalis*. Collegeville: Liturgical, 1982.
Hallinger, Kassius, et al., eds. *Corpus consuetudinum monasticarum*. 12 vols. to date. Siegeburg: Schmitt, 1963–.
de Vogüé, Adalbert. "The Cenobitic Rules of the West." *Cistercian Studies* 12 (1977): 175–83.
———. *Les règles monastiques anciennes (400–700)*. Turnhout: Brepols, 1985.
Hallinger, Kassius. "Consuetudo, Begriff, Formen, Forschungsgeschichte." *Untersuchungen zu Kloster und Stift. Max-Planck-Institut für Geschichte, Veröffentlichungen* 68 (1980): 140–66.

MONASTICISM. From its origins in the Egyptian desert in the second half of the 3rd century, monasticism quickly spread throughout the Roman Empire. By the 4th century, the *Lives of the Desert Fathers* were being read in the West, and monasticism soon became established there. The semilegendary figure of Martin, Roman soldier, bishop of Tours, and founder of Marmoutier, the first known monastic house in Gaul at the end of the 4th century, was influential in the spread of Frankish monasticism. Although early Egyptian monasticism had emphasized the eremitic life, hermits were rare in Gaul, where monasticism was normally of the cenobitic sort, in which a group of brothers lived together under the direction of an abbot.

Monasticism from the beginning emphasized separation of the individual from secular society, putting him into a setting where prayer and contemplation of God would be his chief concerns. Humility and obedience to the abbot, who himself was expected to be humbly obedient to God, responsible for the souls of the monks entrusted to him, was stressed in all monastic rules. Monks were expected to live in common, with no individual property. They deliberately gave up normal secular pleasures, from sex to red meat to fine clothing, in order to concentrate on the world beyond.

The Merovingian period saw a great variety of monastic practices. Martin's foundation of Marmoutier continued to influence many new houses. The 5th-century foundation of Lérins, in Provence, followed a rule that went back to Cassian. Luxeuil, founded at the end of the 6th century by Irish monks—who had themselves been influenced by monks from Tours fifty years earlier—was another house whose customs, called the *Rule of Columbanus*, were widely imitated. Also influential was Saint-Maurice of Agaune, in the Burgundian Alps. The *Rule of St. Benedict*, written for the monks of Monte Cassino in Italy in the first half of the 6th century, became widely adopted in Gaul. The Life of St. Benedict, written by Pope Gregory I (r. 590–604), did much to popularize this *Rule*. Throughout the 7th and 8th centuries, Benedict's *Rule* was adopted at an increasing number of French houses, replacing the other rules in circulation, including the so-called "mixed" rules, which took elements from several. The combination of strictness with flexibility in Benedict's *Rule* made it both appealing for those looking for a holy way of life and adaptable to a variety of situations. The Benedictines, or Black Monks (so called from the color of their habits), became by far the most common form of the institutionalized religious life in this period.

The Merovingian period witnessed the foundation of a large number of monasteries, the majority, indeed, of all French houses founded before the 11th century. Kings, lords, and bishops all established communities of monks that would receive gifts of property from other wealthy individuals. Most of the monks were settled in existing churches at the edges of the old Roman provincial capitals. The churches, and hence the communities of monks, were most commonly dedicated to a local saint, often one martyred when trying to spread Christianity to a pagan population under the late empire, such as Saint-Marcel of Chalon or Saint-Valérien of Tournus. Other basilicas had been rededicated to a local bishop buried there, such as Saint-Germain of Auxerre or Saint-Remi of Reims, by the time monks were settled there. Still other Merovingian monasteries were founded in what had once been a hermitage, such as Moûtier-Saint-Jean in the diocese of Langres, and were dedicated to the first holy hermit who had lived there. Houses for monks greatly outnumbered those for nuns.

Many of these Merovingian foundations remained small, and some seem to have sheltered monks only intermittently. By the 8th century, however, virtually every French episcopal city had one major monastery, which was in constant if low-level competition with the bishop throughout the rest of the Middle Ages. Such a monastery was usually located just outside the city walls, though sometimes it was slightly farther away. The competition between bishops and monks—expressed in everything from quarrels over monastic immunities to attempts to build more elaborate edifices than the cathedral church—was especially marked if, as at Tours, Auxerre, or Reims, the monastery could claim the influence, or even the body, of an early sainted bishop whom the bishops themselves treated as a font of their spiritual authority.

Founded in large numbers in France in the 6th and 7th centuries, monasteries experienced serious setbacks in the 8th century. Muslim attacks devastated many monasteries, especially in the south but as far north as Burgundy. Both laypeople and bishops seized monastic property as their own; a number of monasteries had received enough generous gifts over the years that a layman was tempted to take the office of abbot and the revenues. Many of the smaller urban and suburban monasteries founded in the Merovingian period remained empty of religious men from the 8th century to the 12th.

Starting in the final years of the 8th century, however, a number of ruined or deserted monasteries were refounded or reformed, usually at the initiative of kings or bishops. The scholar Alcuin, at Charlemagne's court, advocated monastic renewal, and the monk Benedict of Aniane promoted adoption of the *Rule of St. Benedict*. This *Rule*, which had been slowly spreading through France for three centuries, was ordered adopted at all Frankish houses at the Council of Chalon in 813. Louis the Pious even hoped that the monastery of Inde, near Aix-la-Chapelle, would become a royal "model" monastery, which monks from every monastery in the Frankish kingdom would visit, to promote regularity and uniformity. Although his plan was ultimately unsuccessful, the commentary on Benedict's *Rule* composed for Inde by Benedict of Aniane was widely imitated. A house's *consuetudines* would spell out additions and modifications to St. Benedict's slim set of regulations.

Between the 5th and the 9th centuries, French monasticism underwent key changes, from being a form of religious life established in tiny houses at the margins of a predominantly urban society, to being the carriers and continuators of Roman culture in large, agriculturally oriented communities. Benedict's *Rule* had assumed that a monastery would be a family, of maybe a dozen or a score of monks, but by the 9th century it was not uncommon for a monastery to have a hundred or more monks and many servants, and the abbey church to be surrounded by a whole complex of workshops, guest houses, an infirmary, administrative offices, rooms for laborers, and the like. Such a monastery might become one of the largest landowners in its region. Although houses that had adopted Benedict's *Rule* continued to follow its chief outlines, in stressing humility, obedience, and common property, such French houses were no longer the small, withdrawn group of brothers that Benedict had envisioned but rather important economic entities in their own right.

NOTABLE MONASTIC LOCATIONS

□ Benedictine

△ Associated with Cluny

• Cistercian

○ Other religious orders

■ Female religious houses

BRUGES

NIVELLES

ST. OMER   GEMBLOUX

ST. AMAND

TOURNAI

LOBBES

ST. RIQUIER

CORBIE

FÉCAMP   OURSCAMP   PRÉMONTRÉ

ROUEN   ST. WANDRILLE   LAON

ROYAUMONT   SOISSONS

JUMÍEGES   ARGENTEUIL   LONGPONT   REIMS

BAYEAUX   METZ

BEC   CHAALIS   VERDUN

CAEN   IGNY   GORZE

LISIEUX   BERNAY   MEAUX

MANTES   ST.-DENIS   NEUWILLER

MONT-SAINT-MICHEL   DREUX   PARIS

Seine

SAVIGNY   CHARTRES   CLAIRVAUX

BRITTANY   TROYES

SENS   MORIMOND

VENDOME   SAINT-BENOIT-   PONTIGNY   MOLESME   LUXEUIL

SUR-LOIRE   FONTENAY

ANGERS   AUXERRE   FLAVIGNY   LA CHARITÉ

MARMOUTIER   CHARITÉ-SUR-LOIRE   VEZELAY   DIJON

Loire   CUNAULT   TOURS   BURGUNDY

FONTEVRAULT   BOURGES   NEVERS   CITEAUX

BEAUNE   ROMAINMOTIER

AUTUN

LOCHES   TOURNUS

POITIERS   NOIRLAC   CLUNY

SOUVIGNY

AQUITAINE   PARAY-LE-MONIAL

MARCIGNY

CHARLIEU

SAINTES   LIMOGES   RIOM   LYON

SOLIGNAC   CHASE-DIEU   LA GRANDE

SAUXILLANGES   VIENNE   CHARTREUSE

Garonne   Dordogne   LE PUY

Rhône   PROVENCE

AGEN   SÉNANQUE

MOISSAC   ARLES   LE THORONET

MONTPELLIER   SILVACANE

LERINS

TOULOUSE   MARSEILLES

Rhine

In the second half of the 9th century, there again began to be new monastic foundations in France, for the first time in some 150 years. Many of these were founded not on the outskirts of the old Gallo-Roman cities but in the countryside, although they quickly became miniature civic centers in their own right, as small boroughs grew up around them. The monks provided a living, whether by paying wages or buying goods, to a whole group of laypeople established near their gates. Cluny, founded in 909 by the duke of Aquitaine, is the best known of these late Carolingian foundations.

By the 9th and 10th centuries, although the fundamental monastic goals of humility, obedience, common property, and separation from ordinary life remained, monks had taken on a new and central role for broader society. Monastic schools were and continued to be, until the 12th century, the chief places to receive an education, in spite of the establishment of cathedral schools under Charlemagne. Increasingly, the manual work that Benedict had recommended to his monks had been replaced by work copying manuscripts in the scriptorium or by additional prayers and Masses. Monasteries became intermediaries between the secular world and the supernatural. Monks prayed within the cloister for the world outside the cloister walls. When laypeople gave the monastery gifts, which they did with increasing frequency, they specified that they wanted to win the friendship of the saint to whom the house was dedicated. This friendship was often made concrete in prayers and Masses that the monks performed or in lists of lay friends in a book of commemoration. Laypeople were frequently buried at the monastery, near both the saint and the monks. At Cluny, prayers for the dead took a major proportion of the monks' day, and manual labor essentially disappeared.

Although the monastic reaction to the secular world, whether in the time of the Egyptian desert fathers or in the Carolingian period, had always been withdrawal, this reaction meant that monks as a group had much better relations with the world's lords than did members of the secular clergy. Bishops and priests, who saw their duty as conversion of the world rather than withdrawal from it, tended to see the princes who ruled this world as at least potential rivals, whereas the monks sought their friendship and hoped that they would be helpful in areas in which the monks themselves did not care to participate.

If the 9th and early 10th centuries were a period in which the large, wealthy monastery became an established part of society—wealthy overall, even though the monks were individually poor—it was also a period in which the monasteries continued to face threats to their integrity. The Viking incursions in the west of France, the Magyar invasions in the east, and the continuing raids of Muslim pirates in the south ruined a number of monasteries and sent their monks fleeing. Burgundy, where Cluny was located, experienced attacks from all three of these "barbarian" groups. Powerful laypeople and even bishops were still tempted with some frequency to take over the direction and the revenues of a monastery.

In response, the monasteries tried to band together. Benedict of Aniane had been abbot of most of the existing monasteries of Aquitaine at the beginning of the 9th century, and such associations were revived in the late 9th and 10th centuries as a form of protection. Affiliations of prayers were formed among monasteries within a region. A house that had been ruined or lost the regularity of its life might have the abbot of another house become its abbot as well, until the monastic life was fully reestablished. In some cases, two houses might be permanently affiliated under the same abbot, although this practice was less common.

Toward the end of the 10th century, such affiliations became the most common way for a ruined or dissolute monastery to be reformed. A layman or bishop who controlled such a monastery would ask the abbot of a house of undoubted holiness of life to send him a group of monks to reestablish the regular life, sometimes under their own abbot, who would bring with him the *consuetudines* and liturgical practices of the house where he had been trained, or sometimes under the continuing direction of the reforming house. In different parts of France, different monasteries took the lead in this reform movement. In Burgundy, Cluny, which in its initial three generations had

reformed houses primarily in southwest France and in Italy, now became the chief source and model for reform. Gorze played a similar role in Lorraine, as did Montmajour in Provence, Marmoutier in western France, and Brogne in Flanders.

From the 8th through the 11th century in France, Benedictine monasticism was the most visible form of the religious life. It was virtually the definition of a holy and devout way of living, even though most houses followed the *Rule* slightly differently during these "Benedictine centuries." During the 11th century, however, French Benedictine monasticism began to receive its first competition in several centuries. These new forms of institutionalized religion gradually spread north from Italy. Hermits appeared in French forests for the first time since the Merovingian period. Secular canons, small groups of priests who had collectively served some urban churches or castle chapels, began to be replaced by regular canons during the 1050s and 1060s. These regular canons, often called Augustinian canons because their rule was based on a letter originally sent by St. Augustine to his sister, combined the collective life and property of monasticism with the dedication to improving the Christian life in the broader world of parish priests and secular canons.

These new forms of the religious life continued to develop and spread throughout the 11th and 12th centuries; most small urban and suburban monasteries, many of which had had no monks for several centuries, were taken over by regular canons, and in absolute numbers they probably outweighed the Benedictines by the end of the 12th century. But monasticism also continued to flourish. Houses like Cluny were still prosperous and followed their rules and customs as closely as they always had. Some houses, like Chaise-Dieu, founded in the middle of the 11th century on eremitical principles, ended up adopting the Benedictine *Rule*. But for some people, both would-be religious and laypeople who wanted to support the religious life, the Black Monks no longer represented the fullest expression of spirituality. These people turned instead both to such groups as the hermits and regular canons and to the new forms of monasticism.

French monasticism in the 11th and 12th centuries included both Benedictine monks and, for the first time since the early 9th century, monks who followed a rule not based on Benedict's. Among the new foundations where Benedictine monasticism was practiced were Tiron, founded in 1109, and Savigny, founded in 1112; both were in the west of France. But the most influential of the new monastic orders of the high Middle Ages was the Cistercian order, founded in a conscious effort to return to a more literal observance of the *Rule of St. Benedict*. The Cistercians originated at Molesme, itself a house founded in 1075 by monks seeking a rigorous form of monasticism. When Robert, the abbot and founder, decided that even Molesme was not rigorous enough, he and some of the brothers instead moved to the New Monastery of Cîteaux. From the time of Cîteaux's foundation in 1098, the monks deliberately set out to restore Benedict's simplicity in food and clothing and his inclusion of manual labor. While the Cistercians, or White Monks, rejected many of the additions that had been made to the *Rule*, such as the *consuetudines* of Cluny or of Benedict of Aniane, especially the liturgical elaboration, they also made modifications of their own. Cistercian customs forbade the reception of children (oblates) and made provision for *conversi*, adult converts, mostly from lower social classes, without the Latin education to be able to become full choir monks. These *conversi* ended up doing a major part of the monks' agricultural labor.

Additionally, the Cistercians created for the first time a truly permanent, institutionalized form of affiliation among monasteries, in which all new Cistercian foundations—and indeed any older houses affiliated with the order (as was Savigny in 1147)—became the daughter house of an already existing Cistercian monastery. The abbots of the daughter house and of the mother house were supposed to visit each other every year, and the abbots of the entire order met in an annual chapter general at Cîteaux, where regulations were passed in the interests of maintaining unity among the houses.

The Cistercians proved enormously popular. Converts flocked to the order, and knights and nobles made gifts, especially those lords lower on the social scale than those who had supported the Benedictines. From five houses in Burgundy in 1115, the Cistercians by the middle of the 12th century rapidly spread to include hundreds of houses across Europe. The monks' agricultural organization via the grange system, which produced compact estates; their reliance on *conversi* rather than tenant or hired labor; the holiness and simplicity of their life, which attracted large numbers of gifts; and their willingness to lend money against principal all made the Cistercians an extremely wealthy order. The monks' use of *conversi* was copied by other monastic orders, and their annual visitation and chapter general were ordered established for all monks by the Fourth Lateran Council of 1215.

As the Cistercians were becoming established, other new forms of monasticism, not based on the Benedictine *Rule*, were arising in France. The most successful was the Carthusian order, established in the 1080s by St. Bruno on a combination of eremitic and cenobitic elements: each monk had his own cell, but the cells were grouped in a single community. Other new orders of non-Benedictine monks included Grandmont, founded on the principle of extreme poverty ca. 1100, and Fontevrault, founded at the same time by Robert d'Arbrissel, with the purpose of combining apostolic preaching, monks, and nuns in one house.

In the 13th century, monasticism, hitherto the preeminent form of the religious life, began to receive its first serious challenge, in the form of the friars. The Dominican and the Franciscan orders, both of which appealed especially to the culture of the newly developing cities, soon outcompeted the monks. Although the monastic houses founded before the end of the 12th century continued for the most part to flourish, there were far fewer monastic foundations in the 13th century than in the 12th. Only houses of nuns, rare throughout the early and high Middle Ages, multiplied during the late Middle Ages. In this static period, many of the intellectuals who might once have become monks went instead to the universities, and powerful members of secular society almost never sent their sons into the cloister.

In the 14th and 15th centuries, French monasticism went into a slow decline. The austerity that had been the goal throughout the Middle Ages was given up at more and more houses; as one example, meat, earlier reserved for the ill, was eaten several times a week. Communal property was increasingly replaced by the practice of allowing monks and nuns to have a certain amount of money of their own, for their own purchases and expenses. The close, fatherly relationship between an abbot and his monks became much more distant, as the abbot usually left the monastery for a nearby establishment of his own. Increasingly, abbots were not even elected by the monks but were appointed by the popes; bishops and cardinals, even secular magnates, might become titular abbots. By the time of the Reformation, many monasteries housed only a handful of monks.

Constance B. Bouchard

[See also: *BENEDICT, RULE OF ST.*; BENEDICT OF ANIANE; CARTHUSIAN ORDER; CASSIAN, JOHN; CISTERCIAN ORDER; CLUNIAC ORDER; DOMINICAN ORDER; FRANCISCAN ORDER; LÉRINS; MARTIN OF TOURS; MONASTIC RULES AND CUSTOMARIES; NUNNERIES; REGULAR CANONS; ROBERT D'ARBRISSEL; ROBERT OF MOLESME; SCHOOLS, MONASTIC; WOMEN, RELIGIOUS EXPERIENCE OF]

Bouchard, Constance B. "Merovingian, Carolingian, and Cluniac Monasticism: Reform and Renewal in Gaul." *Journal of Ecclesiastical History* 41 (1990): 365–88.

———. *Holy Entrepreneurs: Cistercians, Knights, and Economic Exchange in Twelfth-Century Burgundy*. Ithaca: Cornell University Press, 1991.

———. *Sword, Miter, and Cloister: Nobility and the Church in Burgundy, 980–1198*. Ithaca: Cornell University Press, 1987.

Constable, Giles. "Cluny—Cîteaux—La Chartreuse: San Bernardo e la diversita delle forme di vita religiosa nel XII secolo." In *Studi su S. Bernardo di Chiaravalle nell'ottavo centenario della canonizzazione*. Rome: Editiones Cistercienses, 1975, pp. 93–114.

———. *Medieval Monasticism: A Select Bibliography*. Toronto: University of Toronto Press, 1976.

Knowles, David. *Christian Monasticism*. New York: World University Library, 1969.

———. *The Monastic Order in England*. 2nd ed. Cambridge: Cambridge University Press, 1963.

Lackner, Bede K. *The Eleventh-Century Background of Cîteaux*. Washington, D.C.: Cistercian, 1972.

Lekai, Louis J. *The Cistercians: Ideals and Reality*. Kent: Kent State University Press, 1977.

Little, Lester K. *Religious Poverty and the Profit Economy in Medieval Europe*. Ithaca: Cornell University Press, 1978.

Lourdaux, W., and Daniel Verhelst, eds. *Benedictine Culture, 750–1050*. Louvain: Bibliothèque de l'Université, 1983.

Prinz, Friedrich. *Frühes Mönchtum im Frankenreich*. Munich: Oldenbourg, 1965.

Rosenwein, Barbara H. *Rhinoceros Bound: Cluny in the 10th Century*. Philadelphia: University of Pennsylvania Press, 1982.

————. *To Be the Neighbor of Saint Peter: The Social Meaning of Cluny's Property, 909–1049.* Ithaca: Cornell University Press, 1989.

Southern, Richard W. *Western Society and the Church in the Middle Ages.* Harmondsworth: Penguin, 1970.

Wallace-Hadrill, J.M. *The Frankish Church.* Oxford: Clarendon, 1983.

MONIAGE GUILLAUME. A late 12th-century chanson de geste, extant in two redactions, of which the incomplete shorter version (*Moniage I*; 934 assonanced decasyllables) postdates the longer (*Moniage II*; 6,629 assonanced decasyllables). The poem recounts Guillaume d'Orange's edifying final days, in which he renounces the world after the death of his wife, Guibourc, in order to expiate the sins committed during his knightly career. The text's origin is controversial: there perhaps was a lost original, and the Sinagon episode appears clearly to have come from a different poem; local legends (e.g., Ysoré's tomb in Paris) have also been suggested. But the real source of the *Moniage* is to be found among historical memories of Count Guillaume of Toulouse's retirement to the monastery of Gellone in the year 806. The shorter version is preserved in two manuscripts, both incomplete; the longer version is found in seven manuscripts, of which two are complete.

The *Moniage* demonstrates that, between the chivalric values of the epic hero and the hypocritical practices of the monastic community, Guillaume's status as hermit allows him, without renouncing his glorious past, to strive for perfection. The poem makes the hero a holy personage, sanctioned by miracles but still physically powerful. He can face his enemies in the monastery itself or take up arms to defend the kingdom, as he does in the combat against the giant Ysoré.

If the *Moniage* satirizes monastic life, it also cultivates the ideal relationship, asserted by Thomas Cabham, between *gesta principum* (the deeds of princes) and *vitae sanctorum* (the lives of saints), between epic and hagiography.

François Suard

[See also: GUILLAUME D'ORANGE CYCLE]

Cloëtta, Wilhelm, ed. *Les deux rédactions en vers du "Moniage Guillaume."* 2 vols. Paris: SATF, 1906–11.

Frappier, Jean. *Les chansons de geste du cycle de Guillaume d'Orange.* 3 vols. Paris: SEDES, 1983, Vol. 3, pp. 19–259.

MONTAIGU. Jean, lord of Montaigu-en-Laye and vidame of Laonnais, then "over fifty" years old, was executed at Paris in October 1409. He had risen to a position of great influence through service to the crown. His family, originally from Montaigu-en-Laonnais, first became prominent with his father, Gérard de Montaigu (d. 1391), a royal notary who was ennobled in 1363, served as a royal secretary and keeper of the archives (Trésor des Chartes) for many years, became a *maître des comptes* in 1390, and was a knight and royal councillor when he died.

The family was connected to two important prelates who owed their positions to royal service, Ferry Cassinel, archbishop of Reims, whose sister married Gérard, and Jean de la Grange, cardinal of Amiens, whose niece married Jean. Jean entered royal service as a secretary of Charles VI in the 1380s. Like Cassinel and La Grange, he was associated with the Marmousets and was dismissed from court when the royal uncles ousted them from power in 1392. By May 1393, however, he had resumed his post, and in 1396 he became a councillor of the king, commissioned to oversee the receipt of funds destined for the household expenditures of the king, queen, dauphin, and the duke and duchess of Orléans. In 1398, he was knighted and became a royal chamberlain and *maître d'hôtel* of the queen. He became captain of the Bastille in 1399 and from 1402 until his death was sovereign master of the king's household. Jean and his wife founded a Celestine convent near Marcoussis castle, which Cassinel had given him in 1388. His political influence and ostentatious wealth finally angered John the Fearless, duke of Burgundy, who engineered his destruction.

His brother, a younger Gérard (d. 1420), succeeded his father as custodian of the Trésor des Chartes and became a royal councillor and *maître des comptes*. Bishop of Poitiers by 1404, Gérard moved to the see of Paris in 1409. He served for about five years as the duke of Berry's chancellor (until 1409) and also received a pension from Louis of Orléans. In November 1413, he became president of the Chambre des Comptes.

A third brother, Jean, was evidently named after his brother, a custom sometimes observed in medieval France. He was elected bishop of Chartres in 1390, transferred to the archbishopric of Sens in 1406, and served as a royal councillor and ambassador. In disgrace after the execution of the elder Jean, he became a supporter of the Orléanist faction. In 1413, after the flight of the Burgundians from Paris, he was president of the Chambre des Comptes for a short time. By 1415, he was a councillor of the king and the duke of Guyenne. He was killed at Agincourt in October of that year.

Richard C. Famiglietti

[See also: GRAND MASTER; MARMOUSETS]

Teulet, Alexandre, et al, eds. *Layettes du trésor des chartes.* 5 vols. Paris: Archives Nationales, 1863–1909, Vol. 5, ed. Henri-François Delaborde, 1900.

Famiglietti, Richard C. *Tales of the Marriage Bed from Medieval France (1300–1500).* Providence: Picardy, 1992.

Malte-Brun, Victor Adolphe. *Histoire de Marcoussis, de ses seigneurs et de son monastère.* Paris: Aubry, 1867.

Merlet, Lucien. "Biographie de Jean de Montagu, grand maître de France." *Bibliothèque de l'École des Chartes* 13 (1852): 248–84.

MONTAUDON, MONK OF (fl. 1194–1210). After becoming a monk at Vic near Aurillac (Cantal), then prior of an abbey perhaps located at the place called Montaudou near Clermont-Ferrand, the Monk of Montaudon left the cloister to become a troubadour. In addition to a number of more conventional *cansos*, or love songs, we have among the poems he wrote from 1194 to 1210 a series of witty debates with God; a satirical gallery of troubadours in the tradition established by Peire d'Alvernhe; four *enuegz*, or lists of annoyances, and one *plazer*, or list of pleasures. The genres of the *enueg* and *plazer* were inspired by Bertran de Born but took their definitive form in the hands of the Monk and were later imitated by poets who wrote in Italian, French, Portuguese, Catalan, and English, including Shakespeare (Sonnet 66).

William D. Paden

[See also: TROUBADOUR POETRY]

Montaudon, Monk of. *Les poésies du Moine de Montaudon*, ed. Michael J. Routledge. Montpellier: Centre d'Études Occitanes, 1977.

Riquer, Martín de, ed. *Los trovadores: historia literaria y textos*. 3 vols. Barcelona: Planeta, 1975, Vol. 2, pp. 1024–45.

Routledge, Michael J. "The Monk Who Knew the Ways of Love." *Reading Medieval Studies* 12 (1986): 3–25.

MONTEREAU. The castle of Montereau-faut-Yonne (Seine-et-Marne), at the confluence of the Seine and Yonne rivers about 49 miles southeast of Paris, was a site of a settlement that already existed when the Romans invaded. Eudes II of Blois built a wooden donjon there ca. 1015–20. A stone castle, completed by 1228, replaced this construction and was held in fief from the archbishopric of Sens by the counts of Champagne. Through the marriage of their heiress to Philip IV of France, Montereau passed into the royal family. The castle covered the surfaces of two small islands at the center of the confluence and was joined to the three adjacent river banks by long wooden bridges.

Montereau is best known as the site of the assassination of John the Fearless, duke of Burgundy, on September 10, 1419. The dauphin, later Charles VII, had invited John to come and discuss a final agreement to end the French civil war. They met on the bridge connecting the castle to the town. According to a prearranged plan, John was assassinated while he knelt at the dauphin's feet as the conference began. The fact that part of the bridge was a drawbridge that could be raised from the town's side prevented immediate retaliation by Burgundian men-at-arms garrisoned in the castle. The duke's assassination is of paramount historical importance, for it drove a greater wedge between the dauphin and the royal government and ultimately left the kingdom without the support needed to defeat Henry V of England.

Richard C. Famiglietti

[See also: ARMAGNACS; CHARLES VII; JOHN THE FEARLESS]

Châtelain, André. *Châteaux forts et féodalité en Île de France du XIe au XIIIe siècle*. Nonette: Créer, 1983, pp. 124, 414.

Quesvers, P. "Le château de Montereau-fault-Yonne." *Revue de Champagne et Brie* 3 (1877): 1–14.

Vaughan, Richard. *John the Fearless: The Growth of Burgundy.* New York: Barnes and Noble, 1966. [See plate 8.]

MONTFORT. The lords of Montfort-l'Amaury (Seine-et-Oise) near Mantes were descended from a 10th-century count of Hainaut. Of no more than local importance before the 13th century, the family became prominent internationally when Simon IV (ca. 1150–1218), who first held the title of count, became a leader of the Albigensian Crusade. After defeating the count of Foix near Castelnaudary in 1212, Simon crushed the king of Aragon and a coalition of southern lords at Muret in September 1213 and for a time secured the county of Toulouse. Then the tide turned against him and he was killed before Toulouse in 1218. His younger son, Simon (1206–1265), married Eleanor, a sister of Henry III of England, became earl of Leicester, and died in battle after leading a major baronial revolt in England. The older son, Amaury VI (1192–1241), failed to regain his father's position in Languedoc but served as constable of France the last eleven years of his life. Amaury's great-granddaughter Yolande married Arthur II, duke of Brittany, in 1294. The county of Montfort passed to a cadet line of the Breton ducal house that won control of Brittany in 1364.

John Bell Henneman, Jr.

[See also: ALBIGENSIAN CRUSADE; AURAY; BRITTANY; JEAN IV; MURET]

MONTIER-EN-DER. Site of a Benedictine abbey (*montier*) founded by St. Berchaire in 672 on the banks of the Voire, Montier (Haute-Marne) is the capital of the area of Champagne called Der, from the Celtic word for the oak trees that dominated this plain before the monks harvested them in the Middle Ages. The abbey church and most of the town were destroyed in World War II but have been admirably restored. The oldest portions of the original church dated to the 990s. The sober Romanesque nave consists of eight semicircular bays resting on low rectangular pillars. The Gothic chevet (ca. 1220), which has four levels, is a marvel of Champenois design: large arcades on twin columns, surmounted by a tribune with paired arches separated by a colonnette and oculus, in turn surmounted by a triforium with triple trilobed arcatures, and finally a row of clerestory windows separated by colonnettes.

William W. Kibler/William W. Clark

Arnoult, René. "L'église abbatiale de Montier-en-Der." *Congrès archéologique* (Troyes) 113 (1955): 262–76.

Aubert, Marcel. "À propos du chœur de Montier-en-Der." *Congrès archéologique* (Troyes) 113 (1955): 277–81.

Koppe, Bernhard. *Die frühromanische Emporenbasilika in Montier-en-Der*. Saarbrücken: Saarbrücker Druckerei und Verlag, 1990.

MONTLHÉRY. The fortress of Montlhéry (Seine-et-Oise), just south of Paris, was built in the early 11th century and became a serious threat to the authority of the early Capetian monarchy. Philip I, who said that it "has made me old before my time," arranged for his younger son to marry the daughter of the lord of Montlhéry in 1104, and Louis VI acquired the tower a few years later. When his castellan was murdered by a rival lord, Louis had to regain Montlhéry by force in 1118.

Centuries later, on July 16, 1465, Louis XI fought a battle near Montlhéry against the rebellious magnates known as the *Ligue du Bien Publique*. He overcame his adversaries but missed the chance for a decisive victory and retired to Paris, leaving the magnates in a position to secure a favorable negotiated settlement.

Nothing remains of the infamous 11th-century château, although the site is occupied by ruins of later constructions: fortification walls that date from the reign of Philip II Augustus (1180–1223) and a donjon of the 14th century.

John Bell Henneman, Jr.

Châtelain, André. *Châteaux forts et féodalité en Île de France du XIe au XIIIe siècle.* Nonette: Créer, 1983, pp. 305–10.

Mesqui, Jean. *Île-de-France gothique.* 2 vols. Paris: Picard, 1987–88, Vol. 2, pp. 248–55.

MONTMAJOUR. The former Benedictine abbey of Montmajour (Bouches-du-Rhône) originally consisted of two churches, Saint-Pierre and Notre-Dame. Built at the end of the 10th century, only Saint-Pierre exists in its original form. Notre-Dame was reconstructed in the late 12th century, at which time the cloister, conventual buildings, and a chapel dedicated to the Holy Cross were also constructed. The abbey began to decay as early as the 14th century.

A rock-hewn edifice, Saint-Pierre offers an example of a primitive monastery. One of its most unusual features is a wooden cornice that trims the flat-stoned roof. A rectangular vestibule features barrel vaulting. Although structurally awkward, the nave is not devoid of harmony and el-

Montmajour (Bouches-du-Rhône), abbey. *Photograph courtesy of Whitney S. Stoddard.*

egance. It consists of three Romanesque bays, covered by a vault of different types of stone, that give way to a triumphal arch of the choir and an apse in cul-de-four. Twelve columns support foliated and interlaced capitals. Adorned with an interlaced pilaster, the corridor between the two chapels provides access to a cave in which, according to tradition, the first monks dwelled. In a recessed vault is a stone chair called the "Confessional of St. Trophimus," (d. ca. 280), where the saint is said to have hidden during Roman persecution.

Because of the slope of the hillside, Notre-Dame has an upper church and a lower church on separate levels. With a polygonal-shaped exterior, Notre-Dame was rebuilt at the end of the 12th century, replacing an 11th-century structure. The crypt is composed of a vast transept with apsidioles and an apse surrounded by an ambulatory with radiating chapels. The apse has a rectangular bay with barrel vaulting. Quadrilobed in plan, the chapel of Sainte-Croix features a narthex, a high cupola, and vaulting in cul-de-four. One door carries an inscription that falsely attributes the construction of the chapel to Charlemagne.

E. Kay Harris

Benoît, Fernand. *L'abbaye de Montmajour.* Paris: Laurens, 1928.

Berenguier, R. *Abbayes de Provence.* Paris: Caisse Nationale des Monuments Historiques, 1960.

Labande, L.H. "Abbaye de Montmajour." *Congrès archéologique* (Avignon) 76 (1909): 154–67.

Villard, André. *Art de Provence.* Paris: Arthaud, 1957.

MONTMORENCY. The castellany of Montmorency, northwest of Paris, became the seat of one of France's most influential noble dynasties. The family had originated around Sens, where two of its members held the archbishopric, but after their ouster from this region in the 10th century Bouchard I le Barbu established himself near Paris on the Île-Saint-Denis. From there, he threatened the holdings of the abbey of Saint-Denis until King Robert II (r. 996–1031) intervened and installed him at the *castrum* of Montmorency some distance away.

From this base, the family grew steadily in importance. Bouchard's son Aubry (Alberic) and his grandson Thibaut were constables of France, and another grandson, Hervé, became butler of France. Mathieu I (d. 1160) and Mathieu II (d. 1230) also both served as constable. The second wife of Mathieu II was Emma, heiress to the lordship of Laval in the county of Maine. A son of this marriage succeeded to Laval as Gui VII (d. 1267); Montmorency went to the older son, Bouchard V (d. 1243), who served Louis IX at the Battle of Taillebourg (1242). The Laval branch of the family became politically important in Brittany as well as Maine after Gui VII married the heiress of Vitré.

The senior line of the family continued to produce men who held high positions in the royal government and women who married into the great lineages of Normandy and the Île-de-France. Mathieu IV (d. 1304) was admiral and grand chamberlain. Jean I (d. 1325) served French kings in wars in Flanders. Among his children were Charles de Montmorency, marshal of France, and Jean, bishop of

Orléans. In virtually every generation after 1300, the head of the family was a royal councillor and chamberlain. At length, in the mid-16th century, Montmorency became a duchy and peerage.

John Bell Henneman, Jr.

[See also: LAVAL]

Bedoz, Brigitte. *La châtellenie de Montmorency des origines à 1368: aspects féodaux, sociaux, et économiques.* Pontoise: Société Historique et Archéologique de Pontoise, du Val d'Oise, et du Vexin, 1980.

MONTMORILLON. Montmorillon (Vienne) is located on the Gartempe River in Poitou. La Hire (ca. 1390–1443), companion-in-arms to Jeanne d'Arc, received the seigneurie of Montmorillon from Charles VII on January 7, 1438, and was originally buried here.

In 1093, the bishop of Poitiers gave the chapel of Notre-Dame to the abbey of Saint-Savin-sur-Gartempe. The crypt of the church constructed later houses a 13th-century Romanesque fresco that some sources claim to be the first representation of St. Catherine's "mystical marriage" to Christ. Others contend that it represents the intercession of the Virgin Mary on behalf of the church. Modifications of this second theme since its first appearance in the 9th century, and a representation of the legend of St. Catherine at Alexandria, would then be the causes for the confusion between the two themes.

A 12th-century frieze on the western front of the church of Saint-Laurent, formerly the abbey church of the Augustinian canons, shows the Childhood of Jesus. The most remarkable of the scenes is the Flight into Egypt, in which the Holy Family is trailed by James, who was, according to apocryphal sources, the son of Joseph from an earlier marriage.

The Octogone and Maison-Dieu of Montmorillon were both begun in the first quarter of the 12th century. The Octogone was originally constructed to serve as a sepulchral chapel. At the end of the century, a second chapel was built above it, and the first was all but abandoned, being used for an ossuary.

Kristen E. Sukalec

Duprat, Clémence-Paul. "La peinture romane en France." *Bulletin monumental* 102 (1943–44): 7–12.
Grosset, Charles. "La Maison-Dieu de Montmorillon." *Congrès archéologique (Poitiers)* 109 (1951): 192–206.
Thibout, Marc. "Notre Dame de Montmorillon." *Congrès archéologique (Poitiers)* 109 (1951): 207–19.

MONTPELLIER. Montpellier, first noted in documents of the 10th century as a rural site, is located close to the Mediterranean in Languedoc. By the late 11th century, a bustling town of artisans and merchants had developed under divided political allegiance to the bishop of Maguelone and local lay lords of the Guilhem family. The king of Aragon and Majorca would replace the Guilhem as seigneurs in the 13th century. The king of France made his influence felt in the south increasingly after the Treaty of Meaux-Paris (1229), which brought Languedoc under Capetian domination following the Albigensian Crusade. In 1293, Philip IV the Fair purchased the episcopal quarter of Montpellier, and in 1349 Philip VI would acquire the seigneurial sector from the bankrupt Majorcan king James III for 120,000 *écus*.

The economic heyday of Montpellier was the 13th century. Northern French and Flemish cloth, dyed scarlet in Montpellier, was exported throughout the Mediterranean world. Spices, drugs, sugar, and silks of the East were imported by Montpelliérains and sold on the local markets or transshipped to centers of demand throughout the western Mediterranean basin and northwestern Europe. Montpellier grew to about 40,000 inhabitants by the early 14th century. Immigrants from Italy, Spain, and central France joined newcomers from the immediate hinterland. In the period 1250–1350, in conjunction with Aigues-Mortes, the major port for Levantine trade, and with Lattes, Agde, Collioure, and other smaller outlets to the sea, Montpellier acted as a fulcrum of trade and finance between the Mediterranean world, the Champagne fairs, and Paris. After the mid-14th century, Montpellier experienced a sharp demographic, economic, and political decline, occasioned by the Black Death, changes in the overall European economy and in Mediterranean trade, and, if one is to believe Petrarch's commentary, by its incorporation into the French kingdom.

Montpellier was celebrated throughout the later Middle Ages for its schools. A medical school, founded by the year 1000, most likely by Jewish or Arab physicians, was incorporated in 1221, and a university uniting it with schools of law and the arts was chartered by Pope Nicholas IV in 1289. Petrarch studied here before going on to Bologna. The present-day school of medicine is located in the converted 14th-century bishop's palace.

A Benedictine abbey was founded in Montpellier by Pope Urban V in 1364. The abbey church, which became the cathedral of Saint-Pierre in 1536 when the diocese of Montpellier was formed, dates in part from the 14th century, although much today is 19th-century neo-Gothic reconstruction. Designed by the Avignon architects Bernard de Manse and Bertrand Nougayrol, it consists of a wide nave without side aisles, but with side chapels in the Languedoc manner. Its unsculpted fortresslike façade has two towers and an awkward porch carried on two thick columns.

Kathryn L. Reyerson

[See also: LANGUEDOC; MEDICAL PRACTICE AND PRACTITIONERS; MEDITERRANEAN TRADE; UNIVERSITIES]

Cholvy, Gérard, ed. *Histoire de Montpellier.* Toulouse: Privat, 1984.
Reyerson, Kathryn L. "Commerce and Society in Montpellier: 1250–1350." Diss. Yale University, 1974.
———. *Business, Banking and Finance in Medieval Montpellier.* Toronto: Pontifical Institute of Mediaeval Studies, 1985.

Thomas, Louis J. *Montpellier, ville marchande: histoire économique et sociale de Montpellier des origines à 1870.* Montpellier: Valat, 1936.

MONT-SAINT-MICHEL. In the bay off the border between Normandy and Brittany, the fortified monastery of Mont-Saint-Michel surmounts a 250-foot tall rock island surrounded by ocean and quicksand. Although a sacred site had occupied the island since the 8th century, the conventual buildings result from a period of over 500 years of construction, with the fusion of monastic and military architecture as the goal.

According to the annals and chronicles of Mont-Saint-Michel, in 708 the archangel Michael came in a vision to Aubert, bishop of Avranches, and told him to build a church on the summit of Mont-Tombe. The first in what was to be a series of ecclesiastical structures took the form of a hollowed-out circular cavern. By the 9th century, the site had become an established pilgrimage center. After the period of Viking invasions, the agreement of Saint-Clair-sur-Epte (911) placed the site in Viking hands. In 965, Richard I, duke of Normandy, replaced the canons with thirty Benedictines and appointed Maynard of the abbey of Saint-Wandrille as abbot. Norman funds initiated several building campaigns.

In 1023, Bishop Hildebert leveled the top of the mount to construct a larger church upon the first cavernous structure and turned the earlier sanctuary into a crypt. The earliest parts of the crypt include the north and south walls and two arches of the central arcade and west wall. In order to support the northwest aisle wall and nave piers of the Romanesque church, the antechamber to the west was built.

With granite from Brittany and the nearby Isles of Chausey, over the course of the 11th and 12th centuries and into the 13th the church came to completion. Its largely Romanesque plan included a seven-bay nave with side aisles, bulky compound piers, transepts with apsidal chapels, a large crossing tower, and a two-bay east end with simple apse. The three-story elevation had a wooden roof. In the later 12th century, Abbot Robert de Torigny added towers to the west front that totally collapsed in 1618; in 1780, three of the seven bays of the nave were pulled down. The 11th-century choir fell in 1421 but was rebuilt in Flamboyant style later in the 15th century by Abbot Guillaume d'Estouteville. An image of the 11th-century church prior to the demise of its east and west ends can be found in the *Très Riches Heures* of John, duke of Berry (fol. 195v.).

In the early 11th century, Abbot Roger II (r. 1106–22) initiated the first set of conventual buildings on the north side of the rock. Under Guy de Thouars, Bretons laid siege to Mont-Saint-Michel and destroyed Roger's buildings. Fears of future invasions together with payment from Philip II Augustus led to the more strongly fortified construction of the monastic buildings known as the "Merveille." During the abbacy of Jourdain (r. 1191–1212) the new monastic plan was initiated and made vertical. Over the period from 1203 to 1264, storage rooms, guest hall, monks' dormitory, refectory, and cloister were stacked on top of one another in three stories on the north face of the rock. The first story held the cellar and almonry, the second level held the *salle des chevaliers* and part of the dormitory, and the third story held the cloister and the refectory. Most of these monastic buildings survive, along with the abbot's lodgings and terraces with gardens south of the church.

Mont-Saint-Michel (Manche), general view. *Photograph courtesy of Whitney S. Stoddard.*

Mont-Saint-Michel, nave. *Photograph courtesy of Whitney S. Stoddard.*

Due to fires and attacks, little evidence of earlier domestic architecture survives, although their changing locations are known. In the 12th century, houses occupied the steep rocks to the east of the abbey. Eventually, the town came to occupy its present position on the south side of the mount. Houses from the 15th and 16th centuries remain.

Until the mid-13th century, the abbey alone was fortified. In 1256, with financial help from St. Louis, walls were built to circle the town, but the present fortifications are largely 15th-century, a product of the Hundred Years' War. The abbey played a heroic role in the early years of the 15th century, holding out against the English for over thirty years, in spite of Abbot Robert Jolivet's capitulation in 1419. During the French Revolution, the abbey was secularized, and it was used as a prison from 1793 to 1863. Recognized as a public monument in 1874, the abbey church and other buildings were restored.

Stacy L. Boldrick

[See also: PILGRIMAGE; ROBERT DE TORIGNY]

Adams, Henry. *Mont Saint Michel and Chartres.* New York: Houghton Mifflin, 1913.

Alexander, J.J.G. *Norman Illumination at Mont-St-Michel.* Oxford: Oxford University Press, 1970.

Froidevaux, Yves-Marie. *Le Mont-Saint-Michel.* Paris: Hachette, 1969.

Gout, Paul. *Le Mont-Saint-Michel.* 2 vols. Paris: Colin, 1910.

Hunt, Edward Francis. *The Architecture of Mont-St-Michel (1203–1228).* Washington, D.C.: Catholic University of America Press, 1928.

MORAL TREATISES. The 13th century saw a considerable production of vernacular moral treatises tailored both to the laity and to those in religious life. Edmond of Abingdon's *Mirour de seinte Eglyse* (1230–40) is a series of prose sermons compiled into a treatise intended to guide religious in meditation in the mode of Hugh of Saint-Victor. The French version of the English *Ancrene Riwle* and the *Vie de gent de religion*, both written near the end of the century, are theological treatises intended to instruct religious.

From the middle of the 12th century, the *Elucidarium* inspired a series of treatises aimed at the laity. Gillebert de Cambres's verse *Lucidaire* was the earliest, followed by the *Lumere as lais* (1266–67) of Peter of Peckham, a much longer work that also relies on the *Quattuor libri sententiarum* of Peter Lombard. More elementary in tone, despite its learned source, is the slightly earlier *Dou pere qui son filz enseigne.* The anonymous *Miroir du monde*, sections of which antedate 1279, consists of four parts: a treatise on virtue, another on the Seven Deadly Sins, ten paragraphs on the precepts of wisdom, and a confession manual. The first two parts were used by Laurent d'Orléans in his *Somme le roi*, composed in 1280 at the request of Philip III the Bold. Jean de Journy's *Dime de penitence* is a confession manual written in 1288.

The few surviving treatises in Occitan are similar and roughly contemporaneous. The *Repentir du pécheur*, written in the second quarter of the 13th century, introduces its confession of sins with a prayer to the Virgin. Raimon de Castelnou's *Doctrinal*, from the second half of the century, is a poetical catechism intended for public recitation. Matfre Ermengaud's *Breviari d'Amor* (1288) is an encyclopedic work broader in scope than the others mentioned here, but its section on the love of God treats the works of mercy, the articles of the creed, and the petitions of the Pater Noster, as well as confession.

Maureen B.M. Boulton

[See also: ANGLO-NORMAN LITERATURE; COUVIN, WATRIQUET BRASSENIEX DE; DIDACTIC LITERATURE (OCCITAN); LAURENT D'ORLÉANS; MATFRE ERMENGAUD; PHILIPPE DE NOVARE]

Brayer, Edith. "Contenu, structure et combinaisons du *Miroir du monde* et de la *Somme le roi.*" *Romania* 79 (1958): 1–38, 433–70.

Langlois, Charles-Victor. *La vie en France au moyen âge du XIIe au milieu du XIVe siècle.* 4 vols. Paris: Hachette, 1926–28, Vol. 4: *La vie spirituelle.*

Lefèvre, Yves. *L'Elucidarium et les Lucidaires: contribution par l'histoire d'un texte à l'histoire des croyances religieuses en France au moyen âge.* Paris: Bibliothèque des Écoles Françaises d'Athènes et de Rome, 1955.

Trethewey, W.H. "The Seven Deadly Sins and the Devil's Court in the Trinity College Cambridge French Text of the *Ancrene Riwle*." *PMLA* 65 (1950): 1233–46.

MORALITY PLAYS. The morality play was one of the major dramatic genres in France during the late Middle Ages. The term *moralité*, long used to designate a moral teaching or doctrine, was applied in the 15th century to plays that taught moral lessons by means of allegory. Though references to allegorical plays survive from the late 14th century, the earliest extant *moralité* was staged at the Collège de Navarre in Paris in 1427. About seventy morality plays written between that date and 1550 have come down to us.

A morality play may be generally defined as an allegorical drama in which the protagonist is required to make a moral choice between good and evil. The plays, however, vary greatly in scope and style. They range from fewer than 200 to more than 30,000 lines. A few have only two or three characters; the longest has more than eighty. Some morality plays, like *Homme Pécheur*, present a single human character who alternates in choosing between good and evil. Others, like *Bien Advisé et Mal Advisé*, have dual protagonists, one good and one bad. Some plays, like *Homme Juste et Homme Mondain*, present the human protagonists on the journey of life from birth to death and confront them with a full range of personified virtues and vices to choose among. Others, like the *Blasphémateurs*, treat only a single vice and cover a short period of time. These four plays bear a superficial resemblance to the Passion plays in that they are quite lengthy, probably requiring several days to perform, and their staging includes both Heaven and Hell with the usual complement of angels and devils. They are essentially different from the Passion plays, however, because their plots are allegorical fictions rather than historical representations. The staging of Hell differs also in that the morality plays show the torments of the sinners inside Lucifer's lair rather than just the Hell-mouth entrance as in the Passion plays. In *Bien Advisé et Mal Advisé*, for example, Hell is depicted as a kitchen in the house of a great lord. Here, sinners are forced to partake of an infernal banquet where every dish is liberally seasoned with sulfur and *sauce d'enfer*.

Some morality plays also bear a superficial resemblance to farces, either in the scenes that provoke laughter or in those that portray the trickery and deception involved in a life of sin. Here, too, though both genres represent fictional worlds, there is a fundamental difference. Dull-witted farce characters are laughable because they are the butt of tricks played by others for material gain. Clever farce characters are comic because they are prisoners of their own venality. If tricks are played in morality plays, it is because evil characters are trying to lure the human protagonists into sin and damnation. The latter do not have to play tricks to gain some paltry material advantage; they need only yield to temptation in order to have all the worldly possessions they desire. When farce characters gain something through deception, they are not punished. They live in an essentially amoral world governed by folly.

Morality-play characters know full well that every action has moral consequences. Those who act virtuously will be rewarded, but those who choose vice will be punished. The world that the morality play represents is ordered, governed by reason, in which there is always a higher power to reward the good and punish the wicked. Indeed, a character named Reason, representing the human ability to distinguish good from evil, appears in a number of morality plays, such as the *Lymon et la terre* and the *Théologastres*. Her function is to guide the protagonist into the path of virtue.

Many morality plays have protagonists who are universalized individuals of the Everyman type. They go by such names as Humanity, Humankind, or Sinful Man. Many others present main characters who exemplify vices—e.g., Poison Tongue—or stages in life. In the latter category are several plays from the 16th century dealing with the problems of youth, especially the children of wealthy bourgeois. The parents in the *Enfant ingrat*, for example, ruin themselves financially in order to give their son every advantage. Morality plays that deal with individuals, whatever the scope, may be termed personal moralities. Some plays, however, deal with the moral condition of particular groups within society and thus have protagonists who personify institutions. These may be termed institutional moralities. One such play is the *Moralité des trois états réformés par Raison*, which shows that institutions as well as individuals can become corrupt when they lose the guidance of reason. Another institutional morality is *Envie, État et Simplesse*, which provides an example of institutional reform by having State expel Envy from his company.

Virtually all morality plays are personification allegories in which ideas and psychological traits are represented as characters on the stage. Their names range from the designation of common virtues and vices like Charity and Pride, or conditions like Poverty, to more fanciful appellations like Ashamed-to-tell-his-sins. One of the principal attributes of these nonhuman characters is that, with few exceptions, they always represent the static concept of their name and therefore never develop or change as would a human character. A few morality plays lack personification of this sort, and they may be called interpretive allegories. Their characters are all human, but the spectator is expected to interpret the play in an allegorical sense. The epilogue to the *Moralité de Pyramus et Tisbee* explains that Pyramus can be understood as the son of God and Thisbe as the human soul. Similarly, André de La Vigne's *Aveugle et le boiteux*, which has the appearance of a farce, can be interpreted as an allegory of the ungainly pairing of soul and body. When the two beggars are miraculously cured, the blind man (soul) accepts God's grace and the cripple (body) rejects it.

There is, finally, a fundamental difference between the morality plays and the dramatic works of later centuries. Renaissance playwrights and their successors fell under the influence of Aristotelian theories concerning the imitation of the physical world, but the authors of morality plays worked largely with Platonic notions of mimesis. If the morality-play protagonist lacks the finely drawn psychological traits of the tragic hero, it is not because medieval playwrights were inept but because they had a different goal. Influenced by a persistent medieval Platonism, they found greater dignity in plays that imitated the "real" world of ideas and concepts than in those that imitated the ephemeral world of material things.

Alan E. Knight

[See also: LA VIGNE, ANDRÉ DE; MIRACLE PLAYS; MYSTERY PLAYS; THEATER]

Helmich, Werner, ed. *Moralités françaises: réimpression fac-similé de vingt-deux pièces allégoriques imprimées aux XVe et XVIe siècles.* 3 vols. Geneva: Slatkine, 1980.
———, and Jeanne Wathelet-Willem. "La moralité: genre dramatique à redécouvrir." In *Le théâtre au moyen âge: actes du Deuxième Colloque International sur le Théâtre Médiéval, 1977,* ed. Gari R. Muller. Montreal: L'Aurore/Univers, 1981, pp. 205–37.
Knight, Alan E. *Aspects of Genre in Late Medieval French Drama.* Manchester: Manchester University Press, 1983.

MORAT. Charles the Bold, duke of Burgundy, at war with a league of Swiss towns in 1476, led his army from Lausanne to besiege the stronghold of Morat (Murten), twenty miles west of Bern. His divisions were poorly positioned and unable to support each other when attacked by a Swiss column on June 22. For the second time in four months, the Swiss defeated the Burgundian army, this time with great slaughter. The battle cost Charles control of Savoy and precipitated the collapse of Burgundian power in the next seven months.

John Bell Henneman, Jr.

[See also: CHARLES THE BOLD]

Vaughan, Richard. *Charles the Bold: The Last Valois Duke of Burgundy.* New York: Barnes and Noble, 1973. [Extensive bibliography.]

MORIENVAL. The abbey church of Morienval (Oise) is a Frankish foundation just north of Paris. The present church is primarily an 11th-century Romanesque structure with a rib-vaulted ambulatory dated ca. 1122. It has three towers, one at the west end and two flanking the apse. A Carolingian flying screen spans the nave with transverse ribs and heavy piers. The groin-vaulted aisles have carved capitals that reflect Byzantine influence. The later ambulatory utilizes diagonal ribs and slightly pointed transverse arches. Although the vaults show experimental construction techniques, they represent important early stages of the Gothic rib-vaulting system.

Karen Gould

MOTET (13TH CENTURY). A musical-poetic genre composed upon a fragment of plainchant. The motet is readily identified by its stylistic and notational differentiation of the tenor from the upper part(s). An upper part, the motetus (or motellus), was notated *cum littera* (texted and in single notes), and the tenor, which carried the plainchant, was notated *sine littera* (untexted and in ligatures subject to modal rhythmic interpretation). The tenor plainchant melisma is the structural foundation of the motet. Throughout the 13th century, tenors develop from simple, literal repetition to more complex patterns, such as the rondeau, but it is the relationship of the upper parts to each other and to the tenor that changed most radically.

In the closing years of the 19th century, Wilhelm Meyer demonstrated that the origin of the motet lay in the discant clausula of the Notre-Dame School. The upper voice (the duplum) of a clausula was notated in rhythmically significant ligature patterns (several notes joined together in one notational symbol) because it had no text. Melodic comparisons of clausulae and early motets showed that many were in fact melodically the same. Thus, when a text was given to the existing duplum of a clausula, the ligature patterns used to notate this part, now called the motetus instead of the duplum, were converted into notation to set individual syllables of text, making use mostly of single notes without rhythmic significance. Meyer thus was able to demonstrate that motets arose from the practice of poetically texting the upper part(s) of clausulae, and this explained the uneven number of syllables and irregular rhyme patterns of the poetry, unlike any other poetry of the time.

For many early motets, a newly composed third voice, the triplum, was added, to which the same text was applied. Such three-part (in rare cases, four-part) compositions with rhythmically organized tenors and a single text for both upper parts are known as conductus motets. Only a few conductus motets have French texts, the repertory being predominantly in Latin. A three-voice motet with one text for the motetus and another for the triplum is called a double motet. Double motets may be completely Latin, completely French, or they may be bilingual, usually with a Latin motetus and a French triplum. The same principles may be applied to triple motets, in which typically a fourth voice, the quadruplum, with its own text, has been added to a double motet. The same language almost always occurs in all parts, and most triple motets are in French.

The largest extant source of the second half of the century for motets is the Montpellier codex, with over 300: triple motets (all French but one in Latin), double motets with Latin moteti and French tripla, Latin double motets, French double motets (some with secular tenors), and a few motets for which the composer is identified as Pierre de la Croix and for others as Adam de la Halle. The use of French texts for tripla or for both tripla and moteti of motets possibly arose in the 1230s. Fifty French-texted motets are included in the *Manuscrit du roi,* which is known primarily as a source for trouvère and troubadour chansons and was inscribed ca. 1250.

It is generally thought that the vertical coincidence of phrase endings among the parts is stylistically earlier than a staggering of phrase endings. An early motet demonstrating the vertical coordination of phrase ending is the three-part conductus motet *Homo quo vigeas/Et gaudebit.* To form the motet, the duplum has been given the text

Homo quo vigeas and a triplum newly composed in note-against-note style. Staggered phrase endings occur especially in double motets, such as *Ypocrite pseudopontifices/ Velut stelle firmamenti/Et gaudebit.* Another double motet that has staggered phrase endings, *O Maria virgo /O Maria maris stella/In veritate*, rhythmically contrasts the parts by setting the tenor in the fifth rhythmic mode, the motetus in the first, and the triplum in the sixth. The end-rhymes of the text for *Beatis nos adhibe/Benedicamus Domino* rhyme with each syllable of the tenor. It is actually an organum prosula that was used in the liturgy as a replacement for or trope to the *Benedicamus Domino.* Like *Beatis nos adhibe,* many of the earliest motet texts maintain a tropic relationship to the text of the tenor from which the clausula has been derived.

The part notation that became the norm in the second half of the century—separate columns of staves for the upper parts with the tenor running along the bottom of the page—led to the abandonment of score arrangement in practical sources. In later 13th-century sources, page turns are sometimes arranged to coordinate with all the parts, indicating that the singers could perform from the manuscript. There is a rhythmic distinction between the long, breve, and semibreve, and rhythm-specific ligatures with modified shapes are introduced. Rests indicated by lines of definite lengths replace the ambiguous rests that had been determined by modal context.

Trends in the continental repertories of motets at the end of the 13th century included a number of other significant developments. The Petronian triplum—after Pierre de la Croix—is characterized by virtuoso declamation of a French text and subdivision of the breve into more than three semibreves, each carrying its own syllable of text. Pierre's own *Aucun vont sovent/Amor qui cor vulnerat/ Kyrieleyson* is a good example. Secular *cantus firmi* were introduced, and binary rhythm is seen in motets like *Amor potest conqueri/Ad amorem sequitur/[Tenor]* in the Montpellier codex. Some late 13th-century French motets tended toward accompanied song, much like *Pucelete bele et avenant/Je languis des maus d'amours/Domino* and some motets of the *Fauvel* manuscript.

Sandra Pinegar

[See also: ADAM DE LA HALLE; ARS ANTIQUA; *CANTUS FIRMUS*; CLAUSULA; CONDUCTUS; ORGANUM; NOTRE-DAME SCHOOL; PIERRE DE LA CROIX; RHYTHMIC MODE]

Everist, Mark. *French Motets in the Thirteenth Century: Music, Poetry and Genre.* Cambridge: Cambridge University Press, 1994.

Huot, Silvia. "Polyphonic Poetry: The Old French Motet and Its Literary Context." *French Forum* 14 (1989): 261–78.

———. "Transformations of Lyric Voice in the Songs, Motets, and Plays of Adam de la Halle." *Romanic Review* 78 (1987): 148–64.

Ludwig, Friedrich. "Über die Entstehung und die erste Entwicklung der lateinischen und französischen Motette in musikalischer Beziehung." *Sammelbände der internationalen Musik-Gesellschaft* 7 (1905): 514–28.

Page, Christopher. "The Performance of Ars Antiqua Motets." *Early Music* 16 (1988): 147–64.

———. *Discarding Images: Reflections on Music and Culture in Medieval France.* Oxford: Clarendon, 1993, pp. 43–111.

Sanders, Ernest H. "The Medieval Motet." In *Gattungen der Musik in Einzeldarstellungen: Gedenkschrift Leo Schrade*, ed. Wulf Arlt, Ernst Lichtenhahn, and Hans Oesch. Bern: Francke, 1973, pp. 497–573.

MOTTO/*DEVISE*. The adoption and use by individual nobles in late-medieval France of a distinctive aphoristic phrase of the type known in Italian and English as the "motto" and in French as the *devise* was probably derived in part from the much earlier use of war cries, or *cris de guerre.* From at least the 12th century, princes and barons in France, as in other parts of Latin Christendom, made use in battle of a distinctive rallying cry. Such cries took a variety of forms, from the simple name of the family (*Châteaubriand!*) through a call for aid to the lord in specific terms (*Louvain au riche duc!*) to an invocation of the patron saint of the dominion (the *Montjoie Saint-Denis!* of the kings of France or the *Notre-Dame de Bourbon!* of the lords of Bourbon) to an exhortation in the most general terms (the *Passavant li meillor!* of the counts of Champagne and the *Place à la banniere!* of the lords of Coucy).

The use of *devises* or mottoes as distinct from cries dates only from the 14th century and was closely associated with the adoption of those figurative cognizances called "badges" in English from the same period. In fact, the earliest mottoes were closely associated with badges, whose significance they often helped to explain, and although the French term *devise* was employed by contemporaries to designate both badges and mottoes separately, and has come to be used in ordinary language especially to designate the latter, scholars now restrict both it and its English derivative "device" to a composition including both a badge and a motto set on or next to it. Ephemeral devices of this sort were employed from ca. 1330, but the first stable devices in Europe seem to have been those of the monarchical orders of knighthood founded by kings and by sovereign dukes in France and the empire between 1347 and 1470. The earliest stable devices were the garter of the English Order of the Garter, bearing the famous motto *Hony soyt ki mal y pense* (1346); the sword of the Cypriot Order of the Sword, with its motto *Pour loyauté maintenir* (1347/59); the love-knot of the Neapolitan Order of the Knot, with its changeable motto *Se Dieu plaist/Il a pleu a Dieu* (1352); and the belt bearing the motto *Esperance* and the golden shield bearing the motto *Allen* created by Duke Louis of Bourbon in 1366 and 1367. The last two may have been the first stable devices in France proper, though they were anticipated by several years by the device adopted at some time between 1352 and 1362 by Amadeus, the "Green Count" of Savoy: a love-knot similar to that of the Neapolitan order, usually accompanied by the motto *Fert.* This motto was also among the first, if not the first, to be used independently of a figural badge.

Promoted in the royal court of Charles VI from 1382, the use of mottoes, typically short and more or less cryptic, spread rapidly among the nobles of France in the last third of the 14th century and enjoyed its greatest vogue in the 15th and 16th centuries. After 1420, indeed, the use of a badge without some sort of motto was rare in France. The use of independent mottoes grew steadily, however, to the point where most great families employed one and commonly displayed it, along with or in place of their *cri de guerre*, as part of their armorial achievement, usually below the shield. In some cases, the motto actually alluded to the figures on the shield of arms whose basic design was common to the whole lineage: thus, the *Sustenant lilia turres* of the Simiane family of Provence, whose arms were semé of lilies and towers. In addition to, or in place of, such familial mottoes, many nobles adopted one or more personal mottoes, some for short periods and some for life. The most famous personal mottoes of this period are those of the four Valois dukes of Burgundy, who bore respectively *Moult me tarde*, *Je le tiens*, *Aultre n'aray*, and *Je l'ay emprins*. In general, the use of mottoes before 1500 closely paralleled the use of both badges and devices. Together, badges, mottoes, and devices formed a loosely structured system of cognizances, which, because of its close association with the traditional heraldic system centered on the arms and crest, is now described as "paraheraldic."

D'A. Jonathan D. Boulton

[See also: ARMS (HERALDIC); LIVERY, BADGES, AND COLORS]

Boulton, D'A.J.D. "Insignia of Power: The Use of Heraldic and Paraheraldic Devices by Italian Princes, c. 1350–1500." In *Art and Politics in Late Medieval and Early Renaissance Italy*, ed. Charles M. Rosenberg. Notre Dame: University of Notre Dame Press, 1990. [Includes a taxonomy of badges and devices.]
Pastoureau, Michel. *Traité d'héraldique*. Paris: Picard, 1979.

MOULINS. Moulins (Allier) originated in the late 10th century as a small settlement of millers who served the needs of the nearby village of Yzeure. Because of its strategic location on the Allier River and at the intersection of Roman roads, Moulins became a favored seat of the lords, later dukes, of Bourbon. An early 15th-century belfry, the Jacquemart, and a concentration of imposing houses in half-timber work and stone testify to the prosperity enjoyed by the town during the heyday of the dukes of Bourbon, from the late 14th century to the early 16th. Portions of the ducal château also survive, including the late 14th-century donjon and the Italianate corps-de-logis added under Pierre II and Anne of Beaujeu ca. 1500.

The collegiate church of Notre-Dame, erected with ducal sponsorship on the site of an earlier chapel, is the city's major monument of the late Middle Ages. Built between 1474 and the early 16th century, it consists of a restrained two-story elevation that may be related distantly to contemporary Parisian architecture. However, Notre-Dame's chief glories are the stained-glass windows of the

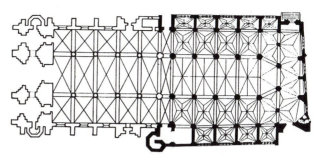

Moulins (Allier), Notre-Dame, plan. After Deshoulières.

chapels, which showcase their aristocratic and bourgeois donors and the splendid triptych ordered by Pierre II and Anne of Beaujeu for the chapel of the Conception and painted by the Master of Moulins in 1498.

Michael T. Davis

Clément, Joseph. *La cathédrale de Moulins: histoire et description*. Moulins: Imprimeries Réunies, 1923.
———. "Moulins." *Congrès archéologique (Moulins et Nevers)* 80 (1913): 3–23.
Guy, André. *La cathédrale de Moulins*. Moulins: Imprimeries Réunies, 1950.
Kurmann-Schwarz, Brigitte. "Les vitraux de la cathédrale de Moulins." *Congrès archéologique* 146 (1988): 21–49.
Legros, Catherine. "La cathédrale Notre-Dame de Moulins." *Congrès archéologique* 146 (1988): 9–19. [Includes a detailed summary of 19th- and 20th-century restorations.]

MOUVANCE. Fiefs were often said to "descend" or "move" (Lat. *movere*) from the person who had granted them and whose permission consequently was required for any abridgment of the fief or its service. Since unauthorized alienations could be met with confiscation, the prudent acquirer of a fief, particularly an ecclesiastic, obtained the approval of the lord in whose *mouvance* it was.

From the 13th century, wealthy princes attempted to increase their influence and prestige by purchasing the *mouvance* of important fiefs and by establishing *mouvance* over allodial lands newly converted into fiefs. When the county of Bar-le-Duc, for example, which consisted of various allodial and feudal lands, was compelled by Philip IV in 1301 to become a fief held from the crown, it entered the royal *mouvance* and henceforth was known as the *Barrois mouvant*, to distinguish it from the rest of the county located in the German empire.

Theodore Evergates

[See also: *ABRÈGEMENT DU FIEF*]

Fourquin, Guy. *Lordship and Feudalism in the Middle Ages*, trans. Iris and A.L. Lytton Sells. New York: Pica, 1976.
Ganshof, François L. *Feudalism*, trans. Philip Grierson. New York: Harper, 1961.

MOZAC. The Benedictine abbey of Saint-Pierre in Mozac (Puy-de-Dôme), founded in 681 by St. Calminus and his wife, St. Namadie, was one of the richest in France until the Reformation, thanks to the transferral here of the relics of St. Austremoine, patron of Auvergne, in the 8th century. The present church, built for the most part during the 12th century in the Romanesque style of Auvergne, incorporates an 11th-century tower on the western façade. The nave and side aisles date from the 12th century and the choir and wooden choirstalls from the 15th. In the treasury is the reliquary of St. Calminus, the largest 12th-century Limousin enamelwork reliquary preserved in France (ca. 1168). It consists of fourteen enamel plaques: on the ends are depicted St. Austremoine and Mary holding the Child Jesus. Within the church, the capitals are the finest examples of Romanesque sculpture in Auvergne. One in particular, that representing Christ's Resurrection, is notable as an important visual source for 12th-century clothing and military equipment.

William W. Kibler/William W. Clark

[See also: ENAMELING; JEWELRY AND METALWORKING]

Luzuy, Abbé. "Mozac." *Congrès archéologique* (*Moulins et Nevers*) 80 (1913): 124–43.
Swiechowski, Zygmunt. *Sculpture romane d'Auvergne.* Clermont-Ferrand: Bussac, 1973.

MULTIPLE-REFRAIN SONGS (*CHANSONS AVEC DES REFRAINS*). Unlike the *chanson à refrain*, where a single refrain reappears at preestablished intervals, the roughly one hundred extant songs with multiple or variable refrains consist of an indeterminate number of stanzas, ranging from two to eight, each followed by a different borrowed or cited refrain (intertextual repetition). The appearance of each refrain entails a metrical and melodic break, since all stanzas are sung to the same melody and have the same rhyme scheme, while each refrain has its own melodic phrase and versification. Nonetheless, the refrain is often integrated into the stanza through a transitional line announcing it. More than one-third of all *chansons avec des refrains* are classified as *pastourelles*.

Eglal Doss-Quinby

Doss-Quinby, Eglal. *Les refrains chez les trouvères du XIIe siècle au début du XIVe.* New York: Lang, 1984, pp. 96–111.

MURBACH. The Benedictine abbey of Murbach (Haut-Rhin) in the Vosges was founded in 727 by St. Firmin and splendidly endowed by Count Eberhard d'Eguisheim. Among its benefactors was Charlemagne, and its abbots were all princes of the Holy Roman Empire. It had the distinction that only members of noble families could join, and its monks were knights as well. Only the east end of the massive, late 12th-century pink-sandstone abbey church of Saint-Sixte survives: choir, transept with twin towers, and flat chevet, flanked by two two-storied chapels. The decoration of the transept and chapels, as at nearby Guebwiller, is of Lombard arcading.

William W. Kibler/William W. Clark

[See also: GUEBWILLER]

Deshoulières, François. "Murbach." *Congrès archéologique* (*Metz, Strasbourg, Colmar*) 83 (1920): 438–47.
Will, Robert. "L'église de Murbach." *Congrès archéologique* (*Haute-Alsace*) 136 (1978): 198–211.

MURET. During the early years of the Albigensian Crusade, Simon de Montfort, a castellan from the Île-de-France, ousted Raymond VI, count of Toulouse, from his lands. Peter II, king of Aragon, intervened in 1213 to support the Occitan lords against the crusaders from northern France. Peter and his allies besieged the town of Muret (Haute-Garonne) on September 10, 1213. Montfort arrived with a much smaller force, hoping to break the siege. Although badly outnumbered, he displayed superior tactical skill in maneuvering his cavalry reserves, who changed formation, charged up a hill, and won a superior position. Montfort then won a decisive victory. The king of Aragon was killed, and the hitherto strong Aragonese political ties to southern France lost their importance.

John Bell Henneman, Jr.

[See also: ALBIGENSIAN CRUSADE; MONTFORT; SAINT-GILLES]

MUSIC THEORY. Systematic reflection on the art of music in the West had its origin in the ancient philosophical tradition that considered mathematical knowledge propaedeutic to the study of philosophy. Ancient mathematics was divided into four disciplines ordered according to two basic divisions of quantity, multitude and magnitude. *Arithmetica* formed the science of multitude *per se*, while *musica* was the discipline treating multitude in ratios; *geometrica* was the subject considering fixed (immobile) magnitudes, and *astronomia* formed the science of magnitude in motion. This fourfold division of mathematical knowledge, the Quadrivium, was transmitted into the Middle Ages by Boethius's *De institutione arithmetica* and *De institutione musica*, and through this foundation a science of rational, systematic reflection on the art of music was established. Cassiodorus's *Institutiones* and Isidore of Seville's *Etymologiae* are two further works of late antiquity that aided in establishing this tradition of musical reflection for the Middle Ages.

As a subject preparatory to philosophy, *musica* stressed "knowing," immutable knowledge in the philosophical sense. That knowing arose from the science of mathematical ratios and from the physical reality that the most basic musical intervals, the consonances of the fourth, fifth, and octave, have their scientific foundation in these ratios. The senses were mistrusted as determinants of musical structures or as the basis of value judgments. The philosophical hero of mythic status was the ancient Greek Pythagoras, who by divine guidance discovered the musical ratios in a smithy. The technique of manipulating the ratios to derive musical systems, or pitch collections, was developed by disciples of Pythagoras, and the application of the ratios to a scientific instrument, the monochord, became the means of determining for the senses an empirical reality based on rational reflection. But the efficacy of rational musical reality was not only revealed in sensual consonance; it was also present in the structure of the universe (*musica mundana*) and in the physical and psychological structure of the human being (*musica humana*).

Boethius's mathematical treatises began to be studied in France during the early 9th century, in monastic communities devoted to the realization of a liturgy that was largely sung. No necessary affinity existed between the rational musical system of antiquity and the practical reality of daily singing the Divine Office and Mass. Nevertheless, the scholar and cantor—often the same person—began to demand a degree of congruence between knowing and doing. During this period, two musical traditions are evident: *cantus* and *musica*, or the art of singing and the discipline of musical theory. Tension between music as a performing art and music as a theoretical discipline is evident in the earliest theoretical and historical sources, yet each played a crucial role in shaping the other during the Middle Ages.

Two traditions are found in the earliest truly medieval theory. On the one hand, a collection of texts associated with the anonymous *Musica enchiriadis* (late 9th c.), while aware of the rediscovery of Boethius and his mathematical basis for musical thought, presents a theory of music largely independent of the ancient tradition. The language of these texts tends toward the qualitative rather than the quantitative, and the myth associated with the collection is that of Orpheus and his inability to bring the mysteries of music into the clarity of day, rather than Boethius's story of Pythagoras and the rational numbers founded on hammers. Basic terminology of these texts is firmly rooted in liturgical practice rather than ancient theoretical tradition, and the linguistic root of much terminology is clearly Byzantine Greek. The tonal and notational system found in these texts is independent of the system transmitted by Boethius. On the other hand, such theorists as Aurelian of Réôme and Hucbald of Saint-Amand had read and somewhat mastered the tradition discovered in Boethius, Cassiodorus, and Isidore and had begun the process of bringing together *cantus* and *musica* in treatises that would form the basis of subsequent musical thought. Many anonymous texts originating sometime between late antiquity and the Carolingian period lie behind these first treatises with named authors, and much terminology found therein seems to be drawn from the same sources as *Musica enchiriadis*.

One of France's most important contributions to the development of musical theory during the Middle Ages is found in the tonary. An important link between the *cantus* and *musica* traditions, the tonary presented a collection of antiphons, and often other chants, of the Office and Mass ordered according to the eight tones for singing the psalms. The fundamental bases for subsequent theoretical discus-

Musica points to the three Boethian levels of music: *Musica mundana, Musica humana,* and *Musica instrumentalis.* MS Pluteo 29, I, facing fol. 1. *Courtesy of Biblioteca Mediceo-Laurenziana, Florence.*

sions of the musical modes is found in these documents. The earliest extant tonary, found in the *Psalter of Charlemagne* (B.N. lat. 13159), originated at the abbey of Saint-Riquier in the late 8th century. A further crucial tonary is that of Metz, known as the *Carolingian Tonary*, which was probably compiled ca. 830 in Metz (preserved in four manuscripts, 9th–11th c.). Perhaps the most important document of this genre is found in the manuscript Montpellier, Bibliothèque de la Faculté de Médecine, H. 159, a source that originated in the abbey of Saint-Bénigne in Dijon, probably under the influence of the monastic reformer William of Volpiano (d. 1031). This source, employing both neumatic notation and an alphabetic notation with roots in the musical system found in Boethius, organized and recorded all the chants of the Mass according to their mode and liturgical genre. Odoranus of Sens (d. 1046) compiled an important tonary, and the *Tonale sancti Bernardi* documents the Cistercian chant reforms.

Monastic houses throughout France were the centers of musical thought during the 10th and 11th centuries.

The abbey of Fleury, judging from the number of theoretical works copied at that abbey around the time of Abbot Abbo (ca. 940–1004), played a notable role in copying and transmitting theoretical works ranging from Boethius to contemporary anonymous treatises. At Fleury, *musica* continued to be taught within the context of the Quadrivium, and both the speculative and practical aspects of music were addressed. Cathedral schools likewise became important centers for the study of *musica*. The cathedral school of Reims, when Gerbert of Aurillac (d. 1003) was master, was an important center for the study of mathematics in general and, within that context, Boethius's *De institutione musica*. But as musical theory became more directed toward problems of musical practice, the intimate relation between music and the remaining mathematical disciplines became strained, and ultimately the separation of music from the other three disciplines forms one of the primary causes of the decline of the Quadrivium during the 11th and 12th centuries.

Four broad topics form the core of musical theory in France from the 9th through the 11th century. (1) For an author, the definition of a tonal system or basic collection of pitches within which music takes place sets the fundamental principles. The Greater Perfect System of Greek antiquity, with the added pitch from the synemmenon tetrachord (b-flat), emerges as the predominant system. The system of *Musica enchiriadis* nevertheless remains in the background of musical thought throughout these centuries, and basic terminology from this complex of texts became integrated into the system inherited from antiquity. The basic systems were taught as abstract collections of pitches and tetrachords, then demonstrated empirically in the division of the monochord. (2) Explanation of the tonal organization of liturgical melodies within the system developed into the medieval theory of the eight modes, four authentic and four plagal. Early theoretical discussions of the modes were based largely on the vocabulary and organization of tonaries. In the course of the 10th and 11th centuries, the theory became more systematic and the modes were explained as species of the octave. (3) Elementary theory of polyphony, that is, organum, formed a part of several treatises, although polyphony never occupied as significant a place in medieval theory as description and analysis of monophonic liturgical melodies. (4) Finally, speculative reflections concerning nonempirical music, from musical mythology to pure mathematics to music of the spheres, continued to form a significant portion of theoretical thought.

Important developments in Italian theory occurred in the early 11th century. The *Dialogus de musica*, formerly attributed to Odo of Cluny, was written around Milan, and Guido d'Arezzo in four treatises developed a concise practical alternative to *Musica enchiriadis*, codified advances in staff notation, and developed a system of solmization. In the late 11th and 12th centuries, these texts were transmitted to France and subsequently exercised critical influence in French musical thought and practice.

Ars Antiqua, Ars Nova. By the 12th century, the harmonic issues of early-medieval theory had been for the most part resolved: a system based on the periodic octave; a theory of consonance organized around the fourth, fifth, and octave; a theory of the liturgical modes systematized on four finals; and an elementary theory of organum or polyphonic voice leading were all set to be recapitulated in later treatises. The all-pervading issue of subsequent musical reflection became the organization of time in music, or the fundamental principles of rhythm. Giving rise to this issue was the rapid development of polyphony during the 11th and 12th centuries and the necessity of bringing some order to two or more voices singing at the same time.

In the late 11th and 12th centuries, intellectual life began to shift from rural monastic centers to urban cathedral schools, which subsequently evolved into the medieval universities. Paris became a center of both intellectual and musical activities during the 12th and 13th centuries, and the musical accomplishments of central France during the period subsequently became known as the Ars Antiqua, a musical movement that witnessed the first great flowering of a polyphonic repertoire with a rational rhythmic foundation. The most outstanding musical theorists of the 13th century, Johannes de Garlandia and Franco of Cologne, were active in Paris, where both *magistri* were probably associated with the University of Paris. Following scholastic traditions of thought, Johannes de Garlandia divided music into genre, species, and divisions in two treatises, *De plana musica* and *De mensurabili musica*. Johannes presented a systematized treatment of rhythmic theory organized around rhythmic modes and defined the three styles of measured polyphony as discant, copula, and organum. Franco of Cologne's *Ars cantus mensurabilis* was widely circulated throughout western Europe during the 13th century; while reflecting scholastic terminology, Franco's work was a thoroughly practical treatise that extended the rational order of rhythmic notation from the various species of organum (*sine littera*) to the texted motets (*cum littera*).

Two remarkable monuments in the history of musical thought grew out of the scholastic culture of Paris during the late 13th and early 14th centuries: Jerome of Moravia's *Tractatus de musica* and Jacques de Liège's *Speculum musice*. The Dominican Jerome of Moravia, in what amounts to a musical *summa*, sought to review as thoroughly as possible the contemporary state of musical thought, drawing on sources as disparate as Boethius, Isidore, Guido, Johannes Affligemensis, al-Farabi, Richard of Saint-Victor, Hugh of Saint-Victor, Johannes de Garlandia, Franco of Cologne, and others. Jerome continued the tradition of discussing music within the context of the Quadrivium, presented the basic theory needed for performance of liturgical chant (*musica plana*), and offered a thorough collection of texts treating the new rhythmic practices (*musica mensurabilis*). The earliest extant treatise developing the theory of rhythmic modes, *Discantus positio vulgaris*, is in fact preserved in Jerome's *Tractatus*. Jerome's musical *summa* is preserved in only one manuscript (B.N. lat. 16663), willed to the Sorbonne by Petrus of Limoges in 1304.

The precedent established by Jerome was followed and even expanded by Jacques de Liège, a canon from Liège active in Paris during the early 14th century. Jacques's

Speculum musice is the largest surviving medieval musical treatise, consisting of seven books (521 chapters) treating every conceivable topic and drawing on virtually every known source. The scholastic nature of the work is evident in the first book, where Jacques draws not only on Boethius in setting the philosophical foundations of the study of music, but on Aristotle, Robert Kilwardby, and Peter Comestor as well. After systematically treating systems, consonances, melodic genres, division of the monochord, solmization, and the modes, Jacques, in the seventh book, turned his attention to the measured music of his time and railed against the musical practices of the 14th century. The conservative Jacques, placing contemporary practices in sharp contrast to the traditional mensural forms and practices of the 13th century, became an important early witness for a historical consciousness within the tradition of music theory. The works of Jerome and Jacques offer eloquent testimony to the wide variety of musical texts available in Paris during the 13th and 14th centuries and to the influence of scholastic culture's demand for the universality of knowledge.

The contrast in style and content between the *summae* of Jerome of Moravia and Jacques de Liège and the carefully wrought treatise of Johannes de Grocheio reflects the stylistic shift in music itself between the Ars Antiqua and the Ars Nova. Johannes de Grocheio explicitly rejected the quantitative, philosophical nature of past theoretical reflections and attempted to develop a musical theory based on empirical observation refined by rational organization. The basis of his work, now known by the title *De musica*, was not ancient authority or even mathematical speculation but the musical life that he experienced in Paris at the beginning of the 14th century. He divided music into *musica vulgaris*, the everyday music of the city; *musica mensurata*, the composed music of musician-scholars; and *genus ecclesiasticum*, the music of the church. His perceptive descriptions of genres within these categories, sometimes offered with commentary on poetic form and social function, transforms his iconoclastic discourse into an invaluable historical record of contemporary musical life.

More representative of the French tradition of musical reflection are the works of two early 14th-century *magistri artium* at the University of Paris, Jehan des Murs and Philippe de Vitry. Both of these scholars were expert in the mathematical disciplines, and their fame and reputation extended well beyond music and music theory. Jehan des Murs's *Musica speculativa secundum Boetium* seems to have functioned as a text in the university curriculum, and his *Opus quadripartitum numerorum*, dedicated to Philippe de Vitry, summarized the state of arithmetical knowledge. The *Notitia artis musice* (formerly known as *Ars nova musice*), remains his most significant theoretical treatise. Written ca. 1320, this work offers a clear, rational approach to the question of duple and triple division of rhythmic values and extended the application of duple and triple divisions to every level of rhythmic organization—*maximodus, modus, tempus*, and *prolatio*. Shortly after Jehan des Murs's work, Philippe de Vitry codified imperfect (duple) mensuration, established the minim as the divisor of the semibreve, and even opened the possibility of dividing the minim into semiminims. The practical clarity of Philippe's thought is most readily seen in his *quatre prolacions*, the four signs that became universally recognized as the fundamental time signatures. The rational, quantitative organization of time in the art of music offered by Jehan des Murs and Philippe de Vitry sets forth the basic principles of rhythmic notation and practice that persisted in western music until the 20th century.

The political instability of the 14th century in France makes it difficult to trace clear developments in musical thought following the first flowering of the Ars Nova. Johannes Ciconia's theoretical works, while written in Padua around the turn of the 15th century, nevertheless reflect French musical thought. Ciconia's broad background in the mathematical disciplines is discerned from his *De arithmetica institutione*, a purely mathematical work cited in his *Nova musica* but since lost. Probably influenced by the ancient theoretical tradition of Liège as well as traditional French musical theory, Ciconia's *Nova musica* is an extended treatise treating traditional theoretical topics, including *musica speculativa*, according to ancient authorities as well as both French and Italian theory of his own day. Ciconia's rhythmic theory draws on the theories of both Jehan des Murs and Marchetto of Padua. His *De proportionibus*, while treating the practical problem of rhythmic proportions, extends his treatment of proportions beyond those normally discussed in rhythmic treatises and closes the work with discussions that are clearly speculative.

Two contemporaries of Ciconia, Egidius de Murino and Philippus de Caserta, are significantly less speculative and thus anticipate the empirical and practical trends of the 15th century. Egidius's *De motettis componendis* offers a practical guide to constructing motets, and Philippus's *Tractatus de diversis figuris* concerns itself wholly with note forms developed in Avignon ca. 1370.

The 15th Century. The medieval theoretical tradition has been defined in large part by its relation to the Quadrivium and its association with speculative as well as practical thinking. A clear departure from that tradition is seen in the theoretical texts of Johannes Tinctoris, the most prolific and accomplished theorist of the 15th century. Tinctoris's twelve treatises return repeatedly to practical problems and specifically to practical problems of musical works written after ca. 1450. Tinctoris looks disparagingly at both music and music theory of the centuries immediately preceding his own and thus represents a fundamental shift in the nature of musical thought. His descriptive analyses of music contemporary to himself are brilliant, but these analyses strike out on new paths. The medieval tradition has essentially ended before Tinctoris, and his works represent the first great flowering of Renaissance theory.

Calvin M. Bower

[See also: ANONYMOUS 4; ARS ANTIQUA; ARS NOVA; AURELIAN OF RÉÔME; CICONIA, JOHANNES; EGIDIUS DE MURINO; FRANCO OF COLOGNE; GROCHEIO, JOHANNES DE; HUCBALD OF SAINT-AMAND; JACQUES DE LIÈGE; JEHAN DES MURS; JOHANNES DE

GARLANDIA; *MUSICA ENCHIRIADIS*; MUSICAL
NOTATION (NEUMATIC); MUSICAL NOTATION
(12TH–15TH CENTURIES); ORGANUM; PHILIPPE DE
VITRY; PHILIPPUS DE CASERTA; RHYTHMIC MODE;
TINCTORIS, JOHANNES]

Barbera, André, ed. *Music Theory and Its Sources: Antiquity and
    the Middle Ages.* Notre Dame: University of Notre Dame
    Press, 1990.
Bernhard, Michael. "Das musikalische Fachschrifttum im
    lateinischen Mittelalter." In *Geschichte der Musiktheorie.*
    Darmstadt: Wissenschaftliche Buchgesellschaft, 1990, Vol.
    3: *Rezeption des antiken Fachs im Mittelalter*, ed. Frieder
    Zaminer, pp. 37–103.
Bower, Calvin M. "The Role of Boethius' *De Institutione Musica*
    in the Speculative Tradition of Western Musical Thought."
    In *Boethius and the Liberal Arts: A Collection of Essays*, ed.
    Michael Masi. Bern: Lang, 1981, pp. 157–74.
Fellerer, Karl G. "Die Musica in den Artes Liberales." In *Artes
    Liberales: Von der antiken Bildung zur Wissenschaft des
    Mittelalters*, ed. Josef Koch. Leiden: Brill, 1959, pp. 33–49.
Huglo, Michel. *Les tonaires: inventaire, analyse, comparaison.*
    Paris: Société Française de Musicologie, 1971.
Klinkenberg, H.M. "Der Verfall des Quadrivium im frühen
    Mittelalter." In *Artes Liberales: Von der antiken Bildung zur
    Wissenschaft des Mittelalters*, ed. Josef Koch. Leiden: Brill,
    1959, pp. 1–32.
Riethmüller, Albrecht. "Probleme der spekulativen Musiktheorie
    im Mittelalter." In *Geschichte der Musiktheorie.* Darmstadt:
    Wissenschaftliche Buchgesellschaft, 1990, Vol. 3: *Rezeption
    des antiken Fachs im Mittelalter*, ed. Frieder Zaminer, pp.
    163–201.
Sachs, Klaus-Jürgen. "Musikalische Elementarlehre im
    Mittelalter." In *Geschichte der Musiktheorie.* Darmstadt:
    Wissenschaftliche Buchgesellschaft, 1990, Vol. 3: *Rezeption
    des antiken Fachs im Mittelalter*, ed. Frieder Zaminer, pp.
    105–61.
Smits van Waesberghe, Joseph. "La place exceptionelle de l'*Ars
    musica* dans le développement des sciences au siècle des
    Carolingiens." *Revue grégorienne* 31 (1952): 81–104.
———. *Musikerziehung: Lehre und Theorie der Musik im
    Mittelalter.* Leipzig: VEB Deutscher Verlag für Musik, 1969.

MUSICA ENCHIRIADIS. An anonymous treatise written
in northern France in the second half of the 9th century,
Musica enchiriadis was one of the most widely read and
influential treatises before the *Dialogus in musica* (Pseudo-
Odo) and Guido's *Micrologus*. The work is preserved in
over forty manuscripts. Two further treatises, *Scolica
enchiriadis* and *Commemoratio brevis de psalmis et tonis
modulandis*, are so closely associated with *Musica enchiriadis* in their theory and in the manuscript tradition that
they should be considered essentially one with it. While
several names have been associated with the text in various
branches of the manuscript tradition, none can be conclusively identified as the author of any of these treatises.

A tonal system built around disjunct tetrachords with
semitone in the central position (T-S-T) lies at the core of
the musical theory of *Musica enchiriadis*. The system thus
repeated itself at the interval of a fifth rather than the octave of the traditional, Boethian system handed down from
Greek antiquity. The terminology of the system relates
directly to musical practice in both the names of notes
(protus, deuterus, tritus, and tetrardus) and the names of
the tetrachords (graves, finales, superiores, excellentes). A
primitive musical notation, *dasia* notation, using transformations of the Greek *prosodia daseia* sign was used in
musical examples within these theoretical texts. Although
the notation never seems to have been used extensively in
practical sources, *dasia* notation represents one of the earliest forms of interval-specific notation.

Musica enchiriadis and its related texts provide some
of the earliest and most extensive witnesses of polyphonic
singing in the West, and the text offers clear theoretical
foundations for voice leading in simple (two-voice) and
compound (three- and four-voice) organum.

During the 10th and 11th centuries, with the renewed
interest in Boethius and a mathematically based tonal system repeating at the octave, the influence of *Musica enchiriadis* waned. Yet the broad influence of the treatise may
be seen in the negative comments of such theorists as Herman the Lame and in the parallels between *Musica
enchiriadis* and Guido's *Micrologus*.

Calvin M. Bower

[**See also:** MUSIC THEORY; ORGANUM]

Schmid, Hans, ed. *Musica et scolica enchiriadis una cum aliquibus
    tractatulis adiunctis.* Munich: Verlag der Bayerischen
    Akademie der Wissenschaften, 1981.
Phillips, Nancy. *"Musica" and "Scolica Enchiriadis": The Liter-
    ary, Theoretical, and Musical Sources.* 2 vols. Diss. New
    York University, 1984.

MUSICAL INSTRUMENTS. Although today we are accustomed to think of musical instruments mainly in terms
of concert or dance music, they played far more varied and
important roles in earlier centuries. Instruments served
the nobility as the very symbol of their authority; they
were essential to the military; they were a frequent companion of the tellers of tales and legends; and they served
their traditional recreational purposes as accompaniment
for song and dance. Literary references like the following
suggest that a sonic kaleidoscope enlivened French villages, courts, and countryside throughout the Middle Ages:

> The joglars began their tale, one took his instru-
> ment and played and the other sang with his
> mouth. . . . Whoever knew new fiddle tunes, or
> *cansos, descorts*, or *lais*, as best he could gave it a
> try. . . . One played harp, another a fiddle; one a
> flute, the other a whistle; one played a giga, another
> the rote; one said the words and another the notes;
> one [played] a pipe, another a panpipe; one the
> bagpipe, the other a shawm; one the mandora, and
> the other struck the psaltery with one string. . . . Two
> hundred joglars, good fiddlers, got in tune with each
> other, two by two they sat scattered about on the

benches, and fiddled the dance, not missing a note . . . [*Flamenca*, mid-13th c.].

When I see unfurled among the orchards banners of yellow, violet, and blue, the neighing of the horses soothes me, and the songs the minstrels sing as they go fiddling from tent to tent, and the trumpets and horns and clarions clear; then I want to compose a *sirventes* for Count Richard to hear [Bertran de Born (1140–1215)].

Few musical instruments survive from the period. Our knowledge of them comes from written and pictorial records, and we can only guess at what sounds they made. Furthermore, their shapes and presumably their sounds changed over the centuries, as they strove to fill the needs of the ever-changing society, and so we can speak only generally of medieval musical instruments. They exhibited a wide variety, and from medieval iconography we also know that, though they can be categorized by type and name, there was no standardization of size, shape, or design. Though no instruments could be considered exclusively "French"—most appear to have been adopted by all of the European countries—some instruments do appear in French sources more frequently than others, as the quotations here, drawn exclusively from French sources, will demonstrate.

Medieval Europe inherited the comparatively simple musical instruments developed during Greco-Roman times: trumpets for warfare and heraldry, plucked harps and lyres to accompany song, and a small pastoral flute. During the Carolingian era in secular centers all over Europe, new instruments were developed as part of feudal society and the beginnings of the courtly traditions celebrated in troubadour and trouvère lyrics. The introduction of many new instruments resulted from the Crusades, which brought Europeans in contact with Arabic and Byzantine musical cultures. The variety of medieval instruments can be seen in Machaut's *Remede de Fortune* (ca. 1340), which by no means includes all of the instruments known to have been popular at the time:

And after the meal you should have seen
The musicians arrive,
All combed and comfortably attired.
They played various harmonies.
For there all in a circle I saw
Violle, rubelle, guiterne,
Leü, morache, micanon,
Cytolle, et le psalterion,
Harpe, tabour, trompes, nacaires,
Orgues, cornes, plus de dis paires,
Cornemuses, flajos, chevretes,
Douceinnes, simbales, clocettes,
Tymbre, la fleüste brehaingne,
Et le grant cornet d'Alemaingne,
Flajos de Scens, fistule, pipe,
Muse d'Aussay, trompe petite,
Buissines, eles, monocorde
Ou il n'a c'une seule corde,

Et muse de blef tout ensemble.
And it certainly seemed to me
That such a melodious sound
Had never been perceived or heard. . . .
And whatever could be played
With finger, pick, or bow [I heard]
In perfect harmony there in the little park
[ll. 3959–88].

Machaut paints a vivid picture of all the instruments playing together, but such an event is unlikely. It is certain that all of the instruments he lists were in use, but they would not have performed simultaneously; the order in which they are listed in the poem has more to do with the poetic needs of line scansion and colorful image than implications of musical ensemble. The poet has mixed together kinds of sounds indiscriminately, but in reality the ensembles in which they played were rigidly set according to types.

The classification of musical instruments in the Middle Ages was different from that of today. Rather than thought of in terms of sound mechanism and material type, such as bowed strings, brass, etc., during the late-medieval period they were divided into two discrete groups according to volume: *haut* and *bas*. Those instruments with loud or shrill sound, *haut*, were considered separate from those whose sound was soft, *bas*, and it was in these groups that they were played. Various combinations were possible within each group, but at no point would the instruments of one group perform in the company of the other. In general, the loud instruments were those used out-of-doors, with the military, or for festive occasions where loud sounds added to the excitement, such as weddings, tournaments, or large feasts. In this group were the trumpets, drums, bagpipes, and a reed instrument known as a shawm. The soft instruments were those that would generally accompany songs and included the voice itself.

Machaut names three percussion instruments as part of the loud ensemble: *tabour*, a large field drum; *nacaires*, a pair of small kettledrums that usually hung from the waist of the drummer; and *simbales*, cymbals. Those were usually found in the company of various sizes of trumpets: some described only as large and small, and others with special names, such as the *buissine*, a large, straight trumpet whose sound is usually described as "bright," "noisy," or "shrill." Trumpets were used in the military, to sound signals and rally the troops throughout a battle; they also added to the color and excitement of festivals and tournaments and lent pomp to civil and religious processions. Trumpets often signaled the changing of courses during large festive banquets, and they are occasionally recorded as having played during Mass at the elevation. But their most frequent duty was as a symbol of nobility, a tradition common to all of Europe, in which pairs of trumpets with banners preceded noblemen through the streets as they went about their official duties, and it was the presence of the trumpets that clearly marked the importance of the noble they accompanied.

To the loud ensemble of percussion and brass instruments were added two woodwinds: the shawm, or *chalumeau*, a loud predecessor of the modern oboe, and the *cornemuse,* a bagpipe. Both instruments came in several sizes. From the time of their introduction to Europe from the East in the 12th century, shawms in the alto and tenor ranges were popular, and in the late 14th century a bass instrument known as the bombard (probably because it resembled a cannon) was added. A great variety of bagpipes is depicted in the iconography: with one or two chanters (melody pipes) in various sizes, with one or two drone pipes, and with no drones at all. Shawms and bagpipes are also occasionally found along with trumpets and drums in military scenes, tournaments, and jousts. But whereas the trumpet had a severely limited range of notes, both shawm and bagpipe could play most of the chromatic scale and therefore were capable of melodies as well as fanfares and heraldic sounds. Two or three shawms, sometimes with bagpipe, are often present in scenes with dancing, and during the 15th century a fairly standard dance ensemble was made up of two or three shawms with a slide trumpet (the slide trumpet was replaced by a trombone at the end of the century).

Of the soft instruments, the *vielle,* or fiddle, is most often mentioned in the performance of many kinds of music. The medieval fiddle was a bowed instrument with four or five strings and is found in the iconography in sizes from soprano to bass. Many of the paintings and sculptures show that it had a flat bridge, suggesting that it could only sound several strings together, but there are also representations of a rounded bridge, which means that some fiddles could have performed single-line melodic passages. The fiddle and another bowed instrument, the smaller three-string rebec, or *rubelle,* were adopted from the East sometime in the late 11th century. Prior to that in Europe, all string instruments were plucked, and of these there was a great variety of sizes, shapes, and numbers of strings.

Principal among the plucked strings were the harp, gittern (or *guiterne*), and lute (*leü*). The harp could have from ten to twenty-five strings; the gittern could have from three to five, either in pairs or single strings; and the lute usually had five pairs. The *cytolle,* a small instrument resembling the gittern, had strings of metal, whereas the lute, the gittern, and usually the harp were strung with gut, which produces a softer sound. Gittern, *cytolle,* and lute were plucked with a plectrum, as was harp on occasion. Another member of this group was the psaltery (*psalterion*), having from ten to twenty metal strings stretched across a wooden sound box. The psaltery came in a number of shapes, it was either plucked with a plectrum or hammered. All of these instruments were seen to be the proper media of the jongleurs and were associated with accompaniment of song and dance.

Less frequently mentioned, but also among the *bas* group associated with the minstrels is the hurdy-gurdy, a string instrument sounded by a turning wheel. A two-player version of this instrument, the organistrum, is often depicted in the hands of church elders on Gothic cathedral tympana, but it is not clear what function it played, if any, in church music. The organ was also a member of the soft group. This term referred not only to the larger church instrument but also to the small portable organ held in the lap, which served as a melody instrument for minstrels.

The soft winds included flutes, flageolets, recorders, and the buzzy reed instruments *cromorne* and *douceinne.* The bagpipe was also sometimes included in the list of *bas* instruments, indicating that one variety of that instrument was suitably modulated in volume to play along with the other members of the soft group. It is probably this type of bagpipe referred to by the 12th-century troubadour Peire d'Alvernhe: "This verse was made to the bagpipe at Puivert with everyone playing and laughing."

Not only were the *haut* and *bas* instruments kept apart for performance purposes, but by and large they were assigned to different classes of performers. Players of trumpets, drums, and shawms were a special group of servant musicians who specialized in those instruments and played only in those groups. They were usually employed by the civic government and assigned specific tasks.

The soft instruments, however, were played by nobles and peasants, masters and servants. Though it is difficult to ascertain if certain instruments were favored by certain social classes, iconographic and literary evidence indicates that until the end of the 14th century most of the soft instruments were played by all classes. It is entirely possible that the music played on them was somewhat different, but we have no information about the repertory of the lower classes. Aristocrats did play these instruments, and their servant entertainers, the minstrels and jongleurs, were also expected to be proficient at several of them.

Beginning in the early 15th century, musical instruments and their playing techniques experienced an important change. As polyphonic music grew in popularity among the noble classes, courtly music required instruments that could play single lines (that is, without drones) and had fairly large ranges that included chromatics. Instruments like bagpipe, hurdy-gurdy, and the flat-bridged fiddle that played drones, and those with a limited range incapable of the new repertory, were less favored by the upper classes and ultimately became associated with the common folk. Some instruments adapted to the new requirements. For example, playing technique for the lute changed from plectrum to fingers in order to facilitate the execution of multiple lines and chords. Other instruments that could easily accommodate this new repertory and especially those that could play multiple lines, such as organ and clavichord, grew in popularity, and new instruments with larger ranges, such as the violin and viol, were developed.

Timothy J. McGee

[See also: *ALTA CAPELLA;* BELLS; DANCE; ICONOGRAPHY OF MUSIC; JONGLEUR; MUSICAL PERFORMANCE PRACTICE]

Aubrey, Elizabeth. "References to Music in Old Occitan Literature." *Acta musicologica* 61 (1989): 110–49.

Bowles, Edmund. "*Haut* and *Bas*: The Grouping of Musical Instruments in the Middle Ages." *Musica disciplina* 7 (1954): 115–40.

Brown, Howard M. "Instruments." In *Performance Practice: Music Before 1600,* ed. Howard M. Brown and Stanley Sadie. New York: Norton, 1989, pp. 15–36.

McGee, Timothy J. *Medieval and Renaissance Music: A Performer's Guide.* Toronto: University of Toronto Press, 1985.

Montagu, Jeremy. *The World of Medieval and Renaissance Musical Instruments.* Newton Abbot: David and Charles, 1976.

Page, Christopher. *The Owl and the Nightingale: Musical Life and Ideas in France 1100–1300.* London: Dent, 1989.

———. *Voices and Instruments of the Middle Ages.* London: Dent, 1987.

Remnant, Mary. *Musical Instruments of the West.* London: Batsford, 1978.

MUSICAL NOTATION (NEUMATIC). The notation used for Gregorian chant and early polyphonic music beginning in the 8th or 9th centuries. The term is derived from the Latin word *neuma*, which referred at first to a short melodic unit but came to be applied to the notational symbols expressing it. In its earlier stages, neumatic notation did not indicate exact pitches but only the number of notes and their relative upward and downward movement. A single note of higher pitch, for example, the *virga*, might take the shape of a slanted stroke like a somewhat lengthened acute accent; a lower single note, the *punctum*, might be written as a dot. A group of two ascending notes, the *podatus* (or *pes*), could be written as a longer stroke than the *virga*, commencing with a hook or a shorter horizontal stroke (the style of neumes varied considerably from region to region, while maintaining a basic familial relationship). Neumes of from one to three notes were common and those of four or more relatively rare. They were written over the text of the chant—later and by a different hand, one concludes, from frequently encountered spacing discrepancies. If deficient because of its vagueness about pitch, neumatic notation served as an effective memory aid to those who were accustomed to sing the chants by heart and was capable of recording subtle nuances of performance. For example, liquescent neumes, variant shapes of the basic neumes, signaled a less straightforward mode of vocalization (not clearly understood today), made necessary by textual peculiarities like double consonants. There were also the "Romanian letters," small letters written in close proximity to the neumes, which could indicate rhythmic nuances: *t*, for example, standing for *trahere* ("to draw out"), and *c*, for *celeriter* ("quickly"), suggesting a slower or faster singing of the affected notes.

Theoretical writers of the 11th century lamented the loss of these subtleties as neumatic notation sacrificed them in its quest to indicate pitch more precisely. The exact notation of pitch was no secret to their predecessors; Carolingian theorists had employed both graphic and alphabetic systems that clearly represented the pitches of short musical examples. These systems were cumbersome, however, compared with the simple addition of neumes to a texted page. Early in the 11th century, in any case, the neumatic notation of Aquitanian manuscripts indicated exact pitches by an expedient known as heightening or diastemmatry. These Aquitanian neumes, written for the most part as separate dots or short strokes for each note and lacking the cursive forms of other neumatic styles, were placed on the page as if on an imaginary graph; while a single drypoint line was inscribed to serve as a basic reference point. Not much later, inked lines began to be drawn in the neumations of several regions; generally, *f* was indicated by a red line and the *c* above it by a yellow line. It was only a matter of time until two more lines were added to create the standard medieval four-line staff. The staff was not particularly hospitable to the graphic eccentricities of the various neumatic styles, and by the 13th century they had coalesced into just two types. The square notation found in modern chant books developed from the French neumes of north-central France. This notation came to be employed throughout France, England, Italy, and Spain; a distinctly different style was common in Germany and to the east, the *Hufnagelschrift*, so called from its *virga*, which has the appearance of a horseshoe nail.

There are three major points of dispute about the early history of neumatic notation. The first involves the date of the first chant books to employ it throughout. It had long been assumed that these were the earliest such books preserved, two graduals and a cantatorium dating from ca. 900. Recently, however, Kenneth Levy has argued that a fully notated gradual must have existed in the time of Charlemagne (d. 814). The second debate has to do with origins. The dominant notion for several decades was that the neumes developed from the classical accents (acute, grave, circumflex, etc.); competing theories see their source elsewhere, for example, in the punctuation of Carolingian manuscripts or in cheironomy, the gestures employed by a cantor directing a group of singers. The third area of controversy is that of the genealogical relationships of the regional neumatic styles. The various French types play a key role in this because of the obvious antiquity of Paleo-Frankish neumes from Picardy and Hainaut and their purported relationship to the later Breton and Lorraine neumes. Kenneth Levy, again, has recently advanced original views on both the origins and genealogy of neumes.

What remains uncontroversial about neumatic notation is its immense significance as the source from which the notation of all western music derives. It can fairly be said to be one of the principal "inventions" of the European Middle Ages.

James McKinnon

	punctum/ tractulus	virga	pes	clivis	torculus	porrectus	scandicus / climacus	
square form								
Palaeo-Frankish (hypothetical archetype)								
St Gall								
French								
Palaeo-Frankish (surviving form)								
Breton								
Lorraine								
Aquitanian								
Catalan								
Beneventan								
North-central Italian								

[See also: GREGORIAN CHANT; MUSIC THEORY; *MUSICA ENCHIRIADIS;* MUSICAL NOTATION (12TH–15TH CENTURIES)]

Apel, Willi. *Gregorian Chant.* Bloomington: Indiana University Press, 1958.
Corbin, Solange. *Die Neumen.* Cologne: Volk, 1977.
Levy, Kenneth. "Charlemagne's Archetype of Gregorian Chant." *Journal of the American Musicological Society* 40 (1987): 1–30.
———. "On the Origin of Neumes." *Early Music History* 7 (1987): 59–90.

MUSICAL NOTATION (12TH–15TH CENTURIES).

During the late 12th and early 13th centuries, square notation became the predominant type of notation in most of western Europe for plainchant (for which it is still used today), secular monophony, and both liturgical and secular polyphony. There are three basic note shapes. The *virga* has a broad, square notehead, and the descending stem is a slender vertical downward extension. The *punctum* differs only by not having a stem. A diamond-shaped "rhomboid," created by setting the nib at a ninety-degree angle, was used to inscribe a descending series of notes, called *currentes* or *coniuncturae.*

Single Notes (*figurae simplices*) of Square Notation.

By the mid-13th century, these three basic notational shapes for single notes acquired temporal significance, the *virga* becoming a long, the *punctum* a breve, and the rhomboid a semibreve, the ancestor of the modern whole note.

Two or more notes linked in the same figure drawn without lifting of the pen comprise a "ligature," a feature of musical notation retained through the 16th century. Ligatures were for melismatic music, that is, melodic lines without text (*sine littera* notation). If a text were given to such a melodic line, the ligatures would be broken up to allow the association of pitches with syllables (*cum littera* notation).

The interpretation of a piece of music preserved in square notation may vary according to its genre, the date at which it was written, and its geographical or cultural point of origin. Modal notation, which originated probably within the Notre-Dame School, organized ligatures into configurations that graphically represented patterns known as "rhythmic modes," a continuous stream of long and short notes. In order to notate more complex rhythms in modal notation, extant sources indicate numerous changes and refinements, some that died out and some that gradually led to a more reliable style of notation, called Franconian after its primary spokesperson, Franco of Cologne. Franco's description of this new notation, the *Ars cantus mensurabilis* (ca. 1280), had such authority and wide circulation that it contributed greatly to a notational standardization by which any piece of rhythmic music could be read, not only in the Parisian circles in which these notations and genres arose but throughout western Europe.

Franconian notation, the earliest true mensural notation, established distinctive graphic elements denoting specific rhythmic values that could either stand in place of a unit within a mode or stand alone and always, unequivocally indicate the same rhythm, both in texted and in melismatic music. Franconian rhythm depends upon equal pulses, each the value of the perfect long, which then could be subdivided in a variety of ways. In succeeding composition, notation, and theory, ever smaller note values were grouped in different ways and in different numbers, always subdividing the equal pulses of the larger note values. Petronian notation (after Pierre de la Croix), which seems to have succeeded Franconian quickly, primarily describes the division of the breve into as many as seven semibreves. To give an idea of the extent to which this process affected western music, by the 16th century it was the semibreve, or *tactus,* that had become the measure of this equal pulse, which was divisible by minims, semiminims, and fusae, known today as half, quarter, and eighth notes.

In Petronian notation, the rhythmic values of the fast semibreves, all equivalent in appearance, were resolved according to certain rules. In France, further revision of Franco's system in the early 14th century resolved the ambiguities of Petronian notation and at the same time allowed for an enormous flexibility in the notation of rhythm. This Ars Nova notation is usually associated with Philippe de Vitry and Jehan des Murs. By means of an additional symbol, the minim (an ascending stem was added to the rhomboid shape of the semibreve), short note values could be indicated precisely and unambiguously. With the admission of duple meter and the rational organization of the entire notational system, the exploitation of the new rhythmic possibilities became a preoccupation of 14th-century composers. The "classic" state of Ars Nova notation, represented in the musical works of Philippe de Vitry and Guillaume de Machaut and in the theoretical treatises of Jehan des Murs, began to expand in the course of the 1370s. By the late 14th century, symbols and note shapes multiplied, allowing the notation of rhythmic complexities to a point not again approached until the 20th century.

In the 15th century, the plethora of notational symbols was reduced, but often, especially in the sacred and ceremonial compositions of such composers as Dufay, Ockeghem, or Busnoys, proportional mensural complexities added a level of number symbolism and signification to the music that only recently has begun to be studied. In addition, the increased utilization of paper instead of parchment led to the creation of hollow note shapes—"white" notation—less apt to penetrate the more fragile surface of the page. The result is closer to the appearance of modern musical notation than the earlier, "black" notation.

Sandra Pinegar/Lawrence Earp

[See also: ANONYMOUS 4; ARS NOVA; ARS SUBTILIOR; FRANCO OF COLOGNE; JEHAN DES MURS; MUSIC THEORY; MUSICAL NOTATION (NEUMATIC); PHILIPPE DE VITRY; PIERRE DE LA CROIX; RHYTHMIC MODE]

Apel, Willi. *The Notation of Polyphonic Music 900–1600.* 5th ed. Cambridge: Mediaeval Academy of America, 1953.

Berger, Anna Maria Busse. *Mensuration and Proportion Signs: Origins and Evolution.* Oxford: Clarendon, 1993.

Gallo, F. Alberto. "Figura and Regula: Notation and Theory in the Tradition of Musica mensurabilis." In *Studien zur Tradition in der Musik: Kurt von Fischer zum 60. Geburtstag,* ed. Hans Heinrich Eggebrecht and Max Lütolf. Munich: Musikverlag Katzbichler, 1973, pp. 43–48.

MUSICAL PERFORMANCE PRACTICE. There is only sketchy evidence of the way in which music was performed during the Middle Ages. It was not the custom to provide directions for performance on the music itself, as in the present century, perhaps because the practices themselves were so commonplace that no one felt the need to write them down. A great deal of latitude was given to the performer concerning aspects of performance, such as tempo, amount and placement of ornamentation, use of instrumental accompaniment, and in some repertories even the actual rhythm of the melody. Some information can be gained from theoretical treatises, literature, and iconography, but in many areas we have an unclear impression of the practices.

The vast majority of sacred music during the Middle Ages was monophonic (single-line) chant, which was entirely sung either by a soloist or by the choir in unison, or by a combination of the two, depending on the service and the item. In the 9th century, a practice arose of providing sacred music with additional lines, hence polyphony. This was performed in a variety of ways, depending upon the type of polyphony and the occasion. In some works, a soloist, or perhaps a small group of soloists, sang a highly ornate top line, accompanied by from one to three others who sang a slower-moving lower line. Other polyphonic compositions, in which the parts were relatively equal, were performed by soloists on each line. On festive occasions, polyphonic sections in either of the above styles were inserted into choral performances of otherwise monophonic chant, taking the place of those lines assigned to the soloist.

By the 13th century, this had given rise to special two-, three-, and four-part settings of liturgical items, and the composition of independent sacred compositions called motets, for performance by soloists during services on special occasions. Most of the sacred polyphony remained the domain of soloists until early in the 15th century, when it was sung by small choruses (six to twelve singers) that developed in some of the larger French churches, such as the cathedral at Cambrai and Notre-Dame in Paris.

Yet another practice that appears to have been carried into the Middle Ages from antiquity was *alternatim* performance: an alternation between two choirs for performance of repetitive items, such as sequences and psalms. This

A *joglaresse* dancing and playing bells, early 12th century. BN lat. 1118. *Courtesy of the Bibliothèque Nationale, Paris.*

performance concept was quickly adapted to include polyphony; at times, it took the all-vocal form of an alternation between polyphonic and monophonic sections, but it could also include sections performed on organ, alternating with either monophonic or polyphonic vocal sections. At such times, the organist might perform rapid treble variations built on the chant.

Scattered references are found to the use of instruments, usually trumpets, in the liturgy, but these are always on special occasions and usually involve fanfares at the elevation. The more common use of instruments in the church was in processions before and after services. There is reason to believe that until the mid-16th century the organ was the only instrument regularly accepted in the celebration of the liturgy.

The largest early secular repertory known is that of the troubadours and trouvères from the 12th and 13th centuries. The rhythmic interpretation of this repertory, like that of early chant, remains controversial, but it is generally accepted that they were solo songs, sometimes sung to improvised accompaniment on instruments like fiddle, harp, or lute. When accompanying solo songs, the instrumentalist, sometimes the same person as the singer, would provide a prelude and postlude, add interludes between verses, and sometimes play decorated versions of the melody as an accompaniment to the song to enhance the performance.

French secular polyphony—motets and chansons—dates from the late 13th century. Recent studies have presented evidence that in general this repertory was also the domain of singers performing one to a part. In some of this repertory, each part has text—sometimes the same poem and sometimes separate poems—but in a substantial part of the repertory vocal performance would have required one or more lower voices to vocalize without text while the poem was sung in the highest voice(s).

Instrumental performance of the secular repertory was also a possibility, either by an ensemble made up solely of instruments, or by instruments in combination with voices, either doubling the voices or substituting for them. Iconographic and documentary evidence indicates that the instruments most frequently associated with courtly life were lute, harp, and fiddle, but Guillaume de Machaut (d. 1377) states in his *Voir dit* that one of his songs may be performed on organ, bagpipes, or other instruments. In two other works, he lists dozens of instruments and implies that minstrels properly entertained on all of them. It is not clear whether they were all equally suitable for polyphonic music, but it does suggest that there were few distinctions about appropriate and inappropriate instruments in courtly secular music.

Except for a small number of dance pieces (*estampies*), no known repertory was written specifically for instrumental performance. Until the end of the 15th century, the instrumental repertory associated with courtly life consisted of the vocal music, improvised performance mostly of dance music, and, beginning in the early 15th century, a combination of written and improvised performance of music for the *basse danse*, in which one or two performers improvised while one instrumentalist played a composed tenor line.

Timothy J. McGee

[See also: *ALTA CAPELLA;* DANCE; MOTET (13TH CENTURY); MUSICAL INSTRUMENTS; RHYTHM]

Brown, Howard M. "Instruments and Voices in the Fifteenth-Century Chanson." In *Current Thought in Musicology*, ed. John W. Grubbs. Austin: University of Texas Press, 1976, pp. 89–137.

———, and Stanley Sadie, eds. *Performance Practice: Music Before 1600.* New York: Norton, 1989.

McGee, Timothy J. *Medieval and Renaissance Music: A Performer's Guide.* Toronto: University of Toronto Press, 1985.

Page Christopher. *The Owl and the Nightingale: Musical Life and Ideas in France 1100–1300.* London: Dent, 1989.

———. *Voices and Instruments of the Middle Ages.* London: Dent, 1987.

MYSTERY PLAYS. During the 15th and 16th centuries, the French term *mystère* was frequently applied to dramatic representations of sacred history and lives of the saints. The word derives from the Latin *ministerium* and

was a synonym of *métier*, meaning craft or trade. It was also used to designate a liturgical office or service. In a dramatic context, it had the meaning of representation or act and was thus analogous to the Italian *sacra rappresentazione* and the Spanish *auto sacramental*. One of the earliest occurrences of the term in this sense is found in the letters patent by which Charles VI established the Confrérie de la Passion (1402) and granted its members the right to play *misterres, tant de saincts comme de sainctes, et mesmement [le] misterre le la Passion*. Over the next two centuries, the term *mystère* appears in the titles of a number of biblical and saint plays, such as Jean Michel's *Mystère de la Passion* and Jean Molinet's *Mystère de saint Quentin*. The term was also applied to the mimed scenes that were staged along the procession routes of noble entries. Gradually, the term was generalized and applied to other types of serious drama. When in 1548 the Parlement de Paris banned the playing of *mystères sacrés* in that city, the staging of *mystères profanes* was permitted to continue.

Alan E. Knight

[See also: MIRACLE PLAYS; PASSION PLAYS; THEATER]

Petit de Julleville, Louis. *Les mystères.* 2 vols. Paris: Hachette, 1880, Vol. 1, pp. 187ff., 412ff.

Runnalls, Graham A. "Form and Meaning in Medieval Religious Drama." In *Littera et Sensus: Essays on Form and Meaning in Medieval French Literature Presented to John Fox*, ed. D.A. Trotter. Exeter: University of Exeter Press, 1989, pp. 95–107.

MYSTICISM. Word now most often used for what would have been called "contemplation" (*contemplatio*) in the medieval Latin tradition. In its narrowest meaning, mysticism involves a personal experience of the unmediated presence of Absolute Reality or, to use the Christian designation, God. Such an experience is described in the literature of religious traditions throughout the world.

Much modern writing on mysticism has focused on "mystical experience," the direct, personal experience of the immediate presence of the divine, which often results in a mental state in which the person is unaware of the ordinary world and aware of only the divine presence ("ecstatic mysticism"). Mystics often describe a process, called the "mystical way," with a variety of stages leading up to the mystical experience. These descriptions generally concern disciplines for the body and the mind to prepare an individual for "mystical experience," as well as with visions, voices, and other extraordinary phenomena that occur as persons follow discipline. Some interpreters, and some mystics, contend that visions and other extraordinary phenomena have little or nothing to do with "mysticism" and can be misleading. If, however, "mystic experience" includes a spectrum of experiences that relate variously to the transcendent divine, present in unmediated mystical experience in one mode but present in a different, mediated form in voices and visions, then "mysticism" must embrace the whole spectrum of experiences recorded by those who have good claim to be counted among the mystics.

Though the Christian tradition draws upon scriptural passages to support interpretations of the mystic way and mystic experience, Jesus is not presented as the archetypal mystic; rather, as one Person of the divine Trinity, he becomes the object of the mystic's experience.

Fundamental lines of Christian mysticism were laid down in late antiquity. Five mystics and theologians had more influence than others on the medieval tradition in France: Origen of Alexandria, Pseudo-Dionysius the Areopagite, John Cassian, Augustine of Hippo, and Gregory the Great. Origen set an important pattern for later biblical exegetes and mystics by taking the relationship of the Bride and Bridegroom in the Song of Songs as a "drama" symbolic of the union between Christ and his church or God and the soul. While Origen paid more attention to this imagery as symbolic of ecclesiastical ideas, he did pursue the symbolism of the mystical experience through the nuptial and erotic imagery of the Song. In this, he was followed by such mystics as Gregory of Nyssa in the Greek East and, much later, Bernard of Clairvaux in the Latin West.

Pseudo-Dionysius the Areopagite claimed to be the 1st-century convert of Paul at Athens but seems to have been a 6th-century Syrian monk. His writings combined Neoplatonism and biblical imagery, stressing on the one hand the material world as a set of partial symbols of the divine realm and on the other an "ascension" from immersion in the material world to a purely spiritual and immaterial apprehension of the divine presence in the "divine darkness" of "unknowing."

Cassian was a monastic author whose *Conferences*, a summary of the teachings of Egyptian desert mystics-ascetics, exerted a decisive influence on Christian spirituality.

Augustine, a great theologian and bishop of the late 4th and early 5th centuries, also combined Neoplatonic philosophy and biblical thought to produce an understanding of the spiritual path as an ascent from the material world, through the world of mind, to a momentary glimpse of Absolute Reality, understood as pure light, beheld in a trembling glance. Augustine's *Confessions* were an enduring personal account of a spiritual journey from Manichaeanism, through Neoplatonism, to Christianity.

Gregory the Great, more than any other author, sums up the Christian spirituality of late antiquity and transmits it to the medieval period. His commentary on the book of Job, *Moralia in Iob*, has sections that are miniature treatises on the mystic way. Gregory's characterization of the contrast between the "active life" of engagement in the world and the "contemplative" life of withdrawal for asceticism and prayer was widely influential, as were his description of the mystical experience as a glimpse of the "unbounded light of divinity" and his conception of the way in which the soul makes a "ladder" of itself to "ascend" from experience of the external world of sense, to the interior world of mind, to the transcendent world of spiritual realities and the "unbounded light" that is God.

As late antiquity gave way to the Middle Ages, the spiritual traditions sketched above were preserved, but little applied or developed. The spirituality of the 6th century to the 11th focused first on missions and expansion, then on the establishment and regularization of the monastic and clerical life. Within monasteries, emphasis was not so much on personal spirituality as on public celebration of the liturgical hours and the Mass. One sees much evidence of "spiritual reading" and reflection on Scripture and earlier authors but little evidence of ecstatic mysticism. However, as the 11th century progressed and reform movements began to gain ground, the spiritual life and the mystical quest began to claim more and more interest.

One of the first "schools" of mysticism to flourish in medieval France was that of the regular canons of the abbey of Saint-Victor at Paris. Two 12th-century canons were among the leading mystical writers of the whole medieval period: Hugh of Saint-Victor and Richard of Saint-Victor. Hugh was one of the first persons in the West to write treatises that offered systematic instruction in the mystic way. According to Hugh's theology, the first humans had been immediately aware of the divine presence and had also been able to perceive the outward, material world as a symbolic manifestation of God's power, wisdom, and goodness. With the Fall, humans lost the inward sense of divine presence and the ability to discern fully the cosmos as symbolic of the divine. In Hugh's powerful image of the "three eyes" with which humans had been created, the Fall produces varying degrees of "blindness": the "eye" of the intellect (which sees God and spiritual things) is totally blinded; the "eye" of reason (which knows the self and those things within the self) is partly blinded; only the "eye of the flesh" functions fully and leads one to a deceptive relationship with the external world of matter. A major aspect of the salvation of human beings is the restoration of the immediate inward awareness of the divine, the "eye" of the intellect. Hugh's treatises on the symbolic meaning of the Ark of Noah and Isaiah's vision of the Lord and the Seraphim (*De arca Noe morali* and *De arca Noe mystica*), and also his treatise *De arrha animae* are complex explorations of the stages by which the soul recovers the immediate awareness of God through discipline of mind and body and the concomitant gift of divine grace. Hugh defines four stages, which correspond to a classic pattern in Christian mysticism: awakening, purification, illumination, union. Each is divided into three degrees, yielding a twelve-stage way. Awakening is divided into stages of fear, sorrow, and love; Purgation, into patience, mercy, and compunction; Illumination, into thinking, meditation, and contemplation; Union, into temperance, prudence, and fortitude. These twelve stages outline advancement in discipline, insight, and experience, culminating in the transformation of the self and experience of God. In *De arrha animae*, Hugh uses the theme of the Bride and Bridegroom from the Song of Songs to develop a long dialogue on the role of love in relation to the world, the self, and the divine, with a focus on the soul's yearning for a unique experience of the divine in intimate relationship, even union. One of the striking aspects of Hugh's spirituality is the use of a visual diagram to present it; his treatises on Noah's Ark describe and use for meditation a drawing that shows in the form of a mandala both the unfolding of the cosmos and history from Christ and the return to union with Christ through the twelve stages of mystical ascent.

Hugh was also crucial in the introduction of the thought of Pseudo-Dionysius the Areopagite into the mystical and theological traditions of the West. His commentary on Pseudo-Dionysius's Greek *Celestial Hierarchy* made that work accessible to his contemporaries and explored such important themes as the role of symbols, the nature of anagogical ascent, and the "divine darkness" in mystical experience (so important in Dionysian thought). Like almost all medieval mystics, Hugh gave attention to the relation of loving and knowing in the mystical quest, concluding that both play central roles but that ultimately it is the "embrace" of love and not the act of knowing that unites the soul with the divine in ecstasy.

Hugh's successor, Richard of Saint-Victor, was interested in the dynamics of development and psychologcal processes. Like Hugh, he depended heavily upon visualizations and personifications to convey his message. In *De arca mystica*, the Ark of the Covenant and its two Cherubim are given a symbolic interpretation that incorporates Richard's understanding of six levels in the epistemological structure of the mystic quest. Contemplation—"beholding" or "apprehending," not analyzing, the object of attention—is possible at all levels of knowing, but contemplating God occurs only in the highest two. Richard offers a complex analysis of the six levels of knowledge (two each for sense, reason, and intellect) including states of mystical ecstasy; he also offers a detailed analysis of the epistemology of prophetic visions; and he presents an analysis of possible ways of entering (or "triggering") the experience of "alienation of mind" or "ecstasy" in which the individual becomes unaware of the external world and the self and is aware only of God and spiritual realities. Richard continued and expanded Hugh's use of Pseudo-Dionysius in his writings.

A second school of 12th-century mysticism was Cistercian, led by Bernard of Clairvaux but developed by other monks, including William of Saint-Thierry and Isaac of Stella in France and Aelred of Rievaulx and John of Ford in England. Just as the Cistercians saw the cloister as a school for the love of God, so their spirituality focused to a great degree on the nature of the mystic's love of God and the reciprocal effect of that love on the individual. Bernard's earliest work, *De gradibus humilitatis et superbiae* reveals the Cistercian revision of Benedictine foundations as Bernard comments on Chapter 7 of Benedict's *Rule*. Cistercian spirituality was shaped in fundamental ways by deep reflection on the bridal imagery of the Song of Songs, transformed for Bernard and others into powerful imagery of the deep union between the self (the soul) and the divine (Christ) in mystical experience. Bernard's eighty-six sermons on the Song of Songs comprise his greatest contribution to the literature of mysticism. William of Saint-Thierry wrote treatises on theological and mystical topics, as well as a commentary on the Song of Songs.

The emergence among the Victorines and Cistercians of intense focus on the nature of the mystic way and experience, and the expression of that way and experience under the symbolism of the marriage bond between two individuals, reflects a new conception of the mystic experience. In the writings of Augustine and Gregory the Great, the mystic experience was primarily a "beholding," usually expressed impersonally in terms of a vision of light. With the 12th century, the mystical experience is conceived in terms of personal and intimate imagery: the relationship between two individuals in the nuptial embrace. Thus, the imagery of love is given full expression in symbolic form in the embrace of the marriage chamber, although the mystics insist that the imagery and experience are purged of all bodily associations and refer to a spiritual union of soul and Christ.

In the 12th century, other movements for monastic and spiritual reform, such as the Carthusians and Premonstratensians, also developed interpretations of the mystic way. A good example is the *Scala claustralum* by the Carthusian Guigo II (d. 1188). In analyzing what he calls "spiritual exercise," Guigo introduces the idea of a ladder that will raise a monk from earth to Heaven. Guigo's ladder has four rungs: reading, meditation, prayer, and contemplation. In this, he owed no small debt to some of the formulations of Hugh of Saint-Victor. Reading, for Guigo, is a careful consideration of Scripture; meditation is a focused search, by reason, for some truth; prayer is primarily petitionary prayer seeking something of God; contemplation is "a certain elevation of the mind above itself, suspended in God, tasting the joys of eternal sweetness." The scheme demonstrates again, in different language, the movement from outer, to inward, to transcendent realities.

With the advent of the mendicant orders in the 13th century came new centers for pursuing ascetic life and contemplative prayer. The Franciscans were influenced by the mystic experiences of their founder, Francis of Assisi, and his devotion to the poor, suffering, crucified Christ. Francis was an extraordinary ecstatic visionary who received, near the end of his life, the stigmata, the presence on his body of the five wounds of Christ, which confirmed for medieval men and women that he was totally conformed to Christ in his life. Franciscan mysticism was given a definitive shape in one of the classics of medieval mystical literature, Bonaventure's *Itinerarium mentis in Deum*. Bonaventure was a Franciscan master lecturing at the University of Paris when he was elected master general of the order in 1257, which was at the time struggling over the true meaning of poverty and other issues. He went for a time of spiritual reflection to Mount Alverna, east of Florence in Italy, where Francis had received the stigmata. While meditating there, Bonaventure realized that the spiritual path of return to God was adumbrated in Francis's vision when he received the stigmata: he had seen the Crucified (Christ) in the form of a six-winged Seraph. Through this image, he understood that the return was accomplished through the humility of the suffering Christ, through burning love of the Crucified, and through six stages of "ascension" from the material world, through the inner world of the mind, to the transcendent world of divine reality. The result of this insight was the *Itinerarium*. Bonaventure here drew upon the six levels of knowing/contemplating as outlined by Richard of Saint-Victor, infusing them with a Franciscan celebration of the divine presence in the world, in the self (through the *imago Dei*), and in the realm of spiritual reality, all considered in light of the significance of the poor, suffering Christ, the emblem of divine self-giving love.

The other major mendicant order, the Dominicans, initially made less of mystical experience, although personal prayer and instruction in ways of praying were both important in the development of a Dominican spirituality. *St. Dominic's Nine Ways of Praying*, accompanied in the manuscript tradition with illustrations showing the nine postures for prayer rooted in the founder's practice, is an example of such instruction. Thomas Aquinas made a theological place for mystical experience in this world and the vision of God (*visio Dei*) in Heaven, but he laid little stress on the former. Just before his death in 1274, he had a profound mystical/visionary experience of Christ, after which he ceased dictating the text of his *Summa theologica* (it was completed by another Dominican) and declared that, next to his vision, all he had written was but straw. However, the real flourishing of mystical experience within the Dominican order occurred in the Rhineland with Meister Eckhart and his disciples Tauler and Suso. Eckhart developed a distinctive mystical way that incorporated ideas of total detachment, emptying the self, and the "birth" of the divine in the soul. Eckhart also evidences a significant development within the Dominican order: the pastoral care of convents of women, both Dominican nuns and others. This involved the friars in the spiritual direction of women who were involved in their own unique kind of spiritual development, often at odds with male patterns of spirituality, especially in the prevalence of visionary experiences, emphasis upon female bodiliness, and a devotional focus on the eucharistic host (as Christ's body). The literature of female spirituality and mysticism receives treatment in another article.

In the late Middle Ages, Jean Gerson (1363–1429) stands out as a figure who combined distinguished leadership as chancellor of the University of Paris, involvement in the ecclesiastical and political aspects of the Great Schism, acute contributions to the development of late-medieval scholastic thought, and a deep sense of the mystical dimension of Christian theology and life. Like his contemporary Nicholas of Cusa, Gerson was drawn to the idea of the coincidence of opposites as a key to understanding and also looked to the mystical writings of Pseudo-Dionysius the Areopagite as significant for guiding one on the way toward an experience of divine presence. Gerson wrote numerous treatises, both technical and "popular," on mysticism and the mystic way. He reached an unusually wide audience, for he wrote and preached in both Latin and French.

Grover A. Zinn

[See also: AQUINAS, THOMAS; BERNARD OF CLAIRVAUX; BONAVENTURE; CISTERCIAN ORDER; DOMINICAN ORDER; FRANCISCAN ORDER; GERSON, JEAN; HUGH OF SAINT-VICTOR; RICHARD OF SAINT-VICTOR; SAINT-VICTOR, ABBEY AND SCHOOL OF; THEOLOGY; WILLIAM OF SAINT-THIERRY; WOMEN, RELIGIOUS EXPERIENCE OF]

Butler, Cuthbert. *Western Mysticism: The Teaching of Augustine, Gregory and Bernard on Contemplation and the Contemplative Life.* 2nd ed. New York: Harper and Row, 1966.

Classics of Western Spirituality, published by Paulist Press, New York, is a series that presents writings of the mystics in new modern translations with introductions. Cistercian Publications, Kalamazoo, Mich., has an extensive series of translations, with introductions, of the writings of Cistercian mystics.

Leclercq, Jean. *The Love of Learning and the Desire for God: A Study of Monastic Culture*, trans. Catharine Misrahi. New York: Fordham University Press, 1961.

McGinn, Bernard, and John Meyendorff, eds. *Christian Spirituality: Origins to the Twelfth Century.* New York: Crossroad, 1985.

Matter, E. Ann. *The Voice of My Beloved: The Song of Songs in Western Medieval Christianity.* Philadelphia: University of Pennsylvania Press, 1990.

Raitt, Jill, ed. *Christian Spirituality: High Middle Ages and Reformation.* New York: Crossroad, 1985.

N

NÁJERA. Battle of Hundred Years' War. Following the ouster of Peter the Cruel from the Castilian throne in 1365 by his French-backed half-brother, Henry of Trastamara, and an army of *routiers* led by Bertrand du Guesclin, Peter sought assistance from the English in Aquitaine. Edward, the Black Prince, agreed to mount an expedition in support of him, and early in 1367 Edward invaded Spain with English, Gascon, and Breton troops. Henry's forces included such French commanders as Du Guesclin and Arnoul d'Audrehem. The armies met at Nájera, a few miles south of the confluence of the Najarerille and Ebro rivers in northeastern Castile, on April 3, 1367. The English gained tactical surprise and managed to surround and defeat Du Guesclin's vanguard. Henry's Castilian main body soon fled in disorder and the Anglo-Gascon victory was complete.

John Bell Henneman, Jr.

[See also: BRIGAND/BRIGANDAGE; GUESCLIN, BERTRAND DU]

Russell, Peter E. *The English Intervention in Spain and Portugal in the Time of Edward III and Richard II.* Oxford: Clarendon, 1955.

NANCY. Founded in the 11th century by Gérard d'Alsace to be the capital of his newly established duchy of Lorraine, Nancy was a small *bourg* composed essentially of the ducal castle and a few monasteries. A fire in 1228 destroyed the town, but it was quickly rebuilt, then surrounded by ramparts in the 14th century, of which only the Porte de la Crafte remains. Nancy was the scene of an important battle between the Burgundian and Swiss armies at the beginning of 1477. Having seized Lorraine from Duke René II in 1475 because it lay between his territories of Burgundy and Flanders, Charles the Bold, duke of Burgundy, suffered two serious defeats at the hands of the Swiss in 1476, and local opposition began to oust Burgundians from Lorraine. Against advice, Charles was determined to take the offensive immediately and regain Nancy. He besieged it in November, but the inhabitants gave stubborn resis-

tance until a Swiss army advanced to their relief at the beginning of January. On January 5, 1477, the Swiss inflicted another terrible defeat on the Burgundians and Charles met his death. His body was found in an icy pond, half eaten by wolves. After his victory over Charles, Duke René rebuilt and enlarged his ducal palace, which had largely fallen into ruins. The present palace, which houses the Historical Museum of Lorraine, is a combination of Flamboyant and Renaissance styles.

John Bell Henneman, Jr.

[See also: CHARLES THE BOLD; LORRAINE]

Cinq-centième anniversaire de la bataille de Nancy (1477): Actes du Colloque . . . Nancy, 22–24 septembre 1977. Nancy: Annales de l'Est, 1979.

Vaughan, Richard. *Charles the Bold: The Last Valois Duke of Burgundy.* New York: Barnes and Noble, 1973.

NANTES. A settlement has existed since the Bronze Age in southeastern Brittany at the tidal limit of the Loire at its confluence with the Erdre. Condevincum was the *civitas* capital of the tribe of Namnetes. Christianity arrived in the late 3rd century, when the town was also enclosed by walls. The cathedral built by Bishop Felix (r. 549–82) is described in a poem by Venantius Fortunatus. Under the Franks, Nantes was part of the March of Brittany, whose most famous holder was the legendary Roland. In 843, the city was sacked by the Vikings, then overrun by the Bretons. The Vikings returned from ca. 920 to 933, but thereafter Nantes remained part of medieval Brittany.

In the 10th and 11th centuries, the counts of Anjou vied with those of Rennes for control. Following the death of Count Mathias (1103), his brother Alain Fergent united Rennes, Nantes, and the other Breton county, Cornouaille, as duke of Brittany (r. 1084–1113). In Nantes, where the duke was later represented by a seneschal, provost, and receiver, he shared rule with the bishop. Bishop Brice (r. 1112–39), adopting an independent Gregorian stance, even sought confirmation of his episcopal rights from Louis VI of France (1123). After the Plantagenêt period of domination in Brittany (ca. 1156–1206), the bishops of Nantes reasserted their rights. Disputes with the duke were frequent, arising particularly from the exercise of regal right during episcopal vacancies. A compromise was reached in 1268, but under Guillaume de Malestroit (r. 1443–62) and Amaury d'Acigné (r. 1462–77) the quarrel violently reerupted.

Until the Breton civil war (1341–65), the inhabitants had little say in government. But the need to involve citizens in all aspects of administration during and after the war allowed them to bargain for privileges. In 1420, Duke Jean V conceded that they could elect ten or twelve burgesses and two proctors to represent them, and the community was born. At the same time, the city was transformed physically: the Roman walls had been extended in the early 13th century to enclose sixty-two acres; they were extensively rebuilt again between 1436 and 1487.

Other major public works included the reconstruction after 1434 of the cathedral of Saint-Pierre-Saint-Paul, built atop a 6th-century crypt that had been reconstructed in the mid-11th. The cathedral houses the exquisite tomb of Duke François II and Marguerite de Foix by Michel Colombe (1499) and has more than a hundred bas-reliefs depicting the story of the Old Testament and parts of the New. The church of Saint-Michel was begun in the 13th century, as was the convent of the Cordeliers, and enlarged in the 14th and 15th. A choir school built for the study of psalms and chorales, the Psalette, dates from the end of the 15th century. The Duke's Castle, constructed in the 10th century over part of the Gallo-Roman wall, was rebuilt in the 13th century and again in 1466 under François II (r. 1458–88); the bridges over the Loire were a constant source of expenditure.

The population of Nantes, living in seven parishes, may have reached a peak of 15,000. The city was a trading rather than industrial center; control of the wine and salt traffic on the Loire can be traced from Carolingian days. Nantes, with Rennes and Vannes, was an administrative center of the duchy. This created wealth and employment. A university was founded in 1460, and the presence of the ducal court encouraged a burgeoning cultural life.

Michael C.E. Jones/Stephen C. Martin

[See also: BRITTANY]

Bois, Paul, ed. *Histoire de Nantes*. Toulouse: Privat, 1977.
Gisler, Claude, and Françoise Oliver-Michel. *A Guide to the Art Treasures of France*, trans. Raymond Rudorff. London: Methuen, 1966.

NANTEUIL CYCLE. One of the lesser-known epic cycles, the Nanteuil Cycle comprises five poems composed between the end of the 12th century and the middle of the 14th: *Doon de Nanteuil, Aye d'Avignon, Gui de Nanteuil, Parise la duchesse,* and *Tristan de Nanteuil.*

The eponymous hero of *Doon de Nanteuil* is identified by the author of *Gaufrey*, a 13th-century chanson de geste, as one of the twelve sons of Doon de Mayence, thus linking this first chanson to the Rebellious Vassal Cycle.

The poem, dating to the end of the 12th century, is preserved only in the 220 nonconsecutive lines copied in the 16th century by Claude Fauchet from a 13th-century *remaniement* by Huon de Villeneuve. The 19th-century scholar Paul Meyer reconstructed the sketchy plot: war breaks out between Doon and Charlemagne; Doon's son, Bérart, is killed by Duke Naime's son, sent as ambassador by the emperor; Doon has to leave Nanteuil and finds refuge in Apulia, where Charles attempts to reach him.

Doon's offspring are the protagonists of the other poems in the cycle. *Aye d'Avignon*, composed between 1195 and 1205, survives in only one complete manuscript (B.N. fr. 2170); two fragments, from two different manuscripts, are also preserved. In 4,132 assonanced and rhymed Alexandrines divided into 179 unequal *laisses*, the author of *Aye d'Avignon* endeavors, superficially, to link his poem to the *Roland* and alludes to episodes from the *Quatre fils Aymon*. There is also evidence that he was familiar with Jehan Bodel's *Chanson des Saisnes* and with the Guillaume d'Orange Cycle. At the same time, the techniques of the romance permeate his poem.

Gui de Nanteuil was composed after *Aye d'Avignon*, of which it is the continuation, and probably before 1207. One almost complete manuscript survives from the 14th century (Montpellier, Fac. de Méd. H 247); another 14th-century manuscript contains a less satisfactory version (Venice, Bibl. Naz. di San Marco fr. 10), and there is also a fragment of 350 lines (Florence, Bibl. Naz. II, IV, 588). The version of the chanson preserved in the Montpellier manuscript has 2,913 rhymed Alexandrine lines.

Gui, the son of Aye and Garnier, goes to Charlemagne's court and is made standard-bearer, which causes spite among Ganelon's relatives; one of them, Hervieu, accuses Gui of murder. Aiglentine, daughter of King Yon of Gascony, falls in love with Gui. The traitors manage to put Gui on bad terms with the emperor, who supports Hervieu for the princess's hand. Gui captures her and flees. Charles and Hervieu set out in pursuit and lay siege to Nanteuil, where Gui and Aiglentine have found refuge. Ganor and Aye come to Gui's rescue, and Hervieu is killed. Peace is made with Charlemagne, who attends the wedding of Gui and Aiglentine.

In addition to *Aye d'Avignon*, the author was familiar with some episodes from the *Quatre fils Aymon* and was also strongly influenced by romance.

Parise la duchesse, composed after 1225 and probably before the middle of the 13th century, is preserved in only one manuscript (B.N. fr. 1374; 3,105 assonanced Alexandrines). Parise, sister of Gui de Nanteuil, is exposed to the hatred of Ganelon's relatives, who accuse her of poisoning her husband's brother, Beuve. She is persecuted and exiled to Hungary, where she has a son, Hugues. He is raised at the royal court of Hungary. After many years of suffering and adventures, Parise meets up again, in Cologne, with her son and with Raymond de Saint-Gilles, her husband. The traitors are caught and executed. This poem is cast in the traditional epic mold but includes many nonepic elements, notably the part played by the bourgeois and the adventures of a woman with her son. The main goal of the chanson is to entertain. It is superficially linked with *Aye* and *Gui* and shows the influence of *Gaidon, Quatre fils Aymon, Doon de la Roche,* and possibly of an older version of *Boeve de Haumtone.*

Tristan de Nanteuil, the last poem of the Nanteuil Cycle, draws some material from the previous poems of the geste and is directly linked to *Gui de Nanteuil.*

Jean-Louis Picherit

[See also: *AYE D'AVIGNON;* CHANSON DE GESTE; *QUATRE FILS AYMON;* REBELLIOUS VASSAL CYCLE; *TRISTAN DE NANTEUIL*]

McCormack, James R., ed. *Gui de Nanteuil, chanson de geste.* Geneva: Droz, 1970. [Based on Montpellier H 247, Venice fr. 10, and Florence fragment.]
Plouzeau, May, ed. *Parise la duchesse, chanson de geste du XIIIe siècle.* Aix-en-Provence: CUER MA, 1986.

NARBONNAIS. The *Narbonnais,* a 13th-century chanson de geste of 8,063 rhyming decasyllables, combines two traditions. The first relates how Aymeri, who considers personal valor to be the basis for acquiring power or land, sends his six older sons away from Narbonne to achieve their preordained functions in life. Sent to Charlemagne's court, Bernard becomes his private adviser, Hernaut his seneschal, William his standard-bearer; Bueves is to win Gascony, Garin Lombardy, and Aïmer Spain, which he will never manage to conquer from the Saracens. The second part reworks an assonanced *Siège de Narbonne,* of which a fragment has survived. The plot is complicated and culminates in the sufferings of Guibelin, Aymeri's youngest son, who is destined to have the fief of Narbonne: imprisoned, the young man is crucified but saved by his father.

The *Narbonnais* is thus a composite text in which moments of epic intensity alternate with the heroic-comic (Hernaut's rages) and the fantastic (Isembart and his black, horned warriors). Revisers have introduced modifications, given their own cyclical propensities: thus, B.N. fr. 1448 reduces the poem to 303 lines (*Département des fils d'Aymeri*) to serve as a prologue to the *Enfances Guillaume,* whereas the "Great Cycle" manuscripts (those combining poems about Guillaume with those about Aymeri), insert the *Enfances Guillaume* at the beginning of the poem and make no mention of Charlemagne's death, so as not to contradict the *Couronnement de Louis.*

François Suard

[See also: GUILLAUME D'ORANGE CYCLE]

Suchier, Hermann, ed. *Les Narbonnais.* 2 vols. Paris: Didot, 1888.
Tyssens, Madeleine. "Le siège de Narbonne assonancé." In *Mélanges Rita Lejeune.* 2 vols. Gembloux: Duculot, 1969, Vol. 2, pp. 891–917.

NARBONNE. In 118 B.C., Rome established the colony of Narbo Martius in southwestern France for war veterans,

and it soon became a flourishing seaport. In 27 B.C., a senatorial province, known as Gallia Narbonensis, was created here by Emperor Augustus. In all Gaul, Narbonne was second only to Lyon in population. In A.D. 413, the Visigoths took Narbonne. In 719, the city fell to the Muslims but was won from them by Franks under Pepin the Short in 759. During the Carolingian period, Narbonne was the capital of the province of Gothia.

From the 9th to the 14th century, Narbonne remained the largest Mediterranean seaport within the kingdom of France. Its vital economic position and the authority of its archbishops made Narbonne a key to Languedoc. Viscounts of Narbonne appear from 821. Rivalry between the secular and ecclesiastical lords intensified in the 11th century, particularly after the accession of the vigorous archbishop Wifred (r. 1019–79). By the 12th century, Narbonne was a co-seigneurie; the archbishops retained jurisdiction over the western half of the city, the viscounts generally over the eastern half and the *bourg.* Narbonne reached the peak of its political power during the remarkable reign of Viscountess Ermessinde (r. 1137–92), who played an aggressive role in the struggles between the counts of Toulouse and Barcelona, often as an ally of the latter. After 1226, the temporal independence of the viscounts and archbishops was circumscribed by the power of the royal seneschalsy of Carcassonne.

The earliest clear reference to the commune and consulates of Narbonne is in 1209. By 1221, consuls functioned in both the *cité* and the *bourg,* and rivalry, sometimes violent, between these two districts remained a constant feature of the society of Narbonne. Until the 14th century, *cité* and *bourg* retained separate consular regimes. In 1309, a long dispute over jurisdiction ended with a *pariage* between the king and viscount. Both consulates were placed under the king's hand and merged in 1338.

Despite early problems with the Inquisition, Narbonne does not appear to have been heavily tainted by Cathar heresy. As at Béziers, the inquisitors recorded few pursuits for Catharism but later serious problems with Spiritual Franciscans and béguines. The economic and political importance of Narbonne declined rapidly in the 14th century, as its prosperity, built on commerce, eroded under pressure of competition from Montpellier and elsewhere, compounded by a shifting and silting of the mouth of the Aude River. The archiepiscopal province of Narbonne was reduced in 1317, and the dynasty of the viscounts ended in 1424.

Alan Friedlander

The present city contains many medieval buildings, among them the basilica of Saint-Paul-Serge (12th–13th c.), the church of the Franciscans, Notre-Dame-de-Consolation (14th–15th c.), and the Archbishop's Palace (13th–14th c.). Saint-Paul-Serge, built on the site of a 4th-century cemetery established by Constantine, houses interesting early Christian sarcophagi.

The cathedral of Saint-Just is the most prominent medieval edifice in Narbonne. Although the current cathedral dates to the 13th century, its history goes back much farther. After the Peace of Constantine in 313, a modest church was erected and subsequently destroyed by fire in 441. In that year, Bishop Rusticius laid the first stone of a new edifice. Completed in 445, the cathedral was dedicated to St. Genes, martyr of Arles. In 782, the church was reconsecrated to the Spanish martyrs Justus and Pastor, two young brothers scourged and beheaded under Emperor Diocletian in the 4th century. The edifice fell into ruin, and reconstruction, under the direction of Archbishop Téodard, commenced in 890. Excavations undertaken in the 1940s revealed the construction to be relatively modest in proportions: 181 feet long and 66 feet wide, consisting of an unvaulted nave extended by a transept and a chevet. Its lopsided belfry still exists.

In 1272, the first stone of the present buidling, sent from Rome by Pope Clement IV, was laid. Built by Jean Deschamps (1286) in the Gothic style of the Île-de-France, the cathedral of Saint-Just features a vast choir with ambulatory and polygonal chapels. By 1354, however, the building reached the city's ramparts and could expand no farther, so no nave or transept was ever built. Stained glass in the triforium bays and in the chapels dates to the 13th and 14th centuries.

A cloister joins the fortified Archbishop's Palace to the cathedral. The palace façade includes three towers dating from the 13th and 14th centuries.

E. Kay Harris

[See also: CATHARS; LANGUEDOC; *PARIAGE*]

Caille, Jacqueline. "Les seigneurs de Narbonne dans le conflit Toulouse-Barcelone au XIIe siècle." *Annales du Midi* 97 (1985): 227–44.

Emery, Richard W. *Heresy and Inquisition in Narbonne.* New York: Columbia University Press, 1941.

Michaud, Jacques, and André Cabanis. *Histoire de Narbonne.* Toulouse: Privat, 1981.

Régné, Jean. *Amaury II, vicomte de Narbonne (1260?–1328): sa jeunesse et ses expéditions, son gouvernement, son administration.* Narbonne: Caillard, 1910.

———. *Étude sur la condition des Juifs de Narbonne du Ve au XIVe siècle.* 1912; Marseille: Lafitte, 1981.

Sigal, Abbé. "Les origines de la cathédrale de Narbonne." *Bulletin de la Commission Archéologique de Narbonne* (1921).

NAVAL POWER. The naval and maritime history of medieval France dates from the Roman occupation of Gaul. Roman vessels utilized the rivers and coastal waters to transport merchandise and military personnel. The early Franks developed fleets for use in trade and war. Their vessels were propelled by oars and probably a single square sail. Charlemagne used a fleet against the Slavs, Saxons, Avars, and others. Because of their Italian interests, the Franks also maintained a small Mediterranean fleet in the 9th century.

The Vikings, who settled in Normandy, influenced the construction of large sailing warships. The Norman invasion of England in 1066 was possible only because Duke William organized a large fleet of Viking-style ships with a single square sail. He shipped horses across the Channel for use by knights in battle against the Anglo-Saxons.

The marriage of Eleanor of Aquitaine to Henry II of England stimulated trade between Gascony and northern Europe after 1154. The English possessions in France led to Anglo-French warfare in the 13th and 14th centuries. The French pieced together a navy for use in the Atlantic and the Channel, often hiring Genoese galleys to fight the English, especially in the Hundred Years' War (1337–1453). France also built a naval base and shipyard, the Clos des Galées, at Rouen. While the French used galleys in warfare, their Castilian allies fought with tall sailing ships that used their advantage in height to rain arrows and stones on their enemies.

Naval power in the Middle Ages did not make possible command of the seas. The ships were few, poorly provisioned, and difficult to keep at sea for long periods, given navigational techniques and weather. The French lost a major naval battle to the English at Sluys in 1340 but were raiding England's south coast in the following few years. In 1350, the English defeated a large Castilian fleet in the Battle of L'Espagnols-sur-Mer off the southeast coast of England, but the Castilians won an important battle off La Rochelle in 1372, a victory that aided the French reconquest of Poitou.

France eventually won the Hundred Years' War, driving the English from all but the port town of Calais by 1453. French fleets consisted mainly of merchant vessels recruited for royal service. Galleys were built or hired to fight, but by the 15th century these were replaced by large sailing ships over a hundred feet in length with carrying capacities of up to 1,000 tons. These included carracks with one or two square sails on a main and foremast and a lateen sail on a mizzenmast. Caravels carried two lateen sails, later a square sail, and were important for Atlantic seafaring.

Ships throughout the medieval period were armed with a combination of weapons. Early open rowing or sailing boats could serve as platforms for shooting arrows or throwing spears. Ships were sometimes used as amphibious assault vessels. During his crusades, Louis IX had towers built on ships so they could be used to bridge town or castle walls adjacent to the water. These evolved into forecastles and aftercastles, which became integrated into a ship's lines over the next two centuries. Topcastles were added to the masts. Guns and cannon appeared aboard ships as they developed in the 14th century. By the early 16th century, gun ports were cut into the hull of a ship so that heavy cannon could be carried lower in the vessel for better stability.

Heading the French navy was an admiral who often was an Italian or an important French noble. The crown long avoided building ships at its own expense and preferred to employ foreigners or rely upon merchant vessels for military service. Advancing technology, however, finally required purpose-built men-of-war with cannon, and these in turn prompted the establishment of a royal navy with a professional officer corps in the 16th century.

Timothy J. Runyan

[See also: ADMIRAL OF FRANCE; HUNDRED YEARS' WAR; SHIPS AND SHIPPING]

Bernard, Jacques. *Navires et gens de mer à Bordeaux (vers 1450– vers 1550)*. 3 vols. Paris: SEVPEN, 1968.

Farrère, Claude. *Histoire de la marine française*. Paris: Flammarion, 1962.

Haywood, John. *Dark Age Naval Power: A Reassessment of Frankish and Anglo-Saxon Seafaring Activity*. London: Routledge, 1991.

La Roncière, Charles de. *Histoire de la marine française*. 5 vols. 3rd ed. Paris: Plon-Nourrit, 1909–32.

Mollat, Michel. *Le commerce maritime normand à la fin du moyen âge*. Paris: Plon, 1952.

———. *La vie quotidienne des gens de mer en Atlantique, IXe –XVIe siècle*. Paris: Hachette, 1983.

Touchard, Henri. *Le commerce maritime Breton à la fin du moyen âge*. Paris: Les Belles Lettres, 1967.

NECROMANCY. Term widely used in the later Middle Ages for the conjuring of demons with the intent to harm enemies, to secure the favor of powerful individuals, to learn future or secret things, to gain wealth, to succeed in romantic exploits, or to create illusions. Necromancers (or "nigromancers") typically stood inside magic circles and recited conjurations, otherwise known as "adjurations" or "exorcisms" and often virtually identical to the exorcisms used for expelling demons; frequently, they used fumigations, astrological symbols, and other elements of the astral magic that had been imported from Arabic culture. They often combined these techniques with image magic— piercing wax images with needles or melting them over fire. Necromancy seems to have been chiefly a clerical form of magic, but clergy who engaged in it appear often to have done so for clients, and frequently these clients were public figures of some prominence.

Important trials for necromancy occurred in France during the early 14th century. In any particular case, it may be questioned whether necromancy was in fact being practiced, whether the charge was a fiction cynically used to attack political adversaries, or whether it expressed the sincere but erroneous apprehensions of potential victims. What we can say is that necromancy was studied (manuscripts survive giving detailed guidelines for conjuring "malign spirits") and surely at least sometimes practiced by members of a kind of clerical underworld.

An important early trial for necromancy was that of Bishop Guichard de Troyes, who was alleged to have used such magic to kill Queen Jeanne in 1305 and was tried on this charge 1308–15. He was said to have consulted both a sorceress and a friar skilled in necromancy. When the friar succeeded in conjuring a demon, the bishop paid the demon homage and heard how they should proceed. All three went in disguise to a hermitage, where they baptized a wax image in the queen's name and then pierced various parts of the image. The queen fell ill, and her physicians could not treat her. But even when the bishop had the sorceress repeatedly pierce the image, the queen still did not die. Exasperated, the bishop broke the image asunder, trampled it, and cast it into a fire, whereupon the queen expired.

Further trials involving the crown occurred in succeeding years. In 1315, Enguerran de Marigny was charged with using image magic, in part to harm Louis X, although his defenders said the magic was intended rather to gain the king's favor. In 1316, Cardinal Francesco Caetani engaged the services of a cleric and a former member of the Templars, who professed expertise in necromancy and who assured him that with the proper equipment and sufficient time they could conjure a demon who would teach the secrets of alchemy; when they informed against Caetani, they charged him with wishing to harm the king and others.

Under Pope John XXII (r. 1316–34), there was a series of cases involving necromancy ostensibly directed against the pope. Bishop Hugues Géraud of Cahors, who was being investigated for simony and other corruption, was tried in 1317 for trying to kill John and his close associates by importing into the papal palace at Avignon wax figures baptized in their names. In the following year, John ordered an investigation of several men, mostly clerics, who allegedly used books of necromancy to invoke evil spirits while standing in circles. By such means, the pope reported, they could ruin people's health, or they could make demons captive in mirrors and other objects so that they might inquire about past or future events. In 1320, the Visconti of Milan were charged with using necromantic image magic against Pope John. Not all the trials for necromancy were political in nature, however. The Carmelite Pierre Recordi confessed in 1329 that he had used wax images and made sacrifices to the Devil for the sake of having sex with women (or, if they refused, doing them harm). A notary named Geraud Cassendi at Carcassonne in 1410 and a priest of Tournai ca. 1472 were accused of invoking demons for the same purpose.

The charge of necromancy recurred sporadically in later decades. When Charles VI became mad in the 1390s, more than one individual was charged with using image magic or other techniques, evidently necromantic, to harm him. Around the turn of the century, concern with necromancy and related arts preoccupied French theologians; the theological faculty at Paris condemned these arts in 1398, and four years later Jean Gerson incorporated the *conclusio* of the Paris theologians in his treatise *De erroribus circa artem magicam*. In 1406, two members of a clerical necromantic conspiracy against Pope Benedict XIII and the king of France, inspired by fear of "diabolical spirits," disclosed the plot to the pope.

While necromancy usually involved a command of Latin and a knowledge of ritual forms expected only among the clergy, the basic concept of invoking demons is found at times among laity as well. For example, one Johanneta Charles was tried at Geneva in 1401 for conjuring a demon to determine the circumstances of a theft. And a trial in the diocese of Soissons in 1460 disclosed that a priest had gone to a sorceress for means to bring vengeance upon his enemies. She had him baptize a toad and feed it a consecrated host. Then she tore the toad to pieces and from it made a poison that caused the enemies to perish.

Yet the cases that attracted most attention were those involving collaboration of clergy and prominent public figures. In 1440, Gilles de Rais, who as marshal of France had fought alongside Jeanne d'Arc at Orléans, was tried for consulting necromancers, most importantly a Florentine priest called François Prelati, in an effort to regain his squandered fortune.

Richard Kieckhefer

[See also: CHARLES VI; JEANNE D'ARC; MAGIC; MARIGNY, ENGUERRAN DE; RAIS, GILLES DE; WITCHCRAFT]

Driscoll, Daniel, trans. *The Sworn Book of Honorius the Magician.* Berkeley Heights: Heptangle, 1983.

Hyatte, Reginald, trans. *Laughter for the Devil: The Trials of Gilles de Rais, Companion-in-Arms of Joan of Arc (1440).* Rutherford: Fairleigh Dickinson University Press, 1984.

Barber, Malcolm. *The Trial of the Templars.* Cambridge: Cambridge University Press, 1978.

Butler, Eliza Marian. *Ritual Magic.* Cambridge: Cambridge University Press, 1949.

Harvey, Margaret. "Papal Witchcraft: The Charges Against Benedict XIII." In *Sanctity and Secularity: The Church and the World*, ed. Derek Baker. Oxford: Blackwell, 1973, pp. 109–16.

Jones, William R. "Political Uses of Sorcery in Medieval Europe." *Historian* 34 (1972): 670–87.

NESSON, PIERRE DE (1383–before 1442). One of the more important late-medieval poets of death. Nesson is known principally for two works: the *Paraphase sur Job* or *Vigiles des Morts*, later published by Vérard, is a powerful and stark meditation on death and human vanity; the *Lai de guerre*, an answer to Alain Chartier's *Lai de paix*, expounds on the political thinking of his patroness, Marie de Berry, widow of John, duke of Berry.

Earl Jeffrey Richards

Piaget, Arthur, and Eugénie Droz, eds. *Pierre de Nesson et ses œuvres.* Paris: Jeanbin, 1925.

Champion, Pierre. "Pierre de Nesson, le poète de la mort." In *Histoire poétique du XVe siècle.* 2 vols. Paris: Champion, 1923, Vol. 1, pp. 167–225.

NEUSTRIA. The northwestern part of Gaul during the Frankish period. There really were two Neustrias. Merovingian Neustria stretched from the Loire to the Meuse; Carolingian and post-Carolingian Neustria was smaller, comprising the area between the Loire and the Seine, excluding Brittany. The name appears ca. 642 and is of uncertain etymology, but it designated the western lands of the kingdom, whereas "Austrasia" designated the eastern lands. In contrast to Austrasia, Neustria was predominantly Gallo-Roman in population, and the form of Latin spoken there, affected by Celtic and Germanic influences, came to be called "Langue d'oïl," the ancestor of modern French. "Languedoil" also came to refer to the region of Neustria, distinguished from southern France ("Languedoc") by its language and its use of unwritten, customary law influenced by Germanic practices. In France during the high and late Middle Ages, a "Frank" generally meant a Neustrian and "Francia" meant Neustria. As the region that gave birth to the French language and formed the power base of the Capetian dynasty, Neustria was in many ways the birthplace of France.

The first Neustria, with its chief royal residence at Paris, was the kingdom given to Chilperic I upon the death of Clotar I in 561, and it passed to his son Clotar II and grandson Dagobert I. It generally dominated Frankish politics from the mid-6th to the late 7th century. The rise of the Austrasian Carolingians ended this first Neustria.

The threat of attacks from Brittany led Charlemagne to recreate a second and smaller Neustria as a subkingdom for his son Charles, and this second Neustria maintained its existence as a kingdom or subkingdom through successive partitions of royal land in the 9th century. The need for an adequate defense against the Vikings led Charles the Bald to grant Neustria as a march to Robert le Fort, and the region continued to be held by his descendants, King Eudes, King Robert I, Hugues le Grand, and Hugh Capet, with their capital at Paris. From the 930s and 940s, the title of marquis of Neustria came to be overshadowed by that of duke of the Franks (*dux Francorum*), given to Hugues le Grand by Louis IV. Both titles were extinguished when Hugh Capet became king in 987 and Neustria ceased to form an administrative unity within the kingdom.

Steven Fanning

[See also: AUSTRASIA; FRANKS; LANGUEDOIL]

Boussard, Jacques. "Les destinées de la Neustrie du IXe au XIe siècle." *Cahiers de civilisation médiévale* 11 (1968): 15–28.

———. "L'ouest du royaume franc aux VIIe et VIIIe siècles." *Journal des savants* (January–March 1973): 3–27.

Joris, André. "On the Edge of Two Worlds in the Heart of the New Empire: The Romance Regions of Northern Gaul During the Merovingian Period." *Studies in Medieval and Renaissance History* 3 (1966): 3–52.

McKitterick, Rosamond. *The Frankish Kingdoms Under the Carolingians, 751–987.* London: Longman, 1983.

Werner, Karl-Ferdinand. "Les origines de la Neustrie." In *La Neustrie: les pays au nord de la Loire de Dagobert à Charles le Chauve (VIIe–IXe siècles)*, ed. Patrick Périn and Laure-Charlotte Feffer. Rouen: Les Musées et Monuments Départementaux de Seine-Maritime, 1985, pp. 29–38.

NEUWILLER-LÈS-SAVERNE. All that remains of the once fortified Benedictine abbey of Neuwiller (Bas-Rhin), founded in 723, is the church of Saint-Pierre-et-Saint-Paul. An early church was enlarged in the 9th century to welcome the many pilgrims attracted by the relics of St. Adelphus, bishop of Metz. The oldest part of the structure is the crypt. Two superimposed chapels in the chevet are 11th-century. The flat Romanesque east end, with rectangular side chapels and transept, was reconstructed in the 12th century. The choir, transept, and east bay of the nave are Romanesque but with later rib vaulting; the rest of the nave and side aisle are 13th-century Gothic in the style of neighboring Champagne. The choir, crossing, tower, and first bay of the nave are decorated with Lombard arcading. The portal of the north façade contains a sculpted tympanum showing Christ with his hand raised in blessing.

William W. Kibler/William W. Clark

Blanchereau, Jules. "Neuwiller." *Congrès archéologique* (*Metz, Strasbourg, Colmar*) 83 (1920): 251–75.

NEVERS. One of several stations called Novidium by the Romans, Nevers (Nièvre) became a bishopric under Clovis (506). Later, it was the capital of the Nivernais, the countship of which was held by several eminent families, including the dukes of Burgundy and the house of Clèves.

The cathedral, Saint-Cyr-et-Sainte-Juliette, represents every period of medieval French architecture. The building is unusual in having an apse at both its east and its west ends. Of the original Romanesque structure (begun ca. 1028), only the west apse and transept remain. Devastated by a fire in the early 13th century, the nave was reconstructed in the Gothic style of the Île-de-France. In the trefoil-arched triforium, colonnettes rest on lively carved human figures. The chevet, with choir, ambulatory, and seven radiating chapels, was rebuilt after another fire in the early 14th century. At the same time, work was begun on the tower. The church was consecrated in 1331 and finished in the 15th and 16th centuries with the addition of Flamboyant lateral chapels, the southern portal, and the completion of the tower.

The Romanesque church of Saint-Étienne, begun under Count Guillaume I of Nevers, became a Cluniac priory in 1068. Constructed mostly between 1083 and 1097,

Nevers (Nièvre), Saint-Étienne, chevet. *Photograph courtesy of Whitney S. Stoddard.*

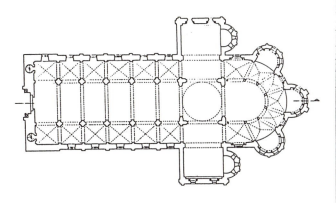

Nevers, Saint-Étienne, plan, isometric section and long section. After Duret.

Nevers, Saint-Étienne, nave. *Photograph courtesy of Whitney S. Stoddard.*

Saint-Étienne is mature Romanesque, contemporary with both the pilgrimage group of churches, such as Conques and Toulouse, and the beginnings of Cluny III.

The east end of Saint-Étienne is three-storied: arcade, triforium arcade, and clerestory with its semidome considerably lower than the nave. In the nave, five bays in length, the elevation has an arcade surmounted by a gallery, vaulted with half-barrel vaults. This format resembles Conques, Toulouse, and churches in Auvergne, but in Saint-Étienne a clerestory is inserted between gallery and nave barrel vault. Thus, direct light into the nave from clerestory windows, a feature adopted in the 11th century in Burgundy, transforms the usual Romanesque elevation.

The multiple planes established by the rounded responds, the square matrix of the piers, and the columnar supports of the nave arcade all give a unity to the interior surfaces. Verticality is emphasized by the nave responds, which extend up through gallery and clerestory and support the capitals from which the transverse arches and the barrel vaults spring.

A dome, supported by squinches, crowns the crossing of the single-vessel transept. To stabilize the cupola and support the crossing tower, diaphragm arches separate nave from transept arms and arms from choir. This treatment of the crossing area is influenced by such churches as Clermont-Ferrand, Issoire, and Saint-Nectaire in the Auvergne, which is southwest of Burgundy.

This creative amalgam of architectural forms derived from the pilgrimage churches, Burgundian structures, and the unusual vaulting of the crossing from Auvergne points up the importance of geography in Romanesque architecture.

Also in Nevers stand the porch of the early 12th-century church of Saint-Sauveur (destroyed in 1838) and the chapel of the convent of Saint-Gildard.

Whitney S. Stoddard/Nina Rowe

Anfray, Marcel. *Architecture religieuse du Nivernais au moyen âge: les églises romanes*. Paris: Picard, 1951.

——. *La cathédrale de Nevers et les églises gothiques du Nivernais*. Paris: Picard, 1964.

Lasteyrie, R. de. *L'architecture religieuse en France à l'époque romane*. Paris: Picard, 1929.

Locquin, Jean. *Nevers et Moulins; Charité-sur-Loire; Saint-Pierre-le-Moûtier; Bourbon-l'Archambault; Souvigny*. Paris: Laurens, 1913.

Serbat, Louis. "Nevers." *Cahiers archéologiques* (Moulins-Nevers) 80 (1913): 300–73.

Stoddard, Whitney S. *Art and Architecture in Medieval France*. New York: Harper and Row, 1972.

NICOLAS DE VERDUN (fl. late 12th c.). A metalworker, goldsmith, and enameler active in the last quarter of the 12th century, Nicolas de Verdun was one of the most original and important artists of his generation. Although his name indicates that he was born in Verdun and elements of his style suggest that he was trained in the Mosan region and northern France, his works are international in scope and demonstrate a wide-ranging interest in and knowledge of both contemporary Byzantine art and western styles. His three most famous surviving works, all of which are different in style, are the Klosterneuburg altarpiece, originally an ambo, inscribed with his name and dated 1181, at Klosterneuberg, Austria; the Shrine of the Three Kings, dated to the 1190s, in Cologne cathedral; and the Shrine of the Virgin, dated 1204, in Tournai cathedral. His son is mentioned as a glass painter at Tournai in the early 13th century.

William W. Clark

[See also: ENAMELING; TOURNAI]

Buschhausen, Helmut. *Der verduner Altar*. Vienna: Tusch, 1980.

Fillitz, Hermann. "Studien zu Nicolaus von Verdun." *Arte medievale* 2 (1984): 79–91.

Swarzenski, Hanns. "The Style of Nicholas of Verdun: Saint-Amand and Reims." In *Gatherings in Honor of Dorothy E. Miner*, ed. U.E. McCracken, L.M.C. Randall, and R.H. Randall, Jr. Baltimore: Walters Art Gallery, 1974, pp. 111–14.

NICHOLAS OF CLAMANGES (of Poillevain; ca. 1360–1437). Nicholas was educated in the Collège de Navarre, Paris, where he gained an excellent knowledge of Latin literary tradition and developed his own elegant style. By 1393, he was rector of the University of Paris, a man of learning, with a talent for friendship. He traveled to Avignon to pursue a career at the (anti)papal court and in 1397 was secretary to Benedict XIII. Until the last years of his life, he continued to be involved with the antipopes, and although he pressed for a solution to the western Schism, his life was blighted by his associations. In 1432, he returned to the Collège de Navarre, where he remained, writing, until his death. Nicholas is best remembered for 151 extant letters combining elegance and Christian learning.

Lesley J. Smith

[See also: AVIGNON PAPACY]

Nicholas of Clamanges. *Opera omnia*, ed. Johannes Martini Lydius. 2 vols. Leiden, 1613. [There exist numerous modern editions of individual letters or groups of letters.]

Coville, Alfred. *Recherches sur quelques écrivains du XIVe et du XVe siècle*. Paris: Droz, 1935, pp. 208–317.

Ouy, Guy. "Le Collège de Navarre, berceau de l'humanisme français." In *Actes du 95e Congrès des Sociétés Savantes*. 2 vols. Paris: Bibliothèque Nationale, 1975, Vol. 1, 283–98.

NICOPOLIS. The Battle of Nicopolis (September 25, 1396), between Crusaders and Ottoman Turks, was one of the greatest military disasters encountered by French cavalry in the 14th century. Under Bayazid I (r. 1389–1402), the Turks had captured Nicopolis, a Bulgarian fortress on the Danube, in 1393. Sigismund, king of Hungary, appealed to the West for assistance against the Turkish advance. England and France agreed to a joint crusading expedition, to be led by the dukes of Burgundy, Orléans, and Lancaster, but after a series of delays these three experienced princes dropped out. The expedition of 1396, largely a Burgundian project, was led by the duke's inexperienced son, John the Fearless, then count of Nevers. Although accompanied by some of the most prestigious French military commanders, John was unable to maintain a unified command and was too readily influenced by younger lords who placed personal glory ahead of strategic objectives. After some minor victories, the crusaders approached Nicopolis, where the French rejected Sigismund's prudent battle plan and insisted on leading a cavalry charge. Inflicting many casualties at first, they were lured into an ambush and crushed by the Turks, who thereby secured for centuries their position in the Balkans. A few of the most notable French leaders were held for ransom, but most were massacred.

John Bell Henneman, Jr.

Atiya, Aziz S. *The Crusade of Nicopolis.* London: Methuen, 1934.

Delaville le Roulx, Joseph M.A. *La France en orient au XIVe siècle: expéditions du maréchal Boucicaut.* 2 vols. Paris: Bibliothèque des Écoles Françaises d'Athènes et de Rome, 1886.

Palmer, John J.N. *England, France, and Christendom, 1377–99.* Chapel Hill: University of North Carolina Press, 1972.

NIEDERHASLACH. An abbey was founded at Niederhaslach (Bas-Rhin) in the 6th century by St. Florent and converted to the Benedictine *Rule* under Louis the Pious in the 9th century. The present church of Saint-Florent, begun in 1274, was burned except for the choir in 1287; reconstruction was completed ca. 1300–85.

The exterior is notable for its three-level rectangular tower—an Alsatian feature—dominating the western façade. The lower level frames the sharply arched portal; the second level has a small but delicate rose window; and the upper level is composed of two immense blind windows. The portal sculptures (ca. 1310) are related to those of western portals of Strasbourg cathedral. The pure lines of the interior are characteristic of Rayonnant style. The stained-glass windows (ca. 1360–75) of the nave are among the most beautiful in Alsace.

William W. Kibler

Bruck, Robert. *Die elsässische Glasmalerei vom Beginn des XI. bis zum Ende des XVII. Jahrhunderts.* Strasbourg: Heinrich, 1902.

Schumacher, L. *Die Sankt-Florentius Kirche zu Niederhaslach.* Strasbourg, 1901.

NÎMES. The ancient Celtic and Roman city of Nîmes in southern France was joined to the kingdom of the Franks in 754. By 900, it formed a viscounty under the counts of Toulouse. The marriage of its heiress Gauziane (ca. 956) to Bernard-Aton II, viscount of Albi, united Nîmes to the fiefs of the family later known as Trencavel. In 1130, a division of their patrimony separated the viscounty of Nîmes, under Bernard-Aton V, from the other Trencavel domains. During the dynastic struggles that followed, Nîmes capitulated to Raymond VI of Toulouse, to whom Bernard-Aton VI ceded his rights in 1184. In 1214, Simon de Montfort, first commander of the Albigensian Crusade, entered Nîmes without struggle, and in 1226 Nîmes became a royal city, thereafter administered by a *viguier* under the seneschal of Beaucaire-Nîmes.

The social history of Nîmes is dominated by the precocious development of its consulate and the influence of the knights of the Arena. As early as the 6th century, the Roman amphitheater had been transformed into a fortress. By 1100, it was equipped with a moat, towers, and chapels dedicated to SS. Martin and Peter. The knights of the Arena, *milites castri Arenarum* (numbering thirty-one in 1100, approximately a hundred in 1226), held their lodgings within the fortress as fiefs of the viscount for whom they guarded the city. In 1155, four knights of the Arena appear as the first consuls of Nîmes. In 1198, they were joined by four burghers, whose privileges were ratified by Count Raymond VI. Raymond's subsequent attempts to restrict these privileges led to the rebellion of 1207, which saw the burghers occupy the city and murder the count's *viguier* in his palace. The alliance formed then between the burghers and the knights brought Nîmes its greatest degree of civil autonomy and represents the height of its consular regime. In 1226, the knights of the Arena were dispersed by Louis VIII; their consulate was suppressed definitively in 1353. Nîmes's prosperity declined during the crises of the 14th century. Its region was devastated most severely by the rural revolt of the Tuchins in 1382.

Alan Friedlander

[**See also:** BEAUCAIRE; LANGUEDOC; SAINT-GILLES; TRENCAVEL]

Dupont, André. "L'évolution sociale du consulat nîmois du milieu du XIIIe siècle au milieu du XIVe siècle." *Annales du Midi* 72 (1960): 187–308.

Huard, Raymond. *Histoire de Nîmes.* Aix-en-Provence: Edisud, 1982.

Ménard, Léon. *Histoire civile ecclésiastique et littéraire de la ville de Nismes.* 7 vols. 1750–58; repr. Marseille: Lafitte, 1975.

Michel, Robert. "Les chevaliers du château des arènes de Nîmes aux XIIe et XIIIe siècles." *Revue historique* 102 (1909): 45–61.

Rogozinski, Jan. "The Counsellors of the Seneschal of Beaucaire and Nîmes, 1250–1350." *Speculum* 44 (1969): 421–39.

NIORT. In Roman times, a "new ford" (Novum Ritum) over the River Sèvre, Niort (Deux-Sèvres) is the site of a castle built by Henry II Plantagenêt and his son Richard the Lionhearted. Only the twin-towered keep, joined by a 15th-century building, remains. The Flamboyant Gothic church of Notre-Dame was built by Berthomé between 1491 and 1560. The spire of its impressive bell tower soars to over 250 feet.

William W. Kibler

Bily-Brossard, Jeanne. *Le château de Niort*. Niort: Privately printed, 1958.

NITHARD (d. after 843). The most detailed information about the division of the Carolingian empire in 840, upon the death of Louis the Pious, and the first years (840–43) of the reign of Charles II the Bald, is found in the contemporary *Histories* of Nithard. Nithard's mother, Bertha, was a daughter of Charlemagne, and he served his cousin Charles the Bald, both in court and at war, and wrote at the king's suggestion. Much of his work was a glorification of the Franks and a justification of Charles's actions, especially his wars against his older brother Lothair.

Constance B. Bouchard

[See also: CHARLES II THE BALD; *STRASBOURG, OATHS OF*]

Nithard. *Histoire des fils de Louis le Pieux*, ed. Philippe Lauer. Paris: Champion, 1926.

Scholz, Bernard S., trans. *Carolingian Chronicles*. Ann Arbor: University of Michigan Press, 1970.

Nelson, Janet L. *Politics and Ritual in Early Medieval Europe*. London: Hambledon, 1986, pp. 195–237.

NOBILITY. One form of nobility or another dominated the society of Gaul and France from the Bronze Age to the Revolution of 1789. Most scholars now believe that the nobility of landed magnates that presided over the western Frankish kingdoms between ca. 620 and 1200 (designated *potentes*, *proceres*, *magnates*, or *principes* as commonly as *nobiles*) was formed in the 6th and early 7th centuries by the fusion of the premigration nobility of the Frankish and other Germanic tribes who settled in Gaul with the remnant of the Roman senatorial nobility already established there. The united nobility of the later Merovingian and Carolingian eras had no privileges enshrined in law, but its members were distinguished from inferior orders not only by the possession of villa-estates and the luxurious lifestyle their income made possible but by the rights of lordship they exercised over their extensive households, free tenants, and clients and by the virtual monopoly they enjoyed over the higher offices of the palace, the provincial administration, and the church. During the first seven centuries of Frankish rule, the nobility remained a small group closed in principle to any but the descendants of its original members. In practice, it was probably not completely closed, for the united nobility of the Frankish kingdom abandoned both the patrilineal structure and the surnames characteristic of the Roman senatorial *gentes* in favor of the amorphous and shifting "sibs" of the Germans, which were marked only by sets of latinized German "leading names" and traced their noble ancestry as much in female as in male lines. This arrangement must have permitted the occasional admission into the nobility of both men and women with only one noble parent of either sex.

Kings could and regularly did confer rank within the nobility by granting the temporary tenure of a high office or "dignity" (*honor* or *dignitas*), such as those of duke, count, and bishop. During the civil wars of the 9th century, the leading nobles succeeded in making the gubernatorial dignities hereditary in principle in a single lineage, thereby depriving the king even of the power of promotion and demotion except in extraordinary circumstances. Between ca. 987 and 1193, the kings of France conferred no important lay dignities outside of their own immediate family.

The emergence first (between ca. 850 and ca. 950) of hereditary duchies, counties, and viscounties and then (between 990 and ca. 1100) of hereditary castellanies carved from their territories, changed both the nature of noble power and the structure of the noble kin group, for the transmission of these dominions to sons by primogeniture soon led to the reemergence of patrilineal "houses" that normally took both their identity and (from ca. 1050) their new, hereditary surname, from the dominion held by their chief. The indivisibility of the family dominion (derived from its official origin or feudal condition or both) tended to affect the transmission of all other patrimonial property in noble houses, and not only daughters but younger sons of nobles tended to receive much smaller shares of their parents' estate than had been the case before 1000. After ca. 1150, the patrilineal surname was increasingly reinforced by a patrilineal emblem, the "arms."

The years between 1180 and 1220 witnessed an even greater change in the structure and more particularly the size of the nobility of France. The much larger class of simple knights that had emerged between 950 and 1050 and had recruited most of its members from ignoble freemen rather than the lesser nobility, succeeded in usurping most of the privileges and attributes usurped in the previous century by the castellans, in closing itself to persons not descended from knights, preferably in the male line, and in being recognized as the lowest stratum of the emerging noble "estate." By 1180, most knights had become petty landlords of the manors they had received in fief from their noble lords, and the members of the old nobility, who had always thought of themselves as warriors as well as rulers, had come to identify with the newly developed ideology of knightliness, or "chivalry," and had adopted the custom of receiving *adoubement* to knighthood on coming of full age. The rise of the knights increased the number of noble persons in France from perhaps 5,000–10,000 in 1180 to perhaps 200,000 in 1220 (about 2 percent of the total population) and converted the nobility into a status group defined on the basis of descent from knights of any rank. In consequence, from ca. 1220 to ca. 1500 the nobility was more often referred to as the *chevalerie*, or "knightage," than the *noblesse*.

The period between ca. 1220 and ca. 1370 saw the emergence of the legal definition, distinctive tenurial obligations, fiscal privileges, and representative institutions that together converted the newly expanded nobility into a juridical "estate" of society. At first, membership in the new nobility was acquired immediately by any nonnoble or *roturier* who secured for himself either the status of knight or possession of a noble fief; but provincial courts, dominated by nobles, came to deny noble status and most of its attendant privileges not merely to those *roturiers* who themselves acquired noble fiefs by purchase or marriage but to their heirs unto the third generation. Louis IX ruled, contrary to long-established usage, that only the king had the right to confer knighthood on a man not descended from knights. This decision led logically to the conferral of the right to receive knighthood, along with the other rights currently characteristic of noble status, by formal letters of ennoblement (*lettres d'anoblissement*), a practice initiated by Philip IV ca. 1290. The average number of such letters of ennoblement issued annually rose from 1.5 in 1308–14 to ten in 1316–22, and fluctuated between five and nearly forty between 1322 and 1350, in response to the pressures of the war with England. Thereafter, it tended to grow as long as the war continued, and from 1372 whole categories of people—typically the mayor, *échevins*, and councilors of a town—were simultaneously ennobled to secure or reward their loyalty to the crown. In the 14th century, nobility came to be sought by rich bourgeois and civil servants both for the honor and for the growing number of privileges it entailed—though in the same century the liabilities of noble status were also increased. In the majority of provincial customary laws, growing numbers of which were committed to writing from ca. 1200, all those who were recognized as noble either by birth or by royal ennoblement were subjected to special rules regarding succession to property (movable and immovable), wardship, payment of debts, and eventually taxes.

Although all nobles in late-medieval France had certain rights and obligations in common, the nobility remained a stratified estate. From ca. 1200, juridical distinctions were drawn on four distinct bases: (1) the extent of the judicial power or "justice" a noble exercised over his nonnoble subjects; (2) the nature and standing of the most important dominion a noble held; (3) the level of the newly crystallized feudal hierarchy on which that dominion was held in fief; and (4) the nobleman's personal military status. Stratification lines were drawn first between the mass of petty manorial lords with only low or middle justice on the one hand, and the much smaller group of lords with high justice on the other. Among those with high justice, called *seigneurs haut justiciers*, the line was drawn between the lesser lords without a proper castle and the greater lords with one or more, and among the latter the line was usually drawn between "castellans" and "barons." Barons were in their turn divided on the basis of their tenurial status into barons of principalities and barons of the realm, and on the basis of whether or not they possessed a dignity into "simple" barons and greater barons, or "princes" (*princes*). Among the princes who were barons of the realm, a distinction was drawn between those who were not and those who were peers (*pairs*) of the realm, holding their principalities as *pairies*, and enjoying extensive privileges.

All but the last of these statuses were developed and transmitted with little or no royal control down to 1296, but from 1193 the kings of France occasionally conferred countships by donative enfeoffment, primarily upon their own sons, and between 1296 and 1314 Philip IV laid the groundwork for the later practice of conferring all of the other dominical statuses, both by regranting existing dominions in fief and by "erecting" new castellanies, baronies, viscounties, counties, duchies, and *pairies* by a legal process usually involving the consolidation of several existing dominions of lower rank. Around 1300, dukes and other peers of France typically had annual incomes in excess of 10,000 *livres tournois*, and most lesser counts and greater viscounts had incomes in excess of 1,000 *livres*; the vast majority of nobles below the rank of castellan had incomes between one and fifty *livres* a year. Since the latter group made up roughly 99 percent of the nobility, the average noble income was not high.

D'A. Jonathan D. Boulton

[See also: ARMOR AND WEAPONS; BARON/BARONY; CASTELLAN/*CHÂTELAIN*; COUNT/COUNTY; DUKE/DUCHY; KNIGHTHOOD; PEER/PEERAGE; PRINCE/PRINCIPALITY]

Boulton, D'A.J.D. *Grants of Honour: The Origins of the System of Nobiliary Dignities of Traditional France, ca. 1100–1515.* Forthcoming.

Contamine, Philippe. *La noblesse au moyen âge, XIe au XVe siècle: essais à la mémoire de Robert Boutruche.* Paris: Presses Universitaires de France, 1976.

Guilhiermoz, Paul. *Essai sur l'origine de la noblesse en France au moyen âge.* Paris: Picard, 1902.

Lucas, Robert H. "Ennoblement in Late Medieval France." *Mediaeval Studies* 39 (1977): 239–60.

Martindale, Jane. "The French Aristocracy in the Early Middle Ages: A Reappraisal." *Past and Present* 75 (1977): 5–45.

Reuter, Timothy. *The Medieval Nobility: Studies on the Ruling Classes of France and Germany from the Sixth to the Twelfth Century.* Amsterdam: North-Holland, 1978.

NOËL. The modern French word for a Christmas carol and Christmastide itself, *noël* was commonly used in late-medieval France as a joyous acclamation; associations with the Christmas season date from the 13th century. In the late 15th century, *noël* also came to denote a strophic poem dealing with the events surrounding the Nativity, usually imitating French or Latin models. *Noëls* were sung, often as *contrafacta*, with the word *noël* a frequent refrain. The earliest literary collection was compiled during the reign of Charles VIII (1483–98), and *noëls* remained popular during the 16th century. Some Latin motets by 15th-century Franco-Burgundian composers feature *noël* refrains set in a distinctive rhythmic sequence, such as Nicolas Grenon's isorhythmic motet *Nova vobis gaudia* (ca. 1420).

J. Michael Allsen

Block, Adrienne F. *The Early French Parody Noël.* 2 vols. Ann Arbor: UMI, 1983.

NOGARET, GUILLAUME DE (ca. 1260–1313). A native of the region of Toulouse, Nogaret was a professor of law at Montpellier in 1282. By 1295, he was a member of Philip IV the Fair's council in Paris. In 1301, Philip arrested Bernard Saisset, bishop of Pamiers, on charges of treason and prepared to try him in his royal court. Pope Boniface VIII forbade him to do so and, in 1302, issued the bull *Unam sanctam*, which declared that all who refused to obey the Roman pontiff would be excluded from salvation. In response, Nogaret publicly charged Boniface with heresy and other crimes and appealed him to a trial before a church council. To execute his plan, Nogaret took an armed guard into Italy in the late summer of 1303 to seize Boniface and return him to France for such a trial.

Face to face with the pope in his native village of Anagni, Nogaret doubted the success of his mission and fled, leaving a shaken pontiff who died a few weeks later. The "attempt" at Anagni became the most famous episode in Philip's campaign to free his monarchy from church control, and it gave Nogaret an enduring fame and notoriety. But Nogaret also played the major role in Philip's crushing of the Templars, the confiscation of Jewish wealth and their ultimate expulsion from France, and several other schemes, all designed to create a centralized secular monarchy.

Franklin J. Pegues

[See also: PHILIP IV THE FAIR]

Pegues, Franklin J. *The Lawyers of the Last Capetians*. Princeton: Princeton University Press, 1962.

NOIRLAC. The Cistercian abbey of Noirlac (Cher), founded by St. Bernard's cousin Robert de Clairvaux, is first mentioned in 1136. After difficult beginnings, the abbey flourished following a generous gift in 1150 from Count Ebbes V of Charenton. The white-stone church, measuring 195 feet in length and having eight bays with aisles, transept, and two-bay chevet, was constructed between 1150 and 1250 and shows the transition in Cistercian architecture from Romanesque to Gothic. In the austere Cistercian manner, there is no sculpture on the capitals or façade and no stained glass.

The conventual buildings, grouped south of the church in typical Cistercian fashion, include cloister, chapter house, and the monks' dortoir (with a wooden ceiling), refectory, and warming room (*chauffoir*). The particularly harmonious chapter house (late 12th c.) has six bays spanned by ogival vaulting resting on polygonal pillars. The rectangular cloister (125 feet by 109 feet), although much mutilated, still preserves its six-part vaulting, which requires alternating strong and weak supporting columns. Structurally, this is solved by colonnettes dividing the arches into two lancets surmounted by an oculus. Its rich ornamentation, including sculpted capitals with floral motifs, contrasts with the austerity of the church.

William W. Kibler/William W. Clark

[See also: CISTERCIAN ART AND ARCHITECTURE]

Aubert, Marcel. *L'abbaye cistercienne de Noirlac*. Paris: Société Générale d'Imprimerie et d'Édition, 1932.

Crozet, René. *L'abbaye de Noirlac et l'architecture cistercienne en Berry*. Paris: Leroux, 1932.

Meslé, Émile, and Jean-Marie Jeun. *L'abbaye de Noirlac*. Paris: CNMHS, 1980.

NORBERT OF XANTEN. *See* Prémontré

NORMANDY. The medieval duchy of Normandy dates from the early 10th century, when the king of the Franks granted territory in the lower Seine Valley to the Viking chieftain Rollo (or Rolf), who had settled with his followers around the city of Rouen. In the century that followed, Normandy (i.e., "Northmannia," the lands of the Northmen) gradually expanded until it stretched east of the Seine to the River Epte and west to the Atlantic shore of the Cotentin. The area ruled by the Norman dukes conformed roughly to the diocesan boundaries of the ecclesiastical province of Rouen, which had been drawn in the days of the Roman Empire. Political, ecclesiastical, and economic development accompanied this expansion, so that by the mid-11th century a dynamic and coherent state had emerged in this corner of northwestern France. In 1066, the duke of Normandy conquered England, laying the foundations for a cross-Channel realm that fused Norman customs and language with Anglo-Saxon, marking a turning point in the history of both the French duchy and the English kingdom. But the Normans did not restrict their ambitions to France and England. In the 11th and 12th centuries, Norman adventurers sought their fortunes and carved new kingdoms in southern Italy and Sicily and in the Holy Land. In the long view, however, it was the conquest of England that had the greatest impact on the duchy, placing Normandy at the center of the rivalry between the kings of England and France for the rest of the Middle Ages.

The initial stages of Norman settlement in France are obscure. According to Norman tradition, the Viking leader Rollo met King Charles III the Simple at Saint-Clair-sur-Epte in 911 to accept baptism, perform homage, and become the first duke of Normandy. This version of the duchy's foundation is shrouded in legend. A charter dated 918 indicates that the king granted to Rollo and his men only some unspecified territory around Rouen, most likely hoping to pacify Rollo's band and to use them as a bulwark against rival French lords and other Viking groups. Grants in 924 and in 933 gave royal sanction to Norman expansion west to the Vire River and then to the sea, but royal concession meant little in this period: the Viking counts of Rouen had to extend their authority gradually over the territory that would become Normandy through an interplay of alliances and force. The new duchy that took shape in the 11th century enjoyed important strategic and commercial advantages, controlling the lower Seine, the gateway to Paris, and facing the English Channel, with easy access to the political and economic world of the northern seas.

The newcomers adopted the French language and religion; they intermarried with the French and with other Scandinavian settlers. Rollo's son and successor, William Longsword, entered the treacherous world of Frankish

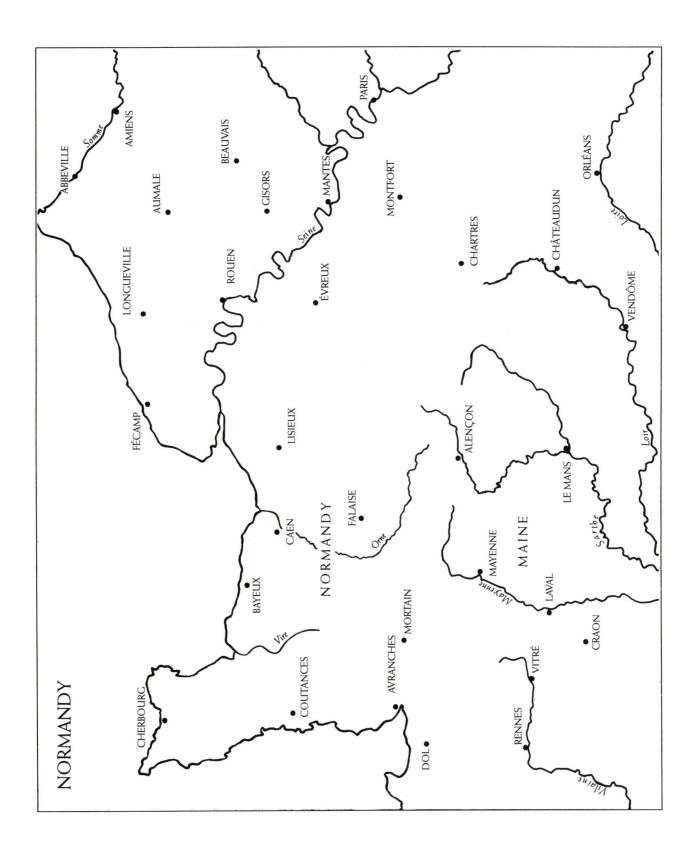

NORMANDY

ABBEVILLE

Somme
AMIENS

BEAUVAIS

AUMALE
GISORS

PARIS

MANTES

MONTFORT

ORLÉANS

LONGUEVILLE

Seine

ROUEN

ÉVREUX

CHARTRES

CHÂTEAUDUN

Loire

VENDÔME

FÉCAMP

LISIEUX

ALENÇON

Loir

FALAISE

Orne

MAINE

LE MANS

Sarthe

NORMANDY

MAYENNE

LAVAL

CAEN

BAYEUX

Vire

Mayenne

CRAON

COUTANCES

MORTAIN

VITRÉ

CHERBOURG

AVRANCHES

RENNES

DOL

Vilaine

politics, performing homage to three successive kings and taking sides in the petty wars of territorial lords. Expansion and assimilation received a setback when he was assassinated in 942 by the count of Flanders, and two years later the Normans faced a two-pronged attack by King Louis IV and Hugues le Grand, duke of the Franks. In the 960s, the counts of Anjou, Flanders, and Blois-Chartres attacked the province with King Lothair. But the Normans of Rouen resisted these aggressions, and during the reigns of William Longsword's son Richard I (r. 942–96) and grandson Richard II (r. 996–1026) the duchy emerged as a permanent territorial entity whose institutions and traditions fused its Scandinavian and French heritage. By the turn of the century, the six bishoprics under Rouen's authority were reestablished and active and important monasteries were restored. Both Richard I and Richard II encouraged this ecclesiastical revival, inviting respected churchmen from outside Normandy to participate in the recovery and reform of churches in their duchy. During the reign of Richard II, the secular administration also took shape. A network of counts and viscounts emerged, bound together by ties of kinship and by their common allegiance to the duke.

Richard II was followed as duke by his sons Richard III (r. 1026–27) and Robert the Magnificent (r. 1027–35). Robert's untimely death returning from pilgrimage to Jerusalem threw the duchy into political disorder, as rival lords and kinsmen opposed the succession of his illegitimate seven-year-old son, William (r. 1035–87). But the young duke survived his minority and overcame his opponents, most notably in 1047 at the Battle of Val-ès-Dunes, in 1054 at the Battle of Mortemer, and in 1057 at the Battle of Varaville. In 1063, Duke William became lord of Maine, pressing the claim of his son Robert Curthose, who had been betrothed to the sister of Count Herbert of Maine. Three years later, on October 14, 1066, William defeated Harold Godwinsson at the Battle of Hastings and seized the crown of England.

The conquest of England enriched the Norman aristocracy, since the new king rewarded his supporters with the lands and titles of the defeated Anglo-Saxon nobility. Their new lands were not to be plundered as war booty but were instead to be held conditionally, in exchange for a specified number of knights to serve the king. This principle of contractual military tenure, the underpinning of feudalism, had existed in the duchy before 1066, but after the Norman Conquest knight service came to be assessed more precisely and systematically in William's lands on both sides of the Channel. The conquest of England thus brought wealth to Normandy, as well as more exact definitions of vassalage and military obligations.

The 11th century was the heyday of Norman expansion to the south and to the north, although this was the work of independent adventurers rather than a ducal program. In southern Italy and Sicily, Norman mercenaries led by Robert Guiscard (d. 1085) carved out a state from Byzantine and Muslim holdings. In the next century, this Norman kingdom of Sicily became a rich and cosmopolitan realm during the reign of Robert's nephew Roger II the Great (d. 1154), one that fused Muslim, Byzantine, and

Latin traditions under the Norman rule. Warriors from Normandy also fought Muslims in Spain and in the Holy Land, where the fall of Jerusalem to the First Crusade (1095–99) brought the creation of four crusader states, including the Norman principality of Antioch, whose first ruler was Bohemund, a son of the same Robert Guiscard. Although these conquests in the Mediterranean had little impact on the duchy itself, the Normans in Normandy boasted of the exploits of their fierce cousins in the south, and a few Norman churches received presents that their members sent back from Italy.

When William the Conqueror died in 1087, the realm was divided between his two eldest sons, Robert Curthose, who received Normandy, and William Rufus, who became king of England. To finance his participation in the First Crusade, Robert entrusted the duchy to his brother in 1096 for a loan of 10,000 marks of silver. When Robert returned in 1100, William II Rufus was dead and their younger brother, Henry I, had seized England and was prepared to fight for Normandy. The subsequent fratricidal war divided the Anglo-Norman aristocracy until Henry took Robert prisoner in 1106 at Tinchebrai. England and Normandy were thus again united under Henry I, who kept his older brother captive for twenty-eight years. The government of Normandy under Henry I became more elaborate and more centralized, as royal justice extended its scope and as the first Norman exchequer kept systematic account of royal revenues, but when Henry died in 1135 with no surviving male heir anarchy broke out. Both the kingdom and the duchy were contested between Henry's daughter, Matilda, and her first cousin Stephen of Blois. Although Stephen won the throne, civil war continued for nineteen years. In 1141, Matilda's husband, Geoffroi d'Anjou, invaded Normandy and spent three years crushing King Stephen's party in the duchy before he was received in Rouen as duke of Normandy. In 1150, Geoffroi passed the ducal title on to his seventeen-year-old son, Henry Plantagenêt. When Geoffroi died in 1151, Henry inherited Anjou as well, and he acquired Aquitaine and Poitou by marriage in 1152. The following year, King Stephen acknowledged the young Plantagenêt as his heir in England. To King Henry II (r. 1154–89), therefore, Normandy represented only one small part of his vast cross-Channel collection of principalities.

Ever since the reign of William the Conqueror, the French kings had tried to undermine the unity of the Anglo-Norman realm. Philip I had supported Robert Curthose in rebellion against his father, and Louis VI had backed William Clito, Robert's son, against Henry I. The Angevin empire of Henry II represented an even greater threat to the French monarchy, and Louis VII (r. 1137–80) and his son, Philip II Augustus (r. 1180–1223), resolved to dismantle it. Henry II's son Richard I the Lionhearted (r. 1189–99) managed with difficulty to check the ambitions of the French king, building the famous Château-Gaillard upstream from Rouen on the Seine and defeating the royal forces decisively at Courcelles in 1198. But Richard's younger brother, John Lackland, succeeding him in 1199, was no match for the determined and resourceful Philip Augustus, who soon found a legal pretext to invade

DUCAL HOUSE OF NORMANDY

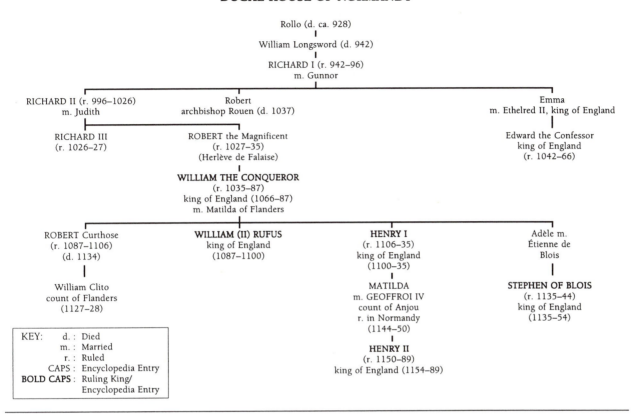

Rollo (d. ca. 928)

William Longsword (d. 942)

RICHARD I (r. 942–96)
m. Gunnor

RICHARD II (r. 996–1026)
m. Judith

Robert
archbishop Rouen (d. 1037)

Emma
m. Ethelred II, king of England

RICHARD III
(r. 1026–27)

ROBERT the Magnificent
(r. 1027–35)
(Herlève de Falaise)

Edward the Confessor
king of England
(r. 1042–66)

WILLIAM THE CONQUEROR
(r. 1035–87)
king of England (1066–87)
m. Matilda of Flanders

ROBERT Curthose
(r. 1087–1106)
(d. 1134)

WILLIAM (II) RUFUS
king of England
(1087–1100)

HENRY I
(r. 1106–35)
king of England
(1100–35)

Adèle m.
Étienne de
Blois

William Clito
count of Flanders
(1127–28)

MATILDA
m. GEOFFROI IV
count of Anjou
r. in Normandy
(1144–50)

STEPHEN OF BLOIS
(r. 1135–44)
king of England
(1135–54)

HENRY II
(r. 1150–89)
king of England (1154–89)

KEY:
d. : Died
m. : Married
r. : Ruled
CAPS : Encyclopedia Entry
BOLD CAPS : Ruling King/
Encyclopedia Entry

Normandy. Since the English king technically held his French lands as the French king's vassal, John was bound by feudal law to come to Philip's court when summoned. When, in 1202, John defied Philip's order to appear in court to answer charges, his disobedience justified confiscation of his fiefs. Philip attacked Normandy that year and by 1204 had wrenched the duchy from the English crown. Anjou and most of the rest of John's French lands soon followed suit. Lords who held lands on both sides of the Channel had to forfeit their domains on one side or the other, and the severance of England from the Continent received its final seal with the defeat of John's allies in 1214 at the Battle of Bouvines.

England refused to acknowledge the French conquest of Normandy until the Treaty of Paris in 1259, but the Normans themselves adjusted to the new order. During the 13th century, peace under the Capetians brought prosperity to the duchy, although increasing royal taxation rankled townsmen. Rebellion broke out over this issue in the next century, leading King Louis X to issue the Norman Charter of 1315, which guaranteed against excessive taxation and promised the duchy a sound currency. The Norman Charter was later seen as a symbol of political liberties and rights—in effect, Normandy's Magna Carta.

The 14th century also witnessed the resumption of the Anglo-French rivalry in the Hundred Years' War (1337–1453). For Normandy, the war began in earnest in 1346,

when Edward III of England invaded the duchy at the invitation of the Norman lord and rebel Godefroi de Harcourt, his army laying waste to the countryside of the Cotentin and making its way to Caen, which suffered a three-day sack. By the 1350s, the English and their allies held the major castles between the Orne and the Vire, and Godefroi confirmed the English king's commitment to conquest by bequeathing his Norman lordships to him. In the next century, after Henry V's defeat of the French at Agincourt in 1415, the English redoubled their efforts to take Normandy. By spring 1418, all lower Normandy was in their hands; Rouen surrendered in January the following year, after a seige of almost six months, and the rest of Normandy then fell swiftly. The English occupation of Normandy lasted for thirty years, during which time the Normans were taxed heavily to support the English war effort. By the 1430s, however, the English position was beginning to slip. The brief career of Jeanne d'Arc, burned in 1431 in the marketplace of Rouen, inspired a groundswell of French patriotism, and twenty years later, by August 1450, all Normandy again belonged to the French.

A pattern of conquest and assimilation runs through the history of medieval Normandy. The Scandinavians who created the realm in the 10th century lost much of their Norseness in the following 150 years, conquering England in 1066 as Christians, speaking French and observing

French customs, yet they remained aware of their own distinct origins. Under the Conqueror and his heirs, the Norman duchy and the English kingdom were at times united, but gradually the Normans of England became more English as the Normans of France became more French. The conquest of Normandy by Philip II Augustus in 1204 confirmed this growing trend of separation, placing the duchy directly under the French crown and forcing the Anglo-Norman aristocracy to choose one side of the Channel or the other. By the Hundred Years' War, the English king's declaration that Normandy was his rightful legacy was in fact the thin excuse of a foreign power to invade—and the Normans, after four centuries, were prepared to defend their right to be French.

Cassandra Potts

[See also: BEDFORD, JOHN OF LANCASTER, DUKE OF; CAEN; CHÂTEAU-GAILLARD; HARCOURT; HENRY I; HENRY II; HUNDRED YEARS' WAR; JOHN I LACKLAND; NORMANS IN SICILY; PHILIP II AUGUSTUS; RICHARD, DUKES OF NORMANDY; RICHARD I THE LIONHEARTED; ROUEN; WILLIAM I THE CONQUERER; WILLIAM II RUFUS]

Bates, David. *Normandy Before 1066.* London: Longman, 1982.

Bois, Guy. *The Crisis of Feudalism: Economy and Society in Eastern Normandy c. 1300–1550.* Cambridge: Cambridge University Press, 1984.

Bouärd, Michel de, ed. *Histoire de la Normandie.* 2nd ed. Toulouse: Privat, 1987.

Douglas, David C. *William the Conqueror: The Norman Impact upon England.* Berkeley: University of California Press, 1964.

Haskins, Charles Homer. *Norman Institutions.* Cambridge: Harvard University Press, 1925.

Jouet, Roger. ... *Et la Normandie devint française.* Paris: Mazarine, 1983.

Le Patourel, John. *The Norman Empire.* Oxford: Clarendon, 1976.

Powicke, Maurice. *The Loss of Normandy, 1189–1204.* 2nd ed. Manchester: University of Manchester Press, 1960.

Searle, Eleanor. *Predatory Kinship and the Creation of Norman Power, 840–1066.* Berkeley: University of California Press, 1988.

Strayer, Joseph Reese. *The Administration of Normandy Under Saint Louis.* Cambridge: Mediaeval Academy of America, 1932.

Tabuteau, Emily Zack. *Transfers of Property in Eleventh-Century Norman Law.* Chapel Hill: University of North Carolina Press, 1988.

NORMANS IN SICILY. In 1016, Norman pilgrims returning from the Holy Land disembarked at Bari, then in revolt against the Byzantine emperor. Hiring themselves out as mercenaries, first to one and then to another side in the wars waged between and among Byzantines in Apulia and Lombards in Campania, both of whom were threatened by Arabs in Calabria and Sicily, they enriched themselves and invited their friends and relatives to join them from Normandy, where many lesser nobles had landless younger sons.

Of the Normans who came south, twelve brothers of the Hauteville family gradually got the upper hand, finally annexing the principality of Capua in 1078. William Iron Arm, Drogo, and Humphrey had conquered northern Apulia. William was elected count of all the Normans in Italy, a position inherited by Drogo in 1046. Their younger brother Robert, surnamed Guiscard ("wily"), a virtual brigand in Calabria, where he and his followers maintained themselves by pillaging the inhabitants, succeeded Humphrey as count in 1057. Robert and his youngest brother, Roger, completed the conquest of southern Italy by capturing Bari, the last Byzantine stronghold, on April 16, 1071. The Byzantines could not effectively resist them because most of their army had to face the Seljuk Turks, who crushed them at Manzikert in August of that year.

In 1053, at Civitate, the Normans captured Pope Leo IX, who had opposed their encroachments on the papal states. Pope Nicholas II used the Normans as allies against local enemies as well as the German and Byzantine emperors. He made Robert Guiscard a duke and his vassal in 1059. The Norman-papal alliance bore fruit in 1084, when Robert responded to the appeals of his suzerain and routed the emperor Henry IV, who was besieging Pope Gregory VII in the Castel Sant'Angelo in Rome. Robert himself died in 1085, during a three-year campaign against the Byzantines and Venetians, during which he seized Avelona and Durazzo and penetrated as far as Thessaly. By that time, his brother Roger had nearly completed the conquest of Sicily, which he had invaded from Calabria, seizing Messina in 1061. Noto, the last Arab outpost, fell to him in 1091.

During the First Crusade, Robert's oldest son, Bohemund, seized Antioch and took the title of prince in the face of Byzantine claims to the city. Hostility between the Hautevilles and Constantinople undermined cooperation between crusaders and Byzantines. Antioch remained a Latin principality until 1287. Roger's younger son, Roger II of Sicily (r. 1105–54), inherited Apulia in 1127 from his cousin, Bohemund's son William, and added Capua and Naples (1139) and Abruzzi (1140). In 1130, he received the crown of Sicily at Palermo from the antipope Anacletus II. Roger continued his father's policy of romanizing the Orthodox and protecting Greek, Arab, Jew, and Lombard in his French-speaking court, which promulgated documents in Arabic and Greek as well as in Latin. He combined Arab and Byzantine autocratic law, taxes, and bureaucratic traditions with Norman feudalism. Normans came to Sicily from England, the other most developed Catholic monarchy of the 12th century. The institutions of each kingdom influenced the other's, but the Sicilian realm was more advanced. Its economy was more monetized, its trade more valuable, its cities larger and richer, and its culture more sophisticated. Roger II occupied Malta and Tripoli and made Tunis pay him tribute. He divided his diverse kingdom into judiciarates.

Under Roger's son William I the Bad (r. 1154–66), domestic revolts and governmental ineptitude caused the loss of Roger's African conquests. His successor, William

II the Good (r. 1166–89), supported Pope Alexander III against the German and Byzantine emperors. Both Williams sought to dominate the Mediterranean from Tunisia and the Adriatic from their possessions at Corfu, Durazzo, and Cephalonia.

William II's marriage to Joan, the daughter of Henry II of England, proved childless, and his death was followed by civil war. His preferred successor, his aunt Constance, was married to Henry VI, soon to become emperor. Her half-brother, Roger II's illegitimate son Tancred, seized the throne and ruled with the support of Norman barons, but at his death in 1194 Henry VI dispossessed his son William III, bringing an end to the Hautevilles' rule. At the death of Henry (1197) and Constance (1198), their child, Frederick II, inherited the throne under the guardianship of Pope Innocent III. The population and prosperity of Sicily continued to grow until the 1190s. Roger II was the richest sovereign in Catholic Europe, and William II's revenues rivaled those of the king of England. En route to the Third Crusade, Richard the Lionhearted wintered in Sicily with his cousin Tancred. Along with Spain, Sicily became the chief conduit of Arabic knowledge to the West. Roger II and his successors patronized translators of Jewish and Arabic works into Latin. Its Jewish physicians and Arabic learning made the old Lombard capital of Salerno Europe's leading medical center, considered by some to be the oldest university. St. Benedict's abbey of Monte Cassino, on the border between the *Regno* and the papal states, and the Basilian monasteries of southern Italy, were centers of learning. To Monte Cassino came Constantine the African, a monk who translated treatises by Greek and Arabic doctors into Latin. Nowhere else did Arabic, Greek, and Latin culture coexist together in such peace and toleration, and no kingdom contributed more to the cultural renaissance of the 12th century. Roger II and his ministers, such as his grand-admiral, George of Antioch, endowed churches built in the Arabo-Byzantine style peculiar to the island, although the Gothic style predominated later with the cathedrals at Palermo and Monreale. The court of Frederick II (r. 1197–1250) witnessed the culmination of Norman scholarship.

William A. Percy, Jr.

[See also: ANJOU, HOUSES OF; CRUSADES; NORMANDY]

Bruhl, Carl Richard, ed. *Rogerii II regis diplomata Latina.* Cologne: Bohlau, 1987. [*Codex diplomaticus regni Siciliae sub auspiciis Academiae Panormitanae Scientiarum Litterarum et Artium.*]

Douglas, David C. *The Norman Achievement.* Berkeley: University of California Press, 1969.

Matthew, Donald. *The Norman Kingdom of Sicily.* Cambridge: Cambridge University Press, 1992.

Norwich, John Julius. *The Normans in the South.* 2 vols. London: Longman, 1967.

NOTARIES. Notaries existed in medieval France primarily in the south in the high and late Middle Ages, as a result of the written law tradition inherited from the Romans. Au-thorized by a variety of political authorities—royal, municipal, episcopal, papal—notaries operated as registrars of public and private law transactions given legal validity by their office. Notaries recorded minutes or drafts of instruments in registers, some of which have survived by the dozens, even hundreds, in such towns as Perpignan, Manosque, Marseille, Toulouse, and Montpellier for the late Middle Ages; other towns, like Narbonne, are not favored with the survival of notarial registers from the medieval era. When called upon, the notary would draw up an extended form of a transaction, filling out formulaic abbreviations, which abounded in the minutes of the registers.

Notaries, strategically positioned on busy squares and streets, attracted as clientele a cross-section of the urban population, who sought written records of last wills and testaments, sales and rentals, emancipation, acquittal, apprenticeship, litigation, and other business and legal engagements. Age and residency requirements protected access to the profession. Paralegal instruction or apprenticeship in the notariate was governed by statute in such towns as Marseille and Tarascon. Thoroughly professional and essential to the process of business and law, notaries garnered a certain social standing in medieval southern France.

Kathryn L. Reyerson

[See also: LAW AND JUSTICE; LEGAL TREATISES; *TABELLIONS*]

Giraud Amalric. *Business Contracts of Medieval Provence: Selected Notulae from the Cartulary of Giraud Amalric of Marseilles, 1248,* ed. and trans. John H. Pryor. Toronto: Pontifical Institute of Mediaeval Studies, 1981.

Aubenas, Roger. *Étude sur le notariat provençal au moyen âge et sous l'ancien régime.* Aix-en-Provence: Aux Éditions du Feu, 1931.

Emery, Richard W. *The Jews of Perpignan in the Thirteenth Century: An Economic Study Based on Notarial Records.* New York: Columbia University Press, 1959.

Gouron, André. "Les archives notariales des anciens pays de droit écrit au moyen âge." In *Recueil de mémoires et travaux publié par la société de l'histoire du droit écrit et des institutions des anciens pays de droit écrit.* Montpellier: Faculté du Droit et des Sciences Économiques, 1966, Fasc. 5, pp. 47–60.

NOTRE-DAME SCHOOL. When Maurice de Sully became bishop of Paris in 1160, he launched the construction of the cathedral of Notre-Dame, which was largely completed by 1250. An abundance of polyphonic music for the Masses and Offices of major feasts of the liturgical year was created during this period to enhance the ceremonies at the cathedral. This musical repertory developed in two phases. The first involved the compilation of the *Magnus liber organi* by Léonin, named by the music theorist Anonymous 4 as the earliest member of this school. This new polyphony, the most advanced music then devised, introduced modal rhythm into segments of the polyphony known as discant clausulae, which were composed in note-against-note style to the plainchant melismas, in contrast to the lengthy and mellifluous lines improvised or composed to the syllabic sections of the chant. The innovation of a musical notation for these clausulae proved a turning point in western music. The clausulae grew in importance, as composers explored ways to expand, extend, and notate increasingly complex rhythms; numerous independent clausulae apparently intended to substitute for the original sections in the *Magnus liber organi* survive in the Notre-Dame sources *W1* and *F*. Some of these clausulae may have been a factor in the *abbreviatio* ("abbreviation" or "revision") of the *Magnus liber organi* that Anonymous 4 attributed to Pérotin, whom he called *optimus discantor*.

The second phase consisted of revisions and additions introduced by Pérotin, whom Anonymous 4 named as Léonin's successor. It is probable that the notation if not much of the music of the *Magnus liber organi* itself was revised and that new organum was added over time, so that the three extant versions of the *Magnus liber organi* reflect three layers, all of which apparently postdate the *abbreviatio* attributed to Pérotin. The version in the Florence manuscript *(F)* may be closer to the liturgical practice of Notre-Dame and is both larger and later than that in *W1*. Craig Wright has proposed, therefore, that the version in *F* may be closer to Léonin's *Magnus liber organi* and that dissemination from Paris was selective rather than additive, as had previously been thought. Anonymous 4 also implied a distinction between the two phases that is valuable in understanding their musical styles. Léonin's polyphony is predominately two-part organum, whereas Pérotin's is generally discant in two, three, or four parts. This liturgical polyphony quickly spread throughout Europe, notably in England and Spain, and manuscript fragments in other northern regions indicate an even wider diffusion. As it spread, however, the spirit of innovation that had imbued its formation was increasingly swept up in the vernacular tide that began in the early 13th century, culminating in the French-texted motet that dominated the second half of the century.

According to Anonymous 4, Pérotin also composed four- and three-part polyphony for the Graduals and Alleluias of Masses for Christmas, Easter, and the Nativity of the Virgin Mary, and several conductus. The notational and rhythmic innovations of Pérotin and his colleagues in the cathedral were probably the basis of the earliest systematic theoretical writings on the rhythmic modes, those attributed to Johannes de Garlandia, which formed the "key" by which Friedrich Ludwig in the early decades of the 20th century unlocked an understanding of the obscure notation of the Notre-Dame organa and clausulae.

Sandra Pinegar

[See also: ANONYMOUS 4; CLAUSULA; LÉONIN; ORGANUM; PÉROTIN; RHYTHMIC MODE]

Handschin, Jacques. "Was brachte die Notre-Dame Schule Neues." *Zeitschrift für Musikwissenschaft* 6 (1924): 545–58.

Ludwig, Friedrich. *Repertorium organorum recentioris et motetorum vetissimi stili.* Halle am Salle: Niemeyer, 1910.

Page, Christopher. *The Owl and the Nightingale: Musical Life and Ideas in France 1100–1300.* London: Dent, 1989.

Wright, Craig. *Music and Ceremony at Notre Dame of Paris 500–1550.* Cambridge: Cambridge University Press, 1989.

NOVAS. Occitan term (meaning "novel, story, argument") that described a range of works, including a late 12th- or early 13th-century discussion of amorous casuistry by Raimon Vidal, the *Judici d'amor* (1,698 octosyllabic lines), the 13th-century courtly romance *Flamenca* (more appropriately called the *Novas de Guillem de Nivers*), Arnaut de Carcassès's courtly tale *Novas del papagai* (309 octosyllabic lines), and a 14th-century piece of Catholic propaganda, *Novas de l'heretje* by Izarn (approximately 800 Alexandrine lines).

Wendy E. Pfeffer

[See also: *FLAMENCA*; TROUBADOUR POETRY]

Cornicelius, Max, ed. *So fo el temps c'om era iays: Novelle von Raimon Vidal nach vier bisher gefundenen Handschriften zum ersten Mal herausgegeben.* Berlin: Feicht, 1888.

Huchet, Jean-Charles, ed. and trans. *Nouvelles occitanes du moyen âge.* Paris: GF-Flammarion, 1992.

Meyer, Paul. "Le débat d'Izarn et de Sicart de Figueiras." *Annuaire-Bulletin de la Société de l'Histoire de France* 16 (1879): 233–84.

NOYON. Located due west of Laon, Noyon (Oise) lies just outside the 12th-century boundaries of the royal domain and just over sixty miles north of Paris. Here, Charlemagne was crowned king of the Franks and Hugh Capet was elected the first Capetian monarch in 987. Noyon, centered in the Oise River basin, is surrounded by rich agricultural land. Traffic into the Seine via the Oise and on the two major routes north and south from Paris to Flanders, and east and west from the channel ports to the fairs of Champagne, made the location of Noyon of paramount importance. Taxes imposed on goods entering and leaving Noyon augmented the treasury of the chapter and the all-important bishop-counts.

The kings of France usually backed the bishop-counts of Noyon. Louis VII made five visits to Noyon, and Philip II Augustus confirmed the city charter in 1181. The chapter,

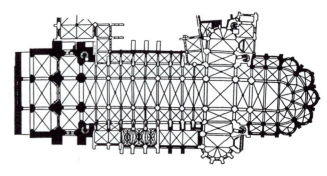

Noyon (Oise), plan of Notre-Dame. After Seymour.

Noyon, Notre-Dame, south transept. *Photograph courtesy of Whitney S. Stoddard.*

consisting of sixty-nine canons, with vast holdings that included mills, vineyards, and forests, was closely associated with the building campaigns for the cathedral. The body of St. Éloi, a 7th-century bishop, was a prize possession of the chapter of Noyon and greatly augmented revenue.

Between 1145 and 1150, following a fire of 1131, a decision was reached to construct a new cathedral. By 1155 or 1160, the five radiating chapels of the choir were completed and a decade later the ambulatory and choir were finished. These early campaigns consisted of a four-story elevation: nave arcade, gallery, blind triforium (no passageway), and clerestory. These campaigns were conservative in design when contrasted with the daring elegance of the Saint-Denis choir (1140–44).

By 1185, the upper choir, the unusual transepts, and the first bay of the nave were completed. The transepts have an arcade of windows above a blind arcade, a triforium with inner passageway, a gallery with passageway, and a clerestory with exterior passageway under embryonic flying buttresses. Reversing the gallery and the triforium is a design detail of extraordinary quality. Blocks of stone extend from exterior to interior walls stabilizing the solidity of the structure, as Norman master masons had done. The nave of Noyon emphasizes the alternation of piers and columns to support the six-part vaulting system, which was replaced in the 13th century by four-part vaults.

The exterior of Noyon, with its rounded aisleless transepts and its choir with radiating chapels and flanking towers and massive western towers, is quite different from the cathedral of Sens and the choir of Saint-Denis. Indeed, Noyon is very unlike all other Early Gothic cathedrals. It possesses an intimacy of scale, consistency of forms, and, especially in the design of the transepts, moments of great creativity.

Until recently, little was known about the monumental sculpture of Noyon except the presence of a fine seated Virgin and Child, badly damaged in 1918. However, in a 1992 article Charles T. Little connected stylistically three other life-size, seated figures to the Noyon Virgin and Child: Moses (The Cloisters, New York), Prophet (Lugano, Baron von Thyssen-Bornemisza Collection), and upper torso of John the Baptist (?) (Duke University). All these statues are distinguished by heavy, swirling folds that reveal contours of arms, elbows, knees, and legs. In style, they display marked similarities to the sculpture of the west portal of Senlis (ca. 1170). Further, Little, in a photomontage, has successfully placed this sculpture in the south-transept portal of the cathedral.

Whitney S. Stoddard

[See also: GOTHIC ARCHITECTURE]

Little, Charles T. "*Resurrexit*: A Rediscovered Sculptural Program from Noyon Cathedral." In *The Cloisters: Studies in Honor of the Fiftieth Anniversary*, ed. Elizabeth C. Parker. New York: Metropolitan Museum in association with the International Center of Medieval Art, 1992, pp. 235–59.

Seymour, Charles, Jr. *Notre-Dame of Noyon in the Twelfth Century: A Study of the Early Development of Gothic Architecture.* New Haven: Yale University Press, 1939.

Stoddard, Whitney S. *Art and Architecture in Medieval France.* New York: Harper and Row, 1972.

NUNNERIES. Throughout the early Middle Ages, religious women had many fewer opportunities for the cloistered life than did men. Nunneries were far outnumbered by male monasteries, and most nuns had not entered the religious life as children, as had the oblates in houses of Benedictine monks. Rather, the majority of nuns had taken the veil as widows, although there were always a certain number of girls, usually from wealthy families, who joined such houses. Although in the early Middle Ages, both in Britain and on the Continent, double monasteries were sometimes found, where a male monastery and a nunnery might be joined under the direction of a single abbess, such institutions tended to become male-only houses.

In the 11th and early 12th centuries, while every French town was surrounded by houses for monks, there might be only one nunnery in a region. Such a nunnery could, however, become an important center for women's intellectual life, and most women writers of this period were nuns. As the new monastic orders began to spread in the 11th century, nunneries were founded specifically to take the wives of men who had decided to enter the cloister; Marcigny, affiliated with Cluny, was such a house, as was Tart, established for the wives of Cistercian converts. But many women's religiosity had to be channeled in other directions before the end of the 12th century; women might establish themselves in small cells attached to male monasteries or decide to follow wondering preachers. Robert d'Arbrissel, for example, had a large group of women followers whom he was persuaded to make settle down as nuns at Fontevrault.

But religious houses for women began to multiply in the 13th century, including Benedictine nunneries but also establishments for canonesses and for such new orders as the Poor Clares, the female wing of the Franciscan order. Because the women of such orders were expected to follow a strict cloistered life, it was sometimes hard to distinguish them from more traditional nuns. By the end of the Middle Ages, there were many more nunneries than monasteries in France.

Constance B. Bouchard

[See also: BENEDICTINE ORDER; FONTEVRAULT; MONASTICISM; ROBERT D'ARBRISSEL; WOMEN, RELIGIOUS EXPERIENCE OF]

Johnson, Penelope D. *Equal in Monastic Profession: Religious Women in Medieval France.* Chicago: University of Chicago Press, 1991.

Wemple, Suzanne Fonay. *Women in Frankish Society: Marriage and the Cloister, 500–900.* Philadelphia: University of Pennsylvania Press, 1981.

Wischermann, Else Maria. *Marcigny-sur-Loire: Gründungs- und Frühgeschichte des ersten Cluniacenserinnenpriorates (1054–1150).* Munich: Fink, 1986.

O ANTIPHONS. These antiphons, sung with the Magnificat at First Vespers on the days preceding Christmas, are so named because they all begin with the exclamation "O." In the Middle Ages, they were sometimes known as the "great antiphons" (*antiphonae maiores*). The texts, charged with Old Testament messianic symbolism, begin with a divine epithet that is elaborated by subsequent phrases and end with an invitation beginning *veni* ("come"). The coherence of the basic group of seven found in medieval antiphoners (*O sapientia, O adonai, O radix Jesse, O clavis David, O oriens, O rex gentium, O Emmanuel*) is attested by the acrostic formed by the first letters of the divine epithets read in reverse: ERO CRAS ("I will be [here] tomorrow"). All of the texts are sung to a solemn melody in the second mode, which is not used outside this group. The number of O antiphons grew to as many as twelve in some sources, with the addition of other texts (*O virgo virginum, O Thoma Didyme*) to the original seven. The starting date of the cycle, which had to conclude on December 23, depended on the number of antiphons traditional in a particular locale.

A 7th-century Roman origin has been proposed by Callewaert, who traces their dissemination through England to the Continent. The Venerable Bede (d. 735) is said to have sung the antiphon *O rex gloriae*, a piece modeled after the O antiphons of Advent, on his deathbed, and in the late 8th century the English poet Cynewulf paraphrased the antiphons in *The Christ*. Alcuin (d. 804) lists ten O antiphons in his *De laude Dei*. Amalarius of Metz devoted a chapter of *De ordine antiphonarii* (837) to a discussion of these antiphons, but neither his ordering of the chants nor that of other French sources conforms to the arrangement suggested by the acrostic. Since Amalarius's antiphoner has been lost, the antiphoner of Compiègne (B.N. lat 17436), from the last third of the 9th century, represents the first appearance of the O antiphons in a liturgical book. Here, as elsewhere, they are entered as a group, not distributed according to the days on which they were to be sung.

These antiphons drew the attention of several medieval commentators on the liturgy (Berno, Jean Beleth, Honorius of Autun, Guillaume Durand, Reinerius of Liège),

and their solemn singing at the close of Advent broke to a certain degree with the penitential character of the season. The honor of intoning them before the Magnificat was reserved to dignitaries of the monastery or cathedral chapter. At Fleury, *O clavis* was assigned to the cellarer; at Rouen, it fell just as appropriately to the cathedral treasurer. In some places, these officials had to provide a treat for their colleagues when it was their turn to sing the O antiphon.

Joseph H. Dyer

[See also: ANTIPHON; MAGNIFICAT]

Liber Usualis. Tournai: Desclée, 1956, pp. 340–42.
Callewaert, Camillus. "De groote Adventsantifonen O." In *Sacris erudiri*. Steenbrugghe, 1942, pp. 405–16.
Rankin, Susan. "The Liturgical Background of the Old English Advent Lyrics: A Reappraisal." In *Learning and Literature in Anglo-Saxon England: Studies Presented to Peter Clemoes on the Occasion of His Sixty-fifth Birthday*, ed. Michael Lapidge and Helmut Gneuss. Cambridge: Cambridge University Press, 1985.
Thurston, Herbert. "The Great Antiphons, Heralds of Christmas." *The Month* 106 (1905): 616–31.
Weber, A. "Die sieben O-Antiphonen der Adventsliturgie." *Pastor bonus* 19 (1906–07): 109–19.

OCCITAN LANGUAGE. The indigenous language of roughly the southern third of what is now France. Occitan is not "a dialect of French" or of any other language. Like the other Romance tongues, it is derived from the spoken form of Latin that spread throughout the Roman Empire. After the conquest of Gallia Cisalpina, or northern Italy, completed shortly after 200 B.C., Rome soon extended its influence across the Alps into Gallia Transalpina. At that time, southern Gaul was inhabited by peoples whose languages are little known to us, notably Ligurians in the southeast, in the southwest tribes referred to variously as Iberians, pre-Basques, or Aquitanians, and an overlay of Gauls throughout the area. A few Greek colonies had been established along the coast beginning ca. 600 B.C.

The Roman military penetration of Occitania began ca. 125 B.C., when Roman forces were called on to repel a Celtic attack against the Greek colony of Massilia (now Marseille). Around 120 B.C., a Roman colony was founded farther west along the coast at Narbonne, which gave the name Gallia Narbonensis to the coastal territory between the Alps and Pyrénées, forming a link between Italy and the Roman provinces of Hispania. It was from southern Gaul, later known simply as Provincia, that in 58 B.C. Julius Caesar launched his conquest of "all Gaul." Latin gradually spread through Gaul, where Gaulish, a language of the Celtic family, became extinct by the 5th century A.D. (except, possibly, in Brittany).

The Occitan language developed its distinctive features from around the 5th to the 8th century. Texts of that time were written only in Latin, but we can suppose that by the 8th and 9th centuries religious works, such as hymns, religious dramas, and sermons (as recommended by the Council of Tours in 813), were being produced in spoken Occitan. Isolated Occitan words and expressions begin to appear in the late 10th century in oaths of fidelity written in Latin. The earliest known text entirely in Occitan, the *Boeci*, a Limousin fragment of the life of Boethius adapted from a Latin original, probably dates from shortly after the year 1000. Also from ca. 1000 dates the Occitan refrain to an *alba* (dawn song) otherwise written in Latin. The *Canço(n) de santa Fe* (probably written in Languedoc, in or near Narbonne) dates from the mid-11th century, followed by other religious works. Admixtures of Occitan occur in 11th-century Latin documents, and the first non-literary document entirely in Occitan, an act of donation, dates from 1102, followed by sixteen other documents before ca. 1120. Though French has earlier texts, Occitan has more documents from before 1200 than any other Romance language, probably because of active municipal life and commercial exchanges. The first known troubadour, Guilhem IX, must have begun to produce his verses shortly before 1100, since he was born in 1071, but the surviving manuscripts of troubadour poetry date only from the 13th century on. The Early Occitan period is generally considered to extend from ca. 800 to 1000, Old Occitan from 1000 to 1350, and Middle Occitan from 1350 to 1550.

In the Middle Ages, Provincia gave its name to Provence, which eventually became the southeastern province of the French kingdom, roughly bordered by the Alps, the Mediterranean, and the Rhône and Durance rivers. The corresponding adjective, *provincialis*, or "Provençal" in its modern French form, became used ca. 1280 for the language of southern France. However, it was not the first such term for that language. *Lengua romana* or *roma(n)*, meaning roughly "vernacular language," was used much earlier, and *lemosi(n)*, derived from the province of Limoges, came in ca. 1200, while *lenga d'oc*, derived from the distinctive affirmative particle *oc*, came into use ca. 1290.

The term "Provençal" (which American scholars tend to pronounce /pRovāsál/ as in French, though some prefer the anglicized version /prəvéntsəl/) began to predominate in the 16th century and was given further impetus by the late 19th-century literary revival centered in Provence known as the *felibrige* movement and by the translations and essays through which Ezra Pound made the troubadours into an important influence on 20th-century poetry. Today, however, most scholars consider that "Provençal" should be reserved for the dialect of the southeast, and that "Occitan" (attested from ca. 1300 under the form *occitanus*) is the most appropriate overall term for this language, whose identity history has cast into confusion by denying it a national state.

From the preliterary period until ca. 1200, Occitan was the chief language of everyday communication in Occitan territory. Latin was known to all educated persons and was spoken, at least on formal occasions, by clerics and intellectuals, but as a written language it was increasingly displaced by the vernacular. In the 12th century, French remained a foreign tongue, compared by at least one troubadour to the barking of dogs. But beginning with the French penetration of Occitania under the guise of the Albigensian Crusade in the early 13th century, the Occitan language has been in almost constant recession. Although Occitan persevered as the standard administrative and judicial language into the 15th century, the prestige of the conquering French culture and the centralizing linguistic tendencies of the Renaissance monarchy and of all subsequent French regimes have fragmented Occitan into a scattering of oral "patois." Almost all of the several million speakers of its various dialects are now bilingual in French, and most inhabitants of Occitania know nothing of the Occitan language. Occitan speakers today fall into two chief groups: inhabitants of remote villages and mountainous areas, and a small number of intellectuals largely connected to Languedocian universities. In the 1980s, Occitan entered the "program" of the French *baccalauréat* and is now studied in certain universities as both a living and a medieval language. Literary expression continues to be torn between the Provençal dialect in the late 19th-century tradition established by poets like Frederi Mistral, and Languedocian, notably as codified by the Institut d'Estudis Occitans in Toulouse.

Because the romanization of southern Gaul began so early and was nearly complete, the form of Latin that came to be spoken in Occitania, the linguistic territory of Occitan, was more conservative, that is, closer to the language of Rome, than in most other areas of the empire. In addition, Occitania was less affected than northern France by the Germanic influence that spread through Gaul in the 5th and 6th centuries, primarily by the Visigoths (particularly in Aquitaine), Burgundians, and Franks, who at times controlled all of what is now France and more.

Still, Occitan and French have enough in common, owing mainly to the common Celtic influence, to be generally considered the two main components of the Gallo-Romance family. That family also includes a group of "Franco-Provençal" dialects around Geneva, Mâcon, Lyon, Saint-Étienne, and Grenoble, which comprise a separate language showing linguistic traits of both Occitan and French. (Gallo-Romance, according to many scholars, also includes the scattered Rheto-Romance areas of Switzerland and northeastern Alpine Italy.)

Occitania is usually divided into three groups of dialects. The southwestern group, Gascon, lies roughly between the Pyrénées, the Atlantic, and the Garonne River. Gascon, considered a separate Romance language by a few specialists, includes the geographical curiosity of Aranais, spoken in the Aran Valley on the southern slopes of the Pyrénées, adjoining the Catalan domain. The southern Occitan dialects are (1) in the southeast, Provençal, whose border runs roughly from the Alps slightly north of Menton, west to include Digne and Orange, across the Rhône, then south to include Nîmes and the Rhône delta; and (2) in the central south, Languedocian, whose large area includes Montpellier, Béziers, Narbonne, Carcassonne, Toulouse, Albi, Agen, Cahors, Rodez, Aurillac, Mende, and nearby points. The northern Occitan dialects are (1) Limousin in the areas of Limoges, Périgueux, and Tulle; (2) Auvergnat in the center of the Massif Central, including the areas of Clermont-Ferrand and Le Puy; and (3) Alpine Provençal from slightly west of the Rhône (including Privas and Valence) east along the Isère River and on farther east to encompass the Piedmontese slopes of the Alps.

Looking at a different set of linguistic traits, however, one can also attach Languedocian to Gascon and Provençal to the northern Occitan dialects. Further debate is fueled by some Occitanists who prefer to attach Occitan and Gascon to Catalan as a "Occitano-Romance" family; it is certainly true that Occitan and Catalan, at least in the Middle Ages, are far closer to each other linguistically than to French and Spanish.

An area of mingled French and Occitan dialect, known as the "Crescent," includes parts of the provinces of La Marche and Bourbonnais, north of Limoges and Clermont-Ferrand. Debate continues as to whether the Occitan domain once included, or at least influenced and was influenced by, southern Poitou, especially since the work of the first troubadour, Guilhem IX of Aquitaine and VII of Poitiers, shows several traits of Poitevin, which can be considered his native tongue.

Medieval Occitan is known through a wealth of deeds, charters, oaths, troubadour poetry, and other literary texts, as well as through treatises on the language, beginning ca. 1200 with Raimon Vidal de Besalú's *Razos de trobar*. These contemporary treatises, like the documents, the troubadours' use of rhyme, and other evidence, reveal greater linguistic standardization than in the French of that period. It is usual to speak of literary Occitan as being a koine, a supradialectal language of general communication. Although the Occitan koine accepts some traits of various dialects, its origin lies probably in Languedoc.

Medieval Occitan shares some phonetic characteristics with French but is closer to Catalan and Italian. Since it has a fairly strong expiratory stress affecting at least one syllable in most words, intertonic and posttonic vowels usually fall (DELICATUM > *delgat* 'delicate'), except that *a* remains (rather than being weakened as in French): MIRABILIAM > *meravelha* 'wonder.' Stressed *e* and *o* tend to diphthongize less than in French and only in certain phonetic contexts and dialects (MEUM > *meu, mieu* 'my'; FOLIAM > *folha, fuelha* 'leaf'), though more frequently than in most other Romance idioms. Vowels are, at least in the Middle Ages, not perceptibly nasalized before a nasal vowel. The Vulgar Latin prosthetic vowel before *s* + consonant remains as *e* (SCHOLAM > *escola* 'school').

Intervocalic consonants or consonants that become word-final generally do not drop, though they are often altered in various ways. Notably, single intervocalic unvoiced consonants generally become voiced : RIPAM > *riba* 'shore,' VITAM > *vida* 'life,' AMICAM > *amiga* 'friend' (f.), PRESENTEM (with /s/) > *presen* (with /z/) 'present.' Some consonants become palatalized in certain positions; for example, *g* before *e* or *i* (SIGILLUM > *sagel* 'seal') or, dialectally, before *a* (*amija*, also reduced to *amia*, for *amiga*). The initial sounds /g/ and /k/ are palatalized to /dʒ/ and /tʃ/ before *a* only in northern Occitan (CANTUM > *can, chan* 'song').

Unlike the case in French, intervocalic *n* that becomes word-final can optionally drop without leaving any trace (FINEM > *fi(n)* 'end'). Many consonants vocalize in certain positions (e.g., ALBAM > *alba, auba* 'dawn'), though not always following the same patterns as in French; the result is a series of diphthongs and triphthongs that is even richer than in Old French. The combination CT has two principal dialectal outcomes, /tʃ/ and /jt/: NOCTEM > *nuech, nueit* 'night.' The behavior of certain groups, notably those ending in /j/ and /w/, is complex and in some cases surprising: BRACHIUM > *bratz, bras* 'arm,' DEBUIT > *dec* 'he/she owed.'

The consonant *h*, whether derived from Latin or Germanic *h*, is not pronounced and there is no Occitan version of French "*h* aspiré" (however, *h* is used in various combinations representing the affricative /tʃ/, and Gascon *h*, derived from Latin *f*, represents a strong /h/ sound).

Occitan vocabulary is almost entirely derived from Latin, without the influx of Germanic and Arabic words that marked French and Spanish, respectively. The few Germanic words are largely widespread Romance borrowings in the expected semantic areas, denoting colors (BLANK > *blanc* 'white'), military objects (HELM > *elm* 'helmet'), geography (BUSK > *bosc* 'forest'). There is also the usual assortment of learned terms derived from Greek: *filosophia, propheta*.

The "classical" (late 12th-c.) literary language contains the following twenty-five consonant phonemes: /p/, /t/, /k/, /b/, /d/, /g/, /ts/, /tʃ/, /dz/, /dʒ/, /f/, /s/, /ʃ/, /v/, /z/, /ʒ/, /r/, /rr/, /l/, /ʎ/, /ʎ/, /m/, /n/, /ɲ/, /ŋ/. The vowels were /i/, /y/, /e/, /ɛ/, /a/, /a̧/, /o̧/, /o̧/, /u/ (there were no /ø/ and /œ/ as in French), and semivowels were /j/, /w/, and /ɥ/. Combinations of these yield about sixteen distinct diphthongs and four triphthongs. All of these categories contain more phonemes than in Old French. As in Old French, authors and scribes render these sounds in varied and confusing ways, and modern editors use different conventions to represent the medieval spellings and pronunciations. On the whole, the modern reader with a basic knowledge of the Old Occitan spelling can make a pretty good attempt at pronouncing as the troubadours did. However, it takes some sophistication to determine the location of tonic stress, and often only a knowledge of etymology can distinguish between the open and closed *e* and *o*.

Like Old French, Old Occitan has a two-case declension of nouns and adjectives that is most prominent and regular in masculines: *murs, mur, mur, murs* 'wall' (cited in the conventional order: nominative singular, oblique singular, nominative plural, oblique plural). Some feminine nouns follow a similar pattern (*flors, flor, flors, flors* 'flower'), but most merely distinguish singular and plural: *domna* 'lady,' *domnas* 'ladies.' A number of masculine nouns and a couple of feminine ones show shifting stress, a changing number of syllables, or both: *bar, baro(n), baro(n), barons* 'noble.' Several other patterns exist, while some nouns and adjectives are invariable.

The verb system has forms corresponding to the active and passive voices; the indicative, subjunctive, conditional, imperative, infinitive, and participial moods; the future, present, imperfect, preterit, future perfect, compound past, pluperfect, and past anterior tenses; three persons; and two numbers. Verbs can be divided into three conjugations, characterized by the thematic vowels *a, e,* and *i.* The most idiosyncratic feature is perhaps the "strong" preterits, which follow patterns like, for *penre* 'to take,' *pris, prezist, pres, prezem, prezetz, preiro(n).* The large number of irregular verbs—on the whole, the most frequently used ones—pose a continuous challenge to the reader.

Further challenges are word order, which is fairly free given that the functions of most nouns, adjectives, and verbs within a sentence are adequately revealed by their endings, and the plentiful use of masculine, feminine, and neuter personal pronouns, whose forms and functions often overlap in ways that give room to the interpreter's imagination. Naturally, with the license encouraged by the constraints of rhyme and syllabification, poetry is harder to interpret than prose, which is closer to the presumed but irretrievable language of everyday life in medieval Occitania.

Nathaniel B. Smith

[See also: FRENCH LANGUAGE; TROBAIRITZ; TROUBADOUR POETRY]

Bec, Pierre. *La langue occitane.* 5th ed. Paris: Presses Universitaires de France, 1986.

Brun, Auguste. *Recherches historiques sur l'introduction du français dans les provinces du Midi.* Paris: Champion, 1923.

Brunel, Clovis, ed. *Les plus anciennes chartes en langue provençale.* Paris: Picard, 1926; *Supplément,* 1952.

Jensen, Frede. *The Old Provençal Noun and Adjective Declension.* Odense: Odense University Press, 1976.

———. *The Syntax of Medieval Occitan.* Tübingen: Niemeyer, 1986.

Klingebiel, Kathryn. *Bibliographie linguistique de l'ancien occitan (1960–1982).* Hamburg: Buske, 1986.

Levy, Émil. *Petit dictionnaire provençal-français.* 5th ed. Heidelberg: Winter, 1973.

Smith, Nathaniel B. "The Normalization of Old Provençal Spelling: Criteria and Solutions." In *Studia occitanica in memoriam Paul Remy,* ed. Hans-Erich Keller et al. Kalamazoo: Medieval Institute, 1986.

———, and Thomas G. Bergin. *An Old Provençal Primer.* New York: Garland, 1984. [With bibliography.]

Tenso: Bulletin of the Société Guilhem IX. [Includes bibliographical updates.]

OCKEGHEM, JOHANNES (ca. 1420–1497). Franco-Flemish composer, active mainly in France. According to recently discovered documents, he was born in Saint-Ghislain, a village near Mons in the Belgian province of Hainaut. His career is first traced in Antwerp, where he was a singer at the church of Notre-Dame in 1443/44. From 1446 to 1448, he was singer in the chapel of Charles I, duke of Bourbon, at Moulins. He became a member of the French royal chapel under Charles VII ca. 1450 and continued to serve that institution under Louis XI and Charles VIII. Named as first chaplain in 1454, he was subsequently cited as master of the chapel (1464) and counselor to the king (1477). In 1459, Charles VII, who was hereditary abbot of Saint-Martin of Tours, appointed Ockeghem to the important post of treasurer of Saint-Martin. Sometime before 1472, possibly in 1464, he was ordained a priest at Cambrai. The only journey he is known to have undertaken outside France and the Low Countries is one to Spain in 1470. In 1484, he revisited his native country when he and other members of the royal chapel traveled to Damme and Bruges in Flanders. He eventually retired to Tours, where he died on February 6, 1497.

Among his pupils may have been Antoine Busnoys, a cleric at Saint-Martin of Tours in 1465 and subsequently singer in the chapel of Charles the Bold, duke of Burgundy. Busnoys honored Ockeghem in his motet *In hydraulis,* calling him the "true image of Orpheus." At Cambrai, Ockeghem met Guillaume Dufay, his greatest musical contemporary, who in 1464 entertained him at his house. The Flemish music theorist Johannes Tinctoris dedicated his treatise on the modes (1476) jointly to Ockeghem and Busnoys, and in his treatises on proportions and counterpoint he cited Ockeghem as "the most excellent of all the composers I have ever heard." In his last treatise, *De inventione et usu musicae* (ca. 1481), Tinctoris describes him not only as a distinguished composer but as the finest bass singer known to him.

Ockeghem's personal appearance and manner, as well as his musicianship, were often praised by his contemporaries. Guillaume Crétin wrote a *Déploration sur le trespas de feu Okergan,* praising his "subtlety" and calling on his mourning colleagues, led by Dufay and Busnoys, to sing his music, including his "exquisite and most perfect Requiem Mass." The poet Jean Molinet also wrote a *déploration* on his death, which was set to music by Josquin des Prez, the great master of the next generation of French composers. An *epitaphium* for Ockeghem by Erasmus of Rotterdam was set by Johannes Lupi in the 16th century.

Ockeghem composed in all genres, but his most important works are his fourteen Masses. A single Credo and only five motets by him are known, but they are each highly individual works. Twenty-two secular songs, all but one in French, come down to us. The exception is a Spanish song, probably a memento of his visit to Spain.

In his time and throughout subsequent centuries, Ockeghem was renowned for his contrapuntal skill, especially in canonic writing. His masterpiece in this technique is his *Missa prolationum,* consisting almost entirely of double canons at all intervals within the octave, and in four different "prolations" (meters) simultaneously. Almost legendary in his time was a thirty-six-voice canon mentioned by Crétin and others, the identity of which remains controversial. His Requiem Mass, which may have been written on the death of Charles VII (1461), is the earliest surviving example of its kind.

The most distinctive features of Ockeghem's music are its varied, unpredictable rhythms and long-breathed, overlapping phrases. Its texture of equally important though highly independent melodic lines and its exploration of the bass register are progressive features, but in many respects its unpredictable, "mystical" character, which virtually defies analysis, evokes a Late Gothic spirit rather than displaying the clarity of the emerging Renaissance style of his contemporaries.

Martin Picker

[See also: BUSNOYS, ANTOINE; CYCLIC MASS; DUFAY, GUILLAUME; TINCTORIS, JOHANNES]

Ockeghem, Johannes. *Collected Works*, ed. Dragan Plamenac and Richard Wexler. 3 vols. N.p.: American Musicological Society, 1947–92.

Goldberg, Clemens. *Die Chansons Johannes Ockeghems.* Laaber: Laaber, 1992.

Lindmayr, Andrea. *Quellenstudien zu den Motetten von Johannes Ockeghem.* Laaber: Laaber, 1992.

Perkins, Leeman L. "The *L'homme armé* Masses of Busnoys and Ockeghem: A Comparison." *Journal of Musicology* 3 (1984): 363–96.

Picker, Martin. *Johannes Ockeghem and Jacob Obrecht: A Guide to Research.* New York: Garland, 1988.

Sparks, Edgar H. *Cantus Firmus in the Mass and Motet, 1420–1520.* Berkeley: University of California Press, 1963.

Thein, Wolfgang. *Musikalischer Satz und Textdarbeitung im Werk von Johannes Ockeghem.* Tutzing: Schneider, 1992.

OCKHAM, WILLIAM OF (William Occam; ca. 1285–1347). Born in Ockham in Surrey, England, William entered a Franciscan convent at an early age. In 1306, he was ordained subdeacon at Southwark in London and began his education at Oxford, where he lectured on Peter Lombard's *Sentantiae* from 1317 to 1319. John Luttrell, the chancellor at Oxford, opposed Ockham's views. Pope John XXII called him to Avignon in 1323/24. A committee investigated Ockham's works and censured fifty-one propositions but did not formally condemn him. In 1327, he met Michael of Cesena, the minister-general of the Franciscan order and leader of the Spiritual Franciscans. Cesena requested Ockham to examine John XXII's constitutions on Franciscan poverty. Ockham declared them full of error and the following year fled Avignon with Cesena and others. He was excommunicated in 1328. He joined the emperor Louis of Bavaria in his dispute with the pope and in 1330 settled at the Franciscan convent in Munich. In 1331, Ockham was expelled from the order and sentenced to imprisonment. He died in Munich in 1347, still under Louis's protective care.

Ockham's writings fall into three stages corresponding to his major residences: Oxford (1306/07–23), Avignon (1323–28), and Germany (1330–47). At Oxford and Avignon, his writings include his commentary on the *Sententiae*, later published in two parts: the *Ordinatio*, his lectures on the first book, and the *Reportatio*, comprising notes taken at his lectures. He also composed commentaries on Aristotle's *Organon*; *Summa logicae*, his major statement on logic; seven quodlibetals; and treatises on the Body of Christ, on the eucharist, and on predestination. After his departure from Avignon in 1328, he wrote works against the Avignon papacy, the chief ones being *Opus nonaginta dierum*, about papal errors regarding poverty; *Dialogus inter magistrum et discipulum* (1333–47); eight *quaestiones* on papal authority (1340); and a treatise on the respective powers of emperor and pope (ca. 1347).

Ockham was principally a theologian, vigorously exploring the philosophical limits of each epistemological, logical, or metaphysical issue, often to see more clearly the theological application. He rejected the older Platonic Realism and the *via antiqua* of the Aristotelians to pursue a *via moderna*, a path of demonstration and the near-autonomy of faith. He insisted upon a method of economy of explanation, later termed "Ockham's razor." With the nominalists, he contested the reality of universals and affirmed the fundamental reality of particulars for the human mind. His own solution to the relationship between universals and particulars is often called "conceptualist" instead of "nominalist," because he viewed concepts not merely as creatures of the mind but rather as entities identical with the abstractive cognition by which the mind considers individual objects in a certain way. With Duns Scotus, he asserted the utter transcendence and unique necessity and freedom of God in contrast with the contingency of all else, including so-called natural and moral laws. He argued the distinction between God's absolute power and that of his ordained power, manifest in his decrees, by which God limits himself to operate within ordinations he established. Ockham also contributed to medieval and early-modern political theory and ecclesiology. He influenced conciliarism, and his theological legacy reached to Pierre d'Ailly, Gabriel Biel, and Martin Luther. He attacked the wealth of the church, challenged the notions of papal infallibility and plenitude of power, upheld the right of imperial election apart from papal interference, and conceded to the emperor the responsibility to depose a heretical pope. He maintained that the papacy was not established by Christ, that the general council was superior to the papacy, but that the pope possessed an ordinary executive authority unless he were heretical.

H. Lawrence Bond

[See also: AVIGNON PAPACY; D'AILLY, PIERRE; DUNS SCOTUS, JOHN; PHILOSOPHY; SCHOLASTICISM; THEOLOGY; UNIVERSITIES]

Ockham, William of. *Opera philosophica*, ed. Philotheus Boehner et al. 3 vols. St. Bonaventure: Editiones Instituti Franciscani Universitatis S. Bonaventurae, 1974–85.

———. *Opera theologica*, ed. Gedeon Gál et al. 10 vols. St. Bonaventure: Editiones Instituti Franciscani Universitatis S. Bonaventurae, 1967–86.

———. *Opera politica*, ed. Jeffrey G. Sikes et al. 3 vols. Manchester: University of Manchester Press, 1940– .

———. *William of Ockham. Philosophical Writings: A Selection*, ed. and trans. Philotheus Boehner. rev. ed. Stephen F. Brown. Indianapolis: Hackett, 1990.

Adams, Marilyn McCord. *William Ockham.* 2 vols. Notre Dame: University of Notre Dame Press, 1987.

Baudry, León. *Guillaume d'Occam: sa vie, ses œuvres, ses idées sociales et politiques.* Paris: Vrin, 1949, Vol. 1: *L'homme et les œuvres.*

Boehner, Philotheus. *Collected Articles on Ockham,* ed. Eligii M. Buytaert. St. Bonaventure: Franciscan Institute, 1958.

McGrade, Arthur Stephen. *The Political Thought of William of Ockham: Personal and Institutional Principles.* London: Cambridge University Press, 1974.

Moody, Ernest A. *The Logic of William Ockham.* London: Sheed and Ward, 1935.

ODILO (961–1049). One of the long-lived abbots of Cluny who helped establish the monastery's authority and prestige (r. 994–1049), Odilo was from a noble family of Auvergne, son of a couple named Berald and Gerberge. Odilo's brother Berald became provost of Le Puy. Odilo himself had been a canon at Brioude, in Auvergne, before coming to Cluny. As prior of Cluny, he governed the house during the final years of his predecessor, Maiolus. In the final years of Odilo's own life, his prior and eventual successor, Hugues, similarly governed for him.

Under Odilo, Cluny reformed a number of monasteries to a regular life, especially in Burgundy. Some, like Paray-le-Monial, became Cluniac priories; others, like Saint-Germain of Auxerre and Saint-Bénigne of Dijon, retained their own abbots while following Cluniac customs.

Constance B. Bouchard

[**See also:** CLUNIAC ORDER; ODO]

Jotsaldus. *Vita Odilonis. PL* 142.897–940.

Bouchard, Constance B. *Sword, Miter, and Cloister: Nobility and the Church in Burgundy, 980–1198.* Ithaca: Cornell University Press, 1987.

Hourlier, Jacques. *Saint Odilon, abbé de Cluny.* Louvain: Bibliothèque de l'Université, 1964.

Rosenwein, Barbara H. *To Be the Neighbor of Saint Peter: The Social Meaning of Cluny's Property, 909–1049.* Ithaca: Cornell University Press, 1989.

ODO (d. 944). Cluny first became an important monastic center under Abbot Odo (r. 926–44), who was from an aristocratic family, probably of the region of Berry. In his youth, he had served in the household of Duke William I the Pious of Aquitaine, Cluny's founder, before becoming a monk at Saint-Martin of Tours. Later, he moved to the stricter monastery of Baume, where Berno was abbot, a house founded by disciples of Benedict of Aniane. Berno also became abbot of four other houses, including Cluny when it was founded in 909, and upon his death Odo was chosen to succeed him at Cluny. In the 12th century, the Cluniacs considered Odo rather than Berno their true founder.

As abbot, Odo took over the direction of eleven houses, most located some distance from Cluny. The most important of these was Romainmoutier, in the trans-Saône kingdom of Burgundy, but his reforms also included houses in Auvergne and southern France, in the west (Tours), and even in Italy. Some of these houses were governed again in later generations by their own abbots, but some stayed under the direction of Cluny's abbot. In all cases, the purpose was to restore the monastic life to regularity, by ejecting dissolute monks if necessary, and to make sure that future monks followed Cluniac customs. As well as his reforms, Odo is well known for his *vita* of Gerald of Aurillac, which became a model for the holy life a layman might follow, without becoming a monk, yet acting as an important protector of monks.

Constance B. Bouchard

[**See also:** CLUNIAC ORDER; HAGIOGRAPHY]

John of Salerno. *Vita sancti Odonis. PL* 133.43–86.

Odo. *De vita sancti Geraldi. PL* 133.630–704.

Sitwell, Gerard, ed. and trans. *St. Odo of Cluny: Being the Life of St. Odo of Cluny by John of Salerno and the Life of St. Gerald of Aurillac by St. Odo.* London: Sheed and Ward, 1958.

Rosenwein, Barbara H. *Rhinoceros Bound: Cluny in the 10th Century.* Philadelphia: University of Pennsylvania Press, 1982.

———. "St. Odo's St. Martin: The Uses of a Model." *Journal of Medieval History* 4 (1978): 316–31.

ODO OF DEUIL (d. 1162). A monk of Saint-Denis who succeeded the famous Suger as abbot in 1152. Odo's reputation is due mainly to his chronicle of the unsuccessful Second Crusade. He served as chaplain to Louis VII on this expedition, and his *De profectione Ludovici VII in orientem* is a firsthand account of events from the time Louis took the cross in 1146 until he sailed from Adalia to Antioch in March 1148.

John Bell Henneman, Jr.

Odo of Deuil. *Odo of Deuil: De profectione Ludovici VII in orientem/The Journey of Louis VII to the East,* ed. and trans. Virginia G. Berry. New York: Columbia University Press, 1948.

OGIER LE DANOIS. *See* **CHEVALERIE OGIER**

OLORON-SAINTE-MARIE. The exterior of the church of Sainte-Croix (begun ca. 1070) in Oloron-Sainte-Marie (Pyrénées-Atlantiques) is disappointing: the defensive-looking tower is heavy, the walls and chevet visibly remodeled, and the doorway a ruin. The Romanesque interior, however, is intact: nave of three bays with side aisles, short transept, apse, and two apsidal chapels. Notable are the octagonal cupola, ribbed in a stellate pattern, and the rich carving of the sanctuary capitals.

The former cathedral of Sainte-Marie (begun ca. 1102) is essentially Gothic: the nave and side aisles are 13th-century; the pentagonal choir, ambulatory, and five radiating chapels were reconstructed in the 14th. The iconography of the celebrated sculpture of the Romanesque portal has been variously interpreted. Remarkable are the marble Deposition of the tympanum, the chained captives of the trumeau, and the wealth of contemporary and anecdotal detail (musical instruments, daily occupations, culinary customs) in the images of the archivolts.

Jean M. French

Allègre, Victor. *Les vieilles églises du Béarn: étude archéologique.* Toulouse: Imprimerie Régionale, 1952.

Andral, Gabriel. "Oloron-Sainte-Marie." *Congrès archéologique (Bordeaux et Bayonne)* 102 (1939): 415–25.

Bartal, Ruth. "Le programme iconographique du portail occidental de Sainte-Marie d'Oloron et son contexte historique." *Cahiers de Saint-Michel de Cuxa 18* (1987): 95–113.

Durliat, Marcel, and Victor Allègre. *Pyrénées romanes.* La Pierre-qui-vire: Zodiaque, 1969.

Lacoste, Jacques. "Le portail roman de Sainte-Marie d'Oloron." *Revue de Pau et du Béarn* 1 (1973): 45–78.

ORBAIS. The Benedictine abbey of Saint-Pierre, Orbais (Marne), was founded in the later 7th century by St. Réole, archbishop of Reims. Construction of the present church was inaugurated ca. 1165, and the initial project, which realized the five radiating chapels and hemicycle piers, may have envisioned a four-story elevation influenced by Laon and Noyon. Modified into a three-story scheme during the second campaign, ca. 1195, the straight bays and upper levels of the choir were indebted primarily to Saint-Remi, Reims, and the new work at Soissons cathedral. The bar tracery of the clerestory windows of the nave, of which only a single bay remains, was adopted ca. 1220 soon after its appearance at the cathedral of Reims. Although not an innovative structure, Orbais reflects the contemporary developments in northern France, and its combination of such features as the linkage of triforium and clerestory and bar tracery anticipate later compositions of the Rayonnant period of Gothic architecture.

Michael T. Davis

[See also: GOTHIC ARCHITECTURE; LAON; NOYON; REIMS; SOISSONS]

Dubout, Nicolas. *Histoire de l'abbaye d'Orbais*, ed. Étienne Héron de Villefosse. Paris: Picard, 1890.

Héliot, Pierre. "Deux églises champenoises méconnues: les abbatiales d'Orbais et d'Essomes." *Mémoires de la Société d'Agriculture, Commerce, Sciences et Arts de la Marne* 80 (1965): 86–112.

Kimpel, Dieter, and Robert Suckale. *Die gotische Architektur in Frankreich, 1130–1270.* Munich: Hirmer, 1985.

Prache, Anne. *Saint-Remi de Reims: l'œuvre de Pierre de Celles et sa place dans l'architecture gothique.* Geneva: Droz, 1978.

Villes, Alain. "L'ancienne abbatiale Saint-Pierre d'Orbais." *Congrès archéologique (Champagne)* 135 (1977): 549–89.

ORCIVAL. The 12th-century pilgrimage church of Notre-Dame at Orcival (Puy-de-Dôme) was constructed in a single campaign out of grey volcanic rock and is distinguished by its austerity and gravity. The church lies at the foot of a hill that constrains it on the west side. As a result, the primary portal is on the south side of the church and the nave is shorter than it should have been in proportion to the rest of the building. Crossed by a transept, it has a semicircular chevet and an ambulatory with four radiating chapels and is preceded by a narthex. Three diaphragm arches support a square cupola over the crossing. A crypt extends beneath the sanctuary.

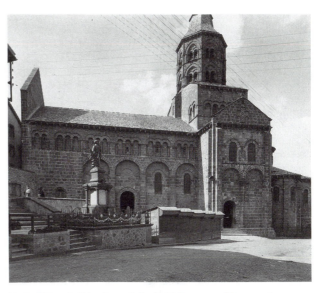

Orcival (Puy-de-Dôme), south flank, 12th century. *Photograph courtesy of Whitney S. Stoddard.*

Almost every column in the church is crowned by a foliate capital. A noteworthy exception depicts a usurer tormented by demons. The church houses a celebrated Virgin reliquary in silver-gilt wood (12th c.).

Nina Rowe

Craplet, Bernard. *Auvergne romane.* La Pierre-qui-vire: Zodiaque, 1955.

Ranquet, Henri du. "Orcival." *Congrès archéologique (Clermont-Ferrand)* 87 (1924): 384–405.

ORDERIC VITALIS (d. ca. 1142). A monk of mixed Anglo-Norman parentage, Orderic Vitalis joined the monastery of Saint-Évroult, in Normandy, ca. 1085. The other monks found his Saxon name, Orderic, barbaric and renamed him Vitalis. His fame is due to his *Historia ecclesiastica.* This work covers the history of Normandy, England, and northern France from the late 11th century to 1141 and is one of the best sources of information on Anglo-Norman society.

Constance B. Bouchard

Orderic Vitalis. *Historia ecclesiastica*, ed. and trans. Marjorie Chibnall. 6 vols. Oxford: Clarendon, 1969–80.

Chibnall, Marjorie. *The World of Orderic Vitalis.* Oxford: Clarendon, 1984.

ORESME, NICOLE

ORESME, NICOLE (ca. 1320/25–1382). A writer known mainly for his mathematical, scientific, and economic treatises and for his vernacular translations of Aristotle. Educated in arts and theology at the Collège de Navarre in Paris, Oresme was in 1356 appointed its grand master. During this period, his long association with the royal family began; he may have been tutor of John II's son, the future Charles V. Partly because of his royal connections, Oresme obtained church offices, becoming canon at Rouen (1362), canon at the Sainte-Chapelle (1363), dean of the cathedral of Rouen (1364), and bishop of Lisieux (1377).

Oresme's writings demonstrate his wide learning. His mathematical and scientific works, such as *De proportionibus proportionum*, *De configurationibus qualitatum et motuum*, and *De commensurabilitate vel incommensurabilitate motuum celi*, are important for their treatment of fractional exponents, their graphic representation of mathematical functions, and their sophisticated discussions of mechanics and astronomy. Oresme also used his learning, in such treatises as *Contra judiciarios astronomos*, *Livre de divinacions*, and *De causis mirabilium*, to attack the "misuse" of science, especially by the astrologers.

Certain of Oresme's works were written explicitly for the royal family. His economic treatise, *De mutationibus monetarum*, was composed during the 1350s for John II. In the late 1360s, Charles V asked Oresme to translate the Latin versions of four Aristotelian texts, the *Ethics*, the *Politics*, the pseudo-Aristotelian *Economics*, and *De caelo et mundo*. Oresme's vernacular translations helped to create a flexible French prose and to expand the French vocabulary, introducing as many as 1,000 new words.

Oresme has often been seen as anticipating modernity: in certain ways, his astronomy foreshadows Copernicus, Galileo, and Kepler, and his mathematics Descartes; his economics may anticipate Gresham's Law. But Oresme is perhaps most impressive in his ability to summarize and synthesize logically and intelligently, all the while advancing the important theories of his age.

Steven F. Kruger

[See also: CHARLES V THE WISE; CURRENCY; TRANSLATION]

Oresme, Nicole. *De proportionibus proportionum and Ad pauca respicientes*, ed. and trans. Edward Grant. Madison: University of Wisconsin Press, 1966.

———. *Le livre de politiques d'Aristote*, ed. Albert Douglas Menut. Philadelphia: American Philosophical Society, 1970.

———. *Nicole Oresme and the Medieval Geometry of Qualities and Motions: A Treatise on the Uniformity and Difformity of Intensities Known as Tractatus de configurationibus qualitatum et motuum*, ed. and trans. Marshall Clagett. Madison: University of Wisconsin Press, 1968.

Hansen, Bert, ed. and trans. *Nicole Oresme and the Marvels of Nature: A Study of His De causis mirabilium with Critical Edition, Translation, and Commentary*. Toronto: Pontifical Institute of Mediaeval Studies, 1985.

Menut, Albert Douglas. "A Provisional Bibliography of Oresme's Writings." *Mediaeval Studies* 28 (1966): 279–99; supplementary note, 31 (1969): 346–47.

ORGANUM

ORGANUM. During the 12th century, improvised and composed or notated vocal polyphonic music began to take on a distinct stylistic change that ultimately divided it into two types. In discant, one or more parts were added mostly note-against-note to a plainchant melody, possibly moving in parallel motion but often in contrary motion with it; in organum, one part embellished with many notes each note of the plainchant, thus slowing it down considerably and making it, at its most ornate, unrecognizable. The limitation to which organum, described as an "infinitely flexible" art, was subject was that there could be but one performer of the added part, and therefore it would have been impossible to coordinate adequately between two or more singers. Organum was an almost perfect medium for virtuoso solo singing and improvising, in contrast to discant, in which interaction among singers (one to a part), a sense of ensemble, was the primary requirement. The singer of the plainchant played a role of support by sustaining each note of the chant until he coordinated the next one with the soloist, and organum that survives in notation is always in score so that the correlation of the two parts can more readily be seen.

These two different styles of polyphony, discant and organum, were nevertheless generically called "organum," and thus the polyphony for the Graduals, Alleluias, and Responsories of the Notre-Dame repertory are termed "organa," including the organa for three and four parts. Theorists of the 13th century who discussed "measurable music" (*musica mensurabilis*) divided this generic organum into three categories, most often discant, copula, and organum, the last being called *organum purum* or *organum in speciali*. These are not three types of pieces of music, however, but the three styles or musical textures that could be found within the polyphony for a Gradual, Alleluia, or Responsory. In time, genres became categorized as species of discant—e.g., the motet—and there seem to be such ties between copula and hocket that need further elucidation. The *Magnus liber organi* for the cathedral of Notre-Dame in Paris was, in its original form, apparently mostly in organum style, since its compiler, Léonin, was called *optimus organista*. Léonin's successor Pérotin, called *optimus discantor*, possibly revised much of the *Magnus liber organi*, replacing many of the passages in organum style with discant; and he composed the two known *organa quadrupla*, which were for the Graduals of the Masses of Christmas and the feast of St. Stephen of the day following. These organa are in discant style, because the three embellishing parts are rhythmically and melodically coordinated in the manner of discant.

Sandra Pinegar

[See also: LÉONIN; MUSIC THEORY; NOTRE-DAME SCHOOL; PÉROTIN]

Atkinson, Charles M. "Franco of Cologne on the Rhythm of *Organum purum.*" *Early Music History* 9 (1989): 1–26.

Reckow, Fritz. "Das Organum." In *Gattungen der Musik in Einzeldarstellungen, Gedenkschrift Leo Schrade.* Bern: Francke, 1973, pp. 434–96.

Roesner, Edward H. "The Performance of Parisian Organum." *Early Music* 7 (1979): 174–89.

Sanders, Ernest H. "Consonance and Rhythm in the Organum of the 12th and 13th Centuries." *Journal of the American Musicological Society* 33 (1980): 264–86.

Yudkin, Jeremy. "The Rhythm of Organum Purum." *Journal of Musicology* 2 (1983): 355–76.

ORIFLAMME. A forked-tongue scarlet banner embroidered with golden flames, the Oriflamme was believed to have originated as Charlemagne's standard; it represented a flaming lance with which he could save the Holy Land from the Muslims. Hugh Capet later deposited it at the monastery of Saint-Denis, where it remained largely unheralded until Louis VI used it as his royal standard in battle in 1124 against Henry I of England. A century later, Louis IX received the Oriflamme from the abbot of Saint-Denis before going on his crusades. Although traditionally to be unfurled only in the face of enemies of Christianity, by the 14th and 15th centuries the Oriflamme had become the military standard of the French kings. It appeared frequently on the battlefield during the Hundred Years' War. It was present both at French victories, as at Mons-en-Pévèle in 1304 (where it was nearly destroyed), Cassel in 1328, and Roosebeke in 1382, and at defeats, like Crécy in 1346, Poitiers in 1356, and Agincourt in 1415. After 1418, the use of the Oriflamme diminished, and it was returned to the monastery of Saint-Denis.

Kelly DeVries

[See also: PRESLES, RAOUL DE]

Contamine, Philippe. *L'oriflamme de Saint-Denis aux XIVe et XVe siècles.* Nancy: Université de Nancy II, Institut de Recherche Régionale, 1975.

Hallam, Elizabeth M. *Capetian France, 987–1328.* London: Longman, 1980.

Keen, Maurice H. *The Laws of War in the Late Middle Ages.* Toronto: University of Toronto Press, 1965.

Lewis, P.S. *Later Medieval France: The Polity.* London: Macmillan, 1980.

Liebman, C.J. "Un sermon de Philippe de Villette, abbé de Saint-Denis, pour la levée de l'oriflamme (1414)." *Romania* 68 (1944–45): 444–70.

ORLÉANS. Ancient city situated at the crossing of the Loire closest to the Seine, the place called Cenabum was the chief trading post of the ancient Carnutes. By the early 4th century, it had become the Roman Aurelium, the seat of a Christian bishop. Subjected to the full impact of the Germanic invasions because of its location, Orléans was defended against Attila in 451 by Aetius and by its bishop, St. Aignan. Clovis I took the town in 498 and convened the first Gallic council of the church there in 511. It became the capital of one of the Merovingian successor states, had an important colony of Syrians and Jews, and was the site of a series of church councils.

Talented bishops, such as Jonas and the poet Theodulf, made the Orléanais a center of the Carolingian renaissance, to which the oratory of Germigny-des-Prés still bears witness. The town's site on the Loire made Orléans vulnerable to Viking raids, against which it found defenders in the Robertian family. With the accession of Hugh Capet as king in 987, Orléans became a royal city and its bishop, Arnulf, proved one of the Capetians' chief supporters.

Under the first four Capetians, Orléans rivaled Paris as a center of royal government. Philip I (r. 1060–1108) established a royal mint there. The seat of a royal *prévôté* and then a *bailliage*, Orléans received a communal charter in 1137. A commercial crossroads, it witnessed an outbreak of heresy in 1022 and developed as a distinguished center for the study of law. Granted university status in 1306 by Pope Clement V, its school attracted distinguished scholars from all over Europe.

After 1344, Orléans became the apanage of a series of royal cadets, first Philip (d. 1375), the younger son of Philip VI, and then (after 1392) Louis, the brother of Charles VI. Until his assassination in 1407, Louis led the anti-Burgundian faction in French politics later known as the Armagnacs. His son Charles d'Orléans, the noted poet, was taken at Agincourt in 1415 and remained a captive in England until 1440. When the English attacked his lands, they were defended by his illegitimate half-brother Jean, comte de Dunois, and Jeanne d'Arc first achieved fame when the English had to raise the siege of Orléans in 1429. Charles d'Orléans lived to sire a son, Louis, who became king of France in 1498.

As a result of the Hundred Years' War and the Wars of Religion, little remains of Orléans' medieval architectural heritage. The cathedral of Sainte-Croix is almost entirely a 17th- and 18th-century structure; only the churches of

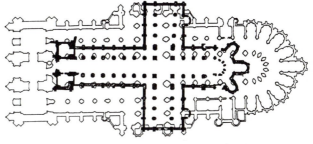

Orléans, Sainte-Croix, 10th-century plan and current plan. After Nivet.

Saint-Pierre (12th–13th c.) and Saint-Aignan (15th c.) retain their medieval character.

R. Thomas McDonald

[See also: CHARLES D'ORLÉANS; DUNOIS, JEAN, COMTE DE; GERMIGNY-DES-PRÉS; HERESY; JEANNE D'ARC; LOUIS, DUKE OF ORLÉANS; ORLÉANS CAMPAIGN; THEODULF OF ORLÉANS]

Bautier, Robert-Henri. "L'hérésie d'Orléans et le mouvement intellectual au début du XIe siècle, documents et hypothèses." *Comité des Travaux Historiques. Section de Philologie et d'Histoire* (1975): 63.
Crozet, René. *Histoire de l'Orléanais.* Paris: Boivin, 1936.
Illiers, Louis d'. *Histoire d'Orléans.* Orléans: Houze, 1954.

ORLÉANS CAMPAIGN. The English defeat at Orléans marks the decisive campaign of the Hundred Years' War. After their victory at Verneuil in 1424, English armies pushed steadily southward from Normandy and subdued Maine by 1428. In October 1428, the earl of Salisbury secured bridgeheads across the Loire above and below the city of Orléans, beginning a siege that threatened Valois control of the Loire Valley. Salisbury was killed in November but was quickly replaced by Suffolk and Talbot. French failure to cut off an English supply train at the Battle of the Herrings, February 12, 1429, seemed to confirm the doom of the Valois citadel.

Jean de Dunois, in command of the garrison, contemplated surrender, but a relief force led by Jeanne d'Arc entered the city on April 29, restoring both supplies and courage. A week later, the French counterattacked and the English withdrew in panic. Revitalized Valois forces inflicted a major defeat on English arms at Patay, June 18, 1429, and, emboldened by this success, Charles VII traveled to Reims in July for the coronation that confirmed his title. The failed seige, heroic defense, and brilliant counterattack proved to be the turning point of the war. After Orléans, the English remained permanently on the defensive.

Paul D. Solon

[See also: BEDFORD, JOHN OF LANCASTER, DUKE OF; DUNOIS, JEAN, COMTE DE; HUNDRED YEARS' WAR; JEANNE D'ARC; ORLÉANS; TALBOT, JOHN]

Burne, Alfred Higgins. *The Agincourt War.* London: Eyre and Spottiswoode, 1956.
Pernoud, Régine. *La libération d'Orléans, 8 mai 1429.* Paris: Gallimard, 1969.
Perroy, Edouard. *The Hundred Years' War.* Bloomington: Indiana University Press, 1951.

OURSCAMP. The Cistercian abbey of Ourscamp (Oise) is one of the largest monastic complexes remaining in northeastern France. Founded in 1129 by Simon de Vermandois, bishop of Noyon, the abbey prospered from its first years and became a well-known foundation. Four bishops of Noyon were buried in the abbey church. Ourscamp founded two daughter houses, Beaupré and Froidmont, and accepted a third, Mortemer, when it affiliated with the Cistercian order. The monastery now presents an imposing façade with two monumental 18th-century wings, which conceal behind them the ruins of the medieval church.

The first small church at the site was dedicated in 1134. Beginning in 1154, this modest structure was replaced by a much larger church. After the Revolution, most of the second church was destroyed, but the entrance bay and the east wall of the transept survive. The remains indicate that the building had a two-story elevation with ribbed vaults. Drawings made of the abbey prior to its demolition indicate that the vaults were supported by flying buttresses; one such buttress survives encased in later masonry at the west end of the church on the north side. The architectural details indicate that, although the church was not consecrated until 1201, most of the structure was erected by the mid-1160s. The flying buttresses were integral to the design from the outset.

In ca. 1234, the eastern end of the church was replaced by a new choir with ambulatory and radiating chapels erected in a simplified version of the Rayonnant style. Although the new choir retained the two-story elevation of the nave, and matched the height of the earlier vaults of the 12th-century church to the west, its forms were much lighter and more delicate. Large windows in the clerestory and in the radiating chapels once flooded the new chevet with light. The Rayonnant choir was deliberately transformed into a picturesque ruin in the mid-19th century by the removal of the outer chapel walls and the webbing of the rib vaults.

Caroline A. Bruzelius

[See also: CISTERCIAN ART AND ARCHITECTURE; CISTERCIAN ORDER]

Bruzelius, Caroline. "Cistercian High Gothic: Longpont and the Architecture of the Cistercians in the Early Thirteenth Century." *Analecta cisterciensia* 35 (1979): 3–204 (esp. 110–28).
———. "The Twelfth-Century Church at Ourscamp." *Speculum* 56 (1980): 28–40.
Héliot, Pierre. "Le chœur de l'abbatiale d'Ourscamp et le groupe de Longpont dans l'architecture cistercienne." *Bulletin de la Société Nationale des Antiquaires de France* (1957): 146–62.
Lefèvre-Pontalis, Eugène. "Ourscamp." *Congrès archéologique* (Beauvais) 72 (1905): 165–68.

OUTREMEUSE, JEAN D' (1338–1400). Notary and master historian of Liège, Jean has left its story in three distinct versions: a relatively short and sober *Chronique en bref*, which may constitute his notes for the more extensive works; a highly romanticized, unfinished poetic text, the *Geste de Liège*, in the form of a chanson de geste (some 53,000 Alexandrine lines extant!); and the three-volume *Myreur des histors* in prose. The latter may originally have been projected for four volumes. His *remaniement* of the chanson de geste *Ogier le Danois* in four books has been lost. Also in four books, his immense lapidary, the *Trésorier de philosophie naturelle des pierres précieuses*, contains practical information on cutting and polishing gems, as well as descriptions in alphabetical order of 256 stones. The French version of Jean de Mandeville's *Voyages* has been incorrectly attributed to Jean d'Outremeuse.

William W. Kibler

[See also: *CHEVALERIE OGIER*; LAPIDARY; MANDEVILLE, JEAN DE]

Outremeuse, Jean d'. *Ly myreur des histors, chronique de Jean des Preis dit d'Outremeuse*, ed. Adolphe Borgnet and S. Bormans. 7 vols. Brussels: Hayez, 1864–87.

Goosse, A. "*Ogier le Danois*, chanson de geste attribuée à Jean d'Outremeuse." *Romania* 86 (1965): 145–98.

———. "La chronique abrégée de Jean d'Outremeuse." *Revue belge de philologie et d'histoire* 32 (1954): 5–50.

Lejeune, Jean. "Une source méconnue: la 'chronique en bref' de Jean d'Outremeuse." *Revue belge de philologie et d'histoire* 34 (1956): 985–1020.

OVID, INFLUENCE OF. When the name of the sophisticated Roman poet of the Augustan age is mentioned in conjunction with medieval France, most scholars think of the *Ovide moralisé*, a text from the first half of the 14th century. In fact, Ovid's works—from the mainly mythological miracles narrated in the *Metamorphoses* to the early erotic elegiacs—were copied, imitated, glossed, and interpreted throughout the Middle Ages. While the 12th century is often referred to as an Ovidian era (*aetas Ovidiana*), the majority of the principal surviving Ovid manuscripts were copied from the 9th to the 11th century. Dozens of *Metamorphoses* manuscripts with commentaries, however, survive from the 12th and 13th centuries.

The prodigious influence of Ovid as a model in 12th-century imaginative literature is obvious in troubadour, Goliardic, and Latin school verse; in the early Romances of Antiquity; and in the works of Chrétien de Troyes (who himself claims to have translated the *Ars amatoria*) and other French romances; and it can be perceived in minor works like the Latin *Love-Council of Remiremont* (*Veris in temporibus sub Aprilis idibus*), a 12th-century poetical debate, and the *De vetula*, a pseudo-Ovidian tale. More specifically, it is through complex love metaphors that Ovid's presence may be gauged in narratives like the Old French *Roman d'Énéas*, an anonymous, free mid-12th-century adaptation of Virgil's *Aeneid*. In Chrétien de Troyes's *Cligés*, both the psychological penetration of the extended love analyses and the irony derive from Ovid's elegiac poems. The same holds true for a poignant text like Marie de France's *Guigemar*, one of her brief *lais* that is unquestionably suffused with Ovidian imagery.

Ovid's daringly original poetry, at once cosmological in scope and trivial in grasp, dominates western vernacular tradition. For Chaucer, he was "Venus' Clerk"; the notion of romantic love, which arises from the medieval idea of courtly love, goes back in large part to the Roman poet's conception of the mutually transforming power of this human emotion. Ancient Ovidian stories, such as those of Pyramus and Thisbe, Narcissus, and Philomela, help to establish the new narrative medieval genre in the vernacular: they were adapted into Old French, then appeared in German, Dutch, Italian, and early English versions. The vogue continued into Renaissance art and poetry.

While reworkings of Ovid's multifaceted *Metamorphoses* began before the Carolingian period, the most ambitious and elaborate treatment is found in two anonymous French translations, which were then vigorously amplified into Christian exegetical moralization, the *Ovide moralisé*. This 72,000–line poem, with its complex web of allegorical interpretation, may be said to attempt a reconciliation of the *Metamorphoses* with orthodox Christian doctrine. It is in this special dress that Ovid reached Boccaccio, Chaucer, Gower, Christine de Pizan, and numerous other later poets. Indeed, Pierre Bersuire, one of Ovid's translators (from the Old French back into Latin), calls the *Metamorphoses* a bible of pagan gods.

Raymond J. Cormier

[See also: ANTIQUITY, ROMANCES OF; *OVIDE MORALISÉ*; OVIDIAN TALES; TRANSLATION]

Cormier, Raymond J., ed. and trans. *Three Ovidian Tales of Love* (*Piramus et Tisbé, Narcisus et Dané*, and *Philomena et Procné*). New York: Garland, 1986.

Munari, Franco. *Ovid im Mittelalter*. Zurich: Artemis, 1960.

Rand, Edward Kennard. *Ovid and His Influence*. Boston: Jones, 1925.

OVIDE MORALISÉ. A poem of some 72,000 lines in octosyllabic couplets, composed between 1316 and 1328 by an anonymous cleric, probably a Franciscan. The language suggests that the writer was of Burgundian origin. The poem survives in nineteen manuscripts, one of which contains only a fragment.

The *Ovide moralisé* is a translation and paraphrase of Ovid's *Metamorphoses*, augmented by extensive commentary on the Ovidian text. The commentary offers moral, allegorical, and theological interpretations of Ovid's tales. Each tale of the *Metamorphoses* is translated and then expounded, the division between tale and exposition usually signaled by an interjection like "Now I would like briefly to expound the meaning of this fable." The expositions are rarely brief, however: they are typically as long as the paraphrases of the Ovidian narratives themselves. Plainly, the exegetical function takes precedence. The *Ovide moralisé* in effect presents a vernacular synthesis of sacred and secular exegetical traditions. The sources of the poem, aside from the *Metamorphoses*, are the Bible, biblical commentary, Ovidian commentary of the 12th and 13th centuries (e.g., the allegorical commentary by Arnulf of Orléans, the *Integumenta Ovidii* by Jean de Garlande, and many anonymous glosses), Ovid's other works (*Heroides, Fastes*), the tradition of mythography from late antiquity and the earlier Middle Ages (Servius, Fulgentius, Hyginus, Vatican mythographers), as well as medieval Homeric lore

(*Ilias Latina, De excidio Trojae historia*). The *Ovide moralise* also incorporates French material: for the tale of Pyramus and Thisbe, the poet inserts a version in Norman French, which he acknowledges as the work of another; and for the tale of Philomela, he uses a version that he attributes to a "Chrestiiens li Gois," whom some scholars identify as Chrétien de Troyes.

There are many reasons for the popularity of this poem among medieval readers, not the least of which was the vernacular access that it gave to a tradition of classical learning. Later vernacular poets, among them Guillaume de Machaut, Eustache Deschamps, Geoffrey Chaucer, John Gower, and Christine de Pizan, derived mythographic information from this French poem. At least three French prose abridgments were made during the 15th century, including one printed by Colard Mansion of Bruges in 1484; another of these prose versions was translated into English prose by William Caxton in 1480. The *Ovide moralise* also found a learned audience. The Benedictine monk Pierre Bersuire used it for the second redaction (1342) of his Latin prose *Ovidius moralizatus* (originally Book 15 of his *Reductium morale*), an important mythographic reference into the early 16th century. By any account, the *Ovide moralise* is the most extensive and influential medieval French treatment of Ovid.

The poem's method of commentary is a mixture of learned exegetical tradition and popular didacticism. The *Ovide moralise* is most indebted to learned tradition in its allegorical approach to pagan myth: since late antiquity, Neoplatonist exegetes had interpreted mythical or fabulous narratives as allegorical "covers" for moral or philosophical truths. The *Ovide moralise* combines such moral readings with theological interpretations of Ovid's text, discovering signs and symbols of Christian history and spirituality in Ovid's text. The poet never implies that Ovid himself was a Christian. Rather, he exploits the Pauline doctrine that "all that is written is for our instruction." He suggests that it is God who puts divine meaning in all writing, that Ovid told the stories, and that a good and inspired exegete like himself can discover the moral and spiritual profit that these stories contain. Thus, for example, the story of Phaeton (*Metamorphoses* 2.1–328) is treated as follows. First is the narrative itself, with some amplification of details; then a historical explanation of the Phaeton myth interpreted as the memory of a summer heat that devastated Ethiopia; then a euhemeristic explanation of Phaeton himself as an astronomer whose writings were destroyed and who threw himself off a high mountain. The fall of Phaeton is then compared with that of Lucifer, so that the Phaeton myth is read as moral advice against the dangers of pride in great undertakings. But the interpretation shifts to a theological theme. The palace of the sun is the throne of glory, where the holy Trinity sits. The sun is Christ; the chariot represents Christian doctrine; the horses are the Evangelists; the driver is the pope, who must not aspire to that office through ambition. Phaeton is also read as the Antichrist, who tries to corrupt humanity but is foiled by God.

In this pluralistic system of interpretation, we have the textual attitude of Neoplatonist mythography, where the text is seen as polyvalent, that is, capable of yielding up many meanings. The popularity of the *Ovide moralise* lies largely in the poet's success in adapting the critical system of moral mythography to vernacular literary interests in Ovid's stories. The poem at once provides a comprehensive rendering of Ovidian lore and elaborates a moral justification for such pagan fictions.

Rita Copeland

[See also: BERSUIRE, PIERRE; LEFÈVRE, RAOUL; OVID, INFLUENCE OF; OVIDIAN TALES]

de Boer, Cornelius, ed. *Ovide moralise*. 5 vols. Amsterdam: Koninklijke Akademie van Wetenschappen, 1915–38.

Demats, Paule. *Fabula: trois études de mythographie antique et médiévale*. Geneva: Droz, 1973.

Engels, Joseph. *Études sur l'Ovide moralise*. Groningen: Wolters, 1945.

Panofsky, Erwin. *Renaissance and Renascences in Western Art*. New York: Harper and Row, 1969.

Tuve, Rosemond. *Allegorical Imagery: Some Mediaeval Books and Their Posterity*. Princeton: Princeton University Press, 1966.

OVIDIAN TALES. Throughout the Middle Ages, Ovid was read, glossed, imitated, and translated. It is not surprising that the 12th century, the *aetas Ovidiana*, should have produced, among other works based on Ovid, French versions of some of his *Metamorphoses*. Those that survive, all from the second half of the century, are *Piramus et Tisbé*, *Narcisse*, and *Philomena*, corresponding, respectively, to *Metamorphoses* 4.55–166, 3.339–512, and 6.426–74; in addition, a fragment of some 120 lines of a hitherto unknown 13th-century rival version of *Piramus* has recently been published. Like the related Romances of Antiquity, these brief stories tend to elaborate the feelings of the characters in long lyric and dramatic monologues and dialogues, based on Ovidian writings on love but having no equivalent in the immediate source. They tend to reduce the role of the pagan gods and (except for *Philomena*) the idea of metamorphosis. All are written in couplets of octosyllabic lines, though *Piramus* has some *vers libres* in the added monologues.

Piramus, which expands Ovid's 112 hexameters into some 920 lines as published, is preserved in three independent manuscripts as well as in the influential early 14th-century compilation *Ovide moralise*, whose author used the poem instead of translating the metamorphosis himself. (Via a later prose version of the *Ovide moralise*, the poem indirectly influenced several authors, including Shakespeare and Théophile de Viau.) Freely and with fine lyrical monologues and dialogues, *Piramus* retells the story of the young Babylonian lovers separated by their parents and imprisoned in neighboring houses; through a chink in the wall they converse and agree to meet by Ninus's tomb under a mulberry tree; Tisbé arrives first and is frightened away by a lion, which bloodies a veil she lets fall; Piramus draws the wrong conclusion, stabs himself, and dies in the arms of Tisbé, who commits suicide with the same sword.

Ovid's metamorphosis of the mulberries' color is omitted. The French poem, unlike Ovid, motivates the separation of the lovers by a quarrel between their fathers, a detail that probably underlies the *Romeo and Juliet* story.

Narcisse, just over 1,000 lines long and preserved in four manuscripts, develops Ovid's story of the youth who scorns the love of the nymph Echo and many others, one of whom prays that he himself may suffer unrequited love. Seeing his reflection in a pool, Narcisse falls in love with himself, wastes away, and dies. The French poem concentrates narratively and psychologically on the anonymous girl, giving her a name, Dané, and letting her take the place of Echo (whose role is reduced to echoing Narcisse's cries). Dané, like Tisbé, decides to die after Narcisse. This poem, too, is written in a richly rhetorical style, with far more emphasis on motivation than in Ovid's version.

In his prologue to *Cligés*, among other Ovidiana he claims to have written, Chrétien de Troyes mentions the subject of *Philomena*. This work appears to survive only in the *Ovide moralisé*, where it is attributed to "Chrestiiens li Gois." The story (1,468 lines), related with all Chrétien's psychological insight and technical skill, tells of the illicit love of King Tereus for Philomena (Philomela in Ovid), sister of his wife, Progné. Having persuaded their father, King Pandion, to let him take Philomena over the sea to visit her sister, Tereus rapes her and cuts out her tongue to prevent her accusations; she embroiders her story on a tapestry that she sends to Progné. The latter rescues Philomena, kills her own son, Itis, and serves his cooked body to her husband. When Tereus seeks to avenge himself, he is miraculously transformed into a hoopoe, Progné into a swallow, and Philomena into a nightingale. The story is reasonably close to Ovid but, again, much expanded, especially in the physical description of Philomena, in analysis of feelings, and in dialogue.

The three surviving tales and the *Piramus* fragment no doubt represent a small fraction of the production of such poems, reworkings of the *Metamorphoses* in the romance style of the 12th century.

Wolfgang G. van Emden

[See also: ANTIQUITY, ROMANCES OF; IDYLLIC ROMANCE; *LAI*, NARRATIVE; OVID, INFLUENCE OF; *OVIDE MORALISÉ*

Branciforti, Francesco, ed. *Piramus et Tisbé*. Florence: Olschki, 1959.

Chrétien de Troyes. *Philomena, conte raconté d'après Ovide*, ed. Cornelius de Boer. Paris: Geuthner, 1909.

Cormier, Raymond, ed. and trans. *Three Ovidian Tales of Love* (*Piramus et Tisbé, Narcisus et Dané, and Philomena et Procné*). New York: Garland, 1986.

Thiry-Stassin, Martine, and Madeleine Tyssens, eds. *Narcisse, conte ovidien français du XIIe siècle*. Paris: Les Belles Lettres, 1976.

Cadot, A.M. "Du récit mythique au roman: étude sur *Piramus et Tisbé*." *Romania* 97 (1976): 433–61.

van Emden, Wolfgang G. "A Fragment of an Old French Poem in Octosyllables on the Subject of Pyramus and Thisbe." In *Medieval French Textual Studies in Memory of T.B.W. Reid*, ed. Ian Short. London: Anglo-Norman Text Society, 1984, pp. 239–53.

Vinge, Louise. *The Narcissus Theme in Western European Literature up to the Early 19th Century*. Lund: Gleerup, 1968.

PALEOGRAPHY AND MANUSCRIPTS. Before the invention of the printing press and movable type in the 15th century, books were hand-produced by scribes trained to copy literary texts, documents, or both. The scribes in many cases would also add minor decoration consisting of running titles, penwork initials, and headings in red and other colors. In the most elaborate volumes, scribes were assisted by illuminators who executed intricate initials, borders, and miniatures and frequently used gold leaf for dramatic visual effect.

The format, script, decoration, and binding of manuscript books depended upon their date and place of origin as well as upon their function within society. Volumes intended for use by a community of monks in 9th-century Tours would differ significantly from those written for a university student in 13th-century Paris.

The disintegration of the Roman Empire in the West saw the rise of "national hands" across Europe. These hands, tied to geographical locations, gradually superseded the widely used Roman system of scripts. In Merovingian Gaul, the local scripts were derived ultimately from the later Roman cursive, or running hand, used for official documents, but with an admixture of letterforms from the more formal bookscripts also used in the Roman Empire.

Among the monastic or cathedral scriptoria (writing places) that produced a distinctive French national hand is the abbey of Luxeuil in Burgundy. Founded ca. 590 by the Irishman St. Columbanus, Luxeuil was one of the most influential centers of Merovingian culture in the 7th and 8th centuries; its scriptorium produced fine manuscript books in a spidery style of writing today termed "Luxeuil minuscule." The first illustration reproduces a leaf of a manuscript of St. Augustine's *Sermons* copied at Luxeuil in the second half of the 7th century (Beinecke 481, no. 2). The minuscule script retains many features of its cursive models: letters were often run together; the words and sentences were usually not distinguished by spaces or by punctuation. Luxeuil minuscule differed from Roman cursive, however, in that the sprawling loops of the earlier running script were replaced by neatly clubbed shafts on such letters as *b, d,* and *l*; the Roman cursive was subdued into a style of writing suitable for copying Latin manuscript books. Other distinctive types of French national hands developed at the monasteries of Corbie and Laon and the convent at Chelles.

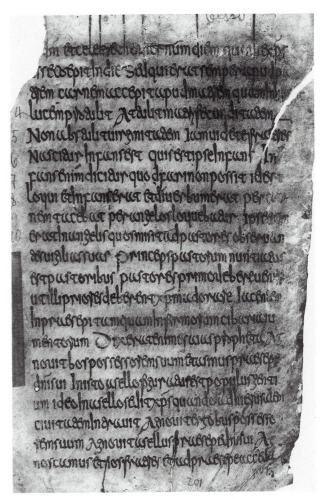

Luxeuil minuscule. Yale MS 481, 2v. *Courtesy of Beinecke Library, Yale University.*

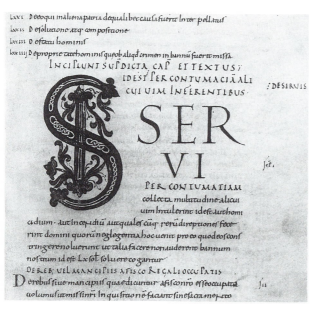

Carolingian minuscule, ca. 873. Yale MS 413, fol. 55. *Courtesy of Beinecke Library, Yale University.*

Late Carolingian minuscule, early 12th century. Yale MS 414, fol. 1. *Courtesy of Beinecke Library, Yale University.*

Latin translation of Aristotle for the university student in Paris, third quarter of the 13th century. Yale Medical Historical, MS 12, fol. 261. *Courtesy of Yale University.*

During the period of Charlemagne (r. 771–814), a new script evolved that is now called "Carolingian minuscule"; during the late 8th and the 9th centuries, it gradually superseded the local styles of writing throughout France. Although the precise origins of the script are still subject to debate, its development and eventual acceptance were related to cultural and historical phenomena affecting the production of manuscripts: the interest of Charlemagne and Alcuin, the abbot of Tours, in promoting Christianity; Charlemagne's commitment to the advancement of education and scholarship; the political advantage of employing a single script and model for books throughout the empire.

The second illustration (above left) reproduces a page from a manuscript containing the *Capitularies* of Charlemagne, of his son Louis the Pious, and of Charles the Bald (Beinecke 413). Produced in northeastern France ca. 873, it is an impressive example of well-developed Carolingian script and book production. The text and decoration are neatly arranged on the page, with broad margins and well-defined interlinear spaces; the decorative initial and the elegant capitals used for headings help the reader to focus attention on the beginning of the chapter. The script itself is easy to decipher, especially when compared with Luxeuil minuscule: Carolingian letterforms, well proportioned and uniformly written, sit firmly on the text line; regular word division and clear punctuation enhance legibility. Whether the texts being copied were biblical, liturgical, or patristic, the standardization of graphic conventions and book production ensured that every Carolingian manuscript would be intelligible.

The Carolingian empire did not endure past the 9th century; yet Carolingian minuscule survived in France well into the 12th century, as it continued to be the preferred style of writing in monastic book production. The script, however, changed and developed over time, so that its overall appearance and individual letterforms were significantly altered in the 11th and 12th centuries. Illustration (bottom left) shows the late, transitional stage of Carolingian minuscule; Beinecke 414 is the second part of a two-volume Bible produced in Aquitaine or Limousin in the early 12th century. The script appears to be compressed laterally, so that letterforms are taller, less round, and more oval. Ascenders, as in the letters *b*, *d*, and *l*, have short horizontal finishing strokes added to their tops. Words are frequently abbreviated, so that more text is accommodated on each page. As in the earlier phase of Carolingian script, distinct portions of text are signaled by rows of calligraphic capitals. Fine polychrome initials are a hallmark of this final stage of Carolingian book production.

Before ca. 1200, monks in monasteries produced most of the manuscript books, transmitting texts from one generation of readers to the next; in the period ca. 1200–1500, book production shifted to professional workshops associated with wealthy patrons or to stationers who marketed university textbooks. In both instances, there was increasing demand for books in the vernacular languages as well as in Latin.

The university at Paris was a main center of textbook production throughout the later Middle Ages. As the university prospered, large numbers of students required texts for study. University books copied in Parisian workshops differed significantly from books written in monasteries in the preceding centuries; the layout, script, and method of production all changed to meet the needs of the students and teachers who used the books. Two 13th-century manuscripts from Paris illustrate the dramatic transformation of medieval books and the way that they were produced.

The works of Aristotle in Latin translation were standard texts in the university curriculum at Paris; after 1255, many were required reading. Illustration (opposite right) reproduces a fine Aristotle manuscript, attributed to Paris in the third quarter of the 13th century (Yale Medical Historical 12). The text of Aristotle occupies a narrowly defined central space; the remainder of each leaf has ample margins ready to receive notes and diagrams. Attractive historiated initials begin each treatise; paragraph marks in red or blue denote internal divisions. The text is written in a Gothic bookhand that developed from the late Carolingian minuscule. The lateral compression noted earlier in the 12th century (bottom left) is now pronounced, with letterforms often touching and joined together. The fusion, or "biting," of letters is characteristic of formal Gothic script. The oval shape of such letters as *o* has become more angu-

Pecia manuscript of St. Thomas Aquinas with scribe's note, Paris, ca. 1270. Yale MS 207, fol. 46. *Courtesy of Beinecke Library, Yale University.*

lar and compact. The annotations surrounding the text were written by at least two individuals in less formal styles of Gothic writing that are characterized by cursive elements and an abundance of abbreviations; both of these features allowed the script to be written more rapidly and permitted the commentary to be squashed into the margins close to the relevant passage being discussed.

Because of the increased demand for inexpensive university books in 13th-century Paris, special bookdealers, or university stationers, developed a system of mass production for selected works. In the *pecia*, or piece, system of transcribing manuscripts, the stationer's "fair" copy (exemplar) of the text was divided into numbered pieces, each of which could be rented out to individuals for copying. The system helped to guarantee accuracy, since every new manuscript was made directly from the stationer's exemplar, and accelerated book production, since several scholars or scribes could copy from the one complete work at the same time.

Among the many works copied and marketed according to the *pecia* system were those of St. Thomas Aquinas (ca. 1224–1274), a Dominican friar who was master of theology at the University of Paris. Aquinas's commentary on Peter Lombard's *Sentences* was composed ca. 1254–56 but was probably revised later in his life. On page 693 is a portion of Aquinas's commentary from a manuscript of the third book, produced in Paris ca. 1270 (Beinecke 207). Recent scholarship has proven that this manuscript was transcribed from an exemplar of the stationer William of Sens, who lived and worked on the rue Saint-Jacques; this shop, conveniently located down the street from the Dominican house of studies, assumed a significant role in the dissemination of Aquinas's works. Beinecke 207 bears internal evidence that it was a product of the *pecia* system. The lower edges of some leaves contain notes where the scribe recorded the number of the piece just completed; most of these numbers, however, were trimmed when the volume was bound or rebound. In addition, the manuscript contains a remarkable statement by the scribe in the lower margin, just below an unsightly erasure: *Nota confundatur stacionarius qui me fecit deturpari librum alicuius probi uiri* ("Take note! Confound the stationer who made me disfigure the book of some worthy man.")

The scribe blamed the stationer for the sloppy appearance of the erasure and superimposed corrections.

In 13th-century Paris, the everyday spoken language was French rather than the Latin language used in the Bible, liturgical texts, and philosophical discourse. Although it is still debated at what precise time vernacular language was regularly used, it is clear that secular texts were being composed in French and transcribed and illuminated in manuscript books by the mid-13th century. It was during the later Middle Ages that a wealthy and literate lay audience, fascinated by the Arthurian and other romances, created a demand for deluxe manuscripts of vernacular prose and poetry.

A splendidly illuminated volume of the Arthurian romances, produced in France in the late 13th century, graphically illustrates the type of expensive book produced by professional scribes and artists in a secular context (below left; Beinecke 229). The French text was copied in an elegant Gothic bookhand, with several small decorative initials to demarcate text divisions. What is most remarkable about this genre of manuscripts is the number of beautifully painted pictures throughout the volume that visually re-

Arthurian romances in Gothic script (Vulgate version), late 13th century. Yale MS 229, fol. 272v. *Courtesy of Beinecke Library, Yale University.*

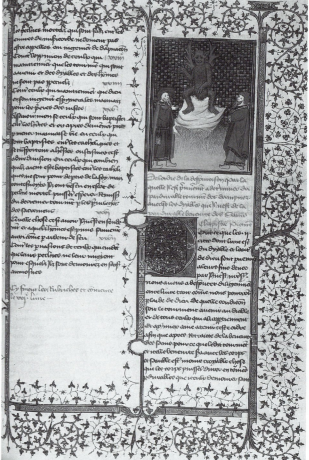

French translation of Augustine's *De civitate Dei (The City of God)*, ca. 1400. Yale MS 215, fol. 145. *Courtesy of Beinecke Library, Yale University.*

Caesar's *Commentaries*, French translation by Jean de Chesne, Bruges, 1476. Yale MS 226, fol. 67. *Courtesy of Beinecke Library, Yale University.*

create the narrative account. For readers already familiar with the text, it would be possible to follow the story through the images without actually reading the prose. The Beinecke manuscript alone contains more than 160 miniatures and historiated initials.

By the mid-14th century, there was a great demand for manuscript books of Latin texts that had been translated into French. The audience for these volumes comprised primarily members of the court, aristocrats who could afford elegantly written and illuminated texts of classical and medieval authors. This genre of French manuscript was generally produced in folio format on parchment of excellent quality and transcribed in distinctive styles of Gothic script characterized by a variety of cursive letterforms. Because of the combination of letterforms from more formal Gothic scripts (as illustrated in Plate 6) with cursive features derived from the chancery, the spiky styles of French Gothic script are often termed "bastard" (*bâtarde*) or "hybrid."

Among the many Latin texts rendered into French was St. Augustine's monumental *De civitate Dei*. Beinecke 215 (opposite right) contains the complete work in four volumes, originally bound as two. Produced in a Parisian workshop ca. 1415, it is illustrative of manuscripts popu-

lar among the French nobility during the 14th and 15th centuries. The spiky style of Gothic script seen here is characterized by decorative shading of such letters as the tall *s* and loops on *d, h,* and *l.*

The tradition of transcribing and illuminating vernacular literary manuscripts flourished throughout 15th-century France to the extent that hundreds of copies still survive today of the popular French works, such as the *Roman de la Rose* and the texts of Christine de Pizan. Many of these manuscripts were copied in an elegant grade of *bâtarde* script with fewer cursive features, a style associated with deluxe book production of the Burgundian court and often termed *lettre bourguignonne*. The overall appearance of the script is calligraphic, though it exhibits some of the prickly aspects of Gothic cursive script.

Beinecke 226 (opposite) is a beautifully illuminated copy of Julius Caesar's *Commentaries*, translated into French by Jean de Chesne. The script, regular and relatively devoid of loops on tall letters, retains many features of the formal Gothic bookhand but also incorporates selected cursive features. The manuscript is a large luxury book containing ten half-page and three smaller miniatures. *Lettre bourguignonne*, as illustrated here, survived into the 16th century as a popular choice for deluxe manuscripts.

Barbara A. Shailor

[See also: LIBRARIES; MANUSCRIPTS, HEBREW ILLUMINATED; MANUSCRIPTS, PRODUCTION AND ILLUMINATION; UNIVERSITIES]

Bischoff, Bernard. *Latin Palaeography: Antiquity and the Middle Ages*, trans. D.O. Cróinin and D. Ganz. Cambridge: Cambridge University Press, 1990.

Boyle, Leonard E. *Medieval Latin Palaeography: A Bibliographical Introduction*. Toronto: University of Toronto Press, 1984.

Brown, Michelle P. *A Guide to Western Historical Scripts from Antiquity to 1600*. Toronto: University of Toronto Press, 1990.

Ganz, David. "The Preconditions for Caroline Minuscule." *Viator* 18 (1987): 23–44.

McKitterick, Rosamond. *The Carolingians and the Written Word*. Cambridge: Cambridge University Press, 1989.

Reynolds, Leighton D., and Nigel G. Wilson. *Scribes and Scholars: A Guide to the Transmission of Greek and Latin Literature*. 2nd ed. Oxford: Oxford University Press, 1974.

Rouse, Richard H. and Mary A. "The Commerical Production of Manuscript Books in Late Thirteenth- and Early Fourteenth-Century Paris." In *Medieval Book Production: Assessing the Evidence*, ed. Linda L. Brownrigg. Los Altos Hills: Anderson-Lovelace/Red Gull, 1990, pp. 103–15.

Shailor, Barbara A. *The Medieval Book*. New Haven: Yale University Press, 1988.

PAMIERS, STATUTES OF. During the Albigensian Crusade, in late November 1212, Simon de Montfort, having become viscount of Carcassonne, held an assembly of prelates and barons at Pamiers for the purpose of establishing his rule and the basis of authority in his new domains. The results, forty-six articles and a brief rider, are known as the Statutes of Pamiers. The statutes aim primarily to accomplish three goals: to strengthen the church against heresy; to reconstitute strict feudal obligations between Simon and his vassals; to apply to all persons the testamentary practices of the custom of Paris (*usus Francie circa Parisius*), which favored the eldest heir and eliminated the southern custom of joint succession or equal division, especially of noble fiefs upon whose service Simon relied. The Statutes of Pamiers, particularly their most radical provisions transplanting into the Midi elements of northern customary law, did not survive the Montforts. Except for the obligations of certain noble families, they were abandoned by Louis IX and Alphonse of Poitiers.

Alan Friedlander

[See also: ALBIGENSIAN CRUSADE; MONTFORT]

Bisson, Thomas N. *Assemblies and Representation in Languedoc in the Thirteenth Century.* Princeton: Princeton University Press, 1964.

Timbal, Pierre. *Un conflit d'annexion au moyen âge: l'application de la coutume de Paris au pays d'Albigeois.* Toulouse: Privat, 1950.

Vaux-de-Cernay, Pierre des. *Historia Albigensis*, trans. Pascal Guébin and Henri Maisonneuve. Paris: Vrin, 1951, pp. 141–44.

Vic, Claude de, and Joseph Vaissète. *Histoire générale de Languedoc.* 16 vols. Toulouse: Privat, 1872–1904, Vol. 8, cols. 623–35. [Text of statutes.]

PARAY-LE-MONIAL. Paray-le-Monial (Saône-et-Loire) is a Romanesque priory belonging to Cluny III, the mother church of the Cluniac order, and located some 13 miles west of Cluny. The design of Paray-le-Monial is based directly on that of Cluny III, yet the sizes are vastly different: Cluny was originally 609 feet long and 97 feet high, with nave, four aisles, two aisleless transepts, choir, and five chapels radiating from an ambulatory, while Paray-le-Monial is 206 feet long and 71 feet high, with nave, two aisles, one aisleless transept, and three radiating chapels.

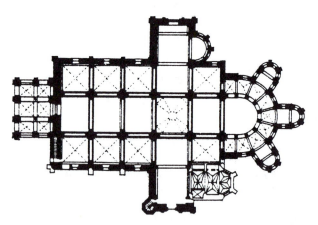

Paray-le-Monial, abbey church, plan, early 12th century. After Losowska.

Paray-le-Monial (Saône-et-Loire), Notre-Dame, nave. *Photograph courtesy of Whitney S. Stoddard.*

The interior spaces of the two monuments are similar: tall, narrow naves capped by pointed barrel vaults and strengthened by pointed transverse arches. The interior elevation of Paray-le-Monial consists of a pointed nave arcade, a blind triforium of three recessed arches separated by fluted pilasters, and a clerestory with three windows framed by arches. The precocious nature of the structure is stated by the clerestory and pointed barrel vaults supported by thick walls but no flying buttresses.

The unusual feature of Paray-le-Monial, as well as of Cluny, is the use of Roman decorative elements, fluted pilasters, that appear on nave piers capped by Corinthian-type capitals, which also decorate the triforium and clerestory. This use of the classical order with base, shaft, and capital is based on Roman monuments, such as the gates at Autun. In spite of this influence, the Romanesque master mason violated the Roman classical proportions by attenuating the pilaster, especially on the nave arcade.

Light plays a strong role in the nave of Paray-le-Monial by the clerestory and more dramatically in the east end, with light admitted in four vertical levels and four planes in space. Light penetrates the choir in three windows in

Paray-le-Monial, Notre-Dame, ambulatory. *Photograph courtesy of Whitney S. Stoddard.*

the upper wall, separating the forechoir from the choir, in the nine clerestory windows beneath the semidome, in the high windows of the ambulatory, and in the five low windows in each of the three radiating chapels.

The west towers and narthex of Paray-le-Monial are an earlier, smaller campaign than the church proper, with the south tower earlier than the north one. The west end dates from the second half of the 11th century; the church proper was constructed in the early decades of the 12th.

Sculpture at Paray-le-Monial consists of floral capitals throughout the church, and geometric and abstract ornament on the two transept portals.

Whitney S. Stoddard

[See also: AUTUN; CLUNY]

Armi, C. Edson. *Masons and Sculptors in Romanesque Burgundy.* 2 vols. University Park: Pennsylvania State University Press, 1983, pp. 171–76; figs. 216–22.
Stoddard, Whitney S. *Monastery and Cathedral in France.* Middletown: Wesleyan University Press, 1966, pp. 39–47, 52, 56; figs. 40, 45–46, 48, 51–52, 54–55.
———. *Sculptors of the West Portals of Chartres Cathedral.* New York: Norton, 1987 [Transept portals, pp. 48–49; Plate XXXIV, 1, 2.]

Virey, Jean. *Paray-le-Monial et les églises du Brionnais.* Paris: Laurens, 1926.

PARENS SCIENTIARUM. This papal bull, issued in 1231 by Gregory IX, was a major step in establishing the independence of the corporation of masters vis-à-vis the bishop of Paris and the chancellor of the cathedral school of Notre-Dame in Paris. After earlier papal statements giving support to the masters in regulating the lives and duties of masters and students, *Parens scientiarum* made much clearer the freedom and right to self-regulation of the corporation of masters. The chancellor was obliged to bestow the license to teach (*licentia docendi*) upon anyone the masters judged worthy; the masters' right to regulation of teaching conditions, clothing, and the like was recognized, and the right to suspend classes in certain situations was confirmed. The publication of *Parens scientiarum* followed the return to Paris of masters and students after the cessation of classes and scattering of students and masters after riots in 1229.

Grover A. Zinn

[See also: GREGORY IX; PHILIP THE CHANCELLOR; UNIVERSITIES]

Leff, Gordon. *Paris and Oxford Universities in the Thirteenth and Fourteenth Centuries.* New York: Wiley, 1968.
Thorndike, Lynn. *University Records and Life in the Middle Ages.* New York: Columbia University Press, 1949.

PARIAGE. When two lords agreed to share the administration of certain lands belonging to one of them, and to divide the nonlanded revenues equally, they drew up a contract called variously in Latin a *conventio, pactio,* or *pariagium.* The party furnishing the land often simply "associated" (*associare*) the other over his land. In either case, the terms of association were stated with precision. *Pariages* were common from ca. 1150 to ca. 1300 and are best known in the royal domain, Champagne, Burgundy, and the Midi.

Pariages could serve several purposes, but we know most about the agreements between powerful secular lords and ecclesiastics, who usually furnished the land and preserved the contracts in their archives. Economic interests prevailed when a monastery desired to develop raw land into new villages by attracting colonists more willing to settle under an enlightened secular lord than a monastic one. The Cistercians often resorted to *pariages* in the 13th century when they were unable to find sufficient lay converts to work their lands. Where villages already were shared by two lords, *pariages* simplified the administration under a single mayor responsible to both parties.

Pariages also served political and military purposes. Louis VII and Philip Augustus extended royal influence southward by *pariages,* and Philip IV consolidated his grip on the Midi by forcing bishops and abbots to accept *pariages,* whereby they created common courts and jointly appointed judges. The modern principality of Andorra continues to embody the medieval *pariage* established in 1278 by the count of Foix and bishop of Urgel to end their longstanding dispute; today, their successors, the president of France and the bishop of Urgel, share the administration of that principality.

Theodore Evergates

Evergates, Theodore. *Feudal Society in the Baillage of Troyes Under the Counts of Champagne, 1152–1284.* Baltimore: Johns Hopkins University Press, 1975.

Gallet, Léon. *Les traités de pariage dans la France féodale.* Paris: Sirey, 1935.

Higounet, Charles. "Les types d'exploitation cisterciennes et prémontrées du XIIIe siècle et leur rôle dans la formation de l'habitat et des paysages ruraux." *Annales de l'Est: mémoires* 21 (1959): 260–75.

Richard, Jean. *Les ducs de Bourgogne et la formation du duché du XIe aux XIVe siècle.* Dijon: Bernigaud et Privat, 1954.

Strayer, Joseph R. *The Reign of Philip the Fair.* Princeton: Princeton University Press, 1980.

PARIS. The development of the actual site of Paris began with the Celtic settlement on the island in the River Seine known today as the Île-de-la-Cité. The Roman city, known as Lutetia or Lutece, grew up on the left bank, where vestiges of the Roman baths and arena can still be seen. The site, a large natural basin ringed by hills and close to the confluence of the Marne, the Bièvre, and, farther downstream, the Oise, was on one of the major north-south Roman roads. Lutece was a major market center for agricultural goods grown in the swampy lowlands, the *marais*, running in an arc around the north side along the old course of the Seine.

The late-antique city consisted of three parts, the Île-de-la-Cité, fortified to protect the commercial docks; the old Roman quarter on the left bank, where the forum was enclosed behind protective walls; and the newly established commercial quarter on the right bank, also behind walls. Bridges connected the three sections. Archaeological finds indicate that the Île-de-la-Cité may have been divided even then between the religious sector to the east and the seat of secular power, site of later royal palaces, to the west. Christianity reached Lutece in the 3rd century with the arrival of Denis, the Apostle of Gaul and first bishop of Paris. Tradition and practice suggest the earliest church was outside the Roman city, perhaps on the site of the first Christian cemetery, later Saint-Marcel. The discovery in 1964 during excavations in front of the present cathedral of Notre-Dame of the bottom of a glass cup with the chi-rho indicates the presence of a church on the site by ca. 360, about the same time that the Roman name, Lutece, was replaced by the place-name Paris, derived from the old Celtic tribe of the Parisi.

By the early 6th century, four churches made up the cathedral group, including the basilica of Saint-Étienne, whose western foundations have been excavated under the square in front of Notre-Dame, the baptistery of Saint-Jean-le-Ronde (destroyed) to the north of Saint-Étienne, the church of Saint-Denis-du-Pas (destroyed) east of the

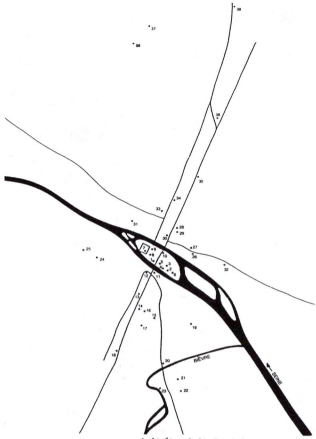

1 - Saint-Étienne ; 2 - Sainte-Marie ; 3 - Saint-Jean-le-Rond ; 4 - Saint-Germain-le-Vieux ; 5 - Saint-Christophe ; 6 - Saint-Denis-du-Pas ; 7 - Le Palais ; 8 - Saint-Martial-Saint-Éloi ; 9 - Saint-Barthélémy-Saint-Malgloire ; 10 - Saint-Denis-de-la-Chatre. La rive gauche : 11 - Saint-Julien ; 12 - Saint-Séverin ; 13 - Saint-Serge-Saint-Bacchus ; 14 - Saint-Étienne-des-Grés ; 15 - Saints-Apôtres-Sainte-Geneviève ; 16 - Saint-Symphorien-des-Vignes ; 17 - Saint-Michel ; 18 - Notre-Dame-des-Champs ; 19 - Saint-Victor ; 20 - Saint-Médard ; 21 - Saint-Martin ; 22 - Saint-Marcel ; 23 - Saint-Hippolyte ; 24 - Saint-Germain-des-Prés ; 25 - Saint-Père. La rive droite : 26 - Saint-Gervais-Saint-Protais ; 27 - Saint-Jean-de-Grève ; 28 - Saint-Merri ; 29 - Sainte-Colombe ; 30 - Saint-Jacques-de-la-Boucherie ; 31 - Saint-Germain-l'Auxerrois ; 32 - Saint-Paul-des-Champs ; 33 - Sainte-Opportune ; 34 - Saint-Georges ; 35 - Saint-Martin-des-Champs ; 36 - Saint-Laurent ; 37 - Saint-Denis-de-Montmartre ; 38 - Saint-Martyre ; 39 - Sainte-Geneviève-de-la-Chapelle.

Paris (Seine), plan of early medieval sites. After Périn et al.

present cathedral, and Notre-Dame under the chevet of the present cathedral. The foundations of Saint-Étienne are generally said to be 6th-century, although a late 4th-century date has recently been proposed because of the five-aisled plan and its resemblance to similar plans found in early Christian Rome. Excavated marble columns and a capital suggest a late 4th- or early 5th-century date, with possible Theodosian models in Constantinople and Milan.

The most important event in the early history of Paris was the arrival of Clovis and the Franks. Beginning shortly after his accession to the kingship in 481 or 482, Clovis began systematically moving the power base of the Franks from Tournai to the south, first only as far as the River Loire but later as far as Bordeaux and Toulouse. In 507 or 508, Clovis was named consul by the emperor Anastasius and established his capital at Paris. The first king of the Franks to adopt Roman Christianity, Clovis set about building a church to serve as the royal necropolis. Dedicated to the Holy Apostles, in imitation of Constantine's burial church in Constantinople, the church later came to be known as Sainte-Geneviève, after its most famous interee. Clovis died and was buried in the Holy Apostles in 511; his daughter Clotilde was buried at his side in 531. His queen, Clotilde, died at Tours in 544 but was buried in Paris at the side of her husband. Of this early church we have no trace, nor were any tombs of the royal family positively identified among the many investigated during the destruction of Sainte-Geneviève in the 19th century.

The situation is similar for the other Merovingian structures known either from texts or from archaeological evidence. The Musée Carnavalet survey lists some thirty-five to thirty-eight Merovingian religious sites identified within the limits of the modern city of Paris; yet because of later rebuilding, not one has been fully recovered in plan. We know, however, that Saint-Étienne was a five-aisled building some 118 feet wide with a probable length of 165–200 feet extending under the nave of the present cathedral of Notre-Dame. Saint-Étienne was largely rebuilt in the 6th century, reusing marble capitals and columns possibly from an earlier structure on the site.

A similar situation exists for the abbey of Saint-Vincent/Sainte-Croix, now Saint-Germain-des-Prés. Founded by Childebert after his 542 campaign in Spain, the church was dedicated December 23, 558, the day the king died. St. Germain, bishop of Paris, was buried there in 576. Excavations in the 19th century recovered Merovingian sarcophagi on the site, marble capital and column fragments, and the foundations of apsidal chapels in the end walls of the transept arms. Excavations in the 1960s demonstrated that the present nave, aisles, and transept were built directly on the 6th-century foundations. Of the original chevet plan, we have no trace. Most of the other Merovingian churches are known only from documents or from archaeological finds, usually sarcophagi and burial goods, occasionally architectural fragments.

The 6th century saw the establishment of most of the important Parisian abbeys, which included, in addition to Holy Apostles/Sainte-Geneviève and Saint-Vincent/Saint-Germain-des-Prés, Saint-Marcel, Saint-Martin (later Saint-Martin-des-Champs), and the church of Saint-Denis, now Saint-Pierre de Montmartre. In addition, the oldest parishes were all established in the course of the 6th, 7th, and early 8th centuries, as were a number of churches beyond the walls. The importance of the city as a trade center is marked by the establishment of the Lendit fair under Dagobert I (d. 638). It is estimated that the population of Paris was 20,000–30,000 by the 8th century. In the later 8th century, the rise of the Carolingians marked a shift in the center of power. The future of Neustria and of the Paris region lay with the Robertian family of counts, who became the principal representatives of public authority under the 9th-century Carolingians.

Settlements on major waterways were particularly vulnerable to Viking attacks in the 9th century, and Paris was victimized more than once. Eudes, the Robertian count of Paris, won great prestige for his vigorous defense in 885–86, when the Vikings failed to take Paris despite a long siege. Soon thereafter, Eudes won elevation to the kingship, and his family remained thereafter the principal rival of the Carolingians in the West Frankish kingdom, gain-

ing the throne permanently with the accession of Hugh Capet in 987.

The rise of the new Capetian monarchy, while it returned the political center of gravity to Neustria, did not immediately bring renewed importance to Paris. The ruling family had several centers of power in the Île-de-France, and Robert II (d. 1031), who was preoccupied with the conquest of Burgundy, made Orléans his principal base. Even within Paris, the Capetians had rivals. Only in the last years of the reign of Henry I (d. 1060) does the charter evidence suggest that Paris was becoming the center of the royal estates and religious foundations. Yet Henry and his son Philip I had their authority further circumscribed by the rise of powerful castellans who held important strongholds in the vicinity of Paris and chose not to reside in Paris for long periods. Influential monasteries and the area's commercial importance probably had more to do with the growth of Paris in the 11th century than did the monarchy. The shift of power under the Carolingians and the difficulties of recovery in the early years of Capetian rule are marked by the absence of major building between the late 7th and early 12th centuries. The texts mention important repairs and some rebuilding after the Viking devastation, but there is little indication of either new foundations or new building activity until the reconstruction of the nave of Saint-Germain-des-Prés in the first half of the 11th century, which is the only surviving example of Romanesque architecture in Paris.

The pacification of the Île-de-France by Louis VI and the greater profitability of the royal domain increased the prestige and effectiveness of royal government and with it the importance of Paris, especially after Louis VI took up residence there ca. 1130. The presence of royal government became an important factor in the city's expansion during the 12th century. The religious establishments, with their increasingly important schools and the continuing expansion of trade, maintained their demographic impact. The schools and the retail establishments that served them accounted for much of the growing population of the left bank, while the merchant community occupied the right bank, expanding rapidly beyond the limits of the old city. In addition, the Capetians found Paris a strategic point from which to check Angevin power to the west and the aspirations of the house of Champagne to the east. Under Louis VI (d. 1137) and during the long reigns of Louis VII (d. 1180) and Philip II Augustus (d. 1223), Paris experienced an unparalleled period of growth and expansion that far surpassed any previous epoch in the city's history. Indeed, the period sets the character of all future growth into the 19th century: rather than tear down and rebuild the old parts of the city, the tendency was always to expand in new directions, to build in new areas, and to push agriculture farther out. This policy is exemplified by Louis VII's grant of lands on the right bank to the order of Knights Templar, whose new "Temple" became their European headquarters and the center of their banking operations. From this time until the end of the 13th century, the royal treasury was housed in the Temple's keep. The round church, built ca. 1140, and the impressive keep were destroyed after the French Revolution.

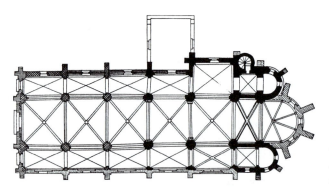

Paris, Saint-Pierre de Montmartre, plan. After Sauvegeot.

Although it was under Louis VI that the building boom in Paris began, little remains prior to the reign of Louis VII. The records and charters are filled with important royal donations from Louis VI, such as the foundation in 1112 of Saint-Victor with William of Champeaux, one of the great teachers of his day, as its head, and the refoundation of Saint-Pierre de Montmartre as a house for nuns in 1134. Saint-Victor is destroyed; but Saint-Pierre de Montmartre, dedicated in 1147, survives in part.

Traditionally the site of at least one large non-Christian temple, Montmartre is also associated with the spot where St. Denis suffered martyrdom. A chapel dedicated to St. Denis no doubt existed on Montmartre by the 6th century. The property passed to Louis VI and his queen, Adelaide of Maurienne, in 1133 and was refounded as a community for nuns the following year. The nave was completed after the church's dedication in 1147, and the main apse was rebuilt ca. 1170, perhaps to increase the space around the burial site of Queen Adelaide, who had retired to the community in 1153 and was buried there in 1154. In 1435, the nuns were forced to abandon the convent, ruined by the Hundred Years' War.

The original plan of Saint-Pierre consisted of a four-bay nave, flanked by aisles, a slightly projecting transept, and a three-apse east end with a tower constructed above the bay preceding the apse on the north side. Despite the damages, rebuildings, and restorations, the original three-story elevation, including main arcades, subdivided and articulated openings into the roof space over the aisle vaults, and low clerestory windows, can still be seen in the eastern bays. Rib vaults were used in the transept and main-apse bays. The capitals of the church are of particular interest, beginning with the reused Merovingian marble columns and capitals against the west façade and in the main apse flanking the altar.

The oldest surviving part of the abbey church of Saint-Martin-des-Champs is the tower on the south side of the chevet, which dates probably from shortly after the abbey was given to Cluny in 1079, while the chevet itself is generally dated to the abbacy of Hugues I (1130–42). The plan of the chevet, the only surviving ambulatory and chapel

scheme in Paris earlier than the chevet of Saint-Denis, is very complex and highly irregular, because the two rows of supports appear to have been aligned with each other without regard for the peripheral wall. This would also explain the extreme irregularity of the vaults. Many of the capitals appear to have been recut in the 19th century and are now noticeably smaller than the piers on which they sit. In style, these capitals have few counterparts in Parisian 12th-century sculpture, other than the second-story capitals in the chevet of Saint-Germain-des-Prés, which are much closer in date to 1150. The elevation of the hemicycle is only two-storied, with small but deeply splayed windows above the richly molded arcades. The broad wood-roofed nave of Saint-Martin is probably contemporary to the only surviving monastic building on the site, the beautiful mid-13th-century refectory that now serves as the library for the Conservatoire des Arts et Métiers.

The peace and prosperity resulting from the efforts of Louis VI led to an increase in the number of monks at Saint-Germain-des-Prés, which in turn meant the need for a larger liturgical area. Coupled with the desire to remind the king of their illustrious history as a royal necropolis and recipient of royal patronage, especially in the face of the efforts of Abbot Suger at Saint-Denis, the monks commissioned the rebuilding of their chevet on a new and much larger plan with four straight bays and a hemicycle surrounded by aisles and ambulatory and a series of five radiating and four rectangular chapels. One of the most interesting features of the original design is the way that it highlighted the Merovingian marble shafts set in the center of each opening in the second story. This deliberate, prominent reuse of Merovingian marbles parallels that at Saint-Pierre de Montmartre, Saint-Denis, and, if old accounts are trustworthy, Sainte-Geneviève and Saint-Marcel. It must have served to emphasize both the antiquity of the foundations and the continuity of their religious life.

The chevet of Saint-Germain-des-Prés is also noteworthy for the sensitive handling of the architectural elements that reflects the three distinctive spaces of the structure: chapels, ambulatory, and choir space. It should probably be understood as a reaction to the new chevet at Saint-Denis (dedicated in 1144), as well as a statement of the importance of Saint-Germain-des-Prés as a royal foundation and necropolis. The new chevet must have been finished by the mid-1150s, even though the solemn consecration was accomplished by Pope Alexander III only in the spring of 1163, by which time the new royal tombs for the Merovingian founders must have been placed in the

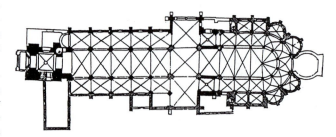

Paris, plan of Saint-Germain-des-Prés. After Lefvre-Pontalis.

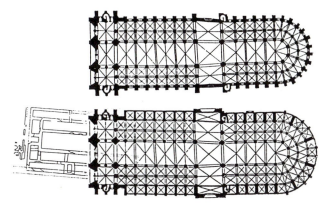

Paris (Notre-Dame), first nave section and present nave section. After Clark/Leconte.

new chevet. The new 12th-century chevet at Saint-Germain-des-Prés was accompanied by a new sculpted portal, the lintel and capitals of which are still in place, added to the old west tower.

The present cathedral of Notre-Dame was begun during the reign of Louis VII, probably not later than the mid-

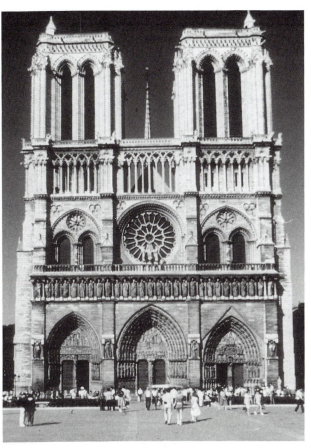

Paris, Notre-Dame, façade. *Photograph courtesy of Grover A. Zinn.*

Paris, Notre-Dame, nave. *Photograph: Clarence Ward Collection. Courtesy of Oberlin College.*

1150s. Designed at prodigious scale, no doubt as a reflection of the prestige of the capital and the wealth of the cathedral chapter, the new church dwarfed the earlier cathedral group. The double-ambulatory scheme without radiating chapels, like the enormous length of the chevet east of the crossing, was clearly intended to surpass in size and scale any previous Romanesque or Gothic structure in the region. Perhaps it is this very size that caused construction of the east end to proceed slowly, although in an orderly fashion. The chevet was finished only after 1177, perhaps even after 1182, sometime after the nave had been begun. The original elevation marked a significant increase in height over any previous Gothic building, although there is evidence that it may not have been initially planned to reach the present height of nearly 100 feet. The elevation had four stories; the double side aisles and single aisle-width vaulted galleries above them were succeeded by round oculi filled with carved tracery that gave into the gallery roof space and, finally, clerestory windows. The prevailing architectural aesthetic is an expression of thinness without depth, of surface without mass, that is uniquely Parisian. In spite of the vast height of the new chevet, there is no evidence that the first builder intended to use flying buttresses to brace the upper structure against wind pressures. In fact, that may well explain the slowdown in construction just as the clerestory was reached.

However, flying buttresses were certainly part of the scheme devised by a second builder for the newly enlarged and expanded nave. And it is likely that it was this second builder who actually completed the main vaults of the chevet, which may have been beyond the capabilities of the first builder. The second builder increased the width of the nave over that of the chevet and made the wall both physically thinner and more open than had his predecessor. His scheme in fact depends on flying buttresses, the external bracing system that is the visual hallmark of Gothic cathedrals. Although the flying buttresses of the nave of Notre-Dame de Paris may not be the first examples, they are unquestionably the most influential, the ones that proved the efficacy of the system. By the time the nave was nearing completion in the late 1190s, flying buttresses had become standard features in the schemes of countless Gothic structures.

The west façade of Notre-Dame was undertaken ca. 1200 and may represent yet another aggrandizement of the earlier plan. It has long been recognized that not only was it started before the last bays of the nave were constructed but that it contains in the south, or Sainte-Anne, portal sculpture that was prepared for a west-façade scheme beginning in the 1150s but that was placed in the present façade only ca. 1210. The most famous sculptural feature of the façade, the gallery of kings—representations of the kings of France from Merovingian times to the early 13th century—may be a commemoration of the victory of Philip II at the Battle of Bouvines in 1214, after which he was known as "Augustus." Thus, the façade of Notre-Dame might equally be read as the triumphal arch of Philip Augustus.

The three sculpted portals of Notre-Dame were probably undertaken simultaneously. Although the sculpture was badly damaged during the French Revolution—all of the statue columns in the three portals and all of the kings in the gallery were destroyed—enough original material remains for us to determine that the figure of Christ and one of the flanking angels in the tympanum of the center portal had to be replaced ca. 1230. While work was still continuing on the towers of the west façade, work began again in the chevet and nave, ca. 1225/30. The decision was made to enlarge the clerestory windows downward in order to increase the interior light. The main effort of this undertaking, however, was the systematic replacement of the earlier flying buttresses by new ones that abutted the wall at a higher level.

Almost on the heels of the rebuilding of the flying buttresses and enlargement of the clerestory windows came the construction of the first chapels between the buttresses of the nave and the decision to extend the transept arms by one bay on each side and to add sculpted portals. The

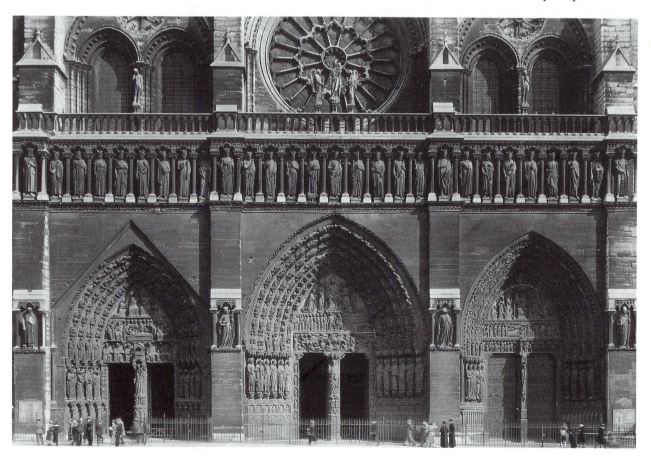

Paris, Notre-Dame, west portals. *Photograph: Clarence Ward Collection. Courtesy of Oberlin College.*

Paris, Saint-Julien-le-Pauvre. *Photograph: Clarence Ward Collection. Courtesy of Oberlin College.*

north side was begun ca. 1246/47 by Jean de Chelles, who also began the south in 1257/58 but was shortly succeeded by Pierre de Montreuil. The elaborate tracery screens and enormous rose windows, the latter in imitation of the rose of the west façade, are clearly in the Rayonnant style. Work continued with the addition of lower chapels on the nave and ultimately around the chevet, as well as with the decoration of the interior by means of the choir enclosure and the transept interiors late in the 13th and into the 14th century.

The present church of Saint-Julien-le-Pauvre, dating from ca. 1170, is the sole surviving 12th-century parish church in Paris. Its three-apse east-end plan, with a tower over the south bay before the apse, is close to the plan of Saint-Pierre de Montmartre but lacks the transept. The church was founded in the 6th century, and its plan type is representative of the conservative tradition found in Paris under Louis VII. In spite of its old-fashioned look, the details indicate that it is contemporary with the upper level of the east end of the cathedral. Construction of Saint-Julien dragged on slowly; the upper parts of the east end may not have been completed before ca. 1210, and construction was finally abandoned ca. 1250. The present façade wall dates from the mid-17th century.

Other sites known to have been founded in the Merovingian period were rebuilt under Louis VI and Louis VII, marking the reestablished prosperity of the city. Further indications of conditions in the city are provided by the transfer of the Grève market to Les Champeaux, ap-proximately on the site of Les Halles, and the concession of the Grève port to the newly established "Marchands de l'Eau" in 1141. Most scholars of Paris believe that the wall on the north bank was rebuilt farther out, perhaps in the first half of the 12th century, to protect the city's commerce; but no archaeological evidence has been found. But the most famous indication of conditions on the Cité is the petition by the monks of Saint-Barthélémy/Saint-Magloire to exchange properties with the king. The Cité, they alleged, was too crowded for the monks to live in peace. Thus, in 1138, they moved to the chapel of Saint-Georges beside the Rue Saint-Denis and began to build their new convent, dedicated to St. Magloire. Their bucolic peace, however, was to be short-lived.

If the ages of Louis VI and Louis VII were devoted largely to the rebuilding of monuments, which would include the old royal palace on the Cité (now the Palais de Justice), then the age of Philip Augustus marks the beginning of what we might term civic projects. Under Philip, Paris truly came into its own as the capital of a strong monarchy and the center of a flourishing French civilization. In 1183, Philip ordered the reconstruction of the great market center, later known as Les Halles, to support the growing mercantile community. Some years later, he began the task of paving the city's more important streets and squares. When he left on crusade in 1190, Philip underscored the importance of the capital by naming six bourgeois of Paris to take charge of royal finances, auditing accounts at the Temple. At about the same time, he ordered the fortification of the city by the construction of walls regularly punctuated by defensive towers. More than three miles of new city walls encircled the sprawling suburbs to the north and the old Roman areas to the south. Protected by the new fortress, the Louvre, to the west and by fortified bridge heads within, the town, now encompassing more than 620 acres, was for the first time unified. The left bank was still underpopulated, and grapes could still be grown on the slopes almost to the Seine. Still, this side of the city was rapidly changing, as the schools of Saint-Victor and the nucleus of the university began to attract students from all over Europe. The intellectual leadership of Paris was sealed with the incorporation of the masters and students as the University of Paris, beginning with recognition of the rights of students by Philip Augustus in 1200 and culminating with papal recognition in 1209/10. Indeed, at Philip's death in 1223, Paris was a rich, flourishing walled city, Europe's foremost administrative and intellectual center, a position that it maintained through the next century. The renowned cultural and intellectual brilliance of Paris in the age of Louis IX (r. 1226–70) was in fact the creation of his grandfather.

This period also marked a time of brilliant achievements in music. A movement dubbed Ars Antiqua by modern scholars and associated in its earliest stages with composers at Notre-Dame, saw the first development of a large repertory of rhythmically measured polyphonic music. Both the repertory—including the genres organum, conductus, and motet—and the body of music theory describing the music had enormous and lasting influence on the subsequent history of music in the West. Paris maintained

Paris, Sainte-Chapelle. *Photograph courtesy of Whitney S. Stoddard.*

its leading role into the 14th century with the further musical innovations of Ars Nova. Paris was also a center of activity for minstrels. The statutes of the Confrérie de Saint-Julien des Ménétriers was signed by thirty-seven *ménestrels* and *ménestrelles* in 1321. Royalty and bourgeoisie alike hired minstrels on the Rue aus Jogleurs, located off the rue Saint-Martin midway between the churches of Saint-Merri and Saint-Nicolas.

The coming of age of Louis IX in 1233 marks the beginning of the Rayonnant style in Paris, perhaps best represented by the splendid new royal chapel, the Sainte-Chapelle, which Louis built in the Cité palace to house the collection of relics, including the Crown of Thorns, bought from the Latin emperor in Constantinople in 1239 and 1241. From the conception of the project, the Sainte-Chapelle was viewed as a gigantic reliquary. Built between 1241 and 1246, possibly by an architect brought from Amiens, the chapel was consecrated in 1248. On the one hand, it is but the latest in the series of two-storied royal chapels that begins with Charlemagne's chapel of Aix-la-Chapelle; on the other, it marks a significant departure from previous chapels. Lavish interior painting makes the stone architecture look more like metalwork than building. The setting of paintings on glass in the wall recalls the

incorporation of cameos and enamels on gilded reliquaries. The statues of the Apostles, their billowing draperies painted to resemble rich silks and brocades, the hemlines studded with jewels, set against the piers in the upper chapel are the quintessential examples of the new court art of Paris associated with the age of Louis IX.

The lower chapel has a secondary row of thin columns set away from the wall so that it could be vaulted without the ribs resting directly on the floor. The effect is to create an interior network of delicate architectural members screening the wall, itself richly decorated with tracery and moldings that seem to peel back layers of ornament to reveal the stained-glass windows. But it is in the upper chapel that the stained glass makes its most dramatic effect. The tall, narrow proportions of the jewellike windows, nearly 50 feet tall, negate any feeling of mass and contribute to the transcendental, ecstatic sense of space. The relics were displayed in a giant gilded and jeweled reliquary above and behind the altar, a shrine within a shrine.

Although no other monument quite equaled the splendor of the Sainte-Chapelle, it set new standards of design in architecture, sculpture, painting, and stained glass that dominated French art for more than a century. Branner termed it the "Court style," but it is really the art of Paris and is not limited to the court, as is demonstrated by the new transept façades of Notre-Dame and many other nonroyal projects in the city.

Louis IX continued some of the ambitious urban projects of his grandfather, including enlarging the markets and, as early as 1240, granting permission for construction beyond the city walls on the right bank. The draining of the surrounding swamps continued with the construction of the Fossés-le-Roi in 1260, and vegetables replaced grain as the principal crop. The king reorganized the administration of Paris in 1261, dividing authority between the royal *prévôt,* who exercised the king's authority and jurisdiction from the Châtelet on the right bank, and the *prévôt des marchands,* who served as the leader of the bourgeois and merchant community. The crown and bourgeoisie collaborated in promoting their common interests in the local economy, regulating the many trades that were represented by guilds of various kinds. These measures, intended to protect consumers from shoddy products and skilled craftspeople from ruinous competition, eventually had a stultifying effect on economic growth, and after the disastrous plagues of 1348 and later, they were relaxed in many ways. The royal archives (Trésor des Chartes) and the chancery, then the judiciary (Parlement) became established bodies requiring more officials and transacting more business.

The fame of the university and its teachers attracted more and more students from afar. The left bank proliferated with privately endowed residential colleges and convents for students and with the houses of the new mendicant orders, maintained for those members who studied and taught in Paris. The preeminence of the city was sealed on the one hand by the university, on the other by Louis IX himself. The process begun by Louis VI's decision to settle in Paris was completed in the age of Louis IX; the role of Paris as the capital, as the seat of national government, dominated by Parisian bureaucracy, was completed in the 13th century.

In the 14th century, Paris grew to a population, estimated from the surviving fiscal registers, of over 80,000, a quarter of whom may have been students. Royal administration grew apace in both size and organization and provided documents concerning households, taxpayers, and tithes. By 1352, nearly 80 percent of the city's taxpayers and taxable wealth was on the right bank, which remains today the financial center of the city. Great lords, both lay and ecclesiastical, acquired houses in Paris as their business and capital increased. Corporate bodies like towns and monasteries often had to maintain representatives there for extended periods. Later examples of some of these structures remain: the Hôtel de Sens (1475–1519) and the Hôtel de Cluny (1485–98), for example. The houses of noble and bourgeois families engaged in royal and city bureaucracy proliferated, although traces of only a few now remain: the portal of the Hôtel de Clisson, built by the king's future constable after 1371, or the Tower of John the Fearless (ca. 1400), all that remains of the residence of the dukes of Burgundy.

The bourgeoisie of Paris began to produce families of great wealth, among them the Arroude, Barbette, Bourdon, Coquatrix, Marcel, de Pacy, Pizdoue, and Sarrazin. Such families grew wealthy practicing a trade, but they also were speculators who stockpiled goods in anticipation of shortages. In addition, some of them became moneychangers, farmed royal offices or municipal taxes, or became purveyors to the growing royal household. Prominent Parisians sometimes gained important positions in the royal government, especially in areas of finance. Others studied law and served in the Parlement. By the 14th century, some of those who had won royal favor were receiving patents of nobility.

Despite the growth of sedentary organs of the royal government, the kings themselves maintained an itinerant style of life until the mid-14th century. When not on crusades or other military campaigns, they generally resided at favored monasteries or royal manors, most of them in the region around Paris and close to forests with good hunting. John II the Good finally began to alter this pattern, spending more time in the royal palace on the Cité than had his predecessors. Charles V also spent much time in Paris but preferred to reside on the right bank, either in the Louvre or his new Hôtel de Saint-Pol. The latter was also the favored residence of Charles VI. In the 15th century, by contrast, the kings were often absent from Paris. Charles VII did not set foot there from the Burgundian occupation of 1418 until the expulsion of the English conquerors in 1436. Even thereafter, he preferred the Loire Valley as a residence, and so did his son, Louis XI (d. 1483), who had been born in that region and harbored a dislike for the Parisians.

Despite considerable loss of population from the Black Death of 1348–49, the right bank had acquired such a large population outside the walls of Philip Augustus—some fifty-one streets by 1300—that Étienne Marcel, *prévôt des marchands* (1354–58), in 1356 began construction of a new wall, which was continued by Charles V. With the 430 acres added by this wall, Paris now covered 1,084 acres. An integral part of the new wall was the construction of six small fortresses at the gates. The most important of these was the one on the eastern side, known as the Bastille Saint-Antoine, whose captain was an important figure in the defense of the city.

The once-close collaboration between the king and the Parisian bourgeoisie was marred by intermittent conflict from the early 14th century. What generally triggered popular uprisings was royal fiscal policy, especially as it concerned the currency. The first explosion of opposition occurred in 1306. Fifteen years later, when the crown sought a tax in peacetime to standardize weights and measures and buy out nonroyal coinage rights, the king's advisers blamed the Parisians for the plan's rejection and even talked of moving the capital to Orléans. A sharply deflationary reform of the currency in 1343 provoked new opposition from the poorer classes.

Parisian hostility to the monarchy reached revolutionary proportions in the next decade. The crown's tampering with the alloy of the currency was but one of the factors in this crisis. Étienne Marcel was a major player in a complex political drama involving both a movement for governmental reform and the personal animosities of the great bourgeois families. Those who had grown rich in royal service were the special targets of Marcel's party. He supported the Jacquerie of 1358 largely because of his hostility toward former members of the Parisian bourgeoisie who had won noble titles. Marcel's Parisians and the Jacques in the countryside introduced an element of class conflict that split a reforming party already disorganized by the fickle, self-seeking adventurism of its putative leader, Charles the Bad, king of Navarre (r. 1332–87). The future Charles V successfully recruited to his cause most of the noble reformers and regained Paris in the summer of 1358, when Marcel was murdered.

Charles V (r. 1364–80), a great patron of the arts, had the most important architects, sculptors, and painters working on his projects. His most famous undertaking, directed by Raymond du Temple, was the rebuilding of the Louvre that effectively changed its character from stern military fortress to sumptuous royal residence at the height of the Hundred Years' War. Its famous spiral staircase, decorated with statues of royalty, was the wonder of his contemporaries; but all that remains are contemporary descriptions and, quite plausibly, the statues of the king and queen now in the Louvre. Charles V also rebuilt the palace on the Cité, which had been remodeled earlier in the century by Philip IV the Fair, the Bastille Saint-Antoine, and the castle at Vincennes.

Class interests were apparent again in 1382, when a new uprising in Paris, that known as the Maillotins, resisted the imposition of the *aides*, indirect royal taxes that bore mainly on the urban populations. Charles VI's government punished this rebellion severely and abolished the office of *prévôt des marchands*. Although the behavior of Charles of Navarre had wrecked his credibility as a leader of reformers, he and his family, the Évreux branch of the royal house, made one enduring contribution to the cause

Paris, Saint-Séverin, ambulatory. *Photograph courtesy of Whitney S. Stoddard.*

of reform by endowing the Collège de Navarre at the University of Paris. Established early in the 14th century and patronized by successive members of the Évreux family, this institution produced a series of brilliant intellectuals who attracted others to a circle of reformers that wielded influence in three successive reigns after 1350. Eloquent preachers associated with this circle espoused such causes as a stable coinage, lower taxes, honest government, and (unusual for this period) the suppression of noble violence against unprotected peasants.

When competing princely factions (Burgundy vs. Orléans and then Armagnac) disrupted French politics in the early 15th century, it was John the Fearless, duke of Burgundy (r. 1404–19), whose success in posing as a reformer won over the Parisian bourgeoisie and important elements at the university. The next major uprising in Paris, that of the Cabochiens in 1413, led to a major ordinance of reform, but the excesses of the rebels antagonized most of the princes, and the ordinance did not survive the suppression of the uprising. The duke of Burgundy, isolated politically by this incident, had to flee Paris, but his forces regained the city in 1418 and massacred his rivals. His murder the following year pushed his son into alliance with England, and the Treaty of Troyes (1420) recognized Henry V as heir to the French throne. During the lifetime of this alliance (to 1435), Paris remained under Anglo-Burgundian control. Charles VII's troops finally recaptured the city for the Valois monarchy in 1436, but several more decades would pass before Paris regained its former stature as the undisputed political and intellectual center of the realm.

The difficulties imposed by the economic hardships of the Hundred Years' War in Paris are illustrated by the parish church of Saint-Séverin on the left bank. The west end and first three nave bays date from the mid-13th century. The church was enlarged laterally to the south in the 14th century because there was no room to expand to the east. The property was acquired in 1445, but construction was delayed by the need to rebuild the nave. The chevet foundations were laid in 1489, but the east end was not finished until ca. 1520, and it is the work of the 15th century that governs the character of the church. Its broad double-aisled plan, at first the result of lack of space to expand longitudinally, came to resemble the double-aisled plan of the cathedral after the 15th-century rebuilding. It is a broad, laterally expansive space that is filled with light, even with the added nave chapels. The restrained Flamboyant of the east end, with its extraordinary piers that contribute to the dynamic sense of movement, sets the conservative tone characteristic of Late Gothic architecture in Paris.

An analogous situation exists for the church of Saint-Germain l'Auxerrois, another old foundation, located on the right bank near the western port of Paris and adjacent to the Louvre. Engulfing an eastern tower of the first half of the 12th century, a 13th-century chevet, and a west portal, it was almost entirely rebuilt in the first half of the 15th century. With tall aisles and a low central vessel consisting simply of broad arcades and clerestory windows, Saint-Germain also has a sense of lateral expansiveness and architectural restraint. What decoration that does exist is concentrated in the window tracery or in the Burgundian-style porch added 1435–39.

Broad, expansive spaces are found in other Parisian churches of the 15th century, even in those like Saint-Laurent, Saint-Médard, and Saint-Merri, with its elegant Flamboyant façade, that do not have double-aisled plans. The one Late Gothic church in Paris that returns to an emphasis on the vertical, the parish church of Saint-Gervais/Saint-Protais, located adjacent to the Porte de Grève and behind the Hôtel de Ville, is frequently attributed to the most prodigious architect working in the late 15th and early 16th century, Martin Chambiges, who is known to have worked on the Hôtel de Ville. The church was begun in 1494, but the nave was not constructed until after 1600. Yet the interior is remarkable for the uniformity and continuity of the first design and for the restraint of the window tracery, as well as for its tall, narrow proportions that look back to nearby Notre-Dame rather than to its immediate 15th-century predecessors. When the Renaissance style is introduced in Paris, with the remodeled chevet of Saint-Nicholas-des-Champs or the extraordinary church of Saint-Eustache, which challenged even the cathedral in its grandeur, it will be, interestingly enough, characterized by the tall, narrow proportions of Saint-Gervais, which itself has a famous Renaissance façade, rather than the more laterally expansive spaces of the early 15th century.

William W. Clark/John Bell Henneman, Jr.

Paris, Saint-Eustache, chevet. *Photograph: Clarence Ward Collection. Courtesy of Oberlin College.*

[See also: *AIDES*; CABOCHIENS; CAPETIAN DYNASTY; CAROLINGIAN DYNASTY; CHAMBIGES, MARTIN; CHARLES V THE WISE; CLOVIS I; EUDES; GENEVIÈVE; JACQUERIE; JEAN DE CHELLES; JOHN II THE GOOD; JOHN THE FEARLESS; LOUIS VI THE FAT; LOUIS VII; LOUIS IX; MARCEL, ÉTIENNE; MEROVINGIAN DYNASTY; MUSIC THEORY; NOTRE-DAME SCHOOL; *PARENS SCIENTIARUM*; PARLEMENT DE PARIS; PHILIP II AUGUSTUS; PIERRE DE MONTREUIL; *PRÉVÔT/PRÉVÔTÉ*; *PRÉVÔT DE PARIS*; SAINT-VICTOR, ABBEY AND SCHOOL OF; TEMPLARS; TRÉSOR DES CHARTES; UNIVERSITIES]

Berry, Maurice, Michel Fleury, et al. *L'enceinte et le Louvre de Philippe Auguste.* Paris: Hachette, 1988.

Boussard, Jacques. *Nouvelle histoire de Paris, de la fin du siège de 885–886 à la mort de Philippe Auguste.* Paris: Hachette, 1976.

Branner, Robert. *Saint Louis and the Court Style in Gothic Architecture.* London: Zwemmer, 1965.

Bruzelius, Caroline A. "The Construction of Notre-Dame de Paris." *Art Bulletin* 69 (1987): 540–69.

Cazelles, Raymond. *Nouvelle histoire de Paris, de la fin du règne de Philippe Auguste à la mort de Charles V, 1223–1380.* Paris: Hachette, 1972.

Clark, William W. "The Early Capitals of Notre-Dame at Paris." In *Tribute to Lotte Brand Philip*, ed. William W. Clark, Colin Eisler, William Heckscher, and Barbara Lane. New York: Abaris, 1985, pp. 34–42.

———. "Spatial Innovations in the Chevet of Saint-Germain-des-Prés." *Journal of the Society of Architectural Historians* 38 (1979): 348–65.

Couperie, Pierre. *Paris Through the Ages.* New York: Braziller, 1968.

Deshoulières, François. "L'église Saint-Pierre de Montmartre." *Bulletin monumental* 77 (1913): 5–30.

Dumolin, Maurice, and Georges Outardel. *Les églises de France: Paris et la Seine.* Paris: Letouzey, 1936.

Duval, Noël, Patrick Périn, and Jean-Charles Picard. "Paris." In *Topographie chrétienne des cités de la Gaule des origines au milieu du VIIIe siècle*, ed. Nancy Gautier and Jean-Charles Picard. Paris: Boccard, 1992, Vol. 8: *Province ecclésiastique de Sens*, pp. 97–129.

Egbert, Virginia W. *On the Bridges of Medieval Paris.* Princeton: Princeton University Press, 1974.

Erlande-Brandenburg, Alain. *Notre-Dame de Paris.* Paris: Nathan, 1991.

Fleury, Michel, Alain Erlande-Brandenburg, and Jean-Pierre Babelon. *Paris monumental.* Paris: Flammarion, 1974.

Gillerman, Dorothy. *The Clôture of Notre-Dame and Its Role in the Fourteenth Century Choir Program.* New York: Garland, 1977.

Gushee, Lawrence. "Two Central Places: Paris and the French Court in the Early Fourteenth Century." In *Bericht über den internationalen musikwissenschaftlichen Kongress Berlin 1974*, ed. Hellmut Kühn and Peter Nitsche. Kassel: Bärenreiter, 1980, pp. 135–51.

Hardy, Chantal. "Les roses dans l'élévation de Notre-Dame de Paris." *Bulletin monumental* 149 (1991): 153–99.

Lefèvre-Pontalis, Eugène. "Église de Saint-Martin-des-Champs à Paris." *Congrès archéologique* (Paris) 82 (1919): 106–26.

———. "Étude historique et archéologique sur l'église de Saint-Germain-des-Prés." *Congrès archéologique* (Paris) 82 (1919): 301–66.

Leniaud, Jean-Michel, and Françoise Perrot. *La Sainte-Chapelle.* Paris: Nathan, 1991.

Périn, Patrick, Philippe Velay, and Laurent Renou. *Collections mérovingiennes.* Paris: Carnavalet, 1985.

Plagnieux, Philippe. "Le portail du XIIe siècle de Saint-Germain-des-Prés à Paris: état de la question et nouvelles recherches." *Gesta* 28 (1989): 21–29.

Velay, Philippe. *From Lutetia to Paris: The Island and the Two Banks.* Paris: CNRS, 1992.

Wright, Craig. *Music and Ceremony at Notre-Dame of Paris 500–1550.* Cambridge: Cambridge University Press, 1989.

PARLEMENT DE PARIS. As the central law court of the French monarchy from 1250 to its suppression by the French Revolution in 1790, the Parlement de Paris grew slowly out of the medieval tradition that the king was the source of justice. The early Capetian kings could provide justice only for those of the royal domain, but with the expansion of the royal domain in the 12th and 13th centuries, and with the increase of royal authority and prestige, ecclesiastical and secular lords as well as towns and lower nobility brought disputes before the king for a more certain and impartial justice.

By 1250, the king's court, which had always moved with him in his travels, became resident at Paris, and a professional body of clerical and lay specialists in law gradually appeared to administer justice in the king's name. The great success of this law court came from Louis IX's decision to allow appeals from the lower courts of *bailliages* and *sénéchaussées*, administrative subdivisions of France established by Philip II Augustus after 1190. The greater part of the Parlement's work would henceforth involve appeals rather than cases in original jurisdiction.

In 1278, Philip III the Bold issued the earliest surviving regulations for operation of the Parlement, and in the following half-century the court assumed most of the organization and procedure that it would retain for the remainder of the medieval period. It found its physical habitat within the royal palace at the western end of the Île-de-la-Cité in Paris. Its personnel accomplished their work within three judicial departments, the Grand'Chambre, the Chambre des Requêtes, and the Chambre des Enquêtes.

The Grand'Chambre was the original Parlement from which the two other chambers emerged. It was also called the Chamber of Pleas, for the great cases of the realm were pleaded there. It also heard pleas involving the death penalty and criminal cases involving corporal punishment. It directed and gave oversight to the work of the other chambers, but its most important responsibility was the issuance of the final legal decree, or *arrêt*, in all cases.

The Chambre des Requêtes heard petitions from persons who wished to initiate suits in the Parlement. If this chamber granted permission to cite one's adversary before the court, letters were issued to this effect and a commissioner was sent to the locality of the dispute to gather testimony and to create a file of written documentation, which was brought back as an *enquête* to the Grand'Chambre.

The Grand'Chambre examined the materials of the *enquête* to determine that the investigation had been properly conducted and then sent it to the Chambre des Enquêtes for extended examination and judgment. There was no pleading in this chamber; litigants never appeared before it. The written documentation of the case was thoroughly discussed and analyzed by the masters and returned with their conclusions to the Grand'Chambre. There, the masters of the Grand'Chambre decided upon final judgment in the case and then issued it as a definitive *arrêt*, or decree. From the mid-13th century, secretaries, or *greffiers*, of the Parlement kept records of its decisions, called the *Olim*, and in the 14th century and thereafter they produced series of records of most of the Parlement's work.

Franklin J. Pegues

[See also: LAW AND JUSTICE]

Aubert, Félix. *Le Parlement de Paris de Philippe le Bel à Charles VII (1314–1422).* 2 vols. Paris: Picard, 1886–90.
Autrand, Françoise. *Naissance d'un grand corps de l'état: les gens du Parlement de Paris (1345–1454).* Paris: Université de Paris I, Panthéon-Sorbonne, 1981.
Bougnot, Arthur. *Les Olim ou registres des arrêts rendus par la cour du roi.* 3 vols. in 4. Paris: Imprimerie Royale, 1839–48.
Bontaric, Edgard. *Actes du Parlement de Paris, première série, de l'an 1254 à l'an 1328.* 2 vols. Paris: Plon, 1863–67.
Mangis, Édouard. *Histoire du Parlement de Paris.* 3 vols. Paris: Picard, 1913–16.

PARTHENAY. Capital of the Gâtine, Parthenay (Deux-Sèvres) is the site of a castle that dominates a wide bend in the River Thouet. In the Middle Ages, Parthenay was an important stopover on the pilgrimage road to Santiago de Compostela, at the juncture of the roads from Thouars and Angers. One can still enter the city from the north along the picturesque medieval Rue Saint-Jacques, after crossing over the 13th-century Pont Saint-Jacques and through the Porte Saint-Jacques. Parts of the 12th-century ramparts and three towers of the 13th-century stronghold remain. The city was given to Richemont, constable of France, in the 15th century and passed, after his death in 1458, to Dunois.

The 12th-century church of Sainte-Croix and the church of Notre-Dame-de-la-Couldre, with its splendid portal in Poitevin Romanesque style, are further reminders of Parthenay's role in the medieval pilgrimage to Santiago. At nearby Parthenay-le-Vieux, the 12th-century church of Saint-Pierre, founded by monks from Chaise-Dieu, possesses a beautiful façade in Poitevin Romanesque style. The tympanum carving of Samson and the lion, the cat heads (representing devils) along the cornice, and the carved animal capitals are all worthy examples of Romanesque sculpture.

William W. Kibler

PARTONOPEU DE BLOIS. Written probably ca. 1182–85, *Partonopeu de Blois* is an enormous romance whose popularity is attested by its many medieval imitations, translations, and adaptations. Ten manuscripts feature three forms of the romance: *V* (Vatican, Palatinus latinus 1971) ends after 10,358 lines, with the marriage of Partonopeu and Melior, followed by the romancer's promise to continue his story, if his lady so commands; *A* (Paris, Arsenal 2986) reworks that ending to eliminate any continuation; and five manuscripts offer selections from the Continuation (only Tours 939, with 14,493 lines, contains both the Anselot and the Sultan Margaris episodes).

The anonymous romancer combines elements from classical, Celtic, and oriental matter to shape the story of Partonopeu of Blois, the nephew of Clovis, king of France, and Melior, empress of Byzantium. Like the fairy mistresses of Celtic *lais*, Melior arranges to lure thirteen-year-old Partonopeu to Chef d'Oire (modeled on Constantinople), where she plans to keep him secretly for two and a half years, until he can be knighted and presented to her barons as a suitable husband. Partonopeu enjoys the pleasures of love with Melior each night, on condition that she remain invisible to him (the Cupid and Psyche story with sex roles reversed). But betrayal follows, and, once she has been seen, Melior's magic powers are destroyed. Seeking death in the Ardennes Forest, Partonopeu is discovered by Urraque, Melior's sister, who persuades him with false news of Melior's pardon to go to Salence. There, Partonopeu recovers his health and prepares for the three-day tournament arranged by Melior's barons to choose her husband. Winner of the tournament, for both his prowess and his beauty, Partonopeu is finally married to a forgiving Melior.

The Continuation offers two unsuccessful love stories, and the narrator tells us that he could write yet another book about the goodness of his lady, Passe-Rose. His desire to win her love motivates the entire romance project and appears in many personal interventions, when he compares the characters' love story and his own. This lyric persona of the narrator, one of the major innovations of *Partonopeu*, begins with the springtime opening evoked in the prologue. The genealogy that follows, linking the French monarchy to Trojan ancestors, establishes the narrator in the clerkly tradition of romance writing as well. Chansons de geste, Romances of Antiquity, *lais*, Chrétien de Troyes's romances, contemporary travelogues, bestiaries, school debates—the author of *Partonopeu de Blois* exploits and reinvents all the literary and historical resources of his day. Reflecting the medieval view of fabulous Byzantium, where goods, peoples, religions, and cultures meet in a rich mix, this romance fuses the real and the marvelous, combines fantasies of the East and lessons on contemporary French politics, as it prolongs the pleasure of a love story skillfully told and enticingly opened to the public's desire for more. A measure of its success can be calculated by the translations of *Partonopeu* into English, Spanish, German, Icelandic, Dutch, and Danish between the 13th and early 16th centuries.

Matilda T. Bruckner

[See also: GRECO-BYZANTINE ROMANCE]

Gildea, Joseph, ed. *Partonopeus de Blois: A French Romance of the Twelfth Century*. 2 vols. Villanova: Villanova University Press, 1967.

Bruckner, Matilda T. *Narrative Invention in Twelfth-Century French Romance: The Convention of Hospitality (1160–1200)*. Lexington: French Forum, 1980.

Fourrier, Anthime. *Le courant réaliste dans le roman courtois en France au moyen âge*. Paris: Nizet, 1960, pp. 315–440.

Hanning, Robert W. *The Individual in Twelfth-Century Romance*. New Haven: Yale University Press, 1977.

Newstead, Helaine. "The Traditional Background of *Partonopeus de Blois*." *PMLA* 61 (1946): 916–46.

PASCHASIUS RADBERTUS (ca. 790–865). Born near Soissons, Paschasius Radbertus was raised in a women's monastery there by Theodrada, sister of Adalard and Wala of Corbie and cousin of Charlemagne. He entered the monastery of Corbie ca. 820, assisted in the founding of Corvey in Saxony in 822, and was ordained deacon. He was elected abbot of Corbie in 844. An active church leader, Radbertus attended the councils of Paris (847) and Quierzy (849), where he signed the condemnation of Gottschalk.

Following a dispute in the abbey of Corbie, he resigned the abbacy and moved to Saint-Riquier (Centula) in 851 but returned to Corbie before his death. Paschasius Radbertus wrote the *vitae* of Adalard and Wala and local saints; commentaries on Psalm 44, Lamentations, and the Gospel of Matthew; and important treatises on theology and the Virgin Mary. He is most famous today for *De corpore et sanguine Domini*, the first Latin treatise on eucharistic theology. The work was written (831) for the Saxon novices of Corvey and revised (844) for Charles the Bald. The second edition is in direct response to his fellow monk, Ratramnus, as is the defense of Mary's perpetual virginity in *De partu Virginis*. Radbertus's eucharistic theology, which strictly identifies the historical body of Christ with the sacrament of the altar, was influential in the later definition of Transubstantiation at the Council of Trent. However, the most popular work of Paschasius Radbertus in medieval France was *Cogitis me*, a letter on the Assumption of the Virgin Mary written under the name of Jerome. In other sermons on the Assumption and in his life of the Virgin Mary, Radbertus shows the importance of the influence of apocryphal literature, such as the *Protevangelium of James*, on the development of medieval Christian thought.

E. Ann Matter

[See also: CORBIE; MARY, DEVOTION TO; RATRAMNUS OF CORBIE]

Paschasius Radbertus. *Opera*. PL 120. CCCM 16, 56, 56A, 56B, 85, 94, 96, 97 (all ed. Beda Paulus), and 56C (ed. E. Ann Matter). Turnhout: Brepols, 1969–93.

Bonano, S. "The Divine Maternity and Eucharistic Body in the Doctrine of Paschasius Radbertus." *Ephemerides mariologicae* 1 (1951): 379–94.

Maus, Cyrin. *A Phenomenology of Revelation: Paschasius Radbert's Way of Interpreting Scripture*. Dayton: St. Leonard College, 1970.

Peltier, Henri. *Paschase Radbert, abbé de Corbie: contribution à l'étude de la vie monastique et de la pensée chrétienne aux temps carolingiens*. Amiens: Duthoit, 1938.

PASSION DES JONGLEURS. An anonymous narrative poem in octosyllabic couplets from the late 12th or early 13th century recounting the events of Christ's last days. Based largely on the biblical accounts, the poem also draws on the apocryphal *Gospel of Nicodemus* for such episodes as the Descent into Hell. Recited publicly by jongleurs, the poem served as the principal source for the early Passion plays. Its popularity is attested by some twenty-six extant manuscripts.

Alan E. Knight

[See also: APOCRYPHAL LITERATURE; PASSION PLAYS]

Perry, Anne Amari, ed. *La Passion des jongleurs*. Paris: Beauchesne, 1981.

PASSION DU CHRIST. A 10th-century inspirational poem of 516 lines that includes Christ's Passion, beginning with the events of Palm Sunday and concluding with Pentecost. Its language, difficult to localize, is remarkable for its many heterogeneous forms. The work survives in a single manuscript (Clermont-Ferrand 189), which also contains the only extant text of the *Vie de saint Léger*.

Thelma S. Fenster

Avalle, D'Arco Silvio. *Cultura e lingua francese delle origini nella "Passion" di Clermont-Ferrand.* Milan: Ricciardi, 1962. [Edition and Italian translation.]

PASSION PLAYS. Dramatizations, often on a large scale, of the life and especially the Passion of Christ, performed throughout France during the late Middle Ages. The essential elements in any mystery play called a "Passion" were the events of Holy Week, starting with Christ's entry into Jerusalem and concluding with his resurrection and appearances; but many later plays extended this portrayal of Christ's life backward, adding first his public life, then his nativity and childhood; some include Old Testament episodes, especially the Creation and the Fall. These longer "cyclical" Passions were often placed within the framework of the *Procès de paradis*, the trial in Heaven in which God finally accedes to the requests of Mercy to send his son to earth to save fallen humanity.

Passion plays were based on numerous sources, including, in addition to the Bible, Gospel commentaries, and apocryphal gospels, especially the *Gospel of Nicodemus*, the *Legenda aurea*, and the *Meditationes beatae Mariae*. But the most important source of the earliest plays was a widely circulated narrative poem, the *Passion des jongleurs*, which provided a lively account of the events of Holy Week and whose numerous passages of dialogue lent themselves easily to dramatization.

The earliest complete Passion play, the *Passion du Palatinus*, dates from the end of the 13th century, and Passion plays were still being written as late as 1549. More than a hundred performances of Passions are recorded from the late 14th to the late 16th century, in all parts of France. The later plays tend to be much longer than the early ones, the shortest being about 2,000 lines and the longest about 60,000. The earliest plays were performed in one session (one *journée*, or day); some took four or eight; the longest were spread out over twenty to twenty-five *journées* of about 2,000 lines each. This increasing length is due not only to the inclusion of pre–Passion Week material but to the expansion of secondary episodes, the increase in the number of minor characters, more explicitly didactic passages (sermons, prayers), and the introduction of popular or comic elements (devils, torture scenes, fools). Whereas the earlier texts are content to show the public the events upon which its faith is founded, later texts show a greater urge to explain or moralize.

In spite of the frequency of recorded performances, barely a dozen complete or nearly complete texts survive. A new text was not necessarily composed for each performance, and manuscripts often circulated among towns in a given region. Several of the surviving texts are related to others; this suggests that the normal practice was to revise, often considerably, an existing Passion play rather than write an original one. Thus, only seven Passion plays have survived, and even among these critics have traced varying degrees of influence and filiation. The most satisfactory way of grouping French Passion plays is according to a mixture of chronology and province of origin.

The *Passion du Palatinus* (Burgundy, late 13th or early 14th c.; 2,000 lines), the oldest complete Passion, dramatizes only the events of Holy Week and is heavily based, especially in the first half, on the *Passion des jongleurs*; but it has an unusual Harrowing of Hell and includes lengthy lamentations by the Virgin Mary and the three Marys. Except for these lyrical passages, the play is fast-moving and depends much on mime. The system of mnemonic rhyme used in other 13th-century plays and in all other Passion plays is absent here. Variants of the text are found in the 15th-century manuscript of the *Passion d'Autun* and in the *Fragment de Sion*. Though it clearly influenced several later plays, the view that the *Passion du Palatinus* was the single source of all Passions is contradicted by the recent discovery, in the Leiden University Library, of a fragment of a different version of the Crucifixion, also dating from the late 13th century.

The Passion play in the Paris Sainte-Geneviève Library, usually referred to as the *Passion Sainte-Geneviève* (Paris, ca. 1380; 4,500 lines), though covering largely the same events as the *Passion du Palatinus*, reveals little direct influence of the latter. Its text, often based closely on the Bible and on the *Gospel of Nicodemus*, has episodes not in *Palatinus*: the raising of Lazarus, Lazarus's account of his visit to Hell, the Veronica episode, and the allegorical debate between Ecclesia and Synagoga. The manuscript that preserves this text contains other religious plays and is probably the repertoire of a *confrérie*. The Confrérie Sainte-Geneviève du Mont is a more likely candidate than the Parisian Confrérie de la Passion. A fragment of a revision of the *Passion Sainte-Geneviève* has also been found in Troyes.

The *Passion de Semur* (Semur-en-Bourgogne; 9,000 lines; two days) survives in a manuscript of 1488, the last in a series of reworkings of an original text that goes back probably to the early 15th century. General resemblances and textual echoes encourage some critics to see the influence of the *Passion du Palatinus*, also Burgundian. The present revised text is divided into two days, though earlier versions were not. The first day includes the Creation and some other Old Testament episodes, the marriage of the Virgin Mary, and the Nativity and ends with the temptation of Jesus. Day 2 takes us from the summoning of the Apostles, through several of Jesus's miracles, the events of Holy Week, concluding with Jesus's appearances to his disciples. The most notable feature of the *Passion de Semur* is its wide range of register; juxtaposed to sermons, Latin hymns, and allegorical episodes are scenes of comedy and great vulgarity, the most striking example of which is the character of Rusticus, a transformation of one of Noah's sons, who reappears at regular intervals throughout the play and engages in foul-mouthed conversations with well-established Passion play characters.

The *Passion d'Arras* (Arras, 1430–40; 25,000 lines; four days), usually attributed to Eustache Marcadé, is the first to extend over four long days and to use the framework of the *Procès de paradis*. It uses no Old Testament material. Day 1 deals with the nativity and childhood of Christ, Day 2 with the public life, Day 3 with the Passion, and Day 4 with the Resurrection and Ascension. The length of the text is due mainly to the author's natural prolixity, to sermons, and to the expansion of secondary episodes. The surviving manuscript also contains a three-day *Vengeance* play, which would sometimes have been performed after the *Passion d'Arras*.

The *Passion* by Arnoul Greban (Paris, ca. 1450; 35,000 lines; four days) is probably the best-known French Passion play, often considered the masterpiece of the genre. Its style is more lyrical than that of most others and its structure the result of careful planning; Greban eschews the extremes of popular and vulgar elements and achieves a greater uniformity of tone. It is arguable, however, whether this makes Greban's play the best Passion play or merely an exceptional one. It is also unusual in that it has survived in three complete and virtually identical manuscripts and a number of fragments—it is extremely rare to find more than one copy of any mystery play. The fame of Greban's work was established early. Abbeville borrowed it in 1452, Jean Michel adapted it in 1486, and a revised version was performed several times in Troyes ca. 1490. Greban's play is held by some critics to be influenced by the *Passion d'Arras*; textual resemblances are few, but the four-day pattern, the *Procès de paradis* setting, and the selection and ordering of episodes are common to both. Greban, however, starts with a brief dramatized prologue, showing the Creation and the falls of Lucifer and of Adam; Day 1 proper begins with the *Procès de paradis,* leading into the Annunciation, the Nativity, and the childhood of Christ. Day 2 includes the sermons of John the Baptist, Jesus's public life, his entry into Jerusalem, and his arrest. Day 3 shows the Crucifixion up to the setting of the guards at the tomb. Day 4 deals with the Resurrection and Ascension.

Jean Michel's *Passion* (Angers, 1486; 30,000 lines; four days) is a revision and expansion of Greban's Days 2 and 3, and most of Greban's text of these two days is preserved intact or with superficial change. Despite the impression of derivativeness, Maurice Accarie has shown what a thorough reworking Michel has carried out. His expansions, additions, new sermons, and especially his prologues reflect major innovations. The main difference is that Michel seeks to replace Greban's continuing emphasis on the visual (his first line reads, *Ouvrez voz yeulx et regardez!* "Open your eyes and behold!") with his own stress on explanation, commentary, and moral and spiritual didacticism. The principal vehicle he uses to this end is the character of Mary Magdalene, the repentant sinner, whose sins (her *mondanité*) and repentance (the anointings) are especially elaborated. She and several other normally secondary characters, like Judas and Lazarus, are given detailed "biographies" that underline Michel's moral message. Michel's Passion play was influential not only because its approach reflected better the spirit of its age but be-

cause it was the first to be printed; no manuscript survives. The number of copies available enabled it to become known far beyond its province of origin. It was used, in conjunction with Greban's Days 1 and 4, as the basis of a text performed in Mons in 1501; and later in the 16th century it was plundered in such distant places as Valenciennes and the Savoy.

The *Passion d'Auvergne* (Clermont-Ferrand, 1477; seven days of about 1,500–2,000 lines each) bears no relation to the Marcadé-Greban-Michel group. Originating in a southern province where many working-class people still did not speak French, it has a structure and an approach to the Passion material that are original. Although only three of the seven days have survived, the manuscripts and archival evidence enable us to reconstruct a detailed picture of the complete play, which was performed in 1477 on six successive Sundays preceding Whitsun and on Whit Monday. Each day's performance was short compared with the Greban-Michel *journée*, probably between 1,500 and 2,000 lines, and would have taken hardly more than three hours. Day 1 depicts John the Baptist and the Temptation of Christ; Days 2 and 3, Christ's public life; Days 4 and 5, the Passion proper; Day 6, the Resurrection; Day 7, the Ascension. The play is distinctive in that it has several violent and vulgar scenes, especially during the Crucifixion; a comic episode written in the lower Auvergne dialect; and, most important, an unusual treatment of the Virgin Mary. Each surviving day ends with a meeting between Jesus and his mother, regardless of whether the traditional sources allow for such a scene. Thus, at the end of Day 5, after the Harrowing of Hell but before the Resurrection, the Virgin Mary is miraculously raised to Heaven to see Jesus. Local archival material suggests that a version of this play was performed not only in 1477 but in 1452 and at the very beginning of the 16th century, perhaps reflecting a custom, attested elsewhere, of performances every twenty-five years.

No original Passion plays have survived from the 16th century. Frequent performances are recorded well after the middle of the century, but the texts, to judge by those that have come down to us, were heavily derivative. The so-called *Passion cyclique* (Paris; 55,000 lines; six days), printed by Geoffroy Marnef in 1507, is a compilation based on Jean Michel's four days, preceded by a *Conception* partly attributed to Greban and followed by Greban's Resurrection, a similar type of text to the one used at Mons in 1501. Of the two texts usually called the *Passion de Valenciennes,* the earlier (Valenciennes, 1547; 45,000 lines; twenty-five days) and the later (Douai, 1549; 40,000 lines; twenty days), though more carefully reworked than the Marnef edition, are both freely based on Marcadé, Greban, Michel, the *Actes des Apôtres,* and other sources.

Passion plays were organized and staged no differently from other mystery plays. If the earliest dramas were put on by *confréries,* later plays required the cooperation of a whole village or town. The expense and the planning were such that a performance of a Passion play was an exceptional event for a town to undertake. A remarkable spectacle designed for public entertainment, it confirmed, illustrated, and explained the Christian faith better than any church service or sermon. The organization involved such a wide range of participants—intellectuals to compose and copy the text, bourgeois and priests to act the main roles, artisans to build and paint the theater and props, and almost everyone to watch it—that the performance emphasized the social cohesion of the community. Moreover, it was often inspired in part by commercial aims, attracting merchants and paying spectators from nearby towns. Passion plays in late-medieval France were neither simply religious plays nor a literary genre; they were major public events, with far-reaching social implications.

Graham A. Runnalls

[See also: APOCRYPHAL LITERATURE; GREBAN, ARNOUL; MICHEL, JEAN; MYSTERY PLAYS; *PASSION DES JONGLEURS*; POPULAR DEVOTION; STAGING OF PLAYS; THEATER]

Durbin, Peter T., and Lynette Muir, eds. *The Passion de Semur.* Leeds: University of Leeds, 1981.

Elliott, John R., and Graham A. Runnalls, eds. *The Baptism and Temptation of Christ.* New Haven: Yale University Press, 1978.

Frank, Grace, ed. *La Passion du Palatinus.* Paris: Champion, 1922.

Greban, Arnoul. *Le mystère de la Passion,* ed. Omer Jodogne. 2 vols. Brussels: Palais des Académies, 1965, 1983.

Marcadé, Eustache. *Le mystère de la Passion, texte du manuscrit 697 de la Bibliothèque d'Arras,* ed. J. M. Richard. Arras: Imprimerie de la Société du Pas-de-Calais, 1893.

Michel, Jean. *Le mystère de la Passion,* ed. Omer Jodogne. Gembloux: Duculot, 1959.

Runnalls, Graham A., ed. *Le mystère de la Passion Nostre Seigneur du manuscrit 1131 de la Bibliothèque Sainte-Geneviève.* Geneva: Droz, 1974.

———, ed. *La Passion d'Auvergne.* Geneva: Droz, 1982.

Accarie, Maurice. *Le théâtre sacré de la fin du moyen âge.* Geneva: Droz, 1979.

Frank, Grace. *The Medieval French Drama.* 2nd ed. Oxford: Clarendon, 1960.

Konigson, Élie. *La représentation d'un mystère de la Passion à Valenciennes en 1547.* Paris: CNRS, 1969.

Petit de Julleville, Louis. *Les mystères.* 2 vols. Paris: Hachette, 1880.

Simon, Eckehard, ed. *The Theatre of Medieval Europe.* Cambridge: Cambridge University Press, 1991, pp. 151–68.

PASTOUREAUX. In Flanders and northern France in 1251, bands of rustics called *pastoureaux* ("shepherds") began to join together under the inspiration of a leader known as the Master of Hungary, a man of obscure origins who claimed to have the blessing of the Virgin Mary. The bands marched under the banner of the Triumphant Lamb. No trustworthy estimate of their number exists, but it was large; and such evidence as there is suggests that shepherds contributed only a fraction to the composition of the bands as finally constituted. Their avowed purpose was to go to the Holy Land to help Louis IX in his crusade. At first tolerated, even encouraged, by the government of Louis's mother, Blanche of Castile, the bands began to threaten local and royal authorities in Rouen, Paris, and Bourges, among other places, ultimately doing violence against prelates, the rich, and Jews. The royal government succeeded in suppressing them in the summer of 1251.

There is no direct filiation between the *pastoureaux* of 1251 and the second movement that bears the name in 1320, but there are striking parallels. Again, throughout the north of France in the aftermath of the great famine (1315–17), people responded eagerly to the call of Philip V for a crusade. When the expedition was not mounted, bands of rustics coalesced around popular leaders, some of whom seem to have been renegade priests, to do the job on their own. Violence ensued. Paris saw angry mobs attack the Châtelet, the seat of the royal *prévôt* of Paris. And greater violence followed in the wake of the arrival of the *pastoureaux* in other towns in the southwest and south. More than one hundred Jews were killed in Toulouse alone before the uprising was suppressed. Those *pastoureaux* who escaped across the Pyrénées were dispatched by the Aragonese army.

William Chester Jordan

[See also: MILLENNIALISM]

Barber, Malcolm. "The Crusade of the Shepherds in 1251." *Proceedings of the Tenth Annual Meeting, 1981, of the Western Society for French Historical Studies* (1984): 1–23.

———. "The Pastoureaux of 1320." *Journal of Ecclesiastical History* 32 (1981): 143–66.

Dickson, Gary. "The Advent of the *Pastores* (1251)." *Revue belge de philologie et d'histoire* 66 (1988): 249–67.

PASTOURELLE/PASTORELA. Medieval lyric genre that developed in the 12th century in Occitan (*pastorela*), flourished during the 13th in French (*pastourelle*), and was imitated in Latin, German, Italian, Galician-Portuguese, Castilian, English, Welsh, Gascon, and Franco-Provençal; it survives in folksongs in various languages. The word means "shepherdess," by synecdoche "poem about a shepherdess"; the French form reveals linguistic influence from Occitan in the retention of the *s* (cf. French *pâtre* 'shepherd') and in the treatment of the stressed vowel (cf. French *pasteur*).

In the most frequent type, a male speaker narrates his encounter with a young woman, often a shepherdess, and his attempt to seduce her. The prototype by Marcabru, *L'autrier jost'una sebissa*, combines elements that are found in medieval Latin compositions and in scattered analogues in other languages (in Chinese, in the Romance of the *kharjas*, perhaps in French); the dialogue follows the man's increasing efforts at hyperbole, and ends with the girl mocking him in his defeat. The context of Marcabru's other satires invites reading the man as a symbol of the decadence of courtly culture (perhaps as a figure of Guilhem IX, the first troubadour), and the girl as a representative of sound peasant morality. Marcabru's tone evolved quickly into the erudite libertinage of Walter of Châtillon's Ovidian *pastourelles*. The French poems, many of them anonymous, run the gamut from sexual farce to rape. In the late 13th century, Guiraut Riquier created a series of *pastourelles* in which he meets the same shepherdess six times over a period of more than twenty years, and the genre entered the *dolce stil nuovo* with Guido Cavalcanti and Dante. In the *serranillas* of the *Libro de buen amor*, Juan Ruiz turned the shepherdess into a folkloric wildwoman of autochthonous strength.

Related forms include the augmented *pastourelle*, in which the cast of characters is increased by adding a peasant lover who often drives the narrator away; the *bergerie*, in which the narrator encounters peasants dancing or quarreling; and the *pastoureau*, in which he talks with a shepherd.

William D. Paden

Audiau, Jean, ed. *La pastourelle dans la poésie occitane du moyen âge.* Paris: Boccard, 1923.

Bartsch, Karl, ed. *Romances et pastourelles françaises des XIIe et XIIIe siècles: Altfranzösische Romanzen und Pastourellen.* Leipzig: Vogel, 1870.

Paden, William D., ed. and trans. *The Medieval Pastourelle.* 2 vols. New York: Garland, 1987.

Bec, Pierre. *La lyrique française au moyen âge (XIIe–XIIIe siècles): contribution à une typologie des genres poétiques médiévaux.* 2 vols. Paris: Picard, 1977–78, Vol. 1, pp. 119–36.

Zink, Michel. *La pastourelle: poésie et folklore au moyen âge.* Paris: Bordas, 1972.

PATHELIN, FARCE DE MAISTRE. Written in the 1460s, *Pathelin* is the earliest of the many farces surviving from the late-medieval period. It is unusual in both its length and its complexity. The play's 1,600 octosyllabic lines make it twice as long as any other farce and three times longer than the average. Whereas most other farces are constructed around a single trick, the anonymous author of *Pathelin* has woven an intricate web of mutual deception. Pierre Pathelin, a down-and-out pettifogging lawyer, purchases cloth on credit from Guillaume the clothier, who cheats him on the price. Guillaume's attempt to collect his money is thwarted by Pathelin, with his wife's complicity, in an inspired scene of comic delirium. Because Guillaume has also cheated his shepherd on his wages, the latter kills and eats a number of the sheep. Accused of the slaughter, the shepherd hires Pathelin to defend him in court. The latter deceives the judge by having the shepherd reply "Baa" to all his questions. Finally, when Pathelin asks to be paid, the shepherd dutifully replies "Baa" to all his entreaties. The theme of trickster tricked (*à trompeur, trompeur et demi*) is thus exemplified several times over.

The length of the play allows the author to develop the characters to an extent not possible in other farces, and some have called *Pathelin* the first comedy of character. The play's comic dimension derives also from its clever situations, its telling gestures, and especially its verbal acrobatics. In such a tissue of deceptions, the words of the characters are like the gold they promise in payment: empty of meaning and devoid of reality. The playwright's satire is far more radical than a simple attack on the venality of merchants and lawyers; it puts into question language itself and its ability to convey the mutual trust on which society depends.

Alan E. Knight

[**See also:** FARCE]

Holbrook, Richard T., ed. *Maistre Pierre Pathelin.* 2nd ed. Paris: Champion, 1937.

Dufournet, Jean, and Michel Rousse. *Sur "La farce de maître Pierre Pathelin."* Paris: Champion, 1986.

Maddox, Donald. *Semiotics of Deceit: The Pathelin Era.* Lewisburg: Bucknell University Press, 1984.

PÂTURAGE. Use of pasture for domestic animals in the forest and common lands of a village; the word also refers to the grazing lands themselves. Originally public rights vested in Carolingian officials, rights to *pâturage* came to be part of the seigneurial or banal rights of lords, who began in the central Middle Ages to exact fees for or to limit use of and access to such grazing lands. Such pasture rights also included rights to graze animals on fallow, to allow pigs into the forest to eat acorns and other nuts, to collect bedding for animals, and other forest uses essential to the village economy. Pasture lands (generally, *pascua* in Latin) should not be confused with meadows (Lat. *prata*, Fr. *prés*), which were much more valuable holdings in particularly well watered, sometimes even irrigated, locations along streams, where they would produce multiple cuttings of hay each summer.

Constance H. Berman

[**See also:** AGRICULTURE; ANIMALS (DOMESTIC); TRANSHUMANCE]

Duby, Georges. *Rural Economy and Country Life in the Medieval West*, trans. Cynthia Postan. Columbia: University of South Carolina Press, 1968.

———, and Armand Wallon, eds. *Histoire de la France rurale des origines à 1340.* Paris: Seuil, 1975.

Slicher van Bath, Bernard H. *The Agrarian History of Western Europe: A.D. 500–1850*, trans. Olive Ordish. London: Arnold, 1963.

PEACE OF GOD. A popular conciliar movement combining lay and ecclesiastical legislation on the regulation of warfare and the establishment of social peace, the Peace of God has been considered the first popular religious movement of the Middle Ages.

The practice of holding peace councils began in the late 10th century in southern France, in Auvergne, Aquitaine, and Rouergue. During an initial phase of strong enthusiasm, it spread rapidly through most of France and survived in some form until at least the 13th century. The early councils typically took place in large open fields to which relics of saints had been ceremonially paraded. The *seniores* (high nobility, bishops, abbots) would proclaim peace legislation designed to protect civilians, such as unarmed clerics, peasants, merchants, pilgrims, and women, from the violence and expropriations of the warrior class of lords, castellans, and knights. This proclamation often took the form of an oath, sworn on relics by the fighting classes in the presence of the assembled crowd.

The peace movement's almost messianic expectations (regulating warfare through collective voluntary commitments), generated enthusiasm at the councils themselves but in the long run failed to eliminate the violence of the landholding and weapon-bearing classes. As a result, despite the initial determination to hold peace councils at regular intervals of five years, the practice gradually declined. By the later 11th century, more effective and long-lasting movements, such as papal reform, the communal movement, and the Crusades, replaced the Peace of God at the center of European concerns. Each of these later developments deployed characteristic elements of the Peace (collective oaths, sanctified violence) to more limited and effective ends. All of them share with the Peace elements that suggest they are all part of a larger social transformation at work in the 11th and 12th centuries—the importance of an informed and active public, autonomy of popular initiatives, and collective religious enthusiasm.

Richard Landes

[See also: ASSEMBLIES; CONCILIAR MOVEMENT; MILLENNIALISM; TRUCE OF GOD]

Cowdrey, Herbert E.J. "The Peace and Truce of God in the Eleventh Century." *Past and Present* 46 (1970): 42–67.

Duby, Georges. *The Chivalrous Society*, trans. Cynthia Postan. Berkeley: University of California Press, 1977, pp. 123–33.

Goetz, Hans Werner. "Kirchenschutz, Rechtswahrung und Reform: Zu den Zielen und zum wesen der frühen Gottesfriedensbewegung in Frankreich." *Francia* 11 (1983): 193–239.

Head, Thomas, and Richard Landes, eds. *Essays on the Peace of God: The Church and the People in Eleventh Century France.* Special edition of *Historical Reflections/Réflections historiques* 14 (1987).

Huberti, Ludwig. *Studien zur Rechtsgeschichte der Gottesfrieden und Landfrieden.* Ansbach: Brugel, 1892.

PEER/PEERAGE. The term "peer" (Lat. *par*, OFr. *per, pair*) was applied in the 11th century in the region between the Seine and the Meuse to all co-vassals in their capacity as suitors to the court of their lord. In recognition of the vast and increasing difference in wealth between greater and lesser vassals, the legal terminology of a growing number of courts began to draw a distinction early in the 12th century between two classes of peers, and by 1150 the title "peer" had come in some dominions to be restricted to a small number of greater vassals, between six and twelve in number, most commonly twelve. By 1200, this usage was normal in northeastern France, and the status of peer had been converted into a dignity permanently and exclusively attached to the possession of one of the six to twelve fiefs (always counties, viscounties, or castellanies within a principality, and knight's fees within a castellany) that had

been recognized as parial fiefs or "parities" (Lat. *paritas, parria, perreria,* Fr. *pairie*). The parities of principalities were normally either selected from or "identical" with the fiefs that in the same period came to be regarded as "baronies" of the principality. The principal privilege of parial status was the right to be tried in all cases touching either the person or parity of the peer in a court in which at least some members of the relevant corps of peers or "peerage" were present.

The peerage of France as a whole seems to have been created on the model of the peerages of the principalities in or shortly before 1202. Its early history is obscure, but there is reason to think that Philip II Augustus, probably invoking the legend of the "twelve peers" attributed to the court of Charlemagne, called the historical peerage into being—possibly to deal with the judgment of his most dangerous vassal, John, king of England, duke of Normandy and Aquitaine—and that he deliberately selected the twelve original parities from among the baronies of the realm. These included six lay (the duchies of Burgundy, Normandy, and Aquitaine or Guyenne, and the counties of Toulouse, Flanders, and Champagne) and six clerical (those held by the archbishop of Reims and the bishops of Laon and Langres, Beauvais, Châlons, and Noyon). Of these twelve, however, two, the duchies of Normandy and Aquitaine, were almost immediately declared confiscate, and although the latter was legally restored in 1259 it was again declared forfeit in 1294; Toulouse was definitively annexed to the royal domain in 1274 and Champagne in 1285. For most of the century, the effective number of peers was thus no higher than ten, and in 1294 it was reduced to eight—six clerical and two lay.

It was in these circumstances that Philip IV in September 1297 inaugurated the practice of conferring peerships by creating or "erecting" three new parities: Anjou, Artois, and Brittany. Philip's successors continued to erect new lay parities, down to 1424 exclusively for members of the royal house, and after 1305 the number of lay peers fluctuated between six and ten. After 1318, parial status lost its strict attachment to a major fief, and some peers secured parial condition for almost all of the lands they held from the crown. The peers also secured the exemption of all of their parial lands from the jurisdiction of all courts save the Grand'Chambre of the Parlement de Paris sitting as a "Court of Peers," so that parities constituted vast immunities within the structure of royal administration.

D'A. Jonathan D. Boulton

[See also: NOBILITY]

Boulton, D'A.J.D. *Grants of Honour: The Origins of the System of Nobiliary Dignities of Traditional France, ca. 1100–1515.* Forthcoming.

Feuchère, Pierre. "Pairs de principauté et pairs de château: essai sur l'institution des pairies en Flandre. Étude géographique et institutionelle." *Revue belge de philologie et d'histoire* (1953): 973–1002.

———. "Essai sur l'institution des pairs entre Seine et Meuse." *Revue du Nord* 36 (1954): 78–79.

Sautel-Boulet, Marguerite. "Le rôle juridictionnel de la cour des pairs au XIIIe et XIVe siècles." *Recueil . . . Clovis Brunel.* Paris: Société de l'École des Chartes, 1955, pp. 507–20.

Valon, François de. *Les pairs de France et leur cour.* Toulouse: Cléder, 1931.

PEIRE CARDENAL (ca. 1180–ca. 1272). One of the most prolific troubadours and the longest-lived, Peire Cardenal composed *sirventes*, or satires, on moral and religious subjects. He left some ninety-six poems. Born in Le Puy, he was employed as a clerk by Raymond VI of Toulouse and frequented the courts of Les Baux, Rodez, Auvergne, and (according to his *vida*) of Aragon. He may have died in Montpellier.

As a satirist, Peire is distant from Marcabru but closer to Bertran de Born, whom he imitated in a number of compositions, sometimes equaling the sting of Bertran's invective, on other occasions echoing his technique of martial description the better to express his disapproval of Bertran's eagerness for combat. Peire imitated the metrical and musical form of preceding compositions in at least 80 percent of his own songs, exploring the possibilities of an increasingly strict sense of contrafacture with impressive technical inventiveness.

As a moralist, Peire praises good actions and blames the bad but laments that he is understood by no one, as though he spoke a foreign language. He tells a fable, *Una ciutatz fo*, in which rain falls on a city and drives everyone mad except one man who has been sheltered; when he goes out into the street, he sees that everyone else is crazy, but they think him mad and drive him away. Thus, worldly spirits reject the man who hears the voice of God. In a few poems, Peire criticizes the worldly love sung by other troubadours and anticipates the *dolce stil nuovo* with his claim that *fin'amors* is born in a *franc cor gentil*, "a noble, gentle heart."

During the extended period of the Albigensian Crusade (1209–29), Peire expressed vigorous anticlericalism at the expense of Dominican inquisitors and severely criticized the French army led by Simon de Montfort. He did not, however, defend the cause of the Albigensians, regarded as heretics by the church, but rather championed the political cause of the counts of Toulouse, whose lands were invaded by the crusaders. In his religious poems, he expresses an orthodox belief in Catholic doctrine.

William D. Paden

[See also: *ESTRABOT*; TROUBADOUR POETRY]

Peire Cardenal. *Poésies complètes du troubadour Peire Cardenal*, ed. René Lavaud. Toulouse: Privat, 1957.

Marshall, John Henry. "Imitation of Metrical Form in Peire Cardenal." *Romance Philology* 32 (1978): 18–48.

Riquer, Martín de, ed. *Los trovadores: historia literaria y textos.* 3 vols. Barcelona: Planeta, 1975, Vol. 3, pp. 1478–518.

Wilhelm, James J. *Seven Troubadours: The Creators of Modern Verse.* University Park: Pennsylvania State University Press, 1970, pp. 173–95.

PEIRE D'ALVERNHE (fl. ca. 1150–70). Praised by his biographer as the best troubadour before Giraut de Bornelh and later hailed by Dante (*De vulgari eloquentia* 1.10) as one of the *antiquiores doctores* of Romance lyric expression, Peire d'Alvernhe saw himself as ushering in a new kind of poetry, or *vers entiers*. A practitioner of the obscure style, Peire was one of the first to use the term *clus* in a technical sense. His legacy consists of twenty songs, including a prayer, a crusade song, a *tenso* with Bernart de Ventadorn, and a satirical poem about his contemporaries, *Cantarai d'aquestz trobadors*.

Elizabeth W. Poe

[See also: TROUBADOUR POETRY]

Peire d'Alvernhe. *Peire d'Alvernha: liriche: testo, traduzione e note*, ed. Alberto Del Monte. Turin: Loescher-Chiantore, 1955.

PEIRE VIDAL (fl. ca. 1187–1205). Son of a furrier in Toulouse, the troubadour Peire Vidal led a colorful life. According to the *vidas*, he had his tongue cut out by the husband of his first lady, was banned from Marseille by the husband of a second on account of a stolen kiss, and was chased and mauled by dogs, as he, disguised as a wolf, tried to enter the castle of a third. The biographer reports that Peire married a Cypriot princess, which made him think that he had a legitimate claim to the Byzantine empire. Though undoubtedly based more on poetic metaphor than on fact, such stories convey the spirit of this often whimsical troubadour, who was constantly on the move, spending time in places as far away as Spain, Italy, Hungary, and Malta. Peire's surviving work consists of approximately fifty *cansos* and *sirventes*, for twelve of which melodies have been preserved. His protectors included Barral de Baux, with whom he exchanged the *senhal Rainier*, Raimon V of Toulouse, Alphonso II of Aragon, and Boniface of Montferrat. It would appear that Peire made a collection of his own songs, which he arranged in roughly chronological order.

Elizabeth W. Poe

[See also: TROUBADOUR POETRY]

Peire Vidal. *Peire Vidal: poesie*, ed. D'Arco Silvio Avalle. 2 vols. Milan: Ricciardi, 1960.

———. *Les poésies de Peire Vidal*, ed. Joseph Anglade. Paris: Champion, 1923.

PÈLERINAGE DE CHARLEMAGNE. See *VOYAGE DE CHARLEMAGNE À JÉRUSALEM ET À CONSTANTINOPLE*

PEPIN. Frankish leaders of the Carolingian family. Among Charlemagne's ancestors, three named Pepin were especially distinguished by their political authority among the Franks. Pepin I of Landen (Pepin the Old or the Elder; d. ca. 640) founded the family of the Arnulfings or the

Pippinids, later known as the Carolingians, through the arranged marriage of his daughter, Begga, to Ansegisel, the son of Arnulf of Metz (d. ca. 645). Pepin was named mayor of the palace (*major domus*) of Austrasia by the Merovingian king Clotar II of Neustria (r. 584–629), for having assisted the monarch to unite the kingdoms of Austrasia and Neustria. During his mayoralty, the office grew into the most powerful position in the Frankish territories, equaling or surpassing the royal throne in importance.

After the murder of Pepin's son and successor, Grimoald in 656, the Pippinids lost control of the Austrasian mayoralty; but in 687, Pepin II of Heristal, duke of Austrasia and Grimoald's nephew, led the Austrasian army to victory over the Neustrians and became mayor of the palace in both regions. From this post, he gradually strengthened his authority over all the Merovingian kingdoms, through his support of the church, manipulation of ecclesiastical posts, and military campaigns.

Pepin III (the Short; d. 768) and Carloman I (d. 754), grandsons of Pepin II, each inherited half the Frankish territories on the death in 741 of their father, Charles Martel, mayor in the united realm. The two brothers cooperated closely in governing their lands; in 743, they together placed another Merovingian, Childeric III, on the royal throne, empty since 737. In 747, however, Carloman felt called to a religious life and abdicated; Pepin became mayor of the entire kingdom. Having deposed Childeric, a move supported by Pope Zachary I, Pepin was acclaimed king in November 751. During a visit to Francia in 754, Pope Stephen II anointed the new monarch along with his wife and sons, Charles (later Charlemagne; 742–814) and Carloman II (d. 771). In recognition of the hope that the new monarchy would protect the Roman church, the pope used the occasion to name Pepin and his sons "patricians of the Romans."

As ruler of the Franks, Pepin III oversaw reform of the secular government and, with the aid of the Irish missionary Boniface, of the ecclesiastical organization. His efforts in the latter regard, especially, provided the foundation for the cultural and intellectual revival known as the Carolingian renaissance, under Pepin's son Charlemagne.

Celia Chazelle

[See also: CARLOMAN; CAROLINGIAN DYNASTY; FRANKS; MAYOR OF THE PALACE]

Hlawitschka, Eduard. "Die Vorfahren Karls des Grossen." In *Karl der Grosse: Lebenswerk und Nachleben*, ed. W. Braunfels et al. 5 vols. Düsseldorf: Schwann, 1965, Vol. 1, pp. 51–82.

McKitterick, Rosamond. *The Frankish Kingdoms Under the Carolingians, 751–987*. London: Longman, 1983.

Miller, David Harry. "Sacral Kingship, Biblical Kingship, and the Elevation of Pepin the Short." In *Religion, Culture, and Society in the Early Middle Ages: Studies in Honor of Richard E. Sullivan*, ed. Thomas F.X. Noble and John J. Contreni. Kalamazoo: Medieval Institute, 1987.

Noble, Thomas F.X. *The Republic of St. Peter: The Birth of the Papal State, 680–825*. Philadelphia: University of Pennsylvania Press, 1984.

Riché, Pierre. *The Carolingians: A Family Who Forged Europe*, trans. Michael I. Allen. Philadelphia: University of Pennsylvania Press, 1993.

PERCEFOREST. Middle French prose romance composed ca. 1337–44 for Count William I of Hainaut, perhaps by an author attached to the monastery of Saint-Landelin at Crespin in Hainaut. This immense work, divided into 531 chapters in six books (it will fill some 6,000 to 7,000 octavo pages when fully edited), treats the history of Britain from Alexander the Great to King Arthur. It exists complete in only one manuscript (Paris, Arsenal 3483–94), compiled by the scribe David Aubert in 1459–60 for Philip the Good, duke of Burgundy. Three other partial manuscripts survive, all from the third quarter of the 15th century, as well as two 16th-century printed editions. The romance was translated into Italian and Spanish in the 16th century.

Unlike many prose romances of its time, *Perceforest* is not an adaptation of an earlier verse romance but presents new materials, though incorporating traditional themes and motifs. After a brief geographical excursus on the island of Britain, the anonymous author traces its history from its founding by the legendary Brutus after the fall of Troy, as recounted in Geoffrey of Monmouth. The romance proper begins with Chapter 15 of Book 1 and is marked by inventiveness, exuberant style, and complex interlacing. The first three books tell of England before Julius Caesar's conquest. The author links England to the glories of Alexander the Great, who arrives in Britain at the beginning of the romance with two companions, Bétis and Gadifer, whom he appoints kings of England and Scotland, respectively. Together, they overcome the evil superstitions of the magician Darnant. Bétis, after slaying Darnant and freeing the forests of the island from his curse, takes the new name Perceforest and is crowned king of Britain by Alexander. In Book 2, Gadifer and Perceforest each organizes his twelve best knights into teams to free the island from chaos and superstition and bring it to culture and chivalry. It ends with the creation of Perceforest's Franc Palais, in which are displayed the shields of the knights who have distinguished themselves. Book 3 relates twelve tournaments held at the Chastel aux Pucelles, each won by the suitor of the girl from whom it was held.

In Book 4, Caesar conquers Britain and destroys the courtly civilization that had been so painstakingly established by Perceforest. This tragedy is overcome, however, as civilization is gradually restored in Books 5 and 6. Book 5 narrates a second series of twelve tournaments, organized by the daughter of King Gadifer to teach the art of chivalry. In Chapter 12 of Book 5, the author traces the ancestry of King Lot of Orkney. He goes on to recount the arrival of Joseph of Arimathea in Britain and alludes frequently to the Arthurian Grail materials. Book 6 tells of the christianization of Britain, before and after the Danish and Saxon invasions, by Gallafur, the grandson of both Gadifer and Perceforest. The final chapter of this final book tells of the adoration of the Holy Grail and recounts the episode of the *roi mehaingne* ("maimed king") in close imitation of the *Queste del saint Graal*.

The didactic themes of the romance are the fragility of civilized life and the importance of religious renewal. The author seeks to show that the gains of civilization, represented by chivalry, religion, and political stability, are constantly being menaced by threats of war and invasion. Between the paganism of Alexander and the Christianity of Arthur are many vicissitudes, but after each trial Britain is able to pick itself up again and continue, refortified, on the road to becoming a civilized Christian kingdom.

William W. Kibler

[See also: AUBERT, DAVID; GRAIL AND GRAIL ROMANCES; ROMANCE]

Roussineau, Gilles, ed. *Troisième partie du roman de Perceforest.* 3 vols. Geneva: Droz, 1988–93.

———. ed. *Perceforest: quatrième partie.* 2 vols. Geneva: Droz, 1987. [Based on MS *B* (B.N. fr. 106–09).]

Taylor, Jane H.M., ed. *Le roman de Perceforest: première partie.* Geneva: Droz, 1979. [Edits about half of Book 1, based on MS *A* (B.N. fr. 345–48).]

Flutre, Louis Fernand. "Études sur *Le roman de Perceforêt.*" *Romania* 70 (1948–49): 474–522; 71 (1950): 374–91, 482–508; 74 (1953): 44–102; 88 (1967): 475–508; 89 (1968): 355–86; 90 (1969): 341–70; 91 (1970): 189–226.

Lods, Jeanne. *Le roman de Perceforest: origines, composition, caractères, valeur et influence.* Geneva: Droz, 1951.

PERCEVAL CONTINUATIONS. Chrétien de Troyes's *Perceval,* or the *Conte du Graal* (ca. 1181–90), which breaks off in mid-sentence, inspired a series of four continuations within the following half-century. Of the fifteen manuscripts containing Chrétien's poem, eleven have one or more of the continuations, and in most there is no break indicated and the handwriting of the continuations is identical to that of Chrétien's work. The most common pattern, found in six manuscripts, is to have Chrétien's *Perceval* followed by the *First Continuation,* the *Second Continuation,* and the *Manessier Continuation.* In two manuscripts, the *Gerbert de Montreuil Continuation* is intercalated between the *Second Continuation* and *Manessier.*

Composed in the late 12th century, the *First Continuation* (also known as the *Pseudo-Wauchier Continuation* or *Gawain Continuation*) exists in three distinct versions, ranging from about 9,500 lines to 19,600. All three, however, tell essentially the same story, centering the action on Gawain, Arthur's nephew, whose adventures in search of the Grail castle were being recounted when Chrétien's poem was interrupted. It opens with Gawain's defeat of Guiromelant, who is spared at the urging of Gawain's sister Clarissant, who loves him. When Arthur weds Clarissant to Guiromelant without obliging him to retract his charge of treason against Gawain, his nephew leaves court in a huff and rides to the Grail castle, where he observes a Grail procession that differs in important details from that described by Chrétien. Most significantly, he sees a bier covered by a silk cloth; there is a body in the bier and a broken sword upon the cloth; he who can perfectly mend the sword would know all the secrets of the Grail castle.

But Gawain falls asleep and fails. The next morning he rides off to Escavalon to do battle with Guinganbresil, who had accused Gawain of treason for killing his lord. But before combat begins, Arthur arrives and makes peace by marrying his granddaughter to Guinganbresil. At this point are interpolated the adventures of Sir Carados, which form essentially an independent romance bearing no direct relationship to the Grail quest. It includes a beheading game similar to that in the English romance *Sir Gawain and the Green Knight,* an enchanted serpent that attaches itself to Carados's arm, and a chastity test with a magic drinking horn. Later in the romance, Gawain, mysteriously returned to the Grail castle, learns that the Bleeding Lance was the one with which Longinus pierced Christ's side at the Crucifixion. Once again, he fails to mend the sword and falls asleep before he can hear the other secrets of the castle. The following morning, he awakens beside the sea and discovers the land to be once again green and fertile. The final episode involves Gawain's brother Guerrehet in an adventure with a swan-drawn boat, in which is found a corpse with the broken end of a lance sticking in his chest that only Guerrehet can remove.

Although it effects a smooth transition from Chrétien's text, the *First Continuation* soon charts new territory: it loses track of the Gawain-Perceval parallel pursued by Chrétien to concentrate on Gawain and his brother Guerrehet; it christianizes the Grail and Bleeding Lance; and it stresses the magical aspects of the story at the expense of Chrétien's psychological realism.

The 13,000 lines of the *Second Continuation* (also called the *Wauchier de Denain Continuation* or *Perceval Continuation*) were composed in the last decade of the 12th century by Wauchier de Denain, known for his free translation of the *Vitae patrum* for Philippe de Namur (r. 1196–1212). Attention shifts back to Perceval's adventures. After defeating the Lord of the Horn, Perceval plays chess on a magical chessboard and falls in love with a maiden who will return his love only if he brings her the head of a white stag; she lends him her dog for the hunt, but the head and dog are stolen from him. Seeking to recover the head and dog, Perceval meets with a long series of adventures, in which he slays a giant, defeats a White Knight, and fights Gawain's son, the "Fair Unknown," to a draw. After a brief interlude with his lady, Blancheflor, Perceval must continue the quest. He returns to his mother's castle ten years after having first left it; there, he sees his sister for the first time and learns how his mother had died at his departure. With his sister, Perceval returns to the hermit uncle he had met in Chrétien's romance, who gives him a lesson on repentence. He finally recovers the stag's head and dog and sets out to return them to the maiden. En route, he encounters another maiden, who gives him her magic ring and white mule to lead him to the Grail castle. But he turns aside to attend a tournament at Proud Castle, where Arthur and his knights will also be. Perceval in disguise defeats all of Arthur's greatest knights, culminating with Gawain. Diverted by the tournament from reaching the Grail castle, Perceval must return the ring and mule. The poem continues with Gawain's adventures for several thousand lines, including an encounter with his son,

Guiglain, the "Fair Unknown," before returning to Perceval, who finally reaches the Grail castle and joins the two pieces of the broken sword, leaving just a tiny nick; the *Second Continuation* then breaks off before the Fisher King can explain the meaning of the Grail symbols.

Like the *First Continuation*, the *Second Continuation* seeks to avoid closure by multiplying adventures and introducing new themes and motifs; even more directly than its predecessor, it insists on the Christian significance of the Grail, which has become the vessel into which Christ's blood flowed at the Crucifixion.

Most manuscripts continue immediately with Manessier's *Third Continuation* (ca. 11,000 lines), composed between 1214 and 1227 (or between 1233 and 1237, according to Corley) for Jeanne de Constantinople, countess of Flanders and Hainaut, the grandniece of Philippe de Flandre, for whom Chrétien wrote his *Conte du Graal*. Manessier's continuation begins with the Fisher King's explanation of the Grail mysteries: the Lance is that of Longinus; the Grail was used by Joseph of Arimathea to catch Christ's blood; the trencher covered the Grail so that the Holy Blood would not be exposed; the sword had been broken when the traitor Partinial of the Red Tower slew the Fisher King's brother, and in his grief the Fisher King crippled himself with the broken pieces. Perceval sets out to avenge the Fisher King and soon joins up with Sagremor, whom he helps to defeat ten knights. The story continues with Sagremor's adventures, and then Gawain's, before returning to Perceval, who in a chapel battles the Devil himself, in the form of a detached hand and black arm, and finally defeats him by making the sign of the cross. He overcomes other demons and, eventually, in the company of the Coward Knight, triumphs over Arthur's knights at yet another tournament. Perceval finally reaches the Red Tower and slays Partinial, then hastens to inform the Fisher King, who is immediately healed and discovers that he is Perceval's maternal uncle. Perceval returns in triumph to Arthur's court but is soon summoned to reign after the Fisher King's death. He restores the land in seven years, then retires to a hermitage, where he lives another ten years, sustained only by the Grail. When he dies, the Holy Grail, Lance, and trencher accompany his soul to Heaven and will never again be seen on earth.

Manessier finally brings to a close the adventures of the Grail, stamping them with a religious tone even more marked than in the earlier continuations: demons assume a real presence as physical adversaries of the hero; Perceval retires to a hermitage and eventually becomes a priest; religious symbolism pervades the whole. It has been suggested that Manessier's continuation influenced the long version of the *First Continuation* in its treatment of the Grail as a relic of the Last Supper and Crucifixion.

In addition to the four continuations, two manuscripts offer a preface of 1,282 lines, composed late in the 13th century, of which the first 484 lines are called the *Elucidation* and the rest *Bliocadran*. The former is a rhymed "table of contents" to the Grail story; while the latter tells of the death of Perceval's father and brothers in pursuit of chivalry.

William W. Kibler

[See also: CHRÉTIEN DE TROYES; GAWAIN ROMANCES; GERBERT DE MONTREUIL; GRAIL AND GRAIL ROMANCES; REALISTIC ROMANCES

Montreuil, Gerbert de. *La continuation de Perceval*, ed. Mary Williams. 2 vols. Paris: Champion, 1922–25.

Roach, William, ed. *The Continuations of the Old French Perceval of Chrétien de Troyes*. 5 vols. Philadelphia: American Philosophical Society, 1949–83.

Wolfgang, Lenora, ed. *Bliocadran: A Prologue to the* Perceval *of Chrétien de Troyes*. Tübingen: Niemeyer, 1976.

Bryant, Nigel, trans. *Perceval, The Story of the Grail*. Cambridge: Brewer, 1982. [Includes translations of excerpts from all four continuations.]

Corley, Corin F. *The Second Continuation of the Old French Perceval: A Critical and Lexicographical Study*. London: Modern Humanities Research Association, 1987.

———. "Manessier's Continuation of *Perceval* and the Prose Lancelot Cycle." *Modern Language Review* 81 (1986): 574–91.

Gallais, Pierre. *L'imaginaire d'un romancier français de la fin du XIIe siècle: description raisonnée, comparée et commentée de la* Continuation-Gauvain. 4 vols. Amsterdam: Rodopi, 1988–89.

Marx, Jean. *Nouvelles recherches sur la littérature arthurienne*. Paris: Klincksieck, 1965, pp. 239–59.

PÉRIGUEUX. Périgueux (Dordogne), the capital of old Périgord, resulted from the union in 1240 of two contiguous cities: Gallo-Roman Vésone, an early episcopal see, and Puy-Saint-Front, a bustling commercial center that had developed around the tomb and monastery of Saint-Front, the apostle of the Périgord. Vésone was the principal *oppidum* of the Gallo-Roman Petrocores, who gave their name to the medieval city and province. Under the Romans, the city became one of the most beautiful in Aquitaine, with temples, a forum, villas, baths, and an arena. Although the Roman town was overrun by the Alemanni in the 3rd century, and later by Visigoths, Franks, and Vikings, it retains many impressive Roman ruins. In 1360 Périgueux was ceded to the English, but it soon rallied to the cause of Charles V, and it

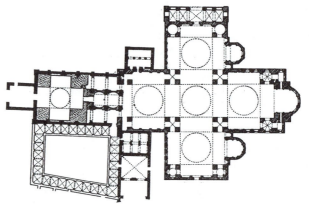

Périgueux, Saint-Front, plan. After Secret.

Périgueux (Dordogne), Saint-Front. *Photograph courtesy of Whitney S. Stoddard.*

was from Périgueux that Bertrand du Guesclin launched his raids against English strongholds in Guyenne.

Architecturally significant are the domed churches, Saint-Étienne-de-la-Cité and Saint-Front. The origin and chronology of this distinctive type of church architecture are controversial. Returning crusaders have been credited with the inspiration, and the former cathedral of Saint-Étienne-de-la-Cité is usually considered the prototype.

Despite the loss of its western tower-porch and two domed western bays, Saint-Étienne is striking for the purity and harmony of its simple geometric forms. The present western bay is an original 11th-century construction; its broad pointed arches, supported by massive piers, carry a hemispherical dome on pendentives. Blind arcades, once surmounted by open passageways as in the eastern bay, relieve the severity of the nave walls. The design of the elegant eastern bay, lit by a triplet of windows in each wall, dates from the second quarter of the 12th century. After the Huguenot destruction of 1577, this bay, with its high cupola, was rebuilt following the original plan. The structure, nevertheless, remained truncated, and in 1669 the former monastic church of Saint-Front became the cathedral of Périgueux.

Saint-Front, celebrated for the exotic profile of its domes and lanterns, was almost entirely reconstructed by Abadie and Boeswillwald in the 19th century. The cathedral is composed of two churches. To the west are the remains of the "old church" of Bishop Frotaire (consecrated 1047), which had succeeded that of the 6th century built over the tomb of St. Front. The spacious new domed church was largely built after the fire of 1120, although some have attempted to date its earliest bays to the 11th century. Greek-cross in plan and surmounted by five domes, it was oriented toward the tomb of St. Front; the beautiful bell tower, largely restored on the exterior but conserving much of its interior configuration, marked the juncture of the two churches. The new church acquired its eastern orientation with the addition of apsidioles, a 14th-century Gothic chapel, and Abadie's apse. The lapidary gallery of the Musée du Périgord contains capitals, corbels, and decorative sculpture that survived the 19th-century restorations.

Jean M. French

[See also: GUESCLIN, BERTRAND DU; HUNDRED YEARS' WAR; ROMANESQUE ARCHITECTURE]

Secret, Jean. *Périgord roman.* La Pierre-qui-vire: Zodiaque, 1979.

———. "La restauration de Saint-Front au XIXe siècle." *Monuments historiques de la France,* n.s. 2 (1956): 145–59.

Soubeyran, Michel. "Catalogue raisonné des éléments de sculpture provenant de la cathédrale Saint-Front de Périgueux et conservé au Musée du Périgord." *Bulletin de la Société Historique et Archéologique du Périgord* 94 (1967): 166–200.

PERLESVAUS. Dating from the early 13th century, perhaps from its first decade, *Perlesvaus* is a French Arthurian prose romance that reworks the story of Perceval, with the hero renamed Perlesvaus (explained as *perd-les-vaus,* or "lose the vales" of Camelot). The work, also known as the *Haut livre du Graal,* is preserved in three manuscripts (Bodl. Lib., Hatton 82; Brussels, Bibl. Roy. 11145; Chantilly 626) and two fragments, as well as a 14th-century Welsh translation.

Divided into eleven branches, and running to more than 10,000 lines of printed prose in the Nitze-Jenkins edition, *Perlesvaus* offers a dense and complex narrative that emphasizes in particular the adventures of Gawain, Lancelot, and Perlesvaus. The first two fail in their Grail quests: Gawain sees the Grail but does not ask the question; Lancelot finds and enters the Grail castle, but, owing to his sinful love for the queen, the Grail does not appear; Perlesvaus, in Branch 9, eventually succeeds. His success consists, however, of his liberating the Grail castle; there is this time no Grail procession, and since the Fisher King is now dead the anticipated Grail question is not asked.

The spirit of the work is militantly religious, and the intense action is characterized by liberal bloodshed, often in the interests of Christianity and often to hasten the process by which the New Law supplants the Old. The pervasive symbolism of the romance is generally explicit, as when the author announces that a certain damsel represents Fortune; elsewhere, symbolic meanings may be indicated, effectively but without subtlety, by the names borne by characters, such as Perlesvaus's mother Yglais (suggesting "Church"; cf. Fr. *église*), and the Fisher King Messios ("Messiah").

Colophons in two manuscripts claim that the *Perlesvaus* had its origin in the "Island of Avalon," assumed to be Glastonbury; its modern editors describe it as "Glastonbury propaganda," doubtless related to, if not inspired directly by, the purported 1191 discovery of Arthur's and Guenevere's bodies at Glastonbury abbey.

An original and important recasting of the Grail material and a masterpiece of early French prose, the *Perlesvaus* was soon overshadowed by the great 13th-century Vulgate Cycle. Its continuing appeal is indicated, however, by the fact that it was printed twice during the 16th century (1516 and 1523) as part of an Arthurian trilogy that also included the Vulgate *Estoire del saint Graal* and the *Queste del saint Graal*.

Norris J. Lacy

[See also: GRAIL AND GRAIL ROMANCES; PROSE ROMANCE (ARTHURIAN); VULGATE CYCLE]

Nitze, William A., and T. Atkinson Jenkins, eds. *Le haut livre du Graal: Perlesvaus*. 2 vols. Chicago: University of Chicago Press, 1932–37, Vol. 1: *Texts, Variants, and Glossary*; Vol. 2: *Commentary and Notes*.

Bryant, Nigel, trans. *The High Book of the Grail*. Ipswich: Brewer, 1978.

Kelly, Thomas E. *Le haut livre du Graal: Perlesvaus. A Structural Study*. Geneva: Droz, 1974.

Nitze, William A. "*Perlesvaus*." In *Arthurian Literature in the Middle Ages: A Collaborative History*, ed. Roger Sherman Loomis. Oxford: Clarendon, 1959, pp. 263–73.

PÉROTIN (Perotinus; fl. late 12th–early 13th c.). Because he composed liturgical vocal polyphony at Notre-Dame for two, three, and four parts (each part sung by a soloist) and employed the rhythmic modes, sophisticated devices of repetition and voice exchange, unprecedented length, and important notational innovations, Pérotin was the most significant musical figure of the early 13th century. His achievements profoundly influenced the course of Western music. The music theorists Johannes de Garlandia and Anonymous 4 mention "Magister Perotinus," but only the latter lists seven of his musical compositions and chronologically places him as "the best discantor" among other singers, composers, and notators working in Paris from the late 12th to late 13th century. Anonymous 4 credits Pérotin with the polyphony found today at the beginning of each of the three major extant Notre-Dame sources (*W1*, *F*, and *W2*): the Graduals *Viderunt omnes* and *Sederunt principes*, both for four voices, and adds to the list three-part polyphony for the Alleluia *Posui adiutorium* and Alleluia *Nativitas*, and three conductus, the three-part *Salvatoris hodie*, the two-part *Dum sigillum*, and the mono-

phonic *Beata viscera*. On the basis of stylistic affinity with these works, several other works in the Notre-Dame sources have been credited to him. Anonymous 4's statement that Pérotin made many clausulae and edited, revised, or shortened Léonin's *Magnus liber organi* has led many to attribute to him one or more of the series of independent discant clausulae that survive in *W1* and *F*.

Petrus, succentor (subcantor) of the cathedral ca. 1207–38, has been proposed as the most probable identity for Anonymous 4's "*Perotinus optimus discantor*," partly because responsibility for the daily services at the cathedral would have fallen to the succentor rather than the cantor, whose post had become largely administrative. Petrus' dates seem to correlate with Anonymous 4's description of Léonin's *Magnus liber organi*, which he stated was in use until the time of Pérotin, while Pérotin's "book or books" were used in the cathedral of Notre-Dame in Paris up to Anonymous 4's own time, probably the 1280s. Hans Tischler and others have maintained, however, that Pérotin lived ca. 1155/60–1200/05, largely on the basis that ordinances issued in 1198 and 1199 by Odo de Sully, bishop of Paris, sanctioned performance of three- and four-part organum at Notre-Dame during Christmas Week. That Pérotin's composition of the four-part polyphony for *Viderunt omnes* and *Sederunt principes* might have elicited these decrees can only be conjectured. The dating of Pérotin's polyphony is particularly important to a history of the musical style of the period. If it dates generally before 1200, that would mean that the rhythmic modes and their notation as well as the discant clausula and consequently the early motet were well advanced at the very beginning of the 13th century.

Sandra Pinegar

See also: ANONYMOUS 4; CLAUSULA; LÉONIN; NOTRE-DAME SCHOOL; ORGANUM; PHILIP THE CHANCELLOR; RHYTHMIC MODE]

Pérotin. *Works*, ed. Ethel Thurston. New York: Kalmus, 1970.

Tischler, Hans. "Perotinus Revisited." In *Aspects of Medieval and Renaissance Music: A Birthday Offering to Gustave Reese*, ed. Jan LaRue. New York: Norton, 1966, pp. 803–17.

Wright, Craig. *Music and Ceremony at Notre Dame of Paris, 500–1550*. Cambridge: Cambridge University Press, 1989, pp. 288–94.

PERPIGNAN. Founded in the 10th century, Perpignan (Pyrénées-Orientales) became the capital of Majorca from 1276 to 1344; it was later incorporated into the principality of Catalonia, in which it was second in importance only to Barcelona. It was here that King Philip III the Bold died while at war with Peter III of Aragon. In the 13th and 14th centuries, Perpignan was an important center of the textile industry. The Palace of the Kings of Majorca, begun in 1276 in Catalan Gothic style on a rectangular plan, is eloquent testimony to the wealth and prestige of Perpignan. It opens onto a large central courtyard with, on two sides, arcades supporting elegant loggias. A third side has superimposed chapels of the 14th century with 15th-century murals. Further witness to the military importance of the town is the Castillet, an imposing rose-brick fort with machicolations and battlements erected in 1367 and enlarged in 1483. The citadel dates from the 16th century.

The cathedral of Saint-Jean was begun in 1324 in Catalan Gothic style but completed only in 1509. It has a broad aisleless nave and a spacious apse with polygonal radiating chapels. Within these are a series of 15th- and 16th-century altar frontals in Catalan style. The earlier church of Saint-Jean-le-Vieux, begun in the 11th century, has a spacious nave from the early 13th century. The Romanesque sculpture on the main portal, with its elegant statue of Christ, is noteworthy.

William W. Kibler/William W. Clark

Ponsich, Pierre. "Saint-Jean-le-Vieux de Perpignan." *Études Roussillonnaises* 3 (1953): 105–36.

———. "Saint-Jean-le-Vieux de Perpignan" and "La cathédrale Saint-Jean de Perpignan." *Congrès archéologique* (*Roussillon*) 112 (1954): 31–86.

Verrier, Jean, and Sylvain Stym-Popper. "Perpignan: le palais des rois de Majorque." *Congrès archéologique* (*Roussillon*) 112 (1954): 9–30.

PERSONAL NAMES. Among the aristocracy in medieval France, one's personal name was an integral part of one's identity. The name attached the person firmly to a group of relatives. Between late antiquity and the end of the 11th century, a person had only one name, that given at baptism. In the late 11th century, when noble men and women began to adopt *cognomina*, so that someone who might previously have been known simply as "Milo" might now be known as "Milo of Noyers," the personal name was still the person's chief identification. The *cognomen* was not a last name in the modern sense. If a loconym, as most were, it changed if a noble changed his residence and was held by everyone living in the same place, whether or not they were related. Throughout the 12th century, someone might appear in some charters with a *cognomen* and in other charters without it.

In the early Middle Ages, both Roman and Germanic names were in circulation among the aristocracy; a secular lord sometimes had a Germanic name while his ecclesiastical brother had a Roman name. Whatever type of name a person was given, it seems in most cases to have been either the name or a variation of the name of a close relative. Until the 9th century, Germanic names commonly had two elements; parents could recombine elements of their own and their relatives' names in assigning names for their children. For example, at the end of the 8th century, the noble couple Witburgis and William, ancestors of the dukes of Aquitaine, named two of their children Witcher and Helimburgis. The recombination of name elements resulted in an enormous number of personal names in circulation.

From the 9th to the 12th centuries, noble children were generally given complete names that identified them with close relatives. No generalized naming "rules" obtained, even within a single lineage, but a child was much more likely to be named for some people than for others. In most cases,

parents chose the names of people they had known personally, rarely related more distantly than an aunt or uncle.

In by far the majority of cases, at least through the 11th century, both boys and girls were given names identifying them with their father's side of the family. Only if the mother's lineage was more important than the father's were any of a couple's boys named for her male relatives. Girls, too, were routinely named for their fathers' mother, sisters, and aunts. Among the upper aristocracy of the 9th and 10th centuries, the only group whose naming patterns can be clearly discerned, girls were almost never named for their own mothers. New women's names nevertheless constantly entered noble lineages, for even if a woman did not name a daughter for herself, each of her sons might name a daughter for her. In the 11th and 12th centuries, however, it became more common for a man to name a daughter for his own wife, or even in some cases for that wife's mother, an unheard-of practice earlier.

The oldest children were named the most assiduously for relatives. The oldest boy was generally named for his father or paternal grandfather. As a result, many lineages consisted of men all having the same personal name, or an alternation of two names, if boys were named for grandfathers with names different from their fathers'. The father's or grandfather's name, an integral part of the lineage's inheritance, was important enough that it was usually given to another son if the oldest died. Younger sons might be named for their paternal uncles or great-uncles or, if he was a particularly important man, for their maternal grandfather. In some cases, younger sons might also be named for important allies. Less powerful members of the aristocracy commonly named their sons, often even the oldest ones, for their lords rather than their own relatives. These lords may often have served as godfathers. The oldest girl was most commonly named for her father's mother; her sisters were named for their paternal aunts and great-aunts and, increasingly in the 11th and 12th centuries, for their own mother or maternal grandmother. Children destined for a clerical life were frequently named for relatives already in the church.

The decision what to name a child could be a difficult one for medieval parents. With no set rules to follow, all parents had to decide individually what names to give their children, names that would identify them with close relatives at the same time as they were an integral part of the children's own identity.

Constance B. Bouchard

Beech, George T. "Les noms de personne poitevins du 9e au 12e siècle." *Revue internationale d'onomastique* 26 (1974): 81–100.

Bouchard, Constance B. "Family Structure and Family Consciousness Among the Aristocracy in the Ninth to Eleventh Centuries." *Francia* 14 (1986): 639–58.

———. "The Migration of Women's Names in the Upper Nobility, Ninth–Twelfth Centuries." *Medieval Prosopography* 9:2 (1988): 1–19.

———. "Patterns of Women's Names in Royal Lineages, 9th–11th Centuries." *Medieval Prosopography* 9:1 (1988): 1–32.

Clark, Cecily. "Women's Names in Post-Conquest England: Observations and Speculations." *Speculum* 53 (1978): 223–51.

Morlet, Marie-Thérèse. *Les noms de personne sur le territoire de l'ancienne Gaul du VIe au XIIe siècle.* 2 vols. Paris: CNRS, 1968.

Störmer, Wilhelm. *Früher Adel: Studien zur politischen Führungsschicht im Fränkisch-Deutschen Reich vom 8. bis 11. Jahrhundert.* Stuttgart: Hiersemann, 1973, chap. 2.

Wenskus, Reinhard. *Sächsischer Stammesadel und fränkischer Reichsadel.* Göttingen: Vandenhoeck und Ruprecht, 1976.

Werner, Karl Ferdinand. "Liens de parenté et noms de personne: un problème historique et méthodologique." In *Famille et parenté dans l'Occident médiévale,* ed. Georges Duby and Jacques Le Goff. Rome: École Française de Rome, 1977.

PETER COMESTOR (ca. 1000–1178). Born in Troyes, Peter became in 1147 dean of the cathedral there. Sometime before 1159, he went to Paris, where he studied under Peter Lombard and later taught theology. He became chancellor of the cathedral of Notre-Dame between 1164 and 1168. He died in 1178 and was buried at the abbey of Saint-Victor. Although known primarily for the *Historia scholastica,* Peter wrote other works, including some 150 sermons, the *Summa de sacramentis* (based on Peter Lombard's *Sententiae*), some *quaestiones,* and commentaries on the Gospels, as well as glosses on the *Glossa ordinaria,* on the *Magna glossatura* of Peter Lombard, and perhaps on Lombard's *Sententiae.* The *Historia scholastica,* used in the schools and later in the university curriculum, was a narrative presentation of biblical history from Creation through the life of Jesus. Peter here sought to counteract what he saw as the destruction of the connected literal-historical sense of the text through the practice of a spiritual exegesis that tended to divide the text into brief "fragments" for symbolic interpretation. Peter not only drew upon traditional patristic authors for the historical sense; he also used Josephus's *Jewish Antiquities* and the commentaries on the *Octateuch* by Andrew of Saint-Victor. In a practical way, Peter continued the emphasis on reading Scripture according to the literal-historical sense that had been established at the abbey of Saint-Victor by Hugh of Saint-Victor.

Grover A. Zinn

[See also: ANDREW OF SAINT-VICTOR; BIBLE, CHRISTIAN INTERPRETATION OF; HUGH OF SAINT-VICTOR]

Peter Comestor. *Historia scholastica; Sermons. PL* 198.1045–844.

———. *Summa de sacramentis,* ed. Raymond M. Martin. In *Maître Simon et son groupe: De sacramentis,* ed. Heinrich Weisweiler. Louvain: "Spicilegium Sacrum Lovaniense," 1937, appendix.

Smalley, Beryl. *The Study of the Bible in the Middle Ages.* 3rd ed. Oxford: Blackwell, 1983.

PETER DE BRUYS (d. ca. 1140). Peter de Bruys seems to have been a priest from the area of Embrun (Hautes-Alpes), who, deprived of his office, took to idiosyncratic preaching. He moved from his parish of Embrun through Languedoc and farther west. Peter's antiecclesiastical message attracted large crowds. The sources of his ideas are unclear, although they may be related to those of the Bogomils. He died at Saint-Gilles, near Nîmes, thrown into a fire in which he was burning crucifixes.

The beliefs of Peter's followers, the Petrobrusians, are known to us from the *Tractatus adversos Petrobrusianos haereticos* of Peter the Venerable and the *Introductio ad theologiam* of Peter Abélard. Believing in the spiritual unity of the church, they rejected what they saw as the merely external. Hence, they denied sacraments, especially infant baptism and the Mass, prayers for the dead, church buildings (*all* places belonged to God), veneration of crucifixes (as recrucifying Christ), the authority of the church (as having no foundation), and a large part of the Bible, especially the Old Testament. Although they rejected these external things as encumbrances, they did not, unlike many sects of the time, embrace apostolic poverty. Petrobrusians took a literalist view of the Gospels as depicting historical events, such as the Last Supper, that could have no greater value through reenactment.

The Petrobrusians believed in direct action: they forced monks to marry, abused priests, ate meat on fast days, and burned crucifixes. Unsurprisingly, Peter's teaching was frequently condemned, as at the Second Lateran Council (1139).

Lesley J. Smith

[See also: HERESY; POPULAR DEVOTION; SAINT-GILLES]

Colish, Marcia L. "Peter of Bruys, Henry of Lausanne, and the Façade of Saint-Gilles." *Traditio* 28 (1972): 451–60.

Lambert, Malcolm. *Medieval Heresy: Popular Movements from Bogomil to Hus.* London: Arnold, 1976.

Wakefield, W.L., and A.P. Evans. *Heresies of the High Middle Ages: Selected Sources Translated and Annotated.* New York: Columbia University Press, 1969.

PETER LOMBARD (ca. 1100–1160). The "Master of the *Sentences,*" born and educated in Novara, Lombardy, arrived in Paris via Reims (ca. 1135) with a letter of recommendation from Bernard of Clairvaux to Abbot Gilduin of Saint-Victor. While he apparently never taught at the abbey, Peter did preach there, and he maintained close ties with Saint-Victor throughout his life.

The Lombard soon made himself a reputation as a formidable theologian. By 1142–43, he had the dubious distinction of being named by Gerhoch of Reichersberg as a dangerous innovator; in 1148, he was summoned by Pope Eugenius III to the Consistory of Reims to help judge the orthodoxy of another innovator, Gilbert of Poitiers, whose christology Peter found lacking. Teaching at Notre-Dame by 1143, he was a canon by 1145 and steadily rose in rank (subdeacon by 1147, deacon by 1150, archdeacon by 1157). In 1158, his years of service were crowned by his election as bishop of Paris; this honor was short-lived, as he died in 1160.

The earliest works of the Lombard are his commentaries on the Psalms (before 1138) and on the epistles of Paul (by 1142). Though Herbert of Bosham reports that Peter meant them for his personal edification only and that he never finished them, they were swiftly and widely circulated, often even replacing the marginal-interlinear glosses for the Psalms and epistles in the *Glossa ordinaria*. Known as the *Magna glossatura*, they became the most frequently cited works of Scripture exegesis in the Middle Ages. Peter based his two commentaries on a close reading of Anselm of Laon's glosses and Gilbert of Poitiers's biblical commentaries. He kept the *Glossa*'s patristic and Carolingian base, took over Gilbert's organization scheme and hermeneutic principles, and consistently worked out doctrinal positions and current theological issues in connection with the scriptural text.

Even more central to the history of medieval theology and philosophy is the Lombard's *Quattuor libri sententiarum*, or the *Sententiae*. Sentence collections proliferated in the 12th century, as theologians strove to systematize and professionalize their field. Peter Lombard's *Sententiae* (1155–57) became an instant and enduring success throughout Europe (legislated into the theological curriculum of the University of Paris in 1215) and remained without serious competition until replaced by the *Summa* of Thomas Aquinas in the 16th century. It was second only to the Bible in importance in theological training; hundreds of theologians wrote commentaries on the *Sententiae*. The reasons for its success have recently been set forth in a effort to restore the luster to the Lombard's tired reputation. Its comprehensive coverage of topics, logical order, lack of dependence on or promotion of any elaborate philosophical system, sensitivity to the need for clarity and consistency in theological language, and readiness to address controversial issues while acknowledging contemporary consensus, all ensured the utility of the *Sententiae* to generations of theologians and philosophers. In addition, Peter's christology avoided many of the semantic pitfalls that plagued contemporary theologians; his Trinitarian views were solemnly ratified at the Fourth Lateran Council in 1215.

Theresa Gross-Diaz

[See also: BIBLE, CHRISTIAN INTERPRETATION OF; *GLOSSA ORDINARIA*; PETER OF POITIERS (d. 1205); PHILOSOPHY; SCHOLASTICISM; SENTENCE COLLECTIONS; THEOLOGY]

Peter Lombard. *Commentarius in psalmos davidicos*. *PL* 191.55–169.

———. *Collectanea in omnes b. Pauli epistolas*. *PL* 191.1297–696 and *PL* 192.9–520.

———. *Sententiae in IV libris distinctae*, ed. Ignatius Brady. 3rd ed. rev. In *Spicilegium Bonaventurianum*. Grottaferrata: Editiones Collegii S. Bonaventurae ad Claras Aquas, 1971–81, Vols. 4–5.

———. *Sermons* (printed under the name of Hildebert of Lavardin). *PL* 171.339–964. [See list in J. de Ghellinck, "Pierre Lombard." In *Dictionnarie de théologie catholique*, Vol. 12 (1935), cols. 1961–62.]

Bertola, Ermenegildo. "Pietro Lombardo nella storiografia filosofica medioevale." *Pier Lombardo* 4 (1960): 95–113.

Colish, Marcia L. *Peter Lombard*. Leiden: Brill, 1993.

———. "Systematic Theology and Theological Renewal in the Twelfth Century." *Journal of Medieval and Renaissance Studies* 18 (1988): 135–56.

———. "From *sacra pagina* to *theologia*: Peter Lombard as an Exegete of Romans." *Medieval Perspectives* 7 (1991): 1–19.

———. "*Psalterium Scholasticorum*: Peter Lombard and the Emergence of Scholastic Psalms Exegesis." *Speculum* 67 (1992): 531–48.

Delhaye, Philippe. *Pierre Lombard: sa vie, ses œuvres, sa morale*. Montreal: Institut d'Études Médiévales, 1961.

PETER OF CELLE (d. 1182). Born in the early 12th century in Aunoy-les-Minimes, Peter probably studied in the schools of Paris before entering the monastery of Montier-la-Celle, where he eventually became abbot. While Peter was at Celle, John of Salisbury visited him and dedicted the *Policratus* to him. In 1162, Peter was made abbot of the monastery of Saint-Remi in Reims, and in 1180 he became bishop of Chartres.

A supporter of monastic reform and strict observance of the monastic rule, Peter corresponded with leading monastic figures of his day and was appointed by Pope Alexander III to mediate quarrels and press for reform. He had an especially close relationship with the Carthusian house of Mont-Dieu and was a promoter of the Carthusians. He supported Alexander III in the dispute over papal succession. Some 175 of Peter's letters survive, in addition to ninety-six sermons and a number of treatises. His letters reveal him as involved in many of the major events and crises of his day, including the Becket affair, while his sermons and treatises address matters of theology, worship, clerical responsibility, and the monastic life.

Grover A. Zinn

[See also: ALEXANDER III; JOHN OF SALISBURY]

Peter of Celle. Works in *PL* 202.

———. *Commentaris in Ruth; Tractatus de Tabernaculo*, ed. Gérard de Martel. *CCCM* 54. Turnhout: Brepols, 1983.

———. *Peter of Celle: Selected Works*, trans. Hugh Feiss. Kalamazoo: Cistercian, 1987.

Leclercq, Jean. *La spiritualité de Pierre de Celle*. Paris: Vrin, 1946.

PETER OF POITIERS (d. 1205). Master in theology at Paris from ca. 1167, successor (1169) to the chair in theology held by Peter Comestor, and chancellor of the schools of Paris from 1193. Peter of Poitiers (to be distinguished from another contemporary Peter of Poitiers, a regular canon of the abbey of Saint-Victor at Paris) was a leading figure in the Parisian schools in the last third of the 12th century. A student under Peter Lombard and a strong supporter of the Lombard's theology when it came under attack in the last decades of the 12th century, Peter of Poitiers was a determined advocate of the usefulness of dialectics in theology.

He was also influenced by the Victorine tradition, represented by Hugh and Richard of Saint-Victor, Peter Comestor, and Peter the Chanter, that emphasized both historical study and the importance of biblical allegory. Four of Peter's works reveal these influences and also Peter's distinctive contributions to theological, historical, and exegetical-homiletic studies in the schools of Paris.

Peter's *Sententiarum libri quinque* (probably before 1170) is modeled directly on the dialectical method as used by Peter Lombard in his *Quattuor libri sententiarum* and also draws upon its content. Peter's work is not, however, a commentary on the Lombard's but is his own formulation of a "compendium of theology" to instruct those who are beginning the study of Scripture. Peter's faithfulness to the Lombard's thought earned him the distinction of being included with the Lombard, Gilbert of Poitiers, and Abélard as one of the "four labyrinths of France" in Walter of Saint-Victor's antidialectical polemic.

Three of Peter's works on scriptural interpretation deserve mention. *Allegoriae super tabernaculum Moysis* explicates the four senses of scriptural interpretation (history, allegory, tropology, and anagogy) and presents a detailed allegorical interpretation of the materials, construction, associated objects, and other aspects of the Tabernacle of Moses. *Compendium historiae in genealogia Christi* is a work of historical explication in service of biblical exegesis. By means of a grand genealogical schematic, with accompanying text, extending from Adam and Eve to Jesus Christ, Peter sketched out the essentials of biblical history for beginning students. Tradition held that he was the first to draw genealogical "trees" on animal skins and hang them on classroom walls in order to instruct students. Finally, *Distinctiones super psalterium* is part of a move within the schools to make resources for biblically based preaching more accessible to students and preachers. The *Distinctiones* takes a word from a psalm and gives a set of meanings, the *distinctio*, all supported by references to other passages of Scripture. Thus, the reader had ready at hand a compendium of many symbolic interpretations of such words as "bed," "fire," or "stone." Some manuscripts present the work as a continuous prose text; others have a schematic structure, with the "key word" in the margin and a series of red lines connecting with the meanings. Such a handbook would be of great use to preachers searching for allegories, and Peter's book is similar in its intent to Peter the Chanter's *Summa Abel* and Praepositinus of Cremona's *Summa super psalterium*.

Grover A. Zinn

[See also: BIBLE, CHRISTIAN INTERPRETATION OF; HUGH OF SAINT-VICTOR; PETER COMESTOR; PETER LOMBARD; PETER THE CHANTER; SCHOLASTICISM; THEOLOGY; WALTER OF SAINT-VICTOR]

Moore, Philip S. *The Works of Peter of Poitiers, Master in Theology and Chancellor of Paris (1193–1205)*. Notre Dame: University of Notre Dame Press. 1936.
———, and James Corbett, eds. *Petri Pictaviensis Allegoriae super tabernaculum Moysis*. Notre Dame: University of Notre Dame Press, 1938.
———, and Mathe Dulong, eds. *Petri Pictaviensis Sententiarum libri quinque*. Notre Dame: University of Notre Dame Press, 1943, Vol. 1.
———, Joseph N. Garvin, and Marthe Dulong, eds. *Petri Pictaviensis Sententiarum libri quinque*. 2 vols. Notre Dame: University of Notre Dame Press, 1950.

PETER OF POITIERS (of Saint-Victor; d. after 1216). Not to be confused with Peter of Poitiers, chancellor of the cathedral of Notre-Dame in Paris, or Peter of Poitiers, secretary to Peter the Venerable, this Peter was a regular canon of the abbey of Saint-Victor at Paris charged with the responsibility of hearing confessions, especially of students in the schools. Essentially nothing is known of his life. About 1215, he wrote a *summa confessorum*, or handbook for confessors, entitled *Compilatio praesens*, to guide priests in administering the sacrament of penance. Peter of Poitiers frequently used the works of Peter the Chanter and cited his *Summa de sacramentis*, thus making Peter of Poitiers one of the masters and ecclesiastics who may be counted in the "circle of Peter the Chanter." Peter's *Compilatio praesens* was part of the literature of handbooks for confessors that became necessary after the Fourth Lateran Council decreed, in canon 21, that every person should commune once per year and should confess to a priest before communing. An introduction, conclusion, and other additions to the text were provided by James of Saint-Victor several years after Peter completed his work.

Grover A. Zinn

Peter of Poitiers. *Summa de confessione: "Compilatio praesens,"* ed. Jean Longère. *CCCM*, 51. Turnhout: Brepols, 1980.
Baldwin, John W. *Masters, Princes, and Merchants: The Social Views of Peter the Chanter and His Circle*. 2 vols. Princeton: Princeton University Press, 1970, esp. pp. 33–34.
Longère, Jean. "La fonction pastorale de Saint-Victor à la fin du XIIe et au début du XIIIe siècle." In *L'abbaye parisienne de Saint-Victor au moyen âge*, ed. Jean Longère. Turnhout: Brepols, 1991, pp. 291–313.

PETER RIGA (ca. 1140–1209). Born in Reims and later canon in the cathedral there, Peter composed one of the most popular versified Bibles of the Middle Ages. Entitled *Aurora*, this work went through three successive versions, in which Peter continually expanded the contents. In its final form, the poem comprised over 15,000 verses, most in couplets but with rhymed hexameters for the Acts of the Apostles, Song of Songs, and Job. It combines versified texts, narratives, and commentaries on texts, demonstrating Peter's skill as a poet and his ability to put both narratives and commentary into verse. *Aurora* was immediately used by other poets in their works: Jean Malkaraume utilized passages in his versified Bible; Macé de la Charité translated it for his French Bible; in England, it was used in the Middle English *Cursor mundi* and by John Gower in *Vox clamantis*. Peter also wrote *Floridus aspectus*, containing an "art of poetry" and a collection of poems based on biblical texts.

Grover A. Zinn

[See also: BIBLICAL TRANSLATION]

Peter Riga. *Opera*. PL 171.1381–442.

————. *Aurora: Petri Rigae Biblia versificata: A Verse Commentary on the Bible*, ed. Paul E. Beichner. 2 vols. Notre Dame: University of Notre Dame Press, 1965.

PETER THE CHANTER (d. 1197). Born near Beauvais, Peter studied at Reims and by ca. 1173 was a master in theology in the schools of Paris. In 1183, he was named chanter of the cathedral of Notre-Dame in Paris. Peter was judge delegate for the pope on a number of occasions, including the divorce trial of Philip II Augustus (1196). He was elected dean of the cathedral of Reims in 1196, but he became ill and was unable to take the position. He entered the Cistercian abbey of Longpont as a monk and died there.

As a teacher in the schools, Peter exerted a remarkable influence on both students and peers. He was at the center, with Peter Comestor and Stephen Langton, of what Beryl Smalley (following Grabmann) called the "biblical moral school," a group of masters in the late 12th-century schools who followed the emphasis on biblical study developed at the abbey of Saint-Victor by Hugh, Richard, and Andrew of Saint-Victor.

While most masters of the day commented only on the Psalms and Gospels, Peter, like Stephen Langton, commented on all the books of the Old and New Testaments. Moreover, Peter was critical of those masters who devoted themselves to seeking out details of the text and its interpretation rather than focusing on the important matters of moral teaching and behavior.

In addition to his lectures on Scripture (which were taken down as *reportationes* by his students), the Chanter devoted much of his time to lecturing and disputing on moral questions; he found the 12th-century church desperately lacking when compared with gospel injunctions and Paul's teaching. Dedicated to testing present practice against the straightforward teaching of Scripture, he was, however, a realist who saw that seriously embracing scripturally based reform could lead to criticism of accepted practices in the church of his day. He raised and resolved hundreds of moral "questions," which were incorporated in his *Summa de sacramentis et animae consiliis*. The questions, with numerous exempla to illustrate situations and conclusions, were grouped according to the sacraments of the church (baptism, confirmation, extreme unction, consecration of churches, the eucharist, and penance). All systematization seems to have given way in the section on penance, for it is a vast collection of case after case for analysis and resolution. Peter's *Verbum abbreviatum* is also directed toward moral concerns, this time with copious citations of passages from "authorities" (Scripture, Christian writers, classical authors) and exempla to discourage vice and promote virtue. Although Peter was recognized as a preacher, no sermons have survived. He was tireless in his devotion to ecclesiastical duties and to the work of a master in lecturing on Scripture, posing questions for resolution through disputation, and providing in his writings the outcome, in a text, of his labors in the classroom.

Grover A. Zinn

[See also: BIBLE, CHRISTIAN INTERPRETATION OF; PETER COMESTOR; SCHOLASTICISM; SCHOOLS, CATHEDRAL; STEPHEN LANGTON]

Peter the Chanter. *Summa de sacramentis et animae consiliis*, ed. Jean-Albert Dugauquier. 3 vols. in 5. Louvain: Nauwelaerts, 1954–67.

————. *Verbum abbreviatum*. PL 205.1–554. [Short version.]

Baldwin, John W. *Masters, Princes, and Merchants: The Social Views of Peter the Chanter and His Circle*. 2 vols. Princeton: Princeton University Press, 1970.

Smalley, Beryl. *The Gospels in the Schools c. 1100–c. 1280*. London: Hambledon, 1985, pp. 101–18.

————. *The Study of the Bible in the Middle Ages*. 3rd ed. rev. Oxford: Blackwell, 1983, chap. 5.

PETER THE VENERABLE (1092/94–1156). Born into the noble Montbossier family in Auvergne, Peter was dedicated by his mother as a child oblate to the Cluniac monastery of Sauxillanges, where he was educated. He became a monk of Cluny not long before 1109. Four of his six brothers also entered ecclesiastical careers; one became archbishop of Lyon while the other three were abbots of Vézelay, La Chaise-Dieu, and Manglieu. Peter served as prior of Vézelay and of Domène before being elected abbot of Cluny in 1122. He proved to be a skillful administrator of a vast monastic organization comprising over 1,000 dependent monasteries and priories; he was also an influential ecclesiastical leader, had scholarly interests, and was a strong defender of Cluniac customs against Cistercian criticisms. His extensive correspondence with notables throughout the western church (193 extant letters) is a rich source of information about various matters, both ecclesiastical and secular, including the world of learning and spirituality. Although Peter and Bernard of Clairvaux were in opposition on matters of monastic discipline and practice, they remained friends throughout life, as their letters reveal. Peter's health was never good, and he probably suffered from malaria on several occasions and from chronic bronchitis.

Peter's election to the abbacy of Cluny came at a time when the order needed a firm hand, following the disastrous abbacy of Pons de Melgueil and the brief four-month abbacy of Hugues II. Monastic discipline was lax; finances needed attention; the large sprawling Cluniac order needed an effective leader. Peter rose to the occasion. He began to enforce a more strict discipline, attended to finances, and traveled often to deal with problems within the order. He was moderate in demands, conservative in outlook, conciliatory in approach, and thoughtful in controversy. Peter became enmeshed in the controversy between Cistercians and Cluniacs, which was marked by heated exchanges on both sides. Peter's Letter 28, a response (if not directly, at least in effect) to Bernard of Clairvaux's *Apologia ad Guillelmum* as well as the general Cistercian attack on

Cluniac laxity in discipline and departure from the *Rule* of St. Benedict, is a carefully reasoned defense of the Cluniac way of life and offers one of the best sources for understanding both the conflict and the Cluniac point of view. Peter was no idle defender of the *status quo*, however; he actively reformed and strengthened Cluniac discipline.

Peter wrote against both heresy (the Petrobrusians [*Tractatus adversos Petrobrusianos haereticos*]) and non-Christian religions (Judaism [*Adversos Judaeorum inveteratum duritiem*] and Islam [*Epistola de translatione sua; Summa totius haeresis Saracenorum*]). After a journey to Spain in 1142, he commissioned a translation of the Qur'an, the first into Latin, and other Arabic texts, so that he might better understand Islam in order to refute it with reason rather than force. In writing against Judaism, he respected the Hebrew version of Scripture and argued without special pleading from Christian Scripture, i.e. the New Testament.

In addition to his numerous journeys in France, Peter traveled to England (1130 and 1155), Spain (1142; perhaps 1124 and 1127), and Rome (1139 [Lateran Council], 1144, 1145, 1147, 1151–52, 1154). He extended the hospitality of Cluny to Peter Abélard after Abélard's condemnation at Sens in 1140. Peter the Venerable wrote to Héloïse a sensitive letter giving a detailed account of Abélard's last days. In addition to the works mentioned above, his writings include sermons, liturgical texts (including an Office of the Transfiguration), hymns, and a treatise recounting holy lives (*De miraculis*). He was an exemplar of the best of the Benedictine tradition.

Grover A. Zinn

[See also: ABÉLARD, PETER; ARABIC INFLUENCE ON LITERATURE; BERNARD OF CLAIRVAUX; CISTERCIAN ORDER; CLUNIAC ORDER; CLUNY; HÉLOÏSE; PETER DE BRUYS; VÉZELAY]

Peter the Venerable. *Opera omnia. PL* 189.61-1054.
———. *The Letters of Peter the Venerable*, ed. Giles Constable. 2 vols. Cambridge: Harvard University Press, 1967.
Constable, Giles, ed. *Petrus Venerabilis, 1156–1956: Studies and Texts Commemorating the Eighth Centenary of His Death*. Rome: Herder, 1956.
Knowles, David. *The Historian and Character*. Cambridge: Cambridge University Press, 1963, pp. 50–75.

PETROBRUSIAN HERESY. *See* **PETER DE BRUYS**

PHILIP I (1052–1108). King of France, 1059–1108. The son of Henry I (r. 1031–60) and Anne of Kiev, Philip was crowned king on May 23, 1059, and was still a child when his father died the following year. Baudouin V, count of Flanders (r. 1035–67), Philip's uncle by marriage, administered the royal government until Philip attained his majority in 1066. In that year, Baudouin's son-in-law, William the Conqueror, duke of Normandy, seized the throne of England.

During the next twenty-five years, Philip strove to assert his control over the royal domain and to expand it.

He acquired Corbie, the Gâtinais, and the French Vexin; developed the system of *prevôts* to administer his holdings; and saw the central administration transformed from a curial to a palatial system, as the great officers of the crown and local castellans replaced the major territorial lords and prelates in validating royal acts. As reform swept the church, the king was under increasing pressure to forgo investiture of clergy and the profits of simony, while the ecclesiastical controversy surrounding Berengar of Tours (condemned in 1080) attested to new intellectual vigor in the kingdom. Philip also was able to exploit the conflicts among William the Conqueror's sons to acquire Gisors in 1090.

After 1092, everything focused on the scandal arising from the king's repudiation of his wife, Queen Bertha, and his bigamous marriage with Bertrade de Montfort, the fourth wife of Foulques IV, count of Anjou. Excommunications and absolutions alternated between 1094 and 1104, when Philip finally achieved normal relations with the papacy. During this time, his son, the future Louis VI, took more and more responsibility for ruling and for defending the Vexin against the attacks of William II Rufus of England (r. 1087–1100). The crown acquired another addition to the royal domain with the purchase of the viscounty of Bourges in 1101. Philip died at the end of July 1108 and was interred in the abbey of Saint-Benoît-sur-Loire (Fleury).

R. Thomas McDonald

[See also: BERENGAR OF TOURS; BERTHA OF HOLLAND; BERTRADE DE MONTFORT; LOUIS VI THE FAT; VEXIN]

Fliche, Augustin. *Le règne de Philippe Ier, roi de France (1060–1108)*. Paris: Société Française d'Imprimerie et de Librairie, 1912.
Prou, Maurice. *Recueil des actes de Philippe Ier, roi de France (1059–1108)*. Paris: Imprimerie Nationale, 1908.

PHILIP II AUGUSTUS (1165–1223). King of France, 1180–1223. Philip II was the first great architect of the medieval French monarchy. Building upon the accomplishments of Louis VI and Louis VII, he began the process of converting feudal into national monarchy, expanding the crown's political and geographical influence, by his death in 1223, far beyond what they had been at his accession in 1180.

As was common in the case of kings ascending as children to the throne, Philip was initially dominated by powerful relatives, in his case the influential and wealthy ruling family of Champagne. His early struggle to assert royal influence was supported by his father's rival, Henry II of England, who denied himself the pleasure of taking advantage of the fifteen-year-old king's apparent weakness. A few years later, Henry probably wished that he had not been so honorable, since Philip utilized the traditional patricidal conflict traditional in the Angevin family against his former protector. This policy saw the French king triumphant over his father's ancient adversary and his sons by 1204, when the luckless King John saw the Angevin territories in France dissolve. By the end of his reign, Philip II had increased his territory nearly fourfold. The English loss of territory north of the Loire augmented the French ruler's lands, but he also added to his acquisitions by the forfeitures of contumacious vassals, by political duplicity, by cleverly arranged marriages, and by manipulation of the confusion over land possession arising from the Albigensian Crusade. Philip Augustus was not a great military leader; he was an astute politician.

Philip was the founder of the centralized bureaucratic state. He chose bourgeois administrators, as well as men from the lower nobility, to run his kingdom, men whose primary loyalty was to their king rather than to their class or to their families. Their offices were remunerated by salary rather than farmed. Philip used feudal rights to enhance his royal position; in his reign, the authority of the king began shifting slowly from his rights exercised as feudal suzerain to his rights exercised as sovereign; he was becoming less a private, feudal lord than a public figure of authority. This obviously contributed to a decline in the functional importance of the feudal structure (it was never a feudal *system*), as did the growing commutation of lord-vassal relationships from mutually exchanged personal obligations into money payments. The administrators of Philip's domains, *baillis* and *prévôts*, were essentially estate managers, men with wide-ranging fiscal, judicial, military, and other responsibilities. Philip's financial administration improved greatly, his policies based upon the model of his newly conquered province, Normandy. He also made Paris what we moderns would call the capital of France.

Philip Augustus was, then, the monarch under whom French monarchy became more a practical than a theoretical concept. His domain, larger than the fief of any vassal, was to remain the dominant power base in France in succeeding generations. As Luchaire wrote, at Philip's death "the [Capetian] dynasty was solidly established, and France founded."

James W. Alexander

[See also: *BAILLI/BAILLIAGE*; BOUVINES; CAPETIAN DYNASTY; FLANDERS; HENRY II; JOHN LACKLAND; LOUIS VIII; NORMANDY; *PRÉVÔT DE PARIS*]

Baldwin, John W. *The Government of Philip Augustus*. Berkeley: University of California Press, 1986.
Bautier, Robert-Henri, ed. *La France de Philippe Auguste: le temps des mutations*. Paris: CNRS, 1982.
Bordonove, Georges. *Philippe Auguste*. Paris: Pygmalion, 1983.
Fawtier, Robert. *The Capetian Kings of France*. London: St. Martin, 1960.
Hallam, Elizabeth. *Capetian France, 987–1328*. London: Longman, 1980.

PHILIP III THE BOLD (1245–1285). King of France, 1270–85. As a boy, Philip appears to have been easygoing and easily influenced, especially by his mother, Marguerite of Provence. As a king, he was dominated at the outset by the counsels of Pierre de la Broce, a former adviser of his father, Louis IX. Later, he came under the influence of his uncle Charles, count of Anjou. Philip became king while on crusade to Tunis with his father, who died of illness during the siege of the city. Philip is the first king whose regnal years begin with the burial of his predecessor rather than the coronation of the new king, which in his case was delayed until 1271.

Although most scholars regard Philip's reign as a hiatus in the development of the monarchy, it was marked by important events. The death, childless, of his uncle and aunt, Alphonse of Poitiers and Jeanne de Toulouse, in 1271 on the way back from crusade brought their vast holdings in the south of France into the royal domain despite the importunities of Charles of Anjou, who coveted the fiefs. The acquisition of these lands by the crown sealed the ascendancy of the French in Languedoc. Philip carried on an active foreign policy. With the support of Charles of Anjou, he briefly put forward his candidacy to the imperial throne. He made efforts to draw neighboring German principalities under French influence. He aggressively defended Capetian family interests in Castile and Aragon. And he intervened with military success in Navarre when a succession crisis there in the mid-1270s threatened French interests.

Philip was drawn into war in Spain again toward the end of his reign when the Aragonese supported the rebellion of the Sicilians against Charles of Anjou (the Sicilian Vespers, 1282). Charles's pleas for support and the blessing of the pope led to the French crusade against Aragon, an ill-fated expedition across the Pyrénées in 1285, in which the French were routed. During the retreat, Philip III himself died.

Philip was married twice: first (1262) to Isabella of Aragon, who died in 1271 on the return from the crusade to Tunis. She was the mother of Philip's son and successor, Philip IV the Fair. In 1274, Philip III married Marie de Brabant, whose party at court was responsible for bringing an end to the influence of Pierre de la Broce; charged with treason, he was executed in 1278. Philip the Fair seems always to have had a strong dislike of Marie, about whom Pierre had spread ugly rumors. These included allegations that she and her party wanted to displace the children of her husband's first marriage by her own in the line of succession and that she had even poisoned Philip IV's older brother as part of her plan. No such conspiracy was ever proved, however, and the succession proceeded smoothly even under the difficult circumstances of the crusade against Aragon.

William Chester Jordan

[See also: CHARLES I; MARGUERITE OF PROVENCE; PHILIP IV THE FAIR; SICILIAN VESPERS]

Langlois, Charles-Victor. *Le règne de Philippe III le Hardi*. Paris: Hachette, 1887.

PHILIP IV THE FAIR (1268–1314). King of France, 1285–1314. Philip expanded royal power within the kingdom and dominated the ecclesiastical and secular affairs of western Europe. The grandson of St. Louis, whose canonization he achieved in 1297, he imitated and attempted to surpass Louis's achievements. Served devotedly by a series of powerful ministers, he imposed his own stamp on governmental policies, instituting widespread consultation of his subjects, issuing a host of reform charters, canceling and returning taxes when the causes that prompted them ceased, and subordinating to his authority the dukes of Aquitaine/Guyenne (also kings of England) and the counts of Flanders. Attentive to matters of conscience and believing in his role as God's minister, he upheld Christian orthodoxy against Pope Boniface VIII and the Knights Templar, appealing to a general council against the pope and destroying the Templars; he obtained papal bulls forgiving him for sins he feared he might commit; he magnified the importance of the royal power to cure; in 1306, he expelled the Jews from France. Anxious to establish the full legitimacy and the glory of the Capetian house, he encouraged the reinterpretation of the Capetians' history. Upholding the highest standards of morality and publicizing his own scrupulosity, in 1314 he presided over the trial and execution of two knights charged with adultery with his own daughters-in-law, thus casting doubt on the legitimacy of his grandchildren.

Born between April and June 1268, while Louis IX was still ruling, Philip, second son of Philip III the Bold and Isabella of Aragon (d. 1271), had a troubled childhood, dominated by the scandals that erupted at court after his father's marriage in 1274 to Marie de Brabant, suspected of poisoning Philip's elder brother, who died in 1276, shortly before the death of his third brother. In 1284, Philip was knighted and married to Jeanne, heiress of Champagne and Navarre; he became king in 1285 after his father's death on a crusade against Aragon. Having extricated himself from the ill-fated venture, Philip avoided conflict for nine years, but in 1294 he precipitated war against the mighty Edward I of England, duke of Aquitaine/Guyenne. Settled in 1303, the fruitless episode strained the kingdom's finances and led to manipulation of the currency. It resulted in the marriages of Philip's sister Marguerite to Edward in 1299 and of his daughter Isabella to Edward II in 1308; the latter union would give Edward III grounds for claiming the throne of France. The war also initiated a conflict with the Flemings, Edward I's allies and Philip's subjects, which, settled in 1305, broke out again in 1312 because of the harsh peace terms Philip imposed. Clerical taxation imposed for the war occasioned Boniface VIII's controversial bull *Clericis laicos* in 1296. From then until Boniface's death in 1303, Philip and the pope were locked in sporadic but bitter struggles involving the limits of secular jurisdiction over ecclesiastics. In the spring of 1303, Philip presided over assemblies in Paris that charged Boniface with heresy and immorality; in September 1303, the pope was violently attacked in Anagni when Philip's minister Guillaume de Nogaret summoned him to submit to the judgment of a council. Clement V, the Gascon-born cardinal who became pope in 1305, was more to the king's liking; he granted Philip many privileges and in 1311 accepted the suppression of the Knights Templar, the crusading order whose assets Philip had seized

in 1307, again because he believed them guilty of heresy and immorality.

Philip failed to achieve some of his ambitions. He never succeeded in placing a relative on the imperial throne; his visionary scheme after his wife's death in 1305 to become ruler of the Holy Land was abortive. The power he exercised within the kingdom led, at the end of his reign, to the formation of leagues of disgruntled subjects protesting his fiscal and monetary policies and demanding the restoration of old customs; his eldest son and successor, Louis X (r. 1314–16), issued numerous charters to pacify them, and he sacrificed Philip's minister Enguerran de Marigny and other officials to their princely enemies at court. Philip used his three sons and his daughter to advance his own goals. Isabella married Edward II of England; Louis married Marguerite, daughter of the duke of Burgundy; Philip's wife, Jeanne, brought to the crown the county of Burgundy; Jeanne's mother, Mahaut of Artois, offered a dowry of 100,000 *livres* to persuade Philip to accept another daughter, Blanche, as the wife of his youngest son, the future Charles IV. The imprisonment of Marguerite and Blanche for adultery in 1314 was the first of a series of tragedies suffered by Philip's direct descendants. Because of the death of Louis X's posthumous son, John I, the product of a second marriage, the throne passed to Philip V (r. 1316–22); because he left no male heir, he was succeeded by Charles IV (r. 1322–28), at whose death without male heir the rule of the direct Capetians ended and the crown passed to the house of Valois.

Elizabeth A.R. Brown

[See also: CHARLES OF VALOIS; JEANNE OF NAVARRE; MARIGNY, ENGUERRAN DE; NOGARET, GUILLAUME DE]

Bautier, Robert-Henri. "Diplomatique et histoire politique: ce que la critique diplomatique nous apprend sur la personnalité de Philippe le Bel." *Revue historique* 259 (1978): 3–27.

Brown, Elizabeth A.R. *The Monarchy of Capetian France and Royal Ceremonial*. London: Variorum, 1991.

———. *Politics and Institutions in Capetian France*. London: Variorum, 1991.

Favier, Jean. *Philippe le Bel*. Paris: Fayard, 1978.

Strayer, Joseph R. *The Reign of Philip the Fair*. Princeton: Princeton University Press, 1980.

PHILIP V THE TALL (1290/91–1322). King of France, 1316–22. Known as *Magnus* and *Le Long*, Philip succeeded his brother Louis X and Louis's posthumous son, John I, in 1316. Second son of Philip IV the Fair and Jeanne of Champagne and Navarre, Philip in January 1307 married Jeanne, daughter of Count Otto of Burgundy and Countess Mahaut of Artois. Because of a marriage contract concluded with Philip IV in 1295, Jeanne brought to France the county of Burgundy, held of the empire. From 1307, Philip was count of Burgundy and in 1311 was made count of Poitiers, but he had little power until Philip IV died. Louis X increased Philip's apanage and in August 1315 revoked Philip IV's deathbed restriction of Poitiers to male heirs. At Louis's death, Philip was in Lyon pressing for the election of a pope. As "first brother of the king" he received pledges of fidelity before returning to Paris for a second funeral service for Louis, which enabled him, as possible successor, to be present at a ceremony of interment. A solemn agreement regarding the succession, concluded on July 16, 1316, made Philip regent. It was vitiated by the birth and death of Louis's posthumous son in November 1316, and Philip was crowned on January 9, 1317.

Philip was a popular king. His wife had been cleared of adultery charges, and the couple had four daughters, and a son who died in February 1317. Philip showered his wife with property, including in September 1318 full rights to the county of Burgundy. During his reign, Philip instituted reform of central and local administration, reclaimed alienated crown lands, pacified the leagues that had disrupted Louis X's reign, received the homage of his brother-in-law Edward II of England, and achieved peace with Flanders. In 1321, he made an unprecedented, far-seeing, though finally abortive effort to secure the realm's financial support for reforming the coinage and weights and measures and for recovering crown lands.

Philip died on January 2/3, 1322, after a wasting illness. In the absence of a male heir, the crown passed to his brother, Charles of La Marche.

Elizabeth A.R. Brown

Lehugeur, Paul. *Histoire de Philippe le Long, roi de France (1316–1322)*. Paris: Hachette, 1897.

——. *Philippe le Long, roi de France, 1316–1322: le mécanisme du gouvernement*. Paris: Sirey, 1931.

Brown, Elizabeth A.R. *The Monarchy of Capetian France and Royal Ceremonial*. London: Variorum, 1991.

——. *Politics and Institutions in Capetian France*. London: Variorum, 1991.

PHILIP VI (1293–1350). First Valois king of France, 1328–50. The son of Charles of Valois (brother of King Philip IV the Fair) and Marguerite, daughter of Charles II of Naples, Philip did not become an important figure until he inherited the counties of Valois, Anjou, and Maine from his father in 1325. By that time, the reigning monarch was Philip's first cousin Charles IV, who had no son or surviving brother. When Charles died at the end of January 1328, he left a pregnant queen, and the French magnates named Philip of Valois regent, with the understanding that he would become king if the queen gave birth to a daughter.

When a daughter was indeed born on April 1, Philip VI became king. He was crowned at Reims late in May, and then, at the behest of an important supporter, Louis I of Flanders, he led a French army against Flemish rebels and won a resounding victory at Cassel in August.

Throughout his reign, Philip VI had to maneuver among conflicting political groupings whose ability to cause him trouble was enhanced by the existence of other descendants of St. Louis who might claim the French throne. Philip IV the Fair, Louis X, and Philip V all had grandsons who were disqualified by the decision to exclude princes whose claims were through their mothers. Two of these,

Edward III of England and the future Charles II of Navarre (r. 1349–87), presented malcontents with attractive alternatives to whom to give allegiance. To avoid alienating the count of Flanders and duke of Burgundy, Philip had to rule against his friend and cousin Robert of Artois in the disputed succession to Artois, and Robert then gave his allegiance to Edward III. When Philip ruled in favor of his nephew Charles de Blois in the disputed Breton succession (1341), the opposing claimant, Jean de Montfort, also turned to Edward. Many nobles of the north and west felt more closely tied to England than to the Valois, and they disliked Philip's queen, Jeanne of Burgundy. Perhaps because of her influence, Philip tended to distrust this important regional aristocracy and to draw a disproportionately large number of his advisers from regions like Auvergne and Burgundy.

Amid growing discontent in the north and west, Philip's relations with England steadily deteriorated. The two monarchies could not resolve differences over Aquitaine, and Philip supported Scottish opposition to Edward, while the latter built up an anti-Valois coalition in the Low Countries. In 1337, the Hundred Years' War began, with the first years marked by expensive preparations and little military action. Edward then defeated the French fleet at Sluys in 1340 and gained a valuable new fighting front the next year with the disputed succession in Brittany. Always short of money, Philip gave great power to the leaders of the Chambre des Comptes, whose aggressive fiscal measures did not produce the military success needed to offset the antagonism they caused.

In 1345, the military situation began to deteriorate seriously. The English victory at Auberoche that autumn secured important gains in Aquitaine. The next year, Edward III invaded Normandy, threatened Paris, and then crushed Philip's army at Crécy. In 1347, the English in Brittany won a major victory at La Roche-Derrien, while Philip could not save Calais from capitulating to Edward III in August.

At the end of 1347, the Estates General convened in Paris and demanded governmental reforms before endorsing plans for each region to raise large taxes to pay for an effective army. Before this initiative could achieve results, France began to be ravaged by the Black Death, which eventually claimed the lives of Philip's queen and daughter-in-law and left government and society in disarray. The plague also produced a lull in the war, but when he died in August 1350, Philip left behind many problems for his son and successor, John II the Good.

John Bell Henneman, Jr.

[See also: BLACK DEATH; CHARLES OF VALOIS; CRÉCY; EDWARD III; HUNDRED YEARS' WAR; VALOIS DYNASTY]

Cazelles, Raymond. *La société politique et la crise de la royauté sous Philippe de Valois*. Paris: Argences, 1958.

Henneman, John Bell. *Royal Taxation in Fourteenth Century France: The Development of War Financing, 1322–1356*. Princeton: Princeton University Press, 1971.

Viard, Jules. "La France sous Philippe VI de Valois." *Bibliothèque de l'École des Chartes* 59 (1896): 337–402.

———. "Itinéraire de Philippe de Valois." *Bibliothèque de l'École des Chartes* 74 (1913): 74–128, 524–92; 84 (1923): 166–70.

PHILIP THE BOLD (1342–1404). The first of the Valois dukes of Burgundy, Philip the Bold was the fourth son of King John II of France and Bonne de Luxembourg. Born at Pontoise on January 17, 1342, he fought beside his father at the age of fourteen and was captured with him at the Battle of Poitiers (1356). After he and the king secured release in 1360, he became duke of Touraine, but he surrendered this duchy in 1363 when John II made him duke of Burgundy and first peer of France. In May 1364, the new king, Philip's brother Charles V, confirmed these titles.

After complex diplomatic maneuvering, Philip became an international figure with his marriage, in 1369, to Marguerite, daughter of the count of Flanders and heiress to five counties in northern and eastern France. The deaths of her grandmother (1382) and father (1384) brought these lands to her and Philip, but they needed military force to secure the most important of them, Flanders, which had been in rebellion since 1379. Marguerite also had a claim to the duchy of Brabant, and in 1385 she and Philip arranged the marriage of their son and daughter to members of the Wittelsbach family that ruled the counties of Hainaut, Holland, and Zeeland, thereby laying the foundations for a Burgundian state that eventually included most of the Low Countries.

Despite his expanding role in the Netherlands, Philip was above all the most powerful French prince of his generation. At the death of Charles V in 1380, he led a coalition that ousted from the regency his older brother Louis of Anjou, and he dominated the French government for the next eight years. He played an active diplomatic role in the Anglo-French war, the papal Schism, and imperial politics, and he secured the services of the French royal army to crush the Flemish rebels at Roosebeke in 1382 and to intimidate his enemy the duke of Guelders in 1388.

Philip supported his projects with vast sums drawn from the receipts of the French crown, as did his brother, John, duke of Berry. In the fall of 1388, Charles VI dismissed his uncles from the royal council at the urging of a reforming coalition of royal officials and military commanders, known as the Marmousets. Four years later, Charles VI's first attack of mental illness enabled the duke of Burgundy to regain his dominant position, which he held for another decade before gradually losing power at court to his nephew Louis of Orléans. He died near Brussels on April 27, 1404.

Besides establishing Burgundian power in the Netherlands, Philip the Bold began the tradition of lavish support for the arts by the Burgundian dukes. He also was the primary organizer of the abortive crusade of 1396 led by his eldest son, John, count of Nevers. His great achievements were to a large degree accomplished at the expense of the French taxpayers, but he gave his native land nearly twenty years of statesmanlike, if sometimes self-serving, leadership.

John Bell Henneman, Jr.

[See also: BURGUNDY]

Nieuwenhuysen, Andrée van. *Les finances du duc de Bourgogne Philippe le Hardi (1384–1404)*. Brussels: Éditions de l'Université de Bruxelles, 1984.

Palmer, John J.N. *England, France and Christendom, 1377–99*. London: Routledge and Kegan Paul, 1972.

Petit, Ernest. *Ducs de Bourgogne de la maison de Valois, I: Philippe le Hardi*. Paris: Champion, 1909.

Richard, Jean. *Les ducs de Bourgogne et la formation du duché*. Paris: Les Belles Lettres, 1954.

Vaughan, Richard. *Philip the Bold: The Formation of the Burgundian State*. Cambridge: Harvard University Press, 1962.

PHILIP THE CHANCELLOR (ca. 1160/85–ca. 1236). An influential theologian, a preacher of considerable stature, and an accomplished poet, Philip was born into ecclesiastical circles: he was the illegitimate son of Archdeacon Philip of Paris and was related through his father to Bishop Étienne of Noyon (d. 1211) and Bishop Pierre of Paris (d. 1218), both of whom favored Philip's career. After studying theology and law, he appears in the historical record no later than 1211 as archdeacon of Noyon.

As chancellor of the University of Paris, a position that he held from 1217, Philip had authority over the fledgling university. Philip's chancellorship came in an era of discontent and controversy, and in a combative move early in his tenure (1219) he excommunicated the masters and students—a move that Pope Honorius III ordered him to reverse. During the strike initiated in 1229, Philip sided with the pope and the university against William of Auvergne, bishop of Paris, and Blanche of Castile, regent during Louis IX's minority. The papal bull *Parens scientiarum* of Gregory IX ended the university strike in 1231. Not long after Philip's death, Henri d'Andeli wrote a *Dit du chancelier Philippe*, in which he is associated with jongleurs, chansons, and vielle playing.

As a master of theology, Philip composed a treatise on moral theology, the *Summa de bono*, that had considerable influence on the earliest generation of Franciscan masters. It was organized into two main parts, *De bono naturae* and *De bono gratiae*, with the latter subdivided into three: *gratia gratum faciens, gratia gratis data, gratia virtutum* (both theological and cardinal). Philip is also credited with 723 sermons, which reveal a preacher vigorously calling both the clergy and the laity to a just and holy way of life.

Of the fifty-eight monophonic conductus attributed to Philip, at least twenty-one texts are confirmed as his. *Angelus ad virginem* was made famous by Chaucer: in *The Miller's Tale*, the scholarly but impoverished cleric Nicholas sings it. Medieval sources ascribe nine polyphonic conductus to Philip, and among four possible textings of conductus caudae at least *Bulla fulminante* (and its contrafact *Veste nuptiali*) and *Minor natu filiu* definitely can be counted as his; *Anima lugi lacrima* and *Crucifigat omnes* (which has two contrafacts: *Mundum renovavit* and *Curritur ad vocem*) are suspected of also being his. He penned the four known tropes to Pérotin's two great organa quadrupla: *Vide prophecie*, *Homo cum mandato dato*, *De Stephani roseo sanguine*, and *Adesse festina*. Philip and Pérotin appear to have known one another and may have collaborated. Since so many of Philip's texts were tropes or contrafacts for music that already had been composed, it would seem that he was not a composer himself. Although his defense of accumulating benefices earned him the displeasure of the Dominicans, he remained a friend of the Franciscans throughout his life and was buried in their church.

Mark Zier/Sandra Pinegar

[See also: CONDUCTUS; HYMNS; *PARENS SCIENTIARUM*; PARIS; PÉROTIN; UNIVERSITIES; VERSUS]

Dreves, Guido Maria, ed. *Lateinische Hymnendichter des Mittelalters*. Leipzig: Reisland, 1907. *Analecta hymnica medii aevi*. Vol. 50, pp. 528–32.

Paine, Thomas. "*Associa tecum in patria*: A Newly Identified Organum Trope by Philip the Chancellor." *Journal of the American Musicological Society* 39 (1986): 233–54.

Principe, Walter H. *The Theology of the Hypostatic Union in the Early Thirteenth Century, IV: Philip the Chancellor's Theology of the Hypostatic Union*. Toronto: Pontifical Institute of Mediaeval Studies, 1975.

Steiner, Ruth. "Some Monophonic Songs Composed Around 1200." *Musical Quarterly* 52 (1966): 56-70.

Wright, Craig. *Music and Ceremony at Notre Dame of Paris 500–1550*. Cambridge: Cambridge University Press, 1989, pp. 249–99.

Wicki, Nikolaus. "La *pecia* dans la tradition manuscrite de la *Summa de bono* de Philippe le Chancelier." In *The Editing of Theological and Philosophical Texts from the Middle Ages*, ed. Monika Asztalos. Stockholm: Almqvist and Wiksell, 1986, pp. 93–104.

PHILIP THE GOOD (1396–1467). Duke of Burgundy, 1419–67. The son and successor of John the Fearless, duke of Burgundy and count of Flanders, Philip was twenty-three years old when the assassination of his father in 1419 made him the mightiest peer of France and the most important prince of the Low Countries. His reign of forty-seven years brought prosperity, prestige, and territorial expansion to his lands. He guided the ill-fated Burgundian state to the peak of its power, but its greatness, dependant on the weakness of the French monarchy, dissipated after the end of the Hundred Years' War.

An astute diplomat and judicious in the use of force, Philip sought to overcome ducal Burgundy's status as a French apanage by enmeshing it in an independent polity in the territories between France and Germany. The Treaty of Troyes (1420) allied him with Henry V of England, secured his French holdings, and allowed him to concentrate on the Low Countries. His second (1422) and third (1430) marriages secured political allies and territorial claims. Conquests of Holland (1425–33) and Luxembourg (1443), and the peaceful acquisitions of Namur (1420) and Brabant (1430) doubled the size of his lands. Philip

eventually sought the crown of a restored Lotharingia from the emperor Frederick III in 1447. His failure to obtain a crown had no immediate political consequences, but it foreshadowed the doom of the Burgundian polity, which remained an overextended Franco-imperial principality in an age of emerging sovereign states. Within France, Philip provided minimal support for the government of Henry VI of England and later realigned himself with Charles VII in 1435 (Treaty of Arras). Fearing a revitalized monarchy, Philip abstained from the decisive campaigns of the Hundred Years' War and sheltered the fugitive dauphin after 1456. The failure of such efforts became manifest when his son, the future Charles the Bold, assumed control of Burgundy in 1464 and launched the *Guerre du bien publique* against Louis XI. Philip's rule thus ended as it began, with Valois France and Valois Burgundy inextricably locked in mortal conflict.

Philip's most celebrated achievement was to make chivalric culture an instrument of policy. The creation of the Order of the Golden Fleece in 1430 provided a diplomatic tool linking the nobility of his disparate territories and precluding their affiliation with any other prince. Even such ostentatious festivals as the Pheasant Banquet in 1454 had political value, for through such devices the prestige of the Valois dukes reached its zenith. Philip himself was a model of late-medieval chivalry: handsome, courageous, pious, self-indulgent, extravagant. He maintained mistresses and bastards throughout his lands yet made heartfelt, albeit unfulfilled, promises to go on crusade. He is remembered as "the Good" above all for the talented artists who gave him the accolade and immortalized Burgundy in tapestries, the paintings of van Eyck, and literature ranging from the *Cent nouvelles nouvelles* to the histories of Chastellain. He may seem less successful in retrospect than he did at the time, but Burgundy was a phantasm and Philip sustained it the best of all his line.

Paul D. Solon

See also: ARISTOCRATIC REVOLT; BEDFORD, JOHN OF LANCASTER, DUKE OF; BURGUNDY; CHARLES VII; CHARLES THE BOLD; CHASTELLAIN, GEORGES; GOLDEN FLEECE; HENRY V; HUNDRED YEARS' WAR; VALOIS DYNASTY; VAN EYCK, JAN]

Bonenfant, Paul. *Philippe le Bon*. Brussels: La Renaissance du Livre, 1955.

Cartellieri, Otto. *The Court of Burgundy: Studies in the History of Civilization*. New York: Askell House, 1970.

Huizinga, Johan. *The Waning of the Middle Ages: A Study of the Forms of Life, Thought and Art in France and the Netherlands in the Dawn of the Renaissance*. London: Arnold, 1924.

Vaughn, Richard. *Philip the Good: The Apogee of Burgundy*. London: Longman, 1970.

———. *Valois Burgundy*. London: Lane, 1975.

PHILIPPE D'ALSACE (1144–1191). The son of Thierry d'Alsace, count of Flanders, Philippe d'Alsace assumed power in the county when his father went to Palestine in

1157. He promoted clearance and new settlements and furthered the cities' economic interests while refusing them any role in the governance of Flanders. His marriage to Elizabeth, daughter of Raoul V de Vermandois, was childless, but he became count of Vermandois in 1163 and thereby ruled the largest territory ever held by a Flemish count.

The bonds between the count of Flanders and the French crown became intimate under Philippe. His heir was the son of his sister Marguerite, wife of Baudouin V of Hainaut. As head of the regency for the young king Philip Augustus, Philippe d'Alsace arranged for the king to marry his niece, Isabelle de Hainaut, in 1180, with Artois as her dowry. When his own wife, Elizabeth, died in 1182, Philippe d'Alsace refused to give up her lands in the Vermandois and so damaged his relations with the crown. In 1185, with the Treaty of Boves, the count had to give in, and he lost practical influence in Vermandois. When Queen Isabelle died in 1190, the county of Artois, her dowry, passed to her child, the future Louis VIII.

Philippe d'Alsace joined the Third Crusade and died in Palestine in 1191. He was succeeded by his nephew Baudouin of Hainaut, who became Baudouin VIII of Flanders.

David M. Nicholas

[See also: ARTOIS; FLANDERS; PHILIP II AUGUSTUS; VERMANDOIS]

Caenegem, R.C. van. "Criminal Law in England and Flanders Under King Henry II and Count Philip of Alsace." *Actes du Congrès de Naples (1980) de la Société Italienne d'Histoire du Droit* (1980): 231–54.

Verhulst, Aadrian, and T. de Hemptinne. "Le chancelier de Flandre sous les comtes de la maison d'Alsace." *Bulletin de la Commission Royale d'Histoire* 141 (1975): 267–311.

Werveke, Hans van. *Een Vlaamse graaf van Europees formaat: Filips van de Elzas.* Haarlem: Fibula-Van Dishoeck, 1976.

PHILIPPE DE NOVARE (ca. 1195–ca. 1265). A native of Lombardy, Philippe de Novare lived as a knight, legal expert, and diplomat in the Latin kingdoms of Cyprus and Jerusalem. His prose memoirs, which incorporate three crusade poems and an episode modeled on the *Roman de Renart*, recount his life in the East from 1218 until 1243 and detail the war between Emperor Frederick II and the Ibelins. In the *Livre a un sien ami en forme de plait*, part of the *Assises de Jérusalem*, he compiled and explained customary law in the courts of Outremer. When he was over seventy, Philippe wrote *Des quatre tens d'aage d'ome* (ca. 1265; five manuscripts), a prose treatise on childhood, youth, middle age, and old age that dispenses moral counsel, derived largely from personal experience, at each stage to both sexes. More personal in its tone than some other didactic works, the *Quatre tens* conveys a pessimistic view of human nature and advocates particularly restrictive roles for women.

Roberta L. Krueger

[See also: MORAL TREATISES; *RENART, ROMAN DE*]

Philippe de Novare. *Livre a un sien ami en forme de plait*. In *Assises de Jérusalem: recueil des ouvrages de jurisprudence composés pendant le XIIIe siècle dans les royaumes de Jérusalem et de Chypre*, ed. Arthur Auguste Beugnot. 2 vols. Paris: Imprimerie Royale, 1841–43, Vol. 1: *Assises de la Haute Cour*, pp. 469–571.

——. *Des quatre âges de l'homme: traité de moral de Philippe de Novare*, ed. Marcel de Freville. Paris: Didot, 1888.

——. *Mémoires (1218–1243)*, ed. Charles Kohler. Paris: Champion, 1913.

Langlois, Charles-Victor. *La vie en France au moyen âge de la fin du XIIe au milieu du XIVe siècle*. 4 vols. Paris: Hachette, 1926–28, Vol. 2: *D'après des moralistes du temps*, pp. 141–75.

PHILIPPE DE THAÜN (fl. late 11th–early 12th c.). Author of the earliest surviving scientific works in French. Philippe's Anglo-Norman dialect, which he helped establish as a literary medium, probably indicates that he was born in England, but he was of continental parentage originating in Thaon in lower Normandy, 13 miles northwest of Caen. His *Cumpoz* (probably 1113) is dedicated to an uncle, Humphrey (Honfroi) of Thaon, chaplain to Eudo Fitz-Hubert, also known as Eudo Dapifer, steward of Henry I of England, whose royal court was a center of learned activity. Philippe's two signed works, the *Cumpoz* and the *Bestiaire*, are in hexasyllabic rhymed, occasionally assonanced, couplets, but the *Bestiaire* ends with an octosyllabic lapidary. Several anonymous works have also been attributed to him.

The *Cumpoz* ("computus") is a practical treatise on the calendar that tells how to predict the dates of Easter and the movable feasts governed by Easter. The problem is reconciliation of the lunar calendar, which determines the date of Easter by its association with Passover, with the Julian solar calendar. Along with accurately detailed computational material, Philippe gives free rein to an allegorical bent in discussions of the zodiac and the names of the days and the months. He twice uses the year 1113 as an example for computing, once implying that it is the current year; in any case, the *Cumpoz* was dedicated before Eudo's death in 1120, for he is referred to as though still alive.

The *Bestiaire* (ca. 1125) is a "Book of Nature" divided into three sections: land animals and sea creatures, birds, and precious gems; it draws on traditional bestiary material from ancient myth and biblical sources. An article on a creature or stone generally opens with a physical description, often incorporating drawings with the text, followed by discussion of specific properties or habits. Allegorical commentary derived from the descriptive material then demonstrates the revelation of God in the natural world. The articles in the first two sections are arranged hierarchically, from the "kings" of each species (the lion, the eagle), which signify Christ, to the "lower" (land-bound birds, and fish), which refer to Satan; precious gems, beginning with their "king," the diamond, are associated with the powers of good. The *Bestiaire* is dedicated to Adeliza (Aaliz de Louvain), whom Henry I married in 1121; she retained the title of queen four years after Henry's death in 1135. Scholars tend to date the *Bestiaire* from early in Adeliza's marriage because of the date of the *Cumpoz*. One manuscript of the *Bestiaire* bears a rededication to Eleanor of Aquitaine, Henry II's queen, written after 1154.

The anonymous *Livre de Sibile* (1135–54), dedicated to the empress Matilda, Henry I's daughter, is a book of prophecies. Authorship has been ascribed to Philippe primarily because the text bears striking linguistic and stylistic resemblances to the signed works; in addition, personal content in the dedication parallels information found in the rededication of the *Bestiaire* to Eleanor of Aquitaine. On the basis of less convincing evidence, two early Anglo-Norman lapidaries, the *Alphabetical* and the *Apocalyptic*, an Anglo-Norman allegorical *Desputeisun del cors e de l'arme*, and a geographical treatise, *Les Divisiuns del mund*, have also been attributed to Philippe.

Rupert T. Pickens

[See also: BESTIARY; *COMPUTUS;* LAPIDARY]

Philippe de Thaün. *Le bestiaire de Philippe de Thaün*, ed. Emanuel Walberg. Paris: Plon, 1900.
———. *Li cumpoz*, ed. Émile Mall. Strasbourg, 1873.
———. *Le livre de Sibile by Philippe de Thaon*, ed. Hugh Shields. London: Anglo-Norman Text Society, 1979.
Legge, M. Dominica. *Anglo-Norman Literature and Its Background*. Oxford: Clarendon, 1963.
McCulloch, Florence. *Mediaeval Latin and French Bestiaries*. Chapel Hill: University of North Carolina Press, 1960.
Pickens, Rupert T. "The Literary Activity of Philippe de Thaün." *Romance Notes* 12 (1970–71): 208–12.
Shields, Hugh. "Philippe de Thaon, auteur du *Livre de Sibylle?*" *Romania* 85 (1964): 455–77.
———. "More Poems by Philippe de Thaon?" In *Anglo-Norman Anniversary Essays*, ed. Ian Short. London: Anglo-Norman Text Society, 1993, pp. 337–59.
Studer, Paul, and Joan Evans. *Anglo-Norman Lapidaries*. Paris: Champion, 1924.

PHILIPPE DE VITRY (1291–1361). Official of the French court under Charles IV, Philip VI, and John II; bishop of Meaux from 1361; poet; and the most important composer of the early Ars Nova. Philippe's many services to the Valois included appointment as one of the nine reformers-general of 1357. Although Philippe's contributions to poetry and music have been difficult to establish unequivocally due to the state of the sources, his authority and reputation, extending into the 15th century, were enormous. As a young man, he probably contributed to the new developments in Ars Nova notation (ca. 1315–20) and probably taught the new techniques to others; he seems not to have written a theoretical treatise himself. Philippe was possibly the inventor of the isorhythmic motet, and there is evidence that he helped to establish the *formes fixes* as the preeminent musical-lyrical forms of the 14th century. Guillaume de Machaut probably numbered him-

self among Philippe's musical pupils. Philippe's most influential work of poetry was the *Dit de Franc Gontier*, which in the 15th century elicited a companion work by Pierre d'Ailly and a parody by François Villon.

Lawrence Earp

[See also: ARS NOVA; *FAUVEL, LIVRES DE; FORMES FIXES;* ISORHYTHMIC MOTET; MUSIC THEORY]

Coville, Alfred. "Philippe de Vitri: notes biographiques." *Romania* 59 (1933): 520–47.
Leech-Wilkinson, Daniel. *Compositional Techniques in the Four-Part Isorhythmic Motets of Philippe de Vitry and His Contemporaries*. 2 vols. New York: Garland, 1989.
Wathy, Andrew. "The Motets of Philippe de Vitry and the Fourteenth-Century Renaissance." *Early Music History* 12 (1993): 119–50.
Wimsatt, James I. *Chaucer and His French Contemporaries: Natural Music in the Fourteenth Century*. Toronto: University of Toronto Press, 1991.

PHILIPPE MOUSKÉS (b. ca. 1193). Fourth son of aristocratic parents, Juliane Mouskete and N. Mouskés of Tournai, Philippe Mouskés wrote before 1243 a *Chronique rimée* (15,628 octosyllabic couplets) of the French kings, from the legendary Marcomire, grandson of Priam of Troy and first king of the Gauls, to the middle of the reign of Louis IX. He is remembered primarily for having used a now lost French translation (related to B.N. fr. 2137 and 17203) of the Latin Pseudo-Turpin chronicle for the almost 5,000 couplets dealing with the history of Charlemagne and for preserving otherwise unknown chansons de geste by borrowing extensively from them. His other sources are French and Norman chronicles; on the reigns of Philip II Augustus, Louis VIII, and Louis IX, he often reports as an eyewitness. His *Chronique* reflects the 13th-century tendency toward popularized history and differs from other chronicles by the fact that Mouskés worked without a patron, simply to amuse himself (*pour resgoïr*).

Hans R. Runte

[See also: BIOGRAPHY; *GORMONT ET ISEMBART;* HISTORIOGRAPHY; PSEUDO-TURPIN]

Philippe Mouskés. *Chronique rimée de Philippe Mouskes*, ed. Frédéric-Auguste-Ferdinand-Thomas, baron de Reiffenberg. 3 vols. Brussels: Commission Royale d'Histoire, 1836–45. [Edition of B.N. fr. 4963.]
Walpole, Ronald N. "Philip Mouskés and the *Pseudo-Turpin Chronicle*." *University of California Publications in Modern Philology* 26 (1947): 327–471.

PHILIPPUS DE CASERTA (fl. ca. 1370). Italian composer of French chansons, represented in the Chantilly codex (Chantilly, Musée Condé 564) by six ballades and possibly one rondeau. Some of his works borrow bits of text from ballades of Machaut. Philippus was active in the papal choir at Avignon in the 1370s, and one of his ballades celebrates Pope Clement VII. His works feature complex and irregular rhythms, and he is possibly the author of the *Tractatus de diversis figuris* on complex Ars Subtilior note shapes. Johannes Ciconia quoted both text and music of three of Philippus's ballades in his virelai *Sus un' fontayne*, perhaps in homage to his teacher.

Benjamin Garber

[See also: ARS SUBTILIOR; CICONIA, JOHANNES; COMPOSERS, MINOR (14TH CENTURY); EGIDIUS DE MURINO; MUSIC THEORY]

Strohm, Reinhard. "Filippotto da Caserta, Ovvero I Francesi in Lombardia." In *In cantu et in sermone: For Nino Pirrotta on His 80th Birthday*, ed. Fabrizio Della Seta and Franco Piperno. Florence: Olschki, 1989, pp. 65–74.
Tomasello, Andrew. *Music and Ritual at Papal Avignon, 1309–1403*. Ann Arbor: UMI Research Press, 1983.

PHILOSOPHY. As the Roman Empire was crumbling in Gaul, so too was the classical tradition of both pagan and Christian Greek and Latin learning. The age of the Latin fathers ended effectively with the death of Augustine of Hippo in North Africa in 430, and the heritage of classical thought was summed up and passed on to the western Middle Ages largely in the philosophical and theological works of "the last Roman," Boethius, who was executed at the Pavian court of King Theodoric in 524. It was not until the Carolingian period, and especially the era of intellectual contacts with Muslim and Jewish Arabic scholars in southern Europe, that more classical texts, particularly by Greek authors, became available.

Traditionally, Latin Europe from the 6th to the 9th century is thought of as barren of philosophy and theology, but as *Romanitas* was being replaced by *Christianitas* in the Gaul of the 5th century, there are sporadic signs of continuing literary and philosophical learning in a world otherwise fraught with a lack of intellectual activity. Thus Sidonius Apollinaris (ca. 432–ca. 485), bishop of Clermont-Ferrand, kept alive the humanist arts of letter writing and historical narrative. Philosophically important for this period is the exchange between Faustus of Riez in Provence (d. ca. 495) and Claudianus Mamertus of Vienne (d. ca. 474) on the locality and materiality of the soul. Merovingian culture continued to evince love for traditional classical culture, especially among Romano-Gallic aristocrats and the bishops who were related to them. The Council of Vaison (529), besides reforming church liturgy, played an important role in this conservation by prescribing the teaching of Latin to ensure the education in arts (philosophy in a broad sense) and in theology of future clerics.

The establishment of monasteries at Annegray, Luxeuil, and Fontaines by the Irish *peregrinus* Columbanus (fl. 600) and the Benedictine *Rule*, introduced into France from Italy at the end of the 7th century, both created a new emphasis in studies. Secular classical learning was downgraded in favor of exegetical studies of the Bible and the organization of the liturgy. Especially illustrative of this period is the dispute between Pope Gregory the Great (ca.

540–604) and Desiderius (Didier) of Vienne (fl. 596–601) on the love for and merits of pagan classical, particularly Greek, literature, grammar, and rhetoric. Gregory set the stage for medieval intellectual life by claiming that the liberal arts and what we today would call philosophical methodology are indispensable for the correct interpretation of the written Word of God but that they should be used for that purpose alone. Elements of the classical tradition were, however, preserved in the works of men like Gregory of Tours (d. 594) and Venantius Fortunatus (540–600), who died as bishop of Poitiers.

It must be noted, too, that the role of women in the preservation of classical education in Merovingian Gaul was not insignificant. Regrettably, few sources have survived. An indicative example, though, is a letter from Caesaria, abbess of the convent at Arles, to King Clotar I's wife, Radegund, who was establishing a house at Poitiers. Caesaria enjoins Radegund to allow no nun to enter who does not learn the liberal arts.

The contribution of Merovingian culture to the history of philosophy was basically that of preserving the scholarship of the ancients. Carolingian scholars and philosophers were generally intent on the classification of what is and can be known about the world. The foundation for intellectual life in the Carolingian era was laid by Alcuin of York (ca. 735–804), who had been invited by Charlemagne to become the head of his palace school at Aix-la-Chapelle. Here, Alcuin revitalized teaching in the Trivium by writing textbooks like *De grammatica* (which has a Boethian introduction entitled "De vera philosophia"), *De rhetorica et virtutibus*, and *De dialectica*; he was also intent on giving rules for the correct transcription of manuscripts. As abbot of Tours for the last eight years of his life, he was especially interested in building up the library and in developing the Liberal Arts with a view to exegetical studies of the Scriptures, which were to provide *sapientia*, or true philosophy.

The early 9th century witnessed some philosophical discussion of Aristotle's methodology, as well as discussion of the relation between grammar and ontology; of the perennial question of the exact status of the soul; and even, in the realm of political theory, of the duties of princes. But without doubt the greatest philosophical impact was made by the gift of the Greek text of the works of Pseudo-Dionysius the Areopagite (the *Corpus areopagiticum*) from the Byzantine emperor Michael the Stammerer to Louis the Pious in 827. Charles the Bald (r. 840–77) can be seen as France's first great patron of philosophy, for in 860 it was he who asked Johannes Scottus Eriugena (d. 877) to translate this collection of Neoplatonic works into Latin. Perhaps most noteworthy in Pseudo-Dionysius's work is the idea that evil *qua* evil is nonexistent; evil must be regarded merely as a lack of goodness, and it can therefore be described only in negative terms. On the other hand, God as Essence *par excellence* can never be adequately described in nonessential language. In this way, the foundation was laid down for the reception of ideas of learned ignorance that played an important role especially in medieval philosophical and theological mysticism, such as that of the Victorines in the 12th century and the Parisian Lullists of the late 14th. Thus, Greek Christian texts by

Pseudo-Dionysius and later by Maximus the Confessor, Gregory of Nyssa, and perhaps Epiphanius of Salamis (Cyprus) entered into Latin European thought, strongly influencing such later thinkers as Bonaventure, Thomas Aquinas, and Nicholas of Cusa. The influence of Eriugena's work has not yet been fully traced, but it is safe to say that it had a wide circulation especially through *florilegia* and glosses in manuscripts of his text. A nexus seems to have been the school of Auxerre, with scholars like Heiric (841–ca. 876) and Remigius (ca. 841–ca. 908). Remigius also wrote many commentaries on grammar (Donatus, Priscian, Eutyches, Phokas), on style (Bede), and on the arts in general (Martianus Capella). Though not very innovative, they did serve to keep alive in France and the rest of northern Europe the tradition of the Liberal Arts on which philosophy must build.

Philosophy in 10th- and early 11th-century France was limited. There is some teaching of logic, mathematics, and astronomy and discussion of the problem of how reason is to be used, notably by Gerbert of Aurillac at Reims (ca. 945–1003), who may have had access to Arabic learning through his studies in the Catalan monastery of Ripoll. But it is not until the middle of the 11th century that philosophy in France receives new impulses, especially from debates on the relationship of logic and grammar to theology and biblical exegesis, such as that between Berengar of Tours (ca. 1010–1088) and Lanfranc of Bec (ca. 1005–1089) on the interpretation of the wording of the eucharist. The stage was being set for the development of the scholastic method of solving intellectual problems that is the hallmark of medieval philosophy.

The scholastic method, the central method of medieval philosophy, is a technique of teaching and interpreting texts by using a system of distinctions, definitions, and disputation deriving from the logic of Aristotle and Boethius. In the 11th and 12th centuries, this narrow basis was broadened to include other authors, and later the scholastic method developed a terministic and semantic logic that made its work in discovering meaning ever more subtle. Many of the important developments of the scholastic method took place in France. Thus, Anselm of Bec (1033–1109), who hailed from Aosta in northern Italy, can be called the "father of scholasticism" on the basis of the treatises he wrote at the Benedictine monastery of Bec in Normandy on how grammar and logic should be used to study the Scriptures.

Three important elements of the scholastic method are the textual commentary, the *quaestio* (or *disputatio*), and the harmonization of authoritative texts. Hugh of Saint-Victor's (ca. 1096–1141) *Didascalicon* defined the commentary as a combination of *lectio* (reading) and *meditatio* (understanding). Peter Abélard (1079–1142), working in Paris, helped calibrate the scholastic method by the structure of his famous *Sic et non*, in which arguments for and against theological and philosophical statements are systematized. The great standard-bearers of the value of the *quaestio* in scholarship are the masters of the so-called school of Chartres. Gilbert of Poitiers (ca. 1075/80–1154) and Clarembald of Arras (ca. 1110–after 1170) stressed how important it was that the *quaestio* be structured in

terms of statement and contradiction. The masters of Chartres used their method especially in the interpretation of Platonic texts, notably Plato's *Timaeus* and Boethius's *De consolatione Philosophiae*. Peter Lombard (ca.1100–1160), at Paris, wrote the standard harmonization of theological and philosophical knowledge, *Quattuor libri sententiarum*, whose influence as the official textbook of theology in the Middle Ages can hardly be exaggerated.

One of the most sustained developers and applicators of scholasticism is Thomas Aquinas (ca. 1224–1274), who taught at Paris in 1256–59 and again after 1269. His *Summa theologica*, the second part of which he wrote at Paris, is a model of medieval methodology. Medieval philosophers themselves had the highest regard for Henry of Ghent (ca. 1217–1293), a secular master of theology at Paris from 1276; his practice of philosophy, too, is a good example of scholastic method.

Even if philosophical discussions were generally structured along the lines of the scholastic method, there was speculation on the borderlines between philosophy and theology on the one hand and cosmology and mysticism on the other. A literary style was employed that was far removed from the clear distinctions of the *quaestio*. An example of poetic cosmology is Bernard Silvestris's (fl. 1147–77) *Cosmographia*. This work has been rightly called an epic poem. In it, Silvestris made a brilliant synthesis of Chartrian understanding of the Platonism of the *Timaeus*, Calcidius, Macrobius, Martianus Capella, and Boethius. The *Cosmographia* combines 12th-century knowledge of science and medicine—often derived from Arabic sources—with Platonism to form a veritable encyclopedia in literary style.

A scholastic who practiced the scholastic method but also tried his hand at literary style when writing on mystical topics is Bonaventure (ca. 1217–1274), who taught at Paris in 1248–55. His *Itinerarium mentis in Deum* shows how philosophy functions in the ascent of the soul from the visible world to the unificatory mystical experience where scholastic *distinctiones* and *quaestiones* are no longer necessary or possible. Here, the text does not impart information or provide analysis but becomes itself part of the process toward illumination.

The basic presupposition of the scholastic method is that knowledge can be acquired only on the basis of the interpretation of authoritative *texts*. The late 13th and 14th centuries saw a shift to the critical examination of how *words* have meaning, how they function in propositions and in wider contexts, and what their relations are to the external world. Important French names in these discussions are Lambert of Auxerre (fl. 1250) and the Parisian masters Jean Buridan (ca. 1295–after 1358) and Marsilius of Inghen (d. 1396). Not all philosophers in France during the Middle Ages used the scholastic method. Through the influence of the Catalan thinker Ramon Lull (ca. 1232–1316), a way of doing philosophy entered into France and especially Paris in the 14th century that leads into the mystical and even alchemical aspects of Renaissance thought.

Debate and discussion are the life's blood of philosophy, and the liveliness of philosophers in medieval France can be illustrated by mentioning three controversies: the debate between Anselm of Bec and Gaunilo, a Benedictine monk of Marmoutier (d. 1083), on proving the existence of God; the acrimonious interchange between Peter Abélard and William of Champeaux (ca. 1070–1121) on the status of universal terms; and the attack of Nicholas of Autrecourt (ca. 1300–after 1350) on Aristotelian scholasticism.

Anselm wrote two works that on philosophical grounds argue for the existence of God. In the *Monologion* (1076), he uses traditional Platonic and Aristotelian arguments to prove the existence of a single supreme nature that is self-sufficient and causes all other things to be. All this is couched in an analysis of the way that language works and constantly employs metaphors, examples, and models derived from Augustine. This makes for a complicated and difficult argument. So, in the *Proslogion* (1077–78) he sets out to find a single, self-evident argument to demonstrate God's existence and to describe a number of his attributes. Anselm begins from the definition of the word "God" as "that than which no greater can be thought." Using only this definition, he demonstrates that it entails God's existence both in the mind of the person who thinks on God's existence and in the real world. In the history of philosophy, this argument is called the "ontological proof" of God's existence. Although the monk Gaunilo did not deny the existence of God in replying to Anselm, he felt that Anselm's proof was philosophically unsound on the grounds that it appears to confuse conventional language (*voces*) and logic with the real world. For Anselm, however, real language (*verbum*) is the structure itself of the created world and serves as the connecting link between the human being who contemplates God and God's answer to his prayer for the enlightenment of his intellect to show that God really exists. This debate can be closely examined today because Anselm instructed manuscript copyists always to add Gaunilo's objections and his own replies to them as appendices to the *Proslogion*.

The bitter controversy between Peter Abélard and William of Champeaux concerned the problem of the status of "universals," terms or concepts like "man" or "animal." William holds the view that genera and species exist ontologically in a real world beyond sense experience; his position can be described as an extreme sort of Platonist realism. Abélard makes a careful distinction between thought and language on the one hand and reality on the other. Genera and species exist as concepts in the mind but they also signify the same real things that particular concepts represent. Insofar as they are words, they are corporeal and sensible; but insofar as they are able to signify many individual things, they are incorporeal, for sense experience does not show them to us. Aristotle is correct when he says that universals exist in sensible things as their forms, but at the same time Plato is also right to believe that universals exist independently of the sensible world when they are abstracted from it by the mind that thinks about the empirical world or as they exist in the Divine Mind. Abélard also asks whether universals continue to have meaning if the individual things that they signify stop existing. His answer is that indeed they have meaning in the mind, because it makes sense to say that something that has existed no longer exists.

These views of Abélard's became especially controversial when he began applying them to theological doctrines, such as that of the Trinity. For example, an analysis of the the word "God" in Abélard's terms as a universal concept signifying the three individual divine persons but itself not existing in the real world, could easily lead to the heresy of tritheism or alternatively to the idea of the three persons as mere modes of the single God. Small wonder, then, that Abélard was several times condemned at church councils: at Soissons in 1121, and especially through the efforts of Bernard of Clairvaux and William of Saint-Thierry again at Sens in 1140. The issues that Abélard raised were of great importance because they helped set the stage for later discussions on the status of language and meaning. Besides, Abélard's way of reasoning and the style of his writing contributed in an important way to the development of the scholastic method, especially to its ahistorical character.

A third philosophical debate that moved the minds of many theologians and philosophers in medieval Paris centered on the Parisian master Nicholas of Autrecourt. Nicholas seems to have been regarded by the university as the leader of a group of philosophers who questioned the authority of Aristotle in philosophical matters. Nicholas held that Aristotle was mistaken about the principle of causation, on which rests the entire system of scholastic theology. According to Nicholas, certitude in scientific demonstration depends only on the principle of contradiction. It is the application of this principle that makes syllogisms viable, and syllogisms are the building blocks of science. Now, the premises of syllogisms are derived from sense experience, but sense experience tells us nothing about substances, only about appearances. Thus syllogisms—and science—can tell us nothing about either substances or about any causal connections between them. Only analytic propositions make sense, and for this reason it is obvious that any traditional proof, whether cosmological or physico-teleological, for the existence of God does not stand up to scrutiny.

Nicholas's philosophy put the ax to the very roots of scholasticism, and his contemporaries fully understood this. In 1346, under Pope Clement VI, his teachings were condemned and his degrees revoked, and he was forced to recant his doctrines; a year later, he had to burn his writings at the University of Paris. He then fled to Germany but later was appointed dean of the cathedral of Metz. Nicholas's ideas, however, were not lost: toward the end of the 14th century, much of his analysis of propositions found its way into the writings of nominalist and realist theologians alike. He was more or less rehabilitated by Pierre d'Ailly (1350–1420), who had studied at Paris and himself debated vehemently against causal connections with regard to future contingent truths.

Arjo Vanderjagt

[See also: ABÉLARD, PETER; ALCUIN; ANSELM OF BEC; AQUINAS, THOMAS; ARABIC PHILOSOPHY, INFLUENCE OF; ARISTOTLE, INFLUENCE OF; *BENEDICT, RULE OF ST.*; BERENGAR OF TOURS; BOETHIUS, INFLUENCE OF; BONAVENTURE; CHARLES II THE BALD; CLAREMBALD

OF ARRAS; D'AILLY, PIERRE; ERIUGENA, JOHANNES SCOTTUS; FAUSTUS OF RIEZ; GERBERT OF AURILLAC; GILBERT OF POITIERS; GREGORY OF TOURS; HEIRIC OF AUXERRE; HENRY OF GHENT; HUGH OF SAINT-VICTOR; LATIN POETRY, MEROVINGIAN; PETER LOMBARD; PSEUDO-DIONYSIUS THE AREOPAGITE; RADEGUND; REMIGIUS OF AUXERRE; SCHOLASTICISM; THEOLOGY; UNIVERSITIES; WILLIAM OF CHAMPEAUX]

Armstrong, A.H., ed. *The Cambridge History of Later Greek and Early Medieval Philosophy*. Cambridge: Cambridge University Press, 1970.

Kretzmann, Norman, Anthony Kenny, and Jan Pinborg, eds. *The Cambridge History of Later Medieval Philosophy*. Cambridge: Cambridge University Press, 1982.

Schmitt, Charles B., Quentin Skinner, and Eckhard Kessler, eds. *The Cambridge History of Renaissance Philosophy*. Cambridge: Cambridge University Press, 1988.

Dronke, Peter, ed. *A History of Twelfth-Century Western Philosophy*. Cambridge: Cambridge University Press, 1988.

Katz, Joseph, and Rudolph H. Weingartner. *Philosophy in the West: Readings in Ancient and Medieval*, with new translations by John Wellmuth and John Wilkinson. New York: Harcourt, Brace and World, 1965.

McKeon, Richard, ed. and trans. *Selections from Medieval Philosophers*. New York: Scribner's, 1929–30.

Shapiro, Herman, *Medieval Philosophy: Selected Readings from Augustine to Buridan*. New York: Modern Library, 1964.

PIERRE DE BEAUVAIS

PIERRE DE BEAUVAIS (fl. early 13th c.). Little is known of Pierre de Beauvais other than what can be surmised from his writings. In the early part of the 13th century, he lived at the abbey of Saint-Denis outside Paris and in the city of Beauvais. There, he found protectors in the Dreux family, with Philippe, bishop of Beauvais, and his brother, Count Robert. In the episcopal palace, Pierre de Beauvais was able to devote himself to writing, composing saints' lives and other works of theological or moral inspiration. He is best known for his prose *Bestiaire divin*, dedicated to Philippe de Dreux, which is a close translation of the Latin *Physiologus*. Two versions of the *Bestiaire divin* are known. The shorter and earlier version (before 1206) comprises thirty-eight chapters in which the nature and attributes of beasts and birds, not all of them real, are used to teach lessons in Christian morality. This didactic approach is also used in the seventy-one chapters of the longer version, whose attribution to Pierre is not certain. At about the same time, Pierre completed a translation of the *Iter Hierosolymitanum*, the *Voyage de Charlemagne en Orient*.

In verse, Pierre de Beauvais composed a *Mappemonde* (954 lines) dedicated to Robert. It claims to be based on the *De naturis rerum* of Solinus (3rd c.), which Simon de Boulogne had translated in the late 12th century, but is actually a translation of Honorius of Autun's *Imago mundi*. Other verse works include Lives of SS. Eustache, Germer, and Josse; a treatise on the Psalms; a celebration of Christ the Physician; and a poem on the Three Marys.

Claude J. Fouillade

[**See also:** BESTIARY; GUILLAUME LE CLERC; PHILIPPE DE THAÜN]

Bianciotto, Gabriel, trans. *Pierre de Beauvais, Guillaume le Clerc, Richard de Fournival, Brunetto Latini, Corbechon: bestiaires du moyen âge*. Paris: Stock, 1980.

Langlois, Charles-Victor. *La vie en France au moyen âge, du XIIe au milieu du XIVe siècle*. 4 vols. Paris: Hachette, 1926–28, Vol. 3: *La connaissance de la nature et du monde*, pp. 122–34. [Summary of *Mappemonde*.]

PIERRE DE CHELLES

PIERRE DE CHELLES (fl. late 13th–early 14th c.). In royal accounts for 1307, Pierre de Chelles was paid for six months of work on the tomb of Philip III and its delivery to the abbey of Saint-Denis. However, Pierre's contribution is uncertain: did he continue sculptural work of Jean d'Arras (d. 1298/99) on the effigy of the late king, or did he make its black-marble base and the canopy framing the recumbent figure? Whatever the ambiguities of his activity as a sculptor, Pierre de Chelles indisputably pursued a career as a master mason. The 1316 report at Chartres cathedral qualifies him as master of the fabric at Notre-Dame, Paris, while other texts name him as "master of the work of Paris" and "master of the city and suburbs of Paris." During his tenure at Notre-Dame, ca. 1296 to ca. 1318, Pierre supervised construction of the fifteen chapels that ring the eastern extremity of the chevet and the north wall of the sculpted choir enclosure. He may also have been responsible for the design of the Virgin Chapel at Saint-Mathurin, Larchant. Pierre based his chapels, with their huge windows and delicate gables, on the work of his predecessors, Jean de Chelles and Pierre de Montreuil. At the same time, his emphasis on the contrast of a robust armature of piers and arches with flat surfaces of tracery as well as his syncopated formal rhythms anticipate directions explored by later generations of Gothic builders.

Michael T. Davis

Aubert, Marcel. "Les architectes de Notre-Dame de Paris." *Bulletin monumental* 72 (1908): 427–41.

———. *Notre-Dame de Paris: sa place dans l'histoire de l'architecture du XIIe au XIVe siècle*. Paris: Laurens, 1929.

Erlande-Brandenburg, Alain. *Le roi est mort: étude sur les funerailles, les sépultures, et les tombeaux des rois de France jusqu'à la fin du XIIIe siècle*. Geneva: Droz, 1975.

Gillerman, Dorothy. *The Clôture of Notre-Dame and Its Role in the Fourteenth Century Choir Program*. New York: Garland, 1977.

Henriet, Jacques. "La chapelle de la Vierge de Saint-Mathurin de Larchant: une œuvre de Pierre de Chelles?" *Bulletin monumental* 136 (1978): 35–47.

Mortet, Victor. "L'expertise de la cathédrale de Chartres en 1316." *Congrès archéologique (Chartres)* 67 (1900): 309–29.

PIERRE DE LA CROIX

PIERRE DE LA CROIX (Petrus de Cruce; fl. 1280–1310). Composer and music theorist. Pierre's treatise *Tractatus de tonis* deals with plainchant. The English theorist Robert de

Handlo in his *Regule* (1326) attributed a treatise on mensural theory to him, which has not survived. Documents of the royal treasury indicate that a *maître Pierre de la Croix d'Amiens* completed an *hystoria* of St. Louis in 1297, the year Louis IX was canonized. The sole source for his plainchant treatise also described Pierre as being from Amiens. Jacques de Liège commented in the seventh book of his *Speculum musicae* upon two of Pierre's motets, *S'amours eust/Au renouveler du joli tans/Ecce* and *Aucun ont trouvé/Lonc tans me sui tenu/Annuntiates*, both of which appear at the beginning of the seventh fascicle of the Montpellier codex. Petronian notation, characterized as the first modification of Franconian mensural notation because it allowed as many as seven semibreves to be sung in the time of a breve, has been viewed at times as merely ornamental and at others as an evolutionary basis for the Ars Nova. Identification of Pierre de la Croix with the Petrus Picardus to whom Jerome of Moravia attributed the Franconian treatise *Ars motettorum* is doubtful, and there is no evidence that the anonymous *Ars cantus mensurabilis secundum Franconem* is his lost treatise on mensural theory.

Sandra Pinegar

[See also: FRANCO OF COLOGNE; JACQUES DE LIÈGE; MOTET (13TH CENTURY); MUSICAL NOTATION (12TH-15TH CENTURIES]

Lefferts, Peter M., ed. *Robertus de Handlo, Regule and Johannes Hanboys, Summa*. Lincoln: University of Nebraska Press, 1991, pp. 17–20.
Pierre de La Croix. *Petrus de Cruce Ambianensi, Tractatus de tonis*, ed. Denis Harbinson. N.p.: American Institute of Musicology, 1976.
Huglo, Michel. "De Francon de Cologne à Jacques de Liège." *Revue belge de musicologie* 34–35 (1980–81): 44–60.
Rokseth, Yvonne, ed. *Polyphonies du XIIIe siècle: le manuscrit H 196 de la Faculté de Médecine de Montpellier*. Paris: Oiseau Lyre, 1933–39, Vol. 4, p. 79 n. 5.

PIERRE DE MONTREUIL (d. 1267). Pierre de Montreuil is the most celebrated French master mason of the 13th century. He has been credited with the construction of every major building in Paris between 1230 and 1270, including the abbey of Saint-Denis and the Sainte-Chapelle. Unquestionably the master mason of the refectory, begun in 1239, and the Virgin Chapel, built from 1245, of the abbey of Saint-Germain-des-Prés, Pierre created an architecture marked by spatial unity, luminosity, and rich rhythms of tracery forms meticulously organized in depth. In the Virgin Chapel, his combination of fully colored windows with *grisaille* glass was the first example of a concept of glazing generalized in the later 13th century. A 1247 document naming Pierre as a *cementarius* (or stone mason) at Saint-Denis suggests that, although active at the abbey, he did not head its workshop and cannot be credited with the design of the Rayonnant structure. Referred to as "mason, master of the works at Notre-Dame of Paris" (*cementarius, magister operum Beate Marie Parisiensiis*) in 1265, Pierre built the cathedral's south-transept façade.

This brilliant work was inspired by Jean de Chelles's north transept but achieved greater unity through the physical linkage of different zones and the formal relationships produced by new motifs, such as the pointed trilobe. Pierre de Montreuil died March 17, 1267. The inscription from his tomb in the Virgin Chapel of Saint-Germain-des-Prés, which lionizes him as " a teacher of masons," testifies to contemporary recognition of his architectural abilities.

Michael T. Davis

Aubert, Marcel. "Pierre de Montreuil, architecte de Saint-Germain-des-Prés et de Notre-Dame de Paris, de Saint-Denis et de la Sainte-Chapelle." In *Festschrift für Karl M. Swoboda*. Vienna, 1959, pp. 19–21.
Branner, Robert. *Saint-Louis and the Court Style in Gothic Architecture*. London: Zwemmer, 1965.
———. "A Note on Pierre de Montreuil." *Art Bulletin* 45 (1963): 355–57.
Bruzelius, Caroline A. *The 13th-Century Church at St-Denis*. New Haven: Yale University Press, 1985.
Grodecki, Louis. "Pierre, Eudes, et Raoul de Montreuil à l'abbatiale de Saint-Denis." *Bulletin monumental* 122 (1964): 269–74.
Prache, Anne. "Pierre de Montreuil." *Histoire et archéologie. Dossiers* 47 (1980): 26–39.
Suckale, Robert. "Pierre de Montreuil." In *Les bâtisseurs des cathédrales gothiques*, ed. Roland Recht. Strasbourg: Éditions les Musées de la Ville de Strasbourg, 1989, pp. 181–85.

PIERRE DE PROVENCE ET LA BELLE MAGUELONNE. A short hagiographical account in prose of the founding of a hospital at Maguelone, south of Montpellier. Cast as an idyllic romance, *Pierre de Provence* was composed in the first half of the 15th century. It exists in two Middle French redactions (the second and longer dated 1453), a 1480 printed edition, as well as several German adaptations.

William W. Kibler

[See also: IDYLLIC ROMANCE]

Biedermann, Adolphe, ed. *Pierre de Provence et la Belle Maguelonne*. Paris: Champion, 1913.

PIERRE DE SAINT-CLOUD (fl. late 12th c.). This skillful and cultured poet brought the adventures of Renart the Fox, known previously only in Latin, to a wider, French-speaking public. The two earliest branches of the *Roman de Renart*, II and Va (ca. 1174–77), which relate the love affair of Renart and Hersent the she-wolf, are attributed to him. Though he imitated *Ysengrimus* for three episodes ("Renart and Chantecler," "Renart and the Titmouse," "Renart and Hersent") and Marie de France for another ("The Fox and the Crow"), "Renart and Tibert the Cat" is his own invention. He pokes fun at the legal system, pontifical legates and certain religious institutions, princes and nobles, through a subtle parody, intended largely to evoke laughter, of the chansons de geste and Arthurian romance. He was read and imitated by French and foreign authors of beast epics, such as Jacquemart Gielée, Heinrich der

Glîchezâre, and Chaucer), by fabulists and writers of exempla (Eudes de Cheriton, Nicole Bozon, Jacques de Vitry), and by Philippe de Novare. After 1180, he assisted Alexandre de Paris in reworking the *Roman d'Alexandre* into dodecasyllabic *laisses*.

Jean Dufournet

[See also: *RENART, ROMAN DE*]

Flinn, John. *Le roman de Renart dans la littérature française et dans les littératures étrangères au moyen âge.* Toronto: University of Toronto Press, 1963.

PIERRE MAUCLERC (ca. 1189/90–1250). Pierre de Dreux (or de Braine), better known as Pierre Mauclerc, was a member of the distinguished Dreux family, a cadet branch of the Capetian line. He was a younger son of Louis VII's nephew Robert II, count of the small fiefs of Dreux and Braine. Although not a landless baron, Pierre's original endowment of lands from his father was small, the villas and manors of Fère-en-Tardenois, Brie-Comte-Robert, Chilly, and Longjumeau. By his marriage in 1212 to Alix, the heiress of Brittany and claimant to the English honor of Richmond, however, he became titular earl of Richmond and titular duke of Brittany (or count, in the view of French authorities unwilling to acknowledge Brittany's ducal status).

Pierre immediately set about imposing his will on the fiercely independent Breton baronage, exacting reliefs and wardships contrary to custom, despoiling or seizing seigneuries whose lords resisted, and commencing a concerted attack against the privileges of the episcopate. This last action precipitated his excommunication and, in retaliation, his expulsion of six of the seven bishops of Brittany. Although his wife died in 1221, he continued as guard (*custos*) and effective ruler of Brittany until his son came of age in late 1237.

Knighted in 1209 by Philip II Augustus, Pierre was secure in his position as ruler of Brittany as long as Philip, with whom he got along well, continued to reign. But with the old king's death in 1223, Pierre became a less trustworthy ally of the new king, Louis VIII (r. 1223–26), although he did take part in crusading expeditions against the Albigensian heretics led by Louis as prince (1219) and king (1226). His emerging lack of devotion to royal policies originated partly from his claims to land in England, claims that made him always eager to cultivate the Capetians' traditional enemy, the Plantagenêts. His own overweening ambition to be the preeminent baron in northwest Europe fueled his political maneuvering. After the death of his first wife, he aspired to the hand of the countess of Flanders in 1226 and the queen of Cyprus (who had claims in the great fief of Champagne) in 1229, only to be thwarted by the king and the pope, who had their own interests to preserve in the disposition of the heiresses and their fiefs. He was reduced to marrying a minor baroness, Marguerite de Montaigu, in 1230; and his resentment was strong. He had already become an open rebel in 1227 because of the failure of the regent, Blanche of Castile, to submit to his influence or cede the regency of the young Louis IX. He was instrumental in 1229 in attacking the count of Champagne, a supporter of the regent whose fief Pierre coveted. He courted the favor of the English king, received military support and large subsidies from him, and rebelled against the French crown again in 1230–31 and still again briefly in 1234. In all of these efforts, his forces were soundly thrashed, though never completely eliminated, by the royal troops.

In November 1237, after his son reached majority and took over control of Brittany, Pierre succeeded in consolidating a small lordship around the nucleus of his wife's lands in the Breton-Poitevin march. His subsequent career saw him active as a crusader against the Muslims, an effort that achieved a reconciliation with the papacy (1235) if not with local clerics, whom he continued to harass whenever he was in a position to do so. He served with distinction on the crusade of Thibaut de Navarre (1239–40) and died of illness and wounds in 1250 on the return home from St. Louis's crusade.

William Chester Jordan

[See also: BLANCHE OF CASTILE; BRITTANY; DREUX]

Painter, Sidney. *The Scourge of the Clergy: Peter of Dreux, Duke of Brittany.* Baltimore: Johns Hopkins University Press, 1937.

PILGRIMAGE. Pilgrimage—journeying from one's home to a hallowed site—has a long tradition. In ancient and modern times, and in many cultures and religions, adherents have traveled to venerate holy places, to visit tombs of holy persons or heroes, to seek counsel from oracles or cures.

Although the earliest Christian pilgrimages seem to have been to the Holy Land, the practice of pilgrimage soon expanded to include sites of veneration of the Virgin, martyrs, and saints. Of particular importance for early Christian pilgrimage and its development in France was the growth of the cult of saints. Early Christianity introduced the concept of Heaven and Earth joined at the tomb of a saint, who was a martyr or holy person seen as able to intercede with God on behalf of humans. The bodies of saints, left on earth to aid the living, could work miracles, just as the saint, or Christ himself, had done while alive. Thus, relics—the physical remains, or closely associated objects, of the holy person—formed the *sine qua non* of the shrine to which pilgrims journeyed.

Well over 1,000 centers of pilgrimage existed in France from the Gallo-Roman period to the end of the Middle Ages. Relics at shrines varied greatly, and many shrines, such as Aix-la-Chapelle, contained a large number. Cultic shrines also developed around miraculous statues of the Virgin (Rocamadour [12th c.] and Mauriac [13th c.]), as well as at sites designated as holy through supernatural apparitions (the Virgin at Rocheville [14th c.] or the archangel Michael at Mont-Saint-Michel [8th c.]).

A number of important shrines are located at places of great height (Le Puy) or near springs (Conques). Some were erected over pagan sanctuaries and Gallo-Roman healing centers. Some Christian shrines were known as particularly efficacious for specific healing, such as Sainte-Foy at Conques for eye ailments and the church of John the Baptist at Saint-Denis for epilepsy.

Pilgrimage was motivated by a variety of reasons. Besides being an act of piety and veneration, a pilgrimage might be undertaken for remission of sins or for purification and absolution and, from the 6th century at least, could be imposed as penance. Many went on pilgrimage seeking miracles and cures or to give thanks for divine assistance. Some went to shrines to die in the presence of relics.

Kings, queens, nobles, and high ecclesiastics have been recorded as pilgrims through the centuries, but shrines attracted untold numbers of ordinary folk, especially in times of calamity like plagues and civil unrest. For the ordinary pilgrim, a journey to a shrine within France had the advantages of requiring less cost and less time than the great international pilgrimages to the Holy Land, Rome, or Santiago de Compostela.

By the 12th century, pilgrims set out from their home parishes after receiving special blessings, and they wore clothing that identified them as pilgrims. Customary garb was a cloak, a low-crowned and broad-brimmed hat, a pouch (called a "scrip"), and a pilgrim's staff. Pilgrims carried letters from ecclesiastical authorities to identify them officially for their protection, although their efficacy was not always certain.

Most pilgrimages were made on foot, but those wealthy enough could travel by horse. Walking barefoot was not common, although some penitents and pious pilgrims did so. Louis IX is said to have walked barefoot about 15 miles to Chartres. Travel on roads was especially dangerous in some periods (the 7th to mid-11th centuries, in particular) due to civil unrest, invasions, and robbery.

Food and water could be brought from home if the pilgrimage was for only a few days, but if the pilgrim was away longer resources had to be found along the roads. During periods of civil unrest and invasions, this was not always easy, nor were accommodations always to be found. A system of hospices for pilgrims within France is not apparent before the late 11th century, when the Augustinians were active in establishing shelters, especially in inhospitable regions. The Templars, by the 12th century, also provided assistance to pilgrims, and by the 13th century many confraternities were organized to help. By the 12th century, inns were no longer so difficult to find. Accommodations could be difficult even when the shrine was reached. Pilgrims to Rocamadour were frequently sheltered in tents because the town was so small; in other towns, like Vézelay, conflict arose between the inhabitants and the abbey over pilgrims' accommodations.

Pilgrims brought gifts and tokens with them to shrines. In keeping with the practice at pre-Christian healing centers in Gaul, pilgrims seeking a cure for an illness might bring to the saint's shrine a representation of the afflicted part of the body, frequently crudely made of wood, wax, or metal. If Christian pilgrims were making their pilgrimage to thank the holy patron for a cure, they might also bring such a token as well as gifts (frequently money, gold, gems, or oil). Pilgrims to Saint-Léonard-de-Noblat who were freed from prison after praying to St. Léonard brought their chains to hang near the saint's tomb.

In addition to leaving offerings at shrines, pilgrims brought away objects in some way sanctified by relics. In some instances, these relics-by-association were thought to possess the power of the saint. While on pilgrimage to the shrine of St. Julian of Brioude, Gregory of Tours broke off a piece of the tomb and brought it back to Tours, where it was reported to have worked miracles. Pilgrims also brought away badges to indicate they had been to shrines. These had images symbolic of the shrine visited, as the head of John the Baptist for Amiens, the Virgin for Rocamadour, Le Puy, and other Marian sanctuaries. Trade in pilgrims' badges was so extensive and open to abuse that it was regulated by legal and episcopal decrees by the 13th century.

The earliest Christian pilgrimages were those to the Holy Land to retrace the footsteps of Christ (2nd c.) and to Rome to visit the tombs of Peter, Paul, and the martyrs. Pilgrimage within France was enhanced by these distant journeys, because pilgrims from the British Isles, Spain, and the Low Countries traveled through France on the way to Rome, and Marseille and Saint-Gilles-du-Gard were major ports of embarkation for ships to Rome and the Holy Land. One of the earliest extant itineraries of a Jerusalem pilgrimage was left by a Gallo-Roman from Bordeaux traveling ca. 333. He gives the route taken from Bordeaux to the Holy Land, indicating the stopping places along the way.

Pilgrimage to shrines within France was well established in the Gallo-Roman and Merovingian periods. Most early sanctuaries seem to be centered in established Gallo-Roman towns with Christian communities, or those where early missionary-martyrs preached. The best-documented early shrine is that of St. Martin (d. 397/400) at Tours. Known for miracles worked during his lifetime, his *vita* was written while he was still alive by his friend Sulpicius Severus (ca. 360–420/25) but was not published until after Martin's death. So many pilgrims came to his tomb that the small chapel built after his death was replaced by a larger church within a century. An account of his miracles was written by Gregory of Tours (ca. 539–594), and by the end of the 6th century Martin's tomb contained the inscription "Here lies Martin the Bishop, of holy memory, whose soul is in the hand of God; but he is fully here, present and made plain in miracles of every kind." The town, and especially the saint's shrine, remained a major pilgrimage center throughout the Middle Ages.

Another Gallo-Roman city with important shrines was Lyon, which had an active Christian community from the end of the 2nd century. The city had early bishops' shrines (St. Irenaeus, St. Justus) as well as sanctuaries of martyrs (Epipodius, Alexander). Nearby at Fourvières was a shrine dedicated to the Virgin, where previously a statue of Mercury had been venerated. Limoges had a sanctuary dedicated to St. Martial (known from the 4th c.), and other shrines were located in the cities of Arles, Auxerre, Marseille, Dijon, Clermont, Cahors, Agde, and Paris. During this early period, relics were also imported from Rome. In 397, Victor of Rouen brought relics of twenty-three martyrs from Rome to Rouen.

Relics were so important in the conversion of pagan Gaul that parts, and entire bodies, of saints were bought, sold, and stolen. Augustine mentions relic sellers in the 5th century, and Gregory of Tours writes about Syrian relic mongers in France in the 6th. In the 7th century, the body of St. Benedict of Nursia was stolen from Monte Cassino after the abbey was destroyed by the Lombards and brought to Fleury (which became Saint-Benoît-sur-Loire), where his relics attracted pilgrims until the 11th century, when the monks of Monte Cassino claimed to have found the true relics still at their abbey.

The establishment of sanctuaries and pilgrimages to shrines continued throughout the tempestuous reigns of the Merovingians, who supported such shrines. Clovis (d. 511) had a shrine built over the tomb of St. Geneviève (d. ca. 500) in Paris, and Dagobert (d. ca. 639) has been credited with revitalizing the shrine of St. Denis, who became the patron saint of France. It is also from the Merovingian period that the early Marian pilgrimage to Ambronay in Burgundy is dated (7th c.), and we begin to see the establishment of shrines in rural monastic settings.

The ever-increasing interest in sanctuaries and pilgrimages received impetus during the Carolingian dynasty. Charlemagne was an ardent collector of relics, which were kept at Aix-la-Chapelle (Aachen). The most important, the swaddling clothes and loincloth of Christ, were exhibited once every seven years and attracted hordes of pilgrims. Carolingian aristocrats also donated relics: Charles the Bald gave the Virgin's tunic to Chartres in 876, from which time the pilgrimage to the cathedral can be dated.

Even more important for the history of pilgrimage, the Carolingian hierarchy reinstated the ruling, first decreed at the Fifth Council of Carthage in 401, that required all altars to contain relics. This necessitated the procuring of more relics than were present in the Frankish kingdoms, and Carolingian ecclesiastics were major movers in procuring saints' bodies and other relics, especially from Rome but also from Spain. For example, in the early 9th century, Abbot Hilduin acquired the body of St. Sebastian from Rome for Saint-Médard in Soissons.

Trade in relics flourished, and the frequency of theft increased, with more than fifty documented instances from 800 to 1100. Among the most famous of these thefts in the Frankish lands were that of St. Foy's body, stolen from Agen by a monk of Conques in the 860s, and that of Mary Magdalene's, said to have been stolen from Provence and brought to Vézelay in the late 9th century. Both became objects of major pilgrimages.

Despite the political fragmentation after the collapse of the Carolingian empire and the incursions of the Vikings, pilgrimage to sites of cultic worship increased during the 9th and 10th centuries. By the 11th century, the cult of relics and pilgrimage were major aspects of religious practice, and they provided important sources of financial support for French monasticism. Funds brought in by pilgrims helped in the ambitious building projects begun in the 11th century by many monastic houses.

Typical of this development is Mont-Saint-Michel. Pilgrimage to this sanctuary began after an apparition of the archangel Michael to Aubert of Avranches while the bishop slept (708). The archangel directed the bishop to build a sanctuary at the top of Mont-Tombe, a granite rock some 550 feet high in the bay near Avranches. A small sanctuary was built and relics were received from the archangel's shrine on Monte Gargano in Italy. By the 11th century, the structure at the top of the mountain was inadequate for pilgrims, and construction of the massive hilltop abbey was begun. By the 12th century, additional lodgings were added, and the lower town began to grow. The 13th century saw Gothic additions to the monastery. The town increased in size each successive century, moving farther up the mount to meet the abbey perched on top.

The 12th century saw ever-greater numbers of people going on pilgrimage. Without doubt, the Crusades popularized the idea of pilgrimage. It was, however, the enormous popularity of the pilgrimage to Santiago de Compostela in Spain that increased the numbers of pilgrims traveling through France and visiting shrines on the route. The tomb of St. James, discovered at Compostela in the northwest corner of Spain in the 9th century, saw its first recorded French pilgrim, Godescalc of Le Puy, in 950–51. Large numbers of pilgrims from all over Europe were arriving by the end of the 11th century, and except for those traveling by sea almost all had to go through France.

The earliest western European guidebook for pilgrims was written by a Frenchman (ca. 1135–39) for those going from France to Compostela. The author gives four routes through France toward Spain, mostly following old Roman roads. Each route began at a major cultic center: Paris, Vézelay, Le Puy, or Arles. The three westernmost routes met at Ostabat and crossed the Pyrénées at Roncevaux, while the route from Arles crossed the Somport pass farther east. Hospices at both passes existed from the late 11th or early 12th century.

A forerunner of the modern travel guide, the text of this guidebook provides information on where to find provisions and drinking water, describes the characteristics of the peoples to be encountered along the way, and provides cautionary tales on the location of thieves and other hazards, as well as instruction on the proper treatment of pilgrims. Of importance for French pilgrimage is a long chapter describing twenty-one shrines in France (and four in Spain) to be visited along the way. It is clear that those on long pilgrimages would visit many shrines and that shrines with important relics located on major pilgrimage routes could benefit greatly. Competition for pilgrims and the funds they donated was so strong during the 12th century that some institutions resorted to advertising to attract pilgrims. The Norman abbey of the Trinity at Fécamp had a vial of Christ's blood by 1120, which they advertised in a poem: ". . . remember that you are never far from Fécamp, where the Lord has sent his precious blood for your benefit. . . ."

The late 11th, 12th, and 13th centuries appear to have been the high point of pilgrimage in France, coinciding with a period when roads were safest and travel most se-

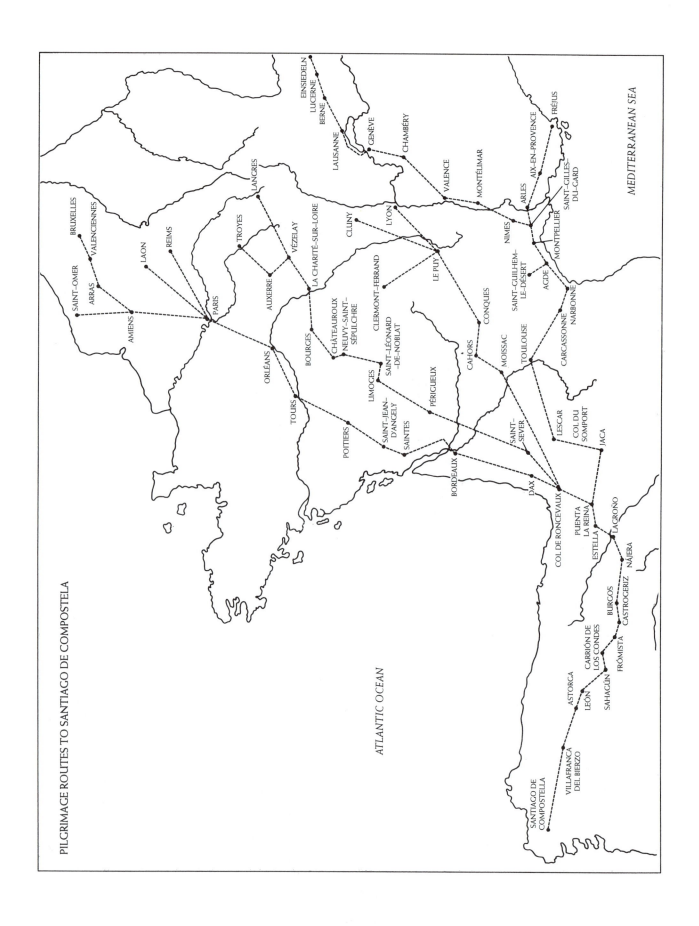

PILGRIMAGE ROUTES TO SANTIAGO DE COMPOSTELA

MEDITERRANEAN SEA

ATLANTIC OCEAN

EINSIEDELN
LUCERNE
BERNE
LAUSANNE
GENÈVE
CHAMBÉRY
FRÉJUS
AIX-EN-PROVENCE
ARLES
SAINT-GILLES–DU-GARD
VALENCE
MONTÉLIMAR
NÎMES
MONTPELLIER
LYON
CLUNY
LANGRES
BRUXELLES
VALENCIENNES
REIMS
TROYES
VÉZELAY
LA CHARITÉ-SUR-LOIRE
LE PUY
SAINT-GUILHEM-LE-DÉSERT
AGDE
NARBONNE
SAINT-OMER
ARRAS
LAON
AMIENS
PARIS
AUXERRE
BOURGES
CHÂTEAUROUX
NEUVY-SAINT-SÉPULCHRE
CLERMONT-FERRAND
CONQUES
CARCASSONNE
SAINT-LÉONARD–DE-NOBLAT
CAHORS
MOISSAC
TOULOUSE
ORLÉANS
LIMOGES
PÉRIGUEUX
TOURS
SAINT-JEAN-D'ANGELY
SAINTES
SAINT-SEVER
LESCAR
COL DU SOMPORT
JACA
POITIERS
BORDEAUX
DAX
COL DE RONCEVAUX
PUENTA LA REINA
LOGROÑO
ESTELLA
NÁJERA
BURGOS
CASTROGERIZ
FRÓMISTA
CARRIÓN DE LOS CONDES
SAHAGÚN
LEÓN
ASTORGA
VILLAFRANCA DEL BIERZO
SANTIAGO DE COMPOSTELA

cure. The Hundred Years' War impeded traffic on roads, and while pilgrimage remained an important aspect of late-medieval religion, private devotion seems to have offered greater consolation.

The later Middle Ages witnessed a decline in the cult of saints and an increasing veneration of the Virgin. Relics of Mary, discovered with greater frequency from the 12th century on, stimulated pilgrimages. Relics of the Virgin's hair were found at, or acquired by, Coutances, Saint-Omer, Mâcon, Sainte-Chapelle, and Saint-Denis. In addition to Mary's tunic at Chartres (9th c.), one finds her slipper at Soissons, as well as other pieces of clothing at Marseille, Toulon, and Arles. Relics at other sanctuaries included the Virgin's milk and nail parings. While pilgrimages to sites of the apparition of the Virgin are known in the later Middle Ages (as at Rocheville, 1315), they are a much more common manifestation of postmedieval religiosity.

Paula L. Gerson

[See also: AGDE; CHARTRES; CONQUES; COUTANCES; LE PUY; *LIBER SANCTI JACOBI;* MARSEILLE; MARTIN OF TOURS; MARY, LITURGICAL VENERATION OF; MARY MAGDELENE; MONT-SAINT-MICHEL; PARIS; POPULAR DEVOTION; RELICS AND RELIQUARIES; ROCAMADOUR; SAINT-DENIS; SAINTS, CULT OF; SOISSONS; TOURS/TOURAINE; TRAVEL; VÉZELAY]

Gregory of Tours. *The History of the Franks*, trans. Lewis Thorpe. Harmondsworth: Penguin, 1974.

Brown, Peter. *The Cult of the Saints: Its Rise and Function in Latin Christianity*. Chicago: University of Chicago Press, 1981.

Cohen, Esther. "*In haec signa*: Pilgrim Badge Trade in Southern France." *Journal of Medieval History* 2 (1976): 193–214.

Davidson, Linda K., and Maryjane Dunn-Wood. *Pilgrimage in the Middle Ages: A Research Guide*. New York: Garland, 1993.

Gauthier, Nancy, and Jean-Charles Picard, eds. *Topographie chrétienne des cités de la Gaule: des origines au milieu du VIIIe siècle*. 8 vols. Paris: Boccard, 1986–90.

Geary, Patrick J. *Furta Sacra: Thefts of Relics in the Central Middle Ages*. 2nd ed. Princeton: Princeton University Press, 1990.

Sivry, Louis de, and Jean-Baptiste-Joseph Champagnac. *Dictionnaire géographique, historique, descriptif, archéologique des pèlerinages anciens et modernes et des lieux de dévotion les plus célèbres de l'univers*. 2 vols. Paris: Migne, 1850–51.

Sumption, Jonathan. *Pilgrimage: An Image of Mediaeval Religion*. Totowa: Rowman and Littlefield, 1975.

Turner, Edith and Victor. *Image and Pilgrimage in Christian Culture: Anthropological Perspectives*. New York: Columbia University Press, 1978.

PLAGUE. *See* BLACK DEATH

PLANH/COMPLAINTE. Dating from 1137 to 1343, over forty *planhs*, or Occitan funeral laments in lyric form, have survived. Most of them are on the death of a powerful man, a few on the death of a relative or friend of the poet, and a few on the death of his lady. The topoi of the genre are ritualized in a tradition descending from the Latin *planctus*, but the grief that the songs express need not be considered insincere. In some *planhs*, the poet grieves for the loss of his patron, but he almost never praises the expected successor, as he might do if his motivation were thoroughly materialistic. In other *planhs*, the poet's grief is disinterested, as when the nobleman Guilhem de Berguedà grieves generously for his enemy Pons de Mataplana, or when Bertran de Born grieves for Henry, the Young King. The practice of metrical imitation, by which one song was set to the tune and metrical form of another (most often a *canso*, or love song), originated in the *sirventes*, or satire, and spread to the *planh* but was never considered obligatory. The generic status of the *planh* is ensured by its codification in the *Doctrina de compondre dictatz* (ca. 1290–1300) and in the *Leys d'Amors* (1341).

The French *complainte*, unlike the *planh*, is not a lyric genre but a thematic one in didactic or narrative form, written in nonlyric stanzas or in octosyllabic couplets and often influenced by the *Vers de la Mort* of Hélinant de Froidmont (ca. 1193–97). The *complainte* is attested from 1226 (Robert de Saincériaux on the death of Louis VIII) through the anonymous *Regrés de la mort saint Loys* (1270), several poems by Rutebeuf, and Alain Chartier's lament for the death of his lady, among other texts; it continued to be cultivated as late as the Grands Rhétoriqueurs.

The theme of the funeral lament has also been studied in its occurrences in narrative verse, both epic and romance.

William D. Paden

[See also: HÉLINANT DE FROIDMONT; PRAYERS AND DEVOTIONAL MATERIALS]

Schulze-Busacker, Elisabeth. "Étude typologique de la complainte des morts dans le roman arthurien en vers du 12e au 14e siècle." In *An Arthurian Tapestry: Essays in Memory of Lewis Thorpe*, ed. Kenneth Varty. Glasgow: French Department of the University of Glasgow, 1981, pp. 54–68.

Stäblein, Patricia H. "New Views on an Old Problem: The Dynamics of Death in the *Planh.*" *Romance Philology* 35 (1981): 223–34.

Thiry, Claude. "De la mort marâtre à la mort vaincue: attitudes devant la mort dans la déploration funèbre française." In *Death in the Middle Ages*, ed. Herman Braet and Werner Verbeke. Leuven: Leuven University Press, 1983, pp. 239–57.

———. *La plainte funèbre*. Turnhout: Brepols, 1978.

PLATO, INFLUENCE OF. The Athenian philosopher Plato (427–347 B.C.), pupil of Socrates and teacher of Aristotle, is undoubtedly the most influential non-Christian thinker in the history of Christian philosophy. Although Plato's own works were not well known—by the 13th century, only his *Timaeus* (translated by Calcidius) and *Phaedo* and *Meno* (both translated by Aristippus) were available in Latin—Platonic ideas and style were endemic in all learned minds, made known by Calcidius's *Commentary on the Timaeus,* Apuleius's *Golden Ass,* Macrobius's commentary on the *Somnium Scipionis,* and the works of Boethius, especially his *De consolatione Philosophiae.*

Two early Christian authors in particular, Augustine and Pseudo-Dionysius the Areopagite, were highly influenced by Platonist thinkers, especially Plotinus (*Enneads*), Porphyry (*Isagoge*), and Proclus. Plotinus (ca. A.D. 205–270) was responsible for a development of Plato's ideas in specifically religious, although non-Christian, terms, and it is his system, known as Neoplatonism, that spread Platonic ideas throughout Christianity. Neoplatonism held there to be a dualism between thought and reality, which could only be unified in God, who is One, a being with its center everywhere and its circumference nowhere. This being could be known by mystical experience.

Augustine's work is suffused with Neoplatonic ideas. His early Manichaean beliefs, with their emphasis on the division of body and spirit, light and darkness, are Platonic in content as well as tone, as is Pseudo-Dionysius's *Celestial Hierarchy.* In this Christian Platonism, Creation is seen as patterned after the Ideas in the mind of God. Their earthly forms are mere shadows of their real selves, existing in the divine intellect.

The largest single outcrop of Neoplatonism is usually said to have occurred in the works of the scholars of Chartres, in the 12th century; but the ideas had been kept alive in the Carolingian renaissance, especially by Johannes Scottus Eriugena, whose use of Maximus the Confessor and the *Celestial Hierarchy* created a somewhat singular and unorthodox Christian cosmology and anthropology. The Chartrians are usually said to have promulgated a Neoplatonic cosmology, but what exactly this may mean is a moot point. Orthodox Christian teaching did not allow for a separation between body and spirit, or indeed of any of the Platonic divisions between light and darkness, good and evil, and the like. Rather, in typical medieval fashion, Chartrian cosmology attempts to express the unity of Truth and Creation. "Oneness" is crucial to being: in Boethius's words, "everything that is, is because it is one."

There are particular difficulties in tracing the influence of Plato in the Middle Ages. Patristic writers were saturated with Platonic influences, which were often inseparable from the rest of the usual, classically educated mind; and although some Platonic distinctions, such as that highlighted by Calcidius among the supreme God, the mind of God (the place of Ideas), and the World Soul (fate; identified by William of Conches with the Holy Spirit), were identifiable, much that is Platonic can be seen only in style and tone rather than content. Perhaps as influential as its content was the *form* of the *Timaeus*—philosophy by myth and metaphor. Plato, with his language of surface and integument, of fable and hidden truth, supported the rationale of Christian biblical exegesis. And Chartrian cosmology was intended, in Platonist fashion, to prefigure a new moral order: from the macrocosm of the universe to the microcosm of the soul.

The long-running debate over universals—whether general concepts ("universals") have reality (a view called "realism") or are simply convenient names ("nominal-ism")—originated in Neoplatonism and the question of Forms. Translation of the works of Aristotle and the introduction of Arabic philosophy, Neoplatonist in style, into the early 13th-century University of Paris did not bring about a corresponding decrease in the influence of Plato. Augustine continued to be the most influential Christian theologian, and some "Aristotelian" works, in particular the *Isagoge* of Porphyry and the *Liber de causis* (pure Proclus), were themselves infused with Neoplatonist ideas.

Lesley J. Smith

[See also: ARISTOTLE, INFLUENCE OF; CHARTRES; PHILOSOPHY; PSEUDO-DIONYSIUS THE AREOPAGITE]

POIRE, ROMAN DE LA. Composed ca. 1250 by an unknown poet who calls himself Tibaut, the *Roman de la Poire* (3,034 lines) is a lyrical romance strongly influenced by the *Roman de la Rose* of Guillaume de Lorris. The author tells how he falls secretly in love, how Love sends his heart to his lady, how she reciprocates, and how they further their love through an exchange of lyric pieces. The oldest *Poire* manuscript, B.N. fr. 2186, presents the poem as a complete audiovisual experience in which paintings and music complement the text and its word games.

Mary B. Speer

[See also: GUILLAUME DE LORRIS]

Marchello-Nizia, Christiane, ed. *Le roman de la Poire par Tibaut.* Paris: Picard, 1984.

POISSY. The origins of Poissy (Yvelines) lie in the Merovingian period, according to finds in the cemetery, but precise dates are lacking. Helgaud's biography of Robert II the Pious names three churches at Poissy (Notre-Dame, Saint-Jean, and Saint-Martin) and describes the lavish rebuilding of Notre-Dame begun by the king. The new building was dedicated in 1061. The interior of the west tower dates from the later 11th century, and Viollet-le-Duc found bases and fragments of capitals and abacus blocks below the present floor. The present church was begun ca. 1140 by a builder who had worked with the first 12th-century builder at Saint-Denis. The original plan called for an ambulatory with a single axial chapel on a rectangular plan around a deep choir flanked by two chapels set beyond the side aisles. The liturgical choir included three nearly square bays and the apse. The straight bays were marked by heavy compound piers and a three-story elevation (arcades, subdivided openings into the roof space, and low clerestory windows) that recall the west bays at Saint-Denis.

Construction of the nave proceeded slowly toward the west tower. The two westernmost bays were rebuilt in the French Renaissance style, although the contemporary portal opening into them is one of the finer Flamboyant ensembles of the region. Chapels were added to the nave in the 15th century.

Until the Revolution, Poissy also had a famous priory church dedicated to St. Louis, constructed west of Notre-Dame. The choice of Poissy was intentional: Louis IX was born there in 1215, and it was in the church of Notre-Dame that he was baptized. Philip IV the Fair probably decided on Poissy even prior to the bull of canonization in August 1297, because work was already in progress by November 1297. It went quickly, because the church was said to be finished when the monks took possession in 1304. The charters suggest, however, that this was not the case and that construction of the church and the monastic buildings was still ongoing after Philip's death in 1314; the church was solemnly dedicated only in 1331. Plans and drawings made prior to its destruction give a general sense of the building as an intentional look back to buildings directly associated with Louis IX, such as Royaumont and the nave of Saint-Denis. The south transept contained statues of the six children of St. Louis, as well as figures of the king and his queen placed on either side of the choir enclosure. The two remaining ones can be identified by comparison with the Gaignières drawings as Isabelle and Pierre d'Alençon. Two statues of angels, one in the Louvre and the other in the Musée National du Moyen Âge, stood atop columns flanking one of the altars on the eastern side of the jubé.

William W. Clark

[See also: LOUIS IX]

Erlande-Brandenburg, Alain. "La priorale Saint-Louis de Poissy." *Bulletin monumental* 129 (1971): 85–112.

Prache, Anne. *Île-de-France romane*. La Pierre-qui-vire: Zodiaque, 1983.

Saint-Paul, Anthyme. "Poissy et Morienval." *Mémoires de la Société Historique et Archéologique de l'Arrondissement de Pontoise et du Vexin* 16 (1894): 1–21.

Salet, Francis. "Notre-Dame de Poissy." *Congrès archéologique* (*Paris-Mantes*) 104 (1946): 221–68.

POITIERS. The Roman city of Limonum, later Poitiers (Vienne), became the capital of the area corresponding to the tribal lands of the Pictones, who had been conquered by Rome in the first century B.C. Early Christians appeared in the city in the 3rd and 4th centuries, and their first great bishop was St. Hilary (d. 368). A second important early Christian was St. Radegund, the wife of Clotar I, who founded the monastery of Sainte-Croix after retiring to Poitiers ca. 550. It was at Moussais near Poitiers in 732 that Charles Martel met and defeated a Muslim raiding party that was pushing northward into France after having conquered Spain. The advance of the Muslims into southern France threatened the Aquitanians, whose duke, Eudes, having been crushed at Bordeaux, appealed to Charles for aid. The Muslims burned the church of Saint-Hilaire but were decimated by the Frankish cavalry and were eventually chased by Charles Martel and his army back across the Pyrénées. Poitiers and much of Aquitaine passed into Frankish hands as a result.

One of the most important historical, religious, and intellectual centers in France, Poitiers is exceptionally rich

Poitiers (Vienne), Baptistry of Saint-Jean, east side. *Photograph courtesy of Whitney S. Stoddard.*

in monuments, the oldest of which are the hypogeum of Abbot Mellébaude in the Faubourg Saint-Saturnin (7th c.) and the former baptistery of Saint-Jean, a 7th-century Merovingian structure on 4th-century foundations (pre-Romanesque narthex, Romanesque frescoes). The majority of the city's extant churches date from the Romanesque period.

The plans of both Saint-Hilaire-le-Grand and Sainte-Radegonde were determined in part (elevated sanctuary above the crypt, ambulatory, and radiating chapels) by their early prominence as pilgrimage shrines. The oldest portions of the church of Saint-Hilaire-le-Grand (dedicated 1049), built over the tomb of the celebrated bishop, are the lower part of the once isolated bell tower and the transept. The present chevet and eastern-transept apsidioles followed, the tower was incorporated into the structure, and the width of the original nave (alternating columns and piers) was reduced by the erection of additional supports to carry the curious stone cupolas. Remarkable are the vaulting of the tower, the carved corbels and metopes, the 11th-century capitals, and the frescoes of the bishops of Poitiers (12th c.). The crypt (ambulatory, three radiating chapels) of the church of Sainte-Radegonde (1099) houses the venerated tomb of the queen of the Franks. A 13th-century aisleless nave with Angevin vaults links the Romanesque chevet (carved capitals) with the majestic tower porch. The present portal is Flamboyant Gothic; within the porch are two reliefs (Christ blessing and a seated St. Radegund or the Virgin). Stained-glass windows include episodes from the life of St. Radegund.

Despite its name, the former collegiate church of Notre-Dame-la-Grande (late 11th–early 12th c.) is relatively small, yet its lavishly sculptured screen façade and harmoniously proportioned crossing tower are among the most famous in western France. In typically "Poitevin" format, the pronounced horizontals of the three-storied façade are framed by vertical clusters of columns supporting open-arcaded corner turrets with conical roofs. A frieze of Old and New

Poitiers, Notre-Dame-la-Grande, façade. *Photograph courtesy of Whitney S. Stoddard.*

Testament scenes and personages, evoking the Fall and the Incarnation, fills the area above the three elaborately decorated arches of the lower story. Between the corbel tables, a large central window separates two rows of superimposed arcades containing Apostles and bishops. Within the almond-shaped mandorla of the gable are the Triumphant Christ with symbols of the four Evangelists, the sun, and the moon. The beautiful arcading, the richly carved radiating voussoirs, and the ornamental masonry of gable, roofs, and crossing tower enrich the decorative effect. The remains of Romanesque frescoes decorate both the choir and the small crypt.

The cathedral of Saint-Pierre (begun ca. 1162) is a "hall church," with ribbed vaults and flat chevet enclosing three apsidioles, whose construction spans several centuries. The tripartite façade with a central rose, like the tympana of the portals, reflects northern Gothic influence. The cathedral contains fine stained-glass windows, the most outstanding of which is a magnificent Crucifixion (ca. 1150–70), with the Ascension above and the crucifixion of St. Peter below. The choirstalls with carved misericords are among the oldest in France (ca. 1235–57).

The former abbey church of Saint-Jean de Montierneuf (1076–96) was mutilated following the partial collapse of the crossing tower in 1640. The disposition of the original chevet, similar to that of Saint-Hilaire-le-Grand, is never-theless striking in its amplitude: apse with ambulatory and radiating chapels, a broad transept with eastern apsidioles. The superstructure of the choir is Gothic.

All that remains of the Romanesque church of Saint-Porchaire that housed the relics of the 6th-century abbot of Saint-Hilaire-le-Grand is the impressive three-storied tower porch (11th c.) built against a primitive façade. The arcading of the porch rests on sculptured capitals; above the portal is a relief of Christ in Majesty surrounded by the four Evangelists and two angels. The body of the church is 16th-century. In the tower hangs the old bell of the university, founded in 1431.

Now a book depot for the university library, the former abbey church of Saint-Hilaire-de-la-Celle (late 12th c.), built over the foundations of St. Hilary's house, retains its deep choir and semicircular apse, strongly projecting transept with eastern apsidioles, and the remarkable octagonal ribbed cupola of the crossing.

The remains of the palace of the counts of Poitiers consist of a 12th-century donjon rebuilt under John, duke of Berry, and a large hall of the late 12th–early 13th century. The wall with monumental triple chimney was also rebuilt under John of Berry, whose statue accompanies those of Charles VI, Isabeau of Bavaria, and Jeanne de Boulogne.

Jean M. French

[See also: CHARLES MARTEL; POITIERS, BATTLE OF; POITOU; RADEGUND; ROMANESQUE ARCHITECTURE]

Blomme, Yves. "La construction de la cathédrale Saint-Pierre de Poitiers," *Bulletin monumental* 152 (1994): 7–65.
Camus, Marie-Thérèse. "La sculpture romane à Poitiers." *Archaeologia* 117 (1978): 53–66.
Crozet, René. *L'art roman en Poitou.* Paris: Laurens, 1948.
Dez, Gaston, Paul Deschamps, Marcel Aubert, et al. *Congrès archéologique (Poitiers)* 109 (1951): 9–143.
Labande-Mailfert, Yvonne. *Poitou roman.* 2nd ed. La Pierre-qui-vire: Zodiaque, 1962.
Oursel, Raymond. *Haut-Poitou roman.* 2nd ed. La Pierre-qui-vire: Zodiaque, 1984.
Rhein, André. "Poitiers." *Congrès archéologique (Angoulême)* 79 (1912): 240–332.

POITIERS, BATTLE OF. Poitiers was the site of a major English victory in the Hundred Years' War (September 19, 1356). In 1355, peace negotiations between France and England broke down. In response, Edward, the Black Prince, led what has come to be known as the *grande chevauchée* from Bordeaux to Narbonne and back. This expedition, a great success with considerable booty taken, added to the difficulties faced by the French king, John II, then embroiled in a political controversy with Charles the Bad, king of Navarre.

The English took advantage of John's continuing political problems the following year when they planned a threefold attack on north-central France. The Black Prince was to lead his troops from Bordeaux; Henry, the duke of Lancaster, was to lead his from Normandy; and Edward III was to lead his from Calais. The French army, in an effort to protect this part of France, including Paris itself, moved to stop the English advance and met the Black Prince's force outside of Poitiers on September 17, 1356. The English army numbered 6,000, the French 20,000. As at the Battle of Crécy (1346), it looked as if the larger French numbers might easily defeat the English. Early on the morning of September 19, after a day of maneuvering and attempts by papal mediators to arrive at a peaceful solution, the battle began. The English, being the smaller army, dismounted and took a defensive position behind a hedge facing the road to Poitiers. The French also dismounted, formed into four divisions, and faced the English troops. After some ineffective English archery fire, the first French column, led by the dauphin, later Charles V, attacked the English line. The two armies engaged in hand-to-hand combat until the dauphin's soldiers were forced to retreat. Other soldiers then fled the battlefield, leaving only John II's own force, the largest and freshest of the French contingents, to continue the battle. John moved his troops forward, but at the same time the Black Prince remounted his army and began his own offensive attack on the French, who were unprepared for this mounted assault. Hit with both a frontal and a flank attack, they were caught by the English knights in complete disarray. French losses were high, numbering nearly 4,000 dead or captured. Among those captured was John II himself.

Kelly DeVries

[See also: EDWARD, THE BLACK PRINCE; HUNDRED YEARS' WAR; JOHN II THE GOOD]

Barber, Richard. *Edward, Prince of Wales and Aquitaine.* London: Lane, 1978.

Burne, Alfred Higgins. *The Crécy War.* London: Oxford University Press, 1955.

Carpentier, Elisabeth. "L'historiographie de la bataille de Poitiers au quatorzième siècle." *Revue historique* 263 (1980): 21–58.

Hewitt, Herbert J. *The Black Prince's Expedition of 1355–1357.* Manchester: Manchester University Press, 1958.

Oman, Charles W. *A History of the Art of War in the Middle Ages.* 2nd ed. 2 vols. Boston: Houghton Mifflin, 1924, Vol. 2, pp. 160–78.

POITOU. One of the largest counties of France, Poitou played a role of major importance in medieval history. Poitiers, its capital and most influential town, was the seat of a large diocese, mostly coterminous with the county, and its bishops figured prominently in councils of international scope in the 11th and 12th centuries. Two of the earliest and most famous French monasteries, Saint-Hilaire and Sainte-Croix (Sainte-Radegonde), were also located in the town and attracted pilgrims in large numbers throughout the medieval period. So also did the beauty of its striking Romanesque churches—Notre-Dame-la-Grande, Saint-Hilaire-le-Grand, Sainte-Croix, Saint-Jean de Montierneuf, among others—which made Poitiers an artistic center of the first order, a development helped by its location on one of the principal pilgrimage routes to Santiago in Spain.

Its schools—Saint-Hilaire and Saint-Pierre, the cathedral—never attained quite the same fame, although they were among the best in France south of the Loire; in 1431, Charles VII approved the foundation of a university in Poitiers. During the lifetime of Eleanor of Aquitaine, and possibly even earlier under her grandfather the troubadour Duke Guilhem IX, Poitiers became a center for courtly-love poetry in Occitan, the first of its kind in France. The city was also commercially important for trade both on an international scale (Poitevin wines were well known in England, Normandy, and the Low Countries) and within the province. Finally, from the mid-10th to the mid-12th century, Poitiers ranked as one of the political centers of gravity in France as the capital of the vast duchy of Aquitaine, which comprised a dozen counties in addition to Poitou and covered nearly a third of the southwestern part of the country from the Loire to the Pyrénées.

Territorially, the medieval county corresponded to the tribal lands of the Pictones conquered by Rome in the first century B.C. Under Roman administration, Poitiers, then called Limonum, became the capital, and it was here that Christian conversion began in the 4th century. The earliest monastic foundation in France was at Ligugé just south of Poitiers, in the 360s. After coming briefly under Visigothic rule in the the 5th century, Poitou became the vital northern outpost of the duchy of Aquitaine, which fell to the Franks in the late 8th century. Charlemagne appointed the first known count of Poitou. One of the greatest aristocratic dynasties of medieval France was that of the counts of Poitou/dukes of Aquitaine, eight of whom, all named William, ruled from the 950s to 1137. Briefly allied with the Capetians through the marriage of Eleanor of Aquitaine to Louis VII (r. 1137–52), Poitou then became part of the Angevin empire through her second marriage, to Henry II of England, in 1154. English rule lasted only a short time. The Capetian kings conquered and absorbed Poitou into the royal domain in the 13th century, and its history as an independant county came to an end.

George T. Beech

[See also: AQUITAINE; ELEANOR OF AQUITAINE; GUILHEM IX; POITIERS]

Dez, Gaston. *Histoire de Poitiers.* Poitiers: Société des Antiquaires de l'Ouest, 1966.

Favreau, R. *La ville de Poitiers à la fin du moyen âge: une capitale régionale.* 2 vols. Poitiers: Société des Antiquaires de l'Ouest, 1977–78.

Garaud, Marcel. *Les châtelains de Poitou et l'avènement du régime féodal, XIe et XIIe siècles.* Poitiers: Société des Antiquaires de l'Ouest, 1967.

Labande, Edmond-René, ed. *Histoire du Poitou, du Limousin et des pays charentais.* Toulouse: Privat, 1976.

Richard, Alfred. *Histoire des comtes de Poitou, 778–1204.* 2 vols. Paris: Picard, 1903.

PONTIGNY. The Cistercian abbey of Pontigny (Yonne) was founded in 1114 as the second daughter house of

Pontigny (Yonne), Notre-Dame, nave. *Photograph: Clarence Ward Collection. Courtesy of Oberlin College.*

Cîteaux by Hugues de Mâcon. It was itself the mother house of thirty-four French abbeys and priories. In the Middle Ages, it served as a refuge for three successive archbishops of Canterbury. Thomas Becket fled here in 1164 and remained until Henry's threat to expel the Cistercians from England forced him in 1166 to move to Sens. Four years later, he would be assassinated at Canterbury. Stephen Langton sought refuge here from 1208 to 1213 during his struggles with King John Lackland; and Edmund Rich was buried here in 1240.

The abbey's most generous benefactor was Thibaut II le Grand of Champagne, who in 1150 gave the abbey the means to build its current church (ca. 1150–1210) and to surround its properties with a 13-foot stone wall. The church is an imposing if severe example of Burgundian Gothic style; its long nave with seven bays is the earliest example of Cistercian rib vaulting. The early 13th-century choir, with its ambulatory and eleven radiating chapels, is especially elegant. Little remains of the other conventual buildings.

William W. Kibler/William W. Clark

[See also: CISTERCIAN ART AND ARCHITECTURE; THIBAUT]

Aubert, Marcel. "Abbaye de Pontigny." *Congrès archéologique* (*Auxerre*) 116 (1958): 163–68.

Fontaine, Georges. *Pontigny, abbaye cistercienne.* Paris: Leroux, 1928.

Kinder, Terryl N. "Architecture of the Cistercian Abbey of Pontigny, the Twelfth-Century Church." Diss. Indiana University, 1982.

PONTOISE. Saint-Maclou, the only surviving medieval church of Pontoise (Val-d'Oise), was raised to the status of cathedral in 1966. The first church of Saint-Maclou was built ca. 1145–60 by a builder who had worked for Abbot Suger on the chevet of Saint-Denis. The plan of the chevet of Saint-Maclou, a shallow choir bay surrounded by an ambulatory with five contiguous chapels, is in fact an attempt to simplify the ambitious plan of the upper level of the chevet of Saint-Denis. At Saint-Maclou, the deep chapels and the ambulatory bays in front of them are covered by single five-part rib-vault units, the design of which is based on the vaults of the Saint-Denis chapels. The projecting transept arms flank a crossing tower and announce the height of the nave of six bays. The original nave elevation may have had three stories, but the Flamboyant redecoration left only the clerestory windows and their flanking columns and capitals in place. The 1453 enlargement also resulted in the splendid but incomplete Flamboyant façade. The north nave aisle was doubled in the 16th century and remains one of the gems of early French Renaissance architecture.

Pontoise also housed the important Benedictine abbey of Saint-Martin, founded by St. Gautier (d. 1099). The church disappeared without a trace after the Revolution, although old plans and views confirm that it too had a chevet plan based on the work of Abbot Suger at Saint-Denis.

William W. Clark

Lefèvre-Pontalis, Eugène. *Monographie de l'église Saint-Maclou de Pontoise.* Pontoise: Amédée Paris, 1888.

———. "Pontoise, église Saint-Maclou." *Congrès archéologique* (*Paris*) 82 (1919): 76–99.

Régnier, Louis. "L'abbaye de Saint-Martin de Pontoise." *Excursions archéologiques dans le Vexin français* 1 (1922): 134–48.

———. "Notre-Dame de Pontoise." *Excursions archéologiques dans le Vexin français* 1 (1922): 1–17.

POPULAR DEVOTION. Until recently, studies of medieval spirituality and devotion have concentrated on the ascetic and mystical writings of a monastic or clerical elite. However, the emergence of a broader understanding of the spirituality of a people as the dynamic unity of the content of a faith, and the manner in which that faith is lived and expressed by people in a given historical and cultural setting, has led to a recognition that the inarticulate and illiterate might have a spiritual life. Efforts are now being made to uncover the ideas implicit in devotional actions and to recover a spirituality written in bodies rather than books. Recent studies show that devotional practices and attitudes cut across the lines separating aristocrat and peasant, clerical and lay persons, literate/elite and illiterate/masses, and other social distinctions. Devotional practices were shared rituals, gestures, and attitudes reflecting group and individual piety.

Christianity came to France in many ways, but perhaps the most public was the conversion of Clovis, king of the Franks, ca. 497, as narrated by Gregory of Tours. At a critical moment in a battle, when defeat seemed imminent, Clovis appealed to the God favored by his Catholic wife, Clotilde, and the sudden and complete victory that followed persuaded him to accept her faith. One thought, however, gave him pause. How would the Franks react when their ruler abandoned their ancestral gods? But before Clovis could even begin to address his people, they cried in unison: "We will give up worshiping our mortal gods, pious King, and are prepared to follow the immortal God about whom Remi preaches." And so, in a church adorned with white hangings, perfumed tapers, and clouds of incense, Clovis and his warriors were baptized by the holy Remi, bishop of Reims.

With this act, the Franks officially became Catholic, the first of the Germanic peoples to do so. Their conversion indicates the character of their religion: formal, public, gestural, perhaps superficial; a religion defined by actions and objects rather than by belief. Indeed, what belief was involved, beyond the conviction that God was powerful and acted for the Franks? The notion of spirituality, the interior dimension of the religious life, seems foreign to such a religion.

The conversion of the Franks suggests the difficulties inherent in any attempt to treat this religion as "popular" devotion. No cultural distinction separated Clovis from the mass of the populace; given the general illiteracy of the Germanic peoples, the greatest lords were as uneducated as any of their followers and fully shared their oral culture. That culture was distinct from the written, Latin, Catholic culture of Gallo-Roman bishops like Remi—distinct, but not detached. To reach the Frankish (and Gallo-Roman) populace, Remi and the other Gallo-Roman bishops had to be effectively bicultural, able to communicate in terms of the general culture. The "popular" devotion of the Franks and the learned culture of the ecclesiastical leadership developed in a continuous dialogue.

The monks who first spread Christianity to the countryside encountered a folk religion localized in springs, rocks, trees, and statues of the gods. They often attacked these objects: Martin of Tours (d. 397/400) induced some pagans to chop down their sacred tree by promising that he would let it fall on him; St. Gall (d. ca. 627) smashed statues and threw the pieces into Lake Constance. But they also followed guidelines proposed by Pope Gregory the Great in 601: the idols should be destroyed, but the temples themselves purified with holy water and converted to Christian use; pagan sacrifices should be replaced by Christian festivities. In short, existing holy places and times were to become christianized and so remain holy.

The holiest objects at these new Christian shrines were the bodily remains of people like Martin of Tours. Crowds flocked to their tombs to ask these friends of God to intercede on their behalf, and the keepers of their shrines recorded and proclaimed their miracles. Oaths sworn on relics became a normal part of judicial procedure, and at the beginning of the 9th century relics were declared an essential element of all churches in the Frankish realm: altars lacking them were to be destroyed, and any newly consecrated churches had to contain them. Access to the necessary relics became an important element in the alliance between the Carolingian rulers and the papacy, since Rome was the great repository of the bones of saints and martyrs; and from Rome these relics flowed north to France, as items of legitimate commerce or objects of pious theft.

In the 11th century, a renewed interest in the lives of Jesus and the Apostles redirected devotion and inspired new forms of piety. Pilgrims continued to frequent local shrines, but increasingly they plied the routes that led across France to Rome or Santiago de Compostela in northwestern Spain, stopping along the way to visit the shrine of Mary Magdalene at Vézelay or the statue of the Virgin at Le Puy—or worship at any of the hundreds of other churches dedicated to Mary. Others set off for the Holy Land, where they could follow the footsteps of Jesus himself. Concern for these holy places helped inspire those armed pilgrimages known as the Crusades. Returning crusaders brought back a fresh harvest of relics: a lumberyard's worth of fragments of the True Cross and the crown of thorns for which Louis IX (r. 1226–70) built that great reliquary known as the Sainte-Chapelle.

Renewed interest in the apostolic life also encouraged reverence for those living holy men who best embodied the evangelical ideal, which was increasingly defined in terms of apostolic poverty. Making a striking contrast to the gold and jewels that adorned the relics of the saints, popular preachers like Robert d'Arbrissel, Bernard de Tiron, and Vitalis de Savigny abandoned secure clerical livelihoods, dressed in rags, and withdrew to the wilderness. But paradoxically, those who most resolutely renounced the world found that an awestruck world pursued and enfolded them. Throngs of admirers gathered around hermits like Eon de l'Étoile in Brittany or followed Peter the Hermit to disaster on the First Crusade. Occasionally, these unstable groupings achieved a more regular and enduring structure, as when Norbert of Xanten (d. 1134) and his followers gave rise to the Premonstratensian order; far more often, these holy hermits left no trace in the historical record, beyond a brief and disapproving notice from some ecclesiastical chronicler.

Of much greater concern to the authorities was the spread of heresy, which in the 12th century, for the first time since the conversion of the Franks, evoked a broad popular response. Some heretics reacted violently to what they saw as an excessive materialization of worship. Peter de Bruys attacked the central elements of Catholic worship, rejecting infant baptism, the doctrine of the Mass as a sacrifice, the value of intercessory prayers for the dead, and even the use of church buildings; he trampled on the cross, and eventually was consigned to a bonfire that he had prepared to consume crucifixes. But for the most part, heterodox spirituality was informed by the same apostolic and ascetic ideals that inspired orthodox movements of reform and religious revival. Between 1116 and 1145, Henry, a renegade monk from western France, called for simplicity of worship and poverty of life, much like other wandering preachers; a few decades later, a rich merchant from Lyon named Waldo gave up his worldly goods and embarked on an apostolic life of preaching and poverty. Both ran afoul of ecclesiastical authorities when their personal ideals led them to denounce clerical immorality, question the church's accumulation of property, and challenge the efficacy of sacraments performed by a wealthy and corrupt clergy.

Even more numerous were the Cathars, or Albigensians, who believed in the existence of two equal and eternal divine powers. Their dualist theory opposed spirit, goodness, and light to matter, evil, and darkness and replaced the Catholic version of sacred history with an elaborate mythology of cosmic struggle between the forces of good and evil. It may be that the Cathar heresy owed its success less to the inherent drama of its theology than to the heroic asceticism of its leaders. Whatever the reason, the Cathars attracted many adherents in southern France and northern Italy and even developed an ecclesiastical structure that rivaled the Catholic church in such regions as Languedoc until it was smashed by crusaders and inquisitors.

The triumph of orthodoxy in the 13th century owed something to the elaboration of ecclesiastical structures and the calculated application of force, but even more to the proliferation of opportunities for the faithful to take an active part in religious life. The spread of the mendicant orders meant more, better, and longer sermons for laity to hear. Prolonged or repeated elevation of the host during the Mass, the use of monstrances to display the consecrated eucharist, and the introduction of Corpus Christi processions all served to satisfy the laity's fervent desire to see the body of Christ, made present by the priest's words and the miracle of Transubstantiation. Urban parishes paraded the relics of their saints in annual processions; villagers followed their priests each spring as they blessed the fields.

In addition to more or less passive attendance at Mass, sermons, and processions, the laity formed religious guilds or confraternities, thousands of which were founded in the late Middle Ages. Every village had its confraternity, and each city had several; there were thirteen confraternities in Aix-en-Provence by 1400, and thirty in Dijon by the end of the 15th century. These pious associations were an important source of charity: they fed the hungry, clothed the poor, dowered young women, visited the sick, and buried the dead. Confraternities staged religious processions or performances on major festivals and met for private devotions. At their weekly or monthly meetings, the members heard Mass or listened to sermons. They also performed devotional exercises—prayer, the singing of hymns, penitential flagellation—according to the bent of the group. Confraternities thus provided an institutional framework within which laypeople could appropriate such monastic practices as flagellation and meditative prayer. Not all of their activities were equally edifying. The Confraternity of the Madonna of Le Puy, founded in 1182 by

a carpenter, was intended to be a devout militia that would preserve the peace and defend the faith against heretics; but it had to be suppressed when it turned its arms against some of the local barons. Councils at Avignon (1326) and Lavaur (1368) condemned confraternities for engaging in acts of brigandage. A more common though less serious problem was simple rowdiness. Confraternities typically spent substantial sums on wine for their annual feast, and what was supposed to be a celebration of Christian brotherhood could degenerate into a drunken brawl or raucous gallop through the forest.

An increasingly literate laity made use of a variety of religious books, whose numbers were further multiplied with the introduction of printing at the end of the 15th century. Luxury items, such as the *Très Riches Heures,* a magnificent book of hours commissioned by the duke of Berry, matched the religious tastes of the wealthy, while the populace at large relied on cheap handbooks designed for mass consumption. Vernacular literacy normally began with the memorization of simple prayers and psalms and continued with the reading of catechisms, saints' lives, and moral tracts.

In their testaments, laypeople often left considerable sums to endow Masses for the benefit of their souls and the souls of their ancestors. In much the same way that prayers to the Virgin were multiplied to the point that rosaries had to be used to keep track of them, this investment in the afterlife could lead to an obsessive multiplication of Masses: in the region of Bordeaux, Bernard d'Escoussans, lord of Langoiran, stipulated in 1338 that 25,000 Masses be said for the repose of his soul, while some thirty years later another nobleman, Jean de Grailly, endowed 50,000. To fulfill the terms of such bequests, church aisles filled with side chapels, where squadrons of chantry priests, a sort of clerical proletariat without pastoral responsibilities or secure incomes, celebrated private Masses without pause.

While the majority of people rested their hopes for salvation on the ministrations of the clergy, some sought to dispense with priestly intercession. In the wake of the Black Death of 1348, processions of flagellants spread through parts of northern France, Flanders, Germany, and Austria. Flagellation had long been accepted as a penitential practice when performed in monasteries or lay confraternities; but when performed like this in public, and by people who rejected clerical supervision and themselves assumed the authority to preach and hear each other's confessions, conflict with ecclesiastical authorities was inevitable. Opposition from the pope, resident in Avignon, and the king of France prevented the flagellant movement from penetrating deeply into French territory.

A more subtle challenge to ecclesiastical authority came from the mystics and visionaries, many of them women, who assumed greater prominence in the 14th and 15th centuries. A few were condemned as heretics, but most managed to convince the suspicious authorities that their inspiration was authentic and their teachings orthodox and so escaped being burned at the stake like Marguerite Porete (d. 1310), Na Prous Boneta (d. 1325), and Jeanne d'Arc (d. 1431). What made even the most orthodox mysticism subversive was its claim of direct and unmediated access to God, without the need for priestly intercession or institutional guidance. In this, as in the emotional intensity of their devotion to the person of Jesus, the mystics were simply extreme examples of a more general interiorization of devotional life. The solitary recitation of the rosary, the multiplication of side chapels and private Masses, and the proliferation of confraternities were other signs of the fragmentation of the Christian collectivity at the end of the Middle Ages.

These later developments, however, were added to earlier ones without replacing them. What we see is an overlay of devotions, in which the early dedication to such objects as relics and shrines was supplemented first by reverence for those living holy men and women who best embodied the evangelical ideal, and then by an effort to sanctify one's own self through the performance of charitable and pious acts. Those acts were often directed toward the most traditional of sacred objects; the cult of relics was as important at the end of the Middle Ages as it was at the start. And for many of the French, the powerful hand of God was as clearly visible in the victories of Jeanne d'Arc as it had been, nearly a millennium earlier, in Clovis's triumph.

Daniel E. Bornstein

[See also: ALBIGENSIAN CRUSADE; CATHARS; CLOVIS I; CONFRÉRIE DE LA PASSION; CRUSADES; DOMINICAN ORDER; FOLKLORE; FRANCISCAN ORDER; GREGORY OF TOURS; HERESIES, APOSTOLIC; HERESY; JEANNE D'ARC; LIMBOURG BROTHERS; MARTIN OF TOURS; MYSTICISM; PETER DE BRUYS; PILGRIMAGE; PREACHING; PRÉMONTRÉ; RELICS AND RELIQUARIES; ROBERT D'ARBRISSEL; SAINTS, CULT OF; WALDO/WALDENSES; WOMEN, RELIGIOUS EXPERIENCE OF]

Adam, Paul. *La vie paroissiale en France au XIVe siècle.* Paris: Sirey, 1964.

Brooke, Rosalind, and Christopher Brooke. *Popular Religion in the Middle Ages: Western Europe 1000–1300.* London: Thames and Hudson, 1984.

Chiffoleau, Jacques. *La comptabilité de l'au-delà: les hommes, la mort et la religion dans la région d'Avignon à la fin du moyen âge.* Turin: Bottega d'Erasmo, 1980.

Delaruelle, Étienne. *La piété populaire au moyen âge.* Turin: Bottega d'Erasmo, 1980.

Geary, Patrick J. *Furta Sacra: Thefts of Relics in the Central Middle Ages.* 2nd ed. Princeton: Princeton University Press, 1990.

Gurevitch, Aron. *Medieval Popular Culture: Problems of Belief and Perception.* Cambridge: Cambridge University Press, 1988.

Hilgarth, J.N., ed. *Christianity and Paganism, 350–750: The Conversion of Western Europe.* rev. ed. Philadelphia: University of Pennsylvania Press, 1986.

Kieckhefer, Richard. *Magic in the Middle Ages.* Cambridge: Cambridge University Press, 1989.

Lambert, Malcolm. *Medieval Heresy: Popular Movements from the Gregorian Reform to the Reformation.* 2nd ed. Oxford: Blackwell, 1992.

Schmitt, Jean-Claude. *The Holy Greyhound: Guinefort, Healer of Children Since the Thirteenth Century.* Cambridge: Cambridge University Press, 1983.

Vauchez, André. *The Laity in the Middle Ages: Religious Beliefs and Devotional Practices,* ed. Daniel E. Bornstein, trans. Margery G. Schneider. Notre Dame: University of Notre Dame Press, 1993.

POPULATION AND DEMOGRAPHY. All demographic figures from the Middle Ages are approximate, but about general trends and sizes a consensus is developing, except in regard to sex ratios and age at marriage. From a high of perhaps 5.7 million ca. A.D. 165, the population of Gaul fell to fewer than 4 million by 500. Germanic tribes raided Gaul in the 3rd century and occupied it in the 5th, becoming a majority in sparsely populated Flanders, where their language predominated, but remaining a minority of less than 10 percent in distant Aquitaine. The population reached its nadir despite their influx and that of British refugees to Armorica (Brittany). Villages that grew from Gallic settlements or Roman villas predominated over hamlets and isolated farmsteads, except in hilly or mountainous regions too poor to support denser settlement.

In the 6th century, the population grew somewhat, but the Arab conquests in the Mediterranean world between 636 and 732 disrupted external trade and hastened urban decay. Gold coinage ceased, merchants from the eastern Mediterranean no longer appear in the sources, and cities that were walled during the chaos of the 3rd century became so depopulated that they reduced the circuits of the walls, sometimes enclosing little more than a fortified cathedral.

Like his father and grandfather, Charlemagne (d. 814) pushed back the Muslims, creating the Spanish March. He annexed Lombardy and Germany, creating a large, safe, and prosperous empire with a good silver coinage. Gaul's population regained 5 million, and for the first time the region surpassed Italy as Europe's most populous. It remained almost entirely rural. A modest revival of some towns ended with the disintegration of the Carolingian empire in the face of Viking raids. Population suffered a new decline in the 9th and 10th centuries, as Danes seized Normandy and destroyed the Flemish ports; Muslims attacking from the south established a base at La Garde Freinet in Provence. Survivors fled to the interior, often to hills, where local lords could defend them more easily against raiders following the river valleys.

After the raids ended, improved agricultural technology by the 11th century made the deep, well-watered fields of northern and western France much more productive than the shallow, sandy soils of the Mediterranean valleys south of the Massif Central. In the north, the French augmented plowlands by clearing forests that may have come to cover three-fourths of the surface. Three centuries of expansion followed, and Europe's population doubled, while that of France nearly quadrupled, from about 4 to 15 million. A royal census of 1328, which did not cover the entire kingdom, listed 23,800 parishes and 2,470,000 hearths. Adding 893,752 hearths to cover the rest of the kingdom, Ferdinand Lot used a multiplier of five per hearth (except for Paris, where he used 3.5) and calculated that the French king then ruled 17.6 million people. Other authorities have since argued for a lower coefficient and a population of 15 million.

Pirenne has described the urbanization of these centuries, as a revival of trade and industry coincided with the agricultural revolution. Although over 90 percent still lived in rural settlements, town populations soared. Abandoned Roman sites were reoccupied and new ones formed under castle walls, *faubourgs,* or suburbs (*burg* means fortress), where merchants wintered. Most of the *villeneuves* founded during the *grands défrichements* remained merely large agricultural villages, although sometimes as large as true towns of 2,000–3,000 people who lived mainly on commerce and industry. Except for the great towns of Flanders, and Paris (which may have grown from 25,000 in 1200 to 210,000 by 1328), only Marseille, Montpellier, Lyon, and Bordeaux ever attained a population of 30,000. Few other French towns, even important trading or administrative centers, reached as many as 10,000 people. Because of congestion and poor sanitation, towns always had a higher mortality rate than rural areas. In spite of considerable emigration, some areas of Normandy and Burgundy contained as many people ca. 1300 as they do today.

In the wake of the Black Death of 1348 and extended periods of warfare, France's population plunged to about 10 million by 1450, recovering gradually thereafter as plague recurred less frequently. By 1500, it had still not regained the pre–Black Death level. After the first visitation wiped out over half their population, some villages and towns were abandoned and never recovered, but fresh immigrants from the countryside repopulated most communities, raising the urban percentage of the entire population. Paris and other cities soon exceeded their preplague totals. The ensuing shortage of rural labor brought lower rents, higher wages, and a drastic reduction in the number of bondsmen, from about 50 percent to about 10 percent of the rural population.

Perhaps a third of all medieval infants failed to reach the age of six, half of these dying in the first year. Death tolls for both sexes remained high until the mid-teens. Those who survived the dangerous childhood diseases gained a basic immunity from the most common scourges, and most who reached maturity could expect to live until fifty, although most of those in their forties were decrepit and disease-ridden. Average nuclear-family size was perhaps only four, because children left the hearth early (seven to twelve years of age) to become apprentices or domestic servants.

Diet, hygiene, and living standards improved after the waves of plague carried off the excess population, but for most of the Middle Ages average life expectancy was only about thirty-four for males and twenty-eight for females. Many more females were exposed or killed at birth, and the mortality of women in childbirth may have exceeded that of men in war, hunting, and accidents. The sex ratio was between 6:5 and 4:3. David Herlihy, who has studied some major demographic documents of the Middle Ages, has argued that more female than male servants may have eluded the enumerators, but this factor alone cannot explain the preponderance of males indicated in virtually all surveys of population in Europe before the 18th century.

Like most slaves, perhaps one-third of the free or freed men could never afford to marry, as in 19th-century Ireland or the Roman Empire. That fact, along with the sex ratio, may have encouraged situational homosexuality, while many exclusives joined the clergy, the celibacy of which held down the population. The newly created orphanages became charnel houses whose horrors and deprivations few survived.

Except for royalty and aristocracy—whose members often married young, boys of eighteen to girls of fifteen or younger—most French people seem to have waited to marry. After plagues or other disasters, when heirs came prematurely into their inheritances, the marriage ages of even common males plunged. Contrariwise, on the overcrowded farms before the Black Death, marriages were postponed. Merchants often waited until they had established their fortunes, or professionals until their careers flourished. We encounter marriages of a "Mediterranean type" (twenty-four-year-old men who could afford their own dwelling marrying fourteen- or fifteen-year-old girls), intermediate between the "European type" that has prevailed in the West since ca. 1500 (men in their late twenties marrying women in their mid-twenties) and the "eastern type" (males at puberty taking women of about twelve and continuing to live with the groom's family).

France had Europe's largest population from Charlemagne to Napoleon, but its rate of growth has since been the slowest in Europe.

William A. Percy, Jr.

Boswell, John. *The Kindness of Strangers: The Abandonment of Children in Western Europe from Late Antiquity to the Renaissance.* New York: Pantheon, 1988.

Herlihy, David. *Medieval Households.* Cambridge: Harvard University Press, 1985.

Lot, Ferdinand. "L'état des paroisses et des feux de 1328." *Bibliothèque de l'École des Chartes* 90 (1929): 51–107.

Pirenne, Henri. *Medieval Cities: Their Origins and the Revival of Trade,* trans. F.D. Halsey. Princeton: Princeton University Press, 1925.

Russell, Josiah Cox. *Medieval Regions and Their Cities.* Bloomington: Indiana University Press, 1972.

PORTS ET PASSAGES. See **CUSTOMS DUTIES**

POST-VULGATE ROMANCE. The popularity of the Arthurian Vulgate Cycle (ca. 1215–35) is attested in part by varied literary continuations, among them the Post-Vulgate Arthuriad (also known as the Post-Vulgate *Romance of the Grail,* or *Roman du Graal,* or the Pseudo–Robert de Boron Cycle; ca. 1230–40). This anonymous corpus of prose narratives follows roughly the structure of the Vulgate romances, providing versions of the *Estoire del saint Graal,* the *Merlin,* the *Queste del saint Graal,* and the *Mort le roi Artu* but omitting the lengthy *Prose Lancelot,* which constitutes nearly half of the Vulgate corpus. To bridge the narrative gap between his *Merlin* and *Queste*, the Post-Vulgate continuator recast selected scenes from the Agravain section of the Vulgate *Lancelot*, combining them with elements from the first version of the *Prose Tristan* and other material of his own invention.

The resultant "text" is nowhere preserved *in toto*; it has been reconstructed from French fragments and from Portuguese and Spanish translations. To judge from the translations, the Post-Vulgate *Estoire del saint Graal* probably differed little from its predecessor in the Vulgate Cycle. The Post-Vulgate *Merlin* (known commonly as the Huth *Merlin* or the *Suite du Merlin*) reduplicates the prose rendering of Robert de Boron's verse text that constitutes the first part of the Vulgate *Merlin* but adds to this base narrative a new elaboration. Whereas the Vulgate *Merlin* expands Robert de Boron's account by chronicling the military exploits of King Arthur, the Huth *Merlin* provides an elaborate scenario of more fantastic incidents. The text is found in two manuscripts, both incomplete at the end: the Huth manuscript, B.L. Add. 38117 and Cambridge Univ. Lib. Add. 7071. The Post-Vulgate *Queste* and *Mort Artu* offer completely remodeled versions of their predecessors in the Vulgate Cycle.

E. Jane Burns

[See also: PROSE ROMANCE (ARTHURIAN); VULGATE CYCLE]

Bogdanow, Fanni, ed. *La folie Lancelot: A Hitherto Unknown Portion of the Suite du Merlin Contained in MSS. B.N. fr. 112 and 12599.* Tübingen: Niemeyer, 1965.
———, ed. *La Queste del Saint Graal et la Mort Artu Post-Vulgate, Troisième partie du Roman du Graal.* Paris: Didot, 1991.
Lacy, Norris J., ed. *Lancelot-Grail: The Old French Arthurian Vulgate and Post-Vulgate in Translation*, trans. Norris J. Lacy et al. 5 vols. New York: Garland, 1993– .
Bogdanow, Fanni. "The *Suite du Merlin* and the Post-Vulgate *Roman du Graal*." In *Arthurian Literature in the Middle Ages: A Collaborative History*, ed. Roger Sherman Loomis. Oxford: Clarendon, 1959, pp. 325–35.
———. *The Romance of the Grail: A Study of the Structure and Genesis of a Thirteenth Century Arthurian Prose Romance.* Manchester: University of Manchester Press, 1966.

PRAGMATIC SANCTION OF BOURGES. Promulgated by Charles VII in 1438, the royal decree known as the Pragmatic Sanction of Bourges regulated the relationship among the crown, the French church, and the papacy. The crown reformed church governance stressing French independence from papal authority: it suppressed papal taxation, subjected church courts to royal courts, and reaffirmed the right of local clerical bodies to elect or appoint ecclesiastical dignitaries. The occasion for the decree was the meeting of a French synod in support of the Council of Basel, which had asserted the supremacy of the council over the papacy.

The twenty-three articles of the decree represent the fulfillment of the Gallican tradition in development since the reign of Philip IV. It was issued in the Roman-law form of a "Pragmatic" to emphasize historical sources of secular authority in this domain. Clergy and crown shared an interest in rejecting papal authority, but the vexatious question of whether the king could impose his will on the clergy remained unresolved. Political circumstance led both Louis X and Charles VIII to suspend the decree, but Louis XII insisted on its enforcement after 1499, and it remained the basis of church governance in France until superseded by the Concordat of Bologna in 1516.

Paul D. Solon

[See also: CONCORDAT OF AMBOISE; GALLICANISM]

Delarulle, Étienne, Edmonde-René Labande, and Paul Ourliac, eds. *L'église au temps du Grand Schisme et de la crise conciliaire, 1378–1449.* Paris: Bloud et Gay, 1962.
Lewis, P.S. *Later Medieval France: The Polity.* New York: St. Martin, 1968.
Martin, Victor. *Les origines du gallicanisme.* Paris: Bloud et Gay, 1939.
Valois, Noel. *Histoire de la Pragmatique Sanction de Bourges sous Charles VII.* Paris: Picard, 1906.

PRAGUERIE. *See* **ARISTOCRATIC REVOLT**

PRAYERS AND DEVOTIONAL MATERIALS. Prayers and devotional materials in Old French belong to two broad categories: those derived from the liturgy and those of more literary and personal inspiration. The liturgical works include French versions of the *Te Deum*, the Kyrie, the Gloria, the Sanctus, and the Agnus Dei; translations and paraphrases of the Credo and the Pater Noster, including the commentaries by Maurice de Sully; and formulae for confession. The liturgical collection deemed most suitable for the laity was the psalter, which explains its early translation into the vernacular. The oldest psalters were in Latin, however, as were most of the books of hours (consisting of the Penitential psalms and the Office of the Dead), but these were sometimes combined with prayers in the vernacular. The earliest prayerbook containing vernacular prayers, the *Psalter of Lambert de Bègue*, was produced early in the 13th century in the vicinity of Liège.

Vernacular prayers, more independent of Latin models than the liturgical pieces, address the heavenly hierarchy: God, Jesus, the Virgin, and the saints. The *Ave Maria* appears in French only in the 13th century and is not included in a psalter until the 14th, but paraphrases of the prayer were composed by such well-known authors as Baudouin de Condé, Rutebeuf, Gautier de Coinci, and Philippe de Beaumanoir. The *Saluts* to the Virgin are derived from the *Aves*, but the Marian chansons, especially those by Rutebeuf and Gautier de Coinci, are more closely related to the secular lyric. Another popular genre was the *complainte* portraying the Virgin's suffering during the Passion. Some of these are based on the Latin *Stabat mater*, others, such as the *Regrets de Nostre Dame* by Huon le Roi de Cambrai, the *Débat de la Vierge et de la Croix*, and the

Plainte Nostre Dame, are longer and more complex. Related to these materials, but different in genre, are the works that combine biblical and apocryphal materials in narrative form.

Maureen B.M. Boulton

[See also: BOOK OF HOURS; DIDACTIC LITERATURE (OCCITAN); GAUTIER DE COINCI; HYMNS; MARY, DEVOTION TO; MARY, LITURGICAL VENERATION OF; MORAL TREATISES; *PLANH/COMPLAINTE*]

Brayer, Edith, and A.M. Bouly de Lesdain. "Les prières usuelles annexées aux anciennes traductions françaises du Psautier." *Institut de Recherche et d'Histoire des Textes: Bulletin* 15 (1969): 69–120.

Sinclair, Keith V. *Prières en ancien français: nouvelles références, renseignements complémentaires . . . du Répertoire de Sonet.* Hamden: Archon, 1978.

———. *French Devotional Texts of the Middle Ages: A Bibliographic Manuscripts Guide.* Westport: Greenwood, 1979. [Supplements, 1982, 1988.]

Sonet, Jean, ed. *Répertoire d'incipit de prières en ancien français.* Geneva, Droz, 1956.

PREACHING. The Frankish church inherited from late antiquity a range of pastoral acts identified with preaching and an ecclesiological framework by means of which these acts were authorized. Patristic preaching was centered on the address of the faithful, which occurred within worship on Sundays and feast days, an address centered on exegesis of biblical readings by which the preacher articulated Christian belief and cult on the one hand, Christian life and practice on the other.

Little is known of the preaching practice of the Frankish church during the Merovingian period (ca. 450–751). Its episcopate was filled largely by scions of the old Roman provincial aristocracy, who tended to maintain the rhetorical and theological traditions of the patristic world. Few monuments to their early homiletic effort survive. The sermons of Caesarius of Arles represent an exception that allows one to see both the continuity of context and pastoral intent between his preaching and that of his patristic predecessors, even while noting the considerable changes in circumstance and a heightened awareness of the countryside and of the enormous dislocations of the day.

The pastoral situation of the Merovingian church was poorly fitted to the rhetorical and institutional framework evolved in the ancient church, which had concentrated pastoral (preaching) efforts in the hands of a bishop and the clergy who made up his immediate household. Merovingian dioceses were sprawling affairs whose sheer physical size necessitated the development of subdiocesan centers of pastoral care, that is, parishes endowed with clerical communities. Who were these parish priests to be? How were they to be trained to pastoral office? And how was their pastoral activity to relate to that carried on by the bishop and his household clergy?

Clear attempts to answer such questions survive only in Carolingian sources (751–989), such as capitularies.

The *Admonitio generalis* (789) established doctrinal ends of preaching—faith in the Trinity, Incarnation, Passion, and Resurrection. It recommended that preachers make use of the Articles of Faith, the list of sins contained in Galatians 5, and the spiritual counsels found in the Sermon on the Mount. At Tours in 813, bishops were admonished to preach to their subjects concerning the Last Things and to do so in the vernacular. At Attigny in 822, they were exhorted to establish assistants within their dioceses who would be competent to help them fulfill their preaching office. The capitulary of Haito, bishop of Basel, demanded that parish priests have in their possession all books requisite to the administration of their responsibilities, among which was to be a collection of sermons covering all Sundays and feast days.

This legislation suggests that by the 8th and 9th centuries the Frankish church had begun to adjust to the logistics of its situation. While the identification of the church's "order of preachers" with the episcopacy remained current, the bishop's office, including his preaching ministry, was assumed to be carried on with a fair degree of autonomy by clerical delegates at the parish level. Preaching was for the most part conceived in terms of the public worship of the faithful. The bishop's preaching, to be carried on in the vernacular, was intended to instruct the faithful in the obligations of membership in the community, obligations of both word and deed.

Haito of Basel's capitulary alludes to another Carolingian initiative. Bishops and clerics became increasingly busy with the compilation and dissemination of homiliaries, collections of sermons covering the readings of the liturgical year. Many were produced in a monastic context with the contemplative *lectio divina* in mind; others were produced primarily for the edification of the clergy. Some, however, were compiled in response to the desire recorded in Haito's capitulary that every parish priest have access to a collection of sermons covering the readings of the entire liturgical year.

This survey of early-medieval preaching must be modified somewhat by pointing to a revival of kerygmatic preaching in the Frankish church. The Gallo-Roman domination of the episcopacy gave way in the latter half of the 7th century. The new willingness of the Frankish nobility to pursue ecclesiastical careers went hand in hand with the wanderings of St. Columbanus and the establishment of Irish monasticism throughout the Frankish lands. A new missionary spirit emerged among Frankish ecclesiastics that culminated in a move to evangelize the Germanic peoples of the Rhineland and Frisia, a mission that culminated in the mid-8th-century missions led by St. Boniface.

The history of preaching takes a significant turn in the 11th century. The advent of the eremetical movement ca. 1000, the birth and spread of the movement of regular canons in the middle decades of the century, and the policies of the reform popes at the century's close all gave voice to a new spirit that sought to dissociate preaching from certain of its old moorings and associate it with new spiritual aims. The episcopal care of the Frankish centuries had addressed communities rather than persons. Its form and focus were adapted accordingly, expressing themselves in large-scale events constituted by highly stylized acts in public liturgical settings. Bishops could be counted on to maintain the required pomp in their preaching in the vernacular, but not so their proxies in the country parishes. Consequently, it would seem that the preaching of the latter remained in the Latin of the homiliaries themselves. Such a preaching, because it was literally unintelligible, addressed the community with a verbal mystery, a fitting adumbration of the subsequent mystery of Word-made-Flesh on the altar at the climax of the Mass.

Many of the French hermits, taking John the Baptist as their patron and model, returned to the edges of the settled land to preach a message of repentance to individuals. In the Frankish church, repentance had been the special concern of the monastic order, which shouldered the burden of a constant repentance on behalf of the faithful as a whole. In the preaching of the 11th-century itinerant preachers, however, the penitent life was democratized and addressed to each of the faithful. As a result, the 11th and 12th centuries can be seen as a great age of religious and lay preaching, and as an age of immense institutional and pastoral ferment, as the church struggled to adapt to this outburst of new needs and feelings. The earliest of these wandering preachers remain largely nameless, but we know the names of many who came to be allied with the movement of reform emanating from and under the auspices of the popes of Rome: Peter the Hermit (1050–1115), Robert d'Arbrissel (1060–1115), St. Norbert of Xanten (1082–1134), to name only a few.

From the 11th century, Benedictine houses began staffing their dependent parishes with monks of the community. Orders of regular canons proliferated, several of which, such as the Premonstratensians, took on pastoral care in rural churches or, like the Victorines in northern France, the care of women religious, including the office of preaching. Nor should one forget the extensive use made of preachers and preaching missions by the popes of the 11th and 12th centuries. One thinks of the Cistercians Bernard of Clairvaux and Alain de Lille commissioned to preach the Second and Third Crusades, of religious sent to preach against heretics in southern France, of the dispirited troop of Cistercians whom St. Dominic met and encouraged in 1206. Examples of lay preaching and preachers are equally plentiful. In particular, one thinks of the career of Peter Waldo.

Just as the hermits of the early 11th century had taken on a biblical exemplar in John the Baptist, so too did lay preachers take on exemplars: the Apostles and the apostolic life described in Matthew 10. In emulation of the Apostles, they moved about two by two, barefoot and penniless, preaching the coming of the Kingdom of God. This flowering of lay preaching, this apostolic movement, by its embrace of mendicancy also drew strength from a development within the rapidly urbanizing regions of Europe: the embrace of a life of voluntary poverty in response to the blatant excesses of monied wealth among townsfolk.

All this ferment provoked anxiety in many quarters. A controversy broke out in the 12th century as to the very possibility of a religious office of preaching: was not the "order of preachers" the episcopacy and those whom bishops delegated to carry out their pastoral functions in parish churches? How was the increasingly widespread claim among religious to an intrinsic preaching office, much less the swarming groups of lay "apostles," to be accommodated to the pastoral institutions of the western church?

The pontificate of Innocent III (r. 1198–1216) would create a framework transforming the church's pastoral care that won the adherence of the majority of religious and lay preachers. In a first phase, Innocent created space for lay and religious preachers by his efforts to reconcile groups of heretical preachers, the Humiliati (1201) and Waldensians (1208 and 1210). His work with St. Francis in Italy and with Bishop Foulques of Toulouse and St. Dominic in southern France went far to establishing the two greatest mendicant orders, the Franciscans and Dominicans. He narrowed the definition of properly clerical preaching (*praedicatio*) by splitting off from it two activities formerly bound to it: the telling of one's faith to another (*professio fidei*) and the defense of orthodoxy in debate with heretics (*defensio fidei*). In a second phase, Innocent crystallized a new pastoral order in the constitutions of the Fourth Lateran Council (1215). He gave universal force to the old Carolingian admonition that bishops recruit preachers competent to preach throughout their diocese. In so doing, however, he associated preaching with the sacrament of penance, for he added that bishops should also recruit competent confessors. In addition, he underscored the importance of confession by establishing a universal obligation to make annual confession to one's "proper priest," further associating this confession with the obligation to receive communion at Easter. The net effect of this legislation was to bind preaching to the sacrament of penance and to institutionalize the spiritual impulses of the previous two centuries by making the sacrament of penance with its prolegomenon, repentance, into an obligatory and annual feature of adult Christian living. This new pastoral axis of preaching-for-confession demanded far-ranging modifications to the church's pastoral institutions.

Preaching could no longer be seen as the preserve of an "order of preachers" identified narrowly with the episcopacy and the homily at Mass celebrated in the cathedral church. Preaching-for-confession assumed a more intimate interaction between preacher and hearer, one more obviously possible at the parish level in the countryside. In the towns, where parish structure was underdeveloped, parish churches needed the supplement of religious oratories open to the faithful. The 13th century saw the formation of many new parishes and the establishment of mendicant priories throughout the towns of Europe.

Preaching-for-confession demanded not only familiarity but also knowledge, a theoretical understanding of what motivated human action. The 13th century saw a considerable expansion of clerical opportunities to study and the proliferation of a vast pastoral literature, much of which was designed to help parish and mendicant priests prepare for their roles as preachers and confessors to the faithful. From the University of Paris especially, there poured forth a torrent of treatises: manuals of confession, guides to confessors, biblical distinctions, collections of model sermons, *summae* of preaching, arts of preaching, biblical postillae, and the like.

By ca. 1300, a new framework of pastoral institutions had been worked out. The locus of pastoral care had been lowered from the cathedral church to the parish church, supplemented in urban areas by the oratories of the religious. The "order of preachers" had been expanded to include parish and religious clergy. Indeed, that old Gregorian term had come to rest upon one order of religious in particular, the Dominican Order of Friars Preachers.

These transformations led to the exclusion of certain possibilities. From the mid-13th century, lay preaching came to be proscribed. Even those lay functions given papal sanction by Innocent III, profession and defense of the faith, came to be viewed with suspicion. The orders founded by Innocent's policy of reconciliation had ceased to be by the end of the century. Nevertheless, a long and uninterrupted tradition of monastic preaching continued with little change. Within the monastery, religious superiors, male and female, preached to their subordinates so as to form them to their religious callings. In France, sermons of the Mistress of Paris's Grand Béguinage are preserved in manuscripts B.N. lat.16481 and 16482.

Literary witnesses to medieval preaching abound. Although they bear a problematic relationship to actual preaching, they do provide some sense of the rhetorical modes that held sway at different periods of medieval history. In general, a patristic mode of preaching predominated in both monastery and public preaching until the close of the 12th century. This mode, the homily (*tractatus, omelia*), represented a more or less continuous commentary on the biblical readings chosen for exposition, whereby the preacher exposited his text by associating it with other biblical passages that shared a significant word or concept. This mode of preaching continued in monastic circles even after it began to give way to other modes outside of monastery walls.

Word-associative approaches to the biblical text crystallized in the course of the 12th century into a set form, the biblical distinction, under the influence of the cathedral schools. The use of biblical distinctions to provide an architectonic for sermons is clearly visible in the sermon collections of late 12th-century bishops like Maurice de Sully. This represents a first step away from the homily tradition and toward a new mode of preaching, the "thematic sermon."

The thematic sermon proper emerges at the dawn of the 13th century and continues to be developed well into the 14th. Here, attention has come to focus upon a single, small passage of the Mass readings. This "theme" is then divided into a number of "parts," usually between two and four. These divisions serve subsequently as occasions for doctrinal, mystical, or moral instruction. Instruction or correction occurs via the process of expansion or dilation by which the meaning of each part is articulated, with or without subdivision, and confirmed by means of "authorities," "arguments," or "examples." The latter category often meant a narrative vignette drawn from a common stock of colorful stories. It could also mean a parallel moment from the nonhuman world, a similitude that drew its power from the assumption of the human microcosm. The more educated the context, the more preachers would be expected to confirm their divisions and subdivisions by recourse to arguments and authorities. When preaching to the ordinary faithful, however, one was expected to use examples and similitudes. The *Sermones vulgares* of Jacques de Vitry show how effectively the thematic sermon could be adapted to the needs of popular preaching.

The 13th-century transformation of preaching in response to the spiritual ferment of the 11th and 12th centuries was largely completed by the mid-14th century. The last two centuries of the medieval era saw a refining and elaboration of the system. Everywhere, there came to be more preachers, more sermon aids of every sort, more opportunities for study. France continued to be blessed with gifted preachers of every stripe, whether a pope like Clement VI, an academic like Jean Gerson, or a mendicant like Vincent Ferrer. None of these gifted men, however, came from an unexpected quarter; the system was firmly in place. There would be no substantial change to the office of preaching until the 16th century, the advent of Calvinist preaching, and the Catholic response inaugurated at the Council of Trent (1563).

Robert Sweetman

[See also: ALAIN DE LILLE; BÉGUINES; BERNARD OF CLAIRVAUX; BERSUIRE, PIERRE; BONIFACE VIII; CAESARIUS OF ARLES; CLEMENT VI; DOMINICAN ORDER; EXEMPLUM; FRANCISCAN ORDER; GERSON, JEAN; GUERRIC D'IGNY; INNOCENT III; JACQUES DE VITRY; MAURICE DE SULLY; POPULAR DEVOTION; PRÉMONTRÉ; ROBERT D'ARBRISSEL; WALDO/WALDENSES]

Bourgain, Louis. *La chaire française au XIIe siècle d'après les manuscrits.* Paris: Société Générale de Librairie Catholique, 1879.

Charland, Thomas-Marie. *Artes praedicandi: contribution à l'histoire de la rhétorique au moyen âge.* Ottawa: Institut d'Études Médiévales, 1936.

D'Avray, David L. *The Preaching of the Friars: Sermons Diffused from Paris Before 1300.* Oxford: Clarendon, 1985.

Lecoy de La Marche, Albert. *La chaire française au moyen âge, spécialement au XIIIe siècle, d'après les manuscrits contemporains.* Paris: Renouard, 1886.

Longhre, Jean. *Œuvres oratoires des maîtres parisiens au XIIe siècle: étude historique et doctrinale.* Paris: Études Augustiniennes, 1975.

———. *La prédication médiévale.* Paris: Études Augustiniennes, 1983.

Schneyer, Johann Baptist. *Repertorium der lateinischen Sermones des Mittelalters, für die Zeit von 1150–1350.* 11 vols. Münster: Aschendorff, 1969–90.

Zink, Michel. *La prédication en langue romane avant 1300.* Paris: Champion, 1976.

PRECARIA. A contract by which land was leased in perpetual usage by ecclesiastics for a nominal annual rent to local knights and lords of castles. The *precaria* was in use throughout the early Middle Ages. The precarial grant frequently was made to knights who would be expected in return to protect the church in question (protofeudal contracts), and it may have been by such contracts that the early Carolingians provided support to the warriors needed to defeat the Muslims. In the upheavals of the 10th and 11th centuries, the precarial grant was often used to regularize a usurpation of church land by knights; in such a case, in return for the church's grant of precarial rights the warrior, who continued to exploit the land, would concede allodial rights to the monks or bishop. Precarial grants could also be used to retrieve for heirs of donors to the church what those heirs considered undue usurpation of family land by ecclesiastics who had persuaded dying men and women to make deathbed grants for their souls.

Constance H. Berman

PREMIERFAIT, LAURENT DE (1388–1420). Humanist and translator from Premierfait, near Troyes. Laurent produced French versions of major Latin and Italian texts, such as Cicero's *De senectute* in 1405 and *De amicitia* in 1410 and Boccaccio's *De casibus virorum illustrium* in 1409 and *Decameron* in 1414. He may also have translated Aristotle's *Economics* into French.

The *Decameron* translation, dedicated to John, duke of Berry, is commonly known as the *Cent nouvelles*. Its popularity is attested by its preservation in fifteen manuscripts and in eight editions of the 1485 Vérard printed text. Laurent's remained the only French version of the *Decameron* for well over a century, until Marguerite de Navarre in 1545 commissioned Anthoine le Maçon to prepare a new translation.

Assessments of Laurent's skill as a translator vary. Evaluation of the *Cent nouvelles* in particular is difficult, both because it still awaits a modern edition and because Laurent, whose command of Florentine was inadequate, translated not Boccaccio's text but a Latin intermediary prepared by Antonio d'Arezzo. Moreover, scholars consulting less than reliable manuscripts have concluded that Laurent was guilty of verbosity and wearisome moralizing. Study of the best manuscripts (e.g., Vatican, Pal. lat. 1989) reveals that he respected his sources far more than has generally been thought, limiting himself to the small interpolations and modifications characteristic of early translators.

Norris J. Lacy

[See also: BERSUIRE, PIERRE; TRANSLATION]

Cucchi, Paolo. "The First French Decameron: Laurent de Premierfait's Translation and the Early French *Nouvelle*." In *The French Short Story*. Columbia: University of South Carolina Press, 1975, pp. 1–14.
Famiglietti, Richard C. "Laurent de Premierfait: The Career of a Humanist in Early Fifteenth-Century Paris." *Journal of Medieval History* 9 (1983): 25–42.

PREMONSTRATENSIAN ARCHITECTURE. The study of Premonstratensian architecture has been dominated by the idea that the churches of Prémontré followed Cistercian plans. The evidence suggests that there were some built on a plan that loosely resembled the so-called "Bernardine" plan: square chevet and projecting transept with contiguous eastern chapels. This is by no means the rule, however, as comparison of the plans of Braine, Dommartin, and Saint-Martin at Laon reveals. The resemblance is strictly confined to the plan. The churches of Prémontré were much more richly decorated and emphatically followed local practices in style and technique, as befits the churches of regular canons. Very few of them seem to have accepted Cistercian austerity in architecture and decoration.

William W. Clark

[See also: BRAINE; DOMMARTIN; LAON]

Clark, William W. "Cistercian Influences on Premonstratensian Church Planning: Saint-Martin at Laon." In *Studies in Cistercian Art and Architecture*. Kalamazoo: Cistercian, 1984, Vol. 2, ed. M. Lillich, pp. 161–88.

PRÉMONTRÉ. Located in the wilderness near Laon, Prémontré (Aisne) was the site of a community of regular canons and lay persons and the mother house of the Premonstratensian order, founded ca. 1120 by Norbert of Xanten. A wealthy and worldly cleric associated with the imperial court, Norbert was converted to a life of eremitic asceticism in 1115. After an abortive attempt to reform the priests at Xanten, Norbert received papal authorization as an itinerant preacher. He proved to be a gifted preacher whose attacks on ecclesiastical abuses and calls for spiritual reform attracted many followers. He was finally persuaded to found a community composed of clerical and lay, male and female members in the isolation of Prémontré. From the beginning, this group was dedicated to poverty, manual labor, personal asceticism, and contemplative prayer, much in line with the other movements of reform— lay, clerical, and monastic—of the day. Norbert also incorporated clerical functions and isolation from the world into the communal ideal. In 1126, Norbert left Prémontré to become archbishop of Magdeburg, where he continued his efforts to reform the clergy and to launch missionary efforts in northern Germany, until his death in 1134. As a wandering preacher, Norbert, like Robert d'Arbrissel, attracted numerous female followers. He organized these women into convents alongside the male monasteries of the order, and initially they shared a church while living in separate buildings. Later, in the 1130s, the separation of communities of women from communities of men was initiated, a move that led to the gradual decline of houses of canonesses.

The Premonstratensians followed the *Rule of St. Augustine* but amplified and modified it with their own *Statutes*, first drawn up (1131–34) under Hugh of Fosses, who succeeded Norbert in 1126. These statutes and later versions were significantly indebted to Cistercian customs with regard to the details of daily life and discipline. Premonstratensians also adopted the Cistercian practice of an annual chapter-general. Communities were soon to be found not only in France, England, and Italy but also in Palestine and eastern Europe. The White Canons, as they were called because of their white (i.e., undyed) wool habits, became known especially for their dedication to poverty, to the care of the poor, to quiet (as a result of communal isolation and/or individual discipline), and to the clerical responsibility for the cure of souls.

Grover A. Zinn

[See also: *AUGUSTINE, RULE OF ST.*; PREACHING; REGULAR CANONS; ROBERT D'ARBRISSEL]

Petit, François. *La spiritualité des Prémontrés aux XIIe et XIIIe siècles.* Paris: Vrin, 1947.
————. *Norbert et l'origine des Prémontrés.* Paris: Cerf, 1981.
Ulm, Kaspar, ed. *Norbert von Xanten: Adliger, Ordensstifter, Kirchenfürst.* Cologne: Wienand, 1984.

PRESLES, RAOUL DE (1316–1382). After legal studies at Orléans, Raoul was attached to the Châtelet in Paris and eventually to the household of Charles V, where he enjoyed considerable royal favor. His works include a Latin *Compendium morale de re publica* (1363), a French *Discours de l'oriflamme* (1369), and the *Muse*, an imaginary quest for a solution to France's contemporary problems. Raoul is best known for his translation (1371–75) of Augustine's *De civitate Dei* (*Cité de Dieu*), with his own important commentary. Many illustrated manuscripts, including the king's own copy of this text, still exist. He began a translation of the Bible at the request of Charles V, but it remained incomplete at his death.

Charity Cannon Willard

[See also: TRANSLATION]

Bossuat, Robert. "Raoul de Presles." In *Histoire littéraire de la France.* Paris: Imprimerie Nationale, 1974, Vol. 40, pp. 113–86.
Leroux de Lincy, Antoine, and L.M. Tisserand. *Paris et ses historiens.* Paris: Imprimerie Impériale, 1867, pp. 83–115.
Willard, Charity C. "Raoul de Presles' Translation of St. Augustine's *De civitate Dei.*" In *Medieval Translators and Their Craft*, ed. Jeanette Beer. Kalamazoo: Medieval Institute, 1989, pp. 329–46.

PRÉVÔT/PRÉVÔTÉ. *Prévôt* (Lat. *praepositus*) was one of several titles given to seigneurial officers involved in managing rural estates. The first Capetian kings used *prévôts* to administer the scattered parts of the royal domain. At a local level, they were responsible for justice, military defense, and collection of the king's seigneurial revenues. In the 11th century, the *prévôts* tended increasingly to make their positions hereditary and thus became more difficult to control. One of the king's "great officers," the seneschal, became their supervisor. In the 12th century, the office of *prévôt* was put up for bidding, and henceforth the *prévôts* were farmers of revenues. To monitor their performance and curtail abuses, the crown established roving justices, *baillis*, to hear complaints against them. The office of seneschal was vacant after 1191, and in the next few years the *baillis* became established in geographical regions as powerful officials superior to the *prévôts*. The district for which a *prévôt* was responsible was called the *prévôté*, and there were half a dozen of these in each *bailliage*.

John Bell Henneman, Jr.

[See also: *BAILLI/BAILLIAGE; PRÉVÔT DE PARIS*]

PRÉVÔT DE PARIS. The *prévôt de Paris* was the official charged with protection of royal rights, oversight of royal administration, and execution of royal justice in the *prévôté* or *vicomté* of Paris throughout the late Middle Ages. It is not known precisely when the first *prévôt* was appointed (probably not before the 11th century), but the office was similar to that held by administrators of noble and royal estates elsewhere in Europe, many of whom, like the *prévôt de Paris*, were originally farmers of income. The Parisian *prévôt* became important because Paris became the principal seat of government for the realm in the late 12th century. Sometime in the reign of Philip II Augustus (r. 1180–1223), another official, salaried, was appointed to supervise the *prévôt de Paris*. Technically, he may have had the title of *bailli*, but the sources ordinarily call him *prévôt* as well. Consequently, in the first half of the 13th century there were two *prévôts de Paris*. No precise line of demarcation has been drawn between their powers, although the *prévôt-bailli* was probably a delegate of the royal court, Parlement, and the judicial superior of the two. In general, they acted jointly and with a single seal. Louis IX, ca. 1260, combined the two positions into one, assigned a huge salary to it, and appointed Étienne Boileau to the new office, a man whom Jean de Joinville praised for his probity.

The court of the *prévôt(s)* was the Châtelet, and though always subordinate to the Parlement de Paris it had extensive criminal and civil jurisdiction; by 1274, it was providing a forum for private registering of acts (voluntary or gracious jurisdiction). It came to exercise even greater powers in the troubled 14th and 15th centuries, when treason cases were frequently tried there. Mercantile jurisdiction in the city, however, lay largely with the *prévôt des marchands*, a "private" official, but one usually under the close supervision of the royal *prévôt* of Paris or of Parlement.

William Chester Jordan

[See also: PARIS; PHILIP II AUGUSTUS; *PRÉVÔT/PRÉVÔTÉ*]

Jordan, William. *Louis IX and the Challenge of the Crusade: A Study in Rulership.* Princeton: Princeton University Press, 1979.
Serper, Arié. "L'administration royale de Paris au temps de Louis IX." *Francia* 7 (1979): 123–39.

PRÉVÔT DES MARCHANDS. See PARIS; *PRÉVÔT DE PARIS*

PRINCE/PRINCIPALITY. The Old French words *prince* and *princ(h)ier*, the Old Occitan *prince(p)/princi(p)* and *princeer*, and the English "prince" are all derived from the Classical Latin *princeps* (pl. *principes*), whose basic sense was "first in order." Throughout the classical and medieval periods, *princeps* was applied to men both as a specific and as a generic title indicative of high political and social rank, but the range of statuses with which it was associated in both senses changed significantly over time.

As a specific and formal title, applicable to the holders of particular political dignities as such rather than as members of broad social categories, *princeps* was used between 500 and 1100 only with the juridical sense it had acquired by 300 in Roman law: "ruler with full monarchical powers" or "sovereign territorial lord." In Gaul, after the collapse of Roman power, it was progressively usurped (before 1020, only as an additional or alternative title) by ever lesser rulers as a sign of their effective independence of higher authority: by the Frankish kings in the 6th century; by their mayors of the palace, ca. 700–51; by the official dukes governing the peripheral provinces of the Frankish kingdom, ca. 700–80; by the rulers of the new marches and duchies and of certain counties (in alternation or combination with other titles in such phrases as *princeps et dux Normannorum*), ca. 900–1100; and by the rulers of certain of the newly formed castellanies, ca. 1020–1120. To both the personal status and the jurisdictional territory of all of these French "princes," the term "principate" (Lat. *principatus*, OFr. *princié, princé(e)*, Old Occitan *principat*) was commonly applied, but before 1020 only as a secondary title.

Between 1120 and 1481, no lord in France is known to have made any regular use of *prince* as a title of lordship, but the title was born throughout this period by a handful of great lords of French origin in Italy (from 1062), the Holy Land (from 1099), and Greece (from 1204), all of whom ruled dominions whose primary title was "principate." Between 1481 and 1515, seven relatively minor barons, six of them in Angoumois or Saintonge and one in Picardy, usurped the title of *prince*. The first titular principality to be officially erected in France was that of Joinville, elevated in April 1552 for the duke of Guise, and thereafter the dignity was occasionally conferred on members of houses that were already princely in the generic sense.

In their generic sense, *princeps* and its vernacular derivatives were applied informally, and usually in the plural, to the members of some loosely defined class of "leading men" within a community or dominion. *Principes* was applied in this sense to the leading members of the Frankish tribe, of the kingdom of the Franks as a whole, and of the duchies, marches, counties, and castellanies down to ca. 1150. In Latin documents before ca. 1150, it was normally employed in alternation or combination with such other generic terms as *magnates, proceres,* and *potentes,* all roughly synonymous; but of these terms, only *princeps* gave rise to a vernacular derivative, so it must have prevailed in the spoken language. During the 12th century, both the Latin word and its vernacular derivatives were largely replaced in France in the generic sense of "leading man" by the newly synonymous title *baron,* but *prince* continued to be used, to 1500 and beyond, of the greater barons of the kingdom who were not only the "leading men" of the realm but virtually sovereign rulers. In consequence, the titles "principate" and "principality" were used as generic titles for the dominions of greater barons, the former before and the latter after ca. 1300. A feminine version of the personal title, *princess,* first appeared only ca. 1320.

From 1441, the generic title *prince* was employed with gradually increasing frequency in the expression *princes du sang (royal),* or "princes of the blood (royal)," to designate the members of the royal house. As all such princes were rulers of major baronies, however, this did not at first alter the basic sense of the title *prince* itself, and the royal princes were just as often referred to at first as "seigneurs" or "lords of the blood." Not until the 16th century did the generic title *prince* and its feminine equivalent, *princess,* begin to acquire their modern sense, "member of the lineage of a sovereign lord," when used by themselves. In France, unlike England, royal princes were always distinguished by the phrase "of the blood."

D'A. Jonathan D. Boulton

[**See also:** NOBILITY]

Boulton, D'A.J.D. *Grants of Honour: The Origins of the Systems of Nobiliary Dignities of Traditional France, ca. 1100–1515.* Forthcoming.

Jackson, Richard A. "Peers of France and Princes of the Blood." *French Historical Studies* 8 (1971): 27–46.

Kienast, Walther. *Der Herzogstitel in Frankreich und Deutschland (9. bis 12. Jahrhundert).* Vienna: Oldenbourg, 1968.

Werner, Karl Ferdinand. "Les principautés périphériques du monde franc du VIIIe siècle." In *Structures politiques du monde franc (VIe–XIIe siècles).* London: Variorum, 1979.

PRISE D'ORANGE. A post-1160 imitation of a lost *Siège d'Orange,* this chanson de geste of 1,888 assonanced decasyllables recounts the exploits that bring together in the Guillaume d'Orange Cycle the name of the hero and that of his city. The lost text, known principally through the *Vita sancti Wilhelmi* (1125), told of the siege of Orange by the Saracens after the conquest of the city (and undoubtedly of its queen, Orable, as well) by Guillaume de Toulouse. This story, perhaps linked to memories of Guillaume de Provence, victor over the Muslims in 972, marks the point of encounter between the traditions relative to Guillaume de Toulouse and the Occitan region.

The reworked version, found in nine cyclical manuscripts, is directly tied to the *Charroi de Nîmes,* which serves as its point of departure. Once installed in Nîmes, Guillaume becomes bored: the Saracens are no longer rebellious, there are no women or minstrels around. Thus, when Guillebert de Laon, who has just escaped from Orange, praises the charms of the town and the beautiful Orable, the hero determines to win them both. He reaches Orange in disguise, with Guillebert and his nephew Guielin, and manages to speak with Orable. Unmasked by a fugitive from Nîmes, he locks himself within the tower Gloriete, convinces Orable to arm the Christians, but is captured. Orable is given charge of the prisoners while a deputation is sent to her husband Thibaut, who, except in a single late manuscript, never arrives. Orable frees the prisoners, who are recaptured but manage to escape again and send Guillebert to Nîmes for help. Guillaume's nephew Bertrand arrives with an army, and after a short battle the Christians are victorious and Guillaume weds Orable.

Borrowing certain motifs from the *Charroi*, such as the use of disguise that allows the hero to praise himself before Orable, the *Prise* is a courtly and humorous, rather than parodic, retelling of a knightly expedition. Love pangs torment Guillaume from the moment he hears Guillebert's tale, and if in his desire for conquest he constantly associates Orange and Orable it seems clear that he undertakes to win the city *par amistié* ("for love," l. 1,564). Related to the theme of the amorous Saracen princess, the hero's conduct, constantly mocked by his two companions, shows his character in a new light and gives the poem a heroic-comic tone.

François Suard

[See also: CHANSON DE GESTE; *CHARROI DE NÎMES*; GUILLAUME D'ORANGE CYCLE]

Régnier, Claude, ed. *Les rédactions en vers de* La prise d'Orange. Paris: Klincksieck, 1968.

Frappier, Jean. *Les chansons de geste du cycle de Guillaume d'Orange.* 2 vols. Paris: Société d'Édition d'Enseignement Supérieur, 1965, Vol. 2, pp. 255–317.

Lachet, Claude. *La prise d'Orange ou la parodie courtoise d'une épopée.* Paris: Champion, 1986.

PRIVATE WAR. The phenomenon of private war reveals essential aspects of medieval French society and government, particularly those relating to chivalry, violence, and the growth of royal sovereignty. Private war in fact existed long before it took on codified form in law. The ancient Germanic feud generated a thriving medieval offspring that flourished in the post-Carolingian decay of royal authority and blossomed into a recognized *droit de guerre* during what Marc Bloch called the "first feudal age." The chivalric ethos glorified the defense of honor through violence. As the legal writer Philippe de Beaumanoir acknowledged in the late 13th century, "Gentlemen may make war according to our custom." It was a cherished right, insisted upon as a sign of noble status and freedom, exercised vigorously by lords who viewed fighting as one of the chief joys and most meaningful occupations of life. The nobles of Picardy and Burgundy insisted on writing their right to private war into the charters they secured from Louis X in the movement of 1314–15.

So important was private war to the demonstration of privileged status and the securing of its material advan-tages that collectivities of townsmen claimed and exercised the right whenever possible. Their wars were as frequent, lasting, and legal as those between lords of fiefs. Feudal lords indeed often treated towns as collective lordships, formally defied them, and fought them in the most accepted style of private war.

The later Capetian kings, however, busily moving their power in the direction of sovereignty, looked on control of lordly violence, and its bourgeois imitation, within their realms as an essential attribute of royal authority. They could scarcely abolish by fiat a custom so old and deeply rooted, but they tried by a wide range of measures to bring it under royal regulation. Royal *ordonnances* periodically prohibited private wars during the king's war and in general portrayed private wars as regulated affairs. Royal *asseurements* forced peace upon quarrelsome parties. Royal *panonceaux*, batons embellished with the fleur-de-lis, theoretically spread the king's protection wherever they were placed, on homes, ships, and so on. Royal charges of *port d'armes* (illegal use of weapons) brought hundreds of cases into the king's jurisdiction.

Yet private war survived throughout the Middle Ages. The efforts of emerging royal sovereignty were significant, but the privileged very slowly yielded the right to violence within the realm of France.

Richard W. Kaeuper

[See also: *CAS ROYAUX*; PEACE OF GOD; *SAUVEGARDE*; WARFARE]

Dubois, P. *Les asseurements au XIIIe siècle dans nos villes du nord.* Paris: Rousseau, 1900.

Ducoudray, Gustave. *Les origines du Parlement de Paris et la justice aux XIIIe et XIVe siècles.* Paris: Hachette, 1902.

Kaeuper, Richard W. *War, Justice, and Public Order: England and France in the Later Middle Ages.* Oxford: Clarendon, 1988.

Keen, Maurice. *The Laws of War in the Later Middle Ages.* London: Routledge and Kegan Paul, 1965.

Perrot, Ernest. *Les cas royaux.* Paris: Rousseau, 1910.

PRIVILEGE. When applied to medieval France, "privilege" is difficult to separate from such terms as "liberties" or "franchises," which implied protection against arbitrary, capricious, or exploitative treatment. "Privilege" could have the same connotation, but it usually tended to confer on someone a special or superior position in society.

Liberties that afforded protection could evolve into what we would recognize as privilege. A document protecting a church and its lands from arbitrary treatment by royal officials might be cited, much later, to justify oppressive treatment of its tenants or exemption from obligations to which the population as a whole was subject. Privileges or liberties might be defined in documents or claimed as part of the customary law of the land. Those with privileges might be corporate bodies (towns, universities, monasteries), members of some occupational or social group, such as students, moneyers, nobles, or royal officials, or even individuals. Individuals generally claimed privileges by virtue of being members of some privileged group or corporate body.

It was not always clear what privileges of a corporate body extended to its members, nor was it clear how privileges applied in situations not foreseen when granted or not provided for in customary law. Regional differences in customary law created further complications. Since France did not have a common customary law, lawyers and judges trained in Roman and canon law often invoked principles from these legal systems to describe what and when privileges might be overriden and what procedures were required to override them. Not surprisingly, privileges and liberties gave rise to much litigation.

When privileges or liberties afforded protection against arbitrary power, they might place one under a jurisdiction other than that of royal officials or authorize one to exercise jurisdiction that normally belonged to the king. Conversely, they might entitle one to come under royal jurisdiction instead of that of a town or seigneur. Those placed under royal protection could escape the jurisdiction of others, but this type of protection did not spare one from arbitrary treatment by the crown. Foreign merchants enjoyed this ambiguous royal "protection" and were prepared to invoke it in court, but they were vulnerable to exactions from their royal protector that could be ruinous.

Many privileges or liberties had fiscal implications. Members of some corporate body or occupational group would gain exemption from royal or seigneurial exactions by paying a lump sum or a nominal annual fee. By the end of the 13th century, however, expensive wars led the monarchy to introduce taxation based on the principle, from Roman law, that the common utility and "evident necessity" justified overriding fiscal privileges. Rarely did courts uphold objections by taxpayers claiming privileges, but the crown usually needed money quickly and often preferred to "settle out of court," getting an immediate payment in return for "letters of nonprejudice" specifying that the payment did not constitute a precedent that could damage alleged privileges. This policy made future litigation a virtual certainty. So also did another royal policy, that of negotiating lump-sum payments from a region or a town, which then had to levy taxes of its own in order to raise the money. People with exemptions from local taxes usually resisted paying those that contributed to royal ones until a court required them to do so.

Such litigation is our best source as to what groups claimed privileges. In 1353, for example, a court required clergy, nobles, moneyers, sergeants, notaries, and other officers of the crown to contribute to a tax they had resisted. Communities like communes, *bastides*, and *villeneuves* had charters dating from the 11th or 12th century exempting them from royal exactions. When the 14th century produced new taxes under new conditions, these privileges ran counter to the doctrine of "evident necessity." Numerous court decisions attempted to resolve the issue, but the matter remained contentious until the French Revolution.

The church desired primarily to establish its right to give consent each time a tax ran counter to its privileges. If proper procedures were followed, the clergy generally were prepared to pay. The right to consent, however, did not in this period imply a right to withhold consent, and most royal subjects resisted taxes on the grounds of precedent or insufficient necessity.

The nobles were the most privileged of all in medieval France, and their concern was to be treated as a separate caste. They might demand the right to render personal military service (the "tax in blood") instead of paying to finance a war. They might be willing to pay a tax based on some established feudal obligation, such as funding the ransom of a captured king. They even acquiesced, reluctantly, in taxes designed exclusively to pay military salaries. If possible, however, they wanted to make their contributions in a different way from others so that their separate status might be underscored.

In general, noble claims of privileges exempting them from taxation were increasingly denied in court by the third quarter of the 14th century, but the political turmoil of Charles VI's reign improved the bargaining position of the nobility. Ordinances of 1388 and 1393 granted nobles exemption from the *taille* and the *aides*, respectively, subject to certain conditions. In the end, the most important of these conditions required that they "live nobly" and avoid actions, such as engaging in trade, incompatible with noble status. Failure to "live nobly," known as *dérogeance*, could in principle cause a loss of fiscal exemptions. Nobles with fiscal exemptions were defined strictly at first, but by the mid-15th century the exemption was broader and few nobles could fail to qualify.

Fiscal privileges were an important matter to nobles who lacked great wealth, as many did by 1450, but it had real significance only when royal taxes became heavy and regular. The nobles had many other privileges, however, some deeply rooted in custom; these included judicial privileges, those attached to certain offices, honorific privileges, and many rights associated with the medieval lordship, or *seigneurie*. The real heyday of privileges, especially those of the nobles, was not the medieval period but the three centuries that ended in 1789.

John Bell Henneman, Jr.

[**See also:** *AIDES*; COMMUNE; NOBILITY]

Bush, Michael L. *Noble Privilege*. London: Holmes and Meier, 1983.

Dravasa, E. "'Vivre noblement': recherches sur la dérogeance de noblesse du XIVe au XVIe siècle." *Revue juridique et économique du Sud-Ouest* (1965): 7–260.

Henneman, John Bell. "Nobility, Privilege and Fiscal Politics in Late Medieval France." *French Historical Studies* 13 (1983): 1–17.

Timbal, Pierre C., et al. *La guerre de cent ans vue à travers les registres du Parlement, 1337–1369*. Paris: CNRS, 1961.

PROCESSION. The ceremonial procession is a common ritual element of virtually all religions. Biblical processions that might have affected Christian practice are those that were held with the Ark of the Covenant and that of Christ's entry into Jerusalem on Palm Sunday. There is already frequent mention of processions in the patristic period, and by the early Middle Ages they are firmly established in the liturgy. The pope, attended by Roman officials and clergy, was conducted in solemn procession to the stational church on each of some ninety dates throughout the year; upon arrival, he vested and was led again through the nave of the church to the sanctuary as the Introit antiphon and psalm were chanted. Several liturgical dates called for processions; among these are Palm Sunday, Candlemas Day (February 2), and the Rogation Days (the day of the Greater Litany, April 15; and the lesser Rogation Days, the three days before Ascension Thursday). During the Rogation processions, and many others as well, the Litany of All Saints was chanted, accounting for use of the word *litania* as a synonym for "procession."

In addition to processions required by the liturgical calendar, it was customary to arrange for them in special circumstances, for example, to pray for rain, peace, or relief from plague. Processions might be held within the confines of the church, and in fact the ambulatories and aisles of the great French Romanesque and Gothic churches must have been planned with this in mind. Saint-Denis saw a marked proliferation of processions after the 13th-century additions to Suger's early Gothic east-end ambulatory. Rogation processions, and others of agricultural significance, moved out into the countryside, while the late-medieval Corpus Christi procession made its way through the streets of the town in a carnival-like atmosphere. Processions were led by an individual carrying the processional cross; originally associated with the movement of some ecclesiastical dignitary, this was simply a cross or crucifix mounted on a long staff so that it would be easily visible.

James McKinnon

[See also: ENTRIES, ROYAL; LITURGICAL YEAR; MASS, CHANTS AND TEXTS]

Bailey, Terence. *The Processions of Sarum and the Western Church*. Toronto: Pontifical Institute of Mediaeval Studies, 1971.

Robertson, Ann Walters. *The Service-Books of the Royal Abbey of Saint-Denis*. London: Oxford University Press, 1991.

PROCESSIONAL THEATER. Processions have been an integral part of culture from the earliest times. In medieval France, they were associated with many ritual and ceremonial activities, taking the form of religious processions, royal and princely entries, funeral cortèges, and carnival parades. There were also processions of petition in times of plague and war, processions of thanksgiving for prayers answered, and processions of joy for royal weddings and births. In addition, jousters and their retinues processed into the lists at tournaments, and players advertised the Passion plays with *montres* in which they paraded through the streets in costume.

All such activities had a theatrical aspect about them, but they were not plays in the modern sense. In the late Middle Ages, however, plays were routinely integrated into many civic and religious processions. The practice of staging biblical or allegorical scenes at royal entries, for example, seems to have begun in northern France in the second half of the 14th century. Such scenes were often *tableaux vivants* or mimed actions, but in many cases they were fully developed plays. In Tournai in 1368, *histoires* were played before the king at a royal entry, but only after the procession. The earliest record of plays or *tableaux vivants* staged along the route of an entry procession is from the entry of Charles VI into Paris in 1380. The custom spread throughout France in the course of the 15th century.

In the northern French provinces, dramatic spectacles were often staged on horse-drawn wagons similar to the pageant wagons of England. This permitted mimed plays and *tableaux vivants* to move with a procession and thus be seen by a greater number of spectators. From the early 15th century, the Corpus Christi procession in the town of Saint-Omer, for example, included a *mystère* that preceded the Sacrament. Staging practice varied from one city to another in the region, but generally the silent spectacles were presented either on fixed stages along the route of march or on moving stages in the procession. The spoken plays were then presented after the procession.

The best-documented example of processional theater comes from the city of Lille, which had a "Grand Procession" every year on the second Sunday after Pentecost. Founded in 1270 as a religious procession in honor of the Virgin Mary, it came to include the trade guilds and other civic institutions. In the 14th century, neighborhood groups began to stage plays at the procession, and prizes were given for the best ones. In the course of the next century, the contest was organized by the Bishop of Fools, a dignitary elected each Twelfth Night by the canons of the collegiate church of Saint-Pierre. In 1463, the "bishop" issued a proclamation calling for new plays to be written for the procession based on the Bible, Roman history, or the lives of the saints. He called for farces as well. Each neighborhood group presented a serious and a comic play, and prizes were given for the best of each. All were staged on pageant wagons. On the morning of the procession, the edifying plays were mimed at designated intervals along the route of march as the procession passed. In the afternoon, all the wagons were brought to the main square, where the plays were performed with spoken dialogue. In the evening, the crowds were entertained with the farces.

A remarkable collection of seventy-two plays written for the Grand Procession of Lille has been preserved in a manuscript in the Herzog August Library in Wolfenbüttel, Germany. The anonymous plays, ranging from 200 to 1,900 lines of verse, were most likely written by clerics attached to the church of Saint-Pierre. Of the sixty-four biblical plays, forty-three derive from the Old Testament and twenty-one from the New Testament. The former treat events in the lives of Abraham, Moses, Joseph, Ruth, David, and Esther, among others. Five of the plays are drawn from the Roman histories of Livy and Valerius Maximus and deal with heroes like Actilius Regulus and Mucius Scaevola. In addition, there are a morality play on the Assumption of Mary, a play on the life of St. Euphrosina, and a miracle play based on the story of the pregnant abbess. The manuscript was written in the 1480s, but plays of this kind continued to be performed at the procession in Lille through most of the 16th century.

Alan E. Knight

[See also: ENTRIES, ROYAL; STAGING OF PLAYS; THEATER]

Guenée, Bernard, and Françoise Lehoux. *Les entrées royales françaises de 1328 à 1515*. Paris: CNRS, 1968.

Knight, Alan E. *Aspects of Genre in Late Medieval French Drama*. Manchester: Manchester University Press, 1983, pp. 117–40.

———. "Processional Theater in Lille in the Fifteenth Century." In *Le théâtre et la cité dans l'Europe médiévale*, ed. Edelgard E. DuBruck and William C. McDonald. Stuttgart: Heinz, 1988, pp. 347–58.

PROPHÉCIES DE MERLIN. Not to be confused with Geoffrey of Monmouth's *Prophetiae Merlini*, with which it has nothing in common beyond the title, the *Prophécies de Merlin* dates from the 1270s and is attributed to Maistre Richart d'Irlande. The prose work, purporting to record Merlin's conversations with his scribes, has the magician make prophecies that are actually references to political events of the 12th and 13th centuries. It is found in at least a dozen late medieval manuscripts and was first printed in 1498 by Vérard.

Norris J. Lacy

[See also: ARTHURIAN COMPILATIONS]

Bertholet, Anne, ed. *Les prophesies de Merlin (Cod. Bodmer 116)*. Geneva: Droz, 1992.

Paton, Lucy, ed. *Les prophecies de Merlin*. 2 vols. New York: Heath, 1926–27.

PROSE ROMANCE (ARTHURIAN). The turn of the 13th century marks a crucial shift in the writing of Arthurian romance, when, due to reasons not yet fully understood, prose becomes a viable medium for telling stories of love and adventure. Previously, Old French prose, like its Latin counterpart, had been reserved largely for recording legal and religious truths. It appeared in juridical texts, charters, religious writings, translations of the Bible, and sermons. Prose was also used to document historical events in the chronicles of Villehardouin, Robert de Clari, and Henri de Valenciennes. But fictive tales of Arthurian knights had before this time appeared only in verse. By the 13th century, the Arthurian adventure story had undergone significant thematic changes, incorporating within the realm of chivalric exploits the spiritual quest for the Holy Grail. Following the examples set in Chrétien de Troyes's verse *Perceval* (ca. 1181–90) and Robert de Boron's even more christianized *Joseph d'Arimathie* (ca. 1200), the Arthurian adventure story moved into the 13th century with an expansive prose format that matched its expanded narrative scope.

As Robert de Boron's *Joseph* and the fragmentary verse *Merlin* appended to it were recast into prose beginning ca. 1210, they emerged sometimes in a trilogy, the *Roman du Graal*, that recounts the history of the Grail vessel (*Joseph d'Arimathie*), its arrival in Great Britain along with the discovery of the future King Arthur (*Merlin*), the quest for the Holy Grail, and the subsequent demise of Arthur's world (*Perceval*, known as the Didot *Perceval*). This basic pattern is followed with variation in subsequent prose rewritings of the ever-popular Grail material. The Arthurian Vulgate Cycle (ca. 1215–35) offers an expanded version of the literary scenario, transforming the *Joseph* into the *Estoire del saint Graal*, the *Merlin* into the Vulgate *Merlin*, and the prose *Perceval* into the *Queste del saint Graal* and *Mort Artu*. To these, the Vulgate adds an elaborate and lengthy version of the Lancelot story. Known generally as the *Prose Lancelot*, this cyclic romance must be distinguished from the noncyclic *Prose Lancelot* conceived, it is thought, in a more secular vein to stand independently of the highly religious *Queste del saint Graal*. A noncyclic and highly elaborated version of the Perceval story is found in the early 13th-century *Perlesvaus*, a tale that mixes familiar exploits of Gawain, Lancelot, and Perceval with political intrigue and savage bloodshed.

The Vulgate *Merlin*, characterized by a historical "suite" that details Arthur's military successes under Merlin's guidance, is rewritten with a more fanciful "suite" in the Post-Vulgate *Roman du Graal* (ca. 1230–40). Formerly known as the Pseudo-Robert de Boron Cycle, this corpus contains a remodeled Vulgate *Estoire*, *Queste*, and *Mort Artu*, portions of the Vulgate *Lancelot*, and the revised *Merlin* (known as the Huth *Merlin*).

Dating from the second and third quarters of the 13th century, the *Prose Tristan* expands the earlier Grail narratives by adding to the world of Arthur's knights King Marc, his wife, Iseut, and nephew, Tristan. Another character introduced here is Palamedes, who also appears in a prose romance called either *Palamedes*, *Meliadus*, or *Guiron le Courtois*. This romance, which predates the cyclic version of the *Prose Tristan*, chronicles the deeds of an older Arthurian generation, following the fathers of Palamedes, Arthur, Tristan, and Erec. In the 14th century, the Middle French *Perceforest* details the pre-Arthurian history of Britain from the time of Alexander the Great, including the arrival of Joseph of Arimathea in Britain and incidents involving the Holy Grail.

E. Jane Burns

[See also: ARTHURIAN COMPILATIONS; GRAIL AND GRAIL ROMANCES; *PERCEFOREST*; *PERLESVAUS*; POST-VULGATE ROMANCE; *PROSE TRISTAN*; ROBERT DE BORON; VULGATE CYCLE]

Bogdanow, Fanni, ed. *La Queste del Saint Graal et la Mort Artu Post-Vulgate, Troisième partie du Roman du Graal*. Paris: Didot, 1991.

Curtis, Renée L., ed. *Le roman de Tristan en prose*. 3 vols. Munich: Hueber, 1963 (Vol. 1); Leiden: Brill, 1976 (Vol. 2); Cambridge: Brewer, 1985 (Vol. 3).

Frappier, Jean, ed. *La mort le roi Artu: roman du XIIIe siècle*. Geneva: Droz, 1954.

Guiron le Courtoys. Paris: Vérard, 1501; repr. with intro by Cedric E. Pickford. London: Scolar, 1980.

Hucher, Eugène, ed. *Le Saint-Graal.* 3 vols. Le Mans: Monnoyer, 1875–78.

Ménard, Philippe, et al., eds. *Le roman de Tristan en prose.* Geneva, Droz, 1987– . (5 vols. to date).

Micha, Alexandre, ed. *Lancelot: roman en prose du XIIIe siècle.* 9 vols. Geneva: Droz, 1978–83.

Nitze, William A. and T. Atkinson Jenkins, eds. *Le haut livre du Graal: Perlesvaus.* 2 vols. Chicago: Chicago University Press, 1932–37.

Pauphilet, Albert, ed. *La Queste del Saint Graal.* Paris: Champion, 1923.

Roussineau, Gilles, ed. *Troisième partie du roman de Perceforest.* 3 vols. Geneva: Droz, 1988–93.

———, ed. *Perceforest, quatrième partie.* 2 vols. Geneva: Droz, 1987.

Taylor, Jane H.M., ed. *Le Roman de Perceforest, première partie.* Geneva: Droz, 1979.

PROSE TRISTAN. Composed ca. 1230, the *Prose Tristan*, with all its successive versions in numerous manuscripts and 15th-century printed editions, is nothing less than a *summa* of the Matter of Britain. A highly developed technique of compilation in effect led to the progressive unification of the story of Tristan and his ancestors with that of King Arthur, the Grail quest, and the loss of Arthur's and Tristan's worlds.

In a smooth and effective prose, the *Prose Tristan* presents in a single text nearly all modes of literary discourse: lyric insertions, love monologues, letters, descriptions, political discourses. It perfects the art of dialogue and debate and skillfully exploits the most diversified techniques for organizing romance narratives.

Its authors, the Pseudo-Luce del Gast and the Pseudo-Hélie de Boron, reformulating and integrating into their story the episodes inherited from Béroul and Thomas d'Angleterre, refashioned the love story on that of Lancelot and Guenevere, making Tristan a knight-errant seeking adventure, a member of the Round Table, a Grail knight. The "sad" knight becomes above all a knight in search of love's "joy," experienced fully if briefly only in the Arthurian world. However, the tradition of the poetic versions, and the power of the theme of love and death, posed an obstacle to this radical transformation of Tristan and his destiny. The most evident sign of this resistance is the systematic degradation of King Mark, who ends by slaying his nephew. The interest of the *Prose Tristan* resides in this tension, between a myth of fatal passion and the sentimentalism and chivalric idealism of the *Prose Lancelot*, between the hero's desire to stay in Cornwall with Iseut and the need he feels to live in the Arthurian world to achieve glory. The lovers underestimate these tensions, which nonetheless reshape the narrative and explain the hero's lengthy sojourns in Arthur's kingdom. But the secondary characters, such as Kaherdin, Palamedes, and Dinadan, underscore through their words and actions the vanity of knight-errantry and of chivalric deeds, the absurdity of the Arthurian world and its customs, and the tragic misunderstandings of passion.

Revised and expanded as late as the 15th century, translated and assimilated into such compilations as the Italian *Tavola Ritonda*, the Spanish and Portuguese *Demandas* (or *Questes del saint Graal*), the *Compilation* of Rusticien of Pisa, Malory's *Morte Darthur*, and other works, and preserved in manuscripts that are often richly decorated, the *Prose Tristan* was immensely popular into the 15th century and beyond. Until the rediscovery of the poetic texts in the 19th century, the story of the love of Tristan and Iseut was known only through its prose versions.

Emmanuèle Baumgartner

[See also: BÉROUL; PROSE ROMANCE (ARTHURIAN); THOMAS D'ANGLETERRE; VULGATE CYCLE]

Curtis, Renée L., ed. *Le roman de Tristan en prose.* 3 vols. Munich: Hueber, 1963 (Vol. 1); Leiden: Brill, 1976 (Vol. 2); Cambridge: Brewer, 1985 (Vol. 3).

Ménard, Philippe, et al., eds. *Le roman de Tristan en prose.* Geneva, Droz, 1987– . (5 vols. to date).

Baumgartner, Emmanuèle. *Le Tristan et prose: essai d'interprétation d'un roman médiéval.* Geneva: Droz, 1975.

———. *La harpe et l'épée: tradition et renouvellement dans le "Tristan" en prose.* Paris: Société d'Édition d'Enseignement Supérieur, 1990.

PROSTITUTION. Prostitution was not an important social phenomenon in France until the urban revival of the high Middle Ages, when the use of the term *meretrix publica* allowed the clear distinction of the professional prostitute from the privately "loose" woman, and when towns began to regulate the profession. In the south of France, prostitutes were generally banned from the centers of towns in the 12th and early 13th centuries but by the late 13th and 14th centuries official red-light districts were protected by the public authorities and sometimes guaranteed as zones where no arrests for adultery could be made. These districts were generally reduced to one house, often owned by the municipality or by the great bourgeois, and sometimes protected by seigneurial or royal safeguard, in the late 14th and 15th centuries. At the same time, repression of competition (procuring and freelance prostitution) was intensified, as was that of concubinage and adultery. These houses were finally closed under Protestant influence in the 16th century.

The prostitute enjoyed full legal capacity in the late Middle Ages and was protected under rape laws. She had to observe regulations concerning dress and behavior and toward the end of the Middle Ages was virtually cloistered in the official brothel under the direction of the person who "farmed" the brothel (paid a fixed sum to the owner yearly in exchange for rights to all profits). In the bigger towns, religious communities of repentant women, founded by clerics and bourgeois, welcomed retired or penitent prostitutes.

Leah L. Otis-Cour

Otis, Leah. *Prostitution in Medieval Society: The History of an Urban Institution in Languedoc.* Chicago: University of Chicago Press, 1985.

Rossiaud, J. *La prostitution médiévale.* Paris: Flammarion, 1988.

PROSULA. A new text added to a preexisting melody, often to a melismatic portion of a chant (i.e., to those places where a single vowel sound is prolonged for many notes) or sometimes to an entire chant. Prosulae are found chiefly for Proper and Ordinary chants that contain significant melismas: Alleluias, Offertories (usually for melismas of final verses), Kyries, Glorias (in particular at the "Regnum"), and some Great Responsories. Prosulae were written by the Franks in the 9th–11th centuries, with important repertories existing in southern France. The prosulae from the area around Limoges edited by Odelman are extreme in that they are texts for entire Alleluia melodies; more typically, prosulae are short texts, interposed only for a single melisma within a longer chant. The literary quality of these texts is often high.

Margot Fassler

[See also: SEQUENCE (EARLY); TROPES, ORDINARY; TROPES, PROPER]

Marcusson, Olof, ed. *Corpus troporum II: Tropes de l'alleluia.* Stockholm: Almqvist and Wiksell, 1976.

Odelman, Eva, ed. *Corpus troporum VI: Les prosules limousines de Wolfenbüttel.* Stockholm: Almqvist and Wiksell, 1986.

Björkvall, Gunilla, and Ruth Steiner. "Some Prosulas for Offertory Antiphons." *Journal of the Plainsong and Mediaeval Music Society* 5 (1982): 13–35.

Fassler, Margot. *Gothic Song: Victorine Sequences and Augustinian Reform in Twelfth-Century Paris.* Cambridge: Cambridge University Press, 1993, pp. 34–37.

Kelly, Thomas Forrest. "Melisma and Prosula: The Performance of Responsory Tropes." *Liturgische Tropen: Referate zweier Colloquien des Corpus Troporum in München (1983) und Canterbury (1984),* ed. Gabriel Silagi. Munich: Arbeo-Gesellschaft, 1985, pp. 163–80.

———. "Neuma Triplex." *Acta musicologica* 60 (1988): 1–30.

PROVENCE. For some medieval writers, "Provence" was that vast area of southern France where the Langue d'oc was spoken. Most, however, used the name in a more restricted way to identify an area of approximately 18,700 square miles in the southeastern corner of France, bounded on the east by the Alps, on the south by the Mediterranean, and on the west by the Rhône. Because of its easy access both to Italy and to northern Europe, Provence played an active role during the Roman Empire and in medieval Europe. Kings, emperors, popes, merchants, and pilgrims regularly passed through this region to conduct their affairs.

The ties of Provence to the Roman Empire and Roman traditions were deeper and more lasting than anywhere else in the West outside of Italy. By the end of the 5th century, as the Germanic tribes established themselves throughout most of the empire, "Provence" came to identify the last province in Gaul to remain under imperial control.

During the early 6th century, several Germanic peoples competed for control of Provence, with the Ostrogoths ultimately becoming dominant. In 536, confronted with the invasion of the emperor Justinian's armies, the Ostrogoths withdrew, thereby permitting the Franks to enter unopposed. Although Provence would remain under Frankish control well after the breakup of the Carolingian empire, it was only when Charles Martel succeeded in crushing local rebellions between 735 and 738 that this region was finally incorporated into the Carolingian state.

Following the death of Louis I, by the Treaty of Verdun Provence became part of the middle kingdom of Lothair I. As was the case for much of Europe, Provence during the late 9th and 10th centuries fell victim to the ambitions of rival aristocratic factions. The ensuing civil strife exposed Provence to attacks by Greek, Viking, and Muslim pirates. The most serious of these began ca. 884, when Muslims established a base at Garde Freinet and launched a series of raids throughout much of the region. It was only in 972 that Count William II, the *pater patriae*, drove them from Provence.

This event marked the beginning of a social and economic revival. Benefiting both from increased Mediterranean trade and from the Crusades, the major Provençal cities, particularly Marseille and Arles, became among the most vibrant and wealthy commercial centers in the West.

Although technically part of the kingdom of Burgundy until 1032 and then part of the Holy Roman Empire, Provence was in fact ruled until the end of the 11th century by the heirs of William II. During the early 12th century, the counts of Toulouse and Barcelona struggled to control Provence, finally agreeing in 1125 to divide the county. As a result, Raymond-Berenguer I of Barcelona acquired the entire region south of the Durance. The house of Barcelona ruled Provence until 1246, when the daughter and heiress of Raymond-Berenguer IV married Charles of Anjou, the brother of Louis IX. This event marked not only the beginning of Angevin rule that would continue until 1481 but also the prolonged involvement of Provence in the ultimately disastrous Angevin policies in southern Italy. The resulting drain on its resources produced an extended economic decline for Provence. After the death of the last Angevin ruler, Charles III (1481), Louis XI incorporated Provence into the kingdom of France.

Stephen Weinberger

[See also: ANJOU, HOUSES OF; DIDACTIC LITERATURE (OCCITAN); LANGUEDOC; OCCITAN LANGUAGE; TROUBADOUR POETRY]

Février, Paul-Albert. *Le développement urbain en Provence de l'époque romaine à la fin du XIVe siècle.* Paris: Boccard, 1964.

Fontana, Mireille. *La réforme grégorienne en Provence orientale.* Aix-en-Provence: Pensée Universitaire, 1957.

Manteyer, Georges de. *La Provence du Ier au XIIe siècle.* Paris: Picard, 1905.

Poly, Jean-Pierre. *La Provence et la société féodale: 879–1166.* Paris: Bordas, 1976.

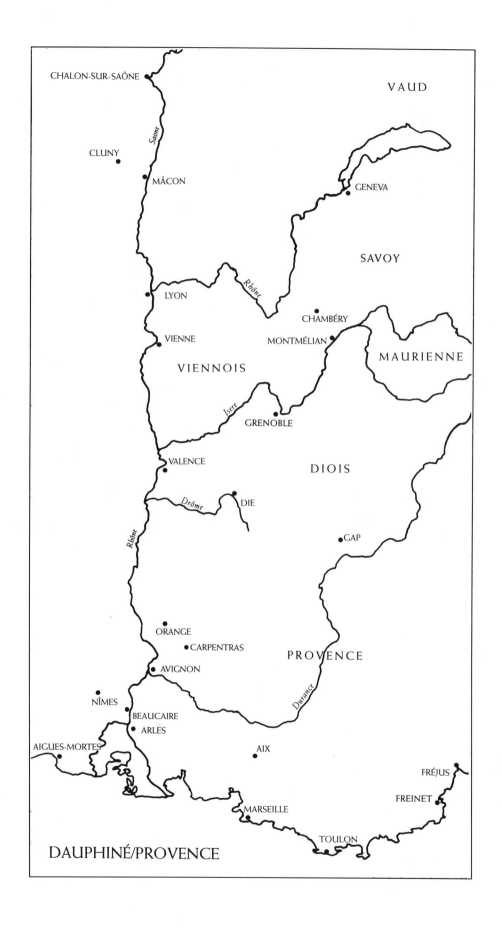

DAUPHINÉ/PROVENCE

PROVERB. Although nearly impossible to define, proverbs—statements of a universal nature borrowed from philosophers, the fathers of the church, the Bible, or popular wisdom—are found in every genre of medieval literature. The Middle Ages collected proverbs, with little care as to their origin. Widely used as a textbook in medieval schools, the *Disticha Catonis*, a proverb collection wrongly attributed to Cato, was paraphrased in Occitan (two 12th-c. fragments extant) and translated by three Anglo-Norman authors, each of whom appended commentary to the text. There are also two Francien versions of the *Disticha*, one of the most widely diffused works of the Middle Ages. Another collection, actually an anthology of biblical and medieval sententious statements attributed to classical authors, the *Moralium dogma philosophorum*, was translated into French in the 13th century, again by three different authors, including Alard de Cambrai.

Popular proverbs were also collected. The first of these collections is the *Proverbia magistri Serlonis* (1150–70), an anthology of French proverbs with Latin translations. The *Proverbes Seneke le philosophe* (1278–81) uses a similar format, attributing to Seneca proverbs from a variety of sources. In a more developed vein is the *Proverbes au vilain* (1174–91), composed of *sixains* that explain a proverb, followed by the proverb itself, which acts as commentary on the preceding verses. The *Proverbes de Marcoul et de Salemon* (early 13th c.) present a dialogue between the wise King Solomon and the boorish peasant Marcoul, the whole punctuated with proverbs. Eight manuscripts preserve three distinct versions, the first two being obscene and scatological, while the third is quite proper. Proverb collections were also assembled for preachers; these anthologies include an allegorical commentary on each proverb. Some 2,500 French proverbs are recorded prior to 1400.

Medieval authors mined anthologies for proverbs to insert into their works. The fabliaux, in particular, are notable for the use of proverbial material as commentary on the story. By the 15th century, use of the proverb had become so fashionable that there are poems composed entirely of proverbs, such as Villon's *Ballade des proverbes*.

Wendy E. Pfeffer

Morawski, Joseph, ed. *Les diz et proverbes des sages.* Paris: Presses Universitaires de France, 1924.

———. *Proverbes français antérieurs au XVe siècle.* Paris: Champion, 1925.

Ruhe, Ernstpeter, ed. *Les proverbes Seneke le philosophe.* Munich: Hueber, 1969.

Schulze-Busacker, Elisabeth, ed. *Proverbes et expressions proverbiales dans la littérature narrative du moyen âge français: recueil et analyse.* Paris: Champion, 1985.

Tobler, Adolf, ed. *Li proverbe au vilain: Die Sprichwörter des gemeinen Mannes. Altfranzösischen Dichtung nach den bisher bekannten Handschriften herausgegeben.* Leipzig: Hirzel, 1895.

Jauss, Hans Robert, and Erich Köhler, eds. *Grundriss der romanischen Literaturen des Mittelalters.* Heidelberg: Winter, 1970, Vol. 6: *La littérature didactique, allégorique et satirique*, tome 2: *Partie documentaire*, ed. Jürgen Beyer and Franz Koppe, pp. 151–61.

Mieder, Wolfgang. *International Proverb Scholarship: An Annotated Bibliography.* New York: Garland, 1982; First Supplement, 1990; Second Supplement, 1993.

PROVINS. Founded during the Merovingian period around a Benedictine priory, Provins (Seine-et-Marne) became one of the leading commercial centers, after Paris and Rouen, of medieval France and was the site of two of the principal Champagne fairs (the first in May–June, the second in September–October). Provins was a favorite residence of the counts of Champagne, notably the trouvère Thibaut IV, and counted over 10,000 inhabitants in the 13th century. Ruined by the 1373 plague and the loss of its fairs in the same century, due in large measure to the Hundred Years' War, Provins is one of the best-preserved medieval cities in France.

The 12th- and 13th-century ramparts, with their impressive twin-towered Porte Saint-Jean, are an important example of medieval military architecture. A wide dry moat precedes the crenellated walls, which average about 10 feet thick. The massive church of Saint-Quiriace, begun under Henri le Libéral in the 1160s, boasts an Early Gothic choir and ambulatory, opening onto three rectangular chapels on the flat east end. The 13th-century nave remains incompleted. The church of Saint-Ayoul preserves its 11th-century transept. After a fire in 1157, the nave and aisles were rebuilt, as was the large projecting façade with its three portals. The church of Sainte-Croix has a Romanesque transept, Gothic nave, and south side aisles from the 13th century and a Flamboyant façade, choir, ambulatory, and double north aisle from the 16th.

The most characteristic building of Provins is the Tour de César, a 12th-century keep erected on a motte that was once the site of a Roman fortress. It consists of an octagonal donjon with four angle turrets built upon a square base. The curtain wall that now surrounds its base was constructed by the English during the Hundred Years' War as an artillery site. The octagonal guard room on the first level has an impressive vault formed of four ogival arches ending in an eye through which arms and provisions could be hoisted to the levels above.

Other medieval vestiges in Provins include a Romanesque house (possibly 11th c.) in the Rue du Palais; the Hôtel de Vauluisant and Hôtel de la Croix-d'Or of the 13th century; and the celebrated Grange aux Dîmes (tithe barn) of the 12th and 13th centuries. Originally rented to merchants by the canons of Saint-Quiriace, after the demise of the fairs it served to store the tenth-part (*dîme*) of the harvest destined for the church.

William W. Kibler/William W. Clark

Maillé, La Marquise de. *Provins.* 2 vols. Paris: Éditions d'Art et d'Histoire, 1939.

Mesqui, Jean. *Provins, la fortification d'une ville au moyen âge.* Geneva: Droz, 1979.

PSEUDO-DIONYSIUS THE AREOPAGITE (fl. ca. 500). A collection of treatises and letters concerning mysticism and theology circulated in the medieval period under the name of Dionysius the Areopagite, a convert of St. Paul in Athens. Modern scholarship has concluded that the works were not written in the 1st century but rather ca. 500, probably by a Syrian monk well versed in Christian and Neoplatonic thought. The author sought "apostolic" credentials by writing under a pseudonym.

The Pseudo-Dionysian writings comprise four treatises in Greek (*Celestial Hierarchy, Ecclesiastical Hierarchy, Divine Names, Mystical Theology*) and ten letters, with internal references to other works that were probably never written. The author conceives of a mystical quest with three basic stages: purgation, illumination, and union. The material world is seen as both a barrier to and a "ladder" for ascent toward the divine. On the one hand, all concepts and images must be purged from the mind in order to arrive at a state of darkness and "unknowing" in which God, who is beyond all concepts and images, will be experienced in the "dazzling darkness" of divine presence. On the other hand, the world is conceived as a series of partial symbols of the divine. These two "theologies," one negative or "apophatic" and the other positive (symbolic) or "cataphatic," exerted a powerful effect upon western Latin theology and spirituality from the 12th century forward. Pseudo-Dionysius also conceived of a hierarchy of spiritual beings linking material and spiritual worlds and the divine. Nine "ranks" of angels were arranged in three "orders" of three ranks each in a descent from God to seraphs through the hierarchy to ordinary angels. The earthly ecclesiastical hierarchy echoed this threefold division in the orders of bishops, priests, and deacons. The sacraments, being a material mediation of divine presence, effected a participation in the divine under the ministry of the ecclesiastical hierarchy. Especially influential in the work of Pseudo-Dionysius was the notion that evil *qua* evil was nonexistent; evil was merely a lack of goodness that can only be described in negative terms.

In the medieval period, "Dionysius the Areopagite" (Fr. "Denis") came to be identified with other persons. He was taken to be a missionary to Gaul who was martyred outside of Paris and whose remains became the major relic at the royal abbey of Saint-Denis. In 827, the Byzantine emperor Michael the Stammerer sent a manuscript of Pseudo-Dionysius's works to Louis the Pious. The abbot of Saint-Denis, Hilduin, produced a rough translation. Later, Johannes Scottus Eriugena translated the works again and wrote a commentary on the *Celestial Hierarchy* that was destined to be influential but had little effect in Eriugena's own day. In the 12th century, Hugh and Richard of Saint-Victor brought Pseudo-Dionysian thought into the mainstream of mystical and theological writing. In the 13th century, new translations appeared. The influence of Pseudo-Dionysius was felt in the analysis of the attributes of God, the ideas of symbolism that informed art and writing about art, sacramental theology, and mysticism. Albert the Great and Thomas Aquinas wrote commentaries on Pseudo-Dionysian works, and Bonaventure made extensive use of Pseudo-Dionysian ideas in his mystical writings. In the 14th century, Jean Gerson and Nicholas of Cusa were much influenced by Pseudo-Dionysius, especially Cusa's ideas of the "coincidence of opposites."

Grover A. Zinn

[See also: ALBERT THE GREAT; AQUINAS, THOMAS; BONAVENTURE; DENIS; ERIUGENA, JOHANNES SCOTTUS; GERSON, JEAN; HILDUIN OF SAINT-DENIS; HUGH OF SAINT-VICTOR; MYSTICISM; PHILOSOPHY; RICHARD OF SAINT-VICTOR; SAINT-DENIS; THEOLOGY]

Pseudo-Dionysius the Areopagite. *Opera omnia. PG* 3.
———. *The Complete Works*, trans. Colm Luibheid with notes and collaboration by Paul Rorem. New York: Paulist, 1987.
———. *The Divine Names and Mystical Theology*, trans. John D. James. Milwaukee: Marquette University Press, 1980.
———. *The Ecclesiastical Hierarchy*, trans. Thomas L. Campbell. Washington, D.C.: University Press of America, 1981.
———. *La hiérarchie céleste*, trans. René Roques, Gunter Heil, and Maurice de Gandillac. 2nd ed. Paris: Cerf. 1970.
———. *Dionysiaca: recueil donnant l'ensemble des traductions latines des ouvrages attribués au Denys de l'Aréopagite*, ed. Philippe Chevallier. 2 vols. Paris: Desclee, 1937.
———. *Œuvres complètes du Pseudo-Denys l'Aréopagite*, trans. Maurice de Gandillac. Paris: Aubier, 1943.
Gersh, Stephen. *From Iamblichus to Eriugena: An Investigation of the Prehistory and Evolution of the Pseudo-Dionysian Tradition*. Leiden: Brill, 1978.
Roques, René. *L'univers dionysien: structure hiérarchique du monde selon Pseudo-Denys*. Paris: Aubier, 1954.
Rorem, Paul. *Biblical and Liturgical Symbols Within the Pseudo-Dionysian Synthesis*. Toronto: Pontifical Institute of Mediaeval Studies, 1984.

PSEUDO-TURPIN. In the first half of the 12th century, an unidentifiable cleric composed in Latin prose an alleged eyewitness *Historia Caroli Magni et Rotholandi* under the assumed name of Archbishop Turpin, borrowed from the *Chanson de Roland*. His Pseudo-Turpin chronicle was extensively copied (more than 200 manuscripts are known) and was translated into all major languages and admitted into official hagiography and historiography. It found its way into the famous *Liber sancti Jacobi* and into the biography of Charlemagne; the *Grandes chroniques de France* of Saint-Denis, among others, relies on it.

The French translations of the *Historia* and their numerous manuscripts have been divided into seven groupings. Version I was written between 1195 and 1205 by Nicolas de Senlis. Version II (sometimes called the Turpin III) by a certain Johannes (before 1206) and Version III by Pierre de Beauvais (ca. 1212) are closely intertwined. The Anglo-Norman Version IV was written ca. 1216–18 by William de Briane. Version V, usually referred to as the Turpin I, dates from 1210–20 and has been contaminated, in six of nine manuscripts, by the Johannes translation. In two manuscripts, Version V forms part of the *Chronique française des rois de France*. A now lost manuscript related to Paris manuscripts B.N. fr. 2137 and 17203 of Version VI (the Turpin II; before 1243) was used by Philippe Mouskés in his *Chronique rimée;* in five manuscripts, Version VI has been integrated into the *Chronique de Baudouin d'Avesnes*. Version VII is a translation in the Burgundian dialect dating from the latter part of the 13th century. There is also an Occitan version.

The *Historia* begins with the conquest of Spain by Charlemagne, who christianizes the country under the patronage of St. James of Compostela and, upon his return to France, founds churches in the saint's name. There follows a new series of successful wars against King Aigolandus, Altumaior of Cordova and Furre of Navarre, the giant Ferracutus, and Ebrahim of Seville. Having reaffirmed his supremacy, Charlemagne undertakes a pilgrimage to St. James's tomb in Compostela. The remainder of the chronicle recounts the Spanish campaign of Charlemagne, Roland, Oliver, and Turpin against Marsile and Baligant, known from the *Chanson de Roland*. After the defeat at Roncevaux, Charlemagne elevates the abbey of Saint-Denis to the rank of most important church in France and builds a basilica in honor of the Virgin Mary in Aix-la-Chapelle. Some time later, Turpin learns in a vision of Charlemagne's death and of the intervention of St. James, who saves the emperor's soul from a horde of black devils.

One of the reasons for the great success of the *Historia* is the ingenious combination of the powerful medieval legends of St. James and Charlemagne and the attempt at subsuming the former under the latter. As a work of church propaganda, the *Historia* promotes Saint-Denis as the center of French political and ecclesiastical power, equal, and ideally superior, to St. James's at Compostela. But the chronicle also marks the transition, in the cultural and literary spheres, from rhymed epic and hagiography, considered unreliable, to authoritative historiography in prose and based on Latin prose. The amalgam of legendary, historic, and didactic elements that is the Pseudo-Turpin marks the demise of hagiography, the birth of historiography, and the conception of the prose romance.

Hans R. Runte

[See also: ANONYMOUS OF BÉTHUNE; CHANSON DE GESTE; HISTORIOGRAPHY; *LIBER SANCTI JACOBI;* LIBERAL ARTS; PHILIPPE MOUSKÉS; PIERRE DE BEAUVAIS; *ROLAND, CHANSON DE*]

Mandach, André de, ed. *Chronique dite saintongeaise: texte franco-occitan inédit "Lee": à la découverte d'une chronique gasconne du XIIIe siècle et sa poitevinisation.* Tübingen: Niemeyer, 1970. [Edition of Version I based on National Library of Wales 5005B (Lee MS).]

Schultz, Oscar, ed. "*Der provenzalische* Turpin." *Zeitschrift für romanische Philologie* 14 (1890): 467–520. [Edition of Provençal version based on B.L. Add. 17920, fol. 6^b–19^b.]

Short, Ian, ed. *The Anglo-Norman* Pseudo-Turpin Chronicle *of William de Briane.* Oxford: Blackwell, 1973. [Edition of Version IV based on B.L. Arundel 220.]

Walpole, Ronald N., ed. *An Anonymous Old French Translation of the* Pseudo-Turpin Chronicle: *A Critical Edition of the Text Contained in Bibl. Nat. fr. 2137 and 17203 and Incorporated by Philippe Mouskés in his* Chronique rimée. Cambridge: Medieval Academy of America, 1979. [Edition of Version VI.]

——, ed. "The Burgundian Translation of the *Pseudo-Turpin Chronicle* in Bibliothèque Nationale (French MS. 25438)." *Romance Philology* 2 (1948–49): 178–215; 3 (1949–50): 83–116. [Edition of single manuscript of Version VII.]

——, ed. *The Old French Johannes Translation of the* Pseudo-Turpin Chronicle. Berkeley: University of California Press, 1976. [Edition of Version II based on B.N. fr. 2464.]

——, ed. *Le Turpin français, dit le Turpin I.* Toronto: University of Toronto Press, 1985. [Edition of Version V based on B.N. fr. 1850.]

PUCELLE, JEAN (d. 1334). An artist documented as producing the seal of the confraternity of Saint-Jacques-aux-Pèlerins in Paris between 1319 and 1324 and whose name appears in marginal notes along with two other illuminators in the *Belleville Breviary* (B.N. lat. 10483–84), dated 1323–26. His name is also mentioned with two other illuminators in the Bible written by Robert de Billyng (B.N. lat. 11935), and inventory entries of the collection of John, duke of Berry, have suggested that between 1325 and 1328 he made the book known as the *Heures de Jeanne d'Évreux* (New York, The Cloisters) with miniatures and marginalia in *grisaille*. The styles of the miniatures in these manuscripts, however, are all different, and their authorship is the subject of ongoing controversy. At best, one can speak of a "Pucelle style" that manifests a new sense of three-dimensionality in modeled figures and architectural space in manuscripts produced for the royal court in the second quarter of the 14th century.

Robert G. Calkins

Annunciation, *Hours of Jeanne d'Évreux,* by Jean Pucelle, 1325–28. Fol. 16. *Courtesy of The Cloisters Collection, Metropolitan Museum of Art, New York.*

[See also: MANUSCRIPTS, PRODUCTION AND ILLUMINATION]

The Hours of Jeanne d'Évreux Queen of France, intro. James J. Rorimer. 2nd ed. New York: Metropolitan Museum of Art, 1965.

Blum, Rudolf. "Jean Pucelle et la miniature Parisienne du XIVe siècle." *Scriptorium* 3 (1949): 211–17.

Deuchler, Florens. "Jean Pucelle—Facts and Fictions." *Metropolitan Museum of Art Bulletin* 29 (1971): 253–56.

Morand, Kathleen. *Jean Pucelle.* Oxford: Clarendon, 1962. [With bibliography.]

PULLOYS, JOHANNES (ca. 1420–1478). Composer, master of the boys at Antwerp cathedral (1444–47), singer in the papal chapel (1447–68/69), thereafter apparently in Antwerp. Pulloys's motet *Flos de spina* reappears in manuscripts to the end of the century. The one Mass cycle ascribed to him so closely reflects the English style of the time that some question its authorship. Of his ten songs, which appear in several mid-century sources, *S'ung bien peu d'esperance* seems to have had the greatest impact.

David Fallows

Gülke, Peter, ed. *Johannes Pulloys: opera omnia.* N.p.: American Institute of Musicology, 1967.

PURGATORY. Over the course of late antiquity and the Middle Ages, Christians developed an understanding of life after death that included the idea of a purification (purgation, purgatorial fires) of the soul for sins committed, with the gradual definition of a place, Purgatory, where this takes place. From earliest times, Christians spoke of a Last Judgment when Christ would return to judge the living and the dead, with evil persons condemned to Hell and the good established in Heaven. Concern for the fate of the soul immediately after death led to varied ideas, but Augustine's position became generally accepted: the truly good, martyrs especially, went directly to Heaven at death; the truly evil went directly to Hell; all other souls, the great majority, remained, until the Last Judgment, in places vaguely described but divided into two categories: places of punishment with fire for the "not completely evil" and places of rest for the "not completely good." These two groups can be helped by the living, who may offer "suffrages" on their behalf: prayers, alms, and the sacrifice of the eucharist. Such suffrages can mitigate punishment, but not ultimate condemnation, or diminish the time waiting for admission to Heaven. By the time of Pope Gregory the Great (d. 604), it was clearly defined that Heaven as a place for the souls of the dead had not been "opened" until Christ's resurrection, hence the good dead of the pre-Christian era had been waiting in the upper reaches of Hell for Christ's advent and their deliverance.

A number of "visions" of the otherworld in the form of "dream" or "out-of-body" journeys were reported in medieval texts and conveyed a vivid understanding of the sufferings of those in Hell and especially in the upper regions thereof, the place where those being purified for eventual entry into Heaven were enduring appropriate torment. Among these were three visions recorded in Gregory the Great, *Dialogues,* 4. 36; the vision of Drythelm (in Bede, *Historia ecclesiastica gentis anglorum*); the *Visio Wettini* by Walafrid Strabo; visions associated with St. Patrick's Purgatory in Ireland; and the Vision of Tundal recorded in numerous works, including Vincent de Beauvais's *Speculum historiale.*

Biblical commentators and theologians gradually began a clarification of the nature of purification, the definition of the place of purgation, and the relation of this to the penitential system of the church, and eventually to the system of indulgences granted by papal decree or initiative. In France, the Parisian theologians Hugh of Saint-Victor (d. 1141) and Peter Lombard (d. 1160) continued with the Augustinian fourfold division of the dead, the necessity of purgation, and the vagueness of the place for that purification. The late 12th and 13th centuries saw the development in the writings of the Parisian theologians of a clearer definition of the place for purgation and something of a recasting of the division of the dead into three groups: they now became the entirely good (to Heaven), the entirely damned (to Hell, with no possibility of deliverance), and the medium (*mediocriter*) good, who have confessed and done penance but need further purification. Purgatory now becomes a place in which souls that have begun to work out punishment in this world for sins, through the sacrament of penance, can continue that process beyond the grave. Augustine's idea that various suffrages could benefit the good souls in Purgatory continued to bear rich fruit in the numerous actions, especially the endowment of Masses, carried out on behalf of the dead. The requirement promulgated by the Fourth Lateran Council (1215) that all faithful Christians had to confess yearly to a priest and the continuing "quantification" of penitential punishment for sins in handbooks for confessors, books developed by masters at Paris and elsewhere especially in light of the decision of the Lateran Council, led to both a more specific measure for and a more thorough presence of penance in this life and a deeper concern with the continuation of penitential suffering in the place of purification after death. Beginning with the call for the First Crusade and continuing throughout the later Middle Ages, the doctrine of indulgences, the specific forgiveness of all or part of the assigned penitential punishment due for sin, led to the development of a complex process in which an ecclesiastically sanctioned grant might mitigate the time in Purgatory. In the 15th century, the papacy declared that the treasury of merits applicable to the living for indulgences might be applied to those in Purgatory as well, thus widening again the field of interaction between the living and the dead in Purgatory.

Grover A. Zinn

[See also: DIGULLEVILLE, GUILLAUME DE; HUGH OF SAINT-VICTOR; INDULGENCES; MARIE DE FRANCE; PETER LOMBARD; WALAFRID STRABO]

Gardiner, Eileen, ed. *Visions of Heaven and Hell Before Dante*. New York: Italica, 1989.

Le Goff, Jacques. *The Birth of Purgatory*, trans. Arthur Goldhammer. Chicago: University of Chicago Press, 1984.

Turner, Victor, and Edith Turner. *Image and Pilgrimage in Christian Culture: Anthropological Perspectives*. Oxford: Blackwell, 1978, pp. 104–39.

PUY. *Puys* were poetic societies that thrived mainly in northern French towns, some from as early as the 11th century, most from the 13th and 14th centuries. The earliest surviving records are those of the Confrérie des Jongleurs et des Bourgeois d'Arras, written in 1194, with later additions. These tell of the miraculous origin of the society, in which the Virgin gave two jongleurs a holy candle with powers to heal plague victims. The other two oldest *puys*, those of Rouen (1072) and Valenciennes (1229), share some details with the Arras foundation story: Rouen by having a similar legendary origin in a miracle of Notre Dame, Valenciennes by claiming to possess its own candle formed from wax gathered from the holy candle at Arras. Most of the *puys* from this region, such as Douai (1330), Amiens (1388), Abbeville (late 14th c.), Dieppe (15th c.), and Caen (1527), were dedicated to the Virgin. *Puys* are also known to have existed at Lille, Tournai, Cambrai, and Béthune; *princes des sots* were elected in Ath, Bouchain, Denain, and Condé. A poetic *companhia* was founded at Toulouse in 1323, which drew up its own rules of poetry known as the *Flors del gay saber*. Further allusions to southern *puys* occur in poems by 12th-century troubadours, such as Peire d'Alvernhe. We also possess detailed records from the end of the 13th century of a *puy* at London.

It is not always easy to distinguish the puys from other kinds of poetic and charitable fraternities, such as professional guilds, the *chambres de rhétorique*, and the (perhaps imaginary) Courts of Love. For instance, Arras possessed a separate Puy de Notre-Dame as well as the Confrérie, and Abbeville has references not only to a Puys d'Amours, but also a Puy de la Conception, to a feast where a *prince des sots* was elected, and a minstrel contest on Mardi Gras at the Fosse-aux-Ballades. Douai had both a Confrérie and a Chambre de Rhétorique. Paris has no records of a *puy* as such, only of a corporation of musicians founded in 1321; of a huge series of plays sponsored between 1339 and 1382 by the Goldsmiths' Guild, which also gave prizes for *serventois*; and of a Cour d'Amour, instituted in 1400 or 1401, with apparently over 600 members.

The *puys* usually have several features in common: a major annual festival, often on the feast of the Conception of the Virgin (December 8), with a dinner at which a *maître* would be elected and a contest held for the best song (*chant royal*, ballade, *serventois, fatras divin*, or rondeau). All the entries would be performed in front of the company (with music, according to the London *puy* regulations), the winner receiving a silver crown and the title *prince du puy*. The poems had to be written on a set refrain, which was composed by the old *maître* and given out some days before the feast. Certain *puys* specialized in a single lyric genre; others, such as Amiens and Dieppe, gave a range of prizes for a variety of genres. Many *puy* poems have survived, identifiable from their refrains, internal allusions, or, if they won, from being marked in the manuscript with a crown.

Ardis T.B. Butterfield

[See also: *CANTUS CORONATUS; SIRVENTES*]

Breuil, Auguste. "La Confrérie de Notre-Dame du Puy d'Amiens." *Mémoires de la Société des Antiquaires de Picardie* 2nd ser. 3 (1854): 485–680. [Also has information on Abbeville, Rouen, Caen, Dieppe, Valenciennes, and Douai.]

Cavrois, Louis, ed. *Cartulaire de Notre-Dame-des-Ardents à Arras*. Arras: Bradier, 1876.

Potvin, Charles. "La charte de la Cour d'Amour de l'année 1401." *Bulletins de l'Académie Royale des Sciences, des Lettres et des Beaux-Arts de Belgique* 3rd ser. 12 (1886): 191–220.

Riley, Henry Thomas, ed. "Regulations of the Feste de Pui." In *Liber custumarum: munimenta gildhallae Londoniensis*. 3 vols. London: Longman, 1859–62, Vol. 2.1, pp. 216–28.

QUAESTIO. *See* SCHOLASTICISM

QUARREL OF THE *BELLE DAME SANS MERCI.* Nothing attests so accurately to the continuing popularity of Alain Chartier's poem (1424) as the debate and the imitations it continued to inspire for more than a century. It is doubtful, however, that it caused as much of a scandal as has sometimes been claimed; the debate rather suggests a literary game like those that continued to be popular into the 17th century. At the court of the dauphin Charles (the future Charles VII), where the poem was written, some courtiers and ladies reproached Chartier for the attitude toward women reflected in the poem. He replied with his *Excusacion aux dames*, in which the God of Love defends the ladies, accusing the poet of heresy. Neither this nor the ladies' complaints can be taken too seriously.

Chartier's *Excusacion*, ca. 1430, inspired an exchange of poems by members of a literary group in Tournai, the most important of which were Baudet Herenc's *Parlement d'Amour*, the anonymous *Dame loyale en amours*, Achille Caulier's *Cruelle femme en amours*, and the *Hôpital d'amour*. The latter, preserved in twenty-one manuscripts and inspired in large part by the *Roman de la Rose*, was long attributed to Chartier himself. Other poems in the same vein debating the merits of the lover or the lady, or presenting a trial of the lovers, usually in Love's court, are the anonymous *Belle dame qui eut merci*, the *Jugement du povre triste amant banni*, and the *Amant rendu cordelier*. The suits of the rejected lover in the God of Love's court would lead eventually to Martial d'Auvergne's *Arrêts d'Amour* (1450), in which the lover's debates of the earlier poems have been transformed into court trials.

Chartier's poem was copied (thirty-four known manuscripts), refuted, approved, and imitated with varying degrees of talent. It was translated into Italian, English, and Catalan and was turned into a series of rondeaux by Anne de Graville in the 16th century, when the debate was also mentioned in Marguerite de Navarre's *Heptameron*.

Charity Cannon Willard

[See also: AUVERGNE, MARTIAL D'; CHARTIER, ALAIN; HERENC, BAUDET; LE FRANC, MARTIN]

Chartier, Alain. *La belle dame sans merci et les poésies lyriques*, ed. Arthur Paiget. Geneva: Droz, 1949.
———. *The Poetical Works of Alain Chartier*, ed. J.C. Laidlaw. Cambridge: Cambridge University Press, 1974.
Champion, Pierre. *Histoire poétique du XVe siècle*. Paris: Champion, 1923, pp. 60–73.
Piaget, Arthur. "La belle dame sans merci et ses imitations." *Romania* 30 (1901): 23–24, 314–51; 31 (1902): 315–49; 33 (1904): 179–208; 34 (1905): 421–560, 575–88.

QUARREL OF THE *ROMAN DE LA ROSE.* Although it is no longer believed that Christine de Pizan's *Épistre au Dieu d'Amour* (1399) launched the debate over the merit of Jean de Meun's continuation of the *Roman de la Rose*, she publicized the affair by presenting copies of the letters it inspired to the queen of France and the provost of Paris (1402). The debate was begun by Jean de Montreuil (1401). He and colleagues at the royal chancellery enjoyed literary debates, as his correspondence shows. They underestimated Christine de Pizan's reaction when they engaged her participation, although she had already criticized Jean de Meun's attitude toward women and his questionable influence on young contemporaries.

The letters grew out of a conversation by Jean de Montreuil with Christine and a "notable clerk" who seems to have shared Christine's views. Later, Jean de Montreuil sent them both a treatise insisting on the poem's merits. Christine's polite reply expressed support for the other person. Her tone changed only after others entered the debate. For Christine, the most important of these was Jean Gerson, who on August 25 preached a sermon taking Jean de Montreuil's views to task. Gontier Col then wrote to Christine playfully expressing his astonishment that anyone should attack such a learned man as Jean de Meun and suggesting that her views merely reflected those of others more wise than she. In reply, Christine, like Gerson, questioned the propriety of some of Jean de Meun's language, suspecting his motives in using it, and even more those of his admiring disciples. Col's patronizing reply annoyed Christine and perhaps encouraged her to make the correspondence public. For her, the issue had become Jean de Meun's unjust slander of women.

On May 18, 1402, Gerson attacked Jean de Meun in an allegorical *Vision*, where he referred to obscene illustrations in some contemporary manuscripts of the poem. Although Gerson and Christine were not objecting to exactly the same things, together they formed a powerful opposition.

In the debate's final round, Pierre Col took issue with both Gerson and Christine in an even more offensive tone, which Christine reproved in her reply. Gerson expressed his disapproval to Col in Latin, suggesting that his ideas skirted heresy and that a canon of Notre-Dame cathedral should turn his mind to more serious matters. The debate ended at once, although there is a final echo in some sermons on Penitence preached by Gerson the following December.

An examination of the documents shows that the quarrel was less between Christine and the Cols than between Jean de Montreuil and Gerson concerning Jean de Meun's influence on public morality. The antifeminist aspect was perhaps accidental but attracted lasting attention, for although Christine's position has sometimes been misrepresented, for the first time a woman dared to defend her sex against traditional clerical misogyny.

Charity Cannon Willard

[See also: ANTIFEMINISM; CHRISTINE DE PIZAN; GAUTIER LE LEU; JEAN DE MEUN; LE FRANC, MARTIN; *ROSE, ROMAN DE LA*]

Baird, Joseph L., and Kane, John R., eds. *La querelle de la Rose: Letters and Documents.* Chapel Hill: University of North Carolina Press, 1978.

Hicks, Eric, ed. *Le débat sur Le roman de la Rose.* Paris: Champion, 1977.

Badel, Pierre-Yves. *Le roman de la Rose au XVIe siècle: étude de la réception de l'œuvre.* Geneva: Droz, 1980.

QUATRE FILS AYMON (or *Renaut de Montauban*; 18,489 Alexandrines; early 13th c.). The most popular epic of the Rebellious Vassal Cycle, as evidenced by the great number of manuscripts and versions in verse and prose composed during the 13th century, as well as numerous allusions to it. Renaut (Rinaldo) also became, with Roland (Orlando), the protagonist of the chivalric romances *Orlando Innamorato* by Boiardo (1495) and *Orlando Furioso* by Ariosto (1516–21); Tasso wrote a *Rinaldo* (1562) and utilized this character in an episode of *Gerusalemme liberata* (1580).

After Renaut has killed Charlemagne's nephew Bertolai in a brawl, he and his three brothers, sons of Aymon of Dordogne, flee the royal court. With the help of their cousin, the sorcerer Maugis, and their wonderful horse, Bayard, they first take refuge in the Ardennes, then in Gascony, where the king marries his daughter to Renaut but later betrays him under pressure from the king of France. Charlemagne pursues the brothers relentlessly; only after many tribulations does he consent to make peace, on condition that Renaut go to Jerusalem and Bayard be surrendered. The horse, thrown into the Meuse by the emperor himself, escapes into the Ardennes. Returning from Palestine with Maugis, whom he met in Constantinople, Renaut learns of the recent death of his wife and, while Maugis retires to a hermitage, leaves his family in order to expiate his faults, which had caused the death of the duchess. He is killed by jealous colleagues while helping carry stones for the construction of the cathedral of St. Peter at Cologne; but his body, thrown into the Rhine, is miraculously saved and returns by itself to be enshrined in Renaut's castle in Dortmund.

Hans-Erich Keller

[See also: CHANSON DE GESTE; NANTEUIL CYCLE; REBELLIOUS VASSAL CYCLE]

Castets, Ferdinand, ed. *Les quatre fils Aymon, chanson de geste.* Montpellier: Coulet, 1909.

Verelst, Philippe, ed. *Renaut de Montauban: deuxième fragment rimé du manuscrit de Londres, British Library, Royal 16 G II ("B"), édition critique.* Romanica Gandensia 21 (1988).

———, ed. *Renaut de Montauban: édition critique du ms. de Paris, B.N., fr. 764 (R).* Ghent: Faculteit van de Letteren en Wijsbegeerte, 1988.

———. "*Renaut de Montauban*, textes apparentés et versions étrangères: essai de bibliographie." Romanica Gandensia 18 (1981): 199–234.

QUERCY. This large and important county, dominated by the city of Cahors, extended over much of southwestern France transected by the River Lot. To the north of the river, the region of Haut-Quercy included the towns of Gourdon, Figeac, and Martel and the viscounty of Turenne. The Bas-Quercy, south of the Lot, extended to the valleys of the Tarn and Garonne and to the new city of Montauban.

From the 9th century, Quercy remained in the hands of the counts of Toulouse, who held it against frequent pressure from the dukes of Aquitaine, later kings of England. The death in 1249 of the last count, Raymond VII, who was succeeded by his son-in-law Alphonse of Poitiers, brother of Louis IX, commenced the long dispute over Quercy between the kings of France and England. The Treaty of Paris in 1259 established the latter in possession of Haut-Quercy and provided for his eventual succession in Bas-Quercy, but its terms remained imperfectly fulfilled. In 1286, Edward I of England yielded Bas-Quercy to France in exchange for guaranteed revenues. The seeds of the dispute, however, lingered through the Hundred Years' War.

Quercy's advantageous geographic position assured it an important economic role. By the close of the Middle Ages, it possessed two major centers of commerce, Montauban, founded in 1144, and Cahors. Cahors especially capitalized on the local resources of wool and wine and its position on the axis linking Languedoc to France and to England through Bordeaux to the west. By the 13th century, the Cahorsins had established trading colonies in Italy, Provence, and Bordeaux as well as England. To their commercial activities, they joined those of banking. The name "Cahorsin" became by the end of the century synonymous with "usurer" and Cahors with sin, as Dante expressed in the *Inferno* 11.50: "the smallest round stamps with its seal both Sodom and Cahors."

Quercy suffered extensively in the campaigns of the Hundred Years' War. The commerce of Cahors, already declining, was badly reduced. The last English troops were not expelled from Haut-Quercy until 1443.

Alan Friedlander

[See also: CAHORS]

Lacoste, Guillaume. *Histoire générale de la province de Quercy.* 4 vols. Cahors: Girma, 1883–86.

Lartigaut, Jean. *Les campagnes du Quercy après la guerre de cent ans (vers 1440–vers 1500).* Toulouse: Université de Toulouse-le-Mirail, 1978.

Ligou, Daniel. *Histoire de Montauban.* Toulouse: Privat, 1984.

Ombret, Antoine, Jean-Claude Fau, and René Touron. *Le Bas-Quercy et les pays limitrophes aux XIVe et XVe siècles.* Montauban: Centre Départemental de Documentation Pédagogique, 1976.

Renouard, Yves. "Les Cahorsins, hommes d'affaires français du XIIIe siècle." *Transactions of the Royal Historical Society* 5th ser. 2 (1961): 43–67.

QUIMPER. Capital of Cornouaille. Founded, according to tradition, in the 5th century by King Gradlon, who brought with him from England the name "Cornwall," the city was made a bishopric in the 6th century. Walled in the 13th, it suffered during the Breton civil war, being sacked by Charles de Blois in 1344 and besieged the following year by Jean de Montfort.

Quimper's cathedral of Saint-Corentin, named for the city's first bishop, is the most representative Gothic church in Brittany, in spite of unfortunate 19th-century additions and "restorations." The choir and ambulatory are 13th-century; the nave, side aisles, and transept—all on an axis different from that of the choir—are 15th-century, as is the Flamboyant façade with towers. Between the towers is an equestrian statue of King Gradlon. Some 15th-century glass is preserved.

The nearby Romanesque church of Sainte-Croix (12th c.) at Quimperlé is notable for its trefoil plan with central rotunda, which is reminiscent of the church of the Holy Sepulcher in Jerusalem.

William W. Kibler

[See also: BRITTANY]

Masseron, Alexandre. *Quimper, Quimperlé, Locronan, Penmarc'h.* Paris: Renouard, 1928.

Waquet, Henri. "Quimper." *Congrès archéologique (Cornouaille)* 115 (1953): 9–14.

QUINZE JOIES DE MARIAGE. Nominally inspired by the genre of devotional poetry praising the "joys" of the Virgin—her attributes or celebrated episodes in her life—the *Quinze joies de mariage* portrays the miseries of married life through satirical vignettes. Four complete manuscripts of the work survive, all from the late 15th century: *R* (Rouen, Bibl. mun. 1052), *C* (Chantilly, Musée Condé 686), *L* (Leningrad, Saltykov-Chtchedrin State Lib. f. fr. p. XV. 4), and *P* (London, Phillipps 8338). The author and date remain uncertain. References to costume and events in the Hundred Years' War situate composition in the early 15th century. The author confesses in the prologue that he has never been married but that he has entered another type of servitude, presumably holy orders. Language and textual allusions suggest that the *Quinze joies* was composed in west-central France, and most of the vignettes are set in a small-town, bourgeois milieu.

Framed by prologue and epilogue, each of the fifteen "joys" recounts a stage of married life. The vantage throughout is that of the afflicted husband; the advantage is nearly always that of the demanding or conniving wife. Material and financial concerns—the need to furnish a new household, to keep the wife in finery, to finance her "pilgrimages"—are one testimony to the obvious vein of bourgeois realism in the work. Although the fifteen vignettes do not constitute a continuous narrative, the first ten progress chronologically through the expected stages of marital development and dilemma. The first "joy" shows the newlywed husband straining to keep his young wife well dressed and to satisfy her every whim. In the second, the husband is already hoodwinked into providing for the wife's visits to various "relatives." By the third "joy," the *ménage* is well established, a child is expected, and the poor husband waits obediently on his pregnant wife, only to find himself later excluded as the women of the family cluster around the mother and newborn. Subsequent episodes depict the disarray of the household after the birth of five or six children, the fatigue and responsibility weighing on the husband, the agonizingly separate aspirations of husband and wife, and the predicaments of various mismatched couples. The eleventh through fifteenth "joys" seem to be case studies of less usual situations, such as the remarriage of a woman who thinks her husband has died in combat and his ill fortune to discover her remarriage.

All fifteen "joys" bear similar refrains of condemnation and despair, reminiscent of the Old Woman's discourse in Jean de Meun's *Roman de la Rose* (ll. 13,967ff.): the husband is the fish caught in the net, doomed to finish his days in pain and anguish, without hope of escape from his miserable condition. Both prologue and epilogue to the *Quinze joies* offer context for the fifteen "joys," on the one hand justifying an antimatrimonial stance by a defense of human liberty and of the exercise of common intelligence, and on the other rationalizing marriage as Christian penance.

The *Quinze joies* seems to have contributed less to the formal development of narrative prose genres at the close of the Middle Ages and more to the popularity of fictional inventories of misfortunes. The work's anecdotal character and its satirical stance on domesticity guaranteed its appeal both in England and France. In shortened and liberally adapted versions, the *Quinze joies* continued to be popular in printed editions from the late 15th through the 18th century.

Janice C. Zinser

[See also: ANTIFEMINISM]

Rychner, Jean, ed. *Les .XV. joies de mariage.* Geneva: Droz, 1967.

Pitts, Brent A., trans. *The Fifteen Joys of Marriage.* New York: Lang, 1985.

Rizk, Nazli. "Didactisme et contestation dans *Les quinze joies de mariage.*" *Moyen français* 1 (1977): 33–89.

Söderhjelm, Werner. *La nouvelle française au XVe siècle.* Paris: Champion, 1910, pp. 29–72.

R

RABANUS MAURUS (Hrabanus, Rhabanus, also known as Magnentius; ca. 780–856). Born in Mainz of a noble family, Rabanus (which means "raven" in Old High German) received the best education available in his day. A favorite pupil of Alcuin, he was called "Maurus" after a disciple of St. Benedict. Rabanus moved in the highest circles of power of the Carolingian world. He became abbot of Fulda in 822 and solicited the patronage of Lothair I to make this one of the outstanding monastic foundations of the age. Rabanus supported Louis the Pious in the political turmoil of the 830s and 840s, and Lothair I on Louis's death. The victory of Louis the German in 840 forced him into exile for about a year; upon his return to German lands, he retired to the abbey of Petersburg until named archbishop of Mainz in 847.

Rabanus was a prolific author and the teacher of some of the most outstanding of the Carolingian scholars, among them Walafrid Strabo. Many of his works have a pedagogical intent. *De institutione clericorum* (before 819) covers ecclesiastical grades, liturgy, liturgical vestments, catechetical instruction, and the Liberal Arts. *De rerum naturis* (after 840; also known as *De universo*) is an encyclopedic work in the style of Isidore of Seville but with an allegorical level of interpretation. His extensive corpus of poetry includes a number of *carmina figurata*, in which the words of poems are arranged in designs to illustrate them. However, it is for his biblical interpretation that Rabanus was most famous in the Middle Ages and early-modern period, even though this material has not been widely studied by modern scholars.

Rabanus wrote commentaries on most books of the Bible: all of the historical books of the Old Testament, many of the books of wisdom literature (significantly, not the Song of Songs), the Major Prophets, Maccabees, the Gospel of Matthew, the Acts of the Apostles, and the Pauline epistles. These are composites of patristic sources, but the extracts from the various patristic works are carefully arranged so as to present allegorical interpretations, mostly having to do with Christ and the church, in a coherent and easily accessible form. These interpretations were widely read before the modern period; they survive in many manuscripts and in printed versions through the 16th century. For his role as a Christian educator, Rabanus earned the title *praeceptor Germaniae*.

E. Ann Matter

[See also: ALCUIN; BIBLE, CHRISTIAN INTERPRETATION OF; CAROLINGIAN ART; LOUIS I THE PIOUS; WALAFRID STRABO]

Rabanus Maurus. *Omnia opera*. PL 107–12.
———. *Liber de laudibus sanctae crucis*. In *Vollständige Faksimile-Ausgabe im Original-format des Codex Vindobonensis 652 der Österreichischen Nationalbibliothek*, commentary by Kurt Holter. 2 vols. Graz: Akademische Druck- und Verlagsanstalt, 1972–73.
———. *The Life of Saint Mary Magdalene and of Her Sister Saint Martha: A Twelfth-Century Biography*, trans. David Mycoff. Kalamazoo: Cistercian, 1989.
———. *Martyrologium*, ed. John McCulloh, and *Liber de computo*, ed. Wesley M. Stevens. *CCCM* 44. Turnhout: Brepols, 1979.
———. *Poems*. MGH Poetae 2.154–258.
Kottje, Raymund, and Harald Zimmermann. *Hrabanus Maurus: Lehrer, Abt und Bischof*. Mainz: Akademie der Wissenschaften und der Literatur, 1982.
Laistner, Max Ludwig Wolfram. *Thought and Letters in Western Europe, A.D. 500 to 900*. London: Methuen, 1957.
Müller, Hans-Georg. *Hrabanus Maurus: De laudibus sancta crucis. Studien zur Überlieferung und Geistesgeschichte mit dem Faksimile-Textabdruck aus Codex Reg. Lat 124 der vatikanischen Bibliothek*. Ratingen: Henn, 1973.
Szoverffy, Josef. *Weltliche Dichtungen des lateinsichen Mittelalters: Ein Handbuch*. Berlin: Schmidt, 1970, Vol. 1.
Turnau, Dietrich W. *Rabanus Maurus, der Praeceptor Germaniae*. Munich: Lindauer, 1900.

RADEGUND (ca. 525–587). This "queen saint," born a Thuringian princess, was captured in 531 by the Franks and betrothed to Clotar I. The polygamous king raised her at Athies as his future spouse. In her twenties, Radegund left her husband to found the monastery of Sainte-Croix at Poitiers, which was eventually richly endowed by Clotar.

Her life at the convent is marked by the often violent political fighting among members of the royal family, but also by an appreciation for learning and literary pursuits. The poet and apologist Venantius Fortunatus (ca. 530–600) became her friend and eventually wrote one of her biographies, the others being composed by Baudonivia, a sister nun, and Gregory of Tours (ca. 538–594). In the biographies, Radegund is praised as an ardent ascetic and exemplary leader of her religious house. The monastery, organized according to the rule of Caesarius of Arles, stressed strict enclosure and education. Radegund left three lengthy verse epistles (perhaps in part coauthored with Venantius Fortunatus) addressed to the emperor Justin II and the empress Sophia of Byzantium, and to her cousin Hamalafred and her nephew Artachis. All three texts testify to Radegund's extensive education in classical Latin and Germanic poetry and her skillful use of the genres.

Ulrike Wiethaus

[See also: CAESARIUS OF ARLES; LATIN POETRY, MEROVINGIAN; PHILOSOPHY; POITIERS; WOMEN, RELIGIOUS EXPERIENCE OF]

Radegund. *De excidio Thoringiae; Ad Iustinum et Sophiam Augustos; Ad Artachin.* In *Monumenta Germaniae Historica: Auctores Antiquissimi,* ed. Friedrich Leo. Berlin, 1881, Vol. 4, part 1, pp. 271–75.

McNamara, Jo Ann, John E. Halborg, and E. Gordon Whatley, eds. and trans. *Sainted Women of the Dark Ages.* Durham: Duke University Press, 1992.

Cherewatuk, Karen. "Radegund and Epistolary Tradition." In *Dear Sister: Medieval Women and the Epistolary Genre,* ed. Karen Cherewatuk and Ulrike Wiethaus. Philadelphia: University of Pennsylvania Press, 1993, pp. 20–46.

Lippert, W. "Zur Geschichte der hl. Radegunde von Thuringen." *Geschichte und Altertumkunde* 7 (1890): 16–38.

RAIMBAUT D'AURENGA (ca. 1144–1173). In his short life, the troubadour Raimbaut, count of Orange, composed some forty lyrics distinguished by their originality and idiosyncrasy. As a follower of the "difficult style," or *trobar clus,* Raimbaut experimented with new forms, developed an unusual vocabulary, and cultivated obscurity. He opposed his fellow poet and friend Giraut de Bornelh by defending *trobar clus* in a debate over the relative virtues of the clear, accessible style known as *trobar leu.* Raimbaut's preoccupation with formal refinement anticipates the rich style and technical virtuosity of *trobar ric* in Arnaut Daniel.

Roy S. Rosenstein

[See also: GIRAUT DE BORNELH; TROUBADOUR POETRY]

Keller, Hans-Erich, et al. *Studia Occitanica.* 2 vols. Kalamazoo: Medieval Institute, 1986.

Pattison, Walter T., ed. *The Life and Works of the Troubadour Raimbaut d'Orange.* Minneapolis: University of Minnesota Press, 1952.

RAIMBAUT DE VAQUEIRAS (fl. 1180–1205). A troubadour adept in many styles, genres, and languages, Raimbaut de Vaqueiras participated in the Fourth Crusade under his patron, Boniface de Montferrat. Twenty-six lyrics of certain attribution survive, in addition to his letter in epic laisses addressed to Boniface in 1205. His songs include the *estampida Kalenda maia,* a bilingual debate with a Genoese woman and another with the trouvère Conon de Bethune, a multilingual and a monolingual *descort,* other debates and *cansos,* a *sirventes,* a crusade song, an *alba,* a woman's song, and examples of other, lesser genres. These reflect the composite portrait of a polished versifier and ironic wit who balanced his commitment to chivalric causes with an attitude of detached amusement toward courtly styles.

Roy S. Rosenstein

[See also: TROUBADOUR POETRY]

Linskill, Joseph, ed. *The Poems of the Troubadour Raimbaut de Vaqueiras.* The Hague: Mouton, 1964.

Bertolucci [Pizzorusso], Valeria. "Posizione e significato del canzoniere di Raimbaut de Vaqueiras nella storia della poesia provenzale." *Studi mediolatini e volgari* 11 (1963): 9–68.

Brugnolo, Furio. *Plurilinguismo e lirica medievale da Raimbaut de Vaqueiras a Dante.* Rome: Bulzoni, 1983.

Rostaing, Charles, and Jean B. Barbaro. *Raimbaut de Vaqueiras.* L'Isle sur la Sorgue: Scriba, 1989.

RAIMON DE MIRAVAL (ca. 1160–after 1229). Born near Carcassonne, the troubadour Raimon de Miraval ruled over the small castle of Miraval. Protected by Raymond VI of Toulouse, whom he addressed as "Audiart," Miraval lost his castle to French troops and fled to Catalonia after the Battle of Muret (1213). A favorite of the Catalan lord and troubadour Uc de Mataplana, who directed a *sirventes* against Raimon criticizing him for the uncourtly dismissal of his wife, Miraval died in Lérida sometime after 1229. His surviving work includes thirty-seven *cansos* and five *sirventes.* His clear statements about the mutual responsibilities binding him and his lady, Mais d'Amic, earned him the respect of other poets, notably Raimon Vidal, who considered him the ultimate authority on love.

Elizabeth W. Poe

[See also: TROUBADOUR POETRY]

Raimon de Miraval. *Les poésies du troubadour Raimon de Miraval,* ed. Leslie T. Topsfield. Paris: Nizet, 1971.

RAIS, GILLES DE (1404–1440). Gilles de Laval, lord of Rais (now Retz) in Brittany, and marshal of France from 1429, was born at Champtocé castle in Anjou and executed at Nantes on October 26, 1440, after a spectacular trial. His parents were heirs to the important lordship of Rais in southern Brittany as well as that of Marchecoul, part of the Laval family holdings and those of the La Suze branch of the Craon family. Gilles's wife, Catherine de

Thouars, was the heiress of important lands in Poitou. While still in his teens, therefore, Gilles de Rais was one of the richest men in Europe.

Already well known as a brutal warrior and a man of extravagant tastes, Gilles de Rais rose to favor at the court of Charles VII thanks to the influence of his cousin Georges de La Trémoille, and he was named marshal of France in 1429, when he was not yet twenty-five years old. In that year, he served on campaigns with Jeanne d'Arc. Toward 1432, Gilles withdrew to his estates, surrounded himself with unsavory henchmen, and began abducting, sexually abusing, and murdering local children. More than thirty of his victims are known; their number may have approached 150.

When Gilles extended his extravagant behavior to alchemy and to practices that looked suspiciously like witchcraft, the duke of Brittany and the bishop of Nantes decided to move against him, perhaps also with a view to confiscating his strategic possessions. Long after his trial and execution, Gilles de Rais was associated in Breton oral tradition with the story of Bluebeard, although that legendary figure has come down to us in folklore as a killer of successive wives, not children.

John Bell Henneman, Jr.

[See also: NECROMANCY]

Bataille, Georges. *Le procès de Gilles de Rais*. Paris: Pauvert, 1972.

Benedetti, Jean. *Gilles de Rais*. New York: Stein and Day, 1972.

Bossard, Eugène. *Gilles de Rais maréchal de France dit Barbe Bleue, 1404–1440*. Paris: Champion, 1886.

Bourdeaut, A. *Chantocé, Gilles de Rais et les ducs de Bretagne*. Rennes: Société d'Histoire et d'Archéologie de Bretagne, 1924.

Hérubel, Michel. *Gilles de Rais, ou, la fin du monde*. Paris: Picollec, 1993.

Hyatte, Reginald, trans. *Laughter for the Devil: The Trials of Gilles de Rais, Companion-in-Arms of Joan of Arc (1440)*. Rutherford: Fairleigh Dickinson University Press, 1984.

RALPH OF LAON (d. 1134/36). Brother and collaborator of Anselm of Laon, Ralph shares in the authorship (or, perhaps more accurately, editorship) of the commentary on the Bible that eventually became known as the *Glossa ordinaria*. Certain other commentaries on the Psalms and the epistles of Paul also bear his name. Ralph appears to have assisted as well in the task of collecting theological opinions, some touching dogma, but most dealing with contemporary pastoral concerns, used for clerical instruction in the cathedral school at Laon.

Mark Zier

[See also: ANSELM OF LAON; BIBLE, CHRISTIAN INTERPRETATION OF; *GLOSSA ORDINARIA*]

Landgraf, A. "Familienbildung." *Biblica* 13 (1932): 65–72.

———. "Untersuchungen." *Recherches de théologie ancienne et médiévale* 8 (1936): 345–47.

RAMPILLON. Situated on a gentle rise in a fertile plain and surrounded by farms, the church of Saint-Éliphe at Rampillon (Seine-et-Marne) is a High Gothic cathedral in miniature. It is 122 feet long, and the vaults rise only 46 feet, about a third the height of Reims. Following the High Gothic format, the nave is divided into three stories (nave arcade, triforium, and clerestory), yet because of its smallness the triforium is the same height as the clerestory and only half the size of the nave arcade. Since the triforium is a passageway related to human size, its height establishes the scale of the church. Thus, by this change in the relative size of the three zones of the elevation, the master builder distinguishes the parish church from the cathedral.

The choir of Rampillon is a single vessel illuminated by windows with oculi above. The oldest part of the church is the bay in the south tower that supports a clock tower. Work progressed from east to west with larger windows in the nave, which was completed around the middle of the 13th century. The springing of the ribs from capitals below the top of the triforium is markedly different from High Gothic cathedrals, where the vaults spring from a point a third of the way up the clerestory.

The simple flank of Rampillon is animated by flying buttresses with a single flier and by the earlier clock tower. The façade is simply composed; the width of the nave is echoed in the central bay, with its splayed portal and large round-headed clerestory window flanked by wall buttresses. The central bay is flanked by the flat terminations of the aisles and on the northwest corner by the squat, circular tower. The portal, containing the Last Judgment in its tympanum and twelve Apostles on the jambs, is clearly related to the sculpture of Reims.

Rampillon is more than a country simplification and reduction of a cathedral. Features derived from the High Gothic cathedrals, such as Reims, are combined with regional traditions of transeptless plan (Paris area) and unusual handling of clerestory (Burgundy). The homogeneity and clarity of statement and the imaginative transformation of High Gothic ideas at Rampillon point up the universal quality of High Gothic, whether in the great cathedrals or in a little church on the fertile plain of Brie.

Whitney S. Stoddard

Carlier, Achille. *L'église de Rampillon*. Paris: Privately printed, 1930.

Stoddard, Whitney S. *Art and Architecture in Medieval France*. New York: Harper and Row, 1972.

RANSOMS. Prisoners captured in medieval warfare were spoils. Roman law had established that prisoners taken in a just war became slaves of the enemy. But canon law later altered this to declare that Christians taken by other Christians were not to be slaves but were to be freed on the payment of a ransom. During the Middle Ages, the capture of prisoners, especially noble prisoners, became one of the most valuable gains of warfare.

In battle, if one man was captured by another, the prisoner had the right to purchase his freedom with a ransom. A payment was agreed upon, depending on the wealth and nobility of the prisoner, and the captor then kept the prisoner until this payment was made. During this imprisonment, the captor could do whatever he needed to ensure due payment of the agreed-upon sum, although he could not threaten the prisoner with death. The prisoner then became a noncombatant, and his lands, from which the ransom revenues must come, became technically immune from war.

The ransoming of prisoners was practiced in most military engagements of the Middle Ages. In some battles, however, this course of action was seen as detrimental to an army, as a large number of soldiers might choose to withdraw with their prisoners rather than keep fighting. In these instances (for example, the Battle of Agincourt in 1415), the military leader would command the killing of prisoners.

Perhaps the most famous medieval ransom was that agreed to by the French king John II after his capture at the Battle of Poitiers in 1356. It was set initially at the exorbitant amount of 4 million crowns, and only a partial sum was eventually paid, even though the amount was later decreased to 3 million crowns by the Treaty of Brétigny. Although John was eventually freed, the ransom remained unpaid and, bound by his ransom agreement, he later returned to England, where he died.

Kelly DeVries

[See also: FEUDAL AIDS; JOHN II THE GOOD; WARFARE]

Contamine, Philippe. *War in the Middle Ages*, trans. Michael Jones. New York: Blackwell, 1984.
———. "Rançons et butins dans la Normandie anglaise (1424–1444)." In *Actes du 101e Congrès National des Sociétés Savantes*. Lille, 1976; Paris, 1978, pp. 241–70.
Henneman, John Bell. *Royal Taxation in Fourteenth Century France: The Captivity and Ransom of John II, 1356–1370*. Philadelphia: American Philosophical Society, 1976.
Keen, Maurice H. *The Laws of War in the Late Middle Ages*. London: Routledge and Kegan Paul, 1965.

RAOUL DE CAMBRAI. This 8,726-line chanson de geste in the Rebellious Vassal Cycle, aside from a manuscript fragment and brief 16th-century extracts, has survived in one complete manuscript (B.N. fr. 2493). Dated ca. 1180–1200, it is a revision of one or more earlier texts now lost. The first 5,555 lines, in rhyme, tell of feudal rebellion and clan feuding. The remainder, in assonance, treat largely of love and adventure, with Saracen motifs. The majority of scholars consider the first part to be the genuine *Chanson de Raoul de Cambrai*, and the romantic second half to be a sequel, a *Raoul II* or *Chanson de Bernier*.

Young Raoul, wrongly disinherited of the Cambrésis by King Louis, demands his patrimony; the king offers him instead the first fief to become vacant. Herbert, count of Vermandois, dies, and Raoul takes up the challenge by invading the Vermandois. Herbert's sons, defending their inheritance, include the father of Raoul's squire, Bernier, born out of wedlock. Bernier eventually quarrels with his lord and takes refuge with the Vermandois. In the ensuing battle, he slays Raoul. War flares up again when Raoul's kin seek to avenge his death. The poem ends with a reconciliation of sorts between the former enemies, who then turn upon King Louis and burn Paris.

Raoul de Cambrai treats the problems that beset society and questions the old heroic values: it depicts a world in chaos, with barons driven to assault each other and the king in senseless battles where no one can prevail. The poet explores in a powerful manner the issues of feudal law, the role of the family, and the reality of the quest for land and power in a time, and for a social class, in a state of crisis.

William C. Calin

[See also: CHANSON DE GESTE; LORRAINE CYCLE; REBELLIOUS VASSAL CYCLE]

Kay, Sarah, ed. and trans. *Raoul de Cambrai*. Oxford: Clarendon, 1992.
Meyer, Paul, and Auguste Longnon, eds. *Raoul de Cambrai, chanson de geste*. Paris: Didot, 1882.
Calin, William. *The Old French Epic of Revolt: Raoul de Cambrai, Renaud de Montauban, Gormond et Isembard*. Geneva: Droz, 1962.
Matarasso, Pauline. *Recherches historiques et littéraires sur Raoul de Cambrai*. Paris: Nizet, 1962.

RAOUL DE HOUDENC (fl. 1210–20). Radulfus de Hosdenc, *miles*, of Hodenc-en-Bray (Beauvaisis), was the author of an Arthurian romance of 5,938 octosyllabic lines, *Meraugis de Portlesguez*, and three short didactic poems, the *Songe d'enfer*, the *Roman des eles*, and a *Dit*. A second Arthurian romance, the *Vengeance Raguidel* (6,182 lines), whose author names himself as "Raols" is probably also by Raoul de Houdenc. Raoul is one of the most talented of the Chrétien epigones, and *Meraugis de Portlesguez*, concerned with the rivalry of two friends for the love of the fair Lidoine, is one of the best examples of the genre. Both *Meraugis* and the *Vengeance Raguidel*, which is concerned with the avenging of a murdered knight called Raguidel, can best be seen as the work of an author coming to grips with the specter of Chrétien de Troyes. All kinds of humor abound in the two romances, as well as in the short didactic pieces. The *Songe d'enfer* is a vision of Hell notable for a particularly gruesome banquet and some allegorical heraldry; the *Roman des eles* is a guide to *courtoisie*. Raoul was acknowledged, along with Chrétien, to be one of the greatest French poets by Huon de Méry in the *Tournoiement Antécrist* (ca. 1230).

Keith Busby

[See also: ARTHURIAN VERSE ROMANCE; CHRÉTIEN DE TROYES; COURTESY BOOKS; GAWAIN ROMANCES; ROMANCE]

Raoul de Houdenc. "Li dis Raoul Hosdaing," ed. Charles H. Livingston. *Romanic Review* 13 (1922): 292–304.
———. *The Songe d'enfer of Raoul de Houdenc*, ed. Madelyn Timmel Mihm. Tübingen: Niemeyer, 1984.

————. "*Le roman des eles*": *The Anonymous "Ordene de Chevalerie,"* ed. Keith Busby. Amsterdam: Benjamins, 1983.

————. *Sämtliche Werke*, ed. Mathias Friedwagner. 2 vols. Halle: Niemeyer, 1897–1909, Vol. 1: *Meraugis de Portlesguez;* Vol. 2: *La vengeance Raguidel.*

Schmolke-Hasselmann, Beate. *Der arthurische Versroman von Chrestien bis Froissart.* Tübingen: Niemeyer, 1980, pp. 106–15, 117–29.

RAOUL DE VERMANDOIS (d. 1152). Seneschal of France. An ardent supporter of the Capetian monarchy, Raoul was the eldest son of Adèle, heiress of Herbert IV, count of Vermandois, and Hugues le Grand (d. 1102), brother of Philip I of France. He became count of Vermandois in 1117, answered the royal summons to oppose an imperial invasion in 1124, lost an eye in royal service in 1128, and was the sole supporter of Louis VI against the revolt of the Garlande family in 1131. In that year, he first appears as royal seneschal. In 1137, he and his archrival, Thibaut II le Grand, count of Champagne, led the entourage that escorted the future Louis VII to Bordeaux for his marriage to Eleanor, heiress of Aquitaine.

Raoul's influence continued under Louis VII (r. 1137–80). His repudiation in 1142 of Thibaut II's niece Eleanor to wed Petronilla (Alix), the queen's sister, led not only to his excommunication but also to war in Champagne. He refused to put Petronilla aside, even after the burning of Vitry led to the king's accommodation with the church. He became co-regent with Suger, abbot of Saint-Denis, during the king's absence on the Second Crusade (1147–49). Upon the death of Suger in 1151, Raoul was replaced as royal seneschal, and he died the following year.

Raoul left three children by Petronilla: Raoul le Lépreux, count of Vermandois (r. 1152–67); Elizabeth (d. 1183), whose husband, Philippe d'Alsace, count of Flanders, ruled Vermandois until 1191; and Eleanor, who was forced to divide the inheritance of Vermandois with the king, Philip II Augustus, who acquired the remainder on her death in 1213.

R. Thomas McDonald

[See also: CHAMPAGNE; ELEANOR OF AQUITAINE; GARLANDE; LOUIS VI THE FAT; LOUIS VII; VERMANDOIS]

RAOUL GLABER (ca. 985–ca. 1046). Born in Burgundy, perhaps out of wedlock, Raoul entered the monastery of Saint-Germain of Auxerre when he was about twelve. By nature restive and averse to discipline, he wandered from monastery to monastery, where, thanks to his literary talents, he was welcomed. From ca. 1015 to 1031, he was the traveling companion of William of Volpiano, abbot of Saint-Bénigne of Dijon and one of the foremost monastic reformers of the day. At William's command, he began a history of the prodigies and wonders surrounding the advent of the year 1000, which he kept with him and added to for the rest of his life. After William's death,

Raoul spent time at Cluny (ca. 1031–35), then briefly at Bèze, finally returning to Auxerre.

In addition to his Latin *Five Books of Histories*, Glaber wrote a hagiographical *vita* of William and some epigraphy that, due to the jealousy of the monks, was destroyed. He seems to have had difficult relations with a number of people, including his mentor, William, and some of his independence of mind shows up in his writing. His history, dedicated in a later recension to Odilo of Cluny, began with the year 900 and presented the history of the German emperors and French kings, which, as it reached Raoul's own time (Books 3–4), included events from all over the known world and, in his old age (Book 5), included a brief autobiography and anecdotes about anonymous people. Several accounts of the same global material also appear in the independently composed but contemporary history of Adémar de Chabannes.

Often criticized for inaccuracy, gossip, disorganization, and prodigy mongering by modern political historians, Raoul has proven a rich source for social history and mentalities; his theology of history, though crude, prefigures such 12th-century historians as Hugh of Saint-Victor, Otto of Freising, and Joachim of Fiore. Raoul is best known for his apocalyptic interpretation of the two millennial dates 1000 (Incarnation) and 1033 (Passion), which he linked to mass manifestations of religious fervor—heresy, church building, pilgrimage (especially to Jerusalem), and the Peace of God movement. He has accordingly suffered from polemical treatment at the hands of modern historians opposed to the romantic notion of the "terrors of the year 1000."

Richard Landes

[See also: ADÉMAR DE CHABANNES; HISTORIOGRAPHY; HUGH OF SAINT-VICTOR; MILLENNIALISM]

Raoul Glaber. *Les cinq livres de ses histoires (900–1044),* ed. Maurice Prou. Paris: Picard, 1886.

————. *Rodulfus Glaber opera,* ed. John France, Neithard Bulst, and Paul Reynolds. Oxford: Clarendon, 1989.

————. *Rodolfo il Glabro: Cronche dell'anno mille (storie),* ed. Guglielmo Cavallo and Giovanni Orlandi. Milan, 1989.

France, J. "Rodulfus Glaber and the Cluniacs." *Journal of Ecclesiastical History* 39 (1988): 497–507.

Iogna-Prat, D., and R. Ortigues. "Raoul Glaber et l'historiographie clunisienne." *Studi medievali* 3rd ser. 26 (1985): 437–72.

RATRAMNUS OF CORBIE (d. ca. 875). Born in the early 9th century, Ratramnus became a monk at the abbey of Corbie, where he died. One of the most original thinkers of medieval France, he was a friend of Paschasius Radbertus, Gottschalk, and Lupus of Ferrières. A spirited author, he directly confronted Paschasius Radbertus on the eucharist and the virginity of Mary *in partu* (i.e., during and after Jesus's birth) and Hincmar of Reims on predestination, the nature of the soul, and (in a lost work) the Trinity. Ratramnus warned against "gross corporeality" in eucharistic thought, maintaining the continued reality of the bread and wine, while also asserting the real presence of Christ in the sacrament. His eucharistic treatise was championed by Berengar of Tours and the Protestant Reformers. He was a favorite of Charles the Bald, and he wrote the *Contra Graecorum* for Pope Nicholas I, in defense of papal primacy, clerical celibacy, and the use of the *filioque* (the procession of the Holy Spirit from both the Father and the Son) in the Creed. Ratramnus ridiculed superstition in his treatise on the virginity of Mary and in his *Epistola de cynocephalis*, concerning the "dog-man" mentioned by Augustine in *City of God* (*De civitate Dei* 16.8).

E. Ann Matter

[See also: BERENGAR OF TOURS; CORBIE; GOTTSCHALK; HINCMAR OF REIMS; PASCHASIUS RADBERTUS]

Ratramnus of Corbie. *Opera omnia*. PL 121.

———. *De corpore et sanguine Domini: Texte original et notice bibliographique*, ed. Jan N. Bakhuizen Van Den Brink. Amsterdam: North-Holland, 1974.

Bouhot, Jean-Paul. *Ratramne de Corbie: histoire littéraire et controverses doctrinales*. Paris: Études Augustiniennes, 1976.

Delhaye, Philippe. *Une controverse sur l'âme au IXe siècle*. Namur: Centre d'Études Médiévales, 1950.

REALISTIC ROMANCES. Term that designates disparate verse romances that, from the late 12th to the late 13th century, shunned the fantastic, lingered on the depiction of everyday *realia*, and made reference to contemporary persons or situations. They are not, however, "realistic" in the modern sense. No author claimed, like Stendhal, "to hold a mirror to reality"—a notion foreign to a literature that had no preoccupation with mimesis.

Gautier d'Arras, no doubt to set himself apart from his rival Chrétien de Troyes, as well as from Marie de France, whose work inspired him, claimed that his romance *Ille et Galeron* had no "phantoms" or "lies," by contrast with the *lais*, which gave their audience the impression of having slept or dreamed (ll. 931–36). Several years later, Jean Renart, the first of the "realistic" writers of the 13th century, expressed himself in similar terms in the prologue to *Escoufle*: his heart, he says, cannot accept many stories he has heard, because his reason prevents it; lies ought not to prevail over truth in a tale (ll. 12–23). Jean's reflections on the art of romance are headed confusedly toward what a later age will call "verisimilitude."

In fact, the "realistic romances" are each more improbable than the other, though they do avoid the Arthurian world and the supernatural. Forgoing the Breton love of the fantastic appears sufficient in their eyes to satisfy reason. Yet if their plots, which often develop folklore motifs, do not seek verisimilitude, they nonetheless seek some foundation in everyday reality. They offer their aristocratic public a reflection of courtly life, sympathetic but also faithful, sometimes detailed and precise. They are concerned with geographical setting and occasionally evoke contemporary people or events. In *Guillaume de Dole*, Jean Renart uses several of his contemporaries as characters, although the romance is set in the distant past. The procedure's lack of verisimilitude, almost ostentatious, but

nonetheless dependent on the "real," invites us to question not only the sort of acceptance medieval romances required of their readers but, more generally, the value of anachronism. The projection of the present onto the past is often deliberate.

To Jean Renart are attributed two romances, *Escoufle* (ca. 1200–02) and the *Roman de la Rose* (ca. 1210–12 or ca. 1228), today called *Guillaume de Dole* to distinguish it from the more illustrious romance of that name, as well as the *Lai de l'ombre* (ca. 1221–22). Born in Dammartin-en-Goële and undoubtedly a *clerc*, Jean spent most of his life in the courts in the northern part of the Francophone region and seems to have been linked to the French-speaking Guelf milieu, as John Baldwin has shown. He dedicated *Escoufle* to Count Baudouin VI of Hainaut, future emperor of Constantinople, and *Guillaume de Dole* to Milon de Nanteuil, bishop of Beauvais. *Guillaume* evokes numerous people connected with the principality of Liège and the entourage of Archbishop Hugues de Pierrepont. With an original turn of mind and a malicious sense of humor, the author hides behind his persona the better to impose his presence. In a style both spontaneous and convoluted, he gives an unexpected twist to commonplace motifs.

After a lengthy prologue devoted to the exploits of Count Richart de Montivilliers, here made duke of Normandy, *Escoufle* recounts the star-crossed love affair of Richart's son Guillaume and Aelis, daughter of the Emperor of Rome. The two young lovers run off together. In a forest in Lorraine, while Aelis is asleep, a kite (OFr. *escoufle*) flies off with her red silk alms purse. Guillaume becomes lost while seeking it; Aelis awakens in the interval and thinks she has been abandoned. The separated lovers are reunited after many wanderings at the court of the Count of Saint-Gilles. In *Guillaume de Dole*, the young German emperor Conrad, a confirmed bachelor, hears his jongleur Jouglet singing the praises of Guillaume de Dole and his sister, the beautiful Liénor, and promptly falls in love. He becomes friendly with her brother, telling him of his intention to wed Liénor. His seneschal, jealous of Guillaume's good fortune, goes to Dole and learns from Liénor's naive mother that the young girl has a rose-shaped birthmark on her thigh. In a version of the wager story, popular in the Middle Ages, he uses this information to lead others to believe he has obtained her favors. But Liénor comes to court and easily proves him wrong. In the prologue, Jean Renart boasts of being the first to include lyric selections in a romance. Indeed, he uses this procedure, which was to become enormously successful in succeeding generations, with a remarkable aptness, sense of citation, and mirror-like effect. The *chansons de toile* that he places in the mouths of Liénor and her mother have been particularly admired.

The *Roman de la Violette* (or the *Roman de Gérard de Nevers*) by Gerbert de Montreuil, possibly the author of a *Perceval* continuation, was written between 1227 and 1229. Although the plot is more like that of the *Roman du comte de Poitiers*, the romance is also imitative of *Guillaume de Dole*, with its inserted lyrics, including a *chanson de toile*; and its use of the wager motif (in its usual form, a wager between the hero, sure of the faithfulness of his beloved, and the traitor); and the birthmark (here, a violet on the breast rather than a rose on the thigh), the traitor's knowledge of which, thanks to the indiscretion of an evil duenna, is interpreted as proof of his success. Convinced of Eurïaut's infidelity, Gérard, who has lost his lands by losing the wager, wishes to kill her but decides to abandon her in the forest after she saves his life. He lives the life of a wanderer, while Eurïaut, rescued by the Duke of Metz, becomes the object of his attentions. The lovers finally are reunited, and Eurïaut's innocence is proven through trial by combat.

The anonymous *Galeran de Bretagne* (ca. 1220) develops the theme already treated by Marie de France in *Fresne*. A woman slanders a neighbor who has given birth to twin sons, claiming that she must have known two men. Shortly afterward, the slanderer herself gives birth to twin daughters. Caught in her own trap, she has one infant abandoned outside a nunnery, where she is found and baptized Fresne, for the ash-tree in which her cradle was hung. She is raised alongside the abbess's nephew, Galeran, son of the count of Brittany, and as they grow older they fall in love. But Galeran, who has become count after his father's death, must set off on adventures that take him to the home of Fresne's parents, while she, mistreated and despised, is driven from the nunnery. A general recognition, pardon, and marriage end the romance.

The *Roman du castelain de Coucy et de la dame de Fayel* by Jakemés (second half of the 13th c.) has as hero the trouvère of the preceding century known as the Châtelain de Coucy and quotes from his songs. This lengthy romance, which uses the traditional situations and peripeties of courtly love, ends with the well-known motif of the eaten heart. It is one of the few medieval romances that do not have a happy conclusion. The author, who presents himself as a dilettante, is perhaps from the region of Saint-Quentin.

Joufroi de Poitiers (after ca. 1250) is a bizarre and unselfconscious romance that demonstrates the mingling, characteristic for its period, of personal outpourings and narrative fiction. A lengthy prologue gives voice to the plaints of a bashful lover, without in the least seeking to introduce the work that follows. Throughout the romance, the author's confessions and comments on his own love affair and on the story disrupt the rambling and disjointed episodes, devoted mostly to the good fortune of the hero, who is inspired by the first troubadour, Count Guilhem IX of Poitiers and Aquitaine. The historical figures appear in happy confusion: Joufroi's mother is named Eleanor, the English king is Henry, and the troubadour Marcabru has a cameo role. The story unfolds with a cynical wit that reminds one of the Occitan romance *Flamenca*.

La Manekine and *Jehan et Blonde* are today generally attributed not to the jurist Philippe de Remi, lord of Beaumanoir and author of the *Coutumes du Beauvaisis* (ca. 1283), but to his father, also named Philippe de Remi. *La Manekine* is one of the many works known throughout all Europe that develop the motif of "The Maiden Without Hands." A princess must flee in disguise to escape the incestuous love of her father; she is taken in by a king who marries her, but later her wicked mother-in-law falsely tells her son that his wife has given birth to a monster and

tries to have her killed. Her only salvation is to flee once more. Finally, she is reconciled with her husband and her father and, in *La Manekine*, also with her left hand, which she had cut off herself, hoping the deformity would discourage her father's wicked intentions. In this romance, the heroine Joie's father is king of Hungary and her husband king of Scotland; the reconciliation occurs in Rome. *Jehan et Blonde* tells in great detail how Jehan, a penniless young noble from Dammartin, wins the love of Blonde, daughter of the Count of Oxford, by his valor. He is able to marry her even though her father had promised her to the Count of Gloucester.

Jean Maillart's *Roman du comte d'Anjou* (1316) treats the same theme as *La Manekine* but shows more moderation in the choice of episodes, if not in style. The heroine is the daughter of the Count of Anjou, her husband is the Count of Bourges, and the wicked mother-in-law is replaced by a wicked aunt, the Countess of Chartres.

All these romances are very similar yet at the same time different. Paradoxically, it is their very banality, their whimsical and hackneyed plots—indeed, their lack of verisimilitude—that focuses attention on the settings, the customs, the everyday activities, and the geographical and historical allusions. Would we be aware of their "realism" if it were not grafted onto a fairy-tale universe? The true originality of these romances and their most remarkable common trait is the important place the writers give to themselves. Whether they intervene directly or show their virtuosity through intertextual effects born of lyrical insertions, they never let their presence be forgotten.

Michel Zink

[See also: BEAUMANOIR, PHILLIPE DE REMI, SIRE DE; *COMTE DE POITIERS, ROMAN DU*; COUCY, CHÂTELAIN DE; *JEHAN DE PARIS, ROMAN DE*; *JOUFROI DE POITIERS*; MAILLART, JEAN; *PERCEVAL CONTINUATIONS*; ROMANCE]

Fay, Percival B., and John L. Grigsby, eds. *Joufroi de Poitiers: roman d'aventures du XIIIe siècle*. Geneva: Droz, 1972.

Gerbert de Montreuil. *Le roman de la Violette ou de Gerart de Nevers par Gerbert de Montreuil*, ed. Douglas L. Buffum. Paris: SATF, 1928.

Jakemés. *Le roman du castelain de Couci et de la dame de Fayel par Jakemés: édition établie à l'aide des notes de John E. Matzke*, ed. Maurice Delbouille. Paris: SATF, 1936.

Jean Renart. *L'escoufle: roman d'aventures*, ed. Franklin Sweetser. Geneva: Droz, 1974.

———. *Galeran de Bretagne: roman du XIIIe siècle*, ed. Lucien Foulet. Paris: Champion, 1925.

———. *Le roman de la Rose ou de Guillaume de Dole*, ed. Félix Lecoy. Paris: Champion, 1966.

———. *The Romance of the Rose or Guillaume de Dole*, trans. Patricia Terry and Nancy Vine Durling. Philadelphia: University of Pennsylvania Press, 1993.

Maillart, Jean. *Le roman du comte d'Anjou*, ed. Mario Roques. Paris: Champion, 1931.

Boulton, Maureen B.M. *The Song in the Story: Lyric Insertions in French Narrative Fiction, 1200–1400*. Philadelphia: University of Pennsylvania Press, 1993.

Lejeune, Rita. *L'œuvre de Jean Renart: contribution à l'étude du genre romanesque au moyen âge.* Paris: Droz, 1935.

Paris, Gaston. "Jehan Maillart." *Histoire littéraire de la France* 31 (1893): 318–50.

Shepherd, M. *Philippe de Remi's "La Manekine" and "Jehan et Blonde": A Study of Form and Meaning in Two Thirteenth-Century Old French Verse Romances.* Amsterdam: Rodopi, 1990.

Zink, Michel. *Roman rose et rose rouge: Le roman de la Rose ou de Guillaume de Dole de Jean Renart.* Paris: Nizet, 1979.

REBELLIOUS VASSAL CYCLE. Cycle of chansons de geste that depict the struggles of a feudal baron and his family against another house or the king. This is the third cycle defined by Bertrand de Bar-sur-Aube in a passage from *Girart de Vienne.* The King Cycle concerns the exploits of Charlemagne and Roland as defenders of the faith; in the Guillaume d'Orange Cycle, the warriors defend the southern frontier. In these first two *gestes*, texts were composed following the principles of medieval cycle formation: epic poets composed sequels to famous poems, telling the early exploits (*enfances*) of a renowned warrior or those of his ancestors. Such was seldom the case in the third cycle. Only in the 13th century were the rebel heroes gathered into a "clan" of their own, known as the Rebellious Vassal (or "Doon de Mayence") Cycle, which then took its place beside the other two.

Epics belonging to the Rebellious Vassal Cycle reflect cultural tensions in the medieval world, especially the crisis of the aristocracy at a time when the barons sensed, in the face of increasing royal power, that for the first time since Charlemagne they were no longer the dominant force in society. The best epics of revolt, *Girart de Roussillon, Raoul de Cambrai, Garin le Lorrain, Chevalerie Ogier,* and *Quatre fils Aymon* (or *Renaut de Montauban*), strove to come to grips with the malaise of their society. They portray a situation in which a weak and tyrannical king is readily swayed by traitors, preferring his favorites to the barons of the realm. Disinherited and insulted, the nobles are forced into rebellion or civil war. Although selfish, vindictive barons are criticized as much as the king, the author takes the side of the aristocracy; and the poor, exiled count or duke, who in the end wins (back) prerogatives and land, is perhaps a projection of the landless petty nobility, the *povres bachelers*, whose aspirations are not at all the same as those of the great barons and the king. The enthusiasm and spontaneity that it was possible to idealize in the *Chanson de Roland* became dangerous in the context of a more complex national society. Valor, so prized in older epics, can be exercised only against one's own people, and good in the individual becomes a social curse, for individual and group interests enter into conflict.

The solutions arrived at by the epic poets are more than a little ambiguous. In most of these texts, the rebel yields to the king even though he is in the right, then sets out on a crusade or pilgrimage to the Holy Land. He fails because the ultimate lesson of the chanson de geste is one of order and harmony, an all-inclusive peace that goes beyond individual, family, and feudal honor to preach submission to authority. Even in *Raoul de Cambrai* and the Lorraine Cycle, although the emperor is humiliated, his life and office remain sacrosanct. None of the rebels could have dreamed of abolishing the kingship, assassinating the king, or even forcing him to abdicate. Rebellion results in no program for reform. The poet asks questions; he provides no easy answers.

William C. Calin

[See also: CHANSON DE GESTE; *CHEVALERIE OGIER; GIRART DE ROUSSILLON;* LORRAINE CYCLE; *QUATRE FILS AYMON; RAOUL DE CAMBRAI*]

Bender, Karl-Heinz. *König und Vasall: Untersuchungen zur Chansons de Geste des XII. Jahrhunderts.* Heidelberg: Winter, 1967.

Calin, William. *The Old French Epic of Revolt: Raoul de Cambrai, Renaud de Montauban, Gormond et Isembard.* Geneva: Droz, 1962.

De Combarieu du Grés, Micheline. *L'idéal humain et l'expérience morale chez les héros des chansons de geste, des origines à 1250.* 2 vols. Aix-en-Provence: Université de Provence, 1979.

RECLUS DE MOLLIENS (fl. early 13th c.). Identified as Barthélémy, monk of the abbey of Saint-Fuscien-au-Bois who went into seclusion at the church of Sainte-Marie de Molliens-Vidame, the Reclus de Molliens wrote two didactic poems in the first third of the 13th century, the *Roman de carité* and *Miserere.* Twenty-one manuscripts and six fragments are extant for *Carité*, twenty-six complete and ten partial manuscripts for *Miserere.* The poems have octosyllabic twelve-line stanzas, rhyming aab/aab/bba/bba, a form found earlier in Hélinant de Froidmont's *Vers de la Mort. Carité* (ca. 1224) recounts in 242 stanzas the poet's abortive quest for Charity amid all the social orders in Christendom. *Miserere* (ca. 1230), in 273 stanzas, adopts the mode of catechism to expound upon the Deadly Sins and the five senses, among other questions. Skillful allegorization, alliteration, assonance, and word play enliven the Reclus de Molliens's stern condemnation of human foibles. In 1360, the city of Amiens offered a copy of both poems as a gift to King Charles V.

Roberta L. Krueger

[See also: ÉTIENNE DE FOUGÈRES; HÉLINANT DE FROIDMONT; LI MUISIS, GILLES]

Van Hamel, Anton Gerardus, ed. *"Li romans de Carité" et "Miserere" du renclus de Moiliens, poèmes de la fin du XIIe siècle.* 2 vols. Paris: Vieweg, 1885.

Langlois, Charles-Victor. *La vie en France au moyen âge de la fin du XIIe au milieu du XIVe siècle.* 4 vols. Paris: Hachette, 1926–28, Vol. 2: *D'après des moralistes du temps,* pp. 141–75.

RECONQUEST OF FRANCE. The Valois campaigns of 1449–53 ended in triumph for Charles VII, with the English expelled from Normandy and Guyenne. In July 1449, armies under Dunois had entered Normandy, meeting feeble resistance. His troops were welcomed as liberators. Although English reinforcements landed in March 1450, on April 15 the French won a decisive victory at Formigny. More formidable resistance came in Guyenne. Dunois's main force entered the region in April 1451, and, after a series of sieges the final Lancastrian citadel at Bayonne fell on August 20, 1451. The English returned in autumn 1452 with considerable local support, and a second Valois army was dispatched. The destruction of Talbot's army at Castillon, July 17, 1453, effectively ended the war, though the threat of renewed English incursions troubled France for many decades.

These campaigns revealed not only the bankruptcy of Lancastrian government but the wisdom of the recent French reforms that had professionalized the army, mobilized a popular militia, and regularized an effective artillery force. The real genius of Charles VII, however, was to be revealed not in his reforms and conquests but in the subsequent retention of these territories and the reconciliation of their people to Valois rule.

Paul D. Solon

[See also: DUNOIS, JEAN, COMTE DE; HUNDRED YEARS' WAR; RICHEMONT, ARTHUR DE; TALBOT, JOHN]

Allmand, Christopher T. *Lancastrian Normandy, 1415–1450.* Oxford: Clarendon, 1983.

Burne, Alfred Higgins. *The Agincourt War.* London: Eyre and Spottiswoode, 1956.

Perroy, E. *The Hundred Years War.* Bloomington: Indiana University Press, 1951.

Vale, Malcolm G.A. *English Gascony, 1399–1453.* London: Oxford University Press, 1970.

REFRAIN. A recurring segment, from one word to a verse or more, that sets off a strophic form. Music for a refrain, if present, also recurs. In *Guillaume de Dole* and other 13th-century narratives with lyrical insertions, refrains appear as parts of convivial dance songs, or *caroles.* They may also appear isolated—courtly amorous aphorisms—sometimes with melody. Refrains apparently form part of a vast, for the most part orally transmitted repertory and were not always connected to the dance. Besides narratives with lyrical insertions, refrains also appear in *chansons à refrain* and *chansons avec des refrains,* and with music in many 13th-century motets. In the 14th and 15th centuries, refrains are essential components of the *formes fixes.*

Lawrence Earp

[See also: BALLADE; DANCE; *FORMES FIXES*; MOTET (13TH CENTURY); MULTIPLE REFRAIN SONGS (*CHANSONS AVEC DES REFRAINS*); RONDEAU; VIRELAI]

Bec, Pierre. *La lyrique française au moyen-âge (XIIe–XIIIe siècles): contribution à une typologie des genres poétiques médiévaux.* 2 vols. Paris: Picard, 1977.

Boogaard, Nico van den. *Rondeaux et refrains du XIIe siècle au début du XIVe.* Paris: Klincksieck, 1969.

Doss-Quinby, Eglal. *Les refrains chez les trouvères du XIIe siècle au début du XIVe.* New York: Lang, 1984.

REGALE/REGALIA. Legal historians describe as "regalian" those rights, powers, and prerogatives associated with royal sovereignty, such as minting money, collecting taxes, punishing or pardoning criminals, or making war. In theory, these were, or should have been, a royal monopoly, but through most of the Middle Ages many great seigneurs exercised and profited from some regalian rights. In most cases, their ancestors had acquired these by delegation or usurpation and had transmitted them to their heirs as inheritable private property. Although only the greater territorial lords wielded significant regalian powers by the end of the Middle Ages, some private exercise of these rights survived until the French Revolution.

Prelates and religious bodies were among the seigneurs with some regalian powers, generally as a result of "immunities" granted to churches as far back as Merovingian times. When exercised by ecclesiastics, regalian rights formed part of the temporal possessions ("temporalities") of the church. Yet while the crown had conferred rights on churches, it also took from them, the most famous example being Charles Martel's appropriation of church lands to provide income to support his warriors. Kings had long been accustomed to intervening in the temporal affairs of the church, often to the consternation of ecclesiastical reformers. Because of the assumption that the lands and temporalities of the church derived ultimately from the crown, these were known as "regalia."

The term "regale" came to refer to a special regalian right over the temporalities of a bishopric or monastery when the position of bishop or abbot was vacant. Although some lords other than the king exercised the regale, it was much less widely dispersed than other regalian powers, was gradually becoming a royal monopoly, and was not granted to princes with apanages. The expanding royal control of the regale was one measure of the growth of royal authority under the Capetian monarchy, but it was never a universal right exercised in every diocese.

The regale entitled the king to collect the revenues of (typically) a bishopric after the bishop died, was promoted to cardinal, resigned, was translated to another bishopric, or engaged in public rebellion. This enjoyment of ecclesiastical revenues, known as the "temporal regale," gave the king incentive to prolong a vacancy. A newly installed bishop had to request that the king deliver to him the regalia before he could have access to the revenues of his episcopacy. The king would sometimes seek to delay doing so.

A more controversial part of the regale was the king's right of appointment to ecclesiastical benefices in a diocese during an episcopal vacancy, the so-called "spiritual regale." This right concerned only benefices without cure of souls, but it occasioned serious friction between the French crown and the papacy, especially in the 14th and 15th centuries, when each wanted control of as many benefices as possible.

The regale was most important economically when the crown's ordinary revenues were proving inadequate and the temporalities of the church still generated considerable wealth (i.e., ca. 1250–1350). Thereafter, as royal taxation grew to maturity and the profits of ecclesiastical estates were in decline, it was not an important source of royal income, and in 1465 Louis XI assigned the profits of the temporal regale to the Sainte-Chapelle in Paris.

John Bell Henneman, Jr.

Lot, Ferdinand, and Robert Fawtier. *Histoire des institutions françaises au moyen âge.* 3 vols. Paris: Presses Universitaires de France, 1957–62, Vol. 3: *Institutions ecclésiastiques.*

REGIS, JOHANNES (ca. 1425–1496). Composer. From 1451 until his death, Regis was at the church of Saint-Vincent in Soignies, first as master of the boys and then, from 1462, as canon and *escollastre* (master of the school). In the 1440s, he appears to have been a singer at Cambrai cathedral and acted as *clerc* for the most famous composer of the day, Dufay. His two known Mass cycles are unusual in both texture and structure, as are his two known songs. But Regis's main success appears to have been as a composer of motets; with their flowing lines, rich chording, and ambitious design, those in five and six voices on a *cantus firmus* line may be the first of their kind and were certainly among the works that generated a new style in the 1470s.

David Fallows

Regis, Johannes. *Johannes Regis: opera omnia,* ed. Cornelis Lindenburg. 2 vols. N.p.: American Institute of Musicology, 1956.
Fallows, David. "The Life of Johannes Regis." *Revue belge de musicologie* 43 (1989): 143–72.

RÉGNIER, JEAN (ca. 1390–ca. 1467). The author of the *Fortunes et adversitez de Jean Régnier* was born into an influential family of Auxerre. The *Fortunes* refers to numerous crucial episodes of his life. As a young squire, he was educated in music, art, and letters in preparation for his years of service to the dukes of Burgundy. In 1403, when he was about thirteen, Régnier participated in an expedition to Jerusalem, most likely a spiritual pilgrimage, with the Marshal Boucicaut. Later in the service of Philip the Good, duke of Burgundy, to whom the English had given the Auxerrois, Régnier was named *bailli* of Auxerre in 1424. He served as the duke's delegate there and took part in negotiations with the French during the next several years. On January 14, 1432, near Beauvais, while on a mission to Normandy, Régnier was taken captive by brigands (*les compagnons de la feuillée*). Realizing his importance, they turned him over to the French for ransom. Held in the episcopal prison in Beauvais, then under the infamous Pierre Cauchon, and later in Lisieux, Régnier was unable to arrange for his release. At one point, enemies close to the dauphin asked for Régnier's execution, but La Hire and others intervened. As Charles d'Orléans

had done, Régnier turned to poetry, composing and assembling most of his *Fortunes* while a prisoner. At last, on May 1, 1433, he was released, having paid a third of his ransom and leaving his wife, Isabeau Chrétien, and his eldest son as hostages until the remaining 2,000 *écus* were paid. Restored to his duties by the duke and eventually recovering financially, in 1441 Régnier purchased the castle of Guerchy and its land, becoming lord of Guerchy. He continued his official duties as *bailli* until 1465, shortly before his death.

No manuscript of the *Fortunes et adversitez de Jean Régnier* is extant. Its 1526 printed edition by Jean de la Garde survives in only five copies. The major portion of the work, the *Livre de la prison,* nearly 5,000 lines, seems to have been composed during Régnier's imprisonment. The *Livre* may have been significantly edited by the author after his release, since he explicitly reserves the right to revise his work and to say things he could not while in prison (ll. 4,299–302). The *Livre de la prison* combines narrative verse with short lyric pieces and draws generously on previous lyric tradition both formally and thematically. His debt to Charles d'Orléans and Alain Chartier is noticeable. Translating the captive Régnier's changing frame of mind, the work moves from his own dilemma to the vast disarray of the French nation. The *Livre* contains a testament suggestive of Villon's, although Régnier's is in a more serious vein. An enumeration of poignant adieux draws an impressive panorama of Régnier's world, conveying both the intensity of his feeling and a keen sense of his political surroundings.

Janice C. Zinser

[See also: CHARLES D'ORLÉANS; CHARTIER, ALAIN]

Régnier, Jean. *Les fortunes et adversitez de Jean Régnier, texte publié par E. Droz.* Paris: Champion, 1923.
Champion, Pierre. *Histoire poétique du XVe siècle.* 2 vols. Paris: Champion, 1923. Vol. 1, pp. 227–84.

REGULAR CANONS. When applied to a person, the term "canon" generally means a member of a group of priests attached to a larger church, usually a cathedral; "regular canon" indicates a priest living in a community in obedience to a rule. (Priests who did not live in a community under a rule came to be called "secular" priests or canons.) During the 9th century in the Carolingian empire and again during the 11th and 12th centuries in Europe generally, there were attempts to organize clerics into communities governed by a rule, much like monks. In the early 9th century, Chrodegang, bishop of Metz, composed for the clergy of his cathedral a *Rule* that expected some elements of a common life but allowed private property and private houses for the canons. This *Rule* was sanctioned by the Synod of Aachen in 816.

In the mid-11th century, communities of regular canons began to appear in Italy and southern France and then to spread throughout Europe in the 12th century. In some cases, these groups were the result of stricter discipline for the clergy of a cathedral; other instances represented the decision of a group of clergy to embrace a life of communal discipline, even apart from an extant church. In contrast to their 9th-century counterparts, these new groups of priests rejected all personal possessions and embraced a fully common life, eating and sleeping in common, like monks. The rise of regular canons as a form of religious life coincided with the general wave of ecclesiastical reform and spiritual renewal that produced the Gregorian Reform movement associated with the papacy, varied attempts by individuals and groups to chart new kinds of "apostolic life" (*vita apostolica*) modeled on concepts associated with the "primitive church" (*ecclesia primitiva*), and such monastic reforms as the founding of Cîteaux and the Cistercian order.

Among significant independent foundations of communities of regular canons in France were Prémontré (near Laon), Arrouaise, Saint-Victor (Paris), and Saint-Ruf (Avignon). Each of these began as a distinctive new foundation, and each became the mother house of an order. The intentions and purposes of these early foundations varied. Prémontré was founded in a forest for purposes of discipline and prayer in a community of priests; Saint-Victor, established just outside Paris by William of Champeaux when he left the schools of Paris, was a center of liturgical piety, scholarly inquiry and instruction, and ecstatic mystical experience; Saint-Ruf was begun by four priests who dedicated themselves to a life of community and discipline in an abandoned church outside Avignon. Arrouaise began with three hermits. By way of contrast, Ivo, bishop of Chartres and himself formerly abbot of a house of regular canons in Beauvais, failed in his attempt to reform his cathedral clergy in Chartres and had to be content with establishing a group of regular canons in the parish church of Saint-André.

While looking to the early church for inspiration, and especially to the sharing of possessions in the Jerusalem community as described in Acts 4:32ff., the regular canons could also call upon Augustine of Hippo as a model and guide (parallel to the place of Benedict of Nursia as the authority, via his *Rule*, for Benedictines and Cistercians). In his episcopal household in Hippo, Augustine had required of his priests personal poverty and a fully common life together. Moreover, he had written a letter (no. 211) instructing a group of female ascetics. By the 12th century, there existed a *Rule of St. Augustine* that consisted of a preface, entitled *Ordo monasterii*, and the body of the *Rule*, the so-called *Praeceptum*.

Regular canons found support and acceptance especially among bishops and clerics dedicated to the Gregorian Reform, with its insistence on clerical celibacy. Monks were sometimes hostile, being opposed to the regular canons' claim to have ancient authority through Augustine for their "new" form of disciplined life that was much like a monastic regimen in almost all respects, save for priestly ordination and responsibilities. Moreover, as the 12th century progressed, ordination of monks to the priesthood, with responsibilities for preaching and the cure of souls, became more and more widespread, so that this was no longer a significant differentiating factor. Nor did all communities of regular canons seek actively to have parish respon-

sibilities. If a differentiating factor can be found for canonical spirituality, it may well be encapsulated in the phrase: "to teach by word and example" (*docere verbo et exemplo*), implying responsibility for teaching others, while Benedictines and Cistercians tended to emphasize the idea of the monk embarking as a learner on a way dedicated to individual salvation.

As one of the three major types of medieval religious orders (the others being monks and mendicant friars), the canons proved to be something of a mediating group. They drew on examples of monastic practice to shape their lives, while in turn providing the basis for St. Dominic's formation of the mendicant Order of Preachers (Dominicans) on the basis of his life as a regular canon.

Grover A. Zinn

[See also: CHRODEGANG OF METZ; CISTERCIAN ORDER; DOMINICAN ORDER; GREGORIAN REFORM; MONASTICISM; PRÉMONTRÉ; SAINT-VICTOR, ABBEY AND SCHOOL OF]

Bynum, Caroline Walker. Docere verbo et exemplo: *An Aspect of Twelfth-Century Spirituality.* Missoula: Scholars, 1979.
———. *Jesus as Mother: Studies in the Spirituality of the High Middle Ages.* Berkeley: University of California Press, 1982.
Dickinson, John Compton. *The Origins of the Austin Canons and Their Introduction into England.* London: SPCK, 1950.
Verheijen, Luc. *La règle de Saint-Augustin.* 2 vols. Paris: Études Augustiniennes, 1967.
Zumkeller, Adolar. *Augustine's Ideal of the Religious Life,* trans. Edmund Colledge. New York: Fordham University Press, 1986.

REIMS. Throughout the Middle Ages, Reims (Marne) played a significant role in the political, religious, and artistic history of western Europe. As Durocortorum, it served as the administrative capital of the Roman province of Belgica Secunda, and its presumed population of approximately 20,000 would have ranked it with Lyon, Nîmes, or Narbonne. The city's importance as a provincial center is attested by the monumental gateway, the Porte de Mars, a spacious forum and cryptoporticus, villas embellished with rich mosaic pavements, and extensive cemeteries. Christianity, established during the second half of the 3rd century, weathered the successive assaults of Germanic tribes, although Bishop Nicasius was martyred on the threshold of his cathedral by the Vandals in 406/07.

In an effort to win a greater measure of security amid the political turmoil of the 5th century, the bishops of Reims established ties to the local Frankish kings. This rapprochement culminated with the conversion to Christianity of Clovis. His baptism at the cathedral on Christmas day in 498 or 499 by St. Remi (459–ca. 530) became the basis for later royal coronation rituals, beginning with that of Louis the Pious at Reims in 816 and persisting into the 19th century. Raised to the rank of archbishopric in the mid-8th century, Reims ecclesiastics were major figures in Carolingian politics: Ebbo (r. 816–35) backed the deposition of Louis the Pious; his successor, Hincmar (r.

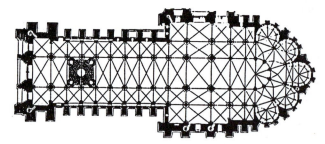

Reims (Marne), Notre-Dame plan. After Deneux.

Reims, Notre-Dame, façade. *Photograph courtesy of Alinari/Art Resources.*

siastical courts at the end of the 14th century completed the secularization of Reims's civic institutions.

The 14th and 15th centuries were a period of crisis for Reims, along with the rest of Champagne. Stagnation in the textile industry and the collapse of the Champagne fairs in the years immediately after 1300 led to a new network of relationships with the Low Countries that was to have enormous consequences during the Hundred Years' War. Located strategically between the two poles of Burgundian power in Burgundy and Flanders, Reims was pulled toward England through its economic ties, while its continuing identity as the site of French royal coronations formed an unbreakable link to Paris. The political impor-

Reims, Notre-Dame, west façade, central portal, Annunciation and Visitation. *Photograph courtesy of Whitney S. Stoddard.*

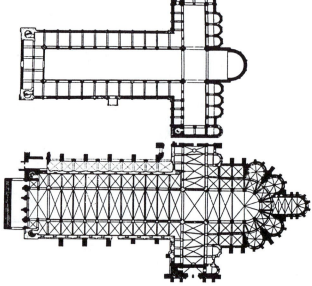

Reims, Saint-Remi, plan of 11th-century church (above) and present plan (below). After Ravaux and Deneux.

845–882), served as chief counselor to Emperor Charles the Bald. Hincmar's *Vita Remigii*, by promoting the primacy of the saint, sought to elevate the archbishop to the status of a protector of the Frankish kingdom.

The power of the archbishops in the city remained uncontested until the 12th century, when Reims entered a period of dynamic development as a center of cloth production. Rapid population increase resulted in the urbanization of the area between the Roman *cité*, centered on the cathedral, and the settlement that had grown up around the abbey of Saint-Remi to the south. Industrialization led to a growing secular presence in the city, and the rising bourgeoisie established a communal government in 1139. Clashes with church authorities over matters of taxation and jurisdiction grew frequent; civic unrest chased the cathedral clergy out of Reims between 1234 and 1237. The abolition of eccle-

tance of Reims in this struggle is illustrated by the coronation of Charles VII at the cathedral on July 17, 1429, following a three-month march from Orléans led by Jeanne d'Arc. Erasing doubts about Charles's legitimacy, the ceremony provided a powerful stimulus for the French, who were able to expel hostile forces from Champagne within a decade.

The works of art and architecture produced in Reims between the 9th and the 13th centuries testify to the luster of its ecclesiastical institutions and their intimate connections with royal power. During the Carolingian era, a brilliant school of manuscript painting, flourishing at the nearby abbey of Hautvillers, produced the incomparable *Ebbo Gospels* (Épernay, Bibl. mun. 1) and *Utrecht Psalter*. Closely allied to the imperial scriptorium at Aix-la-Chapelle, the energetic, classically based style of the Reims school typified the innovative retrospection of the Carolingian *renovatio*. In the realm of architecture, the nave and sections of the transept of the abbey of Saint-Remi survive from a vast Romanesque project (1005–49) intended as a shrine for the saint's relics as well as a storehouse for the miraculous oil delivered for the baptism of Clovis and used in royal unctions. Its T-shaped basilican plan may recall St. Peter's in Rome; the tall three-story elevation of arcade, gallery, and clerestory, originally wooden-roofed, sounds an emphatic note of spacious verticality. An expanded choir, erected ca. 1170–90 under Abbot Peter of Celle, reflects the new Gothic style in its ground plan with a series of contiguous radiating chapels around an ambulatory and a diaphanous four-story elevation stayed by flying buttresses.

A fire on May 6, 1210, destroyed the cathedral of Notre-Dame, a heterogeneous assemblage of 9th- and 12th-century campaigns. Reconstructed beginning in 1211, the new edifice absorbed and modernized elements of Saint-Remi within the framework of a uniform, three-story bay structure influenced by ideas from Chartres and Soissons. A similar barometer of architectural change is seen at the parish church of Saint-Jacques, where the late 12th-century phases of construction in the transept were shaped by Saint-Remi, whereas the later nave was conceived as a simplified version of the cathedral scheme. The glory of the cathedral, however, is its sculptural decoration. From the angels placed on the choir chapels and the north-transept portals of the 1220s and 1230s, which reveal a clear dependency on ancient Roman art, one witnesses the development of a vital naturalism in the work of the Joseph Master and his successors on the west façade and inner west wall, ca. 1255–70. The elegant animation and expressive intensity of these figures set a tone and provided models that inspired artists for the next two centuries. The architecture of the west façade, with its screen of gables, is connected with that of the Benedictine abbey of Saint-Nicaise, begun in 1231 and demolished during the Revolution. Its architect, Hugues Libergier, combined the precious effects of metalwork with the monumentality of the twin-towered triple-portal format to create one of the most innovative frontispieces of the Gothic age.

Michael T. Davis

Reims, Saint-Remi, chevet. *Photograph courtesy of Whitney S. Stoddard.*

[See also: BURGUNDY; CHAMPAGNE; CLOVIS I; GOTHIC ARCHITECTURE; GOTHIC ART; HINCMAR OF REIMS; HUGUES LIBERGIER; HUNDRED YEARS' WAR; JEANNE D'ARC; MANUSCRIPTS, PRODUCTION AND ILLUMINATION; TEXTILES]

Bideault, Maryse, and Claudine Lautier. "Saint-Nicaise de Reims: chronologie et nouvelles remarques sur l'architecture." *Bulletin monumental* 135 (1977): 295–330.

Branner, Robert. "Historical Aspects of the Reconstruction of Reims Cathedral." *Speculum* 36 (1961): 23–37.

Caviness, Madeline Harrison. *Sumptuous Arts at the Royal Abbeys in Reims and Braine: ornatus elegantiae, varietate stupendes.* Princeton: Princeton University Press, 1990.

Congrès archéologique 78 (1911). 2 vols.; and 135 (1977). [Contains articles on monuments of the city and surrounding region. The 1911 volumes are of particular value, for they predate the extensive damage inflicted on Reims and its monuments in World War I.]

Desportes, Pierre. *Reims et les Rémois aux XIIIe et XIVe siècles.* Paris: Picard, 1979.

———. *Histoire de Reims.* Toulouse: Privat, 1983.

Kurmann, Peter. *La façade de la cathédrale de Reims: architecture et sculpture des portails: étude archéologique et stylistique.* 2 vols. Paris: CNRS, 1987.

Le Goff, Jacques. "Reims, ville du sacre." In *Les lieux de mémoire,* ed. Pierre Nora. 3 vols. Paris: Gallimard, 1986, Vol. 2: *La nation,* pp. 89–184.

Prache, Anne. *Saint-Rémi de Reims: l'œuvre de Pierre de Celle et sa place dans l'architecture gothique.* Geneva: Droz, 1978.

Reinhardt, Hans. *La cathédrale de Reims: son histoire, son architecture, sa sculpture, ses vitraux.* Paris: Presses Universitaires de France, 1963.

Salet, Francis. "Le premier colloque international de la Société Française d'Archéologie: chronologie de la cathédrale." *Bulletin monumental* 125 (1967): 347–94.

Sauerländer, Willibald. *Gothic Sculpture in France, 1140–1270,* trans. Janet Sondheimer. New York: Abrams, 1973.

RELICS AND RELIQUARIES. Relics are the remains of a dead holy person or objects closely related to that person. The Middle Ages recognized three classes of relics: the body, or parts of the body, of the holy person; objects closely related to the person, such as garments; and objects that touched these remains, as oils from the tomb collected in ampullae. While relics constituting the whole bodies of holy persons were placed in tombs, from the early Christian period on fragmentary parts of these bodies or objects closely related to the dead person were placed in smaller receptacles called reliquaries, usually crafted of ivory, precious metals, enamelwork, and gems.

The most important relics were those of Christ. Because Christian belief held that Christ was resurrected and ascended into Heaven, nothing of his adult body remained as a relic, although "relics" of his foreskin were recorded at Conques (9th c.), at Charroux in Poitou (from the end of the 11th c.), and at Boulogne (15th c.). Some relics of his clothing are found in France, such as his swaddling clothes and loincloth at Aix-la-Chapelle (by the 9th c.) and the Holy Cloak at Argenteuil (13th c.). By far the most numerous relics are those of the Passion (pieces of the True Cross, nails from the Crucifixion, thorns from the Crown of Thorns). The most famous group of Passion relics in France was that acquired by King Louis IX in the mid-13th century. The expense of creating the gold and jeweled receptacles to hold these relics was actually greater than the cost of the Sainte-Chapelle, which was built to house them.

Relics of the Virgin were next in importance. As she, too, was believed to have been assumed bodily into Heaven, her relics tend to be objects closely related to her, such as the tunic she wore at Christ's birth (at Chartres by the 9th c.) and other garments at Soissons, Marseille, and Arles. Also venerated were her hair (Coutances, Saint-Omer, Saint-Denis), nail parings, and milk.

Relics of the Apostles and saints remain the largest category. Between the 3rd and 6th centuries, veneration of saints became a major part of Christianity, and by the 6th century it was generally believed that the relics of deceased Apostles and saints have been left on earth for the benefit of the living, and specifically that these relics could perform miracles. Relics were not only objects of veneration in and of themselves but were also appealed to for miraculous cures, assistance in childbirth, or help in coping with the woes of life.

From the early Christian period through the Middle Ages, relics were the object of pilgrimage. Under the Merovingians, relics and their miraculous properties were used to convert pagans. In the Carolingian period, the role

Conques, reliquary of Sainte Foy (10th century with later additions). *Photograph courtesy of Alinari/Art Resources.*

Casket-type reliquary. Martyrdom and Burial of Thomas Becket (Limoges, early 13th century). *Courtesy of the Allen Memorial Art Museum, Oberlin College, Oberlin, Ohio. Gift of Baroness René de Kerchove, 1952.*

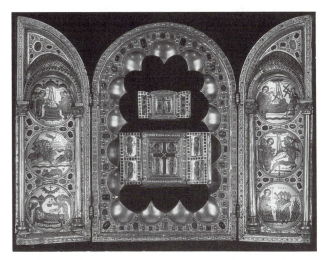

Stavelot triptych. True Cross reliquary, Mosan, 12th century. *Courtesy of Pierpont Morgan Library, New York.*

Arm reliquary (Mosan, c. 1230). *Courtesy of The Cloisters Collection, Metropolitan Museum of Art, New York.*

Gothic metalwork, Saint-Elizabeth Shrine, Paris. *Courtesy of The Cloisters Collection, Metropolitan Museum of Art, New York.*

Saint-Étienne, Mosan. *Courtesy of The Cloisters Collection, Metropolitan Museum of Art, New York.*

While the stone sarcophagi of saints were heavy and not easily moved, from at least the 7th century on we also find in France smaller reliquaries that could be carried in liturgical processions or brought to ecclesiastic councils. These reliquaries are made of gilded copper, sometimes set with enamels or precious gems, the workmanship of the 7th- and 8th-century examples showing the influence of northern European Migrations art. They are most frequently shaped like miniature sarcophagi (reliquary casket of St. Maurice d'Agaune, 7th c.; reliquary casket of St. Mommola, 8th c., Saint-Benoît-sur-Loire; reliquary casket with Christ blessing between the archangels Michael and Gabriel, 8th c., church of Saint-Évrault, Mortain), or they were fashioned like purses (purse reliquary of Saint-Bonnet-Avalouze, 7th c.; purse reliquary with Virgin and Child between SS. Peter and Paul, 8th c., now in the Cluny Museum).

During the Carolingian period, the demand for relics increased. Although dead bodies were supposed to remain intact for the Final Resurrection, after considerable negotiation the ecclesiastic hierarchy in Rome agreed to the dismemberment of saints' bodies, having placed them in a special category. Relic fragments in this period found their way into altars and reliquaries of the casket and purse type.

It is during the Carolingian period that a new type of reliquary appears in France, one that imitates the shape of the body part within. The tradition of body-part reliquaries may have originated in the East: the Piacenza pilgrim (ca. 570) saw a gold-encased and jeweled head reliquary of St. Theodota in Jerusalem. The earliest record of a body-part reliquary in the West is the 9th-century Carolingian head reliquary of St. Mauritius, given to Vienne cathedral by King Boso of Provence (d. 887). Head reliquaries become common in the Middle Ages, with many French examples. In addition to head reliquaries (Alexander head, 12th c.; St. Yrieux, 13th c.), there are bust reliquaries (St. Baudine, St. Césaire, St. Chaffre, all from the 12th c.) and a considerable number of arm reliquaries and some foot reliquaries, which seem to have been most popular during the 12th and 13th centuries.

Whole-figure reliquary statues in France are found from at least the 10th century. The only extant reliquary of this type from this period is that of St. Foy in Conques (probably assembled ca. 984), but Bernard of Angers writes of four such figure reliquaries brought to a synod at Rodez in the early 11th century. A surviving 13th-century example is the St. Stephen reliquary now at The Cloisters in New York.

By the 12th century, many types of reliquaries can be found, most of which continue to be made to the end of the Middle Ages. In addition to the casket, purse, body-part, and figure reliquaries, a number of relics of the True Cross are placed within cross-shaped reliquaries (Cross of Clairmaris, Saint-Omer, 13th c.) and reliquaries in the shape of a miniature church (reliquary of St. Romain, Rouen, and of St. Taurin at Évreux, both 13th c.) became popular. Monstrance reliquaries, known from at least the 12th century, become popular in the late Middle Ages. These reliquaries are in many shapes, but all include a

of relics was extended when Charlemagne decreed that all oaths had to be sworn on or over them.

During the Gallo-Roman period and throughout the Merovingian period, when entire bodies of French saints were intact they were placed in rectangular stone sarcophagi, following Roman burial tradition. Such sarcophagi were used for the lay population as well as for saints. A 6th-century example is the sarcophagus of St. Clarus, bishop of Euze (d. ca. 510). Many more are extant from the 7th and 8th centuries, including the sarcophagus of St. Raimundus (7th c.) at Moissac, the sarcophagus of St. Drausius, bishop of Soissons (7th c.), now in the Louvre, and the extraordinary group at the abbey of Jouarre (St. Theodechilde, late 7th–early 8th c.; St. Agilbert, 7th c., with scenes of the Last Judgment; St. Agilberta, 7th c.). By the 12th century, many stone sarcophagi of saints were replaced by those made of precious metals and gems.

glass or crystal compartment in which the relic can be clearly seen (reliquary of the hand of St. Attale, Strasbourg, 12th–15th c.; carriage reliquary, Orléans, 13th c.; reliquary of the Holy Thorn, Arras, 13th c.). Reliquaries with the contemplative aid of narrative scenes can also be dated from the 12th century on (Stavelot Triptych with relics of the True Cross and scenes of the finding of the True Cross, Pierpont Morgan Library, 12th c.; reliquary of the Virgin and Child with scenes of Christ's infancy, The Cloisters, 14th c.).

Paula L. Gerson

[See also: ENAMELING; GOTHIC ART; MIGRATIONS ART; PARIS; PILGRIMAGE; POPULAR DEVOTION; ROMANESQUE ART; SAINTS, CULT OF]

Gauthier, Marie-Madeleine. *Highways of the Faith: Relics and Reliquaries from Jerusalem to Compostela*, trans. J.A. Underwood. Secaucus: Wellfleet, 1986.

Lasko, Peter. *Ars Sacra: 800–1200*. Harmondsworth: Penguin, 1972.

Legner, Anton, ed. *Ornamenta ecclesiae: Katalog zur Ausstellung des Schnügen-Museums in der Josef-Haubrich-Kunsthalle.* 3 vols. Cologne: Stadt Köln, 1985, esp. Vol. 3.

Taralon, Jean, ed. *Les trésors des églises de France: Musée des Arts Décoratifs.* 2nd ed. Paris: CNMHS, 1965.

REMIGIUS OF AUXERRE (ca. 841–ca. 908). Carolingian grammarian and teacher, first at the Benedictine school of Saint-Germain of Auxerre, where he studied with Heiric, later at the cathedral schools of Reims and Paris. Through Heiric, Remigius was influenced by both Haimo of Auxerre and Johannes Scottus Eriugena; his life and works represent both the traditional and the innovative in Carolingian thought and span the change from monastic to cathedral schools as the primary centers of learning. Among his students at Paris was Odo, later abbot of Cluny. Remigius wrote commentaries on grammatical and rhetorical works by Bede, Martianus Capella, and Boethius, as well as commentaries on biblical books, including Genesis, the Psalms, the Gospels, and perhaps the Pauline epistles. The biblical exegesis of Remigius has long been intertwined with that of Haimo of Auxerre and is just now being systematically sorted out. Seen by modern scholars as a protoscholastic, Remigius was in the vanguard of the gloss tradition of biblical learning.

E. Ann Matter

[See also: BIBLE, CHRISTIAN INTERPRETATION OF; ERIUGENA, JOHANNES SCOTTUS; HAIMO OF AUXERRE; HEIRIC OF AUXERRE; ODO; PHILOSOPHY]

Remigius of Auxerre. *Opera. PL* 131. [Many writings attributed to Remigius in this volume are not his.]

————. *Commentum in Martianum Capellam*, ed. Cora E. Lutz. 2 vols. Leiden: Brill, 1962–65.

————. Commentary on Bede's *De arte metrica et de schematibus et tropis*, ed. Calvin B. Kendall and M.H. King. *CCSL* 123A. Turnhout: Brepols, 1975.

Leonardi, Claudio. "Remigio di Auxerre e l'eredità della scuola carolingia." In *I classici nel medioevo e nell'umanesimo.* Genoa: Universita di Genova, Istituto di Filologia Classica e Medievale, 1975.

RENART, ROMAN DE. The twenty-six "branches" of the *Roman de Renart* were composed by some twenty authors of varying talent between ca. 1174 and 1250. This episodic narrative in octosyllabic verse has come down to us in thirteen major manuscripts. Ceaselessly modified by oral and written transmission, it is a fluid work that reflects the constant interaction of language, imagination, and reality—so much so that its component parts are difficult to date with precision. It is possible to identify three principal collections, differing in organization, content, and length. To designate the parts of each collection, the term *branche* is used. Each episode grows from the main Renardian trunk like the branch of a tree, and one can sense here a bit of mischievous fun, for until its use in the *Renart*, the comparison had been found in religious and moral literature to designate the good qualities flowing from a cardinal virtue or the vices from a mortal sin.

The earliest branches (II and Va; ca. 1175) show the trickster Renart the fox impelled by an all-devouring hunger, both physical and sexual, triumphing over such opponents as Tibert the cat, Chantecler the rooster, and Tiecelin the crow. They also narrate Renart's rape of the she-wolf Hersent, the cause of the enmity between Renart and Isengrin the wolf. Branches I and Ia recount the consequences of these actions, whereby Renart is summoned to judgment at the court of Noble the lion. Branch IV (ca. 1177) tells the delightful tale of Renart and Isengrin in the well. Other early branches, composed 1180–90, develop the themes of these first branches into a lighthearted parody of contemporary society. Seven branches composed between 1190 and 1205 round out the beast epic; similar in spirit but introducing new episodes, they present a full picture of contemporary peasant society. A series of ten later branches (1205–50) is inferior in inspiration, full of contradictions, and tending toward heavy-handed satire.

Renart is the man-beast of unbridled violence and sexuality; like the bear and the wolf, he symbolizes the destructive forces at work in creation; he incarnates the primitive forces of nature, which, goaded by voracious physical and sexual appetites, violate and mutilate both animals and men. Beyond these mythemes, one finds, in the movement from orality to textuality, a folktale structure, as in the episodes with Tibert the cat. But the cultured clerics who first wrote down these tales, only a few of whom—Pierre de Saint-Cloud, Richard de Lison, the Priest of La Croix-en-Brie—we know by name, have also drawn from French and Latin literary sources (Aesop's fables in prose and verse, *Ecbasis captivi*, and especially *Ysengrimus*). *Renart* has close ties to the Tristan material, which likewise uses division into branches and whose hero, also a trickster, is in the same triangular relationship with Iseut and his uncle Mark as Renart is with Hersent and his uncle Isengrin. In Branch XIII, the animals search for Renart in the castle in a scene reminiscent of Chrétien's *Yvain*; in other branches, they go on pilgrimage to the hen Pinte's tomb as they do to Muldumarec's in Marie de France's *Yonec*; and the fox and the wolf wage war on one another like the feudal barons of the chansons de geste; Branch IX ends in an apocalypse of the chivalric world reminiscent of the *Mort Artu*.

Rewriting is also present within the *Roman de Renart*, both in a single branch that exists in multiple versions and between branches, through repetition of formulae and motifs or structure: Branch XII is grafted on Branch XV, Branch VII on IV, with a subtle play of variations, inversions, and amplifications. Moreover, the *Roman de Renart* was rewritten through the centuries: in Rutebeuf's *Renart le bétourné*, in the 13th-century *Couronnement de Renart*, in Jacquemart Gielée's *Renart le nouvel* (late 13th c.), in the Priest of Troyes's *Renart le contrefait* (1319–28), in Jean Tenessax's *Livre de maistre Renart* (15th c.), as well as in modern adaptations.

An animal behaving like a man, Renart plays a wide variety of roles, changing his name (to Galopin or Chuflet) and his color (red, yellow, black); he is a genius at ruse and metamorphosis who makes a mockery of all taboos, seeking adventure like a knight-errant, compelled ever onward by his insatiable desires. What creates the charm of the work and of its central character is the constant interplay between the animal and the human worlds, as the former, increasingly anthropomorphic, apes the feudal world. The animals mimic human gestures—they speak, ride horses, assault castles, pray to God—in metaphors that the reader accepts without ever losing sight of their underlying animal nature. Renart's world is one of physical joy, of nonintellectual relaxation, of the triumph of instinct. A joyful work paradoxically abounding in death, injury, and mutilation, the *Roman de Renart* depicts a cruel universe where action is motivated by hunger and danger. But the reader senses a feeling of physical, moral, and religious liberation, and the laughter, both satiric and parodic, is also the anarchic and amoral expression of the feast of fools. It is a desacralized universe that holds all conduct to be folly and rests finally on the reality of nature, as does Jean de Meun's *Roman de la Rose*. The greatest value in Renart's world is life, and to survive is to triumph.

Jean Dufournet

[**See also**: *ECBASIS CAPTIVI*; FABLE (*ISOPET*); JACQUEMART GIELÉE; PIERRE DE SAINT-CLOUD; *RENART LE CONTREFAIT*; *YSENGRIMUS*]

Dufournet, Jean, ed. and trans. *Le roman de Renart*. 2 vols. Paris: Flammarion, 1985. [Modern French translation.]

Fukumoto, Naoyuki, Naboru Harano, and Satoru Suzuki, eds. *Le roman de Renart édité d'après les manuscrits C et M*. 2 vols. Tokyo: France Tosho, 1983–85.

Roques, Mario, ed. *Le roman de Renart*. 6 vols. Paris: Champion, 1951–63.

Bossuat, Robert. *Le roman de Renart*. Paris: Hatier, 1957.

Dufournet, Jean, et al. *Le goupil et le paysan*. Paris: Champion, 1990.

Flinn, John. *Le roman de Renart dans la littérature française et dans les littératures étrangères au moyen âge*. Toronto: University of Toronto Press, 1963.

Foulet, Lucien. *Le roman de Renart*. Paris: Champion, 1914.

Jauss, Hans-Robert. *Untersuchungen zur mittelalterlicher Tierdichtung*. Tübingen: Niemeyer, 1959.

Scheidegger, Jean. *Le roman de Renart ou le texte de la dérision*. Geneva: Droz, 1989.

Subrenat, Jean, and M. de Combarieu du Gres. *Le roman de Renart: index des thèmes et des personnages*. Aix-en-Provence: CUER MA, 1987.

RENART LE CONTREFAIT. It was an unnamed priest of Troyes, defrocked for bigamy, who composed this final avatar of the *Roman de Renart*, in eight branches, of which we have two redactions. The first (*A*: 32,000 lines) was composed between 1319 and 1322, and the second (*B*: 41,150 lines) appeared between 1328 and 1342. There is also a prose section. The whole is an incoherent but rich monster, a lively reflection of its age, as well as a conglomeration of tales, incidents, reflections, and commentaries of every sort.

A virulent satire of the monarchy, aristocracy, ecclesiastical abuses, and vices of women, this defense of the weak is above all a compendium of medieval moral and philosophical thought that bears witness to the wide-ranging culture of its author as well as to the influence of Jean de Meun. The poet makes explicit much of what was only hinted at in the earlier *Roman de Renart*. Renart is at times the mischievous fox of the early branches, at other times the symbol of evil in all its manifestations, and even the repentent philosopher commenting on human vices under the guise of Reason, Nature, and God.

Jean Dufournet

[See also: *RENART, ROMAN DE*]

Raynaud, Gaston, and Henri Lemaître, eds. *Le roman de Renart le contrefait*. 2 vols. Paris: Champion, 1914.

Flinn, John. *Le roman de Renart dans la littérature française et dans les littératures étrangères au moyen âge*. Toronto: University of Toronto Press, 1963, pp. 364–441.

RENAUT DE BEAUJEU (de Bâgé; ca. 1165–1230). Author of an Arthurian verse romance of over 6,000 lines, the *Bel Inconnu*, written ca. 1185–90. The hero of the poem is Gawain's son, Guinglain, who releases Esmeree, daughter of the King of Wales, from the enchantment of two sorcerers, who had transformed her into a serpent. Guinglain marries Esmeree after liberating her and resisting seduction by a supernatural woman. Many narrative elements of the *Bel Inconnu* are traditional and occur elsewhere in romance: the sparrowhawk contest, the seduction of a mortal by a fairy, the *fier baiser*, and so on. Even the primary plot of the *Bel Inconnu* recurs as the basis of other romances, such as the Middle English adaptation of Renaut, *Libeaus Desconus*, the Italian *Carduino*, and the Middle High German *Wigalois*. There are grounds for believing that the story of the Fair Unknown was associated originally with Gawain, as part of a complex of tales about him; later versions probably transferred it to his son.

Renaut de Beaujeu presents his poem in a personal manner, saying that he is writing it for his own beloved. This personal touch in some ways exemplifies the differences between the *Bel Inconnu* and the romances of Chrétien de Troyes. Chrétien is concerned with issues of human existence and courtly values, whereas Renaut is more intent on telling a good story. This seems to have been Renaut's way of responding to Chrétien's reputation. Nevertheless, the latter's influence, on both verbal and narrative levels, is clear in the *Bel Inconnu*. The prologue, for example, is worded in such a manner as to recall that of *Lancelot,* and the sparrowhawk episode inevitably calls to mind *Erec et Enide.*

The *Bel Inconnu* seems to be the only full-length Arthurian romance written in the two decades following the death of Chrétien de Troyes.

Keith Busby

[See also: ARTHURIAN VERSE ROMANCE; GAWAIN ROMANCES]

Renaut de Beaujeu. *Le Bel Inconnu,* ed. G. Perrie Williams. Paris: Champion, 1929.

———. *Renaut de Bâgé: Le Bel Inconnu* (*Li Biaus Descouneüs; The Fair Unknown*), ed. Karen Fresco, trans. Colleen P. Donagher. New York: Garland, 1992.

Fierz-Monnier, Antoinette. *Initiation und Wandlung: Zur Geschichte des altfranzösischen Romans im zwölften Jahrhundert von Chrétien de Troyes zu Renaut de Beaujeu.* Bern: Francke, 1951.

RENAUT DE LOUENS (fl. 1330s). A Dominican friar from Poligny in the Jura Mountains, Renaut wrote the *Livre de Mellibee et Prudence* in 1336 or 1337. Renaut's *Mellibee,* in French prose, is a loose translation of the *Liber de consolationis et consilii* by Albertano of Brescia (1246). Albertano's book was translated also into Italian, German, and Dutch. Of the four versions in French, the earliest, from the second half of the 13th century, was a close translation of the Latin prose; two others, one in prose and one in verse, are of unknown authorship and date. The fourth version, by Renaut de Louens, was the most popular, surviving in at least twenty-six manuscripts, and was Chaucer's source for the *Tale of Melibee.* Renaut de Louens also produced a verse translation of Boethius's *De consolatione Philosophiae* during the same period (1336–37) that he wrote the *Mellibee.* He undertook both of these books of consolation for an unnamed lady's benefit and instruction.

The *Livre de Mellibee et Prudence* is a moral allegory. The house of Melibeus is attacked while he is away; his wife, Prudence, is beaten and his daughter, Sophie, is wounded. Melibeus calls for revenge and plans to make war on his enemies, but Prudence convinces him to control his anger, maintaining that war is terrible and useless and that reconciliation and peace are altogether more desirable. Arguing from biblical and philosophical authorities, she succeeds in counseling him to pardon his enemies.

Rita Copeland

[See also: TRANSLATION]

Renaut de Louens. *Le livre de Mellibee et Prudence,* ed. J. Burke Severs. In *Sources and Analogues of Chaucer's Canterbury Tales,* ed. W.F. Bryan and Germaine Dempster. Chicago: University of Chicago Press, 1941, pp. 560–614.

Roques, Mario. "Traductions françaises des traités moraux d'Albertano de Brescia: *Le livre de Melibee et de Prudence* par Renaut de Louhans." In *Histoire littéraire de la France.* Paris: Imprimerie Nationale, 1936, Vol. 37, pp. 488–506.

RENÉ D'ANJOU (1409–1480). Son of Louis II, duke of Anjou, and Yolande of Aragon, the "Good King René" is known for his accomplishments in several areas. This second son of the politically ambitious Yolande was, for strategic reasons, adopted by the duke of Bar. He was married in 1420 to Isabelle of Lorraine. He became duke of Bar in 1430 and duke of Lorraine in 1431, but his claim to the latter title cost him five years in prison. At the death of his elder brother Louis in 1434, René inherited the duchy of Anjou and the family claim to the kingdom of Naples. Although he lost the latter throne to Alfonso of Aragon in 1442, René's prestige and influence nonetheless continued to grow at the court of his brother-in-law, Charles VII, and in France generally. After the death of Isabelle in 1453, he married Jeanne de Laval. René, whose titles derived from the circumstances of aristocratic inheritance, was one of the last obstacles to the unification of France by Louis XI. Deprived of Bar and Anjou by Louis, René retreated in his later years to Provence.

Despite his political reversals, René d'Anjou was known as a good strategist in battle and an expert in warfare. He wrote a treatise on tournaments, the *Traictié de la forme et devis d'un tornoy* (1445–50), and organized several celebrated tournaments on Charles VII's behalf. He was a generous patron of the arts and himself a painter and writer. He composed two richly illuminated allegorical works in verse and prose: the *Mortifiement de vaine plaisance* (1455) and the *Livre du cuer d'amours espris* (1457).

Janice C. Zinser

[See also: *ABUZÉ EN COURT;* ANJOU, HOUSES OF; LORRAINE]

René d'Anjou. *Le livre du cuer d'amours espris,* ed. Susan Wharton. Paris: Union Générale des Éditions, 1980.

———. *King René's Book of Love* (*Le cueur d'amours espris,* intro. and commentary F. Unterkircher, trans. Sophie Wilkins. New York: Braziller, 1975. [Reproduces sixteen illuminations attributed to René.]

Des Garets, Marie Louyse. *Un artisan de la Renaissance française du XVe siècle, le roi René, 1409–1480.* Paris: Éditions de la Table Ronde, 1946.

Lyna, Frédéric. *Le mortifiement de vaine plaisance de René d'Anjou: étude du texte et des manuscrits à peintures.* Brussels: Weckesser, 1926.

RENNES. Condate, at the confluence of the small rivers Ille and Vilaine in east-central Armorica, or Brittany, was the chief city of the Redones. It was fortified in the late 3rd century; an important abbey commemorated the cult of an early bishop, St. Mélaine (d. ca. 530). Frankish influence was strong, and with Nantes, Rennes formed part of the March of Brittany. In 831, however, Emperor Louis the Pious, unable to defeat the Bretons by force, appointed Nominoe *missus* of both the Celtic and Frankish parts of Brittany, and Rennes came under Breton political control. Factional disputes and Viking invasions allowed a new comital dynasty to emerge; ties with royal France remained strong. The 10th and 11th centuries witnessed an intense rivalry with the counts of Nantes for the ducal title, which Conan I of Rennes (d. 992) obtained. A family quarrel allowed Eudo, brother of Alain III (r. 1008–40), to seize Rennes after his death. From 1084, Alain Fergent (r. 1084–1113) reunited it with the rest of the ducal domain. With Nantes and Vannes, Rennes remained a center of ducal administration.

The court of the seneschal at Rennes received appeals from other Breton *sénéchaussées*, with the exception of Nantes. The city, politically and strategically important, was frequently attacked. Its Roman walls, which had enclosed 22 acres, were strengthened by a ducal castle after the late 10th century. Henry II of England took the town in 1182 and destroyed the castle. During the Breton civil war (1341–64), Rennes was held for Charles de Blois and Jeanne de Penthièvre; it withstood a nine-month siege by the English (1356–57). But the need to defend new suburbs and a total population of around 14,000, living in nine parishes, led between 1421 and 1476 to the construction of two further *enceintes*. Some 155 acres were eventually enclosed, including the abbey of Saint-Georges, a ducal foundation (ca. 1030) for Benedictine nuns, and low-lying quarters south of the Vilaine, where small craft industries, notably textile and leatherworking, had developed. The defenses were tested for the last time by a French siege in 1491, before Duchess Anne married Charles VIII and delivered Rennes, and Brittany, into royal hands. Among the distinguished bishops of Rennes may be noted the poet and reformer Marbode (r. 1096–1120) and Étienne de Fougères (r. 1168–78), author and servant of Henry II of England. St. Yves Helory (d. 1303) was briefly the bishop's official. A Franciscan convent was established ca. 1238; the Dominicans arrived in 1368 and the Carmelites in 1448. Printing was introduced in 1483. Medieval Rennes was almost totally destroyed in a great fire in 1720. The church of Saint-Mélaine has some Romanesque portions but was poorly rebuilt in the 14th, 15th, and 17th centuries.

Michael C.E. Jones

[See also: BRITTANY; ÉTIENNE DE FOUGÈRES; LATIN LYRIC POETRY; MARBODE OF RENNES; NANTES]

Leguay, Jean-Pierre. *La ville de Rennes au XVe siècle à travers les comptes des miseurs*. Paris: Klincksieck, 1968.
Meyer, Jean, ed. *Histoire de Rennes*. Toulouse: Privat, 1972.

REQUÊTES, MAÎTRE DES. The name Requêtes de l'Hôtel, or "Requests of the Household," was first given in the reign of Philip III (r. 1270–85) to the informal judicial sessions at which the king presided in person, earlier known as the Plaids de la Porte, or "Pleas of the Doorway." The king had long been assisted on these occasions by officers who, because they never left his side, had been called *poursuivants du roi,* and when the new name for these proceedings began to prevail, the *poursuivants* began to bear the new designation *maîtres des requêtes de l'hôtel.* Under Philip IV (r. 1285–1314), the king gradually ceased to attend the sessions of the tribunal traditionally identified with him, and from ca. 1300 the *maîtres* normally presided alone. This raised some difficulties about the competence of the Court of Requests, and these were finally settled by an ordinance of 1346 that limited the number of *maîtres* to five and limited their competence to cases concerned with disputes over a royal office and personal claims against royal officers. The Court of the Requests of the Household was thus largely reduced to a kind of domestic court, though from 1344 it also had the right to judge charges of error against *arrêts* of the Parlement.

D'A. Jonathan D. Boulton

[See also: *HÔTEL DU ROI*]

Lot, Ferdinand, and Robert Fawtier. *Histoire des institutions françaises au moyen âge*. 3 vols. Paris: Presses Universitaires de France, 1957–62, Vol. 2: *Institutions royales.*

RESVERIE. A nonsense genre practiced in 13th-century Picardy. The *resverie* alternates long and short verses; the short verse simultaneously provides the logical conclusion to the thought introduced in the previous verse and establishes the rhyme for the following verse, which otherwise has no logical connection with it. Only three *resveries* survive: *Oiseuses* by Beaumanoir, and the anonymous *Dit des traverses* and *Resveries.*

Elizabeth W. Poe

[See also: BEAUMANOIR, PHILIPPE DE REMI, SIRE DE; *FATRAS/FATRASIE; SOTTE CHANSON*]

Bec, Pierre. *La lyrique française au moyen-âge (XIIe–XIIIe siècles): contribution à une typologie des genres poétiques médiévaux*. 2 vols. Paris: Picard, 1977–78, Vol. 1: *Études*; Vol. 2: *Textes.*

REVERDIE. A northern French lyrico-narrative genre of the 13th century. The *reverdie* is a joyful song celebrating springtime greenery and recounting an amorous meeting between poet-knight and lady. The loosely defined genre, of which eight specimens survive, is characterized by stanzaic structure, dialogue, and the conspicuous use of diminutives, such as *roussignolet, praelet, matinet.*

Elizabeth W. Poe

Bec, Pierre. *La lyrique française au moyen-âge (XIIe–XIIIe siècles): contribution à une typologie des genres poétiques médiévaux*. 2 vols. Paris: Picard, 1977–78, Vol. 1: *Études*; Vol. 2: *Textes.*

RHETORIC. *See* LIBERAL ARTS

RHYMED OFFICE. Poetic texts and chants were written in the thousands during the later Middle Ages, both for newly instituted feasts of the Lord and for saints' feasts. The development of this genre of liturgical poetry and music reflects the increasing use of rhymed, accentual texts, until after the 12th century, when this style predominated. This vast repertory of poetic texts and music, although often reflective of the most intense spiritual or political drives of individual regions, religious orders, monasteries, and churches, is not comprehensively catalogued, edited, or even much studied.

The versified texts are primarily antiphons and great responsories as sung in First and Second Vespers, Matins, and Lauds; the little Hours commonly repeat the antiphons of Lauds, and new material is not usually fashioned for Compline. The long series of antiphons and responsories sung at Matins was often compiled so that the chants, which were commonly adapted for the new texts from earlier sources, were arranged in modal order.

Margot Fassler

[**See also:** DIVINE OFFICE]

Crocker, Richard. "Matins Antiphons at St. Denis." *Journal of the American Musicological Society* 39 (1986): 441–90.

Dolbeau, François. "Hagiographie latine et prose rimée: deux exemples de vies épiscopales rédigées au XII siècle." *Sacris erudiri* 32 (1991): 223–68.

Epstein, Marcy J. "'Ludovicus decus regnantium': Perspectives on the Rhymed Office." *Speculum* 53 (1978): 283–333.

Hughes, Andrew. "Late Mediaeval Rhymed Offices." *Journal of the Plainsong and Mediaeval Music Society* 8 (1985): 33–49.

———. "Modal Order and Disorder in the Rhymed Office." *Musica disciplina* 37 (1983): 29–52.

———. "Word Painting in a Twelfth-Century Office." In *Beyond the Moon: Festschrift Luther Dittmer*, ed. Bryan Gillingham and Paul Merkley. Ottawa: Institute of Mediaeval Music, 1990, pp. 16–27.

Jonsson, Ritva. *Historia: études sur la genèse des offices versifiés.* Stockholm: Almqvist and Wiksell, 1968.

RHYTHM. The question of whether rhythm was essential or even appropriate to the performance of the songs of the troubadours and trouvères before the graphic means of notating it developed in the 13th century occupied a large and often contentious part of early 20th-century scholarship in medieval music. Central to the issue was the *Modaltheorie* developed by Friedrich Ludwig and his students Pierre Aubry and Jean Beck. According to the *Modaltheorie*, the accentual patterns of poetic texts of trouvère and troubadour chansons paralleled the six rhythmic modes prevalent in early 13th-century theoretical works, and thus the musical rhythm of a chanson could be determined from the poetic accents of its text.

Hendrik van der Werf rejected *Modaltheorie* in the 1960s, initiating a reassessment of the question of applying 13th-century modal rhythm, which arose in the context of untexted liturgical polyphony, to texted monophony in secular and usually courtly settings. Since that time, many editions of medieval monophony have notated the melodies with rhythmically undifferentiated notes (note heads without stems) when the notation of the source is indubitably nonmensural.

Current scholarship is exploring rhythmic distinctions among the genres of secular monophony. The supposition that the declamatory rhythm of the troubadour and trouvère *grand chant* has a different style and origin from that of the dance song, like the *estampie* or *carole*, seems reasonable.

Sandra Pinegar

[**See also:** RHYTHMIC MODE; TROUBADOUR POETRY; TROUVÈRE POETRY]

Parker, Ian. "The Performance of Troubadour and Trouvère Songs: Some Facts and Conjectures." *Early Music* 5 (1977): 184–207.

Stevens, John. *Words and Music in the Middle Ages.* Cambridge: Cambridge University Press, 1986.

van der Werf, Hendrik. *The Chansons of the Troubadours and Trouvères.* Utrecht: Oosthoek, 1972.

RHYTHMIC MODE. Rhythmic patterns governing some music of the Notre-Dame School, which were probably modeled on poetic metrics of ancient Greek and Latin. A series of rhythmic modes most likely predated the graphic notation, developed in the early 13th century within the Notre-Dame School, providing the earliest western musical notation indicating rhythm. The earliest systematic

The Six Garlandian Rhythmic Modes

	Ligature Configuration	Modern Notation
Mode 1		♩ ♪♩ ♪♩ ♪♩ ♪♩ 𝄾
Mode 2		♪♩ ♪♩ ♪♩ ♪♩ ♪𝄾
Mode 3		♩. ♪♩ ♩. ♪♩ ♩. ♪♩ ♩. 𝄾
Mode 4		♪♩ ♩. ♪♩ ♩. ♪♩ ♩. ♪♩𝄾
Mode 5		♩. ♩. ♩. 𝄾.
	or	♩. ♩. ♩. 𝄾.
Mode 6		♫♫ ♫♫ ♫♫ ♫♫ ♪𝄾
	or	♫ ♫ ♫ ♫ ♪𝄾

theoretical treatment of rhythmic modes was probably a distillation of performance practices at the cathedral, subsequently edited and revised by Johannes de Garlandia (not the English poet and scholar of the same name). Garlandia provided notational patterns for six rhythmic modes, all intended for untexted music, and undoubtedly developed for the discant clausulae composed at Notre-Dame as parts of organa, the polyphonic embellishment of the liturgical service. Such modally rhythmized discant clausulae gave rise to the motet early in the 13th century.

Sandra Pinegar

[See also: ARS ANTIQUA; CLAUSULA; FRANCO OF COLOGNE; MOTET (13TH CENTURY); MUSIC THEORY; NOTRE-DAME SCHOOL; RHYTHM]

Frobenius, Wolf. "Modus (Rhythmuslehre)." In *Handwörterbuch der musikalischen Terminologie*, ed. Hans Heinrich Eggebrecht. Wiesbaden: Steiner, 1972–. 8 pp. (1974).
Treitler, Leo. "Regarding Meter and Rhythm in the Ars Antiqua." *Musical Quarterly* 65 (1979): 524–58.

RICHARD (DUKES OF NORMANDY). Richard I the Fearless (r. 942–96) was the grandson of the Viking chieftain Rollo, the founder of Normandy. A child when his father William Longsword was murdered by Arnulf of Flanders, Richard barely survived an alliance of King Louis IV and Hugues le Grand against him during his minority. He faced another crisis in the 960s, when King Lothair joined forces with the counts of Anjou, Blois-Chartres, and Flanders to invade Normandy. Peace was settled at Gisors in 965. Richard then concentrated on strengthening his position within his lands, allying his family with other Scandinavian clans in the region through marriage ties, and gaining ecclesiastical support for his rule by rebuilding churches and promoting reform.

Richard I's son and heir, Richard II (r. 996–1026), also used family ties and the church to bolster his authority. The duke's brothers and cousins staffed the secular and ecclesiastical administration through which he governed, and the marriages of his female relatives secured alliances with neighboring lords. His powerful uncle Count Rodulf effectively put down a peasant rebellion early in Richard II's reign. In 1013–14, Richard II waged a successful campaign against Eudes II of Blois-Chartres, which helped secure the duchy's southern border along the River Avre, and he also allegedly supported King Robert II the Pious against Burgundy. His son Richard III reigned less than a year.

Cassandra Potts

[See also: NORMANDY]

Bates, David. *Normandy Before 1066.* London: Longman, 1982.
Boüard, Michel de, ed. *Histoire de la Normandie.* 2nd ed. Toulouse: Privat, 1987.
Douglas, David C. "The Earliest Norman Counts." *English Historical Review* 61 (1946): 129–56.

Searle, Eleanor. *Predatory Kinship and the Creation of Norman Power, 840–1066.* Berkeley: University of California Press, 1988.

RICHARD I THE LIONHEARTED (1157–1199). King of England (r. 1189–99). Richard I, second son of Henry II of England and Eleanor of Aquitaine, was installed as duke of Aquitaine in 1172 and played a nominal role in the rebellion of his brother and mother against his father in 1173–74. His first independent exercise of political authority came later in the 1170s, when he put down a number of Aquitanian revolts. From 1182, Richard became involved in wars between Henry and his sons over plans for the succession to the various parts of the vast Angevin empire, which included England, Normandy, Anjou, Brittany, and Aquitaine. In 1188, Richard allied with his father's enemy Philip II Augustus of France, and their successful opposition to the dying Henry brought Richard all the Angevin holdings on Henry's death in 1189.

Richard, like Philip, departed for the Third Crusade in 1190. On the way, at Messina in 1191, the two made a treaty that redefined the relationship of Richard's fiefs with the French crown. Richard's capture in Germany when returning from crusade in 1192 allowed Philip to attempt the dismemberment of the Angevin possessions, with the collusion of Richard's younger brother John. Ransomed in 1194, Richard began a set of campaigns against Philip that consumed the next five years. Richard pursued two strategies: conquest of the strategic Vexin from his newly built fortress of Château-Gaillard and the detachment of the counts of Toulouse and Flanders from alliance with Philip. Despite the overall success of these policies and two victories over Philip personally on the battlefield, Richard had not yet regained all of Normandy when he died in 1199 while putting down a revolt in the Limousin.

Richard was the friend of many troubadours and trouvères and is himself credited with two French lyrics. The more famous, a *rotrouenge* composed while he was a prisoner in Germany, complains of Philip's perfidy and the inconstancy of his own friends; the second, a *sirventes* of 1196, reproaches his vassal the troubadour Dalfin d'Alvernhe and his cousin for not having come to his aid against Philip.

Donald F. Fleming

[See also: CHÂTEAU-GAILLARD; NORMANDY; PHILIP II AUGUSTUS; VEXIN]

Gillingham, John. *The Angevin Empire.* New York: Holmes and Meier, 1984.
———. *Richard the Lionheart.* New York: Time Books, 1978.
Powicke, F.M. *The Loss of Normandy, 1189–1204: Studies in the History of the Angevin Empire.* 2nd ed. Manchester: University of Manchester Press, 1961.
Pernoud, Régine. *Richard Cœur de Lion.* Paris: Fayard, 1988.

RICHARD II (1367–1399). King of England (r. 1377–99). Richard was born at Bordeaux, the only son of Edward, the Black Prince, and the grandson and successor of Edward III. He came to the throne in 1377, as a minor, inheriting a war with France that by the 1370s had turned against England and seemed unending. His turbulent reign, which ended with his violent overthrow and murder, was characterized by two policies, peace abroad and quasiabsolutism at home, which drew from the English nobility and especially his uncles a stubborn resistance. Domestically, his reign virtually began with the Peasants' Revolt of 1381, the greatest popular uprising of English history, sparked largely by the unprecedented taxation required by the war with France. If it was not this event that convinced Richard to end the war, he might have found many other reasons to do so; since the early 1370s, France under Charles V had been on the offensive, retaking all the gains of Richard's father and grandfather and threatening England itself with invasion. Despite the obvious necessity of peace, this policy was stubbornly opposed by the most important figures of the English nobility: Richard's uncles, John of Gaunt and the duke of Gloucester; Gaunt's son Henry, earl of Derby (the future Henry IV); and the earls of Arundel, Warwick, and Nottingham.

These same men were little enamored of Richard's domestic policy of autocratic kingship and his exalted view of the royal prerogative. In 1386, with Gaunt out of the country pursuing, literally, castles in Spain, the remaining five magnates, incensed at the result of Richard's first few months of personal rule, temporarily took over the government of the realm and resumed the war. Richard regained power in 1389, and in 1390 Gaunt negotiated a treaty with France, heralding the first significant period of peace with that country since the Treaty of Brétigny in 1360. The new state of relations between the two kingdoms was sealed by Richard's marriage in 1396 with Isabella, the seven-year-old daughter of the king of France. Richard used this respite from foreign commitments to secure his position at home, but his autocratic methods caused a resentment that, when the exiled Henry of Derby returned in 1399, left him alone and without support. He was forced to abdicate in Derby's favor, and later that year he was murdered in his prison at Pontefract castle.

Monte L. Bohna

Barron, Caroline, and Du Boulay, F.R., eds. *The Reign of Richard II*. London: Athlone, 1971.

Goodman, Anthony. *The Loyal Conspiracy: The Lords Appellant Under Richard II*. London: Routledge and Kegan Paul, 1971.

Jones, Richard H. *The Royal Policy of Richard II: Absolutism in the Later Middle Ages*. Oxford: Blackwell, 1968.

Mathew, Gervase. *The Court of Richard II*. London: Murray, 1968.

Palmer, John J.N. *England, France and Christendom, 1377–1399*. London: Routledge and Kegan Paul, 1972.

RICHARD DE FOURNIVAL (1201–before 1260). Poet, canon, and chancellor at Amiens cathedral and canon of Rouen, Richard de Fournival produced a rich and varied corpus, composing songs in the trouvère style, the prose

Bestiaire d'amours and its fragmentary verse redaction, and the Latin *Biblionomia*, the catalogue of his remarkable library. Three other prose treatises, the *Commens d'amours*, the *Consaus d'amours*, and the *Poissance d'amours*, are of questionable attribution.

It is for the *Bestiaire d'amours* that Richard is chiefly known. In this adaptation of the bestiary format, birds and animals represent aspects of the love experience. The text, immediately popular, has been transmitted in numerous manuscripts, richly illuminated. It inspired several literary responses, all anonymous. The earliest is the *Response au bestiaire*, in which the lady to whom the *Bestiaire d'amours* was addressed supposedly replies, turning each of the bestiary examples into an illustration of her need to take care to protect herself against male sexual advances. A verse adaptation, different from the fragmentary verse redaction apparently by Richard himself, also survives; although the author gives his name, he does so in an anagram of such complexity that it remains unsolved. In two 14th-century manuscripts, the *Bestiaire d'amours* is given a narrative continuation, in which the lover captures the lady and receives from her a red rose. In another 14th-century manuscript, the *Bestiaire* and its *Response* are embedded in a sequence of prose texts that form a dialogue between lover and lady; although none is a bestiary, all refer to the *Bestiaire*, which clearly inspired the sequence.

We know from the *Biblionomia* that Richard owned some unusual books, including the only known complete copy of the poems of Tibullus. At his death, his library passed to Gérard d'Abbeville and then to the Sorbonne.

Sylvia Huot

[See also: BESTIARY; LAPIDARY]

Fournival, Richard de. *Le bestiaire d'amour rimé*, ed. Arvid Thordstein. Lund: Ohlssons, 1941.[The anonymous verse adaptation of the *Bestiaire d'amours*.]

———. *Li bestiaires d'amours di maistre Richart de Fornival e Li response du bestiaire*, ed. Cesare Segre. Milan: Riccardi, 1957.

———. *Biblionomia*, ed. Léopold Delisle. *Cabinet des Manuscrits* 2 (1874): 520–35.

———. *Richard de Fournival. l'œuvre lyrique de Richard de Fournival*, ed. Yvan G. Lepage. Ottawa: University of Ottawa Press, 1984.

RICHARD OF SAINT-VICTOR (d. 1173). A major writer on mysticism in the second half of the 12th century, Richard joined the regular canons of the abbey of Saint-Victor at Paris sometime near the middle of the century (certainly by the early 1150s but perhaps before the death of Hugh of Saint-Victor in 1141). He may have been born in Scotland. He served as subprior and was elected prior in 1161. His writings on the contemplative life were widely known and influenced Bonaventure's treatise *Itinerarium mentis in Deum*.

Richard followed the tradition of Victorine spirituality established by Hugh, but he concentrated more on the stages of development in the mystical life and on what today would be called the psychological aspects of that development. Two of his major mystical writings are symbolic interpretations of biblical persons, objects, and narratives. *De duodecim patriarchiis* (also called *Benjamin minor*) interprets the births and lives of the twelve sons and one daughter of Jacob, recorded in Genesis, as representing the stages of ascetic practice, mental discipline, and spiritual guidance that lead to contemplative ecstasy. *De arca mystica* (also called *Benjamin major*) presents the Ark of the Covenant and the two cherubim that stood on either side of it, described in Exodus, as symbolic of the six kinds or levels of contemplation. Books 4 and 5 of *De arca* give a subtle and influential analysis of types of visionary and ecstatic experience. Richard's *De IV gradibus violentae caritatis* analyzes the stages of the love of God and the transformation of the self by love in the mystical quest. Richard also wrote a commentary on the Book of Revelation, a treatise on the Trinity, mystical comments on various Psalms, a handbook for the Liberal Arts and the study of history (*Liber exceptionum*; digested primarily from works by Hugh of Saint-Victor), a collection of allegorical sermons, and treatises on biblical and mystical topics.

Grover A. Zinn

[See also: BONAVENTURE; HUGH OF SAINT-VICTOR; MYSTICISM; REGULAR CANONS; SAINT-VICTOR, ABBEY AND SCHOOL OF]

Richard of Saint-Victor. *Opera omnia.* PL 196.
———. *De Trinitate*, ed. Jean Ribaillier. Paris: Vrin, 1958.
———. *Liber exceptionum*, ed. Jean Châtillon. Paris: Vrin, 1958.
———. *Selected Writings on Contemplation*, trans. Claire Kirchberger. London: Faber, 1957.
———. *The Twelve Patriarchs, The Mystical Ark, and Book Three on the Trinity*, trans. Grover A. Zinn. New York: Paulist, 1979.
———. *Les quatre degrés de la violente charité*, ed. Gervais Dumeige. Paris: Vrin, 1955.
Dumeige, Gervais. *Richard de Saint-Victor et l'idée chrétienne de l'amour.* Paris: Presses Universitaires de France, 1952.
Zinn, Grover A. "Personification Allegory and Visions of Light in Richard of St. Victor's Teaching on Contemplation." *University of Toronto Quarterly* 46 (1977): 190–214.

RICHARS LI BIAUS. Preserved by a single manuscript (Turin, Bibl. Univ. L 13), *Richars li biaus* was composed by an otherwise unknown "maistre Requis" in the second half of the 13th century in the extreme northern part of Picardy or in Walloonie. Realistic rather than courtly in tone, the romance combines in 5,454 octosyllabic rhyming couplets two important folklore motifs: "The Son Who Sets Out to Find His Parents" and "The Grateful Dead."

William W. Kibler

Holden, Anthony J., ed. *Richars li biaus, roman du XIIIe siècle.* Paris: Champion, 1983.

RICHEMONT, ARTHUR DE (1393–1458). Constable of France and duke of Brittany. The second son of Jean IV, duke of Brittany, Arthur inherited title to his father's English earldom of Richmond in 1399 and for most of his life was known by its French form, *comte de Richemont*, until he finally became duke of Brittany as Arthur III near the end of his life. A title derived from English lands was singularly ill suited for the man who would mold and command the Valois armies that reconquered France for Charles VII. Captured at Agincourt (1415), Richemont won freedom in 1420 by helping persuade his brother, Duke Jean V of Brittany, to support the Treaty of Troyes. The ambitious Richemont married a sister of Philip the Good but abandoned Burgundy to accept the office of constable of France when his brother reconciled Brittany to the Valois cause in 1425.

Despite his office, Richemont's importance was more administrative and diplomatic than military. He was as proud and fractious a counselor as might be expected from one of his lineage. He sought to dominate Charles's court and was involved in the assassination of counselors who opposed his interests. A bitter struggle for favor with Georges de La Trémoille led to his exile from court after 1428. Though he fought at Patay, he returned to court only in 1433 to work for a reconciliation with Burgundy, which, after the Treaty of Arras, made possible his entry into Paris at the head of Charles's army in 1436.

Richemont's greatest achievement was to draw on his familiarity with English military administration in directing the French military reforms of 1445. He dispersed many undisciplined companies and prepared the remainder for the final victories of 1449–53. During the Norman campaign, Richemont commanded the armies entering lower Normandy. His timely arrival at Formigny clinched the decisive victory of the campaign. After 1450, Richemont became regent of Brittany but continued to serve Charles as constable and military governor of lower Normandy. He unexpectedly became duke himself in 1457 but died a year later without legitimate heirs.

Paul D. Solon

[See also: BRITTANY; CHARLES VII; HUNDRED YEARS' WAR; RECONQUEST OF FRANCE; TRÉMOILLE, LA]

Gruel, Guillaume. *Chronique d'Arthur de Richemont*, ed. Achille Le Vavasseur. Paris: Renouard, 1890.
Beaucourt, Gaston du Fresne de. *Histoire de Charles VII.* 4 vols. Paris: Librairie de la Société Bibliographique, 1881–91.
Cosneau, Eugène. *Le connétable de Richemont.* Paris: Hachette, 1886.
Pocquet du Haut-Jussé, B.A. "Le connétable de Richemont, seigneur bourguignon." *Annales de Bretagne* 7 (1935): 309–36; 8 (1936): 7–30, 106–38.
Vale, Malcolm G.A. *Charles VII.* Berkeley: University of California Press, 1974.

RIGAUT DE BERBEZILH (fl. 1150s–1160s). Long misassigned to the late 12th century, the troubadour Rigaut de Berbezilh's extant work—consisting of nine *cansos*, including the famous *Atressi con l'orifanz*—stands out for its overt reference to Ovid, its allusion to Perceval and the Grail, and its striking animal imagery.

Elizabeth W. Poe

[See also: TROUBADOUR POETRY]

Rigaut de Berbezilh. *Liriche*, ed. Alberto Varvaro. Bari: Adriatica, 1960.

———. *Le canzoni, testo e commento*, ed. Mauro Braccini. Florence: Olschki, 1960.

RIGORD (ca. 1150–ca. 1209). Chronicler. Born in Languedoc, this monk of Argenteuil and then of Saint-Denis, who gave up practicing medicine in 1186, described himself as *Regis francorum chronographus*. Besides a brief chronicle of the kings of France from the earliest times, only fragments of which survive, he wrote the *Gesta Philippi Augusti*, covering the period 1179–1206, of which the later part flatters the king much less than the earlier part. Rigord inserted in his chronicle Philip's arrangements of June 1190 for the government by his mother and the archbishop of Reims during his absence on crusade, indicating that *baillis*, who were ordered to hold monthly assizes and to supervise the *prévôtés*, already administered the royal domain. Guillaume le Breton abridged and continued the *Gesta* to 1220.

Pedro J. Suarez

Delaborde, Henri-François, ed. *Œuvres de Rigord et de Guillaume le Breton, historiens de Philippe-Auguste*. 2 vols. Paris: Renouard, 1882–85.

RIOM. Founded in the 5th century by St. Amable, Riom (Puy-de-Dôme) was a sleepy town clustered around its church until Philip II Augustus made it his administrative capital for Auvergne in the early 13th century. In 1360, Riom passed with the rest of Auvergne to John, duke of Berry, who built a magnificent castle here that has since disappeared, but for its chapel. It was in this 14th-century Sainte-Chapelle, with its beautiful stained glass, that John married Jeanne de Boulogne in 1389 and, in 1410, the poet Charles d'Orléans wed Bonne d'Armagnac. The much-restored collegiate church of Saint-Amable (begun 1160) has preserved its Romanesque 12th-century nave and transept in Auvergnat style. The nave has a pointed barrel vault without cross-arches; its bay arches are likewise pointed. Above the groin-vaulted aisles are galleries that open onto the nave through twin arcades. The Gothic choir, of the early 13th century, shows Parisian influence. The church of Notre-Dame-du-Marthuret is notable for its Flamboyant Gothic façade as well as for a beautiful 15th-century sculpture, Our Lady with Child and Bird, within.

William W. Kibler/William W. Clark

Gauchery, Paul. "Riom." *Congrès archéologique (Moulins, Nevers)* 80 (1913): 144–73.

ROADS. *See* TRAVEL

ROBERT (COUNTS OF FLANDERS). Name of three counts of Flanders. Robert I the Frisian (r. 1071–93), the younger son of Count Baudouin V, usurped the countship from his nephew Arnulf III in 1071. Robert had married the widow of Count Florence I of Holland and Frisia, hence his nickname. Robert quickly repaired his diplomatic fences by marrying his stepdaughter, Bertha, to King Philip I of France, who had supported Arnulf III, and by supporting Philip against William of Normandy and England. Robert I and his son Robert II (r. 1093–1111) extended their influence in the bishopric and city of Cambrai, detaching the diocese of Arras from it in the interests of having a purely Flemish archbishopric outside the empire. The first significant evidence of the Flemish central administration comes from the period of Robert I, with the attachment of the chancery to the provostship of the church of Saint-Donatien of Bruges.

Robert II, known as Robert of Jerusalem for his participation in the First Crusade, became an active church reformer under the influence of his wife, Clementia, whose brother would become Pope Calixtus II. The Cluniac rule was introduced at Saint-Martin de Tournai, Saint-Bertin, and Bergues-Saint-Winoc. Robert proclaimed a peace in 1111, shortly before he died, forbidding the construction of fortifications without his authorization. He extended the local governmental organizations based on the castellanies introduced by Baudouin V.

Robert III de Béthune (r. 1305–22), the son of Gui de Dampierre, had to implement the Peace of Athis, which provided a huge indemnity to France in return for the restoration of the Dampierres to governance in Flanders. Realizing that the financial terms were impossible, Philip IV agreed to take the towns and castellanies of Lille, Douai, and Orchies from Flanders in exchange for part of the indemnity. This caused resentment, as did the demand that the Flemings indemnify Francophile patricians who had fled in 1302 and demolish their fortifications. The issue of further concessions to the French divided Robert's sons Louis I de Nevers and Robert de Cassel. To secure his position in Flanders, Robert III became more independent of the crown and was condemned by the court of peers in 1315. Rains that autumn prevented an invasion by the French and their Avesnes allies in Hainaut and Holland. Robert de Béthune was succeeded by his grandson Louis I (II de Nevers) in late 1322.

David M. Nicholas

[See also: DAMPIERRE; FLANDERS]

de Hemptinne, T. "Vlaanderen en Henegouwen onder de erfgenamen van de Boudewijns, 1070–1244," and Vandermaesen, M. "Vlaanderen en Henegouwen onder het Huis van Dampierre, 1244–1384." In *Algemene Geschiedenis der Nederlanden*. 2nd ed. Haarlem: Fibula-Van Dishoeck, 1982, Vol. 2, pp. 372–440.

Ganshof, François L. *La Flandre sous les premiers comtes*. Brussels: Renaissance du Livre, 1943.

Pirenne, Henri. *Histoire de Belgique*. Brussels: Lamertin, 1922–1929, Vols. 1–2.

Verlinden, Charles. *Robert Ier le Frison, comte de Flandre: étude d'histoire politique*. Antwerp: De Sikkel, 1935.

ROBERT (DUKES OF NORMANDY). The Viking war leader Rollo, founder of the Norman ducal dynasty, assumed the name Robert when he accepted baptism ca. 911. Although he was technically no more than the first Norman count of Rouen, later writers often referred to "Duke Rollo" or, occasionally, "Robert."

Rollo's great-great-grandson, Robert the Magnificent, was the father of William the Conqueror. He became duke in 1027, suspected of having poisoned his brother, Richard III, and in conflict with his powerful kinsmen Robert, archbishop of Rouen, and Hugh, bishop of Bayeux. William of Bellême soon threatened Robert's authority along the southern border, and later, in the 1030s, Alain of Brittany struck in the west. Robert the Magnificent met these challenges successfully and gained the southern part of the French Vexin from King Henry I in 1033. In his mid-twenties, Robert resolved to journey on a pilgrimage to Jerusalem. He died during his return in 1035, leaving the duchy in the unsteady hands of his seven-year-old illegitimate son, William, the future conqueror of England.

Robert Curthose, William the Conqueror's eldest son, was twice designated heir of all his father's dominions, but he destroyed that prospect through open rebellion. In exile when his father died in 1087, Robert nevertheless became duke of Normandy. A weak and prodigal ruler, he attempted unsuccessfully in 1088 to overthrow his brother William II Rufus, who had inherited the kingdom of England. In 1096, he joined the First Crusade, pledging the duchy to William Rufus for a loan of 10,000 marks of silver. When he returned in 1100, his youngest brother, Henry, had succeeded Rufus in England. Robert made another unsuccessful attempt to gain the English crown in 1101, then returned to Normandy, only to lose the duchy to Henry I in 1106 at the Battle of Tinchebrai. Imprisoned by his brother in Cardiff, Wales, Robert Curthose died in 1134.

Cassandra Potts

[See also: HENRY I; NORMANDY (genealogical table); WILLIAM I THE CONQUERER; WILLIAM II RUFUS]

Bates, David. *Normandy Before 1066*. London: Longman, 1982.

David, Charles W. *Robert Curthose, Duke of Normandy*. Cambridge: Harvard University Press, 1920.

Douglas, David C. "Rollo of Normandy." *English Historical Review* 57 (1942): 417–36.

———. *William the Conqueror: The Norman Impact upon England*. Berkeley: University of California Press, 1964.

Searle, Eleanor. *Predatory Kinship and the Creation of Norman Power, 840–1066*. Berkeley: University of California Press, 1988.

ROBERT II THE PIOUS (972–1031). King of France (r. 987–1031). The son of Hugh Capet, Robert II was the second king in the Capetian line. He was crowned at Orléans in December 987 and reigned jointly with his father until Hugh's death in 996. At that point, he left his first wife, Susanna of Denmark, and married his cousin Bertha, a recent widow of the count of Blois. This ill-advised move aroused the hostility of his father's allies, especially the count of Anjou, Foulques Nerra, and Pope Gregory V, who condemned the incestuous union and excommunicated the king. Robert resisted, apparently from passionate love for Bertha, until sometime between 999 and 1001, when she was repudiated. He subsequently married Constance of Arles ca. 1005, and the couple had three sons, Hugh (joint king 1017–25), Henry (his successor), and Robert (later duke of Burgundy).

Trends appearing under Hugh Capet became more pronounced in his son's long reign. Royal authority and prestige among the lay aristocracy continued to decline, and late in the reign one disgruntled bishop even spoke of the king's impotence (*imbecillitas*). On the other hand, by the mid-1010s Robert's reputation for piety had gained him such strong support among ecclesiastics that even places that had resisted his father's accession accepted his hereditary claim to the throne, acknowledging the failure of the Carolingian line. His renowned piety (he was the first Capétian reputed to have healing powers), as well as his policies of supporting Cluny, encouraging pilgrimage, sponsoring the Peace of God, and appointing learned nonaristocratic bishops, all earned him the enthusiastic support of the laity and the reforming church. In 1010, he had a Jew burned outside Orléans for allegedly plotting the destruction of the Holy Sepulcher; and in 1022, at the prompting of his ecclesiastical advisers, Robert had thirteen convicted heretics burned at Orléans, the first official execution of heretics in western Europe. His final years were complicated by the death of his chosen heir, Hugues (1026), and the battle for succession between his choice, Henry, and his wife's candidate, Robert.

Richard Landes

[See also: CAPETIAN DYNASTY; CONSTANCE OF ARLES; HENRY I; HUGH CAPET]

Helgaud de Fleury. *Vie de Robert le Pieux/Epitoma vitae regis Rotberti Pii,* ed. and trans. R.H. Bautier and Gillette Labory. Paris: CNRS, 1969.

Newman, William M. *Catalogue des actes de Robert II roi de France*. Paris: Sirey, 1937.

Pfister, Christian. *Études sur le règne de Robert le Pieux (996–1031)*. Paris: Vieweg, 1885.

ROBERT D'ARBRISSEL (ca. 1047–1117). Born in Brittany, the son of a priest, Robert became known as a preacher supporting Gregorian clerical reform in Rennes in 1089. Soon thereafter, he became a forest hermit, practicing extreme asceticism. He attracted many followers from all levels of society and formed them into a community, but he soon left this group to become a popular and powerful wandering preacher in France. He again attracted many followers, especially women, and in 1101 he decided to found a community for them. The site selected was at Fontevrault (Maine-et-Loire), near the Loire River in the diocese of Poitiers. The result was a "double monastery" of women and men, living in separate buildings but sharing a church. As finally organized, the community was ruled by an abbess, with the women following a modified Benedictine *Rule* and the men, who provided manual labor and sacramental services for the abbey, under the Augustinian *Rule*. Robert founded a number of priories dependent upon Fontevrault and was effective in attracting donations from the nobility in support of the resulting Order of Fontevrault. Robert was buried in the church at Fontevrault, which also was the burial site for Henry II Plantagenêt, Eleanor of Aquitaine, and Richard I the Lionhearted of England.

Grover A. Zinn

[See also: *AUGUSTINE, RULE OF ST.*; FONTEVRAULT; MONASTICISM]

Bienvenu, Jean-Marc. *L'étonnant fondateur de Fontevraud, Robert d'Arbrissel.* Paris: Nouvelles Éditions Latines, 1981.
Dalarun, Jacques. *L'impossible sainteté: la vie retrouvée de Robert d'Arbrissel (v. 1045–1116) fondateur de Fontevraud.* Paris: Cerf, 1985.
Picard, Louis Auguste. *Le fondateur de l'ordre de Fontevrault: Robert d'Arbrissel, un apôtre du XIe siècle, son temps, sa vie, ses disciples, son œuvre.* Saumur: Girouard et Richou, 1932.

ROBERT DE BLOIS (fl. mid-13th c.). The little we know about this author can be deduced from his works: he most likely lived during the second third of the 13th century and exercised his talents in several literary domains. The two most nearly complete manuscripts to have transmitted his works contain two Arthurian romances, *Floris et Lyriopé* and *Beaudous*, as well as poetry and moralistic and didactic works. The fullest manuscript, B.N. fr. 24301, presents the opening section of *Beaudous*, followed by the insertion, under the guise of advice given by Beaudous's mother, of Robert's complete works, after which the romance is taken up again—an apparent attempt to put all of one's works in one neat package. His lyrical pieces appear in various chansonniers. Robert's didactic works have been particularly appreciated in modern times, with the *Chastoiement des dames* and the *Enseignement des princes* finding their way into anthologies. In the *Chastoiement*, under the guise of moralistic instruction, Robert has written a work imbued with humor. And this ambiguity extends to other works, such as *Floris et Lyriopé*.

Robert's most extensive works are his two Arthurian romances. The more modest one, *Floris et Lyriopé* (1,758 lines), clearly shows what an educated writer of the period had learned: one portion of the tale is based on the Latin "comedy" *Alda*, the other on the Narcissus legend from Ovid's *Metamorphoses*. The two sections are united genealogically and through a common moralistic theme: the evil of pride. Though some feel the work is contrived and derivative, most agree that Robert shows skill in weaving strands of different tales into a neat whole. His longest poem, *Beaudous* (4,829 lines), is marked throughout by

the influence of other writers of romance, chiefly Chrétien de Troyes; indeed, some of the most important features of the romance are derived from Chrétien's works, especially the *Conte du Graal*. The hero leaves his mother to seek adventure at Arthur's court; his mother treats him to words of wisdom as he departs (Robert's complete works!); after many adventures and tourneys, he will be wed, to the delight of his mother, Amie, and his father, Gawain. Along the way, we encounter most of the principal knights of the Round Table. The very end of the romance, which probably consists of a few closing remarks, is missing.

Among Robert's other works are poems on the Creation, on confession, and on the joys of Paradise and pains of Hell.

Paul Barrette

[See also: CHRÉTIEN DE TROYES; COURTESY BOOKS; GAWAIN ROMANCES; MORAL TREATISES]

Robert de Blois. *Sämtliche Werke Robert von Blois*, ed. J. Ulrich. 3 vols. Berlin: Meyer und Müller, 1889–95.
——. *Robert de Blois, son œuvre didactique et narrative: Étude suivie d'une édition critique . . . de l'Enseignement des princes et du Chastoiement des dames*, ed. John Fox. Paris: Nizet, 1950.
——. *Floris et Lyriopé*, ed. Paul Barrette. Berkeley: University of California Press, 1968.
Shapiro, Norman. *The Comedy of Eros.* Urbana: University of Illinois Press, 1971. [Includes a translation of much of the *Chastoiement des dames*.]

ROBERT DE BORON (fl. 1180s–1190s). The few facts known about the most important early Grail poet after Chrétien de Troyes are inferred from the epilogue of Robert's *Joseph d'Arimathie*, also called the *Roman de l'estoire dou Graal*, where he names himself and the nobleman in whose company he was writing, Gautier de Montbéliard. Montbéliard is in northern Franche-Comté; Boron is a small village about 12 miles to the northeast. Robert's verse bears traces of his eastern dialect. Gautier left on crusade in 1201, to remain in Palestine until his death in 1212; Robert must have finished the *Joseph* at or before the turn of the century. Robert's incorporation of material from Chrétien's *Conte du Graal* indicates that he wrote after the early 1180s. Other evidence suggests that the *Joseph* might be dated after 1191: Joseph foretells that the Grail will be taken to the "vales of Avaron [Avalon]"— that is, Glastonbury in Somerset; association of the Grail and of Arthurian matter with the abbey was not widespread before 1190–91, when the discovery there of a grave marked as Arthur's was announced.

Joseph d'Arimathie is a verse romance (3,500 octosyllables) that recounts the history of the Grail from the Last Supper and the Descent from the Cross, when Joseph used it to collect Christ's blood, through the imprisonment of Joseph, whom Christ visits and comforts with the holy vessel, until the moment when Joseph's brother-in-law, Bron (or Hebron), the Rich Fisher, is poised to take the Grail from a place of exile outside Palestine to Great Britain. As the *Joseph* draws to a close, the narrator announces that he will relate stories of adventures that Joseph has foretold, including that of the Rich Fisher, if he has time and strength and if he can find them written down in Latin; meanwhile, he will continue with the matter he has at hand.

Robert thus seems to project a complex work consisting of the *Joseph/Estoire*, the narrative to which he will pass immediately, and the fulfillment of Joseph's prophecies. The only manuscript to transmit Robert's verse *Joseph* (B.N. fr. 20047) in fact continues with the fragment of a *Merlin* romance (504 octosyllables), apparently the beginning of the second part; no more of Robert's original work survives.

However, a prose adaptation of the *Joseph*, by an anonymous author referred to as the Pseudo-Robert de Boron, was executed within a few years, and this is linked to a *Merlin* in prose, conjoining the history of the Grail and the history of Britain, that is found complete in a large number of manuscripts (forty-six) and fragments. Two manuscripts also contain a third prose romance, which portrays the Rich Fisher: the Didot *Perceval* (so called because one of the manuscripts was in the Firmin Didot collection). Unlike the first two romances, the Didot *Perceval* is never ascribed to Robert de Boron, nor is there any proof that a verse original of this text existed, yet it is clear that the Didot *Perceval* logically concludes the trilogy. It resembles one of the works projected at the end of the *Joseph/Estoire* and recounts the fulfillment of God's prophecy in the *Joseph* that the Rich Fisher will not die until he is visited by his son's son; it is also closely linked to the prose *Merlin*: finally succeeding at the Grail castle with Merlin's help, Perceval replaces his uncle as Rich Fisher; the hero's triumph coincides with the downfall of the Arthurian kingdom, the founding of which the *Merlin* had recounted.

In the *Joseph/Estoire* and what must have been the original verse *Merlin*, Robert de Boron in effect rewrites the *Conte du Graal* of Chrétien de Troyes. He expands the religious content of the original to provide the Grail's "sacred history," identifying it for the first time with the cup of the Last Supper. In addition, he extends Chrétien's references to pre-Arthurian Britain, which echo Wace's *Brut*, to provide the Grail's "secular history."

Robert's most important contribution is the generative power that infuses his verse. Not only are the prose adaptations of the *Joseph/Estoire* and *Merlin* among the earliest examples of literary prose in French, they also stand at the head of a long tradition that promoted the "translation" of imaginative and historical works written in "unreliable" verse into the "more stable" and "more authoritative" medium of prose. The better-known, more highly respected, Pseudo-Robert de Boron who was thus created, the one to whose authorship the more widely transmitted prose works are attributed, became in the early 13th century an even stronger literary force. He inspired the "completion" of Chrétien de Troyes's unfinished *Conte du Graal* in the anonymous Didot *Perceval*, and he is ultimately responsible for the germination of the Vulgate Cycle.

Rupert T. Pickens

[**See also:** CHRÉTIEN DE TROYES; GRAIL AND GRAIL ROMANCES; *PERCEVAL CONTINUATIONS*; PROSE ROMANCE (ARTHURIAN); VULGATE CYCLE]

Robert de Boron. *Merlin, roman du XIIIe siècle*, ed. Alexandre Micha. Geneva: Droz, 1979.

———. *Le roman de l'estoire dou Graal*, ed. William A. Nitze. Paris: Champion, 1927.

———. *Le roman du Graal*, ed. Bernard Cerquiglini. Paris: Union Générale d'Éditions, 1981.

Roach, William, ed. *The Didot* Perceval *According to the Manuscripts of Paris and Modena*. Philadelphia: University of Pennsylvania Press, 1941.

Cerquiglini, Bernard. *La parole médiévale*. Paris: Minuit, 1981.

O'Gorman, Richard F. "The Prose Version of Robert de Boron's *Joseph d'Arimathie*." *Romance Philology* 23 (1969–70): 449–61.

———. "La tradition manuscrite du *Joseph d'Arimathie* en prose de Robert de Boron." *Revue d'histoire des textes* 1 (1971): 145–81.

Pickens, Rupert T. "Histoire et commentaire chez Chrétien de Troyes et Robert de Boron: Robert de Boron et le livre de Philippe de Flandre." In *The Legacy of Chrétien de Troyes*, ed. Norris J. Lacy, Douglas Kelly, and Keith Busby. 2 vols. Amsterdam: Rodopi, 1988, Vol. 2, pp. 17–39.

———. "'Mais de ço ne parole pas Crestiens de Troies . . .': A Reexamination of the Didot *Perceval*." *Romania* 105 (1984): 492–510.

ROBERT DE CLARI (fl. early 13th c.). Chronicler. The *Conquête de Constantinople* (ca. 1219) of Robert de Clari is a valuable source for the Fourth Crusade. Robert begins with Foulques de Neuilly's preaching of the crusade in 1198 and continues in detail to 1205; from 1205 to 1219, he summarizes the events. Robert was neither well educated nor privy to the councils of the mighty; we cannot understand the politics of the crusade from him. His strength is his rendering of ambient rumors and his brilliant descriptions of what ordinary knights experienced, such as the marvels of Constantinople. The single manuscript (Copenhagen, Bibl. roy. 487) was copied in the 13th century at Corbie, to which Robert gave relics he had stolen in Constantinople.

Leah Shopkow

[**See also:** CRUSADES; HISTORIOGRAPHY; VILLEHARDOUIN, GEOFFROI DE]

Robert de Clari. *La conquête de Constantinople*, ed. Philippe Lauer. Paris: Champion, 1924.

———. *The Conquest of Constantinople*, trans. Edgar Holmes McNeal. New York: Columbia University Press, 1936.

Dufournet, Jean. *Les écrivains de la IVe croisade: Villehardouin et Clari*. 2 vols. Paris: Société d'Édition d'Enseignement Supérieur, 1973.

ROBERT DE COURÇON (ca. 1160–1219). Robert, a sometimes brusque and unpopular Englishman, studied with Peter the Chanter toward the end of the 12th century at Paris. Within a few years of Peter's death (1197), Robert was teaching in Paris, where he composed a theological *Summa* and served on several missions as papal judge-delegate. On March 15, 1212, Pope Innocent III named him cardinal and the following year charged him with the task of making preparations in France for the Fourth Lateran Council, which was held in 1215. At the same time, Robert was to rally support for another Crusade to the Holy Land. During these years, Robert also accompanied the Albigensian Crusade, confirming in 1214 the conquests of Simon de Montfort.

In August 1215, in perhaps his most lasting contribution, Robert promulgated a papal charter for the University of Paris (a royal corporation since 1200) that set out the relationship between the schools and the cathedral chapter, regulated the number of chairs in theology, and stipulated the qualifications of masters in theology. Of special interest here is the prohibition of the arts faculty to teach the *Metaphysics* of Aristotle; the arts masters, especially in the medical faculty, were thought to have exceeded the limits of their expertise in dealing with this subject.

In the fall of the same year, at the beginning of the Lateran Council, Robert was recalled to Rome, where he remained until 1218, when he joined the Fifth Crusade. He died the following year at the siege of Damietta.

Mark Zier

[See also: ALBIGENSIAN CRUSADE; ARISTOTLE, INFLUENCE OF; INNOCENT III; UNIVERSITIES]

Robert de Courçon: The Paris statutes, in *Chartularium universitatis Parisiensis*, ed. Denifle and Chatelain, Vol. 1.20, pp. 78ff. (ET in Lynn Thorndike, *University Records and Life in the Middle Ages* (1944), pp. 27–30.)
———. *Le traité De usura de Robert de Courçon*, ed. G. Lefèvre. *Travaux de l'Institut Catholique de Lille* (1902).
Dickson, M. and C. "Le cardinal Robert de Courson: sa vie." *Archives d'histoire doctrinale et littéraire du moyen âge* 9 (1934): 53–142.
Kennedy, V.L. "Robert Courson on Penance." *Medieval Studies* 7 (1945): 291–336.
———. "The Contents of Courson's Summa." *Medieval Studies* 9 (1947): 81–107.

ROBERT DE GRETHAM (fl. first half of the 13th c.). An English cleric, Robert de Gretham wrote two didactic works. The *Corset* is a treatise of 2,400 octosyllabic lines on the sacraments of penance, marriage, holy orders, and extreme unction, presumably incomplete. The *Miroir*, or *Évangiles des domnées*, is a sermon cycle of some 19,000 lines, each sermon consisting of a translation of the day's gospel, a doctrinal explanation, and an exemplum.

Maureen B.M. Boulton

[See also: MORAL TREATISES; PRAYERS AND DEVOTIONAL MATERIALS; SERMONS IN VERSE]

Robert de Gretham. *Miroir ou Les évangiles des domnées*, ed. S. Panunzio. Bari: Adriatica, 1974.
Aitken, M.Y.H. *Étude sur Le miroir ou Les évangiles des domnées de Robert de Gretham*. Paris: Champion, 1922.

ROBERT DE LUZARCHES (fl. early 13th c.). The labyrinth set into the nave pavement of Amiens cathedral states that Robert de Luzarches was the first master mason, succeeded by Thomas de Cormont and his son Renaud. Robert began his work at Amiens ca. 1220. He was responsible for the plan and construction of the lower level of the nave and western bays of the chevet. Robert's origins and early work are obscure, but details at Amiens are close to such earlier Picard churches as Laon, Soissons, and Longpont. Although he probably died before the upper levels at Amiens were begun in the 1230s, his architectural design formed the basic characteristics of this great Gothic cathedral.

Karen Gould

[See also: AMIENS; CORMONT; LAON; LONGPONT; SOISSONS]

Murray, Stephen. "Looking for Robert de Luzarches: The Early Work at Amiens Cathedral." *Gesta* 29 (1990): 111–31.

ROBERT OF TORIGNY (d. 1186). Robert entered the Benedictine abbey of Bec in 1128. He became prior of Mont-Saint-Michel in 1149, and in 1154 he was elected abbot. Robert was both an able administrator and enthusiastic bibliophile. Among his collected works is a revision and continuation of the *Gesta Normannorum ducum* of Guillaume de Jumièges; Robert added material that pertained to the reigns of Henry I and Henry II. His principal work, however, is the continuation of the chronicle of Sigebert de Gembloux for the years 1100 to 1182. Contemporaries praised the work for its literary style, and despite its suspect chronology it remains an important source of Anglo-French history. Robert's narratives are replete with accounts of the marvelous, and he was careful to avoid incorporating into his histories any matter that would jeopardize the church, his monastery, or the reputations of kings Henry I and Henry II. He was responsible for the annals of Mont-Saint-Michel from 1135 to 1173, and he contributed significantly to the abbey's collection of cartulary documents.

E. Kay Harris

[See also: HISTORIOGRAPHY; MONT-SAINT-MICHEL; SIGEBERT DE GEMBLOUX]

Robert de Torigny. *Chronique et opuscules religieux*, ed. Léopold Delisle. 2 vols. Rouen: Société de l'Histoire de Normandie, 1872–73.
———. *Gesta Normannorum ducum*. In Guillaume de Jumièges, *Gesta Normannorum ducum*, ed. Jean Marx. Rouen: Lestringant, 1914, pp. 199–334.
Chibnall, Marjorie. "Orderic Vitalis and Robert of Torigni." In *Millénaire monastique du Mont-Saint-Michel*. 4 vols. Paris: Lethielleux, 1967, Vol. 2, pp. 133ff.

ROBERT LE DIABLE. Hagiographical legend. Identified in medieval French literature as the son of a Norman duke and duchess, Robert is Satan's liege from birth because his mother, long barren, had in desperation asked the Devil to give her a child. After a youth filled with violent crimes, Robert suddenly repents and spends the rest of his life expiating his sins. In the earliest French version, a hagiographical romance composed in the late 12th century (5,078 lines in octosyllabic couplets; two manuscripts), he dies a holy hermit. In the 14th-century *Dit de Robert le diable* (1,016 Alexandrines in 254 monorhymed quatrains; three manuscripts), Robert marries the daughter of a Roman emperor after completing his penance. From the *Dit* derive the later 14th-century *Miracle de Robert le diable* (2,279 verses, with speeches in octosyllabic couplets ending in a four-syllable cue-line) and a 15th-century French prose rendering extant in a dozen editions printed between 1496 and 1600, as well as adaptations in English, German, Dutch, and Spanish. Another version in French prose, composed probably in the late 13th century, supplies the opening chapters of the *Chroniques de Normandie*, found in numerous manuscripts and early printed editions. The legend also appears among the Latin exempla collected by the 13th-century Dominican, Étienne de Bourbon in his *Tractatus de diversis materiis predicabilibus*.

Mary B. Speer

[See also: MIRACLE PLAYS]

Breul, Karl, ed. "Le dit de Robert le diable." In *Abhandlungen Herrn Prof. Dr. Adolf Tobler . . . .* Halle: Niemeyer, 1895, pp. 464–509. [Based on MS *A* (B.N. fr. 24432).]
Löseth, Eilert, ed. *Robert le diable, roman d'aventures.* Paris: Didot, 1903. [Based on MS *A* (B.N. fr. 25516).]
Paris, Gaston, and Ulysse Robert, eds. *Miracle de Robert le dyable.* In *Les miracles de Nostre Dame par personnages.* 8 vols. Paris: Didot, 1876–93, Vol. 6, pp. 1–77. [Based on B.N. fr. 820, a collection of miracles written for the Paris guild of goldsmiths.]

ROBERT LE FORT (d. 866). Count of Anjou, Blois, Tours, Auxerre, and Nevers; the earliest known ancestor of the Capetians. First called "the Strong" (*vir strenuus*) by the chronicler Regino of Prüm, who wrote a generation later, Robert was a powerful count best known for leading the fight against the Vikings. He was one of the great lords whose power was nearly as well established as that of the Carolingians.

The sources are virtually silent on Robert's ancestry, but there have been many ingenious attempts to determine his origins. It seems most likely that he was from the Rhine region, but the family trees proposed for him by modern scholars have persuaded few but their creators. When he died fighting the Vikings, his sons, Eudes and Robert I, were still too young to succeed, although both later became kings of the Franks.

Constance B. Bouchard

Bouchard, Constance B. "The Origins of the French Nobility: A Reassessment." *American Historical Review* 86 (1981): 501–32.
Glöckner, K. "Lorsch und Lothringen, Robertiner und Capetinger." *Zeitschrift für die Geschichte des Oberrheins* 89 (1937): 301–54.
Levaillain, Léon. "Essai sur le comte Eudes, fils de Harduin et de Guérinbourg, 845–871." *Moyen âge* 47 (1937): 153–82, 233–71.
Werner, Karl Ferdinand. "Important Noble Families in the Kingdom of Charlemagne." In *The Medieval Nobility: Studies on the Ruling Classes of France and Germany from the Sixth to the Twelfth Century*, ed. and trans. Timothy Reuter. Amsterdam: North-Holland, 1978, pp. 137–202.

ROBERT OF FLAMBOROUGH (ca.1135/80–ca. 1219/33). Born probably in Flamborough, Yorkshire, Robert became a canon regular and later subprior at the Parisian abbey of Saint-Victor early in the 13th century. Contemporary documents refer to him as a canon penitentiary, and indeed his only known work is the *Liber poenitentialis*. Robert's penitential was the first such work to make available to ordinary priests the important 11th- and 12th-century developments in canon law on the matter of penance. The *Liber poenitentialis* was soon followed by similar handbooks for confessors. Completed between 1208 and 1213, Robert's penitential is in the form of a dialogue, a confession between a priest and a penitent. Although criticized by contemporaries for relying heavily and uncritically on outdated decretals, the penitential was nevertheless influential and survives in a number of manuscripts.

E. Kay Harris

Robert of Flamborough. *Liber poenitentialis: A Critical Edition*, ed. J.J. Francis Firth. Toronto: Pontifical Institute of Mediaeval Studies, 1971.
Kuttner, Stephen, and Eleanor Rathbone. "Anglo-Norman Canonists of the Twelfth Century: An Introductory Study." *Traditio* 7 (1949–51): 279–358.

ROBERT OF MELUN (d. 1167). Born in England, Robert studied in the schools of Paris. He succeeded Peter Abélard in the school at Mont-Sainte-Geneviève in Paris, where he taught John of Salisbury, who mentions him in the *Metalogicon*. Sometime ca. 1142, Robert moved to Melun, where he taught theology. He returned to England ca.1160 and was elected bishop of Hereford in 1163.

Robert's main theological writings were three: an unfinished *Sententiae, Quaestiones de divina pagina*, and *Quaestiones de epistolis Pauli*. In each of these works, Robert draws upon two of the great theologians of the immediate past, Abélard and Hugh of Saint-Victor, and in so doing represents the tendency of later 12th-century authors to draw together viewpoints that would have been more clearly opposed in the early to mid-12th century. One can see the influence of Hugh's thought in the structure of Robert's *Sententiae*. At the same time, Robert mounted a spirited defense, in opposition to Bernard of

Clairvaux, of Abélard's description of the Trinity in terms of predicating power of the Father, wisdom of the Son, and love of the Holy Spirit.

Grover A. Zinn

[See also: ABÉLARD, PETER; HUGH OF SAINT-VICTOR; SCHOLASTICISM; SCHOOLS, CATHEDRAL; SENTENCE COLLECTIONS]

Horst, Ulrich. *Die Trinitäts- und Gotteslehre des Robert von Melun.* Mainz: Matthias-Grünewald, 1964.

Luscombe, David. *The School of Peter Abelard: The Influence of Abelard's Thought in the Early Scholastic Period.* Cambridge: Cambridge University Press, 1970, pp. 281–98.

Martin, Raymond-Marie, and R.-M. Gallet, eds. *Œuvres de Robert de Melun.* 3 vols. in 4. Louvain: Spicilegium Sacrum Lovaniense, 1932–52.

ROBERT OF MOLESME (ca. 1027–1111). The founder of the monasteries of both Molesme and Cîteaux, Robert had spent much of his life trying to find or to establish a house where he thought the Benedictine *Rule* was being practiced with sufficient rigor. He spent time in the abbey of Moutier-la-Celle, in the diocese of Troyes; was briefly abbot of Saint-Michel of Langres, then prior of Saint-Ayoul of Provins; and for a period lived as a hermit. In 1075, deciding to try an entirely new Benedictine house, he and a small group of monks founded Molesme, of which he became first abbot (r. 1075–1111). In 1098, believing that even this house was not sufficiently rigorous, he left with a few brothers to found the New Monastery of Cîteaux. Although the monks at Molesme, feeling destitute, had the pope order Robert back to their house in the following year, Cîteaux flourished even without him and became in the 12th century the head of a large and influential order. Molesme, meanwhile, although overshadowed by Cîteaux, also acquired numerous gifts of property, including many priories and cells.

Constance B. Bouchard

[See also: BENEDICTINE ORDER; CISTERCIAN ORDER; CÎTEAUX]

Bouton, Jean de la Croix, and Jean Baptiste Van Damme, eds. *Les plus anciens textes de Cîteaux.* Achel: Commentarii Cistercienses, 1974.

Laurent, Jacques, ed. *Cartulaires de l'abbaye de Molesme.* 2 vols. Paris: Picard, 1907–11.

Lackner, Bede K. *The Eleventh-Century Background of Cîteaux.* Washington, D.C.: Cistercian, 1972.

Spahr, Kolumban. *Das Leben des hl. Robert von Molesme: Eine Quelle zur Vorgeschichte von Cîteaux.* Freiburg: Paulusdruckerei, 1944.

ROBERT PULLEN (ca. 1080–1146). A noted English theologian of the first half of the 12th century, Robert Pullen enjoys the distinction of being the first cardinal to have been born in the British Isles. He is known to have studied at Paris under the tutelage of William of Champeaux, sometime after 1103. In 1133, Robert moved from Exeter to Oxford, where he lectured on the Bible for five years. From 1134, he held the prebend of the archdeaconry of Rochester. Bernard of Clairvaux encouraged him to go to Paris to teach, which he did ca. 1142; but his travels soon took him to Rome as a cardinal, appointed by Pope Lucius II (r. 1144–45). Robert published several sermons and the *Sententiarum libri VIII* (composed at Oxford before 1142). This latter work seems to have had no apparent influence on Peter Lombard, the author of the most famous sentence collection of the day. Robert died at Viterbo in September of 1146.

Mark Zier

[See also: THEOLOGY]

Robert Pullen. *Opera.* PL 186.

Courtney, Francis. *Cardinal Robert Pullen: An English Theologian of the Twelfth Century.* Rome: Universitatis Gregorianae, 1954.

ROCAMADOUR. From the 12th century to the end of the 14th, the pilgrimage to Our Lady of Rocamadour (Lot) was one of the most famous in Christendom. The holy city is set in tiers up a rugged rock face rising 500 feet above the Alzou Canyon. The Great Stairway (216 steps) leads from the lower town to the sacred precinct, where a small parvis, formerly a cemetery, is enclosed by seven sanctuaries, the majority of which underwent extensive restoration and rebuilding in the 19th century. The heart of Rocamadour is the Miraculous Chapel of Our Lady, a small oratory (Gothic portal) that houses the famous "Black Virgin," an austere, 12th-century wooden reliquary statue, once covered with silver and decorated with gold. On the façade are painted fragments of the Three Living and Three Dead (15th c.). Two 12th-century sanctuaries virtually intact are St. Amadour's Crypt, below the basilica, and the funerary chapel of St. Michael, perched like a watchtower set into the cliff. In the apse are vestiges of a Majestas Domini (13th c.); on the exterior façade are frescoes of St. Christopher (14th c.) and a fine 12th-century Annunciation and Visitation (supposedly unrestored), akin to Limousin reliquaries. Above the sacred precinct, 14th-century ramparts enclose the 19th-century castle; below, the reconstruction of the bishops' palace is a Neo-Gothic fantasy.

Jean M. French

[See also: PILGRIMAGE]

Albe, Edmond. *Les miracles de Notre-Dame de Roc-Amadour au XIIe siècle: texte et traduction d'après les manuscrits de la Bibliothèque Nationale.* Paris: Champion, 1907.

Koster, Kurt. *Pilgerzeichen und Pilgermuscheln von mittelalterlichen Santiagostrassen: Saint-Léonard, Rocamadour, Saint-Gilles, Santiago de Compostela.* Neümunster: Wachholtz, 1983.

Rocacher, Jean. *Rocamadour et son pèlerinage: étude historique et archéologique.* 2 vols. Toulouse: Privat, 1979.

Rupin, Ernest. *Roc-Amadour: étude historique et archéologique.* Paris: Baranger, 1904.

RODEZ. Perched on a butte some 400 feet above the Aveyron, Rodez was once the capital of the Rouergue. Originally a Gallo-Roman center named Segodunum, it was overrun by the Romans and renamed Ruthena. It was made a bishopric in 401. Much of the medieval history of the town involves the struggle between the bishops, who controlled the *cité*, and the counts of Rouergue, who dominated the *bourg*. The enmity was so intense that it led to the creation of adjacent walled communities. The town fell briefly into English hands at the start of the Hundred Years' War (1360–68), and later its bishop was suspected of collaboration.

The red-sandstone cathedral of Notre-Dame dominates the old town. The earliest part is the eastern end, begun in 1277, with an ambulatory in Parisian style. The fortified western façade (15th c.), with its massive twin towers, has no porches or portals, since it projected beyond the city walls and served itself as part of the ramparts. The Flamboyant Gothic bell tower on the northeast corner rises nearly 290 feet. The interior, spare but impressive for its size and proportions (560 feet by 119 feet), is notable for its quatrefoil-shaped pillars with ring capitals. Within can be found two marble sarcophagi of early bishops (5th–6th c.) and a 10th-century altar table.

William W. Kibler/William W. Clark

Bousquet, Louis. "Rodez, cathédrale." *Congrès archéologique* (Figeac, Cahors et Rodez) 100 (1937): 360–86.
de Gauléjac, Bernard. "Rodez, monuments civils et militaires." *Congrès archéologique* (Figeac, Cahors et Rodez) 100 (1937): 387–93.

ROGATION DAYS. *See* LITURGICAL YEAR

ROHAN. The small Breton community of Rohan (Morbihan) gave its name to a noble family that has remained prominent in Brittany for nearly nine centuries. The family was founded by Alain I, younger son of a 12th-century count of Porhoet. Known as viscounts of Rohan, his descendants were prominent figures by 1300, with important rights over the religious houses of the region and an administrative center at Pontivy, where their 15th-century castle remains intact.

The wealth and influence of the Rohan family grew enormously in the late 14th and early 15th centuries as a result of favorable marriages. Viscount Jean I (r. 1352–95) married Jeanne, heiress to the important lordship of Léon in Brittany. Their son, Alain VIII (d. 1429), married Beatrix de Clisson, daughter and principal heiress of the fabulously wealthy Olivier de Clisson, constable of France, whose second wife was Jean I's sister. Jean I also was remarried, to a sister of Charles II of Navarre and aunt of the duchess of Brittany. In 1407, when they came into the Clisson inheritance, Alain VIII and Beatrix arranged for

their son, Alain IX (d. 1452), to marry a sister of Duke Jean V of Brittany. These brilliant marriages made the Rohan family the most powerful in central Brittany. Rohan became a duchy and peerage in 1603.

John Bell Henneman Jr.

[See also: BRITTANY; CLISSON]

Gicquel, Yvonig. *Alain I de Rohan (1382–1462): un grand seigneur de l'âge d'or de Bretagne.* Paris: Picollec, 1986.
Halgouet, Hervé du. *La vicomté de Rohan et ses seigneurs.* Paris: Champion, 1921.

ROI FAINÉANT. The last Merovingian kings, in the first half of the 8th century, are frequently referred to as *rois fainéants*, or "do-nothing" kings. This image owes a great deal to Einhard, contemporary biographer of Charlemagne, who stressed their weakness in order to help justify the Carolingians' assumption of the Frankish throne; Einhard even described the kings as going about, degraded, in ox carts rather than riding horses. Even aside from Einhard's picture, the last Merovingians did little that left any historical record. Childeric III, the final king of his line, was deposed, shaved of his symbolically uncut hair, and put in a monastery in 751 by Pepin the Short, who became the first Carolingian king. Childeric was the first king in the West to be deposed not for tyranny or for injustice but for incompetence.

Constance B. Bouchard

[See also: MEROVINGIAN DYNASTY]

Einhard. *The Life of Charlemagne*, trans. Samuel E. Turner. Ann Arbor: University of Michigan Press, 1960.
Geary, Patrick J. *Before France and Germany: The Creation and Transformation of the Merovingian World.* New York: Oxford University Press, 1988.
Wallace-Hadrill, J.M. *The Barbarian West: The Early Middle Ages,* A.D. *400–1000.* rev. ed. New York: Harper and Row, 1962.
———. *The Long-Haired Kings and Other Studies in Frankish History.* London: Methuen, 1962.

ROI FLORE ET LA BELLE JEANNE. A mid-13th-century anonymous prose romance found in a single manuscript (B.N. fr. 24430; dated 1290), *Roi Flore et la belle Jeanne* is really two distinct stories forcibly combined. Written in Picard-Wallon dialect, the tale relates the adventures of Jehane, first as third wife of Flore, then as cross-dressed squire to her husband, Robert.

Wendy E. Pfeffer

Moland, Louis, and Charles d'Héricault, eds. *Nouvelles françoises du XIIIe siècle.* Paris: Jannet, 1856, pp. 83–157.
Krueger, Roberta. "Double Jeopardy: The Appropriation of Women in Four Old French Romances of the 'Cycle de la Gageure.'" In *Seeking the Woman in Late Medieval and Renaissance Writings: Essays in Feminist Contextual Criti-*

cism, ed. Sheila Fisher and Janet E. Halley. Knoxville: University of Tennesse Press, 1989, pp. 21–50.

ROLAND, CHANSON DE. Bearing the marks of the enthusiasm engendered by the First Crusade, the *Chanson de Roland* is probably the earliest preserved chanson de geste, and the masterpiece of the genre. It seems to have been composed ca. 1100 by an anonymous poet (unless the mysterious Turoldus of the last line is considered to be the author—a controversial matter), who may well have been a Norman. Like other chansons de geste, it was certainly intended for singing, to a stringed instrument called a vielle, by a jongleur; whether this performer was also the composer is a debated question.

The earliest extant version, 4,002 decasyllabic lines grouped into some 290 assonanced laisses (stanzas of irregular length; the exact divisions are in some cases a matter of editorial controversy), is preserved in one Anglo-Norman manuscript of the second half of the 12th century, Oxford, Bodl., Digby 23 (*O*). Another manuscript, the Franco-Italian *V⁴*, preserves an assonanced text of the same type down to a line corresponding to line 3,683 of *O*, after which it joins the rhymed versions. Ms *O* came to the Bodleian in 1634, having belonged to Sir Kenelm Digby; it was rediscovered in the early 19th century by Francisque Michel, who published the *editio princeps* in 1837 and who gave the poem its modern title (it has none in the manuscript). This edition undoubtedly contributed to the resurgence of the study of medieval literature in the 19th century: the poem, with other chansons de geste, inspired Victor Hugo for parts of his *Légende des siècles*, and Gaston Paris chose to lecture on it at the Sorbonne in 1871 as a contribution to the restoration of French national feeling and morale after the Franco-Prussian war.

Although isolated, the Oxford *Roland* was a poem of great influence. It is imitated stylistically by many other chansons de geste, and its main personages play important roles elsewhere. Thus, *Girart de Vienne*, by Bertrand de Bar-sur-Aube, sets out, some eighty years later, to explain how the hero came to be the sworn comrade of Oliver and the betrothed of the latter's sister Aude, as he is in the *Chanson de Roland*. Roland, Charlemagne, Oliver, and even Ganelon are important figures in *Fierabras*, the *Voyage de Charlemagne*, the *Chanson d'Aspremont*, and other poems that make up the King Cycle (the cycle of epics devoted to Charlemagne and his exploits), but also in epics of the Rebellious Vassal Cycle, such as the *Quatre fils Aymon* and *Girart de Vienne*, in which Charlemagne ceases to be idealized as he is in the *Chanson de Roland*.

Toward the end of the 12th century, there was an important rhymed *remaniement* (twice as long as *O*), based on the assonanced version and preserved in five major manuscripts, the end of *V⁴*, and some fragments. This version, which seems to have largely replaced the assonanced version (summarized below), has lengthy extra episodes recounting an escape by Ganelon on the return journey to France and the death of Aude, the latter being much expanded with exploitation of the link with *Girart de Vienne*, a premonitory dream, and a death preceded by a conver-

sation with her brother, whose corpse speaks and invites her to join him and Roland in Heaven. Later, the material goes into prose versions, such as that compiled or written by David Aubert in 1458 (*Croniques et conquestes de Charlemaine*). It is no doubt a sign of the popularity of the subject that from the early 13th century there was a college of the twelve peers of France, magnates (six ecclesiastical, six lay) who took part in the *lits de justice* of the Parlement.

The poem's influence is also to be seen in non-French versions of the subject. It was adapted into Middle High German (the *Ruolandes liet* by the Pfaffe Konrad, whose version was used by Der Stricker for his *Karl der Grosse* and by an anonymous author for *Karl Meinet*), Old Norse (the *Karlamagnús saga*), Middle English (*Song of Roland* fragment), medieval Welsh (*Cân Rolant*), and Dutch (fragments only); there are related Latin texts in verse (*Carmen de prodicione Guenonis*) and prose (the Pseudo-Turpin chronicle); others in Occitan (*Ronsasvals*) and Spanish; later, via the Franco-Italian tradition, the subject reaches Pulci, Boiardo, and Ariosto, not to mention the Italian puppet theater, which survives to this day. Three of these texts were most likely composed in France. The Latin *Carmen de prodicione Guenonis* (482 lines) has been the subject of controversies over both dating and localization but was certainly composed after the Oxford text and probably in France. Preserved in a single manuscript, it is a school exercise in rhetoric that focuses on Ganelon's treason and the battle proper. The anonymous Occitan *Ronsasvals* (1,802 lines; one 14th-c. manuscript, in Apt) likewise centers the action on the battle itself. Although it alters characterizations and introduces Oliver's son Galien into the battle, it is a well-constructed and emotionally elevated work. In the same manuscript with *Ronsasvals* is the heroic-comic *Rollan a Saragossa*, which recounts in 1,410 lines Roland's amorous encounter with Bramimonde in Saragossa and his ensuing rift and conciliation with Oliver.

The poem is based ultimately on the historical ambush by Christian Basques or Gascons that destroyed Charlemagne's baggage train on August 15, 778, during his return from an unsuccessful campaign in Spain. It recounts the heroic death of the emperor's nephew Roland in an unequal fight with an enormous host of Spanish Saracens and Charlemagne's vengeance and imposition of Christianity on the vanquished. Faced with inevitable defeat in the last Saracen stronghold left after a campaign of seven years by Charlemagne, King Marsile of Saragossa sues for peace, giving false guarantees. In anger at being nominated by his hated stepson Roland for the dangerous peace negotiations, Count Ganelon persuades the Saracens to commit their 400,000 men to overwhelm the French rearguard of 20,000, to be led by Roland, whom he describes as the Frankish "hawk." In spite of Charlemagne's fears, provoked by prophetic dreams, the French host sets off, leaving the rearguard behind. When Roland's comrade Oliver hears the Saracen army's approach, Roland emphatically rejects his friend's advice to sound his elephant-tusk horn (the *olifant*) to recall the main army; he fears personal and family dishonor, a point of view that Oliver does not accept. After great deeds and initial successes by the French, led by Roland, Oliver, and the battling archbishop Turpin, the weight of numbers reduces the Christians to sixty survivors; Roland now at last decides to sound the horn, but Oliver angrily says that this would indeed be dishonorable now that the battle is on, and he accuses Roland of a monumental error of judgment, motivated by recklessness. Turpin points out that it can no longer be a matter of help, only of vengeance and Christian burial for the dead, so that no dishonor is involved. Roland's sounding of the *olifant* brings the army back but fatally injures the arteries of his temple. After witnessing the deaths of Oliver, with whom he is reconciled at the last, and Turpin, Roland himself dies as a conqueror, the Saracens having fled on hearing the trumpets of the returning army. Angels bear his soul to Heaven. Charles returns and, with the aid of a divine miracle that prolongs the daylight, catches up with the Saracens and kills all of Marsile's surviving men.

As the emperor prepares next day to leave for *dulce France* with the bodies of Roland, Oliver, and Turpin, we suddenly learn that Marsile's overlord, the emir Baligant, summoned seven years earlier, when Charles had first invaded, has arrived. (This development has not been prepared in any way, and the status of this long episode is a subject for controversy.) Charles fights a second great battle, in which he finally kills Baligant. Saragossa is taken, and the remaining Saracens are converted or killed. Charles returns to Aix-la-Chapelle, where Oliver's sister Aude, whom Roland was to have married, dies at the news of his death. Ganelon, accused by Charlemagne of treason, is protected by his powerful kinsman Pinabel, who nearly secures his acquittal by his threatening influence; but Tierri d'Anjou proves by judicial combat against Pinabel that Ganelon has committed treason, against the emperor as much as against Roland, and Ganelon is quartered by horses. As he sits alone at night, discouraged and desolate, Charles is summoned by the Archangel Gabriel, who is throughout the poem God's messenger to the patriarchal figure of the emperor, to further efforts against the Muslims far away. Charles is deeply unwilling to go, but we know that he will not fail.

However he himself composed, the poet of the *Chanson de Roland* drew on what were surely well-worn formulaic expressions and metric techniques belonging to a tradition of sung epic. How he uses these expressions and techniques is what sets him apart. His exploitation of the laisse is particularly striking: in the *Roland*, the laisses remain relatively short, fewer than fourteen lines on average, so that most have a unity that is often absent in later poems. Each is like a good paragraph, dealing comprehensively with one motif or unit of narration; the first and last lines often link thematically across the boundaries of the laisses and are frequently lapidary and memorable. Although epic is primarily a narrative genre, the laisses are sometimes grouped in twos or threes (*laisses similaires* and *laisses parallèles*), where a single event or conversation is repeated on different assonances to produce an emphasis on important elements of story or motivation, as well as to provide a lyrical pause. Other poems have such

devices, but the *Roland*-poet is a particularly skillful exponent of the technique: see, for example, the first horn scene, which is formally perfect in a static mode, or the three laisses leading up to the death of Roland, where the technique is used in a more dynamic way. The poet is a master of concise, evocative use of words, within the limitations imposed by the formulaic epic tradition; he rarely uses formulae in a mechanical way, and his use of repetition links laisses and episodes with recall and echo. Flashback techniques are sometimes reminiscent of the cinema, as when Roland sounds his horn and we see the effect alternately on the main army and on him. The poet revels in colors, bright light reflecting from armor and weapons, the sound of trumpets and horns. His sober, economical, yet vivid descriptions give an immediacy to his scenes; hearers or readers feel that they are spectators of events. This remains true in spite of the omnipresent epic idealization—exaggeration of numbers of combatants and the power of blows, the emphasis on single combats and battle scenes.

Executed with precision, variety, and evocative language, this poem, like other chansons de geste, nevertheless exploits to a considerable extent essentially dramatic techniques. Some 40 percent of the text consists of direct speech; we learn about the characters by what they say and do rather than by the poet's analysis. Although we do not usually expect to find detailed psychological analysis in epic poetry, the characters of the *Chanson de Roland* ring remarkably true, at least over the range of emotions and beliefs the poet needs to show. They express themselves in dialogue that is concise, telling, and suitable. The traditional formulaic style does not prevent the individualization of the characters; compare, for example, the first words of Roland with those of Ganelon. This characterization remains subordinate to the development of the action, but it is done with precision.

The importance of the issues that the poem addresses, and the passion with which they are debated; the precision and affectivity of the language; the dignity, order, and sober understatement of the most moving moments; the dramatic technique that involves the hearer—all this makes the *Chanson de Roland* one of the great epics of the world and a brilliant opening to the rich 12th century.

In spite of its clarity, the *Roland* provokes debate. One of its liveliest controversies is over the interpretation of the moral conception of the subject. Traditional exegesis held that Roland's decision not to recall his uncle is caused by pride, by *desmesure*, the epic fault of failing to keep a proper sense of proportion, which leads to fatal consequences; when he sees the slaughter caused by his decision, he repents or at least changes course to remedy his mistake as far as possible by recalling Charlemagne, and his self-inflicted death leads to his apotheosis and to the Christian revenge. More recently, scholars have questioned this view, seeing Roland as being right in his decision; on this hypothesis, he deliberately sacrifices his men and himself in order to ensure that Charles, who is seen as being ready to abandon the war prematurely because weary of it, achieves the final victory. Roland is seen either as a fervent Christian saint and martyr, an imitator of Christ, or, on the contrary, as exhibiting the pagan virtues of a Germanic tradition of heroism, with a thin veneer of Christianity.

The Baligant episode has also caused controversy. It is not prepared for earlier in the poem, and many scholars believe it to have been added by the *remanieur* to whom we owe the Oxford version, while others argue for its authenticity as part of the conception of the subject at an earlier stage of development; some find it stylistically different from the rest of the epic, while others see homogeneity. What can be said is that the episode adds to the Christian dimension of the poem, reflecting the structure of some saints' lives, in which the death of the saint is put in the context of the struggle of the Church Militant. This does not mean, however, that the view of the hero as profoundly religious in his actions is necessarily the right one: it is a matter of deciding whether Roland attains his apotheosis by his original merits or by repentance.

A final controversy over the *Chanson de Roland*, and the other chansons de geste, concerns origin and method of composition. The old question as to how the kernel of historical truth underlying the poem could have reached the author, and in so distorted a form, has in the last thirty years been associated with the problem of oral as against written composition. This controversy, between "Traditionalists" and "Individualists," is discussed in the article on CHANSON DE GESTE.

Wolfgang G. van Emden

[See also: *ASPREMONT*; AUBERT, DAVID; CHANSON DE GESTE; *FIERABRAS*; JONGLEUR; KING CYCLE; PSEUDO-TURPIN; *QUATRE FILS AYMON;VOYAGE DE CHARLEMAGNE À JERUSALEM ET À CONSTANTINOPLE*]

Brault, Gerard J., ed. and trans. *The Song of Roland: An Analytical Edition*. 2 vols. University Park: Pennsylvania State University Press, 1978. [Conservative edition, with controversial detailed commentary and annotation.]

Segre, Cesare, ed. *La chanson de Roland*. Milan: Ricciardi, 1971; rev. trans. (into French) by Madeleine Tyssens. Geneva: Droz, 1989. [Most scholarly and detailed modern edition, with many references to other versions.]

Burgess, Glyn, trans. *The Song of Roland*. Harmondsworth: Penguin, 1990.

Burger, André. *Turold, poète de la fidélité: essai d'explication de La chanson de Roland*. Geneva: Droz, 1977. ["Individualist" approach.]

Cook, Robert Francis. *The Sense of the Song of Roland*. Ithaca: Cornell University Press, 1987.

Crist, Larry S. "À propos de la desmesure dans la *Chanson de Roland*: quelques propos (démesurés?)." *Olifant* (1974): 10–20.

Duggan, Joseph J. *A Guide to Studies on the Chanson de Roland*. London: Grant and Cutler, 1976.

Faral, Edmond. *La chanson de Roland: étude et analyse*. Paris: Mellottée, 1934.

Le Gentil, Pierre. *La chanson de Roland*, trans. Frances F. Beer. Cambridge: Harvard University Press, 1969.

Menéndez Pidal, Ramón. *La chanson de Roland et la tradition épique des Francs*, trans. (from Spanish) by the author and I.-M. Cluzel. 2nd ed. Paris: Picard, 1960. ["Traditionalist" approach.]

Owen, Douglas David Roy. "The Secular Inspiration of the *Chanson de Roland*." *Speculum* 37 (1962): 390–400.

Vance, Eugene. *Reading the Song of Roland*. Englewood Cliffs: Prentice-Hall, 1970.

van Emden, Wolfgang G. "'E cil de France le cleiment a guarant': Roland, Vivien et le thème du *guarant*." *Olifant* 1 (1974): 21–47.

ROMANCE. In Old French, the term *roman*, used as early as 1150 in the Romances of Antiquity, originally designated a work in French as opposed to Latin. Even when Chrétien de Troyes employs an expression like *entreprendre/faire un roman* ("to embark on/to make a *roman*"), a usage that emphasizes the writer's creative activity, *roman* still maintains its primary meaning of a "story composed in French," intended for a lay courtly public that did not know Latin. Only later did the term take on the generic meaning of "romance" (and, even later, "novel") associated with it today.

With the important exception of the *Roman d'Alexandre*, written in epic laisses, romances of the 12th century were composed in octosyllabic rhyming couplets, a form used also in didactic and scientific literature of the period, as well as in historical chronicles in French. In the 13th century, with the appearance of literary prose, romances in verse and prose existed side by side. Only in the course of the 14th century did prose become the preferred medium of romance.

Unlike chansons de geste and lyric poetry, which were sung, romances were intended to be read, aloud and before a select company, from manuscript books. Their prologues often insist upon the talent of the writer and generally give the author's name and the title of the work. Romances assert their status as a written product.

The first text considered a "romance" is the Alexander fragment by Albéric de Pisançon (first third of the 12th c.). In the decade after 1150, the Romances of Antiquity and vernacular chronicles, which evoked Britain's past, appeared simultaneously (Geffrei Gaimar's *Estoire des Engleis*, Wace's *Brut* and *Rou*, Benoît de Sainte-Maure's *Chronique des ducs de Normandie*). Both romances and chronicles sought to celebrate the past for the benefit of the men and women of their day. The act of writing, above all an act of remembering, also represents the diffusion of knowledge and wisdom. Several romances open with references to classical, pagan, or biblical wisdom and repeatedly invoke the writers' obligation to exploit their God-given talent. Blessed by their historical situation, writers of romance could build upon the inherited Latin sources and interpret them in a definitive manner, giving them, in Marie de France's words, a *surplus de sens* ("an abundance of meaning"). Writers of romance thus saw themselves as the privileged heirs of a secular *translatio* of learning and chivalry, from Greece through Rome to France and Norman England, whose destiny and deeds they were to celebrate.

Jehan Bodel's famous distinction among the Matter of France (chansons de geste), the Matter of Rome (Romances of Antiquity), and the Matter of Britain:

N'en sont que trois materes a nul home vivant:
De France et de Bretaigne et de Ronme la grant;
Ne de ces trois materes n'i a nule samblant.
Li conte de Bretaigne si sont vain et plaisant,
E cil de Ronme sage et de sens aprendant,
Cil de France sont voir chascun jour aparant. (*Saisnes*,
ed. A. Brasseur, ll. 6–11)

masks a continuity that the romances themselves exploit between the Matter of Rome and that of Britain: Brutus and the British nation are, in the fiction of the chronicles, both the descendants of Aeneas and his Trojans and also the ancestors of King Arthur. This distinction nonetheless takes into account the two principal sources of romance inspiration in the 12th century and the differences in their expression.

Composed in the continental domains of Eleanor of Aquitaine after 1150, the Romances of Antiquity (*Thèbes*, *Énéas*, *Troie*, *Alexandre*, and the Ovidian tales) are on one level a vulgarization of myths, legends, and historical figures of classical antiquity. Their didactic intent is evident in the role accorded to descriptions, which offer scientific knowledge (as in Alexandre de Paris's third branch of the *Roman d'Alexandre*) as well as idealized models of the beautiful (portraits, descriptions of towns, art objects). It is also seen in extensive discourses on politics and on love, notably in the *Roman de Troie*.

The Matter of Britain is represented in the 12th century principally by the Arthurian romances of Chrétien de Troyes and by the verse romances about Tristan and Iseut. The anonymous Breton *lais* and those by Marie de France exploit a wide variety of motifs and legends, in which the Fairy Mistress and the rivalry between the otherworld and this world play an essential role. Originally transmitted orally, the Matter of Britain was first written down in French in Wace's *Brut*. The account he gave of Arthur's reign and deeds provided the setting and time frame for key characters and motifs—Arthur and Guenevere, Merlin, Gawain, Kay, the Round Table—exploited by Chrétien and his immediate followers and, in the 13th century, by the Vulgate and Post-Vulgate cycles. Better than the Matter of Rome, which was seen as more or less historical, the Matter of Britain was the ideal locus, with its blend of the real and the fantastic, in which to explore other modes of structuring romance materials (focused on the knight-errant and the quest for adventure) and to test a complex meditation upon the nature of love and its relation to bravery. Exemplified in the "Breton romance," this meditation reached its highest expression in the Grail.

Introduced by Chrétien de Troyes in the *Conte du Graal*, where it was attached to the person of Perceval, the motif of the Grail offered an alternative to the quest for earthly love. But it quickly became, with the story of Grail origins launched by Robert de Boron in the verse *Roman de l'estoire dou Graal*, a myth of origins relating simultaneously to the central figure of Joseph of Arimathea, the holy vessel, and chivalry itself. The interrelated stories of the Grail and Arthur's kingdom became, in the first third of the 13th century, the subject of immense cyclical prose romances: the trilogy of the Pseudo–Robert de Boron (*Joseph*, *Merlin*, the Didot *Perceval*), the *Perlesvaus*, and above all the Vulgate Cycle, or *Lancelot-Grail*. Organized around the motif of the Grail quest, these works function as a *summa* of the Matter of Britain and as a rewriting of the Arthurian "pre-text." They also offer a reflection on "courtly" chivalry and on its relation to royal authority and its ability to penetrate the sphere of the sacred (*Perlesvaus*, the *Queste del saint Graal*). The choice of prose is explained by the belief in its greater veracity and by the very form of these stories, which were written to resemble historical chronicles. Above all, prose was the medium most suitable to a form of writing that sought to saturate narrative time and space and capture its fictional universe in its fullness and complexity.

Similarly attached to a Celtic framework, but with less emphasis on the fantastic (the love potion is but another name for carnal lust) and with a biographical structure, the 12th-century Tristan romances by Béroul and Thomas d'Angleterre present a more realistic but also darker view of the passion of love, which cuts off the individual from society and admits of no outcome other than death.

The Britain of King Arthur remained the favorite setting for romance throughout the Middle Ages (*Perceforest*, *Ysaie le Triste*, Froissart's *Méliador*). But after 1150, a number of works were set in an equally imaginary Near East. Prime among these are the idyllic romance of *Floire et Blancheflor*, Chrétien's "Byzantine" romance *Cligés*, and, at the end of the 12th century, poems like *Florimont*, *Ipomedon*, and *Partonopeu de Blois*. These substitute for the wonders of the fairy otherworld the more concrete marvels of Byzantium, a city that becomes, in Gautier d'Arras's *Eracle*, a story that hovers between hagiography and romance, the site of an exemplary and creative past.

Gautier's other romance, *Ille et Galeron*, which though based on Marie de France's *lai* of *Eliduc* locates the adventures of its heroes in a "real" world, is one of the first examples, in the late 12th century, of a new form of romance writing, sometimes termed "realistic." The most representative writer of realistic romances is Jean Renart (*Guillaume de Dole*, *Escoufle*, *Lai de l'ombre*). Also of this type are texts that, like *Galeran de Bretagne*, the *Roman de la Violette*, *Joufroi de Poitiers*, the *Roman du castelain de Coucy et de la dame de Fayel* by Jakemés, the Occitan romance *Flamenca*, and others, strive for the illusion of reality. But the narrative cohesiveness of these works comes primarily from preexisting literary traditions, such as popular stories and courtly lyrics.

The interpenetration of the lyric and the romance occurs first in the form of lyric inserts in *Guillaume de Dole*, then in the *Violette*, the *Castelain de Coucy*, and other works. But it is the very source of the *Roman de la Rose* of Guillaume de Lorris, a poem that works the motifs of the courtly lyric into a narrative while using the methods of allegorical writing to create an exemplary erotic quest that is also an art of love. It is this latter dimension that Jean de Meun prefers to exploit, turning the second *Roman de la Rose* into a "Mirror for Lovers," a didactic locus of philosophical reflections with encyclopedic pretentions, on the relation of humankind to love and nature.

Also significant among 13th-century romances are tales of extraordinary adventures, such as Adenet le Roi's *Cleomadés* and Girart d'Amiens's *Meliacin*, or of edifying adventures (Philippe de Beaumanoir's *La Manekine* or *Belle Helaine de Constantinople*), or tales, like *Amadas et Ydoine* and *Jehan et Blonde*, that develop the theme of social climbing by a hero, either a bastard or of lower rank, who triumphs over all obstacles and wins the hand of his lady.

From its appearance in the 12th century, medieval romance gives an impression of astonishing diversity, with stories that examine both mythical and historical regions and time. One theme that stands out, however, is that of the bride quest, which is a vehicle for exploring the relationship of love with independence and power, love being the means by which the hero achieves that ideal model of civilization that the 12th century called courtliness. The romance transforms the warrior hero of the chanson de geste into a bold but courtly knight, worthy of inspiring love and ensuring his power over his own world.

Emmanuèle Baumgartner

[See also: ADENET LE ROI; ALEXANDER ROMANCES; ANGLO-NORMAN LITERATURE; ANTIQUITY, ROMANCES OF; ARTHURIAN VERSE ROMANCE; BEAUMANOIR, PHILIPPE DE REMI, SIRE DE; CHRÉTIEN DE TROYES; GAUTIER D'ARRAS; GAWAIN ROMANCES; GRAIL AND GRAIL ROMANCES; IDYLLIC ROMANCE; MARIE DE FRANCE; OVIDIAN TALES; *PERCEVAL CONTINUATIONS*; PROSE ROMANCE (ARTHURIAN); REALISTIC ROMANCES; ROBERT DE BORON; TOURNAMENT ROMANCES; TRISTAN ROMANCES; VOW CYCLE; VULGATE CYCLE; WACE]

Bruckner, Matilda Tomaryn. *Shaping Romance: Interpretation, Truth, and Closure in Twelfth-Century French Fictions.* Philadelphia: University of Pennsylvania Press, 1993.

Chênerie, Marie-Luce. *Le chevalier errant dans les romans arthuriens en vers des XIIe et XIIIe siècles.* Geneva: Droz, 1986.

Fourrier, Anthime. *Le courant réaliste dans le roman courtois en France au moyen âge.* Paris: Nizet, 1960.

Frappier, Jean, and R. Grimm, eds. *Le roman jusqu'à la fin du XIIIe siècle.* Part IV of *Grundriss der romanischen Literaturen des Mittelalters.* 2 vols. Heidelberg: Winter, 1978, 1984.

Köhler, Erich. *L'aventure chevaleresque: idéal et réalité dans le roman courtois.* Paris: Gallimard, 1974.

Lacy, Norris J., Douglas Kelly, and Keith Busby, eds. *The Legacy of Chrétien de Troyes.* 2 vols. Amsterdam: Rodopi, 1987–88.

Ménard, Philippe. *Le rire et le sourire dans le roman courtois en France au moyen âge.* Geneva: Droz, 1969.

Payen, Jean-Charles. *Le motif du repentir dans la littérature française médiévale, des origines à 1230.* Geneva: Droz, 1967.

———, and F.N.M. Diekstra, eds. *Le roman.* Typologie des sources 12. Turnhout: Brepols, 1975.

Petit, Aimé. *Naissances du roman: les techniques littéraires dans les romans antiques du XIIe siècle.* Paris: Champion, 1985.

Zink, Michel. *La subjectivité littéraire: autour du siècle de saint Louis.* Paris: Presses Universitaires de France, 1985.

ROMANESQUE ARCHITECTURE. Romanesque architecture of the 11th and 12th centuries represents a fusion of two architectural traditions from late antiquity—that of the massively vaulted structure, such as the basilica of Constantine in Rome, and that of the huge wooden-roofed building, characterized by vast interior spaces, such as Old St. Peter's in Rome, now destroyed, and St. John Lateran. Both traditions survived from late antiquity to the pre-Romanesque period. Basilical structures in the larger towns and wealthier abbeys generally followed the Old St. Peter's model, although the old Roman tradition of brick-faced concrete was abandoned. These monuments, found mostly in the river valleys of France, were of impressive size and constructed of large, carefully dressed stones. The style they reflect at the beginning of the 11th century has come to be known as the Early Romanesque of the North, the *zone septentrionale* as defined by the French scholar Henri Focillon, who contrasted this northern Early Romanesque to that of the southern, mountainous regions of France and Europe. Northern Early Romanesque monuments of major significance and interest, military architecture excepted, are almost exclusively churches.

Monuments found in the poorer, mountainous areas of the south were usually of the vaulted type, without transept, compact, smaller in scale, and constructed of small, semidressed stones. External walls were invariably decorated with shallow, irregular arcades framed by flat pilasters engaged onto roughly coursed walls and towers. This style, European in scope, was labeled *le premier art roman*

Anzy-le-Duc (Saône-et-Loire), Romanesque vaulting. *Photograph courtesy of Whitney S. Stoddard.*

by the Catalan scholar J. Puig i Cadafalch, who gave it its art-historical identity. Such churches have survived in relatively large numbers. Their counterparts in the wealthier cities and abbeys of France, however, were almost always remodeled or replaced in later times, but their characteristics can often be determined from excavations, from archaeological traces surviving in the remodeled structure, or from old drawings and photographs.

Early Romanesque in the south flourished in the Alps, in the Pyrénées, in the Languedoc, and in other mountainous regions of southern France. Fine examples can be seen at Saint-Michel-de-Cuxa and Saint-Martin-du-Canigou in the Pyrénées, or at Saint-Guilhem-le-Désert in the Languedoc. Important churches in this style can also be found in the plains and river valleys, or in small villages, such as Chapaize in Burgundy. Perhaps even more surprising, because of its northern location, is Saint-Vorles at Châtillon-sur-Seine, between Dijon and Troyes. The decorative vocabulary of southern Early Romanesque was so pervasive that scholars often overlook its vital contribution to the fully developed Romanesque structure, in particular, the vaulting of major spaces.

North of the Alps, in addition to the early Christian tradition of the unvaulted structure, as at Old St. Peter's or St. John Lateran, there is the indigenous tradition of timber architecture. Although none of these great structures survive, they are described in such sources as *Beowulf* and the writings of Fortunatus, bishop of Poitiers. This tradition of the great public building in wood facilitated the acceptance of the early Christian wood-roofed basilica during the early-medieval, Carolingian, and Ottonian periods. The great unvaulted basilicas of the Loire Valley from the end of the 10th century and beginning of the 11th were in harmony with this tradition.

Two major innovations distinguish the emerging Romanesque basilica in the north: the twin-towered façade, which replaced the Carolingian westwork, and the choir with ambulatory and radiating chapels, which reflected new liturgical practices. These stylistic characteristics are found only in the major cathedral and abbey churches of the first half of the 11th century: Orléans cathedral, Saint-Aignan in Orléans, Saint-Martin in Tours, Notre-Dame at Jumièges, and Bishop Fulbert's cathedral in Chartres. These great monuments are known to us in varying degrees through excavations, old drawings, and significant surviving fragments. They were vast, unvaulted thin-wall structures, often provided with tribunes or galleries over side aisles and with large, spacious transepts—monuments that reflected the immense agricultural wealth of the Loire Valley, Normandy, and the region to the south and east of Paris.

A fascinating example of the evolution of the twin-towered façade out of the Carolingian westwork is still to be seen in the church of Notre-Dame at Jumièges. Magnificent twin towers some 165 feet in height flank an atrophied westwork, which projects slightly on the exterior in the Carolingian manner, as at Corvey in Germany. Inside, a truncated platform remains, a downsizing of the elaborate Carolingian type, an example of which is still extant at Corvey. The nave at Jumièges, covered as always in large 11th-century buildings with a wooden roof, had galleries over the side aisles, in the manner of the Loire examples at Orléans and Tours, and was rhythmically subdivided into compartments by great transverse arches.

The nave and transept of the fine abbey church of Saint-Étienne at Caen, founded by William the Conqueror and destined to be his resting place, is well known. It still boasts its original though subsequently remodeled twin-towered façade, by which one enters this great structure. Although the nave was vaulted in the 12th century, and underwent major restoration subsequently, its original 11th-century form can be easily reconstructed: a vast, thick-wall structure with vaulted tribune galleries over the side aisles, surmounted by a wall passage at the base of the clerestory windows. All three levels were lit by exterior windows. The church of Saint-Remi at Reims followed the same general architectural design in the first half of the 11th century: a thin-wall, wooden-roofed nave with galleries over side aisles, intersecting a transept of equal width and height, also unvaulted. Throughout the region to the north of the Loire this avant-garde building type prevailed. As we would expect, smaller structures were more conservative in nature and did not adhere to the format of the great monuments that were instrumental in the evolution of the 12th-century, fully developed Romanesque style.

The so-called High Romanesque style resulted from the slow and idiosyncratic fusion of the two Early Romanesque traditions. To the southern tradition, High Romanesque owes the practice of integrating and vaulting high spaces; to the northern, it owes the predilection for expanded, generous, and open spaces, especially as represented by the fully developed transept. Often, vaulting would be introduced under the original wooden roofs of Early Romanesque naves and transepts, and rectangular bays of choirs. A good example is the nave of the great abbey church of Saint-Philibert at Tournus, where transverse barrel vaults have been introduced under the original wooden roof. Even with the resulting contraction of volume, the nave of Tournus seems enormous. One can imagine how much more vast the original 11th-century vessel would have been.

The Romanesque style in France is habitually subdivided into a plethora of local styles, or "schools." This manner of classifying 12th-century production is most instructive in clarifying regional differences. We must not lose sight, however, of what these seemingly disparate monuments have in common. No longer are they constructed of small, irregularly shaped, and coursed stones; rather, fine ashlar walls are the rule in virtually all major monuments. Wooden roofs were replaced by superbly planned stone vaults over the high spaces of naves, transepts, and rectangular bays of choirs.

Only a small portion—the south arm of the major transept—of the great Burgundian abbey church at Cluny III survives, but it represents French Romanesque architecture at its finest. Some 109 feet in height, this stunning space anticipates French Gothic architecture in its vertical thrust and intricate wall design. The church itself was immense: a double-aisled nave with two transepts, barrel-vaulted, with two magnificent crossing towers, and an ambulatory with radiating chapels. Already, a century ear-

PRINCIPAL CENTERS OF ROMANESQUE ARCHITECTURE

lier, the abbey church of Cluny II was vaulted throughout. Such churches reflected the wealth amassed and sometimes flaunted by the monastic order of Cluny. The abbey church at Vézelay, more modest in architectural scope, offered a luxury of sculptural decoration that was the only equal to Cluny.

A special type of Romanesque architecture prevailed in the southwest of France, the cupola church. The cathedral of Périgueux is an outstanding though abusively re-stored example of this architectural type. What is so exceptional about this cupola church is that the walls are not articulated by engaged half-columns, which are the rule in French Romanesque architecture. Rather, they are flat in the Byzantine manner, and the filiation from Byzantium via Venice is certain. The nearby cathedral of Angoulême is much more "Gallicized" in this regard.

Another important Romanesque substyle is that associated with the Cistercian order. In contrast with that

Saint-Guilhem-le-Désert, abbey church. *Photograph courtesy of William W. Kibler.*

of Cluny, this style is sparse, minimalist, and often associated with St. Bernard, who fulminated against luxuriously decorated churches: "O vanity of vanities, yet no more vain than insane! The church is resplendent in her walls, beggarly in her poor. She clothes her stones in gold, and leaves her sons naked. . . ." (*Apologia ad Guillelmum Abbatem* 28). The fine abbey church of Le Thoronet, in Provence, shows the Bernardin approach to church design, where austerity is the rule and decoration suspect.

Finally, there is another important Romanesque style that is linear in form and constituted by the great pilgrimage churches. Saint-Sernin at Toulouse is a superb example of the type. Other well-preserved examples can be seen at Compostela in Spain and at Sainte-Foy, Conques, in Auvergne. Two other celebrated examples are now lost: Saint-Martial at Limoges and Saint-Martin at Tours. All were characterized by two elements typical of the major monuments of French Romanesque architecture: their major spaces were covered with barrel vaults throughout, and their choirs were furnished with ambulatory and radiating chapels. In addition, the aisles of the nave, the transept arms, and the rectangular bays of the choir were surmounted with galleries, or tribunes, as was the practice in such northern Early Romanesque monuments as Saint-Martin at Tours or Orléans cathedral. The pilgrimage churches represent, like Cluny III, Romanesque architectural practice at its apogee.

The developing Gothic style in the region around Paris was much indebted to the Romanesque in its formative years and in fact adopted many of the features of Romanesque structures, such as the ambulatory with radiating chapel, the use of high vaults throughout, fine ashlar masonry, and the placing of galleries above the aisles to counteract the thrust of high vaults. In much of the rest of Europe, however, the earlier Carolingian and Ottonian approaches to architectural design prevailed down to Gothic times. In France, the Romanesque charted new directions in the design of great monuments. French Gothic continued this development.

John B. Cameron

[See also: CAEN; CHARTRES; CISTERCIAN ART AND ARCHITECTURE; CLUNY; CONQUES; GOTHIC ARCHITECTURE; JUMIÈGES; LIMOGES; ORLÉANS; PÉRIGUEUX; REIMS; ROMANESQUE ART; ROMANESQUE SCULPTURE; SAINT-AIGNAN-SUR-CHER; SAINT-MICHEL-DE-CUXA; THORONET, LE; TOULOUSE; TOURNUS; TOURS/TOURAINE; VÉZELAY]

Armi, C. Edson. *Masons and Sculptors in Romanesque Burgundy: The New Aesthetic of Cluny III.* 2 vols. University Park: Pennsylvania State University Press, 1983.
Aubert, Marcel. *Romanesque Cathedrals and Abbeys of France,* trans. Cuthbert Girdlestone. London: Vane, 1966.
Focillon, Henri. *The Art of the West in the Middle Ages,* trans. Donald King. 2 vols. 2nd ed. London: Phaidon, 1969.
Grodecki, Louis. *L'architecture ottonienne: au seuil de l'art roman.* Paris: Colin, 1958.
Kahn, Deborah, ed. *The Romanesque Frieze and Its Spectator.* London: Harvey Miller, 1992.
"La nuit des temps" collection published by Zodiaque at La Pierre-qui-vire (Yonne) has a valuable series of regional studies on Romanesque architecture: *Auvergne roman, Bourgogne roman, Haut-Languedoc roman, Poitou roman, Val-de-Loire roman,* etc.

ROMANESQUE ART. Romanesque painting and sculpture gave vibrant, expressive life to the pilgrimage churches and cathedrals in mid-11th to late 12th-century France. Invented by 19th-century archaeologists to describe medieval works of crude Roman derivation, the term "Romanesque" remains in use due to the relationship between the medieval world and its antique past from the middle of the 11th to the third quarter of the 12th century.

Ideas and images of the ancient Roman Empire, the development of trade routes and urban areas, the growth of pilgrimage roads, the Crusades, and the continuity of the Capetian line all contributed to the production of Romanesque art. In certain areas of France, classical remains directly inspired the revival of monumental sculpture. Fixed within architectural and liturgical contexts, monumental painting and sculpture appeared to the roaming pilgrim as a series of moving images.

Painting and sculpture were often interdependent media, as in the case of portable devotional objects like wooden statues of the enthroned Virgin and Child, painted with polychromy on gesso. Architectural sculpture was often painted, and both painting and sculpture depicted similar themes. Yet fundamental differences in technique and other circumstances of production distinguish the two media. While both Romanesque sculpture and painting were intended to be didactic, the two media present their messages in different ways. Sculpture graced entrances, such as exterior portals and inner narthex portals, piers in cloisters, or capitals in parts of monasteries, and presented scenes and figures to the pilgrim. Wall painting occupied

Pentecost, Cluny lectionary, late 11th century. Nouv. Acq. Lat. 2246, fol. 79v. *Courtesy of the Bibliothèque Nationale, Paris.*

Saint-Augustine (Marchiennes), mid-12th century, Douai. MS 250, vol. 1, fol. 2. *Courtesy of the Bibliothèque Municipale, Douai.*

areas that shape space—vaults, walls, and interior focal points—and thus could convey narrative to the processing pilgrim differently than did sculpture.

Other than illuminated manuscripts, wall paintings were the dominant and most accessible form of painting in Romanesque France. Apart from antependia from Catalonia and altar frontals from other European countries, few Romanesque panel paintings survive in France, although many must have been produced. Remains of French monumental painting abound. Compared with other regions in western Europe, French wall painting is diverse. Early scholarship formulated inadequate categories of workshops and schools that have led to a recent focus on the synthesis of painting styles of individual workshops and use of a variety of media. The lack of a recent in-depth survey or overview of French Romanesque wall painting may be at-

tributed to the poor state of preservation and destructive postmedieval "restorations."

Classical fresco technique remained in use throughout the 8th and 9th centuries, and by the 11th century fresco in western Europe largely resembled the Byzantine technique. Generally, three stages had to take place before painting began. First, painters established construction lines to indicate registers and axes of symmetry on the architectural fabric. Then, geometric diagrams of figures were drawn on the ground, and finally the preparatory drawings were laid down. Unlike Byzantine incised drawings, Romanesque drawings were visible up to the final stage of execution. Many Romanesque preparatory drawings remain on the surface underneath flaking fresco.

Rather than follow an iconographic canon, Romanesque artists must have started from *similia*—iconographic models from illuminations or in albums—and personal collections of notes and drawings. Model books served only as points of departure, for elaboration took place *in situ* on the wall.

The basic process involved fresco finished with lime or occasionally tempera. Writings of Theophilus (first half

Christ in Majesty, Sacrementary of Saint-Étienne at Limoges, ca. 1100. Lat. 9438, fol. 58v. *Courtesy of the Bibliothèque Nationale, Paris.*

Annunciation, Mont-Saint-Michel Sacrementary, late 11th century. M 641, fol. 24. *Courtesy of the Pierpont Morgan Library, New York.*

of the 12th c.) and Pierre Saint-Audemar (late 12th c.) describe the process of wall painting as true fresco with lime later added to dry walls to fix the color by carbonization. Pierre Saint-Audemar writes about the use of oil and tempera on walls, possibly a later development in technique. Variations of binders for certain colors may have given rise to a style of wall painting that favors flat areas of color and no modeling. Contemporary sources do not mention the application of paint, but generally western European mural paintings have thin layers of paint and are more opaque than Byzantine murals.

Many of the Romanesque mural cycles in French churches followed a set iconographical scheme. A Christ in Majesty or enthroned Virgin with either Magi or Holy Women frequently adorned the apse, the longitudinal focal point of the basilican church. The vaulted ceiling often received a celestial design, in contrast to the lower part of the wall surface, which was painted in *trompe l'oeil* with architectural motifs or with other earthly decorations ranging from embroiderylike designs to grotesques. Crossings tended to carry more architectonic designs, and the tran-

septs received no set subject. Figures in arches and spandrels usually turned toward the central scene in the apse. The west wall often held the acceptance and refusal of sacrifices or the Last Judgment. In the nave, a main narrative, such as the miracles and death of Christ or the Old and New Testament, occupied the upper part of vaults. Generally, smaller spaces, galleries, porches, and crypts held more articulate and systematic decoration.

Two examples of the diverse types of wall painting are found at the vast abbey church of Saint-Savin-sur-Gartempe and the grange at Berzé-la-Ville. The murals at Saint-Savin display the effects of wall painting on a large scale, while the paintings of Berzé-la-Ville are experienced in intimate space.

The abbey church of Saint-Savin contains the most comprehensive scheme of wall painting. Although much restored, the columnar piers in the nave are painted in *trompe l'oeil* to resemble colorful variegated marble. Four areas of the building—the west gallery, the barrel-vaulted nave, the crypt, and the porch—contain scenes from the life of Christ, thirty-six scenes from the Old Testament (including the Creation and the stories of Noah, Abraham, Joseph, and Moses), saints' legends, and the Apocalypse, respectively. Earth tones predominate, with red ocher, yellow ocher, green, and occasionally black. Demus, Deschamps, and Thibaut agree that several artists, or teams of artists with similar styles, accomplished the painting in a short period, sometime from the late 11th century to the early 12th.

Seven miles from the abbey of Cluny in Burgundy, the dependent grange of Berzé-la-Ville also possesses extensive wall painting in rich reds, greens, purples, and whites against a deep-blue background. In the semidome of the apse of the chapel, Christ in Majesty resides in a mandorla, with his right hand raised in blessing St. Paul and his left hand giving a scroll to St. Peter. Peter and Paul, who lead a group of six Apostles to either side of Christ, were associated with Cluny, whose domains were dedicated to the two saints. The apse painting also includes the chapel patrons, SS. Vincent, Lawrence, and Blaise.

The rest of the chapel contains portrait busts of saints venerated at Cluny on the dado, two martyrdoms (of SS. Blaise and either Vincent or Lawrence) in blind niches, and figures of female saints in the spandrels of the arcade beneath the vault. Of ornamental painting, part of the dado has *trompe l'oeil* curtains, and a pattern of flowers and leaves defines the arch framing the apse. These paintings, displaying a strong Byzantine influence on style, iconography, and format, have been dated to the early 12th century.

Later Romanesque wall painting was influenced by other media and in some instances incorporated embellished reliefs. At the chapel of St. Michael in Rocamadour, the intense blue background and linearity of the Annunciation and Visitation paintings show the influence of Limoges enamels. In the Salle des Morts at the cathedral of Notre-Dame, Le Puy, a wall painting of the Crucifixion in a large lunette covers the south wall. The presence of prophets and philosophers bearing texts on the sacrifice of Christ and his victory over death is unique. On a technical level, the use of embellished reliefs suggests enamels and mosaic work.

Stacy L. Boldrick

[See also: BERZÉ-LA-VILLE; GOTHIC ARCHITECTURE; GOTHIC ART; LE PUY; MANUSCRIPTS, PRODUCTION AND ILLUMINATION; MOISSAC; POITIERS; ROCAMADOUR; ROMANESQUE ARCHITECTURE; SAINT-CHEF; SAINT-GILLES-DU-GARD; SAINT-SAVIN-SUR-GARTEMPE; VÉZELAY; VICQ]

Cahn, Walter. *Romanesque Bible Illumination.* Ithaca: Cornell University Press, 1982.

Demus, Otto. *Romanesque Mural Painting,* trans. Mary Whittall. New York: Abrams, 1970.

Deschamps, Paul, and Marc Thibaut. *La peinture murale en France: le haut moyen âge à l'époque romane.* Paris: Plon, 1951.

Kupfer, Marcia. *Romanesque Wall Painting in Central France: The Politics of Narrative.* New Haven: Yale University Press, 1993.

Schapiro, Meyer. *Romanesque Art.* New York: Braziller, 1977.

Seidel, Linda. *Songs of Glory: The Romanesque Façades of Aquitaine.* Chicago: University of Chicago Press, 1981.

Stoddard, Whitney S. *Art and Architecture in Medieval France.* New York: Harper and Row, 1972.

Wettstein, Janine. *La fresque romane: la route de Saint-Jacques, de Tours à Léon. Études comparatives II.* Paris, 1978.

ROMANESQUE SCULPTURE. A major aspect of the "Renaissance of the Twelfth Century" was the resurgence of monumental sculpture in stone. Production of luxury objects had never ceased (Limoges became a center of *champlevé* enameling), and wooden cult images of the Virgin and Child were popular, especially in the Auvergne. The outstanding innovations of the Romanesque period, however, were the proliferation of historiated capitals and the appearance of great sculptured church portals.

The earliest attempts at façade decoration occurred in the first half of the 11th century in the Roussillon, where traditional techniques of marble carving (altar tables and other ecclesiastical furniture) were applied to church exteriors (Saint-André-de-Sorède; Saint-Genis-des-Fontaines). It was not until the turn of the century that monumental portals evolved in Languedoc, northern Spain, and Burgundy.

This sculpture is architectonic in character, international in style, and often epic in iconography. It is an art of power, of energy in tension, imaginative, expressive, with a love of variation and decorative effect and of geometric, stylized, and even fantastic forms. Despite a certain homogeneity fostered by artistic exchange along trade routes and pilgrimage roads, distinctive regional tendencies may also be discerned.

The "school of Languedoc" comprises several related styles emanating from workshops at Toulouse and Moissac. The leading early sculptor was Bernard Gilduin, credited

Crucifixion, Reims Sacrementary (Reims), mid-12th century. MS 28, fol. 6v. *Courtesy of the Walters Art Gallery, Baltimore.*

Toulouse (Haute-Garonne), Saint-Sernin, Christ in Majesty, ambulatory relief. *Photograph courtesy of Whitney S. Stoddard.*

Saint-Étienne) may be studied in the Musée des Augustins in Toulouse.

The great church of Cluny III was among the earliest and most influential centers of Burgundian Romanesque sculpture. The dating of the choir capitals (ca. 1095), with their subtle carving, lively figures, and sophisticated iconography, has long been controversial. The great west portal, largely destroyed, was roughly contemporary with the Porte Miègeville in Toulouse. Characteristic of Cluniac ateliers is the distinctive plate drapery, possibly derived from German sources. Two outstanding sculptors, thought to have been trained at Cluny, developed individual styles that mark the apogee of Burgundian Romanesque: Gislebertus of Autun and the anonymous master of Vézelay. At Saint-Lazare, Autun, the style of Gislebertus, both lyrical and expressive, imparts a unity to the capitals of the choir and nave, the gigantic Last Judgment of the west doorway, and the fragments of the north portal. The "Mission of the Apostles" of the central doorway of the inner narthex of La Madeleine at Vézelay is charged with an energy unparalleled in Burgundian sculpture. The "multilinear" style is activated with rhythmic patterns and swirls; the figures are elongated and angular, agitated in pose and gesture. It is a dynamic style, somewhat akin to the frescoes of Berzé-la-Ville. Later Burgundian portals are characterized by luxuriant foliage, detailed ornamentation, and by movement, almost restlessness, in the composition. Particularly important and complex are the rapports between Burgundian Romanesque and the first Gothic sculpture of the Île-de-France.

The flourishing culture of western France (Poitou, Saintonge, Angoumois) is reflected in the elaborate decoration of its screen façades. The focus is not on a central carved tympanum but on the multiplicity of richly carved archivolts, embellishing doorways, niches, windows and arcades, which activate the façade. At Saint-Pierre at Aulnay, two systems of carving the archivolts led to significantly different results in embellishment. The earlier method (south portal), imitated even in Spain and England, consists of small repetitive motifs (Elders of the Apocalypse, fantastic animals, etc.) placed radially, one motif to each voussoir. The alternative method (west portal), adopted at Saint-Denis and subsequent Gothic portals, allowed large figures (Virtues and Vices) to be placed along the curve of the arch, converging toward the keystone. At the cathedral of Angoulême and Notre-Dame-la-Grande at Poitiers, the sculptural program was expanded over the entire façade. The cumulative effect of multiple archivolts, superimposed arcades, friezes, and figures in niches is one of lavish decorative richness.

The Auvergne possesses some impressive capitals but few carved portals (see, however, Clermont-Ferrand), due in part to the intractable nature of the local stone. The most interesting series are those of Notre-Dame-du-Port (Clermont-Ferrand), Saint-Nectaire, Mozat, and Brioude, where motifs from Gallo-Roman art, such as centaurs, sirens, and griffins, are juxtaposed with Christian themes and with subjects from local folklore. The heavy figures with large heads approximate the appearance of Gallo-Roman bas-reliefs. Related to the Auvergne in style and

with the altar table (ca. 1096) of the church of Saint-Sernin, Toulouse, capitals in the tribunes, and the large marble reliefs now in the ambulatory. The fullness of his forms, suggestive of polished ivory carving, was further developed in the Porte Miègeville (ca. 1110–15); a similar style developed along the pilgrimage route in northern Spain (Jaca, León, Compostela).

The first Moissac workshop was responsible for the cloister capitals and pier reliefs (ca. 1100) of the abbey of Saint-Pierre, the oldest of the historiated cloisters that survives relatively intact. There is a new spirit at work, however, in the famous south portal, where a decorative richness suggestive of Islamic Spain is combined with Burgundian elements and with a more dynamic treatment of the figure. The resultant visionary effect was widely imitated; the characteristic elongated figures, in cross-legged and dancing poses, were repeated at Beaulieu (Corrèze) and culminated in the ecstatic image of the prophet Isaiah at Souillac (Lot). The sculpture of later Toulousan ateliers (La Daurade and the chapter house of

format (stocky figures and triangular lintel) is the immense Last Judgment at Conques (Rouergue). The inventiveness of its demons and punishments and the diagrammatic layout, reinforced by explanatory text carved on banderoles and frames, make it one of the most accessible, and didactic, of Romanesque tympana.

Large sculptured ensembles made their appearance later in Provence than in Languedoc and Burgundy. Provence was rich in classical remains, and Romanesque sculptors made full use of a classical vocabulary, including decorated cornices, Corinthian capitals, friezes, and figures in niches set between fluted pilasters. The façade of Saint-Gilles-du-Gard resembles Roman stage architecture; the figures and draperies, more classically conceived than elsewhere in France, display a distinctly Roman feel for monumental form. The Apostles of the west portal of Saint-Trophime at Arles have an equally classicizing flavor.

In the north of France, where a regional Romanesque was never as fully developed, the masters at Saint-Denis, Notre-Dame at Étampes, and Chartres were free to appropriate elements, and even craftsmen, from other regions. The result of this assimilation and experimentation was a revolutionary deployment of the figure and a new approach to the entire portal format.

The Royal Portal of Chartres, in which the triple portals and supporting elements are integrated within an iconographic whole, has been viewed as the culmination of the Romanesque, as Early Gothic, or as a unique transitional style. The serene column figures placed on the jambs of the portals assume the shape of architectural members lining the three entrance portals and embody a rare fusion of sculpture and architecture. In comparison with the reliefs of the jambs and trumeaux of Moissac and Vézelay, from which they ultimately descend, they are at the same time statues in their own right and integral parts of the structural columns.

Jean M. French

[See also: ANGOULÊME; AULNAY-EN-SAINTONGE; AUTUN; BEAULIEU-SUR-DORDOGNE; BRIOUDE; CHARTRES; CLERMONT-FERRAND; CONQUES; ENAMELING; GISLEBERTUS; GOTHIC ART; MOISSAC; POITIERS; ROMANESQUE ARCHITECTURE; ROMANESQUE ART; SAINT-DENIS; SAINT-GILLES-DU-GARD; SAINT-NECTAIRE; SOUILLAC; TOULOUSE; VÉZELAY]

For regional Romanesque, see the multivolume series "La nuit des temps" (*Bourgogne roman, Auvergne roman,* etc.) published by Zodiaque at La-Pierre-qui-vire (Yonne).

Armi, C. Edson. *Masons and Sculptors in Romanesque Burgundy: The New Aesthetic of Cluny III.* 2 vols. University Park: Pennsylvania State University Press, 1983.

Borg, Alan. *Architectural Sculpture in Romanesque Provence.* Oxford: Oxford University Press, 1972.

Focillon, Henri. *L'art des sculpteurs romans: recherches sur l'histoire des formes.* Paris: Leroux, 1931.

Forsyth, Ilene H. *The Throne of Wisdom: Wood Sculptures of the Madonna in Romanesque France.* Princeton: Princeton University Press, 1972.

Hearn, M.F. *Romanesque Sculpture: The Revival of Monumental Stone Sculpture in the Eleventh and Twelfth Centuries.* Ithaca: Cornell University Press, 1981.

Lyman, Thomas W. *French Romanesque Sculpture: An Annotated Bibliography.* Boston: Hall, 1987.

Mâle, Emile. *Religious Art in France. The Twelfth Century: A Study of the Origins of Medieval Iconography,* ed. Harry Bober, trans. Marthiel Mathews. Princeton: Princeton University Press, 1978.

Porter, Arthur K. *Romanesque Sculpture of the Pilgrimage Roads.* 10 vols. Boston: Marshall Jones, 1923.

Schapiro, Meyer. *Romanesque Art.* New York: Braziller, 1977.

Scher, Stephen K. *The Renaissance of the Twelfth Century.* Providence: Rhode Island School of Design, Museum of Art, 1969.

Seidel, Linda. *Songs of Glory: The Romanesque Façades of Aquitaine.* Chicago: University of Chicago Press, 1981.

RONDEAU (13th c.: *rondet* or *rondel*). A popular dance form of the 13th and 14th centuries and one of the *formes fixes* of the late 14th and 15th. The name perhaps derives from a round dance. The simplest fully developed form comprises eight lines in the pattern ABaAabAB, in which capital letters indicate the two refrain verses and lowercase letters are new text with the same rhyme scheme and syllable count as the corresponding refrain lines (musical settings have two sections that repeat as necessary, one for the A-sections and the other for the B-sections). Unlike the *carole*, and the later ballade and virelai, the rondeau refrain is partially repeated within the stanza. In the 15th century, rondeaux were enormously popular, with refrains three, four, or five lines long. How much of these long refrains recurred after the opening is still debated.

Lawrence Earp

[See also: FORMES FIXES; REFRAIN]

Bec, Pierre. *La lyrique française au moyen-âge (XIIe–XIIIe siècles): contribution à une typologie des genres poétiques médiévaux.* 2 vols. Paris: Picard, 1977.

Boogaard, Nico van den. *Rondeaux et refrains du XIIe siècle au début du XIVe.* Paris: Klincksieck, 1969.

Cerquiglini, Jacqueline. "Le rondeau." In *La littérature française aux XIVe et XVe siècles.* Heidelberg: Winter, 1988, Vol. 1: *Partie historique,* ed. Daniel Poirion, pp. 45–58.

ROSE, ROMAN DE LA. Allegorical poem composed in the course of the 13th century by Guillaume de Lorris and Jean de Meun. For a description of the poem, see the articles under the names of its two authors; for an account of the literary debate occasioned by the *Rose,* see the article under QUARREL. The response to the *Rose* in the 14th and 15th centuries was phenomenal. It survives in over 250 manuscripts, more than exist for any other work of Old or Middle French literature. Most of these manuscripts are illuminated, many lavishly. Most are also equipped with extensive rubrics, occasionally in rhymed couplets, that chart the thematic and narrative structure of the poem.

Some manuscripts, perhaps one-tenth of the surviving corpus, have marginal glosses and annotations added by medieval readers; a great many more have had memorable lines identified with the inscription *Nota*. These annotations are invaluable in assessing the interests of medieval readers of the *Rose*. Reactions to the poem can also be gauged from the numerous literary responses and rewritings that it generated. These in turn range from interpolated passages to extensive revisions and reworkings of the text to the composition of entirely new texts. Finally, the influence of the *Rose* spread well beyond France: by the end of the 14th century, it had been translated into Italian, Dutch, and English.

The number of miniatures varies considerably from one manuscript to another, ranging from none at all to well over a hundred. Most manuscripts have at least one miniature representing the Dreamer in bed at the beginning of the poem. Many begin with a large four-part miniature that takes up most of the first page and, with some variation, illustrates the opening scenes of the poem: the Dreamer sleeping, rising, going out of doors, arriving at the garden wall. Aside from the opening miniature, other favorite motifs are the anticourtly images on the garden wall, nearly always represented in a series of miniatures; Idleness admitting the Lover to the garden; the *carole*; Narcissus at the fountain; the interactions of the Lover and the God of Love; and an author portrait at the beginning of Jean de Meun's continuation. Many manuscripts feature an illustration at the beginning of each of the major discourses, illustrating the character about to speak; many illustrate mythological exempla, especially Narcissus and Pygmalion; and many depict the events of the narrative. In addition to their aesthetic value, the illustrations can be useful as a guide to ways in which the poem was understood by its medieval readers.

Equally important are the numerous rubrics that, in most manuscripts, chart the narrative and thematic divisions of the poem. Rubrics, too, vary considerably; there was no standardized program. Most manuscripts, however, do use rubrics to identify which character is speaking throughout the poem; and by identifying the first-person voice as either *Amant* ("Lover") or *Acteur* ("Narrator"), according to the context, these rubrics allow us to study medieval readings of the complex narrative voice of the *Rose*. Rubrics identifying thematic divisions are often elaborate and show what different medieval readers found important in the poem. In some cases, rubrics even offer a moral gloss on the text. Such is the case, for example, in the late 13th-century manuscript B.N. fr. 1569, in which a series of rhymed rubrics establishes the allegorical framework for the poem as a celebration of love, stressing the values of joy, love, and beauty. In the 14th-century manuscript B.N. fr. 1574, on the other hand, the rubrics establish a moralizing critique of the erotic Garden of Delight, stressing the Lover's folly. The comparative study of these and other rubricated manuscripts shows that there was no single way of reading the *Rose* in the Middle Ages.

Rubrics indicate the formal structures perceived in the *Rose* by copyists; the reactions of other readers are revealed in marginal glosses and annotations. Even the terse comment *Nota* tells us that the line so marked was judged worthy of memory; and, as might be expected, different readers were attracted to different aspects of the poem. *Nota* often appears next to antifeminist passages, bearing out Christine de Pizan's assertion that the *Rose* fostered negative attitudes toward women. Some readers additionally focused on the satirical portrayal of marriage, courtship, and erotic love, annotating most heavily the discourses of Friend and the Old Woman; others, however, concentrated on the more erudite sections of the poem, such as the discourses of Reason and Nature. Where annotations are more extensive than the simple word *Nota*, they typically consist of literary citations and proverbs in either French or Latin. The author most frequently cited is Ovid, although one also finds citations of Seneca, Aristotle, *Pamphilus*, Gratian's *Decretum*, and others. Such glosses indicate that the *Rose* reached an educated readership, one interested in its character as a vernacular compendium drawing on the Latin tradition.

The *Rose* inspired several projects of revision, or *remaniements*, as well as numerous interpolations, some of which appear in as many as one-fourth of the 116 manuscripts collated by Ernest Langlois. The earliest is probably the brief anonymous conclusion, predating Jean de Meun's longer and far more famous continuation, that allows Guillaume de Lorris's lover to spend a night of bliss with the Rose. The most extensive *remaniement* and the only one that is not anonymous is that executed by Gui de Mori in the late 13th century. Gui suppressed allusions to pagan mythology, added considerable didactic material, and attempted to replace the ring structure that characterizes several of Jean de Meun's major discourses with a linear progression. Another important *remaniement* is that designated by Langlois as the *B* text, which survives in several recensions. The *B remanieur* in general sought to recast Jean de Meun's continuation in the more courtly framework of Guillaume de Lorris, suppressing in part or in whole both philosophical digressions and bawdy or satirical passages. But while these are the two most important and most widely diffused *remaniements*, the manuscript tradition contains other examples of both abridgment and interpolation, sometimes considerable. Among the passages most frequently rewritten are Reason's defense of plain speech, the discourse of False Seeming, and the discourse of Genius; but every part of the poem shows at least some variation.

Literary responses to the *Rose* are many and varied. Few medieval poets attempted to match the scope of the *Rose*, but a great many adopted aspects of it, such as first-person narrative, the dream-vision format, the garden setting, or mythological and allegorical characters and motifs. The most explicit imitation of the *Rose* is the late 14th-century *Échecs amoureux*. Evrart de Conty's voluminous prose commentary on the *Échecs* (ca. 1400) cites the *Rose* repeatedly and is one of the most important sources for late-medieval readings of that poem. Poets as diverse as Nicole de Margival, Guillaume de Digulleville, Christine de Pizan, René d'Anjou, and François Villon also cite the *Rose* explicitly. Guillaume de Machaut and Jean Froissart were profoundly influenced by it. Indeed, it would be impossible to imagine Middle French literature without the *Rose.*

The *Rose* continued to be popular well into the Renaissance. It went through several printed editions in the 15th century and, in the modernization attributed to Clément Marot, was printed several times in the 16th century as well. Jean Molinet's prose redaction, accompanied by an idiosyncratic reading of the text as sacred allegory, was also printed in the 16th century.

Sylvia Huot

[See also: *ÉCHECS AMOUREUX.*; GUI DE MORI; GUILLAUME DE LORRIS; JEAN DE MEUN; MOLINET, JEAN; QUARREL OF THE *ROMAN DE LA ROSE*]

Arden, Heather M. *The* Roman de la Rose: *An Annotated Bibliography.* New York: Garland, 1993.

Badel, Pierre-Yves. *Le roman de la Rose au XIVe siècle: étude de la réception de l'œuvre.* Geneva: Droz, 1980.

Bourdillon, Francis W. *The Early Editions of the* Roman de la Rose. London: Chiswick, 1906.

Huot, Sylvia. *The* Romance of the Rose *and Its Medieval Readers: Interpretation, Reception, Manuscript Transmission.* Cambridge: Cambridge University Press, 1993.

Langlois, Ernest. *Les manuscrits du* Roman de la Rose: *description et classement.* Paris: Champion, 1910.

ROTROUENGE. A poetic form. Little is known regarding the *rotrouenge,* and the few extant examples differ from one another in versification; yet the designation of a given song as a *rotrouenge* often appears in the text, a fact that has led scholars to postulate that the genre's underlying formal structure is perhaps musical rather than textual. The text consists of an indeterminate number of stanzas, two to eight lines each, with a one- to two-line poststrophic refrain. The most representative rhyme scheme is aaa . . . (b) + (A)B / (B)B.

Eglal Doss-Quinby

Bec, Pierre. "Note sur la rotrouenge médiévale." In *Mélanges de langues et de littératures romanes offerts à Carl Theodor Gossen,* ed. Germán Colón and Robert Kopp. 2 vols. Bern: Francke, 1976, Vol. 1, pp. 127–35.

Gennrich, Friedrich. *Die altfranzösische Rotrouenge.* Halle: Niemeyer, 1925.

ROUEN. On the Seine between Paris and the English Channel, the city of Rouen (Seine-Maritime) was the starting point of the medieval duchy of Normandy. During the late Roman Empire, it had been the head of the secular and ecclesiastical province Lugdunensis Secunda, and it remained an important port in the Frankish territory of Neustria until Viking raids disrupted its political and religious life. Ceded to the Viking chieftain Rollo ca. 911, Rouen was the base of his authority, and it served as the capital of upper Normandy under Rollo's heirs. The city prospered in the later 10th and 11th centuries as a great trade center; the church, ruled by Rouen's archbishop,

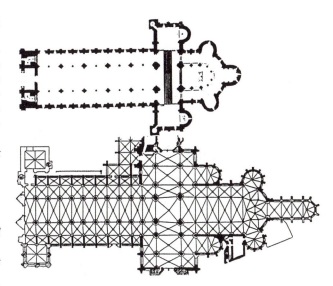

Rouen (Seine-Maritime), Notre-Dame, plan of 11th century, present plan. After Lanfrey.

regained its former jurisdictional boundaries. The Norman conquest of England in 1066 added to Rouen's wealth. The following century witnessed the rise of its commune and other bourgeois associations to protect common economic and judicial privileges.

In 1204, Rouen surrendered swiftly when Philip II Augustus conquered Normandy, and the French king confirmed important monopolies and liberties for the town. Until the resumption of war with the English in the mid-14th century, the city's trade and textile industries made Rouen one of the richest cities in France. The 13th and early 14th centuries witnessed the apogee of Gothic architecture; workers began to rebuild the cathedral of Rouen and the great abbey church of Saint-Ouen. But the Hundred Years' War brought higher taxes and disrupted trade. In 1418, King Henry V of England besieged Rouen for six months, reducing the population to starvation, before it surrendered. The English occupation of Rouen continued for over thirty years, in the course of which, in 1431, nineteen-year-old Jeanne d'Arc was executed in Rouen's marketplace. Eighteen years later, in 1449, King Charles VII of France entered the city victoriously.

Cassandra Potts

Rouen has many medieval monuments, of which the most important are the cathedral of Notre-Dame, the Benedictine abbey church of Saint-Ouen, and the church of Saint-Maclou. All date from the Gothic period, although some remains of earlier Romanesque structures are preserved in the cathedral (Tour Saint-Romain and crypt) and Saint-Ouen (Tour des Clercs).

The cathedral was rebuilt following a fire in 1200. Construction began at the west end under the direction of the architect, Jean d'Andelys. Work continued during the 13th and 14th centuries, with additional construction on the towers in the 15th and 16th centuries. The nave has eleven bays with side aisles opening onto chapels. The

Rouen, Notre-Dame, nave and aisle. *Photograph: Clarence Ward Collection. Courtesy of Oberlin College.*

Rouen, Saint-Ouen. *Photograph courtesy of Whitney S. Stoddard.*

transept has three bays with aisles and a chapel on the east side of each transept arm. The choir has five bays with ambulatory, two small radiating chapels, and a central chapel dedicated to the Virgin. The three-story elevation is elegantly proportioned, especially in the choir. Stained-glass windows of the 13th century are in the ambulatory, and 14th-century windows representing archbishops and saints of Rouen are in the Virgin Chapel. The cathedral houses tombs of several dukes of Normandy and the 15th-century duke of Bedford. The south-transept chapel is dedicated to Jeanne d'Arc.

The imposing west façade has three sculpted portals surmounted by gables, galleries, and a rose window. The left and right portals dedicated to St. John the Baptist and St. Stephen contain 13th-century sculpture; the Tree of Jesse in the central-portal tympanum dates from the 16th century. The Tour Saint-Romain with its Romanesque base on the north and the 15th-century Tour de Beurre on the south flank the façade. The transept portals, the Portail des Libraires on the north and the Portail de la Calende on the south, have interesting sculpture, especially the early 14th-century tympanum on the south transept representing the Passion.

The Benedictine abbey church dedicated to St. Ouen, a Merovingian bishop of Rouen, replaced an earlier Ro-

manesque building. Construction began in 1318 at the east end and continued into the 15th century. The long, narrow structure is composed of ten bays in the nave with single aisles, three bays in the choir with radiating chapels, and a compact transept. The three-story elevation is filled with eighty bays of stained glass dating from the 14th and 15th centuries.

The church of Saint-Maclou, just east of the cathedral, is the third edifice on this site. Built between 1436 and 1520, it is a beautiful example of Flamboyant Gothic style as seen in the exterior silhouette with crocketed gables, arcades, and pinnacles with openwork tracery. The plan of nave, transept, and choir with surrounding aisle chapels forms a cross with equal arms that center on the crossing. The convex five-bay western porch echoes the curve of the eastern radiating chapels. Wooden door panels are carved with an extensive iconographic program.

Karen Gould

[See also: HENRY V; JEAN D'ANDELYS; JEANNE D'ARC; NORMANDY; PHILIP II AUGUSTUS]

Blois, Guy. *The Crisis of Feudalism: Economy and Society in Eastern Normandy ca. 1300–1550.* Cambridge: Cambridge University Press, 1984.

Cheruel, Adolphe. *Histoire de Rouen sous la domination anglaise.* 1840; repr. Geneva: Slatkine-Megariotis, 1976.

Lanfry, Georges. *Cahiers de Notre-Dame de Rouen.* Rouen: Cerf, 1956–63.

Lefrançois-Pillon, Louise. *Les portails latéraux de la cathédrale de Rouen.* Paris: Picard, 1907.

Masson, André, *L'église abbatiale Saint-Ouen de Rouen, avec une étude sur les vitraux par Jean Lafond.* Paris: Laurens, 1927.

Mollat, Michel. *Histoire de Rouen.* Toulouse: Privat, 1979.

Naillon, Edgard. *Églises de Rouen.* Rouen, 1941.

Périaux, Nicetas. *Histoire sommaire et chronologique de la ville de Rouen.* Brionne: Manoir de Saint Pierre de Salerne, 1874.

ROUERGUE.

From the period of the Carolingians, the region of the Rouergue formed an important and extensive county. Centered on the city of Rodez, it reached north to Conques, south to the towns of Saint-Félix-de-Sorgues and Sylvanès, west to include Najac and the viscounty of Saint-Antonin, and east to include the viscounty of Millau. In the 9th century, the Rouergue came under the authority of the counts of Toulouse. Separated from the Toulousain by a division of inheritance in 919, it was recovered by Raymond de Saint-Gilles in 1066 and reunited with the other domains of the elder branch of the family.

At the end of the 11th century, two centers of power emerged in the Rouergue: the viscounty of Millau and the county of Rodez. Viscounts of Millau appear as early as 920. By 1080, they had added to their possessions the Gévaudan, Carlat, and Lodève. Viscount Gilbert (r. 1092–1108), through his marriage to the heiress Gerberge, added the county of Provence, and his daughter, Dulcia, passed these extensive domains to her husband, Raymond-Berenguer, count of Barcelona. Until 1222, Millau and its territories formed a spearhead for the penetration of the house of Barcelona into Languedoc. At the same time, Richard de Lodève, brother of viscount Gilbert, was recognized as the first count of Rodez (ca. 1112).

The crisis of the Albigensian Crusade had little impact on the Rouergue, where Count Henri I of Rodez submitted to Simon de Montfort in 1214. Control of the Rouergue and Millau passed to Alphonse of Poitiers and thence to the crown of France. The line of the counts of Rodez continued until 1312, when its heiress, Cécile, was succeeded by her husband, Bernard VI, count of Armagnac. The Treaty of Brétigny in 1360 assigned the Rouergue to the English, who administered it until 1368. The downfall of the counts of Armagnac in 1473 prepared the way for the restoration of the county of Rodez to the crown, a reunion consummated with the accession of King Henry IV.

Alan Friedlander

[See also: LANGUEDOC; SAINT-GILLES]

Artières, J. "Les vicomtes de Millau (916–1272)." *Mémoires de la Société des Lettres, Sciences et Arts de l'Aveyron* 21 (1921): 487–551.

Enjalbert, Henri. *Histoire de Rodez.* Toulouse: Privat, 1981.

———. *Histoire de Rouergue.* Toulouse: Privat, 1979.

Ourliac, Paul, and Anne-Marie Magnou. *Le cartulaire de La Selve, La Terre, les hommes et le pouvoir en Rouergue au XIIe siècle.* Paris: CNRS, 1985.

Rouquette, Joseph. *Le Rouergue sous les Anglais.* Millau: Artières and Maury, 1887.

ROYAL ADMINISTRATION AND FINANCE.

Although the Merovingian kings made some effort to preserve Roman institutions, early Frankish culture tended to think of government in private, personal terms. When movable wealth changed hands, the Franks understood gifts, booty, and tribute but not taxes and salaries. The Carolingians not only came from the least romanized part of the Frankish world but also took power at a time when the economy had become very local, warfare had disrupted administrative practice, and few laymen could write. Charlemagne tried to govern a large territory through family members, supportive clergy, household officials, and followers bound to him by a personal oath of loyalty. His strong personality and military prowess made the system work for awhile, but even he found that inadequate public institutions of government had to be supplemented by private, personal arrangements.

For nearly three centuries after the death of Charlemagne, monarchs, territorial lords, and many lesser nobles governed their lands in much the same way—deriving income mainly from the profits of rural estates and staffing military and judicial posts with household officers and men bound to service through private contracts of vassalage. The king's theoretical position at the apex of the social order and his ability to control more ecclesiastical appointments than other lords provided him with resources that others lacked, but royal administration and finance long involved little more than the management of those lands, rights, and jurisdictions that collectively made up the royal domain.

Under Philip I, obscure household officials emerged as important figures in the making and executing of royal policies. These were the earliest "great officers" of the crown—the seneschal, butler, chamberlain, and constable—to whom we should add the chancellor, who supervised those who wrote and authenticated royal documents. In this same period, the late 11th century, increasing urbanization, population, and trade made the revenues of the royal domain more substantial, but these were farmed by officials called *prévôts*, who were difficult to control and often corrupt.

Several modest achievements in the 12th century laid the basis for important developments in royal administration and finance. Louis VI forcibly pacified the unruly castellans of the Île-de-France, and these henceforth formed a pool of reliable men to fill administrative and military posts. The reduction of violence in the region also made the royal domain more profitable. Under the next two kings, the introduction of itinerant *baillis* helped bring the *prévôts* under better control, and the crown began building up a significant treasure, housed in the Temple and subject to audit by the *curia regis*.

The stage was now set for the large territorial additions to the royal domain under Philip II Augustus and his successors. The 13th-century *bailli* became more of a provincial governor, wielding judicial, financial, and military power over a group of *prévôtés*. When a great fief or large territorial block, such as Anjou, Normandy, or Languedoc, came into royal possession, the king left intact whatever local administrative structure he found, especially if it seemed superior to that existing in his other lands. Normandy, for instance, had an exchequer to monitor the revenues of the domain, so Philip left that in place and his Norman *baillis* were concerned more with military and judicial matters. In other lands, where the chief political officer had been the seneschal of the previous lord, the crown used this title, instead of *bailli*, for its chief local representative. In Languedoc, which had more developed judicial institutions, the crown preserved and enhanced these, leaving the seneschals with functions that were mainly military and financial. Thus, the field administration did not achieve uniformity. It adapted royal practices in the old domain to traditions and practices already present in newly acquired lands, thereby smoothing the process of absorbing these lands but reinforcing regional differences that would later hamper centralization. This administration was not always honest or efficient, and Louis IX, who sent out *enquêteurs* to receive complaints of official malfeasance, enacted many improvements in his ordinance of 1254.

In the central government, the great officers of the crown entered a period of eclipse under Philip II, who allowed the powerful office of seneschal of France to remain vacant after 1191 and made increasing use of salaried officers. Because he lost his archives in a battle in 1194, we lack details about royal governmental operations in the preceding decades, but that debacle did lead Philip to establish permanent archives, the Trésor des Chartes, in Paris. The daily operations of the government were in the hands of the *curia regis*, which in the 13th century increasingly came to be called the "king's council" (*conseil*). This small body consisted of prelates and nobles in frequent attendance on the king, as well as household officers and trusted salaried officials. For important occasions, the king expanded this council into a much larger body by summoning his important vassals from farther afield. When such an assembly dealt with a matter of political policy, such as planning a crusade, it was called a "great council," but when its work was largely judicial it was called a "court" (*curia*).

The everyday *curia/conseil* contained (or had added to it when needed) experts specializing in law, finance, or the currency. The king named six bourgeois of Paris, for instance, to oversee finances when he went on crusade in 1190. Gradually, those with special expertise became detached from the council and achieved the status of a permanent, separate body. The judicial experts were functioning as a separate entity after 1254, becoming the Parlement de Paris, the kingdom's highest court. The financial experts, after operating somewhat separately for decades, received official status as the Chambre des Comptes in 1320. By this time, the royal council itself acquired a different character. To maintain authority in the difficult political environment of the 14th century, the

king had to include on his council representatives of powerful political interests whose agenda might differ from his own. As the council became more of a political forum, the kings made greater use of the royal household (*hôtel du roi*), where their most trusted followers served as *maîtres des requêtes* or *chambellans*.

Royal finances long remained the revenues of a great seigneur, including those from high justice, coinage, treasure-trove, forests and fisheries, fairs and markets, and mineral rights, which only the greatest lords possessed. Philip II built an abundant treasure from these "ordinary" revenues, but under Philip IV they were becoming insufficient because of the demands of more frequent war. By this time, the 1290s, evolving military technology was making warfare on any scale much more expensive. The reign of Philip IV was of great importance for the emergence of "extraordinary" revenues as a supplement to traditional ones, and although it ended in rebellion over this issue, the momentum toward extraordinary revenues slowed only briefly. The reign of John II, fifty years later, was critical for the evolution of these extraordinary revenues into a system of taxation, while that of Charles VII, especially after 1435, would mark a third step: the taxes became, for all intents and purposes, permanent.

Intermittent war with England or Flanders, beginning in 1294, eventually gave way to the Hundred Years' War, which involved several extended periods of intense fighting. Successive kings, beginning with Philip IV, tried various expedients to augment revenues—expanding the feudal aids, manipulating the currency, squeezing money out of foreign residents—but they repeatedly had to ask their subjects for "war subsidies" to pay for the realm's defense. The frequency of these demands provoked growing opposition, particularly at moments when hostilities were suspended or at a low level. Underfinanced and poorly led French forces suffered severe defeats in the 1340s and 1350s, culminating in the capture of John II. The treaty that secured his release required payment of a heavy ransom. It was financed by indirect taxes, the *aides* and *gabelle*, which were collected in the years 1361–80 and 1382–1417 before being revived permanently in the 1430s.

The truce following the king's capture left thousands of soldiers unemployed; their violent behavior led the government in 1363 to impose the *fouage*, or graduated hearth tax, to pay an army that would both provide employment for the unruly military class and enable the crown to maintain order. This tax lasted seventeen years, began reappearing some years later as the *taille*, and continued as a recurrent extraordinary levy through the early decades of the 15th century. Charles VII and his successors levied the *taille* permanently after 1439, often raising the rate to suit escalating royal needs, and it became the major source of revenue.

The requirements of warfare and the accompanying rise of taxation had a significant impact on institutions of government but did not lead to any permanent role for the Estates General. Once persuaded that taxes were justified, French subjects showed little interest in a formal mechanism for consenting to them. They were, however, extremely suspicious of the officials who collected them, and the government had to develop a separate administration for those extraordinary revenues that became regular taxes. Supervising collection at the local level were *élus*, who themselves reported to a board of *généraux*. After 1390, the latter acquired institutional status as the Cour des Aides.

To ensure that tax receipts financed an effective army, the crown had to devise a system that made captains responsible for mustering their retinues regularly in the presence of designated officials. The *généraux* entrusted tax receipts to a war treasurer, who paid the captains on orders from the marshals of France after the muster had been recorded. Ordinances sought to develop and to enforce these rules and prevent corruption in the paying of troops. The most famous and successful was that of Charles VII in 1445, which established permanent *compagnies d'ordonnance* consisting of 100 "lances"—six-man tactical units headed by a heavy cavalryman. This professionalization of the army, which had been in progress for more than a century, was the final step in restoring truly public institutions in lieu of those based on private, feudal arrangements.

John Bell Henneman, Jr.

[See also: *AIDES; BAILLI/BAILLIAGE;* CHAMBRE DES COMPTES; *COMPAGNIES D'ORDONNANCE; CONSEIL; CURIA REGIS;* CURRENCY; CUSTOMS DUTIES; ELECTION; *ÉLU;* ESTATES (GENERAL); FEUDAL AIDS; *GABELLE; GÉNÉRAUX; HÔTEL DU ROI;* HUNDRED YEARS' WAR; *JUGE-MAGE; JUGE-ORDINAIRE; REQUÊTES, MAÎTRE DES; MISSI DOMINICI; PRÉVÔT/PRÉVÔTÉ;* ROYAL DOMAIN; SEIGNEUR/SEIGNEURIE; SENESCHAL; *TAILLE;* TRÉSOR DES CHARTES]

Bournazel, Éric. *Le gouvernment capétien au XIIe siècle, 1108–1180: structures sociales et mutations institutionelles.* Paris: Presses Universitaires de France, 1976.

Henneman, John Bell. *Royal Taxation in Fourteenth Century France: The Captivity and Ransom of John II.* Philadelphia: American Philosophical Society, 1976.

Lot, Ferdinand, and Robert Fawtier. *Histoire des institutions françaises au moyen âge.* 3 vols. Paris: Presses Universitaires de France, 1958, Vol. 2: *Institutions royales.*

Strayer, Joseph R. *On the Medieval Origins of the Modern State.* Princeton: Princeton University Press, 1970.

ROYAL DOMAIN. Historians apply the term "royal domain" (*domaine, demesne*) to the lands, rights, and revenues directly controlled by the king, beginning in the 10th century, when it amounted to little. It has been described as the king's patrimony or as his personal seigneurie. No single synonym or brief description captures precisely the meaning of the term. It consisted of lands, revenue-producing rights, jurisdiction, and what we might call patronage. Contemporaries viewed the domain largely in economic terms, as that which provided the king with the revenues he required, but it also had a political aspect that had to do with power rather than wealth.

Nowadays, historians tend to view the royal domain from a territorial perspective, as the area in which the king exercised direct authority, contrasted with such lands as territorial principalities, great fiefs, or certain apanages, in which he lacked such authority. It has become customary to portray on maps the growth of the royal domain. For all its convenience, this territorial approach is probably the least accurate way to portray the domain. If the king tightened control over his local officials, suppressed public disorder, and compelled his nominal vassals to honor their obligations, he might derive sharply increased resources, and therefore power, from his domain without adding territory. If, on the contrary, he acquired direct control over a large but poorly organized territory, its addition to the domain might add little to his effective wealth and power.

The first Capetian kings controlled some remnants of the old Carolingian holdings, mostly around Laon and Soissons, as well as lands and rights in and around Paris, Orléans, Étampes, Corbeil, and other places in the Île-de-France. They also possessed rights of patronage over about one-fifth of the kingdom's bishoprics and around a dozen monasteries. They were continually adding to this domain and also giving away parts of it. In the 11th century, the crown added Dreux, Sens, Melun, the Gâtinais, and the French Vexin, plus scattered places of lesser importance. Philip I purchased the viscounty of Bourges ca. 1100. Louis VI, by contrast, added little territory, but his vigorous measures made the existing domain far more profitable, as did a favorable economy. Louis VII got little but trouble from his temporary acquisition of Aquitaine through his first marriage to Eleanor. He made more modest but enduring additions in the later years of his reign.

Philip II Augustus inherited a domain that made him at least the equal of such lords as those who ruled Flanders, Burgundy, or Normandy. His wealth and power were nevertheless dwarfed by the French resources of Henry II of England, who held Normandy, Anjou, Maine, Poitou, and the *mouvance* of most of southwestern France. Philip, however, secured Artois from Flanders as his wife's dowry, and in a series of steps acquired the counties of Amiens, Valois, and Vermandois following a disputed succession. His legal proceedings against King John of England in 1203 led to his conquest of Normandy, Anjou, and Maine. Louis VIII occupied Poitou in 1224 and laid the groundwork for the settlement of 1229 that secured lower Languedoc for the crown. In just twenty-five years, the territorial extent of the royal domain had increased explosively.

Louis VIII granted out much of the new territory other than Normandy and Languedoc as apanages to his younger sons, but dynastic marriages and fortuitous deaths brought much of this land back into royal hands along with additional territories like the county of Toulouse (1271). Philip IV, by marrying the heiress of Champagne, added that county to the domain of his successors. The accession of Philip VI in 1328 returned to the crown the vast holdings of the Valois family. Serious reversals during the Hundred Years' War reduced the domain substantially, but the crown finally made good these losses, seizing the last of Aquitaine in 1453 and the duchy of Burgundy in 1477. In 1481, the king regained the lands of the house of Anjou, including Provence, which lay outside the medieval French kingdom. The marriage of successive kings to the heiress of

Brittany finally brought that stubbornly autonomous region under royal control.

This superficial survey of the most important territorial acquisitions does not take into account the steady gains of royal jurisdiction, the acquisition of scattered rights and properties all over France, and the administrative improvements that steadily augmented royal wealth and power throughout the 13th and early 14th centuries.

John Bell Henneman, Jr.

[See also: APANAGE; CAPETIAN DYNASTY; ROYAL ADMINISTRATION AND FINANCE]

Fawtier, Robert. *The Capetian Kings of France*, trans. L. Butler and R.J. Adam. London: Macmillan, 1960.

Lot, Ferdinand, and Robert Fawtier. *Histoire des institutions françaises au moyen âge.* 3 vols. Paris: Presses Universitaires de France, 1958, Vol. 2: *Institutions royales.*

Newman, William M. *Le domaine royal sous les premiers capétiens (987–1180).* Paris: Sirey, 1937.

ROYAUMONT. The Cistercian abbey of Royaumont (Oise) was founded in 1228 by King Louis IX in fulfillment of his father's will. Although Louis VIII had stipulated a Victorine foundation, the execution of the will redirected the endowment to the Cistercians, perhaps as a result of the influence of the queen regent, Blanche of Castile. The new abbey was richly endowed by Louis and his noblemen, which permitted the rapid construction of the church, probably essentially complete by its dedication in 1236. The abbey figures prominently in narratives about King Louis and was the site for several of the king's pious deeds early in his life. After the burial in 1234 of the king's younger brother, Philip Dagobert, it also became the necropolis for Louis's own children, several of whom died in infancy.

Disaffected in 1791, the church was the victim of its historic association with the royal family. Shortly after its acquisition by the Marquis de Travannet, it was pulled down, and only the eastern corner and stairtower of the north transept survive. The conventual buildings were not demolished, however, and now function as a conference center. Of particular note among the monastic buildings is the large 13th-century latrine.

It has been suggested that the foundation of Royaumont in 1228 was inspired by Longpont, the dedication of which Louis IX and his mother had attended in 1227 on their return from the young king's coronation at Reims. Both churches have a three-story elevation with simple cylindrical supports in the arcade, but at Royaumont the triforium consisted of two pairs of trefoil arches surmounted by a trilobe and enclosed in a relieving arch. The triforium at Longpont is blind, but that at Royaumont included a passage. In spite of the differences in the design of the two elevations, the scale of the two churches was almost identical: the width of each church was about 86 feet; the height of the elevation at Longpont was 88 feet, at Royaumont 91 feet; the diameters of the cylindrical supports were also the same, 3½ feet. In each case, the width of the nave and aisles equaled the total height of the vaults, dimensions that correspond with the proportions of Cistercian churches of the 12th century, such as the abbey of Fontenay.

Caroline A. Bruzelius

[See also: LONGPONT]

Branner, Robert. *St. Louis and the Court Style in Gothic Architecture.* London: Zwemmer, 1965, pp. 31–37.

Bruzelius, Caroline. "Cistercian High Gothic: Longpont and the Architecture of the Cistercians in the Thirteenth Century." *Analecta cisterciensia* 35 (1979): 3–204, esp. 90–110.

Duclos, Henri-Louis. *Histoire de Royaumont, sa fondation par St. Louis et son influence sur la France.* 2 vols. Paris: Douniol, 1867.

Gouïn, Henry. *L'abbaye de Royaumont.* Paris: Laurens, 1932.

RURAL SOCIAL STRUCTURE. Medieval rural social structure was based on the patriarchal family unit, which was most frequently the nuclear or stem family. Occasionally, because castles and other "feudal" properties were held by groups of siblings, a more complicated family structure might be temporarily maintained. Although the patriarchal family involved obvious inequalities of power, family members generally had the same status as the head of the household. In the relatively fluid rural society of the early Middle Ages, marriage was the main means of social mobility—by marriage or concubinage, for instance, slaves became Merovingian queens. By marriage to heiresses of higher social status, knights associated themselves with ancient lineages and legitimized their power. Similarly, as unfree peasant men married free women, their children then had the free status of their mother. In such fashion, the lowest level of servile status seems to have disappeared in many regions by ca. 1000.

It was the early-medieval world, almost entirely a rural society, that was most characterized by the tripartite division into those who fight, those who pray, and those who work the land. Through the Merovingian and Carolingian eras, moreover, there was little differentiation in economic status between men and women or between a lord and his dependents: all were poor and living not far from starvation. Although there were a few independent peasants who worked their own land for subsistence, or soldier-peasants who might be called up for Carolingian military service, the rural population was made up almost entirely of peasants tied to the villa or manor and their lords, whether simple knights living off the revenues of a single estate, or more important secular lords and ladies owning many estates and moving from one to the next throughout the year, or important ecclesiastics, particularly monks and abbots. In addition, the growing religious fervor and social change after the Carolingian era gave rise to increasing numbers of religious hermits and other marginal peoples—charcoal producers, poachers, thieves, beggars, outcasts—living in the forests on the edge of the cultivated lands.

Relations between a rural lord and his peers were by military ties of feudalism or mutual defensive pacts often recorded in *convenientia* contracts. Relations between lords and peasants were basically those of lord and man, with the peasants expected to work and produce for their lords in return for military protection; historians call this rural economic organization "manorialism." Manorialism had its roots in the old Roman estate system of landlords with dependent tenant cultivators, in the emperor Diocletian's legislation that tied free peasants to the land, in the settlement of Roman and barbarian troops in territories devastated by invasion or peasant revolt, and in the commendation of free peasants to aristocrats who promised to protect them from late-imperial tax collection. In the 8th- and 9th-century polyptichs of the Carolingian church, these varying origins of the peasant population are still visible. Those documents differentiate among *liberi* (free peasants), *coloni* (free men who had been tied to the land by tax legislation), *laeti* (probably barbarian settlers), and *servi* (serfs). Serfs were descendants of slaves allowed by their Roman masters to settle on tenancies and marry. Their servile origins were reflected in the requirement that they perform several days of agricultural labor each week on the lands of their lord and in certain limitations on their freedom, in particular on the freedom to leave their holding, the right to marry outside of the lord's estate, and the right to bequeath property without interference. Often, such manors were also immune from royal control, and serfs on them were required to use their lord's rather than public courts.

Distinctions among peasants of the Carolingian era were blurred in the centuries that followed. As the power of the kings, emperors, and their officials waned, free and unfree alike became increasingly subject to the economic exploitation based on force imposed by lords of castles, particularly after the year 1000. In the name of their *bannum*, such lords introduced "new and evil customs" that effectively captured a growing share of the expanding agricultural production of this period. Such customs as requiring peasants to use their newly installed water mills or the village ovens for a fee, to contribute to upkeep of castle walls, and to allow the lord to sell his wine before their own were imposed not just on serfs belonging to a particular landlord but on all the inhabitants of the district around a castle. Payments for such new customs were often more onerous than any previously paid rents and dues, and the universal application of such exactions tended to erase earlier distinctions among peasants. Although documentation is sparse for the earlier period, by ca. 1100 most peasants were either free or unfree, some richer or poorer, but all increasingly dependent on the new castle lords.

This tendency to flatten distinctions among the peasantry does not mean that peasant status necessarily declined during this period. First of all, because agricultural production was increasing, peasants could afford higher rents. Moreover, competition for experienced agricultural laborers often increased as new villages were founded in the forested pockets of rural France, as new agricultural frontiers opened up in Spain and the German east, as the new monastic orders sought lay brothers, and as the cities beckoned as havens of freedom and craft labor. Lords who were instigators of new village foundations made concessions of liberties in order to attract settlers to their new villages, and lords who held older estates were forced to make similar concessions—to grant or sell liberties, to allow peasants to buy themselves out of servitude, or to allow peasants to create new fields and additions to their holdings in the waste adjoining the older cultivated area.

By the 12th and 13th centuries, lordship was no longer a purely rural affair. Lords themselves had also felt the attraction of towns and new frontiers and deserted the countryside. *Demesnes*, often not all that profitable, were converted into peasant holdings, labor services were commuted into payments in money or kind, and serfdom became increasingly a legal category having little effect on the economic circumstances of peasants. In the 13th century, lords in some regions, apparently faced by increasing costs and creeping inflation, tried to squeeze the last drop of profit out of the legal disabilities of serfdom by selling liberties and enfranchisements to their rich peasants or peasant villages or attempting to extort payment for legal disabilities long forgotten. Generally, however, it was the disappearance of labor services that ended the great division within the peasantry between free and unfree. Although not everyone owed the same rent, all were henceforth virtually equal inasmuch as none had to spend time working on the lord's land. The rural classes of the years after 1300 were increasingly impoverished, by famine, warfare, plague, and excessive division of property among a population growing beyond the means of European lands to support it. Yet because there were fewer to share remaining wealth, the condition of those peasants who survived the Black Death of 1348 and subsequent pandemics must have improved temporarily.

By the end of the Middle Ages, most distinctions in the rural world were economic. Rich peasants took land at farm from powerful lords for large sums and proceeded to hire laborers to work it, but there were also impoverished rural families whose names were entered on the abbey rolls of those entitled to a daily dole. In between were the masses of peasants whose economic condition varied considerably from one generation to the next, depending not so much on external economic circumstances as on bad luck, too-great fecundity (necessitating an overdivision of inheritance), or the good chance of having only one surviving heir to marry and bring property to the patrimony. After the 14th century, lords abandoned the countryside to live in cities as *rentiers* and seigneurs, as they would until the French Revolution.

Constance H. Berman

[See also: AGRICULTURE; *CONVENIENTIA;* FAMILY AND GENDER (PEASANTRY); FEUDALISM; GRANGE; POPULATION AND DEMOGRAPHY; SERFDOM/SERVITUDE/SLAVERY; *VILLENEUVE*]

Bloch, Marc. *French Rural History: An Essay in Its Basic Characteristics*, trans. Janet Sondheimer. Berkeley: University of California Press, 1966.

Duby, Georges. *Rural Economy and Country Life in the Medieval West*, trans. Cynthia Postan. Columbia: University of South Carolina Press, 1968.

———. *The Early Growth of the European Economy: Warriors and Peasants from the Seventh to the Twelfth Century*, trans. Howard B. Clarke. Ithaca: Cornell University Press, 1979.

Herlihy, David. *Medieval Households.* Cambridge: Harvard University Press, 1985.

Jordan, William C. *From Servitude to Freedom: Manumission in the Sénonais in the Thirteenth Century.* Philadelphia: University of Pennsylvania Press, 1986.

RUTEBEUF (fl. 1248–85). The Parisian Rutebeuf composed works in a greater variety of genres than any other medieval poet. Known from a dozen manuscripts, his fifty-five extant pieces illustrate the range of medieval urban poetry. Rutebeuf composed in every vernacular genre except those especially cultivated in the provincial courts of 13th-century France: chivalric epics, romances, and songs of courtly love. At a time when manuscript compilations grouped lyric, dramatic, and narrative pieces separately, Rutebeuf, like his contemporary Adam de la Halle, imposed such a vivid and coherent poetic identity on all his compositions that they were gathered as a corpus in three contemporary compilations. Unlike the vagabond Goliards or jongleurs who traveled from castle to court, Rutebeuf remained in Paris, where he wrote to please many patrons—the royal family, the university, the higher clergy, the papal legate—and to amuse a public in city streets and taverns. While the aristocratic provincial courts were attuned to the refined art of the chanson and the idealizing fantasies of Arthurian romance, Rutebeuf's heterogeneous urban public relished topical works that spoke to issues of the day, such as the Crusades and the proliferation of mendicant orders in Paris. Rutebeuf's political verse follows historical events closely and presupposes familiarity with Parisian topography, personalities, and issues. The notable variety of genres and the historical content that characterize Rutebeuf's poetry are inseparable from Paris, the city that was its essential and nurturing environment, and from the colorful figure of the poet himself.

Although no document preserves any record of Rutebeuf's life, his poems reveal much about his background, training, and relations with patrons. He may have come from the region of Champagne; his earliest polemical poem, the *Dit des Cordeliers* (1249), favors the rights of Franciscan monks in Troyes. Throughout his career, Rutebeuf composed eulogies of nobles from Champagne, although mostly in connection with his role as a Parisian propagandist of papal crusade policy, as in his *complaintes* for Count Eudes de Nevers (1266) and Count Thibaut V of Champagne (1279). Rutebeuf's *Vie de sainte Elysabel* (ca. 1271) was commissioned for Isabelle, daughter of King Louis IX and wife of Thibaut V. Rutebeuf's most prominent benefactors were members of the royal family, such as Alphonse of Poitiers, brother of Louis IX, whom he addresses in his request poem *Complainte Rutebeuf* and in his crusade piece *Dit de Pouille* (ca. 1265) and whom he eulogizes in 1271. The poet also appeals repeatedly to King Philip III the Bold to replace generous benefactors lost on the Crusades. Like the eulogies and commissioned devotional works, Rutebeuf's political poems and appeals for largesse mark his status as a skilled professional poet and his relations with patrons in the highest ecclesiastical and aristocratic circle.

Rutebeuf composed a number of comic pieces like those described in minstrel repertoires. His *Dit de l'herberie* is one of several examples of a dramatic monologue by a quack who amuses an audience with rapid enumerations of coins, exotic places, stones, and herbal remedies. All of Rutebeuf's fabliaux are known in other medieval versions: the story of the Franciscan who enrolls a girl in his monastic order (*Frère Denise*); the tale of the wife who pretends that her midnight rendezvous with the priest is a devotional exercise (*Dame qui fist trois tours autour du moutier*); the account of the bishop who gave Christian burial to a donkey who left him twenty pounds (*Testament de l'âne*). The theme of the obscene *Pet au vilain* is reused in André de la Vigne's farce, the *Meunier de qui le diable emporte l'âme en enfer* (1496).

Rutebeuf also had sufficient clerical training to read Latin and know the student's life. His *Dit de l'université* is a sympathetic account of a peasant boy come to study in Paris who soon squanders his hard-earned funds on pretty city girls. Though not a vulgarizer of philosophical and scientific concepts like his contemporary Jean de Meun, he draws on Latin sources for his saints' lives, miracles, polemical poems, and requests for largesse. In the *Dit d'Aristote*, he translates a passage from the epic *Alexandreis* by Walter of Châtillon; in *Sainte Elysabel*, he abridges a Latin *vita*; in his miracle of the *Sacristain et la femme au chevalier*, he expands an exemplum from the early 13th-century *Sermones vulgares* of the preacher Jacques de Vitry. Rutebeuf's lives of exemplary penitents combine French and Latin sources in the narrative *Sainte Marie l'Egyptienne* and the *Miracle de Théophile*, which dramatizes versions by Gautier de Coinci and Fulbert of Chartres. He even translates and glosses lines from Ovid's *Metamorphoses* in his allegorical *Voie de paradis*.

Rutebeuf's clerical training not only led him to rich literary sources, it also determined his subjects and his style. Rutebeuf's moral poems contribute to the ecclesiastical effort, inspired by the Fourth Lateran Council (1215), to instruct laypeople in religious doctrine: his *Voie de paradis* is an allegorical catechism of confession; three works, the *Etat*, *Vie*, and *Plaies du monde*, adapt the conventional estates satire of Latin preachers and moralists for a lay public. In contrast with the self-reflective mode of contemporary courtly lyric and moral verse, Rutebeuf's poetry often seeks to turn its hearers toward the outer world of history painted in dramatic moral colors.

Commissioned by supporters of the crusade policies of Louis IX and the pope, Rutebeuf's eleven crusade poems incorporate estates satire and rhetorical techniques of moral persuasion from the didactic tradition to rouse public opinion in favor of increasingly unpopular crusades against Charles of Anjou's Christian rival for the Sicilian throne (1265) and against the Muslims in Tunis (1270). As a professional pamphleteer, Rutebeuf does not express personal opinions in his poems. He advocates the differing views of the two causes he served in order to sway public opinion and encourage partisans to action; he is an ardent supporter of papal policies in his crusade verse, a fiery Gallican in his defense of university autonomy.

In his fourteen poems supporting the secular university masters against their Franciscan and Dominican rivals and the pope, Rutebeuf again recasts the motifs of didactic poetry to new, polemical ends. Dream allegories, battles of vices and virtues, animal satires, complaints attributed to the church personified—all the resources of the Latin and French satirical tradition are brought to bear on partisan concerns. Knowledge of historical circumstances is essential to the understanding of Rutebeuf's topical poems: the proliferation of mendicant orders in Paris (*Ordres de Paris*, *Chanson des ordres*, *Des béguines*); the struggle between mendicants and secular clergy for parish privileges and university chairs (*Discorde de l'université et des Jacobins*, *Des règles*, *Dit de sainte Église*, *Bataille des vices et des vertus*, *Des Jacobins*); the writings of William of Saint-Amour, banished leader of the university masters (*Dit* and *Complainte de Guillaume*). Out of this factional literature rises a new allegorical figure, Hypocrisy, which comes to overshadow earlier concern with pride and avarice and dominate moral literature of the late 13th and 14th centuries. Personified in Rutebeuf's *Du Pharisien* and *Dit d'Hypocrisie*, hypocrisy is central to Jean de Meun's character False Seeming in the *Roman de la Rose* as well as in late animal satires, such as *Renart le contrefait* and the *Livres de Fauvel*.

Polemical, pious, or entertaining in topic and nonlyric in form, Rutebeuf's poems have a style and shape that owe little to prevailing courtly modes. His characteristic form is the first-person nonmusical *dit*, a rambling, open form, most often cast in octosyllabic couplets or tercets, that accommodates all the topical themes of contemporary history that found little place in courtly song, romance, or epic. In spite of their rhetorical embroidery and rich rhymes, Rutebeuf's poems give an overall impression of artless simplicity and directness. His verses are engaging and amusing: enlivened with frequent irony, animated with proverbs, touched with realistic details. Lively, colloquial direct discourse and dialogue characterize both Rutebeuf's poems and the tableaux of his *Miracle de Théophile*. Often shaped as *complaintes*, Rutebeuf's *dits* pass easily from one subject to another via apostrophes and exclamations that are united more by appeal to emotion than by rigorous logic.

The figure of the poet himself, however, is the element that unifies Rutebeuf's works. Identified by a signature pun as *Rustebeuf qui rudement œvre* ("Rutebeuf who works crudely"), the persona of the poet is protagonist in many of his moral, political, and comic pieces: "Rutebeuf" is the pilgrim in the allegorical *Voie de paradis*; he is the character who goes to Rome in a dream vision to hear news of the election of Pope Urban IV (*Dit d'Hypocrisie*, 1261). It is in his own name that Rutebeuf accuses church prelates of caring less for the Crusades than for "good wine, good meat, and that the pepper be strong" (*Complainte*

d'Outremer, ll. 94–95). It is he who witnesses the chaste speech of Alphonse of Poitiers in his eulogy and who is called to judge the comic debate between Charlot and the barber.

Characterization of his poetic persona is most vividly developed in Rutebeuf's best-known works, his ten poems of personal misfortune. His poetic "I" is based on the conventional character type of the poor fool that figures in medieval request verse by Goliards and minstrels and later in the poetry of Eustache Deschamps and François Villon. Picturesquely personal rather than autobiographical in content, his poems of misfortune dramatize an exaggerated, grotesque self, deserted by friends, grimacing with cold and want, and martyred by marriage and a weakness for gambling. In the plaintive or ironic tones of the *Dit d'Aristote*, the *Paix de Rutebeuf*, and *De Brichemer*, the poet reminds his patrons of the virtue of largesse and prompt payment. The *Repentance Rutebeuf* gives a solemn subjective resonance to the conventional poetry of remorse found in his saints' lives and miracles. Furthermore, in his *Griesche d'hiver*, *Griesche d'été* and *Dit des ribauds de Grève*, Rutebeuf shows the reader a social world excluded from courtly song, romance, and epic, that of a homeless urban proletariat, stung by white snowflakes in winter and by black flies in summer.

Appreciatively collected by contemporaries, Rutebeuf's poetry was forgotten after his time. But in his works we discover a poetic voice that dramatizes and particularizes the subjective lyric while it speaks with satirical wit and ethical fervor about concerns of the urban world of medieval France.

Nancy F. Regalado

Rutebeuf. *Œuvres complètes de Rutebeuf*, ed. Edmond Faral and Julia Bastin. 2 vols. Paris: Picard, 1959.

———. *Œuvres complètes*, ed. and trans. Michel Zink. 2 vols. Paris: Bordas, 1989–90.

Cerquiglini, Jacqueline. "'Le clerc et le louche': Sociology of an Esthetic." *Poetics Today* 5 (1984): 479–91.

Huot, Sylvia. *From Song to Book: The Poetics of Writing in Old French Lyric and Lyrical Narrative Poetry*. Ithaca: Cornell University Press, 1987, pp. 213–19.

Regalado, Nancy Freeman. *Poetic Patterns in Rutebeuf: A Study in Noncourtly Poetic Modes of the Thirteenth Century*. New Haven: Yale University Press, 1970.

Rousse, Michel. "Le mariage Rutebeuf et la fête des fous." *Moyen âge* 88 (1982): 435–49.

Zink, Michel. "Time and Representation of the Self in Thirteenth-Century French Poetry." *Poetics Today* 5 (1984): 611–27.

———. *"La subjectivité littéraire autour du siècle de saint Louis.* Paris: Presses Universitaires de France, 1985, pp. 47–74.

SAINT ALEXIS, VIE DE. Considered a masterpiece among the early saints' lives, the *Alexis* tells the story of a young man who vows himself to God and a life of poverty. The hero flees from Rome on his wedding night, leaving his new bride behind with his father and mother. In exile, Alexis earns a reputation as a holy man but disdains the worldly attention it brings. He returns to Rome, where, unrecognized, he lives out a life of penury and degradation under a staircase of his parents' house. Not until his death do those around him realize that he was a holy man. The abnegation Alexis practices is that of an *imitator Christi*, a person who heeds Christ's injunction, as reported in the Gospels, to renounce worldly position, wealth, and family.

The Old French poem is part of a European legendary tradition of unknown origin centering upon the "Man of God." According to a near contemporary account, this nameless individual died in Edessa in Mesopotamia ca. 430. An early Greek account gave him the name Alexis and has him return to Rome to die. His feast is July 17. The story passed through Syriac, Greek, and Byzantine stages, reaching Rome in the 10th century. The French work is based on a Latin composite source and is generally thought to have been written in the mid-11th century.

Alexis is often praised for its spare beauty and formal perfection. Apparently a popular story, it survives in numerous manuscripts and in different versions. The redaction in manuscript *L* (Lamspringe, now Hildesheim) is generally considered the best. It contains 125 stanzas, each of five assonating decasyllabic lines (625 lines total). A second important manuscript, the Ashburnham, ends with stanza 110, omitting mention of the salvation of Alexis's family. Both manuscripts, derived from a common source, date from the 12th century.

Thelma S. Fenster

[See also: SAINTS' LIVES]

Paris, Gaston, and L. Pannier, eds. *La vie de saint Alexis: poème du XIe siècle et renouvellements des XIIe, XIIIe et XIVe siècles*. Paris: Franck, 1872.

Storey, Christopher, ed. *La vie de saint Alexis*. Geneva: Droz, 1968.

————. *An Annotated Bibliography and Guide to Alexis Studies*. Geneva: Droz, 1987.

Uitti, Karl D. *Story, Myth, and Celebration in Old French Narrative Poetry 1050–1200*. Princeton: Princeton University Press, 1973, pp. 3–64.

SAINT LÉGER, VIE DE. Leodegard, or Léger in French (ca. 616–678), abbot of Saint-Maixent, then bishop of Autun, was declared a martyr, primarily on political grounds, after the death in 681 of his enemy, Ebroin. By the 10th century, when the French *Vie* was composed, his cult was widespread. The 240-line strophic poem, probably from the northeast, exists in a unique 11th-century manuscript at Clermont-Ferrand, which also contains the sole copy of the *Passion du Christ*.

Thelma S. Fenster

[See also: SAINTS' LIVES]

Linskill, Joseph, ed. *Saint Léger: étude de la langue du ms. de Clermont-Ferrand, suivie d'une édition critique du texte avec commentaire et glossaire*. Paris: Droz, 1937.

SAINT PLAYS. About fifty extant plays in French and Occitan are based on the lives of the saints, ranging from a few hundred to many thousands of lines. Three main groups of saints are featured in these plays: the Apostles and other New Testament figures, especially Peter, Paul, and Mary Magdalene; well-known saints of the early church, most of them martyrs like Barbara, Margaret, and Lawrence; and the most original and interesting group, the saints of France, from the patronal St. Denis to the medieval St. Louis, canonized in 1297, and Jeanne d'Arc, already treated as sanctified in the mid-15th-century *Mystère du siège d'Orléans*. The most contemporary saint play of all was that of St. Catherine of Siena, performed in Metz in 1468, only seven years after her canonization. The text, however, has not survived.

The model for most hagiographic drama is the life of Christ. There is occasionally a nativity scene, as for St.

Geneviève, patron saint of Paris, and almost always a death scene, violent for the martyrs like St. Barbara, peaceful for the confessors like St. Martin of Tours, and edifying for all. Although the pattern of ministry, miracles, and martyrdom is established by the Gospels, the sources for the lives and especially the deaths of the saints are largely New Testament apocrypha or, more usually, the *legenda*, Latin lectionaries used in the liturgy for the relevant saint's day. Consequently, the plays exhibit much greater freedom in the treatment of the subject matter than do the biblical plays, and there is less ready-made amplification in the form of allegory, typology, and exegesis. As a result, most saint plays are fairly short, with few surpassing 10,000 lines.

A saint may have been chosen as the subject of a play because he or she was the patron of a community or a church, a trade guild or religious confraternity, or even an individual. Some plays were linked with local relics or statues, and some were performed in thanksgiving for safe delivery from pestilence or other disaster. In a number of cases, we have no explanation for a particular performance in a particular place. In the civic plays, a comparison of performance records suggests that, whereas a small community might produce a play about its patron on one or two occasions, the larger towns generally had regular productions that intermingled the shorter, and therefore cheaper, saint plays with the elaborate and expensive Passion plays. Although evidence exists for plays being put on in many parts of France, they are most common in the northern area and in the southeastern provinces of Savoy and Dauphiné.

Comedy provides an important contrast to the elevated mixture of sermons and suffering that make up many saint plays. *Diableries*, or devil scenes, are as common as in the Passion plays. There are also many instances of the introduction of a single character, a simpleton (*fou, sot*) or peasant (*vilain, rusticus*), who acts as a humorous, sometimes satirical, often obscene chorus to the action or who takes part in comic scenes of misunderstanding with messengers. Comic also are the jailers and torturers, who figure largely in the popular martyrdom plays and who work the complicated special effects for beheading, boiling in oil, or tearing apart by wild horses.

The more historical type of play features the saint preserving his or her native city from pagan invaders. The two surviving plays on St. Louis, king of France, provide interesting contrasts here. The anonymous 15th-century play stresses the king's conflict with the English, an obviously appealing subject in the aftermath of the Hundred Years' War; the early 16th-century play by Pierre Gringore lays greater emphasis on Louis's defense of the church against the German emperor Frederick. Plays like the *Mystère de saint Bernard*, on the founding of the famous hospice at the Great Saint-Bernard Pass, probably reflect the importance of travel and pilgrimage in the 15th century. Numerous scenes depict journeys by boat or on horseback and offer other touches of contemporary realism, even in the plays that purport to be set in biblical times. It is this element of personal, local, or national involvement that gives the saint plays their unique flavor and justifies treating them as a distinct dramatic genre.

Lynette R. Muir

[See also: GRINGORE, PIERRE; MIRACLE PLAYS; MYSTERY PLAYS; PASSION PLAYS; SAINTS' LIVES; THEATRE]

Muir, Lynette R. "The Saint Play in Medieval France." In *The Saint Play in Medieval Europe,* ed. Clifford Davidson. Kalamazoo: Medieval Institute, 1986.

Petit de Julleville, Louis. *Les mystères.* 2 vols. Paris: Hachette, 1880.

SAINT-AIGNAN-SUR-CHER. From the 10th century, Saint-Aignan-sur-Cher (Loir-et-Cher) was the center of an important castellany dependent on the counts of Blois. Eudes I, count of Blois (r. 976–96), constructed a castle here in the 9th century. Conflicting sources date the church of Saint-Aignan to either the 8th or 9th century, with one source suggesting the consecration of a church by monks from Saint-Martin of Tours.

In the 12th century, the church at Saint-Aignan housed a chapter of secular canons as well as a parish and was dependent on the archbishop of Bourges. The crypt mirrors the upper church, with ambulatory and three apsidal chapels, and extends one bay in length, with side aisles. Romanesque and some Gothic wall paintings survive from the last quarter of the 12th century on the upper walls and vaults of the axial and south chapels and in the main apse. With its white ground and lighter color scheme, the main apse contains an enthroned Christ who gives keys and a scroll to SS. Peter and James the Lesser, and cripples surround them. In contrast to the main apse, the frescoes elsewhere, in highly saturated colors, illustrate the life of St. Gilles, the Glory of the Lamb, the raising of Lazarus, and the life of Christ. With origins in the 13th century, the château consists mostly of 15th- and 16th-century construction; it is not open to the public.

Stacy L. Boldrick

Baylé, Maylis. "Saint-Aignan-sur-Cher." *Congrès archéologique (Blésois)* 139 (1981): 334–36.

Devailly, Guy. *Le Berry du Xe siècle au milieu de XIIIe: étude politique, religieuse, sociale, et économique.* Paris: Mouton, 1973.

SAINT-BENOÎT-SUR-LOIRE. Founded at Fleury (Loiret) in 651, the abbey of Saint-Benoît-sur-Loire followed the *Rule* of St. Benedict of Nursia. Between 690 and 707, the remains of Benedict were brought from the Italian monastery of Monte Cassino, then in ruins, to Saint-Benoît, underscoring the growing dedication to Benedict and his *Rule* in France. An elaborate account of the search for and return with Benedict's remains is given in Adrevald of Fleury's *Historia translationis sancti Benedicti.* Adrevald tells of an expedition from Saint-Benoît to Monte Cassino being joined by citizens of Le Mans seeking the remains of St. Scholastica. The monks from Saint-Benoît arrive at Monte Cassino first,

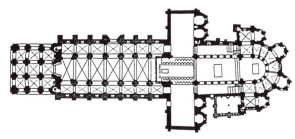

Saint-Benoît-sur-Loire (Loiret), plan of church. After Rousseau.

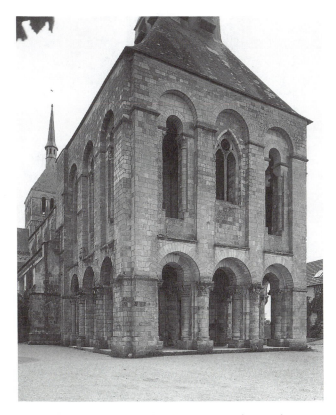

Saint-Benoît-sur-Loire, abbey church, west tower. *Photograph courtesy of Whitney S. Stoddard.*

while the Le Mans group stops in Rome. Led to the tomb of Benedict and Scholastica by miraculous signs, the monks rush back with the remains of both saints. The Le Mans group soon arrives at Saint-Benoît and demands Scholastica's remains, which are given to them. Adrevald's account of the *translatio* of the relics of these two widely venerated saints became a model for the literary description of many later translations, or thefts, of relics of saints in the medieval period.

Saint-Benoît was an important intellectual center with scriptorium throughout the early Middle Ages, especially under Abbot Abbo of Fleury (r. 988–1004). Successive parts of the abbey church span the Romanesque through Early Gothic periods. The western-tower porch was constructed during the abbacy of Gauzlin (r. 1004–30). The

transept and choir, begun under Abbot Guillaume (r. 1067–80), were complete by 1108. The late 12th-century nave was dedicated in 1218.

The two-story porch has nine vaulted compartments. The foliate and historiated column capitals and sculpted plaques on the north wall were carved by Umbertus and his followers. The rib-vaulted nave has seven bays with single groin-vaulted aisles. The transept with two chapels on the eastern side of each arm has a square tower over the crossing. A tunnel-vaulted choir terminates in a faux-transept with single chapels and an ambulatory with two radiating chapels. The choir and apse have a blind-arcaded triforium and clerestory whose carved capitals reflect later Romanesque sculpture. An Early Gothic portal dated ca. 1200 is on the north side of the nave. Above six jamb figures is a tympanum with Christ enthroned surrounded by the four Evangelists and the translation of St. Benedict's relics on the lintel. This monument attests to the abbey's religious and intellectual importance during the central Middle Ages.

Karen Gould

[See also: ABBO OF FLEURY; MONASTICISM]

Geary, Patrick. *Furta Sacra: Thefts of Relics in the Central Middle Ages.* 2nd ed. Princeton: Princeton University Press, 1990, pp. 118–22.

Vergnolle, Éliane. *Saint-Benoît-sur-Loire et la sculpture du XIe siècle.* Paris: Picard, 1985.

Ward, Benedicta. *Miracles and the Medieval Mind: Theory, Record, and Event, 1000–1215.* Philadelphia: University of Pennsylvania Press, 1982.

SAINT-CHEF. Abundant documentation reveals the long history of the monastery of Saint-Chef (Isère), well known today for its wall paintings. According to the letters of St. Adon, archbishop of Vienne (r. 860–75), a local saint, Théodore, founded in the 6th century an abbey church dedicated to the Virgin. After his death in 575, the church was rededicated to both Théodore and the Virgin. By 837, conventual buildings had been built, and in 890–91 Bishop Barnoin de Vienne restored the abbey church after Vikings had destroyed the cloister. At about the same time, the Vikings brought monks from Montier-en-Duc here to Saint-Théodore. By the end of the 9th century or the beginning of the 10th, the monks returned to Montier-en-Duc and the abbey fell into a state of neglect.

In the second half of the 10th century, archbishops Thibaud de Vienne (r. 952–1000) and Leodegar (r. 1030–70) restored the church. Sometime in the 14th or 15th century, the name of the monastery was changed from Saint-Théodore to Saint-Chef. At the beginning of the 15th century, a fire severely damaged the abbey, and in 1423 a new cloister was built. Later fires brought reconstruction in the 19th century.

Of the abbey church, the *petit appareil* (small-stone) masonry of the seven-bay nave with side aisles has Norman single-light windows and a wooden roof. Regular supports end at the transept and east end of ashlar masonry, where a larger compound pier leads to the large apse with two smaller apsidal chapels to either side. Each arm of the transept contains one of the apsidal chapels and is barrel-vaulted.

The apses and conventual chapel of SS. Michael and George in the upper story of the north transept of the abbey church contain remains of a comprehensive scheme of mid-11th to mid-12th-century decoration. (Overpainting makes dating the work problematic.) Christ in Majesty and standing figures of saints occupy the apse, and the conventual chapel carries an enthroned Christ in the center of a high domical vault with four sides. Surrounded by four triangular compartments holding the Virgin, Apostles, angels, saints, and a holy city, Christ occupies the apex of the Heavenly Jerusalem.

Stacy L. Boldrick

[See also: ROMANESQUE ART]

Cahansky, Nurith. *Die romanischen Wandmalereien der ehemaligen Abteikirche Saint Chef (Dauphine).* Bern: Franke, 1966.

Oursel, Raymond. "L'architecture de l'abbatiale de Saint-Chef." *Bulletin monumental* 119 (1962): 49–70.

Varille, M., and D. Loisin. *L'abbaye de Saint Chef en Dauphiné.* Lyon: Masson, 1929.

SAINT-DENIS. The abbey church of Saint-Denis, just north of Paris, one of the oldest and most prestigious monastic foundations in northern France, marks the final resting place of St. Denis (Dionysius), Apostle of Gaul and first bishop of Paris, who died during the persecutions of Diocletian. A church was built here at the initiative of St. Geneviève before 500, but associations with royalty are said to have begun only with King Dagobert (r. 629–39). The legend is that Dagobert, fleeing the wrath of his father, sought refuge in the church and fell asleep on the tomb of St. Denis. His vengeful father tried several times to enter the church but each time was prevented from so doing. In gratitude, Dagobert built a new church that was miraculously consecrated by Christ, Peter, Paul, and Denis and his two companions the night before its dedication.

Dagobert's basilica was decorated with marble columns and capitals, some of which survive and most of which were reused when Fulrad rebuilt and enlarged the church, beginning ca. 750, with the patronage of the Carolingian dynasty. When Pepin III the Short died in 768, he was buried, according to his wishes, face down outside the west doors to atone for the sins of his father, Charles Martel. Charlemagne, Pepin's son, is said to have paid for a new west structure that extended the consecrated space of the church over his father's burial site. The Carolingian kings followed the example of Pepin, who had not only enriched the church with lavish donations but also employed its abbot, Fulrad, for diplomatic missions, and frequently included the abbots among their trusted advisers. Thus, it is no surprise that Fulrad's church, as revealed in Crosby's excavations, was a splendid structure composed of a nine-bay nave with aisles, a projecting tran-

Saint-Denis (Seine-Saint-Denis), nave isometric. After Violet-le-Duc.

sept, and a two-level apse with *confessio* around the burial sites of Denis and his two companions. The east end was surrounded by a crypt chapel of three parallel aisles (ca. 830) during the abbacy of Hilduin.

The 12th-century abbacy of Suger (r. 1122–51), the next great age of the abbey, is also marked by close ties with royalty, in this case the Capetians Louis VI and Louis VII. This is perhaps the best-known moment in the history of the abbey, thanks to the preservation of Suger's history of his abbacy and of his building efforts, culminating with the consecration of the enlarged church in 1144. From Suger's writings, we learn not only of the two architectural additions, the nave extension and western bays and the two-level chevet, but also of their embellishment with sculpture and bronze doors, with stained glass and bejeweled liturgical vessels intended to complement, even to surpass, such venerated treasures as the Cross of St. Éloi (7th c.), the so-called throne of Dagobert (9th c.), and the now lost altar frontal of Charles the Bald depicted by the Master of St. Gilles.

Saint-Denis, abbey church, west façade. *Photograph: Clarence Ward Collection. Courtesy of Oberlin College.*

Saint-Denis, abbey church, chevet. *Photograph by J. Herschman.*

Saint-Denis, abbey church, crypt. *Photograph by S. McK. Crosby.*

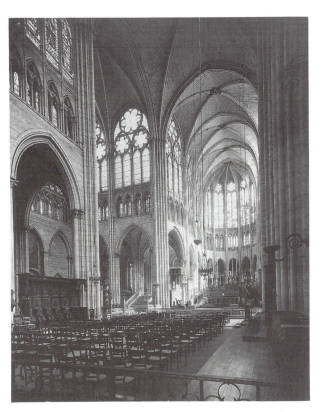

Saint-Denis, abbey church, nave. *Photograph: Clarence Ward, Collection. Courtesy of Oberlin College.*

The architectural additions of Abbot Suger include a westwork three bays wide and two deep, as well as the four bays necessary to join the old nave and a two-level chevet. The lower level consists of ambulatory and chapels wrapped around both the old apse and Hilduin's chapel to create a level platform for the upper ambulatory and seven radiating chapels. These eastern additions mark a significant change in medieval French art and gave rise to a new style that is still (erroneously) called "Gothic." The upper level of the new chevet of Saint-Denis, dedicated with pomp and ceremony in 1144, is universally recognized as the first example of the new style. In reality, both levels of the chevet, crypt as well as upper level, mark the beginning of a new conception of the organization of architectural space that differs profoundly from the Romanesque style.

Equally important in the history of Gothic art are the three west-façade portals, mutilated in the 18th century; the Porte de Valois, a 12th-century portal now installed in the 13th-century north transept; the remaining stained-glass windows; and the lavish liturgical objects commissioned by Abbot Suger. From his writings and such later documents as survive, lost works like the bronze doors, the Great Cross, and the Tomb of the Martyrs can be at least partly reconstructed by scholars.

Although Crosby's excavations revealed that Abbot Suger ultimately intended to rebuild even the 8th-century nave, this was not accomplished until the 13th century. Beginning on the north side in 1231, the church was progressively enlarged to its present width and height. The expansion of the transept created a new space that by its lateral extension almost seemed to include Abbot Suger's chevet, rather than setting it apart. The process was completed by rebuilding the upper stories and heightening them to match the new height of the transept. In plan, this church has an eight-bay nave with the monks' choir in the first two, which is why the transept has double-aisle bays on the west side. Work on this church, one of the finest examples of the Rayonnant style, continued almost to the end of the century.

It was this 13th-century church that became the burial site of the kings of France as a result of the efforts of Louis IX. Kings had been buried at Saint-Denis since the time of Dagobert and probably long before that—the intact tomb of Queen Arnegund, mother of Chilperic, dates to the mid-6th century, and the cemetery has yielded still earlier nonroyal burials. Prior to the 13th century, none of the royal tombs was indicated by more than an engraved floor slab. At the instigation of Louis IX, all of the royal tombs were opened and the bodies transferred to new, raised sarcophagi topped by carved effigies. The new tombs were grouped by dynasties along the sides of the crossing, except for such patrons as Charles the Bald, who as lay abbot was buried in the monks' choir; Dagobert, who was buried on the south side between the two altars; Philip II Augustus, Louis VIII, and Louis IX (until his canonization), who were buried in the center of the crossing.

The importance of Saint-Denis continued into the early 14th century, when the abbey became the fountainhead in collecting, writing, and disseminating such works as the *Grandes chroniques de France* and the *Vie de saint Denis*.

The privileged position of the abbey in relation to royalty produced such splendid gifts as the Virgin and Child, now in the Louvre, given by Queen Jeanne d'Évreux.

All of these works suffered enormous damage and destruction, especially in the aftermath of the Revolution and in the early, misguided attempts at preservation and restoration. Modern scholarship nonetheless continues to piece together the evidence to give an understanding of the complexities that distinguish the works of art associated with this prestigious foundation, just as recent excavations have revealed other churches on the abbey site.

William W. Clark

[See also: DENIS; GOTHIC ARCHITECTURE; GOTHIC ART; *GRANDES CHRONIQUES DE FRANCE*; HILDUIN OF SAINT-DENIS; HISTORIOGRAPHY; PIERRE DE MONTREUIL; SUGER]

Blum, Pamela Z. *Early Gothic Saint-Denis: Restorations and Survivals*. Berkeley: University of California Press, 1992.

Bouttier, Michel. "La construction de l'abbatiale de Saint-Denis au XIIIe siècle." *Bulletin monumental* 145 (1987): 357–86.

Brown, Elizabeth A.R. "La généalogie capétienne dans l'historiographie du moyen âge." In *Religion et culture autour de l'an mil: royaume capétien et Lotharingie*, ed. Dominique Igona-Prat and Jean-Charles Picard. Paris: Picard, 1990, pp. 199–214.

Bruzelius, Caroline A. *The Thirteenth Century Church at Saint-Denis*. New Haven: Yale University Press, 1985.

Bur, Michel. *Suger: abbé de Saint-Denis, régent de France*. Paris: Perrin, 1991.

Clark, William W., and Charles M. Radding. "Abélard et le bâtisseur de Saint-Denis: études parallèles d'histoire des disciplines." *Annales: Économies, Sociétés, Civilisations* 43 (1988): 1263–90.

Cothren, Michael W. "Suger's Stained Glass Makers and Their Workshop at Saint-Denis." In *Paris: Center of Artistic Enlightenment*, ed. George Mauner. University Park: Pennsylvania State University Press, 1988, pp. 46–75.

Crosby, Sumner McKnight. *The Royal Abbey of Saint-Denis from Its Beginnings to the Death of Suger, 475–1151*, ed. Pamela Z. Blum. New Haven: Yale University Press, 1987.

Foley, Edward B. *The First Ordinary of the Royal Abbey of St. Denis in France*. Fribourg: Fribourg University Press, 1990.

Gerson, Paula L., ed. *Abbot Suger and Saint-Denis*. New York: Metropolitan Museum, 1986.

Grodecki, Louis. *Les vitraux de Saint-Denis I*. Paris: Arts et Métiers, 1976.

Hedeman, Anne D. *The Royal Image*. Berkeley: University of California Press, 1991.

Kidson, Peter. "Panofsky, Suger and St. Denis." *Journal of the Warburg and Courtauld Institutes* 50 (1987): 1–17.

Panofsky, Erwin. *Abbot Suger on the Abbey Church of St. Denis and Its Art Treasures*. Princeton: Princeton University Press, 1979.

Romero, Anne-Marie. *Saint-Denis: Emerging Powers*. Paris: CNRS, 1992.

Rudolph, Conrad. *Artistic Change at St. Denis: Abbot Suger's Program and the Early Twelfth-Century Controversy over Art*. Princeton: Princeton University Press, 1990.

SAINT-GELAYS, OCTAVIEN DE (1468–1502). Writer and translator. Born into an important family in Cognac, Saint-Gelays studied law in Paris, was introduced to the royal court, and in 1494 became bishop of Angoulême. His extensive literary production was as varied as his life. During the reign of Charles VIII, he was notable as a poet of circumstance, inspired among other events by the death of the king, but he also wrote a *Débat de l'homme de cour et de l'homme des champs*. His most important work, the *Séjour d'Honneur* (1490–94) is a combination of verse (8,794 lines) and prose reflecting a remarkable array of literary traditions, from Ovid and Jean de Meun to Boccaccio and Charles d'Orléans, including contemporary history and autobiographical elements, as the poet makes his way from the bower of Vain Hope to the House of Understanding, passing through the Séjour d'Honneur (the court). Its popularity is shown by four printed editions before 1526.

Equally successful were his translations: the *Ystoire de Eurialus et Lucresse* of Aeneas Sylvius Piccolomini in verse (1493), Terence (ca. 1500), Virgil's *Aeneid* (published in 1509), and especially Ovid's *Heroides* (1496), one of the great successes of the period. For his brief thirty-four years, his accomplishment is extraordinary.

Charity Cannon Willard

[See also: GRANDS RHÉTORIQUEURS; TRANSLATION]

Saint-Gelays, Octavien de. *Le séjour d'Honneur*, ed. Joseph A. James. Chapel Hill: University of North Carolina Press, 1977.

Cigada, Sergio. "Introduzione alla poesia di Octavien de Saint-Gelais." *Aevum* 39 (1965): 244–65.

Guy, Henri. "Octavien de Saint-Gelays: *Le séjour d'Honneur*." *Revue d'histoire littéraire de la France* 15 (1908): 193–321.

SAINT-GÉNÉROUX. This small church, dating from the 9th–10th centuries, belonged to the priory of Saint-Jouin-de-Marnes and was dedicated (ca. 682) to St. Généroux,

Saint-Généroux (Deux-Sèvres), east end. *Photograph courtesy of Whitney S. Stoddard.*

abbot of Saint-Jouin-de-Marnes. With the exception of its façade, Saint-Généroux offers an almost complete example of pre-Romanesque architecture. Although subjected to brutal restoration, the church has not lost all its interest. In the sanctuary, a central apse and two smaller ones precede long bays on the right and display intercalated and reticulated stonework. They are linked to one another by doubled bays and by the lateral passages of a large room with three arcades surmounted by an unusual clerestory. Originally a rectangular room, the nave was subdivided in the 13th century into three spaces; the division consists of a double series of arcades in broken arches on rectangular pillars.

E. Kay Harris

Crozet, René. "La restauration de l'église de Saint-Généroux." *Bulletin de la Société Historique et Scientifique des Deux-Sèvres* 40 (1961).

SAINT-GENIS-DES-FONTAINES. The small church of Saint-Genis (Pyrénées-Orientales) is noted for its carved marble lintel above the entrance. The rectangular slab, dated

Saint-Genis-des-Fontaines (Pyrénées-Orientales), lintel of west door. *Photograph courtesy of Whitney S. Stoddard.*

1020–21 by inscription, depicts Christ in a mandorla supported by two angels with three Apostles standing under horseshoe arches to each side. Decorative details and the apocalyptic subject suggest Spanish influence. The flat, linear carving and compressed figural proportions reflect lack of sculptural expertise. Although the lintel was incorporated in a 12th-century remodeling of the church, it is significant as a precursor of Romanesque architectural sculpture.

Karen Gould

Durlait, Marcel. "Les premiers essais de decoration de façades en Roussillon au XIe siècle." *Gazette des beaux arts* 67 (1966): 65–78.

SAINT-GERMAIN-EN-LAYE. In 1124, Louis VI built a fortress overlooking the Seine on the hillside of Saint-Germain (Yvelines), on the site of the present château. The keep, often attributed to Charles V, belongs to this first phase of construction. Between 1230 and 1238, Louis IX added to the castle and had its Sainte-Chapelle built. Burned by Edward, the Black Prince, during the Hundred Years' War, the fortress was restored by Charles V ca. 1368. In 1539, Francis I razed the entire castle with the exception of the its keep and the chapel built by St. Louis. Perhaps the work of Pierre de Montreuil, this Sainte-Chapelle recalls the style of the apsidal chapels of the cathedral of Reims. The nave, spanned by slender columns and illuminated by tall windows (without their stained glass, unfortunately), is 80 feet long and 33 feet wide. The western façade, including its rose window, was covered over by Francis I with a symmetrically angled turret. The carved keystones of the vaulting provide one of the most interesting ornamental details. In these stones, one seems to recognize the heads of St. Louis; his wife, Marguerite de Provence; his mother, Blanche of Castile; and his brothers.

E. Kay Harris

Poisson, Georges. *Évocation du Grand Paris, la banlieue nord-ouest.* Paris: Minuit, 1956.

SAINT-GERMER-DE-FLY. The abbey church of Saint-Germer-de-Fly (Oise), undertaken ca. 1150, represents an attempt to combine the ambulatory and radiating-chapel plan from Senlis or Saint-Denis with the compound-pier tradition of the Vexin. The four-story elevation here consists of aisles, groin-vaulted gallery, rectangular slots opening into the gallery roof space, and clerestory windows with a narrow, corbeled ledge below them, suggesting a regional interpretation of the Anglo-Norman clerestory wall passage. The galleries of the chevet and nave are connected by a wall passage around the transepts. The elaborate west end, of which only the east wall remains, was a western transept resembling that built slightly later at Noyon. Saint-Germer has suffered disasters over the centuries and is in poor condition, but most of the architectural decoration is intact and confirms the dating to the third and last quarters of the 12th century. The beautiful abbot's chapel added beyond the axial radiating chapel was clearly patterned after the upper chapel of the Sainte-Chapelle in Paris.

William W. Clark

Saint-Germer-de-Fly (Oise), chevet section. After Pessin and Besnard.

[**See also:** NOYON; PARIS; SAINT-DENIS; SENLIS]

Besnard, André. *L'église de Saint-Germer de Fly (Oise) et sa Sainte-Chapelle.* Paris: Lechavalier, 1913.

Héliot, Pierre. "Remarques sur l'abbatiale de Saint-Germer et sur les blocs de façade du XIIe siècle." *Bulletin monumental* 114 (1956): 81–114.

Henriet, Jacques. "Un édifice de la première génération gothique: l'abbatial de Saint-Germer-de-Fly." *Bulletin monumental* 143 (1985): 93–142.

Lohrmann, Dietrich. "Saint-Germer-de-Fly und das anglo-normannische Reich." *Francia* 1 (1973): 193–256.

Régnier, Louis. "Excursion à Gournay-en-Bray et Saint-Germer." *Annuaire normand* (1903): 67–110.

SAINT-GILLES. The house of Saint-Gilles, or the "Raimondin" family, was associated with the county of Toulouse for centuries. The first member of the family to govern Toulouse was Fredelon, who received the title of *marchio* from Charles the Bald in 849. His son Odo recovered Toulouse and the Rouergue from the count of Auvergne in 885 and established the dynasty, dividing the two counties between his sons, a division that lasted until 1065.

By 924, the family was claiming supremacy over all Septimania and, for a few decades, over the duchy of Aquitaine as well. Guilhem Taillefer (961–1037) extended the family's interests to the Rhône when he married Emma, one of the heiresses to Provence. By the middle of the 11th century, the counts had built a castle at Saint-Gilles on the Petit Rhône. The port quickly became a major trading center, and from the time of Guilhem's grandson Raymond IV the heads of the family were often called "counts of

Saint-Gilles," since the Rhône Valley was their main source of wealth and the home of their most important followers.

After Raymond IV conquered the Rouergue (1065), he took the title of marquis of Provence and invented that of duke of Narbonne. One of the leaders of the First Crusade, he ended his life as count of Tripoli. His niece Philippa married Duke Guilhelm IX of Aquitaine, allowing her granddaughter Eleanor of Aquitaine and her successive husbands, Louis VII of France and Henry II of England, to lay claim to Toulouse.

Count Raymond V (r. 1148–94) contracted marriage alliances that extended his power to the Alps in the east and put pressure on the count of Barcelona in Occitania. His alliances made and broken with various powers made him for a while the most powerful lord in Occitania but eventually mired him in endless unsuccessful warfare. In the last decades of his life, the town of Toulouse became a virtually independent city-state. In 1177, hoping to find an additional ally in the church, he brought the attention of the Cistercians to the spread of heresy in his lands, inviting armed intervention that presaged the Albigensian Crusade to come.

His son, Raymond VI, reaped the consequences. In 1208, he was accused of plotting the death of Peter of Castelnau, the papal legate. Raymond adroitly directed against the Trencavel family the crusade that was sent to punish him, but in 1211 Simon de Montfort turned his army against Toulouse and gained possession of the city after his victory at Muret in 1213. The Fourth Lateran Council (1215) made Simon count of Toulouse, took Avignon and the Comtat Venaissin for the papacy, and left only a portion of Provence for the future Raymond VII. When Louis VIII took over leadership of the crusade in 1226, the family's fate was sealed. The Treaty of Meaux-Paris (1229) provided that Raymond's daughter would marry Louis's son Alphonse of Poitiers, giving all political claims in Occitania and the inheritance of Toulouse to the Capetians. Raymond VII, the last count of Saint-Gilles, died in 1249.

Frederic L. Cheyette

[**See also:** ALBIGENSIAN CRUSADE; LANGUEDOC; ROUERGUE; TOULOUSE; TRENCAVEL]

SAINT-GILLES CYCLE. *Aiol* (10,983 lines; pre-1173) and *Élie de Saint-Gilles* (2,671 lines; early 13th c.), which constitute the Saint-Gilles epic cycle, both sing of a poor knight struggling to make his way in society. *Aiol*, whose methodical composition suggests a single author, is distinguished by an aristocratic outlook opposed to the emergence of the enterprising bourgeoisie. *Élie*, a true adventure romance by a different poet, combines contemporary chivalric preoccupations with folklore and fantasy.

Bernard Guidot

Normand, Jacques, and Gaston Raynaud, eds. *Aiol*. Paris: Didot, 1877.
Raynaud, Gaston, ed. *Élie de Saint-Gille*. Paris: Didot, 1879.

SAINT-GILLES-DU-GARD. The largest exterior ensemble of Romanesque sculpture is the façade of Saint-Gilles-du-Gard (Gard). The superstructure of the façade was destroyed during the religious wars in the 16th century. Because of the presence of many Roman monuments, Provençal Romanesque architecture and sculpture both exhibit strong Roman influences. The design of the Saint-Gilles portals resembles both Roman triumphal arches and procenia of theaters.

The three portals of Saint-Gilles depict major events in the life of Christ. Twelve larger-than-life Apostles flank the central portal. The Virgin and Child adored by the Magi occupy the left tympanum, and the Entry into Jerusalem decorates the frieze and lintel. The upper frieze to the left of the central portal contains such scenes as Christ Cleansing the Temple and the Raising of Lazarus. The central tympanum, now modern, may have depicted the Last Judgment above the damaged Last Supper on the lintel. The frieze continues to the right, with Christ being led before Pilate, undergoing the Flagellation, and Carrying the Cross. The final scenes of Christ's Passion are located on the right portal; the Crucifixion is in the tympanum, and the Holy Women buying perfume and the Angel appearing to the Holy Women after the Resurrection are on the lintel.

The iconographic programming of the façade was controlled by the clergy. The depiction of the Crucifixion, a rare subject to appear in a tympanum, reflects the strong stand taken by the clergy against a heretical sect led by Peter de Bruys, who had denied the validity of the Mass and the need for church structures. To emphasize his feelings, he and colleagues stole the wooden crosses from Saint-Gilles, and on Good Friday they roasted pork in front of the abbey over a fire made of the crosses. A few days later, Peter and his companions were burned as heretics on the same spot. This event, which took place ca. 1136, did not

Saint-Gilles-du-Gard (Gard), west façade. *Photograph courtesy of Whitney S. Stoddard.*

end this heretical movement; St. Bernard spent summers preaching against it in the 1140s.

Much evidence in the construction of the portal leads to the conclusion that the design changed as work progressed. Blocks of limestone were inserted under the small marble columns flanking the side portals and under the monumental figures across the entire façade, resulting in the raising of all three portals. Five sculptors were responsible for most of the façade sculpture: Brunus (Matthew [signed Brunus], Bartholomew, James Major, and Paul); Thomas Master (Thomas, James the Less, Peter, and bases of central portal); Soft Master (two Apostles and left-portal Virgin and Child of tympanum, Preparation and Entry into Jerusalem); Hard Master (two Apostles, right portal, Crucifixion, and lintel); Michael Master (Angel Michael, Archangel, and parts of left and right portal). Soft Master, Hard Master, and Michael Master divided up the carving of the upper frieze of the central portal.

The four Apostles by Brunus exhibit a massiveness and an anatomical articulation of the body that result from the influence of Roman and early Christian sculpture. In spite of this classical impact, the Apostles are placed either between pilasters or under friezes so that they remain part of the wall (Romanesque), not added to the wall (Roman).

There is no agreement about the dating of the façade: dates from the late 11th century to the early 13th have been proposed. Based on historical, architectural, iconographical, and stylistic evidence, as well as relationships between Saint-Gilles and dated monuments outside Provence, the accumulated evidence seems to point to the 1140s as the most logical date.

The 16th century witnessed the destruction of the superstructure of Saint-Gilles. The large Cluniac choir with ambulatory and radiating chapels exists only as a fragment. The nave capitals, bases, and sections of the northern part of the choir have preserved their 12th-century sculpture.

The crypt of Saint-Gilles, begun in 1116, was constructed to protect the tomb of St. Gilles and to facilitate access for pilgrims to his grave. Because of the slope of the site from northeast to southwest, the crypt is three aisles wide in the two western bays and two aisles in the four eastern bays. A groin vault covers the central bay, containing the tomb. The crypt has a western extension under the central portal. On this extension and on the western wall of the crypt are burial inscriptions, dated ca. 1129. A study of the articulation of the piers and the design of the ribs reveals that the nave of the crypt was built from west to east, with the groin vault over St. Gilles's tomb constructed first. The Saint-Gilles crypt is an impressive Romanesque statement, and its powerful ribbed vaults, a Gothic structural system, are meant to crown the low, rectangular spaces and support the church above, not to light the interior.

Whitney S. Stoddard

[See also: MEDITERRANEAN TRADE]

Hamann, Richard. *Die Abteikirche von St. Gilles und ihre Nachfolge.* 3 vols. Berlin: Akademie, 1955.
Horn, Walter. *Die Fassade van St. Gilles.* Hamburg: Evert, 1937.
Lassalle, Victor. "L'influence antique dans l'art roman provençal." *Revue archéologique Narbonnaise* 2 (1970): 73–74, 69–79, 90–92, 99–102.
Schapiro, Meyer. "New Documents on St. Gilles." *Art Bulletin* 17 (1935): 415–31.
Stoddard, Whitney S. *The Façade of Saint-Gilles-du-Gard.* Middletown: Wesleyan University Press, 1973.

SAINT-GUILHEM-LE-DÉSERT. Founded in 804 as the Benedictine abbey of Gellone by St. Guilhem d'Aquitaine, the count of Toulouse who was the hero of the Guillaume d'Orange epic cyle, the monastery was renamed later for its founder. Thanks to the relics of the saintly Guilhem, his place in epic history, and the monastery's location along the pilgrimage route to Santiago de Compostela, Saint-Guilhem prospered and reached its apogee in the 11th and 12th centuries, when the present Romanesque abbey church, the third on the site, was built. The church was built in three phases: the nave and side aisles were finished ca. 1075, in time for the church's consecration in 1076; the transept and the chevet, with its three apsidal chapels, were constructed between 1077 and the end of the century; the narthex was built in the second half of the 12th century. A bell tower was added in the 15th century. The exterior is decorated with Lombard bands. The sober four-bay nave, 59 feet high but only 20 feet wide, is covered by plain barrel vaulting supported by wide doublures that rest on pilasters extending directly to the floor, emphasizing the sense of verticality. The interior is lit by large windows above each of the bays. Some remains of the cloister, which originally had galleries on two levels, flank the south side of the church; others can be found at the Cloisters in New York City.

William W. Kibler

Alzieu, Gérard, and Robert Saint-Jean. *Saint-Guilhem le Désert.* La Pierre-qui-vire: Zodiaque, 1973.
Lugand, Jacques. *Languedoc roman: le Languedoc méditerranéen.* La Pierre-qui-vire: Zodiaque, 1985.

SAINT-JOUIN-DE-MARNES. Saint-Jouin-de-Marnes (Deux-Sèvres), renowned for the relics of the 4th-century hermit Jovinus, was one of the oldest abbeys of the Poitou. The transept of the present church, crowned by an octagonal dome on squinches, and the first bay of the choir date from the late 11th century. The complex Angevin vaults of the seven eastern bays of the long nave are 13th-century, as are those of the choir, ambulatory, and three radiating chapels. The south transept, facing the keep of Moncontour, retains part of the 14th-century fortifications; to the north are the remains of the Gothic cloister.

In the high gable of the west façade, Christ sits in majesty before a cross potent, flanked by angels. Thirty small figures converge in two groups toward the Virgin beneath his feet. Other sculptures frame the windows of the three bays of the twin-turreted façade. Although enigmatic in detail, the general theme of both sculpture and architecture is one of triumph.

Jean M. French

Labande-Mailfert, Yvonne. *Poitou roman.* La Pierre-qui-vire: Zodiaque, 1957.

Maillard, Elisa. "La façade de l'église romane de Saint-Jouin-de-Marnes en Poitou." *Gazette des beaux-arts* 5th ser. 9 (1924): 137–50.

Oursel, Raymond. *Haut-Poitou roman.* La Pierre-qui-vire: Zodiaque, 1975.

Rhein, A. "Saint-Jouin-de-Marnes." *Congrès archéologique (Angers et Saumur)* 77 (1910): 108–19.

SAINT-LÉONARD-DE-NOBLAT. The picturesque town of Saint-Léonard-de-Noblat (Haute Vienne), retaining some medieval houses, recalls the 6th-century hermit and savior of prisoners whose cult spread throughout the medieval West. The collegiate church presents complex problems for the architectural historian due to the many discrepancies in plan, supports, and vaulting. The walls of the nave and transept are 11th-century; the nave supports and vaulting, the domes of the crossing and transept arms, and the impressive choir were modified or rebuilt in the 12th century; the façade is Gothic. The problems of chronology have been compounded by later restorations. Nevertheless, the high and ample choir, with its elegant columns, ambulatory and seven radiating chapels, the "limousin" belfry (restored), and the 11th-century domed "Sepulcher" attest to the importance of Saint-Léonard as a pilgrimage site.

Jean M. French

[See also: PILGRIMAGE]

Fage, René. "Saint-Léonard." *Congrès archéologique (Limoges et Brive)* 84 (1921): 89–116.

Koster, Kurt. *Pilgerzeichen und Pilgermuscheln von mittelalterlichen Santiagostrassen: Saint Léonard, Rocamadour, Saint-Gilles, Santiago de Compostela.* Neumünster: Wachholtz, 1983.

Maury, Jean, et al. *Limousin roman.* La Pierre-qui-vire: Zodiaque, 1959.

Saint-Léonard et les chemins de saint Jacques en Limousin: XIe–XVIIIe siècles: exposition du 15 juin au 18 août, 1985. Saint-Léonard-de-Noblat: L'Association, 1985.

SAINT-LEU-D'ESSERENT. The Cluniac priory church of Saint-Leu d'Esserent (Oise) has a mid-12th-century narthex and south tower. The lower story of the narthex is an open porch in the Norman manner; the second story is a vaulted tribune gallery. Abutting the east side of the narthex are traces of the earlier church, which has been excavated. In plan, the church has a nave and aisles, no transept, and a chevet consisting of two flanking towers, an ambulatory, and five radiating chapels. The shallow plans of the chapels perhaps reflect the dramatic site of the church on the bluffs above the Oise. The ambulatory and radiating chapels were built in the later 1150s or early 1160s, with the upper parts of the chevet following a decade or so later. The three-story elevation of the nave shows influence from Paris, as do the flying buttresses added around the whole of the church at the time of the nave construction late in the 12th century. One interesting feature is the double-

Saint-Leu-d'Esserant (Oise), mid-12th-century façade. *Photograph courtesy of Whitney S. Stoddard.*

story axial radiating chapel. More may have been intended, since the interior-wall design suggests a gallery elevation, but no others were constructed.

William W. Clark

Durvin, Pierre. *Le millénaire d'un sanctuaire: Saint-Leu d'Esserent.* Amiens: Centre Régional de Recherche et de Documentation Pédagogiques, 1975.

———, and Jean Hubert. "Les fouilles de l'église de Saint-Leu d'Esserent." *Bulletin de la Société Nationale des Antiquaires de France* (1959): 70–73.

Fossard, Albert. *Le prieuré de Saint-Leu d'Esserent: abbaye bénédictine de Cluny.* Paris: Imprimerie du Réveil, 1934.

Lefèvre-Pontalis, Eugène. "Saint-Leu-d'Esserent." *Congrès archéologique (Beauvais)* 72 (1905): 121–28.

Paquet, Jean-Pierre. "La restauration de Saint-Leu d'Esserent: problèmes de stabilité." *Monuments historiques de la France* 1 (1955): 9–19.

Racinet, Philippe. "Construction, reconstruction et aménagement du prieuré clunisien de Saint-Leu-d'Esserent." *Groupe d'Études des Monuments et Œuvres d'Art du Beauvaisis* 13 (1982): 17–25.

SAINT-LOUP-DE-NAUD. The village of Saint-Loup-de-Naud (Seine-et-Marne) stands on a ridge not far from the fortified medieval town of Provins. Of medieval buildings, the rural village retains only a parish church with a formidable history. Some type of ecclesiastical building dedicated to St. Loup existed even before the foundation of the Benedictine monastery ca. 980.

Founded as a dependency of the abbey of Saint-Pierre-le-Vif in Sens, Saint-Loup maintained a close relationship with its mother house. In 1161, Archbishop Hugues de Tourcy brought the body of the patron saint to Saint-Loup from the abbey of Sainte-Colombe, much to that abbey's dismay. The theft of the relics reinforced the strong cult of St. Loup and initiated a 200-year-long controversy over the rightful ownership of the relics. Little documentary evidence survives about the church in the 13th and 14th centuries, but the structure suffered much in the Hundred Years' War and Wars of Religion.

Open on three sides, the single-bay, rib-vaulted porch leads into the six-bay, 12th-century nave, initially barrel-vaulted but partially restored with rib vaults in the first few bays. Irregular alternating supports carry an arcade and blocked windows. The slightly projecting transept arms stand to either side of the crossing tower and barrel-vaulted east end.

Recent scholarship suggests that the portal complex is probably entirely medieval and dates to the mid- to late-12th century. The sculpted portal is protected by a porch tower with round-headed windows and a simple gable. Similar to the royal portal at Chartres, the program includes a tympanum with Christ in Majesty and Evangelist symbols, the Virgin and Apostles on the lintel, a trumeau statue of St. Loup, and figures on piers and jambs. Maines suggests that the composition is a composite integration of sculpture from Sens designed for another location (*spolia*) and sculpture designed for the portal of St. Loup.

Original frescoes were damaged and overly restored in the 19th century, although Salet suggests that the figure of St. Savinien, bishop of Sens, escaped restoration and dates to the middle of the 12th century. Other medieval remains inside the church include a 14th-century stone Virgin in the right apsidal chapel and a 12th-century font.

Stacy L. Boldrick

Droulers, Charles. *Saint-Loup-de-Naud.* Provins: n.p., 1934.

Lefèvre-Pontalis, Eugène. "Église de Saint-Loup-de-Naud." *Congrès archéologique (Troyes et Provins)* 69 (1902): 82–85.

Maines, Clark. *The Western Portals of Saint-Loup-de-Naud.* New York: Garland, 1979.

Salet, Francis. "Saint-Loup-de-Naud." *Bulletin monumental* 92 (1933): 129–69.

SAINT-MICHEL-DE-CUXA. The present church of the Benedictine abbey of Saint-Michel-de-Cuxa (Pyrénées-Orientales), founded in 878 at the foot of Mount Canigou in Roussillon, combines the pre-Romanesque church of Abbot Garin (dedicated 974), characterized by distinctive horseshoe arches, and the "first Romanesque" additions of Abbot Oliba (r. 1009–40): rectangular ambulatory with three chapels, two magnificent Lombard bell towers (one remains), and the centralized Trinity chapel (demolished 16th c.) above the unusual crypt of the Virgin of the Manger (circular chapel with a vault of rough stone supported by a massive central column).

Two major sculptural programs (elements of both later dispersed) were undertaken in the 12th century: a large cloister (ca. 1130–40), with vigorously carved capitals, and a richly ornamented marble tribune (ca. 1140–45). Two galleries of the cloister have been recreated at Cuxa; reliefs from the tribune have been mounted around the north portal. Other cloister capitals, as well as elements from the tribune, form the nucleus of the Cloisters collection of the Metropolitan Museum of Art in New York City. Contemporaneous with the tribune is the recently recovered commemorative relief of Abbot Gregory (d. 1146), founder of the Cuxa cloister. Both Cuxa ateliers were influential throughout the Roussillon (Serrabone ensemble, cloister of Espira de l'Agli, portals of Villefranche-de-Conflent and Brouilla) and beyond the Pyrénées as well.

Jean M. French

Cazes, Daniel, and Marcel Durliat. "Découverte de l'effigie de l'abbé Grégoire créateur du cloître de Saint-Michel de Cuxa." *Bulletin monumental* 145 (1987): 7–14.

Durliat, Marcel. *La sculpture romane en Roussillon.* 3rd ed. Perpignan: Tramontane, 1959, Vol. 1.

———. *Roussillon roman.* 3rd ed. La Pierre-qui-vire: Zodiaque, 1975.

Ponsich, Pierre. "Chronologie et typologie des cloîtres romans roussillonais." *Cahiers de Saint-Michel de Cuxa* 7 (1976): 75–97.

Simon, David. "Romanesque Sculpture in North American Collections. XXIV. The Metropolitan Museum of Art. Part IV: Pyrenees." *Gesta* 25 (1986): 245–76.

SAINT-NECTAIRE. Built of local volcanic stone that harmonizes with the rugged landscape, Saint-Nectaire (Puy-de-Dôme) belongs to a distinctive group of Auvergnat Romanesque churches. Contributing to its special character are the picturesque setting, the retention of the original westwork, the substitution of columns for the characteristic nave piers, and the richness of its sculptural ensemble. Striking are the sense of monumentality, despite its relatively modest dimensions, and the purity of the interior volumes (no additions or restorations). The towers of the heavily weathered façade are modern, as is the octagonal crossing tower (copied from Saint-Saturnin). The celebrated historiated capitals are the most important in the Auvergne. Treasures include the 12th-century Notre-Dame du Mont-Cornadore and the bust of St. Baudime, a masterpiece of Limoges workmanship.

Jean M. French

[See also: ISSOIRE]

Craplet, Bernard. *Auvergne romane.* La Pierre-qui-vire: Zodiaque, 1962.

Deshoulières, François. *Congrès archéologique (Clermont-Ferrand)* 87 (1924): 265–86.

Fayolle, le Marquis de. "Le trésor de l'église de Saint-Nectaire." *Congrès archéologique (Clermont-Ferrand)* 62 (1895): 292–306.

Ranquet, Henri du. "L'église de Saint-Nectaire." *Congrès archéologique (Clermont-Ferrand)* 62 (1895): 239–71.

Swiechowski, Zygmunt. *Sculpture romane d'Auvergne.* Clermont-Ferrand: Bussac, 1973.

SAINT-OMER. Saint-Omer (Pas-de-Calais) has its origins in the Merovingian villa of Sithiu, a rural domain conferred upon St. Omer, the missionary bishop of Thérouanne, by one of his converts ca. 650. There, on the River Aa surrounded by marshland, St. Omer and his followers, monks from Luxeuil, built a monastery dedicated to St. Peter, later known as Saint-Bertin, destined to become the largest and most powerful in the region. In 663, St. Omer built the church of Sainte-Marie, later Notre-Dame, at the highest point of Sithiu and gave it to the monastery, requesting that he be buried there.

The surprising transformation of the rural, monastic Sithiu of the Carolingian period into the bustling Flemish market town known as Saint-Omer (*villa Sancti Audomari*) has played a major role in the debate over the origins of medieval towns. By 1042, the church of Sainte-Marie, which had been fortified against the last Viking attack in 891, was flanked on the one side by the *castellum* of the counts of Flanders, seigneurs of the region from 892, and on the other by a marketplace and a parish church. The early communal charter, granted by Count William Clito in 1127, is believed to confirm privileges that the burghers already enjoyed.

With Saint-Omer linked to the channel port of Gravelines by the canalization of the Aa, local merchants dominated the Anglo-Flemish wool trade in the 12th century, and the town became a major center for the production of cloth, as well as an important market for grain, wine, and fish. Urban prosperity continued under the Capetians, as Prince Louis (later Louis VIII) inherited Saint-Omer, along with the Artois, from his mother, Isabella of Hainaut, in 1190. Reclaimed by Flanders in 1200, Saint-Omer became part of the French crown lands in 1212, ruled by the counts of Artois from 1237.

The town came to be governed by an increasingly repressive merchant elite, which led to workers' revolts in 1280 and 1306. In the 14th century, Saint-Omer was devastated by the plague and war. At the boundary of Flanders and Artois, Saint-Omer remained loyal to the king of France during the Franco-Flemish War (1297–1305) and the Hundred Years' War. In 1384, Philip the Bold, duke of Burgundy, became count of Flanders and Artois through marriage, and Saint-Omer enjoyed another period of prosperity, in spite of the decline in the cloth industry, as part of the Burgundian state.

The church of Sainte-Marie, founded by St. Omer in 663, belonged to the monks of Saint-Bertin until Abbot Fridugisus (r. 820–34) replaced the monks with canons. Later known as Notre-Dame, this church became a cathedral in 1559, after the destruction of Thérouanne. It is now a parish church. The present Gothic building replaces a Romanesque church, under construction in 1052, of similar dimensions. The new Gothic east end was begun between 1191 and 1207. By ca. 1225, the choir, ambulatory, radiating chapels, and detached octagonal tower were complete. The original transept was completed by 1263, but it was extended by two bays on the south in 1375–89 and two bays on the north in 1449–72. The nave and aisles date from ca. 1400–44. The chapels flanking the north aisle were undertaken ca. 1379–1403; those on the south, from 1378 to the beginning of the 16th century.

The 13th-century east end is an important Flemish example of the Gothic style also found at Saint-Yved at Braine and typified by a three-story elevation with relatively short clerestory, diagonal chapels placed at the intersection of choir and transept, and an exterior clerestory passage or loggia. At Saint-Omer, these features appear along with a tall triforium typical of Flanders and triplet clerestory windows known from the cathedrals of Arras and Cambrai.

Also dating from the 13th century is the poorly preserved sculptural decoration of the main south-transept portal. Reassembled in the 14th century, this decoration (ca. 1250–75) includes a Last Judgment tympanum and socle reliefs of the life of St. Omer. The cenotaph of St. Omer (ca. 1250), now in the nave, was originally in the ambulatory. Other significant works of sculpture preserved in the interior of Notre-Dame are the monumental Last Judgment group (ca. 1230) from the south-transept gable of the cathedral of Thérouanne and an early 13th-century Sedes Sapientiae from the chapel of Notre-Dame-des-Miracles, Saint-Omer.

The entire east end of Notre-Dame, including the transept, was covered with an elaborate incised stone pavement encrusted with colored cement, completed in 1263, depicting religious, secular, and decorative subjects of which only fragments remain.

The monastery of Saint-Bertin, the major landholder in the region during the Merovingian and Carolingian periods, fell under the domination of the counts of Flanders in 892. Under the counts, who frequently served as lay abbots, Saint-Bertin became the center of Flemish historiography and one of the necropolises of the house of Flanders. The monastery was reformed by Gérard de Brogne in 944, by a pupil of Richard of Saint-Vanne in 1021, and by Cluny in 1099.

Excavations undertaken in 1831 and 1845 revealed the foundations of two earlier churches beneath the present ruins of the Gothic building. These are the 8th- and 9th-century church of Saint-Martin, in which St. Bertin was buried (ca. 700), which replaced St. Peter's as the main abbey church by the 10th century, and the Romanesque church begun ca. 1045, dedicated in 1105, and repaired after a fire in 1152.

The Gothic abbey church was begun between 1311 and 1326. Almost finished in 1350, the choir was rebuilt from 1396 to 1429. The transept and nave date from ca. 1420 to ca. 1473. The single-tower west façade, typical for the region and serving as a model for Notre-Dame, was built between 1431 and ca. 1500. The church was elegant but conservative in style, with only the west façade and tower expressing the Flamboyant Gothic of the 15th century. It was sold to speculators in 1799, and all that remains are the ruins of the west façade and tower, the north transept, and aisles of the nave.

Rosemary Argent

[See also: BRAINE; GOTHIC ARCHITECTURE; HUNDRED YEARS' WAR; LOUIS VIII; PHILIP III THE BOLD; WOOL TRADE]

Derville, Alain, ed. *Histoire de Saint-Omer.* Lille: Presses Universitaires de Lille, 1981.
Giry, Arthur. *Histoire de la ville de Saint-Omer et de ses institutions jusqu'au XIVe siècle.* Paris: Vieweg, 1877.
Héliot, Pierre. *Les églises du moyen âge dans le Pas-de-Calais.* 2 vols. Arras: n.p., 1951–53.
Pas, Justin de, and Pierre Héliot. "Saint-Omer." *Congrès archéologique (Amiens)* 99 (1936): 475–545.

SAINT-QUENTIN. As the Roman city Augusta Veromanduorum, Saint-Quentin (Aisne), was an important crossroads and commercial center. Its present name is derived from the missionary St. Caius Quintinus, beheaded here in 287. His remains are preserved in the 11th-century crypt beneath the choir of the collegial church of Saint-Quentin. This complex Gothic structure (13th–15th c.) is built on an unusual double-transept plan; one was rebuilt in 1350, the other in the 15th century. The church features a spacious nave with three-story elevation, a choir with double ambulatory, and a labyrinth set in the floor (1495). The south portal (Porche Lamoureux) is Flamboyant. The Late Gothic town hall (14th–15th c.) is constructed in the Flemish civic style.

William W. Kibler/William W. Clark

Héliot, Pierre. "Chronologie de la basilique de Saint-Quentin." *Bulletin monumental* 117 (1951): 7–50.
———. *La basilique de Saint-Quentin.* Paris: Picard, 1967.

SAINT-RIQUIER. A Merovingian abbey dedicated to St. Riquier, a hermit-saint converted in the reign of Dagobert, was founded ca. 645 at Centula (Somme). Among several medieval churches built here, the Carolingian and Gothic structures are especially important.

The Carolingian abbey church was built ca. 790 under Abbot Angilbert, a pupil of Alcuin and member of the inner circle of Charlemagne's court. Engravings made after a drawing of the church in an 11th-century manuscript show a six-bay nave with single aisles, transepts at east and west, and a projecting semicircular apse. Its multiple towers and massive westwork, which incorporated atrium, narthex, and western transept with vaulted chapel, formed significant precedents for Carolingian and Romanesque architecture.

The present Gothic church was begun in the second half of the 13th century but completed and rebuilt in the

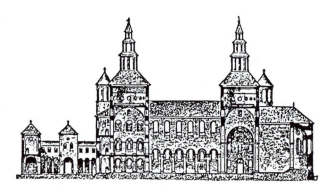

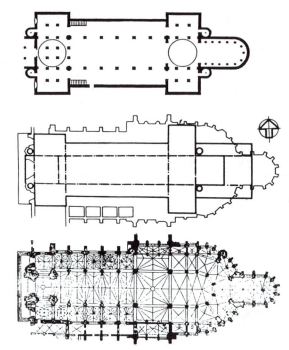

Saint-Riquier at Centula (Somme). Bottom to top: present church, excavations tracing Carolingian church, restored plan of Carolingian church, restored long section of Carolingian church. After Durand, Bernard, Heitz, and Effman.

late 15th and 16th. The spacious plan of a nave with six bays, single aisles, slightly projecting transept, choir, and ambulatory with nine chapels, as well as parts of the transept, date from the 13th century. The two-story elevation and multipartite rib vaults reflect the late Flamboyant Gothic style, as does the west façade, with central tower and screenlike sculptural decoration.

Karen Gould/E. Ann Matter

Conant, Kenneth John. *Carolingian and Romanesque Architecture, 800–1200.* 2nd ed. Harmondsworth: Penguin, 1978, pp. 43–46.
Durand, Georges. "Saint-Riquier." *Congrès archéologique (Amiens)* 99 (1936): 96–124.
Hénocque, Jules. *Histoire de l'abbaye et de la ville de Saint-Riquier.* 3 vols. Amiens: Douillet, 1880–88.

Parsons, David. "The Pre-Romanesque Church of Saint-Riquier: The Documentary Evidence." *Journal of the British Archaeological Association* 130 (1977): 21–51.

SAINT-SARDOS. Saint-Sardos (Lot-et-Garonne) in the Agenais was a priory of the abbey of Sarlat. In December 1322, the Parlement de Paris authorized the conversion of this priory into a fortified *bastide* to be held jointly by the abbey and the French crown. The plan was opposed by the Gascon lord of Montpézat, who destroyed the place on October 16, 1323, and hanged a royal officer. The action precipitated a brief Anglo-French war because Charles IV, already impatient over Edward II's delay in rendering homage for Guyenne, believed that the incident at Saint-Sardos had the tacit support of Ralph Basset, the English seneschal of Gascony. The "war of Saint-Sardos" was halted by a truce late in 1324 and ended by a treaty the following summer.

John Bell Henneman, Jr.

[See also: GASCONY]

Chaplais, Pierre. *The War of Saint-Sardos (1323–1325): Gascon Correspondence and Diplomatic Documents.* London: Royal Historical Society, 1954.

SAINT-SAVIN-SUR-GARTEMPE. From its position on the River Gartempe, the abbey church of Saint-Savin dominates the skyline with its well-preserved Romanesque exterior. Founded ca. 800 by Abbot Badilon of Marmoutier, the abbey was named for the 5th-century martyr St. Savinus, interred nearby. Enlarged by Louis the Pious, who placed it under the care of Benedict of Aniane, Saint-Savin became a center of monastic reform from the 9th to the 11th century, as it reestablished observance of the Benedictine *Rule* there and in other houses. The community of Saint-Savin suffered repeated sackings during the Hundred Years' War and Wars of Religion. Today, the 11th-century abbey church is a parish church, and monastic buildings house municipal offices.

No medieval documentary evidence on the building survives, but scholarship places most construction in the late 11th century, with painting following from ca. 1095 to 1115. The abbey church has a barrel-vaulted nave with groin-vaulted side aisles and columnar supports with carved capitals. A gallery in the west tower opens toward the nave, and below the choir with apsidal chapels is a barrel-vaulted crypt.

Although wall painting in the transepts and choir is fragmentary, extensive paintings survive in the west gallery, the nave, the crypt, and the porch. The subject of the murals in the west gallery is Christ's Passion and Resurrection, with the Entombment occupying a central position over the west window. The wall and the roof carry figures of saints, and elaborate ornamentation resides in the borders and dado. In the nave, despite much restoration, columnar piers painted to resemble marble illustrate the practice of applying paint to architectural members to

Saint-Savin-sur-Gartempe, abbey church. *Photograph courtesy of Whitney S. Stoddard.*

heighten the decorative effect and to project the idea of wealth. Above, the vaulting carries thirty-six scenes representing an Old Testament cycle. From the Creation of Adam and Eve to the stories of Noah, Abraham, Joseph, and Moses, the scenes are arranged in four tiers that extend longitudinally along the nave ceiling, and the spandrels contain fragments of prophet figures. The narrative meanders, possibly due to artists working around incomplete sections in the east end. In addition to figural work, medallions and ornament cover one of the western transverse vaults. In the crypt, the entire wall surface sports longitudinal tiers of scenes from the legends of SS. Savinus and Cyprian. On the east wall, symbols of the Evangelists surround an enthroned Christ. The porch contains apocalyptic scenes: Christ in Majesty above the door, with angels bearing instruments of the Passion below. Divided into

Saint-Savin-sur-Gartempe, nave. *Photograph courtesy of Whitney S. Stoddard.*

three sections, the barrel vaults carry six scenes from Revelation.

Stacy L. Boldrick

[See also: ROMANESQUE ART]

Dubourg-Noves, Pierre. "Aux origines de l'architecture de Saint-Savin." *Bulletin de la Société Nationale des Antiquaires de France* (1984): 197–208.
Maillard, *L'église de Saint-Savin-sur-Gartempe.* Paris: Laurens, 1927.
Yoshikawa, Itsuji. *L'Apocalypse de Saint Savin.* Paris: Éditions d'Art et d'Histoire, 1939.

SAINT-SULPICE-DE-FAVIÈRES. Saint-Sulpice (Essonne) is a pilgrimage church located in a small village south of Paris. Large in relation to the community around it, the church was built to honor the relics of St. Sulpice, bishop of Bourges (d. ca. 647), who resuscitated a young child of the region. His feast is celebrated the first Sunday in September. When the chapel commemorating the saint became too small, a new sanctuary was constructed beginning ca. 1180. Parts of this structure, which survive as the "Chapelle des Miracles" off the north side of the present church, preserve an ancient well, perhaps of pre-Christian origins, the *sinopia* for wall paintings of the 14th century, and niches that may originally have contained relics.

A new church was begun at the site ca. 1245–50. Consisting of six bays and a polygonal apse, the new building was designed in the fashionable Rayonnant style that prevailed in Paris under Louis IX. The elevation has three stories, with passageways at the triforium level and on the exterior of the clerestory. Characterized by superimposed screens of wall penetrated by the wall passages, the tracery is cut in thin elements, thus giving the chevet the brittle grace and delicacy typical of Rayonnant style. Certain elements recall the Rayonnant parts of Meaux cathedral, as well as the Sainte-Chapelle in Paris and Saint-Denis.

The church retains some of its medieval decoration. Most striking are the 13th-century windows in the chapel at the east end of the south aisle and a battered but handsome Gothic portal with St. Sulpice on the trumeau.

Caroline A. Bruzelius

[See also: GOTHIC ARCHITECTURE]

Branner, Robert. *Saint Louis and the Court Style in Gothic Architecture.* London: Zwemmer, 1965, pp. 74–75.
Sjöberg, Yves. "Saint-Sulpice-de-Favières." *Congrès archéologique (Île-de-France)* 103 (1944): 246–64.

SAINT-THIBAULT-EN-AUXOIS. Site of an ancient priory, the little town of Saint-Thibault (Côte-d'Or) boasts one of the most graceful examples of Burgundian Gothic architecture. Built through the generosity of Duke Robert II and his wife, Agnès de France, daughter of Louis IX, to house the relics of St. Thibault, who died here in 1247, the church was begun in 1297. The nave crumbled in the 17th century, but the surviving choir, apsidal chapel, and sculpted portal are of rare beauty. The tympanum is dedicated to the Virgin, surrounded in the arches by the Wise and Foolish Virgins. Five full-sized statues in the portal, remarkable for their expression, represent St. Thibault, Duke Robert II, his son Hugues V, the duchess Agnès, and Bishop Hugues d'Arcy of Autun. A 14th-century altarpiece within is dedicated to the life of St. Thibault.

William W. Kibler/William W. Clark

Freigang, Christian, and Peter Kurmann. "L'église de l'ancien prieuré de Saint-Thibault-en-Auxois, sa chronologie, ses restaurations, sa place dans l'architecture gothique." *Congrès archéologique (Auxois-Châtillonnais)* 144 (1986): 271–90.
Gillerman, Dorothy. "The Portal of Saint-Thibault-en-Auxois: A Problem of Thirteenth Century Burgundian Patronage and Founder Imagery." *Art Bulletin* 68 (1986): 567–80.

SAINT-VICTOR, ABBEY AND SCHOOL OF. Established in 1108 by William of Champeaux when he resigned as archdeacon of Paris and retired from teaching in the cathedral school, this community of regular canons who adopted the *Rule* of St. Augustine became one of the preeminent religious communities of Paris in the 12th century. Generously supported as a royal abbey by the king, associated with ecclesiastical reform, in the forefront of theological developments, and home to a distinguished series of canons who contributed to religious and intellectual life, Saint-Victor left an indelible mark on the medieval church.

Although Abélard suggested that William had left the schools of Paris because Abélard bested him in debate, a more accurate interpretation associates William's move with other instances of the decision by a cleric, or group of clerics, to reform a cathedral chapter or to found a community of regular canons. When William withdrew from the life of the cathedral chapter and schools, he moved to a chapel dedicated to St. Victor located just outside the walls of Paris on the left bank of the Seine. He gathered there a small group of students and others. In 1113, William went to Châlons as bishop. In the same year, Louis VI made a significant gift of property and income to William's nascent community and school, now described by the king as the community of regular canons that he intended to install in the church of Saint-Victor at Paris. In the same year, the community elected its first abbot, Gilduin, who led the community astutely and guided it to a leading place in French ecclesiastical life.

Construction of adequate buildings for the abbey began in the second decade of the 12th century. The necrology of the abbey indicates that one Hugh, canon of Halberstadt and uncle of Hugh of Saint-Victor, joined the community at Paris and contributed to the building of the church. Royal documents also show that Louis VI made major gifts toward the erection of the church and cloister. The 12th-century buildings were pulled down in the 16th century, and Francis I built a new church for the canons. That church lasted until the 19th century, when, following the breakup of the Victorine order in the French Revolution, the buildings were destroyed to make way for a modern metro station. Unfortunately, no detailed descriptions of the church and other buildings exist; the layout of the altars and some other details have been determined, however. Before its destruction in the 19th century, the church was praised as having one of the grandest collections of medieval stained glass in Paris.

In the 12th century, the abbey school attracted students from all of Europe and was for several decades open to students from outside the abbey. The intellectual traditions of the abbey school took shape under the leadership of Hugh of Saint-Victor, one of the major exegetes, theologians, and mystics of the 12th century. Andrew of Saint-Victor pursued Hugh's emphasis on the literal sense of Scripture, and Richard of Saint-Victor developed the Victorine mystical tradition. Adam of Saint-Victor was the greatest of the 12th-century sequence writers, and the Victorine sequence repertory became in the late 12th century a magnificent theological and liturgical construction. Godefroi and Achard of Saint-Victor continued the earlier combination of theological, philosophical, and contemplative emphases; Walter of Saint-Victor represented a different spirit with his attack on Peter Lombard and other scholastic theologians. In the 13th century, the Victorine school showed little of the vigor and creativeness that marked it in the 12th, but the abbey continued to be a center for dedicated religious life, while the canons functioned especially as confessors for the students of the schools, later the University, of Paris. The medieval library of the abbey survives fairly intact today in the Bibliothèque Nationale, Paris.

Grover A. Zinn

[See also: ACHARD OF SAINT-VICTOR; ADAM OF SAINT-VICTOR; GILDUIN OF SAINT-VICTOR; GODEFROI OF SAINT-VICTOR; HUGH OF SAINT-VICTOR; MYSTICISM; REGULAR CANONS; RICHARD OF SAINT-VICTOR; SCHOOLS, MONASTIC; THEOLOGY; WALTER OF SAINT-VICTOR; WILLIAM OF CHAMPEAUX]

Bonnard, Fourier. *Histoire de l'abbaye royale et de l'ordre des chanoines réguliers de Saint-Victor de Paris.* 2 vols. Paris: Savaete, 1905–07.

Jocqué, Luc, and Ludo Millis, eds. *Liber ordinis Sancti Victoris Parisiensis.* CCCM 61. Turnhout: Brepols, 1984.

Longère, Jean, ed. *L'abbaye parisienne de Saint-Victor au moyen âge.* Turnhout: Brepols, 1991.

Ouy, Gilbert, et al. *Le catalogue de la bibliothèque de l'abbaye de Saint-Victor de Paris de Claude de Grandrue 1514.* Paris: CNRS, 1983.

SAINT-WANDRILLE. One of a number of medieval foundations located on the right bank of the Seine, the Benedictine abbey of Saint-Wandrille remains distinct from the group as an active, surviving monastery. Founded by St. Wandrille (d. 688) in 649, and sacked by the Vikings in the mid-9th century, Saint-Wandrille, also known as Fontenelle, was rebuilt and restored after 966 by Abbot Maynard. A prosperous monastery in the Middle Ages, Saint-Wandrille was suppressed at the Revolution and fell into disrepair, only to be revived after 1931.

Ruins of the medieval abbey church reveal several building campaigns. Most of the building, including the two-bay transepts aligned with the side aisles of the nave, and radiating chapels (alternating with polygonal and rectangular chapels), was built between 1255 and 1288. The seven-bay nave with side aisles and regular compound piers was not completed until the 14th century.

Unlike the church, many of the conventual buildings survive. The 11th- and 12th-century refectory has large round-headed windows and blind arcading, and the 14th-century cloister has intriguing bits of architectural sculpture: the eastern wall holds a standing Virgin and Child (14th c.), the vault boss depicts a king with what may be Wisdom and Folly, and over the cloister entrance the badly damaged tympanum features the Coronation of the Virgin, with bishops and abbots in the voussoirs.

North of the abbey, the chapel of Saint-Saturnin retains its early 11th-century pre-Romanesque plan, rectangular with a trefoil-shaped east end. At the crossing, fantastic carved creatures inhabit the impost capitals.

Stacy L. Boldrick

Aubert, M. Marcel. "Saint Wandrille." *Congrès archéologique (Rouen)* 89 (1926): 550–72.

Musset, Lucien. *Normandie romane.* 2 vols. La Pierre-qui-vire: Zodiaque, 1974.

SAINTE EULALIE, SÉQUENCE DE. A composition in twenty-nine lines commemorating the passion of Eulalia of Mérida, in Spain, a 4th-century martyr. The heroine, refusing to abjure Christianity, is decapitated by the Romans. Her soul ascends to Heaven in the form of a dove. Composed ca. 878–82 in northeast France, *Eulalie* is the earliest surviving saint's life in the vernacular.

Thelma S. Fenster

[See also: SAINTS' LIVES; SEQUENCE (EARLY)]

Aspland, Clifford W., ed. "Sequence of Saint Eulalia." In *A Medieval French Reader*. Oxford: Oxford University Press, 1979, pp. 4–6.
Wagner, Robert Leon. *Textes d'étude*. Geneva: Droz, 1964.

SAINTE FOY, CHANSON DE. A melody for this Occitan saint's life, composed ca. 1060 in the Cerdagne/Roussillon region (between Narbonne and the Pyrénées), is preserved with the text in a single manuscript (University of Leiden, Cod. Vossianus Lat., in Octavo, No. 60, ca. 1100). With 593 octosyllabic lines in fifty-five rhymed laisses, the *Chanson* has great linguistic and literary importance as one of the earliest surviving narratives in the Langue d'oc, and the first rhymed poem in the vernacular in France.

The opening lines name oral and written sources: first, "a Latin book" read "under a pine-tree"; second, a song with a melody "fine for dancing," a "Spanish story," and a "French style"; and third, a written "Passion." The narrator's references to himself singing and to the audience listening give immediacy to the song.

He recounts Fides's comfortable early life at Agen, her choice of poverty and piety, then her eloquent refusal to worship Roman gods. Broiled alive and decapitated, with angels attending, her remains give eyesight to the blind and speech to the mute. Her pagan persecutors end by destroying themselves.

Amelia E. Van Vleck

[See also: SAINTS' LIVES]

Hoepffner, Ernest, and Prosper Alfaric, eds. and trans. *La chanson de sainte Foy*. Paris: Les Belles Lettres, 1926. [Facsimile of manuscript, critical edition, introduction, modern French translation.]
Zaal, Johannes W.B. *"A lei francesca" (Sainte Foy, v. 20): étude sur les chansons de saints gallo-romanes du XIe siècle*. Leiden: Brill, 1962.

SAINTES. An important center in Roman times and capital of the Gaulish Santones, Saintes (Charente-Maritime) was a bishopric from the 3rd century. It flourished under the dukes of Aquitaine and passed, with that duchy, to England. Louis IX won a victory over England here in 1242, and in the Treaty of Saintes (1259) Henry III rescinded his claim to Normandy. The town passed to English hands again under the Treaty of Brétigny (1360) but in 1371 was reclaimed by Bertrand du Guesclin.

Little remains of the original late 12th-century cathedral of Saint-Pierre. Under the direction of three successive bishops (1426–1503), this church was reconstructed in the Flamboyant Gothic style. Owing to the devastations during the Wars of Religion, it underwent further (and unfortunate) restorations in the 17th and 18th centuries. The building has a polygonal apse and a long choir with an ambulatory and radiating chapels. The transept follows the original Romanesque foundations; the nave is short, and additional chapels line the south side of the building. At the western entrance to Saint-Pierre is an unusually large bell-tower porch. The arched molding around the great portal contains figures of angels, musicians, doctors of the church, saints, and prophets.

The Cluniac priory church of Saint-Eutrope (dedicated 1096), built over the remains of an early Christian church, was a recommended stopping place for travelers en route to the pilgrimage church of Santiago de Compostela. The building, divided into upper and lower sections, was designed to accommodate visitors to the tomb of the city's first bishop, housed in the lower church or crypt. The crypt retains its original form. The wide and squat proportions of the aisles, apse, ambulatory, and radiating chapels convey a sense of weight and massiveness. In the upper church, part of the ambulatory and apse were reconstructed in the 15th century in Flamboyant Gothic style; however, the Romanesque character can still be found in the choir and transept. The columns in the upper church are surmounted by lions, griffins, tritons, acrobatic figures, and biblical subjects. In the last years of the 15th century, Louis XI funded the construction of a great bell tower on the north arm of the transept. The nave was demolished in 1803, and the original choir now serves this purpose.

Additional medieval buildings in Saintes include the Benedictine Abbaye aux Dames (11th c. with 15th-c. additions); the remains of a 14th-century Gothic cloister; the church of Saint-Pallais, which combines Romanesque and Gothic elements; and the Chapelle des Jacobins (1446), distinguished by an immense Flamboyant Gothic window.

Nina Rowe

Crozet, René. "Saint-Eutrope de Saintes," "L'abbaye-aux-Dames de Saintes," and "Ancienne cathédrale Saint-Pierre à Saintes." *Congrès archéologique (La Rochelle)* 114 (1956): 97–125.
Grenier, Albert. *Manuel d'archéologie gallo-romaine*. Paris: Picard, 1958, p. 650.

SAINTES-MARIES-DE-LA-MER. Originally a small pilgrimage church housing the relics of St. Hippolytus (first mentioned mid-6th c.), Saintes-Maries-de-la-Mer (Bouches-du-Rhône), under its original name, Notre-Dame-de-Radeau, became a priory of the Benedictine abbey at Montmajour (1078). The high altar is dedicated to Mary Cleophas, the sister of the Virgin, and Mary Salome, the mother of five Apostles. Tradition holds that these two Marys, along with their maid Sarah, Mary Magdalene, St. Martha, and St. Lazarus landed at this spot ca. A.D. 40, having fled from persecution in the Holy Land. A new

Saintes-Mairies-de-la-Mer (Bouches-du-Rhône), 12th-century nave. *Photograph courtesy of Whitney S. Stoddard.*

Aubert, Marcel. *L'art roman en France.* Paris: Flammarion, 1961, pp. xi, 401, 416–17.

Benoît, Fernand. "Église des Saintes-Maries-de-la-Mer." *Bulletin monumental* 95 (1936): 145–80.

Chaillan, Marius. *Les Saintes-Maries-de-la-Mer.* Aix: Dragon; Marseille: Tacussel, 1926.

SAINTS, CULT OF. The veneration of those people deemed to be saints lay at the heart of the practice of late-antique and medieval Christianity. Saints were "holy people" (*sancti, -ae*) who had lived a life of heroic virtue and had posthumously been judged by God to be worthy of entrance to the Kingdom of Heaven. In theory, all who resided in the divine court were saints, but in practice Christian churches accorded a relatively small number of people the title of saint and public veneration. The first Christians to be so honored were martyrs, who had died for giving witness to the faith during the Roman persecutions. With the official acceptance of Christianity, ascetics—and, still later, bishops, teachers, and others—came to be considered saints under the rubrics of "confessor" and "doctor," that is, those who preached or were learned in the faith.

A person could not become a saint in isolation: he or she had first to be accepted as an embodiment of holiness by a community of Christians and then recognized by ecclesiastical authority. During the Middle Ages, there was no single canon of saints universally observed in western Christendom. Indeed, the canon differed widely from region to region and even from period to period, although many feasts (such as that of the Apostle Peter or of the first martyr, Stephen) were standard. Following traditions established in Roman North Africa, bishops were charged with control of the canon of saints to be venerated and liturgically celebrated in their diocese, but from the 12th century on the papacy exerted ever more control over the processes of canonization.

The public honor, or *cultus*, accorded saints took many forms. One pervasive mode was liturgical. The memory of those admitted to the canon of saints was celebrated on a feast that commemorated the day of that saint's death, that is, the day on which he or she had been born into eternal life. Such commemoration could be as simple as the inclusion of the saint's name in the recital of the martyrology—the list of martyrs and other saints whose feasts fell on a given day, as part of the Mass or monastic office. A variety of martyrologies circulated during the Middle Ages, the most influential of which was the *Martyrologium Hieronymianum*, falsely attributed to Jerome. Saints of significant stature, either universally or locally, were provided more elaborate commemoration on their feasts, ranging from readings taken from the saint's life to processions bearing their relics. Monastic communities celebrated a round of feasts on which they not only commemorated the saints but prayed for their intercession. Liturgical calendars specific to dioceses, monasteries, or religious orders abound in medieval manuscripts, most particularly in Sacramentaries and in those collections of hagiographic readings known as "legendaries."

church was built in the latter half of the 12th century. Its official name, Notre-Dame-de-la-Mer, was soon transformed by pilgrims to "Saintes-Maries" or "Trois-Maries."

The church is simple in plan. It has no transept, and its aisleless nave is covered by a slightly pointed barrel vault. The choir has a semicircular apse and columns ornamented with decorative capitals. A scarcity of windows keeps the interior in perpetual shadow. From the exterior, the church resembles a fortress. A polygonal tower, situated over the apse, is topped by a gabled belfry. A room inside the tower once housed arms for the defense of the church. In the 15th century, it became a high chapel dedicated to St. Michael.

In 1448, King René d'Anjou sponsored excavations that led to the "discovery" of what he claimed were the relics of Mary Cleophas, Mary Salome, and Sarah. In addition, he sponsored the construction of a new crypt and extended the church by two bays (constructed in the same style as the rest of the church). In this period, and still today, Saintes-Maries was an important pilgrimage church for gypsies.

Nina Rowe

[See also: RENÉ D'ANJOU]

The other most important form that the veneration of saints assumed was the cult of relics. These were physical objects associated with the saints. The most important relics were the saints' corpses, or fragmentary parts of their bodies. They were literally, in Latin, that which the saint had left behind (*reliquiae*) or pledges of the saints' sacred power (*pignora*). Tokens, such as bits of cloth (*brandea*) or vials of water that had touched the body or its shrine, also assumed the status of relics, while objects that a saint had possessed, such as a crozier, might likewise become important memorials. Relics were not a representation of the saint but his or her physical presence. This was most true of corporal relics, for the saint's body was the part of a saintly person that remained in this world awaiting resurrection at the time of the Last Judgment. Relics thus provided a physical link between the Kingdom of Heaven, where the soul of the saint resided, and this world, where the shrine guarded the saint's bodily remains.

The purpose of the cult of saints was to aid Christians of lesser stature in their search for salvation. As members of the divine court, the saints possessed God's favor and could mediate on behalf of the souls of the deceased, helping them to procure entrance into Heaven. This idea is graphically depicted on the tympanum of the church of Conques: Christ sits in majesty overseeing the final Judgment, while the figure of St. Foy, whose relics were enshrined within the church, kneels next to his ear, pleading the case of those who have sought her powers of intercession. The powers of the saints were not confined to the afterlife. Since disease and other afflictions were seen in part as punishment for sin, pilgrims came to the shrines of the saints in search of miraculous cures. The saints served as patrons who provided benefits to their clients, although the manner in which they dispensed patronage varied according to changing social norms.

The origins of the cult of relics in the western Roman Empire are to be found in the care lavished by Christian families on the tombs of their ancestors in the cemeteries located outside urban centers. Particular attention was given to the tombs of martyrs and other people considered holy. In time, churches were erected over these spots, attracting pilgrims who sought miraculous cures and families who wished to have members of their clans interred in or near these same churches (*ad sanctos*) in the hope that they would share in the bodily resurrection of the saints on the Day of Judgment. Communities of monks came to serve these churches, their patron saints, and their clientele. Such suburban monastic shrines became an important characteristic of the topography of the cities of the late empire.

Little is known about the veneration of saints' relics in Gaul prior to the last decade of the 4th century, when it underwent a significant revival, at least partially in response to the Germanic migrations. Although there was no direct connection between the Greco-Roman cult of heroes and the Christian cult of saints, the shrines of Christian saints may well have filled an important gap when pagan shrines devoted to curing deities, such as Asclepius, were closed. Some of Gaul's relics were imported from distant provinces, such as those of varied Roman martyrs whose reception at Rouen in 396 was recorded by Bishop Victricius in

a panegyric. But many of the province's most prominent saints were its martyred bishops, such as Julian of Brioude, Trophimus of Arles, and, most important of all, Martin of Tours. As Martin's reputation grew over the course of the 5th century, pilgrims flocked in increasing numbers to his tomb outside of Tours, where an important new church was built over the shrine in the 460s.

The Gallo-Romans regarded their saints as one of their chief bulwarks against the invading Germans. As they converted to Christianity, however, the Franks themselves enthusiastically adopted the cult of relics. Clovis, for example, allegedly endowed the church that housed the relics of Martin. The greatest chronicler of the cult of saints in the early Frankish kingdom was Gregory of Tours (d. 594). In addition to the anecdotes provided in his monumental *Liber historiae Francorum*, Gregory composed eight linked collections of hagiographic tales (*Life of the Fathers*), in which he provided the miraculous history of the holy men of his native Gaul. Gregory's work confirms that the veneration of relics had become central to the practice of Christianity, and one of his goals was to endow the cults of local saints with trustworthy histories. The shrines of the saints were special places: their walls were adorned with ornate hangings and murals depicting scenes from the lives of the saints; candles and incense burned ceaselessly before the shrine; pilgrims jostled one another for physical contact with the holy tomb. One common practice was incubation, that is, sleeping on the grating that covered the tomb. People came not only to be cured; they also swore oaths in an attempt to end feuds or begged the saint's aid at the Last Judgment. Gregory himself hoped that on that day the angels would say of him, "This is a man on whose behalf St. Martin petitions."

By the Carolingian period, as communities of monks and canons gained control of most important shrines, these became central to the identity and to the economy of the monastic houses. Legal documents specified Fleury, for example, as "the place where St. Benedict rests." When noble families donated lands to a monastery, the charters claimed that the gift was made not to the monks, but to their patron saint. This was not a legal fiction, for the patron saint of a monastery was the owner of its lands. The number of pilgrims who came to monastic shrines could be large, particularly on the feast day of the saint. Monks had to provide hospices and even elaborate, if meatless, feasts for their guests. Most monastic churches, however, remained closed to women, and special arrangements, such as the construction of wooden tribunes outside the cloister, had to be made in order to allow female pilgrims access to reliquaries. Saints not only provided cures and mediation to their friends, they also were thought capable of wreaking miracles of chastisement on those who stole their property. Adrevald of Fleury, for example, recorded how his fellow monks had brought the relics of St. Benedict to Count Odo of Orléans in a vain attempt to stop him from plundering their lands. When Odo died in battle, his demise was interpreted as the judgment of God.

The reforms instituted by Carolingian rulers and bishops at synods like those held at Frankfurt (994) and Mainz (813) did much to transform the cult of saints. First, attempts to regulate liturgical practice resulted in the composition of many new martyrologies by such figures as Florus of Lyon, Ado of Vienne, Rabanus Maurus, and Notker the Stammerer. The most influential of these was the work of Usuard, which eventually formed the basis of the Roman martyrology compiled in the 16th century by Caesar Baronius. Second, attempts made to regulate the veneration of relics provided each bishop control over the cult of saints in his diocese and led indirectly to the composition of numerous hagiographic works concerning traditionally venerated saints, such as Denis of Saint-Denis and Remi of Reims. Third, a number of canons required that every consecrated altar in a Christian church must contain relics and suggested that oaths be sworn over reliquaries. These decrees increased the demand for fragmentary relics. Indeed, relics came to be encased not only in altars but in such objects as the throne of Charlemagne and the hilt of Durendal, the legendary sword of Roland.

The social and political order of France was radically reshaped in the decades ca. 1000. During the following two centuries, many ancient monastic houses were reformed, and in the process the cults of their traditional patron saints were renewed. Frequently, as part of this process, the churches that housed the relics of the saints were rebuilt. Raoul Glaber (d. ca. 1046), describing a profusion of church building in Italy and France during the first decade of the new millennium, commented that it was as if "the world itself, shaking off the old, had covered itself with a shining robe of churches." In the 1130s, Abbot Suger of Saint-Denis argued that it was necessary to rebuild his abbey's church because of crowding caused by the throng of pilgrims who "spilled out of every door."

During this revival of the cult of saints, the concept of saintly patronage was based on the evolving social practices of vassalage, feud, and gift exchange. Devout Christians gained the protection and intercession of the holy dead by bringing them gifts or providing them with services. A detailed picture of this process can be found in the stories gathered in numerous miracle collections composed by monks at this time. The "family" of a patron saint included many people: the monks or canons of the community, the serfs who worked the lands of that community, the nobles who donated land to the saint, the pilgrims who brought offerings or simply their prayers to the shrine. In exchange for their services and gifts, the saint provided his or her friends with intercession in the divine court and protection against disease and enemies in this world. The power of the saints was also portrayed by monastic authors as an effective deterrent to the saint's enemies. A story from Anjou told how a son of a knight had injured himself while riding illegally on the property of the monastery of Saint-Albinus. The boy began to curse the saint and was struck dumb. His friends, attracted by his tears, led him back to his father. On the advice of the monks, the boy came to their church, where he lay prostrate in supplication before the relics of Albinus. Eventually, he rose and told how the saint had appeared to him and loosed his tongue on the condition that he warn others not to treat the saints irreverently.

The relationships between saint and servants were reciprocal, for the saints became obligated to their servants, as can be seen in a story told by the monks of Conques about a man who had been punished by his master for having attended the feast of their patron, St. Foy, by having his eyes gouged out; the saint then appeared to the man and promised him a cure. In times of trouble, when they thought that their patron had deserted them, monastic communities sometimes performed a ritual humiliation of that saint's relics, in which the relics were taken out of their shrine, scattered on the floor of the church or in some cases buried, and cursed as a means of forcing the saint to reverse the sagging fortunes of the community.

While the relics served as a focus for the charismatic power of the saints, the miracles were thought to be performed not by the relics but by the saints themselves or, as the hagiographers themselves insisted, by God working through the saints. The relics themselves could be put to good use. One group of monks dunked a casket containing relics of their patron into a vat of wine from Sancerre and then drank its contents in an attempt to combat an outbreak of disease. When a nobleman tried to steal some vineyards that belonged to the monastery of Glanfeuil, its abbot threatened the malefactor with a reliquary of the monastery's patron, saying, "Omnipotent God through the merits of Blessed Maurus and other saints, whose relics are venerated and preserved in this small box, will claim punishment and vengeance from those who are scornful of his own and their servants, and most especially he will extract it from you, who, devoted to the evil of pillage, causes such robbery to occur." Reliquaries were also brought forth from their shrines for other important occasions: processions to mark a feast day, journeys undertaken by representatives of a monastic community in search of donations, episcopal councils held as part of the movement known as the Peace of God, and even battles fought to protect monastic property. The unscrupulous sometimes used falsified relics for the sake of religious sensationalism or profit. Raoul Glaber recorded how a "swindler" sold "the bones of some anonymous man from the lowest of places" as the relics of a martyr named Just.

Over the course of the later Middle Ages, traditional monastic shrines declined in importance. Such reformed orders as the Cistercians and Grandmontines were founded on an ideal of greater separation from society; their members specifically prayed to Bernard of Clairvaux and Stephen of Muret that those saints refrain from performing miracles at their tombs that would attract unwanted pilgrims. The mendicant orders, on the other hand, were dedicated to pastoral care. Although they made use of relics and prayers to the saints in this task, in France (unlike in Italy) they did not become the custodians of significant shrines.

This period was marked by the recognition of contemporary figures as saints shortly after their deaths. The tombs of some new saints, such as Bernard of Tiron (d. 1117) and Louis of Anjou (d. 1297), enjoyed brief vogues in attracting pilgrims, but more common were such figures as Louis IX (d. 1270) and Jeanne-Marie de Maillé (d. 1414), whose importance was linked to their holy example and powers of intercession rather than to shrines. This does not mean that the physical remains of these holy men and women were not prized. The Dominican confessor of Margaret of Ypres (d. 1237) asked the saint's mother to provide him with some of her possessions, such as head-dresses and shoelaces, after the young girl's death.

Relics came to be displayed more prominently in the churches of the later Middle Ages than they had been in earlier periods. New fragments of saintly bodies were eagerly sought and placed in ornate reliquaries. Many relics were brought back to France as spoils both from Jerusalem during the Crusades and from Constantinople after the sack of 1204. In 1248, that vigorous crusader Louis IX had the Sainte-Chapelle dedicated as a form of relic treasury: the building even imitated a reliquary in its shape. Other forms of church ornamentation also celebrated the cult of saints, as hagiographic legends were prominently displayed in stained-glass windows and painted triptychs. Moreover, the old relic shrines never completely lost their allure: the head of St. Martial, for example, was displayed in Limoges both in 1364, on the occasion of the visit of the English prince Edward, and again in 1388, as part of an attempt both to end the Great Schism and to alleviate local famine.

Traditional shrines of local importance were to some degree replaced in the later Middle Ages by shrines of international significance, such as that of St. James in Compostela, those of the martyrs in Rome, that of Thomas Becket in Canterbury, and, most important, the holy places around Jerusalem. No shrine of comparable importance was located in France, although the abbey of Mont-Saint-Michel did attract long-distance pilgrimage. French pilgrims flocked to distant lands in search of the miracles and intercession many had once found closer at hand.

This period also witnessed a steady growth in the importance of shrines dedicated to the Virgin Mary and to Christ himself. Both figures had been of great devotional importance throughout the history of Christianity, but from the 12th century onward the faithful came to approach them more directly. Because of the doctrines of the Assumption of Mary and the Ascension of Christ, corporal relics of the usual sort were lacking. The cathedral of Chartres claimed to possess the Virgin's tunic, which made it one of the earliest and most prominent Marian sanctuaries in France. More common were statues of the Virgin that acquired miraculous reputations. One of the earliest was fashioned from gold in Clermont at the end of the 10th century. By the end of the next century, others could be found at Coutances, Bayeux, and elsewhere. Still later, Marian statues came to be painted black: the first mention of the Black Virgin of Rocamadour was in 1235, and Louis IX brought a similar statue from Palestine to Le Puy in 1254. Since devotion to the relics of Christ centered on bits of the Savior's body discarded before his death and resurrection, it took on a sometimes bizarre quality. The monks of Saint-Médard displayed one of the Savior's milkteeth; the abbeys of Charroux and Coulombs both claimed to possess his foreskin. The eucharist, the real presence of the body and blood of Christ, came to be treated like a relic in many forms of devotion.

Even as its forms changed, the cult of saints continued to be important to the lay practice of Christianity in the later Middle Ages. Preachers used exemplary stories gleaned from the lives of the saints to spice up their sermons. Prominently displayed works of art, works of vernacular hagiography, and translations of such works as the *Legenda aurea* brought the stories of the saints to a wider audience. Glass-fronted reliquaries made bits of holy bodies visible to the faithful. Confraternities adopted appropriate saints as their patrons and celebrated their feasts in elaborate fashion. Books of hours promoted the observance of many feasts, as well as the cult of the Virgin Mary, in the home. Individuals and communities sought the aid of "specialist" saints with particular problems, such as St. Roch for the plague and St. Margaret for difficult childbirths. During the Hundred Years' War, St. Martial developed a reputation among both armies for the ability to liberate prisoners. Saintly intercession came to be institutionalized in the granting of indulgences.

The 16th-century Reformation brought with it a radical reaction against such practices. Reform theologians and preachers in particular rejected the idea of saintly intercession, which was thought in Lutheran terminology to constitute a reliance on works rather than on faith. John Calvin composed a systematic critique of the cult of relics in the vernacular (*Traité des reliques*, 1547), in which he rejected the veneration of relics on theological grounds and delighted in such absurdities as the multiple heads of John the Baptist enshrined in churches throughout Europe. Theological opposition often turned to violent iconoclasm on the part of Huguenots during the Wars of Religion. Relic collections were destroyed and the statues of the saints in many French churches still bear the scars of attack. The Council of Trent took steps to reorganize the practice of the cult of saints and the means by which saints were canonized within early-modern Catholicism.

Thomas Head

[See also: BOOK OF HOURS; CHARTRES; CONQUES; GREGORY OF TOURS; HAGIOGRAPHY; *LEGENDA AUREA*; MARTIN OF TOURS; PILGRIMAGE; RELICS AND RELIQUARIES; SAINTS' LIVES]

Brown, Peter. *The Cult of the Saints: Its Rise and Function in Latin Christianity*. Chicago: University of Chicago Press, 1981.

Dubois, Jacques. *Les martyrologes du moyen âge latin*. Turnhout: Brepols, 1978.

Farmer, Sharon. *Communities of Saint Martin: Legend and Ritual in Medieval Tours*. Ithaca: Cornell University Press, 1991.

Geary, Patrick J. *Furta Sacra: Thefts of Relics in the Central Middle Ages*. 2nd ed. Princeton: Princeton University Press, 1990.

Head, Thomas. *Hagiography and the Cult of Saints: The Diocese of Orléans, 800–1200*. Cambridge: Cambridge University Press, 1990.

Patlagean, Evelyne, and Pierre Riché, eds. *Hagiographie, cultures, et sociétés: IVe–XIIe siècles*. Paris: Études Augustiniennes, 1981.

Philippart, Guy. *Les légendiers latins et autres manuscrits hagiographiques*. Turnhout: Brepols, 1977.

Rousselle, Aline. *Croire et guérir: la foi en Gaule dans l'antiquité tardive*. Paris: Fayard, 1990.

Schmitt, Jean-Claude. *The Holy Greyhound: Guinefort, Healer of Children Since the Thirteenth Century*. Cambridge: Cambridge University Press, 1983.

Sigal, Pierre-André. *L'homme et le miracle dans la France médiévale (XIe–XIIe siècle)*. Paris: Cerf, 1985.

Vauchez, André. *La sainteté en occident aux derniers siècles du moyen âge d'après les procès de canonisation et les documents hagiographiques*. Rome: École Française de Rome, 1981.

Wilson, Stephen, ed. *Saints and Their Cults*. Cambridge: Cambridge University Press, 1983.

SAINTS' LIVES. Hagiographic literature in Old and Middle French—stories about Christ, the Virgin, biblical figures, authentic or apocryphal, and above all the lives of the saints—is rich and varied. Unlike most other writing in the vernacular, to which the church was either indifferent or hostile, hagiographic literature was encouraged by ecclesiastical authorities, especially after the Fourth Lateran Council (1215), which insisted on the necessity of preaching in the vernacular tongues. Hagiography is one of the most fecund of Old French genres, as well as the most ancient. There exist in verse more than 240 versions of the Lives of over a hundred saints and an even higher number in prose. Most of this literature is unedited. The first extant French literary composition, the *Séquence de sainte Eulalie*, dates to 878–82. Another early work, the *Vie de saint Léger*, is from the 10th century.

The main source for the French saints' lives is the "official" Latin hagiographic literature, often going back to latinized Byzantine and other eastern Christian writings. Though most of the Lives date from the early centuries of Christianity, many told the stories of more recent saints. Thus, the popular cult of St. Thomas Becket (1118–1170) found its French expression in at least three *vies* in verse, contemporary with his martyrdom. The same can be said of the Lives of SS. Dominic, Francis of Assisi, and Elizabeth of Hungary. But hagiography was also capable of finding its inspiration in history, folklore, romances, and even in truly adventitious sources. *Barlaam et Josaphat* is apparently a Christian recasting of the legend of Buddha. Conversely, saints' lives profoundly influenced other genres of medieval French literature, particularly the very concept of the hero. Not only Roland, Oliver, and Guillaume d'Orange but also Perceval, Lancelot, and Galahad became, so to speak, "canonized." Countless pilgrims visited the purported graves of these epic and romance heroes, who grew increasingly idealized and saintly with the development of Arthurian romance.

The Lives do not exhibit a specific literary form but adopt the formal properties of other popular genres. The oldest extant version of the *Vie de saint Alexis* (ca. 1050), a masterpiece of verse hagiography, is in five-line decasyllabic monoassonanced stanzas closely resembling the basic form of the chanson de geste. In the 13th century, when most of the verse saints' lives were composed, not only the prevailing meter (rhymed octosyllabic couplets) but also the prevailing novelistic tone were shared by hagiographic and romance narratives.

The distinction between the verse and prose Lives is not merely formal. Those in verse are generally older and of greater literary value, taking more liberty with their sources and tending to stress the marvelous character of the narration. Many hagiographic verse narratives exist in more than one version. The *Alexis*, as well as the Lives of SS. Bon, Brendan, Eustace, George, Laurent, Agatha, Catherine of Alexandria, Elizabeth of Hungary, Mary the Egyptian, Margaret, and Thaïs—to name but a few—were recast in verse several times. Some of them were later prosified, transformed into dramatic forms in the miracle and saint plays, or both.

Most of the earlier verse Lives were composed as isolated works, but some were later gathered in collections called "legendaries" (*légendiers*); the majority of prose Lives in the legendaries appeared in the first half of the 13th century. Some of the prose Lives are simply recastings of earlier poems, but most are new translations from more authentic Latin texts or reworkings of those translations. With the prose translations came a marked concern for the "truth," with less "romantic" and fabulous versions of the stories, more closely resembling the Latin texts.

Parallel to their Latin counterparts, the legendaries were organized either in the traditional generic "hierarchical" groupings (Apostles, doctors, martyrs, virgins, widows, etc.) or were arranged in the order of the liturgical year, with a prescribed legend (i.e., reading) for a specific calendar day of the commemoration of the given saint. The most famous of such collections is the *Legenda aurea*, compiled ca. 1261–67 by Jacobus of Voragine and translated into French by Jean Beleth sometime in the 14th century and by Jean de Vignay in 1348. Beleth's version became the basic text of the incunabula; Jean's was a veritable bestseller, with a large number of manuscripts extant.

The spiritual or ideological content, clearly visible in the formal aspects of the French saints' lives, is shared with all Christian hagiography, which narrates a personal road to salvation and thus presents narrative patterns basic to all the genres. Despite their heterogeneity and their differing aesthetic values, all hagiographic stories present strikingly similar narrative patterns: unusual birth, followed by a precocious childhood in the presence of pious parents and/or teachers, separation from the family, life of temptation and/or sin, conversion, repentance and/or good works, martyrdom and/or pious death. With the death, often followed by the visible signs of sainthood (miracles), begins the liturgical (i.e., literary) existence of a saint, a life having become The Life. These patterns are spiritually and historically explainable. All saints are *imitatores Christi*, and those patterns are clearly discernible in the biblical accounts of Christ's life.

Peter F. Dembowski

The heyday of French hagiography was the 13th century, but approximately twenty-five verse texts presenting the Lives of saints were composed as late as the 15th century. Among the saints whose Lives were written in this period are Anthony (of the desert), Anthony of Padua, Barbara, Catherine, Christine, Denis, the 10,000 crucified, Eustace, Fiacre, John the Baptist, Josse, Margaret, Mathurin, Onuphre, Opportune, Quentin, Reine, René, Roch, Sauveur, and Winifrid. We find the same blend as in previous centuries: there are saints from the early years of Christianity (Eustace, Catherine, Onuphre), for whom the paucity of documentation has been made up for by invention; some from more recent times, for whom there is credible source material (Anthony of Padua); and still others who were near-contemporaries (Roch). There is also the usual blending of pan-Christian saints with saints more closely associated with France, such as Denis (bishop of Paris), Fiacre (connected to the abbey of Breuil, near Meaux) Josse (Toulouse), Mathurin (Sens), Opportune (Normandy), Reine (Autun), René (Angers), and Roch (Montpellier). Saints not immediately identified as French are found to have some connection with the country, like Christine, transported miraculously to the neighborhood of Béthune, or Anthony of Padua, who lived briefly in France.

One-third of these works are in the long-popular narrative form of the octosyllabic couplet (Christine, Josse, Margaret, Mathurin, Onuphre, Opportune, Quentin, René). The rest show variety in their verse forms, harmonizing with those popular for the transmission of secular texts. A good number of these Lives are stanzaic: those of Barbara, Catherine, Denis, Eustace, and Sauveur, for example, have quatrains of Alexandrines, a common form in the 14th century. Other Lives use various stanzaic forms, ranging from octosyllabic *sizains* (Denis), *septains* (Catherine), and *huitains* (Christine, Fiacre) to eleven-lined stanzas of decasyllables (Reine). When the spirit of the age calls for feats of rhyming virtuosity, as at the time of the Grands Rhétoriqueurs, these texts, like the Life of Reine, provide examples of unusually rich rhyme configurations. The poems range from the fairly short (Christine's 278 lines) to the more extended (Mathurin's 1,294 lines). Incunabula texts tend to be in the middle range, approximately 400–600 lines in length.

These works carry on a rich French hagiographic tradition (over 240 hagiographic verse texts). The genre's popularity is explainable partly by its appeal to a broad audience, rich and poor, male and female, young and old, active and contemplative, with portrayals of individuals bright, independent, and virtuous, who all show the way to eternal felicity. Furthermore, the saints were believed to perform valuable aid in times of danger or distress, such as childbirth (Margaret) or plague (Roch).

Paul Barrette

[See also: ANGLO-NORMAN LITERATURE; *BARLAAM ET JOSAPHAT*; BENEDEIT; GAUTIER DE COINCI; HAGIOGRAPHY; *LEGENDA AUREA*; MIRACLE PLAYS; *SAINT ALEXIS, VIE DE*; *SAINT LÉGER, VIE DE*; SAINT PLAYS; *SAINTE EULALIE, SÉQUENCE DE*; *SAINTE FOY, CHANSON DE*; SAINTS, CULT OF; *SERMONS JOYEUX*; *VIES DES ANCIENS PÈRES*; WACE]

Montaiglon, Anatole de, and James Rothschild, eds. *Recueil de poésies françoises des XVe et XVIe siècles, morales, facétieuses, historiques.* Paris: Daffis, 1877, Vol. 12.

Barrette, Paul. "Fifteenth-Century Hagiographic Poems in French." In *Le gai savoir: Essays in Linguistics, Philology, and Criticism, Dedicated to the Memory of Manfred Sandmann*, ed. Mechthild Cranston. Madrid: Turanzas, 1983, pp. 55–68.

Bowen, Willis H. "Present Status of Studies in Saints' Lives in Old French Verse." *Symposium* 1 (1947): 82–86.

Cazelles, Brigitte. *Le corps de sainteté, d'après Jehan Bouche d'Or, Jehan Paulus et quelques vies des XIIe et XIIIe siècles.* Geneva: Droz, 1982.

Dembowski, Peter F. "Literary Problems of Hagiography in Old French." *Medievalia et humanistica* 7 (1976): 117–30.

Johnson, Phyllis, and Brigitte Cazelles. *Le vain siècle guerpir: A Literary Approach to Sainthood Through Old French Hagiography of the Twelfth Century.* Chapel Hill: University of North Carolina Press, 1979.

Meyer, Paul. "Légendes hagiographiques en français." *Histoire littéraire de la France* 33 (1906): 328–458.

SALIC LAW. The body of laws promulgated by Merovingian and Carolingian kings for the Salian Franks and those living within their territory of Neustria. The first version of the *Lex Salica*, the *Pactus legis Salicae* was probably issued by Clovis I between 507 and 511. Although it and all later versions were written in Latin, the law was based on Frankish customary practices, which makes it an invaluable source for early Frankish legal and social life. Major modifications and additions were made from the mid-6th century to the mid-9th. The extant manuscripts are confusing and difficult to understand, as they represent many redactions and were subjected to innumerable revisions and efforts at correction. To the Carolingians, Salic Law was probably primarily of antiquarian interest. It continued to be studied long after the Carolingian period and was influential in the development of law in northern France up to the French Revolution.

The provisions of Salic Law do not constitute a comprehensive or even orderly collection of Frankish law. They do not form a true code of law. Rather, they concern matters that needed to be repeated, reinforced, clarified, or amended. Moreover, a king might issue laws merely so as to be seen as a lawgiver. The *Pactus legis Salicae* is the oldest written version of laws concerning a West Germanic people, and it is the most Germanic of such written law on the Continent, displaying virtually no evidence of a Christian or a Roman influence.

The society seen in Salic Law, overwhelmingly rural and agricultural, is based on the strong ties of an extended family and the cohesion of tightly knit communities. Salic Law deals chiefly with private law and is concerned primarily with property and inheritance and the peaceful resolution of disputes that arise over everyday crimes—theft, property damage, personal injuries, sexual offenses, and homicide. Wergelds, monetary compensations for injuries, ties of kinship, and the feud dominate its provisions.

One of the most famous "provisions" is the so-called Salic Law of Succession. In the 14th and 15th centuries, it was alleged that Salic Law forbade women to inherit property or to succeed to the throne or even to transmit such a claim to succession to their descendants. However, there is no factual basis to these claims.

Steven Fanning

[See also: FRANKS; LAW AND JUSTICE; WERGELD]

Rivers, Theodore John, trans. *The Laws of the Salian and Ripuarian Franks*. New York: AMS, 1986.

Murray, Alexander Callander. *Germanic Kinship Structure: Studies in Law and Society in Antiquity and the Early Middle Ages*. Toronto: Pontifical Institute of Mediaeval Studies, 1983, pp. 115–33.

Wallace-Hadrill, J.M. *The Long-Haired Kings and Other Studies in Frankish History*. London: Methuen, 1962.

SALUT D'AMOR. Verse love letter. Also called *domnejaire*, the Occitan *salut d'amor* incorporates standard courtly themes in the five-part structure prescribed in medieval Latin letter books. Arnaut de Mareuil composed five of the twenty surviving *saluts*. Whereas the Occitan *salut* is typically nonstrophic, the genre developed in northern France into a stanzaic piece with refrain, sometimes called *complainte d'amour*.

Elizabeth W. Poe

Bec, Pierre. *Les saluts d'amour du troubadour Arnaud de Mareuil*. Toulouse: Privat, 1961.

SARLAT. A picturesque city with numerous Renaissance façades, Sarlat (Dordogne) grew up around the Benedictine abbey of Saint-Sacerdos. The Romanesque church was demolished in 1504 in favor of the present cathedral, which was completed in the 17th century. The sole remains are the western bell tower (upper stage is 17th-c.), a Romanesque window and wall fragments in the chevet, and the restored chapel of St. Benoît, south of the cathedral. The sacristy with ogive vaulting was a 14th-century chapter house. Most remarkable is the Lanterne des morts, a two-storied cylindrical tower capped by an elaborate tiered cone, at the head of the terraced Jardin des enfeus (ancient cemetery of the monks). According to legend, it commemorates the miracles worked by St. Bernard during his visit to Sarlat in 1147.

Jean M. French

Deshoulières, M. "Sarlat." *Congrès archéologique* (*Périgueux*) 90 (1927): 271–95.

Secret, Jean. "La chapelle Saint-Benoît de Sarlat," and "La lanterne des morts de Sarlat." *Congrès archéologique* (*Périgord Noir*) 137 (1979): 9–17.

SAULIEU. The church of Saulieu (Côte-d'Or), dedicated to St. Androche, who was martyred in A.D. 177 by order of Emperor Marcus Aurelius, is best known for its Romanesque capitals, both historiated and ornamental. However, in spite of the loss of the east end by fire set by the English in 1359 and its subsequent rebuilding in 1704, probably over the remains of Carolingian structures, and the destruction of the façade portal during the French Revolution, the church is a fine example of Cluniac architecture based on the elevation and vaulting of Cluny III— pointed nave arcade, arcaded triforium, clerestory, pointed barrel vaults strengthened by transverse arches, and groin-vaulted aisles. In Saulieu, the nave piers and arcade of the triforium are not animated by fluted pilasters (influence of Roman architecture), like Cluny III, Paray-le-Monial, and Autun. Rather, the Saulieu master builder employed the pier system of Vézelay with a rounded outer respond over a rectangular one. The design of Vézelay thus seems to have influenced that of Saulieu.

The nave capitals of Saulieu, which include the Flight into Egypt, the Hanging of Judas, the Appearance of Christ to Mary Magdalene, and other figured capitals as well as numerous ornamental ones, based on Romanesque variants of the Roman Corinthian capital, are of high quality and relate most closely in iconography, design, and treatment of drapery to the sculpture of Autun. Some of the ornamental capitals appear to be by the same sculptor involved in decorating the outer narthex of Autun. This stylistic relationship to Autun seems to negate the significance of the 1119 dedication, which did not specify what was being dedicated. The sculpture, like the nave, appears to date from the 1130s.

Whitney S. Stoddard

[See also: AUTUN]

Baudry, Jean, et al. *Bourgogne roman*, La Pierre-qui-vire: Zodiaque, 1962, pp. 120–50.

Oursel, Charles. *L'art roman de Bourgogne: études d'histoire et d'archéologie*. Dijon: Venot, 1928.

Porter, A. Kingsley. *Romanesque Sculpture of Pilgrimage Roads*. 2 vols. Boston: Marshall Jones, 1923, Vol. 1, pp. 87–88, 113–14; Vol. 2, figs. 55–61.

Sapin, Christian. *La Bourgogne préromane*. Paris: Picard, 1986, pp. 121–22.

SAUMUR. Until the Revolution, Notre-Dame-de-Nantilly was the only parish in Saumur (Maine-et-Loire). Its name appears for the first time in 849. Its Romanesque nave is composed of five bays with barrel vaulting on rectangular beams (12th c.). Lateral walls are reinforced by arcades. The windows display semicircular Romanesque arches. The transept, with a narrow crossing, and the south aisle are in Flamboyant Gothic style (15th c.). The choir of two bays with cylindrical vaulting is followed by an apse in cul-de-four. A simple façade, with a single door and window, is surmounted by a slightly raised tower.

The principal church in Saumur today is Saint-Pierre, begun in 1162. The choir, the oldest part of the building, comprises one apse and two bays with ribbed vaulting. Large niches punctuate the lower part of the walls; two-story windows illuminate the church. Twin pillars support beams. The transept is covered by a ribbed cupola, and the arms display ribbed vaulting. An apse, vaulted in cul-de-four, opens on each arm. The 13th-century façade has a door ornamented with statues.

A castle, founded probably in the 10th century, is one of the most impressive medieval monuments in Saumur. A massive rectangular fortress with corner towers, it displays the transition from military to domestic architecture. Despite its early foundation, no part of the castle is older than the 13th century. An illustration painted by the Limbourg brothers is found in the *Très Riches Heures* of John, duke of Berry, for the month of September.

E. Kay Harris

Landais, Hubert. *Saumur et sa région.* Paris: Delmas, 1959.

Mussat, A. *Le style gothique de l'ouest de la France, XIIe–XIIIe siècles.* Paris: Picard, 1963.

Rhein, André. "Saumur." *Congrès archéologique (Angers et Saumur)* 77 (1910): 3–32.

SAUVEGARDE. The French crown issued *lettres de sauvegarde* in order to place some person, group, corporate body, or land under its protection. The concept of royal protection had distant roots in the king's proprietary rights of the Frankish period. The late-medieval royal safeguard, however, was an adaptation of a concept appearing in 13th-century canon law—the *conservator*, who protected someone against injuries. Acceptance of royal safeguard amounted to a recognition of royal sovereignty; violation came to be regarded as a serious crime, a *cas royal* that would come directly under the king's jurisdiction. To signify that a place, such as a church, had come under the crown's protection, royal officers would affix batons embellished with the fleur-de-lis. Known as *panonceaux*, these became the recognized symbols of royal safeguard. By the 14th century, the crown extended safeguard to those who were appealing to the royal court. Because of its implications for royal power and jurisdiction, expanding use of royal safeguard came under fire, and Philip VI had to promise to restrict it to those who were weak and defenseless.

John Bell Henneman, Jr.

[See also: CAS ROYAUX; PRIVATE WAR]

Cheyette, Frederic. "The Royal Safeguard in Medieval France." *Studia Gratiana* 15 (1972): 631–52.

Kaeuper, Richard. *War, Justice, and Public Order: England and France in the Later Middle Ages.* Oxford: Clarendon, 1988.

SAVOY. The county, then duchy (1416) of Savoy formed part of the kingdom of Burgundy during the Middle Ages and was never a part of the French kingdom, but the inhabitants were French in language and culture. Members of the ruling family, originally known as the counts of Maurienne, were often allies, vassals, and spouses of French princes. Adelaide of Savoy was the wife of Louis VI and mother of Louis VII; Louis IX's wife, Marguerite de Provence, was the granddaughter of Count Thomas of Savoy, as was the wife of Charles of Anjou, king of Sicily (r. 1266–85). In the later Middle Ages, Savoyard princes intermarried with the princely houses of Bourbon, Berry, and Burgundy, and both the wife of Louis XI and the mother of Francis I were Savoyard princesses.

Geographically, Savoy comprised the region of the French Alps centering on the basin of Lake Le Bourget and the Isère Valley from Montmélian to the confluence with the Arc; but politically, from an early date, it included the upper Isère watershed and the Valle d'Aosta, the Arc Valley (Maurienne) and the Val di Susa, and the Swiss Valais, to which were later added the Pays de Vaud (1263), Bresse (1285), Nice (1388), the Genevois (1401), and the Italian Piedmont (1418), which had long been ruled by a cadet branch of the house of Savoy. Savoy was the principal gateway to Italy for medieval French rulers, merchants, and pilgrims. Under Duke Amadeus VIII (1391–1451), who became the antipope Felix V (r. 1440–49), the court of Savoy was a center of patronage for French artists, writers, and musicians. According to the *Chanson de Roland*, it was in the "vales of Moriane" (Maurienne) that Charlemagne gave Roland his famous sword Durendal.

Eugene L. Cox

[See also: ADELAIDE OF SAVOY]

Bautier, Robert-Henri, and Janine Sornay. *Les sources de l'histoire économique et sociale du moyen âge.* Paris: CNRS, 1968, Vol. 1: *Provence, Dauphiné, et états de la maison de Savoie.*

Brondy, Rejane, Bernard Demotz, and Jean-Pierre Leguay. *La Savoie de l'an mil à la réforme.* Évreux: Herissey, 1984.

Cox, Eugene L. *The Green Count of Savoie: Amadeus VI and Transalpine Savoie in the Fourteenth Century.* Princeton: Princeton University Press, 1967.

———. *The Eagles of Savoie: The House of Savoie in Thirteenth-Century Europe.* Princeton: Princeton University Press, 1974.

Prévité-Orton, C.W. *The Early History of the House of Savoie 1000–1223.* Cambridge: Cambridge University Press, 1912.

SCHISM, GREAT. Between 1378 and 1417, western Christendom experienced almost four decades in which there were two, and then three, simultaneous claimants to the papal throne, each of whom could rightfully claim to have been elected by a legitimate authority. Earlier, there had been periods in which there were two claimants, but never before had the same electoral body (the College of Cardinals) repudiated one election and then proceeded to elect another pope while the first claimant still exercised power. Moreover, with the assertion of the right of a council to elect the pope (Council of Pisa, 1409–10) and the continuation of the other claimants in office, there were suddenly three, not two, popes claiming to be the legitimate leader of the one true church. The crisis was institutional, sacramental, and moral. The struggle to resolve the crisis summoned the best efforts of kings, emperors, ecclesiastics of all ranks, and university masters. Roman politics, national rivalries, ecclesiastical and secular conflicts, and entrenched positions of power within and without the church all contributed to the divisiveness of the crisis and the difficulty of resolving it.

The schism arose in the aftermath of the return in 1377 of Gregory XI to Rome from Avignon (thus ending the long [1309–77] residence of the bishop of Rome in another city, with the exception of 1367–70, when Urban V returned briefly to Rome), his death in the next year, and the election of Urban VI by the sixteen cardinals who were then in Rome. The cardinals were actively threatened should they fail to elect an Italian, rather than a French, pope; they elected Bartolomeo Prignano, archbishop of Bari. An experienced member of the papal court, Prignano, as Urban VI (r. 1378–89), immediately attacked the privileges, wealth, and moral failings of the cardinals. The French cardinals especially took offense and left Rome. Others followed and in August, four months after electing Urban, the College of Cardinals (less the three Italian cardinals) declared Urban's election invalid because it was carried out under threat of violence and elected Robert of Geneva, who was related to the French king, as Pope Clement VII (r. 1378–94).

While Clement, supported by the French king, the Spanish realms, Scotland, Sicily, and some parts of the empire, sought to enter Rome with the support of French troops, Urban began to consolidate power in Rome and Italy while the emperor, England, Ireland, Poland, Hungary, Scandinavia, and most of Italy declared their loyalty to the "Roman" as opposed to the "Avignon" pope. Clement, having failed to enter Rome by force, took up residence in the papal palace in Avignon. Each pope claimed to have a legitimate College of Cardinals (three Italian cardinals went with Urban, the rest with Clement) and established parallel papal curias. With Europe divided into two distinct "obediences," attempts to end the schism began to materialize. Calling a council was briefly entertained as a possibility, especially by the theologians and canon lawyers of the University of Paris, particularly Henry of Langenstein and Conrad of Gelnhausen, but early on in the schism the way of a council, which was finally to be the path to an ultimate solution, proved unattractive.

After more than a decade with a divided church, a new "way" was proposed by French leaders: the *via cessionis*, which called for both claimants to resign their positions, followed by the election of a successor. King Charles VI, with his advisers the dukes of Berry and Burgundy, the University of Paris (led by Jean Gerson and Pierre d'Ailly), and the French clergy (influenced by Simon de Cramaud), actively promoted this strategy. Benedict XIII (r. 1394–1417), a French cardinal elected to succeed Clement, and Boniface IX (r. 1389–1404), Urban's successor in Rome, both rejected the idea of abdication, for each thought his line to be legitimate. In order to force compliance with the *via cessionis*, the French introduced the idea of "subtraction of obedience," which sought to limit papal authority and revenues in order to force the two claimants to resign. "Subtraction of obedience" to Benedict XIII was declared by the French clergy on July 27, 1398, with Simon de Cramaud as the chief architect of the policy, which he articulated in *De subtraccione obediencie*. Both popes and their successors remained obdurate, however, even in light of pressures that included a provision in the elections that the successors of Boniface IX would abdicate if Benedict XIII or one of his successors should abdicate.

The idea of calling a general council of the church (*via consilii*, or "conciliarism") began to gain prominence again in the 1390s, but the general councils of the church in the 11th, 12th, and 13th centuries (Clermont, the third and fourth Lateran councils, and the councils of Vienne, for example) had all been called by the pope. The University of Paris, led by Gerson and d'Ailly, urged that a general council of the church be called, if need be by the civil power, because the earliest councils had been summoned by Constantine and other emperors. The two colleges of cardinals were finally persuaded to unite and to call a council, which met in Pisa in 1409. Bishops and others from both "obediences" attended, and the two claimants were deposed and a new pope was chosen, Alexander V (r. 1409–10). The supposed solution served only to complicate matters, for the popes in the Avignon and Roman lines refused to accept the judgment of the council. Benedict XIII and Gregory XII (r. 1406–15) continued to claim legitimacy, although in reality most leaders in Europe gave allegiance to the new "Pisan" pope, Alexander. Finally, a new council, supported by the emperor Sigismund and called by the cardinals and Alexander's successor, John XXIII (r. 1410–15)—not recognized in the accepted line of popes, so a name/number reused in the 20th century—assembled at Constance in 1414. This major gathering of European leaders, ecclesiastical and secular, determined to end the schism and to reform the church "head and members." The "way of the council" (*via concilii*) succeeded in restoring the unity of the headship of the church by deposing two claimants (Benedict XIII and John XXIII), accepting the abdication of the Roman one (Gregory XII) and electing Odo Colonna as Martin V (r. 1417–31). The council also addressed the question of heresy (it executed Jan Hus), established the idea of the reform of the church through regularly scheduled councils (the decree *Frequens*), and declared the superiority of a council over the pope (the decree *Haec sancta synodus* [or *Sacrosancta*]). Martin V immediately established concordats with the major European leaders that effectively limited papal power in significant ways within the various European kingdoms, thus establishing in France certain of the sought-for Gallican liberties. Martin's successors succeeded in overcoming the impetus for full-blown "conciliarism" in the church, and the papal monarchy gradually reasserted itself over the claims of conciliarists.

Grover A. Zinn

[See also: CONCILIAR MOVEMENT; D'AILLY, PIERRE; GALLICANISM; GERSON, JEAN; SUBTRACTION OF OBEDIENCE; URBAN V]

Crowder, C.M.D. *Unity, Heresy and Reform, 1378–1460: The Conciliar Response to the Great Schism*. New York: St. Martin, 1977.

Oakley, Francis. *Council over Pope? Towards a Provisional Ecclesiology*. New York: Herder and Herder, 1969.

————. *The Western Church in the Later Middle Ages.* Ithaca: Cornell University Press, 1979.

Spinka, Matthew. *Advocates of Reform from Wyclif to Erasmus.* Philadelphia: Westminster, 1953.

Swanson, Robert N. *Universities, Academics and the Great Schism.* Cambridge: Cambridge University Press, 1979.

Ullmann, Walter. *The Origins of the Great Schism.* London: Burns, Oates and Washbourne, 1948.

SCHOLASTICISM. Name commonly given to the system of thought and teaching used in the early universities (or "schools"), especially those of Paris and Oxford. Scholasticism begins in the belief that God's truth can and ought to be known by rational understanding as well as by revelation. It draws a distinction between an understanding of God based on "simple" belief based on revelation, and an understanding drawn from questioning and argument, resolved by means of logic (the "scholastic method"). The Schoolmen's method of proceeding can be characterized as argumentative, authoritative, and additive.

(1) *Argumentative:* Truth can be found by argument, which is to say by the asking and answering of questions. Although these questions (*quaestiones*) originally arose from issues in a biblical text that were separable from and wider than the general run of commentary, they expanded to encompass the great philosophical-theological issues of Christianity, such as the nature and number of God, the number and purpose of sacraments, or the typology of sin. A "classic" scholastic question runs according to a set form. First the question is posed, with a formulaic *Quaeritur utrum . . . , An . . . ,* or *Videtur quod . . .* ("It is asked whether . . . ," "Whether . . . ," or "It seems that . . ."). Then the arguments for the proposition are given ("And it seems that it is, because . . ."), followed by the arguments against, *sed contra* ("on the other hand") or *objectio* ("it is objected . . ."). The writer then makes his judgment *for* the proposition (almost never against: that is simply the way the questions are posed) in a *Solutio* ("solution") or *Respondeo quod* ("I answer that . . .") and completes the question by answering each of the objections in turn *Ad quod . . .* ("to that which was objected . . ."). The meat of the arguments pro and con is culled from acknowledged "authorities," the second characteristic of the method.

(2) *Authoritative:* Truth should be sought in the opinions of the authorities of the past. Preeminent among these is the Bible, but since Scripture can be self-contradictory it cannot be relied upon to provide the solution itself. The next "level" of authority is the writings of the Latin and Greek fathers, in particular Augustine and Jerome: these are regarded as almost as authoritative as the Bible itself. Finally, more "modern" writers, closer to contemporaneous, may be adduced as secondary evidence, but their opinions are frequently given anonymously.

(3) *Additive:* Truth is additive: one system is not to be replaced by another, but rather each single truth can be added to all others to give a fuller picture. The classic epigrammatic statement of this belief is found in Bernard of Chartres, repeating what was even then a truism, that the scholars of his day were like dwarfs standing on the shoulders of giants: they saw farther than the giants, not through their own efforts but from their higher vantage point. Thus, reading a succession of medieval authors addressing the same question we find identical points used in argument for and against the issue. The difference between them will almost always be a difference in weighting of the same evidence rather than something new or different. This approach arises not from a lack of imagination or originality but from a worldview that thought that most "truth" had already been discovered by the authorities of the past.

This method is a means of exposition, not of deliberation. The method is not used in order to arrive at the truth—that is done by a prior and inner appeal to traditional doctrine, experience, and common sense with reason. The method is simply the means of stating, in convincing fashion, what the solutions are and what the arguments might be.

Lesley J. Smith

[**See also:** PHILOSOPHY; THEOLOGY]

Landgraf, Artur Michael. *Introduction à l'histoire de la littérature de la scholastique naissante,* ed. Albert M. Landry, trans. Louis B. Geiger. Montreal: Institut d'Études Médiévales, 1973.

Flint, Valerie I.J. "The 'School of Laon': A Reconsideration." *Recherches de théologie ancienne et médiévale* 43 (1976): 89–110.

Chenu, Marie Dominique. *La théologie au douzième siècle.* Paris: Vrin, 1957.

————. *Nature, Man, and Society in the Twelfth Century: Essays on New Theological Perspectives in the Latin West,* ed. and trans. Jerome Taylor and Lester K. Little. Chicago: University of Chicago Press, 1968. [Selected chapters from *La théologie au douzième siècle.*]

————. *Toward Understanding St. Thomas,* trans. Albert-M. Landry and Dominic Hughes. Chicago: Henry Regenery, 1964.

Colish, Marcia L. "Systematic Theology and Theological Renewal in the Twelfth Century." *Journal of Medieval and Renaissance Studies* 18 (1988): 135–56.

Gilson, Étienne. *History of Christian Philosophy in the Middle Ages.* New York: Random House, 1955.

Grabmann, Martin. *Die Geschichte der scholastischen Methode.* 2 vols. Freiburg-im-Breisgau: Herder, 1909–11.

SCHOOLS, CATHEDRAL. Although precedents for cathedral schools can be found from the early Middle Ages, they did not acquire a firm institutional base until 8th- and 9th-century Carolingian legislation required that arrangements be made for the proper education of clergy. Most cathedral schools aspired to little more, essentially dedicating themselves to ensuring that parish clergy and cathedral canons had sufficient education to perform their assigned tasks; what little we know about the education they provided suggests that they concentrated on the basics of Latin grammar and Christian doctrine. But cathedral schools occasionally did furnish an institutional forum to masters whose ambitions were higher and who drew students from outside the immediate region, although this role scarcely ever outlived the master whose eminence it reflected. In the 11th century especially, it was generally cathedral schools that employed the masters who were responsible for redefining the objectives of higher education to include the extension as well as the transmission of knowledge. Indeed, the 12th-century *studium* of Paris originally grew up under the auspices and legal protection provided by the cathedral of Paris.

In the 9th century, cathedral schools were generally less prominent in the movement known as the "Carolingian renaissance" than their counterparts in the monasteries. Toward the end of the century, however, the cathedral at Laon under the patronage of Charles the Bald became a center for Irish scholars active in France; the schoolmaster appears to have been a certain Martin Hiberniensis (819–875), and Johannes Scottus Eriugena was also affiliated with the school. Much of the actual education provided, however, must have been at a fairly elementary level; its character is suggested by the contents of Laon manuscript 468. This manuscript, which is too large (12.4 inches by 8.4 inches) to be a student's notebook and which was apparently corrected by Martin himself, consists of a life of Virgil, some glosses on Virgil's poetry, several pages of comments on the Liberal Arts, and Alcuin's Latin grammar. The material on the Liberal Arts, especially, is rudimentary; the longest discussions address ethics and logic, with the invention of ethics being attributed to Socrates and that of logic to Plato, with the author noting the divisions of the different arts and the names of the principal textbooks. In short, it is a compilation whose material is intended to be memorized as an end in itself rather than to serve as an initiation into more advanced studies.

The eminence of the school of Laon did not survive into the 10th century. Indeed, the only French cathedral school of note in this century was that of Reims, whose archdeacon Gerranus's reputation in logic drew both Abbo of Fleury and Gerbert of Aurillac. Gerbert (later Pope Sylvester II) stayed on to become master at Reims from 972 to 982, returning to his post in 983 after a brief failed abbacy at Bobbio; he remained master until 989.

Gerbert himself enjoyed a reputation for logic and astronomy, and we are fortunate in having an account by his student Richer of the course of studies that he taught in logic. According to Richer, Gerbert began with the *Isagoge* of Porphyry, which he taught with Boethius's commentary; he then taught Aristotle's *Categories* and *On Interpretation*, proceeding afterward to Aristotle's *Topics* in Cicero's translation, which he also taught with Boethius's commentary. This account of Gerbert's curriculum has often been regarded as showing a revival of logical studies before the year 1000, but there are reasons for being more cautious. In the first place, Richer's statement that Cicero's *Topics* was a translation of Aristotle is incorrect—a fact that is explicit in both the *Topics* itself and in Boethius's commentary; Richer's acquaintance with those works must therefore have been far less thorough than he wished to imply. Richer's account also bears a family resemblance to the synopsis of logic contained in Laon manuscript 468, a

coincidence suggesting that Richer may have been borrowing traditional definitions of dialectic instead of describing his own experience. Finally, citations of Aristotle do not become at all frequent in works of French scholars until after 1050; Gerbert's own learning in the subject, which is attested by his short treatise *De rationali et ratione uti*, does not appear to have been systematically conveyed to any of his students.

No teacher of comparable importance took Gerbert's place after his departure from Reims. Basic instruction doubtless continued to be available, but it was now of only regional significance. The same pattern was to be repeated at other schools throughout the 11th and early 12th centuries, because a cathedral school rarely had two consecutive masters of more than regional importance. Chartres, Anjou, Liège, Laon, and Paris all had their moments of importance at different times in the 11th century, but none established an institutional tradition of scholastic excellence, and the importance of the school did not outlast the death or departure of its famous master.

In the early 11th century, the center for French education was the cathedral school of Chartres under Fulbert. Fulbert's prestige is attested by the fact that, although many of his students were evidently drawn from regions near Chartres, others came from as far away as the Rhineland to study with him. The pattern of students traveling great distances to study with a distinguished master was not new; but it is harder to state with certainty where Fulbert's academic expertise lay. It does not seem to have been in the Trivium; the mnemonic poems that he left in this area are elementary, and this impression is confirmed by the fact that Fulbert's students, most notably Berengar of Tours, neither reveal any extensive knowledge of Aristotle nor do they often invoke arguments from the Liberal Arts. But Fulbert's works and those of his students do reveal a measured and analytical approach to questions of Christian doctrine, as well as an ability to recognize and anticipate multiple points of view on contested issues. It was probably, therefore, a broadly based learning rather than any advanced technical expertise in the Liberal Arts that drew students to Fulbert's school at Chartres.

Most of Fulbert's students returned to their home cathedrals or monasteries after finishing their studies with him, often themselves becoming masters. But at least two of Fulbert's students, Berengar of Tours and Adelman of Liège, followed more complex careers, serving as schoolmasters at more than one cathedral, and this shift in career pattern marks a quickening of the intellectual pace of cathedral schools. Not every cathedral schoolmaster was swept up in the movement; most remained essentially grammar masters, introducing students to the basics of Latin grammar and literature, often with an ethical or Christian overlay. But a handful of later 11th-century masters began the exploration of more speculative issues in the Trivium and in Christian doctrine, and although this movement did not leave monastic schools untouched it was generally in cathedral schools that these masters found an institutional home. The increasingly advanced character of the instruction is revealed not just by the sophistication of some of the theoretical analyses but also by the fact that masters now began to discuss the views of their contemporaries as well as the ancients. The basic texts (Priscian on grammar; Cicero on rhetoric; Porphyry, Aristotle, and Boethius on logic) continued to be expounded, but the glosses and commentaries increasingly took up "questions" where doctrine was unsettled. Masters could make reputations—and, apparently, fortunes—by their skill at expounding the standard texts.

During the decades ca. 1100, the two preeminent masters of cathedral schools in France were William of Champeaux in Paris and Anselm in Laon. William was better known for his work in the Liberal Arts, Anselm for his commentaries on the Bible; but neither was as specialized as later masters would be, and both appear to have taught a wide range of subjects. Students in this period, moreover, frequently traveled themselves, spending considerable amounts of time with a series of masters. Thus, for example, Peter Abélard spent time as a student of both William and Anselm before he launched his own career as a master.

After the 1120s, the cathedral schools gradually lost their role as centers of scholarship and teaching to the concentration of masters at Paris; students who went to Paris could study with several masters at once instead of being limited to the resources of a cathedral school. Although both Thierry of Chartres and Gilbert of Poitiers had ties to Chartres, both did most of their teaching in Paris. Despite the competition, cathedral schools continued to play a significant though reduced role in French education until the end of the century. Peter the Chanter studied at Reims, while Orléans was apparently a center of composition (*ars dictaminis*). Yet comparatively little is known about either center, and after 1200 any person intending to pursue a scholarly career would have sought his training in Paris or one of the other universities rather than in any local school.

Charles Radding

[See also: ABBO OF FLEURY; ABÉLARD, PETER; ALCUIN; ANSELM OF LAON; ARISTOTLE, INFLUENCE OF; BERENGAR OF TOURS; BOETHIUS, INFLUENCE OF; CHARTRES; EDUCATION; ERIUGENA, JOHANNES SCOTTUS; FULBERT OF CHARTRES; GERBERT OF AURILLAC; GILBERT OF POITIERS; LIBERAL ARTS; OVID, INFLUENCE OF; PETER THE CHANTER; PLATO, INFLUENCE OF; SCHOOLS, MONASTIC; THIERRY OF CHARTRES; UNIVERSITIES; VIRGIL, INFLUENCE OF; WILLIAM OF CHAMPEAUX]

Contreni, John. *The Cathedral School of Laon from 850 to 930: Its Manuscripts and Masters.* Munich: Arbeo, 1978.

Merlette, Bernard, and Suzanne Martinet. *Enseignement et vie intellectuelle (IXe–XVe siècle [Actes du 95e Congrès National des Sociétés Savantes]).* Reims, 1970.

Radding, Charles. "The Geography of Learning in Early Eleventh-Century Europe: Lanfranc of Bec and Berengar of Tours Revisited." *Bullettino dell'Istituto Storico Italiano per il Medio Evo e Archivio Muratoriano.* Forthcoming.

———, and William W. Clark. *Medieval Architecture, Medieval Learning: Builders and Masters in the Age of Romanesque and Gothic.* New Haven: Yale University Press, 1992.

Southern, Richard W. "Lanfranc of Bec and Berengar of Tours." In *Studies in Medieval History Presented to Frederick Maurice Powicke*, ed. R.W. Hunt et al. Oxford: Clarendon, 1948, pp. 27–48.

SCHOOLS, MONASTIC. The education of Greek and Roman society was highly developed, but Christianity, having become the state religion in A.D. 380, faced a dilemma—how to marry the two strands of its tradition: that of the illiterate fishermen-Apostles with the bookish, classical training of its apologists. The tradition of learning was strong, and a number of patristic writers, especially Jerome, were associated with education, although we still see Augustine, for example, questioning the legitimacy of his use of his pagan, classical education for Christian ends. The first Christian, nonclassical religious schools date from the 4th century and were associated with monasteries.

The fate of these schools varied with the political situation of their times and places, so that in mainland Europe around the 5th–8th centuries few schools taught anything but the absolute basics of reading and writing. In the insular and insulated territories of Ireland and Britain, however, a brighter light burned, and monastic schools taught grammar and singing to their oblates and perhaps to secular children as well. Bede tells us of his education at Wearmouth-Jarrow, and famous schools existed at York, Canterbury, and Irish centers.

The Carolingian revival of education under Charlemagne drew heavily on insular scholars and included the importation of Alcuin from York. In 797, Theodulf of Orléans introduced parish schools into his diocese and laid down their mandate for teaching. From this time onward, schools spread throughout the Frankish empire and beyond, and from the beginning of the 9th century all the more famous monasteries had two distinct schools—one for its oblates, one for outsiders. The Council of Aix (817) decreed a separation of monastic and secular pupils at monastic schools. Although their histories vary at different periods, there were famous schools at most of the important Benedictine monasteries of the 9th–12th centuries, such as Bec, Fulda, and Reichenau.

Although the history of this period remains misty, at some time during the 11th century "secular" religious schools, based around cathedrals with nonmonastic foundations, grew fashionable. In particular, Notre-Dame in Paris, Reims, Laon, and Chartres had famous masters and pupils. They were perceived as offering a less traditional and accepting, more argumentative style of learning, with debate as well as lecturing as a teaching practice. Leclercq has characterized seven major differences between monastic and secular learning: the intended audience of the teaching, the subjects dealt with, the pastoral tendency of the writers, an interest in the reform of the church, the sources employed, the intellectual methods of the writers, and finally their modes of expression. This is perhaps too generalizing to be wholly convincing; however, it is true that some subjects, such as commentaries on the Song of Songs, are largely the province of "monastic" rather than secular authors, as is a preference for the Gospel of John over the Synoptics as a source of authority. And it is true that until the advent of the university *any* school of this period was only as famous as the master heading it at the time.

In 1108, William of Champeaux, former master of the cathedral school in Paris, opened a school at the abbey of Saint-Victor. A house of Augustinian canons (clergy who lived under a rule in a community), Saint-Victor occupied a point midway between secular clergy and cenobites. It has been suggested that Saint-Victor tried to hold just such a position in the spectrum of learning, blending monastic exegesis with scholastic as the latter became more occupied with theological questioning. But the picture is complicated, and we must not think that books of *Sententiae,* or theological questions, were not also produced and read in monasteries. Nor must we forget that the famous books produced *from* monastic learning, such as the works of Bernard of Clairvaux, Anselm, or Rupert of Deutz, were works produced *for* monastic learning. The day-to-day teaching in monastic schools was the usual round of basic literacy, followed by the Trivium and Quadrivium, with textbooks by Priscian, Donatus, Boethius, Aristotle, and Euclid. Indeed, the learned monks of the 12th century were influential despite the decline in influence of monastic schools and learning.

Although monastic schools continued into the 13th century and later, they were used only as sources of primary education: any ambitious pupil went to a secular school or university.

Lesley J. Smith

[See also: EDUCATION; SAINT-VICTOR, ABBEY AND SCHOOL OF; SCHOOLS, CATHEDRAL; UNIVERSITIES]

Leach, A.F. *The Schools of Medieval England.* London: Methuen, 1915.

Leclercq, Jean. *The Love of Learning and the Desire for God,* trans. Catherine Misrahi. New York: Fordham University Press, 1974.

Smalley, Beryl. *The Study of the Bible in the Middle Ages.* 3rd ed. Oxford: Blackwell, 1983.

SCIENCE. We begin with a distinction between what the medievals called "science" (*scientia*) and what, if anything, corresponds to our modern understanding of the term. *Scientia,* following Aristotle (ἐπιστήμη), meant systematic knowledge, organized through principles, so that philosophy and theology were "sciences" along with physics and mathematics. Prior to the 12th century, "science" meant the Quadrivium (arithmetic, geometry, music, and astronomy) and the Trivium (grammar, rhetoric, and logic), which together comprised the notion of Liberal Arts. In the 12th and 13th centuries, translations into Latin from the Arabic (by Gerard of Cremona [d. 1187]) and from the Greek (by William of Moerbeke [d. ca. 1286]) brought an explosion of "new" knowledge, information, and disciplines into the mainstream of medieval intellectual life: Aristotle, Euclid, Alkindi, Avicenna, Averroes, Al Farabi, Galen,

Alexander of Aphrodisias, and Proclus, among others. These texts provided both authoritative sources and the impetus for extension and expansion of the "sciences of nature" (called "natural philosophy" [*philosophia naturalis* or *physica*]). While the whole is called "philosophy" (from the Greek, φιλία [love]] and σοφία [wisdom]), classification of the parts differed. Hugh of Saint-Victor (d. 1141) divided philosophy into theoretical, practical, mechanical, and logical. He listed medicine among the mechanical arts and declared it a suitable occupation for manually adept members of the lower classes. Being concerned with a product, health, which it borrows from nature, disqualifies medical knowledge from inclusion among the higher, more speculative branches of knowledge. Dominicus Gundissalinus (fl. 1140) divided philosophy into two parts: theoretical and practical. The first is further divided into physical science, mathematics, and the highest speculative science, known variously as theology, first philosophy, or metaphysics. The second is divided into political science, family ordering, and ethical or moral science. Gundisalvo includes medicine among the physical sciences.

When we look for areas of knowledge cognate with our modern understanding of science, we find mathematics, physics (including theory of weight, motion, kinetics, dynamics, magnetism, optics), astronomy and astrology, chemistry and alchemy, geography, oceanography, zoology and botany, and medicine (including anatomy, physiology, and pharmacology; medical diagnosis, treatment, and surgery). (The inclusion of astrology and alchemy in the list suggests the affinity that medieval science had to "magic.") There is also great concern to provide a theoretical account of the structure and dynamics of the universe (cosmology) as well as some attempts to reflect upon methods.

The generally accepted cosmology rested on the assumption of an immobile earth at the center of the universe, with the stars and planets revolving about the earth within concentric spheres—as proposed by Ptolemy (fl. A.D. 127–51) and systematized in Aristotle's physical treatises. Arguments on behalf of a rotating earth were known to the Medievals (e.g., Ptolemy himself, Jean Buridan [b. ca. 1300] and Nicole Oresme [b. ca. 1320/25]) but were not accepted as conclusive. Even in rejecting those arguments, however, both Buridan and Oresme recognized that, on the assumption of a moving earth, the heavenly phenomena would appear to us just as they do on the assumption of a stationary earth.

This cosmology provided the theoretical basis for astrology. Actually, "astronomy" and "astrology" were often used interchangeably; for example, Albert the Great (ca. 1200–1280) says there are two parts to astronomy, the second of which we would be inclined to call "astrology." In general, "astronomy 1" is the science of the stars, the reasons for their relations to one another and to the earth; "astronomy 2" (astrology) is the science of describing the position of the stars for obtaining "a knowledge of the times." The basis for the latter is the causal influences exercised by the former throughout the concentric spheres of the universe down to the region under the moon. Astrological judgments may seem to contradict human free will inasmuch as they seem to place in the hands of the astrologer (astronomer) who understands the causal connection of the movements of heavenly bodies to the events in the sublunar world, a knowledge of necessity and determinism that appears to be at odds with human freedom. But the apparent contradiction, Albert maintains, is not real. Astrological knowledge concerns not human actions directly but dispositions to actions that are always subject to whether the act will or will not actually be done. Persons remain masters of their fate by using their intellect. A person can avert much evil from the effects of the operations of the stars if he knows the influence to be exerted and can prepare to receive it. Choosing the favorable hour expresses both the astrological influence and human freedom. On the other hand, casting horoscopes, although not condemned by Albert, is recognized as emphasizing the potential conflict between astrological horoscopes (as, e.g., when the length of a life is predicted from the constellations) and free will.

As far as methods were concerned, Robert Grosseteste (b. ca. 1168) may serve as a good example. Grosseteste based his approach to scientific knowledge on Aristotle's *Posterior Analytics:* a two-stage process. Beginning with an observed fact, the scientist "resolves" the fact into the principles or elements that constitute it; the second stage consists of "composing," that is, reconstructing the fact on the basis of its "reasons" or "causes." This approach assumed both a uniformity in nature and a principle of economy that chose between competing explanations on grounds of needing the fewer number of suppositions. Because of these "extra-demonstrative" assumptions, Grosseteste's approach yielded probable rather than strictly scientific knowledge of the natural world, since the observed facts would be deduced from more than one explanatory theory without contradiction. In providing scientific knowledge of the heavens or of the behavior of light in optics, Grosseteste recognized that he was providing the formal cause (from the four-cause explanatory structure of explanation provided by Aristotle: formal, material, efficient, and final causes), but he could not provide the material or efficient causes—nor, within natural science—the final cause either. The formal cause could be deduced mathematically (say, geometric epicycles and eccentrics in astronomy); but the material and efficient causes required knowledge of natures—the subject matter of other, higher sciences. Because of his metaphysical theory that light was the basic nature of physical reality, Grosseteste regarded optics as the foundation of physical science; but optics required the mathematics of lines, figures, and angles. Grosseteste was, thus, one of the first to link mathematics directly to the study of natural phenomena beyond the movements of the heavenly bodies.

Grosseteste wrote *Commentaries* on the *Physics* and the *Posterior Analytics* of Aristotle and produced some original treaties on optics. Perhaps no one, however, better expresses the impact of the full corpus of Aristotle's works (and their Arabic commentaries) made available by the 12th- and 13th-century translations than Albert the Great. His voluminous writings include detailed commentaries on Aristotle's physical and biological treatises, to which he added extensive examples of his own observations of flora and fauna gained on his travels on foot in Germany, France, and Italy. What characterized Albert's approach to science and set him apart from many of his contemporaries was his continuous insistence on his own observations and on the need to return to what in Latin is *experimentum*. The term "experiment" cannot be understood in the modern sense. More often than not, the term indicates a careful, scrutinizing process of observing, describing, and classifying. At the same time, natural magic was considered a branch of science: the science that dealt with "occult virtues" (or hidden powers) within nature. God acts through natural causes in the case of natural phenomena, says Albert; and while we would not presume to investigate the causes of the divine will, we are free to investigate—in detail and specifically—the natural causes that are instruments of the divine will. It is in the spirit of what Albert reads in Aristotle (and in pseudo-Aristotelian texts) that he seeks concrete, specific, detailed, accurate knowledge of everything in nature. There are many powers of stones and plants that are learned by experience, and magicians, as well as natural philosophers, investigating these powers, work wonders with them.

Albert's reputation for magic was probably based on two things: 1) there are many references to magic scattered throughout Albert's writings, many of them expressing approval, and some include explicit treatments of the special case of magic, astrology; and 2) the prodigious accumulation of factual (and reportedly factual) knowledge of the natural world, including the medicinal powers of herbs, the folklore about the powers of stones and minerals together with theories of the structure of natural substances and the organization of the universe: all contributed to a Faustian characterization of this one man of the 13th century to be called "Great."

The association of science and the magical arts is evidenced in several ways. The *Libellus de alchimia*, for example, lists several ("scientific"?) precepts for the alchemist to follow:

1) the alchemist/scientist should work silently and secretly; if many know what he is doing, the secret will not be kept and when it is divulged, it will be repeated with error; 2) the scientist should have a laboratory—a special house away from the sight of others in which to carry out his procedures; 3) the scientist must observe the time and the seasons; 4) the scientist must be sedulous, persevering, untiring—a constant worker; if he begins and does not persevere, he will lose both materials and time; 5) in all procedures, the scientist must have and follow a protocol; 6) all vessels should be made of glass; 7) the scientist should stay away from administrators; if you are committed to your work, they will bother you with questions about how you are coming and when will you be finished, and if you take too long they will regard your work as trifling and you will experience great dissatisfaction. Of course, if you do not succeed, you will be humiliated; if you do succeed, they will give you

something else to do; 8) finally, the scientist should have plenty of money.

Medieval science, then, was comprehensive and holistic, both in the sense of embracing all areas of human knowledge and in the sense of a hierarchy of interrelated knowledges. It was profoundly aware of and deferential to the great minds and intellectual traditions of preceding ages, pagan as well as religious, without mistaking authority for reasons. "Science" only slowly differentiated itself from "magic," since both concerned natural phenomena. Mathematics provided a deductive discipline, a source of theoretical explanation of bodies in motion, and the beginnings of what would become an essential constituent of later science.

Frank Catania

[See also: AGRICULTURE; ALBERT THE GREAT; ALEXANDER NECKHAM; ARABIC PHILOSOPHY, INFLUENCE OF; ARMOR AND WEAPONS; ARTILLERY; ASTRONOMICAL AND NAVIGATIONAL INSTRUMENTS; BERNARD SILVESTRIS; CLOCKS AND TIMEKEEPING; CONSTRUCTION TECHNIQUES; ENAMELING; HEALTH CARE; JEWELRY AND METALWORKING; LAPIDARY; LIBERAL ARTS; MAGIC; MARBODE OF RENNES; MEDICAL PRACTICE AND PRACTITIONERS; MILITARY ARCHITECTURE; MILLS AND MILLING; MINING AND METALS; ORESME, NICOLE; SHIPS AND SHIPPING; STAINED GLASS; TAPESTRY; TEXTILES; VITICULTURE; WEIGHTS AND MEASURES]

Clagett, Marshall. *The Science of Mechanics in the Middle Ages.* Madison: University of Wisconsin Press, 1959.
Crombie, A.C. *Augustine to Galileo: Medieval and Early Modern Science.* 2 vols. 2nd ed. Cambridge: Harvard University Press, 1959.
———. *Science, Optics, and Music in Medieval and Early Modern Thought.* London: Hambledon, 1990.
Grant, Edward, ed. *A Source Book in Medieval Science.* Cambridge: Harvard University Press, 1974.
Thorndike, Lynn. *A History of Magic and Experimental Science.* New York: Macmillan, 1923.

SCROFULA. Glandular tuberculosis in general (*scrofule*), a systemic infection of the skin and various organs, was apparently widespread in medieval France as a result of dietary deficiencies, contagion, and bovine tuberculosis, to which it is related. One form that drew particular attention is an inflammation of the lymph glands in the neck (*écrouelles*). Medical encyclopedists, such as Bernard de Gordon and Gui de Chauliac, described scrofulous abscesses in detail among the apostemes caused by phlegmatic humor, and they noted correctly that the young were the most common victims. Physicians prescribed an improved diet as the first phase of therapy. Next, softening salves or plasters were applied; a "French remedy" was cited by the 12th-century Syrian traveler Usamah. Surgery was to be used only if medicaments failed, as stipulated in a contract by which a Toulouse barber in 1400 promised

a cure for the price of eight *écus* payable after doctors certified success. A last resort was the noisome application of caustics. Patients who found no help in medical treatment might make a pilgrimage to St. Marcoul, whose specialized cult spread after 1300. They could also seek the ceremonial royal touch for the "King's Evil." Remissions, often spontaneous, were celebrated as miracles. Claims to healing power were made by French kings from the Capetians to the Bourbons and contested by English dynasties. Ironically, scrofula may have claimed the lives of several members of the house of Valois.

Luke Demaitre

[See also: DISEASES; HEALTH CARE; MEDICAL PRACTICE AND PRACTITIONERS]

Barlow, Frank. "The King's Evil." *English Historical Review* 95 (1980): 3–27.
Bloch, Marc. *The Royal Touch: Sacred Monarchy and Scrofula in England and France,* trans. J.E. Anderson. London: Routledge and Kegan Paul, 1973.

SEALS AND SIGILLOGRAPHY. From the 13th through the 15th century, the use of seals in France was a generalized phenomenon that involved the society as a whole and crossed boundaries of gender, age, religion, and social and professional status. All persons and corporations could, and most did, legally commit themselves by affixing their seals to charters recording their transactions and decisions. The seal's function as a means of documentary validation should not obscure its broader implications as a cultural phenomenon.

The seal presents a dualistic aspect. The seal matrix, made of metal, such as brass, bronze, latten, or gold and silver for the ruling elites, was carved in the negative and designed to impress repeatedly a raised image, the seal impression, upon a secondary surface, most often of wax or lead. Seals thus evoked notions both of being (matrix) and of becoming (impression) and projected a creative capacity analogous to life itself, which may account for the intense psychosocial identification of medieval individuals with their seals. For the seal was a personal object incorporating both a text—the legend—and an image. The legend identified the sealer by name and by rank, and the importance of identity, repeatedly declared under a wide variety of circumstances, rendered the choice of title significant. The image, however, dwelt less on individuality than on status and sociopolitical function, less on subjective than on group consciousness. Persons appeared on their seals within such categories as kings, queens, knights, abbesses, artisans, even peasants and Jews. Moreover, when displaying coats of arms individuals defined their locus within their family, since heraldic emblems expressed the identity of a kindred in relation to its subbranches and other groups. Underlying conventions therefore dictated that sealers be represented by conceptual images and not as individuals and that seal iconography foster a symbology of power, articulating and probably authenticating the organizing principles of French medieval society.

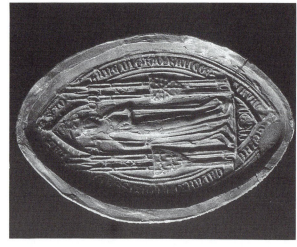

Jeanne of Navarre, queen of Philip the Fair (1300). Standing queen under canopy, with regalia and coats of arms (France and Navarre). *Photograph courtesy of Archives Nationales, Paris.*

Humbert II, dauphin of Viennois (1343). A view of the city of Vienne (Isère). *Photograph courtesy of Archives Nationales, Paris.*

Philip the Fair, king of France (1286). King enthroned, with regalia. *Photograph courtesy of Archives Nationales, Paris.*

Simon de Montfort (1211). Hunting equestrian. *Photograph courtesy of Archives Nationales, Paris.*

Childeric, king of the Franks (d. 482). Royal bust, with imperial dalmatic and long hair. *Photograph courtesy of Archives Nationales, Paris.*

Raymond VII, count of Toulouse (1218). Equestrian in arms. *Photograph courtesy of Archives Nationales, Paris.*

Abbey of the Trinity at Fécamp (1204). Blessing Christ, in bust. *Photograph courtesy of Archives Nationales, Paris.*

Jeanne the grocer (1315). A woman holding two scales. *Photograph courtesy of Archives Nationales, Paris.*

Chapter of Notre-Dame of Xehun-sur-Yère (Cher, 1308). A Gothic church. *Photograph courtesy of Archives Nationales, Paris.*

Moissac (Tarn-et-Garonne, 1243). A walled city. *Photograph courtesy of Archives Nationales, Paris.*

Peter Lombard, bishop of Paris (1159). Standing bishop in vestments. *Photograph courtesy of Archives Nationales, Paris.*

Hugues X, lord of Lusignan (1224). A coat of arms (a barruly). *Photograph courtesy of Archives Nationales, Paris.*

Seals drew their power as effective agents of authentication from a dual legacy. The first results from a specific pattern of diffusion. From ca. 450 to ca. 1050, documentary sealing had remained an exclusively royal prerogative, an as yet unchallenged expression of public authority, which thereafter spread to magnates, male and female, ecclesiastical and lay. From ca. 1050 to ca. 1200, nonroyal seals were used solely by such elites in emulating, claiming, and exercising ruling status, arrogating to themselves regalian rights, among them that of seal usage. The second legacy involves the tradition, unbroken since the early Middle Ages, of exchanging symbolic objects, such as knives, whips, and handles, as evidence of agreement or transaction. As legal titles came to depend increasingly on written records by the early 13th century, the seal provided both an authoritative guarantee derived from its previously royal character and the tangibility of a symbolic object that had regulated the oral and ritual system of property transfers and judicial settlements. The medieval seal, thus standing at the junction of literate and oral tradition, encouraged trust in the written word by incorporating participatory, tactile, and iconic practices associated with an orality that remained throughout the Middle Ages the framework in which literacy and documentation functioned.

Brigitte Bedos-Rezak

Bedos-Rezak, Brigitte. "The Social Implications of the Art of Chivalry: The Sigillographic Evidence (France, 1050–1250)." In *The Medieval Court in Europe*, ed. Edward R. Haymes. Munich: Fink, 1986, pp. 142–75.

———. "Suger and the Symbolism of Royal Power: The Seal of Louis VII." In *Abbot Suger and Saint Denis*, ed. Paula L. Gerson. New York: Metropolitan Museum of Art, 1986, pp. 95–103.

———. "Women, Seals and Power in Medieval France, 1150–1350." In *Women and Power in the Middle Ages*, ed. Mary Erler and Maryanne Kowaleski. Athens: University of Georgia Press, 1988, pp. 61–82.

Candilhon, René, and Michel Pastoureau. *Bibliographie de la sigillographie française*. Paris: Picard, 1982.

Pastoureau, Michel. *Les sceaux*. Turnhout: Brepols, 1981.

SÉES (Séez). The present cathedral of Notre-Dame at Sées (Orne) replaces one burned in 1174 by Henry II Plantagenêt. Among the finest examples of Norman Gothic architecture, it was begun from the west side in the early 13th century. The well-proportioned nave with three stories—arcades, triforium, and high pointed arches—reflects English influence. The transept and choir with clerestory and ambulatory, begun ca. 1280 under Bishop Jean de Bernières (r. 1278–94), were inspired by Paris. They are lit by 13th-century square-framed rose windows, remarkable for their finely carved tracery. The façade with porch and bell towers dates from the 14th century; its main portal has an impressive tympanum of the Virgin.

William W. Kibler/William W. Clark

Gobillot, René. *La cathédrale de Séez*. Paris: Laurens, 1937.

———. "Sées." *Congrès archéologique* (Orne) 111 (1953): 39–58.

Lafond, Jean. "Les vitraux de la cathédrale de Sées." *Congrès archéologique* (Orne) 111 (1953): 59–83.

SEIGNEUR/SEIGNEURIE. By the end of the Middle Ages, various kinds of people were called "lord" (Lat. *dominus*, Fr. *seigneur*, *sire*), including members of the old military aristocracy and people of humble origins who had acquired a privileged occupation or title. Most commonly, however, the term continued to refer to those who possessed a seigneurie, or lordship, generally but by no means always rural in character. Those who possessed a seigneurie might be the lord of different kinds of people: (1) those who were their tenants; (2) those who were subject to their jurisdiction or *ban*; and (3) those who owed them homage for a fief. To the first group, the seigneur was landlord; to the second, he was judge and political ruler; to the third, he was the superior in a feudal relationship but often the social equal. The feminine form, "lady" (Lat. *domina*), often referred to the wife or widow of a lord but could also refer to a woman who exercised lordship over one or more of these groups in her own right, usually as a result of inheritance. A corporate body, such as a monastery or cathedral chapter, could also be a seigneur.

Although the term seigneurie could mean "lordship" in an abstract sense, most commonly it referred to the persons and territory subject to one or both of the first two types of lordship indicated above. In the first, and much older of these, the seigneur was the proprietor of an agricultural operation, deriving his income, in cash or kind, from the rents paid by his peasant farmers, who also often had to perform obligatory labor services (*corvées*) on the lord's own farmland, the produce of which was an important part of his revenue. The seigneurie in this sense had ancient roots, and with it went a certain amount of petty jurisdiction that came to be called "low justice." This kind of seigneurie was able, for a time, to support the lord as a mounted warrior, but in the 12th century its economic value began to decline relative to the revenues obtainable from the second type of lordship, sometimes called the *seigneurie banale*.

The *seigneur banal* was the political and judicial ruler of those who were his dependents. With respect to some of these, he might also exercise the traditional role of landlord, but he might wield banal powers also over people who were the tenants of a lesser landlord. The seigneur of this type possessed "high justice," a far more lucrative jurisdiction that covered most serious felonies. He could demand exactions that came to be associated with serfdom. He could require his subjects to use his mill, winepress, or oven and pay him a fee. He might hold extensive rights over the forests and waterways, from which he could exact fees or tolls. Lordships of this sort provided the basic financial support for the higher nobility of France. When they encountered economic difficulties in the 14th century, the nobility suffered a serious crisis.

The seigneurie has sometimes been described as the exercise of formerly public powers by private individuals, since the *ban* was the symbol of public authority. The Frankish kings had adopted the practice of granting charters of "immunities" to ecclesiastical lords, promising that royal officers would not enter their lands to exercise their military or judicial functions. The holder of such a charter had the right and duty to take over these functions in lieu of the royal officials. When they were incompatible with clerical status, the church would have an important local layman act as *vidame* or "advocate" and perform the functions associated with the *ban*.

In time, immunities were extended to important lay lords who could exercise the *ban* on their own behalf. Finally, ca. 1000, the growing importance of the castle brought further changes, as castellans used their positions to usurp banal powers from the counts and impose their *ban* on lesser landlords and their tenants. By the 11th and 12th centuries, the seigneurie was the principal unit of government and political power at the local level, but in later centuries, as territorial princes and kings reasserted their own public powers, it became primarily an economic unit again.

John Bell Henneman, Jr.

[See also: ADVOCATUS/*AVOUÉ*; *BAN/BANALITÉ*; *CENS*; *FORMARIAGE*; GRANGE; *MÉTAYER/MÉTAYAGE*; NOBILITY; PRECARIA; RURAL SOCIAL STRUCTURE; SERFDOM/SERVITUDE/SLAVERY]

Cheyette, Frederic L., ed. *Lordship and Community in Medieval Europe.* New York: Holt, Rinehart and Winston, 1968.
Duby, Georges. *Rural Economy and Country Life in the Medieval West*, trans. Cynthia Postan. London: Arnold, 1968.
Fourquin, Guy. *Lordship and Feudalism in the Middle Ages.* New York: Pica, 1976.

SEINTE RESURECCION. A late 12th-century play fragment (522 lines) in the Anglo-Norman dialect, based on the Gospel narratives of the Resurrection. Its style is more closely related to the historical realism of the late-medieval Passion plays than to the liturgical and lyrical character of the near-contemporary *Jeu d'Adam.* The text is found in two manuscripts, both fragmentary: B.N. fr. 902 and B.L. Add. 45103.

Alan E. Knight

[See also: *JEU D'ADAM*; STAGING OF PLAYS; THEATER]

Jenkens, Thomas Atkinson, et al., eds. *La seinte Resureccion.* Oxford: Blackwell, 1943.

SÉLESTAT (Schlettstadt). An early residence of the Frankish monarchs, Sélestat (Bas-Rhin) is situated on the left bank of the River Ill. In the 13th century, it was granted its charter as a free imperial city. It preserves its late-medieval town center and two towers of its fortifications, the Tour des Sorcières and the Tour de l'Horloge (14th c.). The magnificent triple-naved priory church of Sainte-Foy (12th c.), in red sandstone and Vosges granite, is one of the finest Romanesque buildings in Alsace. Its decoration aban-

dons the Rhenish style and Lombard arcading of other Alsatian churches (Murbach, Guebwiller, Neuwiller) in favor of French foliated capitals. The massive west end consists of a porch between two square towers decorated with arcades on colonnettes. The octagonal lantern tower over the transept with arcatures and a stone spire rising to 142 feet is also original. The central nave has early rib vaulting supported on alternating strong and weak Romanesque columns; the flanking aisles have groin vaulting.

The Gothic church of Saint-George was built from the 13th to the 15th century. An unusual 13th-century narthex runs the entire length of the façade and opens to the south with an elegant portal and rose window representing the Ten Commandments. The four windows in the façade are 13th-century; the vaulting of the nave is 14th-century; and important 15th-century stained glass represents the lives of SS. Catherine and Agnès.

William W. Kibler/William W. Clark

Dorlan, Alexandre. *Histoire architecturale et anecdotique de Schlestadt.* 2 vols. Paris: Tallandier, 1912.
Duraud, Georges. "Sélestat." *Congrès archéologique* (Metz, Strasbourg, Colmar) 83 (1920): 461–85.

SÉNANQUE. With Le Thoronet and Silvacane, Sénanque (Vaucluse) is one of the "three Cistercian sisters of Provence." Founded in 1148, it was attacked by the Waldensians in 1544 but remained active until the Revolution,

Sénanque (Vaucluse), mid-12th-century Cistercian abbey. *Photograph courtesy of Whitney S. Stoddard.*

then was reoccupied and restored by the order between 1854 and 1969 (with a hiatus from 1900 to 1927). Its 12th-century conventual buildings—church, cloister, chapter house, dormitory, and warming room—are typically simple and austere, according to the dictates of the order's founder, St. Bernard of Clairvaux. Due to its site in a narrow glen, the church is oriented north-south. Its nave is spanned by an impressive continuous barrel vault without cross-arches.

William W. Kibler/William W. Clark

[See also: CISTERCIAN ART AND ARCHITECTURE; SILVACANE; THORONET, LE]

Thibout, Marc. "L'abbaye de Sénanque." *Congrès archéologique* (*Avignon et Comtat-Venaissin*) 121 (1963): 365–76.

SENESCHAL. The seneschal (Lat. *dapifer*) originated as an officer of the royal household concerned with keeping the king's itinerant entourage properly supplied with the produce and revenues of scattered royal estates. When, after a period of obscurity, the seneschal emerged in the 11th century as one of the "great officers of the crown," he quickly became the senior royal official. In this sense, his role can be traced back to the Merovingian mayor of the palace and forward to the grand master of the household in the later Middle Ages.

The king's household was still the principal organ of the central government in the 11th and 12th centuries, and the seneschal enjoyed great importance. He was the leading military commander and the one to whom the *prévôts*, the principal domainal officers in the field, were supposed to report. Three important men held the position of seneschal for much of the 12th century, Anseau de Garlande, Raoul de Vermandois, and Thibaut de Blois, each from a more prestigious family than his predecessor. Thibaut, as count of Blois, was a major territorial lord. When he died in 1191, Philip II Augustus allowed the position to remain vacant.

Meanwhile, important territorial lords had their own staffs of major household officers, with the seneschal holding senior rank. In many great fiefs, he acted as lieutenant in the lord's absence, being in charge of military, judicial, and financial matters. When the French kings began to absorb great fiefs into the royal domain, they preferred to retain existing institutions that had proven workable. The seneschals, now royal appointees, continued to be the chief administrative officers of such territories, and the lands under their control became known as *sénéchaussées*. By the second half of the 13th century, these officers, found mostly in southwestern France, were roughly comparable with the bailiffs (*baillis*) who served as the king's chief regional officers in the northern part of the kingdom. In the late Middle Ages, the realm contained between thirty and forty districts governed by a bailiff or a seneschal. By that time, both types of officer had largely military responsibilities, as their former judicial and financial duties were performed by specialized subordinates.

John Bell Henneman, Jr.

Fesler, James W. "French Field Administration: The Beginnings." *Comparative Studies in History and Society* 5 (1962–63): 76–111.

Lot, Ferdinand, and Robert Fawtier. *Histoire des institutions françaises au moyen âge.* 3 vols. Paris: Presses Universitaires de France, 1958, Vol. 2: *Institutions royales.*
Michel, Robert. *L'administration royale dans la sénéchaussée de Beaucaire au temps de saint Louis.* Paris: Picard, 1910.
Rogozinski, Jan. "The Counsellors of the Seneschal of Beaucaire and Nîmes 1250–1350." *Speculum* 44 (1969): 421–39.

SENLIS. Senlis (Oise) is best remembered for an event that took place relatively late in its history, the election of Hugh Capet as king of France in 987. A favorite royal city of both the Merovingians and Carolingians, Senlis takes its name from its first Gallic inhabitants, the Sulbanectes (later the Sylvanectes), and not from its Roman name, Augustomagus. The thriving Gallo-Roman town was destroyed in the 3rd century, an event that led to the first city walls, the only ones of their date still preserved in France. Christianity reached Senlis probably in the late 3rd century, although the first bishop we know by name, St. Rieul, was probably active in the mid-4th century. Early references to the cathedral give two names, Notre-Dame and Saints-Gervais-et-Protais, suggesting an episcopal group of two or three (including the baptistery of Saint-Jean). The double vocable is still preserved; the cathedral is Notre-Dame and the two-storied octagonal chapel (later 10th or early 11th century) is Saints-Gervais-et-Protais.

The present cathedral, underway by 1153, owes its inspiration to the chevet of Saint-Denis. Comparison of the details of capitals and other architectural elements indicates that the west façade, also based on Saint-Denis, was begun at the same time as the east end, which was completed by 1167. The whole building was dedicated in 1195. A transept was inserted in the 13th century, as were

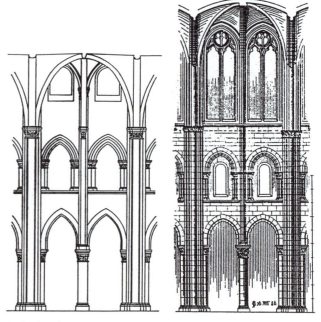

Senlis (Oise), Notre-Dame, nave elevations, 12th century and present. After Aubert and Vermand.

Senlis, west portal, Coronation of the Virgin. *Photograph courtesy of Whitney S. Stoddard.*

Senlis, Notre-Dame, ambulatory and chapels. *Photograph: Clarence Ward Collection. Courtesy of Oberlin College.*

lateral chapels. A major fire in 1504 resulted in a dramatic increase in the height of the clerestory and the addition of new vaults.

The original plan called for a deep chevet of five bays under two sexpartite vaults; the last straight bay is vaulted with the hemicycle. The main vessel is flanked by aisles and ambulatory with five radiating chapels. The plan of the east end of Senlis is irregular, the result of the builder having to insert the chevet in the space close to the Gallo-Roman city walls, which included a chapel used by the canons.

The 12th-century design of Senlis cathedral is one of the first to include vaulted galleries in the Gothic style, a feature also found at nearby Noyon. The third story of the elevation was a single low window, the height of which can be reconstructed from the level of the 12th-century vault between the west towers. Because the original plan was based on compound piers, the plan of the rebuilt vaults repeated the original, although at a higher level. The smallest of the major 12th-century Gothic buildings, Senlis is marked by an elegance in execution that befits its importance in a major royal city.

The west façade was planned to have three portals, but only the center one was decorated with figure sculp-

ture. The design and composition of this portal are among the major innovations of the period, as is the choice of subject matter. Here, for perhaps the first time, the theme of the tympanum is given over to the Coronation of Mary as Queen of Heaven. Already enthroned, Mary turns toward Christ, who was shown reaching out to crown her—his hands and the crown are missing. The lintel below, which has been dropped into the zone of the jambs, is divided into two scenes in parallel compositions. On the left, the mourning Apostles surround Mary's deathbed while angels convey her soul to Heaven; on the right, an ecstatic group of angels raise the body of Mary so that it might join her soul. The four ranks of archivolts show her earthly genealogy, the Tree of Jesse, together with those sibyls and Prophets who predicted the Virgin Birth. The eight statue columns are the Christophores, those Old Testament prefigurations of salvation, arranged in pairs of historical sequences. On the right, the sequence runs from the outside to the door: David, Isaiah, Jeremiah, and Simeon; on the left, it runs out from the door: Abraham, Moses, Aaron, and John the Baptist. The cycle of time is completed by the Labors of the Months flanked by mythical beasts.

The parish church of Saint-Pierre, converted to a covered market in the 19th century, has recently been excavated and restored with a semblance of its Flamboyant elegance intact. Saint-Aignan, until recently a movie theater, is also under excavation and restoration. The collegial church of Saint-Frambourg was closed after the Revolution and converted to other use. Begun in 1177 and completed by the end of the century, this remarkably homogeneous single-nave building has also been carefully restored and now serves as a concert hall. Excavations in the course of the restorations of all three churches have revealed the plans of earlier structures.

Senlis preserves three other significant buildings associated with its medieval past: the bishop's palace with its chapel; the Hôtel Vermandois, a 12th-century seigneurial residence built by Raoul de Vermandois, first cousin and seneschal to Louis VI; and the royal palace at Senlis, a favorite residence of Louis VI and Louis VII, both of whom made additions to it. The ruins of the palace complex include a two-storied great hall and royal chapel; the Hôtel Vermandois has vestiges of its great hall intact (and under restoration). In addition, Senlis has a number of 15th- and 16th-century residences of nobility and wealthy citizens.

William W. Clark

[**See also:** GOTHIC ARCHITECTURE]

Aubert, Marcel. *Senlis*. Paris: Laurens, 1933.
Bianchina, Nicole. "Saint-Frambourg de Senlis: étude historique et archéologique." *Revue archéologique de l'Oise* 20 (1980): 5–16; 22 (1981): 13–31.
Crépin-Leblond, Thierry, and Dominique Vermand. "L'ancien hotel de Vermandois à Senlis." *Mémoires de la Société d'Histoire et d'Archéologie de Senlis 1986–89* (1991): 123–56.
Fontaine, Anne, and Jacques Fontaine. *Senlis*. La Pierre-qui-vire: Zodiaque, 1985.
Vermand, Dominique. "La cathédrale Notre-Dame de Senlis au XIIe siècle: étude historique et monumentale." *La cathédrale Notre-Dame de Senlis au XIIe siècle*. Senlis: Société d'Histoire et d'Archéologie de Senlis, 1987, pp. 3–107.

SENS. Sens (Yonne) takes its name from the Senones, the Celtic tribe who first settled on the island in the Yonne River, rather than from its Roman name, Agendicum. After the Roman conquest, the town became an important center of trade owing to its location at the junction of two important roads, east-west from Troyes to Orléans and north-south from Lyon to Paris. Sens was a major center by the 4th century, with extensive city walls. Nothing of the early city remains above ground—the last Roman gate was demolished in the 1840s—although extensive archaeological finds of sculpture and architecture, today in the municipal museum, attest to its importance.

Christianity probably reached Sens in the 3rd century. The 7th-century *vita* of St. Loup repeats the legend that the first cathedral was built by St. Savinien on the site of a pagan temple. Of the many parish churches and abbeys, only the cathedral and the 13th-century church of Saint-Jean, now on the grounds of the hospital, survive.

The early episcopal group at Sens consisted of Saint-Jean (the baptistery), Saint-Étienne, and Notre-Dame. The three portals of the Gothic cathedral commemorate these three early churches. In the 9th century, Archbishop Wénilon

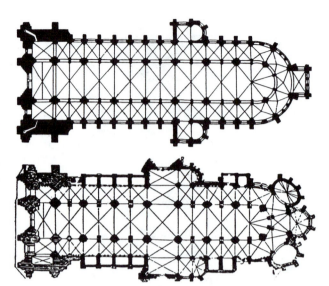

Sens (Yonne), Saint-Étienne, plans of 12th-century and present church. After Clark/Bouy and Bégule.

Sens, Saint-Étienne, nave aisle. *Photograph courtesy of Whitney S. Stoddard.*

Sens, Saint-Étienne, choir from the south. *Photograph courtesy of Whitney S. Stoddard.*

rebuilt Saint-Étienne, which again was destroyed by fire in 968. The third church, built 968–82, survived until it was torn down to give way to the present Gothic cathedral.

This building was undertaken by Archbishop Henri Sanglier (r. 1122–42) ca. 1140. The south chapel was in use by 1151, and Pope Alexander II dedicated the altar of Peter and Paul in the completed chevet on April 19, 1164. The burning of the city in 1184 must have damaged the new façade, although most of the work postdates the fire.

The building history is complicated by the collapse of the south tower of the façade in 1268, which necessitated rebuilding it, the vault between the towers, and the first bay of the nave and several aisle vaults. This occurred after the construction of a new axial chapel and the enlargement of the clerestory windows in the east end of the building, 1230–40. Chapels were added between the buttresses of the nave in the late 13th and early 14th centuries, but the most profound changes occurred after 1490, when Martin Chambiges began construction of the south-transept arm. The new arm was vaulted in 1498 and the north-transept arm constructed in 1500–17.

The original plan of Sens belonged to that small series of medieval buildings without transepts, which in part accounts for the axial regularity and for the commanding sense of continuous space. The chevet had an ambulatory with a single rectangular chapel. Two side chapels beyond the ambulatory complete the chevet plan. The main vessel is extremely wide (49 feet) and tall (nearly 80 feet). The resulting space is on a grand scale. That sense of scale is

reinforced by the huge domical six-part main vaults erected over double nave bays.

The elevation consisted of three stories, two of which, arcades and triforium, remain. The second story consisted of double units of subdivided arcading opening into the roof space. In the 19th century, a back wall was erected in each bay, although there is no communication between bays. The clerestory was enlarged in the 13th century.

Construction of the present building started with the erection of the chapel of Saint-Jean on the north side, followed by the outer wall of the ambulatory. Construction proceeded at a regular pace up to the level of the windows, where there are several visible changes in the design, largely a matter of an increase in first the width and then the height of the windows. The north ambulatory wall preserves evidence of two, probably three, such enlargements. The lower tails of groin vaults can still be seen in several bays. This lowest course, on the same block as the transverse-arch capital, had already been prepared when the decision to incorporate rib vaults was made. The late addition of rib vaults explains the little corbels stuck in to take the ribs. The masks and grotesques on the corbels, together with the capitals, confirm the presence of workers brought to Sens from the abbey of Saint-Denis, which also explains the changes in window sizes and the decision to use rib vaults. The accompanying change in attitude toward the architectural space makes Sens the first Gothic cathedral.

The abbey of Saint-Jean, of which only the chevet of the church remains, was founded in 500. The chevet was nearing completion when Abbot Simon Galtier died in 1245. The church was heavily damaged in the Hundred Years' War and again by the Calvinists in 1567. The ruined chevet was restored and completed by the Maurists between 1672 and 1684 in a manner harmonious with the surviving ambulatory. The 13th-century church, inspired both by Sens cathedral and by Auxerre cathedral, is a fine example of Burgundian Gothic.

William W. Clark

[See also: GAUTIER DE VARINFOY; GOTHIC ARCHITECTURE]

Bégule, Lucien. *La cathédrale de Sens: son architecture, son décor.* Lyon: Rey, 1929.

Bruand, Yves. "Église Saint-Jean de Sens." *Congrès archéologique (Auxerre)* 116 (1958): 383–91.

Henriet, Jacques. "La cathédrale Saint-Étienne de Sens: le parti du premier maître et les campagnes du XIIe siècle." *Bulletin monumental* 140 (1982): 81–168.

Kurmann, Peter, and Dethard von Winterfeld. "Gautier de Varinfroy: Ein 'Denkmalpfleger' im 13. Jahrhundert." In *Festschrift für Otto von Simson zum 65. Geburtstag*, ed. L. Griesbach and K. Renger. Frankfurt: Propyläen, 1977, pp. 101–59, esp. 121–43.

Salet, Francis. "La cathédrale de Sens et sa place dans l'histoire de l'architecture médiévale." *Académie des Inscriptions et Belles-Lettres, comptes-rendus des séances* (1955): 182–87.

Severens, Kenneth W. "The Early Campaign at Sens, 1140–1145." *Journal of the Society of Architectural Historians* 29 (1970): 97–107.

———. "The Continuous Plan of Sens Cathedral." *Journal of the Society of Architectural Historians* 34 (1975): 198–207.

SENTENCE COLLECTIONS. Originally, *sententia* was the term for a scriptural text under consideration, but it came to mean the interpretation of that text. *Sententiae* is a Latin word meaning "opinions," and sentence collections, sometimes called *florilegia* ("bunches of flowers"), are gatherings of the opinions of the church fathers, arranged around topics. Sentence collections could be more popular than the original works, and patristic authorities might well be quoted from these collections rather than from the complete work. Sometimes, sentence collections feature the opinions of only one author: Gregory the Great was popular in this respect. Early sentence collections were compiled by Prosper of Aquitaine and Isidore of Seville.

Biblical exegesis was most commonly done book by book, following the text of any one book straight through. But certain questions that arose out of the text could be detached from it and continue life as separate topics, with the opinions of their patristic authorities in attendance. Grouped together, these formed collections of sentences and are the progenitors of the great *summae*, or summaries, of theology that are the characteristic product of the scholasticism of the high Middle Ages.

Some of the famous collections of the Middle Ages are associated with Anselm of Laon, especially the *Sententiae divinae paginae* and the *Sententiae Anselmi*, both collected together after his death. The anonymous *Summa sententiarum*, probably by Otto of Lucca, was used by Peter Lombard for his own *Sententiae;* but most collections are both anonymous and more ordinary than these, for they represent the "commonplace books" of readers and preachers, rather in the manner of books of *distinctiones*. Other famous collections are the *Liber Pancrisis*, the *Sententiae Atrebatensis*, and the *Sententiae* of Robert Pullen and of Rolando Bandinelli. It has been argued that sentences are a particular production of the "School of Laon," under Anselm, and that they form a bridge between the output of the monasteries and the more combative work of the schools. However, as so often in the Middle Ages, our understanding is hampered by a confusion of terms, both modern and medieval. We may attempt to deal with centuries of tradition in different contexts with the same word; they recognized the changes in meaning of the same term used in a different situation. Named collections of sentences are extant from monastic sources as diverse as that of Defensor of Ligugé in the 7th century to Hélinant de Froidmont at the beginning of the 13th, and sentence collections are found in large numbers in south German monastic libraries. The apogee of the sentence collection was reached ca. 1155, when Peter Lombard, master of the schools at Paris and later bishop of Paris, published his *Quattuor libri sententiarum*. This work of largely patristic opinions, with heavy prevalence given to Augustine, is arranged under headings and questions, with the minimum of linking commentary by Peter himself. The four books cover God in Trinity, the Creation and Sin, the In-carnation and Virtue, and Sacraments and the Eschaton. The extracts, chosen with skill, produce a wide range of question and opinion in the minimum of space. When in the 1220s Peter's sentences became the textbook for the theology faculty of the University of Paris, each doctoral student had to write a commentary on the work as part of his training. No additional important sentence collections *per se* were then produced, merely more commentaries on Lombard.

Lesley J. Smith

[See also: ANSELM OF LAON; PETER LOMBARD; SCHOLASTICISM; SCHOOLS, MONASTIC; THEOLOGY]

Colish, Marcia L. "Another Look at the School of Laon." *Archives d'histoire doctrinale et littéraire du moyen âge.* 53 (1983): 7–22.
Flint, Valerie I.J. "The 'School of Laon': A Reconsideration." *Recherches de théologie ancienne et médiévale* 43 (1976): 89–110.
Ghellenck, Joseph de. *Le mouvement théologique du XIIe siècle.* 2nd ed. Bruges: De Tempel, 1948.
Lottin, Odin. *Psychologie et morale aux XIIe et XIIIe siècles.* 6 vols. Louvain: Abbaye du Mont César, 1942–60.

SEPTIMANIA. The Mediterranean coastal region between the Rhône and the Pyrénées, stretching from Avignon to Perpignan and comprising the modern French departments of the Gard, Hérault, Aude, and Pyrénées-Orientales, was known as "Septimania" in the early Middle Ages. The name (first attested in the 5th c.) is derived from the 7th Roman legion, which was settled in the area of Béziers (Colonia Iulia Septimanorum Baeterrae) in the 1st century A.D. Septimania, part of the Roman province of Transalpine Gaul (later Gallia Narbonensis), was thoroughly romanized. In the 4th century, it was separated from the region east of the Rhône and formed into the province of Narbonensis Prima. The Visigoths gained control of it in the late 5th century but did not colonize it intensively. Under Visigothic rule to the mid-8th century, Septimania was not part of Merovingian Gaul; it was, rather, a barrier to direct Merovingian access to the Mediterranean and was the object of repeated unsuccessful Frankish efforts to conquer it in the 6th century, by Childebert I, Theuderic I, and Guntram.

After the victory of Clovis I over Alaric II in 507, Septimania remained in the Visigothic kingdom of Spain as the province of Septimania (sometimes also called Gallia or Gallia Narbonensis) and often exhibited strong separatist feelings. The Muslims did not conquer Septimania when they took the rest of the Visigothic kingdom in 713, but it was exposed to frequent attacks until it was taken over by Pepin the Short in the 750s. Its nobility and population continued to see itself as Gothic and Gothic law was enforced there. Under the Carolingians, the name "Gothia" came to be used for the region, although for over a century "Septimania" continued to be used as well.

Steven Fanning

[See also: GOTHIA]

Abadal y de Vinyals, Ramón. "El paso de Septimania del dominio godo al franco a través de la invasión sarracena, 720–768." *Cuadernos de historia de España* 19 (1953): 7–54.

Rivert, A.L.F. *Gallia Narbonensis.* London: Batsford, 1988.

Rouche, Michel. *L'Aquitaine des Wisigoths aux Arabes, 418–781: naissance d'une région.* Paris: École des Hautes Études en Sciences Sociales, 1979.

Thompson, E.A. *The Goths in Spain.* Oxford: Clarendon, 1969.

SEQUENCE (EARLY). Sequences, also known as "proses," were long chants sung at Mass on high feast days after the singing of the Alleluia and before the intoning of the Gospel. They were apparently first conceived as verses to be set to long melismas (textless vocalizations upon a single vowel sound, called *melodiae* or *sequentiae* in the sources) sung at the end of the Alleluia. Although sequences quickly became an independent genre, whose melodies were sometimes related to a "parent" Alleluia and sometimes not, early-medieval sequences always looked as if they were texted *melodiae*. Manuscripts both east and west of the Rhine consistently preserved sequences in two forms, with and without texts; the untexted form probably aided in reading the notation of the texted form, which required that the neumes be broken down into simple virgae and puncta to accommodate individual syllables. The music of early sequences, except in beginning and closing lines, is often made up of repeating couplets, which cause the text to unfold in paired versicles: a, bb, cc, dd, ee, ff, g.

Although the origins of the early-medieval sequence are still in dispute, most scholars believe that the genre began in West Frankish lands, especially in what is now northern France, probably during the first half of the 9th century, with models later inspiring poets and musicians in other regions; the East Frankish repertory was established in the second half of the 9th century, with Notker of Saint-Gall (ca. 840–912) a major creative force. Sequence repertoires in southern France and in England, both of which developed in the 10th century, were dependent primarily upon the northern French tradition, whereas Italian sequences, also developing in the 10th century, drew upon both East and West Frankish traditions. Manuscripts are extant in each tradition from one or two generations after the repertoires were first created: the earliest complete, liturgically ordered collections of sequences, for example, date from the second half of the 10th century and were copied in southern France.

Although each geographical region had its own style of sequence, these differences have been little studied. The texts are written in art prose, carefully constructed and commonly using such poetic devices as assonance and rhyme, yet following no presently understood rules. The melodies of early-medieval sequences—simple, forceful, and strongly reliant upon the modes—are different in style from the Alleluias themselves, and from other Gregorian chants as well. Some early sequence melodies were frequently reset or readapted for new texts. The late 10th and early 11th centuries in southern France witnessed a sec-

ond flourishing of early sequences, and here one can find an increasing dependence upon rhyme.

Margot Fassler

[See also: *ANALECTA HYMNICA MEDII AEVI; SAINTE EULALIE, SÉQUENCE DE*; SEQUENCE (LATE)]

Dreves, Guido, ed. *Analecta hymnica medii aevi.* Leipzig: Fues's Verlag, 1889, vol. 7.

Björkvall, Gunilla. "En marge des plus anciennes séquences médiévales." *Revue bénédictine* 88 (1978): 170–73.

Crocker, Richard. *The Repertoire of Proses at Saint Martial de Limoges (Tenth and Eleventh Centuries).* 2 vols. Diss. Yale University, 1957.

———. *The Early Medieval Sequence.* Berkeley: University of California Press, 1977.

Elfving, Lars. *Étude lexicographique sur les séquences limousines.* Stockholm: Almqvist and Wiksell, 1962.

Fassler, Margot. *Gothic Song: Victorine Sequences and Augustinian Reform in Twelfth-Century Paris.* Cambridge: Cambridge University Press, 1993, pp. 38–57.

SEQUENCE (LATE). The late 11th and early 12th centuries were witness to a minor revolution in poetic taste in northern Europe. Study of medieval treatises *de rithmis* reveals that rules for writing rhythmic poetry were standardized during this period, just as great quantities of liturgical poetry began to be written in this style: sequences, versus, conductus, rhymed offices, some ordinary tropes, and liturgical plays. As Dag Norberg has argued, the patterns predominating in rhythmic poetry are based on those found in quantitative verse but depend on word accent rather than duration. Lines are governed by the number of syllables they contain, and rhyme is used to underscore caesurae and ends of lines and strophes.

Medieval France was an early fountainhead of liturgical rhythmic poetry, and this is manifested particularly in the rise of the late sequence. Sequences with rhyming, accentual texts, called "late sequences" or "second-epoch sequences," were written only in small numbers in the late 11th century but in ever greater numbers as the 12th century progressed. By the second quarter of the 13th century, significant numbers of late sequences were sung in cathedrals and monasteries throughout France, with only the strictest monastic orders (Carthusians, Cistercians, and most Franciscans) not adopting them. The late sequences were first championed by the Augustinian canons regular, particularly by those at the abbey of Saint-Victor in Paris, where late in life the poet Adam made his home. The sixty or so late sequences that survive from 12th-century Paris were the first substantial group of late sequences and the first sequence poems west of the Rhine to be consistently unified by historical narratives depending upon Old Testament typology. Although it is impossible to state categorically how many of these works are by Adam, a significant number are calls to the common life as advocated by the *Rule of St. Augustine* and develop themes that seem to relate to the struggles in which Adam and other reformers from the first half of the 12th century were engaged. There are far greater numbers of late-sequence texts than of melodies, and many individual pieces are *contrafacta*.

Margot Fassler

[**See also:** ADAM OF SAINT-VICTOR; *ANALECTA HYMNICA MEDII AEVI*; SEQUENCE (EARLY)]

Adam of Saint-Victor. *Les proses d'Adam de Saint-Victor: texte et musique précédées d'une étude critique*, ed. Eugène Misset, and Pierre Aubry. Paris: Welter, 1900.

Bannister, Henry, and Clemens Blume, ed. *Analecta hymnica medii aevi.* Leipzig: Reisland, 1915–22, Vols. 54–55.

Fassler, Margot. *Gothic Song: Victorine Sequences and Augustinian Reform in Twelfth-Century Paris.* Cambridge: Cambridge University Press, 1993.

Hesbert, René-Jean. *Le prosaire d'Aix-la-Chapelle, XIIIe siècle, début.* Rouen: Imprimerie Rouennaise, 1961.

———. *Le prosaire de la Sainte-Chapelle: manuscrit du chapitre de Saint-Nicolas de Bari (vers 1250).* Mâcon: Protat, 1952.

Husmann, Heinrich. "Notre-Dame und Saint-Victor: Repertoire-Studien zur Geschichte der gereimten Prosen." *Acta musicologica* 36 (1964): 98–123, 191–221.

SERFDOM/SERVITUDE/SLAVERY. Roman Gaul knew chattel slavery, and chattel slavery of the classical type persisted in the households and on the estates of the Gallo-Roman and Merovingian aristocracy long after the fall of imperial administration. Under the Carolingians, classical slavery rapidly declined, and one of the common Latin words for slave, *servus* (Fr. *serf*), was detached in the process from its original meaning. It came to represent a still debased but more elevated status than slave, although slaves properly so called continued to exist. Historians debate whether serfs, in the new meaning of the word, were primarily the ameliorated descendants of slaves or whether they constituted a new group of people and their descendants, who entered or commended themselves voluntarily into debasing but not slavish dependency, ostensibly for protection in the unsettled political and social conditions under the later Carolingians.

The period roughly from the death of Charles the Bald (877) to the 11th century sees weakness in central institutions and a confusion in terminology, so that it is difficult to determine at times the precise distinctions among slaves, serfs, and free rustics. They were all usually under heavy obligations to local lords. The question is whether these obligations debased personal status and in effect isolated individuals from the fiscal demands and judicial protections of royal authority. And that question, though never unimportant, became crucial only later, when the monarchy and other central institutions regained strength. Precise legal definitions of serfdom derive primarily from 12th- and 13th-century records, long after the varied social configurations we call "serfdom" came into existence.

The legal precision in the French sources ca. 1200 owes much to the concern of jurists for determining litigants' access to royal or princely courts reserved for "free people." Certain obligations owed to lords or restrictions on personal power were said by the jurists to debase personal status and thus to block access to courts of free people, especially for the defense of property. These included subjection to an arbitrary capitation, or head tax, often called *chevage*; the requirement to pay the token of lordship known as the *taille*; the incapacity to inherit, termed *mainmorte*; the prohibition of marriage outside the lordship, or *formariage*; restrictions on residence and free movement; liability to forced labor, or *corvée*. Because serfdom differed from region to region, it was not unknown for one or more of these obligations to be absent in practice. Moreover, liability to any one of them did not necessarily make an individual a serf. Burghers in a seigneurial town could be under the restriction of *formariage* or subject to the *taille*, for example. But one effect of the sharpening of legal categories in the late 12th and 13th centuries was the tendency of "free" people to buy themselves out of obligations whose vocabulary or content raised any presumption of servile status.

It is still an open question whether most French rustics at any time in the Middle Ages should be considered serfs, given the welter of names applied to varying forms of dependence and changes in the nature of dependence even when the words remained the same; *homme de corps* is a case in point. Some regions, like Normandy, never knew serfdom, however we define it, as an important social or economic institution. Finally, it is difficult to assess the economic and social impact of serfdom even in regions where there is no doubt that the majority of rustics lived under theoretically debasing obligations. The authority of lords, although expressed in the powerful language of obligations owed to them, was never absolute and always contested. This helps explain why so many of the obligations, theoretically arbitrary or at the pleasure of the lord, were in fact rigorously regulated by custom.

In the most general sense, manorial courts—courts that adjudicated property and other disputes involving servile tenants—were as bound by customary restraints on arbitrary lordship as the courts of free people. More specifically, debasing obligations were usually mitigated in practice. Negotiation led to *chevage* and even the *taille* (though less systematically) becoming levies collectible only at regular intervals and, indeed, at fixed sums whose burden was gradually eroded by inflation. *Mainmorte* might be resolved into a system that permitted the serf to inherit as long as the lord received the "best beast" in the legacy. Marriages between serfs of different lords or between a serf and a free person could be accomplished by the payment of a fine or fines to the appropriate lord or lords, and the relationship of the children of these marriages to the lord could frequently be worked out by negotiation. Serfs could purchase permission to take up residence in other lordships. And lords sometimes commuted *corvées* to fixed monetary sums, sometimes required very limited amounts of labor as the *corvée*, or sometimes even "paid" for the labor by giving workers a superabundance of food and drink during the period of the *corvée*.

Where political factors had led to a situation in which the obligations of serfs were radically mitigated, where they became mere licensing fees, it made little economic sense on the part of lords to perpetuate the system. Since the language of servile obligations remained pejorative ("vile and unnatural" is what the records call serfdom), serfs sought to be manumitted and lords frequently responded favorably for a price. The 13th and early 14th centuries were the most active periods for manumission. King Louis X in 1315 freed all royal serfs. The demographic catastrophe of the middle decades of the 14th century went farther to undermine traditional serfdom, as peasants whose labor was in demand were able to escape the strictures of the system. On the other hand, the conservatism of lords in several regions and the attempt to enforce servile obligations as a hedge against the labor unrest of the 14th and 15th centuries ensured that in some areas of France serfdom would persist until the end of the *ancien régime*.

It should be added, finally, that even where manumission was widely practiced or the demographic crisis undermined traditional forms of dependence, serfdom vanished, not lordship. Many obligations therefore remained in being that were not considered debasing of status at all. The most important of these were the so-called banalities, the requirement that rustics living in a seigneurie bake their bread for a fee in the lord's oven, grind their grain at his mill, press their grapes at his winepress, and perhaps concede a privileged place in the market to the lord's produce. Although often contested, these obligations remained largely intact until well into the modern period.

William Chester Jordan

[See also: *AFFRANCHISEMENT; BAN/BANALITÉ; FEUDALISM; FORMARIAGE; MAINMORTE;* SEIGNEUR/SEIGNEURIE]

Bernard, Pierre. *Étude sur les esclaves et les serfs d'église en France du VIe au XIIIe siècle.* Paris: Sirey, 1919.

Bloch, Marc. *Rois et serfs: un chapitre d'histoire capétienne.* Paris: Champion, 1920.

Dockès, Pierre. *Medieval Slavery and Liberation,* trans. Arthur Goldhammer. Chicago: University of Chicago Press, 1982.

Sée, Henri. *Les classes rurales et le régime domanial en France au moyen âge.* Paris: Giard et Brière, 1901.

SERGEANT. The word "sergeant" (Lat. *serviens*/OFr. *sergent*) described people of various types and duties. In the military context, sergeants were lightly armed fighting men who served and supported knights. In other contexts, sergeants acted as guards, ushers, policemen, messengers, process servers, jailkeepers, all-purpose functionaries of administrators in provincial districts like *bailliages* or *sénéchaussées*, and simply as servants within noble households. Mounted sergeants charged with executing judgments, levying fines, confiscating property, or apprehending malefactors were perhaps the governmental officials most frequently encountered by ordinary citizens. Understandably, they were unpopular, and sometimes the king responded to demands that their number be reduced.

John Bell Henneman, Jr.

SERMONS IN VERSE. A number of 12th- and 13th-century poems were called "sermons" by their authors, but the term seems to have referred as much to their oral mode of presentation as to their religious content. The eight extant 12th-century "sermons," including the Norman *Grant mal fist Adam,* are mostly in stanzaic form and urge contempt for the world. In contrast to the others, Thibaut de Marly's *Vers* (ca. 1182–85) was addressed to court circles, recalling its audience to chivalric as well as Christian virtues. At the end of the century, the *Poème moral,* a systematic moral treatise in the form of a sermon that dealt in turn with penitence, salvation, and vigilance, was addressed to a popular audience.

In the 13th century, Gautier de Coinci addressed two sermons to a convent of nuns. Hélinant de Froidmont's *Vers de la Mort,* a meditation on death as the culmination of the Christian life, was the earliest of a series of such sermons. Other cycles of sermons were written by Robert de Gretham and Nicole Bozon.

Maureen B.M. Boulton

[See also: BOZON, NICOLE; GAUTIER DE COINCI; HÉLINANT DE FROIDMONT; PREACHING; ROBERT DE GRETHAM]

SERMONS JOYEUX. Among the dramatic monologues or one-character plays of the late Middle Ages are parodies of wills, mandates, prognostications, and especially of sermons. About thirty of these *sermons joyeux* have survived from the 15th and early 16th centuries. Short, comic pieces (150–400 octosyllabic lines), carnivalesque in their bacchic and alimentary themes and obscenity, they were usually performed in festive contexts, such as weddings, trade-guild banquets, or monastic holidays.

Some of the *sermons joyeux* are parodies of saints' lives. Instead of the saint whose feast it is, they tell of carnivalesque saints, using the same rhetorical eloquence prescribed by the *artes praedicandi.* The actor who "preaches" the sermon relates the saint's life, describes the martyrdom, and reveals the miracles worked by the saint. Typical subjects are St. Oignon, who makes people cry; St. Hareng, who was martyred on the grill; and the priapic St. Billouard, who repopulated the earth after the Flood. Other sermons, based on nuptial folklore, give rudimentary (and comic) instruction in sexual behavior to newlyweds. Still others, from monastic and school milieux, have a goliardic character. One treats the great deeds of Nemo (Nobody), who, taken as a person, is all-powerful. Another is the polemical sermon of La Chopinerie, in which the students of Paris defend their privileges and vaunt their drinking prowess.

The *sermon joyeux* depends for its basic meaning and comic effect on the opposition between its serious form, derived from the sermon tradition, and its comic content, based on carnival themes. Often, however, the imagery of the piece suggests another level of meaning. The *Sermon de saint Jambon et sainte Andouille,* for example, may be read as an erotic allegory. Moreover, the actor may inject a topical meaning derived from historical circumstances. In this way, St. Jambon came to denote a certain Joannes Bonus (or Jean le Bon), who was incarcerated in Paris for having recited on All Soul's Day a *sermon joyeux* inviting the audience to indulge in public drunkenness.

Most of the texts are anonymous, though the *Sermon de saint Billouard* was written by Jean Molinet and the *Sermon pour une nopce* by Roger de Collerye. Much of the humor of these short pieces is accessible to readers today, despite the fact that many allusions remain unexplained. Products of an era when preaching flourished, the *sermons joyeux* cast light on the festive spirit in France on the threshold of modern times.

Jelle Koopmans

[See also: MOLINET, JEAN; THEATER]

Koopmans, Jelle, ed. *Quatre sermons joyeux.* Geneva: Droz, 1984.
———, ed. *Recueil de sermons joyeux.* Geneva: Droz, 1988.
Aubailly, Jean-Claude. *Le monologue, le dialogue et la sottie.* Paris: Champion, 1976.

SESTINA. Invented by the troubadour Arnaut Daniel, the sestina is composed of six six-line stanzas and a three-line *tornada*. The first stanza establishes six rhyme words which are repeated according to a fixed structure: stanza *a* rhymes 1 2 3 4 5 6; the next stanza rhymes 6 1 5 2 4 3; subsequent stanzas repeat the permutation. Were there to be a seventh stanza, it would repeat the rhyme-word order of the first. All six rhyme words are repeated in the *tornada*. Though a creation of Occitania, the genre found its greatest audience in Italy, where Dante and Petrarch were master practitioners.

Wendy E. Pfeffer

[See also: VERSIFICATION]

Riesz, János. *Die Sestine: Ihre Stellung in der literarischen Kritik und ihre Geschichte als lyrisches Genus.* Munich: Fink, 1971.

SEVEN SAGES OF ROME. The Seven Sages of Rome is an antifeminist frame tale that generated many variations and continuations in France and became enormously popular throughout medieval Europe. It derives from an unknown version of an eastern romance, the *Book of Sindbād*, which probably originated in India in the 5th century B.C. Like the oriental archetypes of two other ostensibly didactic frame narratives that won favor in Old French adaptations, *Barlaam et Josaphat* and the *Chastoiement d'un pere a son fils*, the *Sindbād* moved westward; it was translated into Persian, Arabic, Greek, and Hebrew and reached Europe by the mid-12th century, with significant changes to both the frame and the intercalated stories having occurred along the way. The oldest text in the western Seven Sages tradition is the Old French verse romance *Sept Sages de Rome*, composed in octosyllabic couplets by a Norman poet between 1155 and 1190. A compelling example of the jongleresque romance style, this poem survives in two redactions, each preserved by a single 13th-century manuscript, B.N. fr. 1553 (*K*: 5,068 lines) and Chartres, Bibl. Mun. 620 (*C*: 2,078 lines; the second half only of the poem).

In the romance, a learned masculine community of clerics and their pupil just barely outwits an unscrupulous woman who threatens to disrupt the legitimate lineage of the empire. The widowed emperor Vespasian of Constantinople charges the Seven Sages of Rome to educate his son, aged seven. After he remarries, he summons the prince, now fourteen, home to meet his stepmother. The youth remains silent on returning to court because he has read in the stars that he will die if he speaks before the eighth day; each of his tutors pledges to defend him for one day. But his father, expecting a well-spoken heir apparent, is distressed by his son's muteness. The queen then offers to make the prince talk. In her bedchamber, she tries to seduce him and proposes poisoning Vespasian. When the prince rebuffs her advances, she accuses him of attempted rape and treason and persuades the emperor to condemn his own son to death. For the next seven days, the sages win a stay of execution by telling stories that often emphasize the wickedness of women, while the queen rekindles the emperor's anger with tales featuring untrustworthy counselors or sons. On the eighth day, the prince tells a story proving his innocence. Father and son are reconciled, and the queen is burned at the stake. Although virtue triumphs through the prince's speech, the narrator emphasizes that the sages, despite their learning, are consistently checkmated by the queen. They subsequently join Samson, Constantine, and Aristotle as often-cited examples of great men humiliated by women.

Based on the verse *Sept Sages* are two derhymed versions. The A redaction in Old French prose is affiliated with the *K* verse text; composed in the first quarter of the 13th century, it appears in twenty-nine manuscripts of the 13th, 14th, and 15th centuries with a complex and contaminated filiation. The Middle French *D* redaction, affiliated with *C*, was prosified probably in the 15th century; it exists in one manuscript. The widely known A prose redaction was the source of Seven Sages texts in Italian, Middle English, Swedish, Dutch, and Welsh, as well as of a much imitated *Historia Septem Sapientum Romae* in Latin prose of the 14th century. A also generated two Old French prose reworkings later in the 13th century: the L redaction, which offers a thirteen-tale duel, with some different stories, and ends with a judiciary combat; and the *Ystoire de la male marastre*, which expands the frame narrative and adds six new stories to nine traditional ones. Seven manuscripts contain L; *Marastre* survives in four manuscripts.

In addition to these derhymings, translations, and reworkings, the A prose redaction inspired six anonymous continuations in Old French prose. The first, *Marques de Rome*, was composed ca. 1250–60; the romances of *Laurin*, *Cassidorus*, *Helcanus*, *Pelyarmenus*, and *Kanor*, all apparently by different authors, followed by the end of the century. Over twenty manuscripts for *Marques* survive, most containing at least one other Seven Sages romance; eight for

Laurin; six for *Cassidorus* and *Helcanus*; and five for *Pelyarmenus* and *Kanor* (both still unpublished). Four manuscripts compile the entire cycle. Besides renewing themes and plot devices from the *Sept Sages*, the continuations incorporate material from Arthurian, oriental, and adventure romances of the period. The Seven Sages reappear as virtuous secondary characters in *Marques*, but in *Laurin* they become evil and die dishonored. In the sequels, the chief male protagonists are Marques, son of the sage Cato, and his descendants, who inherit the throne of Constantinople through their mother. After *Marques*, overt antifeminism fades from the cycle, but the themes of wisdom, kingship, lineage, and the role of women remain central.

The "Dolopathos" tradition, which constitutes a second family of medieval Seven Sages texts, comprises two texts: a Latin prose romance composed in the last quarter of the 12th century by Johannes, a Cistercian monk at the abbey of Alta Silva, who dedicated his work to Bertrand, bishop of Metz; and an Old French verse romance of nearly 13,000 lines in octosyllabic couplets written in the first quarter of the 13th century by a clerk named Herbert, who freely translated and amplified Johannes's composition. Both Johannes and Herbert seem to have known the rhymed version of the *Sept Sages*; they include four of its stories and a similar frame narrative. One of the Dolopathos tales not borrowed from the *Sept Sages* offers an early version of the Swan Knight legend. In *Dolopathos*, the prince accused of rape is the son of Dolopathos, king of Sicily; his tutor in Rome is Virgil. The tale sequence defending him comprises only eight stories, seven told by seven nameless sages and a final one told by Virgil. After his youthful adventures, the prince converts to Christianity and devotes himself to pious works.

In both families, the Seven Sages romances illustrate the power of narrative to instruct, persuade, and captivate. Like the king who is the pivotal figure in the tale sequences, medieval audiences evidently enjoyed the intercalated stories as much as they relished the downfall of the crafty woman who foiled the sages. This fascination with storytelling, together with the adaptability of the frame and the possibility of substituting new tales for those that were lost or ceased to entertain, helped ensure an active and varied life for the French Seven Sages tradition over more than four centuries.

Mary B. Speer

[See also: *BARLAAM ET JOSAPHAT*]

Alton, Johann, ed. *Le roman de Marques de Rome.* Tübingen: Laupp, 1889.

Herbert. *Li romans de Dolopathos*, ed. Charles Brunet and Anatole de Montaiglon. Paris: Jannet, 1856.

Johannes de Alta Silva. *Dolopathos or The King and the Seven Wise Men*, trans. Brady B. Gilleland. Binghamton: Center for Medieval and Renaissance Studies, State University of New York, 1981.

Niedzielski, Henri, ed. *Le roman de Helcanus: édition critique d'un texte en prose du XIIIe siècle.* Geneva: Droz, 1966.

Palermo, Joseph, ed. *Le roman de Cassidorus.* 2 vols. Paris: Picard, 1963–64.

Paris, Gaston, ed. *Deux rédactions du Roman des Sept Sages de Rome.* Paris: Didot, 1876. [Critical edition of *D* (B.N. fr. 5036) and of a Middle French translation of the Latin *Historia Septem Sapientum Romae*.]

Runte, Hans R., ed. *Li ystoire de la male marastre.* Tübingen: Niemeyer, 1974. [Based on *T* (Ashburnham 52).]

Speer, Mary B., ed. *Le roman des Sept Sages de Rome: A Critical Edition of the Two Verse Redactions of a Twelfth-Century Romance.* Lexington: French Forum, 1989.

Les Sept Sages de Rome: roman en prose du XIIIe siècle, ed. Section de Traitement Automatique des Textes Littéraires Médiévaux. Nancy: CRAL de l'Université de Nancy II, 1981. [Transcription of the A redaction from B.N. fr. 2137 in a computer-facilitated format.]

Thorpe, Lewis, ed. *Le roman de Laurin, fils de Marques le sénéchal: Text of MS. B.N. f. fr. 22548.* Cambridge: Heffer, 1960.

Runte, Hans R., Keith Wikeley, and Anthony Farrell. *The Seven Sages of Rome and the Book of Sindbād: An Analytical Bibliography.* New York: Garland, 1984.

SHIPS AND SHIPPING. In the Middle Ages, boats allowed the movement of relatively large amounts of goods and troops less expensively than did land transport, which

Ships being loaded for transport, from a 14th-century manuscript. BN fr. 4274, fol. 6. *Courtesy of the Bibliothèque Nationale, Paris.*

was unwieldy and costly. Although the crown lacked access to them in the early Capetian period, France had vast coastlines with many ports. Royal fleets, notably under the Carolingians and later Capetians, played an important role in military engagements, such as the hostilities before Bouvines or in the crusades of St. Louis.

For North Sea and Atlantic travel, medieval sailors used the cog, a clinker-built ship with single mast and square sail. In the Mediterranean, galleys and carvel-built round ships (*nefs*) having two masts with lateen sails were common, though there was some technology transfer between north and south in the high and late Middle Ages. The cog with a lateen sail came to be used in both areas. Shipping via the Atlantic between the Mediterranean and North Sea ports was recorded in the late 13th century. Ship technology underwent considerable evolution in the 15th century, with the addition of masts on a vessel called a carrack, which carried upward of 1,500 tons. River transport involved smaller river barges, which plied the Seine, Loire, Somme, Rhône, Garonne, Oise, Saône, and lesser arteries. While more convenient than overland transport, rivers, like roads, were plagued by toll stations.

Kathryn L. Reyerson

[See also: MEDITERRANEAN TRADE; NAVAL POWER]

Mollat, Michel. *Études d'histoire maritime.* Turin: Bottega d'Erasme, 1977.
Pryor, John. *Commerce, Shipping and Naval Warfare in the Medieval Mediterranean.* London: Variorum Reprints, 1987.
Waghenaer, Lucas. *The Mariners Mirrour.* London: Charlewood, 1588. Repr. Amsterdam.

SICILIAN VESPERS. On Easter 1282, when the French sergeant Drouet molested a young Sicilian woman in Palermo just before Vespers, her husband stabbed him. The incident provoked a bloody rebellion throughout the island against the monarchy of Charles I of Anjou, in which Sicilians slaughtered some 4,000 Frenchmen and went so far as to rip the fetuses believed to have been fathered by Frenchmen from the wombs of women who had consorted with the hated foreigners.

The result of this uprising was to remove the island of Sicily from the control of the house of Anjou and to precipitate many years of war, during which the French monarchy and the Angevin king at Naples were unable to dislodge from Sicily the royal house of Aragon, whose king, Peter III, the Sicilians invited to rule them.

Historians have attributed the uprising to various foreign conspiracies: one involving John of Procida, a Sicilian exile, and Peter of Aragon, whose wife had a claim to Sicily; or one involving Michael Paleologus, the Byzantine emperor whose lands Charles of Anjou had hoped to invade. Whatever the truth of these theories, such conspiracies alone could not have produced so spontaneous a mass uprising. The real cause was desperation over extraordinarily high taxation, which produced revenues greater than those of England, France, and the papacy combined. In the end, the Sicilian Vespers permanently dismembered the most precocious medieval monarchy and undermined the crusading movement in western Christendom. After twenty years of war, during which the last foothold of the crusaders in the Holy Land was lost, the old Sicilian kingdom remained in two much weakened parts, and the leadership of the pope, an Angevin supporter, was badly compromised.

William A. Percy Jr.

[See also: ANJOU, HOUSES OF; CHARLES I]

Geneakopolos, Deno J. *Emperor Michael Paleologus and the West, 1258–1282: A Study in Byzantine-Latin Relations.* Cambridge: Harvard University Press, 1959.
Percy, William A. "The Earliest Revolution Against the "Modern State": Direct Taxation in Medieval Sicily and the Vespers." *Italian Quarterly* 22.84 (1981): 69–83.
———. "The Indirect Taxes of the Medieval Kingdom of Sicily." *Italian Quarterly* 22.85 (1981): 73–85.
———. "A Reappraisal of the Sicilian Vespers and the Role of Sicily in European History." *Italian Quarterly* 22.86 (1981): 77–96.
Runciman, Steven. *The Sicilian Vespers.* Cambridge: Cambridge University Press, 1958.

SIDRAC, ROMAN DE. The work of an anonymous compiler of the 13th century, *Sidrac* is a wisdom book in French prose, probably the imitation of an oriental model, in the form of alternating questions and answers. Although its prologue gives the date 1243, it was more likely composed late in the century, perhaps at Lyon, by an author who had probably visited the Latin kingdoms in the Middle East. Numerous manuscripts and three principal redactions survive, with the number of questions ranging from about 600 to over 1,200. The work touches on theology, astronomy, obstetrics, geography, zoology, medicine, precious stones, and history.

William W. Kibler

Langlois, Charles-Victor. *La vie en France au moyen âge, du XIIe au milieu du XIVe siècle.* 4 vols. Paris: Hachette, 1925–28, Vol. 3: *La connaissance de la nature et du monde,* pp. 198–275.

SIGEBERT DE GEMBLOUX (ca. 1030–ca. 1112). Sigebert was both raised and educated in the Benedictine monastery of Gembloux. After completing his education there, he became a schoolmaster at Saint-Vincent in Metz, where he remained for twenty years. Sigebert was one of the most prolific and versatile writers of the 11th century. His interests included hagiography, history, and relations between ecclesiastical and secular authorities. In the Investiture conflict, for example, he argued persuasively for imperial authority despite the claims made for the papacy by Gregory VII. Although Sigebert's literary career began at Metz, his major works were completed at Gembloux after he returned there in 1070. Access to Gembloux's excellent library enabled him to write two important histories. In the *Chronica,* a work colored by his views on investiture,

Sigebert sought to establish a precise chronology of historical events from 381 to 1111. The *Chronica* was widely disseminated and was subsequently continued by others. Sigebert's *Gesta abbatum Gemblaciensium* supplies many important details regarding the Investiture conflict of the 11th century. The *De viris illustribus*, a catalogue of 172 important ecclesiastical writers beginning with Marcellus, a disciple of St. Peter, and ending with himself, is an important compendium listing many Christian writers of the Middle Ages who would have otherwise been unknown. Among Sigebert's others works are the *Passion of St. Lucia* and the *Passion of the Theban Martyr Legion*.

E. Kay Harris

[See also: ROBERT DE TORIGNY]

Sigebert de Gembloux. *Chronica*. PL 160 (188).57–834. [Includes the continuations.]

——. *Sigeberti Gemblacensis. Chronographiae auctarium Affligemense*, ed. P. Gorissen. Brussels: Paleis der Academiën, 1952.

Dekkers, Eligius. "Sigebert van Gembloux in zijn *De viris illustribus*." *Sacris eruditi* 26 (1983): 57–102.

SIGER DE BRABANT (ca. 1240–ca. 1284). A member of the Picard "nation" at Paris, Siger was by 1266 a teaching master of arts in Paris and canon of Saint-Paul, Liège. He was a leading exponent of Aristotle, known largely through the works of Averroes. He and scholars of similar mind are known as "Latin Averroists." As is usual for the 12th and 13th centuries, they knew Aristotle mostly through the interpretations of Averroes, Proclus, and particularly Avicenna. This tendency made Siger suspect, and in 1270 he was involved in bishop Étienne Tempier's condemnation of thirteen theological errors at Paris. In the same year, Thomas Aquinas wrote *De unitate intellectus contra Averroistas*, directed chiefly against Siger and his followers.

The controversy continued until 1276, when Siger and two others were indicted for heresy by the French inquisitor Simon du Val, but Siger had already fled the country, apparently to make an appeal to the papal court. According to John Peckham, Siger was killed at Orvieto ca. 1284.

Siger was an Aristotelian in believing that Aristotle's meaning should not be concealed, even if it conflicted with revealed truth. The two Aristotelian doctrines that caused constant consternation for philosopher-theologians at this time were the eternity of the world, which Aristotelians held to be true but theology knew to be false, and the unity of the intellect, which denied the possibility of the resurrection of the individual, since every mind was subsumed into one unified intellect after death. This did not endear Siger to many, although he himself believed that truth was always on the side of faith and that in cases of apparent conflict between faith and reason one should always decide for revelation rather than reason. Critics accused him of holding to "double truth," that is, that some things were true in philosophy but false in theology. He himself may have felt as confusion and uncertainty that which outsiders took for lack of belief.

His main works are commentaries and questions on Aristotle, especially on the *De anima*, the *Physics*, and the *Metaphysics*, and shorter treatises on, for example, the eternity of the world.

Lesley J. Smith

[See also: AQUINAS, THOMAS; ARABIC PHILOSOPHY, INFLUENCE OF; ARISTOTLE, INFLUENCE OF; ÉTIENNE TEMPIER; PHILOSOPHY; SCHOLASTICISM; THEOLOGY]

Steenberghen, Fernand van. *Siger de Brabant d'après ses œuvres inédites*. 2 vols. Louvain: Éditions de l'Institut Supérieur de Philosophie, 1931–42.

——. *Maître Siger de Brabant*. Louvain: Publications Universitaires, 1977.

SILVACANE. One of the "three sisters of Provence," with Le Thoronet and Sénanque, the Cistercian abbey of Silvacane (Bouches-du-Rhône) was founded in 1144 when the land was deeded to St. Bernard, one of the order's founders. It prospered until a devastating fire in 1357. The Romanesque church, begun in 1175, is simple and austere in Cistercian fashion, with a wide nave and transepts spanned by pointed barrel vaulting, and typically flat chevet. The chapter house, *armarium* (book locker), and rectangular cloister were all constructed in the Gothic style (13th c.). The large 15th-century refectory is ornate and well lighted by a row of upper windows and a fine rose.

William W. Kibler/William W. Clark

[See also: CISTERCIAN ART AND ARCHITECTURE; SÉNANQUE; THORONET, LE]

Esquieu, Yves. "L'abbaye de Silvacane." *Congrès archéologique* (*Le pays d'Aix*) 143 (1985): 284–96.

Fixot, Michel, and Jean-Pierre Pelletier. "Découvertes archéologiques récentes à l'abbaye de Silvacane." *Congrès archéologique* (*Le pays d'Aix*) 143 (1985): 297–99.

Pontus, Paul. *L'abbaye de Silvacane*. Paris: CNMHS, 1982.

SIRVENTES. An Occitan lyric genre including personal invective, political satire, and moralizing verse, contrasted with the dominant *canso*, or love song. Etymologically, *sirventes* means "servantlike." This meaning may have been applied literally to satirical songs because they were sung by servants (Rieger), but historical evidence is weak. We have firmer grounds for a figurative interpretation: the *sirventes* was considered the "servant" of the *canso* because the poet composing one would adopt a preexisting *canso*'s metrical form. The *sirventes* could then be sung to the melody of the *canso*, facilitating its diffusion. The *sirventes* is thus an example of contrafacture, or melodic appropriation, a special kind of intertextuality.

Such imitation developed gradually. The first great satirist among the troubadours, Marcabru, never used the term *sirventes* but called his own songs *vers*; in only one poem is it certain that he imitated a form by another poet, and he did so in an answer to his model. The word *sirventes* was first applied to the text that contained it ca. 1150 by the minor Gascon troubadour Marcoat, who seems to refer to contrafacture. Bertran de Born, ca. 1180–1200, practiced demonstrable imitation in about one-third of his *sirventes* (calling them by this name, though he used no generic term for his love songs), and extended imitation to include the choice of rhyme sounds as well as stanzaic shape. In the 13th century, Peire Cardenal composed at least 80 percent of his *sirventes* in imitative forms. All in all, about two-thirds of the 500-odd extant *sirventes* are demonstrable imitations. In troubadour practice, imitation was never obligatory; a *sirventes* could have a new melody or could imitate a song that was of a genre other than the *canso*, even another *sirventes*. Imitation became the rule for composition of *sirventes* in treatises written in the late 13th and 14th centuries (*Doctrina de compondre dictats, Leys d'Amors*).

Subgenres include the *sirventes-joglaresc*, or *sirventes* addressed to a *joglar*, which is mentioned several times among the *vidas*; the *sirventes-ensenhamen*, in which a troubadour lists the repertory that a *joglar* should know; and the *canso-sirventes*, in which themes of satire and love are commingled and which is named once in a song by Folquet de Romans. None of these narrower types achieved the well-established generic status of the *sirventes*.

William D. Paden

[See also: BERTRAN DE BORN; MARCABRU; PEIRE CARDENAL; TROUBADOUR POETRY]

Chambers, Frank M. "Imitation of Form in the Old Provençal Lyric." *Romance Philology* 6 (1952–53): 104–20.
———. *An Introduction to Old Provençal Versification.* Philadelphia: American Philosophical Society, 1985.
Rieger, Dietmar. *Gattungen und Gattungsbezeichnungen der Trobadorlyrik: Untersuchungen zum altprovenzalischen Sirventes.* Tübingen: Niemeyer, 1976.
Riquer, Martín de, ed. *Los trovadores: historia literaria y textos.* 3 vols. Barcelona: Planeta, 1975, Vol. 1, pp. 53–59.
Thiolier-Méjean, Suzanne. *Les poésies satiriques et morales des troubadours du XIIe siècle à la fin du XIIIe siècle.* Paris: Nizet, 1978.

SLUTER, CLAUS (ca. 1345–1405/06). Artist who also achieved prominence as one of Philip the Bold of Burgundy's *valets de chambre*, a position he acquired after the death of his master, Jehan de Marville. Sluter was born in Haarlem in Holland; after working in Brussels from 1379 to 1385, he became an assistant to Marville, then *valet de chambre* to Philip, in Dijon. The Chartreuse de Champmol in Dijon, a project begun by Marville and his workshop, features one of Sluter's and the workshop's finest accomplishments, the *Well of Moses* (ca. 1395–1406). Sluter also finished the tomb of Philip the Bold, now in the Musée des Beaux-Arts in Dijon, which had been begun by his predecessor. His primary achievement in his art was to free sculpture from its purely structural function, enabling the figures to dominate the architectural setting. Sluter

infused his work with energy and an emotive quality unsurpassed by his contemporaries.

Michelle I. Lapine

[See also: DIJON]

Morand, Kathleen. *Claus Sluter: Artist at the Court of Burgundy.* Austin: University of Texas Press, 1991.
Snyder, James. *Northern Renaissance Art.* New York: Abrams, 1985.

SOISSONS. An important center during the Merovingian period, Soissons (Aisne) was the site of a key battle in which Clovis I defeated the Romans under Syagrius in 486. Clovis's son Clotar I made it his capital, as did Chilperic, the king of Neustria and husband of the notorious Fredegunde. And it was in Soissons that Pepin III the Short was proclaimed the first Carolingian king in 751.

Soissons was a bishopric in the archdiocese of Reims by the 5th century, but the history of its early cathedrals is unknown. A cathedral was built in the 12th century, beginning with a Romanesque nave in the 1130s or 1140s, and an Early Gothic choir in the 1150s. Between ca. 1170 and ca. 1190, a new transept was built, of which only the four-story, rounded-plan south arm now survives. The 12th-century north arm was replaced in the mid-13th century and has an elegant Court Style terminal.

The cathedral of Saint-Gervais-et-Saint-Protais at Soissons is one of five French High Gothic cathedrals begun

Soissons (Aisne), Saint-Gervais-et-Saint-Protais, nave. *Photograph courtesy of Whitney S. Stoddard.*

during the period ca. 1190–ca. 1220. The choir and nave of Soissons feature an interior elevation of three stories consisting of main arcade, triforium, and clerestory that matches the height of the main arcade. The four-part vaults (100 feet tall) are sustained by an early example of the two-tiered flying-buttress system. The nave of Soissons was completed by ca. 1220/25, and the west façade was built in several stages and completed ca. 1300. The traditional view is that the High Gothic choir of Soissons was begun slightly later than and was influenced by the cathedral of Chartres, begun in 1194. However, the Soissons chapter began to use the new choir on May 13, 1212, so Soissons may in fact have been begun slightly earlier than Chartres.

Soissons cathedral suffered extensive damage to its stained glass during the religious wars of the 16th century, and the west façade portals were stripped of their sculpture in the 18th century. The nave was extensively damaged by German artillery fire during World War I and was conscientiously rebuilt in the 1920s and 1930s.

The former abbey of Saint-Jean-des-Vignes in Soissons, founded in 1076, was one of the largest and most prestigious in medieval France. The magnificent abbey church of the 13th through 15th centuries was destroyed in the early 19th century, except for its façade, which features two graceful Flamboyant towers. Other reminders of the abbey include the 13th-century double-naved refectory, two galleries of the 14th-century cloister, and the ribvaulted cellar beneath the refectory.

Carl F. Barnes, Jr.

[See also: CHARTRES; CLOVIS I; GOTHIC ARCHITECTURE; MEROVINGIAN DYNASTY]

Barnes, Carl F., Jr. *The Architecture of Soissons Cathedral: Sources and Influences in the 12th and 13th Centuries.* Diss. Columbia University, 1967.

———. "The Twelfth-Century Transept of Soissons Cathedral: The Missing Source for Chartres?" *Journal of the Society of Architectural Historians* 28 (1969): 9–25.

Lefèvre-Pontalis, Eugène. "Soissons." *Congrès archéologique* (*Reims*) 78 (1911): 315–37.

Poquet, Abbé, and Abbé Daras. *Notice historique et archéologique de la cathédrale de Soissons.* Soissons: Voyeux-Solin, 1848.

SOLIGNAC. The first act of consecration of the abbey church of Saint-Pierre in Solignac (Haute-Vienne) was signed by St. Éloi (631/32). It was taken by the Muslims in 793 and by the Vikings in 860. Almost completely ruined in 922, the present structure, consecrated in 1143, utilized the foundation of the 10th-century bell tower. This fine example of Romanesque Périgordine architecture has a nave with two square bays, a transept with chapels on the east wall of each arm, and a semicircular apse with three radiating chapels. The porch dates from the early 13th century. Twelve steps descend into the nave. The church is roofed by four cupolas (initially five; the south transept has been revaulted).

Throughout the church are granite capitals carved with palmettes, personages in mandorlas held by angels, inter-

lace designs, and heads of monsters. Two rows of oak choir-stalls (1479) and misericords are playfully ornamented with Gothic motifs. On the eastern side of the north crossing, a damaged limestone frieze shows Christ in Majesty. The church houses a gilt copper reliquary of St. Théau (14th c.). Among surviving fragments of apse windows is the Miracle of St. Valérie presenting her head to St. Martial.

The conventual buildings, long occupied by a porcelain factory, were the first workshop for the production of Limoges enamels, founded by St. Éloi in 631.

Nina Rowe

Fage, René. "Église de Solignac." *Bulletin monumental* 74 (1910): 75–106.

———. "Solignac: église abbatiale." *Congrès archéologique* (*Limoges et Brive*) 84 (1921): 237–59.

Maury, Jean, Marie-Madeleine S. Gauthier, and Jean Porcher. *Limousin roman.* Paris: Zodiaque, 1906.

SONE DE NAUSAY. A long verse romance (over 21,300 lines) of the late 13th century, *Sone de Nausay* (or *Nansai*) is the story of a young man who, rebuffed by the woman he loves, seeks adventures throughout the world. Eventually, Sone repudiates the woman and becomes king of Norway by marrying Odee, the daughter of the deceased king. Though not essentially an Arthurian romance, the poem includes several Arthurian episodes and motifs, notably the Grail and Bleeding Lance. Only one manuscript is known (Turin 1626).

Norris J. Lacy

Goldschmidt, Moritz, ed. *Sone von Nausay.* Tübingen: Bibliothek des litterarischen Vereins in Stuttgart, 1899.

Langlois, Charles-Victor. *La vie en France au moyen âge du XIIe au milieu du XIVe siècle*, 4 vols. Paris: Hachette, 1926–28, Vol. 1: *D'apres les romans mondains du temps*, pp. 286–319.

SONGE DU VERGIER. An important political tract of the 14th century, the *Songe du vergier* may be seen as a statement of the views prevailing at the court of Charles V in the late 1370s, particularly among those royal advisers who became known as the "Marmousets."

In the spring of 1374, Charles V commissioned a member of his household with legal training to prepare a document setting forth the position of the French crown on such subjects as the relationship of ecclesiastical and secular power, the position of the monarch *vis à vis* the emperor and the pope, and the nature of royal sovereignty over the kingdom. The tract first appeared on May 16, 1376, under the Latin title *Somnium viridarii*. The author then revised the work before translating it into French as *Songe du vergier* in 1378.

Scholars have long debated the authorship of the *Songe*, but there is now considerable evidence that the person responsible was Évrart de Trémaugon, a cleric from the region of Saint-Brieuc in Brittany who had studied with the distinguished Italian legist John of Legnano and was a member of the royal household in the 1370s before becoming bishop of Dole. The *Songe* takes the form of a lengthy debate between a priest and a knight (a literary device then popular in France). The views expressed by the knight include a powerful statement of royal sovereignty, possibly ahead of its time, and are a valuable guide to the policies and programs of the Marmousets during their period of greatest influence at the French court (1374–92).

John Bell Henneman, Jr.

[See also: CHARLES V THE WISE; CHARLES VI; MARMOUSETS]

Schnerb-Lièvre, Marion, ed. *Le songe du vergier (édité d'après le manuscrit royal 19 C IV de la* British Library). 2 vols. Paris: CNRS, 1982.
Coville, Alfred. *Évrart de Trémaugon et le Songe du vergier.* Paris, 1933.
Lièvre, M. "Note sur les sources du Somnium viridarii et du Songe du vergier." *Romania* 81 (1960): 483–91.
Quillet, Jeannine. *La philosophie politique du Songe du vergier (1378): sources doctrinales.* Paris, 1977.

SONGE VÉRITABLE. Written in 1406, the *Songe véritable* is a political pamphlet in verse. The 19th-century editor of the poem concluded that the author was not Laurent de Premierfait, as some had thought, but was definitely a resident of Paris in royal service.

The poem (3,174 lines) describes a dream that begins with a glimpse of the king of France living in an impoverished state. Allegorical personifications take over as Poverty leads the common people toward Patience. The narrator is replaced by Everyman, who seeks counsel because his eldest daughter Money has been raped and his other daughter is threatened.

The central theme is the corruption of princes and royal officials. Apology says that royal servants of lower rank serve the king well, but they are mistreated by the powerful and do not receive benefices. The poem features the allegorical figures Fortune and Reason. Reason addresses long letters, quoted in full, to the most vilified personages discussed: Queen Isabeau, the dukes of Berry and Orléans, Jean de Montaigu (grand master of the *hôtel du roi*), and Clignet de Brébant (admiral of France). The poem levels accusations against more than 120 institutions and individuals, most of them identified by Moranvillé.

Richard C. Famiglietti

Moranvillé, H., ed. "*Le songe véritable,* pamphlet politique d'un parisien du XVe siècle." *Mémoires de la Société de l'Histoire de Paris et de l'Île-de-France* 17 (1890): 217–438.
Famiglietti, Richard C. *Royal Intrigue: Crisis at the Court of Charles VI, 1392–1420.* New York: AMS, 1986.

SORDEL (Sordello; ca. 1200–ca. 1270). Immortalized by Dante (*Purgatorio,* Cantos 6–8), the troubadour Sordel was born in Mantua. After seducing Cunizza, whom he had abducted at the request of her brother, Ezzelino da Romano, Sordel fled in the late 1220s to Provence, where he was supported by Blacatz, Raymond-Berenguer IV, and Charles of Anjou, among others. Although he composed *cansos,* he was more interested in other forms, especially *sirventes* and *partimens*; he is best known for his *planh* on the death of Blacatz.

Elizabeth W. Poe

[See also: TROUBADOUR POETRY]

Sordello. *Le poesie,* ed. Marco Boni. Bologna: Palmaverde, 1954.
———. *The Poetry of Sordello,* ed. and trans. James J. Wilhelm. New York: Garland, 1987.

SOTTE CHANSON. Popular in northern France from the 13th through the 15th century, the *sotte chanson* is a systematic parody of the troubadour *canso,* in which *fin'amor* is reduced to animal lust; the courtly lady, to a depraved shrew; the ethereal joy of love, to postprandial or postorgasmic contentment. Two manuscripts preserve twenty-six *sottes chansons* from the 13th and early 14th centuries. The genre had gained respectability by the 15th century, as evidenced by its inclusion in several treatises on poetry. Froissart, Deschamps, and, most notably, Villon, with his *Ballade de la Grosse Margot,* experimented with the genre.

Elizabeth W. Poe

[See also: FATRAS/FATRASIE; RESVERIE]

Bec, Pierre. *La lyrique française au moyen-âge (XIIe–XIIIe siècles): contribution à une typologie des genres poétiques médiévaux.* 2 vols. Paris: Picard, 1977–78, Vol. 1: *Études;* Vol. 2: *Textes.*

SOTTIE. Short comic plays in verse whose characters, usually five in number, are *sots* ("fools") or the equivalent. Approximately twenty-five comic plays from late-medieval France have in their title the terms *sots* or *sottie* (or *sotie*). In addition, a number of plays called *farces* by their earliest text are similar enough to be grouped with these *sotties* by modern scholars. Although there is still disagreement on the number of *sotties* remaining, or even on a definition of the genre, scholars generally accept about sixty plays as *sotties*. These plays, whose average length is about 400 lines, date from ca. 1450–1550 and show a great variety of dramatic techniques.

The *sot* (roughly translated "fool" or "jester") was one of a large family of foolish characters that fascinated the late Middle Ages and Renaissance: "Aujourd'uy Toult le Monde est fol," remarks a fool in *Tout le Monde*; the cry of Gringore's *Jeu du Prince des Sots et Mère Sotte* summons fifty-seven kinds of *sots* and *sottes* to the play. Fools appeared in both serious and comic literature, at noble courts and the great fairs, in the church holiday called the *fête des fous,* in art and music, and in the theater. By the end of the 15th century, *compagnies joyeuses*, or societies of fools, had formed in the major towns of France, made up of respectable citizens who assembled regularly to perform *sotties* and other dramatic amusements. The most important of these societies were those of Paris (whose "fools" made up the Enfants-sans-souci), Rouen, Dijon, and Lyon.

In the past, scholars have disagreed about whether the term *sottie* referred to the internal characteristics of a dramatic genre or the external properties of the *sot*, such as costume. That is, was the *sottie* simply any play performed by a company of fools? Most scholars now propose a definition of the *sottie* based on the plays rather than the players, but no definition has been universally accepted. Part of the problem is caused by the apparently inconsistent use of generic terms by the texts, which sometimes label *farce* or *moralité* plays that appear to be *sotties*. *Farce* seems to have been a general term that included a variety of comic plays. Furthermore, the *sottie* is similar to the morality play in its use of allegorical characters.

The problem is made more difficult by the complex nature of the fool in the Middle Ages and Renaissance, a paradoxical creature who had three principal facets: he was a clown, an entertainer often using absurd or obscene forms of humor; he was a foolish person, unable to refrain from wrongdoing; and he was a speaker of the truth, who could strip away appearances to reveal the underlying reality, showing himself wiser than the reputedly wise. The fools of the *sottie* combine these characteristics in varied ways. The plays themselves can be grouped according to their relation to these three facets of the fool, for the *sotties* are either primarily comic plays in which the *sots* are clowns, or they have a social and political significance, through the relation of the *sots* to evil—either doing evil (the *sot* as malicious fool) or revealing it (the *sot* as speaker of truth).

Only a few *sotties* fall into the category of simple, humorous sketches with no political overtones. The *Sottie de Trotte-Menu et Mire-Loret* involves little more than a scatalogical joke; the *Sottie des coppieurs et lardeurs* is a lively exchange between two groups of *sots* who attempt to make fools of each other. In a number of *sotties* (the *sotties de bande*), the fools make fun of themselves as a group or type of character. In the *Vigilles Triboullet*, for example, a band of fools holds a mock funeral to bury one of their heros, whose eulogy recalls above all how well he could drink. Even the simplest *sotties,* however, usually have some satiric significance, just as the satiric fools are still clowns.

Many *sotties* put on stage a group of fools (usually three) who criticize the way the world is going; they speak about hidden evildoers, though prudence (the fear of censorship or punishment) usually forces them to do so in veiled terms. The *Menus propos* simply has three *sots* speak one after another, mixing absurd, outrageous statements with allusions to social reality: *Se m'aist Dieu, tout ce qu'on promet/Maintenant n'est pas verité* ("May God help me, everything they promise these days isn't true"). Other plays, such as the *Croniqueurs* of Gringore, are more open in their political commentaries. The structure of a court case

or investigation is sometimes used to allow the fools to reveal wrongdoing by professions or social classes, as in *La mère de ville*. When the *sots* are faced with the agents or the victims of wrongdoing, they may act out the situations that fools like the "Chroniclers" only describe. In Gringore's *sottie* of the *Prince des Sots et Mère Sotte*, a play that combines both truth-speaking and evildoing fools, we watch the evil pope as he attempts to corrupt the king's loyal supporters but is unmasked by the wise fools.

In the third group of *sotties*, most or all of the characters act out satirical portraits of foolish wrongdoers, such as those who attempt to step outside their social roles or status. The plot of these *sotties* is often an enactment of a general idea, such as the use of a card game in the *Sots ecclésiastiques* to show the insatiable avarice and duplicity of certain prelates. In some plays, such as the *Gens nouveaux*, only wicked fools appear; the voice of morality is either expressed by their victim (Le Monde) or is silent. (Alan Knight [1983] has suggested grouping this kind of play in a separate category, the *farce moralisée*, to distinguish it from the *sottie*, in which the fools speak for a moral point of view.)

Through this variety of dramatic structures and characters, the *sotties* express humorous dismay at society's increasing immorality. This satiric view, which is often conservative, makes of the *sotties* a powerful and intriguing expression of late-medieval popular thought.

Heather M. Arden

[See also: FARCE; GRINGORE, PIERRE; MORALITY PLAYS; THEATER]

Droz, Eugénie, ed. *Le recueil Trepperel.* 2 vols. Paris: Droz, 1935, Vol. 1: *Les sotties.*
Picot, Emile, ed. *Recueil général des sotties.* 3 vols. Paris: Didot, 1902–12.
Arden, Heather M. *Fools' Plays: A Study of Satire in the "Sottie."* Cambridge: Cambridge University Press, 1980.
Aubailly, Jean-Claude. *Le monologue, le dialogue et la sottie.* Paris: Champion, 1976.
Garapon, Robert. *La fantaisie verbale et le comique dans le théâtre français du moyen âge à la fin du XVIIe siècle.* Paris: Colin, 1957.
Knight, Alan E. "The Medieval Theater of the Absurd." *PMLA* 86 (1971): 183–89.
———. *Aspects of Genre in Late Medieval French Drama.* Manchester: Manchester University Press, 1983.

SOUILLAC. Reclaimed from marshland in what is now the department of the Lot by Benedictine monks, Souillac (from *souille*, a wallowing place of wild boars) boasts one of the purest examples of the domed churches of southwest France and important fragments of Romanesque portal sculpture. Only the 12th-century abbey church of Sainte-Marie, remarkable for its harmonious proportions and unity of style, escaped the destruction of the wars of religion. The plan—single nave with domes on pendentives over two bays and a third over the crossing, projecting transepts with a polygonal chapel off each arm, and an ambu-

Souillac (Lot), church of Sainte-Marie. Isaiah. *Photograph courtesy of Whitney S. Stoddard.*

latory with three radiating chapels—is a smaller, more refined version of the plan of the cathedral of Cahors.

The sculpture now mounted on the interior west wall of the nave is one of the highlights of Romanesque carving. Above the entrance, and flanked by seated figures of SS. Benedict and Peter, is one of the oldest representations of the legend of Theophilus. To the left of the present door is Joseph or Hosea and to the right, the masterpiece of the Souillac sculptors, the expressive "dancing" figure of Isaiah. The former trumeau is carved on three faces. On the right lateral face, three pairs of figures either struggle or embrace; on the central face, a medley of gripping, devouring beasts culminates in a tortured human; on the left lateral face is the redemptive scene of Abraham and Isaac. On a second pilaster, a lion and lioness, suggestive of the crossed pairs of the Moissac trumeau, devour a ram. Both the original disposition of the sculpture and its iconography have been the subject of controversy.

Jean M. French

[See also: PÉRIGUEUX]

Aubert, Marcel. "Souillac." *Congrès archéologique* (*Périgueux*) 90 (1927): 261–70.
Labourdette, Régis. "Remarques sur la disposition originelle du portail de Souillac." *Gesta* 18 (1979): 29–35.
Schapiro, Meyer. *Romanesque Art.* New York: Braziller, 1977, pp. 102–30.
Thirion, Jacques. "Observations sur les fragments sculptés du portail de Souillac." *Gesta* 15 (1976): 71–72.
Vidal, Marguerite. "Souillac." In *Quercy roman.* La Pierre-qui-vire: Zodiaque, 1959.

SOUVIGNY. Control of the church of Saint-Pierre at Souvigny (Allier) passed to Cluny in 915, making it one of the oldest and most important possessions of the Burgundian abbey. The growth and prosperity of Souvigny are the result of, first, the death and burial there of Abbot Maiolus of Cluny in 994 and, later, the burial there in 1049 of his successor at Cluny, Abbot Odilo. The tomb of the canonized abbots became a pilgrimage site in the region. The church of Saint-Pierre has a complicated history, with important building periods in the 11th and 12th centuries and significant rebuilding (the Flamboyant façade) in 1433–45. The new façade destroyed the early Galilee porch; the Revolution saw the destruction of the church of Notre-Dame des Avents, which was probably the Infirmary chapel. The 12th-century sculptures, in the past called the "Tomb of Maiolus," are actually from the jubé. The 12th-century church of Saint-Marc, built north of the abbey church to serve the parish, has recently been restored. Initially receptive to Burgundian influences, the abbey of Souvigny soon became a regional center, as Cahn puts it, "a regional Cluny on a small scale."

William W. Clark

[See also: CLUNY]

Cahn, Walter. "Souvigny: Some Problems of Its Architecture and Sculpture." *Gesta* 27 (1988): 51-62.
Vergnolle, Éliane. "L'ancienne priorale Saint-Pierre de Souvigny." *Congrès archéologique* (*Bourbonnais*) 146 (1988): 399–431.
Wu, Fang-cheng. "Église Saint-Marc de Souvigny." *Congrès archéologique* (*Bourbonnais*) 146 (1988): 432–41.

SPANISH MARCH. In order to secure the Carolingian realm against invasions from Spain, Charlemagne (742–814) created a march, or defensive zone organized on a military basis, along the Spanish border. Frankish conquests in the 790s and early 9th century enabled the establishment of such a region between the Pyrénées and the Ebro, with Barcelona its capital. The march belonged to the kingdom of Aquitaine, ruled during Charlemagne's lifetime by his son, the future emperor Louis the Pious (778–840), and was the origin of the area later known as Catalonia.

After the crisis of 830 at Louis's court, the emperor allocated the march to his son Charles the Bald (823–877).

Its last count commissioned by a Frankish king was Guifred le Velu (d. 897), whose descendants ruled Catalonia for more than half a millennium. When the Umayyad caliphate in Spain fell in the early 11th century, the area became part of the group of Christian states that gravitated around the count of Barcelona.

Celia Chazelle

[See also: MARCH]

Bonnassie, Pierre. *La Catalogne du milieu du Xe à la fin du XIe siècle: croissance et mutations d'une société.* 2 vols. Toulouse: Association des Publications de l'Université de Toulouse–Le Mirail, 1975–76.

Riché, Pierre. *The Carolingians: A Family Who Forged Europe,* trans. Michael I. Allen. Philadelphia: University of Pennsylvania Press, 1993.

SPONSUS. An 11th-century Latin music drama based on the parable of the Wise and Foolish Virgins. Forty of its eighty-seven verses are in Occitan, making it the earliest dramatic work with vernacular passages. The text, found in a unique manuscript from Saint-Martial of Limoges (B.N. lat. 1139), also includes stage directions. The play is set to a small number of non-liturgical melodies in heighted Aquitanian neumes.

Lynette R. Muir

[See also: LITURGICAL DRAMA; STAGING OF PLAYS]

Thomas, Lucien-Paul, ed. *Le sponsus: mystère des Vierges Sages et des Vierges Folles.* Paris: Presses Universitaires de France, 1951.

SQUIRE. See Esquire/Escuier

STAGING OF PLAYS. A large amount of material on medieval staging in France has survived in the form of stage directions in play manuscripts, lists of stage properties in municipal records and account books, and eyewitness descriptions in memoirs and letters. Most of it, however, relates to the staging of mystery plays, with little information existing on the staging of farces and *sotties*.

The commonest method of staging described is that usually known as "*mansion* and *platea*": that is, a series of identifiable locations (or *lieux*), sometimes raised on scaffolds, combined with an anonymous central playing area. This arrangement, found already in the 12th-century *Jeu d'Adam* and *Seinte Resureccion*, is specified in the prologues and stage directions of several 15th-century plays. Performances might take place in a town square, the courtyard of a religious house, an amphitheater, or any open space where scaffolding could be erected. There are few references to indoor stages, notably for the Confrérie de la Passion in Paris. Many contracts survive for the construction of stages, some of which include audience stands and private, lockable spectator boxes. Depending on the type of theater, the audience might face the playing area or surround it. The illustration of the stage for the Valenciennes Passion play and the Fouquet miniature depicting the martyrdom of St. Apollonia show both types of theater, but their exact interpretation is a matter of debate. Performances on pageant wagons drawn by horses or oxen, recorded from northern France and the Burgundian Netherlands, normally involved only small-scale plays.

Most plays were organized by trade guilds, religious confraternities, or municipalities, with a few known instances of small groups of individuals binding themselves by contract to stage plays. Records of the staging of guild and confraternity plays are scarce, and most of the detailed information relates to the large-scale municipal and civic dramas, notably the play texts, expense accounts, and production records from Mons (1501) and Romans (1509). Since the big Passion plays and saint plays were expensive to produce, cities often tried to recoup some of their costs by charging admission to the enclosed playing area. Prices varied for standing room, regular seats, or seats in a box. At Romans, the church contributed half the costs and took half the income; at Valenciennes, the actors, who signed contracts guaranteeing their good behavior and attendance, could choose to contribute to the costs in exchange for a share in the possible profits.

A specialist might be brought in from outside the town and paid a fee to prepare and oversee the "secrets" or special effects, which might include trapdoors, lifting machinery, false bodies, and fireworks. The list of such *feintes* for the *Actes des Apôtres* played at Bourges in 1536 is many pages long. A recently discovered manuscript from Provence gives not only a list of devices required but precise instructions on how to create, for example, a fire-breathing devil.

Although the *lieux* that lined the turf-covered stage at Mons were merely labeled to indicate their changing identity from day to day, two locations were always fixed and elaborate: Heaven and Hell. The former was normally elevated and decorated with clouds, curtains, and revolving wheels or artificial angels. It had contrivances for the fire at Pentecost and the dove of Noah and sometimes included a concealed lift for the Ascension as well. Hell was at ground level, with its entrance through the animal jaws of Hellmouth. One could see instruments of torture and mechanical devils or weird tree roots on the exterior and smoke issuing from every orifice. At Mons, it took seventeen men, with their own special cue sheet, to work the infernal thunder machines, cannon, and fireworks. Music, which reflected the harmony of Heaven, was an important part of the plays, though the instruments, as well as the furniture, curtains, and plate for the court scenes, might be borrowed rather than purchased.

In contrast to the stage and decor, we know little about the costumes used in the plays. Because they were normally provided by the actors, they do not figure in the expense accounts. In 1535, Jean Bouchet warned the citizens of Issoudun, who were rehearsing a Passion play, against having characters like the Pharisees dressed as richly as Pilate, which suggests that elaborate rather than appropriate costumes were worn. This is supported by the account of the *montre*, or preperformance parade, from Bourges, which describes rich costumes adorned with gold and jewels.

The actors in the civic plays were drawn from all walks of life—nobility, clergy, bourgeois, and artisans. Virtually all of them were men, playing both male and female roles. There are a few recorded instances, however, when women took part in plays. The first such occasion was in Metz in 1468, when a young girl of eighteen played the title role in a play of St. Catherine of Siena.

Preparations and rehearsals usually took several months, and the performances were mostly in the summer. Though not usually linked with any special feast day, plays might be staged on several successive days, during which the shops and workplaces were closed. They might also be played on Sundays and feast days only, over a period of some weeks. Notices of productions and invitations were sent to many neighboring communities. During the performance, guards were increased at the town gates and in the playing area, and other precautions were taken against civil disorder. Children under twelve, pregnant women, and the infirm were barred from the theater at Mons, but the theater at Romans had a special railing on the boxes to prevent children from falling.

The amount of money taken at the entrances suggests that audiences of several thousand attended each performance of the big plays. Money was also made from the sale of materials and properties after the event. Despite this, Mons, Romans, and Bourges all lost money on their plays, though Issoudun and Valenciennes both made a profit. There were other advantages, however, for the plays brought trade, fame, and visitors to the towns and provided employment for the local craftsmen. Above all, there were many spiritual benefits for the organizers, artisans, actors, and spectators who "with divine help and all being done devoutly and for the instruction of the people" took part in the "play of God."

Lynette R. Muir

[**See also:** THEATER]

Meredith, Peter, and John E. Tailby, eds. *The Staging of Religious Drama in Europe in the Later Middle Ages*. Kalamazoo: Medieval Institute, 1983.

Muir, Lynette R. "Audiences in the French Medieval Theatre." *Medieval English Theatre* 9 (1987): 8–22.

———. "Women on the Medieval Stage: The Evidence from France." *Medieval English Theatre* 7 (1985): 107–19.

Rey-Flaud, Henri. *Le cercle magique*. Paris: Gallimard, 1973.

Tydeman, William. *The Theatre in the Middle Ages*. Cambridge: Cambridge University Press, 1978.

STAINED GLASS. Suger, the mid-12th-century abbot of Saint-Denis, described the new ambulatory of his church as shining "with the wonderful and uninterrupted light of most luminous windows, pervading [its] interior beauty" (*De consecratione* 4). Filled with richly colored and painted glass, the round-headed windows of the Saint-Denis ambulatory chapels transformed natural sunlight into a re-

Chartres (Eure-et-Loir), Notre-Dame, west façade lancet, Tree of Jesse. *Photograph courtesy of Grover A. Zinn.*

splendent gloom interpreted to reveal the Divine Presence. This association of God with light, critical to the understanding of medieval stained glass, was grounded in the Gospels (e.g., John 1: 4–9; 8:12) and was further elaborated in the writings of the early church fathers. While Bernard of Clairvaux (1090/91–1153), the founder of the Cistercian order, similarly embraced early Christian analogues of God as light, Cistercian glazings eschewed color, using instead uncolored glass arranged in symmetric interlace patterns. Whether colored or not, these hovering windows of light altered the very nature of a church interior from substance to the immaterial, mirroring the transmutation of the corporeal to the spiritual, thereby creating a vision for the worshiper and a paradise in which to encounter the Divine. Just as Suger recalled "dwelling" in meditation within "some strange region of the universe that neither exists entirely in the slime of the earth nor entirely in the purity of Heaven" (*De administratione* 33), stained-glass windows were construed as a mystical conduit for the illumination of the soul. Stained glass, the preeminent form of monumental painting of the Gothic period, was inexorably tied to its ecclesiastical and architectural context, the juncture intended to reveal Heaven on earth. Within this medieval construct of the Heavenly Jerusalem, glass and stone could not be separated but were conceived of as mutually dependent components of a whole: just as architectural masonry articulated the shape of a Gothic church, so light transmitted through its glazing defined and unified its sacred space.

Modern knowledge of medieval stained-glass production is indebted to the step-by-step instructions provided by a German monk writing under the pseudonym of Theophilus (ca. 1100). Current use of the term "stained glass" technically refers to pot-metal glass, that is, molten glass colored by the addition of metallic oxides. Glass itself is a fluid material composed of sand with additions of potash as a flux. In his manual, *De diversis artibus*, Theophilus recommends that scaled designs for windows be drawn on a flat whitewashed board, which could serve both as a surface for cutting and a workbench for assembly. The molten glass was blown either into an open cylinder shape (called "muff") or crown, a process in which the glass was transferred from the blowpipe to a pontil iron and spun into a circle. Once a flat surface was obtained, individual pieces of glass were cut by tracing the desired shape with a hot iron, followed by tracing the pattern with cold water, thus causing the glass to crack. The piece was subsequently shaped by edging bits of glass off the rim with the aid of a grozing iron (a handle with a small hook at the end) and pincers. The pieces of colored glass were in turn painted with a vitreous paint composed of iron filings and ground glass, bound by either wine or urine. Painting was used to indicate facial features, drapery folds, or intricate design patterns. Depending on the amount used, the liquid binder could make a thick black paint used for detailing or it could create a light grey wash for modeling. The pieces were then fired, affixing the paint to the glass surface. Theophilus suggests that the painter work in a three-layered process, beginning by laying down a wash and working up to the details.

With the introduction of silver stain at the beginning of the 14th century, this process changed dramatically. Composed of silver-oxide, silver stain is a paint that turns a range of hue from pale yellow to fiery orange depending on the length of time it is fired. The advantage of this painting technique was the ability to obtain a varied palette without having to cut and join different colors together with lead strips. Flashed glass (clear glass laminated with color) also gained popularity in the later Middle Ages, although this process had always been used for red, as the color is too opaque for light to penetrate when made of pot-metal glass. Once the painting was fired, pieces of glass were joined to one another by flexible lead cames, H-shaped strips grooved with channels to accommodate the edges. The panel was assembled by sequentially pinning each piece of glass to the board. Lead joints were soldered

and an encircling frame of iron provided to give the panel stability. The completed panel was puttied for weatherproofing and fixed within the armatures, the iron skeletal frame set within the masonry of the window.

Glazing windows with patterns of colored glass was an ancient Roman tradition that continued into the early Middle Ages. Prior to the 9th century, numerous documents speak of decorative compositions in windows installed as far afield as Constantinople, Rome, Syria, and Northumberland. As early as the 5th century, the French bishop Sidonius Apollinaris described such a decorative glazing in the church of the Maccabees at Lyon. Yet the art of painting on glass, a distinctly medieval invention, survives in only a handful of fragments dated prior to the cycle of prophets at Augsburg cathedral (ca. 1130). The extensive ambulatory glazing (1144) at Saint-Denis is the earliest surviving stained-glass program in France. With this masterly ensemble and the nearly contemporaneous windows of the west façade of Chartres cathedral (ca. 1150), painted stained glass was firmly entrenched as a defining component of French Gothic art. The placement of windows was carefully considered within the architectural complex. For example, the axial choir bay glazed with the

Chartres, Notre-Dame, Good Samaritan and Genesis window. *Photograph courtesy of Whitney S. Stoddard.*

Chartres, Notre-Dame, north transept windows. *Photograph courtesy of Whitney S. Stoddard.*

tive, similar to those in the west façade windows at Chartres, or on emblematic discourse, such as the Allegories of St. Paul window at Saint-Denis and the typological Crucifixion from the abbey church of Orbais (1190?). The pictorialization of Isaiah's prophecy of Christ's lineage, known as the Tree of Jesse, had also been well established by 1200. Hagiographical narrative appeared in the 12th century, as in the St. Nicholas panels from Troyes (ca. 1170–80) or the legend of St. Catherine from Angers (ca. 1180). In the 13th century, historiated windows were increasingly devoted to the depiction of saints' lives, Marian narrative, and Old Testament cycles. While 13th-century legendary windows could be expansively discursive (at the Sainte-Chapelle, the story of Esther and Ahasuerus is recounted in 129 scenes), by the early 14th century narrative was reduced to only the most crucial scenes.

Clerestory windows were most often glazed with single figures to facilitate being read at a distance. The range of subject matter was wide, including the genealogy of Christ, as at the abbey church of Saint-Yved at Braine (ca. 1200); prophets, Apostles, and bishops, like those at Bourges cathedral (ca. 1220–30); or saints, as at Beauvais (1340s). Occasionally, these large standing figures would be cast in narrative tableaux, as in the choir at Chartres (1210–25), while historiated scenes, as at Tours (ca. 1255–60), were adopted by the second half of the 13th century.

Marking the interior termini of ecclesiastical space, rose windows were glazed with eschatological or cosmological themes, such as the Last Judgment at Mantes (ca. 1220), the Apocalypse at Chartres south (1221–30) and at the Sainte-Chapelle (ca. 1485), or the west rose (ca. 1220) at Notre-Dame in Paris, with its portrayal of the zodiac, Virtues, and Vices surrounding the Virgin and Apostles. In keeping with the widespread Marian dedication of Gothic cathedrals, the Glorification of the Virgin, as at Laon (1210–15), was also a popular theme. The 15th century witnessed the introduction of new themes as well, such as the Apostles' Creed at Riom (ca. 1460) and Signs of the End of the World in the north rose at Angers cathedral (1451).

What do we know about the artists of these windows? Not only are signatures virtually unknown, but written documentation is sparse until the end of the 13th century. The only portrait of a glass painter from this time comes from the German abbey of Arnstein (ca. 1160; now in Münster), showing the painter Gerlachus holding his brush and paint pot, praying for the gift of light. A signature of a certain Clement of Chartres survives on a banderole in the Joseph window (ca. 1235) from the cathedral of Rouen. Stylistic evidence tells us that several painters sometimes worked on the same window, while other windows indicate a single, coherent style. Though a window was often the product of more than one individual, not enough is known about how artists prior to the 15th century collaborated or about how the labor was divided. While archival records list artists, such as a certain Étienne who lived in Bourges ca. 1220, it is impossible to link these names with extant windows. Late-medieval tax rolls provide additional demographic information, including the names of women, such as Jehanne la Verrière and Ysabellot la Verrière. Guild records offer lists of members, as well as

Crucifixion (ca. 1180) from the abbey church of Saint-Remi in Reims and the Crucifixion-Ascension window (ca. 1165–70) in the axial bay of the chevet at Poitiers are both painted in monumental scale commanding the longitudinal vista from the nave. Placement could also be governed by the precious regard for certain stained-glass windows, as witnessed by the retention and reinstallation of early compositions into renovated or new architectural contexts. The "Notre-Dame de la Belle Verrière" (ca. 1180) from Chartres was recovered after the fire of 1194 and reset into the new 13th-century cathedral. Portions of the original nave glazing of Rouen, the so-called "Belles Verrières" (ca. 1200), were salvaged in the late 13th century and reinstalled into newly constructed nave-chapel windows. The admiration for stained glass also prompted concern for its upkeep. Suger mentions that a master glazier was appointed to maintain the windows at Saint-Denis (*De administratione* 34 A).

Stained-glass imagery was often conditioned by window placement. Historiated subjects, predominantly located in nave-aisle windows, contrasted with large standing or seated figures generally depicted in the upper reaches of the clerestory or with eschatological and cosmological subjects portrayed in rose windows. Early historiated windows in France generally focused on christological narra-

Paris (Seine), Sainte-Chapelle, upper chapel. *Photograph courtesy of Whitney S. Stoddard.*

Paris, Saint-Germain-des-Prés, St. Vincent. *Courtesy of the Walters Art Gallery, Baltimore.*

transcribe regulations governing the practice of glass painting. In the 15th century, the names of glass painters, like other artists, survive with increasing frequency in conjunction with their windows, such as the court painter André Robin, who worked at Angers.

Throughout the Middle Ages, the status of the patron eclipsed that of the artist. Seeking to elucidate sacred or theological precepts associated with a site or to express personal devotion, remembrance, political prestige, or a combination of these qualities, patrons of stained-glass windows encompassed a broad spectrum of French society. Donor portraits testify to this diversity, whether monastic, episcopal, noble, or lay. They are shown in supplication, as in the depiction of Suger at the feet of the Virgin, or holding a model of their window, like the portrait of Canon Raoul de Ferrières in Évreux (ca. 1325). The beguiling representations of artisans at the base of windows, such as the shoemakers, wine carriers, furriers, and bakers at Chartres, attest to the influence wielded by laypeople as well. Heraldry, too, was a major means for importing the patron's identity. The fleurs-de-lis and castles of Castile filling the interstices of the north rose at Chartres (ca. 1235) signify the royal sponsorship of Blanche of Castile and her son Louis IX, while the arms below the cathedral's south rose indicate the prestige of the noble Dreux-Bretagne family.

The style and appearance of medieval French windows were directly related to the window design. The round-headed lancet openings of the later 12th century demanded an orthogonal arrangement for armatures, with the panels frequently arranged in sequential rows of circles or in alternating patterns of circles and squares, as in the west-façade windows at Chartres. Blue and red contrasting backgrounds predominated, as in the expansive setting of the Ascension (ca. 1140–45) from the cathedral of Le Mans, where brilliantly alternating blocks of diaphanous blue and ruby-red backgrounds accent the upward motion of the composition. The preciousness associated with color was emphasized by Suger, who extolled the resonant blue used at Saint-Denis as "sapphire glass" (*De administratione* 34), a reference to its inestimable luminous quality. Typically, a vivid palette of greens, pinks, yellows, and blues complemented this emphasis. Wide jewellike borders, evoking contemporary metalwork, customarily framed these 12th-century compositions. The painting style of later 12th-century windows varied, depending on its regional origin. It can generally be characterized as bearing a stylized, graphic approach to the delineation of elongated figures and drapery folds and the rendering of often highly expressive facial features.

With the introduction of double-lancet windows in the early 1200s, the organization of window designs, particularly historiated windows in the nave aisles, was increasingly defined by armatures molded into highly complex, centrifugal patterns of alternating squares and circles. Epitomized by the windows of Chartres and Bourges, these molded armatures played an integral role not only in window design but also in directing the eye in reading the composition. Dispensing with single grounds of color, historiated scenes were surrounded by mosaic grounds linked by ornamental bosses. The Saint-Chéron window (1220–25) in the ambulatory of Chartres departed from this model by returning to an orthogonal arrangement of its armatures with its scenes arranged in horizontal registers. By the mid-13th century, window designs varied. Molded armatures were still employed at the Sainte-Chapelle (1244–48), while the orthogonal arrangement was contemporaneously used for the Lady Chapel glazing at the abbey of Saint-Germain-des-Prés (ca. 1247). The Sainte-Chapelle, built by Louis IX to house the sacred relic of the Crown of Thorns, represents the culminating effect of deeply saturated light created by 13th-century windows. Virtually a reliquary "turned outside in," the Sainte-Chapelle interior is lit by walls of glass windows whose narrative both glorifies the relics acquired by Louis and chronicles the course of human history recounted in the Bible. In the second half of the 13th century, orthogonal armatures and simplified compositions were favored, as windows became increasingly elongated and subdivided. Similarly, the painting style became open and summary, with a few salient lines sufficing to delineate gesture, drapery folds, and facial expressions. Bold color backgrounds again distinguished these compositions, replacing mosaic grounds popular in the earlier part of the century. Ornamentation was also simplified, with thinner borders composed of abstracted foliate motifs. Blue and red continued to dominate the color palette, with light pinks, purples, blues, and yellows used for contrast.

Grisaille windows, compositions of cut glass in its natural green, pink, or white state arranged into intricate patterns and painted, were also integral components of glazings at this time. Distinct from ornamental windows created with colored glass, grisaille windows are characterized by interlocking floral or geometric designs often set against dense cross-hatching. Favored by Cistercian foundations, such as Obazine (ca. 1150), grisaille windows were also adopted by other ecclesiastical foundations, as at Saint-Jean-aux-Bois (ca. 1230s). Colored bosses and borders were incorporated into grisaille windows toward the middle of the 13th century. Ensembles of grisaille and saturated glass were also combined at this time, as at Saint-Germain-des-Prés, where the colored hemicycle windows of the Lady Chapel contrasted with grisaille in the straight bays of the nave. By the third quarter of the 13th century, a new attitude was evident. In tandem with increasing ornamentation of interior church surfaces and window tracery, glazings contained greater amounts of grisaille glass, juxtaposing uncolored and colored figural panels in the same window. At the abbey church of Saint-Père at Chartres (second half of the 13th c.), grisaille and colored lights were installed vertically side by side, while at Tours (ca. 1260) figural panels were placed as a horizontal register between the grisaille (called band windows). The great masterpiece of this style is the collegiate church of Saint-Urbain (ca. 1270) in Troyes. Built by Pope Urban IV on the site of his birthplace, the church and its glazing

are a resplendent ensemble of luminosity, pattern, and color—far different from the mysterious ambience that so moved Abbot Suger.

As so many of France's 14th- and 15th-century windows have been destroyed, it is difficult to study them in any kind of comprehensive fashion. In general, stained glass of the later Middle Ages in France became increasingly pictorial and painterly in style. To a large degree, this approach was facilitated by the advent of silver stain around the beginning of the 14th century. With the thin window lancets of the Late Gothic period, mixed glazings of grisaille and colored glass became the norm. Historiated scenes were simplified to only one episode or figure per lancet. Architectural canopies became increasingly important as an organizing compositional device. The mixed glazing of the abbey church of Saint-Ouen (1318–39) in Rouen is among the most arresting programs of the period. Its historiated panels, framed by elaborate arcades and backed by damascene grounds, are elegantly delineated with mannered line and light, vibrant colors. The bordering grisaille panels are composed of clear, white glass enlivened with botanically accurate plant renderings, including periwinkle, strawberry, columbine, and buttercup. The technical mastery of glass painters in the subsequent century, as well as the pervasive influence of Netherlandish painters like Jan van Eyck, is evident in the Annunciation window (1448–50) presented by Jacques Cœur to Bourges cathedral.

Our knowledge of medieval French stained glass relies on only a tiny fraction of the number of windows actually produced. Victims to changes in taste as well as iconoclasm and political revolt, stained-glass windows were destroyed in vast quantities during the 18th century and in the aftermath of the Revolution. Modern warfare reduced their number even more. Today, pollution continues to threaten these irreplaceable monuments of French patrimony.

M.B. Shepard

[See also: ANGERS; BOURGES; BRAINE; CHARTRES; CISTERCIAN ART AND ARCHITECTURE; GOTHIC ARCHITECTURE; GOTHIC ART; LAON; MANTES; ORBAIS; PARIS; REIMS; RIOM; ROUEN; SAINT-DENIS; SUGER; TOURS/TOURAINE; TROYES; VAN EYCK, JAN]

Brisac, Catherine. *A Thousand Years of Stained Glass*, trans. Geoffrey Culverwell. Garden City: Doubleday, 1986.

Brown, Sarah. *Stained Glass: An Illustrated History*. London: Studio Editions, 1992.

———, and David O'Connor. *Glass-Painters*. London: British Museum, 1991.

Caviness, Madeline H. "Biblical Stories in Windows: Were They Bibles for the Poor?" In *The Bible in the Middle Ages*, ed. Bernard S. Levy. Binghamton: Medieval and Renaissance Texts and Studies, 1992, pp. 103–47.

———. *Sumptuous Arts at the Royal Abbeys in Reims and Braine*. Princeton: Princeton University Press, 1990.

———, with Evelyn Ruth Staudinger. *Stained Glass Before 1540: An Annotated Bibliography*. Boston: Hall, 1983.

Cothren, Michael. "Suger's Stained Glass Masters and Their Workshop at Saint-Denis." In *Paris: Center of Artistic En-*

lightenment. Papers in Art History from the Pennsylvania State University, Vol. 4 (1988), pp. 46–75.

Grodecki, Louis. *Le vitrail roman*. Fribourg: Office du Livre, 1977.

———, and Catherine Brisac. *Gothic Stained Glass, 1200–1300*, trans. Barbara Drake Boehm. Ithaca: Cornell University Press, 1985.

Kemp, Wolfgang. *Sermo Corporeus: Die Erzählung der mittelalterlichen Glasfenster*. Munich: Schirmer/Mosel, 1987.

Lautier, Claudine. "Les peintres-verriers des bas-côtés de la nef de Chartres au début du XIIIe siècle." *Bulletin monumental* 148 (1990): 7–45.

Lillich, Meredith Parsons. "Gothic Glaziers: Monks, Jews, Taxpayers, Bretons, Women." *Journal of Glass Studies* 27 (1985): 72–92.

——— . "Monastic Stained Glass: Patronage and Style." In *Monasticism and the Arts*, ed. Timothy G. Verdon. Syracuse: Syracuse University Press, 1984, pp. 207–54.

———. *Rainbow Like an Emerald: Stained Glass in Lorraine in the Thirteenth and Early Fourteenth Centuries*. University Park: University of Maryland Press, 1991.

———. *The Armor of Light: Stained Glass in Western France 1250–1325*. Berkeley: University of California Press, 1993.

Panofsky, Erwin, ed. and trans. *Abbot Suger on the Abbey Church of St. Denis and Its Art Treasures*. Princeton: Princeton University Press, 1979.

Raguin, Virginia. *Stained Glass in Thirteenth-Century Burgundy*. Princeton: Princeton University Press, 1982.

Williams, Jane Welch. *Bread, Wine & Money: The Windows of the Trades at Chartres Cathedral*. Chicago: University of Chicago Press, 1993.

Zakin, Helen Jackson. *French Cistercian Grisaille Glass*. New York: Garland, 1979.

The volumes produced under the sponsorship of the Corpus Vitrearum Medii Aevi, an international group of scholars dedicated to the study and documentation of stained glass, are essential to the study of medieval French stained glass. Relevant titles include: Marcel Aubert et al., *Les vitraux de Notre Dame et de la Sainte-Chapelle de Paris* (Paris, 1959), and Jean Lafond with the assistance of Françoise Perrot and Paul Popesco, *Les vitraux de l'église Saint-Ouen de Rouen*, Vol. 1 (Paris, 1970). In the series *Études*: Louis Grodecki, *Les vitraux de Saint-Denis: étude sur le vitrail au XIIe siècle* (Paris, 1976); Colette Manhes-Deremble with the assistance of Jean-Paul Deremble, *Les vitraux narratifs de la cathédrale de Chartres: étude iconographique* (Paris, 1993). In the series *Recensements des Vitraux Anciens de la France*, sponsored in conjunction with the Inventaire Général: *Les vitraux de Paris, de la région parisienne, de la Picardie, et du Nord-Pas-de-Calais*, Vol. 1 (Paris, 1978); *Les vitraux du Centre et des Pays de la Loire*, Vol. 2 (Paris, 1981); *Les vitraux de Bourgogne, Franche-Comté et Rhône-Alpes*, Vol. 3 (Paris, 1986); *Les vitraux de Champagne-Ardenne*, Vol. 4 (Paris, 1992).

STATIONS OF THE CROSS. An exercise of Christian devotion known also as the Way of the Cross, in which the faithful move around the interior of a church, stopping to pray and meditate at representations of events from the Passion of Christ. The practice had its origins in the visits of Christian pilgrims to the places in Jerusalem traditionally associated with the sufferings and death of Jesus Christ. These pilgrimages are attested to as early as the 4th century, and a series of five stational shrines was erected in the church of San Stefano in 5th-century Bologna. The idea was given considerable impetus in the 12th and 13th centuries by the increase in devotion to the Passion of Christ that was encouraged by veterans of the Crusades returning from the Holy Land. The Franciscans in particular took it up and saw to the installation of stations in the churches under their care. Still, the practice did not become universal in Catholic churches, nor was the number of stations standardized at fourteen until the 18th century.

James McKinnon

[See also: MASS, CHANTS AND TEXTS; PROCESSION]

Thurston, Herbert. *The Stations of the Cross*. London: Burns and Oates, 1906.

STEPHEN HARDING (d. 1134). Born in England, Stephen entered the Benedictine abbey of Molesme and was one of the monks who accompanied Robert of Molesme when he left to found the new monastery of Cîteaux and thus set in motion the reform movement that produced the Cistercian order. Harding was subprior and prior before being elected the third abbot of Cîteaux in 1109. He was abbot when Bernard of Clairvaux and a group of his followers joined the community. He was the author of the early text of the *Carta caritatis* (ca. 1119), which formed the basic constitution of the order and established the General Chapter and the pattern of yearly visitations of daughter houses by the abbot of the mother house. The *Exordium parvum*, a brief history of the founding of Cîteaux, is probably by Stephen. He produced, with the assistance of a converted Jew whom he consulted, a revision of the Vulgate translation of the Bible that sought to be more faithful to the Hebrew text.

Grover A. Zinn

[See also: BERNARD OF CLAIRVAUX; *CARTA CARITATIS*; CISTERCIAN ORDER; ROBERT OF MOLESME]

Douglas, David C., and W. Greenaway, eds. *English Historical Documents*. London: Eyre and Spottiswoode, 1953, Vol. 2, pp. 687–91. [Translation of *Carta caritatis*.]

STEPHEN LANGTON (ca. 1155–1228). Stephen Langton and his brother Simon were two of the most influential figures of their age. Stephen was born in Langton-by-Wragby, near Lincoln. His early education was probably at the Lincoln cathedral school, but ca. 1170 he moved to Paris and studied and then taught, for about twenty years, around the Petit Pont, probably at the school of Peter the Chanter. Like the Chanter and Peter Comestor, Stephen was interested in practical moral questions and in biblical studies. He was at his best when discussing, in a common-sense way, the problems of everyday life. He sided most definitely with the active rather than the contemplative life.

Stephen's fame came not from his theology but from his preaching and biblical commentaries. He was known as *Linguatonans*—thundering tongue. About 500 of his sermons survive. He is credited with the division of the Bible into more or less its present chapters; he was well known for his corrections to the text; and he commented on most of the Bible according to both the literal and spiritual senses. His commentaries circulated in a number of forms, some with only one sense, some with both. He also wrote commentaries on Peter Comestor's *Historia scholastica*.

While in Paris, he was a close friend of Lothar of Segni, who as Pope Innocent III made him a cardinal in 1206. In December 1206, Stephen was elected archbishop of Canterbury; but owing to disputes over his election between King John Lackland and the Canterbury chapter (backed by Innocent III), he was not allowed to take his seat until 1213. Until then, he lived in exile at the abbey of Pontigny.

Stephen was closely involved with Magna Carta and may have been its author. He worked hard to maintain the role of mediator during the events that led to 1215 and saw the charter not as innovation but as restatements of the rights and duties of kingship. Innocent read Langton's mediation with the barons as an indirect challenge to himself and suspended him as archbishop for two years. The dispute was eventually settled by the deaths of John and Innocent, and Stephen returned to England in 1218.

He attended the Fourth Lateran Council in 1215 and was very much in sympathy with its reforming principles. Back in England, he avidly pursued church reform, holding the first provincial council to legislate in England in 1222 in Oxford. He himself was active in administration of his see. He presided over the translation of the relics of Thomas Becket at Canterbury in 1220. He played a major role in the coronation of the boy-king Henry III (1220) and became his adviser. He died in Sussex in 1228.

Lesley J. Smith

[See also: BIBLE, CHRISTIAN INTERPRETATION OF; INNOCENT III; PETER COMESTOR; PETER THE CHANTER; PREACHING]

Stephen Langton. *Commentary on the Book of Chronicles*, ed. Avrom Saltman. Ramat-Gan: Bar-Ilan University Press, 1978.

——. *Der Sentenzenkommentar des Kardinals Stephan Langton*, ed. Artur Michael Landgraf. Münster: Aschendorff, 1952.

——. *Selected Sermons of Stephen Langton*, ed. Phyllis Barzillay Roberts. Toronto: Pontifical Institute of Mediaeval Studies, 1980.

Baldwin, John W. *Masters, Princes, and Merchants: The Social Views of Peter the Chanter and His Circle*. 2 vols. Princeton: Princeton University Press, 1970, Vol. 1, pp. 25–31.

Longère, Jean. *Œuvres oratoires de maîtres parisiens au XIIe siècle: étude historique et doctrinale*. Paris: Études Augustiniennes, 1975.

Powicke, Frederick Maurice. *Stephen Langton: Being the Ford Lectures Delivered in the University of Oxford in Hilary Term 1927*. Oxford: Clarendon, 1928.

Roberts, Phyllis Barzillay. "Master Stephen Langton Preaches to the People and Clergy: Sermon Texts from Twelfth-Century Paris." *Traditio* 36 (1980): 237–68.

——. *Stephanus de Lingua-Tonante: Studies in the Sermons of Stephen Langton*. Toronto: Pontifical Institute of Mediaeval Studies, 1968.

STEPHEN OF BLOIS (ca. 1100–1154). King of England. Stephen of Blois, the third son of Adèle, daughter of William the Conqueror, and Étienne de Blois, rose to prominence through the patronage of his uncle Henry I of England. Stephen acquired his French lands by grants from Henry: the county of Mortain (by 1113), and the county of Boulogne through marriage to the heiress Matilda in 1125. Despite significant holdings in France, Stephen played a limited role in French politics. As an active member of Henry's court, Stephen had little time for independent action in France, though he did lead an unsuccessful Flemish campaign in 1127 against Henry's rival to the throne, William Clito, who was supported by Louis VI. His assumption of the English throne in December 1135 led to a civil war that was waged primarily in England.

Stephen fought to establish his control in Normandy from March to November of 1137. After formal recognition as duke of Normandy by Louis VI in May, Stephen put down several rebellions but failed to regain control of territories seized by Geoffroi d'Anjou. He returned to England to quell a baronial rebellion, leaving the situation in Normandy unsettled.

Stephen continued to play an indirect role in French politics through a marriage alliance in 1140 between his son, Eustache, and Louis VII's sister, Constance. This alliance fell into abeyance when Geoffroi d'Anjou, who had married Henry I's daughter Matilda, brought Normandy under his control in 1144 and won Louis's support through the cession of Gisors and the Norman Vexin. When he returned from crusading in 1149, Louis, alarmed by Geoffroi's power, revived the alliance with Stephen. Louis and Eustache, with limited success, campaigned against the Angevins in the summer of 1151 and again in 1152 after the marriage of Geoffroi and Matilda's son Henry, count of Anjou and duke of Normandy, to Eleanor of Aquitaine. Stephen's indirect role in French politics ended with the failure of these campaigns, Eustache's death in August 1153, and the negotiated settlement with Henry, who would succeed Stephen as Henry II.

Heather J. Tanner

[See also: HENRY II; MATILDA]

Davis, Ralph H.C. *King Stephen, 1135–54*. Berkeley: University of California Press, 1967.

Warren, Wilfred L. *Henry II*. Berkeley: University of California Press, 1973.

STRASBOURG. Because of its location on the Rhine River at the border between French and German lands, Strasbourg (Bas-Rhin) has since Roman times been a crossroads; its very name means "city of roads." While the resulting multicultural influences enriched its artistic heritage, the ravages of numerous wars have damaged many of Strasbourg's medieval monuments.

The best-preserved and best-restored medieval edifice is the cathedral of Notre-Dame. This church illustrates a progressive stylistic shift from Ottonian Romanesque to French Gothic. Its plan and proportions follow those of a Romanesque church begun on this site in 1015. Rebuilding in the choir and transept ca. 1200 continues Romanesque features, such as the apse opening directly to the transept, an elongated crypt, and an octagonal tower over the crossing. Some of the Romanesque stained-glass windows are reemployed in the glazing program of the transept.

French Gothic architecture and sculpture began to predominate at Strasbourg ca. 1200. A new atelier, possibly from Chartres, vaulted the south transept and was responsible for sculpture of the Last Judgment pillar inside and portal sculpture, including tympana of the Death and Coronation of the Virgin and pillar statues representing Church, Synagogue, and Solomon outside the south transept. These sculptures are masterpieces of the damp-fold, expressive style developed in the transepts of Chartres cathedral.

From ca. 1240–75, the nave was rebuilt in the Rayonnant style of Parisian Gothic architecture. The nave of seven bays with single aisles has a three-story elevation with glazed triforium. The stained glass from the mid-13th to mid-14th century features standing saints in the clerestory, Christ's genealogy in the triforium, seated emperors in the north aisle, and scenes from the lives of the Virgin and Christ in the south aisle. The main addition to the nave was the mid-14th-century chapel of Sainte-Catherine.

The final phase of construction was the west façade, begun ca. 1275, purportedly under Erwin de Steinbach, and completed in the 15th century. It is famous for its "harp string" effect of vertical lines and pointed gables in a Rhenish Gothic style. The lower story with three sculpted portals, whose tympana represent Christ's infancy, Passion, and the Last Judgment in a French Gothic style, was completed before a fire in 1296. On the gable of the central portal is the throne of Solomon, surrounded by a dozen lions representing the Twelve Tribes of Israel; the whole is surmounted by a statue of the Virgin and Child. The sculptures show an expressive combination of French Gothic and Germanic mannerist styles. Surviving drawings for the façade show that two towers of equal height were planned; however, only the north tower, completed in the 15th century, was built.

Four other medieval churches attesting to the economic prosperity of Strasbourg merit notice. Of Sainte-Aurélie, founded in the 8th century, there remains only the 12th-century tower of the west façade. The collegial church of Saint-Thomas, constructed in the 13th and 14th centuries, betrays the influence of the cathedral in its capitals and façade. The church of Saint-Étienne was largely destroyed during World War II; the medieval transept and choir have been restored, but the nave is modern. The Protestant church Saint-Pierre-le-Jeune was founded in the

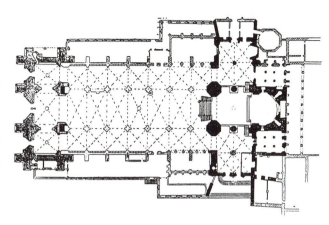

Strasbourg (Bas-Rhin), Notre-Dame, plan. After Walter.

11th century as an abbey church in Romanesque style. Rebuilt in Gothic style in the late 13th and early 14th centuries, it retains its Romanesque tower (lower three levels), cloister, and conventual buildings.

Karen Gould

[See also: ERWIN DE STEINBACH; GOTHIC ARCHITECTURE]

Beyer, Victor, Christiane Wild-Block, and Fridtjof Zschokke. *Les vitraux de la cathédrale Notre-Dame de Strasbourg* (*Corpus Vitrearum. . . .*, France IX-1). Paris: CNRS, 1986.

Haug, Hans. *La cathédrale de Strasbourg.* Strasbourg: Dernières Nouvelles, 1957.

Reinhardt, Hans. *La cathédrale de Strasbourg.* Paris: Arthaud, 1972.

Schmitt, Otto. *Gotische Skulpturen des Strasburger Münsters.* 2 vols. Frankfurt, 1924.

STRASBOURG, OATHS OF. The earliest written evidence of French or of any Romance language, as recorded by the chronicler Nithard, the Oaths were sworn at Strasbourg in 842 by Charles II the Bald and Louis the German in alliance against their brother Lothair, who sought sole control of their grandfather Charlemagne's empire. Each swore in his brother's language, Louis in *romana lingua*, Charles in *teudisca lingua.*

The linguistic interest of the Oaths is considerable, although it has been difficult to localize their dialect. Old French elements include the new future tense, diphthongs formed from palatalization, the monophthongization of the Latin diphthong AU, as well as evidence for the so-called mute *-e.* Nevertheless, certain uncharacteristic features have suggested either that the Oaths may have been written in a southwestern dialect or that they were composed in a chancery Latin, then translated into French. The Oaths have cultural and literary interest as well. Of particular note is the pair of words *podir* 'might' and *savir* 'wisdom,' which figures importantly in later descriptions of the knightly ideal.

The texts exist today in a single manuscript (B.N. lat. 9768) of the second half of the 10th century.

Thelma S. Fenster

[See also: CAROLINGIAN DYNASTY; FRENCH LANGUAGE; NITHARD]

Paris, Gaston, ed. *Les plus anciens monuments de la langue française (IXe, Xe siècles). Album.* Paris: Didot, 1875.

SUBTRACTION OF OBEDIENCE.

SUBTRACTION OF OBEDIENCE. The Great Schism of the papacy entered a new phase in 1394 with the election of Benedict XIII, the second pope of the Avignon obedience. The French government adopted a policy that it would follow, with minor interruptions, for fifteen years—advocating the *via cessionis* as the means to end the Schism. Under this policy, France would no longer support the use of force to impose the Avignon pope on Rome or any judicial proceeding to determine which contender was the sole true pope. Instead, both popes were to abdicate and a single successor elected in their place.

Neither pope was willing to consider this approach to union, and the French developed sanctions aimed at forcing compliance on Benedict XIII. The principal sanction was called "subtraction of obedience," a term that meant cutting off the revenues of a pope recognized in France as the legitimate one. One could subtract obedience without casting any aspersion on the papacy as an institution or on the legitimacy of the pope in question. In French ecclesiastical politics, however, subtraction could have at least two meanings. Partial subtraction, which denied the papal government certain powers over the French church, was the policy favored by proponents of "Gallican liberties," whose stronghold was the University of Paris. They sought to make the policy permanent, thus presumably returning to an earlier time, before the popes had supposedly appropriated powers that properly belonged to the bishops. The cardinals, and others who found the existing system beneficial, naturally opposed the Gallican solution of permanent partial subtraction, but many of them were prepared to take more drastic short-term action to force compliance with the *via cessionis*. Thus was born the concept of *total* subtraction of obedience from a particular pope who, by refusing to abdicate, was perpetuating the Schism, thereby falling into heresy and losing the capacity to perform any papal function. Total subtraction would in no way diminish the powers of the papacy but, by removing them from a particular pope, could be invoked to hasten the end of the Schism.

The driving force in France behind total subtraction of obedience was Simon de Cramaud, patriarch of Alexandria, a protégé of the duke of Berry, the French prince most dedicated to ending the Schism. At a first council in Paris, early in 1395, the French prelates, under prodding from the government, finally endorsed the *via cessionis*. A second council, meeting in Paris in the summer of 1396, debated ways of enforcing this policy, and the university made a determined bid to have the government adopt its Gallican program, which included partial subtraction. The effort failed, but in the process papal supporters launched a counterattack against the *via cessionis* itself.

Neither Cramaud nor Berry was present for the second council of Paris, and in the months that followed Cramaud, who was no Gallican, produced his treatise *De subtraccione obediencie*, a powerful argument for total subtraction that was destined for wide circulation. His purpose was to head off a papalist reaction without alienating the Gallican supporters of partial subtraction. A third Paris council, in 1398, voted for subtraction of obedience, and for three years the Avignon papacy was denied much of its authority in France and Castile.

Because of international political factors, however, Cramaud and the French cessionists were not able to get wide European backing at this time, and in 1401 the government abandoned the policy of subtraction. Five years later, the climate was more auspicious. At a fourth Paris council, in 1406–07, even the University of Paris favored full subtraction. In the end, unilateral subtraction of obedience by France failed to coerce Benedict XIII, but the French debate and the wide circulation of Cramaud's treatise produced many conversions to the *via cessionis*. As it happened, only a general council of the church could bring to bear enough pressure to end the Schism. At Pisa, in 1409–10, Cramaud had the satisfaction of presiding at a gathering that declared both popes deposed on the basis of doctrines he had been espousing.

John Bell Henneman, Jr.

[See also: AVIGNON PAPACY; SCHISM, GREAT]

Cramaud, Simon de. *De subtraccione obediencie*, ed. Howard Kaminsky. Cambridge: Medieval Academy of America, 1984.
Kaminsky, Howard. *Simon de Cramaud and the Great Schism.* New Brunswick: Rutgers University Press, 1983.

SUGER

SUGER (1081–1151). Abbot of Saint-Denis from 1122 to 1151, Suger is one of the most interesting representatives of French monastic culture in the 12th century, combining an extraordinary devotion to his monastery with an understanding of the weaknesses and potential strengths of the kings of France. He was an ardent administrator and builder, and, if he is best remembered for his desire to adorn his church, he also reformed the liturgy and improved the life of the community, earning the praise of Bernard, abbot of Clairvaux.

Suger also stands out from most of his contemporaries because of the much clearer picture we have of his personality and achievements. He himself wrote a Latin *vita* of Louis VI, in which he gives a vivid picture of the king's attempts to subdue the turbulent aristocracy in the Paris region, his own role in this process, and the king's special devotion to St. Denis. He also wrote two works concerning his administration of the monastery's lands and the building and consecration of the new church. A small number of his charters and letters survive, and his image and his words are preserved in several places in the church of his abbey.

Suger's chalice, Saint-Denis. *Courtesy of the National Gallery of Art, Washington, D.C.*

Suger's eagle vase, Saint-Denis. *Courtesy of the Louvre, Paris, Réunion des Musées Nationaux.*

Suger was born of a modest knightly family probably not too far from Saint-Denis and was given as an oblate to the abbey. During his early years, he seems to have realized how the abbey had lost prestige, power, and wealth since the time of Charlemagne and Charles the Bald; how the reciprocal devotion of saint and king had been a strength to both; and how the church's small size and decayed furnishings no longer served the needs of the monks or the crowds of pilgrims coming there. Throughout his long life and particularly during his abbacy, it was his purpose to remedy these three lacks.

Suger tells us how as a youth he used to look at the abbey's muniments and how he was aware not only of its lost domains, but also how through mismanagement it was receiving much less revenue than it should. The first portion of his book on the administration of the abbey, *De rebus in administratione sua gestis*, described how he carefully and painstakingly tried to recover what was owed to the abbey and to increase its revenues. For example, increases came from getting more revenues from the town of Saint-Denis or acquiring a wealthy priory like Argenteuil,

but they also came from clearing forests, planting new crops and vines, settling new inhabitants on the land, enforcing ancient rights against the encroachments of local lords, building houses, granges, and courts, establishing new churches, and converting cash rents into payments in kind.

Suger also learned from the monastery's history that it had been a frequent beneficiary of royal munificence. Lands, money, and precious objects had been given to Saint-Denis by kings of France from Dagobert on. He knew, too, that it was in times of peace and harmony that Saint-Denis had prospered most. An opportunity to recreate that special harmony between king and abbot arose from the fact that Louis VI, once a pupil at the abbey, had a particular devotion to the martyrs and confidence in Suger. Although Suger was to become regent while Louis VII was on crusade, and it was then that he acted as a royal "minister" of the king, it was really during the reign of Louis VI (d. 1137) that troublesome enemies of both king and abbey, like the lords of Le Puiset, were brought to heel. The ancient relationship between *regnum* and *monasterium* was not only enhanced but refashioned when Louis VI returned the crown of his father, Philip I, to Saint-Denis; took the royal standard from the abbey's altar as he left for war in 1124, declaring that if he were not king he would do homage to the abbey; granted the fair of the Lendit what amounted to an immunity from royal justice; and declared that the kings of France should be buried at Saint-Denis.

The more rigorous administration of the monastic lands and the creation of symbols that emphasized Saint-

Denis's special importance for the French were antecedent to Suger's intention to tear down the old church and replace it with a larger one with more splendid hangings, stained glass, altars, crosses, and other objects. Though this must have long been planned for, Suger tells in his *De consecratione ecclesie sancti Dionisii* that once construction started the work proceeded quickly, the western narthex and towers being consecrated in 1140, and the translation of the saints to their new reliquaries and the construction of the eastern end with the new ambulatory and stained-glass windows completed in 1144. If stylistically the chevet anticipates many features of the Gothic churches of the Île-de-France, the church also incorporates many of Suger's major concerns: the preservation of the past, a harmonious adaptation of the old to the new, an emphasis on the liturgy, and most of all the exaltation of the saints.

Suger was inventive and eclectic. He reshaped and adorned objects that had been in the church; if he was not given the precious stones he needed, he bought them. So, too, he found the sources for his conception of the church in writings as diverse as saints' lives, liturgical texts, biblical commentaries, chronicles, and the writings of Pseudo-Dionysius the Areopagite, as well as in buildings he had seen.

Suger was a small man and an assertive one, and on behalf of his church he considered any means legitimate. In his last years, as regent, he had had to spend much of his time away from Saint-Denis, and money that had been intended for the rebuilding of the nave he used for the king's needs. He died at Saint-Denis in 1151.

Thomas G. Waldman

[See also: ARGENTEUIL; DENIS; GOTHIC ARCHITECTURE; GOTHIC ART; LOUIS VI THE FAT; LOUIS VII; SAINT-DENIS]

Suger. *Vie de Louis VI le Gros* (*Vita Ludovici VI*), ed. and trans. Henri Waquet. Paris: Les Belles Lettres, 1929.
————. *Abbot Suger on the Abbey Church of Saint-Denis and Its Art Treasures*, ed. and trans. Erwin Panofsky. 2nd ed. Princeton: Princeton University Press, 1979. [*Liber de rebus in administratione sua gestis*, chs. xxiv–xxxiv; *Libellus de consecratione Sancti Dionysii; Ordinatio.*]
Bur, Michel. *Suger, abbé de Saint-Denis, régent de France*. Paris: Perrin, 1991.
Cartellieri, Otto. *Abt Suger von Saint-Denis, 1081–1151*. Berlin: Ebering, 1898.
Gerson, Paula L., ed. *Abbot Suger and Saint-Denis: A Symposium*. New York: Metropolitan Museum of Art, 1986.

SUMPTUARY LAWS. As in other countries, towns in France in the late Middle Ages enacted sumptuary legislation—laws forbidding the wearing of excessively elegant clothing—largely in the hopes of discouraging the blurring of social distinctions through elegant dressing by the humbler classes (e.g., prostitutes), but also sometimes for moral and/or economic reasons. As there is no synthesis to date dealing with this problem, the scholar must consult the legislation of each town.

Leah L. Otis-Cour

[See also: CLOTHING, COSTUME, AND FASHION]

T

TABELLIONS. Officials, found especially in northern France, who recorded and preserved the acts of judicial bodies. For a long time, *tabellion* was almost a synonym for notary, as those who recorded judicial acts were called scribes, notaries, or *tabellions* without much distinction. Toward the end of the Middle Ages, however, a distinction finally began to appear. Henceforth, notaries were the ones who transcribed the record of official actions, while *tabellions* filled the archival function—preserving the record and delivering documents when called upon.

John Bell Henneman, Jr.

[See also: NOTARIES]

TAILLE. The word *taille* ("tallage" in English) referred originally to exactions that seigneurs demanded from people under their power, but it also came to describe a method of assessment—apportionment among households on the basis of their presumed ability to pay. The seigneurial *taille*, from the 11th century on, was arbitrary in nature and thus the most onerous obligation imposed on peasants. By the 13th century, many began to win enfranchisement, which eliminated the *taille* or converted it to a fixed annual payment.

When whole communities, such as towns, became enfranchised, they owed a fixed *taille* that they funded by levying taxes of their own choosing on their inhabitants. For the taxpayers, the *taille* was now territorial rather than personal. Town governments needed money for other purposes, such as fortifications, and in the late Middle Ages it was common to call most municipal taxes *tailles*. Technically, however, the term applied only to direct taxes assessed by *répartition*, that is, apportioned on the basis of ability to pay ("the strong carrying the weak").

The word *taille* began to appear in royal taxation only toward the end of the 14th century, when it grew out of the *fouages,* taxes on "hearths" (households), levied in the years 1364–80. In Languedoc, the towns of a district paid royal taxes as lump sums apportioned among them mostly on the basis of households and raised through municipal *tailles* of their own choosing. In the 15th century, this system of *fouages* began to be called the *taille*, and lawyers called it the *taille réel* because the "hearth" in the Midi had come to refer to a certain type of property holding that was *roturier* (i.e., neither noble nor clerical) rather than to actual households.

In northern France, the *fouage* was directly linked to households and, while it was reckoned at three francs, actual payments per household varied from one to nine francs according to wealth. Charles V canceled it in 1380, but in a few years the government began resorting to occasional special taxes. These were apportioned direct taxes not unlike the old *fouage*, but they were called *tailles*. After fifty years of intermittent *tailles*, the Estates General of 1439 authorized a *taille* that the crown continued to collect year after year, adjusting the amount as it saw fit. Under Louis XI (r. 1461–83), the proceeds of the *taille* soared from 1.2 to 3.9 million pounds. It was reduced sharply in 1484 but remained thereafter the basic tax of the French monarchy.

John Bell Henneman, Jr.

[See also: *FOUAGE*]

Henneman, John Bell. *Royal Taxation in Fourteenth Century France: The Development of War Financing, 1322–1356.* Princeton: Princeton University Press, 1971.

———. *Royal Taxation in Fourteenth Century France: The Captivity and Ransom of John II, 1356–1370.* Philadelphia: American Philosophical Society, 1976.

Rey, Maurice. *Le domaine du roi et les finances extraordinaires sous Charles VI, 1388–1413.* Paris: SEVPEN, 1965.

Stephenson, Carl. *Medieval Institutions: Selected Essays*, ed. Bryce D. Lyon. Ithaca: Cornell University Press, 1954, pp. 41–103.

TAILLEVENT, MICHAULT (LE CARON) (ca. 1390–ca. 1458). Born in Saint-Omer, the prolific and versatile poet Michault le Caron dit Taillevent served some twenty-five years at the Burgundian court as an actor in farces, as the duke's valet, and as court poet. His work includes occasional poems; numerous short lyrics (some arranged into longer pieces) and satirical, political, and reflective poems; and a morality play. The *Psautier des vilains* (1440), the *Passe temps de Michault Taillevent* (ca. 1440), and the *Débat du cœur et de l'œil* (ca. 1444) are his best-known works. Of these, the *Passe temps* is the most appreciated for its vivid evocation of his personal history and anxieties as well as its announcement of Renaissance preoccupations with the quick passage of time and the *carpe diem* "solution." Taillevent's technical mastery of verse, the adaptable registers of his poetic voice, and his blend of didacticism and personal reflections place him in the tradition of Charles d'Orléans and Alain Chartier.

Janice C. Zinser

Deschaux, Robert, ed. *Un poète bourguignon du XVe siècle: Michault Taillevent*. Geneva: Droz, 1975.

Champion, Pierre. *Histoire poétique du XVe siècle.* 2 vols. Paris: Champion, 1923, Vol. 1, pp. 285–338.

TALBOT, JOHN (ca. 1388–1453). John Talbot, first earl of Shrewsbury, was the chief Lancastrian commander in the late Hundred Years' War. He derived wealth and power from his high birth and fortunate marriage. Though summoned to Parliament in 1409 and made Lord Lieutenant in Ireland in 1414, he was to gain fame as a soldier rather than as a statesman. Talbot fought in the Welsh and Irish wars from 1404 and on the Continent after 1420. He received the Order of the Garter after distinguishing himself at Verneuil in 1424. He shared command of the failed English siege of Orléans in 1429 and was captured at the subsequent Battle of Patay.

The years following his release in 1433 he devoted to defending Henry VI's continental possessions. Despite his recapture of Harfleur in 1440 and defense of Pontoise in 1441, he could not prevent the eventual loss of Normandy and Guyenne after 1449. Talbot's heroic death in a superbly ill-conceived assault against French artillery at Castillon in 1453 confirmed the final defeat of English pretensions to French holdings outside of Calais. Brave but harsh and intemperate, Talbot was a better warrior than a general. Feared and respected by his contemporaries, he is remembered as England's last chivalric hero.

Paul D. Solon

[See also: HUNDRED YEARS' WAR; ORLÉANS CAMPAIGN; RECONQUEST OF FRANCE]

Allmand, Christopher T. *Lancastrian Normandy, 1415–1450: The History of a Medieval Occupation*. Oxford: Clarendon, 1983.

Brill, Reginald. *An English Captain of the Later Hundred Year's War: John Lord Talbot, c. 1388–1444*. Diss. Princeton University, 1966.

Pollard, A.J. *John Talbot and the War in France, 1427–1453.* London: Royal Historical Society, 1983.

Talbot, Hugh. *The English Achilles: An Account of the Life and Campaigns of John Talbot*. London: Chatto and Windus, 1981.

TAPESTRY. The word "textile" stems from Latin *texere* "to weave," and the weaving process remains central to production of medieval tapestries. Throughout the Middle Ages, political, technological, and economic changes continued to shape the textile industry. From their origins in China and Coptic Egypt, fabrics made of such fibers as silk, linen, hemp, cotton, and wool changed in quality, character, and design as the weaving process changed along with trade routes and the rise of mercantilism in Europe. Technological innovations took weavers out of the domestic and monastic environment and into the professional urban workshop. In the later Middle Ages, tapestry production became a separate industry, and major tapestry centers tended to be located near centers of political and economic power. Tapestries and other wall hangings served architectural, social, and practical purposes, as they colored space with images or scenes that were objects of conversation, and provided insulation. Textiles used as banners, ecclesiastical and liturgical materials, clothing, furniture accessories, napkins and towels, and even horse trappings survive.

In the early Middle Ages, weavers worked with the vertical warp-weighted loom, which rested against a wall. Warp threads tied to an upper crossbar were secured to the ground by weights. The wefts were attached to rods and woven through warps in a variety of ways that resulted in differently patterned weaves. In the mid-11th century, the invention of the horizontal treadle-operated loom sped up the process immensely and initiated the change in workers and working environment. Before the horizontal loom, workers were predominantly women who operated within the domestic sphere. After this invention, professional, mostly male, workshops were established, and the industry became more export-oriented. In the mid-13th century, the invention of the broadloom, a loom twice as broad as the horizontal treadle loom, allowed two people to work at one loom and so heightened productivity.

Apart from wool, other fibers, such as linen, silk, and satin, were either produced or imported. Linen production apparently was widespread but poorly documented, with such varieties as *dowlas* and *poldavy* from Brittany, sieve cloth from Rennes, and fuller linens, such as bysse and cambric, originally from Cambrai. Silk from Byzantium, Islamic Spain and other Islamic countries, Italy, and even central Asia was brought to western Europe and woven into damask, lampas, and satin, often in elaborate patterns. Ecclesiastical embroideries of silver-gilt thread on colored silk or linen could be used for copes, altar frontals, and orphreys. In the domestic realm, embroidered napkins, towels, tablecloths, and pillow covers were popular.

While the textile industry flourished in medieval France, the 14th century brought the establishment of tapestry workshops to urban centers. The specialized trade of tapestry introduced new steps to production. Artists produced small drawings called *petit patrons*, designers transformed the compositions into cartoons (*patrons*) for the tapestry, and weavers translated the cartoons into tapestry. The weaving method involved weft threads that cover short spaces with different colors as specified by the design and hide the warp threads in the finished fabric. Only wool warp threads could be used, but wool wefts could be used in combination with different fibers, such as gold and silk threads.

The *Livre des métiers* (ca. 1263), initiated by the provost of Paris Étienne Boileau, contains the earliest references to tapestries. In medieval Paris, three groups of textile workers—*tapissiers notrez*, *tapissiers sarazinois*, and *tapissiers de la haute lisse* (high-warp weavers)—were documented, the *tapissiers sarazinois* being most closely associated with Islamic techniques. An agreement from 1303 allowed high-warp weavers to practice their technique, and by the end of the 14th century Paris workshops were firmly established. Later in the 14th century, references to tapestries and carpets became interchangeable.

To a great extent, patrons controlled the rise and fall of tapestry production. In the late 13th century, Arras was the principal center of production, but soon Paris, then Tournai in the 14th century, became leading centers due to changes in patronage. From 1350 on, King John II the Good acquired 237 *tapis*, intended for his own quarters and his sons, probably supplied by Parisians. In the 15th century and the beginning of the 16th, workshops in the Loire region benefited from its proximity to the court.

Initially, high-warp tapestries had simple designs, such as geometric patterns and heraldic devices, followed later by depictions of birds and small animals. Around 1370, subject matter included religious and secular scenes, figure compositions, landscapes, and genre scenes. Over the course of the 15th and 16th centuries, the number of secular themes grew, and portrayal of the narrative became more complex and subtle. Tapestries depicted the Nine Heroes and Heroines, scenes from the Trojan War, and the Labors of Hercules. Manuscripts often served as the basis for complicated projects. For the design of the Apocalypse Tapestry, the duke of Anjou provided one of his illuminated manuscripts as a model.

A category of tapestries known as *millefleurs* was produced in the Loire region ca. 1500. With their delicately depicted flowers and foliage on blue or pink grounds, *millefleurs* tapestries helped transform the interior into a world of sensual pleasure and provided the patron, who could name the vast array of plants, with conversation pieces.

Long after the Middle Ages, the tapestry industry continued to flourish. Many late-medieval tapestries survive along with a fair amount of documentary information about artistic activity, patronage, and tapestry merchants.

Stacy L. Boldrick

[See also: APOCALYPSE TAPESTRY; ARRAS; TEXTILES; UNICORN TAPESTRIES]

Burnham, Dorothy. *Warp and Weft: A Dictionary of Textile Terms.* New York: Macmillan, 1981.

Chorley, Patrick. "The Cloth Experts of Flanders and Northern Europe During the Thirteenth Century: A Luxury Trade?" *Economic History Review* 40 (1987): 349–87.

Geijer, Agnes. *A History of Textiles.* London: Sotheby, 1979.

Lepinasse, R. de. *Les métiers et corporations de la ville de Paris.* 3 vols. Paris, 1879–97.

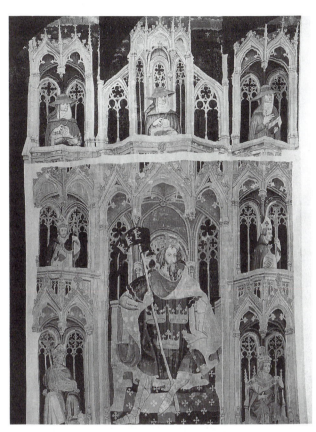

Nicolas Bataille. King Arthur tapestry, end of 14th century, 14' x 9'9". *Courtesy of The Cloisters Collection, Metropolitan Museum of Art, New York.*

The Unicorn Brought to the Castle, The Hunt of the Unicorn, tapestry, late 15th century, 12' x 12'9". *Courtesy of The Cloisters Collection, Metropolitan Museum of Art, New York.*

Weibel, A.C. *Two Thousand Years of Tapestry Weaving: A Loan Exhibition*. London: Wadsworth Atheneum, 1951.

Weigert, Roger-Armand. *French Tapestry*, trans. Donald and Monique King. London: Faber and Faber, 1962.

TAPISSIER, JOHANNES (Jean de Noyers); (ca. 1370–ca. 1410). Burgundian court composer in the early 1390s and teacher of choirboys in Paris in the early 15th century. Tapissier, along with Carmen and Cesaris, was mentioned as one of the composers who "astonished all of Paris" in Martin Le Franc's *Champion des dames* (ca. 1440). Surviving compositions include an isorhythmic motet and two Mass compositions.

Benjamin Garber

[See also: CESARIS, JOHANNES; COMPOSERS, MINOR (15TH CENTURY); *CONTENANCE ANGLOISE*]

Wright, Craig. *Music at the Court of Burgundy, 1364–1419: A Documentary History*. Henryville: Institute of Mediaeval Music, 1979.

TEMPLARS. Founded in 1120 in the Holy Land to defend Jerusalem and protect Christian pilgrims, the Knights Templar was a crusading order whose members took vows of poverty, chastity, and obedience. Their name is derived from the fact that Baudouin II, the crusader king of Jerusalem (r. 1118–31), turned over to them a portion of his palace on the site of the Temple of Solomon. Within nine years of their founding, they had received significant grants in France from such distinguished nobles as Thibaut de Blois, Thierry d'Alsace, and William Clito of Flanders. From humble beginnings, the order developed by ca. 1300 a network of some 870 castles, preceptories, and subsidiary houses. In the 13th century, the Templars may have had as many as 7,000 knights, sergeants, brothers, and priests, with perhaps 2,500 serving in the Holy Land. The order developed a powerful Mediterranean fleet to transport men, food, and clothing to the Holy Land, and its international structure and extensive resources made the Templars ideal bankers and financial agents.

The regulations of the order, largely inspired and perhaps actually written by Bernard of Clairvaux, were drawn up at the Council of Troyes (1129). They provided for an ascetic, celibate, and antimaterialistic order closely modeled on the Cistercians. Like the Hospitalers, who had been founded in the Holy Land ca. 1080, the Templars were organized into provinces reflecting geopolitical realities. There were three categories of members: knights, sergeants, and chaplains. The knights, who wore white garments with a red cross, were originally free to leave at will but eventually could leave only to join a stricter order. The sergeants were bourgeois associates and/or servants; the chaplains were priests who served for life, administering to the spiritual needs of the knights.

By 1150, the order had a strong presence in northern France, Provence, England, Aragon, Portugal, and Italy, but its recognized center was France, and nearly all of the twenty-two grand masters between the founding of the order and its dissolution in 1312 were Frenchmen. The Templars were recognized as a distinct order in three papal bulls between 1139 and 1145, by Innocent II, Celestine II, and Eugenius III, exempting them from paying tithes and even from the effects of ordinary papal decrees. In spite of papal recognition and a strong defense by Bernard of Clairvaux in his *De laude novae militae* (ca. 1136), the privileges granted the Templars and their increasing wealth and influence aroused the virulent opposition of such contemporary moralists as John of Salisbury, William of Tyre, Walter Map, and Isaac of Stella.

As long as the crusading spirit was strong, attacks on the Templars were unsuccessful. However, the fall of Jerusalem to the Muslims in 1187 signaled the beginning of the decline of the order. As repeated crusades failed to recapture the city, crusading fervor began to wane and support for the Templars and other military orders, whose primary *raison d'être* was defense of the Holy Land, declined. After the fall of Acre in 1291, many Templars hired themselves out as mercenaries to the highest bidders. The order maintained a strong presence in France, centering their activities in Paris, where their Temple became the depository of the royal treasury. Relations with King Philip IV the Fair (r. 1285–1314) remained normal for some twenty years, although the king was constantly debt-ridden and no doubt jealous of the Temple's wealth. Sometime ca. 1306, for reasons that have continued to evoke debate among historians, Philip determined to bring them down. He blamed the Templars for the loss of the Holy Land, accused them of heretical practices and obscene acts, notably in their highly secret initiation rites, and persuaded Pope Clement V (r. 1305–14), who owed his election to Philip, to investigate the entire order. Without waiting for papal adjudication, Philip ordered all the Templars in France, about 2,000 of them, arrested on the same day, October 13, 1307, and their property confiscated. After stirring up public opinion against them, Philip's royal ministers, nominally under the leadership of the inquisitor for France but actually acting on royal orders, brought the Templars to trial. Using torture, they extracted confessions from the leading Templars, including the grand master, the Burgundian Jacques de Molay. Although Templars in all other countries were judged innocent of all charges and the Council of Vienne (1311) voted overwhelmingly against suppression of the order, in France and in all areas under French domination (Provence, Naples, and even the papal states), they were found guilty as charged, and a vacillating and weak Clement V dissolved the order by papal decree in 1312. Still not satisfied, Philip had Jacques de Molay and other leading Templars burned at the stake on March 18, 1314. It was popularly believed that Jacques repudiated his confession and summoned Philip and Pope Clement to meet him within the year before the judgment seat of God. The Temple's vast holdings, being church property, were turned over to the Hospitalers, who in 1318 settled Philip's claims for compensation and expenses. The Templars' archival records were lost in their entirety, perhaps when the Ottoman Turks overran Cyprus in 1571. A disaster for historians, this has been a boon for students of the occult and conspiracy theorists.

Grover A. Zinn

[See also: BERNARD OF CLAIRVAUX; CRUSADES; ISAAC OF STELLA; JOHN OF SALISBURY; KNIGHTHOOD; NOGARET, GUILLAUME DE; PHILIP IV THE FAIR]

Barber, Malcolm. *The Trial of the Templars.* Cambridge: Cambridge University Press, 1978.

———. *The New Knighthood: A History of the Order of the Temple.* Cambridge: Cambridge University Press, 1994.

Delisle, Léopold. *Mémoire sur les opérations financières des Templiers.* Paris: Académie des Inscriptions et Belles Lettres, 1889.

Demurger, Alain. *Vie et mort de l'ordre du Temple, 1118–1314.* Paris: Seuil, 1985.

Forey, Alan J. *The Military Orders from the Twelfth to the Early Fourteenth Centuries.* Toronto: University of Toronto Press, 1992.

Lizerand, Georges, ed. and trans. *Le dossier de l'affaire des Templiers.* 2nd ed. Paris: Les Belles Lettres, 1964.

Partner, Peter. *The Murdered Magicians: The Templars and Their Myth.* Oxford: Oxford University Press, 1982.

TENSO/DÉBAT. Debate poetry in the medieval vernaculars of France begins with the Provençal *tenso,* a symmetrical exchange of stanzas between friendly rivals. At best, the *tenso* resembles a *sirventes* in dialogue and at worst an exchange of personal invectives, as its name (meaning "dispute") indicates. The earliest example is the *tenso* between Cercamon and Guilhalmi, datable to 1137. In the later *partimen* (or *joc partit,* Fr. *jeu-parti*), a troubadour presents an antithetical topic for debate and allows his interlocutor to choose a position, leaving the first poet to defend the alternative. Unlike the Latin *conflictus* and the French *débat,* the *tenso* and *joc partit* generally put poets, not abstractions, on stage. These poets may represent differing social groups or political stances, but often their debates treat issues of crude seduction or more subtle love casuistry. The poet may also debate with himself in a variation on the mind-body separation, or he may present anthropomorphized animals as in some *débats.* The metrical structure and music are sometimes borrowed from an existing song.

Roy S. Rosenstein

[See also: *JEU-PARTI;* TROUBADOUR POETRY]

Bonnarel, Bernard, ed. *Las 194 cançons dialogadas dels trobadors.* Paris: Bonnarel, 1981.

Bossy, Michel-André, ed. and trans. *Medieval Debate Poetry: Vernacular Works.* New York: Garland, 1987.

Långfors, Arthur, Alfred Jeanroy, and Louis Brandin, eds. *Recueil général des jeux-partis français.* 2 vols. Paris: Champion, 1926.

Jones, John David. *La tenson provençale.* Paris: Droz, 1934.

TEXTILES. The most important industrial commodities in medieval regional and international trade were textiles, whose leading producers during most of this era were found in France, especially the northern provinces. During the high Middle Ages, the majority of French textiles, manufactured in a wide variety, were cheap to medium-priced: fairly coarse, generally light worsted, woolens, linens, and mixed fabrics, particularly worsted-woolen *says* and linen-cotton or linen-woolen *fustians* and *tiretaines,* sold chiefly in Mediterranean markets. The upper price ranges comprised more finely textured, heavier, pure linens and woolens; and the most luxurious woolens were densely woven from the finest English wools. The most expensive French textile was the woolen *escarlate* (*écarlat, scarlet;* first documented ca. 1030–50), whose distinctive red color was produced by *kermes* (or *grain*), a dyestuff composed of rare Mediterranean oak-infesting insects (*Coccus ilicis*). Rivaling the finer Italian silks, a late-medieval French *escarlate* (about 80 by 5 ft.) could cost as much as three years' pay for a master mason or carpenter in Paris or Rouen.

Of all these textiles, the most important were wool-based. From the first evidence for commercial production in the later Carolingian era until perhaps the 12th century, worsted-type fabrics seem to have predominated. They were distinguishable by their lozenge or diamond-twill weaves, composed of strong, long-fibered wool yarns, woven on the vertical warp-weighted loom of great antiquity. A fashion and industrial revolution took place with the emergence and subsequent victory of the long, heavy, felted woolen broadcloth, composed of short-stapled, finer wools whose yarns were woven on the new horizontal foot-operated treadle loom. First so described by Rashi of Troyes (ca. 1040–1105), it was subsequently much enlarged and improved by the 13th century as the famous broadloom. If that loom was the most crucial innovation for the new long broadcloths, their cohesion and durability also depended upon extensive fulling (unlike worsteds), with water, chemicals, pressure, and heat: to force the fine, curly, but weak wool fibers to interlock and be felted into a highly compressed and thus heavy fabric, whose fiber-ends were then repeatedly raised or "napped" with teasels (a thistle plant) and shorn with razor-sharp, foot-long shears, until all visible trace of weave was obliterated and the texture had become as smooth as silk.

Three other labor-saving innovations of the late 12th and 13th centuries were also particularly well suited to producing woolens: carding the wool fibers with two wired brushes, which also facilitated subsequent felting; spinning carded wools or cotton with a hand- or foot-operated wheel that rotated the spindle; and mechanical fulling, with water-powered wooden hammers to pound, scour, and felt the woven cloth. While the rival and younger Italian and English cloth-making establishments, called "draperies," soon adopted these innovations, the more prominent Franco-Flemish draperies long resisted them, for fear of impairing the quality of their woolens. Many required the traditional techniques of hand-combing the wool fibers and then spinning them with the drop-spindle and distaff to produce both the warps (the strong yarns stretched on the loom) and the wefts (the weaker yarns passed

Women carding, spinning, and weaving wool, from a 14th-century manuscript. B.N. fr. 12420, fol. 71. *Courtesy of the Bibliothèque Nationale, Paris.*

manufacturing processes of this era were performed there and almost everywhere by women. Even in the fully developed export-oriented woolen draperies of the high and later Middle Ages, female workers still outnumbered males; but throughout western Europe, men had succeeded in decisively dominating this industry.

In the commercially oriented Franco-Flemish draperies, production became organized by a "putting-out" system under the supervision of entrepreneurs known as *drapiers*, almost always men, the exception typically being their widows. Some *drapiers* might also be wool merchants; but most purchased wools from such merchants, who often delivered them already sorted by staple length, beaten, cleansed, greased, and sometimes partially dyed in the wool, usually woad-blue as the foundation for other colors. Under the *drapier*'s supervision, these wools were "put out" to combers and carders, almost exclusively female, who prepared them for spinning in their own homes—often rural cottages, for piecework wages. Thus prepared, such wools were then similarly "put out" to spinners, again females, whether using the distaff or the wheel, also working in their own homes or cottages. The warp and weft yarns so spun were then delivered to the weavers, who were almost exclusively male by the high or late Middle Ages—all the more so since the master weaver was frequently also the *drapier*.

The broadloom required two weavers, one on each side, to operate the treadles for separating the warps and to pass the weft-bearing shuttle back and forth through the warps; their assistants, who wound and fitted the warps and wefts, were usually females. The woven cloth was then delivered to the fullers, who were again almost exclusively male, as were the other artisans in the finishing processes. After the cloth had been thoroughly scoured, degreased, felted, and subjected to a preliminary napping (teaseling) and "wet-shearing," it was hung by tenterers on large frames, to be dried and stretched so that no wrinkles remained, and then returned to the *drapier*. He might choose to sell this broadcloth, whose manufacture had taken over two weeks, to cloth finishers or merchants, who might then commission shearers and dyers to finish the cloth; or the *drapier* himself might send the cloth to the shearers and dyers; or the woolens might be exported to Italian towns, Florence especially, for such finishing.

In the leading Franco-Flemish draperies, formal guild organization by the later Middle Ages was confined largely to the four major urban-based and male-dominated crafts: the master weavers, who as *drapiers* depended on profits for their incomes, while their journeymen weavers received wages; the master fullers, dependent piecework employees of the *drapiers*; and the master shearers and dyers, most of whom were independent fee-earning craftsmen.

The ultimate, late-medieval commercial preeminence of the luxury-quality woolens was due not just to changes in fashion or technology but more particularly to adverse economic changes that sharply raised transportation and marketing costs in international trade to a prohibitive level for the cheaper textiles. Most of these rising costs resulted from the widespread, prolonged warfare—and associated fiscal, monetary, and commercial policies pursued by the combatants—that afflicted so much of western Europe and

through the warps), although some grudgingly permitted carding and wheel-spinning for the wefts alone. Above all, they insisted upon the laborious, traditional method of foot-fulling, which took three or four days for each cloth.

Some of these changes involved in the evolution of the medieval felted woolen broadcloth also involved changes in the sexual division of labor, which, however, were more related to the commercialization and urbanization of the French woolens industry. A growing dependence on competitive export markets required greater specialization of labor to provide both lower-cost efficiency and better quality. Insofar as early-medieval and Carolingian cloth production was much more oriented to local consumption, it had been a largely rural domestic or household craft with little formal division of labor, except in the large workshops of manorial estates and religious orders, called *gynaecia*. As that term indicates, the cloth-

the entire Mediterranean basin, Christian and Muslim, from the later 13th to the mid-15th centuries. Europe was also seriously afflicted, during the last hundred years of this era, by plagues and famines; but in France the industrial and commercial transformations were readily apparent well before these later calamities.

The most graphic evidence can be found in the rapid decline of the Champagne fairs during the late 13th and early 14th centuries. Most of the textile industries scattered across central and northern France, the Low Countries, and the adjacent Rhineland had been vitally dependent upon these fairs, which had long served as the hub of western European and especially Mediterranean-oriented commerce. During the mid-13th-century apogee of these fairs, and in the famous Hanse of the Seventeen Towns, producers of the cheaper, lighter textiles well outnumbered those of luxury woolens. The great majority of the draperies were then francophone; and even in Flanders, a French county, francophone draperies then predominated over the *draperies flamigantes*. But by the mid-14th century, the big urban *draperies flamigantes* of Ypres, Ghent, and Bruges had gained a decisive ascendancy by specializing more and more in those luxury woolens whose commerce could better withstand rising marketing costs; in stark contrast, dozens of the smaller, cheaper-line French draperies in French Flanders (annexed to the royal domain), Tournai, Artois, Ponthieu, Vermandois, Champagne, and the Île-de-France had either disappeared or were relegated to a much more modest existence in supplying purely local or regional markets. Of the linen industries in this region, only the luxury producers, chiefly at Reims, survived and prospered. The supremacy of those urban Flemish draperies was short-lived, however, as they encountered increasingly severe competition in luxury woolens from quasirural *nouvelles draperies* within Flanders itself and from draperies in neighboring imperial Brabant, Holland, Florence and other north Italian towns, and England. Within France, by the late 14th and early 15th centuries, several new Norman draperies also provided some competition in the luxury field, while in the south new draperies in Languedoc and Catalonia sold cheap to medium-priced woolens in Mediterranean markets that the northern draperies could no longer effectively service. Finally, in 1470, with the dawning of the early-modern era, France gained a new textile industry, when Louis XI successfully established an Italian-style silk-making craft at Tours.

John H. Munro

[See also: CHAMPAGNE; CLOTHING, COSTUME, AND FASHION; FAIRS AND MARKETS; FLANDERS; TAPESTRY; VESTMENTS, ECCLESIASTICAL; WOOL TRADE]

Carus-Wilson, Eleanora M. "The Woollen Industry." In *Cambridge Economic History of Europe*, ed. M.M. Postan and Edward Miller. 2nd ed. Cambridge: Cambridge University Press, 1987, Vol. 2: *Trade and Industry in the Middle Ages*, pp. 613–90.

Chorley, Patrick. "The Cloth Exports of Flanders and Northern France During the Thirteenth Century: A Luxury Trade?" *Economic History Review*, 2nd ser., 40 (1987): 349–87.

Coornaert, Émile. "Draperies rurales, draperies urbaines: l'évolution de l'industrie flamande au moyen âge et au XVIe siècle." *Revue belge de philologie et d'histoire* 28 (1950): 59–96.

De Poerck, Guy. *La draperie médiévale en Flandre et en Artois: techniques et terminologie.* 3 vols. Bruges: De Tempel, 1951.

Harte, Negley B., and Kenneth G. Ponting, eds. *Cloth and Clothing in Medieval Europe: Essays in Memory of Professor E.M. Carus-Wilson.* London: Heinemann, 1983.

Munro, John. "Scarlet," "Silk," "Textile Technology," and "Textile Workers." In *Dictionary of the Middle Ages*, ed. Joseph Strayer et al. New York: Macmillan, 1988, Vol. 11, pp. 36–37 [correction of publisher's error in "Errata," Vol. 13, p. 612], 293–96, 693–715.

———. "Industrial Transformations in the North-West European Textile Trades, c. 1290–c. 1340: Economic Progress or European Crisis?" In *Before the Black Death: Studies in the "Crisis" of the Early Fourteenth Century*, ed. Bruce M.S. Campbell. Manchester: Manchester University Press, 1991.

———. *Textiles, Towns and Trade: Essays in the Economic History of Late-Medieval England and the Low Countries.* London: Variorum, 1994.

Van der Wee, Herman. "Structural Changes and Specialization in the Industry of the Southern Netherlands, 1100–1660." *Economic History Review*, 2nd ser., 28 (1975): 203–21.

THEATER. Medieval theater originated in the 10th century in the Latin liturgical drama that was associated with the Easter rites of the church. New forms of dramatic expression were developed over the next 200 years, one example of which is *Sponsus*, a play based on the parable of the Wise and Foolish Virgins. By the late 12th century, plays were being written in French, though a few nonliturgical Latin plays were also performed. The earliest play whose dialogue is entirely in French is the *Jeu d'Adam*. Another biblical play from this period is the *Seinte Resureccion*. Around this time also, there appeared the narrative *Passion des jongleurs*, which later served as a principal source for the *Passion du Palatinus*.

The 13th century saw a significant development of theatrical activities in the wealthy commercial centers of northern France, particularly in Arras, where Jehan Bodel wrote his *Jeu de saint Nicolas*, Adam de la Halle his *Jeu de la feuillée*, and an anonymous author his *Courtois d'Arras*, a play based on the parable of the Prodigal Son. The record of dramatic activity in the 14th century is sparse, though an important collection of miracle plays, written for the Guild of Parisian Goldsmiths, has survived.

The vernacular plays surviving from this early period are not numerous, but their quality is high. The pattern of survival suggests that dramatic activity was limited to certain urban centers, not only in France but in other countries as well. In the 15th century, however, the theater burst into prominence everywhere as a significant feature of European life. The cycle plays of England, the Passion plays of France, the *Fasnachtspiele* of Germany, and the *sacre rapresentatione* of Italy were all part of a general theatricalization of European culture. Plays were usually performed on feast days and general holidays; were written by clerics, law clerks of the Basoche, rhetoricians, and students; and were acted by amateurs belonging to trade guilds, rhetorical societies, schools, and municipal organizations. Techniques for the staging of plays ranged from simple to spectacular, with performances taking place in halls, courtyards, or town squares. Plays were acted on small trestle stages or in large open-air theaters built specially for the occasion. The presentation of plays on pageant wagons was the custom in northern France, where processional theater was a frequent component of public ceremony.

The theater of the late Middle Ages played a central role in the life of the community. Biblical plays, history plays, and saint plays reinforced people's identity as children of God by teaching the history of the world and the community's place in that history. At the same time, morality plays taught Christian ethics by showing the consequences of good and bad behavior. Farces and fools plays, called *sotties*, provided collective release by making satirical thrusts at social abuses. Perhaps the simplest of the comic pieces were the dramatic monologues, which required only a single actor. Among these, one finds the *sermons joyeux*, festive parodies of the sermons heard in church on Sundays.

The serious plays treating historical subjects were often called mystery plays. The most important type of mystery play in French was that which dramatized the Passion of Jesus. In Paris, the staging of these plays was the exclusive right of the Confrérie de la Passion. Elsewhere, it was usually the municipalities that subsidized these lengthy and costly plays. Though most of the surviving medieval plays are anonymous, the authors of several of the Passion plays are known. Eustache Marcadé is the presumed author of a *Mystère de la Passion* from the first part of the 15th century. Arnoul Greban wrote the best known of the Passion plays ca. 1452, then collaborated with his brother, Simon Greban, in writing the *Mystère des Actes des Apôtres*. Toward the end of the century, Jean Michel wrote another important Passion play. André de La Vigne wrote a *Vie de saint Martin* and two other plays that were staged in the Burgundian town of Seurre in 1496. Guillaume Coquillart, a writer of comic debates and dramatic monologues, was also active around this time. The masterful *Farce de Maistre Pathelin*, however, despite the sleuthing of many scholars, remains resolutely anonymous.

One of the well-known dramatic writers of the early 16th century was Pierre Gringore, who attacked Pope Julius II in his *sottie* of 1512 and who later wrote a lengthy *Vie monseigneur saint Louis* for the stage. The Renaissance seems to have had little impact on the continued writing and performance of late-medieval dramatic genres. All of them flourished until about mid-century. In 1548, however, the playing of biblical plays was forbidden in Paris, and the subsequent religious wars effectively stopped all such productions in most parts of France. Morality plays, which were not affected by the ban, continued to be played, showing some signs of development toward the newly introduced genre of tragedy. Even at the beginning of the century, the delightful morality play *Condamnation de*

Banquet, pointed toward a new secularism. Farces also continued to be played, changing little throughout the period. Because of their stability as a genre, the farces of the early 17th century were able to transmit the medieval comic tradition to the young Molière.

Alan E. Knight

[See also: ADAM DE LA HALLE; BASOCHE; CONFRÉRIE DE LA PASSION; COQUILLART, GUILLAUME; *COURTOIS D'ARRAS;* FARCE; GREBAN, ARNOUL; GREBAN, SIMON; GRINGORE, PIERRE; HISTORY PLAYS; JEHAN BODEL; *JEU D'ADAM;* LA VIGNE, ANDRÉ DE; LITURGICAL DRAMA: MARCADÉ, EUSTACHE; MICHEL, JEAN; MIRACLE PLAYS; MORALITY PLAYS; MYSTERY PLAYS; *PASSION DES JONGLEURS;* PASSION PLAYS; *PATHELIN, FARCE DE MAISTRE;* PROCESSIONAL THEATER; SAINT PLAYS; *SEINTE RESURECCION; SERMONS JOYEUX; SOTTIE; SPONSUS;* STAGING OF PLAYS; THEATER, LATIN]

THEATER, LATIN. Secular Latin plays were produced in the 12th century alongside religious and liturgical drama. Their appearance seems to depend on two factors, the high standard of learning in the period and the change in conception of the value of the human being, epitomized in Anselm of Bec's *Cur Deus homo* and exemplified in the autobiographies of Guibert de Nogent and Peter Abélard. Latin being a learned language, these plays were associated almost entirely with the schools, particularly those of the Loire Valley. Only comedies are extant, the earliest of which (ca. 1130) would appear to be the anonymous *Panphilus*, based loosely on an Ovidian theme and written in Ovidian style. As if to assert the real origins of comedy, Vitalis of Blois wrote two plays: *Geta* (ca. 1150), an update of Plautus's *Amphytrion*, and *Aulularia* (ca. 1155), based on the pseudo-Plautine comedy of the same name. *Geta*, with its satire of the rival Parisian schools and Abélard's philosophy, was an enormous success and immediately became a set-text studied in all the schools of Europe; almost a hundred manuscripts are extant. Vitalis's success inspired others to follow his example. While in Sicily in 1168, William of Blois wrote the *Alda*, an updated version of a play by Menander with a Norman setting. Other teachers from the Loire region tried different sources. Matthieu de Vendôme's *Milo* is based on an eastern motif; the plays of his archenemy Arnulf of Orléans, the *Lydia* and the *Miles gloriosus* (despite its Plautine title), are more closely linked to fabliau material. Among the remaining "comedies" whose links with the theater are not so obvious, but which might be more accurately termed "dramatic monologues," one deserves mention: *Panphilus, Glycerium et Birria*, associated with an episcopal or royal court in Normandy, combines a vernacular interlude structure with the characters of Roman comedy, thus firmly stating its theatrical nature.

Although limited in time (ca. 1130–80), probably because of changes in the French educational system, these comedies continued to have an influence elsewhere in Europe, first in England, where the *Babio* (ca. 1175) stands out as a supreme example of Latin *récupération* of the vernacular, and then in Italy in the 13th century with texts like the *Uxor Cerdonis* and *De Paulino et Polla*. The *Panphilus* was also to influence the vernacular, especially the English *Dame Siriz* and the Spanish *La Celestina*. Even religious drama was not immune. The Beauvais *Ludus Danielis* (ca. 1175) acquired the synopsis and prologue of comedy that are absent from the earlier *Historia Danielis* (ca. 1140) of Hilarius.

Keith Bate

[See also: LITURGICAL DRAMA; THEATER]

Bertini, Ferruccio, ed. *Commedie Latine del XII e XIII secolo.* 6 vols. Genoa: Istituto di Filologia Classica e Medievale, 1976–.
Elliott, Alison G., trans. *Seven Medieval Latin Comedies.* New York: Garland, 1984.
Bate, Keith. "Twelfth-Century Latin Comedies and the Theatre." In *Papers of the Liverpool Latin Seminar: Second Volume, 1979*, ed. Francis Cairns. Liverpool: School of Classics, 1979, pp. 249–62.
Roy, Bruno. "Arnulf of Orleans and the Latin 'Comedy.'" *Speculum* 49 (1974): 258–66.

THEODULF OF ORLÉANS (ca. 760–821). Born in Spain of Visigothic parents, Theodulf became a member of the Carolingian court in the latter part of the 8th century. He was abbot of Saint-Benoît-sur-Loire and then Saint-Aignan before becoming bishop of Orléans. Removed from episcopal office for plotting against Louis the Pious, he was exiled to Angers in 817. Among his theological writings is a defense of the *filioque* (the procession of the Holy Spirit from both Father and Son) in the Creed, a work on baptism, and possibly expositions of the Creed and the Mass. Theodulf concerned himself with producing a corrected text of the Vulgate Bible, even consulting (or inspiring his disciples to consult) a Hebrew text. However, his corrected text had little influence; Alcuin's Bible would be the accepted Vulgate text of the Carolingian period. Theodulf was a poet of note, composing verses for various occasions and purposes: an introduction to his Bible text; a description of a plaque portraying the seven Liberal Arts, virtues, etc.; vivid descriptions of personalities at Charlemagne's court; and religious poetry, including hymns. While bishop of Orléans, Theodulf ordered priests to establish schools for the instruction of children, gave attention to the liturgy, and showed a deep appreciation of art and its essential role in the church. As author of the *Libri Carolini*, Theodulf responded to Byzantine icon veneration as sanctioned by the Second Council of Nicaea (787).

Grover A. Zinn

[See also: CAROLINGIAN ART; GERMIGNY-DES-PRÉS; LATIN POETRY, CAROLINGIAN; *LIBRI CAROLINI*]

Theodulf of Orléans. *Opera omnia. PL* 105.187–380.
Freeman, Ann. "Theodulf of Orléans and the *Libri Carolini*." *Speculum* 32 (1957): 664–705.

THEOLOGY. Term from the Greek, Θεολογία ("theologia"), "the knowledge of God." For Christians, theology proceeds from "evidence" provided by God via forms of revelation—biblical, experiential, creational. The classic medieval statement of the nature of theology is Anselm of Bec's "faith seeking understanding" (*fides quaerens intellectum*), which illustrates both the medieval given starting point of religious belief and simultaneously the trust in reason, "understanding," as a way to God.

Theological orthodoxy is decided by the consensus of the community of the faithful. In the Christian case, this was settled at general councils of the church, which considered and formulated statements about the nature of God and God's relationship with Creation and pronounced on their validity.

Sources of theology are various and debated among theologians. The Bible stands in a unique place as the authoritative word of God and holds primacy among means of revelation. However, God is believed not to be limited to revelation to those intelligent or learned enough to be able to read Scripture and interpret it, using the tools of reason. Hence, there has always been a special place in Christian theology for direct revelation—God speaking directly to the faithful believer. For Christians, direct revelation is the life, death, and resurrection of Jesus Christ, and after his ascension the communication of tradition has been carried on by the Holy Spirit. A third method of revelation of God to humankind is by observation of the created order. We can infer the nature of God from the world around us and from our relationships with other human beings.

Theology as a subject in itself did not exist until the establishment and flourishing of the universities. Until then, theological speculation had taken place in a wide variety of settings and writings: biblical commentary, sermons, treatises, liturgy, hymns, works of spiritual revelation. Indeed, any attempts to make generalizations about the nature of God and Creation, drawn from the various forms of revelation, are the stuff of "theology." Theology exists even in the Gospels, notably in the Gospel of John, where the writer makes inferences about God and Creation from the experience of the life of Christ, against the background of the Hebrew Scriptures. The basic theological doctrines of Christianity were framed at general (or ecumenical) councils of the church: Nicaea I (325, on the divinity of Christ), Constantinople I (381, on the dual nature of Christ), Ephesus (431, on the singularity of the person of Christ), Chalcedon (451, on the dual nature of Christ), Constantinople II (553, on the persons of God), Constantinople III (680–81, on the existence of both divine and human wills in Christ), and Nicaea II (787, on the iconoclastic controversy). These doctrines, formulated from the writings of the church fathers, were made orthodox by the agreement of the general councils, representing the consensus of the whole church. The underlying theological theme was the nature of Christ as one person with two natures and wills, divine and human, and the relations of the three persons of the Trinity.

During the revival of interest in theology in the Carolingian schools, the main topics of debate were predestination and the nature of the eucharist. Neither of these subjects was new, but they were given fresh impetus by such scholars as Johannes Scottus Eriugena, Gottschalk, and Paschasius Radbertus. "Predestination" concerned the belief that some people were divinely and infallibly led to salvation. Gottschalk's extreme view of the matter, "double predestination," held that others were similarly led to damnation. This opinion was condemned, since it limited the actions of God. The nature of the eucharist had provoked surprisingly little disagreement among the early fathers. But Paschasius Radbertus questioned the identity of the Eucharistic Body of Christ with his True Body in Heaven. His opinion was not influential in the 9th century, but it resurfaced in the thought of Berengar of Tours (11th c.) whose opposition to the doctrine of the Real Presence provoked a finely wrought defense by Lanfranc of Bec.

The heyday of theology as an academic subject was in the late 12th and 13th centuries in Paris. The University of Paris was famed as the leading center for the study of theology in the West, and its scholars were listened to by the highest members of the church. Indeed, they often took those positions themselves: from the 13th century, a university education became a well-established route to ecclesiastical and political preferment. It was in the mid-13th century, too, that we first encounter questions as to whether theology is a science, which is to say, a suitable topic for reasoned investigation. The corollary to this was to ask who could make theological statements. The Christian principle that the means of salvation must be available to every believer implied that any faithful person, no matter how simple or uneducated, must be able to understand enough of the nature of God—theology—to follow a path to eternal life. This meant that direct revelation had to be admitted as a means of knowledge about God. But it was understood to be partial. Opinion among the theological doctors leaned toward professional specialization: their methods were the only foolproof way to higher knowledge about the nature of God and the principles of religion.

The precise definition of certain theological issues was heightened by the "question" form of scholasticism, and it was at this time that a number of topics were honed to sharpness. For example, the number and definition of the sacraments were settled at this period. It is perhaps no coincidence that this was also the era of persecution of heretics and Jews—those who put themselves outside defined orthodoxy. Theology was influenced by the new availability of translations of the metaphysical works of Aristotle. Although the impact of Aristotle on the Latin West has been much discussed, it is not clear that any issues of orthodoxy were affected by the use of his philosophy by Christian scholars. They rebutted his ideas on the eternity of the world (as against Creation) and the unity of the Intellect (which denied the bodily resurrection of the individual). What they did take to, coming as it did in the right place at the right time, was Aristotle's method. His division of substance and accident, for instance, enabled a precise formulation of the changes wrought by the eucharist as transubstantiation.

No less interesting than the issues faced by speculative theologians in the 12th and 13th centuries were those

developments in moral and practical theology, particularly associated with Peter the Chanter and his circle in the 12th century and some of the mendicant theologians in the 13th century. The Franciscans were especially plagued by the debate over apostolic poverty and theological questions about the ownership of property.

How, if at all, did any of this "high theology" discussed in the universities make its way down to ordinary people, or even the less educated clergy? The obvious medium is in sermons, and the theological content of preaching is the subject of much new research, difficult as it is to study a phenomenon that is essentially oral, context-specific, and transitory. Nevertheless, the high percentage of mendicants among Paris theologians from almost their foundations is striking; the orders recognized the importance of theological training and research to their preaching aims.

The question of who might make theological statements was heightened by vernacular translations of the Bible. "Heretical" groups of laypeople, such as Lollards, or groups living in community and following an abbreviated rule, like béguines, made their own interpretations of orthodox theology. Often condemned by the official church, they represented a desire by ordinary devout believers to formulate a deeper understanding of God that yet took into account the everyday experiences of the majority of the faithful.

It is only with hindsight that we make "theology" into a medieval concern, as though it were somehow in opposition or juxtaposition to the study of sacred scriptures. *Theologia* is not a term much used by medieval writers. They prefer to concentrate on the texts they used for basic knowledge and call themselves not "masters of theology" but "masters of the sacred page" or "masters of sacred scripture." These terms illustrate how, as so often, our attempts to formalize and distinguish reflect our own views of order and fitness, not those of medieval scholars themselves.

Lesley J. Smith

[See also: ARISTOTLE, INFLUENCE OF; BERENGAR OF TOURS; ERIUGENA, JOHANNES SCOTTUS; GOTTSCHALK; HERESY; LANFRANC OF BEC; PASCHASIUS RADBERTUS; PETER THE CHANTER; PHILOSOPHY; RATRAMNUS OF CORBIE; SCHOLASTICISM]

THIBAUT. Name of five counts of Champagne and several counts of Blois. The Thibaudian counts of Blois-Champagne ranked among the leading princely families of northern France from the 10th through the 13th century. Thibaut le Vieux, viscount of Tours, founded the dynasty, and his son Thibaut le Tricheur, count of Blois, Chartres, and Tours (r. 940–ca. 977) gave it a territorial base. The proximity of their lands to the Capetian domain, however, often strained relations with the royal house, especially after Eudes II (r. 996–1037) acquired lands in Champagne and Berry that threatened to encircle the royal domain. Although Blois-Chartres remained the Thibaudian heartland until 1152, the counts were drawn eastward after the loss of Tours (1044) and the acquisition of additional counties in Champagne by Thibaut III (I of Champagne; r. 1037–89).

Thibaut IV (II of Champagne, r. 1102–52) shifted the center of the dynasty to Champagne, which passed to his eldest son, Henri I (r. 1152–81); younger sons held Blois-Chartres and Sancerre as fiefs from the count of Champagne. In the second half of the 12th century, the Thibaudians became intimately tied to the royal family. Henri and his brother Thibaut (V of Blois; r. 1152–91) married Louis VII's daughters by Eleanor of Aquitaine, while the king married their sister Adèle (of Champagne; queen 1160–79). Thibaut also served as royal seneschal (1154–91). The youngest brother, Guillaume, rose quickly in the church as bishop of Chartres (1165–68), then archbishop of Sens (1168–75) and Reims (1175–1202). Another sister married the count of Bar-le-Duc and introduced the name Thibaut into that lineage.

The Thibaudians almost redrew the political map of France under Eudes II; they nearly established a royal dynasty in England when Stephen of Blois became king (1135–54) with the aid of his brother Henry, bishop of Winchester (r. 1129–71); and they might have dominated the Capetians into the 13th century had it not been for Philip II's resistance. Thibaudian influence waned in the 13th century. Although Champagne remained an important and prosperous county under Thibaut III, Thibaut IV, and Thibaut V, it came under direct royal control with the marriage of its last heiress, Jeanne, to the future Philip IV (1284). Since the counts of Blois had already ended in their male line in 1218, only Sancerre survived as a minor lordship until the 15th century. The name Thibaut was never adopted by the royal family, and it failed to survive in the comital lineages of Sancerre and Bar-le-Duc.

Theodore Evergates

[See also: CHAMPAGNE; THIBAUT DE CHAMPAGNE]

Arbois de Jubainville, Henri d'. *Histoire des ducs et des comtes de Champagne*. 6 vols. Paris: Durand, 1859–66.

Bur, Michel. *La formation du comté de Champagne, v. 950–v. 1150*. Nancy: Mémoires des Annales de l'Est, 1977.

Davis, Ralph H.C. *King Stephen, 1135–54*. Berkeley: University of California Press, 1967.

Dunbabin, Jean. *France in the Making, 843–1180*. Oxford: Oxford University Press, 1985.

THIBAUT DE CHAMPAGNE (1201–1253). The most illustrious of the trouvères and one of the most prolific, Thibaut IV, count of Champagne and king of Navarre, grandson of the great patroness of poets Marie de Champagne, was also an important political figure. After several years' education at the royal court of Philip II Augustus, young Thibaut began his life as a ruler under the regency of his mother, Blanche of Navarre. He later took part in the war of the newly crowned Louis VIII against the English, appearing at the siege of La Rochelle in 1224, and continued to serve the king, his overlord, thereafter. In 1226, however, he withdrew his support during the royal siege

of Avignon and returned home in secret. Upon the king's death a few months later, Thibaut was accused of having poisoned him, but nothing came of this apparently groundless charge. The following year, he allied himself with other feudal powers in an attempt to dethrone Blanche of Castile, widow of Louis VIII and regent for their son Louis IX, but the queen succeeded in detaching him from the rebellious group and making him her defender. Attacked by his erstwhile allies, Thibaut was saved by the royal army.

Thibaut's relations with the crown, however, were unsteady, particularly after 1234, when he succeeded his uncle Sancho the Strong as king of Navarre, and it was not until 1236 that a final peace was achieved, based on the vassal's submission. Three years later, he left for the Holy Land as head of the crusade of 1239; the undertaking was marked from the start by discord among the Christian leaders and by Muslim military superiority, the result of which was Thibaut's decision in 1240 to withdraw from his charge and return to France. There, armed struggles engaged his attention through the following years, and in 1248 he made a penitent's pilgrimage to Rome. He died in Pamplona. He had been betrothed twice, married three times, divorced once, widowed once, and had fathered several children. The rumor has persisted since his day that the great love of his life was none other than Blanche of Castile, but apart from offering a tempting key to his political shifts, it seems to have no merit.

As a trouvère, Thibaut was immediately successful, seen as equaled only by his great predecessor Gace Brulé. Dante was to consider him one of the "illustrious" poets in the vernacular, and the medieval songbooks that group their contents by composer place his works before all others. The over sixty pieces ascribed to him with reasonable certainty, almost all preserved with music, show a majority of courtly chansons, none anticonventional in theme or form but most marked by an unusual development of imagery, especially allegorical, use of refrains, or self-confident lightness of tone. The other works, revealing a style similarly characteristic of Thibaut, are *jeux-partis* (among the earliest known), debates, devotional songs (including one in the form of a *lai*), crusade songs, *pastourelles*, and a *serventois*.

Samuel N. Rosenberg

[See also: CHAMPAGNE; GACE BRULÉ; THIBAUT; TROUVÈRE POETRY]

Brahney, Kathleen J., ed. and trans. *The Lyrics of Thibaut de Champagne*. New York: Garland, 1988.

van der Werf, Hendrik, ed. *Trouvères-Melodien II*. Kassel: Bärenreiter, 1979, pp. 3–311.

Wallensköld, Axel, ed. *Les chansons de Thibaut de Champagne, roi de Navarre*. Paris: Champion, 1925.

Bellenger, Yvonne, and Danielle Quéruel, eds. *Thibaut de Champagne, prince et poète au XIIIe siècle*. Lyon: La Manufacture, 1987.

THIERRY D'ALSACE (d. 1168). Grandson of the Flemish Count Robert I the Frisian, and himself count of Flanders from 1128, Thierry became the candidate of the Flemish cities for the countship in 1128 after they renounced their allegiance to William Clito, son of Robert Curthose of Normandy, who was preferred by most Flemish nobles in the succession quarrel after the assassination of Count Charles the Good in 1127. Thierry was recognized throughout Flanders after William died on June 28, 1128. After repairing his relations with the nobles, Thierry in 1134 married Sybilla, daughter of Foulques V, count of Anjou and king of Jerusalem. Evidently in the hope of conquering a principality, Thierry went on crusade four times. Despite his frequent absences, the Flemish administration functioned well. Thierry also fostered economic growth by founding settlements, promoting land clearance, and avoiding foreign conflicts except for his continued effort to extend Flemish influence in the Cambrésis. When he returned to Palestine in 1157, he left Flanders in the care of his fourteen-year-old son and heir, Philippe, whom he installed formally as count, and apparently thought seriously of remaining in the East. He returned in 1159, went again to Palestine in 1164, and died in 1168, shortly after his return. The prestige of Thierry d'Alsace, owing to his conspicuous piety and international diplomacy, seems to have exceeded his achievement.

David M. Nicholas

[See also: FLANDERS; PHILIPPE D'ALSACE]

de Hemptinne, T. "Vlaanderen en Henegouwen onder de erfgenamen van de Boudewijns, 1070–1244." In *Algemene Geschiedenis der Nederlanden*. 2nd ed. Haarlem: Fibula-Van Dishoeck, 1982, Vol. 2, pp. 372–98.

Pirenne, Henri. *Histoire de Belgique.* Brussels: Lamertin, 1929, Vol. 1.

Verhulst, Aadrian, and T. de Hemptinne. "Le chancelier de Flandre sous les comtes de la maison d'Alsace." *Bulletin de la Commission Royale d'Histoire* 141 (1975): 267–311.

THIERRY OF CHARTRES (d. after 1151). A Breton by birth, Thierry was probably not the younger brother of Bernard of Chartres, as is sometimes asserted. He studied arts at Chartres and was master of the schools there in 1121. He went ca. 1124 to teach in Paris, where John of Salisbury was one of his pupils. He continued in a conventional ecclesiastical career, becoming archdeacon of Dreux in 1136 and archdeacon and chancellor of Chartres in 1141. In 1148, he was a member of the synod of Reims that condemned Gilbert of Poitiers and in 1149 was present at the Diet of Frankfurt. Sometime between 1151 and 1156, however, he retired into a monastery, and we know nothing more of his life.

Thierry lays claim to be the most interesting Neoplatonist of Chartres. His interpretation of Genesis 1, a commentary on Plato's *Timaeus* called *De sex dierum operibus*, contains his statement of divine formalism: that God is the form of all created things. Thierry also displays the influence of Aristotelian logic. In the *De sex dierum* and in his three commentaries on Boethius's *De Trinitate*, he attempted to develop a rational justification for the Trinity,

describing it in terms of Aristotle's four causes: Father as efficient cause, Son as formal cause, Holy Spirit as final cause, and divinely created matter as material cause. His other works include a commentary on Cicero's *De inventione* and a textbook for the Trivium and Quadrivium, the *Heptateuchon*.

Lesley J. Smith

[See also: CHARTRES; PHILOSOPHY; PLATO, INFLUENCE OF]

Thierry of Chartres. *Commentaries on Boethius by Thierry of Chartres and His School*, ed. Nikolaus M. Häring. Toronto: Pontifical Institute of Mediaeval Studies, 1971.

———. *The Latin Rhetorical Commentaries by Thierry of Chartres*, ed. Karin M. Fredborg. Toronto: Pontifical Institute of Mediaeval Studies, 1988.

Dronke, Peter, ed. *A History of Twelfth-Century Western Philosophy*. Cambridge: Cambridge University Press, 1988, pp. 358–85.

THIRTY, COMBAT OF THE. In 1351, the English garrison at Ploermel in Brittany was attacked by a French force under Jean de Beaumanoir. To forestall a siege, Richard Bamborough, the garrison commander, suggested a tournament-style combat on the open field in front of the castle of Ploermel between thirty men-at-arms from each side. The fight was to be to the death. Bamborough's knights, who included Breton and German mercenaries as well as English soldiers, were determined to fight so well that the legacy of such a chivalric battle would be mentioned often among nobles. All fought on foot with swords, daggers, axes, and war hammers. The battle was long and exhausting. A recess was taken, but battle soon recommenced. In the end, after a diligent fight by the English, they were defeated when one of the French knights unchivalrously mounted his horse and rode into them. Nine English were killed, including Bamborough, and the rest were taken prisoner; six French knights were slain.

Kelly DeVries

Froissart, Jean. *Chroniques*, ed. Siméon Luce et al. 15 vols. Paris: Renouard, 1869–1975, Vol. 4, pp. 110–15.

Jean Le Bel. *Chronique*, ed. Jules Viard and Eugène Déprez. 2 vols. Paris: Renouard, 1904–05, Vol. 2, pp. 194–97.

Brush, Henry R. "La bataille de trente anglois et de trente bretons." *Modern Philology* 9 (1911–12): 511–444; 10 (1912–13): 36–90.

THOMAS D'ANGLETERRE (fl. 2nd half of the 12th c.). Eight fragments totaling 3,146 octosyllabic lines, distributed among five manuscripts, are all that remain of Thomas's *Tristan*, composed ca. 1175 for the nobility of Norman England. The author may have been a clerk at the court of Henry II Plantagenêt in London. The fragments of Thomas's *Tristan* preserve essentially the last part of the story, from Tristan's exile in Brittany to the lovers' deaths. Line 3,134 of the epilogue, the adaptations by Brother

Robert (Old Norse) and Gottfried von Strassburg (Middle High German), and the Oxford *Folie*, however, all indicate that Thomas had composed a complete version, one that followed the biographical structure and general movement of the original legend, though Thomas made numerous modifications to it.

Placing Arthur in the mythic past and situating the story in an England ruled over by King Marc, Thomas's reworking is dominated by rationality; the poet tones down the fantastic elements and shows a certain logic in the ordering of events and in the behavior and motivation of the characters. It is possible to suppose that Thomas would have described the *amur fine e veraie* experienced by the protagonists when Tristan first came to Ireland (see l. 2,491), with the love potion only confirming that love. In keeping with the milieu for which he wrote, Thomas eliminated or reworked overly "realistic" episodes (harp and lyre, Iseut and the lepers, life in the forest of Morois), bringing the story into line with the new courtly ideals. A master hunter, Tristan (like his "pupil" Iseut) is also a musician and poet as well as an artist capable of creating the marvelous statues of the Hall of Images.

The principal contribution of Thomas, as scholar and moralist, is in his minute analysis of of love and the other mysteries of human nature. Characters reveal themselves through monologues, debates, and lyric laments; and their self-examination is analyzed through the narrator's long interventions. The action is motivated less by exterior agents than by *inner* adventure, the wanderings of the protagonists' consciences, which alone seems to interest Thomas. The paradox in Thomas's version is thus the narration, within the story of a love seen as absolute and perfect, of an analysis of love that shows Tristan's desire for change (*novelerie*) and his fundamental dissatisfaction. This analysis is coupled with reflections on jealousy and on Tristan's obsession with taking the place of the Other (Iseut or Marc) and feeling himself the pleasure experienced (or not) by the Other. Iseut's role is to express, in actions and lyric laments, her passion, tenderness, and pity for her lover's plight. Thomas uses the technique of "gainsaying": the quarrel between Iseut and Brangain allows the queen to reveal the positive side of *fin'amor*, which had been depicted by Brangain as folly and lechery. Characters like Cariado, Iseut of the White Hands, Tristan the Dwarf, and, undoubtedly, the faithful Kaherdin in the lost episodes, are there to fill out this "mirror" of the multiple faces of love.

The language available to Thomas was not yet as subtle and supple as his analyses. Words like *desir*, *voleir*, *poeir*, even *raisun*, whose meanings seem still too imprecise or overcharged, are significant less in themselves than through the systems of oppositions into which they fit. Repetitions bordering on redundancy, anaphora, antitheses, and rhetorical questions occur almost too frequently. Thomas, however, is capable of realistic depiction, as in the description of London, the doctors who treat Tristan, or the storm. The death scene is characterized by a rhythm wedded to the circularity of desire that conveys, in the echoing of certain rhyme pairs (*confort/mort*, *amur/dulur*, *anguissus/desirus*), the very essence of love.

Thomas makes good the ambitious program articulated in the epilogue: to complete a narrative (*l'escrit*) in which all lovers, whatever their manner of loving, can find pleasure, recall their own passion through the exemplary destiny of Tristan and Iseut, and perhaps escape—for that seems to be the moralist's ultimate goal—the torments and deceits of passion.

Emmanuèle Baumgartner

[See also: BÉROUL; *FOLIES TRISTAN*; *PROSE TRISTAN*; TRISTAN ROMANCES]

Thomas d'Angleterre. *Le roman de Tristan par Thomas*, ed. Joseph Bédier. 2 vols. Paris: SATF, 1902–05.
——. *Les fragments du roman de Tristan, poème du XIIe siècle*, ed. Bartina H. Wind. Geneva: Droz, 1960.
——. *Thomas of Britain: Tristran*, ed. and trans. Stewart Gregory. New York: Garland, 1991.
Baumgartner, Emmanuèle. *Tristan et Iseut: de la légende aux récits en vers*. Paris: Presses Universitaires de France, 1987.
Fourrier, Anthime. *Le courant réaliste dans le roman courtois en France au moyen âge*. Paris: 1960, pp. 19–109.
Hunt, Tony. "The Significance of Thomas' *Tristan*." *Reading Medieval Studies* 7 (1981): 41–61.

THOMAS GALLUS (d. 1246). A regular canon of the abbey of Saint-Victor, Paris, Thomas went to Italy in 1218 or 1219 to assist in the creation of a community of regular canons at Saint-André at Vercelli. He was elected prior of Saint-André in 1224 and abbot in 1226. In 1243, he was forced to leave Saint-André due to the Guelf-Ghibelline conflict. He took refuge at Ivré, where he died in 1246.

Gallus was above all else a commentator on biblical texts and on the works of Pseudo-Dionysius the Areopagite, thus following in the path laid down by two illustrious predecessors at Saint-Victor, Hugh and Richard. He wrote three commentaries on the Song of Songs and over the course of two decades produced glosses, commentaries, and translations concerned with the works of Pseudo-Dionysius. He glossed the *Celestial Hierarchy* and *Mystical Theology*, made an *Extractio* of the entire corpus, and then wrote *Explanationes* for the whole corpus as well. His work on the Pseudo-Dionysian writings continued the earlier work of Hugh of Saint-Victor and made the works and thought of Pseudo-Dionysius accessible to western thinkers at the high tide of scholasticism in the 13th century.

Grover A. Zinn

[See also: BIBLE, CHRISTIAN INTERPRETATION OF; HUGH OF SAINT-VICTOR; PSEUDO-DIONYSIUS THE AREOPAGITE; RICHARD OF SAINT-VICTOR]

THORONET, LE. Founded in 1136 in the diocese of Fréjus, the Cistercian abbey of Le Thoronet (Var) is with Sénanque and Silvacane one of the "three sisters of Provence." Its austere Romanesque church of Saint-Laurent (1160–90), similar to that at Sénanque, features four apses at the east end. To the north, the trapezoidal cloister with its barrel-vaulted galleries is constructed on three levels. Particularly noteworthy is the six-sided lavabo (washing room). The Gothic chapter house surmounted by the monks' dortoir, the tithe barn, the cellar, the warming room, the *armarium* (book locker), and a house for postulants (*convers*), complete the foundation. The refectory has been destroyed.

William W. Kibler/William W. Clark

[See also: CISTERCIAN ART AND ARCHITECTURE; SÉNANQUE; SILVACANE]

Bérenguier, Raoul. *L'abbaye du Thoronet.* 5th ed. Paris: CNMHS, 1964.
Roustan, F. *Monographie de l'abbaye du Thoronet.* Toulouse, 1924.

TINCTORIS, JOHANNES (ca.1435–1511). Composer, musician, and music theorist, Tinctoris was born in the village of Braine-l'Alleud, near Nivelles in present-day Belgium. In 1460, he was briefly in Cambrai, where he served as a *petit vicaire* under Guillaume Dufay. By 1463, and probably earlier, he was a succentor at the cathedral of Orléans. In the later 1460s, Tinctoris was apparently in Chartres, serving as instructor of the cathedral choirboys. He spent much of his later career, from ca. 1472 onward, in the service of the Aragonese court in Naples, as a singer and eventually first chaplain and adviser to Ferdinand I. It was while in Aragonese service that he took a hand in editing and compiling the "Mellon" chansonnier (Yale University, Beinecke Rare Book and Manuscript Library 91), a central source of late 15th-century Burgundian chansons. The details of the last twenty years of his life are largely unknown, although his death in 1511 is documented by the transferral of Tinctoris's prebend at the church of Sainte-Gertrude in Nivelles to another man.

Nearly twenty of Tinctoris's musical works survive, along with several additional works that he composed as musical examples for his treatises. His Masses and motets feature complicated counterpoint and occasional experimentation with very low voice ranges; most of his secular pieces are chanson reworkings based on tenors from Burgundian chansons by Binchois, Morton, and others. The most prominent French music theorist of his generation, Tinctoris was the author of at least a dozen treatises, covering virtually every aspect of late 15th-century music: notation (*Proportionale musices* and others), compositional procedure (*Liber de arte contrapuncti*), practical matters of solmization and performance (*Expositio manus* and *De inventione et usu musicae*), and the aesthetics and uses of music (*Complexus effectuum musices*). His *Terminorum musicae diffinitorium*, one of two treatises published during Tinctoris's lifetime, is the earliest printed dictionary of musical terms. Respected by his contemporaries as a humanist and as an authority on music, Tinctoris is also recognized by modern scholars as the single most important witness to later 15th-century musical thought.

J. Michael Allsen

[See also: BINCHOIS, GILLES; DUFAY, GUILLAUME; MUSIC THEORY]

Tinctoris, Johannes. *Opera omnia,* ed. William Melin. N.p.: American Institute of Musicology, 1976.
———. *Opera theoretica,* ed. Albert Seay. 3 vols. N.p.: American Institute of Musicology, 1975–78.
Woodley, Ronald. "Iohannes Tinctoris: A Review of the Documentary Biographical Evidence." *Journal of the American Musicological Society* 34 (1981): 217–48.

TONGRES. Founded by members of Julius Caesar's army in 57 B.C. as Atuatuca-Tungrorum, Tongres (Limburg) is with Tournai one of the oldest settlements in modern-day Belgium. An important fortified city at the crossing of the Roman roads from Bavay to Cologne and from Arlon to Nijmegen, it was largely overrun by the Franks and Vikings between the late 3rd and 6th centuries and declined under the Merovingians. Gradually, under the protection of Liège, it regained some momentum between the 9th and 13th centuries, when it built new city walls.

The Gothic collegial church of Notre-Dame, on a cultic site that goes back at least to the 4th century A.D., was begun in 1240 and completed 300 years later. On a basilical plan, Notre-Dame has three naves of six bays, crossed by a transept, but without an ambulatory. The choir, transept, and eastern parts of the nave, all with three levels, date from the 13th century; the apse was added in the 14th, side aisles and chapels in the 15th, and the massive western tower between 1442 and 1541.

The treasury is the richest in Belgium, remarkable for the age, variety, number, and splendor of its objects. Notable are a Merovingian enamelwork buckle; a 9th-century ivory book cover; a triptych of the Holy Virgin (ca. 1380); important reliquaries; fourteen silver statuettes from the 14th–16th centuries; and a fine collection of ecclesiastical vestments.

William W. Kibler

Paquay, Jean. *Monographie illustrée de la collégiale de Tongres.* Tongres, 1911.

TONNERRE. The Gallo-Roman city of Tornodorum was situated among the pleasant farmland and vineyards on the left bank of the Armaçon. Today, Tonnerre (Yonne) is dominated by the towers of the churches of Notre-Dame and Saint-Pierre. The choir of the former dates from the 13th century, that of the latter from the early 14th. Except for its choir and 15th-century square tower, Saint-Pierre was rebuilt in 1556 after the town burned.

The real interest of Tonnerre is in its hospital, founded in 1293 by Marguerite of Burgundy (d. 1308), the widow of Louis IX's brother Charles of Anjou, and virtually unchanged to our day. It consists of a large oak-vaulted ward (*salle des malades*) terminating in a polygonal apse. Its forty beds were arranged in wooden alcoves along the side walls, as at the more famous hospital of Beaune, which is 150 years later. In the hospital's chapel is a moving sculptural group (15th c.) representing Christ being placed in his tomb. Similar groupings can be found at Semur-en-Auxois and Dijon.

William W. Kibler/William W. Clark

[See also: BEAUNE; HOSPITALS]

Quénée, Noel. *L'hôpital Notre-Dame des Fontenilles à Tonnerre.* La Pierre-qui-vire: Zodiaque, 1956.

Salet, François. "L'église Saint-Pierre de Tonnerre." *Congrès archéologique (Auxerre)* 116 (1958): 214–24.

———. "L'hôpital Notre-Dame des Fontenilles à Tonnerre." *Congrès archéologique (Auxerre)* 116 (1958): 225–39.

TOUL. Capital of the Gallo-Roman Civitas Leucorum, Toul (Meurthe-et-Moselle) was with Verdun, Metz, and Trier one of the principal cities of Belgica Prima. For most of the Middle Ages, Toul was ruled by its bishop, who had the right to appoint the count; the county of Toul depended directly on the Holy Roman Empire. From the mid-13th until the mid-15th century, there were frequent and bloody conflicts between the bishop's forces and the townspeople, punctuated in 1366 by the grant of a charter of freedoms to the town by the emperor Charles IV, counter to the bishop's claims.

A church dedicated to the Virgin and St. Stephen was founded in the 5th century on the site of the present cathedral, and several successive structures occupied the site. Construction of the Gothic cathedral of Saint-Étienne began with the chevet in 1221; the west façade by Master Jacquemin was completed between 1460 and 1496. This façade, one of the most distinctive of its period, features three portals in Flamboyant style with flanking towers 214 feet high; the original matching towers for the chevet have been lowered due to structural weaknesses, and the statues that originally stood in the portals were destroyed in the Revolution. Gables over each portal, over the western rose, and on each tower give a strong vertical thrust to the whole. This effect is echoed by a multiplicity of pinnacles and spires.

The church is composed of an eight-bayed nave flanked by side aisles with chapels between the buttresses, an unusually wide transept, a choir with two square flanking chapels, and a seven-sided apse. The beauty of the nave, which rises to 100 feet, derives from the simplicity of its two-story elevation—clerestory windows above wide arcades—and the soaring vertical lines joining arcades to vaulting. Details of the elevation, the interior decoration, and the sculpture on the capital of the northeast pillar of the crossing all show the influence of Reims cathedral.

A graceful cloister flanks the south side of the cathedral. It is formed of three long galleries of square rib-vaulted bays; the fourth gallery, against the church, is interrupted by a chapel and the chapter house.

The collegial church of Saint-Gengoult, in Champenois Gothic style, was begun in the mid-13th century. Like the cathedral, construction began with the chevet and concluded in the 15th century with the elevation of the west façade. A remarkable Gothic cloister was added in the 16th century. The influence of the cathedral of Saint-Étienne is manifest in the gabled façade, exterior towers, two-story elevation, projecting transept, and interior decoration.

William W. Kibler

Vallery-Radot, Jean. "Toul: cathédrale," "Toul: église Saint-Gengoult." *Congrès archéologique (Nancy, Verdun)* 96 (1933): 229–74.

TOULOUSE. The principal metropolis of Languedoc, whose counts came to dominate much of the region between the Rhône and Garonne, Toulouse (Haute-Garonne) owed its greatness to a strategic position on the routes of trade and to the political and economic energy of its citizens. Founded, according to legend, before Rome itself, the ancient city of Tolosa was capital of the Roman province of Narbonensia and later of the Visigothic kingdom. It fell to the Franks in 507, and in the 8th century the Frankish dukes of Aquitaine ruled as virtual sovereigns from Toulouse. The great dynasty of the counts of Toulouse began with Fredelon in 849 and despite the rivalry of the houses of Barcelona and Aquitaine continued paramount in Languedoc until the death of Count Raymond VII in 1249.

The power of the counts over their wide domains was matched, however, by that of the burghers over Toulouse itself. More than any other great city of Languedoc, Toulouse saw its citizens take and hold real authority from its overlords. The burghers' rise was facilitated by the counts' external struggles, which both distracted them and forced from them concessions favorable to the townsmen, whose loyalty they needed. In 1119, Count Alphonse-Jourdain owed his survival to the aid of the Toulousans after his defeat by Guilhem IX of Aquitaine; in 1141 and 1147, Alphonse-Jourdain issued the charters that founded the liberties of the burghers of Toulouse. By 1175, the consuls (*capitouls*) of Toulouse exercised wide authority and by 1189 achieved practical autonomy from the count. For the next half-century, their power reached out not only over the *cité* and *bourg* of Toulouse but over the towns and countryside of the Toulousain. The counts of Toulouse were implicated in the Cathar heresy, and the city was the scene of much fighting during the Albigensian Crusade (1208–29).

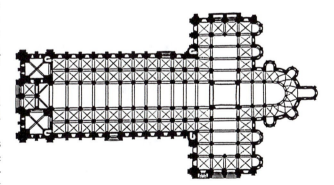

Toulouse (Haute-Garonne), Saint-Sernin, plan. After Radding, Clark.

Toulouse, Saint-Sernin, aerial view. *Courtesy of the French Government Tourist Office.*

Toulouse, Saint-Sernin. *Photograph by V. Jansen.*

The unrestricted dominance of the citizens over their city and its region was reduced finally by the successive seneschals who served Count Alphonse of Poitiers (r. 1249–71) and governed on behalf of the king after 1271. The Toulousain suffered from the devastation of the Hundred Years' War, and Toulouse was implicated in the peasant revolt of the Tuchins in 1384. In 1420, however, its support was essential for rallying the Midi to the dauphin Charles; in 1444, Charles VII established permanently the Parlement of Languedoc at Toulouse.

Alan Friedlander

Toulouse has two of the finest religious structures in the south of France, the Romanesque basilica of Saint-Sernin, and the church of the Jacobins, a masterpiece of southern Gothic style. Saint-Sernin was founded by the late 4th century as the burial site of St. Sernin (Saturninus), the apostle of the Languedoc and first bishop of Toulouse, who was martyred in 257 by being dragged behind a wild bull. Enriched by Charlemagne, it became a key pilgrimage center on the route to Santiago de Compostela. Its treasure includes the relics of 128 saints, among them six Apostles, a piece of the True Cross, and a thorn from the Crown of Thorns. The present building, the largest and one of the finest Romanesque buildings in France, was begun ca. 1060 in response to the masses of pilgrims. It measures 380 feet long by 211 feet at the transept, and its vaulting rises to nearly 70 feet. Saint-Sernin is built in a mixture of stone and brick, with stone predominating in the 11th-century choir (dedicated in 1096 by Pope Urban II) and deambulatory, and brick in the later nave. The chevet encompasses five radiating chapels, and each wing of the transept has two. The nave is flanked by double aisles, the first surmounted by a gallery. Saint-Sernin's deambulatory and multiple semicircular apses, huge transept with aisles, and double aisles flanking the nave are all concessions to the needs of the crowds of pilgrims. A splendid octagonal lantern tower rises for five tiers of arcades above the crossing. The three lower levels have rounded Romanesque arcades (early 13th c.); the upper levels were built in Gothic style (late 13th c.). Its steeple is 14th-century. The tower exercised a profound influence on the architecture of the surrounding region. Saint-Sernin was also a center for the revival of sculpture in the late 11th century. Its south portal (Porte Miègeville; ca. 1120) has a celebrated tympanum representing the Ascension. Other important Romanesque sculptures at Saint-Sernin are the main altar (1096) and the numerous carvings in the deambulatory.

The fortified brick monastery church of the Jacobins was begun in 1230 in response to the Albigensian Crusade. St. Dominic founded the Dominican order (also known as Jacobins because of the location of their Parisian house on the Rue Saint-Jacques) in 1215 to combat the Cathars, and by 1216 Dominicans were present in Toulouse, where they founded the university in 1229 as part of their campaign against the Cathars. The exterior of the church of the Jacobins is strongly buttressed, with large blind arcades between them supporting a *chemin de ronde*. Its graceful octagonal tower was the original bell tower of the university. The church was completed in the second half of the 14th century, in time to receive the relics of St. Thomas Aquinas (d. 1274). Its interior features a double nave, divided by a row of seven slender cylindrical columns rising 72½ feet, and beautiful fan vaulting in the east end. Each nave ends in a rose window, which still has its 14th-century stained glass. The monastery buildings have for the most part been destroyed, except for the capitulary, the chapel of St. Antonin, with important murals in italianate style, and two wings of the cloister.

Other medieval churches in Toulouse include the cathedral of Saint-Étienne and Notre-Dame-du-Taur. The former was rebuilt in 1211, with a wide aisleless nave; its late 13th-century choir shows the influence of northern Gothic. Saint-Étienne is particularly noteworthy for its lack of symmetry: the choir does not align with the nave, nor does the western rose align with the portal below. The church of Notre-Dame-du-Taur was constructed in the 14th and 15th centuries to replace the church erected on the spot where St. Sernin was dragged to death by the bull (OFr. *taur*).

William W. Kibler

[See also: ALBIGENSIAN CRUSADE; CATHARS; FOLQUET DE MARSELHA; LANGUEDOC; SAINT-GILLES]

Durliat, Marcel. *Saint-Sernin de Toulouse*. Toulouse: Eche, 1986.
Gilles, Henri. *Les coutumes de Toulouse (1286) et leur premier commentaire (1296)*. Toulouse: Espic, 1969.
Mundy, John H. *Liberty and Political Power in Toulouse (1050–1230)*. New York: Columbia University Press, 1954.
———. *The Repression of Catharism at Toulouse: The Royal Diploma of 1279*. Toronto: Pontifical Institute of Mediaeval Studies, 1985.
Rey, Raymond. *La cathédrale de Toulouse*. Paris: Laurens, 1929.
Wolff, Philippe. *Commerces et marchands de Toulouse (vers 1350–vers 1450)*. Paris: Plon, 1954.
———. *Histoire de Toulouse*. Toulouse: Privat, 1974.

TOURNAI. The oldest city in present-day Belgium, Tournai (Hainaut) was founded by the Romans as Turris Nerviorum and became the cradle of the Merovingian dynasty. It was evangelized by St. Piat in the 3rd century and, because of its key position controlling the lower Scheldt River, it became the first capital of the Salian Franks (ca. 431–40). French kings looked to Tournai as the cradle of their monarchy, for it was the birthplace of Clovis in 465, and Childeric died there in 481. However, it lost some prestige when Clovis transferred his capital to Soissons in 486. Philip II Augustus visited Tournai in 1187, when it was at the height of its wealth and prestige, thanks to its tapestry and stonecarving industries, to gain the support of the local bishop. He granted the city charters in 1188 and 1211, ensuring its independence under the protection of the French monarchy. It was the only city in Belgium that remained loyal to France throughout the Hundred Years' War, even sending gold to aid Jeanne d'Arc during her captivity.

In Merovingian times, then again in the 13th century, Tournai was an important metalworking center. In the Carolingian period, its abbey of Elnone was one of the most famous centers of Carolingian manuscript illumination and production. From the 12th century, the fine-grained local grey stone was widely exported, both in its natural state and sculpted. In the late-medieval period, Tournai was the birthplace of the important painters Robert Campin (d. 1444) and Rogier van der Weyden (1399/1400–1464).

The 12th and 13th centuries marked Tournai's apogee and saw the construction of its cathedral, as well as the churches of Saint-Piat, Saint-Brice, Saint-Jacques, Saint-Quentin, Sainte-Marie-Madeleine, Saint-Nicolas-du-Bruille, and Saint-Jean-des-Chauffours, as well as the abbey of Saint-Médard or Saint-Nicolas des Prés. The cathedral of Saint-Étienne-et-Notre-Dame was founded during the Merovingian period by St. Éleuthère (d. 531), destroyed by the Vikings, reconsecrated after 1070, then completely rebuilt in the 12th and 13th centuries. It is one of the largest and most innovative churches in Belgium. The nave was built ca. 1110–41 in Romanesque style and the transept between ca. 1150 and 1171; the four transept towers and the lantern at the crossing were constructed in the late 12th century; rib vaulting was installed in the transept and lantern in the early 13th century; and the choir was completely rebuilt in Gothic style between 1243 and 1255.

The nine-bay nave with side aisles is one of the most imposing in Romanesque architecture. It measures 165 feet in length and 30 in width and rises to a height of 86 feet in four distinct levels, which, for the harmony of its superposed arcades, has been compared to a Roman aqueduct. The exterior, with its three levels of windows, is equally remarkable. The enormous transept measures 33 by 221 feet, culminating in magnificent semicircular ends with ambulatories that continue the play of arcades and galleries of the nave, but now more open to the light under Gothic influence. The later choir contrasts sharply with the western portions of the cathedral. At 221 by nearly 40 feet, it is longer and wider than the nave; its vaults rise some 30 feet higher than those of the nave. Much influenced by the International Gothic style found in the roughly contemporary cathedrals of Beauvais or Soissons or the Saint-Chapelle in Paris, it appears to be all stained glass. Built of seven bays, it ends in a broad ambulatory with five apsidal chapels.

The cathedral and its treasury are a tribute to local artists. Of the original three sculpted Romanesque portals of the western façade, two remain, although largely restored. The capitals throughout the cathedral are notable for their variety and skill. In the treasury, the reliquary of St. Éleuthère is one of the richest examples of the 13th-century goldsmith's art, and numerous other reliquaries, chalices, and ecclesiastical vessels testify to the importance of Tournai as an artistic center.

William W. Kibler

[See also: JEWELRY AND METALWORKING; NICOLAS DE VERDUN]

Genicot, L.-F. *La cathédrale de Tournai*. Gembloux, 1969.
Héliot, Pierre. "La cathédrale de Tournai et l'architecture du moyen âge." *Revue belge d'archéologie et d'histoire de l'art* 31–33 (1962–64): 1–139.
Rolland, Paul. *Les églises paroissales de Tournai*. Brussels: Nouvelle Société d'Édition, 1936.
———. *Tournai, noble cité*. Brussels: Renaissance du Livre, 1944.

TOURNAMENT. In the early 12th century, as military conflict in France became less common than it had been earlier, much martial energy was turned toward tournaments, which functioned both as training grounds for and as substitutes for war. Young nobles and knights could make a career of tournaments, where the victors won the weapons and armor of those they defeated.

The original tournaments were fought as *mêlées*, open battle among many mounted knights. Although the weapons were supposed to be blunted, participants were sometimes killed. In 1183, Prince Henry, son of Henry II of England, died in a French tournament after his father had forbidden tournaments in England. One could be excommunicated for participating in a tournament, but this did not reduce their popularity.

By the end of the Middle Ages, tournaments had become much more elaborate and ritualized encounters. Paired in two-man jousts, knights tried to unhorse each other with their lances. Late-medieval jousters had to provide "proofs" of their nobility before they could be admitted to a tournament. The heavy plate armor they now wore meant they were rarely killed. Tournaments remained popular long after the 14th-century invention of gunpowder, but as occasions for display, not mock battles.

Constance B. Bouchard

[See also: ARMS (HERALDIC); CHIVALRY; HERALD/HERALDRY; KNIGHTHOOD; TOURNAMENT ROMANCES]

Barber, Richard. *The Knight and Chivalry*. New York: Harper and Row, 1970.

Duby, Georges. *The Chivalrous Society*, trans. Cynthia Postan. Berkeley: University of California Press, 1977.

Keen, Maurice. *Chivalry*. New Haven: Yale University Press, 1984.

Painter, Sidney. *French Chivalry: Chivalric Ideas and Practices in Mediaeval France*. Baltimore: Johns Hopkins University Press, 1940.

TOURNAMENT ROMANCES. The *Roman du Hem* (1278) by Sarrasin and the *Tournoi de Chauvency* (1285) by Jacques Bretel (or Bretex) recount contemporary tournaments featuring historical personages in a singular mixture of literary invention and documentary concerns. *Hem*, a text of 4,624 octosyllabic lines, survives in one mutilated manuscript (B.N. fr. 1588) written shortly after 1278. The polemical-allegorical framework has Prowess, Largesse, and Valor lament Philip III's interdiction of tournaments, which is detrimental to both honor and the economy. Two young noblemen nevertheless plan a tournament that has the principals disguised as characters from Chrétien de Troyes's romances and reenacts scenes from Arthurian romance. *Chauvency* (4,563 lines) survives in three manuscripts (Oxford, Bodl., Douce 308; Mons, Bibliothèque de la Ville 330–215; Florence, Bib. Laurenziana, Pal. CXVIII). It opens with an encounter between the minstrel Jacques and the German Conrad Warnier (with a linguistically interesting accent), who informs him of the great tournament about to take place at Chauvency. Jacques wants to cover this event and, once at the castle, identifies the participants with the help of a herald (a profession he denigrates). The bulk of the romance is taken up by countless jousts and musical soirées that feature songs with refrains from contemporary poets, games, and storytelling.

Tournaments become literary events in these romances, which intriguingly blur the line between history and fiction.

Renate Blumenfeld-Kosinski

[See also: CHRÉTIEN DE TROYES; HUON D'OISY; ROMANCE; TOURNAMENT]

Bretel, Jacques. *Le tournoi de Chauvency,* ed. Maurice Delbouille. Paris: Droz, 1932.

Sarrasin. *Le roman du Hem*, ed. Albert Henry. Brussels: Éditions de la Revue de l'Université de Bruxelles, 1939.

Duvernoy, Émile, and René Harmand. *Le tournoi de Chauvency en 1285: étude sur la société et les mœurs chevaleresques au XIIIe siècle*. Nancy: Berger-Levrault, 1905.

———. *Histoire littéraire de la France* 23 (1856): 469–83.

TOURNUS. A Celtic city that became a Roman *castrum*, Tournus (Saône-et-Loire) has preserved remains of its Roman fortifications. One of France's earliest monastic sites, the city was evangelized by St. Valérien, who gave his name to a Merovingian foundation. In the late 9th century, monks from Noirmoutier, fleeing the Vikings, arrived with relics of St. Philibert, the founder of the abbey of Jumièges. After destruction by Hungarian raiders in 937, the abbey was rebuilt after 949.

The Benedictine church of Saint-Philibert in Tournus is a complex structure approximately 265 feet in length. A twin-towered façade stands on the western bay of the 10th-century narthex, itself a museum of Romanesque vaulting techniques. Downstairs, the central vessel is covered with groin vaults and its flanking aisles with transverse barrel vaults. Upstairs, the central vessel has a longitudinal barrel vault and the aisles quadrant vaults. Adjacent to the narthex is an aisled nave, with walls carried on massive cylindrical piers and originally a wooden roof. This nave

Tournus (Saône-et-Loire), Saint-Philibert, narthex. *Photograph courtesy of Whitney S. Stoddard.*

Tournus, Saint-Philibert, aisle and nave vaults. *Photograph courtesy of Whitney S. Stoddard.*

was modified in the 12th century, when the present transverse barrel vaults were added. All of the 11th-century parts of the church, vast in scale, are of small-stone construction.

The nave abuts a transept that was originally designed to support a wooden roof. The transept arms were barrel-vaulted in the 12th century, and at the crossing is a cupola carried on squinches. The choir, with ambulatory and radiating chapels, rests on a crypt of the same plan.

The church was consecrated in 1120, but documents recording places of burials indicate that the south wall of the nave was probably complete in 1056 and the south transept by ca. 1105. The crossing has Brionnaise capitals, a type not found in Burgundy after ca. 1120.

Saint-Philibert brought to Burgundy many of the distinctive elements of the northern Early Romanesque style found in the great Loire Valley churches of the 11th century, such as the cathedral of Orléans or Saint-Martin at Tours: vast wood-roofed basilicas constructed in ashlar masonry, whose choirs had ambulatories with radiating chapels. The architects of Tournus adopted the type but used the small-stone construction technique characteristic of the more compact churches of southern Early Romanesque.

John B. Cameron

[See also: ORLÉANS; ROMANESQUE ARCHITECTURE; TOURS/TOURAINE]

Armi, C. Edson. *Masons and Sculptors in Romanesque Burgundy: The New Aesthetic of Cluny III.* 2 vols. University Park: Pennsylvania State University Press, 1983.

Henriet, Jacques. "Saint-Philibert de Tournus: l'œuvre du second maître: la galilée et la nef." *Bulletin monumental* 90 (1992): 101–64.

Vergnolle, Éliane. "Recherches sur quelques series de chapiteaux romans bourguignons." *Information de l'historie de l'art* 20 (1975): 55–79.

TOURS/TOURAINE. Tours (Indre-et-Loire) was the chief town of the Turones, the Roman Caesarodonum, capital of Lugdunensis Tertia. It had a flourishing Christian community by the time of St. Martin (bishop 372–97), founder of Marmoutier, whose tomb became a major pilgrimage site. It fell under Visigothic, then Frankish rule. Its bishop Gregory (r. 573–94) chronicled Merovingian Gaul, and its treasures attracted the Muslim razzia turned back by Charles Martel in 732.

An intellectual center whose scriptorium helped develop Carolingian minuscule under Alcuin (d. 804), Tours was subject to numerous Viking raids (853–911), leading to the fortification of the suburbs and abbey of Saint-Martin as the *châteauneuf.* The region furnishes some of the earliest examples of feudal usage, of the use of radial chapels, and of stone architecture, both secular and ecclesiastical.

The countship and the lay abbacy of Saint-Martin fell to the ancestors of Hugh Capet, and the countship then passed to the house of Blois (940/41) and to that of Anjou (1044), although the king retained the right of episcopal appointment. Site of a stone bridge and a flourishing *bourg,* including a Jewish community, Tours experienced renewed intellectual life. Berengar of Tours (d. 1088) initiated a eucharistic controversy that led to the definition of Transubstantiation.

After 1154, Tours became a crossroads of the Plantagenêt empire, where the *livre tournois* (set at four to the English pound) became ubiquitous. Prosperity continued after the French conquest of 1204–05, when a *bailli* at Tours and *prévôts* at other key points integrated Touraine into the royal domain. By 1300, serfdom had virtually vanished.

Under the Valois kings (1328–1498), Touraine became an apanage and suffered from financial exploitation, the Black Death (post-1351), and the Hundred Years' War (1337–1453). The enforced residence of Charles VII (r. 1422–61) on the Loire led to the location of the Chambre des Comptes and a royal mint at Tours, where the Estates often met and which was a bastion of the monarchy during the worst days of the war. Touraine was a preferred royal residence in the late Middle Ages and a center of political and artistic life that transformed its châteaux-forts into the châteaux for which the region remains renowned.

R. Thomas McDonald

In Tours, the stone bridge across the Loire meets the bridge across the River Cher at the Rue Nationale, a street that today neatly divides the city in half. The two areas retain much of the fabric of the medieval city, as well as fragmentary monuments of the thriving early Christian communites. The east quarter holds the cathedral of Saint-Gatien, the abbey church of Saint-Julien, the remains of the castle of Henry II Plantagenêt, the archbishops' palace, 15th-century gabled houses, and remains of a late-medieval castle. The area west of the Rue Nationale grew around the tomb of St. Martin and now contains the remains of a medieval cemetery, 12th–18th-century houses, and the 15th-century church of Notre-Dame-la-Riche.

Partial collapse and a fire in the Romanesque church of Saint-Gatien necessitated rebuilding after 1239, which continued until the Flamboyant façade was completed in 1484. The north and south towers were finished in 1507 and 1550, respectively. Stained-glass windows in the transepts and east end, which illustrate the Passion of Christ and legends of the saints, have been dated to ca. 1260. The abbey of Saint-Julien consisted of a Romanesque tower and 13th-century chapter house and cellars, but only a 16th-century dormitory still stands.

Although early-medieval Tours flourished as a pilgrimage site and had a well-known scriptorium, comparatively little architecture survives, especially as regards the once massive basilica of Saint-Martin. Vikings destroyed the original sanctuary, and a new basilica was built over the course of the 11th–13th centuries. During the Revolution, the church fell into disrepair and was pulled down in 1802. Two of the Romanesque towers, the Tour Charlemagne and the north-transept Tour de l'Horloge, remain, as well as the crypt, now located below the modern basilica. In the Tour Charlemagne, a restored wall painting of St. Florentius survives from the mid-12th century.

Some 12th-century remains in the largely 17th- and 18th-century archbishops' palace include the Ecclesiastical Tribunal, which now houses the Musée des Beaux Arts. Of the old city gates and castle built by Henry II, only two towers, including the Tour de Guise, survive. In Place Foire-le-Roi, 15th-century gabled houses surround the square where medieval food fairs and mystery plays took place. A wing of brick and stone remains from Louis XI's nearby château of Plessis-lès-Tours from 1463. Recent excavations have revealed a medieval cemetery in the tiny square of Saint-Pierre-le-Puelier.

Stacy L. Boldrick

[See also: MARTIN OF TOURS]

Farmer, Sharon. *Communities of Saint Martin: Legend and Ritual in Medieval Tours.* Ithaca: Cornell University Press, 1991.

Leseur, Frédéric. "Saint Martin de Tours." *Congrès archéologique (Tours)* 106 (1948): 9–28.

Leveel, Pierre. *Histoire de la Touraine.* Paris: Presses Universitaires de France, 1967.

Rand, E.K. *A Survey of the Manuscripts of Tours.* 2 vols. Cambridge: Mediaeval Academy of America, 1929.

TOWNS. As the Roman Empire declined after A.D. 165, all cities, stricken by high taxes and plague, decayed, but unevenly. As interprovincial trade diminished, Marseille shrank, but Lyon, a capital as well as emporium, was buttressed by increasing bureaucratization. After 406, Germanic invasions threatened urban life, but under the Merovingians eastern merchants continued to function until the Muslims seized the Mediterranean, after which gold coinage and papyrus virtually disappeared. Although shrunken walls protected cathedrals and their adjuncts, trading towns and secular administrative centers virtually disappeared. Muslim occupation diminished Bordeaux, Toulouse, and Narbonne on the Garonne route. With about 20,000 inhabitants, only Paris, which held off the Norsemen

in 885, and Orléans, another river port as well as a monastic center, escaped significant disruption. Near Tours, downstream from Orléans, the Franks stopped the Muslims in 732, but Norsemen sacked the place in 853 and 903.

In the short-lived Carolingian revival, Duurstede and Quentovic developed along the Scheldt and Rhine estuaries, formerly *limes* but now imperial arteries. Their trading with England and Scandinavia sparked a revival that better coinage and a "renaissance" attest, but the fragmentation of the empire and the Viking raids destroyed them and all other important ports, while Muslims wrecked southern commerce. Feudalization of coinage in the 10th century also impeded trade. Peddlers conveyed salt, metals, and a few luxury items that seeped from Venice. Territorial principalities developed around Rouen in Normandy and Bordeaux in Aquitaine, but no town surpassed 10,000 inhabitants between the 8th century and the year 1000.

Cessation of invasions, greater political stability, warmer climate, and an agricultural revolution thereafter fostered trade and urban growth. Old Roman sites revived, as itinerant merchants wintered under their protective walls or those of propitiously located castles. They gradually established settled mercantile communities that outstripped the adjacent fortified area. The merchants profited from oriental goods, available after Christian shipping reopened the Mediterranean, and northerners brought Baltic products to Flanders to trade for eastern luxuries at the fairs of Champagne. Though Flemish weavers surpassed other craftsmen and Lombard bankers excelled Jewish pawnbrokers, French towns also developed guilds. Unlike their Italian counterparts, French communes, backed by guilds, rarely included nobility. Before the disasters of the 14th century, the general population trebled but many towns multiplied tenfold, although three-quarters of them still had fewer than 2,000 inhabitants. Among them were thirty-nine bastides founded by Alphonse of Poitiers and the more significant centers of Aigues-Mortes and Carcassonne established by his brother Louis IX. By the 14th century, Paris attained a population of perhaps 200,000; Bordeaux, Marseille, Montpellier, and Lyon, 30,000; and Béziers, Bourges, Dijon, Narbonne, Reims, Rouen, Toulouse, and Troyes, about 10,000.

Plagues in the 14th century carried off half the townspeople, but rural immigrants quickly replaced many of them. Although recurrent plagues prevented urban populations from rising, the townspeople became a larger percentage of the population. Shortage of rural labor encouraged emancipation and rising wages, so more peasants could afford manufactured goods and richer ones a few luxuries. Yet some merchants evaded the high costs of guild labor by "putting out" wool to be spun and woven by peasants in their homes.

Although only churches, castles, and municipal buildings used masonry before 1150, when Gothic architecture supplanted Romanesque, after 1300 guildhalls and patrician *palazzos* did, more in the south than in the north, thereby reducing fire hazards and blocking rats, which had spread disease after gnawing through wood. Laws regulated leprosaries, hospitals, tanneries, and slaughter-houses, along with cemeteries outside the walls. Better planning, paving, water supplies, and waste disposal also ameliorated conditions in richer quarters, as *faubourgs*, or suburbs, proliferated. Universities arose, first at Paris and then at Toulouse, Montpellier, Avignon, Orléans, and Grenoble. Forging enduring alliances with towns, although he taxed them heavily, Louis XI (r. 1461–83) fostered silk production at Lyon and also a fair that diverted much business from Geneva as well as the commerce through Marseille and other ports, Aigues-Mortes having declined since its harbor had silted up.

William A. Percy, Jr.

[See also: AIGUES-MORTES; BASTIDE; BOURGEOISIE; CHAMPAGNE; *CITÉ*; COMMUNE; FAIRS AND MARKETS; POPULATION AND DEMOGRAPHY; TEXTILES]

TRADE ROUTES. Medieval France was crisscrossed by little roads of mud foundation that linked towns of secondary importance, creating a dense network in contrast to the older Roman road system, still partially functional, which favored straight, paved thoroughfares between major urban sites. The main river systems—the Seine, Loire, Garonne, and Rhône (the boundary between southern French territory and the empire)—and lesser rivers like the Saône served as important arteries of trade in an era when water transport was substantially less expensive than overland carting. Cross-Channel and Atlantic trade connections linked Normandy and Brittany to the British Isles. North Sea ports, such as Montreuil-sur-Mer, Boulogne, and Calais, were jumping-off points for trade via Frisia and Denmark to Hanseatic centers farther east. Access to central and southern France by land from the east was a matter of Vosges and Jura crossings and Alpine passes. With the Spanish peninsula, commercial links with southern France might be overland across the Pyrénées or, more frequently, by sea. Mediterranean ports, such as Collioure, Agde, Aigues-Mortes, and Marseille, facilitated trade with the western and eastern basins of the Mediterranean.

The Champagne fairs were a significant international commercial destination in the era of caravan trade, functioning as a crossroads of interaction between merchants of northern and southern Europe. Italians traveled by boat to southern France and then north by two main arteries, the Rhône Valley route involving travel partly on land, partly on water; and the Regordane, stretching within medieval France from Montpellier or Nîmes to Alès and north across the Cévennes to Le Puy, Brioude, Issoire, Clermont, and beyond to Paris or east into Champagne. There was also another, more westerly, passage to Paris from Montpellier, north through Lodève, Millau, Rodez, Figeac, Aurillac, La Force, and Clermont. Italians could opt for an overland route to Champagne using the Mont-Cenis and Saint-Bernard passes in the Alps. The Saint-Gothard pass, opened in 1237, made possible overland travel between northern Italy and Flanders via the Rhine, eliminating passage through Champagne. The Atlantic sea route, inaugurated in 1277, provided an alternative route from the Mediterranean to England and Flanders, further encouraging the decline of Champagne as a European commercial hub.

Kathryn L. Reyerson

[See also: CHAMPAGNE; FAIRS AND MARKETS; MEDITERRANEAN TRADE; SHIPS AND SHIPPING; TRAVEL; WINE TRADE]

Bautier, Robert-Henri. "Recherches sur les routes de l'Europe médiévale." *Bulletin philologique et historique des sociétés savantes 1960* (1961): 99–143.

Boyer, Marjorie N. "A Day's Journey in Medieval France." *Speculum* 26 (1951): 597–608.

Combes, Jean. "Transports terrestres à travers la France centrale à la fin du XIVe siècle et au commencement du XVe siècle." *Fédération historique du Languedoc-Roussillon* (1955): 3–7.

Lopez, Robert S. "The Evolution of Land Transport in the Middle Ages." *Moyen âge* 69 (1963): 479–90.

Renouard, Yves. "Les voies de communication entre pays de la Méditerranée et pays de l'Atlantique: problèmes et hypothèses." In *Mélanges Louis Halphen*. Paris: Presses Universitaires de France, 1951, pp. 587–94.

TRANSHUMANCE. Nomadic animal husbandry involving seasonal migration of flocks and herds. Transhumance maximized pastoral resources by moving animals to where the grass was most abundant. In the Middle Ages, it was used especially in the Midi, where changes in elevation and season of grass growth occur over short distances, to support larger flocks and herds. Animals were pastured during the winter in lowlands having their rainy season then, as along the Languedoc coast; in spring and early summer, they were moved to the high mountain pastures (*estives*, *montagnes*, or *alpes*) of the Pyrénées, the Massif Central, and the Alps and were brought down again to the lowlands in the fall. Because of the many passage, feeding, and watering concessions involved, medieval transhumance was practiced most extensively on a large scale by the great monastic houses; those of Bonneval and Bonnecombe in Rouergue, for instance, were well known for bringing sheep and cattle from Quercy up into the high elevations of Rouergue; the animals, numbering in the thousands, included not only those belonging to the monks but many others tended under contract. The transhumance practiced by the great religious corporations is well documented in the many surviving charters recording controversy and agreement about dates of coming and going to the *estives*; amounts of time to rest, feed, and water animals en route; numbers of animals; the building of shepherds' huts; and the division of pasture and water in the *estives*. There is evidence from coastal Provence of transhumance practiced by peasant villages since Roman times; only by such seasonal migration could these villagers survive in that hostile environment. Most transhumance in France was conducted by specialized shepherds and cowherds who migrated from the lowlands up into the high summer pastures to tend their animals and make butter and cheese from their milk during the summer. Standard routes, dates, and ceremonies for the movements of cattle and sheep developed; walled sheep roads called *drailles* (or *drayas*) can still be seen in the higher elevations of the Massif Central, like the Aubrac plateau, still famous for its transhumance. Although friction always existed between stock raisers and cereal cultivators, there is little indication for medieval France of the widespread disruption that accompanied transhumance in medieval Spain and Italy.

Constance H. Berman

[See also: ANIMALS (DOMESTIC); *CONVENIENTIA*]

Berman, Constance H. *Medieval Agriculture, the Southern French Countryside, and the Early Cistercians.* Philadelphia: American Philosophical Society, 1986.

Bousquet, Jacques. "Les origines de la transhumance en Rouergue." In *L'Aubrac: étude ethnologique, linguistique, agronomique, et économique d'un établissement humain.* Paris: CNRS, 1971, Vol. 2, pp. 217–55.

Sclafert, Thérèse. *Cultures en Haute-Provence: déboisements et pâturages au moyen âge.* Paris: SEVPEN, 1959.

TRANSLATION. Translations into Old French from classical and late Latin texts can be divided, for the sake of descriptive taxonomy, into three large categories: translations and imitations of major classical literary models, translations of historical and political texts, translations of sentential and educational texts.

Of all literary translations from Latin sources, Boethius's *De consolatione Philosophiae* and the works of Ovid have the longest and most complex histories. This is not surprising, since Boethius and Ovid were major authors of the arts curriculum and their work exerted great influence on vernacular literary culture. Though Virgil's *Aeneid* was also a central curricular text, its influence was felt through the particularly medieval Romances of Antiquity rather than through direct formal imitation and translation. Boethius's *Consolatio*, however, proved congenial to vernacular literary interests in poetic form; and Ovidian materials could be assimilated directly into vernacular interests in mythology and into conventions of erotic literature.

The Occitan *Boeci* (ca. 1000–30) is the oldest literary text preserved in the language. The earliest French version of the *Consolatio* is an incomplete Anglo-Norman paraphrase composed in verse by Simon de Freine ca. 1180. From the early 13th century to the late 15th, at least thirteen versions of the *Consolatio* were produced in French. Some of these were simply revisions of earlier versions. The five earliest of these translations are in prose, suggesting that translators were initially more interested in the philosophical content than in the literary character of Boethius's prosimetrum text. These five prose translations, which seem to have been produced independently of each other, are by an anonymous Burgundian (early 13th c.; one manuscript), an anonymous Wallonian (late 13th c.; one manuscript), Bonaventure da Demena (late 13th or early 14th c.; one manuscript), Pierre de Paris (1305–09;

one manuscript), and Jean de Meun (probably after 1285; eighteen manuscripts). Except for the Wallonian version, these prose translations can be associated with academic interests through their incorporation of medieval commentaries and glosses on the *Consolatio.* Jean de Meun's version achieved considerable currency for a number of reasons: Jean's literary reputation, which was founded not only on the *Roman de la Rose* but on other translations he had made (as well as on works attributed to him), including translations of Abélard's *Historia calamitatum* and Vegetius's *De re militari*; the clarity and rigor of his translation of the *Consolatio*, which also incorporated glosses by the philosopher William of Conches; and Jean's preface to his translation, in which he dedicates the work to Philip IV, thus identifying his vernacular text with a cosmopolitan court culture and the very center of political power. Chaucer consulted Jean de Meun's version for his own Middle English translation of the *Consolatio.*

Jean's prologue became better known than his translation: his dedicatory preface was affixed to another translation of the *Consolatio*, made in the mid-14th century, a prosimetrum version that, though less rigorous than Jean's prose, achieved enormous success, surviving in at least sixty-four manuscripts, mainly of the 15th century. This version, composed probably 1350–60, is actually a revision of a prosimetrum translation that had been composed ca. 1330, known in only four manuscripts. The revised prosimetrum exists in two forms, glossed and unglossed: the glossed version incorporates commentary, translated into French, from a redaction of William of Conches's commentary. The success of the revised prosimetrum translation is probably the result of two factors: its attribution to Jean de Meun because Jean's prologue was affixed to it in most manuscripts, and its attention to the formal properties of Boethius's text, which identifies the translation as much with vernacular literary interests as with learned academic concerns.

The middle and late 14th century produced four verse translations of the *Consolatio*. One of these, by an anonymous author from Meun (date uncertain), exists complete in only one manuscript; this translation, consisting of over 12,000 lines of verse, is interesting for its encyclopedic and mythographic interests. In 1336 or 1337, the Dominican friar Renaut de Louens composed a verse translation that incorporated glosses from the commentary on the *Consolatio* by a 14th-century English Dominican, Nicholas Trevet. Renaut's version, surviving in over thirty manuscripts, was twice revised in the late 14th century; one of these revisions, by an anonymous Benedictine, achieved great popularity on its own, also extant in over thirty manuscripts. Two further prosimetrum translations were composed in the 15th century: one of these was a partial revision of the Benedictine's version of Renaut's verse translation, and the other was printed by Colard Mansion in 1477 and again by Antoine Vérard in 1494.

The history of Ovid translations is also complicated, because the Ovidian tradition was deeply enmeshed in vernacular literature. The *Ars amatoria* was readily assimilated into courtly convention, where it had a contemporary analogue in Andreas Capellanus's *De amore.* From the early 13th to the late 14th century, there were no less than five independent translations or adaptations of the *Ars amatoria*, four in verse and one in prose. Chrétien de Troyes claimed (*Cligés*, ll. 1–3) to have translated the *Ars amatoria*, as well as a work called the *Commandemenz Ovide*, perhaps the *Remedia amoris*. Chrétien's translations are not extant. Four of the surviving translations, which are in verse, date from the 13th century. The earliest, the "Maistre Elie" version, was composed probably early in the 13th century; its unique 14th-century manuscript covers only the first two books of the *Ars amatoria*, and its method is both to amplify and to abbreviate its source. It also substitutes contemporary French cultural and geographical references for Ovid's Roman culture and locales, medievalizing the text in a way that was conventional in vernacular literary imitations of ancient sources, especially the Romances of Antiquity. The *Art d'amors* of Jakes d'Amiens, also of the early 13th century, extant in five manuscripts and an incunabulum, uses Andreas Capellanus's *De amore* as a literary model for the translation of Ovid's text. The other two verse translations, the *Clef d'amors* (written possibly 1280; one manuscript) and the version by Guiart (one manuscript), similarly medievalize Ovid's text: the *Clef d'amors* presents a framework of a dream narrative in which the God of Love appears to the poet; and the adaptation by Guiart combines Ovid's *Ars amatoria* with elements from the *Remedia amoris* and medieval religious motifs.

A prose translation of the *Ars amatoria* from the late 14th century (conserved in four 15th-c. manuscripts) offers a fairly literal translation of Ovid's text, with extensive glosses and a prologue to the text based on Latin academic models (*accessus ad auctores*). Some of the glosses contain proverbs and quotations from French lyrics. In three of the manuscripts, the translation covers only Books 1 and 2 of the *Ars amatoria*; Book 3 appears only in one manuscript and seems to have been a later addition to the French text. This translation is interesting for its synthesis of vernacular literary materials and academic exegetical conventions.

There are also French translations of the *Remedia amoris*, *Metamorphoses*, and *Heroides*. Three translations of the *Remedia amoris* are extant: one from the 13th century, attributed to Jakes d'Amiens in two manuscripts that also contain his version of the *Ars amatoria*, and two from the 14th century. The tradition of the *Metamorphoses* is best considered with reference to the *Ovide moralisé*, which translates the entire *Metamorphoses*, incorporating earlier translations of individual tales and which also formed the basis of at least two 15th-century prose redactions (1466 and the Colard Mansion edition of 1484). Finally, a number of versions of the *Heroides* have come down to us. Two of these date from the 15th century: one is by Octavien de Saint-Gelays (1496), extant in fifteen manuscripts and an incunabulum; the other, anonymous, is extant in only one manuscript. But there is also a prose adaptation of the *Heroides*, probably from the 13th century, of which only parts are now extant: some parts of this translation survive embedded in the second redaction of the *Histoire ancienne jusqu'à César* (1364–80), and other parts survive separately under the title *Epistles que les dames de Grece*

envoierent a leur maris qui estoient devant Troies et les responses d'icelles.

Although Virgil and Terence were standard curricular authors, their works were not translated into French until the 15th century. Terence's comedies were translated twice: a prose translation of 1466 by Guillaume Rippe (two manuscripts) and a verse translation by Gilles Cybille, which survives only in an incunabulum (ca. 1500). For the tradition of Virgil's *Aeneid*, we must preserve a distinction betwen the popular courtly imitation of Virgil's epic, the *Roman d' Énéas* (ca. 1160), and actual translation of the work. Of the latter, we have only one version, a translation by Octavien de Saint-Gelays, composed ca. 1500 (three manuscripts and two early printed editions).

Some translations of historical and political texts had wide circulation, and some ancient works were of sufficient interest to undergo more than one translation. One influential text, found in over sixty manuscripts, was a compilation known as the *Fet des Romains* (1213–14), which combined materials from Sallust's *De coniuratione Catilinae*, Suetonius's *De vita Caesarum*, Lucan's *Pharsalia*, and Caesar's *Bellum Gallicum*. But these historical sources were also translated individually in the later Middle Ages. Of the two 15th-century translations of Caesar's *Bellum Gallicum*, one is by Jean Duchesne (ca. 1473; nine manuscripts) and the other by Robert Gaguin (late 15th c.; four manuscripts and three incunabula). Sallust's *De coniuratione Catilinae* and *Bellum Iugurthinum* were translated in 1417 by Jean le Bègue (extracts in a unique manuscript). Part of Suetonius's *De vita Caesarum* was also translated separately. Lucan's *Pharsalia* (properly called *Bellum civile*) was translated in the late 14th century by Nicolas de Vérone (2 manuscripts).

To judge from manuscript circulation or multiple translations, the historical and political works that commanded greatest interest were Livy's history of Rome, *Ab urbe condita*, and Vegetius's *De re militari*, a manual of Roman military institutions composed in the late 4th century A.D. *Ab urbe condita* was translated by the Benedictine monk Pierre Bersuire between 1352 and 1356; this translation survives, either complete or in part, in at least eighty manuscripts and an incunabulum. It was received as a preeminent example of the transformation of French into a learned language: Bersuire equipped it with a prefatory dictionary of all the French terms he had coined out of Latin in order to render Livy's text, and he also made use of a commentary on Livy by Nicholas Trevet. Bersuire undertook the translation at the request of King John II the Good, and indeed this text became a kind of "mirror of princes," a treatise on politics, warfare, and morality. Many aristocratic libraries possessed copies, notably those of Charles V, John of Berry, and the dukes of Burgundy. It circulated widely through the 15th century, and later in printed editions. Part of Livy's history, the third decade, was retranslated by Robert Gaguin ca. 1493 (one printed edition, 1508). Vegetius's *De re militari* was translated six times in the 13th and 14th centuries. Jean de Meun's version, made for Jean de Brienne, count of Eu, in 1284, is extant in over twenty manuscripts and was revised twice: once in verse by Jean Priorat between 1284 and 1290 for

Jean de Châlon-Harlay, an influential noble, and again in the 15th century, with some substantive changes to preserve its relevance for later audiences. Jean de Vignay, a prolific translator, produced a version of Vegetius ca. 1320 for Philip VI (nine manuscripts). An anonymous translation was made in 1380 (two manuscripts), and an Anglo-French translation ca. 1272, attributed in one of the four extant manuscripts to a "Maistre Richard"; this translation seems to have been directed to the future Edward I of England.

Translations of several minor historical and tactical writings may be mentioned here. Vasque de Lucène translated in 1468 Quintus Curtius Rufus's *De rebus gestis Alexandri*, written in the 1st century A.D.; his version survives in at least thirty-six manuscripts and an incunabulum. The *Breviarium ab urbe condita* by Eutropius, a 4th-century historian, was translated twice in the 13th century, once by an unknown author (one manuscript), and once by Jofroi de Watreford and Servais Copale (one manuscript). The *Strategemata* of Frontinus (1st c. A.D.), a manual of historical examples of Greek and Roman military strategy composed for officers, was translated for Charles VII by Jean de Rouroy ca. 1439 (nine manuscripts).

Translations of sentential and theoretical or educational texts, though representing the smallest category in terms of the authors translated, circulated widely. These translations, like those of historical and military sources, are often associated with royal patronage. This is the case with the translation of the *Facta et dicta memorabilia* of Valerius Maximus (1st c. A.D.), a collection of rhetorical exempla grouped under moral and philosophical topics, which Simon de Hesdin undertook ca. 1375 for Charles V, the great royal patron of learned culture and vernacular translation. Simon de Hesdin died in 1384, leaving the translation unfinished; it was completed in 1404 by Nicolas de Gonesse at the request of John of Berry, the brother of Charles V. This translation greatly amplifies the source with commentary, new divisions and subdivisions, and borrowings from a host of other sources, classical and medieval, pagan and Christian. In partial or complete form, the translation survives in at least seventy-five manuscripts and five incunabula.

Two of Cicero's works, *De senectute* and *De amicitia*, were translated in 1405 and 1416, respectively, by Laurent de Premierfait, a *clerc* from Champagne associated with the intellectual circles of the papal court of Avignon. Laurent's literary activity was extensive: among other works, he translated Boccaccio's *Decameron* and *De casibus illustrium virorum*. He undertook the translation of *De senectute* (extant in twenty-five manuscripts) at the request of Duke Louis of Bourbon; the *De amicitia* (fifteen manuscripts) was presented to John of Berry. A number of other translations of Cicero's works also survive, among them an anonymous translation of the *Pro Marcello* (uncertain date; one manuscript), a translation of the *Epistola ad Quintum* by Jean Miélot (1468; two manuscripts); and three 15th-century translations of the *De officiis* (two manuscripts and one incunabulum, one incunabulum, and one manuscript, respectively). There is also a translation of the Ciceronian *rhetorica* (Cicero's *De inventione* and

the pseudo-Ciceronian *Ad Herennium*), completed in 1282 by Jean d'Antioche (known also as Jean de Hareng), which survives in one manuscript. The translation of the Ciceronian rhetorics is interesting for a number of reasons: its stylistic aim at technical precision; its prologue, which offers a classification of the sciences; and two appendices, which offer a theoretical discussion of logic, translation, and linguistic difference. The translation is directed to Guillaume de Saint-Étienne, who in 1296 was in charge of the order of St. John of Jerusalem on Cyprus; Jean d'Antioche's work seems to have emerged from an Italian rather than a French literary milieu (cf. Brunetto Latini's *Rettorica*, an Italian version of the *De inventione*, written ca. 1260).

The moral works associated with Seneca the Younger received some attention, although their circulation never compared with that of the translation of Valerius Maximus. Seneca's *Epistolae ad Lucilium* were translated by an unknown author ca. 1310 (extant in six manuscripts). The pseudo-Senecan *De remediis fortuitorum* was translated in the 13th century by an anonymous author (two manuscripts) and again in the late 14th century by Jacques de Bauchant, who, like Simon de Hesdin, worked under the patronage of Charles V. The Jacques de Bauchant translation survives in five manuscripts. Translations of the *Epistolae ad Lucilium*, the *De remediis fortuitorum*, and Seneca's *De brevitate vitae* are found, along with other pseudo-Senecan texts, in an incunabulum from ca. 1500, the colophon of which attributes the translations to Laurent de Premierfait. Though this attribution has not been verified, it is evidence that the value of a translation could depend as much on the celebrity of the translator as on the prestige of the author of the original work; we compare the enormous popularity of Jean de Meun's translation of Boethius's *Consolatio* and of the later translation associated with his name.

We may also note two other works of the sentential tradition. There is an anonymous translation (uncertain date) of the *Sententiae* of Publilius Syrus, a text from the 1st century B.C. that was one of Seneca's sources for the *Epistolae ad Lucilium*. The *Distichs of Cato* (3rd or 4th c. A.D.) was a popular sentential text in the medieval schools. At least seven versions exist in French: in Anglo-Norman, by Everard of Kirkham and Elie of Winchester (12th c.); by Jean de Paris (ca. 1280); by Adam de Suel (mid-13th c.); by Jean Lefèvre (14th c.); and two anonymous versions from the 15th century.

Many aspects of the history of translation in medieval French lie beyond the scope of this survey: translations of patristic sources, the Bible, Greek authors (from Latin versions), legal documents, and medieval Latin sources. We can, however, draw some general conclusions. No correlation necessarily exists between the importance of a curricular author and translation of that author. Horace, for example, was widely read in the medieval schools as part of the basic curriculum in *grammatica*; yet there is no extant French translation of the *Ars poetica*, the best known of Horace's texts. The reason is not difficult to see: the *Ars poetica* was important for instruction in reading Latin poetry, especially classical texts, but offered little that was directly relevant to vernacular poetic traditions, which generated their own arts of poetry. Similarly, it might be surprising that the *Aeneid* received so little attention from translators; but this suggests that vernacular writers were more interested in developing themes and narratives from the *Aeneid* than in imitating it as a formal entity. The same may be said of the *Thebaid* of Statius, the primary narrative source of the *Roman de Thèbes*, which was not directly translated into French. Boethius's *Consolatio*, on the other hand, inspired considerable formal interest as a literary model; in fact, the most successful translations of Boethius are those that emphasize its poetic features over its difficult philosophical content. But if translation of poetry is shaped largely by the tastes of vernacular literary milieux, translation of historical and political texts seems determined by the interests of royal patrons, whose ideological purposes might be served by possession of texts that had relatively little currency in academic and literary circles. The translation of classical texts is conditioned less by the norms of classical study in the medieval schools than by the concerns of vernacular literary production and of contemporary politics.

Rita Copeland

[See also: ANTIQUITY, ROMANCES OF; BERSUIRE, PIERRE; *BOECI*; BOETHIUS, INFLUENCE OF; *FET DES ROMAINS*; GAGUIN, ROBERT; GOLEIN, JEAN; MIÉLOT, JEAN; ORESME, NICOLE; *OVIDE MORALISÉ*; OVIDIAN TALES; PREMIERFAIT, LAURENT DE; PRESLES, RAOUL DE; RENAUT DE LOUENS; SAINT-GELAYS, OCTAVIEN DE; *VIES DES ANCIENS PÈRES*; VIGNAY, JEAN DE; VIRGIL, INFLUENCE OF]

Bossuat, Robert. "Traductions françaises des *Commentaires* de César à la fin du XVe siècle." *Bibliothèque d'Humanisme et Renaissance* 3 (1943): 253–411.

Buridant, Claude. "Translatio medievalis: théorie et pratique de la traduction médiévale." *Travaux de linguistique et de littérature* 21 (1983): 81–136.

Chavy, Paul. *Traducteurs d'autrefois, moyen âge et Renaissance: dictionnaire des traducteurs et de la littérature traduite en ancien et moyen français (842–1600).* 2 vols. Geneva: Slatkine, 1988.

Copeland, Rita. *Rhetoric, Hermeneutics, and Translation in the Middle Ages: Academic Traditions and Vernacular Texts.* Cambridge: Cambridge University Press, 1991.

Dwyer, Richard A. *Boethian Fictions: Narratives in the Medieval French Versions of the Consolatio Philosophiae.* Cambridge: Medieval Academy of America, 1976.

Kelly, F. Douglas. "*Translatio Studii*: Translation, Adaptation, and Allegory in Medieval French Literature." *Philological Quarterly* 57 (1978): 287–310.

Lucas, Robert H. "Mediaeval French Translations of the Latin Classics to 1500." *Speculum* 45 (1970): 225–53.

Lusignan, Serge. *Parler vulgairement: les intellectuels et la langue française aux XIIIe et XIV siècles.* Paris: Vrin, 1986, pp. 129–71.

Minnis, Alistair J., ed. *The Medieval Boethius: Studies in the Vernacular Translations of De consolatione Philosophiae.* Cambridge: Brewer, 1987.

Monfrin, Jacques. "Humanisme et traductions au moyen âge." *Journal des savants* 148 (1963): 161–90.

———. "Les traducteurs et leur public en France au moyen âge." *Journal des savants* 149 (1964): 5–20.

Palmer, Nigel F. "Latin and Vernacular in the Northern European Tradition of the *De consolatione Philosophiae*." In *Boethius: His Life, Thought, and Influence*, ed. Margaret Gibson. Oxford: Blackwell, 1981, pp. 362–409.

TRAVEL. The Roman Empire required ease of communication for its governance. Travelers benefited from an immense network of surfaced roads, a high level of security, and the existence of a variety of vehicles developed especially for passengers and available for hire in Rome. The medieval period, however, saw many changes in the conditions of travel. Some of these began to become apparent in the 5th century, as the imperial government lost control of Gaul. The roads became unsafe, and there was less trade. Meanwhile, early-medieval government itself became itinerant because of the small number of officials, the paucity of royal resources, and the personal nature of loyalty. The period also had its own particular reasons for travel that were inherent in certain aspects of medieval Christianity, such as the requirements of church administration and the popularity of pilgrimage.

Where the Romans had been famous for their roads, people in medieval France considered bridges of primary importance. Beginning in the 11th century, bridge building became a pious work on the grounds that it saved lives in times of flood, and the enthusiasm for construction meant that by the early 14th century France had been provided with an impressive network of bridges. Some of them were built on difficult sites, but construction and maintenance were hampered by a shortage of money and of workers, and travelers were glad to be informed whether such and such a bridge were passable at any given time.

During the Middle Ages, the orientation of the network of roads changed. In Roman times, it had centered on Lyon, but as the Capetians gradually expanded their power all the roads in France came to lead to Paris. Only one system of rivers led to the capital, and the direction of the routes may have had something to do with the concentration of travelers on land routes. Evidence shows that only if the entire journey were between points on the same river, as on the Loire or downstream on the Rhône between Lyon and Avignon, were travelers tempted to take a boat. It was not quicker, and if one had already hired one's horses it was also more expensive to pay for river travel.

Methods of travel likewise shifted between ancient and medieval times. In late antiquity, the favorite and most prestigious conveyance was the carriage. Beginning in the 5th century, however, more and more people rode on horseback, and by 700 mentions of carriages are rare. By the 9th century, passenger vehicles as such had disappeared, and for a king or warrior to ride in any type of vehicle was considered a disgrace. Only illness or old age excused his failure to mount his steed. For nobles and warriors, this situation continued at least into the late 15th century, when the king made ceremonial entries riding in a carriage. On the other hand, by 1200 it was not only permitted but required that queens and duchesses should each own two gorgeously decorated chariots, one for their own and one for their ladies' use on ceremonial occasions, such as entries into their towns. Though passenger vehicles disappeared in the Carolingian period, carts and wagons continued in use over long distances by the tenants of the great abbeys to carry produce, like wine and lumber, either to the convent or to fairs.

The Middle Ages saw technological improvements in travel and transportation. The shaft cart, little used in antiquity, became common. The stirrup was introduced from the East early in the medieval period, and later we find nailed-on horseshoes, the harnessing of horses in tandem, and an improved horse collar. Suspended carriages reached France in the 14th century, when artists at last take sufficient interest in depicting the undercarriage of chariots so that it is possible to prove that the pivoted front axle was in common use. (It was known in Hallstatt times and during the Roman Empire, but how widely it was employed is difficult to determine before the 14th century.)

Despite these advances in traction, riding on horseback remained popular and seems to have been preferred to riding in vehicles. Improvements were made in horse breeding. Varieties of horses were bred for specialized purposes, like the *destrier*, strong enough to carry a knight in full plate armor, and the palfrey, a saddle horse with a comfortable, ambling gait. Both types were luxuries, and many all-purpose horses continued in use as mounts and as plow and draft horses. Throughout the Middle Ages, it was common for pilgrims to walk, for they were believed to acquire additional merit if they performed their pious journeys on foot and especially barefoot. Poor folk and servants were frequently pedestrians. In southern France, in the 14th and 15th centuries, if an official hired a horse to make a journey to transact town business, he was accompanied by a groom on foot to care for the animal. There were foot messengers but more mounted couriers, particularly in northern France. Even in the case of mixed companies of horsemen and pedestrians, travelers could maintain a speed of at least 30 miles a day over a period of several days.

Hospitality was an important obligation, and the church had a particular duty to furnish it. Abbeys built visitors' quarters and housed their guests according to rank, the great nobly and pilgrims and wayfarers simply. By the 13th century, a favorite charity was the foundation of hospices for the ill and the aged and for pilgrims, wanderers, and indigent travelers. The kings of France were entertained by their officials, by churchmen, and by various towns. (Evidently, the municipalities felt that it was a productive investment, but officials and some churchmen attempted to procure documents exempting them from this honor.) Most of the French kings' travels seem to have been from one of their châteaux to another. Royalty offered foreign dignitaries hospitality in castles with or without furnishings and food. French kings and nobles employed a household official, the harbinger, to travel ahead and arrange for quarters, food, and fodder; they ensured the provision of sufficient bedsteads, collecting from the neighborhood an adequate supply of mattresses, straw, featherbeds, sheets, and cushions, and saw that the tapestries were hung before royalty's arrival.

All classes stayed at inns. Even royalty found the accommodations at some inns adequate, doubtless after the king's harbinger had seen to it that the furnishings and provisions were what they should be. Those in modest circumstances ate at the landlord's table, but travelers with a servant frequently bought food and firewood from the innkeeper and the servant cooked the meal. This custom enabled persons seeking favors from government officials to entertain them in a suitable style. The provisions so purchased sometimes lasted several meals. At inns, a noble would sleep in a bed in a private room, less important people on pallets in the main room, and grooms frequently on straw in the stable with their charges.

In the course of the 15th century, some of the peculiarly medieval values that had given prestige to travel in France began to decline. There were no longer the same reasons for travel to the Roman curia, because many of the appointments to offices and much of the litigation formerly decided there were now determined in France. Pilgrims had been objects of charity, because they were engaged in a pious mission, and students studying at French universities had been a cause of pride. Now, pilgrims began to be classed with vagabonds, and English students, because of the Hundred Years' War, were no longer welcome in France. German students preferred the newly founded universities in their own region. Despite this contraction, however, in the 15th century we find for the first time explicit expressions of pleasure in travel.

Marjorie N. Boyer

[See also: PILGRIMAGE; SHIPS AND SHIPPING; TRADE ROUTES]

TREASON. The political concept of treason developed in France during the 13th and 14th centuries and was closely interrelated with the increasingly defined notions of sovereignty, obedience, and just war. Before the 13th century, loyalty to the king was often conditional and formal defiance possible; customary law assigned treason the meaning of "treachery." By the second half of the century, however, Roman ideas of treason and *lèse-majesté* (literally, to "injure majesty") had been resurrected. Unlike the English, who in 1352 received their Statute of Treason, there was no such single enactment for the French. Legislation was constructed as circumstances required, often against the pretensions of seigneurs, towns, and church, all of which claimed degrees of legal autonomy. Though the principal features of treason law were in place by the early 14th century, it was not until the outbreak of the Hundred Years' War that earnest prosecution began. By the reign of Louis XI (r. 1461–83), the charge of treason could be a serious political weapon.

Treason law itself, as a means to punish and deter, embodied a wide definition. Virtually all treason came under the heading of *lèse-majesté:* crimes against the king, the crown, or the kingdom. Among the offenses were regicide, attempted assassination, war against the king, consorting with the enemy, breaches of loyalty, crimes disregarding the king's sovereignty, and treason by word.

Treasonable offenses could be tried in a number of ways, most commonly by the king and his council, or, by the late 14th century, the Parlement de Paris. The 15th century saw the creation of the Grands Jours and provincial parlements, courts that were also competent to try treason.

The penalties for treason included fines, the confiscation of all movable and immovable property by the crown, and the capital punishments of decapitation, hanging, and drawing and/or quartering. It was possible to receive a royal pardon for treasonable offenses, though it could be challenged and did not necessarily provide for a full restitution.

Through the middle of the 17th century, French treason law remained heavily based on late-medieval precedents, and was an important part in the consolidation of royal authority.

Robert A. Bennett

Beaumanoir, Philippe de. *Coutumes de Beauvaisis,* ed. Amédée Salmon. 2 vols. Paris: Picard, 1899–1900.
Bellamy, John G. *The Laws of Treason in England in the Later Middle Ages.* Cambridge: Cambridge University Press, 1970.
Cuttler, Simon H. *The Laws of Treason and Treason Trials in Later Medieval France.* Cambridge: Cambridge University Press, 1981.

TRÉMOILLE, LA. The lordship of La Trémoille (Vienne) in Poitou produced one of the longest-lived noble houses in France. A lord of La Trémoille is first attested in the mid-11th century, but the family passed through twelve generations before achieving national prominence with Gui VI and his brother Guillaume, both of whom were important 14th-century royal commanders and chamberlains of Philip the Bold, duke of Burgundy. They both died on the crusade to Nicopolis. Gui VI made his family's fortune by marrying Marie de Sully, heiress not only to the lordship of Sully but to the important lordship of Craon in Anjou. Their son, Georges de La Trémoille (1385–1446), did not follow his father's Burgundian allegiance but became grand chamberlain of Charles VII and was the most influential figure at court until his ouster in 1433. His hostility to Jeanne d'Arc and Arthur de Richemont, the principal French heroes of their day, and his participation in the Praguerie of 1440 have left him with a bad reputation among historians. His sons, Louis de La Tremoille and Georges, lord of Craon, although hereditary chamberlains of Burgundy, generally served Louis XI, of whom Georges II was a particular favorite, holding important military commands and serving as bailiff of Touraine. The son of Louis de La Trémoille, Louis II (1460–1525), was an illustrious French commander, serving Anne de Beaujeu in Brittany in the 1480s and, with younger members of the family, playing an important role in the Italian wars of the early 16th century.

John Bell Henneman, Jr.

La Trémoille, Georges de. *Archives d'un serviteur de Louis XI,* ed. Louis, duc de La Trémoille. Nantes: Grimaud, 1888.
La Trémoille, Louis, duc de. *Les La Trémoille pendant cinq siècles.* 5 vols. Nantes: Grimaud, 1890–96.

TRENCAVEL. Possession of five great fiefs—Albi, Nîmes, Béziers, Agde, and Carcassonne—established the power of the family of Trencavel in the 12th century. The origins of the family may be traced to the viscounts of Albi, who appear in the 10th century. Bernard-Aton II (r. 956–74) added through marriage the viscounty of Nîmes. In 1066, the marriage of Raymond-Bernard, surnamed Trencavel, viscount of Albi and Nîmes, with Ermengarde, heiress of the counties of Béziers and Agde, assembled the vast domains that constituted the patrimony of the Trencavels. After her husband's death in 1074, she seized control also of the county of Carcassonne. The reign of Bernard-Aton IV (1074–1129), under the strong hand of his mother, Ermengarde, saw the height of the Trencavels' power.

The viscounts' indulgence of the Cathar heresy precipitated their downfall in the 13th century. In 1179, Roger II suffered excommunication, and in 1209 the full weight of the Albigensian Crusade fell on his son Raymond-Roger. In 1240, the last viscount, Raymond Trencavel II, attempted to recover his lands by invasion. His forces were stopped at the siege of Carcassonne, and in 1247 he ceded his rights to the king. Granted several small fiefs within his old domains, Raymond Trencavel was still alive in 1263. His son, Roger de Béziers, died on crusade at Tunis. The last of the Trencavels, Béatrix de Béziers, died sometime after 1322, possessing the small towns of Cesseras and Belvèze.

Alan Friedlander

[See also: ALBI; ALBIGENSIAN CRUSADE; BÉZIERS; CARCASSONNE; LANGUEDOC]

Cheyette, Frederic L. "The 'Sale' of Carcassonne to the Counts of Barcelona (1067–1070) and the Rise of the Trencavels." *Speculum* 63 (1988): 826–64.
d'Alauzier, Louis. "L'héritage des Trencavels." *Annales du Midi* 62 (1950): 181–86.
Dupont, André. "Le vicomte Bernard-Aton IV (1074–1129)." *Mémoires de l'Académie de Nîmes,* 7th ser., 56 (1965–67): 153–77.
Guilaine, Jean, and Daniel Fabre. *Histoire de Carcassonne.* Toulouse: Privat, 1984.
Rouillan-Castex, Sylvette. "Bernard-Aton Trencavel et les Carcassonnais." *Carcassonne et sa région: fédération historique du Languedoc méditerranéen et du Roussillon* (1970): 147–51.

TRÉSOR DES CHARTES. According to legend, Philip II Augustus established the Trésor des Chartes as a repository for crown papers following the loss of important documents during his flight from Fréteval in 1194. The Trésor's documented history dates from 1231, when it was already housed near the Sainte-Chapelle. The archive was under the control of the chancellor and the chancellery was its primary source of documents. Philip IV created an office of *garde des chartes* in 1307. Between 1371 and 1391, Gérard de Montaigu completed the first inventory, which divided the collection into *layettes* of charters and chronological *régistres*. Not only were state papers, such as treaties and *ordonnances*, preserved, but lesser materials like pardons and ennoblements were synopsized (for a fee) in the registers as well. Supplanted by court and agency archives in the 16th century, the Trésor virtually ceased acquisitions by 1600. In 1808, it entered the Archives Nationales as series J and JJ.

Throughout its history, the archive proved an invaluable source of documentation for royal spokesmen and legists. Gallican theorists drew on it in producing the *Somnium viridarii* (a tract known in its French translation as the *Songe du vergier*) in the 14th century, and Dupuy and Godefroy used it in extending the doctrine of inalienability to justify Bourbon conquests in their *Traité des droits du roy* in the 17th. The riches of the archive inspired a vital tradition of medieval scholarship highlighted by Dom Mabillon's *De re diplomatica* of 1681. This French archival tradition climaxed with the establishment of the Archives Nationales after 1789 and the École des Chartes in 1821.

Paul D. Solon

Favier, Jean, ed. *Les archives nationales, état général des fonds.* Paris: Archives Nationales, 1978, Vol. 1.

Kelley, Donald R. *Foundations of Modern Historical Scholarship.* New York: Columbia University Press, 1970.

Laborde, H. François de. "Étude sur la constitution du Trésor des Chartes." In *Layettes du Trésor des Chartes,* ed. Alexandre Teulet. Paris: Plon, 1863–1909, Vol. 5, pp. i–ccxxiv.

TRISTAN DE NANTEUIL. The last chanson de geste in the Nanteuil Cycle. Dating to the mid-14th century, *Tristan de Nanteuil* is found in one manuscript of the 15th century (B.N. fr. 1478) and comprises 23,361 rhymed Alexandrines.

The poem begins with Gui de Nanteuil and Aiglentine leaving Nanteuil to rescue Aye d'Avignon and her husband, Ganor. Aiglentine is captured and sold to the Sultan of Babylon. Her son, Tristan, is separated from her but is saved by a siren, who feeds him her miraculous milk. A hind also absorbs some of that milk and reaches a monstrous size. It carries away Tristan and rears him in the wilds. While living in savage state, Tristan captures Blanchandine, daughter of the king of Armenia, and has a son, Raimon, by her. Blanchandine is eventually baptized and marries Tristan, but later, while disguised as a knight, she is forced to marry Clarinde. Thinking Tristan has died, Blanchandine, before the wedding night, allows herself to be changed into a man by an angel. Clarinde and Blanchandin(e) have a son, Gilles. Gui and Aiglentine, on their way to reclaim their fief of Nanteuil, are killed by the traitors Persant and Macaire. Aye d'Avignon dies of grief. Charlemagne agrees to return the fiefs of Avignon and Nanteuil to the rightful heir, Raimon. Tristan is killed by Garcion, his illegitimate son.

The author knew the previous poems of the cycle, since several of the well-known members of the Nanteuil family participate in the poem's multifarious adventures. Although cast in the traditional epic mold, *Tristan de Nanteuil* is a complex poem that includes many supernatural and fantastic elements and many important romance themes, such as the Change of Sex, the Handless Maiden, and the Hermit Saint. In addition to the poems of the Nanteuil Cycle, the author of *Tristan* must have known the *Vie de saint Gilles* by Guillaume de Berneville, *Guillaume de Palerne, Huon de Bordeaux,* Chrétien's *Erec,* the *Roman de la Violette,* the *Vie de saint Jean Bouche d'or,* the *Estoire de Merlin,* and *Lion de Bourges.*

Jean-Louis Picherit

[See also: CHANSON DE GESTE; *HUON DE BORDEAUX;* LATE EPIC; NANTEUIL CYCLE]

Sinclair, Keith V., ed. *Tristan de Nanteuil, chanson de geste inédite.* Assen: Van Gorcum, 1971.

———. *Tristan de Nanteuil: Thematic Infrastructure and Literary Creation.* Tübingen: Niemeyer, 1983.

TRISTAN ROMANCES. In the obscure origins of the Tristan legend, which forms an important branch of the Matter of Britain, one can distinguish several strata. The hero is possibly of Pictish origin: Drust, son of Talorc, who in Celtic became Drystan or Trystan. His story, linked to that of Arthur and his earliest companions (see, e.g., the Welsh *Triads,* where Tristan is also the lover of Essylt, King Marc's wife), may have been elaborated by Celtic storytellers on the model of a famous Irish elopement tale, the story of Diarmaid and Grainne; set and developed in Cornwall, at Tintagel, it might have become associated there with traditions about King Marc. But the subsequent influence of Brittany was significant, providing, among other motifs, the story of the hero's parents and the episode of Tristan and Iseut's marriage. Other motifs, such as the dragon fight, the search for the golden-haired princess, and the man torn between two women, can be traced more generally to popular tales, classical mythology, and other sources.

It was in the Plantagenêt domains, both insular and continental, that Breton and other Celtic storytellers transmitted the legend to their French counterparts. It was profoundly remodeled, owing to the demands of a different society—feudalism gave new meaning to the conflict between love and moral, societal, and religious principles—and a new cultural and literary context, marked by the ethos of *fin'amor* and the first manifestations of troubadour poetry and the courtly romance. From allusions in troubadour lyrics (ca. 1130–50), iconographic testimony, and references to sources, it is possible to deduce a sort of standard, or "vulgate," version of the lovers' story, organized along biographical lines and relating the hero's youthful adventures, from his birth to the scene of the love potion; love's trials, from the potion to the return from the Forest of Morois; and the hero's exile, marriage, return trips to Cornwall, and Liebestod. More satisfactory than Bédier's rigid archetypal reconstitution, the notion of a "vulgate" version (Béroul's *estoire*?) explains both the relative stability of the main story and the important variations from poet to poet. It is important to recall that the famous pun on Tristan/*triste* 'sad' cannot go back beyond the "French" stage of the legend.

The only complete 12th-century version based on the "vulgate" is that in Middle High German by Eilhart von Oberg (ca. 1170–80). Béroul's fragment (ca. 1180), the first part of which is closely parallel to Eilhart, is also faithful to the "vulgate," unlike that of Thomas d'Angleterre (ca. 1175), which moves consciously away from it. Thomas's version, summarized in the Norwegian prose of Brother Robert (ca. 1130), was freely adapted ca. 1210 in Gottfried von Strassburg's unfinished poem. The motif of Tristan returning to see Iseut was used again in the two anonymous *Folies* and in Marie de France's *Chievrefoil*. Some elements of the legend reappeared in the *Donnei des amanz* (ca. 1200) and in Gerbert de Montreuil's continuation of Chrétien de Troyes's *Perceval*. The 13th-century *Prose Tristan* is the only complete version of the legend preserved in French.

But the influence of the Tristan story goes well beyond the group of texts that narrate it and the adaptations that it inspired in nearly every western language. Accepted, attacked (notably by Chrétien), reformulated to accord with the courtly ethic (in the *Prose Tristan*), this legend of a fatal passion became one of the primary representations of love, influencing western thought up to our own time. The lovers were frequently represented in medieval art, especially in ivories and manuscript miniatures. Thirty-five scenes from the Tristan legend are illustrated on the Chertsey Abbey tiles (ca. 1270).

Emmanuèle Baumgartner

[See also: BÉROUL; *DONNEI DES AMANZ*; *FOLIES TRISTAN*; MARIE DE FRANCE; *PROSE TRISTAN*; THOMAS D'ANGLETERRE]

Walter, Philippe, and David Lacroix, eds. and trans. *Tristan et Iseut: les poèmes français, la saga norroise*. Paris: Livre de Poche, 1990. [Includes editions and modern French translations of all the medieval French poems, and a translation of the Norse saga.]

Baumgartner, Emmanuèle. *Tristan et Iseut: de la légende aux récits en vers*. Paris: Presses Universitaires de France, 1987.

Ferrante, Joan M. *The Conflict of Love and Honor: The Medieval Tristan Legend in France, Germany and Italy*. Paris: Mouton, 1973.

Shirt, David J. *The Old French Tristan Poems: A Bibliographical Guide*. London: Grant and Cutler, 1980.

TRIVIUM/QUADRIVIUM. *See* LIBERAL ARTS

TROBAIRITZ. Although the term has been found only once in Old Occitan (in *Flamenca*, a 13th-c. romance), in English "trobairitz" answers the need for a feminine alternative to "troubadour," which has been naturalized in En-

glish since the 18th century. The root is *trobar* 'to compose,' and the suffix expresses the agent, either female (*-airitz*) or male (*-ador*). Thus, "trobairitz" means "woman who composes" (Occitan lyric poetry).

We know about twenty trobairitz by name, and their corpus includes some thirty-two songs. (These figures are vague because of the difficulty in distinguishing real trobairitz from fictional characters, either named or anonymous, who speak in dialogue poems.) Only two trobairitz left more than one song apiece: the Comtessa de Dia, who sings of passionate love, happy or unhappy, in four *cansos*, or love songs, and Castelloza, who adopts a melancholy, even masochistic, tone in three *cansos* of certain attribution and a fourth that is anonymous in the manuscript. In another *canso*, Beatritz de Romans addresses Lady Maria in language that seems warmly affectionate to some readers, while others consider it lesbian. In a *sirventes*, or satire, Gormonda de Montpellier responds vigorously to a diatribe against the Roman church by Guilhem Figueira, matching his stanzaic form, his rhyme scheme, and many of his rhyming words while reversing his polemical intention. In the genres in dialogue, the trobairitz debate questions of amorous casuistry, usually with men, and often show greater willingness than the troubadours to depart from courtly conventions in order to gain satisfaction in love or demonstrate their independence. In one strikingly realistic exchange of *coblas*, or couplets, the sisters Alais and Iselda ask Carenza whether they should marry, and she advises them to become brides of Christ.

The trobairitz are fewer in number than troubadours (about 5 percent as many), and their extant compositions are fewer still (about 1 percent as many as we have by the men), although far more important than such a comparison would suggest for our understanding of medieval poetry and life. Most of the trobairitz about whom we have information were active during the period from ca. 1180 to 1260, that is, they began later and stopped earlier than the troubadours, whose recorded activity begins with Guilhem IX ca. 1100 and continues to 1300 or later. This disparity may reflect the evolution of the status of women, who briefly regained during this period some of the rights they had earlier enjoyed, before their situation continued its long decline toward a legal status comparable with that of minors.

Stylistically, the trobairitz address the beloved directly more often than do troubadours; they prefer more negative language, in order to express frustration, deprivation, or strong feelings in general; and they tend to use more verbs in the subjunctive mood, expressing uncertainty or desire, or in the past tense, referring to real relationships that have a past, whereas the troubadours tend more toward factual statements about the present. The trobairitz provide a dramatic corrective to the image of the lady in many male songs of *fin'amors*, since they are neither distant, unapproachable, nor speechless. Their songs provide a key to understanding *fin'amors*, both male and female, more adequately than it has traditionally been understood.

The male lyrics of courtly love that echoed across Europe were rarely interrupted by a female voice. Marie de France was a contemporary author of narrative poetry, but among the trouvères, or lyric poets of the *Langue d'oïl*, we find scarcely any women, although the trouvères left as many songs as did the troubadours. Nor do we find women writers of medieval lyric in Galician, Castilian, German, or English. It is probable that one Italian woman, the "Compiuta Donzella," wrote during the period of the *dolce stil nuovo*, but she left us only three sonnets. The fictional women's songs, or *chansons de femme*, in French, Galician, and German seem to have been written by men. Most medieval women who wrote did so in Latin (Héloïse, Hildegard of Bingen) or, if in the vernacular, on religious subjects (Catherine of Siena, Marguerite Porete); women began to write on secular subjects in other languages only in the 15th century (Florencia Pinar, Christine de Pizan). The trobairitz provide a rare avenue of approach to secular female experience in the 12th and 13th centuries.

William D. Paden

[See also: TROUBADOUR POETRY; *VIDAS* AND *RAZOS*; WOMEN'S SONGS]

Bruckner, Matilda Tomaryn, Laurie Shephard, and Sarah White, eds. *Songs of the Women Troubadours: An Edition and Translation*. New York: Garland, 1995.

Rieger, Angelica, ed. *Trobairitz: Der Beitrag der Frau in der altokzitanischen höfischen Lyrik: Edition des Gesamtkorpus*. Tübingen: Niemeyer, 1991.

Schultz[-Gora], Oscar, ed. *Die provenzalischen Dichterinnen: Biographien und Texte nebst Anmerkungen und einer Einleitung*. Leipzig: Fock, 1888.

Bogin, Meg. *The Women Troubadours*. New York: Paddington, 1976.

Paden, William D., ed. *The Voice of the Trobairitz: Perspectives on the Women Troubadours*. Philadelphia: University of Pennsylvania Press, 1989.

TROPES, ORDINARY. Texted compositions written to supplement Ordinary chants for the Mass (Kyrie, Gloria, Sanctus, Agnus Dei). Although the Credo was rarely troped, a small repertoire of tropes for the Benedicamus Domino, the piece sung at the close of the hours of the Office and at the close of Mass during Lent, exists as well. Because chants for the Ordinary were being composed during the 9th and 10th centuries, the same period in which Ordinary tropes were first written, there has been argument over the extent to which Ordinary chants were originally conceived with their tropes.

True Kyrie tropes, to be distinguished from the syllabically texted Latin Kyrie, are rare and originated early, with French sources containing even fewer of them than manuscripts from east of the Rhine and from Italy. The music of these chants is distinguished in style from that of Kyrie chants in general; the tropes are added to Kyries with greater flexibility than is found with many Proper chants. Gloria tropes comprise a larger and more varied repertory of texts and music. Some of the verses of Gloria tropes, the "wandering verses," are used in a variety of positions and combinations and may have been derived from Gallican chants, especially the litanies. Sanctus and

Agnus Dei tropes were often of two types: those that introduce the chant and help establish the feast (making an Ordinary chant Proper) were of special importance in southern French sources; other trope elements were interpolated within the petitions of the chant, and, within the Agnus Dei, created a piece resembling a litany. Iversen has found that Sanctus and Agnus Dei tropes dating from the 11th century and written in northwestern France and England often develop trinitarian themes. In the following example of a Sanctus trope, from a 12th-century source from the Norman abbey of Saint-Évroult, the trope transforms the chant, causing each statement to be addressed to a particular member of the Trinity:

> SANCTUS,
> Pater, ex quo omnia, deus.
> SANCTUS,
> Filius, per quem omnia, deus.
> SANCTUS
> Spiritus, in quo omnia, colendus,
> DEUS SABAOTH.
> PLENI SUNT CAELI ET TERRA GLORIA TUA, etc.

Margot Fassler

[See also: TROPES, PROPER]

Iversen, Gunilla, ed. *Corpus Troporum VII: Tropes du Sanctus*. Stockholm: Almqvist and Wiksell, 1990.

———. *Corpus Troporum IV: Tropes de l'Agnus Dei*. Stockholm: Almqvist and Wiksell, 1980.

Bjork, David. "The Kyrie Trope." *Journal of the American Musicological Society* 33 (1980): 1–41.

Crocker, Richard. "The Troping Hypothesis." *Musical Quarterly* 52 (1969): 183–203.

Falconer, Keith Andrew. *Some Early Tropes to the Gloria*. Diss. Princeton University, 1989.

Husmann, Heinrich. *Tropen- und Sequenzenhandschriften: Répertoire International des Sources Musicales*. Munich: Henle, 1964, Sec. B, Vol. 5, pt. 1.

TROPES, PROPER. Beginning in the 9th century, several Proper chants for the Mass (Introits, Alleluias, Offertories, Communions) were commonly ornamented with supplemental texted compositions in centers both east and west of the Rhine; great responsories for Matins also were provided with tropes, only much more rarely. These later additions to Proper Gregorian chants, both the texts and the music, are known today as Proper tropes, and in medieval manuscripts as *tropi*. Proper tropes served several functions: they expanded the chants to which they were attached, thus allowing more time for ceremonial action and communal reflection; they commented upon both the original chants and the particular parts of the liturgy to which they belonged; they helped establish the significance of individual feasts and seasons of the church year; and they further defined the offices of the clergy. Like the first sequences, tropes were created by the Franks, on both sides of the Rhine, and early examples may preserve elements of the varied Gallican liturgical traditions that were suppressed throughout the second half of the 8th century. Tropes and sequences were never standardized, and each source reflects the liturgical taste and religious ideals not only of the geographical region in which it originated but of an individual monastic community or church. The repertoire of each source is somehow unique, even though it may resemble those of other sources from the same region, containing many of the same pieces.

Each genre of Proper tropes is distinctive, having been created to ornament a particular kind of chant and to explain its liturgical function. The most extensive repertoire of Proper tropes comprises those for the Introit, the first Proper chant of the liturgy. Introit tropes consist of either individual lines, which often comprise sets or groups of lines interpolated into a particular chant. Thus, the Introits of highly ranked feasts would characteristically be sung with an introductory trope, perhaps the longest of all individual lines; the Introit antiphons were subdivided in conventional ways as well, and yet other trope lines would preface each of the divisions. Both the psalm verses for this chant as well as the doxology might also have an introductory trope. Further, each time the Introit antiphon was repeated, a new set of tropes might well be sung. In the example below, taken from a 13th-century Gradual from Chartres cathedral, the text of the Introit, taken from Isaiah 9:6, is written in capitals and the trope texts in lower case.

Gaudeamus hodie quia deus descendit de celis et
    propter nos in terris
[PUER NATUS EST NOBIS]
Quem prophete diu vaticinati sunt
[ET FILIUS DATUS EST NOBIS]
Hunc a patre iam novimus esse missum in mundum
[CUIUS IMPERIUM SUPER HUMERUM EIUS ET
    VOCABITUR NOMEN EIUS]
Admirabilis consiliarius deus fortis princeps pacis
[MAGNI CONSILII ANGELUS.]

Let us rejoice today because God descended from
    heaven to earth for our sakes
[A boy is born to us]
Whom long the prophets predicted
[and a son is given to us]
Now we know that this child was sent into the world
    by the father
[upon whose shoulder dominion rests and his name
    will be called]
wonderful counselor, mighty God, prince of peace
[angel of great counsel].

The interrelationships among the many trope manuscripts continue to pose difficulties: texts and music were transmitted throughout the late 9th and early 10th centuries both orally and in early, no longer extant written records. Consistent patterns of variants capable of sustaining theories of transmission have not been uncovered as yet. Most repertoires of Proper tropes died out during the 12th century in France and England, but a few pieces survived this watershed in regions east of the Rhine.

Margot Fassler

[See also: TROPES, ORDINARY]

Björkvall, Gunilla, ed. *Corpus Troporum V: Les deux tropaires d'Apt, mss. 17 et 18: inventaire analytique des mss. et édition des textes uniques.* Stockholm: Almqvist and Wiksell, 1986.

Björkvall, Gunilla, Gunilla Iversen, and Ritva Jonsson, eds. *Corpus Troporum III: Cycles de Pâques.* Stockholm: Almqvist and Wiksell, 1982.

Reier, Ellen J., ed. *The Introit Trope Repertory at Nevers: MSS Paris B.N. lat. 9449 and Paris B.N. n.a. lat. 1235.* Diss. University of California at Berkeley, 1981.

Evans, Paul. *The Early Trope Repertory of Saint Martial de Limoges.* Princeton: Princeton University Press, 1970.

Jonsson, Ritva. *Corpus troporum I: Cycle de Noël.* Stockholm: Almqvist and Wiksell, 1975.

Planchart, Alejandro. *The Repertory of Tropes at Winchester.* 2 vols. Princeton: Princeton University Press, 1977.

TROUBADOUR POETRY. The lyric poets who wrote in Occitan (also called Provençal), the language of southern France, during the 12th and 13th centuries left an extensive corpus of songs remarkable for their diversity, quality, and influence. The troubadours made *fin'amors*, or "true love," known now also as "courtly love," their subject of choice, and by singing of it with passionate intensity inspired imitation across Europe: in northern France among the trouvères (the word is the French form corresponding to "troubadour"); twice in Italy, first in the Sicilian School of Frederick II Hohenstaufen early in the 13th century, then again in the *dolce stil nuovo* of Dante and his friends; in Germany among the Minnesinger; in Portugal and England. The troubadours were not the first poets who wrote in a medieval vernacular: Mozarabic poets in Spain had composed *kharjas* (vernacular strophes in Romance dialect concluding songs in Arabic) for more than a century; there survives an extensive body of poetry in Old English and Old High German; and love poetry had long been written in Latin and continued to be. Indeed, it has been argued that courtly love is a universal tendency of the human heart that has appeared independently in widely scattered cultures from ancient Egypt to medieval Georgia. But the poetic tradition launched by the troubadours represents a high point of medieval secular culture and provided impetus for the transition into the Renaissance.

The Occitan word *trobador* is a compound of the root *trobar* 'to compose' with the suffix expressing agent, and thus means "one who composes," presumably a man. The feminine suffix produces *trobairitz* 'a woman who composes.' The origin of the verb *trobar* has been sought in classical Latin, medieval Latin, and Arabic, but no consensus has emerged, just as agreement on the origin of *fin'amor* has not been reached. There were contacts with the Mozarabic culture of Spain, but no literary influence has been established; closer yet were the Latin clerical poets of the "Loire school," such as Baudri of Bourgueil and Marbode of Rennes. It is not certain whether the earliest preserved troubadour texts followed a large body of songs that have been lost, or whether the first troubadour we know was one of the first poets to use the vernacular in the Midi. In any case, we know that Eble, viscount of Ventadorn, wrote songs contemporary with the earliest ones preserved, although none of his work has survived.

The earliest troubadour whose works we have is Guilhem IX, duke of Aquitaine and count of Poitiers (1071–1126), who left a small number of love songs, some courtly, others bawdy, and a song of departure from the world. In the following generation, Marcabru, a *joglar*, or performer, of Gascon origin, excoriated the decadence of courtly society in satirical songs but also created the prototypical *pastorela*, in which a witty and sensible shepherdess fends off the advances of the narrator. Around the middle of the 12th century, Peire d'Alvernhe and Raimbaut d'Aurenga developed the concept of *trobar clus*, or "closed composition," in contrast to *trobar leu*, the "easy style." Troubadour love song reached a peak in the poetry of Bernart de Ventadorn, who continued the "school" of Eble de Ventadorn with intensely personal lyrics depicting the joy and torment of the lover buffeted by desire and frustration. Toward the end of the century, Bertran de Born sang of his delight in combat, developed the satirical tradition stemming from Marcabru, and took a skeptical or mocking attitude toward *fin'amor*.

The 13th century witnessed the crusade against the Albigensians (1209–29, with sporadic continuations to 1244), carried out by a French army at the instigation of Pope Innocent III in an effort to extirpate heretical tendencies that had taken root in Languedoc. Peire Cardenal wrote songs critical of unworthy clergy and defended the interests of Count Raymond of Toulouse, whose lands were invaded and eventually subjected to the king of France; but Peire professed an orthodox Catholic faith himself and did not defend the Albigensian creed. Scholars have explained the decline of troubadour poetry as the effect of destruction of courtly society during the crusade, but the explanation is unsatisfactory: the crusade ravaged Languedoc but not Provence to the east or the Limousin to the north, and troubadours continued to compose until the end of the century. Among those who did were some of the most prolific, including Peire Cardenal, Guiraut Riquier, and the Catalan Cerverí de Girona. Poetry continued to be composed in Occitan, though with little distinction, through the 14th and 15th centuries. Those who wrote it are referred to as "poets," not as "troubadours"; they composed written verse, not songs, for academic competitions organized by the *Consistòri de la Subregaya Companhia del Gai Saber*, or "Academy of the Most Joyful Company of the Joyful Wisdom," at Toulouse. The rules for this competition were formulated as the *Leys d'Amors*, or "Laws of Love" (where love is understood as referring to love poetry), a massive codification of approved usage compiled by Guilhem Molinier in 1341.

The medium of troubadour expression seems to have evolved from an original one that emphasized live performance with musical accompaniment and permitted a significant oral component in performance, transmission, and possibly composition, toward written composition with or without musical accompaniment or live performance, and with a correspondingly reduced role for orality. Evidence for such an evolution, necessarily indirect, includes the fluidity, or *mouvance*, of both text and music, especially in early compositions, and the decreasing frequency of reference to the *joglar*, or performer of the troubadour's work.

By the end of the 12th century, Occitan poetry had attained sufficient prestige to produce a treatise by the Catalan Raimon Vidal called the *Règles de trobar*, or "Rules of Composition," and the tradition was continued, perhaps ca. 1240, by Uc Faidit in his *Donatz proensals*, or "Provençal Donatus," named after the author of a standard Latin grammar. In the early 13th century, the songs began to inspire prose commentaries called *razos*, or "reasons" for their composition, and biographical sketches of the troubadours called *vidas*, or "lives." The ninety-five extant manuscripts of troubadour composition represent a late stage in this evolution, beginning with the earliest manuscript, dated 1254 in the colophon, and continuing into the 14th century. The transmission of earlier troubadour compositions into these manuscripts must have involved written forms that are not preserved, perhaps parchment rolls, and may have involved oral transmission. The notation of melodies, which is found in only four of the manuscripts, is nonmensural, taking no account of rhythm or duration of the individual note. The choice of such notation rather than the mensural notation employed at the same time for other kinds of music seems to imply that troubadour musical performance was declamatory, that is, that the rhythm was determined in performance by the singer on the basis of linguistic or poetic considerations. It follows that performance was probably not accompanied, since the rhythmic structure was not standardized.

The genres of lyric composition took shape during this evolution of the medium. The earliest troubadours, such as Guilhem IX and Marcabru, made no generic distinctions but called their work collectively *cansos* or *vers*, simply "songs." Toward the end of the 12th century, the term *canso*, under the influence of the increasing prestige of the theme of *fin'amor*, became specialized in the sense "love song," in contrast with *sirventes*, or "satire," which could be personal, political, or moralizing. Less frequent genres include the *pastorela*, the *alba* (dawn song), the *planh* (funeral lament), the crusade song, and the *tenso* (debate). These terms were integrated into an elaborate taxonomy in the poetic treatises. The preserved corpus of troubadour songs includes about 2,500 compositions by about 450 known poets, of whom perhaps twenty rank as major figures. Some twenty others are women (*trobairitz*). About 1,000 songs are *cansos*; about 500 are *sirventes*; about 500 more are *coblas*, a genre first attested ca. 1190 comprising independent stanzas; and the remaining 500 are *pastorelas*, *albas*, *planhs*, crusade songs, *tensos*, and minor genres. The music is preserved for about 250 songs.

William D. Paden

[See also: *ALBA/AUBE*; ARNAUT DANIEL; BERENGUER DE PALAZOL; BERNART DE VENTADORN; BERTRAN DE BORN; CERCAMON; CERVERÍ DE GIRONA; COURTLY LOVE; FOLQUET DE MARSELHA; GAUCELM FAIDIT; GIRAUT DE BORNELH; GUILHEM IX; GUILHEM DE MONTANHAGOL;

GUIRAUT RIQUIER; JAUFRE RUDEL; *LEYS D'AMORS;* MARCABRU; MONTAUDON, MONK OF; *NOVAS;* *PASTOURELLE/PASTORELA;* PEIRE CARDENAL; PEIRE D'ALVERNHE; PEIRE VIDAL; *PLANH/COMPLAINTE;* RAIMBAUT D'AURENGA; RAIMBAUT DE VAQUEIRAS; RAIMON DE MIRAVAL; RHYTHM; RIGAUT DE BERBEZILH; *SIRVENTES;* SORDEL; *TENSO/DÉBAT;* TROBAIRITZ; TROUVÈRE POETRY; VERSIFICATION; *VIDAS* AND *RAZOS*]

Hill, Raymond Thompson, and T.G. Bergin, eds. *Anthology of the Provençal Troubadours.* 2nd ed. rev. by T.G. Bergin with Susan Olson, William D. Paden, Jr., and Nathaniel Smith. 2 vols. New Haven: Yale University Press, 1973.

Riquer, Martín de, ed. *Los trovadores: historia literaria y textos.* 3 vols. Barcelona: Planeta, 1975.

Boase, Roger. *The Origin and Meaning of Courtly Love: A Critical Study of European Scholarship.* Manchester: Manchester University Press, 1977.

Chambers, Frank M. *An Introduction to Old Provençal Versification.* Philadelphia: American Philosophical Society, 1985.

Davenson, Henri (pseudonym of Henri-Irénée Marrou). *Les troubadours.* Paris: Seuil, 1961.

Jeanroy, Alfred. *La poésie lyrique des troubadours.* 2 vols. Toulouse: Privat, 1934.

Taylor, Robert A. *La littérature occitane du moyen âge: bibliographie sélective et critique.* Toronto: University of Toronto Press, 1977.

van der Werf, Hendrik. *The Chansons of the Troubadours and Trouvères: A Study of the Melodies and Their Relation to the Poems.* Utrecht: Oosthoek, 1972.

TROUVÈRE POETRY. Well over 2,000 strophic songs for single voice have survived from the rich production of the 12th- and 13th-century trouvères of northern France, preserved in about two dozen chansonniers and other manuscript sources dating from the 13th and 14th centuries. Almost half of the texts are unique, while the rest occur in up to ten or more versions; about two-thirds survive with their music. The trouvères, like their Provençal counterparts, the troubadours, were poet-composers who singlehandedly created both poem and melody as a unified whole. However, the vagaries of oral and written transmission, producing intended or unintended changes by performers (jongleurs) or scribes, have left us numerous instances of significant variation among redactions. For the same reasons, but also and more strikingly as a result of deliberate imitation or borrowing among trouvères, we have many a poem with two or more musical settings and many a melody accompanying two or more poems; in particular, many devotional songs, contrafacta of secular compositions, fall into this last category. Opening with the earliest known French lyrics, the 150-year span of the trouvère repertory closes with the abandonment of its principal genres, the emergence of "fixed" forms, and the advent of a verbal lyricism not tied to music.

About half the corpus shows some kind of authorial ascription, but many of the roughly 250 trouvères identified are otherwise unknown; many of the attributions are uncertain; and the distribution is extremely uneven, running from over 130 trouvères credited with one or two pieces each to only a dozen with more than twenty, but four of these—Gace Brulé, Thibaut de Champagne, Jehan Bretel, and Adam de la Halle—with upward of sixty. Socially, the trouvères were quite diverse, including men better remembered for other literary achievements, such as Chrétien de Troyes (the earliest known composer of lyric in French), Guiot de Provins, Richard de Fournival, and Adam de la Halle; powerful feudal lords, such as Thibaut de Champagne; and even artists who doubled as itinerant jongleurs, such as Colin Muset and Rutebeuf. But most of them seem to have belonged to some rank of the nobility, especially in the early, "classical," decades that produced illustrious figures like Blondel de Nesle, Gace Brulé, and the Châtelain de Coucy; or, particularly in the 13th century, to the bourgeoisie of the commercial north, a group including, among others, Guillaume le Vinier, Jehan Bretel, and Perrin d'Angicourt, as well as Adam de la Halle. Though the activity of the first group was centered in aristocratic courts, the artistic arena of the trouvères of Artois and Picardy tended to be poetic guilds (*puys* or *confréries*), notably the Puy d'Arras. Communication among the court-centered trouvères appears to have been just as intense as among the bourgeois, and to a great extent the two milieux were in contact with each other, elaborated the same lyric themes, and cultivated the same genres.

With few exceptions, their subject was love, and in the first-person *chanson d'amour*, or *grand chant courtois*, which celebrated—but less ecstatically—much the same courtly idea of true love that the troubadours had developed as *fin'amors*, they brought to the subject a high seriousness that made the genre, like the troubadours' *canso*, the ultimate expression of their artistic abilities. They sang of amorous longing and of the interplay between desire and creativity in terms that, for all their depersonalizing abstractness and conventional vocabulary, could yet reveal individual inventiveness, even virtuosity, and communicate an intense human experience. Different from the *canso*—never venturing into the hermeticism of *trobar clus*, for example, and veering away from the southern emphasis on *joy*, youth, and the power of love and the beloved to refine the sensibilities of the lover—the *grand chant* is nevertheless of the same genre and clearly a product of Provençal inspiration.

The prosody of the *grand chant*, as of the other genres, with the notable exception of the *lai-descort*, allows great freedom within the fundamental constraint of isostrophic form: that all stanzas be set to the same melody and therefore show not only the same number of lines but also an unvarying succession of (syllabically measured) line lengths. Most poems are five or six stanzas long, with stanzas normally comprising eight to ten lines and lines tending to be hepta-, octo-, or decasyllabic. Isometric stanzas are more usual than heterometric, which, though frequent, are more restrained in shape than the heterometric stanzas of lighter genres, such as the *pastourelle*. As for homophony, it is rhyme rather than assonance. Rhyme scheme reveals much the same stanza-to-stanza invariability as line-length succession, though the array of rhyme words in a given text rarely shows any repetition. The rhymes themselves, that is, the sounds that rhyme, may be repeated through all stanzas (*coblas unissonans*), change after every pair of stanzas (*coblas doblas*), or, much less commonly, change with each stanza (*coblas singulars*); other arrangements occur, too, as well as smaller rhyme-based devices serving to structure the text. The modern principle of alternating masculine (oxytonic) and feminine (paroxytonic) rhymes is unknown. A further structuring is sometimes achieved, though only rarely among the classical trouvères, through the adjunction of a refrain, normally invariable, at the end of each stanza. The initial stanza of a *grand chant* is always marked as introductory, whether by an evocation of nature or the desire to sing or by other exordial material. The conclusion is usually marked as well, whether in the last stanza or in a following partial stanza (the *envoi*), by a statement that "sends" the song to the beloved or some other auditor. The intervening stanzas tend toward an inherently lyrical semantic discreteness, a result of which is that it is not uncommon for the several manuscript redactions of a given poem to present them in different sequences. The usual internal structure of the *grand chant* stanza is bipartite, the first section (*frons*) being divided into two subsections (*pedes*, sing. *pes*) that are identical in meter and rhyme, and the second section (*cauda*) showing a freer sequence, as in: 8a 8b / 8a 8b // 8b 8a 8a 8b or 10a 10'b / 10a 10'b // 10a 10a 4'b 7c 7c.

This structure is widely paralleled by the overall melodic form AAB, in which musical *pes* and prosodic *pes* coincide, but in which the line-by-line development of B may readily diverge from the pattern suggested by the corresponding rhymes. The melodic construction of the *grand chant*, as of the other genres, is modal. Compared with other such music, the trouvère corpus is unusually rich in accidentals, including not only B-flat and B-natural but also E-flat, F-sharp, and C-sharp; extensive in range, with most melodies developed within the range of a seventh to a tenth, but others within considerably narrower or broader intervals; and ample in both its choice of finals and its ways of relating the final to the melodic ambitus. The *grand chant* is variable in its overall density of melismatic ornamentation, but it is infrequent for a given ornament to include more than four notes. In all these respects, there is broad variation from songbook to songbook, each of which, or each family of which, tends to show stylistic individuality; a consequence is the often marked diversity within multiple redactions of the same melody. But the most striking feature of the trouvères' melodies, and the one that has not ceased to generate heated controversy, is that, with only few exceptions, the manuscripts transmit them in nonmensural neumatic notation, that is, with no indication of rhythm. Theories have been proposed to fill the void—an undertaking essential to any performance of the music. Their spectrum moves from a strict application of the principles of modal rhythm, which would apparently deny the text, to the advocacy of a free declamatory rhythm that would reduce the importance of the music; propositions between these poles argue for a modal usage somehow responsive to poetic rhythm or a sort of isosyllabism effectively eliminating the ebb and flow of rhythm altogether. Cutting across all these theories are such questions as whether all lyric genres, including dance songs, are to be treated in the same fashion and, if not, how to differentiate among them, or whether certain melodic features point to particular rhythmic interpretations.

From the deep source of Provençal lyric, the trouvères derived not only the *grand chant* but also, in combination with local materials, the related crusade song and the heterostrophic *lai-descort*, both of which are well represented in the French corpus. The political or religious *serventois*, however, is of only passing importance compared with the southern *sirventes*, and the troubadours' *planh* is barely reflected in the few, heterogeneous death laments of the trouvères; much the same may be said of the *alba/aube*. The Provençal debate songs, on the other hand, proved a popular model, with the *jeu-parti* in particular showing a much greater development among the trouvères, especially in the bourgeois circle of Arras; similarly, the *pastourelle*, documented first in Provençal, came to be cultivated above all by the trouvères.

In addition to the lyric types deriving wholly or in part from the troubadours, the trouvère repertory includes genres indigenous to northern France. Though the Provençal-inspired tend toward a certain aristocratic tone, the natively French types incline, relatively speaking, toward a popular, even folkloric, character; while the former, moreover, are almost exclusively masculine in poetic voice, the latter give prominence to the feminine voice. Indeed, women's songs, embracing the *chanson de toile* and other types, form a significant segment of the trouvère corpus. Other purely French genres, certain of which came to be represented in Provençal as well, include some defined chiefly by their content, such as the *chanson pieuse* (devotional), *sotte chanson* (parodic), *reverdie* (springtime reverie), satirical songs, and songs of jongleur life, and others defined by their prosodic/musical form, sometimes reflecting a dance function, like ballette, *rondet* (or rondeau), *rotrouenge*, *estampie*, motet. Frequently occurring throughout this repertory—and in some genres, such as the ballette and rondeau, constituting a structural *sine qua non*—is the refrain, an apparently independent one- or two-line utterance that, like its modern counterpart, is invariable, cited recurrently at fixed intervals through the song (*chanson à refrain*), or else is variable, one of a succession of such utterances strung through the song at fixed intervals (*chanson avec des refrains*).

Samuel N. Rosenberg

[See also: ADAM DE LA HALLE; *ALBA/AUBE*; AUDEFROI LE BÂTARD; BALLADE; BALLETTE; BLONDEL DE NESLE; *CHANSON DE TOILE*; CHRÉTIEN DE TROYES; COLIN MUSET; CONON DE BÉTHUNE; COUCY, CHÂTELAIN DE; COURTLY LOVE; CRUSADE SONGS/*CHANSONS DE CROISADE*; GACE BRULÉ; *JEU-PARTI*; JONGLEUR; *LAI-DESCORT*; MULTIPLE REFRAIN SONGS (*CHANSONS AVEC DES REFRAINS*); PASTOURELLE/PASTORELA; *PUY*; *RESVERIE*; *REVERDIE*; RHYTHM; RUTEBEUF; *SIRVENTES*; THIBAUT DE CHAMPAGNE; TROUBADOUR POETRY; VERSIFICATION; *VERSUS*; WOMEN'S SONGS]

Bec, Pierre, ed. *La lyrique française au moyen âge (XIIe–XIIIe siècles): contribution à une typologie des genres poétiques médiévaux.* 2 vols. Paris: Picard, 1977–78, Vol. 1: *Études;* Vol. 2: *Textes.*

Boogaard, Nico H.J. van den, ed. *Rondeaux et refrains du 12e siècle au début du 14e.* Paris: Klincksieck, 1969.

Rosenberg, Samuel N., and Hans Tischler, eds. *Chanter m'estuet: Songs of the Trouvères.* Bloomington: Indiana University Press, 1981.

van der Werf, Hendrik, ed. *Trouvères-Melodien I–II.* Kassel: Bärenreiter, 1977–79.

Dragonetti, Roger. *La technique poétique des trouvères dans la chanson courtoise.* Bruges: De Tempel, 1960.

Linker, Robert W. *A Bibliography of Old French Lyrics.* University: Romance Monographs, 1979.

Mölk, Ulrich, and Friedrich Wolfzettel. *Répertoire métrique de la poésie lyrique des origines à 1350.* Munich: Fink, 1972.

Sadie, Stanley, ed. *The New Grove Dictionary of Music and Musicians.* 20 vols. London: Macmillan, 1980, Vol. 19, pp. 189–208.

Spanke, Hans. *G. Raynauds Bibliographie des altfranzösischen Liedes.* Leiden: Brill, 1955.

Zumthor, Paul. *Essai de poétique médiévale.* Paris: Seuil, 1972.

TROYES. One of the major commercial cities of Capetian France, Troyes (Aube) developed from the Roman *castrum* of Augustobona. Sited on a loop of the Seine in northeastern France, it was located near the intersection of major roads that linked it with Flanders to the north, Lyon and Italy to the south. Evangelized during the 3rd century, the city was saved from devastation by the Huns in the 5th century by the heroism of its bishop, St. Loup. Despite the rebuilding of the city's walls, Troyes and its cathedral were ruined during the period of Viking raids in the later 9th century. The city was long ruled by its bishops and as-

Troyes, Saint-Urbain, chevet. *Photograph: Clarence Ward Collection. Courtesy of Oberlin College.*

sumed importance only after the 10th century, when its counts (of Vermandois, then Blois) began assembling important territories to form the province of Champagne.

The city entered its heyday under Thibaut II le Grand (r. 1125–52) and Henri le Libéral (r. 1152–81). Thibaut shifted the center of the dynasty from Blois-Chartres to Troyes-Champagne, which at his death passed to his son Henri. Younger sons held Blois-Chartres as a fief from the count of Champagne. Under comital protection, the great fairs of Troyes flourished in the 12th century and stimulated the development of an extensive suburb west of the older *cité.* With the wealth derived from tolls on fair business, the counts, rather than the bishops, became the major sponsors of ecclesiastical and charitable institutions. Henry I, for example, established the collegiate church of Saint-Étienne adjacent to his palace, founded the Hôtel-Dieu, and supported the Benedictine convent of Notre-Dame-aux-Nonnains.

Because of its prominence as a commercial and financial center, Troyes was home to a sizable Jewish populace, concentrated at the western edge of the suburb, as indicated by such modern street names as the Rue de la Juiverie and Rue de la Synagogue. While the counts governed Troyes, the Jewish community seems to have prospered in a relatively tolerant atmosphere, engaging in active moneylending and entering other occupations as well. A Talmudic school established by Rashi (ca. 1039–1104) flourished in Troyes from the late 11th to the 13th century. With the advent of Capetian rule after 1284, their situa-

Troyes (Aube), Saint-Urbain. *Photograph courtesy of Whitney S. Stoddard.*

Troyes, Saint-Urbain, chevet vaults. *Photograph: Clarence Ward Collection. Courtesy of Oberlin College.*

tion deteriorated. In 1288, thirteen Jews were framed and executed for the murder of a Christian, and in 1306 the entire community was banished as a result of Philip IV's general expulsion of the Jews from the royal domains.

The 13th century was a period of energetic church construction in Troyes, and the variety of architectural styles visible in the major edifices reflects the city's diverse horizons. The nave and transept of La Madeleine (ca. 1200) adopt a Burgundian idiom, while the contemporaneous choir of the catheral of Saint-Pierre-Saint-Paul seems to have been begun by a Champenois master. By ca. 1230, the cathedral workshop was under the direction of an Île-de-France mason, often identified as the Master of Saint-Denis, who introduced the glazed triforium and elaborate tracery effects into the upper levels of the choir. Saint-Urbain (1262 and ca. 1280), erected as a shrine at the birthplace of Pope Urban IV (r. 1261–64), achieved an opulent complexity through a play of gables and tracery that drew upon the latest Parisian and northern French developments.

With the waning importance of the fairs at the end of the 13th century and the opening years of the 14th, the Black Death, and the Hundred Years' War, Troyes endured a century and a half of economic stagnation and political instability. As a result of the Treaty of Troyes (1420), Henry

V of England, recognized as heir to the French throne, married Catherine of France, daughter of King Charles VI, at Saint-Jean-au-Marché. Anglo-Burgundian forces finally were expelled in 1429, when the city opened its gates to Jeanne d'Arc and the dauphin, the future Charles VII. The city recovered its fortunes and population during the later 15th and early 16th centuries, a period marked by another burst of building. Sustained work on the cathedral's nave, which had suffered a disastrous collapse in 1389, was pursued from 1450, and the monumental west façade, designed by the Parisian mason Martin Chambiges, was raised beginning in 1502. A host of parish churches were built and decorated, including the choirs of La Madeleine (ca. 1490–1550), Saint-Remi (ca. 1500), and Saint-Jean-au-Marché (1508–55), Saint-Nizier (ca. 1500–75), Saint-Pantaléon (1517–52), and Saint-Nicolas (begun 1526). In conjunction with this Late Gothic architectural activity, renowned schools of glass painting and sculpture flourished in Troyes.

Michael T. Davis

[See also: BLOIS; CHAMPAGNE; CHARLES VI; FAIRS AND MARKETS; JEWS; NECROMANCY; REIMS]

Art et archéologie des Juifs en France médiévale. Paris: Commission Française des Archives Juives, 1980.

Bautier, R.-H. "Les foires de Champagne, recherches sur une évolution historique." *Receuils de la Société Jean Bodin* 5 (1953): 97–147.

Bur, Michel. *La formation du comté de Champagne, v. 950–v. 1150.* Nancy: Université de Nancy II, 1977.

Chapin, E. *Les villes de foires de Champagne, des origines au début du XIVe siècle.* Paris: Champion, 1937.

d'Arbois de Jubainville, H. *Histoire des ducs et des comtes de Champagne.* 7 vols. Paris: Durand, 1859–69.

Jordan, William C. *The French Monarchy and the Jews.* Philadelphia: University of Pennsylvania Press, 1989.

Murray, S. *Building Troyes Cathedral: The Late Gothic Campaigns.* Bloomington: Indiana University Press, 1987.

Roserot, Alphonse. *Dictionnaire historique de la Champagne méridionale (Aube) des origines à 1780.* 4 vols. in 3. Angers: Éditions de l'Ouest, 1942–48.

TRUCE OF GOD. The movement known as the Peace of God spawned a new movement, in which councils shifted emphasis from protecting classes of people at all times to banning all military activity at certain times of the year (Lent) or week (Thursday sunset to Monday sunrise). The Truce of God placed less emphasis on popular enthusiasm and more on the attempts of committed elements of the warrior and clerical orders to restore peace: enforcement tended to fall into the hands of the counts, the dukes, and their allies. Although juridically distinguishable, the Truce and the Peace were considered virtually synonomous by contemporaries. Beginning in the late 1020s in the south, the movement found favor among the rulers of western Europe from Spain to Germany during the later 11th century and throughout the 12th.

Had it ever been fully effective, the Truce of God would have severely limited feudal warfare, since any sustained campaign could only operate half the week, and the warriors' traditional Fields of March would be transformed into the pilgrims' Lenten road. Even when frequently transgressed, the Truce maintained an important place in public opinion and discourse, and many a ruler could clothe his rivalry with the aristocracy in the rhetoric of enforcing the peace. In fact, by permitting the use of designated armies (comital, ducal, royal) to enforce the Truce, the movement directly contributed to a distinction between public and private rights to the use of violence that, *mutatis mutandis*, would lead to the formation of that institution with a monopoly on violence: the modern state.

Richard Landes

[See also: PEACE OF GOD]

Cowdrey, Herbert E.J. "The Peace and the Truce of God in the Eleventh Century." *Past and Present* 46 (1970): 42–67.

Erdmann, Carl. *The Origin of the Idea of Crusade*, trans. Marshall W. Baldwin and Walter Goffart. Princeton: Princeton University Press, 1977.

Grabois, Aryeh. "De la trêve de Dieu à la paix du roi: étude sur les transformations du mouvement de la paix au XIIe siècle." In *Mélanges d'histoire médiévale dédiés à René Crozet*, ed. Pierre Gallais and Yves-Jean Riou. 2 vols. Poitiers: Société d'Études Médiévales, 1966, Vol. 1, pp. 585–96.

Hoffmann, Hartmut. *Gottesfriede und Treuga Dei*. Munich: Deutsches Institut für Erforschung des Mittelalters, 1964.

TUCHINS. *See* BRIGAND/BRIGANDAGE

U

UNAM SANCTAM. Issued in 1302, while Pope Boniface VIII was engaged in his second unsuccessful struggle with Philip IV the Fair of France, the constitution *Unam sanctam* contained some of the medieval papacy's strongest statements about its supremacy in temporal, as well as spiritual, affairs. The text was based on previous papalist writings, including those of Bernard of Clairvaux, and on the papalist reading of the Pseudo-Dionysian doctrine of hierarchy. Much of its wording was figurative, making the exact nature of its assertion of papal temporary supremacy ambiguous; but the French monarch saw through the wording to the essential demand for obedience. The heart of the argument was the close identification of Christendom with the church, outside of which there was no salvation. Submission to the papacy as the visible head of the church also was necessary for salvation. The pope was described as holding the spiritual sword but having the temporal sword exercised for the church by kings and knights. Failure to wield it as the spiritual power directed, however, could lead to condemnation of the king by the pope. Even after Boniface's death in 1303, Philip remained eager to have *Unam sanctam* revoked. In 1306, Clement V replied in the bull *Meruit* with an ambiguous declaration that *Unam sanctam* made the French king, realm, and people no more subject to the papacy than it had been before. *Unam sanctam* never found a place in the official collections of canon law, but it was cited frequently by papal apologists in later centuries.

Thomas M. Izbicki

[See also: BONIFACE VIII; CLEMENT V; PHILIP IV THE FAIR]

Luscombe, David. "The *Lex divinitatis* in the Bull *Unam sanctam* of Pope Boniface VIII." In *Church and Government in the Middle Ages: Essays Presented to C.R. Cheney on His 70th Birthday*, ed. Christopher Brooke. Cambridge: Cambridge University Press, 1976, pp. 205–21.

Tierney, Brian. *The Crisis of Church and State, 1050–1300.* Englewood Cliffs: Prentice-Hall, 1964, pp. 180–92.

UNICORN TAPESTRIES. Both sets of unicorn tapestries, those at the Cloisters in New York and at the Musée Cluny in Paris, were woven ca. 1500. The unicorn had been an object of fascination for encyclopedists and poets since antiquity, and in the Middle Ages it acquired more symbolic meanings as it took on christological qualities. Included in innumerable writings about fantastic creatures, such as the *Physiologus*, the unicorn also gained fame in romances and lyric poetry, such as the famous *Auxi con l'unicorn sui* by Thibaut, count of Champagne (1201–1253).

The seven Cloisters tapestries (all about 12 feet 1 inch by anywhere from 8 feet to 14 feet) feature seven scenes depicting the narrative of the hunt for the unicorn. The first tapestry shows a scout in the distance calling to huntsmen equipped with such accessories as plumed hats, spears, and dogs on leashes. The next tapestry depicts the discovery of the unicorn in a forest clearing between a fountain and a stream. The unicorn is in the process of purifying the water for the thirsty animals who wait nearby, and the huntsmen stand unabashedly around the unicorn. In the third scene, the unleashed dogs run and huntsmen thrust spears, but the unicorn leaps over the stream away from the hunters. The fourth scene features the unicorn kicking huntsmen and goring a dog. The two fragments of the fifth scene show the second and more successful method of unicorn hunting, entrapment by a maiden. In the sixth tapestry, huntsmen bring the dead unicorn in triumph back to the lord and lady of the castle. The last piece in the series shows the unicorn resurrected and peacefully captive, tied to a pomegranate tree and surrounded by a fence and a dazzling array of flowers and foliage. Despite the dense quality of the compositions, the unicorn occupies the central position in most of the scenes, and all subsidiary elements point to it.

At the Museé Cluny, the five "Lady with the Unicorn" tapestries represent five allegories of the senses. In each scene, the heraldic devices of lion and unicorn support banners of the Le Viste family and interact with the lady who stands in the center of the composition. In *Sight*, the lady shows the unicorn on her left its reflection in a hand-held mirror. The lady plays a portable organ decorated with lion and unicorn in *Hearing*, and in *Taste* the unicorn wears a flying cape with the Le Viste coats of arms while a maidservant offers sweetmeats to her lady. In *Smell*, the lady makes a bouquet of carnations, and in *Touch* she holds a banner in her right arm and with her left hand touches the horn of the unicorn. The last tapestry in the series, *A Mon Seul Desir* (a phrase that appears on the edge of the tent), consists of a lady inspecting her jewels and framed by the opening into the tent.

Both sets of tapestries have been assigned to a variety of workshops and patrons, but recent scholarship suggests that the Cloisters tapestries were made in Brussels, while the Museé Cluny tapestries were commissioned by Jean le Viste between 1484 and 1500. Reasons behind the commissioning of the tapestries remain matters for speculation, but the Museé Cluny set may have been produced in honor of a marriage or, as Erlande-Brandenburg suggests, to glorify the family name.

Stacy L. Boldrick

[See also: TAPESTRY (photo)]

Erlande-Brandenburg, Alain. *La dame à la licorne.* Paris: Éditions de la Réunion des Musées Nationaux, 1978.
Freeman, Margaret. *The Unicorn Tapestries.* New York: Metropolitan Museum of Art, 1976.
Williamson, John. *The Oak King, the Holly King and the Unicorn: The Myths and Symbolism of the Unicorn Tapestries.* New York: Harper and Row, 1986.

UNIVERSITIES. In the Middle Ages, the term for a university was *studium* or *studium generale*, with the word *universitas* referring to the institutional or corporate shell enclosing and regulating the communities of masters and students. The most important university in medieval France was that of Paris, whose origins can be found in the 12th century; also of 12th-century origin was the medical school of Montpellier. By the end of the 15th century, however, the model of these early universities had inspired the foundation of many universities throughout France.

In the late 11th century, the school of William of Champeaux had been located in Paris. After William left the city for the nearby community of Saint-Victor, his absence permitted his former student Peter Abélard to establish his own school outside the city on Mont-Sainte-Geneviève; later, in the 1130s, when Abélard again resumed teaching after the interruption prompted by his castration and entry into monastic life, it was again to Mont-Sainte-Geneviève that he returned. The attractions of Paris were several: it was well provided with food and wine; it was the capital of the king of France; there were numerous regional schools that could provide students; and the bishop and cathedral chapter generally failed to exercise much control over teaching in the city.

By the time Abélard left Paris for the last time, in 1141, the city was the center of a considerable community of masters and students: sources regarding the schools of Paris in the early 1140s mention not only Abélard but Albéric de Monte, Robert of Melun, Peter Helias, Adam du Petit-Pont, Gilbert of Poitiers, Thierry of Chartres, and Peter Lombard. Other towns may have boasted masters who were worthy of this company, but none could match the concentration of talent that Paris offered an aspiring student. Students naturally came in large numbers and often from considerable distances; how many there were is impossible to say with any certainty, but the rapid settlement of the Left Bank—the area between the cathedral and Mont-Sainte-Geneviève where scholars settled in large numbers—suggests that the academic community may have numbered 3,000 or 4,000 by the end of the 12th century. Whatever the precise number, by 1200 Paris was the leading center in Europe for the study of the Liberal Arts and theology.

The texture of the intellectual community, however, was also changing by the 1140s. John of Salisbury recalled having come to Paris as a young man in the 1130s and hearing Abélard lecture, but students in the 1140s were studying with John, a student himself who used the money he earned to finance his own studies. The growing size of the academic community perhaps contributes to the fact that we know the names of comparatively few masters for the second half of the 12th century; it must have been harder to stand out from the crowd. But it was also in this period that one sees the first steps toward defining the legal context in which the masters and students operated.

The first issue to arise was the *licentia docendi*, or license to teach. Pope Alexander III, in 1166–67 and later in conjunction with the Third Lateran Council (1179), barred the chancellor of Paris from exacting a fee for the right to teach at Paris. The prohibition apparently was not entirely effective, for it had to be repeated in the early 13th century. At that time, Pope Innocent III and then his legate (and Paris master) Robert de Courçon assigned the right to assess the qualifications of candidates for the license to teach to the masters themselves. This provision of Courçon's statutes, moreover, confirmed the formation of the masters into a corporation that could act jointly on issues of university governance. The masters may in fact have been acting collectively as early as the mid-12th century, but a corporation, or *universitas*, of masters was not specifically mentioned until 1208. By the early 13th century, therefore, the University of Paris had both achieved corporate status and won independence from local supervision by the chancellor of Paris.

In practice, the University of Paris consisted of several institutions that managed different aspects of university life. The *universitas* to which Innocent III addressed his letter in 1208 comprised all the masters of theology, canon law, and the arts. Already they were exercising authority over their members in such matters as dress and the order of lectures, as well as more internal issues, such as the duty of masters to attend the funerals of dead colleagues. Courçon's statutes of 1215, moreover, also assigned the masters jurisdiction over crimes involving one of their members, as well as control over such issues as the prices to be charged for lodging. The independence of the university of scholars from local (but not papal) supervision was made still more explicit by Gregory IX in 1231, when the bull *Parens scientiarum* commanded the chancellor of

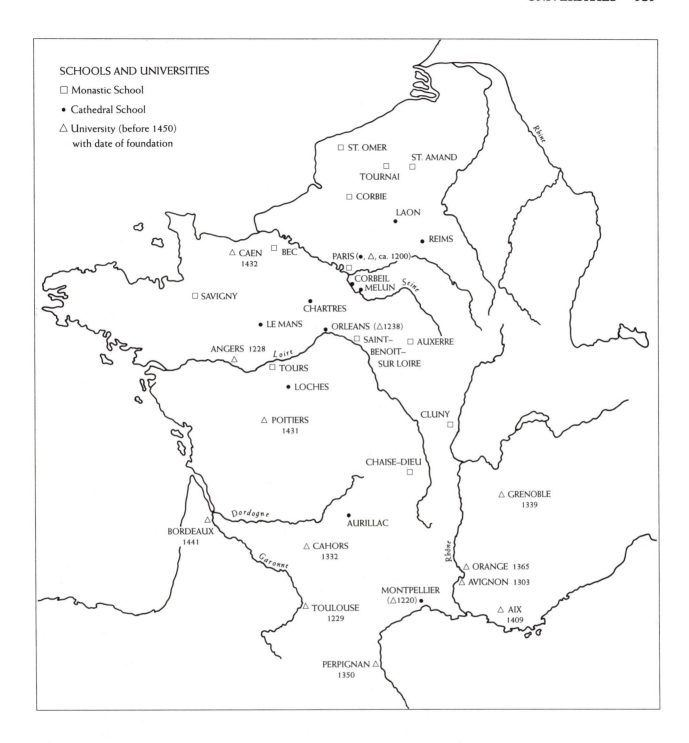

SCHOOLS AND UNIVERSITIES

□ Monastic School

• Cathedral School

△ University (before 1450)
  with date of foundation

□ ST. OMER

ST. AMAND

□ TOURNAI   □

□ CORBIE

LAON

• REIMS

△ CAEN   □ BEC
  1432

PARIS (•, △, ca. 1200)

□ CORBEIL
MELUN

Seine

□ SAVIGNY

CHARTRES •

• LE MANS   ORLEANS (△1238)

ANGERS 1228   Loire   □ SAINT-   □ AUXERRE
  △   BENOIT-
□ TOURS   SUR LOIRE

• LOCHES

△ POITIERS   CLUNY
  1431   □

CHAISE-DIEU
□

△ GRENOBLE
  1339

△   Dordogne
BORDEAUX   AURILLAC •
1441

△ CAHORS   Rhône
  1332   △ ORANGE 1365
                    △ AVIGNON 1303

            MONTPELLIER
            (△1220) •   △ AIX
△ TOULOUSE   1409
  1229

Garonne

PERPIGNAN △
  1350

Paris to swear to respect the rights of the university, that is, the corporation of masters.

The superior faculties of theology, medicine, and law were headed by "regent" masters. The faculty in these faculties were quite few—e.g., eight for theology—and the great bulk of the masters taught in the arts. In the 13th century, there are also references to the university of artists and its rector, an official whose role would grow in the later Middle Ages. The membership of the medieval faculty of arts was also subdivided according to each member's country of origin into several groupings known as "nations": French, for those from the Île-de-France and the Mediterranean, Norman for those from Normandy and Brittany, Picard for those from Picardy and the Low Countries, and English for those from England, Germany, and Scandinavia. Each nation possessed its own seal and operated as an independent organization, meeting regularly and being responsible for the examinations for the license to teach the arts. The importance of the nations declined at the end of the Middle Ages, as Paris itself became less international in its composition as a result of competition from other newly founded universities.

Also operating within the ambit of the university were colleges. These were foundations intended to support the studies of poorer scholars. The most famous of them was that founded by St. Louis's chaplain Robert de Sorbon ca. 1257.

Although the course of studies at Paris before 1150 appears to have been fluid, with masters and students both able to move from one discipline to another, by the 13th century it had become traditional that the youngest scholars would study arts, only later advancing to the superior faculties of law, medicine, or theology. This sequence is already enshrined in the statutes of Robert de Courçon, who specifies twenty-one as the minimum age for lecturing in the arts (by which time a scholar should have heard lectures himself for six years), while the minimum age for theologians was to be thirty-five.

Lecturing took the form of expositions of standard texts; the master would explain each passage, noting as well the issues surrounding the passage that were currently being discussed. The list of texts remained remarkably stable for centuries: for example, students read Priscian for grammar, Aristotle for logic, Peter Lombard's *Sententiae* for theology. The fixed place in the curriculum held by some of these texts does not, however, mean that the education received at the university was unchanging. In the first place, even while lecturing on traditional texts, masters generally discussed whatever issues were more *professionally* important at the time; these issues changed constantly, as some questions were settled and scholars' attention turned to new ground. The curriculum also evolved, especially in the 13th century, by the introduction of lectures on newly translated works, such as Aristotle's *Metaphysics* and *Ethics*, that brought with them a variety of concepts apparently in conflict with Christian doctrine. Several times in the course of the century, popes attempted to ban the teaching of certain doctrines or books, but these prohibitions were only sporadically effective, at least until a doctrine had actually been formally proclaimed to be heretical.

Medieval universities did not grant formal degrees, but there were events that marked a student's progress through his studies. Mid-13th-century statutes of the English nation use the term "bachelors" to describe students who had been licensed to take the exam known as "determination." To take this exam, they had to be at least twenty years old and to have listened to lectures for five years; the exam itself consisted of a series of disputations, after which a student would be expected to participate in disputations for another year. A student who had "determined" could continue his studies and receive a license to teach, a further step known as "inception," which like determination involved disputations and public ceremonies; inception functioned as the examination for master in the faculty of arts.

A student who qualified to teach in the faculties of law, medicine, or theology at Paris was known as a "doctor." In law and medicine, candidates typically would have been about twenty-five years old; the age for incepting in theology was thirty-five. Although master and doctor designate a person who has demonstrated a level of competency worthy of a license to teach, in practice few graduates of the university taught for long. The world outside the university also acknowledged the value of the learning certified by these titles, and graduates continued to claim their status as masters and doctors long after leaving academic life.

As part of its control of the academic environment, the University of Paris claimed the right to regulate the book trade as well as the price of classroom rentals and tuition. The university's objective was both to control prices and to certify the accuracy of texts. University stationers had official copies of works, whose sections, however, had not been bound into a codex; copyists then worked from these sections, known as *pecia*, to produce multiple copies.Using this method, several copyists could work together to reproduce a book quickly; indeed, one reason for the ascendancy of Gothic script was the fact that Gothic tended to be more uniform from one scribe to another. Students could also borrow *pecia* rather than an entire book. Both the wages of the copyists and the fees charged by the stationers were regulated by the university, although the stationers did not always comply completely or happily.

Also having roots in the 12th century, the University of Montpellier originally centered on medicine, which may have been taught there before 1150. In 1220, a papal legate confirmed university statutes for the *universitas medicorum*. Law had also been taught at Montpellier in the 12th century, most notably by the great Italian jurist Placentinus, and legal teaching was firmly established by the second third of the 13th century. A collection of statutes for the faculty of arts dates from 1242. Formal acknowledgment that the schools at Montpellier constituted a *studium generale* came from Pope Nicholas IV in 1289.

By the 13th century, there was a concept of *studium*, or university, that was sufficiently well defined to permit the founding of new universities as deliberate acts. The University of Toulouse was founded in 1229, by treaty between the king of France and the count of Toulouse, as part of the settlement of the Albigensian heresy. The count promised to pay the salaries of fourteen professors—four in theology, two in canon law, six in the arts, and two in grammar. The idea clearly was to promote the teaching of orthodox learning as a way to counter heretical doctrines. An effort was made to attract doctors from Paris to staff the new university, but when the count reneged on the salaries he had promised the *studium* quickly foundered. At this point, however, the pope intervened with a bull guaranteeing the privileges of the masters, and the university seems to have been functioning successfully by the 1240s.

Other, smaller *studia* can also be documented for the 13th century, and there was a continuous string of foundations in the 14th and 15th centuries, often under the sponsorship of the local bishop. Having a university could be a matter of local pride, and successions of masters from existing universities could provide recruits out of which faculties could be formed. Most of these universities were small compared with Paris, however, and many offered training only or mainly in law. This was a field that saw a steady demand for university graduates, and after the mid-14th century an increasing percentage of French lawyers were laymen with university degrees.

Charles Radding

[See also: ABÉLARD, PETER; ADAM DU PETIT-PONT; ARISTOTLE, INFLUENCE OF; EDUCATION; GILBERT OF POITIERS; INNOCENT III; JOHN OF SALISBURY; MONTPELLIER; PALEOGRAPHY AND MANUSCRIPTS; *PARENS SCIENTIARUM;* PARIS; PETER LOMBARD; ROBERT DE COURÇON; ROBERT OF MELUN; SCHOLASTICISM; SCHOOLS, CATHEDRAL; SCHOOLS, MONASTIC; THIERRY OF CHARTRES; WILLIAM OF CHAMPEAUX]

Baldwin, John W. "Masters at Paris from 1179 to 1215: A Social Perspective." In *Renaissance and Renewal in the Twelfth Century*, ed. Robert L. Benson and Giles Constable with Carol D. Lanham. Cambridge: Harvard University Press, 1982, pp. 138–72.

———. *Masters, Princes and Merchants: The Social Views of Peter the Chanter and His Circle.* 2 vols. Princeton: Princeton University Press, 1970.

Ferruolo, Stephen. "Parisius-Paradisus: The City, Its Schools, and the Origins of the University of Paris." In *The University and the City: From Medieval Origins to the Present*, ed. Thomas Bender. New York: Oxford University Press, 1988, pp. 22–43.

———. *The Origins of the University: The Schools of Paris and Their Critics, 1100–1215.* Stanford: Stanford University Press, 1985.

Kibre, Pearl. *The Nations in the Medieval Universities.* Cambridge: Mediaeval Academy of America, 1948.

Leff, Gordon. *Paris and Oxford Universities in the Thirteenth and Fourteenth Centuries.* New York: Wiley, 1968.

Post, Gaines. "Alexander III, the *Licentia docendi* and the Rise of the Universities." In *Anniversary Essays in Mediaeval History by Students of Charles Homer Haskins*, ed. John L. La Monte and Charles H. Taylor. Boston: Houghton Mifflin, 1929, pp. 255–77.

———. "Parisian Masters as a Corporation, 1200–1246." *Speculum* 9 (1934): 421–45.

Rashdall, Hastings. *The Universities of Europe in the Middle Ages*, ed. Frederick M. Powicke and Alfred B. Emden. new ed. 3 vols. Oxford: Clarendon, 1936.

Rouse, Richard H., and Mary A. Rouse. "The Book Trade at the University of Paris, ca. 1250–ca. 1350." In *Authentic Witnesses: Approaches to Medieval Texts and Manuscripts*, ed. Mary A. Rouse and Richard H. Rouse. Notre Dame: University of Notre Dame Press, 1991, pp. 259–338.

Southern, Richard W. "The Schools of Paris and the School of Chartres." In *Renaissance and Renewal in the Twelfth Century*, ed. Robert L. Benson and Giles Constable with Carol D. Lanham. Cambridge: Harvard University Press, 1982, pp. 113–37.

Thorndike, Lynn. *University Records and Life in the Middle Ages.* New York: Columbia University Press, 1944.

URBAN IV (r. 1261–64). Pope. After the death of Alexander IV in 1261, the eight surviving cardinals were unable to elect one of themselves pope. At last, they selected Jacques Pantaléon, titular patriarch of Jerusalem, who was on a mission to the Holy Land. Jacques, of low birth but a protegé of Innocent IV, had wide experience but no ties to Italian politics. As Pope Urban IV, he gained control of the papal states and rebuilt the Guelf alliance against the Hohenstaufen. Urban created a substantial French bloc in the College of Cardinals and renewed his ties with Louis IX of France. Although the king refused to campaign against Manfred, the illegitimate son of Frederick II, he permitted Urban to approach a younger brother, Charles of Anjou. This was the first step toward Angevin domination of the papacy. Urban's successor, Clement IV, would support Charles's wars against the Hohenstaufen with all of the papacy's resources. Urban neglected the affairs of the Holy Roman Empire; but he negotiated with Emperor Michael VIII Paleologus, who had recaptured Constantinople from the Latins, for recognition of the Roman primacy. Urban, who had been exposed to the feast of Corpus Christi in the north, attempted to extend the feast to the entire western church, thus reaffirming the doctrine of transubstantiation; and the name of Thomas Aquinas is associated with the office for that feast, which only later became universally popular, and only later would the story of a miracle at Bolsena be used to explain Urban's effort.

Thomas M. Izbicki

[See also: LOUIS IX]

Rodríguez de Lama, Ildefonso, ed. *La documentación pontificia de Urbano IV (1261–1264)*. Roma: Instituto Español de Historia Ecclesiástica, 1981.

Hampe, Karl. *Urban IV und Manfred, 1261–64.* Heidelberg: Winter, 1905.

Rubin, Miri. *Corpus Christi: The Eucharist in Medieval Culture.* Cambridge: Cambridge University Press, 1991.

URBAN V (r. 1362–70). Pope. When Pope Innocent VI died in 1362, the dominant Limousin party in the College of Cardinals became divided and could not elect a pope from within its own ranks. At last, Guillaume de Grimoard, abbot of Saint-Victor, Marseille, was chosen, although he was absent on a mission in Italy. Upon his return to Avignon, the new Roman pontiff, who chose to reign as Urban V, adopted an austere life within the papal palace. Urban was especially concerned with the welfare of the universities, founding two colleges at the University of Montpellier. Praised for combining love of learning and zeal for reform with generosity, he was, however, imprudent about money and inclined to appeasement, even of the Milanese tyrant Bernabò Visconti and of the mercenaries who terrorized France. In 1367, having concluded that the work of Cardinal Albornoz to pacify the papal states could be consummated only by returning the papacy to Rome, Urban left part of the curia in Avignon and departed for Rome with the rest. Although the pope regretted leaving the peace and quiet of Avignon for the perils of Rome, he completed his journey. In the Eternal City, he crowned Charles IV of Luxembourg Holy Roman Emperor; and he received the Byzantine Emperor John V Paleologus, who sought aid against the Turkish threat. In 1370, Urban returned to Avignon, where he died in an odor of sanctity. He was beatified by Pius IX in 1870.

Thomas M. Izbicki

[See also: AVIGNON PAPACY]

Urban V. *Urbain V (1362–1370): lettres communes*, ed. Marie-Hyacinthe Laurent and members of the École Française de Rome. 12 vols. Paris: Boccard, 1954–89.

———. *Urbain V (1362–1370): lettres secrètes et curiales du Pape Urbain V (1362–1370): se rapportant à France*, ed. Paul C.N.M.J. Lecacheux et al. 4 vols. Paris: Fontemoing, 1902–55.

de Lanouvelle, Edgar. *Le bienheureux Urbain V et la Chrétiente au milieu du XIVe siècle.* Paris: Letouzy et Ané, 1911.

USURY. Medieval jurists and moralists defined usury as any predetermined charge for a loan of money or goods. The taking of usury was a canonical offense punishable by excommunication. In France, usurers were subject to banishment and their property to confiscation by the crown. The ban on usury did not apply to ordinary business profits or to penalties for overdue loans.

The usury prohibition originated in the early church but was not applied to the laity until Charlemagne forbade lending at interest to all subjects of the empire at the Council of Aix-la-Chapelle (789). The increase in moneylending generated by the growth of trade after 1100 provoked a series of papal and conciliar decrees between 1179 (Third Lateran Council) and 1311 (Council of Vienne) that reiterated the traditional ban and strengthened the canonical penalties for usurers. Local councils in most regions of France followed suit and adopted antiusury canons in the course of the 13th century.

Although lending at interest was strictly forbidden by Louis IX in decrees of 1230 and 1254, political and fiscal considerations generally dictated French royal policy on usury. Philip IV effectively legalized usury in 1311, when he abolished penalties for lenders who charged annual rates of less than 20 percent. The crown frequently granted *ad hoc* exemptions from the usury ban. Exemptions conceded to Châteauneuf (1181) and Poitiers (1222) favored towns in the royal domain; similar concessions to the fairs of Champagne and Brie (1349) and to Lyon (1419) were designed to encourage international trade. As early as the last quarter of the 12th century, the crown and local authorities permitted Jewish and foreign, usually Italian, moneylenders to lend at annual rates as high as 43 percent a year (two *deniers* per *livre* per week) on payment of an annual fine. Nevertheless, the position of such public usurers was precarious. Jewish moneylenders were subjected to frequent expulsions and expropriations throughout the 13th and 14th centuries. Italian moneylenders and financiers, many of whom were creditors of the crown, were banished and their assets seized in 1277, 1291, 1311, and 1331.

From the reign of Charles V, the economic effects of the Hundred Years' War dictated a less erratic policy on usury, and moneylenders were authorized by letters patent to lend in most French cities at an annual rate of 16 percent. Licensed usury became a virtual monopoly of Italian moneylenders after 1394, when Charles VI revoked privileges previously granted to Jewish lenders. The later Middle Ages also saw a moderation of the ecclesiastical position on usury as a result of the development of titles to compensatory interest by canonists and theologians.

Lawrin D. Armstrong

[See also: BANKING AND MONEYLENDING]

Dumas, Auguste. "Intérêt et usure." In *Dictionnaire de droit canonique*, ed. Raoul Naz. 7 vols. Paris: Letouzey et Ané, 1935–65.

Gilchrist, John. *The Church and Economic Activity in the Middle Ages.* New York: Macmillan, 1969.

LeGoff, Jacques. *Your Money or Your Life: Economy and Religion in the Middle Ages*, trans. Patricia Ranum. New York: Zone, 1988.

McLaughlin, T.P. "The Teaching of the Canonists on Usury (XII, XIII, and XIV Centuries)." *Mediaeval Studies* 1 (1939): 81–147; 2 (1940): 1–22.

Noonan, John T. *The Scholastic Analysis of Usury.* Cambridge: Harvard University Press, 1957.

Shatzmiller, Joseph. *Shylock Reconsidered: Jews, Moneylending, and Medieval Society.* Berkeley: University of California Press, 1990.

VALENCIENNES. The church of Notre-Dame-la-Grande at Valenciennes (Nord) was another of the large buildings of northern France destroyed in the years following the French Revolution. We know the building only from documents, as the site has not been excavated and no fragments are known to have survived. It was an interesting variation on the trefoil plan, in which the chevet and each transept arm were polygonal in plan and surrounded by an ambulatory and gallery. The axial chapel of the ambulatory was two-storied, and both transept arms had two-story polygonal chapels on the east side. Above the gallery was a wall passage and clerestory windows. If the visual evidence and descriptions are trustworthy, Notre-Dame-la-Grande, which was built in the last quarter of the 12th century, was richly decorated on the interior with dark Tournai stone. It may have been known to William of Sens before he went to Canterbury.

William W. Clark

Serbat, Louis. "L'église Notre-Dame-la-Grande à Valenciennes." *Revue de l'art chrétien* 53 (1903): 366–83; 56 (1906): 9–21, 242–52.

———. "Quelques églises anciennement détruites du nord de la France." *Bulletin monumental* 88 (1929): 365–435.

Thiébaut, J. "Quelques observations sur l'église Notre-Dame-la-Grande de Valenciennes." *Revue du Nord* 62 (1980): 331–44.

VALENTINOIS. Until its annexation to the French kingdom in the 15th century, this region, bounded by the Rhône, the Isère, the Drome, and the Diois, constituted a virtually independent principality centering on the city of Valence. Imperial charters gave the bishops, who ruled the city, secular authority over the diocese as well, but their claims were challenged repeatedly by the counts of Valentinois. In 1189, Raymond V of Toulouse ceded his rights in the Diois to Aymar II de Poitiers, count of Valentinois, who thereafter intensified his efforts to create a unified state at the expense of the bishops in both regions. During the Albigensian Crusade, Simon de Montfort attacked Aymar's citadel at Crest because of Aymar's alli-

ance with Raymond VI of Toulouse. In 1396, Valence was placed under the protection of the king of France, and in 1452 a university was founded there. In 1404, the king of France purchased the county of Valentinois, and in 1499 Louis XII erected it into a duchy-peerage for Cesare Borgia.

Eugene L. Cox

[**See also:** DAUPHINÉ/VIENNOIS]

Chevalier, Jules. *Mémoires pour servir à l'histoire des comtes de Valentinois et de Diois.* Paris: Picard, 1897.

VALET/*VARLET.* See Esquire/Escuier

VALOIS DYNASTY. Family that ruled France from 1328 to 1589. At the death of the last great Capetian monarch, Philip IV the Fair (r. 1285–1314), the throne passed rapidly among his sons, who all died young. When the posthumous son of Louis X (r. 1314–16), John I, died shortly after his birth in 1316, Louis's brother Philip V (r. 1316–22) seized the crown and the magnates agreed to exclude female heirs from the royal succession. Therefore, when Philip V died leaving only daughters, his brother Charles IV (r. 1322–28) succeeded him. He too left only daughters and his closest male heir was his sister's son, Edward III of England. The magnates preferred that the throne pass to the late king's cousin, Philip, count of Valois, and they ruled that a valid claim to the throne could not be inherited through a woman. The reign of Philip VI (r. 1328–50) thus inaugurated the Valois line of kings, descended from Charles, the second son of Philip III. The throne passed through seven generations of Valois until the death of Charles VIII (r. 1483–98) and thence to a younger branch of the family that ended with the murder of Henry III in 1589.

During its first 170 years, which encompassed all the catastrophes accompanying the waning of medieval civilization, the Valois dynasty overcame the greatest series of challenges to confront the monarchy before 1789. The most direct challenge was military: Plantagenêt claims to the

VALOIS DYNASTY

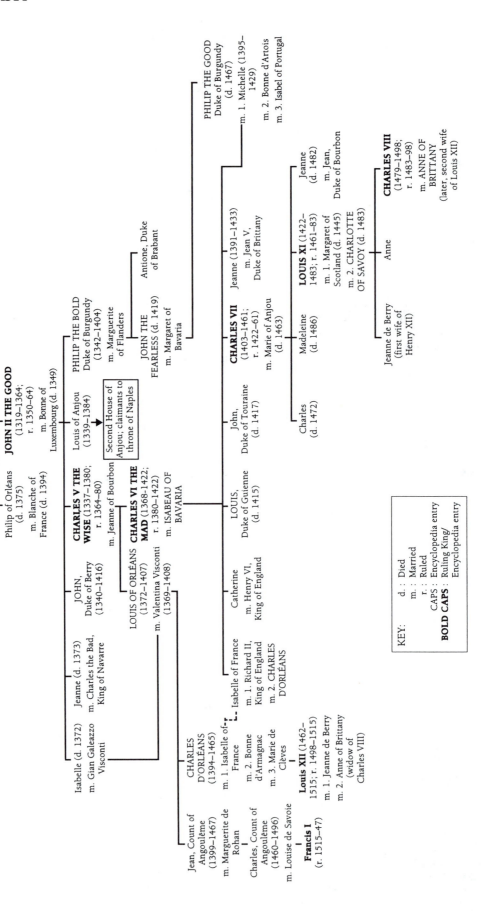

KEY:

d. :	Died
m. :	Married
r. :	Ruled
CAPS :	Encyclopedia entry
BOLD CAPS :	Ruling King/ Encyclopedia entry

throne produced military disasters et Crécy (1346) and Poitiers (1356). Desperate expedients, such as the grant of Burgundy in apanage to John II the Good's son, Philip the Bold, and reliance on mercenary companies led to military chaos and aristocratic defiance. Though Charles V (r. 1364–80) revitalized the monarchy, the unfortunate Charles VI (r. 1380–1422) almost destroyed it. Charles VII (r. 1422–61) required a lifetime to discipline his forces and expel the English, but by the time of Louis XI (r. 1461–83) and Charles VIII (r. 1483–98) the dynasty was able to acquire Burgundy and Brittany and even forcefully press its claims south of the Pyrénées and the Alps.

Nonetheless, the most profound Valois challenge was to preserve the Capetian constitutional legacy. Philip VI and his immediate heirs, dependent on their magnate allies, did little. Only after a century of chaos would France allow Charles VII and Louis XI to consolidate their bureaucratic governance of France through such devices as the imposition of the Pragmatic Sanction of Bourges, the establishment of the *ordonnance* companies, the regularization of the *taille*, and the expansion of the parlements. As a result, Charles VIII was able to pass a clearly acknowledged sovereignty and political ascendency on to the "Renaissance Monarchs" of the later Valois era. Despite setbacks, the early Valois not only preserved but ultimately expanded their Capetian inheritance by defeating military adversaries, consolidating political power, expanding crown domain, and extending French frontiers beyond those of the medieval monarchy.

Paul D. Solon

[See also: CHARLES OF VALOIS; EDWARD III; HUNDRED YEARS' WAR; PHILIP VI; RECONQUEST OF FRANCE]

Cuttler, Simon H. *The Law of Treason and Treason Trials in Later Medieval France.* Cambridge: Cambridge University Press, 1981.
Deneuil-Cormier, Anne. *Wise and Foolish Kings: The First House of Valois, 1328–1498.* Garden City: Doubleday, 1980.
Famiglietti, Richard C. *Royal Intrigue: Crisis at the Court of Charles VI, 1392–1420.* New York: AMS, 1986.
Fowler, Kenneth A. *The Age of Plantagenet and Valois: The Struggle for Supremacy, 1328–1498.* New York: Putnam, 1967.
Lewis, Peter S. *Later Medieval France: The Polity.* London: Macmillan, 1968.
Vaughn, Richard. *Valois Burgundy.* London: Lane, 1975.

VAN DER WEYDEN, ROGIER (1399/1400–1464). Flemish painter, a student of Robert Campin, known in his day as second only to Jan van Eyck, Rogier van der Weyden was born in Tournai in French-speaking Hainaut, but the economic life of the area depended heavily on Flanders rather than France. In the 1430s, rather than seek employment at the Burgundian court, he moved to Brussels as the head of a large workshop. As a guild member, he catered heavily to Germanic circles of patronage, which did not, however, prevent his appreciation of the achievements of the court painter van Eyck. The influence of his predecessor can be detected in early works such as the *Annunciation* of ca. 1435, now in the Louvre, from his attention to detail in the patterning of the floor and fabrics to the symbolic objects filling the panel with meaning. Simultaneously, van der Weyden began to move beyond van Eyck's stylistic accomplishments to create a style of his own, as exemplified by his *Lamentation* (ca. 1435–38) in the Prado. In a shallow, undefined space, van der Weyden focuses the viewer's attention upon the monumental figures actively demonstrating their grief. He rejects the disguised symbolism so favored by van Eyck in order to explore more fully the emotive capabilities of composition. Van der Weyden, although not employed directly by the Burgundian court, did produce some works for its most prominent members. An example is his *Altarpiece of the Seven Sacraments* (ca. 1453–55) in the Musée Royal des Beaux-Arts of Antwerp, executed for Jean Chevrot, bishop of Tournai, in which he expanded the Gothic cathedral interior as depicted in van Eyck's earlier *Madonna in the Church.* He and van Eyck shared a client in the person of Nicolas Rolin, chancellor of Flanders. Van der Weyden also painted a nativity altarpiece (1452–55), now in Berlin, for Pieter Bladelin, who was the chief tax collector in Flanders for Philip the Good.

Michelle I. Lapine

[See also: CAMPIN, ROBERT; VAN EYCK, JAN]

Davies, Martin. *Rogier van der Weyden.* London: Phaidon, 1972.
Panofsky, Erwin. *Early Netherlandish Painting.* New York: Harper and Row, 1971.
Snyder, James. *Northern Renaissance Art.* New York: Abrams, 1985.

VAN EYCK, JAN (ca. 1380–1441). As one of the most famous painters of his day, van Eyck had the special privilege of being a *valet* to Philip the Good, duke of Burgundy. His role as court painter extended into the realm of diplomacy, as van Eyck was one of Philip's emissaries to Spain between 1424 and 1430. Van Eyck began his career in the Burgundian court after the death of his former patron, John of Bavaria. Although he served Philip directly, his production of panel painting for him went unrecorded. However, accounts of patronage do exist for members of Philip's circle. Van Eyck's reputation as a great master emerged from his superrealistic and sensual treatment of the panel, his rich and precise handling of clothing and jewels. Van Eyck fully exploited oil paint as his medium, evidenced by his exquisite details and nearly invisible brushwork. As was practiced by the majority of northern painters, van Eyck infused the objects in his world with secondary, allegorical, and christological meanings. The most obvious expression of his disguised symbolism can be found in his treatment of the Virgin and Child, a subject van Eyck repeatedly explored. His *Madonna in the Church* (ca. 1437–38), now hanging in the Gemäldegalerie-Staatliche Museen in Berlin, represents a beautifully executed example of his style and iconographic approach: the large size of the Virgin in comparison with her surroundings emphasizes her status. The *Ghent Altarpiece* (1432), which has sparked many a debate concerning attribution and assemblage, was done in collaboration with his brother Hubert and represents the only painting known by van Eyck prior to 1433.

Van Eyck produced his most renowned work for the members of the Burgundian court or people closely linked to it, particularly the two-thirds of his paintings that contain portraits. The *Arnolfini Wedding Portrait*, which rivals the altarpiece in reputation, was painted for Giovanni Arnolfini in 1434. Arnolfini settled in Flanders with his half-French wife after Philip the Good appointed him to a position at court. Baudouin de Lannoy, lord of Molembaix, commissioned a work in honor of his membership in the order of the Golden Fleece, founded by Philip in 1430. The inclusion of the order's collar in his portrait of 1435 advertises his newly acquired status. Van Eyck served Philip and the court of Burgundy for a sixteen-year stint that ended with his death in 1441. It was during his tenure as artist of the court that van Eyck developed the detailed, naturalistic style that had such a great impact on all who followed him.

Michelle I. Lapine

[See also: GHENT; VAN DER WEYDEN, ROGIER]

Dhanens, Elisabeth. *Hubert and Jan van Eyck*. New York: Alpine, 1970.

Henbison, Craig. *Jan van Eyck: The Play of Realism*. London: Reaktion, 1991.

Panofsky, Erwin. *Early Netherlandish Painting*. New York: Harper and Row, 1971.

Snyder, James. *Northern Renaissance Art*. New York: Abrams, 1985.

VASSAL. In modern usage, anyone who performed homage, swore fealty, and received a fief. Such a generic sense of "vassal," however, was unknown in medieval France, although the lack of a systematic history of the term precludes a definitive summary of its evolution.

Vassus and *vassalus* are latinized forms of Celtic terms for "servant." In Salic Law, a vassal was a slave, but by the 8th century he could be a legally free man who had commended himself to a landlord. Carolingian kings extended the term to middle-level landlords who received royal benefices in return for administrative services; these royal vassals (*vass[all]i dominici*) swore fealty to the king in the hands of the royal *missi*. Thus, two distinct levels of vassals were linked hierarchically to the king and subsequently, after the collapse of royal authority, to the counts.

In the 10th century, "vassal" was applied to the retainers of counts and barons and often was synonymous with "knight," but thereafter it rarely appeared in Latin texts. Although *vavassor* later denoted low-level feudal tenants, perhaps the descendants of 10th-century vassals, contemporaries generally referred to anyone who had performed homage (*hominium*) to a lord as the latter's "man"

(*homo*). Fulbert of Chartres (1020) and Galbert de Bruges (1127) spoke not about vassals but rather about men who had done homage and sworn fealty. Administrative bureaus later compiled lists of knights, homages, military service, and fiefs, rather than of vassals.

It was in the vernacular, principally in the chansons de geste, that "vassal" survived in the sense of warrior and was associated with the qualities of courage and loyalty, although the earliest vernacular historians, such as Villehardouin, who can be assumed to reflect current usage, did not employ the term.

Theodore Evergates

[See also: FEUDALISM; FIEF HOLDING]

Dunbabin, Jean. *France in the Making, 843–1180*. Oxford: Oxford University Press, 1985.

Fourquin, Guy. *Lordship and Feudalism in the Middle Ages*, trans. Iris and A.L. Lytton Sells. New York: Pica, 1976.

Ganshof, François L. *Feudalism*, trans. Philip Grierson. New York: Harper, 1961.

Poly, Jean-Pierre, and Eric Bournazel. *La mutation féodale, XIe–XIIe siècles*. Paris: Presses Universitaires de France, 1980.

Woledge, Brian. "Bons vavasseurs et mauvais sénéchaux." In *Mélanges offerts à Rita Lejeune*. 2 vols. Gembloux, 1969, Vol. 2, pp. 1263–77.

VAUX-DE-CERNAY. The abbey of Vaux-de-Cernay was founded 2 miles from Cernay-la-Ville (Yvelines) by monks from Savigny in 1118 and, like the other houses of the Savigniac order, passed under Cistercian control in 1147. Partly destroyed after the Revolution, the property was bought by the Rothschilds in 1873 and recently has become an exclusive resort hotel. The site is dominated by the ruins of an imposing 12th-century church some 205 feet long. The plan was determined and the lower walls of the chevet, transept, and nave aisles partly built before the abbey came under the Cistercians. In plan, it consisted of a large square chevet, a projecting transept with pairs of eastern chapels, and a lengthy nave with aisles. Although the nave was completed in the second half of the century, the church was groin-vaulted throughout. The west wall of the façade has a large rose window, some 22 feet in diameter, flanked by two smaller oculi. Taken under royal protection in 1142, the abbey of Vaux-de-Cernay had a long and distinguished history in the 12th and 13th centuries, with a number of its abbots serving in royal administrations. The most famous was Thibaut de Marly (r. 1235–47), a descendant of the Montmorency family later canonized as St. Thibaut.

William W. Clark

Aubert, Marcel. "L'abbatiale de Vaux-de Cernay." *Bulletin monumental* 92 (1933): 397–418.

———. *L'abbaye des Vaux-de-Cernay*. Paris: Laurens, 1934.

Morize, L. *Étude archéologique sur l'abbaye de Notre-Dame des Vaux de Cernay*. Tours: Deslis, 1889.

VENDÔME. The *pagus Vindocinensis* was located around the Gallo-Roman *oppidum* of Vinocium. In the 10th century, Vendôme (Loir-et-Cher) fell into the hands of the Robertian family, and Hugh Capet granted it, along with Paris, Melun, and Corbeil, to Count Bouchard le Vénérable (d. 1007), who retired to the abbey of Saint-Maur-des-Fossés. Eudes, one of his fellow monks, wrote his *vita* ca. 1050. By the end of the 11th century, Vendôme was endowed with a castle on the plateau above the Loir, which was substantially altered in the 14th century and again in the 17th. Within its walls are the foundations of the 11th-century church of Saint-Georges, which was destroyed in the Revolution. The most important vestige of the 14th-century fortifications is the Porte Saint-Georges, a gateway flanked by two semicircular towers with battlements and machicolations. Vendôme's abbey of La Trinité, founded possibly in the 9th century by Geoffroi Martel, became the focus of a major pilgrimage to venerate a tear that Christ shed at the tomb of Lazarus.

The counts of Vendôme by the mid-11th century had become vassals of the counts of Anjou and thus, a century later, of the kings of England. They took part in the crusade of 1101 and in the first expedition of Louis IX. In 1212, the town was the center of the children's movement to save the Holy Land, led by Étienne de Cloyes. On the death of Count Bouchard VII in 1374, Vendôme was carried to the house of Bourbon by the marriage of the count's sister, Catherine, to Jean I, count of La Marche (r. 1361–93). The counts remained loyal to the crown during the dark years of the Hundred Years' War, with Louis of La Marche/Vendôme (1393–1446) serving as a principal royal commander. The town with its castle was an important frontier site between French and English territories during the conflict. The county returned to the crown with the accession of the Bourbon king Henry IV in 1589.

The history of Vendôme illustrates several steps in early feudal development, with its records furnishing some of the earliest examples of primogeniture and liege homage, with a clear assignment of castle guard appearing by the early 11th century. Its counts also led the way in rural development with the founding of a *villeneuve*, a market, and a church in the forest in the 10th century; the introduction of vines from Saintonge in 1055–60; and the foundation of rural *bourgs* in the 12th century.

The former abbey church of La Trinité preserves transept walls from the original 11th-century Romanesque structure, and the stained-glass window of the Virgin in one of the chapels off the ambulatory is 12th-century. However, the vaulting is 13th-century, the windows of the clerestory are 14th-century, and the façade is Flamboyant Gothic. Near the church is a detached belfry with a 12th-century stone spire that rises 260 feet and is considered the prototype of the Romanesque south tower at Chartres. Of the conventual buildings, there remain the sacristy (14th c.), chapter house (14th c.), a wing of the cloister (14th–15th c.), and the abbot's lodgings (15th–16th c.).

R. Thomas McDonald

Barthélemy, Dominique. *La société dans le comté de Vendôme: de l'an mil au XIVe siècle.* Paris: Fayard, 1993.

Eudes de Saint-Maur-des-Fossés. *Vie de Bouchard-le-Vénérable, comte de Vendôme, de Corbeil, de Melun, et de Paris* (*Xe et XIe siècles*), ed. Bourel de la Roncière. Paris: Picard, 1892.

Plat, Gabriel. *L'église de la Trinité de Vendôme.* Paris: Laurens, 1934.

VERDUN. The Gallo-Roman fortress Virodunum Castrum occupied a strategic location along the Meuse River. Verdun (Meuse) was elevated to the rank of bishopric in the 3rd century and was an active port and commercial outpost from the 8th century. The city gave its name to the treaty of 843, which divided Charlemagne's empire among his three grandsons. From the 12th century on, the French kings battled with the Holy Roman emperor for jurisdictional rights over the city. It later became one of the "Three Bishoprics" (with Toul and Metz) that were united to France in 1552.

Outside of the city walls, Saintin, an early Christian apostle, erected the first sanctuary dedicated to St. Peter (ca. 350). In the 10th century, the Benedictine abbey of Saint-Vanne was founded upon this site. By the early 11th cen-

Vendôme (Loir-et-Cher), La Trinité, façade. *Photograph courtesy of Whitney S. Stoddard.*

tury, it was one of the most celebrated in the West. Only a 12th-century tower, incorporated into Vauban's 17th-century citadel, remains. In the 13th century, Verdun hosted communities of Dominicans, Franciscans, and Victorines.

Upon an original 6th-century foundation, the cathedral of Notre-Dame was rebuilt and expanded under the Teutonic bishop Thierry the Great (r. 1047–89) after fire destroyed the previous building in 1048. The church was further developed under Bishop Albéron de Chiny (r. 1132–52). In the style of the great Carolingian churches of Saxony, the basilica structure has transepts and apses at both its east and its west ends. Each transept is capped by two towers. (Today, the eastern towers are razed at roof level.) In the 13th and 14th centuries, ribbed vaults were constructed over the aisles, transepts, choirs, and nave. The monumental northern portal and porch date from the 14th century, and the Gothic chapels along the aisles from the 15th.

The Rhenish tendencies of the overall structure are complemented by elements typical of the Burgundian Romanesque. The polygonal structure of the eastern apse is similar to that at Autun, and the sculpture of the eastern portal, showing Christ in Majesty, recalls the style of the tympanum at Vézelay.

Nina Rowe

[See also: CAROLINGIAN DYNASTY]

Aimond, Charles. *La cathédrale de Verdun: étude historique et archéologique.* Nancy: Royer, 1909.
Fels, Étienne. "Verdun." *Congrès archéologique* (Nancy et Verdun) 96 (1933): 391–418.
Grodecki, Louis. *L'architecture ottonienne: au seuil de l'art roman.* Paris: Colin, 1958.
Ventre, André, and Marcel Delangle. "Les fouilles de la cathédrale de Verdun." *Monuments historiques de la France* 2 (1937): 9–17.

VERMANDOIS. By the Carolingian period, the Roman *civitas Vermanduorum* had been split into two parts, of which the one centered on the towns of Saint-Quentin and Péronne was alone called the *pagus Vermanduensis.* Situated on the plateau that served as a source to the Scheldt, the Oise, and the Somme, and crossed by Roman roads, it became of great economic and strategic value. It was one of the earliest areas to develop a feudal vocabulary (*vassi* and *fideles* used in 948 and *fevum* as the equivalent of *beneficium* by 1036/43) and to collect a money *cens* (pre-1018–40). Saint-Quentin, named for a 3rd-century martyr, received one of the oldest communal charters in 1080 from count Hugues le Grand (ca. 1068–1102). Along with Lower Lorraine, it was the region of the chansons celebrating Raoul de Cambrai and Ibert de Ribemont.

In the late 9th and early 10th centuries, Vermandois was ruled by descendants of Charlemagne in the male line, of whom the most prominent was Count Herbert II (900–943). He attempted to expand his holdings by conquest and by making his five-year-old son, Hugues, archbishop of Reims. Though he was the captor of King Charles III the

Simple (r. 893–922) from 923 to 929, first at Château-Thierry and then at Péronne, Herbert's influence had deteriorated by the time of his death, when his sons divided his remaining lands. Vermandois was eventually united to Valois and the two countships passed to a collateral Capetian line by the marriage of their heiress, Adèle, to Hugues, a younger son of King Henry I (r. 1031–60) and a brother of Philip I (r. 1060–1108). Hugues participated in the First Crusade and died in 1102 at Tarsus on his second expedition to the Levant.

On the death of Count Raoul le Lépreux (r. 1162–67), Vermandois/Valois passed to the elder of his two sisters, Elizabeth (d. 1183), wife of Philippe d'Alsace, count of Flanders. Philippe disputed her inheritance with King Philip II Augustus. The Treaty of Boves (1185) gave the king Amiens and sixty-five castles in western Vermandois. After Philippe's death, the king acquired the rest by the Treaty of Arras (1192), except for Saint-Quentin proper and Valois, which both went to Eleanor, Elizabeth's younger sister, reverting to the crown on her death in 1213.

R. Thomas McDonald

VERSIFICATION. The rhythm of poetry in medieval French is based on a fixed number of syllables in a line. Longer lines are frequently divided by a pause, called a caesura, into parts called hemistiches. Although examples exist of lines from one to fifteen syllables, the commonest lines in medieval French poetry are of eight, ten, and twelve syllables. The octosyllabic line, the oldest meter in French verse, appeared in the 10th century in the *Passion du Christ* and in the 11th-century *Vie de saint Léger* and was the meter of the epic poem *Gormont et Isembart.* The octosyllabic line, arranged in rhyming couplets (*rimes plates* or *suivies*) became the meter of narrative poetry and drama in the 12th century. The decasyllabic line was first used in the 11th-century *Vie de saint Alexis* and was the meter of most of the older chansons de geste, such as the *Chanson de Roland* and *Chanson de Guillaume.* It predominated in the poetry of the 14th and 15th centuries. The dodecasyllabic line began to displace the decasyllabic in 13th-century epic (e.g., *Voyage de Charlemagne*); used in the *Roman d'Alexandre* (ca. 1179), it became known as the Alexandrine.

The first vernacular poems, beginning with the *Séquence de sainte Eulalie* (9th c.), were assonanced. Assonance consists of the identity of sound of the final accented vowel of successive verses; this identity need not extend to preceding or following sounds. The chansons de geste were typically composed of laisses, groups of lines constructed on a single assonance.

The first rhymed poem in the vernacular was the Occitan *Chanson de sainte Foy* (11th c.). Other early rhymed poems were the *Voyage de saint Brendan* (ca. 1112) and the *Bestiaire* of Philippe de Thaün (ca. 1125). Beginning with the 12th-century Romances of Antiquity (*Thèbes, Énéas, Troie*), poems were regularly rhymed in French. By 1200, assonance had given way to rhyme almost completely. Rhyme consists of the identity of the final tonic vowel of two or more verses and any following articulations. If the words end in a tonic vowel

aimé : chanté

favori : ami

then rhyme and assonance are identical, and the rhyme is called *rime pauvre*.

If the tonic vowel is followed by one or more consonants

mort : sort

passanz : granz

then the rhyme is both *suffisante* and *pauvre*.

When the identity of sound extends to articulations preceding the tonic vowel

vers : divers

main : demain

then the rhyme is *riche*.

If the identity of sound extends to the vowel that precedes the tonic vowel and includes all the following sounds

ressentir : repentir

acier : glacier

then the rhyme is called *léonine* (also *double* or *superflue*).

If the identity of sound extends farther back to include the consonant

félicité : férocité

utilité : tranquillité

then the rhyme is *riche léonine*.

Rhyme is divided into *rimes masculines* and *féminines*. Words that end in a mute *e* are feminine and the rest are masculine. Masculine and feminine rhymes did not have to alternate in medieval French poetry. A word could rhyme with itself and did not have to have different meanings or derivations as in modern French poetry.

Rhymes that included homonyms

partira : part ira

à mordre : amordre

are called *rimes équivoques*.

Sequences of rhymes involving variations on the same word

avez : savez, savons : avons

are called *rimes grammaticales* and were frequent in Old French poetry.

In the 15th century and later, with the Grands Rhétoriqueurs, other rhyme forms were much favored, such as *rime batelée* (the last word of a line rhymes with the word at the caesura in the following line); *rime renforcée* (the caesura of a line rhymes with the end of the line); *rime brisée* (words rhyme at the caesura); *rime couronnée* (the last syllable of a line is repeated twice); *rime emperière* (a sound is repeated three times at the end of a line); *rime fratrisée* or *enchaînée* (the last word of a line is repeated at the beginning of the next line); *rime entrelacée* (part of the last word of a line is repeated in the next line); *rime annexée* (the word at the end of a line has the same root as the word at the beginning of the next line); *rime rétrograde* (a series of words could be inverted word for word or syllable for syllable); *rime senée* (all the words of each line begin with the same letter); and *rime en écho* (the last word of a line is used alone as the following line).

The lyric strophe, or stanza, is formed by a fixed number of lines, rarely more than fourteen. The more common strophes comprise two lines (the *couplet* or *distiche*); four lines (the quatrain); six lines (the *sixain*); eight lines (the *huitain*); and ten lines (the *dixain*). Some poems with fixed strophe forms, the *formes fixes*, that were popular in the later Middle Ages were the rondeau, ballade, *chant royal*, chanson, *sirventes*, virelai, *lai lyrique,* and *pastourelle*.

The earliest treatise to distinguish between quantitative and syllabic accentual verse was by the Englishman Bede, *De arte metrica* (ca. 725). Other medieval treatises in Latin were collected by Faral, especially those by Matthieu de Vendôme, Geoffroi de Vinsauf, Gervais de Melkley, Evrard l'Allemand, and Jean de Garlande). The first vernacular work on versification was by the Catalan troubadour Raimon Vidal, the *Razos de trobar* (ca. 1200). The most important collection of Provençal *arts poétiques* was the *Leys d'Amors*, or *Flors del gay saber* (1341). The first treatise in French was the *Art de dictier* (1392) of Eustache Deschamps. Important 15th-century treatises on versification were collected by Langlois (Jacques Legrand, Baudet Herenc, Jean Molinet, and four anonymous treatises). Also important in the development of verse forms are the *Prologue* (1370) of Machaut's *Dit du vergier* (ca. 1330) and the *Intermedes lyriques* of his *Remede de Fortune* (ca. 1340). The theorist of the Grands Rhétoriqueurs was Jean Molinet, author of the *Art de rhétorique vulgaire* (1493).

Lenora D. Wolfgang

[See also: *ARTS DE SECONDE RHÉTORIQUE*; BALLADE; CHANSON DE GESTE; DESCHAMPS, EUSTACHE; *FORMES FIXES*; FRENCH LANGUAGE; GRAND RHÉTORIQUEURS; HERENC, BAUDET; *LAI-DESCORT*; *LEYS D'AMORS*; MACHAUT, GUILLAUME DE; MOLINET, JEAN; *PASTOURELLE/PASTORELA*; RONDEAU; SESTINA; *SIRVENTES*; TROUBADOUR POETRY; TROUVÈRE POETRY; VIRELAI]

Elwert, W. Theodor. *Traité de versification française des origines à nos jours.* Paris: Klincksieck, 1965.

Faral, Edmond. *Les arts poétiques du XIIe et du XIIIe siècle.* Paris: Champion, 1924.

Grammont, Maurice. *Le vers français.* 5th ed. Paris: Delagrave, 1964.

———. *Petit traité de versification française.* Paris: Colin, 1965.

Kastner, Leon Emile. *A History of French Versification.* Oxford: Clarendon, 1903.

Langlois, Ernest. *Recueil d'arts de seconde rhétorique.* Paris: Imprimerie Nationale, 1902.

Lote, Georges. *Histoire du vers français.* 6 vols. Paris: Boivin, 1949–51, Vols. 1–3: *Le Moyen âge*; and Aix-en-Provence: Université de Provence, Vols. 4–6: *Le XVIe et le XVIIe siècle.*

Tobler, Adolphe. *Le vers français ancien et moderne,* trans. Karl Breul and Léopold Sudre. Paris, 1885.

VERSUS. Monophonic and polyphonic songs with both sacred and secular texts, written in significant numbers from the late 11th through the early 13th century, especially in southern France. The versus belonged to the late-medieval flourishing of rhythmic, accentual Latin poetry that affected several genres of liturgical song, and they undoubtedly influenced the development of troubadour song as well. When sacred versus became important in the north, most notably in Paris in the late 12th and early 13th centuries, they were called "conductus" and were frequently set polyphonically.

The major sources of the Aquitanian repertory are nine versaria—collections of versus—contained in four manuscripts, which embody a chronological history of the genre. Texts for the versus, although sharply marked and sometimes strophic, were set to both simple melodies with clear phrase structures and to melodies with lengthy melismas, especially toward the ends of lines.

Margot Fassler

[See also: CONDUCTUS]

Gillingham, Brian, ed. *Paris, Bibliothèque Nationale, fonds latin 1139, fonds latin 3719, fonds latin 3549 and London, B.L. Add. 36,881.* 3 vols. Ottawa: Institute of Mediaeval Music, 1987.

Arlt, Wulf. "'Nova cantica': Grundsätzliches und Spezielles zur Interpretation musikalischer Texte des Mittelalters." *Basler Jahrbuch für historische Musikpraxis* 10 (1986): 13–62.

Fassler, Margot. "Accent, Meter, and Rhythm in Medieval Treatises 'De rithmis.'" *Journal of Musicology* 5 (1987): 164–90.

Grier, James. "Scribal Practices in the Aquitanian Versaria of the Twelfth Century: Towards a Typology of Error and Variant." *Journal of the American Musicological Society* 45 (1992): 373–427.

Spanke, Hans. "St. Martial-Studien: Ein Beitrag zur frühromanischen Metrik." *Zeitschrift für französische Sprache und Literatur* 54 (1931): 282–317, 385–422.

Treitler, Leo. *The Aquitanian Repertories of Sacred Monody in the Eleventh and Twelfth Centuries.* 3 vols. Diss. Princeton University, 1967.

VESTMENTS, ECCLESIASTICAL. Ecclesiastical vestments and insignia originated for the most part as the customary secular garb of Greco-Roman antiquity but were retained when standards of dress changed during the centuries of barbarian ascendancy and took on symbolic significance in the early Middle Ages.

The most important vestments are the six worn by the priest at Mass: the amice, alb, cincture, maniple, stole, and chasuble. The amice is a white rectangular cloth draped over the upper back and shoulders and secured in place by tapes around the waist; it is thought by most to have originated as a sort of scarf, although some maintain it was a kerchief protecting the head. The alb is a white floor-length garment with long sleeves; it appears to be descended from the Roman undergarment called the *tunica*. The alb is belted in at the waist by the cincture, a long white cord with tassels at each end. The maniple, perhaps a handkerchief originally, is a narrow band of material draped over the left forearm. The stole, of uncertain origin, is a similarly narrow, but much longer, band of cloth draped about the neck of the priest with its ends hanging down his front to about knee length. Worn also by the deacon, but over his left shoulder like a sash and secured under his right arm, it came to be looked upon as the distinctive vestment of the deacon. The chasuble, worn over the other vestments, owes its origins to a cloak called the *planeta*, like a small tent with a hole in the middle for the head. Symbolic meaning was attached to priestly vestments during the Carolingian period: for example, the cincture standing as a bond of chastity and the alb as a sign of innocence. The alb was worn also by the newly baptized on Holy Saturday and throughout Easter Week until the following Sunday, the *Dominica in albis depositis*.

Other important vestments are the dalmatic, tunicle, pallium, cope, and surplice. The dalmatic and tunicle are outer garments of varying design worn, respectively, by the deacon and subdeacon at Mass. They, as well as the maniple, stole, and chasuble were originally made from white wool but came in the later Middle Ages to be of silk decorated with bands of ophrey (cloth woven with gold thread). They came also to assume the colors associated with the different liturgical occasions. White (also gold) was the color of most important festivals; red was associated with Apostles, martyrs, and the Holy Ghost; black (later purple) was the color of penitential occasions and green that of ordinary Sundays. The pallium is a narrow woolen band marked with six purple crosses; derived from imperial insignia, it was worn by the pope and shared by him with bishops of special importance. The cope, or *pluviale*, is an outer garment similar to the chasuble but open in the front; it was worn by priests and bishops at functions other than the Mass and by cantors in choir. In the late Middle Ages, it was often richly decorated. The medieval surplice was a knee-length white linen shirt with wide sleeves worn by clerics in choir and also on many nonofficial occasions; its Latin name, *superpelliceum* ("over a fur garment"), betrays its origins as something worn over fur coats in northern European countries as a replacement for the tighter-fitting alb.

James McKinnon

[See also: CHURCH, INTERIOR; CLOTHING, COSTUME, AND FASHION; EUCHARISTIC VENERATION AND VESSELS]

Braun, Joseph. *Die liturgische Gewandung.* Freiburg im Breisgau: Herder, 1907.

Norris, Herbert. *Church Vestments: Their Origin and Development.* London: Dent, 1949.

Pocknee, Cyril E. *Liturgical Vesture: Its Origins and Development.* London: Mowbray, 1960.

VEXIN. The Gallo-Roman *pagus Veliocassinus*, located strategically on the north bank of the Seine between the Oise and the Andelle, incorporated the towns of Mantes-la-Jolie, Meulan, and Pontoise along with the fortress of Gisors. The countship, established by the reign of Hugh Capet (r. 987–96), may have grown out of the advocacy of the lands of the royal abbey of Saint-Denis, which dominated the region. Its banner, the *oriflamme*, supposedly that of Charlemagne, became the standard of the French kings in the 12th century in their capacity as counts and vassals of the abbey. At some time, however (traditionally in 911), the *pagus* was divided at the Epte into eastern and western parts (French and Norman Vexin, respectively), and it became a vital strategic march for both the dukes of Normandy and the kings of France.

The original line of counts was drawn into close ties with England as early as the 1030s, when Count Dreux married a sister of Edward the Confessor (r. 1042–66), and Henry I of France (r. 1031–60) was to cede the French Vexin to Duke Robert of Normandy in return for aid in securing his throne. Philip I (r. 1060–1108) wrested it back from Count Simon between 1076 and 1077 to bestow it upon his son the future Louis VI (r. 1108–37), who even occupied the Norman Vexin until his defeat at Brémule (1119).

Henry II of England (r. 1154–89) did homage for the Norman Vexin, and the French Vexin was made the dowry of two daughters of Louis VII (r. 1137–80), married and betrothed successively to two of Henry's sons. The latter marriage, to Richard I the Lionhearted (r. 1189–99) never having taken place, Philip II Augustus (r. 1180–1223) waged war against him from 1195 to 1199, losing most of the French Vexin in the process. But after Richard's death, the annexation of Normandy in 1204, confirmed by the Battle of Bouvines in 1214, rendered moot the question of the frontier. Philip II was to grant communal charters to several towns in the Vexin, which quickly became integrated into the royal domain.

R. Thomas McDonald

[See also: NORMANDY; ROYAL DOMAIN]

Barroux, Robert. "L'abbé Suger et la vassalité du Vexin en 1124." *Moyen âge* 64 (1958): 1–26.

Grierson, Philippe. "L'origine des comtes d'Amiens, Valois et Vexin." *Moyen âge*, 3rd ser., 2 (1939): 81–125.

VÉZELAY. The stormy history of Vézelay (Yonne) and its monastery spans most of the Middle Ages. Founded in Carolingian times, the first monastery, not on the hill, was destroyed in 886–87 by Vikings whom Charles III The Fat had allowed to pillage in Burgundy. It was soon rebuilt on the hill above, which was fortified. Belief in the presence of remains of the body of Mary Magdalene grew, and in 1058 Pope Stephen IX confirmed the relics and pilgrimages began.

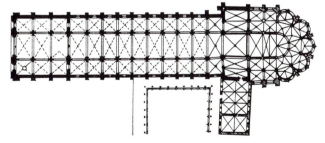

Vézelay (Yonne), La Madeleine, plan and elevation of narthex and nave. After Salet and Losowska.

Given the vast numbers of pilgrims, Abbot Artaud decided in 1096 to replace the Carolingian church with a larger structure, whose choir and transept were consecrated on April 21, 1104. Two years later, the townspeople, overwhelmed by taxes to finance the construction, assassinated Artaud. His successor, Renaud de Semur, rebuilt the Carolingian nave, which had been destroyed by a fire on the feast of Mary Magdalene (July 21, 1120) in which over 1,000 worshipers perished. The new church was dedicated by Pope Calixtus II in 1132. It was at Vézelay on Easter Sunday of 1146, on the north slope of the monastery, that Bernard of Clairvaux preached the Second Crusade and here that Thomas Becket excommunicated King Henry II in 1166; from here, Richard I the Lionhearted and Philip II Augustus set off in 1190 for the Third Crusade. Just a few years earlier, ca. 1185, Abbot Girard d'Arcy had rebuilt the choir in Gothic style.

The Romanesque nave presents spatial shapes and systems of construction different from those of pilgrimage churches like Conques and Toulouse. Interior volumes are much squatter and are crowned with domical groined vaults. This allows clerestory windows to penetrate into the vaults. The transverse arches of alternating stones and the domical vaults give each bay greater independence.

The elevation of nave arcade, blank wall, and clerestory seems to have derived from the priory of Anzy-le-Duc, although the nave of Vézelay is more decorative and coloristic. Anzy-le-Duc, with no flying buttresses, helps one visualize the exterior of Vézelay in its original appearance.

The continuity of the masonry along the north flank of Vézelay may indicate that the first campaign from 1096–1104 included the outer walls of the nave and narthex up to the sills under the nave and narthex windows. By 1004, more of the Romanesque east end was probably finished. The burning of the small, wooden-roofed Carolingian church in 1120 could not have damaged the Romanesque choir, narthex, and nave walls. Thus, the sculptural programs of nave façade or narthex portals and outer façade could have begun before 1120.

The three portals inside the narthex of Vézelay comprise one of the most impressive sculptural ensembles in Romanesque art. The large central portal depicts the Ascension of Christ combined with the Mission of the Apostles. The tympanum shows Christ flanked by the Apostles. His power to save humankind (left side with quiet clouds and open books) and condemn (right side with stormy clouds and closed books) is clearly revealed; the lintel, showing Lydians, Greeks, Africans, and others, manifests Christ's goal to preach and convert. Archivolts, containing the signs of the zodiac and occupations of the months, frame Christ as the supreme ruler of space and time. Side portals include the Adoration of the Magi, Annunciation, Visitation, and Nativity (south portal) and Ascension and Christ meeting Apostles on the road to Emmaus (north portal). The freeing of the Holy Land as a result of the First Crusade of 1095 and the necessity of the Second Crusade, 1146–47, are both reflected and prophesied in the central portal.

Vézelay, La Madeleine, narthex portal. *Photograph courtesy of Whitney S. Stoddard.*

Vézelay, La Madeleine, nave. *Photograph courtesy of Whitney S. Stoddard.*

Originally, the tympanum and lintel were planned to rest on the short columns and the trumeau (John the Baptist). The portal, however, was raised by adding the two pairs of Apostles and a new base under John.

A northern dynamic intensity permeates the narthex sculpture. Christ is pushed into the block with frontal chest, transfixed head, and thin legs suspended diagonally. A hierarchy of sizes, keyed to the hierarchy of importance, is accompanied by an increase in the amount of relief to make the sculpture more readable and more meaningful.

According to Armi, the three portals were carved by two sculptors: the Avenas Master carved the altar in Avenas, worked at Mâcon and at Perrecy-les-Forges, and created two of the jamb capitals of the side portals and tympanum of the north portal at Vézelay. The second sculptor, named the Perrecy Master, collaborated with the Avenas Master at Perrecy-les-Forges and was responsible for two jamb capitals, the lintel and tympanum of the south portal, and all of the Vézelay central portal. These two sculptors also carved the Cluny choir capitals. Gislebertus, who signed his name on the lintel of the portal of Autun, was involved in two sculptural projects at Vézelay: the outer-façade portal and the mausoleum of Mary Magdalene.

In 1793, figures of most of the sculpture of the outer façade were hacked off. In 1840, Viollet-le-Duc, at the age of twenty-six, was placed in charge of restorations. Because the condition of vaults, roofs, and buttresses was so precarious, the restoration of the west façade was postponed until the 1850s. The tympanum and lintel of the central portal were removed to the south of the church, and damaged capitals were replaced by new ones. The distinctive drapery style of the preserved details of the tympanum, with narrow, flat planes, shifting inward at the bottom and separated by rounded ridge folds and wind-blown terminations, can be seen also in the fragments of the mausoleum of Mary Magdalene, now housed in the museum in the monastic dormitory. These fragments are identical in style to the capitals and tympanum at Autun by Gislebertus. Since his hand can be seen in the portal of Cluny, he has a career as sculptor at Cluny, Vézelay, Autun, and perhaps beyond.

In its encyclopedic scope, the Vézelay portal (narthex and façade), together with the capitals of nave and narthex, has a powerful effect on the modern visitor. For groups of pilgrims gathered at Vézelay to start toward Spain or Jerusalem, the impact must have been even more vital and moving.

The choir of Vézelay is Early Gothic, begun ca. 1185. It has a three-storied elevation like Sens cathedral. Indeed, by studying Vézelay, which has not been altered by enlarging the clerestory windows and raising the vaults as at Sens, one can imagine the original appearance of Sens. The plan consists of crossing, short transept arms, single ambulatory with five radiating apsidioles, and four square chapels in the forechoir. These nine chapels are separated at the bottom level only, so that space is continuous around the periphery of the choir. The treatment of the ribs and vaults exhibits fascinating Early Gothic inconsistencies. The happy juxtaposition of Early Gothic choir and Romanesque nave imparts a visual vibrancy to Vézelay.

Whitney S. Stoddard

[See also: ANZY-LE-DUC; GISLEBERTUS; MARY
MAGDALENE; ROMANESQUE ARCHITECTURE; SENS]

Armi, C. Edson. *Masons and Sculptors in Romanesque Burgundy: The New Aesthetic of Cluny III.* 2 vols. University
Park: Pennsylvania State University Press, 1983.

Salet, Francis. *La Madeleine de Vézelay.* Melun: Librairie
d'Argences, 1948.

Saulnier, Lydwine, and Neil Stratford. "La sculpture oubliée de
Vézelay." *Bibliotheque de la Société d'Archéologie* 17 (1984):
27–29, 33–37.

Stoddard, Whitney S. *Monastery and Cathedral in France.*
Middletown: Wesleyan University Press, 1966.

———. *The Sculptors of the West Portals of Chartres Cathedral.* New York: Norton, 1987.

VICQ. Located within the diocese of Bourges, the parish
of Vicq (Indre) was one of many highly desirable sites in
the 11th and 12th centuries. Although little specific documentation survives about the Benedictine abbey church of
Saint-Martin at Nohant-Vicq, the parish of Vicq is often
mentioned as a possession of Déols, in relation to surrounding areas and possessions. By the later 12th century,
a dispute arose over parish rights between the priory of
Aureil, which had acquired many possessions in the parish, and Déols. In the end, Déols kept the abbey.

Sometime between the last quarter of the 11th century and the early 12th, the church of Saint-Martin at Vicq
was constructed and later painted. (It was transformed
into a barn in 1700.) No architectural sculpture but much
wall painting survives. Inside, each of the three successive
spaces grows increasingly small. Within the rectangular
nave, the transverse wall contains a small entrance into the
choir and an enthroned Christ in mandorla, Apostles, and
scenes from the life of Christ and the Virgin. Small windows illuminate the wall paintings of the life of Christ and
scenes from the Old and New Testaments in the cubic
choir and half-round apse. Around the apsidal arch are
paintings of biblical and saintly figures and within the apse
a Christ in Majesty.

Stacy L. Boldrick

[See also: ROMANESQUE ART]

Hubert, Jean. "Vic." *Congrès archéologique* (*Bourges*) 94 (1931):
556–76.

Kupfer, Marcia. *The Romanesque Frescoes in the Church of
Saint-Martin at Nohant-Vicq.* Diss. Yale University, 1982.

———. "Spiritual Passage and Pictorial Strategy in the Romanesque Frescoes at Vicq." *Art Bulletin* 68 (1986).

VIDAME. Term (Lat. *vice-dominus*) that originally referred
to the lieutenant or stand-in of the lord of a great seigneurie.
Rather early, it acquired a more specialized meaning: the
man responsible for the temporal possessions of a religious house or bishopric. His tasks involved administering
justice and defense, as well as leading the troops whom the
bishop or monastery had to send if the king summoned

them to military service. A *vidame* thus resembled the *avoué*
of a monastery. The position soon became a hereditary
fief, with a bishop's *vidame* being one of the important
nobles of the diocese.

John Bell Henneman, Jr.

[See also: *ADVOCATUS/AVOUÉ*]

VIDAS AND RAZOS. Commonly referred to jointly as
the "biographies of the troubadours," the Provençal *vidas*
and *razos* are brief accounts in prose. The *vidas* were rarely
more than a few sentences long, reporting who the troubadour was, whence he came, whom he loved, what kind of
songs he composed, and where he died; the *razos* ("reasons"), usually several paragraphs long, attempted to explain how a given troubadour happened to write a certain
song. *Vidas* survive for about a hundred troubadours; *razos*,
for about twenty-five.

The *vidas* and *razos* are preserved in some twenty
chansonniers, most of which were compiled in northern
Italy. Four of these collections date from the 13th century;
virtually all the rest, from the 14th. In the 13th-century
manuscripts, the *vidas* and *razos* are placed immediately
before (or, in the case of the nineteen Bertran de Born
razos, immediately after) the poem or poems to which
they pertain; in the 14th-century codices, the biographical
texts stand detached from the poems, in a section unto
themselves.

Two of the biographies are signed: the *vida* for Peire
Cardenal, by a certain Miquel de la Tor, and one of the
razos for Savaric de Mauleon, by the troubadour Uc de
Saint-Circ, who identifies himself as having written *estas
razos.* The common errors, cross-references, and stylistic
similarities among the texts make it apparent that there
was one primary biographer, undoubtedly Uc. Even if Uc
"wrote" the biographies, he did not necessarily invent them.
The abundance of accurate geographical detail in the *vidas*
suggests that they were composed originally by jongleurs,
who, as traveling performers, knew the southern French
countryside well and who would have invented these narratives on the spot as a means of enlivening their recital of
troubadour songs.

The *vidas* and *razos* follow a variety of narrative patterns: some resemble miniature saints' lives; others are like
fabliaux; still others are reminiscent of the Latin *accessus
ad auctores*; most of them are simply humorous expansions on metaphors drawn from troubadour poems.

Both the virtual absence of *razos* (with the exception
of those pertaining to Bertran de Born) from the earliest
chansonniers and the relative narrative simplicity of the
typical *vida* compared with the *razo* made scholars for a
long time assume that the *vidas* predated the *razos.* The
opposite, however, is true. None of the information reported in the *razos* postdates the year 1219, whereas some
of what is contained in the *vidas* does. Uc did not produce
the *razos* as a single block. He wrote the *razos* for Bertran
de Born first. These texts remained detached from the others. Uc referred to them once in a *razo* about Folquet de

Marseille as *l'autr'escrit*, thus acknowledging that he wrote them at an earlier time.

The distinction between *vida* and *razo* is not always clear-cut. There are at least a dozen mixed texts spread throughout the chansonniers. Within the biographies themselves, the term *razo* is applied indiscriminately and the word *vida* never occurs as a generic designation. *Vida* first appears in the rubrics of certain 14th-century chansonniers.

Elizabeth W. Poe

[See also: BERTRAN DE BORN; TROUBADOUR POETRY]

Boutière, Jean, and Alexander H. Schutz, eds. *Biographies des troubadours: textes provençaux des XIIIe et XIVe siècles.* 2nd ed. rev. with Irénée-M. Cluzel. Paris: Nizet, 1964.

Egar, Margarita, ed. and trans. *The Vidas of the Troubadours.* New York: Garland, 1984.

Favati, Guido, ed. *Le biografie trovadoriche, testi provenzali dei secoli XIII e XIV: edizione critica.* Bologna: Palmaverde, 1961.

Poe, Elizabeth W. *From Poetry to Prose in Old Provençal.* Birmingham: Summa, 1984.

VIENNE. Under the name of Vienna Senatoria, Vienne (Isère) became a Roman colony and the capital of the province of Gaul shortly after Julius Caesar's death. Later, it was capital of the kingdom of Burgundy (413–534) and from 879 to 1032 was the capital of the so-called kingdom of Arles. Its archbishops, who from 1119 bore the title of primate of Gaul, divided its territory with the dauphins of the Viennois until the accession of Louis IX, when it was absorbed by the province of Dauphiné. In 1311, the city hosted the fifteenth ecumenical council, at which Clement V pronounced the suppression of the Templars.

The former cathedral of Saint-Maurice was begun in the early 11th century and completed in the 15th. In the 13th century, the choir, apse, and aisles were reconstructed around the original Romanesque nave. In the 14th century, chapels were built along the length of the church. In the 15th century, the church was extended to twelve bays, and the vaulting, western façade, and two flanking towers were completed. The absence of a transept and the uninterrupted garland of the triforium exaggerate the low (82 feet at its highest point) and long (297 feet) proportions of the structure. The Flamboyant western front (14th and 15th c.) is preceded by a broad flight of steps descending toward the Rhône River. The three gabled portals of the façade are surrounded by richly sculpted moldings. On the upper story is a grand rose window, as large as the central doorway it surmounts. The arms of the antipope Clement VII (r. 1378–94) appear sculpted in the portal to the right of the façade.

The church of the abbey of Saint-Pierre-de-Vienne, founded in the first half of the 6th century, was built upon the foundation of a 4th-century Christian basilica. Until the 12th century, it was the burial place of the archbishops of Vienne. Rebuilt in the 10th and 12th centuries, it has a nave with aisles and an apse. At the front of the church stands a square Romanesque bell tower (12th c.), and on the south portal is a sculpted tympanum (12th c.).

The church of Saint-André-le-Bas was founded in 542. Ravaged by Muslims and Franks, it was restored in the 9th century. Originally belonging to an order of nuns, it was given to the Benedictines in the 10th century. Reconstructed ca. 1152, the building has no aisles and is only 45 feet long. The extensive decorative program of the interior includes an ornamental frieze and columns capped by historiated capitals. Bulging cross-ribbed vaults are supported by flying buttresses, perhaps the first instance of this structure more typical of the 13th and 14th centuries. On the exterior is a three-story bell tower like that at Saint-Pierre.

Nina Rowe

Albrand, Emilie. *L'église et le cloître de Saint-André-le-Bas à Vienne.* Lyon: Presses des Audin, 1951.

Bégule, Lucien. *L'église Saint-Maurice, ancienne cathédrale de Vienne en Dauphiné: son architecture, sa décoration.* Paris: Laurens, 1914.

Bretocq, Abbé Gabriel. "L'ancienne cathédrale Saint-Maurice de Vienne." *Bulletin monumental* 110 (1952): 297–364.

Formigé, Jules. "Vienne." *Congrès archéologique* (*Valence et Montélimar*) 86 (1923): 7–127.

VIES DES ANCIENS PÈRES. In the 6th century, a collection of Lives of monks and saints who lived in the desert of Egypt was translated into Latin from Greek and formed, in ten books and an appendix, what was collectively known as the *Vitae patrum.* This collection was frequently translated into medieval French, the most interesting version being that by Wauchier de Denain for Philippe, marshal of Namur (d. 1212). However, the title *Vies des anciens pères* refers more specifically to a 13th-century collection of pious tales, totaling over 30,000 octosyllabic lines and found, in one of its several forms, in more than fifty manuscripts and fragments. The first forty-two tales, from the early 13th century, are largely oriental in inspiration. Well written, each has a prologue and focuses on humanity's role in its own salvation. The later tales, from mid-century, are more closely related to the Miracles of the Virgin, lack prologues, and are generally set in contemporary France. The straightforward narratives of the early group are replaced by convoluted rhetoric, word play, and metrical intricacies in the manner of Gautier de Coinci.

Claude J. Fouillade

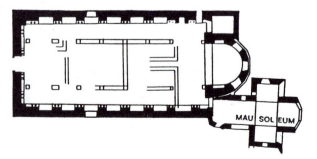

Vienne (Isère), Saint-Pierre, restored plan. After Reynaud.

[See also: GAUTIER DE COINCI; HAGIOGRAPHY; MIRACLE PLAYS; MORAL TREATISES; SAINT PLAYS; SAINTS' LIVES; TRANSLATION]

Lecoy, Félix, ed. *Vies des Pères*. Paris: SATF, 1988. [Edition of Tales 1–21.]
Schwan, E. "La vie des anciens pères." *Romania* 13 (1884): 233–63.

VIGNAY, JEAN DE (ca. 1282/85–1350). Translator. Born near Bayeux, Vignay was a monk of the order of Saint-Jacques-du-Haut-Pas in Paris. Eleven of his twelve translations from the Latin (one is lost) are preserved in magnificent illuminated manuscripts made for King Philip VI (r. 1328–50); his widow, Jeanne of Burgundy; and their eldest son, the future John II the Good. His most important translations are of Vegetius's *De re militari* (*De la chose de la chevalerie*), Vincent de Beauvais's *Speculum historiale* (*Miroir historial*), Hugues de Saint-Cher's *Speculum Ecclesiae* (*Miroir de l'Église*), Jacobus of Voragine's *Legenda aurea* (*Légende dorée*), and Jacques de Cessoles's *Liber super ludo scaccorum* (*Livre des eschez*). The latter two were translated into English and printed by William Caxton. The *Livre des eschez* was the second book to be printed in the English language (1475). Jean de Vignay's Latin was rudimentary and his French style halting; moreover, his extreme faithfulness to the vocabulary and syntax of his originals frequently makes his translations difficult to follow.

Lenora D. Wolfgang

[See also: TRANSLATION]

Knowles, Christine. "Jean de Vignay: un traducteur du XIVe siècle." *Romania* 75 (1954): 353–83.
Meyer, Paul. "Les anciens traducteurs français de Végèce, et en particulier Jean de Vignai." *Romania* 25 (1896): 401–23.

VIGNEULLES, PHILIPPE DE (1471–1528). All the works of this rich bourgeois deal with Lorraine and, more specifically, with his beloved city of Metz. Vigneulles left us a *Journal*, a long *Chronique de Metz, de Lorraine et de France*, the epic *Garin le Lorrain* (translated *de ancienne rime en prouse*), and a collection of *contes à rire*: the *Cent nouvelles nouvelles*. His *Journal* gives a vivid picture of Metz and describes his education, Italian voyage, capture by brigands and payment of a ransom, the ravages of the plague, and so on. The *Chronique* begins with Adam and ends in 1525. The *Nouvelles* and the prose *Garin* (unedited) were completed in 1515.

The *Nouvelles* are preserved in a unique manuscript, now in Bowdoin College. The lascivious character of the stories accounts for the severe mutilation of the manuscript, probably by Philippe's heirs. Of the 110 stories (Phillipe added ten stories to the original hundred, without bothering to change the title), about forty are incomplete and fourteen are missing altogether.

Several models influenced Philippe's compilation. He was inspired by its more famous 15th-century namesake, the anonymous *Cent nouvelles nouvelles*. He also drew on, sparingly, the *Decameron*, Poggio's *Liber facetiarum*, and other Italian storytellers. But his chief sources were the ubiquitous fabliau tradition, with its insistance on the salacious, and oral stories heard by him in his native Lorraine or on his voyages. The stories, placed in a concrete milieu, constitute a priceless document preserving the daily life of the bourgeoisie of Metz at the waning of the Middle Ages.

Peter F. Dembowski

[See also: *CENT NOUVELLES NOUVELLES, LES*; FABLIAU; METZ]

Vigneulles, Philippe de. *La chronique de Philippe de Vigneulles*, ed. Charles Bruneau. 4 vols. Metz: Société d'Histoire et d'Archéologie de la Lorraine, 1927–33.
——. *Gedenkbuch des Metzer Bürgers Philippe von Vigneules*, ed. Henri Michelant. Stuttgart: Literarischer Verein, 1852. [Edition of Philippe's *Journal*.]
——. *Les cent nouvelles nouvelles*, ed. Charles H. Livingston with Françoise R. Livingston and Robert T. Ivy, Jr. Geneva: Droz, 1972.

VIGNORY. Founded ca. 1000, the church of Saint-Étienne of Vignory (Haute-Marne) is one of the earliest Romanesque structures in France. Built largely between 1032 and 1057, it consists of a nine-bay nave under an open-timber roof, separated from the side aisles by a two-story arcade: wide arcades, a false tribune of twin bays with sculpted capitals,

Vignory (Haute-Marne), Notre-Dame, nave. *Photograph courtesy of Whitney S. Stoddard.*

and high windows. A high triumphal arch separates the nave from the vaulted choir with ambulatory, Gothic radiating chapels, and twin flanking towers, which are 12th-century. The church contains some beautiful 14th- and 15th-century statuary in Champenois style. The most remarkable are an altar frontal showing the Crowning of Mary between SS. Peter and Paul and an altar frontal of the Passion flanked by donors presented by John the Baptist and St. Catherine.

William W. Kibler/William W. Clark

Aubert, Marcel. "L'église de Vignory: essai sur les dates de sa construction." *Mémoires de la Société Nationale des Antiquaires de France* 83 (1954): 165–69.

Ronot, Henry, and Philippe Dautrey. *L'église de Vignory*. Paris: Éditions du Cerf, 1951.

VIGUIER. In the government of the Frankish kings and the Carolingian empire, the title *vicarius* (Fr. *viguier*) designated widely the principal local deputy of the counts or dukes. After the breakdown of royal authority in the 10th century, these *viguiers* continued to function, particularly in the south, as officials under the regime of their hereditary overlords. The status and power of the *viguiers* increased with the advent of royal government in Languedoc in the 13th century. Although many of their judicial functions were assumed by judges, they were endowed with broad executive powers in the administration of districts (*vicariae*) under the royal seneschals. They received salaries that, for the greater *viguiers*, afforded a handsome revenue. Until it was broken up in 1352, the *viguerie* of Béziers remained the largest in the Midi, encompassing four episcopal cities, Béziers, Narbonne, Agde, and Lodève. Few *viguiers*, nonetheless, advanced to the rank of seneschal; most appear to have been recruited from the lesser nobility or in some cases from among the nonnoble inhabitants of the region.

Alan Friedlander

[See also: ROYAL ADMINISTRATION AND FINANCE; SENESCHAL]

Dognon, Paul. *Les institutions politiques et administratives du pays de Languedoc du XIIIe siècle aux guerres de religion*. Toulouse: Privat, 1895.

Michel, Robert. *L'administration royale dans la sénéchaussée de Beaucaire au temps de Saint Louis*. Paris: Picard, 1910.

Sivéry, Gérard. "La rémunération des agents des rois de France au XIIIe siècle." *Revue historique de droit français et étranger* 28 (1980): 587–607.

Strayer, Joseph R. "Viscounts and Viguiers Under Philip the Fair." *Speculum* 38 (1963): 242–55.

VIKINGS. The raids of the Vikings struck terror into those living near the Atlantic coast or on the rivers leading to the Atlantic in the 9th and early 10th centuries. The Norsemen were Scandinavians who for the most part lived on coastal farms. In the late 8th century, they developed sails for their longships, and many a Viking lord, frequently an unsuccessful claimant to the throne of one of the numerous Scandinavian principalities, began leading raids southward. Their first attack took place in England in 793, and raiding intensified over the 9th century. The Carolingian trading center of Duurstede, sacked repeatedly, lost all real importance. Vikings found monasteries, with their treasure and wine cellars, an especially appealing target; some monks, such as those of Saint-Philibert, had to flee repeatedly as each place they settled turned out to be subject to Viking attack.

The inability of the Carolingians to deal with the Viking raids was one of the signs of governmental weakness in the second half of the 9th century. Lords who could resist them were able to use this success in their efforts to establish strong principalities. In 885–86, the Vikings besieged Paris; Count Eudes, son of Robert le Fort, led the defense and was elected king (r. 888–98) shortly afterward.

But the Vikings were more than raiders. They established centers for trading fur, honey, and pitch; the "Rus" branch of the Vikings established long trade networks across what later became Russia, reaching eventually to Constantinople. Vikings made permanent settlements in Ireland and in the eastern part of Great Britain. In 911, the French king Charles III the Simple granted Normandy (named for the Normans, or Northmen) to their leader Rollo on the condition that he be baptized a Christian.

Constance B. Bouchard

[See also: NORMANDY; ROBERT (DUKES OF NORMANDY)]

Hodges, Richard, and David Whitehouse. *Mohammed, Charlemagne and the Origins of Europe*. Ithaca: Cornell University Press, 1983.

Randsborg, Klavs. *The Viking Age in Denmark*. London: Duckworth, 1980.

Sawyer, P.H. *Kings and Vikings: Scandinavia and Europe, A.D. 700–1100*. London: Methuen, 1982.

Zettel, Horst. "France, Norse in." In *Medieval Scandinavia*, ed. Phillip Pulsiano et al. New York: Garland, 1993.

VILLANDRANDO, RODRIGO DE (ca. 1380–ca. 1455). Born in Castile, Rodrigo de Villandrando traveled to France to pursue a career in arms. He began in Burgundian service but joined the dauphin Charles after establishing his own company in 1420. Able but unreliable, he won fame after 1435 for his command of a formidable band of *écorcheurs*. His undisciplined troops ravaged France by living off the land and extorting money from the cities and estates of Languedoc. As the greatest mercenary of his era, Villandrando incarnated the need for military reform. He returned to Castile once reform began in 1439 and died there in retirement.

Paul D. Solon

[See also: BRIGAND/BRIGANDAGE]

Contamine, Philippe. *Guerre, état et société à la fin du moyen âge: étude sur les armées des rois de France, 1337–1494.* Paris: Mouton, 1972.

Quicherat, Jules. *Rodrigue de Villandrando.* Paris: Hachette, 1879.

Tuetey, Alexandre. *Les écorcheurs sous Charles VII.* Montbéliard: Barbier, 1874.

VILLARD DE HONNECOURT (Wilars dehonecort; Vilars dehoncort; fl. 1220–30). Picard artist now known only through a portfolio of thirty-three parchment leaves of drawings in Paris (B.N. fr. 19093). Some leaves have been lost from the portfolio; the maximum number that can be proven to be lost is thirteen, with the possible loss of two additional leaves.

Villard addressed his drawings to an unspecified audience, saying that his "book" contained "sound advice on the techniques of masonry and on the devices of carpentry . . . and the techniques of representation, its features as the discipline of geometry commands and instructs it." The subjects of Villard's drawings are animals, architecture, carpentry, church furnishings, geometry, humans, masonry, mechanical devices, recipes or formulae, and surveying.

Villard traveled extensively, and most of the identifiable monuments that he drew date to the first quarter of the 13th century. He drew, and perhaps visited, the cathedrals of Cambrai, Chartres, Laon, Meaux, Reims, and the abbey of Vaucelles in France; the cathedral of Lausanne in Switzerland; and the abbey of Pilis in Hungary.

There is no documentary evidence that Villard designed or built any church anywhere or that he was in fact an architect. It has been proposed that he may have been "a lodge clerk with a flair for drawing" or that his training may have been in metalworking rather than masonry. It may be that Villard was not a professional craftsman but rather an inquisitive layman who had an opportunity to travel widely.

Carl F. Barnes, Jr.

[See also: CAMBRAI; CHARTRES; LAON; MEAUX; REIMS]

Barnes, Carl F., Jr. "Le 'problème' Villard de Honnecourt." In *Les bâtisseurs des cathédrales gothiques,* ed. Roland Recht. Strasbourg: Éditions les Musées de la Ville de Strasbourg, 1989, pp. 209–23.

———. *Villard de Honnecourt: The Artist and His Drawings, A Critical Bibliography.* Boston: Hall, 1982.

———, and Lon R. Shelby. "The Codicology of the Portfolio of Villard de Honnecourt (Paris, Bibliothèque nationale, MS fr. 19093)." *Scriptorium* 40 (1988): 20–48.

Hahnloser, Hans R. *Villard de Honnecourt: Kritische Gesamtausgabe des Bauhuttenbuches ms. fr. 19093 der Pariser Nationalbibliothek.* Vienna: Schroll, 1935; rev. ed. Graz: Akademische Druck- und Verlagsanstalt, 1972. [Best facsimile edition.]

VILLEHARDOUIN, GEOFFROI DE (ca. 1150–before 1218). Author of the *Conquête de Constantinople,* one of the earliest historical works written in French prose, and one of two eyewitness accounts of the Fourth Crusade. Villehardouin was born into a noble Champenois family. He served the count of Champagne, Thibaut III, as marshal after 1185. In this capacity, Villehardouin developed the mediating abilities that would serve him so well. We know of three disputes he mediated, one involving the count himself.

Count Thibaut III of Champagne (d. 1202) was one of the organizers of the Fourth Crusade, so Villehardouin was at the heart of the planning. He was one of the six ambassadors sent to Venice in 1201 to negotiate passage in Venetian ships. In 1203, he was sent to Isaac II, whom the crusaders had restored to the throne of Constantinople, to see that the Latins would be paid as agreed. He carried out negotiations between the emperor Baudouin and Boniface of Montferrat, the new leader of the crusade, when the two fell out. Because of his outstanding services, Villehardouin was made marshal of Romania in 1205. The rest of his life is obscure. He last appears in the records in 1212 and was certainly dead by 1218, when his son arranged a memorial for him.

The *Conquête,* which begins with the preaching of the crusade by Foulques de Neuilly and ends suddenly in 1207, was composed after the events it relates, although Villehardouin probably made notes and certainly used documentary sources. The prose is straightforward and unrhetorical. The story is told in excellent chronological order.

Villehardouin seems to have intended his work as a defense of the crusade against critics who pointed out that the crusaders attacked only the Christian cities of Zara and Constantinople and never got to Jerusalem at all. Villehardouin lays chief blame for these unfortunate facts on those who failed to join the crusade at Venice and help pay for passage, forcing the crusaders to repay Venice by attacking Zara, and those who deserted later, leaving too small a fighting force for a real holy war. He does not, however, hold blameless those who participated or remained; their sins, particularly their greed, caused further disasters and offended God.

Villehardouin's narrative was more widely read than Robert de Clari's, the other eyewitness account of the Fourth Crusade. Six manuscripts of the *Conquête* are extant, and two more were used in early editions before they disappeared. In addition, two manuscripts of an abbreviation exist. Villehardouin's work was also incorporated in the *Chronique de Baudouin d'Avesnes,* a 13th-century compilation that circulated widely.

Leah Shopkow

[See also: CRUSADES; HISTORIOGRAPHY; ROBERT DE CLARI]

Villehardouin, Geoffroi de. *La conquête de Constantinople,* ed. Edmond Faral. 2 vols. 2nd ed. Paris: Les Belles Lettres, 1937.

Joinville and Villehardouin. *Chronicles of the Crusades,* trans. Margaret Shaw. Harmondsworth: Penguin, 1963.

Beer, Jeanette M.A. *Villehardouin, Epic Historian.* Geneva: Droz, 1968.

Dufournet, Jean. *Les écrivains de la IVe croisade: Villehardouin et Clari.* 2 vols. Paris: SEDES, 1973.

VILLENEUVE. Newly founded village on reclaimed land. Although there had been earlier waves of depopulation and resettlement in France, from ca.1000 to 1250 a great surge of village foundation coincided with the great movements of clearance and reclamation. These new villages in areas that had previously been forest or waste were called by such names as *villeneuves, neuvilles, neufbourgs,* or *sauvetés.* Except for rare instances when squatters successfully cooperated to found such villages, the *villeneuves* were founded by the economic and political efforts of the lay and religious lords who were owners of wide tracts of forest and waste. These lords founded such villages in order to increase their rents and dues, or to extend their power into march and border areas, or to settle previously bandit-invested stretches along pilgrimage routes. Some *villeneuves* were set out along either side of a long street with holdings stretching far out behind each farmstead (the herringbone plan); others were compact villages of farmsteads set out on a grid with fields surrounding them. In Aquitaine, such new villages, called *sauvetés,* were sited near chapels or priories protected by the Peace and Truce of God and whose safeguard extended to crosses that enclosed and protected the new inhabitants. Frequently, the *villeneuves* were founded cooperatively by lay and ecclesiastical lords, one providing legal rights over the land, the other the laborers or the capital for startup costs. The tendency of such lords to invest capital in such new villages, providing mills, churches, and ovens, demonstrates not only the effort to increase political power but the increase in rural production of this era, in which such lords wished to share. Settlers for such *villeneuves* came from older, generally extremely overpopulated villages, often not far from the new settlements. Expansion of village foundations generally improved the condition of peasants throughout a region; since favorable terms were offered in the new villages, lords of older settlements had to improve conditions and grant charters of liberties in order to maintain their labor force. Such settlements on previously unoccupied land should not be confused with later transformation of granges into bastides by the Cistercians and others.

Constance H. Berman

[**See also:** BASTIDE; *DÉFRICHEMENT*]

Bloch, Marc. *French Rural History: An Essay in Its Basic Characteristics,* trans. Janet Sondheimer. Berkeley: University of California Press, 1966.

Duby, Georges. *Rural Economy and Country Life in the Medieval West,* trans. Cynthia Postan. Columbia: University of South Carolina Press, 1968.

Higounet, Charles. *Paysages et villages neufs du moyen âge.* Bordeaux: Fédération Historique du Sud-Ouest, 1975.

Lyon, Bryce. "Medieval Real Estate Developments and Freedom." *American Historical Review* 63 (1957): 47–61.

VILLENEUVE-SUR-YONNE. A "new town" founded in 1163 by Louis VII, Villefranche-le-Roy (now Villeneuve-sur-Yonne in the department of Yonne) preserves at either end of its main street the massive Gothic town gates (Porte de Sens; Porte de Joigny). Portions of the original ramparts are also standing, as well as the 12th-century cylindrical keep (Tour Louis-le-Gros) and 12th-century bridge. The church of Notre-Dame, begun in 1240, shows both Burgundian and Champenois influence. The choir and ambulatory were constructed first, followed by the wide nave and side aisles. The façade is pure Renaissance.

William W. Kibler/William W. Clark

[See also: *VILLENEUVE*]

Lafond, Jean. "Les vitraux de l'église Notre-Dame à Villeneuve-sur-Yonne." *Congrès archéologique* (Auxerre) 116 (1958): 378–82.

Vallery-Radot, Jean. "Villeneuve-sur-Yonne." *Congrès archéologique* (Auxerre) 116 (1958): 370–77.

VILLON, FRANÇOIS (1431–1463). Of all the lyricists of late-medieval France, Villon is the most celebrated among both scholars and general readers. Students of premodern literature inside and outside the francophone world have encountered him in his original Middle French; and thousands of people who have little or no French have read versions of his poems in the major European languages.

It was not always thus. The circle of contemporaries who knew of Villon's literary abilities was a modest one. He tells us in his *Testament* that an earlier work, the *Lais,* is already in circulation and being referred to by a title not of his choosing. On the other hand, the number of early sources preserving his poems is small; and his readers were in general not found among the rich and powerful. Although some such personages come in for mention in his verses, it is usually in the context of appeals for money, or of distant, uneasy, or downright irreverent allusion; Villon was not a success with well-off patrons of literature. The fame he sought eluded him. He seemingly hoped for a career as a court poet and exerted himself to catch the eye of such highly placed connoisseurs as Charles d'Orléans; but for unknown reasons, he did not achieve more than a small gift of money here and there. Greater success in his lifetime, however, might well have spelled later obscurity; his *poésies de circonstance,* composed, we must assume, to curry favor, competent though they are, are by and large forgettable. Rather than spend much of his career in turning out pleasing official verse, he was driven by circumstance, and perhaps also by a jarring personality, to live by expedients, know misery, reflect on it, and write amateur poetry of a unique stamp.

The body of Villon's works is of moderate dimensions: some 3,300 lines. It comprises independent pieces in fixed form (ballades and rondeaux) and two unified compositions, the *Lais* and the *Testament.* The *Lais,* dated 1456, is a series of burlesque legacies occasioned by being, as Villon asserts, crossed in love, and consequently deciding to quit Paris, perhaps never to return. The *Testament*

(1461) takes up again the legacy pattern but refines it into the articles of a last will and testament, complete with legal clauses and phraseology, the fiction now being that the author is near death and bethinking himself of soul and body as well as of worldly goods. This, Villon's major work, written in octaves (eight-line strophes of octosyllabic verse), contains fixed-form pieces as well, some of which may antedate or even postdate 1461. The whole amounts to a personal literary anthology as well as the poet's artistic testament and monument. The rest of his *œuvre* is made up of a fulsome *Louange* of Princess Marie d'Orléans, with attached double ballade and much Latin adornment; a *Ballade franco-latine*, even more latinate; a number of difficult poems in the jargon of the medieval French underworld; and some ballades made up of the rhetorical devices dear to the schoolroom and fashionable court. Jumbled in with them are some pieces so intensely felt, so personal, so perfectly marrying form and content, that they belong by right to the greatest world literature. Among these are the *Épître à ses amis*, Villon's *De profundis*; the yes-and-no meditation on fate and individual responsibility best called *Débat de Villon et de son cœur*, and the *Ballade des pendus*, with its unbearable yet inescapable vision of legally executed bodies (including the poet's?) and its reiterated solicitation of prayer for their souls. Villon's last poems appear to fit into the interval between his last imprisonment and appeal, the commutation of his death sentence to a ten-year exile, and his departure in 1463 to an unknown end.

Villon was born into a poor family (*Testament*, ll. 273–75) in 1431, the year marked by the death of Jeanne d'Arc, celebrated in the *Testament* (ll. 351–52) as . . . *Jehanne la bonne Lorraine/Qu'Engloys brulerent a Rouen* ("Joan, the brave girl from Lorraine/Burned by the English at Rouen"). The Hundred Years' War was dragging on; disease, food-shortages, and protracted spells of cold, wet weather afflicted everyone, the poor especially. It was out of harsh necessity, no doubt, that the future poet's mother entrusted her child to a presumed relative, Guillaume de Villon, the kindly chaplain of the Parisian church of Saint-Benoît-le-Bétourné not far from the Sorbonne, who would be the boy's *plus que père* (*Testament*, l. 849).

Young François, originally called de Montcorbier or des Loges, took the surname of his adoptive father, and much else besides: security, relative comfort, clerical status, and the opportunity for the best formal education then available. In 1449, he obtained the baccalaureate degree and three years later the License and the degree of Maître ès Arts. This and his connections ought to have smoothed Villon's path into the learned professions; but these were overpopulated in the mid-15th century. To enter the secular or regular clergy was apparently not for him a viable choice; nor, in the absence of an independent income or a patron, was it possible for him to become a professional writer. He turned to living by his wits, in the company of other unemployed *clercs* and even more lowly individuals; and this led him into repeated brushes with the law, mainly for theft but once for manslaughter. As an *écolier*, he was entitled to the church's protection from the full rigor of secular justice; but it looks as if he lost the

benefit of clergy, as well as many months of freedom, when he was condemned to prison at Meung-sur-Loire in 1461 by the bishop of Orléans.

It was his long police record, rather than one final and spectacular crime, that drove the exasperated secular authorities in late 1462 to pass a capital sentence; the Parlement, on appeal, commuted this to a ten-year banishment from Paris and its environs. Sadly, it is owing to his activities as part-time criminal that much of the information about Villon has come to us, for the abundant records have been preserved in the Paris archives. They supplement the hints, half-truths, special pleading, and downright lies that bestrew the poet's own writings.

Such a biographical excursus is particularly indicated in Villon's case, for much of his work is highly personal without always being informative or even candid. His feelings take precedence over the exact cause for them, his hatred for his enemies overshadows the ways whereby the latter have earned his resentment, and the possibility that the poet himself might somehow have provoked or deserved rough handling is pushed far into the background. Yet the interweaving of concrete if unreliable allusions to persons and events on the one hand, of passionate response on the other, makes of Villon an autobiographical lyricist to an unusual degree.

His themes, though, are universal ones, colored by his cultural milieu and his own subjectivity. Adversity, suffering, insecurity, the hunger for love, the transitoriness of youth and of all good things, the approach of death, the faith that sees beyond it—these are the timbers of which his work is built. Through the 2,000 lines of the *Testament*, he turns these notions over and over, in a composition structured by association of ideas and shifting moods rather than logical or formal progression. This begins as early as the first stanzas, which move with great rapidity from the testator's age and mental condition to his state of health and thence to his recent hardships and the person responsible for them; and with the name of Bishop Thibaut d'Aussigny, the memory of the preceding summer's incarceration, and probable degradation from clerical status, comes flooding back, making him sacrifice syntax to sarcasm: yes, he will pray for his enemy—with a cursing psalm. For good measure, he adds a prayer for Louis, *le bon roy de France*. On he goes, intermingling complaint, piety, and half-admissions of unsatisfactory behavior. Yet a sinner in his situation is pardonable: *Neccessité fait gens mesprendre/Et fain saillir le loup du boys* ("It's need drives folks to go astray,/And hunger, the wolf to leave the woods"; ll. 167–68). He has abundant grounds for lamentation. His youth has flown; he is prematurely old, poor, rejected by his kin, disappointed in love, regretting his old friends (where are they now?), knowing that death will come for him as it has for the lovely ladies and great potentates of the past. These are themes to which he returns, obsessively but not uninterruptedly; for a great number of bequests remain to be formulated and the whole apparatus of the fictitious testament to be worked in.

There is a good deal of humor in all this, of a rough, pun-filled, scabrous character; and the poet takes advantage of the safety afforded by the last-will-and-testament schema to take verbal revenge on the individuals and classes who have earned his disapproval; after all, the document, according to the poetic fiction, will not be read until after his decease. We are led once again to the theme that underlies the *Testament* as a whole. It sometimes is expressed with gentle gravity, as in the *Ballade des dames du temps jadis*; in grimmer moments, the poet's thought turns to scenes commonly beheld in Paris: the piled-up and anonymous bones in the Cemetery of the Innocents, the cadavers of executed criminals dangling from the Montfaucon gibbet, the last agony awaiting each man and woman. In the Europe of the 15th century, the body's death was but a stage in the soul's journey; prayers and allusions to Heaven and Hell throng the octaves and fixed-form pieces. In the intervals of anxiety about death and what is in store for himself and all humankind, Villon repeatedly turns to common experience, particularly its darker side. Happiness is rare and fleeting; sorrow, fear, physical discomfort, and decrepitude—these are the lot of the human race. Why had Villon, why had so many men and women known suffering? Why does a just God permit malevolent Fortune to afflict the innocent? The poet's own stance, at least as early as the independent *Épître à ses amis* (presumably composed during the 1461 incarceration at Meung-sur-Loire) is that of a blameless victim, and he cries out with the words of the archetypical righteous sufferer, Job (ll. 1–2): *Ayez pictié, ayez pictié de moy/A tout le moins, s'i vous plaist, mes amis!* ("Have pity, do have pity upon me,/You at least, if you please, who are my friends"). This explicit kinship with Job is affirmed repeatedly through the *Testament*; it has become the poet's characteristic way of making sense of what has befallen him, of understanding, as well, the human condition.

Villon's themes are by no means original, nor is his use of archetypes in working them out. As an educated man, he was steeped in the Latin classics and in the Bible, those storehouses of human experience and its literary expression; to allude to traditional topoi, stories, and personages was second nature for him, as it was for other writers of the day. His preoccupation with death and decay, his frequent melancholy, his startling coarseness, his mingling of jest and seriousness, are also features common in late-medieval writing, and in the visual arts as well. What sets him apart is the immediacy of his communication with the reader. His verse revivifies the notion of lyric: not poems to be sung, but poems expressive of feeling. Unlike the conventional and impersonal *je* of much contemporary writing, Villon's *je* most frequently is his unique and unruly self, temporarily brought to order by the discipline of his octaves and his fixed-form pieces. Much 15th-century poetry treats of love, again in courtly and stereotyped ways, for the stylized worship of the lady was still very much alive. Villon writes of love, too, but mostly from his own limited experience: it is a snare and a delusion, at best a fleeting joy. By and large, women are sensual and venal (but not to be condemned, for it is *nature femeninne* [*Testament*, l. 611] that moves them), and in any case their attractiveness soon withers. Indeed, woman's charms, such a staple among mainstream masculine writers of the period, do not feature much here except in the context of bitter reminiscence and of regret for the transitoriness of all things desirable. It would in fact not be easy to find another major poet so indifferent to beauty; but then visual description of any sort does not stand out in Villon's verses. He inclines to naming persons and places, to evoking action and speech and gesture, rather than to painting word pictures. Even his self-description is limited to a few qualifiers: *sec et noir; plus maigre que chimere* ("skinny and dark"; "thinner than a wraith"). What he does give us is his reactions to his experience, and a sketch of late-medieval France as he knew it. This is a world of people living by their wits and not hampered by scruples: entertainers, prostitutes, counterfeiters, tavern keepers and tavern haunters, jailers and moat cleaners, peddlers, beggars, dissolute monks—Villon's poetry opens the door upon a teeming world, lacking in grace or nobility but intensely alive. Most vital of all are the poet's own self and experience, given expression that transcends his own time and milieu so as to be at once personal and universal.

Villon's works have been preserved in a number of manuscripts and fragments, and in a printed edition of 1489. These early sources vary in completeness, from the *Lais*, the *Testament*, and numerous independent pieces, down to two or three ballades; they differ also in degree of reliability. The manuscript copies, the incunabulum, and also the many 16th-century printings of his works attest to a moderate readership over the course of about a century. Villon then, like most medieval writers, underwent an eclipse, with one edition at the end of the 1600s and three in the 1700s. The years from 1832 onward have seen an increasing flow of editions, translations, historical notes, and interpretive essays; and the stream shows no sign of drying up. Villon continues to be subject to much critical scrutiny, some of it closer to creative writing than to explication of the texts, but much of it responsible and serious. We can now read Villon's often difficult and allusive verses with a fair approximation to his own meaning.

Barbara N. Sargent-Baur

[See also: ALEXIS, GUILLAUME; BAUDE, HENRI; CHARLES D'ORLÉANS]

Villon, François. *Complete Poems*, ed. and trans. Barbara N. Sargent-Baur. Toronto: Toronto University Press, 1994.

———. *Le lais Villon et les poèmes variés*, ed. Jean Rychner and Albert Henry. 2 vols. Geneva: Droz, 1977.

———. *Le Testament Villon*, ed. Jean Rychner and Albert Henry. 2 vols. Geneva: Droz, 1974–85.

———. *François Villon: Œuvres*, trans. André Lanly. 2 vols. Paris: Champion, 1969.

———. *François Villon: ballades en jargon*, trans. André Lanly. Paris: Champion, 1979.

———. *The Poems of François Villon*, trans. Galway Kinnell. New York: New American Library, 1965.

Burger, André. *Lexique complet de la langue de Villon*. 2nd ed. Geneva: Droz, 1974.

Champion, Pierre. *François Villon: sa vie et son temps*. 2nd ed. 2 vols. Paris: Champion, 1934.

Fox, John Howard. *The Poetry of Villon*. London: Nelson, 1962.

LeGentil, Pierre. *Villon*. Paris: Hatier, 1967.

Peckham, Robert D. *François Villon: A Bibliography.* New York: Garland, 1990.

Sargent-Baur, Barbara N. *Brothers of Dragons: Job dolens and François Villon.* New York: Garland, 1990.

Siciliano, Italo. *François Villon et les thèmes poétiques du moyen âge.* Paris: Nizet, 1934.

Sturm, Rudolf. *François Villon, bibliographie et matériaux littéraires (1489–1988).* Munich: Saur, 1990.

Vitz, Evelyn Birge. *The Crossroad of Intentions: A Study of Symbolic Expressions in the Poetry of François Villon.* The Hague: Mouton, 1974.

Ziwès, Armand, and Anne de Bercy. *Le jargon de maître François Villon interprété.* 2nd ed. 2 vols. Paris: Puget, 1960.

VINCENNES. The castle of Vincennes, just northeast of Paris, was a favorite residence of the Capetian and Valois kings. Philip II Augustus built a hunting lodge here, and Louis IX is reported to have dispensed justice beneath the giant oaks of the nearby forest. The castle, constructed on a rectangular plan with square towers, was begun by Philip VI, continued under John II the Good, and completed by Charles V in 1369. Only one tower and the impressive 185-foot-tall keep remain. Flanked at the corners by turrets, the keep remains an outstanding example of 14th-century military architecture, although its battlements and machicolations have been destroyed. Within the walls of the later classical fortress (17th c.), the Flamboyant Chapelle Royale, an elegant Gothic single-nave structure begun in the late 14th century under Charles V in imitation of the Sainte-Chapelle in Paris, was completed by Philibert de l'Orme in the 16th.

William W. Kibler

Fossa, François de. *Le château historique de Vincennes.* 2 vols. Paris: Daragon, 1908.

VINCENT DE BEAUVAIS (ca. 1190–ca. 1264). The author of a most spectacular encyclopedia of medieval culture and thought, Vincent de Beauvais joined the Dominican house at Paris ca. 1220, shortly after its founding, and probably moved to the new Dominican house in his native region of Beauvais toward the end of the same decade. Vincent served as lecturer to the monks of the nearby Cistercian abbey of Royaumont, founded by King Louis IX in 1228 and through this association, mediated by Abbot Ralph, won the favor of the king and ultimately the support of the royal purse for his scholarly projects.

The first half of the 13th century was a time of intellectual "consolidation," when several scholars, Vincent among them, felt the need to integrate the results of the intellectual explosion of the 12th century with the traditional learning of western civilization. Vincent entitled his work *Speculum maius,* a mirror to the world and its truths, which he compares implicitly with earlier attempts, perhaps the *Imago mundi* of the 12th century, sometimes attributed to Honorius of Autun. The *Speculum* originally comprised two parts: the *Naturale* and the *Historiale.* The *Naturale* beings with a treatise on theology (the triune

God, archetype and creator of the universe; angels; demons; account of Creation and the exitus of all reality from God), proceeds to a consideration of the Fall, Redemption, and the sacraments of the church, and concludes with a summation of natural philosophy, including a description of the physical universe and the nature of human being. The *Historiale* gives an account of history from the Creation story of Genesis to 1244 in his earliest edition, and extended to 1254 in his later version. Its popularity is attested by several translations into the vernacular, including French, Catalan, and Dutch verse. After revising and reorganizing his work, Vincent produced a third volume, the *Doctrinale,* that contained a treatise on knowledge and the arts, including all the fields of science, from grammar and mechanics to politics, law, and medicine: in short, all that is useful to know to live a fruitful and productive life, both public and private. Although Vincent had intended to publish a fourth part, the *Morale,* he never accomplished his goal. The tract entitled *Morale* that began to circulate in the 14th century with the first three parts is in fact an anonymous compilation drawn from the *Summa theologica* of Thomas Aquinas.

In the last years of his life, Vincent composed treaties for the royal court. On the death of the dauphin Louis in January 1260, he wrote his *Epistola consolatoria super morte filii.* Within the next year or so, he published at the request of Queen Marguerite a tract on the education of princes, *De eruditione filiorum nobilium,* for the tutors of Prince Philip. Finishing this work, Vincent returned to his treatise concerning royal government requested by Louis IX. Sometime before Pentecost 1263, he presented the first part, *De morali principis institutione,* to his patron. But as with his *Speculum,* Vincent never finished this work: the second part was only supplied at a later date by a fellow Dominican, William Peraldus.

Mark Zier

Vincent de Beauvais. *De eruditione filiorum nobilium,* ed. Arpad Steiner. Cambridge: Mediaeval Academy of America, 1938.

Gabriel, Astrik. *The Educational Ideas of Vincent of Beauvais.* 2nd ed. Notre Dame: University of Notre Dame Press, 1962.

Lusignan, Serge, A. Nadeau, and M. Paulmier-Foucart, eds. *Vincent de Beauvais: Actes du Colloque de Montréal, 1988.* Montreal, 1990.

McCarthy, Joseph M. *Humanistic Emphases in the Educational Thought of Vincent of Beauvais.* Leiden: Brill, 1976.

Paulmier-Foucart, M., and Serge Lusignan. "Vincent de Beauvais et l'histoire du *Speculum majus.*" *Journal des Savants* 1990, pp. 97–124.

VINCENT OF LÉRINS (d. before 450). A monk of the monastery of Lérins, Vincent contributed to theological argumentation in his day. A vigorous opponent of Augustine's ideas on grace and predestination (which he saw as a deviation from true tradition), he may be identified as a Semi-Pelagian. His *Commonitorium* offers the famous rule for determining what is to be believed as Catholic truth: *quod ubique, quod semper, quod ab om-*

nibus creditum est ("what has been believed everywhere, always, by all"). The three characteristics of universality, antiquity, and unanimity represented a line of defense against heretical, or at least deviant, developments in matters of belief.

Grover A. Zinn

[See also: LÉRINS]

Vincent of Lérins. *Commonitorium*, ed. R. Demeulenaere. *CCSL* 64. Turnhout: Brepols, 1985.
———. *Commonitorium*, trans. George E. MacCracken. In *Early Latin Theology*. Philadelphia: Westminster, 1957.

VIRELAI. While in the 14th century the virelai has a recognizable *forme fixe*, its origins and development are obscure and controversial. The first references to the *vireli* or *virenli* occur in the mid-13th century in the context of dance-song, but at this date it is difficult to distinguish it from the ballette: in effect, both are expansions of the *rondet*. There are resemblances between the *vireli* and the Occitan *dansa*, the Spanish *villancico*, and the Italian *lauda*.

By the 14th century, the term "virelai" becomes more common, although it is then redefined by Guillaume de Machaut as *chanson baladee*. The first known poems of the type, composed by Jehannot de Lescurel (d. 1303), feature an opening refrain; strophes in two sections, the second corresponding to the meter and rhyme of the refrain lines; and the repetition of the refrain after each strophe. The number of refrain lines varies from one to eight, and the first strophic section can have a distinct rhyming and metrical scheme. The music has the pattern: I II II I etc. Of Machaut's thirty-three virelais set to music, twenty-five are monodic (like Lescurel's). Never common, virelais are increasingly rare by the 15th century.

Ardis T.B. Butterfield

[See also: BALLADE; LESCUREL, JEHANNOT DE; MACHAUT, GUILLAUME DE; RONDEAU; VERSIFICATION]

Wilkins, Nigel, ed. *One Hundred Ballades, Rondeaux and Virelais from the Late Middle Ages.* Cambridge: Cambridge University Press, 1969.
Apel, Willi. "Rondeaux, Virelais, and Ballades in French Thirteenth-Century Song." *Journal of the American Musicological Society* 7 (1954): 121–30.
Bec, Pierre. *La lyrique française au moyen âge (XIIe–XIIIe siècles): contribution à une typologie des genres poétiques médiévaux.* 2 vols. Paris: Picard, 1977–78, Vol. 1: *Études*; Vol. 2: *Textes.*

VIRGIL, INFLUENCE OF. Among all the Latin poets, Virgil (ca. 70–19 B.C.) was the most "classical"—in the literal sense. Students read and relished his writings, copied and interpreted the Latin, and memorized and canonized his ideas from the earliest period. Those who followed the master imitated his style unashamedly: Ovid, Lucan, and Claudian, for example, allude to his works constantly. Medieval authors found in his works inspirational and exemplary inducements to pursue virtue. Both Virgil's own person and his work became magical touchstones of prophecy.

Virgil left to the Latin West three influential texts, each providing a unique allegorical matrix and unique perspective on life's stages: the *Eclogues*, the *Georgics*, the *Aeneid*. The youthful, nostalgic, and pastoral mood of the *Eclogues* gives way to an adult husbandman's deep concern for nature in the *Georgics*.

In his mature years, Virgil composed a national epic in imitation of Homer, among other sources. The work was in many ways a perfect vehicle to be taken up by the medieval mind. Half allegory, half history and legend, Virgil tells of Aeneas's flight from the burning citadel of Troy, wanderings in the Mediterranean, and struggles in Italy to found a new home. From the horrendous storm in Book 1 to the plangent melancholy of the Dido episode; from the marvelous underworld visit in Book 6 to the martyrdom of the young prince Pallas in Book 11—the poem became in the hands of interpreters a kind of three-part invention that fused the mythic past and mythic present to an imagined future. Bitter political irony often intrudes as well, because Caesar Augustus's poet at once ambiguously reifies and decries the unspeakably violent and unscrupulous power games necessary to create and control a world empire.

Once the magic and prestige of this material was absorbed by visionary rulers like Charlemagne or William the Conqueror, there was no end to attempts to link up one's royal dynasty with the lineage of the Trojans. With Julius Caesar and other grand emperors as your ancestors (and King Priam of the fifty sons behind them), any upstart baron could convince his liege or perhaps even the papacy of his imperial pretensions.

Studying Virgil's Latin, like reading the Bible and savoring Ovid's rhetorical trivialities, is what educated people have done for nearly 2,000 years. Throughout the Middle Ages, for church fathers like Jerome and Augustine, or for Christian poets like Prudentius, grammar study meant reading the *Aeneid*. Geoffrey of Monmouth used Virgil extensively.

Of the 1,500 or so surviving Virgil manuscripts—of which perhaps two-thirds were copied in France—many date from the crucial *aetas Virgiliana*, the 9th–11th centuries. Of those, some 170 carry ancient commentary from Servius, Fulgentius, and others, which were absorbed *en passant* by the mid-12th-century anonymous *Énéas* poet, who freely adapted Virgil's *Aeneid* into the vernacular Norman French for a noble audience. This fascinating early romance combines many diverse elements that were used by subsequent French authors, such as Benoît de Sainte-Maure, Chrétien de Troyes, Guillaume de Machaut, and Jean Froissart. The *Énéas* features rich descriptions of scientific marvels as well as a strong Ovidian intertextuality. The protracted love story of Lavine and Énéas provides interlaced counterpoint for the violent feudal battles. Little Virgilian texture remains, but much adventure and romance charmed both medieval listeners and future imitators.

Another thinker residing in France at this time, Bernard Silvestris, composed a keen allegorical interpretation of the first six books of the *Aeneid*. His commentary, a kind of *Virgile moralisé*, replaced the older treatise by Fulgentius and remained a standard reference work throughout the Middle Ages.

Stylistically and axiologically, the works of Virgil exerted a profound influence upon much of the new vernacular literature of medieval France as well as in the intellectual and latinate culture of monastic scriptoria and cathedral schools.

Raymond J. Cormier

[See also: ANTIQUITY, ROMANCES OF; BERNARD SILVESTRIS; OVID, INFLUENCE OF]

Cardwell, R.A., and J. Hamilton, eds. *Virgil in a Cultural Tradition: Essays to Celebrate the Bimillennium.* Nottingham: Nottingham University Press, 1986.

Cormier, Raymond J. *One Heart One Mind: The Rebirth of Virgil's Hero in Medieval French Romances.* University: Romance Monographs, 1973.

———. "The Present State of Studies on the *Roman d'Énéas.*" *Cultura Neolatina* 31 (1971): 7–39.

Jones, Julian Ward, and Elizabeth Ward Jones, eds. *The Commentary on the First Six Books of the "Aeneid" Commonly Attributed to Bernardus Silvestris.* Lincoln: University of Nebraska Press, 1977.

Lectures médiévales de Virgile. In *Actes du colloque organisé par l'École Française de Rome, 1982,* ed. J.-Y. Tilliette. Rome: École Française, 1985.

VISCONTI. The Visconti family, which ruled Milan between the mid-13th and mid-15th centuries, concluded two important marriage alliances with the French monarchy in the 14th century. In 1360, when the Milanese state was divided between two Visconti brothers, Bernabo and Galeazzo, the latter arranged for his son, Gian Galeazzo, to marry Isabelle, the daughter of John II, furnishing the French king with a large sum of money needed for his ransom from captivity in England. In 1387, Gian Galeazzo's daughter Valentina (1371–1408) married Louis, duke of Orléans, the younger brother of Charles VI. She became involved in the political intrigues of the French court, particularly her husband's Italian ambitions. After his assassination in 1407, she demanded justice from the French government but died without obtaining satisfaction. Her son, Charles d'Orléans, then only fourteen years old, eventually became the father of the future Louis XII, who, as Valentina's grandson, claimed the duchy of Milan and conquered it in 1499.

John Bell Henneman, Jr.

VISCOUNT/VISCOUNTY. The English word "viscount" and its Old French cognate, *visconte,* are derived from the Latin word *vicecomes* 'vice-count,' coined ca. 790 specifically as the title of a new type of officer appointed in a growing number of counties to serve as the deputy of the count. By ca. 850, virtually every county in the new West Frankish kingdom seems to have been provided with a viscount, who, in addition to performing certain administrative functions peculiar to his office, assumed all of the normal duties of the count during his frequent absences from the county. By 1000, the office was hereditary in virtually every province except Normandy, where it always remained appointive. From ca. 1020, "viscountess" (Lat. *vicecomitissa,* OFr. *viscontesse*) was sometimes employed by the wives, widows, and heiresses of hereditary viscounts, but it seems to have been rare before 1150.

The collapse of the traditional administration in most counties between ca. 980 and 1050 deprived the viscount of most of his original duties, but the dignity and title were at first retained by the heirs of most of the viscounts, and in the 11th century they were gradually attached to the principal dominion or dominions that each vicecomital lineage (or in some counties each branch of that lineage) succeeded in creating. Thus, for example, the viscount of (the county of) Poitou at Thouars became the viscount of Thouars, and his barony came to be known as the "viscounty" (Lat. *vicecomitarus,* OFr. *visconté*) of Thouars. In northern France, the new viscounties were generally minor, castellanial baronies, so small that when the last remaining functions of the vicecomital office disappeared in the 12th century their lords often abandoned the title "viscount." In the lands south of the Loire, by contrast, and especially in Gascony and Gothia, many of the new viscounties were relatively large principalities, representing either entire counties whose government had been taken over by the viscount (like Narbonne), or major partitions of such counties (like Turenne). The vicecomital dignity was thus more honorable as well as more common in the south (where the corresponding titles were written *vescomte, vescomtesa,* and *vescomtat*).

In 1200, about ninety viscounties were left in the kingdom, and a similar number of viscounts, and between that date and 1500 the number of both viscounties and viscounts seems to have declined slowly as a result of consolidation and annexation to the royal domain.

D'A. Jonathan D. Boulton

[See also: COUNT/COUNTY; NOBILITY]

Boulton, D'A. J.D. *Grants of Honour: The Origins of the System of Nobiliary Dignities of Traditional France.* Forthcoming.

Sickel, Wilhelm. *Die fränkische Vicecomitat.* N.p. [Strasbourg?], 1907.

VISIGOTHS. A group of Germanic peoples, composed primarily of Goths and known as the Visigoths ("Noble Goths"), entered Gaul after their sack of Rome in 410 and settled in Aquitaine. With the decline of the Roman Empire in the second half of the 5th century, the Visigoths expanded their control over all Gaul south of the Loire and across the Pyrénées over most of Spain. The rise of the Franks challenged Visigothic power, however, and the victory of Clovis I in 507 was followed by the Frankish conquest of most of the Visigothic territories in Gaul, establishing the dominance of Gaul by the Merovingians and Carolingians. In Gaul, the Visigoths retained Septimania, which preserved a distinct Gothic character even after its incorporation into the kingdom of the Franks by the Carolingians, when it became known as Gothia. Thus, a Visigothic legacy was preserved in Gaul into the 10th and 11th centuries.

After their initial entry into Gaul in 412, the Visigoths were defeated by the Roman general Constantius, who settled them in the province of Aquitania Secunda, between the Garonne and the Loire, as self-governing federates (treaty partners) of the empire on the basis of hospitality, either land sharing with the Roman senatorial class or receiving Roman tax revenues. Toulouse was the center of the Visigothic settlement. Roman officials like Aetius were able to keep the Visigoths under imperial control, and they were prominent in the defeat of Attila in 451. After the murder of Emperor Valentinian III in 455, the Visigoths, along with Gallo-Roman aristocrats, began to control the affairs of Gaul and were even able to place their own candidate, Avitus, on the imperial throne (r. 455–56).

The weakness of the Roman government led to a period of Visigothic expansion under King Euric (r. 466–84), who came to hold Gaul south of the Loire and west of the Rhône, and all of Spain except for the Suevic territories in the northwest. Euric held the largest state of any Germanic king, and it appeared as if the Visigoths were the destined masters of the West. But the accession of the Frankish King Clovis I in 482 and Euric's death in 484 changed the future of Gaul and of the West. In alliance with Catholics of southern Gaul, Clovis won a great victory over the Arian Visigoths at Vouillé, near Poitiers, in 507 and conquered the Gallic portions of the Visigothic kingdom, except for Septimania. The Visigoths left Gaul for Spain, and their kingdom was thenceforward predominantly an Iberian state. Septimania, however, remained part of their kingdom until the Muslims conquered southern and central Spain (711–13). It was then incorporated into the rest of Gaul by Pepin the Short. The remnant of the Visigothic kingdom of Spain was the origin of the later kingdom of Asturias.

Steven Fanning

[See also: GOTHIA; SEPTIMANIA]

Goffart, Walter. *Barbarians and Romans: Techniques of Accommodation.* Princeton: Princeton University Press, 1980.
Heather, Peter. *Goths and Romans, 332–489.* Oxford: Clarendon, 1991.
Thompson, E.A. *The Goths in Spain.* Oxford: Clarendon, 1969.
———. *Romans and Barbarians: The Decline of the Western Empire.* Madison: University of Wisconsin Press, 1982, pp. 38–57.
Wallace-Hadrill, J.M. *The Barbarian West, 400–1000.* 4th ed. London: Hutchinson University Library, 1961, pp. 115–39.
Wolfram, Herwig. *History of the Goths,* trans. Thomas J. Dunlap. Berkeley: University of California Press, 1988.

VITICULTURE. The production of wine in France has its origins in the 6th century B.C., with the founding of the Greek colony at Marseille. For the next several centuries, viticulture flourished in the warm, dry Mediterranean regions of France. The northern expansion of this industry occurred largely as a result of two distinct dynamic forces—one political, the other religious. For the Romans, the vine was a sacred plant (*sacra vitis*), and as they extended their empire beyond the Mediterranean, great vineyards were introduced as far north as the Seine, the Moselle, and the Rhine. What seems to have allowed for the successful introduction of vines in the colder and moist regions of the north was the earlier experience of Mediterranean vintners along the slopes of the Alps. Likewise, the spread of Christianity had an equally important effect on the northern expansion of the vine, since wine was central for the celebration of the Mass. As a result, the founding of each new church and monastery saw vineyards appearing soon afterward.

The most important period for medieval French viticulture occurred during the economic revival of the 11th–13th centuries. The resulting growth in population, commerce, and urban life encouraged landowners to increase productivity, and no area of agriculture was more affected than was viticulture. It was during these centuries that the regions of Anjou, Arbois, Beaune, Bordeaux, Épernay, and Hautvilliers established their reputations for producing fine wines.

The documents of this period are filled with references to the *métayage* and *medium vestum* agreements. By the terms of *métayage*, a cultivator would give the landowner a fixed percentage of his harvest in return for the use of the land. Under *medium vestum*, the cultivator agreed to clear lands and make them productive. Once this was accomplished, usually after five to seven years, the land would then be evenly divided, with the cultivator now becoming a small landowner.

If those involved in viticulture made significant investments in labor and materials, they could feel confident that the demand for their product would more than justify their expenses. Throughout the Middle Ages, wine was not simply the preferred beverage of rich and poor alike. In a period when water was often hazardous, wine offered the consumer the dual benefits of pleasure and security.

Stephen Weinberger

[See also: AGRICULTURE; BEVERAGES; *MÉTAYER/ MÉTAYAGE;* WINE TRADE]

Berlow, Rosalind Kent. "The 'Disloyal' Grape: The Agrarian Crisis of Late-Fourteenth-Century Burgundy." *Agricultural History* 56 (1982): 426–38.
Dion, Roger. *Histoire de la vigne et du vin en France des origines au XIXe siècle.* Paris: The Author, 1959.
Grand, Roger. "Le contrat de complant depuis les origines jusqu'à nos jours." *Nouvelle revue historique de droit français et étranger* 40 (1916): 169–228, 337–82, 555–89.

VOTIVE MASS. Mass offered for a special intention (a *votum*), such as for peace (*pro pace*) or for the dead (*pro* *defunctis*), as opposed to a Mass called for by the liturgical calendar. Votive Masses are already mentioned during the patristic period, and the early-medieval Sacramentaries make ample provision for them. They grew in popularity throughout the Middle Ages, even though the increasingly full liturgical calendar left few days without their appointed Mass and Office. The situation was circumvented by having the prescribed Mass celebrated once each day on the high altar, while individual priests offered their private Masses as votive Masses. In some localities, it was customary to say a weekly series of votive Masses: Sunday, of the Trinity; Monday, for charity; Tuesday, for wisdom; Wednesday, of the Holy Ghost; Thursday, of the angels; Friday, of the Cross; and Saturday, of the Blessed Virgin.

James McKinnon

[See also: MASS, CHANTS AND TEXTS]

Jungmann, Josef. *The Mass of the Roman Rite: Its Origins and Development*, trans. Francis X. Brunner. 2 vols. New York: Benziger, 1951–55.

VOW CYCLE. A cluster of verse romances that center on the concept of making and fulfilling elaborate vows—representing a tradition that stretches back to the boastings and verbal warfare of Germanic warriors—appeared in the early 14th century. The *Vœux du paon* (ca. 1310) with its two continuations, *Restor du paon* and *Parfait du paon*, form a late entry into the Alexander romance cycle; the *Vœux de l'épervier* and the *Vœux du héron* derive their substance from historical events. The *Vœux du faisan* by Philip the Good, duke of Burgundy, is based on the festivities at Lille, February 17, 1454, when vows were made to reconquer Constantinople from the Turks.

The *Vœux du paon*, by Jacques de Longuyon, was by far the most popular. An independent poem (despite its insertion into the Alexander canon) of some 8,500 rhymed Alexandrine lines, it has survived in thirty-four manuscripts and five fragments, along with two modern transcriptions and a 15th-century prose adaptation. The poem can be divided into two parts: the prelude to the vows, the vows and their accomplishment. In the first part, Clarus besieges the castle of Epheson in order to force Gadifer's sister Fesonas to marry him. Gadifer's ally Casamus has obtained the succor of Alexander in the conflict. After several clashes, the lords and ladies end by amusing themselves in the castle at games. The second part begins with a résumé of the preceding events, as if there were a new start, a second poem. At this point, Porrus kills Fesonas's peacock, causing her some consternation, but the venerable Casamus calms emotions by proposing that the peacock be the centerpiece of vows, so that all can show their prowess. After a series of a dozen or so vows directed against the enemy besieging them, the knights accomplish them. Ladies, too, make vows, to seek a husband of Alexander's choice. After the battle is won, Alexander distributes husbands according to the ladies' wishes, the dead are buried, and so ends the poem.

The *Restor du paon* is a continuation of some 2,800 Alexandrines written by Jean le Court de Brisebarre shortly after the completion of the *Vœux du paon*—at least before 1338, the date of the earliest manuscript. Jean composed several pious works: *Escole de foy*, a *serventois*, chansons, and the *Dit de l'esvesque et de droit*, the latter strongly influenced by the *Roman de la Rose*. The *Restor du paon* exists only in manuscripts that also contain the *Vœux*. The *Parfait du paon* has been preserved in two manuscripts, one of which lacks some 100 lines at the end. Its author, Jean de le Mote, who leaves his name in an acrostic near the end, claims in his explicit to have completed this sequel to the *Vœux* in 1340.

Far more important than these appendages to the *Vœux du paon*, however, are the *Vœux de l'épervier* and the *Vœux du héron*. Though derivative, they exploit the qualities that the Vow Cycle seems to represent. Both are short and feature as their centerpiece a vowing session. Of the *Vœux de l'épervier*'s 562 Alexandrines, 425 are devoted to the pronouncement of vows. This obscure and slender piece, composed to commemorate Henry of Luxembourg's 1310 expedition to Rome, recounts his assassination. Wolfram, who edited the poem, suggested that Simon de Marville, treasurer of the cathedral chapel at Metz, was the author. Since he died before 1326, we can conjecture that it was created 1310–26, probably nearer the later date. The poem survived in a single 15th-century manuscript (Metz Mun. Libr. 831; destroyed in 1944).

The *Vœux du héron* (ca. 1340) purports to dramatize in 422 rhymed Alexandrines an event in 1338 that led to the Hundred Years' War. Robert d'Artois has been banished from France by Philippe de Valois, who also imprisoned his family. Robert publicly labels Edward III of England a coward for failing to maintain control over France and instigates a vowing session in which the English king promises to invade France and renounce the treaty he had concluded in his naive youth. The bird chosen to be honored is the heron, the symbol of cowardice, captured by Robert to antagonize Edward. The text has been preserved in five manuscripts, two 19th-century transcriptions, and four critical editions. Nothing is known about the author, but he was obviously familiar with the events he related and in fact might have been present if the vows were actually pronounced. A comment by Froissart on Gautier de Magny (Walter of Manny) hints that something of the sort occurred.

John L. Grigsby

[See also: ALEXANDER ROMANCES; LE MOTE, JEAN DE; PHILIP THE GOOD]

Grigsby, John L., ed., and Norris J. Lacy, trans. *The Vows of the Heron (Les Vœux du Héron)*. New York: Garland, 1992.

Le Mote, Jean de. *Le parfait du paon*, ed. Richard Carey. Geneva: Droz, 1966.

Longuyon, Jacques de. *Les vœux du paon*, ed. Camillus Casey. Diss. Columbia University, 1956.

Bertoni, Giulio. "I Vœux du Hairon (ms. di Berna, no. 323)." *Archivum romanicum* 5 (1921): 426–36.

Blumenfeld-Kosinski, Renate. "The Poetics of Continuation in the Old French Paon Cycle." *Romance Philology* 39 (1985–86): 437–47.

Coville, Alfred. "Les vœux du héron." In *Histoire littéraire de la France*. Paris: Imprimerie Nationale, 1949, Vol. 38, pp. 268–82.

Gégou, Fabienne. "Du Roi de Sicile aux Vœux de l'épervier." In *Jean Misrahi Memorial Volume: Studies in Medieval Literature*, ed. Hans Runte et al. Columbia: French Literature, 1977, pp. 71–88.

Thomas, Antoine. "Jacques de Longuyon, Trouvère." In *Histoire littéraire de la France*. Paris: Imprimerie Nationale, 1927, Vol. 36, pp. 1–35.

Wolfram, Georg, and François Bonnardot, eds. *Les vœux de l'épervier*. *Jahrbuch der Gesellschaft für Lothring: Geschichte und Altertumskunde* 6 (1894): 177–280.

VOYAGE DE CHARLEMAGNE À JÉRUSALEM ET À CONSTANTINOPLE.

A chanson de geste belonging to the King Cycle. Few of the many critics who have studied the *Voyage* (also known as the *Pèlerinage de Charlemagne*) agree on its date of composition, although most would place it in the 12th century. The unique manuscript disappeared from the British Museum in 1879 or 1880. Since then, critical editions have been based on E. Koschwitz's editions, particularly on his diplomatic transcription. First edited and published by Francisque Michel in 1836, the *Voyage* comprises 870 twelve-syllable lines.

Charlemagne, with his twelve peers and many knights, leaves Paris for Jerusalem and Constantinople, after the queen has publicly stated that Hugo the Strong, emperor of Constantinople, has more presence when wearing his crown than does her royal husband. Full of anger, Charles decides to prove her wrong and to avenge himself. Riding mules and carrying staffs, the Franks first stop at Jerusalem, where the patriarch gives them many relics. Charles and his retinue finally reach Constantinople, where they are bedazzled by Hugo's wealth and power. At a banquet, Oliver is struck by the beauty of Hugo's daughter. In their chambers at night, the Franks boast drunkenly of being able to carry out incredible feats of strength and skill. A spy hidden in the chamber reports to Hugo. Enraged, the emperor decides to force the Franks to carry out their boasts or be executed. The Franks pray to God, who sends an angel to reprimand them but also to assure them they will be successful. Oliver, who has said he will make love a hundred times during the same night to Hugo's daughter, is the first to be asked to comply. He succeeds thanks to a false statement made by Hugo's daughter. Two more boasts are fulfilled before Hugo agrees to become Charlemagne's liegeman. As both kings proceed side by side, it becomes apparent that Charles wears his crown a little higher than Hugo. Returning to Saint-Denis with many relics, Charles forgives the queen.

Though literary critics have divergent interpretations of this chanson, many agree that it is a comical work exploiting the heroic tradition. The poet, it seems, wants to entertain his audience, using humor and a bantering tone. Several critics consider the *Voyage* to be a caricature and a parody of other chansons de geste. The poet may have been familiar with a chronicle, the *Descriptio qualiter Karolus Magnus clavum et coronam Domini a Constanti-* nopoli Aquisgrani detulerit qualiterque Karolus Clavus hec ad Sanctum Dionysium retulerit, that describes the relics of the Passion and tells how they reached the treasury of Saint-Denis.

Jean-Louis Picherit

[See also: *FIERABRAS*; *GAB*; KING CYCLE]

Aebischer, Paul, ed. *Le voyage de Charlemagne à Jérusalem et à Constantinople*. Geneva: Droz, 1965.

Burgess, Glyn S., and Anne E. Colby, eds. and trans. *The Pilgrimage of Charlemagne and Aucassin and Nicolette*. New York: Garland, 1988.

Picherit, Jean-Louis, ed. and trans. *The Journey of Charlemagne to Jerusalem and Constantinople*. Birmingham: Summa, 1984.

Horrent, Jules. *Le pèlerinage de Charlemagne: essai d'explication littéraire avec des notes de critique textuelle*. Paris: Les Belles Lettres, 1961.

VULGATE CYCLE.

Known by many titles, the Arthurian Vulgate Cycle (ca. 1215–35) derives its most common name from the first, and only complete, edition of the cycle, undertaken by H. Oskar Sommer between 1908 and 1916. Using British Museum Additional manuscripts 10292–10294, Sommer provides a text of the *Estoire del saint Graal* (Vol. 1), *Estoire de Merlin* (Vol. 2), *Estoire de Lancelot del Lac* (known commonly as the *Prose Lancelot*, Vols. 3–5), *Queste del saint Graal* (Vol. 6), and *Mort le roi Artu* (Vol. 7). More rigorous editions have been undertaken subsequently for all volumes except the *Estoire del saint Graal*. French scholars of the Vulgate romances refer typically to their material as the Lancelot-Grail Cycle, although this appelation generally includes only the last three works of the series, omitting the *Merlin* and sometimes also the *Estoire del saint Graal*. Attribution of the *Queste* and *Mort Artu* to Walter Map has fostered occasional reference to the whole corpus as the Pseudo-Map Cycle. The diverse titles all reflect 13th-century French prose composition through their common use of the term "cycle," depicting thereby an expansive narrative structure that chronicles the deeds of whole generations of knights across numerous volumes of text.

Taking as their subject the entire history of the Grail from its origin in the Passion of Christ to the successful accomplishment of the quest by the chosen hero, the Arthurian prose texts adopt the comprehensive scale of literary and theological *summae* of the 13th century, such as Jean de Meun's *Roman de la Rose*, Vincent de Beauvais's *Speculum naturale*, and Thomas Aquinas's *Summa theologica*. One of the earliest literary examples of this *effet totalisant* is found in the *Roman du Graal* (ca. 1210), a prose trilogy attributed to Robert de Boron, which recounts the history of the Grail vessel (*Joseph d'Arimathie*), its arrival in Great Britain along with the discovery of the future King Arthur (*Merlin*), and the quest for the Holy Grail and subsequent demise of Arthur's world (*Perceval*).

The Vulgate Cycle offers a more elaborate version of this narrative scenario, expanding the prose *Perceval* into two separate tales, the *Queste del saint Graal* and the *Mort le roi Artu*, and adding a lengthy rendition of the Lancelot story to make a total of five roughly sequential narratives. The *Lancelot propre* (or *Lancelot en prose*), the *Queste*, and the *Mort Artu* were written first, then supplemented by the *Estoire del saint Graal* and the *Estoire de Merlin* (or the Vulgate *Merlin*), although the latter two are designed to head the sequence in terms of narrative chronology.

As we move from the classic Arthurian verse romances of the 12th century, which tend to focus on the chivalric exploits of a single knight, to protracted prose accounts of the Grail quester's complex heritage and inheritors, the scope of the Arthurian adventure story becomes simultaneously more historical and more religious. Appeal is made to two distinct traditions of authority: historical chronicle and the Divine Book. The *Queste* and *Mort* are attributed to Walter Map, a scribe at the court of the English king Henry II (r. 1154–89). Throughout the Vulgate Cycle, fictive genealogies claim that the tale we read descends from eyewitness testimony of events in the Arthurian past. As knights-errant completed feats of heroism in the Arthurian forest, we are told, they returned to Arthur's court, where royal scribes recorded in writing their tales of adventure. The story we read is presented as an accurate transcription or historical documentation of events that actually occurred. But while posing as historiography, the adventure story also claims descent from an authoritative tradition of scriptural writings. The *Merlin* results ostensibly from Merlin's dictation to his scribe, Blaise, who combines accounts of the Arthurian past with those of Christ's miracles. The *Estoire* claims to issue directly from the mouth of God and from a book that Christ, the divine author, gave the vernacular "author" to copy.

An elaborate matrix of cross-references involving prophecy and family lineage thematizes the conjunction of spiritual and chivalric modes cultivated throughout the cycle. The *Lancelot* announces at its beginning that Lancelot was given the baptismal name of Galahad, thus forging a crucial link between the archetypical knight-lover and the chosen hero of the *Queste del saint Graal*. At the end of the *Lancelot*, we learn that Lancelot is in fact Galahad's father, having engendered the Grail hero during a visit with King Pelles's daughter at Corbenic, although the son far surpasses the more courtly Lancelot in spiritual achievement. Galahad represents the ideal conjunction of religious and chivalric modes and of past and future epochs. Descending from King David on his father's side and from Joseph of Arimathea and the Grail kings on his mother's, he is the embodiment of biblical history destined to cure the ills of the Arthurian world.

The belated prologue to the Vulgate Cycle supplied by the *Estoire del saint Graal* recasts this father-son scenario in a yet more religious vein. A highly christianized version of Robert de Boron's *Joseph*, this tale adds to the story of the Grail keeper, Joseph of Arimathea, the narrative of his son, Josephe, whose purity and chastity qualify him to become the first bishop. Joseph catches Christ's blood in the holy vessel after the Crucifixion, but it is Josephe who has a privileged vision of Christ while con-

templating the Grail and later becomes the spiritual leader of the Christians. The evangelization of East and West ensues through a series of miraculous conversions and a final voyage to Great Britain. When Josephe dies, he confers the Grail on Alain, the first Fisher King, who places it in Corbenic castle to await the arrival of the *bon chevalier*.

In the *Estoire de Merlin*, the most chroniclelike of the Vulgate stories, Merlin as prophet and enchanter becomes the nexus where chivalric and sacred threads of the narrative cross. With a knowledge of the past inherited from his incubus father and a divine gift of foresight, Merlin confounds onlookers with his ability to explain mysterious events and predict the future. He uses his magic to engineer the conception of the future King Arthur, to ensure Arthur's success at pulling the sword from the stone, and to devise military strategies that ensure the king's power. Arthur's military exploits are detailed in a narrative *suite* (the *Suite-Vulgate*, *Suite du Merlin*, or historical *suite*) that links the *Merlin* proper to the *Lancelot*.

The *Lancelot*, which alone accounts for half of the Vulgate Cycle, narrates the adventures of its most popular, if flawed, chivalric hero. Different from the Lancelot story provided by Chrétien de Troyes's *Chevalier de la charrette*, the quintessential Arthurian hero's chivalric prowess is here marred significantly by his adulterous liaison with Guenevere. The cemetery scene, which in Chrétien's version proclaimed Lancelot as the future liberator of Gorre, now contains two tombstones that the hero must lift. Lancelot's failure to remove the second stone predicts his subsequent exclusion from the Grail quest. His cousin Bohort joins Perceval and Galahad on the final quest of the Grail.

The *Queste* begins with a description of Galahad's uncanny powers as chosen hero and ends with his privileged viewing of the mysterious Grail vessel. But the bulk of the tale is concerned with attempts of less successful knights: Lionel, Hector, and Gawain, who form the elite of earthly questers, and Perceval and Bohort, who are chosen but less accomplished than Galahad. The adventures of these knights along with their visions and dreams are routinely interpreted by hermits who offer to tell the *senefiance* and *verité* of what we read.

Providing a *suite* for the *Queste* and a conclusion for the entire cycle, the *Mort le roi Artu* recounts the final holocaust on Salisbury Plain in which Arthur and his bastard son, Mordred, kill each other. This violent finale, marking the end of the cycle of tales by signaling the end of the whole Arthurian world, results from an inexorable chain of cause and consequence set in motion by the renewed love affair between Lancelot and Guenevere. Despite its emphasis on chronological sequence, this chronicle of Arthur's last days does not come to a definitive close. Arthur, though dead and buried, is also conveyed out to sea by fairies from the isle of Avalon, thus leaving open the possibility of his return and the return of the adventure story that bears his name.

E. Jane Burns

[**See also:** CHRÉTIEN DE TROYES; GRAIL AND GRAIL ROMANCES; *PERCEVAL CONTINUATIONS;* POST-VULGATE ROMANCE; PROSE ROMANCE (ARTHURIAN); ROBERT DE BORON; ROMANCE]

Frappier, Jean, ed. *La mort le roi Artu.* Geneva: Droz, 1964.
Micha, Alexandre, ed. *Merlin: roman du XIIIe siecle.* Geneva: Droz, 1979.
————, ed. *Lancelot: roman en prose du XIIIe siecle.* 9 vols. Geneva: Droz, 1978–83.
Pauphilet, Albert, ed. *La queste del saint Graal.* Paris: Champion, 1921.

Sommer, H. Oskar, ed. *The Vulgate Version of the Arthurian Romances.* Washington, D.C.: Carnegie Institute, 1908–16.
Lacy, Norris J., ed. *Lancelot-Grail: The Old French Arthurian Vulgate and Post-Vulgate in Translation,* trans. Norris J. Lacy et al. 5 vols. New York: Garland, 1993– .
Burns, E. Jane. *Arthurian Fictions: Rereading the Vulgate Cycle.* Columbus: Ohio State University Press, 1985.
Frappier, Jean. *Étude sur* La mort le roi Artu. Geneva: Droz, 1961.
Kibler, William W., ed. *The Lancelot-Grail Cycle: Text and Transformations.* Austin: University of Texas Press, 1994.

W

WACE (ca. 1100–after 1174). Born on the island of Jersey, Wace received his training first at Caen, then at Paris or, less likely, at Chartres; the influence of Hugh of Saint-Victor on his work is evident. Early in the 1130s, *maistre* Wace returned to Caen, where he occupied the position of *clerc lisant* (this term, used by Wace himself, most likely meant "reader of the lessons in the church service"); between 1165 and 1169, King Henry II of England rewarded him for his literary work with the prebend of a canon at Bayeux. He must have sojourned in England, since he knew the English language and gives precise geographical details of that country, especially of the Dorset area. Charters at Bayeux that bear his signature are not helpful in more precisely dating his life, which is known exclusively from personal remarks in his *Roman de Rou*.

Wace began his literary career with a series of hagiographical poems, of which three, signed by him, are preserved. From his stay in England, the center of St. Margaret's cult, he probably brought back a *Vie de sainte Marguerite* (742 lines), the first and stylistically by far the best of thirteen verse adaptations of this legend into French. His *Conception Nostre Dame* (1,810 lines) was designated as propaganda in favor of the establishment of the feast of the Immaculate Conception, as furthered by Abbot Anselm of Bury-Saint-Edmunds (r. 1121–46) against formidable opposition, especially from St. Bernard of Clairvaux. As a Norman, Wace would have had great interest in the life of the Virgin, for the Normans were among the first in France to establish the feast of the Immaculate Conception, which was often called the *fête aux Normands*. In the *Conception Nostre Dame*, Wace introduces the technique of grouping different episodes in one poem, in this case five that lead from the establishment of the feast to the Assumption of the Virgin. The same technique is found in his *Vie de saint Nicolas* (1,563 lines), written probably for a citizen of Caen, Robert, son of Tiout; containing twenty-three independent episodes, without any advancement in time, it testifies to the popularity of the saint in Normandy in the first half of the 12th century. The three poems, all in rhymed octosyllabic lines, can be dated ca. 1135–50.

Wace's reputation as an adapter of Latin works on popular topics might have brought him the commission by Eleanor of Aquitaine, newly wed to Henry II, to "translate" Geoffrey of Monmouth's *Historia regum Britanniae* (ca. 1136). Wace could not immediately locate a copy of this text and consequently based most of his adaptation on the *Britannici sermonis liber vetustissimus* (possibly by the archdeacon Walter of Oxford, a close friend of Geoffrey of Monmouth who is mentioned by Geffrei Gaimar), written in the early 1130s with the intent of ingratiating the Celtic part of the population with the new Norman rulers by stressing the Britons' claim to Britain, tracing its history back to the Trojans, in particular to Aeneas, with the help of early Welsh chronicles and Nennius. According to these sources, Brutus (folk etymology of *Brytt* 'Briton'), Aeneas's great-grandson, led the Trojans out of Greek captivity to Britain; the *Liber vetustissimus* then depicted the legendary history of Brutus's descendants on this island through the 8th century, when the Celts had to abandon all hope of reconquering the country from the Anglo-Saxons. It was this text that Geoffrey reedited and brought to renown thanks to the interest of the Norman dynasty in the predecessors of the Anglo-Saxons, renown that also had its repercussions on Wace's *Roman de Brut*, or *Geste des Bretons* (1155), since scribes of later manuscripts constantly altered the text by increasingly modeling it on Geoffrey's work. In the critical edition, the *Roman de Brut* is narrated in 14,866 octosyllabic verses; the manuscript Durham Cathedral C. iv. I (Anglo-Norman; 13th c.) inserts 670 decasyllabic verses containing the prophecies of Merlin related by a certain Elias; Lincoln Cathedral 104 (Anglo-Norman; 13th c.) adds 640 Alexandrines of the same prophecies by a certain William; and B.L. Add. 45103 (Anglo-Norman; 13th c.) contains yet another version of the prophecies, also in Alexandrines, and anonymous. B.N. fr. 1450 (Picard; 13th c.) goes even further and inserts between lines 9,798 and 9,799 Chrétien de Troyes's romances *Erec*, *Perceval*, *Cligés*, *Yvain*, and *Lancelot*, in that order.

Wace is remarkably critical of his source, frequently stressing that he is not certain of a fact; conversely, he romanticizes the dry events of history in order to make them palatable to an audience of noble laypersons. In particular, his work contains several episodes that presage the spirit of courtly love, such as King Aganippus's love "from afar" for

Cordeïlle, King Leïr's youngest daughter, or Uther Pendragon's love from reputation only for Ygerne; but he also stresses the catastrophic consequences of passion, illustrated, for example, by the episodes of Locrin's and Mordred's adulterous relationships. Though he eliminates the most fantastic elements in his source, such as Merlin's prophecies, he adds many picturesque details, among them a mention of the institution of the Round Table, a detail that to date has not been satisfactorily explained. Wace's work was enormously popular (twenty-six manuscripts have preserved it in complete or fragmented form), and ca. 1200 the priest Layamon of Raston in Worcestershire adapted it into Middle English, swelling it to nearly 30,000 lines; it is Layamon who reports that Wace had dedicated his work to Eleanor, which is possible though not mentioned in the text.

While in the *Roman de Brut* Wace was highly successful in converting pseudohistory into narrative fiction, he was less so in the *Roman de Rou* (i.e., Rollo), or *Geste des Normands* (11,440 octosyllabic lines; plus a prologue of 315 lines and the first 4,425 lines of the work, in Alexandrines; in addition, there exists the first draft of a prologue in 750 octosyllabic lines). The work was commissioned by Henry II, who wanted a poem similar to the *Brut* with respect to the history of Normandy. Wace especially had recourse to Dudo de Saint-Quentin's unreliable *De moribus et actis primorum Normanniae ducum*, from the first years of the 11th century, Guillaume de Jumièges's *Gesta Normannorum ducum* of 1071, Guillaume de Poitiers's *Gesta Guillelmi* (ca. 1078), and William of Malmesbury's *Gesta regum Anglorum* of the first half of the 12th. Wace began the project in 1160. He was uncomfortable with real history and its sources, excelling only when he narrated legendary material, such as stories about Duke Richard I, the Richard of Normandy in the *Chanson de Roland*, and events during the reigns of kings William II Rufus and Henry I (r. 1100–35), where he was a historian in his own right, drawing from personal information. Occasionally, he also gives firsthand information concerning the reign of the Conqueror, such as details about William's fleet in 1066, having as a small child heard his father comment on it. The commission did not excite Wace: for a while, he even attempted another meter, the Alexandrine (one of the first authors, if not the first, to do so); the work thus advanced so slowly that Henry II grew impatient and commissioned the much younger Benoît de Sainte-Maure, whose *Roman de Troie* (ca. 1165) had superseded the *Brut* as a literary success, with the same task. Wace, bitterly disappointed, interrupted his work after having narrated the Battle of Tinchebrai, in which Henry I defeated his older brother Robert Curthose and annexed Normandy (1106). Since he mentions Henry II's siege of Rouen in 1174, it is assumed that he died soon after that date.

Wace is undoubtedly the most brilliant author of the first period of Norman literature; the modern reader is also struck by his conscientiousness, honesty, and—for the period—highly critical, even scholarly approach to literature.

Hans-Erich Keller

[See also: ANGLO-NORMAN LITERATURE; BENOÎT DE SAINTE-MAURE; GEFFREI GAIMAR; HISTORIOGRAPHY]

Wace. *Le roman de Brut de Wace*, ed. Ivor Arnold. 2 vols. Paris: SATF, 1938–40.
———. *The Conception Nostre Dame of Wace*, ed. William Ray Ashford. Chicago: University of Chicago Libraries, 1933.
———. *Le roman de Rou de Wace*, ed. Anthony J. Holden. 3 vols. Paris: Picard, 1970–73.
———, ed. *Wace: La vie de sainte Marguerite*, ed. Hans-Erich Keller. Tübingen: Niemeyer, 1990.
———. *La vie de saint Nicolas par Wace, poème religieux du XIIe siècle*, ed. Einar Ronsjö. Lund: Gleerup, 1942.
Keller, Hans-Erich. *Étude descriptive sur le vocabulaire de Wace*. Berlin: Akademie, 1953.
———. "The Intellectual Journey of Wace." *Fifteenth Century Studies* 17 (1990): 185–207.
Pelan, Margaret. *L'influence du "Brut" de Wace sur les romans français de son temps*. Paris: Droz, 1931.

WALAFRID STRABO (ca. 808–849). A Carolingian scholar and poet, Walafrid (Strabo means "the squinter") was born in Swabia and educated at Reichenau and later at Fulda under Rabanus Maurus. He served from 829 to 838 as tutor to Louis the Pious's youngest son, Charles the Bald. After 838, he was the abbot of Reichenau; for political reasons, he was expelled by Louis the German in 840 but reinstated in 842. Walafrid died on August 18, 849, crossing the Loire to visit his former student, Charles the Bald.

To modern readers, Walafrid's most famous works are his poems, including the *Visio Wettini*, a hexameter treatment of visions of Hell, Purgatory, and Paradise written at the age of eighteen and dedicated to his former teacher, Wettin of Reichenau; and *De cultura hortorum* (or *hortulus*), a medicinal description and allegorical interpretation of twenty-three herbs and flowers. Other poems include hagiography and praises of important people (including Louis the Pious and the empress Judith, mother of Charles the Bald). In the Middle Ages, he was also famous for his exegesis, much of it based on the longer works of Rabanus Maurus, including commentaries on the Pentateuch, the Psalms, and the canonical epistles. This exegesis remains in need of further critical study. The *Glossa ordinaria*, published as a work of Walafrid in Migne's *Patrologia Latina*, Vols. 113–14, is now known to have been written in the 12th century and erroneously ascribed to Walafrid in the 15th.

E. Ann Matter

[See also: BIBLE, CHRISTIAN INTERPRETATION OF; CHARLES II THE BALD; *GLOSSA ORDINARIA*; LATIN POETRY, CAROLINGIAN; LOUIS I THE PIOUS; PURGATORY; RABANUS MAURUS]

Walafrid Strabo. *Poems*. MGH Poetae 2.259–473.
Traill, David A., ed. and trans. *Walahfrid Strabo's Visio Wettini: Text, Translation and Commentary*. Bern: Lang, 1974.
Duckett, Eleanor Shipley. *Carolingian Portraits: A Study in the Ninth Century*. Ann Arbor: University of Michigan Press, 1962, pp. 121–60.
Godman, Peter. *Poets and Emperors: Frankish Politics and Carolingian Poetry*. Oxford: Clarendon, 1987.

Onnerfors, Alf, Johannes Rathofer, and Fritz Wagner, eds. "Über Walahfrid Strabos Psalter-Kommentar." In *Literatur und Sprache im europaischen Mittelalter: Festschrift für Karl Langosch zum 70. Geburtstag.* Darmstadt: Wissenschaftliche Buchgesellschaft, 1973, pp. 75–121.

WALDO/WALDENSES. The Waldenses, or "Poor of Lyon," were members of a lay spiritual movement founded on three principal points: the adoption of voluntary poverty, access to the Scriptures through a vernacular translation, and public preaching. In many ways, the form that this movement took is a product of the developing "profit economy" of the 12th century. The founder was a certain Waldo, a rich merchant of Lyon, who, upon hearing a jongleur sing the *Vie de saint Alexis*, had a conversion experience ca. 1173. He then had two priests translate the Bible into French and decided upon the apostolic life: giving away his wealth and placing his wife and daughters in convents, he memorized his translated Bible and began to preach. He quickly gained a following of laymen who called themselves "the poor" and traveled in pairs, begging and preaching repentance.

Doctrinally orthodox, Waldo and his followers preached against Cathar heretics, but their ostentatious poverty and public preaching soon roused clerical opposition. Waldo sought the pope's approval of his mission and his vernacular Bible (1179), but the clergy proved both contemptuous of these unlettered laymen and unalterably opposed to their preaching, despite their usefulness in combating the church's primary concern—Catharism. Waldo disobeyed rather than forsake the Lord's command to preach the gospel, and by 1184 the group was condemned as heretical. In response, some Waldensians (especially the Lombards) claimed that the church had become the "Whore of Babylon." Rejecting clerical sacraments, prayers for the dead, and relic cults, they established their own church of *perfecti*, who administered sacraments and confession. Waldo himself never gave up hope of a reconciliation, and some followers, such as Durand of Huesca and the "Catholic Poor," returned to the church. Radical Waldensianism spread rapidly throughout Europe from the Pyrénées to central Europe, developing a parallel ecclesiastical structure while maintaining a commitment to evangelical Christianity. Despite inquisitorial persecution, they survived into the modern period, providing fertile ground for Protestantism in the 16th century. A Waldensian church survives in Italy to this day.

Richard Landes

[See also: HERESIES, APOSTOLIC; HERESY; INQUISITION; PREACHING; *SAINT ALEXIS, VIE DE*; WITCHCRAFT; WOMEN, RELIGIOUS EXPERIENCE OF]

Audisio, Gabriel, ed. *Les Vaudois des origines à leur fin (XIIe–XVIe siècles).* Turin: Meynier, 1990.
Biller, P. "Thesaurus absconditus: The Hidden Treasure of the Waldensians." In *The Church and Wealth*, ed. W.J. Sheils and Diana Wood. Oxford: Blackwell, 1987, pp. 139–54.
Gonnet, Jean, and Amedeo Molnar. *Les Vaudois au moyen âge.* Turin: Claudiana, 1974.
Lerner, Robert E. "A Case of Religious Counter-Culture: The German Waldensians." *American Scholar* 55 (1986): 234–47.
Marthaler, B. "Forerunners of the Franciscans: The Waldenses." *Franciscan Studies* 18 (1958): 133–42.
Patchovsky, Alexander, and Kurt-Victor Selge. *Quellen zur Geschichte der Waldenser.* Gümüterscloh: Mohn, 1973.
Selge, Kurt-Victor. *Die ersten Waldenser.* Berlin: De Gruyter, 1967.
Thouzellier, Christine. *Catharisme et Valdéisme en Languedoc à la fin du XIIe et au début du XIIIe siècle.* Louvain: Nauwelaerts, 1969.
Wakefield, Walter, and Austin Evans, eds. *Heresies of the High Middle Ages.* New York: Columbia University Press, 1969, pp. 200–42, 278–89, 346–51.

WALTER. *See also* GAUTIER

WALTER OF SAINT-VICTOR (d. after 1180). Prior of the abbey of Saint-Victor at Paris, Walter is known chiefly for his harsh attack on the dialectical method in *Contra quatuor labyrinthos Franciae*, which singled out Peter Abélard, Peter Lombard, Peter of Poitiers (canon of Notre-Dame), and Gilbert of Poitiers for sharp criticism. Walter is also the author of some twenty sermons, which exhibit a rather ordinary piety and none of the spirituality of his predecessors Hugh and Richard of Saint-Victor.

Grover A. Zinn

[See also: ABÉLARD, PETER; GILBERT OF POITIERS; HUGH OF SAINT-VICTOR; PETER LOMBARD; PETER OF POITIERS; RICHARD OF SAINT-VICTOR; SAINT-VICTOR, ABBEY AND SCHOOL OF]

Walter of Saint-Victor. *Le Contra quatuor labyrinthos Franciae de Gauthier de Saint-Victor*, ed. Palémon Glorieux. *Archives d'histoire littéraire et doctrinale du moyen âge* 19 (1953): 187–335.
Chatillon, Jean. "De Guillaume de Champeaux à Thomas Gallus: chronique d'histoire littéraire et doctrinale de l'école de Saint-Victor." *Revue du moyen âge latin* 8 (1952): 139–62.
———. "Sermons et prédicateurs victorins de la seconde moitié du XIIe siècle." *Archives d'histoire littéraire et doctrinale du moyen âge* 23 (1965): 7–60.
Glorieux, Palémon. "Mauvaise action et mauvais travail: le *Contra quatuor labyrinthos Franciae* de Gauthier de Saint-Victor." *Recherches de théologie ancienne et médiévale* 21 (1954): 179–93.

WARFARE. Warfare was a dominant feature of medieval French history. After the late 4th century, Germanic tribes penetrated the western Roman Empire in force, bringing important changes to the military system. Roman discipline and organization gave way to badly organized forces with poor training, few arms, and almost no discipline.

Military recruitment and payment for services were based on the amount of booty a leader could provide his soldiers, and loyalty to this leader was dependent on the continued success of his conquests. Soldiers generally were equipped with only a rudimentary shield and helmet, and their arms consisted of a sword, ax, or spear. These militaristic barbarians had an almost Homeric sense of heroism and revered martial skills. Their names, both male and female, reflected the omnipresence of war, and warriors were the elite of Germanic society, placed at the top of the wergeld system of compensation and given elaborate burials with their equipment and booty.

By the 6th and 7th centuries, the Merovingian Franks, who required military service of all free men, had an effective army based on infantry. Their special weapon was the *francisca*, a throwing ax. They adopted body armor only gradually. Their fortifications, other than those inherited from Rome, were simple earth and wood ramparts.

When the Carolingians came to power in the 8th century, the requirements of a large empire led to new military institutions that presaged the feudalism of a later time. Rulers granted income-producing estates to followers who promised to render full-time military service at their own expense. The expanding role of the stirrup gradually encouraged the development of heavy cavalry and the archetypical medieval knight.

This system of land grants and oaths of loyalty enabled Charlemagne to muster an effective cavalry force almost annually. His armies were not large, but they were powerful and dominated their opponents. He generally led them himself, and although there were few "formal" military tactics, they were successful in most engagements.

The Capetian monarchy in France gradually emerged from the fragmentation of the Carolingian empire. The survival of the early Capetians depended on their military capabilities, and some of them suffered serious reversals. Recruitment of soldiers increasingly depended on feudal institutions in the 11th and 12th centuries, and the kings sometimes could not muster sufficient troops. As they began to acquire more resources, they began to supplement feudal troops with paid professionals. The king himself or a designated noble lieutenant generally commanded these armies.

Mounted knights were still the core of the army. With improved weapons and armor and mounted upon expensive warhorses, they usually decided the course of each battle, fighting with couched lance in a tournament-like fashion. Most knights by the 13th century were nobles supported by fiefs. Large battles were infrequent and those that were fought often included only rudimentary tactical combinations.

While knights were the core of the army, the most numerous forces were still the infantry. Levied from among the free men of the kingdom, these troops were armed much less well than their mounted counterparts. While some were protected by a helmet, a small shield, and a leather hauberk, infantry soldiers frequently served without armor. Offensive infantry weapons included the spear, sword, lance, and pike, with little standardization among these weapons. Archers also served in infantry contingents,

initially being equipped with short bows. In the course of the 12th century, these began to be replaced with the more powerful crossbow.

In the Capetian period, the siege replaced the battle as the primary form of military engagement. Though Charlemagne had effectively altered the standard of battlefield fighting, he and his successors tended to neglect fortifications, leaving the empire vulnerable to the raids of Vikings and Hungarians. In the 11th century, local rulers led in the construction of fortifications, at first small earth and wood motte-and-bailey castles, but soon larger and stronger structures of masonry. These more intricate and costly fortifications provided valuable defenses. Although mining, sapping, and stone-throwing engines were used against them, a castle or town with strong stone walls could generally be reduced only by starvation.

In the late Middle Ages, five significant developments altered warfare. First, armies fighting on foot began again to predominate. The stunning defeat of French knights by Flemish infantry at Courtrai in 1302 showed that a strong unified infantry line could halt the charge of cavalry. The Scots similarly defeated English knights at Bannockburn in 1314, and Swiss infantry defeated Austrian cavalry at Mortgarten in 1316. French cavalry suffered serious defeats over the next century at the hands of English armies dominated by footsoldiers and longbowmen. The second development was the continual fighting that beset France between 1337 and 1453, the period misnamed the "Hundred Years' War." The long struggle exhausted the French military and required a stricter and often less noble military bureaucracy. The emergence of *routiers* and *condottieri*, paid mercenaries without feudal ties, weakened traditional military institutions. The third factor was the Black Death of 1348–49, which significantly reduced the numbers available to fight on the battlefield and defend French towns and castles. The fourth was the advent of frequent and often violent popular rebellions by French peasants and townspeople, the suppression of which required changes in military tactics.

Finally, warfare was changed by the advent and proliferation of missile weapons employing gunpowder. Appearing initially in the early 14th century, they began influencing warfare by the 1380s, when they were used effectively against fortifications and also on the battlefield. By 1400, no siege was free of their use, as they reduced substantially the time needed to destroy walls. No longer was it necessary to rely on starvation to force the capitulation of castles or towns. By the 1430s, hand-held gunpowder weapons began to take their place among infantry contingents, changing the face of battlefield engagements. By the Swiss and Burgundian wars of 1475–77, one third of the infantry on each side was outfitted with handguns. These late-medieval changes brought an end to feudal methods of warfare and encouraged the development of states capable of financing modern armies.

Kelly DeVries

Allmand, Christopher T. *The Hundred Years War: England and France at War c1300–c1450*. Cambridge: Cambridge University Press, 1988.

Contamine, Philippe. *Guerre, état et société à la fin du moyen âge: étude sur les armées des rois de France, 1337–1494*. Paris: Mouton, 1972.

———. *War in the Middle Ages*, trans. Michael Jones. New York: Blackwell, 1984.

Kaeuper, Richard W. *War, Justice and Public Order: England and France in the Later Middle Ages*. Oxford: Clarendon, 1988.

Verbruggen, J.F. *The Art of Warfare in Western Europe During the Middle Ages: From the Eighth Century to 1340*, trans. Sumner Willard and S.C.M. Southern. Amsterdam: North-Holland, 1977.

WARHORSE. The warhorse (OFr. *destrier*) was the most important military equipment owned by a medieval knight. The ownership of a horse not only indicated the knight's military status, but the expense of ownership and upkeep also established the knight's status within medieval feudal society. So important and expensive was the warhorse that often the French king provided some compensation or reimbursement for one that was killed or injured on the battlefield or in a tournament.

Although many barbarian tribes used the warhorse in the early Middle Ages, it was not until the more frequent use of the stirrup, nailed horseshoe, and saddle with cantle (ca. 1100) and the establishment of heavy cavalry units that the horse became a dominant force in medieval armies. From then until 1300, victory in nearly every French military engagement was tied to the heavy cavalry and its tactical use of mounted shock combat. Even after the infantry victories against the French cavalry at Courtrai, Crécy, Poitiers, and Agincourt, the mounted knight remained the dominant part of the French army.

Off the battlefield, among the noble (or chivalric) class of Europe, the warhorse also played an important role. A knight was expected to own not only his horses for military engagement but also large, expensive horses on which he rode during jousts and tournaments.

Kelly DeVries

[See also: CAVALRY; WARFARE]

Contamine, Philippe. *War in the Middle Ages*, trans. Michael Jones. New York: Blackwell, 1984.

Bachrach, Bernard S. "Charles Martel, Mounted Shock Combat, the Stirrup, and Feudalism." *Studies in Medieval and Renaissance History* 7 (1970), 47–75.

———. "Animals and Warfare in Early Medieval Europe." In *L'uomo di fronte al mondo animale nell'alto medioevo*. Spoleto: Presso la Sede del Centro, 1985, pp. 707–63.

Vale, Malcolm. *War and Chivalry: Warfare and Aristocratic Culture in England, France and Burgundy at the End of the Middle Ages*. London: Duckworth, 1981.

Verbruggen, J.F. *The Art of Warfare in Western Europe During the Middle Ages: From the Eighth Century to 1340*, trans. Sumner Willard and S.C.M. Southern. Amsterdam: North-Holland, 1977.

White, Lynn, Jr. *Medieval Technology and Social Change*. Oxford: Oxford University Press, 1962, pp. 1–38.

WAUQUELIN (DE MONS), JEAN (fl. 1441–52). Translator, scribe, and editor of manuscripts for the library of Philip the Good, duke of Burgundy. Notable among his accomplishments is the *Chroniques de Hainaut* (Brussels, Bibl. Roy. 9242), a translation of the Latin *Annales Hannoniae*, whose dedication miniature is a landmark in Burgundian illumination. Other masterpieces from his workshop are a *Chronique d'Alexandre* (B.N. fr. 9342), *Girart de Roussillon* (Vienna, Nationalbibliothek 2549), a *Gouvernement des princes* (Brussels Bibl. Roy. 9043), as well as a number of lesser-known manuscripts. He is also responsible for prosifications of the *Belle Helaine de Constantinople* (1448) and of Philippe de Beaumanoir's *La Manekine*.

Charity Cannon Willard

[See also: *BELLE HELAINE DE CONSTANTINOPLE*; TRANSLATION]

Delaissé, L.M.J. *La miniature flamande, le mécénat de Philippe le Bon*. Brussels: Bibliothèque Royale, 1959.

———. "Les 'Chroniques de Hainaut' et l'atelier de Jean Wauquelin à Mons, dans l'histoire de la miniature flamande." In *Miscellanea Erwin Panofsky*. Brussels: Patrimoine des Musées Royaux des Beaux-Arts, 1955.

Van Buren, Anne. "Jean Wauquelin de Mons et la production du livre au Pays-Bas." *Publication du Centre Européen d'Études Burgondo-Médianes* 23 (1983): 53–66.

WAVRIN, JEAN DE (1395–1475). Natural son of a Burgundian nobleman, officially legitimatized in 1437, Wavrin eventually became an official at the Burgundian court. A veteran of the Battle of Agincourt (1415), he nevertheless remained pro-English in his political orientation, writing the *Chroniques et anciennes istoires de la Grande Bretaigne, à présent nommé Engleterre* about events in France, Normandy, and Burgundy up to 1469. A notable bibliophile, he sponsored a workshop in Lille where manuscript copies were illustrated by a highly original artist known as the Wavrin Master.

Charity Cannon Willard

Wavrin, Jean de. *Recueil des croniques et anciennes istoires de la Grande Bretaigne, à présent nommé Engleterre*, ed. William Hardy. 5 vols. London: Rolls Series, 1864–91.

Crone, H.-R. "Neue Studien zum Maître de Wavrin." *Scriptorium* 23 (1969): 320–32.

Nabur, Antoinette. "Les goûts littéraires d'un bibliophile de la cour de Bourgogne." In *Courtly Literature: Culture and Context*, ed. Keith Busby and Erik Kooper. Amsterdam: Benjamins, pp. 459–68.

WEIGHTS AND MEASURES. Medieval France had a multitude of weights and measures typical of premetric Europe. This condition was due primarily to the fierce provincialism of duchies, counties, royal and aristocratic estates, cities, and manors. By the 16th century, France had more than 1,000 units of measurement accepted as standards in Paris and the provincial capitals, with approximately 250,000 local variations. Unit names were often superfluous and confusing, and physical standards bore little relationship to one another. Hundreds of ambiguous and misleading decrees and laws had been issued, beginning with the modest reforms of Charlemagne in the late 8th century. Control over weights and measures belonged to feudal lords, churchmen, guildsmen, judges, city officials, and others as part of their administrative rights, and, since taxes were based on units of measure, it was to their best interests to establish their own systems and standards.

Medieval French weights and measures varied depending on whether they were used in retail or wholesale trade. There were special units employed at warehouses, harbors, ports, foundries, mines, and workshops. They differed on the highways, the seas and waterways, inside and outside town walls, and in the forests. Product variations abounded especially for grains, liquors, and textiles. Units based upon a complex array of numbers, multiples, submultiples, accounts, coinages, wages, prices, land functions, time allotments, production spans, and labor needs were commonplace. Many other types flourished, but certain weights and measures could be considered national standards by the later Middle Ages.

Among linear measures, for example, the *aune, lieue, perche, pied,* and *toise* were of paramount importance. The *aune,* a textile measure, was 3 *pieds,* 7 *pouces,* 10⁵/₆ *lignes,* or 526⁵/₆ *lignes* (1.188 meters) in all. For road and sea measurements, the *lieue* had six official standards ranging from 2,000 to 3,000 *toises* (3,898.08 to 5,847.12 meters). The *perche* employed in agriculture was either 18, 20, or 22 *pieds* (5.847, 6.497, or 7.146 meters). The *pied* was 12 *pouces* (0.325 meters) or 144 lignes, while the *toise* was 6 *pieds* (1.949 meters).

For area measurement, the *arpent de Paris* was 32,400 square *pieds* (34.189 *ares*); the *arpent de commun,* 40,000 square *pieds* (42.208 *ares*); and the *arpent des eaux et forêts,* 48,400 square *pieds* (51.072 *ares*). All were 100 square *perches,* but the length of the *perche* was different in each standard.

In capacity measurement, the *boisseau, mine, muid,* and *setier* dominated. The *boisseau* contained 655.78 cubic *pouces* (13.008 liters), but had different subdivisions for wheat, oats, charcoal, and plaster. The *mine* totaled 3,934.68 cubic *pouces* (78.05 liters) for all dry products except salt, oats, and coal. The *muid* had six recognized standards for liquids and dry products. The *setier* was 4 *quartes* (7.45 liters) for most liquids and two *mines* (156.10 liters) for most dry products.

The *livre* was the principal unit of weight. During the late 8th century under Charlemagne, the *livre esterlin* was fixed at 5,760 grains (367.1 grams) and consisted of 20 *sous,* 12 *onces,* 240 *deniers,* 480 *oboles.* This *livre* was the first national standard; it was retained until the middle of the 14th century, when the government of King John II the Good authorized the employment of a new, heavier, *livre* called the *livre poids de marc.* Totaling 9,216 grains (489.506 grams), it was subdivided for valuable goods, such as gold and silver, into 2 marks or 16 *onces* and for cheaper goods into 2 *demi-livres* or 16 *onces.* There were other official *livres* for pharmacists, physicians, and merchants.

Further diversification and proliferation of these weights and measures continued after 1500, especially in the wake of increasing industrialization. Prior to the late 18th century, significant progress in French metrology took place only in the manufacture of physical standards. The French Revolution and its radically new metric system replaced these weights and measures by the early 19th century.

Ronald Edward Zupko

Guilhiermoz, Paul. "Note sur les poids du moyen âge." *Bibliothèque de l'École des Chartes* 67 (1906): 161–233, 402–50.

———. "Remarques diverses sur les poids et mesures du moyen âge." *Bibliothèque de l'École des Chartes* 80 (1919): 5–100.

Zupko, Ronald E. *French Weights and Measures Before the Revolution: A Dictionary of Provincial and Local Units.* Bloomington: Indiana University Press, 1978.

———. *Revolution in Measurement: Western European Weights and Measures Since the Age of Science.* Philadelphia: American Philosophical Society, 1989.

WERCHIN, JEAN DE (ca. 1375–1415). Seneschal of Hainaut. Werchin is cited in the *Livre des faits de Jacques de Lalaing* as an especially valiant knight of the region. He was also sufficiently versed in poetry to be a minister of the *cour amoureuse* founded in Paris in 1401. He was the author of a long allegorical poem, the *Songe de la barge* (1404; ca. 3,500 lines), and a series of ballades exchanged with his squire, Guillebert de Lannoy. His exploits were celebrated in a ballade by Christine de Pizan, who also dedicated to him her *Livre des trois jugemens.* After his death at the Battle of Agincourt, he was nostalgically remembered by Achille Caulier in the *Hôpital d'amour* in the company of Tristan and Lancelot.

Charity Cannon Willard

Piaget, Arthur, ed. "*Le songe de la barge* de Jean de Werchin, sénéchal de Hainaut." *Romania* 38 (1909): 71–110. [Partial edition, with summaries of omitted episodes.]

———. "Ballades de Guillebert de Lannoy et Jean de Werchin." *Romania* 39 (1910): 324–68.

Willard, Charity Cannon. "Jean de Werchin, Seneschal of Hainaut: Reader and Writer of Courtly Literature." In *Courtly*

Literature: Culture and Contexts, ed. Keith Busby and Erik Cooper. Philadelphia: Benjamins, 1990, pp. 595–603.

WERGELD. Germanic law codes required a sum known as "wergeld" (literally, "man money") to be paid to the relatives (or in the case of a slave, the master) of one who was killed. The amount of the wergeld varied with the legal status, ethnic background, occupation, sex, and age of the victims, thus representing their social standing.

The taking of life was not technically a violation of Germanic laws and the victim's relatives could seek an eye-for-an-eye vengeance, which often led to a bloody cycle of retaliatory deaths. Payment of the wergeld to the kinsfolk of the victim provided an honorable compensation for the death, and a vendetta could thus be avoided. However, a killer could refuse to pay the wergeld or the victim's kin could refuse to accept it, and either refusal would initiate the blood feud.

Exact values varied among the law codes. In the Salic Law, the wergeld of the typical freeman (*leudis*) normally was 200 *solidi*, that of a member of the king's entourage was 600, but a slave's was only thirty-five. In the Burgundian Code, nobles had a wergeld of 300 *solidi*, lower classes 150, and slaves thirty. (By comparison, the Ripuarian Code equated the value of a stallion with seven *solidi*, a cow with one, and a sword with three.)

The payment of one's wergeld or a portion of it could sometimes be imposed as a penalty for certain crimes.

Steven Fanning

[See also: SALIC LAW]

Fischer, Katherine, trans. *The Burgundian Code*. Philadelphia: University of Pennsylvania Press, 1949.
Rivers, Theodore John, trans. *The Laws of the Salian and Ripuarian Franks*. New York: AMS, 1986.
Murray, Alexander Callander. *Germanic Kinship Structure: Studies in Law and Society in Antiquity and the Early Middle Ages*. Toronto: Pontifical Institute of Mediaeval Studies, 1983, pp. 135–55.
Wallace-Hadrill, J.M. *The Long-Haired Kings and Other Studies in Frankish History*. London: Methuen, 1962.

WIDOWS AND WIDOWHOOD. When a medieval woman was widowed, she was able to act independently for one of the few times in her life, rather than being under the tutelage of a father, brother, or husband. Since women normally married men much older than themselves, widows were more common than widowers.

A widow could live singly, remarry, or enter a nunnery. A dowry that she had brought to the marriage was usually hers for her lifetime, and she could also support herself from any dower her husband had fixed on her at the time of their marriage. A woman with young children, it was assumed, would take over her husband's property at least until her sons had grown up. In practice, especially in the early Middle Ages, this meant that the widow of a powerful lord was treated almost like an heiress, and a man might marry her seeking her late husband's property.

A well-placed woman could marry and be widowed several times during her life. Older widows and those who had already had several husbands usually retired eventually to the cloister; medieval French nunneries recruited at least as many widows as young girls.

Constance B. Bouchard

WILLAME DE WADINGTON (fl. mid-13th c.) The *Manuel des péchés*, written in Anglo-Norman verse ca. 1250–70, is commonly ascribed to Willame de Waddington, though he may have been simply its scribe. The work is a confession manual addressed to the laity and deals first with the most common breaches of the Ten Commandments, then with the Seven Deadly Sins; there follow a series of exempla on the sin of sacrilege, a discussion of the sacraments, and instructions for making a good confession. The whole work is interlarded with saints' legends, accounts of visions, and exempla, which constitute nearly half its bulk. The *Manuel* was translated into English verse ca. 1300 with the title *Handlying Synne*, then later into English prose. Its popularity is attested by fifteen complete manuscripts, averaging 1,200 lines.

Maureen B.M. Boulton

Allen, Hope Emily. "The *Manuel des pechiez* and the Scholastic Prologue." *Romanic Review* 8 (1917): 434–62.
Arnould, Émile-Jules François. *Le manuel des péchés: étude de littérature religieuse anglo-normande*. Paris: Droz, 1940.
Laird, Charlton "Character and Growth of the *Manuel des pechiez*." *Traditio* 4 (1946): 253–306.

WILLIAM. *See also* GUILHEM; GUILLAUME

WILLIAM I THE CONQUEROR (1028–1087). Prior to his conquest of England in 1066, William I had been duke of Normandy. Prime factors behind the success of the Conquest had been the stability he had established in Normandy and the freedom from attack that the duchy had enjoyed since the deaths of Geoffroi Martel of Anjou and the Capetian king Henry I. Such stability and safety could not have been predicted in 1035, when William, then called "the Bastard" because of his illegitimate birth, inherited the duchy at age seven from his father, Robert I the Magnificent. The young duke survived several internal challenges and through successful military campaigns and judicious alliances was able to assert his authority in the duchy and in relation to the other powers of northern France. He conquered Maine and established Norman hegemony over eastern Brittany. One of his earliest and most important triumphs outside the duchy was not a military one at all, but marriage to Matilda (d. 1083), daughter of Count Baudouin I of Flanders. The 1050/51 marriage, though initially forbidden by the papacy on grounds of consanguinity, allied William with the richest principality in northern France and related him through marriage to both the German emperors and the kings of France. Matilda bore him three sons and four daughters before 1066 and seems to have been a supportive and valuable companion. She founded La Trinité, a convent for nuns, near William's Saint-Étienne in Caen, and it is in these abbey churches that the two are buried.

William I's conquest of England established a cross-Channel dominion that altered the balance of power in northern France. William's rivals were quick to exploit his difficulties in ruling the far-flung, multifrontier Anglo-Norman empire, and he would spend the rest of his life fighting off a powerful alliance of French princes. Maine rebelled in 1069, and rebels there invited Foulques le Rechin of Anjou to be their count. William and King Philip I of France supported rival claimants in the succession crisis in Flanders in 1070–71, and an anti-Norman pact between Philip, Foulques, and Count Robert of Flanders resulted. Security in William's empire was further compromised by vassals who held land both on the Continent and in England. Raoul de Gael rebelled against William in 1075 and continued his struggle from his Breton lands. Philip came to relieve the besieged Raoul at Dol in 1076 and formed a Breton-Angevin-Capetian alliance. William's rivals were also able to exploit tensions within his own family. In 1078, his eldest son, Robert Curthose, demanding independent control of Normandy and Maine, rebelled and fled Normandy. He retained considerable support within the duchy and found immediate allies in Flanders and France. Robert defeated his father at Gerberoi in 1079, but a Scottish invasion of England that same year forced a speedy reconciliation. Robert rebelled again in 1083 and again became the tool of all those who opposed William.

In 1087, William took ill on campaign in the Vexin, a region of particular contention between Normandy and France. He died outside Rouen that same year, leaving Normandy and Maine to Robert but England to his second son, William II Rufus (himself succeeded by his younger brother, Henry I). Both William II and Robert spent the rest of their lives trying to attain full possession of the empire their father had created.

Robert S. Babcock

[See also: CAEN; HENRY I (OF ENGLAND); NORMANDY; ROBERT (DUKES OF NORMANDY); VEXIN]

Bates, David. *Normandy Before 1066*. London: Longman, 1982.
————. *William the Conqueror*. London: Longman, 1989.
Chibnall, Marjorie. *Anglo-Norman England 1066–1166*. New York: Blackwell, 1986.
Douglas, David C. *William the Conqueror*. Berkeley: University of California Press, 1964.
LePatourel, John. *The Norman Empire*. Oxford: Clarendon, 1976.

WILLIAM II RUFUS (d. 1100). The second son of William I the Conqueror, William II acquired England in 1087 when his father left the duchy of Normandy and the county of Maine to his eldest surviving son, Robert Curthose, and England to William (called "Rufus" for his ruddy complexion). William II faced some opposition in the kingdom but devoted much of his English resources to trying to win the continental lands from his brother. Most often these attempts were in the form of bribes to Robert's vassals. William II finally did gain possession of the continental dominions, though not the title of duke or count, in return for financing Robert's participation in the First Crusade in 1096. Robert had been a weak duke, so William II took possession of territories near to the point of anarchy. Through quick military action and judicious bribery, William II was able to quell the baronial wars that had become commonplace in Normandy and to restore Norman power in Maine. Determined to hold all that his father had held, he launched unsuccessful campaigns to retake the French Vexin from Philip I in 1097–98 and 1098–99. William II died in a hunting accident in England, but during his brief reign he had managed to maintain royal power in England, restore ducal authority in Normandy, and reunite his father's empire, which fell to his younger brother, Henry I.

Robert S. Babcock

[See also: ROBERT (DUKES OF NORMANDY); WILLIAM I THE CONQUERER]

Barlow, Frank. *William Rufus*. Berkeley: University of California Press, 1983.
Freeman, Edward A. *The Reign of William Rufus and the Accession of Henry*. Oxford: Clarendon, 1882.

WILLIAM OF AUVERGNE (William of Paris; 1180/90–1249). Born in Aurillac in the Auvergne, William was canon of Notre-Dame in Paris by 1223, regent master at Paris in 1225, and bishop of Paris in 1228. A secular master himself, William was, however, an early champion of the mendicant orders, allowing Roland of Cremona to hold the first Dominican chair in theology (1229). Known for his fairness and good sense, he was confessor to Blanche of Castile and friend and adviser to Louis IX.

William left a vast corpus of works in encyclopedic style, including a series of tracts sometimes called his *Magisterium divinale* (1123–40), which included *De universo*, *Cur Deus homo*, *De fide et legibus*, and *De Trinitate*. His *De vitiis et virtutibus* rivaled that of William Peraldus (the two men were often confused) in popularity. One of the first theorists of Purgatory, he was also among the first theological users of Aristotle in Paris, and he sought out texts of Avicenna, Maimonides's *Guide*, Avicebrol, and others in the service of orthodox belief.

Lesley J. Smith

[See also: ARABIC PHILOSOPHY, INFLUENCE OF; ARISTOTLE, INFLUENCE OF; MAGIC; PURGATORY; THEOLOGY; UNIVERSITIES]

William of Auvergne. *Opera omnia*. 2 vols. Paris: Andraeas Pralard, 1674; repr. Frankfurt am Main: Minerva, 1963.
————. *De Trinitate*, ed. Bruno Switalski. Toronto: Pontifical Institute of Mediaeval Studies, 1976.

———. *The Immortality of the Soul = De immortalitate animae*, trans. Roland J. Teske. Milwaukee: Marquette University Press, 1991.

———. *The Trinity, or, The First Principle = De Trinitate, seu De primo principio*, trans. Roland J. Teske and Francis C. Wade. Milwaukee: Marquette University Press, 1989.

Bernstein, A.E. "Esoteric Theology: William of Auvergne on the Fires of Hell and Purgatory." *Speculum* 57 (1982): 509–31.

Marrone, Steven P. *William of Auvergne and Robert Grosseteste: New Ideas of Truth in the Early 13th Century*. Princeton: Princeton University Press, 1983.

Quentin, Albrecht. *Naturkenntnisse und Naturanschauungen bei Wilhelm von Auvergne*. Hildesheim: Gerstenberg, 1976.

Rohls, Jan. *Wilhelm von Auvergne und der mittelalterliche Aristotelismus: Gottesbegriff und aristotelische Philosophie zwischen Augustin und Thomas von Aquin*. Munich: Kaiser, 1980.

Valois, Noël. *Guillaume d'Auvergne, évêque de Paris (1228–1249), sa vie et ses ouvrages*. Paris: Picard, 1880.

WILLIAM OF AUXERRE (ca. 1150–1231). Little is known of the career and works of this influential secular master of Paris, although he was teaching in Paris by 1189. A useful administrator as well as theologian, William was made archdeacon of Beauvais by Pope Honorius III sometime between 1216 and 1227; he was a member of the commission appointed by Gregory IX in 1231 to examine and amend the physical treatises of Aristotle, whose use had been forbidden at Paris in 1210. He was himself among the first users of these Aristotelian treatises.

William's chief work, called the *Summa aurea* (1215–20) by admiring contemporaries, takes the form of a loose commentary on the *Sententiae* of Peter Lombard but shows much of William's originality of thought and reformist tendencies. He often introduces specific, contemporary examples and is concerned for the moral reform of the church.

Lesley J. Smith

[See also: ARISTOTLE, INFLUENCE OF; THEOLOGY; UNIVERSITIES]

William of Auxerre. *Summa aurea*, ed. J. Ribaillier. 7 vols. Grottaferrata (Rome): Collegio S. Bonaventura, 1980–87.

Principe, Walter H. *The Theology of the Hypostatic Union in the Early Thirteenth Century*. 4 vols. Toronto: Pontifical Institute of Mediaeval Studies, 1963–75, Vol. 1: *William of Auxerre's Theology of the Hypostatic Union*.

St. Pierre, Jules A. "The Theological Thought of William of Auxerre: An Introductory Bibliography." *Recherches de théologie ancienne et médiévale* 33 (1966): 147–55.

WILLIAM OF CHAMPEAUX (ca. 1070–1121). Much of our information about William comes from Abélard and so cannot be judged uncritically; little of his writing is extant. It seems that William studied philosophy and theology with Anselm of Laon, probably with Roscelin at Compiègne, and possibly with Manegold of Lautenbach at Paris. He became archdeacon of Paris and head of the cathedral school (ca. 1100), where Abélard was one of his pupils; but he left the schools, probably because of Abélard's hostility, in 1108.

William established a religious community at a site dedicated to St. Victor just outside the walls of Paris, organized it according to the new rule of Augustinian regular canons, and laid the foundations of the school there. The abbey flourished under his direction, and it attempted to bridge the widening gulf between monks and schoolmen. In 1113, William became bishop of Châlons-sur-Marne, remaining as a reforming bishop until his death in 1121.

William's thought has been characterized (through Abélard's depiction) as "exaggerated realism" (a Neoplatonic view that held that concepts as much as individuals have existence), so that William regarded the individuals in the same species as having an identical reality.

Lesley J. Smith

[See also: ABÉLARD, PETER; ANSELM OF LAON; PHILOSOPHY; SAINT-VICTOR, ABBEY AND SCHOOL OF]

Green-Pedersen, Neils J. "William of Champeaux on Boethius' *Topics* According to Orléans Bibl. Mun. 266." *Cahiers de l'Institut du Moyen Âge Grec et Latin* 13 (1974): 13–30.

Fredborg, Karin M. "The Commentaries on Cicero's *De inventione* and *Rhetorica ad Herennium* by William of Champeaux." *Cahiers de l'Institut du Moyen Âge Grec et Latin* 17 (1976): 1–39.

Jolivet, Jean. "Données sur Guillaume de Champeaux dialecticien et théologien." In *L'abbaye parisienne de Saint-Victor au moyen âge*, ed. Jean Longère. Turnhout: Brepols, 1991, pp. 235–51.

Tweedale, Martin M. "Logic (i): From the Late Eleventh Century to the Time of Abelard." In *A History of Twelfth-Century Western Philosophy*, ed. Peter Dronke. Cambridge: Cambridge University Press, 1988, pp. 196–226.

Weisweller, Heinrich. "L'école d'Anselme de Laon et de Guillaume de Champeaux." *Recherches de théologie ancienne et médiévale* 4 (1932): 237–69, 371–91.

WILLIAM OF CONCHES (ca. 1085–ca. 1154). Named by John of Salisbury as one of his teachers, William is most often associated with the so-called School of Chartres, as a student of Bernard of Chartres and a master there, although Richard W. Southern has called into question whether William actually taught at Chartres, as opposed to Paris. John of Salisbury calls William a grammarian, and much of William's extant work is in the form of glosses on authoritative texts widely used in the schools. He glossed Boethius's *De consolatione Philosophiae*, Macrobius's *In somnium Scipionis*, Plato's *Timaeus*, Priscian's *Institutiones grammaticae*, and Juvenal. He may be the author of *Moralium dogma philosophorum*. His gloss on *De consolatione* identified the World Soul with the Holy Spirit, although the gloss on the *Timaeus* presents the World Soul as a concept with many hidden meanings. William's glosses on Macrobius and the *Timaeus* analyze the nature of *fabula* and *integumentum* as these apply to the "cloaking" of philosophical and theological truth in words and images in literary texts and imaginative narratives. William's interest in physics and cosmology is revealed in his *Philosophia mundi* (entitled *Dragmaticon* in a later revision), a systematic treatment of physical, cosmological, geographical, and meteorological phenomena and questions, summing up scientific knowledge in the era before the translation of Aristotle's scientific works. He sought to discern the true workings of nature and shunned "miraculous" explanations, even for biblical events, when a more straightforward explanation might be found. William made use of translations-adaptations of medical works from the Arabic, such as Constantine the African's *Pantegni*.

Grover A. Zinn

[See also: BOETHIUS, INFLUENCE OF; CHARTRES; MACROBIUS, INFLUENCE OF; MARTIANUS CAPELLA; PLATO, INFLUENCE OF; SCHOOLS, CATHEDRAL]

William of Conches. *Glosae in Iuvenalem*, ed. Bradford Wilson. Paris: Vrin, 1980.

———. *Glosae super Platonem*, ed. Édouard Jeauneau. Paris: Vrin, 1965.

———. *Philosophia*, ed. Gregor Maurach with Heidemarie Telle. Pretoria: University of South Africa, 1980.

———. *Das Moralium dogma philosophorum des Guillaume de Conches, lateinisch, altfranzösich und mittelniederfrankisch*, ed. John Holmberg. Uppsala: Almqvist and Wiksell, 1929.

Gregory, Tullio. *Anima mundi: la filosofia de Guglielmo di Conches e la scuola di Chartres*. Florence: Sansoni, 1955.

Häring, Nikolaus M. "Commenatry and Hermeneutics." In *Renaissance and Renewal in the Twelfth Century*, ed. Robert L. Benson and Giles Constable with Carol D. Lanham. Cambridge: Harvard University Press, 1982, pp. 173–200.

Jeauneau, Édouard. "Deux rédactions des gloses de Guillaume de Conches sur Priscien." *Recherches de théologie ancienne et médiévale* 27 (1960): 212–47.

———. "*Lectio philosophorum*": recherches sur l'École de Chartres. Amsterdam: Hakkert, 1973.

Parent, Joseph-Marie. *La doctrine de la création dans l'École de Chartres: études et textes*. Paris: Vrin, 1938.

Southern, Richard W. *Platonism, Scholastic Method, and the School of Chartres*. Reading: University of Reading, 1979.

Wetherbee, Winthrop. *Platonism and Poetry in the Twelfth Century: The Literary Influence of the School of Chartres*. Princeton: Princeton University Press, 1972.

WILLIAM OF SAINT-AMOUR (ca. 1200–1272). William is now chiefly remembered for his ferocious campaign against the mendicant orders. We know nothing of his life until he became master of arts in Paris (by 1228). By November 1238, he had received the doctorate in canon law and was also canon of Beauvais and rector of Guerville. He went on to study theology in Paris and ca. 1250 was a regent master.

From about this time, William began his attacks on the mendicant way of life, and it was through his influence that the Dominicans were suspended from teaching in 1254 for having in effect broken the closed shop of masters by ignoring the suspension of classes in the previous year and continuing to teach.

William never substantially amended his views on the mendicants, and his subsequent fate depended on who was pope at the time. Innocent IV (r. 1243–54) was sympathetic, and he flourished. Alexander IV (r. 1254–61) was cardinal protector of the Franciscans, and William was deprived of his privileges and expelled from France. Clement IV, although disagreeing, allowed him to return to Saint-Amour, where he died. His most famous polemical work is *De periculis novissimorum temporum* (1256).

Lesley J. Smith

[See also: DOMINICAN ORDER; FRANCISCAN ORDER; UNIVERSITIES]

Douie, Decima L. *The Conflict Between the Seculars and the Mendicants at the University of Paris in the Thirteenth Century*. London: Blackfriars, 1954.

Dufeil, M.M. *Guillaume de Saint-Amour et la polémique universitaire parisienne, 1250–1259*. Paris: Picard, 1972.

WILLIAM OF SAINT-THIERRY (1070/90–1148). Born in Liège, William of Saint-Thierry studied at the schools of Reims and perhaps at Laon under Anselm of Laon, where he may have met Peter Abélard. For unknown reasons, he renounced his studies and in 1113 became a monk in the Benedictine monastery of Saint-Nicasius in Reims. In 1118, he became abbot of Saint-Thierry, near Reims. As a close friend and admirer of Bernard of Clairvaux, he wished to change orders and become a Cistercian. However, Bernard dissuaded him until 1135, when William became a monk in the newly founded Cistercian monastery of Signy, where he died in 1148.

On several occasions, William encouraged Bernard's literary activities. Bernard's early work, the *Apologia*, a fierce attack on the traditional Benedictine monastic lifestyle, was written at William's request and dedicated to him. About 1138, William, shocked by the theological audacity of Abélard, persuaded Bernard to oppose him, adding to his request a list of Abélard's errors, published as the *Disputatio adversus Abaelardum*. Bernard's intervention resulted in Abélard's condemnation at the Council of Sens in 1141. William was also instrumental in bringing about Bernard's famous series of sermons on the Song of Songs. When both were ill, they spent some time together in the infirmary of Clairvaux, talking about the *Canticle*. William also intended to write a life of Bernard but completed only the first book, the so-called *Sancti Bernardi vita prima*.

William published many works on devotional and exegetical themes, among which are the *Expositio in epistolam ad Romanos* (in reaction to Abélard's commentary on Paul's Epistle to the Romans), the *Expositio super Cantica canticorum* (a commentary on the Song of Songs), as well as two compilations on the Song of Songs from the works of Ambrose and Gregory the Great and a treatise on the relation between body and soul (*De natura corporis et* animae). Author of *De natura et dignitate amoris* and *De contemplando Deo*, William is also considered to be the author of the famous *Epistola ad fratres de Monte Dei*, about the solitary and contemplative life.

For William, the act of faith is part of and subsumed under mystical knowledge and contemplation. Faith is a pretaste of the vision of the divine. Reason helps faith in the process of understanding itself, raising it to the level of full mystical knowledge characterized by love. William supports his reflections on mystical knowledge with quotations from many sources, mainly patristic, while also frequently referring to profane, classical authors. He, like the "monastic theology" he helped to create, can thus be seen as part of the so-called 12th-century renaissance.

Burcht Pranger

[See also: ABÉLARD, PETER; BERNARD OF CLAIRVAUX; CISTERCIAN ORDER; MYSTICISM; THEOLOGY]

William of Saint-Thierry. *Opera.* PL 180, 184, 185.
———. *On Contemplating God,* trans. Sister Penelope. Kalamazoo: Cistercian, 1977.
———. *The Nature and Dignity of Love,* trans. Thomas X. Davis. Kalamazoo: Cistercian, 1981.
———. *On Contemplating God; Prayer; Meditations,* trans. Sister Penelope. Kalamazoo: Cistercian, 1971.
———. *On the Nature of the Body and the Soul,* trans. B. Clark. In *Three Treatises on Man: A Cistercian Anthropology,* ed. Bernard McGinn. Kalamazoo: Cistercian, 1977.
———. *Exposé sur le Cantique des cantiques,* ed. Jean M. Déchanet, trans. Pierre Dumontier. Paris: Cerf, 1962.
———. *The Mirror of Faith,* trans. Thomas X. Davis. Kalamazoo: Cistercian, 1979.
———. *Lettre aux frères de Mont-Dieu (Lettre d'Or),* ed. and trans. Jean M. Déchanet. Paris: Cerf, 1975.
Bell, David N. *The Image and Likeness: The Augustinian Spirituality of William of Saint-Thierry.* Kalamazoo: Cistercian, 1984.
Déchanet, Jean M. *William of Saint-Thierry: The Man and His Work.* Spencer: Cistercian, 1972.

WILLIAM OF SENS (late 12th c.). French builder hired to rebuild the east end of Canterbury cathedral after the fire of 1174. According to the chronicle of the Canterbury monk Gervais, which is the only surviving year-by-year description of a medieval architectural project, William spent five years working at Canterbury and would have continued had he not been injured in a fall from the scaffolding in the crossing. Using an intermediary, he was able to direct the works until the end of the building season in 1179 but then had to give up the project to someone who could be on hand at every phase of the building, an Englishman named William. Although his name indicates he was born in Sens, there is no evidence that William ever worked there. His style and the details of his design suggest that he came to Canterbury from somewhere in northern France, probably the Arras-Valenciennes region.

William W. Clark

Gervais. *The Architectural History of Canterbury Cathedral,* trans. R.W. Willis. London, 1845.
Bony, Jean. "French Influences on the Origins of English Gothic Architecture." *Journal of the Warburg and Courtauld Institutes* 12 (1940): 1–15.

WILLIAM OF VOLPIANO (William of Saint-Bénigne of Dijon; 962–1031). Born into the high aristocracy in Lombardy, William of Volpiano preferred the monastic life to the ecclesiastical career prepared for him and went north to Cluny (987). Abbot Maiolus soon sent him to Saint-Bénigne in Dijon to reform that venerable but undisciplined house (989). He quickly established his talents as an effective if severe reformer, attracting the interest of dukes and kings. He reformed Fécamp (1006) and Jumièges (1015) for Richard of Normandy and Saint-Germain-des-Prés for Robert II the Pious, and founded Fruttuaria (1003) on family property. His monasteries had schools attached that accepted anyone, no matter how poor. After Odilo of Cluny (whom he allegedly "discovered" and sent on to Maiolus as a successor), he founded and reformed more monasteries and priories than anyone of his generation.

He brought Lombard masons and sculptors to Dijon to rebuild the monastic basilica with a huge crypt for relics and a large rotunda modeled on the Holy Sepulcher and an oculus at the top, placed at the east end (1001–18). Although not subsequently copied, the building prefigures Romanesque art in its drive for size, its use of sculpture, and its stone vaults. William traveled a great deal, and sometime in the mid-1010s he added the monk Raoul Glaber to his suite, commanding him to write his history of the "events and prodigies" of the year 1000. In it, Raoul featured William as one of the great geniuses responsible for the renewal of Christian society and for the "white mantle of churches" with which Europe robed itself shortly after the millennium. Attempting to retire to his family monastery in his old age, William was called away to Fécamp, where he died in 1031 in his seventieth year. After his death, his monastic empire vanished; there was apparently little to hold it together beyond his formidable personality. His only important disciple was John of Fécamp.

Richard Landes

[See also: CLUNY; DIJON; FÉCAMP; MILLENNIALISM; ODILO; RAOUL GLABER; ROMANESQUE ARCHITECTURE]

Raoul Glaber. *Vita Willelmi.* In *Rodulfus Glaber Opera,* ed. John France. Oxford: Clarendon, 1989, pp. 254–302.
Bulst, Nithard. *Untersuchungen zu den Kloster-reformen Wilhelms von Dijon (962–1031).* Bonn: Röhrscheid, 1973.
Herval, R. "Un moine de l'an mille: Guillaume de Volpiano, premier abbé de Fécamp." *L'abbaye bénédictine de Fécamp: ouvrage scientifique du XIIIe centenaire.* 3 vols. Fécamp: Durand, 1959, Vol. 1, pp. 27–44, 321–22.
Williams, Watkin. "William of Dijon: A Monastic Reformer of the Early XIth Century." *Downside Review* 152 (1934): 520–45.

WINE TRADE. Much more important in the medieval world than they are today, wines were a part of the everyday life of both rich and poor. In addition, Christianity demanded wine for ritual purposes. The wines were put into barrels within hours (or, at most, days) of being pressed, when they had not yet completed the fermentation process, and were consumed young, generally within a year after production. Since the wines retained unfermented sugars and yeast, they were more nutritional than today's table wines.

The Middle Ages had a variety of solutions to the problem of distributing wines to areas that did not favor their production. One solution was to plant vines over a much greater area than is done today, for example, around Laon, an important medieval center. The wines produced in such areas, however, were barely drinkable. Some monastic institutions not located in regions that favored the production of wines acquired properties in wine-producing regions or maintained friendly relations with lords in those regions, who supplied wine to satisfy their needs. The earliest stages of commerce in wines are obscure, but by the 12th century a clear correlation exists between regions that were famed for their wines, such as Cahors and Pourçain in the Bourbonnais, and centers of early capital accumulation.

Certain geographic regions achieved fame for the quality of their wines at an early date. In the 6th century, Gregory of Tours commented on the wines produced in the area around Dijon in Burgundy, comparing them to the celebrated Falernian wines of ancient Rome. These "wines of Beaune," as they were known in the Middle Ages, were greatly prized, making their way overland to the markets of the north and by river south to the papal court in Avignon. In the 14th century, during the Great Schism, Petrarch declared that one of the causes for the perpetuation of the "Babylonian captivity" was the fondness of the papal court for the wines of Beaune.

The "wines of Burgundy" were those produced in a vast area of central France, of which only a modest portion remains today around Chablis. In the 12th century, the vines stretched as far as Vézelay, the hills of which the crusader Gui de Bazoches described as being covered with vineyards. In the 13th century, the Franciscan Salimbene commented on the quality of these wines, "which gladden the heart." He noted that they were an important item of commerce, being transported by river to the markets of the north, including Paris. Among the most reputed of the medieval "wines of Burgundy" mentioned by Salimbene were those of Auxerre, which were shipped as far as Normandy, Picardy, Flanders, and Hainaut.

The wines produced in the area around Bordeaux were probably the most important commercially from the 12th century on. Sent by boat down the Garonne River to the sea, then across to England, the wines of this region were not known for their quality, being weak and pale, and were sometimes fortified by the heavy, deep wines of Cahors. Nevertheless, the wine trade with England flourished, encouraged by the political connection between Aquitaine and England and the inferiority of English wines. This trade reached its peak in the early 14th century, when more than 100,000 barrels of wine, each containing approximately 250 gallons, were sent to English shores in a single year.

In the later Middle Ages, the procurers for great lay and ecclesiastical lords and the merchants from industrial areas that did not favor the production of wines traveled long distances to the major wine-producing areas, where they found a host of local officials to assist them. Wine brokers guided them to the cellars of local growers and advised them on quality. Measures varied considerably from one community to the next, but local officials inspected the barrels to be sure that the standards of the community were maintained. Finally, official binders saw to it that the barrels were tied in the manner appropriate to that community, a mark that contributed to the diffusion of a locality's reputation. Those who used false measures or mislabeled their wines were fined or suffered confiscation of their wines.

The wines of a previous harvest, called "old wines," were sold at a discount or sometimes discarded when the new harvest was in, and the barrels were reused. Wines could not be stored for any length of time, since the huge wooden barrels, containing around 250 gallons each, were porous, admitting air and bacteria. Only the better-quality wines would be transported any distance. The poorer wines, still unstable when marketed, could not withstand the hazards of the trip. Glass bottles used for the storage of wines were not common in the Middle Ages; they had to await the availability of corks and the invention of the corkscrew in the early-modern period before becoming commercially viable.

The poorer grades of wines were sold in the local taverns "by the pot and by the pint." Almost anyone who had a supply of wine could open a tavern. All one had to do was hang out a green branch to signify that small quantities of wines could be bought there. The taverns' reputation as centers of crime and violence, if court records can be believed, was well deserved. Communities also regulated the retail trade in wines, supervising measures, requiring proper labeling, and, in some of the larger communities, regulating the prices. In Paris, for example, a herald proclaimed publicly the prices charged in the taverns and received a few pennies from each taverner for his pains.

With the availability of commercial supplies of wine, areas that produced substandard grades could transform the land to more suitable crops. In the late Middle Ages, with the decline of the population associated with the Black Death and other social catastrophes, even some of the better vineyards were abandoned for lack of labor.

In the late 14th century, a new varietal type of grape, the Gamay, made its appearance in the back hills of Burgundy. At first, the duke of Burgundy sought to outlaw its use, but since it produced twice the quantity of wine in the same area as the Pinot grape it spread rapidly. With the introduction of the Gamay grape into the hills of the Beaujolais, one is on the threshold of the modern era of wine production in France, marked by the commercial development of table-quality wines in large quantities for the mass markets in Paris and other urban centers.

Rosalind K. Berlow

[See also: BEVERAGES; TRADE ROUTES; VITICULTURE]

Berlow, Rosalind Kent. "The 'Disloyal' Grape: The Agrarian Crisis of Late Fourteenth-Century Burgundy." *Agricultural History* 56 (1982): 426–38.

Dion, Roger. *Histoire de la vigne et du vin en France des origines au XIXe siècle.* Paris: The Author, 1959.

James, Margery K. "The Medieval Wine Dealer." *Explorations in Entrepreneurial History* 10 (1957): 45–53.

Seward, Desmond. *Monks and Wine.* New York: Crown, 1979.

WITASSE LE MOINE. Only one extant manuscript (B.N. fr. 1553) tells the story of this 13th-century French Robin Hood. The anonymous author recounts, in some 2,300 octosyllabic lines, the comic pranks and adventures of Witasse, who confounds his enemy, the Count of Boulogne, notably by his use of disguises. It presents a mixture of folk motifs, internal history of the Boulonnais, and the relations among England, France, and the county of Boulogne in the period 1200–17.

Wendy E. Pfeffer

Conlon, Denis Joseph, ed. *Li romans de Witasse le Moine.* Chapel Hill: University of North Carolina Press, 1972.

WITCHCRAFT. The term "witchcraft" (Fr. *sorcellerie*) can be used for maleficent magic or sorcery, but in France from the 1430s onward this and related terms were applied to an alleged "sect" of conspiratorial Devil worshipers bent on overturning the order of Christendom.

This notion of conspiratorial witchcraft arose in southeastern France and southwestern Switzerland and quickly spread. From ca. 1428 and through the 1430s, large-scale trials occurred from the Dauphiné across to the Valais. The trial records indicate growing concern with a new type of conspiratorial witchcraft, and the concept of this offense was developed especially in writings of the 1430s: the anonymous *Errores Gazariorum*, the chronicler Johann Fründ's report about witches in the Valais, the secular judge Claude Tholosan's treatise regarding the witches he encountered in southeastern France, and (slightly later) Martin Le Franc's more skeptical report of recent witch beliefs in the *Champion des dames.* Also produced in the 1430s was the Dominican friar Johannes Nider's highly influential *Formicarius*, which told of witch trials in Switzerland around the turn of the century. This literature was followed in the 15th century by other important writings on witchcraft; especially important works written in France were Nicolaus Jacquerius's *Flagellum haereticorum fascinariorum* (1458) and Johannes Tinctoris's *Sermo de secta Vaudensium* (1460). These writings told how the witches met at "synagogues" or "sabbaths," where they paid homage and rendered an obscene kiss to the Devil (who often appeared as a black cat), made a pact with the Devil in their own blood, ate their own offspring, had indiscriminate sex with others in attendance. At these assemblies, they received powders and unguents to be used for destroying people and crops. The witches of the Valais were said to claim that they had recruited about 700 members for their "sect" and boasted that within a year they would be so powerful that they could rule Christendom and sit in judgment over it.

The association of witchcraft with the heresy of the Waldensians is reflected in the term *Waudenses* or *Vaudenses* (*Vaudois* in French), used for witches as early as 1437 in Pope Eugenius IV's *Ad nostrum,* alerting inquisitors to them. The term was used regularly in the 1450s, particularly in connection with the affair at Arras beginning in 1459, when thirty-four people were arrested and twelve burned for *Vauderie.* In this case, the ritual elements of witchcraft were accentuated and the role of sorcery (or maleficent magic) was negligible. Yet it is difficult to determine whether the witches spoken of as *Vaudois* had a genuine link to the Waldensian heresy or whether the term was being applied loosely; some of the accused in the 1430s may have been Waldensians, but certainly the *Vaudois* of the 1450s show little sign of having belonged to this sect.

Although witches are occasionally recorded as having confessed without torture, the use or threat of torture was often a major factor in obtaining confessions. It was important in coercing alleged witches to give the names of other people they had seen at the sabbath. The dynamics of prosecution can be seen clearly in the trial of Pierre Vallin at La-Tour-du-Pin in 1438. Vallin was convicted by an episcopal official and an inquisitorial vicar of invoking demons and serving "Belzebut" more than sixty-three years. He had renounced God, defiled the Cross, dedicated his infant daughter to the Devil (who then killed her), aroused storms, ridden to the "synagogue" on a stick, eaten the flesh of infants, and had sexual intercourse with Belzebut (who appeared for the purpose in the form of a twenty-year-old woman). His ecclesiastical judges then released him to the secular court, which demanded to know the names of his associates in the sect; when he claimed to know no names, the judge said it was impossible for him to have belonged to the sect so long and not know names. Instruments of torture were shown him, and he named eight persons; after lunch, the judge had the instruments of torture readied, but Vallin said he could not give further names, no matter what was done to him. The next day, the judge tried to induce him to name priests, nobles, or wealthy men from the area, but he could not oblige.

Prosecution for witchcraft was often encouraged by developing regional governments; when Claude Tholosan tried witches in southeastern France, he did so as agent of the rising regional state of Savoy. The central authority of the royal government, however, sometimes served as a braking influence in the witch trials. It was the Parlement de Paris, for example, that eventually overturned the convictions at Arras. The cautious stance of the national government is perhaps best reflected in a case at Marmande in 1453. In the midst of an epidemic, eleven or twelve women at Marmande were seized by a local mob. Three of them confessed under torture that they had killed children by their sorcery, whereupon the local authorities had them burned. Two others confessed but then recanted, and when the authorities refused to execute them the outraged populace seized and burned them. The rest of the women refused to confess under torture; two of them died from their torture, but the others were eventually released. In the end, the royal government disciplined the consuls of Marmande for having failed to maintain public order during this crisis.

In places like Arras and the diocese of Lausanne, where the ritual and heretical elements of witchcraft remained prominent and the element of sorcery was proportionally less developed, witches were predominantly male. Indeed, one man in the Val de Travers who confessed having attended the sabbath told of several men who had been in attendance, and his judges had to ask him whether there were not women as well. Elsewhere, however, women outnumbered men—by about two to one in the Dauphiné and elsewhere still more strongly.

Occasionally, there is evidence that the women tried as witches were local healers. The vulnerability of such women can be seen in the trial of Catherine de Chynal in the Aosta Valley in 1449. Her personal history was tumultuous: born in Basel, she had moved to the Valais when young, married, left her husband and moved about, and had children by two men. She was accused in part of practicing medicine without having the requisite education; she told of a charm that she had used successfully to keep wounds from becoming inflamed, yet she was accused of harming people with her magic. One of the people she was supposed to have bewitched was a priest who came to her hoping she could relieve a tumor of his, but the medicine she gave him seemed to aggravate his condition and he died soon afterward. She was charged not only with harming people but with causing a cow to stop giving milk, and when the cow's owner beat a pail to restore the flow of milk Catherine was later discovered to have borne the effects of this magical beating. Worst of all, she was accused by one Pierre Proveschy (himself a "heretic" or witch) of having attended a "synagogue," denied God, kissed the Devil on the posterior in the form of a black cat, and spat and trampled on a cross. She denied all these charges, even under repeated torture, and at the demand of her son a local canon undertook her defense, yet the court found her guilty and sentenced her to penance (including a pilgrimage to Rome) and to banishment.

A woman at Villars-Chabod named Antonia, tried in 1477, denied at first that she was a witch, but after being tortured and left in prison over a month she confessed to attending the "synagogue" and paying homage to a demon named Robinet. She had been induced to join the "heresy" because of financial problems; at the synagogue, the demon had given her a purse filled with gold and silver, but when she returned home she discovered that the purse was empty. Amid all the details of the synagogue and of sorcery, there is reference to her having cured people's illnesses with the aid of her demon and with a charm, suggesting that she, too, was established as a kind of local healer.

Women more than men were liable to accusation if they became known as troublesome, and especially if in quarrels with those about them they uttered curses that could be interpreted as having had the intended effect. A woman in the hospital at Provins in 1452 was bitten by a dog kept there, and in her fury she hit the woman in attendance and uttered a curse that she might die in three days, which in fact happened. Imprisoned, the woman attempted to hang herself in her cell, but the jailer resuscitated her. The charges pressed against her soon went well beyond mere sorcery: she was accused of belonging to the sect of *Vaudois*, of standing in circles and invoking demons, of consorting with the Devil in the form of a large black cat, of killing children, and so forth. Eventually, the case was transferred from the provost's court to that of the archbishop of Sens, and then appealed to the Parlement de Paris, as was the case a few years later at Arras. Another person accused of joining the *Vaudois* was the Carmelite theologian William Adeline, who in 1453 confessed that he had done so to curry favor with a knight whose displeasure he had incurred; when the presiding demon saw him at the assembly, he said, "The best one has come," and Adeline allegedly enjoyed great esteem among the *Vaudois*.

Often, a witch's reputation for sorcery and other misconduct was built up over several years before she was finally brought to trial. When a fifty-six-year-old widow named Andrée Garaude was executed for witchcraft at Bressuire in 1475, it became clear that she had long been at odds with the community. About eighteen years earlier, someone had killed all her goslings, and in her rage she called on the Devil for revenge, whereupon he appeared to her as a black dog named Sathanas and agreed to satisfy her desires if she would serve him and attend the sabbath. After some reluctance, she consented. Apart from the usual details of the sabbath, she confessed that she had used a wax image against more than one of her neighbors, she had killed another neighbor's goat by afflicting it with a reddish powder, and she had desecrated the local church, urinating in the holy water fount and defecating in the nave at the Devil's command.

Vulnerability to prosecution was increased if a woman had relatives who had been convicted of witchcraft or if she herself was known for general immorality. When sickness broke out among both the infants and the animals at Boucoiran in 1491, a woman named Martiale Espaze realized that she had been accused of sorcery by other women detained for the same offense, and thus she fled. Her husband asked her if she was in fact a sorcerer, and she told him she was not, yet she was fleeing to Gabriac to stay with her cousins. Her husband later told the authorities he had no reason to think her a sorceress. Others, however, were not so sure. Witnesses told how she and her mother had fled to Boucoiran some years ago when a relative was executed elsewhere for witchcraft and her mother was suspected. Martiale herself was pregnant at the time and claimed to be a widow. In Boucoiran, she had a reputation for sexual promiscuity. Eventually, she was captured at Gabriac and brought back to Boucoiran, where she confessed that she had attended the sabbath. She had killed and witnessed the killing of children; she once did so in the course of a quarrel in which she had been accused of theft. But she had also killed pigs, not out of vengeance but simply in compliance with the Devil's command.

Especially poignant as an example of a woman's vulnerability is the case of Jehanneta Lasne of Vacheresse, who confessed under torture at Fribourg in 1493 that she had attended assemblies of the witches' sect, presided over by a figure who called himself Sathanas. She had been induced into this sect because her husband would beat her, and one night she went into the woods and cried out asking God or the Devil to come to her aid. Sathanas then appeared and told her that if she denied God and took him as her master he would comfort her and her husband would cease beating her.

Richard Kieckhefer

[**See also:** MAGIC; NECROMANCY]

Bonney, Françoise. "Autour de Jean Gerson: opinions de théologiens sur les superstitions et la sorcellerie au début du XVe siècle." *Moyen âge* 77 (1971): 85–98.

Cohn, Norman. *Europe's Inner Demons: An Enquiry Inspired by the Great Witch-Hunt.* London: Chatto and Windus, 1975.

Ginzburg, Carlo. *Ecstasies: Deciphering the Witches' Sabbath,* trans. Raymond Rosenthal. New York: Pantheon, 1991.

Kieckhefer, Richard. *European Witch Trials: Their Foundations in Popular and Learned Culture, 1300–1500.* London: Routledge and Kegan Paul, 1976.

Kors, Alan C., and Edward Peters, eds. *Witchcraft in Europe, 1100–1700: A Documentary History.* Philadelphia: University of Pennsylvania Press, 1972.

Lea, Henry Charles. *Materials Toward a History of Witchcraft.* 3 vols. Philadelphia: University of Pennsylvania Press, 1939.

Levack, Brian, ed. *Articles on Witchcraft, Magic and Demonology.* 12 vols. New York: Garland, 1992, Vol. 2: *Witchcraft in the Ancient World and the Middle Ages.*

Russell, Jeffrey Burton. *Witchcraft in the Middle Ages.* Ithaca: Cornell University Press, 1972.

WOMEN, RELIGIOUS EXPERIENCE OF. In assessing the scope of medieval women's religious experience, it is necessary to consider that the concept "experience" comprises both internal and external factors, only one of which is gender. Other components include theoretical knowledge, access to situational frameworks (e.g., to the opportunity to exercise publicly recognized authority), social and economic status, age, and linguistic skills to express and reflect upon experiential data. All of these variables differ greatly not just between men and women, due to sociological causes, but also among members of one sex. It is difficult to defend an essentialist claim that distinctly female or male core experiences exist; yet the unwillingness of the male medieval-church hierarchy to share its power with women forced religious women on paths that favored certain types of experience and their communication over others. It has been argued, for example, that women's exclusion from the priesthood fostered a uniquely feminine eucharistic piety that stressed an intimate psychophysical union with the human Christ. Furthermore, women's ability to become pregnant, to lactate, and to nurse is said to have caused a specifically feminine "mother-mysticism," in which women visualized these activities vis-à-vis the Christ child in the late Middle Ages. Yet all these "feminine" activities have also been reported for male mystics, albeit with less frequency. And the reverse is also true: women visionaries and mystics, such as Jeanne d'Arc (ca. 1412–1431), appropriated "masculine" patterns of spirituality that stressed activism, or, as in the case of Aldegund (d. ca. 684), the woman's *virilitas,* or manliness. It is more helpful, therefore, to pay attention to the localization of women's spiritual experiences in their specific cultural and economic contexts; as this survey will show, their spirituality changed greatly through the ages. It represents more women's sociologically determined commentaries on pressing issues of their day than an ahistorical, archetypal feminine "essence."

We need to assess our sources critically, since only a small minority of women left written testimonies to their thoughts and lives. Most of our information is filtered through devout or even hostile texts (as in the transcripts of trials conducted by the Inquisition) written by men who either knew the women or merely heard about them. Therefore, we are often confronted with reflections about what women's religious experiences were thought to be rather than with an accurate account of these experiences as authenticated by the women themselves. Finally, the question of what constitutes women's and men's distinctly gendered experiences is not a medieval but a thoroughly modern issue. Medieval women writers who talked about their spiritual lives understood their experiences to be paradigmatic and open to all Christians, no matter what their gender. It is almost impossible *not* to distort their own accounts by attempting to isolate gendered units of meaning.

Medieval France (however difficult to define geographically) produced some of the highest intellectual and artistic religious achievements of its era. Nonetheless, we have the names of only a handful of extraordinary French religious female leaders and authors; not all of them were mystics or used traditional literary genres to channel their interest in religious questions. For example, Héloïse (d. 1163/64), Christine de Pizan (d. ca. 1430), and Marie de France (fl. 12th c.) achieved lasting fame as writers, but little attention has been paid to their religious beliefs. Na Prous Boneta (d. 1325), Jeanne d'Arc, and Marguerite Porete (d. 1310), fascinating innovators and mystics in their own right, were condemned and killed as heretics. Little is known about 14th-century visionaries like Constance de Rabastens or Marie Robine. In comparison with the lasting impact of French male mystics, such as St. Bernard of Clairvaux (1090/91–1153) and the Victorines (fl. 12th and 13th c.), the contributions of women mystics have been largely neglected due to a lack of institutional support and access to a public forum in the medieval period and indifference in the following centuries. Furthermore, women's monasteries, the ideal locus for intensely practiced religiosity, tended on the whole to be poorer than men's houses; nuns were more tightly cloistered than monks; and, with the rise of the universities, all women's access to learning, to publishing, and to participation in culturally relevant discussions drastically declined. By necessity, religious women's creative outlets aligned them more closely to popular culture, the vernacular and heretical movements.

In sum, women's religious achievements became generally possible only under favorable conditions that included access to theological knowledge, freedom from traditional roles related to child rearing and work in a home-based economy (Jeanne-Marie de Maillé [1331–1414] began her career as a visionary recluse after the death of her spouse), institutional support, and a relatively stable, economically thriving, and culturally diverse environment (e.g., the women saints of the Merovingian era tended to live in well-endowed and well-connected monasteries). Therefore, we can locate most medieval French women mystics in regions characterized by the existence of royal houses or important medieval cities, with vibrant trading centers and their potential for cultural exchanges.

Medieval France witnessed three phases of distinguished female religious creativity. In the 6th and 7th centuries, when the Merovingians shaped the three kingdoms of Burgundy, Austrasia, and Neustria, a remarkable number of noble women saints emerged whose biographies testify to their influence on local spiritual culture. In many cases, their cults were promoted by fellow nuns who survived the saint (often the founder of the community) and struggled to keep the monastery financially secure and spiritually alive. Religious experiences cultivated in these monastic environments centered on a mixture of active charity to the community (the saints functioned as "living sermons," to use the felicitous term coined by Jo Ann McNamara) and mediatory roles that highlighted the saints as "mothers" and peacemakers in the community. In the cases of Radegund (ca. 525–587), Aldegund, and Balthild (d. ca. 680), their lives have either been recorded by themselves or other women, thus representing a more accurate view of women's spirituality.

- In these accounts, virginity and ascetical feats appear to be less important than compassionate leadership, the performance of miracles, and love of God and community. Radegund was a Thuringian princess captured by the Franks and married to Clotar I (r. 511–67). With the help of two bishops, Radegund managed to leave Clotar and established a monastery at Poitiers, for which she secured a relic of the Holy Cross. Her male biographer Venantius Fortunatus stressed Radegund's extravagant penitential piety and acts of status reversal, both features more typical of male saints. In contrast, her female biographer Baudonivia, a fellow nun, focused more on miracles that consolidated Radegund's community and her visionary teachings, which Radegund revealed only to a small group of trusted nuns.

Aldegund, also a member of the nobility, was educated at the monastery of Nivelles and later founded her own monastery at Maubeuge. The description in her *vita* of her visions was dictated by Aldegund herself and used as inspirational readings in her own institution, thus establishing a kind of "female lineage" of teachings. Although Aldegund's visionary imagery is traditional (including Christ, the Virgin, angels, the Devil in the form of a wolf and a lion), its message of love is innovative. Balthild was a Saxon slave who eventually became a queen and regent. She founded a monastery for men at Corbie and one for women at Chelles, where she lived from 664/65 until her death. Renowned for her generosity, Balthild, like Radegund, encouraged peacemaking efforts and durable relations between the court and the monastery and promoted her monastery as the location for a royal cult. Feminine spirituality as promoted by early-medieval women saints and their followers is marked by an affirmation of community ties and the continuity of secular and religious identity rather than status reversal and conversion.

From the following centuries, hardly any female voices survived. This is in part due to the fact that women's monastic communities sharply dropped in numbers, a development that did not reverse itself until the 11th century. We have, however, an exceptional testimony from the 10th century, the *vita* of the serf Flothilda of Avenay (d. 942), who died shortly after she received her revelations. The first set of her visions describe Flothilda's persecution by demons and men on horses and her escape to safety, an almost timeless topos reflecting women's fear of sexual violence. The second cycle deals with church-political questions of her community at Reims and the decline of moral standards among the clergy. From the 12th century, the era of Marie de France and Héloïse, we possess a fascinating document depicting the lively cult and rich visionary talents of Blessed Alpais of Cudot (b. ca. 1156 in northern France), a simple peasant woman. At the age of twelve, Alpais became gravely ill and was unable to leave her bed for the rest of her life. Her body was so disfigured with open sores that her brothers decided to let her starve. At this point, Alpais began to receive regular apparitions and visions, proved to be capable of telepathy and vision at a distance, and abstained completely from food, a sign of holiness that reached back to the desert fathers and eventually became a hallmark for later women mystics. The Cistercians supported her cult and, against her strong resistance, the local archbishop built a church adjacent to Alpais's house during her lifetime, since she was recognized as a living saint. Spirituality in the 12th century is marked by a rise in Marian piety and in eucharistic devotion; both trends are well represented in Alpais's visionary accounts. Most remarkable, however, is her vision of the Cistercian abbot Gilduin, who is seen as feeding his monks with milk from his breast—a highly suggestive image preceding that of the younger Italian St. Clare of Assisi (ca. 1193–1253) receiving milk from St. Francis (1181/82–1226) and reminiscent of St. Bernard of Clairvaux, who received milk from the Virgin Mary. Alpais's contribution to eucharistic piety is her account of the heavenly events that parallel each earthly celebration. As the priest conducts the eucharistic rite, she sees a beautiful child being offered by angels to God and then returned to the altar of the church. Visionary participation in the eucharist, often expressed in observing the transformation of the host into the human Christ, miraculous revelations about the worthiness of priests, and revelations surrounding the host became in time characteristic of women's religious experience of the high Middle Ages, the second distinctive phase of medieval women's spirituality.

The other great spiritual theme of the 12th century and late 13th is voluntary poverty, that is, a desire for the apostolic lifestyle of early Christianity and a thorough moral reform of the church. Within the church, this impulse found expression in the new orders of the Franciscans, Dominicans, and Cistercians, which almost immediately had to confront the uncomfortable question of the *cura monialium*, the pastoral care of women attached to the order either as nuns or as tertiaries.

In distinction to the social landscape of early-medieval women's religiosity, we note the inclusion of women of the middle and lower classes, as in the case of Alpais of Cudot. New centers of religious activity and creativity appeared in northern and southern France in the wake of the rise of wealthy cities. Not just women in the reform orders of the Cistercians, Dominicans, or Franciscans but also those women who joined Waldensians or Cathars gained prominence as leaders. Béguines like Marguerite Porete straddled the difficult demarcation between heretical and orthodox groupings, since they had to endure a tumultuous fluctuation in ecclesiastical and civic support.

Inquisitional records provide ample evidence of women's activities among the Cathars and the Waldensians. A survey of such documents from the region of Quercy in the 13th century estimates that 30 percent of active Cathars and 52 percent of active Waldensians were women; in the diocese of Toulouse, which hosted very few Waldensians, 40 percent of the Cathar leaders seem to have been female. In their early phase, Waldensians permitted women to preach, baptize, forgive sins, and celebrate the eucharist. The Cathars, or, as they called themselves, the "good Christians," had a dual message for women. On one hand, they rejected the female body as the representation of the evil material world; nonetheless, women as well as men could reach the status of the "perfect," the highest rank among the Cathars. The "good Christians" also offered monastic institutions for women, the so-called *hospicie*.

In terms of social respectability and visibility, medieval women's mysticism had reached its peak by the end of the 13th century—within rather than outside the church. The following women reached fame for their religious contributions: as representatives of eucharistic piety, Marie d'Oignies (1177–1213) from Nijvel, who is also regarded as one of the founding mothers of the béguines; Juliana of Mont-Cornillon (1193–1258), who initiated the feast of Corpus Christi, first celebrated at Liège in 1247; Ida of Louvain (d. 1260), who received special papal permission to receive the eucharist on a daily basis; and Marguerite d'Ypres (d. 1237), who already showed intense devotion to the eucharist by the age of five. As mystical writers in their own right, the Carthusian prioress Marguerite d'Oingt (ca. 1240–1310) and the Cistercian prioress Beatrijs of Nazareth (1200–1268) deserve mention. St. Douceline de Digne (ca. 1214–1274), who founded two or three béguinages in southern France and whose life was recorded in Occitan by her pupil Philippine de Porcellet, became the subject of a popular local cult. Despite significant differences, all of the religious women of this period share the following features.

Mystical phenomena. These include both charismatic gifts, such as levitation, inedia, visions, locutions, revelations, the reading of hearts, ecstasies, and intellectual transformations like increasing intuitive knowledge of divine reality, interior absorption in God, and contemplative and meditative skills. All of these phenomena are more deeply developed than in the early-medieval period.

Greater dependency upon male sponsors, teachers, and ecclesiastical authorities for spiritual guidance and interpretation of experience. Due to the fluid boundaries between heretical and orthodox reform movements, the unpredictable formation of a new relationship between clergy and laity caused by the shift from agrarian to urban social structures and the concomitant rise of the burgher class, and the growing importance of vernacular languages, women's religious roles needed to be redefined. It has been pointed out that male biographers of religious women's lives, such as Thomas de Cantimpré (1201–1263/72), stressed female innocence and lack of theological training as signs of holiness, thus creating a myth of female spiritual superiority that successfully barred women from demanding equal access to positions of power. Since women of the early Middle Ages tended to belong to royal houses, their religious experiences were not shaped by the attempt to create sharply gendered divisions of power.

Increased sophistication regarding emotional and sensual aspects of devotion to the human Christ and asceticism. Women followed here a larger cultural trend that manifested itself in the secular tradition of courtly love and the bridal mysticism propagated by St. Bernard of Clairvaux in his *Commentaries on the Song of Songs*. Unlike St. Bernard's more cautious teachings, however, women's exploration of psychological dynamics became more concrete and radical, frequently culminating in highly sexualized experiences of spiritual union or intensely celebrated psychosomatic pregnancies.

The final stage of medieval women's religious life is defined by increased repression, decline of institutional support, and marginalization. As Caroline Bynum and other scholars have pointed out, by the 15th century the image of the woman mystic is almost identical with that of the witch. The dramatic biographies of women mystics of the 14th and early 15th centuries illustrate this turn of events. All of the women who were eventually executed as heretics overstepped the limits that kept earlier women mystics in their gendered niche. They claimed for themselves the exclusively male prerogatives—sanctioned as divinely instituted—to pronounce theological teachings (Marguerite Porete, burned 1310), to become publicly active in a male role (Jeanne d'Arc, burned 1431), or to usurp religious authority that rivaled or even canceled out ecclesiastical authority (Na Prous Boneta, burned 1325; Jeanne Daubenton, burned 1372). Those of their contemporaries who were spared the stake followed the pattern of obedience and integration in existing institutions chosen by the women of the 12th and 13th centuries. After the death of her husband, Jeanne-Marie de Maillé (1331–1414) cared for the sick and poor, was eventually forced to retreat to Planche-de-Vaux to live as a recluse, and finally joined the Franciscans in 1386. From within the safe walls of the monastery, she became a revered counselor and visionary, who was even summoned to King Charles VI on several occasions. Coletta Boylet of Corbie (1381–1447) received revelations regarding the Franciscans at the age of nine; as an adult, she first chose the lifestyle of a tertiary, then that of a recluse at Corbie. Motivated by revelations, Coletta asked for papal permission to reform Franciscan monasteries and proceeded to found the remarkable number of seventeen female and at least seven male institutions. Her authority was guarded by an unwavering commitment to church-approved channels for religious activity and intensely mystical phenomena that were identified with femininity rather than masculinity—long-lasting ecstatic states, levitations, revelations from souls in Purgatory, and the like.

In contrast, Jeanne d'Arc's mysticism appears minimalistic. The young woman followed the supernatural voices of SS. Michael, Catherine, and Margaret; there are no other charismatic gifts reported. Like Marguerite Porete, Jeanne d'Arc had no spiritual director, did not live in a community, and moved about freely. Marguerite Porete, Na Prous Boneta, Heilwic Bloemard (d. 1335), and Marie of Valenciennes (fl. end of the 14th c.) all claimed the possibility of transcending the limits of human sinfulness, either by having been elected mother (donatrix) of the Holy Spirit and receiving a glorified body (Na Prous Boneta), or by having achieved the perfection of the âme anéantie, the annihilated and therefore liberated soul. These teachings catapulted the women mystics outside of quantifiable and therefore controllable parameters of social norms and experiential criteria that had been developed in a slow and complex historical process. Women's religious experience in the 14th and 15th centuries reached the limits of what seemed patriarchally tolerable; it was mirrored in the all-consuming annihilation of the stake, a far cry from the community-affirming miracles of a St. Radegund and the peacemaking efforts of a Balthild 900 years earlier.

Ulrike Wiethaus

[See also: BÉGUINES; BERNARD OF CLAIRVAUX; CHRISTINA MIRABILIS; CISTERCIAN ORDER; DOMINICAN ORDER; EUCHARISTIC VENERATION AND VESSELS; FRANCISCAN ORDER; GILDUIN OF SAINT-VICTOR; HADEWIJCH; HÉLOÏSE; HERESY; JEANNE D'ARC; JULIANA OF MONT-CORNILLON; LUITGARD OF AYWIÈRES; MARGUERITE D'OINGT; MARGUERITE PORETE; MARIE D'OIGNIES; MYSTICISM; NUNNERIES; RADEGUND; WALDO/WALDENSES]

Barstow, Anne Llewellyn. "Joan of Arc and Female Mysticism." *Journal of Feminist Studies in Religion* 1 (1985): 29–42.

Bynum, Caroline Walker. *Fragmentation and Redemption: Essays on Gender and the Human Body in Medieval Religion.* New York: Zone, 1991.

Johnson, Penelope D. *Equal in Monastic Profession: Religious Women in Medieval France.* Chicago: University of Chicago Press, 1991.

McNamara, Jo Ann, John E. Halborg, and E. Gordon Whatley, eds. and trans. *Sainted Women of the Dark Ages.* Durham: Duke University Press, 1992.

Maisonneuve, Roland. "L'expérience mystique et visionnaire de Marguerite d'Oingt (d. 1310), moniale chartreuse." In *Kartausermystik und -Mystiker*, ed. James Hogg. Salzburg: Institut für Anglistik und Amerikanistik, 1981, Vol. 1, pp. 81–103.

May, William Harold. "The Confession of Na Prous Boneta, Heretic and Heresiarch." In *Essays in Medieval Life and Thought*, ed. John H. Mundy et al. New York: Columbia University Press, 1955, pp. 3–30.

Mundy, John H. *Men and Women at Toulouse in the Age of the Cathars.* Toronto: Pontifical Institute of Mediaeval Studies, 1990.

Pernoud, Régine. *La femme au temps des cathédrales.* Paris: Stock, 1984.

Schweitzer, Franz Josef. "Von Marguerite von Porete (d. 1310) bis Mme Guyon (d. 1717): Frauenmystik im Konflikt mit der Kirche." In *Frauenmystik im Mittelalter*, ed. Peter Dinzelbacher and Dieter Bauer. Ostfildern bei Stuttgart: Schwabenverlag, 1985, pp. 256–75.

Wemple, Suzanne Fonay. "Female Spirituality and Mysticism in Frankish Monasticism: Radegund, Balthild and Aldegund." In *Peaceweavers: Medieval Religious Women*, ed. John A. Nichols and Lillian Thomas Shank. Kalamazoo: Cistercian, 1987, pp. 39–55.

WOMEN IN TRADE. Case studies have shown that women throughout medieval France were deeply involved in trade, despite limitations placed upon their participation. Their activities, though concentrated in the textile and food trades—the stereotypical spinsters and brewsters—could, depending on the region, be as varied as moneychanger or moneylender (a status noted for Jewish women in northern France), manuscript illuminator, or precious-metal worker. Wives and daughters of craftsmen frequently worked with the male family members in their occupation and continued in the trade as widows. Single women (*femmes soles*) were also often involved in artisanal activities. Some twenty of the forty-one cloth-industry employees of the exploitative Jehan Boinbroke of Douai were women. Numerous wetnurses and midwives and occasional female surgeons have been recorded. Women served as petty merchants but rarely in long-distance commerce, where if they were involved at all it was as sedentary investors. Generally, women in business could appear in court, independent of their husbands, in matters of their trade.

Women were denied access to guild membership in many trades; in others, widows achieved guild membership in their husbands' stead. Some guilds were exclusively female. According to the *Livre des métiers* of Étienne Boileau (1292), drawn up for tax purposes in Paris, six guilds were female only, but women were working in eighty others, out of over 120 in all. In Toulouse, women were admitted to the guilds of weaver, cloth finisher, candlemaker, wax merchant, and *avoir-du-poids* merchant. In Montpellier, there was female guild membership only for the *caritat des fourniers* (bakers), whose regulations were recorded in 1365. In Arras, widows who had not remarried could enjoy membership in the same food trades as their late husbands. Guilds with predominantly female membership usually had male governance.

Wages for women were lower than those for men in comparable employment, a fact that led to the preferential hiring of some women and the disgruntlement of unemployed men. Piecework was usually financially more advantageous for women. In late-medieval France, commercial possibilities for women tended to narrow in the increasingly negative economic climate.

Kathryn L. Reyerson

[See also: STAINED GLASS; TEXTILES]

Dixon, E. "Craftswomen in the *Livre des métiers.*" *Economic Journal* 5 (1895): 209–28.

Jordan, William C. "Jews on Top: Women and the Availability of Consumption Loans in Northern France in the Mid-Thirteenth Century." *Journal of Jewish Studies* 29 (1978): 39–57.

Reyerson, Kathryn L. "Women in Business in Medieval Montpellier." In *Women and Work in Preindustrial Europe,* ed. Barbara Hanawalt. Bloomington: Indiana University Press, 1986, pp. 117–44.

WOMEN'S SONGS. The women's songs, or *chansons de femme,* accounting for a significant part of the Old French lyric corpus, constitute not a genre but a conceptual set identified by female voice and exclusive preoccupation with love. Though limited thematically, their poetic elaboration, like their music, is highly diversified and ranges from products of a precourtly, even pre-Christian, European tradition, as is reflected also in Portuguese or Germanic songs, to compositions variously influenced by the forms and ideology of the troubadour-derived *grand chant* style. From the most archaic, folkloric type to the most aristocratized, it is likely that most pieces extant, transmitted largely by the same chansonniers that preserve the courtly trouvère compositions of the 12th and 13th centuries, were written or rewritten by men; almost all are anonymous. Though noncourtly women's texts were sung in Provençal as well as in French, the Provençal songs are barely represented in the manuscript sources.

Love here tends to be forthright, sensual, shadowed by pain, and unencumbered with the artifices of *fin'amors;* its basic vehicle is the monologue. These characteristics are all subject, however, to considerable modification.

The genres accommodating the *chansons de femme* include only one, the *chanson de toile,* in which formal definition and feminine interest are coterminous. Elsewhere, form is not necessarily identified with a specifically feminine experience of love, and particular experience does not necessarily dictate a given form. A *chanson d'ami,* for example, voicing the amorous longing, joy, or heartbreak of an unmarried girl (rarely, an unwilling young nun), may take the form of a dance piece such as a ballette, or a *rondet/*rondeau, or a more freely defined sequence of refrain-capped stanzas. As a confrontation with an adversary of love, often the girl's mother, it may merge with a debate song or suggest the incipient drama of a *chanson à personnages;* as a farewell to a lover, it overlaps other songs of separation, the crusade songs, for example.

If the unmarried girl stands, as often claimed, at the heart of all women's lyric, the unhappy wife is, in the Old French corpus, even more prominent. These *chansons de malmariée,* too, show many forms and variations, including, in particular, a male poet serving as narrator and occasional interlocutor. An encounter with the poet, for example, may introduce the woman's lament; she may be presented arguing with her husband, debating with another woman, or conversing with her lover.

The *aube,* or dawn song, though not inherently feminine, tends in Old French as in Provençal to be the separation lament of a woman, married or unmarried. It is the only traditional *chanson de femme* better represented in southern manuscripts than northern (eighteen to five, not all of which are in a female voice). The French poems show less formal homogeneity than the others; music is almost wholly wanting in both sets.

Whatever the form of women's songs, they show a widespread incorporation of *refrains,* one- or two-line exclamations that may themselves have originated in women's dances. Songs in the high style of *fin'amors* are extremely rare in Old French, which did not develop a counterpart of the trobairitz.

Samuel N. Rosenberg

[See also: *ALBA/AUBE;* BALLETTE; *CHANSON DE TOILE;* MULTIPLE REFRAIN SONGS (*CHANSONS AVEC DES REFRAINS*); TROBAIRITZ; TROUVÈRE POETRY]

Rosenberg, Samuel N., and Hans Tischler, eds. *Chanter m'estuet: Songs of the Trouvères.* Bloomington: Indiana University Press, 1981.

Bec, Pierre. *La lyrique française au moyen âge (XIIe–XIIIe siècles): contribution à une typologie des genres poétiques médiévaux.* 2 vols. Paris: Picard, 1977–78, Vol. 1: *Études,* pp. 57–119; Vol. 2: *Textes.*

Dronke, Peter. *The Medieval Lyric.* London: Hutchinson University Library, 1968.

WOOL TRADE. During the Middle Ages, a major commodity of French commerce was wool. The cloth-manufacturing industry that had developed in Flanders, Artois, and Picardy had by the 12th century outstripped domestic supplies to meet its needs, and purchasing of English wool had begun. The principal merchants in the 12th century and much of the 13th were the Flemings, who bought the output of monastic houses and that of the laity. It was at times a simple transaction of money for wool. Frequently, wool was purchased by contract, money being advanced for future delivery. Some of the merchants were independent traders; others were agents of major wool towns commissioned to buy wools to meet the towns' needs.

A conflict begun in 1270 between the kings of England, Henry III and Edward I, and Marguerite, countess of Flanders, contributed to the undermining of Flemish dominance in the traffic of English wool. Hostilities lasted for five years, but even peace in 1275 did not end strained relations between the rulers. Reparations sought by aggrieved merchants of both sides for goods seized during the conflict occasioned coolness between Edward I and Gui, Marguerite's successor, and brought intermittent in-

English wool arrived regularly by ship to supply the textile industry of northern France. B.N. fr. 2810, fol. 86v. *Courtesy of the Bibliothèque Nationale, Paris.*

terruptions of trade by the English king to pressure the count to make promised payments. A serious break between England and Flanders occurred in 1304, when Edward I agreed to help Philip IV in his war against Flanders. The response of the Flemings was to give aid to Scotland, then at war with England. This resulted in the devising of a method to prevent the Flemish merchants from direct access to English wool. A compulsory staple (exclusive market for English wool) came into being in 1313. A cross-Channel town was designated in which all wool shipped from England to the Low Countries had to be marketed. The staple was variously at Saint-Omer in Artois and Antwerp in Brabant, being located in Flanders at Bruges only in 1325. The sharp decline in the role of Flemish merchants in its wool trade with England did not result from the staple. Edward II was generous in his exceptions, even giving a license to all merchants of Ypres to buy wool in England. The decline that began with the conflict that occurred from 1270 to 1275 grew sharper when the Flemings lost their contacts with English monastic houses and conditions in England became unsettled. Into their places stepped the Italians, the English, and members of the Hanseatic League. Despite their declining role, Flemings still traded in England, but in far fewer numbers. It was also true that for much of the 14th century Flemish ship owners still carried the bulk of the wool exported from England. Though Flanders had the dominant role, it was not the only French region from which merchants came. Picardy sent frequent buyers to England. The merchants of the southern city of Cahors had a particularly large share in shipping wool from the major eastern ports of England and importing wool for the clothiers of Toulouse. In addition, the source of wool for France changed by the 15th century. Far fewer sacks of raw wool came from England as the English developed their own cloth for export; Germany and, most importantly for Flanders, Spain, replaced England as suppliers.

Robert L. Baker

[See also: TEXTILES; TRADE ROUTES]

Carus-Wilson, Eleanora. *Medieval Merchant Venturers: Collected Studies.* London: Methuen, 1954.

Endrei, Walter. "Changements dans la productivité lainière au moyen âge." *Annales: Économies, Sociétés, Civilisations* 26 (1971): 1291–99.

Espinas, Georges *La draperie dans la Flandre française au moyen âge.* 2 vols. Paris: Picard, 1923.

Poerck, Guy de. *La draperie médiévale en Flandre et en Artois,* 3 vols. Bruges: De Tempel, 1951.

Y

YPRES. The smallest, after Bruges and Ghent, of the "three cities" that dominated Flanders in the Middle Ages, Ypres is first mentioned in written sources of the 11th century, the only "new" or founded town of Flanders that became a major metropolis. Its area was still heavily forested in 1000 but was being cleared rapidly. It was the site of a castle of the Flemish counts and the church of Saint-Martin, on the Yperlee canal at the point where it became navigable to merchants traveling inland from the coast. Ypres was thus at a strategic point linking the hydrographic systems that concentrated on Bruges and Ghent. One of the "five fairs" of Flanders was held at Ypres, and it grew rapidly, playing an important role in the revolutionary events of 1127–28. Ypres received a charter based on that of Arras, probably in 1174, and an annually chosen *échevinage*, or city council, in 1209. By then, it was one of the most important textile centers of Flanders, indeed the most purely industrial of the Flemish cities, with an active overseas trade. With Ghent and Bruges, and before 1305 Lille and Douai, Ypres participated as a "good town" of Flanders in regular consultations with the counts.

Ypres kept this position to the end of the *ancien régime*, despite a severe economic decline after ca. 1315. The famine of that year and a subsequent plague cost Ypres nearly one-sixth of its population, which is thought to have been about 22,000 in 1315, 14,000 in 1360, and 9,390 in 1437. Ypres was also the only one of the "three cities" that faced substantial competition from neighboring smaller towns, particularly Poperinge, in textile manufacture. Although the manufacture of certain types of luxury cloth was forbidden within three comital miles of Ypres, the town was unable to enforce its right, and the result was that the Ypres vicinity and the nearby Lys Valley became known for the production of medium-grade cloth by the late 14th century. The cloth production of Ypres dropped 60 percent between 1312 and 1360, and decline became even more rapid after 1370. The events of 1302 did not involve replacing the French-speaking aristocracy at Ypres, which continued to function except between 1325 and 1329. The walls of Ypres, which still left most of the textile workers in the suburbs, were less extensive than those of the other Flemish towns, for the ruling merchants, fearing rebellion, did not want to have the artisans enclosed within the same set of walls as themselves. The workers of Ypres thus suffered terribly during the wars of the 1380s, and most seem to have emigrated. Despite its continued political importance, Ypres was a secondary center economically thereafter.

David M. Nicholas

[**See also:** BRUGES; FLANDERS; GHENT; TEXTILES; WOOL TRADE]

Merlevede, J. *De Ieperse stadsfinanciän (1280–1330): Bijdrage tot de studie van een Vlaamse stad.* Brussels, n.d.

Mus, Octaaf, and Jan A. van Houtte, eds. *Prisma van de Geschiedenis van Ieper.* Ypres, 1974.

Nicholas, David. *Town and Countryside: Social, Economic, and Political Tensions in Fourteenth-Century Flanders.* Bruges: De Tempel, 1971.

YSENGRIMUS. A Latin poem of some 6,500 dactylic hexameters in seven books, composed ca. 1150 and attributed to the Flemish monk Nivard of Ghent. This first great beast epic, centered on the figure of the wolf, is a coherently constructed work in twelve episodes. Both a fable and an oratorical and satirical text, *Ysengrimus* reflects contemporary life and the problems of the Second Crusade. This somber and pessimistic poem is largely unsympathetic to St. Bernard, Pope Eugenius III, and the monks of Cîteaux and Cluny. It is an excellent reflection of the culture of a 12th-century cleric: well acquainted with Virgil, Ovid, Lucan, Juvenal, and other classical authors; steeped in biblical and liturgical culture; and generally indifferent to popular culture.

Jean Dufournet

[**See also:** *RENART, ROMAN DE*]

Charbonnier, Elisabeth, ed. *Le roman d'Ysengrin.* Paris: Les Belles Lettres, 1991.

Mann, Jill, ed. and trans. *Ysengrimus.* Leiden: Brill, 1987.

INDEX

Page references to encyclopedia entries appear in boldface; page numbers for maps and tabular material are set in italic.

This index is intended to guide the user to treatments of persons, places, events, rituals, musical works, texts, towns and cities, and other concepts discussed in the Encyclopedia, but not included as main entries. Main entries are also listed, with further references as required to other places in the volume where they are discussed. Major monuments (e.g., churches and public buildings) are not usually listed individually since they are treated in the article for the city or area where they are located; they are also often discussed in comprehensive topical articles for time periods and/or geographical regions. Treatises, musical works, plays, and other texts are listed by title and/or author. Minor works (individual lyrics, hymns, fabliaux, etc.) are generally not listed.

In alphabetizing the index, particles (of, de, des, le, etc.) in names of individuals have been ignored. Thus, Bernard of Clairvaux will appear before Bernard Délicieux and Bernard de Soissons.

Used in conjunction with the "See also" listings at the end of each article, the index allows the reader to explore in detail the many facets of life and thought in medieval France.

troubadour poetry, 219–22, 252, 288, 551, 678, 687, **929–31**
troubadours:
and crusade songs, 275
didactic poetry of, 294
and homosexuality, 457
partimen of, 495
rhythm in songs of, 797
role in organizing *Consistòri de la Subregaya Companhia del Gai Saber*, 542
secular repertory of, 651
songs as *cantus versicularis*, 421
and "trobairitz," 927
use of *gab*, 379
See also under specific troubadours
trouvère poetry, 219–22, 252, **931–33**
trouvères:
and bestiary allusions, 119
and *cantus versicularis*, 421
cantus coronatus composed by, 165
and crusade songs, 275
jeux-partis of, 495
rhythm in songs of, 797
secular repertory of, 651
scarcity of women among, 927–28
See also under specific trouvères
Troyes, 192, 259, 402, 445, 455, 794, **933–34**
Troyes, Council/Synod of, 112, 902
Troyes, Treaty of, 203, 443, 466, 477, 706, 731, 800, 934
Trubert (Douin de Lavesne), 304, 333
Truce of God, 24, 182, 278, 417, **934–35**, 958. *See also* Peace of God movement
Truce of Malestroit, 486
True Cross, as relic, 790
trumpets, 647, 651
tuberculosis, 865. *See also* scrofula
Tuchins, 145, 171, 521, 914. *See also* brigand/brigandage
tumors, treatment for, 606
tunic, 236, 238
two-field rotation, 12

Uc de Saint-Circ, 953
Uc Faidit, 930
Ugolino. *See* Gregory IX
Unam sanctam, 88, 135, 230, 394, 668, **937**
underdress, 236, 238
unicorn tapestries, 937–38
unity of intellect, 63, 449
universal chronicles, 451–53
universals, 736
universities, 59, 164, 417, 452–53, **938–39**. *See also specific universities under location of university*
Urbain li courtois, 265
Urban II, 273, 278, 417, 472

Urban IV, 230, 327, 463, 504, **941**
Urban V, 90, 436, 606, **941–42**
Urban VI, 90, 249, 473, 859
urban defenses, 619
urban government, 532
uroscopy, 605
usury, 95, 520, **942**
Utrecht Psalter, 174, 789

Vaillant, Jean, 247
Vair Palefroi, 468, 515
Vaison, Council of, 734
Valence, Council of, 321
Valence, university of, 943
Valenciennes, 438, **943**
Valentin (miracle play), 624
Valentina Viscontia, 564, 963
Valentinois, 308, **943**
Valerius Maximus, 922
Val-ès-Dunes, Battle of, 670
valet, 322. *See also* esquire/escuier
Valognes, Treaty of, 200, 328
Valois dynasty, 207, 246, 729, **943–45**, *944*
van der Weyden, Rogier, 163, 915, **945**
van Eyck, Jan, 151, 393, 731, 892, **945–46**
Varaville, Battle of, 670
variola, 297
vaslet. See valet
vassal, 324, 340–41, 342, 344, 389, 456, 476, **946**
Vaudémont, house of, 561
Vaudois, 982
Vaux-de-Cernay, **946**
Vedast, 435
vegetables, 295, 608
Vegetius, 223, 488, 920, 921, 922, 955
veils, 236, 237
Venantius Fortunatus, 217, 434, 450, 468, 530, 611, 657, 734, 778, 984
Vendôme, 138–39, 364, **947**
Venerable Bede. *See* Bede
Venette, Jean de, 53
vengeance, as punishment, 272
Vengeance de Jésus Christ, 455
Vengeance Nostre Seigneur (Eustache Marcadé), 585
Vengeance plays, 711
Vengeance Raguidel (Raoul de Houdenc), 387–88, 780
Vengement Alixandre (Gui de Cambrai), 25
Veni creator spiritus, 468, 469, 529
Veni redemptor gentium (Ambrose), 468
Venjance Alixandre (Jean Le Névelon), 25
Verbum abbreviatum (Peter the Chanter), 725

Verdun, **947–48**
Verdun, Treaty of, 23, 83, 154, 169, 177, 200, 368, 420, 560, 562, 565, 616
Vergier d'honneur (André de La Vigne), 515
Vermandois, **948**
vernacular writings, 371, 407, 437, 469, 495, 811, 905–6
Verneuil, Battle of, 466, 513, 686
Vers (Thibaut de Marly), 877
Vers de la Mort (Hélinant de Froidmont), 253, 440, 494, 743, 784, 877
Vers de la Mort (Robert le Clerc), 440
vers orphelin, 195
versification, **948–49**
versus, 875, **949–50**
Vespers, 164, 299
vestments, ecclesiastical, **950**
Vexilla regis prodeunt (Venantius Fortunatus), 468, 530
Vexin, **950–51**, 976
Vézelay, 86, 157, 240, 258, 364, 598, 749, 820, **951–53**
via cessionis, 271, 859, 896
via consilii, 859
"vicar of Christ," 473
"vicar of Peter," 473
Vicq, **953**
vidame, **953**
vidas, 930, **953–54**
Vide, Jacobus, 248
Viderunt omnes (Pérotin), 720
Vie de gent de religion, 637
Vie de saint Alexis, 35, 37, 436, 855, 948, 971
Vie de saint Denis, 293, 838
Vie de saint Georges, 37, 294
Vie de saint Gilles (Guillaume de Berneville), 37, 926
Vie de saint Grégoire le Grand (Frère Angier), 37
Vie de saint Honorat (Raimon Féraut), 294
Vie de saint Jean Bouche d'or, 926
Vie de saint Jean l'Aumônier, 37
Vie de saint Laurent, 37
Vie de saint Léger, 710, 855, 948
Vie de saint Louis (Jean de Joinville), 253, 493, 501
Vie de saint Martin (André de La Vigne), 906
Vie de saint Nicolas (Wace), 969
Vie de saint Quentin (Huon le Roi de Cambrai), 468
Vie de saint Thomas Becket (Guernes de Pont-Sainte-Maxence), 422
Vie de saint Trophime, 294
Vie de sainte Agnès (translated by Jean Golein), 399
Vie de sainte Elysabel (Rutebeuf), 830